Literature	*Lit*	**литера**
literary	*lit*	**книжн**
low colloquial	*low CQ*	**грубое**
masculine	*m*	**мужск**
masculine and feminine	*m and f*	**мужско**
Mathematics	*Math*	**математика**
Mechanics	*Mech*	**механика**
Medicine	*Med*	**медицина**
Meteorology	*Meteorol*	**метеорология**
Military	*Mil*	**военное дело**
Music	*Mus*	**музыка**
noun	*n*	**имя существительное**
Nautical	*Naut*	**морское дело**
negative	*neg*	**отрицательный**
neuter	*neut*	**средний род**
nominative	*nom*	**именительный падеж**
noun plural	*npl*	**существительное во множественном числе**
numeral	*num*	**числительное**
obsolete	*obs*	**устаревшее слово, выражение**
official	*off*	**официальный термин**
Optics	*Opt*	**оптика**
Ornithology	*Orn*	**орнитология**
prepositional case	*P*	**предложный падеж**
passive	*pass*	**страдательный залог**
pejorative	*pejor*	**уничижительно**
personal	*pers*	**личный**
perfective	*pf*	**совершенный вид (глагола)**
Philosophy	*Philos*	**философия**
Photography	*Photo*	**фотография**
Physics	*Phys*	**физика**
plural	*pl*	**множественное число**
poetic	*poet*	**поэтический**
Politics	*Polit*	**политический термин**
possessive	*poss*	**притяжательный**
past participle passive	*ppp*	**причастие второе**
predicative	*predic*	**предикативное употребление**
prefix	*pref*	**приставка**
preposition	*prep*	**предлог**
present tense	*pres*	**настоящее время**
pronoun	*pron*	**местоимение**
Psychology	*Psych*	**психология**
Radio	*Radio*	**радиотехника**
Railways	*Rail*	**железнодорожное дело**
reflexive	*reflex*	**возвратный**
Religion	*Rel*	**религия**
relative	*rel*	**относительный**
School	*School*	**школьное выражение**
Scotland	*Scot*	**употребительно в Шотландии**
semelfactive	*semel*	**одноразовый**
Sewing	*Sew*	**швейное дело**
singular	*sing*	**единственное число**
slang	*sl*	**сленг**
somebody	*smb*	**кто-то**
something	*smth*	**что-то**
Sport	*Sport*	**спорт**
Soviet Union	*SU*	**употребительно в Советском Союзе**
superlative	*superl*	**превосходная степень**
Technical	*Tech*	**технический термин**
Telephone	*Tel*	**телефон**
Textiles	*Text*	**текстильное дело**
Theatre	*Theat*	**театр**
transitive	*trans*	**переходный**
Television	*TV*	**телевидение**
Typography	*Typ*	**типографский термин**
United Kingdom	*UK*	**употребительно в Великобритании**
University	*Univ*	**университет**
United States	*US*	**употребительно в США**
usually	*usu*	**обыкновенно**
verb	*vb*	**глагол**
Veterinary medicine	*Vet*	**ветеринария**
verb intransitive	*vi*	**непереходный глагол**
verb transitive	*vt*	**переходный глагол**
verb transitive and intransitive	*vti*	**переходный и непереходный глагол**
vulgar	*vulg*	**вульгарно**
Zoology	*Zool*	**зоология**

THE MODERN RUSSIAN DICTIONARY FOR ENGLISH SPEAKERS

THE MODERN RUSSIAN DICTIONARY FOR ENGLISH SPEAKERS

ENGLISH-RUSSIAN

BY
ELIZABETH A M WILSON
MA OXON

Russian Editor L P POPOVA
Assistant Russian Editor M D LITVINOVA
Assistant Compilers E WILSON
A LEE
J MCNAIR

PERGAMON PRESS
OXFORD • NEW YORK • TORONTO • SYDNEY • PARIS • FRANKFURT

МОСКВА
ИЗДАТЕЛЬСТВО «РУССКИЙ ЯЗЫК»

U.K.	Pergamon Press Ltd., Headington Hill Hall, Oxford OX3 OBW, England
U.S.A.	Pergamon Press Inc., Maxwell House, Fairview Park, Elmsford, New York 10523, U.S.A.
CANADA	Pergamon Press Canada Ltd., Suite 104, 150 Consumers Rd., Willowdale, Ontario M2J 1P9, Canada
AUSTRALIA	Pergamon Press (Aust.) Pty. Ltd., P.O. Box 544, Potts Point, N.S.W. 2011, Australia
FRANCE	Pergamon Press SARL, 24 rue des Ecoles, 75240 Paris, Cedex 05, France
FEDERAL REPUBLIC OF GERMANY	Pergamon Press GmbH, 6242 Kronberg-Taunus, Hammerweg 6, Federal Republic of Germany

First edition 1982

Library of Congress Cataloguing in Publication Data

Wilson, Elizabeth A. M.
The Modern Russian Dictionary for English Speakers.
Bibliography: p. 720
1. English language — Dictionaries — Russian.
I. Popova, L.P. (Lucy P.) II. Title.
PG2640.W54 1981 423'.9171 81—12141
AACR2

British Library Cataloguing in Publication Data

Wilson, Elizabeth A. M.
The Modern Russian Dictionary for English Speakers.
1. Russian language — Dictionaries — English
2. English language — Dictionaries — Russian
I. Title
491.73'21 PG2640

ISBN 0—08—020554—2

Printed in the USSR

In memory of my son David

ACKNOWLEDGEMENTS

My first thanks are due to Professor O. S. Achmanova, Professor of English Linguistics at Moscow University, who in 1969 invited me to help in revising her two small school dictionaries (Russian-English and English-Russian) and thus I was introduced to lexicography. Her approach was not only scholarly, but vivid, human and humorous and I can never forget the hours she generously spent in teaching me from 1969 to 1971.

My thanks are also due to Anna Dmitrievna Mihalchi, Deputy Editor-in-Chief of the Russian Language Publishing House in Moscow. She also taught me much and has shown me unfailing patience and kindness. I am more indebted than I can say to my Russian editors, Lucy Popova and Marina Litvinova. Lucy's problems with a very green author from overseas have been many more than usually fall to the lot of an editor and I must thank her especially for her kindness and patience and trojan hard work. I have also greatly enjoyed working on the literary side with the lively Marina Litvinova who has added much light and colour to the Russian translations. I appreciate very much that she could spare time for this from her busy life of teaching and translation. It has been a great comfort to know that the grammatical problems have all been checked by so careful and knowledgeable a person as Nelly Semyonova. Also I do not forget how much my way has been smoothed by Evgeny Mouzhevlev, who administers the department with unflappable humour, good sense and efficiency. A special word of gratitude is owed to the Russian copyists and typists and to all my Russian colleagues for their welcoming hospitality to me on my sojourns in Moscow. I would like also to thank very warmly successive members of the British Embassy in Moscow for help and hospitality on these visits.

At home, I would like first to thank Miss Irina Kirillova of Newnham College, Reader in Russian at Cambridge University, for her constant encouragement. Without it I don't think I would have dared to go on. Many others have also helped and encouraged me, Professor Wheeler of Belfast University, Professor Stolz of University of Michigan, USA, Professor Raskin of Purdue University, USA, Doctor Barnes of St Andrews University, Joe Dobbs, Felicity Cave, Alexander, Leonard, Olga and many others. Lilian Bainbridge and Ann Symes both helped me with typing for which I am very grateful. Lastly I would like to thank warmly my friend Andrew Phillips who relieved me of much administration.

Now I come to my fellow compilers in England who over three years shared the slog with unfailing patience, persistence and humour. I also am indebted to the very good friend who checked (and indeed often compiled) all the Russian of the first draft. His work was quite indispensable to me. I must here make special mention of the help I had in compiling from Katherine Stidworthy M. A. (Oxon). I thank them all most warmly. The mistakes are mine!

I would also like to thank my publisher Robert Maxwell for trusting me with the work and to thank him and the staff of Pergamon Press for their support, particularly Miss Anna Moon, and the late Howard Warner; and also the photocopying department. Thanks too are due to Director V. I. Nazarov of the Russian Language Publishing House, and to others of his staff, apart from those I have already named.

One more thanks — and a big one — to Doctor Jeffery Jay of Glasgow University who saved my right eye in 1978. And then I come to my family who have borne with me and lived with the dictionary for seven years. My husband read through all the text correcting and suggesting, and my daughter Elizabeth compiled, suggested, corrected, and all of them encouraged.

Elizabeth A. M. Wilson
Cala Na Ruadh
Port Charlotte
Islay, Argyll PA487TS
Scotland

ОТ ИЗДАТЕЛЬСТВА

Настоящий «Англо-русский учебный словарь» предназначается для всех, кто говорит по-английски и изучает русский язык.

Основная задача словаря — оказать помощь читателю в овладении русской устной речью, познакомить его с разговорной лексикой современного русского литературного языка, с построением живой русской фразы.

Как известно, одним из решающих факторов перехода к устному общению в изучении любого языка является овладение повседневной разговорной речью. Усвоив основы грамматики, изучающий стремится в первую очередь овладеть наиболее употребительными в обычной повседневной жизни выражениями, конструкциями, фразами. Чтобы облегчить эту задачу, русский язык в словаре подается читателю через его родной, английский язык. Английский словник представлен словами и словосочетаниями, широко употребительными в повседневной жизни англичан; в словарь вошли также некоторые термины, часто встречающиеся в разговорной и письменной речи. Таким образом словарь будет интересен и для русского читателя, изучающего английский язык. Он может быть полезен и преподавателям английского языка.

В помощь иностранному читателю в словаре дается целый ряд сведений о русской грамматике в виде помет, пояснений, грамматических комментариев. Особое внимание уделяется трактовке вспомогательных глаголов с учетом их практического перевода на русский язык.

Словарь является совместным изданием, результатом международного сотрудничества между советским Издательством «Русский язык» и английским Издательством «Пергамон Пресс». Как автор, так и редакторы словаря максимально стремились к тому, чтобы оба языка — как русский, так и английский — были представлены наиболее живо и соответствовали современным литературным нормам.

При работе над словарем широко использовались словари Collins-Robert French-English English-French Dictionary (1979) и Collins Spanish-English English-Spanish Dictionary by Colin Smith (1975), в которых принципы отбора английского словника близки принципам данного словаря. Орфография английских слов дается также по этим словарям. Использовались в качестве справочников также следующие словари: A. S. Hornby, Oxford Advanced Learner's Dictionary of Current English (1974), «Большой англо-русский словарь» в 2-х томах под ред. проф. И. Р. Гальперина (М., 1980), «Словарь русского языка» С. И. Ожегова (М., 1981), «Орфографический словарь русского языка» (М., 1979).

Замечания и предложения просим направлять в Издательство «Русский язык» по адресу: 103009, Москва, К-9, Пушкинская ул., 23.

BIBLIOGRAPHY

For the English Vocabulary I have relied throughout on the Oxford Advanced Learner's Dictionary of Current English (A. S. Hornby). Later I met Professor Colin Smith; I have made much use of the English side of his English-Spanish Dictionary (Collins) and after 1978 of the English side of the Collins-Robert Dictionary. I was particularly encouraged to find that my own approach to lexicography coincided so closely with that of Professor Colin Smith whom I regard as a pioneer in his approach to modern two-way lexicography. I have also found very helpful Volume I of the Oxford Dictionary of Current Idiomatic English (Cowie and Mackin).

On the Russian side my first acknowledgement must be to the admirable Dictionary of the Russian Language by Professor S. I. Ozhegov. I have also used largely the mammoth two-volume New English-Russian Dictionary of Professor Galperin and his many colleagues. I have found Professor Marcus Wheeler's lucid Oxford Russian-English Dictionary an invaluable check-back, and very helpful in its admirable layout of grammatical points. For grammar and syntax I have made extensive use of Russian Syntax (Borras and Christian) and for quick reference I still use the elementary, but lucid and comprehensive New Russian Grammar of Anna H. Semeonoff (first published in 1934!).

INTRODUCTION

NOTES FOR USERS

INTRODUCTION

1. THE USER

This dictionary is primarily a practical one for the student whose approach to the Russian language will be through English, irrespective of whether he lives in Britain, North America or elsewhere. The vocabulary comprises the words which the average educated man might want to use in speaking or writing Russian, including the simple technical terms in common use.

The criterion for method has been ease in use, or, in the words of James Murray, "eloquence to the eye". Clutter in the text reduces clarity and adds to eyestrain. For this reason cross-references are avoided as far as possible. Much use is made of clearly marked divisions and the dictionary is well provided with indications of style and shades of meaning, and with occasional grammatical notes and cautions. The student should thus be able to find what he wants easily and quickly, without constant recourse either to his grammar or to a Russian-English dictionary.

There is a wealth of illustrative phrases, couched in the language of "everyday" and these should help to give the student the feel of spoken Russian.

2. COVERAGE (LEXIS)

The nature of the dictionary has determined the vocabulary. Very full treatment has been given to the few basic words which figure so largely in our daily use—**do, get, give, go, make, put, way,** etc., as also to prepositions. Special attention is paid to verbs in combination with prepositions or adverbial particles, which are usually translated by Russian verbal prefixes. These are of the first importance to the student. All the commoner senses of the selected English headwords have been covered, but not necessarily rare ones. Thus for instance when a verb is nearly always used in the transitive form, although the intransitive form exists (or vice versa), the rare usage may be ignored.

To save space, abstract nouns and adverbs derived directly from adjectives are not given, e.g. **tender** *adj* не́жный is given, but not **tenderness** *n* не́жность, nor **tenderly** *adv* не́жно.

In groups of cognate words, such as **biological, biologist, biology,** one or more of the terms may be omitted. Similarly English words which are translated by direct transliteration into Russian are often omitted, e.g. **morgue** морг, or **nymph** ни́мфа. In such cases it will be easy for the student to form or find these for himself.

3. THE LANGUAGE

Emphasis has been given to the spoken language — both everyday colloquial uses and more specialized uses, e.g. the language of the committee man. Many of the examples are given in the second person singular indicating exchanges between friends of the same age, or colleagues of the same rank, or members of a family. A strong distinction is made between colloquial expressions and slang, the latter being included only if it is well established, partly because it can date so quickly, partly because it is hard to appreciate its exact tone in a foreign language. Translations are as far as possible stylistically matched. Where there is no true equivalent of an English expression such as **ghost writer,** it has seemed better to omit the term rather than to offer explanations or cumbrous circumlocutions, which the student could equally well form for himself if need arose.

4. ILLUSTRATION

Translation by single words seldom enables the student to use these words in a living context. The illustrations are designed to provide such a context. They also show the difference between the two languages in construction and grammar where rules apply. For example, translation of the English predicative adjective does not always in Russian follow directly from the attributive form, e.g. **unconnected sentences** несвя́зные фра́зы, but **the two events are quite unconnected** э́ти два собы́тия ника́к не свя́заны ме́жду собо́й.

Illustrations also serve to familiarize the student with Russian word combinations and word order, and with the typical flow and rhythm of the Russian sentence, none of which can be deduced a priori. Though word order in both languages is flexible, varying according to emphasis, nevertheless there are standard patterns of order where the two languages differ, e.g. **she walked in her sleep last night** сего́дня [**NB**] но́чью она́ ходи́ла во сне. Again the invariable English cadence is **supply and demand,** but the Russians prefer спрос и предложе́ние.

5. LAYOUT

All English words and phrases are printed in bold type. Indicators (of style, meaning, etc.) are printed in italics. Long entries are divided; each division is numbered, begins on a new line and is inset. But short entries which can be taken in at a glance, may contain no divisions, even when these would be justified semantically.

6. ORDER WITHIN AN ENTRY

Usually an entry or division starts by giving one or more general translations. Examples then follow grouped around the general translations in the order in which these were given; then come examples which are not covered by any of the general translations.

Within an entry or division, direct uses are given first, followed by specialized, colloquial direct, figurative and then figurative colloquial uses. In big entries figurative uses are often treated in a separate division. Attributive uses of a noun come at the end of the entry or of the appropriate division.

The divisions of an entry normally depend on the different shades of meaning in which the English headword is being used, but, exceptionally, divisions may be given over to translations of a single English meaning by particular Russian constructions, if it seems that to do so will make for a clearer understanding by the English learner.

Transitive and intransitive uses of a verb are treated separately. In the case of the larger verbs, uses with prepositions or adverbial particles are given separately as headwords in alphabetical order, and they are similarly divided into transitive and intransitive uses.

7. TRANSLATION OF HEADWORDS

A number of entries open with a colon and proceed straight to the examples. This happens when no sufficiently general translations of the headword suggest themselves. A translation which only suits one use of the headword is always shown in context: it is misleading to give one-time uses in a way that suggests that they can be widely applied.

Again Russian definitions or explanations of the headword are avoided. The student is looking for Russian equivalents usable (when properly inflected) in live context. To translate **some** (*pronoun*) by не́которое коли́чество is an explanation, and it is most unlikely to be the correct translation of **some** (*pronoun*) in any given context. Again приве́тствие is a correct translation of **welcome** (*noun*), but, in the four common examples chosen in the text, it is not used once. In such a case the student is less likely to be misled if the entry opens immediately with translations of the common contexts, or of the set combinations in which the headword is normally used.

8. GRAMMATICAL INDICATIONS

Each headword is followed by its grammatical label in abbreviated form: *n*—noun, *adj*—adjective and so on.

The constructions following a Russian word are always shown, either in abbreviated form, e.g. любо́вь к + *D*, привы́кнуть к + *D or* + *inf*, or they may be shown in examples, and often in both ways.

A number of explanatory notes on grammar and construction are provided in square brackets; or the student's attention may be drawn to an unexpected usage with an **NB** in square brackets.

Knowledge of the aspects of Russian verbs is of such fundamental importance that, even at the cost of much repetition, aspects are noted in all verb entries.

Inflexion and changes of stress are shown for numerals and pronouns which are one-time entries. Otherwise these are not shown, as a Russian word may recur in many entries and repetition of the information under each entry or cross-referencing would alike be uneconomic.

9. STYLISTIC AND FIELD LABELS

Stylistic and field labels are given in italics without brackets, thus: *joc*—jocular, *fig*—figurative, *CQ*—colloquial. Field labels begin with a capital letter, thus: *Bot*—botany, etc. The indication is given immediately after the headword if it applies to the whole entry, otherwise just in front of the appropriate part of the entry. Specifically British, American or Russian uses are marked (*UK*), (*US*) or (*SU*) respectively.

10. INDICATORS OF MEANING

Indicators of meaning are given in italics and round brackets where necessary, to show in which sense an English word or phrase is being used, or which sense of the headword a division covers.

E.g. **affect** *vt* **1** (*influence*)...
2 (*move*)...
3 (*pretend*)...

Indicators are also used to differentiate between shades of meaning where more than one Russian translation is offered, e.g. **deliberately** *adv* (*on purpose*) наро́чно, преднаме́ренно; (*slowly*) неспе́шно; (*cautiously*) осторо́жно.

Translations which are synonyms or "near synonyms" are divided by a comma; if they differ more widely by a semicolon. However, true synonyms are very rare, and every effort has been made to differentiate shades of meaning of Russian words, not only by indicators, but also by examples. Where one or more of the "near synonyms" may be used in an example as alternatives, these are shown.

NOTES FOR USERS

1. ORDER OF THE ENTRIES

Strictly alphabetical order is followed. Grammatical homonyms of words related in meaning are distinguished by their grammatical labels, and are treated as separate headwords in the following sequence: noun, adjective, adverb, preposition, verb, thus:

round *n*
round *adj*
round *adv*
round *prep*
round *vti*

Homonyms of different meaning are distinguished by superior numbers and treated in the same sequence, in the order of their superior numbers, thus:

fast[1] *n Rel*
fast[1] *vi*
fast[2] *adj* (*firm*)
fast[2] *adv*
fast[3] *adj* (*quick*)
fast[3] *adv*

2. PRONUNCIATION

Phonetic transcriptions of English words are not given. Russian pronunciation is indicated by stress marks. Alternative stresses are marked only if both stresses are in current use.

3. USE OF THE TILDE

The tilde sign stands for the whole English headword when repeated in an entry, thus: **face** *n*...; ~ **to** ~ лицóм к лицý (= face to face); **correct** *vt*...; **the teacher ~ed my essay**... (= corrected).

4. USE OF THE HYPHEN, AND OF THE HYPHEN PLUS VERTICAL STROKE

i) In showing the perfective aspects of Russian verbs, a hyphen, when preceded by a prefix, represents the full Russian perfective, thus: писáть (на-) (= написáть).

ii) With Russian words divided by a vertical stroke, the hyphen represents that part of the word which is to the left of the stroke, thus: получ|áть (-и́ть) (= получи́ть); комсомóл|ец, *f*-ка (= комсомóлка).

iii) A stress mark over the hyphen indicates shift of stress to the syllable immediately preceding the vertical stroke, thus: встав|ля́ть (-́ить) (= встáвить); вы|полня́ть (-́полнить) (= вы́полнить); провер|я́ть (-́ить) (= провéрить).

5. USE OF BRACKETS

i) If a word in either English or Russian is enclosed in round brackets but is **not** in italics, it means that that word may be omitted without detriment to the sense of the phrase.

ii) Round brackets are used to enclose the aspectival forms of Russian verbs. Russian italics are not used.

iii) Round brackets in conjunction with (English) italics are used:

a) to enclose indicators of meaning;

b) to enclose abbreviated grammatical indications; e.g. to draw attention to a Russian singular used to translate an English plural or vice versa: **variations in price** изменéние (*sing*) в цéнах (*pl*); or to note the Russian use of an impersonal verb: **I feel sick** меня́ тошни́т (*impers*); or to note the use of a Russian adverb to translate an English noun or adjective: **in the vicinity of the station** побли́зости от/вблизи́ (*advs*) вокзáла; etc.

iv) Square brackets in conjunction with (English) italics are used for brief editorial comment, e.g. to enlarge on a point of grammar, or a construction. They are also used with an

NB to draw attention to an unexpected usage in Russian, e.g. **to bake a lot of pastries** напéчь пирожкóв [**NB** *use of prefix*]; **the market is buoyant** торгóвля оживи́лась [**NB** *tense*].

6. INDICATING ALTERNATIVES: THE DIAGONAL STROKE, THE COMMA AND "OR"

i) **The diagonal stroke** is used:

a) to show different combinations which may be used with the headword and in the corresponding translations, thus: **to get an answer/permission/a prize/recognition/a scolding** получи́ть отвéт/разрешéние/приз/признáние/вы́говор;

b) to show possible alternatives within a phrase in one language only, thus: **the casting/deciding vote** решáющий гóлос; **various forms of transport** рáзные/различ́ные ви́ды трáнспорта.

ii) **A comma** is used:

a) when two separate translations are offered for one English phrase, thus: **in a manner of speaking** в какóй-то стéпени, мóжно сказáть;

b) when English combinations separated by a diagonal stroke require two different Russian translations, thus: **vegetable soup/salad** овощнóй суп, салáт из овощéй.

iii) **Both the diagonal stroke and the comma** may be needed when translating more than two English combinations, thus: **a violent blow/attack of fever/explosion** си́льный удáр/при́ступ лихорáдки, мóщный взрыв.

iv) "*Or*": when an alternative translation is shown within an alternative, the "sub-alternative" is indicated by the English word "*or*" written in italics, thus: **I'm going to visit my sister** я собирáюсь (*to drop in*) зайти́ к сестрé/(*to stay*) навести́ть сестрý *or* погости́ть у сестры́; **bad manners/news** плохи́е *or* дурны́е манéры/вéсти.

7. GRAMMAR: TREATMENT OF NOUNS

A knowledge of basic grammar and permutations of vowels is assumed. Gender is shown only for common nouns, and for masculine nouns ending in the soft sign, or in a non-masculine termination, thus:

левшá (*m and f*)
дождь (*m*)
слугá (*m*)
доми́шко (*m*).

Indeclinable nouns are noted and can be assumed to be neuter, unless a gender is given. Collective nouns are noted, as also are nouns which have no singular or no plural, thus:

кóфе (*m, indecl*)
кинó (*indecl*)
картóфель (*m, collect*)
щипцы́ (*no sing*)
óбувь (*no pl*).

These indications are given every time a noun appears as a general translation of the headword, but not always otherwise, except for (*collect*).

8. GRAMMAR: TREATMENT OF VERBS

i) The imperfective aspect is treated as the basic form of all verbs with its perfective form shown in round brackets. The following are the abbreviations used to give aspectival information:

a) писáть (на-) (= *pf* написáть); сверк|áть (*semel* -нýть) (= *semelfactive pf* сверкнýть);

b) when the verb is for any reason first quoted in its perfective form, the entry runs: получ|и́ть (*impf* -áть);

c) where there is no established corresponding aspect, the verbs are shown thus: рыдáть (*impf*); стерпéть (*pf*);

d) a verb which is used for both aspects is shown thus: эвакуи́ровать (*impf and pf*);

e) when a Russian verb exists in both aspects, but translates an English usage in only one of its aspects, it is shown thus: **believe** *vi* вéрить (*only in impf*), **to talk somebody out of doing something** отговори́ть когó-л от чегó-л (*only in pf*) or thus: **to canvass for votes** вести́ предвы́борную кампáнию (*usu impf*), **to bid somebody good morning** пожелáть комý-л дóброго ýтра (*usu pf*) (= *usually* (*im*)*perfective in this usage*).

ii) Aspectival information is given only in verb entries and only when the verb is offered as a general translation of the headword, or as a translation of an English example given in the infinitive form. It is usually given only once in an entry and is not repeated for the reflexive form of the verb.

iii) In a long entry, where several compounds of a verb may appear, aspectival information is normally shown only for the first appearance of the compound. The student can then deduce the aspectival forms of any further of these particular compounds which may appear in that entry.

9. VERBS OF MOTION WITH TWO IMPERFECTIVES

The terms "indeterminate" and "determinate" are used to distinguish the two imperfectives, thus: ходи́ть (*indet impf of* идти́; по-), е́хать (*det impf of* е́здить; по-) (= *pfs* походи́ть and пое́хать).

Such verbs are fully illustrated to bring out their special meanings, especially the force of the prefix по- in the perfective forms.

The inchoative sense of the perfective of the determinate form is shown in examples, e.g. **it began to rain** пошёл дождь. It is shown how, in order to translate the determinate verb in a true perfective sense, the perfective of one of its compounds must be used, e.g. **he's gone off to bathe/to the theatre** он пошёл купа́ться, он ушёл в теа́тр (= "he set off to bathe", but "he has gone to the theatre").

The perfective of the indeterminate form is illustrated as meaning to do something for a while, without particular purpose or direction. The student will find throughout the dictionary examples showing how perfective verbs, with the prefix по- used in this same sense, can be formed from many imperfective verbs (though they are not held to be aspectivally related), e.g. **to flirt a little** пофлиртова́ть (*pf*).

10. THE TRANSLATION OF "IT"

The entry for "**it**" shows how the correct translation depends on the gender of the antecedent word. By convention, in brief examples where the antecedent is not shown, "**it**" is translated by э́то.

бу́ква «а»; *Mus* ля; (*in school*) *as indecl n*), пятёрка [5 = *highest* *in SU*]; **to get an A for/in** получи́ть пятёрку по геогра́фии; **'s all the time** учи́ться на отли́чно, и́чником; **to know smth from A to** ать что-л от «а» до «я».

a (an) 1 *indefinite article, not translated*: **without a doubt** без сомне́ния; **a lot of money** мно́го де́нег; **a little more** чуть/немно́го бо́льше; **they answered "yes" to a man** все до еди́ного отве́тили «да»; **he's a friend of mine** он мой друг; **a friend of mine told me** оди́н мой прия́тель сказа́л мне

2 (*a certain*) не́кий, како́й-то; **a Mr Smith has called** приходи́л не́кий ми́стер Смит

3 *after "many", "such", "what" with nouns and adjs*: **what a day!** что за день!, како́й день!; **many a man** мно́гие (лю́ди); **what a girl!** кака́я де́вушка!; **such a marvellous painting** така́я удиви́тельная карти́на

4 (= *one*): **a £1** оди́н фунт; **a dozen eggs** дю́жина яи́ц; **wait a minute!** одну́ мину́тку!; **he didn't say a word** он не сказа́л ни сло́ва; **they're all of a size** они́ все одного́ (и того́ же) разме́ра

5 (*distributive*) **i)** в + *A*; **40 miles an hour** со́рок миль в час; **twice a day/a year** два́жды в день/в год; **£40 a week** со́рок фу́нтов в неде́лю; **ii)** по + *A or D* (*see also under* **apiece** *and* **each**); **he gave them an apple each** он дал им по я́блоку; **peaches cost a rouble/2 roubles a kilo** пе́рсики сто́ят рубль/два рубля́ килогра́мм; **the students went in two at a time** студе́нты входи́ли по два челове́ка/по́ двое; **he comes on a Tuesday** он прихо́дит по вто́рникам.

aback *adv*: **he was taken ~** он был поражён, он опе́шил.

abacus *n* счёты (*pl*).

abandon *vt* **1** (*leave*) поки|да́ть (-́нуть); остав|ля́ть (-́ить); *CQ* брос|а́ть (-́ить); **to ~ ship/a town** поки́нуть кора́бль/го́род; **to ~ one's family** оста́вить/бро́сить семью́; **to ~ smb to his fate** бро́сить кого́-л на произво́л судьбы́

2 (*give up*): **we ~ed all hope** мы уже́ ни на что не наде́ялись; **they ~ed the project/the attempt to see him** они́ отказа́лись от прое́кта/от попы́тки уви́деться с ним; **the game was ~ed after 20 minutes' play** че́рез два́дцать мину́т игру́ пришло́сь останови́ть.

abandoned *adj*: **an ~ child/house** поки́нутый ребёнок/дом.

abashed *predic adj*: **she was not a bit ~ at/by this** её э́то ниско́лько не смути́ло.

abate *vi* утих|а́ть, стих|а́ть (*pfs* -́нуть); успок|а́иваться (-о́иться); ослаб|ева́ть (-е́ть *and* -́нуть); **the pain/the wind has ~d** боль ути́хла, ве́тер ути́х/стих/ослабе́л/успоко́ился; **the floods are abating** наводне́ние (*sing*) пошло́ на у́быль [**NB** пошло́ = *started to abate*].

abbreviate *vt* сокра|ща́ть (-ти́ть); **an ~d text** сокращённый текст.

abbreviation *n* сокраще́ние.

ABC *n* а́збука, алфави́т.

abdication *n* отрече́ние.

abdomen *n* брюшна́я по́лость, *CQ* живо́т; (*of insects, etc.*) брюшко́.

abdominal *adj* брюшно́й; **~ pains** боль в брюшно́й по́лости/в животе́; **an ~ operation** полостна́я опера́ция.

aberration *n* (*mental*) рассе́янность; *Opt* аберра́ция; *Tech* отклоне́ние; **in a moment of ~** по рассе́янности.

abeyance *n*: **the question is in ~** рассмотре́ние э́того вопро́са приостано́влено; **this rule has fallen into ~** э́то пра́вило устаре́ло/бо́льше не соблюда́ется.

abhor *vt* ненави́деть (*impf*); (*feel revulsion*) пита́ть отвраще́ние к + *D* (*only in impf*); **I ~ flattery/violence** я ненави́жу лесть, я пита́ю отвраще́ние к наси́лию.

abhorrent *adj* ненави́стный, отврати́тельный.

abide *vti vt* (*tolerate, only used negatively*) терпе́ть, выноси́ть (*only in impfs*); **I can't ~ dogs** я не выношу́/я терпе́ть не могу́ соба́к

vi: **to ~ by the rules/a decision** приде́рживаться пра́вил/реше́ния (*impf*); **I ~ by what I said** я остаю́сь ве́рным тому́, что сказа́л.

ability *n* спосо́бность (*often pl*); **he has great ~ in mathematics** у него́ больши́е спосо́бности к матема́тике (*sing*); **to the best of my ~** по ме́ре свои́х сил и возмо́жностей; *Comm* **~ to pay** платёжеспосо́бность.

abject *adj* жа́лкий; **an ~ apology** жа́лкие извине́ния (*pl*); **~ poverty** нищета́.

ablative *n Gram* твори́тельный паде́ж.

ablaze *predic adj and adv*: **the house was ~ in five minutes** че́рез пять мину́т дом уже́ пыла́л; **they set the barn ~** они́ подпали́ли амбáр; *fig*: **the streets were ~ with lights** ýлицы бы́ли я́рко освещены́; **the garden was ~ with colour** сад полыхáл всéми крáсками (*pl*); **her eyes were ~ with excitement/with anger** её глазá блестéли от возбуждéния/сверкáли гнéвом.

able *adj* **1** спосóбный; (*with one's hands*) умéлый; **an ~ student** спосóбный студéнт; **an ~ carpenter** умéлый плóтник; **an ~ piece of work** талáнтливо сделанная/талáнтливая рабóта

2 to be ~ to + *inf*: **i)** (*can*): **are you ~ to come?** ты мóжешь прийти́?; **I escaped as soon as I was ~** я убежáл, как тóлько появи́лась возмóжность; **ii)** (*know how to*) умéть; **she is ~ to drive now** онá тепéрь умéет води́ть маши́ну.

able-bodied *adj*: **an ~ seaman** матрóс пéрвой статьи́.

ably *adv* умéло, искýсно.

abnormal *adj* ненормáльный, *Med* анормáльный.

aboard *adv*: **he's already ~** он ужé на бортý; **to go ~ a ship** сади́ться на корáбль, поднимáться на борт (корабля́); **to go ~ a plane** сади́ться в самолёт; (*US*) **to go ~ a train/a coach** сади́ться в *or* на пóезд/в автóбус; **all ~!** посáдка начинáется!; **welcome ~!** добрó пожáловать!

abolish *vt* отмен|я́ть (-и́ть); **to ~ slavery** отмени́ть/уничтóж|ить рáбство (*impf* -áть); **to ~ an old custom** упраздн|я́ть стáрый обы́чай (-и́ть).

A-bomb *n* áтомная бóмба.

abominable *adj* отврати́тельный; мéрзкий; **~ weather** отврати́тельная/мéрзкая погóда; **the food here is ~** здесь плóхо кóрмят, *CQ* здесь отврати́тельная едá.

abomination *n*: *CQ* **the new concert hall is an ~** э́тот нóвый концéртный зал прóсто ýжас.

aboriginal *adj* тузéмный, коореннóй.

abortion *n* абóрт; **she got an ~** ей сдéлали абóрт, онá сдéлала абóрт.

abortive *adj fig*: **an ~ plan** неудáчный план; **our attempt was ~** нáша попы́тка не удалáсь, *CQ* мы старáлись впустýю (*adv*).

abound *vi* изоби́ловать + *I* (*impf*); **the sea ~s in fish, fish ~ in the sea** мóре изоби́лует ры́бой.

about *adv* **1** (*approximately*) приблизи́тельно, примéрно; **~ as high as that tree** высотóй приблизи́тельно как/с э́то дéрево; **my coat is ~ your size** моё пальтó примéрно вáшего размéра; **on or ~ the fifth of May** приблизи́тельно пя́того мáя; **he walked ~ three miles** он прошёл ми́ли три [**NB** "*about*" *shown by inversion of noun and numeral*]; **it's ~ six o'clock now** сейчáс навéрно часóв шесть; *CQ*: **I've had just ~ enough** мне (э́того) вполнé достáточно; **it's ~ time you stopped nattering** хвáтит тебé болтáть; **that's ~ the size of it** вот к чемý э́то свóдится; **that's ~ it/right** э́то подойдёт, э́то то, что нáдо

2 (*of place*): **all ~** … **I dropped the key somewhere ~ here** я … здесь урони́л ключ; **don't leave your toy**… не разбрá-сывай свои́ игрýшки; *fig* … **the other way ~** нет, как раз наобо…

3 (*with verbs*): **i)**: **there we**… **~ on the grass** на травé сид… *also verbs* + **about; ii)** *the perfe*… *indet verbs of motion conveys* …ing "*about*" *in the inf and past tense*: … **want to run ~ in the garden** дéти … бéгать в садý/по сáду; **we drove ~** … **town in the morning** ýтром мы поéзд… гóроду; **iii)** *with verb "to be"*: **is Sash**… Сáша здесь?; **he must be ~ somewhere** … дóлжен быть гдé-то здесь; **there's a lot** … **flu ~ just now** сейчáс повсю́ду (хóдит) грипп… **to be ~ again** (*after illness*) быть опя́ть на ногáх; **iv) to be ~ to** + *inf* собирáться + *inf*; **I was ~ to say that...** я как раз собирáлся сказáть, что...; **I was just ~ to leave when he arrived** тóлько что я собрáлся уходи́ть, как он пришёл.

about *prep* **1** (*of place*) по + *D*; **to walk ~ the town** ходи́ть по гóроду; **to do jobs ~ the house** дéлать рабóту (*sing*) по дóму; **I've no money ~ me** у меня́ с собóй нет дéнег

2 *various*: **there's something strange ~ him** он какóй-то стрáнный; **while you're ~ it, could you also bring my spectacles?** поскóльку ты там, заоднó принеси́ мне мои́ очки́; **what are you ~?** что э́то ты задýмал?; **mind what you're ~!** смотри́, что ты дéлаешь!; *CQ* **and ~ time too!** и давнó порá!

3 (*concerning*) о + *P*, из-за + *G*; **tell me all ~ him** расскажи́ мне всё о нём; **they quarrelled ~ money** они́ поссóрились/*CQ* поругáлись из-за дéнег; **how ~ me?** а как же я?; **what ~ it?** (*what of it?*) ну и чтó (из э́того)?, (*what do you say to this?*) ну чтó ты на э́то скáжешь?; **what's all this ~?** в чём дéло?; **what's he so angry ~?** почемý он такóй серди́тый?; **what can I do ~ it?** что я могý подéлать?; **we've got to do smth ~ it** так э́то нельзя́ остáвить; **I came ~ the job** я пришёл по пóводу/насчёт э́той рабóты; **what ~ a song?** давáйте споём чтó-нибудь.

about-face *n fig*: **he did a complete ~** он пóлностью измени́л свою́ пози́цию.

above *adv* наверхý, вы́ше; **the room ~** кóмната наверхý; **as stated ~** как скáзано вы́ше.

above *prep* **1** (*of place*: *over*) над + *I*; (*higher than*) вы́ше + *G*; **~ the horizon** над горизóнтом; **~ sea level** над ýровнем/вы́ше ýровня мóря; **the water came ~ his knees** водá былá емý вы́ше колéн; *fig*: **he is ~ me in rank** он вы́ше меня́ по чи́ну/чи́ном; **that is ~ my head** э́то вы́ше моегó понимáния; **I couldn't hear a word ~ the din** я не расслы́шал ни еди́ного слóва из-за шýма; **she thinks she's ~ doing housework** онá считáет, что рабóта по дóму не для неё; **he is not ~ a bit of blackmail** он инóй раз не гнушáется и шантажо́м; **he is not ~ suspicion** не исключено́, что он винова́т; **I'm not ~ accepting help** я не про́тив, что́бы мне помогли́

2 (*greater, more than*): **the temperature is ~ average today** сего́дня температу́ра вы́ше сре́дней; **there were not ~ twenty people there** там бы́ло не бо́льше двадцати́ челове́к.

aboveboard *adj* откры́тый, че́стный; прямо́й; **it's all plain and ~** э́то всё де́лается че́стно и в откры́тую.

above-mentioned *adj* вышеупомя́нутый.

abrasion *n* (*action*) тре́ние; (*on skin*) сса́дина.

abreast *adv*: **the battleship came ~ of the steamer** линко́р поравня́лся с парохо́дом; *Mil* **to march four ~** марширова́ть в коло́нне по четы́ре; *fig*: **he keeps ~ of the times** он идёт в но́гу со вре́менем; **he keeps ~ of the latest scientific developments** он в ку́рсе после́дних достиже́ний нау́ки.

abridge *vt* сокра|ща́ть (-ти́ть); **an ~d edition** сокращённое изда́ние.

abroad *adv* **1: he lived/travelled ~ for many years** он мно́го лет жил/ча́сто быва́л за грани́цей; **to go ~** е́хать за грани́цу; **visitors from ~** го́сти из-за грани́цы; **people ~ think...** за грани́цей ду́мают, что...

2 (*about*): **there were not many people ~ at that early hour** в э́тот ра́нний час на у́лице бы́ло малолю́дно; **there is a rumour ~ that...** хо́дит слух, что...

abrogate *vt Law* отмен|я́ть (-и́ть), аннули́ровать (*impf and pf*).

abrupt *adj* круто́й, ре́зкий; **an ~ turn in the road** круто́й поворо́т доро́ги; **~ manners** ре́зкие мане́ры; **he was very ~ with me** он был о́чень ре́зок со мной.

abruptly *adv* (*sharply*) ре́зко; (*suddenly*) **he left ~** он внеза́пно вы́шел.

abscess *n* нары́в, абсце́сс.

abscond *vi*: **he ~ed with the cash** он скры́лся/сбежа́л, прихвати́в (с собо́й) де́ньги.

absence *n* отсу́тствие; (*absenteeism, truancy*) прогу́л; **in his ~** в его́ отсу́тствие; **in the ~ of evidence** за отсу́тствием ули́к (*pl*); **~ from a meeting/from court** нея́вка на собра́ние/в суд; **~ from work/school due to illness** невы́ход на рабо́ту/про́пуск заня́тий (*pl*) по боле́зни; *Mil*: **leave of ~** о́тпуск, (*for a few hours*) увольне́ние; **~ without leave** самово́льная отлу́чка; *fig* **~ of mind** рассе́янность.

absent *adj* **1** *attr* отсу́тствующий, *also fig*; **~ friends** отсу́тствующие друзья́; **an ~ look** отсу́тствующий взгляд

2 *predic*: **to be ~ from school** отсу́тствовать на уро́ках, пропуска́ть уро́ки; **to be ~ from work** отсу́тствовать на рабо́те, не вы́йти на рабо́ту, (*of absenteeism, truancy*) прогуля́ть; **he was ~ from the meeting** он отсу́тствовал на собра́нии, он не яви́лся на собра́ние; *Mil* **to be ~ on leave** находи́ться в о́тпуске/(*for a few hours*) в увольне́нии.

absentee *n* отсу́тствующий; (*without leave or good reason*) прогу́льщик.

absenteeism *n* прогу́л.

absent-minded *adj* рассе́янный.

absolute *adj* абсолю́тный; по́лный, соверше́нный; **an ~ majority** абсолю́тное большинство́; **~ proof** бесспо́рное/несомне́нное доказа́тельство; *CQ*: **the man's an ~ idiot** он по́лный идио́т; **that's ~ rubbish** э́то соверше́ннейшая чушь; **it's an ~ scandal** э́то про́сто сканда́л.

absolutely *adv*: **it is ~ forbidden to...** категори́чески запреща́ется + *inf*...; **I deny it ~** я категори́чески/по́лностью отрица́ю э́то; *CQ*: (*as answer*) **~!** коне́чно!, безусло́вно!; **~ right!** соверше́нно ве́рно!; **he ~ refused to do it** он наотре́з отказа́лся э́то сде́лать.

absolve *vt*: **I ~ you from your promise** я освобожда́ю вас от ва́шего обеща́ния; **I ~ you from all blame** я вас ни в чём не виню́; *Law* **the court ~d him from guilt** суд оправда́л его́.

absorb *vt* погло|ща́ть (-ти́ть), впи́т|ывать (-а́ть); **a sponge ~s water** гу́бка поглоща́ет/впи́тывает во́ду; *fig* **he is ~ed in his book/in his work/in thought** он поглощён кни́гой, он весь в рабо́те, он погружён в размышле́ния (*pl*).

absorbent *adj*: **cotton wool is ~** ва́та хорошо́ впи́тывает жи́дкость.

absorbing *adj fig*: **I find history a most ~ subject** для меня́ исто́рия—увлека́тельнейший предме́т.

abstain *vi*: **to ~ from smoking/voting** возде́рж|иваться от куре́ния/от голосова́ния (-а́ться).

abstainer *n*: (*from alcohol*) **a total ~** тре́звенник.

abstemious *adj* уме́ренный, возде́ржанный; **he's ~ over food and drink** он уме́рен/возде́ржан в еде́ и питье́.

abstention *n*: **6 votes for, 3 against and 2 ~s** шесть голосо́в «за», три «про́тив» и два воздержа́вшихся; **the bill was carried with 2 ~s** зако́н был при́нят при двух воздержа́вшихся.

abstract *n* (*summary*) кра́ткий обзо́р; *Philos* **in the ~** в абстра́кции.

abstract *adj* абстра́ктный, *also Art, Gram.*

abstract *vt* извле|ка́ть (ʹчь); **to ~ iron from ore/a paper from a file** извлека́ть желе́зо из руды́, извлека́ть докуме́нт из подши́вки.

abstracted *adj* (*absent-minded*) рассе́янный.

abstraction *n* **1** абстра́кция

2 (*absent-mindedness*) рассе́янность; **with an air of ~** с рассе́янным ви́дом.

abstruse *adj* (*obscure*) нея́сный, малопоня́тный; (*profound*) глубо́кий.

absurd *adj* неле́пый, абсу́рдный; **you look ~ in that hat** ты неле́по/смешно́ вы́глядишь в э́той шля́пе; **what an ~ suggestion!** како́е неле́пое/абсу́рдное предложе́ние!; **how ~!** кака́я неле́пость!, како́й вздор!

abundance *n* изоби́лие; **there is an ~ of fruit in the market just now** сейча́с на ры́нке изоби́лие фру́ктов; **food and drink in ~** еды́ и питья́ вдо́воль (*adv*) [**NB** *G case*].

abundant *adj* оби́льный; **an ~ harvest** оби́льный урожа́й; **a land ~ in minerals** земля́, бога́тая поле́зными ископа́емыми; **we have ~ proof of his guilt** у нас (име́ется) мно́го доказа́тельств (*pl*) его́ вины́.

abuse *n* **1** (*bad language*) ру́гань; (*insulting language*) оскорбле́ние; **he was greeted with a stream of ~** на него́ обру́шился пото́к ру́гани/оскорбле́ний (*pl*)

2 (*misuse*) злоупотребле́ние + *I*; **an ~ of trust** злоупотребле́ние дове́рием; **to put an end to ~s** поко́нчить с злоупотребле́ниями.

abuse *vt* **1** (*scold*) руга́ть + *A* (*pfs* вы́-, от-); (*curse*) обруга́ть (*pf*); **he ~d his secretary for the mistake** он отруга́л секрета́ршу за оши́бку

2 (*misuse*) злоупотреб|ля́ть + *I* (-и́ть); **to ~ one's authority/smb's kindness** злоупотреби́ть свое́й вла́стью/чьей-л добroто́й.

abusive *adj* оскорби́тельный, бра́нный; **an ~ article** оскорби́тельная статья́; **~ language** брань, ру́гань, руга́тельства (*pl*); **he became ~** он стал руга́ться.

abysmal *adj fig*: **~ ignorance** вопию́щее/полне́йшее неве́жество; *CQ* **the play was ~** пье́са была́ чудо́вищно безда́рной.

abysmally *adv fig*, *CQ*: **to fail ~** безнадёжно провали́ться.

abyss *n* бе́здна, *also fig.*

academic *n* учёный.

academic *adj* **1** академи́ческий; **the ~ year** академи́ческий год

2 (*theoretical*) академи́ческий, академи́чный; **the question is entirely ~** э́то вопро́с чи́сто академи́ческий; **his approach is too ~** у него́ сли́шком академи́чный подхо́д.

academician *n* (*SU*) акаде́мик.

academy *n* акаде́мия; (*in Scotland*) шко́ла; **military ~** вое́нная акаде́мия; (*UK*) **the Royal A. of Arts** Короле́вская акаде́мия худо́жеств; (*SU*) **the A. of Sciences** Акаде́мия нау́к.

accelerate *vti vt* ускор|я́ть (-́ить); **the pace of the work was ~d** темп рабо́ты уско́рился, рабо́та пошла́ уско́ренным те́мпом

vi **1** (*of machines*) ускоря́ть ход; на|бира́ть ско́рость (-бра́ть), прибав|ля́ть ско́рость/ход/*CQ* хо́ду (-́ить); (*of stationary machines*: *to "rev up"*) увели́чивать/набира́ть оборо́ты; **the train ~d** по́езд уско́рил ход; **the car ~d to overtake the bus** маши́на приба́вила ско́рости, что́бы обогна́ть авто́бус; **the aeroplane ~d down the runway** самолёт набира́л ско́рость на взлётной полосе́

2 (*of runners*, *drivers*) увели́чи|вать ско́рость (-ть); **the runner ~d on the bend** на поворо́те бегу́н увели́чил ско́рость; *Aut* **I ~d up the hill** я увели́чил ско́рость/*CQ* я приба́вил га́зу на подъёме; *CQ* **~ a bit before you start** дай газ пе́ред тем, как е́хать.

acceleration *n* ускоре́ние; разго́н; **this car has good ~** э́та маши́на бы́стро набира́ет ско́рость.

accelerator *n Aut* акселера́тор; *attr*: **~ pedal** педа́ль акселера́тора.

accent *n* (*of a dialect or of a foreign accent*) акце́нт, *also Mus*; *Ling* ударе́ние; **to speak with a Scottish ~** говори́ть с шотла́ндским акце́нтом.

accent *vt Ling* де́лать ударе́ние (с-); **~ the last syllable** (*in speech*) сде́лайте ударе́ние/(*in writing*) поста́вьте ударе́ние на после́днем сло́ге.

accentuate *vt* под|чёркивать (-черкну́ть).

accept *vt* при|нима́ть (-ня́ть); **to ~ a present/an invitation/delivery of goods** принима́ть пода́рок/приглаше́ние/това́ры; **it is ~ed that...** так при́нято, что...; **I ~ that the proposed motion will be divisive** я допуска́ю, что предложе́ние вы́зовет разногла́сия; **he is ~ed as one of us** мы счита́ем его́ свои́м.

acceptable *adj* прие́млемый; **if the proposal is ~ to you** е́сли предложе́ние прие́млемо для вас/вас устра́ивает; **thank you, tea would be very ~** спаси́бо, от ча́я не откажу́сь; **a book is always an ~ gift** кни́га — хоро́ший пода́рок.

acceptance *n*: **we've had ten ~s for the reception** де́сять челове́к при́няли приглаше́ние на приём

accepted *adj*: **nowadays it's the ~ thing that women wear trousers** сейча́с при́нято, что́бы же́нщины носи́ли брю́ки; **he's the ~ expert in this field** он при́знанный авторите́т в э́той о́бласти.

access *n* **1** (*to a place*) подхо́д к + *D*; (*to people*, *things*) до́ступ к + *D*; **I have ~ to the archives** я получи́л до́ступ к архи́вам; **there's no ~ to the yard from this street** с э́той у́лицы во двор не попадёшь; **this door gives ~ to the garden** э́та дверь ведёт в сад; **he has direct ~ to the Minister** он име́ет пра́во входи́ть к мини́стру без докла́да

2 *Med* при́ступ, *also fig*; **an ~ of coughing/of rage** при́ступ ка́шля/гне́ва.

accessible *adj* досту́пный; **the archives are ~ to students** архи́вы досту́пны для студе́нтов; **our dacha is not ~ by car** к на́шей да́че на маши́не не подъе́дешь; **he is always ~** к нему́ всегда́ попадёшь.

accession *n*: **~ to the throne** вступле́ние на престо́л; **after his ~ to his uncle's estate** вступи́в во владе́ние име́нием дя́ди; **recent ~s to the library include...** но́вые поступле́ния в библиоте́ку включа́ют...

accessory *n* **1** *Law*: **an ~ to a crime** соуча́стник преступле́ния **2** *pl* (**accessories**) принадле́жности, аксессуа́ры.

accident *n* **1** (*chance*) слу́чай, случа́йность; **I came across him by ~** я случа́йно встре́тил его́; **I'm sorry — it was an ~** извини́те, я сде́лал э́то не наро́чно

2 (*misfortune*) несча́стный слу́чай; *Rail*, *Aut*, *Aer* ава́рия; *Rail* (*implying fatalities*) круше́ние; **he met with a climbing ~** с ним произошёл несча́стный слу́чай при восхожде́-

нии; **he broke his leg in a skiing ~** он сломáл нóгу, катáясь на лы́жах; **the scene of the ~** мéсто авáрии; **she had a bad ~ in her car** онá попáла в автомоби́льную катастрóфу; *CQ* **I've had an ~ in the kitchen—I dropped six glasses** я разби́л на кýхне срáзу полдю́жины стакáнов—такáя неприя́тность!

accidental *adj* случáйный.

accidentally *adv* (*by chance*) случáйно; (*unintentionally*) ненарóком.

accident-prone *adj*: **he's ~** с ним вéчно приключáются каки́е-нибудь несчáстья.

acclaim *n*: **the play received great ~ from the critics** пьéса былá с восторгом встрéчена кри́тикой (*collect*).

acclamation *n*: **the cosmonauts drove through Moscow amid the ~ of the crowds** космонáвтов, éхавших по ýлицам Москвы́, востóрженно привéтствовали жи́тели столи́цы.

acclimatize *vt* акклиматизи́ровать (*impf and pf*); **to become ~d** акклиматизи́роваться.

accomodate *vt* **1** (*put up*: *for large party*) разме|щáть (-сти́ть); (*for individuals*) поме|щáть (-сти́ть), устр|áивать (-óить); **the delegates were ~d in hotels** делегáтов размести́ли по гости́ницам; **to ~ a guest in a spare room** помести́ть гóстя в отдéльной кóмнате; **I was ~d in a hotel** меня́ устрóили в гости́нице; *CQ* **I can ~ him for a night in my flat** я могý приюти́ть егó на однý ночь у себя́

2 (*hold*) вме|щáть (-сти́ть); **the hall ~s/can ~ 500 people** зал вмещáет пятьсóт человéк

3 (*supply*): **the bank ~d me with a loan of £100** банк предостáвил мне ссýду в сто фýнтов

4 (*adapt*): **I'll ~ my plans to yours/to fit in with yours** я согласýю свои́ плáны с вáшими; **you'll have to ~ yourself to these conditions** тебé придётся приспосóбиться к э́тим услóвиям

5 (*oblige*): **we always try to ~ our clients** мы старáемся всегдá услужи́ть свои́м клиéнтам.

accomodation *n* **1** помещéние; **there's good ~ for the workers near the factory** для рабóчих пострóены хорóшие домá недалекó от завóда; **I hope to find ~ in a hotel** надéюсь устрóиться в гости́нице; **hotel ~ is scarce here in summer** лéтом здесь не хватáет гости́ниц; **the hotel has ~ for 200 guests** в гости́нице мóжет размести́ться двéсти человéк; **~ is expensive here** кварти́ры/гости́ницы здесь дороги́е

2 (*compromise*): **to come to an ~ with smb** прийти́ к соглашéнию с кем-л.

accompaniment *n Mus* сопровождéние, аккомпанемéнт; **he sang to the ~ of the guitar** он пел под гитáру; *fig* **he finished his speech to the ~ of loud jeers** он закóнчил речь, осыпáемый грáдом насмéшек.

accompanist *n* аккомпаниáтор.

accompany *vt* (*escort*) сопрово|ждáть (-ди́ть); *Mus* аккомпани́ровать + *D*; **accompanied by my brother** в сопровождéнии моегó брáта; **to ~ a singer on the piano** аккомпани́ровать певцý на роя́ле.

accomplice *n*: **an ~ (in a crime)** соучáстник (преступлéния).

accomplish *vt* вы|полня́ть (-́полнить), соверш|áть (-и́ть); **he ~ed in a week what others do in a month** он сдéлал за недéлю то, что у други́х зáняло бы мéсяц; **he ~ed his object** он дости́г своéй цéли.

accomplished *adj* прекрáсный, великолéпный; **an ~ violinist** прекрáсный скрипáч; **he gave an ~ rendering of the Moonlight Sonata** он великолéпно испóлнил «Лýнную сонáту».

accomplishment *n* (*completion*) выполнéние, завершéние; (*achievement*) достижéние; (*artistic and social skills*; *usu pl*) достóинства; **she's a girl of many ~s** онá обладáет мнóгими достóинствами; *CQ* **it's quite an ~ to persuade him to change his mind** вы сдéлали вели́кое дéло—уговори́ли егó измени́ть решéние.

accord *n* (*agreement*) соглáсие; **with one ~** единодýшно, единоглáсно; **of one's own ~** по сóбственной вóле; **the students of their own ~ contributed to the fund for the victims of the fire** студéнты добровóльно сóбрали дéньги для пóмощи пострадáвшим от пожáра; **the little boy brought me a flower of his own ~** малы́ш сам догадáлся преподнести́ мне цветóк; **the problem won't go away of its own ~** проблéма самá собóй не реши́тся.

accord *vti vt*: **they were ~ed the right to vote** им бы́ло предостáвлено прáво голосовáния; **he was ~ed a warm welcome** емý был окáзан тёплый приём

vi согласовáться (*impf*); **what you say now does not ~ with what you said before** вáши словá расхóдятся с тем, что вы говори́ли рáньше.

accordance *n*: **in ~ with** в соотвéтствии с + *I*.

accordingly *adv* поэ́тому, соотвéтственно; **she has had a baby and ~ had to leave her job** у неё мáленький ребёнок, поэ́тому ей пришлóсь остáвить рабóту; **you've been told to be strict and you must act ~** вам скáзано, что необходи́ма стрóгость—поступáйте соотвéтственно.

according to *prep* по + *D*; *more off* соглáсно + *D*; **~ him** по егó словáм; **the books are arranged ~ subject** кни́ги расстáвлены по тéмам; **~ the newspapers/instructions** соглáсно сообщéниям газéт/инстрýкции (*sing*); **~ the treaty** в соотвéтствии с договóром.

accordion *n* аккордеóн.

accost *vt*: **to ~ smb** приста|вáть к комý-л (-́ть); **he ~ed me in the corridor** он пристáл ко мне/поймáл меня́ в коридóре.

account *n* **1** *Fin* счёт (*nom pl* счетá, *when fig* счёты); **current/bank/joint ~** текýщий/бáнковский/óбщий счёт; **to open/close an ~ with a shop/bank** откры́ть/закры́ть счёт в магазúне/в бáнке; **put it down to my ~** запишúте это на мой счёт; **to keep ~s** вестú счетá; **the garage has sent in my ~** мне прислáли счёт из гаражá; **~ rendered** счёт, предъявленный к оплáте; **I've settled ~s with my tailor** я расплатúлся с портным; *fig*: **to settle ~s with smb** сводúть счёты с кем-л; **he turned the occasion to good ~** он сумéл воспóльзоваться слýчаем; *attr*: **~s department** бухгалтéрия

2 (*report*) отчёт; **he gave an ~ of what he had done** он дал отчёт о своúх дéйствиях; **according to the ~ in the papers** по сообщéниям (*pl*) газéт; **she gave an amusing ~ of the incident** онá так забáвно описáла этот слýчай; **by all ~s he was at fault** по мнéнию всех был виновáт он; **by his own ~ he was not speeding** по егó словáм, он не превышáл скóрости; *fig* **he gave a good ~ of himself in the oral examination** он произвёл хорóшее впечатлéние на экзáмене

3 (*consideration, importance*): **to take smth into ~** принимáть что-л во внимáние/в расчёт, учúтывать что-л; **it's of no ~** это не имéет значéния

4 (*reason*): **on this ~** по этой причúне; **on no ~** ни в кóем слýчае, никóим óбразом; **on ~ of** (*because of*) из-за + *G*, (*for the sake of*) рáди + *G*.

account *vt* (*consider*) считáть (счесть); **he is generally ~ed a coward** все считáют егó трýсом; **I should ~ it a great favour if...** я счёл бы велúким одолжéнием с вáшей стороны́, éсли бы...

account for *vti vt*: **three people have not been ~ed for** не досчитáлись трёх человéк/троúх.

vi (*explain*) объясн|ять (-úть); (*justify*) отчúт|ываться (-áться); **that ~s for his absence** это объясняет егó отсýтствие; **I will have to ~ to my father for the money I've spent** я дóлжен бýду отчитáться пéред отцóм за истрáченные дéньги.

accountable *adj*: **I will be held ~ for this** мне придётся за это отвечáть; **I am ~ to the director for the work of the department** я отчúтываюсь пéред дирéктором за рабóту отдéла.

accountancy *n* бухгáлтерское дéло; **he has gone in for ~** он стал бухгáлтером.

accountant *n* бухгáлтер.

account book *n* бухгáлтерская кнúга.

accredited *adj*: **he is the ~ representative** он аккредитóванный представúтель (*m*).

accrue *vi* (*of interest*) нараст|áть (-ú); **how much interest has ~d on my account?** скóлько у меня наросло процéнтов?; **~d interest** нарóсшие процéнты (*pl*).

accumulate *vti vt* на|кáпливать (-копúть); **to ~ knowledge/a mass of facts/debts** накáпливать знáния (*pl*)/большóй фактúческий материáл/долгú

vi накáпливаться; (*of interest*) нараст|áть (-ú); **dust soon ~s** пыль бы́стро накáпливается; **interest ~s slowly** процéнты (*pl*) нарастáют мéдленно.

accumulator *n Elec* аккумулятор.

accuracy *n* тóчность; (*in shooting*) мéткость.

accurate *adj* тóчный; (*in shooting*) мéткий; **he is ~ in his work** он тóчен в рабóте; **are your scales ~?** у вас тóчные весы́?; **he is always ~ in his use of words** он привы́к тóчно выражáться.

accursed, accurst *adj* прóклятый.

accusation *n* обвинéние; **to bring/make an ~ against smb** вы́двинуть обвинéние прóтив когó-л.

accusative *n Gram* винúтельный падéж.

accuse *vt* обвин|ять (-úть); **to ~ smb of a crime** обвинúть когó-л в преступлéнии; **she was ~d of taking money** её обвинúли в крáже дéнег.

accused *n Law* (**the ~**) обвиняемый; (*in court*) подсудúмый.

accuser *n* обвинúтель (*m*).

accustom *vt usu pass or reflex* привык|áть (-нуть); (*train oneself*) приуч|áться (-úться); **I'm not ~ed to a late dinner/to dining so late** я не привы́к так пóздно обéдать; **he's not ~ed to criticism/to being criticized** он не привы́к к крúтике; **I've ~ed myself to live/to living in cold rooms** я приучúл себя жить в хóлоде; **this is not the treatment to which I am ~ed** я к такóму обращéнию не привы́к.

ace *n Cards* туз; (*on dice*) однó очкó; **the ~ of trumps** козырнóй туз; *fig* **to be within an ~ of** быть на волосóк от + *G*; *CQ* **he's an ~ (pilot)** он ас.

acetic acid *n* ýксусная кислотá.

ache *n* боль; **I'm all ~s and pains** у меня всё болúт.

ache *vi* болéть (*impf*); **my head/ear ~s** у меня болúт головá/ýхо; **my heart ~s for her** у меня за неё душá болúт; *CQ* **I'm aching for the holidays** я жду не дождýсь óтпуска.

achieve *vt* дости|гáть + *G* (-́чь); (*of more abstract achievements*) доби|вáться + *G* (-́ться); **he ~d his objective** он достúг своéй цéли; **to ~ success/recognition** добúться успéха/признáния; **he'll never ~ anything** он никогдá ничегó не добьётся.

achievement *n* достижéние.

aching *adj*: **an ~ tooth/back** больнóй зуб, больнáя спинá; **~ limbs** устáлые члéны; *fig* **with an ~ heart** с тяжёлым сéрдцем.

acid *n* кислотá.

acid *adj* кúслый; *fig* **to pass ~ remarks** говорúть кóлкости.

acidity *n* кислотá; кислóтность, *also Med.*

acknowledge *vt* призна|вáть (-́ть); **he ~d his guilt/mistake** он признáл свою винý/ошúбку; **he ~d him as his heir** он признáл егó своúм наслéдником; **they ~d his services by a handsome gift** егó отблагодарúли за услýги дорогúм подáрком; **nowadays they don't even ~ us** тепéрь онú нас дáже/и знать не хотят.

acknowledged *adj* при́знанный.

acknowledgement *n*: **I've had no ~ of my letter** они́ не подтверди́ли получе́ния моего́ письма́; **they gave us a painting in ~ of our help** в благода́рность за ока́занную по́мощь они́ подари́ли нам карти́ну; **these flowers are a small ~ of your kindness** э́ти цветы́—знак призна́тельности за ва́шу доброту́.

acoustics *npl* аку́стика (*sing*).

acquaint *vt* **1** знако́мить (*pfs*: *with facts* о-, *with people or facts* по-); **he ~ed me with the details of the affair** он ознако́мил меня́ с подро́бностями э́того де́ла

2 *pass or reflex*: **I am ~ed with him** я с ним знако́м; **we are already ~ed** мы уже знако́мы; **I'd like you two to be ~ed** я хоте́л бы вас познако́мить; **I have ~ed myself with the outlines of the case** я ознако́мился с де́лом в о́бщих черта́х.

acquaintance *n* **1** (*person*) знако́мый; **he has a wide circle of ~s** у него́ большо́й круг знако́мых, у него́ широ́кий круг знако́мств

2 (*knowledge of people or facts*) знако́мство с + *I*; **do you know her?—Not really, I've just a nodding ~ with her** ты зна́ешь её?—Нет, про́сто ша́почное знако́мство; **to make smb's ~** познако́миться с кем-л.

acquiesce *vi* уступ|а́ть (-и́ть); **I reluctantly ~d in their arrangement** я неохо́тно уступи́л им в э́том.

acquire *vt* приобре|та́ть (-сти́); **to ~ a habit/new friends/a reputation for wit** приобрести́ привы́чку/но́вых друзе́й/репута́цию остряка́; **the word has ~d a new meaning** сло́во приобрело́ но́вое значе́ние; *joc* **I've just ~d a new grandchild** у меня́ неда́вно появи́лся внук.

acquisition *n* приобрете́ние; **there have been some valuable ~s to the museum** музе́й попо́лнился це́нными приобрете́ниями/экспона́тами.

acquisitive *adj*: **an ~ nature** скло́нность к приобрета́тельству; *joc* **my son is very ~—a regular magpie** мой сын та́щит домо́й всё подря́д, как соро́ка.

acquit *vt* **1** *Law*: **to ~ smb** оправда́ть кого́-л (*only in pf*); **he was ~ted of two of the charges** по э́тим двум пу́нктам он был при́знан невино́вным

2: **he ~ted himself well in the first round of the competition/in the interview** он хорошо́ вы́ступил в пе́рвом ту́ре ко́нкурса, с ним была́ бесе́да—он произвёл хоро́шее впечатле́ние.

acquittal *n Law* оправда́ние.

acrid *adj* е́дкий, *also fig*.

acrimonious *adj* язви́тельный.

acrobat *n* акроба́т.

acrobatics *npl* акроба́тика (*sing*); *Aer* возду́шная акроба́тика.

across *adv* **1** (*crosswise*) попере́к; (*in width*) в ширину́; (*in diameter*) в диа́метре, в попере́чнике; (*of crossword clues*) по горизонта́ли; **the lake is more than a mile ~** о́зеро бо́льше ми́ли в ширину́

2 (*of position, movement*): **he came ~ to speak to me** он подошёл поговори́ть со мной; **he is already ~** (*on far side*) он уже́ на той стороне́; **he lives just ~ from us** он живёт как раз напро́тив нас

3 *with verbs, often translated by prefix* пере-: **to walk/drive/swim** *or* **sail ~** перейти́, перее́хать, переплы́ть.

across *prep* **1** (*to the other side*) че́рез + *A*; **a bridge ~ the river** мост че́рез ре́ку; *often translated by prefix* пере- *with verbs*: **to swim ~ a river** переплы́ть (че́рез) ре́ку; **to drive ~ the frontier** перее́хать грани́цу; **he ran ~ the street** он перебежа́л (че́рез) у́лицу; **to fly ~ Canada** пролете́ть над Кана́дой

2 (*on or from the other side*): **the bus stop is ~ the street** остано́вка авто́буса че́рез доро́гу; **somebody called me from ~ the street** кто́-то окли́кнул меня́ с друго́й стороны́ у́лицы; **from ~ the sea** из-за мо́ря

3 (*athwart*): **a tree lay ~ the road** попере́к доро́ги лежа́ло де́рево.

act *n* **1** (*deed*) посту́пок; **a bold ~** сме́лый посту́пок; **an ~ of God** стихи́йное бе́дствие; **to catch smb in the ~** пойма́ть кого́-л с поли́чным; **he fell in the ~ of ascending the steps** он упа́л, поднима́ясь по ле́стнице

2 *Theat* де́йствие, акт; *fig* **it's just an ~!, she's just putting on an ~!** э́то всего́ лишь игра́!

3 *Law* зако́н, постановле́ние.

act *vti vt Theat* игра́ть (сыгра́ть); **to ~ a part** игра́ть роль; **who ~ed Othello?** кто игра́л Оте́лло?

vi **1** (*take action*) де́йствовать (*only in impf*); поступ|а́ть (-и́ть); **he ~ed decisively** он де́йствовал реши́тельно; **they are ~ing on advice** они́ поступа́ют, как им посове́товали

2 (*behave*) вести́ себя́ (*only in impf*); поступа́ть; **he ~ed wisely** он вёл себя́ у́мно́; **he ~ed like a true friend** он поступи́л, как настоя́щий друг

3 (*function*) де́йствовать (по-; *pf not used of people*); **has the medicine ~ed?** лека́рство поде́йствовало?; **he ~ed for his friend/on his friend's behalf** он де́йствовал от лица́/от и́мени своего́ дру́га; **this wire ~s as a lightning conductor** э́тот про́вод слу́жит громоотво́дом; **he ~ed as director for two months** он исполня́л обя́занности дире́ктора два ме́сяца; **he ~ed as our interpreter** он был у нас за перево́дчика; **he ~ed as intermediary** он игра́л роль посре́дника; **the brakes did not ~** тормоза́ отказа́ли/не срабо́тали

4 *Theat* игра́ть (сыгра́ть); **she had always wanted to ~** она́ мечта́ла стать актри́сой; **have you ever ~ed in a film?** ты когда́-нибудь снима́лся в кино́?

acting *n Theat* игра́.

acting *adj*: **the ~ manager** исполня́ющий обя́занности заве́дующего, *abbr* и.о.; **the ~ director** и.о. дире́ктора.

action *n* **1** (*doing*) де́йствие; **a man of ~** челове́к де́йствия; **collective ~** совме́стные де́йствия (*pl*); **to take** ~ принима́ть ме́ры (*pl*)

2 (*deed*) посту́пок; **to judge people by their ~s** суди́ть о лю́дях по их посту́пкам

3 (*functioning*) *Mech* де́йствие; **to put smth out of ~** выводи́ть что-л из стро́я; **the phone is out of ~** телефо́н не рабо́тает; **the ~ of a watch** де́йствие часово́го механи́зма; *Med*: **the ~ of the heart** де́ятельность се́рдца; **the ~ of the medicine upon the kidneys** де́йствие лека́рства на по́чки; **~ of the bowels** де́ятельность/рабо́та кише́чника (*sing*)

4 *Mil*: **to go into ~** вступа́ть в бой; **to be killed in ~** поги́бнуть в бою́

5 *Law* иск; де́ло; **to bring an ~ against smb** возбуди́ть де́ло/иск про́тив кого́-л.

actionable *adj*: **don't send him that letter—it would be ~** не посыла́й ему́ э́то письмо́—он пода́ст на тебя́ в суд.

activate *vt Chem, Phys* активизи́ровать (*impf and pf*).

active *adj* **1** (*energetic*) энерги́чный, де́ятельный, акти́вный; **an ~ man** энерги́чный/де́ятельный челове́к; **an ~ politician/committee/child** акти́вный полити́ческий де́ятель, акти́вно де́йствующая коми́ссия, живо́й *or* шу́стрый ребёнок; **he's very ~ for his years** он о́чень акти́вен/де́ятелен/подви́жен для свои́х лет; *Gram* **the ~ voice** действи́тельный зало́г

2 (*functioning*): **an ~ law/volcano** де́йствующий зако́н/вулка́н

3 *Mil*: **on ~ service** на действи́тельной слу́жбе.

actively *adv* акти́вно; **he is ~ engaged on this project** он акти́вно рабо́тает над э́тим прое́ктом.

activity *n* акти́вность; *pl* (**activities**) рабо́та, де́ятельность (*sings*); **out-of-school activities** внекла́ссная рабо́та; **his activities were much criticized** его́ де́ятельность/рабо́ту си́льно критикова́ли; **there's a lot of ~ on the site** на площа́дке заме́тно оживле́ние.

actor *n* актёр.

actress *n* актри́са.

actual *adj* действи́тельный; факти́ческий; **what was the ~ price?** какова́ действи́тельная цена́?; **in ~ fact** факти́чески, в действи́тельности; **what were his ~ words?** повтори́ то́чно, что он сказа́л; **let's take an ~ case** дава́й возьмём действи́тельный слу́чай.

actually *adv* на са́мом де́ле; в действи́тельности, факти́чески; **he made out he was ill, but ~ he was quite fit** он притворя́лся больны́м, но на са́мом де́ле был соверше́нно здоро́в; **~ I don't like him** по пра́вде говоря́, я его́ не люблю́; **he ~ struck her** он да́же уда́рил её.

acute *adj* о́стрый, си́льный; **~ hearing** о́стрый слух; **his anxiety was ~** он был си́льно обеспоко́ен; **the situation is becoming ~** ситуа́ция обостря́ется; **an ~ observer** то́нкий наблюда́тель.

adamant *adj fig* твёрдый, непрекло́нный.

adapt *vt* **1** приспоса́бливать, приспособля́ть (*pf for both* приспосо́бить); **to ~ oneself to one's environment** приспоса́бливаться к среде́; **to ~ a building for use as a school** переобору́довать зда́ние под шко́лу (*impf and pf*)

2: **to ~ a text** адапти́ровать текст (*impf and pf*); **to ~ a short story for television** инсцени́ровать расска́з для телеви́дения (*impf and pf*); **the play is ~ed from a novel by Scott** э́то инсцениро́вка рома́на В. Ско́тта.

adaptability *n* приспособля́емость.

adaptable *adj* приспособля́емый; **he is very ~** он легко́ приспоса́бливается к обстоя́тельствам.

adaptation *n* (*of mechanism*) приспособле́ние; (*of organism, text*) адапта́ция; **an ~ of a novel for the stage** инсцениро́вка рома́на.

adapter *n Elec, Radio* ада́птер.

add *vt* добав|ля́ть, прибав|ля́ть (*pfs* -ить); **to ~ salt to the soup/sugar to one's tea/a spoonful of sugar** доба́вить со́ли в суп, положи́ть са́хар в чай/ло́жку са́хара; (*with figures, money*): **to ~ some money/10 roubles to the fund** доба́вить де́нег (*partitive G*)/де́сять рубле́й в фонд; **to ~ 2 and/to 7** к семи́ приба́вить два; (*in writing or speech*): **there's nothing to ~ to what's been said** к ска́занному не́чего доба́вить; **to ~ a few lines at the end of a letter** приписа́ть не́сколько строк в конце́ письма́; **they've ~ed on a wing to the house** они́ пристро́или фли́гель к до́му

add to *vi*: **to ~ to our difficulties** в доверше́ние всех на́ших бед; **this has ~ed to our knowledge of primeval man** э́то расши́рило на́ши зна́ния (*pl*) о первобы́тном челове́ке

add up *vti vt*: **to ~ up figures in a column** скла́дывать чи́сла сто́лбиком (сложи́ть)

vi: **the figures ~ up to 200** э́ти чи́сла в су́мме составля́ют две́сти; *fig CQ*: **it just doesn't ~ up** тут я не ви́жу то́лку; **it all ~s up to saying that he doesn't agree** э́то всё равно́ что сказа́ть, что он не согла́сен; **all these little annoyances do ~ up** все э́ти ма́ленькие неприя́тности выраста́ют в пробле́му.

adder *n Zool* гадю́ка.

addict *n*: **drug ~** наркома́н; **he's a TV ~** его́ не отта́щишь от телеви́зора.

addicted *adj*: **I'm afraid of becoming ~ to tranquillizers** бою́сь, что привы́кну к успока́ивающим табле́ткам и без них не смогу́ обойти́сь; **he is ~ to smoking/football** он пристрасти́лся к куре́нию, он поме́шан на футбо́ле.

addiction *n*: **drug ~** наркома́ния.

addition *n* добавле́ние, прибавле́ние; дополне́ние; *Math* сложе́ние; **an ~ to the family** прибавле́ние семе́йства; **an ~ to the report** дополне́ние к докла́ду; **an ~ to my collection** пополне́ние мое́й колле́кции; **the ~ of salt will improve the flavour of the soup** доба́вьте со́ли, и вкус су́па улу́чшится; **in ~ to his salary he earns a bit on the side** он имéет дополни́тельный зáработок на сторонé; **in ~ may I say...** я бы хотéл вдобáвок сказáть...; **he will be a useful ~ to the faculty** он бýдет полéзным приобретéнием для факультéта.

additional *adj* (*supplementary*) дополни́тельный; (*added*) добáвочный; **~ information** дополни́тельная информáция; **~ expenses/taxes** дополни́тельные расхóды/налóги; **an ~ difficulty** добáвочная трýдность.

addled *adj*: **an ~ egg** тýхлое яйцó.

address *n* **1** (*postal*, *etc.*) áдрес; **give your name and ~** скажи́те вáшу фами́лию и áдрес; **write to my office ~** пиши́те мне на слýжебный áдрес; **letters should be sent to the above ~** пи́сьма слéдует направля́ть по вышеукáзанному áдресу; *attr*: **~ book** áдресная кни́га

2 (*speech*): **to deliver an ~** вы́ступить с обращéнием

3 (*skill*): **with ~** лóвко.

address *vt* **1** (*in speech*) обра|щáться к + *D* (-ти́ться); **complaints should be ~ed to the management** с жáлобами обращáться к администрáции; **he ~ed us on economics** он прочитáл нам лéкцию по экономи́ке (*sing*); **the words were ~ed to her** словá бы́ли адресóваны ей

2 (*in writing*) адресовáть (*impf and pf*); **to ~ a letter/parcel to smb** адресовáть письмó/посы́лку комý-л; **to ~ an envelope** написáть áдрес на конвéрте; **~ the letter to him c/o my brother/ c/o the embassy** посылáйте емý письмó на áдрес моегó брáта/чéрез посóльство.

adduce *vt*: **to ~ reasons/proofs** при|води́ть дóводы/доказáтельства (-вести́).

adenoids *npl* аденóиды.

adept *adj* искýсный; **an ~ dressmaker** искýсная портни́ха; *as n*: **he's an ~ at chess** он талáнтливый шахмати́ст; **he's an ~ at getting his own way** он умéет настоя́ть на своём.

adequate *adj* достáточный; **is his strength ~ to the task?** достáточно ли у негó сил, чтóбы спрáвиться с э́тим?; **his wage is not ~ to support a family** он на свою́ зарплáту не мóжет содержáть семью́; **the repair is not good but it's ~ for just now** ремóнт сдéлан не óчень хорошó, но покá и так лáдно/сойдёт; **he doesn't feel ~ to the task** он не считáет себя́ спосóбным вы́полнить э́ту задáчу.

adhere *vi*: **to ~ to** прилип|áть к + *D* (´-нуть) (*with a sticky substance*), приклé|иваться к + *D* (-иться) (*with glue*); *fig*: **to ~ to a (political) party** быть сторóнником какóй-л пáртии; **to ~ to the rules** придéрживаться прáвил (*impf*).

adhesion *n Med* спáйка.

adhesive *adj* ли́пкий; **~ plaster** лейкоплáстырь; **~ tape** клéйкая лéнта, *CQ* скотч.

ad infinitum *adv* до бесконéчности.

adjacent *adj* (*of rooms*) смéжный, *also Math*; (*of buildings*) примыкáющий; (*of fields*, *etc.*) прилегáющий.

adjective *n Gram* и́мя прилагáтельное.

adjoin *vti vt*: **the playground ~s the school** за шкóлой дéтская площáдка; **this room ~s my study** э́та кóмната смéжная с моúм кабинéтом

vi: **the two houses ~** э́ти два дóма примыкáют друг к дрýгу.

adjourn *vti vt* пере|носи́ть (-нести́); **the meeting has been ~ed till next week** собрáние перенесли́ на слéдующую недéлю

vi: **the meeting ~ed** сегóдняшнее заседáние (*session*) кóнчилось; **the meeting ~ed for lunch** объяви́ли переры́в на обéд; **the guests ~ed to the drawing room** гóсти перешли́ в гости́ную.

adjournment *n* (*postponement*) отсрóчка; (*break*) переры́в; **an ~ for a month** отсрóчка на мéсяц.

adjudicate *vti vt Law*: **to ~ a claim for damages** вы|носи́ть решéние об уплáте убы́тков (´-нести)

vi: **who is adjudicating in this competition?** кто (в) жюри́ э́того кóнкурса?

adjudicator *n* (*in competition*) член жюри́; *pl* (**the ~s**) жюри́ (*indecl*); (*in exam*) экзаменáтор.

adjust *vti vt* (*of hair*, *tie*, *etc.*) поправ|ля́ть (´-ить); (*of mechanisms*, *instruments*) регули́ровать (от-); **to ~ wages** регули́ровать зáработную плáту; **I must ~ my watch** я дóлжен прáвильно постáвить часы́; **to ~ oneself to** приспосáбливаться к + *D*, приспособля́ться к + *D* (*pf for both* приспосóбиться)

vi: **he has ~ed well to the time change** он бы́стро приспосóбился к рáзнице во врéмени.

adjustable *adj* регули́руемый; **an ~ spanner** разводнóй ключ; **~ shelves** раздвижны́е пóлки.

adjustment *n* (*of mechanisms*, *etc.*) регулирóвка, регули́рование; **it takes time to make the necessary ~s when living in a new country** нýжно врéмя, чтóбы приспосóбиться к жи́зни в чужóй странé.

adjutant *n* адъютáнт.

ad lib *adv* по желáнию, как угóдно; **I spoke ~** я говори́л экспрóмтом, *Theat* я импрови-зи́ровал.

administer *vti vt* управля́ть + *I*, руководи́ть + *I* (*impfs*); **to ~ a country** управля́ть странóй; **to ~ a ministry/department** руководи́ть министéрством/отдéлом; **to ~ justice** отправля́ть правосýдие (*only in impf*)

vi: **to ~ to old persons' needs** ухáживать за старикáми (*impf*).

administration *n* (**the ~**) (*government*) прави́тельство, (*of offices*, *hotels*, *etc.*) администрáция; (*process*) управлéние + *I*; (*US*) *Polit* **the Reagan ~** администрáция Рéйгана.

administrative *adj* администрати́вный.

administrator *n* администрáтор.

admirable *adj* превосхóдный; замечáтельный; **he displayed ~ self-control** он прояви́л замеча́тельную вы́держку; **an ~ summary** уда́чное резюме́ (*indecl*).

admiral *n* адмира́л.

admiralty *n* адмиралте́йство; *attr* адмиралте́йский.

admiration *n* восхище́ние, восто́рг; **she was the ~ of all** она́ очарова́ла всех; **I was full of ~ for him** я восхища́лся им.

admire *vt* восхи|ща́ться + *I* (-ти́ться); (*of sights*) любова́ться (по-); **I ~ him for his courage** я восхища́юсь/восхищён его́ му́жеством; **to ~ the view** любова́ться ви́дом; **she was admiring herself in the mirror** она́ любова́лась на себя́ в зе́ркало.

admirer *n* покло́нник; **her ~s** её покло́нники, *CQ* её ухажёры; **I'm a great ~ of his** я его́ большо́й почита́тель.

admissible *adj* допусти́мый; прие́млемый; *Law* **it is ~ evidence** э́то мо́жет быть при́нято в ка́честве показа́ния.

admission *n* **1** (*entry*) вход; **~ free/by ticket** вход свобо́дный/по биле́там; **price of ~** входна́я пла́та; **~ to the University is by examination only** что́бы поступи́ть в университе́т, на́до обяза́тельно сдать экза́мены (*pl*)

2 (*confession*) призна́ние; **an ~ of guilt/defeat** призна́ние вины́/пораже́ния; **that was a damaging ~** э́то призна́ние ему́ повреди́т [**NB** *tense*].

admit *vti vt* **1** (*let in*) впус|ка́ть (-ти́ть); **the audience is not yet being ~ted** зри́телей ещё не впуска́ют; **he has been ~ted to the university** его́ при́няли в университе́т; **we were not ~ted to the lecture** нас не пусти́ли на ле́кцию; **this ticket ~s two** э́то биле́т на два лица́

2 (*allow*) призна|ва́ть (-́ть); допус|ка́ть (-ти́ть); **he did not ~ that he'd been wrong** он не признава́л, что был не прав; **I ~ myself beaten** признаю́ себя́ побеждённым; **it's hard, I ~, but it can be done** допуска́ю, что э́то тру́дно, но сде́лать всё же вполне́ возмо́жно; **it's generally ~ted that...** общепри́знано, что...; **I ~ your claim** я принима́ю ва́ше тре́бование

vi: **I ~ to having made a mistake** я признаю́ свою́ оши́бку; **it ~s of no delay** э́то не те́рпит отлага́тельства; **these words ~ of no other interpretation** э́ти слова́ не допуска́ют друго́го/ино́го толкова́ния.

admittance *n* вход; **no ~** вхо́да нет, вход воспрещён; **I was denied ~** меня́ не впусти́ли.

admittedly *adv*: **~ it's not easy** призна́ться, э́то нелегко́.

admixture *n* при́месь.

ad nauseam *adv* до тошноты́, до отвраще́ния.

ado *n*: **without more ~** сра́зу, без вся́ких разгово́ров; **much ~ about nothing** мно́го шу́ма из ничего́.

adolescence *n* ю́ность.

adolescent *n* подро́сток (*used also of girls*).

adolescent *adj* подро́стковый.

adopt *vt* **1** (*a child*) усынов|ля́ть (*boy*), удочер|я́ть (*girl*) (*pfs* -и́ть); **he is ~ed** он приёмный сын

2: to ~ a resolution/new methods при|нима́ть резолю́цию (-ня́ть), примен|я́ть но́вые ме́тоды (-и́ть).

adorable *adj CQ* преле́стный, чуде́сный; **what an ~ little girl!/boy!/kitten!** девчу́шка про́сто пре́лесть!, ма́льчик про́сто чу́до!, како́й преле́стный котёнок!

adore *vt* о́чень люби́ть, *CQ* обожа́ть (*impfs*); **I ~ ice cream** я обожа́ю моро́женое.

adorn *vt* укра|ша́ть (-́сить).

adrift *adv and predic adj*: *Naut* **to be ~** дрейфова́ть, *fig* плыть по тече́нию; *CQ* **the aerial has come ~** анте́нну снесло́ (*impers*).

adroit *adj* иску́сный, ло́вкий.

adult *n* взро́слый.

adult *adj* взро́слый; **~ education** обуче́ние взро́слых.

adulterate *vt*: **I'm sure they ~ the milk with water** я уве́рен, что они́ разбавля́ют молоко́ водо́й.

adultery *n* адюльте́р.

advance *n* **1** продвиже́ние (вперёд); **the ~ of science** прогре́сс нау́ки; **with the ~ of old age** с приближе́нием ста́рости

2 (*of salary*) ава́нс

3 *pl* (**~s**): **to make ~s to smb** заи́грывать с кем-л (*whether amorous or not*); **to make the first ~s** (*after quarrel*) де́лать пе́рвый шаг к примире́нию

4 *phrases*: **i) in ~** вперёд, зара́нее (*advs*); **to send luggage in ~** отпра́вить бага́ж вперёд/за́годя; **to pay in ~** плати́ть вперёд; **I can tell you in ~—it's not on** я вам скажу́ наперёд—э́то невозмо́жно; **let me know a week in ~** дай мне знать за неде́лю; **to book in ~** заказа́ть зара́нее; **ii) in ~ of** (*of place*) впереди́ + *G*; (*of time*) ра́ньше + *G*; **he walked in ~ of the whole party** он шёл впереди́ всех; **he arrived in ~ of the others** он пришёл ра́ньше други́х; **his ideas were in ~ of his time** его́ иде́и опереди́ли его́ вре́мя.

advance *adj*: **an ~ copy** (*of a new book*) сигна́льный экземпля́р; **~ booking office** ка́сса предвари́тельной прода́жи биле́тов; (*station notice*) **A. Luggage** отпра́вка багажа́; **I would like ~ notice of your arrival** я хоте́л бы знать зара́нее о ва́шем прие́зде; *Mil*: **~ guard** головно́й отря́д; **~ party** головна́я похо́дная заста́ва.

advance *vti vt* **1** (*move forward*): *Chess* **he ~d his queen** он дви́нул ферзя́ вперёд; **he has been ~d to the rank of colonel** ему́ присво́или зва́ние полко́вника; **this behaviour won't ~ your interests** тако́е поведе́ние тебе́ то́лько повреди́т; **we ~d the date of departure from the 10th to the 2nd of May** мы перенесли́ отъе́зд с деся́того на второ́е ма́я; **to ~ an opinion/an idea** вы́сказать мне́ние, вы́двинуть иде́ю

2 (*of money*): **to ~ money to smb** ссудить (*by bank*)/одолжить (*by individual*) кому-л деньги (*usu pfs*); **the director ~d him a month's salary** директор дал ему месячную зарплату вперёд

vi (*move forward*) продви|гаться, *also fig*, *Mil* (-нуться); *Mil* наступать (*only in impf*); **the work is advancing nicely** работа идёт/продвигается успешно.

advanced *adj*: **~ in years** пожилой, в годах; **courses for ~ students** курсы для продвинутых учащихся; **~ studies** научная работа; **summer is far ~** лето близится к концу; **he has ~ views** у него передовые взгляды.

advantage *n* **1** (*superiority*): **~ over** превосходство над + *I*, преимущество перед + *I*; **to gain/win an ~ over smb** добиться превосходства над кем-л; **the new house has one ~ over the old** новый дом имеет одно преимущество перед старым; **this method has many ~s** этот метод имеет ряд преимуществ

2 (*profit*) выгода, польза; **he turns everything to his own ~** он всё обращает себе на пользу; **it will be to your ~ to buy a car now** вам выгоднее сейчас купить машину; **he took ~ of my mistake** он воспользовался моим промахом; *pejor* **he took ~ of her good nature** он злоупотребил её добротой; **he showed to good ~ on that occasion** в этом случае он показал себя с лучшей стороны

3 (*in tennis*): **~ in/out** больше/меньше (у подающего).

advantageous *adj* выгодный.

adventure *n* приключение; **we had an ~ on the way here** в пути у нас было приключение; *attr*: **an ~ story** приключенческий роман.

adventurous *adj* (*of person*) смелый, предприимчивый; (*of journeys, etc.*) **an ~ journey** путешествие, полное приключений.

adverb *n Gram* наречие.

adversary *n* противник.

adverse *adj* неблагоприятный; **under ~ circumstances** при неблагоприятных обстоятельствах; **conditions were ~ to the success of our enterprise** обстоятельства не благоприятствовали успеху нашего предприятия; **an ~ wind** встречный ветер.

adversity *n* (*misfortune*) несчастье, беда (*often pl*); **my companion in ~** мой товарищ по несчастью; **to show courage in ~** мужественно переносить беды (*pl*); **~ brings out the best in her** в жизненных испытаниях (*pl*) раскрываются лучшие черты её характера.

advertise *vti vt Comm* рекламировать (*impf and pf*); **to ~ goods** рекламировать товары; **the film is widely ~d** фильм широко разрекламирован; **to ~ a vacancy** объяв|лять о вакансии (-ить)

vi: **it pays to ~** рекламировать выгодно; **to ~ for private pupils** да|вать объявление о частных уроках (-ть).

advertisement, *abbr* **ad, advert** *n* реклама; (*public notice*) объявление; **an ~ for stockings** реклама чулок; **~ of a concert** (*in street*) концертная афиша, (*in newspaper*) объявление о концерте.

advertising *n* реклама; **my brother is in ~** мой брат работает в рекламе; *attr* рекламный.

advice *n* совет; **on his ~** по его совету; **to offer smb ~** давать кому-л советы (*pl*); **I took his ~** я последовал его совету; **take my ~** послушайтесь моего совета; **I took legal ~** я посоветовался с юристом; **I acted on medical ~** я последовал совету врача; *attr Comm*: **~ note** авизо (*indecl*).

advisable *adj* целесообразный; **if you think it ~** если вы считаете это целесообразным; **it's not ~ for you to travel alone** вам не следует путешествовать одному.

advise *vt* **1** советовать + *D* (по-), рекомендовать + *D* (*impf and pf*, *pf also* по-); **where would you ~ me to apply for help?** куда бы вы мне посоветовали/рекомендовали обратиться за помощью?; **he ~d me against accepting the offer** он не советовал мне принимать это предложение; **the doctor ~d a change of air** врач посоветовал/порекомендовал перемену климата; **you'd be well ~d to refuse** с твоей стороны было бы благоразумнее отказаться от этого

2 (*notify*) увед|омлять (-омить); **please ~ us of the time of your arrival/when you have despatched the goods** прошу уведомить нас *or* сообщить нам о времени вашего приезда/об отправке товаров.

advisedly *adv* намеренно.

adviser *n* (*private individual*) советчик; (*professional*) консультант, советник.

advisory *adj* совещательный; консультативный; **he sits on the commission in an ~ capacity** он член комиссии с совещательным голосом; **~ board** консультативная комиссия.

advocate *n Law* адвокат; (*supporter*) сторонник.

advocate *vt*: **what course do you ~?** что вы рекомендуете предпринять? (*impf and pf*, *pf also* по-).

aerate *vt* газировать (*impf*); **~d water** газированная вода.

aerial *n* антенна.

aerodrome *n* аэродром.

aeroplane *n* самолёт.

aerosol *n* аэрозоль (*m*).

aesthetic *adj* эстетический.

afar *adv*: **from ~** издалека, *CQ* издалёка.

affable *adj* любезный.

affair *n* **1** дело; **that's not my ~** это не моё дело; **it's a strange ~** это странное дело; **the wedding will be a big ~** свадьба будет грандиозная; **current ~s** текущие дела; **to put one's ~s in order** уладить свои дела, привести дела в порядок

2 *CQ* роман; **he's having an ~ with Olga** у него роман с Ольгой.

affect *vt* **1** (*influence*) влия́ть на + *A* (по-); **this will ~ her decision/her health** это повлияет на её решение, это скажется на её здоровье; (*concern*) **this ~s me** это касается меня; *Med*: **the tuberculosis is ~ing the lungs** туберкулёз поражает лёгкие; **his shoulder is ~ed by rheumatism** у него плечо поражено ревматизмом

2 (*move*) тро́|гать (-нуть); **we were much ~ed by the play** пьеса нас взволновала/растрогала

3 (*pretend*) притвор|я́ться + *I* (-и́ться); **he ~s indifference** он притворяется равнодушным; **he ~ed not to hear** он делал вид, будто не слышит.

affectation *n* (*pretence*) притворство; *pl* (~s) (*mannerisms*) жеманство (*sing*); **her show of sympathy is sheer ~** её сочувствие—сплошное притворство; **he listened with an ~ of interest** он слушал с притворным интересом; **I don't like her ~s** мне не нравится её жеманство.

affected *adj* жеманный; **to be ~** жеманиться, *CQ* кривляться; **~ manners** жеманные манеры; **he/she is an ~ person** *CQ* он/она кривляка.

affecting *adj* трогательный; **an ~ scene** трогательная сцена.

affection *n*: **he is held in great ~** его все любят; **he is starved of ~** он истосковался по ласке.

affectionate *adj* ласковый, нежный; **an ~ look** ласковый взгляд; **he is very ~** он очень ласков(ый); **an ~ wife** любящая жена.

affectionately *adv* тепло, ласково; **she greeted him ~** она его тепло встретила; (*in letters*) **Yours ~** любящий Вас.

affiliate *vt usu pass*: **we are ~d with an American bank** мы объединены с американским банком.

affinity *n*: **there is some ~ between English and French** существует некоторая близость между английским и французским языками; **there is a strong ~ between them** они очень близки; **I feel no ~ with him** нас с ним ничто не связывает.

affirm *vt* утверждать (*only in impf*).

affirmation *n* утверждение.

affirmative *adj* утвердительный; *as n*: **to answer in the ~** ответить утвердительно.

affix *vt*: **to ~ a signature to a document** ставить подпись на документе (по-); **a seal was ~ed to the agreement** договор был скреплён печатью.

afflicted *adj*: **he is ~ with rheumatism** он страдает ревматизмом.

affliction *n* несчастье; (*physical*) болезнь, недуг; **the ~s of old age** недуги старости.

affluence *n* (*luxury*) роскошь; (*wealth*) богатство; **to live in ~** жить в роскоши.

affluent *adj* роскошный; богатый; **the ~ society** общество всеобщего благоденствия.

afford *vt* **1** (*of money, time*: *usu with* "*can*", "*can't*"): **I can't ~ the trip/to be idle** я не могу позволить себе эту поездку/предаваться лени; **I can't ~ it** мне это не по средствам/по карману; **I can't ~ the time** у меня нет времени на это; **you can't ~ to miss more lessons** тебе больше нельзя пропускать занятия

2 (*give*) достав|ля́ть (-́ить); **this ~ed me great pleasure** это доставило мне большое удовольствие; **this ~ed me a chance to speak out** это давало мне возможность высказать своё мнение.

afforestation *n* лесонасаждение.

affront *n* обида; (*stronger*) оскорбление; **it was an ~ to his pride** это задело/укололо его самолюбие.

affront *vt usu pass*: **I was ~ed by his remark** я был задет его замечанием.

Afghan *n* афганец, афганка.

Afghan *adj* афганский.

afield *adv*: **don't go too far ~** не уходи далеко.

afloat *adv and predic adj*: **to spend one's life ~** провести жизнь на море; **the largest vessel ~** крупнейшее судно на плаву; **by some miracle we were still ~** каким-то чудом наша лодка ещё держалась на поверхности.

afoot *predic adj*: **there's something ~** что-то затевается.

aforesaid *adj* вышеупомянутый, вышесказанный.

afraid *predic adj*: **she's ~ to go alone** она боится идти одна; **I'm ~ not** боюсь, что нет; **I'm ~ we will be late/we may be late** боюсь, что мы опоздаем/, как бы нам не опоздать; **he's not ~ of hard work** он не боится тяжёлой работы.

afresh *adv* снова, заново.

African *n* африканец, африканка.

African *adj* африканский.

aft *adv*: **to go ~** идти на корму; **to be ~** быть на корме.

after *adv* **1** (*of time*) потом, затем, позднее; **you begin supper, I'll come on ~** садитесь ужинать, я приду позднее; **you speak first, I'll speak ~** сначала говори ты, а затем скажу я; **he left soon ~** вскоре после этого он уехал

2 (*of movement*) следом; **I went first, my brother ~** я пошёл первый, мой брат следом.

after *prep* **1** (*in time*) после + *G*; через + *A*, спустя + *A*; **~ breakfast** после завтрака; **~ a year** через/спустя год; **it's just ~ 4** сейчас начало пятого; **time ~ time** раз за разом; **you should get off at the next stop ~ this one** вам нужно сойти через одну остановку

2 (*behind in place, order*) за + *I*; **shut the door ~ you** закрой за собой дверь; **he ran ~ her with her umbrella** он побежал за ней, чтобы отдать зонтик; **~ you!** прошу вас, проходите!; **~ you** (*with the hoover, iron, etc.*) я за тобой/после тебя

3 *various*: **this is ~ my own heart** это мне по душе; **she dresses ~ the latest fashion**

онá одевáется по послéдней мóде; **he takes ~ his father** он похóж на отцá, (*if used pejor*) он весь в отцá; **he asked ~ your health** он спрáшивал о твоём здорóвье; **~ all** (*in the end*) в концé концóв; **I was right ~ all** всё же я был прав; **what's he ~?** что он хóчет?; **he's a painter ~ a fashion** он в нéкотором рóде худóжник; **I mended my watch ~ a fashion** я кóе-кáк починúл свой часы́; **he's named ~ his uncle** он нáзван в честь дя́ди; **the police are ~ him** полúция úщет его́.

after *conj* пóсле тогó как.

after-effect *n* послéдствие.

afterglow *n* зáрево.

aftermath *n see* **after-effect.**

afternoon *n*: **in the ~** днём (*adv*), пóсле полýдня, *CQ* пóсле обéда; **at 3 in the ~** в три часá дня; **in the late ~** к вéчеру; **good ~!** дóбрый день!

aftertaste *n* прúвкус.

afterwards *adv* (*later*) пóзже; (*and then*) потóм, затéм; (*subsequently*) впослéдствии.

again *adv* опя́ть; снóва; ещё раз; (*with negatives*) бóльше; **he's late ~** он опя́ть опáздывает; **try ~** попрóбуйте ещё раз; **~ and ~** снóва и снóва; **he tried time and ~** он стóлько раз пытáлся; **I've told you time and ~** я тебé скóлько раз говорúл; **now and ~** врéмя от врéмени; **as much/as many ~** стóлько же; **twice/half as much ~** вдвóе/в полторá рáза бóльше; **then ~ we must remember...** крóме тогó, слéдует пóмнить...; **never ~** никогдá бóльше; **I shan't go there ~** я тудá бóльше не пойдý.

against *prep* **1** (*indicating opposition*) прóтив + *G*; **I've nothing ~ it** я ничегó прóтив э́того не имéю; **it's ~ our interests** э́то не в нáших интерéсах; **an injection ~ typhus** привúвка прóтив тúфа; **I'm up ~ it as regards money** у меня́ туговáто с деньгáми; **his appearance is ~ him** егó внéшность не располагáет в егó пóльзу

2 (*for*): **to save ~ a rainy day** откладывать на чёрный день; **I'm buying in food ~ the arrival of our relatives** я закупáю продýкты к приéзду рóдственников

3 (*of position*): **the rain beat ~ the window** дождь барабáнил в окнó; **he struck his foot ~ a stone** он ушúб нóгу о кáмень, он удáрился ногóй о кáмень; **he leant ~ a post** он прислонúлся к столбý; **a piano stood ~ the wall** у стены́ стоя́ло пианúно; **the ship ran ~ a rock** корáбль наскочúл на скалý; **the trees were dark ~ the sky** дерéвья темнéли на фóне нéба.

age *n* **1** (*of years lived*) вóзраст; **at the ~ of 10** в вóзрасте десятú лет; **people of all ~s** лю́ди всех вóзрастов; **what is your ~?** скóлько вам лет?; **he's twice my ~** он вдвóе стáрше меня́

2 (*period*) век, эпóха; **the ~ of Shakespeare** эпóха Шекспúра; **the Middle Ages** срéдние векá, средневекóвье (*sing*)

3 (*long time*) *CQ*: **we waited an ~/for ~s** мы ждáли цéлую вéчность; **this building has stood here for ~s (and ~s)** э́тот дом испокóн векóв здесь стоúт; **~s ago** óчень давнó, давны́м-давнó.

age *vti vt* стáрить (со-); **the experience ~d him** э́то переживáние состáрило егó

vi старéть (по-); **he has greatly ~d** он замéтно постарéл.

aged *adj* **1**: **a boy ~ 15** мáльчик/подрóсток пятнáдцати лет

2 (*very old*) престарéлый.

age group *n*: **he's not of our ~** он не нáшего вóзраста; **the children are divided according to their ~** дéти разделены́ по возрастны́м грýппам (*pl*).

ageing *n*: **the process of ~** процéсс старéния.

ageless *adj*: **he seems ~** он как бýдто не стáрится; **the themes of Shakespeare's tragedies are ~** тéмы трагéдий Шекспúра вéчны.

agency *n* агéнтство.

agenda *n* повéстка дня.

agent *n* агéнт, посрéдник; *Chem* (химúческое) веществó; **shipping ~** агéнт пароходства.

aggravate *vt* **1** (*make worse*) усугуб|ля́ть (-úть); отяго|щáть (-тúть); ухудш|áть (-ить); **to ~ an offence** усугубúть винý, отягощáть преступлéние; **to ~ a situation** ухýдшить положéние; **her many worries ~d her illness** многочúсленные забóты ухýдшили её состоя́ние

2 *CQ* (*annoy*) раздражáть (*usu impf*).

aggravating *adj*: **an ~ habit** раздражáющая привы́чка; **he's a very ~ child** он трýдный ребёнок; **how ~!** какáя досáда!

aggregate *n*: **in the ~** в совокýпности, в цéлом.

aggressive *adj* агрессúвный.

aggressor *n* агрéссор.

aggrieved *adj* обúженный.

aghast *predic adj* в ýжасе, потрясённый; **he was ~ at the news/at her behaviour** он был потрясён *or* ошеломлён э́тим извéстием, он был в ýжасе от её поведéния.

agile *adj* подвúжный, провóрный; (*of fingers, etc.*) лóвкий; (*active*) живóй, *also fig*; **he's ~ for such an old man** он óчень подвúжен для своúх лет; **an ~ mind** живóй ум.

agitate *vti vt* (*stir, shake*) взбáлтывать (взболтáть); *fig* (*disturb*) волновáть (вз-); **to be ~d** волновáться

vi: **to ~ for/against smth** агитúровать за что-л/прóтив чегó-л (*only in impf*).

agitation *n* (*emotional*) волнéние, возбуждéние; *Polit* агитáция; **she was in a state of great ~** онá былá в сúльном возбуждéнии/волнéнии.

agitator *n* подстрекáтель (*m*).

ago *adv* (томý) назáд; **a year/a week/two hours ~** год/недéлю/два часá (томý) назáд; **long ~** давнó; **not long ~** недáвно; **I saw her no longer ~ than last Tuesday** я вúдел её не позднéе чем в прóшлый втóрник.

agonized *adj*: **an ~ look** взгляд, по́лный му́ки.

agonizing *adj* мучи́тельный.

agony *n* му́ка; **she was in ~ with her broken leg** сло́манная нога́ причиня́ла ей си́льную боль; **I suffered agonies of doubt/with toothache** я му́чился сомне́ниями (*pl*), у меня́ ужа́сно боле́л зуб.

agree *vti vt*: **the inspector has ~d the accounts** контролёр подтверди́л пра́вильность счето́в

vi согла|ша́ться (-си́ться); быть согла́сным; (*arrange*) догов|а́риваться (-ори́ться); *Gram* согласо́в|ываться с + *I* (-а́ться); **he ~d with me/with the proposal/to the terms** он согласи́лся со мной/с предложе́нием/на усло́вия; **do you ~?** вы согла́сны?; **we all ~d on joining the group/that it's impossible** мы все бы́ли согла́сны присоедини́ться к гру́ппе/, что э́то невозмо́жно; **we ~d on a price/to meet here/that he was to go first** мы договори́лись о цене́/встре́титься здесь/, что он пое́дет пе́рвым; **at the ~d time** в усло́вленное вре́мя; **we'll never ~ about that** нам об э́том никогда́ не договори́ться (*impers*); **we could not ~ as to how it should be done** мы разошли́сь в вопро́се о том, как э́то сде́лать; **~d!** договори́лись!, ла́дно!; **his story does not ~ with the facts** его́ расска́з не соотве́тствует фа́ктам; **the children can never ~** де́ти не уме́ют ла́дить друг с дру́гом; **wine doesn't ~ with me** вино́ мне вре́дно, мне нельзя́ пить вино́.

agreeable *adj* (*consenting*) согла́сный; (*pleasant*) прия́тный; **is that ~ to all?** все согла́сны с э́тим?; **it was an ~ surprise for me to hear that...** я был прия́тно удивлён, услы́шав, что...

agreement *n* соглаше́ние, догово́р; **a disarmament/cultural ~** соглаше́ние о разоруже́нии/о культу́рном обме́не; **to reach ~** прийти́ к соглаше́нию; **a gentleman's ~** джентльме́нское соглаше́ние.

agricultural *adj* сельскохозя́йственный; **an ~ expert** агроно́м.

agriculture *n* се́льское хозя́йство.

aground *adv*: **to run ~** сесть на мель; **to be ~** сиде́ть на мели́.

ah *interj* а!, ах!; **ah—I see** а, понима́ю; **ah, that's what you mean** а, во́т что ты име́ешь в виду́.

aha *interj* ага́!

ahead *adv* впереди́, (*of movement*) вперёд; (*in race*) **the black horse is ~** чёрная ло́шадь впереди́; **we've a very busy time ~** у нас впереди́ мно́го рабо́ты; **to run on ~** забежа́ть вперёд; *Naut* **full steam ~!** по́лный вперёд!; *fig*: **we're going ~ with our plans** мы осуществля́ем заду́манное; **things are going ~ now** тепе́рь дела́ иду́т на лад; **one has to look ~** на́до смотре́ть вперёд.

ahead of *prep*: **he's ~ of the others in his class** он у́чится лу́чше други́х в кла́ссе; **the French are ~ of us in this field** францу́зы опереди́ли нас в э́той о́бласти [**NB** *tense*]; **we finished the job ~ of time** мы зако́нчили рабо́ту досро́чно (*adv*).

aid *n* **1** по́мощь; **by/with the ~ of** с по́мощью + *G*; **in ~ of** в по́мощь + *D*; **to come to smb's ~** прийти́ кому́-л на по́мощь; **economic ~ to Africa** экономи́ческая по́мощь африка́нским стра́нам; *CQ* **what's all this in ~ of?** к чему́ всё э́то?

2 *pl* (~s) (*equipment*) посо́бия, прибо́ры; **audiovisual ~s** аудиовизуа́льные посо́бия; **~s to navigation** посо́бия по навига́ции (*almanacs, etc.*), навигацио́нные прибо́ры (*instruments*).

ail *vi*: **the children are always ~ing** де́ти ве́чно боле́ют; **an ~ing child** боле́зненный ребёнок.

ailment *n* недомога́ние; неду́г.

aim *n* цель, *also fig*; **to take ~ at** прице́литься в + *A*; *fig*: **with the ~ of** с це́лью/с наме́рением + *inf*; **his one ~ in life is to make money** его́ еди́нственная цель—де́ньги.

aim *vti vt*: **he ~ed a blow at me** он замахну́лся на меня́; **that remark was ~ed at me** э́то замеча́ние бы́ло в мой а́дрес

vi (*with gun*) це́литься, прице́ливаться в + *A* (*pf for both* прице́литься); *fig* стреми́ться к + *D or* + *inf* (*impf*); **he's ~ing at perfection/at becoming a doctor** он стреми́тся к соверше́нству, он собира́ется стать врачо́м; **he's ~ing high** он ме́тит высоко́.

aimless *adj* бесце́льный.

air *n* **1** во́здух; (*light breeze*) ветеро́к; **fresh ~** све́жий во́здух; **in the open ~** на откры́том во́здухе, под откры́тым не́бом; **spring is in the ~** в во́здухе пове́яло (*impers*) весно́й; **I must get/let some fresh ~ in here** на́до прове́трить ко́мнату; **I must get some fresh ~** (*go out*) мне на́до прогуля́ться; *Aer* **to travel by ~** лета́ть (самолётом); *Radio* **to be on the ~** (*of person*) выступа́ть по ра́дио, (*of event*) передава́ться по ра́дио; *fig*: **he's a breath of fresh ~** он тако́й живо́й; **to clear the ~** разряди́ть атмосфе́ру; **my plans are still in the ~** мои́ пла́ны всё ещё не ясны́; **that's all hot ~** э́то всё одни́ разгово́ры; **he vanished/disappeared into thin ~** он как сквозь зе́млю провали́лся, он как в во́ду ка́нул; **one can't live on ~** одни́м во́здухом сыт не бу́дешь; **I'm walking on ~!** я ног под собо́й не чу́ю!

2 *Mus* напе́в

3 (*manner*) вид; **with an ~ of importance** с ва́жным ви́дом; **~s and graces** жема́нство (*sing*); **she gives herself ~s** она́ задаётся, она́ ва́жничает.

air *vt*: **to ~ a room/clothes** прове́тр|ивать ко́мнату/ве́щи (-ить); *fig*: **to ~ one's knowledge** выставля́ть напока́з свои́ зна́ния (*pl*) (*usu impf*); **she is always ~ing her grievances** она́ ве́чно жа́луется на судьбу́.

airborne *adj*: **we are now ~** тепе́рь мы в во́здухе; **~ troops** возду́шный деса́нт (*sing*).

air-conditioned *adj*: **the theatre is ~** зда́ние теа́тра кондициони́ровано.

air-cooled *adj* с возду́шным охлажде́нием.
aircraft *n* самолёт.
aircraft carrier *n* авиано́сец.
aircrew *n* экипа́ж самолёта.
air cushion *n* надувна́я поду́шка; (*under hovercraft*) возду́шная поду́шка.
air defence *n* противовозду́шная оборо́на.
air force *n* вое́нно-возду́шные си́лы (*pl*).
air hostess *n* стюарде́сса.
airless *adj* ду́шный.
airlift *n* возду́шный мост, возду́шные перево́зки (*pl*).
airline *n* авиали́ния.
airmail *n*: **by** ~ авиапо́чтой.
airman *n* лётчик.
airport *n* аэропо́рт.
air raid *n* возду́шный налёт; *attr*: **air-raid shelter** бомбоубе́жище; **air-raid warning** сире́на возду́шной трево́ги.
airsick *adj*: **I'm always** ~ меня́ всегда́ ука́чивает (*impers*) в самолёте.
airstrip *n* (*runway*) взлётно-поса́дочная полоса́, поса́дочная площа́дка.
airy *adj* возду́шный; **a large** ~ **room** просто́рная ко́мната.
aisle *n Theat, etc.* прохо́д (ме́жду ряда́ми).
ajar *adv*: **the door is** ~ дверь приоткры́та.
akimbo *adv*: **to stand with arms** ~ стоя́ть подбоче́нясь.
à la carte *adv* на зака́з.
alacrity *n*: **he replied with** ~ он с гото́вностью откли́кнулся/отозва́лся.
alarm *n* трево́га; **in** ~ в трево́ге; **to feel** ~ трево́житься; **to raise the** ~ подня́ть трево́гу; **to sound the** ~ дать сигна́л трево́ги; *attr*: ~ **bell** сигна́л трево́ги.
alarm *vt* трево́жить (вс-, рас-); **his severe manner** ~**ed me** его́ суро́вость встрево́жила меня́; **don't be** ~**ed!** не трево́жься!; **the shot** ~**ed the birds** вы́стрел спугну́л птиц.
alarm clock *n* буди́льник.
alarming *adj*: **the news is** ~ э́то трево́жная но́вость; **I found him** ~ он встрево́жил меня́.
alarmist *n* паникёр.
alas *interj* увы́!
Albanian *n* алба́нец, алба́нка.
Albanian *adj* алба́нский.
albino *n* альбино́с.
album *n* альбо́м.
albumen *n Biol, etc.* бело́к; (*egg white*) яи́чный бело́к.
alcohol *n* алкого́ль (*m*).
alcoholic *n* алкого́лик.
alcoholic *adj* алкого́льный.
alert *n*: **the forces are in a state of** ~ войска́ в состоя́нии боево́й гото́вности; **to be on the** ~ быть начеку́/настороже́ (*advs*).
alert *adj* (*lively*) живо́й; (*watchful*) бди́тельный; **he is mentally** ~ у него́ живо́й ум, он бы́стро сообража́ет.
algebra *n* а́лгебра.
Algerian *n* алжи́рец, алжи́рка.
Algerian *adj* алжи́рский.
alias *adv*: **Tom Smith,** ~ **Ben Brown** Том Смит, он же Бен Бра́ун.
alibi *n* а́либи (*indecl*).
alien *n* иностра́нец, чужестра́нец.
alien *adj* чу́ждый, *also fig*; **an** ~ **environment** чу́ждое окруже́ние; **ambition is** ~ **to his nature** честолю́бие ему́ чу́ждо.
alienate *vt*: **he was completely** ~**d from his family** он оконча́тельно порва́л с семьёй; *Law* **to** ~ **property** отчужда́ть иму́щество (*impf*).
alight[1] *predic adj*: **to be** ~ горе́ть; **to set smth** ~ заже́чь что-л; **is the stove** ~**?** то́пится ли пе́чка?; **the lamps are** ~ ла́мпы горя́т/зажжены́; *fig* **faces,** ~ **with joy** сия́ющие ра́достью ли́ца.
alight[2] *vi* (*get out of*): **to** ~ **from a bus/at a (bus) stop/from a train** вы|ходи́ть из авто́буса/на (авто́бусной) остано́вке, сходи́ть с по́езда (-йти, сойти́); **passengers for Zagorsk** ~ **here** пассажи́рам, е́дущим в Заго́рск, пригото́виться к вы́ходу; (*of birds*) **to** ~ **on a branch** сади́ться на ве́тку (сесть).
align *vt*: **to** ~ **oneself with** объедин|я́ться с + *I* (-и́ться).
alignment *n*: **the chairs are out of** ~ сту́лья стоя́т в ряду́ неро́вно; *fig Polit* расстано́вка сил (в ми́ре).
alike *predic adj* одина́ковый; **you're all** ~**!** все вы одина́ковы!; **they all look** ~ **to me** (*of people*) они́ для меня́ все на одно́ лицо́, (*of things*) они́ все одина́ковые.
alike *adv* одина́ково; **to treat everybody** ~ обраща́ться со все́ми одина́ково; **summer and winter** ~ **she wears the same dress** и зимо́й и ле́том она́ но́сит одно́ и то́ же пла́тье; **share and share** ~ всё по́ровну.
alive *predic adj* **1** жив (*short form only*); **it's a wonder he's still** ~ удиви́тельно, что он ещё жив (*of a sick man*)/, что он оста́лся жив (*after an accident*); **he's kept** ~ **on drugs** он де́ржится на лека́рствах; **it's good to be** ~**!** жизнь прекра́сна!
2 *fig uses*: **the river is** ~ **with fish** река́ киши́т ры́бой; **he's very much** ~ он по́лон жи́зни; **in the country old traditions are still** ~ в дере́вне ста́рые тради́ции ещё жи́вы; **he is** ~ **to the danger of the situation/to the fact that...** он осознаёт опа́сность ситуа́ции, он сознаёт, что...; *CQ* **look** ~**!** пошеве́ливайся!
alkali *n* щёлочь.
alkaline *adj* щелочно́й.
all *pron* **1** всё, *pl* все; ~ **is lost** всё пропа́ло; **that's** ~ э́то всё; **he took** ~ **there was** он взял всё, что там бы́ло; ~ **of us are agreed** все мы согла́сны; **he was the first of** ~ **to object** он пе́рвый возрази́л; **I like her best of** ~ я люблю́ её бо́льше всех; **it cost him** ~ **of £100** э́то ему́ сто́ило все сто фу́нтов; ~ **but three came** не пришли́ то́лько тро́е
2 *in prep and adv phrases*: **i) at all: I don't know him at** ~ я его́ совсе́м не зна́ю; **I'm not at** ~ **tired** я совсе́м/ничу́ть не уста́л;

it's not at ~ expensive это совсе́м не до́рого; **he did not come at ~** он вообще́ не пришёл; **if it's at ~ possible** е́сли э́то вообще́ возмо́жно; **I'll go tomorrow if at ~** е́сли уж пойду́, то пойду́ за́втра; **are you hurt?—Not at ~** ты пора́нился?—Нет, ничу́ть; **thanks!—Not at ~** спаси́бо!—Не́ за что!; **ii) for all: for ~ I know, he may already have left** не зна́ю, мо́жет, он уже ушёл; **for ~ I care he can leave and never come back** мне-то что, пусть ухо́дит навсегда́; **for ~ his learning, he can't change a bulb** то́же мне учёный—ла́мпочку смени́ть не мо́жет; **for ~ that, I do like him** при всём том он мне нра́вится; **once and for ~** раз и навсегда́; **iii) in all: there were 5 of them in ~** их бы́ло всего́ пя́теро; **taken ~ in ~ it's not been easy** в о́бщем/в це́лом, э́то бы́ло нелегко́; **~ in ~ he's right** в о́бщем, он прав; **iv)** *various*: **above ~** пре́жде всего́; **after ~ we decided not to go** в конце́ концо́в мы реши́ли не идти́; **best of ~** лу́чше всего́; **most of ~** бо́льше всего́; **~ in good time** всё в своё вре́мя; **it's ~ to the good** всё к лу́чшему; **it was ~ I could do not to laugh** я чуть не расхохота́лся.

all *adj* весь; **~ day/morning** весь день, всё у́тро; **~ the year round** кру́глый год; **~ day and ~ night** кру́глые су́тки; **~ France** вся Фра́нция; **~ her hair fell out** у неё вы́пали все во́лосы (*pl*); **I wish you ~ happiness** жела́ю вам са́мого большо́го сча́стья; **they come in at ~ hours** они́ прихо́дят когда́ хотя́т; **beyond ~ doubt** вне вся́кого сомне́ния; **with ~ respect** при всём моём уваже́нии; **with ~ speed** со всей ско́ростью; *CQ* **of ~ the idiots, he takes the prize** друго́го тако́го идио́та не сы́щешь.

all *adv* совсе́м; **it's not ~ that far** э́то совсе́м не так далеко́; **I'm ~ in** я совсе́м вы́дохся; **your hands are ~ tar** у тебя́ все ру́ки в смоле́; **he did it ~ alone** он сде́лал э́то оди́н/сам; **~ along the river bank** по всему́ бе́регу/вдоль всего́ бе́рега реки́; **~ the better** тем лу́чше; **you'd be ~ the better for a wash** тебе́ не меша́ло бы помы́ться; **he ~ but drowned** он чуть не утону́л; **it's ~ but done** почти́ всё сде́лано; **I'm ~ for going at once** я двумя́ рука́ми голосу́ю за то, что́бы отпра́виться сра́зу; **~ the same it wasn't right** всё-таки э́то бы́ло неве́рно; **if it's ~ the same/~ one to you** е́сли тебе́ всё равно́; **he's ~ out to get the job** он вовсю́ хлопо́чет, что́бы получи́ть э́ту рабо́ту; **we're ~ set to begin** мы гото́вы нача́ть; **~ of a sudden** вдруг; *CQ*: **he's very much ~ there** он па́рень с голово́й; **it's ~ up with him** его́ пе́сенка спе́та.

allay *vt* успок|а́ивать (-о́ить).

all-clear *n* отбо́й; **to give the ~** дать отбо́й.

allegation *n* заявле́ние, утвержде́ние; **can you support your ~?** вы мо́жете подтверди́ть/обоснова́ть ва́ше заявле́ние?; **that is a very serious ~** э́то о́чень серьёзное обвине́ние.

allege *vt* **1** утвержда́ть (*usu impf*), заяв|ля́ть (-и́ть); **he ~d he didn't see me** он утвержда́л, что не ви́дел меня́; **he is ~d to be wealthy** утвержда́ют, что он бога́т; **the statement ~d to have been made by the accused is clearly untrue** заявле́ние, я́кобы сде́ланное обвиня́емым, не соотве́тствует и́стине; **the ~d thief** предполага́емый вор

2 (*of statements put forward by oneself*): **he ~d illness as his reason for not going to work** он не вы́шел на рабо́ту, сосла́вшись на боле́знь.

allegedly *adv* бу́дто (бы), я́кобы; **he did not go to work—~ he was ill** он на рабо́ту не вы́шел я́кобы по боле́зни (= *so others say*)/, сказа́л, что бу́дто бы бо́лен (= *so he himself said*).

allegiance *n* ве́рность, лоя́льность.

allergic *adj* аллерги́ческий; **I'm ~ to lobster/to flattery** у меня́ аллерги́я к ома́рам (*pl*), я не выношу́ ле́сти.

alleviate *vt* облегч|а́ть (-и́ть).

alley *n* переу́лок.

alliance *n* сою́з; **to form an ~** заключа́ть сою́з.

allied *adj Polit, etc.* сою́зный; (*kindred*) ро́дственный; *fig* **chemistry and ~ subjects** хи́мия и сме́жные нау́ки.

all-in *adj*: (*of hotel, etc.*) **the ~ charge is £ 40 a week** пла́та—со́рок фу́нтов в неде́лю на по́лном пансио́не; **that's an ~ price** э́та цена́ включа́ет всё.

all-night *adj*: **we made an ~ journey** мы е́хали всю ночь; **we had an ~ party** мы весели́лись до утра́; *Rel* **an ~ service** все́нощная.

allocate *vt*: **to ~ money for various projects** ассигно́в|ывать де́ньги на разли́чные объе́кты (-а́ть); (*if for one project*) **to ~ money for building a school** вы́делить де́ньги на строи́тельство шко́лы; **rooms have been ~d to the delegates** делега́там предоста́вили номера́ в гости́нице.

allot *vt*: **we have been ~ted various tasks** нам бы́ли даны́ разли́чные зада́ния; **a flat has been ~ted to you** вам вы́делена кварти́ра; **in the ~ted time** в отведённое вре́мя.

allotment *n* (*of land*) (земе́льный) уча́сток.

allow *vti vt* **1** (*permit*) разреш|а́ть (-и́ть); позвол|я́ть (-и́ть); **I cannot ~ you to do that** я не разреша́ю/позволя́ю вам де́лать э́то; **~ me to introduce my brother** позво́льте/разреши́те предста́вить моего́ бра́та; **I ~ myself two cigarettes a day** я позволя́ю себе́ две сигаре́ты в день; **~ me!** (*to help*) позво́льте мне!; **feeding the animals is not ~ed** корми́ть живо́тных запреща́ется; (*notice*) **smoking is not ~ed** не кури́ть

2 (*give*): **how much are you ~ed for books?** ско́лько де́нег вам выдаю́т на кни́ги?; **that only ~s us 5 minutes to change** в результа́те у нас оста́нется всего́ пять мину́т, что́бы переоде́ться; **I didn't ~ myself enough**

time to get to the station я пло́хо рассчита́л вре́мя и опозда́л на по́езд; **you must ~ half an hour to get home** вам на́до на доро́гу домо́й полчаса́; **she ~s her imagination full play** она́ даёт во́лю воображе́нию; *Comm* **to ~ discount** де́лать ски́дку (с-); *Law* **the judge ~ed him £200 compensation** судья́ назна́чил ему 200 фу́нтов компенса́ции

3 (*admit*) призна|ва́ть (-́ть); **one has to ~ he's no fool** на́до призна́ть, (что) он не дура́к; **let's ~ that...** допу́стим, что...; *Law* **to ~ a claim** призна́ть тре́бование справедли́вым

vi: **the situation ~s of no delay** де́ло не те́рпит отлага́тельства; **one must ~ for unforeseen delays** на́до уче́сть непредви́денные заде́ржки (*impf* учи́тывать).

allowable *adj* допусти́мый; **~ expenses** допусти́мые расхо́ды/затра́ты.

allowance *n* (*payment*) посо́бие; *Fin* (*discount*) ски́дка; **family ~** посо́бие на дете́й; **maternity ~** посо́бие матеря́м; **subsistence ~** команди́ро́вочные (де́ньги); **my father gives me a monthly ~ of £100** оте́ц выдаёт мне сто фу́нтов в ме́сяц; (*ration*): **the ~ of bread is half a kilo per head per day** дневна́я но́рма хле́ба—полкило́ на челове́ка; **what's the ~ per head?** ско́лько полага́ется на ка́ждого?; *pl fig* **one must make ~s for his youth** ну́жно сде́лать ски́дку (*sing*) на его́ мо́лодость.

alloy *n Tech* сплав.

all-purpose *adj* универса́льный.

all right *adj and adv* **1** (*satisfactory, satisfactorily*): **did they arrive ~?** они́ благополу́чно доéхали?; **the work is quite ~** рабо́та сде́лана вполне́ прили́чно; **are you ~ in that room?** тебе́ хорошо́/удо́бно в э́той ко́мнате?; **he's not all that interesting, but he's ~** он не о́чень интере́сный собесе́дник, но челове́к о́чень хоро́ший; **I had a headache, but now I'm ~** у меня́ боле́ла голова́, а тепе́рь прошло́; **is my hat ~?** у меня́ шля́па пра́вильно наде́та?; *CQ*: **it's ~ for you, but it's not your car** тебе́-то хорошо́, э́то не твоя́ маши́на; **I made it ~ with the porter** я всё ула́дил с дежу́рным; **if it's ~ with you, I'll come early** е́сли вас устра́ивает, я приду́ ра́но; **he's a bit of ~** он па́рень что на́до

2 (*in answers*) **i)**: **should I do it again?—No, it's ~ as it is** мне э́то переде́лать?—Нет, и так сойдёт; **do you like the picture?—It's ~** тебе́ нра́вится карти́на?—Да, нра́вится (= *yes*)/—Ничего́ (*without enthusiasm*)/—Та́к себе (*not very much*); **how are you?—I'm ~** как ты себя́ чу́вствуешь?—Ничего́ *or* Норма́льно (*so-so*)/—Та́к себе (*not so well*); **ii)** *used as exclamation*: **~!** хорошо́! (*sense shown by tone of voice*), ну ла́дно!, хорошо́! (*in affirmation*), ничего́! (*without enthusiasm*).

all-round *adj*: **an ~ sportsman** разносторо́нний спортсме́н.

all-time *adj*: **an ~ record** непревзойдённый реко́рд, вы́сшее достиже́ние в спо́рте.

allude *vi*: **to ~ to** ссыла́ться на + *A* (сосла́ться); (*mention*) упом|ина́ть (-яну́ть); (*hint at*) намек|а́ть на + *A or* о + *P* (-ну́ть); (*touch on*) каса́ться + *G* (косну́ться); за|тра́гивать + *A* (-тро́нуть); **he was alluding to his original source** он ссыла́лся на первоисто́чник; **he ~s to him in the footnotes** он упомина́ет о нём в примеча́ниях; **he ~d to this in conversation** он намекну́л на э́то/упомяну́л об э́том в разгово́ре; **he ~d to this question in his speech** в свое́й ре́чи он косну́лся э́того вопро́са/он затро́нул э́тот вопро́с.

alluring *n* (*attractive*) привлека́тельный; (*tempting*) соблазни́тельный.

allusion *n*: **an ~ to** ссы́лка на + *A*, (*hint*) намёк на + *A*; **better not to make any ~ to her marital troubles** лу́чше не упомина́ть о её семе́йных неуря́дицах; **his poetry is full of classical ~s** его́ поэ́зия полна́ класси́ческих аллю́зий.

ally *n* сою́зник, *also Polit*.

ally *vt usu pass or reflex*: **to be allied with, to ~ oneself with** объедин|я́ться с + *I* (-и́ться).

almighty *adj* всемогу́щий; *CQ* **he's an ~ bore** он ужа́сный зану́да.

almond *n* (*tree*) минда́ль (*m*); (*nut*) минда́льный оре́х, минда́ль (*collect*); *attr*: **~ oil** минда́льное ма́сло.

almost *adv* почти́; (*all but*) чуть не, едва́ не; **~ always** почти́ всегда́; **I've ~ finished my novel** я почти́ зако́нчил рома́н; **I ~ missed the train** я чуть не/едва́ не опозда́л на по́езд; **he ~ died of fright** он чуть не у́мер со стра́ху.

alone *predic adj and adv* **1** (*without company*) оди́н, одино́кий; **he lived ~** он жил оди́н/в одино́честве; **it's hard to live ~** тру́дно жить одному́; **in the large city he felt himself ~** в большо́м го́роде он чу́вствовал себя́ одино́ко; **all ~** совсе́м оди́н; **the baby was left ~** ребёнка оста́вили одного́

2 (*and no other*) (то́лько) оди́н; **he ~ survived the fire** он оди́н оста́лся в живы́х по́сле пожа́ра; **you ~ can decide** то́лько ты оди́н мо́жешь реши́ть э́то; **we are not ~ in thinking this** так ду́маем не мы одни́; **his silence ~ is proof of his guilt** его́ молча́ние само́ по себе́ уже́ явля́ется доказа́тельством его́ вины́

3 leave alone: leave her ~! оста́вьте её (в поко́е)!; **leave it ~!** не тро́гай!, оста́вь!

4 let alone *as conj*: **I haven't the time, let ~ the money** у меня́ на э́то нет вре́мени, да и де́нег то́же/не говоря́ уже́ о деньга́х.

along *adv*: **move ~ now!** проходи́те, проходи́те!; **come ~, children!** пошли́, ребя́та!; **I'll be ~ in 10 minutes** я бу́ду че́рез де́сять мину́т; **I'll be ~ at 6** я приду́ в шесть; **he's coming ~ this evening** он зайдёт к нам сего́дня ве́чером; **I knew it all ~** я э́то знал с са́мого нача́ла.

along *prep* по + *D*, вдоль + *G*; **to walk ~ the embankment** идти́ вдоль/по на́бережной; **to sail ~ the coast** плыть вдоль бе́рега;

there are bookcases ~ the walls вдоль стен стоя́т кни́жные шкафы́.

alongside *prep* (*of movement*): **the ship came ~ the quay** су́дно подплы́ло к при́стани; **the dinghy came ~ the steamer** ло́дка подплыла́ к бо́рту парохо́да; (*of position*): **the ships lay ~ one another/~ the quay** суда́ стоя́ли борт о́ борт/вдоль прича́ла; **he walked ~ his brother** он шёл ря́дом с бра́том; **the car stopped ~ the kerb** маши́на останови́лась у тротуа́ра.

aloof *adj*: **I find him rather ~** меня́ порази́л его́ отрешённый вид.

aloof *adv*: **he keeps himself ~ from his colleagues** он сторо́нится свои́х колле́г.

aloud *adv* вслух; гро́мко; **to read/think ~** чита́ть/ду́мать вслух; **he laughed ~** он гро́мко смея́лся.

alphabet *n* алфави́т.

alphabetical *adj* алфави́тный.

alpine *adj* альпи́йский.

already *adv* уже́; **we've ~ fed** мы уже́ пое́ли.

Alsatian *n* (*dog*) неме́цкая овча́рка.

also *adv* то́же, та́кже; (*moreover*) к тому́ же; **they ~ came** они́ то́же пришли́; **the walls need painting and ~ the doors** ну́жно покра́сить сте́ны, да и две́ри то́же; **not only... but ~** не то́лько..., но и/но к тому́ же; **~ I find it boring** к тому́ же я нахожу́ э́то ску́чным.

altar *n* алта́рь (*m*).

alter *vti vt* меня́ть (*impf*); измен|я́ть (-и́ть); **to ~ course** меня́ть курс; **that ~s things/the case** э́то меня́ет де́ло; **I found her very much ~ed** я нашёл её си́льно измени́вшейся; **to ~ a dress** переде́л|ывать пла́тье (-ать)

vi меня́ться, изменя́ться; **the town has ~ed a lot** го́род си́льно измени́лся.

alteration *n* измене́ние; **there's no ~ in the plan** в пла́не нет измене́ний (*pl*); **an ~ in temperature** переме́на температу́ры; **I'm having some ~s done** (*to clothes*) я ко́е-что́ перешива́ю [**NB** *Russian doesn't distinguish whether this is be done by oneself or by a dressmaker*], (*in house*) мы ко́е-что́ переде́лываем в кварти́ре.

altercation *n* ссо́ра, перебра́нка.

alternate *adj*: **on ~ days** ка́ждый второ́й день, че́рез день.

alternate *vti vt* чередова́ть с + *I* (*impf*); **we ~ grain and root crops** мы черед́уем зерновы́е с овощны́ми культу́рами

vi чередова́ться с + *I*; **wet days ~d with fine** дождли́вые дни чередова́лись с я́сными; **cold ~d with sultriness** жара́ сменя́лась прохла́дой.

alternately *adv* по о́череди; сменя́я друг дру́га; **she laughed and cried ~** она́ то смея́лась, то пла́кала.

alternating *adj Elec*: **~ current** переме́нный ток.

alternative *n* альтернати́ва; (*choice*) вы́бор; (*way out*) вы́ход; **I have no ~ but to dismiss you** у меня́ нет друго́го вы́бора/вы́хода, как то́лько вас уво́лить.

alternative *adj* альтернати́вный.

although *conj* хотя́ и, хоть и; **he came, ~ he was two hours late** он пришёл, хотя́ и/хоть и опозда́л на два часа́; **~ he was very tired he came** он пришёл, несмотря́ на уста́лость; *see also* **though.**

altitude *n* высота́; **the plane is gaining ~** самолёт набира́ет высоту́; **the town is at an ~ of 2,000 metres** го́род нахо́дится на высоте́ две ты́сячи ме́тров над у́ровнем мо́ря; **in these ~s** на э́тих высо́тах.

altogether *adv* (*in all*) всего́; (*completely*) совсе́м, соверше́нно; **there are 7 of them ~** их всего́ семь челове́к; **I'm not ~ sure** я не совсе́м уве́рен; **you are ~ wrong** вы соверше́нно не пра́вы; **I don't ~ agree with her** я не совсе́м с ней согла́сен; **the weather was bad and ~ the picnic was a flop** пого́да была́ плоха́я, и вообще́ пикни́к не уда́лся.

aluminium *n* алюми́ний.

always *adv* всегда́; **why must you ~ tease your sister?** почему́ ты всё вре́мя дра́знишь сестру́?

amalgamate *vti vt* объедин|я́ть (-и́ть)

vi: **to ~ with** объединя́ться с + *I*.

amalgamation *n*: **the ~ of the two firms** объедине́ние/слия́ние э́тих двух фирм.

amass *vt*: **to ~ wealth** на|ка́пливать де́ньги/бога́тства (-копи́ть).

amateur *n* люби́тель (*m*); *attr* люби́тельский, непрофессиона́льный; **~ theatricals** люби́тельский спекта́кль (*sing*); **an ~ artist** худо́жник-люби́тель.

amaze *vt* удив|ля́ть (-и́ть), (*stronger*) изум|ля́ть (-и́ть), (*strongest*) пора|жа́ть (-зи́ть); **the news ~d everybody** но́вость удиви́ла/изуми́ла/порази́ла всех; **he was ~d to see us** он о́чень удиви́лся, уви́дев нас.

amazement *n* удивле́ние, (*stronger*) изумле́ние; **to my ~** к моему́ удивле́нию/изумле́нию; **I heard with ~...** с удивле́нием/с изумле́нием я услы́шал...; **he looked at me in ~** он посмотре́л на меня́ с изумле́нием.

amazing *adj* удиви́тельный, порази́тельный.

amazingly *adv* удиви́тельно, *CQ* на удивле́ние.

ambassador *n* посо́л.

amber *n* янта́рь (*m*); *attr* янта́рный.

ambidextrous *adj*: **he's ~** он одина́ково владе́ет ле́вой и пра́вой руко́й.

ambiguity *n* двусмы́сленность.

ambiguous *adj* двусмы́сленный.

ambition *n* честолю́бие; (*aim*) стремле́ние; мечта́; **his ~ knows no bounds** его́ честолю́бие беспреде́льно; **he's achieved his cherished ~** его́ заве́тная мечта́ сбыла́сь; **his sole ~ is to make money** его́ еди́нственное стремле́ние—разбогате́ть.

ambitious *adj attr* честолюби́вый; **~ youths/plans** честолюби́вые молоды́е лю́ди/пла́ны; *predic*: **he is ~ for fame** он стреми́тся к сла́ве/к изве́стности; **she is ~ for her children** она́ о́чень мно́гого ждёт от свои́х дете́й.

ambivalent *adj* дво́йственный; **an ~ attitude to smth** дво́йственное отноше́ние к чему́-л.

amble *vi*: **we ~d round the park** мы прогуля́лись по па́рку; **the horse ~d along** ло́шадь шла ме́дленно.

ambulance *n*: **to send for the ~** вы́звать ско́рую по́мощь; **he was taken away in an ~** его́ увезла́ ско́рая по́мощь.

ambush *n* заса́да; **to lay an ~** устра́ивать заса́ду; **to run into an ~** наткну́ться на заса́ду, попа́сть в заса́ду.

ambush *vt usu pass*: **they were ~ed** они́ попа́ли в заса́ду.

amenable *adj* сгово́рчивый; **he is always ~ to reason** он всегда́ прислу́шивается к го́лосу ра́зума.

amend *vt* измен|я́ть (-и́ть); *Law* **to ~ a bill** вноси́ть измене́ния/попра́вки в законопрое́кт (внести́).

amends *npl*: **to make ~ for an injury** возмеща́ть/компенси́ровать убы́тки; **to make ~ he brought her flowers** что́бы ка́к-то загла́дить вину́, он принёс ей цветы́.

amenity *n usu pl*: **our city has many amenities** в на́шем го́роде есть что посмотре́ть; **our country cottage has no amenities** у нас на да́че нет удо́бств.

American *n* америка́нец, америка́нка.

American *adj* америка́нский.

amiable *adj* любе́зный, ми́лый.

amicably *adv* дру́жески.

amidships *adv*: **our cabin is ~** на́ша каю́та посереди́не су́дна.

amid(st) *prep* среди́ + *G*.

amiss *adv*: **don't take it ~ if I say...** пойми́те меня́ пра́вильно, е́сли я скажу́...; **what's ~?** в чём де́ло?; **there's not much ~ with this engine** с э́тим мото́ром ничего́ стра́шного (нет); **it would not be ~ for him to apologize** ничего́ стра́шного, е́сли он извини́тся; **nothing comes ~ to him** он из всего́ извлечёт по́льзу; **a cup of tea wouldn't come ~** ча́шка ча́ю не помеша́ет.

ammonia *n* аммиа́к; **household ~** нашаты́рный спирт.

ammunition *n* боеприпа́сы (*pl*); *attr*: **~ dump** (полево́й) склад боеприпа́сов.

amnesty *n* амни́стия.

amok *adv*: **to run ~** бу́йствовать (*impf*).

among(st) *prep* среди́ + *G*; из + *G*; ме́жду + *I*; **~ the books** среди́ книг; **my brother was ~ the guests** среди́ госте́й был мой брат; **this is just one example ~ many** э́то лишь оди́н приме́р из мно́гих; **a quarrel arose ~ them** у них произошла́ ссо́ра; **divide it ~ the children** раздели́ э́то ме́жду детьми́.

amoral *adj* амора́льный.

amorphous *adj* амо́рфный, бесфо́рменный.

amount *n* **1** (*quantity*) коли́чество; **in small ~s** в небольши́х коли́чествах; **there's any ~ of food left** оста́лось мно́го еды́; **they have any ~ of money** у них полно́ де́нег; **I can give you any ~ of potatoes** я могу́ вам дать карто́шки ско́лько уго́дно; **this car has given us any ~ of trouble** у нас с э́той маши́ной (бы́ли) сплошны́е неприя́тности

2 (*total*) о́бщая су́мма, ито́г; **what is the ~ of the debt?** какова́ о́бщая су́мма до́лга?; **he owes me money to the ~ of £500** он до́лжен мне пятьсо́т фу́нтов.

amount *vi* (*of figures, money*) состав|ля́ть (-́ить); быть ра́вным + *D*; **what does it ~ to?** каку́ю су́мму э́то составля́ет?; **the expenditure ~ed to £500** расхо́ды соста́вили пятьсо́т фу́нтов; **the bill ~s to 20 dollars** счёт на два́дцать до́лларов; *fig*: **it ~s to the same thing** э́то, в о́бщем, одно́ и то́ же; **what he said didn't ~ to much** его́ слова́ ма́ло что зна́чат; **it ~s to a refusal** э́то равноси́льно отка́зу.

ampère, *abbr* **amp** *n Elec* ампе́р.

amphibian *n Zool* амфи́бия, земново́дное.

amphibious *adj Zool* земново́дный; *Mil* **~ tank/vehicle** танк-/автомоби́ль-амфи́бия.

ample *adj*: **an ~ supply of bread** больши́е запа́сы (*pl*) хле́ба; **~ resources** бога́тые ресу́рсы; **£5 will be ~ for me** мне вполне́ доста́точно пяти́ фу́нтов (*G*); **there's ~ room for all** для всех хва́тит ме́ста; **we've ~ time for the train** вре́мени у нас вполне́ доста́точно—мы не опозда́ем на по́езд.

amplifier *n Radio* усили́тель (*m*).

amplify *vt*: **could you ~ your statement?** могли́ бы вы раскры́ть полне́е э́ту мысль?/(*in court*) э́то положе́ние?; *Radio, etc.* уси́л|ивать (-ить).

amply *adv* вполне́, доста́точно; **you were ~ justified by events** собы́тия показа́ли, что вы бы́ли пра́вы; **we are ~ supplied with books for the journey** чте́нием (в доро́ге) мы вполне́ обеспе́чены.

amputate *vt* ампути́ровать (*impf and pf*).

amuse *vt* (*entertain*) развле|ка́ть (-́чь); (*make laugh*) смеши́ть (рас-); весели́ть (раз-); **he ~d the children/kept the children ~d by telling them stories** он развлека́л дете́й расска́зами; **his funny stories kept us ~d** он смеши́л нас свои́ми анекдо́тами; **I was highly ~d by their escapades** меня́ о́чень смеши́ли/весели́ли их вы́ходки; **the children ~ themselves for hours in the garden** де́ти часа́ми игра́ют в саду́; **he was not ~d to find I'd forgotten the keys** он не о́чень обра́довался, узна́в, что я забы́л ключи́.

amusement *n* развлече́ние, заба́ва; **they do it only for ~** они́ э́то де́лают про́сто ра́ди заба́вы/развлече́ния; **he slipped on a banana skin much to the ~ of the school children** он поскользну́лся на кожуре́ бана́на и чуть не упа́л, что о́чень развесели́ло шко́льников; *attr*: **~ park** парк с аттракцио́нами.

amusing *adj* заба́вный; **an ~ fellow** заба́вный ма́лый; **an ~ story** заба́вный/смешно́й расска́з.

anachronism *n* анахрони́зм.

anaemic *adj* малокро́вный, анеми́чный.

anaesthetic *n* анестезия, наркоз; **a local** ~ местная анестезия, местный наркоз.

analogy *n* аналогия.

analyse *vt* анализировать (про-); *Gram* **to** ~ **a sentence** раз|бирать предложение (-обрать).

analysis *n* анализ; *Gram* разбор; *fig* **in the last** ~ в конечном счёте/итоге.

analytical *adj* аналитический.

anarchy *n* анархия.

anatomy *n* анатомия.

ancestor *n* предок.

ancestral *adj* родовой.

ancestry *n* происхождение.

anchor *n* якорь (*m*); **to be/ride at** ~ стоять на якоре; **to cast/drop** ~ бросить якорь; **to raise/weigh** ~ поднимать якорь, сниматься с якоря.

anchor *vti vt*: **to** ~ **a ship** ставить судно на якорь (по-); **to be** ~**ed** стоять на якоре (*impf*)

vi: **we/the ships** ~**ed at Odessa** мы/корабли стали на якорь в Одессе.

anchorage *n* якорная стоянка.

anchovy *n* анчоус.

ancient *adj* древний; старинный; *CQ* **I've got a very** ~ **car** у меня очень старая машина.

ancillary *adj*: ~ **services** вспомогательные службы.

and *conj* **1** (*general*) и; с + *I* (*usu with personal pronouns*); **nice** ~ **warm** тепло и приятно; **to read** ~ **write** читать и писать; ~ **so on** и так далее, *abbr* и т.д.; **you** ~ **I** мы с тобой/с вами; **my husband** ~ **I will come** мы с мужем придём; **bread** ~ **butter** хлеб с маслом

2 (*with numbers, time*): **three** ~ **a half** три с половиной; **a hundred** ~ **fifty** сто пятьдесят; **a mile** ~ **a half** полторы мили; **an hour** ~ **twenty minutes** час двадцать минут; **an hour/a mile** ~ **a bit** час/миля с небольшим; **two** ~ **two is four** два плюс два—четыре

3 (*repetition, continuation*): **it gets easier** ~ **easier** становится всё легче и легче; **she gets more** ~ **more beautiful** она становится всё красивее; **we talked for hours** ~ **hours** мы беседовали (целыми) часами; **he talked** ~ **talked** он всё говорил и говорил; **time** ~ **time again he is late** он снова и снова опаздывает; **it's miles** ~ **miles away** это за много миль отсюда

4 (*meaning "to"*): **come** ~ **see** приходи посмотреть/посмотришь; **try** ~ **do it** постарайся это сделать

5 (*adversative*) а; **it was on Tuesday** ~ **not on Wednesday** это было во вторник, а не в среду; **turn right** ~ **then left** идите направо, а потом налево; ~ **why not?** (*in agreement*) (а) почему бы и нет?, (*in objection*) а почему нельзя?

anecdote *n* забавный рассказ.

anew *adv* снова, заново.

angel *n* ангел, *also CQ*; **be an** ~ **and fetch my spectacles** будь добр, принеси, пожалуйста, мои очки.

anger *n* гнев.

anger *vt* сердить (рас-); злить (разо-); **he** ~**ed me by his stupidity** он разозлил меня своей глупостью.

angina *n*: ~ **pectoris** грудная жаба [**NB** ангина = *tonsillitis*].

angle[1] *n Math* угол; **an acute/obtuse/right** ~ острый/тупой/прямой угол; **adjacent** ~**s** смежные углы; **at right** ~**s/at a right** ~ **to the wall** под прямым углом (*always sing*) к стене; **at an** ~ **of 40 degrees** под углом сорок градусов; **look at the picture from this** ~ посмотри на картину отсюда; *fig* **consider it from another** ~ посмотри на это под другим углом.

angle[2] *vi* (*fish*) удить рыбу (*impf*); ловить рыбу на удочку/удочкой (*only in impf*); *fig* **he's angling for an invitation** он напрашивается на приглашение.

angler *n* рыболов.

angry *adj* сердитый; **to make smb** ~ рассердить кого-л; **her words made me** ~ её слова рассердили меня; **I was** ~ **with him for being late** я рассердился/был сердит на него за опоздание.

anguish *n* мука, боль; **to be in** ~ мучиться.

anguished *adj*: **with an** ~ **look** с мукой во взгляде.

angular *adj Math, etc.* угловой; *fig* угловатый.

animal *n* животное; **domestic/wild** ~**s** домашние/дикие животные; **wild** ~ зверь; **farm** ~**s** домашний скот (*collect*).

animal *adj* животный; ~ **husbandry** животноводство; ~ **desires** животная страсть (*sing*); ~ **spirits** жизнерадостность (*sing*).

animate *adj Gram* одушевлённый.

animated *adj* (*lively*) оживлённый; живой; **an** ~ **conversation** оживлённый разговор; **an** ~ **cartoon** мультипликация.

animation *n* оживление; воодушевление.

animosity *n*: ~ **towards/against smb** враждебность по отношению к кому-л.

aniseed *n* анисовое семя.

ankle *n* лодыжка; **I've sprained my** ~ я растянул лодыжку, *CQ* я подвернул ногу; **we were** ~ **deep in mud** мы увязли по щиколотку в грязи; *attr*: ~ **sock** носок.

annals *npl* летопись (*sing*); анналы.

annex *vt*: **to** ~ **territory** аннексировать территорию (*impf and pf*); (*attach*) **you will find the list** ~**ed** список прилагается.

annexe *n* (*building adjoining*) пристройка; крыло; (*separate*) флигель (*m*); **an** ~ **to a hotel** крыло здания гостиницы, (*if separate*) другой корпус; (*to document*) **an** ~ **to a treaty** дополнение к договору; **an** ~ **to a book** приложение к книге.

annihilate *vt* полностью уничтож|ать (-ить).

annihilation *n* полное уничтожение.

anniversary *n* годовщи́на; **wedding** ~ годовщи́на сва́дьбы; *attr*: **an** ~ **dinner** торже́ственный обе́д по слу́чаю годовщи́ны.

Anno Domini, *abbr* **A.D.** на́шей э́ры; **A.D. 200** двухсо́тый год на́шей э́ры.

annotate *vt* снаб|жа́ть примеча́ниями/комента́риями (-ди́ть); анноти́ровать (*impf and pf*).

announce *vt* объяв|ля́ть (-и́ть); сообщ|а́ть (-и́ть); **to** ~ **over the radio/at a meeting** объяви́ть *or* сообщи́ть по ра́дио/на собра́нии; **to** ~ **in the papers** опубликова́ть в газе́тах (*usu pf*); **he** ~**d his intention to retire** он объяви́л о своём реше́нии уйти́ в отста́вку; **to** ~ **the arrival of the train** сообщи́ть о прибы́тии по́езда.

announcement *n* сообще́ние; объявле́ние; *Cine* ано́нс; **the** ~ **appeared yesterday** сообще́ние появи́лось вчера́; **according to a recent** ~ согла́сно неда́внему сообще́нию; **an** ~ **of a forthcoming concert** объявле́ние о предстоя́щем конце́рте.

announcer *n Radio* ди́ктор.

annoy *vt* раздража́ть (*usu impf*); надо|еда́ть + *D* (-е́сть); **I got/felt/was** ~**ed with him for being so stupid** он раздража́л меня́ свое́й ту́постью; **he** ~**ed me by/with his questions** он надое́л мне свои́ми вопро́сами.

annoyance *n* (*feeling*) доса́да, раздраже́ние; (*cause of annoyance*) доса́дная неприя́тность; **much to my** ~ к мое́й большо́й доса́де.

annoying *adj* доса́дный; **how** ~! кака́я доса́да!; (*causing annoyance*): **she can be very** ~ она́ быва́ет поро́й несно́сна; **the** ~ **thing is...** са́мое доса́дное/оби́дное, что...

annual *n* (*flower*) однолётнее расте́ние; (*magazine*) ежего́дник.

annual *adj* (*every year*) ежего́дный; (*for one year*) годово́й; *Bot* одноле́тний; ~ **leave/conference** ежего́дный о́тпуск/съезд; ~ **increment** ежего́дная приба́вка (к зарпла́те); ~ **income** годово́й дохо́д.

annually *adv* ежего́дно.

annul *vt*: **to** ~ **a law** отмен|я́ть зако́н (-и́ть); **to** ~ **an agreement** аннули́ровать соглаше́ние (*impf and pf*); **to** ~ **a marriage/a contract** расторг|а́ть брак/контра́кт (-́нуть).

anomalous *adj* анома́льный.

anonymous *adj* анони́мный.

anorak *n* анора́к.

another *pron* **1** друго́й; ~ **might do it differently** друго́й бы э́то сде́лал ина́че; **one after** ~ **they left the room** они́ вы́шли из ко́мнаты оди́н за други́м; **he's just such** ~ и он тако́й же

2 *reflex pron*: **one** ~ друг дру́га (*case of the second word changes according to construction of sentence*); **they love one** ~ они́ лю́бят друг дру́га; **they are always quarrelling with one** ~ они́ ве́чно ссо́рятся друг с дру́гом.

another *adj* **1** (*a different*) друго́й; **in** ~ **room** в друго́й ко́мнате; **that's quite** ~ **matter** э́то совсе́м друго́е де́ло; **I'll do it** ~ **time** я э́то сде́лаю в друго́й раз

2 (*a second or more*) ещё (*adv*); **will you have** ~ **cup of tea?** (хо́чешь) ещё (ча́шку) ча́ю?; **have** ~ **try** попыта́йся ещё раз; ~ **two minutes and I'd have missed the train** ещё две мину́ты, и я бы опозда́л на по́езд; **he left without** ~ **word** он ушёл, не сказа́в бо́льше ни сло́ва.

answer *n* отве́т; (*solution*) реше́ние, *also Math*; **in** ~ **to your question** в отве́т на ваш вопро́с; **the** ~ **to a problem** реше́ние пробле́мы; **he has a complete** ~ **to the charge** у него́ есть исче́рпывающий отве́т на вы́двинутое обвине́ние; *CQ* **he knows all the** ~**s** он за сло́вом в карма́н не поле́зет.

answer *vti vt* **1** (*reply*) отве|ча́ть (-́тить); **to** ~ **smb/a letter/a question** отве́тить кому́-л/на письмо́/на вопро́с; **our prayers have been** ~**ed** на́ши моли́твы бы́ли услы́шаны; **to** ~ **the bell/the door** откры́ть дверь; **please** ~ **the telephone for me** подойди́ за меня́ к телефо́ну; **his secretary** ~**ed the phone** тру́бку взяла́ его́ секрета́рша; **to** ~ **a call/summons** отклик|а́ться на зов (-́нуться)

2 (*fulfil*): **he** ~**s (to) the description** он соотве́тствует описа́нию; **it will** ~ **the purpose** годи́тся для э́той це́ли

vi отвеча́ть; **I can't** ~ **for it/for her** я не могу́ отвеча́ть за э́то/за неё; **he's got a lot to** ~ **for** ему́ за мно́гое придётся отве́тить; **the dog** ~**s to the name of Johnny** соба́ка отклика́ется на и́мя Джо́нни; **the plan has not** ~**ed** план не уда́лся; **don't** ~ **back!** не дерзи́!

answerable *adj*: **I am** ~ **to the director for this** я отвеча́ю пе́ред дире́ктором за э́то.

ant *n* мураве́й.

antagonism *n* антагони́зм.

antagonist *n* проти́вник.

antagonistic *adj attr* (*opposing*) антагонисти́ческий; противоде́йствующий; *predic* (*hostile*): **he is** ~ **to the proposal** он реши́тельно про́тив э́того предложе́ния.

antagonize *vt*: **he manages to** ~ **everybody** он умудря́ется настро́ить про́тив себя́ всех.

antarctic *adj* антаркти́ческий; **the A. Circle** Ю́жный поля́рный круг.

antecedent *n Gram* антецеде́нт.

antedate *vt*: **to** ~ **a letter** дати́ровать письмо́ за́дним число́м (*impf and pf*).

ante meridiem, *abbr* **a.m.: 10 a.m.** в де́сять часо́в утра́.

antenatal *adj*: **an** ~ **clinic** же́нская консульта́ция.

antenna *n* (*of insects*) щу́пальце, у́сик; *Radio* анте́нна.

anthem *n* гимн; **national** ~ госуда́рственный гимн.

ant-hill *n* мураве́йник.

anthology *n* антоло́гия.

anthropology *n* антрополо́гия.

anti-aircraft *adj*: ~ **gun** зени́тное ору́дие.

antibiotic *n* антибио́тик.

anticipate *vt* **1** (*foresee*) предви́деть, (*expect*) ожида́ть + *G* (*impfs*); **I** ~ **that...** я предви́жу, что...; **I** ~ **an interesting lecture** я ожида́ю услы́шать интере́сную ле́кцию; (*with apprehension*) **I ~ a stormy meeting** бою́сь, что собра́ние бу́дет бу́рным; (*with pleasure*) **to ~ success** предвкуша́ть успе́х (*impf*)

2 (*forestall*): **to ~ smb's wishes** предупрежда́ть/предвосхища́ть чьи-л жела́ния (*usu impfs*).

anticipation *n* ожида́ние, предвкуше́ние; **to stock up with coal in ~ of a hard winter** запасти́сь углём, предви́дя суро́вую зи́му; **we enjoyed the holiday in ~ more than anything** предвкуше́ние пра́здника бы́ло бо́лее прекра́сно, чем са́мый пра́здник; (*in letters*): **in ~ of an early reply** в ожида́нии ско́рого отве́та; **thanking you in ~** зара́нее вас благодарю́.

anticlimax *n* спад, разочарова́ние; **today seems an ~ after the concert** сего́дня у меня́ спад по́сле вчера́шнего волне́ния пе́ред конце́ртом; **the ceremony was an ~** э́та церемо́ния всех разочарова́ла.

anticlockwise *adv* про́тив часово́й стре́лки.

antics *npl* ша́лости, проде́лки.

anticyclone *n* антицикло́н.

antidote *n* противоя́дие; **an ~ against/to/for snakebite** противоя́дие от змеи́ного уку́са.

antifreeze *n Aut* антифри́з.

antimissile *adj Mil* противораке́тный.

antipathetic *adj*: **I find him ~** он мне антипати́чен.

antipathy *n* антипа́тия; **he doesn't conceal his ~ to her** он не скрыва́ет свое́й антипа́тии к ней.

antiquarian *adj* антиква́рный.

antiquary *n* (*scholar*) знато́к дре́вностей.

antiquated *adj* устаре́лый, старомо́дный; **his views are a bit ~** у него́ устаре́лые взгля́ды; *CQ* **my ~ bicycle** мой ста́рый велосипе́д.

antique *n* антиква́рная вещь; **he sells ~s** он антиква́р.

antique *adj* антиква́рный; **an ~ shop** антиква́рный магази́н.

antiquity *n* 1 (*old times*) глубо́кая дре́вность; **a city of great ~** дре́вний го́род

2 (*classical*) анти́чность; (*works, etc. of classical period*) **the antiquities of ancient Greece** дре́вности Элла́ды.

antiseptic *n* антисепти́ческое сре́дство.

antisocial *adj* (*of person*) необщи́тельный; (*of behaviour, etc.*) антиобще́ственный; **reading at table is ~** чита́ть во вре́мя еды́ неприли́чно.

antithesis *n Philos* антите́зис; *Lit* антите́за; **there's a marked ~ between...** есть ре́зкий контра́ст ме́жду + *I*.

antler *n* (оле́ний) рог.

anvil *n* накова́льня.

anxiety *n* 1 (*worry*) беспоко́йство; (*alarm*) трево́га; **his health is giving rise to ~** его́ здоро́вье вызыва́ет трево́гу; (*care*): **all these anxieties have tired her out** все э́ти хло́поты/забо́ты совсе́м извели́ её

2 (*desire*): **in his ~ to be gone, he forgot his key** второпя́х он забы́л ключ; **in his ~ to please her** желая доста́вить ей удово́льствие.

anxious *adj* 1 *attr* беспоко́йный, озабо́ченный; **an ~ mother** беспоко́йная мать; **in an ~ voice** озабо́ченным то́ном; **she gave me an ~ look** она́ взгляну́ла на меня́ озабо́ченно

2 *attr* (*causing worry*) трево́жный; **it was an ~ moment** э́то был трево́жный моме́нт

3 *predic*: **to be ~ about** беспоко́иться о + *P* (*about health*), за + *A* (*about success or the future*); **I'm ~ about his health** я беспоко́юсь о его́ здоро́вье (*now*)/за его́ здоро́вье (*in future*); **he's late and I'm ~ about him** его́ ещё нет, и я беспоко́юсь за него́; **I'm ~ about the outcome of this business** я беспоко́юсь за исхо́д э́того де́ла; **don't be ~** не беспоко́йтесь

4 *predic* (*eager*) *usu translated by verb* (о́чень) хоте́ть; **we were ~ to get there early** нам о́чень хоте́лось добра́ться туда́ пора́ньше; **I'm very ~ that she should do less** мне о́чень хоте́лось бы, что́бы она́ поме́ньше устава́ла; **I'm not all that ~ to go** мне не о́чень/осо́бенно хо́чется идти́ туда́; **he is ~ for approval** он хо́чет, что́бы его́ похвали́ли.

anxiously *adv* с волне́нием, с трево́гой, беспоко́йно.

any *pron* 1 *in interrog and conditional sentences* кто́-нибудь, что́-нибудь; **do ~ of you want to come with me?** хо́чет кто́-нибудь из вас пойти́ со мной?; **if you have ~ of this material left** е́сли у вас оста́лось ско́лько-нибудь э́того материа́ла; **few, if ~ of his books, are worth reading** лишь немно́гие из его́ книг интере́сны; **tell me if you like ~ of these books** скажи́ мне, е́сли тебе́ понра́вится кака́я-нибудь из э́тих книг

2 *in negative sentences* никто́, ничто́ [NB *if used with a prep, the prep intervenes between* ни *and pronoun*]; *for special emphasis use* ни оди́н/одна́/одно́; **I haven't talked to ~ of my friends about it** я ни с кем из мои́х друзе́й не говори́л об э́том; **I can't find the quotation in ~ of these books** я не могу́ найти́ э́той цита́ты ни в одно́й из э́тих книг

3 *in affirmative sentences* любо́й; **take ~ of these books you like** бери́те любу́ю из э́тих книг; **~ of them will show you the way** любо́й из них пока́жет вам доро́гу.

any *adj* 1 *in interrog and conditional sentences* i) како́й-нибудь, како́й-либо (*interchangeable, though* -либо *is more official*); **is there ~ hotel here?** есть здесь кака́я-нибудь гости́ница?; **~ questions?** есть ли каки́е-нибудь вопро́сы?; **have you ~ money on you?** есть ли у вас при себе́ ско́лько-нибудь де́нег?; **have you talked to ~ students yet?** вы уже́ говори́ли с ке́м-нибудь из студе́нтов?; **ii)** *in open questions "any" is not always translated*: **have you ~ news of your son?** (*in letter from him*) что пи́шет сын?, (*from a third person*) есть ли у вас каки́е-нибудь но́вости (*pl*) о сы́не?; **are there ~ Englishmen here?**

здесь есть англича́не?; **have you ~ matches?** есть ли у вас спи́чки?

2 *in negative sentences* **i)** никако́й [**NB** *if used with a prep, the prep intervenes between* ни *and* како́й]; (*for emphasis*) ни оди́н/одна́/одно́; **I don't see ~ familiar faces here** я не ви́жу здесь ни одного́ знако́мого лица́ (*sing*); **not in ~ circumstances** ни при каки́х обстоя́тельствах; **ii)** *if "any" not emphatic, it may be omitted*: **he hasn't ~ sisters** у него́ нет сестёр; **this bucket hasn't ~ handle** у э́того ведра́ нет ру́чки; (*with bread, milk, etc. "any" is not translated*): **we haven't ~ sugar in the house** у нас (в до́ме) нет ни куска́ са́хара

3 *in affirmative sentences* ка́ждый, вся́кий (= *every*), любо́й (= *any at all*); **you'll find the book in ~ library** э́ту кни́гу найдёшь в любо́й библиоте́ке; **~ schoolboy knows that** ка́ждый шко́льник э́то зна́ет; **without ~ doubt** вне вся́кого сомне́ния; **choose ~ three cards** вы́бери любы́е три ка́рты; **in ~ case** во вся́ком слу́чае; **come ~ time (you like)** приходи́ в любо́е вре́мя.

any *adv* **1** *in interrog and conditional sentences* ещё, ско́лько-нибудь; **~ more questions?** есть ли ещё вопро́сы?; **have you ~ more of these pens?** есть у вас ещё таки́е ру́чки?; **if you stay ~ longer** если вы ещё оста́нетесь; **is he ~ better?** ему́ хоть ско́лько-нибудь лу́чше?

2 *in negative sentences* ниско́лько, *CQ* ничу́ть; бо́льше; **he isn't ~ the worse for it** ему́ от э́того ничу́ть не ху́же; **he doesn't live here ~ more/longer** он здесь бо́льше не живёт; (*US*) **it didn't help us ~** э́то нам ниско́лько/ника́к не помогло́.

anybody *pron* **1** *in interrog and conditional sentences* кто́-нибудь; *CQ* кто; **is ~ else coming?** кто́-нибудь ещё придёт?; **did you speak to ~?** вы с ке́м-нибудь говори́ли?; **if ~ rings, don't answer** е́сли кто позвони́т, не отвеча́й

2 *in negative sentences* никто́ [**NB** *if used with a prep, the prep intervenes between* ни *and pronoun*]; **there isn't ~ here** здесь никого́ нет; **I haven't spoken to ~ about it** я ни с кем не говори́л об э́том; **I'm not referring to ~ here** я не говорю́ ни о ком из прису́тствующих

3 *in affirmative sentences* **i)** вся́кий (= *everyone*), любо́й, кто уго́дно (= *anyone at all*); **~ can do that** э́то мо́жет сде́лать кто уго́дно/вся́кий/любо́й; **~ who saw him then...** те, кто его́ ви́дели тогда́...; **he does it better than ~** он э́то де́лает лу́чше всех; **ii) hardly anybody: there's hardly ~ there** там вря́д ли кто́-нибудь есть; **I suppose hardly ~ will come/was there** вря́д ли кто́-нибудь придёт/был там

4 (*person of importance*): **he'll never be ~** из него́ ничего́ не вы́йдет; **everybody who is ~ will be there** там бу́дут все, кто име́ет хоть како́й-нибудь вес.

anyhow *adv* (*by any possible means*) любы́м спо́собом; (*if negative*) ника́к; **do it ~ you like** сде́лай э́то любы́м спо́собом/как хо́чешь; **we couldn't open the door ~** мы ника́к не могли́ откры́ть дверь; (*carelessly*) **the work was done ~** рабо́та была́ сде́лана ко́е-ка́к; (*at any rate*) **~ I'll have a try** во вся́ком слу́чае/ка́к бы то ни́ было, я попыта́юсь.

anyone *pron see* **anybody.**

anything *pron* **1** *in interrog and conditional sentences* что́-нибудь; **is there ~ you need?** вам что́-нибудь ну́жно?, *CQ* вам ничего́ не ну́жно?

2 *in negative sentences* ничего́; **he doesn't do ~** он ничего́ не де́лает; **not for ~** ни за что́; **there's hardly ~ left** почти́ ничего́ не оста́лось; **I was ~ but pleased** мне э́то бы́ло совсе́м не прия́тно

3 *in affirmative sentences* всё; (всё) что уго́дно; **I will do ~ I can to help you** я сде́лаю всё, что смогу́; **our dog will eat ~** на́ша соба́ка ест всё, что ей дашь; **what will we do?—A. you like** что же де́лать?—Что хоти́те, то и де́лайте; **I like gardening better than ~** бо́льше всего́ я люблю́ рабо́тать в саду́

4 *intensive use*: **it's as easy as ~** э́то совсе́м/о́чень легко́; **he ran/swore like ~** он бежа́л изо всех сил *or* сломя́ го́лову, он руга́лся на чём свет стои́т.

anyway *adv see* **anyhow.**

anywhere *adv* **1** *in interrog and conditional sentences* (*of position*) где́-нибудь, где́-то; (*of direction*) куда́-нибудь; **if you see him ~, tell him...** е́сли ты где́-нибудь уви́дишь его́, скажи́ ему́...; **does he live ~ near here?** он живёт где́-то здесь побли́зости?; **did you go ~ yesterday?** ходи́ли вы вчера́ куда́-нибудь?

2 *in negative sentences* (*of position*) нигде́; (*of direction*) никуда́; **I can't find my purse ~** я нигде́ не могу́ найти́ свой кошелёк; **I haven't been ~ for ages** я давно́ нигде́ не́ был; **I'm not going ~** я никуда́ не иду́/е́ду

3 *in affirmative sentences* (*of place*) везде́, всю́ду; **you can buy it ~** вы мо́жете э́то купи́ть везде́/в любо́м магази́не; (*of direction*) **I will go ~** я пойду́ куда́ уго́дно; *CQ* **it costs ~ from 5 to 10 dollars** э́то сто́ит что́-то ме́жду пятью́ и десятью́ до́лларами.

apart *adv* **1** в стороне́, в сто́рону; **the house stands ~** дом стои́т в стороне́; **he stood ~ from the others/with his feet ~** он стоя́л в стороне́ от други́х/ расста́вив но́ги; **he took me ~** он отвёл меня́ в сто́рону; **joking ~** шу́тки в сто́рону, кро́ме шу́ток; **I've set some potatoes ~ for seed** я оста́вил немно́го карто́феля на семена́; **his sensitive playing sets him ~ from other pianists** от други́х пиани́стов его́ отлича́ет кака́я-то осо́бая проникнове́нность исполне́ния; **the boards have come ~** до́ски разошли́сь; **my dress has come ~ at the seams** моё пла́тье распоро́лось по швам; **to take a watch ~** разобра́ть часы́; **they live ~** они́ живу́т врозь/отде́льно

2 *as prep*: ~ **from** кро́ме + *G*; **but quite ~ from that, there are other considerations** но, кро́ме того́, есть и други́е соображе́ния; ~ **from that he's nice enough** но при всём (при) том он неплохо́й челове́к.

apartheid *n* апартеи́д.

apartment *n* (*flat*) кварти́ра; (*room*) ко́мната; *CQ iron* апартаме́нты (*pl*); *attr*: **an ~ house** жило́й дом.

apathetic *adj* апати́чный, вя́лый.

ape *n* обезья́на.

aperient *n Med* слаби́тельное.

aperitif *n* аперити́в.

aperture *n* отве́рстие; (*chink, slit*) щель.

apex *n* верши́на, *also fig.*

apiece *adv*: **I paid a rouble/2 roubles/5 roubles ~ for these brooches** за э́ти бро́шки я заплати́л по рублю́/по два рубля́/по пяти́ *or* по пять рубле́й за шту́ку; **fountain pens cost a rouble/2 roubles/5 roubles ~** авторучки сто́ят по рублю́ *or* рубль/(по) два рубля́/(по) пять рубле́й ка́ждая; **he gave them an apple/two apples/six apples ~** он дал ка́ждому по я́блоку/по два я́блока/по шесть я́блок.

apologetic *adj attr*: **an ~ letter** письмо́, по́лное извине́ний; **with an ~ air** с винова́тым ви́дом; *predic*: **he was ~ about his early departure/for leaving early** он извини́лся за ра́нний ухо́д.

apologetically *adv*: **he spoke very ~ about it** он говори́л об э́том таки́м извиня́ющимся то́ном.

apologize *vi* извин|я́ться (-и́ться); **he ~d to us for being late/for keeping us waiting** он извини́лся пе́ред на́ми за опозда́ние/, что заста́вил нас ждать; **you must ~ to her** ты до́лжен попроси́ть у неё извине́ния (*G*) *or* (*for smth serious*) проще́ния (*G*)/извини́ться пе́ред ней.

apology *n* извине́ние; **to make/offer an ~ to smb** извини́ться пе́ред кем-л; **I demand an ~** я тре́бую извине́ния; *CQ* **this is just an ~ for a letter** э́то не письмо́, а како́е-то жа́лкое подо́бие.

apoplectic *adj Med* апоплекси́ческий; *CQ* **he gets ~ if he's contradicted** когда́ ему́ противоре́чат, ка́жется, что его́ вот-во́т хва́тит уда́р.

apoplexy *n* апопле́ксия.

apostle *n* апо́стол.

apostrophe *n Gram* апостро́ф.

appal *vt* ужас|а́ть (-ну́ть); **we were ~led by his appearance** нас ужасну́л его́ вид.

appalling *adj* ужа́сный, ужаса́ющий, *also CQ.*

apparatus *n* прибо́р, аппара́т; **a heating ~** обогрева́тельный прибо́р.

apparent *adj* **1** (*seeming*) ви́димый; **for no ~ reason** без ви́димой причи́ны; **her self-confidence is more ~ than real** она́ не так уве́рена в себе́, как мо́жет показа́ться

2 (*obvious*): **it's quite ~ that...** соверше́нно я́сно, что...; **it is becoming ~ to all that...** всем стано́вится я́сно, что...

apparently *adv* по-ви́димому; ~ **he has already left** по-ви́димому, он уже́ ушёл.

apparition *n* виде́ние; (*ghost*) при́зрак, привиде́ние.

appeal *n* **1** (*official*) обраще́ние; призы́в; **an ~ to the nation** обраще́ние к наро́ду; **to sign an ~** подписа́ть обраще́ние; **to answer an ~ for help** откли́кнуться на призы́в о по́мощи; **to organize an ~ for the flood victims** организова́ть фонд по́мощи пострада́вшим от наводне́ния

2 *Law* апелля́ция; обжа́лование; **there's no ~ from the decision of the court** реше́ние суда́ обжа́лованию не подлежи́т; **Court of A.** апелляцио́нный суд; **to lodge an ~** пода́ть апелля́цию

3 (*attraction*) привлека́тельность; **camping has lost its ~ for me** я бо́льше не хожу́ в похо́ды—э́то потеря́ло для меня́ свою́ привлека́тельность.

appeal *vi* **1** обра|ща́ться (с про́сьбой/тре́бованием) (-ти́ться); **we have ~ed to the management for compensation** мы обрати́лись к дире́кции с тре́бованием возмести́ть убы́тки; **it's no good ~ing to me** бесполе́зно обраща́ться ко мне; **the chairman ~ed for silence** председа́тель призва́л к тишине́; **I ~ to your finer feelings** я взыва́ю к твои́м лу́чшим чу́вствам; **to ~ to smb for help** взыва́ть к кому́-л о по́мощи; *Sport* **to ~ to the referee** обраща́ться к судье́

2 *Law* обжа́ловать (*pf*); апелли́ровать (*impf and pf*); **to ~ to a higher court** апелли́ровать в вы́сшую инста́нцию; **to ~ against a decision/a judgement of the court** обжа́ловать реше́ние/пригово́р суда́

3 (*attract*) нра́виться; **she/this painting ~s to me greatly** она́/э́та карти́на мне о́чень нра́вится.

appear *vi* **1** (*come in sight*) появ|ля́ться (-и́ться); пока́з|ываться (-а́ться); **the sun ~ed from behind the clouds** со́лнце появи́лось/показа́лось из-за облако́в; **he didn't ~ till 9** он пришёл то́лько к девяти́; **his name ~s on the list** его́ и́мя есть в спи́ске

2 *Law* предста|ва́ть (-́ть), яв|ля́ться (-и́ться); **to ~ in court** (*of defendant or prosecution*) представа́ть пе́ред судо́м, явля́ться в суд; **to ~ for the defendant/prosecution** вы|ступа́ть в ка́честве защи́тника/обвини́теля (-́ступить)

3 *Theat, etc.* выступа́ть; **he has ~ed in every concert hall in Europe** он выступа́л во всех конце́ртных за́лах Евро́пы; **he ~ed as Hamlet** он игра́л Га́млета

4 (*of book*): **when will your book ~?** когда́ вы́йдет ва́ша кни́га?

5 (*seem*) каза́ться (по-); (*turn out*) ока́з|ываться (-а́ться); **it ~s (to me) that...** (мне) ка́жется, что...; **it ~ed that nobody knew about it** оказа́лось, что никто́ об э́том не знал; **strange as it may ~ I hadn't heard about it** как ни стра́нно, я об э́том ничего́ не слы́шал; **he ~s ill/upset** у него́ больно́й/

расстро́енный вид; **he ~ed not to know about it** он, по-ви́димому, об э́том не знал.

appearance *n* **1** (*act of appearing*) появле́ние; **to make an ~** появля́ться, пока́зываться, (*on stage*) выступа́ть; **to make one's first ~** (*on stage*) дебюти́ровать; **he put in an ~ towards midnight** он появи́лся то́лько к полу́ночи; *Law* **to make an ~ in court** явля́ться в суд, (*usu not of accused*) выступа́ть в суде́ **2** (*aspect*) (вне́шний) вид, вне́шность; **to judge by ~s** суди́ть по вне́шности/по вне́шнему ви́ду (*sings*); **to all ~s** по всей ви́димости (*sing*); **the child had the ~ of being unwell** ребёнок каза́лся больны́м; **he has a healthy ~** у него́ здоро́вый вид; **to keep up ~s** соблюда́ть прили́чия; **they keep a car just for the sake of ~s** они́ де́ржат маши́ну то́лько для ви́да (*sing*).

appease *vt*: **to ~ an angry man/smb's anger** успок|а́ивать/утихоми́ри|вать разгне́ванного челове́ка (-о́ить/-ть), смягч|а́ть чей-л гнев (-и́ть); **to ~ one's hunger** утол|я́ть го́лод (-и́ть); **to ~ her I brought her some flowers** что́бы её уми́лостивить, я принёс ей буке́т цвето́в (*pf*).

appeasement *n*: **policy of ~** поли́тика умиротворе́ния.

append *vt* (*add*) добав|ля́ть (-́ить); (*attach*) прил|ага́ть (-ожи́ть); **to ~ a clause to a treaty** добавля́ть пункт к догово́ру; **a copy of the inventory is ~ed** ко́пия о́писи прилага́ется.

appendicitis *n* аппендици́т.

appendix *n* (*to document*) приложе́ние; *Anat* аппе́ндикс.

appetite *n* аппети́т; **the cold air gave us a good ~** от хо́лода у нас разыгра́лся аппети́т; **to work up an ~** нагуля́ть аппети́т; **it will spoil/take away your ~** э́то испо́ртит тебе́/отобьёт у тебя́ аппети́т; **they ate with ~** они́ е́ли с аппети́том; *fig* **I've no ~ for quarrelling** я не люблю́ сканда́лов.

appetizer *n* (*food*) заку́ска (*usu pl*); (*drink*) аперити́в.

appetizing *adj* вку́сный, аппети́тный.

applaud *vt*: **to ~ an actor/a pianist** аплоди́ровать актёру/пиани́сту (*impf*); *fig* (*approve*) одобр|я́ть (-́ить).

applause *n* аплодисме́нты (*no sing*).

apple *n* я́блоко; *attr* я́блочный.

applecart *n fig*: **to upset the ~** спу́тать все ка́рты.

apple pie *n* я́блочный пиро́г; *attr*: **in apple-pie order** в безупре́чном поря́дке.

apple tree *n* я́блоня.

appliance *n* (*device*) устро́йство; (*instrument*) прибо́р; (*gadget*) приспособле́ние; **electrical ~s** электроприбо́ры.

applicable *adj*: **is the rule ~ to this case?** э́то пра́вило примени́мо в да́нном слу́чае?; **delete/add where ~** зачеркни́те/запо́лните, где необходи́мо; **this is not ~ to you** э́то к вам не отно́сится.

applicant *n* кандида́т; **are you an ~ for this post?** вы кандида́т на э́ту до́лжность?; **there were 200 ~s** бы́ло по́дано две́сти заявле́ний.

application *n* **1** примене́ние, употребле́ние; *Med* наложе́ние; **the ~ of theory to practice** примене́ние тео́рии на пра́ктике; **the ~ of new methods to industry** примене́ние но́вых ме́тодов в промы́шленности; **for external ~ only** то́лько для нару́жного употребле́ния; **the law has no ~ in such cases** зако́н на подо́бные слу́чаи не распространя́ется; *fig* **she works with great ~** она́ рабо́тает с по́лной отда́чей **2** (*official request*) заявле́ние; (*if made by an official for an official quota*) зая́вка; **to send in an ~ for one's leave** пода́ть заявле́ние об о́тпуске; **your ~ has been accepted/turned down** ва́ше заявле́ние (не) при́нято; **an ~ for a job** заявле́ние о приёме на рабо́ту; **the librarian has sent in an ~ for new books** библиоте́карь по́дал зая́вку на но́вые кни́ги; **details may be had from the administration on ~** за информа́цией обраща́йтесь к администра́тору; *attr*: **an ~ form** анке́та.

apply *vti vt* примен|я́ть (-и́ть); *Med* на|кла́дывать на + *A*, при|кла́дывать к + *D* (*pfs* -ложи́ть); **you'll have to ~ force** на́до примени́ть си́лу; **to ~ a bandage to a wound** наложи́ть повя́зку на ра́ну; **to ~ ice to the forehead** прикла́дывать лёд ко лбу; **~ the ointment twice daily** накла́дывайте мазь два ра́за в день; **to ~ the brakes** тормози́ть (за-); **~ your mind/yourself to what you are doing** ду́май, что де́лаешь

vi **1** (*concern*): **this doesn't ~ in your case** э́то к вам не отно́сится; **delete what does not ~** зачеркни́те что не ну́жно **2** (*request*): **I'm ~ing for a job as librarian** я ищу́ ме́сто библиоте́каря; **to ~ to the university for a grant** обра|ща́ться в декана́т с про́сьбой о предоставле́нии стипе́ндии (-ти́ться).

appoint *vt* **1** назнач|а́ть (-́ить); **at the ~ed time** в назна́ченное вре́мя; **to ~ a day for the meeting** назна́чить день/да́ту собра́ния; **he was ~ed ambassador** он был назна́чен посло́м **2: his office is well ~ed** его́ кабине́т хорошо́ обста́влен.

appointment *n* **1** (*engagement*) встре́ча, свида́ние; **I have an ~ with the director** у меня́ встре́ча с дире́ктором; **I have an ~ with the doctor for 5 o'clock** в пять часо́в я иду́ на приём к врачу́; **~ with a girl friend** свида́ние с де́вушкой; **I've got an important business ~ today** сего́дня у меня́ ва́жное делово́е свида́ние; **I've got an ~ with my sister now** я сейча́с встреча́юсь с сестро́й; **I'm meeting him by ~ at 6** мы договори́лись с ним встре́титься в шесть часо́в **2** (*post*): **to receive an ~ as director** получи́ть назначе́ние на до́лжность/на пост дире́ктора.

apportion *vt* распредел|я́ть, раздел|я́ть (*pfs* -и́ть); **to ~ money** распредели́ть де́ньги; **the**

blame should be ~ed equally among them они́ все винова́ты в ра́вной ме́ре.

apposite *adj* уме́стный.

apposition *n Gram* приложе́ние.

appraisal *n* оце́нка.

appraise *vt* оце́ни|вать (´-ть).

appreciable *adj* заме́тный, ощути́мый, значи́тельный; **an ~ change in temperature** заме́тное измене́ние температу́ры; **an ~ sum** значи́тельная/ощути́мая су́мма (де́нег).

appreciate *vti vt* **1** (*value*) цени́ть (*impf*); **I ~ your kindness** я ценю́ ва́шу доброту́; **after a long winter one really ~s the sun** по́сле до́лгой зимы́ начина́ешь цени́ть со́лнце

2 (*understand*) понима́ть (*usu impf*); **I fully ~ your difficulties** я вполне́ понима́ю ва́ши тру́дности; **I ~ that we have no choice** я понима́ю, что у нас нет вы́бора; **he ~s music** он то́нко чу́вствует/понима́ет му́зыку; **I ~ the distinction** я чу́вствую ра́зницу

vi: **this land has ~d greatly since the war** цена́ на э́ту зе́млю значи́тельно вы́росла по́сле войны́.

appreciation *n* **1** (*assessment*) оце́нка; **he has no ~ of poetry** он ничего́ не понима́ет в поэ́зии

2 (*gratitude*) призна́тельность; **please accept this as a token of my ~** прими́те э́то в знак благода́рности

3 (*rise in value*) повыше́ние в цене́.

appreciative *adj*: **an ~ audience** (*sensitive*) чу́ткая аудито́рия/пу́блика; **he was very ~ of your kindness** он был вам о́чень призна́телен за ва́шу доброту́.

apprehend *vt* **1** (*perceive*) восприн|има́ть (-я́ть)

2 (*anticipate smth unpleasant*): **do you ~ any difficulty/that there will be any difficulty?** вы опаса́етесь каки́х-либо затрудне́ний?

3 (*arrest*) аресто́|вывать (-ва́ть).

apprehension *n* **1** (*perception*) восприя́тие

2 (*fear*) опасе́ние; **I waited for him with some ~** я ждал его́ с не́которым опасе́нием; **I am full of ~ of the outcome** я опаса́юсь за исхо́д

3 (*arrest*) аре́ст.

apprehensive *predic adj*: **to be ~** (*worry*) волнова́ться о + *P*, опаса́ться + *G or* за + *A* (*impfs*); **he's always ~ before an exam** он всегда́ волну́ется пе́ред экза́меном; **I am ~ for her health** я опаса́юсь за её здоро́вье; **I am ~ of failure/that...** я опаса́юсь *or* бою́сь неуда́чи/, что...

apprehensively *adv* со стра́хом, с опасе́нием.

apprentice *n* подмасте́рье (*m*), учени́к.

apprenticeship *n*: **he served his ~ with a carpenter** он был ученико́м у столяра́.

apprise *vt*: **we have been ~d of the date of the meeting** нам сообщи́ли о да́те собра́ния.

approach *n* **1** (*coming*) приближе́ние, *also fig*; (*of seasons*) наступле́ние; **the ~ of winter** наступле́ние/(*when further away*) приближе́ние зимы́; **at his ~** при его́ приближе́нии

2 (*access*) подхо́д, *also fig*; по́дступ; **our house has an easy ~** к на́шему до́му легко́ подъе́хать; *Mil* **at the ~es to the town** на по́дступах к го́роду; *fig*: **one must find the right ~ to the problem/to him** на́до найти́ пра́вильный подхо́д к пробле́ме/к нему́; **he made ~es to her** он уха́живал за ней; *attr*: **an ~ road** подъездно́й путь.

approach *vti vt* **1** (*to a place, also fig*) прибли|жа́ться к + *D* (´-зиться); (*drive up to*) подъе|зжа́ть к + *D* (´-хать); **we are now ~ing the palace** тепе́рь мы приближа́емся/подъезжа́ем к дворцу́; *fig* **her naivety ~es stupidity** её наи́вность грани́чит с глу́постью

2 (*go up to a person, also of trains and fig*) под|ходи́ть к + *D* (-ойти́); **a boy ~ed me in the street** ма́льчик подошёл ко мне на у́лице; **the train ~ed the station** по́езд подошёл к ста́нции; *fig*: **I didn't know how to ~ him** я не знал, как к нему́ подступи́ться; **it's better to ~ the manager about that** с э́тим лу́чше обрати́ться к заве́дующему; **to ~ a question with caution** осторо́жно подходи́ть к реше́нию вопро́са

vi приближа́ться; (*of seasons, etc.*) насту|п|а́ть (-и́ть); **the holidays are ~ing** приближа́ются кани́кулы; **spring/night is ~ing** наступа́ет весна́/ночь.

approachable *adj*: **he is very ~** к нему́ всегда́ мо́жно обрати́ться.

approaching *adj*: **the ~ holiday** приближа́ющийся пра́здник; **~ traffic** встре́чное движе́ние.

approbation *n* одобре́ние.

appropriate *adj* подходя́щий; уме́стный; удо́бный; **choose the ~ moment** вы́бери подходя́щий/удо́бный моме́нт; **his speech was most ~** его́ выступле́ние бы́ло о́чень кста́ти; **I'll repair it if you give me an ~ tool** я э́то починю́, е́сли ты дашь мне подходя́щий инструме́нт; **an ~ remark** уме́стное замеча́ние; **apply to the ~ department** обрати́тесь в соотве́тствующий отде́л; **what would be the ~ dress for this occasion?** како́е пла́тье лу́чше наде́ть для тако́го слу́чая?

appropriate *vt* **1** присв|а́ивать (-о́ить); **my son has ~d my jersey** сын присво́ил себе́ мой сви́тер

2 (*set aside*): **funds have been ~d for a new theatre** на строи́тельство но́вого теа́тра бы́ли вы́делены/отпу́щены сре́дства.

approval *n* одобре́ние; **the proposal met with ~** предложе́ние бы́ло встре́чено с одобре́нием; *Comm* **on ~**, *abbr* **on appro** на про́бу.

approve *vti vt* (*agree*) одобр|я́ть (´-ить); (*confirm*) утвер|жда́ть (-ди́ть); **the council has ~d the plans** сове́т одо́брил/утверди́л пла́ны; **the minutes were read and ~d** протоко́л (*sing*) был зачи́тан и одо́брен

vi: **I ~ of her choice** я одобря́ю её вы́бор; **he doesn't ~ of his wife smoking** он о́чень недово́лен, что его́ жена́ ку́рит.

approved *adj*: **an ~ school** *equiv* исправи́тельная коло́ния для несовершенноле́тних.

approving *adj* одобри́тельный.

approximate *adj* приблизи́тельный.

approximate *vi*: **our output figures ~ to our target** на́ши произво́дственные показа́тели приближа́ются к за́данным.

approximation *n*: **I can only give you an ~ of how long it will take to get to Edinburgh** я могу́ вам то́лько приблизи́тельно сказа́ть, ско́лько е́хать до Эдинбу́рга.

apricot *n* абрико́с (*fruit and tree*); *attr* абрико́совый.

April *n* апре́ль (*m*); *attr* апре́льский.

apron *n* пере́дник, фа́ртук; *Aer* площа́дка пе́ред анга́ром; *attr CQ*: **he's tied to his mother's/wife's ~ strings** он не сме́ет без ма́тери и ша́гу шагну́ть, он у жены́ под башмако́м.

apropos *adv and predic adj*: **his suggestion is very much ~** его́ предложе́ние о́чень кста́ти (*adv*); **~ of your remark...** относи́тельно/по по́воду ва́шего замеча́ния...

apt *adj* **1** *attr*: **an ~ pupil** спосо́бный учени́к; **an ~ remark** уме́стное замеча́ние; **an ~ description** уда́чное описа́ние

2 *predic*: **I am ~ to be out on Tuesdays** по вто́рникам меня́ обы́чно не быва́ет до́ма; **he's ~ to forget that his daughter is only two** он забыва́ет, что его́ до́чери всего́/то́лько два го́да; **he's ~ to get bronchitis** он скло́нен к бронхи́там (*pl*); **the fire is ~ to go out** ого́нь вками́не то и де́ло га́снет; **she's ~ to take offence easily** она́ о́чень оби́дчива.

aptitude *n* спосо́бность (*usu pl*); **I've no ~ for mathematics** у меня́ нет спосо́бностей к матема́тике; *attr*: **an ~ test** прове́рка спосо́бностей уча́щегося.

aqualung *n* аквала́нг.

aquarium *n* аква́риум.

Arab *n* ара́б, ара́бка.

Arabic *n* ара́бский язы́к.

Arabic *adj* ара́бский.

arable *adj* па́хотный.

arbitrary *adj* произво́льный, случа́йный; (*dictatorial*) деспоти́чный.

arbitrate *vi*: **he ~d between the workmen and the management** он выступа́л трете́йским судьёй в конфли́кте ме́жду рабо́чими и администра́цией.

arbitration *n* арбитра́ж; *attr*: **~ tribunal** арбитра́жный суд.

arbitrator *n* арби́тр, трете́йский судья́ (*m*).

arc *n Math* дуга́; *attr*: **~ lamp** дугова́я ла́мпа.

arcade *n* пасса́ж; арка́да.

arch *n Archit* а́рка, свод.

arch *vt* вы|гиба́ть (дуго́й) (´-гнуть); **the cat ~ed its back** ко́шка вы́гнула спи́ну.

archaeology *n* археоло́гия.

archaic *adj* (*obsolete*) устаре́лый, устаре́вший; (*ancient*) дре́вний.

archbishop *n* архиепи́скоп.

archipelago *n* архипела́г.

architect *n* архите́ктор.

architecture *n* архитекту́ра.

archive *n* архи́в.

archway *n* прохо́д/прое́зд под а́ркой.

arctic *adj* аркти́ческий; **the A. Circle** Се́верный поля́рный круг.

ardent *adj* горя́чий, пы́лкий; **an ~ desire** горя́чее жела́ние; **an ~ supporter** я́рый сторо́нник; **an ~ lover** пы́лкий любо́вник.

ardour *n* пыл, горя́чность, страсть; **to damp smb's ~** охлади́ть чей-л пыл.

arduous *adj* тру́дный, тяжёлый, напряжённый; **an ~ climb** тру́дное восхожде́ние; **it's ~ work** э́то тяжёлая/напряжённая рабо́та.

area *n Math* пло́щадь; *Geog* зо́на, райо́н, пло́щадь; **the forest is 1,000 square kilometres in ~** лес пло́щадью в ты́сячу квадра́тных киломе́тров; **the ~ of a triangle** пло́щадь треуго́льника; **sown ~** посевна́я пло́щадь; **the Cambridge ~** Ке́мбридж и его́ окре́стности; **prohibited ~** запре́тная зо́на; *fig*: **the ~ of finance** сфе́ра фина́нсов; **the ~s of disagreement** вопро́сы, по кото́рым существу́ют разногла́сия (*pl*).

arena *n* аре́на; (*in boxing*) ринг.

Argentinian *n* аргенти́нец, аргенти́нка.

Argentinian *adj* аргенти́нский.

arguable *adj*: **it's ~ that...** мо́жно утвержда́ть, что...

argue *vti vt* **1** (*dispute*): **I'd like to ~ that point** я хоте́л бы возрази́ть по э́тому пу́нкту; **his case was well ~d** он хорошо́ аргументи́ровал свои́ до́воды; **he ~d that...** он утвержда́л/дока́зывал, что...

2: **to ~ smb into/out of doing smth** убеди́ть/разубеди́ть кого́-л сде́лать что-л (*usu pfs*)

vi спо́рить (по-); **I ~d with him over/about it for hours** я часа́ми спо́рил с ним об э́том; **don't ~!** не спорь!; **he ~d against/in favour of the proposal** он приводи́л до́воды про́тив/в по́льзу э́того предложе́ния.

argument *n* **1** (*debate, quarrel*) спор; **there was a heated ~** разгоре́лся жа́ркий спор; **he had the better of the ~** он был я́вно сильне́е в э́том спо́ре; **let's have no ~s** дава́йте не бу́дем спо́рить; **you've heard only one side of the ~** вы вы́слушали пози́цию то́лько одно́й стороны́ в э́том спо́ре

2 (*reason*) до́вод, аргуме́нт; **that's a good ~** э́то убеди́тельный до́вод/аргуме́нт; **for the sake of ~, let's say...** допу́стим...; **his ~ is that...** он утвержда́ет, что...; **I don't follow your ~** я не ви́жу/ула́вливаю свя́зи в ва́ших до́водах (*pl*); **I'm open to ~** я го[...] вы́слушать други́е мне́ния (*pl*).

argumentative *adj*: **he's very ~** он [...] лю́бит спо́рить.

arid *adj* сухо́й, *also fig*; засу́ш[...]

aright *adv*: **did I hear you ~**[...] вильно по́нял?

arise *vi* **1** (*come into ex*[...] (´-нуть); **the question do**[...] исключено́, э́тот вопро́с[...]

ка́л; **should the opportunity** ~ е́сли предста́вится слу́чай

2 (*result from*) прои|сходи́ть (-зойти́); **it all arose from a misunderstanding** э́то произошло́ по недоразуме́нию; **arising from the decision of the council** по реше́нию сове́та.

aristocrat *n* аристокра́т.

arithmetic *n* арифме́тика.

arm[1] *n* **1** рука́ (*from shoulder to wrist*); **to take smb by the** ~ взять кого́-л по́д руку; **they walked** ~ **in** ~ они́ шли по́д руку; **to carry a child in one's** ~**s** нести́ ребёнка на рука́х; **to take a child in one's** ~**s** взять ребёнка на́ руки; **to rush into smb's** ~**s** бро́ситься кому́-л в объя́тия; **to welcome smb with open** ~**s** встре́тить кого́-л с распростёртыми объя́тиями; **she put her** ~**s round him** она́ обняла́ его́; **to carry smth under one's** ~ нести́ что-л под мы́шкой; **a babe in** ~**s** грудно́й ребёнок; *fig*: **to chance one's** ~ рискну́ть; **to keep smb at** ~**'s length** держа́ть кого́-л на почти́тельном расстоя́нии

2 (*of a garment or river*) рука́в; **an** ~ **of the sea** морско́й зали́в; *fig* **the** ~ **of the law** кара́ющая рука́ зако́на.

arm[2] *n* **1** *Mil* род во́йск; **the air** ~ вое́нно-возду́шные си́лы (*pl*)

2 *pl* (~**s**) ору́жие (*collect*); **under** ~**s** под ружьём; **to take up** ~**s** взя́ться за ору́жие; **to lay down** ~**s** сложи́ть ору́жие; *fig*: **he was up in** ~**s over/about the remark at once** при э́том замеча́нии он момента́льно ощети́нился; *CQ* **they were up in** ~**s about the introduction of new rules** они́ при́няли в штыки́ но́вые пра́вила; *attr*: ~**s limitation** сокраще́ние вооруже́ний.

arm[2] *vt Mil* вооруж|а́ть (-и́ть); **to** ~ **oneself with** вооружа́ться + *I*, *also fig*.

armaments *npl* вооруже́ние (*collect*); *attr*: **the** ~ **race** го́нка вооруже́ний.

armband *n see* **armlet.**

armchair *n* кре́сло.

armed *adj* вооружённый; **the** ~ **services/forces** вооружённые си́лы; ~ **robbery** вооружённый грабёж; **he was** ~ **to the teeth** он был вооружён до зубо́в.

Armenian *n* армяни́н, армя́нка.

Armenian *adj* армя́нский.

armful *n* оха́пка.

armhole *n* про́йма.

armistice *n* переми́рие.

armlet *n* нарука́вная повя́зка.

armour, (*US*) **armor** *n Hist* доспе́хи, ла́ты (*pls*); (*modern*; *collect*) броня́.

armoured, (*US*) **armored** *adj* брониро́ванный; ~ **car** бронемаши́на.

armoury, (*US*) **armory** *n* арсена́л; (*in Kremlin*) **the A.** Оруже́йная пала́та.

armpit *n Anat* подмы́шечная впа́дина, подмы́шка [*but declines as separate words* под мы́шку, под мы́шкой].

army *n* а́рмия, во́йско (*only in sing*, *pl* = *troops*); **he's in the** ~ он слу́жит в а́рмии, он вое́нный; *fig CQ*: **an** ~ **of tourists/of insects** то́лпы (*pl*) тури́стов, ту́чи (*pl*) насеко́мых; *attr*: ~ **corps** арме́йский ко́рпус; **an** ~ **doctor** вое́нный врач, *abbr CQ* военвра́ч.

aroma *n* арома́т.

aromatic *adj* арома́тный, благово́нный.

around *adv* круго́м; **all** ~ повсю́ду; ~ **all was still** круго́м всё бы́ло ти́хо; **there's no one** ~ здесь/побли́зости никого́ нет; **he's somewhere** ~ он где́-то здесь; *see also verbs* + **around.**

around *prep* вокру́г + *G*; ~ **the house there were many trees** вокру́г до́ма росло́ мно́го дере́вьев; **we walked** ~ **the pond** мы обошли́ пруд круго́м; **the children are playing** ~ **the house** де́ти игра́ют в до́ме (*inside*)/о́коло до́ма (*outside*); **just** ~ **the corner** здесь за угло́м; **she is** ~ **50** ей лет пятьдеся́т [**NB** *approximation best expressed by inversion of noun and numeral*; о́коло пяти́десяти = *nearly* 50, *just under* 50]; **it cost** ~ **5 roubles** э́то сто́ило что́-то о́коло пяти́ рубле́й.

arouse *vt* (*awaken*) буди́ть (раз-), пробу|жда́ть (-ди́ть), *also fig*; *fig* (*of interest, suspicion, curiosity*) возбу|жда́ть (-ди́ть), (*of contempt, indignation, envy, pity, interest*) вы|зыва́ть (-звать); **it** ~**d her maternal instincts** э́то пробуди́ло в ней матери́нский инсти́нкт (*sing*).

arrange *vti vt* **1** (*put in order*): **to** ~ **one's affairs** при|води́ть дела́ в поря́док (-вести́); **to** ~ **books in alphabetical order/by subject** расстав|ля́ть кни́ги в алфави́тном/темати́ческом поря́дке (-́ить); **to** ~ **flowers** расставля́ть цветы́

2 (*fix*) устр|а́ивать (-о́ить); назнач|а́ть (-́ить); **to** ~ **a concert/a party** устра́ивать конце́рт/ве́чер; **the meeting** ~**d for Tuesday is cancelled** заседа́ние, назна́ченное на вто́рник, отменено́; **it was** ~**d that the meeting would be held in Kiev** договори́лись, что встре́ча состо́ится в Ки́еве; **everything is** ~**d for our holiday** всё гото́во к о́тпуску

3 *Mus* переложи́ть (*only in pf*); ~**d for two pianos** в переложе́нии для двух фортепья́но

vi догов|а́риваться (-ори́ться); **I've** ~**d for you to stay with my brother** я договори́лся, что ты остано́вишься у моего́ бра́та; **he** ~**d to call for me at 6** он обеща́л зайти́ за мной в шесть (часо́в); **can you** ~ **for my letters to be forwarded?** ты мо́жешь договори́ться, что́бы мне пересыла́ли мои́ пи́сьма?

arrangement *n* **1** (*order, ordering*): **I like the** ~ **of this room** мне нра́вится, как обста́влена э́та ко́мната; **a flower** ~ компози́ция из цвето́в; ~ **by subject** расстано́вка по те́мам (*pl*)

2 (*agreement*) соглаше́ние, догово́р; **the price is a matter for** ~ цена́ бу́дет согла́сно догово́ру; **salary by** ~ зарпла́та по догово́ру; **we can come to some sort of** ~ **over expenses later** пото́м разберёмся, кто ско́лько потра́тил

3 (*plan*; *often pl*): **I've made all the ~s for my journey** я закóнчил все приготовлéния к поéздке; **I'll make ~s for smb to meet you/for you to be met at the airport** я договорю́сь, чтóбы тебя́ встрéтили на аэродрóме; **I'll make my own ~s** я сам кáк-нибудь устрóюсь

4 *Mus* переложéние.

array *n*: **he has quite an ~ of tools** у негó цéлый набóр вся́ких инструмéнтов; *Mil* **in battle ~** в боевóм поря́дке.

arrears *npl* (*of money*) задóлженность (*sing*); **to collect ~ of rent** взы́скивать задóлженность по квартплáте; **I'm in ~ with my hire purchase instalments** я запáздываю с вы́платой рассрóчки; **I'm in ~ with my correspondence/with my work** я не успевáю отвечáть на пи́сьма/справля́ться с рабóтой.

arrest *n* арéст; **under ~** под арéстом.

arrest *vt* (*by police, etc.*) арестóв|ывать (-áть); **he's been ~ed for murder** егó арестовáли по обвинéнию в уби́йстве; *fig*: **to ~ growth** задéрж|ивать рост (-áть); **the disease has been ~ed** болéзнь былá приостанóвлена; **the sound of steps ~ed my attention** звук шагóв приковáл моё внимáние.

arrival *n* прибы́тие; приéзд (*only of people by transport*); **on our ~ in Moscow** по приéзде в Москвý; **on the ~ of the train** по прибы́тии пóезда; **time of ~** (*of train, plane, person*) врéмя прибы́тия; **"to await ~"** «храни́ть до прибы́тия адресáта»; (*of person*) **have you met the new ~s?** вы встрéтили вновь прибы́вших?

arrive *vi* (*of people*: *on foot*) при|ходи́ть (-йти́), (*by vehicle*) при|езжáть (-éхать); (*of trains, planes and officially of people*) прибы|вáть (-ть); **we ~d at their flat early** мы рáно пришли́ к ним; **the delegation ~d yesterday** делегáция прибылá вчерá; **the train ~d half an hour late** пóезд опоздáл на полчасá; (*of seasons*) **summer has ~d** наступи́ло лéто; *fig*: **to ~ at a decision/conclusion** прийти́ к решéнию/к заключéнию; **to ~ at an understanding** дости́гнуть взаимопонимáния; *CQ* **that artist has ~d at last** в концé концóв э́тот худóжник получи́л признáние.

arrogance *n* высокомéрие, надмéнность; спесь.

arrogant *adj* высокомéрный, надмéнный; спеси́вый.

arrow *n* (*weapon*) стрелá; (*pointer, etc.*) стрéлка.

arsenal *n* арсенáл.

arsenic *n* мышья́к.

arson *n* поджóг.

art *n* **1** искýсство; **fine/applied ~s** изя́щные/прикладны́е искýсства; **folk ~** нарóдное искýсство; **~s and crafts** худóжественные прóмыслы/ремёсла; **a work of ~** произведéние искýсства; *attr*: **~ critic** искусствовéд; **~ gallery** карти́нная/худóжественная галерéя; **~ school** худóжественное учи́лище

2 *pl* (**the ~s**) *Univ* гуманитáрные наýки

3 (*cunning*) хи́трость.

artery *n Anat* артéрия.

artful *adj* хи́трый.

arthritis *n Med* артри́т.

artichoke *n* артишóк; **jerusalem ~s** земляны́е грýши.

article *n* **1** (*object*) предмéт, вещь; **an ~ of clothing** предмéт одéжды; **household ~s** предмéты домáшнего обихóда; **he collected his various ~s** он собрáл свои́ вéщи

2 (*written*) статья́; **the ~ says that...** в статьé говори́тся, что...; **leading ~** передовáя статья́, передови́ца

3 *Law* пункт, парáграф, статья́; **~ 12 of the agreement states that...** пункт двенáдцатый соглашéния гласи́т, что...

4 *Gram* арти́кль (*m*).

articulate *adj*: **he is not very ~** он не óчень я́сно выражáется.

articulate *vi*: **he ~s badly** он неотчётливо/плóхо произнóсит словá (*usu impf*).

articulated *adj*: **an ~ lorry** грузови́к с прицéпом.

artificial *adj* искýсственный; **~ silk** искýсственный шёлк; **~ respiration** искýсственное дыхáние; **an ~ limb** протéз; **an ~ smile/manner** притвóрная улы́бка, жемáнство.

artillery *n* артиллéрия.

artisan *n* ремéсленник.

artist *n* худóжник; *Theat, Cine* арти́ст, *f* -ка.

artistic *adj* худóжественный, артисти́чный.

artless *adj* (*natural*) естéственный; (*simple*) простóй, простодýшный, бесхи́тростный.

arty *adj CQ* (*of clothes, etc.*) экстравагáнтный, *sl* модернóвый.

as *conj, adv and prep* **1** (*in comparisons*) **i) as... as, so... as: he's as tall as his father** он такóй же высóкий, как и егó отéц; **my hair is as long as yours** у меня́ таки́е же дли́нные вóлосы, как и у вас; **as quickly as possible** как мóжно быстрée/скорée; **I'll be as quick as I can** *CQ* я ми́гом, я сейчáс; **as white as snow** бéлый как снег; **the tin's as good as empty** бáнка почти́ пустáя; **he was as good as his word** он как сказáл, так и сдéлал; **this rope is so old as to be useless** верёвка такáя стáрая, что порá ужé её вы́бросить; **I'm not so stupid as to believe that** я не так глуп, чтóбы повéрить э́тому; **ii) as if, as though: he behaved as if/as though he were drunk** он вёл себя́ так, как бýдто был пьян; **he said it as if joking** он сказáл э́то как бы в шýтку

2 (*concessive*): **much as I love you** хотя́ я и óчень люблю́ вас; **be that as it may** кáк бы то ни́ было; **that's as may be, but all the same...** э́то так, но всё же...; **try as he would** как он ни старáлся; **it's all right as far as it goes** в какóй-то мéре э́то неплóхо; **I'm far too busy as it is** я и так/я и без тогó сли́шком зáнят

3 (*in capacity of*) как; **we're going as tourists** мы éдем как тури́сты; **he's treated as one of**

the family к нему́ отно́сятся как к чле́ну семьи́; **it's regarded as an accident** счита́ют, что э́то несча́стный слу́чай; **he accompanied us as an interpreter** он сопровожда́л нас в ка́честве перево́дчика; **it's not bad as a first effort** для пе́рвого ра́за непло́хо; **he works as an engineer** он рабо́тает инжене́ром

4 (*concerning*): **as to that, as regards that, as far as that's concerned** что каса́ется э́того; **as for her, I never want to see her again** что до неё, я не хочу́ её бо́льше ви́деть; **he said nothing as to salary** он ничего́ не сказа́л насчёт зарпла́ты

5 (*of manner*) как; **do as I do** де́лай, как я; **do as you please** де́лай как хо́чешь; **better to leave things as they are** лу́чше оста́вить всё как есть; **as things stand, he's hardly likely to agree** при ны́нешнем положе́нии дел он вря́д ли согласи́тся; **he arranged matters so as to suit everyone** он всё сде́лал так, что́бы никого́ не оби́деть; **as it happens, I was present** (случи́лось так, что) я как ра́з был там

6 (*of time*): **as I was leaving home, it began to rain** когда́ я выходи́л и́з дому, пошёл дождь; **as a child, I lived in Scotland** ребёнком/в де́тстве я жил в Шотла́ндии; **as long as I live** пока́ я жив; **just as he finished speaking** как то́лько он ко́нчил говори́ть; **we left as soon as we could** мы ушли́, как то́лько смогли́

7 (*causal*): **I couldn't phone you as I was busy** я был за́нят и не мог вам позвони́ть; **as I don't sleep well, I tend to get up late** я пло́хо сплю и поэ́тому обы́чно встаю́ по́здно

8 (*introducing relative clauses*): **we drove out by the same road as we came in by** мы верну́лись той же доро́гой, кото́рой прие́хали; **such apples, as we do have, are quite good** те я́блоки, кото́рые у нас есть, совсе́м неплохи́е; **take as much as you like** возьми́ ско́лько хо́чешь

9 (*of purpose*): **keep quiet, so as not to wake the baby** ти́ше, не разбуди́ ребёнка, веди́ себя́ поти́ше, а то разбу́дишь ребёнка

10 (*conditional*): **do what you like, as long as you're back for supper** де́лай что хо́чешь, то́лько не опозда́й к у́жину

11 *various*: **we might just as well do it now** хорошо́ бы сде́лать э́то сейча́с; **would you be so good as to hand her this letter?** бу́дьте любе́зны, переда́йте ей э́то письмо́; **I thought as much** я так и ду́мал; **Igor came as well** Игорь то́же пришёл; **as yet there's no news** пока́ нет никаки́х новосте́й (*pl*); **as usual he was late** он как всегда́ опозда́л; **as per order** согла́сно зака́зу; **the conditions are as follows...** усло́вия сле́дующие...; **as a matter of fact** на са́мом де́ле, факти́чески, (*by the way*) ме́жду про́чим; **as far as I can judge** наско́лько я могу́ суди́ть.

asbestos *n* асбе́ст.

ascension *n Rel* (**the A.**) вознесе́ние.

ascent *n* (*climb*) восхожде́ние; (*climb or gradient*) подъём; **the ~ of Everest** восхожде́ние на Эвере́ст; **a steep ~** круто́й подъём.

ascertain *vt* устан|а́вливать (-ови́ть); **to ~ the cause of the crash** установи́ть причи́ну ава́рии.

ascetic *n* аске́т.

ascribe *vt* припи́с|ывать (-а́ть); **the play has been ~d to Shakespeare** э́ту пье́су припи́сывают Шекспи́ру; **he ~d his failure to bad luck** он объясни́л свой прова́л невезе́нием.

aseptic *adj* стери́льный, асепти́ческий.

ash[1] *n* (*tree*) я́сень (*m*); **mountain ~** ряби́на.

ash[2] *n* (*of fire, cigars, the dead*) пе́пел (*collect*); (*of fire*: *usu pl*) зола́ (*collect*); **a heap of ~(es)** ку́ча пе́пла/золы́; **to burn to ~es** сжига́ть дотла́ (*adv*).

ashamed *predic adj*: **I am ~ of you/of what I've done** мне сты́дно за вас, я стыжу́сь своего́ посту́пка; **I'm ~ to say it's true** сты́дно сказа́ть, но э́то пра́вда/так; **to be ~ of oneself** стыди́ться; **you ought to be ~ of yourself** тебе́ должно́ быть сты́дно, как тебе́ не сты́дно!; **your generosity makes me feel ~** пра́во, я смущён ва́шей доброто́й.

ash-bin, (*US*) **ash can** *n* му́сорное ведро́ (*bucket*), му́сорный я́щик (*bin*).

ashore *adv*: **to come ~** сходи́ть на бе́рег; **they are still ~** они́ ещё на берегу́.

ashtray *n* пе́пельница.

Asian *adj* азиа́тский.

aside *n Theat* ре́плика в сто́рону.

aside *adv* в стороне́; (*of motion*) в сто́рону; **to take smb ~** отводи́ть кого́-л в сто́рону; **to turn ~** сверну́ть в сто́рону; **he stood ~** он стоя́л в стороне́; **I set the book ~ for you** я отложи́л э́ту кни́гу для вас; **to set ~ a verdict** отмени́ть пригово́р; **joking ~** кро́ме шу́ток, шу́тки в сто́рону.

ask *vti vt* **1** (*inquire*) спра́шивать (спроси́ть); **I'll ~ him about it** я его́ спрошу́ об э́том; **I want to ~ you a question** хочу́ зада́ть вам вопро́с; **I ~ed him how to get there** я спроси́л его́, как туда́ пройти́/прое́хать

2 (*request, demand*) проси́ть (по-); **he ~ed my help/me for help/me to help** он проси́л меня́ помо́чь/мое́й по́мощи (*G because not a specific object*); **he ~ed me for (some) money/for £10** он попроси́л у меня́ де́нег (*G because an unspecified amount*)/де́сять фу́нтов; **he ~ed me a favour/a favour of me** он попроси́л меня́ об одолже́нии [**NB** о + *P cannot be used of a specific object*]; **he ~ed his sister to lend him her bicycle** он попроси́л сестру́ дать ему́ велосипе́д, он попроси́л у сестры́ велосипе́д; **he ~ed that we keep it a secret** он попроси́л нас держа́ть э́то в секре́те/в та́йне; **how much are they ~ing for the car?** ско́лько они́ про́сят за маши́ну?; **one shouldn't ~ too much of a 10-year old** нельзя́ сли́шком мно́го тре́-

бовать с десятиле́тнего; **he ~ed us to excuse him** он извини́лся пе́ред на́ми

3 (*invite*) пригла|ша́ть (-си́ть); **let's ~ her to dinner/to dine** дава́й пригласи́м её на обе́д; **shall I ~ him in?** пригласи́ть его́ войти́?; **he ~ed me out tomorrow/for a dance** он пригласи́л меня́ за́втра на прогу́лку/на та́нец

vi **1** (*inquire*) спра́шивать (спроси́ть); **I was only ~ing** я то́лько спроси́л (и ничего́ бо́льше); **to ~ about/after/for smb** спра́шивать/справ|ля́ться о ком-л (-́иться)

2 (*demand*) проси́ть (по-); **he ~ed for advice** он проси́л сове́та; **he ~ed for his pencil back** он попроси́л свой каранда́ш обра́тно; **he ~ed to see my husband** он хоте́л повида́ть моего́ му́жа; *CQ* **he's just ~ing for trouble** он напра́шивается на неприя́тности (*pl*).

askance *adv*: **he looked at me ~** он ко́со/подозри́тельно посмотре́л на меня́.

askew *adv*: **the picture is ~** карти́на виси́т ко́со; **he wore his hat ~** он носи́л шля́пу набекре́нь.

asleep *predic adj*: **to be ~** спать; **he was fast ~** он кре́пко спал; **to fall ~** засну́ть; **I'm half ~** я почти́ сплю.

asparagus *n* спа́ржа.

aspect *n* вид; *fig* аспе́кт, сторона́; **he is a man of stern ~** у него́ тако́й суро́вый вид; **the house has a southern ~** дом выхо́дит на юг; **every ~ of the question** все сто́роны/аспе́кты (*pls*) э́того вопро́са.

aspen *n* оси́на.

asperity *n* ре́зкость; **he spoke with some ~** он говори́л ре́зко.

aspersion *n* клевета́ (*no pl*); **to cast ~s on smb** клевета́ть на ко́го-л.

asphalt *n* асфа́льт.

asphyxiate *vt* (*if murder*) удуши́ть (*pf*); (*by fumes*) **to be ~d** задохну́ться (*pf*).

asphyxiation *n* (*if murder*) удуше́ние; (*by fumes*) уду́шье.

aspic *n approx* сту́день (*m*), холоде́ц; заливно́е; **fish/chicken in ~** заливно́е из ры́бы *or* заливна́я ры́ба, заливно́е из цыплёнка.

aspirate *adj Ling* придыха́тельный.

aspire *vi*: **to ~ to** стреми́ться к + *D or* + *inf* (*impf*); **he ~s to become a writer/famous** он мечта́ет стать писа́телем, он стреми́тся к изве́стности *or* стать изве́стным.

aspirin *n* аспири́н.

ass *n* осёл; *CQ* **you ~!** ты осёл!

assailant *n*: **I didn't see the face of my ~** я не разгляде́л/ви́дел лица́ того́, кто напа́л на меня́.

assassin *n* уби́йца (*m and f*).

assassinate *vt* уби|ва́ть (-́ть).

assassination *n* уби́йство.

assault *n* нападе́ние на + *A*; *Mil* при́ступ, штурм; **an ~ on smb** нападе́ние на кого́-л; **he was charged with indecent ~** его́ суди́ли за изнаси́лование.

assault *vt* напа|да́ть на + *A* (-́сть).

assemble *vti vt*: **to ~ people** со|бира́ть люде́й (-бра́ть); *Tech* (*of large constructions, also in electronics*) монти́ровать (с-), (*of watches, electrical devices*) собира́ть

vi собира́ться; **we ~d in the hall/for the meeting** мы собрали́сь в за́ле, мы пришли́ на собра́ние.

assembly *n* собра́ние, о́бщество; *Tech* (*of large units*) монта́ж, (*of smaller units*) сбо́рка; **General A. of the UN** Генера́льная Ассамбле́я ООН; *attr*: **~ line** сбо́рочный конве́йер.

assent *n* согла́сие.

assent *vi*: **to ~ to a proposal** (*by individuals*) согла|ша́ться на предложе́ние (-си́ться), (*by committees, etc.*) одобр|я́ть предложе́ние (-́ить).

assert *vt* утвер|жда́ть (-ди́ть); **to ~ one's rights** утвержда́ть свои́ права́; **he likes ~ing himself** он лю́бит показа́ть себя́.

assertion *n* утвержде́ние.

assertive *adj*: **in an ~ tone** авторите́тным то́ном; *pejor* **he's very ~** он чересчу́р напо́рист.

assess *vt* оце́н|ивать (-и́ть); **to ~ (the value of) a property at £10, 000** оце́нивать иму́щество в де́сять ты́сяч фу́нтов; **to ~ taxes** определ|я́ть/устан|а́вливать разме́р нало́гов (-и́ть/-ови́ть); *fig* **to ~ smb's character/a situation** оцени́ть чей-л хара́ктер/ситуа́цию.

assessment *n* оце́нка; **~ for taxation** обложе́ние нало́гами.

asset *n usu pl* (**~s**) *Fin* акти́в (*sing*); *fig*: **when they come to make the appointment your teaching experience will be a great ~** при обсужде́нии кандидату́р твой педагоги́ческий о́пыт бу́дет тебе́ больши́м плю́сом; **good health is a great ~** хоро́шее здоро́вье—вели́кое де́ло.

assiduous *adj* приле́жный.

assign *vt* (*fix, appoint*) назнач|а́ть, (*earmark*) предназнач|а́ть (*pfs* -́ить); (*set aside*) от|води́ть (-вести́); **Tuesday has been ~ed as the day for the trial** суд назна́чили на вто́рник; **these rooms have been ~ed to us** э́ти ко́мнаты отведены́ нам/предназна́чены для нас; **I have been ~ed a flat** мне вы́делили/да́ли кварти́ру; **two pupils were ~ed to prepare the display** вы́ставку поручи́ли пригото́вить двум ученика́м.

assignation *n* (*of lovers*) свида́ние.

assignment *n* (*commission*) зада́ние, поруче́ние; (*appointment*) назначе́ние; (*in schools*) зада́ние.

assimilate *vti vt* усв|а́ивать (-о́ить); ассимили́ровать (*impf and pf*); **fish is easily ~d** ры́ба легко́ усва́ивается органи́змом; **America has ~d people of many different nationalities** Аме́рика ассимили́ровала люде́й мно́гих национа́льностей; *fig* **to ~ new ideas** усво́ить/приня́ть но́вые иде́и

vi: **they find it difficult to ~ to new conditions** им тру́дно привыка́ть к но́вым усло́виям.

assist *vti vt* помо|гать + *D* (́-чь); **to ~ smb with money / in his work / in finishing** *or* **to finish his task** помочь кому-л деньгами / в работе / закончить работу

vi (*participate*): **to ~ in smth** прин|имать участие в чём-л (-ять).

assistance *n* помощь; **to render smb ~** оказывать кому-л помощь; **can I be of ~ to you?** могу ли я чем-нибудь помочь вам?

assistant *n* помощник; *Univ* (*to a professor*) ассистент; **laboratory ~** лаборант, *f* -ка; *attr*: **~ manager** заместитель (*m*) начальника.

associate *n* (*in profession*) коллега (m); *Comm* компаньон; (*member*) член; (*in crime*) соучастник; *attr* (*US*): **~ professor** адъюнкт-профессор.

associate *vti vt*: **he is ~d with the new school of painting** он примкнул к новому течению в живописи; **I always ~ spring with tulips** у меня всегда весна ассоциируется / связана с тюльпанами; **I don't wish to ~ myself with that opinion** я не желаю присоединяться к этому мнению; **was he ~d with that scandal?** был ли он замешан в этом скандале?; **my son is ~d with an American firm** мой сын связан по работе с одной американской фирмой

vi (*be in company of*) общаться с + *I* (*impf*); *pejor* связ|ываться с + *I* (-аться); **she ~s mostly with her colleagues** она общается главным образом со своими коллегами; **he ~s with highly undesirable people** он водит компанию с весьма неприятными людьми, он связался с плохой компанией.

association *n* **1** (*group*) общество, объединение; ассоциация

2 (*being with others*) общение; **he benefited greatly from his ~ with your family** общение с вашей семьёй дало ему очень много

3 (*mental connection*) ассоциация; **by an ~ of ideas** по ассоциации; **the word has unpleasant ~s for me** это слово вызывает у меня неприятные ассоциации.

assorted *adj*: **a pound of ~ chocolates** фунт шоколада ассорти (*indecl*); **dresses in ~ colours** платья разнообразных расцветок.

assortment *n* ассортимент; **they carry a wide ~ of goods** у них широкий ассортимент / выбор товаров.

assume *vt* **1** (*take up*): **to ~ office** вступ|ать в должность (-ить); **he has ~d control of the business** он возглавил это предприятие; **she ~d an air of innocence** она приняла невинный вид

2 (*suppose*) предпо|лагать (-ложить); **let us ~ that...** предположим, что...; **assuming that...** предполагая, что...

assumed *adj* (*pretended*) притворный; напускной; **an ~ name** вымышленное имя.

assumption *n* предположение; **on the ~ that...** предполагая, что...

assurance *n* **1** (*promise*) заверение, уверение; **he gave me his ~ that...** он заверил меня, что...

2 (*confidence*) уверенность

3 (*insurance*) страхование.

assure *vt* увер|ять, завер|ять (*pfs* ́-ить); **it is so, I ~ you** это так, уверяю вас / я вас уверяю; **he ~d me of his loyalty** он заверил меня в своей преданности.

assured *adj* уверенный; *Comm* (*insured*) застрахованный; **you may rest ~ that...** будьте уверены, что...; **he has an ~ manner** у него уверенные манеры (*pl*); **he has an ~ income of £1,000 a year** у него твёрдый годовой доход в тысячу фунтов.

assuredly *adv* несомненно; конечно, наверняка.

asterisk *n* звёздочка.

astern *n*: **my cabin is ~** моя каюта на корме; **there's a sailing ship ~ of us** сзади по ходу у нас парусная лодка; **to go ~** плыть / идти задним ходом; **full speed ~!** полный ход назад!

asthma *n* астма.

astonish *vt* удив|лять, (*stronger*) изум|лять (*pfs* -ить); пора|жать (-зить); **I was ~ed at his behaviour** я был удивлён / поражён его поведением, я удивился / изумился его поведению.

astonishing *adj* удивительный, поразительный.

astonishment *n* удивление, изумление; **to everybody's ~** к удивлению всех.

astound *vt* изум|лять (-ить); пора|жать (-зить); **I was ~ed by his insolence** его наглость поразила меня.

astrakhan *n* (*fur*) каракуль (*m*).

astray *adv*: **to go ~** заблудиться (*pf*), сби|ваться с пути (́-ться), *also fig*; *fig* **to lead smb ~** сбить кого-л с пути истинного.

astride *adv*: **to ride ~** ехать верхом; **he sat ~ the chair** он сидел верхом на стуле.

astrology *n* астрология.

astronaut *n* космонавт.

astronomical *adj* астрономический; *fig CQ* **an ~ sum** астрономическая / немыслимая сумма.

astronomy *n* астрономия.

astute *adj* проницательный; сообразительный; *pejor* **an ~ move** хитрый шаг.

asylum *n* **1**: **to seek political ~** просить политического убежища

2 (*mental hospital*) психиатрическая больница.

asymmetrical *adj* асимметричный.

at *prep* **1** (*of place*: *where*) у + *G*, на + *P*; в + *P*; **~ the window, ~ Olga's** у окна, у Ольги; **~ the corner / station / meeting** на углу, на вокзале, на собрании; **get off ~ the second stop** вам выходить через одну остановку; **~ a distance of 50 miles** на расстоянии пятидесяти миль; **~ a height of 10 feet** на высоте десяти футов; **~ the hotel / chemist's / theatre / concert** в гостинице, в аптеке, в театре, на концерте; **there's a museum ~ Zagorsk** в Загорске есть музей; **to arrive ~ Zagorsk** приехать в Загорск;

we have a house ~ the sea у нас есть дом на берегу́ мо́ря; **my son is ~ sea** мой сын моря́к (*is a sailor*)/в пла́вании (*is voyaging*); **we were sitting ~ table/dinner** мы сиде́ли за столо́м, мы обе́дали; **~ hand** под руко́й; **~ the top/bottom of the page** наверху́/внизу́ страни́цы

2 (*of time, order*) в + *A*, в + *P*; **~ any/the same time** в любо́е/в то́ же вре́мя; **~ 3 o'clock** в три часа́; **~ a quarter past 9** в че́тверть деся́того; **~ noon** в по́лдень; **~ half past 8** в полови́не девя́того; **~ the age of 5** в пятиле́тнем во́зрасте; **~ a quarter to 2** без че́тверти два; **~ 10 to 3** без десяти́ три; **~ dawn** на рассве́те; **~ night** но́чью; **~ first** снача́ла; **~ first sight** с пе́рвого взгля́да; **~ last** наконе́ц; **~ once** сра́зу

3 (*of rate, price, etc.*): **~ 30 m.p.h.** со ско́ростью три́дцать миль в час; **~ full speed/gallop** на по́лной ско́рости, во весь опо́р; **I bought strawberries ~ a rouble/~ 2 roubles/~ 5 roubles a kilo** я купи́л клубни́ку по рублю́/по два рубля́/по пять рубле́й кило(гра́мм); **he lent me money ~ 4% interest** он ссуди́л мне де́ньги под четы́ре проце́нта; **to sell ~ a high price** прода́ть по высо́кой цене́; **~ least** по кра́йней/ме́ньшей ме́ре; **~ worst/best** в ху́дшем/лу́чшем слу́чае; **he wasn't ~ his best** он был не в фо́рме

4 *with adjs*: **he's good ~ languages** у него́ спосо́бности (*pl*) к языка́м; **I'm no good ~ sewing** я не уме́ю шить; **he was impatient ~ the delay** заде́ржка раздража́ла его́; **I'm delighted ~ the idea** я в восто́рге от э́той иде́и

5 *with verb "to be"*: **he's ~ work/~ a conference** он на рабо́те, он на конфере́нции; **he's been ~ it for three days** он уже́ три дня э́тим занима́ется; **they're hard ~ it** они́ заняли́сь э́тим всерьёз [**NB** *tense*]; **she's been ~ me all day** она́ весь день меня́ руга́ет; **the children have been ~ me to let them go to the cinema** де́ти приста́ли ко мне, что́бы я их отпусти́л в кино́; **while we're ~ it let me say...** и раз уж мы об э́том заговори́ли, то скажу́...; **the mice have been ~ the cheese** мы́ши добрали́сь до сы́ра; **moths have been ~ my fur collar** моль (*collect*) поби́ла мой мехово́й воротни́к

6 *with other verbs; see also under particular verbs*: **to look ~ smb/smth** смотре́ть на кого́-л/на что-л; **to shout ~ smb** крича́ть на кого́-л; **to laugh ~ smb** смея́ться над кем-л; **she smiled ~ me** она́ улыбну́лась мне; **I'm surprised ~ you** я удивля́юсь вам; **she knocked ~ the door** она́ постуча́ла в дверь

7 *various*: **~ my request/suggestion** по мое́й про́сьбе, по моему́ предложе́нию; **~ the sight of the sea** при ви́де мо́ря; **~ one blow** одни́м уда́ром.

atheist *n* атеи́ст.

athletic *adj* атлети́ческий; **~ sports** лёгкая атле́тика (*sing*).

atlas *n* а́тлас.

atmosphere *n* атмосфе́ра, *also fig*; **a friendly ~** дру́жественная атмосфе́ра.

atmospherics *npl Radio* атмосфе́рные поме́хи.

atom *n* а́том.

atomic *adj* а́томный.

atone *vi*: **to ~ for a misdeed** искупи́ть вину́ (*usu pf*); **in order to ~ for being late** что́бы загла́дить вину́ за опозда́ние.

atrocious *adj* зве́рский; *CQ* ужа́сный, жу́ткий; **~ weather** ужа́сная пого́да.

atrocity *n* зве́рство.

attach *vti vt* **1**: **to ~ smth to smth** (*fasten*) прикреп|ля́ть/(*tie*) привя́з|ывать что-л к чему́-л (-и́ть/-а́ть); (*stick*) **to ~ a label to smth** накле́|ивать этике́тку на что-л (-ить); **to ~ documents to a letter** при|лага́ть докуме́нты к письму́ (-ложи́ть); **please find copy ~ed** ко́пия прилага́ется

2 *fig uses* (*of people*): **we were ~ed to the English group** нас присоедини́ли к гру́ппе англича́н; **he has ~ed himself to this party** он примкну́л к э́той па́ртии; **he ~ed himself to us** он приста́л/*CQ* приби́лся к нам; **I ~ great importance to these facts** я придаю́ э́тим фа́ктам большо́е значе́ние; **I am very ~ed to her** я о́чень к ней привя́зан

vi: **absolutely no blame ~es to him** он в э́том нисколько не пови́нен.

attaché *n* атташе́ (*indecl*).

attaché case *n* пло́ский чемода́нчик для бума́г, *CQ* «диплома́т».

attack *vti vt* **1** напа|да́ть на + *A* (-́сть), *also Mil, fig*; *Mil, fig* атакова́ть + *A* (*impf and pf*); **to ~ a town/an enemy** напа́сть на го́род/на проти́вника *or* атакова́ть проти́вника; **the little boy ~ed his sister with his fists** ма́льчик набро́сился на сестру́ с кула́ками

2 (*affect*) пора|жа́ть (-зи́ть); **woodworm has ~ed the flooring** полы́ (*pl*) поражены́ древе́сным жучко́м; **this disease ~s the nervous system/children** э́та боле́знь поража́ет не́рвную систе́му, э́то де́тская боле́знь; **rust ~s metals** ржа́вчина разъеда́ет мета́ллы; *fig*: **he ~ed our proposals** он подве́рг напа́дкам на́ши предложе́ния; **he was ~ed in the press** его́ подве́ргли кри́тике в газе́тах/в пре́ссе; **he was ~ed by doubts** на него́ напа́ли сомне́ния

vi атакова́ть, *also Sport*.

attain *vt* дости|га́ть + *G* (-́чь); **we ~ed our objective/the summit** мы дости́гли свое́й це́ли/верши́ны горы́.

attainable *adj* достижи́мый.

attainment *n* достиже́ние; **for the ~ of his purpose** для достиже́ния свое́й це́ли; **his ~s are many** он доби́лся успе́ха во мно́гих областя́х.

attempt *n* попы́тка; **I'll make an ~ to come** я попыта́юсь прийти́; **this is my first ~ at painting** э́то моя́ пе́рвая попы́тка в жи́вописи (*P*); **we gave up the ~** мы отказа́лись от попы́ток (*pl*); **he's making an ~ on the record** он попыта́ется поби́ть реко́рд; **they made two ~s on Everest** они́ два́жды пыта́-

лись подня́ться на Эвере́ст; **he made an ~ on his own life** он пыта́лся поко́нчить с собо́й.

attempt *vt* пыта́ться, про́бовать (*pfs* по-); **to ~ to do smth** пыта́ться/про́бовать сде́лать что-л; **don't ~ the impossible** не пыта́йся объя́ть необъя́тное; **I'll ~ it** я попыта́юсь, я попро́бую.

attend *vti vt* **1** (*to nurse, etc.*) уха́живать за + *I* (*impf*); (*of service*) обслу́ж|ивать (-и́ть); (*accompany*) сопрово|жда́ть (-ди́ть); **which doctor is ~ing you?** како́й врач вас ле́чит?; **three secretaries ~ the president on his travels** президе́нта сопровожда́ют в пое́здках три секретаря́

2 (*meeting, etc.*) прису́тствовать на + *P* (*impf*); **to ~ a conference** прису́тствовать/быть на конфере́нции; **the meeting was well ~ed** на собра́нии бы́ло мно́го наро́ду; **to ~ lectures** посеща́ть ле́кции (*only in impf*)

vi: **he didn't ~ to what I said** он не слу́шал, что я ему́ говори́л; **to ~ to business** занима́ться дела́ми; **I'll ~ to the baby** я займу́сь ребёнком; (*in shop, etc.*) **I'll ~ to you in a minute** сейча́с я вас обслужу́.

attendant *n* (*servant*) слуга́ (*m*); (*in lift*) лифтёр; (*in car park, museum, library*) служи́тель (*m*), *f* -ница; **cloakroom ~** гардеро́бщи|к, *f* -ца.

attendant *adj*: **the ~ nurse** дежу́рная сестра́.

attention *n* **1** (*heed*) внима́ние; **to listen with ~** слу́шать внима́тельно; **to attract/distract smb's ~** привлека́ть/отвлека́ть чьё-л внима́ние; **he drew my ~ to the picture** он обрати́л моё внима́ние на э́ту карти́ну; **pay no ~ to what he says** не обраща́й внима́ния на то, что он говори́т; **the old lady receives many ~s from her neighbours** сосе́ди внима́тельны к стару́шке; **a pretty girl gets lots of ~** хоро́шенькие де́вушки (*pl*) избало́ваны внима́нием

2 (*care*) ухо́д; **this plant needs daily ~** э́то расте́ние тре́бует ежедне́вного ухо́да

3 *Mil*: **to stand at ~** стоя́ть сми́рно.

attentive *adj* внима́тельный; **an ~ audience** внима́тельная пу́блика; **he is ~ to his mother** он внима́телен к ма́тери; **he is very ~ to his studies** он о́чень добросо́вестно отно́сится к свои́м заня́тиям.

attic *n* черда́к; манса́рда.

attitude *n* **1** (*pose*) по́за; **he assumed a threatening ~** он при́нял угрожа́ющую по́зу; **he's always ready to strike/take up an ~** он скло́нен к позёрству

2 (*mental*) отноше́ние; **what's your ~ to this problem?** как вы отно́ситесь к э́тому вопро́су?; **if that's your ~ we may as well stop talking** раз вы так к э́тому отно́ситесь, (нам) не́ о чем говори́ть; **that's a stupid ~ to take/adopt** э́то неу́мная пози́ция.

attract *vt* (*of magnets*) притя́гивать (*only in impf*); *fig* привле|ка́ть (-́чь); **a sound ~ed my attention to the garden** како́й-то стра́нный звук в саду́ привлёк моё внима́ние.

attraction *n* (*by magnet*) притяже́ние; *fig*: **I don't fall for her ~s** на меня́ не де́йствуют её ча́ры; **the job has many ~s for me** э́та рабо́та меня́ мно́гим привлека́ет; **the tour offers many ~s** в э́той пое́здке мно́го привлека́тельного.

attractive *adj* привлека́тельный; **what an ~ child!** како́й ми́лый ребёнок!; **I've had an ~ offer of a job in Paris** мне предложи́ли рабо́ту в Пари́же—предложе́ние о́чень зама́нчивое.

attribute *n* ка́чество, сво́йство; *Philos* атрибу́т.

attribute *vt* припи́с|ывать (-а́ть); (*explain*) объясн|я́ть (-и́ть); **the play is sometimes ~d to Shakespeare** э́ту пье́су не́которые припи́сывают Шекспи́ру; **to what do you ~ his failure?** чем ты объясни́шь его́ неуда́чу?

attributive *adj Gram* атрибути́вный.

aubergine *n* баклажа́н.

auction *n* аукцио́н; **to sell by ~** пойти́ с молотка́; **to put smth up for ~** продава́ть что-л с аукцио́на; *attr*: **an ~ sale** прода́жа с аукцио́на.

audacious *n* сме́лый; (*impudent*) де́рзкий.

audibility *n* слы́шимость.

audible *adj* слы́шный; слы́шимый; **he was scarcely ~** его́ едва́ бы́ло слы́шно (*impers*); **a scarcely ~ whisper** е́ле слы́шный шёпот.

audience *n* **1** (*at lecture, etc.*) аудито́рия; *Theat, etc.* пу́блика, зри́тели (*pl*); **there was a big ~** собрала́сь больша́я аудито́рия, бы́ло мно́го пу́блики

2 (*interview*) аудие́нция; **to give/grant smb an ~** дать кому́-л аудие́нцию; **to be received in ~ by smb** получи́ть аудие́нцию у кого́-л.

audio-visual *adj* аудиовизуа́льный.

audit *vt*: **to ~ accounts** провер|я́ть счета́ (-́ить).

audition *n* прослу́шивание, про́ба.

auditorium *n* аудито́рия; зри́тельный зал.

augment *vt* увели́чи|вать (-ть); **he ~s his income by working as a night watchman** он подраба́тывает ночны́м сто́рожем.

augur *vti*: **it ~s ill/well** э́то ничего́ хоро́шего не предвеща́ет *or* не сули́т, э́то хоро́ший знак.

August *n* а́вгуст; *attr* а́вгустовский.

aunt, *CQ* **auntie, aunty** *n* тётя, *CQ* тётка, тётушка.

aural *adj* ушно́й; **an ~ test** прове́рка слу́ха.

auspices *npl*: **under favourable ~** при благоприя́тных обстоя́тельствах; **he is researching under the ~ of Oxford university** он занима́ется иссле́дованиями при Оксфо́рдском университе́те.

auspicious *adj* благоприя́тный.

austere *adj* суро́вый.

Australian *n* австрали́ец, австрали́йка.

Australian *adj* австрали́йский.

Austrian *n* австри́ец, австри́йка.

Austrian *adj* австри́йский.

authentic *adj* (*of antiques, etc.*) по́длинный; аутенти́чный; (*of news, etc.*) достове́рный.

authenticate *vt* удостовер|я́ть (-́ить).

author *n* а́втор; **a book by a French ~** кни́га францу́зского а́втора.

authoritative *adj* авторите́тный.

authority *n* 1 (*quality*) авторите́т; **he's got an air of ~** у него́ вид челове́ка влия́тельного; **he spoke with ~** он говори́л авторите́тным то́ном; **he can make his ~ felt** он иногда́ даёт почу́вствовать свою́ власть

2 (*official power*) полномо́чие; **I've no ~ to take a decision** я не уполномо́чен принима́ть реше́ния; **he was given ~ to sign the agreement** его́ уполномо́чили подписа́ть соглаше́ние; **he did it without ~** он сде́лал э́то, не име́я на то пра́ва

3 (*people*) вла́сти (*pl*); (*department*) управле́ние, отде́л; **the city authorities** городски́е вла́сти; **he's in trouble with the authorities** у него́ неприя́тности с властя́ми; **apply to the proper ~** обрати́тесь в соотве́тствующие инста́нции (*pl*); **those in ~ say...** авторите́тные ли́ца говоря́т...; **the Port of London A.** Управле́ние Ло́ндонского по́рта; **nursery schools come under the Health authorities** я́сли нахо́дятся в ве́дении министе́рства здравоохране́ния

4 (*authoritative source*) авторите́т; **he is an ~ in this field** он авторите́т в э́той о́бласти; **he has Plato's ~ for (stating) this** он утвержда́ет э́то, ссыла́ясь на Плато́на; **I have it on good ~ that...** я зна́ю из надёжного исто́чника, что...

authorization *n* разреше́ние, са́нкция.

authorize *vt* уполномо́чи|вать (-ть); **to ~ smb to do smth** уполномо́чить кого́-л сде́лать что-л; **an ~d translation** авторизо́ванный перево́д.

authorship *n* а́вторство.

autobiography *n* автобиогра́фия.

autograph *n* авто́граф.

automate *vt* автоматизи́ровать (*impf and pf*).

automatic *n* автомати́ческий пистоле́т.

automatic *adj* автомати́ческий; (*done without thought*) машина́льный.

automaton *n* автома́т, *also fig*.

automobile *n* автомоби́ль (*m*).

autonomous *adj* автоно́мный.

autopsy *n* вскры́тие, ауто́псия.

autumn *n* о́сень; **last ~** про́шлой о́сенью; *attr* осе́нний.

autumnal *adj* осе́нний.

auxiliary *adj* вспомога́тельный; **~ troops,** *also as n* **auxiliaries** вспомога́тельные войска́.

avail *n*: **it was of no/little ~** э́то бы́ло бесполе́зно; **to no ~** напра́сно (*adv*).

avail *vt*: **to ~ oneself of smth** по́льзоваться чем-л (вос-).

availability *n*: **it will depend on ~ of spare parts** э́то зави́сит от того́, каки́е бу́дут запасны́е ча́сти.

available *adj* **1: tomatoes aren't ~ at present** сейча́с помидо́ров ещё нет; **is the manager ~ just now?** мо́жно ви́деть сейча́с заве́дующего?; **I made my car ~ to him while his was being repaired** пока́ его́ маши́на была́ в ремо́нте, я предоста́вил в его́ распоряже́ние свою́; **fetch every bucket ~** дава́йте сюда́ все вёдра, каки́е то́лько есть; **by all ~ means** все́ми возмо́жными сре́дствами

2 (*US*) (*valid*): **the ticket is ~ for one month** биле́т действи́телен на оди́н ме́сяц.

avalanche *n* сне́жный обва́л, лави́на.

avarice *n* жа́дность, а́лчность.

avaricious *adj* жа́дный, а́лчный.

avenge *vt* мстить + *D or* за + *A* (ото́-); **to ~ an insult** отомсти́ть за оскорбле́ние; **to ~ oneself/to be ~d on an enemy** отомсти́ть врагу́.

avenue *n* алле́я; (*as street name*) авеню́ (*indecl*); *fig* **to explore every ~** разузна́ть все возмо́жности.

aver *vt* утвер|жда́ть (-ди́ть).

average *n* сре́днее; *Math* сре́днее число́; **his work is above/below (the) ~** его́ рабо́та вы́ше/ни́же сре́днего у́ровня; **on an/the ~** в сре́днем.

average *adj* сре́дний; **the ~ temperature** сре́дняя температу́ра; **the ~ man** обы́чный челове́к; **a man of ~ ability** челове́к сре́дних спосо́бностей (*pl*).

average *vi*: **we ~ 8 hours work a day** мы рабо́таем в сре́днем во́семь часо́в в день; **he ~d 100 kilometres (an hour) all the way** он де́лал в сре́днем сто киломе́тров в час.

averse *adj*: **I am ~ to early rising** я не люблю́ ра́но встава́ть; **I am ~ to answering such letters** я не располо́жен отвеча́ть на подо́бные пи́сьма; **I'm not ~ to an occassional drink** я не прочь иногда́ пропусти́ть рю́мочку-другу́ю.

aversion *n* неприя́знь, отвраще́ние; **I took an immediate ~ to her** у меня́ сра́зу появи́лась к ней неприя́знь; **I have an ~ for garlic** я терпе́ть не могу́ чесно́к; **he/botany is my pet ~** он мне осо́бенно неприя́тен, бота́ника внуша́ет мне отвраще́ние.

avert *vt* от|води́ть (-вести́), от|вора́чивать (-́верну́ть); (*stave off*) предотвра|ща́ть (-ти́ть); **she ~ed her eyes from the corpse** она́ отвела́ взгляд от тру́па; **he ~ed his face** он отверну́лся; **in order to ~ suspicion from himself** что́бы отвле́чь/отвести́ от себя́ подозре́ние; **an accident was narrowly ~ed** ава́рию чу́дом предотврати́ли; **I tried to ~ my thoughts from tomorrow's exam** я стара́лся не ду́мать о за́втрашнем экза́мене.

aviation *n* авиа́ция.

avid *adj* жа́дный, *also fig*; **he is an ~ reader** он глота́ет кни́ги.

avocado (pear) *n Bot* авока́до (*indecl*).

avoid *vt* избе|га́ть + *G or* + *inf* (-жа́ть); укло|ня́ться от + *G* (-ни́ться); **he purposely ~s me** он (наро́чно) избега́ет меня́; **I ~ driving at the rush hours** я избега́ю е́здить в часы́ пик; **the driver couldn't ~ (hitting) the cyclist** води́тель не смог объе́хать велосипеди́ста; **by going this way we ~ London** по э́той доро́ге мы мину́ем Ло́ндон; **he ~ed the question** (*did not raise it*) он обошёл э́тот вопро́с, (*did not answer directly*) он уклони́лся от отве́та на вопро́с; **he ~ed the blow** он уклони́лся от уда́ра; **to ~ paying taxes** уклоня́ться от упла́ты нало́гов.

avowed *adj*: **he has an ~ interest in the deal** он не скрыва́ет, что заинтересо́ван в э́той сде́лке.

await *vt* (*for smth near in time*) ожида́ть + *G*, (*for smth further off in time*) ждать + *G* (*impfs*); **a warm welcome ~s you** тебя́ ожида́ет тёплый приём; **I ~ your reply** я жду ва́шего отве́та.

awake *predic adj*: **I was already ~ at 6** в шесть часо́в я уже́ просну́лся; **the children are still ~** де́ти ещё не спят; **coffee keeps me ~** е́сли я вы́пью ко́фе, я не могу́ засну́ть; **I lay/stayed ~ all night** я не спал всю ночь; *fig* **he is ~ to the danger/to what is going on** он я́сно ви́дит *or* осознаёт опа́сность, он понима́ет, что происхо́дит.

awake *vti vt* буди́ть (раз-); **the noise of voices awoke me** голоса́ разбуди́ли меня́

vi про|сыпа́ться (-сну́ться); **I awoke when it was still dark** когда́ я просну́лся, бы́ло ещё темно́; *fig* **it's time you awoke to the fact that...** пора́ вам наконе́ц поня́ть,/осозна́ть, что...

awaken *vti vt* буди́ть (раз-, *fig* про-); **he ~ed me at 8** он разбуди́л меня́ в во́семь (часо́в); *fig* **he's been ~ed at last to a sense of responsibility/to the urgency of the situation** наконе́ц-то в нём пробуди́лось чу́вство отве́тственности, наконе́ц он по́нял серьёзность положе́ния

vi про|сыпа́ться (-сну́ться); **we ~ed to find the sun already up** мы просну́лись, когда́ со́лнце уже́ взошло́.

awakening *n* пробужде́ние, *also fig*; **a rude ~** возвраще́ние к суро́вой реа́льности.

award *n* (*prize*) награ́да; *Law* реше́ние суда́; *Univ* стипе́ндия.

award *vt* прису|жда́ть (-ди́ть); **he was ~ed first prize** ему́ была́ присуждена́ пе́рвая пре́мия; **he was ~ed the Order of Lenin** его́ награди́ли о́рденом Ле́нина; *Law* **the judge ~ed her £500 damages** судья́ вы́нес реше́ние вы́платить ей пятьсо́т фу́нтов в ка́честве компенса́ции.

aware *predic adj*: **to be ~ of smth** сознава́ть что-л; **I was fully ~ of the danger** я прекра́сно сознава́л опа́сность; **are you ~ that it's already 8 o'clock?** тебе́ изве́стно, что уже́ во́семь часо́в?; **has he gone?—Not that I'm ~ of** он ушёл?—Мне ка́жется, что нет; **I had offended her deeply without being ~ of it** я бо́льно заде́л её чу́вства, сам того́ не сознава́я.

awash *predic adj*: **the decks were ~** па́луба (*sing*) была́ залита́ водо́й.

away *adv* **1: 10 miles ~** в десяти́ ми́лях отсю́да; **~ in the distance** где́-то вдали́/далеко́; **far ~ can be seen the mountains** вдали́ видны́ го́ры; **let's sit well ~ from the fire** дава́йте ся́дем пода́льше от огня́; **~ with you!** (*be off!*) прочь!; **~ with him!** (*down with him!*) доло́й его́!; **I'll come right ~** я сейча́с же приду́; **he's far and ~/out and ~ my best pupil** он бесспо́рно мой лу́чший учени́к; **is the next match at home or ~?** сле́дующая игра́ на своём и́ли на чужо́м по́ле?; *as adj*: **an ~ match** матч, проводи́мый на чужо́м по́ле

2 *with verb "to be"*: **he's ~ from home** его́ нет до́ма; **how long will he be ~?** ско́лько вре́мени его́ не бу́дет?; **the sea is 2 miles ~** до мо́ря отсю́да две ми́ли, мо́ре в двух ми́лях отсю́да

3 *with other verbs; see also particular verbs* **i)** *indicating removal; usu translated by prefix* у-: **he's just this minute gone ~** он то́лько что ушёл/уе́хал; **put your toys ~** убери́ игру́шки; **I'll take ~ the tea things** я унесу́/уберу́ ча́шки; **ii)** *indicating loss, weakening*: **the water has all boiled ~** вся вода́ выкипела; **the sound died ~** шум зати́х; **iii)** *indicating continuity*: **we chatted ~ for hours** мы часа́ми разгова́ривали; **he's still working ~ at his thesis** он всё ещё тру́дится над свое́й диссерта́цией.

awe *n* благогове́ние; **she holds him in ~** она́ благогове́ет пе́ред ним.

awful *adj* ужа́сный, стра́шный, *also CQ*; **it was an ~ moment** э́то был ужа́сный моме́нт; *CQ* **how ~!** како́й у́жас!; **I feel ~** (*ill*) я ужа́сно себя́ чу́вствую; **I feel ~ about it** (*ashamed, sorry*) мне ужа́сно сты́дно!, (*embarrassed*) мне о́чень нело́вко!

awhile *adv*: **stay ~ yet!** погоди́ немно́го!; **I won't be coming yet ~** я ещё не иду́.

awkward *adj* (*clumsy*) неуклю́жий; нело́вкий, *also fig*; *fig* (*inconvenient*) неудо́бный; **my son is an ~ child** мой сын о́чень неуклю́жий/нело́вок; **an ~ silence** нело́вкое молча́ние; **I felt ~** я чу́вствую себя́ нело́вко; **it's an ~ bend** э́то неудо́бный поворо́т; **it's an ~ time for me** э́то для меня́ неудо́бное вре́мя; **he's an ~ customer/~ to deal with** с ним тру́дно име́ть де́ло, с ним лу́чше де́ла не име́ть.

awning *n* (*above doors, windows, etc.*) наве́с, тент.

axe, (*US*) ax *n* топо́р.

axe, (*US*) ax *vt CQ* (*dismiss*) увол|ьня́ть (-́ить).

axiom *n* аксио́ма.

axis *n* ось, *also fig Polit*.

axle *n Tech* ось; **front/back ~** пере́дняя/за́дняя ось.

aye *n*: **the ~s and the noes** (голоса́) «за» и «про́тив»; **the ~s have it** большинство́— «за».

azalea *n* аза́лия.

Azerbaijani *n* азербайджа́нец, азербайджа́нка.

Azerbaijanian *adj* азербайджа́нский.

azure *adj* лазу́рный.

B

B *n Mus* си (*indecl*).

babble *n* (*child's*) ле́пет; (*of water, etc.*) журча́ние; **the ~ of voices** шум голосо́в, го́вор.

babble *vi* лепета́ть (*impf*); (*of water*) журча́ть (*impf*).

baby *n* грудно́й ребёнок/младе́нец; (*of animal*) детёныш; **two/five babies** два грудны́х младе́нца, пять грудны́х младе́нцев; **she's going to have the ~ in hospital** она́ бу́дет рожа́ть в больни́це/(*SU*) в роддо́ме; *fig* **he's just a big ~** он про́сто большо́й ребёнок; *attr*: **a ~ boy/girl** ма́ленький сын, ма́ленькая дочу́рка.

baby carriage *n* (*US*) (де́тская) коля́ска.

baby grand *n* кабине́тный роя́ль (*m*).

babyish *adj*: **~ behaviour** ребя́чество; **don't be so ~** переста́нь ребя́читься.

baby-sit *vi*: **I promised to ~ for her tomorrow** я обеща́ла за́втра посиде́ть с её детьми́/присмотре́ть за её детьми́.

baby talk *n* сюсю́канье.

bachelor *n* холостя́к; *Univ* **B. of Arts/Science** бакала́вр иску́сств/нау́к (*pl*).

bacillus *n* баци́лла.

back *n* **1** *Anat* спина́; (*of animal*) спина́, спи́нка; **the small of the ~** поясни́ца; **a pain in the ~** боль в спине́/в поясни́це; **he's broken his ~** у него́ перело́м позвоно́чника (*spine*); **to lie/sleep/carry smth on one's ~** лежа́ть/спать/нести́ что-л на спине́; **he fell on his ~** он упа́л на́взничь (*adv*)/на́ спину; **they stood ~ to ~/with their ~s to the window** они́ стоя́ли спина́ к спине́/спино́й (*sing*) к окну́

2 (*back part*: *of chair*) спи́нка; (*of material*) изна́нка; (*of knife*) тупа́я сторона́ (ножа́); (*of book*: *spine*) корешо́к; (*of document*) оборо́тная сторона́, оборо́т; **the ~ of the head** заты́лок; **sign on the ~** распиши́тесь на оборо́те; **the index is at the ~ of the book** и́ндекс в конце́ кни́ги; **at the ~ of the stage** в глубине́ сце́ны; **it's in/at the ~ of the drawer** э́то лежи́т в глубине́ я́щика; **the garage is at the ~ of the house** гара́ж позади́ до́ма; **he stood at the ~** он стоя́л позади́ (*adv*); **the house seen from the ~** вид до́ма сза́ди (*adv*)

3 *Sport* защи́тник

4 *fig uses*: **he did it behind her ~** он сде́лал э́то у неё за спино́й/вта́йне (*adv*) от неё; **it's not nice to talk behind people's ~** некраси́во говори́ть за спино́й; **what's at the ~ of it all?** что за э́тим кро́ется?; **to put smb's ~ up** гла́дить кого́-л про́тив ше́рсти; **to put one's ~ into a job** энерги́чно взя́ться за де́ло; **to break the ~ of a job** вы́полнить бо́льшую часть рабо́ты; **with one's ~ to the wall** припёртый к стене́; **we were glad to see the ~ of him** мы бы́ли ра́ды от него́ изба́виться; **the name is at the ~ of my mind** э́то и́мя ве́ртится у меня́ в голове́.

back *adj* **1** за́дний; **the ~ rows** за́дние ряды́; **~ wheel** за́днее колесо́; **~ garden** сад за до́мом; **~ tooth** коренно́й зуб

2 (*overdue*): **~ payment** просро́ченный платёж.

back *adv* **1** (*backwards*) наза́д; **to run ~** бежа́ть наза́д/(*if returning somewhere*) обра́тно; **there and ~** туда́ и обра́тно; **to send smth ~** отосла́ть что-л обра́тно; **he's just ~ from Paris** он то́лько что верну́лся из Пари́жа; **I'll be ~ in a minute** я сейча́с верну́сь; **the house stands ~ from the road** дом стои́т в стороне́ от доро́ги

2 (*of time*) (тому́) наза́д; **a few years ~** не́сколько лет тому́ наза́д; **as far ~ as 1900** ещё в ты́сяча девятисо́том году́.

back *prep* (*US*): **~ of = behind, beyond.**

back *vti vt*: **to ~ (up) smb/a proposal** подде́рж|ивать кого́-л/предложе́ние (-а́ть); **I ~ed the car out of the garage** я вы́вел маши́ну за́дним хо́дом из гаража́; **to ~ a horse** (*move it back*) оса́|живать ло́шадь (-ди́ть), (*bet on*) ста́вить на ло́шадь (по-)

vi дви́|гаться/идти́ наза́д (-нуться/пойти́); **to ~ away from smb** попя́титься от кого́-л; **the car/train is ~ing** маши́на/по́езд даёт за́дний ход; (*to driver*) **you'll have to ~ a little** пода́й немно́го наза́д; **unfortunately I ~ed into a wall** тако́е несча́стье, моя́ маши́на вре́залась за́дом в сте́ну; **our house ~s on to the park** наш дом за́дним фаса́дом выхо́дит в парк; *fig*: **he ~ed down/out at the last minute** в после́днюю мину́ту он пошёл на попя́тную; **you can't ~ out of the invitation now** тепе́рь уж по́здно отка́зываться от приглаше́ния.

backbiting *n* спле́тни, наговоры́ (*pls*).

backbone *n* позвоно́чник; спинно́й хребе́т; *fig*: **such men are the ~ of the country** таки́е лю́ди — опо́ра госуда́рства; **he's English to the ~** он англича́нин до мо́зга косте́й; **he's got no ~** он како́й-то бесхребе́тный.

back-breaking *adj*: **it's a ~ job** э́то ка́торжная рабо́та.

backchat *n*: **I don't want any ~!** не огрыза́йся!

backdate *vt*: **to ~ a letter** дати́ровать письмо́ за́дним число́м; **our pay rise is ~d to June 1st** ра́зница в зарпла́те бу́дет выпла́чиваться начина́я с пе́рвого ию́ня э́того го́да.

back door *n* чёрный ход; *fig* **he got in by the ~** *CQ* он попа́л туда́ по бла́ту.

background *n* **1** фон, за́дний план, *both also fig*; **in the ~ of the picture** на за́днем пла́не карти́ны; **against a dark ~** на тёмном фо́не; *fig*: **against the ~ of recent events** на фо́не неда́вних собы́тий; **to stay in the ~** остава́ться на за́днем пла́не/в тени́

2 (*of person*): **what is his ~?** каково́ его́ происхожде́ние?; **he has a working-class ~** он вы́ходец из рабо́чей среды́; *attr*: **first I'll give you some ~ information** снача́ла я вам дам не́которую необходи́мую информа́цию; ~ **music/noise** музыка́льный фон, шум на за́днем пла́не.

backhand *n* (*in tennis*) уда́р закры́той (раке́ткой).

backhanded *adj fig*: **a ~ compliment** сомни́тельный комплиме́нт.

backing *n* подде́ржка.

backlash *n*: **there may be a ~ to this decision** э́то реше́ние мо́жет вы́звать нежела́тельную реа́кцию.

backlog *n*: **~ of rent due** задо́лженность по квартпла́те; **I've caught up with my ~ of work** я поко́нчил с отстава́нием в рабо́те.

back number *n*: **~ of a magazine** ста́рый но́мер журна́ла; *fig* **he's a ~ these days** с ним тепе́рь уже́ не о́чень счита́ются.

back pay *n* просро́ченный платёж.

back-pedal *vi fig* идти́ на попя́тный.

back seat *n* за́днее сиде́нье; *fig* **he'll have to take a ~ now** тепе́рь ему́ придётся дово́льствоваться вторы́ми роля́ми (*pl*); *attr*: **my wife is a ~ driver** когда́ я за рулём, моя́ жена́ лю́бит учи́ть меня́, как вести́ маши́ну.

backslapping *n CQ*: **I hate all this ~** я терпе́ть не могу́ запанибра́тских отноше́ний.

backstage *adv* за кули́сами; **to go ~** идти́ за кули́сы/за сце́ну.

backstroke *n* (*swimming*): **he was using ~** он плыл на спине́.

backward *adj* (*to the rear*) обра́тный; **he gave a ~ glance** он огляну́лся; *fig*: **a ~ step** шаг наза́д; **a ~ child** (*shy*) ро́бкий/(*retarded*) у́мственно отста́лый ребёнок; **he was not ~ in helping us**/*pejor* **in accepting money** он сра́зу пришёл к нам на по́мощь, он не постесня́лся взять де́ньги.

backward(s) *adv* наза́д; **to fall ~** упа́сть наза́д; **to go ~ and forward(s)** ходи́ть взад и вперёд; **to walk ~** пя́титься, идти́ за́дом наперёд; **she/the horse moved ~** она́/ло́шадь попя́тилась; *fig* **to know a road/a play ~** знать доро́гу/пье́су вдоль и поперёк.

backyard *n* за́дний двор.

bacon *n* бeко́н.

bacterium *n* (*pl* **bacteria**) бакте́рия, микро́б.

bad *n*: **to take the good with the ~** принима́ть и плохо́е и хоро́шее.

bad *adj* плохо́й, нехоро́ший, дурно́й; скве́рный; (*serious*) серьёзный, си́льный; **a ~ man** плохо́й/нехоро́ший/дурно́й челове́к; **~ manners/news** плохи́е *or* дурны́е мане́ры/ве́сти (*pl*); **I'm in a ~ temper** я в плохо́м настрое́нии; **I speak ~ French** я пло́хо говорю́ по-францу́зски; **he's in a ~ way** с ним де́ло пло́хо; **it's a ~ business** де́ло пло́хо; **things aren't all that ~** дела́ не так уж пло́хи; **a ~ smell** скве́рный/проти́вный за́пах; **~ weather** плоха́я/скве́рная пого́да, непого́да; **a ~ word** гру́бое сло́во, руга́тельство; **~ language** ру́гань, скверносло́вие; **you ~ boy—look what you've done!** скве́рный мальчи́шка, посмотри́, что ты наде́лал!; **~ dog!** га́дкий пёс!; **it's too ~ of you** э́то о́чень нехорошо́ с твое́й стороны́; **I've got a ~ cold/cough** у меня́ си́льный на́сморк/ка́шель; **he had a ~ fall** он упа́л и си́льно расши́бся; **a ~ mistake** серьёзная оши́бка; **I feel ~** (*unwell*) я пло́хо/нева́жно себя́ чу́вствую; **I feel ~ about not being able to help you** мне со́вестно, что я тебе́ не могу́ помо́чь; **a ~ apple** гнило́е я́блоко; **~ meat** ту́хлое мя́со; **a ~ tooth** больно́й/гнило́й зуб; **my ~ toe/finger** мой больно́й па́лец; **with a ~ grace** неохо́тно; **he had ~ luck** ему́ не повезло́; **the light is ~ today** (*for painting, etc.*) сего́дня ма́ло све́та; **that's too ~** о́чень жаль, *also iron.*

badge *n* значо́к.

badger *n* барсу́к.

badger *vt* приста|ва́ть (-́ть); **he ~ed me with questions/to tell him** он приста́л ко мне с вопро́сами/с ножо́м к го́рлу, что́бы я рассказа́л ему́.

badly *adv* **1** пло́хо; (*seriously*) си́льно; тяжело́; **my dress fits ~** моё пла́тье пло́хо на мне сиди́т; **he was ~ hurt/wounded** он си́льно ушиб́ся, он был тяжело́ ра́нен; **we were ~ beaten** *CQ* мы с тре́ском проигра́ли

2 (*very much*) о́чень, *CQ* стра́шно; **I ~ need a rest** мне о́чень ну́жен о́тдых, мне обяза́тельно ну́жно отдохну́ть; (*urgently*) **he ~ wants to see you** он сро́чно хо́чет ви́деть тебя́.

baffle *vt* озада́чи|вать (-ть); **the police are ~d** поли́ция озада́чена/в по́лном недоуме́нии.

bag *n* **1** (*lady's*) су́мка, (*smaller*) су́мочка; (*for travelling*) чемода́н, саквоя́ж; (*sack*) мешо́к; **shoulder ~** су́мка че́рез плечо́; **shopping/beach ~** хозя́йственная/пля́жная су́мка; **evening ~** вече́рняя/театра́льная су́мочка; **I've packed my ~** я уложи́л (свои́ ве́щи в) чемода́н; **a ~ of coal** мешо́к у́гля́/с у́глём; **paper/plastic ~** бума́жный/целлофа́новый паке́т; **string/nylon ~** се́тка, *CQ* аво́ська; **diplomatic ~** дипломати́ческая по́чта; *fig*: **~s under the eyes** мешки́ под глаза́ми; *CQ* **we've got ~s of time** у нас у́йма вре́мени

2 *Sport* (*hunting*) добы́ча; *fig* **it's in the ~** де́ло в шля́пе

3 *pl* (**~s**) *CQ* (*UK*: *trousers*) брю́ки.

baggage *n* бага́ж.

baggy *adj*: **~ trousers** мешкова́тые брю́ки.

bagpipes *npl* волы́нка (*sing*).

bail[1] *n Law* зало́г; **to go ~ for smb** заплати́ть зало́г за кого́-л; **to let smb out on ~** отпуска́ть кого́-л под зало́г.

bail[2] *vt Naut*: **to ~ out a boat** вы|че́рпывать во́ду из ло́дки (-́черпать).

bait *n* (*for rod*) нажи́вка; (*for trap*) прима́нка, *also fig*; (*in fishing*): **to rise to the ~** клева́ть; **to take/swallow the ~** клю́нуть, попа́сться на у́дочку, *also fig.*

bait *vt*: **to ~ a hook** наса́|живать нажи́вку/червяка́ (*worm*) на крючо́к (-ди́ть); *fig* **to ~ smb** трави́ть кого́-л (за-).

bake *vti vt* печь (ис-); **to ~ apples/a cake** печь я́блоки/пиро́г; **to ~ a lot of pastries** напе́чь пирожко́в [**NB** *use of prefix*]; **to ~ bricks** об|жига́ть кирпичи́ (-же́чь)

vi (*of bread, cakes, etc.*) пе́чься; *fig*: **we ~d in the sun all day** мы весь день жа́рились на со́лнце; **it's baking hot today** сего́дня си́льно печёт (*only of heat from the sun*).

baker *n* пе́карь (*m*); **the ~'s** (*shop*) бу́лочная.

baking powder *n* пека́рный порошо́к.

baking soda *n* со́да (питьева́я).

balance *n* **1** (*equilibrium*) равнове́сие; **to keep/lose one's ~** сохраня́ть/теря́ть равнове́сие; **~ of power** равнове́сие сил; **after her illness her ~ of mind was disturbed** боле́знь поде́йствовала на её пси́хику

2 (*scales*) весы́ (*no sing*); *fig*: **his future hangs in the ~** его́ бу́дущее поло́жено на весы́; **to weigh smth in the ~** взве́шивать/обду́мывать что-л

3 *Fin* бала́нс; **favourable/unfavourable ~** акти́вный/пасси́вный бала́нс; **~ of payments/trade** платёжный/торго́вый бала́нс; **what's the ~ in hand?** ско́лько остаётся нали́чных (де́нег)?; **the ~ is to be paid by May 1st** оста́ток до́лжен быть вы́плачен к пе́рвому ма́я; **to strike a ~** подводи́ть бала́нс, *fig* найти́ золоту́ю середи́ну; *fig* **on ~ I prefer the first proposal** взве́сив всё, я предпочёл [**NB** *tense*] пе́рвое предложе́ние.

balance *vti vt* **1** баланси́ровать (*only in impf*) [**NB** *Russian verb is intrans*]; **he ~d himself on one foot** он баланси́ровал на одно́й ноге́; **she ~d the basket on her head** она́ несла́ корзи́ну на голове́

2 *Fin*: **to ~ an account/the books** под|води́ть бала́нс (-вести́), баланси́ровать счета́ (с-)

vi **1**: **to ~ on a rope** баланси́ровать на кана́те (*only in impf*)

2 *Fin*: **the accounts don't ~** счета́ не схо́дятся.

balanced *adj* (*of object*) сбаланси́рованный, *also Fin*; *fig* (*of people*) уравнове́шенный; **a ~ judgement** взве́шенное/проду́манное сужде́ние; **a ~ diet** сбаланси́рованная дие́та.

balance sheet *n Fin* сво́дный бала́нс, бала́нсовый отчёт.

balcony *n* балко́н, *also Theat*.

bald *adj* лы́сый; **to go ~** лысе́ть; **a ~ patch** лы́сина; *fig* **~ facts** го́лые фа́кты.

baldly *adv*: **to put it ~** говоря́ пря́мо/без обиняко́в.

bale[1] *n* (*of goods*) ки́па, тюк; **a ~ of hay** тюк се́на.

bale[2] *vi Aer*: **to ~ out of a plane** вы|бра́сываться с парашю́том из самолёта (-бро́ситься).

balk *vi*: **the horse ~ed at the jump** ло́шадь заарта́чилась пе́ред препя́тствием; **my husband ~ed at the expense** мой муж заарта́чился, услы́шав це́ну.

ball[1] *n* мяч; **tennis ~** те́ннисный мяч; **to play ~** игра́ть в мяч; **a ~ of wool/string** клубо́к ше́рсти/верёвки; **the ~ of the foot** поду́шечка ступни́; **to curl up in a ~** сверну́ться клубко́м; *fig*: **he's very much on the ~, he keeps his eye on the ~** он начеку́; **to start the ~ rolling** заводи́ть разгово́р.

ball[2] *n* бал; **to give a ~** дава́ть/устра́ивать бал.

ballast *n* балла́ст.

ball bearing *n* шарикоподши́пник.

ballcock *n* поплаво́к.

ballerina *n* балери́на.

ballet *n* бале́т.

ballet dancer *n* (*male*) арти́ст бале́та, танцо́вщик, *f* балери́на, танцо́вщица.

balloon *n* возду́шный шар/(*toy*) ша́рик.

ballot *n* (*voting*) баллотиро́вка; **to take a ~ on smth** ста́вить что-л на голосова́ние; **there will be a ~ for the remaining tickets** оста́вшиеся биле́ты бу́дут разы́граны; *attr*: **~ box** избира́тельная у́рна; **~ paper** избира́тельный бюллете́нь.

ball-point pen *n* ша́риковая ру́чка.

ballroom *n* ба́льный/танцева́льный зал; *attr*: **~ dancing** ба́льные та́нцы (*pl*).

ballyhoo *n CQ* шуми́ха.

bamboo *n* бамбу́к; *attr* бамбу́ковый.

ban *n* запреще́ние; запре́т; **to be under a ~** быть под запре́том; **to raise the ~ on smth** снять запре́т с чего́-л.

ban *vt* запре|ща́ть (-ти́ть); **to ~ a meeting/a play/a book** запрети́ть собра́ние/пье́су/кни́гу; **he was ~ned from driving** у него́ отобра́ли води́тельские права́.

banal *adj* бана́льный.

banana *n* бана́н (*tree and fruit*).

band *n* **1** (*strip, stripe*) полоса́, *dim* поло́ска; (*ribbon*) ле́нта (*also on hat*); (*edging*) кайма́, (*on plate*) каёмка; (*hoop for barrel*) о́бруч; (**black**) **arm ~** (тра́урная) повя́зка; **the crate was fastened with steel ~s** я́щик был скреплён стальны́ми полоса́ми

2 *Radio*: **wave ~** диапазо́н волн

3 *Mus* орке́стр; **jazz/brass ~** джаз-орке́стр, духово́й орке́стр

4 (*group*) гру́ппа; (*of robbers*) ба́нда, ша́йка.

band *vi*: **to ~ together** (**against**) объедин|я́ться (про́тив + *G*); (-и́ться).

bandage *n* бинт, повя́зка.

bandage *vt* бинтова́ть (за-), на|кла́дывать бинт/повя́зку на + *A* (-ложи́ть).

bandit *n* банди́т.

bandy-legged *adj* кривоно́гий.

bane *n*: **drink/she has been the ~ of his life** пья́нство для него́ смерть *or* поги́бель, он связа́лся с ней на свою́ поги́бель.

bang *n* **1** (*explosion*) взрыв; (*of fireworks*) хлопо́к; **a gun went off with a loud ~** разда́лся гро́мкий руже́йный вы́стрел; **the door shut with a ~** дверь си́льно хло́пнула; **~!** бах!

2 (*blow*) уда́р; **he got a nasty ~ on the head** он си́льно уда́рился голово́й

3 (*of hair*) чёлка.

bang *adv*: **the stone hit him ~ on the forehead** ка́мень попа́л ему́ пря́мо в лоб; *CQ*: **he was ~ on time/target** он пришёл как раз во́время, он попа́л пря́мо в цель; **your guess is ~ on** ты попа́л в то́чку.

bang *vti vt* хло́п|ать + *I*, *CQ* тра́х|ать (*semel for both* -нуть); **he ~ed the door/the lid shut** он хло́пнул две́рью/кры́шкой; **you have to ~ the bonnet to shut it** что́бы капо́т закры́лся, на́до им хороше́нько хло́пнуть; **he ~ed the table with his fist** он тра́хнул кулако́м по столу́; **he ~ed his head on the door** он тра́хнулся голово́й о дверь; **he ~ed the books down on the table** он гро́хнул кни́ги на стол; **he ~ed down the receiver** он бро́сил тру́бку

vi: **the door ~ed shut** дверь хло́пнула; **there's a door ~ing somewhere** где́-то хло́пает дверь.

bangle *n* брасле́т.

banish *vt*: (*person*) **to ~ from/to** вы|сыла́ть из + *G*, ссыла́ть в + *A* (´-слать, сосла́ть); **I tried to ~ all thoughts of my exam** я стара́лся отогна́ть мы́сли об экза́мене.

banister *n usu pl* пери́ла (*no sing*).

bank *n* **1** (*of river, lake*) бе́рег; (*man-made*) вал, на́сыпь; *Naut* (*if submerged all or part of the time*) мель, ба́нка, (*if always visible*) о́тмель; **on the left ~** на ле́вом берегу́; **a ~ of snow/fog/clouds** сугро́б, полоса́ тума́на, гряда́ облако́в

2 *Fin* банк, *also Cards*; **to keep/break the ~** держа́ть/сорва́ть банк.

bank *vti vt*: **they ~ed (up) the snow at the side of the road** они́ сгребли́ снег к кра́ю доро́ги; **to ~ a fire** сгрести́ золу́ в ку́чу, присы́пать у́гли золо́й; **the pilot ~ed his plane** лётчик сде́лал вира́ж; *Fin* **to ~ money** класть де́ньги в банк (положи́ть)

vi: **storm clouds are ~ing up** ту́чи собира́ются; **the plane ~ed** самолёт накрени́лся; *Fin* **I ~ with the bank of Scotland** я держу́ де́ньги в Шотла́ндском ба́нке; *fig* **to ~ on smb/smth** по|лага́ться на кого́-л/на что-л (-ложи́ться).

bank account *n* ба́нковский счёт.

bank-book *n* ба́нковская кни́жка.

banker *n* банки́р.

banking *n* (*of earth*) на́сыпь; *Fin* ба́нковское де́ло.

banknote *n* банкно́т.

bank rate *n* учётная ста́вка ба́нка.

bankrupt *adj*: **to become/be ~** обанкро́титься.

bankruptcy *n* банкро́тство.

banner *n* зна́мя.

banquet *n* банке́т.

baptize *vt* крести́ть (о-).

bar *n* **1** (*rod*: *of metal*) металли́ческий прут, (*wooden*) па́лка; *Naut* о́тмель; *Mus* такт; *fig* (*hindrance*) препя́тствие + *D*, поме́ха + *D*; **a ~ of gold/chocolate** сли́ток зо́лота, пли́тка шокола́да; **behind ~s** (*in prison*) за решёткой; **parallel ~s** паралле́льные бру́сья; *attr*: *Mus* **~ line** та́ктовая черта́

2 *Law*: **the B.** колле́гия адвока́тов, адвокату́ра; **to be called to the ~** стать адвока́том; **prisoner at the ~** подсуди́мый

3 (*in hotel, etc.*) бар; (*counter*) сто́йка; (*in station, theatre, etc.*) буфе́т; **to serve behind the ~** стоя́ть за сто́йкой; **snack ~** заку́сочная.

bar *prep*: **all ~ two** все, кро́ме двух; **all ~ none** все без исключе́ния.

bar *vt* **1** (*fasten*): **to ~ a door** за|пира́ть дверь на засо́в (-пере́ть); **we ~red the windows because of the children/against burglars** мы приколоти́ли решётки на о́кна из-за дете́й/от воро́в

2 (*obstruct*): **a fallen tree ~red the road** упа́вшее де́рево загороди́ло доро́гу; **soldiers ~red our way** солда́ты прегради́ли нам путь

3 (*prohibit*): **he was ~red from entering the race** его́ не допусти́ли к забе́гу.

barbarian *n* ва́рвар; *attr* ва́рварский.

barbecue *n*: **we had a ~ in the garden** мы жари́ли шашлы́к в саду́.

barbed wire *n* колю́чая про́волока.

barber *n* (мужско́й) парикма́хер; **the ~'s** (*shop*) парикма́херская.

barbiturate *n* барбитура́т.

bare *adj* го́лый, *also fig*; обнажённый; **~ to the waist** го́лый/обнажённый до по́яса; **with one's ~ hands** (с) го́лыми рука́ми; **~ feet** бо́сые но́ги; **with one's head ~** с обнажённой голово́й; **~ trees** наги́е/го́лые дере́вья; **to sleep on ~ boards** спать на го́лых доска́х; **the larder is ~** кладова́я пуста́; **a room ~ of furniture** пуста́я ко́мната; *fig*: **~ facts** го́лые фа́кты; **to lay ~ a plot** разоблачи́ть за́говор; **earns a ~ £100 a month** он зараба́тывает каки́х-то сто фу́нтов в ме́сяц; **he got in by a ~ majority** он победи́л (на вы́борах) с незначи́тельным переве́сом/незначи́тельным большинство́м голосо́в.

bare *vt* обнаж|а́ть (-и́ть); **the dog ~d its teeth** соба́ка оска́лила зу́бы.

bareback *adv* без седла́.

barefaced *adj*: **a ~ lie** на́глая ложь.

barefoot(ed) *adj and adv* босико́м (*adv*).

barelegged *adj* с го́лыми нога́ми.

barely *adv* едва́, е́ле-е́ле; **we ~ caught the train** мы едва́/е́ле-е́ле успе́ли на по́езд.

bargain *n* (*deal*) сде́лка; **to make/strike a ~ with smb** (*in business*) заключи́ть сде́лку с кем-л, (*privately*) уговори́ться с кем-л; **you drive a hard ~** ты сли́шком торгу́ешься; **I'm afraid I'm getting the better ~** бою́сь, я вас обделя́ю; **you got a (good) ~/a bad ~ there** вы э́то дёшево купи́ли, вы здо́рово переплати́ли; (*in addition*) **into the ~** в прида́чу; *attr*: **at a ~ price** по дешёвке; **~ sale** распрода́жа.

bargain *vi* (*haggle*): **to ~ with smb for smth** торгова́ться с кем-л из-за чего́-л (*usu impf*); *fig* **he got more than he ~ed for** он получи́л бо́льше, чем рассчи́тывал.

barge *n* ба́ржа́.

barge *vi CQ*: **to ~ into smb/smth** на|тáлкиваться на когó-л/на что-л (-толкнýться); **to ~ into a queue/a conversation** вле|зáть в óчередь/в разговóр (-зть); **to ~ through a crowd** протиснуться сквозь толпý.

bark[1] *n* (*of tree*) корá.

bark[1] *vt*: **he ~ed his shins** он ободрáл себé все нóги.

bark[2] *n* (*of dog*) лай.

bark[2] *vi* лáять (*impf*); **to begin to ~** залáять (*pf*).

barley *n* ячмéнь (*m*); *attr*: **~ sugar/water** ячмéнный сáхар/отвáр.

barmaid *n* официáнтка в бáре.

barman *n* бáрмен.

barn *n* амбáр; сарáй.

barometer *n* барóметр.

baroque *adj* барóчный; **in ~ style** в стиле барóкко (*indecl*).

barrack *n usu pl* казáрма, казáрмы.

barrel *n* бóчка; (*of gun*) ствол; *fig* **if they gave him the job, they must have had to scrape the bottom of the ~** éсли уж они емý дáли эту рабóту, знáчит, у них совсéм плóхо с людьми.

barrel organ *n* шармáнка.

barren *adj* (*of woman or land*) бесплóдный.

barricade *vt* баррикади́ровать (за-); **the streets were ~d** на ýлицах бы́ли сооружены́ баррикáды; **they ~d themselves in** они́ забаррикади́ровались.

barrier *n* барьéр, *also fig*; (*at toll, etc.*) шлагбáум; **show your tickets at the ~** предъявля́йте билéты на контрóле.

barring *prep* крóме + *G*; **I can come any day ~ Monday** я могý прийти́ в любóй день, крóме/за исключéнием понедéльника; **~ accidents** éсли ничегó не случи́тся.

barrister *n* адвокáт, бáрристер.

barrow[1] *n Archaeol* моги́льный холм, кургáн.

barrow[2] *n* (*wheelbarrow*) тáчка; (*for luggage, goods, etc.*) ручнáя телéжка; (*porter's*) носи́лки (*no sing*).

barter *n* мéна, менвáя торгóвля.

barter *vt* обмéн|ивать (-я́ть); **to ~ wheat for machinery** обмéнивать пшени́цу на станки́; *fig* **to ~ away one's freedom (for)** променя́ть своіо свобóду (на + *A*).

base[1] *n* (*of building, etc.*) основáние, *also Math, Chem*; (*stand*) подстáвка; *Mil* бáза; *fig* оснóва.

base[1] *vt* оснóв|ывать на + *P* (-áть); *Mil* бази́роваться на + *P* (*impf*); **these conclusions are ~d on facts** эти вы́воды оснóваны на фáктах; **I ~ myself on official data** я оснóвываюсь на официáльных дáнных; **I am ~d in London** моя́ глáвная контóра—в Лóндоне; *Mil* **the fleet was ~d on Malta** флот бази́ровался на Мáльте.

base[2] *adj* пóдлый, ни́зкий; *Tech* (*of metals*) неблагорóдный.

baseless *adj* необоснóванный.

basement *n* подвáл.

bash *n CQ*: **I'll have a ~ at it** я попрóбую.

bashful *adj* рóбкий; застéнчивый.

basic *adj* основнóй; *CQ* **in the dacha living conditions are pretty ~** на дáче нет почти́ никаки́х удóбств.

basically *adv* в основнóм.

basin *n* (*kitchen bowl*) ми́ска; (*washtub*) таз; (*sink, wash basin*) рáковина; *Geog* бассéйн; (*of harbour*) портóвый бассéйн.

basis *n* оснóва, основáние; **on a sound ~** на разýмной оснóве; **on the ~ of this evidence** на основáнии этих дáнных (*pl*).

bask *vi*: **to ~ in the sun** грéться на сóлнце (*usu impf*).

basket *n* корзи́на, *dim* корзи́нка; **laundry ~** бельевáя корзи́на; **wastepaper ~** корзи́на для бумáг.

basketball *n* баскетбóл.

bass *n Mus* бас; *attr* басóвый.

bassoon *n* фагóт.

bastard *n* незаконнорождённый ребёнок; *pejor* (*in abuse*) **he's a real ~!** какóй же он подóнок!

baste[1] *vt Cook*: **to ~ meat** поли|вáть жаркóе жи́ром (-́ть).

baste[2] *vt Sew* смётывать (сметáть).

bat[1] *n Zool* летýчая мышь.

bat[2] *n* (*baseball, cricket*) битá; (*table tennis*) ракéтка; *fig* **he did it off his own ~** он это сдéлал по своéй/сóбственной инициати́ве.

bat[3] *vt*: **without ~ting an eyelid** (и) глáзом не моргнýв.

batch *n* (*of goods, bread, prisoners, recruits*) пáртия; (*of letters*) пáчка.

bath *n* вáнна; *pl* (**~s**) (*public washing places*) бáня (*sing*), (*for swimming*) бассéйн (*sing*); **Turkish ~s** турéцкие бáни; **to have/take a ~** приня́ть вáнну; *attr*: **~ soap/cap** бáнное мы́ло, купáльная шáпочка.

bath *vt*: **to ~ a baby** купáть ребёнка (вы-, ис-).

bathe *n* купáние; **I'm going for a ~** я идý купáться (*for a long swim*), (я) пойдý искупáюсь (*for a quick dip*).

bathe *vti vt*: **to ~ a wound** промы|вáть рáну (-́ть); **~d in tears** обливáющийся слезáми

vi купáться (ис-).

bather *n* купáльщ|ик, *f* -ица.

bathing *n* купáние; **"No B."** «здесь купáться воспрещáется»; *attr* купáльный; **~ costume** *or* **suit/wrap** купáльный костю́м/халáт; **~ cap/trunks** купáльная шáпочка, плáвки.

bathroom *n* вáнная.

bath salts *npl* аромати́ческие сóли (для вáнны).

bath towel *n* купáльное полотéнце.

bathtub *n* вáнна.

baton *n Mus* дирижёрская пáлочка.

battalion *n* батальóн.

batter *n Cook* взби́тое тéсто.

batter *vti vt* бить (*impf*) *and compounds*; **to ~ a child** бить ребёнка; **the ship was ~ed against the rocks/to pieces by the waves** корáбль разби́лся о скáлы, вóлны разби́ли сýдно в щéпки; **we were badly ~ed by the gale** нас сúльно потрепáло (*impers*) штóрмом

vi: **the waves ~ed against the side of the ship** вóлны бúлись о борт корабля́; **to ~ at a door** колотúть в дверь (*usu impf*).

battered *adj* разбúтый; **a ~ old car/hat** разбúтая стáрая машúна, потрёпанная шля́па; *fig* **I feel ~ after the journey** я чýвствую себя́ разбúтым пóсле э́той поéздки.

battery *n Mil* батарéя; *Elec*, *Aut* аккумуля́тор; (*for torches*) батарéйка; **the ~ is flat** аккумуля́тор сел/разрядúлся; *fig* **he had to face a ~ of questions** егó засыпáли грáдом вопрóсов.

battle *n* **1** бой; (*if named*) бúтва; **he was killed in ~** он пал в бою́; **to join/give ~** давáть бой/сражéние; **to do ~** вестú бой, сражáться; **the ~ of Stalingrad/Borodino/Waterloo** Сталингрáдская/Бородúнская бúтва, бúтва при Ватерлóо; *attr*: **in ~ order** в боевóм строю́/поря́дке

2 *fig uses*: **a ~ royal ensued** разразúлся грандиóзный скандáл; **a ~ of wits** поедúнок умóв; **good health is half the ~** глáвное—здорóвье; **you're fighting a losing ~** ты ведёшь безнадёжную борьбý, тебя́ ждёт вéрный прóигрыш; **let him fight his own ~s** пусть сам за себя́ постоúт.

battle *vi fig* борóться (*impf*); **to ~ against difficulties/the wind** борóться с трýдностями/с вéтром; **to ~ with smb for smth** борóться с кем-л за что-л (*impf*).

battlefield *n* пóле бóя/бúтвы/сражéния.

battleship *n* линéйный корáбль, *abbr* линкóр.

batty *adj CQ*: **she's quite ~** онá совсéм спя́тила.

bawdy *adj CQ* похáбный.

bawl *vti vt CQ*: **to ~ out a song** горлáнить пéсню (*impf*)

vi вопúть, орáть (*impfs*).

bay[1] *n Bot* лáвровое дéрево; *attr*: **~ leaf** лаврóвый лист.

bay[2] *n Geog* бýхта, (*larger*) залúв; **the B. of Biscay** Бискáйский залúв.

bay[3] *n* (*of wolf*) вой; (*of dog*) лай; *fig*: (*in hunting*) **a deer at ~** зáгнанный олéнь; **I'm keeping my creditors at ~ with difficulty** я с трудóм отбивáюсь от моúх кредитóров.

bay[4] *adj* (*colour*) гнедóй; *as n* (**a ~**) гнедáя лóшадь.

bayonet *n* штык.

bay window *n Archit* э́ркер, фонáрь (*m*).

bazaar *n* (*oriental*) востóчный базáр; (*charitable*) благотворúтельный базáр.

be A *as link verb joining subject and predicate usu* быть [**NB "am, is, are"** *usu not translated in present tense*; *in past and future tenses and in imperative the predicate is often in the instrumental case*]

1 *with noun, pronoun predicate*: **he is a doctor** он врач; **he was/will ~ a doctor** он был/бýдет врачóм; **boys will ~ boys** мальчúшки есть мальчúшки; **business is business** дéло есть дéло; **things aren't what they were** тепéрь всё не так, как бы́ло рáньше; **what is the matter?** в чём дéло?; **don't ~ such a fool** не будь такúм дуракóм

2 *with adj predicate* [**NB** *predicative adjs in the nominative are often in the short form*]: **the room is too big** кóмната слúшком великá; **all is ready** всё готóво; **he was very young** он был óчень мóлод; **the play was interesting** пьéса былá интерéсная; **the book was boring** кнúга оказáлась скýчной; **I'll ~ very glad** я бýду óчень рад; **he'll ~ tired after the journey** он вернётся из поéздки устáлым; **he is bored** емý скýчно; **I was hot/cold** мне бы́ло жáрко/хóлодно [*compare*: **the weather was hot** погóда былá жáркая; **he was cold towards me** он был хóлоден со мной]

3 (*of age*): **she is 3** ей три гóда; **she will ~ 10 tomorrow** зáвтра ей (бýдет/испóлнится) дéсять лет

4 *Math*: **2 x 2 is 4** двáжды два—четы́ре; **how much is 6 + 7?** скóлько бýдет шесть плюс семь?

5 (*of possession*): **is it her umbrella?—No, it is mine** э́то её зóнтик?—Нет, э́то мой

6 (*of place*) быть, (*be situated*) находúться, (*be frequently*) бывáть (*impfs*); **where is he?** где он?; **he's in the garden** он в садý; **I was at the concert** я был на концéрте; **the museum is opposite the theatre** музéй (нахóдится) напрóтив теáтра; **are they often in London?** онú чáсто бывáют в Лóндоне?

7 (*of position*) *the verbs* лежáть, стоя́ть, висéть (*impfs*) *are often used in preference to* быть; **the letter was on the table/in my pocket** письмó лежáло на столé/бы́ло у меня́ в кармáне; **to ~ in hospital/in bed** лежáть в больнúце/в постéли; **my shoes are/my suitcase is in the corner** мой тýфли стоя́т/мой чемодáн стоúт в углý; **my dress is in the wardrobe** моё плáтье висúт в шкафý

8 *in more literary contexts "to be" is also translated by* яв|ля́ться + *I* (-úться), представля́ть собóй (*only in impf*); **he is typical of the Oxford school of philosophy** он явля́ется типúчным представúтелем Оксфóрдской филосóфской шкóлы; **what sort of man is he?** что он собóй представля́ет?, что он за человéк?; **a sundial is a disc with an upright pin in the centre** сóлнечные часы́ представля́ют собóй диск с вертикáльным стéржнем в цéнтре

9 *various*: **how are you?** (*how do you do?*) как вы поживáете?, (*how do you feel?*) как вы себя́ чýвствуете?; **how are things?** как делá?; **he wants to ~ a lawyer** он хóчет стать адвокáтом; **she is better** ей лýчше, ей стáло лýчше; **how much is the book?** скóлько стóит э́та кнúга?; **what a time you've been!** как ты дóлго!; **here's to your success!** за ваш успéх!; **my wife to ~** моя́ бýдущая женá

B *as auxiliary verb*

1 *forming continuous tenses, not translated, sense conveyed by use of impf aspect*: **I am reading** я читáю; **I am playing in a concert**

tonight я выступа́ю на конце́рте сего́дня ве́чером; **I will ~ playing with this orchestra next year** (*once, or regularly*) я бу́ду игра́ть с э́тим орке́стром в бу́дущем году́; **I won't ~ coming any more** я бо́льше не бу́ду приходи́ть; *CQ* **will you ~ seeing him tomorrow?** ты уви́дишь его́ за́втра?; **I hadn't been/wasn't expecting him/it** я его́ не ждал, я э́того не ожида́л

2 *forming passive voice, translated* **i)** *by using reflex verbs*: **the question is/was being discussed** вопро́с обсужда́ется/обсужда́лся; **the house is still being built** дом всё ещё стро́ится; **ii)** *by using impersonally 3rd person pl of active verb*: **we were taken to the museum** нас вози́ли в музе́й; **we are being tricked** нас обма́нывают; **he was sacked** его́ уво́лили; **iii) by using** быть + *ppp*: **the question is/has been decided** вопро́с решён; **the question had already been decided** вопро́с был уже́ решён; **the work will ~ completed on time** рабо́та бу́дет вы́полнена во́время

3 *in conditional sentences*: **if I were to tell you what I think** е́сли бы я вам сказа́л, что ду́маю; **if he were agreeable** е́сли бы он был согла́сен

4 *used with "to" + inf, expressing duty, necessity, command, prohibition, possibility, etc.*: **I am to ~ there at 4** я до́лжен быть там в четы́ре (часа́); **the concert was to have been yesterday** конце́рт до́лжен был быть вчера́; **he is to ~ pitied** его́ на́до пожале́ть; **it's to ~ hoped that...** на́до наде́яться, что...; **it's a film not to ~ missed** э́тот фильм нельзя́ пропусти́ть; **I am to inform you that...** мне пору́чено сообщи́ть вам, что...; **you are not to touch my books** не тро́гай мои́ кни́ги; **we are not to have guests in our rooms** нам не разреша́ется приводи́ть госте́й в ко́мнаты; **he said I wasn't to tell anyone** он проси́л меня́ никому́ не говори́ть об э́том; **he's nowhere to ~ found** его́ нигде́ нельзя́ найти́; **what's to ~ done?** что де́лать? (= *nothing can be done*), что ещё де́лать? (= *what needs doing?*); **when is the wedding to ~?** когда́ бу́дет сва́дьба?; **if we are to ~ there in time** е́сли мы хоти́м быть там во́время; **it was not to ~** но э́тому не суждено́ бы́ло сбы́ться; **when am I to ~ there?** во ско́лько мне приходи́ть?; **who is to begin?** кому́ начина́ть?; **the telegram was to say that...** в телегра́мме сообща́лось, что...; *CQ* **what's it to ~?** (*offering drinks*) что бу́дешь пить?

5 *in tag questions and in answers, etc.*: **it's a bit cold today, isn't it?—Yes, it is** сего́дня прохла́дно на у́лице, пра́вда?—Да, прохла́дно; **you're not angry, are you?** ты ведь не се́рдишься?; **you're late.—No, I'm not** ты опозда́л.—Нет, не опозда́л

C *vi* **1** (*exist*) быть, существова́ть (*impf*); **I think therefore I am** я мы́слю, сле́довательно, я существу́ю; **to ~ or not to ~** быть и́ли не быть; **there are such people** есть таки́е лю́ди; **so ~ it** так и быть; **let it ~ so** пусть так бу́дет; **you'll have to take him as he is** ну́жно принима́ть его́ таки́м, како́й он есть; **as things are, I can't come** так сложи́лось, что я не смогу́ прийти́

2 there is/are, *etc.*: **there is/was a hotel not far away** побли́зости есть/была́ гости́ница; **there are/were three churches in the village** в э́той дере́вне (бы́ло) три це́ркви; **there are two cinemas in the town** в го́роде (есть) два кинотеа́тра; **there will ~/was a lecture on Friday** в пя́тницу бу́дет/была́ ле́кция; **there were some brilliant students here last year** в про́шлом году́ у нас бы́ло не́сколько о́чень спосо́бных студе́нтов; **there are always a lot of tourists here** у нас всегда́ (быва́ет) мно́го тури́стов; **is there anyone to replace him?** кто́-нибудь мо́жет замени́ть его́?; **there is/was always something to talk about** всегда́ есть/бы́ло о чём поговори́ть; **who is there to advise us?** кто мо́жет дать нам сове́т?; **there is a strong wind** ду́ет си́льный ве́тер; **there is something about him I don't like** что́-то в нём мне не нра́вится

3 there is/are not: *neg construction is impers—in present* нет + *G*, *in future* не бу́дет + *G*, *in past* не́ было + *G* [**NB** *stress*]; **there is no doctor in the village** в дере́вне нет врача́; **there are/were no apples on the market** на ры́нке нет/не́ было я́блок; **there was nobody at home** до́ма никого́ не́ было; **there will ~ no meeting** заседа́ния не бу́дет; **there's nothing to do here** здесь не́чего де́лать; **there is no one to ask** спроси́ть не́ у кого; **there was no one for me to talk to** мне не́ с кем бы́ло поговори́ть; **there is nowhere/no time for us to rest** нам не́где/не́когда отдыха́ть; **there was not a soul to be seen** не́ было ви́дно ни души́; **there is no telling** нельзя́ сказа́ть; **there is no stopping him** его́ не остано́вишь

4 (*presenting, or indicating*): **here is the book/your gloves** вот кни́га/твои́ перча́тки; **there are your spectacles** вот твои́ очки́; **there he was sitting quietly at home** а он сиде́л себе́ споко́йно до́ма

5 (= *go, come, esp. in perfect tense*) быть; **where has he been?** где он был?; **has anyone/the post been?** кто́-нибудь был?, была́ ли по́чта?; **he has recently been to Paris** он неда́вно был *or* побыва́л в Пари́же/е́здил в Пари́ж

D *as impersonal verb*

1 *with adjs and nouns*: **it is cold today** сего́дня хо́лодно; **it was dark outside** на у́лице бы́ло темно́; **it's possible that...** возмо́жно, что...; **it's probable I'll be late** я наве́рно опозда́ю; **it's my turn** тепе́рь моя́ о́чередь; **it is Tuesday (today)** сего́дня вто́рник; **it's 3 o'clock** сейча́с три часа́; **it's 100 miles to London from here** отсю́да до Ло́ндона сто миль

2 *of supposition*: **if it were not for you,/had it not been for you, I might have drowned** е́сли бы не ты, я бы утону́л

3 *emphatic*: **someone rang yesterday.—It wasn't me** вчера́ кто́-то звони́л.—Э́то не я; **it's not that I want to force you, but...** не то что́бы я хоте́л тебя́ заста́вить, но...; **it's not that I dislike London, but...** не то что́бы мне не нра́вился Ло́ндон, но...; **it was your father I wanted to see, not you** я твоего́ отца́ хоте́л ви́деть, а не тебя́; **how was it you didn't see me?** как случи́лось, что ты меня́ не ви́дел?; **that's women for you** вот они́, же́нщины.

beach *n* пляж.

beach *vt*: **to ~ a boat** вы|та́скивать ло́дку на бе́рег (-тащить).

bead *n* бу́сина; *pl* (**~s**) бу́сы (*no sing*); **~s of sweat** ка́пли по́та.

beady *adj*: **~ eyes** глаза́-бу́синки.

beak *n* клюв.

beam *n* **1** (*ray*) луч, *also Phys*; *Aer* **on/off the ~** по лучу́, с отклоне́нием от луча́

2 (*of wood*) ба́лка; (*squared or rounded*) брус; *Naut* бимс

3 *Naut* (*width of ship*) ширина́ су́дна; *fig CQ* **she's broad in the ~** она́ поперёк себя́ ши́ре.

beam *vti vt Radio*: **to ~ a programme** направ|ля́ть переда́чу (-́ить)

vi (*shine*) сия́ть (*impf*), *also fig*; **he ~ed with joy/at us** он сия́л от ра́дости, он ра́достно улыбну́лся нам.

bean *n* **1** боб; **kidney ~** туре́цкий боб; **French/runner ~s** фасо́ль; **coffee ~s** кофе́йные зёрна

2 *CQ*: **they haven't a ~** у них нет ни гроша́; **the boys are full of ~s** э́ти ма́льчики—ужа́сные шалуны́; **to spill the ~s** проболта́ться.

bear[1] *n* медве́дь (*m*); *Astron* **the Great/Little B.** Больша́я/Ма́лая Медве́дица.

bear[2] *vti vt* **1** (*carry*) носи́ть (*indet impf of* нести́, *pf* по-), нести́ (*det impf of* носи́ть, *pf* по-) *and compounds*; **to ~ arms** носи́ть ору́жие (*sing*); **to come ~ing gifts** при|носи́ть пода́рки (-нести́); **to ~ smth away/off** уноси́ть что-л (унести́); **the stone bore an inscription** на ка́мне была́ на́дпись; **the letter bore his signature** на письме́ стоя́ла его́ по́дпись; *fig*: **to ~ interest at 5%** приноси́ть пять проце́нтов при́были; **to ~ the cost of smth** нести́ расхо́ды по чему́-л; **he must ~ responsibility for the whole affair** он до́лжен нести́ за э́то отве́тственность; **this ~s no relation to the matter in hand** э́то не име́ет никако́го отноше́ния к де́лу; **to ~ a resemblance to** име́ть схо́дство с + *I*; **I ~ him no ill will** я не таю́ зло́бы про́тив него́; **he bore himself courageously** он му́жественно вёл себя́/держа́лся; **finally it was borne in on me that...** наконе́ц до меня́ дошло́, что...

2 (*give birth, yield*): **she bore him a son** она́ родила́ ему́ сы́на; **to be born** роди́ться; **he was born British** он англича́нин по рожде́нию; **to ~ fruit** приноси́ть плоды́, плодоноси́ть (*impf*); *fig* **our plans have borne fruit** на́ши пла́ны принесли́ свои́ ощути́мые результа́ты

3 (*support*) вы|де́рживать (-́держать), *also fig*; **these beams can ~ a heavy load** э́ти ба́лки мо́гут вы́держать большу́ю нагру́зку; **the ice is ~ing sledges now** тепе́рь уже́ лёд вы́держит са́ни; *fig*: **the accounts won't ~ close scrutiny** счета́ не выде́рживают стро́гой прове́рки; **it doesn't ~ thinking about** об э́том и поду́мать стра́шно; **you will ~ me out** ты подтверди́шь мои́ слова́

4 (*endure*) терпе́ть (вы́-), пере|носи́ть (-нести́), вы|носи́ть (-́нести); **he bore the operation well** он хорошо́ перенёс опера́цию; **I can't ~ rudeness** я не выношу́ ха́мства; **I can't ~ her** я её терпе́ть не могу́, я её не выношу́

vi: **to ~ north** направ|ля́ться на се́вер (-́иться); **~ right at the church** у це́ркви сверни́те напра́во; **the ice isn't ~ing yet** лёд ещё то́нкий; **the apple trees are ~ing well** на э́тих я́блонях быва́ет мно́го я́блок; **to bring a telescope/a gun to ~ on smth** на|води́ть телеско́п/ору́дие на что-л (-вести́); *fig* **to bring pressure to ~ on smb** ока́з|ывать давле́ние на кого́-л (-а́ть).

beard *n* борода́.

bearded *adj* борода́тый.

beardless *adj* безборо́дый; **a ~ boy** безу́сый юне́ц.

bearing *n* **1** (*posture*) оса́нка

2 (*relation*) отноше́ние; **this has no ~ on the matter** э́то к де́лу не отно́сится; **to consider a matter in all its ~s** всесторо́нне (*adv*) обсуди́ть вопро́с

3: **it's past ~** э́то уже́ про́сто невыноси́мо

4 *Naut*: **to take/find one's ~s** ориенти́роваться, *also fig*

5 *Tech* опо́ра; подши́пник.

beast *n* (*wild*) зверь (*m*); *Agric* скот (*collect*); *fig* (*of person*) скоти́на (*m and f*); **we have many/500 ~s on our farm** на на́шей фе́рме мно́го скота́/пятьсо́т голо́в скота́.

beastly *adj CQ*: **what a ~ day!** како́й кошма́рный день!; **what ~ weather!** кака́я ме́рзкая пого́да!

beat *n* **1** (*of heart*) бие́ние; *Mus* такт; **to the ~ of the drums** под бараба́нный бой

2 (*of a policeman*) маршру́т; *fig* **it's off my ~** э́то не по мое́й ча́сти.

beat *vti vt* **1** (*hit*) бить (по-, *pf for one blow* уда́рить) *and compounds*; *Cook* (*eggs, cream*) взби|ва́ть (-ть), (*meat*) отби́ть; **his father ~ him** оте́ц поби́л его́; **the bird ~ its wings against the glass** пти́ца би́лась кры́льями о стекло́; **to ~ a drum** бить в бараба́н; **to ~ a retreat** бить отбо́й (*Mil and fig*); **to ~ carpets** вы|бива́ть ковры́ (-́бить); **to ~ time** отбива́ть такт; *fig*: **to ~ one's head against a brick wall** би́ться голово́й о стену́; *CQ* **~ it!** убира́йтесь!

2 (*defeat*) *Mil, Sport* разби|ва́ть (-́ть); побе|жда́ть (-ди́ть); **our army/team was ~en**

на́ша а́рмия была́ разби́та, на́ша кома́нда потерпе́ла пораже́ние; **we were ~en 2—1** мы проигра́ли со счётом 2:1; **he ~ me at chess** он вы́играл у меня́ в ша́хматы; **to ~ a record** поби́ть реко́рд; **I'll ~ you to the summit** я ра́ньше тебя́ дойду́ до верши́ны; *fig*: **the police owned they were ~en** поли́ция призна́ла своё бесси́лие; *CQ*: **this ~s me** сдаю́сь, мне э́то не по зуба́м; **it ~s me why he did it** ума́ не приложу́, почему́ он э́то сде́лал

vi би́ть(ся); **his heart was ~ing fast** у него́ си́льно би́лось се́рдце; **the drums were ~ing** би́ли бараба́ны; **the sun ~ through the window** со́лнце би́ло в окно́; **waves were ~ing on the shore** во́лны би́лись о бе́рег; **rain was ~ing on the windows** дождь стуча́л/бараба́нил в о́кна; **to ~ on a door** колоти́ть в дверь (*usu impf*)

beat back *vt Mil*: **to ~ back an attack/an enemy** отби́ть ата́ку, отбр|а́сывать проти́вника (-о́сить)

beat down *vti vt*: **hail had ~en down the rye** рожь поби́ло (*impers*) гра́дом; **to ~ down a price** сбива́ть це́ну; **I ~ him down** (*in price*) я заста́вил его́ сба́вить це́ну

vi: **the sun was ~ing down mercilessly** со́лнце пали́ло немилосе́рдно

beat out *vt*: **we ~ out the fire** мы сби́ли ого́нь; **I'll have to get the dent in my wing ~en out** мне ну́жно вы́править вмя́тину на крыле́ маши́ны; **to ~ out a rhythm** отбива́ть ритм

beat up *vt*: **to ~ smb up** избива́ть кого́-л.

beater *n Cook* (*whisk*) ве́нчик, взбива́лка.

beating *n* (*thrashing*) по́рка, побо́и (*pl*); (*of drums*) бой; (*of heart*) бие́ние; *Mil*, *Sport* (*defeat*) пораже́ние; **he got a good ~** его́ вы́пороли.

beautiful *adj* краси́вый; (*fine*) прекра́сный; чуде́сный; **what a ~ day!** како́й чуде́сный день!

beauty *n* (*abstract*) красота́; (*of person or horse*, *etc.*): **he/she is a ~** он краса́вец, она́ краса́вица; *CQ* (*usu Sport*: *of stroke*, *goal*, *etc.*): **that was a ~!** э́то был краси́вый уда́р/гол!; **the ~ of it is (that) it cost me nothing** пре́лесть вся в том, что э́то мне ничего́ не сто́ило; *attr*: **~ contest/parlour** ко́нкурс красоты́, космети́ческий кабине́т.

beaver *n* бобр; *attr* бобро́вый.

because *conj* потому́ что, (*for emphasis*) потому́, что; из-за того́, что; **I couldn't come ~ the trains weren't running** я не мог прие́хать, потому́ что поезда́ не ходи́ли; **it was ~ I didn't want to hurt you that I didn't tell you** я не сказа́л тебе́ э́того потому́, что не хоте́л тебя́ оби́деть.

because of *prep* из-за + *G*; **this is all ~ of your laziness** э́то всё из-за твое́й ле́ни; **I said nothing ~ of the children being there** я ничего́ не сказа́л, потому́ что там бы́ли де́ти.

beckon *vti* мани́ть (по-); **he ~ed (me to follow him)** он помани́л меня́ за собо́й.

become *vti vt* (*suit*: *of clothes*, *etc.*) быть к лицу́ + *D*, идти́ + *D* (*only in impf*); **that dress ~s you** э́то пла́тье вам к лицу́/вам идёт; (*befit*) **it ill ~s you to speak like that** вам не подоба́ет (*impers*)/вам не к лицу́ так говори́ть

vi **1 ~ of** (*happen to*): **what's ~ of him?** что с ним ста́ло?, что тако́е с ним сде́лалось?; **what will ~ of the children?** что бу́дет/ста́нется с детьми́? [**NB** ста́нется *special form*, *used only in future or inf*]; **what's ~ of my knife?** куда́ задева́лся мой нож?

2 (*as link verb + noun or adj*) ста|нови́ться + *I* (-ть); *also often translated by verbs formed from the adj*; **he became an actor** он стал актёром; **the days are becoming shorter** дни стано́вятся коро́че; **he became famous** он стал знамени́т(ым); **to ~ better/worse** улучш|а́ться, ухудш|а́ться (*pfs* ́-иться); **to ~ old/pale/dark** старе́ть, бледне́ть, темне́ть (*pfs* по-); **to ~ ill** заболе|ва́ть (́-ть); **to ~ rich** богате́ть (раз-, *more usu in pf*).

bed *n* **1** (*as furniture*) крова́ть, (*as place to sleep*) посте́ль; **I moved the ~ to the other wall** я передви́нул крова́ть к друго́й стене́; **we were in ~ by 10** мы бы́ли в посте́ли в де́сять; **a single/double ~** односпа́льная/двуспа́льная крова́ть; **to make the ~s** застила́ть посте́ли; **to make up a ~ for smb** стели́ть посте́ль кому́-л; **to change the ~s** меня́ть посте́льное бельё; **to go to ~** ложи́ться спать; **to get into/out of ~** лечь в посте́ль, встать с посте́ли; **to take to one's ~** (*if ill*) слечь; **to put a child to ~** уложи́ть ребёнка в посте́ль/спать; **I gave him a ~ for the night** я пусти́л его́ переночева́ть; **I got a ~ with them** я устро́ился/ночева́л у них; **~ and board** ночле́г и пита́ние; *fig*: **he got out of ~ on the wrong side** он не с той ноги́ встал; **life isn't a ~ of roses** жизнь прожи́ть—не по́ле перейти́

2 (*of river*) ру́сло; (*of sea*) дно; (*of ocean*) ло́же; *Archit* основа́ние; *Geol* пласт; (*in kitchen garden*) гря́дка; **a ~ of hay/leaves/nettles** подсти́лка из се́на/из ли́стьев, за́росли (*pl*) крапи́вы (*collect*).

bedbug *n* (посте́льный) клоп.

bedding *n* (*for people*) посте́льное бельё и одея́ла; (*for animals*) подсти́лка.

bedpan *n* подкладно́е су́дно, *CQ* у́тка.

bedridden *adj* прико́ванный к посте́ли.

bedrock *n Geol* материко́вая поро́да.

bedroom *n* спа́льня.

bedside *n*: **she watched at the sick man's ~** она́ сиде́ла у посте́ли больно́го; *attr*: **~ table** прикрова́тная ту́мбочка; **the doctor has no ~ manner** у него́ нет враче́бного та́кта.

bedsore *n* про́лежень (*m*).

bedspread *n* покрыва́ло.

bedstead *n* о́стов крова́ти.

bedtime *n*: **it's ~, children!** де́ти, пора́ спать!; **my ~ is 10 o'clock** я ложу́сь спать в де́сять часо́в.

bee *n* пчела́; **queen ~** пчели́ная ма́тка; *fig* **he's got a ~ in his bonnet about commas** он помеша́лся на запяты́х.

beech *n* (*tree*) бук; *attr* бу́ковый.

beef *n* говя́дина; **roast/salt ~** ро́стбиф, солони́на; *attr*: **~ cattle** мясно́й скот.

beefsteak *n* бифште́кс.

beefy *adj CQ* му́скулистый.

beehive *n* у́лей.

beekeeper *n* пчелово́д, па́сечник.

beekeeping *n* пчелово́дство.

beeline *n*: **he made a ~ for the food/for the blonde** но́ги са́ми понесли́ его́ к столу́/к краси́вой блонди́нке.

beer *n* пи́во.

beet *n Bot* свёкла; **sugar ~** са́харная свёкла.

beetle *n* жук.

beetroot *n* свёкла; *fig* **she went red as a ~** она́ покрасне́ла как рак; *attr*: **~ soup** свеко́льник.

befall *vti vt*: **a strange thing befell him** с ним произошла́ стра́нная исто́рия

vi случ|а́ться (-и́ться).

befit *vt* сле́довать, подоба́ть + *D and inf* (*impfs*; *impers*); **it does not ~ a man in your position to...** челове́ку в твоём положе́нии не сле́дует/не подоба́ет + *inf*.

before *adv* ра́ньше; **I've heard that ~** я э́то слы́шал ра́ньше; **I spent last year in America and the year ~ in Spain** в про́шлом году́ я жил в Аме́рике, а за год до э́того/перед те́м—в Испа́нии; **long ~** давно́; **~ long** вско́ре.

before *prep* **1** (*of place*) пе́ред + *I*; **~ me stretched the steppe** передо мно́й расстила́лась степь; **he appeared ~ the judge** он предста́л пе́ред судьёй; **~ my very eyes** пря́мо у меня́ на глаза́х; *fig* **the proposal is now ~ the committee** предложе́ние сейча́с обсужда́ется комите́том

2 (*of arrangement*) пе́ред + *I*, впереди́ + *G*; **A comes ~ B** А стои́т пе́ред/впереди́ Б; **the theatre is the stop ~ the station** теа́тр бу́дет не доезжа́я одно́й остано́вки до вокза́ла; (*in queue*) **I'm ~ you** я пе́ред ва́ми

3 (*of time*) до + *G* (= *up to, till*); пе́ред + *I* (= *just before*); **~ the war** до войны́; **~ dinner** пе́ред обе́дом; **we won't get home ~ supper** мы прие́дем к у́жину, не ра́ньше; **we still have an hour ~ us** у нас есть ещё час (вре́мени); **that was ~ your time** э́то бы́ло ещё до тебя́; **long ~ my arrival** задо́лго до моего́ прие́зда.

before *conj* до того́ как, пре́жде чем; пе́ред тем как, пока́ не + *past tense*; **put out the lights ~ you go to bed** пе́ред тем как ля́жешь спать, потуши́ свет; **he gave me a ring ~ leaving** он мне позвони́л, пе́ред тем как уйти́; **I reasoned with him a long time ~ he agreed** я до́лго его́ убежда́л, пока́ он не согласи́лся; **~ they built the bridge, we had to cross by ferry** когда́ не́ было моста́, мы переправля́лись на паро́ме; **I'll ring you ~ I leave** я тебе́ позвоню́ пе́ред ухо́дом; **he was gone ~ I could stop him** он ушёл—я не успе́л останови́ть его́; **~ I forget, here's your key** пока́ я не забы́л, вот твой ключ.

beforehand *adv* зара́нее, за́годя.

befuddled *adj*: **I'm thoroughly ~** у меня́ всё в голове́ перепу́талось; **he was ~ by drink** он напи́лся до чёртиков.

beg *vti vt* (*ask*) проси́ть (по-); (*beseech*) умоля́ть, упра́шивать (*usu impfs*); вы|пра́шивать (-просить); кля́нчить (*usu impf*); [**NB** *A for concrete, G for abstract requests*]: **I ~ged him for help/to accompany me/for £5** я проси́л у него́ по́мощи/его́ проводи́ть меня́, я попроси́л у него́ пять фу́нтов, я умоля́л его́ о по́мощи/проводи́ть меня́/дать мне хотя́ бы пять фу́нтов; **he ~ged me for advice** он попроси́л у меня́ сове́та; **he ~ged the director for a week's leave** он вы́просил у дире́ктора неде́лю о́тпуска; **she ~ged me for the brooch** она́ упра́шивала меня́ отда́ть ей э́ту бро́шку, она́ кля́нчила у меня́ э́ту бро́шку

vi **1** (*of a beggar*) ни́щенствовать, (*of dog*) попроша́йничать (*impfs*)

2 (*formal*): **I ~ to report...** (я) осме́люсь/име́ю честь доложи́ть...; **I ~ to differ** позво́лю себе́ не согласи́ться; (*in business letters*): **we ~ to enclose our account** при э́том прилага́ется счёт; **we ~ to remain, yours faithfully...** остаёмся пре́данные Вам...; **we ~ to inform you...** извеща́ем Вас...

beggar *n* ни́щий; *CQ*: **lucky ~!** счастли́вчик!; **poor ~!** бедня́га! (*m and f*).

begin *vti vt* на|чина́ть (-ча́ть); **to ~ work** начина́ть рабо́ту/рабо́тать; **to ~ a new box of chocolates** начина́ть но́вую коро́бку шокола́да (*collect*); **he began his speech with a word of welcome** он на́чал речь приве́тствием/с приве́тствия

vi **1** (*with person as subject*) **i)** *used absolutely* начина́ть; **let's ~!** начнём!; **to ~ at/from the beginning** начина́ть с са́мого нача́ла; **ii)**: **to ~ to** + *inf* начина́ть + *impf inf*; **to ~ to read/to understand** начина́ть чита́ть/понима́ть

2 (*with thing as subject*) начина́ться; **when does the concert ~?** когда́ начина́ется конце́рт?; **dinner began with a fish course** у́жин начался́ с ры́бного блю́да; **to ~ with we had a glass of sherry** для нача́ла мы вы́пили по рю́мке ше́рри; **to ~ with, I didn't have enough money** во-пе́рвых, у меня́ бы́ло ма́ло де́нег

3 *often translated by pf verbs with inchoative prefixes* за- *or* по-, *or by* стать (*only in pf*); **to ~ to talk** заговори́ть (*pf*); **the leaves have begun to turn yellow** ли́стья пожелте́ли/ста́ли желте́ть; **her heart began to thump** се́рдце у неё заби́лось/заколоти́лось; **it began to rain** пошёл/начался́ дождь.

beginner *n* (*novice*) новичо́к; **mathematics for ~s** матема́тика (*sing*) для начина́ющих.

beginning *n* нача́ло; **from ~ to end** с нача́ла до конца́.

beguile *vt*: **to ~ smb with promises/into doing smth** обма́н|ывать кого́-л обеща́ниями (-у́ть), обма́ном уговори́ть кого́-л сде́лать что-л (*usu pf*); **we ~d the time by telling stories** мы корота́ли вре́мя, расска́зывая вся́кие исто́рии.

behalf *n*: **on ~ of** *used as prep* за + *A*, ра́ди + *G*, в по́льзу + *G*; (*in name of*) от и́мени + *G*; **I spoke on his ~** я вы́сказался в его́ подде́ржку; **don't put yourself out on my ~** не беспоко́йтесь (обо мне́); **I am speaking on ~ of my husband** я говорю́ от и́мени моего́ му́жа.

behave *vti* вести́ себя́ (*impf*); **children, ~ yourselves!** де́ти, веди́те себя́ как сле́дует!; **he ~d perfectly** он прекра́сно себя́ вёл; **he ~d disgracefully towards her** он безобра́зно вёл себя́ с ней; **the car is behaving well today** сего́дня маши́на хорошо́ идёт.

behaviour *n* поведе́ние; **he was on his best ~** он вёл себя́ про́сто идеа́льно.

behind *n euph CQ* зад; *joc* мя́гкое ме́сто; **he fell on his ~** он упа́л и уда́рился мя́гким ме́стом.

behind *adv* **1** (*at the back*) позади́; (*from behind*) сза́ди; (*to the back*) наза́д; **he's standing ~** он стои́т позади́/сза́ди; **he came up from ~** он подошёл сза́ди; **look ~!** огляни́сь наза́д!

2 *with verb "to be"*: **we are ~ in our work/with our payments** мы отстаём в/по рабо́те, мы просро́чили платёж (*sing*); **I'm ~ with everything today** я сего́дня ни с чем не справля́юсь; *Sport* **he's ~ on points** он отстаёт по очка́м.

behind *prep* **1** (*of position*) за + *I*; сза́ди + *G*, позади́ + *G*; (*of movement*) за + *A*; **there is a kitchen garden ~ the house** позади́ до́ма/за до́мом есть огоро́д; **put the letter ~ the clock** положи́ письмо́ за часы́ (*no sing*); **with his hands ~ his back** заложа́ ру́ки за́ спину, держа́ ру́ки за спино́й; **they're coming just ~ us** они́ приду́т/иду́т сле́дом за на́ми; **the sun came out from ~ the clouds** со́лнце вы́шло из-за туч

2 *fig uses*: **what's ~ all this?** что за э́тим кро́ется?; **it's all ~ us now** тепе́рь э́то всё позади́; **he left three children ~ him** он оста́вил по́сле себя́ трои́х дете́й; **he's ~ the other boys** он отстаёт от свои́х све́рстников; **his ideas are ~ the times** у него́ отста́лые взгля́ды; **we're all ~ you on this** в э́том мы все вас подде́рживаем.

behindhand *adv see* **behind** *adv* **2**.

beholden *adj*: **I don't want to be ~ to anybody for anything** я никому́ ниче́м не хочу́ быть обя́занным.

beige *adj* бе́жевый.

being *n*: **a human ~** челове́к; **human ~s** лю́ди; **it is not known when the world came into ~** неизве́стно, когда́ возни́к мир.

being *adj* (*only in*): **for the time ~** пока́.

belch *n* отры́жка.

belch *vti vt*: **the volcano was ~ing flames** вулка́н изрыга́л пла́мя (*sing*)

vi рыг|а́ть (*semel* -ну́ть).

belfry *n* колоко́льня.

Belgian *n* бельги́ец, бельги́йка.

Belgian *adj* бельги́йский.

belie *vt*: **his cheerfulness ~d his true feelings** его́ весёлость дава́ла неве́рное представле́ние о его́ и́стинных чу́вствах; **he ~d our hopes** он не оправда́л на́ших наде́жд.

belief *n* ве́ра, *also Rel*; (*conviction*) убежде́ние; **it's my ~ that...** я ве́рю/уве́рен, что...; **I haven't much ~ in his promises/in my doctor** я не о́чень-то ве́рю его́ обеща́ниям/доверя́ю моему́ врачу́; **to the best of my ~** наско́лько мне изве́стно; **it passes ~, it's beyond ~** э́то (про́сто) невероя́тно.

believe *vti vt* ве́рить + *D* (по-); **don't you ~ it** не ве́рьте э́тому; **he is ~d to be in Paris** полага́ют, что он в Пари́же; **I could ~ anything of him** от него́ мо́жно всего́ ожида́ть; **I ~ he's already here** ду́маю, что он уже́ пришёл; **is he coming?—I ~ so/not** он придёт?—Ду́маю, что да/, что нет

vi ве́рить (*only in impf*), *also Rel*; **to ~ in God** ве́рить в бо́га; **do you ~ in ghosts?** ты ве́ришь в привиде́ния?; **I ~ in saying what you think** по-мо́ему, всегда́ на́до говори́ть то, что ду́маешь.

believer *n* **1** *Rel* ве́рующий

2: **he's a ~ in homoeopathy** он ве́рит в гомеопа́тию.

bell *n* (*in church*) ко́локол; (*Tel*, *Elec*, *on door*, *in school*) звоно́к; (*small hand bell*) колоко́льчик, *also Bot*; *Naut* скля́нка; **to ring the ~** позвони́ть, дать звоно́к; **I'll answer the ~** я пойду́ откро́ю дверь; **there's the ~** звоня́т; *Naut* **it's gone 4/8 ~s** проби́ло (*impers*) четы́ре скля́нки/во́семь скля́нок; *fig* **that name rings a ~/doesn't ring a ~ with me** э́то и́мя мне знако́мо/мне ничего́ не говори́т.

bellicose *adj* вои́нственный, агресси́вный.

belligerent *adj*: **the ~ countries** вою́ющие стра́ны.

bellow *vi* (*of bull or child*) реве́ть (*impf*).

belly *n* живо́т; *pejor* брю́хо.

bellyache *vi CQ*: **he's always bellyaching about the grub in the canteen** он ве́чно жа́луется, что в столо́вой пло́хо ко́рмят.

bellyful *n CQ*: **I've had my ~ of meetings** я сыт по го́рло вся́кими заседа́ниями.

belly-landing *n Aer* поса́дка «на брю́хо».

belong *vi* **1** принадлежа́ть + *D* (*impf*); **who does this ~ to?** кому́ э́то принадлежи́т?; **to ~ to a club** быть чле́ном клу́ба; **I hardly know them—they ~ to a different set** я их пло́хо зна́ю—они́ не принадлежа́т к на́шему кру́гу; **he ~s to the North of England** он ро́дом из се́верной А́нглии; **he doesn't ~ here** он нezде́шний

2 (*have as proper place*): **this lid ~s to the milk can** э́та кры́шка от моло́чного бидо́на; **where do these books ~?** где стоя́т э́ти кни́ги?

belongings *npl* ве́щи (*pl*).

beloved *adj* (*of people*) возлю́бленный, *also used as n*; *joc* (*of things*) люби́мый; **he's lost his ~ pipe** он потеря́л свою́ люби́мую тру́бку.

below *adv* (*lower*) ни́же; **the passage quoted ~** отры́вок, приведённый ни́же; **the captain is/has gone ~** капита́н внизу́/спусти́лся вниз.

below *prep* (*lower than*) ни́же + *G*; (*under*) под + *I* or (*of motion*) + *A*; **~ sea level/average/zero** ни́же у́ровня мо́ря/сре́днего/нуля́; **~ the bridge** под мосто́м (*under it*), ни́же моста́ (*downstream from it*); **~ the surface** под пове́рхностью; **put it ~ some books** положи́ э́то под кни́ги.

belt *n* (*lady's*) по́яс; (*man's*) реме́нь (*m*), *also Tech*; *Geog* полоса́, зо́на, по́яс; **fan ~** реме́нь вентиля́тора; **safety ~** *Aut* реме́нь безопа́сности, *Aer* привязно́й реме́нь; **green ~** (*round city*) зелёный по́яс, зелёная зо́на; **black-earth ~** чернозёмная полоса́; **conveyer ~** ле́нта конве́йера; **to hit below the ~** нанести́ уда́р ни́же по́яса, *also fig*, *fig* примени́ть запрещённый приём; *attr*: **~ drive** ремённый приво́д.

bench *n* **1** (*seat*) скамья́, скаме́йка; (*in laboratory*) стол; **carpenter's/work ~** верста́к

2 *Law* (**the B.**) (*court*) суд, (*judges collectively*) су́дьи; **to sit on the ~** *equiv* суди́ть.

bend *n* изги́б, сгиб; (*on racetrack*) вира́ж; **a sharp ~ in the road** круто́й изги́б/поворо́т доро́ги; *fig sl* **it'll drive me round the ~** э́то меня́ докона́ет.

bend *vti vt* (*in one place*) гнуть (по-, со-), (*in several places*) из|гиба́ть (-огну́ть) *and other compounds*; (*incline*) наклон|я́ть (-и́ть); **I've bent the poker** я согну́л кочергу́; **to ~ wire into a ring/into the shape of a star** согну́ть про́волоку в кольцо́, изогну́ть про́волоку в фо́рме звезды́; **~ the end of the wire under the plank** загни́ коне́ц про́волоки под до́ску; **he bent his head** он наклони́л/нагну́л го́лову; **to go down on ~ed knees to smb** преклон|я́ть коле́ни пе́ред кем-л (-и́ть); *fig*: **he is bent on going to the theatre tonight** он вознаме́рился пойти́ сего́дня ве́чером в теа́тр

vi гну́ться *and compounds*; наклоня́ться *and other compounds*; **I can't ~ easily because of my rheumatism** я с трудо́м сгиба́юсь из-за ревмати́зма; **the bough bent but did not break** ве́тка гну́лась, но не лома́лась; **the shelf bent under the weight of the books** по́лка прогну́лась под тя́жестью книг; **the road/river ~s westwards here** здесь доро́га/река́ повора́чивает на за́пад; **he bent towards/over her** он наклони́лся к ней, он склони́лся над ней; **he bent forward to have a word with her** он наклони́лся, что́бы сказа́ть ей не́сколько слов.

beneath *prep* (*of place*) под + *I*; (*of motion*) под + *A*; *fig only* ни́же + *G*, недосто́йно + *G*; **to sit ~ a tree** сиде́ть под де́ревом; **put the bucket ~ the table** поста́вь ведро́ под стол; **she dropped her eyes ~ his gaze** она́ опусти́ла глаза́ под его́ взгля́дом; *fig*: **~ one's breath** вполго́лоса (*adv*); **such conduct is ~ you** тако́е поведе́ние недосто́йно вас; **she thinks housework is ~ her** она́ счита́ет для себя́ зазо́рным занима́ться дома́шним хозя́йством.

benefactor *n* благоде́тель (*m*).

beneficial *adj* (*salutary*) благотво́рный; (*useful*) поле́зный; (*advantageous*) вы́годный; **a ~ influence** благотво́рное влия́ние; **a climate ~ to health** цели́тельный кли́мат.

benefit *n* **1** по́льза; **I did it for your ~** я сде́лал э́то ра́ди тебя́/ра́ди твое́й же по́льзы; **I hope you got some ~ from your holiday** наде́юсь, вы провели́ о́тпуск с по́льзой; **I'll recapitulate for the ~ of latecomers** я повторю́ для опозда́вших; **speak louder for the ~ of those at the back** говори́те гро́мче, что́бы и сза́ди бы́ло слы́шно; **I'll give you the ~ of the doubt this time** на э́тот раз я вам пове́рю; **I had the ~ of a good education** у меня́ бы́ло преиму́щество — я получи́л хоро́шее образова́ние; **we're reaping the ~s of last year's work** мы пожина́ем плоды́ свое́й прошлого́дней рабо́ты

2 (*allowance*) посо́бие; **maternity/sickness/unemployment ~** посо́бие матеря́м/по боле́зни/по безрабо́тице

3 *attr Theat*: **a ~ performance** бенефи́с, бенефи́сный спекта́кль (*m*) [*obsolete in SU*].

benefit *vti*: **the sea air will ~ you, you will ~ from the sea air** морско́й во́здух пойдёт тебе́ на по́льзу; **the new railway will ~ the whole area** но́вая желе́зная доро́га принесёт всему́ райо́ну большу́ю по́льзу; **he ~ed by his uncle's death** по́сле сме́рти дя́ди он получи́л нема́лое насле́дство.

benevolent *adj* доброжела́тельный.

benign *adj Med* доброка́чественный.

bent *n* накло́нность, спосо́бность к + *D* (*both usu pl*); **to follow one's ~** сле́довать свои́м накло́нностям; **he has a ~ for music** у него́ музыка́льные спосо́бности.

bent *adj*: **he was ~ with age** он с года́ми ссуту́лился/сго́рбился; **his fingers are ~ with arthritis** у него́ па́льцы скрю́чены артри́том; **he was ~ over a book** он уткну́лся в кни́гу; **she was sitting on the sofa with her legs ~ under her** она́ сиде́ла на дива́не, поджа́в под себя́ но́ги; **the rear bumper is ~** за́дний ба́мпер по́гнут; **with eyes ~ on the ground** поту́пив взор; **he is ~ on becoming a doctor** он наме́рен стать врачо́м.

benzine *n* бензи́н.

bequeath *vt* завеща́ть (*impf and pf*); **he ~ed me his watch** он завеща́л мне свои́ часы́.

bequest *n* насле́дство; **he left ~s of money to his grandchildren** он оста́вил де́ньги свои́м вну́кам.

bereaved *adj*: **the ~ wife** вдова́; **he is recently ~** он неда́вно потеря́л жену́/овдове́л.

bereavement *n*: **owing to her recent ~** из-за пости́гшего её го́ря; *off* **we send our condolences to you on your recent ~** приму́те на́ши соболéзнования в связи́ с пости́гшим вас несчáстьем.

beret *n* берéт.

berry *n* я́года.

berserk *adj*: **when drunk he would go ~** напи́вшись, он звереéт.

berth *n Naut* (*anchorage*) стоя́нка, мéсто стоя́нки; (*cabin*) каю́та; (*bunk*) кóйка; *Rail* (*sleeper*) спáльное мéсто, пóлка; *fig*: **to give smb a wide ~** обходи́ть когó-л за версту́; *CQ* **I've found myself a snug ~** я нашёл себé тёплое местéчко.

beset *adj*: **he was ~ by doubts** егó одолевáли сомнéния; **a policy ~ with difficulties** поли́тика, чревáтая осложнéниями.

beside *prep* (*side by side*) ря́дом с + *I*; **she sat ~ her mother** онá сидéла ря́дом с мáтерью; **our house is ~ the sea** наш дом ря́дом с мóрем; **she seems dull ~ her sister** ря́дом с сестрóй онá кáжется ску́чной; **the road runs ~ the river** дорóга идёт вдоль реки́; *fig*: **that's ~ the point** э́то не по существу́, э́то не относится к дéлу; **she was ~ herself with rage/grief** онá былá вне себя́ от гнéва/уби́та гóрем.

besides *adv* (*apart from that*) крóме тогó; (*also*) тáкже; (*moreover*) вдобáвок, к тому́ же.

besides *prep* крóме + *G*; **there were four guests ~ myself** крóме меня́/не считáя меня́, бы́ло ещё чéтверо гостéй.

besiege *vt* осаждáть (*usu impf*), *also fig*; **we were ~d by journalists/with questions/requests** нас осаждáли журнали́сты, нас засыпáли вопрóсами/прóсьбами.

besotted *adj*: **he is ~ with drink/with her** он си́льно под му́хой, он без пáмяти от неё.

bespeak *vt* (*rooms, tickets, seats*) брони́ровать (*impf and pf, pf also* за-); (*goods*) закáз|ывать (-áть); **all the rooms are already bespoken** все кóмнаты ужé заброни́рованы.

bespectacled *adj* в очкáх.

best *n* **1** *usu translated by adj* лу́чший; **the ~ of wives** лу́чшая из жён; **the ~ of the day has gone** (*of weather*) сóлнца ужé нет, лу́чшая часть дня ужé позади́, (*bigger part of the day*) дéнь-то ужé прошёл; **the ~ of it is that he didn't recognize his own wife** и что всегó смешнéе—он не узнáл своéй жены́; (*on parting*) **all the ~** всегó сáмого лу́чшего; **I'll have to put on my Sunday ~** придётся надéть наря́дное плáтье

2 *phrases with preps*: **at ~** в лу́чшем слу́чае; **it's all for the ~** всё к лу́чшему; **to the ~ of my knowledge** наскóлько мне извéстно; **I'll do it to the ~ of my ability** я сдéлаю всё, что в мои́х си́лах; **the garden is at its ~ in June** сад краси́вее всегó в ию́не; **he doesn't talk much even at the ~ of times** он и вообщé-то не óчень разговóрчив

3 *phrases with verbs*: **they are doing their ~** они́ дéлают всё, что в их си́лах; **they have the ~ of everything** у них всё сáмое лу́чшее.

best *adj* (наи)лу́чший, сáмый лу́чший; **my ~ friend/dress** мой лу́чший друг, моё сáмое лу́чшее плáтье; **we spent the ~ part of the time arguing** мы проспóрили бóльшую часть врéмени; **for the ~ part of an hour** почти́ час; **with the ~ will in the world I can't arrive any sooner** кáк бы я ни рвáлся, я не смогу́ приéхать рáньше; **he's the ~ man for the job** он наибóлее подходя́щий человéк для э́той рабóты; **to make the ~ use of one's time/opportunities** испóльзовать врéмя/возмóжности наилу́чшим óбразом; **he's among the ~ scholars in this field** он оди́н из сáмых талáнтливых учёных в э́той óбласти.

best *adv* бóльше всегó, лу́чше всегó; **which do you like ~?** что вам нрáвится бóльше всегó?; **I thought it ~ to tell you** я поду́мал, что сáмое лу́чшее—рассказáть тебé об э́том; **you know ~** тебé лу́чше знать; **do as you think ~** поступáй как знáешь.

bestial *adj fig* звéрский.

bestseller *n* бестсéллер.

bet *n* пари́ (*indecl*); **to lay a ~ that...** держáть пари́, что..., *CQ* спóрить, что...; **to win/lose a ~** вы́играть/проигрáть пари́; **that horse is a good ~** стáвить на э́ту лóшадь—вéрное дéло; **we had a ~ whether you'd come** мы поспóрили,/заключи́ли пари́, придёшь ты и́ли нет.

bet *vti vt* (*on horses, cards*) стáвить (по-), держáть пари́ (*impf*); (*between friends, usu not for money*) спóрить (по-), би́ться об заклáд (*impf*) [**NB** спóрить *usu in 1st person pl*]; **he ~ £5 on the black horse** он постáвил пять фу́нтов на чёрную лóшадь; **he ~ that...** он держáл пари́, что...; **I ~ you anything you like/a bottle of brandy he'll be late** (по)спóрим на что угóдно,/на буты́лку коньякá, что он опоздáет; **father disapproved.—I ~ he did!/You bet!** отéц э́то не одóбрил.—Ещё бы!

vi: **I don't ~** я не спóрю на дéньги; **I don't ~ on horses** я не игрáю на скáчках.

betide *vt*: **woe ~ you, if...** гóре тебé, éсли...

betimes *adv*: **we must be up ~ tomorrow** зáвтра нáдо рáно вставáть.

betray *vt* **1** (*a person, one's country*) предa|вáть (-́ть)

2 (*reveal*) вы|давáть (-́дать); **to ~ a secret** вы́дать тáйну; **his eyes ~ed his anxiety** глазá выдавáли егó беспокóйство.

better *n*: **to change for the ~** измени́ться к лу́чшему; **for ~ or worse** к добру́ и́ли ху́ду; **so much the ~** тем лу́чше; **the quicker the ~** чем скорée, тем лу́чше; **she got the ~ of her shyness** онá преодолéла свою́ застéнчивость; **my curiosity got the ~ of me** меня́ одолевáло любопы́тство; **he always gets the ~ of these quarrels** он всегдá выхóдит победи́телем в э́тих спóрах; **I thought all the ~ of him for that** э́то пóдняло егó в мои́х глазáх.

better *adj* лу́чший; **~ houses** лу́чшие домá; **I'm much ~ now** тепéрь мне гóраздо лу́чше;

it's ~ / it would be ~ to wait лу́чше бы́ло бы подожда́ть; **he's no ~ than a thief** чем он лу́чше во́ра?; **he's seen ~ days** он знава́л лу́чшие дни; *joc* **my ~ half** моя́ полови́на, моя́ жена́.

better *adv* **1** лу́чше; **he does it ~ than I do** он э́то де́лает лу́чше меня́; **he did ~ than his word** он сде́лал бо́льше, чем обеща́л; **they're ~ off now** им сейча́с лу́чше живётся, они́ сейча́с лу́чше живу́т; **we're ~ off without his help** лу́чше мы обойдёмся без его́ по́мощи; **he always knows ~** он всегда́ бо́льше всех зна́ет; **you ought to know ~ than to expect help from her** ва́м-то сле́довало бы знать, что от неё не́чего ожида́ть по́мощи; **I know ~ than to believe him** я не так глуп, что́бы ве́рить ему́; **I meant to tell him, but thought ~ of it** я хоте́л сказа́ть ему́ э́то, но переду́мал

2 had better: you'd ~ go yourself вам лу́чше бы пойти́ самому́ [NB *sing after* вам]; **hadn't you ~ take an umbrella?** не лу́чше ли взять с собо́й зо́нтик?; **I'd ~ begin by explaining** я лу́чше начну́ с объясне́ния.

better *vt* улучш|а́ть (-́ить); **to ~ oneself** (*in one's job*) продвига́ться по слу́жбе, получа́ть бо́лее высо́кую зарпла́ту, найти́ рабо́ту полу́чше.

between *adv*, *also* **in ~ 1: he saw his professor in the morning, his parents in the afternoon and in ~ he lunched with us** у́тром он был у профе́ссора, пото́м обе́дал у нас, а ве́чером пошёл к роди́телям; **trains are few and far ~** поезда́ хо́дят о́чень ре́дко

2: the school consists of two buildings with a swimming pool in ~ шко́ла состои́т из двух зда́ний и бассе́йна ме́жду ни́ми.

between *prep* ме́жду + *I*; **she stood ~ them** она́ стоя́ла ме́жду ни́ми; **it's ~ 5 and 6 miles off** э́то приме́рно пять-шесть миль отсю́да; **it happened ~ one and three o'clock** э́то случи́лось ме́жду ча́сом и тремя́; **~ ourselves, ~ you and me** ме́жду на́ми; **they had only £10 ~ the two of them** на двои́х у них бы́ло то́лько де́сять фу́нтов; **~ us we'll do it very quickly** вме́сте мы э́то сде́лаем о́чень бы́стро; **they bought the car ~ the four of them** они́ сложи́лись вчетверо́м и купи́ли маши́ну; **a look passed ~ them** они́ обменя́лись взгля́дами; *fig*: **~ the children, my job and the cooking I haven't a minute** де́ти, рабо́та и хозя́йство не оставля́ют мне ни одно́й свобо́дной мину́ты; **~ one thing and another, I've not got down to it yet** я ещё не добра́лся до э́того—всё дела́/не́когда.

betwixt *adv*: **~ and between** ни то́ ни сё.

beverage *n* напи́ток, питьё.

beware *vi* бере́чься + *G* (*impf*), остере|га́ться + *G* (-́чься); **~ of pick-pockets!** береги́сь воро́в!; **tell her to ~ of strangers** скажи́ ей, что́бы она́ остерега́лась незнако́мых люде́й; **~ when crossing the road** бу́дьте осторо́жны, переходя́ у́лицу; **"B. of the dog!"** «Осторо́жно, зла́я соба́ка!»

bewilder *vt usu pass*: **she was ~ed by the big city** она́ растеря́лась в большо́м го́роде.

bewilderment *n* (*confusion*) замеша́тельство; си́льное изумле́ние.

bewitch *vt* околдо́в|ывать, очаро́в|ывать (*pfs* -а́ть), *both also fig*.

bewitching *adj* плени́тельный, очарова́тельный; **a ~ smile/child** плени́тельная улы́бка, очарова́тельный ребёнок.

beyond *n*: **we live at the back of ~** мы живём на краю́ све́та/*CQ* у чёрта на рога́х.

beyond *adv* вдали́, да́льше; **~ could be seen the lake** вдали́ бы́ло ви́дно о́зеро.

beyond *prep* **1** (*of place*) за + *I*; (*of motion*) за + *A*, да́льше + *G*; **~ the marsh/river** за боло́том, за́ реку; **~ the seas** за моря́ми; **~ the village rise the mountains** за дере́вней начина́ются го́ры; **don't go ~ the school** не уходи́ далеко́ от шко́лы

2 (*of time*): **don't stay out ~ 10** не гуля́й по́зже десяти́ часо́в ве́чера

3 (*in neg or interrog sentences = except*) кро́ме + *G*; **has she anything ~ her pension?** у неё есть ещё каки́е-нибудь дохо́ды, кро́ме пе́нсии?; **I've no reasons ~ those I've already given** у меня́ нет други́х причи́н, кро́ме тех, кото́рые я назва́л

4 (*exceeding, past*): **~ belief/all doubt/praise** невероя́тно (*adv*), вне вся́кого сомне́ния, вы́ше вся́ких похва́л (*pl*); **we succeeded ~ our wildest hopes** успе́х превзошёл на́ши са́мые сме́лые ожида́ния; **to live ~ one's means** жить не по сре́дствам; **the task is ~ him** э́та зада́ча ему́ не по плечу́; **it's ~ me** (*my comprehension*) э́то вы́ше моего́ понима́ния; **the car is ~ repair** э́ту маши́ну уже́ не отремонти́руешь.

bias *n* **1: a ~ against/in favour of** предубежде́ние про́тив + *G*, пристра́стие к + *D*; **without ~** беспристра́стно (*adv*)

2 *Sew*: **to cut on the ~** крои́ть/ре́зать по косо́й ли́нии/по диагона́ли.

bias *vt usu pass*: **he is ~sed against/in favour of it** он предубеждён про́тив э́того, он к э́тому осо́бо располо́жен; **a ~sed opinion** предвзя́тое мне́ние.

bib *n* де́тский нагру́дник, «слюня́вчик».

bible *n* би́блия.

biblical *adj* библе́йский.

bicarbonate of soda *n* со́да (питьева́я).

bicentenary *n* двухсотле́тие.

biceps *n* би́цепс.

bicker *vi*: **they are always ~ing** они́ ве́чно препира́ются/пререка́ются.

bicycle *n* велосипе́д.

bicycle *vi* (*to specific destination*) е́здить (*usu impf*)/(*for pleasure*) ката́ться на велосипе́де (по-).

bid *n* **1** (*at auction sale*): **he made a ~ of £ 40** он предложи́л со́рок фу́нтов; **there's been a ~ of £ 500—any higher?** предлага́ется (цена́ в) пятьсо́т фу́нтов—кто бо́льше?; **final ~** оконча́тельная цена́; *Comm* **a ~ for a**

contract заявка на подряд; *fig* **he made a ~ for the chairmanship** он добивался председательского кресла

2 *Cards*: **whose ~?** кому объявлять?

bid *vti vt* 1 (*at auction sale*) пред|лагать (-ложить)

2 *Cards*: **to ~ two clubs** объявлять две трефы

3 (*say*): **to ~ smb good morning/farewell** пожелать кому-л доброго утра (*usu pf*), про|щаться с кем-л (-ститься)

vi предлагать; **I will ~ up to £5 for the table** я предложу за этот стол самое большее пять фунтов; **he is ~ding against me** он всё набавляет и набавляет сумму—мне за ним не угнаться.

biddable *adj* послушный.

bidding *n* 1 (*at auction*): **~ was brisk** шла бойкая распродажа; **the ~ opened at £5** первое предложение было пять фунтов

2 *Cards*: **to open the ~** объявить первым

3: **to do smb's ~** исполнять чьё-л приказание.

biennial *adj* двухлетний; *as n Bot* двухлетнее растение.

bifocal *adj* двухфокусный, бифокальный.

big *adj* большой; крупный; (*of clothes*; *usu predic*) велик; **he's a ~ boy** он уже большой мальчик; **a ~ sum of money** большая/крупная сумма денег; **a ~ firm** большая/крупная фирма; **~ business/landowners** большой бизнес, крупные землевладельцы; **that's ~ news** это важная новость; **the dress is/these shoes are (too) ~ for me** это платье мне велико, эти туфли мне велики; **he likes to do things in a ~ way** он всё делает с размахом; *CQ iron* **you pay the bill while I get the coats.—That's ~ of you!** ты заплати по счёту, а я возьму пальто.—Какая щедрость с твоей стороны!

big *adv CQ*: **to talk ~** хвастаться; **to think ~** мыслить широко.

bigamy *n* двоежёнство.

bigoted *adj* узколобый; фанатичный.

bigwig *n CQ* важная персона, «шишка».

bike *n and vi CQ see* **bicycle** *n and vi.*

bikini *n* бикини (*indecl*).

bilateral *adj* двусторонний.

bilberry *n* черника (*of plant and collect of berries*).

bile *n Med* жёлчь, *also fig.*

bilge *n Naut* днище; *fig sl* **~!** ерунда!; *attr*: **~ water** трюмная вода.

bilingual *adj* двуязычный.

bilious *adj*: **she's got a ~ headache** у неё тошнота и головная боль; **she had a ~ attack** её тошнило/(*if vomiting*) рвало (*impers*); **I feel slightly ~** меня подташнивает (*impers*).

bill[1] *n* (*bird's*) клюв.

bill[1] *vi*: **to ~ and coo** ворковать, *also CQ of lovers* (*impf*).

bill[2] *n* 1 счёт; **telephone/hotel ~** счёт за телефон/в гостинице; **to make out a ~** выписать счёт; **to pay/*CQ* foot the ~** оплатить счёт/расходы; **put it down on the ~** внесите это в счёт

2 *Fin* (*US*: *banknote*) банкнот; **a 5-dollar ~** банкнот в пять долларов; **a ~ of credit** аккредитив; **a ~ of exchange** вексель

3 *Law* законопроект

4 (*notice*) афиша; (*esp. Polit*) плакат; *fig CQ* **that will fill the ~** это подойдёт

5 *various*: **~ of fare** меню (*indecl*); **the doctor gave me a clean ~ of health** врач сказал, что я совсем здоров; *Comm* **~ of lading** накладная.

bill[2] *vt* 1 (*in hotel, etc.*): **they've ~ed me for three nights instead of two** мне засчитали три ночи вместо двух, с меня взяли за три ночи вместо двух

2 *Theat*: **Chaliapin was ~ed to appear as Boris** было объявлено, что Бориса будет петь Шаляпин.

billiards *npl* бильярд (*sing*).

billion *n* (*UK*) биллион, (*US*) миллиард.

billy goat *n* козёл.

bimonthly *adj and adv* выходящий раз в два месяца.

bin *n* (*chest*) ларь (*m*); (*for corn*) закром; **flour ~** ларь с мукой; **rubbish/litter ~** (*in house*) мусорное ведро, (*outside*) мусорный ящик.

bind *n sl*: **it's an awful ~** это такая обуза; **what a ~ to have to take her along** брать её с собой—такая обуза.

bind *vti vt* 1 вязать (с-), связ|ывать (-ать) *and other compounds*; **to ~ smb hand and foot** связать кому-л руки и ноги/*fig* кого-л по рукам и ногам; **to ~ smth to smth** привязывать что-л к чему-л; **I bound up his finger tightly** я туго завязал/перевязал ему палец; *fig*: **their common interests ~ them together** их связывают общие интересы; **this problem is bound up with many others** эта проблема связана со многими другими

2 *Sew* обши|вать (-ть); **to ~ cuffs with leather** обшить манжеты кожей

3 (*books*) перепле|тать (-сти)

4 (*compel*) обяз|ывать (-ать); **he bound me to secrecy** он взял с меня слово хранить тайну; *Law* **to ~ smb to appear in court** обязать кого-л явиться в суд

vi: **clay ~s when heated** глина твердеет при нагревании; **bananas are ~ing** (*constipating*) бананы крепят.

binding *n* (*of book*: *act and cover*) переплёт; *Sew* (*act and material used*) обшивка.

binding *adj*: **a ~ promise** связывающее обещание; *Law* **that clause has ~ force** этот пункт имеет силу обязательства.

bindweed *n Bot* вьюнок.

binge *n* кутёж; **to go on a ~** кутнуть.

bingo *n* бинго (*indecl*).

binoculars *npl* бинокль (*m*, *sing*).

biochemistry *n* биохимия.

biography *n* биография.

biology *n* биология.

biophysics *n* биофизика (*sing*).

birch *n* (*tree*) берёза; (*rod*) ро́зга; **he got the ~** его́ наказа́ли ро́згами (*pl*); *attr* берёзовый.

bird *n* **1** пти́ца; **~ of prey/of passage** хи́щная/перелётная пти́ца; *fig*: **a little ~ told me** мне соро́ка на хвосте́ принесла́; **to kill two ~s with one stone** уби́ть двух за́йцев (одни́м вы́стрелом); *CQ* **that's strictly for the ~s** э́то для дурако́в; *Theat* **he got the ~** его́ освиста́ли

2 *CQ* (*of person*): **he's a queer ~** он стра́нный тип; **he's a wily old ~** он стре́ляный воробе́й; **he's an early ~** он ра́но встаёт; *sl pejor* (*girl*) деви́ца.

birdcage *n* кле́тка (для птиц).

bird's-eye view *n* (**a ~**) вид с пти́чьего полёта; *fig* о́бщая перспекти́ва.

bird watching *n* наблюде́ние птиц (в есте́ственных усло́виях).

birth *n* рожде́ние, *also fig*; *Med* ро́ды (*pl*); **I'm Scottish by ~** я ро́дом из Шотла́ндии; **to give ~** роди́ть; **she gave ~ to a son** она́ родила́ сы́на; **he weighed seven pounds at ~** при рожде́нии он ве́сил семь фу́нтов; **the father was present at the ~** оте́ц ребёнка прису́тствовал при ро́дах; **cats usually have five-six kittens at a ~** ко́шки обы́чно прино́сят пять-шесть котя́т; *fig* **the ~ of an idea** рожде́ние иде́и.

birth control *n* (*general*) регули́рование рожда́емости; **to practise ~** применя́ть противозача́точные сре́дства.

birthday *n* день рожде́ния; *attr*: **~ present** пода́рок ко дню рожде́ния.

birthmark *n* ро́динка.

birthplace *n* ме́сто рожде́ния.

birth rate *n* рожда́емость.

biscuit *n* сухо́е пече́нье; **water ~** гале́та.

bisect *vt* разрез|а́ть/раздел|я́ть попола́м (-́ать/-и́ть).

bishop *n* еписко́п.

bit[1] *n* (*for horse*) удила́ (*no sing*); *Tech* пёрка, бура́в.

bit[2] *n* **1** кусо́к; *dim* кусо́чек; **have a ~ of cake** съешь кусо́чек то́рта; **a ~ of string** кусо́к бечёвки; **the dog has eaten every ~ of our supper** соба́ка съе́ла весь наш у́жин до кро́шки; **he's torn his trousers to ~s** он изорва́л свои́ брю́ки в кло́чья; **the vase is smashed to ~s** ва́за разби́лась вдре́безги (*adv*); **this table comes to ~s** э́тот стол мо́жно разобра́ть; **unfortunately the box has come to ~s** к сожале́нию, я́щик развали́лся; **the trunk is full of her ~s and pieces** чего́ то́лько нет в её сундуке́!; **I've got odd ~s and pieces of work to finish** мне оста́лось ко́е-что́ доде́лать; **I've a ~ of news for you** у меня́ для тебя́ есть но́вость; **I'll give you a ~ of advice** я дам тебе́ оди́н сове́т; **they've got a ~ of money** у них во́дятся де́нежки; **to do one's little ~** внести́ свою́ ле́пту; **~ by ~ we pieced together the evidence** мы понемно́гу нака́пливали доказа́тельства (*pl*); *fig* **they tore him to ~s** они́ ему́ все ко́сточки перемы́ли

2 *as adv* (*a little*) **a ~: I am a ~ tired** я немно́го уста́л; **I waited a ~** я немно́го подожда́л; **it's a ~ cold today** сего́дня холоднова́то/прохла́дно; **he's a ~ foolish** он глупова́т; **a ~ later/louder/softer/darker** немно́го по́зже/гро́мче/ти́ше/темне́е *or*: попо́зже, погро́мче, поти́ше, потемне́е; **wait a ~!** (*not so fast*) подожди́!, не торопи́сь!; **it was a ~ of a surprise to find she was married** мы слегка́ удиви́лись, узна́в, что она́ за́мужем

3 *various*: **me tired? Not a ~ of it!** я уста́л? Да ни ка́пельки!; **do you mind sitting at the back?—Not a ~!** ничего́, е́сли ты ся́дешь сза́ди?—Коне́чно; **he's every ~ as good as she is** он ни в чём не уступа́ет ей; **the house is a good ~ larger than I expected** дом значи́тельно бо́льше, чем я ожида́л.

bitch *n* су́ка, *also fig low CQ*.

bitchy *adj CQ*: **what a ~ thing to say!** как то́лько язы́к поверну́лся сказа́ть таку́ю па́кость!

bite *n* **1** (*from dog, insects*) уку́с; (*of insects, snakes*) жа́ло; **a mosquito ~** уку́с комара́; **the snake ~ went septic** ра́нка от уку́са зме́и загнои́лась; **adders have a poisonous ~** уку́с гадю́ки (*sing*) ядови́т

2 (*from fish*) клёв; **I haven't had a ~ all day** за весь день ни ра́зу не клю́нуло (*impers*)

3 (*of eating*): **he demolished the tart in two ~s** он откуси́л два ра́за, и пирожка́ не ста́ло; **have a ~** (*to try smth*) на, откуси́; **he took a ~ out of the pear** он надкуси́л гру́шу; **I had a quick ~ before I left** я перекуси́л пе́ред ухо́дом; **there's not a ~ to eat in the house** в до́ме хоть шаро́м покати́.

bite *vti vt* **1** (*general*) кус|а́ть (*semel* -ну́ть), укуси́ть (*pf*) *and other compounds*; (*of birds, fish*) клева́ть (клю́нуть); (*of snakes, insects*) жа́лить (у-); **the dog bit her leg/her in the leg** соба́ка укуси́ла её за́ ногу; **the parrot bit me** попуга́й клю́нул меня́; **a snake has bitten her** зме́я ужа́лила/укуси́ла её; **she's been badly bitten by mosquitoes** её си́льно искуса́ли комары́; **she bit her lip to stop herself from crying** она́ закуси́ла губу́, что́бы не запла́кать; **I've bitten my tongue** я прикуси́л себе́ язы́к; **after I said it I could have bitten off my tongue** сказа́в э́то, я гото́в был откуси́ть себе́ язы́к; **he bit off a hunk of bread** он откуси́л большо́й кусо́к хле́ба; **she bit off the thread** она́ перекуси́ла ни́тку

2 *fig uses*: **I'm very bitten with water-skiing** я о́чень увлёкся во́дными лы́жами; **I bit back the remark just in time** я во́время прикуси́л язы́к; *CQ* **what's biting you?** кака́я му́ха тебя́ укуси́ла?; **I've bitten off more than I can chew** я сли́шком мно́го взял на себя́

vi **1** куса́ться; жа́лить; клева́ть, *also fig*; **the dog bit right through her hand** соба́ка прокуси́ла ей ру́ку; **snakes only ~ if you tread on them** змея́ (*sing*) куса́ет/жа́лит, то́лько когда́ на неё насту́пят; **the fish are biting today** сего́дня есть клёв; *fig* **I suggested it to him but he wouldn't ~** он не клю́нул на моё предложе́ние

2 (*of acids*) разъе|да́ть (́-сть); **acid ~s into metals** кислота́ разъеда́ет мета́ллы.

biting *adj*: **a ~ wind** ре́зкий/прони́зывающий ве́тер; (*of remark, critic, tongue*) язви́тельный.

bitter *n* (*beer*) го́рькое пи́во.

bitter *adj* (*of taste, etc.*) го́рький, *also fig*; **a ~ cold** прони́зывающий/ре́зкий хо́лод; **a ~ disappointment/grief** го́рькое разочарова́ние, си́льное го́ре; (*of person*): **he's very ~** он озло́бленный/ожесточённый челове́к; **a ~ struggle** ожесточённая борьба́.

bitterly *adv*: **it's ~ cold today** сего́дня о́чень хо́лодно/*CQ* соба́чий хо́лод; **I was ~ disappointed** я был го́рько разочаро́ван; **she spoke ~ about the divorce** она́ с го́речью говори́ла о разво́де.

bitterness *n* го́речь, *also fig*; *fig* озлобле́ние; **he spoke with such ~** он говори́л с тако́й го́речью; **there's great ~ between them** в их отноше́ниях накопи́лось мно́го го́речи.

bizarre *adj* стра́нный, чудно́й.

blab *vti CQ vt*: **he ~bed out her secret** он вы́болтал её секре́т

vi: **it was he who ~bed** э́то он на́ябедничал/донёс.

black *n* (*colour*) чёрный цвет; (*person*) негр, черноко́жий; **she was dressed in ~** она́ была́ оде́та в чёрное; *fig* **I worked like a ~** я рабо́тал как вол.

black *adj* чёрный; *fig* мра́чный; **a ~ and white film** чёрно-бе́лый фильм; **get it from him in ~ and white** получи́ э́то от него́ в пи́сьменном ви́де; **~ ingratitude** чёрная неблагода́рность; **~ frost/ice** моро́з без сне́га, гололёд; **to turn ~** черне́ть; **coins ~ with age** моне́ты, почерне́вшие от вре́мени; **it's as ~ as pitch/ink here** здесь темно́ хоть глаз вы́коли, здесь тьма кроме́шная; **he has a ~ eye** у него́ подби́тый глаз/синя́к под гла́зом; **I'm ~ and blue after my fall** я так си́льно упа́л, что всё те́ло в синяка́х; **he gave me a ~ look** он бро́сил на меня́ зло́бный взгляд; **the future looks ~** бу́дущее вы́глядит мра́чным; **he's in ~ despair** он в мра́чном настрое́нии; **he swore till he was ~ in the face that it was so** он кля́лся и божи́лся, что так всё и бы́ло; **everything went ~** всё в глаза́х потемне́ло.

black *vti vt*: **to ~ shoes** чи́стить боти́нки чёрным кре́мом (по-); **to ~ in one's eyebrows** под|води́ть бро́ви (-вести́); **the storm ~ed out the town** из-за грозы́ в го́роде пога́сло электри́чество

vi: **to ~ out** теря́ть созна́ние (по-).

blackbeetle *n* чёрный тарака́н.

blackberry *n* ежеви́ка (*of bush and collect of fruit*).

blackbird *n* чёрный дрозд.

blackcurrant *n* чёрная сморо́дина (*of bush and collect of fruit*).

blacken *vt* черни́ть (за-, *fig* о-); **the walls were ~ed by the fire** сте́ны от пожа́ра почерне́ли; *fig* **to ~ smb's reputation** очерни́ть кого́-л.

blacklist *vt* вноси́ть в чёрный спи́сок (внести́).

blackmail *n* шанта́ж.

blackmail *vt* шантажи́ровать (*impf*).

blackmailer *n* шантажи́ст.

blackout *n* (*in war*) затемне́ние; *fig* **I had a ~** (*fainted*) я потеря́л созна́ние, (*of memory*) на меня́ нашло́ затме́ние.

blacksmith *n* кузне́ц.

bladder *n* пузы́рь (*m*); *Anat* мочево́й пузы́рь.

blade *n* (*of knife, razor, skate*) ле́звие; (*of sword*) клино́к; (*of oar, propeller*) ло́пасть; **the ~ of a saw** полотно́ пилы́; **a ~ of grass** трави́нка.

blame *n* вина́; **he took the ~** он взял вину́ на себя́; **to put the ~ on smb for smth** возложи́ть/свали́ть вину́ на кого́-л за что-л; **where does the ~ lie for our failure?** в чём причи́на на́шей неуда́чи?

blame *vt*: **to ~ smb for smth** вини́ть кого́-л в чём-л (об-) *or* за что-л (*only in impf*); **who's to ~?** кто винова́т?; **I'm to ~ for it all** я во всём винова́т; **you've only yourself to ~** в э́том вы должны́ вини́ть то́лько самого́ себя́; **one can't ~ him for refusing** нельзя́ вини́ть его́ за отка́з; **I ~ you/myself for this** я счита́ю, что ты в э́том винова́т, я виню́ себя́ за э́то; (*in sympathy*) **I don't ~ you!** я могу́ вас поня́ть!

blameless *adj*: **~ conduct** безупре́чное поведе́ние; **he is ~ in this affair** на нём нет никако́й вины́ в э́том де́ле.

blank *n*: **leave a ~ for the date** оста́вьте ме́сто для да́ты; (*in lottery*) **to draw a ~** вы́тащить пусто́й биле́т, *also fig*; *Mil* **to fire ~s** стреля́ть холосты́ми.

blank *adj* пусто́й; **a ~ cheque/page/space** незапо́лненный чек, пуста́я страни́ца, пусто́е ме́сто; **a ~ cartridge** холосто́й патро́н; **his face was ~** его́ лицо́ ничего́ не выража́ло; *fig*: **in ~ dismay** в по́лном отча́янии; **a look of ~ amazement crossed his face** его́ лицо́ вы́разило глубо́кое изумле́ние; **my mind went ~** у меня́ был како́й-то прова́л в па́мяти.

blanket *n* одея́ло; *fig*: **a ~ of snow/fog** сне́жный покро́в, пелена́ тума́на; *CQ* **he's such a wet ~** он всегда́ тако́й уны́лый.

blanketed *adj*: **the valley is ~ in fog** доли́на оку́тана тума́ном.

blankly *adv* ту́по, невырази́тельно.

blare *vi*: **the trumpets ~d** тру́бы труби́ли (*impf*).

blasphemous *adj* богоху́льный, кощу́нственный.

blast *n* (*of wind*) поры́в ве́тра; (*of explosion*) взрыв; *Tech* дутьё; **there was an icy ~ from the window** из окна́ тяну́ло (*impers*) хо́лодом; **the windows were broken by the ~**

óкна бы́ли вы́биты взрывно́й волно́й; *fig* **the work was going full ~** рабо́та шла по́лным хо́дом.

blast *vt* **1** (*blow up*) взрыва́ть (взорва́ть), под|рыва́ть (-орва́ть)

2 (*destroy*): **the frost has ~ed the fruit buds** моро́зом поби́ло (*impers*) плодо́вые по́чки; **the tree was ~ed by lightning** де́рево бы́ло расщеплено́ мо́лнией; *fig* **our hopes were ~ed** на́ши наде́жды ру́хнули

3 *CQ* (*scold, curse*): **the boss ~ed me good and proper** шеф дал мне разго́н; **~ it!** чёрт возьми́!; **what a ~ed nuisance!** кака́я доса́да!, прокля́тье!

blatant *adj* на́глый; **a ~ lie/liar** на́глая ложь, на́глый лжец; **~ injustice** вопию́щая несправедли́вость; **~ colours** крича́щие цвета́.

blaze *n* **1** пла́мя; **the ~ of the campfire** пла́мя костра́; **the heat from the ~** жар от пла́мени; **they had difficulty in extinguishing the ~** пожа́р потуши́ли с трудо́м

2 *fig uses*: **in a ~ of anger** в поры́ве гне́ва; **the garden is a ~ of colour** сад пламене́ет кра́сками; **the town is a ~ of light** го́род сверка́ет огня́ми; **she lives in a ~ of publicity** она́ купа́ется в луча́х сла́вы; *CQ* **go to ~s!** иди́ к чёрту!

blaze *vi* пыла́ть (*impf*), *also fig*; (*of light*) сверка́ть (*usu impf*); **the logs are blazing merrily** дрова́ (в пе́чке) я́рко пыла́ют; **the fire will ~ up in a moment** ого́нь сейча́с вспы́хнет; **in a moment the whole building was blazing** че́рез мину́ту всё зда́ние уже́ пыла́ло; **in the ball room all the lights were blazing** танцева́льный зал сверка́л огня́ми; **the sun was blazing down** со́лнце пали́ло; *fig*: **his eyes were blazing** его́ глаза́ сверка́ли; **he was blazing with indignation** он пыла́л гне́вом.

blazer *n* бле́йзер.

bleach *n* (*for hair*) пе́рекись водоро́да; (*for household*) *CQ* хло́рка.

bleach *vti vt* бели́ть (вы́-); отбе́л|ивать (-и́ть)

vi беле́ть (по-).

bleaching powder *n* хло́рная/бели́льная и́звесть.

bleak *adj*: **a ~ landscape/day/welcome** уны́лый пейза́ж, безра́достный день, холо́дный приём; **~ prospects** мра́чные перспекти́вы.

bleary-eyed *adj* с му́тными глаза́ми.

bleat *vi* (*of sheep, etc.*) бле́ять (*impf*); *fig* **stop ~ing!** переста́нь ныть!

bleed *vti vt Med*: **to ~ smb** пус|ка́ть кровь кому́-л (-ти́ть); *fig* **they bled him for £1,000** они́ вы́манили у него́ ты́сячу фу́нтов

vi кровоточи́ть (*impf*); **his wound is ~ing** ра́на у него́ кровоточи́т; **my nose/finger is ~ing** у меня́ из но́са/из па́льца идёт *or* течёт кровь; **to ~ to death** умере́ть от поте́ри кро́ви; *fig* **my heart ~s for her** у меня́ се́рдце кро́вью облива́ется, когда́ я о ней ду́маю.

bleeding *n* кровотече́ние.

bleeper *n Radio CQ* пища́лка.

blemish *n* пятно́, *also fig*.

blench *vi* (*turn pale*) бледне́ть (по-); (*flinch*) **when he got the injection he didn't ~** он да́же не вздро́гнул от уко́ла.

blend *n* смесь.

blend *vti vt* сме́ш|ивать (-а́ть); **to ~ paints/wine/tea** сме́шивать кра́ски/ви́на/сорта́ ча́я; **to ~ cream and milk** перемеша́ть сли́вки с молоко́м

vi (*mix*) сме́шиваться; (*match*) сочета́ться (*impf and pf*); **oil and water do not ~** ма́сло с водо́й не сме́шивается; **yellow and brown ~ well** жёлтый цвет хорошо́ сочета́ется с кори́чневым; **the two voices ~ well** э́ти два го́лоса хорошо́ звуча́т вме́сте; **the house ~s in well with its surroundings** дом хорошо́ впи́сывается в окруже́ние (*sing*).

blender *n*: **electric ~** электри́ческий ми́ксер.

bless *vt* благослов|ля́ть (-и́ть); **God ~ you!** благослови́ тебя́ бог!; **she was not ~ed with children** судьба́ обдели́ла её—она́ безде́тна; **she is ~ed with good health** здоро́вьем бог её не́ оби́дел; **I ~ the day I bought my washing machine** я благословля́ю тот день, когда́ купи́ла стира́льную маши́ну; *CQ*: **I'm ~ed if I know** будь я про́клят, е́сли я зна́ю; **well I'm ~ed—if it isn't Tom!** не мо́жет быть—да э́то же Том!; **~ you!** (*after a sneeze*) бу́дьте здоро́вы!

blessed *adj Rel* блаже́нный; *CQ*: **the whole ~ day** весь э́тот день; **the whole ~ lot of them** вся их чёртова компа́ния; **we didn't find a ~ thing** мы там ни черта́ не нашли́.

blessing *n Rel* благослове́ние; (*advantage*) бла́го, сча́стье; **we must count our ~s** но есть и хоро́шие сто́роны; **it proved a ~ in disguise** э́то оберну́лось бла́гом; **what a ~ we didn't leave yesterday** како́е сча́стье, что мы вчера́ не уе́хали; **having talent is a mixed ~** тала́нтливым лю́дям нелегко́ живётся.

blight *n Bot* ми́лдью (*indecl*); *fig*: **he cast a ~ over the whole day** он испо́ртил нам весь день; **what a ~!** кака́я доса́да!

blight *vt fig*: **our hopes are ~ed** на́ши наде́жды ру́хнули; **her life is ~ed by rheumatism** ревмати́зм отравля́ет ей жизнь.

blighter *n sl*: **you lucky ~!** ты счастли́вчик!; **poor ~!** бедня́га! (*m and f*).

blind *n* што́ра; **sun/Venetian ~s** жалюзи́ (*indecl*); *fig* **that's only a ~** э́то про́сто обма́н.

blind *adj* слепо́й; *as n* **the ~** слепы́е; **he's ~ in one eye** он слеп на оди́н глаз; **she's ~ as a bat** она́ о́чень пло́хо ви́дит; **to go ~** сле́пнуть; *Aut* **a ~ corner** слепо́й поворо́т; *Aer* **a ~ landing** поса́дка по прибо́рам; *Archit* **a ~ wall/window** глуха́я стена́, фальши́вое окно́; *fig*: **~ obedience** слепо́е повинове́ние; **a ~ alley** тупи́к; **~ with rage** ослеплённый гне́вом; **it's a case of the ~ leading the ~** слепо́й ведёт слепо́го; **to turn a ~ eye to smth** закрыва́ть глаза́ на что-л; *CQ* **~ drunk** пья́ный в сте́льку.

blind *vt* ослеп|ля́ть (-и́ть), *also fig*; **he was ~ed in an accident** он потеря́л зре́ние в результа́те несча́стного слу́чая.

blindfold *vt*: **to ~ smb** завя́з|ывать глаза́ кому́-л (-а́ть).

blinding *adj*: **~ headlights** слепя́щий/ослепля́ющий свет фар; **a ~ flash** ослепи́тельная вспы́шка.

blindly *adv* сле́по, вслепу́ю; **to obey ~** сле́по повинова́ться; **in this matter we're acting ~** на э́тот раз мы де́йствуем вслепу́ю.

blindness *n* слепота́, *also fig*.

blink *vti vt*: **to ~ one's eyes** морг|а́ть (*semel* -ну́ть); *fig* **there's no ~ing the fact that...** нельзя́ закрыва́ть глаза́ на то, что...

vi морга́ть; мига́ть, (*of a light*) мерца́ть (*impfs*).

bliss *n* блаже́нство; *CQ* **a hot bath for me is sheer ~** горя́чая ва́нна для меня́—настоя́щее блаже́нство.

blissful *adj* блаже́нный, счастли́вый; **we spent a ~ day doing nothing** мы провели́ день в блаже́нном ничегонеде́лании; **he was in a state of ~ ignorance** он был в счастли́вом неве́дении.

blister *n* (*on skin*) волды́рь (*m*); (*on paint*) пузы́рь (*m*).

blister *vt* (*rub*) на|тира́ть (-тере́ть); **I ~ed my heel** я себе́ натёр пя́тку; **the paintwork was ~ed** кра́ска пузы́рилась.

blistering *adj*: **~ heat**/*fig* **criticism** паля́щий зной, жесто́кая кри́тика.

blizzard *n* мете́ль, вью́га.

bloated *adj* оплы́вший (жи́ром); **~ with (continuous) overeating** ту́чный от обжо́рства; **I feel ~ after that dinner** я объе́лся, мне тяжело́; *fig* **he's ~ with pride** его́ распира́ет (*impers*) от го́рдости.

blob *n* (*drop*) ка́пля; **a ~ of ink/paint/wax** ка́пля черни́л (*pl*), пя́тнышко кра́ски, ша́рик во́ска.

bloc *n Polit* блок.

block *n* **1** (*of wood*) чурба́н; (*of stone*) глы́ба, блок; (*executioner's*) пла́ха; (*for a pulley*) блок; (*one among several blocks of dwellings*) ко́рпус; **a ~ of flats** многоэта́жный дом; **a ~ of buildings** гру́ппа домо́в/зда́ний, (*group of buildings bounded by four streets, or one side of such an area*) кварта́л; **the theatre is two ~s further on** теа́тр че́рез два кварта́ла; **building ~s** (*toys*) де́тские ку́бики; *Theat* **a ~ of seats** не́сколько ряд́ов

2 (*obstruction*): **there was a ~ in the pipe** труба́ засори́лась; **traffic ~** про́бка, зато́р.

block *vt* прегра|жда́ть (-ди́ть); **cars ~ed the entrance to the car park** маши́ны загороди́ли въезд на стоя́нку; **he ~ed my way** он прегради́л мне доро́гу; **the path was ~ed by snowdrifts** тропи́нку занесло́ (*impers*) сне́гом; **the sink is ~ed** ра́ковина засори́лась; **to ~ up a hole** за|тыка́ть дыру́ (-ткну́ть); **my nose is ~ed** у меня́ зало́жен нос; *Fin* **to ~ an account** замор|а́живать счёт (-о́зить); *fig* **our plans were ~d by the opposition** оппози́ции удало́сь расстро́ить на́ши пла́ны.

blockade *n* блока́да; **to raise/run the ~** снять/прорва́ть блока́ду.

blockade *vt* блоки́ровать (*impf and pf*).

blockage *n* (*of traffic*) про́бка, зато́р; (*of pipes*) засоре́ние; *Med* блока́да.

block capitals, block letters *npl*: **to write in ~** писа́ть печа́тными бу́квами.

bloke *n sl* па́рень, тип; **he's quite a decent ~** он неплохо́й па́рень; **some ~ wants to see you** како́й-то тип хо́чет тебя́ ви́деть.

blond(e) *n* блонди́н(ка).

blond(e) *adj* белоку́р|ый, -ая.

blood *n* кровь; **the ~ rushed to his face** кровь бро́силась ему́ в лицо́; *fig*: **it runs in his ~** э́то у него́ в крови́; **it makes my ~ boil** э́то меня́ бе́сит; **he's out for my ~** он жа́ждет мое́й кро́ви; **my ~ ran cold** у меня́ кровь засты́ла в жи́лах; **~ is thicker than water** кровь не вода́; **to make bad ~ between brothers** се́ять раздо́р ме́жду бра́тьями; **it's like trying to get ~ out of a stone** э́то всё равно́ что во́ду из ка́мня выжима́ть.

blood bank *n* храни́лище кро́ви.

blood count *n Med* гемогра́мма; *CQ* **I'm to have a ~ done** мне сде́лают ана́лиз кро́ви.

blood group *n* гру́ппа кро́ви.

blood heat *n* норма́льная температу́ра те́ла.

bloodhound *n* ище́йка.

blood poisoning *n* зараже́ние кро́ви.

blood pressure *n* кровяно́е давле́ние; **I have high/low ~** у меня́ высо́кое/ни́зкое давле́ние.

blood relation *n* бли́зкий ро́дственник.

bloodshed *n* кровопроли́тие.

bloodshot *adj*: **~ eyes** нали́тые кро́вью глаза́.

blood stream *n* кровообраще́ние.

blood test *n* ана́лиз кро́ви.

blood transfusion *n* перелива́ние кро́ви.

blood vessel *n* кровено́сный сосу́д.

bloody *adj* крова́вый; *fig pejor* прокля́тый.

bloody *adv fig CQ*: **he can ~ well do it himself** он э́то прекра́сно мо́жет сде́лать сам; **not ~ likely!** чёрта с два́!

bloody-minded *adj sl*: **he's just being ~** он э́то де́лает назло́/, что́бы насоли́ть.

bloom *n*: **in full ~** в (по́лном) цвету́; **to come into ~** расцвета́ть.

bloom *vi* цвести́ (*impf*); (*open out*) расцве|та́ть (-сти́), *also fig*; **she is/looks ~ing after her holiday** у неё по́сле о́тпуска цвету́щий вид.

bloomer *n sl*: **to make a ~** допусти́ть про́мах.

blossom *n* цвет, цвете́ние.

blossom *vi* расцве|та́ть (-сти́); *fig* **she was so shy at school, but she ~ed out at University** в шко́ле она́ была́ о́чень засте́нчива, а в университе́те пря́мо расцвела́.

blot *n* (*smudge*) кля́кса; (*mark*) пятно́; *fig* **the new cinema is a ~ on the landscape** но́вый кинотеа́тр по́ртит весь анса́мбль.

blot *vt* (*make smudge*) посади́ть кля́ксу (*usu pf*); (*dry ink, etc.*) промок|а́ть (-ну́ть); **clouds ~ted out the moon** ту́чи закрыва́ли луну́; *fig* **to ~ one's copybook** запятна́ть свою́ репута́цию.

blotting paper *n* промока́тельная бума́га, *CQ* промока́шка.

blouse *n* блу́за, блу́зка.

blow[1] *n* уда́р, *also fig*; **a ~ with a hammer/with the fist** уда́р молотко́м/кулако́м; **he struck him a heavy ~ on the head** (*in boxing*) он нанёс ему́ си́льный уда́р по голове́; **they came to ~s** де́ло дошло́ до дра́ки; **they surrendered without striking a ~** они́ сдали́сь без еди́ного вы́стрела; *fig* **it was a heavy ~ for her** для неё э́то бы́ло тяжёлым уда́ром.

blow[2] *n*: *CQ* **I'm going out for a good ~** я пойду́ прогуля́юсь/прове́трюсь; **give your nose a good ~!** вы́сморкайся хороше́нько!

blow[2] *vti vt* **1** (*of wind*) дуть (*impf*) *and compounds*; **the wind blew the sand in all directions/the ship off course** ве́тром нанесло́ (*impers*) везде́ песка́, из-за си́льного ве́тра кора́бль сби́лся с ку́рса

2 *Mus, etc.*: **to ~ a horn/trumpet/whistle** труби́ть в рог/в трубу́ (*impf*), свист|е́ть в свисто́к (*semel* ´-нуть); *Aut* **to ~ one's horn** сигна́лить (по-)

3 *Aut*: **to ~ a gasket** проби́ть са́льник

4 *various*: **to ~ glass** выдува́ть стекло́ (*usu impf*); **he blew his brains out** он пусти́л себе́ пу́лю в лоб; *fig*: **to ~ one's own trumpet** бахва́литься (*impf*); **I blew him a kiss** я посла́ла ему́ возду́шный поцелу́й; *CQ*: **let's ~ the money on a new car/on a good booze** дава́й ку́пим но́вую маши́ну/дава́й кутнём на э́ти де́ньги; **I'll be ~ed if I'll do it!** будь я про́клят, е́сли я э́то сде́лаю!

vi **1** (*of wind*) ве́ять, (*harder*) дуть (*impfs*); **to ~ a little** поду́ть (*pf*); **to begin to ~** за|дува́ть (-ду́ть); **a light/strong breeze was ~ing** пове́ял *or* поду́л ветеро́к, дул си́льный ве́тер; **it's ~ing a gale outside** на у́лице о́чень си́льный ве́тер, (*at sea*) на мо́ре шторм

2 (*move with wind*): **the door blew open/shut** ве́тром распахну́ло/захло́пнуло (*impers*) дверь

3 *Mus, etc.*: **the trumpets blew** труби́ли тру́бы; **stop when the whistle ~s** останови́тесь по свистку́; **the foghorn is ~ing** гуди́т тума́нный горн

4 (*breathe out*): **the old man was puffing and ~ing** стари́к пыхте́л и отдува́лся; **he blew on his soup** (*to cool it*)/**on his fingers** (*to warm them*) он дул на суп/на па́льцы

5 (*of fuse, etc.*): **a fuse has ~n** перегоре́ла про́бка; **the fuse on the iron has ~n** в утюге́ сгоре́л предохрани́тель; **a tyre has ~n** ши́на ло́пнула

blow about *vti*: **my hair was ~n about by the wind** на ветру́ у меня́ растрепа́лись во́лосы (*pl*); **papers were ~n/~ing about the floor** бума́ги разлете́лись по́ полу

blow away *vti*: **the wind blew my hat away** ве́тер сдул с меня́ шля́пу; **my hat blew away** у меня́ ве́тром сду́ло (*impers*) шля́пу

blow down *vt*: **the tent was ~n down by the wind** ве́тер сорва́л пала́тку; **a lot of trees have been ~n down** ве́тром повали́ло (*impers*) мно́го дере́вьев

blow in *vi*: **a leaf blew in through the window** лист занесло́ (*impers*) в окно́ ве́тром; *CQ* **he blew in for half an hour** он загляну́л к нам на полчаса́

blow off *vti vt*: **to ~ off steam** вы|пуска́ть пар (´-пустить)

vi fig CQ: **he blew off when he heard about it** услы́шав э́то, он пришёл в я́рость и стал ора́ть

blow out *vti vt*: **to ~ out one's cheeks** наду|ва́ть/разду|ва́ть щёки (*pfs* ´-ть); **the storm has ~n itself out** бу́ря ути́хла/улегла́сь

vi: **the candle has ~n out** свеча́ пога́сла

blow over *vi* (*of storm, crisis*) минова́ть (*impf and pf*)

blow up *vti vt*: **to ~ up a tyre** наду|ва́ть/нака́ч|ивать ши́ну (´-ть/-а́ть); **to ~ up a building** взрыва́ть зда́ние (взорва́ть); *fig*: **the incident has been ~n up by the press out of all proportion** э́та исто́рия была́ невероя́тно разду́та пре́ссой; **to ~ up a photo** увели́ч|ивать фо́то (-ить)

vi **1** (*explode*) взрыва́ться, *also fig*

2: the wind is ~ing up ве́тер уси́ливается; **it's ~ing up for rain** ве́тер подня́лся—сейча́с хлы́нет дождь.

blowlamp *n* пая́льная ла́мпа.

blow-out *n*: *Aut* **we had a ~** у нас ло́пнула ши́на; *Elec* **there's been a ~ somewhere** где́-то перегоре́ли про́бки.

blowy *adj* ве́треный.

blue *n* (*light*) голубо́й/(*dark*) си́ний цвет; (*for laundry*) си́нька; **navy/azure/Prussian ~** тёмно-си́ний цвет, лазу́рь, берли́нская лазу́рь; *fig*: **it was a bolt from the ~** э́то бы́ло как гром среди́ я́сного не́ба; **he appeared out of the ~** отку́да ни возьми́сь—он; *Polit* **he's a true ~** он настоя́щий консерва́тор; **he's got (a fit of) the ~s** он хандри́т, на него́ нашла́ хандра́ (*sing*); *pl* **(the ~s)** *CQ* (*jazz*) блюз (*sing*).

blue *adj* голубо́й, си́ний, лазу́рный (*see noun*); *Polit* консервати́вный; **navy ~** тёмно-си́ний; **~ eyes** голубы́е глаза́; **a ~ bruise** синя́к; **~ rings under the eyes** си́ние круги́ под глаза́ми; **he was ~ with cold** он посине́л от хо́лода; **afar the mountains showed ~** вдали́ сине́ли го́ры; *fig*: **~ blood** голуба́я кровь; *CQ* **I feel ~** (*sad*) у меня́ хандра́; **you may talk till you are ~ in the face, he'll not change his mind** мо́жете говори́ть до посине́ния, его́ не переубеди́шь; *CQ* **a ~ film** порнографи́ческий фильм.

bluebell *n* (*wild hyacinth*) полево́й гиаци́нт; (*campanula*) колоко́льчик.

bluebottle *n* тру́пная му́ха.

blue-eyed *adj* голубогла́зый; *fig* **her ~ boy** её люби́мчик.

bluestocking *n*: **she's a ~** она́ си́ний чуло́к.

blue tit *n Orn* лазо́ревка.

bluff *n* (*deception*) блеф, обма́н; **his offer was just ~** его́ предложе́ние оказа́лось бле́фом; **I called his ~** я вы́вел его́ на чи́стую во́ду.

bluff *vti vt*: **he was ~ed into thinking that...** его́ обма́ном уве́рили, что...; **he was caught red-handed but ~ed it out somehow** его́ пойма́ли с поли́чным, но он ка́к-то вы́крутился

vi Cards блефова́ть (*impf*), *also fig*.

blunder *n* про́мах.

blunder *vi* (*make mistake*) допус|ка́ть про́мах (-ти́ть), прома́х|иваться (-ну́ться); (*grope*) **to ~ around in the dark** ша́рить в темноте́ (*only in impf*).

blunt *adj* (*of knives, etc.*) тупо́й; *fig*: **a ~ answer** прямо́й отве́т; **he's a ~ sort of chap** он всегда́ говори́т пря́мо/без обиняко́в (*a plain speaker*), он беста́ктен (*is tactless*).

blunt *vt* тупи́ть (за-); (*a little*) притуп|ля́ть (-и́ть), *also fig*; **to become ~ed** тупи́ться, затупля́ться; *fig* **his feelings have become ~ed** у него́ притупи́лась острота́ чувств.

blur *n* пятно́; (*of ink smudge*) кля́кса; **I can't see you properly, you're just a ~** я не ви́жу отчётливо твоего́ лица́, то́лько како́е-то пятно́; **the print is just a ~ to me** у меня́ все бу́квы слива́ются; **I felt faint—everything became a ~** я чу́вствовал себя́ пло́хо, всё плы́ло перед глаза́ми.

blur *vt*: **the writing is ~red** бу́квы все слива́ются; **her eyes were ~red with tears** слёзы застила́ли ей глаза́; **outlines became ~red** очерта́ния предме́тов расплы́ли́сь; **the windscreen is ~red** ветрово́е стекло́ запоте́ло; *TV* **a ~red picture** расплы́вчатое изображе́ние.

blurt *vt*: **he ~ed out the news/the secret** он вы́палил э́ту но́вость, он вы́болтал та́йну.

blush *n*: **with/without a ~** покрасне́в, не красне́я; **to spare your ~es** что́бы не смуща́ть тебя́.

blush *vi* красне́ть (по-); **I ~ for you/to say** я красне́ю за тебя́, мне сты́дно сказа́ть; **to ~ to the roots of one's hair** покрасне́ть до корне́й воло́с.

bluster *vti*: **he ~ed it out somehow** он ко́е-ка́к отговори́лся; **he raged and ~ed** он рвал и мета́л.

blustery *adj*: **a ~ day/wind** ве́треный день, поры́вистый ве́тер.

boar *n* бо́ров; **wild ~** каба́н.

board *n* **1** (*plank*) доска́; *Theat* (**the ~s**) подмо́стки (*no sing*); **ironing/notice ~** глади́льная доска́, доска́ объявле́ний; **diving ~** трампли́н для прыжко́в в во́ду; *Cards* **to sweep the ~** сорва́ть банк, *fig* преуспе́ть; *fig* **it was all open and above ~** всё бы́ло сде́лано откры́то и че́стно

2 *Naut*: **to be/go on ~** быть на борту́, подня́ться на́ борт; *fig* **that plan has gone by the ~** э́тот план отве́ргли

3: **~ of directors** правле́ние, дире́кция; **~ of examiners** экзаменацио́нная коми́ссия

4 (*food*): **~ and lodging** стол и кварти́ра; **what do you pay for full ~?** ско́лько вам сто́ит ко́мната с по́лным пансио́ном?

board *vti vt* **1**: **to ~ (over) a floor** на|стила́ть пол (-стла́ть); **before they left they ~ed up the windows** пе́ред отъе́здом они́ заколоти́ли о́кна

2: **to ~ a bus/train/ship** сади́ться в авто́бус/в *or* на по́езд/на кора́бль (сесть)

3: **we ~ two students during term** во вре́мя уче́бного семе́стра у нас обы́чно живу́т на всём гото́вом два студе́нта

vi: **to ~ with smb** жить у кого́-л на всём гото́вом.

boarder *n*: **these students are ~s** э́ти студе́нты живу́т в общежи́тии.

boarding *n Aer*: **~ has begun for flight number 5** начала́сь поса́дка на рейс но́мер пять.

boarding house *n* пансио́н.

boarding school *n* (шко́ла-)интерна́т.

board room *n* кабине́т директоро́в компа́нии.

boast *n*: **it is our ~ that...** мы мо́жем похва́статься, что...

boast *vti* хва́стать(ся) + *I*, хвали́ться + *I* (*pfs* по-); **this year we have nothing to ~ of** в э́том году́ нам не́чем похва́статься; **our firm is nothing much to ~ of** на́шей фи́рме не́чем осо́бенно похвали́ться; **he ~ed that...** он похва́стался (тем), что...; **he loves to ~ of his son's success** он лю́бит похва́статься успе́хами (*pl*) своего́ сы́на.

boastful *adj* хвастли́вый.

boasting *n* хвастовство́, *CQ* похвальба́.

boat *n* кора́бль (*m*), су́дно; (*steamer*) парохо́д, теплохо́д; (*small*; *for rowing, sailing or with motor*) ло́дка; **I'm going by ~** я поплыву́ на парохо́де; *fig*: **to miss the ~** упусти́ть слу́чай; **to burn one's ~s** сжечь свои́ корабли́; **we're all in the same ~** мы все в одина́ковом положе́нии.

boat *vi*: **to go ~ing** ката́ться на ло́дке (*usu impf*).

boatman *n* ло́дочник.

bob[1] *vt*: **to ~ one's hair** ко́ротко стри́чься (по-); **she wears her hair ~bed** у неё коро́ткая стри́жка.

bob[2] *vi*: **to ~ about/up and down** (*of cork, boat*) покачиваться (*impf*), (*of a child*) подпры́г|ивать (-нуть); *fig CQ* **he ~s up everywhere** наш постре́л везде́ поспе́л.

bobbin *n Sew* шпу́лька.

bobbysocks *npl* (*US*) коро́ткие носки́.

bobsled, bobsleigh *n* бо́бслей.

bode *vti*: **this ~s no good** э́то ничего́ хоро́шего не предвеща́ет; **that ~s well for us** э́то для нас хоро́ший знак.

bodice *n* лиф.

bodily *adj* физи́ческий, теле́сный.

bodily *adv*: **he lifted her ~ into the car** он по́днял её на́ руки и посади́л в маши́ну.

body *n* **1** те́ло: (*trunk*) ту́ловище, ко́рпус; (*corpse*) труп; **heavenly bodies** небе́сные тела́; *Med* **a foreign ~** иноро́дное те́ло; *CQ*: **he's a decent ~** он хоро́ший челове́к; **she's a dear old ~** она́ ми́лая стару́шка

2 *Tech* ко́рпус; *Aut* ку́зов; (*main part of structure*) **we sat in the ~ of the hall** мы сиде́ли в це́нтре за́ла

3 (*group*): **governing ~** администрати́вный сове́т; **the ~ of the electors** избира́тели; **the ~ politic** госуда́рство; **a large ~ of students marched to the square/think that...** больша́я толпа́ *or* гру́ппа студе́нтов направля́лась к пло́щади, мно́гие студе́нты счита́ют, что...; **the teachers resigned in a ~** преподава́тели все до одного́ по́дали заявле́ние об ухо́де; **he has a large ~ of facts to support his theory** он собра́л мно́го фа́ктов, подтвержда́ющих его́ тео́рию

4 *various*: **he devotes himself ~ and soul to the cause** он целико́м посвяти́л себя́ э́тому де́лу; **this wine has plenty of ~** э́то густо́е вино́; **over my dead ~!** то́лько че́рез мой труп!

bodyguard *n* ли́чная охра́на.

bodywork *n Aut* ко́рпус, ку́зов.

bog *n* боло́то.

bog *vi*: **the lorry got ~ged down in the mud** грузови́к застря́л/увя́з в грязи́; *fig* **the proposal is ~ged down in committee** предложе́ние застря́ло в комите́те.

boggle *vi*: **the imagination ~s!** тру́дно себе́ предста́вить!, *CQ* с ума́ сойти́!; **he ~d at the idea of protesting officially** он побоя́лся протестова́ть официа́льно.

boggy *adj* боло́тистый.

bogus *adj*: **I find his kindness a bit ~** его́ доброта́ мне ка́жется неи́скренней; **I'd say he's rather a ~ poet** он выдаёт себя́ за поэ́та, а, по-мо́ему, никако́й он не поэ́т; **~ science** лженау́ка.

boil[1] *n Med* фуру́нкул.

boil[2] *n*: **to bring water to the ~** доводи́ть во́ду до кипе́ния; **the kettle is coming to the ~/is on the ~** ча́йник закипа́ет/закипе́л; **the soup has gone off the ~** суп уже́ не кипи́т.

boil[2] *vti vt* (*of liquid, clothes*) кипяти́ть (вс-, про-); (*cook*) вари́ть (с-, от-); **to ~ sheets/milk** кипяти́ть (*usu impf*) бельё (*collect*), вскипяти́ть молоко́; **to ~ potatoes/fish/glue** вари́ть карто́шку (*collect*)/ры́бу/клей; *fig* **I'm trying to ~ down the article to 2,000 words** я стара́юсь сократи́ть статью́ до двух ты́сяч слов

vi кипе́ть (вс-, за-); кипяти́ться, вари́ться; **the milk has ~ed away/over** молоко́ вы́кипело/убежа́ло; **the jam has ~ed down** варе́нье увари́лось (*usu pf*); *fig*: **it makes me ~** э́то приво́дит меня́ в бе́шенство; **I'm ~ing with rage** во мне всё кипи́т от я́рости; **it all ~s down to this** де́ло всё сво́дится к сле́дующему; **there's a crisis ~ing up** назрева́ет кри́зис.

boiler *n* котёл, *also Tech.*

boiler house, boiler room *n* коте́льная.

boiler suit *n* комбинезо́н.

boiling point *n* то́чка кипе́ния.

boisterous *adj* (*of weather*) бу́рный, бушу́ющий; (*of children, puppies*) ре́звый.

bold *adj* (*daring*) сме́лый; (*shameless*) на́глый, наха́льный; (*of outlines*) чёткий; **if I may make so ~ as to say** е́сли позво́лите, я осме́люсь заме́тить; **he walked into the room as ~ as brass** он вошёл в ко́мнату с са́мым наха́льным ви́дом; **in ~ relief** чётко, релье́фно; *Typ* **~ (face) type** жи́рный шрифт.

bole *n* (*of tree*) ствол.

bolt *n* **1** (*of door*) засо́в, задви́жка; (*smaller: of window, etc.*) шпингале́т; *Tech* болт; **a ~ of cloth** руло́н тка́ни

2 (*dash*): **he made a ~ for it/for the door** он бро́сился бежа́ть, он рвану́лся к две́ри.

bolt *adv*: **to sit ~ upright** сиде́ть о́чень пря́мо.

bolt *vti vt*: **to ~ the door** за|пира́ть дверь на засо́в/на задви́жку (-пере́ть); **to ~ the window** закры́ть окно́ на шпингале́т; **to ~ together** скреп|ля́ть болта́ми (-и́ть); *fig* **to ~ one's dinner** на́скоро пообе́дать

vi (*escape*) убе|га́ть (-жа́ть); **the horse ~ed** ло́шадь понесла́; **he ~ed for the door** он бро́сился к две́ри.

bomb *n* бо́мба; **atom ~** а́томная бо́мба; **to plant a ~** подложи́ть бо́мбу.

bomb *vt* бомби́ть (раз-); **we were ~ed out** наш дом разбомби́ло (*impers*).

bombard *vt* бомбардирова́ть (*impf*), *also fig*; *fig* **to ~ smb with questions** засып|а́ть/(´-ать)/бомбардирова́ть кого́-л вопро́сами.

bomber *n* (*plane*) бомбардиро́вщик; *attr*: **~ pilot** бомбардиро́вщик.

bombing *n* бомбардиро́вка, бомбёжка.

bombshell *n fig*: **the news was a ~ for us** э́та но́вость была́ для нас как гром среди́ я́сного не́ба.

bond *n* **1** (*agreement*) обяза́тельство, догово́р; *fig* **his word is (as good as) his ~** он хозя́ин своего́ сло́ва

2 *pl* (**~s**) (*fetters*) у́зы; *fig*: **the ~s of friendship** у́зы дру́жбы; **their interest in music is a ~** их свя́зывает интере́с к му́зыке

3 *Fin* облига́ция; *Comm*: **goods in/out of ~** това́ры, оста́вленные на тамо́жне/опла́ченные по́шлиной.

bone *n* кость; **this fish has a lot of ~s** э́то о́чень кости́стая ры́ба; **no ~s broken I trust** наде́юсь, ничего́ не сло́мано; *fig*: **I've a ~ to pick with you** у меня́ к вам (есть) прете́нзия; **he made no ~s about accepting the money** он отню́дь не постесня́лся приня́ть э́ти де́ньги; **a ~ of contention** я́блоко раздо́ра.

bone *vti vt* снима́ть мя́со с косте́й (снять)

vi CQ: **I must ~ up on my geography** мне на́до подзубри́ть геогра́фию (*pf*).

bone-idle *adj*: **he's ~** он стрáшно ленúв, лень-мáтушка рáньше негó родилáсь.

bonfire *n* костёр.

bonnet *n* (*woman's or child's*) кáпор, чéпчик; *Aut* капóт.

bonny *adj*: **what a ~ baby!** какóй мúлый ребёнок!; **a ~ lass** красóтка.

bonus *n* бóнус, прéмия; **cost-of-living ~** надбáвка к зарплáте из-за рóста стóимости жúзни; *fig* **it's a ~ for us that you could come** нам повезлó, что ты смог прийтú.

bony *adj* (*full of bones*) костúстый; (*thin*) костлявый; **a ~ fish** костúстая рыба; **~ hands** костлявые рýки.

boo *vt*: **the actor was ~ed** актёра освистáли.

boob *n CQ* прóмах; **to make a ~** сдéлать прóмах.

booby *n* (*fool*) болвáн, óлух; *attr*: **~ prize** утешúтельный приз.

book *n* **1** кнúга; **a ~ on/about birds** кнúга о жúзни птиц; **a reference ~** спрáвочник; **a cheque/ration ~** чéковая кнúжка, кáрточки (*pl*); **to sit at one's ~s** сидéть над кнúгами; *Comm*: **to do the ~s** вестú счетá; **our order ~s are full** мы бóльше не принимáем закáзов

2 *fig uses*: **to be in smb's good/bad ~s** быть у когó-л на хорóшем/плохóм счетý; **I can read her like a ~** я вúжу её насквóзь; **we must stick to/go by the ~** нáдо дéйствовать соглáсно прáвилам; **I'll take a leaf out of your ~** я послéдую твоемý примéру; **he was brought to ~ for that** за э́то егó привлеклú к отвéту.

book *vti vt* **1** (*reserve*) закáз|ывать (-áть); (*mostly of hotels*) бронúровать (за-); **we ~ed tickets for the plane/concert/theatre** мы заказáли билéты на самолёт/на концéрт/в теáтр; **they ~ed us into the hotel** онú забронúровали для нас кóмнату в гостúнице; **the hotel is ~ed up until May** в гостúнице не бýдет свобóдных номерóв до мáя; **I ~ed a passage to New York** я заказáл билéт на парохóд до Нью-Йóрка; **the actor is ~ed (up) for the whole season** актёр ангажúрован на весь сезóн; **are you ~ed (up) on Tuesday?** вы зáняты во втóрник?

2 *Comm*: **to ~ orders** при|нимáть закáзы (-нять); **we're heavily ~ed for the next six months** мы завáлены закáзами на полгóда вперёд

3 (*fine*): **he's been ~ed for speeding** он был оштрафóван за превышéние скóрости; *Sport* **the referee ~ed him** судья сдéлал емý предупреждéние

vi: **~ well in advance** закáзывать нáдо зарáнее; **I've ~ed through to Odessa** я заказáл билéт до Одéссы.

bookbinding *n* (*business*) переплётное дéло; (*cover*) переплёт.

bookcase *n* кнúжный шкаф.

booking clerk *n Rail* кассúр билéтной кáссы.

booking office *n Rail* (билéтная) кáсса.

bookish *adj* (*of style*) кнúжный; **a ~ person** кнúжник.

book-keeper *n* бухгáлтер.

book-keeping *n* бухгалтéрия.

booklet *n* брошю́ра, буклéт.

bookmaker *n* (*in racing*) букмéкер.

bookmark *n* заклáдка.

book post *n*: **by ~** почтóвой бандерóлью.

bookseller *n* продавéц книг; **secondhand ~** букинúст.

bookshelf *n* кнúжная пóлка.

bookshop *n* кнúжный магазúн.

bookstall *n* кнúжный киóск.

boom[1] *n Naut* гик; *Tech* (*of crane*) стрелá, вы́лет.

boom[2] *n* (*noise*) гул; **the ~ of guns** гул орýдий.

boom[2] *vi* гудéть (*impf*).

boom[3] *n Comm* бум; *attr*: **building is now a ~ industry** в строúтельстве сейчáс бум; **these were the ~ years** э́то бы́ли гóды бýма.

boom[3] *vi*: **business/trade is ~ing** торгóвля процветáет.

boon *n* блáго; *CQ* **I find my washing machine a real ~** для меня стирáльная машúна—прóсто спасéние.

boor *n* грубиян.

boost *vt Tech* усúл|ивать (-ить); *Elec* повы|шáть напряжéние (´-сить); *Comm* **advertising has ~ed their sales** распродáть товáры им помоглá реклáма; (*of people*) **his morale needs ~ing** егó нáдо подбодрúть.

booster *n Tech* усилúтель (*m*); *attr*: **a ~ injection/rocket** добáвочная привúвка, ракéта-носúтель.

boot *n* (*ankle length*) ботúнок, (*high*) сапóг; *Aut* багáжник; *fig CQ*: **to give smb the ~** увóлить когó-л; **he's too big for his ~s** он мнóго о себé мнит.

boot *vt CQ*: **to ~ smb out of the house** вы́гнать когó-л úз дому (*usu pf*).

bootee *n usu pl* (**~s**) (*baby's*) башмачкú, (*lady's*) ботúнки.

booth *n* киóск; **telephone ~** телефóнная бýдка.

bootlace *n* шнурóк для ботúнок.

bootpolish *n* сапóжный крем, крем для óбуви.

booty *n* добы́ча.

booze *n CQ* (*drinks*) спиртнóе (*collect*); **I've brought the ~** я принёс вы́пить; **to have a ~(-up), to go on the ~** выпивáть, устрóить попóйку.

boracic acid *n* бóрная кислотá.

border *n* (*edge*) край; (*on dress*) каймá; (*on wallpaper, material*) бордю́р; *Hort* клýмба; (*frontier*) границa; *attr*: **~ zone** пограничная зóна.

border *vi*: **to ~ on** гранúчить с + *I* (*impf*), *also fig*; *fig* **this ~s on insanity** э́то гранúчит с безýмием.

borderline *n* границá; *attr fig*: **this is a ~ case** (*general*) э́то неясный слýчай, э́то трýдно реши́ть/определи́ть, (*more off*, *of examinees*, *in court*) это тру́дно квалифици́ровать/(*in science*) классифици́ровать.

bore[1] *n* (*tool*) бур; (*of gun*) кали́бр.

bore[1] *vti vt* (*hole*) сверли́ть (про-); (*tunnel*, *etc.*) бури́ть (про-); **to ~ a hole in a plank** сверли́ть отве́рстие в доске́; **to ~ a well** бури́ть коло́дец; **woodworm** (*collect*) **have ~d through the beam** ба́лка исто́чена жучко́м; *fig* **his eyes ~d through me** он сверли́л меня́ взгля́дом

vi: **to ~ for water/oil** бури́ть сква́жину в по́исках воды́/не́фти; **they ~d through 100 metres of granite** они́ пробури́ли сто ме́тров грани́та.

bore[2] *n* ску́ка; (*of people*) зану́да (*m and f*).

bore[2] *vt* надо|еда́ть + *D* (-е́сть), наску́чить + *D* (*pf*); *impers* ску́чно + *D*; **he ~s me stiff** он мне до́ смерти надое́л [**NB** *tense*]; **to be ~d** скуча́ть (*impf*); **I'm ~d doing nothing** мне ску́чно/(*stronger*) то́шно от безде́лья.

boredom *n* ску́ка.

boring *adj* ску́чный.

born *adj*: **he's a ~ poet** он прирождённый поэ́т; **he's a Londoner ~ and bred** он коренно́й ло́ндонец; **never in all my ~ days** ни ра́зу в жи́зни.

borough *n* го́род; (*administratively*) райо́н; *attr*: **~ council** городско́й/муниципа́льный сове́т.

borrow *vt* (*money*) за|нима́ть (-ня́ть), *also Math*; (*money*, *things*) ода́лживать (одолжи́ть); (*ideas*, *words*) заи́мствовать (*impf and pf*); **can I ~ a rouble off you?** одолжи́ мне рубль; **can I ~ your car for an hour?** мо́жете одолжи́ть мне ва́шу маши́ну на часо́к?; **he ~ed this idea from Kant** он заи́мствовал э́ту иде́ю у Ка́нта; **English has ~ed many words from French** в англи́йском мно́го слов, заи́мствованных из францу́зского языка́; **you can ~ four books at a time from the library** вы мо́жете взять в библиоте́ке сра́зу четы́ре кни́ги.

bosom *n* грудь; *fig* **in the ~ of the family** в ло́не семьи́.

boss *n CQ* нача́льник, шеф, гла́вный; нача́льство; **my ~** мой шеф; **who's ~ here?** кто здесь гла́вный?

botany *n* бота́ника.

botch *vt* (*mess up*): **I've ~ed things/it** я испо́ртил всё де́ло; (*repair badly*) **I'll ~ it up somehow** я э́то ка́к-нибудь залата́ю.

both *pron and adj m and neut* о́ба, *f* о́бе, *G/P* обо́их, *f* обе́их, *D* обо́им, *f* обе́им, *I* обо́ими, *f* обе́ими [*followed by the same construction as numerals* **2, 3, 4**]; **~ my friends** о́ба мои́х дру́га; **~ large cups are broken** о́бе больши́е ча́шки разби́лись; **~ of us/we ~ want to go** мы о́ба/о́бе хоти́м пойти́; **they ~/~ of them drive** они́ о́ба уме́ют води́ть маши́ну; **my brother and I ~ smoke** мы с бра́том о́ба ку́рим; **they are pulling down ~ the big houses** э́ти два больши́х до́ма сно́сятся; **for ~ these reasons** по э́тим двум причи́нам; **you can't have it ~ ways** придётся выбира́ть что́-то одно́.

both *adv*: **both... and** и... и; **he plays ~ the flute and the horn** он игра́ет и на фле́йте и на валто́рне; **he knows ~ when to speak and when to hold his tongue** он зна́ет, когда́ говори́ть, а когда́ и промолча́ть; **I find it ~ amusing and at the same time vulgar** по-мо́ему, э́то заба́вно, хотя́ и грубова́то.

bother *n*: **I'm afraid I'm causing you a lot of ~.—It's no ~ at all** бою́сь, что я причиня́ю вам большо́е неудо́бство.—Совсе́м нет, не беспоко́йтесь; **it's not worth the ~** э́то не сто́ит труда́; **did you have any ~ in finding the house?** вы легко́ нашли́ наш дом?; **I'm having some ~ with the car** у меня́ что́-то не в поря́дке с маши́ной; **I had a lot of ~ repairing the fuse** мне пришло́сь повози́ться, что́бы почини́ть про́бку; **this lock is always a ~** с э́тим замко́м ве́чно во́зишься; **silver is such a ~ to clean** с серебро́м хло́потно—всё вре́мя на́до чи́стить; **what a ~!** кака́я доса́да!; **oh ~!** го́споди!; *CQ* **he had a spot of ~ with the police** у него́ бы́ли неприя́тности (*pl*) с поли́цией.

bother *vti vt* беспоко́ить (по-); (*disturb*) меша́ть + *D* (по-); (*pester*) пристава́ть (*usu impf*); **don't ~ yourself about me** не беспоко́йтесь обо мне́; **his bad leg is ~ing him** его́ беспоко́ит больна́я нога́; **does the noise ~ you?** вам шум не меша́ет?; **does it ~ you if I smoke?** вам не помеша́ет, е́сли я закурю́?; **please don't ~ me about it now** не пристава́йте ко мне сейча́с с э́тим; **she very easily gets hot and ~ed** её легко́ вы́вести из равнове́сия; **are you coming?—I can't be ~ed** ты придёшь?—Что́-то не хо́чется

vi беспоко́иться; **don't ~—I'll do it myself** не беспоко́йтесь—я э́то сде́лаю сам; **don't ~ about getting dinner for me** не беспоко́йтесь о моём обе́де; **he didn't even ~ to phone** он да́же не потруди́лся позвони́ть.

bottle *n* буты́лка; (*for scent*) флако́н; **baby's ~** рожо́к; **water ~** фля́га; **hot-water ~** гре́лка.

bottle *vt*: **to ~ wine** разли|ва́ть вино́ по буты́лкам (-́ть); **~d beer** буты́лочное пи́во; *fig* **to ~ up one's feelings** сде́рживать свои́ чу́вства (*usu impf*).

bottle-feed *vt*: **to ~ a baby** корми́ть ребёнка из рожка́ (на-, по-); **he's a bottle-fed baby** э́тот ребёнок на иску́сственном вска́рмливании, *CQ* он «иску́сственник».

bottle-opener *n* открыва́лка (для буты́лок).

bottom *n* (*of sea*, *river*, *cup*, *box*, *etc.*) дно; (*of ship*, *barrel*) дни́ще; (*of slope*) подо́шва; (*of hill*, *monument*) подно́жие; *CQ* зад; **to sink to the ~** идти́ ко дну́; **there's a lake at the ~ of the hill** у подно́жия холма́ есть о́зеро; **at the ~ of the garden** в глубине́ са́да; **at the ~ of the page/table/stairs** в конце́ страни́цы, в конце́ стола́, внизу́ ле́стницы; **he is at the ~ of the class** он после́дний в кла́ссе; *CQ* **~s up!** (пей) до дна́!; *fig*: **at ~ he's a kind man**

вообще́-то он до́брый челове́к; **I think Tom is at the ~ of this** по-мо́ему, заводи́лой-то был Том; **to get to the ~ of a matter** добра́ться до су́ти де́ла; **I thank you from the ~ of my heart** (я) благодарю́ вас от всего́ се́рдца; **the ~ has fallen out of the market** це́ны ре́зко сни́зились/упа́ли.

bottom *adj* (са́мый) ни́жний; **the ~ shelf** ни́жняя по́лка; *CQ* **you can bet your ~ dollar he'll be there** поспо́рим на что уго́дно, что он там бу́дет.

bottomless *adj* бездо́нный.

bough *n* ветвь, сук.

boulder *n* валу́н.

bounce *n* (*of ball*) отско́к; **to catch a ball on the ~** пойма́ть мяч на отско́ке; **these balls have lost their ~** э́ти мячи́ пло́хо отска́кивают; *fig* **he's full of ~** он по́лон эне́ргии.

bounce *vi* от|ска́кивать (-скочи́ть); **the ball ~d off the wall** мяч отскочи́л от стены́.

bound[1] *n* (*leap*) прыжо́к, скачо́к.

bound[1] *vi* (*leap*) пры́г|ать (-нуть), скака́ть (*impf*) *and compounds*; **he came ~ing towards me/upstairs** он прыжка́ми нёсся мне навстре́чу, он бежа́л по ле́стнице, перепры́гивая че́рез ступе́ньки; **the dog ~ed across the fence** соба́ка перепры́гнула/перескочи́ла че́рез забо́р.

bound[2] *n* (*limit*) преде́л, грани́ца, *both also fig*; **beyond the ~s of the city** за городско́й черто́й (*sing*), за преде́лами го́рода; *fig*: **it is not beyond the ~s of possibility that...** вполне́ возмо́жно, что...; **his vanity knows no ~s** его́ тщесла́вию нет преде́ла; **the cinema is out of ~s for us** нас не пуска́ют в кино́.

bound[2] *vt* ограни́ч|ивать (-ить); **the plot was ~ed by a wall** уча́сток был отделён забо́ром; **our garden is ~ed on one side by the park** наш сад с одно́й стороны́ грани́чит с па́рком.

bound[3] *adj* 1 (*destined for*): **the ship was ~ for Odessa** парохо́д направля́лся в Оде́ссу

2 (*certain, obliged*): **he's ~ to come** он обяза́тельно/непреме́нно придёт; **it's ~ to happen** э́то обяза́тельно произойдёт; **I'm ~/I feel ~ to say...** (я) счита́ю ну́жным заме́тить...; **you're not ~ to go if you don't want to** ты не обя́зан идти́, е́сли не хо́чешь; **I'm ~ by contract (to do it)** я свя́зан контра́ктом, я обя́зан э́то сде́лать по контра́кту; **he's ~ up in his work** он с голово́й в рабо́те; **it's ~ up with the question of safety regulations** э́то свя́зано с те́хникой безопа́сности

3 *Law*: **he was ~ over** ему́ да́ли испыта́тельный срок.

boundary *n* грани́ца; (*between fields, etc.*) межа́; *attr*: **~ dispute/stone** пограни́чный спор, межево́й знак.

boundless *adj* безграни́чный, беспреде́льный.

bouquet *n* буке́т (*also of wine*).

bourgeois *adj* буржуа́зный.

bout *n* (*spell*): **I did a good ~ in the garden today** я сего́дня хорошо́ порабо́тал в саду́; **a ~ of coughing** при́ступ ка́шля; **I had a bad ~ of flu** у меня́ был си́льный грипп; **a drinking ~** попо́йка; *Sport* (*boxing, wrestling*) встре́ча.

bow[1] *n* (*archer's*) лук; *Mus* смычо́к; (*knot*) бант; **to tie shoelaces in a ~** завяза́ть шнурки́ ба́нтиком.

bow[2] *n* (*in greeting*) покло́н; **he made her a low ~** он ни́зко ей поклони́лся; **the actor took his ~** актёр раскла́нялся.

bow[2] *vti vt*: **the old man was ~ed with age** стари́к сго́рбился от ста́рости; **the branches were ~ed under the weight of the snow** ве́тки согну́лись под тя́жестью сне́га

vi (*in greeting*) кла́няться (поклони́ться); **he ~ed to me** он поклони́лся мне; *fig* **to ~ to the inevitable** покори́ться неизбе́жности.

bow[3] *n Naut* нос; **in the ~s** на носу́ (*sing*).

bowel *n* кишка́; **have your ~s moved?** у вас был сего́дня стул?; *fig* **the ~s of the earth** не́дра земли́ (*no sing*).

bowl[1] *n* (*small*) ми́ска; (*very large*) таз; **salad ~** сала́тница; **a ~ of flowers** ва́за с цвета́ми; **the ~ of a pipe** ча́шечка тру́бки.

bowl[2] *n* (*for game*) шар; *pl* (**~s**) (*game*) игра́ в шары́.

bowl[2] *vti vt fig*: **she was ~ed over by the news/by him** но́вость ошеломи́ла её, он её покори́л

vi 1 (*to play bowls*) игра́ть в шары́

2: **we ~ed along on our bikes** мы ката́лись на велосипе́де (*sing*).

bow-legged *adj* кривоно́гий.

bowling alley *n* (*US*) кегельба́н.

bow tie *n* (га́лстук-)ба́бочка.

bow window *n Archit* э́ркер.

bow-wow *interj* гав-га́в!

box[1] *n* (*of varying sizes, usu wooden*) я́щик; (*trunk, chest*) сунду́к; (*of cardboard*) коро́бка; *Theat* ло́жа; **letter/money ~** почто́вый я́щик, копи́лка; **a ~ of chocolates** коро́бка шокола́дных конфе́т; **a ~ of eggs/pills** коро́бка яи́ц/пилю́ль; **a ~ of matches** коро́бка/коробо́к спи́чек.

box[1] *vt*: **to ~ smth** укла́дывать что-л в сунду́к, упако́в|ывать что-л в я́щик (уложи́ть, -а́ть).

box[2] *vti vt*: **to ~ smb's ears** да|ва́ть кому́-л затре́щину (-ть)

vi Sport бокси́ровать (*impf*).

box[3] *n Bot* самши́т; *attr*: **a ~ hedge** и́згородь из самши́та.

boxer *n* боксёр.

boxing *n* бокс; *attr* боксёрский.

Boxing Day *n* второ́й день рождества́.

box-number *n*: **address the letter to ~ 100** адресу́й письмо́ на почто́вый я́щик но́мер сто.

box-office *n* театра́льная ка́сса.

box room *n* чула́н.

boy *n* (*up to student age*) ма́льчик; (*youth*) ю́ноша, *CQ* па́рень (*m*); **~s and girls** (*small*) ма́льчики и де́вочки, (*youths*) па́рни и де́вушки; **they have two ~s and a girl** у них два сы́на и дочь; **he's a good ~** он хоро́ший ма́льчик; **let's go, ~s** ну, ма́льчики,/ребя́та, пошли́!; **you nasty ~!** (*usu said by girl*) ты проти́вный мальчи́шка!; **here, my ~, see what I've brought you** смотри́, малы́ш, что я тебе́ принёс; (*to unknown youth*) **come over here, ~!** эй, па́рень, иди́ сюда́!; **he's a wonderful old ~** он чу́дный старика́н; (*irrespective of age*) **look, old ~, you'll have to stay behind** зна́ешь, старина́, тебе́ придётся оста́ться; **my dear ~, you can't say that!** (*to adult*) послу́шай, прия́тель,/(*to child*) ма́льчик, не на́до так говори́ть; **he's one of the ~s now** тепе́рь он наш/с на́ми; *attr*: **you can only get things done through the old ~ network** то́лько че́рез друзе́й/че́рез свои́х ребя́т и мо́жно чего́-нибудь доби́ться.

boycott *vt* бойкоти́ровать (*impf*).

boyfriend *n*: **Olga's ~** дружо́к О́льги.

boyhood *n*: **in his ~ he lived in France** де́тство он провёл во Фра́нции.

boyish *adj* мальчи́шеский.

bra *n CQ* (*abbr of* **brassière**) ли́фчик, бюстга́льтер.

brace *n* **1** (*tool*): **~ and bit** дрель, *Aut* (*for changing wheel*) коловоро́т

2 (*a pair*) па́ра

3 *pl* (**~s**) (*for trousers*) подтя́жки.

brace *vt* (*support*) под|пира́ть (-пере́ть); *fig* **I ~d myself to lift the heavy box/to tell her the truth** что́бы подня́ть э́тот тяжеле́нный я́щик, пришло́сь хороше́нько поднату́житься, я всё-таки собра́лся с ду́хом и сказа́л ей пра́вду.

bracelet *n* брасле́т.

bracing *adj* бодря́щий.

bracken *n Bot* па́поротник-орля́к.

bracket *n* **1** (*support for shelf, etc.*) подпо́рка, кронште́йн

2 *pl* (**~s**) ско́бки; **in square/round ~s** в квадра́тных/кру́глых ско́бках; **to open/close the ~s** откры́ть/закры́ть ско́бки.

bracket *vt* (*fasten together, fasten to*) скреп|ля́ть, прикреп|ля́ть (*pfs* -и́ть); *Gram* ста́вить в ско́бки (по-); *fig*: **Tom and John were ~ed first in the exam/in the competition** Том и Джон получи́ли «отли́чно» на экза́мене/вы́шли на пе́рвое ме́сто; **I'd ~ those subjects under one heading** я бы объедини́л э́ти те́мы под одни́м заголо́вком.

brackish *adj* солонова́тый.

brag *vi*: **to ~ of** хва́статься + *I* (по-).

braggart *n* хвасту́н.

braid *n* (*of cord*) шнуро́к, (*of ribbon*) тесьма́; (*of hair*) коса́; *Mil* галу́н.

brain *n* мозг; *Cook* (**~s**) мозги́; *fig usu pl*: **I racked my ~s over that problem** я лома́л себе́ го́лову над э́той пробле́мой; **I've got that tune on the ~** э́та мело́дия пресле́дует меня́; **I want to pick your ~s** я хочу́ с тобо́й посове́товаться; *CQ* **he has no ~s** у него́ не хвата́ет мозго́в; **use your ~s!** шевели́ мозга́ми!

brainless *adj* безмо́зглый.

brainwash *vt fig*: **to ~ smb** «промы|ва́ть» мозги́ кому́-л (-́ть).

brainwave *n* гениа́льная/блестя́щая иде́я.

brainy *adj CQ* мозгови́тый, башкови́тый.

braise *vt* туши́ть (*impf*); **~d meat** тушёное мя́со.

brake *n* то́рмоз; **foot/hand ~** ножно́й/ручно́й то́рмоз *or CQ* ручни́к; **to put on the** (*foot*) **~s** затормози́ть; **to take off the hand ~** снять с ручно́го то́рмоза; **leave her on the hand ~** поста́вь маши́ну на ручно́й то́рмоз/*CQ* на ручни́к; *attr Tech*: **~ drum/lever/fluid/lining/shoe** тормозно́й бараба́н/рыча́г, тормозна́я жи́дкость/накла́дка/коло́дка; **~ lights** стоп-сигна́л, тормозно́й сигна́л (*sings*); **~ pedal** педа́ль ножно́го то́рмоза.

brake *vt* тормози́ть (*pfs*: *so as to stop* за-, *in order to slow down* при-).

braking *n* торможе́ние; *attr*: **~ distance** тормозно́й путь.

bramble *n* ежеви́ка (*of bush or collect of fruit*).

bran *n* о́труби (*pl*).

branch *n* ветвь, *also fig*; ве́тка, *also Rail*; (*side shoot*) ответвле́ние (*also of Rail, road, pipe*); (*of mountain range*) отро́г; (*of river*) рука́в; (*of shop, bank*) отделе́ние; (*of institution*) филиа́л; (*of administration*) отде́л; **a ~ of learning/industry** о́трасль зна́ния/промы́шленности; **a ~ of the Tudor family** ветвь дина́стии Тюдо́ров; **some ~ of our family settled in America** не́которые на́ши ро́дственники осе́ли в Аме́рике; *attr Rail*: **a ~ line to Oxford** (железнодоро́жная) ве́тка, веду́щая в О́ксфорд.

branch *vi* (*of road, river*) разветв|ля́ться (-и́ться); **the road ~es here** здесь разви́лка доро́ги; **we ~ed off at Zagorsk to reach the village** мы поверну́ли к дере́вне у Заго́рска; *fig*: **our firm/he has ~ed out in new directions** на́ше предприя́тие расши́рило свою́ де́ятельность, у него́ появи́лись но́вые интере́сы; **he's ~ing out into philosophy** у него́ появи́лось [**NB** *tense*] но́вое увлече́ние—филосо́фия; **he has ~ed out on his own** он отдели́лся, у него́ тепе́рь своё де́ло.

brand *n Comm* сорт, ма́рка; (*on cattle*) клеймо́; **a good ~ of tea** хоро́ший сорт ча́я.

brand *vt* клейми́ть (за-), *also fig*; **he was ~ed as a liar** его́ заклейми́ли лжецо́м; *Comm* **~ed goods** сорти́рованный това́р (*collect*).

brandish *vt* разма́х|ивать + *I* (*semel* -ну́ть).

brand-new *adj* соверше́нно но́вый; **a ~ suit** костю́м с иго́лочки.

brandy *n* бре́нди (*indecl*), конья́к.

brash *adj* наха́льный.

brass *n* лату́нь, жёлтая медь; *Mus* (**the ~**) *collect* ме́дные духовы́е инструме́нты; *fig sl* (*cheek*) на́глость, наха́льство; **he's got some ~** ему́ наха́льства не занима́ть; *CQ* **the top ~** большо́е нача́льство; *attr* ме́дный; *CQ* **to get down to ~ tacks** перейти́ к де́лу.

brassière *n* бюстга́льтер, *CQ* ли́фчик.

bravado *n* брава́да; **he did it out of sheer ~** он сде́лал э́то то́лько для брава́ды.

brave *adj* хра́брый.

brave *vt*: **he ~s death every time he flies that plane** летя́ на э́том самолёте, он ка́ждый раз риску́ет жи́знью; **as a war correspondent he ~d danger all the time** как вое́нный корреспонде́нт он постоя́нно подверга́лся опа́сности; **I decided to ~ the storm and go out** несмотря́ на бу́рю, я реши́л вы́йти на у́лицу; **we must ~ the press** нам придётся вы́держать на́тиск журнали́стов.

bravo *interj* бра́во!

brawl *n* дра́ка, потасо́вка.

brawl *vi* дра́ться (по-).

brazen *adj* (*of brass*) ме́дный; *fig* на́глый.

brazen *vi*: **he ~ed it out** он вы́крутился благодаря́ свое́й на́глости.

breach *n* **1** (*of wall, embankment, Mil*) брешь; *fig* **to step into/fill the ~** закры́ть/прикры́ть брешь

2: **a ~ of promise/***Law* **contract** наруше́ние обеща́ния/догово́ра.

breach *vt* проби|ва́ть брешь (-́ть).

bread *n* хлеб; **rye/black ~** ржано́й/чёрный хлеб; **brown ~** се́рый хлеб; **~ and butter** хлеб с ма́слом; **help yourself to ~** бери́те хлеб; **to earn one's ~** зараба́тывать себе́ на жизнь; **daily ~** хлеб (наш) насу́щный.

breadbin *n* хле́бница.

breadboard *n* хле́бная доска́.

bread-crumb *n* хле́бная кро́шка; *Cook* (**~s**) толчёные сухари́.

breadknife *n* хле́бный нож.

breadth *n* ширина́; **the street is 10 metres in ~** ширина́ у́лицы де́сять ме́тров; *fig* **~ of mind** широта́ взгля́дов.

breadwinner *n*: **she's the ~ of the family** она́ в семье́ корми́лец.

break *n* **1** (*split*) разры́в, *also fig*; (*breach*) проло́м; *Med* перело́м; **a ~ in a pipe/a wall** разры́в трубопрово́да, проло́м в стене́; *fig*: **a ~ in diplomatic relations** разры́в дипломати́ческих отноше́ний; **there's been a ~ between them/in the weather** ме́жду ни́ми произошёл разры́в, пого́да измени́лась

2 (*interval*) переры́в; **there will be a ~ of 10 minutes for a commercial** (*on TV*) в програ́мме бу́дет переры́в на де́сять мину́т для переда́чи рекла́мы; **there was a ~ in the conversation** разгово́р прерва́лся; **let's take a ~** дава́й устро́им переры́в; **at school we have half an hour's ~ at 11** в шко́ле в оди́ннадцать часо́в получасова́я переме́на; **without a ~** беспреры́вно (*adv*); **she's unwell and needs a ~** она́ больна́ и нужда́ется в о́тдыхе; **a ~ in the clouds** просве́т в ту́чах

3 (*chance*): **I had a lucky ~** мне повезло́/посчастли́вилось (*impers*)

4 (*getaway*): **let's make/he made a ~ for it** дава́й сбежи́м, он бро́сился бежа́ть *or* он пусти́лся наутёк (*adv*).

break *vti vt* **1** (*of things which snap across*) лома́ть (с-); (*in several pieces*) раз|ла́мывать (-лома́ть); *fig* сломи́ть (*pf*); **he broke his walking stick/his leg** он слома́л свою́ трость/(себе́) но́гу; **to ~ smth in two** перелома́ть что-л (попола́м); **to ~ (open) a lock/a door/a drawer** взла́мывать замо́к/дверь/я́щик (взлома́ть); *fig* **they broke the enemy's resistance** они́ сломи́ли сопротивле́ние врага́

2 (*crockery, etc.*) бить, разбива́ть (*pf for both* разби́ть); **to ~ a cup/dishes** разби́ть ча́шку, бить посу́ду (*collect*); **my watch is broken** мои́ часы́ слома́лись/разби́лись/(*doesn't go*) не хо́дят; *fig*: **her heart is broken** у неё се́рдце разби́то; **to ~ a record** поби́ть реко́рд (*usu pf*)

3 (*interrupt*) пре|рыва́ть (-рва́ть); *Tel* **the connexion has been broken** связь прервала́сь; *fig*: **to ~ a journey/the thread of thought** прерва́ть путеше́ствие/ход мы́слей; **to ~ a strike** срыва́ть забасто́вку; *Cards* **to ~ the bank** сорва́ть банк

4 *other fig uses*: **to ~ a contract/law/promise** наруш|а́ть усло́вия контра́кта/зако́н/обеща́ние (-́ить); **he broke the news of her father's death to her** он сообщи́л ей о сме́рти отца́; **I'm trying to ~ him of the habit of biting his nails** я стара́юсь отучи́ть его́ от привы́чки куса́ть но́гти

vi лома́ться, разбива́ться, прерыва́ться, *etc.*; **my son's voice is ~ing** у моего́ сы́на лома́ется го́лос; **the mirror broke** зе́ркало разби́лось; **her voice broke with emotion** её го́лос прерыва́лся от волне́ния; **the trees were (almost) breaking under the weight of the apples** ве́тви я́блонь ломи́лись под тя́жестью плодо́в; **the hawser broke** трос ло́пнул; *fig*: **dawn/day broke** рассвело́; **the clouds/storm/weather broke** в ту́чах появи́лся просве́т, разрази́лась бу́ря, пого́да испо́ртилась; **the frost has broken** моро́з ослабе́л

break away *vi*: **he broke away from his family** он ушёл из семьи́; **two states have broken away from the federation** два шта́та отдели́лись от федера́ции; **the prisoner broke away from the convoy** пле́нный убежа́л от конво́йных (*pl*)

break down *vti vt*: **to ~ down a door/***fig* **resistance** взлома́ть дверь, сломи́ть сопротивле́ние; **to ~ down expenditure** да|ва́ть дета́льный отчёт о расхо́дах (-ть), анализи́ровать расхо́ды (*impf*)

vi: **the car broke down** маши́на слома́лась/вы́шла из стро́я; **she/her health broke down** её здоро́вье сда́ло/пошатну́лось; **our plans/negotiations broke down** на́ши пла́ны ру́хнули *or* провали́лись, перегово́ры бы́ли со́рваны; **he broke down in the middle of his speech** он запну́лся в середи́не (свое́й) ре́чи; **she broke down and wept/confessed** она́ не вы́держала и распла́калась/и призна́лась

break even *vi Comm* покры|ва́ть свои́ расхо́ды (-́ть); *CQ* (*in gambling*) оста́ться при свои́х (*usu pf*)

break in *vti vt*: **to ~ in a horse** объезжа́ть ло́шадь (*only in impf*) *vi*: **thieves broke in and robbed the shop** во́ры влéзли в магази́н и обчи́стили его́; **"But how?" he broke in** «Но как?»—переби́л он

break into *vi*: **to ~ into a house/a safe** вломи́ться в дом, взлома́ть сейф; **to ~ into a conversation** вмéш|иваться в разгово́р (-а́ться); **to ~ into roars of laughter** расхота́ться (*pf*); **he broke into a run** он пусти́лся бего́м/бежа́ть; **to ~ into a £ 5 note** разменя́ть пятифу́нтовую бума́жку

break off *vti vt*: **to ~ off a branch/a flower** слома́ть вéтку, сорва́ть цвето́к; **he broke off the handle of the cup/a piece of chocolate** он отби́л ру́чку у ча́шки, он отломи́л кусо́чек шокола́да; **she's/they've broken off her/their engagement** она́ порвала́ с ним, их помо́лвка расстро́илась; **to ~ off talks/relations with** прерва́ть *or* сверну́ть перегово́ры, прерва́ть отношéния с + *I*; **to ~ off a conversation/work** прерва́ть бесéду/рабо́ту; *Tel* **our call was broken off** нас прерва́ли

vi: **a leg of the chair broke off** у сту́ла отломи́лась но́жка; **she broke off immediately he came in** как то́лько он вошёл, она́ прикуси́ла язы́к

break out *vi* **1** (*of fire, war, riots, strike, epidemic*) вспы́х|ивать (-нуть); **cholera has broken out** вспы́хнула эпидéмия холéры; **a rash has broken out on his chest** у него́ вы́сыпала/появи́лась сыпь на груди́; **my face has broken out in a rash** у меня́ всё лицо́ покры́лось сы́пью; **a fierce argument broke out** завяза́лся горя́чий спор

2: **to ~ out of prison** бежа́ть из тюрьмы́

break over *vi*: **heavy seas were ~ing over the bows** огро́мные валы́ нака́тывались на нос корабля́

break through *vi*: **the enemy broke through our defences** проти́вник прорва́л на́шу ли́нию оборо́ны (*sing*); **the sun broke through** со́лнце проби́лось сквозь ту́чи

break up *vti vt* разби|ва́ть (-́ть); **we're ~ing up boxes for firewood** мы разла́мываем я́щики на дрова́; **we broke up the pupils into groups** мы разби́ли уча́щихся на гру́ппы; **the estate was broken up** имéние раздели́ли; **the police broke up the meeting** поли́ция разогнала́ ми́тинг

vi: **the ship broke up on the rocks** кора́бль разби́лся о ска́лы; **the party broke up late** го́сти разошли́сь по́здно; **their marriage has/they have broken up** они́ разошли́сь, их брак распа́лся; **school broke up early this term because of the epidemic** из-за эпидéмии шко́льников в э́той чéтверти распусти́ли ра́но.

breakable *adj* ло́мкий; (*brittle*) хру́пкий.

breakage *n*: **we'll have to pay for ~s** нам придётся заплати́ть за поло́манные вéщи.

breakdown *n* **1** (*mechanical*) поло́мка; *Aut, Rail* ава́рия; *Med* **he's had a (nervous) ~** его́ здоро́вье пошатну́лось, у него́ нéрвное истощéние; *attr*: *Aut* **~ service** авари́йная слу́жба

2 (*analysis*) ана́лиз; **a ~ of expenses** ана́лиз затра́т.

breaker *n* буру́н, вал.

breakfast *n* за́втрак.

breakfast *vi* за́втракать (по-).

breaking-point *n Tech* то́чка разрушéния; *fig* **I've reached ~** *CQ* я дошёл до ру́чки.

breakneck *adj*: **to move at ~ speed** нести́сь сломя́ го́лову.

breakthrough *n Mil* проры́в; *fig* **they've made an important ~ in cancer research** они́ далеко́ шагну́ли в изучéнии приро́ды ра́ка.

breakwater *n* волноре́з.

breast *n* грудь; (*of chicken*) **do you like ~ or leg?** вам что—гру́дку и́ли но́жку?; *fig* **to make a clean ~ of it** чистосердéчно призна́ться во всём.

breast-feed *vt*: **to ~ a baby** корми́ть ребёнка гру́дью (на-, по-); **a breast-fed baby** грудно́й ребёнок.

breast-pocket *n* нагру́дный карма́н.

breast-stroke *n* (*swimming*) брасс.

breath *n* дыха́ние; **to hold one's ~** затаи́ть дыха́ние; **to be out of ~** запыха́ться; **to take a deep ~** глубоко́ вздохну́ть; **to recover one's ~** отдыша́ться; **he is short of ~** он страда́ет оды́шкой; **bad ~** неприя́тный за́пах изо рта́; **with bated ~** затаи́в дыха́ние; **he said it all in one ~** он э́то вы́палил одни́м ду́хом; **under one's ~** вполго́лоса (*adv*); **in the very next ~ he said...** и в ту́ же секу́нду он приба́вил...; **there wasn't a ~ of air/wind** нé было ни ветерка́; **I'm going out for a ~ of fresh air** пойду́ подышу́ свéжим во́здухом; *fig*: **she's like a ~ of fresh air** она́ как глото́к свéжего во́здуха; **it took my ~ away** от э́того у меня́ дух захвати́ло (*impers*); **you're wasting your ~** ты броса́ешь слова́ на вéтер; **the least ~ of scandal and I'll lose my job** малéйший намёк на сканда́л—и я вы́лечу с рабо́ты.

breathe *vti vt*: **to ~ fresh air** дыша́ть свéжим во́здухом; **I ~d a sigh of relief** я с облегчéнием вздохну́л; *fig* **don't ~ a word of this to anybody** никому́ ни сло́ва об э́том

vi дыша́ть (*impf*); **to ~ in/out** вдыха́ть, выдыха́ть (вдохну́ть, вы́дохнуть); **well, that's over—we can ~ again** дéло сдéлано, тепéрь мо́жно вздохну́ть свобо́дно.

breather *n* передь́шка; **let's have a ~** дава́й передохнём.

breathing *n* дыха́ние; *attr*: **~ space** переды́шка.

breathless *adj* (*of person*) запыха́вшийся, задыха́ющийся; *fig* **a ~ hush/calm** мёртвая тишина́, мёртвый штиль.

breath-taking *adj*: **with ~ speed** с головокружи́тельной быстрото́й; **the view from there was ~** вид отту́да потряса́ющий—дух захва́тывает.

breeches *npl* бри́джи (*no sing*); **riding ~** верховы́е бри́джи.

breed *n* порóда; **what ~ of dog is that?** какóй порóды э́та собáка?

breed *vti vt* раз|водить (-вести́); **to ~ cattle** разводи́ть (рогáтый) скот; **he's a town bred boy** он городскóй мáльчик; *fig*: **dirt ~s disease** все болéзни (*pl*) от грязи; **war ~s poverty** войнá несёт с собóй нищету́

vi размнож|áться (-́иться), плоди́ться (рас-).

breeding *n Agric* разведéние; *Biol* размножéние; (*of person*) воспитáние; **good ~** воспи́танность; *attr Agric*: **the ~ season** случнóй сезóн.

breeze *n* (лёгкий) ветерóк; **a sea ~** бриз.

breeze *vi CQ*: **he ~d in for half an hour** он заглянýл к нам на полчасá.

breezy *adj* вéтреный; (*of person*) живóй, бóйкий.

brevity *n* крáткость, недолговéчность.

brew *vti vt*: **to ~ beer** вари́ть пи́во (с-); **to ~ tea** завáр|ивать чай (-и́ть); *fig* **these boys are ~ing some mischief** э́ти мальчи́шки затевáют какýю-то шáлость

vi fig: **trouble is ~ing** ну и завари́лась [**NB** *tense*] кáша.

brewery *n* пивовáренный завóд.

bribe *n* взя́тка.

bribe *vt*: **to ~ smb** подкуп|áть когó-л (-и́ть), да|вáть взя́тку комý-л (-ть).

bribery *n* (*taking bribes*) взя́точничество; (*giving bribes*) пóдкуп.

brick *n* кирпи́ч (*sing and collect*); **~s** кирпичи́ *or* кирпи́ч, (*toys*) кýбики; **an ice-cream ~** брикéтморóженого; *fig CQ*: **to drop a ~** сдéлать ля́псус/прóмах; **he came down on us like a ton of ~s** он нас ругáл на чём свет стои́т; **you're a ~!** ты молодéц!, ты молотóк!

bricklayer *n* кáменщик.

brickwork *n* кирпи́чная клáдка; **~s** кирпи́чный завóд (*sing*).

bridal *adj* свáдебный.

bride and bridegroom *ns* невéста и жени́х.

bridesmaid *n* подрýжка невéсты.

bridge[1] *n* мост; *dim* мóстик; (*of nose*) перенóсица; *Naut* (капитáнский) мóстик; (*of a stringed instrument*) подстáвка; **a ~ over the Neva** мост чéрез Невý.

bridge[1] *vt* стрóить/наводи́ть мост чéрез + *A* (по-/навести́); *fig* **I'm just bridging a gap till the new accountant comes** я прóсто затыкáю брешь, покá не придёт нóвый бухгáлтер.

bridge[2] *Cards* бридж.

bridle *n* уздá; **to put a ~ on a horse** взнуздáть лóшадь.

brief *n* **1** (*summary*) крáткое изложéние дéла; *Law* (*case*) дéло; **to take a ~** принимáть ведéние дéла в судé; *fig* **I hold no ~ for him** я не поддéрживаю егó

2 *Comm*, *Mil* (*instructions*) инстрýкции (*pl*); **to go beyond one's ~** превы́сить полномóчия (*pl*)/инстрýкции

3 *pl* (**~s**) (*pants*) трусы́.

brief *adj* крáткий; **be as ~ as possible** будь по возмóжности крáток; **in ~** вкрáтце (*adv*); **for a ~ moment I thought that...** на какóй-то миг я подýмал, что...

brief *vt* (*instruct*) инструкти́ровать (*impf and pf*, *pf also* про-); **he ~ed me on this** он вкрáтце описáл мне ситуáцию/рассказáл мне, в чём дéло; *Law* **to ~ a lawyer** поруч|áть дéло адвокáту (-и́ть).

briefcase *n* портфéль (*m*).

briefing *n Mil* инструктáж.

briefly *adv* крáтко, вкрáтце.

brier *n* **1** *Bot* шипóвник

2 (*pipe*) (кури́тельная) трýбка (из вéреска).

brigade *n Mil* бригáда.

brigadier *n Mil* (*UK*, *US*) бригади́р.

brigand *n* банди́т, разбóйник.

bright *adj* **1** (*of colour*) я́ркий; **a ~ light** я́ркий свет; **~ red** я́рко-крáсный; **a ~ room** свéтлая кóмната; **~ eyes** блестя́щие глазá; **a ~ smile** сия́ющая улы́бка; *Meteorol*: **a ~ sky** я́сное нéбо; **cloudy with ~ intervals** пáсмурно с прояснéниями

2 *fig uses*: **a ~ idea/future/pupil** блестя́щая идéя, свéтлое бýдущее, смышлёный учени́к; **~ prospects** рáдужные перспекти́вы; **to look on the ~ side of things** ви́деть свéтлую стóрону/положи́тельные стóроны (*pl*) жи́зни; **she's always ~ and cheerful** онá всегдá бодрá и веселá.

brighten *vti vt* ожив|ля́ть (-и́ть); **the flowers ~ the room** цветы́ оживля́ют кóмнату

vi проясн|я́ться (-и́ться); *fig* оживля́ться; **the sky ~ed** нéбо проясни́лось; **he ~ed up after her visit** он оживи́лся пóсле её посещéния.

brilliance *n* блеск; (*of colour*) я́ркость; (*of person*) блеск умá.

brilliant *adj* блестя́щий, *also fig*; (*of light, etc.*) я́ркий; **a ~ idea/success/victory** блестя́щая идéя, замечáтельный успéх, блистáтельная побéда; **he is ~** он человéк блестя́щего умá.

brilliantly *adv* я́рко; *fig* блестя́ще; **the sun shone ~** сóлнце я́рко свети́ло; *fig* **he passed his exam ~** он блестя́ще сдал экзáмен.

brim *n* край; (*of hat*) поля́ (*pl*).

brim *vi*: **to ~ over** перели|вáться чéрез край (-́ться); **he's ~ming over with high spirits** жизнь бьёт в нём чéрез край.

brimful *adj* пóлный до краёв.

brine *n Cook* рассóл.

bring *vt* **1** *with person as subject*: (*smth by hand*) при|носи́ть (-нести́); (*smb on foot*) при|води́ть (-вести́); (*smb, smth in car, etc.*) при|вози́ть (-везти́); **I've brought you an article to read** я принёс тебé статью́, почитáй; **my husband will ~ the children and the luggage** (*in the car*) мой муж привезёт детéй и багáж; **may I ~ my sister with me?** (*on foot*) мóжно мне прийти́ с сестрóй?; **may I ~ my dog?** могý я взять с собóй собáку?

2 *with things as subject*: (*object a thing*) приноси́ть, (*object a person*) приводи́ть; **his paintings ~ him a small income** егó карти́ны прино́сят ему́ небольшо́й дохо́д; **what ~s you here at this hour?** что вас привело́ сюда́ в таку́ю по́ру? [**NB** *tense*]; **this will ~ you luck** э́то принесёт вам уда́чу; **it brought us nothing but trouble** э́то нам ничего́ не принесло́, кро́ме неприя́тностей (*pl*)

3 (*cause*) вы|зыва́ть (-звать), застав|ля́ть (-ить); **it brought tears to her eyes/a blush to her cheeks** она́ не могла́ сдержа́ть слёз, э́то вогна́ло её в кра́ску; **he couldn't ~ himself to apologize** он не мог заста́вить себя́ извини́ться; **to ~ pressure/influence to bear on smb** ока́з|ывать на кого́-л давле́ние/влия́ние (-а́ть)

bring about *vt*: **what brought about this quarrel?** чем была́ вы́звана э́та ссо́ра?

bring against *vt Law*: **to ~ a case/a charge against smb** возбу|жда́ть де́ло про́тив кого́-л (-ди́ть), предъяв|ля́ть кому́-л обвине́ние (-и́ть)

bring away *vt* уноси́ть, уводи́ть, увози́ть; **I brought away very pleasant impressions** я увёз с собо́й са́мые прия́тные воспомина́ния

bring back *vt* приноси́ть/приводи́ть/привози́ть обра́тно; возвра|ща́ть (*pfs* -ти́ть, верну́ть); **don't forget to ~ it/the knife back** не забу́дь э́то верну́ть/принести́ нож обра́тно; **to ~ back capital punishment** сно́ва ввести́ сме́ртную казнь; **the snapshot brought back to me my childhood** э́тот сни́мок напо́мнил мне моё де́тство

bring before *vt*: **the proposals will be brought before the committee tomorrow** за́втра э́ти предложе́ния бу́дут пе́реданы на рассмотре́ние коми́ссии; **he was brought before the committee** он предста́л пе́ред коми́ссией

bring down *vt*: **the gale brought down the telephone wires/the old oak** ве́тром сорва́ло (*impers*) телефо́нные провода́, ста́рый дуб свали́ло (*impers*) бу́рей; **I brought down a snipe** я подби́л/подстрели́л бека́са; **the enemy brought down five of our aircraft** проти́вник сбил пять на́ших самолётов; **to ~ the house down** вы́звать бу́рные аплодисме́нты (*win applause*)/взрыв сме́ха (*cause laughter*); **that brought him down to earth with a bump** ну и пришло́сь ему́ спусти́ться с небе́с на зе́млю; **to ~ down prices** сни|жа́ть це́ны (-зить)

bring forward *vt*: **to ~ forward a proposal** вы|двига́ть предложе́ние (-двинуть); **the meeting has been brought forward to the 7th** собра́ние бы́ло перенесено́ на седьмо́е (число́); *Math* **to ~ forward** перенести́

bring in *vt*: **to ~ in the wounded** вноси́ть ра́неных; **to ~ in a bill** вноси́ть законопрое́кт; **to ~ in an income** приноси́ть дохо́д; **we brought in an expert to advise** мы консульти́ровались со специали́стом

bring into *vt* вводи́ть (ввести́); **to ~ a ship into harbour/troops into action** вводи́ть су́дно в га́вань/войска́ в бой; **to ~ into fashion/force/use** вводи́ть в мо́ду/в де́йствие/в употребле́ние; **to ~ a new factory into production** ввести́ в строй но́вый заво́д; **the company he keeps has brought him into disrepute** он обя́зан дурно́й сла́вой свои́м дружка́м; **my work ~s me into contact with many Russians** я по рабо́те ча́сто встреча́юсь с ру́сскими

bring off *vt*: **they brought all the passengers off safely** пассажи́ры бы́ли благополу́чно сня́ты с корабля́; **we brought off the deal** мы дости́гли соглаше́ния

bring on *vt*: **the warm weather is ~ing on the vegetables nicely** така́я тёплая пого́да благоприя́тствует созрева́нию овоще́й; **I brought it on myself** я сам э́то на себя́ навлёк

bring out *vt*: **he brought out his wallet** он вы́нул бума́жник; **to ~ out a new book** изда|ва́ть но́вую кни́гу (-ть); **the Ford company is shortly ~ing out a new model** автомоби́льная компа́ния Фо́рда ско́ро вы́пустит но́вую моде́ль маши́ны; **the lecturer brought out clearly the differences between...** ле́ктор я́сно показа́л ра́зницу (*sing*) ме́жду + *I*; **she ~s out the best in him** она́ пробужда́ет в нём всё са́мое лу́чшее

bring round *vt*: **do ~ them round to see us** приведи́ их к нам; *Med* **to ~ smb round** приводи́ть кого́-л в созна́ние; **he brought the conversation round to his favourite topic** он перевёл разгово́р на свою́ люби́мую те́му; **we brought them round to our point of view** мы их убеди́ли

bring to *vt*: **that will ~ the total to £ 5** э́то доведёт су́мму до пяти́ фу́нтов; **it has been brought to my attention that...** до моего́ све́дения дошло́, что...

bring together *vt*: **we were brought together by fate** нас свела́ судьба́; **the birth of their son brought them closer together** рожде́ние сы́на сбли́зило их

bring up *vt*: **to ~ up children** (*educate*) воспи́т|ывать/(*rear*) вы́растить дете́й (-а́ть/*only in pf*); **he brought up his dinner** его́ вы́рвало (*impers*) по́сле обе́да; *Mil* **to ~ up reserves/the rear** под|тя́гивать резе́рвы (-тяну́ть), замыка́ть ше́ствие (*impf*); *fig*: **to ~ up a question** под|нима́ть вопро́с (-ня́ть); **to ~ smb up to date** ввести́ кого́-л в курс де́ла; **why ~ that up now?** заче́м э́то сейча́с вороши́ть?

brink *n* (*edge*) край; (*shore*) бе́рег; *fig*: **on the ~ of the grave** на краю́ моги́лы; **on the ~ of war/ruin** на гра́ни войны́/разоре́ния.

briny *adj* солёный.

brisk *adj* бы́стрый; (*of people*) энерги́чный, живо́й; **I'm going for a ~ walk** пойду́ на у́лицу прогуля́юсь; *Comm* **trade is ~** в торго́вле оживле́ние.

bristle *n* щети́на.

bristle *vi* (*of cat, dog*) ощети́ниться (*usu pf*), *also fig*; *fig*: **the problem ~s with difficulties** в э́том де́ле тру́дностей хоть отбавля́й; **he ~s criticism** он огрыза́ется на замеча́ния (*pl*).

bristly *adj* щети́нистый.

British *adj* брита́нский; *as n* (**the ~**) брита́нцы.

brittle *adj* хру́пкий, ло́мкий.

broach *vt*: **to ~ a bottle/a barrel** откры|ва́ть буты́лку/бо́чку (́-ть); *fig* **to ~ a subject** под|нима́ть вопро́с (-ня́ть), на|чина́ть диску́ссию (-ча́ть).

broad *adj* широ́кий; **the river is 10 metres ~** ширина́ реки́ де́сять ме́тров; *fig*: **a ~ hint/accent** я́сный намёк, си́льный акце́нт; **in a ~ sense it's true** в бо́лее широ́ком смы́сле э́то ве́рно; **he gave a ~ grin** он широко́ улыбну́лся; **~ humour** грубова́тый ю́мор; **it's about as ~ as it's long** то́ же на то́ же выхо́дит *or* что в лоб, что по́ лбу.

broadcast *n Radio* переда́ча.

broadcast *vti vt Radio*: **to ~ a play** передава́ть пье́су по ра́дио (*usu impf*); **the concert will be ~ live** конце́рт бу́дет трансли́роваться прямо́й переда́чей; *fig* **I don't want it ~ everywhere** я не хочу́, что́бы об э́том трезво́нили по всему́ го́роду

vi: **the president will be ~ing at 9** президе́нт бу́дет выступа́ть по ра́дио в де́вять часо́в.

broadcasting *n* радиовеща́ние, трансля́ция; (*on TV*) переда́ча по телеви́дению; *attr*: **~ station** радиоста́нция.

broaden *vti* расшир|я́ть(ся) (́-ить(ся)).

broad-gauge *adj Rail* ширококоле́йный.

broadly *adv*: **~ speaking** вообще́ говоря́; **it's ~ true that...** в о́бщем ве́рно, что...; **a ~ based coalition** широ́кая коали́ция.

broad-minded *adj* с широ́ким кругозо́ром; **a ~ man** челове́к широ́ких взгля́дов.

broadside on *as adv*: **the ships collided ~** корабли́ столкну́лись борта́ми.

brocade *n* парча́.

brochure *n* брошю́ра.

broil *vti* жа́рить(ся) (на откры́том огне́) (за-, под-).

broiler *n* бро́йлер.

broke *adj*: **the firm has gone ~** фи́рма обанкро́тилась; *CQ* **I'm ~ just now** у меня́ сейча́с нет ни копе́йки, я сейча́с на мели́.

broken *adj* (*of sticks, bones*) сло́манный; (*of glass, etc. and fig*) разби́тый; (*of law, promise, silence*) нару́шенный; (*intermittent*) преры́вистый; **a ~ heart/marriage** разби́тое се́рдце, разби́тая семья́; **they are children of a ~ marriage/from a ~ home** роди́тели э́тих дете́й разошли́сь; **a ~ man** ко́нченый челове́к; **a ~ sleep** сон уры́вками (*adv*); **~ weather** неусто́йчивая/переме́нная пого́да; **~ ground** пересечённая ме́стность; **he spoke ~ English** он говори́л на ло́маном англи́йском (языке́).

broken-down *adj*: **a ~ old car** ста́рый разби́тый драндуле́т.

bronchial *adj* бронхиа́льный.

bronchitis *n* бронхи́т.

bronze *n* бро́нза; *attr* бро́нзовый; **the B. Horseman** (*statue of Peter the Great in Leningrad*) Ме́дный вса́дник.

brooch *n* брошь.

brood *n* (*of chickens*) вы́водок; *fig* **she arrived with a whole ~ of children** она́ пришла́ со всей свое́й ора́вой.

brood *vi* (*of bird*) сиде́ть на я́йцах (*impf*); *fig*: **he was ~ing over his problems** он лома́л го́лову над свои́ми пробле́мами; **try not to ~ about it** стара́йся об э́том не ду́мать.

brood mare *n* племенна́я кобы́ла.

broody *adj*: **a ~ hen** насе́дка; *fig* **whenever I see a baby I go all ~** *approx* когда́ я ви́жу ма́ленького ребёнка, становлю́сь сама́ не своя́.

brook *n* руче́й.

broom *n* (*brush*) метла́; *Bot* раки́тник; *fig* **a new ~ (sweeps clean)** но́вая метла́ (чи́сто метёт).

broth *n* (*with vegetables, etc.*) суп; **chicken ~** кури́ный бульо́н.

brother *n* брат; *fig* **he and his ~ officers** он и его́ това́рищи по полку́.

brother-in-law *n* (*wife's brother*) шу́рин; (*sister's husband*) зять (*m*); (*husband's brother*) де́верь (*m*); (*husband of wife's sister*) своя́к.

brotherly *adj* бра́тский.

brow *n* (*forehead*) лоб; (*eyebrow*) бровь; **the ~ of a hill/cliff** верши́на холма́, вы́ступ утёса.

browbeat *vt*: **to ~ smb into doing smth** прину|жда́ть кого́-л сде́лать что-л (́-дить).

brown *n* кори́чневый цвет.

brown *adj* кори́чневый; (*sunburnt*) загоре́лый; **~ sugar** кори́чневый са́хар; **chestnut ~ hair** кашта́новые во́лосы; **a person with ~ hair** шате́н(ка); **~ eyes** ка́рие глаза́; **~ paper** обёрточная бума́га; **a ~ bear** бу́рый медве́дь; **she's ~ as a berry** она́ о́чень загоре́лая; *fig* **he is in a ~ study** он погружён в свои́ мы́сли.

brown *vti vt Cook* поджа́р|ивать, подрумя́н|ивать (*pfs* -ить); *fig CQ* **I'm ~ed off with my job** мне надое́ла моя́ рабо́та [NB *tense*]

vi Cook поджа́риваться, подрумя́ниваться; (*with sun*) загор|а́ть (-е́ть).

browning *n Cook* (*process*) жа́рение; (*for gravy*) кори́чневая припра́ва для со́уса.

browse *vi* (*of sheep, etc.*) пасти́сь (*impf*); *fig* **he was browsing through some journals** он просма́тривал каки́е-то журна́лы.

bruise *n* уши́б; (*esp. if blue*) синя́к.

bruise *vti vt* (*of people*) ушиб|а́ть (-и́ть); **he ~d his elbow** он уши́б ло́коть; **to ~ oneself** ушиба́ться

vi: **peaches ~ easily** пе́рсики легко́ мну́тся.

brunette *n* брюне́тка.

brunt *n*: **the infantry bore the ~ of the attack** всю тя́жесть бо́я вы́несла на свои́х плеча́х пехо́та; **we bore the ~ of the expense/work/his anger** на нас легла́ вся тя́жесть затра́т, нам доста́лась са́мая тру́дная часть рабо́ты, его́ гнев обру́шился на нас.

brush *n* **1** щётка; (*broom*) метла́; **scrubbing/clothes/tooth ~** полова́я/платяна́я/зубна́я щётка

2 (*act*): **your coat needs a good ~** пальто́ на́до хороше́нько почи́стить щёткой

3 (*clash*) схва́тка, (*in words*) перепа́лка, сты́чка; *CQ* **I had a ~ with the boss** у меня́ бы́ли сты́чки (*pl*) с нача́льством.

brush *vt* чи́стить (щёткой) (по-, на-, вы́-); **to ~ clothes/teeth/shoes** почи́стить щёткой оде́жду/зу́бы/о́бувь; **to ~ the floor/the carpet** под|мета́ть пол/ковёр (-мести́); **to ~ smb's/one's (own) hair** при|чёсывать кого́-л (-чеса́ть), причёсываться

brush against *vi*: **I ~ed against the table as I passed** я шёл по ко́мнате и заде́л бо́ком о стол

brush aside *vt fig*: **he ~ed aside their complaints** он отмахну́лся от их жа́лоб

brush away *vt*: **to ~ away flies/snow/a tear** отма́хиваться от мух (*usu impf*), счи|ща́ть снег (-́стить), смахну́ть слезу́ (*usu pf*)

brush off *vti vt*: **to ~ smth off a table** (*accidentally*) сма́х|ивать что-л со стола́ (-ну́ть); **to ~ fluff off one's sleeve/crumbs off the table** стряхну́ть пуши́нку с рукава́ (*usu pf*), сме|та́ть кро́шки со стола́ (-сти́)

vi: **the mud will ~ off easily when it's dry** грязь легко́ отчи́стить, когда́ она́ вы́сохнет

brush up *vt*: **to ~ up broken glass off the floor** подме|та́ть оско́лки с по́ла (-сти́); *fig* **I must ~ up my French** мне на́до подзаня́ться францу́зским.

brush-off *n*: *CQ* **she gave him the ~** он получи́л у неё отста́вку.

brush-up *n*: **I need a wash and ~** мне ну́жно привести́ себя́ в поря́док.

brushwood *n* за́росли (*pl*), куста́рник.

brusque *adj* (*of voice, manner*) ре́зкий.

brutal *adj* (*cruel*) жесто́кий; (*bestial*) зве́рский.

brute *n* (*animal*) живо́тное; (*wild*) зверь (*m*); *CQ* (*person*): **you ~!** скоти́на!; **they are utter ~s** они́ про́сто ското́/сви́ньи; *fig* **it's a ~ of a problem** э́то черто́вски сло́жная пробле́ма.

brute *adj*: **by ~ force** гру́бой си́лой.

bubble *n* пузы́рь (*m*), *dim* пузырёк; **to blow ~s** пуска́ть мы́льные пузыри́.

bubble *vt*: **the kettle was bubbling** ча́йник кипе́л; **the spring ~s out of the rock** родни́к бьёт ключо́м из скалы́; *fig* **she was bubbling over with high spirits** она́ горе́ла воодушевле́нием.

buck *n* **1** (*deer*) оле́нь-саме́ц; (*of hare, rabbit*) саме́ц; **I have two rabbits—a ~ and a doe** у меня́ два кро́лика—саме́ц и са́мка; *attr*: **he's got ~ teeth** у него́ зу́бы торча́т вперёд

2 (*US*) *sl* до́ллар; *sl* **to pass the ~** свали́ть отве́тственность на друго́го.

buck *vi*: **this horse ~s** э́та ло́шадь ляга́ется.

bucket *n* ведро́; (*toy*) ведёрко; *Tech* (*scoop*) ковш; **a ~ of sand/water** ведро́ с песко́м/воды́; *CQ* **the rain came down in ~s** дождь лил как из ведра́.

bucketful *n*: **I need a ~ of sand** мне пона́добится ведро́ песку́ (*partitive genitive*).

buckle *n* пря́жка.

buckle *vti vt*: **to ~ (on) sandals/a belt** за|стёгивать санда́лии/пря́жку на ремне́ (-стегну́ть)

vi (*of metal*) гну́ться (по-); *fig* **to ~ down to work** бра́ться за рабо́ту (взя́ться).

buckwheat *n* (*plant*) греча́ха; *Cook* гре́чневая крупа́ (*collect*), *CQ* гре́чка.

bud *n* по́чка; (*of flower*) буто́н; **the trees/roses are in ~** на дере́вьях набу́хли по́чки, на куста́х роз появи́лись буто́ны; *fig* **to nip smth in the ~** пресе́чь что-л в ко́рне, подави́ть что-л в заро́дыше.

bud *vi* дава́ть по́чки (*usu impf*); *fig* **a ~ding poet** начина́ющий поэ́т.

buddy *n* (*US*) *CQ* дружо́к.

budge *vti* (*usu vi*) сдви|га́ть(ся) (-́нуть(ся)); шевел|и́ть(ся) (-ьну́ть(ся)); **the piano hasn't ~d an inch** роя́ль не сдви́нулся ни на сантиме́тр; **he didn't dare to ~** он не смел/боя́лся пошевельну́ться; *fig* **he wouldn't ~ (an inch)** он не хоте́л ни в чём уступи́ть.

budget *n* бюдже́т.

budget *vi*: **we hadn't ~ed for such large heating bills** мы не предусмотре́ли таки́х затра́т на отопле́ние; **to ~ for every eventuality** предусмотре́ть всё; **we'll have to ~ for four people now/for the coming year** тепе́рь у нас расхо́ды бу́дут на четверы́х, нам на́до соста́вить бюдже́т на бу́дущий год.

buffalo *n* бу́йвол.

buffer *n Rail* бу́фер; *attr fig*: **a ~ state** бу́ферное госуда́рство.

buffet[1] *n* (*place for buying snacks*) буфе́т; *attr*: **a ~ supper** у́жин «а-ля фурше́т».

buffet[2] *vt usu pass*: **the ship was ~ed by the waves** кора́бль броса́ло (*impers*) на волна́х.

buffet car *n Rail* ваго́н-рестора́н.

buffoon *n* шут; **to play the ~** пая́сничать.

bug *n* клоп; *CQ* **he's got some ~ or other** у него́ кака́я-то инфе́кция; *fig* **he's got the travel ~** он помеша́лся на путеше́ствиях; *sl* **he's a big ~** он ва́жная персо́на, он «ши́шка».

bug *vt CQ*: **this room is ~ged** в э́той ко́мнате устано́влены потайны́е/скры́тые микрофо́ны.

buggy *n* (*US*: *pram*) де́тская коля́ска.

bugle *n* горн.

build *n* (тело)сложе́ние; **a man of sturdy ~** челове́к кре́пкого сложе́ния; **they're of the same ~** они́ одина́ково сложены́.

build *vt* (*house, road, plans*) стро́ить (по-); **the old churches were built of wood** ста́рые це́ркви стро́ились из де́рева; **these ships are Polish built** э́ти суда́ бы́ли постро́ены в По́льше; **to ~ a fire** раскла́дывать костёр (разложи́ть)

build in(to) *vt* встра́ивать (встро́ить); **this cupboard has been built in/into the wall** э́тот шкаф встро́ен в сте́ну; *fig* **an allowance for travel has been built into your salary** ва́ша зарпла́та включа́ет и расхо́ды на пое́здки

build on *vt*: **we've built on a new wing/a third storey** мы пристро́или но́вый флигель, мы надстро́или тре́тий эта́ж; *fig* **don't ~ any hopes on him/on his promises** не возлага́йте наде́жд на него́, не ве́рьте его́ обеща́ниям

build up *vti vt*: **this area is being built up** сейча́с э́тот райо́н застра́ивается; **I'm ~ing up a library** я собира́ю дома́шнюю библиоте́ку; **the enemy are ~ing up their reserves** враг нака́пливает резе́рвы; **the sea air built up her strength** морско́й во́здух укрепи́л её здоро́вье; **he built up a good business/reputation** он основа́л соли́дную фи́рму, он со́здал себе́ хоро́шую репута́цию

vi: **pressure is ~ing up** давле́ние растёт; **in summer traffic ~s up along the coast roads** ле́том движе́ние на доро́гах вдоль побере́жья увели́чивается и образу́ются про́бки; **he began training with a mile a day and gradually built up to ten** он на́чал тренирова́ться с одно́й ми́ли в день и постепе́нно дошёл до десяти́.

builder *n* строи́тель (*m*).

building *n* (*act*) строи́тельство; (*act or thing built*) (по)стро́йка; **a ~** зда́ние; *attr*: **he's in the ~ trade** он строи́тель.

build-up *n*: *Mil* **a ~ of forces** сосредото́чение сил; *fig* **he got a good ~ in the press** пре́сса создала́ ему́ рекла́му.

built-in *adj*: **~ cupboards** встро́енные/стенны́е шкафы́

built-up *adj*: **a ~ area** застро́енный райо́н.

bulb *n Bot* лу́ковица; *Elec* ла́мпочка; **the ~'s gone** ла́мпочка перегоре́ла.

Bulgarian *n* болга́рин, болга́рка.

Bulgarian *adj* болга́рский.

bulge *n* (*on surface*) вы́пуклость.

bulge *vi*: **the plaster on the wall ~s near the corner** в углу́ на стене́ отхо́дит штукату́рка; **his pockets were bulging with apples** его́ карма́ны бы́ли наби́ты я́блоками.

bulging *adj*: **he has ~ eyes** у него́ глаза́ навы́кате (*adv*)/вы́пуклые глаза́; **~ pockets** оттопы́ренные карма́ны.

bulk *n* **1** (*volume*) объём; (*greater part*) **the ~ of the students live at home** бо́льшая часть студе́нтов живёт до́ма

2 *Comm*: **to buy in ~** покупа́ть о́птом.

bulky *adj* объёмистый; (*of person*) ту́чный; **a ~ parcel/volume** объёмистый паке́т, то́лстый том.

bull *n* бык; *fig* **to take the ~ by the horns** взять быка́ за рога́.

bulldoze *vt*: **to ~ a site** вы|ра́внивать уча́сток бульдо́зером (-ровнять); *fig* **he ~d his opponents into agreeing** он угро́зами (*approx*) доби́лся усту́пок.

bulldozer *n* бульдо́зер.

bullet *n* пу́ля.

bulletin *n* бюллете́нь (*m*); сво́дка; **a ~ about the president's health** бюллете́нь о состоя́нии здоро́вья президе́нта.

bulletproof *adj* пуленепробива́емый.

bullfight *n* бой быко́в.

bullock *n* вол.

bull's-eye *n* я́блоко мише́ни; **to score a ~** попа́сть в цель, *also fig*.

bully[1] *n* зади́ра (*m and f*).

bully[1] *vt* задира́ть (*impf*).

bully[2] *adj sl*, *usu as interj*: **~ for you!** молоде́ц!

bumblebee *n* шмель (*m*).

bump *n* **1** (*usu translated by verb*): **I gave my head a ~** я сту́кнулся голово́й; **I sat down with a ~** я бу́хнулся/плю́хнулся на стул; (*sound of a blow*) **there was a ~ when the two cars met** вдруг уда́р—две маши́ны столкну́лись

2 (*on people*: *lump*) ши́шка; (*swelling*) о́пухоль; **I've a ~ on my head** у меня́ ши́шка на голове́; *fig* **I've no ~ of locality** я пло́хо ориенти́руюсь на ме́стности.

bump *vti vt* сту́кнуться (*usu pf*); **I ~ed myself/my knee against the table** я сту́кнулся/уда́рился (коле́ном) о стол; *sl* **to ~ smb off** уби́ть кого́-л

vi (*of people*) удар|я́ться (-́иться); на|тыка́ться (-ткну́ться); на|та́лкиваться (-толкну́ться), *also fig*; (*of people or cars*, *also fig*) ста́лкиваться (столкну́ться), налет|а́ть (-е́ть); (*usu of vehicles*) врез|а́ться (-́аться); **I ~ed into the wall/against the table** я наткну́лся на стену́, я налете́л на стол *or* я уда́рился о стол; **his car ~ed into a tree/into ours** его́ маши́на вре́залась в де́рево/столкну́лась с на́шей; **the car ~ed along over the potholes** маши́на трясла́сь по уха́бам; *fig* **I ~ed into him yesterday in the street** вчера́ я столкну́лся с ним на у́лице.

bumper[1] *n Aut* ба́мпер.

bumper[2] *adj*: **a ~ crop** небыва́лый урожа́й.

bumpy *adj* (*of road*: *with lumps*) неро́вный; (*with potholes*) уха́бистый; **we had a ~ journey/flight** в доро́ге/в самолёте нас растрясло́ (*impers*).

bun *n* (*to eat*) бу́лочка; *fig* **to do one's hair in a ~** забира́ть во́лосы в пучо́к.

bunch *n* (*of fruit*) кисть, гроздь; **a ~ of bananas** гроздь бана́нов; **a ~ of flowers** буке́т цвето́в; **a ~ of keys** свя́зка ключе́й; **a ~ of people** гру́ппа люде́й; **he's the best/the pick of the ~** он лу́чший среди́ них; *pejor* (*of people*) **what a ~!** ну и компа́ния!

bundle *n* у́зел; **a ~ of rags/clothes** у́зел ста́рого тряпья́ (*collect*)/оде́жды; **a ~ of sticks/papers** свя́зка ве́ток, сто́пка бума́г.

bundle *vt* (*by tying*) свя́з|ывать в у́зел (-а́ть); (*stuff*): **to ~ things into a suitcase/smb into a taxi** запихну́ть ве́щи в чемода́н, втолкну́ть кого́-л в такси́; **I ~d the children upstairs/off to school** я погна́л дете́й спать, я бы́стро отпра́вил дете́й в шко́лу.

bung *n* вту́лка.

bung *vt*, *also* **~ up** (*plug*) за|тыка́ть (-ткну́ть); **we ~ed up the hole with rags** мы заткну́ли дыру́ тряпьём (*collect*); *CQ* **~ it all into the box** кида́йте всё в я́щик; *fig CQ*: **I've a filthy cold and I'm all ~ed up** у меня́ ужа́сный на́сморк и всё зало́жено; **her eyes**

were all ~ed up with sleep у неё глаза́ слипа́лись.

bungalow *n* бу́нгало (*indecl*).

bungle *vt CQ*: **I've ~d the job/it** я всё де́ло испо́ртил/запоро́л.

bunion *n* ши́шка на большо́м па́льце ноги́.

bunk[1] *n* (*bed*) ко́йка, *also Naut*; *Rail* спа́льное ме́сто, по́лка; *attr*: **~ beds** де́тские крова́ти одна́ над друго́й.

bunk[2] *n sl*: **to do a ~** удра́ть (*only in pf*).

bunker *n Naut* (*for coal*) бу́нкер, у́гольная я́ма; *Mil* бу́нкер.

bunny *n* кро́лик.

buoy *n* буй, *dim* буёк; **life ~** спаса́тельный буй/круг.

buoy *vt*: **to ~ a channel** ста́вить буи́/ба́кены в проли́ве (по-); *fig* **we were ~ed up by the (good) news** э́то изве́стие приободри́ло нас.

buoyant *adj* плаву́чий; *fig* бо́дрый; *Comm* **the market is ~** торго́вля оживи́лась [**NB** *tense*].

burden *n* (*in the hand*) но́ша; (*load*) груз; (*weight*) тя́жесть; *fig* бре́мя; **he bent under the ~** он согну́лся под тя́жестью но́ши; *fig*: **the ~ of taxation** нало́говое бре́мя; **the ~ of proof lies on the accuser** кто обвиня́ет, тот пусть и дока́зывает вину́; **to be a ~ to smb** быть кому́-л в тя́гость, сиде́ть у кого́-л на ше́е; **life became a ~ to her** жизнь ста́ла ей в тя́гость.

burden *vt* обремен|я́ть (-и́ть); **to be ~d with** быть обременённым + *I*.

burdensome *adj* обремени́тельный.

bureau *n* бюро́ (*indecl*); **information ~** спра́вочное бюро́.

bureaucracy *n* бюрократи́зм; **the ~** (*people*) чино́вники, бюрокра́ты.

bureaucratic *adj* бюрократи́ческий.

burglar *n* вор, взло́мщик.

burglary *n* кра́жа со взло́мом.

burgle *vt*: **they've been ~d** их обокра́ли.

burial *n* захороне́ние, погребе́ние.

burial ground *n* кла́дбище; *Archaeol* захороне́ние.

burial service *n* заупоко́йная слу́жба, панихи́да.

Burmese *n* бирма́нец, бирма́нка.

Burmese *adj* бирма́нский.

burn *n* ожо́г.

burn *vti vt* жечь, сжига́ть (*pf for both* сжечь) *and other compounds*; **to ~ papers** сжига́ть бума́ги; **I've ~t a hole in my dress** я прожгла́ дыру́ на пла́тье; **I've ~t myself/my hand with steam/on the oven door** я обжёгся/я обжёг себе́ ру́ки па́ром/о две́рцу духо́вки; **their faces were ~t by the sun** у них бы́ли обожжённые со́лнцем ли́ца; **he was ~t at the stake/to death** (*accidentally*) он был сожжён на костре́, он поги́б в огне́ *or* он сгоре́л; **the house was ~t to the ground** дом сгоре́л дотла́ (*adv*); **I've let the meat ~** у меня́ подгоре́ло мя́со; **the meat tastes ~t** мя́со подгоре́ло; **last winter we ~t three tons/a lot of coal** за про́шлую зи́му мы сожгли́ три то́нны у́гля/мы израсхо́довали мно́го у́гля; **we ~ coal/wood in the stove** мы то́пим у́глем/дрова́ми (*pl*) (*impf*)

vi горе́ть (*impf*) *and compounds*; **a bonfire/house/light/the gas was ~ing** костёр/дом/свет/газ горе́л; **the pie has ~t black/a little** пиро́г сгоре́л/подгоре́л; **the fire ~t up brightly** ого́нь я́рко разгоре́лся; **I left the gas ~ing all night** я жёг газ всю ночь; **my hands are ~ing from the nettle stings** у меня́ ру́ки жжёт (*impers*)—я обжёг их крапи́вой (*collect*); **my throat is ~ing from the liqueur** у меня́ от э́того ликёра жжёт (*impers*) в го́рле; *Elec* **the fuse has ~t out** про́бка перегоре́ла; *fig* **I was ~ing with shame/anger** я сгора́л от стыда́, я пыла́л гне́вом.

burner *n* горе́лка.

burning *adj*: **the ~ house/sun** горя́щий дом, паля́щее со́лнце; **the plates are ~ hot** таре́лки горя́чие; *fig* **~ desire** горя́чее жела́ние.

burp *vi* рыг|а́ть (*semel* -ну́ть).

burrow *n* нора́.

burrow *vti*: **to ~ (a hole)** рыть нору́ (вы́-).

bursar *n* казначе́й.

bursary *n* **1** (*office, esp. Univ*) (**the ~**) канцеля́рия казначе́я

2 (*award*) (**a ~**) стипе́ндия.

burst *n* (*explosion*) взрыв, *also fig*; (*of shells, etc.*) разры́в; **a ~ of thunder** уда́р гро́ма; **a ~ of flame**/*fig* **of anger** вспы́шка пла́мени/гне́ва; *fig* **a ~ of applause** взрыв аплодисме́нтов.

burst *vti vt*: **to ~ a balloon/tyre** про|ка́лывать возду́шный шар/ши́ну (-коло́ть); **the frost has ~ the pipes** от моро́за ло́пнули тру́бы; **the river has ~ its banks** река́ вы́шла из берего́в; *fig* **we ~ our sides with laughing** мы чуть не ло́пнули от сме́ха

vi **1** (*by splitting*) ло́п|аться (-нуть), *also fig*; **the balloon/bubble ~** возду́шный шар/пузы́рь ло́пнул; **a bottle/pipe/tyre has ~** буты́лка/труба́/ши́на ло́пнула; **she's ~ing out of her dress** на неё пла́тье уже́ не налеза́ет; **my case is full to ~ing** мой чемода́н наби́т до отка́за; *fig* **he was ~ing with joy/pride/indignation** он сия́л от ра́дости/от го́рдости, он кипе́л от негодова́ния

2 (*by exploding*) вз|рыва́ться, раз|рыва́ться (*pfs* -орва́ться) *and other compounds*; **the boiler ~** котёл взорва́лся; **the shell ~** снаря́д разорва́лся; **the dam ~** плоти́ну прорва́ло (*impers*); **the abscess ~** нары́в прорва́лся; **the storm ~** разрази́лась бу́ря; *fig* **she ~ into the room** она́ ворвала́сь в ко́мнату

3 *other fig uses*: **to ~ into blossom/flames/song/tears** расцве|та́ть (-сти́), вспы́х|ивать (-нуть), запе́ть (*pf*), распла́каться (*pf*); **the door ~ open** дверь распахну́лась; **to ~ out laughing** рассмея́ться, (*louder*) расхохота́ться; **she is ~ing with vitality** от неё так и ве́яло (*impers*) жи́зненной си́лой; *CQ* **she was ~ing to tell me all about it** ей не терпе́лось всё мне вы́ложить.

bury *vt* **1** (*a person*) хоронить (по-); (*things*) за|кáпывать (-копáть); **he buried the box under a tree** он закопáл ящик под деревом; **the dog buried his bone in the snow** собáка зарыла кость в снег; **the village was buried by an avalanche** деревня былá погребенá под снéжной лавиной

2 *fig uses*: **he buried himself in the country/in his books** он похоронил себя в деревне, он зарылся в книги; **she buried her face in her hands/in a pillow** онá закрыла лицó рукáми, онá зарылась лицóм в подýшку; **let's ~ the hatchet** давáй перестáнем сводить стáрые счёты.

bus *n* автóбус; **to travel by ~** éхать на автóбусе; **I'm going to catch my ~** я пойдý на автóбус; **I will go back by ~** я поéду обрáтно автóбусом; **to get on a ~** сесть/ *CQ* влезть в автóбус; [**NB** *prep is* в + *A when actually entering a bus, but* на + *A if directions are being given*]: **take the Zagorsk ~ and at Pushkino change to a number 2** сядьте на автóбус до Загóрска и в Пýшкино пересядьте на автóбус нóмер два.

bush *n* куст; *pl* (**~es**) кусты, кустáрник (*collect*); **a rose ~** рóзовый куст; **a currant/bramble ~** куст сморóдины/ежевики; **the Australian ~** австралийский буш.

bush telegraph *n CQ*: **I heard it on ~** я узнáл это из трéтьих рук.

bushy *adj* кустистый; **~ eyebrows** кустистые брóви; **a ~ beard** густáя бородá.

busily *adv*: **my little son was ~ scribbling all over my article** мой мáленький сын деловито чертил карáкули на моéй статьé; **she was ~ ironing** онá глáдила бельё.

business *n* **1** *Comm* (*general*) дéло; **big ~** большóй бизнес; **what's his (line of) ~?** чем он занимáется?, что он дéлает?; **he's in the wholesale/retail/publishing/car ~** он занимáется оптовóй торгóвлей/рóзничной торгóвлей/издáтельским дéлом, он торгýет автомобилями; **to set smb up in ~** помогáть комý-л начáть дéло; **he's away on ~** он в командирóвке, он уéхал по делáм; **can I see the director?—What is your ~?** мóжно увидеть дирéктора?—По какóму дéлу?; **I do ~ with him** я с ним сотрýдничаю; **we were talking ~** у нас был деловóй разговóр; (*agenda*) **~ of the day** повéстка дня; (*at a meeting*) **any further ~?** есть ещё чтó-нибудь?; *fig*: **now we're talking ~** вот это другóй разговóр; **there's some funny ~ going on** тут чтó-то нечисто; **he's up to some funny ~** он занимáется какими-то тёмными делишками (*pl*); **~ before pleasure** дéлу врéмя, потéхе час

2 (*a firm*) предприятие, дéло; **he runs three ~es** он управляéт тремя предприятиями; **he's made a lot out of the ~** на этом дéле он нáжил немáлые дéньги; **a family ~** семéйное дéло

3 (*task, duty*) обязанность, дéло; **I'll make it my ~ to help her** я считáю своéй обязанностью ей помогáть; **you've no ~ to do that** вы не имéете прáва так поступáть; **that's no ~ of yours** это не вáше дéло, это вас не касáется; **mind your own ~!** занимáйся своим дéлом!, не вмéшивайся в чужие делá!

4 (*affair*) дéло; истóрия; **what a ~!** ну и делá!; **it's a nasty ~** это сквéрная истóрия; **did you hear about that ~ yesterday?** вы слыхáли об этой вчерáшней истóрии?

5 *attr* деловóй; **~ interests** деловые интерéсы; **~ letter/address** деловóе письмó, служéбный áдрес; **~ hours** рабóчие часы, часы торгóвли/приёма посетителей (*for receiving clients*); **~ trip** командирóвка, деловáя поéздка.

businesslike *adj* деловитый.

businessman *n* коммерсáнт, деловóй человéк.

busload *n*: **every day ~s of tourists arrive to see the castle** кáждый день многочисленные автóбусы привóзят туристов на осмóтр зáмка.

bus-stop *n* остановка автóбуса.

bust[1] *n* грудь, бюст, *also Art*; *attr*: **~ measurement** размéр груди.

bust[2] *n* (*spree*) весéлье; кутёж; **to go on the ~, to have a ~** веселиться, (*if drunken*) кутить (*usu impfs*).

bust[2] *adj sl*: **the firm has gone ~** фирма лóпнула.

bustle *n* (*fuss*) суетá; (*turmoil*) суматóха.

bustle *vi* (*hurry*) торопиться, (*fuss busily*) хлопотáть (*usu impfs*); **she ~d about getting the supper** онá хлопотáла с ýжином.

bust-up *n CQ* скандáл.

busy *adj* **1** (*of people*) занятóй (*only attr*), зáнятый (*usu predic*); **a ~ man/housewife** занятóй человéк, заботливая хозяйка; **are you ~?** ты зáнят?; **I'm ~ with the children for the moment** сейчáс я занимáюсь с детьми; **the children keep me ~** дéти отнимáют у меня всё врéмя; **he's ~ on/at/over his thesis** он зáнят своéй диссертáцией; **she's ~ getting dinner/about the house** онá готóвит обéд, онá хлопóчет по хозяйству; **the director is ~ at a meeting** у дирéктора сейчáс совещáние; **the baby/garden keeps me ~** ребёнок не даёт мне покóя, я мнóго занимáюсь сáдом; **I like to keep myself ~** я не люблю сидéть без дéла/сложá рýки; *pejor* **he's too ready to be ~ in other people's affairs** он лю́бит совáть нос в чужие делá

2 (*of periods of time, streets, etc.*): **the busiest time of year for the gardener is the spring** для садóвника сáмое горячее врéмя—веснá; **it's been a ~ day for me** сегóдня у меня было мнóго дел/хлопóт; **the hospital is very ~ just now** больница сейчáс перепóлнена; **in summer Cambridge is very ~** лéтом в Кéмбридже на ýлицах тóлпы туристов; *Tel* **lines to Paris are ~** парижская линия (*sing*) занятá.

busybody *n*: **she is a ~** онá вездé суёт свой нос.

but *adv*: **he talks ~ little** он мáло говори́т; **he all ~ fell** он чуть не/едвá не упáл; **she did nothing ~ sob** онá всё тóлько рыдáла; **the water is anything ~ hot** водá совсéм не горя́чая; **you can ~ try** что ж, попрóбуй.

but *prep* крóме + *G*; **no one ~ an expert could have seen the difference** никтó, крóме специали́ста, не мог замéтить рáзницы/э́того разли́чия; **any day ~ Thursday suits me** мне подхóдит любóй день, крóме четвергá; **take the next turning ~ two** повернúте чéрез два квартáла; **he arrived the last ~ one** он пришёл предпослéдним; **she buys nothing ~ the best** онá покупáет всё сáмое лýчшее/тóлько вы́сшего кáчества; **he's nothing ~ a country bumpkin** он всегó лишь деревéнский парни́шка.

but *conj* **1** но; **~ why wait?** но зачéм же ждать?; **he's poor ~ honest** он бéден, но чéстен; **true, ~ all the same I disagree** э́то так, но всё же я не соглáсен

2 (*on the other hand*) а; **~ what if he isn't at home?** а что éсли егó нет дóма?; **I'm ready ~ she's not** я готóв, а онá нет; **he gave a cake to her ~ not to me** он дал ей пирожóк, а не мне

3 *various*: **we have no choice ~ to obey** нам остаётся тóлько подчини́ться; **I don't doubt ~ that he'll come** я не сомневáюсь, что он придёт; **I'll have to refuse, not ~ what I sympathize with you** я вы́нужден откáзáться, хотя́ я и сочýвствую вам.

butcher *n* мясни́к; *fig* палáч; **the ~'s** (*shop*) мяснóй магази́н; **I'm going to the ~'s** (я) пойдý куплю́ мя́са.

butler *n* дворéцкий.

butt[1] *n*: **water ~** (большáя) бóчка для воды́.

butt[2] *n* (*end*) (тóлстый) конéц; (*of rifle*) приклáд ружья́; (*of cigarette*) окýрок.

butt[3] *n* (*target*) стрéльбищный вал; *pl* (**the ~s**) стрéльбище (*sing*); *CQ* (*of person*) посмéшище.

butt[4] *vt* (*of goat, etc.*) бодáть (за-)

butt in *vi* (*to conversation*) переби|вáть (-́ть); (*to meddle*) мешáть (по-)

butt into *vt* пре|рывáть (-рвáть).

butter *n* мáсло; *fig* **he looks as though ~ wouldn't melt in his mouth** он вы́глядит пáинькой/таки́м тихóней.

buttercup *n* лю́тик.

butterfly *n* бáбочка.

buttocks *npl* я́годицы.

button *n* **1** пýговица; **I must sew on a loose ~** у меня́ пýговица болтáется, нáдо её приши́ть/укрепи́ть; **I've lost a ~/a ~ has come off my jacket** я потеря́л пýговицу у пиджакá, у меня́ на пиджакé оторвалáсь пýговица

2 (*for bell, etc.*) кнóпка; **press/push the ~** нажми́ кнóпку.

button *vti vt, also* **~ up** за|стёгивать (-стегнýть); *fig* **he's very ~ed up** он зáмкнутый человéк, он застёгнут на все пýговицы

vi застёгиваться; **the blouse ~s at the back/front** блýзка застёгивается на спинé/спéреди (*adv*).

buttonhole *n* пéтля, петли́ца.

buttonhole *vt fig*: **he ~d me after the meeting** он пристáл ко мне с вопрóсами пóсле собрáния.

buxom *adj*: **a ~ girl** пышнотéлая деви́ца, *CQ* пы́шка.

buy *n* покýпка; **a good ~** удáчная покýпка.

buy *vt* **1** покупáть (купи́ть); **he bought her a ring/a ring for her** он купи́л ей кольцó; **we bought two chairs at £10 each** мы купи́ли два стýла по дéсять фýнтов за кáждый; **I bought myself a secondhand car for £100** я купи́л подéржанную маши́ну за сто фýнтов

2 (*bribe*) подкуп|áть (-и́ть); **he can't be bought** он неподкýпен; *CQ* **he'll not ~ that one!** егó на э́том не проведёшь!

buy in *vt*: **to ~ in coal for the winter** закуп|áть ýголь нá зиму (-и́ть)

buy off *vt*: **he bought off his business rival** он подкупи́л конкурéнта, он заплати́л конкурéнту отступны́е

buy out *vt*: **he bought out his partners** он вы́купил дóлю свои́х партнёров; **he bought himself out of military service** он откупи́лся от слýжбы в áрмии

buy up *vt* скуп|áть (-и́ть).

buyer *n* покупáтель (*m*).

buzz *n* (*noise of insects, conversation*) жужжáние; *Tel CQ* **I'll give you a ~ tomorrow** я вам зáвтра позвоню́; *fig CQ* **the ~ went round that...** ходи́л(и) слýх(и), что...

buzzer *n* (*siren*) гудóк; (*internal telephone*) зýммер.

by *adv* **1** (*past*) ми́мо; **they went ~ an hour ago** они́ проéхали ми́мо час назáд; **the bus went ~ without stopping** автóбус проéхал ми́мо, не останáвливаясь

2 *phrases*: **~ and ~** чéрез нéкоторое врéмя, спустя́ врéмя, со врéменем; **~ and large** вообщé; **~ now** ужé.

by *prep* **1** (*denoting agent, instrument*) *I case*; **the palace was built ~ Napoleon** дворéц был пострóен Наполеóном; **the dacha was built ~ him with his own hands** он пострóил дáчу сóбственными рукáми; **the wound was caused ~ a knife** рáна былá нанесенá ножóм; **what do you mean ~ that?** что ты хóчешь э́тим сказáть?

2 (*denoting authorship*) *usu G case*; **a play ~ Shakespeare** пьéса Шекспи́ра; **a picture ~ Repin** карти́на Рéпина; **who is the play ~?** чья э́то пьéса?

3 (*denoting manner, method, means*): **we came ~ car/train/bus** мы приéхали на маши́не/пóездом *or* на пóезде/на автóбусе (*nowadays* на + *P more usual*); **~ air mail** авиапóчтой; **to send ~ post** послáть по пóчте; **your letter arrived ~ return post** вáше письмó пришлó обрáтной пóчтой; **you should see the waterfall ~ moonlight** нáдо/вы должны́ посмотре́ть водопа́д при све́те луны́; **to read ~ electric light** чита́ть при электри́ческом све́те; **to pay ~ cheque** плати́ть че́ком; **to climb ~ easy stages** поднима́ться наве́рх небольши́ми перехо́дами; **two ~ two** по́ двое; **one ~ one** по одному́, оди́н за други́м, поодино́чке (*adv*); **~ accident** случа́йно (*adv*); **~ heart** наизу́сть (*adv*); **he took her ~ the hand** он взял её за́ руку; **he has a son ~ his first wife** у него́ есть сын от пе́рвой жены́; **I know him ~ sight but not ~ name** я его́ зна́ю в лицо́, но не по и́мени; **he goes ~ the name of Smith** он изве́стен под фами́лией Смит [NB *nominative case*]; **he earns his living ~ teaching** он зараба́тывает на жизнь препода-ва́нием

4 (*of time*: *not later than*) к + *D*; **I'll be there ~ five/~ supper time** я приду́ к пяти́ часа́м/к у́жину; **~ that time, ~ then** к тому́ вре́мени; **~ the time that...** к тому́ вре́мени, когда́...; **~ tomorrow** к за́втрашнему дню; **~ the end of the day** к концу́ дня; (*during*) **~ day/night** днём, но́чью

5 (*of place*): **to stand ~ the fire/window** стоя́ть у ками́на/у окна́; **a house ~ the sea** дом у мо́ря/на берегу́ мо́ря; **it's a good thing when you're reading a textbook to have a pencil ~ you** поле́зно чита́ть уче́бник с карандашо́м в рука́х; **he walked ~ her side/~** (*past*) **me** он шёл ря́дом с ней, он прошёл ми́мо меня́; **a path ~ the river** тропи́нка вдоль реки́; **we came ~ Berlin** мы е́хали че́рез Берли́н

6 (*according to*) по + *D*; **~ all accounts** по све́дениям; **judging ~ what he says** по его́ слова́м; **he's cautious ~ nature** он осторо́жен по нату́ре; **~ the terms of the agreement** по усло́виям догово́ра; **~ her request** по её про́сьбе; **he's a lawyer ~ profession** он по профе́ссии юри́ст; **he's English ~ birth** он ро́дом англича́нин; *CQ* **it's O.K. ~ me** (я) не возража́ю

7 (*of measurements, rate, Math*) на + *A*; **the carpet is 8 feet ~ 4** ковёр разме́ром во́семь фу́тов на четы́ре; **it's too short ~ a foot** э́то коро́че на оди́н фут; **he missed ~ inches** он чуть-чу́ть не попа́л; **he's older ~ two years** он ста́рше на два го́да; **to divide/multiply ~ 3** подели́ть/помно́жить на три; **to reduce ~ a quarter** уме́ньшить на че́тверть; **to buy ~ the kilo** покупа́ть килогра́ммами; **to pay ~ the month** плати́ть поме́сячно (*adv*).

bye-bye *interj CQ* пока́!; (*baby talk*: *as n*): **it's time to go to ~s** пора́ идти́ спать.

Byelorussian *n* белору́с, белору́ска; (*language*) белору́сский язы́к.

Byelorussian *adj* белору́сский.

bygone *adj* про́шлый; *as n*: **let ~s be ~s** что бы́ло, то прошло́.

by-law *n* пра́вило, постановле́ние.

bypass *n* объе́зд.

bypass *vt*: **we ~ed Cambridge** мы оста́вили Ке́мбридж в стороне́; **the road ~es Oxford** доро́га огиба́ет О́ксфорд.

by-product *n* побо́чный проду́кт.

by-road *n* просёлочная доро́га.

bystander *n* (*onlooker*) наблюда́тель (*m*), (*witness*) (случа́йный) свиде́тель (*m*); **~s** (*those present*) прису́тствующие.

byway *n* просёлочная доро́га; *fig* **the ~s of history** задво́рки исто́рии.

byword *n*: **he's a ~ for laziness** его́ лень вошла́ в поrightóрку.

C

C *n Mus* до.

cab *n* (*taxi*) такси́ (*indecl*); **~ of a lorry** каби́на грузовика́; *attr*: **~ rank** стоя́нка такси́.

cabbage *n* капу́ста; **sour ~** ква́шеная/ки́слая капу́ста; *attr*: **~ soup** щи (*pl*).

cabin *n* (*hut*) хи́жина; *Naut* каю́та; (*pilot's, or of lorry*) каби́на.

cabinet *n* (*for display*) витри́на; (*for radio, etc.*) ко́рпус; *Polit* кабине́т (мини́стров).

cable *n* (*rope*) кана́т; трос; *Elec, Tel* ка́бель (*m*); (*telegram*) телегра́мма.

cable railway *n* фуникулёр.

cache *n*: **a ~ of stores/arms** та́йный склад запа́сов/ору́жия (*collect*).

cackle *n* (*of hens*) куда́хтанье; (*of geese, and fig* = *laughter*) го́гот; *CQ* **cut the ~!** хва́тит болта́ть!

cad *n* негодя́й, подле́ц.

cadaver *n* (*US*) труп.

caddish *adj* по́длый, гну́сный; **that's a ~ trick** э́то по́длый трюк, э́то гну́сная проде́лка.

cadge *vti vt*: **he's always cadging cigarettes** он ве́чно кля́нчит сигаре́ты; **I ~d five roubles off him** я вы́просил у него́ пятёрку; **can I ~ a meal/a bed off you?** мо́жет, покo̒рмите меня́ обе́дом?, мо́жно у вас переночева́ть?; **I ~d a lift from her** я упроси́л её подвезти́ меня́

vi попроша́йничать (*impf*).

cadger *n* попроша́йка (*m and f*).

café *n* кафе́ (*indecl*).

cafeteria *n* кафете́рий.

cage *n* кле́тка; (*of lift*) каби́на.

cagey *adj CQ*: **he was pretty ~ with me** он не о́чень-то открове́нничал со мной.

cahoots *n sl*: **to be in ~ with smb** быть в сго́воре с кем-л.

cajole *vt* уговори́ть (*only in pf*); **she ~d her father into giving her a car** она́ уговори́ла отца́ купи́ть ей маши́ну.

cake *n* торт; (*small cake, bun*) пиро́жное; (*of soap, etc.*) кусо́к; *CQ* **his records sell like hot ~s** его́ пласти́нки раскупа́ют нарасхва́т (*adv*).

caked *adj*: **my shoes are ~ with mud** у меня́ на боти́нки нали́пли ко́мья гря́зи.

calamity *n* бе́дствие; *CQ* **I've had a ~ in the kitchen** у меня́ на ку́хне катастро́фа/*CQ* чепе́ (*indecl*).

calcium *n* ка́льций.

calculate *vti vt* вы|числя́ть (-́числить); подсчи́т|ывать, рассчи́т|ывать (*pfs* -а́ть); **to ~ a square root** вы́числить квадра́тный ко́рень; **to ~ the cost of a journey** подсчита́ть, ско́лько бу́дет сто́ить пое́здка; **he ~d it would take 10 hours to get there** он рассчита́л, что доро́га туда́ займёт де́сять часо́в; **his remark was ~d to annoy me** э́тим замеча́нием он хоте́л/наде́ялся позли́ть меня́

vi: **I ~ on arriving by supper time** я рассчи́тываю прие́хать к у́жину.

calculated *adj*: **a ~ insult** наме́ренное/умы́шленное оскорбле́ние.

calculating *adj* (*of people*: *pejor*) расчётливый.

calculating machine *n* счётная/вычисли́тельная маши́на.

calculation *n* подсчёт, расчёт; *Math* вычисле́ние; **on a rough ~** по приблизи́тельным подсчётам (*pl*); **by my ~(s) the river shouldn't be far away** по мои́м расчётам река́ (должна́ быть) недалеко́; **that didn't enter into my ~s** э́то не входи́ло в мои́ расчёты; **to be out in one's ~s** ошиби́ться в вычисле́ниях/в расчётах.

calculus *n*: **differential ~** дифференциа́льное исчисле́ние.

calendar *n* календа́рь (*m*).

calf[1] *n* телёнок.

calf[2] *n Anat* икра́ ноги́.

calibre *n Tech* кали́бр, *also fig*; **there are few men of his ~** таки́х люде́й, как он, немно́го.

call *n* **1** (*cry*) крик; *Theat* вы́зов; **~s for help** кри́ки о по́мощи; **the ~ of a thrush** крик дрозда́; **within ~** в преде́лах слы́шимости; **give me a ~ at 7** разбуди́ меня́ в семь часо́в; **she took five (curtain) ~s** её вызыва́ли пять раз; *Cards* **whose ~?** кому́ объявля́ть (масть)?

2 *Tel* звоно́к; **I'll wait your ~** я бу́ду ждать ва́шего звонка́; **I must put through a ~ to him** я до́лжен позвони́ть ему́; (*operator speaking*) **there's a ~ for you from Paris—will you take it?** вас вызыва́ет Пари́ж—бу́дете говори́ть?; (*telephone rings in house or office*) **I'll take the ~** я возьму́ тру́бку

3 (*visit*) визи́т, посеще́ние; **to pay a ~ on smb** навеща́ть кого́-л, *CQ* заходи́ть к кому́-л; **the ambassador returned the Minister's ~** посо́л нанёс отве́тный визи́т мини́стру; **the steamer made a ~ at Yalta** парохо́д сде́лал захо́д в Я́лту; **the doctor has several ~s to make** у врача́ не́сколько вы́зовов

4 (*appeal*) призы́в; *Poet or iron* зов; **a ~ to arms** призы́в к ору́жию; **the ~ of the sea** зов мо́ря

5 (*need*, *demand*): **I have many ~s on my time** у меня́ совсе́м нет свобо́дного вре́мени; **you had no ~ to say that** у тебя́ не́ было причи́ны так говори́ть; *Comm* **there's no ~ for such goods nowadays** на таки́е това́ры тепе́рь нет спро́са.

call *vti vt* **1** (*summon*: *from close to*) звать (по-), (*from further away*) оклик|а́ть (-́нуть); вы|зыва́ть (-́звать); **your mother is ~ing you** тебя́ ма́ма зовёт; **~ your sister to the phone** позови́ сестру́ к телефо́ну; **~ a taxi/a doctor/the ambulance** вы́зови такси́/врача́/ско́рую по́мощь; (*wake*) **~ me at 7** (раз)буди́ меня́ в семь часо́в (утра́)

2 *Tel* звони́ть (по-); **he ~ed me (up) from Paris** он позвони́л мне из Пари́жа

3 (*name*) на|зыва́ть + *A of person and I of name* (-зва́ть), (*less formally*) звать + *A and I or nom* (*only in impf*); (*of things*) **to be ~ed** называ́ться (*only in impf*); **they ~ed the child Ivan after his uncle** ребёнка назва́ли Ива́ном в честь дя́ди; **she is ~ed Irina** её зову́т Ири́на; **what do they ~ him at home?** как его́ зову́т до́ма?; *iron* **he ~s himself an engineer** он называ́ет себя́ инжене́ром; **we stopped at a town ~ed Omsk** мы останови́лись в го́роде О́мске; **what is this ~ed in Russian?** как э́то (называ́ется) по-ру́сски?; **I ~ that an insult** я счита́ю э́то оскорбле́нием; (*in order to insult*) **he ~ed me a liar** он обозва́л меня́ лгуно́м

4 *various*: **to ~ a meeting** со|зыва́ть собра́ние (-зва́ть); **to ~ a meeting to order** при|зыва́ть собра́ние к поря́дку (-зва́ть); **to ~ a strike** объяв|ля́ть забасто́вку (-и́ть); **I know her name, but I can't ~ it to mind** я зна́ю, как её зову́т, но сейча́с ника́к не могу́ вспо́мнить; **it ~ed to mind my childhood** э́то напо́мнило мне (моё) де́тство; (*on parcel*) **"to be ~ed for"** «до востре́бования»; *CQ* **let's ~ it a day** пора́ конча́ть, на сего́дня хва́тит; *Cards* **he ~ed three hearts** он объяви́л три че́рвы

vi **1** (*cry out*) кри|ча́ть (*semel* -́кнуть); **I think I hear smb ~ing** мне ка́жется, кто́-то кричи́т

2 *Tel*: **who's ~ing?** кто говори́т?; **I'll ~ tomorrow** я позвоню́ за́втра

3 (*visit*): (*formal*) **the French ambassador ~ed yesterday** вчера́ францу́зский посо́л нанёс нам визи́т; (*informally*) **he was out when I ~ed** когда́ я зашёл к нему́, его́ не́ было до́ма; **a man has ~ed to read the gas meter** приходи́ли снять показа́ние с га́зового счётчика; **the steamer ~s here twice a week** парохо́д захо́дит сюда́ два ра́за в неде́лю

call back *vti vt*: **she ~ed me back** она́ позвала́ меня́ обра́тно

vi: **I'll ~ back tomorrow** я зайду́/зае́ду за́втра ещё раз; *Tel* **I'll ~ back later** я (вам) по́зже позвоню́

call for *vi*: **to ~ for help** звать на по́мощь (по-́); **what time shall I ~ for you?** когда́ мне за тобо́й зайти́/зае́хать?; **that remark was not ~ed for** не на́до бы́ло э́то говори́ть; **this will ~ for plenty of tact** э́то тре́бует большо́го та́кта; **this ~s for a drink/a celebration** за э́то на́до вы́пить, *CQ* э́то на́до обмы́ть

call in *vt*: **the police were ~ed in** вы́звали поли́цию; **they are ~ing in old banknotes**

ста́рые банкно́ты на́до возвраща́ть в банк

call off *vt*: **~ off your dog!** отзови́ свою́ соба́ку!; **to ~ off a deal** (*before completion*) отка́з|ываться от сде́лки, (*when made*) расторг|а́ть контра́кт (-а́ться, -нуть); **the strike was ~ed off** забасто́вка была́ отменена́/(*if already begun*) прекращена́; **the search was ~ed off** по́иски (*pl*) бы́ли прекращены́

call on *vi*: **the chairman ~ed on me to speak** председа́тель предоста́вил мне сло́во; **the government ~ed on its citizens to save electricity** прави́тельство призва́ло гра́ждан эконо́мить электроэне́ргию

call out *vti vt*: **to ~ out instructions** выкри́кивать кома́нды; **he ~ed out something but I didn't hear** он что́-то прокрича́л, но я не расслы́шал; **to ~ out the fire brigade** вы́звать пожа́рную кома́нду

vi: **he ~ed out to us** он окли́кнул нас; **if you want anything, just ~ out** кри́кни, е́сли тебе́ что́-нибудь пона́добится

call together *vt* со|зыва́ть (-зва́ть)

call up *vt Mil*: **to ~ smb up** призва́ть кого́-л на вое́нную слу́жбу; *Tel* **I'll ~ you up tomorrow** я вам за́втра позвоню́.

callbox *n Tel* телефо́н-автома́т; (*SU*: *in post office*, *for long-distance calls*) каби́на; **I'm speaking from a ~** я звоню́ из автома́та.

caller *n* (*visitor*) посети́тель (*m*); *Tel* (*operator speaking*): **can you hear me, ~?** абоне́нт, вы меня́ слы́шите?

calling *n* (*vocation*) призва́ние; профе́ссия.

callous *adj fig* безду́шный, бесчу́вственный.

callow *adj*: **a ~ youth** зелёный юне́ц.

call-up *n*: **my son has had his ~** моего́ сы́на призва́ли в а́рмию.

callus *n* мозо́ль.

calm *n* зати́шье; *Naut* **a dead ~** мёртвый штиль (*m*).

calm *adj* споко́йный; **he is always ~** он всегда́ споко́ен; **a ~ night** ти́хая ночь; **~ weather** ти́хая/безве́тренная пого́да; **keep ~!** не волну́йтесь!

calm *vti vt*: **to ~ smb (down)** успок|а́ивать кого́-л (-о́ить)

vi: **to ~ down** (*of person*, *wind*, *sea*) успока́иваться.

calorie *n* кало́рия.

calumny *n* клевета́.

camber *n Aut* попере́чный укло́н доро́ги.

camel *n* верблю́д; *attr*: **~ hair** верблю́жья шерсть.

cameo *n* каме́я.

camera *n* **1** фотоаппара́т; *Cine* киноаппара́т

2 *Law*: **in ~** при закры́тых дверя́х.

camomile tea *n* насто́й рома́шки.

camouflage *n* камуфля́ж, маскиро́вка.

camouflage *vt Mil and fig* маскирова́ть (за-).

camp *n* ла́герь (*m*), *also fig*; **concentration ~** концентрацио́нный ла́герь; *Polit* **the opposition ~** ла́герь оппози́ции.

camp *vi*: **to ~ out, to go ~ing** идти́ в похо́д с ночёвкой; **to go for a ~ing holiday** проводи́ть о́тпуск в тури́стском похо́де; **we ~ed by a river** мы поста́вили пала́тки у реки́; *Mil* распо|лага́ться ла́герем (-ложи́ться); (*notice*) **Camping** ке́мпинг.

campaign *n* кампа́ния; **election ~** предвы́борная кампа́ния.

campaign *vi Mil* уча́ствовать в кампа́нии (*impf*); *Polit* **to ~ for/against smb/smth** агити́ровать за кого́-л/за что-л/про́тив кого́-л/про́тив чего́-л (*impf*).

campbed *n* похо́дная/(*folding*) складна́я крова́ть.

campfire *n* костёр.

camphor *n* камфара́.

campstool *n* складно́й стул.

campus *n* (*US*) *Univ* университе́тский городо́к.

can[1] *v modal aux*, *past and conditional* **could** **1** (*be able to*) мочь (с-) [**NB** *Russian inf very rare*]; **I can't swim today** (*am too busy*) сего́дня я не смогу́ пойти́ купа́ться; **~ you come tomorrow?** ты мо́жешь за́втра прийти́?; **he said he couldn't come today** он сказа́л, что не мо́жет сего́дня прийти́; **I'll help if I ~** я помогу́ вам, е́сли смогу́; **I'd help if I could** я помо́г бы, е́сли бы мог; **I would have helped you if I could** я бы помо́г вам, е́сли бы смог; **he could do it if he wanted to** он мог бы э́то сде́лать, е́сли бы захоте́л; **I could have come earlier if you'd told me** я мог бы ра́ньше прийти́, е́сли бы вы мне сказа́ли; **be as quick as you ~** дава́й быстре́е; **I'll mend the trousers as best I ~** я починю́ брю́ки, как суме́ю; **I've mended the trousers as best I could** я почини́л брю́ки, как мог

2 (*indicating possibility*, *in negative—improbability*); **where ~ it be?** где э́то мо́жет быть?; **where could it be?** куда́ э́то могло́ де́ться?; **it could be in the cupboard** э́то мо́жет быть в шкафу́; **it could have been thrown out** мо́жет быть, э́то вы́бросили; **I asked when it could be ready** я спроси́л, когда́ э́то бу́дет гото́во; **it can't/could be true** не мо́жет быть, мо́жет э́то и так; **I knew it couldn't be true** я знал, что э́того не могло́ быть; **he could have changed his mind** он мог переду́мать; **who ~ tell?** кто мо́жет знать?; **how could one have told?** кто мог знать?; **one can't swim today** (*because too rough*) сего́дня нельзя́ пла́вать; **it must be done as soon as ~ be** э́то на́до бу́дет сде́лать как мо́жно скоре́е; **it was done as soon as could be** э́то бы́ло сде́лано сра́зу же/неме́дленно; (*expressing disbelief*): **you can't mean that!** да что́ ты говори́шь?, не мо́жет быть!, неуже́ли?; **~ he really have meant it?** ду́маешь, он мог тако́е сказа́ть?; (*expressing reproach*) **how ~ you say such things?** как ты мо́жешь тако́е говори́ть?

3 (*know how to*) уме́ть (*usu impf*); **he ~ swim** он уме́ет пла́вать; **she could read when she was 4** в четы́ре го́да она́ уже́ уме́ла чита́ть; **she couldn't speak any Russian** она́ совсе́м не говори́ла по-ру́сски

4 (*with verbs of perception usu not translated*): ~ **you see her?** ты ви́дишь её?; **I ~ hear smb whistling** я слы́шу, как кто́-то свисти́т

5 (*in polite requests*): ~/**could you open the door?** откро́й, пожа́луйста, дверь; ~/**could I speak to Ivan?** мо́жно мне поговори́ть с Ива́ном?; ~ **I have the butter please?** переда́й мне, пожа́луйста, ма́сло; **could you tell me the right time?** вы мне не ска́жете, кото́рый час?

6 (*indicating permission*): **Mum says we can't swim today** ма́ма не разреша́ет нам сего́дня купа́ться; **you ~ go now** тепе́рь мо́жешь идти́; **one/you can't smoke here** здесь нельзя́ кури́ть

7 (*in generalizations*): **she ~ be very rude if she wants to** она́ мо́жет быть о́чень гру́бой; **it ~ be very cold here in May** здесь быва́ет о́чень хо́лодно в ма́е

8 (*indicating suggestion*): **you could try phoning** мо́жно попро́бовать позвони́ть; **you could have told me sooner** ты мог бы мне ра́ньше сказа́ть

9 (*could = would like to*): **I could smack your face** *CQ* наби́л бы я тебе́ мо́рду; **I could have smacked his face** *CQ* я чуть не съе́здил/не дал ему́ по физионо́мии.

can[2] *n* (*tin*) ба́нка, жестя́нка; (*for petrol*) кани́стра; (*for milk*) бидо́н.

can[2] *vt* (*food*) консерви́ровать (за-).

Canadian *n* кана́дец, кана́дка.

Canadian *adj* кана́дский.

canal *n* кана́л.

canary *n* канаре́йка.

cancel *vti vt* (*an order, leave*) отмен|я́ть (-и́ть); (*a stamp*) пога|ша́ть (-си́ть); *Math* (*in fractions, equations*) сокра|ща́ть (-ти́ть); **I've ~led my booking** я отмени́л зака́з; **my leave has been ~led** мне перенесли́ о́тпуск; (*dictating to secretary*) ~ **that paragraph** зачеркни́ э́тот абза́ц; **to ~ a debt** аннули́ровать долг (*impf and pf*); **to ~ a subscription** аннули́ровать подпи́ску (*impf and pf*); *Sport* **to ~ a match** отмени́ть матч; *fig* **your second argument ~s out your first** то, что вы сейча́с говори́те, сво́дит на нет то, что вы говори́ли ра́ньше

vi Math сокраща́ться.

cancellation *n* (*of order, etc.*) отме́на; (*of stamp*) погаше́ние; *Math* сокраще́ние; **they'll let me know if there are any ~s on the flight** мне сообща́т, е́сли кто́-нибудь отка́жется лете́ть.

cancer *n Med* рак.

cancerous *adj Med* ра́ковый.

candid *adj* открове́нный; **to be quite ~** открове́нно говоря́.

candidate *n* кандида́т; ~ **for a post** кандида́т на пост; (*in exam*) **~s** экзамену́ющиеся.

candle *n* свеча́; **to light/blow out a ~** заже́чь/погаси́ть свечу́; *fig*: **to burn the ~ at both ends** прожига́ть жизнь; **he can't hold a ~ to her** он ей в подмётки не годи́тся.

candlelight *n*: **by ~** при све́те свечи́.

candlestick *n* подсве́чник.

candy *n* конфе́та.

cane *n* (*for walking*) трость; (*for punishment*) па́лка; *Bot* тростни́к; **sugar ~** са́харный тростни́к; *attr*: ~ **furniture** плетёная ме́бель.

canine *adj* соба́чий; *fig* ~ **tooth** клык.

cannabis *n* марихуа́на.

canned *adj* (*of food*) консерви́рованный; *CQ*: **I hate ~ music in restaurants** терпе́ть не могу́, когда́ в рестора́нах кру́тят магнитофо́нные за́писи; (*drunk*) **he's ~** он пьян.

cannon *n* пу́шка; *collect* (артиллери́йские) ору́дия (*pl*).

canny *adj* осмотри́тельный.

canoe *vi* плыть на байда́рке/на каноэ́ (*indecl*) (*det impf*).

can opener *n* консе́рвный нож/ключ.

cant *n* пусты́е фра́зы (*pl*).

cantankerous *adj* сварли́вый.

canteen *n* столо́вая; (*for snacks, etc.*) буфе́т.

canter *vi* (*of rider*) е́хать/(*of horse*) идти́ ке́нтером/лёгким гало́пом.

canvas *n* (*for sails*) паруси́на; (*artist's*) холст; (*a painting on canvas*) полотно́; (*for cross-stitch*) канва́; (*for tarpaulins*) брезе́нт.

canvass *vti vt*: **to ~ opinion** выявля́ть обще́ственное мне́ние (*usu impf*)

vi: **to ~ for smb** *approx* агити́ровать за кого́-л/за кандида́та (*impf*); **to ~ for votes** вести́ предвы́борную кампа́нию (*usu impf*); *Comm* **to ~ for orders** добива́ться зака́зов (*only in impf*).

cap *n* **1** (*man's*) ке́пка; (*with ear flaps*) ша́пка; (*lady's*) **woollen/knitted ~** шерстяна́я/вя́заная ша́почка; *Mil* (*officer's hard cap*) фура́жка; (*private's soft cap*) пило́тка; *fig* **snow ~** сне́жная ша́пка

2 (*of bottle*) кры́шка; ~ **of petrol tank** кры́шка бензоба́ка; **hub ~** колпа́к колеса́.

cap *vt fig*: **they ~ped each other's jokes** они́ перееки́дывались шу́тками; **he can ~ any story** он зна́ет исто́рии и похле́ще.

capable *adj* спосо́бный; **he is a very ~ boy** он о́чень спосо́бный ма́льчик; **he is ~ of anything/of working day and night** он спосо́бен на всё/рабо́тать день и ночь; (*of things, situations*) **the plan is ~ of improvement** э́тот план мо́жно улу́чшить.

capacious *adj* (*roomy*) вмести́тельный; (*of container*) объёмистый.

capacity *n* **1** (*ability*) спосо́бность (*often pl*); **he has a marked ~ for mathematics** у него́ больши́е спосо́бности к матема́тике (*sing*); **she has a great ~ for making friends** у неё осо́бый дар везде́ заводи́ть друзе́й; **the book is within the ~ of any schoolboy** э́та кни́га поня́тна/досту́пна ка́ждому шко́льнику

2 (*volume*) ёмкость, объём; (*roominess*) вмести́мость; **a can with a ~ of 5 litres** бидо́н ёмкостью (в) пять ли́тров; **cylinder ~** рабо́чий объём цили́ндров; **load ~** грузоподъёмность; **the hall has a seating ~ of 500**

зал вмещáет пятьсóт человéк, в зáле пятьсóт мест; **the hall was filled to ~** в зáле нé было свобóдных мест; **the factory is working to ~** завóд рабóтает на пóлную мóщность; *attr*: **a ~ audience** пóлный сбор, аншлáг

3 (*position*): **in my ~ as chairman, I...** я, как председáтель...

cape[1] *n Geog* мыс.

cape[2] *n* (*cloak*) плащ, накúдка; (*short*) пелерúна; **a ~ with a hood** плащ с капюшóном.

capital *n* **1** (*city*) столúца

2 *Fin* капитáл; **the company has a ~ of £ 100,000** компáния располагáет капитáлом в сто ты́сяч фýнтов

3: a ~ (letter) большáя/заглáвная бýква; **write in block ~s** напишúте заглáвными бýквами.

capital *adj CQ* отлúчный.

capitalism *n* капиталúзм.

capitalize *vti vt Fin* превра|щáть в капитáл (-тúть)

vi fig: **to ~ on the errors of a rival firm** воспóльзоваться ошúбками конкурúрующей фúрмы.

capitulate *vi* сда|вáться (´-ться), *also fig*.

caprice *n* капрúз.

capricious *adj* капрúзный, с причýдами.

capsize *vti* (*of boats*) опрокú|дывать(ся) (-нуть(ся)).

capsule *n Bot* оболóчка; (*of astronauts*) кáпсула, *also Med*.

captain *n Mil, Naut, Sport* капитáн.

captain *vt*: *Naut* **to ~ a ship** быть капитáном кораблá; *Sport* **to ~ a team** возглав|лáть комáнду (´-ить), быть капитáном комáнды.

caption *n* (*of article, chapter*) заголóвок; *Cine* титр; (*to cartoon*) нáдпись.

captious *adj* придúрчивый.

captivate *vt* очарóв|ывать (-áть); плен|я́ть (-úть); **to be ~d by** увле|кáться + *I* (´-чься), плен|я́ться + *I* (-úться).

captivating *adj* очаровáтельный, пленúтельный.

captive *n* плéнный; *fig* плéнник; *attr*: **a ~ lion** пóйманный лев; **a ~ audience** зрúтели/слýшатели поневóле.

captivity *n* (*of people*) плен; (*of animals*) невóля; **to be in ~** быть в пленý; **to keep wild animals in ~** держáть дúких живóтных в невóле.

capture *n* (*act*) захвáт; (*of thieves, etc.*) пóимка; **the ~ of the city/the murderer** захвáт гóрода, пóимка убúйцы.

capture *vt* поймáть (*pf*), захвáт|ывать (-úть); **to ~ a criminal/a giraffe** поймáть престýпника/жирáфа; **to ~ a city/prisoners** захватúть гóрод/плéнных; *fig*: **to ~ the imagination** плен|я́ть воображéние (-úть); **to ~ smb's attention** завладéть чьим-л внимáнием; **the artist has ~d the mood of an autumn day** худóжник сумéл передáть настроéние осéннего дня.

car *n* **1** автомобúль (*m*), машúна; **racing/saloon/estate ~** гóночный автомобúль, автомобúль с закры́тым кýзовом, универсáл; **sports/open ~** спортúвная/откры́тая машúна; **to start a ~** заводúть машúну; **we went by ~** мы поéхали на машúне

2 *Rail, etc.* вагóн; **sleeping/dining ~** спáльный вагóн, вагóн-ресторáн; **tram ~** вагóн трамвáя.

carafe *n* графúн.

caravan *n* (*of camels, nomads*) каравáн; (*gipsies'*) фургóн; (*for holidays*) жилóй автоприцéп.

caraway *n*, *also* **caraway seeds** тмин (*plant and collect = seeds*).

carbohydrate *n* углевóд.

carbolic *adj*: **~ acid** карбóловая кислотá.

carbon *n Chem* углерóд; *Elec* ýгольный электрóд; *attr*: **~ dioxide** углекислотá; **~ monoxide** óкись углерóда, угáрный газ.

carbon copy *n* кóпия (чéрез копúрку); **I want two carbon copies** мне нáдо два экземплáра.

carbon paper *n* копировáльная бумáга, *CQ* копúрка.

carburettor *n* карбюрáтор.

carcass *n* тýша.

card *n* **1: he sent me a ~ from Yalta** он прислáл мне откры́тку из Я́лты; **Christmas/birthday ~** рождéственская/поздравúтельная откры́тка; **visiting/index/library/ration ~** визúтная/каталóжная/абонемéнтная (*user's*)/продовóльственная кáрточка; **invitation/membership ~** пригласúтельный/члéнский билéт; **press ~** журналúстское удостоверéние; **admission ~** (*permit*) прóпуск

2 *Cards* кáрта; **court ~** фигýра (в кáртах); **to play ~s/a high ~** игрáть в кáрты, ходúть со стáршей кáрты; **to lose/win money at ~s** проигрáть/вы́играть в кáрты; *fig*: **to lay one's ~s on the table** раскры́ть кáрты; **that's our strongest/trump ~** э́то наш глáвный кóзырь; **I have a ~ up my sleeve** у меня́ есть кóзырь про запáс; **it's quite on the ~s that...** весьмá верóятно, что...; *CQ* **he's quite a ~** ну он и тúп; *attr*: **~ game/table/trick** кáрточная игрá, кáрточный *or* лóмберный стол, кáрточный фóкус.

cardboard *n* картóн; *attr* картóнный.

cardiac *adj* сердéчный.

cardigan *n* вя́заная кóфта/кóфточка, кардигáн.

cardinal *n* кардинáл.

cardinal *adj* **1** (*important*) основнóй, глáвный; **~ points** (*of compass*) глáвные рýмбы

2: ~ numbers колúчественные числúтельные.

card index *n* картотéка.

card sharper *n* шýлер.

care *n* **1** (*supervision*) попечéние, *also Law*; (*for short periods*) присмóтр за + *I*; (*tending*) ухóд за + *I*; **my nephew has been left in my ~** племя́нник остáлся на моём попечéнии; **the children were left in their granny's ~** дéти бы́ли под присмóтром бáбушки; **she took ~ of the children when their mother died** онá взялá детéй к себé, когдá умерлá их мать;

she is under the doctor's ~ онá под наблю-дéнием врачá; **~ for the sick** ухóд за больны́ми; **hothouse plants need constant ~** теплúчные растéния трéбуют постоя́нного ухóда; (*on letters*) **Mr A ~ of** (*abbr* **c/o**) **Mr B** господúну Б. для господúна А.; **the library is in Ivan's ~** Ивáн завéдует библиотéкой; **he took ~ of the valuables/the luggage** цéнные вéщи хранúлись у негó, он взял на себя́ багáж; **I'll take ~ of that** об э́том я позабóчусь, я э́то возьмý на себя́; **that will take ~ of itself** э́то самó собóй улáдится

2 (*attention*) внимáние; (*caution*) осторóжность; **listen with ~** слýшай внимáтельно; **you should take more ~ over your work** ты дóлжен рабóтать бóлее внимáтельно; **take ~!** осторóжно!, берегúсь!; (*on parcel*) **"with ~"** «осторóжно»; **to be handled with ~** обращáться с осторóжностью; **take ~ not to waken the baby** тúше,/смотрú, не разбудú ребёнка

3 (*anxiety*) забóта; **he hasn't a ~ in the world** у негó никакúх забóт; **the ~s of office** должностны́е забóты.

care *vi* **1** (*mind*): **who ~s?** когó э́то волнýет?; **as if I ~d** как бýдто меня́ э́то волнýет; **I couldn't ~ less** меня́ э́то ничýть не волнýет, *CQ* мне э́то до лáмпочки; **for all I ~** что касáется меня́, что до меня́; **I don't ~ either way** мне всё равнó; **I don't ~ what people may say** мне всё равнó, что лю́ди скáжут; **I don't ~ how it's done** меня́ не интересýет, как э́то дéлается

2 (*be anxious*) **~ about** забóтиться о + *P* (по-); волновáться о + *P* (*impf*); **he doesn't seem to ~ about having failed his exam** егó, кáжется, нискóлько не волнýет то, что он завалúл экзáмен; **he doesn't ~ about his work any more** рабóта стáла емý безразлúчна

3 (*like*): **would you ~ to go for a walk?** не хóчешь пойтú погуля́ть?/прогуля́ться?; **I don't ~ much for dancing** я не óчень люблю́ тáнцы; **I don't ~ for that painting/the idea** э́та картúна/идéя мне не нрáвится

4 (*look after*): **she's caring for the children while their parents are away** в отсýтствие родúтелей онá присмáтривает за детьмú; **she is caring for her sick uncle at home** онá ухáживает за больны́м дя́дей дóма (*impf*).

career *n* **1** карьéра; (*profession*) профéссия; **to make a ~ for oneself** сдéлать себé карьéру; *attr*: **a ~ diplomat** профессионáльный дипломáт

2 (*of movement*): **in full ~** во весь опóр.

career *vi* мчáться, нестúсь (*usu impfs*).

carefree *adj* беззабóтный, беспéчный.

careful *adj* **1** *attr* аккурáтный, тщáтельный, внимáтельный; **a ~ worker/piece of work** аккурáтный рабóтник, тщáтельно вы́полненная рабóта; **a ~ medical examination** тщáтельный медицúнский осмóтр; **after a ~ examination of the engine/manuscript** при внимáтельном осмóтре двúгателя/просмóтре рýкописи; **a ~ housewife** эконóмная хозя́йка; **give ~ attention to this point** отнесúтесь к э́тому пýнкту с осóбым внимáнием

2 *predic*: **to be ~ about one's health** забóтиться о своём здорóвье; **he's ~ with his money** он не лю́бит сорúть деньгáми; **one can't be too ~** осторóжность не помешáет; **be ~ what you say to him** смотрú, не скажú емý ничегó лúшнего; **I was ~ not to offend him** я старáлся не обúдеть егó.

careless *adj*: **~ work** небрéжная/неаккурáтная рабóта; **a ~ mistake** ошúбка по небрéжности; **~ driving** неосторóжная ездá; **I've lost my key.—That was very ~ of you!** я потеря́л ключ.—Какóй ты растя́па!

caress *vt* ласкáть (*impf*).

caretaker *n* стóрож; **she's a ~** онá стóрож.

careworn *adj* измýченный забóтами.

car-ferry *n* автомобúльный парóм.

cargo *n* груз; *attr*: **~ boat** грузовóе/товáрное сýдно.

caricature *n* карикатýра; (*cartoon*) шарж.

carnation *n* гвоздúка.

carp[1] *n* (*fish*) карп.

carp[2] *vi*: **to ~ at** придирáться к + *D* (*usu impf*).

carpenter *n* плóтник.

carpet *n* ковёр; *attr*: **~ slippers** домáшние тýфли; **~ sweeper** щётка для ковpá.

carport *n* навéс для машúны.

carriage *n* **1** (*horse-drawn*) экипáж; карéта; *Rail* вагóн; (*of typewriter, etc.*) карéтка; (*of gun*) лафéт

2 (*bearing*) осáнка

3 (*transport*: *from somewhere to somewhere*) перевóзка, транспортирóвка; (*only of delivery*) достáвка; **~ paid/free/forward** достáвка оплáчена, бесплáтная достáвка, налóженным платежóм.

carrier *n* (*porter*) носúльщик; (*transport firm*; *often pl*) (**~s**) трáнспортное агéнтство (*sing*); (*on motorcycle*) багáжник; *Med* бациллоносúтель (*m*).

carrier-bag *n* сýмка, *CQ* авóська.

carrion *n* пáдаль.

carrot *n* (*single*) *CQ* моркóвка; *pl* (**~s**) моркóвь (*collect*).

carry *vti vt* **1** (*of a person*) носúть (*indet impf*, по-), нестú (*det impf*, по-) *and compounds*; **I normally ~ my money in a wallet** я обы́чно ношý дéньги в кошелькé; **I'm very tired after ~ing the child around for half the day** я óчень устáл, полдня́ поносúв ребёнка на рукáх; **as I was ~ing the shopping home** когдá я нёс покýпки домóй; **you ~ the case now** тепéрь ты понесú чемодáн; **to ~ smth in one's hands/arms/on one's shoulder/back** нестú что-л в рукáх/на рукáх/на плечé/на спинé; **she is ~ing a child** (*pregnant*) онá берéменна; **he carries himself well** у негó хорóшая осáнка; **he ran off as fast as his legs would ~ him** он удирáл со всех ног

2 (*in vehicle, train, ship*) возúть (*indet impf*, по-), везтú (*det impf*, по-) *and compounds*; **our products are carried by rail from the fac-**

tory to Moscow продýкция (*collect*) нáшего завóда перевóзится в Москвý по желéзной дорóге

3 *other direct uses*: **these beams can ~ heavy weights** эти бáлки мóгут вы́держать большýю нагрýзку (*sing*); **the logs are carried downstream by the current** лес сплавляют по рекé вниз по течéнию; **the oil is carried in pipes** нефть подаётся по трýбам; **wires ~ electricity** электрúчество передаётся по проводáм; **this road carries a lot of traffic** на этой дорóге большóе движéние

4 *fig uses*: **the papers carried the news that...** газéты поместúли сообщéние о том, что...; **this newspaper carries a lot of advertisement** в этой газéте печáтается мнóго объявлéний (*pl*); **they ~ their liquor well** онú умéют пить, не пьянéя; **to ~ an election** победúть на вы́борах; **to ~ one's point** добúться своегó (*only in pf*); **his words ~ conviction/weight** егó словá убедúтельны/имéют вес; **the bill was carried** законопроéкт был прúнят; **they always ~ things to extremes** онú всегдá впадáют в крáйности; **how can he ~ all that in his head?** как он мóжет держáть всё это в головé?; *Comm* **we don't ~ much stock** мы не дéржим большúх запáсов (*pl*); *Fin* **to ~ interest** при|носúть процéнты (-нестú); *Math*: **to ~ one** (держáть) одúн в умé; **to ~ 7 forward to the next column** пере|носúть семь в слéдующий столбéц (-нестú); *Mil* **to ~ the war into the enemy's country** перенестú воéнные дéйствия на территóрию протúвника

vi: **peaches do not ~ well** пéрсики плóхо перенóсят перевóзку; (*of sound*): **his voice carries well** егó гóлос хорошó слы́шен; **sound carries well in this hall** в этом зáле хорóшая акýстика

carry away *vt* (*by person*: *from close at hand*) от|носúть, (*to some distance*) у|носúть (*pfs* -нестú); **the mast was carried away by the gale** вéтром снеслó (*impers*) мáчту; *fig* **he was carried away by/with their enthusiasm** емý передалóсь их востóрженное настроéние

carry back *vt* (*take*) отнестú/отвезтú обрáтно, (*bring*) принестú/привезтú обрáтно; *fig* **it carried me back to my childhood** это перенеслó меня в дéтство

carry down *vt*: **they carried the trunk down from the attic** сундýк с чердакá снеслú вниз

carry off *vt* (*in one's arms, etc.*) уносúть, (*in car, etc.*) увозúть; **an eagle carried off a lamb** орёл унёс ягнёнка; **my brother has carried the children off to the dacha** мой брат увёз детéй на дáчу; *fig*: **he carried off all the prizes** он взял все призы́; **he carried it off splendidly** он великолéпно с этим спрáвился

carry on *vti vt*: **to ~ on the work** продолжáть рабóту (*impf*); **to ~ on a conversation/negotiations with smb** вестú разговóр *or* бесéду/переговóры с кем-л; **to ~ on a business** вестú торгóвлю; **to ~ on a tradition/custom** продолжáть *or* хранúть традúцию, соблюдáть обы́чай (*only in impf*)

vi: **~ on!** продолжáй!, продóлжим!, давáй(те)!; **we'll ~ on somehow** (мы) перебьёмся; **he carries on so about the noise** он вéчно жáлуется на шум; **his wife is ~ing on with an officer** у егó жены́ ромáн с какúм-то офицéром; **what a way to ~ on!** кто же так себя ведёт!

carry out *vt*: **to ~ out a threat/one's intentions** исполн|ять угрóзу (ʹ-ить), осуществ|лять свои намéрения (-úть); **to ~ out a promise/instructions** вы́полнить *or* испóлнить обещáние/прикáзы; **to ~ out a sentence** при|водúть приговóр в исполнéние (-вестú); **to ~ out tests** про|водúть испытáния (-вестú).

carrycot *n*: **the baby travelled in the plane in a ~** в самолёте ребёнка везлú (*approx*) в корзúне.

carry-on *n CQ* переполóх, суматóха; **there was a great ~ over the packing** мы собирáлись в дорóгу в такóй суматóхе.

cart *n* телéга.

cart-horse *n* ломовáя лóшадь.

cartilage *n* хрящ.

cartload *n*: **a ~ of wood/hay** воз дров/сéна.

carton *n* (*of cardboard*) картóнная корóбка, картóнка; (*for milk, juice, etc.*) пакéт.

cartoon *n* (*humorous*) шарж; (*satirical*) карикатýра; (*film*) мультфúльм.

cartridge *n* патрóн.

cart-track *n* гужевáя/просёлочная дорóга.

carve *vti*: **to ~ (smth) in** *or* **out of wood/ivory** вы|резáть (что-л) из дéрева/из слонóвой кóсти (ʹ-резать); **to ~ smth in stone** вы|секáть что-л из кáмня (ʹ-сечь); **to ~ one's initials on a tree** вы́резать инициáлы на дéреве; **to ~ the meat** (*all of it*)/**smb a slice of meat** нарез|áть мя́со, отрез|áть комý-л (кусóк) мя́са (*pfs* ʹ-ать).

carving *n* резьбá; (*single object*) резнáя фигýрка; *Cook* нарезáние, рéзка; **he does wood ~** он занимáется резьбóй по дéреву; **to look at ~s** посмотрéть резьбý (*collect*).

carving knife *n* нож для нарезáния/рéзки мя́са.

case[1] *n* **1** (*box of wood, any size*) я́щик; (*cardboard*) корóбка; **packing ~** упакóвочный я́щик; **jewel ~** шкатýлка для драгоцéнностей; **spectacle ~** футля́р для очкóв; **cigarette ~** портсигáр; **show ~** витрúна; **cello ~** футля́р/(*if of soft material*) чехóл для виолончéли

2 (*suitcase*) чемодáн; **overnight ~** дорóжный несессéр; **vanity ~** *CQ* (сýмочка-) косметúчка

3 *Typ* наборная кáсса; *attr*: **lower/upper ~ letters** кáсса строчны́х/прописны́х лúтер.

case[2] *n* **1** (*instance*) слýчай, *also Med*; примéр; (*matter*) дéло; **this is a ~ in point** вот, напримéр, слýчай; **it's a clear ~ of carelessness** вот я́ркий примéр халáтности; **we have five ~s of typhus** у нас пять слýчаев тúфа; **the worst ~s were sent to hospital** сáмые тяжёлые больны́е бы́ли отпрáвлены в больни́цу; **this is a ~ for the director to decide** таки́е дела́ (*pl*) реша́ет дире́ктор; **it's a ~ of conscience** э́то де́ло со́вести; **that alters the ~** э́то меня́ет де́ло; **is it the ~ that the ring has been found?** э́то ве́рно,/пра́вда, что кольцо́ нашло́сь?; **that's not the ~** э́то не так; **it's a sad ~** э́то тяжёлый слу́чай

2 *with preps*: **in any ~** во вся́ком/в любо́м слу́чае; **in most ~s** в большинстве́ слу́чаев; **in no ~** ни в ко́ем слу́чае; **in such a ~** в тако́м слу́чае; **in ~ of fire** в слу́чае пожа́ра; **in your ~ I would advise a change of job** вам и́менно я бы посове́товал смени́ть рабо́ту; **as in the ~ of Igor** как в слу́чае с И́горем; **take an umbrella just in ~** на вся́кий слу́чай возьми́ зо́нтик; *as conj*: **in ~ I forget** в слу́чае, е́сли я забу́ду

3 *Law* (суде́бное) де́ло; **the ~ will be tried tomorrow** де́ло бу́дет слу́шаться за́втра

4 (*arguments, reasoning*) до́воды (*pl*); **he made out a good ~ for his project** он привёл убеди́тельные/ве́ские до́воды в защи́ту/в по́льзу своего́ прое́кта; **let's hear the ~ for and against** дава́йте послу́шаем до́воды за и про́тив; **there's a strong ~ for refusing** есть серьёзные причи́ны (*pl*) для отка́за; **he has a watertight ~** у него́ о́чень про́чная пози́ция—кома́р но́су не подто́чит

5 *Gram* паде́ж.

case history *n Med* исто́рия боле́зни.

cash *n* нали́чные (де́ньги) (*pl*); **~ in hand, hard ~** нали́чные; **to pay ~** плати́ть нали́чными; **I've no ~ on me** у меня́ нет при себе́ де́нег/нет нали́чных; **~ on delivery** нало́женным платежо́м; *attr*: **~ register** ка́ссовый аппара́т.

cash *vt*: **to ~ a cheque** (*of customer*) получ|а́ть де́ньги по че́ку (-и́ть), (*of bank clerk*) опла́|чивать чек (-ти́ть); **my father will ~ a cheque (for you)** дай чек моему́ отцу́, он опла́тит тебе́ его́; *CQ* **to ~ in on smth** обра|ща́ть что-л в свою́ по́льзу (-ти́ть).

cashbook *n* ка́ссовая кни́га.

cashdesk *n* ка́сса; **pay at the ~** плати́те в ка́ссу.

cashier *n* касси́р.

cask *n* бочо́нок.

casserole *n* (*utensil*) гуся́тница, утя́тница; (*food*) **~ of lamb** бара́нина, тушённая в горшо́чке.

cast *n* (*throw*) бросо́к; (*mould*) фо́рма; (*squint*) лёгкое косогла́зие; *Theat* соста́в исполни́телей; *Med* **they put his arm in a plaster ~** ему́ наложи́ли гипс на́ руку; *fig* **he is of a serious ~ of mind** он челове́к серьёзного скла́да ума́.

cast *vti vt* **1** брос|а́ть (-́ить); *Tech* (*of metals*) отли|ва́ть (-́ть); **to ~ lots** броса́ть жре́бий (*sing*); **to ~ a shadow** отбра́сывать тень; (*of horse*) **to ~ a shoe** теря́ть подко́ву (по-); **snakes ~ their skins** зме́и меня́ют ко́жу; **to ~ a vote** пода|ва́ть го́лос (-́ть); *Theat*: **to ~ roles** распредел|я́ть/отда|ва́ть ро́ли (-и́ть/-́ть); **he was ~ as the king** он получи́л роль короля́; **she was badly ~** ей да́ли не ту роль; *Naut* **to ~ anchor/the lead** броса́ть я́корь/лот

2 *fig uses*: **to ~ a slur on smb** броса́ть тень на кого́-л; **to ~ doubt on smth** подверг|а́ть что-л сомне́нию (-́нуть); **she is very ~ down** она́ о́чень удручена́; **can you ~ any light on the matter?** не мо́жешь ли ты проли́ть свет на э́ту зага́дку?

vi (*of fishing*) (*also vt* **to ~ a line**) заки́|дывать у́дочку (-нуть); (*knitting*) **to ~ off/~ on** спус|ка́ть/на|бира́ть пе́тли (-ти́ть/-бра́ть); *Naut* **to ~ off** отдава́ть шварто́вы.

casting *adj*: **~ vote** реша́ющий го́лос.

cast-iron *adj* чугу́нный; *fig* **a ~ excuse/case** уважи́тельная причи́на, неопровержи́мые *or* желе́зные доказа́тельства (*pl*).

castle *n* за́мок; *fig* **to build ~s in the air** стро́ить возду́шные за́мки.

cast-off *adj*: **~ clothing,** *also as npl* **~s** обно́ски (*pl*); **as a child I used to wear my sister's ~s** в де́тстве я ходи́ла в обно́сках сестры́.

castor oil *n* касто́ровое ма́сло.

casual *adj* **1** (*chance*) случа́йный; (*informal*) непринуждённый; бесцеремо́нный; **a ~ encounter** случа́йная встре́ча; **a ~ manner** непринуждённая (*relaxed*)/небре́жная (*off-hand*) мане́ра; **~ clothes** повседне́вная оде́жда; **he's a ~ sort of chap** он дово́льно бесцеремо́нный тип; **from a ~ glance I thought that...** на пе́рвый взгляд мне показа́лось, что...

2: **a ~ worker** вре́менный рабо́тник; **~ labour** вре́менные рабо́чие (*pl*).

casually *adv* случа́йно; небре́жно; **he ~ remarked...** он небре́жно/вскользь заме́тил...; **I said it quite ~** я сказа́л э́то про́сто так; **I was watching the game quite ~ when...** я не о́чень внима́тельно смотре́л матч, как вдруг...

casualty *n* (*victim*) пострада́вший, же́ртва; **there were a lot of casualties** бы́ло мно́го пострада́вших/же́ртв; *Mil* **we suffered heavy casualties** мы понесли́ тяжёлые поте́ри; *attr*: **~ list** спи́сок ра́неных и уби́тых.

cat *n* кот, *f* ко́шка; *fig*: **to let the ~ out of the bag** проговори́ться; **she's like a ~ on hot bricks** она́ сиди́т как на иго́лках; **there isn't room to swing a ~** здесь не́где поверну́ться; *attr fig*: **they lead a ~ and dog life** они́ ве́чно ссо́рятся, они́ живу́т как ко́шка с соба́кой.

catalogue, (*US*) **catalog** *n* катало́г.

catalogue, (*US*) **catalog** *vt*: **to ~ an item/a collection** вноси́ть назва́ние предме́та в катало́г (внести́), состав|ля́ть катало́г колле́кции (-́ить).

cataract *n* (*waterfall*) водопа́д; *Med* катара́кта.

catarrh *n Med* ката́р.

catastrophe *n* катастро́фа.

catcall *vi* освист|ывать (-а́ть).

catch *n* **1** (*quantity caught*: *of fish*) уло́в; *Sport* кетч; *fig* **he's quite a** ~ он зави́дный жени́х

2 (*bolt*) задви́жка; (*part of a lock*) защёлка; (*hook on door*) крючо́к; (*small bolt of window*, *cupboard*, *etc*.) шпингале́т

3 (*trick*) подво́х; **there must be a** ~ **somewhere** здесь где́-то есть подво́х.

catch *vti vt* **1** пойма́ть (*pf*; *impf* лови́ть = *try to catch*); **he caught the ball/a bird/a fish/a runaway prisoner** он пойма́л мяч/пти́цу/ры́бу/беглеца́; **the thief was caught** во́ра схвати́ли/пойма́ли

2 (*grasp*, *seize*) хвата́ть (схвати́ть); **she caught the boy by the hand** она́ схвати́ла ма́льчика за́ руку

3 (*by surprise*) засти́гнуть, пойма́ть, заста́ть (*usu pfs*); **I caught him red-handed/unawares** я его́ пойма́л с поли́чным, я засти́г *or* заста́л его́ врасплох; **we were caught by the rain** мы попа́ли под дождь; *fig*: **I caught myself thinking that...** я пойма́л себя́ на мы́сли, что...; **you'll not** ~ **me that way** меня́ на э́том не проведёшь/не пойма́ешь

4 (*intercept*) перехва́т|ывать (-и́ть); **I caught him on his way home** я перехвати́л его́ по доро́ге домо́й; *fig* **he caught his breath** у него́ перехвати́ло дыха́ние/дух захвати́ло (*impers*)

5 (*be in time for*) успе|ва́ть на + *A* (-́ть), *CQ* захвати́ть; **I caught the last bus** я успе́л на после́дний авто́бус; **you won't** ~ **the post now** ты уже́ опозда́л к после́дней вы́емке пи́сем

6 *Med*: **he caught measles/a cold** он подхвати́л корь, он схвати́л на́сморк

7 (*hear*, *comprehend*): **I didn't quite** ~ **what you said** я не расслы́шал, что ты сказа́л; **I only caught the end of the conversation** я заста́л/захвати́л то́лько коне́ц бесе́ды; **to** ~ **smb's meaning** поня́ть смысл чьих-л слов

8 *fig uses*: **the house caught fire** дом загоре́лся; **to** ~ **a likeness** улови́ть/пойма́ть схо́дство; **I caught his eye** я пойма́л его́ взгляд; **it caught my imagination/attention** э́то порази́ло моё воображе́ние, э́то привлекло́ моё внима́ние; **I caught a glimpse of her at the theatre** я ви́дел её ме́льком в теа́тре; *CQ* **he caught it!** ну ему́ и доста́лось!

vi: **the damp wood caught at last** сыры́е дрова́ (*pl*) наконе́ц загоре́лись

catch at *vi*: **he caught at a branch**/*fig* **at the opportunity** он ухвати́лся за ве́тку/за э́ту возмо́жность

catch in *vt*: **I caught my finger in the door** я прищеми́л себе́ па́лец две́рью

catch on *vti vt*: **she caught her foot on a stone/her stocking on a nail** она́ споткну́лась о ка́мень, она́ зацепи́лась чулко́м о гвоздь; **the blow caught him on the head** уда́р пришёлся ему по голове́

vi: **my dress caught on a briar** у меня́ пла́тье зацепи́лось за колю́чки шипо́вника; *fig* **that fashion never caught on here** э́та мо́да здесь не привила́сь

catch out *vt*: **I caught her out in a lie** я уличи́л её во лжи́, я пойма́л её на вранье́

catch up *vti vt*: **you go on—I'll** ~ **you up** иди́, я тебя́ догоню́; **I've stupidly got caught up in helping them** я заче́м-то ввяза́лся помога́ть им

vi: **to** ~ **up with smb** на|гоня́ть/до|гоня́ть кого́-л (*pfs* -гна́ть); *fig*: **he has caught up with the class** он догна́л свой класс; **I must** ~ **up on my work** я до́лжен подогна́ть рабо́ту; **I've caught up on sleep** мне удало́сь отоспа́ться.

catching *adj* (*infectious*) зара́зный, прили́пчивый.

catchword *n* мо́дное слове́чко.

catchy *adj CQ*: **a** ~ **tune** навя́зчивая/прили́пчивая мело́дия.

categoric(al) *adj* категори́ческий.

category *n* катего́рия.

cater *vi*: **the canteen** ~**s for 100 for lunch every day** столо́вая обслу́живает в день сто челове́к; **this restaurant** ~**s for weddings** в э́том рестора́не мо́жно отпра́здновать сва́дьбу; **this magazine** ~**s for low tastes** э́тот журна́л угожда́ет ни́зменным вку́сам; **they don't** ~ **for beginners here** здесь не подла́живаются к новичка́м.

catering *n*: **who does your** ~**?** (*in hotel*, *etc*.) кто занима́ется ва́шим обслу́живанием?, (*at home*) кто ведёт ва́ше хозя́йство?

caterpillar *n* гу́сеница; *attr*: ~ **tractor** гу́сеничный тра́ктор.

cathedral *n* собо́р; *attr* собо́рный.

catholic *adj Rel* (**C.**) католи́ческий; *fig* **a man of** ~ **interests** челове́к с разносторо́нними интере́сами.

catkin *n Bot* серёжка.

cattle *n* (рога́тый) скот (*collect*).

catty *adj* (*of remark*) ко́лкий, язви́тельный; (*of people*) недоброжела́тельный.

cauliflower *n* цветна́я капу́ста.

causal *adj* причи́нный.

cause *n* **1** (*reason*) причи́на; (*grounds*) основа́ние; (*occasion*) по́вод; ~ **and effect** причи́на и сле́дствие; **without good** ~ без уважи́тельной причи́ны; **the** ~ **of the fire** причи́на пожа́ра; **that was the** ~ **of all our difficulties** э́то бы́ло причи́ной всех на́ших тру́дностей; **there's no** ~ **for alarm** нет причи́ны *or* причи́н/основа́ния *or* основа́ний для беспоко́йства; **to give** ~ **for complaint** дать по́вод недово́льству

2 (*purpose*, *object of effort*) де́ло; **that's a lost** ~ э́то безнадёжное де́ло; **to take up smb's** ~ хлопота́ть за кого́-л; **to make common** ~ **with smb** объединя́ться с кем-л в борьбе́ за о́бщее де́ло; **he did much for the** ~ **of science** он мно́го сде́лал для нау́ки.

cause *vt* причин|я́ть (-и́ть); **she** ~**d me a lot of trouble** она́ причини́ла мне мно́го непри́ятностей (*pl*); **what** ~**d the accident?/his death?** что бы́ло причи́ной ава́рии?, какова́ причи́на его́ сме́рти?; **to ~ a sensation** вы|зыва́ть сенса́цию (-звать).

caustic *adj* е́дкий, *also fig.*

cauterize *vt Med* при|жига́ть (-же́чь).

caution *n* осторо́жность; (*circumspection*) осмотри́тельность; (*warning*) предостереже́ние, предупрежде́ние; *Law* **he was let off with a ~** он отде́лался предупрежде́нием; *CQ* (*usu of a child*) **he's a ~!** он тако́й озорни́к!

caution *vt* предостере|га́ть (-́чь), предупре|жда́ть (-ди́ть); **I ~ed her against being late** я предупреди́л её, что опа́здывать нельзя́; **the judge ~ed him** судья́ сде́лал ему́ предупрежде́ние.

cautionary *adj*: **~ tales** назида́тельные исто́рии.

cautious *adj* осторо́жный; (*circumspect*) осмотри́тельный.

cavalry *n* кавале́рия, ко́нница.

cave *n* пеще́ра.

cave *vi*: **to ~ in** (*of tunnel, etc.*) осе|да́ть (-́сть), *fig CQ* сда́ться (*usu pf*).

caviar(e) *n* (чёрная) икра́.

cavil *vi*: **to ~ at** при|дира́ться к + *D* (-дра́ться).

cavity *n* впа́дина; (*in a tree or tooth*) дупло́.

caw *vi* ка́рк|ать (*semel* -́нуть).

cease *vti vt* прекра|ща́ть + *A or* + *inf* (-ти́ть); переста|ва́ть + *inf* (-́ть); **to ~ work/working** прекрати́ть рабо́ту/рабо́тать, переста́ть рабо́тать

vi прекраща́ться, перестава́ть; остан|а́вливаться (-ови́ться); **the rain has ~d** дождь прекрати́лся/переста́л; **work ~d** рабо́та останови́лась/прекрати́лась.

ceasefire *n Mil* прекраще́ние огня́.

ceaseless *adj* непреста́нный, непреры́вный.

cedar *n* кедр.

cede *vt*: **to ~ territory/rights** сда|ва́ть террито́рию (-ть), уступ|а́ть права́ (-и́ть).

ceiling *n* потоло́к; *fig*: **to fix a ~ for wages** установи́ть максима́льный у́ровень за́работной пла́ты; *CQ* **when he found out he hit the ~** он взбеси́лся, когда́ узна́л об э́том.

celebrate *vti* пра́здновать (от-); **to ~ the first of May/a birthday** пра́здновать *or* отме|ча́ть Пе́рвое ма́я/день рожде́ния (от-/-́тить); *off* **to ~ a victory** торжествова́ть побе́ду (*impf*); **to ~ a wedding** справ|ля́ть сва́дьбу (-́ить); **this district is ~d for its wines** э́та ме́стность сла́вится свои́ми ви́нами; *CQ* **let's ~ (the occasion)** дава́й отпра́зднуем/отме́тим (э́то собы́тие).

celebrated *adj* знамени́тый; просла́вленный; **heroes ~ in song** геро́и, просла́вленные в пе́сне.

celebration *n* пра́зднование; *off* торжество́.

celebrity *n* (*fame*) изве́стность; (*person*) знамени́тость.

celery *n* сельдере́й.

cell *n* (*prison*) тюре́мная ка́мера; (*monk's*) ке́лья; *Biol* кле́тка; (*in honeycomb*) яче́йка; *Elec* элеме́нт.

cellar *n* (*basement*) подва́л; (*under house, pavement*) по́греб; **he keeps a good ~** у него́ всегда́ большо́й запа́с вин.

cellist *n* виолончели́ст.

cello *n* виолонче́ль.

cellophane *n* целлофа́н.

cement *n* цеме́нт.

cement *vt* скреп|ля́ть цеме́нтом (-и́ть); цементи́ровать, *also fig* (*impf and pf*); *fig* скреп|ля́ть (-и́ть).

cemetery *n* кла́дбище.

censor *n* це́нзор.

censor *vt*: **all films have to be ~ed** все фи́льмы должны́ пройти́ цензу́ру; **that book was heavily ~ed** в кни́ге бы́ли больши́е купю́ры; **that paragraph was ~ed** цензу́ра вы́резала/вы́бросила э́тот абза́ц.

censorship *n* цензу́ра.

censure *vt*: **to ~ smb for smth** осу|жда́ть/порица́ть кого́-л за что-л (-ди́ть/*impf*).

census *n* пе́репись; **to take a ~ of** провести́ пе́репись + *G*.

cent *n* цент; **I haven't a ~** у меня́ нет ни гроша́.

centenary *n* столе́тняя годовщи́на, столе́тие; *attr* столе́тний.

centigrade *adj* стогра́дусный; **10 degrees ~** де́сять гра́дусов по стогра́дусной шкале́/по Це́льсию.

centimetre *n* сантиме́тр; **5 ~s higher/less** на пять сантиме́тров вы́ше/ме́ньше.

centipede *n* многоно́жка.

central *adj* центра́льный; **our house is very ~** наш дом в са́мом це́нтре (го́рода).

centralize *vt* централизова́ть (*impf and pf*).

centre, (*US*) **center** *n* центр; (*middle*) середи́на; **dead ~** мёртвая то́чка; **in the ~ of the square** в середи́не пло́щади; **shopping/administrative ~** торго́вый/администрати́вный центр; *Med* **~ of infection** оча́г инфе́кции; *attr Sport*: **~ forward** центр нападе́ния.

century *n* век; столе́тие; **in the twentieth ~** в двадца́том ве́ке/столе́тии; **for centuries** в тече́ние веко́в, века́ми; **many centuries ago** мно́го веко́в (тому́) наза́д; **he lived for a ~** он жил сто лет/це́лый век.

ceramics *n* кера́мика (*collect*).

cereal *n usu pl* (**~s**) хле́бные зла́ки, зерновы́е (*always pl*).

cerebral *adj* мозгово́й.

ceremonial *adj*: **a ~ dinner** торже́ственный обе́д; **~ dress** пара́дная оде́жда.

ceremonious *adj* церемо́нный.

ceremony *n* (*function*) церемо́ния, торжество́; (*rite*) обря́д; (*of behaviour*) этике́т, форма́льность.

cert *n sl*: **to bet on a dead ~** поста́вить на ве́рную ло́шадь; **it's a dead ~ he'll get the job** он наверняка́ полу́чит э́ту рабо́ту.

certain *adj* **1** *predic*: *of facts* (*beyond doubt*): **this much is ~, he won't help** он не помо́жет — в чём, в чём, а в э́том сомне́ния нет; **we don't know for ~ that the match is on** мы то́чно не зна́ем, состо́ится ли матч;

he is ~ to come, he'll come for ~ он обязательно/наверняка́ придёт

2 *predic*: *of people* (*be convinced*): **I'm ~ I've seen her somewhere** я уве́рен, что где́-то ви́дел её; **don't buy it unless you're ~ it's what you want** не покупа́й, пока́ не убеди́шься: э́то и́менно то, что тебе́ ну́жно

3 *attr* (*sure*) ве́рный; надёжный; **to face ~ death** идти́ на ве́рную смерть; **there's no ~ cure for this disease** от э́той боле́зни нет надёжного сре́дства/лека́рства

4 *attr* (*known, but not specified*) определённый; изве́стный; не́который; **to a ~ extent** в изве́стной сте́пени, до не́которой/определённой сте́пени; **for ~ reasons** по не́которым соображе́ниям; **under ~ conditions** при изве́стных/определённых усло́виях; **I'm only free on ~ days** я свобо́ден то́лько по определённым дням

5 *attr*; *sing only*: **a ~ Mr Smith** не́кий г-н Смит, не́кто Смит; **a ~ person told me that...** оди́н челове́к мне сказа́л, что...

6 **to make certain**: **you ought to make ~ when the bus goes** ты до́лжен то́чно узна́ть, когда́ отхо́дит авто́бус; **I'll order tickets so as to make ~ of seats** я закажу́ биле́ты зара́нее, что́бы у нас наверняка́ бы́ли места́; **to make ~ of smb's vote** обеспе́чить себе́ чей-л го́лос.

certainly *adv* 1 (*in answer to questions*) коне́чно, безусло́вно; **~ not!** ни в ко́ем слу́чае!, коне́чно, нет!

2 (*undoubtedly*: *of future*): **I'll ~ come** я наверняка́/обяза́тельно/безусло́вно приду́; (*of past*): **he ~ was there whatever he may say** он наверняка́ там был, что́ бы он ни говори́л; **he ~ should have been there** он наверняка́ до́лжен был быть там.

certainty *n*: **I can't say with ~** я не могу́ сказа́ть с уве́ренностью; **that's a ~** э́то наверняка́; **to know for a ~** знать наверняка́ (*adv*); **we have no ~ of success** мы не уве́рены в успе́хе.

certificate *n* свиде́тельство; спра́вка; *Univ* дипло́м; **death/birth ~** свиде́тельство о сме́рти/о рожде́нии; **health ~** медици́нская спра́вка; **you'll need a ~ from the doctor** *CQ* принеси́ спра́вку от врача́.

certify *vt* (*in writing*) удостовер|я́ть (-́ить); (*less formal*) руча́ться (поручи́ться); **I can ~ to his character** я могу́ поручи́ться за него́; **the doctor certified him as insane** врач призна́л его́ душевнобольны́м.

chafe *vti vt* (*so as to cause a sore*) на|тира́ть (-тере́ть); (*in order to warm*) рас|тира́ть (-тере́ть)

vi fig: **to ~ at/under smth** раздража́ться из-за чего́-л (*usu impf*).

chaff[1] *n* (*of grain*) мяки́на.

chaff[2] *n* (*fun*) насме́шка.

chaff[2] *vt*: **we ~ed him about his snobbery/his girlfriend** *or. CQ* **his latest** мы подшу́чивали над его́ сноби́змом/над его́ (но́вым) увлече́нием.

chaffinch *n* зя́блик.

chain *n* цепь; *dim* цепо́чка; *fig*: **a ~ of mountains** го́рная цепь; **a ~ of events** цепь/ход собы́тий; **a ~ of restaurants** сеть рестора́нов; *attr*: **he's a ~ smoker** он непреры́вно ку́рит, он ку́рит одну́ сигаре́ту за друго́й.

chain *vt*: **to ~ up a dog** сажа́ть соба́ку на цепь (посади́ть); **the cap is ~ed to the petrol tank** кры́шка бензоба́ка на цепо́чке.

chair *n* 1 стул; **to sit (down) on a ~** сесть на стул; **to be sitting on a ~** сиде́ть на сту́ле; **to get up from/fall off a ~** встать/упа́сть со сту́ла; **to offer smb a ~** предложи́ть кому́-л сесть

2 *Univ* ка́федра; **he holds the ~ of mathematics** он руководи́т ка́федрой матема́тики (*sing*); **to be appointed to a ~** получи́ть ка́федру

3 (*at meeting*): **to take the ~ at a meeting** председа́тельствовать на собра́нии.

chairman *n* председа́тель (*m*).

chalk *n* мел; **artist's ~** пасте́ль; *fig*: **he doesn't know ~ from cheese** *CQ* он ни в чём ни у́ха ни ры́ла; *CQ* **he's not the best by a long ~** он далеко́ не са́мый лу́чший/пе́рвый; *attr* мелово́й; **~ cliffs** мелов́ые ска́лы.

challenge *n* (*by sentry*) о́клик; (*to duel, competition*) вы́зов; **to issue a ~ to smb** бро́сить кому́-л вы́зов; **to take up a ~** приня́ть вы́зов; *fig*: **the work is hard but I like the ~** рабо́та тру́дная, но я от тру́дностей не бегу́; **he enjoys the ~ of mountaineering** альпини́зм привлека́ет его́ ри́ском.

challenge *vt* (*to a duel, to compete*) вы|зыва́ть (-́звать); (*of sentry*): **to ~ smb** оклик|а́ть кого́-л (-́нуть); **to ~ smb to (a) race** вы́звать кого́-л на соревнова́ние по бе́гу; **to ~ smb's right to smth** оспа́ривать чьё-л пра́во на что-л (*usu impf*); *Law* **to ~ a will** оспа́ривать завеща́ние.

challenging *adj*: **it's ~ work** э́та рабо́та предъявля́ет больши́е тре́бования.

chamber *n Hist* пала́та; **~ of commerce** торго́вая пала́та; **conference ~** конфере́нц-зал.

chambermaid *n* го́рничная.

chamber music *n* ка́мерная му́зыка.

chamberpot *n* ночно́й горшо́к.

chamois *n* се́рна; *attr*: **~ leather** за́мша.

champagne *n* шампа́нское.

champion *n* чемпио́н; (*of smb*) защи́тник; **tennis/world ~** чемпио́н по те́ннису, чемпио́н ми́ра; *attr*: **a ~ boxer** чемпио́н по бо́ксу; *CQ* **it's ~** э́то замеча́тельно.

champion *vt*: **to ~ smb/a cause** подде́рж|ивать кого́-л (-а́ть), защища́ть де́ло (*only in impf*).

championship *n* пе́рвенство, чемпиона́т; **to win the world ~ at football** завоева́ть пе́рвенство ми́ра по футбо́лу.

chance *n* 1 (*luck, fate*) случа́йность, слу́чай; **by a lucky ~** по счастли́вой случа́йности; **by sheer ~** чи́сто случа́йно; **have you by any ~ a screwdriver?** у тебя́ нет случа́йно отвёртки?; **to leave things to ~** положи́ться на во́лю слу́чая; **he left nothing to ~** он всё предусмотре́л; **it can't have been a matter of ~** э́то не мо́жет быть случа́йностью; **as ~ would have it, I didn't go** случи́лось так, что я не пошёл; **~s are against him** всё про́тив него́; **games of ~** аза́ртные и́гры

2 (*opportunity*) (удо́бный) слу́чай, возмо́жность; **it's the ~ of a lifetime** тако́й слу́чай быва́ет/выпада́ет раз в жи́зни; **now is our ~** сейча́с са́мое вре́мя; **give me a ~ to try again** дай мне возмо́жность попыта́ться ещё раз; **I took the ~ to +** *inf* я воспо́льзовался слу́чаем, что́бы + *inf*; **it's a good ~ to...** э́то удо́бный слу́чай + *inf*; *CQ* **he has an eye for the main ~** он своего́ не упу́стит

3 (*possibility*) шанс, *often pl*; **he has a fair ~ of success** у него́ есть реа́льные ша́нсы на успе́х; **he has no ~ of getting the job** у него́ нет ша́нсов получи́ть э́то ме́сто; **there's no ~ of anyone seeing us** нас наверняка́ никто́ не уви́дит; **the ~s are that...** по всей вероя́тности...; **I looked in on the off ~ of seeing him** я зашёл к нему́ на вся́кий слу́чай, вдруг он до́ма

4 (*risk*): **to take a ~/~s** рискова́ть.

chance *adj* случа́йный.

chance *vti vt* рискну́ть + *inf* (*usu pf*); **let's ~ it/our luck** (дава́й) рискнём, а что е́сли рискну́ть?

vi: **it ~d that...** случи́лось так, что...; **I ~d to see him yesterday** я его́ случа́йно встре́тил вчера́; **I ~d on him/on a rare book in the library** я случа́йно наткну́лся на него́/на ре́дкую кни́гу в библиоте́ке.

chancy *adj CQ* риско́ванный.

change *n* **1** измене́ние; переме́на; (*on a journey*) переса́дка; (*of clothes*) сме́на; **a ~ of plan** измене́ние в пла́не; **to make a ~ in the agenda** внести́ измене́ние в пове́стку дня; **the timetable is subject to ~** расписа́ние мо́жет быть изменено́; **a ~ for the better** измене́ние/переме́на к лу́чшему; **a ~ in the weather** переме́на пого́ды; **you need a ~** (*of scene, etc.*) вам нужна́ переме́на обстано́вки; **there have been many ~s since then** с тех пор мно́гое перемени́лось; **a ~ of underwear** сме́на белья́; **for a ~** для разнообра́зия, разнообра́зия ра́ди; *Med* **~ of life** кли́макс

2 (*money*) сда́ча; **small ~** ме́лочь; **don't forget your ~** не забу́дь взять сда́чу; **can you give me ~ for a rouble?** не мо́жете ли вы разменя́ть мне рубль?; *fig CQ* **you'll get no ~ out of him** от него́ ничего́ не добьёшься, с него́ где ся́дешь, там и сле́зешь.

change *vti vt* **1** меня́ть (по-); (*alter*) измен|я́ть (-и́ть); (*replace*) смен|я́ть (-и́ть); **to ~ the beds/the sheets** смени́ть бельё; **to ~ tyres/one's job** смени́ть ши́ны/рабо́ту; **to ~ one's flat** перемени́ть/поменя́ть кварти́ру; **to ~ places with smb** поменя́ться места́ми с кем-л; **to ~ a 100-rouble note** разме́н|ивать сторублёвку (-я́ть); *Naut* **to ~ course** изменя́ть курс, *also fig*

2 *often translated by prefix* пере- *with appropriate verb*: **to ~ a baby** перепелена́ть ребёнка; **to ~ one's dress** переоде|ва́ть пла́тье (´-ть), переоде|ва́ться (´-ться); **to ~ furniture around** перестав|ля́ть ме́бель (´-ить); **the house has ~d hands** дом перешёл к друго́му владе́льцу; **this car has ~d hands several times** э́та маши́на меня́ла хозя́ина/переходи́ла в други́е ру́ки не́сколько раз; **I've ~d my mind** я переду́мал/разду́мал; **to ~ one's seat** пере|са́живаться (-се́сть); **to ~ trains** де́лать переса́дку (с-); **the time of the meeting has been ~d** вре́мя заседа́ния перенесли́; *Aut* **to ~ gear** переключ|а́ть ско́рость (-и́ть); *fig* **to ~ one's tune** перемени́ть тон

vi меня́ться, изменя́ться, *etc.*; **times ~** времена́ меня́ются; **you haven't ~d at all** вы совсе́м не измени́лись; **his expression ~d** он измени́лся/перемени́лся в лице́; **the weather has ~d** пого́да перемени́лась; (*of clothes*) **don't bother changing** переодева́ться не на́до; (*in trains, buses*): **you will have to ~ twice** вам придётся сде́лать две переса́дки; **all ~!** по́езд да́льше не идёт; *Aut* **to ~ down/up** перейти́ на ни́зшую/вы́сшую ско́рость; **the wind has ~d from north to east** се́верный ве́тер смени́лся восто́чным; **we've ~d over to an estate car** мы смени́ли свою́ маши́ну на универса́л; **we've ~d over from solid fuel to electricity** мы перешли́ с у́гля на электри́чество; **he's ~d over to modern languages** он переключи́лся на изуче́ние совреме́нных языко́в.

changeable *adj* изме́нчивый.

channel *n* проли́в; *Naut* (*fairway*) фарва́тер; (*riverbed*) ру́сло; (*for irrigation*) кана́л, *also fig*; **the English C.** Ла-Ма́нш; **diplomatic ~s** дипломати́ческие кана́лы; **~s of information** исто́чники информа́ции; *TV* **what's on the other ~?** что по друго́й програ́мме?

chaos *n* хао́с, беспоря́док.

chap *n CQ* па́рень; **little ~** ма́лый; **he's a very decent ~** он сла́вный ма́лый; **a ~ I know** оди́н мой знако́мый; **he's nearly blind, poor ~** он почти́ слепо́й, бедня́га; **come on, ~s** пошли́, ребя́та (*of any age*).

chapel *n* часо́вня.

chapped *adj*: **~ hands** обве́тренные/потре́скавшиеся ру́ки.

chapter *n* глава́; *fig* **I've had a ~ of accidents today** у меня́ сего́дня сплошны́е неуда́чи/неприя́тности.

character *n* хара́ктер; *Theat* де́йствующее лицо́; *Lit* геро́й, персона́ж; **the ~ of the soil/climate** хара́ктер по́чвы/кли́мата; **a man of independent ~** челове́к незави́симого хара́ктера; **that's quite in ~ for him** для него́ э́то характе́рно; *Lit*: **a good/bad ~** положи́тельный/отрица́тельный геро́й; **the subsidiary ~ in the novel** второстепе́нный персона́ж рома́на; **a well-drawn ~** хорошо́ вы́веденный о́браз; *CQ* **he's a ~/an odd ~** он оригина́л, он стра́нный тип *or* он чуда́к.

characteristic *n* характе́рная черта́; осо́бенность, сво́йство.

characteristic *adj* характе́рный.

charcoal *n* древе́сный у́голь (*m*).

charge *n* **1** (*cost*) пла́та; **extra ~s** пла́та (*sing*) за дополни́тельные услу́ги; **professional ~s** пла́та за услу́ги; **~ for admission** пла́та за вход

2 (*responsibility*): **who's in ~ here?** кто здесь нача́льник?/заве́дующий?; **who's in ~ meantime?** кто сейча́с за нача́льника?; **the teacher put him in ~ of the books** учи́тель назна́чил его́ отве́тственным за кни́ги; **I'm leaving the children in your ~** я оставля́ю дете́й на ва́ше попече́ние/на вас

3 *Mil*, *Sport* ата́ка; (*explosive*) *Mil*, *Elec* заря́д; *Law* обвине́ние; **to appear on a ~ of** представа́ть пе́ред судо́м по обвине́нию в + *P*; **what's the ~ against him?** како́е ему́ предъя́влено обвине́ние?, в чём его́ обвиня́ют?

charge *vt* **1** (*of prices*): **what did they ~ you for the work?** ско́лько с вас взя́ли за рабо́ту? **how much are they charging for apples?** ско́лько они́ беру́т за я́блоки?; **how much will you ~ for this?** ско́лько э́то бу́дет сто́ить?; **~ it (up) to my account** запиши́те э́то на мой счёт

2 (*order*) поруч|а́ть (-и́ть); **I was ~d to give you this letter** мне пору́чено переда́ть вам э́то письмо́

3 *specialized uses*: *Mil*, *Sport* атакова́ть (*impf and pf*); *Elec* заря|жа́ть (-ди́ть); **is the battery ~d?** аккумуля́тор заряжён?; *Law* **he was ~d with murder** его́ обвини́ли в уби́йстве.

chargeable *adj Fin* подлежа́щий опла́те; *Law*: **this is a ~ offence** э́то подсу́дное де́ло.

charitable *adj* (*kind*) милосе́рдный; **~ work** благотвори́тельная де́ятельность.

charity *n*: **he would never accept ~** он никогда́ не при́мет ми́лостыни; **to live on ~** жить на пода́чки (*pl*).

charm *n* **1** (*attraction*) обая́ние, очарова́ние, ча́ры (*no sing*), пре́лесть; **what ~ she has!** как она́ очарова́тельна!; **to turn/lay on the ~** пусти́ть в ход свои ча́ры; **this valley has a ~ of its own** у э́той доли́ны есть своё осо́бое очарова́ние/своя́ осо́бая пре́лесть

2 (*spell*) ча́ры, (*spoken*) заклина́ние; (*trinket*) амуле́т.

charm *vt* очаро́в|ывать (-а́ть).

charmer *n CQ*: **he is a real ~** в нём бе́здна обая́ния.

charming *adj* очарова́тельный, преле́стный.

chart *n Naut* морска́я ка́рта; (*diagram*) диагра́мма.

charter *n* **1** *Hist* ха́ртия; *Polit* **~ of the UN** уста́в ООН

2 (*hired ship*) (**a ~**) ча́ртер; *attr*: **a ~ flight** ча́ртерный рейс.

charter *vt* (*take on hire*) на|нима́ть (-ня́ть); **we ~ed a bus/plane** мы на́няли авто́бус/самолёт; *Comm* **to ~ a vessel** фрахтова́ть су́дно (за-).

charwoman, *CQ abbr* **char** *n* (приходя́щая) домрабо́тница.

chary *adj*: **he is ~ of strangers/of catching cold** он остерега́ется чужи́х, он бои́тся просту-ди́ться.

chase *n* (*hunt*) (**the ~**) охо́та; **after a long ~ the thief was caught** по́сле до́лгой пого́ни вор был по́йман; **my dog saw a hare and immediately gave ~** моя́ соба́ка уви́дела за́йца и сра́зу погнала́сь за ним; (*search*) **in ~ of** в по́исках + *G*.

chase *vti vt* гна́ться за + *I* (по-); **the police ~d the thief** полице́йские (*pl*) гна́лись за во́ром; **our dog ~d the cat out of the room/away from the chickens** на́ша соба́ка вы́гнала кота́ из ко́мнаты/отогнала́ кота́ от цыпля́т; **the letter ~d me for a week** письмо́ шло за мной це́лую неде́лю

vi: **I ~d after him** я бро́сился вслед за ним; **he's chasing after some girl or other** он всё вре́мя с како́й-нибудь де́вушкой.

chassis *n* шасси́ (*indecl*).

chaste *adj* целому́дренный.

chat *n* разгово́р, бесе́да; **during our ~ he said...** в разгово́ре он сказа́л...; **it's time we had a ~** пора́ бы нам с тобо́й поговори́ть.

chat *vti vt CQ*: **you'll have to ~ up the director** вам придётся испо́льзовать всё своё обая́ние, что́бы уговори́ть дире́ктора; **he was ~ting up a waitress** он улёщивал официа́нтку

vi говори́ть, бесе́довать (*impfs*; *both verbs can be used with* по-, *not as true pfs*, *but* = "*to have a bit of a chat*").

chattels *npl*: **my goods and ~** весь мой скарб.

chatter *n* (*talk*) болтовня́; (*of birds*) щебета́ние.

chatter *vi* болта́ть, (*of birds*) щебета́ть (*impfs*); *fig* **my teeth were ~ing with cold** у меня́ зу́бы стуча́ли от хо́лода, у меня́ зуб на́ зуб не попада́л от хо́лода.

chatterbox *n* болту́н, *f* -ья.

chatty *adj* (*person*) болтли́вый; **I got a ~ letter from her** я получи́л от неё письмо́, по́лное вся́ких новосте́й; **a ~ style** разгово́рный стиль.

chauffeur *n* шофёр.

cheap *adj* дешёвый; **to become ~er** дешеве́ть; **this was a ~ buy,** *CQ as n* **I bought this on the ~** я купи́л э́то по дешёвке; *fig pejor* **that's a ~ remark/trick** э́то неуважи́тельное замеча́ние, э́то нече́стный приём.

cheap *adv* дёшево; **to buy ~ and sell dear** купи́ть подешёвле и прода́ть подоро́же.

cheapen *vti*: **to ~ oneself** роня́ть себя́ (урони́ть); **you ~ yourself by associating with such people** ты опусти́лся до тако́го о́бщества.

cheaply *adv* дёшево, *CQ* по дешёвке; *fig* **he got off ~** он дёшево отде́лался.

cheat *n* (*fraud*) обма́н; (*person*) обма́нщик, (*at cards*) шу́лер.

cheat *vti vt*: **he ~ed me out of 10 roubles** он обману́л/*CQ* обжу́лил меня́ на де́сять рубле́й

vi: **to ~ at cards/in an exam** жу́льничать в ка́рты (*usu impf*), по́льзоваться шпарга́лками (*use a crib*) *or* спи́сывать (*copy*) на экза́мене (*impf*, *usu impf*); (*at games*) **stop ~ing!** переста́нь жу́льничать!

cheating *n* (*at games*) жу́льничество, моше́нничество.

check[1] *n* **1: our advance met with a ~** на́ше продвиже́ние бы́ло приостано́влено; **keep a ~ on your temper** уме́й сде́рживаться; **to hold the enemy in ~** сде́рживать на́тиск врага́

2 (*checkup*) контро́ль (*m*), прове́рка; **I am keeping a ~ on my petrol consumption** я контроли́рую расхо́д бензи́на; **ticket ~** прове́рка биле́тов; **they're giving the carburettor a final ~** они́ прово́дят контро́льную прове́рку карбюра́тора; **she keeps a careful ~ on household expenses** она́ о́чень эконо́мно ведёт хозя́йство

3 (*counterfoil*) тало́н; (*for luggage*) бага́жная квита́нция; (*at cloakroom*) номеро́к; (*bill for food*) счёт; (*US*: *cheque*) чек; **I got a ~ for my case** я получи́л квита́нцию на чемода́н

4 *Chess* шах; **he is in ~** ему́ объя́влен шах; **to put smb in ~** объяви́ть кому́-л шах.

check[1] *vti vt* **1** (*stop*, *hold back*) заде́рж|ивать, сде́рж|ивать (*pfs* -а́ть), приостан|а́вливать (-ови́ть); **the enemy's advance was ~ed** наступле́ние проти́вника бы́ло приостано́влено; **I ~ed myself just in time** я во́время сдержа́лся; **to ~ one's tears/anger** сдержа́ть слёзы/гнев; **the drought has ~ed all growth** за́суха задержа́ла/заме́длила рост расте́ний

2 (*rebuke*): **she ~ed her son for his greed** она́ упрекну́ла сы́на в жа́дности

3 (*examine*) провер|я́ть (-́ить); **to ~ weight/an engine/figures** прове́рить вес/мото́р/ци́фры; **I've ~ed the items off the list/the account** я прове́рил спи́сок по пу́нктам/счёт; **the customs have ~ed my luggage** тамо́женники осмотре́ли мой бага́ж; **I've ~ed in my baggage** (*at airport*) я сдал бага́ж; *Aut* **to ~ the oil** прове́рить у́ровень ма́сла

vi: **to ~ in at/out of a hotel** регистри́роваться/распла́|чиваться в гости́нице (*usu impf*/-ти́ться); **to ~ up on smb/smth** проверя́ть кого́-л/что-л.

check[2] *n* (*criss-cross pattern*) кле́тка; *attr*: **a ~ material** ткань в кле́тку, кле́тчатая ткань.

checkmate *vt* поста́вить кому́-л мат; **~!** (шах и) мат!

checkpoint *n* контро́льный пункт.

checkup *n* прове́рка; *Mech*, *Med* осмо́тр.

cheek *n* щека́; *CQ* (*impudence*) на́глость, наха́льство; **what ~!, of all the ~!** кака́я на́глость!; **to have the ~ to** име́ть на́глость + *inf*.

cheeky *adj* на́глый, наха́льный; **to be ~ to smb** дерзи́ть/груби́ть кому́-л (*pfs* на-).

cheep *n* (*of chicken*) писк; *fig* **there wasn't a ~ out of him, he didn't utter a ~** он да́же не пи́скнул.

cheer *n usu pl*: **the visitors were received with ~s** госте́й встре́тили приве́тствиями; **they gave three ~s for the general** при ви́де генера́ла они́ три́жды прокрича́ли «ура́»; *CQ* **~s!** ва́ше здоро́вье!

cheer *vti vt* **1: the speaker was loudly ~ed** ора́тору отвеча́ли во́згласами одобре́ния/гро́мко аплоди́ровали

2 (*encourage*) под|ба́дривать (-бодри́ть); **your visit has ~ed up the invalid** ва́ше посеще́ние подбодри́ло больно́го; **to ~ on the runners** подба́дривать бегуно́в кри́ками

vi: **~ up!** не унывай́!, не ве́шай но́са!; **she soon ~ed up** она́ вско́ре приободри́лась.

cheerful *adj* весёлый; (*only of people*) бо́дрый; **in a ~ mood** в весёлом настрое́нии; **he looked ~** у него́ был весёлый/бо́дрый вид; **we all felt more ~ when the rain stopped** мы все повеселе́ли, когда́ дождь переста́л; **a ~ fire was blazing in the grate** в пе́чке ве́село горе́л ого́нь.

cheering *adj* ободря́ющий.

cheerio *interj CQ* (**~!**) счастли́во!

cheerless *adj* (*of people*) невесёлый; (*of places or people*) мра́чный.

cheese *n* сыр; **bread and ~** хлеб с сы́ром; **have some ~** поешь сы́ру (*G*); **a whole ~** голо́вка/круг сы́ра; **cottage/grated ~** творо́г, тёртый сыр.

cheesed off *ppp CQ*: **he's pretty ~ with his job** ему́ осточерте́ла его́ рабо́та.

cheeseparing *n* грошо́вая эконо́мия.

cheeseparing *adj* скупо́й, прижи́мистый.

chef *n* шеф-по́вар.

chemical *n usu pl* хими́ческий препара́т, химика́лии (*usu pl*).

chemical *adj* хими́ческий; **~ plant/engineer/fertilizer** хими́ческий заво́д, инжене́р-хи́мик, минера́льное удобре́ние.

chemist *n* (*scientist*) хи́мик; (*in shop*) апте́карь (*m*); **the ~'s** (*shop*) апте́ка.

chemistry *n* хи́мия; *Univ* **the department of ~** хими́ческий факульте́т.

cheque, (*US*) **check** *n* чек; **a blank/crossed/traveller's ~** пусто́й/кросси́рованный/тури́стский чек; **to pay by ~** плати́ть че́ком; *attr*: **~ book** че́ковая кни́жка.

cherish *vt*: **to ~ hopes/illusions** леле́ять наде́жды (*impf*), пита́ть иллю́зии (*only in impf*); **I ~ those memories** я о́чень дорожу́ э́тими воспомина́ниями.

cherry *n* ви́шня (*sing and collect*, *also has pl*); (*large sweet variety*) чере́шня (*collect*); *attr* вишнёвый; **~ brandy/tree** вишнёвый ликёр, ви́шня.

chess *n* ша́хматы (*pl*); **to play ~** игра́ть в ша́хматы; **let's have a game of ~** дава́й сыгра́ем па́ртию в ша́хматы.

chessboard *n* ша́хматная доска́.

chessman *n* ша́хматная фигу́ра.

chessplayer *n* шахмати́ст.

chest *n* **1** (*box*) сунду́к; **linen ~** бельево́й сунду́к; **~ of drawers** комо́д

2 *Anat* грудна́я кле́тка, грудь; **I've a pain in my ~** у меня́ боль в груди́; *fig* **I had to get it off my ~** мне ну́жно бы́ло вы́сказаться/облегчи́ть ду́шу.

chestnut *n* **1** каштáн (*tree or fruit*); *sl* (*stale joke*) избúтый анекдóт
2 (*a horse*) каýрая лóшадь.

chestnut *adj* (*colour*) каштáнового цвéта; ~ **hair** каштáновые вóлосы (*pl*).

chew *vt* жевáть (*impf*); *fig* **to ~ over smth** обдýм|ывать что-л (-ать).

chewing gum *n* жевáтельная резúнка, *CQ* жвáчка.

chic *adj* элегáнтный, шикáрный.

chicken *n* (*if very young*, *also* **chick**) цыплёнок; *Cook* **boiled/roast** ~ варёная/жáреная кýрица; *fig*: **don't count your ~s before they're hatched** цыплят по óсени считáют; *CQ* **she's no** ~ онá ужé не молодá; *sl* **you're ~!** сдрéйфил?; *attr* курúный; ~ **soup** курúный бульóн.

chicken *vi*: *CQ* **he ~ed out at the last moment** он стрýсил в послéдний момéнт.

chicken pox *n* вéтряная óспа, ветрянка.

chicory *n* цикóрий.

chief *n* (*of tribe*) вождь (*m*); (*of department*) начáльник, *CQ* шеф; ~ **of staff/police** начáльник штáба/полúции.

chief *adj* глáвный; ~ **engineer** глáвный инженéр; **the ~ thing to remember is that...** прéжде всегó нýжно пóмнить (о том), что...

chiefly *adv* (*above all*) прéжде всегó; (*mainly*) глáвным óбразом.

chilblain *n* обморожéние пáльцев; **I've got ~s** (*on fingers or toes*) у меня обморóжены пáльцы.

child (*pl* **children**) *n* ребёнок; (*infant*) младéнец; **children** дéти, (*more informal*) ребята; **Madonna and** ~ мадóнна с младéнцем; **they have one** ~ у них одúн ребёнок; **they have two/three/four/five children** у них двóе/трóе/чéтверо/пять *or* пятеро детéй; **he/she is an only** ~ он/онá едúнственный ребёнок; **he's only a small** ~ он ещё мáленький; **she's a perfectly healthy** ~ онá совершéнно здорóвый ребёнок; **the children are doing well at school** дéти/ребята хорошó ýчатся; **no ~ of mine is going to that film** мои дéти на этот фильм не пойдýт; **come on children, let's go** дéти,/ребята, пошлú; **children, no more nonsense!** дéти, хвáтит баловáться; **you naughty ~!** ты неснóсный ребёнок!; **she's with** ~ онá берéменна; **children's hospital** дéтская больнúца; *fig*: **that's ~'s play to him** это для негó дéтские игрýшки (*pl*); **a ~ of his time/of nature** дитя своегó вéка/прирóды; **this novel is as it were his favourite** ~ этот ромáн—егó любúмое дéтище.

childhood *n* дéтство; **from/in** ~ с дéтства, в дéтстве; **he's in his second** ~ он впал в дéтство.

childish *adj* ребяческий.

childless *adj* бездéтный.

childlike *adj* дéтский; младéнческий; **a ~ innocence/belief** младéнческая невúнность, дéтская вéра.

children *npl* дéти, *see* **child**.

chill *n* хóлод; (*illness*) простýда; **to take the ~ off the soup/a room** подогрéть суп, натопúть кóмнату; **to catch a** ~ простудúться; *fig* **his arrival cast a ~ over proceedings** егó приéзд положúл конéц весéлью.

chill *vt* охла|ждáть (-дúть); **to ~ wine** охлаждáть винó; **I was ~ed to the bone** я продрóг до костéй (*pl*).

chilly *adj* холóдный, прохлáдный, *both also fig*.

chime *n*: **the ~ of bells** колокóльный перезвóн.

chime *vti vt*: **the clock ~d six** пробúло (*impers*) шесть
vi звонúть (по-); **the bells are chiming** звонят колоколá; **the doorbell ~d** зазвонúл двернóй звонóк.

chimney *n* дымовáя трубá.

chimney sweep *n* трубочúст.

chin *n* подбóродок; **a double** ~ двойнóй подбóродок.

china *n* (*material and collect = dishes, etc.*) фарфóр.

Chinese *adj* китáйский; **he/she is** ~ он китáец, онá китаянка.

chink[1] *n* (*crack*) щель; (*smaller*) трéщина.

chink[2] *n* (*sound of coins, etc.*) звякáнье.

chintz *n* обúвочный сúтец.

chip *n* (*of wood*) щепá, щéпка; лучúна (*also collect*); (*of stone, glass, etc.*) облóмок; *pl* (**~s**) (*for roads*) щебёнка (*collect*), (*US*: *potato-crisps*) хрустящий картóфель; (*counter for games*) фúшка; **a ~ on the edge of a plate** щербúнка на ободкé тарéлки; **potato ~s** жáреная картóшка; *fig*: **he's a ~ off/of the old block** он весь в отцá; **at school he had a ~ on his shoulder** средú одноклáссников он чýвствовал себя обделённым судьбóй.

chip *vti vt*: **to ~ the edge of a plate** отбúть край у тарéлки (*usu pf*); **the roadmen were ~ping stones** дорóжные рабóчие дробúли кáмни (*impf*); **the sculptor was ~ping out the shoulder of a statue** скýльптор высекáл плечó стáтуи; **chickens ~ their way out of eggs** цыплята проклёвывают яúчную скорлупý
vi: **these cups ~ easily** у этих чáшек бы́стро обивáются краи́; *fig CQ* **he's always ~ping in** он всегдá вмéшивается в разговóр.

chiropodist *n* мозóльный оперáтор.

chirp *vi* чирúкать, щебетáть (*impfs*).

chisel *n* (*for wood*) долотó; (*sculptor's*) резéц.

chisel *vi* рабóтать долотóм/резцóм (*impf*).

chit *n* (*written note*) запúска; (*note of money owed for drinks, etc.*) распúска.

chitchat *n* болтовня.

chivalrous *adj* галáнтный.

chivvy *vt CQ*: **to ~ smb about/along/around/up** гонять когó-л (*only in impf*); **he chivvied me into going to the pub** он затащúл меня в паб.

chloride *n Chem* хлорúд.

chloroform *n* хлорофóрм.

chock-a-block, *also* **chock-full** *adj*: **the room was ~-a-block with/~-full of people** кóмната былá полнá нарóду; **the room is ~-full of furniture** кóмната вся застáвлена мéбелью; **the square was ~-a-block with cars** плóщадь былá запрýжена маши́нами.

chocolate *n* шоколáд (*no pl*); **a cup/bar of ~** чáшка/пли́тка шоколáда; **a box of ~s** корóбка шоколáдных конфéт; *attr* шоколáдный; **a ~ box** корóбка из-под шоколáда.

choice *n* вы́бор (*no pl*); **a wide ~** ширóкий вы́бор; **you made a bad ~** вы сдéлали плохóй вы́бор, вы неудáчно вы́брали; **for ~ I prefer...** вообщé-то я предпочитáю...; **I had no ~ but to go** мне пришлóсь éхать — вы́бора у меня́ нé было.

choice *adj* отбóрный.

choir *n* хор; хоровóй ансáмбль (*m*).

choke *n Aut* подсóс; *CQ* **give her more ~** прибáвь подсóс.

choke *vti vt* **1** (*suffocate*) души́ть (за-); **sobs ~d her** её души́ли рыдáния (*only in impf*); **she ~d back her sobs** онá подави́ла рыдáния

2 (*block up*) засор|я́ть (-и́ть); **the pipe is ~d up again** трубá опя́ть засори́лась; **the chimney is ~d with soot** трубá заби́та сáжей; **the garden is ~d with weeds** сад зарóс сорнякáми; **~ the bonfire with damp leaves** загаси́ костёр влáжными ли́стьями; *CQ* **he wanted to come but I ~d him off** он хотéл прийти́, но я егó отговори́л

vi (*suffocate*) дави́ться (по-); за|дыхáться (-дохнýться); **he ~d on a bone** он подави́лся кóсточкой; **he was choking with anger** он задыхáлся от гнéва; **I swallowed some water the wrong way and ~d** водá не в то гóрло попáла, и я поперхнýлся (*pf*).

cholera *n* холéра.

choleric *adj* вспы́льчивый.

choose *vti vt* вы|бирáть (-брать) *and other compounds*; **I didn't know which to ~** я не знал, что вы́брать; **he was chosen as chairman** егó вы́брали/он был вы́бран председáтелем; **we chose curtains to match the wallpaper** мы подобрáли занавéски под цвет обóев; **I chose the threads I needed from your workbox** я взялá в твоéй шкатýлке ни́тки, котóрые мне нужны́; **there's nothing to ~ between them** выбирáть тут нéчего

vi: **you'll have to ~ between them** вам придётся выбирáть мéжду ни́ми; **he chose to stay at home** он реши́л остáться дóма; **just as you ~** как хоти́те; **I don't ~ to do it** я не хочý э́того дéлать; **I cannot ~ but obey** я не могý не послýшаться.

choosey *adj CQ* разбóрчивый; **he's ~ about his food** он разбóрчив в едé.

chop *n* (*blow*) удáр; *Cook*: **mutton/pork/chump ~** барáнья/свинáя/тóлстая отбивнáя; *CQ* **he got the ~** егó увóлили, егó вы́гнали с рабóты.

chop *vti vt* (*wood or meat, parsley, etc.*) руби́ть (по-, на-); **to ~ up meat** руби́ть мя́со; **to ~ wood** руби́ть дровá (*pl*); **to ~ kindlings** щепáть лучи́ну (*collect*) (*impf*); **to ~ down a tree** сруб|áть дéрево (-и́ть); **to ~ off a branch** обруб|áть вéтку (-и́ть)

vi fig CQ: **he's always ~ping and changing** у негó семь пя́тниц на недéле.

chopped *adj Cook* рýбленый.

chopper *n* (*hatchet*) колýн; *Cook* тя́пка.

chopping block *n* (*for wood*) колóда, (*smaller*) чурбáн.

chopping board *n Cook* доскá для рýбки мя́са, *etc*.

choppy *adj* (*of sea*) неспокóйный.

chord *n Mus* аккóрд; *Math* хóрда; *Anat* **vocal ~s** голосовы́е свя́зки.

chore *n CQ*: **I've got a few ~s to do** мне нáдо сдéлать кóе-чтó по хозя́йству; **it's your turn for the ~s today** сегóдня твоя́ óчередь занимáться домáшними делáми; **I find ironing a real ~** терпéть не могý глáдить.

chorus *n Mus*, *fig* хор; (*refrain*) припéв, рефрéн; *fig* **a ~ of praise/protest** хвалéбный хор, бýря протéстов.

chorus girl *n* хори́стка.

Christ *n* Христóс.

christen *vt* (*perform ceremony*) крести́ть (о-); (*name*): **the child was ~ed Mary after her grandmother** дéвочку назвáли Мари́ей в честь бáбушки.

christening *n* (*rite*) крещéние; (*ceremony and party combined*) крести́ны (*no sing*).

Christian *n* христиани́н.

Christian *adj* христиáнский; **~ name** и́мя.

Christianity *n* христиáнство.

Christmas, *abbr in writing* **Xmas** *n* рождествó; **Father ~** *approx* Дед Морóз; **merry ~!** с рождествóм!; *attr*: **the ~ holidays** рождéственские кани́кулы; **~ day/eve** пéрвый день/канýн рождествá; **~ tree** ёлка.

chromatic *adj* хромати́ческий.

chromium *n* хром.

chromium-plated *adj* хроми́рованный.

chronic *adj* хрони́ческий; **a ~ invalid** больнóй-хрóник; *CQ* **the weather here is ~** погóда здесь ужáсная.

chronicle *n* хрóника; лéтопись.

chronological *adj* хронологи́ческий.

chrysalis *n* кýколка (насекóмого).

chrysanthemum *n* хризантéма.

chubby *adj* пýхлый; **a ~ baby** пýхлый ребёнок.

chuck *vt* (*throw*) брос|áть (-ить), *also fig*; **to ~ away/out old letters** вы́бросить стáрые пи́сьма; *fig*: **to ~ in one's hand** (*give up*) сда|вáться (-ться); **to ~ out gatecrashers** прово|жáть/вы|гоня́ть незвáных гостéй (-ди́ть/-гнать); **to ~ (up) one's job/girlfriend** брóсить рабóту/свою́ дéвушку; *CQ* **~ it!** брóсьте!, перестáньте!

chuffed *adj sl*: **he was pretty ~ about it** он был óчень э́тим довóлен.

chug *vi*: **the train/steamer/lorry ~ged along** пóезд/парохóд пропыхтéл ми́мо, ми́мо протарахтéл грузови́к.

chum *n* прия́тель (*m*); **we were great ~s at school** в шко́ле мы бы́ли закады́чные друзья́.

chum *vi*: *CQ* **to ~ up with smb** подружи́ться с кем-л (*pf*).

chunk *n* (*of cheese, meat, bread, etc.*) большо́й кусо́к; *fig CQ* **I got through a big ~ of work today** я сего́дня у́йму дел переде́лал.

church *n* це́рковь; *attr* церко́вный.

churchyard *n* кла́дбище (при це́ркви), пого́ст.

churlish *adj* гру́бый; **he's ~** он грубия́н.

chute *n* (*for rubbish*) мусоропрово́д; (*for coal, wood, etc.*) лото́к; (*in playgrounds*) го́рка.

cicada *n* цика́да.

cider *n* сидр.

cigar *n* сига́ра.

cigarette *n* сигаре́та; (*Russian, with paper holder*) папиро́са; **a packet of ~s** па́чка сигаре́т; **he lit/put out a ~** он закури́л/погаси́л сигаре́ту; *attr*: **a ~ case/end/holder/lighter** портсига́р, оку́рок, мундшту́к, зажига́лка.

cinch *n sl*: **it's a ~** э́то де́ло ве́рное.

cinder *n*: **~s** зола́, (*industrial*) гарь (*no pls*); **the cake was burnt to a ~** пиро́г си́льно подгоре́л; *attr*: **~ track** га́ревая доро́жка.

cine-camera *n* киноаппара́т.

cinema *n* (**the ~**) кино́ (*indecl*); (*building*) кинотеа́тр.

cinnamon *n* кори́ца.

cipher *n Math* (*zero*) ноль (*m*), нуль (*m*); (*any number*) (ара́бская) ци́фра; (*code*) шифр; **in ~** ши́фром, зашифро́ванный; *fig* **he's just a ~** он пусто́е ме́сто.

circle *n* круг; **the family ~** семе́йный круг; **business ~s** деловы́е круги́; **a study ~** кружо́к; **the students gathered round him in a ~** вокру́г него́ собрали́сь студе́нты; **a ~ of trees** кольцо́ дере́вьев; **a vicious ~** поро́чный круг; **to draw a ~** начерти́ть/нарисова́ть круг; *Theat* **we have seats in the dress/first/upper ~** у нас места́ в бельэта́же/на пе́рвом я́русе/на ве́рхнем я́русе; *Aut* **turning ~** ра́диус поворо́та маши́ны; *fig* **to come full ~** заверши́ть круг; *CQ* **I've been running round in small ~s all day** я сего́дня ношу́сь це́лый день и всё без то́лку.

circle *vti vt* кружи́ть (*impf*); **the aeroplane ~d the town** самолёт кружи́л над го́родом; **to ~ a lake** (*on foot*) об|ходи́ть/(*in car*) объ|езжа́ть о́зеро (-ойти́/-е́хать); **the cosmonaut ~d the Earth several times** космона́вт сде́лал не́сколько витко́в вокру́г Земли́

vi кружи́ться.

circuit *n* (*tour, route*) маршру́т; *Elec* цепь; **the postman's ~** маршру́т почтальо́на; *Sport* **racing ~** го́ночный трек; *Elec* **short ~** коро́ткое замыка́ние.

circuitous *adj*: **by a ~ route** око́льным путём.

circular *n* (*office memo, etc.*) циркуля́р; (*advertisement through post*) **it's only a ~** э́то про́сто рекла́ма.

circular *adj*: **a ~ tower/tour** кру́глая ба́шня, кругово́й объе́зд *or* кольцево́й маршру́т; **~ motion** кругово́е движе́ние; **a ~ saw/letter** циркуля́рная пила́, циркуля́р; **a ~ staircase** винтова́я ле́стница.

circulate *vti vt*: **~ this letter to all the staff** пусть все прочту́т э́то письмо́; **he ~d the letter round the table** он переда́л письмо́ по кру́гу; **to ~ news** распространя́ть но́вости (*pl*) (*usu impf*)

vi (*of air, etc.*) циркули́ровать (*impf*); **rumours are circulating that...** хо́дят слу́хи, что...; **I didn't ~ much at the reception** я ма́ло с кем говори́л на приёме.

circulation *n* (*of air, etc.*) циркуля́ция; **this newspaper has a ~ of 2 million** э́та газе́та име́ет двухмиллио́нный тира́ж; *Fin* **to put into/to withdraw from ~** пуска́ть в обраще́ние, изыма́ть из обраще́ния; *Med* **he's got poor ~** у него́ плохо́е кровообраще́ние; *fig* **he's been out of ~ for a long time because of his illness** он давно́ нигде́ не появля́ется из-за боле́зни.

circumference *n Math* окру́жность; **to have a ~ of 10 metres** (име́ть) де́сять ме́тров в окру́жности.

circumlocution *n*: **without further ~** без дальне́йших околи́чностей.

circumnavigate *vt* плыть вокру́г + *G* (*det impf*); **to ~ the globe** соверши́ть кругосве́тное пла́вание.

circumspect *adj* осмотри́тельный.

circumstance *n* **1** обстоя́тельство; **in/under these ~s** при да́нных обстоя́тельствах; **under no ~s will I go** я ни при каки́х обстоя́тельствах не пойду́ туда́; **he was the victim of ~s** он был же́ртвой обстоя́тельств; **extenuating ~s** смягча́ющие обстоя́тельства

2 *always pl* (**~s**): **they are/live in reduced ~s** они́ сейча́с в весьма́ стеснённых обстоя́тельствах; **he lives in easy ~s** он хорошо́ обеспе́чен, у него́ хоро́шее материа́льное положе́ние (*sing*).

circumstantial *adj* обстоя́тельный.

circumvent *vt*: **to ~ a difficulty** об|ходи́ть затрудне́ние (-ойти́); **their plans were ~ed by the weather** пого́да помеша́ла их пла́нам.

circus *n* **1** цирк; *attr* цирково́й

2 (*in town*) пло́щадь, круг.

cistern *n* бак; (*in W.C.*) бачо́к; **hot-/cold-water ~** бак с горя́чей/с холо́дной водо́й.

cite *vt*: **to ~ a precedent** ссыла́ться на прецеде́нт (сосла́ться); **to ~ an instance** при|води́ть приме́р (-вести́).

citizen *n* (*of a country*) граждан|и́н, *f* -ка; (*of a town*) жи́тель (*m*); **a Soviet ~** сове́тский граждани́н; **the ~s of Cambridge** жи́тели Ке́мбриджа.

citizenship *n* гражда́нство.

citric *adj*: **~ acid** лимо́нная кислота́.

citrus *adj*: **~ fruits** ци́трусовые.

city *n* го́род; *attr* городско́й.

civic *adj* гражда́нский; (*of a town*) городско́й; **~ rights** гражда́нские права́.

civil *adj* **1** (*of state*) госуда́рственный; (*as opposed to military*) гражда́нский; **~ servant** госуда́рственный слу́жащий; **he's a high-ranking ~ servant** он кру́пный чино́вник; **~ disobedience** беспоря́дки (*pl*)

2 (*polite*) ве́жливый; **it was ~ of them to offer to help** с их стороны́ бы́ло о́чень любе́зно предложи́ть нам по́мощь; **keep a ~ tongue in your head!** не дерзи́!, разгова́ривай пове́жливее!

civility *n* ве́жливость.

civilization *n* цивилиза́ция.

civilize *vt* цивилизова́ть (*impf and pf*); (*educate*) воспи́т|ывать (-а́ть); *iron* **my student son is becoming slightly more ~d** мой сын-студе́нт стано́вится всё бо́льше похо́ж на цивилизо́ванного челове́ка.

clad *adj* оде́тый; **~ in white/in silk** оде́тый в бе́лое/в шелка́ (*pl*).

claim *n* **1** притяза́ние, прете́нзия; тре́бование; (*right*) пра́во; **to lay ~ to smth** предъявля́ть прете́нзию/тре́бования к чему́-л, претендова́ть на что-л; **there are too many ~s on my time** сли́шком мно́гого тре́буют от меня́; **his ~ to be a scholar is absurd** его́ прете́нзия на учёность про́сто смешна́; **I put in a ~ for the insurance** я обрати́лся с тре́бованием о вы́плате страхо́вки; **he has no ~ on my help** он не име́ет пра́ва тре́бовать от меня́ по́мощи

2 *Law*: **a ~ to an inheritance** притяза́ния (*pl*) на пра́во насле́дства; **to make/put in a ~ against smb for smth** предъяви́ть кому́-л иск на что-л; **you have no legal ~ to the property** вы не име́ете зако́нного пра́ва на э́то иму́щество.

claim *vt* **1** (*demand as one's due*) тре́бовать + *G* (*impf*); претендова́ть на + *A* (*impf*); **he ~ed exemption from tax** он тре́бовал освобожде́ния от нало́га; **I ~ that the hearing should be postponed** я тре́бую, что́бы рассмотре́ние де́ла бы́ло отло́жено; **he ~ed her attention all evening** он весь ве́чер претендова́л на её внима́ние; **he ~ed the property as his** он претендова́л/предъявля́л права́ (*pl*) на э́то иму́щество; **who ~s these gloves?** чьи э́то перча́тки?

2 (*assert*) утвержда́ть (*only in impf*); **he ~s to be her son/to have seen her** он утвержда́ет, что он её сын/, что ви́дел её; (*used sceptically*) **he ~s to be a doctor** он счита́ет себя́ врачо́м.

claimant *n* претенде́нт.

clamber *vi* кара́бкаться (вс-); **to ~ over rocks** кара́бкаться по ска́лам.

clammy *adj* ли́пкий.

clamorous *adj* шу́мный; крикли́вый.

clamour, (*US*) **clamor** *n* шум; **there was a ~ of protest at the new law** но́вый зако́н вы́звал бу́рные проте́сты (*pl*).

clamour, (*US*) **clamor** *vi* шуме́ть (*impf*); **to ~ against new taxes** протестова́ть про́тив введе́ния но́вых нало́гов (*impf and pf*); **the children were ~ing to be allowed to bathe** де́ти по́дняли тако́й крик—проси́лись купа́ться.

clamp *n Tech* зажи́м.

clamp *vti vt* скреп|ля́ть (-и́ть); за|жима́ть (-жа́ть)

vi fig uses: **to ~ down on the number of visas issued** ограни́ч|ивать число́ виз (-ить); **the police are ~ing down on traffic offenders** поли́ция применя́ет всё бо́лее стро́гие ме́ры к наруши́телям у́личного движе́ния; **the museum is ~ing down on security** музе́й принима́ет ме́ры по усиле́нию охра́ны.

clandestine *adj* та́йный, скры́тый.

clang *n* (*of bell, etc.*) звон; лязг.

clang *vi* (*ring*) звене́ть, (*clank: of metals*) ля́згать (*impfs*); **the gates ~ed shut** воро́та с ля́згом закры́лись.

clanger *n sl*: **to drop a ~** де́лать ля́псус.

clap *n* (*with hands*) хлопо́к; **he gave me a ~ on the shoulder** он хло́пнул меня́ по плечу́; **a ~ of thunder** уда́р гро́ма.

clap *vti vt* **1** (*with hands*) хло́п|ать (по-, *semel* -нуть); **the audience ~ped the singer** пу́блика гро́мко хло́пала певцу́

2 (*put*): **he ~ped his hand to his forehead/over his mouth** он хло́пнул себя́ ладо́нью по лбу/по губа́м; **he ~ped down the lid of the box** он захло́пнул кры́шку сундука́; *CQ*: **they ~ped him in jail** он был бро́шен в тюрьму́, его́ посади́ли; **as soon as I ~ped eyes on him** как то́лько я уви́дел его́

vi (*applaud*) хло́пать, аплоди́ровать (*impf*).

clapper *n* (*of bell*) язы́к.

clapping *n* аплодисме́нты (*pl*), (*sparse*) хлопки́ (*pl*).

claptrap *n CQ* ерунда́, чепуха́; **don't talk ~!** не болта́й ерунды́!

claret *n* бордо́ (*indecl*).

clarify *vt* **1** поясн|я́ть (-и́ть), вы|сня́ть (-́яснить); **I'd like to ~ one or two points with you** я хочу́ вы́яснить с ва́ми не́сколько вопро́сов

2 (*liquids*) очи|ща́ть (-́стить).

clarinet *n* кларне́т.

clash *n* (*noise of metal on metal*) лязг; (*conflict*) столкнове́ние, *also fig*; **a ~ with the police** столкнове́ние с поли́цией; *fig* **a ~ of interests/personalities** столкнове́ние интере́сов/хара́ктеров.

clash *vi* (*make noise: of metals*) ля́зг|ать (*semel* -нуть); (*knock against*) ста́лкиваться с + *I* (столкну́ться), *also fig*; **the two armies ~ed outside the town** две а́рмии сошли́сь у го́рода; **their interests ~ed** их интере́сы столкну́лись; **our views ~** мы расхо́димся во взгля́дах; **the two statements ~** одно́ заявле́ние противоре́чит друго́му; **the dates of the two concerts ~** э́ти конце́рты состоя́тся одновре́менно; **these colours ~** э́ти цвета́ несовмести́мы/не гармони́руют.

clasp *n* **1** (*buckle*) пря́жка, (*of necklace, etc.*) застёжка

2 (*handshake*) рукопожа́тие.

clasp *vt* **1** (*fasten*) заст|ёгивать (-егну́ть)

2 (*hold*) сжимáть (сжать); **to ~ smb in one's arms/smb's hand tightly** сжимáть когó-л в объя́тиях, крéпко пожáть комý-л рýку; **to ~ one's hands** склáдывать ладóни (сложи́ть).

clasp knife *n* складнóй нож.

class *n* **1** (*group, sort*) класс, род; **~ of mammals** класс млекопитáющих; **a hotel of the best ~** гости́ница вы́сшего разря́да, первоклáссная гости́ница; **to travel first ~** éхать пéрвым клáссом; *fig* **he's in a ~ by himself** он еди́нственный в своём рóде; *attr*: **a first ~ ticket** билéт пéрвого клáсса

2 (*social division*) класс; **working ~** рабóчий класс; **middle ~** срéдние слои́ óбщества; **propertied/ruling ~** имýщий/прáвящий класс; *attr*: **~ barriers/divisions** сослóвные барьéры/делéния

3 (*in school*) класс; (*course*) курс; **he's top of the ~** он пéрвый учени́к в клáссе; **I'm attending evening ~es in Russian/in cooking** я посещáю вечéрние кýрсы рýсского языкá/кулинáрии; **what time do ~es begin?** когдá начинáются заня́тия?

class *vt* классифици́ровать (*impf and pf*); **that book should be ~ed as biography** э́ту кни́гу мóжно отнести́ к биографи́ям; **to ~ together** зачисл|я́ть в однý категóрию (-и́ть); **he shouldn't be ~ed with the beginners** егó ужé не посáдишь в оди́н класс с начинáющими.

class consciousness *n* клáссовое сознáние.

classic *n* **1** (*famous author or composer*) клáссик; (*of work*) клáссика; **"War and Peace" is a ~** «Войнá и мир»—класси́ческое произведéние; **that ballet is a ~** э́тот балéт—клáссика

2 *pl* (~s) (*Latin and Greek literature*): **I read ~s at the university** я изучáл анти́чную литератýру в университéте.

classic *adj* класси́ческий.

classicist *n* филóлог-клáссик.

classification *n* классификáция.

classified *adj* классифици́рованный; (*secret*) **~ documents** секрéтные докумéнты.

classify *vt* классифици́ровать (*impf and pf*); **to ~ by subject/by date/by alphabetical order** классифици́ровать по тéмам (*pl*)/по дáтам (*pl*)/по алфави́ту.

classroom *n* класс.

classy *adj CQ* превосхóдный, клáссный.

clatter *n* (*of dishes, hooves, wheels*) стук; (*louder*) грóхот; **the ~ of machinery** грóхот механи́змов (*pl*); **there was a ~ of dishes in the kitchen** на кýхне гремéли посýдой (*collect*).

clatter *vi* (*of hooves, wheels*) стучáть (*impf*); (*of metal, machinery*) громыхáть (*impf*); **the pans ~ed to the floor** кастрю́ли с грóхотом попáдали нá пол.

clause *n Law* статья́, пункт; **~ one, paragraph 4** пункт пéрвый, парáграф четвёртый; *Gram*: **main/subordinate ~** глáвное/придáточное предложéние.

clavichord *n* клавикóрды (*no sing*).

claw *n* (*of bird, cat*) кóготь (*m*); (*of lobster, crab*) клешня́; *CQ* **she's showing her ~s** онá покáзывает коготки́.

clay *n* гли́на; *attr* гли́няный.

clean *adj* **1** (*not dirty*) чи́стый; **a ~ dress** чи́стая одéжда; **~ sheets** чи́стое бельё (*collect*); **a ~ copy** чистови́к, белови́к; **to keep one's house ~** держáть дом в чистотé; *fig* **he got a ~ bill of health** дóктор сказáл, что он здорóв

2 (*pure, etc.*): **a ~ conscience** чи́стая сóвесть; **it was all good ~ fun** всё бы́ло óчень пристóйно; **keep it ~!** не нáдо э́той гря́зи!; *Law* **he has a ~ record/driving licence** он не имéет суди́мости, у негó нет прокóлов

3 (*clearly defined*): **the yacht has lovely ~ lines** у э́той я́хты изя́щные ли́нии; **a sharp knife makes a ~ cut** óстрый нож хорошó рéжет; *fig.* **I've made a ~ cut with my past** я нáчисто порвáл с прóшлым.

clean *adv* совершéнно, совсéм; **I ~ forgot about it** я совсéм/совершéнно/*CQ* нáчисто забы́л об э́том; **he got ~ away** он скры́лся; **the fish jumped ~ out of the water** ры́ба вы́прыгнула из воды́; **we're ~ out of umbrellas** у нас нет ни одногó зонтá; (*open*) **I'll come ~ with you** я тебé скажý начистотý.

clean *vt* чи́стить (по-); (*tidy*) при|бирáть (-брáть); **to ~ shoes/vegetables/one's teeth** чи́стить тýфли/óвощи/зýбы; **to ~ a room** убирáть кóмнату (убрáть); **to ~ a window/the floor** мыть oкнó/пол (по-, вы́-)

clean out *vt*: **to ~ out a kitchen cupboard/stable** мыть буфéт на кýхне, чи́стить конюшню (*pfs* вы́-); *fig*: **the guests ~ed us out of whisky** гóсти вы́пили у нас всё ви́ски; **we were ~ed out** (*in gambling*) мы проигрáлись нáчисто/в пух и прах; **I'm ~ed out after buying the car** я на мели́ пóсле покýпки маши́ны

clean up *vti vt*: **I must ~ up my room** я дóлжен прибрáть кóмнату/прибрáться в моéй кóмнате; **I'm just going to ~ (myself) up** я тóлько приведý себя́ в поря́док; *fig*: **the police are going to ~ up the drug traffic** поли́ция намéрена покóнчить с торгóвлей наркóтиками; *CQ* **we ~ed up £ 50 at the races** мы вы́играли пятьдеся́т фýнтов на скáчках

vi: **to ~ up after smb** убирáть за кем-л.

cleaner *n* убóрщица; **the ~'s** (*shop*) (хим)-чи́стка.

cleaning *n* (*general*) чи́стка, очи́стка; (*of rooms, etc.*) убóрка; **dry ~** химчи́стка.

cleanliness *n* чистотá.

clean-shaven *adj*: **he is ~** у негó нет бороды́.

clear *adj* **1** (*distinct*) я́сный; (*pure*) чи́стый; (*obvious*) я́вный; (*transparent*) прозрáчный; **a ~ day/mind** я́сный день/ум; **a ~ reflection/outline** я́сное отражéние/очертáние; **a ~ sky** я́сное/чи́стое нéбо; **~ water/skin/conscience** чи́стая водá/кóжа/сóвесть; **~ air/sound** чистый во́здух/звук; **it's a ~ case of murder** э́то я́вное уби́йство; **~ ice** прозра́чный лёд; **~ soup** бульо́н; **~ handwriting** чёткий/разбо́рчивый по́черк

2 (*certain*) я́сный; **he made it ~ that...** он я́сно/отчётливо дал поня́ть, что...; **I am not ~ on this question** э́тот вопро́с мне нея́сен; **as ~ as crystal/as day** я́сно как день; **are you ~ that you really do want to buy it?** вы то́чно реши́ли э́то купи́ть?

3 (*free*) свобо́дный; **the motorway is ~ of snow** магистра́ль свобо́дна/очи́щена от сне́га; *fig*: **the road/coast is ~** путь свобо́ден; **we're ~ of debt** мы расплати́лись со всё́ми долга́ми (*pl*); **I'll need three days ~** мне ну́жно по́лных три дня; *Fin* **~ profit** чи́стая при́быль; *Sport* (*of horse jumping or of hurdling*) **he had a ~ round** он чи́сто прошёл всю диста́нцию; *as n*: **I'm in the ~ now** тепе́рь я вне подозре́ния (*no longer suspect*)/я вне опа́сности (*out of danger*), тепе́рь у меня́ нет долго́в (*not in debt*).

clear *adv*: **I heard him loud and ~** я отчётливо слы́шал его́; **when we get ~ of London, you can drive** когда́ вы́едем из Ло́ндона, ты поведёшь маши́ну; **keep ~ of alcohol/of him** не сове́тую тебе́ пить, держи́сь пода́льше от него́; (*in lifts, etc.*) **keep ~ of the gates!** осторо́жно, две́ри закрыва́ются!; **he jumped ~ of the car** (*away from an approaching car*) он успе́л отскочи́ть (с доро́ги).

clear *vti vt* **1** (*remove obstructions, etc.*) убира́ть (убра́ть); **to ~ a room/the yard/stones from the road** убира́ть ко́мнату/двор/ка́мни с доро́ги; **to ~ the table** убра́ть со стола́; **to ~ the streets of snow** очи|ща́ть у́лицы от сне́га (-́стить); **to ~ a site for building** расчи|ща́ть уча́сток для строи́тельства (-́стить); **to ~ a drain** прочи|ща́ть сто́чную трубу́ (-́стить); **to ~ a space for a bed** освобо|жда́ть ме́сто для крова́ти (-ди́ть); **to ~ the court of people** освободи́ть зал суда́ от пу́блики; *Comm* **we're ~ing stock** мы распродаём запа́сы; *fig*: **to ~ the air** разря|жа́ть атмосфе́ру (-ди́ть); **to ~ the way/the decks for action** гото́виться (при-)/быть гото́вым к де́йствиям (*pl*)

2 (*pass, get over without touching*): **the horse easily/just ~ed the fence** ло́шадь легко́/едва́ взяла́ препя́тствие; **the plane just ~ed the treetops** самолёт едва́ не заде́л верху́шки дере́вьев; **I/the car just ~ed the narrow entrance** я е́ле прое́хал/маши́на едва́ прошла́ в у́зкие воро́та; *Fin*: **I ~ed £ 40 on that deal** на э́той сде́лке я вы́ручил со́рок фу́нтов; **I didn't even ~ my expenses** я да́же расхо́дов не оправда́л

3 (*be passed as in order*): **have you ~ed your luggage at/with the customs?** вы прошли́ тамо́женный осмо́тр?; **to ~ a ship at/with/through the customs** произ|води́ть тамо́женный досмо́тр су́дна (-вести́); **he's been ~ed by Security** его́ прове́рили на лоя́льность; **I'll have to ~ the plan/my expenses with the director** я до́лжен утверди́ть план/мои́ расхо́ды у дире́ктора; *Law* **to ~ oneself of a charge of theft** снять с себя́ обвине́ние в кра́же

vi: **the sky is ~ing** не́бо очища́ется от туч/проясня́ется; **the weather soon ~ed (up)** пого́да вско́ре улу́чшилась

clear away *vti vt* убира́ть; **to ~ away the dishes** убира́ть посу́ду (*collect*); **to ~ away leaves/rubble** убра́ть ли́стья/строи́тельный му́сор

vi: **I'll ~ away** (*after meal*) я уберу́ со стола́; **the clouds ~ed away** облака́ рассе́ялись

clear off *vti vt*: **I've ~ed off my debts/my mortgage** я расплати́лся с долга́ми, я вы́платил (*approx*) ссу́ду

vi: **~ off!** убира́йся!; **he ~ed off quickly** он бы́стро скры́лся

clear out *vti vt*: **to ~ out a cupboard** при|бира́ться в шкафу́ (-бра́ться)

vi: **I've had enough and I'm ~ing out** (*leaving family, etc.*) с меня́ дово́льно—я ухожу́; **you'd better ~ out before my father sees you** тебе́ лу́чше уйти́, пока́ мой оте́ц тебя́ не уви́дел

clear up *vti vt* (*tidy*) убира́ть; *fig* **to ~ up a misunderstanding/a question/a mystery** вы|ясня́ть недоразуме́ние/вопро́с (-́яснить), раскры|ва́ть та́йну (-́ть)

vi: **it ~ed up** не́бо проясни́лось.

clearance *n* **1**: **security ~** прове́рка; **certificate of customs ~** тамо́женное свиде́тельство; *attr*: **a ~ sale** распрода́жа

2 *Aut* (*space*) кли́ренс, доро́жный просве́т; **you've only got a ~ of one foot on this side** с э́той стороны́ у вас есть просве́т всего́ в оди́н фут.

clear-cut *adj* чёткий; я́сный; **a ~ distinction** чёткое отли́чие; **~ lines** я́сные ли́нии; **~ features** пра́вильные черты́ лица́.

clearing *n* (*in forest*) поля́на.

clear-sighted *adj* зо́ркий, *also fig*.

clearway *n* автостра́да, где остано́вка тра́нспорта запрещена́.

clef *n Mus*: **alto/bass/treble ~** альто́вый/басо́вый/скрипи́чный ключ.

cleft *n* тре́щина; *attr*: **~ palate** расщеплённое нёбо, во́лчья пасть.

clench *vt* сжима́ть (сжать); **with ~ed fists** со сжа́тыми кулака́ми; **to ~ one's teeth** сти́с|кивать зу́бы (-нуть).

clergy *n collect* (**the ~**) духове́нство.

clergyman *n approx* свяще́нник, священнослужи́тель (*m*).

clerical *adj* (*of the clergy*) духо́вный; (*of clerks*) канцеля́рский; **due to a ~ error** из-за опи́ски.

clerk *n* конто́рский слу́жащий; клерк; **bank ~** ба́нковский слу́жащий.

clever *adj* (*intelligent*) у́мный; (*able*) уме́лый; *pejor* ло́вкий; **a ~ book/speech/student** у́мная кни́га/речь/студе́нтка (*f*); **a ~ workman** уме́лый рабо́тник; **he's ~ with his hands** у него́ уме́лые ру́ки; **a ~ conjuror/trick**

ло́вкий фо́кусник, ло́вкая проде́лка; **a ~ doctor** зна́ющий врач; **how ~ of you to fix my iron** како́й ты у́мница/молоде́ц, что почини́л мой утю́г; **she is ~ at arranging flowers** она́ уме́ет краси́во расставля́ть цветы́, она́ иску́сно ста́вит цветы́.

cliché *n* клише́ (*indecl*).

click *n* щёлканье.

click *vti vt* щёлк|ать (*semel* -нуть); **to ~ one's heels/one's tongue** щёлкать каблука́ми, прищёлк|ивать языко́м (-нуть); **he ~ed the shutter of his camera** он щёлкнул затво́ром фотоаппара́та

vi: *CQ* **they ~ed at once** они́ ми́гом/момента́льно сошли́сь, они́ сра́зу нашли́ о́бщий язы́к.

client *n* клие́нт.

cliff *n* утёс; (отве́сная) скала́.

climate *n* кли́мат; *fig* **it wouldn't be possible given the present ~ of opinion** обще́ственное мне́ние воспроти́вится э́тому.

climax *n* кульмина́ция, вы́сшая то́чка; **to reach a ~** дости́гнуть кульмина́ции/вы́сшей то́чки; **the ~ of the play** кульмина́ция пье́сы; **at the ~ of the battle** в разга́р бо́я; **the fireworks were the ~ of the evening** фейерве́рк (*sing*) был гвоздём ве́чера.

climb *n* подъём; **it's a steep ~ to the village** к дере́вне ведёт круто́й подъём; **Elbrus is a stiff ~** поднима́ться на Эльбру́с нелегко́; (*expedition*) **I'm going on a ~ with my brother** мы с бра́том собира́емся пойти́ в го́ры.

climb *vti vt* [**NB** *in Russian verbs* = "*to climb*" *are intrans, but combined with preps translate English trans uses*] ла́зить (*indet impf*), лезть (*det impf*, по-) *and compouds*; под|нима́ться на + *A* (-ня́ться); взбира́ться на + *A* (взобра́ться); **children love ~ing trees** де́ти лю́бят ла́зить по дере́вьям; **to ~ a tree/a ladder** влеза́ть на де́рево/на ле́стницу (влезть); **to ~ a fence** пере|леза́ть че́рез забо́р (-ле́зть); **to ~ a mountain/the stairs** подня́ться на́ гору/по ле́стнице; **to ~ a rope** взбира́ться/лезть по кана́ту

vi: **the aircraft ~ed steeply** самолёт кру́то набира́л высоту́; **the road ~s to 1,000 metres** доро́га поднима́ется до километро́вой высоты́; *Sport* **do you ~?** вы альпини́ст?; **to ~ down a cliff** слеза́ть/спус|ка́ться со скалы́ (слезть/-ти́ться); **to ~ through a window/into a car** влеза́ть в окно́/в маши́ну; **he managed to ~ out of the well** ему́ удало́сь вы́браться из коло́дца; **he ~ed to the fifth floor** он взобра́лся на шесто́й эта́ж; (*of plants*) **ivy is ~ing up the wall** плющ вьётся вверх по стене́; *fig* **to ~ down** уступ|а́ть (-и́ть).

climber *n* альпини́ст; (*of plant*) вью́щееся расте́ние; *fig pejor* карьери́ст.

climbing *n* альпини́зм; **I like ~** я люблю́ ла́зить по гора́м.

clinch *vt fig*: **to ~ a bargain** заключи́ть сде́лку (*usu pf*); **to ~ matters/an argument** оконча́тельно реши́ть вопро́с (*usu pf*).

cling *vi* (*stick to*) прилип|а́ть к + *D* (-нуть); (*hang on to*) цепля́ться за + *A* (уцепи́ться); **wet clothes ~ to the body** мо́края оде́жда прилипа́ет к те́лу; **a ~ing dress** облега́ющее пла́тье; **the child clung to his mother's hand** ребёнок цепля́лся за ру́ку ма́тери; **they clung to each other** они́ вцепи́лись друг в дру́га, *also fig*; *fig* **he clung to the hope that...** он цепля́лся за наде́жду...

clinic *n* кли́ника; (*approx, corresponding to G.P.'s "surgery"*) поликли́ника; **maternity ~** же́нская консульта́ция.

clinical *adj* клини́ческий; **~ record/history** исто́рия боле́зни; **~ thermometer** медици́нский термо́метр.

clink[1] *n* (*of glass, metal, money*) звон.

clink[1] *vti vt*: **to ~ glasses** (*in a toast*) чо́к|аться (-нуться)

vi: **the keys ~ed in his pocket** ключи́ звене́ли у него́ в карма́не (*impf*); **the glasses ~ed on the tray** стака́ны позвя́кивали на подно́се (*impf*).

clink[2] *n sl*: **he's in ~** он сиди́т (в тюрьме́).

clip[1] *vt* стричь (о́-, под́-); **to ~ a sheep/a poodle/one's hair/one's nails** стричь овцу́/пу́деля/во́лосы/но́гти; **to ~ an article out of a newspaper** вы|реза́ть статью́ из газе́ты (́-резать); **to ~ a ticket** проби|ва́ть биле́т (́-ть); *CQ* **he ~ped him one on the ear** он дал ему́ по́ уху.

clip[2] *n* (*fastener*) скре́пка; **paper ~** канцеля́рская скре́пка.

clip[2] *vt*: **to ~ papers together** скреп|ля́ть бума́ги (-и́ть).

clippers *npl* (*for hair*) маши́нка (*sing*) для стри́жки воло́с; *Hort* садо́вые но́жницы.

clipping *n* (*from newspaper*) газе́тная вы́резка.

clique *n* кли́ка.

cloak *n* плащ.

cloak *vt* покры|ва́ть (́-ть); *fig* (*conceal*) скры|ва́ть (-ть).

cloakroom *n* гардеро́б; *euph* (*W.C.*) туале́т, убо́рная.

clock *n* часы́ (*no sing*); **the ~ is going/has stopped** часы́ иду́т/останови́лись; **to set/wind/repair a ~** ста́вить/заводи́ть/чини́ть часы́; **it's 2 by this ~** по э́тим часа́м сейча́с два (часа́); **the ~ struck 12** часы́ проби́ли двена́дцать; **the ~ is 10 minutes fast/slow** часы́ спеша́т/отстаю́т на де́сять мину́т.

clock *vti vt*: **we ~ed 80 m.p.h. on the speedometer** мы де́лали во́семьдесят миль в час, су́дя по спидо́метру; *Sport* **he ~ed 4 minutes for the mile** он показа́л четы́ре мину́ты на ми́лю

vi: **we ~ in at 9 a.m. and ~ out at 6 p.m.** мы прихо́дим на рабо́ту в де́вять часо́в утра́, а ухо́дим (с рабо́ты) в шесть ве́чера; (*enter time*) **don't forget to ~ in/out** не забыва́йте отмеча́ть вре́мя прихо́да/ухо́да.

clockwise *adv* по часово́й стре́лке.

clockwork *n* часовóй механи́зм; *fig* **everything went like ~** всё шло как по мáслу; *attr*: **~ toy** заводнáя/механи́ческая игрýшка.

clod *n* (*of earth*) ком, глы́ба.

clog *vt* засор|я́ть (-и́ть), заби|вáть (-́ть); **the pipes are ~ged with leaves** вóдостóчные трýбы засоря́ются/забивáются ли́стьями; *fig* **my memory is ~ged with useless information** моя́ головá заби́та вся́кими ненýжными свéдениями.

clogs *n usu pl* деревя́нные башмаки́.

close[1] *n* конéц; **at the ~ of the season/meeting** в концé сезóна/собрáния; **at/in the ~ of his report he said...** в концé доклáда он сказáл...; **to bring a meeting/a discussion to a ~** закры́ть собрáние, прекрати́ть обсуждéние.

close[1] *vti vt* **1** (*shut*) закры|вáть (-́ть); **"Road ~d"** «проéзд закры́т»; **to ~ the door/a suitcase/a drawer** закры́ть дверь/чемодáн/я́щик; **to ~ the curtains** задёр|гивать занавéски (-нуть); *Ling* **a ~d vowel** закры́тый глáсный

2 (*conclude*) заключ|áть (-и́ть); **to ~ a deal/a speech** заключ|áть сдéлку (-и́ть), за|кáнчивать речь (-кóнчить)

vi (*shut*) закрывáться; **the shops ~ at 6** магази́ны закрывáются в шесть часóв; **the meeting will ~ at 7.00 p.m.** собрáние закóнчится в семь часóв вéчера

close down *vti vt*: **the schools are ~d down just now** сейчáс шкóлы закры́ты

vi: **the factory has ~d down** завóд закры́лся; *Radio* **the time is midnight and we are closing down** сейчáс рóвно пóлночь, нáши передáчи окóнчены

close in *vi*: **the days are closing in** дни станóвятся корóче; **night ~d in** наступи́ла ночь; **the police ~d in on the fugitives** поли́ция окружи́ла беглецóв

close up *vti vt*: **the house has been ~d up all winter** дом всю зи́му стоя́л заколóченный

vi: **flowers ~ up at night** нóчью цветы́ закрывáются; **the wound ~d up** рáна закры́лась; **the ranks ~d up** ряды́ сомкнýлись

close with *vi*: **I ~d with the offer** я соглаcи́лся на э́то предложéние; **the boxer ~d with his opponent** боксёры вошли́ в бли́жний бой.

close[2] *adj* **1** (*near*) бли́зкий; **the ~st house to us** ближáйший к нам дом; **the school is ~ to the theatre** шкóла нахóдится недалекó от теáтра; *fig*: **a ~ relation/friend/resemblance** бли́зкий рóдственник/друг, большóе схóдство; **he's very ~ to his father** он óчень бли́зок с отцóм; *fig* **he had a ~ shave** он был на волосóк от смéрти

2 (*close together, tight*) тéсный; плóтный; **we're in ~ contact with** мы в тéсном контáкте с + *I*; **they live at ~ quarters** они́ живýт в теснотé; **a ~ weave/texture** плóтная ткань; **the dress/window frame is a ~ fit** э́то плáтье плóтно облегáет фигýру, окóнная рáма плóтно при́гнана; **~ print** плóтный набóр; **it was a ~ election** за кандидáтов пóдали почти́ рáвное/одинáковое коли́чество голосóв; *Sport*: **a ~ finish** плóтный фи́ниш; (*of football match, etc.*) **it was a ~ thing** рáзница в счёте былá небольшáя; *Mil* **~ formation** сóмкнутый строй; *fig* (*mean*) **he's ~** он скупóй

3 (*stuffy*) дýшный

4 (*thorough, strict*): **on ~ examination/consideration** при ближáйшем рассмотрéнии, тщáтельно взвéсив/обдýмав; **a ~ analysis of the problem** подрóбное рассмотрéние вопрóса; **I'll give it my ~ attention** я уделю́ э́тому вопрóсу осóбое внимáние; **he was kept in ~ confinement** егó держáли в тюрьмé под осóбым наблюдéнием.

close[2] *adv* **1** (*near*) бли́зко, недалекó; **he was sitting ~ to the fire/to me** он сидéл бли́зко кками́ну/ря́дом со мной; **the metro is ~ at hand** метрó óчень бли́зко/совсéм ря́дом, до метрó отсю́да рукóй подáть; **I have the article ~ at hand** статья́ у меня́ под рукóй; **to follow ~ behind smb** слéдовать за кем-л по пятáм; **keep ~ behind me/~ to the wall** слéдуй за мной, держи́сь бли́же к стенé; **to come ~** приближáться; **to sail ~ to the wind** *Naut* идти́ крутóй бейдеви́нд (*adv*), *fig* обходи́ть закóн; *fig*: **that comes ~ to saying that...** э́то всё равнó что сказáть...; **the film keeps ~ to the text of the novel** фильм бли́зко слéдует тéксту ромáна

2 (*nearly*): **it's ~ on 5 o'clock** сейчáс óколо пяти́ (часóв); **he must be ~ on 40** емý, должнó быть, под сóрок.

closed *adj* закры́тый; (*limited*) ýзкий, ограни́ченный; **behind ~ doors** при закры́тых дверя́х, за закры́тыми дверя́ми; **a ~ society** ýзкий круг; **he has a ~ mind** у негó ýзкий кругозóр, он ограни́ченный человéк; *Elec* **~ circuit** зáмкнутая цепь.

closely *adv* **1** (*carefully*): **to look at smb/a text ~** внимáтельно смотрéть на когó-л, внимáтельно *or* тщáтельно рассмáтривать текст; **to question smb ~** подрóбно расспрáшивать когó-л; **the secret was ~ guarded** тáйна стрóго сохраня́лась

2: **to work ~ with smb** тéсно сотрýдничать с кем-л; **the two theories are ~ connected** э́ти две теóрии органи́чески свя́заны мéжду собóй; **she ~ resembles her father** онá óчень похóжа на отцá; **it was a ~ contested election** вы́боры (*pl*) проходи́ли в óчень óстрой борьбé; (*tightly*) **a ~ written page/printed text** убóристо испи́санная страни́ца, мéлко напечáтанный текст.

closet *n* шкаф; **water ~** (*abbr.* **W.C.**) туалéт.

closet *vt*: **he was ~ed with the director for two hours** дирéктор совещáлся с ним два часá.

close-up *n Cine*: **to take a ~** снять крýпным плáном; **then came a ~ of the heroine's face** затéм на экрáне крýпным плáном появи́лось лицо́ герои́ни; (*of snapshot*) **I want to take a ~** я хочу́ снять э́то с бли́зкого расстоя́ния.

closing *n*: **it's early ~ today** сего́дня магази́ны ра́но закрыва́ются.

closing *adj*: **~ remarks** заключи́тельное сло́во (*sing*); **~ date for (sending in) applications** после́дний день пода́чи заявле́ний.

closure *n* закры́тие.

clot *n*: **a ~ of cream** комо́к густы́х сли́вок (*pl*); **a blood ~** сгу́сток кро́ви; *sl* **you ~!** ты, дуби́на!

clot *vi* (*of blood, cream*) сгу|ща́ться (-сти́ться).

cloth *n* мате́рия, ткань; **a length of ~ for a suit** отре́з на костю́м; **table/dish/floor ~** ска́терть, тря́пка, полова́я тря́пка; **tea ~** посу́дное полоте́нце.

clothe *vt* оде|ва́ть (-́ть); **to ~ one's family** одева́ть семью́; **she was ~d in black** она́ была́ оде́та в чёрное; **to ~ oneself** одева́ться.

clothes *npl* оде́жда (*collect*); **to change one's ~** переоде́ться; **she makes her own ~** она́ сама́ шьёт; *attr*: **~ line/peg** бельева́я верёвка, прище́пка для белья́.

clothing *n* оде́жда (*collect*); **article of ~** предме́т оде́жды; **ready-made ~** гото́вое пла́тье (*collect*); *attr*: **~ shop/trade** магази́н оде́жды, торго́вля оде́ждой.

cloud *n* о́блако; (*heavy*) ту́ча; **a small ~** о́блачко, ту́чка; **~s of smoke** клубы́ ды́ма; *fig*: **a ~ of mosquitoes** ту́ча/тьма комаро́в; **he was under a ~** на него́ упа́ла тень подозре́ния (*of suspicion*), он попа́л в неми́лость (*out of favour*); **to have one's head in the ~s** вита́ть в облака́х.

cloud *vti vt fig*: **that is only ~ing the issue** э́то то́лько запу́тывает де́ло

vi: **it/the sky has ~ed over** не́бо покры́лось облака́ми/ту́чами; *fig* **her face/eyes ~ed over** её лицо́ омрачи́лось, её глаза́ затума́нились.

cloudburst *n* ли́вень (*m*).

cloudy *adj* о́блачный; (*of liquids*) му́тный.

clove *n* гвозди́ка (*collect*); **oil of ~s** гвозди́чное ма́сло.

clover *n* кле́вер.

clown *n* кло́ун.

clown *vi* пая́сничать (*not of a professional*).

club *n* **1** (*stick*) дуби́нка; **golf ~** бита́; *pl* (**~s**) *Cards* тре́фы; **the queen of ~s** да́ма треф

2 (*association*) клуб; **tennis ~** те́ннисный клуб.

club *vi*: **they ~bed together to hire a bus** они́ (все) ски́нулись и взя́ли напрока́т авто́бус.

clue *n* ключ; **~ to a puzzle** ключ к реше́нию головоло́мки; **the detective found a ~** детекти́в нашёл ключ к разга́дке; *CQ*: **I haven't a ~** (*don't know*) я не име́ю ни мале́йшего поня́тия; **he hadn't a ~ as to what you were talking about** он ни сло́ва не по́нял из того́, что ты говори́л; **he hasn't a ~** (*is stupid*) он така́я бе́столочь.

clump *n*: **~ of trees** ку́па/гру́ппа дере́вьев; **primroses grow in ~s** при́мулы расту́т куста́ми.

clumsy *adj* (*physically*) неуклю́жий; (*physically, or tactless*) нело́вкий.

cluster *n*: **a ~ of grapes** гроздь/кисть виногра́да; **a ~ of trees/people** ку́па дере́вьев, ку́чка/гру́ппа люде́й.

cluster *vi* расти́ кистя́ми/гро́здьями; *fig*: **the children ~ed round her/the table** де́ти окружи́ли её/сгруди́лись вокру́г стола́ (*usu pf*); **the houses ~ed at the foot of the cliff** до́мики лепи́лись у подно́жия скалы́.

clutch *n* **1**: *fig* **he fell into/got out of their ~es** он попа́л к ним в ла́пы, он вы́рвался из их лап

2 *Aut* сцепле́ние; **to engage** *or* **let in/let out the ~** включа́ть/выключа́ть сцепле́ние.

clutch *vti vt*: **the child ~ed my hand** ребёнок уцепи́лся за мою́ ру́ку/(*in terror*) вцепи́лся в мою́ ру́ку

vi: **he ~ed at a branch as he fell** па́дая, он пыта́лся ухвати́ться за ве́тку; *fig* **a drowning man will ~ at a straw** утопа́ющий хвата́ется за соло́минку.

clutter *n* беспоря́док.

clutter *vt* зава́л|ивать + *I* (-и́ть); **the table was ~ed with papers** стол был зава́лен бума́гами.

coach *n* **1** каре́та, экипа́ж; *Rail* пассажи́рский ваго́н; *Aut* тури́стский авто́бус

2 (*tutor*) репети́тор; *Sport* тре́нер.

coach *vt*: **to ~ smb for an exam** гото́вить кого́-л к экза́мену (*only in impf*); *Theat* **to ~ smb** репети́ровать с кем-л роль (*usu impf*); *Sport* тренирова́ть кого́-л (*usu impf*).

coagulate *vti* сгу|ща́ть(ся) (-сти́ть(ся)).

coal *n* у́голь (*m*) (*collect and also = a piece of coal*); **a small piece of ~** уголёк; *fig* **to haul smb over the ~s** дать кому́-л нагоня́й; *attr*: **the ~ industry** у́гольная промы́шленность; **a ~ fire was burning in the grate** в ками́не горе́ли у́гли; **~ cellar/dust/scuttle** у́гольный по́греб, у́гольная пыль, ведёрко для угля́.

coal-black *adj* чёрный как смоль.

coalfield *n* каменноу́гольный бассе́йн.

coalition *n* коали́ция.

coalmine *n* ша́хта.

coalminer *n* шахтёр.

coarse *adj* (*of material, etc.*) гру́бый; (*of sand, oatmeal, etc.*) кру́пный; *fig* неприли́чный, непристо́йный; **a ~ story/gesture/language** неприли́чный анекдо́т, гру́бый жест, непристо́йные выраже́ния (*pl*).

coast *n* бе́рег; (*area*) побере́жье; **on the ~** на берегу́; **the Black Sea ~** побере́жье Чёрного мо́ря; **there are many caves along the ~** вдоль бе́рега мно́го пеще́р; **we are approaching the ~** мы приближа́емся к бе́регу; **off the ~ of France** у берего́в (*pl*) Фра́нции; *fig* **the ~ is clear** путь свобо́ден.

coast *vi* (*in ship*) пла́вать вдоль побере́жья (*impf*); (*on bike*) спуска́ться с горы́ на свобо́дном ходу́, *Aut* е́хать на нейтра́льной ско́рости (*usu only in impfs*).

coastal *adj*: **~ waters** прибре́жные во́ды; **~ defence** берегова́я оборо́на; **~ shipping** кабота́ж, кабота́жное пла́вание.

coastguard *n* слу́жащий берегово́й охра́ны; *attr*: **the ~ service** берегова́я охра́на.

coastline *n* бе́рег; (*as seen from afar*) берегова́я ли́ния; **a ragged ~** изре́занный бе́рег; **the path follows the ~** тропи́нка идёт вдоль бе́рега.

coat *n* **1** (*overcoat*) пальто́ (*indecl*); (*light raincoat*) плащ; (*man's jacket*) пиджа́к; **sheepskin ~** дублёнка, (*as worn by peasants, etc.*) овчи́нный тулу́п (*long*), полушу́бок (*short*); **tail ~** фрак

2 (*of animal*: *fur*) мех, (*wool*) шерсть, (*hide*) шку́ра; **the horses have glossy ~s** у лошаде́й лосня́щаяся шку́ра (*sing*)

3 (*layer*) слой; **a ~ of paint/dust** слой кра́ски/пы́ли; **a ~ of snow** сне́жный покро́в.

coat hanger *n* ве́шалка, *CQ* пле́чики (*no sing*); **give me a ~/some ~s** дай мне пле́чики.

co-author *n* соа́втор.

coax *vt*: **he tried to ~ her to eat a little** он угова́ривал её пое́сть хоть немно́го; **she just needs ~ing** её то́лько на́до уговори́ть; **they managed to ~ her out of reporting them/into buying a cat** они́ упроси́ли её не говори́ть о них/купи́ть ко́шку.

cobble *vt* (*shoes*) чини́ть (по-); (*streets*) мости́ть булы́жником (*collect*) (за-); **a ~d street** у́лица, мощённая булы́жником.

cobbler *n* сапо́жник.

cobbles, cobblestones *npl* булы́жник (*collect*).

cobweb *n* паути́на.

cocaine *n* кокаи́н.

cock *n* **1** (*bird*) пету́х; *attr*: **the ~ bird of this species** саме́ц э́того ви́да птиц

2: (*tap*) **water/stop ~** кран; **hay ~** стог; (*of gun*) куро́к.

cock *vt*: **to ~ a gun** взводи́ть куро́к (взвести́); **to ~ one's ears** (*of animal and fig*) навостри́ть у́ши (*pf*).

cock-a-hoop *adj*: **to be ~** ликова́ть.

cock-and-bull *adj*: **he produced some ~ story** он рассказа́л каку́ю-то небыли́цу.

cockcrow *n*: **I got up at ~** я встал с петуха́ми.

cock-eyed *adj* (*with a squint*) косогла́зый; *CQ* **it's a ~ scheme** э́то безу́мный план.

cockney *n* ко́кни (*indecl*) (*of person and dialect*).

cocksure *adj pejor* самоуве́ренный.

cocktail *n* кокте́йль (*m*).

cocky *adj CQ*: **a ~ little boy** де́рзкий мальчи́шка.

cocoa *n* кака́о (*indecl*).

coconut *n* коко́с.

cod *n* треска́.

coddle *vt*: **it's right to ~ an invalid** больно́му ну́жно угожда́ть/потака́ть (*impf*); **she ~s the child too much** она́ сли́шком уж трясётся над свои́м ребёнком; **a ~d child** изне́женный ребёнок.

code *n* (*cipher*) код; *Law* ко́декс; **in ~** закоди́рованный; **to break a ~** раскры́ть/расшифрова́ть код; **a moral ~, ~ of honour** мора́льный ко́декс, ко́декс че́сти; **highway ~** пра́вила (*pl*) доро́жного движе́ния.

cod-liver oil *n* ры́бий жир.

co-driver *n* води́тель-сме́нщик (*m*).

coeducation, *abbr* **coed** *n* совме́стное обуче́ние.

coercion *n* принужде́ние; **under ~** по принужде́нию.

coexist *vi* сосуществова́ть (*impf*).

coffee *n* ко́фе (*m, indecl*); **black/white ~** чёрный ко́фе, ко́фе с молоко́м; *attr* кофе́йный.

coffee pot *n* кофе́йник.

coffin *n* гроб.

cog *n* зубе́ц; *fig* **he's just a ~ in the machine** он ме́лкая со́шка.

cogency *n*: **we were convinced by the ~ of his argument** он убеди́л нас мо́щью свое́й аргумента́ции.

cogent *adj* убеди́тельный.

cognac *n* конья́к.

cognate *adj* ро́дственный.

cogwheel *n* зубча́тое колесо́.

cohabit *vi* сожи́тельствовать (*impf*).

coherent *adj*: **a ~ story/argument** свя́зный расска́з, после́довательные до́воды (*pl*).

coiffure *n* причёска.

coil *n* кольцо́; (*contraceptive*) спира́ль, пружи́нка; **the ~s of a snake/of smoke** ко́льца змеи́/ды́ма; **a ~ of rope/wire** бу́хта тро́са/про́вода.

coil *vti vt*: **to ~ a rope** свёртывать трос в бу́хту (сверну́ть)

vi: **to ~ up** свёртываться; **the snake ~ed round a branch** змея́ обвила́сь вокру́г ве́тки.

coin *n* моне́та; **to toss a ~** подбро́сить моне́ту; *fig* **to pay smb back in his own ~** отплати́ть кому́-л той же моне́той.

coin *vt* (*mint*) чека́нить моне́ту (*usu impf*); *fig*: **to ~ new words** созда|ва́ть но́вые слова́ (-́ть); *joc*: **to ~ phrase** как говори́тся; **he must be ~ing money** у него́ де́нег ку́ры не клюю́т.

coinage *n* (*minting*) чека́нка моне́т; **decimal ~** десяти́чная моне́тная систе́ма; **to debase the ~** сни́зить курс.

coincide *vi*: **to ~ with** (*of events, tastes*) совпа|да́ть с + *I* (-́сть); (*correspond to*) **his story ~s with the facts** его́ расска́з соотве́тствует фа́ктам.

coincidence *n* совпаде́ние; **sheer ~** чи́стое/просто́е совпаде́ние.

coke[1] *n* (*US*) *CQ* ко́ка-ко́ла.

coke[2] *n* (*fuel*) кокс.

colander *n* дуршла́г.

cold *n* **1** (**the ~**) хо́лод; **severe ~** сту́жа; **the ~ was intense** был стра́шный/*CQ* соба́чий хо́лод; **I feel the ~ terribly** я обы́чно так мёрзну; *fig* **he was left out in the ~** его́ оста́вили без внима́ния

2 (*in head*) на́сморк, просту́да; **to catch ~** простуди́ться, *CQ* схвати́ть на́сморк; **I've got another ~** я опя́ть простуди́лся.

cold *adj* холо́дный; **it's ~ today** сего́дня хо́лодно; **it's getting ~er** стано́вится холодне́е; **a ~ snap** ре́зкое похолода́ние; **I am/my feet are ~** мне хо́лодно, у меня́ замёрзли но́ги; **your dinner is getting ~** твой обе́д остыва́ет/сты́нет; *fig*: **a ~ reception** холо́дный приём; **he's a ~ man** он чёрствый челове́к; **that's ~ comfort** э́то сла́бое утеше́ние; **I've got ~ feet** мне бо́язно; **he did it in ~ blood** он сде́лал э́то хладнокро́вно; **he poured ~ water on my enthusiasm/on the suggestion** он охлади́л мой пыл, он хо́лодно отнёсся к э́тому предложе́нию; **his words left me ~** его́ слова́ не тро́нули меня́.

cold-blooded *adj* хладнокро́вный.

cold-shoulder *vt*: *CQ* **now that he's gone up in the world he ~s me** он тепе́рь большо́й нача́льник и знать меня́ не хо́чет.

coleslaw *n* капу́стный сала́т.

colitis *n Med* коли́т.

collaborate *vi* сотру́дничать с + *I* (*impf*).

collaboration *n* сотру́дничество; **to work in ~ with smb** рабо́тать в сотру́дничестве с кем-л.

collage *n Art* колла́ж.

collapse *n* (*fall*) паде́ние; (*caving in*) обва́л; *Med* упа́док сил; колла́пс; *Fin* крах, банкро́тство; *fig* (*of plans*) круше́ние, прова́л.

collapse *vi* **1** (*of people*): **he ~d from exhaustion** он свали́лся в изнеможе́нии/от уста́лости; *fig* **we ~d with laughter** мы попа́дали со́ смеху

2 (*of buildings and fig*) ру́шиться (*pfs* ру́хнуть, об-); **the walls/our plans ~d** сте́ны/на́ши пла́ны ру́хнули; **the ceiling ~d** потоло́к ру́хнул/обру́шился/обвали́лся; **the firm ~d** фи́рма разори́лась.

collapsible *adj*: **a ~ dinghy** разбо́рная ло́дка; **a ~ seat** откидно́е сиде́нье; **a ~ bed** складна́я крова́ть, *CQ* раскладу́шка.

collar *n* (*of coat, jacket*) воротни́к; (*of shirt, blouse or separate*) воротничо́к; **a stiff/separate ~** крахма́льный/сме́нный воротничо́к.

collarbone *n* ключи́ца.

collate *vt* слич|а́ть с + *I* (-и́ть).

collation *n* сравне́ние, сличе́ние; (*meal*) **a cold ~** холо́дная заку́ска.

colleague *n* колле́га (*m and f*), сотру́дн|ик, *f* -ица.

collect *vti vt* (*people, data, information, signatures, taxes*) со|бира́ть (-бра́ть); (*stamps, pictures, books*) собира́ть, коллекциони́ровать (*impf*); **to ~ taxes/fines** взима́ть нало́ги/штра́фы (*impf*); **to ~ the post** за|бира́ть по́чту (-бра́ть); **to ~ children from school** забира́ть дете́й из шко́лы; **I'll come and ~ you/the parcel** я зайду́ (*on foot*) *or* я зае́ду (*by car*) за ва́ми/за паке́том; **nylon ~s dust** нейло́н притя́гивает пыль; **to ~ oneself** опо́мниться (*pf*); **to ~ one's thoughts** собра́ться с мы́слями

vi **1** собира́ться; ска́пливаться (скопи́ться); **a crowd soon ~ed** вско́ре собрала́сь толпа́; **dust quickly ~s on bookshelves** пыль бы́стро ска́пливается на кни́жных по́лках; **rainwater ~s in the butt** дождева́я вода́ собира́ется в бо́чке

2: to ~ for the blind собира́ть поже́ртвования в по́льзу слепы́х.

collected *adj* **1: the ~ works of Tolstoy** собра́ние сочине́ний Толсто́го

2: he was calm and ~ он был споко́ен и со́бран.

collection *n* сбор; (*of stamps, porcelain, etc.*) колле́кция; **~ of signatures** сбор по́дписей; **times of ~** (*from postbox*) часы́ вы́емки пи́сем; **the/a ~ of rubbish** (*taking away*) сбор му́сора, (*a heap*) ку́ча му́сора; **a ~ of stories/poems** сбо́рник расска́зов/стихо́в; **to add to a ~ of stamps** попо́лнить колле́кцию ма́рок; **they had an interesting ~ of people there** у них собира́лись интере́сные лю́ди.

collective *adj* коллекти́вный; **a ~ farm** колхо́з; **a ~ farmer** колхо́зн|ик, *f* -ица.

collectively *adv* совме́стно, сообща́.

collector *n* (*of stamps, porcelain, etc.*) коллекционе́р, *CQ* собира́тель (*m*); (*of taxes*) сбо́рщик нало́гов; **ticket ~** контролёр.

college *n* (*SU*) институ́т; (*US, UK*) *Univ* колле́дж; (*UK*) **C. of Surgeons** Корпора́ция хиру́ргов.

collide *vi*: **to ~ with** ста́лкиваться с + *I* (столкну́ться).

collie *n* шотла́ндская овча́рка, ко́лли (*indecl*).

colliery *n* ша́хта.

collision *n* столкнове́ние; **to come into ~ with** столкну́ться с + *I*.

colloquial *adj* разгово́рный.

collusion *n*: **they are acting in ~** они́ (де́йствуют) в сго́воре.

colon *n Gram* двоето́чие.

colonel *n* полко́вник.

colonize *vt* колонизи́ровать (*impf and pf*).

colony *n* коло́ния.

colossal *adj* колосса́льный, *also CQ*.

colour, (*US*) **color** *n* **1** цвет; **sense of ~** чу́вство цве́та; **what ~ is your dress?** како́го цве́та твоё пла́тье?; (*complexion*) **she has very little/a good/a high ~** она́ о́чень бледна́, у неё све́жий цвет лица́, у неё румя́нец во всю щёку; **to change/lose ~** измени́ться в лице́, побледне́ть; *fig*: **to be off ~** нева́жно чу́вствовать себя́; **to give/lend ~ to a story** придава́ть расска́зу правдоподо́бность; *CQ* **let's see the ~ of your money** снача́ла плати́те де́ньги

2 *pl* (**~s**) *Art* кра́ски; **a water ~** акваре́ль; **to paint in water ~s** писа́ть акваре́лью (*sing*); *fig* **to paint smth in bright/dark ~s** представля́ть что-л в ро́зовом/мра́чном цве́те

3 *pl* (**the ~s**) *Mil* зна́мя, флаг (*sings*); *fig*: **to show oneself in one's true ~s** пока-зáть себя́ в и́стинном свéте; **he passed his exam with flying ~s** он блестя́ще сдал/вы́держал экзáмен.

colour *vti vt* (*paint or dye*) крáсить (по-); окрá|шивать (-сить); **to ~ smth red** крáсить что-л в крáсный цвет; *fig* **his wartime experiences have ~ed his views** войнá повлия́ла на егó взгля́ды

vi (*flush*) краснéть (по-); (*of leaves: go yellow*) желтéть (по-).

colour-blind *adj*: **he is ~** он дальтóник.

colour blindness *n* дальтони́зм.

coloured *adj* цветнóй; *fig* **highly ~** си́льно приукрáшенный.

colour film *n* (*for private camera*) цветнáя плёнка; *Cine* цветнóй фильм.

colourful *adj* крáсочный; (*bright*) я́ркий; *fig* **he's a ~ personality** он я́ркая ли́чность.

colouring *n* (*substance*) крáсящее веществó; (*complexion*) цвет лицá.

colourless *adj* бесцвéтный, *also fig*.

colour television *n* цветнóе телеви́дение.

colt *n* жеребёнок.

column *n Archit, Mil* колóнна; (*in newspaper*) столбéц, колóнка; **a ~ of smoke** столб ды́ма; **spinal ~** позвонóчный столб; **a ~ of figures** столбéц/колóнка цифр; *Aut* **steering ~** колóнка управлéния.

columnist *n approx* áвтор статéй в газéте.

comb *n* (*for hair*) гребёнка; (*of cock*) грéбень (*m*), гребешóк; (*for honey*) сóты (*no sing*); *attr*: **~ honey** сóтовый мёд.

comb *vt*: **to ~ one's hair** при|чёсывать вóлосы (-чесáть), причёсываться; **to ~ wool** чесáть шерсть (*impf*); *fig* **to ~ the countryside in search of...** прочёсывать мéстность в пóисках + *G*.

combat *n* схвáтка; **single ~** поеди́нок.

combat *vi* борóться с + *I* (*impf*), *also fig*.

combination *n* сочетáние; **to act in ~ with smb** дéйствовать сообщá с кем-л; **owing to a ~ of circumstances** из-за сложи́вшихся обстоя́тельств; *attr*: **a ~ lock** набóрный замóк.

combine *n Agric* комбáйн; *Comm* объединéние.

combine *vti vt* объедин|я́ть (-и́ть); (*abstract qualities*) сочетáть (*impf and pf*); **to ~ forces** объедини́ть си́лы; **to ~ business and pleasure** сочетáть прия́тное с полéзным; **she ~s good looks and intelligence** в ней ум сочетáется с красотóй

vi объединя́ться, сочетáться; **oil and water will not ~** мáсло и водá не смéшиваются.

combustion *n* горéние, сгорáние; **spontaneous ~** самовозгорáние; *attr*: **internal ~ engine** дви́гатель вну́треннего сгорáния.

come *vi* **1** (*arrive*) при|ходи́ть (*on foot*), при|езжáть (*in vehicle*) (-йти́, -éхать); *off* прибы|вáть (-ть); **the visitors have ~** гóсти пришли́/приéхали *or* съéхались; **who's coming today?** кто сегóдня придёт/приéдет?; **the car/the post has ~** маши́на/пóчта пришлá; **the president's car/the delegation has ~** прибылá *or* подъéхала маши́на президéнта, делегáция прибылá; **people were coming and going all day** одни́ прихóдят, други́е ухóдят — и так цéлый день; **the pain ~s and goes** боль то появля́ется, то исчезáет; (*with inf of purpose*): **the men have ~ to paint the door** пришли́ маляры́ покрáсить дверь; **he came to get a book** он зашёл/заéхал за кни́гой; **do ~ to see us** заходи́те к нам

2 (*approach*) при|ходи́ть (-йти́); (*come up to*) под|ходи́ть к + *D* (-ойти́); наступ|áть (-и́ть); прибли|жáться (-зиться); **spring is coming** веснá идёт, наступи́ла веснá [**NB** *tense*]; **spring ~s early in the South** на ю́ге веснá прихóдит рáно; **the time will ~ when...** придёт врéмя, когдá...; **in the coming year** в наступáющем годý; **the bus/train/car is coming** автóбус идёт, пóезд прибывáет, маши́на подъезжáет; **they came running/hurrying towards us** они́ подбежáли к нам; (*in summons*): **~ here!** иди́ сюдá!; (*answer*) **I'm coming!** идý!; **~ to the window/nearer** подойти́ к oкнý/(по)бли́же; **~ and look at this/and see for yourself** приходи́ посмотрéть на э́то/посмотри́ сам; **~ and see us in Moscow** приезжáйте к нам в Москвý; **~, let's go!/begin!** ну, пошли́!, ну, давáй(те)!

3 (*reach*) до|ходи́ть, (*in car*) до|езжáть до + *G* (-йти́, -éхать); под|ходи́ть, (*in car*) подъ|езжáть к + *D* (-ойти́, -éхать); **when you ~ to the station, take bus No 4** дойди́те до стáнции и сади́тесь на четвёртый автóбус; **when you ~ to London you must change trains** доезжáйте до Лóндона и там дéлайте пересáдку; **they came to a large river** они́ подошли́/подъéхали к большóй рекé; **the forest ~s right to the lake** лес подхóдит к сáмому óзеру; **it came to my hearing that...** до меня́ дошлó, что...

4 (*occur, happen*): **B ~s after A** бýква B слéдует за A; **your turn will ~** твоя́ óчередь придёт; **on what page does it ~?** на какóй э́то страни́це?; **how does it ~ (about)/CQ how ~ that you're so late?** почемý ты так пóздно?; **~ what may** будь что бýдет; **it came as a complete surprise to me** для меня́ э́то бы́ло пóлной неожи́данностью

5 (*result*): **it all came to nothing** всё э́то ничéм не кóнчилось; **it all came right in the end** всё кóнчилось хорошó; **nothing came of it** из э́того ничегó не вы́шло; **no good/harm will ~ of it** э́то ни к чемý хорóшему не приведёт, ничегó плохóго (от э́того) не бýдет; **see what ~s of being too credulous** ви́дишь, к чемý привóдит изли́шняя довéрчивость

6 (*amount to*): **the bill came to £5 for the two of us** за нас двои́х мы заплати́ли пять фýнтов; **his earnings ~ to £ 5,000 a year** егó зáработок составля́ет пять ты́сяч фýнтов в год; **it all ~s to the same thing** всё свóдится к одномý; **what you are saying ~s to this...** в óбщем твои́ словá свóдятся вот к чемý...

7 come to + *noun*, **come into** + *noun* (*see also under particular nouns*): **to ~ to an agreement/a conclusion/an understanding** прийти́ к соглаше́нию/к заключе́нию, дости́гнуть понима́ния; **they nearly came to blows** у них чуть до дра́ки не дошло́; **to ~ into flower** расцве|та́ть (-сти́); **it came into my head that...** мне пришло́ в го́лову, что...; **he didn't do well in the 100 metres, but he came into his own in the mile** он не о́чень хорошо́ пробежа́л стоме́тровку, но на диста́нции одна́ ми́ля он показа́л, на что спосо́бен

8 (*with adjs and advs* = "*be*" *or* "*become*"): **it ~s easy/naturally to him** э́то ему́ легко́ даётся; **that will ~ very expensive** э́то бу́дет о́чень до́рого; **it ~s cheaper if you buy in bulk** покупа́ть о́птом деше́вле; **to ~ true** сбы|ва́ться (-́ться); **my laces/zip came undone** у меня́ шнурки́ развяза́лись/мо́лния расстегну́лась; **this dress ~s in three sizes** тако́е пла́тье есть трёх разме́ров

9 *various*: **~, ~!** (*in contradiction*) ну что́ вы!; **oh ~, he's not that bad** ну что́ вы, он не тако́й уж плохо́й челове́к; **a week ~ Tuesday** во вто́рник на сле́дующей неде́ле; **it'll be a year ~ Tuesday since he left** в бу́дущий вто́рник бу́дет год, как он уе́хал; **to ~ of age** дости́гнуть совершенноле́тия; **he ~s of peasant stock** он из крестья́нской семьи́; **he'll ~ to no good/harm** он добро́м не ко́нчит *or* он пло́хо ко́нчит, с ним ничего́ не случи́тся; **how did you ~ to know about it?** как вы узна́ли об э́том?; **I came to know her in Paris** я познако́мился с ней в Пари́же; **I've forgotten her name—it'll ~ to me in a minute** я забы́л её и́мя—сейча́с вспо́мню; **if it ~s to that, we can always leave** е́сли до э́того дойдёт, мы всегда́ смо́жем уйти́; **if it ~s to that, why didn't you tell him yourself?** раз тако́е де́ло, почему́ ты сам с ним не поговори́л?; **when it ~s to washing-up, he's nowhere to be seen** когда́ ну́жно мыть посу́ду, его́ днём с огнём не сы́щешь; **~ to think of it, it's hardly surprising** е́сли поду́мать, в э́том нет ничего́ удиви́тельного

come across *vi*: **I came across a new letter of Darwin's** мне случа́йно попа́ло в ру́ки неизве́стное письмо́ Да́рвина; **I came across him at the station** я случа́йно встре́тил его́ на вокза́ле

come along *vi*: **he came along with his sister** он пришёл (вме́сте) с сестро́й; **~ along!** иди́!, идём!, пошли́!; **the patient/garden is coming along/on nicely** больно́й поправля́ется, сад хорошо́ разраста́ется

come away *vi*: **I came away at once** я сра́зу же ушёл; **children, ~ away from the stove!** де́ти, отойди́те от пе́чки!; **the handle came away in my hand** ру́чка оста́лась у меня́ в руке́

come back *vi* возвра|ща́ться (*pfs* -ти́ться, верну́ться); **it will ~ back to me soon** я о́чень ско́ро э́то вспо́мню

come before *vi*: **to ~ before the court** предста|ва́ть пе́ред судо́м (-́ть); **my family ~s before everything** для меня́ на пе́рвом ме́сте семья́

come between *vi*: **it's unwise to ~ between husband and wife** никогда́ не на́до встава́ть ме́жду му́жем и жено́й

come by *vi*: **tickets for the ballet are hard to ~ by** биле́ты на бале́т о́чень тру́дно доста́ть

come down *vi*: **to ~ down a mountain/ladder** спус|ка́ться с горы́/с ле́стницы (-ти́ться); **the hydroplane/space capsule came down in the sea** гидропла́н сел на во́ду, косми́ческая каби́на опусти́лась на во́ду; **mist/the curtain came down** опусти́лся тума́н, за́навес опусти́лся; **a chimney pot came down in the gale** трубу́ на до́ме снесло́/свали́ло (*impers*) бу́рей; **these houses are coming down shortly** э́ти дома́ ско́ро снесу́т; **prices have ~ down** це́ны упа́ли/сни́зились; **he's ~ down in the world since then** ему́ тепе́рь гора́здо ху́же живётся, чем ра́ньше; **it ~s down to this** вопро́с сво́дится к сле́дующему

come for *vi*: **I will ~ for you** я зайду́/зае́ду за тобо́й; **the car has ~ for you** за ва́ми пришла́ маши́на

come forward *vi* вы|ступа́ть вперёд (-́ступить)

come from *vi*: **I ~ from Scotland** я ро́дом из Шотла́ндии; **the quotation ~s from Pushkin** э́та цита́та из Пу́шкина; **that word ~s from Arabic** э́то сло́во пришло́ из ара́бского языка́

come in *vi* входи́ть (войти́); **tell her to ~ in at once** скажи́ ей, пусть сейча́с же войдёт; **~ in!** (*in answer to knock*) войди́те!, (*to smb on doorstep, or on threshold of room*) входи́те!, заходи́те!; **he came in first/third** он вошёл пе́рвым/тре́тьим; **the train/plane from Kiev has ~ in** при́был по́езд/самолёт из Ки́ева; **the tide is coming in** начина́ется прили́в; **long skirts have ~ in again** дли́нные ю́бки опя́ть в мо́де/вошли́ в мо́ду; **he came in for a lot of criticism** он подве́ргся ре́зкой кри́тике

come into *vi* входи́ть (войти́); **to ~ into a room/fashion/use** входи́ть в ко́мнату/в мо́ду/в употребле́ние; **to ~ into an inheritance/£ 1,000** получи́ть насле́дство/ты́сячу фу́нтов в насле́дство; **he came into possession of a large estate** он вступи́л во владе́ние кру́пным поме́стьем; **how did this knife ~ into your possession?** как к вам попа́л э́тот нож?; **to ~ into effect/office/conflict with** вступи́ть в си́лу/в до́лжность/в конфли́кт с + *I*

come off *vi*: **he came off his horse** он упа́л с ло́шади; **the wallpaper is coming off** обо́и (*pl*) отхо́дят; **a button/wheel came off** пу́говица оторвала́сь, колесо́ отскочи́ло; *CQ*: **the visit never came off** э́та пое́здка так и не состоя́лась; **the experiment/it came off very well** о́пыт *or* экспериме́нт уда́лся, всё получи́лось хорошо́; **~ off it!** да бро́сь ты!

come on *vi*: **it came on to rain** пошёл дождь; **the work is coming on nicely** рабо́та хорошó продвигáется; ~ **on, pull yourself together!** а ну, соберúсь!; ~ **on!** (*in disbelief*) да чтó ты!, ты шýтишь!; *Theat* **to ~ on to the stage** выходúть на сцéну

come out *vi*: **he came out of the house** он вы́шел из дóма; **the moon came out from behind the clouds** лунá вы́шла из-за облакóв; **the cork/mark won't ~ out** прóбка не вытáскивается, пятнó не схóдит; **a stopping came out of my tooth** у меня́ (из зýба) вы́пала плóмба; **the buds are coming out** пóчки распускáются; **the book came out in the spring** кни́га вы́шла веснóй; **she came out in a rash/with all her troubles** у неё вы́ступила сыпь, онá излилá мне все свои́ печáли и забóты; **he came out well in the photo/top in the exam** он хорошó вы́шел на сни́мке *or* на фóто, он был лýчшим на экзáмене

come over *vi*: **to ~ over a frontier/a mountain pass** переéхать грани́цу/чéрез перевáл; **they came over to our side** они́ перешли́ на нáшу стóрону; **what's ~ over him?** чтó с ним?; **a change came over her** в ней/с ней произошлá перемéна; **his speech did not ~ over well on the radio** егó выступлéние по рáдио бы́ло плóхо слы́шно

come round *vi*: **do ~ round and see us** приходи́/заходи́ к нам; **I came round by Cambridge** я éхал чéрез Кéмбридж; **she came round** (*after fainting*) онá пришлá в себя́/в сознáние; **Xmas will soon ~ round again** скóро рождествó; **he is coming round to our way of thinking** он склоня́ется к нáшей тóчке зрéния; **I think he'll ~ round eventually** я дýмаю, что в концé концóв он передýмает

come through *vi*: **we came through Oxford** мы éхали/проéхали чéрез Óксфорд; **she has ~ through the operation well** онá хорошó перенеслá операцию

come together *vi* (*foregather*) сходи́ться (сойти́сь); (*coincide*): **all the concerts seem to ~ together** все концéрты почемý-то идýт в оди́н и тóт же день

come up *vi*: **he came up to me** он подошёл ко мне; **the water came up to my knees** водá доходи́ла мне до колéн; **the sun came up** сóлнце взошлó; **the seeds have ~ up** семенá взошли́; **he only ~s up to my shoulder** он мне тóлько до плечá; **the president ~s up for reelection in the autumn** президéнт бýдет переизбирáться óсенью; **I came up to Oxford a year ago** я поступи́л в Óксфорд год назáд; **we've ~ up against snags** мы натолкнýлись на препя́тствия; **the problem of his education came up** встал вопрóс о егó образовáнии; **it came up in conversation that...** в разговóре вы́яснилось, что...; **don't worry we'll ~ up with something** не беспокóйся, мы чтó-нибудь придýмаем; **the house is coming up for sale shortly** э́тот дом скóро бýдет продавáться; **he came up with the right answer/with a suggestion/with the idea of building a dam** он нашёл прáвильный отвéт, он вы́ступил с предложéнием, он пóдал идéю пострóить дáмбу; *Law* **the case is coming up tomorrow** дéло бýдет слýшаться зáвтра

come within *vi*: **that doesn't ~ within my jurisdiction** э́то не вхóдит в мою́ компетéнцию.

comeback *n*: **the filmstar made an unexpected ~** кинозвездá неожи́данно снóва вернýлась в кинó; **he made a witty ~** он остроýмно отпари́ровал.

comedian *n* кóмик.

comedown *n*: **it was a great ~ for her to have to take a cleaner's job** ей пришлóсь пойти́ рабóтать убóрщицей—такóй удáр по её самолю́бию.

comedy *n* комéдия.

comer *n*: **the first ~** пришéдший пéрвым; **late ~s** опоздáвшие; **it's for all ~s** э́то для всех.

comet *n* комéта.

comfort *n* **1** (*solace*) утешéние; **that's cold/small ~** э́то плохóе/слáбое утешéние; **you're a great ~ to me** ты для меня́ огрóмное утешéние

2 (*physical*) ую́т; комфóрт; удóбства (*pl*); **he likes his ~s** он лю́бит комфóрт (*sing*).

comfort *vt* утеш|áть (-́ить).

comfortable *adj* удóбный; (*well-equipped*) комфортáбельный; **a ~ hotel/car** комфортáбельная гости́ница/маши́на; **are you ~?** вам удóбно?; **make yourself ~** располагáйтесь поудóбнее; **I never feel ~ with them** (*at ease*) я у них всегдá чýвствую себя́ нелóвко; **he enjoys a ~ income** у негó прили́чный дохóд.

comic *n* (*person*) кóмик; (*paper*) **(the ~s)** кóмиксы (*usu pl*).

comic(al) *adj* коми́ческий; коми́чный; **comic opera** коми́ческая óпера; **a comical situation/dog** коми́чная ситуáция, смешнáя собáка.

comma *n* запятáя; **inverted ~s** кавы́чки.

command *n* **1** (*order: spoken*) приказáние, комáнда, (*usu written*) прикáз; **at the word of ~** по комáнде; **at his ~** по егó прикáзу

2 (*control*): **~ of the seas** госпóдство на мóре (*sing*); *Mil*: **high ~** вы́сшее комáндование; **who is in ~ of the regiment?** кто комáндует полкóм?; **the regiment is in the ~ of...** полк под комáндой + *G*; **to take ~ of a garrison** принимáть комáндование гарнизóном

3 *fig uses*: **he has a good ~ of French** он хорошó владéет францýзским языкóм; **he was in ~ of the situation** он был хозя́ином положéния; **I'm at your ~** я в вáшем распоряжéнии; **all the money at my ~ is yours** все дéньги, котóрыми я располагáю—вáши.

command *vt* (*give order*) прикáз|ывать + *D* (-áть); (*be in command of*) комáндовать + *I* (*impf*); (*to have at disposal*) располагáть + *I* (*only in impf*); **he ~ed his men to attack** он приказáл свои́м солдáтам атаковáть; **to ~ a ship** комáндовать кораблём; *fig*: **to ~**

respect/sympathy внуш|áть уважéние (-и́ть), вызывáть сочу́вствие (*usu impf*); **the castle ~s a fine view** из óкон зáмка открывáется краси́вый вид.

commandeer *vt Mil* реквизи́ровать (*impf and pf*); *CQ* присв|áивать (-óить).

commander *n Mil* команди́р.

commemorate *vt* ознаменóв|ывать (-áть).

commemoration *n*: **in ~ of** в ознаменовáние + *G*.

commence *vti* нач|инáть(ся) (-áть(ся)).

commend *vt* **1** (*praise*): **he was ~ed for his bravery** он был отмéчен за проя́вленное му́жество; **his thesis was highly ~ed** егó диссертáцию óчень хвали́ли

2 (*recommend*) рекомендовáть (*impf and pf*); **I ~ him to you as an excellent teacher** я егó рекоменду́ю вам как превосхóдного педагóга; **I ~ the book to your attention** рекоменду́ю э́ту кни́гу вáшему внимáнию; **the plan does not ~ itself to me** э́тот план мне не нрáвится.

commendable *adj* похвáльный.

commensurable *adj* соизмери́мый.

comment *n* (*remark*) замечáние; (*textual*) комментáрий; (*at a meeting*): **any ~s?** есть замечáния?/добавлéния?; (*answering a reporter, etc.*) **no ~!** я на э́тот вопрóс не бу́ду отвечáть, *CQ iron* комментáрии изли́шни!

comment *vi*: **to ~ on a text/on the international situation** комменти́ровать текст/междунарóдное положéние (*impf and pf, pf also* про-); **critics ~ed unfavourably on his play** кри́тики отрицáтельно отзывáлись о егó пьéсе; **matron ~ed unfavourably on my dress** увидáв, как я одéта, стáршая медсестрá сдéлала мне замечáние.

commentary *n* (*on text, etc.*) комментáрии (*pl*); *Radio* репортáж; **they are giving a running ~ on the match** репортáж о мáтче передаётся по рáдио.

commentator *n Radio* (радио)комментáтор.

commerce *n* торгóвля, коммéрция; **Chamber of C.** торгóвая палáта.

commercial *n Radio* радиорекла́ма, *TV* телерекла́ма.

commercial *adj* торгóвый, коммéрческий; **~ traveller** коммивояжёр.

commiserate *vi*: **I ~d with him on his misfortune** я посочу́вствовал емý в егó бедé.

commissariat *n Mil, etc.* отделéние продовóльственного снабжéния

commission *n* (*order*: *to artist, etc.*) закáз; (*body of people*) (**a C.**) коми́ссия; *Comm* комиссиóнные (*pl*); **he got a ~ for/to paint a portrait of the mayor** он получи́л закáз на портрéт мэ́ра; **to receive/charge a ~ of 10%** получáть/взимáть дéсять процéнтов комиссиóнных; *Mil* **he got a/resigned his ~** емý присвóили офицéрское звáние, он пóдал в отстáвку; *Naut* **the vessel is out of ~** су́дно в ремóнте.

commission *vt* (*of private orders*) закáз|ывать (-áть), поруч|áть (-и́ть); **we ~ed a portrait from him** мы заказáли емý портрéт; **he was ~ed to design a theatre/to head the delegation** емý поручи́ли создáть проéкт нóвого теáтра/возглавля́ть делегáцию.

commissionaire *n* швейцáр, портьé (*indecl*).

commit *vt* **1** (*perform*) соверш|áть (-и́ть); **to ~ a crime/a murder/error** соверши́ть преступлéние/уби́йство, сдéлать оши́бку (*usu pfs*); **to ~ suicide** покóнчить с собóй (*pf*)

2 (*entrust*) поруч|áть (-и́ть); **they ~ted the child to the care of her aunt** они́ поручи́ли ребёнка забóтам тётки; **to ~ smb to prison/to a mental hospital** посади́ть когó-л в тюрьмý, помести́ть когó-л в психиатри́ческую больни́цу (*usu pfs*); **I ~ted my papers to his safe-keeping** я передáл мои́ бумáги емý на хранéние; *fig* **to ~ smth to memory/to paper** *or* **to writing** запом|инáть что-л (-́нить), запи́с|ывать что-л (-áть)

3 (*bind*): **I've ~ted myself to returning on Friday** я обещáл верну́ться в пя́тницу; **I'm ~ted to helping them** я обязáлся им помóчь; **without ~ing myself** без вся́ких обязáтельств с моéй стороны́; **he is deeply ~ted to this policy** он целикóм за проведéние э́той ли́нии.

commitment *n* обязáтельство; **financial ~s** финáнсовые обязáтельства.

committee *n* комитéт (*only on high level*); коми́ссия; **to appoint a ~** назначáть коми́ссию.

commodious *adj* вмести́тельный.

commodity *n* товáр (*sing and collect*).

common *n* **1** (*land*) общи́нная земля́; (*pasture*) общи́нный вы́гон

2: we have nothing in ~ у нас нет ничегó óбщего; **in ~ with many others I dislike this painting** мне, как и мнóгим други́м, не нрáвится э́та карти́на.

common *adj* **1** (*shared*) óбщий; **a ~ bathroom** óбщая вáнная; **by ~ consent** с óбщего соглáсия; **the ~ good** (все)óбщее блáго; *Gram* **~ gender** óбщий род

2 (*widespread*) распространённый; **a ~ error** обы́чная/распространённая оши́бка; **this bird is ~ in Scotland** э́та пти́ца распространенá в Шотлáндии; **this word is in ~ use** э́то слóво óчень употреби́тельно; **it is ~ knowledge that...** общеизвéстно, что...

3 (*ordinary*) **i)** (*of people*) простóй (*complimentary*); **the ~ people** просты́е лю́ди; (*average*) рядовóй; (*mediocre, often pejor*) зауря́дный; (*vulgar*) вульгáрный; **ii)** (*of phenomena*) обы́чный; **such weather is quite ~ in autumn** óсенью такáя погóда—обы́чное явлéние; **it's ~ practice among lawyers to...** у адвокáтов обы́чно при́нято + *inf*; **a ~ or garden sparrow** простóй воробéй

4 *Math*: **~ multiple** óбщий мнóжитель (*m*).

commonplace *adj* зауря́дный.

common sense *n* здрáвый смысл.

commotion *n* шум; (*disorder*) **civil ~** волнéния, беспоря́дки (*pls*).

communal *adj* óбщий, общéственный; (*SU*) коммунáльный.

commune *n* комму́на; *Hist* общи́на.

communicate *vti vt* (*news*, *opinion*, *etc.*) сообщ|а́ть (-и́ть), переда|ва́ть (-́ть); **to ~ a disease to smb** зарази́ть кого́-л (*usu pf*); *Phys* **to ~ heat** передава́ть теплоту́ (*only in impf*)

vi **1** свя́з|ываться (-а́ться); **I'll ~ with him by telephone** я свяжу́сь с ним по телефо́ну; **the young say they can't ~ with their parents** молоды́е говоря́т, что не мо́гут найти́ о́бщий язы́к с роди́телями

2: **the bathroom ~s with the bedroom** ва́нная сообща́ется со спа́льней; **communicating rooms** сме́жные ко́мнаты.

communication *n* (*report or means of communication*) сообще́ние; **to receive a ~** получи́ть сообще́ние; **what are ~s like there?** како́е там сообще́ние? (*sing*); **wireless ~s** радиосвя́зь (*sing*); **I am in ~ with him about this** я подде́рживаю с ним связь по э́тому вопро́су.

communication cord *n Rail* шнур э́кстренного торможе́ния.

communicative *adj* общи́тельный, разговорчи́вый; **he is not at all ~ on the subject** он не хо́чет говори́ть об э́том.

communion *n Rel* прича́стие; **to take ~** причаща́ться.

communiqué *n* коммюнике́ (*indecl*).

communism *n* коммуни́зм.

communist *n* коммуни́ст.

communist *adj* коммунисти́ческий; **the ~ party** коммунисти́ческая па́ртия.

community *n* (*in general*) о́бщество; **the local ~** ме́стные жи́тели (*pl*); **the Italian ~ in London** италья́нская коло́ния в Ло́ндоне; **to work for the good of the ~** рабо́тать для о́бщего бла́га.

commute *vti vt*: **to ~ a death sentence to life imprisonment** замен|я́ть сме́ртную казнь пожи́зненным заключе́нием (-и́ть)

vi: **I ~ to London every day** я е́зжу на рабо́ту в Ло́ндон ка́ждый день.

compact *n* **1** соглаше́ние, догово́р; **we made a ~ not to tell our wives** мы договори́лись ничего́ не говори́ть об э́том на́шим жёнам

2 (*for powder*) пу́дреница.

compact *adj*: **it's a ~ little flat/car** э́то ма́ленькая, но удо́бная кварти́ра, э́то небольша́я, но вмести́тельная маши́на; **a ~ style** (*of writing*) сжа́тый стиль.

companion *n* това́рищ, *f* подру́га; **travelling ~** спу́тн|ик, *f* -ица (*by arrangement*), попу́тч|ик, *f* -ица (*by chance*); **he was my constant ~ at school** в шко́ле мы всегда́ бы́ли вме́сте; **he's an amusing ~** с ним всегда́ ве́село.

companionable *adj* компане́йский (*CQ*).

companionship *n*: **I enjoy his ~** мне хорошо́ в его́ о́бществе; **theirs is a ~ of many years standing** их свя́зывает многоле́тняя дру́жба.

company *n* **1** компа́ния; го́сти (*pl*); о́бщество; **I'll come with you for ~** я пойду́ с тобо́й за компа́нию; **I'll keep you ~** я соста́влю тебе́ компа́нию; **we're expecting ~ tonight** сего́дня ве́чером у нас (бу́дут) го́сти; **the ~ broke up** го́сти разошли́сь; **he's good ~** *CQ* он компане́йский па́рень; **he was seen in the ~ of a pretty blonde** его́ ви́дели в о́бществе краси́вой блонди́нки; **he has fallen into bad ~** он попа́л в дурно́е о́бщество/в плоху́ю компа́нию; **I get bored in his ~** мне с ним ску́чно; **present ~ excepted** о прису́тствующих не говоря́т; **we part ~ here** здесь мы расстаёмся, *fig* здесь мы расхо́димся во взгля́дах

2 *Comm* компа́ния; **an insurance ~** страхова́я компа́ния.

comparable *adj* сравни́мый.

comparative *adj* сравни́тельный, *also Gram*; **to live in ~ comfort** жить в сравни́тельном комфо́рте.

compare *n*: **beyond ~** вне сравне́ния.

compare *vti vt* сра́вн|ивать (-и́ть); **the two pictures can't be ~d** э́ти две карти́ны нельзя́ сра́внивать; **~d with** по сравне́нию с + *I*; *CQ* **let's ~ notes** дава́й поде́лимся впечатле́ниями

vi: **he can't ~ with you** его́ с тобо́й не сравни́ть; **this car ~s very favourably with the other** э́та маши́на вы́годно отлича́ется от той; **how do they ~ for speed?** кака́я у них ра́зница в ско́рости?

comparison *n* сравне́ние; **to make/draw a ~ between** проводи́ть сравне́ние ме́жду + *I*; **by/in ~ with** по сравне́нию с + *I*; **there's no ~ between them** их нельзя́ сра́внивать.

compartment *n* отделе́ние; *Rail* купе́ (*indecl*); *Naut* **watertight ~** водонепроница́емый отсе́к.

compass *n* (*range*) преде́лы (*pl*); *Naut* ко́мпас; **the points of the ~** стра́ны све́та; *Math* **a pair of ~es** ци́ркуль (*m*, *sing*).

compassion *n* сострада́ние; *CQ joc* **take ~ on the last bit of cake!** ну уж съе́шьте после́дний кусо́чек то́рта!

compassionate *adj* сочу́вствующий; сострада́тельный; **~ leave** о́тпуск по семе́йным обстоя́тельствам.

compatible *adj* (*of ideas*, *etc.*) совмести́мый; (*of people*) **they are not ~** они́ не мо́гут ужи́ться (друг с дру́гом).

compatriot *n* соотéчественник.

compel *vt*: **to ~ smb to sign smth** прину|жда́ть/вынужда́ть кого́-л подписа́ть что-л (-́дить/вы́нудить); **I feel ~led to say that...** я вы́нужден сказа́ть, что...

compelling *adj*: **a ~ argument** убеди́тельный до́вод/аргуме́нт.

compensate *vti vt*: **to ~ smb for a loss** возме|ща́ть/компенси́ровать кому́-л убы́ток/поте́рю (-сти́ть/*impf and pf*)

vi: **to ~ for smth** компенси́ровать что-л.

compensation *n Law* возмеще́ние (*abstract*), компенса́ция (*in money*, *kind*); **to claim ~** тре́бовать возмеще́ния убы́тков/компенса́ции; **to receive ~/£1,000 ~ for smth** получи́ть компенса́цию/ты́сячу фу́нтов компенса́ции за что-л; **the weather was bad but in ~ the hotel was very comfortable** пого́да была́ скве́рная, зато́ гости́ница оказа́лась прекра́сной.

compère *n* конферансье́ (*indecl*).

compete *vi*: **to ~ with smb in a race** соревнова́ться/состяза́ться (*usu only Sport*) с кем-л в бе́ге (*impfs*); **to ~ in a (mounted) steeplechase** уча́ствовать в ска́чках (*impf*); **they are both competing for this job** они́ о́ба уча́ствуют в ко́нкурсе на э́то ме́сто; *Comm* конкури́ровать (*impf and pf*).

competence *n*: **he was praised for his ~ in administration** его́ похвали́ли за его́ уме́ние вести́ дела́; **that is not within the ~ of the court** э́то вне компете́нции суда́.

competent *adj* компете́нтный; **he is a ~ authority in this field** он специали́ст в э́той о́бласти; **he's a ~ editor** он о́чень спосо́бный реда́ктор; **the ~ authority to deal with that is the police** э́тим должна́ занима́ться поли́ция.

competition *n* **1** *Comm*, *etc.* конкуре́нция

2 (*event*) ко́нкурс; *Sport* соревнова́ния (*pl*); **a piano/beauty ~** ко́нкурс пиани́стов/красоты́; **entry into the university is by ~** в университе́т принима́ются проше́дшие по ко́нкурсу; **a swimming ~** соревнова́ния по пла́ванию.

competitive *adj*: **~ spirit/examination/prices** дух сопе́рничества, ко́нкурсный экза́мен, конкурентоспосо́бные це́ны; **he is very ~** в нём силён дух сопе́рничества.

competitor *n* уча́стник ко́нкурса/*Sport* соревнова́ний (*pl*); *Comm* конкуре́нт.

compile *vt* состав|ля́ть (-́ить).

complacence, complacency *n* самодово́льство.

complacent *adj*: **he looks so ~** у него́ тако́й дово́льный вид; **he's too ~** он чересчу́р дово́лен собо́й.

complain *vi* жа́ловаться (по-); **she ~ed to me of a headache/about the noise/that...** она́ жа́ловалась мне на головну́ю боль/на шум/, что...

complaint *n* жа́лоба; **we get no ~s about the cooking** у нас нет жа́лоб на ка́чество пригото́вленных блюд; **he's full of ~s** он ве́чно жа́луется; **you've no cause for ~** у вас нет причи́н (*pl*) жа́ловаться; *Law* **to lodge/lay a ~ against smb** подава́ть жа́лобу на кого́-л; *Med* **he suffers from a heart ~** у него́ больно́е се́рдце.

complaisant *adj* услу́жливый.

complement *n* дополне́ние, *also Gram*; *Naut* экипа́ж, соста́в; **with a full ~/a ~ of 400 men** в по́лном соста́ве, в соста́ве четырёхсо́т челове́к.

complement *vt* дополн|я́ть (-́ить).

complementary *adj* дополни́тельный.

complete *adj* **1** (*full*) по́лный; **a ~ edition of Tolstoy** по́лное собра́ние сочине́ний Толсто́го; **if I had a car my happiness would be ~** для по́лного сча́стья мне не хвата́ет то́лько маши́ны

2 (*total*): **he's a ~ stranger to me** он мне соверше́нно незнако́м; **it was a ~ surprise to me** э́то бы́ло для меня́ по́лной неожи́данностью; *CQ*: **he's a ~ fool** он кру́глый дура́к; **the party was a ~ flop** ве́чер не уда́лся

3 (*finished*) зако́нченный, (*on larger scale*) завершённый; **the report/building is not yet ~** докла́д ещё не зако́нчен, строи́тельство ещё не завершено́.

complete *vt* за|ка́нчивать (-ко́нчить), (*on big scale*) заверш|а́ть (-и́ть).

completely *adv* соверше́нно; по́лностью.

completion *n* оконча́ние; заверше́ние; **payment on ~** опла́та по оконча́нии/по заверше́нии рабо́ты; **building is nearing ~** строи́тельство идёт/приближа́ется к концу́.

complex *n* ко́мплекс, *also Psych*; **a vast ~ of buildings** большо́й ко́мплекс зда́ний; *Psych* **an inferiority ~** ко́мплекс неполноце́нности.

complex *adj* сло́жный, *also Gram*.

complexion *n* цвет лица́; **a good/fair/dark ~** хоро́шая/све́тлая ко́жа, сму́глый цвет лица́; *fig* **that puts a different ~ on it** э́то меня́ет де́ло.

complexity *n* сло́жность, усложнённость.

compliance *n* усту́пчивость; **in ~ with your wishes** в соотве́тствии с ва́шими пожела́ниями.

compliant *adj* усту́пчивый.

complicate *vt* усложн|я́ть, осложн|я́ть (*pfs* -и́ть); **to ~ matters further** ещё бо́льше осложни́ть де́ло (*sing*).

complicated *adj* сло́жный; **the situation has become/is ~** положе́ние усложни́лось.

complication *n* сло́жность, тру́дность.

complicity *n* соуча́стие.

compliment *n* **1** комплиме́нт; **to pay a ~** сде́лать комплиме́нт; **a back-handed ~** двусмы́сленный комплиме́нт; **I take it as a ~ that...** я счита́ю за честь, что...; **they paid me the ~ of inviting me to lecture** они́ оказа́ли мне честь, пригласи́в прочита́ть у них ле́кцию

2 *pl* (**~s**) (*greetings*): **give her my ~s** переда́йте ей приве́т; (*on card with flowers, etc.*) **with ~s from...** с наилу́чшими пожела́ниями от...

compliment *vt*: **he ~ed me on my cooking/dress** он наговори́л мне ку́чу комплиме́нтов по по́воду мои́х кулина́рных спосо́бностей, он похвали́л моё пла́тье.

complimentary *adj* (*flattering*) ле́стный; (*congratulatory*) поздрави́тельный; **a ~ ticket** контрама́рка.

comply *vi*: **to ~ with smb's request** исполн|я́ть чью-л про́сьбу (-́ить); **to ~ with the rules** подчин|я́ться пра́вилам (-и́ться).

component *n Phys*, *Tech* компоне́нт; *attr*: **~ part** составна́я часть.

compose *vt* (*constitute*) состав|ля́ть (-́ить); (*poem, music*) сочин|я́ть (-и́ть); **to be ~d of** состоя́ть из + *G* (*impf*).

composed *adj* (*of person*) со́бранный.

composer *n* компози́тор.

composition *n* (*structure*) соста́в; *Lit*, *Mus* сочине́ние, произведе́ние; **the ~ of the soil** соста́в по́чвы.

compositor *n* набо́рщик.

composure *n* самооблада́ние, со́бранность; **he quickly recovered his ~** он бы́стро овладе́л собо́й.

compound *n* (*mixture*) смесь; *Chem* соедине́ние; *Gram* сло́жное сло́во.

compound *adj* сло́жный; **~ fracture** осложнённый перело́м; *Gram* **a ~ sentence** сложносочинённое предложе́ние.

comprehend *vt* (*understand*) пости|га́ть (-́чь), пон|има́ть (-я́ть); (*include*) включ|а́ть (-и́ть); (*used in both senses*) охва́т|ывать (-и́ть); **I can't ~ Hegel's philosophy** я не понима́ю филосо́фии Ге́геля; **the problem is too complicated for me to ~** мне тру́дно охвати́ть всю пробле́му.

comprehensible *adj* постижи́мый.

comprehension *n* понима́ние; **it passes/is beyond my ~** э́то вы́ше моего́ понима́ния.

comprehensive *adj*: **~ insurance** по́лное страхова́ние; **a ~ study** всесторо́ннее изуче́ние/иссле́дование; **a ~ school** *approx* общеобразова́тельная шко́ла.

compress *n Med* компре́сс.

compress *vt* сжима́ть (сжать); **to ~ a spring/one's lips/an article** сжать пружи́ну/гу́бы, сократи́ть статью́.

compressed *adj* сжа́тый; **~ air** сжа́тый во́здух; **a ~ account** сжа́тое изложе́ние.

comprise *vt* включ|а́ть в себя́ (-и́ть); **the flat ~s two rooms, a hall and a kitchen** кварти́ра состои́т из двух ко́мнат, прихо́жей и ку́хни; **the collection ~s 40 songs** в сбо́рник вклю́чены со́рок пе́сен.

compromise *n* компроми́сс; **we settled for a ~** мы согласи́лись на компроми́сс.

compromise *vti vt*: **to ~ oneself** *or* **one's reputation/smb** компромети́ровать себя́/кого́-л (с-)
vi идти́ на компроми́сс (пойти́).

compulsion *n* принужде́ние; **to act under ~** де́йствовать по принужде́нию; **you are under no ~ to answer** вы не обя́заны отвеча́ть.

compulsive *adj*: **a ~ smoker/liar** зая́длый кури́льщик, отча́янный лгун; **she's a ~ eater** она́ всё вре́мя что́-нибудь ест/жуёт, она́ всё вре́мя хо́чет есть.

compulsory *adj* обяза́тельный.

compunction *n*: **she had no ~ in keeping him waiting** она́ без зазре́ния со́вести заста́вила его́ ждать.

computer *n* компью́тер.

comrade *n* това́рищ.

con[1] *n*: **when you weigh up the pros and ~s** е́сли взве́сить все «за» и «про́тив».

con[2] *vt sl*: **we've been ~ned** нас провели́/наду́ли.

concave *adj* во́гнутый.

conceal *vt* скры|ва́ть (-ть); **to ~ the truth/one's feelings/a fugitive** скрыва́ть пра́вду/свои́ чу́вства, укрыва́ть беглеца́; **he ~ed it from his wife** он скрыл э́то от жены́; **to ~ oneself, to be ~ed** скрыва́ться.

concealment *n* укры́тие; **stay in ~ till the danger has passed** спря́чьтесь, пока́ опа́сность не прошла́.

concede *vt* (*yield*) уступ|а́ть (-и́ть); (*admit*) допус|ка́ть (-ти́ть); **to ~ territory/a right** уступи́ть террито́рию/пра́во; **I ~ you that point** в э́том вопро́се я вам уступа́ю; **let us ~ that...** допу́стим, что...

conceit *n* самомне́ние; **he has a good ~ of himself** он о себе́ высо́кого мне́ния.

conceited *adj* самодово́льный; **he is very ~** у него́ тако́й самодово́льный вид.

conceivable *adj*: **we tried every ~ method** мы испро́бовали все мы́слимые сре́дства; **it's hardly ~ that...** тру́дно предста́вить себе́, что..., вряд ли возмо́жно, что...; **it's just ~ that...** не исключено́, что...

conceivably *adv*: **it can't ~ be true** э́то немы́слимо; **he couldn't ~ have done it** исключено́—он э́того не де́лал.

conceive *vti vt* **1** (*a child*) зача́ть, забере́менеть (*pfs*)
2 (*mentally*): **to ~ a plan** заду́мать/замы́слить план (*usu pfs*); **I cannot ~ why...** я не могу́ предста́вить, почему́...; **I ~d a dislike for him/a passion for mushrooms** я его́ невзлюби́л, я пристрасти́лся к гриба́м
vi: **I can't ~ of anything worse** ху́же я не могу́ себе́ и предста́вить.

concentrate *n Chem* концентра́т.

concentrate *vti vt* (*troops*, *thoughts*) концентри́ровать (с-), сосредото́ч|ивать (-ить)
vi концентри́роваться, сосредото́чиваться; **I can't ~ on anything** я не могу́ ни на чём сосредото́читься.

concentrated *adj* (*of food, etc.*) концентри́рованный.

concentration *n* концентра́ция, сосредото́чение; **a ~ of troops** стя́гивание/концентра́ция войск; **he listened with ~** он сосредото́ченно слу́шал; **he has great powers of ~** он уме́ет сосредото́читься.

concentric *adj* концентри́ческий.

concept *n* поня́тие.

conception *n* **1** (*of a child*) зача́тие
2 (*idea*) конце́пция, иде́я; **a bold ~** сме́лая конце́пция/иде́я; **his ~ of the role** его́ конце́пция э́той ро́ли; **he has no ~ of the difficulties involved** он да́же не представля́ет, каки́е мо́гут возни́кнуть тру́дности.

concern *n* **1**: **that's your ~/no ~ of yours** э́то (не) твоё де́ло; **it's of some ~ to us all** э́то в како́й-то ме́ре каса́ется нас всех
2 *Comm* фи́рма, предприя́тие, де́ло; **a paying ~** дохо́дное предприя́тие; **it's a going ~** э́то предприя́тие уже́ де́йствует.

concern *vt* **1** (*affect*, *involve*) каса́ться + *G* (*usu impf*); **the book ~s the problems of education** в кни́ге рассма́триваются пробле́мы образова́ния; **the parties ~ed** заинтересо́ванные ли́ца/сто́роны; **as far as I'm ~ed** что каса́ется меня́; **where the children are ~ed**

he has endless patience в обращéнии с детьмú он проявляéт бесконéчное терпéние; **were you ~ed in this affair?** вы учáствовали в этом дéле?; **he has ~ed himself with the education of the deaf** он заинтересовáлся проблéмами обучéния глухúх

2 (*trouble*) беспокóить (о-); **I'm ~ed that you eat so little** меня́ беспокóит, что ты так мáло ешь; **he was ~ed lest we miss our train** он беспокóился, как бы мы не опоздáли на пóезд; **don't ~ yourself about us** не беспокóйтесь о нас; **your father is very ~ed about your bad marks** отéц óчень встревóжен твоúми плохúми отмéтками.

concerning *prep* о + *P*; относúтельно/касáтельно + *G*.

concert *n* **1** концéрт; **they went to the ~** онú пошлú на концéрт; **he gave a ~** он дал концéрт; *attr* концéртный

2: to act in ~ дéйствовать согласóванно; **they work in ~** онú рабóтают вмéсте.

concerted *adj*: **a ~ effort** согласóванные дéйствия (*pl*).

concerto *n Mus* концéрт.

concession *n* устýпка; *Econ* концéссия; **to make ~s on both sides** пойтú на взаúмные устýпки.

conciliate *vt* (*placate*) умиротвор|я́ть (-úть); **he was very angry, but I did my best to ~ him** он был óчень зол, и я, как мог, старáлся умиротворúть егó.

conciliatory *adj* примирúтельный.

concise *adj* крáткий; **a ~ dictionary** крáткий словáрь; **he was very ~** он был óчень крáток/немногослóвен; **a ~ style** сжáтый/лаконúчный стиль.

conclude *vti vt* за|кáнчивать (-кóнчить), заключ|áть (-úть); **he ~d his speech with a quotation** он закóнчил речь цитáтой; (*of a serial*) **"to be ~d"** «окончáние слéдует»; **to ~ a treaty/a bargain** заключúть договóр/сдéлку; (*deduce*) **from your objections I ~ that...** из вáших возражéний я дéлаю вы́вод, что...

vi: **he ~d by saying that...** в заключéние он сказáл, что...; (*at end of speech*) **to ~ ...** в заключéние скажý...

concluding *adj* заключúтельный; **~ remarks/instalment** (*of a serial*) заключúтельное слóво (*sing*), послéдний вы́пуск.

conclusion *n* заключéние; вы́вод; (*of speech, document*) заключúтельная часть; **in ~** в заключéние; **the ~ of a treaty** заключéние договóра; **at the ~ of the meeting** в концé собрáния; **I came to the ~ that...** я пришёл к заключéнию,/к вы́воду, что...; **it's a foregone ~** э́то неизбéжный вы́вод; **don't jump to ~s** не дéлайте поспéшных вы́водов, не спешú с вы́водами.

conclusive *adj*: **~ evidence** убедúтельные доказáтельства (*pl*).

concoct *vt Cook* стря́пать (со-), *also fig, often pejor* [**NB** *in cooking used usually of smth made of flour*]; **I'll ~ some sort of pie/something for supper** я состря́паю какóй-нибудь пирóг, я придýмаю чтó-нибудь на ýжин; *fig* **to ~ a plot for a novel/an excuse** состря́пать сюжéт ромáна, придýмать отговóрку.

concrete *n* бетóн; *attr* бетóнный; **~ mixer** бетономешáлка.

concrete *adj* (*not abstract*) конкрéтный.

concur *vi* (*agree*) согла|шáться с + *I* (-сúться).

concurrent *adj* совпадáющий.

concurrently *adv* одноврéменно.

concussion *n* сотрясéние мóзга.

condemn *vt* **1** (*morally*) осу|ждáть (-дúть), *also Law*; **he was ~ed to 5 years' imprisonment** егó приговорúли к пятú годáм; *CQ* **I'm ~ed to hang round in London all summer** я обречён торчáть в Лóндоне цéлое лéто

2 (*declare unsafe*): **the inspectors ~ed the tinned meat** контролёры забраковáли все мясны́е консéрвы; **the building has been ~ed** здáние решенó снестú.

condensation *n* конденсáция.

condense *vti vt* (*milk*) сгу|щáть (-стúть); (*gas, vapour*) конденсúровать (*impf and pf, pf also* с-); (*text*) сокра|щáть (-тúть)

vi сгущáться, конденсúроваться.

condescend *vi* сни|сходúть (-зойтú); **he ~ed to see me personally/to hear my request** он мúлостиво соглаcúлся приня́ть меня́ лúчно, он снизошёл вы́слушать мою́ прóсьбу; **he'd never ~ to bribery** он не унúзился бы до взя́тки.

condescending *adj* снисходúтельный.

condescension *n* снисхождéние, снисходúтельность.

condiment *n* припрáва.

condition *n* **1** (*stipulation*) услóвие; **on ~ that...** при услóвии, что...; **on no ~** ни при какúх услóвиях (*pl*); **~s of sale** услóвия продáжи

2 (*state*) состоя́ние; **he's in no ~ to travel** он не в состоя́нии éхать; **the house is in terrible ~** дом в ужáсном состоя́нии; *Sport*: **to be out of ~** быть не в фóрме; **to keep oneself in good ~** сохраня́ть фóрму; *Agric* **these animals are in good ~** у э́тих живóтных ухóженный вид

3 *pl* (**~s**) (*circumstances*): **living/working ~s** жилúщные услóвия, услóвия (для) рабóты; **in such ~s one can't work** в такúх услóвиях невозмóжно рабóтать.

condition *vt*: **prices are ~ed by supply and demand** цéны определя́ются спрóсом и предложéнием (*usu impf*).

conditional *adj* услóвный, *also Gram*; **my promise to help you is ~ on your good behaviour** я обещáю вам помóчь при услóвии, что вы бýдете вестú себя́, как нáдо.

conditioned *adj*: **a ~ reflex** услóвный рефлéкс.

condole *vi*: **I ~d with him on the death of his father** у негó ýмер отéц—я вы́разил емý своё соболéзнование.

condone *vt*: **he took no notice of his wife's infidelity and even appeared to ~ it** он смотрéл сквозь па́льцы на неве́рность жены́ и да́же, каза́лось, проща́л ей.

conducive *adj*: **moisture is ~ to the growth of plants** вла́га спосо́бствует/благоприя́тствует ро́сту расте́ний; **exercise is ~ to health** физи́ческие упражне́ния поле́зны для здоро́вья; **such secretiveness is not ~ to mutual trust** скры́тность не спосо́бствует взаи́мному дове́рию.

conduct *n* (*behaviour*) поведе́ние; (*management*) веде́ние; **they are dissatisfied with the ~ of the war/elections** они́ недово́льны хо́дом *or* веде́нием войны́/проведе́нием вы́боров.

conduct *vti* **1** (*guide*) води́ть (*usu impf*); (*escort*) про|води́ть (-вести́); **she ~s parties round the palace** она́ во́дит гру́ппы тури́стов по дворцу́; **to ~ smb to a seat/across the street** провести́ кого́-л к ме́сту/че́рез у́лицу

2 (*direct*): **to ~ an examination/experiment/meeting** проводи́ть экза́мен/о́пыт/собра́ние; **to ~ a seige** вести́ оса́ду; *Mus* **who is ~ing (the choir)?** кто дирижи́рует (хо́ром)?

3 (*behave*): **he ~ed himself very well** он хорошо́ вёл себя́ (*only in impf*)

4 *Phys*, *Elec*: **to ~ electricity/heat** проводи́ть ток/теплоту́.

conducted *adj*: **a ~ tour** экску́рсия.

conductor *n Mus* дирижёр; (*of bus*) конду́ктор; *Elec* проводни́к; **lightning ~** громоотво́д.

cone *n Bot* ши́шка; *Math* ко́нус; (*for ice cream*) рожо́к.

confectioner *n* конди́тер; **~'s** (*shop*) конди́терская.

confectionery *n* конди́терские изде́лия (*pl*).

confederate *n* (*accomplice*) соуча́стник, соо́бщник.

confederation *n* конфедера́ция; сою́з.

confer *vti vt*: **to ~ a doctorate on smb** (*award*) прису|жда́ть кому́-л сте́пень до́ктора (-ди́ть), (*give personally*) вруч|а́ть кому́-л дипло́м о присужде́нии до́кторской сте́пени (-и́ть)

vi: **to ~ with smb about smth** совеща́ться с кем-л о чём-л (*impf*).

conference *n* конфере́нция, (*on smaller scale, or involving fewer people*) совеща́ние; **press/summit ~** пресс-конфере́нция, совеща́ние на вы́сшем у́ровне *or* в верха́х; **the director is in ~** дире́ктор на совеща́нии.

confess *vti vt* призна|ва́ться в + *P or* + что (-́ться); **to ~ a crime/that...** признава́ться в преступле́нии/, что...

vi: **to ~ to smth** призна́ться в чём-л; **I ~, I don't want to go** признаю́сь, мне не хо́чется идти́; *Rel* испове́доваться (*impf and pf*).

confessedly *adv* по ли́чному призна́нию.

confession *n* призна́ние; *Rel* и́споведь; **he made a full ~** он во всём призна́лся; **I've a ~ to make—it was I who broke the cup** признаю́сь—ча́шку разби́л я.

confide *vti vt*: **he ~d to me that...** он мне сообщи́л по секре́ту, что...; **to ~ a secret to smb** дове́рить кому́-л та́йну (*usu pf*)

vi: **I have nobody to ~ in** мне не́кому дове́риться/откры́ть ду́шу.

confidence *n* **1** (*trust*) дове́рие; **to be in/to enjoy smb's ~** по́льзоваться чьим-л дове́рием; **I haven't much ~ in what he says** я не о́чень доверя́ю его́ слова́м, я не осо́бенно ве́рю тому́, что он говори́т; **I have every ~ in you** я вам по́лностью доверя́ю

2 (*assurance*) уве́ренность; **to speak with ~** говори́ть с уве́ренностью/уве́ренно; **he is gaining ~** у него́ прибавля́ется (*impers*) уве́ренности; **to give smb ~** всели́ть в кого́-л уве́ренность

3 (*secret*) секре́т, та́йна; **we exchanged ~s** мы обменя́лись свои́ми та́йнами; **in strict ~** стро́го конфиденциа́льно.

confidence man, *abbr* **conman** (*US*) *n* моше́нник.

confident *adj* уве́ренный; **I am ~ of success/that...** я уве́рен в успе́хе/, что...

confidential *adj* конфиденциа́льный; секре́тный; **a ~ secretary/talk** дове́ренный секрета́рь, конфиденциа́льный разгово́р; **~ papers** секре́тные докуме́нты.

confidently *adv* уве́ренно, с уве́ренностью.

confiding *adj* дове́рчивый.

confine *vt* **1**: **to ~ wild birds in a cage** держа́ть птиц в кле́тке (*impf*); **he's ~d to the house with/by flu** он сиди́т до́ма с гри́ппом; **he is ~d to bed** он лежи́т, (*if bed-ridden*) он прико́ван к посте́ли

2 (*limit*): **the damage is ~d to the outbuildings** пострада́ли то́лько дворо́вые постро́йки; **I shall ~ myself to the facts/to saying that...** я ограни́чусь фа́ктами/тем, что скажу́...

3 (*of childbirth*): **she expects to be ~d in May** ей роди́ть в ма́е.

confinement *n Med* ро́ды (*pl*); (*in prison*): **solitary ~** одино́чное заключе́ние.

confines *npl* преде́лы, *also fig*; **within/beyond the ~ of** в преде́лах + *G*, за преде́лами + *G*.

confirm *vt* (*uphold*) подтвер|жда́ть, (*ratify*) утвер|жда́ть (*pfs* -ди́ть); **his suspicions were ~ed** его́ подозре́ния подтверди́лись; **to ~ smth by letter** подтверди́ть что-л письмо́м; **his appointment has been ~ed** его́ назначе́ние утверждено́.

confirmed *adj*: **a ~ bachelor/drunkard/invalid** убеждённый холостя́к, неисправи́мый пья́ница, хрони́ческий больно́й.

confiscate *vt* конфискова́ть (*impf and pf*).

conflagration *n* большо́й пожа́р.

conflict *n* столкнове́ние, конфли́кт; **a ~ of interests/opinions/principles** столкнове́ние интере́сов/мне́ний, борьба́ при́нципов; **he is in/came into ~ with his boss** он в конфли́кте *or* он конфликту́ет/он вступи́л в конфли́кт со свои́м нача́льством.

conflict *vi*: **his report ~s with yours** его́ расска́з противоре́чит ва́шему (*impf*).

conflicting *adj* противоречи́вый; **~ evidence** противоречи́вые показа́ния (*pl*).

conform *vi*: **his interpretation of the facts does not ~ with the accepted view** его́ интерпретáция фáктов идёт вразрéз с общепри́нятой тóчкой зрéния; **all new buildings must ~ to the sanitary regulations** все нóвые здáния должны́ отвечáть санитáрным нóрмам; **to ~ to fashion/the rules** подчин|я́ться мóде/прáвилам (-и́ться).

conformity *n*: **in ~ with** в соотвéтствии с + *I*.

confound *vt* пора|жáть (-зи́ть); **we were ~ed by the news of the disaster** нас как грóмом поразилo сообщéние о бéдствии; *CQ*: **~ it!/the man!** проклятье!, чёрт бы егó побрáл!; **what a ~ed nuisance!** вот досáда!

confront *vt*: **to ~ danger** смотрéть опáсности (*D*) в лицó; **the difficulties that ~ us are nearly insuperable** трýдности, стоя́щие перед нáми, почти́ непреодоли́мы; **the government is afraid to ~ the unions** прави́тельство бои́тся конфли́кта с профсою́зами; **they ~ed him with his accusers** емý устрóили óчную стáвку с тéми, кто пóдал [**NB** *sing verb*] на негó в суд; **when ~ed by the evidence he confessed all** под давлéнием ули́к (*pl*) он во всём признáлся; **we were ~ed by a sentry/by unexpected obstacles** мы натолкнýлись на часовóго (*ran into*) *or* нас останови́л часовóй (*were challenged by*), мы натолкнýлись на неожи́данные препя́тствия.

confrontation *n* конфронтáция.

confuse *vt* (*muddle*) пýтать (с-); запýт|ывать (-ать); перепýтать (*usu pf*); (*embarrass*) сму|щáть (-ти́ть); **I always ~ her with her sister** я всегдá пýтаю её с (её) сестрóй; **I got their names ~d** я спýтал/перепýтал их именá; **I was completely ~d** у меня́ в головé всё перемешáлось (*by fatigue, drink, etc.*), я запýтался (*in exams, etc.*), я смути́лся (*in embarrassment*); **he ~d me by his questions** он запýтал/смути́л меня́ свои́ми вопрóсами; **don't ~ the issue** не запýтывайте дéло; **the old man was ~d by all the traffic** при ви́де проноси́вшихся ми́мо маши́н стари́к совсéм растеря́лся.

confusing *adj* слóжный, запýтанный; **the rules seem very ~** э́ти прáвила кáжутся сли́шком слóжными/запýтанными; **London is very ~ for a foreigner** в Лóндоне инострáнцу легкó заблуди́ться; **I find it ~ to drive on the left** мне трýдно привы́кнуть к левостóроннему движéнию.

confusion *n* пýтаница; беспоря́док; (*embarrassment*) смущéние, замешáтельство; **there was some ~ over the dates** былá какáя-то пýтаница в дáтах; **the army retreated in ~** áрмия отступи́ла в беспоря́дке; **in the ~ I forgot my umbrella** в суматóхе я забы́л зóнтик; **their arrival threw our plans into ~** их появлéние спýтало нáши плáны; **she was covered in ~** онá былá сконфýжена.

confute *vt* опроверг|áть (-нуть).

congeal *vt*: **the blood ~ed/was ~ed** кровь запеклáсь; **the fat ~ed on the plates** жир застыл на тарéлках.

congenial *adj* (*of person*) прия́тный, симпати́чный; **~ work** интерéсная рабóта; **a ~ climate** благоприя́тный кли́мат.

congenital *adj* врождённый.

congested *adj*: **~ streets** ýлицы, перегрýженные трáнспортом (*with cars*)/запрýженные *or* перепóлненные нарóдом (*with people*); **a ~ area** перенаселённый/густонаселённый райóн.

congratulate *vt* поздрав|ля́ть (-ить); **I ~ you on winning the competition** поздравля́ю вас с побéдой на кóнкурсе.

congratulations *npl* поздравлéния; **may I offer my ~ on your appointment** прими́те мои́ поздравлéния в связи́ с вáшим назначéнием; **~!** поздравля́ю!

congratulatory *adj* поздрави́тельный.

congregate *vi* со|бирáться (-брáться).

congress *n* конгрéсс; съезд; (*US*) **C.** конгрéсс США.

congressman *n* (*US*) конгрессмéн.

conical *adj* кони́ческий.

conifer *n* хвóйное дéрево.

conjecture *n* предположéние.

conjecture *vt* предпо|лагáть (-ложи́ть); **one can only ~ how things are going** мóжно тóлько предполагáть,/догáдываться, что происхóдит.

conjugal *adj* супрýжеский.

conjugate *vt* *Gram* спрягáть (про-).

conjunction *n*: **in ~ with him** вмéсте/совмéстно с ним; **the two firms acted in ~** э́ти две фи́рмы дéйствовали совмéстно; *Gram* сою́з.

conjunctivitis *n* *Med* конъюнктиви́т.

conjure *vi* (*of conjurer*) покáз|ывать фóкусы (-áть); *fig* **his is a name to ~ with in the ministry** с ним считáются в министéрстве.

conjurer *n* фóкусник.

connect *vti* *vt* (*join*) соедин|я́ть (-и́ть), *also Tel*; (*of smaller thing to larger*) присоединя́ть; (*link*) свя́з|ывать (-áть); **to ~ two parts** (*of mechanism*) соедини́ть две детáли; *Tel* **please ~ me with the manager** пожáлуйста, соедини́те меня́ с управля́ющим; **is the gas/telephone/electricity ~ed?** газ/телефóн подключён?, электри́чество подключенó?; **I have never ~ed these two ideas** я никогдá не свя́зывал вмéсте э́ти две идéи; **the events are not in any way ~ed** э́ти собы́тия никáк не свя́заны мéжду собóй; **he is ~ed with that firm** он свя́зан с э́той фи́рмой; **I'm ~ed with the Smiths by marriage** Сми́ты—мои́ рóдственники со стороны́ жены́

vi: **where does the cooker ~ with the gas-pipe?** где плитá соединя́ется с гáзовой трубóй?; *Rail* **this train ~s with the Aberdeen train at Edinburgh** в Эдинбýрге сойдёте с э́того пóезда и пересáдете на aберди́нский.

connection, connexion *n* **1** связь, *also Tel*; **a causal ~** причи́нная связь; **in this ~** в э́той свя́зи; **in ~ with your request** в связи́ с вáшей прóсьбой; **what is the ~ between**

the two subjects? какая связь между этими двумя предметами?; **there must be a loose ~** здесь где-то ослаблено соединение/(*only Elec*) слабый контакт; *Rail*, *etc.*: **to miss one's ~** не успеть сделать пересадку/пересесть; **the buses run in ~ with the trains** движение/расписание автобусов и поездов согласовано; **in winter the only ~ with the far north is by air** зимой самолёт — единственное средство связи с отдалёнными северными районами

2 *pl* (**~s**) (*of people*) связи; **he has good business ~s** у него большие связи в деловом мире; **family ~s** родственники.

connivance *n*: **with the ~ of** при попустительстве + *G*.

connive *vi*: **to ~ at smth** попустительствовать чему-л (*impf*), смотреть на что-л сквозь пальцы (по-), закры|вать глаза на что-л (-ть).

connoisseur *n* знаток; **a ~ of literature/wine** знаток литературы, ценитель вин.

conquer *vt* (*in war, battle*) побе|ждать (-дить); (*territory, a country*) завоёв|ывать (-ать); (*subjugate a people, an area*) покор|ять (-ить); *fig* (*difficulties, etc.*) преодоле|вать (-ть); **they did not ~ that country** они не смогли завоевать эту страну/покорить этот народ.

conquest *n* завоевание; (*subjugation*) покорение; **the ~ of Siberia** покорение Сибири; *CQ* **she made a ~ of him** она пленила его.

conscience *n* совесть; **I've got a guilty/bad ~ about/towards him** вспоминая его, я чувствую угрызения совести; **it's better to own up and get it off your ~** лучше признаться во всём, чтобы совесть не мучила/была чиста; **it's on my ~ that I've not yet gone to see her in hospital** меня мучит совесть, что я ещё не был у неё в больнице; (*in emphasis*) **I cannot in all ~ agree** по совести говоря, я не могу согласиться.

conscientious *adj* добросовестный; **a ~ worker/piece of work** добросовестный работник, добросовестно выполненная работа.

conscious *adj* **1** *attr* мыслящий; **man is a ~ being** человек — существо мыслящее; **he has made a ~ effort to overcome that failing** он сознательно старался преодолеть этот свой недостаток

2 *predic*: **I am ~ of my folly** сознаю, что сделал глупость; **I became ~ of being/that I was being followed** я почувствовал, что за мной следят; **I became ~ of a pain in my leg** я вдруг почувствовал боль в ноге; *Med* **he was ~ to the last** он был в сознании до последней минуты.

consciously *adv* сознательно.

consciousness *n* сознание, *also Med*; осознание; **to lose/regain ~** потерять сознание, прийти в сознание/в себя; **he suffers from class ~** *approx* он стесняется своего происхождения.

conscript *n* призывник, новобранец.

conscript *vt* при|зывать на военную службу (-звать).

conscription *n* воинская повинность.

consecrate *vt* посвя|щать (-тить).

consecutive *adj translate by adv* подряд; **they made three ~ attacks** они провели три атаки подряд; **for four ~ days** четыре дня подряд.

consecutively *adv* подряд.

consensus *n*: **the ~ of opinion was that...** общее мнение было, что...; **according to the ~ of opinion** по единодушному мнению.

consent *n* согласие; **by common/tacit ~** с общего/молчаливого согласия; **he gave his ~ to the proposal** он дал своё согласие на предложение; **they parted by mutual ~** они расстались по взаимному согласию.

consent *vi*: **to ~ to** согла|шаться на + *A*, *or* + *inf* (-ситься).

consequence *n* **1** (*result*) последствие, результат; **in ~** в результате; **in ~ of** вследствие + *G* (*prep*); **to take the ~s** отвечать за последствия

2 (*importance*): **it's of no ~** это не имеет никакого значения; **a man of some ~** влиятельное лицо.

consequent *adj* последующий; **~ on/upon** следующий за + *I*.

consequently *adv* следовательно; в результате.

conservation *n*: **nature ~** охрана природы.

conservative *adj* консервативный, *also Polit*; *as n Polit* консерватор; (*cautious*): **at a ~ estimate** по скромным подсчётам (*pl*).

conservatoire *n* консерватория.

conservatory *n* (*greenhouse*) оранжерея.

conserve *n usu pl* варенье, джем (*sings*).

conserve *vt*: **to ~ one's strength** сохран|ять силы (*pl*) (-ить).

consider *vt* **1** (*regard as, be of opinion*) считать (*usu impf*); **he is ~ed a brilliant violinist** его считают блестящим скрипачом; **I ~ it my duty to tell you that...** (я) считаю своим долгом сообщить вам, что...; **you can ~ yourself lucky to have escaped alive** ваше счастье, что остались живы; **we ~ that you're not to blame** мы считаем, что вы не виноваты

2 (*think about*) думать (по-) *and compounds*; **have you ever ~ed going by train?** как ты думаешь, а не поехать ли поездом?; **he wouldn't ~ it for a moment** он и думать об этом не станет; **~ your answer carefully** продумай как следует свой ответ; **my ~ed opinion is that...** поразмыслив, я решил, что...; **we are ~ing him for the post** мы обдумываем его кандидатуру на этот пост; **let me ~ a little** дайте мне подумать

3 (*take into account*) считаться с + *I* (*impf*), прин|имать во внимание + *A* (-ять); **to ~ the feelings of others** считаться с чувствами других; **all things ~ed** приняв всё во внимание, всё взвесив.

considerable *adj* значи́тельный; большо́й; **a ~ income** значи́тельный дохо́д; **we had ~ difficulty in finding the house** мы с больши́м трудо́м нашли́ э́тот дом.

considerably *adv* значи́тельно; о́чень.

considerate *adj*: **she is ~ of/to/towards others** она́ внима́тельна к други́м, она́ счита́ется с други́ми.

consideration *n* **1** (*thoughtfulness*) уваже́ние, внима́ние; **out of ~ for her age** из уваже́ния к её во́зрасту; **to show ~ for smb** счита́ться с кем-л (*by thoughtfulness*), ока́зывать кому́-л внима́ние (*by some action*)

2 (*thought*): **he acted without due ~** он поступи́л так, не поду́мав; **he promised to give it serious ~** он обеща́л серьёзно об э́том поду́мать; **the matter is now under ~** э́тот вопро́с сейча́с рассма́тривается

3 (*factor, reason*) соображе́ние; фа́ктор; **leaving aside financial ~s** оставля́я в стороне́/отбро́сив фина́нсовые соображе́ния; **he is above such ~s** ему́ тако́е и в го́лову не придёт; **time is an important ~** вре́мя—ва́жный фа́ктор

4 (*payment*): **he'll do it for a small/modest ~** он сде́лает э́то за небольшо́е/скро́мное вознагражде́ние.

considering *prep and adv*: *prep* **~ his age** принима́я во внима́ние/учи́тывая его́ во́зраст; *adv* **that's not so bad ~** в о́бщем, э́то не так уж пло́хо.

consign *vt Comm* отправ|ля́ть (-́ить); **to ~ goods by sea** отправля́ть това́ры мо́рем; *fig*: **the project has been ~ed to oblivion** прое́кт был пре́дан забве́нию; **the child was ~ed to the care of his uncle** ребёнка поручи́ли забо́там дя́ди.

consignment *n Comm*: **a ~ of goods** па́ртия това́ра, груз.

consist *vi*: **to ~ of/in** состоя́ть из + *G*/в + *P* (*impf*); **the committee ~s of 10 members** комите́т состои́т из десяти́ чле́нов; **the difficulty ~s in this** в э́том и состои́т/заключа́ется тру́дность.

consistency *n* **1** (*density*) консисте́нция; *Cook* **beat the mixture till it reaches pouring ~** взбе́йте смесь до жи́дкого состоя́ния; *fig* (*of person, argument, etc.*) после́довательность.

consistent *adj* (*constant, logical*): **they/the arguments are not ~** их поведе́ние непосле́довательно, их до́воды противоречи́вы; (*in agreement with*) **that is not ~ with what you said to me yesterday** вы противоре́чите са́ми себе́—вчера́ вы говори́ли друго́е.

consistently *adv* (*logically*) после́довательно; (*continuously*) постоя́нно; **he has ~ refused promotion** он постоя́нно отка́зывается [NB *tense*] от повыше́ния по слу́жбе.

consolation *n* утеше́ние; *attr*: **~ prize** «утеши́тельный» приз.

console *vt* утеш|а́ть (-́ить).

consolidate *vt* укреп|ля́ть (-и́ть); *Comm* (*unite*) объедин|я́ть (-и́ть); **to ~ one's position/influence** укрепля́ть своё положе́ние/влия́ние; (*teacher to pupils*) **in order to ~ what we learned last week** что́бы закрепи́ть то, что мы прошли́ на про́шлой неде́ле.

consoling *adj* утеши́тельный.

consommé *n* бульо́н.

consonant *n Gram* согла́сный звук.

consort *vi*: **to ~ with** обща́ться с + *I* (*impf*).

conspicuous *adj* ви́дный, заме́тный, бро́ский; **put them in a ~ place** поста́вь их на ви́дное ме́сто; **he is ~ by his absence** его́ отсу́тствие заме́тно; **I don't want to make myself ~ by being late** я не хочу́ опа́здывать, что́бы не привлека́ть к себе́ внима́ния; **a ~ poster** бро́ская/я́ркая афи́ша; **a ~ tie** я́ркий/бро́ский га́лстук; **he is ~ because of his height** его́ рост всем броса́ется в глаза́; **I felt ~ on the platform** сто́я на трибу́не, я чу́вствовал обращённые на меня́ со всех сторо́н взо́ры.

conspicuously *adv*: **she always dresses ~** она́ всегда́ так бро́ско одева́ется; **he behaves ~** он всё де́лает напока́з, он лю́бит привлека́ть к себе́ внима́ние.

conspiracy *n* за́говор; **a ~ of silence** за́говор молча́ния.

conspirator *n* загово́рщик.

conspire *vi*: **to ~ against smb** устр|а́ивать/состав|ля́ть за́говор про́тив кого́-л (-о́ить/-́ить); **to ~ with smb to do smth** сгова́риваться с кем-л сде́лать что-л (сговори́ться); **events seemed to ~ against me** каза́лось, про́тив меня́ сговори́лось всё.

constable *n* (*UK*) полице́йский; **chief ~** нача́льник поли́ции.

constabulary *n* (*UK*) поли́ция.

constancy *n* ве́рность; постоя́нство; **~ of purpose** постоя́нство це́ли.

constant *n Math, Phys* конста́нта, постоя́нная (величина́).

constant *adj* (*regular*) постоя́нный; **a ~ visitor/friend, ~ rain** постоя́нный посети́тель, ве́рный друг, непреры́вный дождь.

constellation *n* созве́здие.

consternation *n* у́жас; **in ~** в у́жасе; **there was general ~** всех объя́л у́жас.

constipation *n Med* запо́р; **to suffer from ~** страда́ть запо́рами (*pl*).

constituent *n* составна́я часть; (*UK*) *Polit* избира́тель (*m*).

constituent *adj* составно́й; *Polit* **a ~ assembly** учреди́тельное собра́ние.

constitute *vt* **1** (*appoint*) назнач|а́ть (-́ить); (*set up*) учре|жда́ть (-ди́ть); **he was ~d adviser** его́ назна́чили консульта́нтом/сове́тником; **to ~ a committee** учрежда́ть комите́т

2 (*amount to*): **to ~ a precedent** созда|ва́ть прецеде́нт (-́ть); **12 months ~ a year** двена́дцать ме́сяцев составля́ют год; **terrorism ~s a serious threat** террори́зм—серьёзная угро́за; **he is so ~d that he cannot endure contradiction** он не выно́сит, когда́ ему́ противоре́чат—тако́й уж у него́ хара́ктер.

constitution *n* (*code of laws*) конститу́ция; (*structure*) соста́в; (*of person*) телосложе́ние, конститу́ция; **he has a strong ~** он кре́пкого сложе́ния, у него́ кре́пкий органи́зм.

constitutional *adj Law* конституцио́нный; *Med* конституциона́льный.

constitutionally *adv*: **she is ~ delicate**/*fig* **incapable of telling a lie** она́ хру́пкого сложе́ния, она́ по приро́де свое́й не спосо́бна лгать; *Law* по конститу́ции.

constrain *vt*: **to ~ smb to do smth** прину|жда́ть кого́-л сде́лать что-л (-́дить); **I felt ~ed to intervene** я был вы́нужден вмеша́ться.

constraint *n*: **to act under ~** де́йствовать по принужде́нию; **I felt some ~ in the director's presence** я чу́вствовал не́которую ско́ванность в прису́тствии дире́ктора.

constricted *adj* стеснённый.

construct *vt* стро́ить (по-); **to ~ a building**/**sentence**/**theory**/**triangle** стро́ить зда́ние/предложе́ние/тео́рию, начерти́ть треуго́льник.

construction *n* (*process*) строи́тельство; (*process or thing built*) постро́йка; (*thing*) сооруже́ние; констру́кция, *also Gram*; **the school is under**/**in process of ~** шко́ла стро́ится; **that ~ in the workshop takes a lot of room** э́то сооруже́ние занима́ет мно́го ме́ста в цеху́; **the new theatre is a strange ~** зда́ние но́вого теа́тра о́чень стра́нной констру́кции; *fig* **he put a wrong ~ on my words** он непра́вильно истолкова́л мои́ слова́.

constructive *adj* конструкти́вный.

construe *vt*: **his remarks were wrongly ~d** его́ замеча́ния бы́ли непра́вильно истолко́ваны; *Gram* **to ~ a sentence** раз|бира́ть предложе́ние (-обра́ть).

consul *n* ко́нсул; **~ general** генера́льный ко́нсул.

consulate *n* ко́нсульство.

consult *vti vt* консульти́роваться (про-), сове́товаться (по-); **to ~ a doctor**/**a lawyer** консульти́роваться *or* сове́товаться с врачо́м/с юри́стом; **to ~ a dictionary**/**one's diary** справля́ться по словарю́/по календарю́; **he ~ed his watch**/**the map** он посмотре́л на часы́/по ка́рте; **to ~ smb's interests** учи́тывать чьи-л интере́сы (*usu impf*)

vi: **to ~ with smb about smth** консульти́роваться/сове́товаться с кем-л о чём-л.

consultant *n* консульта́нт; *Med* врач-консульта́нт.

consultation *n* консульта́ция; **they are in ~ now** они́ сейча́с на консульта́ции; **it was decided in ~ with the doctor** они́ э́то реши́ли, посове́товавшись с врачо́м; **after some ~ they accepted the offer** посове́товавшись, они́ при́няли предложе́ние.

consultative *adj*: **a ~ committee** консультати́вная коми́ссия.

consulting *adj*: **~ hours** (*at surgery*)/**room** приёмные часы́, кабине́т врача́.

consume *vt* (*eat*) съеда́ть (съесть); **he ~d everything that was put before him** он съел всё, что ему́ бы́ло по́дано; *fig*: **all the papers were ~d by fire** пожа́р уничто́жил все бума́ги; **he was ~d by curiosity** он сгора́л от любопы́тства; **the car ~s a lot of petrol** э́та маши́на потребля́ет/расхо́дует мно́го бензи́на; **we will soon have ~d all our natural resources** мы ско́ро исчерпа́ем все на́ши приро́дные ресу́рсы.

consumer *n* потреби́тель (*m*); *attr*: **~ goods** потреби́тельские това́ры, това́ры широ́кого потребле́ния.

consummate *adj*: **~ skill**/**taste** зако́нченное мастерство́, превосхо́дный вкус.

consummation *n*: **the ~ of a life's work** заверше́ние де́ла жи́зни; **the ~ of a marriage** исполне́ние супру́жеских обя́занностей.

consumption *n* **1** потребле́ние; **what is your petrol ~?** ско́лько бензи́на потребля́ет ва́ша маши́на?; **his ~ of beer is spectacular** он поглоща́ет невероя́тное коли́чество пи́ва; **this food is not fit for human ~** э́то недоброка́чественные проду́кты (*pl*), *joc* э́то есть нельзя́

2 *Med* туберкулёз лёгких, чахо́тка.

consumptive *adj* чахо́точный.

contact *n* **1** (*physical*): **the car came into ~ with the wall** маши́на заде́ла сте́ну; **his hand came into ~ with the electric saw** он прикосну́лся к электропиле́

2 *Med*, *Elec*, *Tech* конта́кт; **he's been in ~ with a case of smallpox** он был в конта́кте с больны́м о́спой; *attr Aut*: **~ points** конта́кты

3 *fig* конта́кт; **I'll be in ~ with him tomorrow** за́втра я уви́жусь с ним; **to make**/**establish ~ with smb** входи́ть в конта́кт/устана́вливать конта́кт с кем-л; **I'm in ~ with him occasionally in the course of my work** я встреча́юсь с ним вре́мя от вре́мени по рабо́те; **he has many business ~s** у него́ мно́го деловы́х конта́ктов; **it's hard to make any ~ with him** с ним тру́дно нала́дить конта́кт.

contact *vt* свя́з|ываться (-а́ться); **I'll ~ you tomorrow** я свяжу́сь с тобо́й за́втра; **where can I ~ the director?** где я могу́ встре́титься с дире́ктором?

contact lenses *npl* конта́ктные ли́нзы.

contagious *adj* зара́зный, инфекцио́нный.

contain *vt* **1** (*hold*) содержа́ть (*impf*); **the book ~s much useful information** кни́га содéржит/в кни́ге соде́ржится мно́го поле́зной информа́ции

2 (*restrain*): **to ~ one's anger**/**laughter** сде́рж|ивать гнев/смех (-а́ть); **I could scarcely ~ myself for joy** я чуть не пры́гал от ра́дости.

container *n* (*general word for packing case, sack, etc.*) та́ра (*collect*); (*vessel for liquids*) сосу́д; *Rail, etc.* конте́йнер.

contaminate *vi* (*infect*) зара|жа́ть (-зи́ть); (*pollute*) загрязн|я́ть (-и́ть); **~d clothing**/**water** заражённая оде́жда, загрязнённая вода́.

contamination *n* (*infection*) зараже́ние; (*pollution*) загрязне́ние.

contemplate *vt* разду́мывать, размышля́ть (*impfs*); **I was contemplating the problem/what would happen if...** я разду́мывал над пробле́мой, я прики́дывал, что мо́жет случи́ться, е́сли...; **I ~ going to Scotland** я ду́маю, не пое́хать ли мне в Шотла́ндию; **she ~d herself in the mirror** она́ смотре́лась в зе́ркало.

contemplation *n Philos* созерца́ние; (*thought*) разду́мье; **sunk in ~** погружённый в глубо́кое разду́мье.

contemporaneous *adj*: **these events were ~ with the reign of Ivan the Terrible** э́ти собы́тия происходи́ли во времена́ Ива́на Гро́зного.

contemporary *n* совреме́нник; (*of same age*) рове́сник; **Pushkin's contemporaries** совреме́нники Пу́шкина; **he and I are contemporaries** мы с ним рове́сники.

contemporary *adj* совреме́нный.

contempt *n*: **~ for smth** презре́ние к чему́-л; **to feel ~ for smb, to hold smb in ~** презира́ть кого́-л; **to incur ~** вызыва́ть к себе́ презре́ние; **he's beneath ~** он не досто́ин да́же презре́ния; **he showed complete ~ of danger** он презира́л опа́сность.

contemptible *adj* презре́нный, ничто́жный.

contend *vti vt*: **to ~ that...** утвержда́ть, что... (*only in impf*)

vi: **to ~ with/against smb for a prize** боро́ться с кем-л за приз; **I have many difficulties to ~ with** я столкну́лся со мно́гими тру́дностями [**NB** *tense*]; **she has enough to ~ with** у неё тру́дностей хвата́ет (*impers*); *Law* **the ~ing parties** спо́рящие сто́роны.

content[1] *n* содержи́мое, *fig* содержа́ние (*no pls*); **the ~s of a jug/pocket** содержи́мое кувши́на/карма́на; **form and ~** фо́рма и содержа́ние; **table of ~s** (*in book*) содержа́ние, оглавле́ние; **the ~ of an article/speech** содержа́ние статьи́/ре́чи.

content[2] *n* (*satisfaction*) удовлетворе́ние; **we swam/talked to our heart's ~** мы накупа́лись/наговори́лись вво́лю (*adv*) [**NB** *use of prefix* на-].

content[2] *adj* дово́льный; **I'm ~ in my job/with that piece of work** я дово́лен свое́й рабо́той/э́той рабо́той; (*willing, ready*): **I am ~ to stay behind** я согла́сен/гото́в оста́ться; **I'd be quite ~ to come with you but I'm not free** я был бы рад вас проводи́ть, но я сейча́с за́нят.

content[2] *vt*: **there's no ~ing him** ему́ ниче́м не угоди́шь; **there's no butter, we'll have to ~ ourselves with dry bread** ма́сла нет, обойдёмся одни́м хле́бом; **he ~ed himself with saying that...** он ограни́чился тем, что сказа́л...

contented *adj* дово́льный.

contention *n* (*quarrelling*) спор; **this is no time for ~** сейча́с не вре́мя для спо́ров (*pl*); (*argument*) **my ~ is that...** я утвержда́ю, что...

contest *n* (*competition*) ко́нкурс; *Sport* соревнова́ние, состяза́ние (*between teams or individuals*).

contest *vti vt* оспа́ривать (оспо́рить); **to ~ a point/a will** оспа́ривать пункт/завеща́ние; **to ~ a seat in Parliament** боро́ться за ме́сто в парла́менте (*impf*)

vi: **they are ~ing for the prize** они́ бо́рются за приз.

continence *n* (*self-control*) сде́ржанность; (*physical*) воздержа́ние.

continent *n* контине́нт; *Geog* (*as opposed to sea*) матери́к; **the ~ of Asia** азиа́тский контине́нт; (*from UK*) **I'm going to the ~** я е́ду в Евро́пу.

continental *adj* континента́льный.

contingency *n* случа́йность, слу́чай; **should the ~ arise that...** в слу́чае, е́сли...; **to provide for every ~** предусмотре́ть вся́кого ро́да нео́жиданности (*pl*).

contingent *n* гру́ппа; *Mil, etc.* континге́нт; **a ~ of tourists/competitors** гру́ппа тури́стов/уча́стников соревнова́ний.

contingent *adj*: **our plans are ~ on the weather** на́ши пла́ны зави́сят от пого́ды.

continual *adj* (*without interruption*) непреры́вный; **he has a ~ cough** он всё вре́мя ка́шляет.

continuation *n* продолже́ние; **the ~ of a story/line/wall** продолже́ние расска́за/ли́нии/стены́.

continue *vti vt* продолжа́ть (*impf*); **"to be ~d"** продолже́ние сле́дует; **~d on page 10** продолже́ние на деся́той страни́це (*written* стр. 10); **he was ~d in the post for another year** он был оста́влен на э́той до́лжности ещё на́ год

vi продолжа́ть(ся) (*impf*); **he ~d to work/working all summer** он продолжа́л рабо́тать всё ле́то; **he ~d with the work** он продолжа́л рабо́ту; **may I ~?** мо́жно продолжа́ть?; **the meating ~d in the afternoon** собра́ние продолжа́лось по́сле обе́да; **we ~d on our way** мы продолжа́ли путь; **the road ~d as far as the eye could see** доро́га тяну́лась наско́лько хвата́ло (*impers*) глаз; **he ~d in office till he was 60** он остава́лся на свое́й до́лжности до шести́десяти лет; **if you ~ to be so obstinate** е́сли и да́льше бу́дешь упря́миться.

continuous *adj* непреры́вный; *Gram* дли́тельный.

contort *vt*: **his face was ~ed with pain** его́ лицо́ искази́лось/искриви́лось от бо́ли.

contour *n* ко́нтур; *attr*: **~ line/map** горизонта́ль, ко́нтурная ка́рта.

contraband *n* контраба́нда; *attr* контраба́ндный.

contraception *n* предупрежде́ние бере́менности; **to practise ~** применя́ть противозача́точные сре́дства, предохраня́ться.

contraceptive *n* противозача́точное сре́дство.

contract[1] *n* догово́р; контра́кт (*usu Comm*); (*subcontract*) подря́д; **to draw up/conclude/break a ~** соста́вить/заключи́ть/нару́шить контра́кт *or* догово́р; **conditions of/breach of ~** усло́вия/наруше́ние контра́кта *or* догово́-

ра; **we are under ~ to that company to supply bricks** у нас контра́кт с э́той компа́нией на поста́вку кирпича́ (*collect*); **to place a ~ for smth, to put smth out to ~** сдать подря́д на что-л; *attr*: **~ law** догово́рное пра́во.

contract[1] *vti vt*: **to ~ an alliance** заключ|а́ть сою́з (-и́ть); **to ~ debts** наде́лать долго́в (*pf*); **to ~ measles** зара|жа́ться ко́рью (-зи́ться); *Law* **the ~ing parties** догова́ривающиеся сто́роны

vi Comm: **to ~ to build a factory** заключа́ть контра́кт/(*if a subcontract*) получ|а́ть подря́д на строи́тельство заво́да (-и́ть); *CQ* **I've ~ed out of the trip** я отказа́лся от пое́здки.

contract[2] *vti vt* (*tighten, shorten*): **to ~ one's muscles/a word** сокра|ща́ть му́скулы/сло́во (-ти́ть)

vi (*of muscles, etc.*) сокраща́ться; **metals ~ when cool** мета́ллы сжима́ются при охлажде́нии.

contraction *n* (*of word, muscle, etc.*) сокраще́ние; (*in childbirth*) родова́я схва́тка.

contractor *n* подря́дчик.

contradict *vt* противоре́чить + *D*, *CQ* (*only if contradicting people*) пере́чить + *D* (*impfs*); **he often ~s himself** он ча́сто противоре́чит самому́ себе́; **the two reports ~ each other** э́ти два сообще́ния противоре́чат друг дру́гу; **don't ~ me!** (ты) не пере́чь мне!; **to ~ rumours** отрица́ть слу́хи (*impf*).

contradiction *n* противоре́чие; (*denial*) отрица́ние; **a ~ in terms** логи́ческое противоре́чие; **to be in ~ with** противоре́чить + *D*.

contradictory *adj* противоречи́вый.

contradistinction *n*: **in ~ to** в отли́чие от + *G*.

contralto *n* контра́льто (*indecl*).

contraption *n CQ*: **what's that ingenious ~?** что э́то за хитроу́мное сооруже́ние?, (*if small*) что э́то за приспособле́ние?

contrarily *adv* своенра́вно, капри́зно.

contrariness *n* упря́мство, своенра́вие.

contrariwise *adv* наоборо́т, напро́тив.

contrary *n*: **on the ~, quite the ~** наоборо́т, как раз наоборо́т; **unless I hear to the ~** е́сли ничего́ не изме́нится; **I know/have heard nothing to the ~** наско́лько мне изве́стно, э́то и́менно так; **the ~ seems to be the case** де́ло вро́де бы обстои́т как раз наоборо́т.

contrary *adj* (*opposite*) противополо́жный; (*obstinate*) упря́мый, своенра́вный; **she's a ~ young woman** она́ своенра́вная осо́ба; **a ~ wind** встре́чный ве́тер.

contrary to *prep* про́тив + *G*; вопреки́ + *D*; **it's ~ to the rules** э́то про́тив пра́вил; **~ to my wishes/expectations** вопреки́ мои́м жела́ниям/ожида́ниям.

contrast *n* контра́ст; **a striking/sharp ~** рази́тельный/ре́зкий контра́ст; **in ~ to/with** по контра́сту с + *I*, в противополо́жность + *D*; **there's a striking ~ between the two brothers** ме́жду двумя́ бра́тьями рази́тельный контра́ст; **her white hair is in sharp ~ to her dark skin** её бе́лые во́лосы ре́зко контрасти́руют со сму́глым цве́том лица́.

contrast *vti vt* сра́вн|ивать (-и́ть); **~ Olga with her sister** сравни́те О́льгу с её сестро́й

vi контрасти́ровать с + *I* (*impf*); (*differ*) отлича́ться от + *G* (*only in impf*); **the reds in the picture ~ well with the blue of the sky** на карти́не кра́сные цвета́ уда́чно контрасти́руют с голубизно́й не́ба; **the two paintings of the sea ~ sharply with each other** э́ти два морски́х пейза́жа рази́тельно отлича́ются друг от дру́га; **his actions ~ sharply with his promises** его́ посту́пки ре́зко расхо́дятся с его́ слова́ми.

contrasting *adj* контра́стный.

contravene *vt*: **to ~ a law** преступ|а́ть/наруш|а́ть зако́н (-и́ть/-́ить).

contribute *vti vt* (*donate*) же́ртвовать (по-); **he ~d £1,000 to the Red Cross/towards the building of a theatre** он поже́ртвовал ты́сячу фу́нтов в фонд Кра́сного Креста́/на постро́йку теа́тра; **to ~ clothing for the refugees** посыла́ть оде́жду в фонд по́мощи бе́женцам; **he ~s regular articles to our magazine** он регуля́рно пи́шет для на́шего журна́ла

vi: **archaeology has ~d greatly to our knowledge of primitive man** археоло́гия расши́рила на́ши позна́ния (*pl*) о первобы́тном челове́ке; **the professor also ~d to the discussion** профе́ссор то́же уча́ствовал в обсужде́нии; **it all ~d to the general chaos** всё э́то то́лько увели́чило сумя́тицу.

contribution *n* (*gift of money or in kind*) поже́ртвование; (*subscription*) взнос; (*article*) статья́; **~s should be sent to the editor** ру́кописи посыла́ть реда́ктору; *fig* **he made a valuable ~ to science** он внёс ва́жный вклад в нау́ку.

contributor *n* (*donor*) же́ртвователь (*m*); (*to magazine*) а́втор; **he is one of our regular ~s** он оди́н из постоя́нных а́второв на́шего журна́ла.

contrite *adj*: **to be ~** ка́яться, (*more seriously*) раска́иваться; **the little boy looks so ~** у ма́льчика тако́й провини́вшийся/винова́тый вид.

contrivance *n* (*gadget*) приспособле́ние; (*invention*) вы́думка.

contrive *vti vt* (*scheme, means*) вы|ду́мывать (-́думать), зате|ва́ть (-́ять)

vi: **he ~d to make matters worse** он ухитри́лся/умудри́лся уху́дшить де́ло (*sing*); **she somehow ~s to make both ends meet** она́ ка́к-то ухитря́ется/умудря́ется своди́ть концы́ с конца́ми.

control *n* **1** (*command*): **the teacher has good ~ over the class** учи́тель де́ржит класс в рука́х; **they have no ~ over their children** де́ти совсе́м их не слу́шаются; **the crowd got out of ~** толпа́ разбушева́лась; **owing to circumstances beyond our ~** по незави́сящим от нас обстоя́тельствам; **to keep one's feelings under ~** сде́рживать свои́ чу́вства; **don't lose ~ of your temper** держи́ себя́ в рука́х

2 (*administrative*) руково́дство + *I*; контро́ль (*m*) над + *I*; **government ~ of industry** контро́ль госуда́рства над промы́шленностью; **production improved under his ~** под его́ руково́дством объём произво́дства увели́чился; **railways are under the ~ of the Ministry** желе́зные доро́ги нахо́дятся в ве́дении министе́рства; **who is in ~ here?** кто здесь руководи́т?/гла́вный?; **~ of the seas** госпо́дство на мо́ре

3 (*check*) контро́ль (*m*); **disarmament ~** контро́ль над разоруже́нием; **passport/customs ~** па́спортный контро́ль, тамо́женный досмо́тр; **the cholera is now under ~** эпиде́мия холе́ры приостано́влена; **traffic/birth ~** регулиро́вка тра́нспорта, регули́рование рожда́емости; **price ~** регули́рование цен, контро́ль над це́нами; *attr*: **~ point** контро́льный пункт

4 *Tech* управле́ние + *I*; **the car got out of ~** маши́на потеря́ла управле́ние; *Aut*, *Aer* **dual ~** двойно́е управле́ние; *Aer* **remote ~** дистанцио́нное управле́ние; *pl* (**the ~s**) контро́льные прибо́ры; *attr*: **~ levers** рычаги́ управле́ния.

control *vt* **1** (*have authority over*): **he knows how to ~ that horse** он зна́ет но́ров э́той ло́шади; **he ~s his class with a firm hand** он де́ржит класс в рука́х; **to ~ oneself** сдержа́ться, сдержа́ть себя́; **to ~ one's temper** владе́ть собо́й (*impf*)

2 (*manage*, *regulate*): **he ~s the export side of the business** он руководи́т отде́лом э́кспорта (в фи́рме); **the government ~s all foreign exchange** госуда́рство контроли́рует обме́н валю́ты; **to ~ traffic/prices** регули́ровать (у́личное) движе́ние/це́ны; **to ~ expenditure** провер|я́ть расхо́ды (-́ить)

3 *Tech*: **this car is easy to ~** управля́ть э́той маши́ной о́чень легко́; **this switch ~s the ignition** э́то выключа́тель зажига́ния; **this knob ~s pressure** э́та кно́пка/ру́чка регули́рует давле́ние.

controller *n Comm* контролёр; *Aer*, *Rail* диспе́тчер.

control panel *n Tech* пульт управле́ния, прибо́рная доска́; *Aut* щито́к управле́ния.

control room *n* (*in factory*) отде́л контро́ля; *Aer* диспе́тчерская.

control tower *n Aer* диспе́тчерская вы́шка; контро́льно-диспе́тчерский пункт.

controversial *adj* спо́рный.

controversy *n* спор, диску́ссия, поле́мика.

convalesce *vi* выздора́вливать, поправля́ться (*only in impfs*).

convalescent *n and adj*: **he is (a) ~** он выздора́вливает, он поправля́ется; **a ~ home** *approx* санато́рий.

convene *vt*: **to ~ a meeting** со|бира́ть собра́ние (-бра́ть).

convenience *n* **1** удо́бство; **it's a great ~ to live near one's work** жить ря́дом с рабо́той— большо́е удо́бство; **come at your ~** приходи́те, когда́ вам удо́бно; **we'll arrange the meeting to suit your ~** назна́чим совеща́ние так, что́бы вам бы́ло удо́бно; **please answer at your earliest ~** про́сим отве́тить как мо́жно быстре́е

2 *pl* (**~s**) удо́бства; **a house with all modern ~s** дом со все́ми удо́бствами

3 *euph* туале́т, убо́рная.

convenient *adj* удо́бный; **I'll come at the first ~ opportunity** я прие́ду при пе́рвом удо́бном слу́чае; **our house is ~ for the station** от на́шего до́ма удо́бно добира́ться до ста́нции; **is it ~ for you to come earlier?** вы смо́жете прие́хать пора́ньше?; **put the hamper on a ~ chair** поста́вь корзи́ну на тот стул, что побли́же.

convent *n* же́нский монасты́рь (*m*).

convention *n* (*conference*) съезд; (*agreement*) конве́нция, догово́р; (*custom*) усло́вность; **she despises the ~s** она́ презира́ет усло́вности.

conventional *adj* традицио́нный; (*accepted*) общепри́нятый; усло́вный; **it's ~ here to dine late** здесь при́нято по́здно обе́дать; **a ~ letter of congratulations** обы́чное поздрави́тельное письмо́; **~ weapons** вооруже́ние (*collect*) обы́чного ти́па; *pejor* **he's very ~** он раб усло́вностей.

converge *vi* (*of lines*, *people*) сходи́ться (сойти́сь); **the armies ~d on the town** войска́ наступа́ли на го́род со всех сторо́н.

conversant *adj*: **I'm not ~ with the rules/with diesel engines** я незнако́м с пра́вилами/с ди́зельными дви́гателями.

conversation *n* разгово́р, бесе́да.

conversational *adj* разгово́рный.

converse[1] *vi*: **to ~ with smb** разгова́ривать/бесе́довать с кем-л (*usu impfs*).

converse[2] *n*: **"hot" is the ~ of "cold"** сло́во «горя́чий»—анто́ним сло́ва «холо́дный»; **that is the ~ of what I said** э́то обра́тное тому́, что я сказа́л.

converse[2] *adj* обра́тный, противополо́жный.

conversely *adv* наоборо́т.

conversion *n* превраще́ние; *Rel* обраще́ние; **the ~ of water into steam** превраще́ние воды́ в пар; **they've done a beautiful ~** (*of their house*) они́ краси́во перестро́или дом; **the ~ of dollars into £s** (*as a calculation*) перево́д до́лларов в фу́нты, (*in money*) обме́н до́лларов на фу́нты.

convert *vt* превра|ща́ть (-ти́ть); *Fin* конверти́ровать (*impf and pf*); **they ~ed the cellar into a bathroom** они́ сде́лали из подва́ла ва́нную; **they live in a ~ed windmill** они́ живу́т в перестро́енной ме́льнице; **he ~ed me to his views** он обрати́л меня́ в свою́ ве́ру

convertible *adj*: **~ currency** обрати́мая/конверти́руемая валю́та.

convex *adj* вы́пуклый.

convey *vt* **1** (*goods*) пере|вози́ть (-везти́); *fig*: **please ~ my thanks to her** переда́йте ей, пожа́луйста, мою́ благода́рность; **the name ~s nothing to me** э́то и́мя мне ничего́ не говори́т; *Law* **to ~ property** передава́ть иму́щество.

conveyance *n* (*carrying*) перево́зка; (*vehicle*) тра́нспортное сре́дство; *Law* докуме́нт о переда́че иму́щества.

convict *n* заключённый.

convict *vt*: **to ~ smb of theft** осуди́ть кого́-л за кра́жу (*usu pf*).

conviction *n* **1** (*belief*) убежде́ние; **it is my ~ that...** я убеждён, что...; **in the full ~ that...** в по́лной уве́ренности, что...

2 (*persuasion*): **his story doesn't carry much ~** его́ расска́з не о́чень убеди́телен; **that is my view, but I'm open to ~** вот моё мне́ние, но меня́ ещё мо́жно переубеди́ть

3 *Law*: **he has had no/three previous ~(s)** у него́ нет/есть три суди́мости.

convince *vt* убе|жда́ть (-ди́ть); **I tried to ~ him that the journey was unnecessary** я стара́лся убеди́ть его́ не е́здить; **he ~d her of his innocence** он убеди́л её в свое́й невино́вности; **I was ~d/I ~d myself that I had failed** я был уве́рен, что провали́лся.

convincing *adj* убеди́тельный.

convivial *adj* весёлый.

convoy *n Naut* конво́й; (*of merchant ships*) карава́н судо́в; **under/in ~** в сопровожде́нии конво́йных судо́в; (*by car*) **we travelled in ~** мы дви́гались коло́нной.

convoy *vt Naut* конвои́ровать (*impf*); вести́ под конво́ем.

convulsed *adj*: **the whole island was ~ by the earthquake** весь о́стров содрога́лся от землетрясе́ния; **we were ~ with laughter** мы смея́лись до упа́ду; **he/his face was ~ with pain** у него́/его́ лицо́ искази́лось от бо́ли.

convulsion *n Med* конву́льсия.

convulsive *adj* су́дорожный, конвульси́вный.

coo *vi* воркова́ть (*impf*), *also fig*.

cook *n* по́вар; **she's a good ~** она́ хоро́ший по́вар.

cook *vti vt* гото́вить еду́ (при-); **to ~ meat/dinner** гото́вить мя́со/обе́д; *fig*: **I've got to ~ up an article before tomorrow** мне ну́жно быстре́нько написа́ть статью́ к за́втрашнему дню; **to ~ accounts** подде́лать счета́

vi: **who ~s for you?** кто вам гото́вит?; **she's busy ~ing** она́ стря́пает на ку́хне; **the meat is ~ing** мя́со гото́вится; **the cabbage is taking a long time to ~** капу́ста ва́рится до́лго; *fig sl* **what's ~ing?** что тут затева́ется?

cooker *n* плита́; **gas/electric ~** га́зовая плита́, электроплита́.

cookery *n* кулина́рия; *attr*: **~ book** кулина́рная/пова́ренная кни́га.

cookie *n approx* пече́нье.

cooking *n* гото́вка; **he does the ~** он гото́вит сам.

cooking *adj*: **~ utensils** ку́хонная посу́да (*collect*); **~ salt** пова́ренная соль.

cool *n*: **the ~ of the evening** вече́рняя прохла́да; *CQ* **he kept his ~** он сохраня́л споко́йствие/хладнокро́вие.

cool *adj* прохла́дный; **it's getting ~er** стано́вится прохла́днее; **the soup is getting ~** суп сты́нет; (*on label*) **"keep in a ~ place"** «храни́ть в прохла́дном ме́сте»; *fig*: **we got a ~ reception** нас при́няли прохла́дно; **he has become very ~ towards us** он охладе́л к нам; **he played it ~** он остава́лся споко́ен; **keep ~!** не горячи́сь!, *CQ* не лезь в буты́лку!; *CQ*: **he lost a ~ thousand at the races** он проигра́л це́лую ты́сячу фу́нтов на ска́чках; *pejor* **he's a ~ customer** он наха́л, он нагле́ц.

cool *vti vt*: **to ~ the soup** студи́ть суп (о-); **the rain has ~ed the air** по́сле дождя́ ста́ло прохла́днее; *fig* **I was left to ~ my heels** меня́ заста́вили ждать

vi сты́нуть, стыть (*pfs* о-), *also fig*; **I'm letting the engine/my tea ~** я жду, пока́ осты́нет мото́р/чай; **I'm going into the sea to ~ down** *CQ* пойду́ в мо́ре охлажу́сь; **the weather has ~ed down a lot** похолода́ло (*impers*); *fig*: **~ down!** осты́нь!; **his enthusiasm has ~ed off** его́ пыл осты́л; **he's ~ed off towards her lately** в после́днее вре́мя он не́сколько к ней охладе́л.

cooler *n sl* (*jail*): **he's in the ~ again** он опя́ть сиди́т.

cooling *adj*: **a ~ drink** прохлади́тельный напи́ток.

coolly *adv* (*calmly*) споко́йно; (*without enthusiasm*) хо́лодно; (*impertinently*) де́рзко.

cooperate *vi* сотру́дничать с + *I* (*impf*).

cooperation *n* сотру́дничество.

cooperative *n* кооперати́в (*of individual farm, shop, etc.*); **agricultural ~s** сельскохозя́йственная коопера́ция (*collect*).

cooperative *adj* (*of societies*) кооперати́вный; (*of people*): **he was very ~** (*on single occasion*) он о́чень нам помо́г; **he's always very ~** он всегда́ гото́в помо́чь/прийти́ на по́мощь.

coopt *vt* коопти́ровать (*impf and pf*).

coop up *vt*: **I was ~ed up in a stuffy office all day** я проторча́л весь день в ду́шном кабине́те.

coordinate *vt* координи́ровать (с-); **to ~ movements/actions** координи́ровать движе́ния/де́йствия; **to ~ policies** согласова́ть полити́ческую ли́нию; *Mil* **a ~d attack** согласо́ванное наступле́ние.

coordination *n* координа́ция.

cope *vt* управ|ля́ться с + *I*, справ|ля́ться с + *I*, (*pfs* -иться); **you get the tickets and I'll ~ with the luggage** вы покупа́йте биле́ты, а я упра́влюсь с багажо́м; **I'll ~ with the visitors/the washing-up** я смогу́ хорошо́ приня́ть госте́й, я упра́влюсь с посу́дой; **can you ~?** ты спра́вишься?; **I'll ~ somehow** я ка́к-нибудь упра́влюсь; **he ~d very well with an awkward situation** он блестя́ще вы́шел из затрудни́тельного положе́ния.

co-pilot *n* второ́й пило́т.

copious *adj*: **a ~ harvest** оби́льный урожа́й; **a ~ writer** плодови́тый писа́тель; **he took ~ notes** он сде́лал ма́ссу заме́ток.

copiously *adv*: **he bled ~** он теря́л мно́го кро́ви.

copper *n* (*metal*) медь; **~s** (*coins*) *CQ* медяки́, медь (*collect*); (*large pan*) таз; **I've no ~s** у меня́ нет ме́ди.

coppice, copse *n* ро́ща.

copy *n* **1** (*facsimile*) ко́пия; **typed ~** машинопи́сная/печа́тная ко́пия; **fair ~** чистови́к, белови́к; **rough ~** чернови́к; **make a carbon ~ of this letter** напиши́те/напеча́тайте э́то письмо́ под копи́рку; **take two copies** (*of letter, etc.*) напеча́тайте два экземпля́ра; **to make a fair ~ of a manuscript** переписа́ть ру́копись на́бело; **to make a ~ of an original letter** снять ко́пию с письма́

2 (*single copy of smth*) экземпля́р; **a secondhand ~ of a book** подёржанный экземпля́р кни́ги; **complimentary ~** а́вторский экземпля́р (*from publisher to author, or from author to friend*); **a ~ of today's "Pravda"** сего́дняшний но́мер «Пра́вды»

3 (*material to be printed*) ру́копись.

copy *vti vt* **1** (*imitate*) подража́ть + *D* (*impf*), копи́ровать (с-); **to ~ smb's way of walking** подража́ть чьей-л похо́дке, копи́ровать чью-л похо́дку; **she copies everything her sister does** она́ во всём подража́ет сестре́

2: **to ~ out smth** перепи́с|ывать что-л (-а́ть)

vi (*in exam*): **to ~ off smb** спи́с|ывать у кого́-л (-а́ть).

copybook *n* тетра́дь.

copying paper *n* копирова́льная бума́га, *CQ* копи́рка.

copyist *n* перепи́счик.

copyright *n* а́вторское пра́во.

coquette *n* коке́тка.

coral *n* кора́лл; *attr* кора́лловый.

cord *n* шнур, шнуро́к; **silk ~** шёлковый шнур; *Anat*: **spinal ~** спинно́й мозг; **vocal ~s** голосовы́е свя́зки.

cordial *adj*: **a ~ welcome** серде́чный/раду́шный приём; **~ greetings** серде́чный приве́т (*sing*).

cordially *adv* серде́чно, раду́шно; **I ~ dislike him** я его́ о́чень не люблю́.

corduroy *n* вельве́т; *pl* (**~s**) *CQ* вельве́товые брю́ки.

core *n* (*of an apple, etc.*) сердцеви́на; *fig*: **the ~ of the problem** суть пробле́мы; **rotten to the ~** насквозь прогни́вший; **he is English to the ~** он англича́нин до мо́зга косте́й; **they represent the hard ~ of the Conservatives** они́ представля́ют/составля́ют ядро́ консервати́вной па́ртии.

co-respondent *n Law* соотве́тчик.

cork *n* (*material and stopper*) про́бка; *attr* про́бковый.

cork *vt* (*stop up*): **to ~ a bottle** за|тыка́ть буты́лку про́бкой (-ткну́ть); (*of wine*): **this wine is ~ed** э́то вино́ отдаёт про́бкой.

corkscrew *n* што́пор.

cork-tipped *adj*: **~ cigarettes** сигаре́ты с фи́льтром.

corn[1] *n* (*grain in general*) хлеб; зерно́ (*collect*); **a field of ~** хле́бное по́ле; **~ on the cob** кукуру́за в поча́тках.

corn[2] *n* мозо́ль; *fig* **to tread on smb's pet ~** наступи́ть кому́-л на люби́мую мозо́ль.

corned *adj*: **~ beef** солони́на.

corner *n* у́гол; (*on a road*) поворо́т; **in the ~** в углу́; **at/on the ~ of the street** на углу́ у́лицы; **he lives just round the ~** он живёт за угло́м; **to turn the ~** заверну́ть за́ угол; **sharp ~!** круто́й поворо́т!; **to watch smb out of the ~ of one's eye** следи́ть за кем-л уголко́м глаз; **to cut a ~** сре́зать у́гол; *Sport* (*football*) **a ~** углово́й уда́р; *fig*: **the four ~s of the earth** четы́ре страны́ све́та; **to be in a tight ~** попа́сть в переде́лку; *attr*: **the ~ house** углово́й дом.

corner *vti vt*: **to ~ smb** за|гоня́ть кого́-л в у́гол (-гна́ть)

vi Aut: **he ~s much too fast** он сли́шком ре́зко повора́чивает (поверну́ть).

cornflakes *npl* кукуру́зные хло́пья.

cornflour *n* кукуру́зная мука́.

cornflower *n* василёк.

corny *adj CQ*: **a ~ joke** изби́тая шу́тка.

corollary *n* сле́дствие, *also Math*.

coronary *adj*: **~ thrombosis** корона́рный тромбо́з; *as n*: **he's had a ~** у него́ был инфа́ркт.

coronation *n* корона́ция.

coroner *n* ко́ронер; **~'s inquest** суде́бный осмо́тр тру́па ко́ронером.

corporal[1] *n* капра́л.

corporal[2] *adj* теле́сный; **~ punishment** теле́сное наказа́ние.

corporate *adj* о́бщий; **~ property/responsibility** о́бщее иму́щество, о́бщая отве́тственность.

corps *n*: **diplomatic ~** дипломати́ческий ко́рпус; **~ de ballet** кордебале́т.

corpse *n* труп.

corpulent *adj* ту́чный.

corpuscle *n*: **white/red ~s** бе́лые/кра́сные кровяны́е тельца́.

correct *adj* (*right*) пра́вильный; (*proper*) корре́ктный; **~!** пра́вильно!; **am I ~ in thinking that...?** прав ли я, ду́мая, что...?; **he's a very ~ young man** он корре́ктный молодо́й челове́к; **can you tell me the ~ time?** вы мо́жете мне сказа́ть то́чное вре́мя?

correct *vt*: **to ~ one's watch by the radio** провер|я́ть часы́ по ра́дио (-́ить); **~ me if I'm wrong** попра́вьте меня́, е́сли я ошиба́юсь; **to ~ a mistake** исправ|ля́ть оши́бку (-́ить); **the teacher ~ed my essay** учи́тель прове́рил моё сочине́ние; **to ~ proofs/a manuscript** пра́вить корректу́ру *or* гра́нки/ру́копись (*impf*); **to ~ a child for rudeness** де́лать ребёнку замеча́ние за гру́бость (с-).

correction *n* (*act*) исправле́ние; (*by teacher*) прове́рка; (*written in*) исправле́ние, попра́вка; (*of proofs*) корректу́ра; **he doesn't like ~** (*rebuke*) он не лю́бит, когда́ ему́ де́лают замеча́ния.

corrective *n* корректи́в, попра́вка, исправле́ние.

corrective *adj* исправи́тельный; *Med* ~ **glasses** корриги́рующие очки́.

correctly *adv* (*rightly*) пра́вильно; (*with propriety*) корре́ктно.

correlation *n* соотноше́ние, взаимосвя́зь, корреля́ция.

correspond *vi* **1** (*agree*) соотве́тствовать + *D* (*impf*); **his story does not ~ with the facts** его́ расска́з не соотве́тствует фа́ктам

2 (*by letter*): **to ~ with smb** перепи́сываться с кем-л (*usu impf*).

correspondence *n* **1** (*similarity*): ~ **between** соотве́тствие ме́жду + *I*

2 перепи́ска; корреспонде́нция; **the ~ of Chekhov** перепи́ска Че́хова; **to keep up a ~ with smb, to be in ~ with smb** вести́ перепи́ску с кем-л; **to read one's ~** чита́ть пи́сьма/корреспонде́нцию; *attr*: ~ **course** зао́чный курс обуче́ния.

correspondent *n* (*press*) корреспонде́нт; **he's the "Pravda" ~** он корреспонде́нт «Пра́вды»; (*private*) **he's a good/bad ~** он ча́сто/ре́дко пи́шет.

corresponding *adj* (**to**) соотве́тствующий (+ *D*).

correspondingly *adv* соотве́тственно; **he works longer hours so his pay is ~ higher** его́ рабо́чий день длинне́е, и он соотве́тственно получа́ет бо́льше.

corridor *n* коридо́р.

corroborate *vt* подтвер|жда́ть (-ди́ть).

corroboration *n* подтвержде́ние; **in ~ of his story** в подтвержде́ние своего́ расска́за.

corrode *vt* разъ|еда́ть (-е́сть).

corrosion *n* корро́зия.

corrugated *adj*: ~ **iron/paper** рифлёное желе́зо, гофриро́ванная бума́га.

corrupt *adj* (*open to bribery*) прода́жный; ~ **practices** корру́пция; (*debased*) **a ~ society** загнива́ющее о́бщество; **a ~ text** искажённый текст.

corrupt *vt* (*bribe*) подкуп|а́ть (-и́ть), да|ва́ть взя́тки (-ть); (*morally*) **to ~ smb/morals** развра|ща́ть кого́-л/нра́вы (-ти́ть).

corruption *n* (*giving or taking bribes*) корру́пция; (*moral*) развращённость; (*of text, language*) искаже́ние.

cosmetic *n* космети́ческое сре́дство; *pl* (**~s**) косме́тика (*collect*).

cosmic *adj* косми́ческий.

cosmonaut *n* космона́вт.

cosset *vt* балова́ть, не́жить (*pfs* из-).

cost *n* **1** цена́; сто́имость; **the ~ of bread/meat** цена́ хле́ба/мя́са; **the ~ of living** сто́имость жи́зни; **the ~ of construction/of freight** сто́имость строи́тельства/перево́зки; **the ~ of grain per ton** сто́имость то́нны зерна́; **at ~** по сто́имости; **below ~** ни́же сто́имости

2 *pl* (**~s**) (*expenses*) изде́ржки; расхо́ды; **production ~s** изде́ржки произво́дства; **legal ~s** суде́бные расхо́ды

3 *fig uses*: **at any ~** любо́й цено́й; **at all ~s** во что́ бы то ни ста́ло; **whatever the ~** чего́ бы э́то ни сто́ило; **at the ~ of his health** цено́ю своего́ здоро́вья; **I learnt this to my ~** я зна́ю [**NB** *tense*] э́то по го́рькому о́пыту.

cost *vt* **1** сто́ить (*impf*), *also fig*; *CQ* об|ходи́ться (-ойти́сь), *also fig*; **to ~ little/a lot** сто́ить дёшево/до́рого; **it ~ him a lot of money/40 roubles** э́то сто́ило ему́ больши́х де́нег/со́рок рубле́й; ~ **what it may, whatever it may ~** ско́лько бы/*fig* чего́ бы э́то ни сто́ило; **it ~ me plenty**/*fig* **dear** э́то сто́ило/*CQ* обошло́сь мне о́чень до́рого, *both also fig*; **what will it ~ to have it repaired?** во ско́лько обойдётся ремо́нт?; *fig* **it ~ him his life/many sleepless nights** э́то сто́ило ему́ жи́зни/мно́гих бессо́нных ноче́й

2 *Comm*: **to ~ articles/goods** оце́н|ивать това́ры (-и́ть); **to ~ a project** определ|я́ть сто́имость прое́кта (-и́ть).

costing *n* расце́нка.

costly *adj* дорого́й, *also fig*; **a ~ apartment** дорога́я кварти́ра; **it was a ~ victory** э́та побе́да доста́лась дорого́й цено́й.

cost price *n*: **to sell at ~** прода́ть по себесто́имости.

costume *n* (*suit*) (же́нский) костю́м; **national ~** национа́льный костю́м; *attr*: ~ **jewelry** *approx* подде́льные драгоце́нности.

cosy *adj* ую́тный; **a ~ room/atmosphere/chat** ую́тная ко́мната, тёплая атмосфе́ра, дру́жеская бесе́да.

cot *n* де́тская крова́тка.

cottage *n* котте́дж; *approx* да́ча (= *summer cottage*); *attr*: ~ **industries** надо́мный про́мысел (*collect*); ~ **cheese** творо́г.

cotton *n* (*raw*) хло́пок; (*fabric*) (хлопчато)бума́жная ткань; (*thread*) (бума́жная) ни́тка; **printed ~** си́тец; *attr* хлопчатобума́жный.

cotton *vi CQ*: **he ~s on quickly** он хорошо́ сообража́ет; **he didn't ~ on to the joke/to what he was supposed to do** он не по́нял шу́тки/, что ему́ полага́лось де́лать.

cotton wool *n* ва́та.

couch *n* дива́н; куше́тка (*also in doctor's surgery*).

cough *n* ка́шель (*m*); **he has a bad ~** у него́ си́льный ка́шель; **to give a slight ~** (*to clear throat*) отка́шляться, (*in order to attract attention or to cough*) ка́шлянуть.

cough *vi* ка́шлять (*impf*), ка́шлянуть (*semel*); **to ~ smth up** отха́ркивать (*usu impf*); *CQ* **in the end he ~ed up a fiver** под коне́ц он всё же вы́ложил пять фу́нтов.

could *see* **can.**

council *n*: **town ~** муниципалите́т, городско́й сове́т; **Security C.** Сове́т Безопа́сности; *attr*: ~ **chamber** зал заседа́ний муниципалите́та; (*UK*) ~ **flat** госуда́рственная кварти́ра.

councillor *n* член муниципалите́та/городско́го сове́та.

counsel *n* **1** (*advice*) сове́т; **to take ~ with smb** сове́товаться с кем-л; **he keeps his own ~** он ни с кем не де́лится; **let's hope that wiser ~s may prevail** бу́дем наде́яться, что одéржат верх бóлее разýмные предложéния

2 *Law* адвокáт; ~ **for the defence** защ́итник подсудúмого; ~ **for the prosecution** (*in criminal cases*) прокурóр, (*in civil cases*) адвокáт истцá.

counsel *vt* совéтовать + *D and inf*, рекомендовáть + *D and inf* (*pfs* по-); **to ~ patience** совéтовать запастúсь терпéнием; **he ~led me to pay the damages** он посовéтовал мне оплатúть причинённый ущéрб/убы́тки; **the doctor ~led him against smoking/going abroad** врач порекомендовáл емý брóсить курúть, врач не совéтовал емý éхать за гранúцу.

counsellor *n Polit, Dipl* совéтник; (*marriage guidance, etc.*) консультáнт.

count *n* **1** счёт; (*counting up*) подсчёт; **to lose/keep ~ of one's debts** потерять/вестú счёт своúм долгáм; **to take a ~ of votes** вестú подсчёт голосóв

2 *Law*: **he was found guilty on all ~s** он был прúзнан винóвным по всем пýнктам обвинéния.

count *vti vt* **1** *Math* считáть (со-); **to ~ 10** считáть до десятú; **to ~ one's money/one's pulse** считáть дéньги/пульс; **to ~ out/up change** отсчúт|ывать/подсчúт|ывать сдáчу (*pfs* -áть)

2 (*include*): **four people live here, not ~ing the visitor** здесь живýт чéтверо, не считáя гóстя; **~ me out for this trip** не включáйте меня́ в э́ту поéздку

3 (*consider*) считáть (счесть); **I ~ him among my best friends** я считáю егó однúм из моúх сáмых лýчших друзéй; **I ~ myself lucky to be here** я считáю за счáстье, что нахожýсь здесь; **his age will ~ against him** он не подойдёт по вóзрасту

vi **1** *Math* считáть (со-); **to ~ up to 100** считáть до ста; **to ~ on one's fingers** считáть на пáльцах; **the third door, ~ing from the corner** трéтья дверь от углá; **2 children ~ as one adult** двóе детéй считáются как одúн взрóслый

2 (*have importance*): **my opinion ~s for very little with them** моё мнéние мáло что знáчит для них; **that ~s for nothing** э́то ничегó не знáчит; **every second ~s** кáждая секýнда имéет значéние; **lack of experience ~ed against him** егó мúнусом был недостáток óпыта

3: **to ~ on** рассчúтывать на + *A* (*only in impf*), по|лагáться на + *A* (-ложúться); **we ~ on dry weather** мы рассчúтываем на сухýю погóду; **one can ~ on her** на неё мóжно положúться.

countdown *n* (от)счёт врéмени.

countenance *vt*: **he won't ~ violence** он прóтив насúлия.

counter[1] *n* **1** (*in shop*) прилáвок; **to sell under the ~** продáть из-под прилáвка

2 (*in games*) фúшка.

counter[2] *adv*: **to act ~ to smb's wishes** дéйствовать вопрекú чьим-л желáниям.

counter[2] *vti vt*: **to ~ an attack** отби|вáть атáку (-́ть); **to ~ aggression with armed force** дать агрéссии вооружённый отпóр (*usu pf*); **they ~ed our proposal with one of their own** онú вы́двинули прóтив нáшего предложéния контрпредложéние

vi: **he ~ed with another question** он отвéтил вопрóсом на вопрóс, в отвéт он сам зáдал вопрóс.

counteract *vt Chem and fig* нейтрализовáть (*impf and pf*).

counter-attack *vt* контратаковáть (*impf and pf*).

counter-attraction *n*: **it's a pity your concert is on Tuesday—the carnival will be a ~** жаль, что твой концéрт во втóрник—карнавáл отвлечёт от негó зрúтелей.

counterbalance *vt* уравновé|шивать (-сить).

counterfeit *n* поддéлка.

counterfeit *adj* (*artificial, forged*) поддéльный; (*false*) фальшúвый.

counterfeit *vt* (*money, signature*) поддéл|ывать (-ать).

counterfoil *n* корешóк (квитáнции/билéта).

countermand *vt*: **to ~ instructions/an order** (*for goods*) отмен|я́ть приказáния/закáз (-úть).

counter-offensive *n* контрнаступлéние.

counterpart *n*: **he is my ~ here** он здесь занимáет дóлжность, соотвéтствующую моéй; **this vase has no ~** э́та вáза уникáльна.

counter-revolution *n* контрреволю́ция.

countersign *vt* стáвить вторýю пóдпись на + *P* (по-).

counterweight *n* противовéс, *also fig*.

countless *adj* бесчúсленный, бессчётный.

country *n* (*of a nation*) странá; (*native land*) рóдина, отéчество; (*as opposed to town*) (**the ~**) дерéвня; *Geog* мéстность; **from all parts of the ~** со всех концóв страны́; **to die for one's ~** умерéть за рóдину; **I live in the ~** я живý в дерéвне; (*just outside a town*) **to spend the day in the ~** провестú день зá городом; **mountainous/wooded ~** гористая/лесúстая мéстность; *attr* деревéнский, сéльский; зáгородный.

countryman *n* (*dweller in country*) сéльский/деревéнский жúтель (*m*); (*peasant*) крестья́нин; **my fellow ~** (*from same district*) мой земля́к, (*of same nation*) мой соотéчественник.

countryside *n*: **we go out into the ~ on Sundays** по воскресéньям мы выезжáем зá город/на прирóду.

county *n* (*UK*) грáфство.

coup *n*: **he brought off a ~** он сдéлал удáчный ход.

couple *n* пáра; **a married ~** супрýжеская пáра; **a ~ of apples** пáра я́блок; **10 ~s took the floor** вы́шли танцевáть дéсять пар; **we stayed a ~ of days** мы остановúлись на пáру дней; *CQ* **we had a ~ in the bar** мы пропустúли по рю́мочке в бáре.

couple *vti vt* соедин|я́ть (-úть); (*of railway coaches*) прицеп|ля́ть (-úть)

vi Zool спáр|иваться (-иться).

coupling *n* соединéние; сцеплéние.

coupon *n* (*voucher*) купóн; (*for food, etc.*) талóн.

courage *n* мýжество, хрáбрость; **to show ~** проявúть мýжество; **I hadn't the ~ to tell her the truth** у менá не хватúло мýжества сказáть ей прáвду; **he has the ~ of his convictions** он твёрд в своúх убеждéниях; **to pluck up ~ to do smth** собрáться с дýхом/набрáться хрáбрости сдéлать что-л.

courageous *adj* мýжественный, хрáбрый.

courier *n* курьéр; (*with travel group*) сопровождáющий.

course *n* **1** (*direction*) курс; **the ship is on/off ~** сýдно дéржит курс/сошлó с кýрса; **to set one's ~ to the south** взять курс на юг; **we followed a northerly ~** мы держáли курс на сéвер; **the ~ of a river** течéние рекú

2 (*process, duration*): **~ of action** óбраз дéйствия; **your best ~ is to accept** вам лýчше всегó согласúться; **there was no ~ open to me but to agree** у менá нé было вы́бора, крóме как согласúться; **what ~ do you advise?** что вы посовéтуете?; **to take a middle ~** проводúть срéдний курс; **the ~ of events** ход собы́тий; **let things take their ~** пусть всё идёт своúм чередóм; **in the ~ of conversation/business** по хóду разговóра/дéла; **the disease ran its ~** течéние болéзни шло как обы́чно; **the theatre is in ~ of construction** здáние теáтра стрóится; **in the ~ of the month** в течéние э́того мéсяца; **in the ~ of nature** в порáдке вещéй (*pl*)

3 (*series*) курс; **a ~ of lectures/treatment** курс лéкций/лечéния; **she's taking a secretarial ~** онá хóдит на секретáрские кýрсы (*pl*)

4 *Sport*: **race ~** (*for horses*) ипподрóм (*whole area*), скаковóй круг (*track*), (*for runners*) дорóжка, дистáнция; **he didn't stay the ~** он сошёл с дистáнции, *also fig*

5 *Cook* блю́до; *attr*: **a 3-~ dinner** обéд из трёх блюд

6 *adv phrases*: **in due ~** в своё/в дóлжное врéмя; **to take smth as a matter of ~** принимáть что-л как самó собóю разумéющееся; **of ~!** конéчно!

court *n* **1** (*yard*) двор; *Sport* площáдка; **tennis ~** тéннисный корт

2 (*royal*) двор

3 *Law* суд; **in ~** на судé; **contempt of ~** неуважéние к судý, оскорблéние судá; **to bring a case/smb to ~** подáть в суд (на когó-л — *in civil cases*), привлéчь когó-л к судéбной отвéтственности (*in criminal cases*); **the ~ sentenced him to...** суд приговорúл егó к + *D*; **to settle affairs out of ~** разрешúть вопрóс/дéло (*sings*) без судá.

court *vti vt*: **to ~ a woman/popularity** ухáживать за жéнщиной (*impf*), добивáться извéстности (*only in impf*); **to ~ disaster** навле|кáть на себá бедý (-́чь), (*by hubristic talk*) наклúкать бедý на себá (*usu pf*)

vi: **they've been ~ing for two years** онú встречáются два гóда; **a ~ing couple** влюблённые.

courteous *adj* вéжливый, учтúвый, обходúтельный.

courtesy *n* вéжливость, учтúвость, обходúтельность; **you might have had the ~ to tell me beforehand** вы моглú сказáть мне э́то порáньше; **by ~ of** по мúлости + *G*.

court-martial *vt* судúть трибунáлом/воéнным судóм.

court room *n* зал судá/судéбных заседáний.

courtyard *n* вну́тренний двор.

cousin *n* двою́родн|ый брат, *f* -ая сестрá; **second ~** трою́родный брат, *etc.*

cove[1] *n Geog* небольшáя бу́хта.

cove[2] *n sl*: **he's an odd/rum ~** он стрáнный какóй-то.

cover *n* **1** (*for bed*) покрывáло; (*lid*) кры́шка; (*hard cover for book*) переплёт, облóжка; (*dust jacket*) суперóблóжка; **loose ~** (*for chair, typewriter, etc.*) чехóл; **to read a book from ~ to ~** прочитáть кнúгу от кóрки до кóрки; **to send under separate ~** послáть в отдéльном конвéрте (*in envelope*)/в пакéте (*in parcel*)

2 (*shelter*) укры́тие; прикры́тие; покрóв; **to take ~ from the rain/one's pursuers** укрывáться от дождá/от преслéдователей; **there was no ~ for miles around** на мúли вокрýг нé было никакóго укры́тия; **under ~ of night** под покрóвом нóчи; **in the north tomatoes have to be grown under ~** на сéвере помидóры прихóдится вырáщивать в теплúцах; *Mil* **under artillery ~** под прикры́тием артиллéрии

3: does your insurance provide ~ against flooding? вáша страхóвка включáет страховáние от наводнéния?

cover *vti vt* **1** покры|вáть (-́ть); **the ground is ~ed with snow** земля́ покры́та снéгом; *Cards* **to ~ a card** покры́ть кáрту; *fig*: **to ~ one's expenses** покры́ть расхóды, оправдáть своú расхóды; **to ~ oneself with glory** покры́ть себá слáвой (*usu pf*)

2 (*put cover on, wrap up*) закры|вáть, укры|вáть (*pfs* -́ть); **to ~ a saucepan** закры́ть кастрю́лю; **to ~ a child with a blanket** укры́ть ребёнка одеáлом; **to ~ bales with a tarpaulin** накры́ть тюкú брезéнтом; **to ~ plants with straw** прикрывáть растéния солóмой; **to ~ a chair with chintz/a book with paper** оби|вáть стул сúтцем (-́ть), обёртывать кнúгу в бумáгу (обернýть)

3 (*protect*): **my insurance ~s me against fire and theft** в мою́ страхóвку вхóдит страховáние от пожáра и крáжи; **he only said that to ~ himself** он сказáл э́то для перестрахóвки

4 (*conceal*) скры|вáть (-ть), *also fig*; **to ~ his confusion** чтóбы скрыть своё смущéние

5 (*of distance*): **he ~ed the distance in an hour** он покры́л (*in car*)/прошёл (*on foot*) э́то расстоя́ние за час; **we ~ed 2,000 miles in a month** чéрез мéсяц мы остáвили позадú/позадú остáлось две ты́сячи миль; *fig*

his thesis ~s a wide field его́ диссерта́ция охва́тывает мно́го пробле́м

6 (*in press*): **the sporting correspondent ~ed the match** спорти́вный коммента́тор дал репорта́ж о ма́тче

vi: *fig* **to ~ up for smb** покрыва́ть кого́-л.

coverage *n* репорта́ж.

covering *adj*: **a ~ letter** сопроводи́тельное письмо́.

covert *adj*: **a ~ threat/sneer** скры́тая угро́за/насме́шка; **a ~ glance** взгляд укра́дкой (*adv*).

covet *vt* зави́довать + *D*, *CQ* за́риться на + *A* (*pfs* по-).

covetous *adj* зави́стливый.

cow[1] *n* коро́ва.

cow[2] *vt* запу́г|ивать (-а́ть).

coward *n* трус.

cowardly *adj* трусли́вый.

cowboy *n* ковбо́й.

cower *vi* съёж|иваться (-иться).

cowshed *n* коро́вник.

coy *adj* засте́нчивый; (*coquettish*) коке́тливый.

crab *n* краб.

crabapple *n* (*tree*) ди́кая я́блоня, дичо́к; (*fruit*) я́блоко-кисли́ца.

crack *n* **1** (*noise*) треск; **the ~ of branches breaking/of rifle shots** треск су́чьев (*G pl of* сук)/вы́стрелов; **the ~ of a whip** щёлканье кнута́/бича́

2 (*split*) тре́щина; (*long, narrow*) щель; (*large, in ground*) рассе́лина; **a ~ in a cup/in a wall** тре́щина на ча́шке/на стене́; **open the window just a tiny ~** приоткро́й окно́; *fig* **at ~ of dawn** с рассве́том

3 (*blow*): **to give smb a ~ on the head** уда́рить/*CQ* тре́снуть кого́-л по голове́; *fig CQ*: **he's always making ~s** он так и сы́плет шу́точками; **I'll have a ~ at translating it** я попыта́юсь э́то перевести́; *attr*: **~ troops** отбо́рные войска́; **he's a ~ shot** он отли́чный стрело́к.

crack *vti vt* **1** (*cause to sound*): **to ~ a whip/one's fingers** щёлк|ать хлысто́м (-нуть), хруст|е́ть па́льцами (´-нуть); *fig* **to ~ a joke** отпус|ка́ть шу́тку/остро́ту (-ти́ть)

2 (*break*): **to ~ nuts** коло́ть оре́хи (*pfs*: *to crack one nut* рас-, *to crack many* на-); **to ~ smb's skull** пролом и́ть кому́-л че́реп (*usu pf*); **he ~ed his skull** ему́ проломи́ло (*impers*) че́реп; **the mirror was ~ed** зе́ркало тре́снуло; **I've ~ed your mirror** я разби́л твоё зе́ркало; **a ~ed plate** тре́снувшая таре́лка; **the vase had already been ~ed** на ва́зе уже́ была́ тре́щина; **boiling water will ~ glass** от кипятка́ стака́н ло́пнет; **my hands are ~ed** у меня́ ко́жа на рука́х потре́скалась; **in a ~ed voice** надтре́снутым го́лосом

3 *fig CQ*: **he's not all he's ~ed up to be** не тако́й уж он тала́нтливый, как о нём говоря́т

vi **1** (*make noise, or break*) треща́ть (*impf*), тре́снуть (*semel*), потре́скивать (*impf*); (*break*) ло́п|аться (-нуть), тре́скаться (по-, *semel* тре́снуть); **a branch/branches ~ed under foot** под нога́ми тре́снула ве́тка/потре́скивали ве́тки; **the ice ~ed** лёд тре́снул; **china will ~ if heated** при нагрева́нии фарфо́р мо́жет ло́пнуть

2 *fig CQ*: **he ~ed under the strain** он не вы́держал напряже́ния; **the old man is ~ing up** стари́к сдаёт; **to get ~ing** взя́ться за рабо́ту/за де́ло; **let's get ~ing** дава́й при́мемся за де́ло; **the police are ~ing down on gambling** поли́ция бо́рется с аза́ртными и́грами.

cracker *n* (*biscuit*) кре́кер; (*firework*) фейерве́рк.

crackers *adj*: *CQ* **he's ~** он чо́кнутый.

crackle *n* (*of wood or of bacon frying*) потре́скивание; (*of shots*) треск; (*of rusk as you eat it or of twigs underfoot*) хруст.

crackle *vi* (*of frying, fire, etc.*) потре́скивать, треща́ть (*impfs*); (*of twigs underfoot*) хруст|е́ть (*semel* ´-нуть).

crackling *n* **1** (*of burning wood*) потре́скивание

2 (*on roast, pork*) шква́рки (*pl*).

cradle *n* колыбе́ль, *also fig*; **from the ~ to the grave** от колыбе́ли до моги́лы.

craft *n* **1** (*skilled trade*) ремесло́; (*skill*) уме́ние, ло́вкость; (*cunning*) хи́трость

2 (*ship*) су́дно; (*collect*) **~ of all kinds** разли́чные суда́.

craftily *adv* хитро́.

craftsman *n* ма́стер, уме́лец.

craggy *adj* скали́стый.

cram *vti vt* **1**: **to ~ one's case with clothes** наби|ва́ть чемода́н веща́ми (´-ть); **I can't ~ any more into my rucksack** в мой рюкза́к бо́льше ничего́ не запихнёшь; **he ~med food into his mouth** он наби́л по́лный рот еды́; **to ~ a child/oneself with cakes** пи́чкать ребёнка/объ|еда́ться пиро́жными (на-/-е́сться); **the hall was ~med** зал был битко́м наби́т/по́лон; **we can't ~ anybody else into the car** маши́на наби́та до отка́за; **the book is ~med with quotations** кни́га перегру́жена цита́тами

2: **to ~ a pupil for an exam**ната́ск|ивать ученика́ к экза́мену (-а́ть); **to ~ (up) history** зубри́ть исто́рию (вы́-)

vi: **we all ~med into the car** мы все наби́лись в маши́ну.

cramp *n*: **I've got ~ in my foot/writer's ~** у меня́ свело́ (*impers*) но́гу/па́льцы.

cramp *vt*: **we're very ~ed for room in our flat** у нас в кварти́ре о́чень те́сно; *CQ* **that will ~ his style** э́то нару́шит его́ стиль.

cranberry *n* клю́ква; *attr* клю́квенный.

crane *n Zool* жура́вль (*m*); *Tech* подъёмный кран.

crank[1] *n Aut* заводна́я ру́чка.

crank[2] *n* (*person*) чуда́к.

crankshaft *n Tech* коле́нчатый вал.

cranny *n* щель.

crash *n* (*noise*) гро́хот; (*accident*) круше́ние; *fig* крах.

crash *vti vt*: **he ~ed his fist on the table** он уда́рил кулако́м по́ столу; **the pilot ~ed**

his plane пилóт разбúлся с самолётом; *CQ* **to ~ a party** явúться в гóсти без приглашéния

vi 1 (*emphasis on noise*): **the dishes/the large picture ~ed to the floor** посýда (*collect*)/картúна с грóхотом упáла нá пол

2 (*crash and break*) разби|вáться (-ться); **the vase ~ed on the stone floor** вáза разбúлась вдрéбезги о кáменный пол; **the plane ~ed** самолёт разбúлся; **the train ~ed at the level crossing** пóезд потерпéл крушéние у переéзда; **the two cars ~ed (into each other)** две машúны столкнýлись; **the bus ~ed into a tree/against a wall** автóбус врéзался в дéрево/в стéну; *Fin* **the business ~ed** предприя́тие разорúлось/потерпéло крах.

crash helmet *n* защúтный шлем.

crash-land *vi Aer* совершúть аварúйную посáдку (*usu pf*).

crass *adj*: **~ ignorance** пóлное невéжество; **he's a ~ idiot** он пóлный идиóт.

crate *vt* паковáть, упакóвывать в я́щик (*pf for both* упаковáть).

crave *vti* 1 (*want*): **he ~s (for) affection** емý так не хватáет лáски; **I'm simply craving for a smoke** я умирáю хочý курúть

2 (*ask*) молúть (*impf*); **to ~ smb's mercy/forgiveness** молúть когó-л о пощáде/о прощéнии.

craven *adj* труслúвый.

crawl *n* **1: in rush hours traffic is reduced to a ~** в часы́ пик машúны éле ползýт; *CQ* **let's go for a pub ~** *approx* давáй пойдём вы́пьем

2 (*swimming*) **(the ~)** кроль (*m*).

crawl *vi* 1 пóлзать (*indet impf*, по-), ползтú (*det impf*, по-) *and compounds*; **snakes/insects ~** змéи/насекóмые пóлзают; **I had to ~ round to pick up the pins** мне пришлóсь попóлзать, собирáя булáвки; **the baby was ~ing on the floor** ребёнок пóлзал пó полу; **the train was ~ing along** пóезд éле полз; **a caterpillar ~ed across the path** гýсеница переползлá чéрез тропúнку; **an ant ~ed into my boot** ко мне в ботúнок запóлз муравéй; **the dog ~ed into/out of his kennel** собáка влéзла в конурý/вы́лезла из конуры́; *fig*: **the weeks ~ed by** недéли тянýлись мéдленно; **to ~ to smb** пресмыкáться пéред кем-л (*impf*)

2: the ground was ~ing with ants земля́ кишéла муравья́ми.

crayfish *n Zool* рак.

crayon *n* цветнóй мелóк (*chalk*)/карандáш (*pencil*).

craze *n*: **he's got a ~ for stamp collecting** он помéшан на мáрках; **long skirts are the latest ~** длúнные ю́бки—послéдний крик мóды.

crazy *adj CQ* сумасшéдший, безýмный; **that's a ~ idea** э́то безýмная идéя; **you're ~ to drive without a spare wheel** ты с умá сошёл—éздить без запаснóго колесá; **to be ~ with pain** обезýметь от бóли; **it's/he's enough to drive one ~** от э́того/от негó мóжно с умá сойтú; **she's ~ about the ballet** онá помéшана на балéте.

creak *vi* скрипéть (*impf*).

creaky *adj* скрипýчий.

cream *n* 1 (*on milk*) слúвки (*no sing*); **whipped/sour ~** взбúтые слúвки, сметáна; *fig* **the ~ of society** слúвки óбщества; *attr*: **~ cheese** слúвочный сыр

2 (*of desserts, cosmetics, polishes*) крем; **chocolate/cold/face/shoe ~** шоколáдный крем, кольдкрéм, крем для лицá/для óбуви.

cream *adj* (*of colour*) крéмовый.

cream *vt*: **to ~ the milk** снимáть слúвки с молокá (снять); *Cook*: **~ the butter and sugar** разотрúте мáсло с сáхаром; **~ed potatoes** картóфельное пюрé (*indecl*).

creamy *adj* слúвочный; **a ~ complexion** нéжная кóжа.

crease *n* склáдка; **trouser ~** отутю́женная склáдка брюк; **my dress is full of ~s** у меня́ плáтье всё измя́лось; **~s on one's forehead** морщúны на лбý.

crease *vti vt* мять (*pfs* из-, с-); **to ~ a bit** помя́ть (*pf*); **to ~ paper/a dress** мять бумáгу/плáтье; **his trousers are beautifully/horribly ~d** егó брю́ки хорошó отглáжены/ужáсно помя́ты

vi мя́ться; **this material ~s easily** э́тот материáл легкó мнётся.

create *vti vt* созда|вáть (-ть); **to ~ a role/difficulties/good working conditions** создавáть роль/трýдности/хорóшие услóвия для рабóты; **he was ~d a peer** (*UK*) он был возведён в пэ́ры (*pl*); **to ~ a bad impression/a sensation** произ|водúть плохóе впечатлéние/сенсáцию (-вестú)

vi CQ под|нимáть шум (-ня́ть).

creation *n* создáние, *also fig*; творéние; **the C.** сотворéние мúра; *fig* **she was wearing the latest ~ from Paris** на ней бы́ло плáтье по послéдней парúжской мóде.

creative *adj* твóрческий.

creativity *n* твóрчество.

creator *n* создáтель (*m*), творéц.

creature *n* существó, создáние; **he's a helpless/strange ~** он беспóмощное/стрáнное существó; **she's a lovely ~** онá прелéстное создáние; **a gazelle is a beautiful ~** газéль—прелéстное творéние прирóды; **dumb ~s** бессловéсные твáри; **poor ~!** бедня́жка!; *attr*: **~ comforts** земны́е блáга.

crèche *n* (дéтские) я́сли (*no sing*).

credentials *npl*: **they will ask you for your ~** у вас потрéбуют удостоверéние (*sing*); *Dipl* **to present one's ~** вручáть верúтельные грáмоты.

credibility *n* веро́ятность; правдоподóбность; *attr*: **with him the ~ gap is pretty large, his ~ rating is not high** емý не осóбенно мóжно вéрить.

credible *adj*: **a ~ rumour** правдоподóбный слух; **~ evidence** достовéрное свидéтельство; **a ~ witness** свидéтель, заслýживающий довéрия; **his story doesn't seem ~** егó расскáз звучи́т неправдоподо́бно; **it's hardly ~ that...** маловероя́тно, что...

credibly *adv*: **I am ~ informed** я получи́л достове́рную информа́цию, я узна́л из достове́рных исто́чников.

credit *n* **1** (*belief*): **I give no ~ to that report** э́тому сообще́нию я не ве́рю

2 (*honour*) честь; **it does you ~** э́то де́лает вам честь; **he's a ~ to his family** он го́рдость семьи́; **to his ~ he refused the money** к че́сти его́ сказа́ть, он не взял де́нег; **he took all the ~ for the committee's work** рабо́тала це́лая коми́ссия, а вся сла́ва доста́лась ему́; **he passed his exams with ~** он сдал экза́мены на «отли́чно»

3 *Comm* креди́т; **to buy on ~** покупа́ть в креди́т; **no ~ is given here** здесь в креди́т не продаю́т; **the bank refused him further ~** банк отказа́л ему́ в дальне́йшем креди́те; **a letter of ~** креди́тное письмо́; *attr*: **~ balance** креди́тный бала́нс; **the bank offers good ~ facilities** банк предлага́ет хоро́шие усло́вия креди́та.

credit *vt* **1** (*believe*) ве́рить + *D* (по-); **you'd never ~ it** вы э́тому не пове́рите

2 *Comm*: **to ~ smb with £10, to ~ £10 to smb's account** запи́с|ывать де́сять фу́нтов (в креди́т) на чей-л счёт (-а́ть); *fig*: **I ~ed you with more sense** я счита́л тебя́ умне́е/благоразу́мнее.

creditable *adj* похва́льный; **the pianist gave a very ~ performance** пиани́ст игра́л о́чень непло́хо.

creditor *n* кредито́р.

credulous *adj* дове́рчивый, легкове́рный.

creed *n* кре́до (*indecl*).

creek *n* бу́хточка; зали́вчик; (*US*: *stream*) руче́й.

creel *n* корзи́на (для ры́бы).

creep *n CQ*: **it gives me the ~s** от э́того у меня́ мура́шки по спине́ бегу́т; *sl* **he's a ~** он подли́за.

creep *vi* **1** (*on all fours*) по́лзать (*indet impf*, по-), ползти́ (*det impf*, по-) *and compounds*; (*stealthily*) кра́сться *and compounds*; **the cat crept along the fence** ко́шка кра́лась вдоль забо́ра; **to ~ about on tiptoe** идти́/(*of burglar, etc.*) кра́сться на цы́почках; **he crept out of the room so as not to wake her** он вы́шел на цы́почках/тихо́нько из ко́мнаты, что́бы не разбуди́ть её; **she crept up to the window** она́ подкра́лась к окну́

2 *fig uses*: **mist crept over the hill** тума́н полз по скло́ну холма́; **a suspicion crept into my mind** у меня́ закра́лось подозре́ние; **some misprints have crept into the text** в текст вкра́лось не́сколько опеча́ток; **old age ~s upon one unnoticed** ста́рость подкра́дывается незаме́тно.

creeper *n Bot* ползу́чее (*along ground*)/выо́щееся (*upwards*) расте́ние.

cremate *vt* креми́ровать (*impf and pf*).

cremation *n* крема́ция.

crematorium *n* кремато́рий.

crêpe, *also* **crepe** *n* (*textile*) креп; (*rubber*) микропо́ристая рези́на, *CQ* микропо́рка; *attr*: **~(-rubber) shoes** *CQ* ту́фли на микропо́рке.

crescent *n* полуме́сяц.

crescent-shaped *adj* серпови́дный, в фо́рме полуме́сяца.

cress *n* кресс-сала́т.

crest *n* (*of cock*) гребешо́к; (*of bird*) хохоло́к; (*of hill, wave*) гре́бень (*m*); *fig* **he's on the ~ of the wave** он на гре́бне сла́вы.

crestfallen *adj*: **he looked ~** у него́ был тако́й удручённый вид.

crevasse *n* рассе́лина, (*very large*) уще́лье.

crevice *n* щель.

crew *n Naut, Aer* экипа́ж, кома́нда; *Aer* **ground ~** поса́дочная кома́нда; *CQ* **a motley ~** пёстрая компа́ния.

crew *vi*: **will you ~ for me tomorrow?** не пойдёшь ли ты за́втра со мной на па́руснике—мне ну́жен помо́щник?

crew-cut *n*: **to have a ~** стри́чься под «ёжик».

crew-neck *adj*: **a ~ sweater** «водола́зка».

crib *n* (*baby's*) де́тская крова́тка; (*for hay*) я́сли (*no sing*); *CQ* (*in school*) шпарга́лка.

crib *vti vt*: **he ~bed the answers from my exercise book** он списа́л отве́ты у меня́ из тетра́дки

vi (*use a crib*) по́льзоваться шпарга́лкой (*impf*).

crick *n and vt*: **I have a ~ in my neck/have ~ed my neck** я растяну́л себе́ ше́йную мы́шцу.

cricket[1] *n* (*insect*) сверчо́к.

cricket[2] *n Sport* кри́кет.

crime *n* преступле́ние, *also fig CQ*; **it would be a ~ not to fish on a day like this!** про́сто преступле́ние не лови́ть ры́бу в тако́й день!; *attr*: **~ fiction** детекти́вные рома́ны, *CQ* детекти́вы (*pls*).

criminal *n* престу́пник (*general word*); *Law* (*smb who breaks criminal law*) уголо́вник.

criminal *adj* уголо́вный; престу́пный; **~ case/law** уголо́вное де́ло/пра́во; **~ code** уголо́вный ко́декс; **~ negligence/gang** престу́пная небре́жность, ша́йка *or* ба́нда престу́пников.

crimson *adj* мали́новый.

cringe *vi*: **the dog was cringing in the corner** соба́ка сиде́ла в углу́, съёжившись; **to ~ with fear** сжа́ться от стра́ха (*usu pf*); *fig* **to ~ to/before smb** пресмыка́ться пе́ред кем-л (*impf*).

crinkly *adj*: **~ hair/paper** вью́щиеся во́лосы, ёлочная бума́га.

cripple *n* кале́ка (*m and f*).

cripple *vt* кале́чить (ис-); **he is ~d with rheumatism** его́ скрю́чило (*impers*) от ревмати́зма; *fig*: **the ship was ~d by the gale** кора́бль си́льно потрепа́ло (*impers*) што́рмом; **our activities are ~d by lack of money** на́ша де́ятельность (*sing*) приостано́влена из-за отсу́тствия де́нег.

crisis *n* кри́зис; **things are coming to a ~** надвига́ется кри́зис; **the patient has passed the ~** больно́й перенёс кри́зис.

crisp *adj*: **~ snow, a ~ lettuce/biscuit** хрустя́щ|ий снег/сала́т, -ее пече́нье; **a ~ day** я́сный моро́зный день; **~ air** бодря́щий во́здух; **~ reply** реши́тельный отве́т; **~ linen** (*sheets*) крахма́льные про́стыни.

crisps *npl*: **potato ~** хрустя́щий карто́фель (*collect*).

criss-cross *adj* перекре́щивающийся.

criss-cross *adv* крест-на́крест.

criterion *n* крите́рий.

critic *n* кри́тик.

critical *adj* **1** крити́ческий; **a ~ article** крити́ческая статья́

2 (*crucial*): **the ~ stage of an illness** крити́ческая/перело́мная ста́дия боле́зни; *Polit* **a ~ situation** крити́ческая ситуа́ция.

critically *adv*: **he looked at it ~** он на э́то посмотре́л крити́чески; **he is ~ ill** он опа́сно бо́лен.

criticism *n* кри́тика; **he can't stand ~** он не выно́сит кри́тики; **he wrote a good ~/ *CQ* crit of the book** он написа́л/дал хоро́шую реце́нзию на э́ту кни́гу.

criticize *vti* критикова́ть (*impf*); **his thesis was ~d for being too long** его́ диссерта́цию критикова́ли за растя́нутость; **people will always ~** кри́тики всегда́ найду́тся.

croak *vi* (*of frog*) ква́к|ать (*semel* -нуть); (*of crows*) ка́рк|ать (*semel* -нуть); (*when hoarse*) хрипе́ть (*impf*).

crochet *n* вы́шивка та́мбуром; *attr*: **a ~ hook** та́мбурный крючо́к.

crock *n* (*pot*) горшо́к; (*old horse*) кля́ча; (*invalid*) кале́ка (*m and f*); *CQ* **I'm/my car is just an old ~ now** я тепе́рь про́сто ста́рая кля́ча, моя́ маши́на тепе́рь про́сто ста́рая колыма́га.

crockery *n collect* посу́да.

crocus *n* кро́кус.

crony *n CQ* дружо́к, *f* подру́жка.

crook *n* (*bend*) изги́б; (*stick*) по́сох; *fig CQ* (*person*) моше́нник.

crooked *adj* (*bent*) криво́й; **a ~ branch** крива́я ве́тка; **a ~ old man** сго́рбившийся стари́к; *fig* (*dishonest*) нече́стный, непоря́дочный.

crooner *n* эстра́дный певе́ц.

crop *n* **1** (*harvest*) урожа́й (*also collect*); (*of what is sown*) посе́вы (*pl*); **rice ~** урожа́й ри́са; **a heavy ~ of apples** бога́тый урожа́й я́блок; **the ~s are late in coming through** посе́вы по́здно взошли́; **the ~s promise well/ have failed this year** в э́том году́ урожа́й обеща́ет быть хоро́шим/урожа́й плохо́й; *fig*: **a short ~** (*of hair*) коро́ткая стри́жка; **a fine ~ of hair** копна́ густы́х воло́с

2 (*of bird*) зоб.

crop *vti vt Agric*: **the sheep had ~ped the grass short** о́вцы объе́ли/съе́ли всю траву́ (под ко́рень); **to ~ a horse's tail** подреза́|ть хвост ло́шади (-́ать); *fig* **to ~ one's hair short** ко́ротко подстри́чься

vi: **the barley ~ped well** в э́том году́ был хоро́ший урожа́й ячменя́; *fig*: **all sorts of difficulties ~ped up** возни́кли вся́ческие затрудне́ния; **it ~ped up in the course of conversation that...** в разгово́ре обнару́жилось,/ вы́плыло, что...; **something has ~ped up and I can't come** возни́кли непредви́денные обстоя́тельства, и я не смогу́ прийти́.

cropper *n CQ*: **I came a ~ on the pavement/*fig* on that question/in the exam** я хло́пнулся на тротуа́р, я сре́зался на э́том вопро́се, я провали́лся на экза́мене.

croquet *n* кроке́т.

croquette *n Cook* кроке́ты (*only in pl*).

cross *n* **1** крест; **to make the sign of the ~** перекрести́ться; *Sew* **to cut on the ~** крои́ть/ ре́зать по диагона́ли

2 по́месь; **this dog is a ~ between a sheepdog and a boxer** э́та соба́ка—по́месь овча́рки с боксёром.

cross *adj* **1** (*transverse*): **~ beams** попере́чные бру́сья; *fig* **~ rhythm** *Mus* перекрёстный ритм, (*in poetry*) перекрёстная ри́фма

2 (*angry*) серди́тый; **to make smb ~** серди́ть кого́-л; **to be ~ with smb** серди́ться на кого́-л; **I was ~ with her for losing her gloves** я рассерди́лся на неё за то, что она́ потеря́ла перча́тки; **I got very ~ about it/with him** я о́чень рассерди́лся на э́то/на него́.

cross *vti vt* **1** (*go across*: *general verbs*) пересе|ка́ть + *A*, переправ|ля́ться че́рез + *A* (*pfs* -́чь, -́иться); (*if on foot*, *in car*, *swimming or sailing*) пере|ходи́ть, пере|езжа́ть, перепл ы|ва́ть + *A or* че́рез + *A* (*pfs* -йти́, -е́хать, -́ть); **to ~ Africa/the Atlantic/the desert** пересе́чь А́фрику/Атла́нтику/пусты́ню; **to ~ the road** (*on foot*) перейти́ доро́гу; **to ~ a mountain ridge** перевали́ть че́рез хребе́т; **we ~ed the river by ferry** мы перепра́вились че́рез реку́ *or* мы переплы́ли реку́ на паро́ме; **to ~ a bridge** перее́хать мост, прое́хать по мосту́; **the railway ~es the main road** желе́зная доро́га пересека́ет шоссе́; *Sport* **to ~ the finishing line** пересе́чь ли́нию фи́ница; *fig*: **to ~ smb's path** перебежа́ть доро́гу кому́-л; **it ~ed my mind that...** мне пришло́ в го́лову, что...

2 (*meet and pass*): **we must have ~ed each other en route** мы, должно́ быть, размину́лись (друг с дру́гом) по доро́ге; **my letter must have ~ed yours** по-ви́димому, моё письмо́ разошло́сь/размину́лось с ва́шим

3 (*place crosswise*): **to ~ one's legs/arms** скре́|щивать но́ги/ру́ки (-сти́ть); *Rel* **to ~ oneself** крести́ться (пере-); *fig*: **to ~ swords with smb** скрести́ть шпа́ги с кем-л; **I'll keep my fingers ~ed!** ни пу́ха ни пера́!

4 (*draw a line through*): **to ~ a cheque** пере|чёркивать/кросси́ровать чек (-черкну́ть/ *impf and pf*); **to ~ off/out** вы|чёркивать (-́черкнуть)

5 (*oppose*): **he ~es me in everything** он мне во всём пере́чит (*impf*); **she was ~ed in love** она́ страда́ла от неразделённой любви́

6 *Biol* скре́|щивать + *A and* с + *I* (-сти́ть)

vi [*see introduction to vt* **1**]: **I ~ed to the**

other side я перешёл/переехал/переплы́л/переправился на другу́ю сто́рону; **we ~ed to the island** (*by boat or swimming*) мы переправились на о́стров; **at the spot where the two roads ~ed** на перекрёстке э́тих двух доро́г; **our letters always seem to ~** на́ши пи́сьма, ка́жется, всегда́ расхо́дятся.

crossbar *n* попере́чная ба́лка; *Sport* перекла́дина.

crossbred *adj* гибри́дный.

cross-country *adj*: **a ~ race/walk** кросс, за́городная прогу́лка.

cross-current *n* попере́чное тече́ние.

cross-examine *vt*: **to ~ smb** подверг|а́ть кого́-л перекрёстному допро́су (-нуть).

cross-eyed *adj* косогла́зый.

crossfire *n* перекрёстный ого́нь (*m*).

crossing *n* перее́зд; пересече́ние; (*of roads*) перекрёсток; *Biol* скре́щивание; *Rail* **level ~** (железнодоро́жный) перее́зд, (*as road sign*) перее́зд!, шлагба́ум!; **pedestrian/zebra ~** (пешехо́дный) перехо́д; **we had a rough ~ from Dover to Ostend** нас си́льно кача́ло во вре́мя перее́зда из Ду́вра в Осте́нд.

cross-legged *adv*: **to sit ~** сиде́ть, положи́в ногу́ на́ ногу/(*on the ground*) по-туре́цки.

cross-purposes *npl*: **we are at ~** мы говори́м о ра́зных веща́х.

cross-reference *n* перекрёстная ссы́лка.

crossroads *npl* перекрёсток (*sing*); *fig* **we've come to the ~** мы стои́м на распу́тье.

cross-saw *n* попере́чная пила́.

cross section *n Archit, Tech* (*drawing*) попере́чный разре́з, (*of subsection*) попере́чное сече́ние; *fig* **we spoke to a ~ of the students** мы разгова́ривали с типи́чными представи́телями студе́нческой молодёжи.

crosswise *adj* попере́чный.

crosswise *adv* (*athwart*) поперёк; (*criss-cross*) крест-на́крест.

crotchet *n Mus* четвертна́я но́та, че́тверть.

crotchety *adj* сварли́вый.

crouch *vi* присе|да́ть (-сть); **the old woman was ~ing by the fire** стару́шка присе́ла у огня́/у камелька́; **the tiger ~ed ready to spring** тигр присе́л пе́ред прыжко́м.

croup *n Med* круп.

crow[1] *n* (*bird*) воро́на; **as the ~ flies** напрями́к (*adv*), по прямо́й.

crow[2] *n* (*noise of cock*) пе́ние/крик петуха́; (*of baby*) гу́канье.

crow[2] *vi* (*of cock*) кукаре́кать (*impf*); (*of baby*) гу́кать (*impf*); **it's nothing to ~ about** здесь не́чему осо́бенно ра́доваться.

crowbar *n* лом.

crowd *n* толпа́; **a ~ soon gathered** ско́ро собрала́сь толпа́; **to get lost in the ~** затеря́ться/потеря́ться в толпе́; **~s of people flocked to see him** лю́ди вали́ли то́лпами посмотре́ть на него́; (*at football match*) **the ~ went wild** трибу́ны (*pl*) неи́стовствовали; *CQ* **I don't care for their ~** мне не нра́вится их компа́ния; *attr Theat*: **~ scene** ма́ссовая сце́на.

crowd *vti vt*: **pedestrians ~ed the streets** на у́лицах бы́ло мно́го пешехо́дов/полно́ наро́ду; **the shop is terribly ~ed** в магази́не ужа́сная да́вка; **the bus was ~ed** авто́бус был наби́т; **the square is ~ed with people/cars** пло́щадь запру́жена наро́дом/маши́нами; **the house is ~ed with guests/furniture** дом по́лон госте́й, дом весь заста́влен ме́белью; **we are very ~ed in the flat** у нас в кварти́ре о́чень те́сно; **we ~ed everything into the cupboard** мы запихну́ли всё в шкаф; **the houses are ~ed together** дома́ стоя́т те́сно друг к дру́гу; **a week ~ed with events** неде́ля, напо́лненная собы́тиями

vi толпи́ться (с-); (*jostle, press*) напира́ть (*usu impf*); **to ~ round smb/smth** толпи́ться вокру́г кого́-л/чего́-л; **we all ~ed into his study** мы наби́лись к нему́ в кабине́т; **the students ~ed through the gates** толпа́ студе́нтов ввали́лась в воро́та; *fig* **memories ~ed in upon me** на меня́ нахлы́нули воспомина́ния.

crown *n* (*royal*) коро́на, *fig* вене́ц; (*of head*) маку́шка; (*of tooth*) коро́нка; (*of hat*) тулья́.

crown *vt* коронова́ть (*impf and pf*); **to be ~ed** коронова́ться; *fig*: **to ~ a tooth** ста́вить коро́нку на зуб (по-); **our efforts were ~ed with success** на́ши попы́тки увенча́лись успе́хом; **to ~ it all** в доверше́ние всего́.

crucial *adj*: **the ~ moment/question** крити́ческий моме́нт, гла́вный вопро́с; **it's of ~ importance** э́то о́чень ва́жно.

crucifix *n* распя́тие.

crucifixion *n* (**the C.**) распя́тие Христа́.

crude *adj* (*raw, unrefined*) сыро́й; *fig* гру́бый; **~ spirit** неочи́щенный спирт; **~ manners/expressions** гру́бые мане́ры/выраже́ния; **a ~ drawing** примити́вный рису́нок.

cruel *adj* жесто́кий; **a ~ woman/fate/disease** жесто́кая же́нщина/судьба́/боле́знь; **he is ~ to animals** он жесто́ко обраща́ется с живо́тными.

cruelty *n* жесто́кость; **~ to children** жесто́кое обраще́ние с детьми́.

cruise *n Naut* круи́з; (*for tourists*): **a Mediterranean ~** круи́з по Средизе́мному мо́рю.

cruise *vi Naut*: **the destroyer is cruising in the Pacific** эсми́нец крейси́рует в Ти́хом океа́не; (*of tourists*) **we ~d round the Greek islands** мы путеше́ствовали по острова́м Гре́ческого архипела́га; *Aut, Aer*: **the plane ~s at 500 miles an hour** ско́рость самолёта—пятьсо́т миль в час; **the car ~s easily at 100 m.p.h.** маши́на легко́ де́лает сто миль в час; *CQ* **we were cruising down the motorway** мы кати́ли по шоссе́.

crumb *n* (*single*) кро́шка; **sweep up the ~s** убери́/смети́ кро́шки; **crust or ~ for you?** тебе́ ко́рку и́ли мя́киш?; **to drop ~s on the floor** кроши́ть хлеб на́ пол; *fig*: **at least it's a ~ of comfort that you passed the exam** по кра́йней ме́ре како́е-то утеше́ние в том, что ты сдал экза́мен; **I picked up a few ~s of information** я раздобы́л ко́е-каку́ю информа́цию.

crumble *vti vt*: **to ~ one's bread** крошить хлеб (ис-, на-, по-)

vi (*of bread*) крошиться; (*of soil, etc.*) осып|áться (́-аться); **the plaster has ~d away** штукатýрка осыпалась.

crumbly *adj* (*of soil*) рыхлый; **these are very ~ biscuits** это печенье (*collect*) сильно крóшится.

crumple *vti vt* (*unintentionally*) мять (*pfs* из-, по-); (*deliberately*) мять, кóмкать (с-); **I've ~d my dress** я помяла платье; **to ~ the sheets** измять прóстыни; **he ~d up the paper** он смял/скóмкал бумáгу

vi мяться.

crunch *n* (*noise*) хруст; *fig CQ* **when it comes to the ~** в критический момéнт.

crunch *vti vt*: **to ~ an apple** грызть яблоко (*impf*)

vi хруст|éть (*semel* ́-нуть); **the snow ~ed under our feet** снег хрустéл под ногáми.

crusade *vi*: **she's crusading for women's rights** онá бóрется за правá жéнщин.

crush *n* **1** *CQ* дáвка; **after the concert the ~ at the cloakroom was unbelievable** пóсле концéрта в раздевáлке былá невероятная дáвка

2: *CQ* (*of juveniles*) **she has a ~ on her teacher—it'll pass** онá влюбилась в учителя—это пройдёт; (*of adults*) **it seems he's got a ~ on me** похóже, что я емý нрáвлюсь.

crush *vti vt* **1** давить (*impf*) *and compounds*; **to ~ grapes** давить виногрáд (*collect*); **to ~ oil out of seeds** давить мáсло из семян; **he was ~ed to death by a lorry** грузовик задавил егó нáсмерть; **to ~ an insect** раздавить насекóмое (*usu pf*); **to ~ sugar** толóчь сáхар (рас-, на-)

2 (*rumple*) мять (из-, с-)

3 (*suppress*): **to ~ a rebellion/one's enemies** подав|ля́ть восстáние (-и́ть), разби|вáть врагóв (́-ть)

vi: **nylon does not ~** нейлóн не мнётся.

crushing *adj*: **a ~ defeat/blow** сокрушительный разгрóм/удáр; **a ~ reply** уничтожáющий ответ.

crust *n*: **~ of a loaf/of ice** кóрка хлéба/льда; **~ of a pie** кóрочка пирогá; **the earth's ~** земнáя корá.

crustacean *n Zool* ракообрáзное.

crutch *n* **1** *usu pl*: **(a pair of) ~es** костыли; **to walk on ~es** ходить на костылях

2 *Anat* промéжность.

crux *n*: **the ~ of the matter** суть дéла.

cry *n* крик; **I heard a ~ for help** я слышал крик о пóмощи; **he gave a ~ for help/of pain** он позвáл на пóмощь, он вскрикнул от бóли; **battle ~** боевóй клич; (*weep*) **to have a good ~** выплакаться; **knowing what you want is a far ~ from getting it** однó дéло—хотéть, другóе дéло—имéть.

cry *vti vt*: **to ~ oneself to sleep** заснýть в слезáх; **to ~ one's eyes out** выплакать все глазá (*usu pf*); **"Help!" he cried** «На пóмощь!/Помогите!»—крикнул он

vi **1** (*shout*) кри|чáть (*semel* ́-кнуть); **to ~ at the top of one's voice** кричáть во весь гóлос/во всё гóрло; **to ~ aloud with pain** вскрик|ивать от бóли (-нуть); *fig*: **to ~ for the moon** желáть невозмóжного; **he promised to come but cried off at the last moment** он обещáл прийти, но в послéдний момéнт отказáлся; **to ~ for mercy** молить о пощáде

2 (*weep*) плáкать (*impf*); **to begin to ~** заплáкать (*pf*); **she cried bitterly over the death of her father** онá гóрько оплáкивала смерть отцá; **there's no use ~ing over spilt milk** слезáми гóрю не помóжешь.

crybaby *n* плáкса (*m and f*).

crying *adj fig*: **~ needs** насýщные потрéбности; **it's a ~ shame** это вопиющее безобрáзие.

crypt *n* склеп.

cryptic *adj* скрытый, тáйный.

crystal *n* кристáлл; (*glass*) хрустáль (*m*); **snow/ice ~s** кристáллы снéга/льда; *attr* (*of crystals*) кристаллический; (*of glass*) хрустáльный.

crystal-clear *adj* прозрáчный, чистый как кристáлл.

crystallize *vti Chem* кристаллизовáть(ся) (за-, *pf fig* вы-); **the jam has ~d** варéнье засáхарилось; **~d fruits** засáхаренные фрýкты; *fig* **our plans gradually ~d/have ~d** нáши плáны постепéнно выкристаллизовались/определились.

cub *n* детёныш.

Cuban *n* кубинец, кубинка.

Cuban *adj* кубинский.

cube *n Math* куб; (*shape*) кýбик; **the ~ of 3 is 27** три в кýбе равняется двадцати семи; **to cut carrots into ~s** нарезáть моркóвь (*collect*) кýбиками; *attr*: **~ sugar** сáхар-рафинáд.

cubic *adj* кубический.

cuckoo *n* кукýшка.

cuckoo clock *n* часы с кукýшкой.

cucumber *n* огурéц.

cud *n*: **to chew ~** жевáть жвáчку.

cuddle *vti vt*: **to ~ a child** при|жимáть ребёнка к груди (-жáть)

vi (*of two people*) прижимáться друг к дрýгу; **to ~ up to smb** прижимáться к комý-л.

cudgel *n* дубина, дубинка.

cudgel *vt* бить/избивáть дубиной (*pfs for both* избить); *fig* **I've been ~ling my brains over it/about how to...** я ломáю себé гóлову над этим/над тем, как + *inf*.

cue *n* **1** *Theat* рéплика; **to give smb his ~** подавáть комý-л рéплику; **I missed my ~** я пропустил своюю рéплику, *fig* я упустил момéнт; *fig*: **I took my ~ from her** я послéдовал её примéру; **that gave me my ~** это было мне намёком

2 (*in billiards*) кий.

cuff[1] *n and vt*: **he gave him a ~/~ed him on the ear** он ударил егó по физионóмии.

cuff[2] *n* (*of shirt, blouse*) манжéта; (*US*: *turn-up of trousers*) отворóт на брюках; *fig*

he spoke off the ~ он говори́л экспро́мтом (*adv*).

cufflinks *npl* за́понки.

cuisine *n*: **the ~ in that hotel is excellent** в э́той гости́нице первокла́ссная ку́хня.

cul-de-sac *n* тупи́к.

culinary *adj* кулина́рный.

culminate *vi*: **to ~ in** заверш|а́ться + *I* (-и́ться); **their quarrels ~d in divorce** их сканда́лы заверши́лись разво́дом.

culpable *adj* вино́вный; *Law* **~ negligence** престу́пная небре́жность/хала́тность.

culprit *n* вино́вник.

cult *n* культ; **the ~ of personality** культ ли́чности.

cultivate *vt* (*soil*) обраб|а́тывать (-о́тать), возде́л|ывать (-ать); (*plants*) раз|води́ть (-вести́); (*soil or plants*) культиви́ровать (*impf*); *fig*: **to ~ the mind** развива́ть ум (*usu impf*); **he ~s friends in high places** он заво́дит друзе́й в высо́ких сфе́рах.

cultivation *n* (*of soil*) обрабо́тка; (*of plants*) разведе́ние; (*of soil or plants*) культива́ция; **fields under ~** обраба́тываемые поля́.

cultural *adj* культу́рный.

culture *n* культу́ра, *also Agric, Biol*; **the ~ of the Romans** культу́ра дре́вних ри́млян; **a ~ of streptococci** культу́ра стрептоко́кков.

cultured *adj* (*of people*) культу́рный; (*mushrooms, pearls, etc.*) культиви́рованный.

cumbersome *adj* тяжёлый.

cumulative *adj*: **the ~ evidence is damning** совоку́пность ули́к (*pl*) говори́т о вино́вности.

cunning *adj* хи́трый, ло́вкий; *pejor* кова́рный.

cup *n* ча́шка; *Bot* ча́шечка; *Sport* ку́бок; **a ~ of tea** ча́шка ча́ю (*G*); *CQ* **he's not my ~ of tea** он не в моём вку́се.

cupboard *n* шкаф; *dim* шка́фчик; **a built-in ~** встро́енный шкаф; *attr fig*: **~ love** коры́стная любо́вь.

cup final *n Sport* фина́л ку́бка.

curb *vt fig*: **to ~ one's passions/one's tongue** сде́рж|ивать свои́ стра́сти (-а́ть), прикуси́ть язы́к (*usu pf*).

curdle *vi* свёртываться (сверну́ться).

cure *n* лече́ние; **a rest/cough ~** лече́ние поко́ем, сре́дство от ка́шля; **to undergo a ~** пройти́ курс лече́ния; **there's no ~ for this disease** от э́той боле́зни нет лека́рства.

cure *vt* **1**: **to ~ a patient/a disease** вы|ле́чивать больно́го (ʹ-лечить), излеч|ивать боле́знь (-и́ть); **he/his cough is completely ~d** он вы́лечился (от ка́шля); **to ~ smb/to be ~d of smoking** отуч|а́ть кого́-л/отуч|а́ться от куре́ния (-и́ть(ся))

2 (*food: by salting*) соли́ть, (*by smoking*) копти́ть (*pfs* за-); **to ~ skins** дуби́ть ко́жу (*collect*) (вы́-); **~d skins** дублёная ко́жа (*sing*), дублёные шку́ры.

curio *n* ре́дкая антиква́рная вещь.

curiosity *n* **1** любопы́тство; **I was dying of/burning with ~** я умира́л/сгора́л от любопы́тства; **I'm filled with ~ about Africa** меня́ о́чень интересу́ет А́фрика

2: **this vase is a ~** э́та ва́за—антиква́рная вещь.

curious *adj* **1** *attr* любопы́тный; курьёзный; стра́нный; **by a ~ coincidence** по любопы́тному совпаде́нию; **a ~ thing happened yesterday** вчера́ произошёл любопы́тный/курьёзный слу́чай; **what a ~ noise!** како́й стра́нный шум!

2 *predic*: **I'm ~ to see what his reaction will be** мне любопы́тно уви́деть его́ реа́кцию; **don't be so ~!** не любопы́тничай!, не суй свой нос куда́ не на́до!

curiously *adv* любопы́тно; **~ enough, I saw her only yesterday** стра́нно сказа́ть, но я как раз вчера́ её ви́дел.

curl *n* (*of hair*) ло́кон, завито́к; **~s** ку́дри (*no sing*).

curl *vti vt* зави|ва́ть (ʹ-ть); **to ~ one's hair** зави́ть во́лосы; **to have one's hair ~ed** зави́ться; **he ~ed his lip in scorn** он презри́тельно скриви́л гу́бы

vi (*of hair, smoke*) ви́ться (*usu impf*); **the smoke ~ed upwards from the chimney/bonfire** дым ви́лся из трубы́/над костро́м; **her hair ~s naturally** у неё вью́щиеся во́лосы; **the leaves ~ed up with the frost** ли́стья скрути́лись от моро́за; **she/the dog ~ed up in the armchair** она́/соба́ка сверну́лась кала́чиком (*adv*) в кре́сле.

curler *n* (*for hair*) бигуди́ (*no sing*); **she had her hair in ~s** во́лосы у неё бы́ли накру́чены на бигуди́.

curly *adj*: **she has ~ hair** у неё кудря́вые/вью́щиеся во́лосы.

currant *n* (*bush, or fresh fruit*) сморо́дина; (*dried*) кори́нка (*collect*); **black/red ~s** чёрная/кра́сная сморо́дина (*collect*).

currency *n Fin* валю́та (*no pl*); **foreign ~** иностра́нная валю́та; *fig* **expressions in common ~** употреби́тельные выраже́ния.

current *n* тече́ние, *also fig*; *Elec* ток; **against/with the ~** про́тив тече́ния, по тече́нию; **a ~ of air** пото́к во́здуха; *Elec* **alternating/direct ~** переме́нный/постоя́нный ток; *fig* **~ of thought/events** тече́ние мы́сли, ход собы́тий.

current *adj*: **the ~ year/issue of a magazine** теку́щий год, но́мер журна́ла за э́тот ме́сяц; **~ events** теку́щие собы́тия; **~ opinion** общепри́нятое мне́ние; **the word is in ~ use** э́то о́чень употреби́тельное сло́во; **her ~ boyfriend** её очередно́й дружо́к/кавале́р; *Fin*: **~ account** теку́щий счёт; **the ~ price/rate of exchange** существу́ющая цена́, курс дня на би́рже.

currently *adv*: **it is ~ reported that...** согла́сно после́дним сообще́ниям...

curriculum *n* уче́бный план; *attr*: **~ vitae** автобиографи́ческие да́нные.

curry[1] *n* (*dish*) кэ́рри (*indecl*); *attr*: **~ powder** (мо́лотая) припра́ва кэ́рри.

curry[2] *vt*: **to ~ favour with smb** заи́скивать пе́ред кем-л (*impf*), подли́зываться к кому́-л (*usu impf*).

curse *n* проклятие; **he seems to be under a ~** на нём как будто лежит проклятие; **to call down ~s on smb** призывать проклятия на чью-л голову; **green fly is a ~ to gardeners** тля—сущее бедствие/наказание для садовников; *CQ* **what a ~!** вот проклятие!, что за наказание такое!

curse *vti vt* прокл|инать (-ясть); **I ~d my stupidity** я проклинал себя за глупость; **she's ~d with a violent temper** уж такой у неё горячий нрав; **when he's drunk he ~s his wife** напившись, он последними словами ругает жену

vi ругаться (*impf*).

cursive *n* курсив; *attr*: **~ script** рукописный шрифт.

cursory *adj*: **after a ~ inspection of the document/the flat** бегло просмотрев документ/осмотрев квартиру; **he gave the letter a ~ glance** он пробежал письмо глазами; **the doctor gave me a ~ examination** врач быстро осмотрел меня.

curt *adj* резкий.

curtail *vt* (*shorten*) сокра|щать (-тить), (*limit*) огранич|ивать (-ить); **we'll have to ~ our visit/our expenditure** нам придётся сократить визит/расходы.

curtain *n* (*of net, lace*) занавеска; (*heavier for door, etc.*) портьера; (*of thick material*) шторы (*pl*); *Theat* занавес; **the ~ rose/fell** занавес поднялся/опустился *or* упал.

curtain *vt* занаве|шивать (-сить); **to ~ a window** занавесить окно; **to ~ off** отдел|ять занавесом (-ить).

curtain call *n*: **he got/took three ~s** он выходил на аплодисменты три раза.

curtain hook *n* крючок для портьер/занавесок.

curtain rail, curtain rod *n* карниз для портьер/занавесок.

curtsy *n* реверанс; **to drop a ~** сделать реверанс.

curvature *n* кривизна; **~ of the spine** искривление позвоночника.

curve *n Math* кривая; (*bend*) изгиб; **a ~ in the road** изгиб/поворот дороги.

curve *vi*: **the road ~s sharply to the left** дорога резко/круто по|ворачивает влево (-вернуть); **the river ~s between the trees/around the town** река вьётся меж деревьев/огибает город (*usu impf*).

curved *adj*: **a ~ beak/surface** изогнутый клюв, изогнутая поверхность; **a ~ line** кривая линия.

cushion *n* (диванная) подушка.

cushion *vt*: **to ~ a blow/a fall** смягч|ать удар/падение (-ить); *fig* **the farmers are ~ed against falling prices by subsidies** чтобы уменьшить ущерб от падения закупочных цен, фермеры получают субсидии.

cushy *adj CQ*: **he has a ~ job** он нашёл себе тёплое местечко.

cussed *adj CQ* упрямый.

custard *n approx* крем.

custodian *n* (*of museum, etc.*) хранитель (*m*).

custody *n* (*guardianship*) опека; (*care*) попечение; (*of documents*) хранение; **the mother has the ~ of the children** дети на попечении матери; **to place one's valuables in safe ~** положить ценности на хранение; *Law* **he was taken into ~** его посадили в камеру предварительного заключения.

custom *n* **1** (*usage: of tribes, etc.*) обычай; (*of individuals*) привычка, обыкновение; **the strange ~s of some tribes** удивительные обычаи некоторых племён; **it's his ~ to walk to work** у него привычка ходить на работу пешком

2 *Comm*: **I shall withdraw my ~ from you** я больше у вас покупать не буду

3 *pl* **(the ~s)** таможня; **to pass through (the) ~s** пройти таможенный осмотр.

customary *adj* обычный, привычный; **as is ~** по обыкновению, как принято.

customer *n* (*in shop*) покупатель (*m*); *Comm* заказчик; клиент; **our ~s** наша клиентура (*collect*); *CQ* **he's a queer ~** он большой чудак.

custom-made *adj* (*US*): **a ~ suit** костюм на заказ.

customs house *n* таможня.

customs officer *n* таможенник.

cut *n* **1** (*on flesh*) порез; (*slit in material, surgical incision*) разрез; (*mark, notch, snip*) надрез; **a ~ after shaving** порез после бритья; **a deep ~ on the finger** глубокий порез на пальце; **the surgeon made a neat ~** хирург сделал аккуратный надрез (*on skin*)/разрез (*deeper incision*)

2: a ~ with a cane/sword (резкий) удар тростью/мечом; *Cards* **whose ~ is it?** кому снимать?; *fig*: **in his speech he got in one or two ~s at me** в своей речи он отпустил в мой адрес пару шпилек; **he enjoys the ~ and thrust of debate** он любит напор и остроту спора

3 (*a piece*): **a ~ of cloth/meat** отрез ткани, кусок мяса

4 (*style*): **I like the ~ of your hair/your coat** мне нравится ваша стрижка/покрой вашего пальто; *fig* **he's a ~ above the others** он на голову выше других

5 (*reduction*): **a ~ in prices/in salary** снижение цен/зарплаты; **there will be a power ~ tomorrow** завтра электричество будет отключено; **they made one or two ~s in the book/film** они сократили кое-что в книге/в фильме; *fig*: **a short ~** прямой путь, путь напрямик (*adv*); **we took a short ~ over the fields** мы пошли напрямик через поля.

cut *vti* **1** резать *and compounds*; **the baby is ~ting/has ~ a tooth** у ребёнка режется/прорезался зуб; **I've ~ my finger** я порезал себе палец; **I've ~ myself on a splinter of glass** я порезался осколком стекла; **the strap ~s (into) my shoulder** ремень режет плечо; **to ~ in two/in pieces/in half** разрезать на две части/на куски/пополам (*adv*); **to ~ the**

pages of a new book разрезать страни́цы но́вой кни́ги; **I've ~ the tablecloth by mistake** я нечаянно разре́зал ска́терть; **to ~ smb's throat** перере́зать кому́-л го́рло; **he ~ his (own) throat** он заре́зался; **to ~ the throat of a wounded animal/horse** прире́зать ра́неного зве́ря/ра́неную ло́шадь; **to ~ (up) the bread/meat** наре́зать хле́ба/мя́са; **please ~ me a slice of bread** отре́жь мне хле́ба, пожа́луйста; **I'll ~ myself a piece of bread** я отре́жу себе́ (кусо́к) хле́ба; **to ~ more bread** наре́зать ещё хле́ба; **to ~ flowers/a spray of lilac** среза́ть цветы́, сре́зать ве́тку сире́ни; **~ me a bite of melon** (*to sample it*) надре́жь мне ды́ню; **to ~ a notch/one's initials on a tree** де́лать надре́з *or* насе́чку, вы|реза́ть свои́ инициа́лы на де́реве (-́резать)

2 (*clip*) стричь (о-́, под-́); **to ~ smb's hair** стричь/(*trim*) подстри|га́ть кого́-л (о-́/-́чь); **to get one's hair ~** подстри́чься; **to ~ one's beard** подстри́чь бо́роду; **to ~ a hedge/a lawn** подстри́чь и́згородь/газо́н; **to ~ hay/grass/corn** коси́ть се́но/траву́, жать хлеб (*pfs* с-)

3 (*chop or fell*) руби́ть (*impf*) *and compounds*; **to ~ meat/parsley small** ме́лко поруби́ть мя́со/петру́шку; **to ~ a carcass into pieces** разруб|а́ть ту́шу (-и́ть); **to ~ a clearing in a forest** вы|руба́ть про́секу (-́рубить)

4 (*cut out of stone*) вы|сека́ть (-́сечь); **to ~ an inscription in/a figure out of stone** вы́сечь на́дпись на ка́мне/фигу́ру из ка́мня; **to ~ steps in a rock** вы́сечь ступе́ни в скале́

5 (*cloth, leather*) крои́ть (с-); **your coat is well ~** ва́ше пальто́ хорошо́ скро́ено

6 *fig* (*reduce*): **to ~ prices/costs of production** сни|жа́ть це́ны/себесто́имость проду́кции (-́зить); **to ~ smb's salary** урез|а́ть кому́-л зарпла́ту (-́ать); **that paragraph will have to be ~** э́тот абза́ц придётся вы́кинуть (*take out*)/сократи́ть (*shorten*); **the film has been ~ a little** в фи́льме сократи́ли ко́е-каки́е места́; **the membership has been ~ to 20** коли́чество чле́нов сократи́ли до двадцати́

7 *other fig uses*: **his remark ~ me to the quick** его́ замеча́ние заде́ло меня́ за живо́е; **you're ~ting your own throat** ты гу́бишь себя́; **he's got everything ~ and dried** у него́ всё по по́лочкам разло́жено; **to ~ the ground from under smb's feet** вы́бить по́чву из-под ног у кого́-л; **~ your coat according to your cloth** по одёжке протя́гивай но́жки; **to ~ a long story short** коро́че говоря́; **to ~ one's losses** отказа́ться от невы́годного де́ла; **to ~ a lesson** пропус|ка́ть уро́к (-ти́ть); **to ~ lessons** прогу́л|ивать уро́ки (-я́ть); *Cards* **to ~ cards** снима́ть коло́ду (снять)

vi: **this knife won't ~** э́тот нож не ре́жет; **cheese ~s easily** сыр легко́ ре́жется; **let the 2 lines ~ at A** пусть две ли́нии пересека́ются в то́чке А; *fig* **it ~s both ways** э́то па́лка о двух конца́х

cut across *vt*: **to save time we ~ across a field** что́бы сократи́ть вре́мя, мы пошли́ по́лем/пря́мо че́рез по́ле; **this ~s across normal procedure** э́то идёт вразре́з с обы́чной процеду́рой

cut away *vt*: **to ~ away undergrowth/a branch** выруба́ть (*hack away*) подле́сок, обреза́ть *or* обруба́ть ве́тку

cut back *vti vt*: **to ~ back shrubs** подреза́ть/обреза́ть кусты́

vi: **to ~ back on expenditure/on fuel** уреза́ть расхо́ды, сокраща́ть расхо́д то́плива

cut down *vt*: **to ~ down a tree/trees** сруб|а́ть де́рево (-и́ть), руби́ть дере́вья (с-); *fig*: **to ~ down expenses** сокраща́ть/уреза́ть расхо́ды; **to ~ smb down to size** поста́вить кого́-л на ме́сто, сбить спесь с кого́-л

cut down on *vt*: **to ~ down on sugar/on staff** есть/потребля́ть ме́ньше са́хара, сокраща́ть шта́ты

cut free from *vt*: **they ~ him free from the wreckage** его́ извлекли́ из-под обло́мков

cut in *vi*: **to ~ in on/into a conversation** вмеш|иваться в разгово́р (-а́ться); *Aut* вкли́н|иваться ме́жду маши́нами (-иться)

cut loose *vi*: **he ~ loose from his family** он порва́л с семьёй

cut off *vt compounds of* ре́зать; **to ~ off 3 metres of material for a dress** отре́зать три ме́тра мате́рии/тка́ни на пла́тье; **to ~ off a bough/a chicken's head** обруби́ть сук, отре́зать го́лову цыплёнку; **to ~ off dead flowers** обреза́ть/среза́ть завя́дшие цветы́; **to ~ the rind off cheese** сре́зать ко́рку с сы́ра; *fig*: **to ~ off smb's retreat** отре́зать кому́-л путь к отступле́нию; **the town is ~ off by floods** го́род отре́зан от ми́ра наводне́нием (*sing*); **to ~ off the enemy/the enemy's supplies** перереза́ть врагу́ путь/ли́нию снабже́ния врага́; **my father has ~ off my dress allowance** оте́ц переста́л дава́ть мне де́ньги на оде́жду; **to ~ smb off with a shilling** лиши́ть кого́-л насле́дства (*G*); *Tel* (*during a call*) **we've been ~ off** нас разъедини́ли; *Elec, etc.* **to ~ off the gas** отключ|а́ть газ (-и́ть)

cut open *vt*: **to ~ open a melon/a carton** разре́зать ды́ню, вскрыть коро́бку

cut out *vti vt*: **to ~ an article out of a magazine** вы́резать статью́ из журна́ла; **to ~ out a dress** скрои́ть пла́тье; *fig*: **I've ~ out tobacco/sugar** я бро́сил кури́ть, я отказа́лся от са́хара; (*omit*) **~ out the details** опусти́те подро́бности; **the editor ~ out two chapters** реда́ктор вы́черкнул/вы́бросил две главы́; **he ~ her out of his will** он вы́черкнул её из завеща́ния; **he's not ~ out to be a doctor** он про́сто не со́здан быть врачо́м; **you'll have your work ~ out to convince him** бу́дет нелегко́ убеди́ть его́

vi Aut: **the engine ~ out** мото́р загло́х; **the heating ~s out by thermostat** отопле́ние отключа́ется термоконтро́лем

cut short *vt*: **she ~ him short as soon as he opened his mouth** она́ переби́ла/обре́зала его́ на пе́рвом сло́ве

cut through *vt*: **to ~ a tunnel through a mountain/a path through the jungle** прорубить туннéль в горé/тропý чéрез джýнгли

cut up *vti vt*: **to ~ up (all) the meat** нарéзать мя́со; **to ~ up a carcass** (*joint it*) разрубить/рассéчь тýшу; **to ~ up logs** (*split*) колóть дровá (*impf*) / (*in quantity*) наколóть дров (*pf*); *fig* **he was very ~ up by the death of his friend** он тяжелó переживáл смерть дрýга

vi: **she'll ~ up rough if I'm late** онá бýдет ругáться, éсли я опоздáю.

cute *adj* (*astute*) хи́трый; *CQ* (*esp US*: *sweet*): **she's ~** онá привлекáтельная дéвушка; **that's a ~ dress** э́то прелéстное плáтьице.

cuticle *n Anat*, *Bot* кути́кула.

cutlery *n collect* (*in shop*) ножи́ (*pl*); (*in household*) ножи́, ви́лки и лóжки.

cutlet *n* отбивнáя (котлéта).

cut-price, cut-rate *n*, *adj*, *adv* по сни́женной ценé; **I get a ~ by buying foodstuffs in bulk** я закупáю продýкты óптом по сни́женной ценé.

cutter *n* (*at tailor's*) закрóйщик; *Naut* кáтер; *pl* **wire ~s** кусáчки (*no sing*).

cut-throat *n* головорéз; *attr*: **~ competition** жестóкая конкурéнция.

cutting *n* (*process*) разрезáние; (*from newspaper*) газéтная вы́резка; *Rail*, *on road*, *etc.* вы́емка; *Hort* черенóк; **to take a ~** срезáть черенóк.

cutting *adj* (*of a tool*) рéжущий; *fig* рéзкий; **a ~ wind/remark** рéзкий вéтер, рéзкое замечáние.

cutting-in *n Aut* вкли́нивание.

cyanide *n Chem* циани́д.

cyclamen *n* цикламéн.

cycle *n* **1** (*series*) цикл; **lunar/song ~** лýнный цикл, цикл пéсен

2 (*bicycle*) велосипéд.

cycle *vi* катáться/éхать на велосипéде (*pfs* по-).

cyclist *n* велосипеди́ст.

cyclone *n* циклóн.

cygnet *n* молодóй лéбедь (*m*).

cylinder *n* цили́ндр.

cymbals *npl Mus* тарéлки.

cynical *adj* цини́чный.

cypher *n see* **cipher.**

cypress *n* кипари́с.

cyst *n Med* кистá.

Czech *n* чех, чéшка; (*language*) чéшский язы́к.

Czech *adj* чéшский.

Czechoslovakian *adj* чехословáцкий.

D

D *n Mus* ре.

dab *n*: **there's a ~ of paint on your dress** на твоём плáтье пятнó крáски; **a ~ of turpentine will clean it** немнóго скипидáру—и пятнó сойдёт.

dab *vt*: **to ~ some iodine on a cut** при|жигáть йóдом царáпину (-жéчь); **to ~ some powder on one's face** слегкá припýдр|ивать лицó (-ить); **to ~ one's eyes with a handkerchief** при|клáдывать платóк к глазáм (-ложи́ть).

dabble *vti vt*: **to ~ one's hands/feet in water** болтáть рукáми/ногáми в водé (*impf*)

vi fig: **to ~ in verse** баловáться стишкáми (*usu impf*); **he has ~d in politics** в своё врéмя он интересовáлся поли́тикой.

dad, daddy *n CQ* пáпа, пáпочка.

daffodil *n* жёлтый нарци́сс.

daft *adj CQ*: **don't be ~!** не глупи́!

dagger *n* кинжáл; *fig*: **to be at ~s drawn with smb** быть на ножáх с кем-л; **to look ~s at smb** смотрéть вóлком на когó-л.

dahlia *n* георги́н.

daily *n* (*paper*) ежеднéвная газéта; (*servant*) (приходя́щая) домрабóтница.

daily *adj* ежеднéвный; (*of routine*) повседнéвный; **~ visits** ежеднéвные посещéния; **my ~ expenditure on food** мой ежеднéвный расхóд на продýкты; **the ~ round** круг повседнéвных заня́тий; **my ~ pay is 10 roubles** мне плáтят дéсять рублéй в день; **the ~ allowance on official business is 5 roubles** командирóвочный получáет пять рублéй в сýтки.

daily *adv* ежеднéвно; кáждый день.

dainty *adj* (*graceful*) изя́щный, грациóзный; (*of clothes*) элегáнтный; (*fastidious*) приверéдливый; **she's ~ over her food** онá приверéдлива в едé.

dairy *n* (*shop*) молóчный магази́н; (*where cows are milked*) дои́льная; *attr* молóчный; **~ farming/cattle** молóчное хозя́йство, молóчный скот; **~ maid** доя́рка; **~ man** (*on farm*) рабóтник на молóчной фéрме.

dais *n* (*for lecturer*) помóст; (*platform*) сцéна.

daisy *n* маргари́тка.

dam *n* плоти́на; **to build a ~** стрóить плоти́ну.

dam *vt* за|прýживать (-пруди́ть); **to ~ (up) a river** запруди́ть рекý.

damage *n* **1** (*physical*) повреждéние; *Comm*, *Law* ущéрб; **was there much ~ to the car?** маши́на си́льно повресденá?; **to cause ~** наноси́ть ущéрб + *D* (*loss*); **the storm did much ~ to the crops** урожáй си́льно пострадáл от бýри; *CQ* **what's the ~?** скóлько я вам дóлжен?

2 *pl* (**~s**) (*compensation*) компенсáция (за убы́тки) (*sing*); **to recover ~s** получи́ть компенсáцию за убы́тки; **to claim £5,000 ~s for the loss of an eye** потрéбовать пять ты́сяч фýнтов как компенсáцию за потéрю глáза; **to claim ~s** взы́скивать убы́тки; **to pay/assess ~s** возмещáть/определя́ть убы́тки.

damage *vt* (*physically*) повре|ждáть + *A* (-ди́ть); (*morally or physically*) вреди́ть + *D* (по-); **he ~d his leg** он повреди́л нóгу; **the mechanism of my watch is ~d** механи́зм мои́х часóв повреждён; **such behaviour is damaging to your reputation** такóе поведéние вреди́т вáшей репутáции; *Aut* **my wing was ~d in the crash** у моéй маши́ны бы́ло си́льно помя́то крылó в авáрии; **the crops were ~d by the**

drought урожа́й пострада́л от за́сухи; **the foodstuffs were ~d in transit** проду́кты испо́ртились при перево́зке; **working in a bad light will ~ your eyes** рабо́тая при плохо́м освеще́нии, ты по́ртишь себе́ зре́ние; **smoking ~d his health** куре́ние губи́тельно сказа́лось на его́ здоро́вье.

damaging *adj*: **it was a ~ admission** э́то призна́ние си́льно повреди́ло (ему́); **this decision is ~ to our interests** э́то реше́ние нано́сит вред/уще́рб на́шим интере́сам.

damn *n CQ*: **I don't give a ~ for his opinion** мне наплева́ть на его́ мне́ние; **it's not worth a ~!** э́то гроша́ ло́маного не сто́ит!

damn *vt* (*condemn*) осу|жда́ть (-ди́ть); **he can't be ~ed just for that** то́лько за э́то его́ не осу́дят; *CQ*: **I'll be ~ed if I'll go!** будь я про́клят,/провали́ться мне на э́том ме́сте, е́сли я пойду́ туда́!; **~ him!** чёрт с ним!; **~ his impudence!** кака́я на́глость!; **~ (it)!** чёрт (побери́/возьми́)!

damnable *adj* (*cursed*) про́клятый; *CQ* прокля́тый; **~ lies** гну́сная ложь (*sing*); **~ weather** ме́рзкая пого́да; **these ~ taxes!** э́ти прокля́тые нало́ги!

damnation *interj* (**~!**) чёрт побери́!, прокля́тие!

damn(ed) *adj CQ*: **some ~ fool of a driver** како́й-то идио́т води́тель; **it's that ~ drain that's choked again** опя́ть э́та прокля́тая труба́ засори́лась; **it's ~ hot here!** здесь черто́вски жа́рко!

damning *adj Law*: **~ evidence** изоблича́ющая/тя́жкая ули́ка.

damp *n* вла́жность, сы́рость.

damp *adj* вла́жный, сыро́й; **these plants like a ~ soil** э́ти расте́ния лю́бят вла́жную по́чву; **~ sheets** вла́жные про́стыни; **a ~ climate/building** сыро́й кли́мат, сыро́е зда́ние; **the grass is ~ with dew** трава́, вла́жная от росы́.

damp, *also* **dampen** *vt* увлажн|я́ть (-и́ть); **~ the soil before planting** поле́йте зе́млю пе́ред поса́дкой; **to ~ clothes before ironing** сбры́знуть бельё пе́ред гла́женьем; **to ~ down a bonfire** присы́пать костёр золо́й (*usu pf*); *fig* **our spirits were ~ed by the rain** дождь нам испо́ртил настрое́ние.

damper *n CQ*: **to put a ~ on things** испо́ртить всё удово́льствие.

dampish *adj* сырова́тый.

damp-proof *adj* влагонепроница́емый.

dance *n* (*steps or music*) та́нец; (*gathering*) бал, ве́чер, та́нцы (*pl*); **country ~** пля́ска; **can I have this ~ with you?** разреши́те пригласи́ть вас на та́нец?; *fig* **she leads him a ~** она́ во́дит его́ за́ нос; *attr* танцева́льный.

dance *vti vt* танцева́ть (*usu impf*); (*of country dancing and joc*) пляса́ть (с-); **to ~ a waltz** танцева́ть вальс; **to ~ a quadrille** пляса́ть кадри́ль

vi танцева́ть; пляса́ть; **shall we ~?** станцу́ем?; **to ~ for joy** пляса́ть от ра́дости; *fig* **to ~ attendance on smb** стоя́ть/ходи́ть пе́ред кем-л на за́дних ла́пках.

dancer *n* танцо́р; **he's a good ~** он хорошо́ танцу́ет, (*of professional*) он хоро́ший танцо́р.

dancing *n* та́нец, та́нцы; **I love ~** я люблю́ танцева́ть; *attr*: **~ school/master** шко́ла/учи́тель та́нцев; **~ partner** партнёр по та́нцу.

dandelion *n* одува́нчик.

dandle *vt*: **to ~ a child in one's arms/on one's lap** кача́ть ребёнка на рука́х/на коле́нях (по-).

dandruff *n* пе́рхоть.

Dane *n* датча́нин, датча́нка.

danger *n* опа́сность; **to be in/out of ~** быть в опа́сности/вне опа́сности; **he's in ~ of losing his job** ему́ угрожа́ет поте́ря рабо́ты; **"D.! High voltage wires!"** «Высо́кое напряже́ние! Опа́сно для жи́зни!»; **there's no ~ here** здесь мы в безопа́сности; **there's no ~ of fire** нет опа́сности пожа́ра; **the hidden reef is a ~ to shipping** подво́дные ри́фы (*pl*) о́чень опа́сны для судо́в; *attr*: **~ signal** сигна́л опа́сности; **~ zone** опа́сная зо́на; **~ money** надба́вка за риск.

dangerous *adj* опа́сный; **drugs are ~ to health** употребля́ть нарко́тики вре́дно для здоро́вья; **bathing here is ~!** здесь купа́ться опа́сно!; **~ driving** опа́сная езда́.

dangerously *adv* опа́сно; **he's ~ ill** он опа́сно бо́лен; **that comes ~ close to cheating** э́то сли́шком похо́же на обма́н; **he likes to live ~** он лю́бит жизнь, по́лную ри́ска.

dangle *vt* болта́ть + *I* (*impf*); **the children were sitting on the fence dangling their legs** де́ти сиде́ли на забо́ре, болта́я нога́ми; **she ~d the key in front of him** она́ помаха́ла ключо́м у него́ пе́ред но́сом.

Danish *n* да́тский язы́к.

Danish *adj* да́тский.

dank *adj* (*of places*) сыро́й; (*of weather*) промо́зглый.

dapper *adj* (*in dress*) оде́тый с иго́лочки; франтова́тый; **he is a ~ little man** он тако́й франт.

dare *vti vt* (*challenge*) *CQ*: **he ~d me to cut the lesson** он подби́л меня́ прогуля́ть уро́к; **I ~ you to say that again!** а ну́-ка, повтори́, что ты сказа́л!

vi **1** сметь (по-); осме́л|иваться (-иться); отва́ж|иваться (-иться); **how ~ you say such things?** как ты сме́ешь говори́ть таки́е ве́щи?; **just you ~!** то́лько посме́й!; **he didn't ~ to dive from the top springboard** он не отва́жился пры́гнуть с ве́рхней вы́шки; **in his position I wouldn't ~ to do it** в его́ положе́нии я не рискну́л бы/не реши́лся бы/не осме́лился бы сде́лать э́то; **I daren't point out his mistake** у меня́ не хва́тит ду́ху/сме́лости указа́ть ему́ на его́ оши́бку; **he actually ~d to ask me for another loan** он име́л на́глость опя́ть проси́ть у меня́ взаймы́

2: I ~ say, but... вероя́тно,/мо́жет быть, но...; **I ~ say he'll come later** вероя́тно, он придёт по́зже.

daredevil *n* смельча́к.

daring *adj* сме́лый, отва́жный.

dark *n* темнота́; **in the ~** в темноте́; **before/after ~** до/по́сле наступле́ния темноты́; *fig* **they kept me in the ~ about it** они́ не посвяща́ли меня́ в э́то.

dark *adj* **1** тёмный; **it's already ~** уже́ темно́; **a ~ night** тёмная ночь; **a ~ day** (*overcast*) хму́рый день; **to get/grow ~** темне́ть; **it's pitch ~ outside** на у́лице тьма кроме́шная/хоть глаз вы́коли; *Photo* **~ room** тёмная ко́мната; **a ~ dress** тёмное пла́тье; **a ~ complexion** сму́глое лицо́

2 *fig* (*gloomy*) мра́чный; **a ~ mood** мра́чное настрое́ние; **to look on the ~ side of things** ви́деть всё в мра́чном све́те; **~ days** чёрные/тяжёлые дни; **a ~ hint** нея́сный намёк; **keep it ~!** никому́ ни сло́ва!; **he's a ~ horse** он «тёмная лоша́дка».

darkly *adv* (*gloomily*) мра́чно; (*in a sinister way*) злове́ще; **he hinted ~ that...** он тума́нно намекну́л, что...

darkness *n* темнота́; мрак; тьма; *CQ* потёмки (*no sing*); **the room was in complete ~** в ко́мнате бы́ло абсолю́тно темно́; *fig* **the powers of ~** си́лы тьмы.

darling *n* дорог|о́й, ми́л|ый, люби́м|ый, *f* -ая, -ая; **my ~** (*endearment*) мой дорого́й/ми́лый; **she's a perfect ~** она́ пре́лесть; **no ~, Mummy's busy** нет, де́точка, ма́ма занята́; **the ~ of all hearts** всео́бщий люби́мец; **the ~ of fortune** ба́ловень судьбы́.

darling *adj* ми́лый; **what a ~ little girl!/hat!** кака́я ми́лая де́вочка!/ми́ленькая шля́пка!

darn *n* зашто́панное ме́сто; *CQ* што́пка.

darn *vt* што́пать (за-).

darning *n* што́панье, што́пка; *attr*: **a ~ needle** што́пальная игла́.

dart *n* **1** (*weapon*) дро́тик

2 (*in game*) стре́лка; *pl* (**~s**) (*game*) мета́ние стре́лок

3 *Sew* вы́тачка

4 (*movement*) рыво́к, бросо́к; **to make a ~** рвану́ться.

dart *vi* стреми́тельно брос|а́ться (-́иться), рвану́ться (*pf*); **to ~ forward** рвану́ться вперёд; **the deer ~ed away into the forest** оле́нь стрело́й умча́лся в лес; **swallows were ~ing hither and thither** ла́сточки стреми́тельно носи́лись взад и вперёд.

dash *n* **1** (*small quantity*): **I'll have a brandy with a ~ of soda** мне конья́к и чу́точку со́довой; **add a ~ of pepper** доба́вить/доба́вьте щепо́тку пе́рца

2 (*in printing*) тире́ (*indecl*)

3 (*rush*): **we can't wait till the rain stops—we'll have to make a ~ for it** у нас нет вре́мени ждать, когда́ ко́нчится дождь—на́до бежа́ть неме́дленно

dash *vti vt*: **she has fainted—~ some water over her face!** она́ потеря́ла созна́ние—бры́зните ей водо́й в лицо́; **the flowers were ~ed by the rain** цветы́ приби́ло (*impers*) дождём; **he ~ed the glass to the ground** он гро́хнул (*CQ*) стака́н о́б пол; **the boat was ~ed against the rocks** су́дно разби́лось о ска́лы; *CQ* **I must ~ off a letter to him** я до́лжен черкну́ть ему́ па́ру строк; *fig* **my hopes were ~ed** мои́ наде́жды ру́хнули

vi **1**: **he ~ed to the door** он бро́сился к две́ри; **he ~ed past us on his bike** он промча́лся/пронёсся ми́мо нас на велосипе́де; *CQ*: **I'll have to ~** мне на́до бежа́ть; **I'm just going to ~ to the market** я сбе́гаю на ры́нок [**NB** *prefix* с- *denotes "and back"*]

2 (*hit violently*) би́ться (*impf*); **huge waves were ~ing against the rocks** огро́мные во́лны би́лись о ска́лы.

dashboard *n Aut* прибо́рная доска́.

dashing *adj* лихо́й.

dashlight *n Aut* ла́мпочка прибо́рной доски́.

data *npl* да́нные, фа́кты.

date[1] *n* **1** да́та; (*on calendar*) число́; **~ of birth/of a battle** да́та рожде́ния/сраже́ния; **what's the ~ today?** како́е сего́дня число́?; **what ~ are you leaving?** како́го числа́ вы уезжа́ете?; **has the ~ for the meeting been fixed?** назна́чен ли день собра́ния?; **we've heard no more to ~** пока́ нам бо́льше ничего́ не изве́стно; **we've received 100 applications to ~** на сего́дняшний день мы получи́ли сто заявле́ний; **at that ~** в те времена́; *fig*: **out of ~** устаре́лый; **to become out of ~** устаре́ть, вы́йти из мо́ды; **we are bringing the catalogue/equipment up to ~** мы дополня́ем катало́г, мы обновля́ем обору́дование/те́хнику

2 *Fin*, *Comm* (*term*) срок; **closing ~** кра́йний срок; **~ of payment** срок платежа́; **by a specified ~** к устано́вленному сро́ку; **he failed to pay by the ~ specified** он пропусти́л срок платежа

3 *CQ* (*appointment*: *with friend*, *on business*) встре́ча, (*with girlfriend*) свида́ние; **we've made a ~ for Tuesday** мы назна́чили встре́чу/свида́ние на вто́рник; (*US*) **who's your ~ tonight?** с кем у тебя́ сего́дня свида́ние?

date[1] *vti vt* дати́ровать + *I* (*impf and pf*); **the letter is ~d the 4th of May** э́то письмо́ дати́ровано четвёртым ма́я; **don't forget to ~ the form** не забу́дьте проста́вить да́ту на бла́нке; **the professor ~s the building from the Roman Empire** профе́ссор отно́сит э́то зда́ние к времена́м Ри́мской импе́рии; *CQ* **he is dating Tanya** он встреча́ется с Та́ней

vi: **the vase/custom ~s back to the first century** э́та ва́за дати́руется пе́рвым ве́ком на́шей э́ры, э́тот обы́чай восхо́дит к пе́рвому ве́ку на́шей э́ры; **this textbook is beginning to ~** э́тот уче́бник начина́ет устарева́ть.

date[2] *n* (*fruit*) фи́ник.

date-line *n Naut*, *Astron* демаркацио́нная ли́ния су́точного вре́мени.

date palm *n* фи́никовая па́льма.

dative *n Gram* да́тельный паде́ж.

daub *n* (*smear*) мазо́к; *CQ* (*bad painting*) мазня́.

daub *vt* ма́зать (*pfs* на-, из-, вы-); **his trousers were ~ed with paint** у него́ брю́ки измázаны крáской / вы́мазаны в крáске; **he just ~ed paint on the wall** он прóсто заля́пал стéну крáской.

daughter *n* дочь, *CQ* дóчка.

daughter-in-law *n* невéстка; (*in relationship to father only*) снохá.

daunt *vt*: **nothing ~s him** егó ничéм не запугáешь; **nothing ~ed** нискóлько не смущáясь.

daunting *adj*: **it was a ~ prospect** э́то былá пугáющая перспекти́ва.

dawdle *vi* мéдлить (*impf*); **don't ~!** давáй побыстрéй!, не мéшкай!

dawn *n* рассвéт; **at ~** на рассвéте; **from ~ till dusk** от зари́ до зари́; **to rise at ~ / with the ~ / at crack of ~** вставáть на рассвéте; *fig* **at the ~ of civilization** на зарé цивилизáции.

dawn *vi* светáть (*impf*), рассветáть (*both used impers*); **it is ~ing** светáет; **the day had already ~ed** ужé рассвелó; **the day ~ed dull and overcast** наступи́л день—хму́рый, óблачный; *fig*: **a new era had ~ed** наступи́ла нóвая э́ра; **it ~ed on me that...** меня́ вдруг осени́ло, что..., мне пришлó в гóлову, что...

day *n* **1** день (*m*); (*24 hours*) су́тки (*no sing*); **break of ~** рассвéт; **a ~'s subsistence** су́точные (дéньги); **what ~ of the week is it?** какóй сегóдня день?; **the ~ I met you** день нáшей встрéчи

2 (*adverbial phrases, uses with preps*): **a few ~s ago** нéсколько дней томý назáд; **a few ~s later** нéсколько дней спустя́; **the other ~** на дня́х; **he came the ~ before / the previous ~** он приéхал наканýне; **the ~ before he came** наканýне егó приéзда; **the ~ before yesterday** позавчерá; **next ~** на другóй / на слéдующий день; назáвтра; **the ~ after tomorrow** послезáвтра; **this ~ week / fortnight** рóвно чéрез недéлю / чéрез две недéли; **in three ~s time** чéрез три дня; **he may be here any ~ now** он приéдет на дня́х, он приéдет не сегóдня-зáвтра; **come any ~ (you like)** приходи́ в любóй день; **one ~** (*in past*) однáжды, (*in future*) когдá-нибудь, кáк-нибудь; **I'll come and see you one ~** я кáк-нибудь зайдý к вам; **one of these ~s** в ближáйшие дни; **one fine ~** (*in fairy tales, etc.*) в оди́н прекрáсный день; **every ~** кáждый день, ежеднéвно (*adv*); **every other / second ~** чéрез день; **twice a ~** два рáза в день; **all ~** весь день; **all ~ long** день-деньскóй; **~ and night** день и ночь, крýглые сýтки; **~ after ~** день за днём; **~ in, ~ out** изо дня́ в дéнь; **for ~s on end / at a time** цéлыми дня́ми, по цéлым дням; **~ by ~** день ото дня́; **by ~** днём [**NB** днём *often = in the afternoon*]; **pay per ~** оплáта зá день; **to work / pay by the ~** рабóтать / плати́ть подённо (*adv*); **from that ~ onwards** (начинáя) с э́того дня; **I'll come for the ~ / for two ~s** я приéду нá день / на два дня; **how is he?—He varies from ~ to ~** как егó здорóвье?—Да так, по-рáзному, день нá день не прихóдится; **he puts off deciding from ~ to ~** он отклáдывает решéние со дня́ нá день; **we live from one ~ to the next** мы живём тóлько сегóдняшним днём; **in these ~s** в э́ти / в нáши дни; **in this ~ and age no one has any domestic help** сейчáс / в нáше врéмя никтó не дéржит прислýгу; **in my ~s we had to walk to school** в моё врéмя мы ходи́ли в шкóлу пешкóм; **early in the ~** ýтром; **in the middle of the ~** в середи́не дня; **late in the ~** в концé дня, *fig* пóздно; **in my school ~s** когдá я учи́лся в шкóле; **in the ~s of old** в прéжние временá; **in the ~s of Ivan the Terrible** во временá Ивáна Грóзного, при Ивáне Грóзном; **she was a beauty in her ~** в своё врéмя онá былá красáвицей; **on that ~** в тот / в э́тот день; **on the same ~** в тóт же день; **on the ~ of her arrival** в день её приéзда; **punctual to the ~** тóчно день в день; **to this very ~** по сей день; **to his dying ~** до концá дней свои́х; **up to the present ~** до настоя́щего врéмени; *fig CQ* **I prefer the train any ~** я в любóм слýчае предпочитáю пóезд

3 (*uses with adjs*): **free / off ~** выходнóй день; **an 8-hour working ~** восьмичасовóй рабóчий день; **good ~!** дóброе ýтро!, дóбрый день!; **the good old ~s** стáрое дóброе врéмя (*sing*); *fig*: **it was a red letter / a black ~ for us** э́то был для нас пáмятный *or* такóй счастли́вый день / такóй несчастли́вый *or* неудáчный день; **for a rainy ~** на чёрный день

4 (*uses with verbs*): **to take each ~ as it comes** жить сегóдняшним днём; **he's seen better ~s** он знавáл лýчшие временá; **my bike has had its ~** моемý велосипéду конéц / кры́шка; **to pass the time of ~ with smb** здорóваться с кем-л; **she's 50 if she's a ~** ей все пятьдеся́т; **it's early ~s yet to say** ещё рáно чтó-нибудь предскáзывать; **you don't look a ~ older** ты всё такóй же, совсéм не постарéл; **can I take a ~ off?** я могý зáвтра не выходи́ть на рабóту?; **his ~s are numbered** егó дни сочтены́; **I'll give you three ~'s grace** я вам дам трёхднéвную отсрóчку; *CQ* **let's call it a ~** на сегóдня хвáтит; *Mil and fig*: **to carry / lose the ~** одержáть побéду, проигрáть сражéние; **to save the ~** спасти́ положéние

5 *attr*: **are you on a ~ or a night flight?** вы лети́те дневны́м и́ли ночны́м рéйсом?; **I'm on ~ shift** я рабóтаю в дневнýю смéну; **it's a 2-~ journey from here** э́то в двух днях пути́ отсю́да.

daybreak *n* рассвéт; **at ~** на рассвéте, с зарёй.

daydream *n* грёза.

daydream *vi* грéзить наявý (*impf*).

daylight *n* дневнóй свет; **in (broad) ~** при дневнóм свéте, средь бéла дня; **can we get home in ~?** попадём ли мы домóй зáсветло (*adv*)?; *fig* **I'm beginning to see ~** наконéц я ви́жу просвéт; *attr*: **~ robbery** грабёж средь бéла дня.

day nursery *n* дéтский сад.

day-to-day *adj*: **the ~ work** повседнéвная рабóта; **we are working on a ~ basis** мы живём сегóдняшним днём.

daze *n*: **I was in a ~** я был как в тумáне.

daze *vt*: **he was ~d by the news/the blow** он был потрясён э́той нóвостью/сражён э́тим удáром.

dazed *adj*: **he had a ~ look** у негó был прóсто обалдéвший вид.

dazzle *vt* слепи́ть (*impf*); ослеп|ля́ть (-и́ть); **the headlights ~d me** автомоби́льные фáры ослепи́ли меня́.

dazzling *adj* ослепи́тельный; **the sun was ~** сóлнце слепи́ло; *fig*: **she is a ~ beauty** онá ослепи́тельна; **~ prospects** блестя́щие перспекти́вы.

dead *n* **1 (the ~)** *collect* мёртвые (*pl*)

2: in the ~ of winter/night глубóкой зимóй/нóчью.

dead *adj* **1** (*of people, slaughtered animals*) мёртвый; (*of animals dying naturally*) дóхлый; **a ~ body** мёртвое тéло; **~ flowers/leaves/matter** увя́дшие цветы́, сухи́е ли́стья, нежива́я матéрия

2 *fig uses*: **he was more ~ than alive** он был ни жив ни мёртв; **a ~ calm/weight** мёртвый штиль/груз; **~ silence/centre/languages** мёртвая тишинá/тóчка, мёртвые языки́; **to come to a ~ end** зайти́ в тупи́к; **my fingers have gone ~** у меня́ онемéли пáльцы; **in a ~ faint** в глубóком óбмороке; **I am in ~ earnest** я э́то говорю́ совершéнно серьёзно; **a ~ failure** пóлный провáл; **she made a ~ set at him** онá вцепи́лась в негó мёртвой хвáткой; **to come to a ~ stop** рéзко останови́ться; **he was ~ to the world** он спал как уби́тый; **he's the ~ spit of his father** он вы́литый отéц; *Tel* **the line has gone ~** телефóн замолчáл/молчи́т; *Sport* **a ~ heat** одновремéнный фи́ниш; *CQ*: **he's ~ from the neck up** он глуп как прóбка; **I wouldn't be seen ~ with that lot** я бы ни за чтó не стал свя́зываться с э́той компáнией.

dead *adv*: **he dropped down ~** он свали́лся зáмертво; *fig*: **he's ~ drunk** он мертвéцки пьян; **I'm ~ tired/beat** я смертéльно устáл, я устáл дó смерти; **I'm ~ against leaving tomorrow** я реши́тельно прóтив тогó, чтóбы éхать зáвтра; **he's ~ straight** он кристáльно чéстен; **he stopped ~ in his tracks** он останови́лся как вкóпанный; **it's ~ easy to arrange this** устрóить э́то—прóще простóго/прóще пáреной рéпы; **I'm ~ certain he'll come** я твёрдо увéрен, что он придёт.

deaden *vt* (*pain*) притуп|ля́ть (-и́ть); (*sound*) заглуш|áть (-и́ть); **to ~ the force of a blow** ослаб|ля́ть си́лу удáра (-ить).

deadline *n* (предéльный) срок; **to meet a ~** успéть с рабóтой к устанóвленному срóку.

deadlock *n*: **to reach a ~** зайти́ в тупи́к.

deadly *adj* смертéльный; **~ poison** смертéльный яд; **the seven ~ sins** семь смéртных грехóв; *CQ* **the play was ~** пьéса былá уби́йственно скучнá.

deadly *adv*: **~ pale** смертéльно блéдный; *CQ* **~ boring** смертéльно/уби́йственно скýчный.

deadpan *adv*: *CQ* **he said it absolutely ~** он сказáл мне э́то с серьёзным ви́дом.

deaf *adj* глухóй; **~ in one ear** глухóй на однó ýхо; **~ and dumb** глухонемóй; **he is a little ~** он глуховáт, он туговáт нá ухо; **~ as a post** глухóй как пень.

deaf-aid *n* слуховóй аппарáт.

deafen *vt* оглуш|áть (-и́ть); **we were ~ed by the noise of the waterfall** шум водопáда оглуши́л нас.

deafening *adj* оглуши́тельный.

deaf-mute *n, adj* глухонемóй.

deal[1] *n* (*fir or pine wood*) елóвые/соснóвые дóски (*pl*), ди́льсы (*pl*); *attr*: **a ~ table** стол из соснóвых дóсок.

deal[2] *n* (*quantity*): **a good ~ of time/money** мнóго врéмени/дéнег; **there's a good ~ of sense in that** в э́том есть смысл; **to take a good ~ of trouble over smth** настóйчиво хлопотáть о чём-л; **they make a great ~ of their grandson** *CQ* они́ нóсятся со свои́м внýком; *as adv*: **to feel a good ~ better** чýвствовать себя́ мнóго/горáздо лýчше; **they see a good ~ of each other** они́ чáсто ви́дятся.

deal[3] *n* **1** (*agreement*) соглашéние; (*transaction, bargain*) сдéлка; **a fair/square ~** чéстная сдéлка; **to do/make a ~ with smb** заключи́ть сдéлку с кем-л; *CQ* **it's a ~!** соглáсен!, идёт!, по рукáм!; *fig*: **he got a raw ~ from the manager** управля́ющий был к немý несправедли́в; **he was given a fair ~** с ним чéстно поступи́ли

2 *Cards* сдáча; **whose ~ is it?** комý сдавáть?

deal[3] *vti vt*: **to ~ smb a blow** на|носи́ть комý-л удáр (-нести́); (*distribute*): **to ~ out gifts** раз|давáть подáрки (-дáть); **to ~ out the takings** распредел|я́ть дохóды (-и́ть); **the question has already been ~t with** э́тот вопрóс ужé решён/*CQ* ужé утрясён; *Cards* **to ~ smb an ace** сдать комý-л тузá

vi **1** (*handle things*): **he's ~ing with this matter** он занимáется э́тим дéлом/вопрóсом; **this chapter ~s with Rome/with the problems of...** в э́той главé говори́тся о Ри́ме/рассмáтриваются проблéмы + *G*; **the manager will ~ with this question** э́тот вопрóс рассмóтрит завéдующий

2 (*handle people*): **she's good at ~ing with children** онá умéет обращáться с детьми́ (*only in impf*); **he ~t very fairly with me** он был óчень коррéктен со мной; *CQ* **I'll ~ with him!** я им займýсь!

3 *Comm*: **he ~s in leather** он торгýет кóжей; **we don't ~ with that firm** мы не имéем дéла с э́той фи́рмой

4 *Cards* сда|вáть (-ть).

dealer *n* (*trader*) торгóвец; *Cards* сдаю́щий (кáрты).

dealing *n* **1: he's well known for honest** ~ его́ все счита́ют поря́дочным челове́ком

2 *pl* (~**s**) (*business relations*) торго́вля (*sing*), (торго́вые) дела́; (*transactions*) сде́лки; *fig* **I wish to have no** ~**s with such a man** я не хочу́ име́ть де́ло с таки́м челове́ком.

dean *n Univ* дека́н.

dear *n* дорог|о́й, ми́л|ый, *f* -а́я, -ая; *CQ*: **isn't she a** ~? ну, не пре́лесть ли она́?; **what a little** ~! како́й он ми́лый!; **certainly, my** ~ ну коне́чно, дорого́й мой/голу́бчик.

dear *adj* **1** (*of people*) дорого́й, ми́лый, люби́мый; **she is very** ~ **to me** она́ мне о́чень дорога́; **a very** ~ **friend of mine** мой большо́й друг; **to hold smb** ~ люби́ть кого́-л

2 (*in letters*: *to friends*) дорого́й; (*formal, Comm*) уважа́емый, глубокоуважа́емый

3 (*of things*) люби́мый, ми́лый, преле́стный, заве́тный; **her** ~**est wish** её заве́тная мечта́; **what a** ~ **little ring!** како́е ми́лое коле́чко!

4 (*expensive*) дорого́й; **to become/get** ~ дорожа́ть; **that shop is always very** ~ в э́том магази́не всё о́чень до́рого.

dear *interj*: **oh** ~!, ~ **me!** бо́же мой!

dearly *adv*: **to love smb** ~ не́жно/о́чень люби́ть кого́-л; **I would** ~ **like to know the truth** я до́рого бы дал, что́бы знать пра́вду; **I paid** ~ **for my mistake** я до́рого заплати́л за свою́ оши́бку/оплóшность.

dearth *n* недоста́ток, нехва́тка.

death *n* смерть; **to die a natural** ~ умере́ть свое́й сме́ртью; **to freeze to** ~ замёрзнуть до́ смерти; **to starve to** ~ умере́ть с го́лоду/от го́лода; **he drank himself to** ~ он спи́лся и у́мер; **to be burnt to** ~ сгоре́ть за́живо; **to put smb to** ~ казни́ть кого́-л; *fig*: **I'm bored to** ~ мне смерте́льно ску́чно; **to work oneself/smb to** ~ рабо́тать на изно́с, выжима́ть из кого́-л все со́ки; *CQ*: **wrap up warmly or you'll catch your** ~ **of cold** оде́нься потепле́е, а то просту́дишься; **this will be the** ~ **of me** э́то меня́ прико́нчит.

death duties *npl* нало́ги на насле́дство.

deathly *adj*: ~ **pale** бле́дный как смерть; **a** ~ **silence** гробово́е молча́ние.

death penalty *n* сме́ртная казнь.

death rate *n* сме́ртность.

debar *vt*: **to** ~ **smb from voting** лиш|а́ть кого́-л пра́ва го́лоса (-и́ть).

debase *vt*: **to** ~ **the coinage** сни|жа́ть курс (валю́ты) (-́зить).

debatable *adj* спо́рный.

debate *n* диску́ссия; пре́ния (*no sing*); **a** ~ **on the findings of the commission** пре́ния по докла́ду коми́ссии; **the matter is under** ~ вопро́с обсужда́ется.

debate *vti vt* обсу|жда́ть (-ди́ть); (*think over*) обду́м|ывать (-ать)

vi: **I am debating with myself whether to stay or go** я обду́мываю,/взве́шиваю, оста́ться и́ли уйти́.

debauched *adj* развращённый, распу́щенный.

debilitating *adj* изнури́тельный.

debit *n Fin* де́бет; *attr*: **a** ~ **balance** пасси́вный бала́нс.

debit *vt*: **to** ~ **£5 against smb's account, to** ~ **smb's account with £5** записа́ть пять фу́нтов на чей-л счёт; **to whom shall I** ~ **this sum?** на кого́ мне записа́ть э́ту су́мму?

debris *n* обло́мки, разва́лины (*pls*).

debt *n* долг; **a** ~ **(to the amount) of £40** долг в разме́ре сорока́ фу́нтов, долг в со́рок фу́нтов; **to be in smb's** ~ быть у кого́-л в долгу́; **to get into** ~ влеза́ть в долги́ (*pl*); **to pay a** ~ отда́ть долг; **a bad** ~ безнадёжный долг; **I'm in your** ~ я вам до́лжен, *fig* я ваш должни́к; *fig* **I am greatly in your** ~ **for your kindness to my son** я так вам обя́зан за доброту́, проя́вленную к моему́ сы́ну.

debtor *n* должни́к.

debunk *vt CQ*: **to** ~ **smb** разве́нч|ивать кого́-л (-а́ть).

debut *n* дебю́т; **to make one's** ~ дебюти́ровать.

decade *n* десятиле́тие.

decadent *adj* упа́дочнический; *Art* декаде́нтский.

decamp *vi fig*: **he** ~**ed with all the money** он скры́лся, прихвати́в с собо́й все де́ньги.

decant *vt*: **to** ~ **wine** перели|ва́ть вино́ (из буты́лки) в графи́н (-́ть).

decanter *n* графи́н.

decay *n* (*decomposition*) разложе́ние; **dental** ~ зубно́й ка́риес; (*of buildings*) **to fall into** ~ ветша́ть, разруша́ться; **the** ~ **of civilization** упа́док цивилиза́ции.

decay *vi* (*decompose*) раз|лага́ться (-ложи́ться); (*of buildings*) ветша́ть (об-); (*of civilizations, etc.*) при|ходи́ть в упа́док (-йти́); ~**ing flesh** разлага́ющаяся плоть; **teeth** ~ **rapidly in old age** зу́бы бы́стро по́ртятся/разруша́ются в ста́рости; **his powers are beginning to** ~ его́ си́лы начина́ют слабе́ть/убыва́ть.

decayed *adj*: **a** ~ **tooth** гнило́й зуб; ~ **wood** гнило́е де́рево; ~ **apples** сгни́вшие я́блоки; **a** ~ **building** обветша́вшее зда́ние.

decease *n* смерть, кончи́на.

deceased *adj* поко́йный; *as n* (**the** ~) поко́йник, поко́йный.

deceit *n* обма́н; ложь.

deceitful *adj* лжи́вый; обма́нный; (*deceptive*) обма́нчивый.

deceive *vt* обма́н|ывать (-у́ть); **to** ~ **oneself** обма́нывать себя́; **to be** ~**d by appearances** быть обма́нутым вне́шностью; **if my memory doesn't** ~ **me** е́сли мне не изменя́ет па́мять; **we were** ~**d in our hopes** мы обману́лись в свои́х ожида́ниях; **we were** ~**d into buying a dud car** нас обману́ли — прода́ли брако́ванную маши́ну.

decelerate *vti* уменьш|а́ть ско́рость (-́ить).

December *n* дека́брь (*m*); *attr* дека́брьский.

decency *n* прили́чие; **to observe the decencies** соблюда́ть прили́чия; **in common** ~ из уваже́ния к прили́чиям (*pl*); ~ **in dress** скро́мность в одéжде; **he hadn't the ~ to say thank you** он дáже спасúбо не сказáл.

decent *adj* **1** прилúчный; (*honest, respectable*) достóйный, порядочный; **~ behaviour** достóйное поведéние; **that story is not ~** это неприлúчный анекдóт; **a ~ suit of clothes** прилúчный костюм

2 *CQ* (*not bad, likable*) слáвный, хорóший, неплохóй; (*of behaviour*) мúлый, любéзный; **he's a ~ chap** он слáвный мáлый; **he was very ~ to me** он óчень хорошó ко мне отнёсся; **quite a ~ lunch** неплохóй зáвтрак; **that's very ~ of you** это óчень любéзно с вáшей стороны; **he's got quite a ~ income** у негó вполнé прилúчный дохóд.

decently *adv*: **to dress ~** прилúчно одевáться; **he treats his employees ~** он хорошó относúтся к своúм подчинённым; *CQ* **he very ~ lent me his flat for a week** он любéзно предостáвил мне свою квартúру на недéлю.

decentralize *vt* децентрализовáть (*impf and pf*).

deception *n* обмáн; **to get smth by ~** добúться чегó-л обмáнным путём/обмáном.

deceptive *adj* обмáнчивый.

decide *vti vt* реш|áть (-úть); **to ~ a question** решúть вопрóс; **that ~s it!/me!** конéц сомнéниям!, тепéрь мне ясно!

vi решúть; **I ~d against inviting him/their proposals** я решúл не приглашáть егó/не принимáть их предложéния; **to ~ to do smth/that...** решúть сдéлать что-л/, что...; **she couldn't ~ what to wear** онá не моглá решúть, какóе плáтье надéть; **she ~d on her black dress** онá решúла надéть чёрное плáтье.

decided *adj* решúтельный; (*definite*) определённый; **he's a very ~ character** он решúтельный человéк; **his ~ opinion was that...** он был непоколебúмо увéрен, что...; **there's been a ~ improvement in his health** егó здорóвье замéтно улучшилось.

decimal *n* десятúчная дробь; **a recurring ~** периодúческая десятúчная дробь.

decimal *adj* десятúчный; **~ currency** десятúчная монéтная систéма.

decipher *vt* (*a code*) расшифрóв|ывать (-áть); **to ~ smb's handwriting** раз|бирáть чей-л пóчерк (-обрáть); **to ~ an inscription** прочéсть (дрéвнюю) нáдпись (*usu pf*).

decision *n* **1** решéние; **to take a ~** принять решéние; **what is your ~?** что вы решúли?, каковó вáше решéние?

2 (*resoluteness*) решúмость, решúтельность.

decisive *adj* решúтельный; (*final*) окончáтельный; **a ~ character/victory** решúтельный человéк, решáющая побéда; **a ~ answer** решúтельный/окончáтельный отвéт; **~ evidence** неопровержúмые улúки (*pl*).

deck *n Naut* пáлуба; **on ~** на пáлубе; **upper/lower ~** вéрхняя/нúжняя пáлуба; **to go on ~** вы́йти на пáлубу; **all hands on ~!** свистáть всех навéрх!; *attr* пáлубный.

deckchair *n* шезлóнг.

declaim *vi* орáторствовать (*impf*).

declaration *n* декларáция, объявлéние, заявлéние; **~ of rights** декларáция прав; **customs ~** тамóженная декларáция; **a ~ of war** объявлéние войны; **to make a ~** сдéлать заявлéние.

declare *vti vt* утверждáть (*only in impf*); *off* объяв|лять, заяв|лять (*pfs* -úть); **to ~ war against/(up)on a country** объявúть войнý какóй-л странé; *Cards* **to ~ trumps** объявúть кóзырь; **to ~ one's love to a girl** объясн|яться дéвушке в любвú (-úться); (*at customs*) **have you anything to ~?** есть ли у вас вéщи, подлежáщие тамóженному сбóру?; **he ~d himself innocent/surprised** он утверждáл, что невинóвен, он сказáл, что óчень удивлён

vi: **well, I ~!** что вы говорúте?, да чтó вы!

declension *n Gram* склонéние.

decline *n* упáдок; спад; **the ~ of civilization/of one's powers, a ~ in trade** закáт *or* упáдок цивилизáции, упáдок сил/торгóвли; **a ~ in the birthrate** снижéние рождáемости.

decline *vti vt* **1**: **to ~ an invitation/a proposal** отклон|ять приглашéние/предложéние (-úть); **he ~d the responsibility** он ушёл от отвéтственности

2 *Gram* склонять (про-)

vi **1** (*refuse*): **he ~d to answer questions** он отказáлся отвечáть на вопрóсы

2 (*go down*): **the sun is declining** сóлнце захóдит; *fig*: **trade is declining** торгóвля идёт на убыль; **his health slowly ~d** егó здорóвье постепéнно ухудшáлось

3 *Gram* склоняться.

decode *vt* расшифрóв|ывать (-áть).

decompose *vi* раз|лагáться (-ложúться).

decontaminate *vt* дезинфицúровать (про-).

décor *n Theat* декорáция.

decorate *vt* **1** (*beautify*) укра|шáть (-сить); **to ~ a room** (*paint*) крáсить стéны в кóмнате (по-)/(*paper*) оклé|ивать обóями кóмнату (-ить)/(*do up*) отдéл|ывать кóмнату (-ать)

2 *Mil* **to ~ smb with an order** награ|ждáть когó-л óрденом (-дúть).

decoration *n* **1** (*adornment*) украшéние; (*of a house*) *usu pl* (**~s**) внýтренняя отдéлка; **the ~s were very costly** отдéлочные рабóты обошлúсь дóрого

2 *Mil* óрден.

decorative *adj* декоратúвный; *CQ* **his wife is very ~** у негó женá óчень эффéктная.

decorator *n* (*painter*) маляр; (*paperer*) обóйщик; **interior ~** худóжник по интерьéру.

decorous *adj* пристóйный, прилúчный.

decoy *n* примáнка, *also fig*.

decrease *n* уменьшéние; **a ~ in population** уменьшéние населéния; **crime is on the ~** престýпность идёт на убыль; **a ~ in the birthrate/in temperature** снижéние рождáемости, понижéние температýры.

decrease *vti vt* уменьш|áть (-ить); убав|лять (-ить); **to ~ speed** сбáвить ход, убáвить скóрость

vi: **the population has ~d** населéние умéньшилось.

decree *n* ука́з, прика́з, декре́т; зако́н; (*court decision*) реше́ние суда́.

decree *vt* постанов|ля́ть (-и́ть), *also Law*; **it has been ~d that...** постанови́ли, что...; **fate ~d otherwise** судьба́ реши́ла/распоряди́лась ина́че.

decrepit *adj* (*of people*) дря́хлый; (*of buildings*) ве́тхий, обветша́лый.

dedicate *vt* посвя|ща́ть (-ти́ть); **to ~ one's life to art** посвяти́ть свою́ жизнь иску́сству; **he is ~d to his work** он весь в рабо́те; **the book is ~d to me** э́та кни́га посвящена́ мне.

dedication *n* посвяще́ние (*also in a book*); **he works with ~** он целико́м отдаёт себя́ рабо́те.

deduce *vt* де́лать вы́вод (с-); заключ|а́ть (-и́ть); **from the tracks I ~d that...** изучи́в следы́, я пришёл к заключе́нию, что...

deducible *adj* выводи́мый.

deduct *vt Math, etc.* вы|чита́ть (-́честь); (*keep back*) уде́рж|ивать (-а́ть); **30% of my salary is ~ed for tax** из мое́й зарпла́ты вычита́ют/уде́рживают три́дцать проце́нтов нало́гов; **after ~ing the cost of transport** за вы́четом сто́имости перево́зки.

deduction *n* **1** (*deducting or amount deducted*) удержа́ние; вы́чет; **~s from salary** вы́четы из зарпла́ты; **he earns £ 100 a week before/after ~ of tax** он зараба́тывает сто фу́нтов в неде́лю без вы́чета/за вы́четом нало́гов

2 (*inference*) вы́вод, заключе́ние.

deed *n* (*act*) де́ло, посту́пок; *Law* акт; **a good ~** хоро́ший посту́пок; **in word and ~** сло́вом и де́лом; **heroic ~s** (герои́ческие) по́двиги; *Law* **~ of purchase** акт о поку́пке.

deep *adj* **1** глубо́кий, *also fig*; (*of colour*) густо́й (*rich*), тёмный (*dark*); **a ~ river/wound/secret** глубо́кая река́/ра́на/та́йна; **a ~ sleep/sigh/interest** глубо́кий сон/вздох/интере́с; **a ~ impression/sorrow/depression** глубо́кое впечатле́ние/го́ре/уны́ние; **with ~ regret** (*in obituary notices, etc.*) с глубо́ким приско́рбием; **~ x-ray treatment** глубо́кая рентгенотерапи́я; **~ grass** высо́кая трава́; **a ~ shelf** широ́кая по́лка; **~ blue** тёмно-си́ний; **a ~ sound/voice** ни́зкий звук/го́лос; **a ~ groan** глухо́й стон

2 (*in measurements*): **10 feet ~** глубино́й (в) де́сять фу́тов; *fig* **to stand three ~** стоя́ть в три ряда́/шере́нги

3 ~ in: ~ in snow покры́тый глубо́ким сне́гом; **to stand knee ~ in mud** быть по коле́но в грязи́; *fig*: **he was ~ in debt** он был по́ уши в долга́х; **~ in the country** в глуши́, в отдалённом ме́сте; **~ in thought/a book** погружённый в размышле́ния (*pl*)/в чте́ние.

deep *adv* глубоко́; **to dig ~** рыть глубоко́; (*to swimmer*) **don't go in too ~** не заходи́те сли́шком глубоко́; **~ in his heart** в глубине́ души́; **to read ~ into the night** чита́ть до глубо́кой но́чи.

deepen *vti vt* углуб|ля́ть (-и́ть); **to ~ a ditch** углуби́ть кана́ву; *fig* **to ~ one's knowledge** углуби́ть зна́ния (*pl*)

vi углуб|ля́ться (-и́ться); **his colour ~ed** (*from indignation, etc.*) он побагрове́л; *fig* **his gloom ~ed** он всё бо́льше мрачне́л.

deep-freeze *n* шкаф-морози́льник; *attr*: **~ compartment** (*in fridge*) морози́льная ка́мера, *CQ* морози́лка.

deep-freeze *vt* замор|а́живать (-о́зить).

deep-fry *vt* прожа́р|ивать (-ить).

deeply *adv* глубоко́; **she feels her mother's death ~** она́ глубоко́ пережива́ет смерть ма́тери; **he is ~ offended** он оби́жен до глубины́ души́, он о́чень оби́жен; **he is ~ interested in philosophy** он глубоко́ интересу́ется филосо́фией.

deep-rooted *adj fig* укорени́вшийся.

deep-sea *adj*: **~ fishing** глуби́нный лов ры́бы.

deep-seated *adj*: **a ~ abscess** глубо́кий нары́в; *fig* **the causes of his depression are ~** причи́ны его́ депре́ссии лежа́т глубоко́.

deep-set *adj*: **~ eyes** глубоко́ поса́женные глаза́.

deer *n* оле́нь (*m*).

deerskin *n* оле́нья ко́жа; лоси́на; (*chamois leather*) за́мша.

deer-stalking *n* охо́та на оле́ней.

deface *vt*: **the statue is ~d** ста́туя обезобра́жена.

de facto *adv* де-фа́кто; факти́чески, на де́ле.

defamatory *adj* клеветни́ческий.

default *n*: **by ~** по небре́жности; за нея́вку; **in ~ of** ввиду́ отсу́тствия, за неиме́нием; **judgement by ~** зао́чный пригово́р.

default *vi* (*not pay*) не плати́ть долго́в (*usu pf*); (*not appear in court*) не яв|ля́ться по вы́зову суда́ (-и́ться).

defaulter *n* (*on payments*) неплате́льщик; *Mil* наруши́тель (*m*) дисципли́ны.

defeat *n* пораже́ние.

defeat *vt Mil, Sport* побе|жда́ть (-ди́ть); на|носи́ть пораже́ние кому́-л (-нести́).

defeatism *n* пораже́нчество.

defeatist *n* пораже́нец.

defecate *vi* испражня́ться (*impf*).

defect *n* недоста́ток; дефе́кт; изъя́н; **he has many ~s** у него́ мно́го недоста́тков/изъя́нов; **there was a serious ~ in the plan** в пла́не был серьёзный просчёт.

defect *vt*: **to ~ to the enemy** перейти́/перемetну́ться на сто́рону врага́ (*usu pf*); **he ~ed to us** он перешёл к нам.

defection *n Polit* ренега́тство, отсту́пничество.

defective *adj*: **he has ~ eyesight/hearing** у него́ дефе́кт зре́ния/слу́ха, (*less formal*) он пло́хо ви́дит/слы́шит; **a mentally ~ child** у́мственно отста́лый ребёнок; **~ goods** брако́ванные това́ры, брак; **~ workmanship/machinery** плоха́я рабо́та, неиспра́вное обору́дование.

defector *n* перебе́жчик.

defence *n* защи́та (*no pl*), *also Law, Sport*; *Mil* оборо́на (*no pl*); *Law*: **the case for the ~** защи́та; **counsel for the ~** защи́тник, адвока́т, защи́та; **witnesses for the ~** свиде́тели защи́ты; **the Ministry of D.** министе́рство оборо́ны; **weapons of ~** оборони́тельное ору́жие (*sing*); **to penetrate the enemy's ~s** прорва́ть оборо́ну/ли́нию оборо́ны проти́вника.

defenceless *adj* беззащи́тный.

defend *vt* защи|ща́ть (-ти́ть), *also Law, Sport*; (*justify*) опра́вд|ывать (-а́ть); *Mil* обороня́ть (*impf*); **to ~ smb/the goal** защища́ть кого́-л/воро́та (*no sing*); **to ~ oneself against/from smb** защища́ться от кого́-л; **to ~ one's point of view/a thesis** защища́ть свою́ то́чку зре́ния/диссерта́цию; **to ~ one's action** опра́вд|ывать свой посту́пок (-а́ть); **to ~ oneself** (*from accusations*) опра́вдываться; **to ~ a town** защища́ть/обороня́ть го́род.

defendant *n Law* (*civil*) отве́тчик, (*criminal*) подсуди́мый, обвиня́емый.

defender *n* защи́тник.

defensible *n* защища́емый.

defensive *n*: *Mil, Sport* **to be on the ~** обороня́ться, защища́ться; *fig* **she's quickly on the ~ if anybody criticizes her children** попро́буй покритику́й её дете́й—она́ их в оби́ду не даст.

defensive *adj* оборони́тельный, *also Sport, fig*; **to play a ~ game** прибе́гнуть к оборони́тельной та́ктике; **~ moves** оборони́тельная та́ктика, защи́тные приёмы; *fig* **when his statement was challenged, he became very ~** когда́ его́ утвержде́ние ста́ли подверга́ть сомне́нию, он оби́делся.

defer[1] *vt* (*put off*) от|кла́дывать (-ложи́ть); отсро́ч|ивать (-ить); **he's ~red his visit till next week** он отложи́л свой визи́т до сле́дующей неде́ли; **to ~ payment** отсро́чивать платёж.

defer[2] *vt*: **to ~ to smb/smb's opinion** уступ|а́ть кому́-л (-и́ть), прислу́|шиваться к чьему́-л мне́нию (-шаться).

deference *n* уваже́ние, почте́ние; **out of ~ to** из уваже́ния к + *D*; **to show ~ to smb** относи́ться к кому́-л почти́тельно; **with all due ~ to the speaker...** при всём моём уваже́нии к докла́дчику...

deferential *adj* почти́тельный.

deferred *adj* (*of meetings*) отло́женный; (*of payments*) отсро́ченный.

defiance *n*: **he acted in ~ of the doctor's/of his director's orders** он не после́довал сове́ту врача́, он нару́шил прика́з дире́ктора; **I set him and his threats at ~** я не бою́сь его́ угро́з, *CQ* плева́л я на его́ угро́зы.

defiant *adj* вызыва́ющий; **his manner was ~** он вёл себя́ вызыва́юще.

deficiency *n* недоста́ток, нехва́тка; **a ~ of protein** недоста́ток протеи́на; **a ~ of raw material** нехва́тка сырья́; **mental ~** слабоу́мие.

deficient *adj*: **he's totally ~ in humour** он соверше́нно лишён чу́вства ю́мора; **a diet ~ in vitamins** недоста́ток витами́нов в пита́нии; **you can't say he's ~ in courage** его́ не обвини́шь в недоста́тке му́жества; **mentally ~** слабоу́мный.

deficit *n* недоста́ча; **a ~ of £100 was discovered** (была́) обнару́жена недоста́ча в сто фу́нтов; **I can't explain a ~ of £10 in my housekeeping accounts** (я) не зна́ю, на что я истра́тил э́ти де́сять фу́нтов.

defile *vt* (*pollute*) загрязн|я́ть (-и́ть).

definable *adj* определи́мый.

define *vt* определ|я́ть (-и́ть).

definite *adj* определённый, *also Gram*; **the time/plan is not yet ~** вре́мя ещё не назна́чено *or* не устано́влено, план ещё не вы́работан оконча́тельно; **he was very ~ about it** он э́то соверше́нно определённо сказа́л.

definitely *adv*: **we are ~ not going** мы то́чно туда́ не пойдём; **it's ~ impossible** э́то соверше́нно невозмо́жно; **did he say so?—Yes, ~** он так и сказа́л?—Да, и́менно так; **you will help me?—D.** вы помо́жете мне?—Коне́чно!; **you will come, won't you?—D.!** ты придёшь?—Обяза́тельно/Безусло́вно приду́!

definition *n* определе́ние.

definitive *adj* (*final*) оконча́тельный; *Lit* **a ~ biography** *approx* по́лная биогра́фия.

deflate *vt* (*let out air*) спус|ка́ть (-ти́ть); **to ~ a tyre** спусти́ть ши́ну; *Fin*: **to ~ the economy** сокра|ща́ть вы́пуск де́нежных зна́ков (-ти́ть); *fig* **he looked ~d** он был как в во́ду опу́щенный.

deflect *vt*: **the bullet was ~ed** пу́ля отскочи́ла рикоше́том; *fig* **to ~ smb from his purpose** отвле|ка́ть кого́-л от поста́вленной це́ли (-́чь).

deforest *vt*: **to ~ an area** обезле́сить ме́стность (*pf*).

deformed *adj* изуро́дованный.

deformity *n* (*state of being deformed or used of a deformed limb, etc.*) уро́дство; (*person*) уро́д.

defraud *vt* обма́н|ывать (-у́ть); **to ~ smb of smth** вы|ма́нивать что-л у кого́-л (-́манить); **he was ~ed of £1,000** у него́ вы́манили ты́сячу фу́нтов; *Law* **with intent to ~** с це́лью обма́на.

defray *vt*: **to ~ expenses** опла́|чивать расхо́ды (-ти́ть).

defrost *vt*: **to ~ a fridge/a chicken** размор|а́живать холоди́льник/ку́рицу (-о́зить); *Aut* **to ~ the windscreen** очи|ща́ть ото льда́ ветрово́е стекло́ (-́стить).

deft *adj* ло́вкий.

defunct *adj* (*of person*) поко́йный; (*of things*) **the law is ~** э́тот зако́н устаре́л.

defy *vt* **1** (*challenge*): **I ~ you to do it** даю́ го́лову на отсече́ние, вам э́того не сде́лать

2 (*resist, ignore*): **he openly defies public opinion/the law** он откры́то броса́ет вы́зов обще́ственному мне́нию, для него́ зако́н не пи́сан; **the pupils defied their teacher** ученики́ вызыва́юще вели́ себя́ с учи́телем; **we defied the weather and picnicked all the same** несмотря́ на плохýю погóду, мы всё же устрóили пикни́к

3 (*present insuperable difficulties*): **the problem defies solution** проблéма неразреши́ма; **the state of the kitchen defied description** беспоря́док на кýхне был/цари́л неописýемый.

degenerate *adj* (*mentally or physically*) дегенерати́вный; *fig* **I do not regard the young today as ~** я не считáю, что молодóе поколéние сейчáс хýже, чем бы́ли мы в своё врéмя.

degenerate *vi* вы|рождáться (-́родиться); *fig* **do not let economy ~ into meanness** пусть бережли́вость не перерастáет в скýпость.

degradation *n*: **he never recovered from the ~** э́то унижéние сломи́ло егó.

degrade *vt*: **to ~ smb in rank** пони|жáть когó-л в чи́не (-́зить); **to ~ oneself** уни|жáться (-́зиться); **don't ~ yourself by telling lies** не унижáйтесь до лжи.

degrading *adj* унизи́тельный.

degree *n* **1** *Math*, *Astron* грáдус; **10 ~s of frost/below zero** дéсять грáдусов морóза/ни́же нуля́; **at an angle of 40 ~s** под углóм в сóрок грáдусов; **~s of latitude/longitude** грáдусы широты́/долготы́

2 (*step*, *stage*) стéпень, *also Gram*; **a ~ of skill** стéпень мастерствá; **by ~s** постепéнно, мáло-помáлу (*advs*); **in some ~** до извéстной/нéкоторой стéпени; **in the highest ~/*CQ* to a ~** в вы́сшей стéпени; **not in the slightest ~** ни в малéйшей стéпени; *Gram* **~s of comparison** стéпени сравнéния

3 *Univ* стéпень.

deign *vi usu iron*: **in the end she ~ed to reply** наконéц онá соблаговоли́ла/соизвóлила отвéтить (*pfs*).

dejected *adj* удручённый, подáвленный.

delay *n* задéржка; **after an hour's ~** пóсле часовóй задéржки; **without ~** без задéржки, *CQ* без проволóчек.

delay *vti vt* задéрж|ивать (-áть); **our departure was ~ed by the weather** мы задержáлись с отъéздом из-за погóды; **the train was ~ed two hours by fog** пóезд опоздáл на два часá из-за тумáна; (*put off*) **the match was ~ed for an hour** матч начался́ на час пóзже

vi мéдлить (*impf*); **don't ~!** не мéдлите!, не мéшкайте!

delayed *adj*: **he's suffering from ~ shock after the accident** он попáл в автомоби́льную авáрию, и у негó тóлько сейчáс наступи́ла реáкция.

delegate *n* делегáт.

delegate *vt*: **he ~d the work to his assistant** он передáл э́ту рабóту своемý помóщнику, он поручи́л э́то сдéлать своемý помóщнику.

delegation *n* делегáция.

delete *vt* вы|чёркивать (-́черкнуть.)

deliberate *adj* (*intentional*) преднамéренный; (*slow*, *cautious*): **~ in speech** нетороплúвый в разговóре; **he entered the room with ~ steps** он не торопя́сь вошёл в кóмнату.

deliberate *vti vt* размышля́ть, обсуждáть (*only in impfs*), раздýмывать (*impf*); **we were just deliberating the question** мы как раз размышля́ли над э́тим вопрóсом/обсуждáли э́тот вопрóс; **we ~d what steps to take** мы раздýмывали, что дéлать дáльше/предприня́ть

vi: **he ~d for a long time whether to go or not** он дóлго колебáлся,/раздýмывал, идти́ емý и́ли нет.

deliberately *adv* (*on purpose*) нарóчно, преднамéренно; (*slowly*) неспéшно; (*cautiously*) осторóжно.

deliberation *n* **1** (*reflection*) размышлéние, обдýмывание; (*discussion*) дискýссия, обсуждéние; **after due ~** пóсле нéкоторого размышлéния; **what was the outcome of your ~s?** какóв результáт вáших обсуждéний?

2 (*care*, *attention*) осмотри́тельность; **with great ~** с величáйшей осторóжностью/осмотри́тельностью.

deliberative *adj*: **a ~ assembly** совещáтельный óрган.

delicacy *n* **1** тóнкость, нéжность; **~ of a material/of features** тóнкость матéрии/черт; **~ of skin** нéжность кóжи

2 (*sensitivity*): **he showed great ~ in leaving us alone** он из деликáтности остáвил нас одни́х; **a situation of some ~** весьмá щекотли́вое положéние; **the violinist played with great ~** скрипáч игрáл с таки́м изя́ществом

3 (*of food*) (**a ~**) лáкомство; **caviare is a great ~** чёрная икрá — большóе лáкомство.

delicate *adj* (*fine*) тóнкий, нéжный; (*fragile*) хрýпкий; **~ lace/work** тóнкое крýжево, тóнкая рабóта; **a ~ aroma/operation** нéжный *or* тóнкий арóмат, тóнкая оперáция; **a ~ plant/skin/shade of blue** нéжное растéние, нéжная кóжа, нéжный оттéнок голубóго; **a ~ child, ~ porcelain** хрýпкий ребёнок/фарфóр; **~ instruments/lungs** высокочувстви́тельные прибóры, слáбые лёгкие; *fig*: **a ~ question/hint** деликáтный вопрóс, тóнкий намёк; **the pianist has a ~ touch** э́тому пиани́сту свóйственна тóнкая манéра исполнéния.

delicious *adj* восхити́тельный, прелéстный; (*of food*) вкýсный; *CQ* **this duckling/dinner is simply ~** э́та ýтка — прóсто объедéние, обéд прóсто восхити́телен.

delight *n* востóрг, восхищéние, удовóльствие; **to my ~** к моемý востóргу/восхищéнию; **it's always a great ~ to be with them** быть с ни́ми — всегдá большóе удовóльствие; **to take ~ in...** получáть удовóльствие от + *G*; **the book is a sheer ~** читáть э́ту кни́гу — однó наслаждéние; **the ~s of country life** прéлести сéльской жи́зни.

delight *vti vt* восхи|щáть (-ти́ть); **his singing ~ed everyone** егó пéние восхищáло всех; **the scenery ~ed them** они́ восхищáлись прирóдой; **the audience were ~ed with his playing** пýблика былá в востóрге от егó игры́/исполнéния; (*answering a suggestion*): **~ed!** с удовóльствием!; **(I'm) ~ed to meet you** (я) óчень рад с ва́ми познако́миться; **we shall be ~ed to come** мы бу́дем о́чень ра́ды прийти́ к вам

vi: **he ~s in music** му́зыка доставля́ет ему́ большо́е наслажде́ние; **he ~s in teasing his sister** он лю́бит дразни́ть сестру́.

delightful *adj* восхити́тельный, очарова́тельный; замеча́тельный; **it was a ~ evening** ве́чер был восхити́тельный — удался́ на сла́ву; **a ~ girl/play** очарова́тельная де́вушка, замеча́тельная пье́са.

delightfully *adv* очарова́тельно; *CQ* **he's ~ vague** он так ми́ло/очарова́тельно рассе́ян.

delinquency *n* престу́пность; **juvenile ~** престу́пность несовершенноле́тних.

delinquent *n*: **juvenile ~** малоле́тний престу́пник.

delirious *adj* (*in fever*): **to be ~** быть в бреду́, бре́дить; *fig* **to be ~ with joy** быть вне себя́ от ра́дости.

delirium *n* бред; **~ tremens** бе́лая горя́чка.

deliver *vt* **1** достав|ля́ть (-́ить); **to ~ letters/goods** доста́вить пи́сьма/това́ры; **to ~ a message** переда|ва́ть поруче́ние (-́ть)

2 (*hand over*): **to ~ smb into the hands of the enemy** отда|ва́ть кого́-л в ру́ки врага́ (-́ть); **the mayor ~ed the keys of the town** мэр переда́л/вручи́л ключи́ го́рода

3 (*speech, etc.*): **to ~ a speech** произ|носи́ть речь (-нести́); **to ~ a lecture** *Univ* чита́ть ле́кцию, (*on special occasion*) выступа́ть с ле́кцией (проче́сть, вы́ступить); **to ~ an opinion** вы|ска́зывать мне́ние (-́сказать)

4 (*a blow, etc.*): **to ~ a blow/an attack** на|носи́ть уда́р (-нести́), атакова́ть (*impf and pf*)

5 *Med*: **to ~ a child** при|нима́ть младе́нца/ро́ды (*pl*) (-ня́ть).

deliverance *n* освобожде́ние; спасе́ние.

delivery *n* **1** (*of letters, etc.*) доста́вка; **~ of a telegram** вруче́ние телегра́ммы; **to pay on ~** опла́чивать при доста́вке; **cash on ~** нало́женным платежо́м, опла́та при доста́вке; *Comm* **bulk ~** ма́ссовая поста́вка; *attr*: **~ note/van** накладна́я, фурго́н для доста́вки

2 (*manner of speaking*) ди́кция

3 (*rescue*) освобожде́ние; спасе́ние

4 *Med* ро́ды (*pl*).

delta *n* де́льта (реки́).

delude *vt* обма́н|ывать (-у́ть); вводи́ть кого́-л в заблужде́ние (ввести́); **he ~d himself into thinking his wife would recover** он те́шил себя́ наде́ждой, что жена́ вы́здоровеет.

deluge *n* (*flood*) пото́п; (*violent rainfall*) ли́вень (*m*); *fig*: **a ~ of words/letters** пото́к слов/пи́сем; **a ~ of questions** град вопро́сов.

deluge *vt* (*flood*) затоп|ля́ть (-и́ть); навод|ня́ть (-и́ть); *fig*: **the editorial office was ~d with letters** реда́кцию завали́ли пи́сьмами; **he was ~d with requests** его́ засы́пали про́сьбами.

delusion *n* заблужде́ние; **he is under a ~** он заблужда́ется; *Psych* **he suffers from ~s** у него́ быва́ют галлюцина́ции.

delusive *adj* обма́нчивый, иллюзо́рный.

de luxe *adj* роско́шный; **a ~ hotel** оте́ль-люкс.

demand *n* **1** тре́бование; **the government turned down the miners' ~s** прави́тельство отве́ргло тре́бования шахтёров; **to meet/satisfy the ~s of the new regulations** удовлетворя́ть тре́бованиям (*D*) но́вых пра́вил; **I have many ~s on my time** у меня́ ка́ждая мину́та на счету́

2 *Comm* спрос; **supply and ~** спрос и предложе́ние; **~ for consumer goods** спрос на това́ры широ́кого потребле́ния; **this material is in great ~** э́та ткань по́льзуется больши́м спро́сом; *fig* **he is in great ~** на него́ большо́й спрос.

demand *vt* (*with concrete object*) тре́бовать + *A* (по-); (*with abstract object*: *ask as of right*) тре́бовать + *G or* + что́бы (по-); **they will ~ a health certificate from you** у вас потре́буют спра́вку о состоя́нии здоро́вья; **he ~ed an explanation from them** он потре́бовал у них объясне́ния; **they ~ that we apologize** они́ тре́буют, что́бы мы извини́лись; **I ~ to know the charge against me** я тре́бую объясни́ть мне, в чём меня́ обвиня́ют.

demented *adj* сумасше́дший; *CQ* **the children will drive me ~** де́ти меня́ с ума́ сведу́т.

demist *vt*: **to ~ the windscreen** включ|а́ть обогрева́тель пере́днего стекла́ (-и́ть).

demobilize *vt* демобилизова́ть (*impf and pf*).

democracy *n* демокра́тия.

democratic *adj* демократи́ческий.

demolish *vt* разруш|а́ть (-́ить); (*buildings only*) сноси́ть (снести́); *fig*: **to ~ smb's argument** разби́ть/опроки́нуть чьи-л до́воды (*pl*); *joc* **he ~ed a plate of potatoes** он уничто́жил таре́лку карто́шки (*collect*).

demolition *n* разруше́ние; снос; **this street is due for ~** дома́ на э́той у́лице подлежа́т сно́су.

demon *n* де́мон, бес; *CQ*: **he's a ~ for work** он рабо́тает как чёрт; (*of a child*) **he's a little ~** он чертёнок, он отча́янный озорни́к.

demonstrably *adv* я́вно.

demonstrate *vti vt* демонстри́ровать (про-); **to ~ a new carpet sweeper** демонстри́ровать рабо́ту но́вого пылесо́са; **to ~ new methods of teaching** демонстри́ровать но́вые ме́тоды обуче́ния; *Math* **to ~ a theorem** дока́з|ывать теоре́му (-а́ть)

vi Polit: **students were demonstrating outside the Embassy** студе́нты устро́или демонстра́цию пе́ред посо́льством.

demonstration *n* (*proof*) доказа́тельство, *also Math*; *Polit* демонстра́ция; **~ of a new aeroplane** пока́з но́вого самолёта.

demonstrative *adj* (*showing feelings*) экспанси́вный; *Gram* указа́тельный.

demonstrator *n* (*in laboratory*) демонстра́тор, лабора́нт; *Polit* демонстра́нт.

demoralize *vt* деморализова́ть (*impf and pf*).

demote *vt* пони|жа́ть по слу́жбе/в до́лжности (-́зить).

demure *adj* скро́мный; **she gave him a ~ smile** она́ засте́нчиво ему́ улыбну́лась.

den *n*: **a lion's/bear's/fox's ~** лóгово льва, медвéжья берлóга, лúсья норá; *CQ joc* **this is my ~** э́то моё лóгово/моя́ берлóга.

denial *n* (*refusal*) откáз; (*repudiation*) отрицáние; *off* опровержéние; **a ~ of help** откáз в пóмощи; **to take no ~** не принимáть откáза; **the government issued a strong ~** правúтельство опубликовáло категорúческое опровержéние; **a ~ of guilt** отрицáние винóвности.

denims *npl CQ* джúнсы.

denominator *n*: *Math* **common ~** óбщий знаменáтель (*m*).

denote *vt* означáть (*impf*), обознач|áть (-́ить); **let x ~ the sum received** допýстим, что x обозначáет полýченную сýмму.

dénouement *n* развя́зка.

denounce *vt*: (*to police*) **to ~ smb** до|носúть на когó-л (-нестú); **to ~ a treaty** денонсúровать договóр (*impf and pf*); **to ~ smb as an impostor** разоблач|áть когó-л как обмáнщика (-úть).

dense *adj* густóй; плóтный, *also Phys*; **a ~ forest/fog/crowd** густóй лес/тумáн, большáя толпá; *CQ* **he's utterly ~** он набúтый дурáк.

densely *adv* гýсто; **it's a ~ wooded/populated district** э́тот рaйóн—сплошны́е лесá, э́то густонаселённый рaйóн.

density *n* плóтность, *also Phys*.

dent *n* вмя́тина; **there's a ~ on the wing** на крылé машúны есть вмя́тина.

dent *vti vt*: **the wing got ~ed in the collision** в авáрии бы́ло помя́то крылó (машúны)

vi гнýться (по-); **this metal ~s easily** э́тот метáлл легкó гнётся.

dental *adj* зубнóй.

dentist *n* зубнóй врач.

denture *n* зубнóй протéз.

denuded *adj* обнажённый; **an area ~ of soil** учáсток землú, почтú лишённый пóчвы; **trees ~ of leaves** гóлые/обнажённые дерéвья; **a hillside ~ of trees** гóлый/безлéсный склон холмá; **rocks ~ of soil** гóлые скáлы; *fig* **he was ~ by his creditors of every penny** кредитóры не остáвили емý ни копéйки.

deny *vt* **1** отрицáть + *A or* + что (*impf*); **to ~ the existence of flying saucers** отрицáть существовáние летáющих тарéлок; **he denied having/using a revolver** он отрицáл налúчие у негó пистолéта/, что стреля́л из пистолéта; **he denied that he was guilty** он отрицáл свою́ винý; **do you ~ being there?/that you were there?** вы отрицáете, что там бы́ли?; **he denied all knowledge of the plot** он утверждáл, что ничегó не знал об э́том зáговоре

2 (*refuse*) откáз|ывать (-áть); **to ~ smb help** отказáть комý-л в пóмощи; **he denies himself nothing** он ни в чём себé не откáзывает.

deodorant *n* дезодорáнт.

depart *vti vt*: **to ~ this life** скончáться (*pf*)

vi **1** (*on foot*) уходúть (уйтú), (*by car, etc.*) уезжáть (уéхать); (*set off*) отправ|ля́ться (-́иться); (*get going*) *off* отбы|вáть (-́ть); (*of trains*) отходúть (отойтú), трó|гаться (-нуться); (*of planes*) улет|áть (-éть); (*of ships*) отплы|вáть (-́ть); **the train for Leningrad ~s at 12** пóезд на Ленингрáд отхóдит/отправля́ется в двенáдцать часóв; **the delegation is ~ing this morning** делегáция отбывáет сегóдня ýтром; **the train has just ~ed** пóезд трóнулся/тóлько что отошёл

2 (*diverge*): **to ~ from** отклон|я́ться (-úться); расходúться (разойтúсь); **to ~ from one's original plans** отклоня́ться от своúх первонáчальных плáнов; **this text ~s from the original** э́тот текст расхóдится с оригинáлом; **to ~ from one's usual routine** отказáться от привы́чного режúма/распоря́дка дня.

department *n* (*within a shop, ministry*) отдéл, (*branch in another place*) отделéние; *Univ* кáфедра; **the export/press ~** отдéл э́кспорта/печáти; **a government ~** *approx* министéрство; (*UK*) **the D. of Industry** министéрство промы́шленности; **the ~ of modern languages** кáфедра нóвых/совремéнных языкóв; *fig* **that's not my ~** э́то не в моéй компетéнции, э́то не по моéй чáсти; *attr*: **~ store** универсáльный магазúн, *abbr* универмáг.

departmental *adj* вéдомственный; *Univ approx* факультéтский.

departure *n* **1** (*on foot*) ухóд, (*by car*) отъéзд; (*of trains*) отправлéние, отхóд; **to take one's ~** уходúть, уезжáть, (*say farewell*) прощáться; **time of ~ 9.00** врéмя отправлéния 9.00; *attr*: **the ~ platform** платфóрма отправлéния

2 (*divergence*): **a ~ from the norm/the rules** отступлéние от нóрмы/от прáвил; **a ~ from tradition** отхóд от традúции; **a ~ from the subject** отклонéние от тéмы; *fig* **this is a new ~ for us** (*in shop, factory*) э́то нáша новúнка, *joc* (*at home, etc.*) э́то у нас нóвшество.

depend *vi* **1** *impers use*: **it ~s on circumstances** э́то завúсит от обстоя́тельств; **~ing what you mean by "common"** смотря́ что ты понимáешь под слóвом «óбщий»; **will you come to supper?—Well, it all ~s** ты придёшь ýжинать?—Не знáю, как полýчится/вы́йдет; **it ~s how I feel** смотря́ по томý, как я бýду себя́ чýвствовать; **it ~s whether my foot is better** э́то бýдет завúсеть от тогó, пройдёт ли моя́ ногá; **as far as it ~s on me** наскóлько э́то от меня́ завúсит

2 (*be conditional on, rely on*) завúсеть от + *G* (*impf*); **the success of the enterprise ~s on us ourselves** успéх дéла завúсит от нас самúх; **prices ~ on supply and demand** цéны завúсят от спрóса и предложéния; **she ~s too much on her mother** онá слúшком завúсит от мáтери; **he ~s on writing for his living** он зарабáтывает на жизнь литератýрным трудóм

3 (*trust*) по|лагáться на + *A* (-ложúться); надéяться на + *A* (*CQ* по-); **you can ~ on him** на негó мóжно положúться; **I was ~ing on him but he let me down** я понадéялся на негó, а он меня́ подвёл; **~ upon it, he'll come** он навернякá придёт.

dependable *adj* надёжный.

dependant *n* иждиве́нец.

dependence *n* зави́симость.

dependent *adj* зави́симый от + *G*; ~ **countries** зави́симые стра́ны; **it's ~ on the weather whether we go or not** пойдём мы и́ли нет, зави́сит от пого́ды; **she is ~ on her daughter** (*financially*) она́ на иждиве́нии у до́чери, (*in other ways*) она́ во всём зави́сит от до́чери; **he's totally ~ on sleeping pills** он не мо́жет засну́ть без снотво́рного.

depict *vt* изобра|жа́ть (-зи́ть).

depilatory *n* сре́дство для удале́ния воло́с.

deplete *vt* истощ|а́ть (-и́ть); **to ~ one's reserves** истощи́ть запа́сы.

deplorable *adj* приско́рбный; плаче́вный; **the cuts on education are quite ~** сокраще́ние расхо́дов на образова́ние кра́йне приско́рбно; **the house is in a ~ state** дом в плаче́вном состоя́нии; ~ **behaviour** отврати́тельное поведе́ние.

deplore *vt* сожале́ть о + *P* (*impf*); **I ~ my son's taste in music** я в отча́янии, что сы́ну нра́вится така́я му́зыка.

deploy *vt Mil* раз|вёртывать (-верну́ть).

depopulated *adj*: **to become ~** обезлю́деть.

deport *vt* вы|сыла́ть (-́слать).

deposit *n* **1** *Fin* депози́т, вклад в ба́нке; (*advance instalment*) зада́ток; (*security*) зало́г; **to place money on ~** внести́ де́ньги в банк на депози́т; *attr*: ~ **account** депози́тный счёт

2 (*sediment*) оса́док, отсто́й; (*of soil*) нано́с; *Geol* отложе́ние; **a ~ of dust** слой пы́ли; **a ~ of lime** известко́вое отложе́ние.

deposit *vt* **1** *Fin* класть в банк (положи́ть); (*pay initial instalment*) да|ва́ть зада́ток (-ть)

2 (*put down*) класть (положи́ть); (*sediment*) на|носи́ть (-нести́), (*if left by river*) намы|ва́ть (-́ть); **he ~ed the parcel on the table** он положи́л паке́т на стол; **the floods ~ed a thick layer of mud on the fields** па́водок (*sing*) оста́вил на луга́х то́лстый слой и́ла.

depositor *n Fin* вкла́дчик, депози́тор.

deposit receipt *n* распи́ска в получе́нии вкла́да.

depot *n* (*warehouse*) склад; храни́лище; *Mil* часть; (*US*) железнодоро́жная ста́нция; **bus/tram ~** авто́бусный/трамва́йный парк; **rail ~** железнодоро́жное депо́ (*indecl*).

depraved *adj* развращённый.

depreciate *vti vt* обесце́ни|вать (-ть); **to ~ the currency** обесце́нить валю́ту

vi обесце́ниваться; **property has ~d** со́бственность обесце́нилась.

depreciation *n* сниже́ние сто́имости; обесце́нка; (*due to wear and tear*) амортиза́ция; **you must allow for ~ when selling your car** продава́я автомаши́ну, учи́тывайте ски́дку на изно́с.

depress *vt* (*a lever, knob*) на|жима́ть (-жа́ть); (*make sad*) угнета́ть (*impf*); **bad weather always ~es me** плоха́я пого́да всегда́ угнета́юще де́йствует на меня́; *Comm* **trade is ~ed just now** сейча́с в торго́вле засто́й/(*more serious*) спад.

depressed *adj* (*in spirits*) уны́лый, пода́вленный; **to become/be ~** впасть в уны́ние, быть пода́вленным, быть в угнетённом состоя́нии; **I feel ~ about life** у меня́ хандра́; *Econ* **when the economy is ~** во вре́мя экономи́ческого засто́я.

depressing *adj* угнета́ющий; гнету́щий; **it's such ~ weather** така́я уны́лая/гнету́щая пого́да; **it's such a ~ book** э́ту кни́гу тяжело́ чита́ть; **it's been a ~ day for me** сего́дня у меня́ был о́чень тру́дный день.

depression *n* (*of mood*) депре́ссия, *also Med*; пода́вленное настрое́ние; *Econ* депре́ссия, засто́й; (*in ground*) лощи́на; *Meteorol* о́бласть пони́женного атмосфе́рного давле́ния; **nervous ~** не́рвное расстро́йство, депре́ссия; **a fit of ~** при́ступ меланхо́лии; **a ~ in industry** засто́й в промы́шленности.

deprivation *n* лише́ние; ~ **of one's political rights** лише́ние гражда́нских прав; **being unable to read is a great ~ to me** невозмо́жность чита́ть — для меня́ большо́е лише́ние.

deprive *vt* лиш|а́ть + *A* (*of person*) *and G* (*of things*) (-и́ть); **to ~ smb of his freedom** лиши́ть кого́-л свобо́ды; **I was ~d of the pleasure of a visit from my grandchildren** меня́ лиши́ли удово́льствия повида́ться с вну́ками.

deprived *adj*: ~ **children** обездо́ленные де́ти.

depth *n* **1** глубина́; **the ~ of a river/well** глубина́ реки́/коло́дца; **the ~ of cupboard** глубина́ шка́фа; **6 feet in ~** шесть фу́тов глубино́й; **don't go out of your ~ children** де́ти, не заходи́те сли́шком глубоко́; **he was out of his ~** *CQ* ему́ бы́ло с голо́вкой; *fig*: **I'm quite out of my ~ in physics** в фи́зике я по́лный профа́н; ~ **of knowledge** глубина́ зна́ний (*pl*); **a study in ~** глубо́кое иссле́дование

2 *pl* (**the ~s**) глубина́, глубь (*usu sing*); **the ~s of the ocean** глуби́ны океа́на; **in the ~s of the forest** в ча́ще ле́са; **she lives in a village in the ~s of the country** она́ живёт в како́й-то глухо́й дереву́шке; **in the ~s of winter** в разга́р зимы́; **in the ~s of despair** в глубо́ком отча́янии.

deputation *n* депута́ция; **let's send a ~ to speak to the head of the department** дава́йте пошлём к заве́дующему на́ших представи́телей (,что́бы они́ с ним поговори́ли).

depute *vt* поруч|а́ть (-и́ть); **he was ~d to act as host/to chair the meeting** ему́ поручи́ли принима́ть госте́й/вести́ собра́ние.

deputize *vi*: **he ~d for me when I was ill** он замеща́л меня́/он исполня́л мои́ обя́занности, когда́ я боле́л (*only in impfs*).

deputy *n* (*second in command*) замести́тель (*m*); **the ~ director** замести́тель дире́ктора, *CQ* замдире́ктора (*m, indecl*); **the director can't come himself but will send his ~/a ~** дире́ктор не мо́жет прийти́ сам, но он пришлёт своего́ замести́теля/представи́теля.

derail *vt usu pass*: **to be ~ed** сходи́ть с ре́льсов (сойти́).

deranged *adj*: **he is mentally ~** у него́ психи́ческое расстро́йство.

derelict *adj*: **a ~ ship/house** бро́шенный кора́бль, забро́шенный дом.

derestrict *vt* *Aut*: **they've ~ed our village** в на́шей дере́вне сня́то ограниче́ние ско́рости.

deride *vt* осме́|ивать (-я́ть), вы|сме́ивать (-смеять).

derision *n* осмея́ние, высме́ивание; **my suggestion was greeted with ~** моё предложе́ние бы́ло вы́смеяно; **he made himself an object of ~** он сде́лал из себя́ посме́шище.

derisive *adj* издева́тельский; **a ~ remark** издева́тельское замеча́ние.

derisory *adj* (*of quantity*): **the compensation offered to me was ~** мне предложи́ли смехотво́рную су́мму в ка́честве компенса́ции.

derivation *n* *Ling* дерива́ция; **a word of Latin ~** сло́во лати́нского происхожде́ния.

derivative *n* *Ling* дерива́т, произво́дное сло́во; *Chem* произво́дное.

derive *vti vt* извле|ка́ть (-́чь); **to ~ profit/benefit/pleasure from smth** извлека́ть дохо́д/по́льзу/удово́льствие из чего́-л

vi: **French ~s from Latin** францу́зский язы́к происхо́дит от лати́нского.

dermatitis *n* дермати́т.

derogatory *adj* пренебрежи́тельный

descend *vti vt* сходи́ть с + *G* (сойти́), спус|ка́ться с + *G* (-ти́ться); **to ~ the stairs/a hill** сойти́ *or* спусти́ться с ле́стницы/с горы́

vi спуска́ться, сходи́ть; *Aer* сни|жа́ться (-́зиться); (*of a balloon*) опус|ка́ться (-ти́ться); (*of origin*) происходи́ть (*impf*); **the road ~ed steeply to the shore** доро́га кру́то сбега́ла к бе́регу; **he ~s/is ~ed from a French family** он по происхожде́нию францу́з; **the estate ~s from father to son** име́ние перехо́дит от отца́ к сы́ну; **the enemy ~ed on them by night** враг напа́л на них но́чью; *CQ* **I ~ed on my friends for the night** я нагря́нул к друзья́м с ночёвкой; *fig* **he would never ~ to lying** он никогда́ бы не уни́зился до лжи.

descendant *n* пото́мок.

descent *n* (*coming down*) спуск; (*slope of a hill*) склон, отко́с, спуск; (*of aeroplane*) сниже́ние; (*ancestry*) происхожде́ние; **a parachute ~** спуск с парашю́том; **the ~ from the mountain to the valley takes two hours** спуск с горы́ в доли́ну занима́ет два часа́; (*attack*) **to make a ~ on** нападать на + *A*.

describe *vt* опи́с|ывать (-а́ть); **he ~s himself as a doctor** он называ́ет себя́ до́ктором; **I wouldn't ~ him as stupid** я бы не сказа́л, что он глуп; *Geom* **to ~ a circle** описа́ть окру́жность.

description *n* **1** описа́ние; **to give a detailed/faithful ~ of a place** дать подро́бное/правди́вое описа́ние ме́стности; **he answers to that ~** он подхо́дит под э́то описа́ние

2 (*sort*): **books of every ~** са́мые ра́зные кни́ги; **people of all ~s** лю́ди вся́кого ро́да и зва́ния, разношёрстная пу́блика.

descriptive *adj* описа́тельный.

desecrate *vt* оскверн|я́ть (-и́ть).

desert *n* пусты́ня; *attr*: **a ~ island** необита́емый о́стров.

desert *vti vt* (*abandon*): **to ~ one's family** поки|да́ть/брос|а́ть свою́ семью́ (-́нуть/-́ить); **his courage ~ed him** му́жество поки́нуло его́; **the streets were ~ed** у́лицы бы́ли пусты́нны; **the village had been ~ed because of the bandits** дере́вня опусте́ла из-за налётов банди́тов

vi Mil дезерти́ровать (*impf and pf*).

deserted *adj* (*empty of people*) пусты́нный, безлю́дный; (*uninhabited*) необита́емый; (*neglected*) забро́шенный; (*abandoned*) поки́нутый.

deserter *n* дезерти́р.

desertion *n* (*of wife, etc.*) ухо́д; *Mil* дезерти́рство; *fig* **~ of duty** невыполне́ние до́лга.

deserts *npl*: **to get one's ~** получи́ть по заслу́гам; **according to one's ~** по заслу́гам.

deserve *vti vt* заслу́ж|ивать + *G or* + *A* (-и́ть) [**NB** *G in more general statements, A in particular cases*]; **such behaviour ~s punishment** тако́е поведе́ние заслу́живает наказа́ния; **he ~d his prize** он заслужи́л э́ту награ́ду; **he ~d his punishment/his success** он понёс справедли́вое наказа́ние, успе́х его́ был заслу́женным; **this picture ~s special attention** э́та карти́на заслу́живает осо́бого внима́ния; **it's more than I ~** э́то бо́льше, чем я заслу́живаю

vi: **they ~ to win/to be helped** они́ должны́ победи́ть, им сто́ит помо́чь; **he ~s to be punished** его́ сле́дует наказа́ть; **he ~s well of his country** у него́ больши́е заслу́ги пе́ред ро́диной.

deservedly *adv* заслу́женно; по заслу́гам, по досто́инству.

deserving *adj* досто́йный + *G*; **a ~ cause** досто́йное де́ло; **she is a ~ case** ей сто́ит помо́чь.

design *n* **1** *Archit, Tech, etc.* прое́кт; (*in engineering*) констру́кция; *Art* компози́ция; (*pattern*) узо́р; **a ~ for a theatre** прое́кт зда́ния теа́тра; **he's working on a ~ for a new carburettor** он разраба́тывает но́вую констру́кцию карбюра́тора; **it's an engine of faulty ~** у э́того дви́гателя неуда́чная констру́кция; **I like the ~ of this camera/dress** мне нра́вится констру́кция э́того киноаппара́та/фасо́н э́того пла́тья; **the ~ of a painting** компози́ция карти́ны; **the carpet has a geometrical ~** на ковре́ геометри́ческий узо́р; **a material with a ~ of flowers** ткань в цвето́чек

2 (*plan, intention*) за́мысел, план; **evil ~s** злы́е/кова́рные за́мыслы; **by ~** наме́ренно, преднаме́ренно (*advs*); **he arrived late, whether by accident or ~** то ли случа́йно, то ли наме́ренно, но он опозда́л; **he has ~s on your daughter** он име́ет ви́ды на твою́ до́чку.

design *vti vt* **1** (*buildings*) проекти́ровать (с-); (*machinery*) конструи́ровать (с-); **to ~ a factory/a washing-machine** проекти́ровать заво́д, конструи́ровать стира́льную маши́ну; **to ~ dresses** созда|ва́ть но́вые фасо́ны пла́тьев (-́ть)

2 (*plan, intend*): **this course is ~ed for foreigners** э́ти ку́рсы (*pl*) предназна́чены для иностра́нцев; **we ~ed this room to be a nursery** мы отвели́ э́ту ко́мнату под де́тскую; (*on architect's plan*) **this room was ~ed to be my study** э́та ко́мната была́ заду́мана как мой кабине́т

vi: **he ~s for a big engineering firm** он рабо́тает констру́ктором на кру́пном промы́шленном предприя́тии; **he ~s for a fashion house** он моделье́р до́ма моде́лей.

designate *vt* (*mark out*): **the boundaries are clearly ~d on the map** грани́цы на ка́рте обозна́чены я́сно; (*appoint*): **I've been ~d his deputy** меня́ назна́чили его́ замести́телем; **he's been ~d ambassador to France** он назна́чен посло́м во Фра́нцию.

designer *n* диза́йнер; (*engineer*) констру́ктор; **a dress ~** модельéр.

designing *adj usu pejor* кова́рный; **a ~ woman** интрига́нка.

desirable *adj* **1** *predic* жела́тельный; **it is ~ that he should be present** жела́тельно, что́бы он прису́тствовал

2 *attr* (*usu in advertisements*): **this ~ property** э́то прекра́сное име́ние.

desire *n* жела́ние; **sexual ~** полово́е влече́ние; **at the ~ of** по жела́нию + *G*; **I have no ~ for fame/to travel** я не стремлю́сь к сла́ве, у меня́ нет охо́ты путеше́ствовать; **he got his heart's ~** его́ жела́ния (*pl*) осуществи́лись; **it was his ~ that we should go** э́то он пожела́л, что́бы мы пошли́.

desire *vt* жела́ть + *G*, + *inf or* + что́бы (по-); **whom do you ~ to see?** кого́ вы жела́ете ви́деть?; **he ~d me to go at once for the doctor** он настоя́л, что́бы я неме́дленно пошёл за врачо́м; **it leaves nothing to be ~d** ничего́ лу́чшего и жела́ть не на́до.

desist *vi* (*stop*): **to ~ from** пере|executава́ть + *inf* (-ста́ть); **could you please ~ from smoking?** не могли́ бы вы не кури́ть?

desk *n* (пи́сьменный/рабо́чий) стол; **he sits at his ~ all day** он весь день сиди́т за столо́м; **school ~** па́рта; *attr*: **~ work** канцеля́рская рабо́та; **I'm stiff after all this ~ work** у меня́ деревене́ет всё те́ло от до́лгого сиде́ния за пи́сьменным столо́м.

desolate *adj*: **a ~ valley** пусты́нная доли́на; **she sat ~ in a corner** она́ одино́ко сиде́ла в уголке́; **she was ~ when her son left** она́ о́чень тоскова́ла/горева́ла, когда́ сын уе́хал.

desolate *vt* опустош|а́ть (-и́ть), *also fig*; **the country lay ~d after the withdrawal of the enemy** отступа́ющий враг оставля́л за собо́й опустошённую зе́млю; *fig* **she is ~d by the death of her father** она́ тяжело́ пережива́ет смерть отца́.

despair *n* отча́яние; **in the depths of ~** в по́лном отча́янии; **he's the ~ of his teachers** он дово́дит учителе́й до отча́яния.

despair *vi* отча́|иваться в + *P* (-яться); **I ~ of success/of ever succeeding** я отча́ялся в успе́хе; **they ~ of his life** его́ состоя́ние безнадёжно.

desperate *adj* отча́янный; **a ~ gambler/remedy** отча́янный игро́к, после́днее сре́дство; **the economy of the country is ~** эконо́мика страны́ на гра́ни разру́хи; **I'm ~ to find any job at all** мне бы найти́ хоть каку́ю-нибудь рабо́ту.

desperately *adv* отча́янно; **he's ~ unhappy** он в по́лном отча́янии; *CQ*: **I was ~ trying to finish cooking before the guests arrived** я мета́лась по ку́хне как угоре́лая, стара́ясь пригото́вить обе́д к прихо́ду госте́й; **I'm ~ trying to finish by Tuesday** я прилага́ю отча́янные уси́лия (*pl*) зако́нчить всё ко вто́рнику.

desperation *n*: **in ~ I rang the doctor** в отча́янии я позвони́л врачу́.

despicable *adj*: **he's thoroughly ~** он настоя́щий подо́нок; **it's ~!** како́й стыд!, како́е безобра́зие!

despise *vt* презира́ть (*impf*); **he was ~d by his classmates** одноклассники его́ презира́ли; **he's an enemy not to be ~d** э́то нешу́точный проти́вник.

despite *prep* несмотря́ на + *A*; **~ the rain we went out** несмотря́ на дождь, мы вы́шли из дому; **~ our warnings** несмотря́ на на́ши предупрежде́ния; **~ what people say, she does sing well** что бы там ни говори́ли, она́ хорошо́ поёт.

despondent *adj* удручённый.

dessert *n* десе́рт; **what is there for ~?** что у нас на десе́рт?

dessertspoon *n* десе́ртная ло́жка.

destination *n* назначе́ние; **they arrived at their ~** они́ при́были к ме́сту назначе́ния; **what is your ~?** куда́ вы е́дете?

destine *vt usu pass* **1** (*be fated*): **his hopes were not ~d to be realized** его́ наде́ждам не суждено́ бы́ло сбы́ться; **they were ~d never to meet** им не судьба́ была́ встре́титься

2 (*be assigned, etc.*): **I hear your son is ~d for Moscow** говоря́т, что ваш сын получи́л назначе́ние в Москву́; **the cargo is ~d for London** груз отправля́ется в Ло́ндон; **his father ~d him for the army** оте́ц определи́л его́ на вое́нную слу́жбу.

destiny *n* судьба́.

destitute *adj*: **they were left ~** они́ оста́лись совсе́м без средств, они́ бы́ли доведены́ до нищеты́; **~ of** лишённый + *G*.

destroy *vt* разруш|а́ть (-ить); **the buildings were all ~ed** все зда́ния бы́ли разру́шены; **to ~ smb's hopes/health** разруша́ть чьи-л наде́жды/чьё-л здоро́вье; **to ~ an army** разби́ть а́рмию; **to ~ the enemy/papers** уничтож|а́ть врага́/бума́ги (-ить); **all his papers were ~ed in the fire** все его́ бума́ги сгоре́ли во вре́мя пожа́ра; **the frost ~ed the crops** моро́з погуби́л урожа́й (*sing*).

destroyer *n Naut* эска́дренный миноно́сец, эсми́нец.

destruction *n* разруше́ние; уничтоже́ние; **the ~ of our hopes** круше́ние на́ших наде́жд; **gambling was his ~** его́ погуби́ла страсть к аза́ртным и́грам.

destructive *adj* разруши́тельный; **~ criticism** убийственная/уничтожа́ющая кри́тика; **children can be very ~** ма́ленькие де́ти лю́бят всё лома́ть; **pigeons are very ~ in the garden** го́луби нано́сят са́ду большо́й уро́н.

desultory *adj*: **he made a few ~ remarks** он бро́сил не́сколько несвя́зных замеча́ний; **~ reading** бессисте́мное чте́ние; **I went for a ~ walk in a park** я бесце́льно броди́л по па́рку.

detach *vt*: **to ~ wires** отсоедин|я́ть провода́ (-и́ть); **I ~ed a key from the ring** я снял ключ с кольца́; **our carriage was ~ed at Minsk** наш ваго́н отцепи́ли в Ми́нске; **you can ~ the collar** воротни́к отстёгивается; **we got ~ed from the rest of the group** мы отдели́лись от гру́ппы; **~ the tear-off slip** оторви́те ни́жнюю часть бла́нка.

detached *adj*: **a ~ house** отде́льный дом; *fig* **I'm trying to be ~ about it** я стара́юсь относи́ться к э́тому объекти́вно.

detachment *n Mil* отря́д; *fig* объекти́вность, беспристра́стность; **he has an air of ~** у него́ отрешённый вид.

detail *n* дета́ль, подро́бность; **in ~** дета́льно, подро́бно (*advs*); **to go into ~** вдава́ться в подро́бности/в дета́ли (*pls*); **an unimportant ~** незначи́тельная *or* ме́лкая дета́ль/подро́бность; **that's a mere ~** э́то (про́сто) ме́лочь; **they worked it out to the last ~** они́ э́то разрабо́тали до мельча́йших подро́бностей (*pl*).

detailed *adj* дета́льный, подро́бный.

detain *vt* заде́рж|ивать (-а́ть); **he was ~ed at the office** он задержа́лся на рабо́те; **don't let me ~ you** я вас не задержу́; **he was ~ed by business/for further questioning** его́ задержа́ли дела́/для дальне́йшего рассле́дования.

detect *vt* обнару́ж|ивать (-ить); **we ~ed a gas leak** мы обнару́жили уте́чку га́за; **he was ~ed in the act of stealing** его́ пойма́ли на кра́же с поли́чным; **submarines can be ~ed by radar** подво́дные ло́дки мо́жно обнару́жить радиолока́тором; *joc* **do I ~ a lack of seriousness in your attitude?** мне ка́жется, вы не о́чень серьёзно отно́ситесь к э́тому.

detectable *adj*: **the sound is hardly ~** звук едва́ различи́м.

detection *n* раскры́тие, разоблаче́ние; **~ of a fraud** разоблаче́ние обма́на; **his absence escaped ~** его́ отсу́тствие прошло́/оста́лось незаме́ченным.

detective *n* детекти́в, сы́щик; *attr*: **~ force** сыскна́я поли́ция; **a ~ story** детекти́вный рома́н, детекти́в.

détente *n Polit* разря́дка (в междунаро́дных отноше́ниях).

detention *n*: **he spent an hour in ~ after school** его́ оста́вили на час по́сле уро́ков; *Law* (*before sentence*) содержа́ние под аре́стом; (*in prison*) тюре́мное заключе́ние.

deter *vt* заде́рж|ивать, уде́рж|ивать (*pfs* -а́ть); **we were ~red by the weather and stayed at home** непого́да задержа́ла нас до́ма; **I was ~red by the cost** цена́ останови́ла меня́.

detergent *n* (*for clothes*) стира́льный порошо́к; (*for dishes*) жи́дкость для мытья́ посу́ды.

deteriorate *vi* (*grow worse*) ухуд|ша́ться (-́шиться); **fruit ~s quickly in hot weather** фру́кты (*pl*) бы́стро по́ртятся на жаре́.

deterioration *n* ухудше́ние.

determinant *n* реша́ющий фа́ктор.

determination *n* **1** (*resolution*) реши́мость; **he showed great ~** он прояви́л большу́ю реши́мость; **he tackled the job with ~** он реши́тельно взя́лся за рабо́ту

2 (*deciding*) определе́ние; реше́ние; **the ~ of the exact meaning of a word can be difficult** быва́ет тру́дно определи́ть то́чное значе́ние сло́ва.

determine *vti vt* **1** определ|я́ть (-и́ть); **to ~ boundaries** определи́ть грани́цы; **to ~ the salinity of sea water** определи́ть/изме́рить солёность морско́й воды́; **prices are ~d by demand** це́ны определя́ются спро́сом; **this ~d us to accept the terms** э́то склони́ло нас приня́ть усло́вия

2 (*decide*) реш|а́ть (-и́ть); **we'll have to ~ what's to be done/whether to go** нам на́до реши́ть, что де́лать/идти́ и́ли нет

vi (*decide*) реша́ть, реша́ться [**NB** *reflex = to have the courage to take a final and considered decision*]; **he ~d to leave tomorrow/to break with his** wife он реши́л е́хать за́втра, он реши́лся порва́ть с жено́й; **we ~d on an early start** мы реши́ли отпра́виться ра́но.

determined *adj* **1** *attr* реши́тельный; **a ~ person** реши́тельный челове́к; **to make a ~ effort to** сде́лать реши́тельную попы́тку + *inf*

2 *predic*: **he's quite ~ to do it** он реши́тельно настро́ен сде́лать э́то; **he's ~ to see the Nile** он хо́чет во что́ бы то ни ста́ло побыва́ть на Ни́ле.

deterrent *n*: **the long journey is a bit of a ~ to me** тако́е дли́нное путеше́ствие немно́го пуга́ет меня́; *Mil* сде́рживающее сре́дство.

detest *vt*: **I ~ getting up early** я терпе́ть не могу́ ра́но встава́ть; **I ~ affectation in a man** мне проти́вна мане́рность в мужчи́нах (*pl*); **I ~ him/sweet wines** мне он о́чень неприя́тен, я не люблю́ сла́дкие ви́на.

detestable *adj* отврати́тельный.

detonate *vt* детони́ровать (*impf*).

detour *n* (*on foot*) обхо́д; (*in car*) объе́зд; **to make a ~** идти́ в обхо́д, е́хать в объе́зд, сде́лать крюк/объе́зд, *CQ* дать крю́ку (*D*); **we had to make a long ~** нам пришло́сь сде́лать большо́й крюк.

detract *vi*: **this does not ~ from his merit** э́то не умал|я́ет/не уменьш|а́ет его́ досто́инств (*pl*) (-и́ть/-́ить).

detriment *n* уще́рб, вред; **to the ~ of** в уще́рб/во вред + *D*; **I know nothing to his**

~ я не зна́ю о нём ничего́ предосуди́тельного.

deuce *n Cards* дво́йка; (*in tennis*) ра́вный счёт, «ро́вно!»; *CQ* **the** ~ *see* **devil 3.**

devaluation *n Fin* девальва́ция.

devalue *vt*: **to** ~ **the currency** про|води́ть девальва́цию (-вести́).

devastate *vt* опустош|а́ть (-и́ть); *fig* **we were simply** ~**d by the news of the defeat** изве́стие о пораже́нии пове́ргло нас в отча́яние.

devastating *adj* (*of storm, etc.*) разруша́ющий; *fig* **the professor's sarcasm could be** ~ профе́ссорский сарка́зм был поро́й уби́йственным.

devastatingly *adv CQ*: **she's** ~ **beautiful** она́ потряса́юще краси́ва.

devastation *n* опустоше́ние.

develop *vti vt* **1** раз|вива́ть (-ви́ть); **to** ~ **one's muscles** развива́ть мускулату́ру (*collect*); **to** ~ **industry/a business** развива́ть промы́шленность, ста́вить де́ло на широ́кую но́гу; **to** ~ **one's mind/an idea** развива́ть ум/иде́ю; **I've** ~**ed an interest in botany** у меня́ просну́лся интере́с к бота́нике; **my car has** ~**ed engine trouble** *CQ* у мое́й маши́ны стал барахли́ть мото́р; **he's** ~**ed a cough/measles/a habit of stammering** у него́ появи́лся ка́шель, он заболе́л ко́рью, он стал заика́ться

2 *specialized uses*: **to** ~ **mineral resources** разраба́тывать месторожде́ния поле́зных ископа́емых (*impf*); (*by building*) **to** ~ **waste land** застр|а́ивать пусты́рь (-о́ить); *Photo*: **to** ~ **a film** прояв|ля́ть плёнку (-и́ть); **the film has not yet been** ~**ed** плёнка ещё не проя́влена; *Mus* **to** ~ **a theme** развива́ть те́му; *Hort* **to** ~ **a new species of rose** вы|води́ть но́вый сорт ро́зы (-вести)

vi **1** (*progress*) развива́ться; **events** ~**ed fast** собы́тия развива́лись стреми́тельно; **how's your thesis** ~**ing?** как продвига́ется ва́ша диссерта́ция?

2 (*grow*): **symptoms of TB have** ~**ed** появи́лись при́знаки/симпто́мы туберкулёза; **plants** ~ **from seeds** расте́ния расту́т из семя́н; **the strike** ~**ed out of an industrial dispute** забасто́вка была́ сле́дствием произво́дственного конфли́кта; **Rotterdam has** ~**ed into one of the world's largest ports** Роттерда́м вы́рос в оди́н из крупне́йших порто́в ми́ра.

development *n* разви́тие; *Mus, Min* разрабо́тка; *Photo* проявле́ние; **what are the latest** ~**s?** каки́е после́дние но́вости?; ~ **of a theory/a plant/industry** разви́тие тео́рии/расте́ния/промы́шленности; **urban** ~ разви́тие городо́в; **a new** ~ **in literature** но́вое тече́ние в литерату́ре; *Hort* ~ **of a new strain** выведе́ние но́вого со́рта.

deviate *vi*: **to** ~ **from one's theme** отклон|я́ться от те́мы (-и́ться); **to** ~ **from tradition/the truth** отступ|а́ть от обы́чая, от|ходи́ть от и́стины (-и́ть, -ойти́).

deviation *n*: **a** ~ **from the norm** отклоне́ние от но́рмы; **a** ~ **from the original/the rules** отступле́ние от оригина́ла/от пра́вил; *Tech* **a** ~ **of the compass** девиа́ция ко́мпаса.

device *n* **1** (*trick*) приём; **the conjuror uses this** ~ **in order to** фо́кусник испо́льзует э́тот приём, что́бы + *inf*; *fig* **leave him to his own** ~**s** пусть он сам справля́ется

2 (*mechanical*) устро́йство; прибо́р; **a safety/nuclear** ~ предохрани́тельное/я́дерное устро́йство; **a labour-saving** ~ бытово́й прибо́р.

devil *n* **1** дья́вол, чёрт, бес

2 *CQ* (*of people*): **poor/lucky** ~**!** бедня́га!, везёт же ему́!; **he's a** ~ **for work** он рабо́тает как чёрт; **that boy is a little** ~ э́тот мальчи́шка—су́щий/настоя́щий чертёнок

3 *CQ* (*in these examples* **the devil** *is interchangeable with* **the deuce**): **where's my pen?—How the** ~ **should I know!** где моя́ ру́чка?—Где, где—отку́да я зна́ю!; **there'll be the** ~ **of a row** бу́дет грандио́зный/жу́ткий сканда́л; **we had the** ~ **of a job to get the wheel off** бы́ло черто́вски тру́дно снять колесо́; **what the** ~ **do you mean?** что вы име́ете в виду́, чёрт побери́?; **it's the** ~ **of a mess** здесь жу́ткий беспоря́док, чёрт но́гу сло́мит; **why the** ~ **didn't you help her?** како́го чёрта ты ей не помо́г?

devilish *adj* дья́вольский, черто́вский.

devilment, devilry *ns*: **he's up to some** ~ он опя́ть что́-то затева́ет; **she's full of** ~ в неё как бу́дто бес всели́лся.

devious *adj*: **we took a** ~ **route to avoid the traffic** мы пое́хали око́льным путём,/ *CQ* мы да́ли крю́ку, что́бы избежа́ть про́бки; *fig* (*of people, methods*) хи́трый; **he got rich by** ~ **means** он на́жил бога́тство нече́стным путём.

devise *vt* приду́м|ывать (-ать); **he** ~**d a gadget for cleaning windows** он приду́мал приспособле́ние для мытья́ о́кон.

devoid *adj*: ~ **of** лишённый + *G* [*often translated by adjs with prefix* без-]; **he's totally** ~ **of humour** он абсолю́тно лишён чу́вства ю́мора; ~ **of fear/shame** бесстра́шный, бессты́дный.

devolution *n Polit* переда́ча полномо́чий; *Econ* децентрализа́ция.

devolve *vi* пере|ходи́ть (-йти́); **if the director is ill, his duties** ~ **upon his deputy** когда́ дире́ктор бо́лен, его́ обя́занности исполня́ет зам (*abbr for* замести́тель).

devote *vt* посвя|ща́ть (-ти́ть); **to** ~ **one's life to music** посвяти́ть свою́ жизнь му́зыке; **he** ~**d himself to working with blind children** он посвяти́л себя́ рабо́те со слепы́ми детьми́; **she is** ~**d to her grandchild** она́ обожа́ет вну́ка.

devoted *adj*: **a** ~ **friend/husband** пре́данный друг, лю́бящий муж; **a** ~ **angler** стра́стный рыболо́в.

devotee *n*: **I'm a great** ~ **of the ballet/of hers** я большо́й покло́нник бале́та, я её большо́й покло́нник; **a** ~ **of football** люби́тель футбо́ла, боле́льщик.

devotion *n* **1** пре́данность + *D*

2 *pl* (~**s**) моли́твы; **he is at his** ~**s** он мо́лится.

devour *vt* (*of animals*) пожира́ть (*only in impf*; *for pf use* сожра́ть); **the lion was ~ing/had ~ed his prey** лев пожира́л/сожра́л свою́ добы́чу; *fig*: **to ~ a novel** проглоти́ть рома́н; **she was ~ed by curiosity** она́ умира́ла от любопы́тства.

devout *adj* благочести́вый.

devoutly *adv*: **I ~ hope** и́скренне наде́юсь.

dew *n* роса́; **wet with ~** мо́крый от росы́.

dextrous *adj* ло́вкий.

diabetes *n* диабе́т.

diabetic *n* диабе́тик; *attr* диабети́ческий.

diabolic(al) *adj* дья́вольский, сатани́нский; **~ cruelty** сатани́нская жесто́кость; **his cunning is ~** он дья́вольски (*adv*) хитёр.

diagnose *vt* диагности́ровать (*impf and pf*); **the doctor ~d diphtheria** врач поста́вил диа́гноз дифтери́и.

diagnosis *n* диа́гноз; **to make a ~** ста́вить диа́гноз; *fig* **my ~ of the situation is as follows...** вот как я объясня́ю сложи́вшуюся ситуа́цию...

diagonal *n* диагона́ль.

diagonal *adj* диагона́льный; **a jumper with ~ stripes** дже́мпер в косу́ю поло́ску.

diagonally *adv* по диагона́ли.

diagram *n* (*drawing*) схе́ма; (*chart*, *table*) диагра́мма; **to make a ~ of a gear box** начерти́ть схе́му коро́бки переда́ч; (*in technical book*) **see ~ number 7** смотри́ рису́нок семь (*abbr* см. рис. 7).

dial *n* (*of clocks*, *instruments*) цифербла́т; *Tel* набо́рный диск.

dial *vti vt Tel* на|бира́ть но́мер (-бра́ть); **~ the number** набери́те но́мер; **what number are you ~ling?** како́й но́мер вы набира́ете?; **~ the fire brigade** позвони́те в пожа́рную охра́ну

vi: **can I ~ direct (to England)?** э́то прямо́й телефо́н?, мо́жно ли отсю́да позвони́ть в А́нглию?

dialect *n* диале́кт, наре́чие; **local ~** ме́стный диале́кт, ме́стное наре́чие; **peasant ~** дереве́нский го́вор.

dialectics *npl* диале́ктика (*sing*).

dialling code *n* телефо́нный код.

dialling tone *n*: **when you hear the ~, dial your number** услы́шав непреры́вный гудо́к, набира́йте но́мер.

diameter *n* диа́метр; **2 feet in ~** два фу́та диа́метром.

diametrically *adv*: **~ opposed views** диаметра́льно противополо́жные мне́ния.

diamond *n* **1** (*uncut*, *and also as used by cutter*) алма́з; (*jewel*) бриллиа́нт, *also* брилья́нт; *attr*: **a ~ mine** алма́зная копь; **a ~ brooch** бриллиа́нтовая брошь; **a ~ wedding** шестидесятиле́тний юбиле́й, бриллиа́нтовая сва́дьба

2 *pl Cards* бу́бны; **the knave of ~s** бубно́вый вале́т.

diaper *n* (*US*: *nappy*) пелёнка.

diaphanous *adj* прозра́чный.

diarrhoea *n* поно́с, диаре́я; **to have ~** страда́ть поно́сом.

diary *n* (*official record or literary journal*) дневни́к; (*for engagements*) календа́рь (*m*); **to keep a ~** вести́ дневни́к; **I've put the date of the meeting down in my ~** я записа́л да́ту заседа́ния в свой календа́рь.

dice *npl* (*sing* **die**[1]) игра́льные ко́сти (*pl*); **I've lost one of the ~** я потеря́л одну́ кость; *attr*: **~ box** коро́бочка для косте́й.

dickens *npl euph for* **"devil"** *in* **"who the ~", "what the ~"**, *etc.*, *see* **devil 3.**

dicky[1] *n CQ* (*shirt front*) мани́шка.

dicky[2] *adj CQ*: **a ~ old man/chair** ве́тхий стари́к/стул; **a ~ old car** драндуле́т; **that table is a bit ~** э́тот стол шата́ется; **he has a ~ heart** у него́ се́рдце поша́ливает; **I feel a bit ~ after the flight** по́сле полёта я чу́вствую себя́ нева́жно.

dictaphone *n* диктофо́н.

dictate *n usu pl*: **the ~s of reason** веле́ние (*sing*) ра́зума; **I was guided by the ~s of conscience** я де́йствовал по веле́нию со́вести.

dictate *vti vt* диктова́ть (про-); **to ~ a letter** диктова́ть письмо́; **to ~ terms to the enemy** диктова́ть проти́внику усло́вия; **common sense ~s that...** здра́вый смысл подска́зывает, что...

vi: **he is dictating to his secretary** он дикту́ет секретарю́; **don't ~ to me!** не дикту́й мне!

dictation *n* (*in school*) дикта́нт; (*to secretary*) дикто́вка; **the teacher gave us ~** учи́тель дал нам дикта́нт; **to take down/write from ~** писа́ть под дикто́вку.

dictator *n* дикта́тор.

diction *n* вы́бор слов; язы́к; **poetic ~** язы́к поэ́зии; (*pronunciation*) ди́кция.

dictionary *n* слова́рь (*m*).

didactic *adj* дидакти́ческий.

die[1] (*sing of* **dice**) *only in fig*: **the ~ is cast** жре́бий бро́шен.

die[2] *vi* **1** умира́ть (умере́ть); погиб|а́ть (-́нуть); (*pass away*) сконча́ться (*pf*); **to ~ of old age/from wounds/by an enemy's hand** умере́ть от ста́рости/от ран, поги́бнуть от руки́ врага́; **to ~ in battle/in poverty** пасть *or* поги́бнуть в бою́, умере́ть в нищете́; **to ~ an early/violent death** ра́но *or* безвре́менно умере́ть/сконча́ться, умере́ть наси́льственной сме́ртью

2 (*of animals only*) до́хнуть (по-, из-); (*of flowers*) за|сыха́ть (-со́хнуть)

3 *fig CQ*: **I'm dying for a drink/to see you** умира́ю от жа́жды, мне до́ смерти хо́чется уви́деть вас

die away/down *vi* (*of wind*) затих|а́ть (-́нуть); (*of sound*) гло́хнуть (за-)

die off *vi*: **in the drought many plants ~d off** мно́гие расте́ния поги́бли от за́сухи

die out *vi* (*become extinct*: *of tribes*, *animals*) вы|мира́ть (-́мереть); (*of customs*) от|мира́ть (-мере́ть).

diehard *n and adj usu Polit* твердоло́бый.

Diesel engine *n* дви́гатель (*m*) Ди́зеля, ди́зель (*m*); *Rail* теплово́з.

Diesel oil *n* ди́зельное то́пливо.

diet *n* диéта; **I'm on a strict ~** я сижý на стрóгой диéте; **I prefer a light ~** я предпочитáю лёгкую пи́щу.

diet *vi*: **I am ~ing very strictly** я придéрживаюсь стрóгой диéты.

differ *vi* **1** отличáться (*only in impf*); различáться (*impf*); **the brothers ~ widely in character** брáтья си́льно отличáются по харáктеру; **the materials ~ in width** э́ти ткáни отличáются/различáются по ширинé; **their views ~** их взгля́ды расхóдятся; **the texts ~** в э́тих тéкстах есть расхождéния; **tastes ~** о вкýсах не спóрят, у кáждого свой вкус, на вкус, на цвет товáрища нет

2 (*disagree*): **I ~ from you there** тут я не соглáсен с вáми, тут нáши мнéния расхóдятся.

difference *n* **1** рáзница; разли́чие; отли́чие; **a ~ in height/temperature/weight** рáзница в рóсте/в температýре/в вéсе; **a ~ of £5** рáзница в пять фýнтов; **to pay/split the ~** уплати́ть рáзницу, подели́ть рáзницу попола́м; **it makes no ~ to me whether I go or not** мне всё равнó, пойдý я и́ли нет; **what ~ does it make?** какáя рáзница?; **a ~ in interpretation** разли́чие в интерпретáции; **this is the ~ between an English actor and his French counterpart** вот в чём отли́чие англи́йского актёра от францýзского, вот в чём рáзница мéжду англи́йскими и францýзскими актёрами; **there's a ~ in character between the brothers** у брáтьев рáзные харáктеры; **they don't get on because of the ~ in their characters** они́ не лáдят из-за несхóдства харáктеров

2 (*disagreement*): **a ~ of opinion** расхождéние во мнéниях; **to settle one's ~s** улáдить спор (*sing*).

different *adj* разли́чный; (*various*) рáзный; (*other*) другóй; **we hold ~ opinions** у нас разли́чные мнéния; **these shirts come in ~ colours** таки́е рубáшки есть рáзных цветóв; **the landscape looks ~ at times** пейзáж вы́глядит по-рáзному в рáзное врéмя; **I rang at three ~ times** я звони́л три́жды в рáзное врéмя (*sing*); **it's surprising how ~ temperatures can be in May** удиви́тельно, каки́е перепáды температýры мóгут быть в мáе; **that's quite a ~ story/matter** э́то совсéм другóе дéло; **I feel a ~ person now** тепéрь я чýвствую себя́ совсéм други́м человéком; **your method is ~ from mine** ваш спóсоб отличáется от моегó.

differential *n Math, Tech* дифференциáл.

differentiate *vti* различ|áть + *A* (-и́ть); отлич|áть от + *G* (-и́ть); разграни́ч|ивать + *A* (-ить); **to ~ poetry from prose/between poetry and prose** отличи́ть поэ́зию от прóзы, различи́ть *or* разграни́чить поэ́зию и прóзу; **to ~ varieties of plants** различáть ви́ды растéний; **this ~s good poetry from bad** э́то и отличáет хорóшие стихи́ от плохи́х; **I can't ~ between cheap and expensive wines** я не отличý дешёвое винó от дорогóго; **languages became ~d through time** языки́ с течéнием врéмени всё бóльше отличáлись друг от дрýга.

difficult *adj* трýдный; **a ~ disposition/child** трýдный харáктер/ребёнок; **it's ~ to choose** трýдно выбирáть; **he's ~ to please** емý трýдно угоди́ть; **she's ~ to get on with** с ней трýдно (лáдить).

difficulty *n* затруднéние; трýдность; **to be in a ~** быть в затруднéнии, быть в затрудни́тельном положéнии; **he's in financial difficulties** у негó дéнежные затруднéния; **the ~ lies in the fact that...** трýдность в том, что...; **with/without ~** с трудóм, без трудá; **I have ~ in breathing** я дышý с трудóм; **we're having ~ in getting enough teachers** у нас трýдно с подбóром учителéй; **I have ~ in understanding Kant** Кант мне трýден (для понимáния); **he's having difficulties with his wife** у негó с женóй нелáды́; **he raised no difficulties** он не возражáл; **he made difficulties when we were late** он нам устрóил из-за опоздáния скандáл.

diffidence *n* (*lack of confidence*) неувéренность в себé; (*shyness*) застéнчивость; **with ~** неувéренно, застéнчиво (*advs*).

diffident *adj* неувéренный (в себé); (*when used of oneself*) **I'm ~ about...** я стесня́юсь + *inf*.

diffuse *adj*: **a ~ light/style** рассéянный свет, многослóвный стиль.

dig *n* **1**: **he gave me a ~ with his elbow** он ткнул меня́ лóктем; *fig*: **to have a ~ at smb** подпусти́ть шпи́льку комý-л; **that was a ~ at me** э́то был кáмешек в мой огорóд

2 *Archaeol*: **I'm going on a ~ in Greece** я éду на раскóпки (*pl*) в Грéцию.

dig *vti vt* копáть (*impf*), рыть (вы́-) *and compounds*; **to ~ a hole/a well** вы́копать *or* вы́рыть я́му/колóдец; **to ~ potatoes** копáть картóшку (*collect*); **a fox has dug his earth in our garden** лиси́ца вы́рыла себé норý в нáшем садý; **the dog dug his teeth into my trousers** собáка вцепи́лась в мои́ брю́ки; **to ~ smb in the ribs** ты́кать когó-л в бок (ткнуть)

vi копáть; **he's ~ging in the garden** он копáет в садý; **to ~ for gold** искáть зóлото (*impf*); *fig* **he had to ~ into his pocket to buy that car** емý пришлóсь вы́вернуть все кармáны, чтóбы купи́ть э́ту маши́ну; *CQ* (*lodge*) **I ~ with my professor's family** я живý в семьé своегó учи́теля

dig down *vi*: **to ~ down to the foundations** рас|кáпывать фундáмент (*sing*) (-копáть); **we had to ~ well down to find the pipe** нам пришлóсь поря́дочно покопáть зéмлю, чтóбы найти́ трýбу

dig in *vt*: **to ~ in manure** вноси́ть удобрéние в зéмлю (внести́); *fig CQ*: **I dug my toes/heels in about that** тут я упёрся; **he's well dug in by now** (*to a job*) он ужé хорошó окопáлся на э́том мéсте

dig up *vt*: **they have dug up the road in order to lay drains** они́ раскопáли дорóгу, чтóбы проложи́ть трýбы; **he dug up a Greek vase** он откопáл грéческую вáзу; *fig* **where did you ~ up that old bicycle?/that scandal?** где ты откопáл э́тот стáрый велосипéд?, как ты разню́хал об э́том скандáле?

digest[1] *n* крáткое изложéние.

digest[2] *vt* (*food*) перевáр|ивать (-и́ть); (*assimilate*) усв|áивать (-óить), *both also fig*; **the body ~s fish more easily than meat** органи́зм усвáивает ры́бу лýчше, чем мя́со; **chicken is easily ~ed** цыплёнок легкó перевáривается; *fig* **I need time to ~ what I have read** мне нýжно врéмя, чтóбы перевари́ть прочи́танное.

digestible *adj* удобовари́мый.

digestion *n* пищеварéние; **he has a poor ~** у негó плохóе пищеварéние.

digestive *adj* пищевари́тельный; **~ trouble** расстрóйство пищеварéния/желýдка, несварéние желýдка.

digging *n* копáние; рытьё.

digit *n* однознáчное числó.

digital *adj*: **a ~ watch** цифровы́е часы́.

dignified *adj* достóйный; **a ~ old lady** достóйная стáрая дáма; **to behave in a ~ way** вести́ себя́ с достóинством/достóйно (*adv*).

dignity *n* достóинство; **it should be beneath your ~ to listen to such gossip** слýшать подóбные сплéтни (*pl*) недостóйно тебя́.

digress *vi* отступ|áть, отклон|я́ться, от|ходи́ть от + *G* (-и́ть, -и́ться, -ойти́); **but I ~** но я отклоня́юсь от тéмы.

digression *n* отступлéние, отклонéние.

digs *npl CQ*: **she didn't like the hostel and is living in ~** ей не понрáвилось общежи́тие, и онá снялá кóмнату; **what are your ~ like?** какáя у тебя́ кóмната?

dike *n see* **dyke.**

dilapidated *adj* вéтхий; **a ~ old house/hat/car** вéтхий дóмик, стáрая, мя́тая шля́па, *CQ* драндулéт.

dilate *vti vt* расшир|я́ть (-́ить); **his pupils were ~d** у негó расши́рились зрачки́, у негó бы́ли расши́ренные зрачки́

vi **1** расширя́ться

2: to ~ on a subject распространя́ться на тéму (*only in impf*).

dilatory *adj* медли́тельный.

dilemma *n* дилéмма; **to be in a ~** стоя́ть пéред дилéммой.

diligence *n* усéрдие, старáтельность; **to work with ~** усéрдно/старáтельно рабóтать.

diligent *adj* усéрдный, старáтельный.

dill *n* укрóп.

dillydally *vi CQ* тянýть, мéдлить (*impfs*); **don't ~!** не тяни́!

dilute *vt* разбав|ля́ть (-́ить); **to ~ wine with water** разбáвить винó водóй.

dim *adj* (*of light*) тýсклый; (*indistinct*) смýтный; **~ lighting** тýсклое освещéние; **~ outlines** смýтные очертáния; **the room was ~** в кóмнате был полумрáк; **his sight is getting ~** у негó слабéет зрéние; **~ memories** смýтные воспоминáния; *CQ* **he's pretty ~** он изря́дный тупи́ца.

dim *vt*: **the stage lights were ~med** освещéние (*sing*) сцéны бы́ло приглушённым; *Aut*: **to ~ one's headlights** включ|áть бли́жний свет (-и́ть); **his headlights were not ~med** у негó был включён дáльний свет; (*passenger to driver*) **~ your lights** переключи́ свет [**NB** *also can mean "turn up your lights", according to situation*].

dimension *n* размéр; *Math* измерéние; **a house of average ~s** дом обы́чных размéров; (*of volume*) **a cistern of large ~s** бак большóго объёма.

diminish *vti* уменьш|áть(ся) (-́ить(ся)).

diminution *n* уменьшéние.

diminutive *adj* (*tiny*) крóхотный, малю́сенький; *Gram* уменьши́тельный; *also as n* уменьши́тельное существи́тельное.

dimple *n* я́мочка.

din *n* шум; **the children are making a terrible ~** дéти ужáсно шумя́т.

din *vt*: **to ~ smth into smb/into smb's head** вдáлбливать что-л комý-л в гóлову (вдолби́ть); **I had it ~ned into me when I was child that...** мне ещё в дéтстве вдáлбливали (в гóлову), что...

dine *vti vt*: **they ~d me very well** они́ угости́ли меня́ хорóшим обéдом; **this table/room ~s 10 comfortably** за э́тим столóм/в э́той кóмнате вполнé мóгут обéдать дéсять человéк

vi обéдать (по-); **we ~d off roast beef** на обéд мы éли рóстбиф; **to ~ out** обéдать не дóма; *fig CQ* **I've been dining out on that funny story of yours** я с больши́м успéхом расскáзываю в гостя́х э́тот твой анекдóт.

diner *n Rail* вагóн-ресторáн.

ding-dong *interj* динь-дóн!; *as adj*: **a ~ argument was in process** шёл шýмный спор.

dinghy *n* мáленькая лóдка; **a rowing/sailing/rubber ~** я́лик, пáрусная/рези́новая лóдка.

dingy *adj* (*of colour*) тýсклый; **a ~ room** (*depressing*) уны́лая/(*dirty-looking*) захламлённая *or* непри́бранная кóмната; **a ~ town** захудáлый городи́шко (*m*).

dining *adj*: **~ room/table** столóвая, обéденный стол; *Rail* **~ car** вагóн-ресторáн.

dinner *n* обéд; **a formal ~** официáльный обéд, банкéт; **to have/take/eat ~** обéдать; **to give a ~** устрóить/дать обéд; **he gave me ~ in a restaurant** он угости́л меня́ обéдом в ресторáне; *attr*: **~ party** обéд; **~ hour** обéденное врéмя, (*break for dinner*) обéденный переры́в; **~ service** обéденный серви́з; **~ jacket** смóкинг.

dint *n*: **by ~ of** посрéдством + *G*.

dip *n* **1** (*slope*) уклóн; **the ~ of the horizon** наклонéние ви́димого горизóнта; **careful, there's a ~ in the road here** осторóжно, здесь дорóга идёт чéрез неглубóкий оврáг

2 *CQ* (*bathe*) купáние; **to take a ~** искупáться; **I'm going for a quick ~** я пойдý искупáюсь; **sheep ~** раствóр для купáния овéц; *fig* **a lucky ~** лотерéя.

dip *vti vt*: **to ~ one's fingers in water**

погру|жа́ть/окун|а́ть па́льцы в во́ду (-зи́ть/-у́ть); **to ~ a spoon into the soup** окуну́ть/опусти́ть ло́жку в суп; **to ~ one's pen in ink** обма́к|ивать перо́ в черни́ла (*pl*) (-ну́ть); **he ~ped his hand into the sack** он запусти́л ру́ку в мешо́к; **to ~ a flag** приспус|ка́ть флаг (-ти́ть); (*dye*) **to ~ a dress** кра́сить пла́тье (по-); *Aut* **to ~ one's headlights** вклю-ч|а́ть бли́жний свет (-и́ть), *see also* **dim** *vt*

vi **1** (*slope down*): **the road ~s towards the shore** доро́га спуска́ется к бе́регу; (*move down*) **the sun ~ped below the horizon** со́лнце ушло́ за горизо́нт; **the birds rose and ~ped as they flew** пти́цы носи́лись вверх и вниз

2 *fig uses*: **to ~ into a book** загляну́ть в кни́гу (*usu pf*); **I had to ~ into my holiday money to pay the electricity bill** что́бы оплати́ть счёт за электри́чество, мне пришло́сь запусти́ть ру́ку в де́ньги, отло́женные на о́тпуск.

diphtheria *n* дифтери́я.

diploma *n* дипло́м; **a ~ in engineering/education** дипло́м инжене́ра/педаго́га.

diplomacy *n* диплома́тия; (*tact*) дипломати́чность, такт; **the dean dealt with the situation with great ~** дека́н о́чень дипломати́чно спра́вился с э́той ситуа́цией.

diplomat *n* диплома́т.

diplomatic *adj* дипломати́ческий; (*tactful*) дипломати́чный, такти́чный.

dipstick *n Aut* указа́тель (*m*) у́ровня ма́сла, *CQ* щуп.

direct *adj* прямо́й, *also Gram*; (*immediate*) непосре́дственный; **a ~ person/reply/heir/descendant** прямо́й челове́к/отве́т/насле́дник/пото́мок; **a ~ hit** прямо́е попада́ние; **~ contact** непосре́дственный конта́кт; **in a ~ line with** на одно́й ли́нии с + *I*; **a ~ contradiction** по́лное противоре́чие; *Gram* **~ statement** пряма́я речь; *Elec* **~ current** постоя́нный ток.

direct *adv* пря́мо; **the train goes ~ to Oxford** по́езд идёт пря́мо до О́ксфорда, переса́живаться не на́до (*without changing*)/без остано́вок (*non-stop*).

direct *vt* **1** направ|ля́ть (-́ить); **he ~ed me the wrong way** он неве́рно указа́л мне доро́гу; **I ~ed the letter to his office** я отпра́вил письмо́ ему́ на рабо́ту; **I'm ~ing all my energies towards finishing the dictionary** я отдаю все свои́ си́лы заверше́нию словаря́; **can you ~ me to the station?** скажи́те, пожа́луйста, как пройти́ на вокза́л?; **to ~ one's gaze towards smth** обраща́ть взгляд/взор на что-л; **may I ~ your attention to a misprint?** позво́льте обрати́ть ва́ше внима́ние на опеча́тку

2 (*manage*) руководи́ть + *I* (*impf*); **to ~ a business** руководи́ть предприя́тием; **to ~ a film/play** быть режиссёром фи́льма, ста́вить пье́су (по-)

3 (*order*): **he ~ed that the baggage be sent in advance** он распоряди́лся отпра́вить бага́ж зара́нее; **I've done as you ~ed** я сде́лал, как вы сказа́ли.

direction *n* **1** направле́ние; **in the ~ of Moscow** по направле́нию к Москве́; **he went off in the opposite ~** он ушёл в противополо́жном направле́нии; **they scattered in all ~s** они́ рассы́пались во все сто́роны; **from all ~s** со всех сторо́н; **they left in different ~s** они́ разошли́сь в ра́зные сто́роны; **he has no sense of ~** он пло́хо ориенти́руется

2 (*management*) руково́дство + *I*; **this department is under the ~ of Ivanov** э́тот отде́л возглавля́ет (това́рищ) Ивано́в; **under the ~ of the new manager the factory increased its output** при но́вом дире́кторе фа́брики вы́пуск проду́кции увели́чился

3 (*instruction*) инстру́кция, указа́ние; (*order*) распоряже́ние; (*written*) предписа́ние; **~s for use** инстру́кция (*sing*), пра́вила по́льзования; **the ~s on the parcel were wrong** посы́лка была́ непра́вильно адресо́вана; *Theat* (*in written play*) **stage ~** (а́вторская) рема́рка.

directive *n* директи́ва.

directly *adv*: **he looked ~ at her** он посмотре́л ей пря́мо в глаза́; **he is ~ descended from Scott** он прямо́й пото́мок Ско́тта; **he is ~ responsible for the export department** он непосре́дственно отвеча́ет за рабо́ту отде́ла э́кспорта; **I work ~ to him** он мой непосре́дственный нача́льник; **we are ~ affected by this rule** э́то пра́вило отно́сится непосре́дственно к нам; **our house is ~ opposite the theatre** наш дом (нахо́дится) пря́мо напро́тив теа́тра; **I'll be with you ~** я сейча́с приду́; **he came ~** он пришёл сра́зу.

directly *conj*: *CQ* **tell me ~ you hear from her** как то́лько полу́чишь от неё письмо́, сра́зу же сообщи́ мне.

directness *n* прямота́.

director *n* дире́ктор; *Theat* режиссёр; **~'s office** кабине́т дире́ктора, дире́кция.

directory *n* спра́вочник; **telephone ~** телефо́нный спра́вочник; **~ enquiries** телефо́нная спра́вочная (*sing*).

dirt *n* грязь; (*loose earth*) земля́ грунт; *fig* **he treats him like ~** он о́чень пло́хо к нему́ отно́сится; *attr*: **a ~ road** грунтова́я доро́га.

dirt-cheap *adj and adv CQ*: **these carpets are ~** э́ти ковры́ на удивле́ние дёшевы; **I bought it ~** я купи́л э́то по дешёвке/за бесце́нок.

dirt track *n Sport* трек для мотоцикле́тных го́нок.

dirty *adj* гря́зный; **~ work** гря́зная/(*of dustmen, etc.*) чёрная рабо́та; **a ~ green** гря́зно-зелёный цвет; (*of weather*) **a ~ night** нена́стная ночь; **~ stories** неприли́чные анекдо́ты; *CQ* (*mean*): **a ~ trick** по́длый посту́пок; *as n*: **to do the ~ on smb** сде́лать кому́-л па́кость.

disability *n*: **he has/suffers from a ~** у него́ есть физи́ческий недоста́ток; *attr*: **he's got a ~ pension** у него́ пе́нсия по нетрудоспосо́бности.

disabled *adj* (*crippled*) искале́ченный; (*unable to work*) нетрудоспосо́бный; **he is ~** он инвали́д; **seats for the ~** места́ для инвали́дов.

disabuse *vt*: **we must ~ him of the idea that...** его́ на́до разуве́рить в том, что...

disadvantage *n*: **this car has two ~s** в э́той маши́не два недоста́тка; **sometimes it's a ~ to be tall** иногда́ высо́кий рост меша́ет; **we sold the house to our ~** мы про́дали дом с убы́тком для себя́; **he's at a ~ here as he can't speak the language** он здесь я́вно в ху́дшем положе́нии, потому́ что он не понима́ет языка́.

disadvantageous *adj* невы́годный; **the terms are ~ to us** э́ти усло́вия нам невы́годны; **it shows him in a ~ light** э́то представля́ет его́ в невы́годном све́те.

disagree *vi* **1** (*quarrel*) спо́рить (по-); **to ~ with** не согла|ша́ться с + *I* (-си́ться); **he and I always ~** мы с ним всегда́ спо́рим; **we ~d about who should pay** мы поспо́рили, кому́ плати́ть; **we ~d about the charge for the room** мы не смогли́ договори́ться о пла́те за ко́мнату; **I ~ with her/with part of the report** я не согла́сен с ней, я не во всём согла́сен с э́тим докла́дом; **we ~ on this point** мы в э́том расхо́димся

2 (*be different*): **the two reports ~** э́ти два отчёта си́льно отлича́ются друг от дру́га; **the circumstantial evidence ~s with the facts** ко́свенные ули́ки (*pl*) противоре́чат фа́ктам; **their evidence ~s with that of the policeman** их показа́ния (*pl*) расхо́дятся с показа́ниями полице́йского

3 (*have bad effects*): **fatty food/the climate ~s with her** жи́рная пи́ща ей вредна́, э́тот кли́мат ей вре́ден *or* противопока́зан.

disagreeable *adj* неприя́тный.

disagreement *n* **1** (*disparity*): **there's a ~ in the evidence of the witnesses** есть разногла́сие в показа́ниях (*pl*) свиде́телей; **there's considerable ~ between the two versions** ме́жду э́тими двумя́ ве́рсиями име́ется значи́тельное расхожде́ние

2 (*failure to agree*): **he expressed his ~ with the decision** он вы́разил несогла́сие с э́тим реше́нием; **he is in ~ with the plan** он не согла́сен с э́тим пла́ном; **there's ~ in the committee on this question** в коми́ссии есть разногла́сия (*pl*) по э́тому вопро́су; **a ~ between husband and wife** семе́йная ссо́ра, ссо́ра ме́жду му́жем и жено́й.

disallow *vt Law*: **to ~ a claim** отклон|я́ть прете́нзию (-и́ть); *Sport*: **the goal was ~ed** гол не́ был засчи́тан.

disappear *vi* исчез|а́ть (-́нуть); **where did you ~ to?** куда́ ты исче́з?; **my ring has ~ed** моё кольцо́ пропа́ло/исче́зло; **he ~ed without trace/into thin air** он бессле́дно исче́з, он как сквозь зе́млю провали́лся; **the snow soon ~ed** снег ско́ро сошёл; **the ship ~ed over the horizon** кора́бль скры́лся за горизо́нтом.

disappearance *n* исчезнове́ние; пропа́жа; **the ~ of the manager/of the money is a mystery** куда́ ушёл заве́дующий — никто́ не зна́ет, пропа́жа де́нег про́сто необъясни́ма.

disappoint *vt* разочаро́в|ывать (-а́ть); **his results have ~ed me** его́ результа́ты меня́ разочарова́ли; **I was ~ed in you/with the book** я разочарова́лся в тебе́/в э́той кни́ге; **she was ~ed with her present** пода́рок разочарова́л её; **I was ~ed not to find/at not finding her at home** я был огорчён, не заста́в её до́ма; **I'm afraid I'll have to ~ you** бою́сь, что придётся тебя́ разочарова́ть/, что я тебя́ разочару́ю.

disappointing *adj*: **the weather was ~ on our holiday** нам не повезло́ (*impers*) с пого́дой во вре́мя о́тпуска; **it's ~ that our son didn't get into Cambridge** оби́дно, что наш сын не поступи́л в Ке́мбридж.

disappointment *n* разочарова́ние; **to my great ~** к моему́ глубо́кому разочарова́нию; **the holiday was a great ~** о́тпуск был сплошны́м разочарова́нием; **he's a big ~ to us** он нас глубоко́ разочарова́л [**NB** *tense*]; **~ in love** разочарова́ние в любви́.

disapproval *n* неодобре́ние; **he expressed his ~ of my decision/of what had been done** он не одо́брил моё реше́ние/того́, что бы́ло сде́лано; **he frowned in ~** он неодобри́тельно нахму́рился.

disapprove *vi* не одобр|я́ть (-́ить); **he ~d of my choice** он не одо́брил мой вы́бор; **I ~ of men using scent** мне не нра́вится,/я не люблю́, когда́ мужчи́ны по́льзуются духа́ми; **I wanted to accept the invitation but father ~d** я хоте́л бы́ло приня́ть приглаше́ние, но оте́ц прояви́л недово́льство.

disapproving *adj* неодобри́тельный.

disarm *vt* обезору́ж|ивать (-ить), *also fig*; *fig* **her smile ~ed me** её улы́бка обезору́жила меня́.

disarmament *n* разоруже́ние; *attr*: **~ talks** перегово́ры по разоруже́нию.

disarray *n*: **in ~** в беспоря́дке.

disaster *n* бе́дствие; **the expedition met with ~** уча́стники экспеди́ции попа́ли в беду́; **to court ~** накли́кать беду́ на себя́; *CQ* **my cake was a ~** мой пиро́г не уда́лся.

disastrous *adj* губи́тельный; **a ~ policy, ~ floods** ги́бельная поли́тика, губи́тельное наводне́ние (*sing*); *CQ* **it was a ~ journey** пое́здка была́ про́сто кошма́рной.

disbelief *n* неве́рие.

disc *n* диск; *Med* **slipped ~** смеще́ние позвонка́.

discard *vt* брос|а́ть (́-ить) *and compounds*; *Cards* сбра́сывать ка́рту (сбро́сить); **we ~ warm clothing in summer** ле́том мы сбра́сываем тёплую оде́жду; **to ~ a hypothesis** отбро́сить гипо́тезу; **she's ~ed her lover** она́ бро́сила любо́вника; **to ~ old friends** переста́ть зна́ться со ста́рыми друзья́ми.

discern *vt* различ|а́ть (-и́ть); **I couldn't ~ her face in the dark** я не мог различи́ть её лица́ в темноте́; **I couldn't ~ any difference between the vases** я не ви́дел никако́й ра́зницы ме́жду э́тими ва́зами.

discernible *adj* различи́мый.

discerning *adj* (*of people*) проница́тельный; **that was a ~ remark of hers** она́ э́то о́чень то́нко подме́тила; **~ taste** то́нкое чутьё.

discharge *n* **1: the ~ of water/steam/electricity/pus** спуск воды́, вы́пуск па́ра, разря́д электри́чества, выделе́ние гно́я

2 (*dismissal*): **the ~ of an employee/a patient** увольне́ние слу́жащего, вы́писка больно́го из больни́цы

3: the ~ of a debt/duty упла́та до́лга, исполне́ние обя́занностей (*pl*).

discharge *vti vt* **1** (*unload, emit*): **to ~ a vessel** разгру|жа́ть су́дно (-зи́ть); **to ~ water from a reservoir** спус|ка́ть во́ду из резервуа́ра (-ти́ть); **to ~ steam/gas** вы|пуска́ть пар/газ (́-пустить); **to ~ electricity** разря|жа́ть электри́ческий заря́д (-ди́ть); **to ~ pus** выделя́ть гной, гнои́ться (*usu impfs*); **it's forbidden to ~ waste into the sea** запрещено́ сбра́сывать отхо́ды в мо́ре (сбро́сить)

2 (*fire*): **to ~ a gun** разряжа́ть ружьё

3 (*dismiss*): **he was ~d from the army/hospital** его́ демобилизова́ли, его́ вы́писали из больни́цы; **to ~ a prisoner** освобо|жда́ть заключённого (-ди́ть)

4 (*pay, perform*): **to ~ a debt/a duty** упла́|чивать долг (-ти́ть), исполн|я́ть обя́занности (*pl*) (́-ить)

vi: **the vessel is discharging** су́дно разгружа́ется; **the sewers ~ into the river** сто́чные во́ды слива́ются в реку́; **this river ~s into lake Baikal** э́та река́ впада́ет в о́зеро Байка́л; **the wound is still discharging** ра́на ещё гнои́тся.

disciple *n* после́дователь (*m*); учени́к; *Bibl* апо́стол.

disciplinary *adj* дисциплина́рный.

discipline *n* дисципли́на, *also Univ* (= *branch of knowledge*); **to keep/maintain ~** подде́рживать дисципли́ну; **the study of Latin is a good mental ~** изуче́ние латы́ни—хоро́шая трениро́вка для ума́.

discipline *vt*: **he doesn't ~ his class** он не приуча́ет класс к дисципли́не; **I've ~d myself to rise early** я приучи́л себя́ ра́но встава́ть; (*punish*) **they were ~d for the offence** они́ бы́ли нака́заны за э́тот просту́пок.

disclaim *vt* отрица́ть (*impf*); **they ~ed all knowledge of the affair** они́ отрица́ли, что зна́ют что́-нибудь об э́том де́ле; **they ~ed responsibility for it** они́ утвержда́ли, что не несу́т за э́то никако́й отве́тственности/, что они́ здесь не при чём; **to ~ a debt** не признава́ть за собо́й до́лга (*only in impf*).

disclose *vt* раскры|ва́ть (́-ть).

disclosure *n* раскры́тие.

discomfiture *n* замеша́тельство.

discomfort *n*: **he's still feeling some ~** он всё ещё чу́вствует не́которое недомога́ние; **the ~s experienced by Arctic explorers** тру́дности, испы́тываемые иссле́дователями Арктики.

discomposure *n* волне́ние, смуще́ние.

disconcert *vt* (*plans, etc.*) расстр|а́ивать (-о́ить); (*person*) сму|ща́ть (-ти́ть); **he was ~ed by her remark** он был смущён её замеча́нием.

disconnect *vt* (*two equal things*) разъедин|я́ть, (*smaller from larger*) отсоедин|я́ть + *A and* от + *G* (*pfs* -и́ть); (*uncouple*) расцеп|ля́ть, отцеп|ля́ть + *A and* от + *G* (*pfs* -и́ть); **we've been ~ed** (*Tel: during conversation*) нас разъедини́ли, (*Tel, Elec, gas for not paying bill*) у нас отключи́ли газ, телефо́н, *etc*.

disconnected *adj* (*of ideas, speech*) несвя́зный.

disconsolate *adj* удручённый.

discontent *n* недово́льство (+ *I*).

discontented *adj* недово́льный; **he's ~ with his job** он недово́лен свое́й рабо́той.

discontinue *vt* прекра|ща́ть (-ти́ть); **to ~ a subscription/subscribing** прекрати́ть подпи́ску; **this publication will be ~d** э́то изда́ние бу́дет прекращено́.

discontinuous *adj* преры́вистый.

discord *n* разла́д; несогла́сие; *Mus* диссона́нс.

discount *n* ски́дка; **at a ~** со ски́дкой; **to give 5% ~** де́лать пятипроце́нтную ски́дку.

discount *vt Fin* дисконти́ровать (*impf and pf*); *fig* **I ~ his opinion** я его́ мне́ние в расчёт не принима́ю.

discourage *vt* обескура́ж|ивать (-ить); **failure ~d him** неуда́ча обескура́жила его́; **I tried to ~ him from taking that job** я отгова́ривал его́ от э́той рабо́ты.

discourse *n*: **he delivered a ~ on the theme of...** он вы́ступил с ре́чью на те́му о + *P*.

discourse *vi*: **to ~ on smth** рассужда́ть о чём-л (*impf*).

discourteous *adj* неве́жливый.

discover *vt* откры|ва́ть, (*after investigation*) раскры|ва́ть (*pfs* ́-ть); обнару́ж|ивать (-ить); **to ~ penicillin/America** откры́ть пеницилли́н/Аме́рику; **to ~ a plot** раскры́ть за́говор; **it was never ~ed how he died** обстоя́тельства его́ сме́рти оста́лись нераскры́тыми; **we ~ed a dump of weapons in an old shed** мы обнару́жили в ста́ром сара́е склад ору́жия (*collect*); **he was ~ed to have been drunk at the time** вы́яснилось, что тогда́ он был пьян.

discovery *n* откры́тие; раскры́тие (*see verb*); **the ~ of radium** откры́тие ра́дия; **the ~ of a plot** раскры́тие за́говора.

discredit *vt* (*throw doubt on*) ста́вить под сомне́ние (по-), подверг|а́ть сомне́нию (́-нуть), дискредити́ровать (*impf and pf*); (*bring into disrepute*) компромети́ровать (с-); **that theory is now ~ed** э́та тео́рия дискредити́рована; **such behaviour will ~ him with the public** тако́е поведе́ние скомпромети́рует его́.

discreet *adj* (*prudent*) осмотри́тельный; благоразу́мный; (*tactful*) такти́чный; **he maintained a ~ silence** он благоразу́мно промолча́л.

discrepancy *n*: **there's a ~ between the two accounts** э́ти два сообще́ния противоре́чат друг дру́гу.

discretion *n* осмотри́тельность; благоразу́мие; **to show ~** прояви́ть осмотри́тельность/благоразу́мие; **to act with ~** де́йствовать осмотри́тельно; **use your own ~** поступа́й по своему́ усмотре́нию; **I leave it to your ~** я оставля́ю э́то на твоё усмотре́ние; **you've reached the age of ~** ты уже́ совершенноле́тний.

discriminate *vti vt* отлич|а́ть, различ|а́ть (*pfs* -и́ть); **to ~ good books from bad** отлича́ть хоро́шие кни́ги от плохи́х.

vi: **to ~ between fact and fancy** отлича́ть фа́кты (*pl*) от вы́мысла; **to ~ against/in favour of smb** предвзя́то относи́ться к кому́-л (*usu impf*), ока́з|ывать предпочте́ние кому́-л (-а́ть); **employers still ~ against women** хозя́ева предприя́тий продолжа́ют ста́вить же́нщин в нера́вное положе́ние по сравне́нию с мужчи́нами.

discriminating *adj* разбо́рчивый; (*treating differently*) дискриминацио́нный; **~ taste, a ~ critic** разбо́рчивый вкус/кри́тик.

discrimination *n* **1** разбо́рчивость; (*taste*) вкус; **he reads every sort of book without ~** он чита́ет все кни́ги без разбо́ра

2 *Polit* дискримина́ция.

discursive *adj*: **he's a ~ talker** он всегда́ так расплы́вчато выража́ется; **a ~ style** расплы́вчатость сти́ля.

discuss *vt* обсу|жда́ть (-ди́ть); **let's ~ the question/what's to be done** дава́й обсу́дим вопро́с/, что де́лать.

discussion *n* обсужде́ние; диску́ссия; **a lively ~ took place** шло живо́е обсужде́ние, шла оживлённая диску́ссия; **the question under ~** обсужда́емый вопро́с; **to have a ~ about smth** обсужда́ть что-л.

disdain *n* презре́ние; пренебреже́ние; **to treat smb with ~** пренебрежи́тельно относи́ться к кому́-л.

disdain *vt* презира́ть (*impf*); пренебре|га́ть + *I* (-́чь); **to ~ flattery** презира́ть лесть; **he ~s advice** он пренебрега́ет сове́тами (*pl*); **he ~ed to notice the insult** он пропусти́л ми́мо уше́й э́то оскорбле́ние.

disease *n* боле́знь.

diseased *adj* больно́й; **a ~ heart** больно́е се́рдце; *fig* **a ~ imagination** больно́е воображе́ние.

disembark *vti vt* (*cargo*) вы|гружа́ть (-́грузить); (*troops, passengers*) вы|са́живать (-́садить)

vi вы|са́живаться (-́садиться).

disenchanted *adj* разочаро́ванный.

disenfranchise *vt*: **to ~ smb** лиш|а́ть кого́-л гражда́нских (*civic rights*)/избира́тельных прав (*voting rights*) (-и́ть).

disengage *vti vt Tech* расцеп|ля́ть (-и́ть); *Aut* **to ~ the clutch** вы|ключа́ть сцепле́ние (-́ключить)

vi Mil вы|ходи́ть из бо́я, отрыва́ясь от проти́вника (-́йти).

disengaged *adj* свобо́дный, неза́нятый.

disentangle *vt* (*wool, knot*) распу́т|ывать (-ать), *also fig*; развя́з|ывать (-а́ть); **to ~ a knot/facts** распу́тать *or* развяза́ть у́зел, разобра́ться в фа́ктах (*only in pf*); **I ~d myself from the barbed wire/from his embraces** я вы́путался из колю́чей про́волоки, я вы́свободилась из его́ объя́тий.

disfavour *n*: **I thus fell into ~** вот так я и впал в неми́лость; **he regarded the idea with ~** он не одо́брил э́ту иде́ю/э́той иде́и.

disfigure *vt* уро́довать (из-); **his face was ~d by a scar** его́ лицо́ бы́ло обезобра́жено/изуро́довано шра́мом; **the statue was ~d by graffiti** ста́туя была́ изуро́дована на́дписями; (*of larger areas*) **the park was ~d by piles of litter** ку́чи му́сора в па́рке по́ртили весь вид.

disgrace *n* позо́р; (*disfavour*) неми́лость; **to be a ~ to one's family** быть позо́ром для семьи́, опозо́рить свою́ семью́; **he brought ~ on himself/his regiment** он опозо́рил себя́/свой полк; **the litter in the streets is a ~ to the city** му́сор на у́лицах—позо́р для го́рода; **I'm in ~ with the director** дире́ктор на меня́ се́рдится, *CQ iron* я в неми́лости у дире́ктора; **he's in ~ and been sent to bed early** он провини́лся, и его́ ра́но отпра́вили спать; *CQ* **go and tidy yourself—you're a ~ and not fit to be seen!** иди́ и приведи́ себя́ в поря́док—на тебя́ сты́дно смотре́ть!

disgrace *vt* позо́рить (о-); **to ~ oneself** опозо́риться.

disgraceful *adj* позо́рный; **~!** позо́р!

disgruntled *adj* недово́льный; (*put out*) расстро́енный; **she is ~ with the children** она́ недово́льна детьми́; **he was ~ at having his working hours disturbed** он был недово́лен (тем), что ему́ меша́ют в рабо́чее вре́мя; **he is ~/in a ~ mood** он в плохо́м настрое́нии.

disguise *n*: **he escaped in ~** он убежа́л, переоде́вшись (кем-л) (*in Russian necessary to state how he was disguised*); **a compliment in ~** скры́тый комплиме́нт; **she made no ~ of her feelings** она́ не скрыва́ла свои́х чувств; **it was a blessing in ~** нет ху́да без добра́.

disguise *vt* (*Mil or for protection, also fig*) маскирова́ть (за-); (*if change of clothes is involved*) переоде|ва́ть (-́ть); **he ~d himself as Father Xmas/as a woman** он переоде́лся де́дом-моро́зом/в же́нское пла́тье; **to ~ one's intentions** маскирова́ть/скрыва́ть свои́ наме́рения; **he couldn't ~ his voice** он не мог измени́ть го́лос; **there's no disguising the fact that...** нельзя́ скрыва́ть того́ фа́кта, что...

disgust *n* (*revulsion*) отвраще́ние; (*annoyance*) доса́да; **I discovered to my ~ that...** я с отвраще́нием обнару́жил, что...; **to my great ~ I found that the car was not yet repaired** к мое́й вели́кой доса́де маши́на ещё не была́ отремонти́рована.

disgust *vt*: **his behaviour ~ed everybody** всех возмути́ло/покоро́било его́ поведе́ние; **he ~s me** он мне проти́вен, он внуша́ет мне отвраще́ние; **I'm ~ed with the referee** меня́ возмуща́ло, как суди́л э́тот судья́/рефери́; **he's ~ed with himself for failing his exam** провали́вшись на экза́мене, он о́чень руга́л самого́ себя́; **the very thought of it ~s me** мне проти́вна сама́ мысль об э́том.

disgusting *adj* отврати́тельный, омерзи́тельный; проти́вный; **how ~!** как отврати́тельно!, как э́то ме́рзко!

dish *n* (*plate or food*) блю́до; *pl* (**the ~es**) посу́да (*collect*); **to wash the ~es** помы́ть посу́ду; **his favourite ~ is roast lamb** его́ люби́мое блю́до — жарко́е из бара́нины; *sl* **she's quite a ~!** она́ де́вочка что на́до!

dish *vt* **1** *also* **~ out/up** (*serve*): **come along, I'm ~ing up the soup/meat** иди́те скоре́й, я уже́ разлива́ю суп/раскла́дываю мя́со; **shall I ~ out/up the vegetables?** мо́жно пода|ва́ть о́вощи? (-́ть)

2 *fig CQ*: **to ~ up other people's ideas/an old joke** препод|носи́ть чужи́е иде́и как свои́/ста́рый анекдо́т под но́вым со́усом (-нести́); **they're ~ing out safety helmets** раздаю́т безопа́сные шле́мы; **our uncle always ~es out £1 each at Xmas** наш дя́дя всегда́ даёт нам по фу́нту (сте́рлингов) к рождеству́; (*thwart*): **that will ~ him** э́то его́ погу́бит, на э́том он погори́т; **that ~ed our plans** э́то спу́тало/разби́ло на́ши пла́ны.

dish cloth *n* (*for washing dishes*) тря́пка (для мытья́ посу́ды), (*for drying*) ку́хонное полоте́нце.

dishearten *vt* обескура́ж|ивать (-ить); **don't be ~ed!** не па́дай ду́хом!

dishevelled *adj* растрёпанный; **to be/get ~** растрепа́ться.

dishonest *adj* нече́стный, непоря́дочный.

dishonour, (*US*) **dishonor** *vt* позо́рить (о-).

dishono(u)rable *adj* (*of a person*) бесче́стный; (*of behaviour*) позо́рный.

dishrack *n* суши́лка для посу́ды.

dishwasher *n* посудомо́йка.

disillusioned *adj* разочаро́ванный; **I was ~ with him/with Rome** он/Рим разочарова́л меня́.

disincentive *n*: **low pay is a ~ to productivity** ни́зкая зарпла́та препя́тствует ро́сту производи́тельности труда́.

disinclination *n*: **his ~ to work/to meet people worries me** его́ нежела́ние рабо́тать/встреча́ться с людьми́ беспоко́ит меня́.

disinclined *adj*: **I feel ~ for work today/to accept the invitation** сего́дня мне что́-то не рабо́тается/не хо́чется рабо́тать, мне не хо́чется принима́ть э́то приглаше́ние.

disinfect *vt* дезинфици́ровать (*impf and pf*).

disinfectant *n* дезинфици́рующее сре́дство.

disingenuous *adj* нейскренний.

disinherit *vt*: **to ~ smb** лиш|а́ть кого́-л насле́дства (*G*) (-и́ть).

disintegrate *vi* рас|пада́ться (-па́сться).

disintegration *n* распа́д.

disinterested *adj* бескоры́стный; **his kindness to me was not altogether ~** его́ расположе́ние ко мне не́ было совсе́м бескоры́стным.

disjointed *adj fig* несвя́зный, бессвя́зный.

disk *n see* **disc.**

dislike *n*: **she doesn't conceal her likes and ~s** она́ не скрыва́ет свои́х симпа́тий и антипа́тий; **I took an instant ~ to him/to the house** я его́/э́тот дом невзлюби́л сра́зу; **he has a marked ~ of jazz** он терпе́ть не мо́жет джа́за.

dislike *vt*: **I ~ gardening** я не люблю́ рабо́тать в саду́; **you'll get yourself ~d if you...** тебя́ не бу́дут люби́ть/невзлю́бят, е́сли ты...; **they ~ each other** они́ недолю́бливают друг дру́га (*impf*); **I ~ her/her manner** она́/её мане́ра мне не нра́вится.

dislocate *vt Med* вы́вихнуть (*usu pf*); **he ~d his shoulder** он вы́вихнул себе́ плечо́; *fig*: **traffic has been ~d by the snow** снегопа́д нару́шил движе́ние; **the strike has completely ~d the factory's schedule** из-за забасто́вки заво́д вы́бился из гра́фика.

dislocation *n Med* вы́вих.

dislodge *vt*: **the rain ~d some tiles** дождём сби́ло (*impers*) черепи́цу (*collect*) с кры́ши; **we ~d a stone from the wall** мы сдви́нули ка́мень у и́згороди; **to ~ the enemy from their position** вы|бива́ть проти́вника с его́ пози́ций (*pl*) (-бить).

disloyal *adj* (*to friends*) неве́рный, вероло́мный; (*to state, etc.*) нелоя́льный.

disloyalty *n* (*to friends*) неве́рность; (*to state, etc.*) нелоя́льность.

dismal *adj* мра́чный; **in a ~ voice** мра́чным то́ном; **the future looks ~** бу́дущее ка́жется мра́чным; **a ~ mood** мра́чное настрое́ние; **~ weather** нагоня́ющая тоску́ пого́да; **a ~ failure** безнадёжный прова́л; **a ~ expression** угрю́мое лицо́.

dismantle *vt*: **to ~ a battleship/an engine/a carburettor** рассна́|щивать кора́бль (-сти́ть), раз|бира́ть дви́гатель/карбюра́тор (-обра́ть).

dismay *n* трево́га; **in ~** в трево́ге; **there was general ~** всех охвати́ла трево́га.

dismay *vt* трево́жить (вс-); **don't be ~ed!** не трево́жьтесь!; **I was ~ed to hear that...** я был встрево́жен, услы́шав, что...

dismiss *vt* **1** увол|ьня́ть (-́ить); **he was ~ed from his post** его́ уво́лили с до́лжности; **he ~ed the class** он отпусти́л ученико́в; **the meeting was ~ed** собра́ние бы́ло распу́щено; *Law* **the judge ~ed the case** судья́ прекрати́л де́ло

2 (*from the mind*): **to ~ doubts** от|бра́сывать сомне́ния (-бро́сить); **I ~ed the matter from my mind** я вы́бросил э́то из головы́; **the chairman ~ed the subject** председа́тель прекрати́л обсужде́ние вопро́са.

dismissal *n* (*from post*) увольне́ние.

dismount *vi* (*from horse*) спе́ш|иваться (-иться); **to ~ from a horse/a bicycle** соскочи́ть с ло́шади, слезть с велосипе́да; **the riders ~ed** вса́дники спе́шились.

disobedience *n* непослуша́ние; *Mil* неповинове́ние.

disobedient *adj* непослу́шный.

disobey *vti* не слу́шаться (по-); *Mil* не повинова́ться + *D* (*impf, past tense also pf*); **to ~ one's parents/an officer** не слу́шаться роди́телей, не повинова́ться офице́ру; **to ~ an order** не подчин|я́ться прика́зу (-и́ться).

disobliging *adj* нелюбéзный.

disorder *n* беспоря́док; **in ~** в беспоря́дке; **civil ~(s)** беспоря́дки (*only in pl*); *Med* **a stomach ~** расстрóйство желу́дка.

disorderly *adj* беспоря́дочный; **a ~ crowd/queue** беспоря́дочная *or* неорганизóванная толпá, беспоря́дочная óчередь; **a ~ room/pile of papers** неу́бранная кóмната, беспоря́дочная гру́да бумáг.

disorganization *n*: **in a state of ~** в беспоря́дке.

disorganized *adj*: **he's a ~ character** он неорганизóванный человéк; **the timetable is ~ because of exams** расписáние нару́шилось из-за экзáменов.

disown *vt*: **he ~ed the pistol** он сказáл, что э́то не егó револьвéр; **he ~s/~ed his son** он не признаёт своегó сы́на.

disparage *vt* умал|я́ть (-и́ть).

disparaging *adj* пренебрежи́тельный.

disparate *adj* несоизмери́мый.

disparity *n* (*inequality*): **~ in rank** разли́чие в рáнгах; (*difference*): **~ in years** рáзница в вóзрасте; **the disparities in the various accounts of the incident are quite remarkable** порази́тельно, как отличáются друг от дру́га опи- сáния э́того происшéствия.

dispassionate *adj* бесстрáстный.

dispatch *n* **1** (*act of sending*): **the ~ of a letter/of troops** отпрáвка *or* отсы́лка письмá, отпрáвка вóйск; *attr*: **~ department** отдéл отпрáвки

2 (*message*) сообщéние; **the editor received a ~ from Paris** редáктор получи́л сообщéние из Пари́жа; *Mil* **mentioned in ~es** упомя́нутый в прикáзе (*sing*)

3 (*speed*): **with ~** бы́стро (*adv*).

dispatch *vt* **1** (*send*): **to ~ troops to the front** отправ|ля́ть войскá на фронт (´-ить); **to ~ a telegram/smb on an errand** по|сылáть телегрáмму/когó-л с поручéнием (-слáть)

2 (*deal with*) исполн|я́ть (´-ить); справ|ля́ться с + *I* (´-иться); **the business was quickly ~ed** с э́тим дéлом бы́стро спрáвились

3 (*kill*): **he ~ed the wounded deer** он прикóнчил рáненого олéня.

dispatch rider *n Mil* мотоцикли́ст свя́зи.

dispel *vt* развé|ивать, рассé|ивать (*pfs* -ять); **the wind soon ~led the fog** вéтер скóро развéял/рассéял тумáн; *fig*: **to ~ gloom/illusions** развéять мрак/иллю́зии; **to ~ doubts** рассéивать сомнéния.

dispensary *n* (*at chemist's shop*) отдéл рецéптов; (*in hospital*) больни́чная аптéка.

dispensation *n*: **~ of justice** отправлéние правосу́дия; **you need a special ~ for that** на э́то ну́жно осóбое разрешéние; **by a ~ of providence, he arrived in time** по вóле судьбы́/провидéния он при́был тóчно вóвремя.

dispense *vti vt*: **to ~ justice** отправля́ть правосу́дие (*only in impf*); **they ~d soup to the refugees** бéженцам раздавáли суп; *Med* **to ~ a prescription** пригот|áвливать лекáрство по рецéпту (-óвить)

vi: **I've ~d with domestic help** я обхожу́сь без домрабóтницы; **let's ~ with formality** давáйте без формáльностей (*pl*).

disperse *vti vt*: **to ~ a crowd** раз|гоня́ть/ рассé|ивать толпу́ (-огнáть/-ять); **the wind ~d the clouds** вéтер разогнáл ту́чи/рассéял облакá

vi: **the crowd/fog ~d** толпá разошлáсь *or* рассéялась, тумáн рассéялся.

dispirited *adj* удручённый.

displace *vt* **1** (*put out of order*): **my books are all ~d** все мои́ кни́ги лежáт не на мéсте; **~d persons** перемещённые ли́ца

2 (*take the place of*): **the chairman has been ~d by/in favour of his deputy** председáтеля смени́л егó замести́тель; **he has ~d Sasha in Tanya's affections** он зáнял Сáшино мéсто в сéрдце Тáни.

displacement *n*: **a ship of 5,000 tons ~** корáбль водоизмещéнием в пять ты́сяч тонн.

display *n* **1**: **a fashion ~** демонстрáция/ покáз мод; **a ~ of goods** вы́ставка товáров; **a gymnastic ~** покáз гимнасти́ческих упражнéний; **they have a marvellous window ~/~ of flowers in the garden** у них óчень краси́вые витри́ны/цветы́ в саду́; **a ~ of feeling/of bad temper** проявлéние чувств, вспы́шка раздражéния

2 (*showiness*): **he did it for ~** он э́то сдéлал напокáз (*adv*).

display *vt* (*in museum, shop window, etc.*) вы|ставля́ть (´-ставить); (*qualities*): **to ~ courage** прояв|ля́ть му́жество, вы|кáзывать хрáбрость (-и́ть, ´-казать); **to ~ affection/bad temper** вы́казать тёплые чу́вства, вспыли́ть; **she ~ed no signs of emotion** онá не прояви́ла/не вы́казала эмóций (*pl*); **don't ~ your ignorance** не выдавáй своегó невéжества.

displease *vt*: **his behaviour ~d me** егó поведéние мне не нрáвилось; **the children have ~d their grandmother** дéти огорчи́ли бáбушку; **she was ~d at my tactlessness/that I was so tactless** моя́ бестáктность вы́звала её недовóльство; **I am ~d with myself for failing to recognize her** я огорчён, что срáзу не узнáл её.

displeasing *adj attr* неприя́тный; *predic*: **the decoration of the room is/is not ~ to me** оформлéние кóмнаты мне не по вку́су/мне нрáвится.

displeasure *n* неудовóльствие; **to incur smb's ~** вы́звать чьё-л неудовóльствие.

disposable *adj*: **~ nappies/handkerchiefs** бумáжные пелёнки/носовы́е платки́.

disposal *n* **1** (*arrangement of ornaments, etc.*) расстанóвка; **the ~ of troops** расположéние войск

2 (*getting rid of*): **the ~ of rubbish** вы́воз (*by carting away*)/сжигáние (*by incineration*) му́сора; **the ~ of radioactive waste** уничтожéние радиоакти́вных отхóдов; **the ~ of property** продáжа (*sale*)/передáча (*Law*: *by conveyance*) сóбственности; **the ~ of that item on the agenda was a matter of minutes** *CQ* с э́тим пу́нктом разде́лались за не́сколько мину́т

3: I am at your ~ я в ва́шем распоряже́нии; **he usually has some extra theatre tickets at his ~** у него́ обы́чно есть два-три ли́шних биле́та на спекта́кль; **the Germans had 200 submarines at their ~** не́мцы располага́ли двумяста́ми подво́дными ло́дками.

dispose *vti vt* **1** (*arrange*) распо|лага́ть (-ложи́ть); **to ~ troops** расположи́ть войска́; *fig* **man proposes God ~s** челове́к предполага́ет, а бог располага́ет

2 (*usu pass* = *be ready or inclined to*): **I am ~d to accept the offer** я скло́нен приня́ть предложе́ние; **he seems well ~d to us** он, ка́жется, к нам располо́жен

vi: **to ~ of rubbish** выбра́сывать (*throw out*)/сжига́ть (*incinerate*) му́сор (вы́бросить/сжечь); **he ~d of £10,000 in 6 months** он истра́тил за полго́да де́сять ты́сяч фу́нтов; **we have ~d of our house** мы про́дали (наш) дом; **they ~d of the incriminating evidence** они́ уничто́жили компромети́рующую ули́ку; **we've ~d of our business for today/of their arguments** мы разде́лались с дела́ми на сего́дня, мы опрове́ргли их до́воды; **the dictator soon ~d of his enemies** дикта́тор бы́стро разде́лался со свои́ми проти́вниками; **I've managed to ~ of the children for the day** я пристро́ил дете́й на сего́дня.

disposition *n* **1** (*placing*): **the ~ of the enemy forces/of the rooms in the castle** расположе́ние сил проти́вника/ко́мнат в за́мке

2 (*temperament*) нрав, хара́ктер; **he has a cheerful/gloomy ~** у него́ весёлый нрав, у него́ мра́чный хара́ктер.

dispossess *vt*: **he was ~ed of his property** его́ лиши́ли по суду́ всей его́ со́бственности.

disproportion *n* несоразме́рность, диспропо́рция.

disproportionate *adj* несоразме́рный с + *I*; **the pay is ~ to the work done** пла́та не соотве́тствует проде́ланной рабо́те.

disprove *vt* опроверг|а́ть (-́нуть).

disputable *adj usu predic*: **it's ~ whether he meant to be rude or not** э́то ещё вопро́с, наме́ренно ли он был груб.

dispute *n* спор; (*on public matters*) ди́спут, диску́ссия; *Law* тя́жба; **beyond ~** вне сомне́ния, бесспо́рно (*adv*); **an industrial ~** произво́дственный конфли́кт; **the territory in ~** спо́рная террито́рия; **that's a matter of ~** э́то спо́рный вопро́с; **to settle a ~** ула́дить спор.

dispute *vti vt* (*discuss*): **to ~ a question** обсу|жда́ть де́ло/вопро́с (-ди́ть); (*call in question*): **to ~ a decision/a fact/an election result** оспа́ривать реше́ние (*usu impf*), ста́вить под сомне́ние факт/результа́ты (*pl*) вы́боров (по-); **I would ~ that** я не согла́сен с э́тим

vi (*quarrel*): **to ~ with/against smb about/over smth** спо́рить с кем-л о чём-л (по-); **they were disputing whether it's quicker to return via Oxford or not** они́ спо́рили, не быстре́е ли бу́дет возврати́ться че́рез О́ксфорд.

disqualification *n* дисквалифика́ция.

disqualify *vt*: **his eyesight disqualified him for military service** по зре́нию он был при́знан него́дным к вое́нной слу́жбе; **our team has been disqualified for the Olympic games/for an infringement of the rules** на́ша кома́нда лиши́лась пра́ва уча́ствовать в Олимпи́йских и́грах/была́ дисквалифици́рована за наруше́ние пра́вил.

disquiet *vt* беспоко́ить (о-); **to be ~ed** беспоко́иться.

disquieting *adj*: **~ news** трево́жные ве́сти (*pl*).

disregard *n*: **the management shows a complete ~ for safety regulations** дире́кция по́лностью пренебрега́ет пра́вилами безопа́сности; **he works till all hours with complete ~ for his own health** он рабо́тает допоздна́, абсолю́тно не ду́мая о со́бственном здоро́вье.

disregard *vt* не обра|ща́ть внима́ния на + *A* (-ти́ть); (*neglect*, *scorn*) пренебре|га́ть + *I* (-́чь); **the children ~ed their mother's call** де́ти не обрати́ли внима́ния на зов ма́тери; **he ~ed our warnings** мы его́ предостерега́ли, но он нас не послу́шал.

disrepair *n*: **the building was in ~** зда́ние бы́ло в запу́щенном состоя́нии; **to fall into ~** ветша́ть.

disreputable *adj*: **a ~ looking fellow** подозри́тельный тип; **you can't go like that—you're too ~** ты не мо́жешь пойти́ в тако́м непригля́дном ви́де; **a ~ pub** сомни́тельного ви́да забега́ловка; **a ~ coat** истрёпанное/поно́шенное пальто́.

disrepute *n* дурна́я сла́ва; **the hotel has fallen into ~** оте́ль приобрёл дурну́ю сла́ву; **to bring smb/smth into ~** навле́чь на кого́-л/на что-л дурну́ю сла́ву.

disrespect *n* неуваже́ние; **I meant no ~, no ~ intended** не сочти́те э́то за неуваже́ние.

disrespectful *adj*: **a ~ attitude** непочти́тельное/неуважи́тельное отноше́ние; **he is ~ to his parents** он непочти́тельно/неуважи́тельно отно́сится к роди́телям.

disrupt *vt* наруш|а́ть (-́ить); **the train service was ~ed by fog** движе́ние поездо́в бы́ло нару́шено из-за тума́на; **my work has been ~ed since the visitors arrived** прибы́тие госте́й помеша́ло мое́й рабо́те.

dissatisfaction *n* недово́льство; **~ among the workers** недово́льство среди́ рабо́чих; **he expressed great ~ with the exam results of his son** он был о́чень недово́лен оце́нками сы́на на экза́менах.

dissatisfied *adj* неудовлетворённый; недово́льный; **he is ~ with his job/his salary** он неудовлетворён свое́й рабо́той, он счита́ет, что ему́ ма́ло пла́тят; **we were ~ with the service at the restaurant** мы бы́ли недово́льны обслу́живанием в рестора́не

dissect *vt Anat* вскры|ва́ть (-ть); *fig* **to ~ a theory/an article** анализи́ровать тео́рию/статью́ (*usu impf*).

dissemble *vti vt* скры|ва́ть (-ть); **he is dissembling his feelings** он скрыва́ет свой чу́вства

vi притворя́ться (*usu impf*); **there's no need to ~** не на́до притворя́ться/де́лать вид.

disseminate *vt* распростран|я́ть (-и́ть).

dissent *n*: **he expressed his ~ from the general view** он вы́разил несогла́сие с о́бщим мне́нием.

dissent *vi*: **to ~ from** не согла|ша́ться с + *I* (-си́ться).

dissertation *n* диссерта́ция.

disservice *n*: **he did me a ~** он оказа́л мне плоху́ю услу́гу.

dissident *n* инакомы́слящий, диссиде́нт.

dissimilar *adj*: **~ from/to** несхо́дный с + *I*; **~ tastes** ра́зные вку́сы.

dissipate *vt*: **to ~ fears** рассе́|ивать стра́хи (-ять); **to ~ one's fortune** пром|а́тывать своё состоя́ние (-ота́ть); **to ~ one's energies** растра́|чивать си́лы/эне́ргию (*sing*) впусту́ю (*adv*) (-тить).

dissipated *adj* (*of person*) распу́щенный; **to lead a ~ life** вести́ разгу́льную жизнь.

dissociate *vt*: **a diplomat has to ~ his public and his private life** диплома́т не до́лжен сме́шивать служе́бные интере́сы с ли́чными; **I wish to ~ myself from what has been said** я хочу́ вы́разить несогла́сие с тем, что бы́ло ска́зано.

dissolute *adj* распу́тный.

dissolve *vti vt* раствор|я́ть (-и́ть); **to ~ salt in water** растворя́ть соль в воде́; **water ~s salt** вода́ растворя́ет соль; *fig*: **to ~ a marriage/a business partnership** расторг|а́ть брак/делово́е партнёрство (-нуть); (*UK*) **to ~ Parliament** распус|ка́ть парла́мент (-ти́ть)

vi растворя́ться.

dissonant *adj* нестро́йный, диссони́рующий.

dissuade *vt*: **to try to ~/to ~ smb from marrying** отгова́ривать/отговори́ть кого́-л от жени́тьбы.

distance *n* **1** (*of space*) расстоя́ние; **within easy ~** на бли́зком расстоя́нии, недалеко́; **within striking ~** на расстоя́нии вы́стрела; **from a ~** издалека́; **at a ~** в отдале́нии; **in the ~** вдали́ (*adv*); **to look into the ~** смотре́ть вдаль (*adv*); **some ~ behind the church there is a lake** немно́го поо́даль/да́льше за це́рковью о́зеро; **from here to London is a ~ of 50 miles** расстоя́ние отсю́да до Ло́ндона—пятьдеся́т миль; **what ~ is it to Zagorsk?** далеко́ ли/ско́лько киломе́тров до Заго́рска?; **the church can be seen from a ~ of 2 miles** це́рковь видна́ с расстоя́ния (в) две ми́ли; **the waterfall is a fair ~ from here** отсю́да до водопа́да поря́дочное расстоя́ние; **the painting looks better from a ~** карти́на лу́чше смо́трится и́здали; **in the middle ~** на сре́днем пла́не; *fig*: **he keeps his ~** он де́ржится весьма́ непристу́пно; **he keeps his staff at a ~** он де́ржит подчинённых на расстоя́нии; *attr Sport*: **a long ~ race** забе́г на дли́нную диста́нцию

2 (*of time*): **at this ~ of time it seems easy but it was not so easy then** сейча́с э́то ка́жется так про́сто, но тогда́ э́то бы́ло совсе́м не легко́; **looking back over a ~ of 40 years** огля́дываясь наза́д по проше́ствии сорока́ лет.

distant *adj* **1** (*in space and time*) далёкий; (*in space*) да́льний; **~ countries** да́льние стра́ны; **a ~ town** далёкий го́род; **we had a ~ view of the Alps** вдали́ бы́ли видны́ А́льпы; **the ~ past/future** далёкое про́шлое/бу́дущее; **the station is some miles ~ from the village** ста́нция в не́скольких ми́лях от дере́вни

2: **a ~ relation/resemblance** да́льний ро́дственник, отдалённое схо́дство

3 *fig* (*reserved*) сде́ржанный; (*cold*) холо́дный.

distaste *n* нелюбо́вь к + *D*; **he has a ~ for travel/for parties** он не лю́бит е́здить, он не охо́тник до вся́ких приёмов.

distasteful *adj* неприя́тный; **it is ~ for me to have to tell you this** мне о́чень неприя́тно говори́ть тебе́ э́то.

distil *vt* дистилли́ровать (*impf and pf*).

distinct *adj* **1** отчётливый; чёткий; (*definite*) определённый; **a ~ sound** отчётливый звук; **the outlines of the mountains are quite ~** очерта́ния гор отчётливо видны́; **a ~ pronunciation/handwriting** чёткое *or* отчётливое произноше́ние, чёткий по́черк; **he speaks with a ~ French accent** он говори́т с заме́тным францу́зским акце́нтом; **there's been a ~ improvement** есть определённое/я́вное улучше́ние; **that was his ~ intention** таково́ бы́ло его́ наме́рение; **there's a ~ chance he'll be here for supper** вполне́ возмо́жно, что он бу́дет здесь к у́жину

2 (*different in kind*) разли́чный; **the two dialects are quite ~** э́ти два диале́кта си́льно различа́ются; **Indian tea is quite ~ from China tea** инди́йский чай си́льно отлича́ется от кита́йского; (*apart*) **you should keep the two ideas ~** не сле́дует сме́шивать э́ти две иде́и.

distinction *n* **1** (*difference*) разли́чие; **without ~** без разли́чия; **~s of rank** разли́чия в чи́не; **a fine ~** то́нкое разли́чие; **to draw/make a ~ between** провести́ разли́чие ме́жду + *I*

2 (*honour*): **you have the ~ of being the first woman barrister** вы име́ете честь быть пе́рвой же́нщиной-адвока́том; **a writer of ~** изве́стный писа́тель; **he has many academic ~s** у него́ мно́го учёных зва́ний; (*exam mark*) **he got a ~ in maths** он получи́л отли́чную оце́нку/вы́сший балл/(*SU*) пятёрку по матема́тике (*sing*).

distinctive *adj*: **~ badges/marks** зна́ки отли́чия; **he has very ~ handwriting/taste** у него́ о́чень характе́рный по́черк/своеобра́зный вкус.

distinctly *adv*: **to write ~** писа́ть отчётливо; **I ~ told you not to do it** я ведь я́сно сказа́л тебе́ не де́лать э́того; **to speak ~** вня́тно говори́ть; **it's ~ awkward** э́то кра́йне неудо́бно; **he's ~ better today** ему́ сего́дня значи́тельно лу́чше.

distinguish *vt* отлич|áть, различ|áть (*pfs* -ить); **it's impossible to ~ the twins from one another/between the twins** невозмóжно отличи́ть одногó близнецá от другóго, э́тих близнецóв невозмóжно различи́ть; **what ~es a rabbit from a hare?** чем отличáется крóлик от зáйца?; **in the dark he could hardly ~ the house** в темнотé он éле различи́л дом; **he ~ed himself in battle** он отличи́лся в бою́.

distinguishable *adj* отличи́мый, различи́мый.

distinguished *adj*: **a ~ guest** почётный гость; **he looks ~** у негó такóй соли́дный вид, (*of position*) он ви́дная фигу́ра; **he's a ~ figure in the world of scholarship/science** у негó есть и́мя в учёном ми́ре, он при́знанный авторитéт в нау́ке; **a ~ doctor** ви́дный/извéстный врач; **he is ~ for his contribution to physics** он извéстен свои́ми откры́тиями в óбласти фи́зики (*sing*); **of ~ birth** знáтного происхождéния; **he had a ~ career** у негó былá блистáтельная карьéра.

distinguishing *adj* отличи́тельный.

distort *vt* искa|жáть (-зи́ть); **her face was ~ed by pain** её лицó искази́лось от бóли; *fig* **to ~ the truth** искажáть и́стину.

distortion *n* искажéние, *also fig*.

distract *vt* отвле|кáть (-́чь); **how can we ~ her from her worries?** как нам отвлéчь её от забóт?; **the boy is easily ~ed** мáльчик бы́стро отвлекáется; **the noise ~ed me from my reading** шум мешáл мне читáть.

distraction *n* (*that which diverts attention*) отвлечéние; (*that which amuses*) развлечéние; **he loves her to ~** он её лю́бит до безу́мия; **the children drive me to ~** дéти сведу́т меня́ с умá [**NB** *tense*].

distraught *adj*: **like one ~** как безу́мный; **she was ~ with anxiety** онá буквáльно потеря́ла гóлову от волнéния.

distress *n* **1** (*sorrow*) гóре; (*misfortune*) бедá; (*calamity*) бéдствие; **we must help those in ~** ну́жно помогáть попáвшим в бедý; **her ~ was such that she could neither eat nor sleep** онá былá уби́та гóрем—не моглá ни спать ни есть; **a ship in ~** су́дно, тéрпящее бéдствие; *attr*: **~ signal** сигнáл бéдствия

2 (*physical*): **the patient is in some ~** больнóй плóхо себя́ чу́вствует; **the runners showed signs of ~** бегуны́ обнару́живали при́знаки устáлости.

distress *vt* огорч|áть (-и́ть); (*upset*) расстр|áивать (-óить); **I am ~ed to hear of your brother's death** я огорчён извéстием о смéрти вáшего брáта; **he is ~ed because his wife is ill** он óчень расстрóен из-за болéзни жены́; **you will ~ your mother if you do that** ты расстрóишь мать, éсли сдéлаешь э́то; **don't ~ yourself!** не огорчáйтесь, не унывáйте.

distressing *adj* неприя́тный; **it's all very ~** всё э́то óчень неприя́тно; **~ news** неутеши́тельная нóвость.

distribute *vt* (*divide and hand out*) распредел|я́ть (-и́ть); (*hand out*) раздa|вáть (-́ть); **he ~d the money fairly** он распредели́л дéньги справедли́во; **to ~ books/plates** раздáть кни́ги, разноси́ть тарéлки; **these tribes are ~d over a wide area of Africa** э́ти племенá расселены́ на обши́рной территóрии в Áфрике.

distribution *n* **1** (*sharing out*) распределéние; (*handing out*) раздáча; **the ~ of profits/of prizes** распределéние при́были (*sing*), раздáча нагрáд

2 (*placing*) размещéние, распространéние; **the ~ of population** размещéние населéния; **this type of pine has a wide ~ in the South** э́тот вид сосны́ широкó распространён на ю́ге; *Mil* **the ~ of troops** расположéние войск.

distributive *adj*: **he works in the ~ trade** он рабóтает в систéме распределéния и достáвки товáров; *Gram* распредели́тельный.

distributor *n Comm* агéнт по продáже; *Aut* распредели́тель (*m*).

district *n* райóн; **the Lake ~** Озёрный край; **electoral ~** избирáтельный учáсток/óкруг; *attr*: **~ council** окружнóй/райóнный совéт.

distrust *n* недовéрие; **he looked at me with ~** он посмотрéл на меня́ с недовéрием; **they have a ~ of foreigners** они́ относя́тся к инострáнцам с недовéрием.

distrust *vt* не доверя́ть + *D* (*only in impf*); **I ~ed him/my own eyes** я емý не доверя́л, я не повéрил сóбственным глазáм.

distrustful *adj* недовéрчивый.

disturb *vt* на|рушáть (-ру́шить); мешáть + *D* (по-); **he ~ed my peace/my train of thought** он нару́шил мой покóй/мой ход мы́слей (*pl*); **I hope I'm not ~ing you?** надéюсь, я вам не помешáю?; **does the TV ~ you?** телеви́зор вам не мешáет?; **sorry to ~ you** извини́те за беспокóйство; **he's sleeping—don't ~ him** он спит—не шуми́; **I'm seriously ~ed by the news** э́та нóвость вы́била меня́ из колеи́; **don't ~ my papers!** не трóгайте мои́ бумáги!

disturbance *n* помéха; (*noise*) шум; *Polit* беспоря́дки (*pl*); **I find the children's practising a bit of a ~ when I'm working** когдá дéти занимáются му́зыкой, мне тру́дно рабóтать; **there was some sort of ~ in the corridor** в коридóре был какóй-то шум; **from the noise, it sounds as if there's a bit of a ~ next door** су́дя по шу́му, нáши сосéди ссóрятся; *Law* **a ~ of the peace** нарушéние общéственного поря́дка.

disturbed *adj*: **I had a ~ night** у меня́ былá беспокóйная ночь; **a ~ child** нéрвный ребёнок.

disuse *n*: **to fall into ~** вы́йти из употреблéния.

disused *adj*: **a ~ well/mine** забрóшенный колóдец, забрóшенная шáхта.

ditch *n* (*in fields*) канáва; (*at side of road*) кювéт; *Mil* ров; **the car went into the ~** маши́на заéхала/съéхала в кювéт; **an anti-tank ~** противотáнковый ров; *attr*: **as dull as ~ water** смертéльно ску́чный.

ditch *vt CQ*: **I'll have to ~ my old car/trousers** порá вы́бросить мой драндулéт на свáлку, мои́ стáрые брю́ки порá вы́бросить; **the pilot had to ~ his plane** пилóт вы́нужден был сдéлать посáдку на мóре; **she's ~ed her boyfriend** онá далá своемý дружкý от ворóт поворóт.

dither *n CQ*: **I'm in a ~/all of a ~** я в нереши́тельности.

dither *vi CQ*: **he's ~ing** он нéрвничает (*is nervous*), он колéблется (*is undecided*).

ditto *n* тó же сáмое; (*the same amount*) стóлько же; **I say ~** я тóже соглáсен, и я так дýмаю, (*if affirming*) и я зá.

divan *n* дивáн, тахтá.

dive *n* прыжóк в вóду; (*of submarine*) погружéние; *Aer* пики́рование; *CQ* **a (low) ~** ви́нный погребóк.

dive *vi* ныр|я́ть (-нýть), *also fig*; (*of submarine*) погру|жáться (-зи́ться); *Aer* пики́ровать (с-); **to ~ for pearls** ныря́ть за жéмчугом (*collect*); *fig*: **the thief ~d into a side street** вор нырнýл в переýлок; **he ~d into his pocket for some change** он сýнул рýку в кармáн за мéлочью.

dive-bombing *n* бомбометáние с пики́рования.

diver *n* ныря́льщик; (*professional, deep-sea*) водолáз; (*bird*) нырóк, гагáра.

diverge *vi* (*of lines, paths*) расходи́ться (разойти́сь), *also fig*; **their paths/opinions ~d** их пути́/мнéния разошли́сь; **we/a path ~d from the main road** мы отклони́лись от магистрáли, от шоссé шла тропи́нка.

divergence *n*: **a ~ of opinion** расхождéние во мнéниях; **a ~ from the norm/from one's theme** отклонéние от нóрмы/от тéмы.

divergent *adj*: **~ paths/opinions** расходя́щиеся пути́, различные мнéния.

diverse *adj* разнообрáзный.

diversify *vt* разнообрáзить (*impf*).

diversion *n* **1** (*of traffic*) объéзд

2 (*amusement*) развлечéние

3 *Mil* лóжная атáка; *fig* **he created a ~ while his mate made off with the money** он отвлёк на себя́ внимáние, а егó прия́тель тем врéменем скры́лся с деньгáми.

diversity *n* разнообрáзие, многообрáзие.

divert *vt* **1**: **the police ~ed the traffic** поли́ция напрáвила движéние в объéзд; **traffic was ~ed through Dover** движéние бы́ло напрáвлено чéрез Дувр; **to ~ the course of a river** измен|я́ть рýсло реки́ (-и́ть); **to ~ water from a river into fields** от|води́ть вóду реки́ в поля́ (-вести́); *fig* **we tried to ~ her thoughts from the impending trial** мы старáлись отвлéчь её от предстоя́щего судá

2 (*amuse*) развле|кáть (-́чь); **in order to ~ the children** чтóбы развлéчь детéй; **to ~ oneself** развлекáться.

diverting *adj*: **a ~ play** развлекáтельная пьéса; **I find it ~ to sit in a café and watch people** иногдá я развлекáюсь тем, что сижý в кафé и наблюдáю людéй.

divide *vti vt* **1** *Math* дели́ть (раз-); **~ 50 by 5, ~ 5 into 50** раздели́те пятьдеся́т нá пять

2 (*share out*) дели́ть (по-), раздел|я́ть (-и́ть), распредел|я́ть (-и́ть); **they ~d the money among themselves** они́ подели́ли/раздели́ли дéньги мéжду собóй; **~ the apples/the apple equally** раздели́те я́блоки пóровну/я́блоко на рáвные чáсти; **they ~d the work between the boys and girls** они́ распредели́ли рабóту мéжду мáльчиками и дéвочками

3 (*separate*) отдел|я́ть (-и́ть); **a wall ~s our garden from his** стенá отделя́ет наш сад от егó сáда

4 (*usu pass = disagree*) расходи́ться (разойти́сь); **opinions are/were ~d** мнéния раздели́лись/разошли́сь; **the meeting was ~d on this point** на собрáнии бы́ли вы́сказаны рáзные мнéния по э́тому вопрóсу

vi (*fork*): **the river/road ~s here** здесь рекá/ дорóга разветвля́ется (*usu impf*); *Math* **5 ~s into 50 without remainder** пятьдеся́т дéлится на пять без остáтка.

dividend *n Fin* дивидéнд; *Math* дели́мое.

dividers *npl* измери́тельный/дели́тельный ци́ркуль (*m*) (*sing*).

dividing line *n* разграничи́тельная ли́ния (*on centre of road, etc., or fig*).

divine[1] *adj* божéственный; **~ being** божествó; *CQ* **she's a ~ cook** онá восхити́тельно готóвит.

divine[2] *vt* угáд|ывать (-áть).

diving *n* ныря́ние; (*of submarine*) погружéние; *attr*: **~ suit/helmet** водолáзный костю́м/шлем.

divinity *n* божéственность; **Doctor of D.** дóктор теолóгии; *attr*: *Univ* **~ school** теологи́ческий факультéт.

divisible *adj* дели́мый.

division *n* **1** (*sharing out*) делéние, разделéние; *Math* делéние; **~ of labour** разделéние трудá; **~ of the spoils** делёж добы́чи

2 (*department*) отдéл; (*if separately housed*) отделéние; *Mil* (*unit*) диви́зия

3 (*dividing line*): **a box with ~s** я́щик с перегорóдками; *fig*: **class ~s** сослóвные/клáссовые разли́чия; **a ~ of opinion** расхождéния во мнéниях (*pl*); **political ~s** полити́ческие разноглáсия.

divisive *adj*: **these issues are ~** э́ти вопрóсы вызывáют нéкоторые разноглáсия.

divisor *n Math* дели́тель (*m*).

divorce *n* развóд; *fig* **the ~ between/of religion and science** отделéние наýки от реЛи́гии.

divorce *vt*: **to ~ one's wife/husband** раз|води́ться с женóй/с мýжем (-вести́сь); **he/she is ~d** он разведён, онá разведенá; *fig* **this question has become totally ~d from reality** э́тот вопрóс чи́сто академи́ческий — не имéет никакóй свя́зи с действи́тельностью.

divulge *vt*: **to ~ a secret** разгла|шáть тáйну (-си́ть).

dizziness *n* головокружéние.

dizzy *adj attr*: **a ~ height** головокружи́тельная высотá; *predic*: **I am/feel ~** у меня́ кру́жится голова́; **it made me ~** от э́того у меня́ закружи́лась голова́.

do A *aux verb forming expanded past and present tenses, not directly translated in Russian* [**NB** *do not, does not, did not* = *CQ don't, doesn't, didn't*]: **i)** *in interrog sentences*: **~ you know her?** ты знако́м с ней?; **did you ~ it?** вы э́то сде́лали?; **ii)** *in neg sentences*: **I don't care** мне всё равно́; **he didn't come** он не пришёл; **iii)** *where inversion occurs*: **so well did they work that...** они́ так хорошо́ рабо́тали, что...; **iv)** *in emphatic affirmatives*: **that's exactly what he did say** э́то и́менно то, что он сказа́л; **~ stop talking** переста́ньте разгова́ривать

B *as verbal substitute to save repetition of main verb; not directly translated in Russian*: **i)** *replacing verb already used*: **she plays better than she did** она́ сейча́с игра́ет лу́чше, чем ра́ньше; **he said he'd come and he did** он сказа́л, что придёт, и пришёл; **ii)** *in interrog sentences*: **he lives in London, doesn't he?** он живёт в Ло́ндоне, не так ли?/ве́рно?; **iii)** *in answers and comments*: **they work hard—Oh, ~ they?** они́ хорошо́ рабо́тают.—Да?/Неуже́ли?; **who lost this pen?—I did** кто потеря́л ру́чку?—Я

C *full verb—vti vt* **1** (*perform, be engaged in*) де́лать (с-); **what are you ~ing?** что вы де́лаете?; **I'll ~ what I can** сде́лаю всё возмо́жное; **~ what you're told** де́лай, как тебе́ говоря́т; **it can't be done** э́то невозмо́жно сде́лать; **what's to be done, what's to ~?** что же де́лать?; **there's nothing to be done about it** тут ничего́ не поде́лаешь; **what should I ~ next?** что мне да́льше де́лать?; **what's ~ing?** что тут происхо́дит?/де́лается?; **for want of anything better to ~** от не́чего де́лать; **are you ~ing anything tomorrow?** ты за́втра за́нят?; **what ~ you ~?** (*what's your job?*) чем вы занима́етесь?; **what does he ~ for a living?** чем он зараба́тывает на жизнь?; **well done!** бра́во!, молоде́ц!, здо́рово!; *fig*: **it's all over and done with** с э́тим всё ко́нчено/поко́нчено раз и навсегда́; *CQ* **done!** (*it's a deal*) идёт!, по рука́м!

2 (*combined with noun*) **i)** (*produce, execute, work at*): **we're ~ing Hamlet just now** (*putting it on*) сейча́с мы ста́вим «Га́млета»; **we'll have to ~ the polite thing and ask them in** из ве́жливости придётся их пригласи́ть; **to ~ one's duty/job** вы|полня́ть долг/рабо́ту (-по́лнить); **he's ~ing his military service** он слу́жит (в а́рмии), он на вое́нной слу́жбе; **I'm ~ing an article for a magazine/a portrait** я пишу́ статью́ для журна́ла, я рису́ю портре́т: **he's ~ing his homework** он сейча́с гото́вит/де́лает уро́ки; **she's ~ing her sewing/some gardening** она́ сейча́с шьёт, она́ рабо́тает в саду́; **I'll ~ the supper** я пригото́влю у́жин; **is the meat done yet?** мя́со гото́во?; **ii)** *Univ, School*: **he's ~ing engineering** он изуча́ет инжене́рное де́ло; **we did French** мы изуча́ли в шко́ле францу́зский; **iii)** (*solve*): **to ~ a crossword** реша́ть кроссво́рд; **children, ~ this sum** де́ти, реши́те э́тот приме́р; **iv)** (*arrange, tidy, clean*): **to ~ the flowers** ста́вить/расстав|ля́ть цветы́ (-и́ть); **to ~ a room/the dishes** убира́ть ко́мнату (убра́ть), мыть посу́ду (*collect*) (вы́-, по-́); **I must ~ my hair** мне на́до причеса́ться; **v)** (*deal with, attend to*): **I'll ~ your hair for you** я сде́лаю тебе́ причёску; **the hair dresser will ~ you next** вы сле́дующий к э́тому ма́стеру; **I must ~ the accounts** мне на́до заня́ться счета́ми; **vi)** *CQ* (*visit, see*): **we must ~ the museum before we leave** пе́ред отъе́здом на́до сходи́ть в музе́й; **one can't ~ Venice in a day** невозмо́жно осмотре́ть Вене́цию за (оди́н) день; **vii)** (*of travel*): **we did the journey in 5 hours** мы проде́лали весь путь за пять часо́в; **we did 300 miles that day** в э́тот день мы прое́хали три́ста миль; **we were/the car was ~ing 60 m.p.h.** маши́на шла со ско́ростью шестьдеся́т миль в час; **viii)** *CQ* (*provide comforts, etc.*): **they ~ one well at this hotel** в э́той гости́нице хорошо́ обслу́живают; **he'll be sure to ~ you very well** он вас наверняка́ о́чень хорошо́ при́мет/угости́т; **he ~es himself very well** он себе́ ни в чём не отка́зывает; **ix)** *CQ* (*cheat*): **I'm afraid you've been done over that** бою́сь, что вас с э́тим наду́ли

vi **1** (*act*) де́лать (с-); поступ|а́ть (-и́ть); **you did well to take his advice** вы пра́вильно сде́лали, что послу́шались его́ сове́та; **you can ~ better than that** ты мог бы сде́лать э́то полу́чше; **~ as you think best** де́лай/поступа́й, как счита́ешь ну́жным; **there's not much ~ing here in August** здесь осо́бенно не́чего де́лать в а́вгусте; *CQ* **can you lend me £5?—Nothing ~ing!** ты не мо́жешь одолжи́ть мне пять фу́нтов?—Нет, ника́к не могу́

2 (*fare*): **how ~ you ~?** (*on introduction*) рад с ва́ми познако́миться; **how's the patient ~ing?** как (себя́ чу́вствует) больно́й?; **roses ~ well in a clay soil** ро́зы хорошо́ расту́т на гли́нистой по́чве; **the wheat is ~ing well** пшени́ца хорошо́ уроди́лась; **he's ~ing well** (*in business*) у него́ хорошо́ иду́т дела́, (*at school*) он хорошо́ у́чится

3 (*various*): **will £5 ~?** пяти́ фу́нтов хва́тит?; **we can make ~ on £100** мы обойдёмся ста фу́нтами; **will this knife ~?** э́тот нож подойдёт?; **that will ~!** хва́тит!, дово́льно!; **that will never ~** э́то никуда́ не годи́тся; **don't throw that shell away—it'll ~ as/for an ashtray** не броса́й э́ту ра́ковину—из неё вы́йдет прекра́сная пе́пельница; **this room/jacket will ~ for me** э́та ко́мната/ку́ртка мне подойдёт; **it won't ~ to keep cadging like this** нельзя́ же так попроша́йничать

do again *vt*: **I've done my thesis again** я переде́лал/перерабо́тал диссерта́цию (*worked it over*), я написа́л диссерта́цию за́ново, я переписа́л диссерта́цию (*again from the start*)

do by *vi*: **his firm did very well by him when he left** фи́рма с почётом проводи́ла его́ на пéнсию; **he felt hard done by** он считáл, что с ним плóхо обошлúсь

do down *vt*: *CQ* **they did us down** онú нас обманýли/надýли (*usu pf*)

do for *vi*: **she ~es for me twice a week** (*cleans*) онá прихóдит ко мне убирáться два рáза в недéлю; **I prefer ~ing for myself** я предпочитáю справля́ться сам; **what did you ~ for water during the drought?** как у вас бы́ло с водóй во врéмя зáсухи?

do in *vt*: *CQ* **to ~ smb in** прикóнчить когó-л (*usu pf*)

do out *vt*: **to ~ out a room/a cupboard** убирáться в кóмнате/в шкафý (убрáться)

do out of *vt*: **he did me out of a fiver/a job** он вы́манил у меня́ пять фýнтов, из-за негó я лиши́лся рабóты

do up *vti vt*: **to ~ up a parcel** паковáть/перевя́з|ывать (*tie up*) посы́лку (у-/-áть); **they are ~ing up their kitchen/derelict cottage** онú дéлают ремóнт кýхни, онú ремонтúруют свою стáрую дáчу; **would you ~ my zip up for me?** застегнú мне, пожáлуйста, мóлнию; **~ up your shoe laces** завяжú шнуркú

vi: **this dress ~es up at the back** э́то плáтье застёгивается сзáди

do with *vi*: **the car could ~ with a wash** не мешáло бы помы́ть машúну; **I could ~ with a beer** я бы вы́пил пúва; **she'll have nothing to ~ with him** онá не желáет имéть с ним ничегó óбщего; **it's nothing to ~ with me** э́то ко мне не имéет никакóго отношéния

do without *vi*: **if we haven't got money we'll have to ~ without** не бýдет дéнег—кáк-нибудь обойдёмся.

docile *adj* послýшный.

dock[1] *n Naut* док; **dry/floating ~** сухóй/плавýчий док; **to be in ~** стоя́ть в дóке; **to put a ship in ~** постáвить сýдно в док; *CQ fig*: **my car's in ~** моя́ машúна в ремóнте.

dock[1] *vti vt*: **to ~ a vessel** вводúть сýдно в док (ввестú); **the ship's been ~ed** корáбль стоúт в дóке

vi: **the vessel ~ed at 3 o'clock** сýдно вошлó в док в три часá.

dock[2] *n Law* скамья́ подсудúмых.

dock[3] *n Bot* кóнский щавéль (*m*).

dock[4] *vt*: **to ~ a horse/a dog** подрез|áть лóшади/собáке хвост (-́ать); **my wages have been ~ed** мне урéзали зарплáту (*permanently*); **they ~ed £ 10 from my wages** у меня́ вы́чли/удержáли дéсять фýнтов из зарплáты (*on one occasion*); **the prisoners were ~ed of part of their rations** плéнным урéзали паёк (*sing*).

doctor *n* врач, дóктор; *Univ* дóктор; **I'm going to see the ~** я идý к врачý; **you ought to see a ~** тебé нáдо пойтú/сходúть к врачý; **I saw the ~ yesterday** вчерá я был у врачá; **to send for a ~** послáть/сходúть за врачóм; **to take one's ~'s degree** получúть стéпень дóктора.

doctor *vt CQ*: **to ~ a cold/a child for a cold** лечúть простýду/ребёнка от простýды (*impf*); **to ~ a cat** кастрúровать котá, стерилизовáть кóшку (*both vbs impf and pf*); **to ~ a horse's food** (*with drugs*) подбав|ля́ть дóпинг в корм лóшади (-́ить).

doctoral *adj Univ*: **~ thesis** дóкторская диссертáция.

doctorate *n* стéпень дóктора.

doctrinaire *adj* доктринёрский.

document *n* докумéнт.

document *vt* документúровать (*impf and pf*); **the case is well ~ed** дéло хорошó документúровано.

documentary *n* документáльный фильм.

doddery *adj*: **a ~ old man** дря́хлый старúк.

dodge *n CQ* (*trick*): **a cunning ~** хúтрая увёртка/улóвка; (*device*): **a good ~ for remembering names** хорóший спóсоб запоминáть именá.

dodge *vti vt*: **to ~ a blow** уклон|я́ться от удáра (-úться); **to ~ the issue** увúливать/уклоня́ться от отвéта на вопрóс; **to ~ work/military service** уклоня́ться от рабóты/от вóинской повúнности; *Sport* **he ~d the full back** он обвёл защúтника

vi: **the thief ~d down an alley** вор юркнýл в аллéю.

doe *n* сáмка олéня (*deer*)/крóлика (*rabbit*).

doer *n*: **he's a ~, not a talker** он не лю́бит болтáть—лю́бит дéло дéлать.

dog *n* **1** собáка, *dim* собáчка (*f*; *but used of both sexes*); *CQ* пёс (*not of a bitch*); **~ fox/wolf** самéц лисы́/вóлка; *CQ* (*of people*): **lucky ~!** везёт емý!; **he's a gay ~** он весельчáк, он весёлый мáлый

2 (*US*): **hot ~** бутербрóд с горя́чей сосúской

3 *phrases*: **he leads a ~'s life** у негó собáчья жизнь; **she leads him a ~'s life** онá емý покóя не даёт; **let sleeping ~s lie** не тронь лúхо, покá спит тúхо; **he likes to be top ~** он лю́бит быть хозя́ином положéния; **he/the school has gone to the ~s** он так опустúлся, шкóла пришлá в упáдок; **he's a ~ in the manger** он как собáка на сéне; *attr*: **I'm in the ~ house with him** я у негó не в честú, он меня́ не жáлует; **I'm ~ tired** я устáл как собáка.

dog *vt*: **to ~ smb/smb's footsteps** неотстýпно слéдовать за кем-л (*usu impf*); *fig*: **he is ~ged by misfortune** егó преслéдуют неудáчи.

dog biscuit *n* галéта для собáк.

dog collar *n* ошéйник.

dog-eared *adj*: **a ~ book** кнúга с зáгнутыми странúцами.

dogged *adj* упря́мый, упóрный.

dogmatic *adj* догматúческий.

dogsbody *n sl*: **he's the ~ at the office** он в контóре на побегýшках.

dog-tooth *n* клык.

doing *n*: **talking is one thing, ~ is another** однó дéло—говорúть, другóе—дéлать; **that will take some ~** над э́тим придётся потрудúться/порабóтать; **this is none of my ~** я не виновáт, э́то не я (сдéлал); **it's all his ~** э́то всё егó продéлки; **tell me all**

about your ~s расскажи́ мне о свои́х дела́х.

do-it-yourself *adj*: **~ kit** набо́р инструме́нтов «Сде́лай сам».

dole *n*: **to be on the ~** получа́ть посо́бие по безрабо́тице.

dole *vt*: *CQ* **to ~ out** разда|ва́ть (-́ть).

doll *n* ку́кла; *dim* ку́колка; (*US*) *sl* де́вушка; **~'s house** ку́кольный дом.

doll *vt*: *CQ* **to ~ oneself up** наря|жа́ться (-ди́ться).

dollar *n* до́ллар; *CQ* **I'd bet my bottom ~ that...** го́лову даю́ на отсече́ние, что...

dolt *n* болва́н, ду́рень (*m*).

domain *n* владе́ние, *usu pl*; *fig* **in the ~ of science** в о́бласти нау́ки.

dome *n* (*arch, vault*) свод; (*of church*) ку́пол.

domestic *n* слуга́ (*m*); (**~s**) прислу́га (*collect*).

domestic *adj* **1** (*family*) семе́йный; (*household*) дома́шний; **he has ~ troubles** у него́ неприя́тности в семье́; **~ service/science** дома́шняя рабо́та, домово́дство; **~ animals** дома́шние живо́тные

2: **the ~ affairs of a country** вну́тренние дела́ страны́.

domesticate *vt* (*of animals*) прируч|а́ть (-и́ть), одома́шнивать (*usu impf*); (*of people*) **she is not at all ~d** она́ не лю́бит занима́ться (дома́шним) хозя́йством.

domicile *n* местожи́тельство.

dominant *adj* (*chief*) гла́вный, домини́рующий; (*basic*) основно́й; **she is the ~ partner in that firm/marriage** она́ гла́вный челове́к в фи́рме, она́ глава́ семьи́; **the ~ idea of the book** гла́вная/основна́я иде́я кни́ги; **a ~ influence** домини́рующее влия́ние; **one question was ~ in all our minds** у всех у нас в мы́слях был оди́н и то́т же вопро́с.

dominate *vt*: **the mountain ~s the valley** гора́ возвыша́ется/госпо́дствует над доли́ной (*impfs*); **he completely ~s the committee** его́ влия́ние в коми́ссии преоблада́ющее, он де́ржит всю коми́ссию в свои́х рука́х.

domineering *adj* вла́стный.

dominion *n* (*power*) власть; *Polit* доминио́н.

domino *n* (*a single domino*) кость домино́; *pl* (**dominoes**) (*game*) домино́ (*indecl*).

don *n* (*UK*) *Univ* преподава́тель (*m*).

donate *vt*: (*money*) **he ~d £1,000/his books to the library** он поже́ртвовал ты́сячу фу́нтов/он переда́л свои́ кни́ги библиоте́ке.

donation *n* (*of money*) поже́ртвование; (*gift*) дар.

done *adj*: **I like my meat well ~** я люблю́ хорошо́ прожа́ренное мя́со; **it's not ~ to read at table** не при́нято чита́ть за столо́м; *CQ*: **this car is ~ (for)** э́той маши́не коне́ц/кры́шка; **I'm ~ in** я вы́дохся.

donkey *n* осёл (*also of person*); *CQ* **I haven't seen him for ~'s years** я его́ не ви́дел бог зна́ет ско́лько вре́мени.

donor *n* (*of money*) же́ртвователь (*m*); (*of things*) дари́тель (*m*); **blood ~** до́нор.

doodle *vi* черти́ть кара́кули (*usu impf*).

doom *n* (*fate*) рок, судьба́; (*ruin, death*) ги́бель.

doom *adj* обре|ка́ть (-́чь); **~ed to failure/to die** обречённый на прова́л/на ги́бель.

door *n* дверь; **front/back ~** пара́дная дверь, чёрный ход; **sliding ~** раздвижна́я дверь; **who lives next ~ (to you)?** кто живёт в сосе́днем до́ме?/ря́дом с ва́ми?; **he lives two/three ~s away** он живёт че́рез дом/че́рез два до́ма отсю́да; **out of ~s** на у́лице, на дворе́, на откры́том во́здухе; **behind closed ~s** за закры́тыми дверя́ми; **the taxi took us from ~ to ~** такси́ довезло́ нас от две́ри до две́ри; **he delivers papers from ~ to ~** он разно́сит газе́ты по дома́м; **to knock at/answer the ~** стуча́ть в дверь, откры́ть дверь; **to show smb to the ~** провожа́ть кого́-л до две́ри; *fig*: **to show smb the ~** вы́ставить кого́-л (за дверь); **he's at death's ~** он при́ смерти/на краю́ моги́лы.

doorbell *n* дверно́й звоно́к.

door-handle *n* дверна́я ру́чка.

doorkeeper *n* швейца́р.

door-knocker *n* дверно́й молото́к.

doormat *n* ко́врик/полови́к у две́ри; *fig* **she makes a ~ of herself** она́ позволя́ет собо́й кома́ндовать.

doorpost *n* дверно́й кося́к; *fig* **deaf as a ~** глух как пень.

doorstep *n* ступе́нька крыльца́; *pl* (**~s**) (*short flight of steps to a house*) крыльцо́ (*in SU can be roofed*).

doorway *n*: **he stood in the ~** он стоя́л в дверя́х (*pl*).

dope *n CQ* (*drug*) нарко́тик; *Sport* до́пинг; *sl*: **give me the ~ on that** введи́ меня́ в курс де́ла; **you ~!** ты, лопоу́хий!/дурачо́к!

dope *vt* (*a person*) да|ва́ть нарко́тики (-ть); *Sport* **to ~ a horse/a runner** дава́ть ло́шади/бегуну́ до́пинг.

dormant *adj*: *Biol* **bears are/lie ~ in winter** зимо́й медве́ди погружа́ются в спя́чку/нахо́дятся в спя́чке; *Fin* **~ capital** мёртвый капита́л; *fig*: **a ~ volcano** спя́щий вулка́н; **they are letting the matter lie ~** они́ отложи́ли э́тот вопро́с в до́лгий я́щик.

dormer *adj*: **a ~ window** манса́рдное окно́.

dormouse *n Zool* со́ня.

dosage *n* дозиро́вка; (*amount of single dose*) до́за.

dose *n* до́за; **to increase the ~** увели́чить до́зу.

dose *vt*: **I ~d him/myself with aspirin** я дал ему́ аспири́н, я при́нял аспири́н.

doss *vi CQ*: **to ~ down for the night somewhere** пристро́иться где́-либо на ночле́г.

doss house *n* ночле́жка.

dossier *n* досье́ (*indecl*).

dot *n* то́чка; **~s and dashes** то́чки и тире́ (*indecl*); *fig CQ* **he arrived/pays on the ~** он пришёл мину́та в мину́ту, он пла́тит то́чно в срок.

dot *vt*: **sheep were ~ted about the field** о́вцы разбрели́сь по по́лю; **there are quite**

a few houses of this type ~ted round the district таких домов довольно много в этой местности.

dotage *n*: **he's in his ~** он впал в детство.

dote *vt*: **she ~s on her grandson** она души не чает в своём внуке; **her husband ~s on her** муж обожает её.

dotted line *n* пунктир, пунктирная линия; *fig* **don't worry—he'll sign on the ~** не волнуйтесь—он сделает всё, что от него потребуют.

dotty *adj CQ*: **she's a little ~** она с приветом.

double *n* (*of quantity*) двойное количество; (*person*) двойник; **she's the ~ of her sister** они с сестрой двойняшки; **the ~ of this vase** вторая такая ваза; (*in tennis*) *pl* (~**s**) парная игра; **mixed/men's ~s** смешанные/мужские пары; *Mil* **at the ~, march!** бегом, марш!

double *adj* двойной; **a ~ chin/room** двойной подбородок, номер на двоих (*in hotel*); **a ~ window** окно с двойной рамой; **the house has one ~ bedroom** в доме одна спальня на двоих; **a ~ tooth/whisky** коренной зуб, двойное виски; **a ~ coat of paint** двойной слой краски; **~ harness** парная упряжь; *fig*: **to work in ~ harness** работать в паре; **that phrase has a ~ meaning** у этого выражения два значения; **he is ~ her age** он вдвое старше её; **his income is ~ what it was** его доходы (*pl*) удвоились.

double *adv* вдвое; вдвойне; **to cost ~** стоить вдвое дороже; **to pay ~** платить двойную плату.

double *vti vt* удв|аивать (-оить); **to ~ one's stake** удвоить ставку; **he was ~d up with pain** он скорчился от боли; *Theat* **he ~s the parts of the king and the general** он играет в пьесе и короля и генерала; *Naut* **to ~ a headland** огибать мыс (обогнуть)

vi: **the population has ~d** население удвоилось; **to ~ back on one's tracks** возвра|щаться (назад) по собственному следу (*sing*) (-титься); **we've only three bedrooms but the children ~ up when we have guests** у нас только три спальни, и детям приходится (*impers*) потесниться, когда приезжают гости.

double-barrelled *adj*: **a ~ gun** двуствольное ружьё.

double bass *n* контрабас.

double-breasted *adj*: **a ~ jacket** двубортный пиджак.

double-cross *vt*: *CQ* **to ~ smb** обман|ывать/наду|вать кого-л (-уть/-ть).

double-dealing *n* обман, двурушничество.

double-decker *n* (**a ~**) двухэтажный автобус.

double entendre *n* двусмысленность; двойной смысл.

double entry *n* двойная бухгалтерия.

double-park *vti* ставить машину во второй ряд (по-).

double spacing *n*: **in ~** через два интервала.

double talk *n*: **that's typical of his ~** это типичное для него лицемерное заявление.

doubly *adv* вдвойне; **be ~ careful crossing the street** будь вдвойне осторожен при переходе улицы/, переходя улицу.

doubt *n* сомнение; **without/beyond ~** без/вне сомнения; **when in ~ consult the doctor** если есть сомнение, обратитесь к врачу; **if you're in any ~ about what to do, ask me** если у вас возникнут какие-то сомнения,/неясности (*pls*), спросите меня; **the result of the election is still in ~** исход выборов всё ещё неясен; **I am in no ~ about his ability** я не сомневаюсь в его способностях (*pl*), у меня нет сомнений (*pl*) насчёт его способностей; **to raise a ~ in smb's mind about smth** возбудить у кого-л сомнение в чём-л; **to throw ~ on smb's statement** подвергнуть сомнению чьё-л утверждение/чьи-л слова.

doubt *vt* сомневаться в + *P* (*impf*); **do you ~ my word?** ты сомневаешься в моём слове?; **I ~ whether he'll come/if that was what she meant** я сомневаюсь, придёт ли он/это ли она имела в виду; **you're sure to win.—I very much ~ it!** ты наверняка выиграешь.—Я сильно сомневаюсь в этом!

doubtful *adj*: **a ~ character** сомнительный тип; **that's a ~ blessing** это палка о двух концах; **your remark is in ~ taste** вы говорите очень неуважительно; **I am ~ what I ought to do** (я) не знаю, как мне поступить; **the weather looks ~** погода сегодня ненадёжная.

doubtless *adv* без сомнения; вполне вероятно.

douche *n Med* промывание.

dough *n* тесто.

doughnut *n* пончик.

dour *adj* (*severe*) суровый; (*gloomy*) мрачный.

dove *n* голубь (*m*).

dowdy *adj*: **a ~ woman, ~ clothes** неряшливая женщина/одежда.

down[1] *n* (*from ducks, on plants, on face*) пух, *dim* пушок.

down[2] *n*: **he's had a lot of ups and ~s** у него в жизни было столько всего/столько взлётов и падений; *CQ* **he has a ~ on me, I don't know why** он за что-то сердится на меня, я не знаю, за что.

down[2] *adv* **1** (*of motion*) вниз, (*of position*) внизу [**NB** *the English adverbial use is often translated by a Russian verb with prefix, see examples and also verbs* + "*down*"]; **I'm going ~ for a minute and I'll be right back** я только схожу вниз и сейчас же вернусь; **he is already ~** он уже внизу; **to go ~ in the lift** спускаться в лифте; **she came ~ to meet the guests** она спустилась к гостям; **the aeroplane is ~** самолёт приземлился; **to go ~ to the country** ехать в деревню; **he's just come ~ from Oxford** (*finally*) он только что окончил Оксфорд, (*for the vacation*) он только что из Оксфорда—приехал на каникулы; *Sport*: **he's ~ and out** (*of boxer*) он в нокауте, *fig* (*destitute*) он разорился; **to be one ~** отстать на один гол (*goal*)/на одно очко (*point*);

fig: **to pay £3 ~** заплати́ть три фу́нта нали́чными; **prices have come ~** це́ны сни́зились; **every man from the general ~** все, от генера́ла до солда́та; **I'm £2 ~** (*on bet, deal, etc.*) я потеря́л два фу́нта; **demand is ~** спрос упа́л; **I'm ~ to my last cigarette** у меня́ оста́лась после́дняя сигаре́та; **he's ~ with flu** он лежи́т с гри́ппом; *CQ*: **it's ~ in black and white** э́то напи́сано чёрным по бе́лому; **she's a bit ~ today** сего́дня она́ в плохо́м настрое́нии; **it suits me ~ to the ground to start early** меня́ вполне́ устра́ивает отпра́виться пора́ньше

2 (*of time*): **~ to the present time** до сих по́р, до настоя́щего вре́мени, по сей день; **right ~ to Shakespeare's time** вплоть до эпо́хи Шекспи́ра

3 *as interj*: (*to dog*) **~!** сиде́ть!; **~ with the oppressors!** доло́й угнета́телей!

down[2] *prep*: **to walk ~ hill** спуска́ться с горы́/по́д гору; **tears ran ~ her face** слёзы текли́ по её лицу́; **her hair hung ~ her back** во́лосы рассы́пались у неё по плеча́м; **to sail ~ river/the Volga** плыть вниз по реке́/по Во́лге; **Oxford is further ~ the river** О́ксфорд нахо́дится ни́же по реке́; **~ wind** по ве́тру; **to walk ~ the road** идти́ по доро́ге; **to go ~ town** идти́ в центр го́рода.

down[2] *vt* (*food or medicine*) глота́ть, прогла́тывать (*pfs for both* проглоти́ть); **he quickly ~ed a glass of beer and left** он бы́стро вы́пил кру́жку пи́ва и ушёл.

downcast *adj* удручённый; **we were all ~ after he left** мы все бы́ли удручены́ его́ отъе́здом; **with a ~ expression** с удручённым ви́дом; **with ~ eyes** опусти́в глаза́.

downfall *n* (*of rain*) ли́вень (*m*); *fig* паде́ние; **his ~ was due to gambling** его́ погуби́ли аза́ртные и́гры.

downgrade *vt* пони|жа́ть по слу́жбе (-зить).

downhearted *adj*: **don't be ~!** не па́дай ду́хом!, не унывай!

downhill *adv* вниз, по́д гору; *fig*: **the business is going ~** дела́ фи́рмы пошли́ [**NB** *tense*] по́д гору; **I fear my grandfather is going ~** бою́сь, мой дед на́чал сдава́ть.

downpour *n* ли́вень (*m*).

downright *adj* (*of person*) открове́нный, прямо́й; **it's ~ nonsense/a ~ lie** э́то абсолю́тная *or* я́вная чепуха́, э́то я́вная ложь.

downstairs *adj* ни́жний; **the ~ rooms** ко́мнаты ни́жнего этажа́

downstairs *adv* (*of motion*) вниз, (*of position*) внизу́; **to go/come ~** сойти́ вниз; **she's ~** она́ внизу́; **to wait ~** ждать внизу́; **he fell ~** он упа́л с ле́стницы; **we live ~** мы живём на пе́рвом этаже́ (*on ground floor*).

downstream *adv* (вниз) по тече́нию.

downtown *adv* (*US*) в це́нтре го́рода.

downtrodden *adj* угнетённый; *fig* **he's a bit ~ at home** с ним до́ма не о́чень счита́ются.

downward *adj*: **a ~ slope** спуск; **a ~ path** тропа́, иду́щая вниз; **prices show a ~ tendency** похо́же, что це́ны на́чали снижа́ться.

downwards *adv* вниз; **she lay face ~** она́ лежа́ла лицо́м вниз; **the monkey hung head ~** обезья́на висе́ла вниз голово́й.

dowry *n* прида́ное.

doze *n* дремо́та; **to have a ~** вздремну́ть.

doze *vi* дрема́ть (по-); **he ~d off in his chair** он задрема́л в кре́сле (*pf*).

dozen *n* дю́жина; **a round ~** ро́вно дю́жина; **by the ~** дю́жинами; **3 ~ eggs** три дю́жины яи́ц; **half a ~** полдю́жины (*f*); *pl CQ*: **~s of people** ма́сса/мно́жество люде́й; **I told you so ~s of times** я ты́сячу раз говори́л тебе́ об э́том; *fig*: **she talks nineteen to the ~** она́ трещи́т как соро́ка; **it's six of one and half a ~ of the other** что в лоб, что по́ лбу.

drab *adj*: **she always wears ~ colours** она́ всегда́ но́сит пла́тья каки́х-то блёклых тоно́в; **life's very ~ just now** жизнь пошла́ така́я се́рая [**NB** *tense*].

draft *n* **1**: **a rough ~** набро́сок; чернови́к; **a final/corrected ~** белови́к; **I've done a rough ~ of the chapter/speech/letter** я написа́л главу́ вчерне́ (*adv*), я наброса́л речь, я написа́л чернови́к письма́; **just type it in ~** печа́тай снача́ла на́черно (*adv*); **my novel is ready in ~** рома́н гото́в в черновике́

2 *other uses*: (*architects', engineers'*) эски́з; *Fin* чек; тра́тта; *Mil* призы́в; набо́р; *Law*, *usu attr*: **a ~ bill/contract** законопрое́кт, прое́кт догово́ра.

draft *vt* **1** (*a document*) состав|ля́ть (-ить); **I have to ~ the agenda/the contract** мне ну́жно соста́вить прое́кт пове́стки дня/прое́кт догово́ра; **he asked me to ~ a letter to the Minister** он попроси́л меня́ подгото́вить письмо́ мини́стру; **I'm ~ing my next chapter** я де́лаю набро́ски сле́дующей главы́

2 *Mil*: **he's been ~ed into the army** его́ призва́ли в а́рмию.

draftsman *n* чертёжник.

drag *n*: **a ~ (net)** бре́день (*m*); (*dredge*) дра́га; *fig* **he is a bit of a ~ on them** он для них обу́за.

drag *vti vt* **1** таска́ть (*indet impf*), тащи́ть (*det impf*) *and compounds*; (*trail*) волочи́ть (*impf*); **to ~ a child along by the hand** тащи́ть ребёнка за́ руку; **he could hardly ~ himself along** он е́ле тащи́лся; **he was ~ging his feet/his bad foot** он е́ле волочи́л но́ги, он приволакивал повреждённую но́гу

2 *with preps*: **we ~ged the dogs apart** мы раста|щи́ли соба́к (*impf* -скивать); **I ~ged her away from the window** я оттащи́л её от окна́; **he was being ~ged down by the current** его́ затяну́ло (*impers*) тече́нием; **to ~ a sack into the shed** втащи́ть мешо́к в сара́й; **they ~ged the box out (of the cupboard)** они́ вы́тащили я́щик (из шка́фа); **to ~ out negotiations** затя|гивать перегово́ры (-ну́ть); **I ~ged the table to the window** я подтащи́л стол к окну́; **he managed to ~ himself to**

the phone он дотащи́лся до телефо́на; *CQ* **we ~ged him off to the theatre** мы вы́тащили его́ в теа́тр

3 (*river, etc.*) драги́ровать (*impf*); **the police ~ged the pond for the corpse** поли́ция драги́ровала пруд в по́исках тру́па

vi: **he ~ged behind the others** он тащи́лся позади́ всех; **our anchor ~ged during the night** у нас но́чью попо́лз я́корь; **the case ~ged on for another month** де́ло тяну́лось ещё ме́сяц.

dragon *n* драко́н.

dragonfly *n* стрекоза́.

drain *n* 1 сток; (*for rain water from roof*) водосто́к; *pl* (**the ~s**) канализа́ция; (*in fields*) дрена́жный ров; (*ditch*) кана́ва; (*at both edges of road*) кюве́т; **the ~ from the sink is blocked** ра́ковина засори́лась; **the ~ is choked with leaves** водосто́к заби́ло (*impers*) ли́стьями; **there's something wrong with our ~s** у нас что́-то не в поря́дке с канализа́цией

2 *fig uses*: **the night work was a great ~ on his health** ночна́я рабо́та подорвала́ его́ здоро́вье; **military expenditure is a ~ on the country's resources** вое́нные расхо́ды истоща́ют эконо́мику страны́; **the brain ~** «уте́чка мозго́в»; **it was just £1,000 down the ~** ты́сяча фу́нтов вы́летела в трубу́.

drain *vti vt Agric, Med* дрени́ровать (*impf and pf*); **to ~ meadows/a wound** дрени́ровать *or* осуша́ть луга́, дрени́ровать ра́ну; **to ~ oil from a tank** вы|пуска́ть нефть из ба́ка (-́пустить); **to ~ a flooded field** от|води́ть во́ду с зато́пленного по́ля (-вести́); **to ~ a swamp** осуш|а́ть боло́то (-и́ть); *fig* **she seemed ~ed of energy** она́ каза́лась соверше́нно обесси́ленной

vi: **the water will soon ~ away from the fields** вода́ ско́ро сойдёт (с поле́й); **the river ~s into the Black Sea** э́та река́ впада́ет в Чёрное мо́ре; **leave the dishes to ~** оста́вь посу́ду (*collect*) со́хнуть

drainage *n* (*sewage system*) канализа́ция; (*from gutters*) водоотво́д; *Agric, Med* дрена́ж; **even the remoter villages now have ~** да́же в са́мых отдалённых деревня́х тепе́рь есть канализа́ция; **the ~ of the marshes will take a long time** осуше́ние боло́т потре́бует мно́го вре́мени.

drainpipe *n* сто́чная/дрена́жная труба́.

drake *n* се́лезень (*m*).

dram *n* (*weight*) дра́хма; *CQ* (*drink*) глото́к спиртно́го.

drama *n* дра́ма.

dramatic *adj* драмати́ческий; *fig* порази́тельный; **~ changes** рази́тельные переме́ны.

dramatics *npl* драмати́ческое иску́сство (*sing*); **are you interested in amateur ~?** вас интересу́ют люби́тельские спекта́кли?

dramatis personae *npl* де́йствующие ли́ца.

dramatist *n* драмату́рг.

drape *vt* драпирова́ть (за-); **he ~d a blanket round himself** он заверну́лся в одея́ло.

drapery *n* (*materials*) тка́ни (*pl*); *attr*: **~ department** отде́л тка́ней.

drapes *n usu pl* (*US*) драпиро́вка (*sing*).

drastic *adj* реши́тельный, круто́й; **~ measures** реши́тельные/круты́е/жёсткие ме́ры; **there have been ~ changes under the new management** при но́вом руково́дстве произошли́ кру́пные переме́ны; **they're selling off old stock at ~ reductions** они́ распродаю́т лежа́лые това́ры с огро́мной ски́дкой.

drat *interj*: **~ it!** чёрт возьми́!; **~ that child!** го́споди, что за несно́сный ребёнок!

draught *n* 1 (*drink*) глото́к; *Med* до́за (лека́рства); **at one ~** за́лпом

2 *Naut* оса́дка (су́дна); **a vessel of shallow ~/with a ~ of 20 feet** су́дно с небольшо́й оса́дкой/с оса́дкой (в) два́дцать фу́тов

3 (*of air*: *in chimney*) тя́га, (*in room*) сквозня́к; **to sit in a ~** сиде́ть на сквозняке́; **there's a howling ~ here** здесь ужа́сный сквозня́к; **there's a ~ from the window** из окна́ (*when open*)/от окна́ (*when open or shut*) ду́ет (*impers*)

4 *pl* (**~s**) (*game*) ша́шки.

draught beer *n* бо́чковое пи́во.

draughty *adj*: **this room is ~** в э́той ко́мнате сквозняки́; **the bus stop is at the most ~ corner of the square** авто́бусная остано́вка (нахо́дится) на са́мой ве́треной ча́сти пло́щади.

draw *n* 1 (*of lots*) жеребьёвка; **when does the ~ take place?** когда́ бу́дет жеребьёвка?

2 *Sport* ничья́; **the game ended in a ~** игра́ ко́нчилась вничью́ (*adv*); **I offer you a ~** предлага́ю вам ничью́

3 *fig uses*: **his appearance will be the ~ of the evening** его́ выступле́ние бу́дет гвоздём програ́ммы; **the new play is proving a great ~** на но́вую пье́су про́сто пало́мничество; *CQ* **he's very quick on the ~** (*ready to quarrel*) он заво́дится с пол-оборо́та/момента́льно.

draw *vti vt* 1 (*pull, tow*) тяну́ть (*impf*); **the tug was ~ing six barges after it** букси́р тяну́л за собо́й шесть барж; **the train was ~n by two engines** соста́в тяну́ли два локомоти́ва; **to ~ the curtains** раздви|га́ть (*open*)/задёр|гивать (*close*) занаве́ски (-́нуть/-нуть); **to ~ blinds** под|нима́ть (*up*)/опус|ка́ть (*down*) што́ры (-ня́ть/-ти́ть)

2 (*draw tight, stretch*): **to ~ a bow** натя́|гивать лук (-ну́ть); **to ~ a knot tight** затя́|гивать у́зел (-ну́ть); **he drew himself up to his full height** он вы́тянулся во весь рост; *fig* **his face was ~n with pain** его́ лицо́ искази́лось от бо́ли

3 (*breath*): **he drew a deep breath** он сде́лал глубо́кий вдох; **the runner stopped to ~ breath** бегу́н останови́лся отдыша́ться/перевести́ дыха́ние *or* дух; **she talked non-stop, without even drawing breath** она́ болта́ла не перестава́я/без у́молку (*adv*)

4 (*extract*) вы|та́скивать (-́тащить); удал|я́ть (-и́ть); **to ~ nails out of** *or* **from a plank/a cork** вы́тащить гво́зди из доски́/про́бку из буты́лки; **to ~ a tooth** удали́ть зуб; **to ~ pus**

вытя́гивать гной; **to ~ beer from a barrel** нали|ва́ть/(*and strain*) нацеди́ть пи́ва из бо́чки (-ть/*pf*); **to ~ a bath** напо́лнить ва́нну; **to ~ water from a well** зачерпну́ть воды́ из коло́дца; **to ~ a fowl** потроши́ть ку́рицу (вы́-); **to ~ money from the bank** брать де́ньги в ба́нке (взять); **to ~ one's salary/rations** получ|а́ть зарпла́ту/паёк (*sing*) (-и́ть); **to ~ money for one's expenses** (*in advance*) получи́ть де́ньги на расхо́ды

5 *fig* (*extract*): **he refused to be ~n** он отказа́лся говори́ть об э́том; **to ~ a conclusion from smth** вы|води́ть заключе́ние/де́лать вы́вод из чего́-л (-вести/с-); **to ~ a distinction/comparison between...** про|води́ть разли́чие/сравне́ние ме́жду + *I* (-вести́); **to ~ a lesson/a moral from smth** извле|ка́ть уро́к/мора́ль из чего́-л (-чь); **to ~ inspiration from nature** че́рпать вдохнове́ние в приро́де (*usu impf*); **his words ~ applause/tears from the audience** его́ слова́ вы́звали аплодисме́нты (*pl*)/слёзы у зри́телей (*pl*) *or* у пу́блики

6 *fig* (*attract*): **he always ~s large audiences** он всегда́ со|бира́ет большу́ю аудито́рию (*sing*) (-бра́ть); **to ~ smb's attention to/away from smth** обра|ща́ть чьё-л внима́ние на что-л (-ти́ть), отвле|ка́ть чьё-л внима́ние от чего́-л (-чь); **I felt ~n to him** меня́ тяну́ло (*impers*) к нему́; **grief drew them closer** го́ре их сблизи́ло

7 (*lots, etc.*): **to ~ lots** тяну́ть жре́бий (*sing*); **to ~ a prize/a blank in a lottery** вы́тянуть счастли́вый/пусто́й биле́т в лотере́е; *fig* **I tried to sound him out but I drew a blank** я пыта́лся узна́ть его́ мне́ние/*CQ* расколо́ть его́, но мне э́то не удало́сь

8 (*with pencil, etc.*) рисова́ть, черти́ть (*pfs* на-) *and compounds*; **to ~ a cat** рисова́ть ко́шку; **to ~ a map/plan** черти́ть ка́рту/план; **to ~ a line** черти́ть/про|води́ть ли́нию (на-/-вести́); *fig* **I drew the line at that** я бы на э́том останови́лся

9 *Naut*: **the ship ~s 40 feet** су́дно име́ет оса́дку (в) со́рок фу́тов

vi **1: let the tea ~** дай ча́ю насто́яться

2: to ~ level with поравня́ться с + *I*, *also Sport*; **the bus is ~ing level with us** нас нагоня́ет/догоня́ет авто́бус; *Sport* **they drew** они́ сыгра́ли вничью́ (*adv*); *Cards* **to ~ for partners** разы́грывать партнёров

3 *Art*: **I love ~ing** я люблю́ рисова́ть

4 (*of air*): **this chimney ~s well** в трубе́ хоро́шая тя́га; **the fire began to ~** ого́нь заня́лся; **the fire/stove won't ~ today** сего́дня ками́н/печь ника́к не раста́пливается; **the sails are ~ing now** тепе́рь паруса́ забира́ют ве́тер/наполня́ются ве́тром

draw ahead *vi Sport* вы|рыва́ться вперёд (-рваться)

draw aside *vti*: **to ~ smb aside** от|води́ть кого́-л в сто́рону (-вести́); **he drew aside to let me pass** он посторони́лся, что́бы дать мне пройти́

draw away from *vi*: **the car drew away from the kerb** маши́на отъе́хала от тротуа́ра; **she drew away from him** она́ отстрани́лась/отшатну́лась от него́; *Sport* от|рыва́ться от + *G* (-орва́ться)

draw back *vti vt*: **he drew back his hand** он отвёл ру́ку

vi от|ходи́ть (-ойти́), отстран|я́ться (-и́ться); (*retreat*) отступ|а́ть (-и́ть), *also Mil*

draw in *vi*: **the evenings are ~ing in** вечера́ стано́вятся коро́че

draw near *vi*: **Xmas is ~ing near** приближа́ется/наступа́ет рождество́; **we drew near to Moscow** мы приближа́лись к Москве́

draw out *vti vt*: **to ~ money out of the bank** брать де́ньги из ба́нка (взять), (*SU equiv*) снима́ть де́ньги со сберкни́жки (*from savings bank*) (снять); *fig*: **she's good at ~ing people out** она́ располага́ет к себе́ люде́й, лю́ди с ней стано́вятся открове́ннее; **he gave some long ~n out explanation** он пусти́лся в до́лгие объясне́ния (*pl*)

vi: **the train drew out of the station** по́езд тро́нулся; **the days are ~ing out** дни стано́вятся длинне́е

draw up *vti vt*: **to ~ up a boat** подтя́|гивать ло́дку к бе́регу (-ну́ть); **to ~ up a chair for a guest** пододви|га́ть стул для го́стя (-нуть); **to ~ one's chair up to the fire** придви́нуть кре́сло к ками́ну; **to ~ up the bedclothes** натя́|гивать на себя́ одея́ло (*sing*) (-ну́ть); **he drew himself up to his full height** он вы́прямился во весь рост; *Mil* **to ~ up troops** вы|стра́ивать войска́ (-строить)

vi: **the bus drew up at the theatre** авто́бус останови́лся у теа́тра.

drawback *n* недоста́ток; **the chief ~ to this plan...** основно́й/гла́вный недоста́ток э́того пла́на...

drawer *n* (*of desk, etc.*) я́щик стола́.

drawing *n* (*the art*) рисова́ние; черче́ние; (*sketch*) рису́нок; *Tech* чертёж; *attr*: **~ board** чертёжная доска́; **~ paper** бума́га для рисова́ния/черче́ния; **~ pin** (чертёжная/канцеля́рская) кно́пка.

drawing room *n* гости́ная.

drawl *n* протя́жное произноше́ние.

drawl *vi*: **he ~s** он говори́т, растя́гивая слова́.

drawn *adj*: **a ~ game** игра́ вничью́ (*adv*); **a face ~ with pain** лицо́, искажённое бо́лью; **she looks ~** она́ осу́нулась, у неё осу́нувшееся лицо́.

dread *n* страх; **to live in constant ~ of smth** жить в постоя́нном стра́хе пе́ред чем-л.

dread *vt* боя́ться + *G*, страши́ться + *G* (*impfs*); **I ~ being ill/illness** я бою́сь заболе́ть/боле́зней (*pl*); **he ~s (taking) responsibility** он страши́тся отве́тственности; **I ~ going to the dentist** я бою́сь идти́ к зубно́му врачу́.

dreadful *adj* стра́шный, ужа́сный, *also CQ*.

dream *n* сон; (*reverie*) мечта́, грёза; **to have a ~** ви́деть сон; **I had a bad ~** мне сни́лся стра́шный сон; **he goes about in a (day) ~** он грёзит наяву́; **it's my ~ to be an actor** моя́ мечта́ — стать актёром; **it succeeded beyond**

my wildest ~s о такóй удáче я не смел и мечтáть / я и не мечтáл; *attr*: **my ~ house / girl** дом, о котóром я мечтáл, дéвушка моéй мечты́.

dream *vti vt* сни́ться (при-) (*impers*); **I ~t that...** мне сни́лось, что...; **I must have ~t it** мне, должнó быть, э́то присни́лось; **I little ~t that I would ever live in Paris** мне и не сни́лось, что я бу́ду жить в Пари́же

vi **1** (*to have a dream*) ви́деть сон (*only in impf*); **I ~t about you** я ви́дел тебя́ во сне; **I ~t about my home / my childhood** мне сни́лся дом, мне сни́лось дéтство

2 (*day-dream*) мечтáть о + *P or* + *inf* (*impf*); **I ~ of love / of returning home** я мечтáю о любви́ / верну́ться домóй; *fig*: **I wouldn't ~ of it!** я об э́том и мечтáть не смéю; **I wouldn't ~ of troubling him** мне и в гóлову не пришлó беспокóить егó.

dreamer *n* мечтáтель (*m*).

dreamily *adv* сóнно, полусóнно; как во сне.

dream land, dream world *n* мир / цáрство грёз.

dreamy *adj* мечтáтельный; **you look ~** у тебя́ мечтáтельный вид.

dreary *adj* мрáчный; **a ~ room** мрáчная кóмната; **~ thoughts** мрáчные мы́сли; **~ weather** ненáстная погóда; **what a ~ programme!** какáя ску́чная прогрáмма!

dredge *n* дрáга.

dredge *vti*: **to ~ (a river)** углуб|ля́ть дно реки́ (-и́ть); **to ~ for oysters** лови́ть у́стриц дрáгой; **to ~ up smth from a pond** вытащить что-л со дна прудá.

dredger *n* (*ship*) землечерпáлка.

dregs *npl* осáдок (*usu sing*); **~ of wine** осáдок в винé; **to drink to the ~** пить до днá; *fig* **the ~ of society** подóнки / отбрóсы óбщества.

drench *vt* (*make wet, usu pass*): **to be ~ed** промок|áть насквóзь (-нуть), вы|мокáть (-мокнуть); **I was ~ed to the skin** я вы́мок до ни́тки, я промóк до костéй.

drenching *adj*: **~ rain** проливнóй дождь.

dress *n* (*clothing*) одéжда; (*one garment*) плáтье; **evening ~** (*lady's*) вечéрнее плáтье, (*man's*) смóкинг; *attr*: (*tails*) **~ clothes** фрак (*sing*).

dress *vti vt* **1** одевáть (одéть); **to ~ a child / a doll** одéть ребёнка / ку́клу; **she was ~ed in white** онá былá в бéлом / одéта в бéлое; **to ~ oneself** одевáться; **to ~ smb up as Father Christmas** наря|жáть когó-л дéдом-морóзом (-ди́ть)

2 (*treat*): **to ~ leather** вы|дéлывать кóжу (-делать); **to ~ one's hair, to have one's hair ~ed** дéлать причёску (с-); **to ~ a shop window** оформ|ля́ть витри́ну (-ить); *Agric* **to ~ a field with lime** вноси́ть в зéмлю и́звесть (внести́); *Cook* **to ~ a salad** заправ|ля́ть салáт (-ить); *Med* **to ~ a wound** перевя́з|ывать рáну (-áть)

vi одевáться; **to ~ for dinner / for the theatre** переод|евáться к обéду /, чтóбы пойти́ в теáтр (-éться); **she ~s well** онá хорошó одевáется; **to ~ up for a ball / in fancy dress** наря|жáться на бал / в маскарáдный костю́м (-ди́ться).

dressing *n Med* перевя́зка; *Cook* приправá.

dressing-down *n CQ*: **he gave me a ~** он отругáл меня́ как слéдует.

dressing gown *n* халáт.

dressing room *n Theat* артисти́ческая.

dressing table *n* туалéтный стóлик.

dressmaker *n* портни́ха.

dressmaking *n* шитьё, поши́в жéнского плáтья.

dribble *vi* **1** (*of babies*) обслюня́виться (*pf*) **2** *Sport* вести́ мяч (*usu impf*).

driblet *n* кáпелька; **in ~s** по кáпле, *fig* понемнóжку.

dribs *npl*: *CQ* **the proofs arrive in ~ and drabs** корректу́ру присылáют в час по чáйной лóжке.

dried *adj* сухóй; **~ fruit / soups** сухофру́кты, сухи́е су́пы.

drier *n* суши́лка, *also Agric*.

drift *n* (*current*) течéние; (*going off course*) *Naut* дрейф, *Aer* снос; (*of sand*) нанóс; (*of snow*) сугрóб; **snow ~s** снéжные занóсы; **the wind must be easterly judging from the ~ of the clouds** су́дя по направлéнию облакóв, вéтер дóлжен быть востóчный; *fig*: **the ~ from the land to the cities** мигрáция населéния из дерéвни в гóрод; **I caught the ~ of what he said** я улови́л смысл егó слов.

drift *vti vt*: **to ~ logs downstream** сплавля́ть лес (*collect*) (*usu impf*); **the wind had ~ed the snow into high banks** (вéтром) намелó (*impers*) высóкие сугрóбы

vi Naut and fig дрейфовáть (*impf*); **to ~ downstream** дрейфовáть по течéнию; **the body ~ed ashore** труп приби́ло (*impers*) к бéрегу; **snow had ~ed over the road** дорóгу занеслó (*impers*) снéгом; **leaves had ~ed into piles** намелó (*impers*) ку́чи ли́стьев; *fig* **he ~s through life** он плывёт по течéнию.

drifter *n Naut* дри́фтер.

drift ice *n* плаву́чая льди́на.

drift wood *n* лес, приби́тый к бéрегу, плавни́к.

drill[1] *n* (*tool*) дрель; (*dentist's*) бормаши́на; *Tech* (*large scale*) бур; **pneumatic ~** отбóйный молотóк.

drill[1] *vti* (*small scale*) сверли́ть, (*large scale*) бури́ть (*pfs* про-); **to ~ a hole / through a plank** просверли́ть отвéрстие / дóску [**NB** *English vt and vi both translated by Russian vt*]; **to ~ for oil** бури́ть (сквáжину) в пóисках нéфти.

drill[2] *n Agric* (*furrow*) боруздá; (*machine*) рядовáя сéялка.

drill[3] *n* (*exercises*) упражнéния (*pl*); *Sport* тренирóвка; *Mil* строевáя подготóвка, учéние; **fire ~** противопожáрная подготóвка; **lifeboat ~** шлю́почное учéние; *CQ*: **you all know the ~** вы все знакóмы с приёмами рабóты; **what's the ~?** (*about a formal occasion*) какова́ процеду́ра?, (*informally*) что да́льше (де́лать)?

drill[3] *vti vt Mil* обуч|а́ть строево́й подгото́вке (-и́ть)

vi Mil занима́ться строево́й подгото́вкой (*impf*).

drill[4] *n* (*material*) тик; *attr*: ~ **trousers** ти́ковые брю́ки.

drilling *n* (*small scale*) сверле́ние; (*for oil, etc.*) буре́ние.

drink *n* питьё; напи́ток; **food and** ~ еда́ и питьё; **soft/strong** ~**(s)** прохлади́тельные/кре́пкие напи́тки; **could I have a** ~ **of water?** дай мне, пожа́луйста, воды́; **you've got hiccups—take a good** ~ **of water** ты ика́ешь—сде́лай большо́й глото́к (*mouthful*) воды́; **will you have a** ~**?** бу́дешь пить?; **he enjoys his** ~ он не прочь вы́пить; **to take to** ~ запи́ть; **he was the worse for** ~ он был уже́ пьян; **it's enough to drive one to** ~ от э́того не хо́чешь, а напьёшься.

drink *vti vt* пить (вы́-); **to** ~ **tea** пить чай; **what will you** ~**?** что бу́дешь пить?; **to** ~ **up/down/off a glass of beer** вы́пить кру́жку пи́ва; **I drank him under the table** я напои́л его́; **he drank himself into a stupor** он напи́лся в сте́льку; **I had too much to** ~ я перепи́л (*and felt ill*), я вы́пил ли́шнего (*and behaved badly*); **these plants need plenty to** ~ э́ти расте́ния тре́буют мно́го вла́ги/воды́; *fig*: **he** ~**s all his earnings** он пропива́ет все де́ньги; **he drank in every word** он жа́дно лови́л ка́ждое сло́во

vi пить (вы́-); **her husband** ~**s heavily** её муж си́льно пьёт; **to** ~ **to smb/to smb's health** пить за чьё-л здоро́вье.

drinkable *adj* го́дный для питья́, питьево́й.

drinker *n*: **he's a heavy** ~ он си́льно пьёт.

drip *n* (*from icicles, thawing snow*) капе́ль; **there's a** ~ **at the end of your nose** у тебя́ ка́пля на носу́; **there's a** ~ **from the ceiling/the tap** ка́пает с потолка́/из кра́на; *CQ* **he's a** ~ с ним така́я ску́ка.

drip *vti vt* ка́п|ать (-нуть); **his finger was** ~**ping blood** у него́ с па́льца ка́пала кровь

vi: **there's a tap** ~**ping in the kitchen** на ку́хне ка́пает из кра́на; **he was** ~**ping with sweat** с него́ лил пот; **rain was** ~**ping from the trees, the trees were** ~**ping with rain** с дере́вьев па́дали ка́пли дождя́; **wine** ~**ped off the table on to the floor** вино́ ка́пало со стола́ на́ пол.

drip-dry *adj*: **this material is** ~ э́та мате́рия не тре́бует гла́жки, э́ту мате́рию гла́дить не на́до

dripping[1] *n* (*fat*) са́ло.

dripping[2] *adj*: **he/his coat is** ~ **wet** он насквозь промо́к, пальто́ всё промо́кло.

drive *n* **1** (*outing*) прогу́лка; пое́здка; **our house is a 2-hour** ~ **from Moscow** мы живём в двух часа́х езды́ от Москвы́; **it's a long** ~ **from here** туда́ далеко́ е́хать; **to go for a** ~ пое́хать поката́ться (на маши́не); **to take smb for a** ~ ката́ть кого́-л (на маши́не)

2 *Sport* (*stroke*) уда́р; (*in tennis*) **forehand/backhand** ~ уда́р откры́той/закры́той (раке́ткой); *Aut*: **front-wheel** ~ приво́д на пере́дние колёса; **a car with left-hand** ~ маши́на с рулём с ле́вой стороны́; *fig*: **he lacks** ~ ему́ не хвата́ет целеустремлённости; **a** ~ **to raise funds** кампа́ния по сбо́ру средств; **an economy** ~ борьба́ за режи́м эконо́мии.

drive *vti vt* **1** (*animals*) гоня́ть (*indet impf*; по- = *to drive round for a while*), гнать (*det impf*; по- = *to start to drive*) [**NB** *the true pf of completed action requires a compound pf, e.g.* пригна́ть]; **dogs love driving cattle** соба́ки лю́бят гоня́ть скот; **after driving his horses round for a while he put them back in the stable** погоня́в немно́го лошаде́й, он отвёл их в коню́шню; **peasants are now driving their cattle to the mountains** крестья́не го́нят скот в го́ры; **he started to** ~ **his horses at a gallop** он погна́л лошаде́й гало́пом (*adv*)

2 (*vehicles*) води́ть (*indet impf*; по- = *to drive a car round for a while*), вести́ (*det impf*; по- = *to start to drive a car*) [**NB** *the true pf of completed action requires a compound pf, e.g.* увести́]; **my father** ~**s a taxi/a tractor** мой оте́ц во́дит такси́/тра́ктор; **let me** ~ **your car for a while** дай мне поводи́ть (твою́ маши́ну); **his mate was driving the train when...** по́езд вёл его́ напа́рник, когда́...; **I drove my first bus when I was 20** я стал води́ть авто́бус, когда́ мне бы́ло два́дцать лет

3 (*to drive smb/smth in a vehicle*) вози́ть (*indet impf*; по- = *to drive smb/smth round for a while*), везти́ (*det impf*; по- = *to start to drive smb/smth*) [**NB** *the true pf of completed action requires a compound pf, e.g.* отвезти́]; **I** ~ **the children to school every morning** я вожу́ дете́й в шко́лу по утра́м; **we drove him round the town for a while** мы повози́ли его́ по го́роду; **it happened when I was driving him home** э́то случи́лось, когда́ я вёз его́ домо́й; **he has** ~**n the children to the museum** он повёз дете́й в музе́й; **he has** ~**n her home** он отвёз её домо́й

4 (*take smb for a spin*) ката́ть (*indet impf*; *pf* по- = *to drive smb round for a while*) [**NB** *det* кати́ть *not used in this sense*]; **in the holidays my father would often** ~ **us into the country for an outing** во вре́мя кани́кул оте́ц, быва́ло, ча́сто ката́л нас за́ город; **yesterday I drove my friends around to see something of London** вчера́ я поката́л друзе́й по Ло́ндону

5 (*of wind, water*) нести́ (*det impf, only the det form + compounds are used in this sense*); **the breakers drove the ship on the rocks** во́лны несли́ кора́бль/кора́бль несло́ (*impers*) прибо́ем (*sing*) на ска́лы; **the gale drove the ship off its course** ве́тер сноси́л су́дно/су́дно сноси́ло (*impers*) ве́тром с ку́рса

6 *specialized uses*: *Tech* **the mechanism/car is** ~**n by electricity** механи́зм приво́дится в де́йствие электри́чеством, у маши́ны электри́ческий дви́гатель; *Agric* **to** ~ **a straight furrow** вести́ ро́вную борозду́ (*for pf use*

про-); *Sport* [**NB** *in English one drives a ball only with a bat, club or racquet; the Russian translations can also mean "kick", or "hit with the hand", the exact meaning only becomes clear with sufficient context*]: (*golf*) **he drove the ball 300 yards** он послáл мяч на трúста я́рдов; (*cricket, baseball, etc.*) **he drove the ball over/to the boundary** он вы́бил мяч за лúнию, он отбúл мяч к лúнии; (*in hunting*) **to ~ game** гнать звéря/дичь (*for pf use* за-)

7 *fig uses*: **he was ~n to stealing by hunger** гóлод толкнýл егó на воровствó; **ambition drove him to work even harder** окрылённый честолюбúвыми мечтáми, он рабóтал ещё упóрнее; **she will ~ me insane** онá сведёт меня́ с умá; **he will ~ himself into the ground** (*by overwork*) он себя́ доведёт, он вгóнит себя́ в гроб

vi **1** (*to ride in a vehicle*) éздить (*indet impf*; по- = *to drive round for a while*), éхать (*det impf*; по- = *to start to drive*) [**NB** *the true pf of completed action requires a compound pf e.g.* вы́ехать]; **it is dangerous to ~ on icy roads** опáсно éздить по обледенéлым дорóгам; **yesterday I drove round the town for a while** вчерá я поéздил по гóроду; **it was pouring when I was driving to London** когдá я éхал в Лóндон, лил проливнóй дождь; **he has just ~n off to the concert** он поéхал на концéрт; **he drove off to Scotland yesterday** вчерá он уéхал в Шотлáндию

2 (*intransitive verbs other than* éздить): **i)** (*as chauffeur*) гоня́ть, гнать [**NB** *when used of cars* гоня́ть, гнать = *to drive at speed*]; **he drove furiously to the airport** он гнал машúну к аэропóрту; **he always ~s at high speeds** он всегдá так гóнит машúну; **ii)** (*as chauffeur*) водúть; **he's learning to ~** он ýчится водúть; **he was driving carefully** он вёл машúну осторóжно; **iii)** *CQ* (*bowl along*: *as driver*) катúть (*det impf*; по- = *to drive fast*); (*as driver or passenger*) катáться (*indet impf*; по- = *to drive round for a while*); **I was driving merrily along to the coast, when...** я беспéчно катúл по дорóге к мóрю, как вдруг...; **in summer I love driving/being ~n around with no special object** лéтом я люблю́ прокатúться/проéхаться кудá-нибудь так, без осóбой цéли

3 (*not of cars*): **clouds were driving across the sky** тýчи неслúсь по нéбу; **the rain was driving in our faces** дождь хлестáл нам в лицó; (*in tennis*) **he ~s well on the backhand** он хорошó бьёт закры́той (ракéткой)

drive across *vti vt*: **he drove a jeep across the desert** он проéхал чéрез пусты́ню на джúпе; **to ~ a road across the mountains** про|клáдывать дорóгу чéрез гóры (-ложúть)

vi: **to ~ across a bridge** пере|езжáть (чéрез) мост (-éхать)

drive as far as *vti vt* до|возúть (-везтú); **I drove the lorry as far as Zagorsk and there I stopped** я довёл грузовúк до Загóрска и там останови́лся; **he drove me as far as the station** он подвёз меня́ до стáнции

vi до|езжáть (-éхать); **~ as far as the church and then turn left** доезжáйте до цéркви и там повернúте налéво

drive at *vi fig*: **what are you driving at?** кудá/к чемý ты клóнишь?

drive away *vti vt* от|гоня́ть (-огнáть); **to ~ away the enemy** отогнáть протúвника; **to ~ a dog away from the door** отогнáть пса от двéри; **the scarecrow will ~ the birds away** пýгало отгóнит птиц; **the demonstrators were ~n away** демонстрáцию/демонстрáнтов разогнáли; **thieves have ~n away the cattle/car** вóры угнáли скот/машúну; **he drove his mother away to Yalta** он увёз мать в Я́лту

vi: **he/the car has just ~n away from the door** он тóлько что уéхал, машúна тóлько что отъéхала

drive back *vti*: **to ~ back a crowd/the enemy** оттесн|я́ть *or* (*more forcibly*) раз|гоня́ть толпý, от|брáсывать протúвника (-úть/-огнáть, -брóсить); **I drove them back to town** я отвёз их обрáтно в гóрод; *fig* **we were ~n back on our own resources** мы должны́ бы́ли обходúться своúми срéдствами

drive by *vi*: **he drove quickly by** он бы́стро проéхал мúмо; **I'll drop the parcel as I ~ by** я бýду éхать мúмо и завезý пакéт

drive from *vt*: **to ~ the enemy from their positions** оттеснúть/отбрóсить протúвника с позúций

drive home *vti vt* **i)**: **the collie ~s the sheep home** кóлли пригоня́ет овéц домóй; **ii)** (*in car*) от|возúть (*from where the speaker is*), при|возúть (*to where the speaker is*) (*pfs* -везтú); **can you ~ me home?** мóжешь ли ты отвезтú меня́ домóй?; **I'll ~ the guests home** я отвезý гостéй домóй; **he's gone to ~ the children home from school** он поéхал, чтóбы привезтú детéй из шкóлы; **he drove all the guests home** он развёз всех гостéй по домáм [*to their various homes*]; **I'll ~ you home on my way to the library** я завезý вас домóй по дорóге в библиотéку; *fig*: **I drove home to him that...** я емý втолкóвывал, что...; **he said little but he drove his point home** он говорúл мáло, но убедúтельно

vi: **he has just driven home** он тóлько что уéхал домóй

drive in/into *vti vt* **i)** за|гоня́ть (-гнáть), вгоня́ть (вогнáть); **to ~ fowls into the henhouse** загоня́ть кур в куря́тник; **to ~ a nail/a wedge into a tree trunk** загнáть *or* вогнáть гвоздь/клин в ствол; **to ~ a stake into the ground** вбить/вогнáть кол в зéмлю; **ii)**: **to ~ the car into the garage** загнáть машúну в гарáж; **I'll ~ you into town** я завезý вас в гóрод; **iii)** *fig*: **to ~ smb into a corner** загнáть когó-л в ýгол; **in the end I drove it into his head that...** в концé концóв я вдолбúл емý в гóлову, что...

vi въезжáть (въéхать); **he drove into the garage** он въéхал в гарáж; **a lorry drove into my car** в мою́ машúну врéзался грузовúк; **the bus drove into a wall** автóбус врéзался в стéну

drive off *vti vt*: **to ~ off an attack/the enemy** отби|ва́ть ата́ку/проти́вника (-́ть); **to ~ off wolves** от|гоня́ть волко́в (-огна́ть); **they were ~n off in a large car** их увезли́ в большо́й маши́не

vi: **he drove off a moment ago** он то́лько что уе́хал; **somebody has ~n off with the car** (*stolen it*) кто́-то угна́л маши́ну; *CQ* **he drove off home at a good lick** он покати́л домо́й

drive on *vti vt fig*: **ambition/his friends drove him on** им дви́гало честолю́бие, друзья́ подбива́ли его́

vi: **~ on!** пое́хали!

drive out *vti vt* вы|гоня́ть (-́гнать); **to ~ cows out to the meadows** вы́гнать коро́в в луга́; **he drove his son out of the house** он вы́гнал сы́на и́з дому; **to ~ the enemy out of their positions** вы́бить проти́вника с занима́емых пози́ций; **I drove the children out of town** я вы́вез дете́й за́ город; *fig* **to ~ smb out of his mind/wits** при|води́ть кого́-л в бе́шенство, с|води́ть кого́-л с ума́ (*pfs* -вести́)

vi: **he drove out of the garage/out of London** он вы́ехал из гаража́/из Ло́ндона

drive over *vi*: **we drove over a river** мы прое́хали че́рез ре́ку; **we drove over a level crossing/the pass** мы прое́хали шлагба́ум/(че́рез) перева́л; **I'll ~ over and collect the books on my way** я по доро́ге зае́ду за кни́гами; *CQ*: **he ~s over to see us now and again** он и́зредка навеща́ет нас; **on Sunday a crowd of my relations drove over to see us** в воскресе́нье к нам нагря́нули ро́дственники

drive past *vti vt*: **he drove us past the palace** он провёз нас ми́мо дворца́

vi: **the bus drove past the stop** авто́бус прое́хал остано́вку (*without stopping or overshot it*); **a large car drove past us** нас обогнала́ больша́я маши́на; **we drove past the theatre** мы прое́хали ми́мо теа́тра

drive round *vi* (*skirt*): **to ~ round a lake** объ|езжа́ть о́зеро вокру́г (-е́хать); **the road is up, we'll have to ~ round by Cambridge** иду́т доро́жные рабо́ты—нам придётся е́хать (в объе́зд) че́рез Ке́мбридж; **I'll just ~ round the corner to park** я то́лько поверну́ за́ угол, что́бы поста́вить маши́ну

drive through *vti vt*: **to ~ a tunnel through a mountain** проби|ва́ть тунне́ль в горе́ (-́ть)

vi: **we drove through Oxford** мы прое́хали че́рез О́ксфорд

drive to *vt*: **he drove the patient to hospital** он отвёз больно́го в го́спиталь; **he drove my things to my new flat** он перевёз мои́ ве́щи на но́вую кварти́ру; *fig* **to ~ smb to despair** до|води́ть кого́-л до отча́яния (-вести́)

drive up *vi*: **the car drove right up to the door** маши́на подъе́хала к са́мому подъе́зду.

drivel *vi* поро́ть чушь, нести́ ерунду́ (*usu impfs*).

driver *n* (*of horse-drawn vehicle*) изво́зчик; (*of car, bus, etc.*) води́тель (*m*), шофёр; *Rail* машини́ст; **L-~** води́тель-учени́к; **racing ~** го́нщик.

driving *n* вожде́ние; **careless ~** неосторо́жная езда́; **his ~ is terrible** он о́чень пло́хо во́дит; *attr*: **to take ~ lessons** брать уро́ки вожде́ния; **~ licence** води́тельские права́ (*pl*); **~ test** (*for driver*) экза́мен на пра́во вожде́ния/по вожде́нию; *Tech* **~ belt/shaft** приводно́й реме́нь/вал.

drizzle *n* ме́лкий дождь (*m*); и́зморось.

drizzle *vi*: **it's been drizzling all day** с утра́ моро́сит (*impers*; *impf*).

drizzly *adj*: **yesterday was ~** вчера́ мороси́ло (*impers*; *impf*).

droll *adj* смешно́й, заба́вный.

drone[1] *n* (*male bee*) тру́тень (*m*), *also fig.*

drone[2] *n* (*of insects*) жужжа́ние; (*of plane in sky*) гуде́ние; (*of noise of talk*) гул.

drone[2] *vi* гуде́ть (*usu impf*); (*of insects*) жужжа́ть (*impf*); **his voice ~d on** его́ го́лос гуде́л.

droop *vi* (*of flowers*) вя́нуть (за-); **we were ~ing from the heat/fatigue** мы изнемога́ли от жары́/от уста́лости; **his head ~ed** его́ голова́ пони́кла, он пове́сил го́лову; *fig* **her spirits ~ed** она́ упа́ла ду́хом/сни́кла.

drop *n* **1** (*of liquid*) ка́пля; **a tiny ~** ка́пелька; **~ by ~** ка́пля за ка́плей, по ка́пле; **to drink to the last ~** вы́пить всё до (после́дней) ка́пли; **take 10 ~s a day** принима́ть по де́сять ка́пель в день; **water with your whisky?—Just a ~** тебе́ ви́ски с водо́й?—Воды́ совсе́м немно́жко; **I never touch a ~** (*of alcohol*) я ка́пли спиртно́го в рот не беру́; *fig* **it's only a ~ in the ocean/bucket** э́то ка́пля в мо́ре

2 (*sweet*) драже́ (*indecl*); **chocolate ~s** шокола́дное драже́

3 (*fall*): **there's a ~ of 30 feet from the window to the ground** от окна́ до земли́—высота́ три́дцать фу́тов; **a 50 foot ~** пятидесятифу́товая высота́; **a ~ in temperature/prices** пониже́ние температу́ры, паде́ние цен; *attr*: *Theat* **~ curtain** опускно́й за́навес.

drop *vti vt* **1** (*let fall*) роня́ть (урони́ть); **to ~ a book** урони́ть кни́гу; **the trees are ~ping their leaves** дере́вья роня́ют ли́стья (*only in impf*); **she ~ped the cup out of her hands** она́ вы́ронила ча́шку из рук (*pf*); (*drop and lose*) **I've ~ped my key somewhere** я где́-то потеря́л/оброни́л ключ (*pf*); **to ~ a letter in the box** брос|а́ть письмо́ в я́щик (-́ить); **to ~ the curtain** опус|ка́ть за́навес (-ти́ть); **to ~ a stitch** спус|ка́ть пе́тлю (-ти́ть); (*in spelling*) **to ~ a letter** пропуска́ть бу́кву; **to ~ bombs** сбра́сывать бо́мбы (сбро́сить); **100 men were ~ped by parachute** бы́ли сбро́шены сто парашюти́стов

2 *fig uses*: **he ~ped his eyes/voice/price** он опусти́л *or* поту́пил взор, он пони́зил го́лос, он сба́вил це́ну; **I ~ped a lot of money on the deal** я потеря́л больши́е де́ньги на э́той сде́лке; **he has been ~ped from the team** он отстранён от игры́ (*for one match*), его́ исключи́ли/*CQ* вы́гнали из кома́нды; **I'll ~ you a line** я тебе́ черкну́ па́ру строк; **he ~ped his studies/his old friends/smoking** он бро́сил учёбу (*sing*)/ста́рых друзе́й/кури́ть

vi **1** па́дать (упа́сть, (*in battle*) пасть); **the leaves are already ~ping** ли́стья уже́ опада́ют/па́дают/облета́ют; **my watch ~ped on to the floor** мои́ часы́ (*no sing*) упа́ли на́ пол; **many soldiers ~ped on the battlefield** мно́го солда́т па́ло в бою́; **I ~ped into an armchair/on a chair/on to my knees** я упа́л в кре́сло/на стул/на коле́ни; **the vase ~ped out of my hands** ва́за вы́пала у меня́ из рук; **the cliff ~ped steeply into the sea** скала́ отве́сно обрыва́лась в мо́ре; **the road ~ped into the valley** доро́га спуска́лась в доли́ну

2 (*of liquids*) ка́п|ать (-нуть); **water was ~ping from the roof of the cave** вода́ ка́пала со сво́дов (*pl*) пеще́ры

3 *fig uses*: **prices have ~ped** це́ны сни́зились/упа́ли; **the temperature has ~ped** температу́ра пони́зилась/упа́ла; **his voice ~ped to a whisper** его́ го́лос перешёл в шёпот; **the wind ~ped** ве́тер ути́х; **to work till one ~s** рабо́тать до изнеможе́ния; **I was ready to ~ with fatigue** я вали́лся от уста́лости

drop back *vi* отступ|а́ть/от|ходи́ть наза́д (-и́ть/-ойти́)

drop in/into *vi* за|ходи́ть (-йти́); (*look in*) загля́|дывать к + *D* (-ну́ть); **to ~ into the library/in to see smb** зайти́ в библиоте́ку/к кому́-л; **do ~ in on us if you are in the neighbourhood** загляни́те к нам, е́сли бу́дете побли́зости (*adv*)

drop off *vti vt*: **to ~ smb off** (*when driving*) вы|са́живать кого́-л (-садить)

vi: **I'll ~ off at the corner** (*out of a car*) я вы́йду на э́том углу́; **the child ~ped off** (*to sleep*) **very quickly** ребёнок мгнове́нно засну́л; **the old man ~ped off in his chair** стари́к задрема́л в кре́сле

drop out *vi* (*of a contest of one's own choice*) вы|ходи́ть из + *G* (-йти); **he ~ped out of the game because of injuries** он вы́был из игры́ из-за тра́вмы (*sing*).

drop-out *n*: **he can't settle to anything—he's becoming a ~** он ниче́м по-настоя́щему не интересу́ется—стано́вится про́сто безде́льником.

dropper *n Med* пипе́тка.

dropping bottle *n* ка́пельница.

droppings *npl* помёт (*sing*).

dropsy *n Med* водя́нка.

dross *n* шлак.

drought *n* за́суха.

drove *n* (*of cattle, etc.*) ста́до; (*of people*) **they came in ~s** они́ приходи́ли то́лпами.

drown *vti vt* топи́ть (у-); **to ~ kittens/oneself** утопи́ть котя́т, утопи́ться; *fig*: **to ~ a noise** заглуши́ть шум; **his voice was ~ed in the hubbub** его́ го́лос потону́л в о́бщем шу́ме; **to ~ one's sorrows in drink** топи́ть го́ре (*sing*) в вине́/в стака́не

vi тону́ть (у-).

drowned *adj* утону́вший; **a ~ person** уто́пленн|ик, *f* -ица.

drowning *n*: *Law* **death by ~** смерть че́рез утопле́ние.

drowse *vi* дрема́ть (*usu impf*).

drowsiness *n* дремо́та, сонли́вость.

drowsy *adj* дремо́тный; дре́млющий; со́нный; **I feel ~** меня́ кло́нит (*impers*) ко сну́.

drudge *vi*: **I've been drudging away all day in the kitchen** я весь день провози́лась на ку́хне/у плиты́.

drudgery *n*: **this is sheer ~** да э́то про́сто ка́торга.

drug *n Med* лека́рство; (*harmful*) нарко́тик; *fig* **a ~ on the market** неходово́й това́р; *attr*: **~ traffic** торго́вля нарко́тиками.

drug *vt*: **they ~ged him/his drink** они́ подмеша́ли ему́ нарко́тики (*pl*) в питьё.

druggist *n* апте́карь (*m*).

drugstore *n* (*US*) апте́ка; (*if food, etc. also sold*) *approx* апте́ка-заку́сочная.

drum *n Mus* бараба́н; *Tech* бараба́н, цили́ндр; **an oil ~** нефтяна́я бо́чка.

drum *vti vt*: **to ~ (with) one's fingers on the table** бараба́нить па́льцами по́ столу (*impf*); *fig*: **to ~ smth into smb's head** вда́лбливать что-л кому́-л в го́лову (вдолби́ть); **to ~ up support for a cause** при|зыва́ть к подде́ржке како́го-л де́ла (-зва́ть)

vi бараба́нить (*usu impf*); **the rain ~med on the window panes** дождь бараба́нил в о́кна; **to ~ (with) one's feet on the floor** стуча́ть нога́ми по́ полу (*only in impf*); **a noise is ~ming in my ears** у меня́ звени́т/шуми́т (*impers*) в уша́х.

drummer *n* бараба́нщик.

drumstick *n* бараба́нная па́лочка; *Cook* кури́ная но́жка.

drunk *n* пья́ница, *CQ* пьянчу́га (*both m and f*).

drunk *adj* пья́ный; опьяне́вший; **~ as a lord** пьян как сапо́жник; **to get/be ~** опьяне́ть, напи́ться; **to get ~ on vodka** напи́ться во́дки; **to make smb ~** спа́ивать кого́-л; **he was charged with driving when ~** его́ обвини́ли в том, что он вёл автомоби́ль в нетре́звом ви́де; *fig*: **~ with success** опьянённый/упоённый успе́хом; **I was ~ with the music** я упива́лся э́той му́зыкой.

drunkard *n* пья́ница (*m and f*).

drunken *adj* пья́ный; **a ~ brawl** пья́ная ссо́ра; **in a ~ stupor** отупе́в от пья́нства.

drunkenness *n* (*habit*) пья́нство; (*state*) опьяне́ние.

dry *adj* сухо́й; **~ weather/clothes/battery** суха́я пого́да/оде́жда/батаре́я; **a ~ cough/dock** сухо́й ка́шель/док; **~ wine** сухо́е вино́; **~ land** су́ша; **~ bread** хлеб без ма́сла, (*stale*) чёрствый хлеб; **a ~ cow** недо́йная/(*barren*) я́ловая коро́ва; (*dried-up*) **a ~ well** вы́сохший коло́дец; **to run ~** пересыха́ть; **I am ~** (*parched*) у меня́ пересо́хло (*impers*) в го́рле; **my lips are ~** у меня́ пересо́хли гу́бы; *fig*: **~ humour** сухова́тый ю́мор;

(*US*) **to go ~** (*prohibit alcohol*) ввести́ сухо́й зако́н.

dry *vti vt* суши́ть (вы́-) *and compounds*; **to ~ out** вы|су́шивать (-́сушить); **to ~ hair/hay/washing** суши́ть во́лосы/се́но/бельё; (*by rubbing*) **to ~ one's hands (on a towel)** вы|тира́ть ру́ки (полоте́нцем) (-́тереть); **to ~ the dishes** вытира́ть посу́ду (*collect*); (*wipe away*) **to ~ one's tears/eyes** утира́ть слёзы (утере́ть), вытира́ть глаза́

vi суши́ться, со́хнуть (*impfs*); **the washing is ~ing outside** бельё су́шится/со́хнет на дворе́; **the rivers are ~ing up because of the drought** ре́ки пере|сыха́ют в за́суху (-со́хнуть); (*after a wetting*) **we sat by the fire till we dried out** мы сиде́ли у пе́чки, пока́ не обсо́хли; **the cows have dried up** коро́вы переста́ли дои́ться; (*of weather*) **at last it's ~ing up** наконе́ц вла́жность ста́ла уменьша́ться; *fig CQ* **do ~ up!** заткни́сь!

dry-clean *vt* чи́стить в химчи́стке (по-); **to have one's suit ~ed** отда|ва́ть костю́м в чи́стку (-́ть).

dry-cleaner's, dry-cleaning *ns* химчи́стка.

dry rot *n* (*of wood*) суха́я гниль.

dry-shod *adv* не замочи́в ног.

dual *adj* двойно́й; **~ nationality** двойно́е по́дданство/гражда́нство; *Aut* **~ control** двойно́е управле́ние; **~ carriage-way** двухполо́сное шоссе́; *Gram as n*: **the ~** двои́ственное число́.

dub *vt*: **he was ~bed "redhead"** его́ прозва́ли Ры́жим; **to ~ a film** дубли́ровать фильм (*impf*).

dubious *adj* **1** *attr* сомни́тельный; **a ~ character/compliment/result** сомни́тельный тип/комплиме́нт/результа́т

2 *predic*: **I am ~ about his honesty/about what to do** я сомнева́юсь в его́ че́стности, я не зна́ю, что де́лать.

duck[1] *n* у́тка; *fig*: **a lame ~** неуда́чник; **like water off a ~'s back** как с гу́ся вода́; **he took to skiing like a ~ to water** он прирождённый лы́жник; **to play ~s and drakes** (*with flat stones*) броса́ть ка́мешки по воде́, «печь блины́».

duck[2] *vti vt*: **to ~ smb (in water)** окун|а́ть кого́-л (в во́ду) (-у́ть); **to ~ one's head** на|гиба́ть го́лову (-гну́ть); *CQ* **to ~ a lesson** прогуля́ть уро́к

vi (*in water*) окуна́ться; (*in order to dodge*) нагиба́ться; (*of boxer*) де́лать «нырóк» (с-).

duck[3] *n* (*cloth*) паруси́на; *pl* (**~s**) паруси́новые брю́ки.

ducking *n*: **they gave him a ~** они́ окуну́ли его́ в во́ду; (*after rain*) **we got a ~** мы промо́кли насквозь.

duckling *n* утёнок.

dud *adj*: **a ~ cheque** него́дный чек; *used as n*: **the bomb was a ~** бо́мба не взорвала́сь.

due *n* **1** *sing only*: **I've paid him his ~** я о́тдал ему́ до́лжное; **he only got his ~** он получи́л по заслу́гам; **to give him his ~, he can sing** на́до отда́ть ему́ до́лжное, он непло́хо поёт

2 *pl only* (**~s**) (*fees, subscriptions*) взно́сы; **harbour ~s** портóвые сбо́ры.

due *adj* **1** (*to be paid*): **when is the rent ~?** когда́ плати́ть за кварти́ру?; **he paid me what was ~ to me** он мне о́тдал всё, что мне причита́лось; **the bill falls ~ on the 4th** ве́ксель подлежи́т опла́те четвёртого числа́

2 (*appropriate*): **after ~ consideration** по́сле внима́тельного рассмотре́ния; **in ~ course** свои́м чередо́м, в своё вре́мя; **with ~ regard/respect** с до́лжным внима́нием/уваже́нием; **in ~ form** по всей фо́рме

3 (*expected*): **he is ~ to broadcast at 10 p.m.** он до́лжен вы́ступить по ра́дио в де́сять часо́в ве́чера; **the train is ~ at 8.10** по́езд прибыва́ет в во́семь де́сять утра́

4: **~ to** (*caused by*): **the accident was ~ to fog** ава́рия случи́лась из-за тума́на; **his absence was ~ to illness** он отсу́тствовал по боле́зни.

due *adv* пря́мо; **to go ~ east** е́хать пря́мо на восто́к.

duel *n* дуэ́ль; **to fight a ~** дра́ться на дуэ́ли.

duet *n* дуэ́т.

duffer *n* тупи́ца (*m and f*).

duke *n* ге́рцог.

dull *adj* **1** (*not clear*) ту́склый; нея́ркий; **a ~ mirror** ту́склое зе́ркало; **a ~ colour** нея́ркий/ту́склый цвет; **~ lighting/light** ту́склое освеще́ние, нея́ркий *or* приглушённый свет; **a ~ surface** ту́склая/ма́товая пове́рхность; **a ~ sound** глухо́й звук; **a ~ day** па́смурный день

2 (*not sharp*) тупо́й; **a ~ edge/pain** тупо́е ле́звие, тупа́я боль; *fig* (*stupid*) **a ~ person** тупо́й/тупова́тый челове́к

3 (*boring*) ску́чный; **a ~ party/person** ску́чный ве́чер/челове́к.

duly *adv*: **he ~ arrived at noon** он при́был, как ожида́лось, в по́лдень; **everybody ~ applauded** все, как и полага́лось, зааплоди́ровали.

dumb *adj* немо́й; **deaf and ~** глухонемо́й; **~ animals** бесслове́сные тва́ри; **to grow/become ~** онеме́ть; **the children were ~ from shyness** де́ти молча́ли от смуще́ния; **to be struck ~ with horror** онеме́ть от у́жаса; *CQ* **he's ~** он тупо́й.

dumbfound *vt* ошелом|ля́ть (-и́ть), *CQ* ошара́ш|ивать (-ить); **he was ~ed at the news** он был ошеломлён/ошара́шен э́тим изве́стием.

dumb show *n*: **he made clear to me in ~ that...** он же́стами дал мне поня́ть, что...

dummy *n*: **tailor's ~** манеке́н (портно́го); **baby's ~** (со́ска-) пусты́шка; *Cards* «болва́н»; *attr*: **a ~ window** ло́жное окно́; **a ~ run** (*trial trip*) испыта́тельный рейс.

dump *n*: **a rubbish ~** (*municipal*) городска́я сва́лка, (*heap*) ку́ча му́сора; *fig CQ*: **this is a terrible ~** э́то жу́ткая дыра́; **to be in the ~s** хандри́ть.

dump *vt* свал|ивать (-ить); **the lorry ~ed the coal right on my doorstep** грузовик свалил уголь прямо у моей двери; **can I ~ this here?** можно мне это здесь оставить?; **I ~ed my old records on him** я отдал ему свои старые пластинки.

dumping *n*: **"D. of rubbish forbidden"** «свалка мусора запрещена».

dumpling *n Cook* клёцка.

dumpy *adj* пухлый; **~ child** пухлый малыш; *CQ* **she's a ~ little woman** она вся такая кругленькая.

dun[1] *adj* серовато-коричневый.

dun[2] *vt*: **he's been ~ning me for that money** он мне все уши прожужжал про эти деньги.

dunce *n* болван, тупица.

dune *n* дюна; **sand ~s** песчаные дюны.

dung *n* навоз.

dungarees *npl* рабочий комбинезон (*sing*).

dungeon *n* темница.

dupe *n* простак, простофиля, *CQ* дурачок.

dupe *vt* дурачить (о-).

duplicate *n* (*typing*) копия; (*second copy of paper, key, etc.*) дубликат; **in ~** в двух экземплярах.

duplicate *adj*: **a ~ key/receipt** дубликат ключа/квитанции.

duplicate *vt* дублировать (*impf*); (*a text, letter*) делать копию/дубликат (с-).

duplication *n* дублирование.

duplicator *n* копировальный/множительный аппарат.

duplicity *n* двуличность.

durability *n* (*of material, or machine*) долговечность.

durable *adj* прочный; **~ cloth** прочная ткань; **~ footwear** ноская обувь; **this is a ~ vacuum cleaner** этот пылесос будет долго работать.

duration *n*: **for the ~ of the war** в течение всей войны, во время войны; **their marriage was of short ~** их брак был недолгим.

during *prep* **1** (*at some point during a period*) в + *P*; *rarely* в + *A*; во время + *G*; на + *P*; **~ childhood I spent my holidays in Yalta** в детстве я проводил каникулы в Ялте; **~ the 19th century there were three outbreaks of cholera** в девятнадцатом веке было три вспышки холеры; **I hope to see her ~ May** надеюсь увидеть её в мае; **~ that year/that period/his latter years I only saw him once** в том году *or* в тот год/в тот период/в последние годы его жизни я виделся с ним только раз; **fire broke out ~ his lecture** во время его лекции начался пожар; **I'll be in London sometime ~ next week** на следующей неделе я буду в Лондоне; **they married ~ their second year at college** они поженились на втором курсе

2 (*throughout the whole of a period*) в + *A*; во время + *G*; в течение + *G*; в продолжение + *G*; на протяжении + *G*; **~ his absence** в его отсутствие; **~ the middle ages** в средние века; **no talking ~ lessons** не разговаривать во время уроков; **~ the war I lived in London** во время войны я жил в Лондоне; **~ all this time we remained friends** в течение/на протяжении всего этого времени мы оставались друзьями; **~ the course I never missed a lecture** в продолжение всего курса я не пропустил ни одной лекции; **~ the whole journey he never spoke a word** за всё время пути он и слова не произнёс

3 (*within a certain period*) за + *A*, за время + *G*; **~ one winter we lost 100 sheep** за одну зиму у нас пало сто овец; **I was in France three times ~ the war** за время войны я был во Франции три раза.

dusk *n* сумерки (*no sing*); **in the ~** в сумерках; **from dawn till ~** от зари до зари [*context must be clear, as this also = "from dusk till dawn"*].

dusky *adj* тёмный; **a ~ complexion** смуглый цвет лица.

dust *n* пыль; **I've got a speck of ~ in my eye** мне в глаз попала соринка; **gold ~** золотой песок; *fig*: **to throw ~ in smb's eyes** пускать пыль в глаза кому-л; *CQ* **to kick up a ~** вспылить, (*stronger*) учинить скандал.

dust *vt*: **to ~ a room/the piano** вы|тирать пыль в комнате, стирать пыль с рояля (´-тереть, стереть); **to ~ oneself with talcum powder** припудриться тальком (*usu pf*); **to ~ a cake with sugar** посыпать торт сахарной пудрой; **to ~ tomato plants with insecticide** опыл|ять помидоры инсектицидом (-ить).

dustbin *n* мусорный ящик.

dustcart *n* фургон для сбора мусора, мусоровоз.

dust cover *n* (*for furniture*) чехол.

duster *n* тряпка; (*for book*) суперобложка; **give me a ~** дай мне тряпку вытереть пыль.

dusting *n*: **the room needs ~** в комнате надо вытереть пыль; **I hate ~** я не люблю вытирать пыль; *Agric* опрыскивание.

dustman *n* мусорщик.

dustpan *n* совок для мусора.

dust sheet *n* чехол.

dust storm *n* пыльная буря.

dust-up *n CQ* скандал.

dusty *adj* пыльный; запылённый; **to get ~** запылиться; *fig CQ* **it's not so ~** это не так уж плохо.

Dutch *adj* голландский; *as n* нидерландский язык.

Dutchman *n* голландец.

Dutchwoman *n* голландка.

dutiful *adj* (*obedient*) послушный; (*attentive*) внимательный.

duty *n* **1** долг; (*obligation*) обязанность; **from a sense of ~** из чувства долга; **to do one's ~** выполнить свой долг; **it's your ~ to do this** сделать это — твой долг; **my duties are various** у меня разнообразные обязанности; **I am in ~ bound to admit...** я вынужден признать...; *attr*: **a ~ visit** визит вежливости

2 on/off ~: who's on ~? кто дежурный?/ дежурит?; **while on ~** во время дежурства;

I am/have come off ~ я свобóден от дежýрства, я тóлько что сменился с дежýрства; *attr*: ~ **roster** расписáние дежýрств

3 (*one's work*) слýжба; рабóта; **in the course of** ~ по дóлгу слýжбы; **to report for** ~ являться на слýжбу; **smoking is not allowed while on** ~ нельзя курить во врéмя дежýрства; *fig* **a box did** ~ **for a table** ящик служил столóм

4 (*tax*) налóг, пóшлина; **death duties** налóги на наслéдство; **stamp** ~ гéрбовый сбор; **customs** ~ таможенная пóшлина; **import/export** ~ ввознáя/вывознáя пóшлина.

duty-free *adj*: **these imports are** ~ эти товáры не облагáются тамóженной пóшлиной.

duty-paid *adj* оплáченный пóшлиной.

duvet *n* большóе пухóвое одеяло.

dwarf *n* кáрлик; *attr*: **a** ~ **plant** кáрликовое растéние.

dwell *vi* (*live in, at*) жить, обитáть (*impfs*); (*linger on*): **he dwelt on the question for a long time** он остановился на этом вопрóсе; **don't** ~ **on it—it won't help** брось об этом дýмать, всё равнó не помóжет; *fig* **he** ~**s in the past** он живёт в прóшлом; *Mus* **to** ~ **on a note** тянýть нóту (*impf*).

dweller *n*: **city** ~**s** городские жители.

dwelling *n* жилище; *attr*: ~ **house** жилóй дом [**NB** *in SU cities* жилóй дом *usu = a block of flats*].

dwindle *vi* уменьш|áться (-иться), убывáть (*usu impf*).

dye *n* крáска; (*stuff*) красúтель (*m*).

dye *vti vt* крáсить (по-, вы-); **to** ~ **a dress red** покрáсить плáтье в крáсный цвет; **to** ~ **a white blouse blue** перекрá|шивать бéлую блýзку в голубóй цвет (-сить)

vi: **this material** ~**s well** эта ткань хорошó крáсится.

dye-works *npl* красúльня (*sing*).

dyke *n* (*ditch*) канáва; (*earthen embankment*) нáсыпь.

dynamic *adj* динамúческий; *fig* динамúчный.

dynamite *n* динамúт.

dynamo *n Elec* динáмо-машúна; *Aut CQ* динáмо (*indecl*).

dysentery *n* дизентерúя.

dyspepsia *n* диспепсúя.

E

E *n Mus* ми.

each *pron* **1** кáждый; ~ **of us/of them expressed his opinion** кáждый (из нас/из них) вы́разил своё мнéние; **the guests arrived,** ~ **bringing a gift** пришлú гóсти, кáждый с подáрком

2 *used distributively* = "*apiece*"; *is translated by* по + *D or* по + *A*; по + *D of the article distributed if it is only one each*: **he gave** ~ **of us an apple/two roubles/five roubles** он дал кáждому (из нас) по (одномý) яблоку/по два рубля/по пяти́ *or CQ* по пять рублéй; **we** ~ **took a book from the pile** мы взя́ли из стóпки по кнúге; **we bought lemons at 30 kopecks** ~ мы купúли лимóны по тридцатú/*CQ* по трúдцать копéек за штýку; **lemons cost 30 kopecks** ~ лимóны стóят трúдцать копéек штýка [**NB** *the verb* стóить *is followed by the accusative, and* по *is not used*]

3: each other друг дрýга (*always m*), одúн другóго [**NB** *the first* друг *is always in the nominative, the case of the second depends on the construction of the sentence*]; **they love** ~ **other** онú лю́бят друг дрýга; **we can help** ~ **other** мы мóжем друг дрýгу помóчь; **the sisters are like** ~ **other** сёстры похóжи друг на дрýга; *also translated by reflex verbs*; **we'll see** ~ **other tomorrow** (мы) зáвтра увúдимся.

each *adj* кáждый; ~ **student has a separate room** у кáждого студéнта отдéльная кóмната; **the fare is £2** ~ **way** билéт стóит два фýнта в одúн конéц; (*distributively—see note on "each" pron* 2): **he gave** ~ **child an apple/two apples/six apples** он дал кáждому ребёнку по (одномý) яблоку/по два яблока/по шестú *or CQ* по шесть яблок.

eager *adj* **1** *attr* энергúчный; (*diligent*) усéрдный; **an** ~ **pupil** усéрдный ученúк; *CQ* **an** ~ **beaver** трýженик, работяга

2 *predic* **i): to be** ~ **for smth** с нетерпéнием ждать чегó-л; **they were** ~ **for the concert to begin** онú с нетерпéнием ждáли начáла концéрта; **to be** ~ **for knowledge** быть любознáтельным; **ii): to be** ~ **to** óчень хотéть + *inf*; стремúться + *inf*; **they were** ~ **to come with me** онú óчень хотéли/им óчень хотéлось (*impers*) пойтú со мной; **they were** ~ **to succeed** онú стремúлись к успéху.

eagerly *adv* (*with impatience*) с нетерпéнием; (*avidly*) жáдно; **they awaited him** ~ онú с нетерпéнием ждáли егó; **they listened to him** ~ онú жáдно слýшали егó.

eagerness *n* (*impatience*) нетерпéние; (*striving for*) тяга к + *D*; **in his** ~ **to reach the door first, he stumbled** он рванýлся к двéри—хотéл быть пéрвым, но споткнýлся.

eagle *n* орёл.

ear[1] *n* **1** *Anat* ýхо; *dim* ушкó; **to prick up one's** ~**s** навострúть ýши, *also fig*; **I couldn't believe my** ~**s** я не вéрил своúм ушáм; **I will have a word in her** ~ **and I think you'll find it's all right tomorrow** я ей шепнý кóе-чтó на ушкó, и зáвтра, дýмаю, всё улáдится; **to listen with half an** ~ слýшать крáем ýха/вполýха (*adv*); **to box smb's** ~**s** дать комý-л пó уху; *fig*: **she was all** ~**s** онá вся обратúлась в слух; **he turned a deaf** ~ **to our requests** он был глух к нáшим прóсьбам; **with him things go in at one** ~ **and out at the other** емý в однó ýхо влетáет, в другóе вылетáет; **I'm up to my** ~**s in work** я зáнят по гóрло; *attr*: ~ **drops** ушны́е кáпли; **a middle** ~ **infection** воспалéние срéднего ýха

2 *Mus* слух; **he has a good ~** у негó хорóший слух; **to play by ~** игрáть на слух/по слýху; *fig* **let's play it by ~** поживём—увúдим.

ear[2] *n* (*of corn, etc.*): **the rye is already in the ~** рожь ужé колосúтся.

earache *n* боль в ýхе.

eardrum *n Anat* барабáнная перепóнка.

early *adj* рáнний; **~ vegetables** рáнние óвощи; **in the ~ morning** рáнним ýтром, рáно ýтром; **he is an ~ riser** он рáно встаёт; **it's too ~ to leave** выходúть ещё рáно; **a man in his ~ fifties** человéк пятúдесяти лет с небольшúм; **in the ~ years of this century** в начáле э́того вéка; **in the ~ chapters of the book** в начáльных глáвах кнúги; **I got an ~ warning** меня́ зарáнее предупредúли; **at the earliest opportunity** при пéрвой же возмóжности; **at your earliest convenience** как мóжно скорée; (*in letter*) **looking forward to an ~ reply** надéюсь на скóрый отвéт; **an ~ death** безврéменная смерть; **an ~ election** досрóчные вы́боры (*pl*); **an ~ manuscript** старúнная/ дрéвняя рýкопись.

early *adv* рáно; (*in good time*) зарáнее, заблаговрéменно; **as ~ as possible** как мóжно рáньше; **earlier on** рáньше, рáнее; **~ in the week** в начáле недéли; **~ one morning** однáжды рáно ýтром; **do come (a bit) ~** приходú порáньше; **it's best to book the tickets ~** лýчше заказáть билéты зарáнее/заблаговрéменно/зáгодя.

earmark *vt*: *fig* **to ~ smth for a special purpose** предназначáть что-л для определённой цéли.

earn *vt* (*salary, etc.*) зараб|áтывать (-óтать); *fig* заслýжи|вать (-ть); **he ~s his living by teaching** он зарабáтывает на жизнь преподавáнием; **if you put your money on deposit it will ~ some interest** éсли вы полóжите дéньги в банк, онú принесýт процéнты (*pl*); **he has ~ed the respect of all/a good rest** он заслужúл всеóбщее уважéние/хорóший óтдых.

earnest *n*: **in ~** серьёзно, всерьёз; **to get down to work in ~** взя́ться за рабóту всерьёз; **are you in ~?** ты э́то серьёзно (говорúшь)?; **it began to rain in ~** дождь припустúл/полúл вовсю́.

earnest *adj* серьёзный; (*painstaking*) усéрдный; (*sincere*) úскренний; **an ~ student** серьёзный/усéрдный студéнт; **it is my ~ wish that this should happen** я úскренне желáю, чтóбы э́то случúлось.

earnings *npl* (*of individual*) зáработок (*only in sing*); (*of factory, etc.*) дохóд.

earphones *npl* наýшники (*pl*).

earring *n* серьгá, серёжка.

earshot *n*: **to be within/out of ~** быть в предéлах/за предéлами слы́шимости.

ear-splitting *adj* оглушúтельный.

earth *n* 1 земля́; (*soil*) земля́, пóчва; *Elec* «земля́»; (*as planet*) **the ~ goes round the sun** Земля́ вращáется вокрýг Сóлнца; **the happiest man on ~** счастлúвейший человéк на свéте

2 (*den*) norá; **to run a fox to ~** загнáть лисúцу в норý; *fig* **I ran him to ~ in his office** я застáл егó в контóре

3 *fig CQ*: **how on ~ did you hear that?** и как э́то ты об э́том узнáл?; **what on ~ is wrong?** что же (такóе) стряслóсь?; **you look like nothing on ~** бог знáет, на когó ты похóж; **it cost the ~** э́то стóило ýйму дéнег, э́то влетéло в копéечку; **he is very down to ~** он óчень практúчный человéк; **to come down to ~** упáсть/спустúться с небéс на зéмлю; **she came down to ~ with a bang** её мечты́ разбúлись вдрéбезги; **he'll move heaven and ~ to get his own way** пусть всем чертя́м стáнет жáрко, он своегó добьётся.

earth *vt Agric, also* **~ up** окýчи|вать (-ть); *Elec* заземл|я́ть (-úть).

earthenware *n* глúняная посýда (*collect*).

earthly *adj* (*terrestrial*) землянóй; *CQ*: **he hasn't an ~ chance** у негó нет ни малéйшей надéжды; **there's no ~ reason why we shouldn't go** у нас нет причúн (*pl*) не пойтú тудá.

earthquake *n* землетрясéние.

earthworm *n* дождевóй/землянóй червь (*m*), *CQ* червя́к.

earthy *adj* землянóй; землúстый; *fig* **~ humour** грубовáтый ю́мор.

ear trumpet *n* слуховáя трýбка.

earwig *n Zool* уховёртка.

ease *n* (*easiness*) лёгкость; (*relief from pain*) облегчéние; **with ~** легкó (*adv*); **her mind is at ~** онá спокóйна; **I feel quite at ~ with them** у них я чýвствую себя́ как дóма/ совсéм свобóдно; **to be ill at ~** (*feel awkward*) чýвствовать себя́ нелóвко, (*feel embarrassed*) смущáться; **she lives a life of ~** ей легкó живётся; *Mil* **(stand) at ~!** вóльно!

ease *vti vt* 1 (*relieve*) облегч|áть (-úть); успок|áивать (-óить); **the tablets have ~d the pain** э́ти таблéтки умéньшили/облегчúли боль; **my talk with the doctor has ~d my mind** разговóр с врачóм успокóил меня́

2 (*slacken*) ослаб|ля́ть (-ить), расслаб|ля́ть (-ить); **to ~ a screw** ослáбить винт; **to ~ a belt/pressure** ослáбить пóяс/нажúм; **to ~ the seams of a dress** распус|кáть швы плáтья (-тúть); *Naut* **to ~ (out) a rope** травúть канáт (*impf*)

vi: **the pain has ~d** боль утúхла; **the rain has ~d** дождь почтú перестáл; **the wind has ~d (off/up)** вéтер стих/уня́лся; **the tension/ situation has ~d** обстанóвка разрядúлась.

easel *n* мольбéрт.

easily *adv* легкó, без трудá; (*decidedly*) бесспóрно, несомнéнно; **he did it ~** он сдéлал э́то без трудá, емý легкó э́то далóсь (*impers*); **the tank holds twelve gallons ~** в бак легкó вхóдит двенáдцать галлóнов; **he is ~ the best pupil in the class** он бесспóрно лýчший ученúк в клáссе; **that may ~ be the**

best thing to do лучше, пожалуй, и не придумаешь.

east *n* восток; *Naut* ост; **the wind is from the ~** ветер дует с востока; **Far/Middle E.** Дальний/Ближний Восток.

east *adj* восточный.

east *adv* на восток, к востоку, в восточном направлении; **Cambridge lies ~ of Oxford** Кембридж находится к востоку от Оксфорда.

Easter *n* пасха; *attr*: **E. Sunday/Monday** первый/второй день пасхи; **E. week** пасхальная неделя.

eastern *adj* восточный.

eastwards *adv* на восток, к востоку.

easy *adj* **1** лёгкий, нетрудный; **it's ~** это легко/нетрудно; **an ~ gradient** лёгкий подъём; **it's ~ to get there** туда легко добраться; **he's ~ to get on with** с ним легко ладить; **she's got an ~ manner** она держится непринуждённо; **if you get an ~ opportunity, ask him about it** спросите его об этом при удобном случае; *Comm* **on ~ terms** на льготных условиях

2 (*free from pain, anxiety, etc.*): **my head is easier now** теперь голова у меня меньше болит; **the pain is a little easier** боль немного утихла; **an ~ conscience** спокойная совесть; **you can be ~ on that score** насчёт этого не беспокойтесь; **what would you like to do?—I'm ~** что ты хочешь делать?—Мне всё равно.

easy *adv*: **~ there!** полегче!, потихоньку!; **take it ~!** (*don't hurry*) не торопитесь!, (*don't worry*) не волнуйтесь!, (*don't overwork*) смотри, не перенапрягайся!; **go ~ with the brandy!** наливай коньяка поменьше!; **the doctor says I must go ~ on sugar/alcohol** доктор посоветовал мне есть меньше сахара/меньше пить; **it's easier said than done** легче сказать, чем сделать.

easy chair *n* кресло.

easy-going *adj* (*easy to get on with*) уживчивый, покладистый; (*compliant*) уступчивый.

eat *vti vt* **1** есть (съ-); **to ~ an apple** есть яблоко; **to ~ one's breakfast/dinner/supper** завтракать/обедать/ужинать (*pfs* по-); **to ~ up** съ|едать (-есть); **to ~ a square meal** плотно поесть; **you should ~ something before you travel** вам надо поесть перед дорогой; **where can we get something/a bite to ~?** где можно перекусить?; **~ up your porridge, children!** (*finish it*) дети, доедайте свою кашу!; *fig* **to ~ smb out of house and home** объедать кого-л

2 (*corrode*) разъ|едать (-есть); (*erode by water*) размы|вать (-ть); **the iron has been ~en away by rust** железо проржавело насквозь; **the river banks have been ~en away** река подмыла берега; *fig* **he is ~en up with pride** его снедает гордость

vi есть *and compounds*; питаться (*impf*); **where shall we ~?** где будем есть?, где бы нам поесть?; **when do you ~ in the evenings?** когда вы ужинаете?; **they ~ very well** они хорошо питаются; **to ~ in/out** обедать (не) дома; *fig* **the extra paper work ~s into my time** бесконечная писанина съедает всё моё время.

eatable *adj* съедобный; *as npl* (**~s**) еда (*sing*).

eating *n* еда; **partridges are good ~** куропатки—вкусная еда; **it's not good to swim after ~** плавать после еды очень вредно; *attr*: **an ~ house** кафе, ресторан.

eats *npl CQ*: **the ~ were excellent** закуска (*collect*) была превосходная.

eaves *npl*: **swallows were nesting under the ~** ласточки свили гнездо под крышей.

eavesdrop *vi* подслуш|ивать (-ать); **he evidently ~ped on our conversation** по-видимому, он подслушал наш разговор.

ebb *n, also* **~ tide** отлив; **the tide is on the ~** начался отлив; *fig* **he is at a low ~** он в подавленном настроении.

ebb *vt*: **the tide is ~ing** начинается отлив.

eccentric *n* чудак; **he's an ~** он (человек) со странностями.

eccentric *adj* эксцентричный, чудаковатый.

eccentricity *n* эксцентричность, чудаковатость; **an ~** *CQ* пунктик.

ecclesiastical *adj* церковный (*to do with the church*); священнический (*to do with priests*).

echo *n* эхо, *also fig*; *fig* отголосок; **the ~ of the old quarrel** отголосок давнего спора; **he was cheered to the ~** он был встречен бурной овацией.

echo *vti vt*: **she ~es everything her husband says** она во всём поддакивает мужу, она, как эхо, всё повторяет за мужем

vi: **the shots ~ed through the hills** звуки выстрелов отдавались эхом в горах; **the valley ~ed with the children's shrieks** долину оглашало эхо детских голосов.

eclair *n* эклер.

eclipse *n Astron* затмение; **a total/partial ~** полное/частичное затмение.

eclipse *vt fig* затм|евать (-ить); **she ~d all the other women there** она затмила своей красотой всех присутствующих там женщин.

economic *adj* (*of economics*) экономический; (*profitable*) выгодный, рентабельный; **~ policy** экономическая политика; **railways are no longer ~** железные дороги больше не рентабельны; **to sell apples at that price is not ~** продавать яблоки за такую цену—себе в убыток.

economical *adj* (*careful*) экономный, бережливый; (*not expensive in use*) экономичный; **to be ~** соблюдать экономию; **to be ~ of one's time** беречь своё время; **an ~ car** экономичная машина.

economics *npl* экономика (*sing*).

economize *vti vt* экономить (с-); **we must ~ our strength** надо экономить силы

vi (*be economical*) соблюдать экономию (*only in impf*); **to ~ on smth** экономить на + *P*; **to ~ on petrol** экономить на бензи́не; **I am economizing by walking to the office** я хожу́ на рабо́ту пешко́м из эконо́мии.

economy *n* **1** (*system*) эконо́мика, хозя́йство; **national** ~ наро́дное хозя́йство, эконо́мика страны́

2 (*avoidance of waste*) эконо́мия; **to practise** ~ соблюда́ть эконо́мию, эконо́мно расхо́довать, эконо́мить; **we are making economies so as to buy a house** мы на всём эконо́мим, что́бы купи́ть дом.

ecstasy *n* экста́з, восто́рг; **he was in** ~ он был в экста́зе; **to be in ecstasies over smth** быть в восто́рге/прийти́ в восто́рг/экста́з от чего́-л.

ecstatic *adj*: **he was** ~ **about the suggestion** он был в восто́рге от э́того предложе́ния.

ecstatically *adv* восто́рженно, восхищённо, с восто́ргом, с восхище́нием.

eddy *n* (*of water*) водоворо́т, (*of wind, air*) вихрь (*m*); **eddies of mist were rising from the fields** с поле́й поднима́лся тума́н (*sing*).

eddy *vi* крути́ться (*impf*).

edge *n* **1** (*cutting edge of knife, etc.*) ле́звие; остриё; *fig* **the** ~ **of criticism** остриё кри́тики

2 (*limit*) край; (*border*) кро́мка; **the** ~ **of a village/a table** око́лица села́, край стола́; **at the** ~ **of a precipice** на краю́ про́пасти; **the** ~ **of material** кро́мка тка́ни; **the** ~ **of the ice/the pavement** кро́мка льда, край тротуа́ра; **the** ~ **of a forest** опу́шка ле́са; **the** ~ **of a road** обо́чина доро́ги; **the** ~ **of a skate** ребро́ конька́; (*in figure skating*) **inside/outside** ~ дуга́ внутрь/нару́жу (*advs*)

3 *fig uses*: **to be on** ~ не́рвничать; **not to put too fine an** ~ **on it** по́просту говоря́; **to have the** ~ **over smb** име́ть преиму́щество пе́ред кем-л; **this scraping sound sets my teeth on** ~ э́тот скре́жет де́йствует мне на не́рвы; **the flu has taken the** ~ **off his appetite** из-за гри́ппа у него́ плохо́й аппети́т; **we had a bite as we came along and it's taken the** ~ **off our appetite** мы перекуси́ли по доро́ге, и э́то переби́ло нам аппети́т.

edge *vti vt* **1: to** ~ **a handkerchief with lace** обши|ва́ть плато́к кру́жевом (-́ть)

2 (*move slowly*): **to** ~ **a chair nearer the fire** пододви|га́ть стул бли́же к огню́ (-́нуть); **to** ~ **one's way through a crowd** про|бира́ться сквозь толпу́ (-бра́ться)

vi: **she** ~**d away from the window** она́ бочко́м-бочко́м отошла́ от окна́.

edgeways, edgewise *advs*: **to place smth** ~ поста́вить что-л ребро́м; *fig* **I couldn't get a word in** ~ мне не удало́сь да́же и слове́чка вста́вить.

edging *n* (*on fabric or wallpaper*) бордю́р; (*piping*) кант; (*facing*) обши́вка; (*trimming of different material*) оторо́чка; (*mount for photo, etc.*) окантóвка; **the lawn needs** ~ ну́жно подровня́ть края́ (*pl*) газо́на; *attr*: ~ **shears** но́жницы для стри́жки бордю́ра.

edgy *adj*: **she's very** ~ **today** сего́дня она́ вся взви́нченная, её сего́дня всё раздража́ет.

edible *adj* съедо́бный.

edict *n* ука́з, эди́кт.

edifying *adj* назида́тельный, поучи́тельный.

edit *vt* (*a book, etc.*) редакти́ровать (от-), (*a newspaper, magazine*) редакти́ровать (*only in impf*); (*to be an editor*) быть реда́ктором; (*a film*) монти́ровать (с-); **she** ~**s scientific journals** она́ редакти́рует нау́чные журна́лы.

edition *n* (*of book*) изда́ние; (*of a newspaper*) вы́пуск; (*collected works of an author*) собра́ние сочине́ний; **popular/pocket** ~ популя́рное/карма́нное изда́ние; **a first** ~ **of 5,000 copies** тира́ж пе́рвого изда́ния пять ты́сяч экземпля́ров; **evening** ~ вече́рний вы́пуск.

editor *n* реда́ктор.

editorial *n* передова́я статья́, *CQ* передови́ца.

editorial *adj* редакцио́нный; (*referring to editors*) реда́кторский; ~ **office** реда́кция; ~ **board** редакцио́нная колле́гия; ~ **comment** редакцио́нное примеча́ние; **an** ~ **slip** реда́кторская оши́бка.

editor-in-chief *n* гла́вный реда́ктор.

editorship *n*: **under the** ~ **of** под реда́кцией + *G*.

educate *vt* да|ва́ть образова́ние (-ть); приуч|а́ть к + *D or* + *inf* (-и́ть); **he was** ~**d to the law** он получи́л юриди́ческое образова́ние; **to** ~ **children to wash their hands before meals** приуча́ть дете́й мыть ру́ки пе́ред едо́й.

educated *adj* образо́ванный; просвещённый; (*well brought-up*) воспи́танный.

education *n* (*training: general*) образова́ние; (*schooling*) обуче́ние; (*upbringing*) воспита́ние; *off* просвеще́ние; **primary/secondary/higher** ~ нача́льное/сре́днее/вы́сшее образова́ние; **the Minister of E./of Higher E.** мини́стр просвеще́ния/вы́сшего образова́ния; **institute of higher** ~ вы́сшее уче́бное заведе́ние, *often abbr* вуз; **I never had a university** ~ я не получи́л вы́сшего образова́ния; [**NB** сре́днее образова́ние *is from 11–17 years*, вы́сшее образова́ние = *education after 17, whether at University or Institute, etc.*]; **a man of** ~ образо́ванный/просвещённый челове́к.

educational *adj* уче́бный; педагоги́ческий; образова́тельный; **an** ~ **film** уче́бный фильм; ~ **qualifications** (*on questionnaire*) образова́тельный у́ровень (*sing*).

education(al)ist, educator *n approx* педаго́г.

eel *n* у́горь (*m*).

eerie, eery *adj* жу́ткий; **I had an** ~ **feeling that...** у меня́ бы́ло жу́ткое/гнету́щее предчу́вствие, что...

efface *vt* стира́ть (стере́ть); **the inscription was** ~**d** по́дпись стёрлась; **I tried to** ~ **myself** я стара́лся быть незаме́тным.

effect *n* **1** (*result*) результа́т, сле́дствие; (*after-effect*) после́дствие; (*action*) де́йствие; (*influence*) влия́ние; **his cough is the** ~ **of whooping cough** его́ ка́шель — после́дствие коклю́ша; **to suffer from the ~s of heat** страда́ть от жары́; **my objections were without ~/of no ~/to no ~** мои́ возраже́ния бы́ли напра́сны; **our arguments had no ~ on him** на́ши до́воды на него́ не поде́йствовали; **has the medicine taken ~?** лека́рство поде́йствовало?; **the new law will take ~/be in ~ from January 1st** но́вый зако́н всту́пит в си́лу с пе́рвого января́; **to carry a plan into ~** осуществля́ть план, претворя́ть план в жизнь; **in ~** в су́щности, факти́чески

2 (*impression*) впечатле́ние, эффе́кт; **his speech had a profound ~ on me** его́ речь произвела́ на меня́ си́льное впечатле́ние; **to do smth for ~** де́лать что-л напока́з

3 (*meaning*): **he said something to the ~ that the meeting would be postponed** он как бу́дто сказа́л, что собра́ние откла́дывается; **the answer was to the ~ that...** он отве́тил в том смы́сле, что...; **I also wrote a letter to the same ~** я то́же написа́л письмо́ подо́бного содержа́ния; **and more to the same ~** и тому́ подо́бное

4 *pl* (*property*) иму́щество (*sing*); (*belongings*) ве́щи; **household/personal ~s** дома́шние/ли́чные ве́щи.

effect *vt* (*accomplish*) достиг|а́ть + *G* (-́нуть); доби|ва́ться + *G* (-́ться); **to ~ one's purpose** доби́ться своего́/свое́й це́ли; **thus they ~ed the desired result** таки́м о́бразом они́ доби́лись/дости́гли жела́емого результа́та; **to ~ a cure** излечи|ва́ть + *A* (-́ть); **by giving up smoking I have ~ed a saving of £100 this year** я бро́сил кури́ть и сэконо́мил сто фу́нтов в э́том году́.

effective *adj* эффекти́вный; (*striking*) эффе́ктный; (*real, actual*) факти́ческий, реа́льный; **it is an ~ medicine** э́то о́чень хоро́шее лека́рство; **the décor was very ~** декора́ции (*pl*) бы́ли о́чень эффе́ктны; **he can be a very ~ speaker** он мо́жет говори́ть о́чень убеди́тельно; **the ~ income of the factory** реа́льный дохо́д заво́да.

effectively *adv* (*efficiently*) де́йственно, эффекти́вно; (*strikingly*) впечатля́юще, эффе́ктно; (*in fact*) факти́чески.

effectual *adj* де́йственный, эффекти́вный.

effeminate *adj* женоподо́бный.

effervesce *vi* (*of drinks*) шипе́ть (*impf*).

effervescent *adj* (*of drinks*) шипу́чий.

efficacious *adj* эффекти́вный, де́йственный; **an ~ remedy for rheumatism** прекра́сное сре́дство от ревмати́зма.

efficiency *n* эффекти́вность, де́йственность; **the ~ of computers depends on their programmers** эффекти́вность компью́теров зави́сит от программи́стов; **in order to increase the ~ of production** в це́лях повыше́ния эффекти́вности произво́дственного проце́сса; **he acted with his usual ~** он де́йствовал как всегда́ о́чень толко́во и расторо́пно.

efficient *adj* **1** (*of persons*: *able*) спосо́бный, уме́лый; (*businesslike*) делово́й, расторо́пный; (*usu of subordinates*) исполни́тельный

2 (*of methods*) эффекти́вный; рациона́льный; **an ~ business** эффекти́вно рабо́тающее предприя́тие

3 (*of machines*: *economical*) экономи́чный, (*reliable*) надёжный, (*in good working order*) испра́вный; **my refrigerator is very ~** у меня́ холоди́льник (о́чень) хорошо́ рабо́тает.

effluent *n* (*of sewage*) сто́чные во́ды (*pl*).

effort *n* **1** (*attempt*) попы́тка; (*exertion*) уси́лие; (*strain*) напряже́ние; **he lifted the box with some ~** он с трудо́м по́днял я́щик; **I will make an ~ to come tomorrow** я попыта́юсь прийти́ за́втра; **I will make every ~ to help you** я приложу́ все си́лы (*pl*)/я сде́лаю всё, что в мои́х си́лах, что́бы помо́чь вам; **it can be done without any special ~** э́то мо́жно сде́лать без осо́бых уси́лий; **to spare no ~** не жале́ть сил (*pl*)

2 *CQ* (*result of effort*): **that's a pretty poor ~** э́то жа́лкая попы́тка; **not bad for a first ~** непло́хо для пе́рвого ра́за; **it's quite a good ~** э́то совсе́м непло́хо.

effrontery *n* на́глость; **he had the ~ to...** он име́л на́глость + *inf*.

effusive *adj*: **her ~ nature** её экспанси́вная нату́ра; **she was ~ in her thanks** она́ рассы́палась в благода́рностях.

egg *n* яйцо́; **hard-/soft-boiled ~** яйцо́ вкруту́ю/всмя́тку (*advs*); **fried ~s** я́ичница (*sing*), (я́ичница-) глазу́нья (*sing*); **scrambled ~s** я́ичница-болту́нья (*sing*); **ham/bacon and ~s** я́ичница с ветчино́й/с беко́ном; *CQ* **he's a bad ~** он негодя́й; *attr* яи́чный.

egg *vt*: *CQ* **to ~ smb on to do smth** подна́чивать/подстрека́ть кого́-л сде́лать что-л (*impfs*), подби|ва́ть кого́-л на что-л (-́ть).

eggbeater *n* взбива́лка (для яи́ц).

eggcup *n* рю́мка для яйца́.

eggplant *n* баклажа́н.

eggshell *n* яи́чная скорлупа́.

egoist *n* эгои́ст.

egoistic *adj* эгоисти́чный.

egregious *adj*: **an ~ ass/idiot** наби́тый дура́к; **an ~ blunder** вопию́щая/грубе́йшая оши́бка; **an ~ liar** закорене́лый лжец.

Egyptian *n* египтя́нин, египтя́нка.

Egyptian *adj* еги́петский.

eiderdown *n* (*quilt*) стёганое пухо́вое одея́ло.

eight *num* во́семь (*G, D, P* восьми́, *I* восьмью́ *and* восемью́) [*see grammatical note under* **five**]; *collect* во́сьмеро [*see grammatical note under* **four**]; **8 years** во́семь лет; **8 beautiful girls** во́семь краси́вых де́вушек; **together with 8 other passengers** вме́сте с восемью́ други́ми пассажи́рами; **there were 8 of us** нас бы́ло во́семь челове́к/во́сьмеро; **an "8"** (*the number* 8, *an* "8" *in cards, also No* 8 *bus, etc.*) восьмёрка; **he is 8 (years old)** ему́ во́семь лет; **8 times 8** во́семью во́семь [NB *stress*]; **volume 8** восьмо́й том; **it's now after 8** сейча́с девя́тый час; **8-year olds** восьмиле́тние де́ти; **800** восемьсо́т (*G* восьмисо́т,

D восьмиста́м, *I* восьмиста́ми, *P* о восьмиста́х); **8,000** во́семь ты́сяч.

eighteen *num* восемна́дцать [*see* **eleven**].

eighteenth *adj* восемна́дцатый.

eighth *adj* восьмо́й; *as n*: **an ~** одна́ восьма́я; **five ~s** пять восьмы́х.

eighty *num* во́семьдесят (*G*, *D*, *P* восьми́десяти, *I* восемью́десятью *or* восьмью́десятью).

either *pron* любо́й; **take ~ of the cakes** бери́те любо́е пиро́жное; **you can take ~ of the two routes** мо́жете пойти́ по любо́й доро́ге; **take both maps — ~ will show you all the local roads** бери́те о́бе ка́рты — и на той и на друго́й обозна́чены все ме́стные доро́ги; **~ of the dresses is suitable** о́ба пла́тья годя́тся.

either *adj* **1** (*one of two*) любо́й/оди́н из двух; тот и́ли друго́й; **take ~ apple — they're both good** бери́те любо́е я́блоко — они́ о́ба вку́сные; **I do not take ~ side in this dispute** в э́том спо́ре я не подде́рживаю ни одну́ из сторо́н; **~ book will answer your purpose** для ва́шей це́ли годи́тся и та и друга́я кни́га

2 (*both of two*): **there is a bus stop at ~ end of the street** авто́бусная остано́вка — в нача́ле и в конце́ у́лицы; **there was a candle at ~ end of the table** на обо́их конца́х стола́ горе́ло по свече́; **you can do it ~ way** мо́жешь э́то сде́лать и так и так.

either *adv* (*in neg sentences*) то́же; **if you don't go, I won't ~** е́сли ты не пойдёшь, то я то́же не пойду́; **I don't like it ~** мне э́то то́же не нра́вится; **I didn't swim ~** я то́же/и я не купа́лся.

either... or *conj* и́ли... и́ли; ли́бо... ли́бо; **don't stand at the door — ~ come in or go out** не стой в дверя́х, и́ли иди́ сюда́ и́ли уходи́; **~ he does the job or I do it** ли́бо он э́то де́лает, ли́бо я.

ejaculate *vt* воскли|ца́ть (-́кнуть).

ejaculation *n* восклица́ние.

eject *vt* вы|гоня́ть (-́гнать); **to ~ a tenant** выгоня́ть/вы|селя́ть жильца́ (-́селить).

eke out *vt*: **to ~ out one's coal by burning driftwood** топи́ть из-за нехва́тки у́гля плавнико́м (*usu impf*); **to ~ out a living** перебива́ться ко́е-ка́к (*usu impf*); **I want to ~ out the meat for three days** я хочу́, что́бы мя́са хвати́ло на три дня.

elaborate *adj* (*complicated*) сло́жный; **an ~ hairdo** замыслова́тая причёска; **they gave us an ~ dinner** они́ угости́ли нас изы́сканным обе́дом.

elaborate *vt* (*work out in detail*): **to ~ a theme** дета́льно/тща́тельно разраб|а́тывать те́му (-о́тать); (*describe in detail*) **please ~ your proposal a little** пожа́луйста, расскажи́те о ва́шем предложе́нии бо́лее подро́бно.

elaborately *adv* (*carefully*) тща́тельно; **the hall was ~ decorated for the occasion** зал был наря́дно укра́шен по э́тому слу́чаю.

elapse *vi* (*generally*) про|ходи́ть (-йти́); (*of a fixed term*: *expire*) исте|ка́ть (-́чь); **six years had ~d** прошло́ шесть лет; **five months of the contract had ~d** пять ме́сяцев контра́кта уже́ истекли́; **not an hour had ~d when...** и ча́са не прошло́, как...

elastic *n* рези́нка; **the ~ in my pants has gone** у трусо́в ло́пнула рези́нка.

elastic *adj* (*of material*) эласти́чный; рези́новый; *fig* **rules here are ~** здесь пра́вила нестро́гие.

elated *adj*: **to be ~** быть в припо́днятом настрое́нии; **~ by his success** окрылённый успе́хом.

elation *n* восто́рг, ликова́ние; **she hugged me in her ~** она́ так обра́довалась, что бро́силась обнима́ть меня́.

elbow *n* ло́коть (*m*); **it's at your ~** э́то у тебя́ под руко́й; **he was at my ~** он стоя́л ря́дом со мной; **my jersey is out at the ~s** моя́ ко́фта протёрлась на локтя́х.

elbow *vt*: **to ~ one's way through a crowd** прота́лкиваться сквозь толпу́ (*only in impf*).

elbow bend *n Tech* коле́но трубы́.

elbow grease *n CQ*: **it'll need some ~ to get these boots to shine!** придётся хороше́нько/как сле́дует потруди́ться, что́бы э́ти боти́нки заблесте́ли.

elbowroom *n*: **there's no ~ in my flat** в мое́й кварти́ре не́где поверну́ться; *fig* **they gave us no ~** нам не да́ли свобо́ды де́йствий.

elder[1] *n Bot* бузина́; самбу́к.

elder[2] *n*: **he is the ~ of the two brothers** он ста́рший брат; **our ~s** ста́ршие.

elder[2] *adj* ста́рший.

elderly *adj* пожило́й.

elect *adj*: **he is president ~** он вновь и́збранный президе́нт (, ещё не заступи́вший на до́лжность).

elect *vt* **1** (*choose by vote*) вы|бира́ть (-́брать), из|бира́ть (-бра́ть); **he has been ~ed (a) member of Parliament/chairman** его́ избра́ли чле́ном парла́мента/вы́брали председа́телем собра́ния

2 (*choose, decide*) выбира́ть, реш|а́ть (-и́ть); (*prefer*) предпо|чита́ть (-че́сть); **he ~ed to stay at home** он предпочёл оста́ться до́ма.

election *n* вы́боры (*pl*); **general ~** всео́бщие вы́боры; *attr*: **~ results** результа́ты вы́боров.

elector *n* избира́тель (*m*).

electoral *adj* избира́тельный.

electorate *n* избира́тели (*m, pl*).

electric *adj* электри́ческий; **~ light** электри́чество, электри́ческое освеще́ние; *fig* **the atmosphere was ~** атмосфе́ра была́ наэлектризо́вана.

electrical *adj* электри́ческий; *fig* порази́тельный; **the effect of these words was ~** впечатле́ние от э́тих слов бы́ло порази́тельное.

electric blue *adj* электри́к (*indecl*).

electrician *n* электроте́хник, эле́ктрик.

electricity *n* электри́чество.

electric-powered *adj*: ~ **saw** электропила́.

electrify *vt* электрифици́ровать (*impf and pf*); *fig* электризова́ть (на-).

electronic *adj* электро́нный.

electronics *npl* электро́ника (*sing*).

elegant *adj* (*of dress, appearance*) элега́нтный; *CQ* шика́рный; **an** ~ **young man/style** элега́нтный молодо́й челове́к/стиль.

element *n* **1** (*force of nature*) стихи́я; **the four** ~**s** четы́ре основны́е стихи́и; *pl* (*of weather*) **the** ~**s** стихи́и; **a house exposed to the fury of the** ~**s** дом, откры́тый всем стихи́ям; *fig* **to be in one's** ~ быть в свое́й стихи́и

2 (*part*) элеме́нт; часть; черта́; (*trace*) части́ца; до́ля; **honesty is a basic** ~ **in his character** че́стность—основна́я черта́ его́ хара́ктера; **there is an** ~ **of truth in what he says** в его́ слова́х есть до́ля и́стины

3 *pl* (*beginnings*) осно́вы; **the** ~**s of geometry** осно́вы геоме́трии

4 *Chem, Elec* элеме́нт.

elemental *adj* стихи́йный.

elementary *adj* (*basic*) элемента́рный; (*of the beginning*) нача́льный; **that's** ~ э́то элемента́рно; **an** ~ **school** нача́льная шко́ла.

elephant *n* слон.

elevate *vt* (*lift*) под|нима́ть (-ня́ть); (*in rank*) воз|води́ть (-вести́); **to** ~ **smb to a bishopric** возвести́ кого́-л в сан епи́скопа.

elevated *adj*: **the speaker stood on an** ~ **dais** ора́тор стоя́л на трибу́не; **an** ~ **railway** надзе́мная желе́зная доро́га; *fig*: **in an** ~ **mood** в припо́днятом настрое́нии; **an** ~ **style** возвы́шенный/высо́кий стиль; *CQ* (*slightly drunk*) подвы́пивший, под му́хой.

elevation *n* (*physical height*) высота́; *Archit* вертика́льная прое́кция; (*in rank*) повыше́ние.

elevator *n* (*apparatus for lifting*) грузоподъёмник; (*grain store*) элева́тор; (*US*: *lift*) лифт.

eleven *num* оди́ннадцать (*G, D, P* оди́ннадцати, *I* оди́ннадцатью) [*in nom, A noun and adj are in G pl; in oblique cases noun and adj are plural, agreeing in case with numeral*]; **11 years** оди́ннадцать лет; **11 large cows** оди́ннадцать больши́х коро́в; **with 11 English soldiers** с оди́ннадцатью англи́йскими солда́тами; **volume 11** оди́ннадцатый том; **it's now after 11** сейча́с двена́дцатый час; **11-year olds** одиннадцатиле́тние; **11,000** оди́ннадцать ты́сяч.

eleventh *adj* оди́ннадцатый; *fig* **at the** ~ **hour** в после́днюю мину́ту.

elfish *adj* (*mischievous*) прока́зливый, озорно́й.

elicit *vt*: **to** ~ **a reply/the truth** доби|ва́ться отве́та/и́стины (-́ться).

eligibility *n*: **his** ~ **for the post has been questioned** сомни́тельно, что он смо́жет занима́ть э́ту до́лжность.

eligible *adj*: **to be** ~ **for election** име́ть пра́во быть и́збранным; **is he** ~ **for membership of the club?** он име́ет пра́во стать чле́ном клу́ба?; **he's an** ~ **young man** он подходя́щая па́ртия.

eliminate *vt* (*remove*) устран|я́ть (-и́ть); (*exclude*) исключ|а́ть (-и́ть); **to** ~ **errors** устрани́ть оши́бки; **to** ~ **a possibility** исключи́ть возмо́жность; **we've** ~**d that candidate** мы сня́ли э́ту кандидату́ру; **we have** ~**d that suspect** подозре́ние с э́того челове́ка бы́ло сня́то; **to** ~ **one's enemies** устраня́ть свои́х проти́вников; (*in competition*) **he was** ~**d in the first round** он вы́был в пе́рвом ра́унде.

elimination *n* устране́ние; исключе́ние; **by a process of** ~ ме́тодом исключе́ния; ~ **of one's rivals** устране́ние проти́вников/сопе́рников.

elite *n* эли́та.

elm *n* вяз; **this table is made of** ~ э́тот стол сде́лан из вя́за.

elocution *n* ора́торское иску́сство; **his** ~ **is bad** у него́ пло́хо поста́влен го́лос.

elope *vi*: **she** ~**d** она́ сбежа́ла с возлю́бленным.

eloquence *n* красноре́чие, ора́торское иску́сство.

eloquent *adj* (*of person or speech*) красноречи́вый; **an** ~ **silence** красноречи́вое молча́ние; ~ **eyes** вырази́тельные глаза́.

else *adv* **1** (*after pronoun*): **i)** (*in addition*): **somebody** ~ **is coming** кто́-то ещё придёт; **I only did what anyone** ~ **would have done** я сде́лал то́лько то, что сде́лал бы любо́й друго́й (на моём ме́сте); **everyone** ~ **had gone** все остальны́е уже́ ушли́; **everything** ~ **is already done** всё остально́е уже́ сде́лано; **he gave me something** ~ **as well** он дал мне ещё ко́е-что́ в прида́чу; **ii)** (*different*): **you'd better ask somebody** ~ **to help you** лу́чше попроси́ кого́-нибудь друго́го помо́чь тебе́; **it must have been somebody** ~ **you saw, not me** э́то был не я—ты, наве́рно, обозна́лся; **we'll have to do that—anything** ~ **is out of the question** мы должны́ э́то сде́лать—у нас нет друго́го вы́бора; **we'll have to think of something** ~ **to do** нам придётся приду́мать что́-то ещё; **I must have left it somewhere** ~ я, должно́ быть, оста́вил э́то где́-нибудь в друго́м ме́сте

2 (*after interrog*) ещё, ина́че; **what** ~ **do you need?** что ещё вам ну́жно?; **is there anything** ~ **to read?** есть ещё что́-нибудь почита́ть?; **where** ~ **can we go?** куда́ же ещё нам пойти́?; **what** ~ **could I have done?** мог ли я поступи́ть ина́че?; **how** ~ **could it have been done?** а как ина́че мо́жно бы́ло э́то сде́лать?; **who** ~ **could have done it but he?** кто ещё мог э́то сде́лать, кро́ме него́?

3 (*after neg pron*) бо́льше; **nothing** ~**, thanks** бо́льше ничего́ не на́до, спаси́бо; **nobody** ~ **knows about it** бо́льше никто́ об э́том не зна́ет; **I don't know anyone** ~ **here** я бо́льше никого́ здесь не зна́ю; **don't tell anyone** ~ бо́льше никому́ не говори́ об э́том; **there's nothing** ~ **to be done** бо́льше не́чего де́лать

4 (*after advs of quantity*): **little ~ remains to be done** о́чень ма́ло остаётся сде́лать; **more than anything ~ I'd like to be able to paint** бо́льше всего́ на све́те я хоте́л бы уме́ть рисова́ть

5 (*alternatively*): **be quiet or ~ leave the room** замолчи́ и́ли вы́йди из ко́мнаты; **he must be joking, or ~ he's mad** он и́ли шу́тит и́ли совсе́м уж рехну́лся; **I choose red or ~ black** я выбира́ю и́ли кра́сное и́ли же чёрное; **go quickly or ~ I'll go myself** иди́ туда́ поскоре́е, а не то я пойду́ сам; *CQ* **you get moving, or ~!** дава́й-ка принима́йся за де́ло, а то ху́же бу́дет!

elsewhere *adv* (*at somewhere else*) (где́-нибудь) в друго́м ме́сте; (*to somewhere else*) (куда́-нибудь) в друго́е ме́сто; **they must have come from ~** они́, наве́рно, пришли́ ещё отку́да-нибудь.

elucidate *vt* поясн|я́ть, разъясн|я́ть (*pfs* -и́ть).

elude *vt* (*escape*) ускольз|а́ть от + *G* (-ну́ть); избе|га́ть (-жа́ть); **to ~ one's enemies/pursuit** ускользну́ть от враго́в/от пресле́дования; **to ~ observation** избежа́ть сле́жки (*G*) (*usu pf*); **the meaning ~s me** смысл ускольза́ет от меня́; **his name ~s me** я не могу́ вспо́мнить его́ и́мя.

elusive *adj*: **an ~ criminal** неулови́мый престу́пник; **happiness is ~** сча́стье обма́нчиво.

emaciated *adj* худо́й, истощённый.

emanate *vi*: (*of light, smell, rumours*) **to ~ from** идти́ из + *G* (*only in impf*), (*of rumours*) исходи́ть от + *G* (*only in impf*).

emancipate *vt* (*slaves, etc.*) освобо|жда́ть от + *G* (-ди́ть); (*women*) эмансипи́ровать (*impf and pf*).

embankment *n* (*stone-built, by river or sea*) на́бережная; (*earthen, by road, railway*) на́сыпь.

embargo *n* эмба́рго (*indecl*), запре́т; **to place an ~ on smth** налага́ть запре́т/эмба́рго на что-л; **to be under an ~** быть под запре́том.

embark *vi* (*board*) сади́ться на кора́бль (сесть); *fig*: **to ~ on smth** на|чина́ть что-л (-ча́ть); бра́ться за что-л (взя́ться), пред-при|нима́ть что-л (-ня́ть); **to ~ on a long novel** взя́ться за дли́нный рома́н (*of either writing or reading*); **to ~ on a 3-year course in English** поступи́ть на трёхгоди́чные ку́рсы англи́йского языка́; **to ~ on a new venture** пус|ка́ться в но́вое предприя́тие (-ти́ться).

embarkation *n* (*of people*) поса́дка; (*of cargo*) погру́зка; *attr*: **my son has a week's ~ leave** мой сын получи́л неде́льный о́тпуск пе́ред отплы́тием; **~ card** поса́дочный тало́н.

embarrass *vt* (*disconcert*) сму|ща́ть (-ти́ть); **to be ~ed** смуща́ться; **to feel ~ed** (*be shy*) стесня́ться, чу́вствовать себя́ нело́вко (*usu impfs*); **he ~ed me** он привёл меня́ в замеша́тельство; **his remarks ~ed me** его́ замеча́ния смути́ли меня́; **he was ~ed by debts** он был обременён долга́ми.

embarrassing *adj* (*awkward*) нело́вкий; (*disconcerting*) смуща́ющий; затрудни́тельный; стесни́тельный; **an ~ silence/situation** нело́вкое молча́ние/положе́ние.

embarrassment *n* смуще́ние; замеша́тельство; **to my ~ he blurted out the whole story** к моему́ смуще́нию он вы́палил всю исто́рию; **financial ~** фина́нсовые затрудне́ния (*pl*); **he's a great ~ to us** он нам о́чень докуча́ет.

embassy *n* посо́льство.

embed *vt*: **the arrow was firmly ~ded/~ded itself in the tree** стрела́ кре́пко засе́ла в де́реве.

embellish *vt* (*dress, room, etc.*) укра|ша́ть (-́сить); *fig* приукра́|шивать (-сить); **he ~ed the story as he went along** он не́сколько приукра́сил свой расска́з.

embellishment *n* (*of dress, etc.*) украше́ние; *fig* (*of story*) приукра́шивание.

ember(s) *n usu pl* тле́ющие у́гли, горя́чая зола́ (*collect*).

embezzle *vt*: **he ~d official funds** он растра́тил казённые де́ньги.

embezzlement *n* растра́та; **he's been arrested for ~** его́ арестова́ли за растра́ту.

embittered *adj* ожесточённый; огорчённый; **he is very ~ about his daughter's marriage** он о́чень огорчён заму́жеством до́чери.

emblem *n* эмбле́ма; си́мвол; **national ~** национа́льная эмбле́ма.

embody *vt*: **the latest model of this car embodies many new features** после́дняя моде́ль э́той маши́ны име́ет мно́го усоверше́нствований.

embrace *n* объя́тие.

embrace *vti vt* **1** (*clasp*) об|нима́ть (-ня́ть); **he ~d her warmly** он не́жно обня́л её

2 (*take*): **to ~ an opportunity** по́льзоваться слу́чаем (вос-); **to ~ a theory/Christianity** при|нима́ть тео́рию/христиа́нство (-ня́ть)

vi: **they ~d** они́ обняли́сь.

embrocation *n* (жи́дкая) мазь.

embroider *vt Sew* вы|шива́ть (-́шить); *fig* **to ~ a story** приукра́|шивать свой расска́з (-сить).

embroidery *n* (*action*) вышива́ние; (*work produced*) вы́шивка; **she loves** (*doing*) **~** она́ лю́бит вышива́ть; **I think her** (*piece of*) **~ is quite beautiful** мне о́чень нра́вится её вы́шивка.

embroil *vt*: **I don't want to get ~ed in their quarrels** я не хочу́ ввя́зываться в их ссо́ры.

embryo *n* заро́дыш; зача́ток, *also fig*; **the project is still only in ~** прое́кт ещё в зача́точном состоя́нии.

emend *vt*: **to ~ a text** исправ|ля́ть текст (-́ить).

emendation *n* исправле́ние.

emerald *n* изумру́д; *attr* изумру́дный.

emerge *vi* (*appear*) появ|ля́ться (-и́ться), *also fig*; пока́з|ываться (-а́ться); (*come out*) вы|ходи́ть (-́йти); (*to surface*) всплы|ва́ть (-ть), *also fig*; **the moon ~d from behind the clouds** луна́ появи́лась/показа́лась/вы́шла из-за облако́в; *fig*: **it ~d that...** вы́яснилось, что...; **what has ~d from the talks?** что вы́яснилось в результа́те перегово́ров?

emergency *n*: **a state of ~ has been declared** бы́ло объя́влено чрезвыча́йное положе́ние; **in an ~, in case of ~** в слу́чае кра́йней необходи́мости; *attr*: **~ exit** запа́сный вы́ход; **~ measures** чрезвыча́йные ме́ры; **an ~ fund** чрезвыча́йный фонд; **an ~ landing** вы́нужденная поса́дка.

emery paper *n* нажда́чная бума́га.

emetic *n* рво́тное сре́дство.

emigrant *n* эмигра́нт, переселе́нец.

emigrate *vi* эмигри́ровать (*impf and pf*).

eminence *n* (*raised ground*) возвыше́ние; возвы́шенность; *fig*: **to win/reach a position of ~** дости́чь высо́кого положе́ния; **a scientist of great ~** выдаю́щийся учёный.

eminent *adj* (*of people and qualities*) выдаю́щийся; **an ~ doctor/talent** выдаю́щийся врач/тала́нт.

eminently *adv* в вы́сшей сте́пени; **he is ~ suitable for the post** он в вы́сшей сте́пени подхо́дит для э́той до́лжности.

emit *vt*: **to ~ rays** испуска́ть лучи́ (*usu impf*); **to ~ light** излуча́ть свет (*usu impf*); **to ~ heat** выделя́ть тепло́ (*usu impf*); **to ~ a smell** распространя́ть за́пах (*pleasant or unpleasant*)/злово́ние (*unpleasant*) (*usu impf*).

emolument *n* жа́лованье; за́работок.

emotion *n* чу́вство; эмо́ция; пережива́ние; (*excitement*) возбужде́ние; (*agitation*) волне́ние; **he spoke with deep ~** он говори́л с больши́м чу́вством; **she gives way too readily to her ~s** она́ сли́шком легко́ даёт во́лю свои́м чу́вствам; **his face showed no ~** его́ лицо́ не вы́разило никаки́х эмо́ций.

emotional *adj* (*given to emotion*) эмоциона́льный; (*rousing emotion*) волну́ющий; **an ~ man/child** эмоциона́льный челове́к, легко́ возбуди́мый ребёнок; **an ~ speech** волну́ющая речь.

emotionally *adv* с чу́вством; с волне́нием; эмоциона́льно; **he is ~ unstable** он эмоциона́льно неусто́йчивый.

emperor *n* импера́тор.

emphasis *n*: **our teacher places great ~ on correct spelling** наш учи́тель придаёт большо́е значе́ние правописа́нию; **special ~ was placed on agriculture** осо́бое внима́ние бы́ло уделено́ се́льскому хозя́йству; **he spoke with great ~** он говори́л о́чень вырази́тельно; *Ling* **the ~ is on the pronoun** логи́ческое ударе́ние па́дает на местоиме́ние.

emphasize *vt* под|чёркивать (-черкну́ть); **he ~d the dangers of infection** он подчеркну́л опа́сность зараже́ния; **I ~d that...** я подчеркну́л, что...; **he ~d his words by thumping the table** в подкрепле́ние свои́х слов он сту́кнул по́ столу; **to ~ the first word** де́лать логи́ческое ударе́ние на пе́рвом сло́ве.

emphatic *adj*: **he expressed his ~ opinion that...** он вы́разил твёрдое убежде́ние (в том), что...; **with an ~ gesture** вырази́тельным же́стом.

emphatically *adv* реши́тельно; си́льно, категори́чески.

empire *n* импе́рия.

empiric(al) *adj* эмпири́ческий, осно́ванный на о́пыте; **~ knowledge** зна́ния (*pl*) на осно́ве о́пыта.

employ *n*: **to be in the ~ of smb** рабо́тать у кого́-л.

employ *vt* **1** (*people*): **he ~s 5 men** у него́ рабо́тает пять челове́к; **the factory ~s 500 men** на фа́брике за́нято пятьсо́т рабо́чих; **to be ~ed by smb** рабо́тать/служи́ть у кого́-л (*usu impf*); **1,000 men are ~ed by this company** в шта́те э́той фи́рмы ты́сяча челове́к

2 (*things*) примен|я́ть (-и́ть); (*time*) занима́ться + *I* (*usu impf*); **he ~ed a new method** он примени́л но́вый ме́тод; **how do you ~ your time/yourself in the evenings?** чем вы занима́етесь вечера́ми?

employee *n* рабо́чий; (*of office worker*) слу́жащий.

employer *n* работода́тель (*m*), нанима́тель (*m*).

employment *n* (*paid work*) рабо́та; (*in an office*) слу́жба; (*occupation, pursuit*) заня́тие; (*trade, profession*) профе́ссия; **full ~** по́лная за́нятость; **he is in ~ just now** тепе́рь у него́ есть рабо́та/он рабо́тает; *attr*: **~ figures** стати́стика (*sing*) за́нятости; **~ exchange** би́ржа труда́.

emporium *n* универма́г.

empower *vt*: **to ~ smb to do smth** уполномо́чить кого́-л сде́лать что-л (*usu pf*); **I have been ~ed to sign this contract** я уполномо́чен подписа́ть э́то соглаше́ние.

empress *n* императри́ца.

empty *n usu pl* (**empties**) (*bottles*) пусты́е буты́лки; (*bottles or jars*) (пуста́я) посу́да, (*containers, crates*) поро́жняя та́ра (*collects*); **empties to be returned** посу́да/та́ра подлежи́т возвра́ту.

empty *adj* пусто́й; **an ~ box/house** пусто́й я́щик/дом; **~ promises** пусты́е обеща́ния; **to travel on an ~ stomach** отправля́ться в путь на голо́дный желу́док; **words ~ of meaning** пусты́е/бессмы́сленные слова́.

empty *vti vt* опор|а́жнивать, опор|ожня́ть (*pf for both* -о́жни́ть); (*liquid*) вы|лива́ть (-лить); (*sugar, etc.*) вы|сыпа́ть (-сыпать), пересы|па́ть (-пать); **to ~ a glass** опоро́жни́ть/вы́пить стака́н; **to ~ wine out of a bottle** вы́лить вино́ из буты́лки; **to ~ smth into smth else** (*of liquids*) перели|ва́ть (-ть), (*of sugar, etc.*) пересыпа́ть; **he emptied the contents of his pockets on to the table** он вы́ложил содержи́мое (*sing*) карма́нов на стол

vi (*of street, etc.*) опусте́ть (*usu pf*); **the streets soon emptied when the rain began** пошёл дождь, и у́лицы бы́стро опусте́ли; **the**

hall emptied quickly after the concert зал бы́стро опусте́л по́сле конце́рта.

empty-handed *adj* с пусты́ми рука́ми.

empty-headed *adj*: **an ~ person** пусто́й челове́к.

emulate *vt*: **I want to ~ my brother's success in his studies** я хочу́ учи́ться так, что́бы не отстава́ть от бра́та.

emulation *n*: **(spirit of) ~** дух соревнова́ния.

enable *vt*: **the money from his uncle ~d him to go to University** благодаря́ дя́дюшкиным деньга́м он смог учи́ться в университе́те; **I am thus ~d to come with you** в тако́м слу́чае я могу́ вас проводи́ть.

enact *vt* (*take place*; *usu pass*): **the place where the murder was ~ed** ме́сто, где бы́ло совершено́ уби́йство; *Law* **it was ~ed that...** суд постанови́л, что...; **to ~ a law** утверди́ть зако́н (*usu pf*).

enamel *n* эма́ль; *Art* эма́ль, фини́фть; **~ on teeth** зубна́я эма́ль; *attr*: **~ paint** эма́левая кра́ска; **~ ware** эмалиро́ванная посу́да (*collect*).

enamel *vt* покры|ва́ть эма́лью (-́ть); *Art* **~led brooches** фини́фтевые бро́шки.

enamour *vt usu pass*: **to be ~ed of smb/smth** быть влюблённым в кого́-л, увле|ка́ться чем-л (-́чься).

encamp *vi* распо|лага́ться ла́герем (-ложи́ться).

encampment *n* ла́герь (*m*).

enchant *vt* (*by magic*) околдова́ть (*usu pf*); *fig* очаро́в|ывать (-а́ть), при|води́ть в восто́рг (-вести́); **she was ~ed with the gift** она́ была́ в восто́рге от пода́рка.

enchanting *adj* очарова́тельный, обая́тельный.

encircle *vt* окруж|а́ть (-и́ть); **we are ~d by the sea/the enemy** мы окружены́ мо́рем/врага́ми (*pl*).

encircling *adj*: *Mil* **an ~ movement** обхо́д.

enclose *vt* (*fence in*) огор|а́живать (-оди́ть); (*in a letter, etc.*) *off* при|лага́ть (-ложи́ть), *usu* по|сыла́ть (-сла́ть); **to ~ a garden with a wall** огороди́ть сад стено́й/забо́ром; **please find ~d the documents in question** прилага́ются необходи́мые докуме́нты; **I ~ a cheque for your birthday** посыла́ю тебе́ чек ко дню рожде́ния.

enclosed *adj* (*shut in*) закры́тый; (*fenced off*) огоро́женный; загоро́женный; **their house is ~ by other buildings** их дом загоро́жен други́ми постро́йками.

enclosure *n* (*place*) огоро́женное ме́сто; (*in letter*) приложе́ние к письму́.

encompass *vt* (*include*) заключ|а́ть (-и́ть); (*encircle*) окруж|а́ть (-и́ть); (*bring about*) причин|я́ть (-и́ть).

encore *n and interj* бис; **the singer gave three ~s** певи́ца три́жды спе́ла на бис; **to give/play an ~** исполня́ть на бис; **~!** бис!

encore *vt*: **the audience ~d the player** исполни́теля вы́звали на бис.

encounter *n* (неожи́данная) встре́ча; *Mil* схва́тка.

encounter *vt* встре|ча́ть + *A* (-́тить); встре|ча́ться с + *I* (-́титься); **to ~ a friend/resistance** встре́тить знако́мого/сопротивле́ние; **to ~ an enemy/difficulties** встре́титься с врато́м/с тру́дностями.

encourage *vt* (*hearten*) ободр|я́ть (-́ить); (*stimulate*) поощр|я́ть (-и́ть); **he is ~d by his success** он ободрён/окрылён свои́м успе́хом; **his efforts must be ~d** его́ уси́лия сле́дует поощря́ть; **the doctor ~d him to take more exercise** до́ктор посове́товал ему́ бо́льше дви́гаться; **would you ~ laziness and fetch my book for me?** мне лень встава́ть, будь добр, принеси́ мне кни́гу; **don't ~ the child's curiosity** не разжига́й у ребёнка любопы́тства; **don't ~ bad habits** не потво́рствуй дурны́м привы́чкам; **don't ~ the dog to beg at table** не приуча́й соба́ку кля́нчить у стола́.

encouragement *n* ободре́ние; поощре́ние; **he didn't give me much ~** он не осо́бенно поддержа́л меня́; **cries of ~** одобри́тельные во́згласы.

encouraging *adj* одобри́тельный; обнадёживающий; **we got an ~ reply** мы получи́ли одобри́тельный отве́т; **the results of the experiment have not been ~** результа́ты о́пыта не о́чень обнадёживали; **he got an ~ report from the doctor** до́ктор дал ему́ обнадёживающее заключе́ние.

encroach *vi*: **to ~ on smb's territory** вторг|а́ться на чью-л террито́рию (-́нуться); **to ~ on smb's time** от|нима́ть чьё-л вре́мя (-ня́ть); **to ~ on smb's rights** посяг|а́ть на чьи-л права́ (-ну́ть); **the sea is ~ing upon the land** мо́ре наступа́ет на су́шу.

encumber *vt usu pass* (*hamper*) меша́ть (*usu impf*); (*burden*) обремен|я́ть (-и́ть); **he could not walk fast as he was ~ed with a heavy suitcase** тяжёлый чемода́н меша́л ему́ бы́стро идти́; **an estate ~ed with debts** име́ние, обременённое долга́ми; **the room was ~ed with furniture** ко́мната была́ загромождена́ ме́белью.

encumbrance *n* поме́ха.

encyclopaedia *n* энциклопе́дия; *fig* **he's a walking ~** он ходя́чая энциклопе́дия.

end *n* **1** (*in physical sense: last part*) коне́ц; **the ~ of a sentence/the street** коне́ц предложе́ния/у́лицы; **~ to ~** концо́м к концу́; **from ~ to ~** из конца́ в коне́ц; **from one ~ of the square to the other** из одного́ конца́ пло́щади в друго́й; **stand the box on its ~** поста́вьте я́щик стоймя́/на попа́ (*vertically*); **at both ~s of the table** на обо́их конца́х стола́; **sign at the ~ of the list** поста́вьте свою́ по́дпись в конце́ спи́ска; **at the far/east ~ of the town** на окра́ине го́рода, в восто́чной ча́сти го́рода; **to fish from the ~ of the pier** уди́ть ры́бу с прича́ла; *Sport* **to change ~s** меня́ться сторона́ми; *attr*: **the ~ carriage/house** после́дний ваго́н/дом

2 (*remnant*) оста́ток; *pl* (**~s**) (*of material*) оста́тки (тка́ни); (*smth torn off*) обры́вок; (*smth broken off*) обло́мок; **an ~ of ribbon** обры́вок ле́нты; (*smth cut off*) **~s of bread/sausage** хле́бные куски́, колба́сные обре́зки; **the box is full of odds and ~s** в э́том я́щике полно́ вся́кого хла́ма (*collect*)

3 (*finish*) коне́ц, оконча́ние; **I don't like the ~ of the story** оконча́ние рома́на мне не нра́вится; **I've read the book to the very ~/from ~ to ~** я прочита́л кни́гу до са́мого конца́/с нача́ла до конца́; **at the ~ of the century/July** в конце́ ве́ка/ию́ля; **towards the ~ of the year/evening** к концу́ го́да/ве́чера; **in the ~** в конце́ концо́в; **the meeting was at an ~/came to an ~** собра́ние зако́нчилось; **he brought the meeting to an ~** он закры́л собра́ние; **their departure put an ~ to the amateur dramatics** их отъе́зд положи́л коне́ц люби́тельским спекта́клям; **as the term drew to its ~** чем бли́же был коне́ц семе́стра, к концу́ семе́стра; **there were difficulties without ~** тру́дностям не́ было конца́; **I'll soon put an ~ to that** я бы́стро поко́нчу с э́тим; **he is nearing his ~** он при́ смерти; **he came to an untimely ~** он безвре́менно сконча́лся

4 (*purpose*) цель; **with this ~ in view, to this ~** с э́той це́лью; **to what ~?** для чего́?; **to the ~ that...** для того́, что́бы...; **to gain/achieve one's ~s** дости́чь (свое́й) це́ли; **the ~ justifies the means** цель опра́вдывает сре́дства

5 *fig uses*: **his hair stood on ~** во́лосы у него́ вста́ли ды́бом; **at the ~/the other ~ of the world** на краю́/на друго́м конце́ све́та; **the ~s of the earth** край (*sing*) све́та; **I'm virtually finished—I've just got to tie up some loose ~s** я факти́чески зако́нчил, оста́лось подчи́стить ко́е-каки́е ме́лочи; **I'm at a loose ~ just now** тепе́рь я ниче́м не за́нят; **he is at the ~ of his tether** он дошёл до то́чки; **to begin at the wrong ~** подойти́ к вопро́су не с того́ конца́; **he always gets hold of the wrong ~ of the stick** он всегда́ всё понима́ет превра́тно; **to keep one's ~ up** держа́ться, не сдава́ться; **to make both ~s meet** своди́ть концы́ с конца́ми; **for three days on ~** три дня подря́д; **she practises** (*the piano*) **for hours on ~** она́ занима́ется часа́ми/мно́го часо́в подря́д; **to be at one's wit's ~** соверше́нно растеря́ться; **and that was the ~ of that** на э́том де́ло и ко́нчилось; **that will be the ~ of me** э́то меня́ доконае́т; **he'll come to a bad ~** он пло́хо ко́нчит; **you'll never hear the ~ of this** э́тому де́лу конца́ не ви́дно; *CQ*: **there were no ~ of high-ups there** там бы́ло полно́ знамени́тостей; **he thinks no ~ of himself** он о́чень высо́кого о себе́ мне́ния.

end *vti vt* конч|а́ть (-ить); за|ка́нчивать (-ко́нчить); ока́нчивать (око́нчить); **to ~ a speech** (о)ко́нчить/зако́нчить речь; **to ~ a meeting** закры́ть заседа́ние; **he ~ed his days in hospital** он око́нчил свои́ дни в больни́це; **he ~ed the programme with a folk song** он зако́нчил програ́мму исполне́нием наро́дной пе́сни

vi конча́ться, зака́нчиваться, ока́нчиваться; *lit and off* заверш|а́ться (-и́ться); **how did the adventure ~?** чем/как ко́нчилось э́то приключе́ние?; **term ~ed last week** семе́стр око́нчился/ко́нчился/зако́нчился на про́шлой неде́ле; **the meeting ~ed late** заседа́ние (о)ко́нчилось по́здно; **the game ~ed in a draw** игра́ око́нчилась вничью́ (*adv*); **the battle ~ed in a victory for the French** бой ко́нчился побе́дой францу́зов; **the undertaking ~ed in success** э́то начина́ние/де́ло успе́шно заверши́лось; **they ~ed up by quarrelling** в конце́ концо́в они́ разруга́лись.

endanger *vt*: **to ~ smth** подверг|а́ть что-л опа́сности (-ну́ть); (*threaten*) угрожа́ть + *D* (*impf*).

endear *vt*: **she ~ed herself to all by her goodness** всех подкупа́ла её доброта́; **his sharp tongue does not ~ him to people** его́ о́стрый язы́к отта́лкивает от него́ люде́й.

endearing *adj* ми́лый, привлека́тельный.

endearment *n* (*caress*) ла́ска; **terms of ~** ла́сковые слова́ обраще́ния.

endeavour *n* (*effort*) стара́ние; (*attempt*) попы́тка; **I'll make every ~ to come** я обяза́тельно постара́юсь прийти́.

endeavour *vi* стара́ться (по-).

ending *n* коне́ц; (*conclusion*) оконча́ние, *also Gram*; **a story with a happy ~** расска́з со счастли́вым концо́м.

endless *adj* бесконе́чный; **~ arguments** бесконе́чные спо́ры; **he bores me with his ~ stories** мне надое́ло слу́шать его́ бесконе́чные исто́рии; **she has ~ patience** её терпе́нию нет преде́ла; **an ~ stream of people** несконча́емый пото́к люде́й.

endorse *vt* (*support*) подтвер|жда́ть (-ди́ть); **I ~ all you say** я подтвержда́ю всё, что вы говори́те; *Comm* **to ~ a cheque/a document** подпи́с|ывать чек/докуме́нт (-а́ть); (*UK*) *Law* **I've had my driving license ~d** я получи́л проко́л [*in SU the militiaman punches a hole in the license on the spot*].

endorsement *n Fin*, *Law* переда́точная на́дпись.

endow *vt*: **to ~ a hospital** же́ртвовать больши́е су́ммы на содержа́ние больни́цы (по-); **he is ~ed with great talents** он наделён больши́ми спосо́бностями.

end product *n* гото́вый проду́кт.

endurance *n* (*hardiness*, *staying power*) выно́сливость, сто́йкость; **he has great powers of ~** он о́чень выно́сливый; **I've come to the end of my ~** у меня́ нет бо́льше никаки́х сил, я бо́льше не могу́; **this waiting is beyond ~!** э́то ожида́ние невыноси́мо!

endure *vti vt* вы|носи́ть (-нести); вы|де́рживать (-держать); терпе́ть (вы́-); пере|носи́ть (-нести́); **to ~ pain** выноси́ть/терпе́ть/переноси́ть боль; **I can't ~ him** я его́ не выношу́; **I can't ~ heat/rudeness** я не выношу́ жары́/гру́бости; **I couldn't ~ it any longer** я не мог э́того бо́льше вы́держать/терпе́ть; **I can't ~ being corrected all the time** я не выношу́, когда́ меня́ без конца́ поправля́ют

vi (*hold out*): **can you ~ a little longer?** ты мо́жешь ещё немно́го продержа́ться?; (*last*): **his fame will ~ for ever** его́ сла́ва оста́нется в века́х; **as long as life ~s** пока́ жив челове́к, до сконча́ния ве́ка.

enduring *adj* про́чный; **an ~ peace** про́чный мир; **~ friendship** кре́пкая/до́лгая дру́жба.

endways, endwise *advs* концо́м вперёд/вверх; **to stand smth ~ (on)** поста́вить что-л стоймя́ (*on its end*).

enema *n* кли́зма.

enemy *n* (*public or private*) враг; не́друг; *Mil*, *Sport* проти́вник; **the ~** *collect* враг, проти́вник, неприя́тель; **he's his own worst ~** он сам себе́ ху́дший враг; **he's an ~ to reform** он проти́вник рефо́рм (*G pl*); *attr* вра́жеский; **~ aircraft** вра́жеские самолёты.

energetic *adj* энерги́чный; акти́вный.

energy *n* эне́ргия, *also Tech*; **he's full of ~** он по́лон эне́ргии; **electrical ~** электроэне́ргия; **he devotes all his energies to his work** он отдаёт все си́лы рабо́те.

enervating *adj* расслабля́ющий; **I find this weather ~** э́та пого́да де́йствует на меня́ расслабля́юще; **an ~ day** жа́ркий, ду́шный день; **an ~ climate** тёплый вла́жный кли́мат.

enfeeble *vt* ослаб|ля́ть (´-ить); **he was ~d by his long illness** он осла́б по́сле до́лгой боле́зни.

enfold *vt* (*embrace*) об|нима́ть (-ня́ть); **I ~ed the shivering child in a blanket** я заку́тал мёрзнущего ребёнка в одея́ло.

enforce *vt* застав|ля́ть (´-ить); прину|жда́ть (´-дить); **to ~ obedience** (*on smb*) принужда́ть (кого́-л) к послуша́нию, заставля́ть (кого́-л) слу́шаться; **he ~d silence on the class** он заста́вил класс замолча́ть; **to ~ a law** наста́ивать на стро́гом исполне́нии зако́на (*only in impf*).

engage *vti vt* **1** (*employ*): **to ~ a guide/smb as a secretary** наня́ть проводника́/кого́-л в ка́честве секретаря́

2 (*book*): **to ~ rooms in a hotel** заброни́ровать номера́ в гости́нице

3 (*attract*): **to ~ smb's attention** привле|ка́ть чьё-л внима́ние (´-чь); **his attention was ~d by the antics of the kittens** он залюбова́лся на игру́ котя́т

4 *various*: *Mil* **to ~ the enemy/battle** завя́з|ывать бой (-а́ть); *Aut* **to ~ first gear** включ|а́ть пе́рвую ско́рость (-и́ть)

vi: **to ~ to do smth** обеща́ть сде́лать что-л (по-); *Tech* зацеп|ля́ться (-и́ться).

engaged *adj* **1** (*busy*, *etc.*) за́нятый; **this seat/the director/***Tel* **the number is ~** э́то ме́сто за́нято, дире́ктор/(э́тот) но́мер за́нят; **they were ~ in conversation** они́ бы́ли за́няты разгово́ром; **I'm ~ in revising my book** я гото́влю кни́гу к переизда́нию

2: **the ~ couple** обручённые, жени́х и неве́ста; **they are ~** они́ помо́лвлены; **he's ~ to her** он собира́ется на ней жени́ться.

engagement *n* **1** (*obligation*) обяза́тельство; **to meet/fulfil one's ~s** выполня́ть обяза́тельства

2 (*of young couple*) помо́лвка, обруче́ние; **they announced their ~** они́ объяви́ли о свое́й помо́лвке; *attr*: **~ ring** обруча́льное кольцо́

3 (*appointment*: *in office*, *etc.*): **I have a lot of ~s this week** э́ту неде́лю я о́чень за́нят, на э́той неде́ле у меня́ мно́го дел; (*socially*) **I'm sorry I can't come I have a previous ~** извини́те, я не могу́ прийти́, я бу́ду за́нят (*with business*)/я уже́ приглашён (*of previous invitation*); **I have no ~s till Friday** до пя́тницы я совсе́м свобо́ден: **I've got an ~ at 7 o'clock** у меня́ встре́ча в семь часо́в

4 *Mil* бой, схва́тка.

engaging *adj* привлека́тельный.

engine *n* (*in steamer*, *factory*) маши́на; *Aut* мото́р, дви́гатель (*m*); *Rail* локомоти́в; **steam ~** парово́з; **diesel ~** теплово́з; **to sit with one's back to the ~/facing the ~** сиде́ть спино́й/лицо́м по хо́ду движе́ния по́езда; *attr*: **~ driver** машини́ст.

engineer *n* инжене́р; **civil ~** инжене́р-строи́тель, гражда́нский инжене́р.

engineer *vt CQ* (*fix*) подстр|а́ивать (-о́ить); **he ~ed it all** он всё э́то подстро́ил.

engineering *n* те́хника; инжене́рное де́ло; **electrical/radio ~** электроте́хника, радиоте́хника; *attr*: **~ sciences** техни́ческие нау́ки.

English *n* (*language*) англи́йский язы́к; (*collect*: *people*) **the E.** англича́не (*pl*); *attr*: **~ teacher** учи́тель англи́йского языка́.

English *adj* англи́йский.

Englishman *n* англича́нин.

Englishwoman *n* англича́нка.

engrave *vt* гравирова́ть (вы́-); *fig* **his words are ~d on my memory** его́ слова́ вре́зались мне в па́мять.

engraving *n* (*on stone*, *etc.*: *process*) гравирова́ние; (*print*) гравю́ра, эста́мп.

engross *vt* завлад|ева́ть + *I* (-е́ть); за|нима́ть (-ня́ть); **he was so ~ed in watching the game that he didn't notice the cold** он был так увлечён игро́й, что не чу́вствовал хо́лода; **he was deeply ~ed in a book** он углуби́лся в чте́ние.

engrossing *adj*: **an ~ book** увлека́тельная/захва́тывающая кни́га.

engulf *vt* погло|ща́ть (-ти́ть); **the boat was ~ed by the waves** кора́бль поглоти́ли во́лны; **the village was nearly ~ed by the floods** дере́вню почти́ всю затопи́ло (*impers*) во вре́мя наводне́ния (*sing*).

enhance *vt*: **the dim light only ~d her beauty** приглушённый свет то́лько подчёркивал её красоту́; **the value of the vase is ~d by age** це́нность э́той ва́зы увели́чивается/повыша́ется с года́ми.

enigma *n* зага́дка; **it remained an ~** э́то оста́лось зага́дкой.

enigmatic *adj* зага́дочный; **his expression was ~** у него́ бы́ло зага́дочное выраже́ние лица́.

enjoin *vt*: **to ~ on smb the necessity for secrecy** вы|нужда́ть кого́-л к молча́нию (-́ну-дить).

enjoy *vt* **1** насла|жда́ться + *I* (-ди́ться); получ|а́ть удово́льствие от + *G* (-и́ть); **I ~ solitude** я наслажда́юсь одино́чеством (*at times*), я люблю́ одино́чество (*in general*); **to ~ a book/a concert** получа́ть удово́льствие от кни́ги/конце́рта; **I ~ed myself very much in Scotland** я получи́л большо́е удово́льствие от пое́здки в Шотла́ндию; **I ~ed my evening with you very much** мне так понра́вился э́тот ве́чер у вас; **he ~ed his dinner** он дово́лен обе́дом; *CQ* **we fairly ~ed your cake** нам о́чень понра́вился ваш торт; **~ yourselves!** жела́ю вам хорошо́ повесели́ться!, (*as parting phrase*) счастли́во вам!

2 (*have use of*) по́льзоваться + *I* (вос-); (*possess*) облада́ть + *I* (*impf*); **to ~ rights/smb's confidence** по́льзоваться права́ми/чьим-л дове́рием; **to ~ good health/a good income** облада́ть хоро́шим здоро́вьем/больши́м дохо́дом.

enjoyable *adj* прия́тный.

enjoyment *n* наслажде́ние, удово́льствие; **to find great ~ in music** наслажда́ться му́зыкой, о́чень люби́ть му́зыку; **he listened with real ~** он слу́шал с больши́м удово́льствием/с восто́ргом.

enlarge *vti vt* (*make larger*) увели́чи|вать (-ть); (*extend*) расшир|я́ть (-́ить); **to ~ a photo/a theatre** увели́чить сни́мок, расши́рить помеще́ние теа́тра; *fig* **to ~ one's horizons** расши́рить кругозо́р (*sing*); *Med* **his heart is ~d** у него́ расшире́ние се́рдца

vi: **to ~ upon a subject/on the danger of smoking** распространя́ться на те́му/о вреде́ куре́ния (*only in impf*).

enlighten *vt* просве|ща́ть (-ти́ть); (*inform*) ос|ведомля́ть (-ве́домить); **he ~ed me on this subject** он просвети́л меня́ в э́том вопро́се; **can you ~ me on/about these rumours?** мо́жете ли вы проинформи́ровать меня́ относи́тельно э́тих слу́хов?

enlightened *adj* (*free from ignorance*) просвещённый; (*modern, progressive*) совреме́нный; **in this ~ age** в наш просвещённый век; **he has a very ~ attitude to such matters** у него́ о́чень совреме́нный подхо́д к подо́бным вопро́сам.

enlightening *adj* (*clarifying*): **his exposition of the subject was very ~** он о́чень я́сно/поня́тно изложи́л суть де́ла; (*revealing*) **that was a very ~ remark** э́то замеча́ние мно́гое разъясни́ло.

enlist *vti vt*: **to ~ support** заручи́ться подде́ржкой (*usu pf*)

vi Mil (доброво́льно) поступ|а́ть на вое́нную слу́жбу (-и́ть).

enliven *vt* ожив|ля́ть (-и́ть); **he much ~ed the party** он о́чень оживи́л о́бщество.

enmity *n* вражда́; вражде́бность; **he lived at/was at ~ with his neighbour** он враждова́л со свои́м сосе́дом.

ennui *n* ску́ка, тоска́.

enormity *n* (*great size*): **it's hard to grasp the ~ of the problem** тру́дно охвати́ть масшта́бы пробле́мы; **does he realize the ~ of his offence?** понима́ет ли он всю тя́жесть соде́янного?

enormous *adj* огро́мный, грома́дный; **an ~ house/success** огро́мный/грома́дный дом/успе́х; **an ~ sum** огро́мная су́мма; *CQ*: **he's ~ fun** с ним так ве́село; **the party was an ~ success** ве́чер уда́лся на сла́ву.

enormously *adv* чрезвыча́йно; невероя́тно; *CQ* о́чень, стра́шно; **I enjoyed the evening ~** ве́чер мне стра́шно понра́вился.

enough *n translated by adv* доста́точно, *or verb* хвата́ть; **have you had ~?** вам хва́тит/доста́точно?; (*of food*) **there's more than ~ for everyone, there's ~ and to spare** у нас всего́ полно́/бо́льше чем доста́точно; **I've ~ to be getting on with** (*of food or work, etc.*) пока́ мне доста́точно/хвата́ет; **we have ~ to live on** нам хвата́ет на жизнь; **I can never have ~ of such music** э́та му́зыка никогда́ мне не надое́ст; **I've had ~ of trailing round museums** я уста́л ходи́ть по музе́ям, *CQ* я уже́ сыт по го́рло музе́ями; **~ is ~** *iron* хоро́шенького понемно́жку; **it was ~ to drive one up the wall** от э́того мо́жно бы́ло на сте́нку поле́зть; **I've had ~ of your impudence** мне надое́ло ва́ше наха́льство; **I've ~ to do without tidying up after you** я не бу́ду убира́ть за тобо́й, у меня́ и без того́ дел хвата́ет; **I've had ~ of him** он мне надое́л.

enough *adj* доста́точный; *usu translated by adv* доста́точно, *or verb* хвата́ть; **have we ~ time for a game of tennis?** у нас есть вре́мя сыгра́ть па́ртию в те́ннис?; **we've ~ petrol/petrol ~ to get home** у нас хва́тит бензи́на дое́хать до до́ма; **I have ~ money** у меня́ доста́точно де́нег (*an adequate sum*), мне хвата́ет де́нег (*plenty*); **I was fool ~ to believe him** я был так глуп, что пове́рил ему́.

enough *adv* **1** доста́точно; дово́льно; **you know well ~ what I mean** вы прекра́сно зна́ете, что я хочу́ сказа́ть; **oddly ~ I knew it would be like that** как ни стра́нно, но я чу́вствовал, что так оно́ и бу́дет; **oddly ~ on this occasion he was late** как ни стра́нно, на э́тот раз он опозда́л; **sure ~ he was there** разуме́ется, он там был; (*in reply*) **sure ~—I'll be there** коне́чно (же), я приду́; **sure ~!** и́менно так!; **you're old ~ to know that** ты уже́ доста́точно взро́слый и до́лжен э́то понима́ть; (*to a dog, child*) **~!** дово́льно!; переста́нь!

2 (*used slightly disparagingly*): **he speaks Russian well ~ to make himself understood**

он доста́точно хорошо́ говори́т по-ру́сски — его́ вполне́ мо́жно поня́ть; **he can be polite ~ when he wants to** он мо́жет быть ве́жливым, когда́ захо́чет.

enrage *vt*: **to ~ smb** серди́ть кого́-л (рас-), злить кого́-л (разо-); **my father was ~d when he heard about it** услы́шав об э́том, оте́ц разозли́лся/пришёл в я́рость.

enrapture *vt* восхи|ща́ть (-ти́ть); при|води́ть в восто́рг (-вести́); **she was ~d by the beauty of the Alps** её восхити́ла/покори́ла красота́ Альп.

enrich *vt* обога|ща́ть (-ти́ть), *also fig*; **to ~ one's diet by adding vitamins** обогаща́ть пи́щу витами́нами; **my vocabulary has been ~ed by reading Chekhov's stories** мой запа́с слов обогати́лся по́сле чте́ния расска́зов Че́хова; **to ~ the soil** удобря́ть по́чву (удо́брить).

enrol(l) *vti vt* запи́с|ывать в + *A* (-а́ть); **to ~ oneself/smb as a member of a club** записа́ться/записа́ть кого́-л в чле́ны клу́ба

vi запи́сываться в + *A*; **I've ~ed in a ballet class** я записа́лся в бале́тный кружо́к.

enrolment *n* регистра́ция, за́пись.

en route *adv* по пути́, по доро́ге; **~ for Oxford** по доро́ге в О́ксфорд.

ensemble *n Mus and of clothes* анса́мбль (*m*).

ensign *n Naut* (*flag*) энси́н, (кормово́й) флаг; (*naval officer*) мла́дший лейтена́нт.

ensnare *vt* (*an animal*) пойма́ть в лову́шку (*only in pf*), *also fig*; *fig* опу́т|ывать (-ать), замани́ть (*usu pf*); **she ~d the innocent youth** она́ замани́ла безу́сого юнца́ в свои́ се́ти.

ensue *vi* сле́довать (по-); **silence ~d** после́довало молча́ние; **many difficulties ~d from this mistake** э́та оши́бка породи́ла нема́ло тру́дностей в дальне́йшем.

ensuing *adj* (по)сле́дующий; **for the ~ year** на сле́дующий год; **the ~ quarrels were beyond belief** разрази́вшиеся вслед за э́тим сканда́лы не поддаю́тся описа́нию [NB *tense*].

ensure *vt* (*provide*) обеспе́чи|вать (-ть); (*guarantee*) руча́ться за + *A* (поручи́ться); **to ~ the best results, cook in a slow oven** э́то блю́до лу́чше гото́вить в духо́вке на сла́бом огне́; **to ~ (*oneself*) against disappointment** что́бы не́ было разочарова́ния; **I can't ~ his success/that he'll be there on time** я не могу́ руча́ться за его́ успе́х/, что он туда́ попадёт во́время.

entail *vt* (*involve*) влечь (по-); (*mean*) означа́ть (*usu impf*); **that will ~ great expense** э́то повлечёт больши́е расхо́ды; **that will ~ an early start** э́то означа́ет, что придётся вы́ехать пора́ньше.

entangle *vt usu pass* запу́т|ывать(ся) (-ать(ся)), *also fig*; впу́т|ываться (-аться), быть заме́шанным в + *P*; **my line got ~d in seaweed** моя́ ле́ска запу́талась в во́дорослях; *fig*: **to get ~d in debt** запу́таться в долга́х; **he got ~d in shady dealings** он был заме́шан в де́нежных махина́циях/афёрах; **don't get ~d in that business** не впу́тывайся ты в э́то де́ло; **he got ~d with some dubious characters** он связа́лся с подозри́тельными ли́чностями.

enter *vti vt* **1** (*go into*) входи́ть в + *A* (войти́); вступ|а́ть в + *A* (-и́ть); **to ~ a room/a forest** войти́ в ко́мнату/в лес; **to ~ a town** вступи́ть в го́род; **the bullet ~ed his heart** пу́ля попа́ла ему́ в се́рдце; **the Dnieper ~s the Black Sea near Odessa** Днепр впада́ет в Чёрное мо́ре недалеко́ от Оде́ссы; **it never ~ed my head that...** мне в го́лову не приходи́ло, что...

2 (*become a member of*): **to ~ school/university/the army** поступ|а́ть в шко́лу/в университе́т/на вое́нную слу́жбу (-и́ть)

3 (*write down*) запи́с|ывать, впи́с|ывать (*pfs* -а́ть); **to ~ smth in one's diary** записа́ть что-л в календа́рь; **to ~ a sum in a ledger** внести́ су́мму в гроссбу́х; **to ~ a word in a dictionary** включ|а́ть сло́во в слова́рь (-и́ть); **this word has been wrongly ~ed** э́то сло́во попа́ло не туда́; **to ~ oneself for an examination** пода́ть зая́вку на сда́чу экза́мена; **to ~ a horse for a race** записа́ть/зарегистри́ровать ло́шадь для уча́стия в ска́чках (*usu pf*)

4 *Law*: **to ~ a suit against smb** возбуди́ть де́ло про́тив кого́-л, пода́ть в суд на кого́-л

vi (*go in*) входи́ть (войти́); **he ~ed and sat down** он вошёл и сел; (*stage direction*) **~ Hamlet** вхо́дит Га́млет

enter for *vi* (*write one's name down*) пода|ва́ть зая́вку на + *A* (-ть); (*take part*) при|нима́ть уча́стие в + *P* (-ня́ть), уча́ствовать в + *P* (*impf*); **to ~ for the 100 metres** пода́ть зая́вку на уча́стие в бе́ге на сто ме́тров; **to ~ for a competition** принима́ть уча́стие/уча́ствовать в ко́нкурсе/в состяза́нии; **to ~ for a race** уча́ствовать/выступа́ть в го́нках

enter into *vi*: **to ~ into detail** вдава́ться в подро́бности (*impf*); **to ~ into negotiations** вступ|а́ть в перегово́ры (-и́ть); **to ~ into an agreement** заключ|а́ть соглаше́ние/догово́р/(*contract*) контра́кт (-и́ть); **to ~ into conversation** вступи́ть в разгово́р, заговори́ть (*usu pfs*); **such a possibility never ~ed into our calculations** таку́ю возмо́жность мы не принима́ли в расчёт; **that simply doesn't ~ into it** э́то к де́лу не отно́сится

enter upon *vi*: **to ~ upon a new career/a new term of office** заня́ться но́вым для себя́ де́лом, на|чина́ть но́вый срок исполне́ния до́лжности (-ча́ть).

enterprise *n* **1** (*undertaking*: *general*) предпринима́тельство; (*particular*) предприя́тие; **private ~** ча́стное предпринима́тельство; **an industrial/a small ~** промы́шленное/ме́лкое предприя́тие

2 (*spirit*) предприи́мчивость; **he is a man of great ~** он исключи́тельно предприи́мчивый челове́к, (*in business*) он челове́к широ́кого разма́ха.

enterprising *adj* предприи́мчивый; **that was ~ of you!** какая предприи́мчивость!/изобретательность!

entertain *vt* **1** (*receive*) при|нима́ть (-ня́ть); (*give a meal to*: *privately*) уго|ща́ть (-сти́ть), *off* устр|а́ивать приём (-о́ить); **we ~ a lot/very little at home** у нас до́ма ча́сто/ре́дко быва́ют го́сти; **they ~ed us very well** они́ нас хорошо́ при́няли; **to ~ friends to dinner** угоща́ть друзе́й обе́дом; **they love to ~** они́ лю́бят (принима́ть) госте́й

2 (*amuse*) забавля́ть (*impf*), (*divert*) развле|ка́ть (-́чь); **he used to ~ us for hours with his stories** он часа́ми забавля́л/развлека́л нас свои́ми расска́зами.

3 (*consider*): **to ~ a proposal** принима́ть предложе́ние во внима́ние; **to ~ doubts about smth** сомнева́ться в чём-л (*usu impf*); **he won't ~ the idea for a moment** он и ду́мать об э́том не ста́нет.

entertaining *adj* заба́вный; развлека́тельный.

entertainment *n* **1** (*diversion*) развлече́ние, (*amusement*) удово́льствие; **the cinema is my favourite ~** кино́—моё люби́мое развлече́ние; **much to the ~ of the small boys** к большо́му удово́льствию мальчи́шек; **the episode afforded us much ~** э́тот эпизо́д о́чень позаба́вил нас

2 (*performance*): **music-hall/light ~** эстра́дный конце́рт, эстра́дное представле́ние; **there will be an official dinner followed by some ~** бу́дет банке́т, а пото́м эстра́дное представле́ние; **to lay on/put on an ~** дава́ть спекта́кль

3 *attr*: **~ allowance** расхо́ды (*pl*) на представи́тельство.

enthralled *adj* си́льно увлечённый; **I was ~ by your novel** меня́ захвати́л ваш рома́н.

enthralling *adj* захва́тывающий.

enthuse *vi CQ*: **to ~ over smth** быть в восто́рге от чего́-л; **the critics ~d over the play** кри́тики с восто́ргом/восто́рженно отзыва́лись о пье́се.

enthusiasm *n* восто́рг; энтузиа́зм; **I can't say I feel any ~ for the project** не могу́ сказа́ть, что отношу́сь к э́тому прое́кту с энтузиа́змом/с больши́м восто́ргом; **a burst of ~ greeted the performance** пье́са прошла́ на ура́.

enthusiast *n* энтузиа́ст.

enthusiastic *adj*: **~ applause** бу́рные аплодисме́нты (*pl*); **I have become ~ about fishing** я пристрасти́лся к ры́бной ло́вле.

enthusiastically *adv* с энтузиа́змом, с восто́ргом, восто́рженно.

entice *vt* (*tempt*) зама́ни|вать, перема́ни|вать (*pfs* -ть); завле|ка́ть (-́чь); **she ~d my cook away** она́ перемани́ла (к себе́) моего́ по́вара; **he ~d his victim into a trap** он замани́л/завлёк свою́ же́ртву в лову́шку.

enticement *n* прима́нка.

enticing *adj* зама́нчивый, соблазни́тельный; **what an ~ prospect!** кака́я зама́нчивая иде́я!; **she prepared a most ~ spread for us** она́ пригото́вила для нас о́чень вку́сное угоще́ние.

entire *adj* по́лный, це́лый, весь; **the ~ world/day** весь *or* це́лый свет/день; **the ~ country** вся страна́; **that is our ~ stock** э́то весь наш запа́с; **he has our ~ confidence** он по́льзуется у нас по́лным дове́рием; **I was in ~ ignorance of what was going on** я соверше́нно ничего́ не знал о происходя́щем.

entirely *adv* **1** вполне́; соверше́нно; совсе́м; **I agree with you ~** я вполне́ согла́сен с ва́ми; **you are ~ right** ты соверше́нно прав; **he is ~ different from his brother** они́ с бра́том совсе́м/соверше́нно ра́зные; **that's not ~ the case** э́то не совсе́м так

2 (*solely*) исключи́тельно; **I say it ~ for your own good** я говорю́ э́то исключи́тельно для твое́й по́льзы; **it's ~ my fault** я сам/оди́н во всём винова́т.

entirety *n* полнота́; **in its ~** во всей полноте́, по́лностью (*adv*).

entitle *vt* **1** (*of a book*): **the book is ~d the "Three Musketeers"** кни́га называ́ется «Три мушкетёра»

2 (*give a right to*): **this pass ~s you to six free visits** э́тот про́пуск даёт пра́во на шесть беспла́тных посеще́ний; **we are ~d to know the reason** мы име́ем пра́во знать причи́ну.

entity *n Philos* бытие́; (*a being*) существо́; **a separate ~** не́что отде́льное.

entourage *n* окруже́ние; **the President and his ~** президе́нт со свои́м окруже́нием.

entr'acte *n* антра́кт.

entrails *npl* кишки́, вну́тренности.

entrance[1] *n* вход; (*door*) дверь; (*for cars*) въезд; (*large gate*) воро́та (*pl*); **front/back ~** пара́дный вход, чёрный ход; **they stood talking in the ~** они́ стоя́ли в пере́дней и разгова́ривали; (*of an actor or of place*) **~ on to a stage** вы́ход на сце́ну; **~ to university** (*going up*) поступле́ние/(*admittance*) приём в университе́т; **"E. free"** «Вход свобо́дный»; *attr*: **~ hall** (*in home*) пере́дняя, (*in public building*) вестибю́ль (*m*); **~ fee** входна́я пла́та; **~ examinations** вступи́тельные экза́мены.

entrance[2] *vt* завор|а́живать (-ожи́ть); **they listened ~d** они́ слу́шали как заворожённые.

entrancing *adj* (*of books*) увлека́тельный; (*of people, scenery, etc.*) очарова́тельный.

entrant *n* (*for exam*) экзамену́ющийся; (*for competition*) уча́стник.

entreat *vt* умоля́ть (*usu impf*); **the children ~ed their father to take them to the circus** де́ти умоля́ли отца́ своди́ть их в цирк.

entreaty *n* мольба́.

entrée *n* **1** (*dish*) пе́рвое блю́до

2 (*access*) до́ступ; **he has the ~ to all the best houses/families** он вхож в лу́чшие дома́.

entrench *vt*: *Mil* **to ~ oneself, to be ~ed** ока́пываться (окопа́ться); *fig* **~ed prejudices** глубоко́ укорени́вшиеся предрассу́дки.

entrust *vt* (*confide*) довер|я́ть, ввер|я́ть (*pfs* ·и́ть); поверя́ть (*impf*); (*give into smb's charge*) поруч|а́ть (-и́ть); **to ~ a secret to smb** дове́рить та́йну кому́-л; **I ~ed the money to him/him with the money** я дове́рил ему́ де́ньги; **I am/have been ~ed to deliver this letter** мне пору́чено доста́вить э́то письмо́; **to ~ one's children to smb** оста|вля́ть дете́й на кого́-л/на чьё-л попече́ние (-вить).

entry *n* **1** (*for pedestrians*) вход; (*for cars*) въезд; *Theat* вы́ход; **"No E."** «Вхо́да/Въе́зда нет», «Вход/Въезд запрещён»; **there were two entries on to the stage** на сце́ну бы́ло два вы́хода

2 (*act*) вступле́ние; поступле́ние; (*of actor*) вы́ход; **the ~ of America into the war** вступле́ние Аме́рики в войну́; **~ into school/university** поступле́ние в шко́лу/в университе́т; **the cosmonauts made/had a triumphal ~ into Moscow** космона́вты торже́ственно въе́хали в Москву́; **the thieves forced an ~ into the building** во́ры прони́кли в зда́ние, взлома́в дверь/окно́

3 (*into notebooks, etc.*) за́пись; **to make an ~ in one's journal/diary** сде́лать за́пись в дневнике́/календаре́; **an ~ into a ledger** внесе́ние/за́пись в гроссбу́х; **an ~ in the minutes** занесе́ние в протоко́л; **an ~ in a dictionary** слова́рная статья́

4 (*for jobs, competitions, etc.*: *application*) зая́вка; **entries must be in by December 1st** срок представле́ния зая́вок до пе́рвого декабря́; **there's a large ~ for this job** на э́ту до́лжность большо́й ко́нкурс; **they expect a large ~ for the 100 metres** (*in running*) в бе́ге на сто ме́тров ожида́ется большо́е число́/коли́чество уча́стников; **an ~ for an exhibition** (*piece of work*) экспона́т.

entry form *n* (*for job, etc.*) анке́та; *Sport* зая́вка на уча́стие.

entwine *vt* плести́ (с-).

enumerate *vt* перечисл|я́ть (·и́ть).

enunciate *vt*: **to ~ words clearly** я́сно/чётко произ|носи́ть слова́ (-нести́); **to ~ a theory** из|лага́ть тео́рию (-ложи́ть).

envelop *vt* (*wrap*) заку́т|ывать (-ать); оку́т|ывать (-ать); **he was ~ed in a blanket** он был заку́тан в одея́ло; **the hills were ~ed in mist** го́ры бы́ли оку́таны тума́ном; **the matter is ~ed in secrecy** де́ло оку́тано та́йной.

envelop(e) *n* конве́рт; **to stick down an ~** закле́ивать конве́рт.

envenomed *adj fig* злой, ядови́тый.

enviable *adj* зави́дный (*not used of people*); **an ~ position** зави́дное положе́ние; **he's an ~ young man** э́тому молодо́му челове́ку мо́жно позави́довать.

envious *adj* зави́стливый; **to cast an ~ look on smth** бро́сить зави́стливый взгляд на что-л; **to be ~ of smb/smth** зави́довать кому́-л/чему́-л.

environment *n* обстано́вка; окруже́ние; **one's home ~** семе́йная/дома́шняя обстано́вка, дома́шнее окруже́ние; **protection of the ~** охра́на окружа́ющей среды́.

environs *npl* окре́стности.

envisage *vt* (*imagine*) представ|ля́ть себе́ (·ить); (*anticipate*) предви́деть (*impf*); **I admit, I had not ~d all the difficulties** признаю́сь, я не предви́дел всех э́тих тру́дностей.

envoy *n* посла́нник; (*special envoy*) полномо́чный представи́тель; (*ambassador*) посо́л.

envy *n* за́висть; **out of ~** из за́вистиı; **his car was the ~ of all** его́ маши́на была́ предме́том всео́бщей за́висти.

envy *vt* зави́довать + *D* (по-); **I ~ you/(you) your good fortune** я зави́дую тебе́/твое́й уда́че; **I ~ you having a trip to the sea** я зави́дую тому́, что ты е́дешь к мо́рю; **he was envied by his friends for his success** друзья́ зави́довали его́ успе́ху.

epic *adj* эпи́ческий; **an ~ (poem)** эпи́ческая поэ́ма; *CQ* **the cup final was ~!** фина́л ку́бка был захва́тывающе интере́сен.

epicentre *n* эпице́нтр.

epidemic *n* эпиде́мия; **a flu ~** эпиде́мия гри́ппа.

epileptic *n* эпиле́птик.

epilogue *n* эпило́г, заключе́ние.

episode *n* слу́чай, происше́ствие; эпизо́д; **there's some shady ~ in his past** в его́ про́шлом есть како́е-то тёмное пятно́.

epitaph *n* эпита́фия; надгро́бная на́дпись.

epithet *n* эпи́тет.

epitome *n*: **she is the ~ of virtue** она́ воплощённая/сама́ доброде́тель.

epoch *n* эпо́ха, э́ра.

epoch-making *adj*: **an ~ discovery** откры́тие мирово́го значе́ния.

equable *adj* ро́вный; **an ~ climate** ро́вный кли́мат; **an ~ character** ро́вный/уравнове́шенный хара́ктер.

equal *n* ро́вня; *or adj* ра́вный *used as n*; **he is not your ~** он вам не ро́вня; **let A be the ~ of B** допу́стим, что А равно́ В; **he has no ~/he is without ~ for courage** он не име́ет ра́вных/ему́ нет ра́вного в хра́брости; **to treat smb as an ~** обраща́ться с кем-л как с ра́вным; *attr*: **the ~ sign** знак ра́венства.

equal *adj* ра́вный; (*identical*) одина́ковый; **with ~ reason** на ра́вных основа́ниях (*pl*); **other things being ~** при про́чих ра́вных усло́виях; **an ~ distance** одина́ковое расстоя́ние; **~ pay for ~ work** ра́вная пла́та за ра́вный труд; **one gallon is ~ to $4^1/2$ litres** оди́н галло́н ра́вен/равня́ется четырём с полови́ной ли́трам; **to divide smth into ~ parts** дели́ть что-л по́ровну (*adv*); **of ~ value** равноце́нный; **to speak French and English with ~ ease** говори́ть по-францу́зски и по-англи́йски одина́ково свобо́дно; (*in recipe*) **add an ~ quantity of sugar** доба́вьте/доба́вить сто́лько же са́хару; **he is not ~ to the task** ему́ не спра́виться с э́тим зада́нием, э́то зада́ние ему́ не по си́лам/не по плечу́; **I don't feel ~ to writing letters today** сего́дня я не в состоя́нии/не могу́ писа́ть пи́сьма.

equal *vt* равня́ться + *D* (*only in impf*); равня́ться (с-); (*compare with*) сра́вни|ваться (-́ться); **3 times 2 ~s 6** три́жды два равня́ется шести́; **nothing can ~ this view** с э́тим ви́дом ничто́ не сравни́тся; **it will all ~ out in the end** в конце́ концо́в всё сравня́ется.

equality *n* ра́венство; **to be on an ~ with smb** быть на ра́вных права́х с кем-л.

equalize *vti vt* ура́вн|ивать (-я́ть); **to ~ incomes** уравня́ть дохо́ды
vi Sport: **they ~d by half time** в конце́ та́йма они́ сравня́ли счёт.

equally *adv* по́ровну; (*likewise*) в ра́вной сте́пени, ра́вным о́бразом; **to divide ~** раздели́ть по́ровну; **it would be ~ wrong to underestimate the risk** в ра́вной сте́пени бы́ло бы непра́вильно не ви́деть ри́ска; **I try to treat all the children ~** я стара́юсь относи́ться ко всем де́тям одина́ково.

equanimity *n* споко́йствие, душе́вное равнове́сие; **he bore his misfortunes with ~** он споко́йно относи́лся к свои́м несча́стьям; **his ~ is not easily disturbed** его́ тру́дно вы́вести из (душе́вного) равнове́сия.

equate *vt* прира́вн|ивать (-я́ть); **to ~ wisdom and/with learning** прира́внивать му́дрость к зна́ниям (*pl*).

equation *n Math* уравне́ние; **the ~ of supply with demand** соотве́тствие спро́са и предложе́ния.

equator *n* эква́тор.

equestrian *n* вса́дник.

equestrian *adj* ко́нный.

equidistant *adj* равностоя́щий.

equilateral *adj* равносторо́нний.

equilibrium *n* равнове́сие, *also fig*.

equinox *n* равноде́нствие; **at the ~** в равноде́нствие.

equip *vt* (*supply with*) снаб|жа́ть + *I* (-ди́ть), обеспе́чи|вать + *I* (-ть); (*to get ready*) снаря|жа́ть (-ди́ть); **we were well ~ped with all we needed** мы бы́ли снабжены́/обеспе́чены всем необходи́мым; **to ~ an expedition with supplies** обеспе́чить экспеди́цию необходи́мыми запа́сами; **to ~ a factory** обору́довать заво́д (*impf and pf*); *Mil* **to ~ an army** (*with arms*) вооруж|а́ть а́рмию (-и́ть), (*with technical equipment*) осна|ща́ть а́рмию (-сти́ть); **to ~ oneself for a journey** снаряжа́ться в путь; **he is well ~ped to succeed in life** он облада́ет всем необходи́мым для достиже́ния успе́ха в жи́зни.

equipment *n* обору́дование, оснаще́ние, снаряже́ние [*all three nouns = act of equipping, or, used collect, = things needed to equip; for differences see "equip"*]; (*small tackle, etc.*) приспособле́ния (*usu pl*); инвента́рь (*m*); **rescue ~** спаса́тельное снаряже́ние; **a factory with modern ~** заво́д с совреме́нным обору́дованием; **I have all the ~ I need for fishing** у меня́ есть все необходи́мые сна́сти/всё необходи́мое для ры́бной ло́вли; **garden ~** садо́вый инвента́рь; **his mental ~ is quite exceptional** его́ мысли́тельный аппара́т соверше́нно исключи́телен.

equitable *adj* справедли́вый.

equity *n* справедли́вость; *Law* пра́во справедли́вости; *pl* (**equities**) *Fin* (*shares*) а́кции.

equivalent *n* эквивале́нт; **I don't know whether there is a Russian ~ for this** я не зна́ю, есть ли в ру́сском языке́ эквивале́нтное выраже́ние; **a kilogram is roughly the ~ of $2^1/_4$ lbs** килогра́мм ра́вен приблизи́тельно двум с че́твертью фу́нтам; **is there an ~ to this medicine in tablet form?** выпуска́ется ли э́то лека́рство в ви́де табле́ток?

equivalent *adj* равноце́нный; **to be ~ to** (*of money, weights, etc.*) равня́ться + *D*; **that's ~ to saying...** э́то всё равно́, что сказа́ть...; **that's ~ to murder** э́то равноси́льно уби́йству; **he gave me an ~ sum in roubles** он дал мне соотве́тствующую су́мму в рубля́х.

equivocal *adj* (*ambiguous*) двусмы́сленный; (*not clear*) нея́сный; (*doubtful*) сомни́тельный; (*evasive*) уклóнчивый; **an ~ reply** укло́нчивый отве́т.

era *n* э́ра, эпо́ха.

eradicate *vt fig* искорен|я́ть (-и́ть).

erase *vt* (*with a rubber*) стира́ть (стере́ть), подчи|ща́ть рези́нкой (-́стить); (*by wiping*) стира́ть, *also fig*; **this has been ~d from his memory** э́то стёрлось в его́ па́мяти.

ere *prep Poet* до + *G*; **~ night** до но́чи; **~ long** вско́ре (*adv*).

erect *adj* прямо́й; *when used predicatively usu translated by adv* пря́мо; **to sit/stand ~** сиде́ть/стоя́ть пря́мо; **with head ~** с по́днятой голово́й; (*of horse, dog, etc.*) **with ears ~** навостри́в у́ши.

erect *vt* (*build*) стро́ить (по-, вы́-), соору|жа́ть (-ди́ть); (*of statues, etc.*) воздвиг|а́ть (-́нуть); **to ~ a house** стро́ить дом; **to ~ a monument** воздви́гнуть па́мятник; **to ~ a fence** стро́ить/ста́вить забо́р.

erection *n* (*of action or of thing erected*) постро́йка, сооруже́ние.

ermine *n* (*animal*) горноста́й; (*fur*) мех горноста́я.

erode *vt* (*corrode*) разъ|еда́ть (-е́сть); (*wash away*) размы|ва́ть (-́ть); **rust ~s iron** ржа́вчина разъеда́ет желе́зо; **the metal has been ~d by acid** мета́лл разъе́ло (*impers*) кислото́й; **the river bank has been ~d by the rains** бе́рег реки́ размы́ло (*impers*) дождя́ми.

erosion *n* эро́зия, разъеда́ние; размыва́ние (*see verb "erode"*).

erotic *adj* эроти́ческий.

err *vi* ошиб|а́ться (-и́ться), заблужда́ться (*impf*); **to ~ is human** челове́ку сво́йственно ошиба́ться; *fig* **it is better to ~ on the generous side** лу́чше переплати́ть, чем недоплати́ть.

errand *n* поруче́ние; **to go on an ~** отпра́виться по поруче́нию; **to send smb on an ~** посла́ть кого́-л с поруче́нием; **he sent**

me on a fool's ~ он послáл меня́ с кáким-то бессмы́сленным поручéнием; **I used to run ~s for him** я был у негó на побегу́шках/на посы́лках.

errand boy *n* мáльчик на посы́лках; посы́льный, рассы́льный.

erratic *adj* **1** (*of things*: *unstable*) неустóйчивый, нерóвный; (*changeable*) перемéнчивый, измéнчивый; **the weather has been very ~ of late** погóда стáла такáя перемéнчивая; **an ~ pulse** нерóвный пульс; **my watch is a bit ~** мои́ часы́ не óчень тóчно хóдят

2 (*of people*, *their behaviour*, *etc.*: *unreliable*) ненадёжный, (*uneven*) нерóвный; **he's an ~ chap** он ненадёжный человéк; **his work is very ~** он óчень нерóвно рабóтает; **his visits are ~** он то зачасти́т, то год не появля́ется.

erratum *n* опечáтка.

erroneous *adj* (*mistaken*) оши́бочный; (*deceptive*) лóжный; (*incorrect*) непрáвильный; **an ~ impression** лóжное впечатлéние.

error *n* оши́бка; заблуждéние; **in ~** по оши́бке, оши́бочно (*adv*); **a spelling ~** оши́бка в правописáнии; **a printer's ~** опечáтка; **an ~ of judgement** просчёт; **to make an ~** сдéлать оши́бку; **to be in ~** ошибáться (*make a mistake*), заблуждáться (*be mistaken*); **I fell into the ~ of underrating my opponent** я допусти́л оши́бку, недооцени́в моегó проти́вника.

ersatz *adj*: **~ coffee** суррогáт кóфе.

erudite *adj* эруди́рованный; **he's an ~ man** он эруди́т.

erupt *vi* (*of volcano*) извергáться (*only in impf*).

eruption *n* (*of volcano*) извержéние; *Med* сыпь.

erysipelas *n Med* рóжа, рóжистое воспалéние.

escalate *vi*: **the conflict ~d into war** конфли́кт перерóс в войну́; **prices are escalating** цéны растýт.

escalation *n* эскалáция.

escalator *n* эскалáтор.

escapade *n* продéлка; эскапáда.

escape *n* **1** (*by flight*) бéгство, побéг; (*deliverance*) спасéние; **he made good his ~** он соверши́л удáчный побéг; **our ~ from shipwreck was nothing short of miraculous** прóсто чýдо, что мы не поги́бли во врéмя кораблекрушéния; **he had a narrow ~ from death** он едвá спáсся, он был на волосóк от ги́бели; *fig* **she reads a lot as an ~ from her worries** онá мнóго читáет—э́то помогáет ей отвлéчься от забóт

2 (*leak*) утéчка; **an ~ of gas** утéчка гáза; *attr*: **an ~ valve** выпускнóй клáпан.

escape *vti vt* (*avoid*) избе|гáть + *G* (-жáть); спас|áться от + *G* (-ти́сь); **to ~ certain death** спасти́сь от вéрной смéрти; **to ~ suspicion/punishment** быть вне подозрéния, избежáть наказáния; **to ~ observation** пройти́ незамéченным; **it ~d my notice that...** от моегó внимáния ускользну́ло, что...; **his name ~s me** я никáк не могу́ вспóмнить егó и́мя

vi **1** бежáть из + *G* (*impf and pf*); убе|гáть из + *G* (-жáть); (*get off with*) отдéл|ываться + *I* (-аться); **he ~d from prison** он бежáл из тюрьмы́; **he ~d with scratches** он отдéлался царáпинами; **they barely ~d with their lives** они́ едвá спасли́сь

2 (*leak*) утекáть (утéчь); **gas is escaping** газ утекáет.

escapism *n Psych* эскапи́зм; *CQ* **it's sheer ~ on your part** ты прóсто ухóдишь от реáльности.

escort *n* (*general*) сопровождéние; (*Mil*, *police*) эскóрт, конвóй; (*group of guards*) охрáна; (*lady's*) кавалéр, партнёр; **under police ~** под конвóем полицéйских; **the president arrived with an armed/a mounted ~** президéнт приéхал в сопровождéнии вооружённой/кóнной охрáны.

escort *vt* сопрово|ждáть (-ди́ть); (*see off*) прово|жáть (-ди́ть); *Mil*, *Naut* конвои́ровать (*impf*); **she was ~ed by a policeman** её сопровождáл полицéйский; **he ~ed her home** он проводи́л её домóй; **~ed by a convoy of ships** в сопровождéнии конвóйных судóв.

Eskimo *n* эскимóс, эскимóска.

Eskimo *adj* эскимóсский.

especial *adj* осóбый; специáльный; **a matter of ~ importance** дéло осóбой вáжности; **I do this for your ~ benefit** я дéлаю э́то специáльно для тебя́.

especially *adv* осóбенно; (*expressly*) специáльно; **the more ~ as...** тем бóлее, что...

Esperanto *n* (язы́к) эсперáнто (*indecl*).

espionage *n* шпионáж.

essay *n* (*written*) óчерк; (*at school*) сочинéние; (*attempt*) попы́тка.

essence *n* **1** существó; сýщность; суть; **the ~ of the matter** существó/суть дéла; **in ~** по существу́, в сýщности.

2 (*extract*) эссéнция, экстрáкт.

essential *adj* необходи́мый; (*obligatory*) обязáтельный; (*indispensable*) непремéнный; (*fundamental*) основнóй; **it is ~ to arrive in time** необходи́мо прибы́ть вóвремя; **an ~ condition** обязáтельное/непремéнное услóвие; **an ~ difference** основнáя рáзница; *as npl* (**the ~s**) всё необходи́мое (*collect*).

establish *vt* **1** (*found*) оснóв|ывать (-áть), учре|ждáть (-ди́ть); (*create*) созда|вáть (-́ть); (*set up*) устан|áвливать (-ови́ть); **to ~ a new state** основáть/создáть нóвое госудáрство; **to ~ a business** основáть дéло/предприя́тие; **the firm was ~ed in 1910** фи́рма существу́ет [**NB** *tense*] с ты́сяча девятьсóт деся́того гóда; **to ~ a commission/organization** учреди́ть коми́ссию, создавáть организáцию; **to ~ a theory/conditions under which ...** создáть теóрию/услóвия, при котóрых...; **this is ~ed by law** э́то установлено закóном; **to ~ relations/communication with** установи́ть отношéния/связь с + *I*; **the custom has been ~ed in the college of dining early on Sundays**

в колле́дже установи́лся обы́чай обе́дать по воскресе́ньям ра́но; **to ~ order** на|води́ть поря́док (-вести́)

2 (*settle in job, flat, etc.*) устр|а́ивать(ся) (-о́ить(ся)); **we are well ~ed in our new house** мы хорошо́ устро́ились в но́вом до́ме; **he is ~ed in the Ministry** он устро́ился на рабо́ту в министе́рстве; **he is ~ed as editor of a newspaper** тепе́рь он рабо́тает реда́ктором газе́ты; **he ~ed his son in a job** *CQ* он нашёл сы́ну рабо́ту; *Hort* **my roses are well ~ed** мои́ ро́зы хорошо́ приняли́сь

3 (*ascertain*) устан|а́вливать (-ови́ть), опреде|ля́ть (-и́ть); **to ~ facts/the cause of death** установи́ть фа́кты/причи́ну сме́рти; **to ~ the degree of kinship** определи́ть/установи́ть сте́пень родства́; **to ~ smb's guilt** установи́ть чью-л вино́вность.

established *adj* (*recognized*) изве́стный, при́знанный; **by now he's an ~ artist** тепе́рь он уже́ изве́стный худо́жник; (*permanent*): **the ~ staff of the ministry** штат министе́рства; **he's one of our ~ staff** он у нас в шта́те.

establishment *n* (*action*) установле́ние; созда́ние; основа́ние; (*institution*) учрежде́ние; (*personnel*) штат; **a scientific ~** нау́чное учрежде́ние; **a research ~** нау́чно-иссле́довательское учрежде́ние; **the ~ of the ministry** штат министе́рства; **the E.** *approx* госуда́рственный аппара́т; (*of household*) **they keep (up) a large ~** у них большо́й штат прислу́ги; *Mil* **peace/war ~** шта́ты ми́рного/вое́нного вре́мени.

estate *n* (*in land*) име́ние, поме́стье; (*country house with land*) уса́дьба; (*property*) иму́щество; **a large ~** кру́пное име́ние/поме́стье; **real ~** недви́жимое иму́щество; **personal ~** дви́жимое иму́щество; (*inheritance*) **he left a large ~** он оста́вил большо́е состоя́ние.

estate car *n CQ* «универса́л».

esteem *n* уваже́ние; почте́ние; **to hold smb in ~** уважа́ть кого́-л; **to be held in ~** по́льзоваться уваже́нием; **after that episode he rose considerably in my ~** по́сле э́того слу́чая он о́чень вы́рос в мои́х глаза́х.

esteem *vt* уважа́ть (*impf*); почита́ть (*impf*); **I'd ~ it a favour if you...** я счёл бы э́то больши́м одолже́нием, е́сли бы вы...

estimable *adj* почте́нный, уважа́емый.

estimate *n* оце́нка; *Comm* сме́та; **to form an ~** оце́нивать, соста́вить мне́ние; **my ~ is** по мои́м оце́нкам (*pl*), я счита́ю, что..., по-мо́ему; **the critics' ~ is that he has a great future** кри́тики предска́зывают ему́ большо́е бу́дущее; **to give an ~ for building costs** соста́вить сме́ту строи́тельных расхо́дов; **can you give me an ~ for it?** ско́лько приблизи́тельно э́то бу́дет сто́ить?

estimate *vti vt* (*judge*) счита́ть (счесть); (*assess*) оце́н|ивать, определ|я́ть (*pfs* -и́ть); **he was ~d to be a good painter** его́ счита́ли тала́нтливым худо́жником; **they ~ the value of the violin to be 5,000 dollars** скри́пку оце́нивают в пять ты́сяч до́лларов; **the cost of repairs is ~d at £500** по предвари́тельным подсчётам ремо́нт обойдётся в пятьсо́т фу́нтов

vi состав|ля́ть сме́ту (-́ить); **I've been asked to ~ for rebuilding the theatre** меня́ попроси́ли соста́вить сме́ту расхо́дов на перестро́йку теа́тра.

estimation *n* **1** (*evaluation*) оце́нка; (*opinion*) мне́ние; **what's your ~ of the situation?** какова́ ва́ша оце́нка сложи́вшейся ситуа́ции?

2 (*esteem*) уваже́ние, почте́ние; **he has sunk in my ~** я потеря́л к нему́ уваже́ние.

Estonian *n* эсто́нец, эсто́нка.

Estonian *adj* эсто́нский.

estrange *vt* отдал|я́ть (-и́ть); **his behaviour ~d all his friends** свои́м поведе́нием он оттолкну́л от себя́ всех друзе́й; **in his later years he was ~d from his family** в после́дние го́ды он совсе́м отдали́лся от семьи́; **they were ~d** они́ жи́ли врозь/отде́льно, они́ разошли́сь (*stronger, can also = "were divorced"*).

estrangement *n* отдале́ние, отчужде́ние, отчуждённость; (*of man and wife*) разры́в; **this caused an ~ between the two brothers/between him and his wife** э́то отдали́ло бра́тьев друг от дру́га, э́то привело́ к разры́ву ме́жду супру́гами.

estuary *n* у́стье.

et cetera, *abbr* **etc. 1** *as adv* и так да́лее, и тому́ подо́бное, *abbrs* и т. д., и т. п.

2 *as npl* **(the ~s)** (*odds and ends*) вся́кая вся́чина; **it was a grand dinner with all the ~s** обе́д был роско́шный—то́лько пти́чьего молока́ не хвата́ло.

etch *vti* гравирова́ть (вы́-).

etching *n* гравю́ра.

eternal *adj* ве́чный, *also fig and CQ*; *CQ* бесконе́чный, нескончáемый; **I'm sick of his ~ questions** мне надое́ли его́ бесконе́чные вопро́сы.

eternally *adv* ве́чно, *also CQ*; **he's ~ telling the same stories** он ве́чно расска́зывает одни́ и те же исто́рии.

eternity *n* ве́чность, *also CQ*; **I waited an ~ for an answer** я ждал отве́та це́лую ве́чность.

ethics *npl* э́тика, мора́ль (*sings*); **to study ~** изуча́ть э́тику; **Christian ~** христиа́нская мора́ль.

ethnic *adj* этни́ческий.

etiquette *n* этике́т; **it's not ~ to leave without saying good-bye** не о́чень ве́жливо/учти́во/не полага́ется уходи́ть не попроща́вшись.

euphemism *n* эвфеми́зм.

Eurasian *adj* еврази́йский.

European *n* европе́ец.

European *adj* европе́йский.

euthanasia *n* безболе́зненная смерть, эйтана́зия.

evacuate *vt* (*people*) эвакуи́ровать (*impf and pf*); (*a town*) остав|ля́ть (-́ить); **we were ~d** нас эвакуи́ровали; **to ~ soldiers** вы|води́ть войска́ (ˊ-вести); **the town was ~d** (*by population*) населе́ние поки́нуло/оста́вило го́род, (*by troops*) войска́ оста́вили го́род.

evacuation *n* (*of population or town*) эвакуа́ция; (*of troops*) вы́вод.

evacuee *n* эвакуи́рованный.

evade *vt* уклон|я́ться от + *G* (-и́ться); **to ~ a blow/a question** уклони́ться от уда́ра/от отве́та на вопро́с; **to ~ paying one's debts/military service** не отдава́ть долги́, уклоня́ться от вое́нной слу́жбы.

evaluate *vt* оце́ни|вать (ˊ-ть).

evaluation *n* оце́нка; **job ~** оце́нка труда́.

evaporate *vti vt* испар|я́ть (-и́ть)

vi испаря́ться; **water ~s in the sun** вода́ испаря́ется на со́лнце; *fig* разве́|иваться (-яться); **his hopes soon ~d** его́ наде́жды ско́ро разве́ялись.

evaporation *n* испаре́ние.

evasion *n* (*of obligations*, *etc.*) уклоне́ние от + *G*; (*ruse*) увёртка; **tax ~** уклоне́ние от упла́ты нало́гов; **his answer was just an ~** его́ отве́т—про́сто увёртка; **~ of the law** обхо́д зако́на.

evasive *adj* укло́нчивый; **an ~ reply** укло́нчивый отве́т; *Mil* **~ action** укло́нчивая та́ктика; *joc* **when he saw his teacher at the concert he took ~ action** уви́дев своего́ учи́теля на конце́рте, он постара́лся не попа́сться ему́ на глаза́.

eve *n* кану́н; **on the ~ (of)** накану́не (*adv or prep* + *G*); **New Year's ~** кану́н Но́вого го́да; **on Christmas ~** накану́не рождества́.

even *adj* **1** (*level*, *regular*, *steady*) ро́вный; (*measured*) ме́рный; (*uniform*) равноме́рный; **an ~ surface/temperature** ро́вная пове́рхность/температу́ра; **~ breathing** ро́вное дыха́ние; **an ~ pulse** ро́вный пульс; **he's a man of ~ temper** у него́ ро́вный хара́ктер; **an ~ voice** ро́вный го́лос; **his work is very ~** он о́чень ро́вно рабо́тает; **at an ~ pace** ме́рным ша́гом, *fig* равноме́рно (*adv*); **an ~ distribution** равноме́рное распределе́ние

2 (*equal*) ра́вный; **~ shares** ра́вные до́ли; **to divide into ~ shares** раздели́ть по́ровну (*adv*); *Sport*: **it was an ~ match** в э́том ма́тче си́лы проти́вников бы́ли равны́; **the score is now ~** счёт сравня́лся; **the two horses are ~ now** э́ти две ло́шади сейча́с иду́т грудь в грудь; *fig*: **I'll be ~ with him yet** я с ним ещё рассчита́юсь; **that makes us ~** тепе́рь мы квиты; (*betting*, *etc.*) **~ money/odds** ра́вные ста́вки/ша́нсы; **to break ~** оста́ться при свои́х.

even *adv* **1** да́же; **he didn't ~ look up** он да́же глаз/головы́ не по́днял; **it's cold in Lapland ~ in July** в Лапла́ндии да́же в ию́ле прохла́дно; **~ now he won't eat fish** да́же и тепе́рь он не ест ры́бы

2: ~ if да́же е́сли; **~ though** хотя́ (бы) и; **I wouldn't say ~ if I knew** я бы не сказа́л, да́же е́сли бы знал; **they won't let you leave ~ if you wanted to** да́же е́сли ты и захо́чешь уйти́, тебя́ не отпу́стят; **they bathed ~ though I warned them it was dangerous** они́ купа́лись, хотя́ я их предупрежда́л, что здесь купа́ться опа́сно

3 (*with comparatives*) да́же, ещё; **and, ~ worse, he forgot his money** и что ещё ху́же, он забы́л де́ньги; **he ran ~ faster** он бежа́л ещё быстре́е

4 *phrases*: **~ as** как раз; **~ as he spoke, the guests arrived** как раз когда́ он говори́л, прие́хали го́сти; **~ so** всё равно́; всё-таки; **this isn't much of a knife, but ~ so one can use it** э́то плохо́й нож, но всё-таки им мо́жно по́льзоваться.

even *vt* вы|ра́внивать (ˊ-ровнять) *and other compounds*; **to ~ (off) the soil with a rake** разровня́ть зе́млю гра́блями; **to ~ the score** сравня́ть счёт (*usu pf*); **she ~ed out the creases in her dress** она́ разгла́дила скла́дки на пла́тье; **to ~ out payments on a monthly basis** выпла́чивать поме́сячно ра́вные су́ммы; **that will ~ things up** э́то вы́ровняет положе́ние.

evening *n* ве́чер; **in the ~** ве́чером; **in the ~s I usually read** по вечера́м я обы́чно чита́ю; **tomorrow/this/on Friday ~** за́втра/сего́дня/в пя́тницу ве́чером; **on the ~ of the 6th** ве́чером шесто́го (числа́); **~ was coming on** вечере́ло (*impers*); *CQ*: **let's make an ~ of it** дава́й пойдём куда́-нибудь (сего́дня) ве́чером; **I work ~s** я рабо́таю по вечера́м/(*on evening shift*) в вече́рнюю сме́ну; **good ~!** до́брый ве́чер!; *attr* вече́рний; **an ~ paper** вече́рняя газе́та; **~ classes** вече́рние ку́рсы.

evenly *adv* **1** (*equally*) по́ровну; **to divide smth ~** подели́ть что-л по́ровну; **the two teams are ~ matched** си́лы обе́их кома́нд равны́

2 (*smoothly*) ро́вно; **to sew ~** шить ро́вно/гла́дко; **he answered ~** он отве́тил споко́йным/ро́вным то́ном.

event *n* **1** (*occurrence*) собы́тие; **the main ~s of this year** гла́вные собы́тия э́того го́да; **in the natural course of ~s** е́сли всё бу́дет норма́льно/в поря́дке; **a happy ~** (*birth*, *marriage*) счастли́вое собы́тие; **that was quite an ~!** э́то бы́ло це́лое собы́тие!

2 (*chance*) слу́чай; **in any ~** в любо́м слу́чае; **at all ~s** во вся́ком слу́чае; **in either ~** в том и в друго́м слу́чае; **in the ~ of his coming** е́сли он придёт

3 (*result*): **in the ~** в коне́чном счёте; **the ~ will prove who's right** собы́тия (*pl*) пока́жут, кто прав; **to be wise/brave after the ~** быть у́мным за́дним число́м, по́сле дра́ки кулака́ми не ма́шут

4 *Sport* соревнова́ние; **in what ~s are you competing?** в каки́х ви́дах соревнова́ний вы уча́ствуете?

eventful *adj*: **it's been quite an ~ day!** день был по́лон собы́тий!; **he leads an ~ life** он живёт по́лной жи́знью.

eventual *adj*: **his ~ failure was predictable** в су́щности его́ прова́л бы́ло нетру́дно предсказа́ть; **the ~ success of the enterprise shows that...** то, что начина́ние в коне́чном счёте оказа́лось уда́чным, говори́т о том, что...; **any ~ profit will be shared equally** возмо́жная при́быль бу́дет поделена́ по́ровну.

eventuality *n* возмо́жность; слу́чай; **in that ~** в том слу́чае; **in the ~ of** в слу́чае + *G or* + е́сли; **we are ready for any ~** мы гото́вы ко всему́.

eventually *adv* в коне́чном счёте; в конце́ концо́в; **we ~ had to compromise** в коне́чном счёте/в конце́ концо́в нам пришло́сь уступи́ть.

ever *adv* **1** (*at any time*) когда́-либо, когда́-нибудь; (*in neg sentences*) никогда́; **have we ~ met before?** ра́зве мы с ва́ми когда́-нибудь ра́ньше встреча́лись?; **I don't think we've ~ met before** мы, ка́жется, никогда́ ра́ньше не встреча́лись; **nothing ~ happens here** здесь никогда́ ничего́ не происхо́дит; **has anybody ~ done this before?** де́лал ли кто́-нибудь что́-либо подо́бное ра́ньше?; **he is seldom, if ~, in London** он почти́ никогда́ не быва́ет в Ло́ндоне

2 (*after comp and superl*): **you look younger than ~!** ты так мо́лодо вы́глядишь!; **it's the coldest day ~** сего́дня ужа́сно хо́лодно; **I'm colder than ~!** мне всё ещё хо́лодно

3 (*in comparisons*): **as ~** как мо́жно + *comp*; **run as fast as ~ you can** беги́ как мо́жно быстре́е; **I'll tell her as soon as ~ I can** я ей э́то скажу́ при пе́рвой же возмо́жности

4 (*at all times*): **they lived happily ~ after** они́ жи́ли счастли́во до са́мой сме́рти; **~ since I had flu** с тех пор, как у меня́ был грипп; **you are ~ in my thoughts** я всё вре́мя о тебе́ ду́маю; **he is ~ ready to help** он всегда́ гото́в помо́чь; (*in letters*) **Yours ~** всегда́ Ваш

5 *CQ* (*to give emphasis*): **who ~ told you that?** кто же мог вам тако́е сказа́ть?; **did you ~ hear such nonsense?** вы когда́-нибудь слы́шали подо́бную чушь?; **what ~ is the dog doing now?** что опя́ть э́та соба́ка натвори́ла?; **where ~ have I put my spectacles?** а куда́ же я дел свои́ очки́?; **why ~ didn't you say so before?** почему́ же вы э́того ра́ньше не сказа́ли?; **as if he would ~ do such a thing!** как бу́дто он мог когда́-нибудь тако́е сде́лать!; **he's ~ so rich, he's ~ such a rich man** он тако́й бога́тый челове́к.

evergreen *n* вечнозелёное расте́ние.

everlasting *adj* ве́чный, *also CQ*; **I'm tired of her ~ complaints** я уста́л от её ве́чных жа́лоб.

evermore *adv* ве́чно, навсегда́; **for ~** навсегда́.

every *adj* **1** ка́ждый, вся́кий; **I heard ~ word you said** я слы́шал ка́ждое ва́ше сло́во; **his ~ movement betrays anxiety** ка́ждое его́ движе́ние выдаёт беспоко́йство; **he saves ~ penny** он бережёт ка́ждую копе́йку; **~ single boy passed the exam** все ма́льчики до одного́ сда́ли экза́мен; **not ~ man finds a rich wife** не вся́кому напи́сано на роду́ жени́ться на бога́той

2 (*all possible*) вся́кий, вся́ческий; **I will help you in ~ possible way** я помогу́ вам, чем возмо́жно; **I wish you ~ success** жела́ю вам (вся́ческого) успе́ха; **he's up to ~ sort of trick** он пойдёт на все уло́вки; **there's ~ reason to believe him** есть все основа́ния пове́рить ему́; (*in letter*) **with ~ good wish** с наилу́чшими пожела́ниями

3 (*denoting time*) ка́ждый; **~ day** ка́ждый день; **~ second day** че́рез день; **he works ~ third day** он за́нят че́рез два дня на тре́тий; **~ few months** ка́ждые два-три ме́сяца; **~ three weeks/hours** ка́ждые три неде́ли/часа́; **I'm expecting him ~ minute** я жду его́ с мину́ты на мину́ту; **~ time he comes, he brings presents** он никогда́ не прихо́дит без пода́рка; **~ time the phone rings I jump** при ка́ждом телефо́нном звонке́ я вска́киваю; **~ year he gets balder** с ка́ждым го́дом он всё бо́льше лысе́ет; **~ now and then, ~ so often** вре́мя от вре́мени

4 *various*: **~ single one of us** мы все до еди́ного; **my sister passed her exam, but ~ other girl in her class failed** моя́ сестра́ сдала́ экза́мен, но все остальны́е де́вочки в кла́ссе провали́лись; **he's ~ bit of 60** ему́ все шестьдеся́т; **she's ~ bit as good as he is** во вся́ком слу́чае она́ ни в чём не усту́пит ему́.

everybody *pron* ка́ждый, вся́кий; все; **~ knows this** все э́то зна́ют, э́то ка́ждый зна́ет; **not ~ can do this** не вся́кий/ка́ждый мо́жет э́то сде́лать.

everyday *adj* (*daily*) ежедне́вный; повседне́вный; (*workaday*) бу́дничный; **an ~ occurrence** повседне́вное явле́ние; **~ clothes** бу́дничная оде́жда.

everything *pron* всё; **art is ~ to her** иску́сство для неё всё.

everywhere *adv* всю́ду, повсю́ду, везде́; **here, there and ~** везде́ и (по)всю́ду; **~ you go you meet tourists** куда́ ни пойдёшь, везде́ тури́сты; **~ in England** по всей А́нглии, повсю́ду в А́нглии.

evict *vt* вы|селя́ть (-́селить); **the tenants of the flat were ~ed for not paying their rent** жильцо́в вы́селили из кварти́ры за неупла́ту.

evidence *n* **1** (*basis*) основа́ние; (*sign*) при́знак; (*facts*) да́нные, фа́кты (*pls*); **historical ~** истори́ческие фа́кты; **there is little ~ for thinking that...** ма́ло основа́ний счита́ть, что...; **what is your ~ for this assertion?** на како́м основа́нии вы э́то утвержда́ете?; **there is ~ of a hasty departure** налицо́ (*adv*) следы́ поспе́шного отъе́зда; **I couldn't believe the ~ of my eyes** я не мог пове́рить свои́м глаза́м; **we have not yet sufficient ~ to say confidently that...** мы ещё не располага́ем доста́точным коли́чеством фа́ктов и не мо́жем утвержда́ть, что...

2 *Law* ули́ки (*usu pl*; *sing = piece of evidence*); свиде́тельства, показа́ния (*usu pls*); (*proof*) доказа́тельство; **circumstantial ~** ко́свенные ули́ки; **documentary/written ~** пи́сьменное доказа́тельство; **to give ~ against smb/that...** дава́ть показа́ния (*pl*) про́тив кого́-л/о том, что...; **to call smb in ~** вызыва́ть кого́-л в ка́честве свиде́теля; **to turn Queen's/King's/(*US*) state's ~** изоблича́ть свои́х соо́бщников; *fig*: **all this is ~ of her conscientiousness** всё э́то свиде́тельствует о её добросо́вестности; **his face bore ~ of his sufferings** страда́ния оста́вили след на его́ лице́

3: he was nowhere in ~ его́ нигде́ не́ было ви́дно; **she was very much in ~** она́ была́ всегда́ на виду́.

evident *adj* очеви́дный, я́вный, я́сный; **it is ~ that...** очеви́дно,/я́сно, что...; **with ~ disgust/pride** с я́вным отвраще́нием, с нескрыва́емой го́рдостью.

evil *n* зло; **the lesser of two ~s** ме́ньшее из двух зол; **to return good for ~** отплати́ть добро́м за зло; **to think ~ of smb** пло́хо ду́мать о ком-л.

evil *adj* злой; дурно́й; (*portending evil*) злове́щий; **an ~ spirit** злой дух; **the ~ eye** дурно́й глаз; **an ~ omen** злове́щий (при́)знак; **an ~ doer** злоде́й; **in an ~ hour** в недо́брый час; **to have an ~ influence on smb** ока́зывать па́губное влия́ние на кого́-л.

evince *vt* обнару́жи|вать (-ть), проявл|я́ть (-и́ть).

evocative *adj*: **for me these are ~ scenes** э́ти сце́ны бу́дят во мне воспомина́ния; **to be ~ of** напомина́ть о + *P*.

evoke *vt* вы|зыва́ть (-́звать); **to ~ admiration/happy memories** вызыва́ть восхище́ние, пробу|жда́ть све́тлые воспомина́ния (-ди́ть).

evolution *n* эволю́ция; (*development*) разви́тие; **theory of ~** тео́рия эволю́ции; **the ~ of drama** разви́тие драматурги́ческого иску́сства.

evolve *vti* разви|ва́ть(ся) (-́ть(ся)); **to ~ a new theory** развива́ть но́вую тео́рию.

ex- *pref* (*former*) бы́вший; **our ~-ambassador in Paris** наш бы́вший посо́л в Пари́же; *CQ* **my ~-husband** мой бы́вший муж.

ex *prep Comm*: **price ~ factory to London** цена́ фра́нко-привоза в Ло́ндон.

exact *adj* то́чный; **~ meaning/size** то́чный смысл/разме́р; **he's five, to be ~ five and a half** ему́ пять, точне́е пять с полови́ной.

exact *vt* (*demand*) тре́бовать + *G* (по-); взыск|ивать (-а́ть); **to ~ obedience from smb** тре́бовать чьего́-л повинове́ния; **to ~ concessions/an apology from smb** тре́бовать от кого́-л усту́пок/извине́ний (*pl*); **to ~ taxes from smb** взима́ть нало́ги с кого́-л (*impf*).

exacting *adj* тре́бовательный, взыска́тельный; **an ~ supervisor** тре́бовательный/взыска́тельный нача́льник; **~ work** рабо́та, тре́бующая большо́го внима́ния.

exactly *adv* (*accurately*) то́чно; (*just, precisely*) и́менно, как раз, ро́вно; **to weigh smth ~** установи́ть то́чный вес чего́-л, то́чно взве́сить что-л; **I'll be there at 5 ~** я приду́ то́чно/ро́вно в пять; **he described the route very ~** он о́чень то́чно описа́л доро́гу; **~ (so)!** вот и́менно!; **that's ~ what I expected** и́менно э́того я и ожида́л; **that's ~ what I want** э́то как раз то, что мне ну́жно; **these shoes fit me ~/are ~ right for me** э́ти ту́фли мне как раз впо́ру; **the situation is not ~ as you describe it** ситуа́ция не совсе́м такова́, как вы её опи́сываете; *CQ* **she's not ~ a beauty** её краса́вицей не назовёшь (= *either "very ugly", or "but all the same nice-looking"*).

exaggerate *vti* преувели́чи|вать (-ть); **to ~ difficulties** преувели́чивать тру́дности; **he always ~s** он всегда́ преувели́чивает.

exaggerated *adj* преувели́ченный; **he's got an ~ sense of his own importance** он сли́шком мно́го о себе́ ду́мает/мнит.

exaggeration *n* преувеличе́ние.

exalted *adj*: **a person of ~ rank** челове́к с высо́ким положе́нием; **~ emotions** возвы́шенные чу́вства.

examination *n* **1** *abbr* **exam** экза́мен; **to sit/go in for/ take an ~** сдава́ть/держа́ть экза́мен, экзаменова́ться; **to pass an ~** вы́держать/сдать экза́мен; **to fail an ~** провали́ться на экза́мене; **to set an ~** соста́вить вопро́сы к экза́мену; **a history ~** экза́мен по исто́рии; **an oral/final ~** у́стный/выпускно́й экза́мен; *attr*: **an ~ paper** (*handed in by examinees*) экзаменацио́нная рабо́та, (*questions set*) вопро́сы (для экзаменацио́нной рабо́ты)

2 (*inspection*) осмо́тр; (*investigation*) обсле́дование; (*check*) прове́рка; (*scrutiny*) рассмотре́ние; **a medical ~** медици́нский осмо́тр, *abbr CQ* медосмо́тр; **to go into hospital for ~** лечь в больни́цу на обсле́дование; **an ~ of the accounts** прове́рка счето́в; **on close ~ of the inscription I noticed...** рассмотре́в внима́тельно на́дпись, я заме́тил...; **on closer ~ of the facts** при ближа́йшем рассмотре́нии фа́ктов; **customs ~** тамо́женный досмо́тр/осмо́тр

3 *Law*: **~ of a witness** допро́с свиде́теля; **~ of evidence** рассмотре́ние ули́к (*pl*).

examine *vt* **1** *Univ, etc.* экзаменова́ть (про-); **I was ~d in maths** меня́ проэкзаменова́ли по матема́тике; **he was ~d on the structure of the spine** на экза́мене его́ спра́шивали о строе́нии позвоно́чника

2 (*inspect*) осм|а́тривать (-отре́ть); (*check*) провер|я́ть (-́ить); (*study*) изуч|а́ть (-и́ть); (*scrutinize*) рассм|а́тривать (-отре́ть); **the doctor ~d the patient carefully** врач тща́тельно осмотре́л больно́го; **I had my eyes/teeth ~d** у меня́ прове́рили зре́ние/зу́бы; **to ~ accounts** прове́рить счета́; **to ~ a picture** внима́тельно рассма́тривать карти́ну; **to ~ a problem** рассма́тривать пробле́му; **to ~ data** изуча́ть да́нные; **to ~ the carburettor** прове́рить карбюра́тор; **my baggage was ~d at the customs** мой бага́ж осмотре́ли в тамо́жне

3 *Law*: **to ~ a witness/evidence** до|пра́шивать свиде́теля (-проси́ть), изуча́ть ули́ки (*pl*).

examinee *n* экзамену́ющийся; **he's a bad ~** как пра́вило, он пло́хо сдаёт экза́мены.

examiner *n* экзамена́тор.

example *n* **1** (*illustration*) приме́р; **for ~** наприме́р (*adv*), *CQ* к приме́ру; **cite an ~** приведи́те приме́р.

2 (*model*) приме́р; **to set an ~** подава́ть приме́р; **to follow smb's ~** сле́довать чьему́-л приме́ру, брать приме́р с кого́-л; **to learn by/from ~** учи́ться на приме́ре/на приме́рах; **to hold smb up as an ~** ста́вить кого́-л в приме́р; **to make an ~ of smb** наказа́ть кого́-л в приме́р други́м; **he became a doctor, following his father's ~** он стал врачо́м по приме́ру отца́

3 (*sample*) образе́ц; **this chapter is a typical ~ of the author's incompetence** э́та глава́—типи́чный образе́ц некомпете́нтности а́втора.

exasperate *vt*: **I get ~d by her stupidity** её ту́пость выво́дит меня́ из себя́/приво́дит меня́ в отча́яние.

exasperating *adj* невыноси́мый; **it's utterly ~** э́то про́сто невыноси́мо; **how ~!** кака́я доса́да!; **I find him ~** он дово́дит меня́ до бе́лого кале́ния, я гото́в его́ уби́ть.

exasperation *n*: **in ~** в по́лном отча́янии.

excavate *vti Archaeol* вести́ раско́пки (*impf*); **to ~ a burial ground** раска́пывать захороне́ние; **we were excavating at Athens** мы вели́ раско́пки в Афи́нах.

excavation *n* (*act*) раска́пывание; (*fieldwork*) *usu pl* (**~s**) раско́пки (*pl*) (*usu of large area*), раско́п (*sing*).

excavator *n* (*machine*) экскава́тор, землечерпа́лка.

exceed *vt* пре|восходи́ть (-взойти́); превы|ша́ть (-́сить); **to ~ expectations** превосходи́ть ожида́ния; **to ~ instructions** превы́сить свои́ полномо́чия; **demand ~s supply** спрос превыша́ет предложе́ние; **to ~ the speed limit** превы́сить ско́рость; **a fine not ~ing £5** штраф не вы́ше пяти́ фу́нтов.

exceedingly *adv* чрезвыча́йно, о́чень, кра́йне, чрезме́рно.

excel *vti vt* пре|восходи́ть (-взойти́); **he ~s us all in courage** он превосхо́дит всех нас му́жеством, он са́мый сме́лый из нас

vi отлич|а́ться в + *P* (-и́ться); *Sport* **he ~s at/in that field** у него́ лу́чшие результа́ты в э́том ви́де спо́рта.

excellence *n* соверше́нство; превосхо́дство; **this hotel is famous for the ~ of its cuisine** э́тот оте́ль изве́стен свое́й превосхо́дной ку́хней; **note the ~ of the carving** обрати́те внима́ние на великоле́пную резьбу́.

excellency *n* (*title*): **His E.** его́ превосходи́тельство.

excellent *adj* превосхо́дный, отли́чный, великоле́пный; прекра́сный; (*of school marks*) отли́чный.

except *prep* **1** кро́ме + *G*; **nobody could swim ~ me** никто́, кро́ме меня́, не уме́л пла́вать; **we work every day ~ Sunday** мы рабо́таем ка́ждый день, кро́ме воскресе́нья; **he does nothing ~ eat** он ничего́ не де́лает, то́лько ест

2: ~ for за исключе́нием + *G*, кро́ме + *G*; е́сли бы не; **the dinner was excellent ~ for the fish** обе́д был прекра́сным, то́лько ры́ба не удала́сь; за исключе́нием ры́бы всё бы́ло пригото́влено прекра́сно; **one could call her a classic beauty ~ for her nose** е́сли бы не нос, её красоту́ мо́жно бы́ло бы назва́ть класси́ческой

3: ~ that кро́ме того́, что; е́сли не счита́ть того́, что; **we had a lovely vac, ~ that it rained almost every day** кани́кулы прошли́ отли́чно, несмотря́ на то, что почти́ ка́ждый день шёл дождь

4 (*in contracts*): **~ as provided in clause 10** за исключе́нием слу́чаев, предусмо́тренных статьёй деся́той; **~ as may be agreed** за исключе́нием тех слу́чаев, кото́рые мо́жно согласова́ть.

except *vt* исключ|а́ть (-и́ть); **present company ~ed** за исключе́нием прису́тствующих, не говоря́ о прису́тствующих; **nobody ~ed** все без исключе́ния.

exception *n* **1** исключе́ние; **without ~** без исключе́ния; **with the ~ of smth/smb** за исключе́нием чего́-л/кого́-л; **to make an ~** де́лать исключе́ние; **an ~ to the rule** исключе́ние из пра́вила

2: she took ~ to what I said/to my presence она́ была́ оби́жена мои́ми слова́ми, она́ была́ недово́льна тем, что я то́же пришёл.

exceptional *adj* исключи́тельный; (*out of the ordinary*) необы́чный, (*usu only of people*) незауря́дный; **an ~ case** исключи́тельный/из ря́да вон выходя́щий слу́чай; **an ~ man** незауря́дный челове́к; **an ~ use of a word** необы́чное употребле́ние сло́ва.

excerpt *n* отры́вок.

excess *n* **1** (*surplus*) избы́ток, изли́шек; **we have bread in ~ of our needs** хле́ба у нас в избы́тке; **this year we have an ~ of apples** в э́том году́ у нас я́блок дева́ть не́куда/*CQ* я́блок про́рва; **in an ~ of enthusiasm** с чрезме́рным восто́ргом; **to ~** сли́шком; **she was generous almost to ~** она́ была́, пожа́луй, сли́шком щедра́; **expenses in ~ of the sum fixed** расхо́ды сверх устано́вленной су́ммы; **last year there was an ~ of imports over exports** в про́шлом году́ това́ров ввози́лось бо́льше, чем вывози́лось; *attr* изли́шний, ли́шний; **~ weight** ли́шний вес, изли́шек ве́са; **~ luggage** изли́шний вес багажа́; **~ profits tax** нало́г на сверхпри́быль; **~ fare** допла́та

2 (*immoderation*) изли́шество; **~ in eating and drinking** изли́шества (*pl*) в еде́ и питье́; **he drinks to ~** он пьёт, не зна́я ме́ры,

CQ он напивáется до чёртиков; (*pl = cruelties*) **the ~es of the enemy will never be forgotten** преступлéния врагá никогдá не бýдут забы́ты.

excessive *adj* чрезмéрный; изли́шний.

exchange *n* **1** обмéн (*usu* + *I*, *rarely* + *G*); **an ~ of views** обмéн мнéниями/мнéний; **an ~ of gifts/civilities/prisoners** обмéн подáрками/любéзностями/плéнными; **in ~ for** в обмéн на + *A*, (*to replace*) взамéн + *G*; **I got a new passport in ~ for my old one** я получи́л нóвый пáспорт в обмéн на стáрый; **to give/to take smth in ~** давáть/брать что-л взамéн; **they took my old car in part ~** они́ при́няли мою́ стáрую маши́ну как часть плáты за нóвую

2 *Fin*: **rate of ~** курс валю́ты; **foreign ~** инострáнная валю́та; *attr*: **the ~ rate is steady** курс устóйчив; **~ control** контрóль дéнежного кýрса

3 (*building*) би́ржа; **the stock ~** фóндовая би́ржа; **labour ~** би́ржа трудá; **telephone ~** телефóнная стáнция.

exchange *vt* **1**: **to ~ smth for smth** меня́ть что-л на что-л (по-), обмéн|ивать что-л на что-л (-я́ть); **I've ~d my house for a flat** я поменя́л/обменя́л свой дом на кварти́ру; **to ~ a library book** обменя́ть кни́гу в библиотéке; *Fin* **to ~ dollars for pounds** обменя́ть дóллары на фýнты

2: **to ~ smth** (*with smb*) обмéниваться + *I*, меня́ться + *I*; **to ~ greetings/glances with smb** обменя́ться привéтствиями/взгля́дами с кем-л; **he ~d places with me** мы поменя́лись с ним местáми; **we ~d a few words** мы обменя́лись/переки́нулись нéсколькими словáми.

exchangeable *adj*: **~ within one week of purchase** подлежáщий обмéну в течéние однóй недéли; **not ~** в обмéн не принимáется, обмéну не подлежи́т.

exchequer *n* (госудáрственная) казнá, казначéйство.

excise[1] *n*, *also* **~ duty** акци́з, акци́зный сбор; *attr*: **~ officer** акци́зный чинóвник.

excise[2] *vt* вы|резáть (-резать), отрез|áть (-ать); *Med* иссе|кáть (-чь); удал|я́ть (-и́ть).

excision *n* вырезáние, отрезáние; *Med* иссечéние, удалéние.

excitable *adj* возбуди́мый.

excite *vt* **1** (*disturb*) волновáть (вз-); возбу|ждáть (-ди́ть); **the children were ~ed at the thought of going to the circus** узнáв, что пойдýт в цирк, дéти óчень обрáдовались; **the patient must not be ~d** нельзя́ волновáть больнóго; **the news of the victory ~d everyone** весть о побéде взволновáла всех; **don't ~ yourselves/don't get ~d!** не волнýйтесь!

2 (*rouse*) возбуждáть; **to ~ interest/curiosity/envy** возбуждáть интерéс/любопы́тство/зáвисть.

excited *adj* возбуждённый; (*agitated*) взволнóванный; **in an ~ voice** взволнóванным гóлосом; **I'm getting ~ about the holidays** у меня́ начинáется предотпускнáя лихорáдка; **I'm so ~ about my new job** я так рад, что мне предложи́ли *or* я получи́л э́ту рабóту, (*if already started to work*) мне так нрáвится моя́ нóвая рабóта; **an ~ crowd** возбуждённая толпá (людéй); **an ~ discussion started** началáсь горя́чая дискýссия; **the child gets too easily ~** ребёнок óчень возбуди́м.

excitement *n* возбуждéние; (*agitation*) волнéние; шум; **in her ~ she...** в возбуждéнии/в волнéнии, онá...; **the children are tired after all the ~s of Christmas** дéти устáли от всех э́тих (*equiv*) новогóдних увеселéний; **what's all the ~ (about)?** что за шум/за переполóх?

exciting *adj* возбуждáющий; волнýющий; **an ~ film/story** волнýющий фильм/расскáз; **oh, how ~!** как э́то чудéсно!

exclaim *vi* воскли|цáть (-кнуть).

exclamation *n* восклицáние; *attr*: **~ mark** восклицáтельный знак.

exclude *vt* исключ|áть (-и́ть); **to ~ smb from membership of a club** исключи́ть когó-л из члéнов клýба; **to ~ all possibility of error** исключáть вся́кую возмóжность оши́бки; **it's been a fine week excluding Sunday** хорóшая былá недéля, éсли не считáть воскресéнья.

exclusion *n* исключéние; **he drinks only claret to the ~ of all other wines** он пьёт тóлько кларéт.

exclusive *adj* **1** (*socially*): **he moves in ~ circles** он вращáется в вы́сших сфéрах; **an ~ hotel** шикáрный отéль

2 (*sole*) исключи́тельный; еди́нственный; **to have ~ rights of sale** имéть исключи́тельные правá продáжи; **an ~ agent** еди́нственный представи́тель; **this has not been my ~ employment** я занимáлся не тóлько э́тим; **he obtained an ~ interview with her** (*of a journalist*) онá далá интервью́ тóлько емý одномý; **he gave the question his ~ attention** он сосредотóчил всё своё внимáние на э́том вопрóсе

3: **~ of** за исключéнием + *G*, не считáя + *G*; **the price of the dinner ~ of wine** стóимость обéда без винá.

exclusively *adv* исключи́тельно; еди́нственно; тóлько.

excrete *vt* вы|деля́ть (-делить).

excruciating *adj* мучи́тельный.

excruciatingly *adv* мучи́тельно; *CQ* **it was ~ funny** мы смея́лись до упáду/до слёз, э́то бы́ло на рéдкость забáвно.

exculpate *vt*: **to ~ smb from a charge** снять обвинéние с когó-л (*usu pf*); **to ~ oneself from a charge** отвести́ от себя́ обвинéние (*usu pf*).

excursion *n* экскýрсия; **to go on an ~** поéхать на экскýрсию; *attr*: **an ~ train/ticket** экскурсиóнный пóезд/билéт

excusable *adj* прости́тельный; **in the circumstances his mistake was ~** в такóй ситуáции егó оши́бка былá прости́тельной.

excuse *n* 1 (*justification*) оправда́ние; (*reason*) причи́на; (*pretext*) отгово́рка, предло́г; **this is no ~** э́то не оправда́ние/не причи́на; **he made all sorts of ~s for his behaviour** он приду́мывал всевозмо́жные оправда́ния своему́ поведе́нию; **he pleaded poverty as an ~** в оправда́ние он ссыла́лся на свою́ бе́дность; **in ~ he said...** в своё оправда́ние он сказа́л...; **a poor/lame ~** пуста́я отгово́рка, неубеди́тельная причи́на; **what's your ~ this time?** кака́я на э́тот раз у тебя́ отгово́рка?; **this gave me an ~ for refusing** э́то (мне) послужи́ло предло́гом для отка́за

2 (*apology*) извине́ние; **I made my ~s** я принёс извине́ния, я извини́лся; **please make my ~s** пожа́луйста, переда́й мои́ извине́ния.

excuse *vt* 1 (*forgive*) извин|я́ть (-и́ть); про|ща́ть (-сти́ть); **~ me!** прости́те!, извини́те!; **~ me for being late** извини́те, что (я) опозда́л/за опозда́ние; **if you'll ~ my language** извини́те за выраже́ние; **~ me, but I don't agree** извини́те, но я с ва́ми не согла́сен; **I must ask to be ~d this time** (*from attending meeting, etc.*) на э́тот раз вам придётся меня́ прости́ть

2 (*justify*) опра́вд|ывать (-а́ть); извин|я́ть (-и́ть); **this does not ~ you** э́то вас не опра́вдывает; **nothing can ~ such behaviour** тако́е поведе́ние ниче́м нельзя́ оправда́ть; **to ~ oneself** опра́вдываться + *I*; **he ~d himself on the grounds of ignorance** он опра́вдывался свои́м незна́нием/свое́й неосведомлённостью

3: to ~ smb from smth отпус|ка́ть кого́-л с чего́-л (-ти́ть); освобо|жда́ть кого́-л от чего́-л (-ди́ть); **the teacher ~d him from attending the class** учи́тель отпусти́л его́ с уро́ка; **he was ~d military service** он был освобождён от вое́нной слу́жбы; **to ~ smb his fees** освободи́ть кого́-л от упла́ты взно́сов.

executant *n Mus, Theat* исполни́тель (*m*).

execute *vt* 1 (*carry out*) исполн|я́ть (-ить); (*fulfil*) вы|полня́ть (-полнить); (*realize*) осуществ|ля́ть (-и́ть); **to ~ a command** испо́лнить прика́з; **to ~ an order (of customer)** вы́полнить зака́з; **to ~ a plan** осуществи́ть план; **to ~ a sonata/a role** испо́лнить сона́ту, сыгра́ть роль

2 *Law* (*draw up*) оформ|ля́ть, состав|ля́ть (*pfs* -ить)

3 (*put to death*) казни́ть (*impf and pf*).

execution *n* 1 (*performing*) выполне́ние; исполне́ние, *also Mus*

2 (*killing*) сме́ртная казнь; **~ by firing squad** расстре́л.

executive *n* (*of a government*): **the ~** исполни́тельная власть; (*in business*): **an ~** *approx* руководи́тель (*m*), администра́тор; **the ~** руково́дство.

executive *adj* исполни́тельный.

executor *n Law* исполни́тель (*m*) завеща́ния, душеприка́зчик.

exemplary *adj* приме́рный, образцо́вый; **an ~ pupil** приме́рный учени́к; **~ behaviour** образцо́вое поведе́ние.

exemplify *vt* (*be an example*) служи́ть приме́ром (по-).

exempt *adj* (*of goods*) не подлежа́щий + *D*; (*of person, institution*) освобождённый от + *G*; **goods ~ from tax** това́ры, не подлежа́щие обложе́нию нало́гом; **pensioners are ~ from tax** пенсионе́ры освобождены́ от упла́ты нало́га; **he's ~ from military service** он освобождён от вое́нной слу́жбы.

exercise *n* 1 (*physical*) упражне́ние; **to take ~** (*by walking*) прогу́ливаться, (*stir*) дви́гаться; **I take very little ~** я ма́ло дви́гаюсь; **dogs need regular ~** соба́к ну́жно регуля́рно прогу́ливать

2 *often pl* (*practical drills: mental or physical*) упражне́ние, трениро́вка; (*physical*) заря́дка, (у́тренняя) гимна́стика; **to do ~s** де́лать заря́дку; **remedial ~s** лече́бная гимна́стика; **~s in translation** упражне́ния по перево́ду; *Mil* **military ~s** вое́нные манёвры, уче́ния

3 (*use of*): **the ~ of rights** осуществле́ние прав.

exercise *vti vt* 1 (*show*) прояв|ля́ть (-и́ть); (*use*) примен|я́ть (-и́ть), испо́льзовать (*impf and pf*); **to ~ patience/self-control** проявля́ть терпе́ние/самооблада́ние; **to ~ one's rights** по́льзоваться права́ми (вос-); **to ~ one's authority** примени́ть власть; **he ~s a strong influence over her** он ока́зывает на неё большо́е влия́ние

2 (*perplex*): **the problem that is exercising us/our minds is this** пробле́ма, кото́рая занима́ет нас, такова́; **I am ~d about my son's future** я беспоко́юсь о бу́дущем моего́ сы́на

3 (*take, give exercise*): **I have to ~ my dog every day** мне на́до ка́ждый день прогу́ливать мою́ соба́ку; **I need to ~ myself more** мне на́до бо́льше дви́гаться/гуля́ть

vi (*be active*) дви́гаться (*usu impf*); (*walk*) гуля́ть, прогу́ливаться (*usu impfs*).

exercise book *n* (*for writing in*) тетра́дь; (*textbook with exercises*) сбо́рник упражне́ний.

exert *vt*: **to ~ pressure/influence on smb** ока́|зывать давле́ние/влия́ние на кого́-л (-а́ть); **he had to ~ all his strength to lift the heavy stone** что́бы подня́ть тяжёлый ка́мень, он напря́г все свои́ си́лы; **to ~ oneself** (*try*) стара́ться (по-); **at your age you shouldn't ~ yourself too much** (*strain*) в тако́м во́зрасте вы не должны́ сли́шком перенапряга́ться; **he ~ed himself on my behalf** он приложи́л все уси́лия, что́бы помо́чь мне; **I must ~ myself and go and dig potatoes** я до́лжен заста́вить себя́ пойти́ копа́ть карто́шку (*collect*).

exertion *n* (*effort*) уси́лие, стара́ние; (*strain*) напряже́ние; **despite all his ~s he couldn't change the wheel** ско́лько он ни стара́лся/ни пыхте́л, он не смог смени́ть колесо́; **he was exhausted after/by all his ~s** он обесси́лел от постоя́нного перенапряже́ния (*sing*); **in that heat it was an ~ even to breathe** така́я жара́, что да́же тру́дно дыша́ть.

exhale *vti* вы|дыха́ть (-́дохнуть).

exhaust *n Tech* вы́пуск; вы́хлоп; (*gases, etc. emitted*) выхлопны́е га́зы (*pl*); *attr Aut*: **~ pipe** выхлопна́я труба́.

exhaust *vt* **1** (*use up*) истощ|а́ть (-и́ть), исче́рп|ывать (-а́ть), *both also fig*; **to ~ the soil** истоща́ть по́чву; **we have ~ed our resources** мы исчерпа́ли свои́ ресу́рсы; **to ~ a subject** исчерпа́ть те́му; **my patience is ~ed** моё терпе́ние ко́нчилось/ло́пнуло; **to ~ a mine** отрабо́тать рудни́к (*only in pf*)

2 (*tire out*) истоща́ть; изнур|я́ть (-и́ть); **he was ~ed by his illness** боле́знь его́ изнури́ла; **I was ~ed by the heat** я изнемога́л от жары́; **I was/felt ~ed by/after the long climb** я вы́бился из сил на э́том бесконе́чном подъёме; **to ~ oneself** изнуря́ть себя́.

exhaustion *n* истоще́ние; изнеможе́ние; **he is in a state of nervous ~** у него́ не́рвное истоще́ние

exhaustive *adj*: **an ~ inquiry** всесторо́ннее/подро́бное рассле́дование.

exhibit *n* (*in museum, etc.*) экспона́т; *Law* веще́ственное доказа́тельство.

exhibit *vti vt* **1** (*in exhibition, etc.*) экспони́ровать (*impf and pf*); вы|ставля́ть (-́ставить); **to ~ one's paintings** выставля́ть свои́ карти́ны

2 (*show a quality*) пока́з|ывать (-а́ть); прояв|ля́ть (-и́ть); **to ~ courage** прояви́ть му́жество

vi (*of artist*) выставля́ться (*only in impf*).

exhibition *n* **1** (*public display*) вы́ставка; **an art ~** вы́ставка карти́н; **an industrial ~** промы́шленная вы́ставка

2 (*of qualities*) проявле́ние; **what an ~ of bad manners!** что за мане́ры!; **don't make an ~ of yourself** не кривля́йся!, не рабо́тай на пу́блику!

exhibitionist *n*: **he's just an ~** он всё де́лает напока́з.

exhibitor *n* экспоне́нт.

exhilarate *vt* бодри́ть (о-); ожив|ля́ть (-и́ть); **we came back from the concert thoroughly ~d** мы возвраща́лись с конце́рта весёлые и оживлённые; **we felt ~d after sailing all day** поката́вшись це́лый день на ло́дке, мы чу́вствовали себя́ о́чень бо́дро; **~d by his success** ободрённый свои́м успе́хом.

exhilarating *adj* бодря́щий; **~ weather** бодря́щая пого́да; **it was an ~ speech** э́то была́ вдохновля́ющая речь; **he's an ~ companion** с ним интере́сно.

exhilaration *n* весёлость, весе́лье, оживле́ние.

exhort *vt* побу|жда́ть к + *D or* + *inf* (-ди́ть); **he ~ed us to work harder** он тре́бовал от нас бо́лее упо́рной рабо́ты.

exhortation *n* побужде́ние.

exhume *vt* вы|ка́пывать (-́копать).

exigency *n*, *usu pl* **exigencies** потре́бности, ну́жды.

exiguous *adj* ску́дный.

exile *n* **1** (*banishment*) ссы́лка; изгна́ние; **to live in ~** жить в изгна́нии, быть в ссы́лке; **to send smb into ~** ссыла́ть кого́-л; **he went into ~** его́ вы́слали из страны́

2 (*person*) изгна́нник, ссы́льный.

exile *vt* из|гоня́ть (-гна́ть), ссыла́ть (сосла́ть).

exist *vi* существова́ть, быть (*impfs*); **does life ~ on Mars?** есть ли жизнь на Ма́рсе?; (*be available*) **a copy of this book ~s in the British Museum** экземпля́р э́той кни́ги име́ется в Брита́нском музе́е; **how can they ~ in such conditions?** как они́ живу́т/существу́ют в таки́х усло́виях?; **she couldn't ~ without television** она́ не мо́жет жить/не мы́слит своего́ существова́ния без телеви́зора.

existence *n* **1** (*being*) существова́ние; **this is the only vase of its kind in ~** э́та ва́за—еди́нственная в своём ро́де; **do you believe in the ~ of ghosts?** ты ве́ришь в привиде́ния?; **it is thought the world came into ~ 4,000 million years ago** при́нято счита́ть, что земля́ существу́ет [NB *tense*] четы́ре миллиа́рда лет

2 (*manner of living*) жизнь, существова́ние; **they lead a happy ~ in the country** они́ живу́т о́чень сча́стливо в дере́вне; **they lead a miserable ~** они́ влача́т жа́лкое существова́ние.

exit *n* (*way out or departure*) вы́ход; (*of actor*) ухо́д; **"No E."** «Нет вы́хода»; **emergency ~** запа́сный вы́ход.

exit *vi Theat*: **~ Hamlet** Га́млет ухо́дит.

exodus *n* ма́ссовый ухо́д (*on foot*)/ отъе́зд (*by transport*); *Bibl* исхо́д.

ex officio *adv and adj* по до́лжности; **he sits on the committee ~, he's an ~ member of the committee** он по до́лжности вхо́дит в э́ту коми́ссию.

exonerate *vt* (*acquit*) опра́в|дывать кого́-л (-да́ть); **to ~ smb from blame** снять обвине́ние с кого́-л (*usu pf*); **he was ~d from all responsibility for what had happened** с него́ сня́та вся́кая отве́тственность за случи́вшееся; **even if he is on crutches, that won't ~ him from appearing personally in court** да́же е́сли он на костыля́х, он всё равно́ до́лжен ли́чно яви́ться в суд.

exorbitant *adj* непоме́рный, чрезме́рный; **they're asking an ~ price for the vase** они́ запра́шивают непоме́рную це́ну за э́ту ва́зу.

exotic *adj* экзоти́ческий.

expand *vti vt* (*broaden*) расшир|я́ть (-́ить); (*develop*) разви|ва́ть (-́ть); **to ~ production** расширя́ть произво́дство; **I'm going to ~ my thesis into a book** я собира́юсь расши́рить свою́ диссерта́цию до моногра́фии; **we are ~ing the export side of the business** мы увели́чиваем э́кспорт на́шей проду́кции

vi **1** расширя́ться; развива́ться; **metals ~**

when heated мета́ллы расширя́ются при нагрева́нии; **trade is ~ing** торго́вля расширя́ется; **our village has ~ed into a large industrial centre** на́ша дере́вня вы́росла/преврати́лась в большо́й индустриа́льный центр

2 (*open*) раскры|ва́ться (-́ться); **flowers ~ in sunshine** на со́лнце цветы́ раскрыва́ются; *fig*: **his face ~ed into a broad smile** его́ лицо́ расплыло́сь в широ́кой улы́бке; **he is taciturn but he can ~ under the influence of alcohol** он обы́чно о́чень сде́ржан, но от вина́ стано́вится разгово́рчивее.

expanse *n*: **a wide ~ of blue sky** огро́мный голубо́й ку́пол не́ба; **the broad ~ of lake Baikal** бескра́йняя во́дная гладь о́зера Байка́л [**NB** *nominative if* о́зера *is used*; *if* о́зера *is omitted*, *then write* Байка́ла].

expansion *n* (*in volume*, *etc.*) расшире́ние; (*by stretching*) растя́жка, *fig* (*growth*) рост; (*development*) разви́тие; (*spread*) распростране́ние; **the ~ of gases when heated** расшире́ние га́зов при нагрева́нии; **the ~ of the electronics industry** расшире́ние электро́нной промы́шленности.

expansive *adj* (*wide*) просто́рный, широ́кий, обши́рный; (*of people*) откры́тый; (*effusive*) шу́мный, экспанси́вный.

expatiate *vi*: **to ~ on a subject** распространя́ться на каку́ю-л те́му (*impf*).

expatriate *n* эмигра́нт, переселе́нец.

expect *vti vt* **1** ждать + *G or* + что, ожида́ть + *G or* + *A*, *or* + что (*impfs*); **they ~ me for supper** они́ меня́ ждут к у́жину; **don't ~ me till you see me** ты осо́бенно меня́ не жди; **he always turns up when least ~ed** он всегда́ появля́ется, когда́ его́ ме́ньше всего́ ждут; **we ~ rain tomorrow** на за́втра ожида́ется дождь; **he was late, just as I ~ed** он опозда́л, как я и ожида́л; **he failed his exam, but it was only to be ~ed after his illness** он не сдал экза́мена, но э́того сле́довало ожида́ть, ведь он то́лько по́сле боле́зни; **an answer can't be ~ed before Thursday** нельзя́ ожида́ть отве́та ра́ньше четверга́

2 (*count on*) рассчи́тывать (*only in impf*); **I ~ to be back by Friday at latest** я рассчи́тываю верну́ться са́мое по́зднее в пя́тницу

3 (*require*) тре́бовать (*only in impf*); **you ~ too much of her** вы тре́буете сли́шком мно́го от неё; **I ~ you to be punctual** я тре́бую, что́бы вы пришли́ во́время; **what am I ~ed to do about it?** что я могу́ сде́лать?

4 (*suppose*) ду́мать, полага́ть (*only in impfs*), *or use adv* вероя́тно, наве́рно(е); **I ~ he'll be there** я ду́маю, (что) он там бу́дет; **I ~ed as much** я так и ду́мал; **prices are ~ed to rise** полага́ют, что це́ны повы́сятся; **I ~ he'll be late** он, вероя́тно, опозда́ет; **I ~ you're ready for bed** вы, наве́рное, хоти́те спать; **one can hardly ~ he'll be pleased** нельзя́ да́же и ду́мать, что э́то ему́ понра́вится

vi: **to be ~ing** ожида́ть ребёнка, быть в положе́нии.

expectancy *n*: **life ~ for a man is about 70 years** сре́дняя продолжи́тельность жи́зни для мужчи́ны приблизи́тельно се́мьдесят лет; **he looked at her with an air of ~** он посмотре́л на неё вопроси́тельно.

expectant *adj*: **an ~ mother** бере́менная же́нщина.

expectantly *adv*: **the children waited for him ~** де́ти с нетерпе́нием ожида́ли его́.

expectation *n* **1** ожида́ние; **according to ~s** как и ожида́лось; (*in letter*) **in ~ of an early reply** наде́юсь на бы́стрый отве́т

2 (*hopes*; *usu pl*) (**~s**) наде́жды; ожида́ния; **to live up to ~s** оправда́ть наде́жды; **to fall short of ~s** не оправда́ть наде́жд/ожида́ний; **beyond ~s** сверх ожида́ния (*sing*); **we have great ~s of you** мы возлага́ем на вас больши́е наде́жды; **he has great ~s** у него́ больши́е перспекти́вы в бу́дущем (*prospects*), его́ ожида́ет большо́е насле́дство (*of an inheritance*).

expectorate *vi* отха́ркивать (*usu impf*).

expedience, expediency *n* целесообра́зность; **on grounds of ~** исходя́ из целесообра́зности.

expedient *adj* целесообра́зный.

expedite *vt* (*speed up*) ускор|я́ть (-́ить); **to ~ delivery/business** уско́рить доста́вку/де́ло.

expedition *n* **1** (*on large scale*) экспеди́ция, *also Mil*; (*trip on foot*) похо́д; прогу́лка; (*by transport*) пое́здка; **an ~ to the North Pole** экспеди́ция на Се́верный по́люс

2 (*speed*): **with ~** бы́стро (*adv*).

expeditionary *adj*: *Mil* **an ~ force** экспедицио́нные войска́ (*pl*).

expeditious *adj* прово́рный.

expel *vt* (*of invaders*, *etc.*) из|гоня́ть (-гна́ть); **to ~ a boy from school** исключи́ть ученика́ из шко́лы.

expend *vt* тра́тить (*pfs* по-, ис-); **to ~ time and money** тра́тить вре́мя и де́ньги; **he ~ed much effort in getting his laboratory equipped** он приложи́л сто́лько уси́лий, что́бы обору́довать лаборато́рию; **they had ~ed all their ammunition** у них вы́шли все боеприпа́сы (*no sing*).

expenditure *n* тра́та, расхо́д (*often pl*); **~ on armaments** расхо́ды на вооруже́ние; **to limit one's ~** ограни́чивать свои́ тра́ты/свои́ расхо́ды/себя́ в расхо́дах; **that will entail an ~ of the order of £10,000** э́то повлечёт расхо́ды поря́дка десяти́ ты́сяч фу́нтов; *fig* **after the ~ of much time and effort** потра́тив мно́го сил и вре́мени.

expense *n* **1** расхо́д; (за)тра́ты (*pl*); счёт; **at public ~** на обще́ственные сре́дства; **at my ~** за мой счёт; **spare no ~** не счита́йтесь с расхо́дами; **regardless of ~** не счита́ясь с затра́тами; **he bought this flat at enormous ~** он заплати́л за э́ту кварти́ру бе́шеные де́ньги; **to be a great ~ to smb, to put smb to great ~** вводи́ть кого́-л в большо́й расхо́д; **to go to great ~** си́льно потра́титься; **don't go to the ~ of buying**

a new car не тра́ться на поку́пку но́вой маши́ны; *fig*: **to profit at smb else's ~** поживи́ться за чужо́й счёт; **at the ~ of one's health** за счёт своего́ здоро́вья; **to laugh at smb's ~** смея́ться над кем-л

2 *pl* (**~s**) расхо́ды; (*costs*) изде́ржки; **travelling ~s** (*for living costs*) командиро́вочные/су́точные (де́ньги), (*for tickets*) доро́жные расхо́ды; **entertainment ~s** расхо́ды на представи́тельство; **overhead ~s** накладны́е расхо́ды; **legal ~s** суде́бные изде́ржки; **to pay smb's ~s** опла́чивать чьи-л расхо́ды.

expense account *n*: **put it down to the ~** отнеси́те э́то за счёт казённых расхо́дов.

expensive *adj* дорого́й; (*valuable*) це́нный; **an ~ car** дорого́й автомоби́ль; **~ jewelry** це́нные ювели́рные изде́лия; **I had an ~ education** моё образова́ние сто́ило о́чень до́рого; **he's got an ~ wife** жена́ ему́ до́рого обхо́дится.

experience *n* **1** о́пыт; **to know by/from ~** знать по о́пыту

2 (*as qualification for jobs*) стаж; **he has 5 years' teaching ~** у него́ пятиле́тний педагоги́ческий стаж; **no ~ necessary** ста́жа не тре́буется; **a workman of ~** о́пытный/квалифици́рованный рабо́чий

3 (*event*) слу́чай; приключе́ние; **an alarming ~** опа́сное приключе́ние; **a strange ~** стра́нный слу́чай; **tell us about your ~s in Africa** расскажи́те о свои́х приключе́ниях в А́фрике.

experience *vt* испы́т|ывать (-а́ть); (*suffer*) пережи|ва́ть (-́ть); **to ~ joy/hardship** испы́тывать ра́дость/тру́дности (*pl*); **to ~ pain** чу́вствовать/испы́тывать боль (*impfs*); **to ~ grief** пережи́ть го́ре.

experienced *adj* о́пытный; (*in one's profession*) со ста́жем, квалифици́рованный.

experiment *n* экспериме́нт (*usu scientific*), о́пыт (*general or scientific*); **as an ~** в поря́дке/в ка́честве экспериме́нта; **to prove smth by ~** доказа́ть что-л на о́пыте; **to conduct a series of ~s** провести́ се́рию/ряд эксперим́ентов; **to carry out an ~ in chemistry** проводи́ть хими́ческий о́пыт.

experiment *vi* эксперименти́ровать (*impf*); про|води́ть о́пыты (-вести́); **to ~ with new materials** эксперименти́ровать с но́выми материа́лами; **to ~ on dogs** проводи́ть о́пыты на соба́ках.

experimental *adj* эксперимента́льный; о́пытный; **an ~ farm** о́пытное хозя́йство.

expert *n* экспе́рт; (*scientific, academic*) специали́ст; (*in fine arts, etc.*) знато́к; **a group of ~s** экспе́ртная гру́ппа; **he's an ~ in economics** он специали́ст в о́бласти эконо́мики; **he's an ~ at dressage** он ма́стер объезжа́ть лошаде́й.

expert *adj* о́пытный; (*skilful*) иску́сный; **an ~ driver** о́пытный/иску́сный води́тель; **an ~ rider** иску́сный нае́здник; **he's an ~ historian** он зна́ющий исто́рик; **an ~ mechanic** о́пытный/высококвалифици́рованный меха́ник; **according to ~ opinion** по мне́нию специали́стов/экспе́ртов.

expiration *n* истече́ние сро́ка; **the ~ of a lease** истече́ние сро́ка аре́нды; **on the ~ of the quarantine period** по оконча́нии (сро́ка) каранти́на.

expire *vi lit* (*die*) сконча́ться (*pf*); (*reach its term*) исте|ка́ть (-́чь); **my driving license has ~d** срок де́йствия мои́х води́тельских прав истёк; **his term of imprisonment has ~d** он о́тбыл срок заключе́ния, срок заключе́ния у него́ ко́нчился.

expiry *n see* **expiration.**

explain *vt* (*elucidate*) объясн|я́ть (-и́ть); (*expound*) из|лага́ть (-ложи́ть); **to ~ the meaning of a word** объясни́ть значе́ние сло́ва; **he ~ed to me what he had in mind** он мне объясни́л, что он име́л в виду́; **how do you ~ the disappearance of the gun?** как вы объясня́ете исчезнове́ние пистоле́та?; **to ~ a theory** изложи́ть тео́рию; **that ~s it!** тепе́рь всё я́сно!; (*to child*) **please ~ yourself!** объясни́ своё поведе́ние, расскажи́, в чём де́ло; **it will be difficult to ~ this away** объясни́ть э́то бу́дет тру́дно.

explanation *n* объясне́ние, поясне́ние, разъясне́ние; (*justification*) оправда́ние; (*reason*) причи́на; **what's the ~ of this?** како́е мо́жет быть э́тому объясне́ние?; **there must be some ~ for his abrupt departure** должно́ быть како́е-то объясне́ние его́ неожи́данному отъе́зду; **in ~ he added that...** в поясне́ние/для я́сности он доба́вил, что...; **I ought to say a few words by way of ~** я до́лжен сказа́ть не́сколько слов в поясне́ние; **in ~ of his behaviour** в оправда́ние своего́ поведе́ния.

explanatory *adj* объясни́тельный; поясни́тельный; **he left an ~ letter** он оста́вил объясни́тельную запи́ску; **~ text** поясни́тельный текст; **an ~ footnote** поясня́ющее примеча́ние, поясне́ние.

expletive *n* руга́тельство, бра́нное сло́во.

explicable *adj* объясни́мый.

explicit *adj* я́сный; определённый; **he was quite ~ that...** он я́сно/определённо дал поня́ть, что...

explode *vti vt* (*of bomb, etc.*) взрыва́ть (взорва́ть); *fig* **to ~ a theory** опроверг|а́ть тео́рию (-́нуть)

vi (*of bomb, etc.*) взрыва́ться, *also fig*; *fig* разра|жа́ться (-зи́ться); **on hearing the lie, he ~d** услы́шав э́ту ложь, он взорва́лся/,он разрази́лся гне́вной тира́дой.

exploit *n* по́двиг.

exploit *vt* эксплуати́ровать (*impf*), *also Polit, Econ*; (*in mining, etc.*) разраб|а́тывать (-о́тать); (*abuse*) злоупотреб|ля́ть (-и́ть); **to ~ a mine** эксплуати́ровать/разраба́тывать рудни́к; **to ~ smb's good nature** злоупотребля́ть чьей-л доброто́й.

exploration *n Geog* иссле́дование, *also fig*; (*reconnaissance*) разве́дка; **the ~ of Africa** иссле́дование А́фрики; **the ~ of the structure of** иссле́дование структу́ры + *G*.

exploratory *adj* исслéдовательский; развéдывательный.

explore *vt Geog* исслéдовать, *also fig* (*impf and pf*); *fig* изуч|áть (-и́ть); **to ~ a problem** изучи́ть вопрóс; **to ~ possibilities** вы|ясня́ть возмóжности (-́яснить).

explorer *n* исслéдователь (*m*).

explosion *n* взрыв, *also fig*; **an ~ of laughter/of anger** взрыв смéха, вспы́шка гнéва; **the population ~** демографи́ческий взрыв.

explosive *n* взры́вчатое веществó, взрывчáтка.

explosive *adj* взры́вчатый; взрывнóй; **~ force/blast** взрывнáя си́ла/волнá; *fig*: **he's got an ~ temper** он вспы́льчивый человéк; **that's an ~ issue** э́то опáсная тéма.

exponent *n* истолковáтель (*m*); **he is an ~ of Kant's philosophy** он истолковáтель филосóфии Кáнта.

export *n* э́кспорт, вы́воз (*no pls*); **our chief ~s to Africa are tractors** основнóй предмéт нáшего э́кспорта в стрáны Áфрики—трáкторы; **last year ~s exceeded imports** в прóшлом годý э́кспорт по объёму превы́сил и́мпорт; *attr*: **~ trade** торгóвля на э́кспорт; **~ figures** отчёт по э́кспорту; **~ duty** э́кспортная пóшлина.

export *vt* экспорти́ровать (*impf and pf*); вы|вози́ть (-везти).

exportable *adj*: **soft fruit is not easily ~** скоропóртящиеся фрýкты трýдно экспорти́ровать; **we must alter the design of our cars if they are to be ~** нам нáдо измени́ть констрýкцию маши́н, éсли мы хоти́м их экспорти́ровать.

expose *vt* **1** (*uncover*) раскры|вáть (-́ть); разоблач|áть (-и́ть); **to ~ a plot** раскры́ть зáговор; **to ~ an impostor** разоблачи́ть обмáнщика

2 (*display*) вы|ставля́ть (-́ставить); **the goods were ~d for view in the shop window** товáр (*sing*) вы́ставили в витри́не

3: to ~ smb/smth to smth подверг|áть когó-л/что-л чемý-л (-́нуть); **the general did not wish to ~ his troops to unnecessary danger** генерáл не хотéл подвергáть войскá ненýжной опáсности; **to be ~d to ridicule** подвергáться насмéшкам; **carpets fade if ~ed to strong sunlight** ковры́ выгорáют на сóлнце; **she's delicate and should not be ~d to infection** у неё слáбое здорóвье, и ей нáдо берéчься от инфéкций

4 *Photo* экспони́ровать (*impf and pf*).

exposed *adj*: *Photo* **an ~ film** экспони́рованная плёнка; **a house in an ~ position/~ to the weather** дом, откры́тый всем ветрáм; **an ~ nerve/flank** обнажённый нерв/фланг.

exposition *n* (*explanation*) объяснéние; (*elucidation*) изложéние; **he gave a clear ~ of his theory** он я́сно изложи́л свою́ теóрию.

expostulate *vi*: **she ~d with him on/about his rash driving** онá старáлась убеди́ть его́ éздить поосторóжнее.

exposure *n* **1** (*baring*) обнажéние; **the ~ of the bone** обнажéние кóсти; **he was brown from ~ to the weather** егó лицó обвéтрилось; **to die of ~** поги́бнуть от хóлода; **to avoid ~ to strong sunlight** избегáть прямы́х сóлнечных лучéй

2 (*unmasking*) разоблачéние; раскры́тие (*not used of people*); **~ of a crime** разоблачéние/раскры́тие преступлéния

3 (*aspect*): **a house with a southern ~** дом фасáдом на юг; **a room with a northern ~** кóмната с óкнами на сéвер

4 *Photo* экспози́ция, вы́держка; *attr*: **~ meter** экспонóметр.

expound *vi* из|лагáть (-ложи́ть); разъясн|я́ть (-и́ть).

express *n Rail* экспрéсс.

express *adj* **1** (*clearly stated*) определённый, я́сный, твёрдый; специáльный; **it was his ~ wish that...** у негó бы́ло вполнé определённое желáние + *inf*; **I came with the ~ purpose of seeing you** я пришёл сюдá специáльно, чтóбы встрéтиться с тобóй; **it was his ~ command, that...** он стрóго приказáл, чтóбы...; **these were the ~ terms of his instructions** таковы́ бы́ли егó тóчные указáния

2 (*urgent, rapid*) срóчный; **an ~ letter** срóчное письмó; **~ train** экспрéсс; **~ messenger** нáрочный, курьéр.

express *adv*: **to send a letter ~** отправля́ть письмó срóчной пóчтой; **to travel ~** éхать экспрéссом.

express *vt* **1** (*make known*) вы|ражáть (-́разить); **to ~ a wish** вы́разить желáние; **an artist ~es himself through his painting** худóжник выражáет себя́ в свои́х карти́нах; **he can't ~ himself well** он не мóжет я́сно излагáть свои́ мы́сли; **he can't ~ himself well in Russian** емý трýдно объясни́ться по-рýсски; **he ~ed himself very strongly on this point** он óчень определённо вы́сказался по э́тому вопрóсу

2: to ~ the juice of a lemon вы|жимáть сок из лимóна (-́жать).

expression *n* (*in words, looks, etc., also Math*) выражéние; **to read with ~** читáть вырази́тельно/с выражéнием; **his grief is beyond ~** егó гóре не вы́разить словáми; **her ~ was full of sorrow** её лицó выражáло скорбь; **his genius found ~ in painting** егó талáнт нашёл выражéние в жи́вописи; **a colloquial ~** разговóрное выражéние; **as an ~ of my thanks** в знак благодáрности.

expressionless *adj* невырази́тельный; без вся́кого выражéния.

expressive *adj* вырази́тельный.

expressly *adv* (*plainly*) определённо; тóчно; я́сно; (*on purpose*) специáльно; намéренно; **I ~ said you were not to do that** я сказáл я́сно, что вы не должны́ э́того дéлать; **these flowers were sent ~ for you** э́ти цветы́ бы́ли пóсланы специáльно для вас.

expulsion *n* (*from one's country, home*) изгнáние; (*from school, club*) исключéние.

expurgate *vt*: **to ~ some passages from a text** вы|чёркивать не́которые места́ из те́кста (-черкнуть); **an ~d edition of Catullus** изда́ние стихо́в Кату́лла с исключе́нием нежела́тельных мест.

exquisite *adj* изы́сканный; исключи́тельный; **with ~ care** с исключи́тельной осторо́жностью; **~ workmanship** удиви́тельное/исключи́тельное мастерство́; **she has ~ taste** у неё о́чень то́нкий/изы́сканный вкус; **an ~ sensibility** необыча́йная чувстви́тельность.

extant *adj*: **this is the only copy still ~** э́то еди́нственный существу́ющий экземпля́р.

extemporary, extempore *adjs* импровизи́рованный.

extempore *adv* экспро́мтом.

extemporize *vi* говори́ть (*speak*)/игра́ть (*act*) экспро́мтом.

extend *vti vt* **1** (*enlarge*) расшир|я́ть (-ить); (*stretch out*) протя́|гивать (-ну́ть); (*lengthen in distance or time*) продл|ева́ть (-и́ть); **to ~ a building** расширя́ть зда́ние; **she ~ed her hand to me** она́ протяну́ла мне ру́ку; **they are ~ing the metro to the airport** ли́нию метро́ продлева́ют до аэропо́рта; **can't you ~ your visit by a few days?** не мо́жете ли вы оста́ться ещё на не́сколько дней?; **the bank won't ~ our credit** банк бо́льше не даёт нам креди́тов (*pl*)

2 (*offer*): **to ~ thanks** вы|ража́ть благода́рность (-разить); **to ~ hospitality** ока́з|ывать гостеприи́мство (-а́ть); **to ~ an invitation to smb** пригласи́ть кого́-л; **they ~ed us a warm welcome** они́ тепло́/раду́шно встре́тили нас

3: he seldom ~s himself он не лю́бит себя́ перетружда́ть

vi (*stretch*) тяну́ться, простира́ться (*usu impfs*); **the garden ~s as far as the river** сад тя́нется до са́мой реки́; **the steppe ~s for hundreds of kilometres** степь тя́нется/простира́ется на со́тни киломе́тров.

extension *n* (*addition*): **an ~ to a building** пристро́йка; **an ~ to a road** продолже́ние доро́ги; **an ~ of a term** продле́ние сро́ка; **an ~ of one's leave** продле́ние о́тпуска; **an ~ for an electric flex** удлини́тель; **a table with an ~** раздвижно́й стол; *Tel* (*extra instrument*) доба́вочный телефо́н; **~ 40** доба́вочный со́рок.

extensive *adj* обши́рный; **an ~ forest** обши́рный лесно́й масси́в; **our house has an ~ view over the river** из о́кон на́шего до́ма открыва́ется широ́кий вид на заре́чные да́ли; **he has an ~ knowledge of this subject** у него́ обши́рные позна́ния (*pl*) по э́тому предме́ту; **we made ~ enquiries** мы повсю́ду навели́ спра́вки; **~ repairs** капита́льный ремо́нт; **we made ~ use of his hospitality** мы ча́сто по́льзовались его́ гостеприи́мством.

extent *n* **1** (*length, area*) протяже́ние; протяжённость; (*dimensions*) разме́ры (*pl*); *fig* широта́; **a race track 1,500 metres in ~** бегова́я доро́жка протяжённостью в полтора́ киломе́тра; **I had no idea of the ~ of the game reserve** я не представля́л себе́ разме́ров запове́дника; **from the grandstand one can see the full ~ of the race course** с гла́вной трибу́ны хорошо́ ви́дно всю диста́нцию; *fig*: **I was amazed at the ~ of his knowledge** я был поражён широто́й его́ позна́ний (*pl*); **the insurance covers us to the ~ of £1,000** мы застрахо́ваны на ты́сячу фу́нтов

2 (*degree*) сте́пень; ме́ра; **to some ~** до не́которой сте́пени; **to a certain ~** в изве́стной ме́ре; **to what ~ can he be trusted?** наско́лько мо́жно ему́ ве́рить?; **he used to exaggerate to such an ~ that in the end no one believed him** он так люби́л преувели́чивать, что в конце́ концо́в все переста́ли ему́ ве́рить.

extenuate *vt*: **nothing can ~ such behaviour** тако́му поведе́нию нет оправда́ния; **extenuating circumstances** смягча́ющие (вину́) обстоя́тельства.

extenuation *n*: **the defence pleaded mental instability in ~ of the crime** защи́тник испо́льзовал в ка́честве смягча́ющего обстоя́тельства психи́ческую неусто́йчивость подсуди́мого.

exterior *n* вне́шность; нару́жность; вне́шний/нару́жный вид; **a decent old man with a rough ~** почте́нный ста́рец с суро́вой вне́шностью; **the ~ of the house was painted blue** снару́жи (*adv*) дом был вы́крашен в си́ний цвет.

exterior *adj* вне́шний; нару́жный; **~ angle** вне́шний у́гол.

exterminate *vt* уничтож|а́ть (-ить).

external *adj* вне́шний, нару́жный; **~ injuries** вне́шние поврежде́ния; (*on medicine bottles*) **for ~ use only** для нару́жного употребле́ния; **~ examiner** приглашённый экзамена́тор; **~ evidence** свиде́тельство со стороны́.

externally *adv* вне́шне, нару́жно; **he was severely concussed, but ~ there was nothing to see** у него́ бы́ло си́льное сотрясе́ние мо́зга без каки́х-нибудь вне́шних поврежде́ний.

extinct *adj*: **an ~ volcano** поту́хший вулка́н; **an ~ species** вы́мерший вид; **to become ~** вымира́ть.

extinction *n* (*of a species, etc.*) вымира́ние; **the ~ of a fire** туше́ние огня́.

extinguish *vt* (*fire, etc.*) туши́ть (по-), гаси́ть (по-); **he ~ed the light** он потуши́л/погаси́л свет; **the fire** (*accidental*) **has been ~ed** пожа́р был поту́шен; **see that the bonfire is ~ed** не забу́дь погаси́ть костёр; *fig* **our hopes have been ~ed** на́ши наде́жды уга́сли.

extort *vt* вы|рыва́ть (-рвать); вымога́ть (*impf*); **to ~ a confession/a promise from smb** вы́рвать призна́ние/обеща́ние у кого́-л; **to ~ money from smb** вымога́ть де́ньги у кого́-л.

extortion *n* вымога́тельство; *CQ* **taxes? I call it sheer ~!** э́то нало́ги? Да э́то про́сто вымога́тельство!

extortionate *adj*: ~ **prices** граби́тельские це́ны.

extra *n usu pl* **1: the dinner costs £3 but coffee and service are** ~**s** обе́д сто́ит три фу́нта, но за обслу́живание и ко́фе придётся доплати́ть; **safety belts are** ~**s** ремни́ безопа́сности выдаю́тся за осо́бую/отде́льную пла́ту

2 *Theat* стати́ст, *f* -ка.

extra *adj* **1** (*additional*) доба́вочный; дополни́тельный; ~ **charges** дополни́тельные расхо́ды; ~ **postage** дополни́тельная почто́вая опла́та; **they are running** ~ **trains over the holiday** на пра́здники вво́дятся дополни́тельные поезда́; ~ **pay** дополни́тельная опла́та; **we need three** ~ **chairs** нам ну́жно ещё три сту́ла; *Sport* ~ **time** доба́вочное/дополни́тельное вре́мя

2 (*spare*) ли́шний; **I've brought an** ~ **towel** я взял с собо́й ли́шнее полоте́нце.

extra *adv* **1** (*especially*) необыча́йно, осо́бенно; **she was** ~ **kind that day** в тот день она́ была́ осо́бенно/необыча́йно любе́зна; **an** ~ **big apple** о́чень большо́е я́блоко

2 (*additionally*): **price £10, packing and postage** ~ цена́ де́сять фу́нтов, не счита́я упако́вки и пересы́лки; **coffee is 20p** ~ за ко́фе—два́дцать пе́нсов сверх счёта; **I'll have to work** ~ **on Saturday** в суббо́ту я бу́ду рабо́тать сверхуро́чно.

extract *n* экстра́кт; **meat** ~ мясно́й экстра́кт; (*from book, etc.*) отры́вок, вы́держка (из текста), вы́писка.

extract *vt* извле|ка́ть (-́чь); (*by squeezing*) вы|жима́ть (-́жать); *Chem* экстраги́ровать (*impf and pf*); **to** ~ **a bullet** извле́чь пу́лю; **to** ~ **a cork** вы́тащить про́бку; **to** ~ **a tooth** удал|я́ть зуб (-и́ть); **to** ~ **juice from an orange** вы́жать сок из апельси́на; **to** ~ **ore from the earth** добы|ва́ть руду́ (-́ть); **I** ~**ed some passages from "Hamlet"** я вы́брал не́которые места́ из «Га́млета»; *Math* **to** ~ **a square root** извлека́ть квадра́тный ко́рень; *fig*: **to** ~ **information from smb** доби́ться све́дений от кого́-л; *CQ* **I managed to** ~ **five roubles out of my aunt** я всё-таки вы́удил пятёрку у мое́й тётки.

extraction *n* **1** извлече́ние; (*by quarrying, etc.*: *of action*) добыва́ние, (*of action or material extracted*) добы́ча; *Chem* экстра́кция; ~ **of a tooth** удале́ние зу́ба

2 (*lineage*): **he is of German** ~ он не́мец по происхожде́нию.

extramarital *adj* внебра́чный.

extraneous *adj* посторо́нний; чу́ждый; ~ **interference** посторо́ннее/чу́ждое вмеша́тельство; **an** ~ **body** иноро́дное те́ло; ~ **considerations** ины́е соображе́ния; **that is** ~ **to our subject** э́то не отно́сится к на́шей те́ме.

extraordinarily *adv* необыча́йно, удиви́тельно; **you are** ~ **kind** вы необыча́йно/удиви́тельно добры́.

extraordinary *adj* необыча́йный; выдаю́щийся; удиви́тельный; стра́нный; **an** ~ **success** необыча́йный успе́х; **an** ~ **talent** выдаю́щийся тала́нт; **it was** ~ **how he managed to escape** удиви́тельно, как ему́ удало́сь убежа́ть; **what an** ~ **taste!** что за стра́нный при́вкус!; **what** ~ **weather!** кака́я необы́чная/стра́нная пого́да!

extrasensory *adj*: ~ **perception** внечу́вственное восприя́тие.

extravagance *n* (*in behaviour*) экстравага́нтность; (*over money, etc.*) расточи́тельство, (*in spending*) мотовство́.

extravagant *adj* экстравага́нтный; (*excessive*) непоме́рный, чрезме́рный; (*over money*) расточи́тельный; **an** ~ **taste/get-up** экстравага́нтный вкус/наря́д; **he has a very** ~ **wife** *CQ* у него́ жена́—транжи́ра; **our cook is very** ~ наш по́вар не уме́ет эконо́мить; ~ **praise** чрезме́рная похвала́.

extreme *n* кра́йность; **in the** ~ в вы́сшей сте́пени, до кра́йности; **to go from one** ~ **to the other** ударя́ться из одно́й кра́йности в другу́ю; **to go to** ~**s** ударя́ться в кра́йности, (*resort to*) прибега́ть к кра́йним ме́рам; **here we get** ~**s of heat and cold** здесь ре́зко континента́льный кли́мат.

extreme *adj* **1** (*farthest possible*) кра́йний; са́мый да́льний; **in the** ~ **north** на кра́йнем се́вере; **at the** ~ **end of the field** в са́мом конце́ по́ля

2 (*in the highest degree*) кра́йний; вы́сший; чрезвыча́йный; ~ **poverty** кра́йняя нужда́/нищета́; **in** ~ **pain** в стра́шных муче́ниях; *fig*: **in** ~ **old age** в глубо́кой ста́рости; **the** ~ **penalty** вы́сшая ме́ра наказа́ния

3 (*immoderate*) кра́йний; **to hold** ~ **views** приде́рживаться кра́йних взгля́дов.

extremely *adv* чрезвыча́йно, в вы́сшей сте́пени; кра́йне.

extremist *n* экстреми́ст; *attr* экстреми́стский.

extremity *n* (*end*) коне́ц; край; оконе́чность; *Anat pl* (**the extremities**) коне́чности; *fig*: **we must help them in their** ~ на́до им помо́чь—они́ в кра́йней нужде́; **they were driven to extremities** они́ бы́ли доведены́ до кра́йности (*sing*).

extricate *vt* вы|свобожда́ть (-́свободить); **to** ~ **a sheep from barbed wire** вы́свободить овцу́, запу́тавшуюся в колю́чей про́волоке; **to** ~ **a lorry from the mud** вы|та́скивать грузови́к из гря́зи (-́тащить); **to** ~ **smb from a predicament** вы́зволить/вы́ручить кого́-л из беды́ (*usu pfs*); **to** ~ **oneself from difficulties** вы́путаться из тру́дного положе́ния (*sing*) (*usu pf*).

extrovert *n Psych* экстрове́рт.

exuberant *adj*: **the children were in** ~ **spirits** де́ти бы́ли возбуждены́.

exude *vti vt* (*sweat, etc.*) выделя́ть (*usu impf*); *fig* **he** ~**s self-confidence** он о́чень самоуве́рен

vi выделя́ться (*usu impf*).

exult *vi* (*rejoice*) ликова́ть (*impf*); (*rejoice over smth*) ра́доваться + *D* (об-); торжествова́ть (*impf*); **the people** ~**ed when they heard**

of the victory народ ликовал, узнав о победе; **the team ~ed in their win** команда радовалась своей победе; **they ~ed in/at/ over the defeat of their opponents** они торжествовали победу над противником (*sing*).

exultation *n* ликование; торжество.

eye *n* **1** глаз; *Poet* око; *dim* глазок; **the whites of one's ~s** белки глаз; **a black ~** подбитый глаз; **the evil ~** дурной глаз; **I've got good ~s** у меня хорошее зрение; **to see with one's own ~s/with the naked ~** видеть собственными глазами/невооружённым глазом; **to measure by ~** мерить/прикидывать на глаз/на глазок; **judging by ~** на глазок; **it happened under his very ~s** это случилось у него на глазах; **I never set ~s on him before** я его в глаза не видел; **when I first set ~s on him** когда я впервые его увидел; **it's 5 years since I set ~s on him** уже пять лет как я не видел его; **the steppe stretched as far as the ~ could see** степь простиралась насколько хватало глаз; **to keep one's ~s glued on smb** не отрывать глаз от кого-л; **he rubbed his ~s in disbelief** он протёр глаза в недоумении; **he couldn't keep his ~s off her** он не мог отвести от неё глаз; **to make ~s at smb** строить глазки кому-л; **I ran my ~ quickly over your article** я пробежал глазами/проглядел вашу статью; *Mil* **~s left!** равнение налево!

2 (*of things like an eye*): **~ of a needle** ушко иголки; **hook and ~** крючок и петелька; (*small ring for threading smth through*) колечко; **the ~ of a potato** глазок картошки; **private ~** частный детектив

3 *fig uses*: **in the ~s of the law** в глазах закона; **in his ~s she's still a child** в его глазах она ещё ребёнок; **I've got my ~ on that violin** у меня давно на примете эта скрипка, я давно заприметил эту скрипку; **he's got a good ~ for a horse** у него на лошадей намётанный глаз, он знает толк в лошадях; **I called on him with an ~ to borrowing some money** я пошёл к нему, собираясь занять немного денег; **I'll keep my ~ on the children for you** я присмотрю за твоими детьми; **I must keep my ~ on the time** мне надо следить за временем; **he's always got one ~ on the clock** он то и дело поглядывает на часы; **one can see with half an ~ he's a foreigner** сразу видно, что он иностранец; **I'm up to my ~s in work** я занят по горло; **to shut one's ~s to smth** закрывать глаза на что-л; **to turn a blind ~ to smth** смотреть на что-л сквозь пальцы; **he married her with his ~s open** он женился на ней, зная на что идёт; **I opened his ~s to the truth** я открыл ему глаза на истину; **to be all ~s** обратиться в зрение, смотреть во все глаза; **there's more in this than meets the ~** это не так просто; **it leaps to the ~, it catches the ~ at once** это сразу бросается в глаза; **I tried to catch the ~ of the auctioneer** я старался обратить на себя внимание аукциониста; **he caught my ~ and gave me a wink** он поймал мой взгляд и подмигнул мне; **it was time to go and I tried to catch my husband's ~** пора было идти, и я старалась подать знак мужу; **she carefully avoided my ~** она старательно избегала моего взгляда; **he's very much in the public ~ these days** теперь он всё время на виду; **I don't see ~ to ~ with him** мы с ним расходимся/не сходимся во взглядах

4 *CQ*: **that's all my ~!** это всё вздор!; **if you keep your ~s skinned, you might spot her in the crowd** если будешь хорошенько смотреть, может быть, и найдёшь её в толпе; **keep your ~s skinned!** гляди в оба!; **that's one in the ~ for him!** это камешек в его огород.

eye *vt* разглядывать, рассматривать (*only in impfs*); **to ~ smb with curiosity** разглядывать кого-л с любопытством; **to ~ smb with suspicion** бросить на кого-л подозрительный взгляд.

eyeball *n* глазное яблоко.

eyebath *n* глазная ванночка.

eyebrow *n* бровь; **to raise one's ~s** поднять брови.

eyeglass *n* линза.

eyelash *n* ресница.

eyelet *n* (*on boots*, *belts*, *etc.*) дырка; (*for a rope*) колечко.

eyelid *n* веко; *CQ* **without batting an ~** не сомкнув глаз (*pl*).

eye-opener *n*: *CQ* **that was an ~ for him** это сразу открыло ему глаза.

eyeshade *n* козырёк (для защиты глаз).

eyeshadow *n* тени (*pl*) для век.

eyesight *n* зрение.

eyesore *n fig*: **that new building is an ~** это новое здание как бельмо на глазу.

eyestrain *n*: **I'm suffering from ~** у меня глаза болят от напряжения.

eyetooth *n* глазной зуб.

eyewash *n*: *CQ* **that's all ~** это всё очковтирательство.

eyewitness *n* очевидец; *Law* свидетель-очевидец.

F

F *n Mus* фа (*indecl*).

fable *n* басня; *fig* выдумка, небылица.

fabric *n* (*cloth*) ткань; **woollen ~s** шерстяные ткани; (*of buildings*) **repairs to the ~ of a building** ремонт здания.

fabricate *vt* (*a document*, *story*) фабриковать (с-); (*a document*) поддел|ывать (-ать); **a ~d will** поддельное завещание.

fabrication *n* фабрикация, фальшивка.

fabulous *adj* легендарный; **~ wealth** неслыханное/сказочное богатство; *CQ* **a ~ dress** потрясающее платье.

façade *n Archit and fig* фаса́д.

face *n* **1** лицо́; *CQ pejor or joc* физионо́мия, ро́жа; **they met/were sitting ~ to ~** они́ столкну́лись лицо́м к лицу́, они́ сиде́ли напро́тив друг дру́га; **he lay ~ down/up** он лежа́л ничко́м (*adv*)/на спине́; **he fell on his ~** он упа́л ничко́м/плашмя́ (*advs*); **he looked me in the ~** он посмотре́л мне в лицо́; **the rain was blowing in our ~s** дождь хлеста́л нам в лицо́ (*sing*); **he told it me to my ~** он сказа́л мне э́то в лицо́; **to make a ~/~s** стро́ить грима́су, ко́рчить ро́жи; **he won't dare show his ~ here** он не посме́ет здесь показа́ться; **his ~ fell** у него́ вы́тянулось лицо́; **I could hardly keep a straight ~** я едва́ уде́рживался от сме́ха

2 (*of cloth, coin, medal, cards*) лицева́я сторона́; (*of a building*) фаса́д; (*of clock, instrument*) цифербла́т; (*in mining*) пло́скость забо́я; **lay the material ~ down/up on the table** положи́те ткань на стол лицево́й стороно́й вниз *or* кни́зу/кве́рху; **to lay a card ~ down/up** положи́ть ка́рту руба́шкой/лицево́й стороно́й вверх

3 *fig uses*: **he will only laugh in your ~** он рассмеётся вам в лицо́; **on the ~ of it** на пе́рвый взгляд; **in the ~ of danger** пе́ред лицо́м опа́сности; **in the ~ of overwhelming odds/of strong opposition** несмотря́ на неимове́рные тру́дности/си́льное сопротивле́ние; **to have the ~ to** име́ть на́глость + *inf*; **he lost ~ when the painting proved to be a forgery** его́ авторите́т си́льно пошатну́лся, когда́ вы́яснилось, что карти́на подде́льная; **the teacher lost ~ when the professor corrected him in front of the students** преподава́тель почу́вствовал себя́ уни́женным, когда́ профе́ссор попра́вил его́ в прису́тствии студе́нтов; **he lost the race, but to save his ~ said he'd hurt his leg** он проигра́л забе́г, но, что́бы спасти́ своё реноме́, сказа́л, что повреди́л но́гу; **he has set his ~ against the proposal** он реши́тельно настро́ен про́тив э́того предложе́ния; **she was very embarrassed but put a brave ~ on it** она́ была́ о́чень смущена́, но де́лала вид, что ничего́ не случи́лось.

face *vti* **1** (*of people, animals*) стоя́ть (*stand*) /сиде́ть (*sit*) лицо́м к + *D* (*impfs*); **they stood facing each other/the light** они́ стоя́ли лицо́м друг к дру́гу/лицо́м к све́ту; **to sit facing the engine** сиде́ть по хо́ду по́езда; **the house/window ~s (towards) the south** дом фаса́дом/окно́ выхо́дит на юг; **the school ~s the theatre** шко́ла нахо́дится напро́тив теа́тра; **see the illustration facing page 5** смотри́ рису́нок к страни́це пять, *abbr* см. рис. к стр. 5

2 (*border with material*): **to ~ a uniform with braid** отде́л|ывать мунди́р шнуро́м (-ать); **to ~ a building with marble** облиц|о́вывать зда́ние мра́мором (-ева́ть)

3 *fig uses*: **he couldn't ~ the disgrace/the thought of parting/another sausage** он не мог вы́нести позо́ра, мысль о расстава́нии терза́ла его́, соси́ски (*pl*) ему́ осточерте́ли; **you'll have to ~ the consequences/up to the facts** вам придётся отвеча́ть за после́дствия/ смотре́ть в лицо́ фа́ктам; **he ~d the situation bravely** он не отступи́л пе́ред тру́дностями; **she won't ~ the fact that ...** она́ не хо́чет призна́ть, что...; **let's ~ it, we haven't the money for a car** согласи́сь, что у нас нет де́нег на маши́ну; **the question facing us** вопро́с, стоя́щий пе́ред на́ми; **when ~d with the evidence/the witnesses he confessed** под давле́нием фа́ктов (*pl*)/по́сле о́чной ста́вки со свиде́телями он призна́лся; **it's time you ~d up to your responsibilities** пора́ бы тебе́ серьёзнее отнести́сь к свои́м обя́занностям; **he was ~d with the threat of dismissal** ему́ грози́ло увольне́ние.

face cloth, face flannel *n* салфе́тка/рукави́чка для обтира́ния лица́ и те́ла.

faceless *adj fig* безли́кий.

face lift *n* пласти́ческая опера́ция лица́; *fig CQ* **our flat has had a ~** мы ко́е-что́ подремонти́ровали в кварти́ре, так, ничего́ осо́бенного—космети́ческий ремо́нт.

facet *n* (*of jewel*) грань; *fig* аспе́кт.

facetious *adj* шутли́вый; **he's in a ~ mood** он настро́ен на шутли́вый лад.

face value *n* (*of money*) номина́льная сто́имость; *fig* **I took his story at its ~** я при́нял его́ расска́з за чи́стую моне́ту.

facial *adj* лицево́й; **~ burns/massage** лицевы́е ожо́ги *or* ожо́ги лица́, масса́ж лица́.

facile *adj*: **a ~ style** бо́йкое перо́; **he's a ~ writer** у него́ бо́йкое перо́; **she has a ~ disposition** у неё мя́гкий/покла́дистый хара́ктер; **he's a ~ liar** он беззасте́нчивый лгун.

facilitate *vt* облегч|а́ть (-и́ть); спосо́бствовать + *D* (*impf*); **in order to ~ the enquiry** что́бы облегчи́ть по́иски (*pl*).

facility *n* **1** (*talent*) спосо́бность (*often pl*); (*ease*) лёгкость; **he has a ~ for languages** у него́ спосо́бности к языка́м; **he writes with ~** он пи́шет легко́

2 *pl* (**facilities**) (*conditions*) усло́вия; **the facilities for research here are excellent** здесь превосхо́дные усло́вия для нау́чных иссле́дований (*pl*).

facing *n Sew* отде́лка; (*on buildings*) облицо́вка, отде́лка.

facing *prep* лицо́м к + *D*; напро́тив + *G*.

facsimile *n* факси́миле (*indecl*).

fact *n* факт; *pl* (**~s**) да́нные; **the ~s are as follows** фа́кты таковы́; **in ~, as a matter of ~** факти́чески *or* на са́мом де́ле; **the ~ is that...** де́ло в том, что..., факт тот, что...; **the ~ that...** тот факт, что...; **is it a ~ that ..?** (э́то) пра́вда, что ..?; **I know for a ~ that...** я то́чно зна́ю,/я зна́ю наверняка́, что...; **the ~s suggest that...** да́нные свиде́тельствуют о том, что...; *Law* **before/after the ~** до/по́сле собы́тий (*pl*).

fact-finding *adj*: **a ~ commission** коми́ссия по рассле́дованию.

faction *n* (*group*) фра́кция; (*discord*) разногла́сия, ра́спри (*usu pls*).

factitious *adj* иску́сственный.

factor *n* **1** фа́ктор; *Math* мно́житель (*m*); **the determining/human ~** реша́ющий/челове́ческий фа́ктор; **the safety ~** фа́ктор безопа́сности

2 (*agent*) аге́нт.

factory *n* заво́д; фа́брика; *attr* заводско́й; фабри́чный.

factotum *n* (*often joc*): **he's our general ~** он у нас ма́стер на все ру́ки.

factual *adj* факти́ческий; **his account was strictly ~** его́ изложе́ние собы́тий бы́ло осно́вано то́лько на фа́ктах; **a ~ error** оши́бка в да́нных.

faculty *n* **1** (*aptitude*) спосо́бность (*often pl*); **a ~ for mathematics** спосо́бности к матема́тике (*sing*)

2 (*powers, mental or physical*): **the ~ of hearing/sight** слух, зре́ние; **the old man is still in full possession of his faculties** стари́к всё ещё о́чень бодр

3 *Univ* факульте́т; **the ~ of law** юриди́ческий факульте́т; (*US: teaching staff of a university*) профе́ссорско-преподава́тельский соста́в университе́та; *attr* факульте́тский.

fad *n* причу́да; *CQ* пу́нктик.

faddy *adj*: **he's ~ about his food** он разбо́рчив в еде́.

fade *vi* (*of colours*) линя́ть (по-); (*of plants*) вя́нуть (за-), увя|да́ть (-́нуть), *both also fig*; *Cine* постепе́нно расплы|ва́ться (-́ться); **this material is guaranteed not to ~** э́та ткань не линя́ет; **daylight was fading** смерка́лось (*impers*), день угаса́л; *fig*: **she gradually ~d away** она́ ме́дленно угаса́ла; **the coast ~d from sight** бе́рег постепе́нно исчеза́л из ви́да/удаля́лся; **the music ~d away into the distance** му́зыка затиха́ла вдали́.

faded *adj*: **~ colours/flowers** блёклые кра́ски, поблёкшие цветы́; **~ curtains** вы́цветшие занаве́ски.

fag *n* **1** *CQ* (*tiresome job*): **what a ~!** кака́я ну́дная рабо́та!

2 *sl* сигаре́та; **have you got a ~?** у тебя́ есть закури́ть?

fag end *n* (*of cigarette*) оку́рок; (*remnant*) оста́ток.

fagged *adj CQ*: **I'm ~ out** я вы́дохся.

fail *n*: **without ~** обяза́тельно, непреме́нно (*advs*).

fail *vti vt* **1** (*in exams*): **to ~ smb in an examination** провали́ть кого́-л на экза́мене (*usu pf*); **to ~ an examination** *see vi* **1**

2 (*let down*): **don't ~ me** не подведи́ меня́; **his heart ~ed him** му́жество поки́нуло его́; **words ~ me** у меня́ нет слов

vi **1** (*not succeed*) прова́л|иваться *absolutely or* на + *P or* по + *D* (-и́ться); (*of exams*) не сдать + *A or* на + *A* (*only in pf*); **he ~ed (in) his examination/in mathematics** он прова-ли́лся на экза́мене/по матема́тике (*sing*), он не сдал экза́мен/матема́тику; **she ~ed (in) her driving test** она́ не сдала́ на (води́тельские) права́ (*pl*); **his attempt ~ed, he ~ed in his attempt** его́ попы́тка не удала́сь; **they ~ed to arrive in time** им не удало́сь (*impers*) прие́хать во́время; **the bank/business ~ed** банк ло́пнул, фи́рма обанкро́тилась/разори́лась

2 (*give out, break down*) не хват|а́ть *used impers* + *G* (-и́ть); **the water supply has ~ed** не хвати́ло воды́; **the potato crop has ~ed this year** в э́том году́ карто́фель (*collect*) не уроди́лся; **his sight is ~ing** его́ зре́ние слабе́ет; **the wind ~ed** не́ было ве́тра; **the old man is ~ing** стари́к сдаёт; **the engine ~ed** мото́р отказа́л/*CQ* сдал; **the electricity ~ed** свет пога́с, электри́чество отключи́ли

3 (*neglect*): **don't ~ to let me know** непреме́нно да́йте мне знать; **he ~ed to remind me about it** он не напо́мнил мне об э́том

4 (*be unable*): **I ~ to understand how...** я не могу́ поня́ть, как...; **they could hardly ~ to see each other** они́ не могли́ не встре́титься.

failing *n* недоста́ток; **for all his ~s I still like him** я люблю́ его́ со все́ми его́ недоста́тками.

failing *prep*: **~ garlic, use onions** е́сли нет чеснока́, возьми́те лук; **~ him invite his brother** е́сли он не смо́жет, пригласи́те его́ бра́та.

failure *n* **1** неуда́ча; (*in exam*) прова́л; **the expedition/play was a ~** экспеди́ция была́ неуда́чной, пье́са провали́лась; **the project ended in ~** прое́кт провали́лся; **I feel such a ~** я чу́вствую себя́ таки́м никчёмным челове́ком/неуда́чником

2 (*neglect, omission*): **~ to pay** неупла́та; **his ~ to appear roused suspicion** его́ отсу́тствие вы́звало подозре́ние; **his ~ to answer irritated the judge** его́ молча́ние раздража́ло судью́

3 (*non-performance*): **heart ~** остано́вка се́рдца; **engine ~** остано́вка дви́гателя; **a ~ of memory** прова́л в па́мяти; **there was an electricity ~ yesterday** вчера́ не́ было све́та/электри́чества

4 *Fin, Comm* разоре́ние, банкро́тство.

faint *n* о́бморок.

faint *adj* **1** (*physically*): **I was/felt ~ with the heat/with hunger** мне бы́ло пло́хо от жары́, я ослабе́л от го́лода

2 (*slight*) сла́бый; **a ~ sound** сла́бый звук; **a ~ resemblance** сла́бое схо́дство; **I haven't the ~est idea why he did it** я не име́ю ни мале́йшего поня́тия, почему́ он э́то сде́лал; **there's not/there's just the ~est chance of my coming** у меня́ нет никако́й возмо́жности прийти́, мо́жет быть я и смогу́ прийти́.

faint *vi* па́дать в о́бморок (упа́сть).

fainthearted *adj* малоду́шный.

faintly *adv* сла́бо; **she was breathing ~** она́ е́ле слы́шно дыша́ла; **he whispered ~**

он ти́хо-ти́хо прошепта́л; **he had a ~ familiar look** он мне отдалённо кого́-то напомина́л.

fair[1] *n* (*trade or village fair*) я́рмарка; **fun ~** аттракцио́ны (*pl*).

fair[2] *adj* **1** (*beautiful*) прекра́сный; **the ~ sex** прекра́сный пол; *fig* (*specious*) **~ promises** пусты́е обеща́ния

2 (*blond*) све́тлый; **~ hair** белоку́рые/све́тлые во́лосы; **a ~ skin** бе́лая ко́жа; **he/she is ~** он блонди́н, она́ блонди́нка

3: a ~ copy чистово́й экземпля́р, *CQ* чистови́к

4 (*just*) справедли́вый; (*honest*) че́стный; **the umpire was ~** судья́ был справедли́в; **to be ~, I should add that...** справедли́вости ра́ди я до́лжен доба́вить, что...; **by ~ means** че́стным путём (*sing*); **it was a ~ deal** э́то была́ че́стная сде́лка

5 (*middling*): **his work is ~** он непло́хо рабо́тает

6 (*quite large or quite good*): **there was a ~ number of spectators** бы́ло дово́льно мно́го зри́телей; **a ~ wage** прили́чная пла́та; **a ~ price** хоро́шая цена́; **he has a ~ chance of winning** у него́ есть серьёзные ша́нсы (*pl*) на побе́ду

7 (*of weather, etc.*) хоро́ший, я́сный, пого́жий; **~ weather** хоро́шая пого́да; **if it's ~ tomorrow** е́сли за́втра бу́дет я́сно/пого́жий день; (*on barometer*) **F.** я́сно.

fair[2] *adv* (*honestly*) че́стно; (*directly*) пря́мо; **to copy smth out ~** переписа́ть что-л на́бело/на́чисто; **to hit smb ~ and square on the chin** уда́рить кого́-л пря́мо в че́люсть.

fair-haired *adj* светловоло́сый, белоку́рый.

fairly *adv* **1** (*justly*) справедли́во, че́стно

2 (*quite*) дово́льно; **he's still ~ young** он ещё дово́льно мо́лод; *CQ* **I was ~ hopping with rage** я был про́сто вне себя́ от я́рости.

fairness *n* справедли́вость; **in all ~ (to him) I must say...** справедли́вости ра́ди, на́до сказа́ть, что (он)...

fairy *n* фе́я; *attr*: **~ tale** ска́зка.

faith *n* **1** ве́ра, *also Rel*; **I have great ~ in him/in this medicine** я в него́ *or* ему́ ве́рю, я о́чень ве́рю в э́то лека́рство; **I'm pinning my ~ on you** я полага́юсь на тебя́; **to keep ~** держа́ть сло́во

2 (*sincerity*): **I acted/spoke in all good ~** я и́скренне ве́рил в то, что де́лал, я э́то сказа́л без зло́го у́мысла; **he acted in bad ~** он де́йствовал вероло́мно/преда́тельски (*advs*).

faithful *adj* ве́рный; **a ~ friend/husband** ве́рный друг/муж; **a ~ account/portrait/translation** ве́рный отчёт/портре́т, то́чный перево́д.

faithfully *adv* ве́рно; че́стно; то́чно; **he ~ carried out instructions** он э́то вы́полнил то́чно по инстру́кции (*sing*); (*in letters*) **yours ~...** с уваже́нием...

fake *n* (*painting, document*) подде́лка; (*document*) фальши́вка; (*person*) притво́рщик; *attr* подде́льный, фальши́вый; сфабрико́ванный.

fake *vt* подде́л|ывать (-ать); фальсифици́ровать (*impf and pf*).

falcon *n* со́кол.

fall *n* **1** паде́ние; **a ~ from a tree** паде́ние с де́рева; **I had a nasty ~** я упа́л и расши́бся; **a heavy ~ of rain** си́льный дождь, ли́вень; **a ~ of snow** снегопа́д; **there was a two-foot ~ of snow yesterday** вчера́ вы́пал снег по коле́но; *fig* **he's riding for a ~** он пло́хо ко́нчит

2 (*decrease*): **a ~ in prices** паде́ние/сниже́ние цен; **a ~ in temperature** паде́ние/пониже́ние температу́ры; **a ~ in the water level of the lake** спад воды́ в о́зере

3 (*waterfall; usu pl*): **the Niagara Falls** Ниага́рский водопа́д (*sing*)

4 (*US: autumn*) (**the ~**) о́сень.

fall *vi* **1** па́дать (упа́сть) *and compounds*; **I fell downstairs/over the cliff/full length** я упа́л с ле́стницы/с обры́ва/плашмя́; **he fell from a window** он вы́валился из окна́; **the cloak fell from his shoulders** плащ спал с его́ плеч; **her hair ~s to her shoulders** во́лосы па́дают/спада́ют ей на пле́чи; **the leaves are already ~ing** ли́стья уже́ опада́ют; **his hat kept ~ing over his eyes** ша́пка всё вре́мя сполза́ла ему́ на глаза́; **the curtain fell** за́навес опусти́лся/упа́л; **the road ~s towards the lake** доро́га спуска́ется к о́зеру

2 (*of rain, etc.*): **rain fell/began to ~** шёл/пошёл дождь; **snow was ~ing/had ~en** па́дал *or* шёл/вы́пал снег; **darkness fell** стемне́ло (*impers*); **a mist fell over the valley** на доли́ну опусти́лся тума́н

3 (*in war*) пасть (*only in pf*); **to ~ in battle/by the sword** пасть в бою́/от меча́; **the town fell (to the enemy)** го́род пал, го́род сда́лся врагу́; *fig* **the government fell** прави́тельство па́ло

4 (*decrease*) (*of barometer, prices*) па́дать (упа́сть); **his voice fell** его́ го́лос упа́л; **the temperature fell** температу́ра упа́ла/спа́ла; **the river has ~en** вода́ в реке́ спа́ла; *fig*: **his spirits fell** он упа́л ду́хом; **he fell in my estimation** он упа́л в мои́х глаза́х; **production fell** произво́дство сни́зилось

5 (*+ predic phrase or + adj* = **become**) *often translated by pf verbs with prefix* за-: **to ~ silent/ ill** замолча́ть, заболе́ть (*pfs*); **to ~ lame** стать хромы́м; **this room will ~ vacant on Monday** э́та ко́мната освободи́тся в понеде́льник; **the rent ~s due on Tuesday** за кварти́ру на́до плати́ть во вто́рник

fall apart *vi* распа|да́ться (-́сться), разва́л|иваться (-и́ться)

fall back *vi Mil* отступ|а́ть (-и́ть); *fig* **we can always ~ back on the old car/the alternative plan/on Tom as a stand-in** мы всегда́ мо́жем воспо́льзоваться ста́рой маши́ной/прибе́гнуть к запасно́му вариа́нту, Том всегда́ мо́жет нас подмени́ть

fall behind *vi* отста|ва́ть (-́ть); **he fell behind the others/in his work/ with his payments**

он отставал от других/в работе, он опаздывал с платежами

fall down *vi* (*of people*) падать (упасть); (*of buildings*) рушиться (об-), рухнуть (*pf*), *also fig*; *fig* **that's where the plan/we fell down** вот почему этот план неудачен, вот на чём мы споткнулись

fall for *vi CQ*: **he fell for her** он влюбился в неё; **I told him it was a bargain and he fell for it (hook, line and sinker)** я сказал ему, что это выгодное дельце, и он клюнул

fall in *vi* **1** (*collapse*): **the walls of the old church fell in** стены старой церкви рухнули/обрушились; **the floor/the tunnel fell in** пол провалился, туннель обвалился; *fig*: **the lease ~s in in May** срок аренды истекает в мае; **I fell in with them at the theatre** я встретил их у театра; **they fell in with our proposal** они согласились с нашим предложением

2 *Mil* строиться

fall into *vi*: **the river ~s into the lake** река впадает в озеро; *fig*: **he fell into a rage/disgrace** он пришёл в ярость, он впал в немилость; **to ~ into bad habits** приобре|тать дурные привычки (-сти); **the book ~s into three parts** книга состоит из трёх частей

fall off *vi*: **he fell off the wall** он упал с забора; **the book fell off the table** книга упала со стола; **all the leaves have ~en off the oak tree** с дуба опали все листья; *fig*: **the number of students has ~en off this year** в этом году число/количество студентов уменьшилось; **his work has ~en off** он стал заметно хуже работать

fall on *vi* падать на + *A*; *Mil* (*attack*) напа|дать на + *A* (-сть); **he fall on his knees** он упал на колени; **the stress ~s on the first syllable** ударение падает на первый слог; *fig*: **suspicion/the lot fell on him** подозрение пало/жребий пал на него; **last year Xmas fell on a Tuesday** в прошлом году рождество пришлось на вторник

fall out *vi*: **he fell out of the boat** он упал с лодки; (*happen*) **it fell out that...** случилось так, что...; (*quarrel*) **we fell out over money** мы поссорились из-за денег

fall through *vi*: **the plan fell through** план провалился

fall to *vi*: **they fell to work/to eating** они принялись за работу/за еду; **it fell to me to...** мне пришлось + *inf*

fall under *vi*: **my pen fell under the table** моя ручка упала под стол; *fig*: **to ~ under suspicion** попасть под подозрение; **to ~ under smb's influence** подпасть под чьё-л влияние.

fallacious *adj*: **a ~ argument** ошибочный/ложный аргумент.

fallacy *n* (*error*) заблуждение; (*false reasoning*) ложный аргумент.

fallibility *n* ошибочность.

fallible *adj*: **all men are ~** людям свойственно ошибаться.

fallout *n*: **radioactive ~** радиоактивные осадки (*pl*).

fallow *n Agric* пар, пары, земля под паром; **to lie ~** быть под паром.

fallow deer *n* лань.

false *adj* **1** ложный; **a ~ alarm, ~ pride/modesty** ложная тревога/гордость/скромность; **the report proved ~** сообщение оказалось ложным; **to give a ~ impression** создать ложное впечатление; **to make a ~ move** сделать ложный шаг; **a ~ friend** неверный друг; *Law* **~ witness** (*person*) лжесвидетель; **to bear ~ witness** лжесвидетельствовать; *Mus* **a ~ note** фальшивая нота; *fig* **his speech struck a ~ note** его речь прозвучала фальшиво

2 (*artificial*): **~ teeth/pearls** искусственные зубы, поддельные жемчуга; (*counterfeit*) **~ coins** фальшивые монеты.

falsehood *n* (*lie*) ложь; (*falseness*) лживость.

falsetto *n*: **to sing ~** петь фальцетом.

falsify *vt* (*facts, text*) фальсифицировать (*impf and pf*); (*accounts*) поддел|ывать (-ать).

falter *vi* (*stumble in speech*) за|пинаться (-пнуться); (*hesitate*) замяться (*pf*); **he/his voice ~ed** он запнулся; **he spoke without ~ing** он говорил без запинки; **he ~ed when I asked him about it** он замялся, когда я спросил его об этом; **with ~ing steps he crossed the road** спотыкаясь, он кое-как перешёл дорогу.

fame *n* слава; известность.

famed *adj* знаменитый, известный; **he is ~ for his poetry/his heroism** он известный поэт, он прославился своими подвигами; **this district is ~ for its wines** эта местность славится/знаменита своими винами.

familiar *adj* **1** знакомый; (*usual*) привычный; **a ~ sight** знакомый/привычный вид; **his face seems ~** его лицо мне кажется знакомым; **these facts are ~ to every schoolboy** эти факты известны каждому школьнику

2: he is ~ with every path in the forest ему знакома каждая тропинка в лесу; **I'm not ~ with the latest discoveries in physics** я не знаком с последними открытиями в физике (*sing*); **to make oneself ~ with details** ознакомиться с подробностями

3 (*intimate*): **are you on ~ terms with him?** вы с ним в приятельских отношениях?; *pejor* фамильярный.

familiarity *n* осведомлённость, знание; *pejor* фамильярность; **his ~ with our history/with the Lake District surprised me** его знание нашей истории/Озёрного края удивило меня.

family *n* семья; *Bot, Zool* семейство; **how's the ~?** как (поживает) ваша семья/*CQ* ваше семейство?; **the whole ~ came** они приехали всей семьёй; **he's a man of good/from a peasant ~** он из хорошей семьи, он родился в крестьянской семье; **it runs in their ~** это у них в роду/наследственное; **he's just like one of the ~** он свой у нас в доме; **we are treating you as one of the ~** мы угощаем вас по-домашнему (*in respect of* *food*); *attr* семейный; (*domestic*) домашний; **the ~ circle** семейный/домашний круг; **a ~ likeness** семейное/фамильное сходство; **a ~ man/estate/tree** семейный человек, родовое имение, родословная; **~ name** (*surname*) фамилия; *CQ* **she's in the ~ way** она в положении.

famine *n* голод; *attr*: **~ years** голодные годы.

famished *adj*: **to be ~** изголодаться; *CQ* **I'm simply ~** я просто умираю с голоду.

famous *adj* знаменитый, известный; **a town ~ for its cathedrals** город, известный своими соборами; *CQ* **that's ~!** великолепно!

famously *adv CQ*: **they get on ~** они отлично ладят.

fan[1] *n* (*hand*) веер; *Tech* вентилятор.

fan[1] *vti vt*: **to ~ oneself** обмахиваться веером (*usu impf*)

vi: **to ~ out** раз|вёртываться веером (-вернуться).

fan[2] *n CQ* (*of people*) поклонник, поклонница; почитатель (*m*); (*of music*) любитель (*m*); *Sport* **a football ~** болельщик (футбола).

fanatic(al) *adj* фанатичный.

fan belt *n* ремень (*m*) вентилятора.

fancied *adj* воображаемый.

fanciful *adj* (*quaint*: *of ideas*, *designs*, *etc.*) причудливый; (*imaginative*: *of stories*, *etc.*) фантастичный.

fancy *n* **1** фантазия; (*whim*) прихоть, каприз, причуда; **it's just a passing ~** это просто очередной каприз; **he works as the ~ takes him** он работает, когда ему вздумается/заблагорассудится; **there was no footstep—it's just your ~** не было никаких шагов (*pl*)—тебе просто почудилось/показалось (*impers*)

2 (*liking*) вкус; **this wine is not to my ~** это вино мне не по вкусу; **the horse took my ~** эта лошадь буквально пленила меня; **the old lady took a ~ to him** он очаровал пожилую даму.

fancy *adj*: **~ patterns** замысловатые/причудливые узоры; **~ buttons** пуговицы причудливой формы; **~ cakes/prices** пирожные, фантастические цены; *CQ* **a ~ shirt** пижонская рубашка.

fancy *vt* **1** (*imagine*) вообра|жать (-зить); (*be inclined to think*) думать (*impf*); **he fancies himself to be Napoleon** он воображает себя Наполеоном; **I ~ he's already left** я думаю,/мне кажется, (что) он уже ушёл; **~ that!** представляешь?; **~ meeting you!** вот это встреча!

2 (*like*): **I don't ~ this car** эта машина мне не нравится; **the patient can eat whatever he fancies** больной может есть всё, что ему захочется; *CQ* **he fancies himself as a singer** он воображает себя певцом.

fancy dress *n* маскарадный/карнавальный костюм.

fancy-dress ball *n* маскарад.

fang *n* (*of dogs*, *etc.*) клык; (*of snakes*) ядовитый зуб.

fanlight *n* веерообразное окно (над дверью).

fanmail *n* письма от почитателей/поклонников.

fantastic *adj* фантастический, *also CQ*; *CQ* **the play was a ~ success** пьеса имела потрясающий/небывалый успех.

far *adj* дальний; далёкий; **at the ~ end of the hall** в дальнем конце зала; **~ countries** далёкие/дальние страны; **on the ~ bank of the river** на другом/на том берегу реки.

far *adv* **1** (*of place*) далеко; **how ~ is it to the town?—Not ~** далеко ли до города?—Недалеко; **~ beyond/~ from the town** вдали/далеко от города; **from ~ away** издалека; **~ away one can see the Alps** вдали видны Альпы; **~ above the clouds** высоко над облаками; **from ~ and near/wide** отовсюду

2 *fig uses* (*with verbs*): **how ~ have you got with your work?** много ли вы сделали?; **he will go ~** он далеко пойдёт; **the reforms didn't go ~ enough** эти реформы мало что изменили, это были куцые реформы; **this money will go ~ towards achieving our object** эти деньги очень помогут нам в достижении цели; **that's going too ~** ну, это уж слишком; **I'd go so ~ as to say that...** я бы даже сказал, что...; **the answer is not ~ to seek** за ответом недалеко ходить; **he's not ~ wrong** он не далёк от истины; **I ~ prefer white bread** я больше люблю белый хлеб

3 *fig uses* (*with advs and preps*): **we went as ~ as the bridge** мы дошли до моста; **as ~ as I know/I am concerned** насколько мне известно, что касается меня; **as ~ as that goes, I could do it myself** если на то пошло, я могу это сделать сам; **as ~ back as I remember** насколько я могу припомнить; **as ~ back as January** ещё в январе; **~ back in history** в далёком прошлом; **she is ~ from beautiful** она далеко не красавица; **~ from agreeing, he wouldn't even listen** он не только не согласился, но даже и слушать не захотел; **do you agree?—F. from it!** вы согласны?—Отнюдь нет!; **~ be it from me to criticize, but...** я отнюдь не собираюсь критиковать, но ...; **~ into the night** далеко за полночь, до глубокой ночи; **Christmas isn't ~ off** скоро рождество; **has he phoned?—Not so ~** он позвонил?—Нет ещё; **so ~ so good!** пока всё в порядке

4 (*with comparatives and superlatives*) гораздо, намного; **it's ~ quicker to go by London** гораздо быстрее поехать через Лондон; **that's ~ better** это гораздо/намного лучше.

faraway *adj* далёкий, дальний, отдалённый; *fig* (*dreamy*) **a ~ look** отсутствующий/рассеянный взгляд.

farce *n* фарс, *also fig*.

farcical *adj* нелепый.

fare *n* **1** (*money for journey*): **what's the ~?** ско́лько сто́ит прое́зд?/биле́т?; **the conductor collected our ~s** конду́ктор взял с нас за прое́зд; **I'll pay your ~** (*train*, *plane*) я оплачу́ ваш прое́зд, (*bus*, *etc.*) я за вас заплачу́

2 (*passenger in taxi*) пассажи́р

3 (*food*) стол, пи́ща; **bill of ~** меню́ (*indecl*); **at home we have very simple ~** у нас до́ма са́мая проста́я еда́; **the peasants have very plain ~** у крестья́н проста́я пи́ща.

fare *vi*: **how did you ~ in Paris?** как вы съе́здили в Пари́ж?; **he didn't ~ badly in the exam** он непло́хо сдал экза́мен.

farewell *n* проща́ние; **to bid ~ to smb** проща́ться с кем-л.

farewell *interj*: **~!** проща́й(те)!

far-fetched *adj*: **a ~ comparison/story** притя́нутое за́ уши сравне́ние, приду́манная исто́рия *or* небыли́ца.

farm *n* фе́рма; (*in SU*) (*state*) совхо́з, (*collective*) колхо́з; **fruit ~** плодо́во-я́годное хозя́йство.

farm *vti vt* (*till*) обраба́тывать (зе́млю) (*usu impf*); **he ~s 2,000 acres** он обраба́тывает две ты́сячи а́кров

vi (*be a farmer*) занима́ться се́льским хозя́йством (*usu impf*).

farmer *n* фе́рмер (*not in SU*).

farming *n* се́льское хозя́йство; (*arable*) земледе́лие; (*of stock*) животново́дство.

farmyard *n* двор фе́рмы.

far-reaching *adj*: **the consequences were ~** э́та исто́рия име́ла далеко́ иду́щие после́дствия.

far-seeing *adj* дальнови́дный.

far-sighted *adj* дальнозо́ркий; *fig* дальнови́дный.

farther *comp adj* [*only of distance*; *see also* **further**]: **on the ~ bank** на том/на да́льнем берегу́.

farther *comp adv* [*only of distance*; *see also* **further**] да́льше; **I can't go any ~** я да́льше не могу́ идти́.

farthest *see* **furthest.**

fascinate *vt* очаро́в|ывать, зачаро́в|ывать (*pfs* -а́ть); (*of a snake*) гипнотизи́ровать (за-); **she ~d him** она́ его́ очарова́ла; **he's simply ~d by ancient history** он до стра́сти увлечён дре́вней исто́рией; **he watched ~d** он смотре́л как зачаро́ванный/заворожённый.

fascinating *adj* (*usu of people*) очарова́тельный; **a ~ job/idea/book** увлека́тельная рабо́та, захва́тывающая иде́я/кни́га; **it's ~ to listen to him** его́ слу́шать необыча́йно интере́сно.

fascination *n* очарова́ние; **it has a strange ~ for me** в э́том есть для меня́ како́е-то осо́бое очарова́ние.

fashion *n* **1** (*manner*) о́браз; **in this ~** таки́м о́бразом; **I've repaired my bike after a ~** я ко́е-ка́к почини́л свой велосипе́д; **he did it in his own ~** он э́то сде́лал по-сво́ему; **he's behaving in a strange ~** он ка́к-то стра́нно ведёт себя́

2 (*vogue*) мо́да; **it's the latest ~** э́то после́дняя мо́да/после́дний крик мо́ды; **to dress in the latest ~** одева́ться по после́дней мо́де; **to be in/out of ~** быть (не) в мо́де; **to come into/go out of ~** входи́ть в мо́ду, выходи́ть из мо́ды; **to set the ~ for smth** ввести́ мо́ду на что-л.

fashionable *adj* мо́дный; (*trendy*) фешене́бельный.

fashion show *n* пока́з/демонстра́ция мод.

fast[1] *n Rel* пост; **to break a ~** разговля́ться; *attr*: **a ~ day** по́стный день.

fast[1] *vi* пости́ться (*impf*).

fast[2] *adj* **1** (*firm*) твёрдый; кре́пкий; **a hard and ~ rule/decision** твёрдое пра́вило/реше́ние; **a ~ grip** кре́пкая хва́тка; **to take (a) ~ hold on a rope** кре́пко ухвати́ться за верёвку; **to make a boat/rope ~** закрепи́ть ло́дку/верёвку

2 (*of colours*): **this material/dye is ~** э́та ткань/кра́ска не линя́ет.

fast[2] *adv* кре́пко; **to be ~ asleep** кре́пко спать; **the door was shut ~** дверь была́ пло́тно закры́та; **to stand ~** не отступа́ть; **to stick ~ in mud** застря́ть в грязи́.

fast[3] *adj* **1** (*quick*) бы́стрый, ско́рый; **a ~ train** ско́рый по́езд; **he's a ~ worker** он бы́стро рабо́тает; **now it's a ~ journey from London to Glasgow** тепе́рь от Ло́ндона до Гла́зго руко́й пода́ть; **my watch is 5 minutes ~** мои́ часы́ спеша́т на пять мину́т; *Photo* **a ~ film** чувстви́тельная (фото)плёнка; *CQ* **to pull a ~ one on smb** надува́ть кого́-л

2 (*dissipated*, *etc.*): **to live a ~ life** вести́ беспу́тную жизнь; **he's one of the ~ set** он гуля́ка.

fast[3] *adv* (*quickly*) бы́стро; ско́ро; **he runs ~** он бы́стро бе́гает; **how ~ can you type?** как бы́стро ты печа́таешь?; *CQ* **put on your coat and make it ~** надева́й пальто́, да побыстре́й/поживе́й.

fasten *vti vt* **1** (*by tying*) вяза́ть, свя́зывать (*pf for both* связа́ть) *and other compounds*; **to ~ two sacks together** связа́ть два мешка́; **to ~ one's shoe laces** завяза́ть шнурки́ (боти́нок); **to ~ (up) a parcel** перевяза́ть паке́т; **to ~ a rope to a tree** привяза́ть верёвку к де́реву

2 (*by nailing*) приби|ва́ть (-́ть), крепи́ть (*impf*), закреп|ля́ть (-и́ть) *and other compounds*; **to ~ a mirror to a cupboard door** приби́ть зе́ркало к две́рце шка́фа; **to ~ a door** (*by locking*) зап|ира́ть дверь (-ере́ть); **to ~ a window** (*with a catch*) закры|ва́ть окно́ на шпинга́лет/на крючо́к (-́ть)

3 (*of clothes*, *etc.*) за|стёгивать (-стегну́ть); **to ~ (up) a shirt/belt/skirt (with buttons/hooks and eyes/zip)** застегну́ть руба́шку/реме́нь/ю́бку (на пу́говицы/на крючки́/на мо́лнию); **~ your seat belts!** пристегни́те ремни́!

4 *fig uses*: **he ~ed his eyes on me** он уставился на меня́; **to ~ one's hopes on smb/smth** воз|лага́ть наде́жды на кого́-л/на что-л (-ложи́ть); *CQ* **they couldn't ~ the crime on him** ему́ не смогли́ приши́ть э́то де́ло

vi: **the door won't ~** дверь не запира́ется; **my dress ~s at the back** моё пла́тье застёгивается сза́ди; **he ~ed on (to) me** он привяза́лся ко мне; *fig* **to ~ on to an idea** ухвати́ться за иде́ю (*pf*).

fastener, fastening *n* (*for dress, necklace*) застёжка; (*paper clip*) скре́пка; (*for door, window*) шпингале́т.

fastidious *adj* разбо́рчивый, приверéдливый; **he's ~ about food** он разбо́рчив/привере́длив в еде́; **he's ~ in his dress/about cleanliness** он о́чень привере́длив в вопро́сах оде́жды, он поме́шан на чистоте́ *or* он чистоплю́й.

fat *n* жир; (*lard, suet*) са́ло; **to fry in deep ~** жа́рить в кипя́щем жи́ре; **he's inclined to run to ~** он скло́нен к полноте́: *fig* **now the ~ is in the fire!** ну, тепе́рь начнётся потéха!; *attr*: **~ content** содержа́ние жи́ра.

fat *adj* (*of person, animal*) жи́рный, то́лстый; *CQ* по́лный; (*excessively*) ту́чный; **a ~ woman** толсту́ха; **~ cheeks** жи́рные/то́лстые щёки; **~ cattle** отко́рмленный/упи́танный скот; **to grow/get/become ~** полне́ть/толсте́ть; **chocolate makes one ~** от шокола́да полне́ют; *fig*: **a ~ wallet** то́лстый бума́жник; **he has a ~ salary** у него́ хоро́шая зарпла́та; *CQ*: **a ~ lot of good that will do!** помо́жет э́то, ка́к же!; **a ~ lot you know about it!/you care!** мно́го ты в э́том понима́ешь *or* смы́слишь, о́чень тебя́ э́то волну́ет!

fatal *adj* фата́льный, рокової; **a ~ mistake** рокова́я оши́бка; (*ending in death*) смерте́льный; *CQ* **it would be ~ to mention it** и не ду́май об э́том говори́ть!

fatalistic *adj* фаталисти́ческий.

fatality *n*: **road fatalities** сме́ртность на доро́гах; **luckily there were no fatalities** к сча́стью, жертв не́ было.

fatally *adv* смерте́льно.

fate *n* судьба́; у́часть; **the Fates** (*Greek*) па́рки, (*Norse*) но́рны; **to decide smb's ~** реши́ть чью-л судьбу́/у́часть; **to leave smb to his ~** оста́вить кого́-л на произво́л судьбы́; **no one knows what ~ has in store for us** никто́ не зна́ет, что нам угото́вано судьбо́й; **to meet one's ~** поги́бнуть; *CQ* **as sure as ~** наверняка́.

fate *vt*: **he was ~d to die young** ему́ бы́ло напи́сано на роду́ умере́ть молоды́м; **they were not ~d to meet** им не суждено́ бы́ло встре́титься.

fateful *adj* рокової.

fathead *n CQ* болва́н, тупи́ца.

father *n* оте́ц; (*priest*) свяще́нник; **like ~ like son** я́блоко от я́блони недалеко́ па́дает; *Rel* **Our F.** (*prayer*) О́тче наш; *fig CQ* **we had the ~ and mother of a row** у нас был ужа́сный сканда́л.

father-in-law *n* (*husband's father*) свёкор; (*wife's father*) тесть (*m*).

fatherland *n* оте́чество, ро́дина.

fatherly *adj* оте́ческий.

fathom *n* морска́я са́жень [*now obs in SU where depth is measured in metres*].

fathom *vt fig* пости|га́ть (-́чь); **to ~ a mystery** пости́чь та́йну.

fatigue *n* уста́лость (*also of metal*); утомле́ние; *Mil, usu pl* хозя́йственная рабо́та (*sing*).

fatigue *vt* утом|ля́ть (-и́ть); **he's ~d** он утомлён, он уста́л.

fatiguing *adj* утоми́тельный.

fatten *vt* (*cattle, etc.*) от|ка́рмливать (-корми́ть).

fattening *adj*: **bread is very ~** от хле́ба полне́ют/толсте́ют.

fatty *adj* жи́рный; *Anat* **~ tissue** жирова́я ткань.

fatuous *adj* глу́пый; **a ~ smile** глу́пая улы́бка.

faucet *n* (*US*) (водопрово́дный) кран.

fault *n* **1** (*error*) оши́бка; (*in wider sense*) недоста́ток, изъя́н; (*mechanical*) неиспра́вность; **a ~ in a sum/an essay** оши́бка в вычисле́ниях (*pl*)/в сочине́нии; **I like him despite his ~s** несмотря́ на все его́ недоста́тки, он мне нра́вится; **a ~ in the electrical system** неиспра́вность в электропрово́дке; **she's generous to a ~** она́ щедра́ до абсу́рда; **to find ~ with smb/smth** придира́ться к кому́-л/к чему́-л; (*in tennis*): **~!** (*in service*) непра́вильная пода́ча!, (*foot fault*) за́ступ!

2 (*blame*) вина́; **whose ~ is it?** чья э́то вина́?, кто в э́том винова́т?; **he is at ~** он винова́т/не прав; **unless my memory is at ~** е́сли мне не изменя́ет па́мять.

fault *vt*: **I couldn't ~ him/his work** мне его́ не́ в чем бы́ло упрекну́ть, к его́ рабо́те нельзя́ бы́ло придра́ться.

faultless *adj* (*irreproachable*) безупре́чный; (*without error*) безоши́бочный.

faulty *adj* (*of work, machines*) с дефе́ктами, с бра́ком; (*of reasoning*) оши́бочный; **~ goods** брако́ванные това́ры.

faux pas *n*: **to make a ~** сде́лать ля́псус, сесть в гало́шу.

favour, (*US*) **favor** *n* **1** (*regard, approval*) расположе́ние; **he won ~ with my aunt** он суме́л расположи́ть к себе́ мою́ тётку; **the suggestion found ~ with the board** сове́т одо́брил э́то предложе́ние; **he's in/out of ~ with the boss** он в хоро́ших/плохи́х отноше́ниях (*pl*) с нача́льством; **to curry ~ with smb** заи́скивать пе́ред кем-л

2 (*act of kindness*) одолже́ние; любе́зность; **do me a ~** сде́лай мне одолже́ние; **do me a ~ and...** бу́дьте любе́зны + *imperative*; **he did it as a ~** он э́то сде́лал из любе́зности; **can I ask a ~ of you?** у меня́ к вам про́сьба

3 (*partiality*): **he showed ~ to applicants from his own town** он оказа́л предпочте́ние кандида́там из своего́ родно́го го́рода

4 (*support*): **he spoke in our ~** он вы́сказался в на́шу по́льзу; **to write a cheque in ~ of smb** вы́писать чек на чьё-л и́мя; **the wind is in our ~** ду́ет попу́тный ве́тер; **I'm in ~ of doing it now** я за то, что́бы сде́лать э́то сейча́с; **are you in ~ of the idea?** ты подде́рживаешь э́ту иде́ю?, ты за?

favour, *US* **favor** *vt* **1** (*approve*) одобр|я́ть (-ить); (*support*) подде́рж|ивать (-а́ть); (*bear out*) подтвер|жда́ть (-ди́ть); **he did not ~ the proposal** он не одо́брил/не поддержа́л э́то предложе́ние; **these facts ~ my theory** э́ти да́нные подтвержда́ют мою́ тео́рию

2 (*show preference*): **the teacher ~ed the clever pupils** учи́тель ока́зывал предпочте́ние спосо́бным ученика́м; **I ~ green wallpaper** мне бо́льше нра́вятся зелёные обо́и; **the weather ~ed our plans** пого́да благоприя́тствовала на́шим пла́нам; *Dipl* **most ~ed nation** наибо́лее благоприя́тствуемая на́ция

3 (*oblige*): (*in business letter*) **please ~ me with a prompt reply** соблаговоли́те отве́тить как мо́жно скоре́е; **she ~ed us with a song** она́ любе́зно спе́ла для нас; *iron* **he even ~ed us with a smile** он да́же соблаговоли́л нам улыбну́ться

4 (*resemble*): **he ~s his father** он похо́ж на отца́.

favourable, (*US*) **favorable** *adj* благоприя́тный; **a ~ answer/opportunity** благоприя́тный отве́т, удо́бный слу́чай; **a ~ wind** попу́тный ве́тер; **he was ~ to the idea** он благоскло́нно отнёсся к э́той иде́е.

favourite, (*US*) **favorite** *n* люби́мец; *Hist, Sport* фавори́т; *CQ pejor* люби́мчик.

favourite, (*US*) **favorite** *adj* люби́мый.

favouritism, (*US*) **favoritism** *n*: **a teacher should not show ~** у учи́теля не должно́ быть люби́мчиков.

fawn[1] *n* (*young deer*) молодо́й оле́нь (*m*); (*colour*) желтова́то-кори́чневый цвет.

fawn[2] *vi*: **the dog ~ed on him** соба́ка ласка́лась к нему́ (*impf*); *fig* (*of people*) **to ~ on smb** подли́з|ываться к кому́-л (-а́ться).

fear *n* страх; боя́знь; **~ of death/loneliness** страх сме́рти, боя́знь одино́чества; **~ of the unknown** страх пе́ред неизве́стным; **from ~** от стра́ха, со стра́ху; **she didn't jump for ~ of hurting herself** она́ не спры́гнула, боя́сь ушиби́ться; *CQ*: **he put the ~ of God into me** он нагна́л на меня́ стра́ху; **there's no ~ of his turning up/of rain today** сего́дня мо́жно не опаса́ться его́ прихо́да, сего́дня дождя́ наверняка́ не бу́дет; **are you going to the lecture?—No ~!** ты пойдёшь на э́ту ле́кцию?—Ни в ко́ем слу́чае!/Ни за что́!

fear *vti vt* боя́ться + *G*, страши́ться + *G* (*impfs*); **to ~ death** боя́ться/страши́ться сме́рти; **to ~ the worst** боя́ться ху́дшего; **there's nothing to ~** не́чего боя́ться; **I ~ (that) I am/may be late** бою́сь, что я опозда́л/, что я могу́ опозда́ть; **I ~ he may change his mind** бою́сь, что он мо́жет переду́мать; **since he's had a better offer, I ~ he may change his mind** он получи́л лу́чшее предложе́ние, и я бою́сь, как бы он не переду́мал; (*in reply*) **I ~ so** бою́сь, что да

vi боя́ться; **she ~ed to speak in his presence/for the children's safety** она́ боя́лась говори́ть в его́ прису́тствии/за дете́й.

fearful *adj* **1** (*timid*) боязли́вый

2 (*frightened*): **she is ~ of waking the baby** (*herself*) она́ бои́тся разбуди́ть ребёнка/, как бы не разбуди́ть ребёнка; **she is ~ lest someone should wake the baby** она́ бои́тся, как бы не разбуди́ли ребёнка

3 (*frightening*) стра́шный, ужа́сный, *also CQ*.

fearfully *adv* боязли́во; *CQ* стра́шно, ужа́сно; *CQ* **he's ~ pleased with himself** он стра́шно/ужа́сно дово́лен собо́й.

fearless *adj* бесстра́шный.

fearsome *adj* гро́зный, стра́шный.

feasible *adj* выполни́мый, реа́льный.

feast *n* банке́т; *Rel* церко́вный пра́здник; *Hist or joc* пир.

feast *vti vt* уго|ща́ть (-сти́ть), по́тчевать (по-); **to ~ one's friends** по́тчевать друзе́й

vi пирова́ть (*impf*).

feat *n* по́двиг.

feather *n* перо́; **as light as a ~** лёгкий как пёрышко; *fig*: **he's in fine ~** он в хоро́шем настрое́нии, он в весёлом расположе́нии ду́ха; **that's a ~ in his cap** он мо́жет э́тим горди́ться; **when I heard of his offer, you could have knocked me down with a ~** я был соверше́нно потрясён, услыха́в э́то его́ предложе́ние; **they're birds of a ~** они́ одного́ по́ля я́года.

feather *vt fig*: **to ~ one's nest** наби|ва́ть себе́ карма́н (-ть).

featherbrained *adj* ве́треный, пусто́й.

featherweight *n Sport* боксёр полулёгкого ве́са/*CQ* в «ве́се пера́».

feathery *adj* пе́ристый.

feature *n* **1** (*of face*) черта́, *also fig*; *fig* осо́бенность; **distinguishing ~s** (*as e. g. asked for on passport*) осо́бые приме́ты; *fig* **geographical ~s** географи́ческие осо́бенности; **a striking ~ of his character** порази́тельная черта́/осо́бенность его́ хара́ктера

2 (*in newspapers*) статья́, (*larger*) о́черк; **the paper made a special ~ of the Queen's visit** газе́та отвела́ визи́ту короле́вы це́лую поло́су; *attr*: *Cine* **a ~ film** худо́жественный фильм.

feature *vti vt Cine* пока́з|ывать (-а́ть); **the film ~s the battle of Britain** в фи́льме пока́зывается би́тва за А́нглию; **this film ~s Smoktunovsky as Hamlet** э́то фильм с уча́стием Смоктуно́вского в ро́ли Га́млета; (*in papers*) **the landing of the cosmonauts was ~d on the front page** пе́рвая страни́ца была́ вся посвящена́ возвраще́нию космона́втов на Зе́млю

vi (*in a story*) фигури́ровать (*impf*); (*in newspapers*) **the report of the match ~d in all the papers** сообще́ние об э́том ма́тче появи́лось во всех газе́тах.

feature writer *n* журнали́ст-очерки́ст.

February *n* февра́ль (*m*); *attr* февра́льский.

feckless *adj* нера́дивый.

federal *adj* федера́льный.

federation *n* федера́ция.

fee *n* пла́та; (*for lawyer, etc.*) гонора́р; **tuition ~s** пла́та (*sing*) за обуче́ние; (*subscription*) **entrance ~** вступи́тельный взнос.

feeble *adj* сла́бый; **to grow ~** ослабева́ть; *CQ* **a ~ joke** несмешна́я шу́тка.

feeble-minded *adj* слабоу́мный.

feed *n Agric* корм; фура́ж; *Tech* пита́ние; *CQ* **she gave the boys a good ~** она́ сы́тно накорми́ла ма́льчиков.

feed *vti* **1** корми́ть (на-, по-); **I've fed the cows/the children** я накорми́л коро́в, я покорми́л дете́й; **they fed us well at the hotel** в гости́нице нас хорошо́ корми́ли; **the pigs are fed on potatoes** свине́й ко́рмят карто́фелем (*collect*); **we fed our left-overs to the pigs** мы скорми́ли объе́дки сви́ньям; **the baby can't ~ himself yet** ребёнок ещё не мо́жет сам есть; **to ~ plants** под|ка́рмливать расте́ния (-корми́ть); *fig CQ* **I'm fed up with your complaints** я сыт по го́рло ва́шими жа́лобами

2 (*maintain*) корми́ть (про-); **he has a family of 7 to ~** он до́лжен корми́ть се́меро ртов; **there's land enough here to ~ 1,000 cattle** здесь хва́тит земли́, что́бы прокорми́ть ты́сячу голо́в скота́

3 *Tech*: **a pipe ~s oil into the engine** ма́сло подаётся че́рез тру́бку в мото́р; *fig*: **the lake is fed by underground springs** о́зеро пита́ется подзе́мными ключа́ми; **to ~ information into a computer** вводи́ть информа́цию в компью́тер; **to ~ a meter** опус|ка́ть моне́ту в счётчик (-ти́ть)

vi (*general*) пита́ться (*impf*); (*of people*) есть (съ-, по-); (*of animals*) корми́ться (*impf*); **in summer we ~ mostly on fruit** ле́том мы в основно́м пита́емся фру́ктами; **the cattle are ~ing in the meadows/on hay** скот пасётся на луга́х, скоту́ даю́т се́но; **have you fed yet?** вы уже́ поéли?; **the sparrow**/*fig* **he ~s out of her hand** она́ ко́рмит воробья́ с ладо́ни *or* воробе́й клюёт корм у неё с ладо́ни, он души́ в ней не ча́ет.

feed-back *n Tech* обра́тная связь.

feeding stuffs *n usu pl* корм (*collect*), корма́ (*pl*).

feel *n*: **cold to the ~** холо́дный на о́щупь; **you can tell it's silk by the ~** мо́жно определи́ть на о́щупь, что э́то шёлк; **I can't bear the ~ of nylon sheets** я не выношу́ нейло́новых просты́нь; **let me have a ~** дай мне потро́гать/пощу́пать; **his study has a homely ~** в его́ кабине́те всегда́ ую́тно по-дома́шнему; **to get the ~ of new surroundings/a new car** осва́иваться в но́вой среде́, осво́ить но́вую маши́ну.

feel *vti vt* **1** (*actively, by contact*) щу́пать (по-); (*touch*) тро́гать (по-); (*grope, palpate*) нащу́п|ывать (-ать); **the doctor felt my pulse/the swelling** врач пощу́пал мой пульс/нащу́пал о́пухоль; **~ how cold my hands are** потро́гай, каки́е у меня́ холо́дные ру́ки; **~ the weight of this box/if the water is warm enough yet** попро́буй, како́й тяжёлый я́щик, потро́гай, доста́точно ли нагре́лась вода́; *fig* **to ~ one's way** зонди́ровать по́чву (про-)

2 (*passively, by sensation*) чу́вствовать (по-); ощу|ща́ть (-ти́ть); (*experience*) испы́т|ывать (-а́ть); **I felt it getting hotter and hotter** я чу́вствовал, что стано́вится всё жа́рче (и жа́рче); **he is ~ing the side effects of the medicine** он ощуща́ет побо́чное де́йствие лека́рства; **I ~ the need of a holiday** мне ну́жно отдохну́ть; **I ~ no interest in this project** я не испы́тываю никако́го интере́са к э́тому прое́кту; **to ~ pity for smb** испы́тывать жа́лость к кому́-л; **he made his authority felt** он дал почу́вствовать свой авторите́т; **earthquake tremors were felt here too** здесь то́же чу́вствовались подзе́мные толчки́; **I ~ a stone in my shoe** у меня́ в боти́нок попа́л ка́мешек; **I can ~ something crawling up my leg** у меня́ по ноге́ кто́-то ползёт

3 (*be sensitive to, suffer from*) пережива́ть (*usu impf*); **he felt the insult deeply** он глубоко́ пережива́л оби́ду; **he felt her death keenly** он тяжело́ пережива́л её смерть; **I ~ the heat very much** я не выношу́ жары́; **to ~ the beauty of nature** чу́вствовать красоту́ приро́ды

4 (*think, believe*) чу́вствовать; счита́ть (*usu impf*); **I ~ he is speaking the truth** я чу́вствую, что он говори́т пра́вду; **I ~ the force of your arguments** я сознаю́ си́лу ва́ших до́водов; **I ~ we ought to accept the proposal** я счита́ю, что нам сле́дует приня́ть э́то предложе́ние; **I felt we wouldn't succeed** я предчу́вствовал, что нам э́то не уда́стся

vi **1**: **~ for** нащу́п|ывать (-ать); **he felt for the switch** он нащу́пал выключа́тель; **he felt in his pocket for the key/around for matches but couldn't find them** он нащу́пал ключ в карма́не, он поиска́л (везде́) спи́чки, но не нашёл

2 + *predic* (= *to be*) быть; чу́вствовать (*usu impf*); **how do you ~?** как вы себя́ чу́вствуете?; **to ~ out of sorts** (*physically*) чу́вствовать себя́ нева́жно; **I ~ guilty leaving her at home** я чу́вствую себя́ винова́тым, оставля́я её до́ма; **I ~ tired** я уста́л; **I ~ cold/hot** мне хо́лодно/жа́рко; **my hands ~ cold** у меня́ холо́дные ру́ки; **she felt sad** ей бы́ло гру́стно; **the room ~s warm** в ко́мнате тепло́; **the stones ~ hot** ка́мни на о́щупь горя́чие; **I know how it ~s to be hungry** я зна́ю, что тако́е го́лод; **I ~ sure that...** я уве́рен, что...; **I ~ strongly that...** я глубоко́ убеждён, что...

3 (*sympathize*): **I ~ for you** я вам сочу́вствую

4 *phrases*: **i) to feel like: do you ~ like a swim?** хо́чешь пойти́ искупа́ться?; **it ~s like silk** на о́щупь э́то похо́же на шёлк; **it ~s like rain** похо́же, что бу́дет дождь;

ii) to feel as if: I ~ as if I'm going to faint я чу́вствую, что вот-во́т упаду́ в о́бморок; **it felt as if the rain would never stop** каза́лось, что дождь никогда́ не ко́нчится; **iii): I don't feel equal (up) to going out today** я сего́дня не в состоя́нии вы́йти и́з дому.

feeler *n* (*of insect*) щу́пальце, у́сик, анте́нна; *fig* **to put out a ~** пусти́ть про́бный шар.

feeling *n* **1** ощуще́ние, чу́вство (*both used for sensation or for emotion*); **a ~ of cold/hunger** ощуще́ние хо́лода, чу́вство го́лода; **I've no ~ in my left arm** у меня́ онеме́ла ле́вая рука́; **a ~ of fear/pride/gratitude** чу́вство стра́ха/го́рдости/ благода́рности; **to speak with ~** говори́ть с чу́вством; **to appeal to ~ rather than reason** взыва́ть скоре́е к чу́вствам (*pl*), чем к рассу́дку; **~s ran high** стра́сти разгоре́лись; **he hurt my ~s** он заде́л/оби́дел меня́; **we've no hard ~s** мы не де́ржим оби́ды, мы не зата́или оби́ды

2 (*sensitivity*) чу́вство; **a ~ for languages** чу́вство языка́ (*sing*); **to play the violin with ~** игра́ть на скри́пке с чу́вством; **he has no ~s for anyone but himself** он не ду́мает ни о ком, кро́ме себя́

3 (*opinion*): **my ~ is that...** мне ка́жется, что...; **I had a ~ that...** у меня́ бы́ло предчу́вствие, что...; **what are your ~s on the matter?** что вы ду́маете по э́тому по́воду?; **the general ~ was that...** о́бщее мне́ние бы́ло, что..., все счита́ли/ду́мали, что...

feign *vt* притвор|я́ться + *I* (-и́ться); **he ~ed illness/indifference** он притвори́лся больны́м/равноду́шным.

feint *n Sport* ло́жный уда́р, финт; *Mil* ло́жная ата́ка.

feline *adj* коша́чий.

fell *vt* (*a tree*) руби́ть (с-), сруб|а́ть (-и́ть), вы|руба́ть (-́рубить); **he ~ed his assailant** он сбил проти́вника с ног.

fellow *n* **1** па́рень (*m*), *CQ* ма́лый; *pejor* тип; **he's a good ~** он хоро́ший па́рень, он сла́вный ма́лый; **poor ~!** бедня́га!; **my dear ~!** мой дорого́й!, голу́бчик!; **there's some ~ at the door asking to see you** како́й-то тип за две́рью хо́чет поговори́ть с тобо́й; **there's that journalist ~ again!** опя́ть э́тот журнали́ст!; **a ~ can't work all day** челове́к не мо́жет рабо́тать весь день; *attr*: **a ~ pupil** однокла́ссник, однока́шник; **a ~ worker** сотру́дник, колле́га; **~ countryman** соотéчественник (*compatriot*), земля́к (*from same district*)

2: I've got one glove but I can't find the ~ у меня́ есть одна́ перча́тка, а друго́й нет

3 (*member*) член; (*UK Univ*) **a ~ of a college** *approx* член-преподава́тель колле́джа; (*SU*) **a ~ of the Academy of Sciences** действи́тельный член Акаде́мии нау́к.

fellow feeling *n*: **he's so tactless—but I've rather a ~ for him** он иногда́ быва́ет беста́ктен, но я его́ понима́ю—я и сам тако́й.

fellowship *n* **1** (*comradeship*) това́рищество, содру́жество

2 (*of a society*: *in UK Univ*) чле́нство.

fellow traveller *n* попу́тчик, *also fig Polit.*

felony *n Law* уголо́вное преступле́ние.

felt *n* фетр; (*coarse*) во́йлок; *attr* фе́тровый; во́йлочный; **a ~ hat** фе́тровая шля́па; **~ slippers** во́йлочные ту́фли; **~ boots** ва́ленки.

female *n* же́нщина; *pejor low CQ* ба́ба; *Zool* са́мка.

female *adj* же́нский, же́нского по́ла; **a ~ insect** са́мка насеко́мого.

feminine *adj* (*female*) же́нский; (*womanly*) же́нственный.

feminist *n* фемини́ст, фемини́стка.

fence *n* **1** забо́р, и́згородь, огра́да; *fig* **to sit on the ~** занима́ть выжида́тельную пози́цию

2 *CQ* (*receiver of stolen goods*) укрыва́тель (*m*) кра́деного.

fence *vti vt* огор|а́живать (-оди́ть); **to ~ in a garden** огора́живать сад; **to ~ off a plot for a playground** отгороди́ть уча́сток под де́тскую площа́дку

vi Sport (*with foils*) фехтова́ть (*impf*); *fig* **he ~d and gave no direct reply** он увильну́л от прямо́го отве́та.

fencing *n* **1** *Agric* (*act*) огора́живание, огражде́ние; (*material*) материа́л для и́згороди

2 *Sport* фехтова́ние.

fend *vti vt*: **to ~ off a blow/an attack** пари́ровать уда́р (*impf and pf*), отра|жа́ть ата́ку (-зи́ть)

vi: **he ought to ~ for himself** он до́лжен сам уме́ть постоя́ть за себя́.

fender *n* (*fireside*) ками́нная решётка; *Naut* кра́нец; (*US*) *Aut* ба́мпер.

fennel *n* сла́дкий укро́п.

ferment *n* (*yeast, etc.*) заква́ска.

ferment *vi* броди́ть (*impf*).

fermentation *n* броже́ние, *also fig.*

fern *n* па́поротник.

ferocious *adj* свире́пый.

ferret *n* хорёк.

ferret *vi*: **to go ~ing** охо́титься с хорько́м (*impf*); *fig*: **he ~ed about in his pockets for some money** он поры́лся в карма́нах, ища́ де́ньги; **to ~ out a secret** вы́ведать секре́т (*only in pf*).

ferroconcrete *n* железобето́н.

ferry *n* (*place*) перево́з; (*boat*) паро́м; **a roll-on-roll-off ~** автомоби́льный паро́м; **we took a ~ over the Rhine** мы перепра́вились че́рез Рейн на паро́ме.

ferry *vt* пере|вози́ть (на паро́ме) (-везти́).

fertile *adj* (*of land*) плодоро́дный; (*of fruit, trees, etc.*) плодонося́щий; (*of people, animals*) плодови́тый, *also fig*; (*rich*) бога́тый, *also fig*; **a ~ writer/imagination** плодови́тый писа́тель, бога́тое воображе́ние.

fertility *n* (*of land*) плодоро́дие; (*of animals*) плодови́тость.

fertilize *vt* (*pollinate*) опыл|я́ть (-и́ть); (*with manure*) удобр|я́ть (-́ить).

fertilizer *n* удобре́ние; **artificial ~** минера́льное удобре́ние.

fervent, fervid *adjs* пы́лкий; горя́чий.

fester *vi* гнои́ться (за-).

festival *n* (*special day*) пра́здник, *also Rel*; *Mus*, *Theat* фестива́ль (*m*).

festive *adj* пра́здничный; **in ~ mood** в пра́здничном настрое́нии.

festivity *n* (*celebration*) пра́зднество, пра́зднование, пра́здник; (*of atmosphere*) весе́лье; **wedding festivities** сва́дьба (*sing*); **May Day festivities** пра́зднование (*sing*) дня Пе́рвого ма́я, пра́здник (*sing*) Пе́рвого ма́я; **we took part in the festivities** мы уча́ствовали в пра́зднествах.

fetch *vti vt* **1** (*bring smth in the hands*) при|носи́ть (-нести́), (*bring smb on foot*) при|води́ть (-вести́); (*bring smb or smth by car*) при|вози́ть (-везти́); (*go and fetch*) сходи́ть/съе́здить (*by car*) за + *I* (*pfs*); (*fetch on one's way*) за|ходи́ть/за|езжа́ть (*by car*) за + *I* (-йти́/-е́хать); **~ me my spectacles** принеси́ мне мои́ очки́; **go and ~ the doctor** сходи́те/съе́здите за врачо́м; **I'll (go and) ~ the bread** я схожу́ за хле́бом (= *from shop*), я принесу́ хлеб (= *from kitchen*); **we'll come and ~ you** мы зайдём/зае́дем за ва́ми; **I'll ~ the children from school (as I pass)** я зайду́/зае́ду за детьми́ в шко́лу, я возьму́/заберу́ дете́й из шко́лы по доро́ге; **I can (go and) ~ the children from school** я могу́ привести́ *or* привезти́ дете́й из шко́лы/сходи́ть *or* съе́здить за детьми́ в шко́лу

2 (*sell for money*): **the house ~ed a lot** они́ *or* мы вы́ручили/получи́ли за дом мно́го де́нег; *CQ* **this car won't ~ much** за э́ту маши́ну мно́го не даду́т

vi: **to ~ and carry for smb** быть у кого́-л на побегу́шках; *CQ* (*arrive*) **we travelled all round Greece and eventually ~ed up in Athens** мы объе́здили всю Гре́цию и вот, наконе́ц, мы в Афи́нах.

fetching *adj*: **a ~ hat/smile** чуде́сная шля́пка, ми́лая улы́бка; **she looks very ~ in that dress** она́ обворожи́тельна/о́чень мила́ в э́том пла́тье.

fettle *n*: **in fine ~** в прекра́сном настрое́нии (*of mood*), в хоро́шем состоя́нии, в хоро́шей фо́рме (*physically*).

feud *n*: **a family ~** (*domestic*) семе́йные ссо́ры (*pl*), (*over generations*) насле́дственная вражда́.

feudal *adj* феода́льный.

fever *n* (*high temperature*) жар; (*disease*) лихора́дка; **he has a high ~** у него́ си́льный жар; **yellow/rheumatic ~** жёлтая/ревмати́ческая лихора́дка; **brain/typhoid ~** воспале́ние мо́зга, брюшно́й тиф; *fig* **in a ~ of excitement/activity** в си́льном возбужде́нии, в состоя́нии лихора́дочной де́ятельности.

fevered *adj*: **he's ~** у него́ высо́кая температу́ра; **a ~ brow** горя́чий лоб; *fig* **a ~ imagination** лихора́дочное воображе́ние.

feverish *adj Med and fig* лихора́дочный; **he's ~** его́ лихора́дит (*impers*).

few *pron and adj* немно́гие; ма́ло + *G*; **a ~, some ~** не́сколько/немно́го + *G*; **a good ~, not a ~, quite a ~** дово́льно мно́го + *G*; **every ~ days** ка́ждые два-три дня; **there are very ~ of us** нас о́чень ма́ло; **only a ~ of us have been in Sweden** то́лько не́которые из нас (по)быва́ли в Шве́ции; **one of his ~ pleasures is smoking** куре́ние—одно́ из немно́гих его́ удово́льствий; **for the last ~ months** за после́дние не́сколько ме́сяцев; **such occasions are ~ and far between** таки́е слу́чаи о́чень редки́.

fewer *adj comp* ме́ньше + *G*; **I saw no ~ than 20 eagles** я ви́дел не ме́ньше двух деся́тков орло́в; **the ~ the better** чем ме́ньше, тем лу́чше.

fiancé *n* жени́х.

fiancée *n* неве́ста.

fiasco *n* прова́л, фиа́ско (*indecl*).

fib *n CQ* вы́думка, враньё; **to tell ~s** привира́ть.

fibre, (*US*) **fiber** *n* волокно́; нить; *fig* **a man of strong moral ~** челове́к высо́ких мора́льных при́нципов.

fibre-glass, (*US*) **fiber-glass** *n* стекловолокно́, стеклова́та; *attr*: **a ~ dinghy** ло́дка из стекловолокна́.

fickle *adj* переме́нчивый; **a ~ character/friend** переме́нчивый хара́ктер, ненадёжный друг.

fiction *n* (*invention*) вы́думка, вы́мысел; фи́кция; *Lit* беллетри́стика, худо́жественная литерату́ра; **to distinguish fact from ~** отлича́ть реа́льность от вы́мысла.

fictitious *adj* вы́думанный, вы́мышленный.

fiddle *n* **1** *Mus CQ* скри́пка

2 *CQ*: **they are engaged on some ~** они́ за́няты каки́ми-то (де́нежными) махина́циями; **a tax ~** махина́ция с нало́гами.

fiddle *vti vt CQ*: **to ~ the accounts** подде́л|ывать счета́ (-ать); **I ~d things so as to be free today** я всё так устро́ил, что́бы быть сего́дня свобо́дным

vi **1** игра́ть на скри́пке (*impf*)

2 *CQ*: **he was fiddling with his motorbike/with the knobs** он вози́лся со свои́м мотоци́клом/с кно́пками; **who's been fiddling with my papers?** кто ры́лся/копа́лся в мои́х бума́гах?

fiddler *n* **1** *Mus CQ* скрипа́ч

2 *CQ* (*cheat*) моше́нник.

fiddling *adj*: **it's a ~ little job** э́то кропотли́вая рабо́та (*tricky*), э́то пустяко́вое де́ло (*futile*).

fidelity *n* ве́рность; **~ to one's friends** ве́рность друзья́м.

fidget *n* (*person*) непосе́да (*m and f*); *pl* **he's got the ~s** он всё вре́мя ве́ртится.

fidget *vi* верте́ться, ёрзать, (*with smth*) теребить (*impfs*); **don't ~!** не верти́сь!, не ёрзай!; **she never stopped ~ing with her pencil/scarf** она́ всё вре́мя верте́ла каранда́ш в рука́х/тереби́ла шарф.

fidgety *adj* вертля́вый.

field *n* **1** по́ле; (*meadow*) луг; *Phys* по́ле; **a ~ of rye** по́ле ржи; **in the ~s** в по́ле (*sing*), на поля́х, на луга́х; ~ **of battle** по́ле сраже́ния/би́твы; **magnetic** ~ магни́тное по́ле; ~ **of vision** по́ле зре́ния; *Sport*: **playing** ~ спорти́вная площа́дка; **the** ~ (*players*) игроки́ (*pl*); **is there a strong** ~**?** мно́го ли у нас сопе́рников? (*Sport*)/конкуре́нтов? (*Comm or for a job*)

2 *fig* (*sphere*) о́бласть; (*of specialization*) специа́льность; **he's a specialist in his** ~ он специали́ст в свое́й о́бласти; **what's your** ~**?** кака́я у вас специа́льность?

field glasses *npl* бино́кль (*m*, *sing*).

field hospital *n* полево́й го́спиталь (*m*), лазаре́т.

field mouse *n* полева́я мышь, полёвка.

fieldwork *n Archaeol*, *Geol*, *etc.* рабо́та в по́ле, полева́я съёмка.

fiend *n* чёрт; (*cruel person*) злоде́й; *CQ* (*of child*) чертёнок; *fig* **he's a fresh air** ~ он пря́мо поме́шан на све́жем во́здухе.

fiendish *adj* дья́вольский, черто́вский, *usu CQ*; **he took a** ~ **delight in teasing his sister** он получа́л осо́бое удово́льствие, дразня́ сестру́; **I had a** ~ **time getting him to agree** мне бы́ло черто́вски тру́дно переубеди́ть его́.

fierce *adj* свире́пый; лю́тый; **a** ~ **look** свире́пый взгляд; **a** ~ **foe/frost/wind** лю́тый враг/моро́з, си́льный ве́тер; **a** ~ **dog/struggle,** ~ **hatred** зла́я соба́ка, ожесточённая борьба́, лю́тая не́нависть.

fifteen *num* пятна́дцать [*see* **eleven**].

fifteenth *adj* пятна́дцатый.

fifth *adj* пя́тый; *as n*: **a** ~ одна́ пя́тая; **two** ~**s** две пя́тых.

fiftieth *adj* пятидеся́тый.

fifty *num* пятьдеся́т (*G*, *D*, *P* пяти́десяти, *I* пятью́десятью); **£50** пятьдеся́т фу́нтов; *as n*: **the fifties** (*of a century*) пятидеся́тые го́ды; *fig* **let's go** ~-~ (*in paying bill*) дава́й запла́тим попола́м.

fig *n* инжи́р (*collect*), фи́га; **green** ~**s** све́жий инжи́р; *fig CQ* **I don't care a** ~ **about it** мне наплева́ть на э́то; *attr*: ~ **tree** фи́говое де́рево, инжи́р; ~ **leaf** фи́говый листо́к.

fight *n* (*between persons*) дра́ка, (*scuffle*) сва́лка; *Mil* сраже́ние, (*skirmish*) схва́тка; (*boxing*) бой; (*quarrel*) ссо́ра; (*argument*) спор; *fig* борьба́; **a street** ~ у́личная дра́ка; **a free** ~ о́бщая сва́лка; **a cock** ~ петуши́ный бой; **the** ~ **against disease/for freedom** борьба́ с боле́знью/за свобо́ду; (*fighting spirit*) **he still has plenty of** ~ **in him** он ещё по́лон боево́го задо́ра.

fight *vti vt* **1**: *Mil* **to** ~ **a battle/a war against** сра|жа́ться с + *I* (-зи́ться), воева́ть с + *I* (*impf*); **to** ~ **off an attack** отби|ва́ть ата́ку (´-ть)

2 (*of individuals*, *animals*) дра́ться с + *I* (по-); **we fought it out** мы дра́лись/би́лись/боро́лись до после́днего, *also fig*

3 *fig* боро́ться с + *I* (*impf*); **to** ~ **a fire/a proposal** боро́ться с огнём/про́тив (приня́тия) предложе́ния; **to** ~ **back tears** сде́рж|ивать слёзы (-а́ть); **to** ~ **off sleep/a cold** боро́ться со сном/с просту́дой; ~ **it out between you** вы́ясните э́то ме́жду собо́й; **to** ~ **one's way through a crowd** проби|ва́ться сквозь толпу́ (´-ться); *Law* **to** ~ **a case** защища́ть де́ло в суде́ (*only in impf*)

vi **1** (*general*) би́ться (*impf*); (*in wars, etc.*) сра|жа́ться с + *I* (-зи́ться), воева́ть с + *I* (*impf*); **Great Britain fought with Russia against Napoleon** Великобрита́ния и Росси́я воева́ли вме́сте про́тив Наполео́на; **did you** ~ **in the war?** вы бы́ли на войне́?, вы воева́ли?; **he went down** ~**ing** он поги́б, но не сда́лся

2 (*of individuals*, *animals*) дра́ться (по-); **two dogs were** ~**ing over a bone** две соба́ки дра́лись из-за ко́сти; **to** ~ **for one's life** боро́ться за жизнь

3 *fig* боро́ться с + *I* (*impf*); **to** ~ **against temptation** боро́ться с искуше́нием; *CQ* **there was such a crowd at the airport we had to** ~ **for our baggage** в аэропорту́ бы́ло так мно́го наро́да, что за багажо́м была́ про́сто настоя́щая сва́лка.

fighter *n* (*warrior*) боец, во́ин; *fig* боре́ц; (*boxing*) боксёр; ~ (**plane**) (самолёт-)истреби́тель; **that dog is a** ~ э́то драчли́вая/зади́ристая соба́ка.

fighter pilot *n* лётчик-истреби́тель (*m*).

fighting *n Mil* бой, сраже́ние, (*skirmish*) схва́тка; ~ **started on the border** завяза́лся бой на грани́це; **there was heavy** ~ **in the town** в го́роде шли тяжёлые бои́ (*pl*); **street** ~ у́личная дра́ка; *attr*: ~ **spirit** боево́й дух; *fig CQ* **he's** ~ **fit** он в хоро́шей фо́рме.

figment *n*: **a** ~ **of the imagination** плод воображе́ния.

figurative *adj Ling* перено́сный; (*metaphorical*) фигура́льный, метафори́ческий; **in a** ~ **sense** в перено́сном смы́сле.

figure *n* **1** *Math* ци́фра, число́; (*sum*) су́мма; **in round** ~**s** в кру́глых ци́фрах; **double** ~**s** двузна́чные чи́сла; **I'm no good at** ~**s** я слаб в арифме́тике; **he named a high** ~ он назва́л большу́ю су́мму

2 (*Geom*, *in skating*, *dancing*) фигу́ра; *attr*: ~ **skating** фигу́рное ката́ние

3 (*diagram*) рису́нок; чертёж, фигу́ра; **see** ~ **2 on page 5** смотри́те рису́нок 2 на страни́це 5 (*abbr* см. рис. 2 на стр. 5)

4 (*human form*) фигу́ра; **she has a good** ~ у неё хоро́шая/стро́йная фигу́ра; **to keep/watch one's** ~ сохраня́ть фигу́ру, следи́ть за фигу́рой; **I saw a** ~ **in the dark** я уви́дел в темноте́ каку́ю-то фигу́ру; **he's a fine** ~ **of a man** он ви́дный мужчи́на

5 (*personage*) фигу́ра; ли́чность; **he cut a poor** ~ он явля́л собо́й жа́лкую фигу́ру; **he was an outstanding** ~ **of his time** он был выдаю́щимся де́ятелем своего́ вре́мени; **a** ~ **of fun** посме́шище

6: a ~ **of speech** ритори́ческая фигу́ра.

figure *vti vt* (*imagine*) представ|ля́ть себе́ (´-ить); (*US*: *think*) счита́ть, ду́мать, полага́ть (*only in impfs*); **that's what we** ~**d** мы так и ду́мали; **to** ~ **out expenses** подсчи́т|ывать расхóды (-áть); **I can't ~ it out** я не могý э́того поня́ть

vi (*appear*) фигури́ровать (*impf*); (*US*: *count on*) рассчи́тывать (*only in impf*); **his name ~s on the list** егó и́мя фигури́рует в спи́ске; **we ~d on your arriving early** мы рассчи́тывали, что вы придёте рáно.

figurehead *n Naut* фигýра на носý корабля́; *fig pejor* **he's only a ~** он не руководи́т, а тóлько чи́слится.

filament *n Elec* нить накáла.

file[1] *n* (*tool*) напи́льник.

file[1] *vt*, *also* **to ~ down** подпи́л|ивать, спи́л|ивать (*pfs* -и́ть); **to ~ one's nails** подпи́ливать нóгти.

file[2] *n* (*folder for papers*) пáпка; (*papers strung together*) подши́вка; **a loose-leaf ~** скоросшивáтель; **card-index ~** картотéка; (*in office*) **the ~s** архи́в (*sing*); **personal ~** досьé (*indecl*); **this bill isn't on the ~** э́того счёта нет в подши́вке; **we've put the correspondence on the ~s** мы подши́ли всю корреспондéнцию.

file[3] *n* колóнна; **to march in single ~** идти́ гуськóм, *Mil* идти́ колóнной по одномý; **in double ~** колóнной пó два; **the rank and ~** рядовóй состáв, *also fig*.

filial *adj* (*of a son*) сынóвний; (*of a daughter*) дочéрний.

filing *n* подши́вка; *attr*: **~ system/cabinet** систéма подши́вки и хранéния документóв, шкаф для хранéния документóв.

fill *n*: **to eat/drink one's ~** наéсться/напи́ться вдóволю *or* до отвáла; *fig CQ* **I've had my ~ of his lies** я сыт по гóрло егó враньём.

fill *vti vt* **1** наполн|я́ть (-́ить); *also translated by using appropriate verbs with prefix* на- *or* за-; **to ~ up** заполн|я́ть (-́ить); **smoke ~ed the room** кóмната напóлнилась ды́мом; **students ~ed the hall** студéнты запóлнили зал; **to ~ (in/up) one's time by reading** запóлнить врéмя чтéнием; **to ~ a bucket with water** напóлнить ведрó водóй, набрáть пóлное ведрó воды́; **~ the glasses** налéйте винó в бокáлы; **to ~ (in/up) a hole with sand** засы́пать я́му пескóм; **the lorry is ~ed with coal** грузови́к нагрýжен углём; **to ~ a tank/car with petrol** зали́ть/напóлнить бак бензи́ном, заправ|ля́ть маши́ну бензи́ном (-́ить); *Cook* **I ~ed the pies with meat** я начини́ла пирожки́ мя́сом

2 *various*: **to ~ a tooth** пломбировáть зуб (за-); **to ~ an exercise book** исписáть тетрáдь (*usu pf*); **we must ~ the post by December** нам нáдо найти́ человéка на э́то мéсто к декабрю́; **he ~s the post very well** он хорошó справля́ется со свои́ми обя́занностями (*pl*); **it ~s a need** э́то отвечáет потрéбностям (*pl*); **I was ~ed with admiration/despair** я был в пóлном восхищéнии/отчáянии

vi наполн|я́ться, заполн|я́ться (*pf* -́иться); **the hall quickly ~ed with people** зал бы́стро запóлнился нарóдом; **her eyes ~ed with tears** в её глазáх заблестéли слёзы; **the sails ~ed** парусá надýлись

fill in *vti vt*: **to ~ in a form/a questionnaire** запóлнить бланк/анкéту; **~ in your name, age and sex** напиши́те/впиши́те вáше и́мя, фами́лию, вóзраст, пол; **~ in the date** простáвьте числó; **I'll ~ in the details** я добáвлю подрóбности; **to ~ in cracks in a wall** заштукатýрить трéщины в стенé

vi: **I'm ~ing in for the director** я замещáю дирéктора (*only in impf*)

fill out *vi* толстéть (по-, рас-)

fill up *vti vt*: **to ~ smth up to the brim** напóлнить что-л до краёв (*pl*); *Aut* **~ her up** заливáй (бак) дóверху (*adv*)

vi Aut заправ|ля́ться (-́иться).

filling *n* (*material*: *in tooth*) плóмба; *Cook* начи́нка.

filling *adj*: **these pies are very ~** э́ти пирози́ óчень сы́тные.

filling station *n Aut* бензоколóнка, заправочная стáнция.

film *n* **1** (*thin skin*) плёнка; (*layer*) слой; **a ~ of oil** нефтянáя плёнка; **a thin ~ of dust** тóнкий слой пы́ли

2 *Photo* фотоплёнка, *CQ* плёнка; **to develop a (colour) ~** прояви́ть (цветнýю) плёнку

3 *Cine* (кино)фи́льм; **full-/short-length ~** полнометрáжный / короткометрáжный фильм; **a sound/silent/documentary ~** звуковóй/немóй/документáльный фильм; **that ~ is showing this week** э́тот фильм идёт на э́той недéле; **to make a ~ of a novel** экранизи́ровать ромáн; *attr* кино-; **~ director** кинорежиссёр; **~ studio** киностýдия; **~ actor/actress** киноактёр, киноактри́са.

film *vti vt* снимáть (фильм) (снять); **they ~ed the match** они́ сня́ли матч; **to ~ an opera** экранизи́ровать óперу (*impf and pf*)

vi **1**: **the story won't ~ well** э́тот расскáз не подхóдит для экранизáции; **they've been ~ing for a month now** они́ ужé мéсяц на съёмках

2 (*mist over*): **the mirror ~ed over** зéркало запотéло.

filming *n* (кино)съёмка.

filter *n* фильтр; **light/oil ~** светофи́льтр, мáсляный фильтр.

filter *vti* (*water*, *air*) фильтровáть(ся) (про-); (*coffee*) процé|живать(ся) (-ди́ть(ся)); *fig* **the news of the defeat ~ed through** дошли́ слýхи (*pl*) о поражéнии.

filter-tipped *adj*: **~ cigarettes** сигарéты с фи́льтром.

filth *n* грязь, гáдость, *both also fig*.

filthy *adj* гря́зный, *also fig*; *fig* гáдкий, мéрзкий; **~ stories** неприли́чные анекдóты; *CQ* **~ weather** мéрзкая погóда.

fin *n* плавни́к; **dorsal/tail ~** спиннóй/хвостовóй плавни́к; *pl* (**~s**) (*for swimming*) лáсты.

final *n Sport* финáл; (*newspaper*) послéдний вы́пуск газéты; *Univ* **to sit one's ~s** сдавáть выпускны́е экзáмены.

final *adj* **1** (*last*) после́дний; коне́чный; заключи́тельный; ~ **day of the competition** после́дний день ко́нкурса; **in the** ~ **analysis** в коне́чном счёте; ~ **chapter** заключи́тельная глава́

2 (*conclusive*) оконча́тельный; **and that's** ~ э́то оконча́тельно.

finale *n Mus* фина́л.

finalize *vt*: **the date has been** ~**d** да́та оконча́тельно определена́; **preparations have been** ~**d** приготовле́ния зако́нчились.

finally *adv* (*in the end*) в конце́ концо́в, наконе́ц; (*to conclude*) в заключе́ние; (*once and for all*) оконча́тельно.

finance *n* (*general*) фина́нсы (*no sing*); *pl* (~**s**) (*money*) дохо́ды; де́ньги; **Ministry of F.** министе́рство фина́нсов; **his** ~**s are in a bad way** у него́ ту́го с деньга́ми/*CQ joc* с фина́нсами; *attr* фина́нсовый.

finance *vt* финанси́ровать (*impf and pf*).

financial *adj* фина́нсовый.

find *n* нахо́дка; (*discovery*) откры́тие.

find *vti vt* **1** на|ходи́ть (-йти́); **the brooch was found on the beach** бро́шку нашли́/бро́шка нашла́сь на пля́же; ~ **the value of X** найди́те значе́ние X; **can you** ~ **your way out?** вы найдёте вы́ход?; **I don't know how it found its way into my bag** я не зна́ю, как э́то попа́ло в мою́ су́мку; **I ran to** ~ **a doctor** я побежа́л за врачо́м; **leave everything as you** ~ **it** оста́вь всё, как есть; **pines are found everywhere in the North** со́сны встреча́ются повсю́ду на се́вере

2 (*to find after search*) оты́ск|ивать (-а́ть) *and other compounds*; [**NB** *with these verbs impfs = try to find, pfs = to find after search*]: **in the end I found the book in the library** наконе́ц я отыска́л/нашёл э́ту кни́гу в библиоте́ке; **I have found a suitable cottage for the summer** я подыска́л/нашёл подходя́щую да́чу на ле́то; **she found a bag to match her shoes** она́ подыска́ла/нашла́ су́мку под цвет ту́фель; **in the end I found him in London** в конце́ концо́в я разыска́л его́ в Ло́ндоне

3 (*discover*) обнару́ж|ивать (-ить); **they found some old graves when excavating** при раско́пках они́ обнару́жили/нашли́ не́сколько дре́вних захороне́ний; **some evidence has been found proving that...** обнару́жились не́которые фа́кты, дока́зывающие, что...; **the detective found that...** сы́щик обнару́жил, что...; **to** ~ **a mistake in the bill** обнару́жить/найти́ оши́бку в счёте

4 (*to come upon smb*) заста|ва́ть кого́-л (-́ть); **I found him at home/sleeping/still in bed** я заста́л его́ до́ма/спя́щим/ещё в посте́ли; **I found no one in** я никого́ не заста́л; **she's never to be found in the office** её невозмо́жно заста́ть на рабо́те

5 (*supply*): **who will** ~ **the money for the expedition?** кто финанси́рует экспеди́цию?; **the pay is £20 a week all found** пла́та—два́дцать фу́нтов в неде́лю на всём гото́вом; **we managed to** ~ **the money to buy a house** мы раздобы́ли де́нег на поку́пку до́ма

6 *reflex*: **he has found himself in his new work** он нашёл себя́ в э́той свое́й но́вой рабо́те; **he found himself at a loss over what to say** он не нашёлся, что сказа́ть; **I found myself in an awkward situation** я очути́лся *or* оказа́лся в нело́вком положе́нии

7 *fig uses*: **I've found the answer/solution** я нашёл отве́т/реше́ние (вопро́са); **how do you** ~ **him?** как ты его́ нахо́дишь?; **I found her well/rather alarming** я нашёл её в до́бром здра́вии, она́ показа́лась мне дово́льно-таки устраша́ющей фигу́рой; **if I** ~ **you doing that again** е́сли я тебя́ ещё раз на э́том пойма́ю; **you'll** ~ **I'm right** уви́дишь, что я прав; **I** ~ **I'll have to leave a day earlier** вы́яснилось, что мне на́до е́хать на день ра́ньше; **I** ~ **it difficult to believe** мне тру́дно в э́то пове́рить; **I found it awkward to tell him about it** мне бы́ло неудо́бно сказа́ть ему́ об э́том; **I can't** ~ **time to see him** я ника́к не могу́ найти́ вре́мя поговори́ть с ним

8 *Law*: **to** ~ **smb guilty** призна́ть кого́-л вино́вным (*only in pf*)

vi Law: **to** ~ **for the plaintiff/for the defendant** реши́ть в по́льзу истца́/ отве́тчика

find out *vti vt* **1** (*learn*) узна|ва́ть, (*make enquiries*) разузна|ва́ть (*pfs* -́ть); **I'll** ~ **out where the station is** я узна́ю,/разузна́ю, где ста́нция

2 (*discover misdeeds*): **to** ~ **smb out** разоблач|а́ть кого́-л (-и́ть); **the real sin is to get found out** не по́йман—не вор; **this affair has really found him out** э́та исто́рия показа́ла его́ и́стинное лицо́

vi: **you'll be for it, if your father** ~**s out** тебе́ доста́нется, е́сли оте́ц узна́ет.

findings *npl* (*conclusions*) вы́воды; *Law* (*verdict*) реше́ние (*sing*).

fine[1] *n* штраф; **a** ~ **of 40 roubles** штраф (в) со́рок рубле́й.

fine[1] *vt*: **to** ~ **smb £100** оштрафова́ть кого́-л на сто фу́нтов (*usu pf*).

fine[2] *adj* **1** (*splendid*) прекра́сный; (*of weather*) прекра́сный, хоро́ший; **he's a** ~ **fellow** он прекра́сный челове́к, *CQ* (*of younger man*) он сла́вный ма́лый; **when it's** ~ (*of weather*) в хоро́шую пого́ду; **a** ~ **day** пого́жий денёк; **to turn** ~ проясня́ться; (*in stories*) **one** ~ **day** в оди́н прекра́сный день; *iron* **that's a** ~ **excuse!** вот прекра́сный предло́г!; **you're a** ~ **one to talk!** не тебе́ бы говори́ть!

2 (*delicate*) то́нкий; (*of small particles*) ме́лкий; **a** ~ **thread/skin** то́нкая нить/ко́жа; **a** ~ **distinction** то́нкое разли́чие; **a** ~ **cutting edge** то́нкое/о́строе ле́звие; ~ **rain/sand** ме́лкий дождь/песо́к; **a** ~ **sieve** ме́лкое си́то; *fig* **not to put too** ~ **a point on it** говоря́ без обиняко́в.

fine[2] *adv* **1** прекра́сно, *also CQ*

2 *Cook*: **to chop smth up** ~ ме́лко наре́зать что-л; *fig*: **he caught the train but cut it** ~ он едва́ успе́л на по́езд; **you've**

cut it a bit ~ ты оста́вил на э́то малова́то вре́мени.

finery *n*: **she was wearing all her** ~ она́ вы́рядилась как на пра́здник.

finesse *n* (*delicacy*) то́нкость, утончённость; **he lacks** ~ он не обу́чен то́нкому обхожде́нию; *Cards* **to take a** ~ проре́зать.

finger *n* **1** па́лец; **index/middle/fourth** ~ указа́тельный/сре́дний/безымя́нный па́лец; **little** ~ мизи́нец; **don't dare lay a** ~ **on the child!** не смей ребёнка и па́льцем тро́нуть!

2 *fig uses*: **you've put your** ~ **on it** вы попа́ли в то́чку; **something's not right, but I can't put my** ~ **on it** что́-то тут не так, но я ника́к не могу́ поня́ть, что; **I'll keep my** ~**s crossed for you!** я бу́ду тебя́ руга́ть!; **his** ~**s are all thumbs** у него́ не ру́ки, а крю́ки; **unquestionably he's got a** ~ **in the pie** он, несомне́нно, заме́шан в э́том де́ле; **she can twist him round her little** ~ она́ из него́ верёвки вьёт; **he got his** ~**s burnt over that** он обжёгся на э́том; **he didn't lift a** ~ **to help** он па́лец о па́лец не уда́рил, что́бы помо́чь; **he slipped through their** ~**s** он ускользну́л от них.

finger *vt*: **to** ~ **cloth** щу́пать ткань (по-); **she** ~**ed her beads** она́ тереби́ла/перебира́ла па́льцами бу́сы; **he** ~**ed the vase** он верте́л в рука́х ва́зу.

fingering *n Mus* аппликату́ра.

fingermark *n* след от па́льца.

fingernail *n* но́готь (*m*) (па́льца руки́).

fingerprint *n* отпеча́ток па́льца.

fingertip *n* ко́нчик па́льца; *fig* **to have smth at one's** ~**s** знать что-л как свои́ пять па́льцев.

finicky *adj* (*of person*) привере́дливый; разбо́рчивый; **it's** ~ **work** э́то кропотли́вая рабо́та.

finish *n* **1** коне́ц; *Sport* фи́ниш

2 (*on goods*) отде́лка; **the table has an oak** ~ стол отде́лан под дуб; *fig* **his playing lacks** ~ его́ игре́ не хвата́ет зако́нченности.

finish *vti vt* **1** (*general*) конч|а́ть (-́ить); ока́нчивать (око́нчить) (*esp. used of periods of time*); до|ка́нчивать (-ко́нчить) (*emphasis on reaching end*); (*finish off*) за|ка́нчивать (-ко́нчить), (*of processes, or large scale operations*) заверш|а́ть (-и́ть) [**NB** *prefix* за- *emphasizing completion*]; **to** ~ **work** (*for the day*) (за)ко́нчить рабо́ту; **to** ~ **a job** зако́нчить/заверши́ть рабо́ту; **I've** ~**ed the portrait** я зако́нчил/написа́л портре́т; **the repairs are not yet** ~**ed** ремо́нт (*sing*) ещё не зако́нчен; **the new building is** ~**ed** но́вое зда́ние уже́ постро́ено; **I've** ~**ed university/military service** я око́нчил университе́т, я отслужи́л свой срок в а́рмии; **to** ~ **a term in prison** отбыва́ть наказа́ние

2 *translated by prefix* до- *with appropriate verb*: ~ **(up) your meat/milk** доеда́й мя́со, допе́й молоко́; **I** ~**ed the novel** я дописа́л (*writing*)/я дочита́л (*reading*) рома́н, я зако́нчил рома́н (*either writing or reading*)

3 *fig CQ* при|ка́нчивать (-ко́нчить), докона́ть (*pf*); **the shock nearly** ~**ed him** э́тот уда́р чуть не докона́л его́; **I'm** ~**ed!** (*tired out*) я вы́дохся!; **as an actor, he's** ~**ed** как актёр он ко́нчился

4 (*by processing*) отде́л|ывать (-ать); **a well** ~**ed cupboard** шкаф краси́вой отде́лки; *fig* **a** ~**ed performance** зако́нченное исполне́ние

vi **1** конча́ться, ока́нчиваться, *etc.* (*see vt* **1**); **the meeting** ~**ed early** собра́ние зако́нчилось ра́но; **you'll** ~ **by losing your job** (де́ло) ко́нчится тем, что вы потеря́ете рабо́ту; **he** ~**ed by saying that...** в заключе́ние он сказа́л, что...; **we** ~**ed up** (*e. g. after theatre*) **at my sister's (flat)** (по́сле спекта́кля) мы зашли́ к мое́й сестре́, посиде́ли; **I've** ~**ed with the screw driver if you need it** мне бо́льше не нужна́ отвёртка, мо́жешь её взять; **he's** ~**ed with her/with politics** он бо́льше с ней не встреча́ется, он отошёл от поли́тики (*sing*)

2 *Sport* финиши́ровать (*impf and pf*).

finishing *adj* после́дний; **the** ~ **touches** после́дние штрихи́; *Sport* ~ **post/line** фи́нишный столб, фи́нишная черта́.

Finn *n* финн, фи́нка.

Finnish *n* фи́нский язы́к.

Finnish *adj* фи́нский.

fiord *n* фио́рд.

fir *n* пи́хта; ель, ёлка; *attr*: ~ **cone** ело́вая ши́шка.

fire *n* ого́нь (*m*), *also Mil*; (*destructive*) пожа́р; (*bonfire*) костёр; **an open** ~ ками́н; **a camp** ~ костёр; **a forest** ~ лесно́й пожа́р; **an electric** ~ электри́ческий ками́н (*fixed in grate*)/обогрева́тель (*portable room heater*); **I'll lay the** ~ **now but won't light it till later** я положу́ дрова́, но раста́пливать ками́н ещё ра́но; **to light/kindle/set a match to a** ~ развести́/разже́чь ого́нь; **to poke the** ~ помеша́ть у́гли; **to mend** *or* **make up the** ~ подложи́ть/подбро́сить у́гля (*G*)/дров (*G pl*) в ого́нь; **to keep up the** ~ поддержа́ть ого́нь; **to sit by the** ~ сиде́ть у огня́/у ками́на; **the house is on** ~ дом гори́т; **the barn/her skirt caught** ~ сара́й загоре́лся, у неё загоре́лась ю́бка; **hooligans have set** ~ **to the barn** хулига́ны подожгли́ сара́й; *Mil* **to be under** ~ быть под огнём/под обстре́лом; *fig*: **to play with** ~ игра́ть с огнём; **everything is hanging** ~ всё пока́ нея́сно, *CQ* всё виси́т в во́здухе.

fire *vti vt* **1** (*kindle*) за|жига́ть (-же́чь); (*if arson*) под|жига́ть (-же́чь); **to** ~ **bricks/pottery** обжига́ть кирпи́ч/посу́ду (*collects*); (*heat*) **we** ~ **the house in winter even when we're not there** зимо́й у нас то́пится печь, да́же когда́ нас нет до́ма; *fig* **his story** ~**d my imagination** его́ расска́з воспламени́л моё воображе́ние

2 *Mil*: **to** ~ **a rifle at smb** стреля́ть/*CQ* пали́ть в кого́-л из винто́вки (*impfs*); **he** ~**d two shots** он вы́стрелил/*CQ* пальну́л два ра́за; **without firing a shot** без еди́ного вы́стрела; **to ~ a volley** да|ва́ть залп (-ть), *CQ* пальну́ть (*pf*); *fig*: **to ~ questions at smb** засып|а́ть кого́-л вопро́сами (-́ать)

3 *CQ* (*dismiss*) увол|ьня́ть (-́ить); **you're ~d!** вы уво́лены!

vi: *Mil* **to ~ at/on smth** стреля́ть *or CQ* пали́ть во что-л (*impf*), вести́ ого́нь по чему́-л (*usu impf*), (*bombard*) обстре́л|ивать что-л (-я́ть); *Aut* **the engine is not firing on one cylinder** в одно́м цили́ндре пропа́ла и́скра; *CQ* **~ away!** (*begin*) начина́йте!, дава́йте!

fire alarm *n* пожа́рная трево́га.

firearms *npl* огнестре́льное ору́жие (*collect*).

fire brigade *n* пожа́рная кома́нда.

fire engine *n* пожа́рная маши́на.

fire escape *n* пожа́рная ле́стница.

fire extinguisher *n* огнетуши́тель (*m*).

firefly *n* жук-светля́к.

fireguard *n* ками́нная решётка.

fire insurance *n* страхова́ние от огня́.

fireman *n* пожа́рник; (*stoker*) кочега́р.

fireplace *n* ками́н.

fireproof *adj* огнеупо́рный.

firewood *n* дрова́ (*no sing*).

firework(s) *n usu pl* фейерве́рк (*sing*).

firing *n Mil* стрельба́, *CQ* пальба́; (*of pottery*) о́бжиг; (*heating*) отопле́ние.

firing line *n* огнево́й рубе́ж.

firm[1] *n* фи́рма.

firm[2] *adj* (*solid*) твёрдый; про́чный; **in a ~ voice** твёрдым го́лосом; **a ~ foundation** про́чное основа́ние; **to keep a ~ grip on smth** кре́пко держа́ться за что-л; *fig*: **a ~ conviction/decision/offer** твёрдое убежде́ние/реше́ние, серьёзное предложе́ние; **be ~ with the children** проявля́й твёрдость с детьми́; **they are ~ friends** они́ больши́е друзья́.

first *n* **1** (*beginning*) нача́ло; **from the very ~** с са́мого нача́ла; **from ~ to last** с нача́ла до конца́; **at ~** снача́ла, сперва́ (*advs*)

2 (*of dates*): **on the ~ of May** пе́рвого ма́я; **we arrive on the ~** мы приезжа́ем пе́рвого числа́

3: we were the ~ to arrive мы при́были/прие́хали пе́рвые

4 *Univ*: **to get a ~ (in history)** *approx* око́нчить с отли́чием, сдать исто́рию на отли́чно.

first *adj* **1** пе́рвый; **~ turn to the right** пе́рвый поворо́т напра́во; **~ violin** пе́рвая скри́пка; **~ name** и́мя; **~ floor** второ́й эта́ж [**NB** *in SU* пе́рвый эта́ж = *ground floor*]; **~ principles** гла́вные при́нципы; **~ lieutenant** ста́рший лейтена́нт; *Sport* **~ half** пе́рвый тайм; *Gram* **the ~ person** пе́рвое лицо́

2 *in adverbial phrases*: **at the ~ opportunity** при пе́рвой возмо́жности; **at ~ sight/glance** с пе́рвого взгля́да; **to do smth for the ~ time** де́лать что-л в пе́рвый раз; **to succeed the ~ time** доби́ться успе́ха с пе́рвого ра́за; **in the ~ place** во-пе́рвых, пре́жде всего́; *CQ* **I'll ring you ~ thing tomorrow** я тебе́ пе́рвым де́лом за́втра позвоню́.

first *adv* снача́ла, сперва́; **~ we had dinner** снача́ла мы пообе́дали; **~ of all, ~ and foremost** пре́жде всего́; **~ you want to go, then you don't** то ты хо́чешь идти́, то хо́чешь оста́ться; **he arrived**/*Sport* **came in ~** он при́был/финиши́ровал пе́рвым; **he got in ~ with his version** он пе́рвый стал объясня́ться; **when did you ~ visit Moscow?** когда́ вы впервы́е/пе́рвый раз посети́ли Москву́?; **I'd die ~!** я скоре́е умру́, чем э́то сде́лаю; **feet/head ~** нога́ми/голово́й вперёд.

first aid *n* пе́рвая по́мощь; **to give smb ~** оказа́ть кому́-л пе́рвую по́мощь.

first-class *adj* первокла́ссный; **a ~ hotel/carriage** первокла́ссная гости́ница, ваго́н пе́рвого кла́сса; **to travel ~** путеше́ствовать пе́рвым кла́ссом.

first cousin *n* двою́родный брат, двою́родная сестра́.

first-hand *adj and adv*: **~ experience** ли́чный о́пыт; **I learnt this (at) ~** я узна́л об э́том из пе́рвых рук.

firstly *adv* во-пе́рвых.

first-rate *adj* первокла́ссный; *CQ* превосхо́дный.

firth *n* (*estuary*) у́стье реки́; (*arm of sea*) морско́й зали́в.

fiscal *adj* фина́нсовый.

fish *n* ры́ба; *fig*: **neither ~ nor fowl** ни ры́ба ни мя́со; **he's like a ~ out of water here** здесь он я́вно не в свое́й таре́лке; *CQ* **he's an odd ~** он чуда́к; *attr*: **a ~ head** ры́бья голова́; **~ market/shop** ры́бный ры́нок/магази́н.

fish *vti vt*: **to ~ a river** лови́ть ры́бу в реке́; *fig* **he ~ed a coin out of his pocket** он вы́удил моне́ту из карма́на

vi лови́ть/уди́ть ры́бу (*impfs*) [**NB** пойма́ть (*pf of* лови́ть) = *to catch fish*]; **to ~ with worms** лови́ть на червя́/на червяка́; *fig* **you're ~ing (for compliments)** ты напра́шиваешься на комплиме́нты.

fishbone *n* ры́бья кость.

fisherman *n* рыба́к, рыболо́в.

fish hook *n* рыболо́вный крючо́к.

fishing *n* ры́бная ло́вля: *attr*: **a ~ boat** рыба́чья ло́дка (*rowboat*), рыболо́вное су́дно (*trawler*); **~ tackle** рыболо́вные сна́сти (*pl*).

fishing line *n* ле́са.

fishing rod *n* (*rod and line*) у́дочка; (*without line*) уди́лище.

fishmonger *n* торго́вец ры́бой; (*shop*) **the ~'s** ры́бный магази́н.

fishpond *n* рыбово́дный пруд; ры́бный садо́к.

fish sauce *n* со́ус к ры́бе.

fishy *adj* ры́бный; **there's a ~ smell here** здесь па́хнет ры́бой; *fig CQ* **this looks/sounds ~** э́то вы́глядит/звучи́т подозри́тельно.

fission *n*: *Phys* **nuclear ~** расщепле́ние ядра́.

fissure *n* тре́щина, (*larger*) щель.

fist *n* кула́к; **to shake one's ~ at smb** грози́ть кому́-л кулако́м.

fistful *n* горсть, при́горшня.

fit[1] *n* (*of clothes*): **to be a good/bad/loose ~** хорошо́/пло́хо/свобо́дно сиде́ть (на ком-л); **this dress is a tight ~** э́то пла́тье пло́тно обтя́гивает; **I've packed everything, but it was a tight ~** я всё умести́л, но чемода́н битко́м наби́т.

fit[1] *adj* **1** (*suitable, good enough*) **~ for, ~ to** + *inf* подходя́щий для + *G or* + *inf*, го́дный/приго́дный к + *D or* для + *G*; (*ready*) гото́вый к + *D or* + *inf*; **this is not a ~ time to** сейча́с не совсе́м подходя́щее вре́мя + *inf*; **he's not ~ company for you** он для тебя́ неподходя́щая компа́ния; **the ground is not yet ~ for sowing** земля́ ещё не гото́ва к се́ву; **this dress is not ~ to wear** э́то пла́тье нельзя́ носи́ть/наде́ть; **this meat is not ~ to eat** э́то мя́со не приго́дно в пи́щу; **I'm not ~ to be seen** я не могу́ показа́ться в тако́м ви́де на́ людях; **he's not ~ to rule the country** он не спосо́бен управля́ть страно́й; **I worked till I was ~ to drop** я рабо́тал до по́лного изнеможе́ния; **do as you think ~** де́лайте, как счита́ете ну́жным

2 (*healthy*) здоро́вый; **he's keeping ~** он здоро́в; **he's not ~ for/to work** он не в состоя́нии рабо́тать; **~ for military service** го́дный к вое́нной слу́жбе; *Sport* **he's very ~** он в хоро́шей фо́рме.

fit[1] *vti vt* **1** (*prepare*) подгот|а́вливать/подгот|овля́ть к + *D* (*pf for both* -о́вить); **to ~ oneself for one's new duties** подгото́виться к исполне́нию свои́х но́вых обя́занностей

2 (*suit, correspond to*) соотве́тствовать + *D* (*impf*), под|ходи́ть к + *D* (-ойти́); **the description ~s the facts/him** э́то описа́ние соотве́тствует фа́ктам, он подхо́дит по описа́нию; **the key didn't ~ the lock** ключ не подошёл к замку́; **this suit ~s you well** э́тот костю́м хорошо́ на вас сиди́т; **these shoes don't ~ me** э́ти ту́фли мне малы́/велики́ (*are too small/too big*)

3 *Sew* пример|я́ть (-ить); **the tailor ~ted my jacket** портно́й приме́рил мне пиджа́к

4 (*put*): **to ~ a key into a lock** встав|ля́ть ключ в замо́к (-ить); **to ~ glass into a frame** под|гоня́ть стекло́ к ра́ме (-огна́ть); **to ~ a plug on to an electric fire** приде́лать ште́псель к электри́ческому обогрева́телю (*usu pf*); (*of people*) **can you ~ me in?** (*to car, etc.*) у вас найдётся для меня́ ме́сто в маши́не?, (*for the night*) я могу́ у вас переночева́ть?, (*for an interview*) вы мо́жете меня́ приня́ть?

5 (*equip, supply*): **to ~ (out) smb/smth with smth** снаб|жа́ть кого́-л /что-л чем-л (-ди́ть); **to ~ a car with a rear windscreen wiper** снабди́ть за́днее стекло́ маши́ны дво́рником; **to ~ out a ship/an expedition** снаря|жа́ть кора́бль/экспеди́цию (-ди́ть); **to ~ out an office/shop** отде́л|ывать кабине́т/магази́н (-ать)

vi **1** (*correspond*) совпа|да́ть с + *I* (-сть); **that ~s in with my plans** э́то совпада́ет с мои́ми пла́нами; **I can't get to my village in one day—the trains don't ~** я не могу́ дое́хать до мое́й дере́вни за оди́н день из-за расписа́ния поездо́в

2 (*of clothes*): **the dress ~s well** пла́тье хорошо́ сиди́т

3 (*suit: of things*) **the lid doesn't ~ on to this pan** кры́шка не подхо́дит к э́той кастрю́ле; **the cupboard will ~ in here** шкаф войдёт сюда́; (*adapt: of people*) **how is he ~ting in at work?** как он вхо́дит в рабо́ту?; **I don't think he'll ~ in well with us** я ду́маю, мы с ним вряд ли пола́дим.

fit[2] *n Med* при́ступ, припа́док, *both also fig*; **a ~ of coughing/hysterics** при́ступ ка́шля, истери́ческий припа́док; **a fainting ~** о́бморок; *fig*: **a ~ of rage** при́ступ гне́ва; **in a ~ of generosity he gave me £5** в поры́ве ще́дрости он дал мне пять фу́нтов; **he worked by ~s and starts** он рабо́тал уры́вками (*adv*); **we were in ~s of laughter** мы умира́ли со́ смеху; *CQ* **he'll have a ~ if he hears of it** его́ хва́тит уда́р, е́сли он об э́том узна́ет.

fitful *adj* поры́вистый.

fitter *n Tech* сбо́рщик; сле́сарь-монта́жник.

fitting *n* **1** *Sew* приме́рка

2 *usu pl* (*equipment*) обору́дование (*collect*); **electric ~s** электрообору́дование; **bathroom ~s** обору́дование для ва́нной; **office ~s** канцеля́рские принадле́жности.

fitting *adj* подходя́щий, надлежа́щий; **a ~ comment** подходя́щее/уме́стное замеча́ние; **is it ~ that we should send our condolences?** сле́дует ли нам посла́ть свои́ соболе́знования?

five *num* пять (*G, D, P* пяти́, *I* пятью́) [*in Nom, A noun and adj are in G pl*; *in oblique cases nouns and adjs are plural, agreeing in case with numeral*]; *collect* пя́теро (*G, A, P* пятеры́х, *D* пятеры́м, *I* пятеры́ми) [*see grammatical note under* **four**]; **5 years** пять лет; **5 gold stars** пять золоты́х звёзд; **in 5 large boxes** в пяти́ больши́х я́щиках; **there were 5 of us** нас бы́ло пять челове́к/пя́теро; **a "5"** (*the number* 5, *a* 5 *in cards, also the school mark, etc.*) пятёрка; **5 times 5** пя́тью пять; **volume 5** пя́тый том; **it's after 5** сейча́с шесто́й час; **a 5-year old boy** пятиле́тний ма́льчик; **a ~-day week** пятидне́вка; **a ~-year plan** пятиле́тний план, пятиле́тка; **500** пятьсо́т (*G* пятисо́т, *D* пятиста́м, *I* пятьюста́ми, *P* о пятиста́х); **5,000** пять ты́сяч; [**NB** *in mathematical usage most numerals are regarded as neutral*] **5 multiplied by 3 = 15** пять, умно́женное на три, равно́ пятна́дцати.

fivefold *adv* впя́теро, в пятикра́тном разме́ре.

fiver *n* (банкно́та в) пять фу́нтов.

fix *n Aer, Radio* (**a ~**) засе́чка; **to take a ~ on smth** засе́чь что-л; *fig CQ* **to get oneself into a ~** попа́сть в переде́лку; *sl* (*of drugs*) **to give smb a ~** дать кому́-л до́зу нарко́тика.

fix *vti vt* **1** (*by fastening down, etc.*) закреп|ля́ть (-и́ть) *and other compounds*; *Photo* фикси́ровать (*impf and pf*); **to ~ a lid on to a box** приде́лать кры́шку к я́щику; (*drive in*) **to ~ a post in the ground** вби|ва́ть кол/столб в зе́млю (-ть); **to ~ a mirror on a wall/on a cupboard door** пове́сить (*hang*) зе́ркало на сте́ну, вде́лать зе́ркало в две́рцу шка́фа; *fig*: **that day is firmly ~ed in my memory** э́тот день хорошо́ мне запо́мнился; **to ~ one's attention/gaze on smb/smth** обра|ща́ть внима́ние/при́стально смотре́ть на кого́-л *or* на что-л (-ти́ть/*only in impf*); **to ~ one's hopes/the blame on smb** возлага́ть наде́жды (*usu impf*)/ возложи́ть вину́ (*usu pf*) на кого́-л

2 (*determine*) реш|а́ть (-и́ть); **nothing is ~ed yet** ещё ничего́ не решено́; **we ~ed a date for the meeting** мы назна́чили день собра́ния; **to ~ prices/ the rent** устан|а́вливать це́ны/ре́нту (-ови́ть); (*Naut and in surveying*): **to ~ one's longitude and latitude** (то́чно) определи́ть долготу́ и широту́

3 *also* **~ up** *mainly CQ* (*arrange, provide for*) устр|а́ивать (-о́ить); **I'll ~ you up for the night/with a job** я устро́ю вас на ночле́г/на рабо́ту; **he'll ~ everything for you** он всё для вас устро́ит; **they ~ed up their quarrel** они́ помири́лись; *CQ*: **I'll ~ you the salad/a meal** я пригото́влю вам сала́т/еду́; **can I ~ you a drink?** что тебе́ нали́ть?; **how are you ~ed for time?/money?** как у вас со вре́менем?/с деньга́ми?; **I'll ~ him!** я ему́ зада́м!

4 (*repair*) чини́ть (по-); исправ|ля́ть (-́ить); **I must ~ that broken chair** мне на́до почини́ть сло́манный стул; **I'll have to get my car ~ed** мне на́до чини́ть маши́ну

5 *CQ* (*rig*) подстр|а́ивать (-о́ить); **the competition/match was ~ed beforehand** о результа́тах соревнова́ний/об исхо́де ма́тча договори́лись зара́нее; **later he ~ed the policeman** а пото́м он ула́дил э́то де́ло с полице́йским; **he ~ed the jury** он подкупи́л прися́жных; **to ~ an election** фальсифици́ровать результа́ты вы́боров (*impf and pf*)

vi: **we ~ed on Tuesday for the next meeting** мы назна́чили сле́дующее заседа́ние на вто́рник; **I've ~ed it up with my son—he'll meet you at the airport** я договори́лся с сы́ном, (что) он встре́тит вас в аэропорту́.

fixed *adj*: **a ~ grin/stare** засты́вшая улы́бка, неподви́жный взгляд; **~ determination** твёрдая реши́мость; **~ prices** твёрдые/устано́вленные це́ны; **a ~ menu** дежу́рное меню́; **of no ~ abode** без определённого ме́ста жи́тельства.

fixture *n* **1** (*immovable equipment*) обору́дование; *fig CQ* **he's a ~ in our department** он у нас в отде́ле для ме́бели

2 *Sport* матч; **~s for the season** календа́рь соревнова́ний сезо́на.

fizz *vi* шипе́ть (*impf*).

fizzle *vi CQ*: **the party/enterprise ~d out** к концу́ ве́чера весе́лье приути́хло, де́ло загло́хло; **his enthusiasm ~d out** его́ энтузиа́зм пропа́л/осты́л.

fizzy *adj* шипу́чий.

flabbergast *vt usu pass CQ*: **I was ~ed by the news** я был потрясён э́той но́востью.

flabby *adj* (*physically*) дря́блый, вя́лый; *fig* сла́бый.

flag[1] *n* флаг; **~ of truce** (бе́лый) флаг парламентёра; *fig*: **to show the white ~** вы́весить бе́лый флаг; **to keep the ~ flying** высоко́ держа́ть зна́мя, не сдава́ться.

flag[2] *n* (*paving stone*) плитня́к, ка́менная плита́.

flag[3] *vi* (*droop*) ни́кнуть (по-, с-), *also fig*; *fig*: **he was ~ging** он сник; **conversation ~ged** разгово́р шел вя́ло/не кле́ился.

flagrant *adj* вопию́щий; **a ~ injustice** вопию́щая несправедли́вость.

flagstaff *n* флагшто́к.

flair *n* чутьё; нюх; **she has a ~ for bargains/for language/for languages** у неё чутьё *or* нюх на вы́годные сде́лки/ о́чень ра́звито чу́вство языка́/спосо́бности (*pl*) к языка́м.

flake *n usu pl*: **soap ~s** мы́льная стру́жка (*collect*); **corn ~s** кукуру́зные хло́пья (*no sing*); **snow ~s** снежи́нки, (*bigger*) хло́пья сне́га.

flake *vi*: **to ~ off** лупи́ться (об-).

flaky *adj* хлопьеви́дный; **~ pastry** слоёное те́сто.

flame *n* пла́мя (*no pl*); **to be in ~s** горе́ть, быть в огне́; **to go up in ~s** сгоре́ть; *fig CQ* **she's an old ~ of his** она́ его́ да́внее увлече́ние.

flame *vi* пыла́ть, горе́ть пла́менем (*impfs*); *fig*: **her cheeks ~d** её щёки запыла́ли; **he was flaming with anger** он пыла́л гне́вом.

flaming *adj*: **~ colours** я́ркие кра́ски; **a ~ sunset** пламене́ющий зака́т; *fig CQ* **a ~ row** ужа́сный сканда́л.

flan *n* откры́тый пиро́г.

flank *n Anat*, *Cook* бок; *Mil* фланг; *attr*: **a ~ attack** ата́ка во фланг (*against enemy's flank*)/с фла́нга (*made from side*).

flannel *n* (*material*) флане́ль; (*for washing*) рукави́чка для обтира́ния лица́/те́ла; *pl* (**~s**) (*trousers*) брю́ки из шерстяно́й флане́ли.

flap *n* **1** (*sound of wings, sails*) хло́панье; *fig CQ*: **to get into a ~** засуети́ться; **there's a ~ on in the office** у нас сейча́с в конто́ре суета́

2 (*cover of an opening*): **~ of a pocket/envelope** кла́пан карма́на/конве́рта; **ear ~s** (*attached to a hat*) у́ши ша́пки; **~ of a tent** пола́ пала́тки; **a table with a folding ~** стол с откидно́й доско́й.

flap *vti vt* (*of movement*) маха́ть, (*of sound*) хло́пать (*usu impfs*); **the birds were ~ping their wings** пти́цы маха́ли/хло́пали кры́льями

vi **1** развева́ться (*only in impf*); маха́ть, хло́пать; **the flags were ~ping** фла́ги развева́лись; **the sails were ~ping in the breeze/against the mast** паруса́ хло́пали на ветру́/би́ли о ма́чту

2 *CQ* суети́ться (за-), волнова́ться (*impf*).

flapjack *n* (*US*) *approx* блин.

flare *n* вспы́шка пла́мени; (*as distress signal*) сигна́льная/освети́тельная раке́та; *Sew* клёш.

flare *vi* я́рко горе́ть (*impf*); **to ~ up** вспы́х|ивать (-нуть), *also fig*, *fig* вспыли́ть (*pf*).

flared *adj*: **a ~ skirt** ю́бка-клёш.

flash *n* (*of flame, light, Photo*) вспы́шка; (*of light*) про́блеск; **a ~ of lightning/from a lighthouse** вспы́шка мо́лнии, про́блесковый ого́нь маяка́; *Radio* **a news ~** сро́чное сообще́ние; (*of time*) **in a ~** мгнове́нно (*adv*); **it came to him in a ~ that...** его́ вдруг осени́ло, что...; *fig*: **a ~ of wit** блеск остроу́мия; **his success was only a ~ in the pan** он был факи́р на час.

flash *vti vt*: **to ~ a torch in smb's eyes** ослеп|ля́ть кого́-л све́том фонаря́ (-и́ть); **to ~ one's headlights** мига́ть фа́рами (*usu impf*)

vi вспы́х|ивать (-нуть), сверк|а́ть (-ну́ть); **lightning ~ed across the sky** небосво́д проре́зала мо́лния; **the lighthouse ~es once every two minutes** мая́к вспы́хивает ка́ждые две мину́ты; *fig* **he ~ed past on his motorcycle** он промча́лся на мотоци́кле.

flashback *n Cine* обра́тный кадр.

flashlight *n Photo* вспы́шка ма́гния.

flashy *adj CQ*: **a ~ shirt/car** пижо́нская руба́шка, шика́рная маши́на; **~ colours** крича́щие цвета́.

flask *n* фля́га, фля́жка.

flat[1] *n* кварти́ра.

flat[2] *n usu pl* **1: mud ~s** боло́та; **the ~ of the hand** ладо́нь

2 *Mus* бемо́ль (*m*)

3 (*US*) *CQ* (*puncture*) (**a ~**) проко́л.

flat[2] *adj* **1** пло́ский; ро́вный; (*of colours*) ма́товый; **a ~ surface** пло́ская/ро́вная пове́рхность; **a ~ chest** пло́ская грудь; **in a ~ voice** глухи́м го́лосом; **~ shoes** ту́фли без каблуко́в; **he has ~ feet** у него́ плоскосто́пие (*sing*); **a ~ pan** ме́лкая кастрю́ля; *Aut* **a ~ tyre** спу́щенная ши́на; **the battery is ~** батаре́я се́ла; *Mus*: **E ~ major** ми бемо́ль мажо́р; **the violin is ~** скри́пка расстро́ена

2 *fig uses*: **life here seems ~ to me** здесь мне о́чень ску́чно; **he felt ~ after playing the concert** он чу́вствовал себя́ соверше́нно разби́тым по́сле выступле́ния на конце́рте; **this beer is ~** пи́во вы́дохлось; **a ~ refusal** категори́ческий отка́з; **and that's ~** э́то оконча́тельно; *Comm*: **a ~ rate** единообра́зная ста́вка; **to buy at a ~ rate** купи́ть всё по одно́й цене́.

flat[2] *adv* пло́ско, ро́вно; **to fall/lie ~** упа́сть/лежа́ть плашмя́; **the tyre has gone ~** ши́на спусти́ла (во́здух); **the tread has worn ~** проте́ктор износи́лся; **the earthquake laid the city ~** землетрясе́ние сровня́ло го́род с землёй; **she sings ~** она́ фальши́во/нечи́сто поёт; *fig*: **he did it in 5 minutes ~** он сде́лал э́то ро́вно за пять мину́т; **the joke fell ~** шу́тка не удала́сь; *CQ* **he's working ~ out** он выкла́дывается на рабо́те.

flat-bottomed *adj*: **a ~ boat** плоскодо́нная ло́дка, плоскодо́нка.

flatly *adv*: **he ~ denied it** он категори́чески отрица́л э́то.

flatten *vt*: **to ~ a road** вы|ра́внивать доро́гу (-́ровнять); **the storm ~ed the crops** урожа́й пострада́л от урага́на; **the town was ~ed (out) by the bombing** при бомбардиро́вке го́род был разру́шен до основа́ния; **to ~ oneself against a wall** прижа́ться к стене́.

flatter *vt* льстить + *D* (по-); **to ~ smb/smb's vanity** льстить кому́-л/чьему́-л самолю́бию; **I ~ myself that...** я льщу себя́ наде́ждой, что...; **I am ~ed by your invitation** мне ле́стно получи́ть ва́ше приглаше́ние; **the snapshot doesn't ~ you** ты пло́хо получи́лся/вы́шел на сни́мке; *iron* **you ~ yourself!** вы себе́ льсти́те!

flatterer *n* льстец, льсти́вый челове́к.

flattering *adj* ле́стный; **that's a ~ portrait of him** на портре́те он лу́чше/краси́вее, чем в жи́зни; **that's a ~ dress** э́то пла́тье тебя́ о́чень кра́сит; **~ words** *pejor* льсти́вые слова́.

flattery *n* лесть; **he's given to ~** он льстив; **to make up to smb by ~** подольсти́ться к кому́-л.

flatulence *n Med* метеори́зм.

flaunt *vt*: **they ~ their riches/liaison** они́ выставля́ют напока́з своё бога́тство, они́ демонстрати́вно афиши́руют свою́ связь/не скрыва́ют свое́й свя́зи.

flautist *n* флейти́ст.

flavour, (*US*) **flavor** *n* (*taste*) вкус; при́вкус, *also fig*; **this soup has a lot of ~/no ~/a ~ of garlic/a strange ~** (э́тот) суп о́чень вку́сный/невку́сный, у э́того су́па чесно́чный/стра́нный при́вкус *or* вкус; **various ~s of ice cream** моро́женое ра́зных сорто́в; *fig* **a ~ of irony** ирони́ческий отте́нок.

flavour, (*US*) **flavor** *vt* приправ|ля́ть + *I* (-́ить); **to ~ a sauce with garlic** припра́вить со́ус чесноко́м.

flavouring, (*US*) **flavoring** *n* припра́ва.

flavourless, (*US*) **flavorless** *adj* пре́сный; безвку́сный.

flaw *n* изъя́н, дефе́кт, *also fig*; *fig* недоста́ток; **a ~ of character/in the evidence** недоста́ток, сла́бое ме́сто в доказа́тельствах (*pl*).

flawed *adj*: **~ goods** това́р (*collect*) с бра́ком/с изъя́ном.

flawless *adj* (*of goods*) без изъя́на; *fig* безупре́чный; **he spoke ~ French** он говори́л на безупре́чном францу́зском языке́.

flax *n* лён.

flea *n* блоха́.

fleabite *n* блоши́ный уку́с; *fig* **to lose £1,000 is a mere ~ to him** для него́ потеря́ть ты́сячу фу́нтов—пустяки́ (*pl*).

fleck *n* кра́пинка.

flecked *adj*: **hair ~ with grey** во́лосы (*pl*) с про́седью/, тро́нутые седино́й; **grey cloth**

~ with red сéрая ткань в крáсную крáпинку.

fledged *adj* оперённый; *fig* **he's a fully ~ doctor now** тепéрь он врач с диплóмом.

flee *vti vt* бежáть (*in this sense impf and pf*), убе|гáть (-жáть); **to ~ the country** бежáть из страны́

vi бежáть, убегáть.

fleece *n* (*of sheep, etc.*) шерсть; (*when cut*) нáстриг с овцы́.

fleece *vt CQ*: **to ~ smb** ободрáть когó-л как ли́пку (*usu pf*).

fleet *n Naut* флот; **the F.** воéнный флот; *fig* **the President was escorted by a ~ of cars** президéнта сопровождáла колóнна маши́н.

fleeting *adj* мимолётный.

flesh *n* плоть; (*meat*) мя́со; (*of fruits*) мя́коть; **in the ~** во плоти́; **he's my own ~ and blood** он моя́ плоть и кровь; **sins of the ~** плóтские грехи́; **it's more than ~ and blood can stand** э́то бóльше, чем обы́чный смéртный мóжет вы́держать/вы́нести.

fleshy *adj* мяси́стый.

flex *n Elec* (ги́бкий) шнур.

flex *vt* (*body, knees*) сгибáть (согну́ть); **to ~ one's muscles** разм|инáть мы́шцы (-я́ть).

flexibility *n* ги́бкость, *also fig.*

flexible *adj* ги́бкий, *also fig*; *fig* (*of person*) устýпчивый; **a ~ policy** ги́бкая поли́тика.

flick *n* **1**: **a ~ of the fingers** щелчóк; **the horse gave a ~ of its tail** лóшадь взмахнýла хвостóм; **with a ~ of her duster she removed the wasp** махнýв тря́пкой, онá отогналá осý

2 *pl CQ* (*UK*): **to go to the ~s** пойти́ в кинó (*indecl*).

flick *vt*: **to ~ ash off a cigarette/ crumbs off a table** стряхнýть пéпел с сигарéты, смахнýть крóшки со столá (*usu pfs*); **to ~ over the pages of/through a book** листáть/перели́ст|ывать страни́цы кни́ги (*impf* /-áть).

flicker *n* (*of light, fire*) мерцáние; *fig*: **without the ~ of an eyelid** глáзом не моргнýв; **a ~ of hope** прóблеск надéжды; **without the ~ of a smile** без тéни улы́бки.

flicker *vi* (*of light*) мерцáть; **the candle ~ed and went out** свечá помигáла и погáсла; **the needle on the speedometer ~ed between 70 and 80 m.p.h.** стрéлка спидóметра дрожáла мéжду семью́десятью и восьмью́десятью ми́лями в час; **a smile ~ed on his lips** у негó на губáх мелькнýла улы́бка.

flight *n* **1** (*action*) полёт; **the ~ of a bird/ bee/bullet/to the Moon** полёт пти́цы/пчелы́/ пýли/на Лунý; **to shoot a bird in ~** стреля́ть пти́цу влёт; **to take to ~** улетéть; **~ path** траектóрия полёта

2 (*flock*): **a ~ of birds/insects** стáя птиц, рой насекóмых; **the first ~s of swallows are here** прилетéли пéрвые стáи лáсточек

3 *Aer* рейс; (*distance flown*) перелёт; **~ number 207 from Moscow to Paris** рейс нóмер двéсти семь Москвá—Пари́ж; **a non-stop ~** беспосáдочный перелёт; **the ~ to Paris takes an hour** самолёт в Пари́ж лети́т час

4: **a ~ of stairs** лéстничный пролёт/марш; **we live three ~s up** нáша кварти́ра на четвёртом этажé

5 (*escape*) бéгство; **to put/take to ~** обращáть/обращáться в бéгство *or* спасти́сь бéгством; *fig Comm* **the ~ of capital** утéчка капитáла.

flighty *adj* вéтреный.

flimsy *adj* (*of cloth, paper*) тóнкий; (*of furniture, etc.*) непрóчный; *fig* **a ~ excuse** сомни́тельный предлóг.

flinch *vi* (*wince*) вздрáгивать (вздрóгнуть); **without ~ing** не дрóгнув; **to ~ from smth** уклон|я́ться от чегó-л (-и́ться).

fling *vti vt* (*throw*) брос|áть (-ить); **to ~ a stone at smth** брóсить кáмень во что-л; **to ~ oneself into a chair** брóситься в крéсло; **to ~ one's arms round smb's neck** брóситься комý-л на шéю; **she flung off her cloak** онá сбрóсила с себя́ *or* с плеч/скинула плащ; **to ~ on one's clothes** набрóсить/накинуть одéжду; **to ~ open a door** распáх|ивать дверь (-нýть)

vi: **she flung out of the room** онá брóсилась вон из кóмнаты.

flint *n* кремéнь (*m*).

flippant *adj* легкомы́сленный; **I was only being ~** э́то не серьёзно, э́то я прóсто так сказáл.

flipper *n* (*of seal or to aid swimmer*) ласт.

flirt *n* (*of woman*) кокéтка; (*of man*) *CQ* ухажёр.

flirt *vi* (*of a woman*) кокéтничать с + *I*, (*of man or woman*) флиртовáть с + *I* (*impfs*); заи́грывать (*only in impf*), *also fig*; **to ~ a little** пофлиртовáть (*pf*); *fig*: **for a while they ~ed with the liberals** однó врéмя они́ заи́грывали с либерáлами; **I am ~ing with the idea of going to Peru** я подýмываю, а не поéхать ли мне в Перý.

flirtation *n* флирт; **to carry on a ~ with smb** флиртовáть с кем-л.

flirtatious *adj* кокéтливая (*only of woman*); **he's very ~** он лю́бит поухáживать/пофлиртовáть.

flit *vi* (*of butterflies, etc.*) порх|áть (-нýть), *also fig*; *fig* **a smile ~ted across his face** по егó лицý пробежáла лёгкая улы́бка; *CQ* (*move house*) пере|езжáть (-éхать).

float *n* **1** (*for fishing, swimmers, also of seaplane*) поплавóк

2 (*vehicle in parade*) платфóрма.

float *vti vt* **1** (*launch*) спус|кáть нá воду (-ти́ть); **to ~ logs downstream** сплав|ля́ть лес вниз по течéнию (-ить)

2 *Fin*: **to ~ a loan** разме|щáть заём (-сти́ть); **to ~ the dollar** вв|оди́ть колéблющийся/ плáвающий курс дóллара (-ести́)

vi плáвать (*indet impf*), плыть (*det impf*) [*see under* **swim** *vi*]; **wood ~s** дéрево не тóнет в водé; **the boat ~ed downstream** лóдка плылá вниз по течéнию; *fig* **clouds**

were ~ing across the sky облака́ плы́ли по не́бу.

floating *adj* плаву́чий; *fig*: **the ~ population** теку́честь населе́ния; **~ voter** избира́тель, не отдаю́щий постоя́нного предпочте́ния ни одно́й па́ртии.

flock *n* (*of animals*) ста́до; (*of birds*) ста́я; **a large ~ of sheep** большо́е ста́до ове́ц, ота́ра; **people came in ~s** лю́ди стека́лись то́лпами.

flock *vi* (*of people or animals*) сгру́диться (*pf*), (*of people*) стека́ться (*usu impf*), *CQ* вало́м вали́ть (*impf*); **crowds ~ed to the exhibition** пу́блика вало́м вали́ла на вы́ставку; **they ~ed round him** они́ сгру́дились вокру́г него́; **people simply ~ed to his performances** на его́ выступле́ниях я́блоку бы́ло не́где упа́сть.

floe *n*, *also* **ice floe** плаву́чая льди́на.

flog *vt* поро́ть (вы-); *fig CQ*: **it's an idea that has been ~ged to death** э́то зата́сканная иде́я; (*UK*) (*sell*) **he's had to ~ his coat to pay his debts** ему́ пришло́сь загна́ть пальто́, что́бы расплати́ться с долга́ми.

flood *n* **1** (*unexpected*) наводне́ние (*usu sing*); (*of annual spring thaw, overspill into meadows*) полово́дье, па́водок; **the road is closed owing to the ~s** э́та доро́га закры́та из-за па́водка; **the river is in ~** река́ разлила́сь, на реке́ па́водок; *Bibl* **the F.** всеми́рный пото́п; *CQ* **we've got a ~ in our bathroom** у нас в ва́нной пото́п

2 *fig* пото́к; **a ~ of callers/lava/words** пото́к посети́телей/ла́вы/слов; **she was in ~s of tears** она́ лила́ пото́ки слёз.

flood *vti vt* зали|ва́ть (ʼ-ть), затоп|ля́ть (-и́ть); **the river ~ed the meadows** река́ затопи́ла луга́; **the meadows were ~ed** затопи́ло (*impers*) луга́; **many people were ~ed out** мно́гие бы́ли вы́нуждены поки́нуть дома́ из-за наводне́ния; *Aut* **to ~ the carburettor** зали́ть карбюра́тор; *fig*: **to ~ the market with goods** наводн|я́ть ры́нок това́рами (-и́ть); **the room was ~ed with light** ко́мната была́ залита́ све́том; **we are ~ed (out) with enquiries** нас засы́пали/заброса́ли вопро́сами

vi: **the river/tide is ~ing** река́ выхо́дит из берего́в, начина́ется прили́в; *fig*: **people were ~ing in to the square** лю́ди шли/стека́лись то́лпами на пло́щадь; **applications are ~ing in** заявле́ния иду́т пото́ком.

flooding *n* затопле́ние.

floodlight *vt* осве|ща́ть проже́ктором (-ти́ть).

floodlighting *n* освеще́ние проже́ктором.

floodlit *adj* освещённый/(*from below*) подсве́ченный проже́ктором.

floodtide *n* прили́в.

floor *n* пол; (*storey*) эта́ж; **to lay a ~** настила́ть пол; **the ground/first/second/top ~** пе́рвый/второ́й/тре́тий/ве́рхний эта́ж; **we live on the same ~** мы живём на одно́м этаже́; **the sea ~** дно мо́ря; *fig* **to take the ~** (*to dance*) пойти́ танцева́ть, (*to speak*) выступа́ть, брать сло́во; *attr*: **~ polisher** полотёр.

floor *vt*: **to ~ a house** на|стила́ть пол в до́ме (-стла́ть); *fig CQ*: **I ~ed him** я поста́вил его́ в тупи́к; **he was ~ed by the question** э́тот вопро́с доконал/оконча́тельно срази́л его́.

floorboard *n* полови́ца.

floorcloth *n* полова́я тря́пка.

flooring *n* насти́л, пол; **what kind of ~ have you got?** како́й у вас пол (в кварти́ре)?

flop *n* : *CQ* **the play was a total ~** пье́са с тре́ском провали́лась.

flop *vi*, *also* **~ down** плю́х|аться (-нуться).

flora *npl* фло́ра (*collect*).

floral *adj* цвето́чный.

florid *adj* (*of face*) багро́вый; (*of style*) цвети́стый.

florist *n* (*shop*) **the ~'s** цвето́чный магази́н.

flounce *n Sew* обо́рка.

flounder[1] *n* (*fish*) ка́мбала.

flounder[2] *vi* (*in water*) бара́хтаться (*impf*); **to ~ in/through deep snow** с трудо́м передвига́ться по глубо́кому сне́гу (*usu impf*); *fig* **he ~ed on in bad French** он продолжа́л объясня́ться на ло́маном францу́зском.

flour *n* мука́.

flour-bin *n* ба́нка для муки́.

flourish *vti vt* взма́х|ивать + *I* (-ну́ть); **he ~ed his sword/the letter** он взмахну́л мечо́м, он помаха́л письмо́м

vi (*thrive*: *of plants*) хорошо́/бу́йно расти́ (*impf*)/разраст|а́ться (-и́сь); *fig* процвета́ть (*impf*); **the country/his business is ~ing** страна́/его́ де́ло процвета́ет; **the children are ~ing** с детьми́ всё в поря́дке; **Socrates/Greek sculpture ~ed in the 5th century B.C.** Сокра́т жил в пя́том ве́ке до на́шей э́ры, расцве́т гре́ческой скульпту́ры прихо́дится на пя́тый век до на́шей э́ры.

floury *adj* мучно́й; **my hands are all ~** у меня́ ру́ки в муке́; **a ~ potato** рассы́пчатая карто́шка.

flout *vt* пренебре|га́ть + *I* (ʼ-чь); **he ~s the conventions** он пренебрега́ет усло́вностями.

flow *n* (*current*) тече́ние, (*stream*) пото́к, *both also fig*; **ebb and ~** (*of tide*) отли́в и прили́в; *fig*: **a ~ of words** пото́к слов; **a steady ~ of exports** постоя́нный пото́к э́кспорта (*sing*).

flow *vi* течь, ли́ться, (*stream*) струи́ться (*impf*); **to begin to ~** поте́чь, поли́ться (*pfs*); **blood ~s through the veins** кровь течёт по жи́лам; **blood was ~ing from the wound** кровь текла́/лила́сь из ра́ны; **water began to ~ from the tap** вода́ потекла́/полила́сь из кра́на; **these rivers ~ into the Black Sea** э́ти ре́ки впада́ют/теку́т в Чёрное мо́ре; *fig*: **money ~ed in** де́ньги поступа́ли; **people ~ed into/out of the stadium** то́лпы люде́й вали́ли на стадио́н/покида́ли стадио́н.

flower *n* (*one flower*) цвето́к; **~s** цветы́; *fig* **the ~ of the army** цвет а́рмии.

flower *vi* цвести́ (*impf*), расцве|та́ть (-сти́).

flower bed *n* клу́мба.

flowerpot *n* цвето́чный горшо́к.

flu *n* грипп.

fluctuate *vi* колеба́ться (*usu impf*); **the price of tea ~s** це́ны (*pl*) на чай коле́блются; **we ~ between hope and despair** мы то полны́ наде́жды, то впада́ем в отча́яние.

flue *n* дымохо́д

fluency *n* (*of speech, piano-playing*) бе́глость; (*of style*) пла́вность, гла́дкость.

fluent *adj* бе́глый; **his Russian is ~** он бе́гло/свобо́дно говори́т по-ру́сски.

fluff *n* пух.

fluffy *adj* пуши́стый.

fluid *n* жи́дкость.

fluid *adj* жи́дкий; *fig* **our plans are still ~** на́ши пла́ны ещё не ясны́.

fluke *n* (*bit of luck*) неожи́данная уда́ча; **I only won by a ~** я вы́играл чи́сто случа́йно, я победи́л по чи́стой случа́йности.

flummox *vt CQ*: **I was completely ~ed** я был соверше́нно сбит с то́лку.

flunk *vt CQ*: **he ~ed his exam** он провали́лся на экза́мене.

fluorescent *adj* флюоресце́нтный.

fluoride *n Chem* фтори́д.

flurry *n*: **a ~ of wind/rain/snow** поры́в ве́тра, до́ждик, внеза́пный снегопа́д; *fig* **the house was in a ~ of excitement** в до́ме подня́лся переполо́х.

flurry *vt*: **don't ~ me!** не дёргай меня́!; **don't get flurried!** не суети́сь!, не волну́йся!

flush[1] *n* (*on face*) румя́нец, (*from embarrassment, anger*) кра́ска; *Med* **hot ~** прили́в кро́ви к лицу́; **the first ~ of dawn** пе́рвые лучи́ зари́; *Cards* **a straight/royal ~** «порядо́к» *or* «стрит», флешь-роя́ль; *fig*: **in the ~ of victory** в упое́нии побе́дой; **she's not in the first ~ of youth** она́ не пе́рвой мо́лодости.

flush[1] *vti vt* **1** *usu pass*: **she was ~ed from the exercise** от прогу́лки у неё разрумя́нились щёки; **his face was ~ed with drink** лицо́ у него́ раскрасне́лось от вы́питого вина́; **he was ~ed with success** он был упоён свои́м успе́хом

2: **to ~ (out) smth with water** смы|ва́ть что-л водо́й/струёй воды́ (-ть); **to ~ the toilet** спус|ка́ть во́ду в убо́рной/в туале́те (-ти́ть)

vi **1** (*blush*) красне́ть (по-); румя́ниться (за-, раз-); раскрасне́ться (*pf*); **he ~ed with shame/anger** он покрасне́л от стыда́/ от гне́ва

2: **the toilet won't ~** вода́ в туале́те не спуска́ется.

flush[2] *adj* **1** (*even*) *usu translated by* вро́вень (*adv*) с + *I*; **the river is ~ with its banks** река́ течёт вро́вень с берега́ми; **the doors are ~ with the walls** две́ри вде́ланы вро́вень/ заподлицо́ (*advs*) со стена́ми

2 *CQ*: **to be ~ (with money)** быть при деньга́х.

fluster *vt* волнова́ть (*impf*); **to be ~ed** волнова́ться, суети́ться.

flute *n* фле́йта.

flutter *vti vt*: **the bird ~ed its wings** пти́ца взмахну́ла кры́льями (*pf*)

vi (*of leaves*) трепета́ть (*impf*); (*of pulse*) неро́вно би́ться (*impf*); **flags ~ed in the breeze** знамёна колыха́лись/развева́лись на ветру́.

fly[1] *n* (*insect*) му́ха; (*for fishing*) (иску́сственная) му́ха; *fig*: **the ~ in the ointment** ло́жка дёгтя в бо́чке мёда; **there are no flies on him** его́ не проведёшь.

fly[2] *n usu pl* (**flies**) (*on trousers*) шири́нка (*sing*).

fly[3] *vti vt* **1**: **to ~ passengers/goods** пере|вози́ть пассажи́ров/гру́зы самолётом *or* по во́здуху (-везти́); **to ~ the Atlantic** перелет|а́ть (че́рез) Атланти́ческий океа́н (-е́ть)

2 (*of pilots*): **to ~ an aeroplane** вести́ (*only in impf*)/пилоти́ровать самолёт, управля́ть самолётом (*impfs*)

3 (*flags*): **the ship was ~ing the French flag** кора́бль шёл/пла́вал под францу́зским фла́гом; **all the embassies were ~ing their flags** все посо́льства вы́весили свои́ фла́ги

4 (*escape from*): **he had to ~ the country** ему́ пришло́сь бежа́ть из страны́

vi **1** (*general of birds, aeroplanes*) лета́ть (*indet impf, pf* полета́ть= *to fly around for a while, rarely used*), лете́ть (*det impf, pf* полете́ть= *to begin/set off to fly*) [*for true pf sense use pf of appropriate compound*]; **swallows ~ swiftly** ла́сточки лета́ют стреми́тельно; **we were ~ing over London during the storm** во вре́мя бу́ри мы лете́ли над Ло́ндоном; **they flew to the Arctic** они́ полете́ли в А́рктику; **he flew to Paris yesterday** вчера́ он улете́л/вы́летел в Пари́ж; **we flew from London to Paris in an hour** мы долете́ли из Ло́ндона в Пари́ж за час; **to ~ blind** (*on instruments*) лете́ть по прибо́рам; **the bird had flown** пти́чка улете́ла, *also fig*; *fig*: **to ~ for one's life/from justice** спас|а́ться бе́гством (-ти́сь), скры|ва́ться от правосу́дия (-́ться); **how time flies!** как лети́т вре́мя!; *CQ* **I must ~ now** я спешу́, я лечу́, я до́лжен бежа́ть

2 (*of flags, etc.*) развева́ться (*impf*); **with her hair ~ing loose** с развева́ющимися волоса́ми

3 *fig uses*: **as the crow flies** по прямо́й, кратча́йшим путём; **to let ~ at smth** (*shoot at*)/**at smb** (*abuse, scold*) стреля́ть во что-л (*impf*), на|бра́сываться на кого́-л с ру́ганью *or* с бра́нью (-бро́ситься); **I sent the vase ~ing** я столкну́л ва́зу; **he flew off the handle/into a rage** он как с цепи́ сорва́лся

4 [**NB** *note the following compounds of* лета́ть *which, although ending in* -ать, *are pf*]: (*to complete a period of flying*) отлета́ть (*pf*); (*to cover a certain distance or period of time flying*) налета́ть (*pf*); (*to fly there and back*) слета́ть (*pf*); **he has flown 5,000 miles/500 hours** он налета́л пять ты́сяч миль/пятьсо́т часо́в; **I flew to Moscow in April** (*and back*) я в апре́ле слета́л в Москву́

fly as far as *vi* долет|а́ть до + *G* (-е́ть); **we flew as far as Paris, but couldn't land** мы долете́ли до Пари́жа, но не смогли́ приземли́ться

fly at *vi* (*attack*) налет|а́ть/брос|а́ться на + *A* (-е́ть/-́иться); **the dog flew at the cat** соба́ка бро́силась на ко́шку

fly away *vi* улет|а́ть (-е́ть), вы|лета́ть (-́лететь); **her hat flew away** с неё слете́ла шля́па

fly by *vi* пролет|а́ть (-е́ть), *also fig*; **we flew by (way of) the North Pole** мы пролете́ли над Се́верным по́люсом; **the weeks flew by** неде́ли пролете́ли

fly in *vi*: **he flew in yesterday** он прилете́л вчера́; **a bird flew in through the window** пти́ца влете́ла в окно́; **to ~ in cargo** достав|ля́ть гру́зы (*pl*) самолётом (-́ить)

fly into *vi*: **we flew into Paris to refuel** мы сде́лали поса́дку в Пари́же для запра́вки горю́чим; **she flew into the room** она́ влете́ла в ко́мнату; **a bird flew into the windscreen** пти́ца уда́рилась о ветрово́е стекло́; **the plane flew into the hillside** самолёт вре́зался в го́ру

fly off *vi*: **the bird flew off the nest** пти́ца вы́летела из гнезда́; **a butterfly flew off that rose** с э́той ро́зы слете́ла ба́бочка; **to ~ off in different directions** разлет|а́ться в ра́зные сто́роны (-е́ться); *fig* **a button flew off** пу́говица отлете́ла

fly open *vi*: **the door flew open** дверь распах|ну́лась (*impf* -́иваться)

fly over *vi* лете́ть/пролет|а́ть над + *I* (по-/-е́ть); **we are now ~ing over London** тепе́рь мы лети́м/пролета́ем над Ло́ндоном

fly past пролет|а́ть (-е́ть), *also fig*; **summer flew past** ле́то пролете́ло; **she/a car flew past me** она́/маши́на промча́лась ми́мо меня́

fly round *vi* облете́ть + *A* *or* вокру́г + *G* (*pf*); **he flew round the lake** он облете́л о́зеро/вокру́г о́зера; *fig*: **rumours flew round the town** слу́хи облете́ли го́род/разлете́лись по го́роду; *CQ* **I'll just ~ round to the shop for a second** я ми́гом слета́ю в магази́н (*pf, implies "and back"*)

fly up *vi*: **sparks flew up** и́скры взлета́ли вверх; *fig* **she flew up to me** она́ подлете́ла ко мне.

flyer *n Aer* лётчик; *fig CQ* **he's a ~** он далеко́ пойдёт.

flying *n* полёт; **high-altitude/blind ~** высо́тный/слепо́й полёт.

flying *adj* лета́ющий; лету́чий; **a ~ fish/saucer** лету́чая ры́ба, «лета́ющая» таре́лка; *Aer* **~ hours** лётные часы́; **F. Fortress** (*aircraft*) «лета́ющая кре́пость»; *fig* **a ~ visit** мимолётный визи́т.

flyleaf *n* фо́рзац.

flyover *n* (*on motorway*) путепрово́д; эстака́да.

flyweight *n* боксёр наилегча́йшего ве́са.

flywheel *n* махово́е колесо́, махови́к.

foal *n* жеребёнок.

foam *n* пе́на.

foam *vi* (*of sea, beer*) пе́ниться (*usu impf*); **the horse was ~ing at the mouth** ло́шадь была́ в мы́ле, у ло́шади на губа́х была́ пе́на; **a ~ing glass of beer** кру́жка пе́нистого пи́ва; *fig* **he was ~ing at the mouth** (*with rage*) он говори́л с пе́ной у рта.

foam rubber *n* пороло́н; *attr*: **~ mattress** поролóновый матра́ц.

fob off *vt*: **he ~bed me off with excuses** он отде́лался от меня́ извине́ниями; **he ~bed defective goods off on his customers** он всучи́л покупа́телям брако́ванный това́р (*collect*); **my sister ~s off her unwanted clothes on to me** моя́ сестра́ навя́зывает мне свои́ нену́жные пла́тья.

focal *adj* (*in optics*) фо́кусный; **~ point** фо́кус.

focus *n* фо́кус, *also fig*; **to be in/out of ~** быть (не) в фо́кусе.

focus *vti vt*: **he ~ed the binoculars on the lighthouse** он навёл бино́кль на мая́к; *fig*: **to ~ one's attention on smth** сосредото́чить внима́ние на чём-л; **all eyes were ~ed on me** все взгля́ды бы́ли обращены́ на меня́

vi фокуси́ровать (с-); **after my operation I can't ~ properly** по́сле опера́ции у меня́ глаза́ пло́хо фокуси́руют.

fodder *n* корм (для скота́).

fog *n* тума́н; **the ~ is lifting/clearing** тума́н поднима́ется; **we ran into a belt of ~** мы попа́ли в полосу́ тума́на.

fogbound *adj*: **the ship was ~** су́дно заде́рживалось из-за тума́на.

fogey *n CQ*: **an old ~** ста́рый хрыч.

foggy *adj* тума́нный; **it's turning ~** ложи́тся тума́н; *fig CQ* **I haven't the foggiest notion of what you mean** я не име́ю ни мале́йшего поня́тия, что ты э́тим хо́чешь сказа́ть.

foghorn *n Naut* сире́на (,подаю́щая сигна́лы во вре́мя тума́на).

foglamp *n Aut* противотума́нная фа́ра.

foible *n* причу́да, капри́з.

foil *n* **1** (*metal wrapping*) фо́льга

2 (*contrast*): **to act as a ~ to smb/smth** служи́ть контра́стом кому́-л/чему́-л.

foist *vt*: **he ~ed the job/the children on to me** он спихну́л на меня́ э́ту рабо́ту/дете́й; **to ~ oneself on smb** навя́з|ываться кому́-л (-а́ться).

fold *n* (*of material*) скла́дка, *also Geol*; **a ~ of the hills** скла́дки (*pl*) холмо́в.

fold *vti vt* **1** (*bend*) скла́дывать (сложи́ть); **to ~ (up) a letter/clothes** сложи́ть письмо́/оде́жду; **with ~ed arms** сложа́/скрести́в ру́ки (на груди́); **to ~ back the bedspread** отки́|дывать покрыва́ло (-нуть); **to ~ down the corner of a page** за|гиба́ть у́гол страни́цы (-гну́ть); **to ~ up an umbrella** сложи́ть зо́нтик; *Cook* **to ~ in beaten egg whites** вме́ш|ивать взби́тые белки́ (-а́ть)

2 (*wrap*) завора́чивать, завёртывать (*pf for both* заверну́ть); **she ~ed her cloak round the baby/round her(self)** она́ заверну́ла ребёнка

/завернулась в плащ; **he ~ed her in his arms** он обнял её

vi: **the divan ~s up/down** этот диван складывается; *CQ* (*close*) **the factory has ~ed up** фабрика закрылась.

folder *n* (*for papers*) папка; **loose-leaf ~** скоросшиватель (*m*); (*giving timetables, etc.*) брошюра, проспект.

folding *adj* складной; **~ chairs/doors** складные стулья/двери; **a ~ table** раздвижной/раскладной стол.

foliage *n* листва.

folk *n collect* народ; люди (*pl*); **old ~** старики; **young ~** молодёжь (*collect*); *attr* народный; **~ dance** народный танец

folklore *n* фольклор.

folksong *n* народная песня.

follow *vti vt* **1** (*move or come after*) следовать за + *I* (по-); идти за + *I or* по + *D* (*usu impf*); (*pursue*) преследовать + *A* (*impf*); **~ me** следуй/иди за мной; **events ~ed in quick succession** события следовали одно за другим; **the enemy are ~ing us** враг преследует нас; **the road/boat ~ed the coast** дорога шла вдоль берега, корабль держался берега; **~ this road as far as the church** идите/поезжайте по этой дороге до церкви; **dinner will be ~ed by a concert** после ужина будет концерт; **he arrived first ~ed by his wife** он прибыл первым, за ним (приехала) его жена; **he ~ed his father as head gardener** он унаследовал от отца место старшего садовника; **to ~ up an advantage/idea** разви|вать успех/мысль (-ть); **we must ~ the job through** надо доводить дело до конца

2 (*to follow watching*) следить за + *I* (*impf*), *also fig*; **we're being ~ed** за нами следят; **to ~ the flight of birds** следить за полётом птиц; *fig*: **I can't ~ his line of thought** я не могу уследить за ходом его мыслей (*pl*); **he ~s international affairs/football** он следит за политикой/за футбольным чемпионатом

3 (*to follow example, etc.*) следовать + *D* (по-); **to ~ smb's advice/a custom/an example/the fashion/the rules** следовать чьему-л совету/обычаю/примеру/моде/правилам; **the police are ~ing up this information** полиция проверяет эти данные (*pl*); **to ~ a diet** соблю|дать диету (-сти); *Cards* **to ~ suit** ходить в масть, *fig* следовать примеру

4: to ~ the law быть/стать юристом

5 (*understand*): **I ~ you** (я) понимаю (вас)

vi **1: we'll ~ on in half an hour** мы выйдем вслед за вами/мы придём через полчаса; (*at meals*) **what's to ~?** что ещё будет?; **to ~ hard behind** ходить за кем-л по пятам; **as ~s** (*in article, etc.*) как следует ниже; **prices are as ~s** цены следующие; **my proposal is as ~s** у меня такое предложение

2 (*result*) следовать (*only in impf*); **it ~s from this that...** из этого следует, что...

3 (*understand*) пон|имать (-ять).

follower *n* последователь (*m*); (*admirer*) поклонник; **he's a ~ of "Dynamo"** (*SU football team*) он болеет за «Динамо»; **she's a great ~ of fashion** она большая модница.

following *n*: **he has a large ~** у него много последователей/поклонников.

following *adj* **1** следующий; **on the ~ day** на следующий день; **a ~ wind** попутный ветер; *as n*: **the ~ should report at 9 o'clock** нижеследующие должны прийти к девяти часам; **he said the ~** он сказал следующее

2 *as prep* после + *G*, вслед за + *I*.

folly *n* глупость, безрассудство.

foment *vt fig*: **to ~ hatred** раз|жигать ненависть (-жечь); **to ~ rebellion** подстрекать (кого-л) к мятежу (*impf*).

fond *adj* (*loving*) любящий; (*tender*) нежный [*both adjs may also = overfond*]; (*of hopes, ambitions*) тщетный; **I'm ~ of her/skating** я люблю её/кататься на коньках.

fondle *vt* ласкать (*impf*).

food *n* пища, еда; (*for animals*) корм; **~ and drink** еда и питьё; **wholesome ~** здоровая пища; *fig* **~ for thought** пища для размышлений (*pl*); *attr*: **~ poisoning** пищевое отравление; **~ value** питательная ценность, питательность.

fool *n* дурак; **what a ~ I was to trust him** какой я был дурак, что доверял ему; **to play the ~** валять дурака; **to make a ~ of oneself/of smb** свалять дурака, одурачить *or* провести кого-л; *CQ* **that ~ of a doctor gave me the wrong pills** этот дурак-доктор прописал мне не то лекарство.

fool *vti vt* одурачи|вать (-ть); провести (*only in pf*); **you can't ~ me** меня не проведёшь; **it didn't ~ him** он не клюнул на эту удочку; **you had me properly ~ed there** тут-то вы меня и поймали; **to ~ smb out of his money** вы|манивать у кого-л деньги (-манить)

vi дурачиться (*impf*); **to ~ about/around** болтаться без дела (*impf*).

foolery *n* дурачество.

foolhardy *adj* безрассудно храбрый; **a ~ person** сорвиголова.

foolish *adj* глупый; **how ~ of you** как глупо с вашей стороны; **that will make him look ~** у него будет такой глупый вид; **don't be ~** не будь дураком/(*f*) дурой.

foolproof *adj*: **this camera is ~** этим фотоаппаратом может снимать каждый.

foot *n* **1** (*of people*) нога (*general word, but also = leg*); стопа, ступня; **the sole of the ~** ступня, подошва ступни; **on ~** пешком; **a slender/broken ~** узкая ступня, перелом стопы; **to get to one's feet** встать на ноги; **I've been on my feet all day** я весь день на ногах; **the children have been under my feet all day** дети весь день вертятся у меня под ногами; **he's light on his feet** у него лёгкая походка; **he trod on my ~** он наступил мне на ногу; **I want to put**

my feet up for an hour мне хо́чется полежа́ть часо́к; **it's wet under** ~ под нога́ми (*pl*) сы́ро; **heavy feet could be heard** послы́шались тяжёлые шаги́; *Aut* **to put one's** ~ **down on the accelerator** нажа́ть на газ; *fig* **I'll never set** ~ **there again** ноги́ моéй там бо́льше не бу́дет

2 *various*: (*of animals*) нога́, (*paw*) ла́па; (*measure*) фут; (*in verse*) стопа́; (*base of a statue*) подно́жие, основа́ние; (*of hill*) подно́жие, подо́шва; **hind feet** за́дние но́ги/ла́пы; ~ **of a stocking** носо́к чулка́; **at the** ~ **of the page** в конце́/внизу́ страни́цы; **he sat at the** ~ **of the table/the bed** он сиде́л в конце́ стола́/в изно́жье крова́ти

3 *fig uses*: **he fell on his feet** ему́ повезло́; **I agreed to do it, but now I've got cold feet** я согласи́лся бы́ло э́то сде́лать, но тепе́рь ста́ло что́-то страшнова́то; **you'll have to put your** ~ **down** вам на́до быть потвёрже; **to stand on one's own feet** стать на́ ноги, стать незави́симым; **he's finding his feet now** он понемно́гу осва́ивается; **to put one's** ~ **in it** сде́лать ля́псус, сесть в кало́шу; **he got off on the wrong** ~ **with the boss** он с са́мого нача́ла че́м-то не угоди́л/ *CQ* не потра́фил нача́льству; **he never puts a** ~ **wrong** он никогда́ не осту́пится; **he's got one** ~ **in the grave** он стои́т одно́й ного́й в моги́ле.

foot *vt CQ*: **he said he'd** ~ **the bill** он сказа́л, что (он) запла́тит (по счёту); **we'll have to** ~ **it** нам придётся идти́ пешко́м.

football *n* (*soccer*) футбо́л; (*ball*) футбо́льный мяч.

footballer *n* футболи́ст.

footbridge *n* пешехо́дный мо́ст(ик).

footfall *n* шаг; по́ступь; (*sound*) звук шаго́в.

foothills *npl* предго́рье, предго́рья.

foothold *n*: **to have a firm** ~ име́ть твёрдую опо́ру под нога́ми.

footing *n*: **to lose/keep one's** ~ оступи́ться, удержа́ться на нога́х; **to be on a friendly/ equal** ~ **with smb** быть с кем-л на дру́жеской/ра́вной ноге́; **on a war** ~ в состоя́нии боево́й гото́вности.

footlights *npl* ра́мпа (*sing*).

footling *adj* пустяко́вый.

footman *n* лаке́й.

footnote *n* сно́ска.

footpath *n* тропи́нка, (пешехо́дная) доро́жка.

footprint *n* след; отпеча́ток ноги́.

footrest *n* подста́вка для ног (*may also* = *extension of chair*).

foot soldier *n* пехоти́нец.

footsore *adj*: **I'm** ~ у меня́ боля́т но́ги.

footstep *n* (*track*) след; (*tread*) шаг; ~**s in the snow** следы́ на снегу́; **I hear** ~**s** я слы́шу шаги́; *fig* **the son followed in his father's** ~**s** сын пошёл по стопа́м отца́.

footstool *n* скаме́ечка для ног.

footwear *n* о́бувь (*no pl*).

for *prep* **1** (*of time*) **i)** *past and present*: *A case*; **I worked** ~ **an hour** я рабо́тал час; **I've not been there** ~ **6 years** я уже́ шесть лет там не́ был; ~ **some time he said nothing** не́которое вре́мя он молча́л; **the play lasts** ~ **two hours** пье́са идёт два часа́; **ii)** *of time subsequent to the action of the main verb*: *usu* на + *A*; **he's going to England** ~ **a year**/ ~ **quite a time** он е́дет в А́нглию на́ год/дово́льно надо́лго; **the meeting is fixed** ~ **tomorrow** заседа́ние назна́чено на за́втра: **he's been elected** ~ **three years** он и́збран на́ три го́да; **he won't be back** ~ **another three days** он не вернётся ещё три дня; **iii)** *during*: ~ **the last three weeks** после́дние три неде́ли; ~ **many years** мно́гие го́ды, в тече́ние/ на протяже́нии мно́гих лет; **iv)** *other expressions concerning time*: ~ **the time being that's all** пока́ всё; ~ **the first and last time** в пе́рвый и после́дний раз; ~ **this once** на э́тот раз; **once and** ~ **all** раз и навсегда́; **it's getting on** ~ **2 o'clock** ско́ро два часа́; ~ **hours on end** це́лыми часа́ми

2 (*of distance*) *A case*; **he walked** ~ **two miles** он прошёл две ми́ли; (*to express distance from a centre*) на + *A*; **there wasn't a house** ~ **miles around** на мно́гие ми́ли вокру́г не́ было ни одного́ до́ма

3 (*of destination*) в + *A*, на + *A*; **to leave** ~ **London**/ ~ **the south** уезжа́ть в Ло́ндон/на юг; **to sail** ~ **New York** плыть в Нью-Йо́рк; **change here** ~ **Oxford!** здесь переса́дка на О́ксфорд!; **passengers** ~ **Kiev** пассажи́ры, е́дущие в Ки́ев

4 (*of purpose*) **i)** для + *G*; **to assign rooms** ~ **lessons** отводи́ть ко́мнаты для заня́тий; **what is this tool** ~?—**It's** ~ **drilling** для чего́ э́тот инструме́нт?—Для сверле́ния; **books** ~ **children** кни́ги для дете́й; **it's** ~ **your own good** э́то для твое́й же по́льзы; **to peel apples** ~ **a pie** чи́стить я́блоки для пирога́; **ii)** ра́ди + *G*; **to read** ~ **pleasure** чита́ть ра́ди удово́льствия; **I did it** ~ **a joke** я э́то сде́лал шу́тки ра́ди; **he works** ~ **his children** он рабо́тает ра́ди свои́х дете́й; *CQ* ~ **God's sake** ра́ди бо́га; **iii)** на + *A*; **to save** ~ **a rainy day** откла́дывать на чёрный день; **to buy coal** ~ **the winter** покупа́ть у́голь на́ зиму; **to peel potatoes** ~ **supper** чи́стить карто́шку (*collect*) на у́жин; **applicants** ~ **the post** претенде́нты на до́лжность; **a good memory** ~ **names** хоро́шая па́мять на имена́; **to go** ~ **a walk** идти́ на прогу́лку, пойти́ погуля́ть; **theatre closed** ~ **repair** теа́тр закры́т на ремо́нт; **orders/demand** ~ **coal** зака́зы/спрос на у́голь; **I'm fit** ~ **nothing at present** я сейча́с никуда́ не гожу́сь; **iv)** за + *A*, за + *I*; **to fight** ~ **freedom** боро́ться за свобо́ду; **I'm going out** ~ **some milk** я иду́ за молоко́м; **v)** под + *A*; **to allocate premises** ~ **a school/ground** ~ **growing vegetables** отводи́ть помеще́ние под шко́лу/уча́сток под огоро́д; **vi)** о + *P*;

the order ~ the attack прика́з о наступле́нии; **a proposal ~ a conference** предложе́ние о созы́ве конфере́нции; vii) *D without prep*; **it's good enough ~ me** э́то мне подойдёт; **this parcel is ~ you** э́тот паке́т тебе́/для тебя́; **to buy flowers ~ smb** покупа́ть цветы́ кому́-л; viii) *interrogatively*: **what did you do that ~?** заче́м ты э́то сде́лал?; **what ~?** заче́м?, к чему́?; ix) + *inf*: **it's time ~ bed/~ dinner** пора́ спать/обе́дать; **I've no time ~ reading** мне не́когда чита́ть

5 (*showing aptitudes, attitudes, inclinations*) к + *D*; **he has ability ~ music** у него́ спосо́бности (*pl*) к му́зыке; **he has a weakness ~ blondes** у него́ сла́бость к блонди́нкам

6 i) (*considering*): **it's warm today ~ January** сего́дня тепло́—совсе́м не янва́рская пого́да; **he's tall ~ his age** он ро́слый не по года́м; **it's cheap ~ nowadays** по на́шим времена́м э́то не до́рого; ii) (*despite*): **~ all his faults** несмотря́ на все его́ недоста́тки; **~ all that, he's a good teacher** несмотря́ на всё э́то, он хоро́ший педаго́г; **~ all you may say** что́ бы вы ни говори́ли; iii) (*concerning*): **I ~ my part** я со свое́й стороны́, что каса́ется меня́, я...; **so much the worse ~ him** тем ху́же для него́

7 i) (*representing*): **member ~ Oxford** член парла́мента от О́ксфорда; **to act ~ smb** де́йствовать от чьего́-л и́мени/лица́; ii) (*as*): **to use a box ~ a table** по́льзоваться я́щиком как столо́м; **they chose him ~ president** они́ вы́брали его́ президе́нтом; **to eat ~ three** есть за трои́х

8 (*in exchange*) i) за + *A*; **payment ~ work** пла́та за рабо́ту; **to pay ~ a ticket** плати́ть за биле́т; **not ~ the world** ни за что на све́те; ii) на + *A*; **to play ~ money** игра́ть на де́ньги; **what can I buy ~ a rouble?** что я могу́ купи́ть на рубль?; **to exchange roubles ~ dollars** обме́нивать рубли́ на до́ллары; **a cheque ~ £3** чек на три фу́нта

9 (*of remedies*) от + *G*, про́тив + *G*; **a cure ~ toothache** сре́дство от зубно́й бо́ли; **medicine ~ a cough** лека́рство от ка́шля; **an injection ~ flu** приви́вка про́тив гриппа

10 (*of cause*): **to condemn/thank/punish/reward smb ~ smth** осужда́ть/благодари́ть/нака́зывать/награжда́ть кого́-л за что-л; **to fear/rejoice ~ smb** боя́ться/ра́доваться за кого́-л; **to shout ~ joy** вскри́кнуть от ра́дости; **he's famous ~ his wit** он изве́стен свои́м остроу́мием; **~ the reason that...** по той причи́не, что...; **I chose this material ~ its colour** я вы́брал э́ту ткань из-за расцве́тки; **~ lack of anything better** за неиме́нием лу́чшего; **we didn't cross the field ~ fear of the bull** мы не пошли́ по́лем—испуга́лись быка́; **~ fear of waking the baby** что́бы не разбуди́ть ребёнка; **~ fear of hurting her feelings he...** боя́сь её оби́деть, он...; **he's much the better ~ his holiday/~ the medicine** он чу́вствует себя́ намно́го лу́чше по́сле о́тпуска/, приня́в э́то лека́рство; **if it weren't ~ you I would have lost my way** е́сли бы не вы, я бы заблуди́лся

11 (*in favour of*) за + *A*; **are you ~ the proposal?—I'm all ~ it** вы за э́то предложе́ние?—Я целико́м за (него́); **he's all ~ leaving tomorrow** он за то, что́бы вы́ехать за́втра

12 (*with infinitive phrases*) *usu D case*; **it's ~ you to decide** вам реша́ть; **it will be good ~ her to rest** ей бу́дет поле́зно отдохну́ть; **he gave orders ~ it to be done** он приказа́л э́то сде́лать; **it's all very well ~ him to say that** ему́-то хорошо́ так говори́ть; **~ this to be possible we need more money** что́бы э́то осуществи́ть, нам ну́жно бо́льше де́нег

13 *various*: **look ~ yourself** посмотри́те са́ми; **to hope ~ the best** наде́яться на лу́чшее; **~ all he cares I could be starving** ему́ всё равно́, да́же е́сли я бу́ду умира́ть/помру́ с го́лоду; **~ certain** наверняка́; **to change ~ the better** измени́ться к лу́чшему; **can I do anything ~ you?** чем я могу́ вам помо́чь?; **~ better or worse** в сча́стье и в несча́стье; *CQ*: **there's nothing ~ it but to go** ничего́ не поде́лаешь—придётся е́хать; **I'm ~ it!** (*a scolding*) мне доста́нется!; **good ~ you!** здо́рово!, молоде́ц!

for *conj* потому́ что, так как; и́бо.

forage *n* фура́ж.

forbear *vi* возде́рж|иваться от + *G* (-а́ться); **I forebore to express my opinion** я воздержа́лся от выска́зываний (*pl*); [**NB** *negative use*]: **I could not ~ expressing/to express my opinion** я не мог не вы́сказать своего́ мне́ния.

forbearance *n* вы́держка; **he showed ~ in a difficult situation** он проявля́л вы́держку в тру́дных обстоя́тельствах.

forbears *n usu pl* пре́дки.

forbid *vt* запре|ща́ть (-ти́ть); **the doctor has ~den me to touch alcohol** врач запрети́л мне прикаса́ться к спиртно́му; **"Walking on the grass is ~den"** «по газо́нам ходи́ть воспреща́ется».

forbidden *adj* запрещённый, (*usu only official*) воспрещённый; запре́тный; **a ~ zone** запре́тная зо́на; **"Smoking/Entry ~"** «кури́ть воспреща́ется», «вход воспрещён».

forbidding *adj* (*of people*) суро́вый; (*threatening*) гро́зный; **he looks ~** у него́ суро́вый/гро́зный вид; **~ cliffs** суро́вые ска́лы.

force *n* **1** (*strength*) си́ла; (*violence*) наси́лие; **the ~ of a blow/an argument** си́ла уда́ра/до́вода; **the ~ of gravity** си́ла притяже́ния; **by ~** си́лой; **by ~ of circumstances/of habit** си́лою обстоя́тельств, в си́лу привы́чки; **with all one's ~** изо всех сил; **brute ~** гру́бая си́ла; **to resort to ~** прибега́ть к си́ле/к наси́лию; **he's a ~ among his fellow students** он авторите́т среди́ свои́х това́рищей; **there's ~ in what you say** в том, что вы говори́те, есть смысл

2 *Law*: **to be/remain in ~** быть/остава́ться в си́ле; **to put a law into ~** вводи́ть зако́н в си́лу

3 (*body of people*): **the police ~** поли́ция; **the fire brigade were there in full ~** пожа́рная кома́нда была́ в по́лном соста́ве (*in full official complement*); **the students came in ~** студе́нты пришли́ толпо́й; **to join ~s** *Mil* объедини́ть си́лы, *Polit* объединя́ть уси́лия; **let's join ~s and go off for a picnic tomorrow** дава́йте все вме́сте съе́здим за́втра куда́-нибудь за́ город.

force *vt* **1** (*use force on smth*): **to ~ an entry into a house** вла́мываться в дом (вломи́ться); **to ~ a lock/door** взла́мывать замо́к/дверь (взлома́ть); **to ~ one's way through a crowd** проби|ва́ться сквозь толпу́ (-́ться)

2 (*constrain*) застав|ля́ть (-́ить), прину|жда́ть (-́дить), вы|нужда́ть (-́нудить); **to ~ smb to do smth** заста́вить/прину́дить/вы́нудить кого́-л сде́лать что-л; **he ~d the money on them/them to take the money** он заста́вил их взять де́ньги; **to ~ smb to confess/a confession from smb** вы́нудить призна́ние у кого́-л; **I am ~d to conclude that...** я вы́нужден заключи́ть, что...; **I ~d myself to get down to work** я заста́вил себя́ взя́ться за рабо́ту [**NB** вы́нудить *not used reflex with* себя́]; (*impose*) **he tried to ~ himself/the dog/the idea on us** он навя́зывался к нам, он навя́зывал нам соба́ку/э́ту иде́ю

3 (*speed up*): **to ~ the pace** ускор|я́ть темп (-́ить); **to ~ plants** вы|гоня́ть расте́ния (-́гнать); *fig* **to ~ pupils** перегру|жа́ть ученико́в (-зи́ть).

forced *adj*: **a ~ landing** вы́нужденная поса́дка; **~ laughter** принуждённый смех; **a ~ smile** натя́нутая улы́бка; **a ~ march** форси́рованный марш; **~ tulips** вы́гоночные тюльпа́ны.

forceful *adj* си́льный; **he is a ~ person** он волево́й/*CQ* (*pushing*) о́чень напо́ристый; **a ~ argument** убеди́тельный аргуме́нт.

forcemeat *n* мясна́я начи́нка.

forceps *npl* хирурги́ческие щипцы́ (*no sing*).

forcible *adj* (*done by force*) наси́льственный; (*of person, style*) напо́ристый; **a ~ entry** наси́льственное вторже́ние.

ford *n* брод.

ford *vt*: **to ~ a river** (*on foot*) пере|ходи́ть ре́ку вброд (*adv*) (-йти́).

fore *n*: **he's very much to the ~ these days** он тепе́рь на виду́.

fore *adj* пере́дний; *Naut* носово́й.

fore *adv Naut*: **~ and aft** на носу́ и на корме́.

forearm *n* предпле́чье.

foreboding *n*: **I have a ~ that...** у меня́ тако́е предчу́вствие, что...

forecast *n* прогно́з; предсказа́ние; **weather ~** прогно́з пого́ды; **~ of next year's trade figures** прогно́з объёма торго́вли на бу́дущий год; **his ~ proved wrong** его́ предсказа́ния (*pl*) не сбыли́сь.

forecast *vt* предска́з|ывать (-а́ть), де́лать прогно́з (с-).

foredoomed *adj*: **the attempt was ~ to failure** попы́тка была́ обречена́ на прова́л.

forefinger *n* указа́тельный па́лец.

forefoot *n* пере́дняя нога́.

forego *vt* отка́з|ываться от + *G* (-а́ться); **she said she'd have to ~ the trip** она́ сказа́ла, что ей придётся отказа́ться от пое́здки.

foregoing *adj* предше́ствующий.

foregone *adj*: **it's a ~ conclusion** э́то предрешено́.

foreground *n* пере́дний план; **in the ~** на пере́днем пла́не, *also fig*.

forehand *n* (*in tennis*) уда́р откры́той (раке́ткой).

forehead *n* лоб.

foreign *adj* **1** иностра́нный; загран́ичный, зарубе́жный; **~ languages** иностра́нные языки́; **Ministry of F. Affairs** (*SU*), **F. Office** (*UK*) министе́рство иностра́нных дел; **~ passport** иностра́нный па́спорт; **passport for ~ travel** (*as issued to SU citizens*) загран́ичный па́спорт; **~ goods** (*made abroad*) и́мпортные това́ры; **~ guests/countries** зарубе́жные го́сти/стра́ны; **~ policy/trade** вне́шняя поли́тика/торго́вля

2: *Med* **a ~ body** иноро́дное те́ло; **deceit is ~ to his nature** прибега́ть к обма́ну не в его́ хара́ктере.

foreigner *n* иностра́нец.

foreknowledge *n* предви́дение; **to have ~ of smth** знать что-л зара́нее.

foreman *n* ма́стер; бригади́р; *Law* **~ of the jury** старшина́ прися́жных.

foremost *adj*: **I consider him the ~ writer of the century** я счита́ю его́ крупне́йшим писа́телем на́шего столе́тия.

foremost *adv*: **head ~** голово́й вперёд; **first and ~** пре́жде всего́, во-пе́рвых.

forensic *adj* суде́бный.

foresee *vt* предви́деть (*impf*).

foreseeable *adj*: **in the ~ future** *approx* в ближа́йшем бу́дущем.

foreshadow *vt* предвеща́ть (*impf*).

foreshorten *vt Art* черти́ть в ра́курсе (на-); **~ed** в ра́курсе.

foresight *n* предви́дение; (*prudence*) предусмотри́тельность.

forest *n* лес; (*for game*) охо́тничий запове́дник; **pine ~** сосно́вый бор; *fig* **a ~ of chimneys** лес труб; *attr* лесно́й.

forestall *vt* (*avert*) предупре|жда́ть (-ди́ть); (*get in first*) опере|жа́ть (-ди́ть); **you ~ed me** ты опереди́л меня́; **to ~ disaster** предупреди́ть несча́стье.

forester *n* лесни́к.

forestry *n* лесово́дство; *attr*: **~ officer** лесни́чий.

foretaste *n* предвкуше́ние.

foretell *vi* предска́з|ывать (-а́ть).

forethought *n* предусмотри́тельность.

forever *adv* навсегда́, наве́ки; ве́чно; **he's ~ pestering me** он ве́чно изво́дит меня́.

forewarn *vt* предостере|гáть (-́чь); **~ed is forearmed** кто предостережён, тот вооружён.

foreword *n* предисло́вие.

forfeit *n* штраф; **to play at ~s** игрáть в фáнты; (*in game*) **to pay a ~** плати́ть штраф.

forfeit *vt* лиш|áться + *G* (-и́ться); **he ~ed his property** он лиши́лся иму́щества; **his driving licence was ~ed** у негó отобрáли води́тельские правá (*pl*); **he has ~ed the respect of his friends** он лиши́лся уважéния друзéй; *Sport* **to ~ a point** потеря́ть очкó.

forfend *vi*: **heaven ~!** не дай бог!, бóже упаси́!

forgather *vi* со|бирáться (-брáться).

forge[1] *n* ку́зница.

forge[1] *vt* **1: to ~ steel** ковáть сталь (*impf*)

2 (*money, documents, signature*) поддéл|ывать (-ать).

forge[2] *vi*: **to ~ ahead** продви|гáться (-́нуться), *Sport* вы|ходи́ть вперёд (-́йти).

forger *n* фальсификáтор; (*of money*) фальшивомонéтчик.

forgery *n* (*act or object*) поддéлка; (*of a document*) подлóг.

forget *vti vt* забы|вáть (-́ть); *CQ* позабы́ть (*usu pf*); [**NB** *present* забывáю *only used continuously*]; **I keep ~ting to buy matches** я всё врéмя забывáю купи́ть спи́чки; **I ~ where I put my spectacles** я забы́л, кудá положи́л очки́; **I forgot that you were leaving tomorrow** я (по)забы́л, что ты уезжáешь зáвтра; **to ~ oneself** (*unselfishly*) забывáть о себé, (*to behave badly*) забывáться; **it was a day never to be forgotten** э́то был незабывáемый день; *CQ*: **and don't you ~ it!** попрóбуй тóлько забы́ть об э́том!; **~ it!** (*it's not important*) э́то невáжно!, (*brushing off thanks*) нé за что!, (*in either sense*) не стóит об э́том говори́ть!

vi забывáть, *CQ* позабы́ть; **I forgot about the time/to ring up** я (по)забы́л о врéмени/позвони́ть.

forgetful *adj* забы́вчивый; **~ of the danger he ran to help her** забы́в об опáсности, он брóсился к ней на пóмощь; **how ~ of me!** какáя забы́вчивость с моéй стороны́!

forget-me-not *n* незабу́дка.

forgivable *adj* прости́тельный.

forgive *vt* про|щáть (-сти́ть); **I forgave him his debts/for forgetting his promise** я прости́л емý егó долги́/, что он забы́л своё обещáние; **~ my interrupting you** прости́те, что я вас перебивáю.

forgiveness *n* прощéние.

forgiving *adj* великоду́шный.

forgotten *adj* забы́тый.

fork *n* ви́лка; *Agric* ви́лы (*pl*); (*in tree*) разветвлéние; (*in road*) разви́лка; **tuning ~** камертóн.

fork *vti vt*: **to ~ over the soil** вскáпывать зéмлю (вскопáть); **to ~ hay** вороши́ть сéно (*usu impf*); **to ~ hay on to a trailer** подавáть сéно ви́лами на прицéп

vi (*branch*) разветвля́ться (*usu impf*); (*turn*) по|ворáчивать (-верну́ть); **the road ~s here** здесь дорóга разветвля́ется; **~ right at the church** у цéркви поверни́те напрáво.

forked *adj*: **a bird with a ~ tail** пти́ца с раздвóенным хвостóм.

forlorn *adj* жáлкий; несчáстный; **a ~ expression** жáлкое/несчáстное выражéние (лицá); **a ~ smile/attempt** жáлкая улы́бка/попы́тка; **a ~ hope** слáбая надéжда.

form *n* **1** (*shape, structure, sort*) фóрма, *also Philos*; вид; **a bowl in the ~ of a rose** чáша в фóрме рóзы; **in sonata ~** в фóрме сонáты; **in abridged ~** в сокращённом ви́де; **medicine in the ~ of powder** лекáрство в ви́де порошкá; **flu takes various ~s** грипп мóжет принимáть рáзные фóрмы; **various ~s of transport** разли́чные ви́ды трáнспорта; **in legal ~** судéбным поря́дком

2 (*figure*) фигу́ра; **her slender ~** её тóнкая фигу́ра

3 (*etiquette*) формáльность; **it's just a matter of ~** э́то чи́стая формáльность; **for ~'s sake** рáди профóрмы; **bad ~** дурнóй тон

4 (*fitness*) фóрма; **the runner is in good ~** бегу́н в хорóшей фóрме; (*of general spirits*) **he was in great ~** он был в удáре

5 (*document*) бланк; (*questionnaire*) анкéта; **a telegraph ~** телегрáфный бланк; **to fill in a ~** запóлнить бланк/анкéту

6 (*in school*) класс

7 (*bench in garden*) скамéйка, (*in school*) шкóльная скамья́.

form *vti vt* **1** (*make, shape*) образóв|ывать (-áть); (*construct*) состав|ля́ть (-́ить); **to ~ the plural/a sentence** образовáть мнóжественное числó, состáвить предложéние; **to ~ smth out of clay/wood/stone** лепи́ть что-л из гли́ны (вы́-), вы|резáть что-л из дéрева (-́резать), вы|секáть что-л из кáмня (-́сечь); *fig* **to ~ a child's character** формировáть харáктер ребёнка (с-)

2 (*take the shape or order of*) образóвывать; **to ~ a circle/a queue** образовáть круг/óчередь; *Mil* **~ fours!** ряды́ вздвой!

3 (*organize*) организó|вывать (-вáть); формировáть (с-); (*create*) созда|вáть (-́ть); **to ~ a club/a choir** организовáть клуб/хор; **to ~ a regiment/a government** сформировáть полк/прави́тельство; **to ~ a committee/a class for beginners** создáть коми́ссию/гру́ппу начинáющих

4 (*constitute*): **the ministers who ~ the government** мини́стры, входя́щие в прави́тельство; **to ~ the basis of/the proof of** яв|ля́ться оснóвой + *G*/доказáтельством + *G* (-и́ться)

5 (*develop*) создавáть, составля́ть; **to ~ a theory/an opinion** создáть теóрию, состáвить мнéние; **I ~ed the impression that...** у меня́ сложи́лось впечатлéние, что...; **he ~ed the habit of walking every day** у негó вы́работалась привы́чка гуля́ть кáждый день

vi образóвываться; формировáться; (*develop*) разви|вáться (-́ться); **ice ~s at minus 4°**

то́лстый слой льда образу́ется при четырёх гра́дусах ни́же нуля́; **crystals ~ed on the glass** на стекле́ образова́лись криста́ллы; **character is ~ed in youth** хара́ктер формиру́ется в ра́нней ю́ности; **an idea was beginning to ~** иде́я начала́ развива́ться/формирова́ться.

formal *adj* форма́льный; **~ logic/politeness** форма́льная ло́гика/ве́жливость; **he is very ~** он стра́шный формали́ст; **a ~ dinner/bow** банке́т *or* официа́льный обе́д, церемо́нный покло́н.

formality *n* форма́льность; **legal formalities** суде́бные форма́льности; **there's too much ~ here** тут сли́шком мно́го форма́льностей (*pl*); **it's just a ~** э́то чи́стая форма́льность.

formally *adv* форма́льно; официа́льно.

formation *n* **1** (*setting up*): **the ~ of a government/a committee** формирова́ние прави́тельства, образова́ние комите́та; **the ~ of a plan** разрабо́тка пла́на; **the ~ of character** становле́ние хара́ктера

2 (*structure*) строе́ние, структу́ра; *Geol* форма́ция; **what is the ~ of this flower?** како́е строе́ние име́ет э́тот цвето́к?; **the ~ of the soil** структу́ра по́чвы

3 *Mil* построе́ние; поря́док; **battle ~** боево́й поря́док.

formative *adj*: **a ~ influence** формиру́ющее влия́ние; **the ~years of a child's life** го́ды, когда́ формиру́ется хара́ктер/ли́чность ребёнка.

former *adj* **1** (*of two*) пе́рвый; **of the two routes the ~ is the shorter** из э́тих двух доро́г пе́рвая коро́че

2 (*earlier*) пре́жний; **in ~ times** в пре́жние/в бы́лые времена́; (*ex-*): **a ~ friend, the ~ president** бы́вший друг/президе́нт.

formerly *adv* пре́жде, ра́ньше.

formidable *adj*: **the admiral is a very ~ person** адмира́л—гро́зная фигу́ра; **it's a ~ task** э́то о́чень тру́дное де́ло; **our teacher was a ~ man** мы поба́ивались на́шего учи́теля.

formless *adj* бесфо́рменный.

formula *n* фо́рмула, *also Math*; формулиро́вка; **a ~ acceptable to all parties** фо́рмула,/формулиро́вка, прие́млемая для всех сторо́н.

formulate *vt* формули́ровать (*impf and pf, pf also* с-).

forsake *vt* (*person, place*) поки|да́ть (-́нуть).

forswear *vt* заре|ка́ться + *inf* (-́чься); **I've forsworn drinking/sweets** я зарёкся пить/есть конфе́ты.

forte *n*: **singing is not his ~** пе́ние не его́ стихи́я.

forth *adv*: **he set ~** он отпра́вился (в путь); **from that day ~** с э́того дня; **and so ~** и так да́лее, и тому́ подо́бное (*abbr* и т.д., и т.п.).

forthcoming *adj* **1** (*approaching*) предстоя́щий; **the ~ elections** предстоя́щие вы́боры; **list of ~ books** спи́сок выходя́щих в свет изда́ний

2 (*available, etc.*): **no answer was ~** не́ было никако́го отве́та; **the money was not ~** де́ньги не поступи́ли

3 (*of people*) *usu predic*: **he was not very ~ when I asked him about his plans/to help** он не сли́шком открове́нничал, когда́ я спроси́л о его́ пла́нах, он не прояви́л осо́бого жела́ния *or* энтузиа́зма, когда́ я попроси́л его́ помо́чь.

forthright *adj* прямо́й, открове́нный.

forthwith *adv* то́тчас.

fortieth *adj* сороково́й; **he's in his ~ year** ему́ ско́ро со́рок; (*in obituary*): **he died in his ~ year** он у́мер на сороково́м году́ жи́зни; *as n* (**a ~**) одна́ сорокова́я (часть).

fortify *vt*: *Mil* **to ~ a town** укреп|ля́ть го́род (-и́ть); *CQ* **to ~ oneself with a good breakfast/with a whisky** пло́тно поза́втракать (*usu pf*), подкреп|ля́ться рю́мкой ви́ски (-и́ться).

fortitude *n* си́ла ду́ха; (*steadfastness*) сто́йкость.

fortnight *n* две неде́ли; **in a ~** че́рез две неде́ли; **a ~ today/next Monday** ро́вно че́рез две неде́ли, в понеде́льник че́рез две неде́ли; **every ~** ка́ждые две неде́ли; **to take a ~'s holiday** брать две неде́ли о́тпуска/двухнеде́льный о́тпуск.

fortress *n* кре́пость.

fortuitous *adj* случа́йный.

fortunate *adj* счастли́вый; **it was a ~ day for us** э́то был счастли́вый день для нас; **I was ~ in finding him at home** к сча́стью, я заста́л его́ до́ма; **he was ~ in life/in his teacher** ему́ всю жизнь везло́ (*impers*), ему́ повезло́ с учи́телем; **it was ~ for you that...** вам повезло́, что...

fortunately *adv* к сча́стью.

fortune *n* **1** (*fate*) судьба́; **to tell smb's ~** предсказа́ть чью-л судьбу́; **to tell ~s by cards/from coffee cups** гада́ть на ка́ртах/на кофе́йной гу́ще

2 (*luck*) сча́стье; **by good ~** к сча́стью, по счастли́вой случа́йности; **I had the good ~ to get a ticket** мне посчастли́вилось (*impers*) доста́ть биле́т

3 (*riches*) (**a ~**) состоя́ние; **to make a ~** нажи́ть состоя́ние; **it's worth a small ~** э́то сто́ит це́лое состоя́ние; **to spend a ~ on clothes** тра́тить у́йму де́нег на оде́жду.

fortuneteller *n* гада́лка.

forty *num* со́рок (*in oblique cases* сорока́); **40 roubles** со́рок рубле́й; **chapter 40** глава́ сорокова́я; **he's in his early/late forties** ему́ со́рок с небольши́м, ему́ под пятьдеся́т.

forward *n Sport* фо́рвард, напада́ющий; **centre ~** центр-фо́рвард, центра́льный напада́ющий.

forward *adj* **1** (*in front, ahead*) пере́дний; **the ~ ranks** пере́дние ряды́; **this seat is too far ~** (*for driving*) сиде́нье сли́шком вы́двинуто вперёд, (*in theatre*) э́то ме́сто сли́шком бли́зко к сце́не; **I am well ~ with my work** моя́ рабо́та успе́шно продвига́ется; **~ plan-**

ning перспекти́вное плани́рование; *Sport* **the ~ line** нападе́ние

2 (*well-advanced*): **a ~ spring** ра́нняя весна́; **the rye is well ~ this year** в э́том году́ рожь хорошо́ уроди́лась; **he's an unusually ~ child** он не по года́м развито́й ребёнок

3 (*familiar*) развя́зный; (*pushing*) напо́ристый

4 *Comm*: **~ prices** це́ны на бу́дущее; **carriage ~** сто́имость перево́зки опла́чивает получа́тель.

forward *adv* **1** (*of motion*) вперёд; **to go ~** идти́ вперёд; **he went backward(s) and ~(s)** он ходи́л взад и вперёд/ туда́ и обра́тно (*over larger distance*); *Mil* **~ march!** вперёд марш!

2: from this time ~ с того́ вре́мени

3 *fig uses*: **no one came ~ to help** никто́ не пришёл на по́мощь; **to bring ~ new evidence** предъявля́ть но́вые доказа́тельства (*pl*); **he's always pushing himself ~** он всё вре́мя стара́ется быть на виду́/ве́ртится на глаза́х у нача́льства.

forward *vt* **1** (*promote*): **to ~ smb's plans** спосо́бствовать осуществле́нию чьих-л пла́нов (*impf and pf*)

2 (*despatch*) : **to ~ a letter/goods** отправ|ля́ть письмо́/това́ры (-́ить); (*on letter*) **"Please ~"** «прошу́ пересла́ть».

fossil *n* окамене́лость; ископа́емое; *CQ* **he's an old ~** у него́ допото́пные взгля́ды, он про́сто ходя́чее «ископа́емое».

foster *vt*: **she has agreed to ~ the orphan** она́ реши́ла взять сироту́ на воспита́ние; **to ~ hope/hatred** пита́ть наде́жду/не́нависть (*only in impf*); **to ~ talent** спосо́бствовать разви́тию тала́нта (*usu impf*).

foster child *n* приёмный ребёнок, *CQ* приёмыш.

foster parent *n* приёмный роди́тель (*m*).

foul *n Sport* наруше́ние пра́вил; фол.

foul *adj* **1** скве́рный; **~ language** скверносло́вие, ру́гань; **to use ~ language** скверносло́вить; **~ weather** скве́рная пого́да; **a ~ smell** дурно́й за́пах, *CQ* вонь; **~ air/water** загрязнённая атмосфе́ра/вода́

2 (*entangled*) *Naut*: **the rope is ~** кана́т запу́тался; **the cable got ~ of the propeller** ка́бель намота́лся на винт; *fig* **he fell ~ of the law/the boss** *CQ* он не в лада́х с зако́ном, у него́ нелады́ с нача́льством

3 *Sport*: **~ play** нече́стная игра́, игра́ не по пра́вилам; *fig* **there's been ~ play here** здесь де́ло нечи́сто.

foul *vt* **1** (*pollute*) загрязн|я́ть (-и́ть)

2 (*entangle*): **the anchor is ~ed** я́корь запу́тался.

found *vt* (*establish*) осно́в|ывать (-а́ть); (*create*) созда|ва́ть (-ть); **to ~ a city/a university** основа́ть го́род/университе́т; **a theory ~ed on facts** тео́рия, осно́ванная на фа́ктах; **to ~ a school of thought** созда́ть филосо́фскую систе́му.

foundation *n* **1** (*act*) основа́ние, *also fig*; (*basis*) осно́ва, *also fig*; (*in building*) *usu pl* (**~s**) фунда́мент (*sing*); **to lay the ~s** заложи́ть фунда́мент/осно́ву; *fig*: **his work laid the ~(s) of our legal system** его́ труды́ (*pl*) заложи́ли осно́ву на́шей правово́й систе́мы; **what ~ have you for this assertion?** на како́м основа́нии вы э́то утвержда́ете?; **this rumour has no ~** э́тот слух ни на чём не осно́ван; *attr*: **~ stone** фунда́ментный ка́мень

2 (*institution*): **our theatre received financial help from the Ford F.** наш теа́тр получи́л де́нежную по́мощь из фо́нда Фо́рда.

founder[1] *n* основа́тель (*m*).

founder[2] *vi Naut* затону́ть (*pf*).

foundry *n* лите́йная, лите́йный цех.

fountain *n* фонта́н.

fountain pen *n* авторучка.

four *num* четы́ре (*G, P* четырёх, *D* четырём, *I* четырьмя́) [**NB** *in Nom and A the noun is in G sing and masc and neut adjs following the numeral are usu in G pl, feminine adjs are in either Nom or G pl; adjs preceding the numeral are usu in Nom pl; in oblique cases nouns and adjs are pl, agreeing in case with numeral*]; *collect* че́тверо (*G, A, P* четверы́х, *D* четверы́м, *I* четверы́ми) [**NB** *the collect form* че́тверо *is used mainly of people; in Nom and A cases the noun is in G pl. It is however the only form which can be used in the nominative with nouns which have no singular, whether animate or inanimate; the collect form is rarely used in the oblique cases, almost never with inanimate nouns in the oblique cases*]; **4 red apples** четы́ре кра́сных я́блока; **the first 4 days** пе́рвые четы́ре дня; **4 big waves** четы́ре больши́е/больши́х волны́; **4 bathrooms** четы́ре ва́нные; **after 4 long days** по́сле четырёх до́лгих дней; **4 sledges** че́тверо сане́й; **with 4 sledges** с четырьмя́ саня́ми; **there were 4 of us** нас бы́ло че́тверо/четы́ре челове́ка; **a "4"** (*the number "4", a 4 in cards, school mark*) четвёрка; **chapter 4** четвёртая глава́; **room (number) 4** ко́мната (но́мер) четы́ре; **it's after 4** сейча́с пя́тый час; **4-year olds** четырёхле́тние (де́ти); **400** четы́реста (*G* четырёхсо́т, *D* четырёмста́м, *I* четырьмяста́ми, *P* о четырёхста́х); **4,000** четы́ре ты́сячи; **the 4 corners of the earth** четы́ре страны́ све́та; **to go on all ~s** ползти́ на четвере́ньках.

four-engined *adj*: **a ~ aeroplane** четырёхмото́рный самолёт.

fourfooted *adj* четвероно́гий.

four-seater *adj*: **a ~ car** четырёхме́стный автомоби́ль.

foursquare *adj* квадра́тный; *fig* (*of person*) прямо́й и че́стный.

fourteen *num* четы́рнадцать [*see* **eleven**].

fourteenth *adj* четы́рнадцатый; *as n*: **one ~** одна́ четы́рнадцатая (часть).

fourth *adj* четвёртый; **for the ~ time** в четвёртый раз; **on the ~ of May** четвёртого ма́я; *as n*: **one ~** одна́ четвёртая (часть); **3 ~s** три че́тверти.

fourthly *adv* в-четвёртых.

fowl *n* (*any bird*) пти́ца; (*poultry*) (~s) дома́шняя пти́ца (*collect*); **to keep ~s** держа́ть пти́цу; **wild ~** дичь.

fox *n* лиса́, лиси́ца; **dog ~** лис, саме́ц лиси́цы; **silver ~** черно-бу́рая лиса́/лиси́ца; *fig* **he's a sly ~** он хи́трая лиса́; *attr* ли́сий; **~ fur** ли́сий мех, лиса́, лиси́ца; **~ hunt** охо́та на лису́.

foxglove *n Bot* наперстя́нка.

foyer *n* фойе́ (*indecl*).

fraction *n Math* дробь; *fig* части́ца, до́ля; **common/vulgar ~** простая дробь; **a ~ of a second** до́ля секу́нды; *CQ* **the dress is a ~ too long** пла́тье чуть-чу́ть длиннова́то.

fractionally *adv* чуть-чу́ть.

fractious *adj* капри́зный; (*irritable*) раздражи́тельный.

fracture *n* перело́м; **simple/compound ~** просто́й/сло́жный перело́м; **a ~ of the skull** тре́щина в че́репе.

fracture *vt* (*of bones*) лома́ть (с-); (*of glass, etc.*) разби|ва́ть (-́ть); **he ~d his leg/skull** он слома́л (себе́) но́гу, у него́ проло́млен че́реп.

fractured *adj*: **a ~ rib** перело́м ребра́; **I've got a ~ rib** я слома́л ребро́.

fragile *adj* (*of china, etc.*) хру́пкий; (*of bones*) ло́мкий; *fig* **a ~ old lady** хру́пкая стару́шка.

fragment *n* (*of stone, etc.*) обло́мок; (*splinter of glass, etc.*) оско́лок; **~s of conversation/paper** обры́вки разгово́ра/бума́ги; **a ~ of a poem/of an ancient urn** отры́вок *or* фрагме́нт из стихотворе́ния, оско́лок дре́вней у́рны *or* ва́зы; *CQ* **just a ~ of cake for me** мне то́лько кусо́чек то́рта.

fragrance *n* арома́т, благоуха́ние.

fragrant *adj* арома́тный, души́стый; **~ flowers** души́стые цветы́.

frail *adj* (*of health*) сла́бый, хи́лый; (*brittle, delicate*) хру́пкий; (*of chair, etc.*) непро́чный.

frame *n* **1** (*in building*) карка́с; скеле́т, о́стов; (*hull, case*) ко́рпус; **the ~ of a building/a boat** карка́с зда́ния, о́стов *or* ко́рпус су́дна; **the ~ of a clock** ко́рпус часо́в

2 (*of man, animal*) те́ло; (*build*) телосложе́ние; (*figure*) фигу́ра; **her whole ~ was shaken by sobs** всё её те́ло содрога́лось от рыда́ний; **he has a large ~** он кру́пного телосложе́ния; **his large ~ appeared in the corridor** в коридо́ре появи́лась его́ кру́пная фигу́ра; *fig* **in a cheerful ~ of mind** в весёлом/припо́днятом настрое́нии

3 (*of pictures, photos, windows, racket, bicycle, Hort*) ра́ма, *dim* ра́мка; (*of spectacles*) опра́ва; *Hort* парни́к; **embroidery ~** пя́льцы (*no sing*); **a cucumber ~** парни́к/ра́ма для огурцо́в.

frame *vt* **1** (*construct*) стро́ить (по-); состав|ля́ть (-́ить); **to ~ a sentence** постро́ить/соста́вить предложе́ние; **to ~ a plan** разра|ба́тывать план (-бо́тать)

2 (*of pictures, etc.*) встав|ля́ть в ра́му/в ра́мку (-́ить); *fig* обрамля́ть (*usu impf*); **his face was ~d by a black beard** лицо́ его́ обрамля́ла чёрная борода́

3 *CQ*: **he said he'd been ~d** он сказа́л, что э́то всё подстро́ено.

frame-up *n CQ* ло́жное обвине́ние.

framework *n* (*of building, etc.*) карка́с, о́стов, скеле́т; *fig* структу́ра; **the ~ of government** структу́ра прави́тельства; **within the ~ of the law** в ра́мках зако́на.

franc *n* франк.

franchise *n* пра́во го́лоса.

frank *adj* открове́нный, откры́тый; **to be ~** открове́нно говоря́; **a ~ opinion/look** открове́нное мне́ние, откры́тый взгляд.

frantic *adj* безу́мный; *CQ*: **despite my ~ efforts to finish in time** несмотря́ на мои́ отча́янные уси́лия ко́нчить во́время; **he drove me ~ with his endless questions** он довёл меня́ до умопомеша́тельства/умопомраче́ния бесконе́чными вопро́сами; **I'm in a ~ hurry** я безу́мно тороплю́сь; **we're ~ in the office just now** у нас сейча́с запа́рка.

fraternal *adj* бра́тский.

fraternity *n* бра́тство.

fraternize *vi*: **to ~ with smb/with the enemy** относи́ться по-бра́тски к кому́-л (*only in impf*), брата́ться с враго́м (по-).

fraud *n* **1** (*deception or act of deception*) обма́н; моше́нничество, *also Law*; (*swindling*) надува́тельство; **by ~** обма́нным путём

2 (*person or thing that deceives*): **he/that advertisement is a complete ~** он настоя́щий моше́нник, э́та рекла́ма—сплошно́е надува́тельство; **he's not ill, he's just a ~** он не бо́лен, он про́сто притворя́ется.

fraudulent *adj* обма́нный, моше́ннический; **by ~ means** обма́нным путём (*sing*), моше́нническими сре́дствами; **~ gains** де́ньги, нажи́тые нече́стным путём.

fraught *adj* (*only predic*): **the atmosphere was ~ with hatred** атмосфе́ра была́ заряжена́ не́навистью; **the situation was ~ with danger/very ~** ситуа́ция была́ о́чень опа́сная/о́чень напряжённая.

fray[1] *n* дра́ка; **to rush into the ~** лезть в дра́ку, *also fig*; *fig* **he is eager for the ~** он рвётся в бой.

fray[2] *vti vt* (*direct use usu in ppp*): **~ed cuffs** обтрёпанные/потёртые манже́ты; **a ~ed collar /rope end** потёртый воротни́к, разлохма́ченный коне́ц кана́та; **the carpet is badly ~ed** ковёр весь вы́терся; *fig* **my nerves are ~ed** у меня́ не́рвы истрепа́лись

vi (*of cuffs, etc.*) обтрепа́ться (*usu pf*).

freak *n* (*of deformed person or animal*) уро́д; **a ~ of nature** оши́бка приро́ды; *attr*: **a ~ storm** чудо́вищный шторм; **~ weather/results** необы́чная пого́да, неожи́данные результа́ты.

freckle *n* весну́шка.

freckled *adj* весну́шчатый; **a ~ face/nose/brow** весну́шчатое лицо́, нос/лоб в весну́шках.

free *adj* **1** свобо́дный; во́льный; **a ~ country, ~ love** свобо́дная страна́/любо́вь; **they were given a ~ choice** им был предоста́влен свобóдный вы́бор; ~ **verse/translation** вóльный стих/перевóд; **you are ~ to decide** вы вольны́ решáть сáми; **of one's own ~ will** по дóброй вóле, добровóльно (*adv*); *Sport* ~ **kick** свобóдный удáр; *Comm*: ~ **of tax** не облагáемый налóгом; **these watches are ~ of duty/duty ~** э́ти часы́ не облагáются пóшлиной; **a ~ port** свобóдный/вóльный порт

2 (*not occupied*) свобóдный, незáнятый; **is this seat ~?** э́то мéсто свобóдно?/не зáнято?; **are you ~ this evening?** вы свобóдны сегóдня вéчером?; **I'm not ~ in the mornings** я не свобóден/я зáнят по утрáм

3 (*costing nothing*) бесплáтный, свобóдный; дáром (*adv*); **entry ~** вход бесплáтный/свобóдный; **a ~ ticket/pass** (*on public transport*) бесплáтный билéт/проéзд; **journalists have ~ passes for the Olympic Games** журнали́сты получи́ли свобóдный прóпуск (*sing*) на все соревновáния Олимпи́йских игр; **I got the ticket ~** *or* **a ~ ticket** я получи́л билéт бесплáтно, мне э́тот билéт достáлся бесплáтно

4 ~ from: свобóдный от + *G*; *often translated by adj + prefix* без-, *or by prep* без + *G*; **~ from care** свобóдный от забóт, беззабóтный, без забóт; **~ from debt/error** свобóдный от долгóв, без оши́бок (*pl*); **the river is ~ from ice** рекá очи́стилась ото льдá; **a day ~ from wind** безвéтренный день; **he's ~ from blame** он не винóвен

5 (*lavish*): **he is ~ with his money/praise** он трáтит дéньги не считáя, он щéдро расточáет похвалы́ (*pl*); *iron* **he's very ~ with his advice/criticism** он лю́бит давáть совéты (*pl*)/критиковáть други́х

6 (*of manners, etc.*): **he's a ~ and easy sort of chap** он прост в обращéнии; *pejor* **his manners are somewhat ~** у негó нéсколько развя́зные манéры; **he is too ~ in his language** он не стесня́ется в выражéниях

7 *predic use with verbs*: **to set smb ~** освободи́ть когó-л; **he let the bird go ~** он вы́пустил пти́цу на вóлю; **to leave the end of a rope ~** остáвить оди́н конéц канáта свобóдным; **they made me ~ of their dacha** они́ предостáвили свою́ дáчу в моё распоряжéние; *joc* **he made ~ with my whisky I see** я ви́жу, он хорошó распоряди́лся мои́м ви́ски; **we're ~ of the guests at last!** наконéц-то гóсти уéхали!; **if I may make so ~ as to say...** éсли мне позвóлено бу́дет сказáть...

free *vt* освобо|ждáть (-ди́ть); (*let out*) вы|пускáть (-пустить); **he was ~d from all his duties/from prison** егó освободи́ли от всех обя́занностей, егó вы́пустили из тюрьмы́; **he has ~d himself from debt** он расплати́лся с долгáми.

freedom *n* свобóда; **~ of speech/of the press/of the will** свобóда слóва/печáти/вóли; **they have never known ~ from fear/want** они́ всегдá жи́ли в стрáхе/в нуждé; **to receive the ~ of a city** получи́ть почётное граждáнство гóрода.

free fight *n*, *also* **free-for-all** *CQ* дрáка, свáлка, потасóвка.

freelance *adj*: **a ~ journalist** внештáтный корреспондéнт.

freelance *vi* рабóтать внештáтно (*impf*).

freemason *n* масóн.

free trade *n Econ* свобóдная торгóвля, фритрéдерство

freewheel *vi* éхать/кати́ться без педáлей (*on cycle*)/ без сцеплéния (*in car*).

freeze *n* **1** морóзы (*pl*); **the ~ has stopped all building** из-за морóзов всё строи́тельство приостанови́лось

2 *Econ*: **price/wage ~** заморáживание цен (*pl*)/зáработной плáты.

freeze *vti vt* **1** скóв|ывать (-áть); **the lake is frozen (over)** óзеро скóвано льдом, óзеро сковáло (*impers*) морóзом, *more usu* óзеро замёрзло, óзеро затяну́лось льдом; **the ship was frozen in the ice** корáбль вмёрз во льды́ (*pl*)

2 (*food*) замо|рáживать (-рóзить), *also fig*; **to ~ meat**/*fig Econ* **prices** заморáживать мя́со/цéны

vi **1** морóзить (*impers impf*); **it is freezing** морóзит, на у́лице морóз; **it froze hard yesterday** вчерá был си́льный морóз; **yesterday it began to ~ /it froze a little** вчерá подморóзило; **it will ~ tonight** сегóдня нóчью бу́дет морóз

2 (*become ice*) за|мерзáть (-мёрзнуть); **the river is freezing over** рекá замерзáет; **the pipes have frozen** водопровóдные тру́бы замёрзли; **the fish in the pond/the climbers froze to death** ры́ба в пруду́ замёрзла, альпини́сты замёрзли в горáх; **the water in the jug has frozen** водá в кувши́не замёрзла; **my gloves froze to the railings** у меня́ перчáтки примёрзли к пери́лам; **the ice cubes have frozen together** ку́бики льда смёрзлись

3 (*get, feel cold*) мёрзнуть, замерзáть (*pf for both* замёрзнуть); (*congeal*) засты|вáть (*pfs* ´-ть *and* ´-нуть); (*be numb with cold*) кочене́ть (о-, за-); **I am/my feet are freezing** я замерзáю, я мёрзну, я замёрз (*past or present tense*), у меня́ нóги мёрзнут/замёрзли/окоченéли/засты́ли; *fig*: **the blood froze in my veins** у меня́ кровь засты́ла в жи́лах; **he froze in his tracks** он зáмер на мéсте; **the smile froze on his lips** у негó на губáх засты́ла улы́бка; **the hare froze when it saw the snake** зáяц оцепенéл, уви́дев змею́.

freezer *n* (*domestic*) морози́льный шкаф (*if separate*); *attr*: **~ compartment** (*of fridge*) *CQ* морози́лка.

freezing *adj* ледянóй, *also fig*; **a ~ wind**/*fig* **look** ледянóй вéтер/взгляд.

freezing point *n* тóчка замерзáния; **5° below ~** пять грáдусов морóза/ни́же нуля́.

freight *n* (*goods*) фрахт, груз, гру́зы; (*carrying goods*) перевóзка гру́зов, фрахт; (*payment*) стóимость перевóзки/фрáхта; **what will the charges be for ~?** скóлько бу́дет стóить перево́зка?; *attr* грузово́й; ~ **rates** грузово́й тари́ф; (*US*) ~ **train** това́рный по́езд.

freighter *n* грузово́е су́дно.

French *n* францу́зский язы́к; **to speak** ~ говори́ть по-францу́зски; **the F.** (*people*) францу́зы.

French *adj* францу́зский.

French door *n* застеклённая дверь, выходя́щая в сад.

French dressing *n Cook* францу́зская припра́ва.

Frenchman *n* францу́з.

French polish *n* шелла́чная политу́ра.

Frenchwoman *n* францу́женка.

frenzied *adj* безу́мный, неи́стовый.

frenzy *n*: **in a** ~ **of despair/delight/enthusiasm/excitement** в безу́мном отча́янии, в бу́рном восто́рге, с неи́стовым энтузиа́змом, в си́льном возбужде́нии; **she was in a** ~ она́ как обезу́мела.

frequency *n* частота́; *Phys* **high/low** ~ высо́кая/ни́зкая частота́.

frequent *adj* ча́стый; **he's a** ~ **visitor in our house** он у нас ча́стый гость; **gales are** ~ **here in winter** зимо́й здесь ча́сты што́рмы; **there are** ~ **trains from here to London** отсю́да в Ло́ндон поезда́ хо́дят ча́сто/(*of tube*) иду́т оди́н за други́м.

frequent *vt* ча́сто посеща́ть (*only in impf*); **he** ~**s the yacht club** он ча́сто быва́ет в яхт-клу́бе, он завсегда́тай яхт-клу́ба.

fresco *n* фре́ска.

fresh *adj* **1** све́жий; ~ **eggs/colours** све́жие я́йца/кра́ски; **a** ~ **wind,** ~ **air** све́жий ве́тер/во́здух; **a** ~ **complexion** све́жий цвет лица́; ~ **flowers** то́лько что сре́занные/со́рванные цветы́; ~ **water** пре́сная вода́; **a** ~ **sheet of paper** чи́стый лист бума́ги; **a** ~ **idea** све́жая/но́вая иде́я; **there's no** ~ **news** пока́ нет никаки́х новосте́й (*pl*); **to make a** ~ **start** нача́ть за́ново

2: ~ **from** то́лько что, пря́мо; **he's** ~ **from school** он то́лько что со шко́льной скамьи́; **bread** ~ **from the oven** хлеб пря́мо из пе́чи

3 (*cheeky*): **to be/get** ~ **with smb** дерзи́ть кому́-л.

freshen *vi*: **the wind is** ~**ing** ве́тер крепча́ет/уси́ливается.

freshman *n Univ* первоку́рсник.

freshwater *adj* пресново́дный.

fret *vti vt*: **he** ~**s himself over trifles** он не́рвничает по пустяка́м

vi волнова́ться о + *P*, беспоко́иться о + *P* (*impfs*); (*be irritable*) не́рвничать (*impf*); **don't** ~**!** не волну́йтесь!, не беспоко́йтесь!; **what are you** ~**ting about?** что вас волну́ет?, о чём вы беспоко́итесь?; **he** ~**s at the slightest delays** мале́йшая заде́ржка — и он уже́ не́рвничает; **the child is** ~**ting for its mother** ребёнок про́сится к ма́тери.

fretful *adj* беспоко́йный, капри́зный; **a** ~ **child** беспоко́йный ребёнок; **the baby is teething and is** ~ ребёнок капри́зничает, потому́ что у него́ ре́жутся зу́бы.

fretsaw *n* ло́бзик.

fretwork *n* резно́е украше́ние.

friction *n* тре́ние, *fig* тре́ния (*pl*); **there's been some** ~ **with the management over the dinner** когда́ устра́ивали банке́т, с администра́цией бы́ли ко́е-каки́е тре́ния (*pl*).

Friday *n* пя́тница; *Rel* **Good F.** страстна́я пя́тница.

fridge *n CQ* холоди́льник.

fried *adj* жа́реный.

friend *n* друг, *f* подру́га; (*less close*) прия́тель (*m*), *f* прия́тельница; (*acquaintance*) знако́мый, *f* знако́мая; **he's a great** ~ **of mine** он мой большо́й друг; **they became great** ~**s** они́ ста́ли больши́ми друзья́ми; **to be/make** ~**s with smb** дружи́ть с кем-л, подружи́ться с кем-л; **intimate/bosom** ~ бли́зкий/закады́чный друг; **he/she is one of my business** ~**s** э́то мой това́рищ по рабо́те, э́то мой колле́га; **my learned** ~ мой учёный колле́га.

friendly *adj* (*of person*) дружелю́бный, приве́тливый; (*of advice, manner, etc.*) дру́жеский; **he's a** ~ **soul** он приве́тливый челове́к, он располо́жен к лю́дям, он откры́тая душа́; **people here are so** ~ здесь таки́е приве́тливые лю́ди; **in a** ~ **manner** по-дру́жески (*adv*); **to be** ~**/on** ~ **terms with smb** быть на дру́жеской ноге́ с кем-л; *off* **a** ~ **power** дру́жественная держа́ва; *Sport* **a** ~ **match** това́рищеский матч.

friendship *n* дру́жба.

fright *n* **1** испу́г; **to scream with** ~ закрича́ть от испу́га; **to run away in** ~ убежа́ть в испу́ге/ с испу́гу; **to give smb a** ~ пуга́ть кого́-л; **to have/get a** ~**, to take** ~ испуга́ться

2 *CQ*: **she looked a** ~ она́ была́ про́сто пу́гало.

frighten *vt* **1** пуга́ть (на-, ис-, пере-) *and compounds*; **to** ~ **away/off** (*by mistake*) спуг|ивать, (*deliberately*) отпу́г|ивать (*pfs* -ну́ть); **how you** ~**ed me!** как ты меня́ испуга́л!; **to** ~ **smb out of his wits** до́ смерти напуга́ть кого́-л; **he** ~**ed me into signing the document** он нагна́л на меня́ тако́го стра́ху, и я подписа́л э́тот докуме́нт

2 *in passive* (**to be** ~**ed**) пуга́ться, боя́ться + *G* (*impf*); **don't be** ~**ed!** не пуга́йтесь!, не бо́йтесь!; **I've never been so** ~**ed in my life** я никогда́ в жи́зни не́ был так испу́ган; **she's** ~**ed of the dark** она́ бои́тся темноты́.

frightening *adj* пуга́ющий.

frightful *adj usu CQ* стра́шный, ужа́сный.

frigid *adj* холо́дный, *also fig*; *Med* фриги́дный; **a** ~ **climate/welcome** холо́дный кли́мат/приём.

frill *n* (*on dress*) обо́рка; *fig*: **she loves preparing dishes with a lot of** ~**s** она́ лю́бит украша́ть блю́да; **he writes without** ~**s** он пи́шет про́сто, без вся́ких выкрута́сов/украша́тельств.

fringe *n* **1** (*on shawl, rug*) бахрома́; (*of hair*) чёлка

2: our dacha is on the ~ of a lake/the forest наша дача на берегу озера/на опушке леса; **I live on the ~ of the city** я живу на окраине (города); **a child was standing on the ~ of the crowd** ребёнок стоял в стороне от толпы; *attr*: **~ benefits** дополнительные льготы.

frisk *vti vt* (*search smb*) обыск|ивать + *A* (-ать)

vi (*frolic*) резвиться (*impf*).

frisky *adj* резвый.

fritter[1] *n* оладья; **apple ~s** яблочные оладьи.

fritter[2] *vt*: **to ~ away time/money/energies** растрачивать *or* тратить время/деньги/силы (*pf for both* растратить).

frivolous *adj* (*of people and things*) легкомысленный; несерьёзный; **a ~ remark/book/objection** легкомысленное замечание, пустая книга, несерьёзное возражение.

frizzy *adj*: **~ hair** жёсткие курчавые волосы.

fro *adv*: **to and ~** взад и вперёд, туда и сюда.

frock *n* платье.

frock coat *n* сюртук.

frog *n* лягушка.

frogman *n* аквалангист.

frolic *n* (*prank*) шалость; (*merry-making*) веселье.

frolic *vi* (*gambol*) резвиться (*impf*).

frolicsome *adj* резвый, игривый.

from *prep* **1** (*of movement*) из + *G* (*from somewhere inside*); от + *G* (*away/out/down from*); с + *G* (*away/down/off from*); из-за + *G* (*out from behind*); **i) to go away ~ home** уехать из дому/из дома; **to sail away ~ the shore** отплыть от берега; **to take a book ~ a shelf** взять книгу с полки; **they arrived ~ the Crimea/the South** они приехали из Крыма/с юга; **turn left ~ the square** поверните с/от площади налево; **to come ~ abroad** приехать из-за границы; **to rise ~ a chair/the table** встать со стула/из-за стола; **people came ~ everywhere** люди приходили отовсюду; **where are you ~?** откуда вы?; **ii)** [**NB** *after verbs with prefix* вы- *always* из + *G*; *after verbs with prefix* от- *usu* от + *G*, *with prefix* с- *usu* с + *G*]: **to take smth ~ one's pocket** вынуть что-л из кармана; **the ship moved off ~ the pier** корабль отплыл от пристани; **he leapt ~ his horse** он соскочил с лошади

2 i) (*of position*) на + *P*, с + *G*; под + *A or I*; **he hung the light ~ the ceiling** он повесил люстру под потолком; **the light hangs ~ the ceiling** люстра висит на потолке; **a spider's web hung ~ the ceiling** паутина свисала с потолка; **ii)** (*of distance*): **we live 5 miles ~ the station** мы живём в пяти милях от станции; **is it far ~ here?/there?** далеко ли это отсюда?/оттуда?

3: from... to (*of place*) [**NB** *the normal Russian pairing of prepositions*] с + *G* ... на + *A*; из + *G* ... в + *A*; от + *G*... к + *D*; от + *G*/с + *G*... до + *G*; **the book fell ~ the table to the floor** книга упала со стола на пол; **he drove ~ London to Cambridge** он поехал из Лондона в Кембридж; **it's 60 miles ~ Cambridge to London** от Кембриджа до Лондона шестьдесят миль; **the deer ran ~ the forest to the river** олень бежал из леса к реке; **~ head to foot** с головы до ног; **I read the book ~ end to end** я прочёл книгу от начала до конца; **~ side to side** из стороны в сторону; **~ place to place** с места на место; **prices run ~ 5 to 10 roubles** цены от пяти до десяти рублей

4 (*of time*) с + *G*; **~ that time** с того времени; **~ childhood** с детства; **~ the start** с самого начала; **starting ~ /as ~ May 5th** начиная/считая с пятого мая; **I'll be there ~ the fifth** я буду там с пятого числа; **5 years ~ now** через пять лет

5: from... to (*of time*) с + *G or* (*rarely*) от + *G*... до + *G or* по + *A*; **~ morning to night** с утра до ночи; **~ spring to autumn** с весны до осени; **~ 3 to 6** с трёх часов дня до шести часов вечера; **~ January to June** с января по июнь; **~ the first of June to the 10th (inclusive)** с первого по десятое июня (включительно)

6: from day to day i) со дня на день (=*from one day to the next*); **to put smth off ~ day to day** откладывать что-л со дня на день; **ii)** день ото дня (*of steady change*); **prices are increasing ~ day to day** цены растут день ото дня; **~ week to week/month to month/year to year his routine never varies** его распорядок дня неделями/месяцами/годами не меняется

7 (*of cause*) (*of physical cause*) от + *G*; (*of emotional cause*) с + *G*, от + *G*; из + *G*; (*owing to*) из-за + *G*; **to die ~ hunger** умереть от голода; **to suffer ~ heat** страдать от жары; **~ grief/joy** с горя, от радости; **~ boredom/fear/shame** со/от скуки, со страху, со/от стыда; **~ jealousy/curiosity** из ревности, из любопытства; **this arose ~ carelessness** это произошло из-за небрежности/по небрежности

8 (*of source*) из + *G*; от + *G*; с + *G*; у + *G*; по + *D*; **he's ~ Minsk** он из Минска; **a quotation ~ Shakespeare** цитата из Шекспира; **I understood ~ the papers that...** я понял из газет, что...; **I learnt of it ~ my brother** я узнал об этом от брата; **a present/letter ~ my father** подарок/письмо от отца; **light ~ a torch** свет (от) фонаря; **nothing was left ~ lunch** от завтрака ничего не осталось; **~ my point of view** с моей точки зрения; **a copy ~ a painting** копия (с) картины; **change ~ a rouble** сдача с рубля; **to translate ~ Russian into English** переводить с русского на английский; **I borrowed 5 dollars ~ him** я занял у него пять долларов; **I took the case ~ her** я взял у неё чемодан; **he bought flowers ~ the girl** он купил у девушки цветы; **to speak ~ memory** говорить по памяти; **to know ~ experience**

знать по о́пыту; **judging ~ appearances** су́дя по вне́шности

9 (*with prices, numbers*): **take 7 ~ 10** вы́честь семь из десяти́; **wine costs ~ £2 a bottle** вино́ от двух фу́нтов за буты́лку и вы́ше; **there were ~ 15 to 20 people there** там бы́ло челове́к пятна́дцать-два́дцать [**NB** *approximation shown by inversion of noun and numeral*]

10 (*with verbs; see also under particular verbs*): **to distinguish good ~ bad** отлича́ть хоро́шее от плохо́го; **to drink ~ a cup** пить из ча́шки; **to brush crumbs ~ one's coat** смахну́ть кро́шки с пиджака́; **to part ~ smb** расста́ться с кем-л; **to write ~ dictation** писа́ть под дикто́вку; **he was absent ~ the meeting** он не́ был на собра́нии; **I prevented him ~ going** я не дал ему́ уйти́, я не пусти́л его́

11 (*combined with other preps and advs*): **~ above/below** све́рху, сни́зу (*advs*); **~ across/beyond/over the sea** из-за мо́ря; **~ afar** издалека́, и́здали (*advs*); **~ behind the door** из-за две́ри; **his head popped out ~ between the curtains** его́ голова́ вы́сунулась из-за занаве́сок; **she is far ~ beautiful** она́ далеко́ не краса́вица; **far ~ helping, he was a positive nuisance** он нам совсе́м не помога́л, а наоборо́т—меша́л; **far be it ~ me to say** я во́все не хочу́ сказа́ть; **the door is locked ~ inside/outside** дверь заперта́ изнутри́/снару́жи (*advs*); **to come in ~ outside** войти́ с у́лицы; **~ round the corner** из-за угла́; **~ under the table** из-под стола́.

front *n* **1** (*of buildings*) фаса́д, лицева́я сторона́; (*foreground*) пере́дний план; (*beginning*) нача́ло; **the west ~ of the cathedral** за́падный фаса́д собо́ра; **in the ~ of the picture** на пере́днем пла́не карти́ны; **the table of contents is at the ~ of the book** оглавле́ние нахо́дится в нача́ле кни́ги; **at the ~ of the stage** на авансце́не; **he's sitting in the ~ (of the car)** он сиди́т на пере́днем сиде́нье (маши́ны); *fig* **we'll have to put a bold ~ on it** нам придётся де́лать хоро́шую ми́ну при плохо́й игре́

2: the sea ~ на́бережная, примо́рский бульва́р

3 *Mil, Polit* фронт; *Meteorol* **a cold ~** холо́дный фронт

4 (*forming advs or preps*): **in ~** (*motion*) вперёд, (*position*) впереди́; **to send smb on in ~** посла́ть кого́-л вперёд; **he's standing in ~** он стои́т впереди́; **in ~ of me/the school** передо мно́й, пе́ред шко́лой; **to march in ~ of the platoon** марширова́ть впереди́ взво́да.

front *adj* пере́дний; **a ~ seat** (*in theatre*) пере́днее ме́сто *or* ме́сто в пе́рвом ряду́, (*in car*) пере́днее сиде́нье; **~ door/hall** пара́дная дверь, пере́дняя; **~ page** (*of book*) ти́тульный лист, (*of newspaper*) пе́рвая полоса́; *Mil* **in the ~ line** на передово́й (ли́нии).

front *vi, also* **to ~ on (to)** выходи́ть на + *A* (*only in impf*); **the house ~s south** дом выхо́дит на юг; **the windows ~ on to the sea** о́кна (до́ма) выхо́дят/смо́трят на мо́ре.

frontal *adj Mil* фронта́льный, лобово́й; *Anat* ло́бный; *Art* **a ~ portrait** портре́т анфа́с.

frontier *n* грани́ца, рубе́ж; *fig* преде́л; **to cross the ~** пересе́чь грани́цу; **a natural ~** есте́ственный рубе́ж; **the ~s of knowledge** преде́лы зна́ния.

front-page *adj*: **it was ~ news all week** э́то бы́ло на пе́рвых страни́цах газе́т всю неде́лю.

front-wheel drive *n Aut* пере́дний приво́д.

frost *n* моро́з; (*hoar-frost*) и́ней; **5 degrees of ~** пять гра́дусов моро́за; **there's ~ on the grass** трава́ покры́та и́неем; **the ~ is holding** стоя́т моро́зы (*pl*); **the roses have been killed by the ~** ро́зы поби́ло (*impers*) моро́зом.

frost *vt*: **the roses are (slightly) ~ed** ро́зы поби́ты моро́зом; **the windscreen was ~ed over** ветрово́е стекло́ заи́ндевело.

frostbite *n* обмороже́ние, обмора́живание.

frostbitten *adj* обморо́женный; **my hands are ~** у меня́ обморо́жены ру́ки.

frostbound *adj*: **the ground is still ~** земля́ ещё мёрзлая.

frosted *adj*: **~ glass** ма́товое стекло́.

frosty *adj* моро́зный; **a ~ sky/morning** моро́зное не́бо/у́тро; **~ ground** мёрзлая земля́; **it's going to be ~ tonight** сего́дня но́чью подморо́зит (*impers*); *fig* **a ~ look/reception** ледяно́й *or* холо́дный взгляд/приём.

froth *n* пе́на.

froth *vi* (*of beer, etc.*) пе́ниться (*impf*); **the dog/the epileptic was ~ing at the mouth** у соба́ки изо рта́ шла пе́на, у эпиле́птика была́ пе́на на губа́х.

frothy *adj* пе́нистый.

frown *vi* хму́риться (на-), (*in concentration*) хму́рить бро́ви; **he ~ed at me** он хму́ро на меня́ посмотре́л; *fig* (*in disapproval*) **he ~ed on the proposal** он с неодобре́нием отнёсся к э́тому предложе́нию.

frozen *adj* (*of food*) заморо́женный; (*of hands or feet*) замёрзший; **his feet are ~** у него́ замёрзли но́ги.

frugal *adj* (*careful*) бережли́вый, эконо́мный; (*scanty*) ску́дный; (*modest*) скро́мный; **a ~ housekeeper** бережли́вая/эконо́мная хозя́йка; **a ~ meal** ску́дный/скро́мный обе́д.

fruit *n* **1** *collect* (*as food*) фру́кты (*pl*); **dried ~** сухофру́кты; **tinned ~** консерви́рованные фру́кты, фрукто́вые консе́рвы; **soft ~** я́годы (*pl*); *attr*: **~ salad** фрукто́вый сала́т

2 *Bot* плод, *also fig*; **to bear ~** приноси́ть плоды́ (*pl*); *fig*: **forbidden ~** запре́тный плод; **to reap the ~s of one's labours** пожина́ть плоды́ свои́х трудо́в.

fruit *vi* при|носи́ть плоды́ (-нести́).

fruit cake *n* кекс (с изю́мом).

fruit farming *n* плодово́дство.

fruitful *adj* плодови́тый; *fig* плодотво́рный.

fruitless *adj* беспло́дный, *also fig*.

fruit tree *n* плодо́вое/фрукто́вое де́рево.

fruity *adj* фрукто́вый; *fig*: ~ **humour** со́чный/сма́чный ю́мор; **a ~ voice/alto/bass** грудно́й го́лос/альт, со́чный бас; **a ~ joke/story** солёная шу́тка, пика́нтный анекдо́т.

frustrate *vt* (*upset*) расстр|а́ивать (-о́ить); (*spoil, ruin*) наруш|а́ть (-́ить); **my plans have been ~d** все мои́ пла́ны бы́ли нару́шены; **I was ~d in my efforts to help** мне не удало́сь помо́чь.

frustrated *adj* неудовлетворённый; **I feel very ~ in my present job** я о́чень неудовлетворён свое́й рабо́той.

frustration *n* неудовлетворённость.

fry[1] *n collect* (*small fish*) мальки́ (*pl*); *fig* **the small ~ sat at the back** ме́нее значи́тельная пу́блика сиде́ла в за́дних ряда́х.

fry[2] *n Cook*: **a ~ of fish/of bacon and eggs** жа́реная ры́ба, яи́чница с ветчино́й.

fry[2] *vti* жа́рить(ся) (на сковороде́) (за-, под-)

frying pan *n* сковорода́, сковоро́дка.

fuddled *adj*: *CQ* **I'm completely ~** у меня́ в голове́ сплошно́й тума́н, (*if from drink*) я окосе́л.

fuel *n* то́пливо; горю́чее; **solid ~** твёрдое то́пливо; *fig* **to add ~ to the fire/flames** подлива́ть ма́сла в ого́нь; *attr* то́пливный; **a ~ tank/pump** то́пливный бак/насо́с; **~ gauge** указа́тель у́ровня то́плива; **~ consumption** расхо́д то́плива/горю́чего.

fuel *vti vt*: **to ~ a lorry/a ship** заправ|ля́ть грузови́к бензи́ном (-́ить), при|нима́ть то́пливо на кора́бль (-ня́ть)

vi заправ|ля́ться (-́иться).

fuelling station *n Aut* автозапра́вочная ста́нция.

fug *n CQ*: **what a ~!** кака́я духота́!

fuggy *adj CQ* ду́шный.

fugitive *n* бегле́ц, бе́глый; (*if escaping invasion*) бе́женец; **a ~ from a workcamp** бе́глый ка́торжник; **~s from an invaded country** бе́женцы из оккупи́рованной страны́.

fulfil *vt* вы|полня́ть (-́полнить); исполн|я́ть (-́ить); **to ~ a promise/one's duty** вы́полнить обеща́ние, испо́лнить свой долг; **to ~ conditions** удовлетворя́ть усло́виям (*only in impf*); **our hopes have been ~led** на́ши наде́жды осуществи́лись; **her work as a nurse has made her feel ~led/that she has ~led herself** рабо́та медсестры́ прино́сит /даёт ей чу́вство глубо́кого удовлетворе́ния.

fulfilment *n* выполне́ние; осуществле́ние; **a sense of (personal) ~** чу́вство удовлетворе́ния.

full *n*: **write your name in ~** напиши́те своё по́лное и́мя; **to tell/pay in ~** рассказа́ть всё, оплати́ть по́лностью (*adv*); **to enjoy smth to the ~** наслажда́ться чем-л в по́лной ме́ре/сполна́ (*adv*).

full *adj* **1: ~ of** по́лный + *G*; **a bucket ~ of water** ведро́, по́лное воды́; **the hall was ~ of people** зал был по́лон наро́ду (*G*); **my coat is ~ of holes** моё пальто́ всё в ды́рах; **he's ~ of the news/of ideas** он по́лон новосте́й (*pl*)/иде́й; **he's ~ of himself/of his own importance** он о́чень ва́жничает

2 (*filled*) напо́лненный, по́лный; **the glass was ~ to the brim** стака́н был по́лон до краёв; **the case is already ~** чемода́н уже́ по́лон; **to live a ~ life** жить по́лной жи́знью; *CQ* **I'm ~** (*with food*) я сыт

3 (*complete*) по́лный; подро́бный; **a ~ account of the accident** подро́бный отчёт об ава́рии; **~ moon** по́лная луна́, полнолу́ние; **the tide is ~** прили́в ко́нчился; **to be on ~ pay** быть на по́лной ста́вке; **we drove a ~ hour/a ~ 6 miles/at ~ speed** мы прое́хали це́лый час/це́лых шесть миль/на по́лной ско́рости; **~ steam ahead!** по́лный вперёд!

4 (*fat*) то́лстый, по́лный; **she has a ~ figure/face** у неё высо́кая грудь, у неё по́лное лицо́; **a ~ skirt** широ́кая ю́бка.

full *adv* пря́мо; **to look smb ~ in the face/eye** смотре́ть кому́-л пря́мо в лицо́/в глаза́; **the branch hit him ~ in the face** ве́тка уда́рила его́ пря́мо по лицу́; **we were driving ~ out** мы е́хали на по́лной ско́рости; **you know ~ well that...** ты о́чень хорошо́ зна́ешь, что...

fullback *n Sport* защи́тник.

full dress *n* по́лная пара́дная фо́рма; *attr*: **a full-dress dinner** пара́дный банке́т; *Theat* **a full-dress rehearsal** генера́льная репети́ция.

full-length *adj*: **a ~ portrait/dress** портре́т в по́лный рост, пла́тье до́ полу; **to fall ~** упа́сть, растяну́вшись во весь рост.

full-scale *adj*: **a ~ model** моде́ль в натура́льную величину́; *Mil* **a ~ attack** наступле́ние по всему́ фро́нту.

full stop *n* то́чка; *fig*: **she/the car came to a ~** она́/маши́на останови́лась; **for the moment my work has come to a ~** сейча́с у меня́ рабо́та засто́порилась.

full-time *adj*: **I've got a ~ job** я рабо́таю по́лный рабо́чий день; *CQ* **it's a ~ job keeping her amused** развлека́ть её — нелёгкое де́ло.

fulsome *adj*: **~ praise** неуме́ренная похвала́; **he was ~ in his thanks** он рассыпа́лся в благода́рностях (*pl*).

fumble *vi* ша́рить (*impf*); **he ~d for the matches in the dark** он ша́рил в темноте́ в по́исках спи́чек; **she ~d in her bag** она́ поры́лась в су́мке; **he ~d with the latch** он вози́лся с замко́м (*impf*).

fume *vi CQ fig*: **he was simply fuming** он так возмуща́лся/кипяти́лся (*only in impfs*); **he ~d at the delay** он зли́лся на заде́ржку (*usu impf*).

fumes *npl* (*in form of smoke*) дым (*sing*); (*from liquids or gases*) пары́, испаре́ния; **poisonous ~** ядови́тые испаре́ния; **to give off ~s** выделя́ть испаре́ния.

fumigate *vt* оку́ривать (*usu impf*).

fun *n*: **what ~!** как ве́село!; **we had lots of ~ yesterday** вчера́ мы хорошо́/*CQ* здо́рово повесели́лись; **he's great ~** с ним о́чень ве́село; **it's no ~ watching football**

in the rain смотре́ть футбо́л под дождём не о́чень большо́е удово́льствие; **I don't see any ~ in that** я не ви́жу в э́том ничего́ заба́вного; **it would be ~ to go to the circus** хорошо́ бы сходи́ть в цирк; **to spoil the ~** испо́ртить всё удово́льствие; **we did it just for ~** мы э́то сде́лали шу́тки ра́ди.

function *n* **1** фу́нкция; (*duty*) обя́занность; **the ~ of the heart/the fan belt** фу́нкция се́рдца, назначе́ние ремня́ вентиля́тора; **it is his ~ to take the minutes** э́то его́ обя́занность вести́ протоко́л; **in his ~ as judge** как судья́, в ка́честве судьи́

2 (*ceremony, reception*) приём; **I'll be late tonight as I've got to attend some ~** я сего́дня опозда́ю, потому́ что я до́лжен прису́тствовать на приёме.

function *vi* рабо́тать, функциони́ровать (*impfs*); **the pump is not ~ing** насо́с не рабо́тает; **the new committee is already ~ing** но́вая коми́ссия уже́ приступи́ла к рабо́те.

functional *adj* функциона́льный.

fund *n* **1** (*store*) запа́с; **he has an inexhaustible ~ of funny stories** у него́ неиссяка́емый запа́с анекдо́тов

2 *Fin* фонд; *pl* (**~s**) фо́нды, де́ньги; **a ~ for the victims of the earthquake** фонд по́мощи пострада́вшим от землетрясе́ния; **this is paid for out of public ~s** э́то опла́чивается из госуда́рственного фо́нда (*sing*); **the museum is out of ~s just now** у музе́я сейча́с нет средств/фо́ндов.

fundamental *adj* основно́й; **a ~ difference** основно́е отли́чие; **maths are ~ to the study of astronomy** зна́ние матема́тики (*sing*) явля́ется непреме́нным усло́вием для изуче́ния астроно́мии.

fundamentally *adv* в осно́ве, в основно́м.

fundamentals *npl* осно́вы (*pl*).

funeral *n* по́хороны (*pl*); *fig CQ* **that's your ~** э́то уж твоя́ забо́та; *attr* похоро́нный.

funereal *adj fig* мра́чный, похоро́нный.

fungus *n Bot* (*generic term*) гриб; (*microorganism*) грибо́к; (*mould*) пле́сень; **a growth of ~** грибови́дный наро́ст.

funicular *n* фуникулёр.

funk *n CQ*: **he's in a blue ~** он тру́сит.

funk *vt CQ* тру́сить (с-); **he ~ed the exam/telling his father** он стру́сил и не пришёл на экза́мен, он побоя́лся сказа́ть об э́том отцу́ (*pf*); **he ~ed it** он побоя́лся/не отва́жился сде́лать э́то.

funnel *n* (*of steamer*) труба́; (*for pouring liquids*) воро́нка.

funnily *adv* смешно́; (*strangely*) стра́нно; **~ enough, I was thinking the same thing** как ни стра́нно, я ду́мал то́ же са́мое.

funny *adj* **1** (*comic*) смешно́й; (*amusing*) заба́вный; *CQ* поте́шный; **a ~ story** анекдо́т, смешна́я исто́рия; **he's such a ~ child** он тако́й заба́вный/*CQ* поте́шный ребёнок; **that's not in the least ~!** э́то совсе́м/во́все не смешно́!; **he's just trying to be ~** (*usu pejor*) он ведь про́сто пая́сничает

2 (*strange*) стра́нный; чудно́й; **~, I thought he'd left** стра́нно, я ду́мал, что он уже́ ушёл; **I've a ~ feeling I've seen him before** у меня́ стра́нное ощуще́ние, бу́дто я когда́-то ра́ньше его́ ви́дел; **there's something ~/some ~ business going on there** тут что́-то не так, (*stronger*) тут де́ло нечи́сто.

funny bone *n Anat* локтево́й отро́сток.

fur *n* **1** мех; *attr* мехово́й; **a ~ coat** мехово́е пальто́, шу́ба

2: **~ on a kettle** на́кипь в ча́йнике; *Med* **~ on one's tongue** налёт на языке́.

furious *adj* я́ростный, бе́шеный, неи́стовый; **he gave me a ~ look** он посмотре́л на меня́ в бе́шенстве; **he's simply ~** он взбешён, он разъярён; **a ~ wind was blowing** неи́стово дул ве́тер; **I'm ~ with him because he...** меня́ бе́сит (*impers*), что он...; **at a ~ pace** с бе́шеной ско́ростью.

furl *vt*: **to ~ sails/a flag** свёртывать паруса́/флаг (сверну́ть); **he ~ed his umbrella** он сверну́л/сложи́л зо́нтик.

fur-lined *adj*: **~ boots** подби́тые ме́хом сапоги́, сапоги́ на меху́.

furnace *n* (*for central heating*) печь; (*industrial*) горн; **the room was like a ~** в ко́мнате бы́ло жа́рко как в ба́не.

furnish *vt* **1** (*provide*) снаб|жа́ть+ *I* (-ди́ть); постав|ля́ть (-́ить); **to ~ the troops with provisions** снабжа́ть войска́ продово́льствием (*sing*), поставля́ть войска́м провиа́нт (*sing*); **to ~ smb with information** снабжа́ть кого́-л информа́цией

2 (*a house*) меблирова́ть (*impf and pf*); обстав|ля́ть ме́белью (-́ить); **I rented a ~ed flat** я снял меблиро́ванную кварти́ру.

furnishings *npl* обстано́вка, меблиро́вка (*sings*); **soft ~** мя́гкая ме́бель (*no pl*).

furniture *n* ме́бель (*no pl*); **~ and fittings** *approx* обстано́вка и обору́дование; *attr*: **~ factory** ме́бельная фа́брика; **~ van** автофурго́н для перево́зки ме́бели.

furore *n* фуро́р; **to create a ~** производи́ть фуро́р.

furrier *n* меховщи́к, скорня́к.

furrow *n Agric* борозда́; (*on face*) морщи́на.

furry *adj* пуши́стый.

further *comp adj of* **far 1** (*of place*) да́льний; **the ~ end of the hall** да́льний коне́ц за́ла; **on the ~ side of the street** на друго́й стороне́ у́лицы

2 (*additional*) дальне́йший; **until ~ notice** до дальне́йшего уведомле́ния; **without ~ difficulties** без дальне́йших тру́дностей; **to give ~ instructions** дать дополни́тельные указа́ния.

further *comp adv of* **far 1** (*of place*) да́льше, да́лее; **it's dangerous to go any ~** да́льше идти́ опа́сно; **it's not ~ than 2 kilometres to the station** до вокза́ла не бо́лее двух киломе́тров; **to move smth ~ back/~ away** отодви́нуть/убра́ть что-л пода́льше; *fig*: **nothing is ~ from my thoughts** ничего́ подо́бного мне и в го́лову не приходи́ло;

to go ~ into a matter подро́бнее разобра́ться в вопро́се, вни́кнуть в де́ло поглу́бже

2 (*more*): **and ~ I believe that...** и ещё/кро́ме того́, я уве́рен, что...; **he said ~ that...** и ещё он сказа́л, что...; **I've heard nothing ~** бо́льше я ничего́ не слы́шал; **don't trouble yourself ~** бо́льше об э́том не беспоко́йся.

further *vt* спосо́бствовать + *D* (*impf*), соде́йствовать + *D* (*impf and pf*); **to ~ the success of an undertaking** спосо́бствовать/соде́йствовать успе́ху предприя́тия; **I did it to ~ his interests** я сде́лал э́то в его́ интере́сах.

furthermore *adv* кро́ме того́, к тому́ же.

furthermost *adj* са́мый да́льний, са́мый отдалённый.

furthest *superl adj and adv of* **far**; *adj* са́мый да́льний; *adv* да́льше всего́.

furtive *adj* (*of a person*) скры́тный; **a ~ glance** взгляд укра́дкой (*adv*); **his ~ behaviour puzzles me** он я́вно что́-то скрыва́ет, и э́то меня́ беспоко́ит.

furtively *adv*: **he looked at her ~** он посмотре́л на неё укра́дкой; **he crept ~ away** он удали́лся кра́дучись.

fury *n* я́рость; неи́стовство; бе́шенство; **to goad smb to ~** доводи́ть кого́-л до бе́шенства; **to be in a ~** быть в я́рости/в бе́шенстве; **he worked himself into a ~** он разбушева́лся.

furze *n Bot* утёсник.

fuse *n* (*for bomb*) запа́л, фити́ль (*m*), взрыва́тель (*m*); *Elec* (пла́вкий) предохрани́тель (*m*), *CQ* про́бка; **to change/mend/replace a ~** смени́ть предохрани́тель *or* про́бку.

fuse *vi Elec*: **the lights have ~d** про́бки перегоре́ли [**NB** *Russians say* "*the fuses have burnt out*"].

fuse box *n Elec* предохрани́тельная коро́бка.

fuselage *n Aer* фюзеля́ж.

fuse wire *n* пла́вкая про́волочка.

fuss *n* суета́; (*row*) шум, сканда́л; **to make a ~** суети́ться, волнова́ться; **what a ~ about nothing** сто́лько шу́му из-за вся́кой ерунды́; **you were quite right to make/*CQ* kick up a ~** ты пра́вильно сде́лал, что по́днял шум; **they made such a ~ of the film star** они́ созда́ли тако́й ажиота́ж вокру́г э́той кинозвезды́.

fuss *vti vt*: **he ~es me with all his questions** он де́йствует мне на не́рвы свои́ми расспро́сами, он надоеда́ет мне свои́ми расспро́сами

vi суети́ться, волнова́ться (*impfs*); **to ~ over/about** носи́ться с + *I* (*only in impf*); **he's always ~ing (about his health)** он ве́чно суети́тся, он ве́чно но́сится со свои́м здоро́вьем; **he ~es over details** он погря́з/увя́з [**NB** *tense*] в мелоча́х; **she ~es over him** она́ трясётся над ним.

fusspot *n CQ*: **he's such a ~** он так суетли́в.

fussy *adj* (*of a person*) суетли́вый, не́рвный; (*of dress, style of writing*) вы́чурный; **he's ~ about his food** он привере́длив в еде́.

fusty *adj* за́тхлый, *also fig*.

futile *adj* (*unavailing*) тще́тный; (*empty*) пусто́й; **a ~ attempt** тще́тная попы́тка; **a ~ play** пуста́я пье́са.

future *n* **1** бу́дущее; **in the ~** в бу́дущем, впредь (*adv*); *attr Gram*: **the ~ (tense)** бу́дущее вре́мя

2 (*prospects*) бу́дущее, бу́дущность; перспекти́ва; **the ~ of industry** перспекти́вы (*pl*) разви́тия промы́шленности; **he has a great ~ in front of him** его́ ожида́ет блестя́щее бу́дущее; *CQ* **there's no ~ in that/it** э́то бесперспекти́вно.

future *adj* бу́дущий.

fuze *n and vti* (*US*) = **fuse.**

fuzzy *adj* (*blurred*) сму́тный; (*fluffy*) пуши́стый; **~ hair** пы́шные/(*crinkly*) вью́щиеся во́лосы.

G

G *n Mus* соль (*indecl*).

gab *n CQ*: **he's got the gift of the ~** он за сло́вом в карма́н не поле́зет.

gabble *vti vt*: **he ~d out an apology** он промя́млил извине́ние

vi: **they were gabbling away in German** они́ болта́ли/тарато́рили по-неме́цки; **I don't understand you when you ~ like that** ты так тарато́ришь — я ничего́ не понима́ю.

gable *n Archit* фронто́н, щипе́ц.

gad *vi CQ*: **we've been ~ding about town/the countryside all day** мы весь день гуля́ли по го́роду/за́ городом.

gadget *n* приспособле́ние; **a ~ for washing windows** приспособле́ние для мытья́ о́кон.

gaffe *n*: **to make a ~** допусти́ть оплошность, сплохова́ть.

gag *n* (*for mouth*) кляп; *CQ* (*joke*) остро́та, *also Theat*.

gag *vti vt*: **to ~ smb** встав|ля́ть/за|со́вывать кляп в рот кому́-л (-и́ть/-су́нуть); *fig* **he'll have to be ~ged** на́до заткну́ть ему́ рот

vi CQ (*of an actor*) вставля́ть отсебя́тину.

gaga *adj sl*: **he's ~** из него́ песо́к сы́плется, он вы́жил из ума́.

gaiety *n* (*general mood*) весе́лье; (*personal mood*) весёлость; **a mood of general ~ prevailed** цари́ло всео́бщее весе́лье; **his ~ seemed artificial** его́ весёлость каза́лась наи́гранной.

gain *n* нажи́ва; при́быль, *also fig*; (*winnings*) вы́игрыш; (*increase*) приба́вка; **he's only interested in ~** он интересу́ется то́лько нажи́вой; **it's pure ~ for us** э́то нам чи́стая при́быль; **he made substantial ~s in the lottery** ему́ доста́лся кру́пный вы́игрыш в э́той лотере́е; **a ~ in weight** приба́вка в ве́се.

gain *vti vt* **1** (*make profit*) получ|а́ть (-и́ть); приобре|та́ть (-сти́); **he ~ed £1,000 on that deal** он зарабо́тал/получи́л ты́сячу фу́нтов на э́той сде́лке; **to ~ an advantage/experience** получи́ть преиму́щество, приобрести́ о́пыт; **he stands to ~ a lot from that** он бу́дет в вы́игрыше от э́того

2 (*increase*): **to ~ height/speed** на|бира́ть высоту́/ско́рость (-бра́ть); **to ~ weight** приба́в|ля́ть в ве́се (-́ить); **he is ~ing strength** он ко́пит си́лы (*pl*); **my watch ~s 5 minutes a day** мои́ часы́ спеша́т на пять мину́т в су́тки

3 (*win, achieve*) доби|ва́ться + *G* (-́ться); **to ~ a victory/a majority** доби́ться побе́ды/большинства́; **what will we ~ by that?** чего́ мы э́тим добьёмся?; **to ~ one's end** доби́ться свое́й це́ли; **to ~ territory** заво|ёвывать террито́рию (-ева́ть); *Sport* **to ~ possession of the ball** овладе|ва́ть мячо́м (-́ть); *fig*: **to ~ smb's confidence** завоева́ть/заслужи́ть чьё-л дове́рие; **the idea is ~ing ground that...** получа́ет всё бо́льшее распростране́ние мысль о том, что...; **to ~ the summit of a mountain** дости́чь верши́ны горы́ (*usu pf*); **to ~ time** вы́играть вре́мя (*usu pf*)

vi **1: my watch ~s** мои́ часы́ спеша́т; **he has ~ed in popularity** его́ популя́рность возросла́; **he has ~ed in weight** он приба́вил в ве́се, он пополне́л

2: to ~ on до|гоня́ть, на|гоня́ть (*pfs* -гна́ть); **the police car is ~ing on us** нас догоня́ет/нагоня́ет полице́йская маши́на; **he ~ed on his pursuers** он оторва́лся от свои́х пресле́дователей; *Sport* **he ~ed on the leader** он догна́л ли́дера, он поравня́лся с ли́дером (*drew level with*), он оторва́лся от ли́дера (*drew away from*).

gainful *adj* (*profitable*) дохо́дный, при́быльный; (*paid*) хорошо́ опла́чиваемый; **~ occupation** при́быльная/ хорошо́ опла́чиваемая рабо́та.

gait *n* похо́дка.

gale *n* си́льный ве́тер, бу́ря; (*at sea*) шторм; **the tree was blown down in the ~** де́рево свали́ло (*impers*) бу́рей; **it was blowing a ~** дул си́льный ве́тер; **~ force 9** шторм в де́вять ба́ллов; *attr*: **a ~ force wind** штормово́й ве́тер; **~ warning** штормово́й сигна́л.

gallant *adj* (*brave*) хра́брый; (*chivalrous*) гала́нтный.

gall-bladder *n* жёлчный пузы́рь (*m*).

gallery *n* (*Art, Archit, in mining*) галере́я; *Theat* балко́н, *CQ* галёрка; **picture ~** карти́нная галере́я; *fig* **to play to the ~** игра́ть на пу́блику.

galley proof *n* гра́нка.

galling *adj*: **it was ~ to/for him to have to apologize** проси́ть проще́ния бы́ло нестерпи́мо для его́ го́рдости/самолю́бия.

gallon *n* галло́н (*= 4,5 ли́тра*).

gallop *vi* скака́ть гало́пом (про-).

gallstone *n* жёлчный ка́мень (*m*).

galore *adv CQ* в изоби́лии.

galosh *n* гало́ша.

galvanize *vt Tech* гальванизи́ровать (*impf and pf*); *fig* **to ~ smb into action** побу|жда́ть кого́-л к де́йствию (-ди́ть), как сле́дует встряхну́ть кого́-л.

gamble *n* риск; **it's a bit of a ~** э́то риско́ванно.

gamble *vi* игра́ть в аза́ртные и́гры (*only in impf*); игра́ть на де́ньги; **to ~ on the stock exchange** игра́ть на би́рже; **he has ~d away his money** он проигра́лся в пух и прах; *fig* **we can't ~ on it's being fine tomorrow** мы не мо́жем рассчи́тывать на хоро́шую пого́ду за́втра.

gambler *n* игро́к.

gambling *n* аза́ртные и́гры (*pl*); игра́ на де́ньги.

game[1] *n* **1** игра́, *also Sport*; (*match*) игра́, встре́ча; **a ~ of cards/football** игра́ в ка́рты/в футбо́л; **a ~ of croquet/chess** па́ртия в кроке́т/в ша́хматы [*but* **NB: (the ~ of) chess** (*general*) игра́ в ша́хматы]; **let's have a ~ of chess** дава́й сыгра́ем в ша́хматы; **he likes ~s** он лю́бит спорти́вные и́гры; **he plays a good ~ of tennis** он хорошо́ игра́ет в те́ннис; **to be on one's ~** быть в фо́рме; **there's a ~ against Cambridge tomorrow** за́втра бу́дет игра́/встре́ча с кома́ндой Ке́мбриджа; **the Olympic Games** Олимпи́йские и́гры; (*in tennis*): **a ~ of tennis** игра́ в те́ннис, (*when scoring*) гейм; **~ all!** счёт ге́ймов 1:1 (оди́н—оди́н); **~, set and match** гейм, сет и встре́ча; **to win two ~s in the first set** вы́играть два ге́йма в пе́рвом се́те

2 *fig uses*: **to play a double ~** вести́ двойну́ю игру́; **I know his little ~** я зна́ю, каку́ю игру́ он ведёт; **I'll spoil his ~ for him** я ему́ всю игру́ испо́рчу; **the ~ is up** де́ло про́играно; **to beat smb at his own ~** победи́ть кого́-л его́ же ору́жием

3 (*in hunting*) дичь (*collect*); **big ~** кру́пный зверь, кру́пная дичь; *fig* **he's easy ~** его́ легко́ провести́, он о́чень дове́рчив.

game[1] *adj*: **he's ~ for anything** он гото́в на всё/на что уго́дно.

game[1] *vi* игра́ть в аза́ртные и́гры (*only in impf*).

game[2] *adj*: **he's got a ~ leg** у него́ покале́ченная нога́.

game reserve *n* запове́дник.

games master *n* учи́тель (*m*) физкульту́ры.

gammon *n* свино́й о́корок.

gander *n* гуса́к.

gang *n* (*of workmen*) брига́да; (*of criminals*) ба́нда, ша́йка; *CQ* компа́ния; **a whole ~ of us are going swimming this afternoon** мы все́й компа́нией по́сле обе́да идём купа́ться.

gangrene *n* гангре́на.

gangway *n Naut* схо́дни (*usu pl*); *Theat, etc.* прохо́д (ме́жду ряда́ми).

gaol *n and vb see* **jail.**

gap *n* **1** (*chink*) щель, (*larger*) проло́м; (*in wall*) брешь, *also Mil, fig*; (*space*) промежу́ток, *also fig*; (*smth missing*) пробе́л, *also fig*; (*passage, pass*) прохо́д; **through a ~ in the wall** че́рез щель/проло́м в стене́; **a ~ in the clouds** просве́т в облака́х; **in the ~ between the houses**/*fig* **the wars** в промежу́тке ме́жду дома́ми/ме́жду во́йнами; **a ~ in a text**

пробе́л в те́ксте; **leave a ~ for the date** оста́вь ме́сто для числа́; **there are ~s in our row of peas** горо́х (*collect*) взошёл недру́жно; *Mil* **a ~ in defences** брешь в оборо́не (*sing*)

2 *fig uses*: **a ~ in one's knowledge/memory** пробе́л в зна́ниях (*pl*), прова́л в па́мяти; **he played another sonata to fill the ~** он испо́лнил ещё одну́ сона́ту, что́бы запо́лнить оста́вшееся вре́мя; **she's filling the ~ while he is away** его́ сейча́с нет, и она́ вме́сто него́; **there's a ~ of 7 years between the children** ме́жду детьми́ ра́зница (в) семь лет; **there was a ~ in the conversation** в разгово́ре наступи́ла па́уза; **a ~ between supply and demand** разры́в ме́жду спро́сом и предложе́нием; **there is a wide ~ between the two theories** име́ется большо́е/суще́ственное расхожде́ние ме́жду э́тими двумя́ тео́риями.

gape *vi* **1** (*of people*: *yawn*) зева́ть (*impf*); (*stare*) *CQ* пя́литься (*impf*); **to ~ at smth** пя́литься на что-л

2 (*of things*) зия́ть (*impf*); **a gaping wound/abyss** зия́ющая ра́на/бе́здна.

gap-toothed *adj* с ре́дкими зуба́ми.

garage *n* гара́ж; (*service station*) ста́нция обслу́живания.

garage *vt*: **to ~ a car** (*put in garage*) ста́вить маши́ну в гара́ж (по-), (*keep in garage*) держа́ть маши́ну в гараже́ (*impf*).

garbage *n* му́сор; *attr*: (*US*) **~ can** му́сорный я́щик.

garbled *adj*: **I only heard a ~ version of the story** я зна́ю э́ту исто́рию, но то́лько в искажённом ви́де.

garden *n* сад; **to sit/stroll in the ~** сиде́ть в саду́, гуля́ть по са́ду; **kitchen/vegetable ~** огоро́д; **nursery ~** пито́мник; **botanical ~s** ботани́ческий сад (*sing*); *attr* садо́вый; **a ~ seat** садо́вая скаме́йка.

gardener *n* садо́вник.

gardening *n* садово́дство; **I'm fond of ~** я люблю́ рабо́тать в саду́; *attr*: **~ gloves** садо́вые перча́тки.

gargle *n* (*medicine*) полоска́ние.

gargle *vi* полоска́ть го́рло (по-, про-).

gargling *n* полоска́ние го́рла; **~ might help** полоска́ние мо́жет вам помо́чь.

garish *adj* крича́щий; *CQ* бро́ский; **~ colours** крича́щие кра́ски; **a ~ tie** сли́шком я́ркий/бро́ский га́лстук.

garlic *n* чесно́к; **a clove of ~** зубо́к/до́лька чеснока́.

garment *n* (*single*) предме́т оде́жды; **~s** оде́жда (*collect*).

garnish *n* украше́ние.

garnish *vt*: **to ~ meat with parsley** по|сыпа́ть мя́со петру́шкой (-сы́пать).

garret *n* черда́к; манса́рда.

garrison *n* гарнизо́н.

garter *n* подвя́зка.

gas *n* **1** газ; **to turn on/light the ~** включи́ть газ; **to turn off/put out the ~** вы́ключить газ; *attr* га́зовый; **a ~ leak** уте́чка га́за

2 (*US*) бензи́н; *Aut CQ* **to step on the ~** дать/приба́вить га́зу.

gas *vti vt* отрав|ля́ть га́зом (-и́ть)
vi CQ болта́ть (*impf*).

gasbag *n CQ* болту́н, *f* -ья.

gas cooker *n* га́зовая плита́.

gash *n* глубо́кий поре́з.

gash *vt* ре́зать (по-); (*badly*) рассе|ка́ть (-́чь); **his face was badly ~ed** лицо́ у него́ бы́ло рассечено́/си́льно поре́зано; **I've ~ed my finger** я поре́зал/рассёк себе́ па́лец.

gaslight *n* (*lighting*) га́зовое освеще́ние; **by ~** при га́зовом све́те.

gas main *n* газопрово́д.

gasman *n* газовщи́к.

gas meter *n* газоме́р, га́зовый счётчик; **to read the ~** снима́ть показа́ния (*pl*) га́зового счётчика.

gasoline *n* (*US*) бензи́н.

gasoline station *n* (*US*) бензозапра́вочная ста́нция, *CQ* бензоколо́нка.

gasp *n*: **at one's last ~** при после́днем издыха́нии; **he gave a ~ of horror/surprise/pain** у него́ перехвати́ло дыха́ние от у́жаса, он за́мер от удивле́ния, он задохну́лся от бо́ли.

gasp *vti vt*: **he ~ed out a few words** он как бы вы́дохнул не́сколько слов
vi за|дыха́ться (-дохну́ться); **he was ~ing for breath/air** он задыха́лся/(*in a very bad way*) он лови́л ртом во́здух; **his impudence left me ~ing** я да́же задохну́лся от его́ на́глости.

gas ring *n* га́зовая пли́тка.

gas tap *n* га́зовый кран.

gastric *adj* желу́дочный.

gastritis *n* гастри́т.

gasworks *npl* га́зовый заво́д (*sing*).

gate *n* **1** (*large, often double gates to factory, stadium, etc.*) воро́та (*no sing*); (*on canal lock*) шлюз; (*at level crossing*) *equiv* шлагба́ум [*in SU always a pole*]; (*wicket gate for people only*) кали́тка

2 (*at football matches, etc.*): **at such matches there's always a big ~** э́ти ма́тчи всегда́ собира́ют мно́го зри́телей *or* боле́льщиков (*a big attendance*)/прино́сят большу́ю вы́ручку (*bring in a lot of money*).

gatecrash *vti*: **to ~ (a party)** при|ходи́ть без приглаше́ния (-йти́).

gatepost *n* столб воро́т.

gateway *n* воро́та (*no sing*); (*under arch or wall into courtyard*) подворо́тня.

gather *n usu pl Sew* сбо́рка; **a dress with ~s** пла́тье в сбо́рку/со сбо́рками.

gather *vti vt* **1** со|бира́ть (-бра́ть); **to ~ a crowd/flowers/information** собира́ть толпу́/цветы́/све́дения (*pl*); *Sew* **to ~ a skirt** собира́ть ю́бку в сбо́рки; **I ~ed up the broken glass off the floor** я подобра́л оско́лки с по́ла; *fig* **to ~ speed/height** на|бира́ть ско́рость/высоту́ (-бра́ть)

2 (*deduce*) заключ|а́ть (-и́ть); **I ~ed from what he said that...** из его́ слов я заключи́л, что...; **I ~ you're leaving us soon** я слыха́л [**NB** *tense*], вы ско́ро от нас уезжа́ете

vi **1** собира́ться; **the children ~ed round the bonfire** де́ти собрали́сь у костра́; **a storm/darkness is ~ing** собира́ется бу́ря, сгуща́ется тьма; **with ~ing speed** с нараста́ющей ско́ростью

2 (*of an abscess*) нарыва́ть (*usu impf*).

gathering *n* **1** (*meeting*) собра́ние; (*social*) встре́ча; **a family ~** семе́йная встре́ча

2 (*abscess*) нары́в.

gauche *adj* нело́вкий.

gaudy *adj* (*of colours*) крича́щий, бро́ский; (*cheap, showy*) **~ jewelry** безвку́сные украше́ния.

gauge *n Tech* кали́бр; (*instrument*) измери́тельный прибо́р; *Rail* колея́; **pressure ~** мано́метр; *Aut* **fuel ~** указа́тель у́ровня то́плива, бензиноме́р; *attr*: **broad/narrow ~ railway** ширококоле́йная/узкоколе́йная желе́зная доро́га.

gauge *vt* (*measure*) измер|я́ть (-́ить); **to ~ the diameter of wire** изме́рить диа́метр про́волоки; *fig*: **it's hard to ~ the speed of the traffic** тру́дно определи́ть (на глаз) ско́рость движе́ния; **he ~d the situation correctly** он ве́рно/пра́вильно оцени́л ситуа́цию.

gaunt *adj* худоща́вый; (*emaciated*) исхуда́лый.

gauze *n* ма́рля.

gawky *adj* неуклю́жий.

gay *adj* весёлый; (*of colours*) я́ркий; *euph CQ* **he's ~** он педера́ст.

gaze *n* взгляд.

gaze *vi*: **to ~ at** гляде́ть на + *A* (*only in impf*), уста́виться на + *A* (*only in pf*).

gazette *n* (*official notice*) бюллете́нь (*m*), ве́стник; (*as newspaper title*): **the Cambridge G.** «Ке́мбридж газе́т».

gear *n* **1** *Tech* (*cogwheel*) шестерня́, зу́бчатое колесо́

2 (*apparatus*) механи́зм; (*drive*) приво́д; **steering ~** рулево́й механи́зм/приво́д; *Aer* **landing ~** поса́дочный механи́зм

3 *Aut* переда́ча, ско́рость; **low/first ~** ма́лая/пе́рвая переда́ча *or* ско́рость; **high/top ~** высо́кая/вы́сшая переда́ча *or* ско́рость; **to change ~** переключа́ть переда́чу/ско́рость; **to engage third/reverse ~** включа́ть тре́тью переда́чу *or* ско́рость/за́дний ход; **the car is not in ~** переда́ча не включена́

4 (*equipment*) принадле́жности (*pl*); *CQ* (*belongings*) ве́щи (*pl*); **fishing/shaving ~** рыболо́вные сна́сти, бри́твенные принадле́жности.

gear *vt* (*adapt to*): **this dictionary is ~ed to the needs of the English speaker** э́тот слова́рь предназна́чен для англи́йского чита́теля; **to ~ production to meet demand** выпуска́ть проду́кцию с учётом спро́са.

gearbox *n Aut* коро́бка переда́ч.

gear lever *n Aut* рыча́г переключе́ния переда́ч.

gelatine *n* желати́н.

gem *n* драгоце́нный ка́мень; драгоце́нность; *CQ* **she's a ~** она́ про́сто сокро́вище.

gen *n CQ* (*facts*) да́нные (*pl*); (*information*) све́дения (*pl*), информа́ция.

gender *n Gram* род; **masculine/feminine/neuter ~** мужско́й/же́нский/сре́дний род; **what is the ~ of this noun?** како́го ро́да э́то существи́тельное?

gene *n Biol* ген.

genealogical *adj* генеалоги́ческий; родосло́вный.

genealogy *n* генеало́гия; (*pedigree*) родосло́вная.

general *n* генера́л.

general *adj* **1** (*universal*) всео́бщий; (*common*) о́бщий; **a ~ strike/election** всео́бщая забасто́вка, всео́бщие вы́боры (*pl*); **~ opinion** о́бщее мне́ние; **a book for the ~ reader** кни́га для широ́кого чита́теля; **there was a ~ panic** всех охвати́ла па́ника; **in ~** вообще́ (*adv*); **as a ~ rule** как пра́вило; **this word is in ~ use** э́то о́чень употреби́тельное сло́во

2 (*not detailed*) о́бщий; **~ impression** о́бщее впечатле́ние; **in ~ outline** в о́бщих черта́х (*pl*); (*not specialized*): **~ hospital** больни́ца о́бщего ти́па; **~ practitioner** *approx* терапе́вт (в поликли́нике)

3 (*in titles*) гла́вный, генера́льный; **~ director/manager** гла́вный/генера́льный дире́ктор.

General Assembly *n* Генера́льная Ассамбле́я.

generalization *n* обобще́ние.

generalize *vi* обобщ|а́ть (-и́ть).

generally *adv* (*usually*) обы́чно; (*in a general sense*) вообще́; **I ~ get up at 7 o'clock** я обы́чно встаю́ в семь часо́в; **~ speaking** вообще́ говоря́; (*widely*) **his proposal was ~ welcomed** его́ предложе́ние все одо́брили.

general staff *n* генера́льный штаб.

general store *n* универса́льный магази́н, *abbr* универма́г.

generate *vt*: **to ~ electricity** *Phys* генери́ровать электри́чество, (*on industrial scale*) производи́ть/вырабатывать электроэне́ргию (*usu impfs*); **to ~ heat** (*industrially*) выраба́тывать тепло́ (*usu impf*); *fig* **to ~ hope/fear** поро|жда́ть наде́жду/страх (-ди́ть).

generating station *n* электроцентра́ль.

generation *n* **1** (*of people*) поколе́ние; **future ~s** бу́дущие поколе́ния; **a ~ ago nobody had television** ста́ршее поколе́ние не зна́ло телеви́зоров (*pl*)

2 *Tech, Phys* генери́рование; (*industrial*) произво́дство.

generator *n* генера́тор.

generic *adj* родово́й.

generosity *n* (*of spirit*) великоду́шие; (*with gifts*) ще́дрость.

generous *adj* (*in spirit*) великоду́шный; (*open-handed*) ще́дрый; **a ~ act/impulse** великоду́шный посту́пок/поры́в; **a ~ gift/helping** ще́дрый пода́рок, больша́я по́рция; **he is ~ with his praises/money** он щедр на похвалы́, он не скупо́й.

genetics *npl* гене́тика (*sing*).

genial *adj* приве́тливый.

genitive *n Gram* роди́тельный паде́ж.

genius *n* **1** (*quality*) гениа́льность, (*talent*) тала́нт; **the contemporaries of Bach did not recognize his ~** совреме́нники Ба́ха не могли́ поня́ть его́ гениа́льности; **this symphony is a work of ~** э́то гениа́льная симфо́ния; **he has a ~ for finding the right word** у него́ осо́бый тала́нт безоши́бочно находи́ть еди́нственно ве́рное сло́во; **she's got a ~ for languages** у неё выдаю́щиеся лингвисти́ческие спосо́бности; *iron* **he has a ~ for arriving at the wrong moment** у него́ пря́мо тала́нт приходи́ть в са́мое неподходя́щее вре́мя

2 (*person*) ге́ний; **he's a ~** он ге́ний, он гениа́льный челове́к

3 (*spirit of smth*): **evil ~** злой ге́ний; **the Russian ~** дух ру́сского наро́да.

gent *n CQ abbr* = **gentleman;** *CQ* **the ~s',** (*as sign*) **"Gents"** мужско́й туале́т.

gentle *adj* **1** не́жный, мя́гкий; ла́сковый; **a ~ look/breeze** не́жный взгляд, ла́сковый ветеро́к; **a ~ character/push** мя́гкий хара́ктер, лёгкий толчо́к

2: of ~ birth зна́тного/дворя́нского происхожде́ния.

gentleman *n* джентльме́н; **he's a real ~** он настоя́щий джентльме́н; **ladies and gentlemen!** (*in official address to or by foreigners in SU*) уважа́емые да́мы и господа́!; (*notice*) **"Gentlemen"** мужско́й туале́т.

genuine *adj* (*not faked*) по́длинный; (*sincere*) и́скренний; **a ~ Rubens** по́длинный Ру́бенс; **they're ~ people** они́ и́скренние/чи́стые душо́й лю́ди; **with ~ pleasure** с и́скренним/нескрыва́емым удово́льствием.

genus *n Biol* род.

geographer *n* гео́граф.

geography *n* геогра́фия.

geologist *n* гео́лог.

geology *n* геоло́гия.

geometric(al) *adj* геометри́ческий.

geometry *n* геоме́трия.

Georgian *n* грузи́н, грузи́нка.

Georgian *adj* грузи́нский.

geranium *n* гера́нь.

germ *n* (*infectious*) микро́б; бакте́рия; баци́лла; *Biol*, *Bot* (*embryo*) заро́дыш; зача́ток; *fig* **the ~ of an idea** заро́дыш иде́и.

German *n* не́мец, не́мка; (*language*) неме́цкий язы́к.

German *adj* неме́цкий.

germane *adj*: **that material is not ~ to our subject** э́тот материа́л не отно́сится к де́лу.

germinate *vi* прораст|а́ть (-и́).

gerrymander *vti*: **to ~ (at) an election** фальсифици́ровать результа́ты вы́боров (*pl*) (*impf and pf*).

gerund *n Gram* геру́ндий.

gesticulate *vi* жестикули́ровать (*impf*).

gesture *n* жест; **he made a ~ of refusal** он сде́лал отрица́тельный жест; **that was a friendly/only an empty ~** э́то был дру́жеский/всего́-на́всего пусто́й жест; **what a nice ~!** как ми́ло!

get *vti vt* **1** (*receive*) получ|а́ть (-и́ть); **to ~ an answer/permission/a prize/recognition/a scolding** получи́ть отве́т/разреше́ние/приз/призна́ние/вы́говор; **to ~ smth for nothing** получи́ть что-л да́ром; **he got a shock/a nasty wound** он получи́л шок/ужа́сную ра́ну; **he has got the support of the directors** он получи́л подде́ржку директоро́в; **you must ~ confirmation in writing** на́до получи́ть пи́сьменное подтвержде́ние; **he got 3 years** (*sentence*) он получи́л три го́да (тюрьмы́); **how much does he ~ a month?** ско́лько он получа́ет в ме́сяц?; **he got a surprise** его́ ждал сюрпри́з; **he ~s it from his father** э́то у него́ от отца́; **this room ~s no sun/all the sun** в э́той ко́мнате не быва́ет со́лнца/всегда́ со́лнце; **she gave him as good as she got** она́ дала́ ему́ сда́чи

2 (*obtain*) доста|ва́ть (-́ть); брать (взять); (*buy*) покупа́ть (купи́ть); доби́ться + *G* (*only in pf*); **I've got tickets for the concert** я доста́л (*managed to get*)/я взял (*bought*)/я получи́л (*tickets reached me or were given to me*) биле́ты на конце́рт; **where did you ~ those apples?** где вы доста́ли/купи́ли э́ти я́блоки?; **I got it cheap** я купи́л э́то дёшево/*CQ* по дешёвке; **I must ~ a new diary** мне на́до купи́ть но́вый дневни́к; **I'll go and ~ some milk.—Get some biscuits too** я схожу́ за молоко́м.—Возьми́ ещё и пече́нья; **I can't ~ any sense out of anyone** я не могу́ доби́ться то́лку (*G*) ни от кого́; **to ~ one's own way** доби́ться своего́; **I got the book I needed** я доста́л/нашёл ну́жную кни́гу; **she got herself a husband** она́ заполучи́ла (*CQ*) себе́ му́жа; **he ~s all his ideas from books** он берёт/че́рпает все свои́ иде́и из книг; **where can we ~ something to eat?** где бы нам доста́ть чего́-нибудь пое́сть?

3 *Radio*, *Tel*: **I can't ~ Paris on my radio** по моему́ приёмнику я не могу́ пойма́ть Пари́ж; *Tel* **~ me the director/the hospital** соедини́те меня́ с дире́ктором/с больни́цей; **I didn't ~ him** (*he was out*) я не заста́л его́, (*could not get through*) я не мог дозвони́ться до него́; **you've/I got the wrong number** вы оши́блись/я оши́бся но́мером *or* вы не туда́ попа́ли/я не туда́ попа́л

4 (*fetch*) при|носи́ть (-нести́); (*take*) брать (взять); **~ me a pencil/a drink of water** принеси́ мне каранда́ш/воды́; **I'll just ~ my coat** я то́лько возьму́ пальто́; **can I ~ you a drink?** вам чего́-нибудь нали́ть?; **hold the line, I'll go and ~ him** не ве́шайте тру́бку, я сейча́с его́ позову́/найду́; **go and ~ a doctor** (*fetch*) сходи́ за врачо́м; **we'll have to ~ the doctor** (*call*) на́до позва́ть врача́

5 (*take*, *put*): **I have to ~ the children to school by 9 o'clock** мне на́до отвести́ (*on foot*)/отвезти́ (*by car*) дете́й в шко́лу к девяти́ часа́м; **how can we ~ him/it home?** как нам доста́вить его́/э́то домо́й?; **they**

managed to ~ him upstairs/into a taxi им удало́сь затащи́ть его́ наве́рх/в такси́; **~ the parcel to me by tomorrow at latest** смотри́, что́бы посы́лка была́ у меня́ са́мое по́зднее за́втра

6 (*catch*) пойма́ть (*only in pf*); **they got the thief** они́ пойма́ли во́ра; **we got a taxi** мы взя́ли (*took*)/пойма́ли (*after search*) такси́; **did he ~ his train?** он успе́л на по́езд?; **I decided to ~ the next train** я реши́л сесть на сле́дующий по́езд; **we'll ~ them yet** мы ещё до них доберёмся; **he got me by the throat** он схвати́л меня́ за го́рло; **the blow got him on the head** уда́р пришёлся ему́ по голове́; **the bullet got him in the arm** пу́ля попа́ла ему́ в ру́ку; (*of pain*) **it ~s me just here** вот тут боли́т/бо́льно; **he got measles/a bad cold** он заболе́л ко́рью, он си́льно простуди́лся *or* он схвати́л си́льный на́сморк; *CQ* **you've got me there!** за́дал ты мне зада́чу!

7 have got (= *have*): у + *G*; **I've got chicken-pox** у меня́ ветря́нка; **I've got earache/a headache** у меня́ боли́т у́хо/голова́; **I've not got much time** у меня́ ма́ло вре́мени; **he has got two dogs/a habit of rubbing his hands** у него́ две соба́ки/привы́чка потира́ть ру́ки; **I haven't got any change** у меня́ нет ме́лочи; *CQ* **he's got it in for me** у него́ зуб про́тив меня́

8 (*cause*): **I'll ~ the porter to bring the luggage** я попрошу́ швейца́ра (*at hotel*) принести́ чемода́ны; **he got her sacked** он доби́лся её увольне́ния; **I got him to reconsider his decision** мне удало́сь уговори́ть (*persuaded*) его́ переду́мать; **he knows how to ~ things done** он уме́ет де́лать дела́; **that affair got me a reputation for obstinacy** из-за э́того я просл́ыл упря́мцем; **don't ~ him on to the subject of horses!** не заводи́ с ним разгово́р о лошадя́х!; **I don't want to ~ you into trouble** я не хочу́ навле́чь на вас неприя́тности (*pl*); **I must ~ the lunch/this finished** мне на́до гото́вить обе́д, я до́лжен э́то зако́нчить; **I'll ~ the papers ready** я пригото́влю бума́ги; **to ~ one's hair cut** подстри́чься; **to ~ one's feet wet** промочи́ть но́ги; **to ~ one's hands dirty** испа́чкать ру́ки

9 (*understand*) по|нима́ть (-ня́ть); (*hear*) расслы́шать (*pf*); **I've got you** я вас понима́ю/по́нял; **~ it?** понима́ешь?, по́нял?; **I got the drift of what he was saying** я улови́л смысл его́ слов; **I didn't ~ what you said/your name** я не расслы́шал вас/ва́ше и́мя

vi [**NB** *verbs used to translate "get" vi are usu in pf aspect, unless translating English continuous tenses*]

1 (*reach*): **I must ~ to London/to the station by 10** я до́лжен быть в Ло́ндоне/на вокза́ле к десяти́ часа́м; **can you ~ there by bus?** мо́жно попа́сть туда́ авто́бусом?; **how did these flowers ~ there?** как э́ти цветы́ попа́ли туда́?; **where did you ~ to yesterday?** где вы бы́ли вчера́?; **where can he have got to?** где он мо́жет быть?; **they should ~ here soon** они́ ско́ро должны́ прийти́/прие́хать; **we got as far as the lake** мы дошли́/дое́хали до о́зера; **we didn't ~ as far as discussing finances** мы не дошли́ до обсужде́ния фина́нсовых вопро́сов; **how far have you got to?** (*in reading a book*) ты до како́го ме́ста дочита́л?; **you won't ~ anywhere with him** ты от него́ ничего́ не добьёшься; **we're ~ting nowhere** у нас ничего́ не получа́ется; **at last we seem to be ~ting somewhere** похо́же, наконе́ц у нас что́-то получа́ется

2 (*become*) ста|нови́ться (́-ть); **he got known** он стал изве́стным; **it got cool towards evening** под ве́чер ста́ло прохла́дно, к ве́черу похолода́ло (*impers*); **I am/was ~ting nervous** я начина́ю/я на́чал *or* я стал не́рвничать; **it got dark** ста́ло темно́, стемне́ло (*impers*); **he got better quickly** ему́ ско́ро ста́ло лу́чше; **he got caught/wounded** его́ пойма́ли, он был ра́нен *or* его́ ра́нило (*impers*); **to ~ old/fat** старе́ть, толсте́ть (*pfs* по-); **to ~ angry** рассерди́ться; **the tea is ~ting cold** чай сты́нет; **I got interested in jazz** я стал интересова́ться джа́зом; **we're ~ting settled at last** наконе́ц мы начина́ем устра́иваться; **to ~ used to** привык|а́ть к + *D* *or* + *inf* (́-нуть); **to ~ wet/soaked** промок|а́ть (́-нуть); *Sport* **~ ready!, ~ set!, go!** пригото́виться!, внима́ние!, старт!

3 + *inf or gerund*: **I got to know him recently** я неда́вно познако́мился с ним; **I'm ~ting to know him now** я его́ узна́ю бли́же; **I got to know about it by chance** я случа́йно узна́л об э́том; **I soon got to like him/to understand the system** он мне ско́ро на́чал нра́виться, я ско́ро на́чал понима́ть э́ту систе́му; **I couldn't ~ to sleep** я не мог засну́ть; **I got to thinking that...** я стал ду́мать, что...; **I got talking to him after the concert** я разговори́лся с ним по́сле конце́рта; **let's ~ going!** (*on foot*) пошли́!, пойдём!, (*by car*) пое́хали!

4 have got to (= *must*): **I've got to be there by five** я до́лжен быть там к пяти́ часа́м; **I've got to make a phone call** мне на́до позвони́ть; [*see also* **have**]

get about *vi*: **I don't ~ about much these days** тепе́рь я ма́ло где быва́ю; **he's ~ting about again** (*after illness*) он опя́ть на нога́х; **he can ~ about on crutches** он мо́жет передвига́ться на костыля́х; **if it ~s about that...** е́сли узна́ют, что...

get across *vti vt*: **I got the idea/it across to them that...** мне удало́сь объясни́ть им, что..., я заста́вил их поня́ть, что...; **to ~ across smb** ссо́риться с кем-л (по-)

vi: **he doesn't ~ across to his pupils** у него́ нет конта́кта с ученика́ми

get at *vi* (*reach*) до|бира́ться (-бра́ться); **I can't ~ at my luggage** я не могу́ добра́ться до свои́х веще́й; **the cat has got at the cream** ко́шка добрала́сь до сли́вок; **to ~ at the truth** добра́ться до и́стины; *CQ*

just let me ~ at him! дай мне то́лько добра́ться до него́!; *fig*: **what are you ~ting at?** к чему́ ты кло́нишь?; **he's always ~ting at me** (*carping*) он ве́чно ко мне приди-ра́ется/цепля́ется

get away *vti vt*: **I want to ~ my mother away for a holiday** я хочу́ увезти́ ма́му от-дохну́ть

vi: **I got away early from work** я ра́но ушёл с рабо́ты; **the bird/fish/prisoner got away** пти́ца улете́ла, ры́ба сорвала́сь с крючка́, пле́ннику удало́сь бежа́ть; **I want to ~ away from it all** я хочу́ порва́ть со всем э́тим; **thieves got away with £1,000,000** во́ры скры́-лись, прихвати́в с собо́й миллио́н фу́нтов; **he got away with it** э́то ему́ сошло́ с рук, он вы́шел сухи́м из воды́; **you'll never ~ away with it** тебе́ э́то да́ром не пройдёт; **you can't ~ away from the fact that...** ни-куда́ не де́нешься от того́ фа́кта, что...; **~ away, you're just flattering me** ну что́ вы, э́то вы мне про́сто льсти́те

get back *vti vt*: **I got my books back from him** он мне отда́л/верну́л кни́ги; **I got my shoes back from mending** я получи́л ту́фли из ре-мо́нта/из почи́нки; **to ~ one's own back (on smb)** взять рева́нш, рассчита́ться с кем-л

vi возвраща́ться (верну́ться)

get behind *vti vt*: **I've got my colleagues behind me on this** в э́том вопро́се мои́ кол-ле́ги подде́рживают меня́

vi: **the cat got behind the cupboard** ко́шка убежа́ла за шкаф; **he got behind with his work/the others** он отста́л в рабо́те/от дру-ги́х (*on walk*, *or in class*)

get by *vi*: **can I ~ by please?** мо́жно мне пройти́?; **he ~s by on £40 a week** он перебива́ется на со́рок фу́нтов в неде́лю; **my essay got by** моё сочине́ние прошло́/ при́нято/*approx equiv* получи́ло проходно́й балл

get down *vti vt*: **to ~ a book down from a shelf** брать кни́гу с по́лки (взять); **I got the medicine down** я проглоти́л лека́рство; (*to secretary*) **did you ~ the last sentence down?** ты записа́л после́днее предложе́ние?

vi: **to ~ down from a train/a ladder/the table** сходи́ть с по́езда (сойти́), спус|ка́ться с ле́стницы (-ти́ться), вста|ва́ть из-за стола́ (-ть); **he got down on his hands and knees** он встал/опусти́лся на четвере́ньки; **let's ~ down to business** дава́й перейдём к де́лу; **to ~ down to work** взя́ться за рабо́ту (*usu pf*)

get in *vti vt*: **to ~ in the harvest** убира́ть урожа́й (убра́ть); **I've got in the week's shop-ping** я сде́лал поку́пки на неде́лю; **~ the chairs in before it rains** унеси́ сту́лья в дом, пока́ нет дождя́; **to ~ the doctor/police in** вы|зыва́ть врача́/поли́цию (-звать)

vi (*on foot*) при|ходи́ть (-йти́), (*of trains, planes, and people*) прибы|ва́ть (-ть); **she/the post got in late** она́/по́чта пришла́ по́здно; **what time do you ~ in from work?** во ско́ль-ко ты прихо́дишь с рабо́ты?; **the train/he got in on time** по́езд/он при́был во́время; **to ~ in smb's way** меша́ть кому́-л (по-); **~ in!** (*to car*) сади́сь!, *CQ* залеза́й!

get into *vti vt*: **to ~ a key into a lock** встав|ля́ть ключ в замо́к (-́ить); **I can't ~ it all into my bag** все э́ти ве́щи не вле́зут в мою́ су́мку; **I couldn't ~ it into his head that...** я не мог вбить ему́ в го́лову, что...

vi (*into car, plane, bus*) сади́ться в + *A* (сесть); **I couldn't ~ into the house** я не мог войти́/попа́сть в дом; **to ~ into bed** ло-жи́ться в посте́ль; **I can't ~ into this dress** э́то пла́тье мне мало́; **he got into debt/ trouble/a mess** он влез (*CQ*) в долги́, он попа́л в беду́, он влип (*CQ*); *Sport* **to ~ into training** нача́ть тренирова́ться

get off *vti vt*: **I can't ~ my boots off** я не могу́ снять сапоги́; **to ~ children off to school** отправ|ля́ть дете́й в шко́лу (-́ить); **I must ~ this letter off today** я до́лжен отпра́вить э́то письмо́ сего́дня; **to ~ a stain off** вы|води́ть пятно́ (-́вести); **I had to ~ it off my chest** мне ну́жно бы́ло облегчи́ть ду́шу; **his lawyer got him off** адвока́т вы́зво-лил его́ из беды́

vi **1** (*alight*) сходи́ть (сойти́); (*off horse or bicycle*) слез|а́ть с + *G* (-ть); **I'm ~ting off at the next stop** я схожу́ на сле́дующей остано́вке

2 (*start*): **we got off early** мы отпра́вились ра́но; **the train got off punctually** по́езд ото-шёл во́время; **the plane was an hour late in ~ting off** самолёт вы́летел с опозда́нием на час

3 *various*: **~ off the grass** сойди́ с газо́на; **he got off doing the dishes** ему́ не пришло́сь мыть посу́ду (*collect*); **he got off with a fine** он отде́лался штра́фом; *CQ* **I told him where he got off** я его́ отши́л

get on *vti vt*: **~ your coat on!** наде́нь пальто́!

vi **1**: **to ~ on (to) a train/bus/bicycle/horse** сади́ться в по́езд/в авто́бус/на велосипе́д/на ло́шадь (сесть); **to ~ on to one's feet** вста|-ва́ть на́ ноги (-ть); **I must be ~ting on** мне пора́ идти́

2 (*advance*): **time is ~ting on** вре́мя идёт, (*it's late*) уже́ по́здно; **it's ~ting on for sup-pertime** ско́ро у́жин; **he's ~ting on for forty** ему́ ско́ро со́рок; **to ~ on in the world** преуспе́ть в жи́зни (*usu pf*); **there were ~ting on for 100 people at the reception** на приёме бы́ло о́коло ста челове́к; **I got on to this by chance** я узна́л об э́том случа́йно

3 (*fare*) *also* **~ along**: **how are you ~ting on?** как вы поплива́ете?, *CQ* как дела́?; **how's the invalid ~ting on?** как больно́й—поправ-ля́ется?; **he is ~ting on well at school** он хорошо́ у́чится; **I ~ on on my own perfectly well** я прекра́сно справля́юсь оди́н; **they ~ on well** они́ прекра́сно ла́дят

get out *vti vt*: **to ~ smth out of one's pockets** вы|нима́ть что-л из карма́на (-́нуть);

I got the book out of the library я взял э́ту кни́гу в библиоте́ке; **~ this out of the way** убери́ э́то; **I didn't ~ much out of his lecture** я ма́ло что вы́нес/извлёк из его́ ле́кции; **he got a lot of money out of selling his pictures** он вы́ручил мно́го де́нег от прода́жи карти́н; **to ~ smb out of a fix** выруча́ть/вы́зволить кого́-л из беды́; **I can't ~ it out of my mind that...** я не могу́ отде́латься от мы́сли, что...; **the children got the secret out of their aunt** де́ти упроси́ли тётку рассказа́ть им секре́т; **I couldn't ~ a word out** я не мог и сло́ва вы́молвить

vi сходи́ть (сойти́); **the rabbit got out of its cage** кро́лик убежа́л из кле́тки; **he's ~ting out of politics** он ухо́дит с полити́ческой аре́ны; *CQ*: **he got out of his lesson** он ушёл с уро́ка (*with or without permission*); **if I can ~ out of the invitation** е́сли я смогу́ отде́латься от приглаше́ния; **I've got out of the habit of getting up early** я отвы́к ра́но встава́ть

get over *vti vt*: **let's ~ it over** дава́й поко́нчим с э́тим

vi: **to ~ over a fence** перелез|а́ть че́рез забо́р (-́ть); **I got over my cold quickly** я бы́стро изба́вился от просту́ды; **he has got over his disappointment** он опра́вился от огорче́ния; **I can't ~ over my shyness/her rudeness** я не могу́ преодоле́ть свою́ ро́бость/прийти́ в себя́ от её гру́бости

get round *vi*: **he ~s round a lot** (*travels*) он мно́го е́здит; **the old man ~s round well for his age** (*moves*) стари́к о́чень ещё подви́жен для свои́х лет; **I'll ~ round to (doing) it some day** я доберу́сь до э́того когда́-нибудь; **I never got round to it** у меня́ до э́того ещё ру́ки не дошли́; **to ~ round a law/difficulty** обходи́ть зако́н/затрудне́ние (обойти́); *CQ* **she knows how to ~ round him** она́ зна́ет, как подъе́хать к нему́

get through *vti vt*: **can you ~ a message through to him?** мо́жете переда́ть ему́ сообще́ние?; **I got through a lot of work/£100 today** сего́дня я мно́го сде́лал/я потра́тил сто фу́нтов; **he ~s through money fast** де́ньги у него́ не заде́рживаются; **we've got through all our supplies/ten bottles of champagne** мы израсхо́довали все на́ши запа́сы, мы вы́пили де́сять буты́лок шампа́нского; **I don't know how I'll ~ through this month** я не зна́ю, как доживу́/дотяну́ до конца́ ме́сяца; **I got through my exam/the customs** я сдал экза́мен, я прошёл тамо́женный досмо́тр *or* осмо́тр

vi: **the news of the crash was a long time ~ting through** сообще́ния об ава́рии до́лго не́ было; **our team got through to the final** на́ша кома́нда вы́шла в фина́л; **I shall ~ through by six** я зако́нчу к шести́; *Tel* **I couldn't ~ through to the doctor/the hospital** я не мог дозвони́ться до врача́/в больни́цу

get together *vti vt* со|бира́ть (-бра́ть)

vi: **let's ~ together before you leave** дава́й встре́тимся (*of two people*)/дава́йте соберёмся (*of more than two*) с тобо́й (с ва́ми) до твоего́ (до ва́шего) отъе́зда; **~ together with him and decide** посове́туйтесь с ним и реши́те

get under *vti vt*: **I've got the fire/my feelings under control** я спра́вился с огнём/со свои́ми чу́вствами

vi: **the cat got under the fence/the bed** ко́шка шмыгну́ла под забо́р/убежа́ла под крова́ть; *Naut* **to ~ under way** отплыва́ть (*only in impf*)

get up *vti vt*: **to ~ up speed** на|бира́ть ско́рость (-бра́ть); **to ~ up a dance** устр|а́ивать та́нцы (*pl*) (-о́ить); **he got himself up as a clown** он наряди́лся кло́уном

vi (*rise*) вста|ва́ть (-ть); **he got up and left the room** он встал и вышел из ко́мнаты; **he got up from his chair** он встал со сту́ла.

getaway *n*: **he made a successful ~** ему́ удало́сь бежа́ть/уйти́.

get-up *n CQ* (*of clothes*) наря́д; **I like your ~** мне нра́вится твой наря́д; **the ~ of a book** оформле́ние кни́ги.

ghastly *adj* (*horrible*) стра́шный, ужа́сный, *also CQ*; (*pale*) **she looked ~** она́ ужа́сно вы́глядела.

gherkin *n* малосо́льный (*slightly salted*)/солёный (*heavily salted*) огуре́ц.

ghost *n* привиде́ние, при́зрак; *fig* **the ~ of a smile** тень улы́бки; *CQ* **there isn't the ~ of a chance** нет ни мале́йшей наде́жды.

ghostly *adj* при́зрачный.

giant *n* гига́нт; велика́н; *attr* гига́нтский.

gibe *n* насме́шка.

gibe *vi*: **to ~ at** насмеха́ться над + *I* (*impf*).

giblets *npl* (кури́ные, гуси́ные, *etc.*) потроха́ (*no sing*).

giddiness *n* головокруже́ние.

giddy *adj*: **I feel ~** у меня́ кру́жится голова́; **a ~ height** головокружи́тельная высота́; (*frivolous*) **a ~ young girl** легкомы́сленная молода́я де́вушка.

gift *n* **1** пода́рок; дар; **I wouldn't take it as a ~** мне э́того и да́ром не на́до

2 тала́нт; (*pl*) спосо́бности; **a ~ for languages** спосо́бности к языка́м; **he made good use of his ~s** он нашёл примене́ние свои́м спосо́бностям/своему́ тала́нту (*sing*).

gifted *adj* одарённый.

giggle *vi* хихи́к|ать (-нуть).

gills *npl* (*of fish*) жа́бры.

gilt *adj* позоло́ченный, золочёный.

gimlet *n* бура́в, бура́вчик.

gimmick *n* трюк; **an advertising ~** рекла́мный трюк.

gin *n* (*drink*) джин.

ginger *n* имби́рь (*m*); *fig* «изю́минка»; (*nickname*) **G.** Ры́жий.

ginger *adj* имби́рный; (*of hair*) ры́жий; **a ~ cat** ры́жий кот.

ginger beer *n* имби́рный лимона́д, имби́рное пи́во.

gingerbread *n* (имби́рный) пря́ник.

gingerly *adv* осторо́жно.

gipsy *n* цыга́н, цыга́нка; *attr* цыга́нский.

giraffe *n* жира́ф.

girder *n* ба́лка.

girdle *n* (*belt*) по́яс; (*sash*) куша́к; (*corset*) корсе́т.

girl *n* (*little*) де́вочка; (*teens onwards*) де́вушка; **what a nice little ~!** кака́я сла́вная де́вочка!; **a lovely ~** хоро́шенькая де́вушка; **you nasty ~!** ты проти́вная девчо́нка!; **there are only ~s working at the factory** у нас на фа́брике рабо́тают одни́ де́вушки; *CQ*: **he's always chasing ~s** он всё бе́гает за де́вочками; **he has a new ~ every week** у него́ ка́ждую неде́лю но́вая симпа́тия/но́вое увлече́ние.

girth *n* 1 (*measure*) обхва́т; **a tree ten feet in ~** де́рево десяти́ фу́тов в обхва́те

2 (*for saddle*) подпру́га.

gist *n* суть; **tell me the ~ of what he said** изложи́те мне суть того́, что он сказа́л.

give *n*: **there's no ~ in a stone floor/this cloth** ка́менный пол не прогиба́ется, э́та ткань не растя́гивается.

give *vti vt* 1 да|ва́ть (-ть) *and compounds*; (*as gift*) дари́ть (по-); **he gave her a doll** он дал/подари́л ей ку́клу; **~ me your hand** дай мне ру́ку; **he was ~n a prize** ему́ вручи́ли приз; **he gave no answer** он не дал отве́та; **to ~ advice/evidence/one's word** дать сове́т/показа́ния (*pl*)/сло́во; **~ your name and address** напиши́те ва́шу фами́лию и а́дрес; **to ~ a lesson/a lecture** дать уро́к, прочита́ть ле́кцию; **to ~ a concert** дава́ть конце́рт, вы|ступа́ть с конце́ртом (-́ступить); **they gave him two years** ему́ да́ли два го́да тюрьмы́; **he was ~n command of the regiment** ему́ поручи́ли кома́ндовать полко́м; **they are giving a dinner/a flat-warming party** они́ даю́т обе́д, они́ устра́ивают новосе́лье; **I gave them dinner** я угости́л их обе́дом (*at hotel*), я накорми́л их у́жином (*at home*); **to ~ smb cause for alarm** дать кому́-л по́вод для беспоко́йства; **~ me something to drink/to do** дай мне попи́ть *or* (*alcoholic*) что́-нибудь вы́пить, дай мне како́е-нибудь де́ло; **I gave him the parcel to deliver** я дал ему́ отнести́ посы́лку; **he gave me to understand that...** он дал мне поня́ть, что...; **to ~ an order/a cry** отда|ва́ть прика́з (-́ть), кри́кнуть; **who'll ~ us a song?** кто нам споёт?; **he's 50, ~ or take a year or so** ему́ лет пятьдеся́т (*sense conveyed by inversion*); *CQ*: **I'll ~ it to him!** я ему́ задам́!; **I don't ~ a damn!** мне наплева́ть!

2 (*hand over*) переда|ва́ть (-́ть); **~ her this letter/my regards** переда́й(те) ей э́то письмо́/приве́т (*sing*) от меня́; **he gave me his cold/his flu** его́ просту́да передала́сь мне, он зарази́л меня́ гри́ппом; **she gave me her watch to look after** она́ дала́/отдала́ мне часы́ на хране́ние; **to ~ one's life to science/for one's country** посвяти́ть жизнь нау́ке, отда́ть жизнь за ро́дину

3 (*provide*) пода|ва́ть (-́ть), (*add*) прида|ва́ть (-́ть); **to ~ an example/a signal** подава́ть приме́р/сигна́л; **who gave you that idea?** кто вам по́дал э́ту иде́ю?; **he gave no sign of having heard** он не по́дал ви́да, что слы́шал; **to ~ smth flavour** придава́ть чему́-л вкус; **the experience gave him confidence** э́то прида́ло ему́ уве́ренности в себе́; **if it would ~ you pleasure** е́сли э́то доста́вит вам удово́льствие; **this lamp doesn't ~ much light** э́та ла́мпа даёт ма́ло све́та; **the apple trees gave a good crop** я́блони да́ли хоро́ший урожа́й

4 (*allow*) дать; **~ me time to think** дай мне поду́мать; **I'll ~ you a week to decide** я вам дам неде́лю на размышле́ние; **to ~ a lot of time/thought to smth** удел|я́ть мно́го вре́мени/внима́ния чему́-л (-и́ть); **the doctors gave him two years** (*to live*) врачи́ сказа́ли, что жить ему́ оста́лось два го́да; **I'll ~ you that (point)** я вам уступа́ю в э́том вопро́се; **you must ~ yourself an hour to get to the station** положи́ на доро́гу до ста́нции час

5 (*pay*): **how much did you ~ for this skirt?** ско́лько ты заплати́ла/отдала́ за э́ту ю́бку?; **I'd ~ a lot to know the answer** я бы мно́го дал, что́бы знать отве́т; *fig* **to ~ him his due, he's very kind** ну́жно отда́ть ему́ до́лжное, он о́чень добр

6 *Tel*: **~ me Paris/the director** соедини́те меня́ с Пари́жем/с дире́ктором, *CQ* да́йте мне Пари́ж/дире́ктора

7 *translated by verb formed from noun*: **to ~ birth** роди́ть (*usu pf*); **to ~ smb a fright/a push** испуга́ть кого́-л, толкну́ть кого́-л; **he gave her a smile/a glance** он ей улыбну́лся, он взгляну́л на неё; **to ~ oneself airs (about smth)** кичи́ться чем-л, ва́жничать (*impfs*); *etc.*

vi (*collapse*) прова́л|иваться (-и́ться); (*bend*) прог|иба́ться (-ну́ться); **the floor gave under the weight of the piano** пол провали́лся/прогну́лся под тя́жестью роя́ля; **the plank gave but did not break** доска́ прогну́лась, но не слома́лась; **the frost is beginning to ~** моро́з ослабева́ет

give away *vt* 1 (*to many people*) разда|ва́ть, (*to one person*) отда|ва́ть (*pfs* -́ть); **to ~ away free samples** раздава́ть образцы́; **I'm not selling it, I'm giving it away** я не продаю́, а про́сто отдаю́

2 (*betray*) вы|дава́ть (-́дать); **to ~ away smb/a secret** вы́дать кого́-л/секре́т; **his face gave nothing away** его́ лицо́ ничего́ не выдава́ло

give back *vt* отда́ть; возвраща́ть (верну́ть); **~ me back my records** отда́й/верни́ мне мои́ пласти́нки; **it gave him back his confidence** э́то верну́ло ему́ уве́ренность в себе́

give in *vti vt* пода|ва́ть (-́ть); **he gave in his resignation** он по́дал в отста́вку; **he gave in an application for leave** он по́дал заявле́ние об о́тпуске *vi* (*surrender*) сда|ва́ться (-́ться); подда́ться; **don't ~ in** не сдава́йся; **you ~ in to her too easily** ты сли́шком легко́ ей поддаёшься

give off *vt*: **to ~ off heat/a smell** выделя́ть тепло́, издава́ть за́пах (*usu impfs*)

give on to *vi*: **my window ~s on to the garden/the yard** моё окно́ выхо́дит в сад/во двор

give out *vti vt* **1** (*distribute*) раздава́ть

2 (*announce*) объяв|ля́ть (-и́ть)

vi истощ|а́ться (-и́ться), иссяк|а́ть (-́нуть); **the supplies had ~n out** запа́сы истощи́лись/иссякли; **my patience gave out** у меня́ исся́кло/ко́нчилось терпе́ние; **the engine gave out** мото́р сдал

give up *vti vt* **1** (*yield*): **to ~ up a town to the enemy** сдать го́род врагу́; **to ~ oneself up** сда́ться; **to ~ up one's seat** уступи́ть ме́сто; **to ~ up a fugitive** вы́дать беглеца́

2 (*abandon*) остав|ля́ть (-́ить), брос|а́ть (-́ить); **to ~ up hope/one's studies** оставля́ть наде́жду, броса́ть учёбу (*sing*); **to ~ up one's job/smoking** броса́ть рабо́ту/кури́ть; **he came so late we'd ~n him up** он пришёл так по́здно, что мы его́ уже́ не жда́ли

vi: **I ~ up!** сдаю́сь!

give way *vi* (*yield*) отступ|а́ть, уступ|а́ть (*pfs* -́ить); подда|ва́ться (-́ться); (*collapse*) не выде́рживать (вы́держать), прова́л|иваться (-и́ться); **to ~ way to force/to demands** отступа́ть пе́ред си́лой, уступа́ть тре́бованиям; **the battalion did not ~ way** батальо́н не отступи́л; **drivers must ~ way to traffic coming from the right** (*in UK*) води́тели обя́заны уступа́ть доро́гу тра́нспорту, иду́щему спра́ва; **the crowd gave way** толпа́ подала́сь наза́д; **to ~ way to despair** предава́ться отча́янию; **the door gave way** (*to pressure*) дверь поддала́сь; **the bench/the roof/the rope gave way** скаме́йка/кры́ша/верёвка не вы́держала; **the ice gave way beneath him/his weight** лёд не вы́держал его́ ве́са; **the bridge gave way** мост ру́хнул/провали́лся; **the clouds gave way to sunshine** ту́чи разошли́сь, и засия́ло со́лнце.

give-and-take *n*: **there must be ~ in a family** в семье́ на́до идти́ на взаи́мные усту́пки.

given *adj*: **under the ~ conditions** при да́нных усло́виях; **at a ~ time** в определённое вре́мя; **~ a fair wind, we'll reach harbour tonight** при попу́тном ве́тре мы дости́гнем га́вани к ве́черу; **~ that...** при том, что...; *Math* **~ the triangle ABC** дан треуго́льник ABC.

glad *adj* **1** *predic* рад + *D*, + *inf or* + что; **I'm very ~ to meet you** я о́чень рад познако́миться (с ва́ми); **I'm very ~ of it** я о́чень рад э́тому

2 *attr* ра́достный; **~ news** ра́достная весть.

gladden *vt* ра́довать (об-); **it ~s the heart to hear the birds singing** пе́ние птиц ра́дует се́рдце.

glade *n* поля́на.

gladly *adv* ра́достно, с ра́достью; (*readily*) охо́тно, с удово́льствием.

glamour *n* блеск, очарова́ние; **the moonlight lent ~ to the scene** лу́нный свет придава́л осо́бое очарова́ние э́той сце́не; **beneath the ~ there's a lot of hard work** за вне́шним бле́ском скрыва́ется тяжёлый повседне́вный труд; *attr CQ*: **a ~ girl** шика́рная деви́ца.

glance *n* взгляд; **at first ~** на пе́рвый взгляд, с пе́рвого взгля́да; **she cast a quick/stealthy ~ at him** она́ бро́сила на него́ взгляд укра́дкой (*adv*).

glance *vi* **1** (*look*): **to ~ at smth** взгляну́ть на что-л (*usu pf*); **he ~d back/over his shoulder** он огляну́лся; **I ~d through the newspaper** я просмотре́л газе́ту

2 (*slip*): **the bullet ~d off his arm** пу́ля то́лько слегка́ заде́ла его́ ру́ку

3 (*gleam*) блесте́ть (*impf*).

gland *n Anat* железа́.

glandular fever *n* воспале́ние желёз.

glare *n* **1** блеск; **the ~ of footlights**/*fig* **of publicity** блеск ра́мпы (*sing*)/сла́вы; **he is blinded by the ~ of the sun/the headlights** он ослеплён бле́ском со́лнца/све́том фар

2 (*look*): **an angry ~** серди́тый взгляд.

glare *vi*: **to ~ at smb/smth** свире́по (*ferociously*)/серди́то (*angrily*)/возмущённо (*indignantly*) смотре́ть на кого́-л/на что-л.

glass *n* **1** (*material*) стекло́; **a pane/splinter of ~** око́нное стекло́, оско́лок стекла́; **to paint on ~** рисова́ть по стеклу́; **to grow tomatoes under ~** выра́щивать помидо́ры в парнике́ (*greenhouse*); *attr*: **a ~ door** стекля́нная дверь; **~ works** стеко́льный заво́д

2 (*tumbler*) стака́н; (*for wine*) бока́л, (*for brandy, or vodka*) рю́мка

3 (*mirror*) зе́ркало; (*barometer*) баро́метр; (*telescope*) *Naut* подзо́рная труба́, *Astron* телеско́п; **to look at oneself in the ~** смотре́ться в зе́ркало; **what's the ~ doing?** что пока́зывает баро́метр?

4 *pl* (**~es**) (*spectacles*) очки́ (*pl*); (*binoculars*) бино́кль (*m, sing*); **to put on/wear ~es** наде́ть/носи́ть очки́; **opera ~es** театра́льный бино́кль.

glass case *n* витри́на.

glasscloth *n* ча́йное полоте́нце.

glasscutter *n* (*person*) стеко́льщик; (*tool*) стеклоре́з; (*diamond*) алма́з.

glasshouse *n* (*UK*) тепли́ца; (*US*) стеко́льный заво́д.

glassware *n* изде́лия (*pl*) из стекла́; (*in household*) стекля́нная посу́да (*collect*).

glassy *adj* (*of surfaces*) зерка́льный; *fig* **a ~ stare** ту́склый взгляд.

glaucoma *n Med* глауко́ма.

glaze *vt* **1**: **to ~ a window** встав|ля́ть стёкла (в окно́) (-́ить), застекл|я́ть окно́ (-и́ть)

2 (*pottery*) покры|ва́ть глазу́рью (-́ть).

glazed *adj* (*fitted with glass*) застеклённый; (*of pottery*) глазуро́ванный; (*of eyes*) ту́склый; **a ~ look** ту́склый взгляд.

gleam *n* луч, про́блеск, *both also fig*; **a ~ of light/hope/intelligence** луч све́та, про́блеск наде́жды/ра́зума; **there was a ~ of mischief**

in his eye у него́ в глаза́х блесну́л хи́трый огонёк.

gleam *vi* блесте́ть, (*fitfully*) мерца́ть (*impfs*).

glean *vti* под|бира́ть коло́сья по́сле жа́твы (-обра́ть); *fig*: **I ~ed some information** я собра́л ко́е-каки́е све́дения (*pl*); **did you ~ anything from him?** ты что́-нибудь у него́ узна́л?

gleeful *adj* весёлый.

glen *n* (го́рная) доли́на.

glib *adj* (*of person*) сладкоречи́вый; (*specious*) благови́дный; **he's got a ~ tongue** у него́ бо́йкий язы́к; **a ~ excuse** благови́дный предло́г.

glide *vi* скользи́ть (*impf*); *Aer* плани́ровать (с-); **to ~ over the ice** скользи́ть по льду; **to ~ into a room** проскользну́ть в ко́мнату.

glider *n Aer* планёр.

gliding *n* плани́рование.

glimmer *n* мерца́ние; *fig* про́блеск.

glimmer *vi* мерца́ть (*impf*).

glimpse *n*: **to catch a ~ of smb/smth** уви́деть кого́-л/что-л ме́льком.

glint *n*: **the ~ of steel** блеск ста́ли; **there was a hard/steely ~ in his eye** в его́ глаза́х сверкну́л недо́брый огонёк.

glisten *vi* блес|те́ть (*semel* -ну́ть); **to ~ with dew** блесте́ть от росы́; **her eyes ~ed with tears** у неё на глаза́х блесну́ли слёзы.

glitter *n* блеск, сверка́ние; **the ~ of gold** сверка́ние зо́лота.

glitter *vi* блесте́ть, сверка́ть (*only in impfs*).

gloat *vi*: **to ~ over the misfortunes of others** ра́доваться чужо́му несча́стью (*only in impf*), злора́дствовать (*impf*); **the miser ~ed over his gold** скря́га ра́довался, гля́дя на своё зо́лото.

global *adj* мирово́й, всеми́рный, глоба́льный.

globe *n* шар; (*the Earth*) земно́й шар; **from all parts of the ~** со всего́ земно́го ша́ра.

globular *adj* шарови́дный.

gloom *n* мрак, тьма; *fig* уны́ние; **his arrival cast a ~ over the company** его́ появле́ние привело́ всех в уны́ние.

gloomy *adj* мра́чный, *also fig*; *fig* угрю́мый, уны́лый.

glorify *vi* прослав|ля́ть (-ить); *iron* **his cottage is a sort of glorified barn** его́ да́ча — про́сто немно́го перестро́енный сара́й.

glorious *adj* сла́вный; (*splendid*) великоле́пный; **a ~ victory** сла́вная побе́да; *CQ iron* **a ~ muddle** жу́ткая неразбери́ха.

glory *n* (*fame*) сла́ва; (*splendour*) великоле́пие.

gloss[1] *n* (*of fur*) блеск; (*of metal, paint*) блеск, гля́нец; (*of hair*) блеск; *fig* лоск; **her presence lent a ~ of respectability to the occasion** её прису́тствие придава́ло всему́ ви́димость прили́чия; *attr*: **~ paint** гля́нцевая кра́ска; *Photo* **~ finish** гля́нец.

gloss[1] *vt fig*: **to ~ over smb's faults** зама́зывать/преуменьша́ть чьи-л недоста́тки (*usu impfs*).

gloss[2] *n* (*marginal note*) заме́тка на поля́х.

glossary *n* глосса́рий; спи́сок слов.

glossy *adj*: **~ hair** блестя́щие во́лосы; **a ~ surface** блестя́щая/глянцеви́тая пове́рхность; **~ paper** лощёная/гля́нцевая бума́га; **a ~ photograph** гля́нцевая фотогра́фия.

glove *n* перча́тка; **a pair of ~s** па́ра перча́ток; *fig* **your dress fits like a ~** э́то пла́тье сиди́т на тебе́ как влито́е; *attr Aut*: **~ compartment** я́щик для ме́лких веще́й.

glow *n* за́рево; (*light*) свет; **the ~ of a campfire/sunset** свет от костра́ *or* ого́нь костра́, за́рево зака́та; **the ~ of a lamp** свет ла́мпы; **the ~ of his cigarette** огонёк его́ сигаре́ты; **a ~ of health** здоро́вый румя́нец; *fig* **a ~ of warmth/satisfaction** тёплое чу́вство, чу́вство удовлетворе́ния.

glow *vi* горе́ть, пыла́ть (*impfs*); (*of hot metal*) раскал|я́ться (-и́ться); **the coal was ~ing brightly** у́гли (*pl*) я́рко пыла́ли/разгора́лись; **her cheeks were ~ing from the frost** её щёки пыла́ли/горе́ли от моро́за; **he ~s with health** он пы́шет здоро́вьем; **he ~ed with pleasure** он сия́л от удово́льствия.

glower *vi*: **to ~ at smb/smth** зло́бно смотре́ть на кого́-л/на что-л.

glowing *adj*: **~ embers/colours** пыла́ющие у́гли/кра́ски; **a ~ sky** пламене́ющее не́бо; *fig* **his book had ~ reviews** на его́ кни́гу бы́ли восто́рженные реце́нзии.

glow-worm *n* светлячо́к.

glucose *n* глюко́за.

glue *n* клей.

glue *vt* кле́ить (с-) *and compounds*; **to ~ together/up** скле́|ивать (-ить); **to ~ a leg on to a chair** прикле́ивать но́жку к сту́лу; *fig*: **he was ~d to the TV all evening** он торча́л у телеви́зора весь ве́чер; **he stood ~d to the spot** он как в зе́млю врос; **he kept his eyes ~d to the door** он не своди́л глаз с две́ри.

glum *adj* мра́чный, хму́рый.

glut *n* изоби́лие; **there's a ~ of tomatoes on the market** на ры́нке полно́ помидо́ров; **we've a ~ of plums this year** в э́том году́ у нас большо́й урожа́й слив — дева́ть не́куда.

glut *vt*: **the market was ~ted with apples** ры́нок был зава́лен я́блоками; **to ~ oneself with strawberries** объе́сться клубни́кой (*collect*).

glutton *n* обжо́ра; *fig* **he's a ~ for work** он жа́ден до рабо́ты.

gluttony *n* обжо́рство.

glycerine *n* глицери́н.

gnat *n* (*mosquito*) кома́р; (*midge*) мо́шка.

gnaw *vt* грызть, глода́ть (*impfs*), *also fig*; **to ~ a bone** грызть/глода́ть кость; *fig* **I am filled with ~ing doubts/anxiety** меня́ грызёт сомне́ние (*sing*), меня́ терза́ет трево́га.

go *n CQ*: **he's full of ~** он по́лон эне́ргии; **I've been on the ~ all day** у меня́ сего́дня бы́ло дел по го́рло; **I had a ~ at steering the boat** я попыта́лся управля́ть ло́дкой; **let me have another ~** да́йте мне ещё раз попыта́ться; **it's your ~ now** тепе́рь о́чередь за тобо́й/твоя́ о́чередь; **he knocked over all the ninepins at one ~** он сбил все ке́гли одни́м уда́ром; **I think we can make**

a ~ of it я ду́маю, что де́ло у нас пойдёт; **it's no ~!** так не пойдёт!; **long skirts are all the ~ now** дли́нные ю́бки сейча́с в мо́де.

go *vti vt*: **to ~ it alone** де́йствовать в одино́чку; *Cards* (*bridge*) **I ~ six clubs** я объявля́ю шестёрку треф; *CQ* **she's five months gone** (*pregnant*) она́ на шесто́м ме́сяце

vi **1** (*of person on foot or of vehicle moving*) ходи́ть (*indet impf, pf* по-), идти́ (*det impf, pf* пойти́) *and compounds* [**NB** походи́ть *is not a true pf, but* = "*to go around for a while*"; пойти́ = "*to begin to/set off to go*"]; **I often ~ to the theatre** я ча́сто хожу́ в теа́тр; **the bus ~es to Zagorsk twice a day** авто́бус в Заго́рск хо́дит два ра́за в день; **we went round the shops for a while till it was time for the train** мы походи́ли по магази́нам до отхо́да по́езда; **where are you ~ing?** куда́ вы идёте?; **this train ~es to Oxford** э́тот по́езд идёт в О́ксфорд; **the car was ~ing very fast** маши́на шла о́чень бы́стро; **he has just gone to buy cigarettes** он пошёл купи́ть сигаре́ты; **are you ~ing to the concert tomorrow?** вы идёте/пойдёте за́втра на конце́рт?; **let's ~!** пойдём!, пошли́!; **we can talk as we ~** мо́жно поговори́ть на ходу́; **the road ~es South** э́та доро́га идёт/ведёт на юг

2 (*of person in car, etc.*) е́здить (*indet impf, pf* по- = "*to go around for a while*"), е́хать (*det impf, pf* по- = "*to begin to go*"); **we usually ~ to the country on Sundays** по воскресе́ньям мы обы́чно е́здим за́ город; **last year we went around in France quite a lot** в про́шлом году́ мы мно́го пое́здили по Фра́нции; **he was ~ing at 60 m.p.h.** он е́хал со ско́ростью шестьдеся́т миль в час; **they've just gone five minutes ago** они́ уе́хали пять мину́т наза́д; **let's ~!** (*in car*) пое́хали!; **he went to Leningrad by sea/by ship** он пое́хал в Ленингра́д на парохо́де/парохо́дом; **to ~ by plane** лете́ть самолётом

3 (*depart*): (*on foot*) уходи́ть (уйти́), (*by car*) уезжа́ть (уе́хать); (*of planes*) улет|а́ть (-е́ть), (*take off*) вы|лета́ть (-́лететь); (*of trains*) от|ходи́ть (-ойти́); (*pass*) про|ходи́ть (-йти́); **it's time for us to ~** нам пора́ идти́/уходи́ть/е́хать; **they've gone South for their holiday** они́ уе́хали в о́тпуск на юг; **don't ~ yet** не уходи́, подожди́ ещё немно́го; **the train ~es from platform three** по́езд отхо́дит от тре́тьей платфо́рмы; **the train has just gone/had gone** по́езд то́лько что отошёл/ушёл; **the plane has/had already gone** самолёт уже́ вы́летел/улете́л

4 (*of purpose*) пойти́, пое́хать + *inf, or* на + *A* (*usu pfs in this sense*); **let's ~ for a walk** пойдём погуля́ем; **to ~ for a trip/a drive** пое́хать на экску́рсию; **she's gone to visit her aunt** она́ пошла́/пое́хала к тётке *or* навести́ть тётку; **to ~ to bed** ложи́ться спать (лечь); **to ~ and do/fetch smth** (*implying return*) сходи́ть (за + *I*) [**NB** *pf*]; **I'll ~ to/and see** (я) пойду́/схожу́ посмотрю́; **he went for/and fetched the doctor** он сходи́л за врачо́м; **to be ~ing to** (*do smth*) собира́ться + *inf* (*usu impf*); **I'm ~ing to change my job** я собира́юсь смени́ть рабо́ту; **it's ~ing to rain** собира́ется дождь; **we're just ~ing to walk in the park** мы собира́емся (*intending to*)/мы идём (*said as one sets out*) в парк погуля́ть

5 (*with gerund*) пойти́, пое́хать (*usu pfs; for impf in this sense use* собира́ться); **they've gone swimming** они́ пошли́/пое́хали купа́ться; **we were ~ing to ~ swimming** мы собира́лись пойти́ купа́ться; **she's gone shopping** она́ пошла́/пое́хала в магази́н за поку́пками

6 (*progress*) идти́, проходи́ть; **we'll see how things ~** посмо́трим, как пойду́т дела́; **how ~es it?** как (иду́т) дела́?; **how did the exam ~?** как прошёл экза́мен?; **I hope all's ~ing well with you** наде́юсь, что у вас всё идёт хорошо́/всё в поря́дке; **if all ~es well** е́сли всё пройдёт благополу́чно; **how did the holiday ~?** как прошёл о́тпуск?; **if I'm not there, everything ~es wrong** без меня́ там всё идёт не так; **things haven't gone well for him** ему́ не повезло́ (*impers*); **it will ~ hard with him** ему́ ту́го придётся

7 (*pass*) идти́, проходи́ть; **summer has already gone** ле́то уже́ прошло́; **it's gone 5** (*o'clock*) уже́ шесто́й час; **he's gone 40** ему́ уже́ за со́рок; **the estate went to his brother** име́ние перешло́ к его́ бра́ту; **the house went for £ 40,000** дом про́дали за со́рок ты́сяч фу́нтов; (*disappear*): **the rash/pain has gone** сыпь/боль прошла́; **when I turned round, he was gone** когда́ я оберну́лся, его́ и след просты́л; **all hope is gone** никако́й наде́жды бо́льше нет; **the money is all gone** де́ньги ко́нчились; **the car will have to ~** маши́ну придётся прода́ть

8 (*function*) ходи́ть, рабо́тать (*impf*); **is your watch ~ing?** ва́ши часы́ иду́т?; **my watch ~es fast/slow** мои́ часы́ спеша́т/отстаю́т; **the engine is ~ing well** мото́р хорошо́ рабо́тает; **the car wouldn't ~** маши́на не шла/(*wouldn't start*) не заводи́лась

9 (*give way*): **his sight/mind is ~ing** он теря́ет зре́ние/рассу́док; (*of invalid*) **he's far gone** он о́чень плох; **the bulb/battery has gone** ла́мпочка перегоре́ла, аккумуля́тор (*of car*) сел, батаре́йка (*of torch*) ко́нчилась

10 (*exist, be available*): **are there any tickets ~ing for tonight's concert?** есть (ли) биле́ты на сего́дняшний конце́рт?; **it's not dear as prices ~ now** при ны́нешних це́нах э́то не так до́рого; **he's not bad as carpenters ~** он не тако́й уж плохо́й пло́тник

11 (*with adjs, etc.*): **to ~ bad/blind/pale/sour** по́ртиться (ис-), сле́пнуть (о-), бледне́ть (по-), прокис|а́ть (-́нуть); **to ~ halves/shares** дели́ть попола́м/по́ровну (*advs*); **it went cheap** э́то бы́ло про́дано дёшево; **to ~ sick** заболе|ва́ть (-́ть); **we missed supper so had to ~ hungry** мы не успе́ли поу́жинать и оста́лись голо́дными; **to ~ slow** (*in factories, etc.*) снижа́ть темп рабо́ты; **~ easy!** (по)ле́гче!, поти́ше!

12 *various*: **as the saying ~es** как говори́тся; **it ~es without saying** само́ собо́й разуме́ется; **it all ~es to show that...** всё э́то говори́т о том, что...; **what he says ~es** как он ска́жет, так и де́лается; **the song ~es like this** вот как э́то поётся; **I can't remember how his argument went** я не по́мню его́ до́водов; **where do you want the piano to ~?** где поста́вить роя́ль?; **to ~ one's own way** идти́ свои́м путём; **here ~es!** ну дава́й!, дава́й начнём!

go about *vi* **1**: **they usually ~ about together** они́ обы́чно хо́дят вме́сте; **the rumour is ~ing about that...** хо́дит слух, что...; **to ~ about one's business** занима́ться свои́ми дела́ми; **how does one ~ about it?** как э́то де́лается?

2 *Naut* по|вора́чивать (-верну́ть)

go across *vt*: **he went across the street** он перешёл у́лицу; **the railway ~es across Siberia** желе́зная доро́га пересека́ет Сиби́рь

go after *vi*: **~ after your father and give him his gloves** догони́ отца́ и дай ему́ перча́тки

go against *vi*: **it ~es against my principles** э́то про́тив мои́х при́нципов; **it ~es against our policy** э́то идёт вразре́з с на́шей поли́тикой; **his looks ~ against him** его́ вне́шность говори́т не в его́ по́льзу; *Law* **the case went against him** де́ло оберну́лось про́тив него́

go ahead *vi*: **you ~ ahead, I'll follow** вы иди́те вперёд, я догоню́; **the work on the new bridge is ~ing ahead** строи́тельство но́вого моста́ продвига́ется (*is getting on*)/продолжа́ется (*is continuing*); **I'll be late for supper, so just ~ ahead (without me)** я опозда́ю к у́жину—не жди́те меня́; **can I use the phone?—Go ahead** я могу́ позвони́ть по ва́шему телефо́ну?—Пожа́луйста

go along *vi*: **to ~ along the street** идти́ по у́лице; **the road ~es along the river** доро́га идёт вдоль реки́; **the work will become easier as you ~ along** чем да́льше, тем ле́гче бу́дет рабо́тать; **I'll ~ along with you as far as the post office** я провожу́ вас до по́чты; *fig* **I don't ~ along with you there** тут я с ва́ми не согла́сен

go as far as *vi* доходи́ть, доезжа́ть до + *G*; **we went as far as the church then turned back** мы дошли́ до це́ркви и поверну́ли обра́тно; **the park ~es as far as the river** парк тя́нется до са́мой реки́; **I wouldn't ~ as far as to say that** я бы всё-таки э́того не сказа́л

go at *vi* (*attack a person*) на|бра́сываться на + *A* (-бро́ситься), *also fig*; **he went at it with a will** он с охо́той/охо́тно взя́лся за де́ло; **he was still ~ing at it three hours later** прошло́ три часа́, а он всё ещё рабо́тал

go away *vi* уходи́ть, уезжа́ть

go back *vi* (*return*) возвра|ща́ться (-ти́ться *and* верну́ться), идти́ обра́тно; *fig*: **these buildings ~ back to the time of Peter the Great** э́ти постро́йки отно́сятся ко вре́мени Петра́ Пе́рвого (*only in impf*); **to ~ back on one's word** отступ|а́ться от свои́х слов (*pl*)/от своего́ обеща́ния (-и́ться)

go behind *vi* заходи́ть; **the sun went behind some clouds** со́лнце зашло́ за ту́чи

go beyond *vi*: **it ~es beyond the bounds of common politeness/of all reason** э́то выхо́дит за ра́мки прили́чий (*pl*), э́то перехо́дит грани́цы разу́много; **he went beyond his brief/authority** он превы́сил свои́ полномо́чия (*pl*); **this ~es beyond a joke** э́то захо́дит сли́шком далеко́

go by *vi* **1** (*on foot, of time*) проходи́ть (*of place* + ми́мо (*adv or prep* + *G*)), (*in car*) проезжа́ть ми́мо; **they went by (our house)** они́ прошли́/прое́хали ми́мо (на́шего до́ма); **the summer went by** ле́то прошло́; **in days gone by** в бы́лые времена́

2 (*use as guide*): **to ~ by appearances** суди́ть по вне́шности (*impf*); **you can't ~ by what he says** нельзя́ полага́ться на его́ слова́; **it's a good rule to ~ by** э́тому пра́вилу поле́зно сле́довать; **to ~ by the rules** подчиня́ться пра́вилам (*usu impf*)

go down *vi* **1** спус|ка́ться с + *G or* по + *D* (-ти́ться); **the canoe was ~ing down stream** челно́к спуска́лся вниз по тече́нию; **the sun went down** со́лнце зашло́; **the ship went down** су́дно тону́ло/шло ко дну́; **the temperature/the swelling/wind has gone down** температу́ра пони́зилась, о́пухоль спа́ла, ве́тер стих

2 *fig uses*: **he has gone down with flu** он заболе́л гри́ппом; **he'll ~ down in history** он войдёт в исто́рию; **prices have gone down** це́ны сни́зились; **his remark didn't ~ down well with my father** его́ замеча́ние бы́ло пло́хо воспри́нято мои́м отцо́м; **he went down from Oxford in June** он око́нчил О́ксфордский университе́т в ию́не э́того го́да; **he's gone down in the world** он потеря́л бы́лое положе́ние

go downhill *vi* идти́ по́д гору; *fig* (*of health*) ухудш|а́ться (-́иться), (*morally*) опус|ка́ться (-ти́ться)

go far *vi* идти́ далеко́, *also fig*; **to ~ too far** заходи́ть сли́шком далеко́; **money doesn't ~ far these days** в на́ше вре́мя де́ньги обесце́нились; **£10 won't ~ far** на де́сять фу́нтов ма́ло что ку́пишь; **that won't ~ far towards buying a car** э́то не намно́го прибли́зит поку́пку маши́ны; **I won't ~ so far as to say that...** я не беру́сь утвержда́ть, что...

go for *vi*: **to ~ for a walk/drive/doctor** пойти́ погуля́ть, пое́хать на прогу́лку, сходи́ть за врачо́м; **to ~ for smb** (*physically or verbally*) на|бра́сываться на кого́-л (-бро́ситься); **the vase went for 5 roubles** ва́за была́ про́дана за пять рубле́й; *CQ* **this ~es for me too** я то́же с э́тим согла́сен

go forward *vi* продви|га́ться (-́нуться), *also fig*; **the prizewinners went forward to receive their awards** призёры вы́шли вперёд для получе́ния награ́д; *fig* **the work is ~ing forward well** рабо́та продвига́ется хорошо́

go from *vi*: **things are ~ing from bad to worse** час о́т часу не ле́гче

go in *vi* входи́ть; **I went in by the back door** я вошёл че́рез чёрный ход; **the piano's too big—it won't ~ in** роя́ль сли́шком вели́к—он сюда́ не войдёт

go in for *vi* (*enter race, etc.*) уча́ствовать в + *P* (*impf*); (*engage in*) занима́ться + *I* (*usu impf*); **are you ~ing in for the 100 metres?** вы уча́ствуете в забе́ге (*running*)/в заплы́ве (*swimming*) на сто ме́тров?; **he ~es in for boxing** он занима́ется бо́ксом; **he's ~ing in for medicine/law** он у́чится на врача́/на юри́ста; **to ~ in for an examination** держа́ть (*impf*)/сдава́ть (*only in impf*) экза́мен; **we don't ~ in for sports clothing** мы не торгу́ем спорти́вной оде́ждой; **I don't ~ in for earrings** я не люблю́/я не ношу́ серёг

go into *vi* входи́ть, *also fig*; **to ~ into the kitchen** входи́ть в ку́хню; **he has gone into hospital/into digs/into the Navy** он лёг в больни́цу [**NB** *accusative*], он снял ко́мнату, он пошёл во флот; **will everything ~ into the boot?** все ве́щи войду́т/*CQ* влезу́т в бага́жник?; *fig*: **to ~ into hysterics/into detail** впа|да́ть в исте́рику (*sing*) (-сть), вдава́ться в подро́бности (*usu impf*); **let's not ~ into that now** не бу́дем пока́ каса́ться э́того

go in with *vi CQ*: **he's gone in with Tom** (*shares flat*) он пересели́лся к То́му, (*into business with*) он стал рабо́тать с То́мом

go near *vi*: **don't ~ near that dog/the fire** не подходи́ к э́той соба́ке/кками́ну

go off *vi* (*depart*) уходи́ть, уезжа́ть, отправ|ля́ться (-́иться); **her husband has gone off with another woman** её муж у́шёл к друго́й же́нщине [**NB** *prep*]; **he went off with the cash** он скры́лся, прихвати́в с собо́й де́ньги; **the train went off the rails** по́езд сошёл с ре́льсов; **the grenade went off by mistake** грана́та случа́йно взорвала́сь; **my alarm went off at 5 a.m.** мой буди́льник зазвони́л в пять часо́в утра́; **the milk has gone off** молоко́ ски́сло; *fig*: **everything went off well** всё обошло́сь/ ко́нчилось благополу́чно; **how did the concert ~ off?** как прошёл конце́рт?; *CQ*: **I've gone off coffee** я тепе́рь стал равноду́шен к ко́фе; **to ~ off one's head** сойти́ с ума́ (*usu pf*), спя́тить (*pf*), свихну́ться (*pf*); *Sport* **he's gone off lately** он в после́днее вре́мя сдал

go on *vi* **1** (*continue*) продолжа́ть (*usu impf*); **afterwards I went on working** пото́м я сно́ва сел за рабо́ту; **I'm ready to ~ on trying** я гото́в продолжа́ть попы́тки; **"Yes", she went on, "I'll come"** «Да,—продолжа́ла она́,—я приду́»; **he went on to say that...** зате́м/пото́м он сказа́л, что...; **how long can this ~ on?** и ско́лько мо́жет э́то продолжа́ться/дли́ться?; **she got stouter as the years went on** она́ пополне́ла с года́ми; **I've enough work to be ~ing on with** пока́ у меня́ доста́точно рабо́ты; **I'd better ~ on, you can come later** я лу́чше пойду́, а ты приходи́ по́зже

2 *various*: **it's ~ing on for 6 o'clock** ско́ро шесть часо́в; **he's ~ing on for 40** ему́ под со́рок; **what's ~ing on here?** что здесь происхо́дит?; **to ~ on stage** выходи́ть на сце́ну; **the teapot ~es on the top shelf** ча́йник стои́т на ве́рхней по́лке; **I'm ~ing on holiday next week** я иду́ в о́тпуск на сле́дующей неде́ле; **the lights went on again** свет опя́ть зажёгся; **there's no real evidence to ~ on** нет доста́точных основа́ний (*pl*); **most of her money ~es on clothes** она́ тра́тит почти́ все де́ньги на оде́жду; **she will ~ on about money** у неё то́лько и разгово́ру что о деньга́х

go out *vi* **1** выходи́ть, *etc.*; **he went out of the room/for a walk** он вы́шел из ко́мнаты/на прогу́лку *or* прогуля́ться; **I'm ~ing out riding/to Australia** я иду́ ката́ться на ло́шади, я е́ду в Австра́лию; **he doesn't ~ out much these days** тепе́рь он ма́ло где быва́ет; **he's ~ing out a lot with Nina** он везде́ появля́ется с Ни́ной; **they've gone out of business** они́ бо́льше не занима́ются торго́влей, (*if because bankrupt*) они́ разори́лись; **the tide is ~ing out** начался́ отли́в; **the tide has gone out** отли́в ко́нчился

2 (*be extinguished*): **the fire's gone out** ого́нь поту́х

3 *fig uses*: **to ~ out of fashion** выходи́ть из мо́ды; **the name has gone out of my head** и́мя вы́летело у меня́ из головы́; **to ~ out of one's mind** сойти́ с ума́; **he's ~ing all out for that job** он всей душо́й стреми́тся к э́той рабо́те

go over *vi* **1** переходи́ть, переезжа́ть; минова́ть (*pf*); **we went over a high pass/the bridge** мы минова́ли высо́кий перева́л, мы перешли́ *or* перее́хали че́рез мост; **they went over to the enemy** они́ перешли́ на сто́рону врага́; **a ferry ~es over to the island once a day** паро́м хо́дит к о́строву/на о́стров раз в день; **we've sold the car and gone over to cycling** мы про́дали маши́ну и ста́ли е́здить на велосипе́де

2 (*check*) просм|а́тривать (-отре́ть), (*work over*) прораб|а́тывать (-о́тать); **we must ~ over the text carefully** мы должны́ тща́тельно просмотре́ть/прорабо́тать весь текст; **I must ~ over my part** (*in play*) я до́лжен пробежа́ть/повтори́ть свою́ роль; **the police went over him thoroughly but found nothing** поли́ция тща́тельно обыска́ла его́, но ничего́ не нашла́

3 (*fare, succeed*): **how did his speech ~ over?** как прошло́ его́ выступле́ние?; **the play went over very well** пье́су при́няли о́чень хорошо́

go past *vi* проходи́ть/проезжа́ть ми́мо + *G* (*on one's way*)/+ *A* (*overshoot*); **we went past the theatre** мы прое́хали ми́мо теа́тра; **the bus went past the stop** авто́бус не останови́лся на остано́вке

go round *vi* (*skirt*) об|ходи́ть (-ойти́), объ|езжа́ть (-е́хать), огиба́ть (обогну́ть); **you must ~ round the lake to reach our house** что́бы дойти́/дое́хать до на́шего до́ма, на́до обогну́ть о́зеро; (*make a detour*) **because of the floods we had to ~ round by Cambridge** из-за наводне́ния (*sing*) нам пришло́сь сде́лать крюк и е́хать че́рез Ке́мбридж; **the Earth ~es round the Sun** Земля́ враща́ется вокру́г Со́лнца; **the visitors are just ~ing round the college** го́сти пошли́ посмотре́ть колле́дж; **she ~es round a lot with my son** она́ повсю́ду появля́ется с мои́м сы́ном; **my head is ~ing round** у меня́ кру́жится голова́; **is there enough to ~ round?** э́того хва́тит (*impers*) на всех?; **the belt won't ~ round my waist** э́тот по́яс на мне не сойдётся; **I'm just ~ing round to my daughter's for half an hour** я собира́юсь загляну́ть к до́чери на полчаса́; **the story went round that...** прошёл слух, что...

go through *vi* проходи́ть, проезжа́ть; **we went through Paris** мы прое́хали Пари́ж; **he went through the crowd** он проби́лся сквозь толпу́; **the bus went through the shop window** авто́бус вре́зался/въе́хал в витри́ну; **the thread won't ~ through the needle** ни́тка не вхо́дит в иго́лку; **the proposal went through** предложе́ние прошло́/бы́ло при́нято; **the novel went through four editions** рома́н вы́держал четы́ре изда́ния; **his appointment has gone through** его́ назначе́ние одо́брено; **the deal did not ~ through** сде́лку не заключи́ли; **he's gone through all his money** он истра́тил все свои́ де́ньги; **she has gone through much** (*suffering*) она́ мно́го пережила́/перенесла́

go to *vi*: **to ~ to sea** (*become a sailor*) стать моряко́м; **he's gone to the front** он пошёл на фронт; **England went to war with Germany** А́нглия вступи́ла в войну́ с Герма́нией; **to ~ to law** обра|ща́ться к зако́ну (-ти́ться); **to ~ to great expense** пойти́ на больши́е затра́ты/расхо́ды; **please don't ~ to any trouble** не беспоко́йтесь,/не затрудня́йтесь,/никаки́х хлопо́т, пожа́луйста; **he went to great lengths to please her** он шёл на всё, что́бы угоди́ть ей; **the brandy/success went to his head** конья́к/успе́х уда́рил ему́ в го́лову; **the dictionary has gone to press** слова́рь печа́тается; **the first prize went to my brother** пе́рвый приз доста́лся моему́ бра́ту; **the lettuce has gone to seed** сала́т зацвёл/пошёл в ду́дку; **12 inches ~ to the foot** оди́н фут равня́ется двена́дцати дю́ймам; **100 kopeks ~ to the rouble** в рубле́ сто копе́ек

go together *vi*: **these colours don't ~ well together** э́ти цвета́ не сочета́ются (*impf and pf*)

go towards *vi*: **the money will ~ towards buying books for the library** э́ти де́ньги пойду́т на поку́пку книг для библиоте́ки

go under *vi* (*sink*) тону́ть (по-), идти́ ко дну́; **the tunnel ~es under the river** тунне́ль прохо́дит под реко́й

go up *vi*: **to ~ up a mountain** под|нима́ться/взбира́ться на́ гору (-ня́ться/взобра́ться); **he went up to London/to Scotland** он пое́хал в Ло́ндон/в Шотла́ндию; **she went up to the professor/the window** она́ подошла́ к профе́ссору/к окну́; **the lift has gone up** лифт пошёл наве́рх; **the glass/the curtain is ~ing up** баро́метр/за́навес поднима́ется; **he's gone up to university** он поступи́л в университе́т; **a new house is ~ing up next door** но́вый дом стро́ится ря́дом с на́шим (до́мом); **to ~ up in flames** сгор|а́ть (-е́ть); **prices are ~ing up** це́ны повыша́ются/расту́т; **the ammunition dump received a direct hit and went up in a huge explosion** бо́мба попа́ла пря́мо в склад боеприпа́сов и вы́звала взрыв огро́мной си́лы; **he's gone up in the world** он пошёл в го́ру

go with *vi*: **he went with her to the station** он проводи́л её до вокза́ла; **the children have gone with their aunt to Novgorod** де́ти пое́хали с тётей в Но́вгород; **the hat ~es well with your dress** э́та шля́пка о́чень идёт к твоему́ пла́тью; **the garden ~es with the house** (*is included for sale*) сад продаётся вме́сте с до́мом; **the party went with a swing** ве́чер прошёл с больши́м успе́хом

go without *vi*: **if we can't get supper here, we'll have to ~ without** е́сли мы здесь не поу́жинаем, то оста́немся вообще́ без у́жина.

goad *vt*: **to ~ smb into action/into doing smth** подби|ва́ть кого́-л сде́лать что-л (-ть); **to ~ smb to fury** при|води́ть кого́-л в бе́шенство/в я́рость (-вести́); **the other boys stood by and ~ed on the hooligans** други́е мальчи́шки стоя́ли вокру́г и подна́чивали хулига́нов.

go-ahead *n CQ*: **we've got the ~ at last** наконе́ц нам да́ли «зелёную у́лицу».

go-ahead *adj CQ*: **he's a very ~ sort of chap** он инициати́вный/предприи́мчивый па́рень.

goal *n* **1** (*purpose*) цель; **to achieve one's ~** дости́чь свое́й це́ли

2 *Sport* (*goal-posts*) воро́та (*no sing*); (*score*) гол; **to score a ~** заби́ть гол; **to win/lose by three ~s** победи́ть, заби́в на три го́ла бо́льше, проигра́ть с ра́зницей в три го́ла.

goalkeeper *n* врата́рь (*m*), голки́пер.

goal-kick *n* (*in soccer*) уда́р от воро́т.

goal-post *n* (*uprights*) бокова́я шта́нга/сто́йка воро́т, (*crossbar*) ве́рхняя шта́нга.

goat *n* коз|ёл, *f* -а́; *fig CQ* **it/he gets my ~** э́то/он мне де́йствует на не́рвы.

gobble *vt CQ* (*eat greedily*) жрать (со-).

go-between *n* посре́дник.

go-by *n CQ*: **to give smth/smb the ~** игнори́ровать что-л/кого́-л; (*break with smb*) порва́ть с кем-л.

god *n* **1 G.** бог; (*in interjections*): **by G.!** ей-бо́гу!; **oh G.!** го́споди!, о бо́же!; **for G.'s sake!** ра́ди бо́га!; **thank G.!** сла́ва бо́гу!; **I hope to G. that's over** дай бог, что́бы э́тим всё ко́нчилось; **G. forbid!** не да́й бог!; **G. willing we'll meet again** даст бог, мы опя́ть встре́тимся; (*after sneeze*) **G. bless you!** бу́дьте здоро́вы!

2: the Greek ~s древнегре́ческие бо́ги; **to make a ~ of smb** боготвори́ть кого́-л

3 *Theat* (**the ~s**) галёрка.

godchild *n* крёстни|к, *f* -ца.

goddess *n* богиня.

godfather *n* крёстный отéц.

godforsaken *adj CQ*: **what a ~ hole!** какáя бóгом забы́тая дырá!

godmother *n* крёстная мать.

go-getter *n CQ approx* делéц, проны́ра (*m and f*).

goggle-eyed *adj* пучеглáзый; *as adv*: **to stare at smth ~** тарáщить глазá на что-л.

going *n*: **it's 20 minutes ~ from here to the school** отсю́да до шкóлы двáдцать минýт ходьбы́ (*on foot*)/ езды́ (*by car*); **it was hard ~ through the bog** бы́ло трýдно идти́ по болóту; **50 m.p.h. is pretty good ~ for my old car** пятьдеся́т миль в час—неплохáя скóрость для моéй стáрой маши́ны; *fig*: **this book is hard ~** э́та кни́га трýдно читáется; **let's cross while the ~ is good** перейдём дорóгу, покá маши́н нет.

going *adj*: **it's a ~ concern** э́то хорошó налáженное предприя́тие; **it's the best car ~** э́то лýчшая из существýющих маши́н.

goings-on *npl*: **what ~!** хорóшенькие делá!

goitre *n* зоб.

gold *n* зóлото; *fig* **she has a heart of ~** у неё золотóе сéрдце; *attr* золотóй; **the ~ standard** золотóй стандáрт; **~ mine** золотóй при́иск/ рудни́к; *fig* **it's a ~ mine** э́то прóсто золотóе дно.

golden *adj* золотóй; (*of colour*) золоти́стый; *fig* **it's a ~ rule/ opportunity** э́то золотóе прáвило, э́то прекрáсная возмóжность.

goldfish *n* золотáя ры́бка.

goldsmith *n* золоты́х дел мáстер.

golf *n* гольф; **to play ~** игрáть в гольф.

gong *n* гонг; *fig sl* медáль; **the ~ has gone/ sounded** прозвучáл гонг.

good *n* **1** добрó; **the ~** блáго, (*collect* = *people*) дóбрые лю́ди; **to do ~** дéлать/ твори́ть добрó; *CQ* **he's up to no ~** он задýмал [**NB** *tense*] чтó-то недóброе

2 (*benefit*) пóльза; **for the ~ of the state** на блáго/ на пóльзу госудáрства; **what ~ will that be?** какáя от э́того пóльза?, какóй от э́того толк?; **what ~ will that do you?** какáя тебé от э́того пóльза?; **it's no ~ talking to him** бесполéзно с ним говори́ть; **has the medicine done you any ~?** э́то лекáрство вам помоглó?; **I'm saying this for your ~** я говорю́ э́то для твоéй же пóльзы; **this box is no ~ for anything now** э́та корóбка ни на что ужé не годи́тся; **it's all to the ~** всё э́то к лýчшему; **we're £100 to the ~** у нас сто фýнтов при́были

3 *adv phrases*: **he's gone for ~ and all** он ушёл навсегдá; **we're settling here for ~** мы посели́лись [**NB** *tense*] здесь навсегдá.

good *adj* **1** (*excellent*, *satisfactory*) хорóший; **~ advice/ sense** хорóший совéт, здрáвый смысл; **a ~ boy** хорóший мáльчик; **be a ~ girl!** будь ýмницей!; **a ~ idea/ job/ memory** хорóшая мысль/ рабóта/ пáмять; **a ~ beginning/ mood, ~ eyesight** хорóшее начáло/ настроéние/ зрéние; **~ manners/ news** хорóшие манéры/ нóвости (*pl*); **did you have a ~ night?** ты хорошó спал?/ вы́спался?; **I had a ~ meal/ breakfast** я плóтно *or* хорошó поéл/ позáвтракал; **is it a ~ thing to be so outspoken?** хорошó ли быть таки́м откровéнным?; **he earns ~ money** он хорошó/ прили́чно зарабáтывает; **I had ~ reason for refusing** у меня́ былá причи́на отказáться; **you're late every day—it's not ~ enough** ты опáздываешь кáждый день—э́то никудá не годи́тся; **it's too ~ to be true!** так хорошó, что и не вéрится!, э́то прóсто невероя́тно!; **~ heavens/ gracious!** бóже мой!

2 (*nice*, *kind*) дóбрый, хорóший; **he's a ~ man/ chap** он дóбрый/ хорóший человéк, он слáвный мáлый; **~ works** дóбрые делá; **he has a ~ name here** о нём здесь дóбрая слáва; **it's very ~ of you** вы óчень любéзны/ добры́; **would you be so ~ as to pass the butter?** бýдьте добры́, передáйте мне мáсло; **he's my ~ friend** он мой большóй друг

3 (*pleasant*) прия́тный; **it's ~ to see you** óчень прия́тно вас ви́деть; (*in greetings*) **~ morning!** дóброе ýтро!; **have a ~ journey!** в дóбрый путь!, счастли́вого пути́!; **~ luck!** счастли́во!, желáю вам удáчи!

4 (*beneficial*) полéзный; **doing exercises is ~ for your health** гимнáстика (*sing*) полéзна для здорóвья; **it's not ~ to swim immediately after a meal** плáвать срáзу пóсле еды врéдно; **this medicine is ~ for coughs** э́то лекáрство помогáет от кáшля

5 (*skilled*, *competent*): **a ~ doctor/ lawyer/ pupil** хорóший врач/ юри́ст/ учени́к; **I'm no ~ at maths/ sewing** я слаб в математи́ке (*sing*) *or* матемáтика мне не даётся, я плóхо шью

6 (*fit*) пригóдный; **is this water ~ for drinking?** э́та водá пригóдна для питья́?; **he's not a ~ man for this post** он не годи́тся на э́ту дóлжность; **throw it away—it's ~ for nothing** вы́броси э́ту вещь—онá ужé ни на что не годи́тся; **all in ~ time** всемý своё врéмя; **we must arrive in ~ time** нáдо порáньше прийти́; **is the meat still ~?** мя́со не испóртилось?; **the fish doesn't smell ~** э́та ры́ба с душкóм

7 (*reliable*, *safe*) надёжный; **~ brakes** хорóшие/ надёжные тормозá; **on ~ authority** из надёжного истóчника; **my car should be ~ for another year or two** моя́ маши́на ещё гóдик-другóй поéздит; **I'm ~ for another 5 miles** я смогý пройти́ ещё пять миль; **he's ~ for another few years** он ещё гóда два протя́нет; **he's ~ for £10** (*contribution*) у негó мóжно вы́удить дéсять фýнтов; **a ticket ~ for 3 months** билéт, действи́тельный на три мéсяца

8 (*thorough*): **he gave her a ~ scolding** он её хорошéнько/ как слéдует отругáл; **we'll have a ~ talk tomorrow** зáвтра мы обо всём поговори́м

9 (*considerable in quantity*): **I learnt a ~ deal at school** в шко́ле я мно́гому научи́лся; **I remember a ~ deal about my childhood** я мно́гое по́мню из своего́ де́тства; **it cost a ~ deal** э́то до́рого сто́ило; **they talked a ~ while** они́ говори́ли дово́льно до́лго; **there were a ~ few people at the lecture** на ле́кции бы́ло дово́льно мно́го наро́ду; **it's a ~ 3 miles from here** туда́ до́брых три ми́ли; **we waited a ~ hour/half hour** мы жда́ли це́лый час/до́брых полчаса́; **we spent a ~ £100 on repairs to the flat** мы угро́хали (*CQ*) сто фу́нтов на ремо́нт кварти́ры

10 as good as: my watch is 6 years old but it's as ~ as new я ношу́ э́ти часы́ шесть лет, но они́ хо́дят, как но́вые; **it's as ~ as settled** э́то в су́щности де́ло решённое; **it's as ~ as saying that...** э́то всё равно́, что сказа́ть...; **he's as ~ a mechanic as his brother/as you'd find** он меха́ник не ху́же бра́та, лу́чшего меха́ника не найти́

11: he made ~ он преуспева́л в жи́зни; **I'll make ~ the loss to you** я вам возмещу́ убы́тки (*pl*); **he made ~ his promise** он сдержа́л обеща́ние.

good *adv*: **we had a ~ long walk** мы хорошо́/как сле́дует прогуля́лись; **it's ~ and hot today** сего́дня о́чень жа́рко, сего́дня жара́; **she told him off ~ and proper** она́ его́ отчита́ла как полага́ется.

good-bye *n* проща́ние; **to say ~ to smb** проща́ться с кем-л.

good-bye *interj* до свида́ния!, *CQ* счастли́во!

good-for-nothing *n* никчёмный челове́к.

good-humoured *adj* доброду́шный.

good-looking *adj* краси́вый; **he/she is ~** он краси́в, она́ хоро́шенькая *or* миловидная.

goodness *n* доброта́; *CQ* (*as interj*): **~ me!** бо́же мой!; **~ knows!** бог зна́ет!; **thank ~!** сла́ва бо́гу!; **I wish to ~ he'd keep quiet** как бы мне хоте́лось, что́бы он замолча́л.

goods *npl* това́р (*collect*), това́ры; **consumer/canned/knitted ~** потреби́тельские това́ры, консе́рвы, трикота́жные изде́лия; *attr*: **a ~ train** това́рный по́езд/соста́в.

good-tempered *adj*: **he's a ~ fellow** у него́ ро́вный/споко́йный хара́ктер.

goose *n* гусь (*m*), *f* гусы́ня; *fig CQ* **you silly little ~** ты, ду́рочка; *attr* гуси́ный.

gooseberry *n* (*bush or fruit*) крыжо́вник (*collect*).

gooseflesh *n*: **I come out in ~ after bathing** у меня́ гуси́ная ко́жа по́сле купа́ния.

gore *vt*: **he was badly ~d by a bull** бык чуть не забода́л его́ на́смерть.

gorge *n* **1** (*ravine*) уще́лье

2 *Anat* го́рло; *fig* **his ~ rose at the sight** э́то вы́звало в нём глубо́кое отвраще́ние.

gorge *vti usu reflex*: **to ~ oneself** на|еда́ться (-е́стьcя); **he ~d himself on pancakes** он нае́лся блино́в (*ate a lot*), он объе́лся блина́ми (*ate to excess*).

gorgeous *adj* великоле́пный, *also CQ*; **we had a ~ time** мы великоле́пно провели́ вре́мя

gory *adj* крова́вый, окрова́вленный.

go-slow *n* (*in industry*) сниже́ние те́мпа рабо́ты.

gospel *n* ева́нгелие; *attr CQ*: **it's ~ truth** э́то и́стинная/су́щая пра́вда.

gossip *n* сплетня; (*person*) спле́тни|к, *f* -ца; *attr*: **~ column** (*in papers*) отде́л све́тской хро́ники.

gossip *vi* спле́тничать (по-, на-); **to ~ about smb** насплéтничать на кого́-л.

gourmand *n* ла́комка (*m and f*).

gourmet *n* гурма́н.

gout *n* пода́гра; **an attack of ~** при́ступ пода́гры.

govern *vt* (*rule*) пра́вить + *I*, управля́ть + *I*, *also Gram* (*impfs*); *fig*: (*be influenced by*) **he is too readily ~ed by the opinions of others** он сли́шком полага́ется на мне́ние други́х; **I'll be ~ed by your advice** я после́дую ва́шему сове́ту.

governess *n* гуверна́нтка.

governing *adj* пра́вящий; **the ~ class/party** пра́вящий класс, пра́вящая па́ртия; **~ principle** руководя́щий при́нцип.

government *n* (*act*) управле́ние + *I*; (*body of people*) (**the ~**) прави́тельство; **the ~ of a state** управле́ние госуда́рством; (*method*) **we have democratic ~** у нас демократи́ческая фо́рма правле́ния; **a member of the ~** член прави́тельства; *attr*: **a ~ official** прави́тельственный чино́вник.

governor *n*: (*US*) **the ~ of a state** губерна́тор шта́та; (*UK*) **the ~ of a prison** нача́льник тюрьмы́; **he's one of the ~s of this hospital** *approx* он вхо́дит в правле́ние э́той больни́цы; *CQ* (*boss*) (**the ~**) шеф.

gown *n* (*lady's*) пла́тье; *Univ* ма́нтия.

grab *vti vt* хвата́ть (схвати́ть)

vi: **to ~ at smth** ухвати́ться за что-л (*pf*), *also fig*; **he ~bed at a branch as he fell** па́дая, он ухвати́лся за ве́тку; *fig* **I ~bed at the chance** я ухвати́лся за э́ту возмо́жность.

grace *n* **1** (*of person, animal, movement*) гра́ция; (*elegance*) изя́щество; (*favour*) ми́лость, *also Rel*; **a girl full of ~** грацио́зная/изя́щная де́вушка; **with ~** грацио́зно; (*in old form of address*) **Your G.** Ва́ша све́тлость/ми́лость

2 *phrases*: **I am in his bad ~s** я у него́ в неми́лости; **to fall from ~** впасть в неми́лость; **at least he had the ~ to apologize** и всё же у него́ хвати́ло та́кта извини́ться; **he accepted his defeat with a good ~** он с досто́инством призна́л своё пораже́ние; **his humour is his saving ~** его́ спаса́ет чу́вство ю́мора

3 (*respite*): **he gave us a week's/month's ~** (*to pay*) он дал нам неде́льную/ме́сячную отсро́чку.

graceful *adj* (*of person, animal*) грацио́зный; (*elegant*) изя́щный; (*of movements*) испо́лненный гра́ции; **the ~ lines of the yacht** изя́щные ли́нии я́хты.

gracious *adj*: **the president's wife was very ~ to all/gave a ~ smile** супру́га президе́нта была́ о́чень любе́зна со все́ми/любе́зно улыбну́лась; **~ me!, goodness ~!** бо́же мой!, бо́же ми́лостивый!

gradation *n* (*transition*) постепе́нный перехо́д; града́ция; (*stage*) ступе́нь (разви́тия); **~s** перехо́дные ступе́ни.

grade *n* **1** (*in scale*) ступе́нь; сте́пень; (*rank*) зва́ние, ранг; (*category*) разря́д; **a major is one ~ higher in rank than a captain** майо́р по зва́нию одно́й ступе́нью вы́ше капита́на; **he's reached the top ~** он дости́г вы́сшего разря́да; *fig CQ* **he won't make the ~ as a pilot** лётчика из него́ не вы́йдет

2 (*in quality*) сорт; **a low ~ of flour** ни́зкий сорт муки́

3 (*US*: *in school*) класс; (*mark*) оце́нка

4 (*US*: *slope*) укло́н; *fig* **business is on the up/down ~** делова́я акти́вность на подъёме/на спа́де.

grade *vt*: **to ~ according to size** сортирова́ть по разме́ру (рас-); **the questions are ~d according to difficulty** вопро́сы подо́браны/даю́тся по сте́пени тру́дности.

gradient *n* укло́н; (*on road signs*) **Steep G.** круто́й спуск (*downhill*)/подъём (*uphill*); *Aut* **a ~ of one in ten** укло́н оди́н к десяти́, (*in road signs*) спуск/подъём 10% (де́сять проце́нтов).

gradual *adj* постепе́нный.

gradually *adv* постепе́нно; ма́ло-пома́лу, понемно́гу.

graduate *n* (*postgraduate*) аспира́нт, *f* -ка; (*UK*: *having first degree*): **he's a ~ (of Oxford)** он око́нчил (Оксфо́рдский) университе́т.

graduate *vi Univ* ока́нчивать университе́т (око́нчить); **he ~d in chemistry** он око́нчил хими́ческий факульте́т.

graduation *n Univ* (*graduating, or having graduated*) оконча́ние университе́та; (*ceremony*) церемо́ния присужде́ния степене́й.

graft[1] *n Hort* (*grafting*) приви́вка; (*grafted shoot*) приво́й, черено́к; *Med* **a bone/skin ~** переса́дка ко́сти/ко́жи.

graft[1] *vt*: *Hort* **to ~ a slip on to a rose bush** приви|ва́ть черено́к к ро́зе (-́ть); *Med* **to ~ bone/skin** переса́живать ко́стную ткань/ко́жу.

graft[2] *n* (*bribery*) взя́точничество; (*bribe*) взя́тка; **some ~ will be needed** на́до дать взя́тку, *CQ* на́до «подма́зать».

grain *n* **1** *collect* (*as crop*) хлеба́ (*pl*); (*cereals generally*) хле́бные зла́ки; (*after thrashing*: *bread grains, wheat, rye*) зерно́ (*collect*), (*other grains, whole or crushed, e.g. barley, buckwheat*) крупа́ (*collect*); *attr*: **the ~ harvest** урожа́й зерна́/хле́ба (*G sing*)

2 (*single seed or particle*) зерно́, *dim* зёрнышко, крупи́нка; **a ~ of gold/salt** крупи́нка зо́лота/со́ли; **a ~ of sand** песчи́нка; *fig*: **there's a ~ of truth in what he says** в его́ слова́х есть зерно́/до́ля и́стины; **there's not a ~ of truth in it** в э́том нет ни ка́пли пра́вды; **he hasn't a ~ of sense** у него́ нет ни ка́пли здра́вого смы́сла

3 (*measure*) гран

4 (*in wood*) волокно́; **against/with the ~** про́тив/вдоль (древе́сного) волокна́; *fig* **it goes against the ~ with me** э́то мне не по душе́/не по нутру́.

grammar *n* грамма́тика; (*textbook*) **a ~** уче́бник грамма́тики.

grammatical *adj* граммати́ческий.

gramme *n* грамм.

gramophone *n* прои́грыватель (*m*); **to play/put on the ~** слу́шать *or* ста́вить пласти́нки; *attr*: **~ record** пласти́нка.

granary *n* амба́р.

grand *adj* вели́чественный; грандио́зный; *CQ* великоле́пный; **in a ~ manner** вели́чественно; **~ schemes** грандио́зные за́мыслы; **a ~ lady** зна́тная да́ма; (*in titles*) **G. Duke** вели́кий князь; (*in chess*) **~ master** гроссме́йстер; *CQ* **that's ~!** великоле́пно!, превосхо́дно!

grandchild *n* внук, *f* вну́чка.

grandfather *n* дед.

grandiose *adj* грандио́зный, *usu pejor*.

grandmother *n* ба́бушка.

grandpa(pa) *n CQ* де́душка, деду́ля.

grand piano *n* роя́ль (*m*).

grandstand *n* центра́льная трибу́на.

granite *n* грани́т; *attr* грани́тный.

granny *n CQ* ба́бушка, бабу́ля, бабу́ся.

grant *n* (*from State to institution, etc.*) дота́ция, субси́дия; (*to individual*) посо́бие; (*to student*) стипе́ндия.

grant *vt* **1** (*give*) да|ва́ть (-ть); (*formal, Hist*) жа́ловать + *A of person and I of gift* (по-); **to ~ rights** дать права́; **the tsars ~ed lands to their courtiers** цари́ жа́ловали свои́х придво́рных поме́стьями; **he was ~ed a pension** ему́ назна́чили пе́нсию; **he ~ed my request** он удовлетвори́л мою́ про́сьбу; **~ me a favour** сде́лайте мне одолже́ние; **to ~ permission** дать разреше́ние

2 (*admit*) допус|ка́ть (-ти́ть), призна|ва́ть (-́ть); **~ed that...** допу́стим, что..., е́сли допусти́ть, что...; **he takes it for ~ed that his father will pay for his car** он счита́ет само́ собо́й разуме́ющимся, что оте́ц запла́тит за его́ маши́ну; **I ~ (you) the force of your argument** признаю́ справедли́вость ва́шего до́вода.

granulated *adj* гранули́рованный; зерни́стый; **~ sugar** са́харный песо́к.

grape *n usu pl* (**~s**) виногра́д (*collect*); **a bunch of ~s** кисть виногра́да; *fig* **that's just sour ~s!** зе́лен виногра́д!; *attr* виногра́дный.

grapefruit *n* гре́йпфрут.

grapevine *n* виногра́дная лоза́; *fig* **I heard on the ~ that...** я слыха́л,/говоря́т, что...

graph *n* гра́фик; *attr*: **~ paper** миллиме́тро́вка.

graphic *adj*: **the ~ arts** гра́фика (*sing*); *fig* (*vivid*) я́ркий, живо́й; **a ~ description** я́ркое/живо́е описа́ние.

grapple *vi*: **to ~ with smb** сцепи́ться/схвати́ться с кем-л (*usu pfs*); *fig* **to ~ with a problem** би́ться над пробле́мой (*impf*).

grasp *n* (*grip*) хва́тка (*see also* **grip** *n* **1**); **she had a firm ~ of my hand** она́ кре́пко держа́ла меня́ за́ руку; *fig*: **he has a good ~ of essentials/of French** он бы́стро схва́тывает суть де́ла, он хорошо́ владе́ет францу́зским; **it's beyond my ~** э́то вы́ше моего́ понима́ния.

grasp *vti vt* хвата́ть (схвати́ть); *fig* схва́тывать (*usu impf*), по|нима́ть (-ня́ть)

vi: **to ~ at smth** хвата́ться за что-л (ухвати́ться).

grasping *adj* жа́дный.

grass *n* **1** трава́; (*as lawn*) газо́н; *Bot* (**a ~, ~es**) злак, зла́ки; *Agric* (*pasture*) па́стбище, (*meadow*) луг; **keep off the ~!** по газо́нам не ходи́ть!; **the ~ is good this year** тра́вы (*pl*) в э́том году́ со́чные; **the cows are out at ~** коро́вы пасу́тся на лугу́; **to put cattle out to ~** выгоня́ть скот на па́стбище; *fig* **he doesn't let the ~ grow under his feet** он не теря́ет вре́мя по́пусту/зря (*advs*)

2 *sl* доно́счик, стука́ч.

grasshopper *n* кузне́чик.

grass widow *n* соло́менная вдова́.

grassy *adj* травяно́й.

grate[1] *n* (*for fire*) (ками́нная) решётка.

grate[2] *vti vt Cook* тере́ть (на-)

vi (*make grating sound*) скрести́ (*impf*); *fig* **his voice ~s on me/on the ears** его́ го́лос де́йствует мне на не́рвы/ре́жет мне слух.

grateful *adj* благода́рный, призна́тельный; **I am most ~ for your advice** я о́чень благода́рен/призна́телен вам за сове́т; **I'm ~ that...** я благода́рен судьбе́, что...; **I'll be most ~ if you would kindly pass on this letter** убеди́тельно прошу́ вас переда́ть э́то письмо́; (*at end of letter*) **with ~ thanks** с благода́рностью (*sing*).

gratefully *adv* благода́рно, с благода́рностью.

grater *n* тёрка.

gratification *n* удовлетворе́ние; **I had the ~ of knowing I had done my duty** я испы́тывал удовлетворе́ние от созна́ния вы́полненного до́лга.

gratify *vt* (*satisfy*) удовлетвор|я́ть + *A* (-и́ть); (*indulge*) потво́рствовать + *D*, потака́ть + *D* (*impfs*); **to ~ smb's desire/whims** удовлетворя́ть чьё-л жела́ние, потака́ть чьим-л капри́зам.

grating *n* решётка.

gratis *adv* да́ром, беспла́тно.

gratitude *n* благода́рность; **I expressed my ~ to him for his help** я благодари́л его́ за по́мощь.

gratuitous *adj* (*unpaid*) беспла́тный; даровóй; (*uncalled-for*) **a ~ insult/remark** незаслу́женное оскорбле́ние, оскорби́тельное замеча́ние.

gratuity *n* (*on retirement, etc.*) посо́бие; (*tip*) чаевы́е (*no sing*).

grave[1] *n* моги́ла.

grave[2] *adj* (*serious*) серьёзный; тяжёлый; (*alarming*) трево́жный; **~ doubts** серьёзные сомне́ния; **he looks ~** у него́ о́чень серьёзный вид; **a ~ situation** серьёзное/тяжёлое положе́ние; **a ~ illness** тяжёлая боле́знь; **there is ~ news from the front** с фро́нта пришли́ трево́жные ве́сти.

gravel *n* гра́вий.

gravestone *n* моги́льная плита́ (*of flat stone*), надгро́бный па́мятник (*of upright stone*), надгро́бие.

graveyard *n* кла́дбище.

gravitate *vi* тяготе́ть к + *D* (*impf*), *also fig*; *fig* тяну́ться к + *D* (*impf*); **young people tend to ~ towards cities** молодёжь притя́гивают больши́е города́.

gravity *n* **1** *Phys*: **centre/force of ~** центр/си́ла тя́жести; **specific ~** уде́льный вес; **law of ~** зако́н всеми́рного тяготе́ния

2 (*seriousness*) серьёзность; **I could hardly keep my ~** мне с трудо́м удало́сь сохрани́ть серьёзный вид.

gravy *n* подли́в(к)а.

gray *adj see* **grey.**

graze[1] *vti* пасти́(сь) (*impf*); **to ~ cattle** пасти́ скот.

graze[2] *n* (*scratch*) цара́пина.

graze[2] *vt* цара́пать (о-, по-); **I ~d my hand/myself on a stone** я оцара́пал ру́ку/оцара́пался о ка́мень.

grease *n* (*animal fat*) жир; (*for engines*) сма́зка.

grease *vt* (*lubricate*) сма́з|ывать (-ать); *fig CQ* **they ~d his palm well** они́ да́ли ему́ взя́тку.

grease gun *n Tech* сма́зочный шприц.

greasepaint *n Theat* грим.

greaseproof *adj* жиронепроница́емый.

greasy *adj* жи́рный, *also of food*; са́льный; **~ hair** жи́рные/са́льные во́лосы; **the roads are ~ today** сего́дня на доро́гах о́чень гря́зно и ско́льзко.

great *adj* **1** (*famed*) вели́кий; **a ~ artist/city/writer** вели́кий худо́жник/го́род/писа́тель; **Peter the G.** Пётр Пе́рвый/Вели́кий; **she was a ~ beauty in her day** в своё вре́мя она́ была́ знамени́той краса́вицей; **the G. War** пе́рвая мирова́я война́

2 (*in quantity, quality*) большо́й; (*intense*) си́льный; **my ~ friend** мой большо́й друг; **a ~ difference/mistake/victory** больша́я ра́зница/оши́бка/побе́да; **a ~ change/distance/future** огро́мные переме́ны (*pl*), большо́е расстоя́ние/бу́дущее; **~ heat/pain** си́льная жара́/боль; **a ~ storm** си́льная бу́ря; **with ~/the ~est pleasure** с больши́м/с огро́мным удово́льствием; **to a ~ extent** в бо́льшей [**NB** *stress*] сте́пени; **the ~/~er part** бо́льшая часть; **he's a ~ gardener/hunter/music lover** он стра́стный садо́вник/охо́тник, он большо́й люби́тель му́зыки; **he's a ~ talker/** *CQ* **a ~ one for talking** он большо́й люби́тель поговори́ть

3 (*to give emphasis*): **see what a ~ big fish I've caught** смотри́, каку́ю здорове́нную/огро́мную ры́бу я пойма́л

4 *CQ*: **we had a ~ holiday** мы чудéсно провели́ óтпуск; **that's ~!** вот здóрово!; **he's ~ at soccer** он здóрово игрáет в футбóл; **he's a ~ chap** он пáрень что нáдо; **he's no ~ shakes** он ничегó осóбенного из себя́ не представля́ет.

greatcoat *n* пальтó (*indecl*); *Mil* шинéль.

great-grandchild *n* прá|внук, *f* -внучка.

great-grandfather *n* прáдед.

great-grandmother *n* прабáбушка.

great-great-grandfather *n* прапрáдед.

greatly *adv* óчень; (*with comparatives*) намнóго; **I would ~ like to come** я бы óчень хотéл прийти́; **he is ~ the better player** он горáздо лу́чше игрáет.

greed *n* жáдность, *lit* áлчность (к + *D*); **~ for money** жáдность к деньгáм; **from/out of ~** от жáдности.

greedy *adj* жáдный к + *D*, на + *A*, до + *G*; (*gluttonous*) прожóрливый; **he's not hungry, he's just ~** он не гóлоден, он прóсто обжóра; *CQ* **you ~ pig!** ну и/вот обжóра!

Greek *n* грек, гречáнка; (*language*) грéческий язы́к.

Greek *adj* грéческий.

green *n* **1** зелёный цвет; **she was dressed in ~** онá былá одéта в зелёное; **a painting in blues and ~s** карти́на в си́них и зелёных тонáх

2 *pl* (**~s**) *Cook* зéлень (*collect*), óвощи.

green *adj* зелёный; (*unripe*) неспéлый, незрéлый, зелёный; **~ apples** зелёные я́блоки; *fig*: **a ~ youth** желторóтый юнéц; **a ~ old age** бóдрая стáрость; **to turn ~ (with envy)** позеленéть (от зáвисти); **he's still ~ at his job** он ещё новичóк в рабóте; **he's got ~ fingers** что он ни посáдит, у негó всё растёт.

greenery *n* зéлень.

greenhouse *n* тепли́ца; (*conservatory*) оранжерéя.

greet *vt* привéтствовать + *A* (*impf*), здорóваться с + *I* (по-); **to ~ the guests** привéтствовать гостéй; **they ~ed one another** они́ поздорóвались; **he was ~ed with applause/with angry shouts** егó встрéтили аплодисмéнтами/гнéвными вóзгласами; **a strange sight ~ed them in the entrance** стрáнный вид откры́лся им при вхóде.

greeting *n* привéт; привéтствие; **with ~s from us all** (*on card with gift*) с привéтом [**NB** *sing*] от всех нас; **they exchanged ~s** они́ обменя́лись привéтствиями.

gregarious *adj* (*of animals*) стáдный; (*of people*) общи́тельный; (*of birds*) **starlings are very ~** скворцы́ живу́т стáями.

grenade *n* гранáта.

grey *n* сéрый цвет; **his hair is touched with ~** егó вóлосы трóнула сединá.

grey *adj* сéрый; (*of hair*) седóй; **a bit ~** серовáтый; **~ hair** сединá; **~ hairs** седы́е вóлосы; **a ~ day** сéрый денёк; **to turn ~ (with worry)** поседéть (от забóт); *fig* **the future looks ~** бу́дущее представля́ется безрáдостным.

grid *n* решётка; *Tech*, *Elec* (*network*) сéтка.

grief *n* гóре; **to die of ~** умерéть от гóря; **his plans came to ~** егó плáны ру́хнули.

grievance *n* оби́да; **to nurse a ~** затаи́ть оби́ду.

grieve *vti vt* огорч|áть (-и́ть); **I was ~d to learn of his death** я с прискóрбием узнáл о егó смéрти

vi горевáть о + *P* (*impf*); переживáть + *A* (*only in impf*); **don't ~** не горю́й; **he is grieving over the death of his mother** он тяжелó переживáет смерть мáтери; **I ~ for your loss** я выражáю вам соболéзнования.

grill *n* (*on cooker*) (электри́ческая/гáзовая) решётка; (*separate appliance*) (электро)гри́ль (*m*); (*dish*) **a mixed ~** ассорти́ (*indecl*) из жáреного мя́са.

grill *vti* (*cook*) жáрить на решётке/в гри́ле (под-); *fig* **to ~ in the sun** жáриться на сóлнце; *CQ* **to ~ smb** допр|áшивать когó-л (-оси́ть).

grilled *adj Cook* жáреный; *fig CQ* **I'm ~** я испёкся.

grilling *adj*: **under a ~ sun** под паля́щим сóлнцем; **it's ~ (hot) today** ну и жарá/*CQ* жари́ща сегóдня.

grim *adj* мрáчный; **~ reality** мрáчная действи́тельность; **he looks ~** у негó мрáчный вид; **what a ~ business!** какáя мрáчная истóрия!; **with ~ determination** с мрáчной реши́мостью; **to hang on like ~ death** вцепи́ться мёртвой хвáткой.

grimace *n* гримáса, (*affected*) ужи́мка.

grimace *vi* гримáсничать (*impf*).

grime *n* (*from soot*) кóпоть; (*from mud, etc.*) грязь.

grimy *adj* (*from soot*) закопчённый; (*dirty*) гря́зный; (*soiled*) запáчканный.

grin *n* усмéшка; *CQ* ухмы́лка; **...he said with a sly ~** ...сказáл он с хи́трой усмéшкой/ухмы́лкой.

grin *vi* усмех|áться (-ну́ться), *CQ* ухмыл|я́ться (-ьну́ться); **to ~ from ear to ear** ухмыля́ться во весь рот.

grind *n CQ*: **it's a frightful ~** э́то кáторжная/ну́дная рабóта.

grind *vti vt* молóть (с-, на-, по-); **to ~ coffee/wheat** молóть кóфе/пшени́цу; (*polish*) **to ~ a lens** шлифовáть ли́нзу (от-); (*sharpen*) **to ~ an axe/a knife** точи́ть топóр/нож (на-); **to ~ one's teeth** скрежетáть зубáми (*impf*); **they were ground down by taxation** их задави́ли налóги

vi: **the train ground to a halt** пóезд с ля́згом останови́лся; *fig CQ*: **he's ~ing away in the garden/at his sums/for his exam** он тру́дится в саду́, он корпи́т над задáчами, он зубри́т пéред экзáменом; **he ground on regardless** он всё нуди́л своё.

grinder *n* мéльница; **coffee ~** кофéйная мéльница, *CQ* кофемóлка.

grindstone *n* точи́ло; *fig* **he keeps our noses to the ~** он нам передохну́ть/разогну́ться не даёт, он нас загнáл [**NB** *tense*].

grip *n* **1** (*hold*) хва́тка; **he has a strong ~** у него́ кре́пкая хва́тка; **he had a firm ~ on/of my arm** он кре́пко держа́л/сжима́л мою́ ру́ку; **don't let go your ~ of the rope** не выпуска́й верёвку из рук; **the tyres have lost their ~** ши́ны стёрлись; *fig*: **to come to ~s with a problem** взя́ться за реше́ние пробле́мы; **he has a good ~ of his subject** он хорошо́ зна́ет свой предме́т; **he was in the ~ of fever** его́ би́ла лихора́дка; **the country was in the ~ of a general strike/of a hard winter** страна́ была́ охва́чена всео́бщей забасто́вкой, повсю́ду стоя́ли си́льные моро́зы

2 (*for travel*) саквоя́ж, су́мка

3 (*handle of suitcase, tennis racquet, etc.*) ру́чка, (*of implement*) рукоя́тка; **my racquet needs a new ~** (*non-slip cover*) у мое́й раке́тки на́до обмота́ть ру́чку.

grip *vti vt* (*squeeze, press*) сжима́ть (сжать); (*catch hold of*) хвата́ть (схвати́ть); **he ~ped my hand** он сжал мою́ ру́ку; **to ~ smb by the arm/hand** хвата́ть кого́-л за́ руку; **he ~ped the banister** он держа́лся (*held*)/ ухвати́лся (*took hold of*) за пери́ла (*pl*); *fig*: **fear ~ped them** их охвати́л страх; **the violinist ~ped the audience** игра́ скрипача́ захвати́ла слу́шателей

vi: **the brakes aren't ~ping** тормоза́ не де́ржат.

gripe *vi CQ* (*grumble*) ворча́ть (*impf*); **what's he griping about?** и что он всё ворчи́т?

gripes *npl CQ*: **I've got the ~** у меня́ ко́лики (*no sing*).

gripping *adj*: **a ~ film** захва́тывающий фильм.

grisly *adj* стра́шный, ужа́сный.

gristle *n* хрящ; **meat with a lot of ~** жи́листое мя́со.

grit *n* (*sand*) песо́к; (*gravel*) гра́вий; **I've got some ~ in my eye/shoe** у меня́ песчи́нка в глаз попа́ла, у меня́ песо́к попа́л в боти́нок; *fig* **he's got ~** у него́ хва́тит (*impers*) вы́держки.

grit *vt*: **to ~ roads** посып|а́ть доро́ги песко́м/гра́вием (-ать); *fig* **we just had to ~ our teeth and get on with the job** мы должны́ бы́ли, сти́снув зу́бы, приня́ться за рабо́ту.

gritty *adj* песча́ный.

grizzled *adj* (*of hair*) седо́й.

groan *n* стон.

groan *vi* стона́ть (*impf*); **to ~ with pain** стона́ть от бо́ли; *fig* **the table was ~ing with food** стол ломи́лся от яств.

grocery *n* продово́льственный/бакале́йный магази́н; *pl* (**groceries**) (*goods*) проду́кты.

grog *n* грог, пунш.

groggy *adj* (*of furniture*) непро́чный, ша́ткий; *fig CQ*: **I feel very ~** я совсе́м раскле́ился [**NB** *tense*]; **the old man is a bit ~ on his legs** стари́к не о́чень уве́ренно де́ржится на нога́х.

groin *n Anat* пах.

groom *n* ко́нюх; (*bridegroom*) жени́х.

groom *vt*: **to ~ a horse** (*general*) ходи́ть/ уха́живать за ло́шадью (*impf*), (*brush*) чи́стить ло́шадь; **his horse was well ~ed** за его́ ло́шадью был хоро́ший ухо́д; *fig* **to ~ smb for the directorship** гото́вить кого́-л на до́лжность дире́ктора.

groove *n* желобо́к; *Tech* паз; *fig* **to get into a ~** войти́ в колею́.

grope *vi* ощу́п|ывать (-ать); **he ~d his way to the door** он о́щупью (*adv*)/на о́щупь пробра́лся к две́ри; **to ~ for smth** иска́ть что-л о́щупью (*impf*).

gross[1] *n* (*measure*) гросс.

gross[2] *adj* **1** (*coarse*) гру́бый; (*flagrant*) вопию́щий, я́вный; (*excessive*) чрезме́рный; **a ~ error** гру́бая оши́бка; **a ~ injustice** вопию́щая/ я́вная несправедли́вость; **a ~ exaggeration** чрезме́рное преувеличе́ние; **she's really ~** она́ про́сто толсту́ха; **a ~ eater** обжо́ра

2 *Econ* валово́й; **~ income/revenue** валово́й дохо́д; **~ amount** валова́я су́мма; **~ weight** вес бру́тто (*indecl adj*).

grossly *adv* гру́бо; чрезме́рно; **the story was ~ exaggerated** э́та исто́рия была́ я́вно преувели́чена, э́ту исто́рию чрезме́рно разду́ли.

grotesque *adj* гроте́скный.

ground[1] *n* **1** (*surface of the earth*) земля́; **above/below ~** над/под землёй: **to lift smth from the ~** поднима́ть что-л с земли́: **to burn to the ~** сгоре́ть дотла́ (*adv*); (*of fox, etc.*): **to go to ~** скры́ться в норе́; **to run a fox to ~** загна́ть лису́ в нору́; *fig* **I ran him to ~ in the library** я нашёл его́ в библиоте́ке; *Aer* **to get off the ~** оторва́ться от земли́; *fig* **the project has not yet got off the ~** прое́кт ещё не сдви́нулся с ме́ста; **to fall to the ~** упа́сть на зе́млю; *fig* **our plans fell to the ~** на́ши пла́ны провали́лись; **we covered a lot of ~** (*by walking*) мы покры́ли большо́е расстоя́ние, *fig* (*at work*) мы мно́го сде́лали, (*in discussion*) мы обсуди́ли мно́го вопро́сов; *Mil* **to give ~** отступа́ть, *also fig*; *Mil* **to stand one's ~** не отступа́ть, *also fig*, *fig* стоя́ть на своём; *Mil* **to shift one's ~** смени́ть пози́цию, *also fig*

2 (*soil*) земля́, по́чва, грунт; **damp/sandy ~** вла́жная/песча́ная по́чва; **to dig the ~** рыть зе́млю; **stony ~** камени́стый грунт; *fig*: **that's delicate ~** э́то делика́тный вопро́с; **to be on sure ~** чу́вствовать твёрдую по́чву под нога́ми

3 (*terrain*) ме́стность; (*area: plot*) уча́сток, (*for sports, etc.*) площа́дка; **uneven ~** неро́вная ме́стность; **the house has extensive ~s** вокру́г до́ма обши́рный уча́сток; **this ~ is owned by the state/school** э́та земля́ принадлежи́т госуда́рству, э́тот уча́сток *or* э́та площа́дка принадлежи́т шко́ле; **football ~** футбо́льное по́ле, (*including stands, etc.*) стадио́н; **to clear the ~ for building** расчи́стить уча́сток/площа́дку под строи́тельство; *fig* **to explore the ~** зонди́ровать по́чву

4 *Art* по́ле, план; (*background*) фон; **on a white ~** на бе́лом фо́не/по́ле; **in the middle ~ of the picture** на сре́днем пла́не карти́ны

5 *pl* (*dregs*): **coffee ~s** кофе́йная гу́ща (*sing*)

6 *usu pl* (*cause*) основа́ние (*usu in sing*); **on what ~s do you say that?** на како́м основа́нии вы так говори́те?, како́е у вас основа́ние так говори́ть?; **I have ~s for thinking that...** у меня́ есть основа́ние ду́мать, что...; **~s for divorce** основа́ние для разво́да.

ground[1] *vti vt* **1** *Naut*: **to ~ one's boat on a sandbank** посади́ть ло́дку на мель (*usu pf*); *Aer*: **he has been ~ed** его́ отстрани́ли от полётов; **the plane was ~ed by fog/for repair** самолёт не мог вы́лететь из-за тума́на, самолёт сня́ли с ре́йса для ремо́нта

2 осно́в|ывать (-а́ть); **I have ~ed my theory on facts** я основа́л свою́ тео́рию на фа́ктах; **to ~ smb in physics** обуча́ть кого́-л фи́зике (*sing*); **to be well ~ed in physics** хорошо́ знать осно́вы фи́зики

vi Naut: **to ~ in shallow water** сади́ться на мель (сесть).

ground[2] *adj* мо́лотый; **~ coffee** мо́лотый ко́фе.

ground crew *n Aer* назе́мный персона́л.

ground floor *n* пе́рвый эта́ж.

ground fog *n* сте́лющийся тума́н.

ground forces *npl Mil* назе́мные войска́.

grounding *n*: **he has a good ~ in mathematics** у него́ хоро́шая математи́ческая подгото́вка.

groundless *adj* необосно́ванный.

ground level *n*: **my office is on ~** мой кабине́т нахо́дится на пе́рвом этаже́.

ground nut *n* земляно́й оре́х.

ground swell *n Naut* до́нные во́лны (*pl*).

groundwork *n* осно́ва; подготови́тельная рабо́та; **to do the ~ for conference** проводи́ть подготови́тельную рабо́ту пе́ред конфере́нцией.

group *n* гру́ппа; **a ~ of buildings/languages** гру́ппа домо́в/языко́в; **they stood around in ~s of 3 or 4** они́ стоя́ли гру́ппами по три-четы́ре челове́ка; **a political/theatre ~** полити́ческая группиро́вка, театра́льная тру́ппа; *attr*: **a ~ photo/project** группово́й портре́т/прое́кт.

group *vti vt* группирова́ть (с-); (*gather*) со|бира́ть (-бра́ть); **he ~ed the children according to age/round him** он раздели́л дете́й на гру́ппы по во́зрасту, он собра́л дете́й вокру́г себя́

vi группирова́ться; собира́ться.

grouse *vi CQ* ворча́ть, брюзжа́ть (*impfs*); **he's forever grousing about the weather** он ве́чно ворчи́т на пого́ду.

grove *n* ро́ща.

grovel *vi fig*: **to ~ before/to smb** заи́скивать пе́ред кем-л (*impf*).

grow *vti vt* (*cultivate*) вы|ра́щивать (-́растить), раз|води́ть (-вести́); **to ~ potatoes/roses** выра́щивать карто́фель (*collect*), разводи́ть ро́зы; **to ~ one's hair/a moustache** отпус|ка́ть во́лосы/усы́ (-ти́ть)

vi **1** расти́ (*impf*); (*grow up*) вы|раста́ть (-́расти); (*increase*) возраст|а́ть (-и́); **vines won't ~ in the north** на се́вере виногра́д не растёт; **the crowd grew** толпа́ росла́; **how you've ~n!** как ты вы́рос!

2 (*become*) ста|нови́ться (-ть), *or translate by verbs formed from adjs*: **the sound was ~ing louder** звук станови́лся гро́мче; **the days are ~ing shorter** дни стано́вятся коро́че; **to ~ dark/light** темне́ть (с-), света́ть (*impf*); **to ~ tired/worse** утом|ля́ться (-и́ться), ухудш|а́ться (-́иться) *or* станови́ться ху́же; **it is ~ing late** уже́ по́здно

grow away from *vi*: **over the years I have ~n away from my school friends** с года́ми я отдали́лся от мои́х шко́льных друзе́й

grow from *vti vt*: **to ~ tomatoes from seed** выра́щивать помидо́ры из семя́н

vi: **their friendship grew from their common interest in botany** их сбли́зил о́бщий интере́с к бота́нике

grow into *vi* вы|раста́ть в + *A* (-́расти); **she has ~n into a beautiful girl** она́ вы́росла/преврати́лась в краси́вую де́вушку; **he'll soon ~ into these trousers** ско́ро э́ти брю́ки бу́дут ему́ впо́ру (*adv*)

grow on *vi*: **money doesn't ~ on trees** де́ньги на доро́ге не валя́ются; **this music ~s on me** э́та му́зыка мне нра́вится всё бо́льше

grow out of *vi* вы|раста́ть из + *G* (-́расти); **this city has ~n out of a few villages** э́тот го́род вы́рос из не́скольких дереве́нь; **she's ~ing out of her clothes** она́ выраста́ет из свое́й оде́жды; **I've ~n out of the habit of going to the theatre** я отвы́к ходи́ть в теа́тр

grow over *vti vt*: **the garden was ~n over with weeds** сад заро́с сорняка́ми

vi: **ivy had ~n all over the wall** плющ уви́л всю сте́ну; **skin has ~n over the wound** ра́на затяну́лась

grow to *vi*: **I've ~n to like/hate him** я полюби́л/возненави́дел его́ (*pfs*)

grow up *vi* вы|раста́ть (-́расти); **he grew up in the country** он рос/вы́рос в дере́вне; **a friendship grew up between them** они́ ста́ли друзья́ми; **it's time he grew up** ему́ уже́ пора́ повзросле́ть (*pf*).

growl *n* рыча́ние.

growl *vti* рыча́ть (*impf*); **to begin to ~** зарыча́ть (*pf*); **the dog ~ed at me** соба́ка зарыча́ла на меня́; **thunder was ~ing in the distance** где́-то вдали́ грохота́л гром (*impf*); **he ~ed out a reply** он что́-то бу́ркнул в отве́т.

grown *adj* взро́слый.

grown-up *adj* взро́слый, *also as n*.

growth *n* **1** (*growing*) рост; (*development*) разви́тие; (*increase*) приро́ст, увеличе́ние; (*spread*) распростране́ние; **a ~ in/of population** рост населе́ния; **a ~ of 2 million in population** приро́ст населе́ния в два миллио́на; **to reach full ~** дости́чь по́лного разви́тия

2 (*what has grown*): **a new ~** молода́я по́росль; **the luxurious ~ of the tropics** роско́шная тропи́ческая расти́тельность; **a thick ~ of weeds** бу́йный рост сорняко́в; **he had**

a 3-day ~ of beard он ужé три дня не брился

3 *Med* (*tumour*) óпухоль.

grub *n* (*larva*) личи́нка; *sl* (*food*) жратвá.

grub *vti vt*: **to ~ up weeds** полóть сорнякú (вы́-)

vi ры́ться в + *P* (*impf*); **pigs were ~bing (about) among the trees** сви́ньи ры́лись под дерéвьями; **he's ~bing about in the garden** он копáется в огорóде.

grubby *adj* гря́зный; **you ~ child!** ты грязнýля! (*m and f*); **wash your ~ hands!** иди́ вы́мой рýки, они́ у тебя́ óчень гря́зные; **a ~ collar** гря́зный воротни́к.

grudge *n*: **he bears me a ~** он на меня́ в оби́де, у негó прóтив меня́ зуб.

grudge *vt*: **he ~s neither time nor effort** он не жалéет ни врéмени, ни сил; **I ~d/didn't ~ the money** мне бы́ло жáлко дéнег, я дéнег не жалéл; **I ~ the money for taxis** мне жáлко трáтить дéньги на такси́; **I don't ~ Nina her success** я не зави́дую успéху Ни́ны.

grudging *adj* скупóй; **~ praise** скупáя похвалá.

grudgingly *adv* неохóтно, нéхотя.

gruel *n* жи́дкая овся́ная кáша.

gruelling *adj* тяжёлый; **~ work** тяжёлая рабóта; **a ~ climate** тяжёлый/ suróвый кли́мат.

gruesome *adj* ужáсный, стрáшный.

gruff *adj* (*of manner*) рéзкий, грубовáтый; **a ~ voice** хри́плый гóлос.

grumble *n* ворчáние; (*complaint*) жáлоба.

grumble *vi* ворчáть (*impf*); **he's always grumbling at me/the weather/that...** он вéчно ворчи́т на меня́/на погóду/, что...

grumbler *n* ворчýн.

grumpy *adj* сварли́вый.

grunt *vi* (*of pig*) хрюк|ать (*semel* -нуть); (*of person*: *if lifting something*, *also in contentment*) кря́к|ать (*semel* -нуть); **he ~ed with satisfaction** он кря́кнул от удовóльствия; **in reply he merely ~ed** в отвéт он тóлько чтó-то пробурчáл.

guarantee *n* гарáнтия; (*pledge*) залóг; **a watch with a two-year ~** часы́ с гарáнтией на два гóда; **he left £100 as a ~** он остáвил сто фýнтов в залóг.

guarantee *vt* гаранти́ровать (*impf and pf*); (*answer for*) ручáться за + *A* (поручи́ться); **to ~ success** гаранти́ровать успéх, ручáться за успéх; **the refrigerator is ~d for a year** холоди́льник имéет гарáнтию нá год; **I will ~ his debts/the truth of the information** я поручýсь за негó/за вéрность информáции; **these pipes are ~d against rust** э́ти трýбы нержавéющие, у них есть гарáнтия; **I can't ~ fine weather tomorrow** я не могý обещáть, что зáвтра бýдет хорóшая погóда.

guarantor *n* поручи́тель (*m*).

guard *n* **1** (*person*: *Mil or police*) часовóй, караýльный; (*group of guards*) охрáна; (*watchman*) стóрож; *Rail* проводни́к; *Mil* (*regiment*) (**the Guards**) гвáрдия (*sing*); **a colonel in the Guards** гвáрдии (*G*) полкóвник; **~ of honour** почётный караýл; **to strengthen the ~** уси́лить охрáну; **he went there under armed ~** он отпрáвился тудá в сопровождéнии вооружённой охрáны

2 (*duty*): **to be on ~** стоя́ть в караýле/ на стрáже/на часáх, нести́ караýл; **to go on ~** заступáть в караýл; **to relieve/change ~** сменя́ть караýл; **to keep smb under ~** держáть когó-л под стрáжей; *attr* караýльный; сторожевóй; **a ~ dog** (*Mil*, *police*) караýльная собáка, (*domestic*) сторожевóй пёс

3 (*watchfulness*): **to be on one's ~** быть начекý/настрожé (*advs*); **to be on one's ~ against smb/smth** остерегáться когó-л/чегó-л; **to catch smb off his ~** застáть когó-л врасплóх (*adv*); **to put smb on his ~ against smth** предостерегáть когó-л от чегó-л.

guard *vt* (*watch over*) охраня́ть, сторожи́ть (*impfs*); *Mil* караýлить (*impf*); **to ~ prisoners of war** караýлить плéнных; **to ~ treasure** охраня́ть клад; **the dog is ~ing the sheep** собáка сторожи́т овéц; **to ~ one's property against thieves** стерéчь имýщество от ворóв

guard against *vt*: **to ~ a town against the enemy** защищáть гóрод от врагá (*usu impf*); **you must ~ against exaggerating/catching cold** нáдо остерегáться преувеличéний (*pl*)/берéчься от простýды (*impfs*).

guard duty *n* караýльная слýжба; **he's on ~** он в караýле.

guarded *adj* осторóжный; **a ~ answer** осторóжный отвéт.

guardian *n* *Law* опекýн; **he was appointed their ~** егó назнáчили их опекунóм; *attr*: **~ angel** áнгел-храни́тель (*m*).

guard's van *n* багáжный вагóн.

guerrilla *n* партизáн; *attr* партизáнский; **~ warfare** партизáнская войнá.

guess *n* догáдка; **a lucky ~** счастли́вая догáдка; **it's anybody's ~** об э́том мóжно тóлько догáдываться; **at a ~ I'd say she was 30** я бы дал ей три́дцать лет; **at a ~ it's a 2-hour journey** дорóга тудá примéрно два часá.

guess *vt* угáд|ывать (-áть); догáд|ываться (-áться); **I ~ed right!** я прáвильно угадáл!, я догадáлся!; **~ what I found!** угадáй, что я нашёл?; **you would never ~ her age** вы никогдá не догадáетесь, скóлько ей лет; **to ~ a riddle** отгáд|ывать загáдку (-áть); (*US*) *CQ*: **I ~ they're right** они́, навéрно, прáвы; **I ~ I'm too old** навéрно, я сли́шком стар.

guesswork *n*: **it was pure ~** э́то бы́ло чистéйшей догáдкой.

guest *n* гость (*m*); **~ of honour** почётный гость; **to be a paying ~** жить у когó-л на пóлном пансиóне; *attr Mus*, *etc.*: **a ~ conductor/artist** приглашённый дирижёр/арти́ст.

guest-house *n* пансиóн.

guffaw *vi* хохотáть, гоготáть (*impfs*).

guidance *n* (*leadership*) руковóдство; (*instructions*) наставлéние; (*advice*) совéт; **we finally**

reached camp under the ~ of a forester наконе́ц лесни́к привёл нас к ла́герю; **he needs his father's ~** ему́ необходи́мы отцо́вские наставле́ния; **give me some ~ as to what I should do** посове́туйте/подскажи́те мне, что де́лать.

guide *n* **1** (*for tourists*) гид, экскурсово́д; (*for climbers, etc.*) проводни́к; (*for the blind*) поводы́рь (*m*); *fig*: **the exam results are no ~ to his ability** по результа́там экза́менов нельзя́ суди́ть о его́ спосо́бностях (*pl*); **instinct is not always a safe ~** не всегда́ мо́жно полага́ться на инсти́нкт; **these figures are only a rough ~** э́то то́лько ориентиро́вочные ци́фры; **allow one table-spoonful per person as a rough ~** приме́рно одна́ ло́жка на челове́ка

2 (*plan, map*) путеводи́тель (*m*) по + *D*; (*textbook*) уче́бник; **a G. to London** путеводи́тель по Ло́ндону; **a ~ to physics** уче́бник фи́зики (*sing*); **a ~ to gardening** спра́вочник/руково́дство по садово́дству.

guide *vt* **1** (*act as guide*) вести́ (по-); **to ~ smb round a museum/over the mountains/through the streets** вести́ кого́-л по музе́ю/по гора́м/по у́лицам; **he ~d us through the dense forest** он провёл нас че́рез чащо́бу

2 (*instruct*) настав|ля́ть (-́ить); да|ва́ть сове́ты (-ть); **he ~d me in my business transactions** он наставля́л меня́/дава́л мне сове́ты в деловы́х опера́циях; **I shall be ~d by your advice** я бу́ду руково́дствоваться ва́шим сове́том.

guidebook *n* путеводи́тель (*m*).

guide dog *n* соба́ка-поводы́рь (*m*).

guile *n* хи́трость; **by ~** хи́тростью.

guileless *adj* бесхи́тростный.

guilty *adj* **1** винова́тый, вино́вный; пови́нный в + *P*; **he is in no way ~** он ни в чём не винова́т/пови́нен; **he is ~ of theft** он вино́вен в кра́же; **he has a ~ look** у него́ винова́тый вид; **I feel ~ about not helping her** я чу́вствую себя́ винова́тым, что не помо́г ей; **a ~ conscience/secret** нечи́стая со́весть, позо́рная та́йна

2 *Law* вино́вный в + *P*; **he was found ~/not ~ of murder** его́ призна́ли вино́вным/невино́вным в уби́йстве.

guinea-pig *n* морска́я сви́нка; *fig* подо́пытный кро́лик.

guise *n*: **under the ~ of friendship** под ви́дом/под личи́ной дру́жбы.

guitar *n* гита́ра; **to play the ~** игра́ть на гита́ре.

gulf *n* (*in sea*) (морско́й) зали́в; (*chasm*) бе́здна; *fig* про́пасть; **there is a wide ~ between them/their views** их/их взгля́ды разделя́ет про́пасть.

Gulf Stream *n* Гольфстри́м.

gull[1] *n* ча́йка.

gull[2] *vt*: **he's easily ~ed** его́ ничего́ не сто́ит обману́ть.

gullet *n* пищево́д.

gullible *adj* легкове́рный.

gully *n* (*ravine*) овра́г; (*drain*) кана́ва.

gulp *n* глото́к; **at a ~** за́лпом, одни́м глотко́м.

gulp *vt* (*food, drink*) прогл|а́тывать (-оти́ть), глота́ть (*impf*); **he quickly ~ed (down) his breakfast/the medicine** он бы́стро проглоти́л за́втрак/лека́рство; (*in emotion*) **to ~ down one's tears/sobs** глота́ть слёзы, сде́рж|ивать рыда́ния (-а́ть).

gum[1] *n Anat* десна́.

gum[2] *n* (*from trees*) гу́мми (*indecl*), каме́дь; (*adhesive*) клей; (**chewing-**) **~** жева́тельная рези́нка.

gum[2] *vt*, *also* **~ together/up** скле́|ивать (-ить); **to ~ down an envelope** закле́ить конве́рт; **to ~ smth to smth** прикле́ить что-л к чему́-л; *fig CQ* **that's ~med up the works** э́то засто́порило всё де́ло (*pf*).

gumboil *n* флюс.

gumboots *npl* рези́новые сапоги́.

gummy *adj* кле́йкий; (*sticky*) ли́пкий.

gumption *n CQ*: **he's got no ~** он тако́й беспо́мощный; **use your ~** шевели́ мозга́ми!

gun *n* ружьё, (*also = hunter's rifle*); *Mil* (*rifle*) винто́вка; (*large, cannon, etc.*) ору́дие, пу́шка; *fig CQ*: **to stick to one's ~s** не скла́дывать ору́жия, не сдава́ться; (*of person*) **he's a big ~** он ва́жная ши́шка, он большо́й нача́льник.

gun *vti vt*: **to ~ smb down** застрели́ть кого́-л (*usu pf*)

vi CQ: **he's ~ning for me** (*generally*) он то́чит на меня́ зуб, (*of a particular remark*) э́то ка́мень в мой огоро́д.

gun crew *n Mil* ору́дийный расчёт.

gunfire *n* артиллери́йский/ору́дийный ого́нь.

gunman *n* (*US*) вооружённый банди́т.

gunner *n Mil* артиллери́ст; *Aer* стрело́к.

gunpoint *n*: **to hold smb at ~** держа́ть кого́-л на прице́ле/му́шке.

gunpowder *n* по́рох.

gurgle *n* (*of water*) бу́льканье.

gurgle *vi* бу́лькать (*impf*); (*of a baby*) *CQ* гу́лить (*impf*).

gush *n* (*of water*) струя́, пото́к; **a ~ of blood/oil** струя́ кро́ви, фонта́н не́фти; **a ~ of tears** пото́к слёз.

gush *vi* бить (струёй) (*usu impf*); **to begin to ~** хлы́нуть (*pf*); **oil ~ed from the broken pipe** нефть би́ла/хлы́нула из сло́манной трубы́; *fig* **she ~ed over the painting** она́ без у́держу восторга́лась э́той карти́ной.

gushing *adj*: **her ~ compliments embarrassed me** мне бы́ло нело́вко от её неуёмных комплиме́нтов; **he was ~ in his thanks** он рассыпа́лся в благода́рностях.

gust *n*: **a ~ of wind** поры́в ве́тра.

gusto *n*: **he ate with ~** он ел с больши́м аппети́том; **he hasn't much voice but he sang with ~** го́лоса у него́ нет, но пел он с больши́м чу́вством (*heartily*).

gusty *adj*: **a ~ day/wind** ве́треный день, поры́вистый ве́тер.

gut *n Anat* кишка́; (*for fishing*) ле́ска; (*for violin, etc.*) струна́; *pl fig CQ* (*of people*): **he's got plenty of/no ~s** он волево́й челове́к, он про́сто тря́пка; **she hadn't the ~s to tell him the truth** у неё не хвати́ло му́жества/сил сказа́ть ему́ пра́вду; **I hate his ~s** я его́ смерте́льно ненави́жу.

gut *vt*: **to ~ fish/a fowl** потроши́ть ры́бу/ку́рицу (вы́-); **the house was ~ted by fire** внутри́ дом весь вы́горел.

gutter *n* (*on street*) сто́чная кана́ва; *pl* (~s) (*on roof*) кро́вельные желоба́; *fig*: **children from the ~** де́ти трущо́б; **to rise from the ~** вы́расти в трущо́бах.

gutter-press *n* бульва́рная пре́сса.

guttural *n Ling* гуттура́льный звук.

guttural *adj* горлово́й; горта́нный; *Ling* гуттура́льный.

guy *n* (*scarecrow*) пу́гало, чу́чело; (*US*) *CQ* па́рень, ма́лый; **he's a nice ~** он сла́вный ма́лый; **that ~ told me that...** э́тот па́рень мне сказа́л, что...; *iron* **a wise ~** у́мник.

guzzle *vt CQ* жрать (со́-).

gymnasium *n* спорти́вный зал, спортза́л.

gymnast *n* гимна́ст.

gymnastics *npl* гимна́стика (*sing*).

gynaecologist *n* гинеко́лог.

gynaecology *n* гинеколо́гия.

gypsum *n* гипс.

gyrate *vi* враща́ться (по кру́гу) (*impf*); дви́гаться по спира́ли (*usu impf*).

H

ha *interj* (*indignation*) ха!; (*triumph*) ага́!; (*laughter*) ~!, ~! ха-ха́!

haberdashery *n* галантере́я.

habit *n* привы́чка; **from ~** по привы́чке; **bad ~s** дурны́е привы́чки; **he's a creature of ~** он в плену́/во вла́сти свои́х привы́чек; **to get into/out of the ~ of** привыка́ть к + *D or* + *inf*, отвыка́ть от + *G or* + *inf*; **this has become a ~ with her** э́то вошло́ у неё в привы́чку; **to cure smb of the ~ of smoking** отуча́ть кого́-л кури́ть/от куре́ния; **he's got into the** (*annoying*) **~ of disturbing my mornings** он завёл себе́ мане́ру беспоко́ить меня́ по утра́м.

habitable *adj* го́дный для жилья́.

habitat *n Zool*, *Bot* ареа́л.

habitation *n* жильё; **the house is not fit for ~** э́тот дом неприго́ден для жилья́; **there was no sign of ~** там не́ было никаки́х при́знаков жилья́.

habit-forming *adj*: **these pills are ~** к э́тим табле́ткам привыка́ешь.

habitual *adj* (*usual*) обы́чный; (*of what has become a habit*) привы́чный; **my ~ time of getting up is 7 o'clock** я обы́чно встаю в семь часо́в; **with his ~ gesture he knocked off his cigarette ash** привы́чным движе́нием он стряхну́л пе́пел с сигаре́ты; *pejor* **a ~ liar/offender** отъя́вленный/закорене́лый лжец, матёрый престу́пник.

habitually *adv* привы́чно; по привы́чке; **he's ~ late for school** он ве́чно опа́здывает в шко́лу.

hack[1] *n* (*notch*) засе́чка; (*blow*): **a ~ on the shins** уда́р по ноге́ (*sing*).

hack[1] *vt* руби́ть (*impf*) *and compounds*; **to ~ down a tree** сруб|а́ть де́рево (-и́ть); **he ~ed his way through the undergrowth** он проруби́л себе́ доро́гу сквозь за́росли (*pl*); **to ~ in pieces** разруб|а́ть (-и́ть); **he ~ed at the log with an axe** он уда́рил/*CQ* рубану́л по поле́ну топоро́м; *joc* **in the old days the surgeon would just have ~ed his leg off** ра́ньше хиру́рг про́сто оття́пал бы ему́ но́гу.

hack[2] *n* ло́шадь; *pejor* кля́ча; *fig* (*writer*) писа́ка (*m*).

hacking *adj*: **a ~ cough** сухо́й ка́шель.

hackneyed *adj*: **a ~ expression** изби́тое/зата́сканное выраже́ние.

hacksaw *n* ножо́вка

haddock *n* пи́кша.

haemorrhage *n* кровоизлия́ние.

haemorrhoids *npl* геморро́й (*sing*).

haggard *adj* измождённый.

hail[1] *n Meteorol* град; *fig* **a ~ of blows** град уда́ров.

hail[1] *vi*: **it is ~ing** град идёт.

hail[2] *n* о́клик.

hail[2] *vti vt* оклик|а́ть (́-нуть); **I ~ed a passer-by** я окли́кнул прохо́жего; **he ~ed me from across the street** он окли́кнул меня́ с друго́й стороны́ у́лицы; **to ~ a taxi** подозва́ть такси́ (*usu pf*)

vi: **where do you ~ from?** отку́да вы ро́дом?

hailstone *n* гра́дина.

hailstorm *n* си́льный град; **there was a ~** прошёл си́льный град.

hair *n* **1** (*single*) во́лос; *dim* волосо́к; *collect or pl* во́лосы; **his ~ is black** у него́ чёрные во́лосы; **she has a few ~s on her chin** у неё не́сколько волоско́в на подборо́дке; **there's a ~ on your coat** у тебя́ како́й-то во́лос на пальто́; **he has a thick head of ~** у него́ густа́я шевелю́ра; **to brush/comb one's ~** причёсываться; **to grow one's ~** отпуска́ть во́лосы; **to have one's ~ done/waved** де́лать себе́ причёску/зави́вку; **she hadn't a ~ out of place** она́ была́ так аккура́тно причёсана; **the old man was tearing his ~ in his grief** стари́к от огорче́ния рвал на себе́ во́лосы; *attr*: **a ~ mattress** волосяно́й матра́ц

2 *fig uses*: **to split ~s** копа́ться в мелоча́х; **he didn't turn a ~** он и гла́зом не моргну́л; **I escaped death/the car missed him by a ~'s breadth** я был на волосо́к от сме́рти, маши́на чуть-чу́ть его́ не сби́ла; **it made my ~ stand on end** от э́того у меня во́лосы вста́ли ды́бом; **he was tearing his ~ over the accounts** счета́ привели́ его́ в отча́яние; **to let one's ~ down** отвести́ ду́шу.

hairbrush *n* щётка для воло́с.

hair-curlers *n usu pl* бигуди́ (*pl only*).

haircut *n* стри́жка; **I like your ~** мне нра́вится твоя́ стри́жка; **I need a ~** мне на́до подстри́чься.

hairdo *n* причёска, *CQ* укла́дка.

hairdresser *n* парикма́хер; (*shop*) **the ~'s** парикма́херская.

hair-drier *n* суши́лка (для воло́с).

hair oil *n* брильянти́н.

hairpin *n* шпи́лька; *attr*: *fig* **a ~ bend** круто́й поворо́т.

hair-raising *adj CQ* кошма́рный.

hair-splitting *n*: **that's just ~** э́то про́сто копа́ние в мелоча́х/ло́вля блох.

hair style *n* причёска.

hairy *adj* волоса́тый.

hale *adj*: **~ and hearty** здоро́вый и бо́дрый.

half *n and adj* **1** полови́на (*n*) + *G*; полови́нный (*adj*); **~ of the apples** полови́на я́блок; **~ the people/the money** полови́на люде́й/де́нег; **3 and a ~** три с полови́ной; **a good ~** до́брая полови́на; **your ~ is larger than mine** твоя́ часть бо́льше мое́й; **return ~** (*of ticket*) обра́тный биле́т; **in ~** попола́м (*adv*); **let's go halves (with the money)** дава́й поде́лим (де́ньги) попола́м; **to cut costs by ~** уме́ньшить расхо́ды вдвое́/наполови́ну (*advs*); **he never does things by halves** он ничего́ не де́лает наполови́ну; **we're on ~ rations** мы на полови́нном пайке́; *CQ* **he's too clever by ~** он сли́шком уж у́мный

2 *Sport*: (*in football*) **first/second ~** пе́рв|ый/втор|о́й тайм, (*in other games*) -ая/-а́я полови́на (игры́)

3 *translated by compound nouns formed by* пол- + *G sing of second noun, from which they take their gender*: **~ a kilometre** полкиломе́тра (*m*); **~ a dozen** полдю́жины (*f*); **~ an hour** полчаса́ (*m*); **~ a minute** полмину́ты (*f*); **~ a year** полго́да (*m*); [**NB** *in nom and A such nouns do not change*; *in oblique cases* пол- *is usu unchanged, but may become* полу- *throughout*; *the second noun declines normally*; *qualifying adjs go in nom or A pl for the nom and A, but in oblique cases agree in number and gender with the second noun*]: **every ~ hour** ка́ждые полчаса́; **for the last ~ year** за после́дние полго́да; **to be taken with ~ a glass of water** (*of pills*) запива́ть полстака́ном воды́; **after the first ~ hour** по́сле пе́рвого получа́са; **he's on ~ pay** он на полста́вки (*indecl*)

4 *translated by compound nouns with* полу- *in the nom* + *second noun in nom*; полу- *remains unchanged throughout*: **a ~ -moon/-circle** полуме́сяц, полукру́г; **in the shape of a ~-moon** в фо́рме полуме́сяца

5 *in expressions of time*: **~ past one/five** полови́на второ́го/шесто́го, *CQ* полвторо́го, полшесто́го [**NB** *rarely abbreviated in oblique cases*]; **I'll come about ~ past 12** я приду́ (приме́рно) в полови́не пе́рвого; **the shops open at ~ past 8** магази́ны открыва́ются в полови́не девя́того/*CQ* в полдевя́того; **from ~ past 6 to ~ past 7** с полови́ны седьмо́го до полови́ны восьмо́го

6: one and a ~ полтора́ (*m and neut*), полторы́ (*f*) [полу́тора *is used for all oblique cases*; *in nom and A the following noun is in G, in oblique cases the following noun is in pl and in same case as* полтора́; *adjs qualifying* полтора́ *in nom and A may be in nom or G pl, in oblique cases are pl and agree in case with* полтора́]: **a year and a ~** полтора́ го́да; **one and a ~ thousand men** полторы́ ты́сячи челове́к; **I waited a good hour and a ~** я ждал до́брые/до́брых полтора́ часа́; **during the last year and a ~** в тече́ние после́дних полу́тора лет; **a day and a ~** полтора́ дня (= 1.5 *working days*), *CQ* по́лтора су́ток (36 *hours*) [**NB** су́тки *has no sing*; *note stress* по́лтора су́ток].

half *adv* **1** наполови́ну; **~ full** напо́лненный наполови́ну/до полови́ны; **he was ~ asleep** он наполови́ну спал; **the work was only ~ done** рабо́та была́ сде́лана то́лько наполови́ну; **it was ~ raining, ~ snowing** шёл не то дождь, не то снег, шёл дождь со сне́гом; **~ laughing, ~ crying** смея́сь и пла́ча; **give me only ~ as much** дай мне вдво́е ме́ньше; **I paid ~ as much again** я (за)плати́л в полтора́ ра́за бо́льше

2 *CQ with neg* **not ~: it wasn't ~ bad** э́то бы́ло о́чень непло́хо; **it didn't ~ rain!** дождь лил как из ведра́; **he didn't ~ swear!** он не выбира́л выраже́ний; **he isn't ~ cunning** он бо́льно хитёр.

half-back *n Sport* полузащи́тник.

half-baked *adj* недопечённый; *fig CQ*: **a ~ idea** глу́пая зате́я; **he's ~** он с при́дурью.

half-circle *n* полукру́г.

half-dead *adj* полумёртвый; **~ with fright** полумёртвый от стра́ха.

half-empty *adj* полупусто́й.

half-fare *n*: **children pay ~** де́тский биле́т (сто́ит) в два ра́за деше́вле.

half-hearted *adj*: **he's rather ~ about the trip** э́та пое́здка его́ не привлека́ет; **he made a ~ attempt to leave/to pay** он реши́л бы́ло уйти́, но оста́лся, он хоте́л бы́ло заплати́ть сам, но не наста́ивал.

half-hour *n* полчаса́ (*m*).

half-kilo *n* полкилогра́мма (*m*), *CQ* полкило́ (*indecl*).

half-length *adj*: **a ~ portrait** поясно́й портре́т.

half-mast *n*: **a flag at ~** приспу́щенный флаг.

half-measure *n* полуме́ра.

half-moon *n* полуме́сяц.

halfpenny *n* полпе́нса (*m*).

half-pound *n* полфу́нта (*m*).

half-price *n* полцены́ (*f*); **I bought it (at) ~** я купи́л э́то за полцены́; **children go/pay ~** де́ти пла́тят полови́ну.

half-ticket *n* биле́т со ски́дкой пятьдеся́т проце́нтов.

half-time *n Sport* переры́в (ме́жду та́ймами).

half-volley *n* (*in tennis*) уда́р с полулёта.

halfway *adj*: **our house is ~ between the school and the theatre** мы живём на полпути́ ме́жду шко́лой и теа́тром; *fig* **~ measures** полуме́ры.

halfway *adv*: **we met ~ between home and the station** мы встре́тились на полпути́/на полдоро́ге ме́жду до́мом и ста́нцией; **we turned back ~** мы верну́лись с полдоро́ги; **~ up/down hill** на середи́не подъёма/спу́ска; *fig* **to meet smb ~** идти́ на усту́пки/компромисс с кем-л, пойти́ кому́-л навстре́чу (*adv*).

half-witted *adj* полоу́мный, придурковáтый.

half-yearly *adj* полугодово́й.

half-yearly *adv* раз в полго́да.

halibut *n* па́лтус.

hall *n* (*entrance*) пере́дняя; (*for concerts, etc.*) зал; (*hostel*) **~ of residence** общежи́тие; **student's dining ~** студе́нческая столо́вая; **town ~** ра́туша, зда́ние муниципалите́та.

hallo *interj see* **hullo.**

hallucination *n* галлюцина́ция.

halo *n Rel* нимб; *Astron* гало́.

halt[1] *n* **1** (*stop*): **we made a ~ halfway** мы сде́лали остано́вку (*in car or on foot*)/прива́л (*on walk*) на полпути́; **the car/work came to a ~** маши́на/рабо́та останови́лась, рабо́та прекрати́лась; **we've come to a ~ in our investigations** на́ше рассле́дование (*sing*) приостанови́лось; **we must call a ~ to this extravagance** на́до прекрати́ть э́то мотовство́; *Mil* **to call a ~** объяви́ть прива́л

2 (*stopping place*: *bus*) остано́вка, *Rail* полуста́нок.

halt[1] *vti* (*stop*) остан|а́вливать(ся) (-ови́ть(ся)); (*cut short*) прекра|ща́ть(ся) (-ти́ть(ся)); *Mil* **~!** стой!

halt[2] *vi* (*vacillate*) колеба́ться (по-); **in a ~ing voice** неуве́ренным го́лосом.

halve *vt* (*divide in half*) дели́ть попола́м (раз-, по-); (*reduce by half*) уменьш|а́ть вполови́ну/вдво́е (-ить); **that will ~ the profits** э́то вдво́е уме́ньшит/сократи́т при́были.

ham *n* (*gammon*) (копчёный) о́корок; (*smoked meat*) ветчина́; *attr*: **a ~ sandwich** бутербро́д с ветчино́й.

hamburger *n* бу́лочка с (ру́бленой) котле́той.

ham-fisted, ham-handed *adj* неуклю́жий.

hamlet *n* дереву́шка.

hammer *n* молото́к; *Mus* (*of piano*) молоточек; **sledge ~** мо́лот; **~ and sickle** серп и мо́лот; **auctioneer's ~** молото́к аукционе́ра; **to come under the ~** продава́ться с молотка́; *Sport* **to throw the ~** мета́ть мо́лот.

hammer *vti vt* **1**: **to ~ in a nail/a wedge** за|бива́ть гвоздь (молотко́м), в|бива́ть клин (*pfs* -би́ть); **to ~ down the lid of a box** заби́ть кры́шку я́щика; **to ~ out a dent** вы|правля́ть вмя́тину (-править)

2 *fig uses*: **I ~ed the idea into his head** я втолкова́л ему́ э́то, я вдолби́л ему́ э́то в го́лову; **we ~ed out the terms of the agreement** мы вы́работали усло́вия догово́ра

vi: **he ~ed away in his shed all day** он весь день стуча́л молотко́м в сара́е; **to ~ at the door** бараба́нить/колоти́ть в дверь (*impfs*); *fig CQ*: **he ~ed away at the point until he got them to agree** он бил в одну́ то́чку, пока́ не уговори́л их; **I ~ed away at my thesis all week** я всю неде́лю, не разгиба́ясь, сиде́л над диссерта́цией; **we ~ed away at the contract all morning** мы би́лись над составле́нием контра́кта всё у́тро.

hammock *n* гама́к.

hamper *n* (больша́я) корзи́на; **a laundry/picnic ~** корзи́на для белья́, корзи́на с едо́й.

hamper *vt*: **the children ~ my work** де́ти меша́ют мне рабо́тать; **the roadworks were ~ed by bad weather** плоха́я пого́да меша́ла доро́жным рабо́там; **his movements were ~ed by his heavy overcoat** тяжёлое пальто́ стесня́ло его́ движе́ния.

hamster *n* хомя́к.

hand *n* **1** рука́; кисть [**NB** рука́ *also* = *arm*; *to distinguish use* кисть руки́]; **I've hurt my ~** я повреди́л себе́ кисть руки́; **the palm of the ~** ладо́нь; **the back of the ~** ты́льная сторона́ руки́; **to drink from cupped ~s** пить во́ду из го́рсти (*sing*); **with one's bare/own ~s** го́лыми/со́бственными рука́ми; **he shook ~s with me** он пожа́л мне ру́ку (*sing*); **I took her by the ~** я взял её за́ руку; **they were holding ~s** они́ взяли́сь/держа́лись за́ руки; **to vote by show of ~s** голосова́ть поднятием руки́ (*sing*); *CQ*: **I've only one pair of ~s!** у меня́ то́лько две руки́!; **wait till I get my ~s on him!** вот попадётся он мне в ру́ки!

2 *phrases with preps*: **I stood at/on his right ~** я стоя́л спра́ва от него́; **near at ~** поблизости (*adv*); **I haven't a pencil at/to ~** у меня́ под руко́й нет карандаша́; **I wrote him by ~** я ему́ написа́л от руки́; **to send a letter by ~** посла́ть письмо́ с на́рочным; **these rugs are made by ~** э́ти ковры́ ручно́й рабо́ты; **to pass smth from ~ to ~** переда́ть что-л из рук в ру́ки; **they walked ~ in ~** они́ шли рука́ о́б руку; **to go down on one's ~s and knees** (в)стать на четвере́ньки; **~s off!** ру́ки прочь!; **~s up!** (*surrender*) ру́ки вверх!, (*in school*) подними́те ру́ки!

3 (*of clock, instrument*) стре́лка

4 (*measure*: *approx* 10 *cm*): **a horse 16 ~s high** ло́шадь в хо́лке сто шестьдеся́т сантиме́тров

5 *Cards*: **to play a ~ of bridge** сыгра́ть па́ртию в бридж; **to win a ~** вы́играть па́ртию; **I've a good ~** у меня́ хоро́шие ка́рты (*pl*)

6 (*writing*) по́черк; **a clear ~** я́сный по́черк

7 (*workman, etc.*): **a lot of ~s are off with flu** о́чень мно́го рабо́чих больны́ гри́ппом; *Naut* матро́с; **all ~s on deck!** все наве́рх!; *fig* **he's a good ~ in committee** у него́ большо́й о́пыт рабо́ты в коми́ссии

8 *fig phrases with preps*: **winter was at ~** зима́ была́ на носу́; **I heard it at first/second ~** я э́то узна́л из пе́рвых/тре́тьих рук; **the work is in ~** рабо́та уже́ ведётся; **the matter in ~** (*agenda*) пове́стка дня; **stick to the matter in ~** не отклоня́йтесь от су́ти де́ла, бли́же к де́лу; **the management have the matter in ~** дире́кция приняла́ необходи́мые ме́ры; **the**

teacher has his class well in ~ учитель держит класс в руках; **the class is quite out of ~** ученики совсем отбились от рук; **he's in good ~s** он в хороших руках; **to take oneself in ~** взять себя в руки; **I'll put that in ~ for tomorrow** я займусь этим завтра; **I'll put it in the ~s of my lawyer** я поручу это моему адвокату; **I took matters into my own ~s** я взял дело (*sing*) в свои руки; **when I get this article/it off my ~s** когда я закончу эту статью, когда я сбуду это с рук; **on every ~, on all ~s** со всех сторон; **on the one ~... on the other ~** с одной стороны... с другой стороны; **he's on ~ if wanted** он на месте, если понадобится; **he's got a big family/job on his ~s** у него на руках большая семья, у него сейчас очень важная работа; **I've time on my ~s** у меня есть время; **he was condemned out of ~** его обвинили огульно, *Law* его приговорили, не разобравшись, в чём дело; *Comm*: **cash in ~** наличные деньги; **your letter of the 20th May to ~** я получил ваше письмо от двадцатого мая

9 *fig phrases with adjs*: **let's give him a big ~** давайте ему как следует похлопаем; **to rule with a firm ~** править твёрдой рукой; **he gave me a free/a helping ~** он предоставил мне свободу действий, он оказал мне помощь; **I've got my ~s full (with those children)** у меня дел по горло (с этими детьми); **he had the upper ~ of me** он одержал/взял надо мной верх

10 *fig phrases with verbs*: **they are ~ in glove** они два сапога пара; **she'll be a good teacher when she gets her ~ in** вот наберётся она опыта и будет хорошим педагогом; **the flat has changed ~s recently** в квартиру недавно въехали новые жильцы; **he never does a ~'s turn** он и пальцем не пошевельнёт [**NB** *tense*]; **he must have had a ~ in this** он наверняка приложил к этому руку; **I had no ~ in it** в этом я не принимал участия; **I can't lay ~s on the map just now** сейчас у меня нет карты под рукой; **he took whatever he could lay ~s on** он брал всё, что попадалось под руку; **they live from ~ to mouth** они перебиваются кое-как; **he makes money ~ over fist** он деньги лопатой загребает; **my ~s are tied** у меня связаны руки; **he can turn his ~ to anything** он на все руки мастер; **I want to try my ~ at embroidery** хочу научиться вышивать; *CQ*: **I wash my ~s of it!** я умываю руки!; **we won ~s down** мы запросто/шутя выиграли.

hand *vt* переда|вать (-ть); вруч|ать (-ить); **he ~ed me the letter** он передал/вручил/отдал мне письмо; **the waiter ~ed me a telegram** официант подал мне телеграмму; *fig CQ* **you've got to ~ it to him for courage** храбрости у него не отнимешь

hand down *vt*: **could you ~ me down that book from the shelf?** пожалуйста, подайте мне эту книгу с полки; **to ~ down a legend/custom** передавать (из поколения в поколение) легенду/обычай; **the picture was ~ed down to me from my grandfather** картина перешла ко мне по наследству от деда

hand in *vt*: **to ~ in an application** пода|вать заявление (-ть)

hand on *vt* передавать

hand out *vt* разда|вать (-ть)

hand over *vt* передавать

hand round *vt*: **to ~ round sweets** пред|лагать конфеты (-ложить).

handbag *n* сумка, (*small*) сумочка.

handball *n* гандбол.

handbook *n* (*manual*) руководство.

handbrake *n* ручной тормоз *or CQ* ручник.

hand cream *n* крем для рук; **I use ~ every night** на ночь я смазываю руки кремом.

handcuff *vt*: **to ~ smb** наде|вать кому-л наручники (-ть).

hand-down *n CQ*: **I don't like wearing my sister's ~s** я терпеть не могу щеголять в обносках сестры.

handful *n* горсть, пригоршня; **a ~ of flour** горсть муки; *fig*: **a ~ of students** горстка студентов; *CQ* **he's a real ~!** он сущее наказание!

handicap *n* **1** (*obstacle*) помеха, препятствие; (*defect*) недостаток; (*physical*) физический недостаток, увечье; **his stutter is a big ~ to him** заикание очень мешает ему в жизни; **his physical ~ prevents him from driving** из-за своего увечья он не может водить машину

2 *Sport* (*in race for bicycles or horses*) гандикап; (*of people racing*) **he was given a ~ of 5 metres** ему дали фору пять метров.

handicapped *adj*: **a physically/mentally ~ child** физически недоразвитый ребёнок, умственно отсталый ребёнок; *as n*: **the physically ~ receive an allowance** инвалиды получают пособие.

handicraft *n* ремесло; **he teaches ~s** он обучает ремеслу (*sing*); **an exhibition of ~** выставка изделий (*pl*) народных промыслов.

handiwork *n* (ручная) работа; **come and see my ~** посмотри мою работу; *fig* **is this your ~?** это твоя работа?, это твоих рук дело?

handkerchief *n* (носовой) платок.

handle *n* ручка; (*of tools*) рукоятка, черенок; **door ~** дверная ручка; **~ of a teapot/suitcase** ручка чайника/чемодана; **~ of a spade/knife/an axe** рукоятка лопаты, черенок ножа, топорище; *fig* **to fly off the ~** выйти из себя.

handle *vt* **1** (*touch*) тро|гать (-нуть); обращаться с + *I* (*only in impf*); **do not ~ the exhibits** экспонаты руками не трогать; **~ the manuscript carefully** обращайтесь с рукописью осторожно; **he was roughly ~d by the hooligans** хулиганы избили его; *Sport* **to ~ the ball** трогать мяч/прикасаться к мячу руками

2 (*control*): **he can ~ a horse/a gun/his subordinates** он знает, как обращаться с лошадью/с автоматом/с подчинёнными; **he couldn't ~ such a large class** он не мог справиться с таким большим классом; **to ~**

a tractor водить трактор (*impf*); **this car is easy to ~** этой машиной легко управлять

3 (*deal with*): **this matter needs to be ~d with care** это дело требует тонкого подхода; **he needs to be gently ~ed** с ним нужно обращаться мягко; **I can't ~ this matter on my own** я с этим сам не могу справиться; **the accounts department will ~ this** это дело будет вести бухгалтерия; **we don't ~ live cargo** мы не занимаемся перевозкой живого груза; **this airport ~s 10,000 passengers daily** этот аэропорт ежедневно обслуживает десять тысяч пассажиров.

handlebar *n* руль (*m*) (велосипеда).

hand-luggage *n* ручной багаж.

handmade *adj*: **this is ~** это ручная работа; **~ furniture** мебель ручной работы.

handout *n*: **(the text of) a press ~** текст заявления для печати.

hand-picked *adj*: **~ troops** отборные войска; **~ apples** яблоки, отсортированные вручную (*adv*).

handrail *n* поручень (*m*), перила (*no sing*).

handshake *n* рукопожатие.

handsome *adj* (*good-looking*) красивый; (*generous*) щедрый; (*considerable*) значительный, большой; **he's very ~** он очень красив, он красавец; **to make a ~ profit** получить большую прибыль.

handwriting *n* почерк.

handwritten *adj*: **the letter is ~** письмо написано от руки.

handy *adj* **1** (*convenient*) удобный; **it's a ~ little cooker/knife** это удобная плитка, этим ножом удобно резать; **that'll come in very ~** это будет очень кстати (*adv*)

2 (*skilful*): **she's ~ with a needle/in the kitchen** она хорошо шьёт, она умеет хорошо готовить

3 (*nearby*): **have you got a bus timetable ~?** у вас есть под рукой расписание автобусов?; **our house is ~ for the station** от нашего дома удобно добираться до станции.

handyman *n*: **he works as a ~** *approx* он выполняет мелкие работы; **my husband is quite a ~** мой муж умеет многое делать сам.

hang *n CQ*: **I didn't get the ~ of what he was saying** я не понял, что он говорил; **I haven't got the ~ of this sewing machine** я не умею обращаться с этой швейной машиной; **I don't give/care a ~** мне наплевать, мне до лампочки.

hang *vti vt* **1** вешать (повесить) *and compounds*; **~ your coat on a peg/in the cupboard** повесь пальто на крючок/в шкаф; **to ~ washing on the line/curtains** вешать бельё на верёвку/занавески (на окна); **to ~ one's head** вешать голову; **to ~ pictures on a wall** повесить картины на стену; **her pictures were hung in the exhibition/are well hung** её картины были на выставке/хорошо развешаны; **the walls are hung with tapestries** стены увешаны гобеленами; **to ~ a door (on its hinges)** наве|шивать дверь (на петли) (-сить); **to ~ wallpaper** окле|ивать стены обоями (-ть); **to ~ meat** подве|шивать тушу (-сить)

2: **he was ~ed for murder** он был повешен за убийство; **to ~ oneself** повеситься

3 *CQ*: **~ it!** чёрт возьми!; **I'm ~ed if I know** я не знаю, хоть убей

vi **1** висеть (*impf*); **the picture ~s on the wall/over the fireplace** картина висит на стене/над камином; **your coat is ~ing on the peg/in the cupboard** ваше пальто висит на крючке/в шкафу; **the lamp ~s from the ceiling** лампа висит под потолком

2 (*of clothes*): **the dress ~s well** платье хорошо сидит; **after her illness her clothes just ~ on her** после болезни платье (*sing*) просто висит на ней

3 *fig uses*: **the work is ~ing fire** работа приостановлена; **his life ~s by a thread** его жизнь (висит) на волоске

hang about *vi* слоняться (*impf*)

hang back *vi*: **she hung back through shyness** из-за своей застенчивости она держалась в сторонке; **everyone is ~ing back till smb gives a lead** все ждут, пока кто-нибудь другой начнёт

hang down *vi* висеть; **her hair hung down to her waist** волосы у неё были до пояса; **your slip is ~ing down** у тебя видна комбинация

hang on *vi*: **he hung on to my hand**/*fig* **to the idea** он держал меня за руку, он ухватился за эту идею; *fig* (*depend on*): **all ~s on his decision** всё зависит от его решения; *CQ* **~ on a moment** подожди минутку; **I'm ~ing on to the ring I found** я храню кольцо, которое нашёл

hang out *vti vt*: **to ~ out washing/flags** вы|вешивать бельё/флаги (-весить)

vi sl (*live*): **where do they ~ out?** где они живут?

hang over *vi*: **clouds hung over the mountains** тучи низко висели над горами; *fig* **exams are ~ing over me** мне предстоят экзамены

hang together *vi fig*: **all will be well if we ~ together** если будем держаться вместе, всё будет хорошо; **his argument ~s together well** все его аргументы (*pl*) логичны/последовательны; **the two parts of the report don't ~ together** эти две части доклада противоречат друг другу

hang up *vti vt* вешать (*see* **hang** *vt* **1**); *Tel* **~ up your receiver** положите трубку; *fig* **we're hung up waiting for raw materials** у нас перебои с сырьём (*collect*)

vi: *Tel* **he hung up (on me)** он положил трубку (,не дав мне договорить).

hangar *n* ангар.

hanger *n* (*for clothes*) вешалка, плечики (*pl*).

hanger-on *n*: **the house is always full of her hangers-on** дом вечно полон её поклонниками.

hanging *n* **1** *pl* (**~s**) (*US*: *curtains*) занавески, драпировки

2 (*for crime*) пове́шение; *attr CQ*: **it's not a ~ matter** за э́то не пове́сят.

hanging *adj* вися́чий.

hangover *n*: **I've got a ~** *CQ* я с похме́лья.

hank *n*: **a ~ of wool** мото́к ше́рсти.

hanker *vi*: **I ~ for a cup of tea/after city life** я мечта́ю о ча́шке ча́ю, я тоску́ю по городско́й жи́зни.

hankie *n CQ* плато́чек.

hanky-panky *n CQ*: **there's evidently some ~ going on here** здесь я́вно каки́е-то ко́зни.

haphazard *adj*: **the choice was ~** э́то был случа́йный вы́бор; **their choice of route was ~** они́ вы́брали доро́гу наобу́м; **his method of working is ~** он рабо́тает без вся́кой систе́мы.

happen *vi* **1** (*occur*) случ|а́ться (-и́ться); прои|сходи́ть (-зойти́); **what ~ed to him?** что с ним случи́лось?; **if anything ~s to me** е́сли со мной что́-нибудь случи́тся; **whatever ~s** что́ бы ни случи́лось; **the accident ~ed through the carelessness of the driver** ава́рия произошла́ из-за небре́жности води́теля; **what ~ed next?** что бы́ло пото́м?

2 (*chance*) ока́з|ываться (-а́ться); *or use adv* случа́йно; **I ~ed to have £10 on me** у меня́ оказа́лось де́сять фу́нтов; **he ~ed to be there** он случа́йно оказа́лся там; **I ~ed to run into him at the concert** я встре́тился с ним на конце́рте соверше́нно случа́йно; **she ~ed on that occasion to be telling the truth** как ни стра́нно, но на э́тот раз она́ сказа́ла пра́вду; **well, I ~ to like him** как ни стра́нно, он мне нра́вится; **as it ~s, I shall be in today** как раз сего́дня я бу́ду до́ма

3: **to ~ on smth** случа́йно найти́ что-л.

happening *n* слу́чай; собы́тие.

happily *adv* счастли́во; **they are ~ married** э́то счастли́вая па́ра; **~ I found her ring** к сча́стью, я нашёл её кольцо́; **the children were playing ~** де́ти ве́село игра́ли.

happiness *n* сча́стье.

happy *adj* **1** *attr* счастли́вый; (*felicitous*) уда́чный; **a ~ day** счастли́вый день; **a ~ choice** уда́чный вы́бор; **what a ~ thought!** кака́я уда́чная/счастли́вая мысль!; **H. New Year!** С Но́вым Го́дом!; **~ birthday!** (поздравля́ю) с днём рожде́ния!

2 *predic* (*pleased*) рад (*no attr form*), сча́стлив [**NB** *stress*]; **I am ~ you can come** я рад/сча́стлив, что вы смо́жете прийти́; **I shall be ~ to do it** я бу́ду рад сде́лать э́то.

happy-go-lucky *adj*: **he has a ~ temperament** у него́ беспе́чный/беззабо́тный хара́ктер.

harangue *vt*: **he ~d us for hours on that subject** он до́лго сиде́л с на́ми и разглаго́льствовал на э́ту те́му.

harassed *adj* задёрганный, заму́ченный.

harbour, (*US*) **harbor** *n* га́вань, порт; *attr*: **~ dues** порто́вые сбо́ры; **~ master** нача́льник по́рта.

harbour, (*US*) **harbor** *vt*: **to ~ an escaped criminal** укры|ва́ть бе́глого престу́пника (-́ть); **feather mattresses ~ fleas** в пухо́вых матра́сах заво́дятся бло́хи; **he ~s a grudge against me** он затаи́л на меня́ оби́ду [**NB** *tense*].

hard *adj* **1** (*firm*) твёрдый; (*rigid*) жёсткий; **~ ground** твёрдый грунт; **a ~ bed/chair** жёсткая крова́ть, жёсткий стул; **~ water** жёсткая вода́; *Rail* **a ~ carriage** жёсткий ваго́н; *Ling* **a ~ consonant** твёрдый согла́сный; *Gram* **the ~ sign** твёрдый знак

2 (*difficult*) тру́дный, тяжёлый; **a ~ task** тру́дное/тяжёлое де́ло; **it's ~ to say** тру́дно сказа́ть; **he's ~ to please** ему́ тру́дно угоди́ть; **it's ~ for me to say good-bye to my parents** мне тяжело́ расстава́ться с роди́телями; **~ times** тяжёлые времена́

3 (*severe*): **a ~ father** стро́гий оте́ц; **he's ~ on his son** он сли́шком строг с сы́ном; **a ~ heart** жесто́кое се́рдце; **~ facts** жесто́кие фа́кты; **a ~ climate/winter** суро́вый кли́мат, суро́вая зима́; **~ frost** си́льный моро́з

4 (*strong, strenuous*): **a ~ blow** си́льный/тяжёлый уда́р; **~ liquor** кре́пкие напи́тки (*pl*); **a ~ worker** усе́рдный (*zealous*)/приле́жный (*diligent*) рабо́тник; **he's a ~ drinker** он си́льно пьёт

5 *phrases*: **~ of hearing** туго́ухий; **he drives a ~ bargain** с ним тру́дно договори́ться о цене́, (*in negotiations*) он нелегко́ идёт на усту́пки; **he's ~ on his shoes** он бы́стро изна́шивает о́бувь; **she had ~ luck** ей не повезло́; **he was sentenced to ~ labour** его́ приговори́ли к ка́торжным рабо́там (*pl*); *Fin*: **~ currency** (обрати́мая) валю́та; **to pay in ~ cash** плати́ть нали́чными.

hard *adv* **1** (*strongly*) си́льно; **to pull ~** си́льно тяну́ть; **it was raining/snowing/freezing ~** шёл си́льный дождь/снег, си́льно подморо́зило; **we were ~ pressed by the enemy/for time** проти́вник нас си́льно тесни́л, нас си́льно поджима́ло вре́мя; **we're ~ at it, we're working ~** мы напряжённо/мно́го рабо́таем; **I tried ~/my ~est** я о́чень стара́лся, я стара́лся изо все́х си́л; **I must think ~ about this** мне э́то на́до хороше́нько проду́мать; **they drank ~ yesterday** они́ вчера́ кре́пко вы́пили

2 (*closely*): **she/the car followed ~ behind** она́/маши́на шла по пята́м; **he's ~ on 40** ему́ ско́ро со́рок; **the school is ~ by our house** шко́ла недалеко́ от на́шего до́ма/ря́дом с на́шим до́мом

3: **I was ~ put to it to choose between them** мне бы́ло тру́дно вы́брать ме́жду ни́ми; **they are very ~ up** у них пло́хо/ту́го с деньга́ми; **he was ~ done by** с ним пло́хо/несправедли́во обошли́сь; **he took it pretty ~** он тяжело́ воспри́нял э́то.

hard-and-fast *adj*: **a ~ rule/decision** твёрдое пра́вило/реше́ние.

hardback *n* кни́га в жёстком переплёте.

hard-bitten *adj*: *CQ* **my landlord is a ~ old devil** мой хозя́ин стре́ляный воробе́й.

hard-boiled *adj*: **a ~ egg** яйцо́ вкруту́ю (*adv*); *fig* **he's ~** он жёсткий челове́к.

hard-earned *adj*: **~ money** с трудо́м зарабо́танные де́ньги.

harden *vti vt*: **to ~ steel**/*fig* **troops** закал|ять сталь, обуч|а́ть войска́ (*pfs* -и́ть); *fig*: **he ~ed his heart and showed her no mercy** се́рдце его́ ожесточи́лось, и он не прояви́л к ней никако́й жа́лости; **a ~ed criminal** закорене́лый престу́пник

vi (*set*) тверде́ть (за-); **the cement has ~ed** цеме́нт затверде́л; *fig* **his expression ~ed** лицо́ у него́ ста́ло суро́вым/посуро́вело.

hard-headed *adj*: **he's a ~ business man** в дела́х у него́ есть хва́тка.

hard-hearted *adj* чёрствый, бессерде́чный.

hardly *adv* **1** (*badly*): **he was ~ treated** с ним обошли́сь несправедли́во

2 (*scarcely*) едва́, е́ле; с трудо́м; почти́ + *neg*; (*suggesting improbability*) едва́ ли, вря́д ли; **we'd ~ left the house when it began to rain** едва́ мы вы́шли и́з дому, как пошёл дождь; **we had ~ time for a snack** мы едва́ успе́ли перекуси́ть; **we ~ recognized him** мы с трудо́м узна́ли его́; **I can ~ believe it** я с трудо́м могу́ пове́рить э́тому; **we ~ know her** мы её почти́ не зна́ем; **~ anybody came** почти́ никто́ не пришёл; **she ate ~ anything** она́ почти́ ничего́ не е́ла; **he'll ~ come now** вря́д ли он придёт сейча́с; **it's ~ worth waiting any longer** едва́ ли сто́ит ещё ждать; **we can ~ ask him to pay** неудо́бно проси́ть его́ заплати́ть за э́то.

hardship *n* тру́дности (*pl*); **to undergo ~s** переноси́ть тру́дности; **it's surely no great ~ for you to get up an hour early** тебе́ не та́к уж тру́дно встать на час пора́ньше; **they suffered many ~s** они́ мно́го пережи́ли.

hardware *n* металли́ческие изде́лия (*pl*); *attr*: **~ shop** *approx* магази́н хозя́йственных това́ров.

hard-wearing *adj*: **this material is ~** э́та ткань хороша́ в но́ске/но́ская.

hardwood *n* твёрдая древеси́на.

hare *n* за́яц.

hare-brained *adj*: **he is ~** у него́ кури́ные мозги́.

harelip *n* за́ячья губа́.

harem *n* гаре́м.

haricot bean *n* фасо́ль (*collect*).

harm *n* **1** (*hurt*) вред; **he/the wine will do you no ~** он/вино́ не причини́т тебе́ вреда́; **what ~ is there in taking a swim?** что стра́шного, е́сли мы искупа́емся?; **they came to no ~** с ни́ми ничего́ плохо́го не случи́лось, от э́того им ху́же не ста́ло; **it would do you no ~ to have a haircut** тебе́ не меша́ло бы подстри́чься; **put the vase out of ~'s way** убери́ ва́зу пода́льше от греха́

2 (*damage*): **the storm did a lot of ~** бу́ря нанесла́/причини́ла большо́й уще́рб.

harm *vt* вреди́ть + *D* (по-); причин|я́ть вред + *D* (-и́ть).

harmful *adj* вре́дный.

harmless *adj* безоби́дный; **a ~ prank** безоби́дная проде́лка; **the dog looks fierce but he's ~** у пса то́лько вид свире́пый, на са́мом де́ле он безоби́дный; **a ~ snake** неядови́тая змея́.

harmonica *n* аккордео́н; гармо́нь, *CQ* гармо́шка.

harmonious *adj* гармони́чный.

harmonize *vti vt Mus* гармонизи́ровать (*impf and pf*)

vi (*of colours, etc.*): **to ~ with** гармони́ровать с + *I* (*impf*).

harmony *n Mus* гармо́ния, *also fig*.

harness *n* у́пряжь.

harness *vt* (*a horse*) запря|га́ть (-́чь); *fig* **to ~ natural resources** испо́льзовать есте́ственные ресу́рсы (*impf and pf*).

harp *n* а́рфа.

harp *vi*: **she's always ~ing on about her grievances** она́ ве́чно жа́луется на свои́ бе́ды.

harpsichord *n* клавеси́н.

harrowing *adj* мучи́тельный.

harsh *adj* ре́зкий; (*severe*) суро́вый; **a ~ voice/contrast/light/wind** ре́зкий го́лос/контра́ст/свет/ве́тер; **~ words** ре́зкие слова́; **a ~ winter/punishment** суро́вая зима́, суро́вое наказа́ние; **a ~ judge** стро́гий судья́.

harum-scarum *adj*: **a ~ child** шалу́н.

harvest *n* урожа́й; **a bumper/poor ~** бога́тый/плохо́й урожа́й; **wheat ~** урожа́й пшени́цы; **everyone is working at the ~** все рабо́тают на убо́рке урожа́я.

harvest *vti* у|бира́ть урожа́й (-бра́ть); **to ~ rice/wheat** убира́ть рис/пшени́цу.

harvester *n* (*man*) жнец; (*machine*) комба́йн.

hash *n* (*meat*): *pejor* **again this ~ for supper!** *approx* опя́ть э́ти котле́ты!; *fig* **he made a ~ of the job/of the accounts** он всё там напу́тал с рабо́той/со счета́ми.

haste *n* спе́шка; **why all this ~?** заче́м така́я спе́шка?; **in my ~ I forgot my umbrella** в спе́шке я забы́л свой зо́нтик; **I made ~ to help her** я поспеши́л ей на по́мощь; **make ~!** потороп́ись!

hasten *vti vt*: **to ~ a process** ускор|я́ть проце́сс (-́ить)

vi спеши́ть, торопи́ться (*pfs* по-); **he ~ed home/to apologize** он торопи́лся домо́й, он поспеши́л извини́ться; **I ~ to add that...** я до́лжен доба́вить, что...

hastily *adv* (*hurriedly*) поспе́шно, торопли́во; второпя́х, на́спех; (*without thought*) опроме́тчиво.

hasty *adj* (*quick*) бы́стрый; (*hurried or injudicious*) торопли́вый, поспе́шный; **a ~ glance/departure/decision** бы́стрый взгляд, поспе́шный отъе́зд, поспе́шное *or* опроме́тчивое реше́ние; **he's got a ~ temper** у него́ горя́чий нрав.

hat *n* (*man's, or woman's large-brimmed*) шля́па; (*woman's, small, close-fitting*) шля́пка; (*soft, warm, for man or woman*) ша́пка; **a fur/knitted/top ~** мехова́я ша́пка, вя́заная ша́почка, цили́ндр; **he raised his ~ to me** уви́дев меня́, он приподня́л шля́пу; *fig*: **to pass round the ~** пуска́ть ша́пку по кру́гу; **to keep smth under one's ~** зама́лчивать что-л; **he is talking through his ~** он несёт чушь; *CQ* **that's old ~** э́то анекдо́т с бородо́й; *attr*:

where is the ~ department? где отдéл головны́х убóров?; **~ box** картóнка для шляп.

hatch *n Naut* люк.

hatch *vti vt*: **to ~ eggs/chickens** (*of sitting hen*) вы|си́живать/(*in incubator*) вы|води́ть цыплят (-сидеть/-вести); *fig* **to ~ a plot** замышля́ть зáговор (*usu impf*)

vi (*of chickens, nestlings*) вы|лупля́ться (-лупиться).

hatchet *n* топóрик.

hate *n* нéнависть.

hate *vt* ненави́деть (*impf*); **I ~ rice/my uncle** я ненави́жу рис/своегó дя́дю; **I ~ getting up early/to bother you** я терпéть не могý *or* ненави́жу рáно вставáть, мне óчень не хóчется вас беспокóить.

hateful *adj* ненави́стный; **that ~ alarm clock** э́тот ненави́стный буди́льник; (*repulsive*) **a ~ crime** отврати́тельное/гнýсное преступлéние.

hatred *n* нéнависть; **~ of/for smb** нéнависть к комý-л.

haughty *adj* надмéнный.

haul *vti vt*: **the steamer was ~ing the barge** парохóд тянýл бáржу (*impf*); **the tractor was ~ing logs/a trailer** трáктор тащи́л брёвна/трéйлер (*impf*); **the goods train was ~ing timber** товáрный состáв перевози́л лес; **to ~ in nets/a boat up the beach** вы|тáскивать сéти/лóдку на бéрег (-тащить); **to ~ down a flag** спус|кáть флаг (-ти́ть); *fig* **to ~ smb over the coals** дать нагоня́й комý-л

vi: **to ~ on a rope** тянýть на канáте.

haulage *n*: **~ is expensive** транспорти́ровка/достáвка обхóдится дóрого.

haunch *n* бедрó (*of man or animal*); **he/the dog was sitting on his ~es** он сидéл на кóрточках (*no sing*), собáка сидéла; *Cook* **a ~ of venison** олéнья ногá.

haunt *vt*: **a ghost is said to ~ this house** в э́том дóме, говоря́т, вóдятся привидéния (*pl*); **a ~ed house** дом с привидéниями; **he is ~ed by remorse** егó мýчит сóвесть; **I am ~ed by memories of the past** меня́ преслéдуют воспоминáния прóшлого.

have *aux verb and vt* **1** *as aux verb forming past tenses*: **he has gone** он уéхал; **~ you seen the film?—Yes, I ~** вы (по)смотрéли э́тот фильм?—Да, (по)смотрéл; **you ought to ~ refused** вам слéдовало бы отказáться; **had I but known it** éсли бы я тóлько знал

2 *vt* (*possess: when owner is a person and object concrete or abstract*) у + *G* + быть; **i)** *in affirmative sentences* (быть *is not usu used in present tense, but 3rd pers sing* есть *may be used for emphasis with both sing or pl subjects*): **he has two sons** у негó два сы́на; **everyone has his problems** у кáждого свои́ проблéмы; **he has a good memory for names** у негó хорóшая пáмять на именá; **we had a visitor yesterday** вчерá у нас был гость; **I will ~ a lot of work tomorrow** зáвтра у меня́ бýдет мнóго рабóты; **all I ~ is at your disposal** всё, что у меня́ есть—в вáшем распоряжéнии; **ii)** *in interrog sentences* (есть *used in present tense*): **~ you a pencil on you?** у вас есть карандáш?; **had you enough money?** у вас бы́ло достáточно дéнег?; **will you ~ time to help me tomorrow?** у вас бýдет зáвтра врéмя помóчь мне?; (*in shop*) **~ you any fish today?** есть ли у вас сегóдня ры́ба?; (*in polite requests*) **~ you a match please?** у вас не найдётся спи́чки?; **iii)** *in neg sentences* у + *G followed by impers* нет, нé было, не бýдет + *G*: **I ~ no words to express my gratitude** у меня́ нет слов, чтóбы вы́разить (свою́) благодáрность; **he had no money** у негó нé было дéнег; **I will ~ no time for reading** у меня́ не бýдет врéмени на чтéние; **iv)** *in neg sentences such as*: **I/you, etc. have nothing to/no one to...**: **I ~ nothing to read** мне нéчего читáть; **I had/will ~ nothing to do on Friday** в пя́тницу мне бы́ло/бýдет нéчего дéлать; **I ~ no one to talk to** мне нé с кем поговори́ть

3 (*possess: when owner is not a person, or when owner is a person and object is abstract*) (не) имéть (*impf*); **I ~ no objection** ничегó не имéю прóтив; **this has nothing to do with me** э́то не имéет никакóго отношéния ко мне; **this building has two entrances** в э́том здáнии (имéются) два вхóда; **the play had a great success** пьéса имéла большóй успéх; **I ~ in mind the famous lines from Hamlet** я имéю в видý знамени́тые стрóки из «Гáмлета»; **our library has a lot of books** в нáшей библиотéке (имéется) мнóго книг; **he had the cheek to say that...** он имéл нáглость сказáть, что...

4 (*possess: other translations*): **he hadn't the courage to refuse** у негó не хвати́ло мýжества отказáться; **the house has three stories** в э́том дóме три этажá; **this hotel has a/has no bar** в э́той гости́нице есть бар/нет бáра; **the box had nothing in it** в корóбке ничегó нé было

5 (*obtain, acquire*): **I had a letter from her** я получи́л от неё письмó; **this is to be had on the market** э́то мóжно купи́ть/достáть на ры́нке; **there's nothing to be had here** здесь ничегó не полýчишь/добьёшься; (*of private deal*) **you can ~ the book for £2** два фýнта—и кни́га твоя́; **can you let me ~ £5?** мóжешь ли ты дать мне взаймы́ пять фýнтов?; **I'll let you ~ my reply tomorrow** зáвтра я дам тебé отвéт; **I ~ it on good authority that...** я знáю из достовéрного истóчника, что...

6 (*of illness*): **he has measles/a bad cold/a headache/a broken leg** он бóлен кóрью, у негó си́льный нáсморк, у негó боли́т головá, он сломáл нóгу

7 (*of food, drink*): **to ~ breakfast/dinner/supper** зáвтракать, обéдать, ýжинать (*pfs* по-); **what will we ~/are we having for dinner today?** что у нас (бýдет) на обéд сегóдня?; (*in restaurant*): **what will you ~ (to eat)?/to drink?** что вы бýдете есть?/пить?; **I'll ~ steak and ice cream** мне, пожáлуйста, бифштéкс и морóженое; **will you ~ some more**

coffee? хоти́те ещё ко́фе?; **do ~ some more meat** возьми́ ещё мя́са; **what wine will you ~ — red or white?** како́е бу́дешь пить вино́ — кра́сное и́ли бе́лое?; **~ a cigarette** хо́чешь сигаре́ту?; **do you ~ sugar?** (*in tea, etc.*) тебе́ с са́харом?

8 (*denoting obligation*): **I ~ to** + *inf* мне на́до/ну́жно + *inf* (= *must, because of external necessity*), мне придётся + *inf* (= *must, but also has sense of "it happens that"*), я до́лжен + *inf* (*it's my duty*), мне обяза́тельно на́до + *inf* (*is imperative*); **does this dress ~ to be ironed?** э́то пла́тье на́до погла́дить?; **you don't ~ to apologize** не ну́жно извиня́ться; **we will ~ to leave early** нам придётся ра́но уе́хать; **we had to get the doctor** нам пришло́сь вы́звать врача́; **I ~ to write to my mother** я до́лжен написа́ть ма́тери; **you don't ~ to book in advance, but it's advisable** зара́нее зака́зывать биле́ты не обяза́тельно, но жела́тельно

9 (*with comparative advs*): **you had better stay in bed** вам лу́чше полежа́ть в посте́ли; **I'd rather/sooner do it myself** я бы лу́чше сде́лал э́то сам

10 (*wish*): **which brooch will you ~?** каку́ю бро́шку ты возьмёшь?; **what more would you ~?** что вы ещё хоти́те?; **I would ~ you know that I'm in charge here** я бы хоте́л, что́бы вы по́мнили — я здесь гла́вный; **as ill luck would ~ it** как назло́

11 (*permit — always in neg sentences*): **I won't ~ it** я э́того не допущу́; **I won't ~ you leave without your breakfast** я не отпущу́ вас без за́втрака

12 (*causative*): **I must ~ my shoes repaired/my hair cut** мне ну́жно почини́ть ту́фли/подстри́чься; **I will ~ the carpenter mend the table** я попрошу́ пло́тника почини́ть стол; **I'm having a dress made** я шью себе́ пла́тье

13 (*as form of passive*): **I had my watch stolen** у меня́ укра́ли часы́; **three students had their names taken** имена́ трёх студе́нтов бы́ли запи́саны

14 (*insist, say*): **he will ~ it that...** он наста́ивает на том, что...; **the papers ~ it that...** газе́ты утвержда́ют, что...; **as Pushkin has it** как ска́зано у Пу́шкина

15 (*with noun phrases: usu use verbs formed from noun; see also noun entries*): **our dog had three puppies yesterday** вчера́ на́ша соба́ка принесла́ трёх щенко́в; **~ you change for a dollar?** ты мо́жешь разменя́ть мне до́ллар?; **I ~ no doubt** я не сомнева́юсь

16 *CQ expressions*: **you've been had** тебя́ обману́ли/провели́/наду́ли; **he had you there** ту́т-то ты ему́ и попа́лся; **I'll let him ~ it!** я ему́ зада́м!; **I've had it** (*I give up, am exhausted*) я сдаю́сь; **if you're going for the 2 o'clock train, you've had it** на двухчасово́й по́езд ты уже́ опозда́л; **I fear my watch has had it** бою́сь, мои́м часа́м коне́ц; **I ~ it!** я по́нял! (*comprehend*), я приду́мал! (*have a bright idea*); **~ it your own way** де́лай, как зна́ешь (*of action*), ду́май, что хо́чешь (*of opinion*); **we've never had it so good** нам никогда́ не́ было так хорошо́; **I'll bring the tent, sleeping bags and what ~ you** я принесу́ пала́тку, спа́льные мешки́, ну и всё остально́е

have in *vt*: **we're having people in tonight** ве́чером к нам приду́т го́сти; **we had them in for supper** мы пригласи́ли их на у́жин; **I ~ a cleaner in on Tuesdays** домрабо́тница прихо́дит ко мне по вто́рникам; *CQ* **I ~ it in for him** у меня́ про́тив него́ зуб

have on *vt*: **she has a hat/spectacles on** она́ в шля́пке/в очка́х; **don't believe him — he's having you on** не верь ему́ — он тебя́ за́ нос во́дит; **~ you anything on tomorrow?** за́втра ты за́нят?; **~ this** (*drink*)/**this round on me** я плачу́

have out *vt*: **I had a tooth out** мне удали́ли зуб; **I had it out with him** мы с ним объясни́лись

have up *vt*: **he was had up for theft** его́ привлекли́ к суду́ за воровство́.

haversack *n* рюкза́к; (*knapsack*) ра́нец.

havoc *n*: **the floods made ~ of the crops** наводне́ние (*sing*) погуби́ло/уничто́жило весь урожа́й (*sing*); **the storm caused terrible ~** бу́ря причини́ла больши́е разруше́ния (*pl*); **the children played ~ in the kitchen** де́ти устро́или на ку́хне каварда́к; **the wind played ~ with my hair** ве́тер растрепа́л мне во́лосы.

hawk *n* я́стреб.

hawker *n* у́личный торго́вец.

hawser *n* трос.

hawthorn *n* боя́рышник.

hay *n* се́но; **to make ~** коси́ть траву́ [NB сено = *grass already cut*]; **make ~ while the sun shines** коси́ коса́, пока́ роса́; *CQ* (*US*) **to hit the ~** ложи́ться спать.

hay fever *n* сенна́я лихора́дка.

hayfield *n* (*while grass is growing*) луг, (*when hay is cut*) ско́шенный луг.

haymaking *n* сеноко́с.

haystack *n* стог се́на.

haywire *adj and adv CQ*: **the television's gone ~** телеви́зор барахли́т.

hazard *n* риск.

hazard *vt* риск|ова́ть + *I or* + *inf* (-ну́ть); **climbers often ~ their lives** альпини́стам ча́сто прихо́дится рискова́ть жи́знью; **I ~ed the remark that...** я рискну́л заме́тить, что...; **I'd ~ the guess that...** я осме́люсь вы́сказать дога́дку, что...

hazardous *adj* риско́ванный.

haze *n* ды́мка, лёгкий тума́н.

hazel *n* (*tree*) оре́шник; (*tree or nut*) лесно́й оре́х.

hazel *adj*: **~ eyes** ка́рие глаза́.

hazelnut *n* (*nut*) лесно́й оре́х.

hazy *adj*: **~ weather** тума́нная пого́да; *fig* **I've a ~ idea I have read the book** мне ка́жется, я чита́л э́ту кни́гу.

he *pers pron* он; **he, who** тот, кто; *see also* **him.**

head *n* **1** голова́; **from ~ to foot** с головы́ до ног; **a blow on the ~** уда́р по голове́; **he fell off his horse ~ first** он упа́л с ло́шади вниз голово́й; **to stand on one's ~** стоя́ть на голове́; **he stumbled and fell ~ over heels** он споткну́лся и полете́л вверх торма́шками; **blood rushed to his ~** кровь бро́силась ему́ в го́лову; **to shake one's ~** (*in negation or disapproval*) отрица́тельно/неодобри́тельно кача́ть голово́й; **they've put a price on his ~** за его́ го́лову назна́чена награ́да; **the wine went to my ~** вино́ уда́рило мне в го́лову; *fig* **success has gone to his ~** успе́х вскружи́л ему́ го́лову

2 (*as measure*): **to win by a ~** опереди́ть на го́лову; **he's taller than his brother by a ~** он вы́ше бра́та на го́лову; *fig* **he's ~ and shoulders above the rest** он на́ голову вы́ше други́х [**NB** *changes of stress*]

3 (*as unit of calculation*): **300 ~ of cattle** три́ста голо́в скота́; **the cook spends 2 roubles a/per ~ per day** по́вар тра́тит по два рубля́ на челове́ка в день; **it cost 6 roubles a ~** э́то сто́ило шесть рубле́й с челове́ка [**NB** с челове́ка *each pays for himself*, на челове́ка *of routine expenditure*]

4 (*of things resembling a head*): **a ~ of cabbage** коча́н капу́сты; **~ of a pin/flower/nail** голо́вка була́вки/цветка́, шля́пка гвоздя́; **~ of an axe** о́бу́х топора́; **a glass of beer with a ~ on it** кру́жка пи́ва с ша́пкой пе́ны; **the abscess has come to a ~** у нары́ва появи́лась голо́вка; *fig* **things have come to a ~** кри́зис назре́л

5 (*front, top part, section*): **at the ~ of the table** во главе́ стола́; **to walk at the ~ of a procession** идти́ во главе́ проце́ссии; **at the ~ of a page/list** в нача́ле страни́цы/спи́ска; **there was a small table at the ~ of the bed** у изголо́вья крова́ти стоя́л сто́лик; **at the ~ of the stairs** на ве́рхней площа́дке ле́стницы (*sing*); **I shall treat my theme under three ~s** я бу́ду рассма́тривать э́ту те́му по трём пу́нктам; *Sport* **to be at the ~ of the field** быть впереди́

6 (*person*) глава́, руководи́тель (*m*); **the ~ of a state/family** глава́ госуда́рства/семьи́; **he is at the ~ of this firm** он стои́т во главе́ э́того предприя́тия; **~ of a department** нача́льник/руководи́тель отде́ла; **~ of the class** пе́рвый учени́к в кла́ссе

7 (*intellect, mind*) ум; **a clear ~** я́сный ум; **to count in one's ~** счита́ть в уме́; **two ~s are better than one** ум хорошо́, а два лу́чше; **he's off his ~** он не в своём уме́, он сошёл с ума́; **it's above my ~** э́то вы́ше моего́ понима́ния; **he has a good ~ on his shoulders** у него́ есть голова́ на плеча́х, он па́рень с голово́й; **use your ~!** поду́май хороше́нько!; **it never entered my ~** у меня́ и в мы́слях тако́го не́ было; **it never entered my ~ to charge them for it** мне и в го́лову не приходи́ло тре́бовать с них де́нег за э́то; **what put that into your ~?** отку́да така́я иде́я?; **it went clean out of my ~** э́то совсе́м вы́летело у меня́ из головы́; **he has an old ~ on young shoulders** он мудр не по лета́м/года́м; **he took it into his ~ to...** он забра́л себе́ в го́лову + *inf*; **let's put our ~s together** дава́й поду́маем вме́сте; **to lose one's ~** теря́ть го́лову

8 *fig uses*: **he has a good ~ for heights** он хорошо́ перено́сит высоту́; **he has a good ~ for figures** арифме́тика даётся ему́ легко́; **he has a strong ~ for drink** он мо́жет мно́го вы́пить; **on your ~ be it** пусть э́то бу́дет на твое́й со́вести; **he spoke to the Minister over the ~ of his director** он обрати́лся к мини́стру че́рез го́лову дире́ктора; **give him his ~** дай ему́ свобо́ду де́йствий (*and all will be well*), ему́ то́лько во́лю дай (*and disaster will follow*); **he's ~ over heels in love** он по́ уши влюблён; *CQ*: **we sat up all night talking our ~s off** мы говори́ли до са́мого утра́; **I've a bit of a ~ this morning** у меня́ сего́дня голова́ боли́т (с похме́лья)

9 *attr*: **the ~ surgeon/cook/waiter** гла́вный хиру́рг, шеф-по́вар, метрдоте́ль (*m*).

head *vti vt*: **he ~ed the boat towards shore/his horse towards home** он напра́вил ло́дку к бе́регу/ло́шадь к до́му; **he ~ed the delegation/expedition/poll** он возглавля́л делега́цию/экспеди́цию, он получи́л большинство́ голосо́в; **his name ~s the list** в спи́ске его́ и́мя стои́т пе́рвым; **to ~ off sheep/the enemy** прегра|жда́ть путь ста́ду ове́ц/врагу́ (-ди́ть); *fig* **~ him off that subject at all costs** то́лько не дава́й ему́ сади́ться на своего́ конька́

vi: **he ~ed southwards/for home** он пое́хал на юг, он отпра́вился домо́й; **he's ~ing for trouble** он напра́шивается на неприя́тности, он ле́зет на рожо́н.

headache *n* головна́я боль; **she has frequent ~s** у неё ча́сто боли́т голова́; **this will relieve your ~** э́то помо́жет тебе́ от головно́й бо́ли; **I have a (splitting) ~** у меня́ боли́т голова́, у меня́ раска́лывается/трещи́т голова́; *fig CQ*: **this is your ~** э́то твоя́ зада́ча; **it will be a real ~** э́то бу́дет про́сто кошма́р.

header *n CQ*: **to take a ~** упа́сть плашмя́.

heading *n* (*of document*) загла́вие, заголо́вок; (*in newspaper*: *headline*) заголо́вок, (*column*) ру́брика; **this article comes under the ~ of Sporting News** э́та статья́ пойдёт под ру́брикой «Но́вости спо́рта»; **does this book come under the ~ of biography or history?** куда́ отнести́ э́ту кни́гу — к биогра́фиям или к истори́ческим сочине́ниям? (*pls*).

headlamp *n see* **headlight.**

headland *n* мыс.

headlight *n Aut* (пере́дняя) фа́ра; **full/dimmed ~s** да́льний/бли́жний свет; **turn your ~s on** включи́ фа́ры/*CQ* да́льний свет; **to dim/dip one's ~s** переключи́ть на бли́жний свет.

headline *n* (газе́тный) заголо́вок; **the earthquake hit the ~s** о землетрясе́нии писа́ли все газе́ты; **this will hit the ~s** э́то вы́зовет сенса́цию.

headlong *adj*: **he set off in ~ flight** он помчáлся сломя́ гóлову.

headlong *adv*: **he fell ~** он упáл головóй вперёд; *fig* **he rushed ~ into danger** он брóсился очертя́ гóлову навстрéчу опáсности.

headmaster, headmistress *n* дирéктор шкóлы.

head-on *adj and adv*: **a ~ collision** столкновéние; **the boys/cars collided ~** мáльчики/машúны столкнýлись лоб в лоб.

headphones *npl* наýшники.

headquarters *npl* (*of department, police*) глáвное управлéние; *Mil* штаб (*sing*).

headroom *n* (*inside*): **there's not much ~ in the cabin/in this car** в каю́те/в машúне нúзкий потолóк; *off Aut, etc.* (*overall outside measurement*) габарúтная высотá.

headscarf *n* головнóй платóк.

headstrong *adj* (*self-willed*) своевóльный; (*obstinate*) упря́мый.

headway *n*: **to make ~ against the wind/***fig* **with one's work** продвигáться прóтив вéтра/в рабóте.

headwind *n* встрéчный вéтер.

heal *vti vt*: **to ~ wounds with herbs** лечúть рáны трáвами (*impf*); *fig* **time ~s all sorrows** врéмя—лýчший лéкарь

vi зажи|вáть (-ть); **the wound ~ed/he ~s quickly** рáна бы́стро зажилá, на нём все царáпины бы́стро заживáют.

healing *adj* лечéбный, целéбный.

health *n* **1** здорóвье; **he is in bad ~** у негó плохóе здорóвье, он нездорóв; **to regain one's ~** вы́здороветь; **the Ministry of H.** министéрство здравоохранéния; *attr*: **~ resort** курóрт

2 (*in toasts*): **to drink to smb's ~** пить за чьё-л здорóвье; **to propose smb's ~** провозгласúть тост за когó-л; **(to) your ~!** (за) вáше здорóвье!

healthy *adj* здорóвый; **it isn't ~ to sit indoors all day** весь день сидéть дóма нездорóво/врéдно для здорóвья; **the climate here is ~ for children** здéшний клúмат целúтелен/полéзен для детéй; **he has a ~ appetite** у негó здорóвый аппетúт.

heap *n* **1** кýча, (*larger*) грýда; **a ~ of sand/stones/books** кýча пескá, грýда камнéй, стóпка книг

2 *fig*, *CQ* (*usu pl*) мáсса, мнóжество, ýйма (*all sing*); **I've ~s of time/money** у меня́ мáсса врéмени/кýча дéнег; **I've ~s to do** у меня́ мáсса/ýйма дел; **there are ~s of books on the subject** на э́ту тéму напúсано мнóжество книг; **I've told her that ~s of times** я говорúл ей э́то ты́сячу раз.

hear *vti vt* **1** слы́шать (у-); **I ~d a knock** я услы́шал стук; **I never ~d such nonsense!** я никогдá такóго вздóра не слы́шал; **I ~ smb playing upstairs** я слы́шу, как наверхý ктó-то игрáет; **I'm glad to ~ that...** я рад слы́шать, что...

2 (*of audience*) слы́шать *and also* слýшать (по-); **last night we ~d a new violinist/a broadcast from Rome/his lecture** вчерá мы слýшали *or* слы́шали нóвого скрипачá/передáчу из Рúма/слýшали егó лéкцию

3 *Law* слýшать (*usu impf*); **to ~ a case** слýшать дéло; **the case was ~d yesterday** дéло слýшалось вчерá

4 слы́шно (*impers*); **he could be ~d snoring** слы́шно бы́ло, как он храпúт; **there was so much noise I could hardly make myself ~d** был такóй шум, что меня́ едвá бы́ло слы́шно; **nothing has been ~d of him** о нём давнó ничегó не *or* нé было слы́шно, о нём давнó ни слýху ни дýху; **speak louder—we can't ~ you** говорúте грóмче—вас не слы́шно

vi **1** слы́шать; **I don't ~ well** я плóхо слы́шу; **I only ~d of it yesterday** я об э́том услы́шал тóлько вчерá; **~! ~!** прáвильно!, прáвильно!

2 слы́шно (*impers*); **can you ~ at the back?** там сзáди хорошó слы́шно?; **we ~ very well from here** отсю́да хорошó слы́шно.

hearer *n* слýшатель (*m*).

hearing *n* **1** (*sense*) слух; **a bit hard of ~** тугoвáт нá ухо

2 (*earshot*): **within/out of ~** в предéлах/вне предéлов слы́шимости; **better not to mention that in the director's ~** лýчше об э́том не упоминáть в присýтствии дирéктора

3 *Law*: **the ~ of a case** слýшание дéла; **he was given a fair ~** егó спокóйно вы́слушали до концá.

hearing aid *n* слуховóй аппарáт.

hearsay *n* слýхи (*pl*); **it's only ~** э́то тóлько слýхи; **by ~** по слýхам.

hearse *n* катафáлк.

heart *n* **1** сéрдце; **he has a bad ~** у негó больнóе сéрдце; **I could feel my ~ beating** я чýвствовал, как у меня́ бьётся сéрдце; **hand on my ~** положá рýку нá сердце; *attr*: **he had a ~ attack** у негó был сердéчный прúступ; **a ~ defect** порóк сéрдца; **~ disease** болéзнь сéрдца

2 *fig uses*: **in the ~ of Africa/the forest** в сéрдце Áфрики, в глубинé лéса; **the ~ of a lettuce** середúнка салáта; **to get to the ~ of the matter** дойтú до сýти дéла

3 *pl* (**~s**) *Cards* чéрвы; **the ace of ~s** червóнный туз; **to play/lead ~s** ходúть с червéй

4: **to learn smth by ~** вы́учить что-л наизýсть (*adv*)

5 (*as symbol of love*): **I lost my ~ to her/to her grandmother** я влюбúлся в неё *or* полюбúл её, я прóсто очарóван её бáбушкой; **he broke her ~** он разбúл её сéрдце

6 (*as seat of emotions*) душá; сéрдце; **in one's ~ of ~s** в глубинé душú; **to one's ~'s content** скóлько душé угóдно, вволю (*adv*); **I poured out my ~ to her** я излúл ей дýшу; **my ~ is not in the job** у меня́ душá не лежúт к э́той рабóте; **he wears his ~ on his sleeve** у негó душá нараспáшку (*adv*); **he's a man after my own ~** он мне по душé/пó сердцу; **with all my ~** всем сéрдцем; **with a light/heavy ~** с лёгким/

тяжёлым сéрдцем; **she has a ~ of gold** у неё золотóе сéрдце; **she took my words to ~** онá принялá мои словá блѝзко к сéрдцу; **I hadn't the ~ to refuse** у меня́ не хватѝло сил отказáться; **to cry one's ~ out** вы́плакаться; **have a ~!** сжáльтесь!

7 (*as symbol of courage*): **with a sinking ~** с замирáнием сéрдца; **his ~ sank** у негó сéрдце упáло; **to lose ~** пáдать дýхом; **to take ~** собрáться с дýхом, набрáться хрáбрости (*G*); **my ~ was in my boots** (*depression*)/**in my mouth** (*fear*) у меня́ бы́ло тяжелó на сéрдце, у меня́ душá в пя́тки ушлá.

heartache *n* душéвная боль, душéвные мýки (*pl*).

heartbreaking *adj*: **it's ~ to see her so unhappy/to have to sell the painting** душá разрывáется вѝдеть её такóй несчáстной, так жáлко продавáть э́ту картѝну—душá разрывáется.

heartbroken *adj* убѝтый гóрем.

heartburn *n* изжóга.

hearten *vt*: **we were ~ed by the news** э́та нóвость обрáдовала нас.

heartfelt *adj* сердéчный.

hearth *n* очáг; *fig* **~ and home** домáшний очáг.

heartily *adv* **1** сердéчно; **I thanked him ~** я сердéчно поблагодарѝл егó; **I ~ agree** я всем сéрдцем соглáсен; **to eat/laugh ~** есть с аппетѝтом *or* жáдно, смея́ться от душѝ

2 (*very*) óчень; **I am ~ glad/sorry that...** я óчень рад,/я óчень сожалéю, что...; **I'm ~ sick of rain** мне дó смерти надоéл дождь, дождь мне осточертéл.

heartless *adj* бессердéчный, бездýшный.

heartrending *adj*: **a ~ cry** душераздирáющий крик.

heart-searching *n*: **after much ~ I decided to tell her the truth** пóсле дóлгих раздýмий (*pl*) я решѝл сказáть ей прáвду.

heart-to-heart *adj*: **to have a ~ talk** говорѝть по душáм.

hearty *adj*: **he has a ~ appetite** у негó прекрáсный аппетѝт; **he gave a ~ laugh/us a ~ welcome** он от душѝ хохотáл, он нас сердéчно прѝнял.

heat *n* **1** теплó; жар; (*of weather*) жарá; **~ from the stove** теплó/жар от пéчи; **to use solar ~ for energy** испóльзовать сóлнечное теплó для вы́работки энéргии; **I can't stand ~** я не выношý жары́; **oppressive ~** зной; **bake at a ~ of 100°** печь/выпекáть при температýре сто грáдусов; **we've no ~ on today** сегóдня у нас не тóпят; *Tech* **white ~** бéлое калéние

2 *fig uses*: **in the ~ of battle/passion** в пылý сражéния/стрáсти; **I said it in the ~ of the moment** я сказáл э́то сгорячá (*adv*)

3 *Zool*: **our dog is on ~** у нáшей собáки тéчка

4 *Sport* (*lap, on foot*) забéг; (*in horse or car racing*) заéзд; **a dead ~** одновремéнный фѝниш.

heat *vti vt* нагре|вáть (-ть), согре|вáть (-ть) *and compounds*; **to ~ some water** нагрéть/согрéть воды́; **to ~ up soup** разогревáть/(*a little*) подогревáть суп; **to ~ (up) an engine** разогрéть мотóр; *fig*: **the argument became ~ed** разгорéлся спор; **they became ~ed with wine/over the argument** винó их разгорячѝло, онѝ горячó заспóрили

vi: **our water ~s slowly** у нас водá мéдленно нагревáется.

heated *adj* нагрéтый; **a ~ flat** квартѝра с отоплéнием; *fig* **a ~ discussion** горя́чий/жáркий спор.

heater *n* обогревáтель (*m*); **an electric ~** электрѝческий обогревáтель; *Aut* **turn on the ~** включѝ вентиля́тор отоплéния.

heath *n* (*plant*) вéреск; (*place*) *approx* вéресковая пýстошь.

heathen *n* язы́чник.

heather *n* вéреск.

heating *n* (*of house, car*) отоплéние; **central ~** центрáльное отоплéние; **the ~ isn't on yet** квартѝра ещё не отáпливается; *attr*: **the ~ system** систéма отоплéния.

heatproof, heat-resistant *adjs* жаростóйкий, жаропрóчный.

heatwave *n*: **we had a ~ in May** в мáе у нас был перѝод сѝльной жары́.

heave *n* (*lift*) подъём; (*pull*) тя́га; (*throw*) бросóк.

heave *vti vt*: **to ~ smth over board**/*Naut* **the lead** бро|сáть что-л за борт/лот (-сить); **to ~ a brick at smb/on to the pile** швырнýть кирпичóм в когó-л/кирпѝч в кýчу; *Naut*: **to ~ up the anchor** под|нимáть я́корь (-ня́ть); **to ~ a boat up on to the shore** вы|тáскивать лóдку на бéрег (-тащить); **to be hove to** лежáть в дрéйфе (*impf*); *fig* **to ~ a sigh** вздыхáть (вздохнýть)

vi: **to ~ in sight** появѝться в пóле зрéния (*usu pf*); *Naut*: **to ~ on a rope** тянýть на канáте; **to ~ to** ложѝться в дрейф (*only in impf*).

heaven *n* **1** нéбо; **the ~s** небесá, нéбо (*sing*); **the kingdom of ~** цáрство небéсное

2 *CQ expressions*: **good/thank ~s!** бóже мой!, слáва бóгу!; **~ forbid!** не дай бог!; **she was in her seventh ~** онá былá на седьмóм нéбе; **I'll move ~ and earth to find it** я переверну́ всё вверх дном, но найдý э́то; **the carcase**/*fig* **this affair stinks to high ~** от э́той тýши ужáсная вонь, от э́той истóрии дýрно пáхнет.

heavenly *adj* небéсный; *CQ*: **what a ~ day!** какóй чудéсный день!; **how ~!** (*of a view, etc.*) какáя красотá!/прéлесть!, (*of a suggestion*) чудéсно!

heaven-sent *adj*: **it was a ~ opportunity for me** э́то былá для меня́ как ниспóсланная бóгом возмóжность.

heavily-built *adj*: **he's ~** он крéпко сложён.

heavy *adj* **1** тяжёлый; **a ~ blow/case/lorry/parcel** тяжёлый удáр/чемодáн/грузовѝк/свёрток; **~ artillery/steps, a ~ fall/breathing** тяжёлая артиллéрия, тяжёлые шагú, тяжёлое падéние/дыхáние; **how ~ are you?/is this box?** скóлько вы вéсите?, скóлько вéсит э́тот я́щик?

2 *fig* тяжёлый; сúльный; крéпкий; **~ industry/food/workload** тяжёлая промы́шленность/пúща/нагрýзка; **~ casualties/responsibilities** тяжёлые потéри, нелёгкие обя́занности; **a ~ defeat/punishment** тяжёлое поражéние/наказáние; **with a ~ heart** с тяжёлым сéрдцем; **I've had a ~ day** у меня́ был тяжёлый день; **~ rain, a ~ cold/snowfall** сúльный дождь/нáсморк/снегопáд; **lilac has a ~ scent** сирéнь сúльно пáхнет; **he's a ~ drinker** он сúльно пьёт; **a ~ wine** крéпкое винó; **he's a ~ sleeper** он крéпко спит, он спит как убúтый; **a ~ sleep** глубóкий сон; **a ~ crop/supper** обúльный урожáй/ýжин; **~ debts/expenses** большúе долгú/расхóды; **~ traffic** большóе движéние; **~ pastry** густóе тéсто; **a ~ fog** густóй тумáн; **~ foliage, a ~ beard** густáя листвá/бородá; **a ~ layer of dust** тóлстый слой пы́ли; **~ soil** жúрная/тýчная пóчва; **~ (*bold*) type** жúрный шрифт; **~ humour** тяжеловéсный ю́мор; **a ~ sea/sky** бýрное мóре, мрáчное *or* хмýрое нéбо; **~ features** крýпные чертьí (лицá).

heavy *adv*: **time hangs ~** врéмя тя́нется мéдленно; **it lies ~ on my conscience** э́то лежúт кáмнем у меня́ на сóвести.

heavyweight *n* (*boxer*) боксёр/(*wrestler*) борéц тяжёлого вéса.

Hebrew *n* (*language*) иврúт.

heckle *vt*: **the students ~d the speaker** студéнты задавáли доклáдчику кáверзные вопрóсы.

hectare *n* (*approx 2.5 acres*) гектáр.

hectic *adj*: **a ~ flush** лихорáдочный румя́нец; *fig* **~ activity** лихорáдочная дéятельность; *CQ*: **I've had a ~ day** у меня́ был сумасшéдший день; **he leads a ~ life** у негó сумасшéдшая жизнь.

hedge *n* (живáя) úзгородь (из кустóв) [*to distinguish from a wire or wooden fence*].

hedge *vt vti*: **to ~ (in/off) a field** огор|áживать/отгор|áживать пóле (*pfs* -одúть); *fig*: **to be ~d in by regulations** быть стеснённым прáвилами; **to ~ one's bets** страховáться от потéрь (за-)

vi fig (*shirk answering directly*) увúл|ивать/уклон|я́ться от прямóго отвéта (-ьнýть/-úться).

hedgehog *n* ёж.

hedgerow *n* живáя úзгородь (*see* **hedge** *n*).

heed *n*: **to take ~ of smth** принимáть что-л во внимáние; **to pay ~ to smb/smth** обращáть внимáние на когó-л/на что-л; **take ~ of what I say** обратúте внимáние на моú словá.

heed *vt*: **he didn't ~ my warning** он пропустúл мúмо ушéй моё предупреждéние.

heedless *adj*: **~ of danger/expense** позабы́в об опáсности, не считáясь с расхóдами.

heel *n* пятá; пя́тка (*also of sock, stocking*); (*of shoe*) каблýк; **I've a hole in the ~ of my sock** у меня́ ды́рка на пя́тке носкá; **high/low ~s** высóкие/нúзкие каблукú; **the ~s of my shoes are badly worn down** у моúх тýфель сúльно стоптáлись каблукú; (*to dog*) **~!** за мнóй!; **he turned on his ~** он рéзко/крýто повернýлся; **to follow hard on smb's ~s** слéдовать/ходúть за кем-л по пятáм; *fig*: **to take to one's ~s, to show a clean pair of ~s** удирáть так, что тóлько пя́тки сверкáют; **he was left locked up to cool/kick his ~s** егó остáвили взапертú (*adv*) поосты́нуть; (*US*) *CQ* **the ~ of a loaf** горбýшка (хлéба); *sl* **he's a ~** он негодя́й, он подóнок.

heel *vt* (*shoes*) стáвить каблукú/набóйки (по-) [набóйка = *extra thickness of rubber or leather fixed on to existing heel*].

hefty *adj CQ*: **a ~ fellow/child/blow/dinner** здоровéнный пáрень, тяжёленький ребёнок, сúльный удáр, сы́тный обéд.

heifer *n* тёлка.

height *n* **1** высотá; **a building 20 metres in ~** здáние высотóй (в) двáдцать мéтров; **to fly at a ~ of...** летéть на высотé + *G*; **to fall from a ~ of...** упáсть с высоты́ + *G*; **the town is at a ~ of 1,000 feet above sea level** гóрод нахóдится на высотé ты́сячи фýтов над ýровнем мóря

2 (*of person*) рост; **what is his ~?** какóй у негó рост?, какóго он рóста?; **a man of average ~** человéк срéднего рóста; **he is over 6 feet in ~** он рóстом вы́ше/бóльше шестú фýтов

3 (*summit*) вершúна; **on the mountain ~s** на гóрных вершúнах

4 *fig uses*: **the ~ of folly** верх глýпости; **he was at the ~ of his fame** он был на вершúне слáвы; **at the ~ of summer/the storm/the battle** в разгáре лéта/бýри/бóя; **the flood had reached its ~** наводнéние достúгло вы́сшей тóчки; **dressed in the ~ of fashion** одéтый по послéдней мóде.

heinous *adj*: **a ~ crime** чудóвищное/гнýсное преступлéние.

heir *n* наслéдник.

heiress *n* наслéдница.

helicopter *n* вертолёт.

hell *n* ад; *CQ*: **oh ~!** чёрт (возьмú)!; **go to ~!** пошёл к чёрту!; **like ~ he helped!** чёрта с два он помóг!; **I'm working like ~** я рабóтаю как чёрт; **he's got the ~ of a lot of money** у негó дéнег до чёрта; **why the ~ should I go?** какóго чёрта я дóлжен идтú?; **the ~ of a noise** áдский шум; **all ~ was let loose** началóсь светопреставлéние; **he gave her ~** он задáл ей жáру; **to raise ~** поднимáть жýткий скандáл; **we had the ~ of a time** мы ужáсно (*bad*)/прекрáсно (*good*) провелú врéмя; **he's the ~ of a chap** он слáвный пáрень, он пáрень что нáдо.

hellish *adj* áдский.

hello *interj see* **hullo.**

helm *n Naut* штурвáл; **to take the ~** стоя́ть за штурвáлом/у руля́, *also fig*.

helmet *n* шлем, ка́ска; **motorcyclist's/crash/safety ~** защи́тный шлем.

helmsman *n Naut* рулево́й.

help *n* **1** по́мощь; **with the ~ of smb/smth** с по́мощью кого́-л/чего́-л *or* при по́мощи чего́-л; **to give/refuse smb ~** оказы́вать кому́-л по́мощь, отка́зывать кому́-л в по́мощи; **to send for ~** посыла́ть за по́мощью; **your map was a great ~ to us** ва́ша ка́рта нам о́чень помогла́; **can I be of any ~?** я могу́ вам че́м-нибудь помо́чь?; **there's no ~ for it** тут уж ниче́м не помо́жешь; **~!** помоги́те!

2 (*of people*): **home ~** домрабо́тница; **we need more ~ in the factory** на заво́де не хвата́ет рабо́чих; **we need some more ~ to move the piano** нам одни́м роя́ль не передви́нуть.

help *vti vt* **1** помо|га́ть + *D* (́-чь); **to ~ smb with money** помога́ть кому́-л деньга́ми; **he ~ed me (to) check/in checking the figures** он помо́г мне прове́рить ци́фры; **this medicine will ~ your cough** э́то лека́рство помо́жет вам от ка́шля; **I am ready to ~ your project in every way** я гото́в вся́чески вам помо́чь в э́том ва́шем начина́нии; **can I have a needle?—H. yourself** ты могла́ бы дать мне иго́лку?—Возьми́ вон там сама́; **God ~ him!** помоги́ ему́ бог!

2 (*at meals*): **may I ~ you to some chicken?** вам положи́ть кусо́к ку́рицы?; **he ~ed himself to some more wine** он нали́л себе́ ещё вина́; **~ yourself to an apple** возьми́ я́блоко; **~ yourselves!** угоща́йтесь,/ку́шайте, пожа́луйста!, прошу́ вас!

3 (*avoid*): **it can't be ~ed** ничего́ не поде́лаешь/попи́шешь; **we couldn't ~ laughing** мы не могли́ удержа́ться от сме́ха; **you/one can't ~ liking her** её невозмо́жно не полюби́ть; **I can't ~ it if it rains** я не винова́т, е́сли пойдёт дождь; **I can't ~ thinking that...** мне всё же ка́жется, что...; **don't spend more than you can ~** не тра́тьте бо́льше, чем необходи́мо

vi: **crying won't ~** слеза́ми го́рю не помо́жешь

help down *vt*: **he ~ed her down from the ladder** он помо́г ей сойти́ с ле́стницы

help off/on *vt*: **he ~ed her off/on with her coat** он помо́г ей снять/наде́ть пальто́

help out *vti vt*: **she ~ed out the soup/the meat** она́ разлила́ суп/она́ разложи́ла мя́со по таре́лкам

vi: **when my mother was ill Granny ~ed out** когда́ ма́ма заболе́ла, (нам) помога́ла/(нас) вы́ручила ба́бушка (*came to the rescue*)

help over *vt*: **he ~ed her over the fence** он помо́г ей переле́зть че́рез огра́ду

help up *vt*: **he ~ed her up** (*rise*) он помо́г ей встать.

helper *n* помо́щн|ик, *f* -ица.

helpful *adj* поле́зный; **your map was very ~ to me** ва́ша ка́рта была́ мне о́чень поле́зна; **inhalation is ~ for sore throats** ингаля́ция помога́ет при анги́не.

helping *n* (*of food*) по́рция; **will you have a second ~?** хоти́те ещё/доба́вки?

helpless *adj* беспо́мощный; **he's a ~ sort of chap** он како́й-то беспо́мощный; **we were ~ in this matter** тут/в э́том мы бы́ли беспо́мощны, мы тут ничего́ не могли́ сде́лать.

hem *n* подо́л; **I must take up/let down the ~ of my skirt** мне ну́жно укороти́ть ю́бку/вы́пустить подо́л ю́бки.

hem *vt* подши|ва́ть (́-ть), подруб|а́ть (-и́ть); *fig* **we were ~med in by the enemy** мы бы́ли окружены́ врага́ми.

hemisphere *n* полуша́рие.

hemline *n*: **is my ~ straight?** у меня́ подо́л подши́т ро́вно?

hemlock *n Bot* болиголо́в.

hemp *n Bot* конопля́; (*fibre*) пенька́.

hen *n* ку́рица; *pl* (**~s**) ку́ры.

hence *adv* **1** (*of time*): **a month ~** че́рез ме́сяц

2 (*of place*: *old use*) отсю́да; **~!** вон (отсю́да)!

3 (*causal*): **~ we may conclude...** отсю́да мы мо́жем заключи́ть..., отку́да мо́жно заключи́ть...

henceforth, henceforward *adv* с э́того вре́мени, с э́тих пор; впредь.

henhouse *n* куря́тник.

henpecked *adj*: **he's ~/a ~ husband** он под башмако́м у жены́.

her *pers pron* (*oblique cases of* **she**) **1** *G*, *A* её, *D* ей, *I* е́ю, *after preps G* неё, *D* ней, *I* не́ю, *P* (о) ней; **I didn't see ~** я её не ви́дел; **he went up to ~** он подошёл к ней; **I'll go with ~** я пойду́ с ней; **I often think about ~** я ча́сто ду́маю о ней

2 *when it refers to the subject of the sentence "her" is translated by reflex pron* себя́, себе́, *etc.*; **she closed the door after ~** она́ закры́ла за собо́й дверь; **she took the book away with ~** она́ унесла́ кни́гу с собо́й

3 *sometimes translated by the nominative* она́; **that's ~** э́то она́; **let ~ try** пусть она́ попыта́ется.

her *poss adj* **1** *use G* её; **~ father/car/behaviour/lips** её оте́ц/маши́на/поведе́ние/гу́бы; **~ eyes are blue** у неё голубы́е глаза́

2 *when the possessor is the subject of the sentence or clause, use reflex poss adj* свой; **she gave me ~ address** она́ дала́ мне свой а́дрес

3 *referring to parts of body use* себе́, *or reflex verb, or omit translation*: **she broke ~ arm** она́ слома́ла себе́ ру́ку; **she hurt ~ foot on a stone** она́ уда́рилась ного́й о ка́мень; **she washed ~ hair** она́ помы́ла го́лову.

herb *n* трава́ (*medicinal or Cook*).

herbal *adj*: **~ tea** отва́р из трав.

herd *n* ста́до, *also fig*.

herd *vti vt* (*gather*): **to ~ cattle** со|бира́ть/сби|ва́ть скот в ста́до (-бра́ть/-ть); (*tend*) пасти́ скот (*impf*)

vi (*of animals*) *also* **~ together** ходи́ть ста́дом, собира́ться в ста́до; (*of people*) **they**

~ed together like cattle они́ сби́лись в ку́чу как ста́до.

herdsman *n* пасту́х.

here *adv* **1** (*place where*) здесь; (*motion to*) сюда́; **I live ~/not far from ~** я живу́ здесь/недалеко́ отсю́да; **I am a stranger ~** я не здесь живу́, я не зде́шний; **from ~ to the school is 2 kilometres** отсю́да до шко́лы два киломе́тра; (*at roll-call*) **~!** здесь!; **come ~!** иди́(те) сюда́!; **bring it ~** принеси́ э́то сюда́; **put it ~** поста́вь э́то здесь/сюда́/тут; **spring is ~** наступи́ла/пришла́ весна́ [**NB** *tense*]

2 (*of time*) здесь, тут, в э́тот моме́нт [**NB** *of present time usu* здесь]; **~ I should add that...** здесь придётся доба́вить, что...; **~ she fell silent** тут она́ замолча́ла

3 (*indicating or offering smth*) вот; **~'s the key** вот ключ, на, возьми́ ключ; **~ comes the bus** вот и авто́бус (идёт/пришёл); **~ he comes** вот и он; **my friend ~ will show you the way** мой друг пока́жет вам доро́гу

4 *phrases*: **~ and there** там и сям, то тут, то там; **~, there and everywhere** везде́ и всю́ду, повсю́ду; **~ goes!** (*before dive, etc.*) ну, пошли́!; **~'s to you!** (за) ва́ше здоро́вье!; **that's neither ~ nor there** э́то к де́лу не отно́сится, э́то ни к селу́ ни к го́роду.

hereabouts *adv* побли́зости; **the school is somewhere ~** шко́ла где́-то побли́зости.

hereafter *adv* (*in future*) в бу́дущем; *Law* **~ called the defendant** в дальне́йшем имену́емый подсуди́мый.

hereby *adv Law* (*in document*): **I ~ declare...** настоя́щим я заявля́ю...

hereditary *adj*: **a ~ disease** насле́дственная боле́знь; **a ~ ruler** насле́дный прави́тель; **~ customs** традицио́нные обы́чаи.

heredity *n* насле́дственность.

heresy *n* е́ресь.

hereupon *adv* по́сле чего́.

herewith *adv*: **cheque is enclosed ~** при сём прилага́ется чек.

heritage *n* насле́дство, *fig* насле́дие.

hermetically *adv*: **~ sealed** гермети́чески закры́тый.

hermit *n* отше́льник.

hernia *n* гры́жа.

hero *n* геро́й; *attr*: **~ worship** культ геро́ев.

heroic *adj* герои́ческий.

heroin *n* герои́н.

heroine *n* герои́ня.

heron *n* ца́пля.

herring *n* (*as caught*) сельдь; (*as eaten, in SU salted raw*) селёдка; **pickled ~** марино́ванная селёдка.

hers *poss pron use G* её; *if referring to the subject of the sentence or clause* свой; **whose is this book—~ or yours?** чья э́то кни́га— её и́ли твоя́?; **he carried my case but she carried ~** он нёс мой чемода́н, а она́ несла́ свой.

herself *pron of emphasis* сама́; **she told me this ~** она́ сама́ мне э́то сказа́ла; **she does all the cooking ~** она́ всё гото́вит сама́; **she did it all by ~** она́ сде́лала э́то одна́/сама́.

herself *reflex pron* **1** себя́, *etc.*, *or use reflex verb*; **she asked nothing for ~** она́ ничего́ не попроси́ла для себя́; **she bought ~ a new dress** она́ купи́ла себе́ но́вое пла́тье; **she's pleased with ~** она́ дово́льна собо́й; **she never thinks of ~** она́ никогда́ не ду́мает о себе́; **she dressed ~ quickly** она́ бы́стро оде́лась

2 *phrases*: **she's not ~ today** сего́дня она́ сама́ не своя́; **she looks quite ~ again** она́ ста́ла опя́ть похо́жа сама́ на себя́; **she keeps ~ to ~** она́ де́ржится особняко́м.

hesitant *adj* неуве́ренный; **he has a ~ manner of speaking** он всегда́ говори́т ка́к-то неуве́ренно; **I am ~ about taking on such responsibilities** я сомнева́юсь, сто́ит ли брать на себя́ таку́ю отве́тственность (*sing*).

hesitantly *adv*: **he answered ~** он отве́тил неуве́ренно/(*indecisively*) нереши́тельно.

hesitate *vi* (*between clear or implied alternatives*) колеба́ться (*impf*); **he didn't ~ for an instant** он ни мину́ты не колеба́лся; **he is hesitating about whether to come or not** он не зна́ет, идти́ и́ли нет; **he ~d over his reply** он отве́тил не сра́зу; **I ~ to blame him—I might have done the same myself** не могу́ его́ осужда́ть—мо́жет, я бы сде́лал то́ же са́мое; **we ~d about what to do next** мы не зна́ли, что де́лать да́льше; **don't ~ to ask** спра́шивайте без колеба́ний/, не стесня́йтесь.

hesitation *n* **1: he answered without ~** он отве́тил без колеба́ний (*pl*)/сра́зу (*at once*); **I have no ~ in stating that...** я могу́ с уве́ренностью утвержда́ть, что...

2: he has a ~ in his speech он заика́ется (*physical defect*).

heterogeneous *adj* разноро́дный.

het up *adj CQ*: **he's all ~ about his exam** он си́льно не́рвничает пе́ред экза́меном.

hew *vt* руби́ть (*impf*) *and compounds*; **he ~ed down a tree/off a large branch** он сруби́л де́рево, он отруби́л большу́ю ве́тку.

hey *interj* (*to arrest attention*) эй!

heyday *n*: **I knew him in his ~** я знал его́ в расцве́те сил.

hi *interj* (*US*) (*in greeting*) приве́т!

hiatus *n* пробе́л.

hibernate *vi*: **bears ~** на́ зиму медве́ди впада́ют в спя́чку.

hiccough, hiccup *n* ико́та; **to have ~s** ика́ть.

hidden *adj*: **~ treasure** клад; **~ meaning** скры́тый смысл.

hide[1] *n* (*skin*) шку́ра.

hide[2] *n* (*for observing birds, etc.*) укры́тие, скра́док.

hide[2] *vti vt* (*conceal*) скры|ва́ть (-ть); (*put out of sight*) пря́тать (с-); **I hid the keys in a drawer** я спря́тал ключи́ в я́щик(е) стола́; **the moon was hidden behind a cloud** ме́сяц скры́лся/спря́тался за ту́чу; **to ~ one's**

intentions скрыва́ть свои́ наме́рения; **I hid the letter from her** я спря́тал письмо́ от неё; **she hid her face in her hands** она́ закры́ла лицо́ рука́ми; ~ **the medicine away from the children** спрячь лека́рство от дете́й

vi пря́таться; (*for a period*) скрыва́ться; **he's hiding in the corner/behind the cupboard/from the police** он пря́чется в углу́/за шка́фом, он скрыва́ется от поли́ции.

hide-and-seek *n*: **to play** ~ игра́ть в пря́тки.

hidebound *adj*: **he is** ~ он о́чень ограни́чен/узколо́бый челове́к.

hideous *adj* (*of person, etc.*) некраси́вый, уро́дливый; *fig* (*of crime, etc.*) гну́сный, отврати́тельный; *CQ* **a** ~ **noise** ужа́сный шум.

hideout *n* укры́тие.

hiding *n*: **he gave his son a good** ~ он хороше́нько вы́драл своего́ сы́на.

hierarchy *n* иера́рхия.

hieroglyphics *npl* иеро́глифы (*pl*).

hi-fi *n* (*abbr of* **high fidelity**) высо́кое ка́чество воспроизведе́ния зву́ка.

higgledy-piggledy *adv CQ*: **his toys lay** ~ **all over the floor** его́ игру́шки валя́лись в беспоря́дке/бы́ли разбро́саны по всему́ по́лу.

high *n Meteorol* (**a** ~) о́бласть повы́шенного давле́ния, антицикло́н; *fig* **exports have reached a new** ~ э́кспорт (*sing*) дости́г небыва́лых разме́ров.

high *adj* **1** высо́кий; **a** ~ **mountain/wall** высо́кая гора́/стена́; **a tree 20 metres** ~ де́рево высото́й (в) два́дцать ме́тров; **how** ~ **is that mountain?** какова́ высота́ э́той горы́?; **the** ~**est floor** ве́рхний эта́ж; **it's** ~ **tide/water at noon today** прили́в сего́дня в по́лдень; **the village is** ~ **above sea level** дере́вня нахо́дится высоко́ над у́ровнем мо́ря; ~ **seas were running** волне́ние на мо́ре бы́ло о́чень си́льное; **a** ~ **wind** си́льный ве́тер; *Mus* **a** ~ **key/voice** высо́кий реги́стр/го́лос

2 *Fin, Comm*: ~ **pay** высо́кая зарпла́та; ~ **interest/taxes** высо́кие проце́нты/нало́ги; **goods of the** ~**est quality** това́ры вы́сшего ка́чества; **the cost of living is very** ~ **here** здесь жизнь дорога́я, здесь всё о́чень до́рого

3 *Tech, etc.*: ~ **frequency** высо́кая частота́; ~ **blood pressure** высо́кое кровяно́е давле́ние; ~ **explosive** си́льное взры́вчатое вещество́; *Aut*: ~ **gear** вы́сшая ско́рость/переда́ча; **to drive at** ~ **speed** е́хать на большо́й ско́рости; *Elec* ~ **tension** высо́кое напряже́ние

4 *fig uses*: **a** ~ **official** вы́сший чино́вник; ~ **command** вы́сшее кома́ндование; **he has a** ~ **position** он занима́ет высо́кое положе́ние; **he moves in** ~ **society** он враща́ется в вы́сшем све́те; ~ **ideals** высо́кие идеа́лы; **I've a** ~ **opinion of him** я о нём высо́кого мне́ния; **he's in** ~ **favour with the director** дире́ктор к нему́ благоволи́т; **I'm in** ~ **spirits today** сего́дня я в хоро́шем/припо́днятом настрое́нии; **he's too** ~ **and mighty** сли́шком уж он ва́жный/ва́жничает; ~ **words were exchanged** они́ обменя́лись весьма́ си́льными выраже́ниями; **he is in the** ~**est degree a responsible person** он в вы́сшей сте́пени обяза́тельный/надёжный челове́к; **he is a patriot in the** ~**est sense of the word** он патрио́т в вы́сшем смы́сле э́того сло́ва; **in** ~ **summer** в разга́р ле́та; **this fish is** ~ э́та ры́ба с душко́м; **it's** ~ **time we left** нам давно́ пора́ идти́; **I knew him when he was so** ~ я знал его́ ещё ребёнком; **she usually has a** ~ **colour** у неё обы́чно я́ркий румя́нец; **they left us** ~ **and dry** они́ оста́вили нас на мели́.

high *adv* высоко́; ~ **in the sky/above our heads** высоко́ в не́бе/над на́шими голова́ми; *fig*: **prices for sheep went as** ~ **as £100 a beast** цена́ (*sing*) на ове́ц подскочи́ла до ста фу́нтов за го́лову; **he's aiming** ~ он высоко́ ме́тит; **we hunted** ~ **and low for him** мы повсю́ду его́ иска́ли; **feelings were running** ~ стра́сти разгоре́лись.

high-altitude *adj*: ~ **flying** высо́тный полёт.

highbrow *adj* интеллектуа́льный.

highchair *n* высо́кий де́тский сту́льчик.

high-class *adj* высо́кого кла́сса; первокла́сный.

higher education *n* вы́сшее образова́ние.

high-grade *adj* высо́кого ка́чества, высокосо́ртный.

Highlander *n*: **Scottish** ~ шотла́ндский го́рец.

highlands *npl* го́рная ме́стность/страна́ (*sings*); **the Highlands of Scotland** го́ры/се́вер Шотла́ндии.

highlight *n fig*: **your concert was the** ~ **of the week for me** твой конце́рт был для меня́ са́мым я́рким собы́тием неде́ли; **they showed only the** ~**s of the match** бы́ли пока́заны то́лько о́стрые моме́нты ма́тча.

highlight *vt fig*: **the report** ~**ed the inadequacy of the measures taken** в докла́де бы́ло осо́бо отме́чено, что ме́ры при́няты недоста́точные.

highly *adv* высоко́; о́чень, весьма́; **a** ~ **paid official** высокоопла́чиваемый чино́вник; **the critics thought** ~ **of his paintings** кри́тики высоко́ оцени́ли его́ карти́ны; **it's** ~ **desirable that...** весьма́ жела́тельно, что́бы...; **a** ~ **amusing story** о́чень заба́вный анекдо́т; **he is a** ~ **strung child** он о́чень не́рвный ребёнок; ~ **polished boots** начи́щенные до бле́ска сапоги́.

highness *n* (*in address*): **Your H.** ва́ше высо́чество.

high-pitched *adj* (*of sound*) высо́кий; пронзи́тельный; (*of roof*) острове́рхий.

high-powered *adj* (*of engines*) мо́щный; *fig* (*of person*) ва́жный, влия́тельный.

high-rise *adj*: ~ **buildings** высо́тные зда́ния.

high-spirited *adj*: **a** ~ **child/young man/horse** весёлый *or* живо́й ребёнок, отва́жный ю́ноша, ре́звый конь.

high-tension *adj Elec* высоково́льтный, высо́кого напряже́ния.

high-up *n CQ* ва́жная персо́на, ши́шка.

highway *n* шоссé (*indecl*); автострáда, автомагистрáль.

hijack *vt*: **to ~ a plane/a train** угнáть самолёт, совершúть налёт на пóезд (*usu pfs*).

hijacker *n* бандúт; (*of plane*) воздýшный пирáт.

hijacking *n* угóн самолёта; (*of lorry, train*) налёт, ограблéние.

hike *n*: **to go for a ~** пойтú на прогýлку (*inside of a day*)/в похóд (*for days*).

hike *vi*: **every summer I go hiking in the mountains** кáждое лéто я отправля́юсь в похóд в гóры.

hiker *n* пéший турúст.

hiking *n*: **I like ~** я люблю́ ходúть в похóды (*pl*).

hilarious *adj*: **we had a ~ time yesterday** мы вчерá веселúлись до упáду; **he tells the most ~ stories** он расскáзывает óчень весёлые/смешны́е истóрии.

hill *n* холм, *dim* хóлмик.

hillside *n*: **sheep were grazing on the ~** óвцы паслúсь на склóне холмá.

hilly *adj*: **~ country** холмúстая мéстность.

him *pers pron* (*oblique cases of* **he**) **1** *G*, *A* егó, *D* емý, *I* им, *after preps G* негó, *D* немý, *I* ним, *P* (о) нём; **I fear ~** я егó бою́сь; **she married ~** онá вы́шла за негó зáмуж; **I'm proud of ~** я им горжýсь; **I don't know ~** я не знакóм с ним

2 *when it refers to the subject of the sentence "him" is translated by reflex pron* себя́, себé, *etc.*; **he took his son with ~** он взял сы́на с собóй; **he left three children behind ~** он остáвил пóсле себя́ троúх детéй

3 *sometimes translated by the nominative* он; **that's ~** вот он; **let ~ do it** пусть он э́то сдéлает.

himself *pron of emphasis* сам; **he said so ~** он сам э́то сказáл; **he had to do all the work ~** емý самомý пришлóсь сдéлать всю рабóту; **can he do it all by ~?** мóжет ли он всё сдéлать сам/одúн?; **he lives by ~** он живёт одúн.

himself *reflex pron* **1** себя́, *etc.*, *or use reflex verb*; **he asked for a copy for ~** он попросúл кóпию для себя́; **he's bought ~ a new car** он купúл себé нóвую машúну; **he's only interested in ~** он интересýется тóлько собóй; **the child can amuse ~ with his toys for hours** ребёнок мóжет часáми занимáться своúми игрýшками

2 *phrases*: **he's not ~ today** сегóдня он сам не свой; **he looks quite ~ again** он опя́ть похóж на себя́; **he keeps ~ to ~** он дéржится особнякóм.

hind[1] *n* (*female deer*) сáмка олéня.

hind[2] *adj* зáдний; **~ leg** зáдняя ногá.

hinder *vt* мешáть + *D* + *inf* (по-); препя́тствовать + *D* (вос-); **don't ~ me in my work** не мешáйте мне рабóтать; **bad weather ~ed the excavations** плохáя погóда мешáла/препя́тствовала раскóпкам; **I was ~ed from writing earlier by having guests** у меня́ бы́ли гóсти, и я не мог написáть вам рáньше.

hindmost *adj* сáмый зáдний; сáмый послéдний.

hindquarters *npl* (*of animals*) зáдняя часть (*sing*).

hindrance *n* помéха, препя́тствие; **I don't want to be a ~ to you** я не хочý быть вам помéхой; **she/the walking stick was more of a ~ to me than a help** онá совсéм не помогáла, скорée наоборóт, от трóсти бы́ло бóльше вредá, чем пóльзы.

hindsight *n*: **it's easy to see with ~ that...** легкó говорúть зáдним числóм, что...

hinge *n* шарнúр; (*of a door*) пéтля; **the door has come off its ~s** дверь сошлá/сорвалáсь с пéтель.

hinge *vi fig*: **everything ~s on the weather/the director** всё завúсит от погóды/от дирéктора.

hinged *adj* (*of door, window, lid*) на пéтлях; **the box has a ~ lid** у корóбки/я́щика кры́шка на пéтлях.

hint *n* **1** намёк; **a broad/gentle ~** я́сный/тóнкий намёк; **to drop/take a ~** обронúть/поня́ть намёк; **~s for car-owners on maintenance** совéты водúтелям по обслýживанию

2 (*trace*): **he said it without a ~ of mockery** он э́то сказáл без тéни насмéшки; *Cook* **add just a ~ of garlic** прибáвьте чуть-чýть чеснокý.

hint *vti vt* намек|áть (-нýть); **I ~ed to her that we ought to leave** я ей намекнýл, что нам порá идтú; **he ~ed that he would accept the job** он дал поня́ть, что соглáсен на э́тот пост

vi: **what are you ~ing at?** на что ты намекáешь?

hip[1] *n* бедрó; **measurement round the ~s** объём бёдер; **she stood with her hands on her ~s** онá стоя́ла подбочéнясь.

hip[2] *n Bot* плод/я́года шипóвника.

hipped *adj CQ*: **he was pretty ~ at being passed over for promotion** он был óчень обúжен тем, что егó обошлú повышéнием/в чúне.

hippie *n* хúппи (*indecl*).

hip-pocket *n* зáдний кармáн.

hippopotamus, *abbr* **hippo** *n* гиппопотáм.

hire *n* (*of workmen*) наём; (*of boats, bicycles, TV, etc.*) прокáт; **the ~ of a building** сня́тие помещéния; **take on ~** *see verb* **to hire; I must pay for the ~ of the hall and the piano** мне придётся платúть за сня́тое помещéние и взя́тый напрокáт (*adv*) роя́ль; **to work for ~** рабóтать по наймý; **I've arranged for the ~ of a TV** я договорúлся, что могý взять телевúзор напрокáт; (*notice*) **"Boats for H."** «Прокáт лóдок».

hire *vt* **1** (*workmen*) на|нимáть (-ня́ть); (*building or hall for special occasion*) снимáть (снять); **we ~ extra labour for the harvest** мы нанимáем дополнúтельных рабóчих для убóрки урожáя; **he was ~d by the day** егó нáняли подённо; **we ~d a hall for the wedding**/

for a temporary office мы сня́ли зал для сва́дьбы/как вре́менное помеще́ние

2 (*piano, TV, car, etc.*) брать напрока́т (взять); **I ~d dress clothes for the dinner** я взял фрак (*sing*) напрока́т для банке́та

3 to hire (out): he ~d us a room for the party он предоста́вил нам зал для проведе́ния ве́чера; **he ~s out bicycles by the day** он даёт велосипе́ды напрока́т.

hired *adj*: **a ~ assassin** наёмный уби́йца; **a ~ car/bicycle** автомоби́ль/велосипе́д, взя́тый напрока́т; (*US*) **~ help** (*in house*) домрабо́тница.

hire purchase *n*: **to buy smth on ~** купи́ть что-л в рассро́чку; *attr*: **he's late with his ~ instalments/payments** он запа́здывает с вы́платой рассро́чки.

his *poss pron use G* его́; *if referring to the subject of the sentence or clause* свой; **this cap is ~** э́та ке́пка его́; **are you a friend of ~?** вы его́ друг?; **this is my pipe— ~ is on the table** э́то моя́ тру́бка, его́—на столе́; **I took my umbrella but he forgot ~** я взял мой зо́нтик, а он забы́л свой.

his *poss adj* **1** *use G* его́; **~ house/coat/future** его́ дом/пальто́/бу́дущее; **these are ~ socks and not mine** э́то его́ носки́, а не мои́; **~ back is aching** у него́ боли́т спина́

2 *when the possessor is the subject of the sentence or clause, use reflex poss adj* свой; **he told me about ~ holiday** он рассказа́л мне о своём о́тпуске; *omit if ownership obvious*: **he took off ~ jacket** он снял пиджа́к

3 *referring to parts of body use* себе́, *or reflex verb, or omit translation*; **he wiped ~ brow** он вы́тер (себе́) лоб; **he fell and hit the back of ~ head** он упа́л и уда́рился заты́лком.

hiss *n* шипе́ние.

hiss *vti vt*: **to ~ an actor (off the stage)/a play** освиста́ть актёра/пье́су (*usu pf*)

vi: **the snake was ~ing/began to ~** змея́ шипе́ла (*impf*)/зашипе́ла.

historian *n* исто́рик.

historic(al) *adj* истори́ческий.

history *n* исто́рия; **ancient/modern/mediaeval/natural ~** дре́вняя/но́вая исто́рия, исто́рия сре́дних веко́в, есте́ственная исто́рия; **the ~ of the case** ход собы́тий, все подро́бности э́того де́ла, *Med* исто́рия боле́зни; **he went down in ~ as a military hero** он вошёл в исто́рию как вели́кий полково́дец; **he read ~ at Cambridge** он изуча́л исто́рию в Ке́мбридже; **this house has a strange ~** у э́того до́ма стра́нная исто́рия.

histrionic *adj* театра́льный, *also fig*; *fig* наи́гранный.

histrionics *npl fig*: **no ~ please!** пожа́луйста, без сцен!

hit *n* **1** (*blow*) уда́р; **he scored a direct ~** он попа́л пря́мо в цель; **that's a ~ at you** э́то вы́пад про́тив тебя́, э́то в твой а́дрес

2 *Mus, Theat, etc.*: **the film was a big ~** фильм име́л огро́мный успе́х; *CQ* **she has made quite a ~ with him** он от неё в восто́рге; *attr*: **~ songs** популя́рные пе́сенки.

hit *vti vt* **1** (*deal a blow*) удар|я́ть (-ить); бить (*for pf use* уда́рить); **he ~ him on the head/in the face** он уда́рил его́ по голове́/по лицу́; **he ~ the ball (with a stick)** он уда́рил по мячу́ (па́лкой); **he ~ him a heavy blow on the chest/shoulder** он нанёс ему́ си́льный уда́р в грудь/в плечо́; **I fell and ~ my head on the pavement** я упа́л и уда́рился голово́й о тротуа́р; **the tree was ~ by lightning** мо́лния уда́рила в де́рево; **don't ~ the child** не бей ребёнка

2 (*of or with missiles*): **he was ~ by a snowball** в него́ бро́сили снежко́м; **the bullet ~ his shoulder** пу́ля попа́ла ему́ в плечо́; **the stone ~ his head** ка́мень попа́л ему́ в го́лову; **to ~ the mark** попа́сть в цель, *also fig*; **the theatre was directly ~ by a bomb** бо́мба попа́ла пря́мо в зда́ние теа́тра

3 (*of collisions*): **the ship ~ a reef** кора́бль натолкну́лся на подво́дный риф; **my car was ~ by a bus** авто́бус столкну́лся с мое́й маши́ной; **the car ~ a tree/a wall** маши́на вре́залась в де́рево/в сте́ну; **he was ~ by a car** его́ сби́ла маши́на

4 *fig uses*: **this will ~ his pocket** э́то уда́рит его́ по карма́ну; **we are ~ by the petrol shortage** мы о́стро ощуща́ем нехва́тку бензи́на; **the crops were badly ~ by the storm** урожа́й си́льно пострада́л от бу́ри; **as you enter the town, the hotel ~s you in the eye** при въе́зде в го́род вам сра́зу броса́ется в глаза́ зда́ние гости́ницы; **we've ~ a problem here** тут мы столкну́лись с пробле́мой; **we ~ the main road at Zagorsk** у Заго́рска мы вы́ехали на автостра́ду; **the portrait ~s him off exactly** он о́чень то́чно изображён на портре́те; *CQ*: **he ~s him off to a T** (*by imitation*) он его́ удиви́тельно то́чно имити́рует; **the discovery ~ the headlines** об э́том откры́тии писа́ли все газе́ты; **they (don't) ~ it off** они́ (не) ла́дят; **it's time to ~ the road** пора́ идти́/е́хать

vi: **he ~ back at him** он нанёс отве́тный уда́р; *fig*: **with him it's a case of ~ or miss** он всё де́лает наута́д; **I ~ on the solution/the right word/an idea** я нашёл реше́ние/то́чное сло́во, мне пришла́ иде́я.

hitch *n* **1** (*knot*) у́зел

2 *fig* (*obstacle*): **there's been a ~ in negotiations** была́ заде́ржка в перегово́рах; **it all went off without a ~** всё прошло́ гла́дко.

hitch *vti*: **I ~ed the rope over/on to a branch** я привяза́л верёвку к ве́тке; **he ~ed up his trousers** он подтяну́л брю́ки; *CQ* **to ~ (a lift)** *see* **hitch-hike.**

hitch-hike *vi* е́здить на попу́тных маши́нах (*usu impf*); **I ~d to Oxford** я дое́хал до О́ксфорда на попу́тных маши́нах.

hitch-hiker *n*: **my son is a great ~** мой сын лю́бит путеше́ствовать на попу́тных маши́нах.

hither *adv arch* сюда́; **~ and thither** туда́ (и) сюда́.

hitherto *adv* до сих по́р (*of present time*); до э́того (*of past time*).

hive *n*, *also* **bee** ~ у́лей; **I lost the whole** ~ (= *all the bees*) **in the winter** зимо́й у меня́ весь рой поги́б; *fig* **our office was a** ~ **of activity last week** на про́шлой неде́ле рабо́та у нас в конто́ре кипе́ла как в у́лье.

hive *vi fig*: **some of the party** ~**d off at Zagorsk** часть компа́нии отдели́лась в Загóрске.

hm, hmph *interj* хм!, гм!

hoard *n* (*store*) запа́с; **a squirrel's** ~ **of nuts** запа́с оре́хов у бе́лки; **a miser's** ~ сокро́вище скря́ги; **I found a** ~ **of banknotes in my aunt's mattress** я обнару́жил ку́чу де́нег в тёткином матра́се.

hoard *vt*: **I'm** ~**ing provisions in case there is heavy snow** я запаса́юсь проду́ктами на слу́чай сне́жных зано́сов; **she** ~**s her money** она́ кладёт все де́ньги в кубы́шку; **he** ~**s all his old journals** он храни́т все ста́рые журна́лы.

hoarding *n* (*for advertisements*) рекла́мный щит.

hoarfrost *n* и́ней.

hoarse *adj* хри́плый, си́плый; **to become** ~ охри́пнуть; **I'm** ~ **today** сего́дня я охри́п; **to talk oneself** ~ договори́ться до хрипоты́; **in a** ~ **voice** охри́пшим/хри́плым го́лосом.

hoax *n* (*trick*) трюк; (*practical joke*) ро́зыгрыш.

hoax *vt*: **he** ~**ed us into believing that...** он разыгра́л нас, и мы пове́рили, что...

hobble *vi* прихра́мывать (*impf*); **he** ~**d along** он шёл прихра́мывая.

hobby *n* хо́бби (*indecl*).

hobby-horse *n* (*toy*) лоша́дка; *fig* конёк; **he's started on his** ~ он сел на своего́ люби́мого конька́.

hobnailed *adj*: ~ **boots** подкóванные сапоги́.

hobnob *vi*: **to** ~ **with smb** якша́ться с кем-л (*impf*).

hock[1] *n* (*of horse*) сухожи́лие.

hock[2] *n* (*wine*) рейнве́йн.

hockey *n* хокке́й на траве́ [**NB** хокке́й = *ice-hockey*]; *attr*: ~ **stick** хокке́йная клю́шка.

hoe *n* моты́га.

hoe *vti* моты́жить (*impf*); **she's** ~**ing in the garden** она́ моты́жит зе́млю в саду́; **to** ~ **the ground** взрыхл|я́ть зе́млю моты́гой (-и́ть).

hog *n* (*pig*) бо́ров; *fig CQ*: **greedy** ~ обжо́ра; **let's go the whole** ~ **and have champagne** гуля́ть так гуля́ть, дава́й вы́пьем шампа́нского.

hog *vt CQ*: **he** ~**ged nearly all the caviare** он сло́пал всю икру́; **he** ~**ged the limelight/the road** он всю сла́ву заграба́стал себе́, он за́нял всю доро́гу.

hoist *n* (*goods lift*) подъёмник.

hoist *vt*: **to** ~ **(up) a sail/a flag** под|нима́ть па́рус/флаг (-ня́ть); **he** ~**ed the child on to the wall/into the saddle** он посади́л ма́льчика на забо́р/в седло́.

hold[1] *n Naut* трюм.

hold[2] *n* **1** (*grasp*): **to take/lay** ~ **of smth** бра́ться за что-л; **to catch/seize** ~ **of smth** хвата́ть что-л, хвата́ться за что-л; **keep** ~ **of my hand** держи́сь за мою́ ру́ку; **I kept a tight** ~ **on the dog('s collar)** я кре́пко держа́л соба́ку за оше́йник; **he let go his** ~ **of the rope** он вы́пустил верёвку (из рук); *CQ*: **where did you get** ~ **of that book?** где ты доста́л э́ту кни́гу?; **it's hard to get** ~ **of him** его́ о́чень тру́дно заста́ть

2 (*influence*, *control*): **his uncle has some sort of** ~ **over him** дя́дя облада́ет како́й-то вла́стью над ним; **I kept a tight** ~ **of myself** я сде́рживался изо всех си́л

3 *Sport* (*in wrestling*) захва́т; (*in climbing*) **there are no** ~**s on the cliff** на скале́ не́ за что уцепи́ться; *fig* **no** ~**s are barred** все сре́дства хороши́.

hold[2] *vti vt* **1** (*grasp*) держа́ть (*impf*); **to** ~ **smth in one's hand/hands/arms/under one's arm** держа́ть что-л в руке́/в рука́х/на рука́х/под мы́шкой; **I held her hand** я держа́л её за́ руку; **they held hands** они́ держа́лись за́ руки; **to** ~ **one's head/a flag high** высоко́ держа́ть го́лову/зна́мя; **to** ~ **oneself erect** держа́ться пря́мо; **the button was held by a thread** пу́говица держа́лась на одно́й ни́тке; **her headscarf was held in place by a brooch** её плато́к был зако́лот бро́шкой; **to** ~ **one's nose** за|жима́ть нос (-жа́ть)

2 (*restrain*) задерж|ивать, удерж|ивать, сдерж|ивать (*pfs* -а́ть); **he could hardly** ~ **the horses** он едва́ уде́рживал/сде́рживал лошаде́й; **there's no** ~**ing him** его́ нельзя́ удержа́ть; **they held the bus till we arrived** они́ задержа́ли авто́бус до на́шего прихо́да; *fig CQ*: ~ **it!** (*keep still for photo*) не шевели́сь!; ~ **your horses!** не торопи́сь!, поду́май хороше́нько!

3 (*keep*, *have*) держа́ть; **he was held prisoner** его́ держа́ли в плену́; **my money is held at the bank** мои́ де́ньги в ба́нке; **he** ~**s the records of the meeting** протоко́л заседа́ния у него́; **the enemy held their ground/the town** проти́вник уде́рживал пози́ции (*pl*)/го́род; **we're** ~**ing the tinned food in reserve** мы де́ржим консе́рвы про запа́с; *fig*: **to** ~ **an office** занима́ть пост (*usu impf*); **he held the floor for two hours** он держа́л речь два часа́; **he can** ~ **an audience** он уме́ет завладе́ть внима́нием аудито́рии; **he can** ~ **his ground with the older boys** он не уступа́ет ста́ршим ма́льчикам; *Sport* **he** ~**s the record for the high jump** он де́ржит реко́рд по прыжка́м (*pl*) в высоту́

4 (*contain*) вме|ща́ть (-сти́ть); **how many people does the hall** ~**?** ско́лько люде́й вмеща́ет э́тот зал?; **our car can** ~ **six people** в на́шей маши́не помеща́ется шесть челове́к; **the kettle** ~**s 2 litres** ча́йник двухлитро́вый; *fig*: **this argument won't** ~ **(water)** э́тот аргуме́нт не вы́держивает кри́тики; **I can't** ~ **all these figures in my head** я не могу́ держа́ть все э́ти ци́фры в голове́; **who knows what the future** ~**s for us?** кто зна́ет, что нас ждёт в бу́дущем/, что нам сули́т бу́дущее?; **the evening held a lot of surprises for us all** ве́чер был по́лон сюрпри́зов для всех

5 (*conduct*): **to ~ talks** вести́ перегово́ры (*only in impf*); **to ~ a meeting/examination/election** про|води́ть заседа́ние/экза́мен/вы́боры (*pl*) (-вести́); **the election was held in May** вы́боры проводи́лись в ма́е; **they held a reception for him** они́ устро́или приём в его́ честь

6 (*consider*) счита́ть (*only in impf*); **I ~ this to be quite impractical** по-мо́ему, э́то соверше́нно нереа́льно, я счита́ю э́то нереа́льным; **we ~ him (to be) a fool** мы счита́ем его́ кру́глым дурако́м; **you will be held responsible** вы за э́то отве́тите; *Law* **he was held (to be) not guilty** он был при́знан невино́вным

vi: **will the ice/rope ~?** вы́держит ли лёд/верёвка?; **if the frost ~s** е́сли моро́з продéржится; **the good weather is still ~ing** всё ещё стои́т хоро́шая пого́да; **this law/my promise still ~s** э́тот зако́н ещё име́ет си́лу, моё обеща́ние ещё в си́ле

hold against *vt*: **he never remembers my birthday, but I don't ~ it against him** он никогда́ не по́мнит моего́ дня рожде́ния, но я на него́ не обижа́юсь

hold back *vti vt*: **they held back the enemy for two days** они́ сде́рживали на́тиск проти́вника два дня; **the police tried to ~ back the crowd** поли́ция стара́лась сде́рживать/удержа́ть толпу́; **I hope we haven't held you back/held back the meeting** наде́юсь, мы вас не задержа́ли/мы не задержа́ли собра́ние; **I held him back from (making) the attempt** я удержа́л его́ от э́той попы́тки; **he's ~ing back information** он что́-то ута́ивает/скрыва́ет

vi: **she held back, not knowing what to say** она́ тяну́ла с отве́том, не зна́я, что сказа́ть; **do help yourselves and don't ~ back** угоща́йтесь, не стесня́йтесь

hold down *vt*: **the invaders couldn't ~ the country down for long** захва́тчики не могли́ до́лго держа́ть страну́ в подчине́нии; **we held down the burglar till the police arrived** мы задержа́ли во́ра до прихо́да поли́ции; **we can't ~ down prices much longer** мы не смо́жем до́лго уде́рживать це́ны на ны́нешнем/существу́ющем у́ровне; **he can't ~ down a job** он не мо́жет удержа́ться ни на како́й рабо́те

hold forth *vi*: **he held forth on the subject at great length** он до́лго разглаго́льствовал на э́ту те́му (*impf*)

hold off *vti vt*: **to ~ off an enemy attack** отра|жа́ть ата́ку проти́вника (-зи́ть)

vi: **if the rain ~s off** е́сли не бу́дет дождя́

hold on *vti vt*: **I had to ~ my hat on** я до́лжен был приде́рживать шля́пу

vi: **~ on to the rope** держи́сь за верёвку; **~ on to your purse** спрячь пода́льше (свой) кошелёк; **~ on to my case for a moment** подержи́ на мину́тку мой чемода́н; **we can ~ on/out for another month** мы мо́жем продержа́ться ещё оди́н ме́сяц; **~ on as far as the bridge and then turn left** иди́те до моста́, а пото́м поверни́те нале́во; *CQ* (*wait*) **~ on!** подожди́те!

hold out *vti vt*: **she held out her hand** она́ подала́/протяну́ла ру́ку; *fig* **the doctor doesn't ~ out much hope of her recovery** у врача́ ма́ло наде́жды на её выздоровле́ние

vi: **as long as our food ~s out** пока́ не ко́нчатся запа́сы еды́/(*of expedition*) продово́льствия; **the garrison can't ~ out much longer** гарнизо́н до́лго не проде́ржится; **we must ~ out for our demands/a better price** ну́жно отст|а́ивать на́ши тре́бования, ну́жно наст|а́ивать на бо́лее вы́годной цене́ (*pfs* -оя́ть)

hold over *vt*: **the matter was held over till the next meeting** обсужде́ние э́того вопро́са отложи́ли до сле́дующего заседа́ния

hold to *vti vt*: **I shall ~ you to your promise** я припо́мню тебе́ э́то обеща́ние

vi: **I ~ to my opinion** я остаю́сь при своём мне́нии

hold together *vt*: **the documents are held together by a paper clip/by string** докуме́нты скреплены́ скре́пкой/свя́заны бечёвкой

hold up *vti vt*: **the ceiling is held up by two beams** потоло́к подде́рживают две ба́лки; **~ the opal up to the light** посмотри́ опа́л на свет(у́); **they were held up by bad weather** они́ задержа́лись из-за непого́ды; **work in the factory has been held up by lack of fuel** рабо́та на заво́де была́ приостано́влена из-за нехва́тки то́плива

vi: **will the weather ~ up?** до́лго ли проде́ржится така́я пого́да?; **he's ~ing up well after his wife's death** у него́ неда́вно умерла́ жена́, но он де́ржится непло́хо

hold with *vi*: **my father doesn't ~ with divorce** мой оте́ц не одобря́ет разво́дов (*pl*).

holdup *n* (*robbery*) грабёж; (*delay*) заде́ржка; (*of traffic*) зато́р, *CQ* про́бка.

hole *n* **1** (*in clothing, etc.*) дыра́, ды́рка; (*slit, cut*) про́резь; **a ~ in a sock/shoe** ды́рка наноске́/в боти́нке; **to wear a jumper into ~s** износи́ть дже́мпер до дыр

2 (*aperture*) отве́рстие; (*in a boat*) пробо́ина; (*a breach*) брешь; **a ~ in a wall/in the roof** отве́рстие в стене́, дыра́ в кры́ше; **a ~ in the ice** (*for fishing*) про́рубь; **a ~ in a tooth** дупло́ в зу́бе; **a ~ in a tree trunk** дупло́ в стволе́ де́рева; **a ~ in the defence** брешь в оборо́не

3 (*in ground*) я́ма, я́мка; (*on putting green, etc.*) я́мка, лу́нка; (*a burrow*) нора́; **a ~ in the road** я́ма/(*pot-hole*) вы́боина на доро́ге

4 *fig uses*: **to get smb out of a ~** вы́вести кого́-л из затрудне́ния, вы́зволить кого́-л из беды́; **I'm in a bit of a ~** я попа́л в беду́; **repairing the car has made a big ~ in my salary** ремо́нт маши́ны проби́л большу́ю брешь в мои́х фина́нсах; **money burns a ~ in his pocket** у него́ де́ньги не де́ржатся;

he's always ready to pick ~s in an argument он любит придираться/задавать каверзные вопросы; **he lives here?—what a ~!** и он здесь живёт, в такой дыре?

hole *vt*: **the ship has ~d her bottom** корабль получил пробоину в днище.

hole-and-corner *adj CQ*: **I don't like his ~ methods** он всё делает украдкой/исподтишка—я это терпеть не могу.

holiday *n* (*public*) праздник; (*day off from work*) выходной (день); (*annual*) отпуск; **school ~s** каникулы; **Sunday is a ~ for most people** для большинства (людей) воскресенье—выходной день; **where are you going for your ~s?** куда вы едете в отпуск (*sing*)/(*school holidays*) на каникулы?; **I need a ~** мне нужно отдохнуть; **I spent my ~/the ~s at the seaside** я провёл отпуск на море; **he's on ~** он в отпуске, у него отпуск; *attr*: **the ~ season** время летних отпусков; **~ centre** турбаза.

holiday *vi* от|дыхать (-дохнуть).

holiday-maker *n* отпускник.

holler *vi CQ* (*call*) кри|чать (-́кнуть); (*wail*) вопить (*impf*).

hollow *n* (*in ground*: *small*) яма; (*big*) лощина; (*cavity*) впадина; **the village lay in a ~ of the hills** село находилось в лощине между холмами.

hollow *adj* **1**: **a ~ bamboo cane/pipe** полая бамбуковая трость/трубка; **a ~ tree (trunk)** дуплистое дерево; **~ cheeks** впалые щёки; **a ~ sound** глухой звук; **he answered in a ~ voice** он ответил глухим голосом; **he gave a ~ laugh** он глухо рассмеялся; **~ words** пустые слова; **a ~ victory** бесполезная победа.

hollow *adv Sport CQ*: **we beat them ~** мы разбили их в пух и прах.

hollow *vt*, *also* **to ~ out** (*with tools*) вы|далбливать (-́долбить); **these rocks have been ~ed out by the action of the waves** эти скалы были подмыты волнами.

hollow-eyed *adj* с ввалившимися глазами.

holly *n Bot* остролист.

holy *adj* святой.

home *n* **1** дом; **is Ivan at ~?** Иван дома?; **he's not at ~** его нет дома; **there was no one at ~** дома никого не было; **he left ~ when he was quite young** он рано ушёл из родительского дома; **he leaves ~ early for the office** он рано уходит (из дому) на работу; **for me this is a ~ from ~** это мой второй дом; **they have a beautiful house, but it doesn't feel like ~** у них прекрасный дом, но чувствуешь себя там как-то неуютно; **they are always at ~ on Wednesdays** они всегда дома по средам; **I hope you will come to our ~ one day** надеюсь, что вы приедете к нам когда-нибудь; **they invited us to their ~** они пригласили нас к себе; **he comes from a poor ~** он из бедной семьи; **he made his ~ in France/with a friend** он поселился во Франции/у приятеля; **I feel most at ~ in the country** лучше всего я себя чувствую в деревне; *fig*: **he's at ~ on any topic** о чём бы ни заговорили, у него всегда есть что сказать; **make yourself at ~** будьте как дома

2 (*place of origin*) родина; **where is your ~?—My ~ is England/Leeds** откуда вы родом?—Моя родина Англия/Я родом из Лидса; **he was far from ~** он был вдали от дома

3 (*institution*) дом; **a ~ for the old** дом для престарелых; **a children's ~** (*orphanage*) детский дом, *abbr* детдом.

4 (*in children's games*) дом; *Sport* **is your match at ~ or away?** вы играете на своём или на чужом поле?

home *attr adj* домашний; **~ address** домашний адрес, (*on forms*) местожительство; **~ cooking** домашняя еда; **~ industry** (*if working independently*) кустарный промысел, (*if connected with factory*) надомная работа, (*as opposed to foreign*) отечественная промышленность; **~ life/comforts** семейная жизнь, домашний уют (*sing*); **one's ~ town** родной город; *Sport* **the ~ team** хозяева поля; *fig* **a ~ truth** горькая правда/истина.

home *adv* **1** (*at home*) дома; (*to home*) домой; **I'm ~ at last** наконец я дома; **I long to be ~** мне хочется домой; **on the way ~** по дороге домой; **to see smb ~** проводить кого-л домой; **to write ~** писать (письма) домой

2 *fig uses*: **in order to drive my point ~** чтобы втолковать это; **the remark went/struck ~** замечание попало в цель; *CQ* **he's nothing to write ~ about** он ничего особенного из себя не представляет.

home-baked *adj*: **~ cakes** домашние сладкие пирожки.

home-brewed *adj*: **~ beer** пиво домашнего приготовления.

home-grown *adj*: **these are ~ vegetables** эти овощи из нашего огорода.

homeland *n* родина, отечество.

homeless *adj* бездомный.

homely *adj*: **a ~ room** уютная комната; **there's such a nice ~ atmosphere with them** у них чувствуешь себя как дома; **~ fare** простая пища; **a ~ old lady** добрая/милая старушка; **she's a ~ girl** она такая простая девушка, (*US*: *plain-looking*) она не красавица.

home-made *adj*: **~ jam** домашнее варенье; **a ~ radio** самодельный радиоприёмник.

homesick *adj*: **to be ~** тосковать по дому (*for family home*)/по родине (*for native country*).

homeward(s) *adv* домой.

homework *n* (*of pupils*) домашние задания (*pl*), домашняя работа; **what ~ have you got today?** что тебе сегодня задали на дом?; *fig* **he hasn't done his ~ for the meeting** он не подготовился к собранию.

homicidal *adj*: **a ~ maniac** убийца-маньяк.

homicide *n* убийство.

homoeopath, (*US*) **homeopath** *n* гомеопат.

homogeneous *adj* однородный.

homonym *n* омо́ним.

homosexual *n* гомосексуали́ст.

honest *adj* че́стный; (*frank*) открове́нный; ~ **dealing** че́стный посту́пок; **he's** ~ **in his dealings** он поря́дочный челове́к; **he's completely** ~ он абсолю́тно че́стен; **he has an** ~ **face** у него́ тако́е откры́тое лицо́; **to be** ~, **I was wrong** че́стно говоря́, я оши́бся; **I'll give you my** ~ **opinion** я вам открове́нно скажу́; *CQ* ~ **to God** че́стное сло́во.

honey *n* мёд; **comb/clover** ~ со́товый/кле́верный мёд; *fig* (*US*: *endearment*) ми́лочка, голу́бушка.

honeycomb *n* пчели́ные со́ты (*no sing*).

honeycombed *adj*: **the coalmine is** ~ **with galleries** ша́хта вся изре́зана галере́ями.

honeysuckle *n* жи́молость.

honk *n*: **the** ~ **of wild geese/of a motor horn** крик ди́ких гусе́й, автомоби́льный гудо́к.

honk *vti Aut*: **to** ~ **(one's horn)** гуде́ть (*impf*).

honorarium *n* гонора́р.

honorary *adj* почётный; **an** ~ **secretary/member** почётный секрета́рь/член.

honour, (*US*) **honor** *n* **1** честь; **a point/debt of** ~ вопро́с/долг че́сти; **a dinner in** ~ **of the president** обе́д в честь президе́нта; **a man of** ~ челове́к че́сти; **the seat of** ~ почётное ме́сто; **roll of** ~ почётный спи́сок; **such feelings do you** ~ таки́е чу́вства де́лают вам честь; **will you do me the** ~ **of dining with me?** окажи́те мне честь отобе́дать со мной; **I hold it an** ~ **to be your chairman** я счита́ю за честь быть ва́шим председа́телем; **I feel in** ~ **bound to tell you that...** счита́ю свои́м до́лгом сказа́ть вам, что...; ~ **among thieves** воровска́я честь

2 *pl*: **military/last** ~**s** во́инские/после́дние по́чести; **to do the** ~**s (of the house)** исполня́ть обя́занности хозя́ина/хозя́йки.

honour, (*US*) **honor** *vt* **1**: **to** ~ **one's parents/smb's memory** почита́ть роди́телей, чтить чью-л па́мять; **I am** ~**ed by your invitation** я польщён ва́шим приглаше́нием; **I** ~ **you for your courageous decision** я вас уважа́ю за ва́ше сме́лое реше́ние

2 (*fulfil*): **to** ~ **one's commitments/one's promise** вы|полня́ть свои́ обяза́тельства (-по́лнить), сдерж|ивать *or* исполн|я́ть своё обеща́ние (-а́ть/-́ить); **to** ~ **a bill/cheque** опла́|чивать счёт/чек (-ти́ть).

honourable, (*US*) **honorable** *adj*: **an** ~ **peace** почётный мир; (*upright*) ~ **intentions** че́стные наме́рения; (*in address*) **my** ~ **colleague** мой уважа́емый колле́га.

hooch *n* (*US*) *CQ* спиртно́е; **I'll bring the** ~ я принесу́ вы́пить.

hood *n* (*of coat*) капюшо́н; *Aut* (*UK*: *roof of open car*) верх, кры́ша; (*US*: *bonnet*) капо́т.

hoodlum *n* (*US*) *CQ* хулига́н.

hoodwink *vt* обма́н|ывать (-у́ть), наду|ва́ть (-́ть).

hooey *n* (*US*) *CQ* чушь, ерунда́.

hoof *n* копы́то.

hook *n* крюк, (*smaller*) крючо́к; *Agric* серп; **I hung my coat on a** ~ я пове́сил пальто́ на крючо́к; **the keys are there on the** ~ ключи́ там, на крючке́; **fish** ~ рыболо́вный крючо́к; *CQ*: **we'll get there on time by** ~ **or by crook** мы бу́дем там во́время, чего́ бы э́то ни сто́ило; **to get/let smb off the** ~ вы́ручить кого́-л из беды́, отпусти́ть кого́-л.

hook *vti vt*: **he** ~**ed a trout but didn't land it** он пойма́л форе́ль на крючо́к, но она́ сорвала́сь; **they** ~**ed two extra wagons on to the train** к соста́ву прицепи́ли ещё два ваго́на; **can you** ~ **up my dress for me?** застегни́ мне, пожа́луйста, пла́тье; **my trousers got** ~**ed on the barbed wire** я зацепи́лся брю́ками за колю́чую про́волоку; *fig CQ*: **she's** ~**ed a husband** она́ подцепи́ла себе́ му́жа; **he's** ~**ed on drugs/on TV** он наркома́н, его́ не оторвёшь от телеви́зора

vi: **the dress** ~**s up at the back** пла́тье застёгивается сза́ди (на крючки́).

hooked *adj*: **a** ~ **nose** крючкова́тый нос.

hooky *n* (*US*) *CQ*: **to play** ~ прогу́ливать (уро́ки) (*usu impf*).

hooligan *n* хулига́н.

hooliganism *n* хулига́нство.

hoop *n* о́бруч; (*croquet*) воро́та (*no sing*); **the child is playing with a** ~ ребёнок ката́ет о́бруч; **to fasten a barrel with** ~**s** наби́ть о́бручи на бо́чку.

hoot *n*: **the** ~ **of an owl** крик совы́; (*of motor horn*, *siren*) гудо́к; **his speech was received with** ~**s of laughter/disapproval** его́ речь была́ встре́чена взры́вами сме́ха/во́згласами неодобре́ния; *sl* **I don't give a** ~**/two** ~**s for what he thinks** мне наплева́ть, что он ду́мает.

hoot *vi* (*of owls*) у́хать (*semel* у́хнуть); (*of sound of siren*, *horn*) гуде́ть (*impf*); (*passenger to driver*) ~ **at the pedestrian/**~ **at the crossing** посигна́льте пешехо́ду/на перехо́де.

hooter *n* (*of car*, *factory*) гудо́к.

hop *n* **1** (*jump*) прыжо́к, скачо́к; *Sport* ~, **skip and jump** тройно́й прыжо́к; *CQ* **he keeps us on the** ~ он не даёт нам поко́я

2 *Aer*: **it's only a short** ~ **from London to Paris** от Ло́ндона до Пари́жа коро́ткий перелёт; **we flew from Moscow to Sydney in three** ~**s** мы лете́ли из Москвы́ в Си́дней с двумя́ поса́дками (*i.e. with two stops*).

hop *vti vt*: *CQ* ~ **it!** убира́йся!, прова́ливай!, кати́сь!

vi пры́гать/скака́ть на одно́й ноге́ (*usu impf*); **I** ~**ped off/on to the bus** я вы́скочил из авто́буса, я вскочи́л в авто́бус; **to** ~ **out of bed** вскочи́ть с посте́ли.

hope *n* наде́жда; **faint/forlorn** ~ сла́бая наде́жда; **I have little** ~**/high** ~**s of success** у меня́ ма́ло наде́жды на успе́х, я о́чень наде́юсь на успе́х; **I haven't the faintest** ~ **of passing the exam** никако́й наде́жды, что я вы́держу экза́мен; **is there any** ~ **that he'll recover?** есть ли наде́жда, что он попра́вится?; **there's not much** ~ **of his being in just now**

ма́ло наде́жды, что он сейча́с до́ма; **we have good ~s of arriving by 9 o'clock** мы наде́емся прие́хать к девяти́ (часа́м); **I went back in the ~ of finding my ring** я пошёл обра́тно, наде́ясь найти́ своё кольцо́; **don't raise her ~s too high!** не сли́шком обнадёживай(те) её; **they put all their ~s on him** они́ возлага́ли на него́ все свои́ наде́жды; *iron* **what a ~!** и не наде́йся!

hope *vti vt*: **to ~ that...** наде́яться, что... (*usu impf*); **I ~ (that) you'll come** наде́юсь, (что) ты прие́дешь [**NB** я *usu omitted*]

vi наде́яться (*impf*); (*of what one hopes of others*) ожида́ть (*impf*); **I ~ so/not** наде́юсь, что да/, что нет; **we ~ to leave on Tuesday** мы наде́емся уе́хать во вто́рник; **let's ~ for the best** бу́дем наде́яться на лу́чшее; **to ~ against hope** наде́яться вопреки́ всему́; **we ~d for better things from him** мы ожида́ли от него́ бо́льшего.

hopeful *adj* **1** *predic only*: **to be/feel ~ that/of** *see verb* **to hope**

2 *predic and attr*: **he has a ~ temperament, he is ~ by temperament** он оптими́ст по нату́ре; **the future doesn't look very ~** бу́дущее вы́глядит безнадёжно; **he is quite a ~ young pianist** он молодо́й пиани́ст, подаю́щий наде́жды (*pl*); *as n*: *joc* **have you met our young ~?** ты знако́м с на́шим молоды́м тала́нтом?

hopeless *adj* безнадёжный; **a ~ situation** безнадёжное/(*desperate*) безвы́ходное положе́ние; (*of illness*) **his case is ~** он в безнадёжном состоя́нии; **we've given up the attempt as ~** мы отказа́лись от э́той попы́тки, как от де́ла безнадёжного; *CQ*: **I'm ~ at remembering names** у меня́ о́чень плоха́я па́мять на имена́; **it's ~ trying to work at home** до́ма не́чего и пыта́ться рабо́тать.

horizon *n* горизо́нт.

horizontal *adj* горизонта́льный.

hormone *n* гормо́н.

horn *n* **1** (*of animal, or as material*) рог; (*of snail*) у́сик; **carved from ~** вы́резанный из ро́га; *fig*: **to be on the ~s of a dilemma** стоя́ть пе́ред диле́ммой; **to draw in one's ~s** (*retract*) пойти́ на попя́тный/на попя́тную, (*cut expenditure*) эконо́мить; *attr* рогово́й

2 (*instrument*: *of hunters*) рог; (*of shepherds and Mus*) рожо́к; *Aut* гудо́к, звуково́й сигна́л; **to blow a hunting ~** труби́ть в охо́тничий рог; *Mus*: **English ~** англи́йский рожо́к; **French ~** валто́рна; **to play the ~** игра́ть на рожке́/на валто́рне; *Aut* **to sound the ~** сигна́лить; **sound your ~!** *CQ* посигна́ль!

horned *adj* рога́тый.

hornet *n* ше́ршень (*m*); *fig* **to stir up a ~'s nest** растрево́жить оси́ное гнездо́.

horn-rimmed *adj*: **~ spectacles** очки́ в рогово́й опра́ве.

horny *adj* (*made of horn*) рогово́й; *fig* **~ hands** мозо́листые ру́ки.

horoscope *n* гороско́п; **to cast a ~** соста́вить гороско́п.

horrible *adj* ужа́сный, *also CQ*; **a ~ accident** (*traffic*) ужа́сная ава́рия; *CQ* **we had a perfectly ~ journey** пое́здка была́ чудо́вищная.

horrid *adj* отврати́тельный, ужа́сный, проти́вный; *CQ*: **~ weather** отврати́тельная/ужа́сная пого́да; **what a ~ idea!** кака́я ужа́сная/ди́кая мысль!; **they were ~ to me** они́ уж так пло́хо обошли́сь со мной; **don't be ~!** не будь таки́м проти́вным!, да ну́ тебя́!

horrific *adj CQ* ужа́сный.

horrify *vt* ужас|а́ть (-ну́ть); **we were simply horrified by the news** э́та но́вость нас про́сто ужасну́ла; **I was horrified when...** я пришёл в у́жас, когда́...

horrifying *adj* ужаса́ющий; *CQ* ужа́сный.

horror *n* у́жас; **to my ~** к моему́ у́жасу; **I have a ~ of rats** я о́чень бою́сь крыс; **we were filled with ~ at the sight** при ви́де э́того нас обуя́л у́жас; *CQ* **that child is a little/perfect ~** не ребёнок, а про́сто наказа́ние; *attr*: **a ~ story/film** рома́н/фильм у́жасов.

horror-stricken *adj* объя́тый/охва́ченный у́жасом; в у́жасе.

hors d'oeuvres *npl approx* заку́ски.

horse *n* **1** ло́шадь; (*male, also of cavalry horses, and in gymnasium*) конь (*m*); (*stallion*) жеребе́ц; (*gelding*) ме́рин; **saddle/race/draught ~** верхова́я/скакова́я/упряжна́я ло́шадь; **to get on/get off/fall off a ~** сесть на ло́шадь, слезть/упа́сть с ло́шади; *fig*: **clothes ~** ра́ма для су́шки оде́жды; **white ~s** (*waves*) бара́шки

2 *fig uses*: **he works/eats like a ~** он рабо́тает как ло́шадь, у него́ во́лчий аппети́т; **I had it straight from the ~'s mouth** я узна́л э́то из пе́рвых рук; **don't look a gift ~ in the mouth** дарёному коню́ в зу́бы не смо́трят; **don't get on your high ~!** не задава́йся!

horseback *adv*: **on ~** верхо́м.

horse-box *n Aut* тре́йлер для лошаде́й.

horse chestnut *n* (ко́нский) кашта́н (*of tree or nut*).

horse-coper, horse-dealer *n* бары́шник.

horse fly *n* слепе́нь (*m*).

Horse Guards *npl* конногварде́йский полк (*sing*).

horsehair *n* ко́нский во́лос; *attr*: **a ~ mattress** волосяно́й матра́ц/тюфя́к.

horsehide *n* ко́нская шку́ра.

horseman *n* вса́дник; (*with reference to horsemanship*) нае́здник; **he's a good ~** он хоро́ший нае́здник.

horseplay *n*: **there was a bit of ~ among the students and a window got broken** студе́нты устро́или возню́ и разби́ли окно́.

horsepower, *abbr* **h.p.** *n* лошади́ная си́ла; *attr Tech*: **a 40 h.p. engine** дви́гатель мо́щностью в со́рок лошади́ных сил.

horse-race, horse-racing *ns* ска́чки (*pl*); (*for horses harnessed, not ridden*) бега́ (*pl*).

horseradish *n* хрен (*plant or sauce*).

horse-sense *n CQ* просто́й здра́вый смысл.

horseshoe *n* подко́ва; *attr* в фо́рме подко́вы, подковообра́зный.

horticultural *adj* садо́вый.

horticulture *n* садово́дство.

hose[1] *n* шланг, рука́в, кишка́ (*used by fire engines*); (*domestic*) шланг.

hose[1] *vt* поли|ва́ть из шла́нга (-́ть); **to ~ down the car** полива́ть маши́ну из шла́нга.

hose[2] *n* (*in shops: stockings*) чулки́ (*pl*), (*socks*) носки́ (*pl*).

hosepipe *n see* **hose**[1] *n.*

hosiery *n attr*: **where is the ~ department?** где отде́л чуло́чных изде́лий?

hospitable *adj* гостеприи́мный; **a ~ family/house/atmosphere** гостеприи́мная семья́, гостеприи́мный дом, атмосфе́ра гостеприи́мства.

hospital *n* больни́ца; *Mil* го́спиталь (*m*); **a maternity/mental ~** роди́льный дом, психиатри́ческая больни́ца; **he's in ~** он лежи́т в больни́це; **how long were you in ~?** ско́лько (вре́мени) вы пролежа́ли в больни́це?; **he was taken to/put in ~** его́ положи́ли/помести́ли в больни́цу; **to go to visit smb in ~** пойти́/пое́хать в больни́цу к кому́-л; *attr*: **~ nurse** больни́чная сестра́.

hospitality *n* гостеприи́мство.

hospitalize *vt* (*US*): **he's been ~d** его́ госпитализи́ровали (*impf and pf*).

host[1] *n* (*of people or things*) мно́жество, *CQ* ма́сса, тьма; **he has a ~ of friends** у него́ мно́жество/ма́сса/тьма друзе́й.

host[2] *n* хозя́ин (*in private house, hotel*; *also Biol*); **he acted as ~** он был за хозя́ина.

hostage *n* зало́жник; **to exchange ~s** обменя́ться зало́жниками.

hostel *n* общежи́тие.

hostess *n* хозя́йка (*at home, or in hotel*).

hostile *adj* **1** (*belonging to the enemy*) вра́жеский; **the ~ camp** вра́жеский ла́герь, ла́герь проти́вника

2 (*unfriendly*) вражде́бный, недружелю́бный, неприя́зненный; **a ~ act/look/tone** недружелю́бный посту́пок, вражде́бный взгляд, неприя́зненный тон; **a ~ crowd** вражде́бно настро́енная толпа́; **he was ~ to our proposal** он при́нял на́ше предложе́ние в штыки́.

hostility *n* **1** вражде́бность, вражда́; **to show ~ towards smb** прояви́ть вражде́бность к кому́-л; **I feel no ~ towards them** я не пита́ю к ним вражде́бных чувств, у меня́ нет к ним вражды́

2: at the outbreak of hostilities в нача́ле войны́; **to open/suspend hostilities** начина́ть/прекраща́ть вое́нные де́йствия.

hot *adj* **1** (*of things hot to touch, feel, taste*) горя́чий; (*of rooms, weather*) жа́ркий; **~ tea/soup** горя́чий чай/суп; **a ~ day** жа́ркий день; **what a ~ room you've got!** как у тебя́ жа́рко в ко́мнате!; **we had a ~ spell** у нас не́сколько дней/неде́ль стоя́ла си́льная жара́; **I got very ~** мне ста́ло о́чень жа́рко; **it's terribly ~ today** сего́дня стра́шная жара́

2 *fig uses*: **he has a ~ temper** у него́ горя́чий нрав, он горя́ч; **he's a ~ supporter of Dynamo** (*football team*) он стра́стный боле́льщик «Дина́мо»; **~ news** са́мые после́дние но́вости (*pl*); **he'll never do it—his threats/promises are all ~ air** он никогда́ э́того не сде́лает, все его́ угро́зы/обеща́ния—про́сто слова́; **my horse is ~ favourite for the Derby** моя́ ло́шадь—фавори́т в де́рби; **he made off in ~ pursuit** он бро́сился вдого́нку (*adv*); **a ~ sauce** о́стрый со́ус; **I got into ~ water because of you** я из-за тебя́ попа́л в хоро́шенькую исто́рию; *sl* **a ~ number** секс-бо́мба.

hot *adv CQ*: **I gave it him ~ and strong** я зада́л ему́ жа́ру; **he's inclined to blow ~ and cold** он то за́, то про́тив, у него́ семь пя́тниц на неде́ле.

hotbed *n Hort* парни́к; *fig* **a ~ of vice** расса́дник поро́ка.

hot-blooded *adj* стра́стный, пы́лкий.

hotchpotch *n* (*soup*) густа́я похлёбка с овоща́ми; *CQ* **his thesis is just a ~ of other people's ideas** его́ диссерта́ция—набо́р чужи́х мы́слей.

hot dog *n* (*US*) бу́лочка с горя́чей соси́ской.

hotel *n* гости́ница, оте́ль (*m*); **to stay/take a room in a ~** останови́ться/снять но́мер в гости́нице.

hothouse *n* оранжере́я; тепли́ца; *attr*: **a ~ plant** оранжере́йное/тепли́чное расте́ние, *also fig.*

hotly *adv*: **they argued ~** они́ горячо́ спо́рили, они́ спо́рили с жа́ром; **he ~ denied the charge** он упо́рно отрица́л обвине́ние.

hotplate *n* (*small cooker*) (электро)пли́тка.

hotpot *n* тушёное мя́со с овоща́ми.

hot-water bottle *n* гре́лка.

hound *n* го́нчая; охо́тничья соба́ка; *pejor* (*of any dog*) пёс; **to ride to ~s** охо́титься (верхо́м) с соба́ками.

hound *vt fig*: **to ~ smb** трави́ть кого́-л (за-).

hour *n* **1** час; **24 ~s** су́тки (*no sing*); **half an ~** полчаса́ (*m*) [*see note under* **half** *n* 4]; **quarter of an ~** че́тверть часа́ [*see* **quarter**]; **an ~ and a half** полтора́ часа́; **the rush ~** час/часы́ пик; *Radio* **children's ~** де́тская переда́ча; *fig*: **to seize the ~** лови́ть моме́нт; **the question of the ~** злободне́вный вопро́с

2 *in expressions of time without preps*: **I was an ~/two ~s late** я опозда́л на час/на два часа́; **two ~s later the snow had gone** че́рез два часа́ снег раста́ял; **he left two ~s before/after lunch** он уе́хал за два часа́ до обе́да/че́рез два часа́ по́сле обе́да; **the meeting lasted an ~/more than an ~ and a half** собра́ние продолжа́лось час/бо́льше полу́тора часо́в; **cement takes four ~s to set** цеме́нт затвердева́ет за четы́ре часа́; **it took us three ~s to get packed** упако́вка заняла́ у нас три часа́; **we have an ~ and a half left till the train goes** (нам) оста́лось/остаётся полтора́ часа́ до отхо́да по́езда; **trains leave for London every ~/every half ~/every two ~s** поезда́ в Ло́ндон иду́т ка́ждый час/ка́ждые полчаса́/ка́ждые два часа́; **the car was doing 70 miles an ~** (*abbr m.p.h.*) маши́на шла со ско́ростью се́мьдесят миль в час; **you can hire a boat for a rouble an ~** мо́жно взять ло́дку напрока́т, пла́та — рубль в час; **to keep late ~s** по́здно ложи́ться спать, сиде́ть допоздна́ (*adv*); **he works long ~s** у него́ дли́нный рабо́чий день; *attr*: **it's a 3 ~ drive/walk from here** э́то отсю́да в трёх часа́х езды́/ходьбы́

3 (*of clocks*): **this clock strikes the ~s (and the half-hours but not the quarters)** э́ти часы́ с бо́ем, э́ти часы́ бьют час и полчаса́, но не че́тверть часа́

4 *in expressions of time with preps*: **this will take about an ~/two ~s** на э́то потре́буется приме́рно час/о́коло двух часо́в; **~ after ~ we waited** мы жда́ли час за ча́сом; **after many ~s** спустя́ мно́го часо́в; **at such an early ~** в тако́й ра́нний час; **they eat at all ~s** они́ едя́т, когда́ придётся; **nobody is here at this ~** в тако́е вре́мя здесь никого́ не быва́ет; **at what ~ is your lesson?** в кото́ром часу́ ваш уро́к?; **at the eleventh ~** в после́днюю мину́ту; **things get worse ~ by ~** час о́т часу не ле́гче; **I am paid by the ~** я на почасово́й опла́те; **I'll be ready in an ~** я бу́ду гото́в че́рез час; **I finished in an ~** я зако́нчил че́рез час; **the Cambridge trains arrive on the ~** поезда́ из Ке́мбриджа прибыва́ют (*approx*) в нача́ле ка́ждого ча́са; **it'll take me over two ~s** э́то займёт у меня́ бо́льше двух часо́в; **I arrived with an ~ to spare** я при́был на час ра́ньше; **he'll be here within the ~** он бу́дет здесь в преде́лах ча́са

5 *usu pl* (*denoting fixed periods*): **office ~s** рабо́чее вре́мя (*for staff*), приёмные часы́ (*for clients, patients*); **during school ~s** во вре́мя уро́ков; **after closing ~s** (*in shops*) по́сле закры́тия магази́нов, (*of pubs*) когда́ закрыва́ются па́бы.

hourglass *n* песо́чные часы́.

hour hand *n* часова́я стре́лка.

hourly *adj*: **there's an ~ bus (service)** авто́бусы отправля́ются/иду́т ка́ждый час; **the ~ rate of pay** почасова́я опла́та; **they live in ~ dread of being caught** они́ живу́т в постоя́нном стра́хе, что их вот-во́т пойма́ют.

hourly *adv*: **2 tablets to be taken ~** принима́ть ка́ждый час по две табле́тки; **we expect news ~** мы ожида́ем сообще́ния с мину́ты на мину́ту.

house *n* **1** (*dwelling*) дом [**NB** *in SU towns* кварти́ра (*flat*) *is equiv of UK* "*house*", *while* дом *usu* = "*block of flats*"]; **a detached ~** особня́к; **prefabricated ~s** сбо́рные дома́; **an apartment ~** многокварти́рный дом; **a country ~** (*manor*) уса́дьба, (*summer cottage*) да́ча; **let's meet at my ~** дава́й встре́тимся у меня́; **come to my ~** приходи́ ко мне; **she keeps ~ for her brother** она́ ведёт хозя́йство в до́ме бра́та; **I've a cold, so I'm keeping (to) the ~** у меня́ на́сморк, и я не выхожу́ (и́з дому); **to move ~** переезжа́ть, меня́ть кварти́ру; **we're going to set up ~ in London** мы собира́емся посели́ться в Ло́ндоне; **they keep open ~** у них гостеприи́мный дом; *fig* **they get on like a ~ on fire** они́ прекра́сно ла́дят

2 *other uses*: (*UK*) **the H. of Lords/of Commons**/(*US*) **of Representatives** пала́та ло́рдов/о́бщин/представи́телей; (*of lineage*) **the H. of Romanov** дом/дина́стия Рома́новых; *Comm* **a fashion ~** дом моде́лей; *Theat* (*audience*) **there was a full/poor ~ last night** вчера́ был по́лный/полупусто́й зал; (*notice*) **"Full H."** «Все биле́ты про́даны»; *Cine* (*showing*) **last ~** после́дний сеа́нс; *fig*: **her appearance brought the ~ down** её появле́ние вы́звало бу́рю аплодисме́нтов; *CQ* (*at hotel bar*) **this one/this round** (*of drinks*) **is on the ~** угоще́ние за счёт хозя́ина *or* угоща́ет хозя́ин

3 *attr* дома́шний; **~ slippers** дома́шние ту́фли; **to be under ~ arrest** быть под дома́шним аре́стом; **a ~ plant** ко́мнатное расте́ние.

house *vt* **1**: **after the war thousands of homeless families had to be ~d** по́сле войны́ ну́жно бы́ло обеспе́чить жильём ты́сячи бездо́мных семе́й; **two families were ~d in one flat** две семьи́ жи́ли в одно́й кварти́ре; **this block of flats can ~ 40 families** в э́том до́ме мо́гут жить со́рок семе́й; **the troops were ~d in a school** солда́т размести́ли в шко́ле; **I can ~ you for a night or two** я могу́ вас приюти́ть на день-два́; **we will ~ the second car in a shed** втору́ю маши́ну поста́вим в сара́й; **the exhibition is temporarily ~d in the school** вы́ставка вре́менно размещена́ в зда́нии шко́лы.

houseboat *n* плаву́чий дом.

household *n* (*people*) дома́шние, домоча́дцы (*pls*); **the royal ~** короле́вский двор; *attr*: **~ chores** дома́шние забо́ты/дела́; **~ expenses** расхо́ды по до́му; **~ goods** хозя́йственные това́ры; (*UK*) **H. Cavalry** гварде́йская кавале́рия.

householder *n* (*owner*) домовладе́лец; (*head of a family*) хозя́ин.

housekeeper *n* (*in private house*) эконо́мка; (*in hospital, hostel*) сестра́-хозя́йка.

housekeeping *n*: **the art of ~** домово́дство; **to do the ~** вести́ хозя́йство; *attr*: **~ money** де́ньги на хозя́йство.

housemaid *n* го́рничная.

house painter *n* маля́р.

house party *n* (*people*) го́сти (*pl*).

house physician *n* врач, живу́щий при больни́це.

house-proud *adj*: **she's very ~** она́ лю́бит, что́бы в до́ме всё блесте́ло.

house-trained *adj*: **my dog is ~** моя́ соба́ка приу́чена жить в до́ме; *fig joc* **my husband is ~** мой муж приу́чен к хозя́йству.

house warming *n*, *often attr*: **I am going to/giving a ~ (party)** я иду́ на новосе́лье, я справля́ю новосе́лье.

housewife *n* домохозя́йка.

housing *n*: **~ is a government priority** жили́щное строи́тельство (*construction*)/обеспе́чение жильём (*providing houses*) — первоочередна́я зада́ча прави́тельства; **more ~ is needed for old people** тре́буется бо́льше кварти́р для одино́ких старико́в; *attr*: **~ conditions** жили́щные усло́вия; **~ estate** жило́й кварта́л; **~ shortage** нехва́тка жилья́.

hovel *n* лачу́га, хиба́рка.

hover *vi* (*of birds*) пари́ть (*impf*); **the helicopter was ~ing above the valley** вертолёт кружи́лся над доли́ной; *fig* **the secretaries ~ed around the president** секретари́ снова́ли вокру́г президе́нта.

hovercraft *n* су́дно на возду́шной поду́шке.

how *adv* **1** (*by what means?*) как?; **~ do you do this?** как э́то де́лается?; **~'s it to be done?** как бы э́то сде́лать?; **~ did it happen?** как э́то случи́лось?; **I know ~ he found this out** я зна́ю, как он узна́л об э́том; **I don't know ~ to play tennis** я не уме́ю игра́ть в те́ннис

2 (*in what state?*) как?; **~ do you do?** как (вы) пожива́ете?; **~ is he?** ну ка́к он?; **~ are things?, ~ goes it?** как дела́?; **~ do you feel?** как вы себя́ чу́вствуете?

3 (*with adjs and advs in questions*): **~ old are you?** ско́лько вам лет?; **~ much does he owe you?** ско́лько он вам до́лжен?; **~ many times have I told you?** ско́лько раз я тебе́ говори́л?; **~ long will it take you to finish your book?** когда́ вы зако́нчите кни́гу?; **~ long is the wall?** какова́ длина́ э́той стены́?; **~ long were you ill?** до́лго ли/ско́лько дней вы боле́ли?; **~ far is it to the station?** далеко́ ли до ста́нции?; **~ often do you see them?** как ча́сто вы ви́дитесь с ни́ми?; **~ else would you describe her?** как бы ина́че её описа́ть?; **~ much are apples today?** ско́лько сто́ят/*CQ* почём сего́дня я́блоки?

4 (*asking for an opinion*): **~ do you like my dress?** как вам нра́вится моё пла́тье?; **~ about a walk?** как насчёт прогу́лки?; *CQ*: **~'s that?, ~ so?** как же та́к?; **~ come?** э́то ка́к же?, ка́к же э́то?; **~ come you're here?** а ты ка́к здесь очути́лся?; **~ the dickens should I know?** отку́да я зна́ю?

5 (*in exclamations*): **~ stupid!** как глу́по!; **~ kind of you!** как любе́зно с ва́шей стороны́!; **~ like him!** как э́то на него́ похо́же!; **~ well you look!** как ты сего́дня хорошо́ вы́глядишь!; **and ~!** ещё как!; **here's ~!** (за) ва́ше здоро́вье!

however *adv* ка́к бы ни; како́й бы ни; **~ that may be** ка́к бы то ни́ было; **you should always repay a debt ~ small** долги́ (*pl*) на́до отдава́ть, да́же са́мые незначи́тельные; **~ much I tried, I never succeeded** ка́к я ни стара́лся, у меня́ ничего́ не получи́лось [**NB** *in past without* бы]; **~ fast he runs, he'll miss the train** как бы он ни торопи́лся, он всё равно́ опозда́ет на по́езд.

however *conj* одна́ко; тем не ме́нее; и всё же; **~ it's all the same to me** мне, одна́ко, всё равно́; **~ he did apologize** тем не ме́нее, он извини́лся; **~ I didn't see the match** и всё же я не посмотре́л матч.

howl *n* (*of wolf, dog, people, wind*) вой (*no pl*); (*expressing pain*) вопль; (*cry*) крик; (*of wind, and CQ of child*) рёв; **with ~s of rage** с я́ростными кри́ками; **the child let out a ~** ребёнок по́днял рёв.

howl *vti vt*: **the speaker/actor was ~ed down** ора́тора заглуши́ли во́пли возмуще́ния, актёра освиста́ли

vi (*of animals, people, wind*) выть, завыва́ть (*impfs*); (*of siren, storm*) реве́ть (*impf*); **to ~ with pain/laughter** взвыть от бо́ли, покати́ться со́ смеху.

howler *n CQ* глупе́йшая/неле́пейшая оши́бка.

howling *adj sl*: **it was a ~ bore/success** э́то бы́ло невероя́тно ску́чно, успе́х был колосса́льный.

hub *n* (*of wheel*) ступи́ца; *fig* **they think their village is the ~ of the universe** они́ все ду́мают, что их дере́вня—центр вселе́нной/мирозда́ния.

hubbub *n* шум, гам.

hub cap *n Aut* колпа́к колеса́.

huddle *vi*: **the children ~d together under the trees** де́ти все столпи́лись под дере́вьями; **the sheep ~d together** о́вцы сби́лись в ку́чу; **she ~d up against her mother to get warm** она́ прижа́лась к ма́тери, что́бы согре́ться; **she sat ~d up on the sofa** она́ сиде́ла на дива́не, сжа́вшись в комо́чек.

hue *n* (*shade*) отте́нок; (*tone*) тон.

huff *n*: **he's in a ~** он оби́жен.

huffy *adj* (*offended*) оби́женный; (*liable to take offence*) оби́дчивый; **don't be ~** не обижа́йся.

hug *vt* об|нима́ть (-ня́ть); **they ~ged each other** они́ обняли́сь; **she was ~ging her doll** она́ прижима́ла ку́клу к груди́; **I'm ~ging myself over selling the car so well** я о́чень дово́лен собо́й, что так уда́чно про́дал маши́ну; *Naut* **to ~ the coast** держа́ться бли́же к бе́регу (*only in impf*).

huge *adj* огро́мный; **a ~ success** огро́мный/*CQ* колосса́льный успе́х.

hulk *n Naut*: **the ~ of a ship-wrecked vessel** ко́рпус затону́вшего корабля́; *fig* (*of a man*) *see* **hulking** *adj*.

hulking *adj*: **he's a great ~ fellow** он про́сто медве́дь.

hull *n Naut* ко́рпус корабля́.

hullabaloo *n*: **what a ~!** что за шум, что за гвалт!

hullo *interj* (*in greeting*) здра́вствуй(те)!, *CQ* приве́т!; *Tel* (*calling*) алло́!, (*answering*) слу́шаю!; (*in surprise*) **~, what's all this?** *CQ* приве́т, что э́то тако́е?

hum *n* (*of insects*) жужжа́ние; (*of traffic, voices*) гул.

hum *vti vt*: **to ~ a tune** напева́ть/мурлы́кать пе́сенку (*impfs*)

vi **1** (*of insects, projectiles*) жужжа́ть (*impf*); (*of person*) **he was ~ming to himself** он мурлы́кал что́-то себе́ под но́с; *fig CQ* **the work is fairly ~ming** рабо́та кипи́т

2: **to ~ and haw** мя́млить (*impf*).

human *n* челове́к; *pl* (**~s**) лю́ди.

human *adj* челове́ческий; **the ~ race** челове́чество, род людско́й/челове́ческий; **it's only ~ to slip up sometimes** челове́ку сво́йственно ошиба́ться.

humane *adj* челове́чный, гума́нный; **he's a ~ man** он гума́нный челове́к.

humanity *n* **1** (*mankind*) челове́чество

2 (*quality*) гума́нность; **they treated the prisoners (of war) with ~** они́ гума́нно обраща́лись с пле́нными

3 *pl* (**the humanities**) гуманита́рные нау́ки, (*classics*) класси́ческие языки́ и литерату́ра.

humble *adj* (*of character*) скро́мный; смире́нный; (*of origin, etc.*) скро́мный, просто́й; **a ~ occupation/dwelling** скро́мное заня́тие, просто́е жили́ще; (*in letter or joc in talk*) **Your ~ servant** Ваш поко́рный слуга́; *iron* **in my ~ opinion** по моему́ скро́мному мне́нию.

humbug *n* **1** *CQ*: **he's just a ~** он про́сто болту́н/обма́нщик; **it's all ~** всё э́то про́сто болтовня́

2 (*sweet*) мя́тная конфе́та.

humdrum *adj*: **I lead a very ~ life** моя́ жизнь весьма́ однообра́зна; **he has a very ~ style** у него́ о́чень ску́чный язы́к.

humid *adj* вла́жный.

humidifier *n* увлажни́тель (*m*) (во́здуха).

humidity *n* вла́жность; **90% ~** девяно́сто проце́нтов вла́жности.

humiliate *vt* уни|жа́ть (́-зить); **I was ~d by the children's behaviour** мне бы́ло о́чень сты́дно за поведе́ние дете́й, де́ти ужа́сно себя́ вели́—я сгоре́ла со стыда́.

humiliating *adj* унизи́тельный.

humility *n* смире́нность, смире́ние; **he accepted the rebuke with ~** он при́нял упрёк безро́потно.

hummock *n* (*hillock*) хо́лмик, приго́рок; (*smaller*) бугоро́к; **he sat down on a ~** он усе́лся на приго́рке.

humorist *n* юмори́ст.

humour, (*US*) **humor** *n* **1** ю́мор; **sense of ~** чу́вство ю́мора; **the story is full of ~** в э́том расска́зе сто́лько ю́мора

2 (*mood*) настрое́ние; **he's in a good/bad ~** он в хоро́шем/плохо́м настрое́нии; **I'm not in the ~ for working** у меня́ нет настрое́ния рабо́тать; **he's out of ~** он не в ду́хе; **he'll talk well when the ~ takes him** когда́ он в уда́ре, он говори́т прекра́сно.

humour, (*US*) **humor** *vt*: **to ~ smb** ублаж|а́ть кого́-л (-и́ть).

humourless, (*US*) **humorless** *adj* без ю́мора.

humourous *adj* юмористи́ческий.

hump *n* (*of camel, man, etc.*) горб; *fig* **we're over the ~ now** бо́льшая часть рабо́ты уже́ сде́лана.

hump *vt CQ*: **I had to ~ the bag of coal upstairs myself** мне пришло́сь самому́ втащи́ть наве́рх мешо́к у́гля.

humpbacked *adj* горба́тый.

humpy *adj*: **~ ground** бугри́стая/неро́вная ме́стность.

humus *n* гу́мус, перегно́й.

hunch *n* горб; *fig* предчу́вствие; **I have a ~ that he won't come** у меня́ предчу́вствие, что он не придёт; **I have a ~ that he is the murderer** мне что́-то подска́зывает, что уби́йца и́менно он.

hunch *vt*, *also* **~ up** го́рбиться (с-); **to ~ one's back/oneself** го́рбить спи́ну, го́рбиться.

hunchback *n* горбу́н.

hunchbacked *adj* горба́тый.

hundred *num and n* **1** сто (*num in oblique cases* ста); **200, 300, 400** две́сти, три́ста, четы́реста; **500, 600,** *etc.* пятьсо́т, шестьсо́т; **101 days** сто оди́н день; **102 girls** сто две де́вушки; **140 trees** сто со́рок дере́вьев; **100 per cent** сто проце́нтов; **it's 100 to one against succeeding** сто про́тив одного́, что э́то не уда́стся; **room number 100** ко́мната (но́мер) сто; **page 100** со́тая страни́ца; **the ~ and twenty second car** сто два́дцать втора́я маши́на; **I've 101 things to do** у меня́ ты́сяча дел

2 (*a hundred of*) со́тня + *G*; сто; **I paid 100 roubles** я заплати́л сто рубле́й/со́тню; **we drove for ~s of miles** мы прое́хали со́тни миль; **to sell by the ~** продава́ть со́тнями/по сто штук; **more than 100 eggs/100 of the eggs were broken** разби́лось бо́льше со́тни яи́ц; **there were ~s of people there** там бы́ли со́тни люде́й; [*but* **NB**]: **there were several ~ people there** там бы́ло не́сколько сот челове́к; **£100** сто фу́нтов; **he has ~s** (*of pounds*) **in the bank** у него́ мно́го де́нег в ба́нке

3: the train departs at six ~ hours по́езд отхо́дит в шесть ноль-ноль.

hundredfold *adv* в сто раз бо́льше.

hundredth *n* (одна́) со́тая; со́тая часть; 3/100, 7/100 три/семь со́тых.

hundredth *adj* со́тый; **he was the ~ to arrive** он при́был со́тым.

hundredweight *n* англи́йский (*= 50.8 kilos*)/америка́нский (*= 45.4 kilos*) це́нтнер [це́нтнер *is Russian measure = 100 kilos*].

Hungarian *n* венгр, венге́рка; (*language*) венге́рский язы́к.

Hungarian *adj* венге́рский.

hunger *n* го́лод; **he is dying of ~** он умира́ет с го́лоду/от го́лода, *also fig CQ*; **to satisfy one's ~** утоли́ть го́лод.

hunger *vi fig*: **the child ~s for affection** ребёнок нужда́ется в ла́ске.

hunger strike *n* голодо́вка; **they've gone on ~** они́ объяви́ли голодо́вку.

hungrily *adv* жа́дно, с жа́дностью; **they ate ~** они́ жа́дно е́ли; **the children eyed the cake ~** голо́дные де́ти смотре́ли на пиро́г с жа́дностью.

hungry *adj* голо́дный; **I'm very ~** я о́чень го́лоден; **they are permanently ~** они́ постоя́нно голода́ют; **to get/grow ~** проголода́ться; **I'm good and ~** я си́льно/здо́рово проголода́лся [**NB** *tense*]; **we went ~ that day** в тот день мы оста́лись голо́дными; **I'm not ~ for breakfast** я не хочу́ за́втракать; **a ~ look** голо́дный взгляд; **digging is ~ work** по́сле того́ как покопа́ешь в огоро́де, поя́вится аппети́т; *fig* **we are ~ for news** мы жа́ждем новосте́й (*pl*); *as n*: **the ~** голода́ющие (*pl*).

hunk *n* (*of bread, meat*) большо́й кусо́к; (*thick slice of bread, pie, cake*) ломо́ть (*m*).

hunt *n* **1** (*for larger game, with dogs, guns*) охо́та; (*for small animals, or birds with nets*) ло́вля; **a fox/rat ~** охо́та на лиси́ц, ло́вля крыс

2 (*search*) по́иски (*pl*); (*police search*) обла́ва, пресле́дование; **after a long ~ I did find the brooch** по́сле до́лгих по́исков я всё-таки нашёл бро́шку; **they organized a big ~ for the escaped convict/for the missing child** на сбежа́вшего престу́пника была́ устро́ена настоя́щая обла́ва, бы́ли организо́ваны по́иски пропа́вшего ребёнка.

hunt *vti vt* **1** (*for animals*) охо́титься на + *A* (*impf*); **to ~ bears** охо́титься на медве́дя (*sing*)

2 (*for people*): **the police are ~ing (for) the thief** поли́ция разы́скивает во́ра; **to ~ a thief down** вы́следить во́ра

3 (*for things*): **we are flat ~ing** мы и́щем кварти́ру; **I'll ~ out the address for you** я разыщу́ вам э́тот а́дрес

vi **1** *Sport* охо́титься; **wolves ~ in packs** во́лки охо́тятся стая́ми; **we went ~ing with dogs** мы пошли́/отпра́вились на охо́ту с соба́ками

2 to ~ for (*people or things*): **we ~ed for you everywhere** мы везде́ тебя́ иска́ли; **I ~ed everywhere for him/for the document and couldn't find him/it** я обыска́лся, не мог его́ найти́/найти́ э́тот докуме́нт.

hunter *n* охо́тник; (*horse*) гу́нтер.

hunting *n* охо́та.

huntsman *n* охо́тник.

hurdle *n Sport* барье́р; *fig* **we've got over the first ~** мы преодоле́ли пе́рвое препя́тствие; *attr*: *Sport* **~ race** барье́рный бег, бег с препя́тствиями.

hurl *vt* швыр|я́ть + *A or* + *I* (-ну́ть); **to ~ stones at smth/smb** швыря́ть ка́мни *or* камня́ми во что-л/в кого́-л; **he ~ed himself at/on his antagonist** он бро́сился на проти́вника; **they ~ed abuse at us** они́ осыпа́ли нас бра́нью (*usu impf*).

hurly-burly *n* сумато́ха.

hurrah *interj* ура́!

hurricane *n* урага́н; *attr*: **~ lamp** фона́рь «мо́лния».

hurried *adj* торопли́вый, поспе́шный; **~ steps** торопли́вые шаги́; **a ~ departure** поспе́шный отъе́зд; **we ate a ~ meal** мы на́спех (*adv*) перекуси́ли; **on a ~ reading I thought that...** прочита́в э́то бе́гло, я поду́мал, что...

hurry *n* **1** спе́шка; **in my ~ I forgot the tickets** в спе́шке/впопыха́х (*adv*) я забы́л биле́ты; **there's no ~** ничего́ спе́шного, не на́до спеши́ть, *CQ* не на пожа́р; **what's the ~?** заче́м така́я спе́шка?, куда́ торопи́ться—нам не́куда спеши́ть; **what's your ~?** ты куда́ спеши́шь?/торо́пишься?; **he was in a ~ to leave** он спеши́л/он торопи́лся уйти́

2 *CQ* (*in neg sentences = soon, willingly*): **I'll not come here again in a ~** я не ско́ро верну́сь сюда́; **you won't see a ring like that again in a ~** вря́д ли вы ещё уви́дите где́-нибудь тако́е кольцо́.

hurry *vti vt* [**NB** *in Russian it is often translated by intrans verb*]: **we must ~ the work along** на́до поторопи́ться с рабо́той; **they hurried him off to hospital** они́ неме́дленно отпра́вили его́ в больни́цу; **this is a project which can't be hurried** э́тот прое́кт нельзя́ осуществи́ть в спе́шке; **don't ~ me!** не торопи́ меня́!, не подгоня́й меня́!

vi спеши́ть (по-), торопи́ться (по-); **we must ~ or we'll be late** на́до поспеши́ть/поторопи́ться, а то мы опозда́ем; **~ up!** торопи́сь!, поспеши́!; **don't ~** не спеши́, не торопи́сь; **she went ahead and I hurried after her** она́ ушла́ вперёд, и я поспеши́л за ней; **they are ~ing to finish the building before the winter** они́ спеша́т/торо́пятся зако́нчить зда́ние к зиме́; **she is ~ing to finish her dress** она́ спеши́т/торо́пится сшить пла́тье; **he hurried to school** он бежа́л в шко́лу; **I will ~ back** я бы́стро верну́сь; **he looked at his watch and hurried out of the room** он посмотре́л на часы́ и поспе́шно вы́шел из ко́мнаты; **~ after her—she's forgotten her gloves** она́ забы́ла перча́тки—догони́ её.

hurt *vti vt* **1** (*of physical injury*) ушиб|а́ть (-и́ть), повре|жда́ть (-ди́ть); **to ~ oneself** ушиба́ться; **I ~ my leg** я повреди́л себе́ но́гу; **it ~s me to cough** мне бо́льно ка́шлять; **my shoes ~ me** у меня́ но́ги боля́т в э́тих ту́флях; **is he seriously ~?** он си́льно ушиб́ся?; **no one was ~ in the crash** в э́той ава́рии никто́ не пострада́л; **don't ~ pussy!** не му́чай ко́шку!

2 (*do harm, damage*) вреди́ть + *D* (по-); **a glass of wine won't ~ anybody** бока́л вина́ никому́ не повреди́т; **it won't ~ you to walk home** тебе́ не вре́дно пройти́сь домо́й пешко́м; **it won't ~ to postpone the matter** ничего́ не случи́тся, е́сли э́то де́ло отло́жим

3 (*offend*) оби|жа́ть (-деть); **you ~ her feelings** вы её оби́дели; **it ~s me that he didn't come to see us** мне оби́дно, что он не зашёл к нам; **to ~ smb's pride** заде|ва́ть чьё-л самолю́бие (-́ть)

vi боле́ть (*impf*); **my eyes ~** у меня́ боля́т глаза́; **stop!—it ~s** переста́нь, мне бо́льно; **where does it ~?** где боли́т?; **he gripped my hand so hard that it ~** он схвати́л мою́ ру́ку и сжал её до бо́ли.

hurt *adj* (*offended*) оби́женный.

hurtle *vi* нести́сь (*usu impf*); **the dog came hurtling towards us** соба́ка несла́сь нам навстре́чу (*adv*); **he ~d down the slope on his sledge** он нёсся с горы́ на са́нках (*pl*).

husband *n* муж; (*formal*) супру́г; **she and her ~ arrived late** они́ с му́жем опозда́ли; **you and your ~ are invited to the dinner** вас с супру́гом приглаша́ют на банке́т.

husband *vt*: **to ~ one's strength/resources** экономить силы (*pl*)/ресурсы (с-).

hush *n* тишина; (*silence*) молчание; **a ~ fell on the company** все замолчали.

hush *vti vt*: **the scandal/affair was ~ed up** скандал замолчали, дело замяли

vi: **~!** тише!, замолчи!

hush-hush *adj CQ* тайный, секретный.

hush money *n*: **they paid him ~** они дали ему взятку, чтобы он молчал.

husk *n* лузга, шелуха (*collects*).

husk *vt*: **to ~ rice** очи|щать рис от шелухи (-стить) (*in factory, etc.*); **to ~ sunflower seeds** (*to eat raw*) лузгать семечки (*impf*).

husky *adj* (*hoarse*) сиплый; (*of jazz singer*) **she has a ~ voice** у неё хрипловатый голос; (*US*) *CQ* (*sturdy*) **he's a big ~ fellow** он здоровенный малый.

hussy *n CQ*: **a brazen ~** наглая девица.

hustle *n* сутолока; суета.

hustle *vti vt* **1** (*push*) толк|ать, пих|ать (*pfs* -нуть) *and compounds*; **the boys were ~d out of the yard** мальчишек вытолкали со двора; **the police ~d him into a car** полицейские впихнули/затолкали его в машину **2** (*hurry*): **don't ~ me!** не торопи меня!, не подгоняй меня!; **I was ~d into the decision** меня торопили принять решение

vi толкаться; **people ~d round the exit** люди толкались у выхода.

hut *n* хижина; (*shack*) лачуга, хибарка.

hutch *n* (*for rabbits, etc.*) клетка.

hyacinth *n* гиацинт.

hybrid *n* гибрид.

hydraulic *adj* гидравлический.

hydroelectric *adj*: **~ station** гидро(электро)-станция.

hydrofoil *n* судно на подводных крыльях.

hydrogen *n* водород.

hydrophobia *n Med* водобоязнь, бешенство.

hygiene *n* гигиена.

hygienic *adj* гигиенический.

hymn *n* гимн.

hypersensitive *adj* (*of apparatus, etc.*) сверхчувствительный; *Med* с повышенной чувствительностью; **she's ~** она такая ранимая/чувствительная.

hyphen *n* дефис.

hyphenated *adj*: **this word is ~** это слово пишется через дефис.

hypnotize *vt* гипнотизировать (за-).

hypochondriac *n* ипохондрик.

hypocrisy *n* лицемерие, ханжество.

hypocrite *n* лицемер, ханжа (*m and f*).

hypocritical *adj* лицемерный, ханжеский.

hypodermic *adj*: **a ~ syringe** шприц для подкожных впрыскиваний.

hypothesis *n* гипотеза.

hypothetic(al) *adj* гипотетический.

hysterectomy *n Med* удаление матки.

hysteria *n* истерия.

hysterical *adj* истерический, истеричный.

hysterics *npl* истерика (*usu sing*); **a fit of ~** истерический припадок; **she has ~** у неё/с ней истерика, она в истерике; **she is liable to go into ~** у неё бывают истерики (*pl*); *CQ* (*of laughter*) **we were in ~** с нами была просто истерика, на нас напал истерический смех.

I

I *pers pron* (*see also* **me**) я; **who is coming?—I for one/—Not ~!** кто придёт?—Я приду/—Только не я!; **my wife and ~ went to the zoo** мы с женой ходили в зоопарк; **you and ~ know better** нам с тобой лучше знать; **neither my sister nor ~ know anything about it** ни я, ни моя сестра ничего не знаем об этом; **~ am cold** мне холодно; **~ have a headache** у меня болит голова; **I've no time** у меня нет времени; (я *often omitted with* надеяться, бояться): **~ hope/fear that...** надеюсь,/боюсь, что...

ice *n* лёд; **my feet are like ~** у меня ледяные ноги; *fig*: **in order to break the ~** чтобы растопить лёд/сделать первый шаг, (*in conversation*) чтобы нарушить молчание; **to skate on thin ~** ходить по тонкому льду; **this project has been put on ~ meantime** этот проект на время заморожен; **his explanation cut no ~ with me** его объяснение не убедило меня.

ice *vti vt*: **to ~ a cake** глазировать торт (*impf and pf*)

vi: **to ~ over/up** обледенеть (*pf*); **the windscreen ~d up** ветровое стекло обледенело; **the pond ~d over** пруд замёрз.

ice age *n* ледниковый период.

ice axe *n* ледоруб.

iceberg *n* айсберг.

icebound *adj*: **the ship was ~** корабль был затёрт/затёрло (*impers*) льдами.

icebox *n* ледник; (*US = fridge*) холодильник.

icebreaker *n* ледокол.

ice cream *n* мороженое.

iced *adj*: **~ water** вода со льдом (*with ice cubes*); **~ coffee** охлаждённый кофе; **an ~ cake** глазированный торт.

ice hockey *n* хоккей [**NB** *UK hockey* = травяной хоккей].

Icelander *n* исландец, исландка.

Icelandic *n* исландский язык.

Icelandic *adj* исландский.

ice rink *n* каток.

icicle *n* сосулька.

icing *n Cook* глазурь, глазировка; *attr*: **~ sugar** сахар для глазировки.

icon *n* икона.

icy *adj* ледяной, *also fig*; **an ~ wind** ледяной ветер; **~ roads** обледенелые дороги; **it's ~ cold today** сегодня собачий холод; *fig*: **his speech was received in ~ silence** его речь была встречена ледяным молчанием; **he gave her an ~ look** он холодно посмотрел на неё.

idea *n* **1** идéя; **the ~ of the good** идéя добрá

2 (*mental picture*) представлéние; **now I have an ~ of how you live** тепéрь у меня есть представлéние, как ты там живёшь; **your description gives me a good ~ of the setup** ты хорошó описáл обстанóвку; **the ~ of sitting here for three hours is not attractive** мне не óчень-то хóчется просидéть/*CQ* проторчáть здесь три часá

3 (*thought*, *suspicion*, *understanding*) мысль, идéя; **that's not a bad ~** э́то неплохáя мысль/ идéя; **don't put ~s into her head** не говорú ей такúх вещéй; **once he gets an ~ into his head he won't budge** éсли ему́ что взбредёт в гóлову, переубедúть егó невозмóжно; **what gave you the ~ that..?** с чегó вы взя́ли, что..?; **he hit on the ~ of...** ему́ пришлó в гóлову + *inf*; **I'd no ~ it was so late** я и не ду́мал, что так пóздно; **I've an ~ it may not be so easy** мне кáжется, э́то бу́дет не так прóсто; *CQ*: **I haven't the foggiest ~ what you mean/ where he is** я никáк не пойму́, что ты хóчешь сказáть, я поня́тия не имéю, где он; **this is not my ~ of fun** у меня́ другóе поня́тие о весéлье; **the very ~!** поду́мать тóлько!; **what's the big ~?** что э́то ты заду́мал?

4 (*intention*) намéрение; **he came here with the ~ of finding work** он приéхал сюдá с намéрением найтú рабóту.

ideal *n* идеáл.

ideal *adj* идеáльный.

idealist *n* идеалúст.

idealize *vt* идеализúровать (*impf and pf*).

ideally *adv* идеáльно, *CQ* в идеáле; **~ we should book in advance** идеáльным вариáнтом бы́ло бы заказáть местá зарáнее.

identical *adj* (*the same*) тóт же (сáмый); (*exactly alike*) одинáковый, такóй же, идентúчный; **this is the ~ bird that nested here last year** э́то тá же сáмая птúца, у котóрой бы́ло здесь гнездó в прóшлом году́; **your shoes are ~ with mine** у тебя́ такúе же ту́фли, как у меня́, у нас одинáковые ту́фли; **the fingerprints of no two people are ~** нет двух людéй с одинáковыми/идентúчными отпечáтками пáльцев; **~ twins** близнецы́, двойня́шки.

identification *n* опознáние, опознавáние; **~ of a corpse** опознáние тру́па; **~ of the victims of an air crash** опознавáние жертв авиакатастрóфы; **~ of aircraft** опознавáние самолётов; **~ of a disease** распознавáние болéзни; **~ of a plant** определéние вúда растéния; *attr*: **~ mark** опознавáтельный знак.

identify *vt* опозна|вáть, распозна|вáть (*pfs* -ть); **he was identified by his fingerprints** он был опóзнан по отпечáткам пáльцев; **to ~ a body** опознáть труп; **he identified him as the man who...** он опознáл/узнáл в нём человéка, котóрый...; **to ~ a plant by its leaves** опредéл|я́ть растéние по лúстьям (-úть); **he identified himself with the hero of the novel** он отождествля́л себя́ с герóем ромáна.

identity *n*: **mistaken ~** ошúбочное опознáние; **to prove smb's ~** установúть лúчность когó-л; *attr*: **~ card** удостоверéние лúчности.

ideological *adj* идеологúческий.

ideology *n* идеолóгия.

idiocy *n* идиотúзм, *Med and CQ*; *CQ* идиóтство.

idiom *n* идиóма; (*language*): **Tolstoy's ~** язы́к Толстóго; **the local ~** мéстный диалéкт.

idiomatic *adj* идиоматúческий; **he knows how to use ~ English** егó англúйская речь идиоматúчна.

idiosyncrasy *n* причу́да, *CQ* пу́нктик.

idiot *n* идиóт, *Med and CQ*: **village ~** деревéнский дурачóк.

idiotic *adj* дурáцкий, идиóтский; **~ behaviour** дурáцкое/идиóтское поведéние; **how ~!** какóй идиотúзм!

idle *adj* **1** *attr* прáздный, досу́жий; ленúвый; **~ talk/gossip** пустáя/прáздная болтовня́, досу́жие сплéтни (*pl*); **to indulge in ~ speculation** пустúться в досу́жие рассуждéния (*pl*); **he's an ~ fellow** он ленúвый пáрень, он лентя́й; **we had an ~ holiday** в óтпуске мы бездéльничали; **I never have an ~ moment** у меня́ нет ни однóй свобóдной минýты

2 *predic*: **I'm seldom ~** я рéдко быва́ю без дéла; **to be ~** бездéльничать; **the men were ~ during the power cut** рабóчие не рабóтали, покá нé было тóка; **many machines stood ~** бездéйствовало/простáивало мнóго машúн; **it's ~ to expect him to help** пóмощи от негó ждать не прихóдится.

idle *vti vt*: **to ~ away one's time** трáтить врéмя пóпусту (*usu impf*)

vi (*of engine*) рабóтать на холостóм ходу́ (*impf*).

idleness *n* прáздность, лень, бездéлье; **he lives in ~** он живёт в прáздности.

idler *n* бездéльник, лентя́й.

idly *adv* прáздно, ленúво; (*aimlessly*) бесцéльно; **I cannot stand ~ by while...** я не могу́ оставáться безучáстным, когдá.../безучáстно смотрéть на + *A*.

idol *n* úдол, кумúр, *also fig*.

idolize *vt fig* боготворúть (*impf*).

idyllic *adj* идиллúческий.

if *conj* **1** éсли; (*in open conditions*: *of present*): **~ he's here, I want to see him** éсли он здесь, я хочу́ егó вúдеть; (*of past*): **~ you thought so, why didn't you say so?** éсли ты так ду́мал, почему́ ты не сказáл об э́том?; (*of future*): **~ it rains, I won't go** éсли бу́дет дождь, я не пойду́; **we'll come at 6, ~ only he arrives in time** мы придём в шесть, éсли тóлько он не опоздáет [**NB** *Russian future tense after* éсли]; *CQ* **~ ever you're in town, drop in** éсли ты когдá-нибудь бу́дешь в гóроде, заходú ко мне; (*in general statement*) **~ you think of it, he's not a bad chap** éсли поду́мать, он не такóй уж плохóй пáрень

2 (*in unreal conditions*) éсли бы; (*in past*): **~ I hadn't left early, I'd have met him** éсли бы я не ушёл так рáно, я бы встрéтил егó;

~ **it hadn't been for him, I would have left** если бы не он, я бы ушёл; (*in present*): ~ **my sister were here, she'd help** если бы моя́ сестра́ была́ здесь, она́ бы помогла́; ~ **I were you, I wouldn't speak to him** на ва́шем ме́сте я бы не стал говори́ть с ним; (*in future*): ~ **they were to consult me, I'd suggest they buy a smaller house** е́сли бы (они́) меня́ спроси́ли, я бы посове́товал (им) купи́ть дом поме́ньше

3 (*concessional*): **even** ~ хотя́, пусть; да́же е́сли; **a good film, (even)** ~ **(it is) rather long** хоро́ший фильм, хотя́ и длиннова́тый; **even** ~ **he's wrong, don't argue with him** пусть он не прав, но ты с ним не спорь; **she's attractive,** ~ **not beautiful** она́ не краса́вица, но о́чень мила́/привлека́тельна; **I wouldn't know her (even)** ~ **I saw her** я её не узна́л бы, да́же е́сли бы уви́дел

4 (*in indirect questions = whether*) ли; **I don't know** ~ **he'll agree** я не зна́ю, согласи́тся ли он; **let me know** ~ **you're coming** скажи́ мне зара́нее,/дай мне знать, придёшь ли ты

5 *other uses*: **i) as if: he behaves as** ~ **he didn't trust us** он ведёт себя́ так, как бу́дто не доверя́ет нам; **it looks as** ~ **we won't make our train** похо́же, что мы не успе́ем на по́езд; **it isn't as** ~ **he were stupid** он вро́де бы не дура́к; **it isn't as** ~ **we wanted it** не то, что́бы мы э́того хоте́ли; **ii) if any: complaints,** ~ **any, should be lodged with the manager** жа́лобы, е́сли таковы́е име́ются, направля́йте/подава́йте заве́дующему; **iii) if not: be here by 6**—~ **not, I'll leave without you** приходи́ не поздне́е шести́, а то я уйду́ без тебя́; **are you coming? Phone me** ~ **not** ты придёшь? Е́сли нет, позвони́ мне; **whom can I ask** ~ **not you?** е́сли не тебя́, то кого́ же я могу́ попроси́ть?; **iv) if only:** ~ **only I knew/had known!** е́сли бы то́лько я знал!; ~ **only he'd go away** то́лько бы он ушёл; **v)** *various*: **well,** ~ **it isn't my old friend!** поду́мать то́лько, ведь э́то мой ста́рый друг!; **she's 40** ~ **she's a day!** да ей все со́рок!

ignite *vti* воспламен|я́ть(ся) (-и́ть(ся)), за|-жига́ть(ся) (-же́чь(ся)).

ignition *n Tech*, *Aut* зажига́ние; *Aut* **put the key into the** ~ вставь ключ в зажига́ние; *attr*: ~ **key/switch** ключ/выключа́тель зажига́ния.

ignoble *adj* (*of behaviour*) неблагоро́дный, ни́зкий; ~ **motives** ни́зменные побужде́ния.

ignominious *adj* позо́рный; **an** ~ **defeat** позо́рное пораже́ние.

ignominy *n* позо́р.

ignoramus *n* неве́жда (*m*), не́уч.

ignorance *n* (*lack of education*) неве́жество; (*not knowing*) неве́дение; **the extent of his** ~ **is amazing** глубина́ его́ неве́жества порази́тельна; **I don't want to reveal my** ~ **of music** я не хочу́ показа́ть себя́ профа́ном в му́зыке; **I acted in** ~ я сде́лал э́то по неве́дению/незна́нию; **we kept him in** ~ **of our plans** мы не посвяща́ли его́ в на́ши пла́ны; **I was in a state of blissful** ~ я пребыва́л в блаже́нном неве́дении.

ignorant *adj* (*generally*) необразо́ванный, *pejor* неве́жественный; несве́дущий в + *P*; **I'm** ~ **of their plans** я не зна́ю их пла́нов.

ignore *vt* игнори́ровать (*impf and pf*); **he** ~**d me/the invitation** он игнори́ровал меня́, он пренебрёг приглаше́нием.

ill *adj* **1** *usu predic* больно́й; **he's seriously** ~ он тяжело́ бо́лен; **to be taken** ~ заболе́ть; **I feel** ~ я пло́хо себя́ чу́вствую

2 *attr uses*: ~ **health** плохо́е здоро́вье; **it's a place of** ~ **repute** э́то ме́сто по́льзуется дурно́й сла́вой/репута́цией; **as** ~ **luck would have it** как назло́.

ill *adv* пло́хо; **to speak/think** ~ **of smb** пло́хо говори́ть/ду́мать о ком-л; **he took it** ~ **that I left early** он был недово́лен (тем), что я ра́но ушёл; **it** ~ **becomes her to criticize** не ей бы критикова́ть; **at present I can** ~ **afford a new coat** сейча́с я не могу́ позво́лить себе́ но́вое пальто́; **we can** ~ **afford to lose him** нам без него́ не обойти́сь; **he felt** ~ **at ease** он чу́вствовал себя́ нело́вко/не в свое́й таре́лке.

ill-advised *adj*: **you'd be** ~ **not to accept the invitation** вам не сле́дует отка́зываться от э́того приглаше́ния.

ill-bred *adj* пло́хо воспи́танный.

ill-considered *adj* необду́манный; (*rash*) опроме́тчивый.

ill-disposed *adj*: **he is** ~ **towards me/the idea** он не располо́жен ко мне, он неодобри́тельно отно́сится к э́той иде́е.

illegal *adj* незако́нный, нелега́льный, противозако́нный.

illegible *adj* (*of handwriting, etc.*) неразбо́рчивый.

illegitimate *adj* (*illegal*) незако́нный; (*of child*) незаконнорождённый, внебра́чный.

ill-fated *adj* злосча́стный, злополу́чный.

ill-feeling *n* неприя́знь; **there's a lot of** ~ **over his appointment** его́ назначе́ние бы́ло встре́чено неприя́зненно/при́нято в штыки́; **there's a lot of** ~ **between the two families** э́ти две семьи́ не ла́дят ме́жду собо́й.

ill-founded *adj* необосно́ванный.

ill humour, (*US*) **ill humor** *n* плохо́е настрое́ние.

illiterate *adj* негра́мотный, безгра́мотный.

ill-judged *adj* (*unwise*) неблагоразу́мный; (*ill--considered*) необду́манный.

ill-mannered *adj* невоспи́танный, неве́жливый, некульту́рный.

ill-natured *adj* (*of person, remark*) злой.

illness *n* боле́знь, заболева́ние; (*ill health*) нездоро́вье; **it is/he has a dangerous** ~ э́то опа́сная боле́знь, он тяжело́ бо́лен; **there's a lot of** ~ **about this winter** э́той зимо́й мно́го просту́дных заболева́ний (*pl*); **he excused himself because of** ~ он сосла́лся на нездоро́вье/боле́знь.

illogical *adj* нелоги́чный.

ill-omened *adj* злополу́чный.

ill-tempered *adj* (*of person*) раздражи́тельный, сварли́вый; (*of remark*) злой.

ill-timed *adj* несвоевре́менный.

ill-treat *vt*: **to ~ smb** гру́бо об|ходи́ться с кем-л (-ойти́сь).

illuminate *vt* (*light*) осве|ща́ть (-ти́ть); (*for festivities*) устр|а́ивать иллюмина́цию (-о́ить); *Hist* **an ~d manuscript** ру́копись, укра́шенная рису́нками.

illuminating *adj fig*: **that was an ~ remark** э́то замеча́ние пролива́ло свет на мно́гое.

illumination *n* (*lighting*) освеще́ние; *pl* (**~s**) (*of festivities*) иллюмина́ция (*sing*).

illusion *n* иллю́зия; **I have no ~s about their true motives** у меня́ нет никаки́х иллю́зий относи́тельно их и́стинных наме́рений; **an optical ~** опти́ческий обма́н.

illusory *adj* иллюзо́рный.

illustrate *vt* иллюстри́ровать (*impf and pf*); **an ~d book/talk** иллюстри́рованная кни́га, ле́кция с демонстра́цией диапозити́вов; **he ~d his theory by examples/diagrams** он подкрепи́л свою́ тео́рию приме́рами/диагра́ммами.

illustration *n* иллюстра́ция, *also fig*; рису́нок, карти́нка; *fig* (*example*) поясне́ние, приме́р; **by way of ~** к приме́ру; **in ~ of his point he quoted...** подкрепля́я своё положе́ние, он процити́ровал...

illustrative *adj* иллюстрати́вный; поясни́тельный; **~ material** иллюстрати́вный материа́л; **this is ~ of his views** э́то отража́ет его́ взгля́ды.

illustrious *adj* просла́вленный, знамени́тый.

ill will *n*: **I bear you no ~** я не держу́ зла на тебя́.

image *n* **1** *Lit* о́браз; *Art*, *Lit* изображе́ние; *Art* (*sculpture*) изваяние, скульпту́ра; **to think in ~s** мы́слить о́бразами

2 (*likeness*) ко́пия, подо́бие; (*reflection*) отраже́ние, *also Photo*; **a mirror ~** зерка́льное изображе́ние; **he's the living/very ~ of his father** он вы́литый оте́ц, он как две ка́пли воды́ похо́ж на отца́

3 (*public face*): **he thinks too much of his ~** он сли́шком забо́тится о том, како́е впечатле́ние он произво́дит на окружа́ющих.

imagery *n Lit* о́бразность ре́чи.

imaginable *adj*: **we had the greatest difficulty ~ in finding her house** вы не представля́ете себе́, с каки́м трудо́м мы нашли́ её дом.

imaginary *adj* вообража́емый, мни́мый, *also Math*; **her illness is just ~** её боле́знь — про́сто плод воображе́ния; **he lives in an ~ world** он живёт в вы́думанном ми́ре.

imagination *n* воображе́ние; фанта́зия; **a lively ~** живо́е воображе́ние; **his ~ has run away with him** его́ воображе́ние разыгра́лось; **it's all ~!** э́то чи́стая фанта́зия!

imaginative *adj*: **he's an ~ child** у ребёнка бога́тое воображе́ние.

imagine *vt* вообра|жа́ть (-зи́ть), представ|-ля́ть себе́ (-́ить); **don't ~ it will make you rich** не вообража́й, что ты на э́том разбогате́ешь; **just ~!** предста́вь себе́!, то́лько вообрази́!; **he wasn't the least as I'd ~d him (to be)** он оказа́лся совсе́м не таки́м, как я его́ себе́ представля́л; **I ~ we're expected at 6** я полага́ю, нас ждут к шести́.

imbecile *n Med* слабоу́мный; *CQ* дура́к, идио́т.

imbibe *vt* (*drink*) пить (вы́-); (*absorb*) впит|ывать (-а́ть), *also fig*.

imitate *vt* подража́ть + *D* (*impf*); копи́ровать, имити́ровать (*usu impfs*), изобра|жа́ть (-зи́ть); (*usu of children*) передра́знивать (*usu impf*); **he unconsciously ~s his father's gestures** он бессозна́тельно подража́ет же́стам отца́; **you should see him imitating his professor!** ну́жно ви́деть, как он изобража́ет своего́ профе́ссора; **the children cruelly ~d the boy's stutter** де́ти передра́знивали за́йку [= *the stutterer*]; **the wall is painted to ~ marble** стена́ покра́шена под мра́мор; **they use this material to ~ wood** э́тот материа́л испо́льзуют как имита́цию де́рева.

imitation *n* подража́ние; (*of material, etc.*) имита́ция; (*of goods*) имита́ция, подде́лка; (*of painting*) ко́пия; **in ~ of his father's example** подража́я отцу́, по приме́ру отца́; **he does a good ~ of her laugh** он так заба́вно передра́знивает её смех; **that's a good ~ of marble** э́то уда́чная подде́лка под мра́мор; *attr*: **~ pearls** иску́сственный же́мчуг (*collect*).

immaculately *adv* безупре́чно, безукори́зненно; **he was ~ dressed** он был безупре́чно оде́т.

immaterial *adj*: **it's ~ to me** э́то для меня́ несуще́ственно/не име́ет значе́ния, мне всё равно́.

immature *adj* незре́лый, недозре́лый, *also fig*; **an ~ gull** молода́я ча́йка.

immeasurable *adj* неизмери́мый, безме́рный.

immediate *adj* (*direct*) непосре́дственный; (*near*) ближа́йший; (*urgent*) неме́дленный, *off* незамедли́тельный; **in the ~ proximity of the theatre** в непосре́дственной бли́зости от теа́тра; **our ~ aim** на́ша ближа́йшая цель; **my ~ superior** (*in office*)/**family** мой непосре́дственный нача́льник, мои́ ближа́йшие ро́дственники (*pl*); **in the ~ future** в ближа́йшем бу́дущем; **an ~ reply is requested** про́сьба отве́тить незамедли́тельно; **to take ~ action** де́йствовать без промедле́ния.

immediately *adv* (*of place and fig*) пря́мо, непосре́дственно; (*of time*) неме́дленно, сра́зу, то́тчас (же), незамедли́тельно, *CQ* сейча́с (же); **~ next to the wall** пря́мо у стены́; **I am ~ responsible to the President** я подчиня́юсь непосре́дственно президе́нту; **he came ~** он пришёл неме́дленно/то́тчас же; **I'll go ~** я сейча́с же пойду́; **it was ~ apparent that...** сра́зу бы́ло ви́дно, что...

immediately *conj* как то́лько; **let me know ~ he appears** дай мне знать, как то́лько он поя́вится.

immemorial *adj*: **from time ~** с незапа́мятных времён, испоко́н веко́в.

immense *adj* огро́мный, грома́дный; **~ buildings** огро́мные/грома́дные зда́ния; **it gave**

me ~ pleasure я получи́л огро́мное удово́льствие от э́того.

immensely *adv CQ*: **he's ~ rich** он стра́шно бога́т; **did you enjoy the play?—I.!** тебе́ понра́вилась пье́са?—О́чень!

immensity *n* безме́рность, необъя́тность; **the ~ of the problem** необъя́тность пробле́мы; **we were appalled by the ~ of the disaster** мы бы́ли потрясены́ разме́рами бе́дствия.

immerse *vt* погру|жа́ть (-зи́ть), *also fig*; **to ~ smth in water** погружа́ть что-л в во́ду; *fig* **he was ~d in a book** он углуби́лся в кни́гу.

immersion heater *n* водообогрева́тель (*m*).

immigrant *n* иммигра́нт.

immigrate *vi* иммигри́ровать (*impf and pf*).

imminent *adj*: **revolution/a storm is ~** надвига́ется револю́ция/гроза́; **the ~ elections** предстоя́щие вы́боры; **he is in ~ danger of losing his job** он мо́жет в любу́ю мину́ту потеря́ть рабо́ту; **the roof is in ~ danger of collapsing** кры́ша вот-во́т провали́тся.

immobile *adj* неподви́жный.

immobilize *vt*: **lack of fuel ~d the army/the tanks** де́йствия а́рмии бы́ли парализо́ваны/та́нки стоя́ли из-за отсу́тствия горю́чего; **my broken leg has ~d me** сло́манная нога́ лиши́ла меня́ спосо́бности передвига́ться.

immoderate *adj* непоме́рный, чрезме́рный; **~ ambition/demand** непоме́рное честолю́бие/тре́бование; **~ charges** чрезме́рно/непоме́рно высо́кие це́ны; **~ drinking was his ruin** неуме́ренное потребле́ние спиртно́го сгуби́ло его́.

immodest *adj* нескро́мный; (*indecent*) неприли́чный.

immoral *adj* амора́льный, безнра́вственный.

immortal *adj* бессме́ртный.

immune *adj*: **he is ~ from smallpox** у него́ иммуните́т про́тив о́спы; *fig*: **~ against attack** защищённый от нападе́ния; **diplomats are ~ from taxation** диплома́ты освобождены́ от нало́гов.

immunity *n*: **~ from chicken pox** иммуните́т про́тив ветря́нки, невосприи́мчивость к ветря́нке; **diplomatic ~** дипломати́ческая неприкоснове́нность; **~ from taxation** освобожде́ние от нало́гов.

immunization *n*: **~ against smallpox** приви́вки (*pl*) про́тив о́спы.

immunize *vt*: **to ~ smb against cholera** де́лать приви́вку кому́-л про́тив холе́ры (с-).

imp *n* чертёнок, бесёнок; *fig* **he's a little ~** он стра́шный озорни́к/прока́зник.

impact *n* уда́р, столкнове́ние; **at the moment of ~** в моме́нт столкнове́ния/уда́ра; **he reeled from the ~ of the blow/the wave** он пошатну́лся от уда́ра/от уда́ра волны́; *fig*: **the ~ of new ideas on society** возде́йствие но́вых иде́й на о́бщество; **the book had a great ~ on its readers** кни́га произвела́ глубо́кое впечатле́ние на чита́телей.

impair *vt* ухуд|ша́ть (́-шить); **his sight is ~ed** его́ зре́ние уху́дшилось; **his health was ~ed by overwork** тяжёлая рабо́та подорвала́ его́ здоро́вье.

impart *vt* (*news, secret, etc.*) сообщ|а́ть (-и́ть).

impartial *adj* (*of person*) беспристра́стный; (*of opinion*) непредвзя́тый.

impassable *adj* (*on foot and fig*) непроходи́мый; (*for cars*) непрое́зжий; **the roads are ~ here in spring** весно́й у нас бездоро́жье/доро́ги непрое́зжие.

impasse *n* тупи́к; **negotiations have reached an ~** перегово́ры зашли́ в тупи́к.

impassive *adj* бесстра́стный.

impatience *n* нетерпе́ние, нетерпели́вость.

impatient *adj* нетерпели́вый; **to grow/get ~** проявля́ть нетерпе́ние; **he is ~ to be off** ему́ не те́рпится (*impers*) уйти́; **he was ~ with me/the children** он был ре́зок со мной/нетерпели́в с детьми́; **he is ~ of interruption** он терпе́ть не мо́жет, когда́ его́ прерыва́ют (*while speaking*)/отрыва́ют от де́ла (*while working*).

impatiently *adv* нетерпели́во, с нетерпе́нием.

impeach *vt*: *Law* **he was ~ed for taking bribes** его́ обвини́ли во взя́точничестве; *fig* **do you ~ my honesty?** вы сомнева́етесь в мое́й че́стности?

impeccable *adj* безупре́чный.

impede *vt* меша́ть + *D* (по-), препя́тствовать + *D* (вос-); **our progress was ~d by the procession** проце́ссия меша́ла нам пройти́; **lack of raw material has ~d our progress** рабо́ты приостано́влены из-за нехва́тки сырья́.

impediment *n*: **an ~ to** поме́ха + *D*, препя́тствие; **an ~ in speech** дефе́кт ре́чи.

impel *vt* вы|нужда́ть (́-нудить); **I feel ~led to say that...** я вы́нужден сказа́ть, что...

impending *adj* надвига́ющийся, предстоя́щий; **the ~ elections** предстоя́щие вы́боры; **in view of my ~ retirement** ввиду́ моего́ предстоя́щего ухо́да на пе́нсию.

impenetrable *adj*: **an ~ forest** непроходи́мый лес; **~ darkness** непрогля́дная тьма; *fig* **he wore an ~ expression** у него́ бы́ло непроница́емое выраже́ние.

impenitent *adj*: **he was quite ~** он ни в чём не раска́ялся.

imperative *n Gram* повели́тельное наклоне́ние.

imperative *adj* (*of voice, manner*) повели́тельный, вла́стный; (*essential*) **it is ~ to start now/that you should be here** необходи́мо сейча́с же отпра́виться/, что́бы вы бы́ли здесь.

imperceptible *adj* (*to touch*) неощути́мый; незаме́тный.

imperfect *adj* несоверше́нный; (*faulty*) дефе́ктный; **an ~ reproduction** несоверше́нная репроду́кция; **~ goods** дефе́ктные това́ры; **~ vision** плохо́е зре́ние; *Gram* **the ~ tense** импе́рфект, проше́дшее несоверше́нное вре́мя.

imperfection *n* недоста́ток, изъя́н.

imperfective *n Gram* несоверше́нный вид.

imperil *vt*: **he did not wish to ~ the other climbers/the success of the expedition** он не хотéл подвергáть опáсности други́х альпини́стов/сорвáть экспеди́цию.

imperious *adj* влáстный, повели́тельный; (*arrogant*) надмéнный.

impersonal *adj* (*of people*) безли́кий; *Gram* безли́чный; **an ~ construction** безли́чный оборóт.

impersonate *vt* изобра|жáть (-зи́ть); **he escaped by impersonating a street cleaner** он сбежáл, переодéвшись двóрником.

impersonation *n*: **he did a good ~ of his teacher in the skit** он забáвно изобрази́л своегó учи́теля в капýстнике.

impertinence *n* дéрзость; нáглость, нахáльство; **what ~!** какáя дéрзость!/нáглость!; **he had the ~ to...** он имéл нахáльство + *inf*.

impertinent *adj* дéрзкий; нáглый, нахáльный; **he was ~ to me** он был дéрзок/нагл со мной; **he's an ~ fellow** он нахáл.

imperturbable *adj* невозмути́мый.

impervious *adj*: **rubber is ~ to water** рези́на водонепроницáема; *fig* **he is ~ to criticism** он не реаги́рует на кри́тику.

impetuous *adj*: **an ~ nature** поры́вистая натýра; **~ remarks** необдýманные замечáния.

impetus *n* и́мпульс; скóрость; *fig* толчóк; **the ~ of the car was such that...** скóрость маши́ны былá таковá, что...; **the agreement will give a big ~ to trade** э́то соглашéние даст мóщный толчóк разви́тию торгóвли.

impiety *n* нечести́вость.

impinge *vi*: **the 20th century has scarcely ~d upon our older universities** в нáших стáрых университéтах забывáешь, что на дворé ужé двадцáтый век.

impish *adj* прокáзливый.

implacable *adj*: **an ~ enemy** неумоли́мый враг.

implant *vt*: **to ~ doubt in smb's mind** всел|я́ть сомнéния (*pl*) в когó-л (-и́ть); **the idea was firmly ~ed in his head that...** в егó мозгý прóчно засéло, что...

implausible *adj* невероя́тный, неправдоподóбный.

implement *n Agric* орýдие; (*of smaller tools*) инструмéнт.

implement *vt*: **to ~ a promise/an agreement** исполн|я́ть обещáние, вы|полня́ть соглашéние (´-ить, ´-полнить).

implicate *vt* вовле|кáть (´-чь); **he tried to ~ three others** он пытáлся вовлéчь (в э́то дéло) ещё трои́х; **he is ~d in the scandal** он замéшан в э́том скандáле.

implication *n*: **do you understand the full ~s of what you are saying?** ты понимáешь ли в пóлной мéре, что говори́шь?; **in accusing him, you are by ~ also accusing me** обвиня́я егó, ты кóсвенно обвиня́ешь и меня́.

implicit *adj*: **~ faith/obedience** слепáя вéра, безоговóрочное повиновéние; **it was ~ in what he said that...** из егó слов мóжно бы́ло заключи́ть, что..., подразумевáлось, что...

implore *vt* умоля́ть (*usu impf*); **to ~ smb for help/to come** умоля́ть когó-л о пóмощи/прийти́.

imply *vt* подразумевáть (*impf*); **what do you ~ by that?** что вы хоти́те э́тим сказáть?, что вы под э́тим подразумевáете?; **his answer implied a certain reluctance** в егó отвéте сквози́ло нежелáние (сдéлать э́то); **he implied that he was unhappy** он дал поня́ть, что несчáстлив; **that will ~ a lot of work for me** э́то означáет, что мне придётся мнóго рабóтать.

impolite *adj* невéжливый; **he was ~ to her** он был невéжлив с ней.

impolitic *adj* неблагоразýмный.

imponderable *adj as npl*: **there are many ~s here** здесь мнóго трýдно учи́тываемых фáкторов.

import *n Comm* (*action*) и́мпорт, ввоз товáров; *pl* (**~s**) и́мпортные товáры; **~s and exports** и́мпорт и э́кспорт (*sings*); *attr*: **~ duty/licence** ввознáя пóшлина/лицéнзия; **~ trade** торгóвля и́мпортными/ввозны́ми товáрами.

import *vt Comm* импорти́ровать (*impf and pf*).

importance *n* вáжность; значéние; **that is of no ~** э́то не имéет значéния, э́то невáжно; **he is a person of ~** он вáжное/влия́тельное лицó; **he is full of his own ~** он испóлнен сознáния своéй значи́тельности.

important *adj* вáжный, значи́тельный.

imported *adj*: **~ goods** ввозны́е/и́мпортные товáры.

importunate *adj* (*of person, demands, etc.*) назóйливый.

impose *vti vt*: **the government has ~d a tax on tobacco** прави́тельство ввелó налóг на табáк/обложи́ло табáк налóгом; **I hesitate to ~ any further burdens on you** я не хочý обременя́ть тебя́ нóвыми поручéниями; **I wouldn't like to ~ myself on them any longer** я не хочý им бóльше навя́зываться

vi: **it's not fair to ~ upon her good nature** нехорошó злоупотребля́ть её добротóй.

imposing *adj* внуши́тельный, впечатля́ющий; импозáнтный; **the colonel is an ~ figure** полкóвник весьмá внуши́тельная фигýра; **an ~ building** вели́чественное здáние.

imposition *n*: **the ~ of a new tax** введéние нóвого налóга; **the tax was regarded as an unfair ~** введéние э́того налóга бы́ло расцененó как очереднáя несправедли́вость; *fig* **it would be an ~ for you if we were all to come** у вас бýдет мнóго хлопóт, éсли мы все к вам придём.

impossibility *n* невозмóжность; **owing to the ~ of reaching agreement** из-за невозмóжности прийти́ к соглашéнию; **it's a sheer ~** э́то совершéнно/абсолю́тно невозмóжно.

impossible *adj* невозмóжный; *CQ* невыноси́мый; *CQ*: **an ~ situation** невыноси́мое положéние; **you're ~!** ты прóсто невыноси́м!; *as n*: **don't ask the ~ of me** не трéбуй от меня́ невозмóжного.

impostor *n* шарлата́н, моше́нник; **he a doctor?—he's just an ~!** како́й он врач—он про́сто шарлата́н!

impotence *n* бесси́лие; *Med* импоте́нция, полово́е бесси́лие.

impotent *adj* бесси́льный; *Med* импоте́нтный.

impoverish *vt* разор|я́ть (-и́ть), до|води́ть до нищеты́ (-вести́); **we have all been ~ed by heavy taxation** нало́ги про́сто разори́ли нас; **they are much ~ed since their father's death** их материа́льное положе́ние уху́дшилось по́сле сме́рти отца́; *Agric* **to ~ the soil** истощ|а́ть по́чву (-и́ть); *fig* **our language is becoming ~ed** наш язы́к обедня́ется.

impracticable *adj* неосуществи́мый.

impractical *adj* непракти́чный.

impregnate *vt* пропи́т|ывать (-а́ть); **the wood is ~d with oil** древеси́на пропи́тана ма́слом.

impresario *n* импреса́рио (*m*, *indecl*).

impress *vt* **1** (*affect*) произ|води́ть впечатле́ние (-вести́); **I was not particularly ~ed by her/by her book** она́/её кни́га не произвела́ на меня́ осо́бого впечатле́ния; **the scene ~ed itself on my memory** э́та сце́на запечатле́лась в мое́й па́мяти

2 (*bring home*): **I must ~ on you that...** я хочу́ внуши́ть тебе́, что...; **I tried to ~ on him what this would lead to** я хоте́л, что́бы он по́нял, к чему́ э́то приведёт.

impression *n* **1** (*of seal*) о́ттиск; **an ~ in wax** о́ттиск на во́ске; *Typ* **first/third ~** пе́рвый/тре́тий о́ттиск

2 (*effect*) впечатле́ние; **to make an ~ on** производи́ть впечатле́ние на + *A*; **I was under the ~ that...** у меня́ бы́ло тако́е впечатле́ние, что...; **he seemed to make no ~ on that pile of letters** похо́же, что он и не притро́нулся к э́той па́чке пи́сем.

impressionable *adj* впечатли́тельный; **at that age children are very ~** в э́том во́зрасте де́ти о́чень впечатли́тельны.

impressionist *n* импрессиони́ст.

impressive *adj* впечатля́ющий.

imprint *n* отпеча́ток.

imprint *vt fig*: **his last words are ~ed on my memory** его́ после́дние слова́ запечатле́лись в мое́й па́мяти.

imprison *vt* заключ|а́ть под стра́жу (-и́ть), сажа́ть (в тюрьму́) (посади́ть); **he was ~ed for 5 years** его́ посади́ли на пять лет (*usu pf*).

imprisonment *n* (тюре́мное) заключе́ние; **life ~** пожи́зненное заключе́ние; **he was sentenced to 5 years' ~** его́ приговори́ли к пяти́ года́м.

improbable *adj* невероя́тный, неправдоподо́бный.

impromptu *n* экспро́мт, *also Theat*, *Mus*.

impromptu *adj* импровизи́рованный.

impromptu *adv* экспро́мтом.

improper *adj* (*out of place*) неуме́стный; (*indecent*) неприли́чный; **an ~ remark** неуме́стное замеча́ние; **such behaviour is ~ at a funeral** тако́е поведе́ние неуме́стно на похорона́х; **to tell ~ stories** расска́зывать неприли́чные анекдо́ты.

improve *vti vt* улучш|а́ть (´-ить); **to ~ conditions/land** улу́чшить усло́вия, повы|ша́ть плодоро́дие по́чвы (´-сить); **to ~ one's English** соверше́нствовать свой англи́йский; **I'm reading a lot to try to ~ my mind** я сейча́с мно́го чита́ю для о́бщего разви́тия

vi **1** улучша́ться; **her writing/the patient is improving** её по́черк улучша́ется, больно́й поправля́ется; **his mathematics have ~d** он сде́лал успе́хи в матема́тике (*sing*); **this book ~s on reading** чем да́льше, тем кни́га интере́снее

2: **his exposition of the subject cannot be ~d on** он превосхо́дно излага́ет свой предме́т, нельзя́ себе́ предста́вить лу́чшего изложе́ния предме́та; **surely you can ~ on that** ты наверняка́ мо́жешь сде́лать э́то ещё лу́чше.

improvement *n* улучше́ние; **there's a noticeable ~ in the patient's condition/in the situation** в состоя́нии больно́го наблюда́ется заме́тное улучше́ние, ситуа́ция заме́тно улучша́ется; **my new car is an ~ on the old** моя́ но́вая маши́на гора́здо лу́чше ста́рой; **that's better, but there is still room for ~** э́то хорошо́, но мо́жно сде́лать ещё лу́чше; **we're making ~s to our house** мы де́лаем ко́е-каку́ю перестро́йку.

improvident *adj* (*short-sighted*) непредусмотри́тельный; (*thriftless*) небережли́вый, расточи́тельный.

improvisation *n* импровиза́ция.

improvise *vti* импровизи́ровать (*impf*), *also Theat*; **to ~ a lunch** пригото́вить обе́д на ско́рую ру́ку; **to ~ on the piano** импровизи́ровать на роя́ле.

imprudent *adj* неосмотри́тельный, неосторо́жный.

impudence *n* на́глость, наха́льство; де́рзость; **he had the ~ to say that...** у него́ хвати́ло на́глости/наха́льства сказа́ть, что...; **the teacher sent him out of the room for ~** учи́тель вы́гнал его́ из кла́сса за де́рзость.

impudent *adj* на́глый, наха́льный; де́рзкий.

impulse *n* побужде́ние, и́мпульс; поры́в; **my first ~ was to run/to phone him** мои́м пе́рвым побужде́нием бы́ло—бежа́ть, мой пе́рвый и́мпульс был—позвони́ть ему́; **I acted on ~** я де́йствовал, подда́вшись поры́ву; **I was seized by the ~ to hit him** меня́ так и подмыва́ло (*impers*) уда́рить его́.

impulsive *adj* импульси́вный.

impunity *n*: **you cannot do this with ~** тебе́ э́то безнака́занно/так не сойдёт.

impure *adj* нечи́стый; гря́зный, *also fig*; **an ~ breed** нечи́стая поро́да; **~ water** загрязнённая вода́; **~ thoughts** непристо́йные мы́сли.

impurity *n* при́месь; **impurities in food/metals** при́меси в пищевы́х проду́ктах/в мета́ллах.

imputation *n*: **the article contained ~s on his honesty** статья́ прозра́чно намека́ла, что он непоря́дочно вёл себя́.

impute *vt*: **to ~ smth to smb** припи́с|ывать что-л кому́-л (-а́ть).

in *n*: **all the ~s and outs of the problem** все то́нкости пробле́мы.

in *adj CQ*: **it's an ~ subject just now** э́то сейча́с мо́дная те́ма.

in *adv* 1 (*of place*): **is Igor ~?** И́горь до́ма? (*at home*)/у себя́? (*in his room at office*); **he's not ~** его́ нет; **when do you get ~?** во ско́лько ты прихо́дишь домо́й?; **the train was already ~** по́езд уже́ стоя́л у платфо́рмы; **the post isn't ~ yet** по́чты ещё не́ было; **the nurses live ~** медсёстры живу́т при больни́це

2 *various, mainly CQ*: **he's ~ on the secret** он посвящён в э́ту та́йну; **strawberries are ~ now** (сейча́с) в магази́нах/на ры́нке появи́лась клубни́ка (*collect*); **long skirts are ~** дли́нные ю́бки в мо́де/о́чень мо́дны; **is the fire still ~?** ками́н ещё то́пится?; **when the Labour Party was ~** когда́ лейбори́сты бы́ли у вла́сти; **the Tory candidate got ~** в парла́мент был вы́бран кандида́т от консервати́вной па́ртии; **I pay £20 a week all ~** я плачу́ два́дцать фу́нтов в неде́лю за кварти́ру и пита́ние; **he's well ~ with the boss** он на хоро́шем счету́ у нача́льства; **I'm all ~** я вы́дохся, я ко́нчился; **day ~ day out** изо дня́ в де́нь

3 **to be in for: I'm ~ for that job** я кандида́т на э́ту до́лжность; **I'm ~ for the long jump** я уча́ствую в прыжка́х (*pl*) в длину́; **he's ~ for a hard time/a shock** его́ ждут тяжёлые испыта́ния, его́ ожида́ет неприя́тный сюрпри́з; *CQ*: **I didn't know what I was letting myself ~ for** я тогда́ не знал, на что шёл; **it looks as if we're ~ for rain** похо́же, мы попадём под дождь; **the teacher saw us—now we're ~ for it** мы влипли—учи́тель заме́тил нас; **what's he ~ for?** (*in prison*) за что он сиди́т?

in *prep* (*see also verb entries*) 1 (*of place: state*) i) в + *P*; **~ hospital/Russia/Paris** в больни́це, в Росси́и, в Пари́же; **~ Siberia/the Alps/the Crimea** в Сиби́ри, в А́льпах, в Крыму́; **~ the forest/garden/cupboard** в лесу́, в саду́, в шкафу́; **he's ~ here/~ there** он здесь/там; **to stand ~ the corner** стоя́ть в углу́; **to sit ~ the second row** сиде́ть во второ́м ряду́ [**NB** *forms of P in* -у́]; **he's ~ the first form** он в пе́рвом кла́ссе; **~ my hand/arms** в мое́й руке́, в мои́х рука́х; **~ the distance** вдали́ (*adv*); ii) на + *P*; **~ the Urals/Caucasus/Ukraine/Canaries** на Ура́ле, на Кавка́зе, на Украи́не, на Кана́рских острова́х; **~ the north/south** (*etc.*) на се́вере, на ю́ге; **~ the street/market** на у́лице, на ры́нке; **he works ~ a factory** он рабо́тает на заво́де; **iii)** в *or* на + *P*; **~ the kitchen/sky/fields** в *or* на ку́хне/не́бе/поля́х; **he travelled ~ a/my car** он пое́хал на маши́не/в мое́й маши́не; **he was killed ~ battle/a duel** он поги́б в бою́/на дуэ́ли; **to play ~ the yard** игра́ть во дворе́ [на дворе́ = *outside*]; **iv)** (*of place: if motion implied*) в + *A*; **put them ~ the box/your pocket/~ here/~ there** положи́ их в я́щик/в карма́н/сюда́/туда́; *but* **NB: he set off ~ a northerly direction** он отпра́вился на се́вер

2 (*of time*) **i)** (*of point, duration of time*): **~ May/childhood/the past** в ма́е, в де́тстве, в про́шлом; **~ the thirties** в тридца́тых года́х; **~ 1902** в ты́сяча девятьсо́т второ́м году́; **~ that year** в тот год, в том году́; **I'll be ~ London ~ the week beginning the 10th of May** я бу́ду в Ло́ндоне по́сле деся́того ма́я; **~ summer/the morning** ле́том, у́тром; **at 8 ~ the morning** в во́семь часо́в утра́; **~ the mornings I do the housework** по утра́м я занима́юсь убо́ркой; **I'll do it ~ my own time** я э́то сде́лаю в своё вре́мя; **I've seen a lot ~ my time** я мно́го повида́л на своём веку́; **~ war** на войне́; **~ the war** (*during*) во вре́мя/в го́ды войны́; **he was killed ~ the war/~ the first World War** он поги́б на войне́/в пе́рвую мирову́ю войну́ [в + *A*, *if war is particularized*]; **~ the first half/the fifth minute of the game** в пе́рвом та́йме, на пя́той мину́те игры́; **~ the reign of Ivan the Terrible** при Ива́не Гро́зном; **I haven't seen him ~ years** я его́ не ви́дел мно́го лет; **a lot has changed ~ the course of this century** мно́гое измени́лось в тече́ние э́того столе́тия/в э́том столе́тии; **ii)** (*within a certain period*): **I'll be back ~ an hour/~ less than an hour** я верну́сь че́рез час/ра́ньше чем че́рез час; **he finished the job ~ a week** он зако́нчил рабо́ту за неде́лю; **five times ~ one week** пять раз в неде́лю

3 (*in respect of*): **broad ~ the shoulders** широ́кий в плеча́х; **three metres ~ length** три ме́тра длино́й/в длину́; **equal ~ size/rank** одина́ковые по разме́ру/по ра́нгу; **young ~ appearance** молодо́й на вид; **blind ~ one eye** слепо́й на оди́н глаз; **a rise ~ prices** повыше́ние цен; **I'm happy ~ my work** я дово́лен свое́й рабо́той; **research ~ physics** иссле́дования (*pl*) в о́бласти фи́зики; **he's weak ~ maths** он слаб в матема́тике (*sing*); **an interest ~ history** интере́с к исто́рии

4 (*of manner, form*): **to pay ~ cash/~ dollars** плати́ть нали́чными/до́лларами; **they arrived ~ groups/~ their thousands** они́ прибыва́ли гру́ппами/ты́сячами; **he spoke ~ Russian** он говори́л по-ру́сски; **it's written ~ Russian/~ pencil** э́то напи́сано на ру́сском языке́/карандашо́м; **he told me ~ secret/~ a few words** он мне сказа́л по секре́ту/в не́скольких слова́х; **he did it ~ secret** он э́то сде́лал тайко́м (*adv*); **to speak ~ jest/~ earnest/~ turn** говори́ть в шу́тку/всерьёз (*adv*)/по о́череди; **~ despair/tears/anger/silence** в отча́янии, в слеза́х, в гне́ве, в молча́нии; **if ~ doubt** е́сли сомнева́етесь

5 (*of weather*) в + *A*, на + *P*; **~ good weather** в хоро́шую пого́ду; **to go out/walk ~ the rain** выходи́ть в дождь, гуля́ть под дождём; **~ the cold/heat** в хо́лод, в жару́; **don't**

stand ~ the cold не стой на хо́лоде; **~ the sun/open air** на со́лнце, на откры́том во́здухе

6 (*of dress*): **the girl ~ red/~ the big hat** де́вушка в кра́сном/в большо́й шля́пе; **she's dressed ~ silk/~ blue** на ней шёлковое пла́тье, она́ оде́та в голубо́е; **I want something ~ cotton** я хочу́ что́-нибудь из хло́пка; **have you that dress ~ my size?** у вас есть тако́е пла́тье моего́ разме́ра?

7 (*with numbers*): **one man ~ 3** оди́н челове́к из трёх; **a reduction of 10p ~ the pound** ски́дка де́сять пе́нсов на фунт; *Aut*, *etc*. **a gradient of 1 ~ 7** укло́н оди́н к семи́

8 (*with gerund*): **he said ~ passing that...** он сказа́л как бы ме́жду про́чим/мимохо́дом, что...; **~ crossing the street** при перехо́де у́лицы, переходя́ у́лицу; **~ saying this I wish to...** говоря́ э́то, я хочу́...; **there's no sense ~ waiting** нет никако́го смы́сла ждать; **don't waste time ~ talking** не трать вре́мя на разгово́ры

9 in that: the theme is interesting ~ that... те́ма интере́сна тем, что...

10 *various*: **a fork ~ the road** разви́лка доро́ги; **the ring is worthless ~ itself** само́ по себе́ кольцо́ не представля́ет це́нности; **what would you do ~ my place?** что бы ты сде́лал на моём ме́сте?; **I didn't know he had it ~ him** я не знал, что он на э́то спосо́бен; **~ my absence/presence** в моё отсу́тствие, в моём прису́тствии; **he's/a man ~ his forties** ему́ за со́рок, челове́к сорока́ с ли́шним лет; **he's ~ the clothing business** он занима́ется торго́влей гото́вым пла́тьем; **he travels ~ refrigerators** он аге́нт по прода́же холоди́льников; **this is the latest thing ~ bicycles** э́то после́дняя моде́ль велосипе́да (*sing*); *CQ* **he's got it ~ for me** у него́ про́тив/на меня́ зуб.

inability *n* уме́ние; (*incapability*) неспосо́бность; **~ to read/to shoot/to count** неуме́ние чита́ть/стреля́ть, неспосо́бность к счёту; **their ~ to reach an agreement is delaying matters** они́ ника́к не мо́гут прийти́ к соглаше́нию, и из-за э́того всё заде́рживается.

inaccessible *adj* (*of place*, *person*) недосту́пный.

inaccuracy *n* нето́чность.

inaccurate *adj* нето́чный; **he is ~ in his work** он невнима́телен в рабо́те.

inaction *n* безде́йствие.

inactive *adj*: **I hate to be ~** я не люблю́ сиде́ть без де́ла; **an ~ volcano** безде́йствующий вулка́н.

inactivity *n* безде́ятельность.

inadequate *adj* недоста́точный; *Psych* неадеква́тный; **these measures are ~** э́ти ме́ры недоста́точны; **the canteen is ~ for such a large factory** э́та столо́вая мала́ для тако́й большо́й фа́брики; **I feel so ~ as a mother** я чу́вствую себя́ тако́й беспо́мощной в ро́ли ма́тери; **he proved ~ for the job** э́та рабо́та оказа́лась ему́ не по плечу́; **an ~ excuse** неубеди́тельная отгово́рка.

inadmissible *adj* недопусти́мый, неприе́млемый.

inadvertence *n*: **due to ~** по недосмо́тру.

inadvertently *adv* неумы́шленно.

inadvisable *adj*: **it is ~ to** не рекоменду́ется + *inf*.

inalienable *adj* неотъе́млемый.

inane *adj* пусто́й; **what an ~ remark!** како́е глу́пое/пусто́е замеча́ние!

inanimate *adj* неодушевлённый, *also Gram*; безжи́зненный; **~ matter** неодушевлённая мате́рия.

inapplicable *adj*: **that rule is ~ in the present case** э́то пра́вило в да́нном слу́чае неприме́нимо; **this clause is ~ to you** э́тот пункт к вам не отно́сится.

inappropriate *adj* неуме́стный; неподходя́щий; **that remark is ~** э́то замеча́ние неуме́стно/некста́ти (*out of place*); **that dress is ~ for a formal dinner** э́то пла́тье не годи́тся для торже́ственного обе́да; **that word is ~ to describe her** э́тот эпи́тет к ней не подхо́дит.

inarticulate *adj*: **he can only make ~ noises** он издаёт то́лько нечленоразде́льные зву́ки; *fig*: **he is a bit ~** он не уме́ет выража́ть свои́ мы́сли; **he was ~ with rage** он задохну́лся от я́рости.

inartistic *adj* нехудо́жественный; **he is ~** у него́ нет (худо́жественного) вку́са.

inasmuch *conj*: **~ as** (*since*) поско́льку.

inattention *n* невнима́ние; **~ to detail** невнима́ние к дета́лям.

inattentive *adj* невнима́тельный.

inaudible *adj* неслы́шный; **he was almost ~** его́ едва́ бы́ло слы́шно.

inaugural *adj*: **~ lecture/address** вступи́тельная ле́кция/речь; **~ flight** пе́рвый рейс.

inaugurate *vt*: **to ~ reforms/a President** вводи́ть но́вые рефо́рмы/президе́нта в до́лжность (ввести́).

inauspicious *adj* неблагоприя́тный.

inborn *adj* врождённый, приро́дный.

incalculable *adj* неисчисли́мый; **~ losses** неисчисли́мые поте́ри; **the storm did ~ damage** бу́ря нанесла́ огро́мный уще́рб.

incapable *adj* неспосо́бный; **he is ~ of telling a lie** он не спосо́бен лгать; *Law* **he was drunk and ~ in charge of a car** он вёл маши́ну в состоя́нии опьяне́ния.

incapacitate *vt*: **the accident ~d him for work** он потеря́л трудоспосо́бность в результа́те несча́стного слу́чая; **he was ~d by a bad fall** он так неуда́чно упа́л, что надо́лго вы́шел из стро́я.

incarnate *adj*: **he is a devil ~** он воплощённое зло.

incautious *adj* неосторо́жный, неосмотри́тельный.

incendiary *adj* зажига́тельный, *also fig*.

incense *n* ла́дан.

incense *vt*: **his obstinacy ~d me** его́ упря́мство привело́ меня́ в я́рость.

incentive *n* сти́мул; **it will be an ~ for him to work hard** э́то бу́дет для него́ сти-мулом рабо́тать не покладая рук; **they are going to pay us a bonus as an ~** они́ бу́дут плати́ть нам пре́мию в ка́честве дополни́тельного сти́мула.

incessant *adj* непреры́вный; **the ~ crying of the child** непреры́вный плач ребёнка; **~ complaints/rain** бесконе́чные жа́лобы, непреры́вный дождь.

incest *n* кровосмеше́ние.

inch *n* дюйм; **6 ~es long** длино́й в шесть дю́ймов; **he is 6 feet 2 ~es tall** он ро́стом шесть фу́тов два дю́йма; *fig*: **I won't yield an ~** я не уступлю́ ни на йо́ту; **the bullet missed my ear by ~es** пу́ля пролете́ла в миллиме́тре от моего́ у́ха; **he edged forward ~ by ~** он ма́ло-пома́лу продвига́лся вперёд; **he's every ~ a man/soldier** он настоя́щий мужчи́на, он солда́т до мо́зга косте́й.

incidence *n*: **the ~ of measles among children is increasing** всё бо́льше слу́чаев заболева́ния ко́рью среди́ дете́й.

incident *n* слу́чай, происше́ствие; эпизо́д; *Mil*, *Dipl* инциде́нт; **a strange ~** стра́нный слу́чай, стра́нное происше́ствие; **we got there without ~** мы дое́хали без вся́ких происше́ствий (*pl*); **the ~ in the novel where...** эпизо́д в рома́не, где...

incidental *adj* (*chance*) случа́йный; (*secondary*) дополни́тельный; **an ~ meeting** случа́йная встре́ча; **~ expenses** дополни́тельные/непредви́денные расхо́ды; **the ~ advantages of this job** дополни́тельные преиму́щества э́той рабо́ты; *Cine* **~ music to a film** му́зыка к кинофи́льму; **problems ~ to adolescence** пробле́мы подро́сткового во́зраста.

incidentally *adv* (*by chance*) случа́йно; (*by the way*) **~, I wanted to tell you...** кста́ти,/ ме́жду про́чим, я хоте́л вам сказа́ть...

incinerate *vt* сжига́ть (дотла́) (сжечь).

incinerator *n* мусоросжига́тель (*m*).

incipient *adj* начина́ющийся; **the ~ rebellion** начина́ющееся восста́ние; **you've got ~ dental decay** у вас начина́ют разруша́ться зу́бы.

incision *n* надре́з; (*slightly larger*) разре́з; **to make an ~ in smth** де́лать надре́з на чём-л.

incisive *adj* (*of words, tone, criticism*) ре́зкий; **an ~ mind** о́стрый/проница́тельный ум.

incisor *n* (*tooth*) резе́ц.

incite *vt usu pejor* подстрека́ть + *inf* (*usu impf*).

inclement *adj*: **~ weather** нена́стная пого́да.

inclination *n* **1** (*slope*) накло́н, укло́н; **the ~ of the road/roof** укло́н доро́ги, накло́н кры́ши; **with an ~ of the head** кивко́м головы́

2 (*desire*) скло́нность; **I have no ~ to help him** я не скло́нен помога́ть ему́; **my first ~ was to agree** мое́й пе́рвой мы́слью бы́ло согласи́ться; **he showed no ~ to leave** он не прояви́л никако́го наме́рения уйти́; **to follow one's ~s** сле́довать свои́м влече́ниям.

incline *n* (*of hill*) склон, (*of roof*) скат; (*gradient*) укло́н.

incline *vti vt* (*bend*) наклон|я́ть (-и́ть); *fig* склон|я́ть к + *D* *or* + *inf* (-и́ть); **he ~d his head** он наклони́л го́лову; **his letter ~d me to think that...** его́ письмо́ склони́ло меня́ к мы́сли, что...; **I am ~d to believe you** я скло́нен ве́рить вам; **I'm half ~d to refuse** я почти́ гото́в отказа́ться; **if you are so ~d** е́сли вам так хо́чется; **he's ~d to get colds** он располо́жен к просту́де

vi: **the road ~s steeply here** здесь доро́га кру́то идёт под укло́н; **I ~ to the opinion that...** я склоня́юсь к мы́сли, что...

include *vt* включ|а́ть (-и́ть); **he's ~d in the team** он включён в кома́нду; **does that invitation ~ me?** я то́же приглашён?; **her duties ~ answering the phone** в её обя́занности вхо́дит отвеча́ть на телефо́нные звонки́; **the article ~s much useful information** в статье́ мно́го поле́зной информа́ции.

including *as prep* включа́я; **tickets cost £10 ~ supper** биле́ты сто́ят де́сять фу́нтов, включа́я сто́имость у́жина; **up to and ~ the 7th of July** по седьмо́е ию́ля включи́тельно; **all staff, ~ cleaners and porters, must...** все сотру́дники, в том числе́ убо́рщицы и швейца́ры, должны́ + *inf*.

inclusive *adj*: **are their terms ~?** у них цена́ включа́ет всё?; **£100 ~ of interest** сто фу́нтов, включа́я проце́нты; **from Tuesday to Friday ~** со вто́рника по пя́тницу включи́тельно.

incognito *adv* инко́гнито.

incoherent *adj* бессвя́зный; несвя́зный; **his lecture was ~** его́ ле́кция была́ бессвя́зной; **he gave an ~ account of the accident** из его́ несвя́зного расска́за о происше́дшем нельзя́ бы́ло ничего́ поня́ть; **he was ~ with rage** от я́рости он потеря́л дар ре́чи.

income *n* дохо́д; **the ~ from the shop is low** магази́н не даёт большо́го дохо́да; **annual/gross/net ~** годово́й/валово́й/чи́стый дохо́д; **tax is payable on ~s over £1,000** дохо́д (*sing*) вы́ше ты́сячи фу́нтов облага́ется нало́гом; **I can't live on my ~** моего́ за́работка не хвата́ет на жизнь; **to live beyond one's ~** жить не по сре́дствам; *attr*: **~ tax** подоходный нало́г.

incomparable *adj* несравни́мый, несравне́нный.

incompatibility *n* несовмести́мость; **to divorce on the grounds of ~** развести́сь из-за несхо́дства хара́ктеров.

incompatible *adj*: **~ with** несовмести́мый с + *I*; **they are ~** они́ соверше́нно ра́зные лю́ди, они́ не сошли́сь хара́ктерами [**NB** *tense*].

incompetent *adj* неспосо́бный; (*of specialists*) некомпете́нтный; **he is ~ as head of department** он не спосо́бен быть руководи́телем отде́ла; **he is an ~ mechanic** он плохо́й/*CQ* никуды́шный меха́ник; **she's so ~** она́ ни к чему́ не спосо́бна.

incomplete *adj* непо́лный; **an ~ answer** непо́лный отве́т; **~ knowledge** недоста́точные зна́ния (*pl*).

incomprehensible *adj* непоня́тный; (*unintelligible*) невразуми́тельный; **an ~ message** непоня́тное сообще́ние; **the lecture was quite ~ to me** я в э́той ле́кции ничего́ не по́нял.

inconceivable *adj* невообрази́мый, немы́слимый.

inconclusive *adj*: **~ arguments/evidence** неубеди́тельные до́воды, недоста́точные доказа́тельства (*pl*); **the investigation was ~** сле́дствие ни к чему́ определённому не привело́.

incongruous *adj* неподходя́щий; (*absurd*) неле́пый; **what an ~ place to meet!** како́е неподходя́щее ме́сто для встре́чи!; **it seems ~ that...** как неле́по, что...

inconsequent *adj* непосле́довательный.

inconsiderable *adj* незначи́тельный.

inconsiderate *adj* невнима́тельный; **he is ~ to her/of her feelings** он невнима́телен к ней, он не счита́ется с её чу́вствами.

inconsistency *n* непосле́довательность; несоотве́тствие; **there are many inconsistencies in the article** в статье́ мно́го противоречи́вого.

inconsistent *adj* непосле́довательный; **his arguments are ~** его́ до́воды противоречи́вы; **your evidence is ~ with the facts** ва́ши показа́ния (*pl*) расхо́дятся с фа́ктами; **his work is very ~** (*uneven*) его́ рабо́та о́чень неро́вная.

inconsolable *adj* безуте́шный, неуте́шный.

inconspicuous *adj* незаме́тный; **the figures are ~ against the dark background** э́ти фигу́ры незаме́тны на тёмном фо́не.

incontinence *n Med* недержа́ние мочи́.

incontrovertible *adj* неопровержи́мый, неоспори́мый.

inconvenience *n* неудо́бство; **it's a great ~ living so far from the centre** большо́е неудо́бство жить так далеко́ от це́нтра; **to cause smb ~** причиня́ть кому́-л неудо́бство, стесня́ть кого́-л; **I was put to great ~ by their visit** их прие́зд был о́чень некста́ти (*adv*).

inconvenience *vt*: **to ~ smb** причин|я́ть кому́-л неудо́бство (-и́ть), затрудн|я́ть кого́-л (-и́ть).

inconvenient *adj* неудо́бный; затрудни́тельный; **an ~ time** неудо́бное вре́мя; **I find it ~** мне э́то неудо́бно; **Cambridge is an ~ place to get to** до Ке́мбриджа дово́льно сло́жно добира́ться.

incorporate *vt* включ|а́ть (-и́ть).

incorrect *adj* (*wrong*) непра́вильный; **an ~ answer** непра́вильный отве́т; **~ behaviour** некорре́ктное поведе́ние.

incorrigible *adj* неисправи́мый; **an ~ liar** неисправи́мый/закорене́лый лгун; **an ~ smoker** *CQ* завзя́тый кури́льщик; **you're ~!** ты неисправи́м!

incorruptible *adj* неподку́пный.

increase *n* рост, увеличе́ние; **an ~ in population/in the number of students** рост населе́ния/числа́ студе́нтов; **an ~ in trade/power/income** увеличе́ние *or* рост торго́вли, укрепле́ние мо́щи, возраста́ние дохо́дов (*pl*); **an ~ in the tax on tobacco** повыше́ние нало́га на таба́к; **an ~ in wages** повыше́ние зарпла́ты, приба́вка к зарпла́те; **crime is on the ~** престу́пность растёт.

increase *vti vt* увели́ч|ивать (-ить); **to ~ speed** увели́чить ско́рость; **the tax on petrol has been ~d** повы́сился нало́г на бензи́н

vi увели́чиваться, расти́ (вы́-); **our difficulties are increasing** на́ши тру́дности всё расту́т; **the pace of work ~d** темп рабо́ты ускорился; **my weight has ~d** я приба́вил в ве́се.

increasing *adj* возраста́ющий.

increasingly *adv*: **an ~ dangerous sport** вид спо́рта, кото́рый стано́вится всё бо́лее опа́сным.

incredible *adj* невероя́тный, *also CQ*; **to an ~ degree** до невероя́тности; **~!** невероя́тно!

incredulity *n* недове́рие; **in/with ~** с недове́рием.

incredulous *adj* недове́рчивый.

increment *n*: **an ~ in salary** приба́вка к зарпла́те; **an ~ of 30 roubles a month** приба́вка в три́дцать рубле́й в ме́сяц.

incriminate *vt*: **don't say anything that might ~ your friends** не говори́ ничего́, что могло́ бы повреди́ть твои́м друзья́м; **the accused may refuse to give evidence that might ~ himself** обвиня́емый име́ет пра́во отказа́ться от да́чи показа́ний (*pl*), кото́рые мо́гут быть испо́льзованы про́тив него́; **the evidence looked incriminating, but he was acquitted** показа́ния бы́ли я́вно про́тив него́, и всё-таки он был опра́вдан; **he tried to ~ Igor** он стара́лся свали́ть всю вину́ на И́горя.

inculcate *vt*: **to ~ ideas in smb** внуш|а́ть кому́-л иде́и (-и́ть).

incumbent *adj*: **it is ~ upon me to help his widow** я обя́зан помо́чь его́ вдове́; **it is ~ on you to appear in court tomorrow** вам надлежи́т за́втра яви́ться в суд.

incur *vt*: **to ~ wrath/displeasure** навле|ка́ть на себя́ гнев/недово́льство (-́чь); **to ~ debts** наде́лать долго́в; **to ~ heavy losses** нести́ больши́е убы́тки (*Fin*)/тяжёлые поте́ри (*Mil*); **I shall reimburse any expenses ~red** я возмещу́ все расхо́ды; **you will ~ a fine if...** тебя́ оштрафу́ют, е́сли...

incurable *adj*: **an ~ invalid/optimist** неизлечи́мо больно́й, неисправи́мый оптими́ст.

indebted *adj*: **I am ~ to you for your help** я у тебя́ в долгу́/я так тебе́ обя́зан за твою́ по́мощь; **I am eternally ~ to you** я у тебя́ в неопла́тном долгу́.

indecency *n* неприли́чие, непристо́йность.

indecent *adj* неприли́чный, непристо́йный; **~ behaviour** неприли́чное/непристо́йное поведе́ние; **~ language** скверносло́вие.

indecipherable *adj*: **an ~ code** код, не поддаю́щийся расшифро́вке; **~ handwriting** неразбо́рчивый по́черк.

indecision *n* нереши́тельность.

indecisive *adj* нереши́тельный; **an ~ answer** нереши́тельный отве́т; **his manner was ~** он вёл себя́ нереши́тельно; **the results of the experiment were ~** результа́ты о́пыта бы́ли не окончáтельными; ~ **evidence** неубеди́тельное доказáтельство; **the battle was** ~ бой никомý не принёс побéды.

indeclinable *adj Gram* несклоня́емый.

indecorous *adj* неблагопристóйный.

indeed *adv* в сáмом дéле, действи́тельно; **that's praise** ~ э́то в сáмом дéле/действи́тельно похвалá; **are you pleased with his progress?—Yes,** ~ вы довóльны егó успéхами (*pl*)?—Ну, конéчно; **thank you very much** ~ огрóмное (вам) спаси́бо; **it is very kind** ~ **of you** вы действи́тельно óчень любéзны; **but I may** ~ **be wrong** но, мóжет быть, я и ошибáюсь; **I never speak to him,** ~ **why should I?** я с ним не разговáриваю, да и о чём мне с ним говори́ть?; **he didn't want to do it,** ~ **he only agreed on one condition** сначáла он и слы́шать об э́том не хотéл, но потóм всё-таки согласи́лся при однóм услóвии.

indefatigable *adj* неутоми́мый.

indefensible *adj*: **an** ~ **theory** несостоя́тельная теóрия; **such behaviour is** ~ такóе поведéние ничéм не опрáвдано; **an** ~ **position** бездоказáтельная пози́ция, *Mil* пози́ция, не удóбная для оборóны.

indefinable *adj*: **she has an** ~ **charm** в ней есть какóе-то очаровáние.

indefinite *adj* неопределённый, *also Gram*; **he was very** ~ **about when he would be coming** он ничегó определённого не сказáл о том, когдá смóжет приéхать.

indefinitely *adv* бесконéчно; **these meetings go on** ~ э́ти собрáния длáтся бесконéчно; **we can carry on** ~ мы мóжем продолжáть так до бесконéчности; **the meeting has been postponed** ~ собрáние отложи́ли на неопределённый срок.

indelible *adj* несмывáемый, *also fig*; *fig* неизглади́мый; **an** ~ **impression** неизглади́мое впечатлéние; ~ **shame** несмывáемый позóр; ~ **pencils/ink** хими́ческие карандаши́/черни́ла (*no sing*).

indemnity *n Law* возмещéние, компенсáция.

indent *vti vt*: *Typ* **to** ~ **the first line** на|чинáть пéрвую строкý с абзáца (-чáть); **to** ~ **5 places** отступ|áть на пять знáков (-и́ть) *vi*: *Comm* **to** ~ **for goods** сдéлать закáз на товáры.

indented *adj*: **an** ~ **coastline** изрéзанная береговáя ли́ния.

independence *n* незави́симость; (*of character, etc.*) самостоя́тельность; (*US*) **I. Day** День незави́симости.

independent *adj* незави́симый; (*of character, etc.*) самостоя́тельный; **I walk to work and am** ~ **of transport** я не зави́шу от трáнспорта—хожý на рабóту пешкóм; **an** ~ **nature/organization** незави́симая *or* самостоя́тельная натýра/организáция; **a man of** ~ **means** человéк, имéющий незави́симое состоя́ние.

independently *adv* незави́симо; самостоя́тельно; **I came to that conclusion** ~ **of what you told me** я пришёл к э́тому заключéнию незави́симо от тогó, что ты мне сказал; **he works** ~ он рабóтает самостоя́тельно.

indescribable *adj* неописýемый, *also CQ*.

indestructible *adj* неразруши́мый.

indeterminate *adj* неопределённый, *also Gram*; неопредели́мый, *also Phys*.

index *n* и́ндекс, указáтель (*m*); (*in library*) каталóг; *Math* показáтель (*m*); **price** ~ и́ндекс цен; **the** ~ **is at the back of the book** указáтель—в концé кни́ги; *attr*: ~ **finger** указáтельный пáлец.

index *vt*: **to** ~ **a book** снаб|жáть кни́гу указáтелем (-ди́ть); **to** ~ **a word** вноси́ть слóво в и́ндекс (внести́); **the book is badly** ~**ed** в э́той кни́ге плохóй указáтель; **it is** ~**ed under "sport"** э́то вы найдёте под заголóвком «Спорт».

Indian *n* (*from India*) инди́ец (*m*); (*Red Indian*) индéец (*m*); *f* (*of both*) индиáнка.

Indian *adj* (*from India*) инди́йский; (*Red Indian*) индéйский; *fig*: **in** ~ **file** гуськóм; **an** ~ **summer** бáбье лéто.

indiarubber *n* лáстик, рези́нка.

indicate *vt* (*point to*) укáз|ывать, (*show*) покáз|ывать (*pfs* -áть); (*mark*) обознач|áть (-ить); (*signify*) означáть (*impf*), обозначáть (*only in impf*); **he** ~**d a notice on the wall** он указáл на объявлéние на стенé; **the needle** ~**s the oil level** стрéлка покáзывает ýровень мáсла; **these figures** ~ **a fall in production** э́ти ци́фры свидéтельствуют о спáде произвóдства; **his smile** ~**s approval** егó улы́бка означáет одобрéние; **churches are** ~**d on the map by a cross** цéркви обознáчены на кáрте крéстиком; **he** ~**d that I should follow him** он пóдал мне знак/(*in words*) он велéл мне слéдовать за ним.

indication *n* при́знак, знак; **is there any** ~ **of a change in the weather?** есть каки́е-либо при́знаки (*pl*) изменéния погóды?; **there is every** ~ **that...** имéются все при́знаки тогó, что...; **it is an** ~ **of their disapproval** так они́ выражáют своё неодобрéние; **did he give you any** ~ **of his intentions?** сказáл/сообщи́л ли он о свои́х намéрениях?; **he gave no** ~ **of having heard** он как бýдто ничегó не слы́шал.

indicative *adj*: **to be** ~ **of smth** свидéтельствовать о чём-л; *Gram* **the** ~ **mood** изъяви́тельное наклонéние.

indicator *n* (*arrow*) стрéлка; (*at railway, airport, etc.*) указáтель (*m*); *Chem* индикáтор; *Aut* указáтель/сигнáл поворóта, *CQ* мигáлка; **your** ~ **is still on** у вас указáтель (поворóта) не вы́ключен.

indict *vt*: **he was** ~**ed on a charge of treason** он был обвинён в госудáрственной измéне.

indictable *adj*: **an** ~ **offence** уголóвное преступлéние.

indictment *n* (*charge*) обвинéние, *also fig*; (*speech*) обвини́тельная речь; (*bill*) обвини́тельный акт; *fig* **the play is an** ~ **of modern morality** пьéса выносит обвинéние совремéнной морáли.

indifference *n* безразли́чие, равноду́шие; **to show ~ to smth** проявля́ть безразли́чие/равноду́шие к чему́-л; **it is a matter of ~ to me** мне безразли́чно, мне всё равно́.

indifferent *adj* равноду́шный, безразли́чный; **an ~ audience** равноду́шная пу́блика; **he is ~ to me** он безразли́чен/равноду́шен ко мне; **it is ~ to me whether you go or stay** мне безразли́чно, уйдёшь ты и́ли оста́нешься; (*mediocre*) **an ~ pianist** посре́дственный/нева́жный пиани́ст.

indifferently *adv* (*not caring*) равноду́шно, с равноду́шием, безразли́чно; **he played ~** он игра́л посре́дственно/нева́жно.

indigenous *adj* тузе́мный, ме́стный.

indigestible *adj* неудобовари́мый, *also fig.*

indigestion *n* несваре́ние/расстро́йство желу́дка; **I've got a touch of ~** у меня́ лёгкое расстро́йство желу́дка; *fig* **his writing gives me mental ~** меня́ от его́ писани́ны тошни́т (*impers*).

indignant *adj* негоду́ющий, возмущённый; **he was ~ with me/at my criticism** он был возмущён мной/мое́й кри́тикой; **the suggestion made him ~** э́то предложе́ние вы́звало у него́ негодова́ние; **he got ~ about the article** он возмуща́лся э́той статьёй.

indignantly *adv* с негодова́нием, с возмуще́нием.

indignity *n*: **he was subjected to many indignities** он подве́ргся мно́гим униже́ниям.

indirect *adj* непрямо́й; око́льный, *also fig*; ко́свенный, *also Gram*; **an ~ answer/route** укло́нчивый отве́т, обходно́й/око́льный путь; **~ taxes/evidence** ко́свенные нало́ги/доказа́тельства (*pl*); *fig* **an ~ approach** око́льные пути́ (*pl*).

indirectly *adv* непря́мо, ко́свенно; **he answered ~** он не дал прямо́го отве́та, он отве́тил укло́нчиво; **he referred ~ to your case** он ко́свенно сосла́лся на ва́ше де́ло; **I only heard about it ~** я узна́л об э́том не из пе́рвых рук.

indiscreet *adj* нескро́мный; **an ~ remark** нескро́мное/беста́ктное замеча́ние.

indiscretion *n*: **she was sacked for ~** её уво́лили за изли́шнюю болтли́вость.

indiscriminate *adj* неразбо́рчивый; **an ~ reader** неразбо́рчивый чита́тель; **he was ~ in his choice of friends** он был неразбо́рчив в вы́боре друзе́й.

indiscriminately *adv* без разбо́ра; **he condemned them all ~** он осужда́л всех без разбо́ра; **you can't blame everyone ~** нельзя́ всех обвиня́ть подря́д; **he hit out ~** он бил куда́ придётся.

indispensable *adj* (*of things*) необходи́мый; (*usu of person*) незамени́мый; **your attendance is ~** вы непреме́нно должны́ прийти́.

indisposed *adj*: **she is ~** она́ нездоро́ва, ей нездоро́вится; **he seems ~ to help us** похо́же, что он не располо́жен/не наме́рен нам помо́чь.

indisposition *n* недомога́ние.

indisputable *adj* бесспо́рный, неоспори́мый, неопровержи́мый.

indistinct *adj* нея́сный; (*of sounds*) невня́тный; **~ muttering** нея́сное/невня́тное бормота́ние; **~ recollections** нея́сные/сму́тные воспомина́ния.

indistinguishable *adj*: **they are ~ from each other** их невозмо́жно отличи́ть друг от дру́га.

individual *n* ли́чность, индиви́дуум; **the right of the ~** права́ (*pl*) ли́чности; **the role of the ~ in society** роль ли́чности/индиви́дуума в о́бществе; **he's a cheerful ~** он весёлый челове́к; **who's that strange-looking ~?** кто э́та стра́нная ли́чность?

individual *adj* индивидуа́льный; **an ~ style of dress** индивидуа́льный стиль в оде́жде; **to give each pupil ~ attention** подходи́ть к ка́ждому ученику́ индивидуа́льно.

indivisible *adj* недели́мый, неразделим́ый.

indoctrinate *vt*: **they had been ~d with strange ideas** им бы́ли препо́даны стра́нные иде́и.

indolent *adj* лени́вый.

indomitable *adj*: **an ~ will** неукроти́мая во́ля; **~ courage** непобеди́мое му́жество.

indoor *adj*: **~ games** (*children's*)/**plants** ко́мнатные и́гры/расте́ния; **an ~ aerial** ко́мнатная анте́нна; **~ sport/games** спорти́вные и́гры в закры́том помеще́нии; **an ~ swimming pool** закры́тый пла́вательный бассе́йн.

indoors *adv*: **I stayed ~** я оста́лся до́ма; **the rain kept us ~** из-за дождя́ мы сиде́ли до́ма/никуда́ не выходи́ли.

indubitable *adj* несомне́нный.

induce *vt* застав|ля́ть (-́ить); **what ~d you to go there?** что тебя́ заста́вило пойти́ туда́?; *Med* **to ~ labour** стимули́ровать ро́ды (*impf and pf*).

inducement *n* сти́мул, побужде́ние; **as an ~ to work** как сти́мул/побужде́ние к рабо́те; **if you'll be there it would be an added ~ for me to go** е́сли ты там бу́дешь, для меня́ э́то бу́дет ещё оди́н сти́мул, что́бы пойти́.

indulge *vti vt* потво́рствовать + *D*, *CQ* потака́ть + *D* (*impfs*); (*spoil*) балова́ть (из-); **he ~s her whims/her in everything** он потво́рствует/потака́ет её капри́зам/ей во всём; **they ~ the child too much** они́ сли́шком балу́ют ребёнка

vi: **on Sundays I often ~ in a long lie** по воскресе́ньям я позволя́ю себе́ полежа́ть подо́льше; (*of drinking*) **he ~s too much** он сли́шком ча́сто прикла́дывается к спиртно́му.

indulgence *n*: **she treats him/his failings with ~** она потво́рствует ему́; **cigars are my one ~** сига́ры—еди́нственное, что я позволя́ю себе́.

indulgent *adj*: **~ parents** нестро́гие/нетре́бовательные роди́тели; **an ~ boss** снисходи́тельный нача́льник; **he's an ~ husband** он балу́ет свою́ жену́.

industrial *adj* промы́шленный, индустриа́льный; (*technically viewed*) произво́дственный; **an ~ estate** промы́шленный/индустриа́льный райо́н; **the ~ revolution** промы́шленная револю́ция; **~ training/insurance** произво́дственное обуче́ние/страхова́ние; **an ~ accident** несча́стный слу́чай на произво́дстве.

industrialist *n* промы́шленник.

industrialize *vt* индустриализ|и́ровать *or* -ова́ть (*both impf and pf*).

industrious *adj* трудолюби́вый, прилё́жный.

industry *n* **1** (*production*) промы́шленность; **heavy/light ~** тяжёлая/лёгкая промы́шленность; **the tourist ~** тури́зм; **cottage industries** ремёсла

2 (*industriousness*) трудолю́бие, приле́жность.

inebriated *adj* опьяне́вший; **to become ~** опьяне́ть.

inedible *adj* несъедо́бный.

ineffective *adj*: **an ~ person** неуме́лый/неспосо́бный челове́к; **~ measures** неэффекти́вные ме́ры.

ineffectual *adj* недействи́тельный, неэффекти́вный.

inefficient *adj*: **~ methods** неэффекти́вные ме́тоды; **these machines/my assistants are very ~** э́ти маши́ны о́чень пло́хо рабо́тают, мои́ помо́щники о́чень неисполни́тельны.

ineligible *adj*: **he is ~ to vote/for unemployment benefit** у него́ нет пра́ва го́лоса/на получе́ние посо́бия по безрабо́тице.

inept *adj* (*of remark*) неуме́стный; (*of phrase*) неподходя́щий; (*of person*) неуме́лый.

ineptitude *n* (*of remark*) неуме́стность; (*of person*) неуме́ние.

inequality *n* нера́венство; **~ of pay between men and women** нера́вная опла́та труда́ мужчи́н и же́нщин; **social inequalities** социа́льное нера́венство (*sing*).

inequitable *adj* несправедли́вый.

ineradicable *adj* неискорени́мый.

inert *adj* ине́ртный, *also fig*; **~ matter** ине́ртное вещество́; **he lay ~ on the floor** он лежа́л неподви́жно на полу́.

inertia *n* ине́рция, *also fig*; *fig* ине́ртность.

inescapable *adj* неизбе́жный.

inessential *adj* несуще́ственный; *as npl* **(the ~s)** несуще́ственные дета́ли.

inestimable *adj* неоцени́мый; **your help was of ~ value to me** ва́ша по́мощь была́ про́сто неоцени́мой.

inevitable *adj* неизбе́жный, немину́емый; неизме́нный; *CQ*: **there was the ~ row** разрази́лся неизбе́жный сканда́л; **a tourist with his ~ camera** тури́ст с неизме́нным фотоаппара́том.

inexact *adj* нето́чный.

inexcusable *adj* непрости́тельный.

inexhaustible *adj*: **he's ~** он неутоми́м; **~ supplies** неиссяка́емые/неистощи́мые/неисчерпа́емые запа́сы; **my patience is not ~** моему́ терпе́нию есть преде́л.

inexpedient *adj* нецелесообра́зный.

inexpensive *adj* недорого́й.

inexperienced *adj* нео́пытный, неискушённый; **she was an ~ typist/~ in the ways of the world** она́ была́ нео́пытной машини́сткой/неискушена́ в жи́зни.

inexplicable *adj* необъясни́мый.

inexpressible *adj* невырази́мый.

inextricable *adj*: **~ confusion** немы́слимая пу́таница; **an ~ situation** безвы́ходное положе́ние.

infallible *adj* непогреши́мый; надё́жный, безоши́бочный; **he thinks he's ~** он счита́ет себя́ непогреши́мым; **an ~ argument/method** неотрази́мый до́вод, надёжный ме́тод; **an ~ proof/~ remedy** неопровержи́мое доказа́тельство, надёжное сре́дство; **nobody is ~** никто́ не застрахо́ван от оши́бок.

infamous *adj*: **an ~ traitor** по́длый преда́тель; **an ~ crime** позо́рное преступле́ние.

infancy *n* младе́нчество, *also fig*; *Law* несовершенноле́тие (*applies also to juveniles*); **from ~** с младе́нчества; **in ~** в младе́нчестве; *fig* **the state is still in its ~** госуда́рство ещё нахо́дится в пери́оде становле́ния.

infant *n* младе́нец, ребёнок; *Law* малоле́тний.

infant *adj* де́тский, младе́нческий; **~ mortality** де́тская сме́ртность.

infantile *adj* де́тский; **~ diseases/paralysis** де́тские боле́зни, де́тский парали́ч; *pejor* **don't be so ~!** не будь таки́м младе́нцем!

infantry *n collect* пехо́та; **two regiments of ~** два пехо́тных полка́.

infatuated *adj*: **he's ~ with her/with jazz** он без ума́ от неё, он бре́дит джа́зом.

infect *vt* зара|жа́ть (-зи́ть), *also fig*; **he ~ed them with flu/with his enthusiasm** он зарази́л их гри́ппом/свои́м энтузиа́змом; **an ~ed wound** инфици́рованная ра́на.

infection *n* инфе́кция, зараже́ние; **flu spreads by ~** грипп распространя́ется путём инфе́кции; **an ~ of the ear** воспале́ние у́ха.

infectious *adj* инфекцио́нный, зара́зный; *fig* зарази́тельный.

infer *vt*: **I ~red from his remarks that...** из его́ замеча́ний я сде́лал вы́вод/заключи́л, что...

inference *n* вы́вод, (умо)заключе́ние.

inferior *n* (*in office, etc.*) подчинённый; **he is intellectually/socially her ~** она́ вы́ше его́ по разви́тию/по социа́льному положе́нию.

inferior *adj* (*in rank, etc.*) (бо́лее) ни́зкий; **an ~ position** бо́лее ни́зкое положе́ние; **he is ~ in rank to me** он ни́же меня́ по чи́ну/по положе́нию; **he felt ~ to them** он чу́вствовал, что во мно́гом им уступа́ет; **he's an ~ character** *CQ* он примити́в; **~ coffee** ко́фе ни́зкого ка́чества.

inferiority *n* (*of goods*) ни́зкое ка́чество; *attr Psych*: **~ complex** ко́мплекс неполноце́нности.

infernal *adj* а́дский, *also fig*.

inferno *n* ад, *also fig*; **the hall was like an ~** в за́ле бы́ло жа́рко, как в аду́.

infertile *adj Biol*, *Agric* беспло́дный, *also fig*; *Agric* неплодоро́дный.

infertility *n Agric* неплодоро́дность, беспло́дность; *Biol* беспло́дие.

infest *vt*: **his clothes are ~ed with lice** его́ оде́жда киши́т вша́ми; **the beans are ~ed with green fly** на фасо́ль напа́ла тля.

infidelity *n* неве́рность.

infiltrate *vt* проник|а́ть (-́нуть), *also fig*; **to ~ headquarters/the enemy lines** прони́кнуть в штаб, перейти́ ли́нию (*sing*) фро́нта (*usu pf*).

infinite *adj* бесконе́чный, безграни́чный, беспреде́льный; **~ gratitude** бесконе́чная благода́рность; **~ love** безграни́чная любо́вь; **the ~ expanse of the steppes** беспреде́льные степны́е просто́ры; **he took ~ pains over his drawings** он необыча́йно стара́тельно труди́лся над свои́ми рису́нками.

infinitesimal *adj* бесконе́чно ма́лый.

infinitive *n Gram* инфинити́в; *attr* инфинити́вный.

infinity *n* бесконе́чность, *also Math.*

infirm *adj* не́мощный; **aged and ~** ста́рый и не́мощный.

infirmary *n* больни́ца.

inflame *vt* воспламен|я́ть (-и́ть); **~d eyes** воспалённые глаза́; **his throat is ~d** у него́ воспалённое го́рло; **~d with anger** распалённый гне́вом.

inflammable *adj*: **petrol is highly ~** бензи́н легко́ воспламеня́ется; *fig* **an ~ situation** напряжённая ситуа́ция.

inflammation *n Med* воспале́ние.

inflammatory *adj*: *fig* **an ~ speech** подстрека́тельская речь.

inflatable *adj* надувно́й.

inflate *vt* (*with air*) наду|ва́ть (-́ть), (*tyres*) нака́ч|ивать (-а́ть); *fig* разду|ва́ть (-́ть); **~d with pride** наду́тый от го́рдости; *Econ*: **~d prices** взви́нченные це́ны; **to ~ the economy** проводи́ть поли́тику инфля́ции в эконо́мике (*only in impf*).

inflation *n Econ* инфля́ция.

inflationary *adj*: **an ~ policy** поли́тика инфля́ции.

inflected *adj Gram* флекти́вный.

inflexible *adj* неги́бкий, жёсткий, *also fig*; *fig* несгиба́емый; **an ~ iron rod** неги́бкий/жёсткий желе́зный прут; **an ~ will** несгиба́емая во́ля; **an ~ timetable/rule** жёсткое расписа́ние/пра́вило; **he is ~ on this point** он неги́бок в э́том вопро́се.

inflexion *n* (*of voice*) модуля́ция; *Gram* фле́ксия.

inflict *vt*: **to ~ a penalty/damage/suffering on smb** на|лага́ть на кого́-л штраф (-ложи́ть), причин|я́ть кому́-л уще́рб/страда́ние (-и́ть); **to ~ one's views/oneself on smb** навя́зывать кому́-л свои́ взгля́ды, навя́зываться кому́-л.

influence *n* влия́ние, возде́йствие; **use your ~ with him** повлия́й на него́; **he used his ~ with the Ministry in order to...** он испо́льзовал своё влия́ние в министе́рстве, что́бы + *inf*; **he has a lot of ~ in the Ministry** он по́льзуется больши́м влия́нием в министе́рстве; **he is/he did it under her ~** он нахо́дится/он сде́лал э́то под её влия́нием/возде́йствием; **a man of ~** влия́тельный челове́к; *CQ* **he was fined for driving under the ~** (*of drink*) он был оштрафо́ван за вожде́ние в нетре́звом ви́де; **he's under the ~** (*of drink*) он в подпи́тии.

influence *vt* ока́з|ывать влия́ние/возде́йствие на + *A* (-а́ть); име́ть влия́ние/возде́йствие на + *A* (*impf*); влия́ть (по-); (*of person only*) возде́йствовать (*impf*); **his words ~d me greatly** его́ слова́ произвели́/оказа́ли на меня́ си́льное возде́йствие, его́ слова́ си́льно повлия́ли на меня́; **as a poet he was ~d by Byron** поэ́зия Ба́йрона оказа́ла на него́ си́льное влия́ние; **what factors ~d your decision?** каки́е фа́кторы повлия́ли на ва́ше реше́ние?; **he is easily ~d** он легко́ поддаётся влия́нию.

influential *adj* (*of person*) влия́тельный.

influenza *n* грипп.

influx *n* прито́к; (*of people*) напль́ів; **an ~ of foreign exchange/tourists** прито́к валю́ты, напль́ів тури́стов.

inform *vti vt* сообщ|а́ть + *D* (-и́ть); *off* (*notify*) освед|омля́ть (-́омить), изве|ща́ть (-сти́ть), информи́ровать (*impf and pf*); ста́вить в изве́стность (по-); **they have been ~ed of their pay rise** им сообщи́ли о повыше́нии зарпла́ты; **he is well ~ed about the whole situation** он хорошо́ информи́рован обо всём; **to ~ oneself about smth** осведомля́ться о чём-л; **I ~ed him that I was resigning/of my resignation** я поста́вил его́ в изве́стность о моём ухо́де; **keep me ~ed (of developments)** держи́ меня́ в ку́рсе де́ла

vi: **to ~ against smb** до|носи́ть на кого́-л (-нести́).

informal *adj* неофициа́льный; **an ~ meeting/dinner/talk/atmosphere** неофициа́льное собра́ние, неофициа́льный обе́д, неофициа́льная бесе́да, непринуждённая атмосфе́ра; **~ dress** непара́дная оде́жда; **the President is very ~** президе́нт де́ржится о́чень про́сто.

informally *adv* неофициа́льно; без ли́шних церемо́ний; **everyone was dressed ~** все бы́ли оде́ты про́сто.

informant *n*: **my ~ was the Minister himself** я слы́шал э́то от самого́ мини́стра.

information *n* **1** информа́ция; све́дения (*pl*); **a piece of ~** сообще́ние, (*in reply to query*) спра́вка; **statistical ~** статисти́ческие да́нные (*pl*); **to give/receive ~ about smth** дать/получи́ть информа́цию/све́дения о чём-л; **apply for ~ to the administration** обрати́тесь за спра́вкой к администра́ции; **he's a mine of ~** он настоя́щий кла́дезь зна́ний (*pl*); *Law* **to lodge ~ against smb** донести́ на кого́-л.

informative *adj* (*of books, etc.*) содержа́тельный; (*educative*) поучи́тельный; **an ~ article** содержа́тельная статья́; **he was very ~** он нам мно́го всего́ сообщи́л.

informer *n* доно́счик, осведоми́тель (*m*).

infra-red *adj*: **~ rays** инфракра́сные лучи́.

infrequent *adj* ре́дкий.

infringe *vti vt* (*law, copyright*) наруш|а́ть (-́ить)

vi: **to ~ on smb's rights** посяг|áть на чьи-л правá (-нýть).

infringement *n* нарушéние; посягáтельство (на + *A*).

infuriate *vt* бесúть (вз-); **his obstinacy ~s me** егó упря́мство бéсит меня́; **I was ~d** я взбесúлся, я был взбешён; **I was ~d by his insinuations** я пришёл в я́рость от егó намёков.

infuse *vti vt*: **to ~ tea** завáр|ивать чай (-úть)

vi: **the tea is infusing** чай завáривается/настáивается.

infusion *n*: **an ~ of tea/herbs** завáрка чáя, настóйка трав.

ingenious *adj* изобретáтельный, нахóдчивый, хитроýмный; **he's very ~** он такóй изобретáтельный/нахóдчивый; **an ~ invention/solution** хитроýмное изобретéние/решéние; **an ~ plan** хитроýмный план.

ingenuity *n* изобретáтельность, нахóдчивость.

ingenuous *adj* простодýшный, бесхúтростный.

ingrained *adj*: **~ honesty** врождённая чéстность; **his habits are deeply ~** у негó глубокó укоренúвшиеся привы́чки; *pejor* **~ prejudices** закоренéлые предрассýдки.

ingratiate *vt*: **to ~ oneself with smb** заискивать пéред кем-л (*impf*).

ingratitude *n* неблагодáрность (к + *D*).

ingredient *n* составнáя часть; ингредиéнт, *also Cook.*

ingrowing *adj*: **an ~ nail** врастáющий нóготь (*m*).

inhabit *vt* населя́ть (*impf*); обитáть в/на + *P* (*impf*); **Eskimos ~ this territory** э́ту территóрию населя́ют эскимóсы; **these caves were ~ed by prehistoric man** в э́тих пещéрах обитáл доисторúческий человéк.

inhabited *adj* населённый; **an ~ region** населённый райóн; **is this castle/island ~?** в э́том зáмке живýт?, э́тот óстров обитáем?

inhalation *n* вдыхáние; *Med* ингаля́ция; (*in smoking*) затя́жка.

inhale *vti vt Med* дéлать ингаля́цию (с-); **to ~ tobacco** затя|гиваться (-нýться); **it's dangerous to ~ petrol fumes** дышáть бензúном врéдно; (*to smoker*) **do you ~?** ты затя́гиваешься?

vi: **he ~d deeply** он глубокó вздохнýл.

inharmonious *adj* негармонúчный, нарушáющий гармóнию, нестрóйный; (*of colours*) несочетáющийся, негармонúрующий.

inherent *adj* присýщий + *D*; **the situation with its ~ difficulties** ситуáция с присýщими ей слóжностями.

inherit *vti vt* наслéдовать, *also fig* (*impf and pf*, *fig pf* у-), получ|áть по наслéдству/в наслéдство (-úть); **she ~ed her mother's good looks/generosity** онá унаслéдовала красотý мáтери, онá щедрá—э́то у неё от мáтери

vi: **if he dies, who ~s?** éсли он умрёт, кто полýчит наслéдство/кто наслéдник?

inheritance *n* наслéдство, *also fig*; **to leave smb an ~** оставля́ть комý-л наслéдство; **the right of ~** прáво наслéдования; *fig* **it's an ~ from the last government** э́то остáлось в наслéдство от прéжнего прáвительства.

inhibit *vt*: **his presence ~ed us/the discussion** егó присýтствие стесня́ло нас/мешáло свобóдно вестú дискýссию; **his modesty ~ed him from asking for toilet paper** он постесня́лся попросúть туалéтной бумáги.

inhibited *adj* стеснúтельный.

inhibition *n Psych* торможéние.

inhospitable *adj* (*of people, behaviour*) негостеприúмный.

inhuman *adj* (*cruel*) бесчеловéчный; (*superhuman*) нечеловéческий.

inhumane *adj* негумáнный, бесчеловéчный.

inimitable *adj* неподражáемый.

iniquitous *adj* чудóвищный, ужáсный.

initial *n* (*person's*) (**~s**) инициáлы; **what do these ~s stand for?** что означáют э́ти бýквы?

initial *adj* (перво)начáльный, исхóдный; **the ~ period** (перво)начáльный перúод; **~ attempts** пéрвые попы́тки; **the ~ stage** исхóдный рубéж, отправнáя тóчка.

initial *vt*: **to ~ a document** парафúровать докумéнт (*impf and pf*).

initially *adv* вначáле; первоначáльно; *CQ* поначáлу.

initiate *vt*: **to ~ a reform** вводúть рефóрму (ввестú); **to ~ a new policy** на|чинáть проводúть нóвую полúтику (-чáть); **I was ~d into my new duties** меня́ ввелú в курс моúх нóвых обя́занностей; **to ~ smb into a secret** посвя|щáть когó-л в тáйну (-тúть); **to ~ smb into the principles of Buddhism** знакóмить когó-л с основны́ми идéями буддúзма (о-, по-); *Law* **to ~ proceedings against smb** возбу|ждáть дéло прóтив когó-л (-дúть).

initiative *n* инициатúва; почúн; **on one's own ~** по сóбственной инициатúве, по сóбственному почúну; **to show ~** проявúть инициатúву; **to take the ~ in smth** брать на себя́ инициатúву в чём-л.

inject *vt*: **to ~ smb with penicillin** дéлать комý-л инъéкции (*pl*) пеницилл́ина (с-).

injection *n* инъéкция, укóл; (*into vein*) вливáние; **an ~ against cholera** укóл от холéры; **he has to have penicillin ~s twice a day** емý дéлают укóлы пеницилл́ина/*CQ* емý кóлют пеницилл́ин два рáза в день.

injudicious *adj* неблагоразýмный, неразýмный.

injure *vt* повре|ждáть (-дúть); (*by a knock*) ушиб|áть (-úть), (*by a cut*) рáнить (по-); **to ~ one's leg** повредúть/порáнить себé нóгу, ушибúть нóгу; **to ~ oneself** ушибúться, порáниться; **he was ~d playing football** он получúл трáвму, игрáя в футбóл; *as n*: **the ~d** рáненые (*pl*); *fig*: **to ~ smb's pride** оскорб|ля́ть чьё-л достóинство (-úть); **an air of ~d innocence** вид оскорблённой невúнности; **the ~d party** пострадáвшая/потерпéвшая сторонá.

injurious *adj*: ~ **to** вре́дный/губи́тельный для + *G*.

injury *n* поврежде́ние; *Sport, etc.* тра́вма; **to do smb an** ~ наноси́ть кому́-л поврежде́ние; **he sustained an** ~ **at the factory** он получи́л тра́вму на произво́дстве; **to do oneself an** ~ ушиби́ться, пора́ниться.

injustice *n* несправедли́вость; **you do me an** ~ ты ко мне несправедли́в.

ink *n* черни́ла (*no sing*); **to write in** ~ писа́ть черни́лами; **invisible/Indian/printer's** ~ симпати́ческие черни́ла, тушь, типогра́фская кра́ска; *attr*: **an** ~ **stain** черни́льное пятно́.

inkling *n* (*notion*) поня́тие; представле́ние; **I have no** ~ **of what is happening** я поня́тия не име́ю, что вокру́г происхо́дит; **he had no** ~ **of it** он не име́л никако́го представле́ния об э́том.

inlaid *adj*: **an** ~ **table** инкрусти́рованный стол; **an** ~ **floor** парке́тный пол.

inland *adj* вну́тренний; ~ **towns** города́ центра́льных/удалённых от мо́ря райо́нов страны́; ~ **sea** вну́треннее мо́ре; *Fin* ~ **revenue** вну́тренние бюдже́тные поступле́ния (*pl*).

inland *adv*: **they live 10 miles** ~ **from Dover** они́ живу́т в десяти́ ми́лях от Ду́вра; **to march** ~ дви́гаться вглубь/внутрь страны́.

in-laws *npl* родня́ (*collect*) со стороны́ му́жа/жены́.

inlet *n* небольшо́й зали́в; *Mech* впуск; *attr*: ~ **pipe** впускна́я труба́.

inmate *n* (*of house, monastery*) обита́тель (*m*); (*of hospital*) больно́й; (*of prison*) заключённый.

inmost *adj* (*farthest*) са́мый отдалённый; (*deepest*) глубоча́йший; ~ **thoughts** сокрове́нные мы́сли.

inn *n* (*tavern*) тракти́р; (*hotel*) гости́ница.

innards *npl CQ* вну́тренности.

innate *adj* врождённый, прирождённый.

inner *adj* вну́тренний.

innermost *adj see* **inmost.**

innocence *n Law* невино́вность; **to prove one's** ~ доказа́ть свою́ невино́вность; **in all** ~ ненаме́ренно.

innocent *adj* неви́нный; (*not guilty*) невино́вный; ~ **victims/pleasures** неви́нные же́ртвы/удово́льствия; **he was declared** ~ он был при́знан невино́вным; **an** ~ **young girl** нео́пытная молода́я де́вушка.

innocuous *adj*: **it's an** ~ **drink** э́то сла́бый напи́ток; **an** ~ **remark** безоби́дное замеча́ние.

innovation *n* нововведе́ние; но́вшество; **to make** ~**s** вводи́ть но́вшества.

innovator *n* нова́тор.

innuendo *n* ко́свенный/скры́тый намёк.

innumerable *adj* бесчи́сленный; **there are** ~ **books on the subject** есть бесчи́сленное мно́жество книг на э́ту те́му; **there are** ~ **reasons for it** на э́то есть мно́го причи́н.

inoculate *vt*: **to** ~ **smb against smth** де́лать кому́-л приви́вку от чего́-л (с-).

inoculation *n* приви́вка.

inoffensive *adj* безоби́дный, безвре́дный.

inoperable *adj Med* неопера́бельный.

inoperative *adj* (*of rules, etc.*) недействи́тельный.

inopportune *adj*: **he came at an** ~ **moment** он пришёл в неуда́чный моме́нт; **his intervention was most** ~ его́ вмеша́тельство бы́ло о́чень некста́ти (*adv*).

inordinate *adj* чрезме́рный, непоме́рный.

in-patient *n* стациона́рный больно́й.

input *n*: **the** ~ **of information to a computer** ввод/пода́ча информа́ции в вычисли́тельную маши́ну.

inquest *n* суде́бное сле́дствие/рассле́дование.

inquire *vti vt* спра́шивать (спроси́ть); **to** ~ **smb's name/the price of bananas** спроси́ть чьё-л и́мя/о цене́ бана́нов; **we** ~**d the way from the farmer** мы спроси́ли у фе́рмера доро́гу/как пройти́.

vi: **to** ~ **about smth** освед|омля́ться/справ|ля́ться о чём-л (-оми́ться/-иться); **he was inquiring about the arrival of the train/after the patient/for you/for a copy of the inventory** он осведомля́лся *or* справля́лся о прибы́тии по́езда, он справля́лся о больно́м, он разы́скивал тебя́, он спра́шивал ко́пию о́писи; **I'll** ~ **into the matter** я рассле́дую э́то де́ло.

inquiring *adj*: **an** ~ **look/mind** вопроси́тельный взгляд, пытли́вый ум.

inquiry *n* **1** (*question*) вопро́с; **in answer to my** ~ **he said...** отвеча́я на мой вопро́с, он сказа́л...; **to make inquiries about smb/smth** наводи́ть спра́вки о ком-л/чём-л; **"all inquiries to the secretary"** «за спра́вками обраща́ться к секретарю́»

2 (*investigation*) рассле́дование; **there will have to be an** ~ **into this** э́то на́до бу́дет рассле́довать; **to set up an** ~ **into the accident** нача́ть рассле́дование обстоя́тельств ава́рии; **a scientific** ~ нау́чное иссле́дование; **a court of** ~ сле́дственная коми́ссия.

inquiry office *n* спра́вочное бюро́ (*indecl*).

inquisitive *adj pejor* любопы́тный.

inroads *npl fig*: **their visit made** ~ **on our time** их визи́т о́тнял у нас мно́го вре́мени; **we have had to make** ~ **on our savings** нам пришло́сь потра́тить часть на́ших сбереже́ний.

insalubrious *adj* нездоро́вый.

insane *adj* сумасше́дший, безу́мный; **an** ~ **plan** сумасше́дший/безу́мный план; **that hammering is driving me** ~ э́тот стук сведёт меня́ с ума́ [**NB** *tense*].

insanitary *adj* антисанита́рный, негигиени́чный.

insanity *n* безу́мие, *also fig*; **he pleaded** ~ он испо́льзовал психи́ческое заболева́ние подзащи́тного как смягча́ющее обстоя́тельство; **it would be** ~ **to go out in this blizzard** чи́стое безу́мие выходи́ть в таку́ю мете́ль.

insatiable *adj* ненасы́тный.

inscribe *vt* надпи́с|ывать (-а́ть); **the author has** ~**d my copy** а́втор надписа́л мне экземпля́р свое́й кни́ги; **their names are** ~**d on the**

memorial их имена́ начёртаны на па́мятнике; *Math* **to ~ a circle in a square** вписа́ть круг в квадра́т.

inscription *n* на́дпись.

inscrutable *adj* (*enigmatic*) зага́дочный; (*impenetrable*) непроница́емый.

insect *n* насеко́мое; *attr*: **an ~ bite** уку́с насеко́мого.

insecticide *n* инсектици́д.

insecure *adj* ненадёжный; **this ladder is ~** э́та ле́стница ненадёжна; **his job is ~** он не зна́ет, до́лго ли продёржится на э́той рабо́те; **he had an ~ hold on the rock** он едва́ уде́рживался за вы́ступ скалы́; **the child felt ~** ребёнок чу́вствовал себя́ незащищённым.

insemination *n*: **artificial ~** иску́сственное осемене́ние.

insensible *adj* **1: he lay ~** он лежа́л без созна́ния; **the blow knocked him ~** он потеря́л созна́ние от уда́ра; **to drink oneself ~** пить до бесчу́вствия

2 (*unaware*): **~ of the danger he pushed forward** не подозрева́я об опа́сности, он продвига́лся вперёд

3: by ~ degrees неощути́мо.

insensitive *adj* (*of person*) бесчу́вственный; **he is ~ to beauty/to our feelings** он нечувстви́телен к красоте́, ему́ безразли́чны на́ши чу́вства.

inseparable *adj* неотдели́мый; **the two questions are ~** э́ти два вопро́са взаимосвя́заны; **~ friends** неразлу́чные друзья́.

insert *vt* встав|ля́ть (-́ить); вкла́дывать (вложи́ть); **to ~ a key into a lock/a new paragraph into an article/lace into a dress** вста́вить ключ в замо́чную сква́жину/но́вый абза́ц в статью́, сде́лать к пла́тью кружевну́ю вста́вку; **to ~ a letter into an envelope** вложи́ть письмо́ в конве́рт; **to ~ coins into a machine** опус|ка́ть моне́ты в автома́т (-ти́ть); **to ~ an advert in a newspaper** поме|ща́ть объявле́ние в газе́те (-сти́ть).

insertion *n*: **an ~ in a book/dress** вста́вка в кни́ге/в пла́тье.

inshore *adj*: **~ fishing** прибре́жный лов ры́бы.

inshore *adv* у бе́рега; (*of motion*) к бе́регу.

inside *n* **1** вну́тренность; вну́тренняя часть/сторона́; (*of clothing*) изна́нка; *CQ* нутро́; **the ~ of the building needs repair** вну́тренние помеще́ния (*pl*) нужда́ются в ремо́нте; **the ~ of the coat is frayed** пальто́ протёрлось с изна́нки; **have you seen the ~ of the castle?** вы бы́ли внутри́ за́мка?, вы ви́дели за́мок изнутри́?; **there's a crack on the ~ of the cup** внутри́ ча́шки есть тре́щина; **the door is bolted on the ~** дверь заперта́ изнутри́; **to walk on the ~ of the pavement** идти́ по вну́тренней стороне́ тротуа́ра; **I'll be away for the ~ of a week** меня́ не бу́дет о́коло неде́ли [**NB** о́коло *always = less than*]; *Aut* **it's forbidden to overtake on the ~** запреща́ется обгоня́ть спра́ва/(*UK*) сле́ва; *CQ*: **my ~ is playing up** у меня́ боли́т живо́т; **I know all this from the ~** я зна́ю всю подного́тную/подоплёку э́того де́ла

2 inside out *as adv*: **she put her dress on ~ out** она́ наде́ла пла́тье наизна́нку; **the wind blew my umbrella ~ out** у меня́ вы́вернуло (*impers*) зо́нтик ве́тром; *fig* **he knows his subject ~ out** он зна́ет свою́ те́му вдоль и поперёк; **we turned the room ~ out looking for the book** мы переверну́ли всю ко́мнату в по́исках кни́ги.

inside *adj* вну́тренний; **~ pockets** вну́тренние карма́ны; **~ information** вну́тренняя информа́ция; *CQ* **an ~ job** кра́жа с наво́дчиком.

inside *adv* внутри́; (*of motion*) внутрь; **what's ~?** что внутри́?; **let's look ~** дава́й загля́нем внутрь; **wear it with the fur ~** э́то ну́жно носи́ть ме́хом внутрь; **he wouldn't come ~** он не хоте́л входи́ть; **come ~!** заходи́!; *sl* **he's ~** (*in jail*) он сиди́т (в тюрьме́).

inside *prep* внутри́ + *G*, в + *P*; (*of motion*) внутрь + *G*, в + *A*; **~ the house it is cool** в до́ме хо́лодно; **have you been/seen ~ the palace?** вы бы́ли внутри́ дворца́?; **to go ~ the house** войти́ внутрь до́ма/в дом; **I'll be there ~ an hour** я бу́ду там приме́рно че́рез час.

insidious *adj* кова́рный.

insight *n*: **a man of ~** проница́тельный челове́к; **an ~ into political affairs** понима́ние полити́ческой обстано́вки (*sing*); **our trip gave us an ~ into the life of the country** на́ша пое́здка познако́мила нас с жи́знью э́той страны́.

insignificant *adj* незначи́тельный.

insincere *adj* нейскренний.

insinuate *vt* **1** (*imply*) намек|а́ть (-ну́ть); **what are you insinuating?** на что ты намека́ешь?; **do you ~ I'm lying?** ты хо́чешь сказа́ть, что я лгу?

2: to ~ oneself into smb's good graces вкра́сться к кому́-л в дове́рие (*usu pf*).

insipid *adj* (*of food*) пре́сный; *fig* ску́чный; **an ~ conversation/girl** ску́чная бесе́да/де́вушка.

insist *vi* наст|а́ивать (-оя́ть); **if you ~** е́сли уж ты так наста́иваешь; **he ~ed on his own way/on his rights/that...** он настоя́л на своём, он отста́ивал свои́ права́, он наста́ивал на том, что́бы...

insistence *n*: **I did it at his ~** я э́то сде́лал по его́ настоя́нию; **his ~ on punctuality annoys me** он тре́бует от всех быть пункту́альными, и э́то раздража́ет меня́.

insistent *adj* насто́йчивый; настоя́тельный; **an ~ demand** настоя́тельное тре́бование; **he is ~ about it** он наста́ивает на э́том.

insole *n* сте́лька.

insolent *adj* де́рзкий, на́глый, наха́льный.

insoluble *adj Chem* нераствори́мый; (*of problem*) неразреши́мый.

insolvent *adj* несостоя́тельный, некредитоспосо́бный, неплатёжеспосо́бный.

insomnia *n* бессо́нница.

inspect *vt* осм|а́тривать (-отре́ть); прове-р|я́ть (-́ить); *off* инспекти́ровать (*impf*); **to ~ luggage** осмотре́ть бага́ж; **to ~ smb's work** проверя́ть/инспекти́ровать чью-л рабо́ту; **they ~ed the school** они́ инспекти́ровали шко́лу; **to ~ the troops** про|води́ть смотр войск (-вести́); **to ~ tickets** проверя́ть биле́ты; **all goods are ~ed** вся проду́кция (*collect*) прохо́дит че́рез контро́ль.

inspection *n* осмо́тр, прове́рка; **an ~ of brakes/baggage** осмо́тр тормозо́в/багажа́; **a medical ~** медици́нский осмо́тр; **~ proved the notes were forged** эксперти́за показа́ла, что де́ньги фальши́вые; **(have) all tickets ready for ~!** пригото́вьте биле́ты (для прове́рки); **~ of schools** инспе́кция школ.

inspector *n* инспе́ктор, ревизо́р; **police/school ~** полице́йский/шко́льный инспе́ктор; **customs ~** тамо́женник; **ticket ~** контролёр.

inspiration *n* вдохнове́ние; **to draw ~ from nature** че́рпать вдохнове́ние в приро́де; **he is an ~ to us all** он всех нас вдохновля́ет; **I had a sudden ~** на меня́ вдруг нашло́ вдохнове́ние.

inspire *vt* вдохнов|ля́ть (-и́ть); внуш|а́ть (-и́ть); всел|я́ть (-и́ть); **it ~d him to write a poem** э́то вдохнови́ло его́ на созда́ние поэ́мы; **he ~d me with fear** он внуши́л мне страх; **to ~ smb with hope/confidence** всели́ть в кого́-л наде́жду/уве́ренность.

inspired *adj* вдохнове́нный; **an ~ speech/guess** вдохнове́нная речь, счастли́вая дога́дка; **~ by smb** вдохновлённый кем-л.

instability *n* (*of relationships, etc.*) непро́чность, нестаби́льность; (*of character*) неуравнове́шенность.

install *vt* устан|а́вливать (-ови́ть); **to ~ a gas cooker/TV** устана́вливать га́зовую плиту́/телеви́зор; **to ~ central heating** про|води́ть центра́льное отопле́ние (-вести́); **to ~ a new bath** ста́вить но́вую ва́нну (по-); **to ~ oneself in a new flat/in an armchair** устр|а́иваться в но́вой кварти́ре/в кре́сле (-о́иться); **to ~ a rector** официа́льно вводи́ть ре́ктора в до́лжность (ввести́).

installation *n* **1** (*act: of machines, etc.*) устано́вка; (*of rector, etc.*) официа́льное введе́ние в до́лжность

2 (*apparatus*): **a heating ~** отопи́тельная систе́ма.

instalment, *US* **installment** *n* **1: the novel will be published in monthly ~s** рома́н бу́дет публикова́ться в журна́ле отде́льными частя́ми раз в ме́сяц

2 *Comm* взнос при рассро́чке; **to buy/pay by ~s** покупа́ть/плати́ть в рассро́чку (*sing*); **my monthly ~ is due next week** на сле́дующей неде́ле я вношу́ очередно́й ме́сячный взнос.

instance *n* **1** (*case*) слу́чай, (*example*) приме́р; **in this ~ he was wrong** в э́том/в да́нном слу́чае он оши́бся; **take an actual ~** возьми́ к приме́ру...; **for ~** наприме́р; **in the first ~** в пе́рвую о́чередь

2: at the ~ of smb по чьей-л про́сьбе.

instant *n* мгнове́ние, моме́нт; **at that ~** в то мгнове́ние, в тот моме́нт; **for an ~** на мгнове́ние/на секу́нду; **come here this ~!** иди́ сюда́ сейча́с же!; *as conj*: **I'll tell you the ~ I see him** я вам сообщу́, как то́лько уви́жу его́.

instant *adj* неме́дленный; незамедли́тельный; **an ~ reply** неме́дленный/незамедли́тельный отве́т; **~ dismissal** неме́дленное увольне́ние; **the medicine brought him ~ relief** лека́рство сра́зу помогло́ ему́; **~ coffee** раствори́мый ко́фе; *Comm* **your letter of the 5th ~** (*abbr* **inst.**) ва́ше письмо́ от пя́того числа́ теку́щего ме́сяца.

instantaneous *adj* мгнове́нный, момента́льный; **death was ~** смерть была́ мгнове́нной; **his recognition of her was ~** он момента́льно её узна́л.

instead *adv* **1** *use prep* вме́сто + *G*; взаме́н (*adv or prep* + *G*); **if he can't go, take me ~** е́сли он не мо́жет пойти́, возьми́ меня́ вме́сто него́; (*in shop*) **we haven't a biro like that—will you take this one ~?** у нас нет тако́й ру́чки, возьми́те э́ту взаме́н; **we've no beer, will you take lemonade ~?** у нас нет пи́ва, не хоти́те ли вы́пить лимона́ду?

2: ~ of *as prep* вме́сто + *G*; **it's better to use oak ~ of beech** лу́чше испо́льзовать дуб вме́сто бу́ка; **~ of lunching at home we had a picnic** мы не обе́дали до́ма, а устро́или пикни́к.

instep *n* подъём (ноги́).

instigate *vt* подстрека́ть (*usu impf*); **to ~ a strike/rebellion** *or* **mutiny** подстрека́ть к забасто́вке/к бу́нту; **to ~ students to demonstrate** подстрека́ть студе́нтов к выступле́ниям.

instigation *n*: **at her ~** по её науще́нию.

instil *vt* внуш|а́ть (-и́ть); **to ~ in smb a respect for the law** внуша́ть/прив|ива́ть (-и́ть) кому́-л уваже́ние к зако́ну.

instinct *n* инсти́нкт; **an ~ for self-preservation** инсти́нкт самосохране́ния; **by ~** инстинкти́вно (*adv*).

instinctive *adj* инстинкти́вный; **an ~ feeling for colour** врождённое чу́вство цве́та.

institute *n* (*educational*) институ́т; (*association*) о́бщество, ассоциа́ция, организа́ция; (*administrative body*) учрежде́ние, организа́ция.

institute *vt* (*found*) основа́ть (*usu pf*); **to ~ new procedures** вводи́ть но́вые поря́дки (ввести́); **to ~ an inquiry into smth** назнач|а́ть рассле́дование чего́-л (-́ить); *Law* **to ~ proceedings against smb** пода|ва́ть в суд на кого́-л (-́ть).

institution *n* **1** (*act: setting up*): **the ~ of a new committee** учрежде́ние но́вой коми́ссии

2 (*organization*) учрежде́ние, институ́т; **educational ~s** уче́бные заведе́ния

3 (*custom, etc.*): **the annual dinner is a long-established ~** дава́ть раз в год торже́ственный обе́д—о́чень ста́рый обы́чай; *CQ* **he's**

become an ~ here он стал здесь чем-то вроде непременного атрибута.

instruct *vt* (*teach*) обучать, учить (*pf for both* обучить); (*give instructions*) инструктировать (про-); **to ~ smb in maths/in driving** обучать кого-л математике, учить кого-л водить машину; **he ~ed us what to do in case of fire** он проинструктировал нас, что делать в случае пожара; **the major ~ed his men to wait by the bridge** майор приказал солдатам ждать у моста; **I shall ~ my solicitor to sue** я поручу своему адвокату предъявить иск.

instruction *n* **1** (*teaching*) обучение; **to give smb ~ in swimming** обучать кого-л плаванию **2** *pl* (**~s**) распоряжение, инструкция (*sings*); **we were given ~s to wait** мы получили распоряжение ждать; **I acted on ~s** я действовал согласно полученной инструкции; **"~s for use"** (*on packet, etc.*) инструкция по применению, *Tech* руководство по эксплуатации.

instructive *adj* поучительный.

instructor *n* (*teacher*) учитель (*m*); *Mil, etc.* инструктор.

instrument *n* инструмент; прибор; **stringed/surgical ~s** струнные/хирургические инструменты; **scientific ~s** научные приборы; **to fly by ~s** летать по приборам; *attr*: **~ panel** *Aut, Aer* приборная доска.

instrumental *adj Mus* инструментальный; *Gram* творительный; *fig* **he was ~ in finding me this job** он нашёл мне эту работу.

instrumentalist *n* инструменталист.

insubordinate *adj* непокорный, непослушный.

insubstantial *adj*: **~ evidence** несущественные доказательства (*pl*); **an ~ meal** лёгкая закуска.

insufferable *adj* невыносимый, нестерпимый; несносный; **~ pain** невыносимая боль; **~ heat/rudeness** нестерпимая жара, недопустимая грубость; **the child is ~** он несносный ребёнок; **he's an ~ bore** он ужасный/невыносимый зануда.

insufficient *adj* недостаточный.

insular *adj* островной; *fig* ограниченный.

insulate *vt* изолировать (*impf and pf*).

insulating tape *n* изоляционная лента.

insulation *n Tech* изоляция; (*material*) изоляционный материал; **heat ~** теплоизоляция.

insult *n* оскорбление; **to swallow an ~** проглотить оскорбление; **it's an ~ to our intelligence** они нас за дураков принимают.

insult *vt* оскорб|лять (-ить); **I felt ~ed** я чувствовал себя оскорблённым; **do have some—don't ~ my cooking!** ешь, не обижай меня!

insulting *adj* оскорбительный.

insuperable *adj* непреодолимый, неодолимый.

insurance *n* (*act*) страхование; (*premium or amount paid*) страховая сумма, *CQ* страховка; **life ~, ~ against fire** страхование жизни/от огня; **national ~** социальное страхование; **how much is your car ~?** сколько вы платите страховки (*G*) в год за вашу машину?; **she received £10,000 ~** она получила десять тысяч фунтов страховки; *CQ* **I'm taking an umbrella as an ~** я беру зонтик на всякий случай; *attr*: **~ company** страховая компания.

insure *vt* страховать (за-); **to ~ smth/oneself against theft** застраховать что-л/своё имущество от кражи; **to ~ oneself** страховать свою жизнь.

insurgent *n usu pl* (**the ~s**) *Hist* (*as heroes*) повстанцы, *pejor* бунтовщики.

insurrection *n* восстание.

intact *adj* целый; **not a window was left ~** ни одно окно не уцелело; **the contents of the parcel arrived ~** содержимое посылки прибыло в целости и сохранности; **his capital remained ~** его капитал остался целым.

intake *n*: **what is the annual ~ of students?** каков годовой приём студентов?; *Tech* впуск.

intangible *adj fig* неуловимый.

integer *n* целое.

integral *adj Math* интегральный; (*inseparable*) **an ~ part** неотъемлемая часть.

integrate *vti*: **~ (into)** объедин|ять в + *A* (-ить); *Math* интегрировать (*impf and pf*).

integrated *adj* цельный; **an ~ personality** цельная натура.

integration *n* объединение; *Math* интегрирование, интеграция; **racial ~** расовая интеграция.

integrity *n*: **he is a man of ~** он неподкупен.

intellect *n* интеллект, ум.

intellectual *adj* интеллектуальный; умственный; **an ~ play** интеллектуальная пьеса; **~ efforts** усилия ума.

intelligence *n* **1** (*understanding*) интеллект, ум, умственные способности (*pl*); **high/low ~** высокий/низкий интеллект; **he had the ~ to report the incident** у него хватило ума сообщить о происшествии; *attr*: **an ~ test** проверка умственных способностей **2** (*news*) сведения (*pl*); **according to the latest ~** по последним сведениям; *attr Mil*: **the ~ service, an ~ report** разведывательная служба/сводка; **an ~ officer** разведчик.

intelligent *adj* умный, разумный; **an ~ person/question/dog** умный человек/вопрос, умная собака; **an ~ approach to smth** разумный подход к чему-л.

intelligible *adj* понятный; **it is scarcely ~ that...** едва можно разобрать, что...

intemperate *adj* (*over drink*) невоздержанный.

intend *vt* намереваться + *inf* (*impf*), со|бираться + *inf* (-браться); **I ~ to leave tomorrow** я намереваюсь/собираюсь уехать завтра; **this book is ~ed for you** эта книга предназначена для вас; **he ~ed no harm/no offence/it as a joke** он не хотел причинить зла/никого обидеть, он пошутил; **is that remark ~ed for me?** это замечание в мой адрес?

intense *adj* сильный; **~ heat/anger** сильная жара, сильный гнев; **~ pain** острая боль;

to my ~ regret к моему́ вели́кому сожале́нию; **~ stupidity** вопию́щая глу́пость; **he is very ~** он о́чень серьёзно настро́ен; **an ~ gaze** при́стальный взгляд.

intensely *adv* си́льно; глубоко́; **I'm ~ unhappy/grateful** я глубоко́ несча́стен/благода́рен; **it was ~ cold** стоя́ли си́льные холода́ (*pl*); **she feels very ~ about women's lib** она́ горя́чий побо́рник же́нского равнопра́вия.

intensify *vti* уси́л|ивать(ся) (-ить(ся)).

intensity *n*: **the ~ of the cold kept everyone indoors** из-за си́льных холодо́в (*pl*) все оста́лись до́ма; **he spoke with ~** он говори́л с чу́вством.

intensive *adj* интенси́вный; *Gram* усили́тельный.

intent *n* наме́рение; **to all ~s and purposes** факти́чески, на са́мом де́ле; *Law*: **with ~ to kill** с у́мыслом уби́ть; **with malicious ~** со злым у́мыслом.

intent *adj*: **he's ~ on his book/the game** он погружён в кни́гу, он увлечён игро́й; **he's ~ on proving her wrong** он стреми́тся доказа́ть её неправоту́.

intention *n* наме́рение; (*object*) цель; **good ~s** до́брые наме́рения; **my ~ is to leave tomorrow/to study English** я наме́рен уе́хать за́втра, моя́ цель—вы́учить англи́йский язы́к; **I have every ~ of coming** я твёрдо наме́рен прийти́.

intentional *adj* (пред)наме́ренный.

intently *adv* внима́тельно; **he listened to her/looked at her ~** он внима́тельно слу́шал её, он при́стально посмотре́л на неё.

interact *vi* взаимоде́йствовать (*impf*).

interbreed *vti* скре́|щивать(ся) (-сти́ть(ся)).

intercede *vi*: **I will ~ with the director on your behalf** я заступлю́сь/хода́тайствую за вас пе́ред заве́дующим.

intercept *vt* перехва́т|ывать (-и́ть), *also Aer, Sport*.

intercession *n* хода́тайство.

interchange *vt* обме́н|иваться (-я́ться); **we ~d gifts/views** мы обменя́лись пода́рками/взгля́дами.

interchangeable *adj*: **the parts are ~** э́ти ча́сти взаимозаменя́емы.

intercom *n* вну́тренняя телефо́нная связь, селе́ктор; **to call smb on the ~** вызыва́ть кого́-л по селе́ктору.

intercommunicate, interconnect *vi* сообща́ться (*only in impf*); **the rooms ~** ко́мнаты сообща́ются/сме́жные.

intercontinental *adj* межконтинента́льный.

intercourse *n* (*social*) обще́ние; *Comm* свя́зи (*pl*); **sexual ~** половы́е сноше́ния (*pl*).

interdependent *adj* взаимозави́симый; зави́сящий (друг от дру́га).

interest *n* **1** интере́с; **I do it just for/from ~** я де́лаю э́то про́сто для интере́са; **it is of great ~ to me** э́то мне о́чень интере́сно; **to take/show/begin to take an ~ in smth** интересова́ться чем-л, прояв|ля́ть интере́с к чему́-л (-и́ть), заинтересова́ться чем-л; **his main ~ is football** футбо́л—его́ гла́вное увлече́ние

2 (*advantage*) *often pl*: **in the ~s of safety** в интере́сах безопа́сности; **this is in your own ~** э́то в ва́ших же интере́сах; **to act in smb's ~s** де́йствовать в чьих-л интере́сах; **he'll look after his own ~s** он своего́ не упу́стит

3 *Fin* проце́нты (*pl*); **to yield/bear ~** приноси́ть проце́нты; **simple/compound ~** просты́е/сло́жные проце́нты; **a high/low rate of ~** высо́кий/ни́зкий проце́нт; **to lend money at an ~ of 5%** одолжи́ть де́ньги под пять проце́нтов; **the ~ on his capital comes to £1,000** проце́нты/дохо́ды с его́ капита́ла достига́ют ты́сячи фу́нтов; *fig* **he repaid us with ~** он нас отблагодари́л с лихво́й, *pejor* он нам отплати́л с лихво́й

4 (*stake*): **a material ~** материа́льная заинтересо́ванность; **to have a financial ~ in a company** име́ть до́лю в предприя́тии.

interest *vt* интересова́ть (за-); заинтересо́в|ывать (-а́ть); **his idea ~s me** его́ мысль заинтересова́ла меня́ [**NB** *tense*]; **he tried to ~ me in his plan** он пыта́лся заинтересова́ть меня́ свои́м пла́ном; **to ~ oneself in smth** интересова́ться чем-л; **I am ~ed in the theatre** я интересу́юсь теа́тром, меня́ интересу́ет теа́тр; **I am ~ed to know where you met him** интере́сно знать, где вы с ним познако́мились; **he is financially ~ed in this** он материа́льно заинтересо́ван в э́том; **the company is ~ed in buying 100 new cars from you** компа́ния заинтересо́вана в поку́пке у вас ста но́вых маши́н.

interested *adj*: **an ~ audience** внима́тельная аудито́рия; *Comm, Law* **an ~ party** заинтересо́ванная сторона́.

interesting *adj* интере́сный.

interfere *vi* вме́ш|иваться в + *A* (-а́ться); меша́ть + *D or inf* (по-); **don't ~ in my business/in what doesn't concern you/between husband and wife** не вме́шивайся в мои́ дела́/не в свои́ дела́/в ссо́ры ме́жду му́жем и жено́й; **who asked you to ~?** кто проси́л тебя́ вме́шиваться?; **don't ~ with my papers/my work** не тро́гай мои́ бума́ги, не меша́й мне рабо́тать.

interference *n* вмеша́тельство; *Radio* поме́хи (*pl*); **there has been some ~ with this machine** кто́-то неуме́ло по́льзовался э́тим прибо́ром.

interfering *adj*: **she's always ~** она́ ве́чно во всё вме́шивается.

interim *n*: **in the ~** ме́жду те́м, тем вре́менем; *attr*: **an ~ report/committee** предвари́тельное сообще́ние, вре́менный комите́т; **~ measures** вре́менные ме́ры.

interior *n* (*of box, etc.*) вну́тренняя часть; (*of the house*) интерье́р; **Department of the I.** министе́рство вну́тренних дел.

interior *adj* вну́тренний; **~ decorators** оформи́тели интерье́ров.

interjection *n* восклица́ние; *Gram* междоме́тие.

interlude *n* (*of time*) промежу́ток; *Theat* антра́кт; *Mus* интерлю́дия; **in the ~s of sunshine** когда́ быва́ет/выгля́дывает со́лнце.

intermarriage *n* (*between families*) брак ме́жду ро́дственниками; (*between nationalities*) сме́шанный брак.

intermediary *n* посре́дник.

intermediate *adj* промежу́точный.

interminable *adj* бесконе́чный.

intermittent *adj* преры́вистый; **an ~ tapping** преры́вистый стук; **~ fever** перемежа́ющаяся лихора́дка.

intermittently *adv* с переры́вами, с промежу́тками; **it rained ~** дождь шёл с небольши́ми переры́вами.

intern *n* (*US*) врач, живу́щий при больни́це.

intern *vt* интерни́ровать (*impf and pf*).

internal *adj* вну́тренний; **an ~ injury** вну́треннее поврежде́ние; **an ~ combustion engine** дви́гатель вну́треннего сгора́ния; **not for ~ use** внутрь не принима́ть.

international *adj* междунаро́дный.

interpolate *vt*: **this passage has been ~d in the text** э́тот абза́ц был вста́влен в текст поздне́е.

interpose *vt* вкли́ни|ваться ме́жду + *I* (*of people*), в + *A* (*in a quarrel*) (-ться); (*a remark*) встав|ля́ть (-́ить).

interpret *vti vt* толкова́ть (*impf*), истолко́в|ывать (-а́ть); **to ~ a text/dreams** толкова́ть текст/сны; **to ~ events** истолко́вывать собы́тия; **her actions were ~ed as an admission of guilt** её де́йствия истолкова́ли как призна́ние вины́; **how am I to ~ that remark?** как мне понима́ть э́то замеча́ние?; *Theat* **to ~ the role of Hamlet** трактова́ть/интерпрети́ровать роль Га́млета

vi (у́стно) пере|води́ть (-вести́); **to ~ for the President** быть перево́дчиком президе́нта.

interpretation *n* толкова́ние, истолкова́ние; *Theat, Art, Mus* интерпрета́ция, тракто́вка; (*translation*) (у́стный) перево́д; **the play is open to various ~s** пье́су мо́жно толкова́ть по-ра́зному, пье́са поддаётся ра́зным толкова́ниям.

interpreter *n* перево́д|чик, *f* -чица.

interrelated *adj* взаимосвя́занный.

interrogate *vt* (*a prisoner*) допр|а́шивать (-оси́ть).

interrogation *n* допро́с.

interrogative *adj* вопроси́тельный, *also Gram.*

interrogator *n Law* сле́дователь (*m*), производя́щий допро́с.

interrupt *vti vt* пре|рыва́ть (-рва́ть); (*a person*) переби|ва́ть (-́ть); **he ~ed his journey** он прерва́л своё путеше́ствие; **play was ~ed because of rain** игра́ была́ пре́рвана из-за дождя́; **don't ~ me when I'm talking/working** не перебива́й меня́, когда́ я говорю́, не отрыва́й меня́ от рабо́ты; **traffic was ~ed** движе́ние бы́ло остано́влено

vi: **don't ~!** не перебива́й!

interruption *n* переры́в; **the ~ of the broadcast was due to a technical fault** переда́чу пришло́сь прерва́ть из-за техни́ческих непола́док (*pl*); **I don't want any ~s while I'm working** я не хочу́, что́бы мне меша́ли, когда́ я рабо́таю; **numerous ~s prevented me from finishing my work** меня́ всё вре́мя отрыва́ли, и я не успе́л зако́нчить рабо́ту.

intersect *vti* пересе|ка́ть(ся) (-́чь(ся)), *also Math.*

intersperse *vt* раз|бра́сывать (-броса́ть), рассып|а́ть, пересып|а́ть (*pfs* -́ать); **his speech was ~d with anecdotes** он пересыпа́л свою́ речь анекдо́тами; **violets ~d with primroses** при́мулы, расту́щие вперемешку (*adv*) с фиа́лками.

interstate *adj* (*US*): **~ relations** отноше́ния ме́жду шта́тами.

interval *n* **1** (*in time*) промежу́ток; переры́в, интерва́л; (*in school*) переме́на; (*at theatre, etc.*) антра́кт, переры́в; *Mus* интерва́л; **we see each other at ~s/at rare ~s** мы вре́мя от вре́мени/ре́дко ви́димся; **at yearly/monthly ~** ежего́дно, ежеме́сячно; **at ~s of 2 weeks** ка́ждые две неде́ли; **tomorrow will be dull with sunny ~s** за́втра бу́дет па́смурно с проясне́ниями; **buses leave at short ~s** авто́бусы иду́т с небольши́ми интерва́лами **2**: **trees planted at ~s of 10 metres** дере́вья, поса́женные на расстоя́нии десяти́ ме́тров друг от дру́га.

intervene *vi* (*of people*) вме́ш|иваться (-а́ться); вступ|а́ться (-и́ться); **to ~ in an argument** вмеша́ться в спор; **to ~ on smb's behalf** вступи́ться за кого́-л; **I shall leave tomorrow if nothing ~s** е́сли ничего́ не помеша́ет, я уе́ду за́втра.

intervening *adj*: **in the ~ period** в промежу́тке.

intervention *n* вмеша́тельство; (*mediation*) посре́дничество; **armed ~** вооружённое вмеша́тельство; **military ~** вое́нная интерве́нция; **thanks to her ~ they were reconciled** благодаря́ её посре́дничеству они́ помири́лись.

interview *n* интервью́ (*indecl*); бесе́да; (*appointment*) встре́ча; **a press ~** интервью́; **a television ~** телевизио́нное интервью́; **I had an ~ yesterday for the job** вчера́ со мной бесе́довали о приёме на рабо́ту; **I have an ~ with the Minister at 9** встре́чу с мини́стром мне назна́чили на де́вять часо́в утра́; **the President granted him an ~** президе́нт дал согла́сие приня́ть его́.

interview *vt*: **a journalist ~ed me** журнали́ст взял у меня́ интервью́; **he was ~ed on the radio** он дал интервью́ по ра́дио; **she was ~ed by a member of the board** с ней бесе́довал оди́н из чле́нов правле́ния; **he was ~ed by the Minister** у него́ была́ встре́ча/был разгово́р с мини́стром.

intestate *adj*: **to die ~** умере́ть, не оста́вив завеща́ния.

intestinal *adj* кише́чный.

intestine *n Anat* кишка́; *pl* (**~s**) кише́чник (*sing*); **small/large ~** то́нкая/то́лстая кишка́.

intimate *adj*: **an ~ friend/talk** бли́зкий друг, инти́мная бесе́да; **we're quite ~ with them** мы дово́льно близки́ с ни́ми; **to have an ~**

knowledge of smth хорошо́ знать что-л; *euph* **to be ~ with smb** быть в инти́мных отноше́ниях с кем-л.

intimate *vt* объяв|ля́ть, заяв|ля́ть (*pfs* -и́ть); **he ~d his approval/that...** он объяви́л о своём согла́сии/, что...

intimation *n* объявле́ние, заявле́ние; **the first ~ we had of it was from the French ambassador/from you** мы в пе́рвый раз об э́том услы́шали из заявле́ния францу́зского посла́/от вас; (*in paper*) **"~s"** «Сообще́ния».

intimidate *vt* запу́г|ивать (-а́ть); **are you trying to ~ me?** вы пыта́етесь меня́ запуга́ть?; **he ~d me into remaining silent** он угро́зами заста́вил меня́ молча́ть.

intimidation *n* запу́гивание.

into *prep* **1** (*with verbs of movement*) в + *A*; **to go ~ the wood/house/shop** входи́ть в лес/в дом/в магази́н

2 (*with other verbs*): **to get ~ a car** сади́ться в маши́ну; **he thrust his hand ~ his pocket/belt/jacket** он засу́нул ру́ку в карма́н/за по́яс/за па́зуху; **to translate ~ Russian** переводи́ть на ру́сский; **to divide ~ 5 parts** дели́ть на пять часте́й

3 *Math*: **3 ~ 12 = 4** двена́дцать, делённое на три, равно́ четырём.

intolerable *adj* (*of person or thing*) невыноси́мый, нестерпи́мый; (*of person*) несно́сный.

intolerant *adj* нетерпи́мый; **he is ~ of criticism** он нетерпи́м к кри́тике.

intoxicate *vt* опьян|я́ть (-и́ть), *also fig*; **he was/got ~d** он опьяне́л; **he was ~d by success** он был опьянён успе́хом.

intoxication *n* опьяне́ние; *Med* интоксика́ция.

intractable *adj* (*of person*) несгово́рчивый, упря́мый; **an ~ girl/problem** упря́мая де́вушка, тру́дная пробле́ма.

intransitive *adj Gram*: **an ~ verb** непереxо́дный глаго́л.

intravenous *adj* внутриве́нный.

in-tray *n* я́щик для входя́щих пи́сем/бума́г.

intrepid *adj* бесстра́шный, отва́жный.

intricate *adj* сло́жный, запу́танный.

intrigue *n* (*plot or love affair*) интри́га; *pl* (**~s**) ко́зни, интри́ги.

intrigue *vti* (*plot*) интригова́ть (*impf*); (*interest*) интригова́ть (за-); **to ~ against smb** интригова́ть про́тив кого́-л; **she/it ~s me** она́/э́то интригу́ет меня́; **I am ~d to know what he said** мне не те́рпится узна́ть, что он сказа́л.

intriguing *adj* (*scheming*) интригу́ющий; *CQ* (*fascinating*) интере́сный.

intrinsic *adj* прису́щий; **his ~ honesty** прису́щая ему́ прямота́; **the ~ value of the brooch is small** сама́ по себе́ брошь сто́ит недо́рого.

intrinsically *adv* в су́щности.

introduce *vt* **1** (*bring in*) вводи́ть (ввести́); вноси́ть (внести́); **to ~ reforms/a fashion/a law** вводи́ть рефо́рмы/мо́ду/зако́н; **to ~ a bill** вноси́ть законопрое́кт; **to ~ a topic for discussion** пред|лага́ть те́му на рассмотре́ние (-ложи́ть); **tobacco was ~d into England from America** таба́к был завезён в А́нглию из Аме́рики; *Radio* **the announcer ~s each programme** ка́ждая програ́мма объявля́ется ди́ктором

2 (*people*) знако́мить (по-), предста|вля́ть (-́вить); **may I ~ Mr Smith to you** разреши́те предста́вить вам господи́на Сми́та; **I ~d them to each other/him to Igor** я их познако́мил, я познако́мил его́ с И́горем

3 (*acquaint smb with smth*) ознаком|ля́ть (-́ить); **we must ~ him to our customs** на́до ознако́мить его́ с на́шими обы́чаями; **I will ~ the subject briefly** я кра́тко ознако́млю вас с те́мой; **I was ~d to chess/to Pushkin at an early age** я на́чал игра́ть в ша́хматы/чита́ть Пу́шкина в ра́ннем де́тстве.

introduction *n* **1** (*process*) введе́ние; (*preface*) предисло́вие, введе́ние; *Mus* интроду́кция; **the ~ of new measures/of a probe into a wound** введе́ние но́вых мер/зо́нда в ра́ну; **my ~ to life in France** моё знако́мство с жи́знью Фра́нции; **in the ~ of the book/to the lecture** в предисло́вии к кни́ге, в вво́дной ча́сти ле́кции; **"An I. to Physics"** «Введе́ние в фи́зику»

2 (*of people*): **to make ~s all round** всех познако́мить/предста́вить друг дру́гу; **a letter of ~** рекоменда́тельное письмо́; **could you give me an ~ to Petrov?** не могли́ бы вы порекомендова́ть меня́ Петро́ву?

introductory *adj* вво́дный, вступи́тельный.

introspective *adj* интроспекти́вный.

introvert *n Psych* интрове́рт.

intrude *vi*: **journalists ~d shamelessly on her privacy** журнали́сты бесцеремо́нно вторга́лись в её ча́стную жизнь; **in his novels a note of sentimentality sometimes ~s** в его́ рома́нах иногда́ слы́шатся сентимента́льные но́тки; **I hope I'm not intruding** наде́юсь, я вам не меша́ю.

intrusion *n*: **sorry for the ~, but could I use your phone?** извини́те за вторже́ние/за беспоко́йство, но не мог бы я воспо́льзоваться ва́шим телефо́ном?; **I resent these ~s on my time** (я) терпе́ть не могу́, когда́ у меня́ отнима́ют вре́мя.

intuition *n* интуи́ция.

intuitive *adj* интуити́вный; **~ knowledge** интуити́вное зна́ние; **women are often ~ in their judgements** же́нщины в свои́х сужде́ниях зачасту́ю полага́ются на интуи́цию.

inundate *vt*: **the fields were ~d** поля́ бы́ли за́литы/зато́плены водо́й; *fig*: **we were ~d with applications/invitations** нас засы́пали заявле́ниями/приглаше́ниями; **the town is ~d with tourists** го́род наводнён тури́стами.

inure *vt*: **he had ~d himself/was ~d to cold** он приучи́л себя́/был приу́чен к хо́лоду; **he had become ~d to mockery** он научи́лся переноси́ть насме́шки.

invade *vt* вторг|а́ться (-́нуться), напа|да́ть (-́сть); **the enemy ~d our country** враг напа́л на на́шу страну́; *fig*: **we are ~d by guests most Sundays** по воскресе́ньям нас осажда́ют го́сти.

invader *n* захва́тчик, оккупа́нт.

invalid[1] *n* инвали́д, больно́й.

invalid[1] *adj* больно́й; **an ~ diet** дие́та для больны́х; **an ~ chair** кре́сло/коля́ска для инвали́дов.

invalid[1] *vt*: **he was ~ed out of the army** его́ освободи́ли от вое́нной слу́жбы по состоя́нию здоро́вья.

invalid[2] *adj* недействи́тельный; **an ~ document/passport/cheque** недействи́тельный докуме́нт/па́спорт/чек; **to declare a marriage ~** объяви́ть брак недействи́тельным; **an ~ argument** несостоя́тельный аргуме́нт; **an ~ excuse** неубеди́тельная отгово́рка.

invalidate *vt*: **the new will ~s the old one** но́вое завеща́ние де́лает ста́рое недействи́тельным; **that ~s your argument** э́то сво́дит ва́ши аргуме́нты (*pl*) на нет.

invaluable *adj fig* бесце́нный; **his ~ contribution to archaeology** его́ бесце́нный вклад в археоло́гию; **your help has been ~** ва́ша по́мощь была́ про́сто неоцени́ма.

invariable *adj* неизме́нный.

invariably *adv* всегда́; **he is ~ late** он всегда́/ве́чно опа́здывает; **I am ~ ill on holiday** я неизме́нно/всегда́ заболева́ю во вре́мя о́тпуска.

invasion *n* вторже́ние, нападе́ние; **Napoleon's ~ of Russia** вторже́ние Наполео́на в Росси́ю.

invective *n*: **a stream of ~ fell from his lips** он разрази́лся пото́ком бра́ни/руга́тельств (*pl*).

inveigle *vt*: **he ~d me into selling him the painting** он уговори́л меня́ прода́ть ему́ карти́ну; **he was ~d into taking a part in the fraud** его́ втяну́ли в э́ту афе́ру.

invent *vt* изобре|та́ть (-сти́); **to ~ a new machine/method** изобрета́ть но́вую маши́ну, вводи́ть но́вый ме́тод (ввести́); *fig*: **he ~ed an excuse for not going** он приду́мал отгово́рку, что́бы не идти́ туда́; **he ~ed every word of it** он всё э́то вы́думал/сочини́л.

invention *n* изобрете́ние; *fig* **his story is pure ~** э́та его́ исто́рия—чи́стая вы́думка/чи́стый вы́мысел.

inventive *adj* (*of person, mind*) изобрета́тельный.

inventor *n* изобрета́тель (*m*).

inventory *n* инвентариза́ция; (*list*) инвентаризацио́нная о́пись; **to take/make an ~** проводи́ть инвентариза́цию; **to enter smth on the ~** заноси́ть что-л в инвентаризацио́нную о́пись.

inverse *adj*: **in ~ proportion to** в обра́тной пропо́рции к + *D*.

invert *vt* пере|вора́чивать/ста́вить вверх дном (-верну́ть, по-); **to ~ the order of words** меня́ть поря́док слов.

invertebrate *adj* беспозвоно́чный; *as n* беспозвоно́чное.

inverted commas *npl* кавы́чки.

invest *vti vt* **1** *Fin* вкла́дывать (вложи́ть), инвести́ровать (*impf and pf*); **he ~ed £1,000 in the firm** он вложи́л в э́ту фи́рму ты́сячу фу́нтов

2 (*endow*) обле|ка́ть (-́чь); надел|я́ть (-и́ть); **he was ~ed with full authority** его́ облекли́ всей полното́й вла́сти

vi Fin: **to ~ in a firm** вкла́дывать капита́л/де́ньги в предприя́тие; *fig joc* **we're ~ing in a new car** мы покупа́ем но́вую маши́ну.

investigate *vt* (*of police, etc.*) рассле́довать, (*of research*) иссле́довать (*impfs and pfs*); **to ~ a crime/a case/the causes of an accident** рассле́довать преступле́ние/де́ло/причи́ны ава́рии; **to ~ the effects of a new drug** изуч|а́ть де́йствие (*sing*) но́вого лека́рства (-и́ть); **to ~ the causes of an illness** устана́вливать причи́ны боле́зни (*usu impf*).

investigation *n* (*inquiry*) рассле́дование; *Law* сле́дствие; (*scientific*) иссле́дование; **the matter/his case is under ~** э́то де́ло/его́ де́ло рассле́дуется; **to hold an ~** проводи́ть рассле́дование; *attr*: **~ bureau** конто́ра ча́стного детекти́ва.

investment *n Fin* вклад капита́ла; капиталовложе́ние; **an ~ of £1,000** вклад в разме́ре ты́сячи фу́нтов; **there is not enough ~ in industry** капиталовложе́ния (*pl*) в промы́шленность недоста́точны; **it proved a bad ~** э́то бы́ло неуда́чным помеще́нием/вложе́нием капита́ла.

investor *n* вкла́дчик.

inveterate *adj*: **an ~ bachelor** убеждённый холостя́к; **an ~ gambler/smoker** зая́длый игро́к/кури́льщик; **an ~ liar** закорене́лый лжец; **an ~ drinker** беспробу́дный пья́ница; **~ prejudices** глубоко́ укорени́вшиеся предрассу́дки.

invidious *adj*: **don't make ~ distinctions** не проводи́ оби́дных сравне́ний.

invigilate *vti*: **to ~ (at) an exam** наблюда́ть за хо́дом экза́мена (*impf*).

invigorating *adj* бодря́щий; **I find swimming ~** купа́ние бодри́т меня́.

invincible *adj* непобеди́мый.

inviolable *adj*: **an ~ right/law** неотъе́млемое пра́во, незы́блемый зако́н.

invisible *adj* неви́димый; **an ~ seam** неви́димый шов; **the dacha is ~ because of the trees** да́чу не ви́дно (*impers*) из-за дере́вьев; **the ~ man** челове́к-невиди́мка; **the boy wished he could become ~** ма́льчику хоте́лось стать невиди́мкой; *Fin* **~ exports** неви́димый э́кспорт (*sing*).

invitation *n* приглаше́ние; **by ~** по приглаше́нию; **to send out ~s** рассыла́ть приглаше́ния; **I got a letter of ~** я получи́л приглаше́ние по по́чте.

invite *vt* **1** (*socially*) пригла|ша́ть (-си́ть); **to ~ smb to a wedding/to supper** приглаша́ть кого́-л на сва́дьбу/на у́жин; **he ~d me in/out for a drink** он пригласи́л меня́ к себе́/он позва́л меня́ пойти́ куда́-нибудь вы́пить

2 (*request*) просить (по-); **the chairman ~d me to speak/my opinion** председатель попросил меня выступить/высказать своё мнение

3 (*ask for*): **to act now is to ~ defeat** если начать действовать сейчас, поражение неизбежно; **he's inviting trouble** он лезет на рожон, он нарывается на неприятности.

inviting *adj* заманчивый, привлекательный, соблазнительный; **an ~ offer** соблазнительное/заманчивое предложение; **the sea/the food looks very ~** море так и манит купаться, еда выглядит очень аппетитно.

invoice *n Comm* счёт-фактура; **as per ~** согласно фактуре.

invoice *vt* вы|писывать кому-л (счёт-)фактуру на что-л (´-писать).

invoke *vt*: **to ~ the protection of the law** взывать о защите к закону (*usu impf*).

involuntary *adj* невольный, непроизвольный; **an ~ movement** невольное/непроизвольное движение; **an ~ smile** невольная улыбка; **I was an ~ participant in their quarrel** я невольно был вовлечён в их ссору.

involve *vt* вовле|кать (´-чь); **I don't want to ~ you in any unpleasantness** я не хочу вовлекать вас в неприятность; **he's ~d in some shady business/with some criminals** он ввязался в сомнительное предприятие, он связался с какими-то преступниками; **a question of principle is ~d** это вопрос/дело принципа; **what exactly does the job ~?** в чём именно состоит работа?; **it will ~ you in a lot of expense** это введёт вас в большие расходы (*pl*); **my new job ~s living in London** моя новая работа требует, чтобы я жил в Лондоне; **I'm ~d in a new experiment** я занят сейчас новым экспериментом; **I don't want to get too ~d with her** я не хочу слишком связывать себя с ней; **the persons who are ~d aren't here yet** те, кого это касается, ещё не пришли.

involved *adj* сложный; **an ~ style/character** сложный стиль/характер; **the problem gets more and more ~** проблема всё усложняется.

involvement *n*: **we don't know the extent of his ~ in the affair** мы не знаем, до какой степени он замешан в этом деле.

invulnerable *adj* неуязвимый, *also fig.*

inwardly *adv* внутренне; **~ calm** внутренне спокойный; **he groaned ~** он простонал про себя.

inward(s) *adv* внутрь; вовнутрь; **the window opens ~** окно открывается внутрь/вовнутрь.

iodine *n* йод.

iota *n*: **there is not an ~ of truth in the rumour** в этой сплетне нет ни доли/ни грана истины.

Iranian *n* иранец, иранка.

Iranian *adj* иранский.

Iraqi *n* житель Ирака.

Iraqi *adj* иракский.

irascible *adj* раздражительный, вспыльчивый.

irate *adj* гневный; **he got very ~** он пришёл в ярость.

ire *n* гнев, ярость.

iridescent *adj* радужный.

iris *n Anat* радужная оболочка глаза; *Bot* ирис.

Irish *adj* ирландский.

Irishman *n* ирландец.

Irishwoman *n* ирландка.

irk *vt*: **it ~s me to be kept waiting** терпеть не могу, когда меня заставляют ждать.

irksome *adj* надоедливый; **an ~ task** нудная работа.

iron *n* железо; (*for clothes*) (**an ~**) утюг; **cast/corrugated/scrap ~** чугун, гофрированное железо, металлолом; *fig*: **to rule with a rod of ~** управлять железной рукой; **strike while the ~'s hot** куй железо, пока горячо; *attr* железный, *also fig*; **~ ore, an ~ will** железная руда/воля; **~ muscles** стальные мускулы.

iron *vti* гладить (по-, вы-, от-), утюжить (от-); **to ~ out creases/*fig* misunderstandings** отутюживать складки, ула|живать недоразумения (-дить).

ironic(al) *adj* иронический.

ironically *adv* иронически, с иронией; **~ (enough)** по иронии судьбы.

ironing *n* (*act*) глаженье, глажка; **I must do the ~** мне надо гладить бельё; **that dress/these trousers could do with ~** не мешало бы выгладить это платье/отутюжить эти брюки; **there's a pile of ~ on the table** на столе—куча белья для глаженья (*to be ironed*)/стопка выглаженного белья (*already ironed*); *attr*: **~ board** гладильная доска.

ironmonger *n*: **I'm going to the ~'s** (*shop*) я схожу в хозяйственный магазин.

ironmongery *n* металлоизделия (*pl*).

ironworks *npl* чугунолитейный завод (*sing*).

irony *n* ирония; **the ~ of it is that...** вся ирония этого в том, что...

irrational *adj*: **an ~ person** неразумный человек; **~ behaviour/fears** неразумное/глупое поведение, необъяснимые страхи; **that argument is quite ~** этот довод нелогичен.

irreconcilable *adj* (*of people*) непримиримый; (*of ideas, etc.*) несовместимый.

irrecoverable *adj*: **~ losses** невозместимые потери.

irrefutable *adj* неопровержимый.

irregular *adj* неправильный, *also Gram*; нерегулярный, *also Mil*; (*uneven*) неровный; **~ features/verbs** неправильные черты лица/глаголы; **~ breathing, an ~ outline/pulse** неровное дыхание, неровные очертания (*pl*), неровный пульс; **the postal delivery is ~ here** почта приходит сюда нерегулярно; **~ attendance at lectures** нерегулярное посещение лекций; **~ troops** нерегулярные войска.

irrelevant *adj*: **that's an ~ question** этот вопрос к делу не относится; **that's ~ to the present situation** это не имеет отношения к данной ситуации.

irreparable *adj*: **~ damage** непоправимый ущерб; **~ loss** невозместимая потеря.

irrepressible *adj*: ~ **laughter** безу́держный смех; **that child is** ~ како́й неугомо́нный ребёнок!

irreproachable *adj* безукори́зненный, безупре́чный.

irresistible *adj* непреодоли́мый; **the urge to contradict him was** ~ меня́ так и подмыва́ло (*impers*) во всём ему́ пере́чить; **you look** ~! ты сего́дня неотрази́ма!

irresolute *adj* нереши́тельный.

irrespective *adj*: ~ **of the consequences I will risk it** будь что бу́дет, я рискну́; ~ **of what you say, I shall go** что бы ты ни говори́л, я всё равно́ пойду́ туда́.

irresponsible *adj* безотве́тственный.

irretrievably *adv*: ~ **lost** безвозвра́тно поте́рянный.

irreverent *adj* непочти́тельный.

irreversible *adj*: **an** ~ **process** необрати́мый проце́сс; **an** ~ **decision** бесповоро́тное реше́ние.

irrevocable *adj* бесповоро́тный.

irrigate *vt* оро|ша́ть (-си́ть).

irrigation *n* ороше́ние, ирріга́ция; *attr*: ~ **canal** ороси́тельный/ирригацио́нный кана́л.

irritable *adj* раздражи́тельный.

irritably *adv* раздражённо.

irritate *vt* раздража́ть (*usu impf*); **I was** ~**d** я был раздражён; **the smoke** ~**s my eyes** дым ест мне глаза́.

irritating *adj* раздража́ющий; **an** ~ **habit** раздража́ющая привы́чка; **I find him/the book very** ~ он/э́та кни́га раздража́ет меня́; **it is most** ~ **of you to refuse at the last minute** о́чень неприя́тно, что ты отка́зываешься в после́дний моме́нт.

irritation *n* раздраже́ние, *also Med.*

Islam *n* исла́м, мусульма́нство (= *the Islamic world and its religion*).

Islamic *adj* мусульма́нский.

island *n* о́стров; (*in road*) острово́к безопа́сности; *attr* островно́й.

islander *n* островитя́нин.

isolate *vt* изоли́ровать (*impf and pf*); *Chem* вы|деля́ть (-делить).

isolated *adj*: **an** ~ **spot/village** уединённое ме́сто, отдалённая/глуха́я дере́вня; **an** ~ **instance** отде́льный слу́чай.

isolation *n* изоля́ция, *also Med*; (*state of isolation*) изоли́рованность, уединённость; **I love the** ~ **of the dacha** мне нра́вится уединённость жи́зни на да́че; *attr*: ~ **ward** изоля́тор.

isosceles *adj Math*: **an** ~ **triangle** равнобе́дренный треуго́льник.

isotope *n* изото́п.

Israeli *n* израильтя́нин, израильтя́нка.

Israeli *adj* изра́ильский.

issue *n* **1** (*output*): **an** ~ **of coins/stamps/shares** вы́пуск моне́т/ма́рок/а́кций; **the** ~ **of rations** вы́дача пайка́ (*sing*); **these things are all government** ~ э́ти ве́щи все казённые; (*of book: publication*) вы́пуск, (*size of issue*) тира́ж; **a back/the latest** ~ **of a magazine** ста́рый/после́дний но́мер журна́ла

2 (*outcome*) исхо́д, результа́т; **to await the** ~ ожида́ть исхо́да/результа́та (*impf*); **in the** ~ в ито́ге, в результа́те; **to bring smth to a successful** ~ привести́ что-л к успе́шному заверше́нию

3 (*matter*) вопро́с; **a political/side** ~ полити́ческий/побо́чный вопро́с; **the point at** ~ **is that...** вопро́с состои́т в том, что...; **to evade/face the** ~ уйти́ от вопро́са/стоя́ть пе́ред пробле́мой; **to force the** ~ наста́ивать на реше́нии; **he took** ~ **with me on that** он вступи́л в спор со мной по э́тому вопро́су

4 *collect* (*offspring*) пото́мство; **to die without** ~ умере́ть безде́тным.

issue *vti vt* вы|пуска́ть (-пустить), вы|дава́ть (-дать); **to** ~ **coins/stamps/shares** выпуска́ть моне́ты/ма́рки/а́кции; **to** ~ **a certificate/warrant for arrest** выдава́ть удостовере́ние/о́рдер на аре́ст; **they** ~**d a rifle to each man** они́ вы́дали ка́ждому по винто́вке; **the troops were** ~**d with provisions** войска́ снабди́ли продово́льствием (*collect*); **the book was** ~**d last year** э́та кни́га вы́шла в про́шлом году́

vi: **smoke was issuing from the chimney** дым шёл из трубы́; **blood** ~**d from the wound** из ра́ны потекла́ кровь; **a strange sound** ~**d from his lips** он изда́л како́й-то стра́нный звук.

it *pron* [**NB** *for genitive* **its** *see separate entry*] **1** *with a noun as antecedent* он, она́, оно́, его́, её, его́, *after preps* (от) него́, неё, него́, *etc.*; *gender depends on that of antecedent*: **have you seen my knife/book/ring?—Yes,** ~**'s in the kitchen** ты ви́дел мой нож/мою́ кни́гу/моё кольцо́?—Да, он/она́/оно́ на ку́хне; **did you notice where I put my knife/book/ring?—Yes, you put** ~ **on the kitchen table** ты случа́йно не ви́дел, куда́ я положи́л мой нож/мою́ кни́гу/моё кольцо́?—Ви́дел. Ты положи́л его́/её/его́ на ку́хонный стол; **where shall I put the knife/book/ring?—Put** ~ **on the desk** куда́ положи́ть нож/кни́гу/кольцо́?—Положи́ (его́/её/его́) на пи́сьменный стол; **it's an interesting article—** ~ **says in** ~ **that...** э́то интере́сная статья́—в ней говори́тся, что...; **I don't speak Russian but I understand** ~ я не говорю́ по-ру́сски, но понима́ю (*antecedent is an adv, so is not translated*)

2 *with clause or question antecedent* э́то (*or not translated at all*); **is** ~ **true?** э́то пра́вда?; **who's there?—It's me** кто там?—Э́то я; **who was that at the door?—It was the postman** кто приходи́л?—(Приходи́л) почтальо́н; **everyone must go out for an hour—** ~ **applies to you too** все должны́ вы́йти погуля́ть на час—э́то к тебе́ то́же отно́сится; **don't go on the ice—** ~**'s dangerous** (*to do so*) не ходи́ по льду—э́то опа́сно; (*in queue*) **what do you think you're doing? It's my turn** почему́ вы без о́череди? Сейча́с не ва́ша о́чередь, а моя́; **whose turn is** ~**?—It's mine** чья о́чередь?—Моя́; **park at the front—** ~**'s asphalt there** поста́вь маши́ну пе́ред до́мом—там асфа́льт;

Paris is a beautiful city, isn't ~? Париж — красивый город, правда?

3: it's (it is) + *adj and inf, gerund, or clause; usu not translated*: **~'s dangerous to go on the ice** по льду ходить опасно; **~'s useless asking him** бесполезно спрашивать у него; **~'s natural that she was offended** естественно, что она обиделась; **I think ~'s right to punish him** по-моему, его надо наказать; **I think ~'s here they live** думаю, что они живут здесь

4 *introductory* **it is/was...** *of time, distance, weather; usu not translated*; это *used only for emphasis*: **what's the time?—It's 3 o'clock** сколько сейчас времени?—Три часа; **~'s 10 past 4** сейчас десять минут пятого; **~ was already 5 o'clock** было уже пять часов; **~'s Tuesday today** сегодня вторник; (*for emphasis*) **~ was Tuesday** это был вторник; **~'s only a month to Xmas** до рождества всего месяц; **~'s three years since I saw you** три года как я вас не видел; **~'s a long way to the sea** до моря далеко; **~'s raining/snowing** идёт дождь/снег; **~ was very wet last summer** прошлое лето было очень дождливым; **~ was a really lovely day** (*emphatic*) день был чудесный

5 *introductory in general or impersonal expressions or used for emphasis; usu not translated*: **~'s said that...** говорят, что...; **~'s no use complaining** бесполезно жаловаться; **~ distresses me to see you in that state** мне горько видеть тебя в таком состоянии; **~'s Olga I was speaking to, not you** я говорил с Ольгой, а не с тобой; **~ was his wife who persuaded him** только жена смогла убедить его; **~'s the red book I want, not the blue one** мне нужна именно красная книга, а не голубая

6 *idiomatic uses*: **that's just ~!** вот именно!; **he looks as if he's had ~** похоже, что он окончательно сдал *or* ему конец (*is dying*)/он совсем выдохся (*is very tired*); **the worst of ~ is, I've forgotten her name** и (что) хуже всего — я забыл её имя; *as n*: **you're ~!** (*in children's games*) тебе водить!; **she's got ~** (*sex appeal*) в ней есть изюминка; **he thinks he's ~** он думает, (что) он что-то из себя представляет.

Italian *n* итальянец, итальянка; (*language*) итальянский язык.

Italian *adj* итальянский.

italic *adj*: **~ type** курсив.

italicize *vt*: **to ~ a word** вы|делять слово курсивом (-делить).

italics *npl* курсив (*sing*); **in ~** курсивом; **the word in ~** слово, данное курсивом.

itch *n* зуд, *also fig*; чесотка; **I've got an ~ (in my foot)** у меня чешется (нога); *fig* **I've got the ~ to travel** у меня тяга к путешествиям (*pl*).

itch *vi* чесаться (*impf*); *CQ* зудеть; **my leg ~es** у меня нога чешется; **I'm ~ing all over from mosquito bites** у меня всё тело зудит от комариных укусов; *fig* **the boys were ~ing to get out and play** мальчикам не терпелось (*impers*) пойти поиграть на улице.

itchy *adj*: **my leg is ~** у меня чешется нога; *fig*: **he's got ~ feet** ему не сидится на месте; **he's got an ~ palm** он взяточник.

item *n* (*object*) предмет; (*point*) пункт; **an ~ in a catalogue/on a list** название/номер в каталоге/в списке; **the first ~ on the programme/agenda/bill** первый номер программы, первый пункт повестки дня/в счёте; **he answered their objections ~ by ~** он отвечал на их возражения по пунктам; **an important ~ in our programme** важный пункт нашей программы; **an ~ in a newspaper** сообщение в газете; **we disagree on several ~s** мы расходимся по некоторым вопросам.

itemize *vt*: **to ~ an account** состав|лять подробный отчёт о расходах (-ить).

itinerant *adj*: **~ players** странствующие/бродячие актёры.

itinerary *n* маршрут; **to plan one's ~** составлять маршрут.

its *poss pron* **1** *translated by* его, её, его; **here's the name of the club and here's ~ address** вот название клуба, и вот его адрес; **I bought a new car but I'm doubtful about ~ reliability** я купил новую машину, но сомневаюсь в её надёжности

2 *where it refers back to the subject of the sentence or clause,* **its** *is translated by* **i)** *reflex poss adj* свой, своя, своё; **the swan looked at ~ reflexion in the water** лебедь смотрел на своё отражение в воде; свой *is often omitted where ownership is clear*: **the club elects ~ committee annually** клуб избирает правление ежегодно; **ii)** *with parts of the body* **its** *may be translated by* себе *or omitted*: **the cat broke ~ leg** кошка сломала себе лапу; **the dog hurt ~ paw** собака ушибла лапу.

it's = it is

itself *pron* **1** (*emphatic*) сам, сама, само; **the picture in ~ is worthless** сама по себе картина ничего не стоит; (*alone*) **the house stands by ~** дом стоит отдельно

2 (*reflexive*): **the dinghy righted ~** лодка выровнялась; **the team has set ~ a hard task** команда поставила себе/перед собой трудную задачу.

ivory *n* слоновая кость; *pl* (**ivories**) (*in billiards*) шары.

ivy *n* плющ.

J

jab *n* (*poke*) пинок; (*prick*) укол, *also Med*; *CQ* **I had my cholera ~** мне сделали укол от холеры.

jab *vti CQ* тыкать (ткнуть); **he ~bed me in the ribs/(at) the meat with his fork** он ткнул меня под рёбра *or* в бок, он потыкал мясо вилкой; **to ~ smb/smth with a bayonet** колоть кого-л/что-л штыком (*impf*).

jabber *vi*: **they were ~ing away in Italian** они́ болта́ли ме́жду собо́й, они́ тарато́рили по-италья́нски (*impfs*).

jack *n*: **Union J.** госуда́рственный флаг Соединённого Короле́вства; **J. Frost** Моро́з Кра́сный Нос; **before you could say J. Robinson he had jumped into the river** я и а́хнуть не успе́л, как он пры́гнул в ре́ку; *Aut*, *Tech* домкра́т; *Cards* вале́т; *CQ*: **he's a ~ of all trades** он ма́стер на все ру́ки, *joc* он и швец, и жнец, и на дуде́ игре́ц; **every man ~** все до одного́.

jack *vt Aut*: **to ~ up a car** под|нима́ть маши́ну домкра́том (-ня́ть).

jackal *n* шака́л.

jackdaw *n* га́лка.

jacket *n* (*of man's suit*) пиджа́к; (*casual jacket*) ку́ртка; (*lady's*) жаке́т; (*of book*) суперобло́жка; **potatoes cooked in their ~s** карто́фель (*collect*) в мунди́ре (*sing*).

jack-knife *n* складно́й нож.

jackpot *n Cards*, *etc.* банк; **he hit the ~** он забра́л все ста́вки, *fig* он доби́лся реша́ющего успе́ха.

jackstraw *n* (*US*) (*for drinking*) соло́мка.

jade *n* (*stone*) нефри́т; *attr* нефри́товый.

jaded *adj* (*of people*) изнурённый, изму́ченный.

jag *n* о́стрый вы́ступ; *Med CQ* уко́л.

jagged *adj*: **~ rocks** о́стрые/зубча́тые ска́лы.

jaguar *n* ягуа́р.

jail *n* тюрьма́; (*imprisonment*) тюре́мное заключе́ние; **he's in ~** он сиди́т в тюрьме́.

jail *vt* заключ|а́ть/*CQ* сажа́ть в тюрьму́ (-и́ть/посади́ть); **he was ~ed for 6 years/for life** его́ посади́ли на шесть лет *or* он получи́л шесть лет, его́ приговори́ли к пожи́зненному заключе́нию.

jailer *n* тюре́мщик.

jalop(p)y *n CQ* драндуле́т.

jam[1] *n approx* (*large pieces of fruit in thick syrup*) варе́нье; (*purée of fruit*) пови́дло, джем; *fig* **money for ~** лёгкая нажи́ва.

jam[2] *n* (*blockage*) зато́р; (*of people*) да́вка; **traffic ~** зато́р в у́личном движе́нии, *CQ* про́бка; **there was a ~ in the entrance hall** в вестибю́ле была́ да́вка (*of people*), вестибю́ль был весь заста́влен чемода́нами (*of baggage*); **there's a terrible ~ at the bar** в ба́ре полно́ наро́ду; *fig CQ*: **I'm in a bit of a ~** я попа́л [NB *tense*] в переде́лку; **to get smb out of a ~** вы́ручить кого́-л (из беды́).

jam[2] *vti vt* **1** (*block*): **a lorry was ~ming the entrance** грузови́к загороди́л въезд во двор [NB *Russian pf*]; **the river was ~med with logs/boats** река́ была́ запру́жена брёвнами/ло́дками; **the waste pipe is ~med with dirt** сливна́я труба́ заби́та гря́зью; **I ~med my finger in the door** я прищеми́л себе́ па́лец две́рью; *Radio* **to ~ a programme/station** глуши́ть переда́чу/ста́нцию

2 (*pack tight*) впих|ивать, запи́х|ивать (*pfs* -ну́ть); **I ~med my clothes into the case** я запихну́л оде́жду в чемода́н; **he ~med the papers into his pocket** он су́нул бума́ги в карма́н; **the room was ~med with people** в ко́мнате бы́ло полно́ наро́ду—не пропихну́ться

3 (*press hard*): **I ~med on the brakes** я ре́зко нажа́л на тормоза́; **he ~med his hat** он нахлобу́чил шля́пу

vi: **the steering wheel has/the brakes have ~med** руль/тормоза́ зае́ло *or* закли́нило (*impers*); **the desk drawer has ~med** я́щик стола́ застря́л.

jam-full *adj*: **my case/the bus is ~** мой чемода́н/авто́бус наби́т битко́м.

jamjar *n* стекля́нная ба́нка.

jamming *n Radio* заглуше́ние.

jam-packed *adj see* **jam-full.**

jangle *n*: **the ~ of chains/keys** лязг цепе́й, звя́канье ключе́й.

jangle *vti*: **she ~d her keys, her keys ~d** она́ звя́кала ключа́ми; **his chains ~d** он звене́л кандала́ми (*impf*).

janitor *n* дво́рник.

January *n* янва́рь (*m*); *attr* янва́рский.

Japanese *n* япо́нец, япо́нка; (*language*) япо́нский язы́к.

Japanese *adj* япо́нский.

jar[1] *n* ба́нка; **a ~ of honey** ба́нка мёда; **put the flowers into that ~ for just now** пока́ поста́вь цветы́ в э́тот кувши́н (= *jug*).

jar[2] *n* (*jolt*) толчо́к; (*shaking*) сотрясе́ние; *fig* **his letter gave me a nasty ~** его́ письмо́ меня́ неприя́тно порази́ло.

jar[2] *vti vt* (*jolt*) толк|а́ть (-ну́ть); (*shake*) встря́х|ивать (-ну́ть); (*knock slightly*) заде|-ва́ть (-́ть); **I must have ~red the camera** у меня́, должно́ быть, фотоаппара́т дро́гнул в рука́х

vi: **his voice ~s on me** его́ го́лос мне ре́жет слух; **these colours ~** э́ти цвета́ не сочета́ются.

jargon *n* жарго́н.

jarring *adj* (*of sound*) ре́зкий; *fig* раздража́ющий; **~ colours** не гармони́рующие цвета́.

jasmine *n* жасми́н.

jasper *n* я́шма.

jaundice *n* желту́ха.

jaundiced *adj* (*of person*, *Med and fig*) жёлчный; *fig* **he takes a ~ view of life** он мра́чно смо́трит на ве́щи.

jaunt *n* прогу́лка; **let's go for a ~ to Oxford** (*by car*) дава́й прока́тимся в О́ксфорд.

jaunty *adj*: **a ~ young man** бо́йкий молодо́й челове́к; **he wore his cap at a ~ angle** он ли́хо заломи́л ша́пку.

javelin *n Sport*: **to throw the ~** мета́ть копьё.

jaw *n* че́люсть; *pl* (**~s**) рот, (*of animal*) пасть; **he has a firm/weak ~** у него́ волево́й/безво́льный подборо́док; *fig CQ*: **we had a good ~** мы хорошо́ поболта́ли; **the headmaster gave the boys a long ~** дире́ктор прочёл ма́льчикам дли́нную нота́цию.

jawbone *n* челюстна́я кость.

jay *n Orn* сóйка.

jazz *n* джаз; *attr*: ~ **band** джаз-оркéстр; ~ **music** джáзовая мýзыка.

jazzy *adj CQ*: **a** ~ **sports car** шикáрная спортúвная машúна; ~ **curtains** весёленькие занавéски.

jealous *adj* (*of smb's affections*) ревнúвый; (*of material things*) завúстливый; **a** ~ **husband** ревнúвый муж; **a** ~ **nature** завúстливая натýра; **she was** ~ **of her husband's secretary/of our new car** онá ревновáла мýжа к егó секретáрше, онá завúдовала, что мы купúли нóвую машúну; **to make smb** ~ возбудúть чью-л рéвность.

jealousy *n* (*of people's affections*) рéвность; (*of material things*) зáвисть.

jeans *npl* джúнсы.

jeep *n* джип.

jeer *n* издёвка, насмéшка.

jeer *vi*: **to** ~ **at smb/smth** насмехáться/глумúться/издевáться над кем-л/чем-л (*impfs*); **the crowd** ~**ed** из толпы́ послы́шались вы́крики.

jeering *n* насмéшки, издевáтельства (*pls*).

jell *vi CQ*: **our plans/my ideas have not yet** ~**ed** нáши плáны ещё не определúлись, мой идéи ещё не вы́кристаллизовались.

jelly *n* желé (*indecl*); *fig* **my legs were like** ~ у менá нóги бы́ли как вáтные.

jellyfish *n* медýза.

jemmy *n*: **a (burglar's)** ~ (воровскóй) лóмик.

jeopardize *vt*: **I wouldn't wish to** ~ **his chances of success** я не хотéл бы стáвить под угрóзу егó шáнсы на успéх.

jeopardy *n* (*of people*): **he is in** ~ он в опáсности; (*of things*): **his life/job is in** ~ егó жизнь в опáсности, емý угрожáет потéря рабóты.

jerk *n* рывóк; (*twitch*) сýдорога; **he opened the door with a** ~ он рывкóм откры́л дверь; **the train stopped with a** ~ пóезд рéзко затормозúл; **to do physical** ~**s** дéлать зарáдку (*sing*); (*US*) *sl* **he's a** ~ он болвáн.

jerk *vti vt* дёр|гать (-нуть); **he** ~**ed his head** он дёрнул головóй; **he** ~**ed my arm/elbow** он дёрнул менá зá руку (*tugged it to get attention*), он толкнýл менá под лóкоть (*jogged it, causing me to spill smth, etc.*); **he** ~**ed the trigger** он нажáл на спусковóй крючóк; **he** ~**ed his arm away** он отдёрнул рýку

vi дёргаться (*only in impf*); **he/his muscles** ~**ed continuously** он весь дёргался.

jerkily *adv* рывкáми; (*of spastic*) **he moves** ~ он хóдит дёргаясь.

jerky *adj* сýдорожный; (*abrupt*) рéзкий; (*bumpy*) трáский; (*of speech style*) оты́вистый; **it was a very** ~ **ride** нас растряслó (*impers*) в дорóге.

jerry *n sl* ночнóй горшóк.

jerry-built *adj* пострóенный на скóрую рýку.

jersey *n* (*material*) джерсú (*indecl*); (*garment*) свúтер; (*woman's*) кóфточка; *attr*: **a** ~ **suit** костюм (из) джерсú.

jest *n* шýтка; **in** ~ в шýтку, шутá; **for a** ~ шýтки рáди.

jest *vi* шутúть (по-).

jesting *adj* шутлúвый.

Jesuit *n* иезуúт.

Jesus *n* Иисýс.

jet *n* (*stream of liquid, gas*) струá; (*nozzle*) соплó; *Aut, Tech* жиклёр; *Aer* реактúвный самолёт; *attr*: **a** ~ **engine** реактúвный двúгатель.

jet-black *adj* чёрный как смоль.

jettison *vt Naut* (*of ballast, etc.*) вы|брáсывать зá борт (-бросить); *fig* **to** ~ **plans/an old bicycle** отверг|áть плáны (-нуть), выбрáсывать стáрый велосипéд.

jetty *n* прúстань.

Jew *n* еврéй, еврéйка; *Hist* иудéй.

jewel *n* драгоцéнный кáмень (*m*); драгоцéнность, *also fig*; (*of a watch*) кáмень; **the crown** ~**s** драгоцéнности из королéвской казны́; **laden/***CQ* **dripping with** ~**s** вся в драгоцéнностях; *attr*: **a 20** ~ **watch** часы́ на двадцатú камнях; ~ **box/case** шкатýлка/футлáр для драгоцéнностей.

jeweller, (*US*) **jeweler** *n* ювелúр; ~**'s (shop)** ювелúрный магазúн.

jewellery, jewelry *n* драгоцéнности (*pl*); (*on sale*) ювелúрные издéлия (*pl*).

Jewish *adj* еврéйский.

jib *vi* упрáмиться (за-); артáчиться (за-); **my horse** ~**bed at the last fence** моá лóшадь заупрáмилась пéред послéдним барьéром; *CQ* **he** ~**bed at cooking the accounts** он наотрéз отказáлся поддéлывать счетá.

jibe *n see* **gibe** *n*.

jiffy *n CQ* миг, минýтка; **wait a** ~ подождú минýтку; **I'll be back in a** ~ я мúгом вернýсь.

jig *n* (*dance*) джúга; *Tech* (*template*) шаблóн, (*gauge*) калúбр.

jig *vi*: **the little boy was** ~**ging up and down with excitement** мáльчик подпры́гивал от волнéния (*only in impf*).

jig-saw (puzzle) *n* составнáя картúнка-загáдка.

jilt *vt*: **she has** ~**ed him** онá брóсила егó.

jingle *n* (*of keys, coins, etc.*) звáканье, побрáкивание; (*rhyme*) стишóк.

jingle *vti vt* бренчáть, позвáкивать (*impfs*); **he was jingling his keys** он бренчáл/позвáкивал ключáми

vi: **his money** ~**d in his pocket** мéлочь позвáкивала у негó в кармáне.

jinks *npl*: **there were high** ~ **among the students yesterday** вчерá студéнты хорошó повеселúлись.

jinx *n CQ*: **there's a** ~ **on my car** на моéй машúне как бýдто какóе проклáтие лежúт.

jitters *npl sl*: **he's got the** ~ он весь трясётся от стрáха.

jittery *adj*: **she's very** ~ онá óчень нéрвничает.

jiu-jitsu *n* джúу-джúтсу (*indecl*).

job *n* **1** (*post*) рабо́та, *off* до́лжность; **I've got an interesting ~** у меня́ интере́сная рабо́та; **I'm out of a ~** я сейча́с без рабо́ты; **to look for a ~** иска́ть рабо́ту; **he lost his ~** его́ уво́лили, он потеря́л рабо́ту; **I had a ~ as a waitress** я рабо́тала официа́нткой; **the government has created many new ~s** прави́тельство учреди́ло мно́го но́вых должносте́й

2 (*piece of work*) де́ло, рабо́та; **I've got a ~ for you—to peel the potatoes** у меня́ есть для тебя́ рабо́та—чи́стить карто́шку (*collect*); **he does odd ~s around the house** он помога́ет по до́му; **I've got lots of ~s that need doing** у меня́ ма́сса/полно́ вся́ких дел; **he made a good ~ of my car** он хорошо́ почини́л мою́ маши́ну; **my ~ is to sell it** моё де́ло—продава́ть э́то; **it was my ~ to dismiss him** мне пришло́сь уво́лить его́; *sl* (*theft, etc.*): **that warehouse ~** та кра́жа на скла́де; **he's off on a ~** он пошёл на де́ло

3 *CQ*: **it's a bad ~** де́ло пло́хо; **it's just the ~** э́то и́менно то, что ну́жно; **it's a good ~ you came** хорошо́, что ты пришёл; **he apologized at once—and a good ~ too!** он сра́зу извини́лся и пра́вильно сде́лал; **we had quite a ~ finding your house** мы с трудо́м нашли́ ваш дом; **I gave it up as a bad ~** я махну́л руко́й на э́то как на безнадёжное де́ло; *attr*: **these chairs are a ~ lot** э́то па́ртия разро́зненных сту́льев.

jobbery *n* махина́ции (*usu pl*); **there's been some ~ here** здесь не обошло́сь без махина́ций; **he got promotion by a piece of ~** он доби́лся повыше́ния все́ми пра́вдами и непра́вдами.

jobbing *adj*: **a ~ gardener** *approx* приходя́щий садо́вник.

jobless *adj* безрабо́тный.

jockey *n* жоке́й.

jockey *vti vt*: **he ~ed me into agreeing/out of my job** он хи́тростью вы́рвал у меня́ согла́сие, он доби́лся-таки моего́ увольне́ния

vi: **he knows how to ~ for position** он уме́ет де́лать карье́ру.

jocose, jocular *adjs* шутли́вый.

jodhpurs *npl* галифе́ (*indecl*).

jog *n* (*push*) толчо́к, *also fig*; (*slow trot*) рысца́.

jog *vti vt* под|та́лкивать (-толкну́ть); **he ~ged my elbow** он толкну́л меня́ под ло́коть; *fig* **to ~ smb's memory about smth** напом|ина́ть кому́-л о чём-л (-́нить)

vi: **to ~ along** (*of horse*) идти́/(*of rider*) е́хать рысцо́й; *Sport* бежа́ть в разми́ночном те́мпе; *fig* **we just ~ along somehow** мы перебива́емся ко́е-ка́к.

joggle *vt*: **we were ~d about in the cart** мы трясли́сь на теле́ге.

john *n* (*US*) *sl* убо́рная, туале́т.

join *n* соедине́ние; (*by sticking*) скле́йка; *Sew* шов; *Tech* стык, шов; **the ~ couldn't be seen** ме́ста соедине́ния не́ было ви́дно.

join *vti vt* **1** (*of two things*) соедин|я́ть, (*by adding a piece*) присоедин|я́ть (*pfs* -и́ть); (*tie, connect*) свя́з|ывать (-а́ть); *Sew* подши|ва́ть (-́ть); **the bridge ~s the island to the mainland** мост соединя́ет/свя́зывает о́стров с материко́м; **to ~ a pipe to the main** присоедини́ть трубу́ к водопрово́ду; **to ~ a rope and/to a cable** свя́зывать кана́т с тро́сом; **to ~ hands** бра́ться за́ руки (взя́ться); **the track ~s the road here** тут тропа́ выхо́дит на доро́гу; **where does this river ~ the Danube?** где э́та река́ впада́ет в Дуна́й?; *Mil* **to ~ battle** вступ|а́ть в бой (-и́ть); *fig* **to ~ forces** объедин|я́ть уси́лия (-и́ть)

2 (*become a member of*): **to ~ a club/a party** вступа́ть в клуб/в па́ртию; **to ~ one's ship/one's regiment** возвраща́ться на кора́бль/в полк (верну́ться); **to ~ the army** поступ|а́ть на вое́нную слу́жбу (-и́ть)

3 (*associate with*): **may I ~ you?** мо́жно к вам присоедини́ться?; **they ~ed us in protesting** они́ поддержа́ли наш проте́ст; **they will ~ us on Tuesday** они́ прие́дут к нам во вто́рник; **you go on and I'll ~ you later** вы иди́те, я вас догоню́ (*catch up*); **will you ~ me in a drink?** не вы́пьете ли со мной?, дава́йте вы́пьем!

vi (при)соединя́ться; (*of rivers*) сли|ва́ться (-́ться); **we ~ed in the game** мы то́же ста́ли игра́ть; **his garden ~s on to mine** его́ сад грани́чит с мои́м; **the two roads ~ (up) at Zagorsk** э́ти две доро́ги соединя́ются у Заго́рска; **my son has ~ed up** мой сын поступи́л на вое́нную слу́жбу; **we ~ with him in wishing you every success** мы присоединя́емся к нему́ и жела́ем вам вся́ческих успе́хов (*pl*).

joiner *n* столя́р.

joinery *n* столя́рное де́ло; **he does ~** он столя́рничает.

joint *n* **1** *Anat* суста́в; *Tech* соедине́ние; стык; (*seam*) шов; (*hinge*) шарни́р; **I put my knee out of ~** я вы́вихнул себе́ коле́но; **a ~ of meat** кусо́к мя́са; **a universal ~** ги́бкое соедине́ние; **a ball and socket ~** шарово́й шарни́р; *fig* **to put smb's nose out of ~** расстра́ивать кого́-л

2 *sl*: **let's have a drink in this ~** дава́й зайдём в э́ту пивну́ю.

joint *adj* **1** совме́стный; о́бщий; объединённый; **~ action** совме́стные де́йствия (*pl*); **a ~ declaration** совме́стное заявле́ние; **~ efforts** о́бщие/объединённые уси́лия; **~ account** о́бщий счёт

2 *can be translated by use of prefix* со-: **~ authors/owners** соа́вторы, совладе́льцы.

jointly *adv* совме́стно.

joist *n* брус, ба́лка.

joke *n* (*verbal or practical*) шу́тка; (*funny story*) анекдо́т; (*witticism*) остро́та; **by way of a ~** в шу́тку; **for a ~** шу́тки ра́ди; **a ~ at my expense** шу́тка на мой счёт/в мой а́дрес; **he/it is a standing ~** он про́сто посме́шище, э́то деж́урная шу́тка; **to crack a ~** отпусти́ть шу́тку; **to play a ~ on smb** подшути́ть над кем-л; **he made a ~ of it** он свёл всё к шу́тке; **he can't take a ~** он не понима́ет шу́ток (*pl*); **he has carried the ~ too far** он зашёл сли́шком далеко́; **it's getting beyond a ~** э́то уже́ не шу́тка; *CQ*: **it's no ~ having to get up at 5** э́то не шу́тка—встава́ть в пять утра́; **is this your idea of a ~?** тебе́ э́то смешно́?, и э́то ты нахо́дишь смешны́м?

joke *vi* шути́ть (по-); **I was only joking** я про́сто пошути́л; **I'm in no mood for joking** мне не до шу́ток; *CQ* **you must be joking!** да ты шу́тишь!

joker *n* (*person*) шутни́к; балагу́р; *Cards* джо́кер.

joking *adj* шутли́вый.

jokingly *adv* в шу́тку, шутя́, шутли́во.

jollification *n CQ* пиру́шка.

jolly *adj* (*merry*) весёлый; (*amusing*) заба́вный; **we had a ~ time with them** мы хорошо́ повесели́лись у них; **it wasn't so ~ for me** мне бы́ло не о́чень-то ве́село.

jolly *adv CQ* о́чень; здо́рово; **~ good!** о́чень хорошо́!, отли́чно!; **he swims ~ well** он здо́рово пла́вает; **it's ~ hard** э́то черто́вски тру́дно; **you'll ~ well have to go** тебе́ всё-таки придётся туда́ пойти́; **you can ~ well do it yourself** ты прекра́сно мо́жешь спра́виться сам; **you can do it ~ well yourself** ты и сам э́то хорошо́ сде́лаешь.

jolly *vt CQ*: **we jollied him into agreeing to help** он согласи́лся помо́чь нам—мы всё-таки суме́ли его́ улома́ть.

jolt *n* толчо́к; **he gave my elbow a ~** он толкну́л меня́ под ло́коть; *fig*: **he needs a good ~** ему́ нужна́ хоро́шая встря́ска; **the news gave us a ~** но́вость потрясла́ нас.

jolt *vti vt* толк|а́ть (-ну́ть); (*shake*) трясти́ (по-); **we were ~ed about in the bus** нас о́чень си́льно трясло́ (*impers*) в авто́бусе; *fig* **the bad reviews of his play have ~ed him out of his complacency** отрица́тельные реце́нзии на его́ пье́су излечи́ли его́ от изли́шней самоуспоко́енности

vi: **to ~ along** трясти́сь (*impf*); **the bus ~ed over the potholes** авто́бус подбра́сывало (*impers*) на уха́бах.

jolting *n* тря́ска; **I feel sick from the ~** мне пло́хо от э́той тря́ски.

jostle *vti* толк|а́ть (-ну́ть); толка́ться (*usu impf*); **we were ~d by the crowd** нас затолка́ли в толпе́; **people ~d in the square** лю́ди толпи́лись на пло́щади.

jot *n* йо́та; **I wasn't one ~ the wiser** я не поумне́л ни на йо́ту; **there's not a ~ of truth in the rumour** в э́том слу́хе нет ни до́ли и́стины.

jot *vt*: **to ~ down** запис|ывать вкра́тце (-а́ть).

jotter *n* блокно́т.

jottings *npl* запи́ски.

journal *n* (*magazine*) журна́л; (*record of proceedings*) запи́ски (*pl*); (*diary*) дневни́к.

journalese *n* газе́тный стиль/язы́к; *CQ* **that's just ~** э́то газе́тные шта́мпы (*pl*).

journalism *n* журнали́стика; **he's gone in for ~** он стал журнали́стом.

journalist *n* журнали́ст, *CQ* газе́тчик.

journey *n* путеше́ствие; (*shorter*) пое́здка; **the return ~ cost £ 100** биле́т туда́ и обра́тно сто́ил сто фу́нтов; **it's two days'/hours' ~ from here** туда́ е́хать два дня, э́то в двух часа́х езды́ отсю́да; **have a good ~!** счастли́вого пути́!

journey *vi* путеше́ствовать (*impf*).

Jove *n*: **by ~!** ей-бо́гу!

jovial *adj* весёлый.

jowl *n*: **with a heavy ~** с тяжёлым подборо́дком.

joy *n* ра́дость; **to jump for ~** пры́гать от ра́дости; **it's a ~ to see you again** как я рад ви́деть тебя́ сно́ва; *CQ* **you can ask him for a loan but you won't get any/much ~ out of him** ты мо́жешь попроси́ть у него́ в долг, но из э́того ничего́ не вы́йдет; *attr*: **they're off for a ~ ride** они́ пое́хали прокати́ться.

joyful *adj* ра́достный.

joyless *adj* безра́достный, невесёлый.

joyous *adj* ра́достный.

joystick *n Aer CQ* ру́чка управле́ния.

jubilant *adj* лику́ющий; **small wonder he looked ~ after his victory** он победи́л—неда́ром у него́ тако́й лику́ющий вид.

jubilation *n* ликова́ние; **there was general ~ over the home team's win** побе́да ме́стной кома́нды вы́звала всео́бщее ликова́ние.

jubilee *n* юбиле́й; **silver/golden/diamond ~** двадцатипятиле́тний/пятидесятиле́тний/шестидесятиле́тний юбиле́й.

judge *n Law*, *Sport* судья́ (*m*); (*of competitions*) член жюри́; *pl* (**~s**) жюри́ (*indecl*); (*expert*) знато́к; (*connoisseur*) цени́тель (*m*); **he's a good ~ of wines** он большо́й цени́тель/знато́к вин; **he's a poor ~ of horses** он пло́хо разбира́ется в лошадя́х; **you're the best ~ of that** вам лу́чше суди́ть об э́том.

judge *vti vt* суди́ть (*impf*), *also Law*; (*assess*) счита́ть (*impf*); (*estimate*) определ|я́ть (-и́ть); (*decide*) реш|а́ть (-и́ть); **it's hard to ~ his ability/whether he's right or wrong** тру́дно суди́ть о его́ спосо́бностях (*pl*)/, прав он и́ли нет; **don't ~ a man by his looks** по вне́шности не су́дят; **I ~ him a fool/to be very shrewd** по-мо́ему, он про́сто дура́к, я счита́ю, что он о́чень проница́тельный челове́к; **I ~d the distance to be just under a mile** расстоя́ние, на мой взгляд, бы́ло чуть ме́ньше ми́ли; **the question should be ~d on its merits** вопро́с на́до реша́ть по существу́; *Law*: **when will the case be ~d?** когда́ слу́шается де́ло?; **who will ~ the case?** кто судья́ на проце́ссе?

vi суди́ть; **as far as I can ~** наско́лько я могу́ суди́ть; **judging by what you say** су́дя по ва́шим слова́м; **it's not for me to ~** не мне суди́ть; **we asked him to ~ between us** мы попроси́ли его́ рассуди́ть нас; **I am going to ~ at the cattle show** я бу́ду в жюри́ на вы́ставке дома́шнего скота́; **~ for yourself** посуди́ сам.

judgement *n* **1** *Law* приговóр, решéние судá; **to pass/pronounce ~ on a case** объявить приговóр по дéлу; **to reverse a ~** отменять приговóр/решéние судá; **the ~ was in his favour/against him** решéние судá было (не) в егó пóльзу; **to sit in ~ on a case** слýшать/разбирáть дéло

2 (*personal quality*): **he has good/sound ~** он здравомыслящий/благоразýмный человéк; **use your own ~** положись на своё чутьё; **in my ~** по-мóему, на мой взгляд; **an error of ~** ошибочное суждéние; **I rely on his ~** я прислýшиваюсь к егó мнéнию; *Aut* **when it comes to overtaking, he's got good ~** он хорошó чýвствует дистáнцию во врéмя обгóна.

judicial *adj Law* судéбный; **to take/bring ~ proceedings against smb** передáть дéло на когó-л в суд; **a ~ separation** *approx* услóвный развóд.

judiciary *n*: **the ~** корпорáция судéй.

judicious *adj* (благо)разýмный; **a ~ reply** разýмный/толкóвый отвéт; **~ advice** благоразýмный совéт; **a ~ decision** благоразýмное решéние; **by the ~ use of our money** разýмно сократив нáши расхóды; **his statement was very ~** егó замечáние было óчень разýмным.

judo *n* дзюдó (*indecl*).

jug *n* кувшин; **milk ~** молóчник; *sl* **he's in ~** он сидит.

jug *vt Cook* тушить в горшóчке (*impf*); *sl* **he's been ~ged** егó посадили.

juggle *vi* жонглировать (*impf*), *also fig*; **to ~ with balls/facts/words** жонглировать шарáми/фáктами/словáми.

juggler *n* жонглёр.

jugular *adj Anat*: **the ~ vein** ярéмная вéна.

juice *n* (*of fruit, etc.*) сок; *sl* (*petrol*) бензин; **digestive ~s** желýдочный сок (*sing*); *fig* **let him stew in his own ~** пусть он вáрится в сóбственном сокý

juicy *adj* сóчный; *sl* **a ~ bit of gossip** пикáнтная истóрия.

jukebox *n* музыкáльный автомáт.

July *n* июль (*m*); *attr* июльский.

jumble *n* (*pile*) кýча; *CQ* мешанина; пýтаница; **a ~ of clothes lay on the floor** на полý лежáла кýча одéжды; **a ~ of voices/ideas** гул голосóв, пýтаница идéй; *attr*: **~ sale** *approx* благотворительный базáр.

jumble *vt*: **his ties and socks were all ~d up together** егó гáлстуки и носки лежáли все в однóй кýче; **my papers are all ~d up** мои бумáги все перемешáлись.

jump *n* **1** (*act*) прыжóк; скачóк, *also fig*; **at a ~** одним прыжкóм/скачкóм; **a parachute ~** прыжóк с парашютом; *Sport* **high/long ~** прыжки (*pl*) в высотý/в длинý; **a standing/running ~** прыжóк с мéста/с разбéга; *fig*: **a ~ in prices** скачóк цен; **there was a big ~ in temperature** температýра рéзко подскочила; **when I saw her, my heart gave a ~** когдá я увидел её, сéрдце у меня ёкнуло

2 (*in riding*) препятствие, барьéр; **he fell at the first ~** он упáл на пéрвом препятствии/барьéре.

jump *vti vt* перепрыг|ивать, пере|скáкивать чéрез + *A* (-нуть, -скочить); **the horse ~ed the hedge clear** лóшадь чисто взялá барьéр; **he ~ed his horse well** он хорошó взял препятствия; *fig*: **he ~ed the queue** он прошёл без óчереди; **don't ~ the queue** *CQ* не лезь без óчереди.

vi прыг|ать (-нуть), *also Sport*; скакáть (*impf*); **to ~ for joy** прыгать/скакáть от рáдости; **it made me ~** я так и подскочил/подпрыгнул; *CQ* **~ to it!** поживéе!

jump about *vi* подпрыг|ивать (-нуть), под|скáкивать (-скочить)

jump aside *vi*: **I heard the car and ~ed aside** я услышал сзáди машину и отскочил в стóрону

jump at *vi*: **he ~ed at my offer/the chance** он ухватился за моё предложéние/за эту возмóжность

jump down *vi* спрыг|ивать (-нуть); **he ~ed down from/off the roof** он спрыгнул с крыши; *fig CQ* **he ~ed down my throat** он огрызнýлся в отвéт

jump from *vi*: **he ~ed from one subject to another** он перескочил с однóй тéмы на другýю

jump in(to) *vi*: **to ~ into the car** вскáкивать/прыг|ать в машину (вскочить/-нуть); **~ in!** лезь побыстрéй!; **he ~ed into the water/the saddle** он прыгнул в вóду, он вскочил в седлó

jump on *vi*: **he ~ed on to his horse** он вскочил на коня; *fig CQ* **he ~ed on me for saying that** когдá я так сказáл, он так и набрóсился на меня

jump out *vi* вы|скáкивать (-скочить), со|скáкивать (-скочить); **he ~ed out of the window/out from behind a tree** он выскочил из окнá/из-за дéрева; **I ~ed out of bed** я соскочил с кровáти; *CQ* **I nearly ~ed out of my skin with excitement** я чуть не подпрыгнул до потолкá от избытка чувств

jump up *vi* под|скáкивать (-скочить); **the price of butter has ~ed up** ценá на мáсло подскочила; **her temperature ~ed up to 40°** температýра у неё подскочила до сорокá (грáдусов).

jumper *n* **1** *Sport* прыгýн, (*of horse*) скакýн; **he's a good ~** (*of man*) он хорошó прыгает, (*of horse*) это хорóший скакýн

2 (*clothing*) свитер, (вязаная) кóфточка; (*without collar*) джéмпер.

jumping *n Sport* прыжки (*pl*).

jumpy *adj CQ* нéрвный; **I always feel ~ when I fly** я всегдá нéрвничаю в самолёте.

junction *n* соединéние, *also Elec*; (*of rivers*) слияние; *Tech* стык; (*crossroads*) перекрёсток; *Rail* железнодорóжный ýзел, (*station*) узловáя ста́нция; **road ~** пересече́ние доро́г, (*fork*) разви́лка; **T-~** Т-обра́зный перекрёсток.

juncture *n* (*junction*) соедине́ние; *fig* моме́нт; **that was a critical ~ in the affairs of the Roman Empire** э́то был крити́ческий моме́нт в исто́рии Ри́мской импе́рии; **at this ~ it's too early to decide** в настоя́щий моме́нт ра́но принима́ть реше́ние.

June *n* ию́нь (*m*); *attr* ию́ньский.

jungle *n* (*tropical*) джу́нгли (*no sing*); *fig*: **the law of the ~** зако́н джу́нглей; **the garden is a ~ of weeds** сад заро́с сорняка́ми.

junior *n*: **he is my ~ by two years** он на два го́да моло́же/мла́дше меня́; (*UK*) *School* **the ~s** мла́дшие ученики́; (*US*) *Univ* третье-ку́рсник; *Sport* юнио́р.

junior *adj* (*in age or position*) мла́дший; **~ partner/officer** мла́дший партнёр/офице́р; **Robert Fleming Jr** Ро́берт Флеминг сын/мла́дший; **~ school** *approx* нача́льная шко́ла; **~ team** ю́ношеская кома́нда, кома́нда юнио́ров.

junk *n* (*any rubbish*) хлам, старьё, барахло́; (*usu of furniture, etc.*) ру́хлядь; **I must get rid of all this ~** на́до вы́бросить э́тот хлам; *CQ*: **he talks a lot of ~** он говори́т чушь; **this play is a load of ~** э́то дрянна́я пье́са.

junketing *n often pl*, *CQ*: **there were great ~s that night** мы/они́ хорошо́ погуля́ли в тот ве́чер.

junkie *n sl* наркома́н.

junta *n* ху́нта.

jurisdiction *n* юрисди́кция; **such cases fall under the ~ of the city court** таки́е дела́ вхо́дят в ве́дение городско́го суда́, таки́е дела́ рассма́тривает городско́й суд; *fig* **that is not within my ~** э́то не вхо́дит в круг мои́х обя́занностей.

jurisprudence *n* юриспруде́нция; **medical ~** суде́бная медици́на.

jurist *n* юри́ст.

juror *n* присяжный заседа́тель (*m*).

jury *n Law* прися́жные (заседа́тели) (*pl*); (*of competition*) жюри́ (*indecl*); **trial by ~** суд прися́жных; **he was tried by ~** его́ де́ло слу́шал суд прися́жных; *attr*: **~ box** скамья́ прися́жных.

juryman *n see* **juror**.

just *adj* (*fair*) справедли́вый; **a ~ man/sentence** справедли́вый челове́к/пригово́р; **he is always ~ to/towards his subordinates** он всегда́ справедли́в к свои́м подчинённым; **to get one's ~ reward** получи́ть заслу́женную награ́ду; **our suspicions proved to be ~** на́ши подозре́ния оправда́лись.

just *adv* **1** (*exactly*) как раз, то́чно; **our house is ~ opposite** наш дом как раз напро́тив; **he says ~ the opposite** он говори́т как раз противополо́жное; **it's ~ what I need** э́то как раз то, что мне ну́жно; **~ by the station** ря́дом с вокза́лом, пря́мо у вокза́ла; **my car is ~ the same as yours** у меня́ така́я же маши́на, как у вас; **he earns ~ as much as I do** он зараба́тывает сто́лько же, ско́лько я; **I've had ~ about as much of it as I can take** я не могу́ бо́льше э́то терпе́ть; **leave everything ~ as it was** оста́вь всё, как бы́ло; **come ~ as you are** приходи́ в том, в чём ты сейча́с (оде́т); **~ so, that's ~ it** то́чно, вот и́менно; **~ what did he say?** что и́менно он сказа́л?; **~ how many isn't known** ско́лько и́менно — неизве́стно; **that's ~ splendid!** э́то про́сто великоле́пно!

2 (*of time*): **what are you/were you doing ~ now?** что вы де́лаете сейча́с?/сейча́с де́лали?; **I've ~ seen him** я то́лько что его́ ви́дел; **we were ~ talking about you** мы как раз говори́ли о вас; **I was ~ going** я как раз собира́лся уходи́ть; **~ as he started to speak, a shot rang out** в тот са́мый моме́нт, когда́ он заговори́л, разда́лся вы́стрел; **it's ~ 3 o'clock** сейча́с ро́вно три часа́; **lunch is ~ about ready** обе́д почти́ гото́в

3 (*only*) то́лько, про́сто; **it's ~ a joke** э́то то́лько/про́сто шу́тка; **he's still ~ learning** он ещё то́лько у́чится; **have some more?— J. a little, thanks** хоти́те ещё?—Спаси́бо, пожа́луй, ещё немно́жко; **~ one apple!** (*each*) то́лько по одному́ я́блоку!, (*at least*) хотя́ бы одно́ я́блоко

4 (*barely*) едва́, е́ле, е́ле-е́ле; **I ~ caught my plane** я едва́/е́ле-е́ле успе́л на самолёт; **I ~ managed to save him** я едва́ спас его́; **it's only ~ enough for four** э́того е́ле-е́ле хва́тит на четверы́х

5 (*with imperative, actual or implied*): **~ imagine!** поду́мать то́лько!; **~ imagine, he's already a professor!** предста́вь себе́, он уже́ профе́ссор!; **~ listen!** ты то́лько послу́шай!; **~ a second!** одну́ секу́нду!/секу́ндочку!; **~ you wait!** ну погоди́!

6 just as well: it's ~ as well I came with you хорошо́, что я пошёл с тобо́й; **it would be ~ as well if I came with you** пожа́луй лу́чше, е́сли я пойду́ с тобо́й [**NB** *tense*]; **it's ~ as well your house is insured** хорошо́, что ваш дом застрахо́ван; **I might ~ as well have stayed at home** я бы с таки́м же успе́хом оста́лся до́ма

7: I'd ~ as soon stay at home я лу́чше до́ма оста́нусь.

justice *n* **1** справедли́вость; **to do him ~, he is kind** на́до отда́ть ему́ справедли́вость/до́лжное, он добр; **this work does not do you ~** э́та рабо́та не де́лает тебе́ че́сти; **poetic ~** возме́здие судьбы́; *fig*: **he did not do himself ~ at the interview** во вре́мя интервью́ он показа́л себя́ не с лу́чшей стороны́; **you are not doing yourself ~** ты спосо́бен на бо́льшее; **he did ~ to his supper** он возда́л до́лжное у́жину.

2 *Law* правосу́дие; **to administer ~** отправля́ть правосу́дие; **to bring smb to ~** отдава́ть кого́-л под суд; **J. of the Peace** (*abbr* **JP**) мирово́й судья́; (*US*) **Department of J.** министе́рство юсти́ции.

justifiable *adj*: **in the circumstances his behaviour was ~** при таки́х обстоя́тельствах его́ поведе́ние мо́жно оправда́ть.

justifiably *adv*: **he is ~ proud of his son** он не без основа́ний горди́тся сы́ном.

justification *n* оправда́ние; (*ground*) основа́ние; **there can be no ~ for violence** не мо́жет быть оправда́ния наси́лию; **there's no ~ for saying that** нет основа́ния так говори́ть.

justify *vt* опра́вд|ывать (-а́ть); **to ~ oneself** опра́вдываться; **research so far does not ~ such hopes/this theory** пока́ ещё иссле́дования (*pl*) не опра́вдывают таки́х наде́жд/не подтвержда́ют э́ту тео́рию; **am I justified in thinking that...?** впра́ве ли я ду́мать, что...?; **you were quite justified in dismissing him** вы бы́ли соверше́нно пра́вы, уво́лив его́.

justly *adv*: **to act ~** поступа́ть справедли́во; **he was ~ punished** он понёс заслу́женное наказа́ние; **it has been ~ said that...** не без причи́ны погова́ривали, что...

jut *vi* выдава́ться, выступа́ть (*usu impfs*).

juvenile *adj* ю́ношеский, *Law* малоле́тний (*also as n*); (*childish*) де́тский; **~ delinquent/delinquency** несовершенноле́тний престу́пник, де́тская престу́пность.

juxtapose *vt* противопостав|ля́ть (-́ить).

juxtaposition *n* противопоставле́ние.

K

kaleidoscope *n* калейдоско́п.

kangaroo *n* кенгуру́ (*m*) (*indecl*).

kaput *adj CQ*: **my bike is ~** моему́ велосипе́ду коне́ц/капу́т/кры́шка.

Kazakh *n* каза́х, каза́шка.

Kazakh *adj* каза́хский.

kebab *n* (*meat on skewers*) *approx* шашлы́к.

keel *n Naut* киль (*m*).

keen *adj* **1** о́стрый, *also fig*; **a ~ blade** о́строе ле́звие; *fig*: **~ hearing/sight** о́стрый слух, о́строе зре́ние; **a ~ appetite/wind** хоро́ший аппети́т, ре́зкий ве́тер; **a ~ glance/mind** проница́тельный взгляд/ум; **a ~ observer** то́нкий наблюда́тель; **~ disappointment** глубо́кое разочарова́ние; **he has a ~ eye for colour** он то́нко чу́вствует цвет; **there will be ~ competition for the post/***Comm* **contract** на э́то ме́сто бу́дет мно́го кандида́тов, мно́гие бу́дут добива́ться э́того контра́кта; **he showed a ~ interest in my play** он прояви́л большо́й интере́с к мое́й пье́се

2 (*enthusiastic*): **a ~ sportsman/angler** стра́стный спортсме́н/рыболо́в; **he is ~ on her/on football/to help us** он увлечён е́ю, он поме́шан на футбо́ле, он о́чень хо́чет нам помо́чь; **I'm not very ~ on jazz** я не осо́бенно люблю́ джаз.

keenly *adv*: **he looked ~ at me** он при́стально на меня́ посмотре́л; **I am ~ interested in classical music** я о́чень люблю́ класси́ческую му́зыку; **I felt the loss ~** я о́стро ощуща́л э́ту поте́рю.

keep *n*: **to earn one's ~** зараба́тывать себе́ на пропита́ние; **I pay £40 a week for my ~** я плачу́ со́рок фу́нтов в неде́лю за ко́мнату и пита́ние; **he's not worth his ~** ему́ зря де́ньги пла́тят.

keep *vti vt* **1** (*retain, set aside*) держа́ть (*impf*) *and compounds*; оста́в|ля́ть (-́ить); **he kept his hands in his pockets** он держа́л ру́ки в карма́нах; **you may ~ the book** мо́жешь оста́вить э́ту кни́гу себе́; **he's ~ing the (***hotel***) room (on) for another week** он оста́вил [**NB** *tense*] за собо́й но́мер ещё на неде́лю; **~ some lunch/a seat/my seat for me** оста́вь мне что́-нибудь пое́сть, займи́ мне ме́сто, посторожи́ моё ме́сто; **he kept his place in the team** он удержа́л своё ме́сто в кома́нде; **I'd like to ~ the job** я не хоте́л бы уходи́ть с э́той рабо́ты; **he's ~ing (to) his room/the house** (*because ill*) он сиди́т до́ма; **~ me in the picture** держи́ меня́ в ку́рсе де́ла; **he ~s himself to himself** он де́ржится особняко́м; **~ it to yourself** пома́лкивай об э́том

2 (*keep safe, preserve, stock*) храни́ть (со-); сохран|я́ть (-и́ть); **he ~s his valuables in the safe** он храни́т/де́ржит свои́ це́нности в се́йфе; **he ~s all his old magazines** он храни́т все ста́рые журна́лы; **where do you ~ the sugar?** где у тебя́ са́хар?; **do you ~ spare parts?** у вас есть запча́сти?; **to ~ a secret** храни́ть секре́т/та́йну; **I kept my temper/***CQ* **my cool** я сохраня́л хладнокро́вие *or* я сде́рживался

3 (*observe*): **he kept his promise/word** он сдержа́л обеща́ние/сло́во; **to ~ the law/rules** соблю|да́ть зако́н/пра́вила (-сти́); **I've got an appointment to ~ at 3 o'clock** у меня́ свида́ние/встре́ча в три часа́; **he did not ~ his appointment** он не пришёл к назна́ченному ча́су

4 (*detain*): **to ~ smb under arrest/observation** держа́ть кого́-л под аре́стом/под наблюде́нием; **I kept him at home/in bed** я не разреши́л ему́ выходи́ть и́з дому/встава́ть; **I hope I didn't ~ you** наде́юсь, я вас не задержа́л; **flu kept me from the office/off work** из-за гри́ппа я не ходи́л на рабо́ту

5 (*own, maintain, support*): **to ~ a family** содержа́ть семью́ (*impf*); **we can't afford to ~ (up) such a big house** мы не мо́жем содержа́ть тако́й большо́й дом; **to ~ hens/a shop** держа́ть кур/ла́вку; **they ~ a dog** у них соба́ка; **my pay barely ~s me in cigarettes** мое́й зарпла́ты едва́ хвата́ет на сигаре́ты

6 (*diary, etc.*): **to ~ a diary/the score/accounts** вести́ дневни́к/счёт/счета́ (*only in impf*); **I kept a note of the title of the book** я записа́л назва́ние кни́ги

7 (*+ adj, verb, etc.*): **they kept me waiting** они́ заста́вили меня́ ждать; **~ the soup hot** держи́ суп на огне́; **to ~ a room clean/tidy** подде́рживать чистоту́/поря́док в ко́мнате; **his encouragement/the cup of tea kept me going** его́ подде́ржка/ча́шка ча́ю придала́ мне сил; **he kept his eyes fixed on her** он не своди́л с неё глаз; **I kept the engine running** я не вы-ключил мотóра; *CQ* ~ **it clean!** тóлько без непристóйностей!

vi 1 (*continue*): **he kept (on) talking** он продолжáл говорúть; **I ~ forgetting to write to her** я всё забывáю ей написáть; **she ~s crying** онá всё врéмя плáчет; ~ **straight on** идúте прямо; ~ **to the right till you come to the church** держúтесь прáвой стороны́, покá не дойдёте до цéркви

2 (*remain*): **I kept calm** я оставáлся спокóйным; ~ **calm!/still!** спокóйно!, не вертúсь!; **he/the press kept silent** он молчáл, прéсса хранúла молчáние; ~ **together in the forest** держúтесь вмéсте в лесý

3 (*of health*): **how are you ~ing?** как поживáете?; **she's (not) ~ing well** онá хорошó/невáжно себя чýвствует; **he ~s very fit** он всегдá в фóрме

4 (*of food*) хранúться (*usu impf*); **will these apples ~?** эти яблоки дóлго хранятся?; **the fish will ~ up to three days in the fridge** ры́ба хранúтся в холодúльнике до трёх дней; *fig* **that will ~ till tomorrow** это подождёт до зáвтра

keep at *vti*: **he used to ~ us at our studies** он заставлял нас занимáться; **I kept at it and finished by supper time** я сидéл, не разгибáясь, весь день и к ýжину закóнчил всё; ~ **at it!** продолжáй! (*continue*), не сдавáйся! (*don't give up*)

keep away *vti vt*: ~ **the children away from the fire** не подпускáйте детéй к огню́

vi: **I'm ~ing well away from him** я держýсь от негó подáльше

keep back *vti vt*: **to ~ back tears** сдéрж|ивать слёзы (-áть); **have I kept you back?** я вас не задержáл?; **they ~ back £5 from my wages for insurance** у меня из зарплáты удéрживают/вычитáют пять фýнтов на страховáние; **we kept the news back from her** мы скрывáли от неё эту нóвость

vi: ~ **back there!** отойдúте назáд!

keep down *vti vt*: **to ~ down one's head** при|гибáть гóлову (-гнýть); **in summer one can't ~ down the weeds** лéтом трýдно борóться с сорнякáми; **to ~ down prices** сохранять ýровень цен; **he can't ~ anything down** чтó бы он ни съел, егó всё врéмя рвёт

vi: ~ **down or you'll be seen** пригнúсь,/(*if already down*) не выпрямляйся, а то тебя увúдят

keep from *vt*: **he kept me from my work** он не давáл/он мешáл мне рабóтать; **I couldn't ~ myself from crying** я не мог удержáться от слёз

keep in *vti vt*: **we ~ the horses in in winter** зимóй мы дéржим лошадéй в конюшне; **he was kept in at school** егó остáвили пóсле урóков; **I do some typing at nights to ~ my hand in** я немнóго печáтаю на машúнке по вечерáм, чтóбы рукá не отвы́кла

vi: **the stove ~s in all night** печь тóпится всю ночь; **you'd better ~ in with him** ты лýчше с ним не ссóрься

keep off *vti vt*: ~ **the wasps off the jam** отгонú ос от варéнья; **the police kept the fans off the pitch** полúция не подпускáла болéльщиков к пóлю; **I ~ off fats/politics** я не ем жúрного, я держýсь подáльше от полúтики (*sing*); ~ **your hands off!** уберú рýки!

vi: **the rain kept off till evening** дождь пошёл тóлько вéчером; ~ **off the grass** не ходú по травé, (*notice*) «по газóнам (*pl*) не ходúть»

keep on *vti vt*: **I kept my coat on** я не снимáл пальтó; **they kept him on for another year** онú продержáли егó там ещё год

vi CQ: **she ~s on at me about smoking** онá меня заéла из-за курéния; **he will ~ on about his adventures in Africa** он прожужжúт нам все ýши о свойх приключéниях в Áфрике; ~ **your hair on!** не нéрвничай!, спокóйнее!

keep out *vti vt*: **they ~ the cattle out all winter** онú всю зúму дéржат скот под откры́тым нéбом; **I was kept out of the room** меня не впускáли в кóмнату; **the blinds ~ out the light** штóры не пропускáют свет

vi: **I kept out of his way/danger/the argument** я избегáл егó/опáсности/спóра; ~ **out!** не входú!, (*notice*) «вход воспрещён!»

keep to *vti vt*: **I kept him to his promise** я застáвил егó сдержáть обещáние

vi: **to ~ to a strict diet/the subject** соблюдáть стрóгую диéту, придéрживаться тéмы

keep up *vti vt*: **to ~ one's head/spirits up** держáть гóлову высокó, не пáдать дýхом; **they kept me up last night till 2 o'clock** из-за них я вчерá не ложúлся до двух часóв нóчи; **I'm ~ing up my German** я старáюсь не забы́ть немéцкий язы́к; **he kept up an endless flow of small talk** он без концá молóл какýю-то чепухý; **to ~ up paintwork** поднов|лять окрáску (-úть)

vi: **if the weather ~s up** éсли хорóшая погóда ещё продéржится; **I've kept up with them since childhood** я поддéрживаю связь с нúми с дéтства; **he can't ~ up with the others** он отстаёт от другúх (*walking or in work*); **to ~ up with current affairs/the fashion** быть в кýрсе дел, следúть за мóдой; **wages aren't ~ing up with prices** зáработная плáта отстаёт от рóста цен; **to ~ up with the Joneses** быть не хýже соседéй, не отставáть от соседéй.

keeper *n* (*custodian, curator*) хранúтель (*m*); (*of lighthouse, etc.*) смотрúтель (*m*); (*warder*) надзирáтель (*m*); (*gamekeeper*) леснúчий; (*at zoo*) служúтель (*m*) зоопáрка.

keep-fit *adj*: **to do ~ exercises** дéлать зарядку.

keeping *n* **1: it's in his safe ~** это у негó на хранéнии

2: his actions are out of ~ with his promises егó словá расхóдятся с дéлом; **to be in ~ with** соотвéтствовать + *D*.

keepsake *n*: **I gave it her as a ~** я подарúл ей это на пáмять.

keg *n* бочóнок.

kennel *n* конурá.

kerb *n* край тротуáра; **to draw into the ~** остановúться у тротуáра.

kerbstone *n* бордю́рный кáмень (*m*).

kernel *n* (*of nut*) ядрó.

kerosene *n* керосúн; *attr*: **a ~ lamp** керосúновая лáмпа.

kestrel *n* пустельгá.

kettle *n* чáйник; **put on the ~** постáвь чáйник; **the ~ is boiling** чáйник кипúт.

kettle drum *n* литáвра.

key *n* **1** (*to door*) ключ (от двéри); **skeleton/master ~** отмы́чка; **under lock and ~** под замкóм; *fig* **the ~ to the mystery/problem** ключ к разгáдке тáйны/к решéнию проблéмы; *attr*: **a ~ position/industry** ключевáя позúция, ведýщая óтрасль промы́шленности

2 (*on piano, typewriter*) клáвиша; *pl* (**~s**) клавиатýра (*collect*); (*of wind instrument*) клáпан

3 *Mus*: **major/minor ~** мажóрная/минóрная тонáльность; **it's in the ~ of A major** э́то в тонáльности ля мажóр.

keyboard *n* клавиатýра.

keyhole *n* замóчная сквáжина; **to listen at/look through the ~** подслýшивать у двéри, подсмáтривать в/сквозь замóчную сквáжину.

key ring *n* кольцó для ключéй.

keystone *n Archit* замóк, замкóвый кáмень (*m*).

key up *vt usu pass*: **I was all ~ed up before the exam** я сúльно нéрвничал пéред экзáменом.

khaki *n and adj* хáки (*indecl*).

kick *n* удáр; (*of gun*) отдáча; **a ~ on the shins/on the backside** удáр по гóлени, пинóк под зад; *Sport*: **free/penalty ~** свобóдный/штрафнóй удáр; **he took a flying ~ at the ball** он удáрил по мячý с лёта; *fig CQ*: **this drink has a lot of ~** э́тот напúток с ног вáлит; **I do it just for ~s** я дéлаю э́то прóсто рáди удовóльствия; **he needs a good ~ in the pants** егó нáдо хорошéнько вздуть.

kick *vti vt* удар|я́ть ногóй (´-ить); (*of horse*) ляг|áть (-нýть); **he/the horse ~ed me** он удáрил меня́ ногóй, лóшадь лягнýла меня́; **when he fell they ~ed him** когдá он упáл, онú стáли бить егó ногáми; *Sport* **he ~ed the ball over the sideline/above the goal** он вы́бил мяч за боковýю лúнию, он удáрил вы́ше ворóт; *fig*: **don't ~ a man when he's down** лежáчего не бьют; **it's no use ~ing against fate** бесполéзно сопротивля́ться судьбé; *CQ*: **I was ~ing my heels all morning** я всё ýтро прождáл бéз толку; **if you ask too much of him, he'll ~** éсли трéбовать от негó слúшком мнóгого, он начнёт брыкáться; **I could have ~ed myself for forgetting the tickets** я забы́л дóма билéты и был готóв кусáть себé лóкти от досáды

vi: **be careful, this horse ~s** осторóжно, э́та лóшадь лягáется; **the baby lay ~ing in the pram** ребёнок лежáл в коля́ске и дры́гал нóжками; **this gun ~s** у э́того ружья́ большáя отдáча

kick about/around *vti vt*: **let's go and ~ a ball about in the park** пойдём поиграéм в мяч в пáрке; *fig CQ* **don't let yourself be ~ed around** не позволя́й собóй помыкáть

vi: **their toys are always ~ing about/around on the floor** их игрýшки вéчно разбрóсаны где попáло

kick off *vti vt*: **I ~ed off my shoes** я сбрóсил ботúнки

vi Sport CQ: **when do we ~ off?** когдá мы начинáем?

kick out *vt CQ*: **he was ~ed out of his job** егó вы́гнали с рабóты

kick over *vt*: **he ~ed over the pail** он споткнýлся о ведрó и опрокú|нул егó (*impf* -дывать)

kick up *vt*: **to ~ up a fuss** под|нимáть шум (-ня́ть).

kick-off *n Sport CQ*: **~ is at 3 o'clock** начáло мáтча в три часá.

kick-starter *n* (*on motorcycle, lawnmower*) ножнóй стартёр.

kid *n* **1** (*young goat*) козлёнок; (*as meat*) козля́тина

2 (*leather*) лáйка; *attr*: **~ gloves** лáйковые перчáтки

3 *CQ* ребёнок; (*without reference to age*) **come on, ~s, let's go** ну, ребя́та, пошлú!; (*US*) *CQ*: **look here, ~, you've got it coming to you!** смотрú, малы́ш, достáнется тебé на орéхи!; **she's a swell ~!** онá дéвочка что нáдо!; *attr* (*US*): **my ~ brother/sister** мой млáдший брат, моя́ млáдшая сестрá.

kid *vti vt CQ* обмáн|ывать (-ýть); **you can't ~ me** меня́ не обмáнешь/не проведёшь; **we're only ~ding ourselves** мы тóлько обмáнываем себя́

vi: **don't worry, I was only ~ding** не волнýйся, я пошутúл; **no ~ding?** ты серьёзно?

kidnap *vt* похи|щáть (людéй) (´-тить).

kidney *n Anat* пóчка.

kidney bean *n* фасóль.

kill *vt* **1** уби|вáть (´-ть), *also fig*; (*slaughter animals*) заби|вáть (´-ть); *in pass* погиб|áть (´-нуть); **he ~ed his own brother/a pig** он убúл своегó брáта, он забúл свинью́; **he was ~ed in the war** он погúб/был убúт на войнé; **drink ~ed him** егó погубúло пья́нство; **he ~ed himself** он покóнчил с собóй; **the frost ~ed the tulips** морóзом побúло (*impers*) тюльпáны

2 *fig uses*: **I was just ~ing time** я прóсто убивáл врéмя; **this remark ~ed the conversation** э́то замечáние испóртило всю бесéду; **mustard ~s the flavour of the meat** горчúца убивáет вкус мя́са; **he's ~ing himself with work** он изводúт себя́ рабóтой; **the heat is ~ing me** я умирáю от жары́; **to ~ a rumour** пресе|кáть слýхи (*pl*) (´-чь); **she is dressed to ~** онá вызывáюще одéта.

killer *n* убúйца (*m and f*); **rabies is a ~** бéшенство — смертéльная болéзнь.

killing *adj* смертéльный; *fig CQ* **it was ~** вот умóра!

killjoy *n*: **he's a ~** он вéчно отравля́ет други́м удовóльствие.

kilogramme, (*US*) **kilogram,** *CQ* **kilo** *n* килогрáмм, *CQ* килó (*indecl*).

kilometre, (*US*) **kilometer** *n* киломéтр; **40 ~s an hour** сóрок киломéтров в час.

kilowatt *n* киловáтт.

kilowatt-hour *n* киловáтт-час.

kilt *n* ю́бка шотлáндского гóрца.

kin *n collect* родня́; родны́е, рóдственники (*pls*); **next of ~** ближáйший рóдственник.

kind[1] *n* **1** (*race, species*) род; **human ~** человéческий род, род людскóй; **they differ in ~** они́ рáзные по натýре; **it's perfect of its ~** э́то в своём рóде совершéнство

2 (*class, sort, type*) сорт; (*variety*) разнови́дность; (*breed*) порóда; **what ~ of cheese do you want?** какóй сорт сы́ра/какóй сыр вам нýжен?; **what ~ of wheat/dog is that?** какóй э́то сорт пшени́цы?, какóй порóды э́та собáка?; **what ~ of car have you?** какóй мáрки вáша маши́на?; **what ~ of person is he/of rose is this?** что он за человéк?, что э́то за рóза?; **he's not that ~ of person/the ~ of person to refuse** он не такóй человéк, он никогдá не откáжет; **she's the ~ of woman who likes to know everything** онá из тех жéнщин, котóрые хотя́т всё знать; **all ~s of people** сáмые рáзные лю́ди; **these are just the ~ of examples I want** мне нужны́ и́менно таки́е примéры; *iron* **what ~ of soup do you call this?** и э́то ты называ́ешь сýпом?; **they are two of a ~** что оди́н, что другóй

3 *phrases*: **something of the ~** чтó-то/чтó-нибудь в э́том рóде; **I said/I'll do nothing of the ~** я ничегó подóбного не говори́л/не сдéлаю; *CQ*: **she ill? Nothing of the ~!** онá больнá? Да ничегó подóбного!; *pejor* **they gave us coffee of a ~** нам дáли чтó-то отдалённо напоминáющее кóфе

4: a kind of: it's a ~ of box э́то такáя корóбочка; **I had a ~ of feeling it would happen** у меня́ бы́ло такóе чýвство, что э́то произойдёт; *CQ as adv*: **it's ~ of difficult/awkward** э́то трудновáто, э́то кáк-то неудóбно/нелóвко; **aren't you pleased?—Well yes, ~ of** ты довóлен?—Да, как бýдто

5 (*goods as opposed to money*): **payment in ~** оплáта натýрой; *fig* **I repaid her in ~** (*for good deed*) я её отблагодари́л, (*for bad deed*) я ей отплати́л той же монéтой.

kind[2] *adj* дóбрый; **it was a ~ act** э́то бы́ло дóброе дéло; **he was very ~ to me** он был óчень добр ко мнé; **would you be so ~ as to tell me...** бýдьте добры́, скажи́те мне...; **that is very ~ of you** вы óчень любéзны/добры́; **to be ~ to animals** хорошó относи́ться к живóтным.

kindergarten *n* дéтский сад.

kind-hearted *adj* дóбрый.

kindle *vti vt* раз|жигáть (-жéчь), *also fig*; (*a stove*) рас|тáпливать (-топи́ть); **to ~ a fire/a bonfire** затопи́тьками́н, разжéчь костёр; **a spark ~d the dry wood** сухóе дéрево загорéлось от и́скры; *fig* **to ~ passions/the imagination/interest** разжигáть стрáсти, воспламен|я́ть воображéние (-и́ть), возбу|ждáть интерéс (-ди́ть)

vi: **wood won't ~ if it's wet** сыры́е дровá (*pl*) плóхо разгорáются.

kindliness *n* добротá.

kindling *n* растóпка.

kindly *adj* дóбрый.

kindly *adv* любéзно; **she ~ helped me with my luggage** онá любéзно помоглá мне с багажóм; **I feel ~ disposed towards him** я к немý располóжен; **would you ~ pass the butter** бýдьте добры́,/любéзны, передáйте мне мáсло; **~ listen when I'm talking to you** извóль слýшать, когдá я с тобóй говорю́; **he didn't take ~ to that sort of treatment** емý не óчень понрáвилось такóе обращéние; **he doesn't take ~ to work** он не óчень-то лю́бит рабóтать.

kindness *n* (*quality*) добротá; (*act*) **a ~** любéзность; **to do smb a ~** оказáть комý-л любéзность.

kindred *n collect* родня́; родны́е, рóдственники (*pls*).

kindred *adj* рóдственный; **~ tribes/languages** рóдственные племенá/языки́; **~ diseases** схóдные/аналоги́чные заболевáния; *fig* **~ souls** рóдственные дýши.

king *n* корóль (*m*), *also Chess, Cards*; **K. of England** корóль А́нглии; *fig*: **~ of beasts** царь звéрей; **oil ~s** нефтяны́е короли́.

kingdom *n* королéвство; цáрство, *also fig*; **animal/plant ~** живóтное/растúтельное цáрство.

kingfisher *n* зиморóдок.

kink *n* (*in rope, etc.*) перегиб; *fig* **he has some odd ~s** у негó есть свои́ причýды.

kinship *n* родствó, *also fig*.

kinsman *n* рóдственник.

kiosk *n* киóск; *Tel* **I'm calling from a ~** я звоню́ из автомáта.

kip *vi CQ*: **I'm going to ~ down for half an hour** пойдý вздремнý полчасá; **he ~ped down on the floor** он спал на полý.

kipper *n* копчёная селёдка.

Kirghiz *n* кирги́з, кирги́зка.

Kirghiz *adj* кирги́зский.

kiss *n* поцелýй; **to give smb a ~** поцеловáть когó-л; **give her a ~ from me** поцелýй её за меня́.

kiss *vti* целовáть(ся) (по-); **she ~ed my cheek** онá поцеловáла меня́ в щёку; **~ and be friends** поцелýйтесь и помири́тесь.

kit *n* (*belongings, luggage*) вéщи; *Mil* ли́чное обмундировáние и снаряжéние; **skiing ~** лы́жное снаряжéние; **tool ~** набóр инструмéнтов; **shaving ~** бри́твенный прибóр; **first-aid ~** аптéчка; **tropical ~** костю́м для трóпиков.

kitbag *n Mil* вещевóй мешóк.

kitchen *n* кýхня; *attr*: **~ garden** огорóд; **~ range/sink** кýхонная плитá/рáковина.

kite *n Orn* ко́ршун; (*toy*) бума́жный змей; **to fly a ~** пуска́ть змея́/*fig* про́бный шар.

kitten *n* котёнок.

kitty *n* (*cat*) *dim* ки́ска; *Cards* банк; **here ~-~!** кис-ки́с!; *fig CQ* **how much have we in the ~?** ско́лько у нас сейча́с де́нег?

kleptomaniac *n* клептома́н.

knack *n* уме́ние, сноро́вка; **there is a ~ to it** для э́того тре́буется уме́ние/сноро́вка; **he has the ~ to say the right thing** он всегда́ зна́ет, что сказа́ть; **he has a ~ with animals** он уме́ет обраща́ться с живо́тными; **it is easy when you have the ~** легко́, когда́ зна́ешь, ка́к де́лать.

knapsack *n* рюкза́к; *Mil* ра́нец.

knave *n pejor* моше́нник; *Cards* вале́т.

knead *vt* (*dough, clay*) меси́ть (*impf*).

knee *n* коле́но; **to go (down) on one's ~s** станови́ться на коле́ни; **my trousers are out/have gone at the ~s** у меня́ брю́ки протёрлись на коле́нках; **she sat on my ~** она́ сиде́ла у меня́ на коле́нях (*pl*); **I felt weak at the ~s** у меня́ дрожа́ли коле́ни.

kneecap *n Anat* коле́нная ча́шечка.

knee-deep, knee-high *advs*: **he was ~-deep in water** он стоя́л по коле́но в воде́; **the grass was ~-high** трава́ доходи́ла до коле́н.

knee joint *n Anat* коле́нный суста́в.

kneel *vi* (*act*) ста|нови́ться на коле́ни (-ть); (*state*) стоя́ть на коле́нях (*impf*).

kneepad *n Sport* наколе́нник.

knickerbockers *npl* бри́джи.

knickers *npl* тру́сики; (*warm, for winter*) (же́нские) трико́ (*pl, indecl*).

knick-knack *n* безделу́шка, побряку́шка.

knife *n* нож; **the wind cut like a ~** дул ре́зкий ве́тер; *CQ* **he has his ~ into me** у него́ про́тив/на меня́ зуб.

knife *vt*: **he was ~d** его́ уда́рили ножо́м.

knife edge *n* остриё ножа́, *also fig*; (*on mountain*) о́стрый гре́бень (*m*).

knife-grinder *n* точи́льщик.

knight *n Hist* ры́царь (*m*).

knit *vti* вяза́ть (с-); **to ~ a jumper by hand/machine** вяза́ть ко́фточку на спи́цах/на маши́не; *Med* **the bone has ~ted together well** кость хорошо́ срасла́сь; *fig* **to ~ one's brows** сдви́нуть бро́ви (*usu pf*).

knitted *adj* вя́заный.

knitting *n* вяза́нье; **whose ~ is this?** кто э́то вя́жет?; **I was doing my ~** я вяза́ла; *attr*: **~ needle** вяза́льная спи́ца.

knitwear *n* трикота́ж (*collect*), трикота́жные изде́лия (*pl*).

knob *n* кно́пка (*if pushed*), ру́чка (*if pulled or turned*); (*protuberance*) вы́пуклость; (*of door*) ру́чка; (*of walking stick*) набалда́шник; *Aut* **that ~ works the choke** э́то ру́чка подсо́са; *Cook* **a ~ of butter** кусо́к ма́сла.

knobbly *adj* (*of stick, etc.*) шишкова́тый; (*of tree trunk, etc.*) бугри́стый.

knock *n* стук; **I hear a ~** я слы́шал стук [**NB** *tense*]; **there was a ~ at the door** в дверь постуча́ли; **give me a ~ at 8 o'clock** постучи́ ко мне в во́семь часо́в утра́; **a ~ on the head** уда́р по голове́.

knock *vti vt* сту́к|ать (*semel* -нуть); удар|я́ть (-́ить); *also compounds of* бить; **they ~ed him on the head** его́ сту́кнули/уда́рили по голове́; **I ~ed my head against/on a beam** я сту́кнулся/уда́рился голово́й о ба́лку; **to ~ a hole in a wall** проби|ва́ть отве́рстие в стене́ (-́ть); **to ~ the bottom out of a box** выбива́ть дно у я́щика; **she ~ed the ball out of my hand** она́ вы́била мяч у меня́ из рук; **I ~ed the cup flying off the table** я смахну́л ча́шку со стола́; *fig*: **to ~ one's head against a brick wall** би́ться голово́й о сте́ну (*only in impf*); **he ~ed the bottom out of her argument** он опрове́рг её до́воды (*pl*); **her death ~ed the bottom out of his world** её смерть сломи́ла его́; **the news ~ed me flat** э́то изве́стие ошеломи́ло меня́

vi стуча́ть (по-); **do stop ~ing on the table** переста́нь стуча́ть по́ столу; **somebody is ~ing on the door** кто́-то стучи́тся в дверь; **I ~ed for 5 minutes and then went away** я мину́т пять стуча́л в дверь, а пото́м ушёл; *Aut* **the engine is ~ing** мото́р стучи́т

knock about *vti vt*: **the boys are ~ing each other about in the yard** мальчи́шки деру́тся во дворе́; **the car was badly ~ed about** маши́на была́ си́льно помя́та

vi CQ: **he's ~ed about the world quite a bit** где он то́лько ни побыва́л; **he ~s about with some odd characters** он во́дит компа́нию с каки́ми-то стра́нными ти́пами; **the gloves must be ~ing about the room somewhere** перча́тки валя́ются где́-то в ко́мнате

knock back *vt CQ*: **he can easily ~ back six pints** ему́ ничего́ не сто́ит вы́пить полдю́жины кру́жек пи́ва за оди́н присе́ст; **here, ~ this back** на, вы́пей; **our new car ~ed us back a bit** но́вая маши́на весьма́ пошатну́ла на́ши фина́нсы

knock down *vt*: **I/the bus ~ed him down** я сбил/сшиб его́ с ног, его́ сшиб авто́бус; **the horse ~ed down the last fence** ло́шадь сби́ла после́дний барье́р; **they are going to ~ this house down** э́тот дом хотя́т сноси́ть; **this house is due to be ~ed down** э́тот дом предназна́чен на снос; *fig*: (*at an auction*) **the vase was ~ed down for £1** ва́за пошла́ с молотка́ за оди́н фунт; **the assistant ~ed the price down by £5** продаве́ц сба́вил це́ну на пять фу́нтов; *CQ* **I got the price ~ed down by £3** я вы́торговал три фу́нта

knock in *vt*: **to ~ in a nail** в|бива́ть/за|бива́ть гвоздь (*pfs* -би́ть)

knock into *vt fig CQ*: **I ~ed it into his head that...** я всё-таки вбил ему́ в го́лову, что...

knock off *vti vt*: **I ~ed the vase off the shelf** я урони́л ва́зу с по́лки; *fig*: **she ~ed 20p off the price** она́ сба́вила/уступи́ла два́дцать пе́нсов; **he ~ed 10 seconds off the record** он улу́чшил реко́рд на де́сять секу́нд; *CQ* **I want**

to ~ this article off by 6 o'clock я хочу закóнчить э́ту статью к шести́ часа́м

vi fig CQ: **they ~ed off early** они́ кóнчили рабóту рáно; **let's ~ off for half an hour/for today** давáйте устрóим переры́в на полчаса́, давáйте на э́том сегóдня закóнчим

knock out *vt* (*in boxing*) нокаути́ровать (*impf and pf*); **he was ~ed out by the blow** он потеря́л сознáние от удáра; **he ~ed out his pipe** он вы́бил трýбку; *fig* **I ~ed the nonsense out of him** я вы́бил из негó дурь

knock over *vt* (*a person*) сби|вáть/сшиб|áть с ног (-ть/-и́ть); (*a thing*) опроки́|дывать (-нуть)

knock together/up *vt Cook* стря́пать (со-); (*in carpentry*) сбивáть, скол|áчивать (-оти́ть)

knock up *vti vt*: **~ me up at 6 o'clock** постучи́ мне (в дверь) в шесть часóв; **we had to ~ the doctor up in the middle of the night** нам пришлóсь разбуди́ть врачá среди́ нóчи; *CQ* **he was ~ed up for a week with flu** он пролежáл недéлю с гри́ппом; *Sport* **to ~ up points** на|бирáть очки́ (-брáть)

vi: (*in tennis*) **to ~ up** раз|минáться (-мя́ться), разы́гр|ываться (-áться).

knockabout *adj*: **~ comedy** фарс, балагáн; **~ clothes** повседнéвная одéжда.

knockdown *adj*: **they were selling tights at ~ prices** там продавáлись колгóтки по сни́женным цéнам.

knocker *n* двернóй молотóк, двернóе кольцó.

knocking *n* стук.

knockout *n* (*in boxing*) нокáут; *CQ* **the show was a ~** спектáкль был сногсшибáтельный.

knockout *adj Sport*: **~ competition** отбóрочные соревновáния (*pl*), соревновáния (*pl*) с выбывáнием.

knock-up *n* (*in tennis*): **before the match they have 5 minutes ~** пéред игрóй им даётся пять минýт разми́нки; **let's have a ~** давáй устрóим разми́нку.

knoll *n* хóлмик; (*low mound*) бугóр.

knot *n* **1** ýзел, *also Naut*; **a ~ in a shoe lace/thread/rope** ýзел на шнуркé/на ни́тке/на канáте; **to tie/untie a ~** завязáть/развязáть ýзел; *Naut* **the vessel does 20 ~s** сýдно дéлает двáдцать узлóв в час; *fig*: **a ~ of boys** кýчка мальчи́шек; **I got tied up in ~s** я запýтался в словáх

2 (*in wood*) сук, сучóк.

knot *vti vt* завя́з|ывать узлóм (-áть)

vi: **silk thread ~s so easily** шёлковые ни́тки (*pl*) вéчно закрýчиваются в узелки́.

knotty *adj* (*of a rope*) с узлáми; (*gnarled*) узловáтый; (*with knots in grain of wood*) сучковáтый; *fig* **a ~ problem** слóжная проблéма.

know *n*: **he's in the ~** он в кýрсе дéла.

know *vt* **1** знать (*impf*); **do you ~ this place?** ты знáешь э́то мéсто?; **I don't ~ whether to go or not** я не знáю—идти́ и́ли нет; **let me ~** дáй(те) мне знать; **to ~ for sure/from experience** знать навернякá/по óпыту; **to ~ one's job/place** знать своё дéло/своё мéсто; **he doesn't ~ his own mind** он сам не знáет, чегó хóчет; **to ~ what's what** знать что к чемý; **how should I ~?** откýда мне знать?; **as far as I ~** наскóлько мне извéстно; **for all I ~ he might still be in Scotland** откýда мне знать, мóжет быть, он ещё в Шотлáндии; **goodness ~s** бог егó знáет; **you ~ what?** знáешь что?; *CQ*: **what do you ~!** подýмать тóлько!; **I wouldn't ~ him from Adam** да я срóду егó не ви́дел

2 (*of things, techniques*): **he ~s about wine** он понимáет толк в ви́нах; **he doesn't ~ one wine from another** он не отличáет однó винó от другóго; **he ~s all there is to ~ about cars** в маши́нах он знáет толк; **to ~ how to do smth** умéть дéлать что-л; **do you ~ French?** вы знáете францýзский?; **to get to ~ (about) smth** узнáть о чём-л

3 (*be acquainted*): **I don't ~ him but I ~ of him** я с ним не знакóм, но слы́шал о нём; **to get to ~ smb** познакóмиться с кем-л; **now that I ~ him better, I like him** я узнáл егó побли́же, и он мне понрáвился [**NB** *tense*]

4 (*recognize*) узн|авáть (-áть); **I knew him instantly by his voice** я егó срáзу же узнáл по гóлосу; **I ~ him by sight** я знáю егó в лицó.

know-all *n CQ* всезнáйка (*m and f*).

know-how *n* умéние; **for this job one needs some technical ~** для э́той рабóты нýжно немнóго разбирáться в тéхнике.

knowing *n*: **there's no ~ what will happen to us** трýдно сказáть, что с нáми дáльше бýдет; **he is (a man) worth ~** с ним стóит познакóмиться.

knowing *adj*: **he's a ~ fellow** он лóвкий мáлый; **a ~ look** многозначи́тельный взгляд.

knowingly *adv* (*deliberately*) сознáтельно.

knowledge *n* знáние (*often pl*); **he has a good ~ of Shakespeare/Russian** он хорошó знáет Шекспи́ра/рýсский язы́к; **lack of ~** недостáток знáний; **first-hand ~** свéдения (*pl*) из пéрвых рук; **without my ~** без моегó вéдома; **that is common ~** э́то всем извéстно; **it has come to my ~ that...** мне стáло извéстно, что...; **my ~ of him is slight** я егó мáло знáю/почти́ не знáю; **I have a reading ~ of German** я читáю по-немéцки.

knowledgeable *adj*: **he is very ~ about cars** он хорошó разбирáется в маши́нах.

known *adj* извéстный; **~ facts** извéстные фáкты; **it became ~ that...** стáло извéстно, что...; **he is ~ for his collection of stamps** он знамени́т своéй коллéкцией мáрок; **he is ~ to the police** он извéстен поли́ции; **he is ~ under the name of Petrov** егó знáют под фами́лией Петрóва; **he made his views ~** он вы́сказал свои́ взгля́ды; **to make oneself ~ to smb** представля́ться комý-л.

knuckle *n* сустáв/*CQ* костя́шка пáльца; *fig* **to rap smb over the ~s** дать комý-л нагоня́й.

knuckle *vi CQ*: **he ~d down to the task** он энерги́чно взя́лся за дéло; **he had to ~ under** он дóлжен был подчини́ться.

knuckleduster *n* кастéт.

koala (bear) *n* коáла, сýмчатый медвéдь.

Komsomol *n* комсомóл; *attr* комсомóльский; ~ **member** комсомóл|ец, *f* -ка.

kopeck *n* копéйка.

Koran *n* корáн.

Korean *n* корéец, кореянка.

Korean *adj* корéйский.

Kremlin *n* Кремль (*m*).

kudos *n CQ*: **he got all the** ~ вся слáва достáлась емý.

L

label *n* (*tie-on*) бирка; (*sticky*) наклéйка; (*of any kind*) ярлык, *also fig*; (*for identification, on library books, specimens*) этикéтка; **luggage** ~ багáжная бирка/наклéйка; **plant** ~**s** бирки с назвáнием растéний; **price** ~ цéнник; **name** ~ (*at conferences, etc.*) личный знак.

label *vt*: **to** ~ **smth** (*stick on label*) приклé|ивать наклéйку/ярлык на что-л (´-ить), (*tie on*) привяз|ывать бирку/ярлык на что-л (-áть); **all the specimens must be clearly** ~**led** на всех образцáх должнá быть чётко написанная этикéтка; **the bottle is** ~**led "Poison"** на бутылке этикéтка «Яд»; *fig* **the boy was** ~**led a juvenile delinquent** за мальчишкой укрепилась слáва малолéтнего престýпника.

laboratory, *abbr* **lab** *n* лаборатóрия; *attr* лаборатóрный.

laborious *adj* (*of work*) тяжёлый, утомительный; трудоёмкий; *fig* (*of style, wit*) тяжеловéсный; **compiling a dictionary is** ~ **work** составлéние словаря — трудоёмкая рабóта.

labour, (*US*) **labor** *n* **1** (*work*) труд, рабóта; **manual** ~ физический труд; **it was a** ~ **of love for me** это для меня не рабóта, а прóсто удовóльствие; *joc* **gardening is hard** ~ **to me** рабóтать в садý для меня хýже кáторги; *Law* **he got 5 years hard** ~ егó приговорили к пяти годáм принудительных рабóт (*pl*)

2 (*collect = people*) рабóчие (*pl*); **we're short of** ~ у нас не хватáет рабóчих/рабóчей силы; **unskilled/skilled** ~ чернорабóчие, квалифицированные рабóчие; **Ministry of L.** министéрство трудá; *attr Polit*: ~ **movement** рабóчее движéние; (*UK*) **L. Party** лейбористская пáртия

3 (*childbirth*) рóды (*pl*); **to be in** ~ рожáть; **she had a difficult** ~ у неё были тяжёлые рóды; *attr*: ~ **pains/contractions** родовые мýки/схвáтки; ~ **ward** родильная палáта.

labour, (*US*) **labor** *vti vt*: **no need to** ~ **the point** не нýжно останáвливаться на этом пýнкте

vi: **we are** ~**ing under considerable difficulties** мы тепéрь в довóльно тяжёлых услóвиях; *fig* **you're** ~**ing under a delusion** ты заблуждáешься.

laboured, (*US*) **labored** *adj*: ~ **breathing** затруднённое дыхáние; **a** ~ **joke** вымученная шýтка.

labourer, (*US*) **laborer** *n* рабóчий; **farm** ~ сельскохозяйственный рабóчий.

laburnum *n Bot* золотóй дождь (*m*).

lace *n* **1** (*fabric*) крýжево, кружевá; **a dress trimmed with** ~ плáтье, отдéланное крýжевом/кружевáми

2 (*for shoes*) шнурóк.

lace *vt*: **to** ~ **(up) shoes** шнуровáть/зашнурóвывать ботинки (*pf for both* зашнуровáть); *fig* **to** ~ **coffee with brandy** добав|лять коньяк в кóфе (´-ить).

lack *n*: ~ **of** (*insufficiency*) недостáток + *G or* в + *P*, нехвáтка + *G*; (*absence*) неимéние + *G*, отсýтствие + *G*; ~ **of raw material** недостáток/нехвáтка сырья; **for** ~ **of horses** из-за нехвáтки/отсýтствия лошадéй; **for** ~ **of money** за неимéнием дéнег; **there's no** ~ **of money in their family** им-то дéнег хватáет; **I'm getting fat from** ~ **of exercise** я мáло двигаюсь, вот и полнéю; **he's bored for** ~ **of company** он скучáет без компáнии.

lack *vti* не хват|áть + *G* (-ить), недоставáть (*usu impf*) (*both used impers*); **we** ~**ed time to finish** нам не хватило врéмени закóнчить рабóту; **he** ~**ed the will power to give up smoking** у негó не хватило силы вóли брóсить курить; **he** ~**s experience** емý недостаёт óпыта; **what is still** ~**ing?** чегó ещё не хватáет?; **he is** ~**ing in confidence** емý не хватáет увéренности в себé.

lackadaisical *adj* вялый, тóмный.

lacquer *n* лак; *collect* лакирóванные издéлия (*pl*).

lacquer *vt* лакировáть (от-), покры|вáть лáком (´-ть); **to** ~ **one's nails** покрывáть нóгти лáком.

lacuna *n* прóпуск (в тéксте).

lad *n* пáрень (*m*); **he's a good** ~ он хорóший пáрень, он пáрень неплохóй; **he's off with the** ~**s** он гдé-то гуляет с ребятами; **he was only a young** ~ **when the war began** он был ещё совсéм мальчишкой, когдá начáлась войнá; **he's a great** ~ (*of small boy*) он слáвный мальчугáн/*CQ* парнишка, (*of older person*) он слáвный мáлый; (*in address*) **come on,** ~**s, let's go!** ну, ребята,/брáтцы, пошли!

ladder *n* приставнáя лéстница, стремянка; (*in stocking*) спустившаяся пéтля; **folding/rope** ~ складнáя/верёвочная лéстница.

ladder *vti vt*: **I've** ~**ed my tights** у меня на колгóтках спустилась пéтля

vi: **nylon tights** ~ **easily** нейлóновые колгóтки быстро рвýтся.

ladderproof *adj*: ~ **tights** колгóтки с неспускáющимися пéтлями.

laden *adj* (*of ships, etc.*) гружёный, нагружéнный; **the tree is** ~ **with apples** вéтки у яблони лóмятся/гнýтся под тяжестью яблок; **dishes** ~ **with fruit** блюда, пóлные фрýктов (*pl*).

ladle *n* (*for soup*) поло́вник, разлива́тельная ло́жка, *CQ* поварёшка.

ladle *vt* разли|ва́ть (-́ть); **she ~d (out) the soup into bowls** она́ разлила́ суп по ми́скам.

lady *n* да́ма, госпожа́; (*title*) ле́ди (*f*, *indecl*); **an old ~** пожила́я да́ма; **is the ~ of the house at home?** а хозя́йка до́ма?; **ladies' fashions** да́мские мо́ды; *attr*: **~ doctor** же́нщина-врач.

ladybird, (*US*) **ladybug** *n* бо́жья коро́вка.

lag[1] *vi* (*trail*) тащи́ться (*impf*); *fig* отста|ва́ть (-́ть); **the children ~ged behind** де́ти тащи́лись позади́; **he ~s behind the rest of his class** он отстаёт от други́х ма́льчиков в кла́ссе, он в кла́ссе отстаю́щий.

lag[2] *vt*: **to ~ pipes** покры|ва́ть тру́бы термоизоля́цией (-́ть).

lag[3] *n*, *also* **old ~** *CQ* уголо́вник.

lager *n* лёгкое пи́во, «ла́гер».

lagging *n* (*process or material*) термоизоля́ция.

lair *n* ло́говище, *also fig*; нора́.

lake *n* о́зеро.

lamb *n* ягнёнок; бара́шек; (*as dish*) бара́нина, бара́шек; (*endearment*) ягнёночек; **a leg of ~** бара́нья нога́; *fig* **just look at her—mutton dressed as ~!** посмотри́ на неё, вы́рядилась, как моло́денькая!

lambskin *n* овчи́на, ове́чья шку́ра; *attr*: **~ mittens** ва́режки из овчи́ны.

lame *adj* хромо́й; **a ~ man** хромо́й (челове́к); **he's ~ in the left leg** он хрома́ет на ле́вую но́гу; **the horse went ~** ло́шадь ста́ла хрома́ть; *fig*: **a ~ argument/excuse** неубеди́тельный до́вод, сла́бая отгово́рка.

lame *vt* кале́чить (ис-, по-), уве́чить (из-); **he was ~d by a falling tree/during the war** его́ покале́чило (*impers*) упа́вшим де́ревом, он получи́л уве́чье/его́ искале́чило (*impers*) на войне́.

lament *vti vt*: **to ~ the good old days** тоскова́ть по до́брому ста́рому вре́мени

vi: **to ~ over** жа́ловаться на + *A*, се́товать на + *A* (*impfs*); **they were ~ing over their misfortunes** они́ жа́ловались на свои́ несча́стья.

lamentable *adj* плаче́вный, жа́лкий; удруча́ющий; **the house was in a ~ state** дом был в са́мом жа́лком/плаче́вном состоя́нии; **a ~ slovenliness** ужаса́ющая неря́шливость.

laminated *adj* слои́стый; **~ glass** слои́стое/безоско́лочное стекло́; **~ wood** фане́ра.

lamp *n* ла́мпа; (*street lamp, torch, etc.*) фона́рь (*m*); (*with several bulbs*) свети́льник.

lamplight *n* свет ла́мпы; **in the ~** при све́те ла́мпы.

lampoon *n* памфле́т.

lampoon *vt*: **he was viciously ~ed** газе́та зло вы́смеяла его́.

lamppost *n* фона́рный столб.

lampshade *n* абажу́р.

lance *vt Med*: **to ~ a boil** вскры|ва́ть (ланце́том) нары́в/чи́рей (-ть).

lance-corporal *n* мла́дший капра́л.

land *n* **1** (*in most senses*) земля́; (*as opposite to sea*) су́ша; **I'm glad to be on dry ~ again** я дово́лен, что наконе́ц сно́ва на су́ше; **to travel by ~** путеше́ствовать по су́ше; **to sight ~** уви́деть су́шу/зе́млю/бе́рег; **to reach ~** приста́ть к бе́регу; *attr*: **a ~ breeze** берегово́й ве́тер; *Mil* **~ forces** сухопу́тные си́лы/войска́

2 (*soil*) земля́, по́чва; **poor/rich ~** бе́дная/плодоро́дная по́чва; **arable ~** па́хотная земля́; **to work on the ~** занима́ться земледе́лием

3 (*terrain*) ме́стность; **forest ~** леси́стая ме́стность; **the road lay over marsh ~** доро́га шла по боло́тистой ме́стности; **arid ~s** засу́шливые райо́ны; **the steppe ~s of the South** ю́жные сте́пи

4 (*as property*) земля́; *Law* земе́льная со́бственность

5 (*country*) страна́; **the customs of different ~s** обы́чаи ра́зных стран; **native ~** ро́дина, оте́чество

6 *various*: **~ of dreams** ца́рство грёз; **he's no longer in the ~ of the living** его́ уже́ нет в живы́х.

land *vti vt* **1** *Naut* (*people*) вы|са́живать (-́садить), (*cargo*) вы|гружа́ть (-́грузить); **the passengers were ~ed at Odessa** пассажи́ры вы́садились/бы́ли вы́сажены в Оде́ссе; **the timber has been ~ed** лес/древеси́ну вы́грузили на бе́рег

2 *Aer* посади́ть (*only in pf*); **he ~ed the plane safely** он благополу́чно посади́л самолёт; **he ~ed the helicopter on the lawn** он посади́л вертолёт на газо́н

3 (*fish*) пойма́ть (*only in pf*); **we ~ed an enormous pike** мы пойма́ли огро́мную щу́ку

4 *fig CQ*: **he ~ed a good job** он доби́лся хоро́шего ме́ста; **she always ~s the leading role** она́ всегда́ добьётся себе́ гла́вной ро́ли; **you've ~ed me in a nice mess!** ну и впу́тал ты меня́ в весёленькую исто́рию!; **I always get ~ed with the heavy jobs** на меня́ всегда́ сва́ливают са́мую тяжёлую рабо́ту (*sing*); **are we really going to be ~ed again with the whole family?** неу́жто на нас опя́ть сва́лится всё э́то семе́йство?; **these goings-on will ~ you in jail** э́ти твои́ штýчки-дрю́чки до добра́ не доведу́т

vi **1** *Naut* выса́живаться, сходи́ть с + *G* (сойти́); **I ~ed at Dover** я сошёл с парохо́да/я вы́садился в Ду́вре; **the delegation ~ed at the port/airport at noon** делега́ция прибыла́ в порт/прилете́ла в по́лдень

2 *Aer* приземл|я́ться (-и́ться); (*of helicopter, birds, etc.*) опус|ка́ться (-ти́ться); **the rocket ~ed on the Moon** раке́та прилуни́лась; **the bird ~ed on the roof** пти́ца се́ла на кры́шу; *fig* **we ~ed up in Finland** мы оказа́лись/очути́лись в Финля́ндии.

landing *n* **1** *Naut* (*of people*) вы́садка; (*of cargo*) вы́грузка; *Aer* приземле́ние; (*on ground, water, etc.*) поса́дка; *Mil* деса́нт; **the Normandy ~s** вы́садка деса́нта (*here = landing force*) в Норма́ндии; *attr*: ~ **force(s)** деса́нтные войска́

2 (*at top of stairs*) ле́стничная площа́дка.

landing net *n* рыболо́вный сачо́к.

landing stage *n* при́стань, прича́л.

landing strip *n Aer* взлётно-поса́дочная полоса́.

landlady *n* (*who owns or lets property*) домовладе́лица, (*of boarding house, etc.*) хозя́йка.

landlord *n* (*proprietor, lessor*) владе́лец, домовладе́лец; (*of inn, etc.*) хозя́ин; (*of an estate*) землевладе́лец; **the entire street is owned by one** ~ все дома́ на э́той у́лице принадлежа́т одному́ владе́льцу; **the** ~ **was serving behind the bar** хозя́ин стоя́л за сто́йкой.

landmark *n* (назе́мный) ориенти́р; (*boundary*) межево́й знак/столб; **the tower was a** ~ **for travellers** ба́шня служи́ла ориенти́ром для путеше́ственников; **this hill is a** ~ **for miles around** э́тот холм ви́ден отовсю́ду; *fig* ~**s in history** ве́хи в миров́ой исто́рии.

landowner *n* землевладе́лец, поме́щик.

landscape *n Geog* ландша́фт; (*aesthetically viewed*) пейза́ж, *also Art*; **a flat/mountainous** ~ пло́ский/го́рный ландша́фт; **to admire the** ~ любова́ться пейза́жем; *attr*: ~ **painter** пейзажи́ст.

landslide *n* о́ползень (*m*), обва́л; *fig* **the election proved a** ~ **for the left** на вы́борах ле́вые одержа́ли внуши́тельную побе́ду.

lane *n* (*in country*) доро́жка, *also Sport*; (*in town*) переу́лок, у́зкая у́лочка; *Aut* ряд; **fast/slow/inside/outside** ~ скоростно́й/ме́дленный/вну́тренний/вне́шний ряд.

language *n* язы́к; **she speaks several** ~**s** она́ владе́ет не́сколькими языка́ми; **they were speaking their native** ~ они́ говори́ли на родно́м языке́; **bad** ~ брань, руга́тельства (*pl*); **to use bad** ~ скверносло́вить; *fig* **we speak the same** ~ мы нашли́ о́бщий язы́к.

languid *adj* то́мный, вя́лый.

lank *adj* (*of person*) худоща́вый; (*of hair*) прямо́й и гла́дкий.

lap[1] *n*: **she held the baby in/on her** ~ она́ держа́ла ребёнка на коле́нях; *fig*: **they live in the** ~ **of luxury** они́ живу́т в ро́скоши; **the future is in the** ~ **of the gods** челове́ку не дано́ знать бу́дущее.

lap[2] *n Sport* круг (бегово́й доро́жки); (*in relay race*) эта́п; **the cyclist fell halfway round in the second** ~ велосипеди́ст упа́л в середи́не второ́го кру́га; **they are on the last** ~ они́ вы́шли на фи́нишную пряму́ю, *also fig*.

lap[3] *vti vt, also* ~ **up** (*drink*) лака́ть (вы́-); *fig* **he'll** ~ **up any compliment** он принима́ет [**NB** *tense*] любо́й комплиме́нт всерьёз (*adv*)
vi (*of water*) плеска́ться (*impf*).

lapdog *n* боло́нка.

lapel *n* отворо́т, ла́цкан.

lapse *n* **1** (*slip*) про́мах, огре́х; **apart from the odd** ~, **her work is good** есть ко́е-каки́е огре́хи, но в о́бщем её рабо́та неплоха́я; **a** ~ **of memory** прова́л па́мяти; **a moral** ~ нра́вственное паде́ние; **a** ~ **from one's principles** отступле́ние от свои́х при́нципов

2 (*passage of time*): **after a long** ~ **of time** спустя́ мно́го вре́мени; **after a** ~ **of 2 months** че́рез/спустя́ два ме́сяца.

lapse *vi* **1** (*fall*): **to** ~ **from the path of virtue** сби́ться с пути́ и́стинного; **he has** ~**d into second childhood** он впал в де́тство; **he often** ~**s into his native tongue** он ча́сто перехо́дит на родно́й язы́к; **he** ~**d into silence** он замолча́л

2 (*expire*) исте|ка́ть (-́чь); **the term has** ~**d** срок истёк, вре́мя истекло́; **my driving licence has** ~**d** у меня́ просро́чены права́ (*pl*); **the custom has** ~**d** э́тот обы́чай уже́ исчез.

lapwing *n* чи́бис.

larch *n* ли́ственница.

lard *n* лярд, топлёное свино́е са́ло; **to fry in** ~ жа́рить на свино́м са́ле.

larder *n* кладова́я.

large *adj* **1** большо́й; (*substantial*) кру́пный, значи́тельный; **a** ~ **house** большо́й дом; **he lost a** ~ **sum at cards** он проигра́л большу́ю/кру́пную/значи́тельную су́мму (де́нег) в ка́рты; **a** ~ **woman** кру́пная же́нщина, *CQ* по́лная да́ма; **a** ~ **firm** кру́пная фи́рма; **a** ~ **majority of the children can't swim** большинство́ дете́й не уме́ет пла́вать; **there was a** ~ **audience at the concert** на конце́рте бы́ло мно́го наро́ду; **a** ~ **crowd** многолю́дная толпа́; **he deals in cars on a** ~ **scale** торго́вля маши́нами поста́влена у него́ на широ́кую но́гу

2 (*too big*) вели́к (*only in short form*); **this coat is a bit** ~ **for me** э́то пальто́ мне немно́го велико́; **these shoes are on the** ~ **side** э́ти ту́фли великова́ты

3 (*adverbial expressions*): **the murderer is still at** ~ уби́йца всё ещё не по́йман; **ambassador at** ~ посо́л по осо́бым поруче́ниям; **there he was as** ~ **as life** там он был со́бственной персо́ной.

largely *adv* в большо́й/значи́тельной ме́ре/сте́пени; в основно́м, гла́вным о́бразом; **his success was** ~ **due to luck** свои́м успе́хом он обя́зан в значи́тельной ме́ре счастли́вому слу́чаю; **it's** ~ **a question of concentration** э́то гла́вным о́бразом вопро́с внима́ния; **he himself was** ~ **to blame** он был во мно́гом сам винова́т.

large-scale *adj*: **a** ~ **map** ка́рта кру́пного масшта́ба; ~ **reforms/operations** кру́пные рефо́рмы, опера́ции кру́пного масшта́ба.

lark[1] *n* жа́воронок; *fig* **to rise with the** ~ встава́ть с петуха́ми.

lark[2] *n* (*prank*) ша́лость; **just for a** ~ шу́тки ра́ди.

larva *n* личи́нка (насеко́мого).

laryngitis *n* ларинги́т.

larynx *n* горта́нь.

lash *n* **1** (*thong*) плеть; хлыст; (*whip*) кнут

2 (*stroke*) уда́р плётью/кнуто́м, *etc.*; *fig* **he often felt the** ~ **of her tongue** ему́ ча́сто достава́лось от её о́строго язычка́

3 (*eyelash*) ресни́ца.

lash *vti vt* **1** (*whip*) стег|а́ть, хлест|а́ть (*pfs* от-, *semel* -ну́ть); **to ~ a horse** стега́ть ло́шадь кнуто́м; **hail was ~ing the windows** град бил по стёклам; *fig* **the speaker ~ed his hearers into a frenzy** выступа́вший довёл пу́блику до исступле́ния

2 (*tie together*) свя́з|ывать, (*tie to smth*) привя́з|ывать к + *D* (*pfs* -а́ть); (*secure*) прикреп|ля́ть к + *D*, закреп|ля́ть, укреп|ля́ть (*pfs* -и́ть); **the timber was ~ed to the deck** брёвна бы́ли на́крепко привя́заны кана́том к па́лубе

vi: **he ~ed out with his fists** он разма́хивал кулака́ми; **the horse ~ed out with her hind legs** ло́шадь ляга́лась; *CQ*: **he fairly ~ed into me** он зада́л мне взбу́чку; **to ~ out on a new coat** разори́ться на но́вое пальто́.

lass, lassie *n CQ* девчо́нка, девчу́шка.

lassitude *n* вя́лость, уста́лость.

last[1] *n* коне́ц; **at long ~** в конце́ концо́в; **to/till the ~** до конца́; **we'll never hear the ~ of it** э́тому конца́ не бу́дет; **at ~** наконе́ц (*adv*); **are we the ~?** мы пришли́ после́дними?; **to breathe one's ~** испусти́ть после́дний вздох; **that was the ~ I heard of him** я бо́льше о нём ничего́ не слыха́л.

last[1] *adj* **1** (*final*) после́дний; **it's our ~ hope** э́то на́ша после́дняя наде́жда; **the ~/second ~ house in the street** са́мый после́дний *or* кра́йний/второ́й от конца́ дом на э́той у́лице; **the ~ house but two** тре́тий дом с кра́ю/от конца́; **that's the ~ thing to worry about** об э́том ме́ньше всего́ сто́ит беспоко́иться; **he's the ~ person I want to see** его́ мне ме́ньше всего́ хо́чется ви́деть; *fig* **they'll die in the ~ ditch for their proposals** они́ костьми́ ля́гут, отста́ивая свои́ предложе́ния

2 (*previous*) про́шлый; **~ year** в про́шлом году́; **he left ~ Tuesday** он уе́хал в про́шлый вто́рник; **~ May he earned £1,000** в ма́е э́того (*in current year*)/про́шлого (*in previous year*) го́да он зарабо́тал ты́сячу фу́нтов; **I saw her ~ week** я её ви́дел на про́шлой неде́ле; **I spent ~ week in bed** всю ту неде́лю я пролежа́л в посте́ли; **~ winter I broke my leg** я слома́л (себе́) но́гу в про́шлом году́ зимо́й; **in the course of ~ autumn** о́сенью про́шлого го́да; **~ night** э́той но́чью (*during the night*), вчера́ ве́чером (*the evening before*); **the night before ~** позавчера́ ве́чером; **the time before ~** в предпосле́дний раз; **under the ~ government** при пре́жнем прави́тельстве

3 NB *the following uses*: **when did you see him for the ~ time?, when was the ~ time you saw him?** когда́ вы ви́дели его́ (в) после́дний раз?; **the ~ time I saw him was in May** после́дний раз я ви́дел его́ в ма́е [**NB** после́дний *used for the last time either e.g. before death or before specific date or event*]; **~ time I saw him he was looking ill** когда́ я ви́дел его́ в про́шлый раз, вид у него́ был больно́й [*implies you will be meeting again*]; **were you at the ~ meeting** (*of all*)? ты был на после́днем собра́нии?; **at the ~** (*previous*) **meeting we decided to...** на про́шлом собра́нии мы реши́ли + *inf*.

last[1] *adv* **1** (*in order*): **he spoke ~** он говори́л после́дним; **my horse came in ~** моя́ ло́шадь пришла́ после́дней; **~ but not least there's the question of pay** и наконе́ц — вопро́с о зарпла́те

2 (*in time*) (в) после́дний раз; **when did you ~ hear him play?** когда́ ты после́дний раз слы́шал его́ игру́?; **I ~ had a letter from her two years ago** я получи́л после́днее письмо́ от неё два го́да (тому́) наза́д.

last[2] *vi* **1** (*go on*) дли́ться (про-), продолжа́ться (*impf*); **the war ~ed five years** война́ дли́лась пять лет; **I knew it was too good to ~** я знал: так хорошо́ до́лго продолжа́ться не мо́жет; **the play ~s two hours** пье́са идёт два часа́; **the heat wave ~ed a month** си́льная жара́ стоя́ла/держа́лась це́лый ме́сяц (*impfs*)

2 (*of people*: *survive, hold out*) вы|де́рживать (-держать); **he's not expected to ~ till morning** нам сказа́ли, что он до утра́ не доживёт; **his secretaries usually ~ a couple of weeks** секретари́ у него́ обы́чно выде́рживают не бо́льше двух неде́ль; **they just ~ed out till the reinforcements arrived** они́ с трудо́м продержа́лись до прибы́тия подкрепле́ния (*sing*)

3 (*of things*: *suffice*) хват|а́ть (*impers*) + *G* (-и́ть); **will our petrol ~ (out)?** у нас хва́тит бензи́на?; **a packet of cigarettes never ~ me long** па́чки сигаре́т мне хвата́ет ненадо́лго; **their money only ~ed a week** им хвати́ло де́нег то́лько на одну́ неде́лю; **that car has ~ed them for years** э́та маши́на у них о́чень давно́.

last[3] *n* (*cobbler's*) коло́дка.

lasting *adj* про́чный; **a ~ peace** про́чный мир; **to his ~ shame** к его́ вели́кому стыду́; **the illness caused no ~ damage** боле́знь не име́ла серьёзных после́дствий (*pl*).

lastly *adv* наконе́ц; **~ let me remind you...** наконе́ц я до́лжен вам напо́мнить...; **the dog, the cat and, ~, the canary** соба́ка, ко́шка и ещё канаре́йка.

latch *n* **1** (*falling bar operated by lever*) щеко́лда

2 (*stop device on Yale lock*) соба́чка; **the door is on the ~** замо́к на соба́чке.

latch *vti vt* (*lock*) за|пира́ть (-пере́ть)

vi (*lock*): **all the doors ~ securely** все две́ри надёжно запира́ются; *CQ*: **he ~ed on to me** он приста́л ко мне; **he soon ~ed on to the fact that...** пото́м он прицепи́лся к тому́, что...

latchkey *n*: **I've lost my ~** я потеря́л ключ от входно́й две́ри.

late *adj* **1** (*far on in time, season, etc.*) по́здний; **a ~ harvest** по́здний урожа́й; **at this ~ hour** в э́тот по́здний час; **let's have a ~ meal** дава́й поу́жинаем поздне́е/попо́зже; **he made a ~ entry** он по́здно появи́лся; **in ~ autumn** по́здней о́сенью; **in the ~ Middle Ages** в эпо́ху по́зднего средневеко́вья;

in the ~ nineteenth century к концу́ девятна́дцатого ве́ка; **come in the ~ morning/afternoon** приходи́ часа́м к двена́дцати/к ве́черу

2 (*former*) бы́вший; **the ~ president** бы́вший президе́нт; **the ~ government** пре́жнее прави́тельство

3 (*deceased*) поко́йный

4 *predic*: **to be ~** опа́здывать; **to be a bit ~** запа́здывать; **he was ~ for the train** он опозда́л на по́езд (*which he was to catch*)/к по́езду (*if meeting smb off a train*); **we were ~ for the theatre** мы опозда́ли на спекта́кль; **I was half an hour ~ for dinner/for the lecture** я на полчаса́ опозда́л к обе́ду/на ле́кцию; **the train was an hour ~** по́езд при́был с опозда́нием/опозда́л на час; **I'm ~ with the rent** я просро́чил с упла́той за кварти́ру; **I was ~ getting up** я по́здно встал; **another swim will make us ~** е́сли ещё раз пойдём купа́ться, то уж обяза́тельно опозда́ем; **don't let me make you ~** я не хочу́ вас заде́рживать; **of ~** после́днее вре́мя; *impers*: **it's getting ~** (уже́) по́здно; **it's a bit/too ~ to change your mind** переду́мывать по́здно/не́когда.

late *adv* по́здно; **better ~ than never** лу́чше по́здно, чем никогда́; **he worked ~ into the night** он рабо́тал до по́здней/глубо́кой но́чи; **we always sit up ~** мы всегда́ заси́живаемся допоздна́; **we arrived too ~ to see him** мы прие́хали сли́шком по́здно и не заста́ли его́; **I was going to write to you for your birthday, but I thought about it too ~** я собира́лся поздра́вить вас с днём рожде́ния, да по́здно спохвати́лся; **he sat up ~ working** он засиде́лся за рабо́той; **as ~ as 1900** ещё в ты́сяча девятисо́том году́; **~ in the year/in his reign** к концу́ го́да/его́ ца́рствования; **~ last year** в конце́ про́шлого го́да.

latecomer *n* опозда́вший.

lately *adv* в после́днее вре́мя, неда́вно; **have you seen him ~?** вы его́ ви́дели в после́днее вре́мя?; **I've seen him quite ~** я его́ ви́дел совсе́м неда́вно; **it's only ~ that I've started painting** я на́чал рисова́ть неда́вно.

lateness *n*: **his ~ is inexcusable** его́ опозда́ние непрости́тельно; **owing to the ~ of the hour** из-за по́зднего ча́са.

latent *adj Med, Biol* лате́нтный; скры́тый, *also fig*.

later *adj* (бо́лее) по́здний [**NB** *Russian also uses positive and superlative degrees in this sense*]; **the ~ symphonies of Beethoven** бо́лее по́здние симфо́нии Бетхо́вена; **we will reconsider this at a ~ meeting** мы вернёмся к э́тому на одно́м из сле́дующих заседа́ний; **this is the ~/a ~ version** э́то поздне́йшая/бо́лее по́здняя реда́кция; **in his ~ years he lived in Yalta** после́дние го́ды он жил в Я́лте.

later *adv* по́зже, поздне́е; **sooner or ~** ра́но и́ли по́здно, ра́ньше и́ли по́зже; **no ~ than yesterday/8 o'clock** не по́зже, чем вчера́, не по́зже восьми́ часо́в; **not now—~** не сейча́с—пото́м; **a bit ~ on they saw him again** чуть по́зже они́ его́ сно́ва уви́дели; **~ on they often met** впосле́дствии/пото́м они́ ча́сто встреча́лись; **I'll come ~ on/a bit ~** я приду́ попо́зже.

lateral *adj* боково́й.

latest *adj* после́дний; **the ~ news** после́дние изве́стия (*pl*); **it's the ~ thing in electric cookers** э́та электри́ческая плита́—са́мая после́дняя моде́ль; **have you heard the ~ joke?** ты слыха́л но́вый анекдо́т?; *used as n*: **have you met his ~?** ты ви́дел его́ но́вую знако́мую?; **I'll come on Tuesday at (the) ~** я прие́ду са́мое по́зднее во вто́рник.

lathe *n* тока́рный стано́к.

lather *n* (*of soap*) мы́льная пе́на; (*of sweat*) **the horse was in a ~** ло́шадь была́ вся в пе́не/в мы́ле.

lather *vi* мы́литься (*impf*); **the soap wouldn't ~** мы́ло не мы́лилось/не дава́ло пе́ны.

Latin *n* **1** (*language*) лати́нский язы́к, латы́нь; **vulgar ~** вульга́рная латы́нь

2 (*people*): **he's a typical ~** он типи́чный южа́нин.

Latin *adj* лати́нский; **a ~ scholar** латини́ст; **the ~ languages** рома́нские языки́.

Latin American *n* латиноамерика́нец.

latitude *n Geog* широта́; **at a ~ of 30° north** три́дцать гра́дусов се́верной широты́; **high/low ~s** высо́кие/тропи́ческие широ́ты; *fig*: **our terms of reference give us very little ~** на́ши полномо́чия о́чень невелики́/весьма́ ограни́чены; **we are allowed great ~ in choosing our subjects** нам была́ дана́ больша́я свобо́да в вы́боре тем.

latrine *n* отхо́жее ме́сто, убо́рная.

latter *adj* **1** после́дний; **the ~ part of the book** после́дняя часть кни́ги; **in the ~ part of the week/year** в конце́ неде́ли, в после́дние ме́сяцы го́да

2 (*second of two*): **the ~** после́дний, второ́й; **Ivan and Paul arrived, the ~ looking very ill** пришли́ Ива́н с Па́влом, после́дний вы́глядел совсе́м больны́м; **of sparrows and swallows, the former are native, the ~ migratory** возьми́те воробьёв и ла́сточек, пе́рвые—зиму́ющие пти́цы, вторы́е—перелётные.

latterly *adv* (*of late*) за после́днее вре́мя; **~ he was unable to speak** под коне́ц он уже́ про́сто не мог говори́ть.

lattice *n* решётка; *attr* решётчатый.

Latvian *n* латы́ш, латы́шка.

Latvian *adj* латви́йский, латы́шский.

laugh *n* смех; **a loud ~** хо́хот; **to raise a ~** вы́звать смех; **with a ~** со сме́хом; **we had a good/hearty ~ over it** мы от души́ посмея́лись над э́тим; *CQ* **he had the ~ on us** он одержа́л верх над на́ми.

laugh *vti vt*: **we ~ed ourselves silly** мы смея́лись до упа́ду; **the speaker was ~ed down** слова́ ора́тора заглуши́л смех; **one can't just ~ it off** от э́того так не отшу́тишься

vi смея́ться над + *I* (по-); **to ~ aloud at a funny story** хохота́ть над анекдо́том; (*mock*)

to ~ at smb/at danger смея́ться над кем-л/над опа́сностью; **to ~ loudly/quietly** хохота́ть, посме́иваться (*impfs*); **to begin to ~** засмея́ться, (*loudly*) захохота́ть (*pfs*); **to burst out ~ing** рассмея́ться, расхохота́ться (*pfs*); **he ~ed till he cried** он смея́лся до слёз; **he made us ~** он нас о́чень смеши́л; **this is no time to ~** сейча́с не до сме́ха; *CQ* **we killed ourselves ~ing** мы помира́ли со́ смеху; **you've got to ~** смех да и то́лько; *fig* **he looked serious but I could see he was ~ing up his sleeve** вид у него́ был серьёзный, но я чу́вствовал, что про себя́ он посме́ивается.

laughable *adj* смешно́й; (*ridiculous*) смехотво́рный; (*absurd*) неле́пый; **it's just ~!** про́сто смех!, ку́рам на́ смех!

laughing *adj*: **it's no ~ matter** э́то (совсе́м) не смешно́, (тут) не́ над чем смея́ться.

laughing stock *n* посме́шище.

laughter *n* смех, (*loud*) хо́хот; **roars of ~** взры́вы сме́ха; **amid general ~** под о́бщий смех.

launch *n* (*boat*) ка́тер; **pleasure ~** прогу́лочный ка́тер; **motor ~** мото́рный ка́тер, (*if small*) мото́рная ло́дка.

launch *vti vt* (*a boat*) спус|ка́ть на́ воду (-ти́ть); **to ~ a rocket** запус|ка́ть раке́ту (-ти́ть); *Mil* **to ~ an offensive** на|чина́ть наступле́ние (-ча́ть); *fig*: **to ~ an election campaign** нача́ть предвы́борную кампа́нию; **to ~ a new company** открыва́ть но́вое предприя́тие

vi: **he ~ed into a long explanation** он пусти́лся в бесконе́чные объясне́ния (*pl*); **I'd like to ~ out into more independent work** мне хоте́лось бы заня́ться бо́лее самостоя́тельной рабо́той; **he ~ed out on a new career** он на́чал но́вую карье́ру.

launching *n* (*of a ship*) спуск на́ воду; (*of a rocket*) за́пуск; (*of an enterprise*) нача́ло; *attr*: **~ pad** пускова́я устано́вка.

launder *vti*: **the linen is beautifully ~ed** бельё прекра́сно вы́стирано; **this material ~s badly** э́та ткань пло́хо стира́ется.

launderette *n* пра́чечная-автома́т.

laundry *n* **1** (*shop or room*) пра́чечная; **he sends his washing to the ~** он отдаёт бельё в пра́чечную

2 (*things*) бельё; **the ~ hasn't come back yet** бельё ещё не верну́лось из пра́чечной/из сти́рки; **to do the ~** стира́ть бельё; *attr*: **~ basket** бельева́я корзи́на.

laurel *n* (*tree*) ла́вровое де́рево, лавр; *fig pl* (**~s**) ла́вры; **to look to one's ~s** ревни́во оберега́ть свои́ ла́вры; **to rest on one's ~s** почи́ть на ла́врах.

lava *n* ла́ва.

lavatory *n* убо́рная, туале́т.

lavender *n Bot* лава́нда; (*colour*) бле́дно-лило́вый цвет.

lavish *adj* роско́шный; **they gave us a ~ dinner** они́ накорми́ли нас роско́шным у́жином; **~ furnishings** роско́шная меблиро́вка; **she is ~ in her praise/with her money** она́ не скупи́тся на похвалы́, она́ не жале́ет де́нег; **he lives on a ~ scale** он живёт на широ́кую но́гу.

lavish *vt*: **she ~es money/gifts on the children** она́ тра́тит тьму де́нег на дете́й, она́ засыпа́ет дете́й пода́рками.

law *n* **1** зако́н; **according to ~** в соотве́тствии с зако́ном; **it's against the ~** э́то противозако́нно, э́то запрещено́ (зако́ном); **to pass a ~** ввести́ зако́н; **to break a/the ~** наруша́ть зако́н; **to keep on the right side of the ~** не наруша́ть зако́на; **the bill has become ~** законопрое́кт стал зако́ном

2 (*jurisprudence, body of law*) пра́во; **civil/criminal/international ~** гражда́нское/уголо́вное/междунаро́дное пра́во; **to study ~** изуча́ть пра́во; **he's gone into the ~** он стал юри́стом; **doctor of ~** до́ктор юриди́ческих нау́к; *attr*: **~ student** студе́нт юриди́ческого факульте́та

3 (*legal procedure*): **to go to ~** обраща́ться в суд; **to take smb to ~** привлека́ть кого́-л к суду́, пода́ть на кого́-л в суд

4 (*principle, rule*): **the ~s of nature/perspective/harmony** зако́ны приро́ды/перспекти́вы/гармо́нии

5 *expressions*: **he's a ~ unto himself** он сам себе́ зако́н, он счита́ется то́лько с со́бственным мне́нием; **don't try to lay down the ~ to me** не кома́ндуй мной; **to take the ~ into one's own hands** распра́виться без суда́.

law-abiding *adj*: **he's a good ~ citizen** он добропоря́дочный граждани́н, уважа́ющий зако́ны.

lawbreaker *n* правонаруши́тель (*m*), наруши́тель (*m*) зако́на.

law court *n* суд

lawful *adj* зако́нный.

lawless *adj* незако́нный, (*stronger*) беззако́нный.

lawn[1] *n* газо́н; **tennis ~** травяна́я площа́дка для те́нниса.

lawn[2] *n* (*cloth*) бати́ст.

lawnmower *n* газонокоси́лка.

lawsuit *n* суде́бный проце́сс; де́ло; **he brought a ~ against them** он возбуди́л про́тив них де́ло; **they're involved in a ~** они́ су́дятся.

lawyer *n* (*barrister or solicitor*) адвока́т; (*legal expert*) юри́ст; **company/corporation ~** юриско́нсульт.

lax *adj* (*careless*) неря́шливый; хала́тный; (*not strict*) нестро́гий; **he's ~ about his dress/work** он неря́шлив в оде́жде, он хала́тно/неради́во отно́сится к рабо́те; **you're too ~ with the children** ты сли́шком потака́ешь де́тям; **a ~ teacher** нестро́гий учи́тель; **~ discipline** сла́бая дисципли́на; **standards nowadays are ~ among the young** молодёжь в на́ши дни сли́шком про́сто смо́трит на мно́гие ве́щи.

laxative *n* слаби́тельное.

lay *vti vt* **1** (*place, put*) класть (положи́ть) *and compounds*; **to ~ a carpet/bricks** класть ковёр/кирпичи́; **to ~ parquet/lino** на|стила́ть паркéт/линóлеум (-стла́ть); **to ~ a cable/pipes** про|кла́дывать ка́бель/трубопровóд (-ложи́ть); **to ~ foundations** за|кла́дывать фунда́мент (*sing*) (-ложи́ть); **a fire was laid in the grate** дрова́ бы́ли полóжены в ками́н; **to ~ the table for supper** накры|ва́ть (на) стол к у́жину (-́ть); *fig*: **I can't ~ hands on that book** я не могу́ найти́ э́ту кни́гу; **don't dare ~ a finger on her** не сме́йте и па́льцем её трóнуть

2 (*flatten*): **the rain will ~ the dust** дождь прибьёт пыль; **the gale has laid the crops** си́льный ве́тер поби́л посе́вы; **the city was laid flat** гóрод был разру́шен; **the country was laid waste** страна́ была́ разорена́

3 *fig uses*: **we are ~ing the foundations of a new movement** мы закла́дываем оснóвы нóвого движе́ния; **to ~ a tax on smth/a burden on smb** об|лага́ть что-л налóгом (-ложи́ть), взва́ли|вать бре́мя на когó-л (-́ть); **to ~ the blame on smb for smth** воз|лага́ть/вали́ть вину́ за что-л на когó-л (-ложи́ть/с-); **to ~ claim to smth** предъяв|ля́ть прете́нзию к чему́-л (-и́ть); **to ~ plans** состав|ля́ть пла́ны (-́ить); **to ~ a trap for smb** устр|а́ивать кому́-л лову́шку (-óить); **the scene is laid in London** де́йствие происхóдит в Лóндоне; (*wager*) **I'll ~ you a fiver that he won't come** спóрю на пять фу́нтов, что он не придёт

4: to ~ eggs нести́ я́йца (с-)

vi: **the hens are ~ing well** ку́ры хорошó несу́тся

lay about *vi*: **he laid about him with his fists** он разма́хивал кулака́ми

lay aside *vt*: **he laid his book aside** он отложи́л кни́гу в стóрону; **to ~ aside/by money for one's old age** от|кла́дывать де́ньги, чтóбы обеспе́чить свою́ ста́рость (-ложи́ть)

lay down *vt*: **to ~ a book down on the table** положи́ть кни́гу на стол; **to ~ down one's life** сложи́ть гóлову (*only in pf*); **to ~ a field down to grass** засе́|ивать пóле травóй (-ять); **to ~ down wine** вы|де́рживать винó (-́держать); *fig*: **he likes to ~ down the law** он лю́бит кома́ндовать; **follow the procedure laid down in the manual** поступа́йте, как ска́зано в руковóдстве

lay in *vt*: **to ~ in stores for the winter** запас|а́ть прови́зию (*collect*)/запас|а́ться прови́зией на́ зиму (-ти́(сь))

lay into *vi*: **to ~ into smb** на|бра́сываться на когó-л с кулака́ми (*physically*)/с оскорбле́ниями (*verbally*) (-брóситься)

lay low *vt*: *CQ* **he was laid low with flu** егó свали́л грипп

lay off *vti vt*: **a 100 workers were laid off** (вре́менно) бы́ло увóлено óколо сóтни рабóчих

vi: *CQ* **you must ~ off the drink** вы должны́ возде́рживаться от спиртнóго; **~ off!** переста́нь!

lay on *vt*: **he ~s his colours on thickly** он гу́сто кладёт кра́ски; **to ~ one's cards on the table** откры|ва́ть/раскры|ва́ть ка́рты (*pfs* -́ть), *also fig*; *fig CQ* **he ~s it on thick** (*of flattery*) он не скупи́тся на лесть, (*of hard luck story, exaggeration, etc.*) он залива́ет вовсю́

lay open *vt*: **he ~s himself open to criticism/to ridicule** он сам навлека́ет на себя́ кри́тику, он даёт пóвод для насме́шек

lay out *vt*: **the blow laid him out** уда́р оглуши́л егó; **to ~ out a large sum on a scheme** вкла́дывать бóльшие де́ньги в предприя́тие (вложи́ть); **the gardens are well laid out** сад (*sing*) прекра́сно распланирóван; **~ out your clothes ready for the morning** приготóвь оде́жду на у́тро; **to ~ out a corpse** обмы|ва́ть те́ло (-́ть)

lay up *vt*: **to ~ up a ship for repairs/a car for the winter** ста́вить кора́бль на ремóнт (*sing*)/маши́ну на́ зиму (по-); **he's laid up with a broken leg** он лежи́т со слóманной ногóй.

layabout *n CQ* безде́льник; (*tramp*) бродя́га (*m*).

lay-by *n Aut* стоя́нка (на обóчине); **let's pull in to the next ~** дава́й останóвимся на сле́дующей стоя́нке.

layer *n* **1** слой; **a thin ~ of snow** тóнкий слой сне́га; *Cook* **arrange pastry and filling in ~s** положи́ть те́сто и начи́нку слоя́ми

2 (*hen*) несу́шка; **this hen is a good ~** э́та ку́рица хорошó несётся.

layette *n* прида́ное новорождённого.

layman *n* (*not clergy*) миря́нин; (*amateur*) непрофессиона́л.

layout *n* планирóвка, разби́вка, расположе́ние; **~ of a building/park** планирóвка зда́ния, разби́вка па́рка; **I like the ~ of the dictionary** мне нра́вится расположе́ние материа́ла в словаре́; **~ of an exhibition** размеще́ние экспона́тов на вы́ставке, экспози́ция.

laze *vi*: **I ~d in the sun all day** *CQ* я весь день валя́лся на сóлнце.

laziness *n* лень; **out of ~** от ле́ни.

lazy *adj* лени́вый; **to be ~** лени́ться; **she's ~ about getting up/her work** она́ ле́нится встава́ть порáньше/рабóтать; **I feel too ~ to...** мне лень + *inf*.

lazybones *n CQ* лентя́й, лóдырь (*m*).

lead[1] *n* (*metal*) свинéц; *attr* свинцóвый.

lead[2] *n* **1** (*front place*) пе́рвое/веду́щее ме́сто; *Sport*: **to be in the ~/take the ~** лиди́ровать; **he's still in the ~** он продолжа́ет лиди́ровать; **he has a ~ of one kilometre/5 minutes** он опережа́ет други́х на киломе́тр/на пять мину́т; **he lost the ~** он потеря́л ли́дерство; *Cards* **it's your ~** вам начина́ть, ваш ход; *Theat* **to play the ~** исполня́ть гла́вную роль; *fig*: **he gave them a ~** он показа́л им приме́р (*an example*), он им намекну́л (*a hint*); **to take the ~** взять на себя́ инициати́ву; **that gave the police a ~** э́то навелó поли́цию на след; **the police are following several ~s** поли́ция ведёт рассле́дование по не́скольким направле́ниям

2 (*leash*) поводóк, привязь; **the dog was on a ~** собáка былá на поводкé; **put the dog on the ~** возьми собáку на поводóк

3 *Elec* прóвод.

lead[2] *vti vt* **1** (*conduct*) водить (*indet impf*, *pf* по-), вести (*det impf*, *pf* по-) *and compounds*; **he led us round the museum/through the forest/to the director/to a table** он вёл нас по музéю/чéрез лес/к дирéктору/к столу; **she led the child by the hand** онá велá ребёнка зá руку; **he was ~ing his horse** он вёл лóшадь на поводу; **he led the way** он шёл пéрвым, он покáзывал нам дорóгу, *fig* он проклáдывал нам путь; **chance led him to Moscow** слýчай привёл егó в Москвý; **you're too easily led** ты слишком подáтлив; **one thing ~s to another** однó цепляется за другóе; **such talk will ~ us nowhere** такóй разговóр ни к чемý не приведёт

2 (*be leader of*) руководить + *I*, возглавлять (*impfs*); **he led the expedition/the army** он руководил экспедицией, он комáндовал áрмией; **he has led the party for 10 years** он возглавляет пáртию/он руководит пáртией ужé дéсять лет [**NB** *tense*]; **an officer led the mutiny** во главé мятежá стоял офицéр; **he led the procession/the crowd** он шёл во главé процéссии/впереди толпы

3 (*be first in*) опере|жáть (-дить); **they're ~ing us by 10 points** они опережáют нас на дéсять очкóв; *fig* **the Swiss ~ the field in clock-making** швейцáрские фирмы занимáют ведýщее положéние в произвóдстве часóв

4 **to ~ smb to** + *inf*: **his behaviour led me to conclude that...** из егó поведéния я заключил/пóнял, что...; **I've been led to believe that...** мне дáли понять, что...; **the report led me to alter my decision** доклáд застáвил меня изменить решéние

5 (*pass time*) вести (*only in det impf*); **he ~s a quiet life** он ведёт спокóйную жизнь; **he seems to ~ a double life** похóже, что он живёт двойнóй жизнью/ведёт двойнýю жизнь

6 *Cards*: **to ~ hearts** ходить с червéй

vi **1** (*go in front*) идти впереди; *Sport* лидировать (*impf*); **his horse led throughout the race** егó лóшадь шлá пéрвой весь забéг; **the German runner is ~ing** немéцкий бегýн лидирует; **that cyclist is ~ing by 20 metres** велосипедист оторвáлся от сопéрников [**NB** *tense*]/опережáет сопéрников на двáдцать мéтров

2 (*of roads*) вести; **where does this road ~?** кудá ведёт эта дорóга?; *fig* **it led to nothing** это ни к чемý не привелó

lead away *vt* уводить (увести); **we mustn't be led away from the point** не нáдо отвлекáться от сýти дéла

lead back *vti vt* приводить обрáтно; **I led her back** я привёл её назáд/обрáтно; **this ~s us back to my first point** это нас возвращáет к томý, что я сказáл внача́ле

vi: **this road ~s back to the village** эта дорóга ведёт обрáтно в дерéвню

lead in/into *vti vt* вводить в + *A* (ввести)

vi: **this path ~s into the garden** эта дорóжка ведёт в сад

lead off *vti vt* отводить

vi на|чинáть (-чáть); **who will ~ off?** кто начнёт?; **the band led off with a waltz** для начáла оркéстр сыгрáл вальс; **the bedroom ~s off the dining room** спáльня нахóдится за столóвой

lead on *vt*: **she'll ~ any man on** онá когó угóдно соблазнит; **he was led on by the other kids** егó подговорили (на это) другие ребята

lead out *vt* вы|водить (-вести)

lead up *vti vt* приводить/подводить к + *D*; *fig* **he led us up the garden path** он нас обманýл

vi: **the cello entry ~s up to the finale** виолончéль ведёт к финáлу; **in the years ~ing up to the revolution** в предреволюциóнные гóды; **events ~ing up to the war** события, ведýщие к войнé; **he led up to the crucial question gradually** он постепéнно подошёл к глáвному вопрóсу.

leader *n* руководитель (*m*); главá (*m*); лидер; (*of orchestra*) пéрвая скрипка; (*in newspaper*) передовáя (статья), *CQ* передовица; **political ~s** (*in West*) политические лидеры/вожди, (*SU*) руководители пáртии и правительства; **the ~ of the expedition** руководитель экспедиции; **the ~ of the tribe** вождь плéмени; **the ~ of the gang** главáрь шáйки.

leadership *n* руковóдство.

leader writer *n*: **he is a ~** он пишет передовицы.

leading *adj* (*outstanding*) выдающийся, глáвный; **a ~ role** глáвная роль, *also fig*; **~ lady** исполнительница глáвной рóли; **a ~ politician** извéстный/крýпный политический дéятель; *Law* **~ counsel** ведýщий адвокáт; *Sport* **the ~ horse** перéдняя/ведýщая лóшадь; *fig* **a ~ question** наводящий вопрóс.

leaf *n* **1** *Bot* лист (*pl* ́-ья, ́-ьев); **the trees are in ~** дерéвья покрылись листвóй (*collect* = *foliage*); **as the leaves begin to fall** во врéмя листопáда; *attr*: **~ mould** лиственный перегнóй

2 (*in book*) лист (*pl* -ы, -óв); **to turn over the leaves of a book** перелистывать книгу; *fig*: **to turn over a new ~** начáть нóвую жизнь; **you should take a ~ out of his book** ты бы брал с негó примéр

3: ~ of a table откиднáя доскá.

leafless *adj* безлистный.

leaflet *n* (*Bot or a sheet of paper, etc.*) листóк, листик; (*printed*) листóвка.

league *n* лига, союз; **the L. of Nations** Лига Нáций; **in ~ with** в союзе с + *I*.

leak *n* (*of fluid*) течь; (*of gas, etc. and fig*) утéчка; **the boat has sprung a ~** лóдка протекáет/далá течь; **to stop/plug a ~** остановить/задéлать течь; **there's a ~ of gas** здесь есть/имéется утéчка гáза; *fig* **a security ~** утéчка секрéтной информáции.

leak *vti vt*: **the drum is ~ing oil** бак пропускает масло; *fig* **somebody ~ed the information** через кого-то сведения просочились

vi течь (*impf*); (*a bit*) протекать (*only in impf*); (*of liquids and fig*) про|сачиваться (-сочиться); **the roof is ~ing** крыша течёт/протекает; **gas is ~ing in the kitchen** в кухне утечка газа; *fig* **the news has ~ed to the press** новость просочилась в прессу.

leakage *n* утечка, просачивание, *both also fig*; *fig* **the authorities are scared of a ~** власти боятся, чтобы эти сведения (*pl*) не стали известны.

leaky *adj*: **~ boots** дырявые ботинки; **the roof/boat is ~** крыша течёт/(*a little*) протекает, лодка протекает.

lean[1] *n* (*meat*) *CQ* постное мясо; **would you like fat or ~?** вам мясо жирное или попостнее?

lean[1] *adj* **1** худой, тощий; (*wiry*) поджарый; **a ~ horse/athlete** худая/тощая лошадь, спортсмен—одни мускулы; **~ meat** постное/нежирное мясо; **to grow ~** худеть

2 (*not productive*): **a ~ year** неурожайный год; **it was a ~ year academically** в этом году у нас была плохая успеваемость [**NB** успеваемость *used only Univ and School*].

lean[2] *vti vt* прислон|ять (-ить); **he ~t the ladder against the wall** он прислонил/приставил лестницу к стене; **he ~t his back against the wall** он прислонился к стене; **~ your head back** откиньте голову назад; **don't ~ your elbows on the table** не облокачивайтесь на стол

vi прислоняться к + *D*; опираться на/о + *A* (опереться); наклон|яться (-иться); **he ~t against the door** он прислонился к двери, (*exerting pressure*) он навалился на дверь; **he ~t forward to speak to her** он наклонился вперёд, чтобы с ней поговорить; **the post ~s towards the right** столб наклонился вправо [**NB** *tense*]; **he was ~ing on a stick/on his son** он опирался на палку/на плечо сына; **don't ~ out of the window** не высовывайтесь из окна; **she ~t over the sleeping child** она наклонилась над спящим ребёнком; **the trees are ~ing over in the wind** деревья гнутся от ветра; *fig*: **they are ~ing over backwards to be helpful to us** они всячески стараются нам угодить; **he ~s on her for guidance** он полагается на её мнение; **I ~ towards the view that...** я склоняюсь к тому мнению, что...

leaning *n* наклонность, склонность; **he has artistic ~s** у него художественные наклонности; **he has ~s towards journalism** у него есть склонность к журналистике.

lean-to *n* пристройка.

leap *n* прыжок, скачок; **in one ~** одним прыжком; *fig*: **a great ~ forward** большой скачок; **it's a ~ in the dark** это прыжок в неизвестность.

leap *vti vt*: **he ~t the fence** он перепрыг|нул через забор (*impf* -ивать)

vi прыг|ать (-нуть), скакать (по-); **the children ~t for joy** дети прыгали от радости; **he ~t out of the window** он выпрыгнул из окна (*as seen from street*)/в окно (*as seen from room*); **he ~t into the saddle/to his feet** он вскочил в седло/на ноги; **he ~t up (and down) in excitement** он даже подпрыгнул/подскочил от волнения; *fig*: **I'd ~ at the opportunity** я бы с радостью ухватился за эту возможность; **look before you ~** смотри, куда прыгаешь.

leap frog *n* чехарда.

leap year *n* високосный год.

learn *vti vt* изуч|ать (-ить); учиться + *D or inf* (*pfs* вы-, на-); (*memorize*) учить (вы-); (*a trade or skill*) обуч|аться (-иться); (*hear about*) узн|авать (-ать); **what do they ~ at school?** что они изучают в школе?; **he ~t French from his mother** он выучился французскому (языку) у матери; **I've ~t my part** я выучил свою роль; **to ~ a trade** обучаться ремеслу; **we ~t the news from a friend** мы узнали эту новость от друга; **I ~t up all I could about the places we were going to visit** я всё прочитал, что смог, о тех местах, которые мы собирались посмотреть; *fig*: **he's ~t his lesson** он получил хороший урок; *CQ* **I'll ~ him** я его проучу!

vi учиться + *inf or* на + *A*; (*find out*) узнавать; **he's ~ing to drive/to be an engineer** он учится водить (машину)/на инженера; **you must ~ to be patient** ты должен научиться терпению/быть терпеливым; **they are ~ing how to cope** они учатся (,как)/привыкают справляться с трудностями; **we ~ from our mistakes/from experience** мы учимся на ошибках/на собственном опыте; **we ~t about it from the radio** мы узнали об этом по радио; **I soon ~t about his bad temper** я скоро узнал его вспыльчивый нрав.

learned *adj* учёный.

learner *n* учен|ик, *f* -ица; учащийся; *attr*: *Aut* **a ~ driver** шофёр-ученик.

learning *n* (*act*) изучение; (*erudition*) учёность, знания (*pl*); **he's a man of ~** он человек учёный/широко образованный.

lease *n* (*contract*) аренда; (*period of lease*) срок аренды; **according to the terms of the ~** по условиям аренды; **the ~ expires in May** срок аренды истекает в мае; **to renew a ~** продлевать срок аренды; **they have taken/hold/have the house on a 10-year/long term ~** они сняли [**NB** *tense*] дом на десять лет/на долгий срок; *fig*: **your help gave him a new ~ of life** ваша помощь придала ему новые силы; **the overhaul gave the car a new ~ of life** после ремонта машина стала как новая.

lease *vt* (*of landlord*) сдавать, (*of tenant*) брать в аренду *or* внаём (*adv*) (сдать/взять); (*of tenant*) арендовать (*impf and pf*), снимать (снять); **they ~ the flat from their aunt** они снимают квартиру у тётки.

leasehold *n* аренда, наём; *attr*: **~ property** арендованная собственность.

leash *n see* **lead**[2] *n* **2.**

least *n* са́мое ме́ньшее; **that's the ~ we can expect** э́то са́мое ме́ньшее, чего́ мо́жно ожида́ть; **to say the ~ (of it)** мя́гко говоря́; **at ~** по кра́йней ме́ре; **I don't mind in the ~** мне соверше́нно всё равно́; **what is the ~ you'll take for the picture?** за каку́ю минима́льную/са́мую ме́ньшую це́ну вы согла́сны отда́ть ва́шу карти́ну?

least *adj* мале́йший; наиме́ньший; **is there the ~ chance of success?** есть ли хоть мале́йший шанс на успе́х?; **that's the ~ of my worries** э́то наиме́ньшая из мои́х забо́т, э́то меня́ ме́ньше всего́ волну́ет; **he answered without the ~ hesitation** он отве́тил сра́зу/не колеблясь.

least *adv* наиме́нее; **the ~ able pupil** наиме́нее спосо́бный учени́к; **he deserved it ~ of all** он ме́ньше всех э́то заслужи́л; **I'm not the ~ tired** я ничу́ть/нисколько не уста́л; **he wasn't the ~ interested** он был совсе́м не заинтересо́ван.

leastways, leastwise *adv* по кра́йней ме́ре.

leather *n* ко́жа; **patent ~** лакиро́ванная ко́жа; **Morocco ~** сафья́н; *attr* ко́жаный; **~ goods** ко́жаные изде́лия, коже́венные това́ры; **a ~ binding** ко́жаный переплёт.

leathery *adj fig*: **this meat is ~** э́то мя́со жёсткое как подо́шва.

leave *n* **1** (*permission*) разреше́ние, позволе́ние; **by your ~** с ва́шего разреше́ния/позволе́ния

2 (*absence*) о́тпуск; **he's on ~** он в о́тпуске; **he's on sick ~** (*for long period*) он в о́тпуске по боле́зни; (*for short period*) *CQ* он на бюллете́не; **I took 6 months ~** я взял о́тпуск на полго́да/шестиме́сячный о́тпуск; **to take ~ (of one's friends)** проща́ться (с друзья́ми); *fig*: **have you taken ~ of your senses?** ты что, с ума́ сошёл?/спя́тил?; **to take French ~** уходи́ть (с рабо́ты, с уро́ков) без разреше́ния, прогу́ливать.

leave *vti vt* **1** (*allow to remain*) остав|ля́ть (-́ить); **he left his coat in the taxi/his supper** он оста́вил пальто́ в такси́, он не притро́нулся к у́жину; **~ some salad for Dad** оста́вь сала́та отцу́; **~ it to me** предоста́вьте э́то мне; **it was left to me/to chance to decide** э́тот вопро́с пришло́сь реша́ть мне, всё оста́вили на во́лю слу́чая; **it's no good leaving it to him** нельзя́ э́то поруча́ть ему́; **don't ~ me all alone/in the lurch** не оставля́йте меня́ одного́/в беде́; **~ 2 pages blank** оста́вьте две чи́стых страни́цы; **better ~ the window/the question open** лу́чше оста́вить окно́/вопро́с откры́тым; **~ the theatre on your right** у теа́тра поверни́те нале́во; **let's ~ it at that/till tomorrow** дава́й э́то так и оста́вим, дава́й оста́вим э́то на *or* до за́втра; **this ~s much to be desired** э́то оставля́ет жела́ть мно́го лу́чшего; **some things are better left unsaid** о не́которых веща́х лу́чше не говори́ть; **they ~ all the work to her** они́ сва́ливают всю рабо́ту на неё; *fig*: **~ word to say where you'll be** попроси́ переда́ть, где ты бу́дешь; **take it or ~ it** как хоти́те, во́ля ва́ша; **he was left holding the baby** на него́ свали́лась вся отве́тственность

2 (*bequeath, etc.*) оставля́ть; завеща́ть (*impf and pf*); **he left everything to his son** он оста́вил/завеща́л всё сы́ну; **he was left an estate** ему́ доста́лось (в насле́дство) име́ние; **he left one son/an unfinished novel** по́сле него́ оста́лся сын/неоко́нченный рома́н

3 (*remain*) оста|ва́ться (-́ться); **I've no money left** у меня́ совсе́м не оста́лось/не остаётся де́нег; **how many are left?** ско́лько оста́лось/остаётся?; **we've an hour left before the train** до по́езда нам оста́лся/остаётся час [*NB present tense if speaker is anxious about or thinking of result*]; *Math* **7 from 10 ~s 3** от десяти́ отня́ть семь—остаётся три; *fig* **there's nothing left for it but to tell her** ничего́ не остаётся, как то́лько всё ей сказа́ть

4 (*quit*) уходи́ть (уйти́); (*abandon*) брос|а́ть (-́ить); поки|да́ть (-́нуть); **he ~s work/school at 5** он ухо́дит с рабо́ты/из шко́лы в пять часо́в; **they ~ school at 16** они́ ока́нчивают шко́лу в шестна́дцать лет; **I must ~ you** я до́лжен вас оста́вить/поки́нуть; **he left Rome/his post** он поки́нул Рим/пост; **you're a fool to ~ school/that job** ты дура́к, что бро́сил шко́лу/э́ту рабо́ту; **he left his wife** он бро́сил жену́; **can I ~ the table?** могу́ я встать из-за стола́?; **the train left the rails** по́езд сошёл с ре́льсов

vi уходи́ть (уйти́); уезжа́ть (уе́хать); **we ~ for Moscow today** мы сего́дня уезжа́ем в Москву́; **my secretary is leaving** мой секрета́рь ухо́дит с рабо́ты; **the train/flight ~s at 3 a.m.** по́езд отхо́дит/самолёт вылета́ет в три часа́ но́чи

leave about/around *vt*: **don't ~ your toys lying around** не разбра́сывай игру́шки где попа́ло

leave off *vti vt*: **you can ~ off your warm clothes now** тепе́рь мо́жно не надева́ть тёплой оде́жды

vi переста|ва́ть (-́ть); **the rain has left off** дождь переста́л; **~ off arguing!** переста́ньте спо́рить!

leave out *vt*: **you've left out two words** ты пропусти́л два сло́ва; **we left that out of our calculations** мы э́то упусти́ли/не учли́ в на́ших расчётах; **he feels left out** он чу́вствует себя́ ли́шним; **~ me out of this** меня́ в э́то не втя́гивайте

leave over *vt*: **how much will that ~ over?** ско́лько тогда́ оста́нется?; **anything left over can go to the cats** все оста́тки мо́жно отда́ть ко́шкам.

leaven *n* дро́жжи (*no sing*).

leavings *npl* оста́тки; *CQ* (*of food only*) объе́дки, оста́тки.

lecherous *adj* распу́тный, развра́тный; (*of look, etc.*) похотли́вый.

lecture *n* ле́кция; **to deliver a ~** чита́ть ле́кцию; (*reproof*) **I gave him a ~ for that**

я его́ отчита́л за э́то; *attr*: ~ **theatre** аудито́рия; **he's on a ~ tour in France** он е́здит по Фра́нции с ле́кциями.

lecture *vti vt*: **stop lecturing me** да переста́нь ты мне ле́кции чита́ть!

vi: **he ~s on history** он чита́ет (нам) ле́кции по исто́рии (*usu impf*), он преподаёт исто́рию (*only in impf*).

lecturer *n* (*visiting*) ле́ктор; *Univ* (*on staff*) преподава́тель (*m*); **he's a ~ in chemistry** он преподаёт хи́мию в университе́те.

lectureship *n*: **he's got a ~ at Oxford** он получи́л ме́сто преподава́теля в О́ксфордском университе́те.

ledge *n* (*of cliff, wall*) усту́п; (*shelf*) по́лка, по́лочка; **window ~** подоко́нник.

ledger *n* гроссбу́х.

lee *n*: **in our ~** с подве́тренной стороны́ (от нас); **we were in the ~ of the cliff** мы бы́ли защищены́ от ве́тра утёсом; *attr*: **the ~ side** (*of ship*) подве́тренный борт су́дна.

leech *n* пия́вка, *also fig*.

leek *n* лук-поре́й (*also collect*).

leer *vi*: **he ~ed at her** он поеда́л её глаза́ми.

lees *npl* оса́док (*sing*).

leeward *n* подве́тренная сторона́; **the coast lay to ~** бе́рег был с подве́тренной стороны́.

leeway *n Naut* дрейф; *fig* **he has a lot of ~ to make up** ему́ ну́жно мно́гое наверста́ть.

left *n* ле́вая сторона́; **keep to the ~** держи́тесь ле́вой стороны́; **he sat on her ~** он сел сле́ва от неё; **from ~ to right** сле́ва напра́во (*advs*); **turn to the ~ at the crossroads** на перекрёстке поверни́те нале́во (*adv*); *Polit*: **the ~** ле́вые (*usu pl*); **politics of the ~** ле́вая поли́тика.

left *adj* ле́вый, *also Polit, Sport*; **his views are ~ of centre** он дово́льно ле́вых взгля́дов; *Sport* **~ back/wing** ле́вый защи́тник, левое крыло́.

left *adv*: **turn ~** поверни́те нале́во; **he's standing ~ of the pillar** он стои́т сле́ва от коло́нны.

left-hand *adj*: **a car with ~ drive** маши́на с рулём сле́ва; **a ~ turn** ле́вый поворо́т; **a ~ screw** винт с ле́вой резьбо́й.

left-handed *adj*: **he/she is ~** он/она́ левша́.

left luggage office *n* ка́мера хране́ния.

left-overs *npl see* **leavings.**

left-wing *adj Polit* ле́вый.

leg *n* **1** (*of human, horse, cow, etc.*) нога́; (*of bird, dog, bear, etc.*) ла́па; (*of insects, small birds*) ла́пка; (*of furniture*) но́жка; (*of a boot*) голени́ще; **I've been on my ~s all day** я весь день на нога́х; **I must stretch my ~s** мне ну́жно размя́ть но́ги; **give me a ~ up on to the wall** подсади́ меня́ на забо́р; **the horse got up on its hind ~s** ло́шадь вста́ла на дыбы́; **he walked me off my ~s** он меня́ совсе́м загоня́л; **trouser ~** штани́на; *fig*: **he's pulling your ~** он тебя́ разы́грывает; **he hasn't a ~ to stand on** ему́ нет никако́го оправда́ния; *attr*: **there's no ~ room in this car** в э́той маши́не ма́ло ме́ста для ног/не́куда дева́ть но́ги

2 (*stage*: *of journey*) эта́п пути́; *Sport* (*in relay*) круг, эта́п; (*one of a series of matches*) тур.

legacy *n* насле́дство; *fig* насле́дие.

legal *adj* (*lawful*) зако́нный, правово́й; (*juridical*) юриди́ческий; **the ~ owner** зако́нный владе́лец; **a ~ document** правово́й докуме́нт; **the ~ faculty** юриди́ческий факульте́т; **a ~ expert** юри́ст; **~ action** суде́бный иск; **~ costs** суде́бные изде́ржки; **a ~ decision** реше́ние суда́; **I'll take ~ advice** я посове́туюсь с юри́стом; **he took ~ proceedings against them** он на́чал суде́бный проце́сс про́тив них.

legality *n* зако́нность.

legalize *vt* узако́н|ивать (-ить); **they have now ~d the sale of alcohol** сейча́с прода́жа спиртны́х напи́тков разрешена́.

legend *n* леге́нда.

leggy *adj* (*of child, puppy, etc.*) длинноно́гий.

legible *adj* разбо́рчивый.

legislate *vi* изда|ва́ть зако́ны (-́ть).

legitimate *adj* зако́нный; **a ~ child** законнорождённый ребёнок; *fig* **a ~ reason for absence** уважи́тельная причи́на (для) отсу́тствия.

leg-pull *n CQ* ро́зыгрыш.

leisure *n* досу́г; свобо́дное вре́мя; **I'll do it at my ~** я сде́лаю э́то на досу́ге; **he spends his ~ gardening** он в свобо́дное вре́мя рабо́тает в саду́; **I have little ~** у меня́ ма́ло свобо́дного вре́мени; *attr*: **~ hours** часы́ досу́га.

leisurely *adj* нетороплй́вый; **at a ~ pace** неторопли́во; **we had a ~ journey/holiday** мы путеше́ствовали не спеша́, мы провели́ о́тпуск в по́лном безде́лье.

lemon *n* лимо́н; *attr* лимо́нный; **~ squeezer** соковыжима́лка для лимо́на.

lemonade *n* лимона́д.

lend *vt* **1** *Fin off* ссу|жа́ть (-ди́ть); (*privately*) да|ва́ть взаймы́ (*adv*) (-ть); ода́лживать (одолжи́ть); **the bank lent him money** банк ссуди́л ему́ де́ньги; (*privately*) **can you ~ me £1?** мо́жете ли вы одолжи́ть мне/дать мне взаймы́ оди́н фунт?; (*of governments*) **the French lent the Italians a million francs** францу́зское прави́тельство предоста́вило Ита́лии заём в миллио́н фра́нков

2 (*things*): **I'll ~ you that book** я вам дам почита́ть э́ту кни́гу; **I never ~ my car** я никому́ не даю́ води́ть мою́ маши́ну; **can you ~ me a ladder?** мо́жно попроси́ть у вас ненадо́лго/на вре́мя ле́стницу?; *fig*: **would you ~ a hand with my trunk?** помоги́ мне нести́ чемода́н; **the presence of the Rector lent importance to the occasion** прису́тствие ре́ктора придава́ло осо́бую ва́жность э́тому собы́тию

3 *reflexive use*: **the system ~s itself to abuse** при тако́й систе́ме возмо́жны злоупотребле́ния (*pl*); **don't ~ yourself to their schemes** не дава́й себя́ втяну́ть в их махина́ции;

his poetry doesn't ~ itself to translation его́ стихи́ не поддаю́тся перево́ду

lend out *vt*: **he ~s out money at high interest** он ссужа́ет де́ньги под больши́е проце́нты (*pl*).

length *n* **1** (*in space*) длина́; **what ~ is the room?** како́й длины́ э́та ко́мната?; **a plank 3 metres in ~** доска́ длино́й в три ме́тра; **along the whole ~ of the street** на всём протяже́нии у́лицы; **he measured his ~ on the floor** он растяну́лся на полу́ во весь рост; *Sport* **the horse won by 3 ~s** ло́шадь опереди́ла други́х на три ко́рпуса; *fig*: **he keeps everyone at arm's ~** он де́ржит всех на расстоя́нии; **she'll go to any ~s to get her way** она́ пойдёт на всё, лишь бы доби́ться своего́; **he went to great ~s to find them** ему́ сто́ило большо́го труда́ их найти́; **I went to the ~ of inviting him home** я да́же пошёл на то, что́бы пригласи́ть его́ к себе́ (домо́й)

2 (*of time*): **a stay of some ~** дово́льно дли́тельное пребыва́ние; **the ~ of a note/syllable** долгота́ но́ты/сло́га; **in a book/film of this ~** в кни́ге тако́го объёма, в фи́льме тако́го метража́; **at ~** (*finally*) наконе́ц, в конце́ концо́в; (*long*) **he spoke at ~** он до́лго говори́л; (*in detail*) **we discussed it at ~** мы подро́бно обсуди́ли э́то

3 (*section*): **a skirt ~** отре́з на ю́бку; **a ~ of pipe** кусо́к/отре́зок трубы́.

lengthen *vti*: **to ~ a skirt** удлин|я́ть ю́бку (-и́ть); **the days are ~ing** дни стано́вятся длинне́е.

lengthways, lengthwise *adv*: **lay the planks ~** положи́те до́ски вдоль; **cut the plank ~** ре́жьте до́ску в длину́; **I ruled the paper ~** я расчерти́л лист продо́льно.

lengthy *adj* дли́нный; (*protracted*) дли́тельный; **a ~ speech** простра́нная/дли́нная речь; **a ~ holiday** дли́тельный о́тпуск.

lenient *adj* мя́гкий, снисходи́тельный; терпели́вый; **a ~ judge** нестро́гий судья́; **he's ~ with his pupils** он не строг с ученика́ми; [**NB** *used predicatively* не *separates from adj*].

lens *n* ли́нза; *Photo* объекти́в; *Anat* хруста́лик гла́за.

Lent *n Rel* вели́кий пост.

lentil *n* чечеви́ца.

leper *n* прокажённый.

leprosy *n* прока́за.

Lesbian *n* лесбия́нка.

lesion *n Med* пораже́ние о́ргана.

less *adj* ме́ньший (*only attr*); *usu translated by* ме́ньше; **eat ~ sugar** е́шь(те) ме́ньше са́хара; **a sum ~ than £1** су́мма ме́ньше фу́нта; **I have ~ time than you have** у меня́ ме́ньше вре́мени, чем у тебя́; **I'll take whichever helping is the ~** я возьму́ ту по́рцию, что поме́ньше; **no ~ a person than the President** ни бо́льше ни ме́ньше как сам президе́нт; **the pain grew ~** боль уме́ньшилась; **~ noise!** ти́ше!; **it's nothing ~ than a disaster** э́то настоя́щее бе́дствие.

less *adv* **1** (*with adjs and participles*) ме́нее; **that's even ~ likely** э́то ещё ме́нее вероя́тно; **it's getting ~ and ~ easy/interesting** стано́вится всё трудне́е и трудне́е /всё ме́нее и ме́нее интере́сно; **that's more or ~ right** э́то бо́лее и́ли ме́нее ве́рно; **he's ~ well-known than his father** он не так изве́стен, как его́ оте́ц; **the child was ~ hurt than frightened** ребёнок не сто́лько ушиб́ся, ско́лько испуга́лся

2 (*with verbs*) ме́ньше; **the ~ I work, the ~ I earn** чем ме́ньше я рабо́таю, тем ме́ньше зараба́тываю; **still/even ~ do I approve of her** она́ мне всё ме́ньше (и ме́ньше) нра́вится; (*of actor*) **he plays ~ and ~** он всё ре́же появля́ется на сце́не

3 *phrases*: **none the ~** тем не ме́нее; **in ~ than an hour's time** ме́ньше чем че́рез час; **we'll be there in ~ than no time** мы ми́гом там бу́дем.

less *prep* без + *G*; **I was there for a year ~ three days** я там был год без трёх дней; **I have already been in Paris for a month ~ three days** че́рез три дня бу́дет ме́сяц, как я в Пари́же; **I received my salary ~ 10%** у меня́ вы́чли из зарпла́ты де́сять проце́нтов.

lessee *n* съёмщик, аренда́тор.

lessen *vti* уменьш|а́ть(ся) (-́ить(ся)).

lesser *adj* ме́ньший; **the ~ of two evils** ме́ньшее из двух зол.

lesson *n* уро́к; **a maths/singing ~** уро́к матема́тики/пе́ния; **he gives/takes private ~s** он даёт/берёт ча́стные уро́ки; **I'm having driving ~s** я хожу́ на ку́рсы води́телей; *fig*: **that taught him a ~** э́то бы́ло ему́ хоро́шим уро́ком; **I'll teach him a ~** я препода́м ему́ уро́к; **let that be a ~ to you** пусть э́то послу́жит тебе́ уро́ком.

lessor *n* хозя́ин.

lest *conj* (*of purpose*) что́бы... не; (*after verbs of fearing*) как бы... не [**NB** *both constructions followed by inf if subject of both clauses is same person, by past tense if subjects are different*]; **he hid ~ they should see him** он спря́тался, что́бы его́ не уви́дели; **we were anxious ~ we should be late** мы беспоко́ились, как бы не опозда́ть.

let *n* сда́ча внаём; **we can't get a ~ for the house** мы ника́к не мо́жем сдать э́тот дом.

let *vt* **1** (*permit*) разреш|а́ть (-и́ть), позвол|я́ть (-́ить); пус|ка́ть (-ти́ть); дава́ть (дать); **~ me pass/help you** разреши́те пройти́, позво́льте мне вам помо́чь; **don't ~ the fire go out** не дава́йте огню́ пога́снуть; **we wanted to come but father wouldn't ~ us** мы хоте́ли прийти́, но оте́ц нам не разреши́л

2 *uses with noun + verb*: (*let go*) пус|ка́ть (-ти́ть) *and compounds*; (*let be*) остав|ля́ть (-́ить); (*let drop*) роня́ть (урони́ть); **don't ~ the opportunity go** не упуска́й э́ту возмо́жность: **don't ~ go (of) my hand/the rope** не отпуска́й мою́ ру́ку/верёвку; **don't ~ that**

dog go не спуска́й соба́ку с поводка́ (*off leash when walking*), не спуска́й э́ту соба́ку с це́пи/с при́вязи (*when chained up at home*); (*of horse, car*) **right, ~ her go!** ну, а тепе́рь побыстре́й!; **~ him be** оста́вьте его́; **I ~ the cup drop** я урони́л ча́шку; **he ~ drop a hint** он оброни́л намёк; **I'll ~ them know about it** я им сообщу́ об э́том; **~ me know what time you're coming** дай мне знать, когда́/*CQ* во ско́лько ты придёшь; **~ it pass!** а, ла́дно!

3: to ~ blood пуска́ть кровь

4 (*hire out*) сдава́ть (сдать); **the flat is ~** кварти́ра сдана́; **"to ~"** «сдаётся»

5 *as aux verb forming indirect imperative with 1st and 3rd person pronouns; in 3rd person introduced by particle* пусть, *CQ* пуска́й; *in 1st person use pf future with or without* дава́й(те); **~ him wait** пусть он подождёт; **~ them all come** пусть/*CQ* пуска́й они́ все приду́т; **just ~ him try!** пусть то́лько попро́бует!; **~ it be clearly understood that...** мы/вы должны́ я́сно понима́ть, что...; (*as supposition*) **~ AB be equal to CD** пусть AB равня́ется CD; **~'s begin** дава́й(те) начнём; **~'s go** пойдём *or* пошли́, (*by car*) поéдем *or* поéхали; **~'s see what can be done** посмо́трим, что мо́жно сде́лать; **~ me see** (*look*) покажи́ мне; **~ me see, where did I put it?** посто́й, куда́ я э́то положи́л?

6 *used reflexively*: **don't ~ yourself fall/be seen** не упади́, не пока́зывайся; **she never ~s herself go** она́ всегда́ так сде́ржанна; **he has ~ himself go completely** он совсе́м опусти́лся; **you'll ~ yourself in for a lot of trouble** вы нарыва́етесь на неприя́тности; **he doesn't know what he's ~ting himself in for** он не зна́ет, во что ввяза́лся

let down *vt*: **to ~ down the curtain** опус|ка́ть за́навес (-ти́ть); **my skirt/this tyre needs ~ting down** мою́ ю́бку на́до удлини́ть *or* отпусти́ть, ши́ну на́до немно́го спусти́ть; *fig*: **he'll never ~ you down** он никогда́ не подведёт; **the weather/the car ~ us down** нас подвела́ пого́да/маши́на

let in *vt* впус|ка́ть (-ти́ть); **~ me in** впусти́ меня́; **he ~ himself in** он о́тпер дверь и вошёл; **the roof ~s in rain** кры́ша течёт; **the window barely ~s in any light** окно́ е́ле пропуска́ет свет; *CQ*: **shall we ~ her in on this?** расска́жем ей об э́том?; **this has ~ me in for a lot of expense** э́то влете́ло мне в копе́ечку

let off *vt*: **will you ~ me off at the next/first stop?** вы́садите меня́ на сле́дующей остано́вке; **he ~ off the gun** он вы́стрелил (из ружья́); **to ~ off steam** вы́пустить пар, *also fig*; **to ~ off fireworks** устр|а́ивать фейерве́рк (*sing*) (-о́ить); **he was ~ off with a fine** он отде́лался штра́фом; **he's so tired, I ~ him off** он так уста́л, что я отпусти́л его́

let on *vi CQ*: **don't ~ on that we know** не расска́зывай/не говори́ никому́ о том, что мы узна́ли

let out *vt*: **he ~ the cat out** он вы́пустил ко́шку (на у́лицу); **he ~ out a yell** он изда́л вопль/крик; *Sew*: **I ~ out my dress/the waist** я вы́пустила пла́тье в бока́х/в по́ясе; **there's nothing to ~ out** здесь не́чего вы́пустить; *fig* **he ~ the cat out of the bag** он вы́болтал секре́т

let up *vi* переста|ва́ть (-́ть); прекра|ща́ться (-ти́ться); **the rain is ~ting up** дождь перестаёт/прекраща́ется; **he never ~s up** он совсе́м не даёт себе́ переды́шки.

let-down *n CQ* разочарова́ние.

lethal *adj* смерте́льный; **a ~ dose** смерте́льная до́за; **~ gases** отравля́ющие га́зы; **a ~ weapon** смертоно́сное ору́жие.

lethargic *adj* летарги́ческий; (*apathetic*) вя́лый.

letter *n* **1** (*of alphabet*) бу́ква; **capital/small ~** загла́вная *or* прописна́я/строчна́я бу́ква; **to write in block ~s** писа́ть печа́тными бу́квами; **the ~ of the law** бу́ква зако́на; **to carry out orders to the ~** то́чно вы́полнить приказа́ние (*sing*); **he uses four-~ words** он сквернoсло́вит

2 (*missive*) письмо́; **registered ~** заказно́е письмо́; **~ of introduction** рекоменда́тельное письмо́

3 *pl* (**~s**): **a man of ~s** литера́тор.

lettuce *n* сала́т.

leukaemia, (*US*) **leukemia** *n Med* белокро́вие, лейкеми́я.

level *n* **1** (*height, degree*) у́ровень (*m*), *also fig*; **at ground/eye/roof ~** на у́ровне земли́/глаз (*pl*)/кры́ши; **above/below sea ~** над у́ровнем/ни́же у́ровня мо́ря; **the water is on a ~ with the banks** вода́ вро́вень (*adv*) с берега́ми; *Aut* **the car does 100 m.p.h. on the ~** ско́рость маши́ны по ро́вной доро́ге сто миль в час; *fig*: **he has found his own ~** он нашёл себе́ ро́вню, он нашёл себе́ под ста́ть; **he's a professional but not on a high ~** он профессиона́л, но не о́чень высо́кого кла́сса; **they're on the same ~ intellectually** у́мственное разви́тие у них одина́ковое; **talks are going on at government ~** иду́т перего́воры на у́ровне прави́тельств; *CQ* **is he on the ~?** он поря́дочный челове́к?

2 (*instrument*) (**spirit-**)**~** у́ровень (*m*), ватерпа́с.

level *adj* (*even*) ро́вный; (*flat*) пло́ский; **the road runs ~ for miles** доро́га ро́вная на мно́го миль вперёд; **this floor is ~ with the street** э́тот эта́ж на одно́м у́ровне с у́лицей; **make the floor ~** сде́лайте пол ро́вным; **the water is already ~ with the road** вода́ уже́ вро́вень (*adv*) с доро́гой; **add a ~ spoonful of flour** доба́вь ло́жку муки́ без го́рки; **this goal made the score ~** э́тот гол сравня́л счёт; *fig*: **in ~ tones** ро́вным го́лосом; **I'll do my ~ best** я сде́лаю всё, что смогу́; **you'll need a ~ head** тебе́ пона́добится всё твоё хладнокро́вие.

level *adv*: **the plane flew ~ with the mountain tops** самолёт шёл вро́вень с верши́нами гор; **to draw ~ with** поравня́ться с + *I*.

level *vti vt* **1** вы|ра́внивать (-ровнять); **to ~ a road/lawn** вы́ровнять доро́гу/газо́н; **the town was ~led to the ground** го́род был разру́шен до основа́ния

2 (*aim*): **he ~led his gun at the lion** он навёл ружьё на льва; *fig* **accusations were ~led against him** про́тив него́ бы́ли вы́двинуты обвине́ния

vi выра́вниваться; **at 1,000 metres the pilot ~led off** на высоте́ ты́сячи ме́тров пило́т вы́ровнял самолёт; **wages are ~ling off** зарпла́та (*sing*) выра́внивается.

level crossing *n* перее́зд; (*as road sign*) «шлагба́ум!»

level-headed *adj* уравнове́шенный, споко́йный.

lever *n* рыча́г.

lever *vt*: **to ~ open/up/out** откры́ть/подня́ть/сдви́нуть при по́мощи рычага́ (*usu pfs*).

leverage *n*: **there's no ~** (здесь) нет опо́ры.

leveret *n* зайчо́нок.

levity *n* легкомы́слие.

levy *vt*: **to ~ taxes** взима́ть нало́ги (*impf*); **a tax was levied on large incomes** кру́пные дохо́ды бы́ли обло́жены нало́гом; *Mil* **to ~ troops** на|бира́ть ре́крутов (-бра́ть).

lewd *adj* (*of jokes*) непристо́йный; (*of look*) похотли́вый.

lexicographer *n* лексико́граф.

liability *n* **1** (*responsibility*): **I don't accept ~ for my wife's debts** я не отвеча́ю за долги́ жены́; **don't admit ~ for the accident** не бери́ на себя́ вину́ за э́ту ава́рию

2 (*obligation*) обя́занность; **~ to pay taxes/for military service** обя́занность плати́ть нало́ги/отбыва́ть во́инскую пови́нность

3 *usu pl Fin* (*debts*) задо́лженность; **to meet one's liabilities** покры́ть свою́ задо́лженность (*sing*); **we've incurred heavy liabilities** мы взя́ли на себя́ тяжёлые обяза́тельства; *fig CQ* **he's a real ~** он больша́я обу́за.

liable *adj usu predic* **1** (*subject to*): **he's ~ for call-up** он военнообя́занный; **goods ~ to duty** това́р (*sing*), облага́емый по́шлиной; **everyone is ~ to income tax** все обя́заны плати́ть подохо́дный нало́г; **if you park here you'll be ~ to a fine** е́сли ты поста́вишь маши́ну здесь, тебя́ мо́гут оштрафова́ть

2 (*prone to*): **she's ~ to sea-sickness** она́ подве́ржена морско́й боле́зни; **we're all ~ to make mistakes** всем сво́йственно ошиба́ться; **his remarks are ~ to misconstruction** его́ замеча́ния мо́жно непра́вильно/ло́жно истолкова́ть; **we are ~ to get snow here in January** в январе́ у нас быва́ет снег.

liaison *n* связь, *also Mil*; **there's no ~ between departments** ме́жду отде́лами нет свя́зи; **they're having a ~** у них рома́н; *attr*: **~ officer** офице́р свя́зи.

liar *n* лгун, лжец; *CQ* **~!** (ты) врёшь!

libel *n* клевета́; **he was sued for ~** на него́ по́дали в суд за клевету́.

libel *vt*: **to ~ smb** клевета́ть на кого́-л (на-), оклевета́ть кого́-л (*pf*)

libellous *adj* клеветни́ческий; **a ~ article** клеветни́ческая статья́; **that's a ~ remark** э́то клевета́.

liberal *n* либера́л.

liberal *adj* **1** (*generous*) ще́дрый; (*plentiful*) оби́льный; **he's ~ with his promises** он щедр на обеща́ния; **~ entertainment** оби́льное угоще́ние

2 (*of views, etc.*) либера́льный, *also Polit*; **a man of ~ outlook** челове́к либера́льных взгля́дов (*pl*); **a ~ education** гуманита́рное/о́бщее образова́ние; **the ~ arts** гуманита́рные нау́ки; *Polit* (*UK*) **the L. government** прави́тельство либера́лов.

liberate *vt* освобо|жда́ть (-ди́ть).

liberty *n* **1** свобо́да; **he is now at ~** он тепе́рь на свобо́де; **you're at ~ to go** вы мо́жете идти́; **I'm not at ~ to decide** я не во́лен реша́ть

2 (*often pl*; *presumption*]: **I've taken the ~ of writing to you** я взял на себя́ сме́лость обрати́ться к вам; **the translator took liberties with the text** перево́дчик во́льно обошёлся с те́кстом; **don't take liberties with me!** не фамилья́рничай(те) со мной!

librarian *n* библиоте́карь (*m*).

library *n* библиоте́ка; **I'm going to work in the ~** я иду́ рабо́тать в библиоте́ку/в чита́льный зал.

licence, (*US*) **license** *n* **1** (*permit*) разреше́ние, пра́во; *off* лице́нзия; **to issue a ~ to sell tobacco** выдава́ть разреше́ние/лице́нзию на прода́жу табака́; **~ to fish** разреше́ние на ры́бную ло́влю; **to import/manufacture under ~** ввози́ть/производи́ть това́р по лице́нзии; **we have a ~ to manufacture this medicine** у нас есть разреше́ние на изготовле́ние э́того лека́рства; *Aut* **driving ~** води́тельские права́ (*pl*)

2 (*freedom*) во́льность; *pejor* изли́шняя во́льность; **poetic ~** поэти́ческая во́льность; **some ~ can be allowed in translation** в перево́де мо́жно допусти́ть не́которую во́льность.

license *vt*: **this shop is ~d to sell spirits** в э́том магази́не разрешена́ прода́жа спиртны́х напи́тков; **my car isn't ~d** моя́ маши́на не зарегистри́рована.

licentious *adj* распу́щенный.

lichen *n* лиша́йник.

lick *n fig CQ*: **it needs a ~ of paint** на́до поднови́ть кра́ску; **just give the room a ~ and a promise** ты хоть для ви́ду/немно́го убери́ в ко́мнате; **the car was going at the hell of a ~** маши́на несла́сь /лете́ла на сумасше́дшей ско́рости.

lick *vt* **1** лиз|а́ть (-ну́ть); обли́з|ывать (-а́ть); **he ~ed his ice cream** он лизну́л моро́женое; **don't ~ your fingers** не обли́зывай па́льцы; **the dog was ~ing itself** пес обли́зывался; **he ~ed the plate clean** он вы́лизал таре́лку; **the cat ~ed up the spilt milk** ко́шка вы́лизала про́литое молоко́; **he ~ed his lips at the thought** он облизну́лся при э́той мы́сли

2 *fig uses*: **flames were ~ing the wall** языки́ пла́мени лиза́ли сте́ну; *CQ*: **to ~ smb's boots** подхали́мничать пе́ред кем-л (*impf*); **our team was ~ed** нас разби́ли в пух и прах; **we'll ~ the conceit out of him/him into shape** мы собьём с него́ спесь, мы бы́стро приведём его́ в ну́жный вид.

licking *n CQ* (**a ~**) (*beating*) по́рка; (*defeat*) пораже́ние, разгро́м.

lid *n* кры́шка; *fig CQ* **that puts the ~ on our plans** всем на́шим пла́нам кры́шка.

lie[1] *n* ложь; **white ~** неви́нная ложь; **he told a ~** он солга́л; **don't tell ~s** не лги; **this gives the ~ to his story** э́то зна́чит, что он солга́л.

lie[1] *vi* (*deliberately*) лгать (со-); (*gratuitously and wildly*) *CQ* врать *and compounds*; **she ~s unblushingly** *CQ* она́ врёт и не красне́ет.

lie[2] *n*: **the ~ of the land** хара́ктер ме́стности; *fig* **to explore the ~ of the land** зонди́ровать по́чву.

lie[2] *vi* **1** (*of people*) лежа́ть (по-); **to ~ in bed/on the grass** лежа́ть в посте́ли/на траве́; **he lay asleep/sick** он спал, он был бо́лен

2 (*of things*) лежа́ть (*only in impf*); **the book lay unopened** кни́га лежа́ла нераскры́той; **the town ~s before us/in ruins/in the valley** го́род лежи́т пе́ред на́ми/в разва́линах/в доли́не; **our way ~s along the river/to the east** наш путь лежи́т вдоль реки́/на восто́к; **snow lay a metre deep** лежа́л метро́вый слой сне́га; **the fields lay deep in snow** на поля́х лежа́л глубо́кий снег; **the snow didn't ~** снег бы́стро растая́л; **the ships lay at anchor** корабли́ стоя́ли на я́коре; **the factory lay idle** заво́д проста́ивал

3 *fig uses*: **~ low for a bit** затаи́сь на вре́мя; **the choice ~s with him** вы́бор за ним; **where does the problem ~?** в чём и́менно пробле́ма?; **the responsibility/fault ~s with him** отве́тственность/вина́ лежи́т на нём; **he knows where his interests ~** он зна́ет, что ему́ (бо́лее) вы́годно; **to find out how the land ~s** вы́яснить, как обстои́т де́ло; **as you've made your bed, so must you ~ on it** сам завари́л ка́шу—сам и расхлёбывай

lie ahead *vi* предстоя́ть + *D* (*impf*); **a hard winter ~s ahead of us** нам предстои́т суро́вая зима́

lie back *vi*: **he lay back in his chair** он отки́нулся на спи́нку кре́сла

lie behind *vi*: **these days lay far behind** те времена́ оста́лись позади́; **what ~s behind their silence?** что кро́ется за их молча́нием?

lie down *vi* ложи́ться (лечь); лежа́ть; **~ down on the couch** ложи́тесь на дива́н; **he was lying down on the bed** он лежа́л на крова́ти; *fig* **I shan't take such treatment lying down** я не потерплю́ тако́го с собо́й обраще́ния

lie in *vi*: **you can ~ in till 10** (ты) мо́жешь полежа́ть в посте́ли до десяти́ (часо́в)

lie up *vi*: **he lay up for a whole month** он пролежа́л (в посте́ли) це́лый ме́сяц.

lieutenant *n* лейтена́нт.

lieutenant-colonel *n* подполко́вник.

lieutenant-general *n* генера́л-лейтена́нт.

life *n* **1** жизнь; **animal/plant ~** жизнь живо́тных/расте́ний; **there's not much bird ~ here** здесь ма́ло птиц; **there were no signs of ~ in the house** в до́ме не́ было никаки́х при́знаков жи́зни

2 (*as opposed to death*) жизнь; **to fight for one's ~** боро́ться за жизнь; **the doctors were fighting for his ~** врачи́ боро́лись за его́ жизнь; **run for your ~** беги́ изо всех сил; **it's a matter of ~ and death** э́то вопро́с жи́зни и сме́рти; **at the cost of many lives** цено́й мно́гих жи́зней; **many lives were lost** бы́ло мно́го поги́бших; **the surgeon's skill brought him back to ~** иску́сные ру́ки хиру́рга верну́ли ему́ жизнь; **he owes his ~ to you** он вам обя́зан жи́знью; **he barely escaped with his ~** он е́ле спа́сся; **an attempt was made on his ~** бы́ло совершено́ покуше́ние на его́ жизнь, на него́ бы́ло совершено́ покуше́ние; **he took his own ~** он поко́нчил с собо́й

3 (*span of life*) жизнь; **I've lived here all my ~** я всю жизнь живу́ здесь [**NB** *tense*]; **he was lamed for ~** он оста́лся хромы́м на всю жизнь; **country/high/home ~** дереве́нская/све́тская/семе́йная жизнь; **he leads an active/quiet ~** он ведёт де́ятельную/споко́йную жизнь; **at his time of ~** в его́ во́зрасте; **by the fifties TV had become a part of everyday ~** телеви́дение вошло́ в быт в пятидеся́тых года́х

4 (*in special fields*): *Art*: **a portrait from ~** портре́т с нату́ры; **still ~** натюрмо́рт; *Med* **time of ~** климактери́ческий пери́од; *Tech*: **the ~ of a battery/car** срок слу́жбы батаре́йки/маши́ны; **these machines have a long ~** э́ти маши́ны до́лго слу́жат

5 *fig uses*: **there he is, as large as ~** а вот и он со́бственной персо́ной; **the children are full of ~** де́ти полны́ жи́зни; **he was the ~ and soul of the party** он был душо́й о́бщества; **he's like a cat with nine lives** он живу́ч как ко́шка; **I lead a dog's ~** у меня́ соба́чья жизнь; **it scared the ~ out of me** я до́ смерти перепуга́лся; **he's seen ~** он зна́ет жизнь [**NB** *tense*]; *CQ*: **I had the time of my ~** я в жи́зни не получа́л тако́го удово́льствия; **not on your ~!** да никогда́ в жи́зни!; **what a ~!** ну и жизнь!

6 *attr*: **~ tenant/member** пожи́зненный аренда́тор/член.

lifebelt *n* спаса́тельный по́яс.

lifeboat *n* спаса́тельное су́дно; (*on ship*) спаса́тельная шлю́пка.

lifebuoy *n* спаса́тельный круг.

life jacket *n* спаса́тельный жиле́т.

lifeless *adj* безжи́зненный, *also fig*.

lifelike *adj*: **it's a ~ portrait of him** он на портре́те как в жи́зни.

lifelong *adj*: **theirs was a ~ friendship** они́ дружи́ли всю жизнь; **painting was his ~ hobby** он всю жизнь увлека́лся рисова́нием.

life-saving *n*: **a course in ~** курс по спасе́нию утопа́ющих.

life-size *adj*: **a ~ statue** ста́туя в натура́льную величину́.

lifetime *n* (вся) жизнь; **the work of a ~** труд всей жи́зни; **once in a ~** раз в жи́зни; **it won't happen in our ~** э́то при на́шей жи́зни не случи́тся; **in my ~** на моём веку́; **it's the chance of a ~** така́я возмо́жность быва́ет раз в жи́зни; **we waited for what seemed a ~** мы прожда́ли це́лую ве́чность.

lifework *n*: **that book was his ~** э́та кни́га была́ гла́вным трудо́м его́ жи́зни; **the relief of suffering was his ~** облегча́ть страда́ния люде́й ста́ло де́лом его́ жи́зни.

lift *n* **1**: **I'll give you a ~ to the station** я вас подвезу́/*CQ* подбро́шу до ста́нции; *fig* **the news gave us a great ~** э́та но́вость о́чень ободри́ла нас

2 (*elevator*) лифт; (*of baggage, goods, etc.*) подъёмник; *attr*: **~ attendant/shaft** лифтёр, ша́хта ли́фта.

lift *vti vt* **1** под|нима́ть (-ня́ть); **~ the box onto the bench** подними́ я́щик и поста́вь его́ на скаме́йку; **the sick man was ~ed on to the bed** больно́го по́дняли и положи́ли на крова́ть; **she ~ed the child to look at the tiger** она́ подняла́ ребёнка на́ руки, что́бы он мог посмотре́ть на ти́гра; **she ~ed the baby from its cot** она́ взяла́ ребёнка из крова́тки; **I'll ~ your case down from the rack** я сниму́ ваш чемода́н с по́лки; **they ~ed the troops by air** они́ перебро́сили войска́ по во́здуху; **~ the carpet** подними́ (*to clean below*)/убери́ (*to remove it*) ковёр; *Agric*: **to ~ potatoes** копа́ть карто́фель (*collect*) (вы-); **the beetroot crop has been ~ed** урожа́й свёклы уже́ у́бран; *fig*: **the blockade was ~ed** блока́да была́ снята́; **he never ~s a finger** он и па́льцем не пошевельнёт

2 *CQ* (*steal*) красть (у-)

vi: **the mist is ~ing** тума́н поднима́ется/рассе́ивается; **the rain ~ed** дождь переста́л.

ligament *n* свя́зка.

light[1] *n* **1** свет; (*lighting*) освеще́ние; **I got up at first ~** я встал чуть свет; **before the ~ fails** пока́ не стемне́ет; **you're in my ~** вы заслоня́ете мне свет; **I need more ~** мне ну́жно бо́льше освеще́ния; **the picture was hung in a bad/good ~** карти́ну пове́сили в пло́хо/хорошо́ освещённом ме́сте; **look at it in the ~** посмотри́ на свету́; **by the ~ of a candle** при све́те свечи́; **electric ~** электри́ческое освеще́ние; **northern ~s** се́верное сия́ние; *fig*: **you show him in a bad ~** вы пока́зываете его́ в невы́годном све́те; **this casts a new ~ on the situation** э́то пролива́ет но́вый свет на ситуа́цию; **I don't see things in that ~** я ви́жу э́то в ино́м све́те; **in the ~ of this information** в све́те э́той информа́ции; **in whatever ~ we view his action** с како́й бы стороны́ мы ни взгляну́ли на его́ посту́пок; **he's seen the ~** он прозре́л; **to bring to ~** обнару́жить

2 (*lamp*) свети́льник; **ceiling ~** лю́стра; **desk ~** насто́льная ла́мпа; **bedside ~** ночни́к; **wall ~** бра (*indecl*); **street/town ~s** у́личные фонари́, (*as seen from distance*) огни́ го́рода; **put the ~ on/out** включи́/погаси́ свет; **there were ~s in every room** во всех ко́мнатах горе́л свет (*sing*); **the ~s have gone out** (*inside house*) свет (*sing*) пога́с, (*in streets*) у́личные фонари́ пога́сли, (*of town lights seen from afar*) огни́ пога́сли; **I prefer working with an overhead ~** я предпочита́ю рабо́тать при ве́рхнем све́те/освеще́нии; **~s out!** погаси́(те) свет!; *Aut*: **car ~s** (*head lights*) фа́ры маши́ны; **rear/braking ~s** за́дние фонари́ *or* за́дний свет, стоп-сигна́л *or* тормозно́й сигна́л (*sing*); **reversing ~** фона́рь за́днего хо́да; **parking ~** свет стоя́нки; **emergency/flashing ~s** авари́йная сигнализа́ция (*sing*); *Aer* **landing ~s** поса́дочные огни́ (*on aerodrome or plane*)

3 (*road signals*): **stop at the ~s** останови́тесь у светофо́ра (*sing*); **red/green ~s** кра́сный/зелёный свет; **don't cross against the ~s** не переходи́ (у́лицу) при кра́сном све́те

4 (*flame*) ого́нь (*m*); **he put a ~ to the bonfire** он разжёг костёр; **can you give me a ~?** да́йте мне спи́чку (*a match*)/прикури́ть (*for a cigarette*); **he struck a ~** он зажёг спи́чку

5 *fig uses*: **he is one of the leading ~s of our time** он оди́н из са́мых выдаю́щихся люде́й на́шей эпо́хи; **he acted honourably according to his ~s** по его́ поня́тиям он поступи́л че́стно; **the plan was given the green ~** э́тому прое́кту да́ли зелёную у́лицу.

light[1] *adj* све́тлый; **it's ~ in here** здесь светло́; **it's already ~** уже́ рассвело́; **~ hair** све́тлые во́лосы; **she has a ~ complexion** у неё о́чень све́тлая ко́жа; **~ blue/brown/grey** голубо́й, све́тло-кори́чневый, све́тло-се́рый.

light[1] *vti vt* **1** (*ignite*) за|жига́ть (-жёчь); (*esp of heating stove*) за|та́пливать (-топи́ть); **he lit a candle/a bonfire/the stove** он зажёг све́чку, он разжёг костёр, он затопи́л пе́чку; **he lit (up) a cigarette** он закури́л сигаре́ту (*pf*)

2 (*illumine*) осве|ща́ть (-ти́ть), *also fig*; **the house is lit by electricity** дом освеща́ется электри́чеством; *fig CQ* **he is well lit up** (*with drink*) он под гра́дусом

vi **1** (*ignite*) зажига́ться, раста́пливаться; загор|а́ться, разгор|а́ться (*pfs* -е́ться); **the match/stove won't ~** спи́чка не зажига́ется, пе́чка не раста́пливается *or* ого́нь в пе́чке не разгора́ется

2 *usu* **~ up**: **it's time to ~ up** пора́ заже́чь свет, (*in car*) пора́ включи́ть фа́ры; **the clock ~s up at night** но́чью цифербла́т часо́в све́тится (*has fluorescent hands*), но́чью э́ти часы́ светя́тся (*of street clock*); *fig*: **her face lit up** её лицо́ освети́лось/озари́лось;

his eyes lit up with joy его́ глаза́ засвети́лись ра́достью.

light[2] *vi*: **I lit/ ~ed on the manuscript by chance** я случа́йно наткну́лся на э́ту ру́копись; **my eye ~ed on a familiar face** мой взгляд упа́л на знако́мое лицо́.

light[3] *adj* лёгкий; **a ~ cart/diet/load, ~ clothing** лёгкая пово́зка/пи́ща/но́ша/оде́жда; **~ beer/punishment/reading** лёгкое пи́во/наказа́ние, развлека́тельное чте́ние; **~ comedy/music** весёлая коме́дия/му́зыка; **with a ~ heart** с лёгким се́рдцем; **as ~ as a feather** лёгкий как пёрышко; **a ~ railway** узкоколе́йка; **he's a ~ eater** он ма́ло ест; **I'm a ~ sleeper** я сплю чу́тко; **he makes ~ of his injury** он не пока́зывает ви́ду, что ему́ бо́льно; **they gave me ~ weight** *CQ* меня́ обве́сили.

light[3] *adv*: **to travel ~** путеше́ствовать нале́гке́.

light bulb *n* ла́мпочка.

lighten[1] *vti vt* осве|ща́ть (-ти́ть)
vi светле́ть (по-).

lighten[2] *vt* облегч|а́ть (-и́ть); **we must ~ the load on the cart** на́до убра́ть ли́шний груз с пово́зки.

lighter[1] *n Naut* ли́хтер.

lighter[2] *n* (*for cigarettes*) зажига́лка.

light-fingered *adj* (*dexterous*) ло́вкий; (*as pick-pocket*) **that boy is ~** э́тот мальчи́шка—вори́шка.

light-headed *adj* (*frivolous*) легкомы́сленный; **heights make him feel ~** у него́ голова́ кру́жится от высоты́.

light-hearted *adj* весёлый; беззабо́тный; **I feel ~** у меня́ на душе́ легко́.

lighthouse *n* мая́к; *attr*: **~ keeper** смотри́тель (*m*) маяка́.

lighting *n* освеще́ние; *Theat* освеще́ние сце́ны.

lighting-up time *n* вре́мя включе́ния освеще́ния.

lightly *adv* легко́; (*slightly, gently*) слегка́; **~ clad** легко́ оде́тый; **a ~ boiled egg** яйцо́ всмя́тку (*adv*); **to touch smth ~** слегка́ прикосну́ться к чему́-л; **he touched ~ on the question** он слегка́ косну́лся э́того вопро́са; **we got off ~** мы легко́ отде́лались; **the judge let him off ~** судья́ вы́нес ему́ лёгкий пригово́р; **I haven't taken this decision ~** мне нелегко́ дало́сь э́то реше́ние; **you're taking the matter too ~** ты несерьёзно отно́сишься к де́лу; **don't speak so ~ of him** не говори́ так неуважи́тельно о нём.

light meter *n* экспоно́метр.

lightning *n* мо́лния; **summer/sheet ~** зарни́ца; **forked ~** зигзагообра́зная мо́лния; **the tree was struck by ~** мо́лния уда́рила в де́рево; *CQ* **he ran like greased ~!** он пронёсся с быстрото́й мо́лнии!

lightning conductor *n* громоотво́д.

lightship *n* плаву́чий мая́к.

light wave *n* светова́я волна́.

lightweight *n Sport* боксёр лёгкого ве́са.

lightweight *adj* легкове́сный, *also fig*; *pejor* **he's a ~** он несерьёзный челове́к.

like[1] *n*: **we shan't see his ~ again** тако́го челове́ка нам бо́льше не встре́тить; **did you ever see the ~?** вы когда́-нибудь ви́дели что́-нибудь подо́бное?; **and the ~, and such ~** и тому́ подо́бное (*abbr* и т.п.); *CQ*: **I've no time for the ~s of him** у меня́ на таки́х, как он, нет вре́мени; **that hotel is not for the ~s of us** э́та гости́ница не для на́шего бра́та.

like[1] *adj* похо́жий, подо́бный; **they're very ~** они́ о́чень похо́жи (друг на дру́га); **they're ~ as two peas** они́ похо́жи как две ка́пли воды́; **in ~ cases** в подо́бных слу́чаях; **he talks well on this and ~ subjects** он о́чень интере́сно говори́т об э́том и вообще́ о подо́бных веща́х; **~ father ~ son** како́в оте́ц, тако́в и сын; **two dogs of ~ breed** две соба́ки одно́й поро́ды.

like[1] *adv*: **~ enough/very ~ he'll come** скоре́е всего́ он придёт.

like[1] *prep* **1** *with pron*: **the portrait isn't ~ him** в портре́те ма́ло схо́дства с ним; **it's not ~ you to be late** опа́здывать на тебя́ не похо́же; **that's more ~ it** э́то бо́льше похо́же; **what's he ~?** что он за челове́к?; **his house is ~ mine** его́ дом похо́ж на мой; **I never saw anything ~ it** я никогда́ ничего́ подо́бного не ви́дел; **he needs a holiday just ~ anybody else** как и вся́кий друго́й, он нужда́ется в о́тпуске

2 *with noun*: **she's just ~ a sister to me** она́ мне как сестра́; **he swims ~ a fish** он пла́вает как ры́ба; **you've left the room ~ a pigsty** у тебя́ не ко́мната, а свина́рник; **he treats her ~ a servant** он отно́сится к ней как к прислу́ге; **he, ~ his wife, hates cats** он, как и жена́, не лю́бит ко́шек; *joc* **just ~ a man!** что мо́жно ожида́ть от мужчи́ны!

3: like that тако́й; **artists are all ~ that** худо́жники все таковы́/таки́е; **how did somebody ~ that get chosen?** как то́лько могли́ вы́брать тако́го челове́ка?; **is he always ~ that?** неуже́ли он всегда́ тако́й?; **in cases ~ that** в подо́бных/таки́х слу́чаях; **do it ~ that** сде́лай э́то так; **it works ~ this** вот как э́то де́лается

4 *various*: **I felt ~ crying** мне хоте́лось пла́кать; **it looks ~ snow** похо́же, что пойдёт снег; **you look ~ nothing on earth** го́споди, на кого́ ты похо́ж!; **that film is nothing ~ as good as this one** тот фильм совсе́м не тако́й интере́сный, как э́тот; **it's something ~ 3 miles from here** э́то о́коло трёх миль отсю́да; *CQ* **that's something ~ a meal!** вот э́то угоще́ние!, э́то пря́мо пир!

like[1] *conj*: **I don't play anything ~ so well as you** я игра́ю куда́ ху́же вас; **she can't cook ~ her mother does** она́ гото́вит не так вку́сно, как её мать.

like[2] *vt* **1** люби́ть (*impf*); нра́виться (по-) [*with inversion of English subject and object*];

I ~ apples/swimming я люблю́ я́блоки/пла́вать; **he's well ~d here** его́ здесь лю́бят; **I ~ that actor** э́тот актёр мне нра́вится; **I ~d the play** пье́са мне понра́вилась; **I ~ it here** мне здесь нра́вится; **how do you ~ your new neighbours?** как вам нра́вятся но́вые сосе́ди?; **would you ~ a drink?** хо́чешь вы́пить?; **how do you ~ your tea?** како́й чай вы пьёте?, вам покре́пче чай или послабе́е?

2 (*with inf = wish*) хоте́ть, *impers* хоте́ться (*pfs* за-); **(do) as you ~** (де́лай), как хо́чешь; **I'd ~ to see you tomorrow** я хочу́ ви́деть вас за́втра (*order*), хоте́лось бы встре́титься с ва́ми за́втра (*wish*); **I don't ~ / I didn't ~ to disturb her** я не хочу́/мне не хоте́лось её беспоко́ить; **I'd ~ to see Samarkand** я хоте́л бы посмотре́ть Самарка́нд.

likeable *adj* (*of people or things*) симпати́чный.

likely *adj* **1** *attr*: **that's a ~ story** э́то правдоподо́бно, *iron* весьма́ убеди́тельно!; **what's the most ~ time to find him in?** когда́ вероя́тнее всего́ заста́ть его́ до́ма?; **there are several ~ candidates** есть не́сколько подходя́щих кандидату́р; **that looks a ~ place for mushrooms** э́то грибно́е ме́сто, здесь грибы́ должны́ расти́

2 *predic*: **i) is he ~ to come?** он действи́тельно придёт?; **when is he ~ to come?** когда́ он мо́жет прийти́?; **where is he ~ to be?** где он мо́жет быть?; **are you ~ to see him?** а ты его́ уви́дишь?; **that's ~ to be the result** тако́в, вероя́тно,/скоре́е всего́, бу́дет результа́т; **he's the most ~ to win** он наибо́лее вероя́тный победи́тель; **ii)** *with neg* вря́д ли; **we're not ~ to stay** мы вря́д ли оста́немся; **that's not ~ to happen** э́то вря́д ли случи́тся/произойдёт; *iron* **am I ~ to have said that?** ты ду́маешь, (что) я мог тако́е сказа́ть?

likely *adv* вероя́тно; **as ~ as not he'll be there** вполне́ вероя́тно,/возмо́жно, что он там бу́дет; **most ~ he's lost it** вероя́тнее всего́, (что) он э́то потеря́л.

like-minded *adj*: **we're very ~** мы ду́маем одина́ково; **together with a few ~ friends** вме́сте с не́сколькими друзья́ми-единомы́шленниками.

likeness *n* схо́дство; **the portrait is a good ~** в портре́те есть большо́е схо́дство.

likes *npl*: **~ and dislikes** симпа́тии и антипа́тии; **she's difficult with all her ~ and dislikes** ей с её капри́зами угоди́ть тру́дно.

likewise *adv* та́кже.

liking *n* (*for person*): **I took an immediate ~ to her** она́ мне сра́зу/с пе́рвого взгля́да понра́вилась; (*for thing*): **we've developed a ~ for French food** мы полюби́ли францу́зскую ку́хню; **it is/isn't to my ~** э́то мне (не) по вку́су.

lilac *n* сире́нь (*tree and flower*).

lilac *adj* (*of colour*) сире́невый, лило́вый.

lily *n* ли́лия; **water ~** водяна́я ли́лия, кувши́нка; **~ of the valley** ла́ндыш.

limb *n Anat* коне́чность; (*of tree*) ве́тка, сук; *CQ* **he's a real young ~** он настоя́щий чертёнок.

limber *vi*: **to ~ up** раз|мина́ться (-мя́ться).

lime[1] *n Chem* и́звесть; **quick ~** негашёная и́звесть.

lime[2] *n Bot* (*linden*) ли́па.

lime[3] *n Bot* (*citrus tree*) лайм; (*fruit*) плод ла́йма.

limelight *n fig*: **he loves the ~** он лю́бит быть в це́нтре внима́ния; **he tries to avoid the ~** он не и́щет популя́рности.

limestone *n* известня́к.

limit *n* преде́л; грани́ца; **within/beyond the ~s of** в преде́лах + *G*, за преде́лами + *G*; **he's below the age ~** он ещё не дости́г возрастно́го преде́ла; **speed/time/weight ~** преде́льная ско́рость, преде́льный срок/вес; **the speaker was given a time ~** ора́тора ограни́чили во вре́мени; **within certain ~s/a 20 kilometre ~** в определённых преде́лах, в преде́лах двадцати́ киломе́тров; **to set a ~ to expenses** установи́ть преде́л расхо́дов; **he's stretched to the ~** его́ си́лы на преде́ле; **his greed knows no ~s** его́ жа́дность не зна́ет преде́лов; *CQ* **this is the ~!/beyond the ~!** э́то перехо́дит вся́кие грани́цы!

limit *vt* ограни́ч|ивать (-ить); **our time is ~ed** вре́мя у нас ограни́чено; **I ~ myself to 5 cigarettes a day** я ограни́чиваю себя́ пятью́ сигаре́тами в день.

limitation *n* ограниче́ние; **there's no ~ on exports** на э́кспорт (*sing*) ограниче́ний (*pl*) нет; (*shortcoming*) **one must know one's own ~s** на́до пра́вильно оце́нивать свои́ возмо́жности/си́лы; **he has his ~s** у него́ есть свои́ недоста́тки.

limited *adj* ограни́ченный, *also fig*; **~ means** ограни́ченные сре́дства; **he's a ~ person** он ограни́ченный челове́к; **a ~ edition** ограни́ченный тира́ж; **sleeping accomodation is ~** спа́льных мест ма́ло; **a ~ liability company** акционе́рное о́бщество с ограни́ченной отве́тственностью.

limitless *adj* (*of plains or credulity*) безграни́чный; (*unlimited*) неограни́ченный.

limp[1] *n* хромота́; **he walks with a slight/severe ~** он прихра́мывает, он си́льно хрома́ет; **his ~ is improving** он стал ме́ньше хрома́ть.

limp[1] *vi* хрома́ть, (*slightly*) прихра́мывать (*impfs*); **he ~ed to the door** он подошёл, хромая́, к две́ри.

limp[2] *adj* вя́лый; **I feel ~ today** сего́дня я како́й-то вя́лый; **the flowers are ~** цветы́ увя́ли; **a ~ handshake** вя́лое пожа́тие руки́; **let your body go ~** рассла́бься; **his broken arm hung ~** сло́манная рука́ у него́ висе́ла безжи́зненно; **the collar has gone ~** воротни́к потеря́л жёсткость.

line[1] *n* **1** *Geom, etc.* ли́ния, черта́; **boundary/dotted ~** пограни́чная/пункти́рная ли́ния;

~s on the hand ли́нии ладо́ни; **to draw a ~ from A to B** проводи́ть ли́нию от то́чки А до то́чки В; **~ of vision** ли́ния прямо́й ви́димости; **air ~** возду́шная ли́ния; *Tech* **production/assembly ~** пото́чная ли́ния; *Art* **bold/sweeping ~s** сме́лые/стреми́тельные ли́нии; *Sport* **white/starting ~** бе́лая/ста́ртовая черта́; (*football*) **forward ~** пере́дняя ли́ния

2 (*row*) ряд; **to plant trees in a ~** сажа́ть дере́вья в ряд

3 (*rope, etc.*) верёвка; *Naut* линь; **the clothes are on the ~** бельё виси́т на верёвке; **fishing ~** ле́ска

4 *Mil*: **front ~** ли́ния фро́нта; **behind the enemy ~s** в тылу́ (*sing*) врага́; **~ of march/retreat** путь сле́дования/отхо́да; **~ of defence** оборони́тельный рубе́ж; **the soldiers stood in ~** солда́ты постро́ились в шере́нгу/в ряд; *Naut* **ship of the ~** лине́йный кора́бль

5 *Tel, etc.* ли́ния; **the ~'s engaged** ли́ния занята́; **he's on the ~ to them now** он сейча́с говори́т с ни́ми по телефо́ну; **hold the ~** не ве́шайте тру́бку; **it's a bad ~** пло́хо слы́шно; **can you get me a ~ to Paris?** мо́жете меня́ соедини́ть с Пари́жем?; **we're on a party ~** у нас спа́ренный телефо́н; **the ~s are all down after the storm** бу́ря повреди́ла все ли́нии; **hot ~** прямо́й про́вод

6 *Rail* железнодоро́жная ли́ния; **branch ~** железнодоро́жная ве́тка; **cross the ~ by the bridge** перехо́д по железнодоро́жному мосту́; **he fell on to the ~** он упа́л на ре́льсы

7 (*print, writing*) строка́, стро́чка; *Mus* лине́йка; **page 5, ~ 10** страни́ца пя́тая, строка́ деся́тая; **just a ~ to tell you we're here** всего́ не́сколько слов, что́бы сообщи́ть тебе́, что мы здесь; **a ~ of poetry** стро́чка стихо́в; *Theat* **he didn't know his ~s** он пло́хо знал роль (*sing*); *fig* **to read between the ~s** чита́ть ме́жду строк (*G*)

8 (*lineage*) ли́ния, род; **he descends in the male/in an unbroken ~ from Bruce** он пото́мок Брю́са по мужско́й/по прямо́й ли́нии; **he's the last of the royal ~** он после́дний представи́тель короле́вского ро́да; **he's next in ~ of succession** он прямо́й насле́дник; **he came of a long ~ of masons** он происходи́л из пото́мственной семьи́ ка́менщиков

9 *fig uses*: **he doesn't know where to draw the ~** он не зна́ет ме́ры/, где останови́ться; **he draws the ~ at nothing** он ни перед че́м не остано́вится; **I draw the ~ at doing your washing** я отка́зываюсь стира́ть твои́ ве́щи; **he's right all along the ~** он во всём прав; **his ~ of argument/thought** ход его́ мы́слей (*pl*); **the police are following several ~s of enquiry** поли́ция ведёт рассле́дование по не́скольким направле́ниям; **we're on the wrong ~s** мы на неве́рном пути́; **he took the ~ of least resistance** он пошёл по ли́нии наиме́ньшего сопротивле́ния; **something along those ~s** что́-нибудь в э́том ро́де (*sing*); **to take a strong ~** проводи́ть жёсткую ли́нию, занима́ть твёрдую пози́цию; **proceed along the ~s laid down** поступа́йте в соотве́тствии с указа́ниями; **a new ~ in rainwear** но́вый фасо́н плаще́й; *CQ* **what's your ~?** чем вы занима́етесь?; **it's hard ~s on her** для неё э́то большо́е несча́стье; **you'd better toe the ~** лу́чше не вылеза́й.

line[1] *vti vt*: **the road is ~d with trees** доро́га обса́жена дере́вьями; **people ~d the streets** лю́ди толпи́лись на тротуа́рах; **portraits ~d the walls** сте́ны бы́ли уве́шаны портре́тами; **a face ~d with age** лицо́, изборождённое ста́рческими морщи́нами; **~d paper** лино́ванная бума́га

vi: **the troops ~d up on the square** солда́ты вы́строились на пло́щади; **they ~d up outside the box-office** они́ вы́строились в о́чередь пе́ред ка́ссой.

line[2] *vt Sew* (*of warm linings for coats or boots*) подби|ва́ть (-́ть); *Tech* об|кла́дывать, на|кла́дывать (*pfs* -ложи́ть); **to ~ a skirt with silk** подши|ва́ть к ю́бке шёлковую подкла́дку (-́ть); *fig pejor* **they ~d their own pockets** они́ наби́ли себе́ карма́ны.

linear *adj* лине́йный.

linen *n* (*material*) полотно́; (*sheets, etc.*) бельё; *attr* льняно́й.

liner *n* **1** *Naut* ла́йнер

2: bin ~ полиэтиле́новый мешо́к для му́сорного ведра́.

linesman *n Sport* судья́ на ли́нии.

line-up *n Polit, Sport* расстано́вка.

linger *vi* задерж|иваться (-а́ться); **to ~ over a point/a job/supper** заде́рживаться на вопро́се, тяну́ть с рабо́той (*usu impf*), засиде́ться за у́жином (*usu pf*); **some guests ~ed till after midnight** не́которые го́сти засиде́лись за́ полночь; **the illness/he ~ed on for two months** боле́знь дли́лась/он протяну́л ещё два ме́сяца.

lingerie *n* да́мское бельё.

lingering *adj* (*of illness*) затяжно́й; **he had ~ doubts/suspicions** у него́ оста́лись сомне́ния/подозре́ния.

linguist *n* лингви́ст; **he's a good ~** у него́ спосо́бности (*pl*) к языка́м.

lining *n* (*of garment*) подкла́дка; (*material*) подкла́дочный материа́л; (*of box, etc.*) оби́вка; *Tech* облицо́вка; *Aut* **brake ~** тормозна́я накла́дка.

link *n* звено́, *also fig*; *fig* связь; *fig*: **the missing ~** недостаю́щее звено́; **cultural ~s** культу́рные свя́зи.

link *vti vt* свя́з|ывать (-а́ть); соедин|я́ть (-и́ть); *Tech* сцеп|ля́ть (-и́ть); **they are ~ed by common interests** их свя́зывают о́бщие интере́сы; **the two incidents are ~ed** э́ти два происше́ствия свя́заны ме́жду собо́й; **they ~ed arms and set off** они́ пошли́, взя́вшись за́ руки; **the police ~ed arms and held back the crowd** полице́йские образова́ли цепь и оттесни́ли толпу́; **we're ~ed to the mainland by telephone** у нас телефо́нная связь с материко́м; **to ~ theory and practice** соединя́ть тео́рию с пра́ктикой

vi also **~ up** соединя́ться (с + *I*).

linocut *n* линогравю́ра.

linoleum, *abbr* **lino** *n* лино́леум.

lion *n* лев; *fig* **the ~'s share** льви́ная до́ля.

lip *n* губа́; (*of cup, crater*) край; **to bite one's ~(s)** куса́ть себе́ гу́бы; **to smack one's ~s** облизываться; *CQ* **none of your ~!** без де́рзостей (*pl*)!

lipread *vi* чита́ть с губ (*only in impf*).

lipstick *n* губна́я пома́да.

liqueur *n* ликёр.

liquid *n* жи́дкость; *Ling* пла́вный звук.

liquid *adj* жи́дкий; *Fin* **~ assets** ликви́дные акти́вы.

liquidize *vt* превра|ща́ть в жи́дкость (-ти́ть).

liquidizer *n* ми́ксер.

liquor *n* спиртно́й напи́ток (*often in pl*); **the sale of ~** прода́жа спиртны́х напи́тков; **you should keep off ~** тебе́ на́до возде́рживаться от спиртно́го.

lisp *vti* шепеля́вить (про-).

list[1] *n* спи́сок; **shopping ~** спи́сок поку́пок; **he put my name on the ~** он внёс мою́ фами́лию в спи́сок; **he gave a ~ of his requirements** он перечи́слил свои́ тре́бования; *Mil* **he's still on the active ~** он ещё в ка́дровом соста́ве; *attr Comm*: **~ price** цена́ по прейскура́нту.

list[1] *vt* (*draw up a list*) состав|ля́ть спи́сок + *G* (´-ить); (*enter on list*) вноси́ть в спи́сок (внести́); (*enumerate*) перечисл|я́ть (´-ить); **he's not ~ed** его́ нет в спи́ске.

list[2] *n Naut* крен; **the ship has a ~ to port** су́дно даёт крен вле́во.

list[2] *vi Naut* крени́ться (на-).

listen *vi* слу́шать + *A* (по-); **to ~ to music** слу́шать му́зыку; **we ~ed but heard nothing** мы слу́шали, но ничего́ не услыха́ли; **don't ~ to him** не слу́шай его́; **~ carefully to all I say** вы́слушай меня́ внима́тельно; **he never ~s to my advice** он никогда́ не прислу́шивается к мои́м сове́там (*pl*); **to ~ in to a telephone conversation** подслу́ш|ивать телефо́нный разгово́р (-ать).

listener *n* слу́шатель (*m*); **he's a bad ~** он не уме́ет слу́шать други́х.

listless *adj* вя́лый, апати́чный.

literacy *n* гра́мотность.

literal *adj* буква́льный, досло́вный; **a ~ translation** досло́вный перево́д.

literally *adv* буква́льно, досло́вно; **they took her words ~** они́ восприня́ли её слова́ буква́льно; *CQ* **we were ~ starving** мы буква́льно умира́ли с го́лоду.

literary *adj* литерату́рный; **a ~ man** (*writer*) литера́тор, (*well-read*) знато́к литерату́ры; **the ~ profession** литера́торы (*pl*).

literate *adj* гра́мотный; (*well-read*) образо́ванный, начи́танный.

literature *n* литерату́ра.

Lithuanian *n* лито́вец, лито́вка.

Lithuanian *adj* лито́вский.

litmus *n* ла́кмус; *attr*: **~ paper** ла́кмусовая бума́жка.

litre, (*US*) **liter** *n* литр.

litter *n* **1** (*veterinary term*) помёт; **the cat/dog/sow has had a ~ of 10 kittens/puppies/piglets** у ко́шки/у соба́ки/у свиньи́ родило́сь де́сять котя́т/щенко́в/порося́т

2 (*rubbish*) му́сор.

litter *vt* му́сорить (за-), сори́ть (на-); **the room is ~ed with cigarette ends** в ко́мнате всю́ду валя́лись оку́рки; **the table is ~ed with papers** стол зава́лен бума́гами.

little *n* **1** (*with indef article*) немно́го, *CQ* немно́жко; **give me a ~** дай мне немно́жко; **stay for a ~** оста́ньтесь ещё ненадо́лго; **after a ~** че́рез/спустя́ не́которое вре́мя; **he knows a ~ of everything** он зна́ет обо всём понемно́гу

2 немно́гое; **I did what ~ I could** я сде́лал то немно́гое, что мог; **the ~ of his work I've seen** то немно́гое из его́ рабо́ты, что я ви́дел; **every ~ helps** пусть хоть немно́го, всё равно́ по́льза/ на по́льзу

3 ма́ло; **he knows ~** он ма́ло зна́ет; **I see ~ of him** я его́ ма́ло ви́жу; **there was ~ we could do** мы ма́ло что могли́ сде́лать; **I could make ~ of the text/him** я ма́ло что по́нял в те́ксте, я его́ совсе́м не понима́ю; **£5 is too ~** пять фу́нтов— сли́шком ма́ло.

little *adj* **1** ма́ленький, небольшо́й; **a ~ boy/town** ма́ленький ма́льчик, небольшо́й го́род [**NB** небольшо́й *is emotionally neutral*]; **stay a ~ while** оста́нься ещё ненадо́лго; **I've ~ time for reading** у меня́ ма́ло вре́мени для чте́ния; **he got ~ benefit from his trip** пое́здка ма́ло что ему́ дала́

2 *with def article, as distinguishing epithet*: **the ~ finger/toe** мизи́нец; **the ~ ones are asleep** малыши́ спят; **the ~ Smiths** де́ти Сми́тов; **the L. Bear** Ма́лая Медве́дица

3 (*with indef article = some*) немно́го, *CQ* немно́жко; **I know a ~ German** я немно́го зна́ю неме́цкий; **have a ~ soup** съешь немно́го су́па; **not a ~ excitement** нема́лое волне́ние

4 *translated by diminutive, esp in emotive uses*: **a ~ dog/boat/house** собачо́нка, ло́дочка, до́мик; **have a ~ drop/sip** вы́пей ка́пельку/глото́чек; **they're dreary ~ people** они́ таки́е ску́чные лю́дишки; **don't let ~ things like that upset you** не волну́йся из-за таки́х пустяко́в; **that poor ~ girl!** бе́дная де́вочка!; **what a nice ~ man!/car!** како́й ми́лый челове́к!, кака́я сла́вная маши́нка!; **come here you ~ rascal!** поди́ сюда́, него́дный мальчи́шка!/дрянь ты э́такая!; **he's a horrid ~ brat** он стра́шный озорни́к.

little *adv* **1** ма́ло; **he's ~ known** его́ ма́ло зна́ют; **~ by ~** ма́ло-пома́лу; **he's ~ more than a boy** он ещё ма́льчик; **he was here ~ more than an hour ago** он был здесь чуть бо́льше ча́са тому́ наза́д; **I tried to say as ~ as possible** я стара́лся говори́ть как мо́жно ме́ньше; **he's ~ better than a thief** он ниче́м не лу́чше во́ра; *CQ* **it's ~ short of madness** э́то про́сто како́е-то сумасше́ствие

2: a ~ немно́го; **the hat's a ~ large** шля́па немно́го велика́/великова́та; **I'm a ~ afraid** я немно́го поба́иваюсь; **he was not a ~ annoyed** он не на шу́тку рассерди́лся

3 (*with some verbs = not at all*): **I ~ dreamt that...** мне и в го́лову не приходи́ло, что...; **~ did I think that...** я уж ника́к не ду́мал, что...

littoral *n* примо́рье.

live *adj* живо́й; **a ~ fish** жива́я ры́ба; **~ coals** горя́щие у́гли; **~ embers** тле́ющие уголькѝ; **a ~ cartridge** *Mil* боево́й/*Sport* неиспо́льзованный патро́н; *Elec* **a ~ rail/wire** конта́ктный рельс, про́вод под напряже́нием.

live *adv*: **the concert will be broadcast ~** конце́рт бу́дет трансли́роваться пря́мо из за́ла; **the programme comes to you ~** э́то пряма́я переда́ча.

live *vti vt* жить (*impf*, *for pf use* про-); **he ~d an amazing life** он про́жил удиви́тельную жизнь; **he ~d most of his life abroad** он провёл бо́льшую часть жи́зни за грани́цей; **he ~s a double life** он живёт двойно́й жи́знью; **the actor ~s the part** актёр вжи́лся в роль

vi жить (*for pfs use* про-, до-); **he hasn't long to ~** ему́ ма́ло оста́лось жить; **can he ~ through the night?** доживёт/протя́нет ли он до утра́?; **he ~d to a great old age** он до́жил до глубо́кой ста́рости; **as long as I ~ I'll remember** я на всю жизнь запо́мню; **once upon a time there ~d** жил-был; **one ~s and learns** век живи́, век учи́сь; **he ~d and died a bachelor** он так и оста́лся на всю жизнь холостяко́м; **they ~ like lords/pigs** они́ живу́т по-ца́рски/как сви́ньи; **I ~d in Japan for a year** я прожи́л год в Япо́нии

live down *vt*: **he'll never ~ it down** ему́ э́того не забу́дут

live for *vi*: **he ~s for ballet/for pleasure** он живёт одни́м бале́том, он живёт в своё удово́льствие; **she ~s entirely for her children** вся её жизнь в де́тях

live in *vi*: **the nurses/servants ~ in** медсёстры живу́т при больни́це, слу́ги живу́т в до́ме; **the house looks well ~d in** э́тот дом вы́глядит вполне́ обжиты́м

live off/on *vi*: **he ~s on his salary/off his writing/on his wife/on fruit** он живёт на зарпла́ту/литерату́рным трудо́м/ на де́ньги жены́, он пита́ется одни́ми фру́ктами; **she hasn't much to ~ on** ей не́ на что жить; **his memory ~s on** па́мять о нём ещё живёт/жива́

live out *vti vt*: **I'll ~ out the rest of my days here** я проживу́ здесь оста́ток свое́й жи́зни

vi: **all her servants ~ out** у неё вся прислу́га (*collect*) приходя́щая; **they ~ out of tins** они́ пита́ются одни́ми консе́рвами; **we ~ out of suitcases** мы ведём кочеву́ю жизнь

live up *vti vt*: *CQ* **to ~ it up** прожига́ть жизнь (*impf*)

vi: **he doesn't ~ up to his principles** он не сле́дует свои́м при́нципам; **they haven't ~d up to our expectations** они́ не оправда́ли на́ших наде́жд; **he ~s up to his reputation** он опра́вдывает свою́ репута́цию

live with *vi*: **we have to ~ with the situation** прихо́дится мири́ться с обстоя́тельствами.

lively *adj* живо́й; оживлённый; **a ~ child/mind** живо́й ребёнок/ум; **a ~ imagination/description** живо́е воображе́ние/описа́ние; **he takes a ~ interest in their affairs** он проявля́ет живе́йший интере́с к их дела́м; **a ~ argument** оживлённый спор.

liven *vti*, *usu* **to ~ up: the tourists ~ up the town** тури́сты оживля́ют го́род; **the party ~ed up** го́сти заме́тно оживи́лись.

liver *n Anat* пе́чень; *Cook* печёнка.

liverish *adj* жёлчный.

livestock *n* дома́шний скот.

livid *adj*: *fig* **he was ~ with us** он стра́шно на нас разозли́лся.

living *n*: **standard of ~** у́ровень жи́зни, жи́зненный у́ровень; **he makes his ~ by painting** он зараба́тывает на жизнь, рису́я карти́ны; **they're used to gracious/simple ~** они́ привы́кли жить в по́лном доста́тке/про́сто; *attr*: **~ conditions** жили́щные усло́вия; **~ room** гости́ная; **a ~ wage** прожи́точный ми́нимум.

living *adj* живо́й; **one of the greatest ~ experts** оди́н из крупне́йших (совреме́нных) специали́стов; **within ~ memory** на па́мяти живу́щих; **no man ~** никто́ на све́те; *as n* **(the ~)** живы́е.

lizard *n* я́щерица.

load *n* **1** (*on ship*, *etc.*) груз; (*carried by smb*) но́ша; *Tech* нагру́зка; **the ship carried a ~ of coal** кора́бль шёл с гру́зом у́гля; **they've delivered us a ~ of gravel** нам привезли́ грузови́к гра́вия/гра́вий; **he dumped his ~ on the floor** он свали́л свою́ но́шу на́ пол; *Tech* **peak ~** максима́льная нагру́зка

2 *fig uses*: **a teaching ~** педагоги́ческая нагру́зка; **he has a heavy ~ of responsibility** на нём лежи́т тяжёлое бре́мя отве́тственности; **that's a ~ off my mind** гора́ с плеч; *CQ*: **we've ~s of time** у нас у́йма вре́мени; **what a ~ of rubbish!** что за чушь!

load *vti vt* **1** грузи́ть (*pfs* за-, на-, по-); нагру|жа́ть (-зи́ть), *also fig*; **they ~ed sacks on to a cart/mule** они́ погрузи́ли мешки́ на теле́гу/на му́ла; **let's ~ the car and go** дава́й загру́зим маши́ну и пое́дем; **the car is so ~ed it can hardly move** маши́на так нагру́жена, что е́ле е́дет; *fig*: **he ~s work on to his assistants** он нагружа́ет рабо́той свои́х помо́щников; **to ~ smb with honours** осы́пать кого́-л по́честями

2 (*gun*, *camera*) заря|жа́ть (-ди́ть)

vi грузи́ться, нагружа́ться; **we'll start ~ing at 6 o'clock** начнём погру́зку/грузи́ться в шесть часо́в; **the ship is ~ing** су́дно на погру́зке.

loaded *adj* нагру́женный; *fig* **a ~ question** вопро́с с подво́хом.

loaf[1] *n* (*white*) бато́н, (*black*) буха́нка.

loaf[2] *vi* (*idle*) безде́льничать, (*hang about*) слоня́ться (*impfs*).

loafer *n* лентя́й.

loan *n* (*on national level*) заём; (*from bank, etc.*) ссу́да; **the government raised a ~ of a million dollars** прави́тельство получи́ло заём в миллио́н до́лларов; **she/the firm got a ~ from the bank** она́/фи́рма получи́ла ссу́ду в ба́нке; (*among friends*): **I got a ~ from my brother** брат дал мне взаймы́ (*adv*), брат одолжи́л мне де́нег; **I asked for the ~ of his car** я попроси́л его́ одолжи́ть мне маши́ну.

loan *vt off* предостав|ля́ть заём (-́ить); (*of banks*) дава́ть ссу́ду (дать); (*privately*) ода́лживать (одолжи́ть), дава́ть взаймы́ (*adv*).

loath *adj*: **I was ~ to leave** я уе́хал нео́хотно, я не хоте́л уезжа́ть.

loathe *vt* не люби́ть, не выноси́ть (*impfs*); **I ~ housework** я о́чень не люблю́/я терпе́ть не могу́ занима́ться дома́шним хозя́йством; **I ~ him** я его́ не выношу́.

loathsome *adj* отврати́тельный.

lobby *n* (*in house*) пере́дняя; (*in hotel*) вестибю́ль (*m*); *fig* **the antivivisection ~** гру́ппа проти́вников вивисе́кции.

lobby *vti vt*: **they are ~ing the students to support the new proposals** они́ агити́руют студе́нтов, что́бы те поддержа́ли но́вые предложе́ния

vi: **to ~ for /against a bill** агити́ровать в кулуа́рах в по́льзу/про́тив законопрое́кта.

lobe *n* (*of ear*) мо́чка.

lobster *n* ома́р; *fig* **red as a ~** кра́сный как рак.

local *n* (*of person*) (**a ~**) ме́стный жи́тель (*m*); *CQ* (*pub*) (**the ~**) ме́стная забега́ловка.

local *adj* ме́стный.

locality *n* райо́н, ме́стность; **I've no sense/ *CQ* bump of ~** я пло́хо ориенти́руюсь.

localize *vt Med* локализова́ть (*impf and pf*).

locate *vt* **1** (*find*): **I ~d the town on the map** я нашёл э́тот го́род на ка́рте; **the doctor ~d the source of the pain** врач установи́л причи́ну бо́ли

2 (*establish*) распо|лага́ть (-ложи́ть), разме|ща́ть (-сти́ть); **the new factory is to be ~d in the suburbs** но́вый заво́д наме́чено постро́ить в при́городе (*sing*); **the office is ~d in the same building** конто́ра нахо́дится в том же зда́нии.

location *n* ме́сто; **that's a suitable ~ for a factory** э́то подходя́щее ме́сто для но́вого заво́да; **they're discussing possible ~s for a/the new school** они́ обсужда́ют, где стро́ить но́вую шко́лу; **the ~ of the theatre in that area was a mistake** стро́ить теа́тр в э́том райо́не бы́ло оши́бкой; *Cine* **they're on ~ in the Alps** они́ на съёмках в А́льпах.

lock[1] *n* (*of hair*) ло́кон.

lock[2] *n* **1** (*of door, lid, gun*) замо́к; **the documents are kept under ~ and key** докуме́нты храня́тся под замко́м

2 (*on canal*) шлюз; *attr*: **~ gate** шлю́зные воро́та; **~ keeper** нача́льник шлю́за

3 *Aut*: **this car has a good ~** у э́той маши́ны небольшо́й ра́диус поворо́та.

lock[2] *vti vt* за|пира́ть (-пере́ть); **he ~ed the door/up the house/the steering wheel** он за́пер дверь/дом/руль; **I ~ed myself in my room** я за́перся в свое́й ко́мнате; **I've ~ed myself out of my flat** я захло́пнул дверь, и у меня́ нет ключа́—тепе́рь не могу́ войти́ в кварти́ру; *fig*: **they were ~ed in combat/in each other's arms** они́ сцепи́лись в схва́тке, они́ обняли́сь; **his jaws were tightly ~ed** его́ че́люсти бы́ли кре́пко сжа́ты

vi: **this trunk doesn't ~** э́тот чемода́н не запира́ется; **the parts ~ into each other** э́ти ча́сти сцепля́ются ме́жду собо́й.

locker *n* шка́фчик; *Naut* рунду́к.

locket *n* медальо́н.

locksmith *n* сле́сарь (*m*).

lock-up *n CQ* (*for drunkards*) вытрезви́тель (*m*); (*prison*) куту́зка.

locomotive *n* локомоти́в; **a steam ~** паро́во́з; *attr*: *Rail* **~ depot** паровозное депо́.

locust *n* саранча́ (*also collect*).

lodge *n* (*in park, on estate*) *approx* сторо́жка; **hunting ~** охо́тничий до́мик; **porter's ~** вахтёрская; **masonic ~** масо́нская ло́жа.

lodge *vti vt*: **we were ~d with the teacher** мы переночева́ли в до́ме учи́теля; **to ~ a complaint** пода|ва́ть жа́лобу (-́ть);

vi посел|я́ться (-и́ться); **I ~d with a friend** (*temporarily*) я останови́лся/ (*more permanently*) я жил у дру́га; **the bullet ~d in his shoulder** пу́ля застря́ла у него́ в плече́.

lodger *n* жиле́ц; **she takes in ~s** она́ сдаёт ко́мнаты жильца́м.

lodging *n*: **he lives in ~s** он снима́ет ко́мнату; **where can we find a night's ~?** где нам найти́ ночле́г?; **they gave me a night's ~** они́ приюти́ли меня́ на́ ночь; **to have full board and ~** жить на по́лном пансио́не; *attr*: **~ house** *approx* меблиро́ванные ко́мнаты, (*with food*) пансио́н.

loft *n* черда́к; **hay ~** сенова́л; **pigeon ~** голубя́тня.

lofty *adj* (*of building, tree, style*) высо́кий; (*of ideas, ideals*) возвы́шенный; (*haughty*) высокоме́рный.

log *n* бревно́; *Naut* лаг; *fig* **I slept like a ~** я спал как уби́тый.

logbook *n Naut* судово́й журна́л; *Aer* формуля́р.

loggerheads *npl*: **they're always at ~** они́ ве́чно ссо́рятся; **he set them at ~** он натрави́л их друг на дру́га.

logic *n* ло́гика; **a mistake in ~** логи́ческая оши́бка.

logical *adj* (*of analysis, etc.*) логи́ческий; (*rational*) логи́чный; **it's the ~ thing to do** э́то бу́дет логи́чно; **the ~ conclusion is that...** по ло́гике веще́й выхо́дит, что...

loin *n Anat* поясни́ца; (*of meat*) филе́йная часть; **a ~ of lamb** бара́нье филе́ (*indecl*).

loiter *vi* ме́длить (*impf*); **to ~ over a job** ме́длить/тяну́ть с рабо́той; **don't ~, it's getting dark** поторопи́сь, уже́ темне́ет; **to ~ at street corners** *CQ* болта́ться/окола́чиваться на у́лице (*impfs*).

loll *vi* (*sprawl*): **she was ~ing on the sofa** она́ сиде́ла на дива́не, лени́во развали́сь; **it was so hot—the dog's tongue was ~ing out** соба́ка от жары́ вы́сунула язы́к.

lollipop *n* леденец (на па́лочке).

lone *adj* одино́кий; **he's playing a ~ hand** он де́йствует в одино́чку.

lonely *adj* одино́кий; **I felt ~** я чу́вствовал себя́ одино́ким; **a ~ place** уединённое ме́сто; **he leads a ~ life** он живёт уединённо; **a ~ road** пусты́нная доро́га.

loner *n CQ*: **he's a ~** он лю́бит жить оди́н.

long[1] *n*: **before ~** ско́ро, вско́ре; **are you going for ~?** вы е́дете надо́лго?; **don't take ~ getting ready** не тяни́ со сбо́рами; **the ~ and the short of it is that...** коро́че говоря́...

long[1] *adj* **1** (*of size*) дли́нный; **a ~ plank** дли́нная доска́; **how ~ is the plank?** како́й длины́ доска́?; **a plank 3/6 metres ~** трёхметро́вая доска́, доска́ длино́й в шесть ме́тров; **it's a ~ way to school** до шко́лы далеко́; **the street is a mile ~** у́лица тя́нется на це́лую ми́лю; **make a ~ arm for the salt** дотяни́сь до со́ли

2 (*of time*) до́лгий; продолжи́тельный; **a ~ winter/holiday** до́лгая зима́, продолжи́тельный о́тпуск; **how ~ is the lesson?** ско́лько дли́тся уро́к?; **a ~ lease** долгосро́чная аре́нда; **he was ill for a ~ time** он до́лго боле́л; **he's been ill a ~ time** он давно́ боле́ет; **don't be ~ answering** не тяни́ с отве́том; **for a ~ time we heard nothing of him** мы до́лго ничего́ не слы́шали о нём; **I've had a ~ day** у меня́ сего́дня был тяжёлый день

3 *expressions*: **he wasn't the first by a ~ chalk** он был далеко́ не пе́рвым; **we're contending against ~ odds** ша́нсы у нас нера́вны́; **it's a ~ shot, but...** хотя́ наде́жды ма́ло, но всё-таки...

long[1] *adv* до́лго; **~ ago** давно́; **~ before the war** задо́лго до войны́; **all day ~** це́лый день; **~ after that** до́лго по́сле э́того, мно́го лет спустя́; **how ~ will you stay?** ты надо́лго (остаёшься)?; **how long do you mean to stay there?** ско́лько ты ду́маешь пробы́ть там?; **stay as ~ as you like** остава́йтесь сто́лько, ско́лько хоти́те; **I can't wait any ~er** я бо́льше ждать не могу́; **it'll be fine as ~ as he keeps well** всё бу́дет прекра́сно, е́сли то́лько он не заболе́ет; **take the book so ~ as you return it** бери́ кни́гу, то́лько верни́ её; **I said so ~ before you did** я э́то сказа́л гора́здо ра́ньше тебя́; *CQ* **so ~!** пока́!

long[2] *vi* (*want*) о́чень хоте́ть + *inf* (*only in impf*); (*look forward to*) ждать + *G* (*only in impf*); **I'm ~ing for a smoke** мне о́чень хо́чется кури́ть; **I ~ for the day when...** я то́лько и жду того́ дня, когда́...; **we're ~ing to see you** ждём вас с нетерпе́нием; **I ~ to return there** мечта́ю туда́ верну́ться; **I ~ for my mother/for Moscow** я тоску́ю *or* скуча́ю по ма́тери/по Москве́ (*impfs*); **I'm ~ing to sleep** меня́ кло́нит ко сну/в сон.

long-awaited *adj* долгожда́нный.

long-distance *adj Tel* междугоро́дный (*inter-city*); **~ calls can't be made from this box** из э́той бу́дки нельзя́ звони́ть по междугоро́дному телефо́ну; *Sport* **~ race** бег на дли́нные диста́нции.

long division *n* деле́ние сто́лбиком.

long-hand *n*: **he takes notes in ~** он де́лает за́писи обы́чным/не стенографи́ческим письмо́м.

longitude *n* долгота́.

longitudinal *adj* продо́льный.

long-sighted *adj* дальнозо́ркий, *also fig.*

long-standing *adj* да́вний; **a ~ friendship/joke** да́вняя дру́жба, ста́рая шу́тка; **they have a ~ agreement/arrangement that...** они́ давно́ договори́лись, что...

long-suffering *adj* многострада́льный.

long-term *adj* (*of lease, loans, weather forecast*) долгосро́чный; **in the ~ view** рассчи́тывая на дли́тельный пери́од; **do you have any ~ plans?** каки́е у вас пла́ны на бу́дущее?; **~ planning** перспекти́вное плани́рование.

long-winded *adj* (*of person*) многоречи́вый; (*of speech*) многосло́вный.

loo *n CQ* убо́рная.

look *n* **1** (*glance*) взгляд; **he gave me a furious ~** он бро́сил на меня́ я́ростный взгляд; **there was a ~ of suspicion in his eye** в его́ взгля́де сквози́ло подозре́ние; **we got some very odd ~s** на нас дово́льно стра́нно посмотре́ли; **if ~s could kill!** како́й уби́йственный взгляд!

2: **to have/take a ~ at smth** смотре́ть (на) что-л; **he had a ~ round the exhibition/at the picture/at the wound** он посмотре́л вы́ставку/на карти́ну, он осмотре́л ра́ну; **I had a quick ~ at the paper** я бы́стро просмотре́л газе́ту; **they're having a ~ round the town/at the drains** они́ осма́тривают го́род, они́ проверя́ют систе́му канализа́ции; **take a close ~** всмотри́сь хороше́нько, посмотри́ внима́тельно; **to have a ~ for smb/smth** иска́ть кого́-л/что-л

3 (*appearance*) вид; **from the ~ of him** су́дя по его́ ви́ду; **I don't like the ~ of him/of things** мне не нра́вится его́ вид/всё э́то; **by the ~ of things** по-ви́димому; **he has an excited ~** у него́ взволно́ванный вид; **the house had a deserted ~/was given**

a new ~ дом казáлся нежилы́м/был перестрóен; **he has a** ~ **of his father/of a sailor** он похóж на отцá/на матрóса; **you can't go by** ~**s** нельзя́ суди́ть по внéшности; **she was famous for her good** ~**s** онá слáвилась красотóй.

look *vti vt* **1** смотрéть (по-); **I** ~**ed him straight in the face/eye** я посмотрéл емý пря́мо в глазá; *CQ* **he** ~**ed daggers at us** он зло посмотрéл на нас

2 (*attend to*): ~ **what you're doing!/where you're going!** ты смотри́, что дéлаешь!/, кудá идёшь!

vi **1** (*see*) смотрéть, глядéть (*pfs* по-); ~ **this way** посмотри́/взгляни́ сюдá!; *fig* **the house** ~**s south** óкна дóма выхóдят на юг

2 (*with adj or other complement = seem*) вы́глядеть (*impf*); **you** ~ **well** ты хорошó вы́глядишь; **the new building** ~**s hideous** нóвое здáние вы́глядит ужáсно; **you'll** ~ **foolish** ты бýдешь глýпо вы́глядеть; **what does he** ~ **like?** как он вы́глядит?; **he** ~**s his age** емý дашь егó вóзраст; **when she's** ~**ing her best, she's quite something** когдá онá захóчет, онá мóжет вы́глядеть потрясáюще (*adv*); **it** ~**s like rain** похóже, что бýдет дождь; **the photo doesn't** ~ **like him** на сни́мке он не похóж на себя́; **you don't** ~ **yourself** ты на себя́ не похóж; **he** ~**s French** он похóж на францýза; **you** ~ **as if you're in pain** у тебя́ такóй вид, как бýдто у тебя́ чтó-то боли́т; **it doesn't** ~ **to me as if he's coming** мне кáжется, что он не придёт; **it** ~**s like salt to me** по-мóему, э́то соль; **he** ~**s every inch a soldier** у негó вы́правка настоя́щего воéнного; **he** ~**s good in uniform** фóрма емý идёт

look about *vi*: **to** ~ **about one** огля́|дываться вокрýг (-нýться)

look after *vi*: **I'll** ~ **after all that** всё э́то моя́ забóта, всё э́то на мне; **I'm** ~**ing after the children** я присмáтриваю/смотрю́ за детьми́; **she** ~**ed after the tomato plants/the patient** онá ухáживала за помидóрами/за больны́м; ~ **after yourself!** поберегѝ себя́!, будь осторóжен!; **he** ~**s after himself when his wife is away** когдá женá в отъéзде, он сам ведёт хозя́йство

look around *vi*: **I'm** ~**ing around for a new job** я поды́скиваю нóвую рабóту

look at *vi* смотрéть на + *A*; **to** ~ **at him you wouldn't think he was a millionaire** посмотрéть на негó, так и не подýмаешь, что он миллионéр; **she's not much to** ~ **at, but...** онá не так уж хорошá собóй, но...; **he wouldn't** ~ **at the idea** он и слы́шать не хотéл об э́том (предложéнии); **they won't** ~ **at you without a degree** *CQ* они́ и смотрéть на тебя́ не стáнут, éсли у тебя́ нет стéпени; **the mechanic will** ~ **at the brakes** мехáник провéрит тормозá

look away *vi* от|води́ть взгляд (-вести́)

look back *vi* огля́|дываться (-нýться); **we** ~**ed back at the house** мы оглянýлись на дом; ~**ing back, I remember...** огля́дываясь назáд, я вспоминáю...

look down *vi* смотрéть вниз; **don't** ~ **down** не смотри́ вниз; ~**ing down from the window** глядя́ вниз из окнá; **she** ~**ed down in embarrassment** онá смущённо потýпила взор; **the castle** ~**s down on the village** зáмок вы́сится над дерéвней; *fig pejor* **they** ~ **down on us** они́ смóтрят на нас свысокá

look for *vi* искáть + *A or* + *G if object is abstract* (*impf*); **I'm** ~**ing for a job** я ищý/присмáтриваю себé рабóту; **to** ~ **for an opportunity to...** искáть возмóжности/удóбного слýчая, чтóбы...

look forward to *vi*: **I'm** ~**ing forward to the trip/to seeing you/to his leaving** я жду с нетерпéнием э́той поéздки, я жду тебя́ с нетерпéнием, я не дождýсь егó ухóда

look in on *vi* за|ходи́ть, за|езжáть к + *D* (-йти́, -éхать); **I** ~**ed in on her/at the exhibition** я зашёл к ней, *CQ* я забежáл ненадóлго на вы́ставку

look into *vi*: **to** ~ **into a problem** рассмáтривать проблéму, разбирáться в вопрóсе; **will you** ~ **into the question of supplies?** вы занимáетесь вопрóсом снабжéния?; **the police are** ~**ing into the theft** поли́ция расслéдует крáжу

look on *vi* **1**: **they just stood and** ~**ed on** они́ тóлько стоя́ли и наблюдáли

2 (*consider*) считáть (*impf*), смотрéть; **I have always** ~**ed on you as a friend** я всегдá считáл тебя́ дрýгом; **I** ~ **on him as a hero** я смотрю́ на негó как на герóя; **I** ~ **on it as an honour to work with him** для меня́ большáя честь рабóтать с ним; **I** ~ **on that as an insult** я рассмáтриваю э́то как оскорблéние

look on to *vi*: **the window** ~**s on to the park** окнó выхóдит в парк

look out *vti vt*: **I'll** ~ **out some clothes for him** я подыщý емý одéжду

vi: **he** ~**ed out of the window** он смотрéл/(*once*) посмотрéл/(*stuck head out*) вы́глянул в окнó; ~ **out, it's slippery** смотри́, тут скóльзко; **let's** ~ **out for him** давáйте посмóтрим, мóжет, уви́дим егó

look over *vti*: **the brakes need to be** ~**ed over** тормозá трéбуют провéрки/осмóтра; **he** ~**ed over his shoulder/their heads** он посмотрéл чéрез плечó/повéрх их голóв; **to** ~ **over an article** просмáтривать статью́; **to** ~ **over a building/a patient** осмáтривать здáние/больнóго

look through *vi* смотрéть в + *A*; (*read, check*) просмáтривать + *A*; **to** ~ **through a window/a telescope** смотрéть в окнó/в телескóп; *fig* **he** ~**ed through me** (*ignored*) он смотрéл ми́мо меня́

look to *vi*: **I** ~**ed to him for help** я обрати́лся к немý за пóмощью; **no good** ~**ing to them for support** нéчего ждать от них поддéржки

look up *vti vt*: **he ~ed me up and down** он смéрил меня́ взгля́дом; **~ me up tomorrow** зайди́ ко мне за́втра; **~ it up in the dictionary** найди́/посмотри́ э́то сло́во в словаре́

vi: **he ~ed up from his book** он по́днял глаза́ от кни́ги; **they were ~ing up at the sky** они́ смотре́ли на не́бо; *fig*: **things are ~ing up** дела́ иду́т на лад; **I ~ up to him** я уважа́ю его́.

looking-glass *n* зе́ркало.

look-out *n* **1** (*post*) наблюда́тельный пост/пункт; (*man*) наблюда́тель (*m*)

2: **he's on the ~ for talent** он и́щет тала́нты (*pl*); **it's a poor ~ for the harvest/for us** ви́ды на урожа́й плохи́е, для нас перспекти́вы нера́достные; **that's his ~** э́то его́ де́ло.

loop *n* (*in string, etc.*) пе́тля; **the river makes a ~ round the town** река́ огиба́ет го́род; *attr Rail*: **~ line** окружна́я желе́зная доро́га.

loop *vt*: **to ~ a rope around a post** завя́з|ывать верёвку пе́тлей вокру́г столба́ (-а́ть); **the wire had ~ed itself round her foot** она́ зацепи́лась ного́й за про́волоку; *Aer* **to ~ the loop** сде́лать мёртвую пе́тлю.

loophole *n Mil* бойни́ца; *fig* лазе́йка; **I left myself a ~** я оста́вил себе́ лазе́йку.

loose *adj* **1** (*not tightly fixed*): **~ window frames** пло́хо при́гнанные ра́мы; **~ steering** ша́ткий рулево́й механи́зм; **a ~ nail/post** расшата́вшийся гвоздь/столб; **a ~ tooth** шата́ющийся зуб; **a ~ knot** сла́бый у́зел; **the nut/knot/hinge has worked ~** га́йка осла́бла, у́зел осла́б, пе́тля расшата́лась; **the handle/wheel is ~** рукоя́тка пло́хо де́ржится, колесо́ вихля́ет; **the ropes are ~** верёвки завя́заны сла́бо; **the bandage is too ~** бинт недоста́точно туго́й; **there are some ~ pages** не́которые страни́цы вот-во́т вы́падут; *Elec* **a ~ connection** непло́тный конта́кт

2 (*not packed*): **the books can go ~ in the car** кни́ги мо́жно про́сто свали́ть в маши́ну, не упако́вывая; **~ sweets/change/bowels** рассыпны́е конфе́ты, ме́лочь, сла́бый кише́чник (*sing*)

3 (*of clothes, etc.*): **a ~ collar/belt** свобо́дный воротни́к/по́яс; **the elastic is wearing ~** рези́нка осла́бла; **the skirt/button is ~** ю́бка виси́т, пу́говица вот-во́т оторвётся; **this dress should be worn ~** э́то пла́тье не должно́ быть прилега́ющим; **she wears her hair ~** у неё во́лосы всегда́ распу́щены; **a ~ weave/thread** непло́тная ткань, вися́щая ни́тка

4 (*free*) свобо́дный; **oh dear, the hens are ~ in the garden** бо́же мой, ку́ры разбрели́сь по всему́ са́ду; **don't let/leave the dog ~** не спуска́й соба́ку с це́пи, не оставля́й соба́ку непривя́занной; **the dog broke ~ from its chain** соба́ка сорвала́сь с це́пи/с при́вязи; **the children have been turned ~ in the garden** де́ти игра́ют в саду́ без присмо́тра

5 *pejor*: **~ conduct/morals** распу́щенность; **a ~ woman/life** распу́тная же́нщина/жизнь

6 *fig uses*: **a ~ interpretation** свобо́дное толкова́ние; **a ~ translation** во́льный (*free*)/нето́чный (*inaccurate*) перево́д; **to tie up ~ ends** устрани́ть недоде́лки; *CQ*: **he's got a screw ~** у него́ не все до́ма; **we're at a ~ end** нам не́чем заня́ться/не́чего де́лать.

loose cover *n* (*for chairs, etc.*) чехо́л.

loose-leaf *adj* с вкладны́ми листа́ми.

loosen *vti vt* (*of screws, ropes, etc.*) ослаб|ля́ть (-́ить); **~ the bandage/nut/knot** осла́бь бинт/га́йку/у́зел; **he ~ed his hold on the box** он вы́пустил я́щик из рук; **~ your hold** не держи́сь так кре́пко; **~ his collar** расстегни́те ему́ воротни́к; **the medicine ~ed his cough** от э́того лека́рства ка́шель у него́ стал ме́ньше; **~ the soil around the shrub** разрыхли́ зе́млю вокру́г куста́; **wine ~ed his tongue** вино́ развяза́ло ему́ язы́к

vi ослабе|ва́ть (-́ть); **the ropes/bandages/nuts have ~ed** верёвки/бинты́/га́йки осла́бли; *Sport* **to ~ up** раз|мина́ться (-мя́ться).

loot *n* добы́ча.

loot *vti* гра́бить (раз-).

lop *vt, also* **~ away/off** (*branches*) отруб|а́ть (-и́ть).

lop-eared *adj* вислоу́хий.

lop-sided *adj* кособо́кий, кривобо́кий.

loquacious *adj* говорли́вый, словоохо́тливый.

lord *n* (*UK*: *title*) лорд; *Rel* **L.** бог, госпо́дь; **the Lord's prayer** «О́тче наш»; *CQ*: **good ~!** го́споди!; **~ knows where/how** бог зна́ет где/как; *fig* **the press ~s** газе́тные короли́.

lordly *adj* (*haughty*) высокоме́рный, надме́нный.

lorry *n* грузови́к; *attr*: **~ driver** шофёр грузовика́; **a ~ load of coal** грузови́к у́гля.

lose *vti vt* **1** теря́ть (по-); **to ~ a leg/a friend/altitude/interest** потеря́ть но́гу/дру́га/высоту́/интере́с; **he lost his sight/the use of his left leg** он лиши́лся зре́ния, у него́ отняла́сь ле́вая нога́; **she lost her looks** она́ потеря́ла свою́ милови́дность, она́ подурне́ла; **I've lost my place** я потеря́л ме́сто в кни́ге, где чита́л; **I've lost my spectacles somewhere** я куда́-то су́нул свои́ очки́; **~ no time in calling the doctor** сходи́ (*pf*) за врачо́м, не теря́я вре́мени; **there's not a moment to ~** нельзя́ теря́ть ни мину́ты; **the watch ~s a minute a day** часы́ отстаю́т на одну́ мину́ту в су́тки; **they lost sight of land/***fig* **of the fact that...** они́ потеря́ли бе́рег из ви́ду, они́ упусти́ли из ви́ду тот факт, что...; **I lost that remark** я прослу́шал/не расслы́шал э́то замеча́ние; **it lost him his job** э́то сто́ило ему́ ме́ста; **he ~s himself in his work** рабо́тая, он забыва́ет обо всём; **he lost his temper/his head** он рассерди́лся, он потеря́л го́лову; **I lost my heart to them** мне они́ стра́шно понра́вились; **after the third attempt I lost heart** по́сле тре́тьей попы́тки я отча́ялся; **I shan't ~ sleep over it** я не лишу́сь сна из-за э́того; **he's lost his stammer** он изба́вился от заика́ния; **I must ~ weight** я до́лжен сбро́сить ли́шний вес/похуде́ть

2 *passive uses*: **he was lost at sea** он утону́л; **the crew was saved but the ship was lost** кома́нда спасла́сь, а кора́бль затону́л; **they were given up for lost** их счита́ли поги́бшими; **all is lost!** всё пропа́ло!; **a lost art/cause/opportunity** забы́тое иску́сство, прои́гранное де́ло, потёрянная возмо́жность; **she was lost in her book** она́ зачита́лась кни́гой; **the joke was lost on him** шу́тка до него́ не дошла́, он не по́нял шу́тки; **his wit was lost on them** они́ не оцени́ли его́ остроу́мия

3 прои́гр|ывать (-а́ть); **to ~ a game/a war/a lawsuit/money at cards** проигра́ть игру́/войну́/суде́бный проце́сс/де́ньги в ка́рты

vi Sport прои́грывать; **we lost 3—6** мы проигра́ли 3:6; *fig*: **they lost on the deal** они́ потеря́ли на э́той сде́лке; *CQ* **you can't ~** вам не́чего теря́ть.

loser *n*: **he's a good/bad ~** он (не) уме́ет прои́грывать; **you'll come off the ~** ты оста́нешься в про́игрыше; *Sport* проигра́вший.

loss *n* **1** потеря́; **~ of altitude/blood/memory/the ship** потеря́ высоты́/кро́ви/па́мяти/корабля́; **~ of strength** упа́док сил (*pl*); **~ of temperature** паде́ние температу́ры; **the army suffered heavy ~es** а́рмия понесла́ тяжёлые поте́ри; **without ~ of time** не теря́я вре́мени; **he's never at a ~** он никогда́ не теря́ется; **I'm at a ~ for words** я не могу́ найти́ слов; **we're utterly at a ~ to understand how it happened** мы в по́лном недоуме́нии,/мы про́сто не зна́ем, как э́то могло́ случи́ться

2 *Comm* убы́ток; **to sell at a ~** прода́ть с убы́тком; **the car was a total ~** маши́на была́ чисте́йшим убы́тком; *CQ* **this car/he is a dead ~** э́та маши́на—сплошно́е разоре́ние, он пусто́е ме́сто.

lost property office *n* отде́л забы́тых и потёрянных веще́й, бюро́ нахо́док.

lot[1] *n* **1** жре́бий (*sing*); **by ~** по жре́бию; **to cast ~s** броса́ть жре́бий; **they drew ~s as to who should begin** они́ тяну́ли жре́бий, кому́ начина́ть; **the ~ fell on me** жре́бий пал на меня́

2 *fig* до́ля, судьба́; **it fell to my ~ to** мне вы́пало на до́лю + *inf*; **his was a hard ~** ему́ вы́пала тяжёлая до́ля, судьба́ была́ к нему́ нела́скова; **I threw in my ~ with them** я связа́л с ни́ми свою́ судьбу́

3 (*consignment of goods, etc.*) па́ртия; **the goods were sent in three ~s** това́р (*collect*) был по́слан тремя́ па́ртиями; (*at auction*) **~19—two chairs** но́мер девятна́дцать—два сту́ла; *fig* **he's a bad ~** он негодя́й, он мерза́вец

4 (*plot*) уча́сток (земли́); **a vacant ~** пусту́ющий уча́сток; **the ~ is vacant** уча́сток пусту́ет; (*US*) **parking ~** стоя́нка.

lot[2] *n* **1** (*amount*) мно́гое; мно́го + *G*; **a ~ of books** мно́го книг; **quite a ~ of roses** дово́льно мно́го роз; **they haven't got a ~ of money** у них не так мно́го де́нег; **we've got such a ~ to do** у нас сто́лько дел; **I'd give a ~ to know why** я мно́гое бы дал, что́бы знать, почему́; **there's not a ~ we can do about it** мы здесь ма́ло что мо́жем сде́лать; **what a ~ of rubbish you talk!** каку́ю ты чепуху́ несёшь!/городи́шь!; **they have ~s and ~s of money** у них ку́ча/у́йма де́нег; **they're a nice ~ of kids** все они́ симпати́чные ребя́та; **we've a dull ~ of neighbours** у нас ску́чные сосе́ди

2 *CQ* (**the ~**) всё, все; **that's the ~** э́то всё; **take the ~** бери́ всё; **get out, the ~ of you** убира́йтесь вы все; **there was champagne, caviar, the ~!** бы́ло шампа́нское, икра́—всё что хо́чешь!

3 *as adv* (**a ~**): **we (don't) see a ~ of her now** тепе́рь мы её ча́сто/ре́дко ви́дим; **I read a ~** я мно́го чита́ю; **we don't go out a ~** мы ма́ло где быва́ем; **things have changed a ~** мно́гое перемени́лось; (*with comparatives*) гора́здо, намно́го; **he's a ~ better** ему́ гора́здо/намно́го лу́чше; *CQ* **a fat ~ you care!** да тебе́ и де́ла нет!

lotion *n* (*cosmetic*) лосьо́н; **eye ~** примо́чка для глаз.

lottery *n* лотере́я.

loud *adj* гро́мкий; **a ~ voice/laugh/cry** гро́мкий го́лос/смех/крик; *Aut* **I gave a ~ hoot** я гро́мко просигна́лил; *fig pejor*: **she's very ~** она́ вульга́рна; **~ colours** крича́щие кра́ски; *as adv*: **out ~** вслух.

loud-mouthed *adj* горла́стый.

loudspeaker *n* громкоговори́тель (*m*), репроду́ктор; *attr*: **a ~ van** маши́на с радиовеща́тельной устано́вкой.

lounge *n* гости́ная; *attr*: **~ suit** костю́м.

lounge *vi* (*round house, streets, etc.*) шата́ться, слоня́ться (*impfs*); (*on sofa, etc.*) развали́ться (*only in pf*).

louse *n* вошь.

lousy *adj fig CQ* парши́вый, ме́рзкий.

lout *n* грубия́н.

lovable *adj* (*of person, animal*) симпати́чный; (*of trait*) привлека́тельный.

love *n* **1** любо́вь к + *D*; **she shows no ~ for her child** она́ не проявля́ет любви́ к своему́ ребёнку; **~ at first sight** любо́вь с пе́рвого взгля́да; **for the ~ of the thing** из любви́ к иску́сству; **they married for ~** они́ жени́лись по любви́; **he's in ~ with her/with Paris** он влюблён в неё/в Пари́ж; **he fell in ~ with her** он влюби́лся в неё, он полюби́л её; **they are thoroughly out of ~** они́ разлюби́ли друг дру́га; **there's no ~ lost between them** они́ недолю́бливают друг дру́га; **she's always in and out of ~** она́ така́я влю́бчивая; **~ of money/gain** страсть к деньга́м, корыстолю́бие; *fig* **it's not to be had for ~ or money** э́того не доста́ть ни за каки́е де́ньги; *attr*: **~ affair** рома́н, любо́вное похожде́ние

2 (*endearment*: *in family*) мой родно́й, моя́ родна́я, *CQ* (*casually*) ми́лый, ми́лая, миле́к

(*m and f*); **hurry up, ~!** торопи́сь, ми́лый!; **he's ill, poor ~** он бо́лен, бедня́жка

3 (*greetings*) приве́т; **give them my ~** переда́й им от меня́ серде́чный приве́т

4 *Sport* ноль; **~ all** счёт — ноль-ноль; **one ~ to him** один-ноль в его́ по́льзу; *attr*: **a ~ game** «суха́я».

love *vt* люби́ть (по-); **I came to ~ them** я их полюби́л; **I'd ~ to see her** мне бы так хоте́лось её повида́ть; **come and see us sometime.—I'd ~ to** заходи́ к нам ка́к-нибудь.— С удово́льствием.

lovely *adj* (*beautiful*) краси́вый; (*tasty*) вку́сный; (*delightful*) чуде́сный, *CQ* чу́дный, сла́вный; **a ~ face** краси́вое лицо́; **a ~ pie** вку́сный пиро́г; **what ~ view!** како́й чуде́сный вид!; **she's a ~ person** она́ чу́дный челове́к; **he's a ~ little boy** он сла́вный ма́льчик; **we had a ~ evening** мы чуде́сно/сла́вно провели́ ве́чер; **it's ~ and warm here** (*indoors*) здесь так ую́тно и тепло́.

lover *n* **1** любо́вник; **she took a ~** она́ завела́ (себе́) любо́вника; **a pair of ~s** влюблённая па́ра, влюблённые

2 (*of things*) люби́тель (*m*); **a music ~** люби́тель му́зыки.

lovesick *adj*: **he's ~** он томи́тся от любви́.

loving *adj* лю́бящий; (*tender*) не́жный; **a ~ glance** лю́бящий взгляд; **~ words** не́жные слова́; (*in letter*) **your ~ friend** твой ве́рный/пре́данный друг.

low[1] *adj* **1** *attr* ни́зкий, *also fig*; **a ~ price/wage/wall** ни́зкая цена́/зарпла́та/стена́; **~ frequency/ground** ни́зкая частота́/ме́стность, *Geog* ни́зменность; **of ~ birth** ни́зкого происхожде́ния; **a ~ attendance** ни́зкая посеща́емость; **a ~ dress** пла́тье с глубо́ким вы́резом; **~ cards/***Aut* **gear** мла́дшие ка́рты, *Aut* пе́рвая переда́ча *or* ско́рость; **~ water** ма́лая вода́, отли́в; **a ~ whisper** ти́хий шёпот; **~ tastes** гру́бые вку́сы; **I've a ~ opinion of him** я о нём невысо́кого мне́ния; **~ behaviour/cunning** ни́зкое поведе́ние/кова́рство; **it will cost 5 roubles at the ~est** э́то бу́дет сто́ить по кра́йней ме́ре пять рубле́й; *as n*: **prices have reached a new ~** це́ны упа́ли до небыва́ло ни́зкого у́ровня

2 *predic*: **the glass is ~** баро́метр упа́л; **the moon is ~ in the sky** луна́ стои́т ни́зко над горизо́нтом; **the rivers are ~** в ре́ках ма́ло воды́; **we're ~ on coal** у нас ма́ло у́гля; **stocks are running ~** запа́сы истоща́ются; **I'm feeling ~** я в плохо́м настрое́нии.

low[2] *vi* (*of cattle*) мыча́ть (*impf*).

low-brow *n and adj fig*: **he is a ~** он челове́к неинтеллиге́нтный.

low-down *n CQ*: **he gave me the ~ on that case** он знал всю подного́тную э́того де́ла и всё мне рассказа́л.

lower *adj* ни́зший; ни́жний; **the ~ animals/classes/ranks** ни́зшие живо́тные/кла́ссы/чины́; **the ~ school** мла́дшие кла́ссы; **a ~ tooth** ни́жний зуб; **the ~ deck** ни́жняя па́луба, (*the crew*) кома́нда; **~ case letters** строчны́е бу́квы.

lower *vt* **1** (*let down*) опус|ка́ть, спус|ка́ть (*pfs* -ти́ть); **she ~ed the blinds/her eyes/her head** она́ опусти́ла што́ры/глаза́/го́лову; **they ~ed the boat/sails/ladder** они́ спусти́ли ло́дку/паруса́/ле́стницу; **he ~ed himself by the rope** он спусти́лся по верёвке

2 (*make lower*) сни|жа́ть, пони|жа́ть (*pfs* -зить); **to ~ prices** сни́зить це́ны; **to ~ the temperature/one's voice** пони́зить температу́ру/го́лос; **we'll ~ the ceilings** мы сде́лаем потолки́ ни́же; **I wouldn't ~ myself to ask** я не уни́жусь до про́сьбы.

low-grade *adj* (*of quality*) низкосо́ртный; (*of metals*) низкопро́бный.

low-heeled *adj*: **~ shoes** ту́фли на ни́зком каблуке́.

low-level *adj*: *Aer* **a ~ attack/flight** ата́ка с ма́лой высоты́, полёт на ма́лой высоте́; *fig* **a ~ official** ме́лкий чино́вник.

low-paid *adj* (*of work or worker*) низкоопла́чиваемый.

low-powered *adj* маломо́щный.

loyal *adj* ве́рный; (*devoted*) пре́данный; (*to state*) лоя́льный; **a ~ friend** пре́данный друг; **a ~ subject** верноподда́нный.

loyalty *n* (*personal*) ве́рность, пре́данность; (*civic*) лоя́льность.

lubricate *vt* сма́з|ывать (-ать); **lubricating oil/grease** сма́зочное ма́сло, консисте́нтная сма́зка.

lubrication *n* сма́зка.

lucid *adj* я́сный; **a ~ style/mind** я́сный стиль/ум; **he has ~ intervals** у него́ быва́ют пери́оды я́сного созна́ния.

luck *n* (*good*) сча́стье; уда́ча, везе́ние [**NB** везе́ние *rare, more usu in form of impers verb* везёт + *D*; *see examples*]; (*chance*) случа́йность; (*fate*) судьба́; **bad ~** несча́стье; **good ~** уда́ча, сча́стье; **as ~ would have it** (*good*) к сча́стью, (*bad*) как назло́; **let's try our ~** дава́й попыта́ем сча́стья; **take it for ~** возьми́ на сча́стье; **it brought them nothing but bad ~** э́то принесло́ им то́лько несча́стье; **it's a matter of ~** э́то де́ло слу́чая; **to push one's ~** искуша́ть судьбу́; **we must trust to ~** нам придётся положи́ться на судьбу́; **good ~!** счастли́во!, жела́ю (вам) уда́чи!, *CQ* ни пу́ха ни пера́!; **we had the good/bad ~ to be there** к (не)сча́стью, мы как раз бы́ли там; **he has the devil's own ~** ему́ черто́вски везёт; **he's down on his ~** ему́ не везёт; **it was bad ~ we missed you** нам не повезло́, что мы не заста́ли вас; **just my ~!** как всегда́ мне не везёт!; **just beginner's ~!** новичка́м (*pl*) везёт!; **with any ~ he'll be on time** е́сли повезёт, он прие́дет во́время; **better ~ next time** в сле́дующий раз повезёт; **don't say that — it's bad ~** не говори́ так, а то сгла́зишь; **worse ~!** к сожале́нию; **no such ~!** я и не наде́юсь!

luckily *adv* к сча́стью.

lucky *adj* счастли́вый; **a ~ guess** счастливая догáдка; ~ **beggar!/dog!** счастли́вец!; ~ **you!** везёт же тебé!; **he was born** ~ он в рубáшке роди́лся; **we had a** ~ **escape** мы счáстли́во отдéлались; ~ **for you, you didn't go** тебé повезлó, что ты не поéхал тудá; **it's our** ~ **day** нам сегóдня удиви́тельно везёт; **third time** ~**!** на трéтий раз повезёт!

lucrative *adj* дохóдный, при́быльный.

ludicrous *adj* нелéпый.

lug *vt* тащи́ть, волочи́ть (*impfs*; *for pfs use compounds*); **they** ~ **the dog about everywhere** они́ всю́ду таскáют собáку с собóй; **they** ~**ged the trunk upstairs** они́ утащи́ли/уволокли́ сундýк навéрх (*impfs* утáскивать/уволáкивать).

luggage *n* багáж; *attr Rail*: ~ **rack/van** багáжная пóлка *or* сéтка, багáжный вагóн.

lukewarm *adj* чуть тёплый, теплова́тый; **the milk should be** ~ молокó должнó быть чуть тёплым; **the water is** ~ водá теплова́тая; **the sea is** ~ **there** там мóре довóльно тёплое; *fig* **he's** ~ **in his support of the project** он довóльно прохлáдно относи́тся к проéкту.

lull *n* зати́шье; **a** ~ **in the fighting/conversation** зати́шье мéжду боя́ми, пáуза в разговóре; **the** ~ **before the storm** зати́шье пéред бýрей/грозóй, *also fig*.

lull *vt* убаю́к|ивать (-ать); **she** ~**ed the baby to sleep** онá убаю́кала ребёнка; *fig* **he** ~**ed her fears/suspicions** он успокóил её стрáхи, он усыпи́л её подозрéния.

lullaby *n* колыбéльная.

lumbago *n* люмбáго (*indecl*), прострéл.

lumber *n* (*timber*) лесоматериáл; (*junk*) хлам; *attr*: ~ **camp** посёлок на лесозаготóвках; ~ **room** чулáн.

lumber *vti vt* загромо|ждáть (-зди́ть); **the attic is** ~**ed up with furniture** чердáк застáвлен/загромождён мéбелью

vi (*US*: *fell trees*) руби́ть дерéвья (*impf*).

lumberjack *n* лесорýб.

luminous *adj*: **a** ~ **watch** часы́ со светя́щимся цифербл́атом.

lump *n* **1** (*bit*) кусóк, (*malleable*) ком; (*hard, broken*) глы́ба; **a** ~ **of sugar/cake/butter** кусóк сáхара/пирогá/мáсла; **a** ~ **of clay** ком гли́ны; **a** ~ **of ice/stone** глы́ба льда, кáменная глы́ба; *fig* **it was paid in a** ~ **sum** вся сýмма былá вы́плачена срáзу

2 (*swelling*) óпухоль; ши́шка; **a** ~ **on one's knee** óпухоль на колéне; **he has a** ~ **on his forehead from the blow** у негó на лбу ши́шка от удáра; *CQ*: **a** ~ **of a girl** толстýха; **you great** ~**!** ты, медвéдь!; *fig* **a** ~ **in one's throat** комóк в гóрле.

lump *vt*, *also* ~ **together** (*odd things*) вали́ть в кýчу/в óбщую мáссу (с-); **to** ~ **under one heading** объедин|я́ть под однóй рýбрикой (-и́ть); *CQ* **if he doesn't like it he can** ~ **it** нрáвится емý э́то и́ли нет, а проглоти́ть придётся.

lumpy *adj* (*of sauce*) комковáтый.

lunatic *n and adj* сумасшéдший.

lunch *n* (*main meal of day*) обéд (в пóлдень); **I had a light/quick** ~ **at the university between lectures** я перекуси́л в университéте мéжду заня́тиями; **the Minister invited us to** ~ **at 2 o'clock** мини́стр пригласи́л нас к обéду в два часá.

lunch *vi* (*of formal or main meal*) обéдать (по-); (*informally—early, lightly*) зáвтракать (по-); (*informally—at any time*) перекуси́ть (*usu pf*); **we** ~**ed off cheese** мы перекуси́ли сы́ром.

lunchtime *n* (*break*) обéденный переры́в; **it's** ~ порá пообéдать.

lung *n* лёгкое; *attr* лёгочный.

lurch[1] *n*: **he left her in the** ~ он брóсил её в бедé.

lurch[2] *vi*: **a drunk** ~**ed along the street** по ýлице шёл пья́ный и шатáлся; **the lorry** ~**ed to one side** грузови́к накрени́лся.

lure *n* (*bait*) примáнка, *also fig*; *fig* **the** ~ **of the big city** притягáтельная си́ла большóго гóрода.

lure *vt* замáни|вать (-ть); **the spider** ~**d the fly into its web** паýк замани́л мýху в паути́ну; **they were** ~**d into a trap** их замани́ли в ловýшку; **to** ~ **smb away from smth** отвле|кáть когó-л от чегó-л (-́чь).

lurid *adj*: **a** ~ **sunset** пылáющий закáт; *fig* ~ **details** чудóвищные/ужáсные подрóбности.

lurk *vi*: **he is** ~**ing in the bushes** он крадётся в кустáх; **suspicion still** ~**ed in his mind** у негó ещё таи́лось подозрéние.

luscious *adj* (*juicy*) сóчный; (*sweet*) слáдкий; (*tasty*) вкýсный; *CQ* **a** ~ **lovely** (*girl*) сногсшибáтельная красóтка.

lush *adj* сóчный, бýйный; ~ **meadows/vegetation** сóчные лугá, бýйная *or* пы́шная расти́тельность; ~ **surroundings** пы́шное окружéние (*sing*).

lust *n* (*sexual*) пóхоть, вожделéние; *fig* **his only motive was** ~ **for power** егó еди́нственным моти́вом былá жáжда влáсти.

lusty *adj* здорóвый, крéпкий; **a** ~ **voice/infant** си́льный гóлос, здорóвый *or* крéпкий ребёнок.

lute *n* лю́тня.

luxuriant *adj* бýйный, пы́шный; ~ **growth/hair** бýйный рост, пы́шные *or* густы́е вóлосы.

luxuriate *vi*: **to** ~ **in a hot bath** нéжиться в горя́чей вáнне (*usu impf*).

luxurious *adj* роскóшный.

luxury *n* рóскошь; **I can't afford many luxuries** я не могý позвóлить себé роскóшествовать; *attr*: **a** ~ **hotel** роскóшный отéль.

lying-in *n* рóды (*pl*).

lymph gland *n* лимфати́ческая железá.

lynch *vt* (*US*) линчевáть (*impf and pf*).

lynx *n* рысь.

lyre *n* ли́ра.

lyric *adj* лири́ческий; ~ **poet** поэ́т-ли́рик; ~ **poetry** ли́рика.

lyrical *adj* лири́ческий; (*enthusiastic*) востóрженный; **he waxed** ~ **about the play** он востóрженно отзывáлся об э́той пьéсе.

M

macabre *adj* мра́чный, жу́ткий; ~ **humour** чёрный/мра́чный ю́мор.

macadamize *vt*: **to ~ a road** покры|ва́ть доро́гу гудро́ном (-́ть), гудрони́ровать доро́гу (*impf and pf*).

macaroni *n* макаро́ны (*pl*).

macaroon *n* минда́льное пече́нье.

machination *n* махина́ция.

machine *n* маши́на; (*for working wood, metal, etc.*) стано́к; *CQ* (= *car*) маши́на; **sewing/knitting ~** шве́йная маши́нка, вяза́льная маши́на; **drilling ~** сверли́льный стано́к; *fig* **party ~** парти́йный аппара́т; *attr*: **the ~ age** век маши́н, маши́нный век.

machine *vt Sew* шить на маши́нке (с-).

machine gun *n* пулемёт.

machine-made *adj* маши́нного произво́дства.

machinery *n* маши́ны (*pl*), маши́нное обору́дование; *fig* **the ~ of law** суде́бная маши́на.

machine shop *n* механи́ческий цех.

machine tool *n* стано́к: *attr*: **the ~ industry** станкострои́тельная промы́шленность.

mackerel *n* макре́ль, ску́мбрия.

mackintosh, *abbr* **mac** *n* макинто́ш, плащ.

mad *adj* **1** (*insane*) сумасше́дший, безу́мный; **a ~ dog** бе́шеная соба́ка; **you must be ~!** ты что, с ума сошёл?/*CQ* спя́тил?; **to drive smb ~** своди́ть кого́-л с ума́, доводи́ть кого́-л до сумасше́ствия; **he was ~ with jealousy** он обезу́мел от ре́вности; *CQ*: **what a ~ thing to do** како́е сумасше́ствие!; **he's as ~ as a hatter** он совсе́м спя́тил; **he's ~ about her** он по ней с ума́ схо́дит; **she's ~ about tennis** она́ помеша́лась на те́ннисе

2 *CQ* (*angry*): **he was ~ at my extravagance** он рвал и мета́л, узна́в, ско́лько я истра́тил де́нег; **he was hopping ~ with me for being late** моё опозда́ние привело́ его́ в бе́шенство; **don't get ~ at me** не серди́сь на меня́.

mad *adv*: **he ran like ~** он бежа́л как сумасше́дший; **she's ~ keen on becoming a film star** она́ мечта́ет стать кинозвездо́й.

madam, madame, *abbr* **ma'am** *n* мада́м (*only in address*); *CQ* **she's a proper (little) ~** она́ про́сто ба́рыня.

madden *vt* своди́ть с ума́ (свести́); беси́ть (вз-); **I find her ~ing** она́ меня́ бе́сит.

mad-house *n CQ* сумасше́дший дом, *also fig*.

madly *adv*: **he's ~ jealous** он безу́мно/стра́шно ревни́в; **they're ~ in love** они́ безу́мно влюблены́ друг в дру́га.

madman *n* сумасше́дший, безу́мный; *fig* безу́мец.

madness *n* сумасше́ствие, безу́мие.

magazine *n* **1** (*journal*) журна́л

2 *Mil* (*store*) склад боеприпа́сов; (*on gun*) магази́н.

maggot *n* личи́нка.

magic *n* ма́гия, волшебство́; **black ~** чёрная ма́гия; **as if by ~** как по волшебству́; **the medicine worked like ~** лека́рство поде́йствовало маги́чески; *fig* **I'll never forget the ~ of that evening** я никогда́ не забу́ду очарова́ния того́ ве́чера.

magic(al) *adj* маги́ческий, волше́бный.

magician *n* (*in fairy tales*) волше́бник; (*conjuror*) фо́кусник.

magisterial *adj* авторите́тный.

magistrate *n approx* судья́.

magnanimous *adj* великоду́шный.

magnate *n*: **oil ~** нефтяно́й магна́т.

magnesia *n* магне́зия.

magnesium *n* ма́гний.

magnet *n* магни́т.

magnetic *adj* магни́тный; *fig* **a ~ personality** притяга́тельная ли́чность.

magnetism *n* магнети́зм; *fig* притяга́тельность.

magnificent *adj* великоле́пный; *CQ* **~!** великоле́пно!

magnify *vt* увели́ч|ивать (-ить); *fig* **to ~ problems** преувели́чивать тру́дности.

magnifying-glass *n* увеличи́тельное стекло́; лу́па.

magnitude *n* (*size*) величина́; *fig* **commercial enterprises of this ~** предприя́тия тако́го масшта́ба.

magpie *n* соро́ка.

mahogany *n* кра́сное де́рево; *attr* кра́сного де́рева; (*of colour*) краснова́то-кори́чневый.

maid *n* (*servant*) служа́нка, прислу́га; (*in hotels*) го́рничная; **old ~** ста́рая де́ва.

maiden *adj*: **~ aunt** незаму́жняя тётка; **~ name** де́вичья фами́лия; *fig* **~ voyage** пе́рвый рейс.

mail *n* по́чта, пи́сьма (*pl*).

mail *vt* пос|ыла́ть по по́чте (-ла́ть).

mailbag *n* мешо́к с по́чтой.

mailbox *n* (*US*) почто́вый я́щик.

mail-order *n* (*US*) зака́з по по́чте.

maim *vt* кале́чить (ис-, по-); **he was ~ed in the war** его́ искале́чило (*impers*) на войне́; **he was ~ed for life** он оста́лся кале́кой на всю жизнь.

main *n* **1** (*for water, etc.*) магистра́ль; **water ~** водопрово́дная магистра́ль; **to turn the water/gas off at the ~s** перекрыва́ть/отключа́ть во́ду/газ

2 (*the greater part*): **in the ~** в основно́м; **I agree with you in the ~** в основно́м я с ва́ми согла́сен; **the soldiers were in the ~ recruits** солда́ты бы́ли в большинстве́ новобра́нцы

3: **with (all one's) might and ~** изо все́х си́л.

main *adj* (*chief*) гла́вный; (*basic*) основно́й; **the ~ street** гла́вная у́лица; **the ~ thing is to work hard** са́мое гла́вное — хорошо́ рабо́тать; **the ~ course** (*of meal*) основно́е блю́до; **the ~ theme of the lecture** основна́я те́ма ле́кции; *CQ* **he's got an eye to the ~ chance** он никогда́ о себе́ не забыва́ет.

mainland *n* матери́к.

main line *n Rail* железнодоро́жная магистра́ль.

mainly *adv* в основно́м, гла́вным о́бразом.

main road *n* шоссе́ (*indecl*), магистра́ль.

mainspring *n* (*of watch, etc.*) ходова́я пружи́на; *fig* (*motive*) дви́жущая си́ла.

mainstay *n fig* гла́вная опо́ра.

maintain *vt* **1** (*keep up*) подде́рживать, сохраня́ть (*only in impfs*); **to ~ contact/relations with smb** подде́рживать конта́кт/отноше́ния с кем-л; **to ~ law and order/the temperature** подде́рживать поря́док/температу́ру; **the roads are well ~ed** доро́ги подде́рживаются в хоро́шем состоя́нии; **if the improvement is ~ed he can get up on Tuesday** е́сли не бу́дет ухудше́ния, он смо́жет встать с посте́ли во вто́рник; **to ~ the status quo** сохраня́ть существу́ющее положе́ние/ста́тус-кво́ (*indecl*)

2 (*support financially*) содержа́ть (*impf*); **the State ~s the army** а́рмию содéржит госуда́рство; **he can no longer ~ his family** он бо́льше не в состоя́нии содержа́ть семью́

3: to ~ that... утвержда́ть, что... (*only in impf*).

maintenance *n* **1** (*preservation*) поддержа́ние; сохране́ние; *Mech* ухо́д; техни́ческое обслу́живание; **the ~ of public order** поддержа́ние обще́ственного поря́дка; **the ~ of peace** сохране́ние ми́ра; *attr*: **~ costs** расхо́ды по техни́ческому обслу́живанию; *Rail, etc.* **~ crew** брига́да техни́ческого обслу́живания

2 (*keep*): **to pay for smb's ~** опла́чивать чьё-л содержа́ние.

maître d'hôtel *n* метрдоте́ль (*m*).

maize *n* маи́с, кукуру́за.

majestic *adj* велича́вый, вели́чественный.

majesty *n* (*as title*): **Your M.** ва́ше вели́чество.

major *n Mil* майо́р; *Law* совершенноле́тний; *Mus* мажо́р; **the key of C ~** тона́льность до мажо́р.

major *adj* **1** (*larger*) бо́льший; (*chief*) гла́вный; **the ~ part** бо́льшая часть; **this is the ~ problem** э́то гла́вная пробле́ма; **a question of ~ importance** вопро́с первостепе́нной ва́жности; (*large-scale*): **the ~ banks/companies** кру́пные ба́нки/компа́нии; **~ repairs** капита́льный ремо́нт (*sing*)

2 *Mus*: **a ~ key** мажо́рная тона́льность.

major *vi* (*US*): **I ~ed in medieval history** я специализи́ровался по исто́рии сре́дних веко́в (*impf and pf*).

major-general *n* генера́л-майо́р.

majority *n* **1** большинство́; **a small/overwhelming ~** незначи́тельное/подавля́ющее большинство́; **in the ~ of cases** в большинстве́ слу́чаев; **the ~ of speakers were men** большинство́ докла́дчиков бы́ли мужчи́ны [**NB** *pl verb*]; **in our school girls are in the ~** в на́шей шко́ле де́вочек бо́льше, чем ма́льчиков; **they had a ~ in Parliament** они́ получи́ли большинство́ в парла́менте; **he was elected by a narrow ~/by a ~ of 3** он был и́збран незначи́тельным большинство́м/большинство́м в три го́лоса; *attr*: **~ rule** подчине́ние меньшинства́ большинству́

2 *Law* совершенноле́тие; **to reach one's ~** дости́чь совершенноле́тия.

make *n*: **goods of Soviet ~** това́ры сове́тского произво́дства; **what ~ is your car?** како́й ма́рки ва́ша маши́на?; **cameras of all ~s** фотоаппара́ты всех ма́рок; *CQ* **he's on the ~** он карьери́ст.

make *vti vt* **1** (*general*) де́лать (с-); (*create*) созда|ва́ть (-́ть); **they have made a reservoir in the mountains** они́ со́здали иску́сственный водоём в гора́х; *fig*: **they are made for one another** они́ со́зданы друг для дру́га; **to ~ difficulties** создава́ть тру́дности; **they made him ambassador/a general** его́ назна́чили посло́м, ему́ присво́или зва́ние генера́ла; **he made a name for himself** он со́зда́л себе́ и́мя; **this doesn't ~ sense** в э́том нет смы́сла

2 (*produce, manufacture*) произ|води́ть (-вести́); вы|пуска́ть (-́пустить); **to ~ glass/tractors** производи́ть стекло́, выпуска́ть тра́кторы; **this factory ~s 500 cars a day** э́тот заво́д произво́дит/выпуска́ет пятьсо́т маши́н в день; **what's this made of?** из чего́ э́то сде́лано?; **to ~ furniture/a film** де́лать ме́бель, снима́ть фильм (снять); **she made that dress herself** она́ сама́ сши́ла э́то пла́тье; **I must have a coat made for the winter** мне ну́жно отда́ть сшить зи́мнее пальто́; *fig* **to ~ an impression on smb** производи́ть на кого́-л впечатле́ние

3 (*prepare*): **to ~ breakfast/supper/a tart** гото́вить за́втрак/у́жин, печь пиро́г (при-, ис-); **to ~ tea/coffee** завари́ть чай, свари́ть ко́фе; **I'll ~ the beds** я застелю́/(*stow bedding off divan*) я уберу́ посте́ли; **to ~ a bonfire** раскла́дывать костёр (разложи́ть); **to ~ hay** коси́ть траву́ (с-)

4 (*notes, speech, agreement*): **to ~ notes of a lecture** запи́с|ывать ле́кцию (-а́ть); **~ a note of my telephone number** запиши́ мой телефо́н; **I'll ~ a mental note of that** я возьму́ э́то на заме́тку; **to ~ a report** (*write*) написа́ть отчёт, (*prepare*) подгото́вить/(*present*) предста́вить докла́д; **to ~ a statement** сде́лать заявле́ние; **to ~ a speech** вы́ступить с ре́чью; **to ~ a list** состав|ля́ть спи́сок (-́ить); **we made an agreement with the publishing house** мы заключи́ли догово́р с изда́тельством; *CQ* **when shall we meet?—Let's ~ it Thursday** когда́ мы встре́тимся?—Дава́й договори́мся на четве́рг

5 (*cause*): **to ~ a fuss/noise** под|нима́ть шум (-ня́ть); **to ~ a scene** устр|а́ивать сце́ну (-о́ить); **we made him laugh** мы его́ рассмеши́ли; **I made them believe that...** я заста́вил их пове́рить, что...; **it made her more careful** по́сле э́того она́ ста́ла осторо́жней; *CQ*: **the film/he made a great hit** фильм/он име́л огро́мный успе́х; **what ~s him tick?** что им дви́жет?

6 (*accomplish*): **to ~ a journey/a trip** соверш|а́ть путеше́ствие/пое́здку (-и́ть); *Aer* **to ~ a landing** сде́лать поса́дку; **we made the crossing by ferry** мы перепра́вились на паро́ме; *CQ*: **we made it to the station on time** мы добрали́сь до ста́нции во́время; **we made it in time for lunch** мы успе́ли к обе́ду; **he didn't ~ it to the finishing line** он не дошёл до фи́ниша; **he's made it/the grade as a conductor** он доби́лся успе́ха как дирижёр

7 (*acquire*): **he made money** он разбогате́л; **how much do you ~ a month?** ско́лько вы получа́ете в ме́сяц?; **I ~ my living by writing** я зараба́тываю на жизнь перо́м/литерату́рным трудо́м; **he's made a lot of friends/enemies here** он завёл здесь мно́го друзе́й, он на́жил себе́ здесь мно́го враго́в; *CQ* **he made a packet in America** он сколоти́л состоя́ние в Аме́рике

8 (*constitute*, *become*): **2 and 3 ~ 5** два плюс три—пять; **1,000 grammes ~ one kilogram** в одно́м килогра́мме ты́сяча гра́ммов; **how many players ~ a football team?** ско́лько челове́к в футбо́льной кома́нде?; **he'll ~ a good doctor** он бу́дет хоро́шим врачо́м; **the story ~s fascinating reading** э́то захва́тывающий расска́з

9 (*calculate*, *understand*): **what do you ~ the answer?** како́й, по-тво́ему, бу́дет отве́т?; **what do you ~ the time?** ско́лько сейча́с на ва́ших часа́х?; **I don't know what to ~ of her** не зна́ю, что сказа́ть о ней

10 *with nouns*: *perform some action*; *often translated by verbs formed from the noun*; *see also under particular nouns*: **to ~ an answer/a start/a visit** отве|ча́ть (-́тить), нач|ина́ть (-а́ть), посе|ща́ть (-ти́ть); **to ~ arrangements about smth** организо́|вывать что-л (-ва́ть), *etc*.

11: **to ~ smth of smb/smth** *with noun complements*: **to ~ a fuss of smb** носи́ться с кем-л; **he made a mess of things** он всё запу́тал; **I made a fool of myself today** сего́дня я сде́лал глу́пость; **he made a pig of himself at dinner** он перее́л за обе́дом

12 *with predic adj*; *often translated by verbs formed from adj*; *see also under particular adjs*: **to ~ smb angry/glad** серди́ть/ра́довать кого́-л (рас-/об-); **I made myself known to them** я предста́вился им; **he can ~ himself understood in French** он мо́жет объясни́ться по-францу́зски

vi: **he made to hit her, but I grabbed him by the arm** он замахну́лся на неё, но я успе́л схвати́ть его́ за́ руку; **he made as if to escape** он попыта́лся вы́рваться

make away *vi*: **he made away with himself** он поко́нчил с собо́й; **he made away/off with the money** он сбежа́л, прихвати́в с собо́й де́ньги

make do on/with *vt*: **she ~s do on/with £20 a week** она́ обхо́дится двадцатью́ фу́нтами в неде́лю

make for *vi*: **he made for the exit** он пошёл/напра́вился к вы́ходу: **the dog made straight for the cat** соба́ка бро́силась на ко́шку; **it will just ~ for difficulties** э́то лишь созда́ст тру́дности

make out *vti vt*: **~ the cheque out to my father** вы́пишите чек на и́мя моего́ отца́; **I can't ~ out his handwriting** я не могу́ разобра́ть его́ по́черк; **I made out a figure in the dark** я различи́л в темноте́ чью-то фигу́ру; **I can't ~ him out** ника́к не могу́ разобра́ться в нём; **how do you ~ that out?** как ты пришёл к тако́му вы́воду?; **he made out he was ill** он сказа́лся больны́м; **he made out a strong case for the defence** он привёл си́льные аргуме́нты в по́льзу своего́ подзащи́тного; **he's not such a fool as they ~ out** он не тако́й дура́к, каки́м его́ счита́ют

vi: **how is he making out?** как у него́ успе́хи?

make over *vt*: **he made over the estate to his son** он переда́л име́ние сы́ну

make up *vti vt*: **I'll ~ up a bed for you** я вам постелю́/пригото́влю посте́ль; **~ up the fire before you go out** подбро́сь у́гля/подложи́ дров пе́ред ухо́дом; **to ~ up a prescription** гото́вить лека́рство по реце́пту; **I'll ~ up a parcel of books for you** я вам заверну́ не́сколько книг; **we ~ up a majority** мы составля́ем большинство́; **I will make the sum up to 100 roubles** я доведу́ су́мму до ста рубле́й; **to ~ up a game** приду́м|ывать игру́ (-ать); **to ~ up one's mind/face** реш|а́ть (-и́ть), кра́ситься (на-); *Theat* **he was made up as a prince** он был в гри́ме при́нца; **they've made it up** они́ помири́лись

vi: **I'll try to ~ up for my rudeness** я постара́юсь загла́дить свою́ гру́бость; **to ~ up for lost time** наверста́ть упу́щенное вре́мя; **he ~s up to him quite openly** он откры́то подли́зывается к нему́.

maker *n* (*manufacturer*) изготови́тель (*m*); (*craftsman*) ма́стер; (*creator*) созда́тель (*m*), творе́ц.

makeshift *adj*: **this is only a ~ repair** я пока́ э́то так починю́.

make-up *n* (*composition*) соста́в; (*cosmetics*) косме́тика; *Theat* грим; **she doesn't use ~** она́ не по́льзуется косме́тикой.

makeweight *n* дове́сок, *also fig*.

making *n* (*manufacture*) произво́дство, изготовле́ние; **the ~ of cars/glass** произво́дство маши́н/стекла́; *fig*: **the army was the ~ of him** а́рмия сде́лала из него́ челове́ка; **the boy has the ~s of a pianist** у ма́льчика есть зада́тки пиани́ста.

maladjusted *adj*: **a ~ child** *approx* тру́дный ребёнок.

maladministration *n*: **our losses are due to ~** на́ши убы́тки объясня́ются просчётами (*inefficiency*)/злоупотребле́ниями (*corruption*) администра́ции.

malady *n* боле́знь, *also fig*; **the social maladies of today** боле́зни совреме́нного о́бщества.

Malay(an) *n* мала́ец, мала́йка.

Malay(an) *adj* мала́йский.

malcontent *n* недовольный, *Polit* оппозиционер.

male *n* мужчина (*m*); (*animal*) самец.

male *adj* мужской; **the ~ sex** мужской пол; **~ lead** главная мужская роль (в пьесе); **~ cat/dog** кот, кобель (*m*); *Tech* **~ screw** шуруп, винт.

malevolent *adj* злой, злобный.

malformation *n*: **a ~ of the spine** искривление позвоночника.

malice *n* злоба, злость; **to bear smb ~** таить злобу на кого-л, *CQ* иметь зуб на/против кого-л; *Law* **with ~ aforethought** с преступными намерениями (*pl*).

malicious *adj* злой; **~ rumours** злые/недобрые слухи.

malign *adj* пагубный, дурной; **a ~ influence** пагубное влияние.

malign *vt* клеветать (о-).

malignant *adj* злобный; *Med* злокачественный.

malinger *vi*: **he's just ~ing** он просто притворяется больным, он симулирует.

malingerer *n* симулянт.

malnutrition *n* недостаточное питание, недоедание.

malpractice *n* противозаконное действие, беззаконие.

malt *n* солод.

maltreat *vt* плохо обращаться с + *I* (*only in impf*).

mamma *n CQ* мама.

mammal *n* млекопитающее.

man *n* **1** человек (*pl* люди); (*implying manliness*) мужчина (*m*); **the achievements/rights of ~** достижения/права человека; **the ~ in the street** обыкновенный/рядовой человек; **her young ~** её молодой человек, её кавалер; (*in address*) **young ~!** молодой человек!; **be a ~!** будь мужчиной!; **best ~** шафер; **a ladies' ~** дамский угодник; **a ~ of letters** литератор; **men and management** рабочие и дирекция; **officers and men** офицеры и солдаты; **a ~ about town** светский человек

2 *various*: **if you need a carpenter, I'm your ~** если вам нужен плотник, обращайтесь ко мне; **I'm not a drinking ~** я человек непьющий; **he's an Edinburgh ~** он из Эдинбурга; **every ~ for himself** каждый за себя; **good ~!** молодец!; **to a ~** все как один, все до одного; **I've known him ~ and boy** я с ним с детства знаком; **I talked to him as ~ to ~** я поговорил с ним как мужчина с мужчиной.

man *vt*: **to ~ a vessel** на|бирать команду (-брать); **we haven't enough staff to ~ the lifts** у нас не хватает лифтёров.

manage *vti vt* **1** (*direct*) руководить + *I*, управлять + *I*, заведовать + *I* (*impfs*); **to ~ an institution/factory** руководить учреждением/фабрикой; **to ~ a** (*small*) **office** управлять конторой; **to ~ a restaurant** заведовать рестораном; **to ~ a household** вести домашнее хозяйство (*only in impf*); **her brother ~s her affairs** брат ведёт все её дела

2 (*handle*) управ|ляться с + *I*, справ|ляться с + *I* (*pfs* -иться); **I can't ~ the boat alone** я не могу сам управиться с лодкой; **he couldn't ~ the work** он не справлялся с работой; **can you ~ the suitcase?** ты сможешь понести этот чемодан?; **can you ~ dinner on Wednesday?** ты сможешь пообедать с нами в среду?

vi **1** (*get along*) об|ходиться (-ойтись); **one can't ~ without money** без денег не проживёшь; **she ~s on £20 a week** ей хватает двадцати фунтов в неделю; **how are you managing?** как у вас дела?

2 (*succeed in*) **to ~ to** + *inf* удаться (*used impers*), (*be in time*) успеть (*only in pfs*); **I ~d to get through to him** (*on phone*)/**to catch the train** мне удалось дозвониться до него, я успел на поезд; **I ~d to lose the key** я умудрился потерять ключ.

manageable *adj*: **a case of ~ size** чемодан удобных размеров (*pl*).

management *n* (*action*) управление + *I*, руководство + *I*; **the ~ of affairs** управление делами; (*people*) (**the ~**) дирекция, администрация (*in hotels always* администрация).

manager *n* управляющий + *I*, заведующий + *I*; (*in industry or large organization*) директор; (*of performing musicians, etc.*; *not in SU*) импресарио (*indecl*); **the ~ of an estate** управляющий имением; **the ~ of a shop** заведующий магазином, *abbr* завмаг, (*of larger shops*) директор магазина; **the ~ of a canteen** заведующий столовой; **she's a good ~** она хорошая хозяйка; *Sport* **the ~ of a football team** *approx* начальник команды.

managerial *adj* административный.

managing director *n* директор-распорядитель (*m*); (*in SU*) заместитель (*m*) директора, *abbr* замдиректора.

mandarin *n* (*fruit*) мандарин.

mandate *n* мандат; **a territory under ~** подмандатная территория.

mandatory *adj* обязательный; принудительный.

mane *n* грива.

manganese *n* марганец.

mange *n* чесотка, парша.

manger *n* ясли (*pl*), кормушка.

mangy *adj* чесоточный, шелудивый; паршивый, *also fig*; *CQ* **what a ~ dinner!** какой скверный обед!

manhandle *vt*: **the box had to be ~d on to the lorry** ящик пришлось поднимать на грузовик вручную (*adv*); *CQ* **the police ~d the hooligans off the pitch** полиция вытолкала хулиганов с поля.

manhole *n* люк.

man-hour *n* человеко-час.

manhunt *n*: **a ~ for the murderer** розыск убийцы.

mania *n* мáния; **homicidal/persecution ~** мáния убийства/преслéдования; *CQ* **football is a ~ with him** он помéшан на футбóле.

maniac *n* маньяк.

manicure *vt* дéлать маникюр (с-).

manifest *adj* очевидный, явный.

manifest *vt* прояв|лять (-ить), обнарýжи|вать (-ть); **he has ~ed some interest in our project** он проявил интерéс к нáшему прoéкту; **no further symptoms have ~ed themselves** бóльше никаких симптóмов не обнарýжилось.

manifesto *n* манифéст.

manipulate *vt* (*handle*) манипулировать + *I* (*impf*), *also fig*; **to ~ facts** манипулировать фáктами; *Aut* **the gears aren't easy to ~** скóрости трýдно переключáть.

mankind *n* человéчество.

manliness *n* мýжественность.

manly *adj* мýжественный.

man-made *adj* искýсственный; (*of textiles, etc.*) синтетический.

mannequin *n* (*fashion model*) манекéнщица; (*dummy*) манекéн.

manner *n* **1** (*way*) óбраз, манéра; **~ of life** óбраз жизни; **in this/the same ~** таким óбразом *or CQ joc* таким манéром, таким же óбразом; **in such a ~ that...** таким óбразом, что...; **by no ~ of means** никóим óбразом; **in a ~ of speaking** в какóй-то стéпени, мóжно сказáть; **I don't like his ~ of speaking** мне не нрáвится егó манéра говорить; **he paints after/in the ~ of Repin** он пишет в манéре Рéпина; **I've patched it after a ~** я залатáл это кóе-кáк; **he does it as to the ~ born** он как бýдто рождён для этого

2 (*kind*): **all ~ of men** сáмые рáзные люди; **all ~ of tools** всевозмóжные инструмéнты; **what ~ of man is he?** что он за человéк?

3 (*behaviour, usu pl in both languages*) (**~s**) манéры; **he's got good ~s** у негó хорóшие манéры; **mind your ~s** веди себя как слéдует; **the ~s of society at that time** нрáвы óбщества тогó врéмени; **a comedy of ~s** комéдия нрáвов.

mannered *adj* манéрный.

mannerism *n* манéрность; **I don't like his ~s** мне не нрáвится егó манéрность (*sing*); **~s of style** манéра (*sing*) письмá.

mannerly *adj* вéжливый, учтивый.

manoeuvre, (*US*) **maneuver** *n* манёвр, *also Mil*; (*trick*) улóвка; **he got his way by devious ~s** он добился своегó рáзными улóвками; *Mil* **the troops are on ~s** войскá на манёврах.

manoeuvre, (*US*) **maneuver** *vti vt*: **he ~d the car into the garage** он с трудóм завёл машину в гарáж; *fig* **to ~ smb into a good job** устрóить когó-л на хорóшую рабóту

vi Mil маневрировать (*impf*); **to ~ for position** маневрировать для занятия выгодной позиции.

manor, *also* **~ house** *n* дом-усáдьба.

manpower *n* рабóчая сила.

manservant *n* слугá (*m*).

mansion *n* (*in country*) усáдьба, (*in city*) особняк.

manslaughter *n Law* непредумышленное убийство.

mantel, mantelpiece, mantelshelf *ns* каминная доскá; **the clock is on the ~** часы на камине.

manual *n* (*handbook*) учéбник; (*of technical instruction*) руковóдство; *Mus* (*on organ*) мануáл (оргáна); **a shorthand ~** учéбник по стенográфии.

manual *adj* ручнóй; **~ controls** ручнóе управлéние; **~ labour** физический/ручнóй труд; **~ worker** чернорабóчий.

manually *adv* вручнýю; **this machine is operated ~** эта машина управляется вручнýю; **these goods have been produced ~** эти товáры—ручнóго произвóдства.

manufacture *n* произвóдство; **the ~ of steel** произвóдство стáли; **goods of foreign ~** товáры инострáнного произвóдства.

manufacture *vt* производить (*usu impf*); **this factory ~s cars** этот завóд произвóдит/выпускáет машины.

manufacturer *n* производитель (*m*), изготовитель (*m*).

manufacturing *n* произвóдство; *attr*: **~ costs** стóимость произвóдства; **~ town** промышленный гóрод.

manure *n* удобрéние; (*dung*) навóз.

manure *vt* удобр|ять (-ить); унавó|живать (-зить).

manuscript *n* рýкопись; **in ~** в рýкописи; *attr* рукописный.

many *adj and n* **1** мнóгие; мнóго + *G* (*not used in oblique cases*); **~ of those present/of us** мнóгие из присýтствующих/из нас; **in ~ cases** во мнóгих слýчаях; **he helped me in ~ ways** он во мнóгом мне помóг; **he's like his father in ~ ways** он во мнóгом похóж на отцá; **~ people/objects** мнóго людéй/предмéтов; **~ years have passed** прошлó мнóго лет; **~ years ago** мнóго лет (томý) назáд; **~ times** мнóго раз; **for ~ a long day** мнóго дней; **there weren't ~ there** там немнóгие были

2 *phrases*: **I have as ~ as you** у меня стóлько же, скóлько у тебя; **I need as ~ plates again** мне нáдо ещё стóлько же тарéлок; **he has twice as ~ books as she has** у негó книг вдвóе бóльше, чем у неё; **as ~ as that?** так мнóго?; **as ~ as you like** скóлько хотите; **he gave back as ~ as he took** он скóлько взял, стóлько и отдáл; **how ~ people/times?** скóлько людéй/раз?; **however ~ toys he has, he always asks for more** скóлько бы у негó игрýшек ни было, он всё врéмя прóсит нóвые; **I've never seen so ~ birds** я никогдá не видел такóго мнóжества птиц; **I told him that in so ~ words** я именно так это емý и сказáл; **look at**

that — so ~ mistakes! посмотри́ на э́то — сто́лько оши́бок!; **I've got one blanket too ~** у меня́ ли́шнее одея́ло; **he was one too ~ for his opponent** он был сли́шком силён для своего́ проти́вника.

many-coloured *adj* многоцве́тный.

many-sided *adj* многосторо́нний.

map *n* ка́рта; (*of town*) план го́рода; **Underground ~** схе́ма ста́нций метро́; **to make/read a ~** составля́ть/чита́ть ка́рту; **to follow a ~** дви́гаться по ка́рте; *fig*: **our dacha is right off the ~** до на́шей да́чи о́чень тру́дно добира́ться; **oil has put Aberdeen on the ~** нефть принесла́ Аберди́ну изве́стность.

map *vt*: **to ~ a territory** состав|ля́ть ка́рту ме́стности (-ить); **to ~ out a programme/route/one's time** составля́ть програ́мму/маршру́т, плани́ровать своё вре́мя (*usu impf*).

maple *n* клён; *attr*: **~ leaf** кленóвый лист.

mar *vt* по́ртить (ис-); **his character is ~red by greed** жа́дность испо́ртила его́ хара́ктер [**NB** *tense*]; **this will make or ~ him** ли́бо пан, ли́бо пропа́л.

marauder *n* мародёр.

marble *n* мра́мор; (*glass ball*) стекля́нный ша́рик; **a game of ~s** игра́ в ша́рики; **to play ~s** игра́ть в ша́рики; *attr* мра́морный.

marbled *adj* (*variegated*) кра́пчатый; **~ linoleum** лино́леум под мра́мор.

March *n* март; *attr* ма́ртовский.

march *n Mil* марш; **on the ~** на ма́рше; **a 3-day ~** трёхдне́вный марш/перехо́д; **a ~ past** торже́ственный марш; **a forced ~** марш-бросо́к; **the river is a day's ~ from the town** река́ в однодне́вном перехо́де от го́рода; *Mus* **funeral ~** похоро́нный марш; *fig*: **the ~ of events** ход собы́тий; **to steal a ~ on smb** опереди́ть кого́-л.

march *vti vt*: **the general ~ed his army into the town** генера́л ввёл войска́ в го́род; **the criminal was ~ed off to gaol** престу́пника отпра́вили в тюрьму́

vi Mil марширова́ть (*impf*); **forward/quick ~!** ша́гом марш!; **the army ~ed off from camp** а́рмия вы́ступила из ла́геря; **the army ~ed on the town** а́рмия дви́нулась на го́род.

marching orders *npl* прика́з (*sing*) о выступле́нии; *fig* (*dismissal*) **he's got his ~** его́ уво́лили.

marching song *n* похо́дная пе́сня.

mare *n* кобы́ла.

margarine, *CQ* **marge** *n* маргари́н.

margin *n*: **the ~ of a page** поля́ (*pl*) страни́цы; **on the ~ of the lake** на берегу́ о́зера; **with this instrument the ~ of error is very small** у э́того инструме́нта минима́льный преде́л погре́шности; **one must allow for a ~ of error** ну́жно всегда́ учи́тывать возмо́жность оши́бки; **the bill was passed by a narrow ~** законопрое́кт был при́нят незначи́тельным большинство́м голосо́в; **~ of profit** чи́стая при́быль.

marginal *adj*: **~ notes** заме́тки на поля́х; **the difference is ~** ра́зница незначи́тельна; (*borderline*) **a ~ case** э́то нея́сный слу́чай.

marginally *adv*: **~ better** немно́го лу́чше.

marigold *n* ногтки́ (*pl*).

marihuana, marijuana *n* марихуа́на.

marinade *n* марина́д.

marinade, marinate *vt* маринова́ть (за-); **~d vegetables** марино́ванные о́вощи.

marine *n*: **merchant/mercantile ~** торго́вый флот; **the Marines** морска́я пехо́та; *fig CQ* **tell that to the Marines!** расскажи́ э́то кому́ друго́му/свое́й ба́бушке!

marine *adj* (*of the sea*) морско́й; (*of ships*) судово́й; **~ insurance** морско́е страхова́ние; **~ stores** судовы́е припа́сы; **~ artist** худо́жник-марини́ст.

mariner *n* матро́с, моря́к; **~'s compass** судово́й ко́мпас.

marionette *n* марионе́тка.

marital *adj* супру́жеский; **~ status** семе́йное положе́ние.

maritime *adj* (*of the sea*) морско́й; (*coastal*) примо́рский; **a ~ power** морска́я держа́ва; **~ region** примо́рский райо́н, примо́рье.

marjoram *n* майора́н.

mark[1] *n* (*coin*) ма́рка.

mark[2] *n* **1** знак; ме́тка *and compounds*; (*trace*) след; (*stain*) пятно́; **question ~** вопроси́тельный знак; **punctuation ~** знак препина́ния; **quotation ~s** кавы́чки; **as a ~ of my respect for you** в знак моего́ уваже́ния к вам; **laundry ~** ме́тка на белье́; **pencil ~** каранда́шная поме́тка; **high water ~** отме́тка у́ровня прили́ва; **the ~ of a hoof on the sand** след/отпеча́ток копы́та на песке́; **you've got a ~ on your jacket** у тебя́ на пиджаке́ пятно́; **stained fingers are the ~ of a smoker** жёлтые па́льцы — при́знак кури́льщика; **trade ~** фабри́чная ма́рка; *fig*: **he left his ~ on history** он оста́вил след в исто́рии; **this work has the ~ of genius** на э́том произведе́нии лежи́т печа́ть ге́ния; **he quickly made his ~ in his profession** он о́чень ско́ро прояви́л себя́ на э́том по́прище

2 (*target*) цель; **to hit the ~** попа́сть в цель/*fig* в то́чку; **off the ~** ми́мо це́ли, *also fig*; *fig*: **his conclusion was a bit wide of the ~** он сде́лал не совсе́м ве́рное заключе́ние; **he's not so far off the ~** он не так далёк от и́стины

3 *Sport* (*in athletics*): **he was quick to get off the ~** он взял бы́стрый старт, *also fig*; **on your ~s!** на старт!; *fig*: **to overstep the ~** зайти́ сли́шком далеко́; **his work is not up to the ~** его́ рабо́та не на у́ровне; **I'm not feeling up to the ~** я себя́ нева́жно чу́вствую

4 (*in exams*) отме́тка, оце́нка, балл; **to get high ~s** получи́ть отли́чную *or* хоро́шую оце́нку/(*SU*) пятёрку *or* четвёрку [**NB** *SU marking system — one to five*]; **to get low ~s/a pass ~** получи́ть едини́цу *or* дво́йку, получи́ть тро́йку *or* проходно́й балл; *fig*

to give smb top ~s for courage высоко́ оцени́ть чью-л сме́лость.

mark[2] *vt* **1** (*make a mark on*) поме|ча́ть, отме|ча́ть (*pfs* ´-тить); **to ~ sheets with one's name** помеча́ть бельё имённой ме́ткой; **I'll ~ the date in my diary** я поме́чу э́то число́ в своём календаре́; **~ your name with a cross** отме́тьте своё и́мя кре́стиком; **be careful or you'll ~ the table** осторо́жно, а то стол поцара́паешь; **smallpox had ~ed her face** о́спа оста́вила следы́ на её лице́; **I hope your dress isn't ~ed** наде́юсь, что на пла́тье пя́тна не оста́нутся; *Comm* **to ~ goods** (*with price*) ста́вить це́ну на това́рах (по-), (*with trade mark*) маркирова́ть това́ры (*impf and pf*)

2 (*indicate*) ука́з|ывать (-а́ть), вы|ража́ть (´-разить); **the way is ~ed by signposts** придоро́жные столбы́ ука́зывают путь; **he ~ed his approval by a nod** он вы́разил своё одобре́ние кивко́м; **the anniversary was ~ed by a large reception** в честь э́той годовщи́ны был дан большо́й приём; **the decade was ~ed by industrial expansion** э́то десятиле́тие бы́ло отме́чено ро́стом промы́шленного произво́дства; **to ~ time** *Mil* марширова́ть/*fig* топта́ться на ме́сте (*impfs*); *fig* **he's working as an interpreter to ~ time till term begins** пока́ не начали́сь заня́тия и что́бы не пропада́ло вре́мя, он рабо́тает перево́дчиком

3 (*heed*) заме|ча́ть (´-тить); **~ the difference/how he does it** заме́тьте ра́зницу, обрати́те внима́ние, как он э́то де́лает; **~ my words** попо́мни мои́ слова́; **~ you, he could have been right** а зна́ете, возмо́жно, он был прав

4 (*of exams*): **the papers haven't been ~ed yet** экзаменацио́нные рабо́ты ещё не прове́рены

mark down *vt* (*write*) отме|ча́ть (´-тить); *Comm* **to ~ down/up goods** сни|жа́ть/повы|ша́ть це́ны на това́ры (´-зить/´-сить)

mark off *vt* от|води́ть (-вести́); **an area has been ~ed off for a school** под шко́лу отвели́ уча́сток

mark out *vt*: **to ~ out a tennis court** разме|ча́ть те́ннисный корт (´-тить); *Aer*, *Naut* **to ~ out a course** про|кла́дывать курс (-ложи́ть).

marked *adj* (*indicated*) отме́ченный; (*significant*) заме́тный; **I read the ~ pages** я прочита́л отме́ченные страни́цы; **a ~ improvement** заме́тное улучше́ние.

market *n* ры́нок; **the black ~** чёрный ры́нок; **to flood the ~ with goods** завали́ть ры́нок това́рами; **this is the cheapest material on the ~** э́то са́мая дешёвая ткань на ры́нке; **that flat is on the ~** э́та кварти́ра продаётся; **this radio has just come on to the ~** э́тот радиоприёмник то́лько что появи́лся в прода́же; **there's no ~ for goods like that** на таки́е това́ры нет спро́са; **the Common Market** о́бщий ры́нок; **~ price/value** ры́ночная цена́/сто́имость.

market *vti vt* сбы|ва́ть (-ть); **we're ~ing our goods in Sweden** мы сбыва́ем/продаём на́ши това́ры в Шве́ции

vi: **she's gone ~ing** она́ пошла́ на ры́нок.

marketable *adj*: **~ goods** това́ры, по́льзующиеся спро́сом, хо́дкие това́ры.

market place *n* ры́нок.

marking *n* (*on animals*, *plants*, *etc.*) пятно́; **a black dog with white ~s** чёрная соба́ка с бе́лыми пя́тнами; (*for identification*, *on aircraft*, *etc.*) **~s** опознава́тельные зна́ки.

marksman *n* ме́ткий стрело́к.

marmalade *n* апельси́нный/лимо́нный джем.

marmot *n* суро́к.

maroon[1] *adj* тёмно-бордо́вый.

maroon[2] *vt*: **we were ~ed by floods/on a desert island** мы бы́ли отре́заны наводне́нием (*sing*) от вне́шнего ми́ра, мы оказа́лись на необита́емом о́строве.

marquee *n* больша́я пала́тка, шатёр.

marriage *n* **1** брак; **a happy/second ~** счастли́вый/второ́й брак; **a ~ of convenience** брак по расчёту; **she's very happy in her ~** она́ сча́стлива в бра́ке; **he made her an offer of ~** он сде́лал ей предложе́ние; **I'm related to him by ~** он мой ро́дственник со стороны́ му́жа/жены́; **an aunt by ~** тётка жены́/му́жа; *fig* **a ~ of opposites** еди́нство противополо́жностей; *attr*: **~ settlement/licence/certificate** бра́чный контра́кт, разреше́ние на брак, свиде́тельство о бра́ке

2 (*wedding*) сва́дьба, *off* бракосочета́ние, *Rel* венча́ние.

married *adj* (*of man*) жена́тый; (*of woman*) заму́жняя, за́мужем; **they're ~** они́ жена́ты; **a ~ couple** супру́жеская па́ра; **~ life** супру́жество.

marrow[1], *also* **vegetable ~** *n Bot* кабачо́к.

marrow[2] *n* ко́стный мозг; *fig* **to be chilled to the ~** продро́гнуть до мо́зга косте́й; *attr*: **~ bone** мозгова́я кость.

marry *vti* **1** (*take in marriage*) (*of woman*) вы|ходи́ть за́муж за + *A* (*adv*) (´-йти), (*of man*) жени́ться на + *P* (*impf and pf*), (*of couple*) жени́ться (по-); **she married him/is married to him** она́ вы́шла за него́ за́муж, она́ за́мужем (*adv*) за ним; **he married her/is married to her** он жени́лся на ней, он жена́т на ней; **he married for love/for money** он жени́лся по любви́/ра́ди де́нег; *fig* **he married money** он жени́лся на деньга́х

2 (*join in marriage*) (*civil*) жени́ть(ся) (по-); *Rel* венча́ть(ся) (об-); (*give in marriage*) **he married (off) his daughter to a millionaire** он вы́дал дочь за миллионе́ра; **they were married in the palace of weddings** они́ расписа́лись во Дворце́ бракосочета́ний.

marsh *n* боло́то, топь.

marshal *n* ма́ршал; (*US*) *Law* (*approx*) суде́бный исполни́тель (*m*); **air ~** ма́ршал авиа́ции; **field ~** фельдма́ршал.

marshal *vt*: **to ~ soldiers** вы|стра́ивать солда́т (´-строить); **the diplomats were ~led into the hall** диплома́тов провели́ в зал;

fig **to ~ facts/one's thoughts** распол|ага́ть фа́кты в определённом поря́дке (-ожи́ть), привести́ свои́ мы́сли в поря́док (*usu pf*).

marshalling yard *n Rail* сортиро́вочная ста́нция.

marshmallow *n Bot* алте́й апте́чный; (*sweet*) *approx* зефи́р.

marshy *adj* боло́тистый, то́пкий.

marten *n* куни́ца.

martial *adj* (*military*) вое́нный; (*warlike*) вои́нственный; **~ law** вое́нное положе́ние; **~ tribes** вои́нственные племена́.

martyr *n* му́ченик, страда́лец, *also fig*; *fig*: **she's a ~ to asthma** она́ страда́ет а́стмой; **to make a ~ of oneself** изобража́ть из себя́ му́ченика/страда́льца.

marvel *n* чу́до, ди́во; **the ~s of science** чудеса́ нау́ки; *CQ*: **he's a ~** он чу́до; **that's a ~** э́то чуде́сно; **it'll be a ~ if he gets there** бу́дет чу́дом, е́сли он доберётся туда́.

marvel *vi* удив|ля́ться + *D or* + что, изум|ля́ться + *D* (*pfs* -и́ться); **I ~ at his patience/that he's sticking to that job** я удивля́юсь его́ терпе́нию/, что он продолжа́ет там рабо́тать; **I ~led at the beauty of the landscape** я был восхищён красото́й пейза́жа.

marvellous *adj* изуми́тельный, чуде́сный, *also CQ*.

Marxism *n* маркси́зм.

Marxist *adj* маркси́стский.

marzipan *n* марципа́н.

mascara *n* тушь для ресни́ц.

mascot *n* талисма́н.

masculine *adj* мужско́й, *also Gram*; (*manly*) му́жественный; **a ~ character** му́жественный хара́ктер; **he's very ~** он настоя́щий мужчи́на.

mash *n* ме́сиво; (*brewing*) су́сло; *Cook* пюре́ (*indecl*).

mash *vt*: **to ~ potatoes** де́лать карто́фельное пюре́ (с-).

mask *n* ма́ска; **gas ~** противога́з; *fig* **under the ~ of** под ма́ской + *G*.

mask *vt*: **the kidnappers were ~ed** похити́тели бы́ли в ма́сках; *fig* **to ~ one's feelings** скрыва́ть свои́ чу́вства (*usu impf*).

masonry *n* ка́менная кла́дка; (*freemasonry*) масо́нство.

mass[1] *n Rel* (*Orthodox*) обе́дня, (*Roman Catholic*) ме́сса; **high ~** торже́ственная ме́сса; **to say/celebrate ~** служи́ть обе́дню/ме́ссу.

mass[2] *n* **1** (*bulk*) ма́сса, *also Phys*; (*great numbers*) ма́сса, *CQ* у́йма, тьма; **a great ~ of people** ма́сса/у́йма/тьма наро́ду; **~es of books** ма́сса/мно́жество книг; *CQ* **he's a ~ of nerves** он сплошно́й комо́к не́рвов; *attr*: **~ media** сре́дства ма́ссовой информа́ции

2 *pl* (**the ~es**) (*people*) наро́дные ма́ссы.

mass[2] *vti vt*: **to ~ troops** сосредото́ч|ивать войска́ (-ить)

vi со|бира́ться (-бра́ться), ска́пливаться (скопи́ться); (*of troops*) сосредото́чиваться; **clouds were ~ing on the horizon** на горизо́нте собира́лись ту́чи.

massacre *n* ма́ссовое уби́йство, резня́, побо́ище; *Sport CQ* **it was a ~** э́то был по́лный разгро́м.

massacre *vt* зве́рски уби|ва́ть (-ть), устр|а́ивать резню́/побо́ище (-о́ить).

massage *vt* де́лать масса́ж (с-), масси́ровать (*impf*).

masseuse *n* массажи́стка.

massive *n* масси́вный; *fig* огро́мный; **a ~ building** масси́вное зда́ние; **a ~ undertaking** огро́мное предприя́тие; **on a ~ scale** в большо́м масшта́бе.

mass-produced *adj* сери́йного/ма́ссового произво́дства.

mast *n Naut*, *TV*, *Radio* ма́чта; **the flag was at half ~** флаг был приспу́щен.

master *n* **1** хозя́ин; *Naut* капита́н; (*of fishing boats, etc.*) шки́пер; **the ~ of the house** хозя́ин до́ма; **the dog bit its ~** соба́ка укуси́ла хозя́ина; **to be ~ in one's own house** быть хозя́ином в со́бственном до́ме; **he's his own ~** он сам себе́ хозя́ин; **to be ~ of the situation/of one's fate** быть хозя́ином положе́ния/свое́й судьбы́

2 (*expert*) ма́стер; **he's a ~ of his craft/subject** он ма́стер своего́ де́ла; **he's a past ~ at chess** он непревзойдённый шахмати́ст; **paintings of the old ~s** карти́ны ста́рых мастеро́в

3 (*in school*) учи́тель (*m*); (*in school and Univ*) преподава́тель (*m*); **English ~** преподава́тель англи́йского языка́; **~'s degree** сте́пень маги́стра (*not SU*); **~ of a college** глава́ колле́джа; *attr*: **~ mason** квалифици́рованный ка́менщик; **~ plan** генера́льный план; **~ switch** гла́вный выключа́тель.

master *vt*: **to ~ difficulties** преодол|ева́ть тру́дности (-е́ть); **to ~ one's feelings/oneself** владе́ть свои́ми чу́вствами/собо́й (о-); **to ~ a foreign language** овладе́ть иностра́нным языко́м.

master copy *n* оригина́л.

masterful *adj* вла́стный.

master key *n* универса́льный ключ (,подходя́щий ко всем дверя́м зда́ния).

masterly *adj* (*skilful*) ма́стерский; соверше́нный.

mastermind *n*: (*of a scholar*) **he's a ~** он выдаю́щийся учёный; **who is the ~ behind this?** кто стои́т за всем э́тим?; **he was the ~ behind the operation** вся э́та опера́ция заду́мана им.

master of ceremonies *n Theat* конферансье́ (*m*) (*indecl*); (*in court, etc.*) церемонийме́йстер.

masterpiece *n* шеде́вр.

master stroke *n fig* мазо́к ма́стера.

mastery *n*: **~ of the seas** госпо́дство/превосхо́дство на мо́ре; **his ~ of the violin is remarkable** он боже́ственно владе́ет скри́пкой.

mastic *n* масти́ка.

masticate *vi* жева́ть (*impf*).

mat *n* (*of fabric, wool*) ко́врик, полови́к; (*of rush, straw, etc.*) цино́вка; (*in gymnastics, etc.*) мат; (*on table if soft*) салфе́тка, (*of* *cork, etc.*) подставка; *fig CQ* **the boss had him on the ~** шеф вызвал его на ковёр.

match[1] *n* **1:** (*of people*) **as a pianist he has no ~** как пианисту ему нет равных [**NB** *pl*]; **when it comes to a row, he's no ~ for her** когда доходит до скандала, он перед ней пасует

2 (*of colours, etc.*): **this tie is a good ~ for the shirt** этот галстук как раз в тон рубашке; **the colours are a good ~** эти цвета хорошо сочетаются

3 (*marriage*): **she made a good ~** она удачно вышла замуж; **she's a good ~** она хорошая партия

4 *Sport* матч, соревнование; **a football/ice-hockey ~** футбольный/хоккейный матч; **boxing/wrestling ~** соревнования (*pl*) по боксу/по борьбе; **a home/an away ~** матч на своём/на чужом поле; **a return ~** ответный матч.

match[1] *vti vt* **1** (*pit against*): **we must ~ cunning with cunning** на хитрость надо ответить хитростью; **to ~ one's strength against smb** мериться силами с кем-л (по-); *Sport* **the teams are pretty evenly ~ed** силы у этих команд, можно сказать, равные

2 (*equal*): **no one can ~ him in boxing** в боксе с ним никто не сравнится; **how can we ~ their hospitality?** как нам отблагодарить их за гостеприимство?

3 (*of colours, etc.*): **the artist ~es his colours well** художник тонко чувствует гармонию красок; **to ~ socks** раз|бирать носки по парам (-обрать); **they're well ~ed** они подходят друг к другу; **have you a hat to ~ my dress?** у вас есть шляпа в тон моему платью?; **these vases ~ one another** эти вазы хорошо смотрятся вместе

vi: **these colours do not ~** эти цвета не сочетаются.

match[2] *n* спичка; **to strike a ~** чиркнуть спичкой.

matchbox *n* коробка спичек, спичечный коробок.

matching *adj*: **a brown suit with ~ shoes** коричневый костюм с ботинками в тон.

matchmaker *n joc* сваха.

mate *n* (*companion*) товарищ; *CQ* (*in address*) приятель (*m*), друг; (*of animals*) самец, *f* самка; (*workman's assistant*) помощник; *Naut* **first ~** старший помощник капитана.

mate *vti* (*of animals, birds*) спаривать(ся) (*usu impf*).

material *n* материал; **raw ~** сырьё; **building ~s** строительные материалы; **writing ~s** письменные принадлежности; **to collect ~ for a book** собирать материал для книги.

material *adj* **1** материальный, физический; **~ well-being** материальное благополучие; **~ loss/damage** материальный ущерб; **~ needs** физические потребности; *Law* **~ evidence** вещественные доказательства (*pl*)

2 (*relevant*) существенный; **this article is ~ to the discussion** эта статья имеет прямое отношение к дискуссии.

materialize *vi* осуществ|ляться (-иться); **his hopes/plans did not ~** его надежды/планы не осуществились.

materially *adv* (*significantly*) существенно; *Fin* материально; **her situation has altered ~** её положение существенно изменилось; **she is ~ better off** материально она в лучшем положении.

maternal *adj*: **a ~ aunt** тётя/тётка по матери/с материнской стороны; **~ instinct** материнский инстинкт.

maternity *n* материнство; *attr*: **~ dress** платье для беременных; **~ leave** отпуск по беременности и родам.

maternity home *n* родильный дом, *abbr* (*SU*) роддом.

mathematical *adj* математический.

mathematician *n* математик.

mathematics, *abbr* **maths,** (*US*) **math** *n* математика (*sing*).

matinée *n Theat, Cine* дневной спектакль (*m*)/сеанс.

matriculate *vi* поступ|ать в университет (-ить).

matriculation *n* поступление в университет; *attr*: **~ exam** вступительный экзамен.

matrimonial *adj* супружеский, брачный.

matrimony *n* (*marriage*) брак; (*state*) супружество.

matron *n* матрона; (*in hospital*) старшая сестра; (*in hostel, etc.*) *approx* заведующая хозяйством, сестра-хозяйка, кастелянша.

matt *adj* матовый.

matted *adj*: **~ hair** спутанные волосы.

matter *n* **1** (*substance, material*) вещество, материал; *Philos* материя; *Med* (*pus*) гной; **radioactive/colouring ~** радиоактивное/красящее вещество; **grey ~** серое вещество (мозга); **reading ~** материал для чтения; **printed ~** печатный материал; **to send smth as printed ~** посылать что-л бандеролью

2 (*content*) содержание; **form and ~** форма и содержание; **the main ~ of his speech** основное содержание его речи; **the subject ~ of his lecture** предмет/тема его лекции

3 (*affair, concern*) вопрос, дело; **a ~ of opinion** спорный вопрос; **it's a ~ of life and death** это вопрос жизни и смерти; **a ~ of time/money/taste** вопрос времени/денег/вкуса; **the ~ is closed** дело решено; **that's quite another ~** это совсем другое дело; **this is no laughing ~** это не шуточное дело; **it's a ~ for rejoicing/for complaint/for regret** тут радоваться надо, есть на что жаловаться, есть о чём пожалеть; **I accepted it as a ~ of course** я принял это в порядке вещей; **he came as a ~ of course** (само собой) разумеется /ясное дело, он пришёл; **as a ~ of fact, I disagree** вообще-то я не согласен; **this is a ~ of fact, not of opinion** это факт, тут спорить не о чем; **as a ~**

of form формáльности рáди, *CQ* для профóрмы; **we'll only be there for a ~ of days** мы там пробýдем всегó нéсколько дней; **she doesn't know, and for that ~ doesn't care** онá не знáет, и к томý же ей всё равнó

4 (*in pl*: *affairs*): **money ~s** дéнежные делá/вопрóсы; **he's an expert in all ~s of law** он знатóк закóнов/прáва; **I don't know how ~s stand** я не знáю, как обстоя́т делá; **as ~s stand there's nothing we can do** при такóм стечéнии обстоя́тельств мы бесси́льны чтó-нибудь сдéлать; **to make ~s worse** бóлее тогó, в довершéние всегó; **not to mince ~s** говоря́ без обинякóв/напрями́к

5 (*importance*): **no ~!** ничегó!, невáжно!, пустяки́!; **no ~ what he says** чтó бы он ни говори́л; **no ~ how hard he tries** кáк бы он ни старáлся; **we'll come no ~ what the weather (is)** мы придём, какáя бы погóда ни былá

6 (*difficulty*): **what's the ~?** в чём дело?; **what's the ~ with you?** что с тобóй?; **what's the ~ with these scissors?** что такóе с э́тими нóжницами?; **there's something the ~ with the engine** чтó-то с дви́гателем не в поря́дке.

matter *vi* имéть значéние; **it doesn't ~ (at all)** э́то не имéет (никакóго) значéния; **it doesn't ~ to me** мне всё равнó; **what does it ~?** какóе э́то имéет значéние?; **what does it ~ to you?** тебé какóе дéло?; **health ~s more than money** здорóвье важнéе, чем богáтство.

matter-of-fact *adj* (*down to earth*) деловóй, практи́чный; **in a ~ voice** делови́м тóном; **she's very ~** онá óчень деловáя/практи́чная осóба.

mattress *n* матрáс, матрáц.

mature *adj* (*of fruit*) зрéлый, *also fig*; **a ~ work** зрéлое произведéние; **on ~ consideration** по зрéлом размышлéнии; **~ wine** вы́держанное винó.

mature *vti vt*: **to ~ wine** вы|дéрживать винó (-держать)

vi (*of fruit*) зреть (со-); *fig* **he has ~d a lot over the last 3 years** он óчень повзрослéл за послéдние три гóда; *Comm* **when does this policy ~?** когдá кончáется срок вы́платы страхóвки?

maturity *n* зрéлость; **to reach ~** дости́чь зрéлости.

maudlin *adj* плакси́вый.

maul *vt*: **he was ~ed by a bear** он был си́льно помя́т медвéдем.

mausoleum *n* мавзолéй.

mauve *adj* розовáто-лилóвый.

maxim *n* сентéнция, афори́зм, мáксима; (*principle*) при́нцип.

maximum *n* мáксимум; **to the ~** до мáксимума; **this costs a ~ of 100 roubles** э́то стóит мáксимум сто рублéй; *attr* максимáльный.

May *n* май; *attr* мáйский.

may *v modal aux*, *past and conditional* **might 1** (*of possibility*): **it ~ /might rain** мóжет пойти́ дождь; **he ~/might come** он мóжет прийти́; **will you come?—I ~/might** ты придёшь?—Мóжет (быть), придý; **that ~/might be true** возмóжно, э́то и так; **it ~ be (that) he doesn't know** он мóжет э́того не знать; **I ~ have said so** я мог так сказáть; **we arrived at 6, or it ~ have been a bit later** мы приéхали в шесть и́ли, мóжет (быть), немнóго пóзже; **he might have come if he'd had a car** он мог бы приéхать, éсли бы у негó былá маши́на; **we ~ as well leave** мы вполнé мóжем уéхать; **that's as ~ be, but...** пусть э́то так, но...; **come what ~** будь что бýдет; **be that as it ~** кáк бы то ни́ было; **try as he ~, however hard he ~ try** кáк бы он ни старáлся; **you ~ well ask!** спроси́ о чём-нибудь другóм!

2 (*of permission*; **might** *expresses diffidence*) мóжно; **~ I come in?** мóжно мне войти́?; **you ~ be seated** вы мóжете сесть; **I'll begin, if I ~** я начнý, éсли мóжно; **~ we smoke here?** здесь мóжно кури́ть?; **if I ~ say so** éсли мóжно так сказáть; **~ I introduce Mr Smith?** позвóльте/разреши́те мне представить господи́на Сми́та; **~/might I pass please?** позвóльте/разреши́те пройти́

3 (*of suggestion*; *only with* **might**): (*politely*) **you might try writing** вы могли́ бы написáть; (*abruptly*) **you might at least have offered to help** ты бы хоть предложи́л свою́ пóмощь

4 (*after verbs, expressing hope, fear, etc. and in clauses of purpose*): **I hope he ~ recover** надéюсь, что он попрáвится; **I hoped he might come** я надéялся, что он всё же придёт; **she's afraid they ~ be late** онá бои́тся, как бы они́ не опоздáли

5 (*in wishes*): **long ~ he live** желáем емý мнóгих лет жи́зни; **~ you be very happy** желáю вам счáстья

6 (*in questions*): **and who ~/might you be?** а вы кто бýдете?; **how far might that be from here?** и далекó ли э́то отсю́да?

maybe *adv* мóжет быть, возмóжно.

May Day *n* Пéрвое мáя; *attr* первомáйский.

mayonnaise *n* майонéз; **egg ~** яйцó под майонéзом.

mayor *n* мэр.

maze *n* лабири́нт, *also fig*; **a ~ of streets** лабири́нт ýлиц; *CQ* **I'm in a ~** я совсéм запýтался.

me *pers pron* (*oblique cases of* **I**) **1** *G/A* меня́, *D* мне, *I* мной, *P* обо мнé; **he didn't recognize ~** он не узнáл меня́; **they invited ~ and my brother** они́ пригласи́ли меня́ с брáтом; **they are talking about ~** они́ говоря́т обо мнé; **she came up to ~** онá подошлá ко мне

2 *when it refers to the subject of the sentence "me" is translated by reflex pron* себя́, себé, *etc.*; **I shut the door after ~** я закры́л за собóй дверь; **I went for a walk and took**

the dog with ~ я пошёл погуля́ть и взял с собо́й соба́ку

3 *sometimes translated by the nominative* я; **it's** ~ э́то я; **he's older than** ~ он ста́рше, чем я, он ста́рше меня́.

meadow *n* луг.

meagre, (*US*) **meager** *adj*: **a** ~ **repast** ску́дная тра́пеза; **there was a** ~ **attendance at the meeting** на собра́нии бы́ло ма́ло наро́ду.

meal *n* еда́ (*though in Russian meal is usu particularized*): **to invite smb for a** ~ пригласи́ть кого́-л на обе́д/на у́жин; **we have our evening** ~ **at 6** мы у́жинаем в шесть часо́в; **before/after** ~**s** до/по́сле еды́; **during** ~**s/a** ~ во вре́мя еды́; **do stay and have a** ~ **with us** остава́йтесь с на́ми пообе́дать; **I had a light** ~ **in the snack bar** я перекуси́л в буфе́те; **I like a square** ~ **in the middle of the day** я люблю́ пло́тно пообе́дать.

meal ticket *n* тало́н на пита́ние в столо́вой.

mean[1] *adj* (*stingy*) скупо́й; (*petty, low*) по́длый; (*shabby*) жа́лкий, убо́гий; **he's** ~ **with his money** он скупова́т; **that's a** ~ **trick** э́то по́дло; **he's got a** ~ **streak in his character** он спосо́бен сде́лать по́длость; **what a** ~ **thing to say!** как мо́жно говори́ть таки́е па́кости?; **I feel** ~ **for saying that** мне сты́дно/со́вестно, что я э́то сказа́л; **a** ~ **appearance** жа́лкий/убо́гий вид; *fig*: **he's no** ~ **pianist** он неплохо́й пиани́ст; **that should be clear to the** ~**est intelligence** э́то и дураку́ я́сно.

mean[2] *n* (*middle term*) середи́на; **the golden** ~ золота́я середи́на; *Math* сре́днее число́.

mean[2] *adj* (*average*) сре́дний.

mean[3] *vt* **1** (*intend + inf*) собира́ться (*only in impf*), намерева́ться, *CQ* ду́мать (*impfs*); **I** ~ **to leave tomorrow** я собира́юсь/ду́маю отпра́виться за́втра; **he meant to help her** он намерева́лся/ду́мал ей помо́чь; **I kept** ~**ing to write** я всё вре́мя хоте́л написа́ть; **he's impossible—I** ~ **to say, he takes offence so easily** с ним о́чень тру́дно—я хочу́ сказа́ть, он о́чень оби́дчив; **what's that** ~**t to be?** э́то что тако́е?; **it's** ~**t to be a drawing of you** э́то он тебя́ так нарисова́л

2 (*intend + noun*): **you can't** ~ **it!** ты шу́тишь!, ты э́то серьёзно?; **I** ~**t it as a joke** я то́лько пошути́л, я э́то в шу́тку сказа́л; **what do you** ~ **by that?** что вы хоти́те э́тим сказа́ть?; **that's not what I** ~**t** я не то име́л в виду́; **I** ~ **what I say** я э́то серьёзно говорю́; **he** ~**s no harm/well** он не жела́ет зла

3 (*destine*) предназнач|а́ть (-ить); **I** ~**t this for you** я предназна́чил э́то вам; **is that remark** ~**t for me?** э́то замеча́ние в мой а́дрес?/отно́сится ко мне?

4 (*signify*) зна́чить, означа́ть (*impfs*); **what does this word** ~**?** что зна́чит э́то сло́во?; **what does your silence** ~**?** что означа́ет ва́ше молча́ние?; **your friendship** ~**s a lot to me** твоя́ дру́жба мно́го для меня́ зна́чит; **this will** ~ **a lot of expense for him** э́то означа́ет для него́ больши́е расхо́ды; **this** ~**s an early start** э́то означа́ет, что нам на́до пора́ньше вы́йти; **the title** ~**s nothing to me** назва́ние кни́ги ничего́ не говори́т.

meander *vi* (*of river, road*) извива́ться, изгиба́ться (*impfs*); (*of people*) броди́ть (по-).

meaning *n* смысл; значе́ние; **the** ~ **of his words/of that word** смысл его́ слов, значе́ние э́того сло́ва; **that word has a double** ~ у э́того сло́ва два значе́ния; **if you get my** ~ е́сли вы меня́ понима́ете; **what's the** ~ **of this?** что всё э́то зна́чит?

meaningful *adj*: **a** ~ **look** многозначи́тельный взгляд; **such discussions are not very** ~ в таки́х диску́ссиях ма́ло то́лку.

meaningless *adj* бессмы́сленный.

meanness *n* (*stinginess*) ску́пость, ска́редность; (*baseness*) по́длость, ни́зость; (*shabbiness*) бе́дность, ску́дность.

means *npl* (*also treated as sing, see examples*) **1** (*way, method*) сре́дства (*pl*), *also* сре́дство (*sing*); **a** ~**/the** ~ **to an end** сре́дство для достиже́ния це́ли; **the end justifies the** ~ цель опра́вдывает сре́дства; ~ **of communication/production** сре́дства сообще́ния/произво́дства; **we must find a/some** ~ **of raising the money** мы должны́ собра́ть э́ти де́ньги/найти́ э́ти сре́дства; **there is no** ~ **of getting from here to the airport within the hour** нет никако́й возмо́жности добра́ться отсю́да до аэродро́ма за час

2 by this/all/any ~, *etc.*: **by this** ~ **we eventually got home** таки́м о́бразом мы наконе́ц-то добрали́сь до до́ма; **do it by all** ~ обяза́тельно сде́лай э́то; **by all** ~ **take it** обяза́тельно возьми́ э́то с собо́й; **by fair** ~ **or foul** любы́ми сре́дствами; **do it by any** ~ **you can** сде́лай э́то во что́ бы то ни ста́ло; **it's not by any** ~ **easy** э́то отню́дь не легко́; **it's by no** ~ **dear** э́то совсе́м не до́рого; **don't worry—we'll do it by some** ~ **or other** не волну́йся, ка́к-нибудь, да ула́дим э́то

3 *Fin* сре́дства; состоя́ние (*sing*); **a man of** ~ челове́к со сре́дствами; **they live beyond their** ~ они́ живу́т не по сре́дствам; **they have no** ~ **of support** у них нет средств к существова́нию; **has he any private** ~**?** он состоя́тельный челове́к?

means test *n* прове́рка дохо́дов (для получе́ния стипе́ндии, посо́бия и т.д.).

meantime, meanwhile *advs* (**meantime** *also as n* **in the meantime**) ме́жду те́м, тем вре́менем.

measles *n* корь; **German** ~ красну́ха (корева́я).

measly *adj CQ* жа́лкий; **a** ~ **present** жа́лкий пода́рок; **what a** ~ **helping!** кака́я ми́зерная по́рция!

measurable *adj* измери́мый.

measure *n* **1** ме́ра; **cubic/square/metric** ~ куби́ческая/квадра́тная/метри́ческая ме́ра; **dry/liquid** ~ ме́ра сыпу́чих тел/жи́дкостей; **full/short** ~ по́лная/непо́лная ме́ра; **a litre** ~

литро́вый сосу́д, литро́вая ме́ра; **made to ~** (*of clothes*) сши́тый по ме́рке; **to have a coat made to ~** сшить пальто́ на зака́з; **he poured me out a generous ~ of gin** он нали́л мне большу́ю рю́мку джи́на; *fig*: **you've got his ~ all right** ты дал ему́ то́чную характери́стику; **popularity is no ~ of greatness** популя́рность—ещё не мери́ло вели́чия

2 (*degree*) ме́ра; **in great/large ~** в значи́тельной/большо́й ме́ре; **in some ~** в како́й-то ме́ре; **the position has improved beyond ~** положе́ние тепе́рь неизмери́мо лу́чше; **he has a certain ~ of independence** он в изве́стной ме́ре незави́сим; **there's a ~ of truth in that** в э́том есть до́ля пра́вды

3 (*step*) ме́ра, *also Law*; **to take strong/preventive ~s** принима́ть реши́тельные/профилакти́ческие ме́ры.

measure *vti vt* ме́рить, измеря́ть (*pf for both* изме́рить); **to ~ distance** измеря́ть расстоя́ние; **to ~ depth/length/temperature** ме́рить *or* измеря́ть глубину́/длину́/температу́ру; **to ~ smb's height** измеря́ть чей-л рост; (*of tailor*) **to ~ smb** снима́ть с кого́-л ме́рку (снять); *fig* **he ~s his words** он взве́шивает ка́ждое своё сло́во (*sing*)

vi: **this room ~s 6 metres by 12** э́та ко́мната пло́щадью шесть ме́тров на двена́дцать; **what does the garage ~?** каковы́ разме́ры гаража́?; **the rug ~s 2 square metres** ковёр величино́й два квадра́тных ме́тра

measure out *vt* отмер|я́ть (-́ить); **he ~d out a litre of milk to everyone** он нали́л ка́ждому по ли́тру молока́

measure up *vi fig*: **the car didn't ~ up to our expectations** маши́на не оправда́ла на́ших ожида́ний; **he doesn't ~ up to the job** он не подхо́дит для э́той рабо́ты.

measured *adj*: **at a ~ pace** разме́ренным ша́гом; **in ~ tones** сде́ржанным то́ном (*sing*); **a ~ reply** проду́манный отве́т.

measurement *n* ме́ра; *pl* (**~s**) разме́ры; **system of ~** систе́ма мер; **to take smb's ~s** снима́ть ме́рку с кого́-л.

measuring *n* измере́ние; *attr*: **~ glass** мензу́рка; **~ tape** ме́рная ле́нта.

meat *n* мя́со; **do you like your ~ rare or well done?** вам мя́со с кро́вью или прожа́ренное?; *fig* **his work is ~ and drink to him** для него́ рабо́та—всё; *attr* мясно́й; **~ pie** пиро́г с мя́сом.

meatballs *npl* те́фтели, фрикаде́льки, бито́чки, котле́ты.

meaty *adj fig*: **a ~ lecture** о́чень содержа́тельная ле́кция.

mechanic *n* меха́ник; **motor ~** автомеха́ник.

mechanical *adj* механи́ческий; **~ engineer** инжене́р-меха́ник; **~ engineering** машинострое́ние.

mechanically *adv* механи́чески; *fig* машина́льно.

mechanics *n* меха́ника (*sing*).

mechanization *n* механиза́ция.

mechanize *vt* механизи́ровать (*impf and pf*); **~d transport** автотра́нспорт.

medal *n* меда́ль.

meddle *vi* вме́ш|иваться (-а́ться); **don't ~ in my affairs** не вме́шивайся в мои́ дела́; **children, don't ~ with those books** де́ти, не тро́гайте э́ти кни́ги.

meddlesome *adj*: **she's a ~ old woman** она́ назо́йливая стару́ха.

medi(a)eval *adj* средневеко́вый.

mediate *vi* посре́дничать (*impf*); **to ~ in a dispute** быть посре́дником в спо́ре.

mediator *n* посре́дник.

medic *n Univ CQ* ме́дик.

medical *adj* медици́нский; **~ attention/care** медици́нское обслу́живание; **to have a ~ examination** проходи́ть медици́нский осмо́тр (*abbr CQ* медосмо́тр); **~ student** студе́нт-ме́дик; **the ~ profession** врачи́ (*pl*); **army ~ corps** вое́нно-медици́нская слу́жба; **~ treatment** лече́ние.

medicament *n* медикаме́нт.

medicinal *adj*: **~ springs/herbs** целе́бные исто́чники, лека́рственные тра́вы; **I only take brandy for ~ purposes** я пью конья́к исключи́тельно в лече́бных це́лях.

medicine *n* **1** (*science*) медици́на; (*as opposed to surgery*) терапи́я; **to practise ~** рабо́тать врачо́м

2 (*substance*) лека́рство; **take ~ for a cough** принима́ть лека́рство от ка́шля.

medicine box/chest *n* апте́чка.

mediocre *adj* посре́дственный, зауря́дный.

meditate *vti vt* (*plan*): **to ~ revenge** замы|шля́ть месть (-́слить)

vi: **to ~ on smth** размышля́ть над чем-л/о чём-л (*impf*); (*contemplate*) созерца́ть, занима́ться медита́цией (*impfs*).

meditation *n* размышле́ние; (*contemplation*) созерца́ние, медита́ция; **deep in ~** погружённый в размышле́ния (*pl*).

Mediterranean *adj*: **the ~ coast** средиземномо́рское побере́жье; *as n* (**the ~**) Средизе́мное мо́ре.

medium *n* **1** (*pl* **media**) *Phys, Biol* среда́; (*means, channel*) сре́дство; **the media of communication** сре́дства ма́ссовой информа́ции; **bronze is his favourite ~** бро́нза—его́ люби́мый материа́л

2: **the happy ~** золота́я середи́на

3 (*pl* **mediums**) (*in spiritualism*) ме́диум.

medium *adj* сре́дний; **of ~ height** сре́днего ро́ста; *Radio* **~ wave band** диапазо́н сре́дних волн (*pl*).

meek *adj* кро́ткий, мя́гкий; **as ~as a lamb** кро́ткий как ове́чка.

meet *n* (*hunting*) сбор охо́тников; (*US*) *Sport* **tracks/athletic ~** легкоатлети́ческие соревнова́ния (*pl*).

meet *vti vt* **1** (*encounter*) встре|ча́ть (-́тить); **to ~ smb** встреча́ть кого́-л, встреча́ться с кем-л (*reflex form often implies "by arrangement"*); **I met her unexpectedly** я встре́тил её случа́йно; **she met her friend in town** она́ встре́тилась с подру́гой в го́роде; **you don't often ~ people like that** таки́е лю́ди ре́дко встреча́ются; **I've never met that expression before** я ра́ньше не встреча́л э́того выраже́ния; **my efforts met with no success** мои́ уси́лия ни к чему́ не привели́; **the announcement was met with applause** объявле́ние бы́ло встре́чено аплодисме́нтами (*pl*); **he wouldn't ~ my eye** он избега́л моего́ взгля́да; **to ~ smb halfway** идти́ навстре́чу (*adv*) кому́-л

2 (*go to meet*): **we'll ~ you at the station** мы вас встре́тим на ста́нции; **we were met at the hotel by our guide** в гости́нице нас встре́тил экскурсово́д; **a bus ~s the train** к прибы́тию по́езда подаётся авто́бус

3 (*get to know*): **I'd like you to ~ Igor** я бы хоте́л познако́мить вас с И́горем; **pleased to ~ you** рад познако́миться (с ва́ми)

4 (*satisfy, respond to*): **to ~ demands/requirements** отве|ча́ть тре́бованиям/потре́бностям (-́тить); **to ~ objections** отвеча́ть на возраже́ния; **to ~ smb's wishes** удовлетвор|я́ть чьи-л жела́ния (-и́ть); **to ~ expenses** опла́|чивать расхо́ды (-ти́ть); **to ~ a challenge** при|нима́ть вы́зов (-ня́ть)

vi **1** встреча́ться; **have you met?** вы встреча́лись?; **let's ~ /CQ ~ up at the cinema** дава́й встре́тимся у кинотеа́тра; **where the roads ~** где доро́ги пересека́ются; **the society ~s once a month** заседа́ния о́бщества происхо́дят раз в ме́сяц; **when does the council ~?** когда́ собира́ется сове́т?; **my belt won't ~** у меня́ реме́нь не схо́дится; *Sport* **the teams ~ in the final** э́ти кома́нды встреча́ются в фина́ле

2 to ~ with: to ~ with misfortune/approval/resistance попа́сть в беду́, встреча́ть одобре́ние/сопротивле́ние; **I met with difficulties in my work** мне в рабо́те встре́тились тру́дности; **my efforts met with no success** мои́ уси́лия ни к чему́ не привели́.

meeting *n* встре́ча; собра́ние; (*large gathering*) ми́тинг; (*session*) заседа́ние; **~ of heads of government** встре́ча глав прави́тельств; **annual/general ~** годово́е/о́бщее собра́ние; **to hold a ~** проводи́ть собра́ние; **to call/convene a ~** созыва́ть собра́ние/ми́тинг; **faculty ~** заседа́ние ка́федры; *Sport*: (*UK*) **athletics ~** легкоатлети́ческие соревнова́ния (*pl*); **race ~** ска́чки (*pl*).

meeting place *n* ме́сто встре́чи/собра́ния.

megalomania *n* ма́ния вели́чия.

melancholy *adj* меланхоли́ческий, печа́льный.

mellow *vi* (*of fruit*) спеть (*impf*); созре|ва́ть (-́ть); *fig* **he ~ed with age** с года́ми он станови́лся мя́гче.

melodic *adj* мелоди́ческий, мелоди́чный.

melodious *adj* мелоди́чный, певу́чий.

melodramatic *adj* мелодрамати́ческий.

melody *n* мело́дия.

melon *n* ды́ня.

melt *vti vt also* **~ down** (*of metal, etc.*) пла́вить (рас-); (*of fat, etc.*) рас|та́пливать (-топи́ть); (*dissolve*) раствор|я́ть (-и́ть)

vi (*of snow*) та́ять (рас-); (*of metal*) пла́виться; (*of fat*) раста́пливаться; (*dissolve*) растворя́ться; *fig*: **his heart ~ed with pity** его́ се́рдце напо́лнилось жа́лостью/раста́яло; **money just ~s away** де́ньги про́сто та́ют; **one colour ~s into another** оди́н цвет незаме́тно перехо́дит в друго́й.

melting *n* (*one occasion*) пла́вка; (*process*) плавле́ние; (*of ice, etc.*) та́яние; *attr*: **~ point** то́чка плавле́ния.

member *n* член, *also Anat, Math, Gram*; **~ of a family/party** член семьи́/па́ртии; **a full ~** полнопра́вный член; *attr*: **a ~ country of the UN** госуда́рство-член ООН.

membership *n* (*status*) чле́нство; (*members*) чле́ны; (*composition*) соста́в; **our club has a big ~** у нас в клу́бе мно́го чле́нов; **to apply for ~ of a club** пода́ть заявле́ние о приня́тии в клуб; **the ~ of the committee has been settled** вопро́с о соста́ве комите́та решён; *attr*: **~ fee/card** чле́нский взнос/биле́т.

memento *n*: **take it as a ~** возьми́ э́то на па́мять.

memoir *n* автобиографи́ческий о́черк; *pl* (**~s**) мемуа́ры, воспомина́ния.

memorable *adj* па́мятный.

memorandum, *abbr CQ* **memo** *n* докладна́я запи́ска; (*diplomatic*) мемора́ндум; **to send in a ~** предста́вить докладну́ю запи́ску.

memorial *n* па́мятник; **to erect a ~ to smb** устана́вливать па́мятник кому́-л; **war ~** па́мятник па́вшим во́инам.

memorial *adj* па́мятный, мемориа́льный; **~ plaque** па́мятная/мемориа́льная доска́; **~ service** *Rel* заупоко́йная слу́жба, *approx civil equiv* (*SU*) гражда́нская панихи́да.

memorize *vt* запом|ина́ть (-́нить), зау́чи|вать (наизу́сть) (-́ть).

memory *n* **1** па́мять; **a short ~** коро́ткая па́мять; **he's got a good ~ for faces** у него́ хоро́шая па́мять на ли́ца; **I've got a bad ~/CQ a ~ like a sieve** у меня́ плоха́я/*CQ* дыря́вая па́мять; **speaking from ~** наско́лько я по́мню; **if my ~ serves me correctly** е́сли па́мять мне не изменя́ет; **within (living) ~** на па́мяти живу́щих; **in ~ of** в па́мять о + *P*; **to dedicate smth to the ~ of smb** посвяща́ть что-л па́мяти кого́-л

2 (*recollection*) воспомина́ние; **memories of childhood** воспомина́ния де́тства.

menace *n* угро́за; *CQ*: **that child is a ~** наказа́ние, а не ребёнок!; **he's a ~ at the wheel** он опа́сен за рулём.

menace *vt* грози́ть + *D*, угрожа́ть + *D* (*impfs*); **these regions are ~d by famine** э́тим райо́нам угрожа́ет го́лод.

mend *n*: **the ~ was hardly noticeable** ла́тка была́ почти́ незаме́тна; *CQ*: **he's on the ~** он идёт на попра́вку, он поправля́ется; **things are on the ~** дела́ иду́т на лад.

mend *vti vt* чини́ть (по-); (*machines, etc.*) ремонти́ровать (от-); **to ~ clothes/a watch/shoes** чини́ть оде́жду/часы́/о́бувь (*collect*); **to ~ a TV set** ремонти́ровать/чини́ть телеви́зор; **to ~ a water-pipe** чини́ть водопрово́д; *fig*: **to ~ one's ways/manner** исправ|ля́ться (-́иться); **this won't ~ matters** э́тим де́лу не помо́жешь

vi (*of health*) поправ|ля́ться (-́иться); (*improve*) улучш|а́ться (-́иться); **it's never too late to ~** испра́виться никогда́ не по́здно.

mendacious *adj* лжи́вый.

mending *n* почи́нка; ремо́нт; **invisible ~** худо́жественная што́пка.

menial *adj* (*of people*) лаке́йский; *joc* **he never helps me with the ~ tasks** он никогда́ не помога́ет мне по до́му.

meningitis *n* менинги́т.

menopause *n* климактери́ческий пери́од, менопа́уза, *CQ* кли́макс.

menstruate *vi* менструи́ровать (*impf*).

mental *adj* (*of the mind*) у́мственный; (*in the mind*) мы́сленный; **~ ability** у́мственные спосо́бности (*pl*); **~ work** у́мственный труд; **~ arithmetic** счёт в уме́; **a ~ image** мы́сленный о́браз; **to make a ~ note of smth** мы́сленно отме́тить что-л; **~ deficiency** у́мственная отста́лость, слабоу́мие; **~ illness** душе́вная боле́знь; **a ~ patient** душевнобольно́й; *CQ* **he's ~** он псих, он спя́тил.

mental hospital *n* психиатри́ческая больни́ца.

mentality *n*: **he has a low ~** он у́мственно отста́лый; **I don't understand his ~** я не понима́ю его́ о́браза мы́слей; *pejor* **what a ~!** что за о́браз мы́слей!

menthol *n* менто́л.

mention *n* упомина́ние; **no ~ was made of her age** её во́зраст не́ был упомя́нут.

mention *vt* упом|ина́ть (-яну́ть); **I'll ~ it to her** я упомяну́ об э́том в разгово́ре с ней; **to ~ smb in a will** упомина́ть кого́-л в заве́щании; **he was (actually) ~ed by name** его́ и́мя фигури́ровало; **his name was ~ed** его́ и́мя бы́ло упомя́нуто; **don't ~ it!** (*reply to thanks*) не́ за что!, (*reply to apology*) ничего́!, не сто́ит об э́том и говори́ть; *Mil* **he was ~ed in despatches** его́ упомяну́ли в прика́зе.

menu *n* меню́ (*indecl*).

mercenary *n* наёмник.

mercenary *adj* коры́стный; **from ~ motives** из коры́стных побужде́ний.

merchandise *n* това́ры (*pl*).

merchant *n* торго́вец; **wine ~** торго́вец вино́м; *CQ* **speed ~** лиха́ч; *attr*: **~ bank** комме́рческий банк; **~ navy** торго́вый флот.

merciful *adj* милосе́рдный.

merciless *adj* безжа́лостный; беспоща́дный; **~ satire** беспоща́дная сати́ра; **he's quite ~** он соверше́нно безжа́лостен.

mercury *n* ртуть.

mercy *n* **1** (*pity*) милосе́рдие, поща́да; (*kindness*) ми́лость; **sisters of ~** сёстры милосе́рдия; **an act of ~** акт милосе́рдия; **he was found guilty with a recommendation to ~** прися́жные призна́ли его́ вино́вным, но хода́тайствовали пе́ред судьёй о поми́ловании

2 *CQ*: *joc* **I'll leave you to the tender mercies of my wife** я вас оставля́ю на попече́ние мое́й жены́; **we must be thankful for small mercies** мы должны́ дово́льствоваться и э́тим; **what a ~ he came!** сла́ва бо́гу, что он пришёл!; **~ on us!** го́споди!, бо́же мой!

mere *adj*: **she's a ~ child** она́ совсе́м ребёнок; **that's ~ prejudice** э́то про́сто предрассу́док; **by ~/the ~st chance** по чи́стой/чисте́йшей случа́йности; **the ~ thought of it makes me sick** от одно́й мы́сли об э́том меня́ воро́тит (*impers*); **don't quarrel over a ~ trifle** не спо́рьте из-за тако́го пустяка́.

merely *adv* про́сто; **I ~ said...** я про́сто сказа́л...

merge *vti vt*: *Comm* **to ~ two companies** объедин|я́ть/сли|ва́ть две компа́нии/два предприя́тия (-и́ть/-ть)

vi слива́ться; объединя́ться; **the rivers ~ here** здесь ре́ки слива́ются; **the voices ~d into a general hum** голоса́ сли́лись в оди́н сплошно́й гул.

merger *n Comm* объедине́ние, слия́ние.

meringue *n* (пиро́жное-)безе́ (*indecl*).

merino *n* (*sheep*) мерино́с; (*wool*) мерино́совая шерсть.

merit *n* (*worth*) досто́инство; (*worthy conduct*) заслу́га; **the artistic ~s of a film** худо́жественные досто́инства фи́льма; **to judge smb on his ~s** оце́нивать кого́-л по досто́инству; **an award for ~** награ́да за заслу́ги; **to treat a case on its ~s** рассма́тривать де́ло по существу́; **his idea at least has the ~ of being original** его́ иде́я по кра́йней ме́ре оригина́льна.

merit *vt* заслу́жи|вать + *G* (-́ть).

merriment *n* весе́лье, оживле́ние.

merry *adj* весёлый, оживлённый; **to make ~** весели́ться; **the more the merrier** чем бо́льше госте́й, тем веселе́е; *CQ* (*tipsy*) **he was a bit ~** он был навеселе́ (*adv*).

merry-go-round *n* карусе́ль; **to have a ride on a ~** поката́ться на карусе́ли.

mesh *n* (*hole*, *loop*) пе́тля, яче́йка.

mess[1] *n* **1** (*disorder*) беспоря́док; **my desk is in a ~** мой стол в беспоря́дке; **tidy up the ~ in your room** наведи́те поря́док/убери́те у себя́ в ко́мнате; *CQ* **my room's an unholy ~** у меня́ в ко́мнате чёрт но́гу сло́мит

2 (*dirt*): (*to child*) **what a ~ you are in—go and wash** смотри́, на кого́ ты похо́ж, иди́ умо́йся; **the cat's made a ~ on the carpet** ко́шка наде́лала на ковре́

3 *CQ* (*muddle*, *trouble*): **he's made a ~ of it/things** он всё запу́тал; **he's got himself into a ~** он попа́л в переплёт; **to get oneself out of a ~** вы́путаться из неприя́тного положе́ния; **their marriage is in a ~** они́ ме́жду собо́й не ла́дят; **he's made a ~ of his life** ему́ в жи́зни не повезло́ (*impers*); **they made a ~ of cutting your hair** ну тебя́ и обкорна́ли!

mess[1] *vti CQ vt*: **my papers are all ~ed up** мои́ бума́ги все перепу́таны; **the weather ~ed up all our plans** пого́да спу́тала все на́ши пла́ны; **the management is ~ing me about and I don't know what I'm supposed to be doing** моё нача́льство со мной не счита́ется, и я не зна́ю, что мне де́лать

vi: **he loves ~ing about in the garden** он лю́бит копа́ться в саду́ (*usu impf*); **he spent the whole day ~ing about with the car** он це́лый день вози́лся с маши́ной (*impf*); **he's ~ing about with some girl in the office** у него́ рома́н с како́й-то деви́цей на рабо́те.

mess[2] *n Mil*: **officers ~** офице́рская столо́вая; *attr*: **a ~ tin** котело́к.

mess[2] *vi Mil*: **the officers ~ together** офице́ры едя́т вме́сте.

message *n off* сообще́ние; *Dipl* посла́ние; **to transmit a ~ by radio** передава́ть сообще́ние по ра́дио; **a ~ from the Queen** посла́ние короле́вы; (*informal*): **did he leave a ~ for me?** он мне что́-нибудь передава́л?; **can you give him a ~?** мо́жете ему́ переда́ть?; **did you get my ~?** тебе́ переда́ли (то), что я проси́л?; *CQ* **do you get the ~?** ты усёк?

messenger *n* посы́льный; курье́р, *also Dipl*; *Mil* связно́й.

messy *adj*: **you ~ child!** ну и грязну́ля/неря́ха же ты!; **the children's room is always ~** в де́тской всегда́ беспоря́док; **it's a ~ job** э́то гря́зная рабо́та, э́то така́я возня́; **it's a ~ painting—I don't like it** на э́той карти́не сто́лько всего́ накру́чено—мне она́ не нра́вится.

metabolism *n* обме́н веще́ств, метаболи́зм.

metal *n* мета́лл; *attr* металли́ческий.

metallic *adj* металли́ческий; **a ~ sound** металли́ческий звук.

metallurgy *n* металлу́ргия.

metaphor *n* мета́фора; **mixed ~s** сме́шанные мета́форы.

metaphorical *adj* метафори́ческий.

metaphysics *n* метафи́зика (*sing*).

meteor *n* метео́р.

meteoric *adj* метеори́ческий, метео́рный; *fig* **a ~ career** головокружи́тельная карье́ра.

meteorological *adj* метеорологи́ческий; **~ report** метеорологи́ческая сво́дка, *abbr* метеосво́дка.

meteorologist *n* метеоро́лог.

meter *n* счётчик; **gas/electricity ~** га́зовый/электри́ческий счётчик; *attr*: **~ reading** показа́ние счётчика.

methane *n* мета́н.

method *n* (*way*) ме́тод, спо́соб; (*orderliness*) поря́док, систе́ма; **the latest ~s** нове́йшие ме́тоды; **a new ~ of processing** но́вый спо́соб обрабо́тки; **teaching ~s** мето́дика (*sing*) преподава́ния; **a man of ~** челове́к, лю́бящий поря́док *or* пунктуа́льный челове́к; **there's ~ in his madness** в его́ безу́мии есть систе́ма.

methodical *adj* (*of work, etc.*) методи́ческий; (*of person*) методи́чный.

methylated spirits, *abbr* **meths** *n* денатура́т (*sing*).

meticulous *adj* тща́тельный; **he's ~ in his dress** он всегда́ тща́тельно оде́т; **he is noted for the ~ accuracy of his work** его́ рабо́та отлича́ется тща́тельностью исполне́ния.

metre, (*US*) **meter** *n* метр; *Poet* разме́р, метр.

metric(al) *adj* метри́ческий; **the ~ system** метри́ческая систе́ма мер.

Metro *n* (**the ~**) метро́ (*indecl*).

metronome *n* метроно́м.

metropolis *n* столи́ца.

metropolitan *n Rel* митрополи́т.

mettle *n*: **to show one's ~** оказа́ться на высоте́.

mew *vi* мяу́к|ать (*semel* -нуть).

Mexican *n* мексика́нец, мексика́нка.

Mexican *adj* мексика́нский.

mezzo(-soprano) *n* (*voice*) ме́ццо-сопра́но (*indecl*); **she's a wonderful ~** у неё чуде́сное ме́ццо-сопра́но.

mica *n* слюда́.

mickey *n sl*: **the boys take the ~ out of the new teacher** мальчи́шки дово́дят но́вого учи́теля.

microbe *n* микро́б.

microbiology *n* микробиоло́гия.

microphone *n* микрофо́н.

microscope *n* микроско́п.

microscopic *adj* микроскопи́ческий.

mid, *also* **mid-** *adj*: **by ~ July** к середи́не ию́ля; **in ~ winter** в середи́не зимы́; **in ~-Atlantic** посреди́ Атланти́ческого океа́на; **the acrobat seemed to float in ~ air** акроба́т как бу́дто плыл по во́здуху; **the bomb exploded in ~ air** бо́мба взорвала́сь в во́здухе; **the ~-morning coffee break** у́тренний переры́в.

midday *n* по́лдень (*m*); **at ~** в по́лдень; **by ~** к полу́дню; *attr*: **the ~ sun** полу́денное со́лнце; **a ~ snack** по́лдник.

middle *n* середи́на; **in the ~ of the day/century/August** в середи́не дня/ве́ка/а́вгуста; **in the ~ of the room/table** посереди́не ко́мнаты/стола́; **in the ~ of the field/square** посреди́ по́ля/пло́щади; **in the ~ of a meal/a speech** во вре́мя обе́да/выступле́ния; **I'm in the ~ of writing the letter now** я сейча́с как раз пишу́ письмо́.

middle *adj* сре́дний; **~ finger** сре́дний па́лец; *Anat* **~ ear** сре́днее у́хо; *Art* **~ distance** сре́дний план; *fig* **to steer/take a ~ course** держа́ться середи́ны, занима́ть уме́ренную пози́цию.

middle-aged *adj*: **a ~ woman** же́нщина сре́дних лет.

Middle Ages *npl* сре́дние века́.

middle-class *adj*: **a ~ residential area** райо́н, где живу́т сре́дние слои́ населе́ния.

middleman *n* (*intermediary*) *Comm* посре́дник.

middleweight *adj Sport*: **a ~ boxer** боксёр сре́днего ве́са; **~ wrestling** борьба́ в сре́днем ве́се.

middling *adj* (*medium*) сре́дний; (*mediocre*) посре́дственный; **of ~ size** сре́днего разме́ра; **as an actor he's fair to ~** он дово́льно сре́дний актёр.

middling *adv*: **~ tall** дово́льно высо́кий; **how are you feeling?—Middling** как самочу́вствие?—Та́к себе, сре́дне.

midge *n approx* кома́р.

midget *n* ка́рлик; лилипу́т; *attr*: **a ~ submarine** сверхма́лая подво́дная ло́дка.

Midlands *npl* (**the ~**) центра́льные райо́ны А́нглии.

midnight *n* по́лночь; **after ~** по́сле полу́ночи; *attr* полу́но́чный.

midst *n*: **in/from our ~** среди́ нас, из на́шей среды́; **in the ~ of all the confusion** посреди́ всей э́той сумато́хи.

midway *adv* на полпути́, на полдоро́ге; **~ between the two towns** на полпути́ ме́жду двумя́ города́ми; **we turned back ~** мы верну́лись с полпути́/с полдоро́ги.

midweek *adj and adv*: **it's cheaper to travel ~** биле́ты на тра́нспорт по вто́рникам, среда́м и четверга́м деше́вле.

Midwest *n* (*US*) (**the ~**) среднеза́падные шта́ты США.

midwife *n* акуше́рка.

might *n* мощь, могу́щество; *fig* **she screamed with all her ~** она́ закрича́ла во весь го́лос/изо всех си́л.

might *v see* **may.**

mighty *adj*: **a ~ nation** могу́щественная на́ция; **a ~ ocean** могу́чий океа́н; **a ~ blow** мо́щный уда́р; *CQ*: **he's very high and ~ these days** он после́днее вре́мя зава́жничал [NB *tense*]; **he was in a ~ hurry** он стра́шно спеши́л.

mighty *adv* (*US*) *CQ*: **that's ~ awkward** э́то ужа́сно неудо́бно.

migraine *n* мигре́нь.

migrant *n* (*nomad*) коче́вник; *Orn* перелётная пти́ца.

migrate *vi* пересел|я́ться (-и́ться), мигри́ровать (*impf*); **these birds ~ to the south in winter** зимо́й э́ти пти́цы улета́ют на юг.

migration *n* мигра́ция, *also Orn*; *Orn* перелёт.

mike *n CQ* микрофо́н.

mild *adj* мя́гкий; **a ~ character/climate/sentence** мя́гкий хара́ктер/кли́мат/пригово́р; **~ cheese/tobacco** мя́гкий сорт сы́ра, не-кре́пкий таба́к; **a ~ evening** тёплый ве́чер; **a ~ spell** пого́жие дни (*pl*); (*slight*): **~ surprise** лёгкое удивле́ние; **a ~ form of flu** лёгкая фо́рма гриппа.

mildew *n* (*on plants*) ми́лдью (*indecl*); (*on leather, etc.*) пле́сень.

mildly *adv* мя́гко; **to put it ~** мя́гко говоря́/выража́ясь; **I was ~ surprised** я был слегка́ удивлён.

mile *n* ми́ля (= 1609,33 *m*); **a nautical ~** морска́я ми́ля (= 1852 *m*); **he was doing 30 ~s an hour** он де́лал три́дцать миль в час; **my car does 30 ~s to the gallon** мое́й маши́не галло́на бензи́на хвата́ет на три́дцать миль; *CQ*: **it's ~s away** э́то о́чень далеко́; **we walked for ~s** мы шли и шли; **they live ~s from anywhere** они́ живу́т в глуши́; **I was ~s out in my reckoning** я намно́го оши́бся в расчётах; **she's ~s better** ей в ты́сячу раз лу́чше; **he sticks out a ~ among them** он среди́ них (как) бе́лая воро́на; **he's a scoundrel—you can tell it a ~ off** он него́дя́й, э́то за версту́ ви́дно.

mileage *n Aut, etc.*: **what ~ has the car done?** како́е расстоя́ние/ско́лько прошла́ э́та маши́на?; **what was your ~ yesterday?** ско́лько ты вчера́ нае́здил?; *attr*: **~ indicator** счётчик про́йденного пути́.

milestone *n* доро́жный ка́мень; *fig* **a ~ in the history of Europe** ве́ха в исто́рии Евро́пы.

milieu *n* окруже́ние, среда́.

militant *n* активи́ст.

militant *adj*: **the students are less ~ now** тепе́рь у студе́нтов нет того́ боево́го пы́ла.

military *n*: **the ~ were called in** бы́ли вы́званы войска́; **the ~ are against this decision** вое́нные круги́ про́тив э́того реше́ния.

military *adj* вое́нный; (*of, for the forces*) во́инский; **~ service** вое́нная слу́жба; **~ train** во́инский соста́в/эшело́н.

militate *vi*: **these factors will ~ against our success** э́ти фа́кторы бу́дут препя́тствовать на́шему успе́ху.

militia *n* (*UK*) *Hist* наро́дное ополче́ние; (*SU*) мили́ция.

militiaman *n* (*UK*) *Hist* ополче́нец; (*SU*) милиционе́р.

milk *n* молоко́; **condensed/evaporated ~** сгущённое молоко́; **skimmed ~** снято́е молоко́; **powdered ~** порошко́вое молоко́; *attr* моло́чный.

milk *vt* дои́ть (по-).

milk bar *n* моло́чная, моло́чное кафе́.

milk-bottle *n* моло́чная буты́лка.

milking *n* доéние, до́йка; *attr*: **~ machine** до́йльная маши́на.

milkman *n* (*delivery man*) продаве́ц молока́.

milk shake *n* моло́чный кокте́йль.

milksop *n* пла́кса (*m and f*).

mill *n* (*of windmill, watermill, etc.*) ме́льница; (*factory*) фа́брика; **coffee ~** кофе́йная ме́льница, *CQ* кофемо́лка; **cotton/paper ~** хлопкопряди́льная/бума́жная фа́брика; *fig*: **to put smb through the ~** испы́тывать кого́-л; **she's been through the ~ lately** ей мно́го пришло́сь испыта́ть в э́ти дни.

mill *vti vt* (*grain, coffee*) моло́ть (с-, по-); **to ~ steel** прока́тывать сталь (*impf*)

vi: *fig* **people were ~ing about the square** лю́ди толпи́лись на пло́щади.

millennium *n* тысячеле́тие; *fig* (**the ~**) золото́й век.

millet *n* про́со.

milligram(me) *n* миллигра́мм.

millinery *n* да́мские шля́пы (*pl*).

million *num, n* миллио́н (+ *Gpl*); **three ~ men** три миллио́на челове́к; *CQ*: **there were ~s of people there** там была́ тьма наро́ду; **he's worth ~s** у него́ у́йма де́нег; **he is one in a ~** таки́х люде́й — оди́н на миллио́н; (*US*) **I feel like a ~ dollars** я от ра́дости ног под собо́й не чу́ю.

millionaire *n* миллионе́р.

millpond *n* ме́льничный пруд.

millstone *n* жёрнов; *fig* **she's a ~ round his neck** она́ ему́ — ка́мень на ше́е.

mime *n Theat* пантоми́ма; (*actor*) мим.

mime *vt*: **to ~ smth** изобра|жа́ть что-л ми́микой (-зи́ть).

mimic *n*: **she's such a clever ~** она́ так заба́вно подража́ет.

mimic *vt* подража́ть + *D*, копи́ровать (*impfs*).

mimicry *n* ми́мика; *Zool* **protective ~** мимикри́я.

mince *n* фарш, ру́бленое мя́со.

mince *vti vt* (*meat*) про|вёртывать че́рез мясору́бку (-верну́ть); *fig* **let's not ~ matters/words** дава́йте говори́ть пря́мо/без обиняко́в

vi (*of gait*) семени́ть (*impf*).

mincer *n*, *also* **mincing machine** мясору́бка.

mind *n* **1** (*intellect*) ум; (*as opposed to matter*) душа́, дух; **he has a brilliant ~** у него́ блестя́щий ум; **the great ~s of our time** вели́кие умы́ на́шего вре́мени; **~ and body** душа́ и те́ло; **a triumph of ~ over matter** побе́да ду́ха над пло́тью; **to be of sound ~** быть в здра́вом уме́; **he's not in his right ~** он не в своём уме́; **it's driving him/he is out of his ~** э́то его́ с ума́ сведёт, он с ума́ сошёл; **she was out of her ~ with fear** она́ обезу́мела от стра́ха

2 (*conscious thoughts, feelings*) ум, голова́, душа́; **it never even crossed my ~** э́то мне да́же и в го́лову не пришло́; **I can't get it out of my ~** я не могу́ э́то вы́бросить из головы́; **what's on your ~?** что тебя́ беспоко́ит?; **I'm uneasy in my ~** у меня́ неспоко́йно на душе́; **frame of ~** настрое́ние; **I can see it in my ~'s eye** я так и ви́жу э́то мы́сленным взо́ром; **it will take your ~ off your worries** э́то отвлечёт тебя́ от забо́т

3 (*opinion*) взгляд, мне́ние; **to my ~** на мой взгляд, по-мо́ему; **she's got a ~ of her own** у неё на всё своё осо́бое мне́ние; **I'm keeping an open ~ on this** я пока́ не соста́вил об э́том мне́ния; **he always speaks his ~** он всегда́ говори́т то, что ду́мает, он никогда́ не криви́т душо́й; **I will speak my ~** я всё вы́скажу; **I'm still in two ~s about this** я всё ещё не реши́л, что с э́тим де́лать; **I'm of the same ~** (*as you*) я разделя́ю твоё мне́ние; **she doesn't know her own ~** она́ сама́ не зна́ет, чего́ хо́чет; **I'll give him a piece of my ~!** ну я ему́ зада́м!

4 (*attention*): **give your ~ to what you're doing** ду́май, что де́лаешь

5 (*memory*): **it slipped my ~** э́то вы́скочило у меня́ из головы́; **it went clean out of my ~** я на́чисто забы́л об э́том; **this brings/calls to ~ the occasion when...** э́то напомина́ет тот слу́чай, когда́...; **he puts me in ~ of my father** он напомина́ет мне моего́ отца́; **bear in ~ that...** име́й в виду́/не забу́дь, что...

6 (*intention*): **I've a ~ to come** я собира́юсь прийти́; **I've a good ~ to tell him what I think of him** я собира́юсь сказа́ть ему́, что я о нём ду́маю; **I've half a ~/I have it in ~ to go to the exhibition** я поду́мываю, а не сходи́ть ли на вы́ставку; **he was going to come but changed his ~** он собира́лся прийти́, но переду́мал; **I've something in ~ for his birthday** я уже́ (приблизи́тельно) зна́ю, что я ему́ подарю́ на день рожде́ния; **he's set his ~ on becoming a doctor** он твёрдо реши́л стать врачо́м.

mind *vti* **1** (*heed, mark*) обра|ща́ть внима́ние на + *A* (-ти́ть); **never ~ him/the expense** не обраща́й на него́ внима́ния, не ду́май о расхо́дах; **don't ~ me** не обраща́й на меня́ внима́ния; **never ~!** ничего́!; **~ what I say** слу́шай, что я говорю́; **~ what you're doing** ду́май/смотри́, что ты де́лаешь; **~ you don't catch cold** смотри́ не простуди́сь!; **I don't ~ the cold** я не бою́сь хо́лода; **I don't object, ~ you, but...** я, коне́чно, не возража́ю, но...; **he denied it, ~ you** и заме́ть, он э́то отрица́л; **~ out!** береги́сь!, осторо́жно!; **~ the steps!** осторо́жно, ступе́ньки!

2 (*oversee*): **who's ~ing the baby?/the shop?** кто присма́тривает за ребёнком?/за магази́ном?

3 (*object to*): **do you ~ if I smoke?** вы не возража́ете, е́сли я закурю́?; **she ~s very much the way you behaved** ей о́чень не понра́вилось, как ты себя́ вёл; **do you ~ the TV being on?** вам меша́ет телеви́зор?; **some tea?—I don't ~ if I do** хо́чешь ча́ю? — Не откажу́сь; **where shall we eat?—I don't ~** где мы бу́дем обе́дать? — Мне всё равно́; **would you ~ opening the door?** не откро́ешь ли дверь?; **children, would you ~ keeping quiet?** де́ти, мо́жете поти́ше?

minded *adj*: **if she were so ~** е́сли она́ захо́чет.

mindful *adj*: **we must be ~ of our duties** мы должны́ по́мнить о свои́х обя́занностях.

mine[1] *poss pron* мой, моя́, моё, *pl* мои́; *if referring to the subject of the sentence or clause* свой; **this is ~** э́то моё; **whose book is this?—Mine** чья э́то кни́га? — Моя́; **a friend of ~ told me** оди́н мой прия́тель сказа́л мне; **it's no business of ~** э́то не моё де́ло; **he's always been good to me and ~** он всегда́ был добр ко мне и мои́м родны́м; **luckily she had her key, as I'd forgotten ~** я забы́л свой ключ, но, к сча́стью, у неё оказа́лся свой.

mine[2] *n* рудни́к, (*coal*) ша́хта; **copper ~** ме́дные ко́пи (*pl*); **a gold ~** золото́й при́иск; *fig* **he's a ~ of information** он ходя́чая энциклопе́дия.

mine[2] *vti vt*: **to ~ (for) coal** добы|ва́ть у́голь (-ть) *vi* вести́ го́рные рабо́ты (*usu impf*).

mine[3] *n* (*explosive*) ми́на; **land** ~ фуга́с; **to lay** ~**s** мини́ровать; **the lorry hit a** ~ грузови́к наскочи́л на ми́ну.

mine[3] *vt*: **to** ~ **a bridge** мини́ровать мост (за-); **the destroyer was** ~**d** эсми́нец подорва́лся на ми́не.

mine detector *n* миноиска́тель (*m*).

minefield *n* ми́нное по́ле.

minelayer *n* ми́нный загради́тель (*m*).

miner *n* горня́к, рудоко́п; (*of coal*) шахтёр.

mineral *n* минера́л; *attr*: ~ **water** минера́льная вода́; ~ **deposits**/**resources** месторожде́ния минера́лов, поле́зные ископа́емые.

minesweeper *n* ми́нный тра́льщик.

mingle *vti vt*: **his respect was** ~**d with a certain awe** к его́ уваже́нию приме́шивался почти́тельный страх

vi: **to** ~ **with the crowd** сме́ш|иваться с толпо́й (-а́ться).

mingy *adj CQ* (*of people*) скупо́й; (*of things*) ску́дный.

miniature *n* миниатю́ра; **in** ~ в миниатю́ре; *attr* миниатю́рный.

minibus *n* микроавто́бус.

minim *n Mus* полови́нная но́та.

minimal *adj* минима́льный.

minimize *vt* преуменьш|а́ть (-́ить); **he** ~**d the difficulties** он преуме́ньшил тру́дности.

minimum *n* ми́нимум; **he earns a** ~ **of 100 roubles** он зараба́тывает ми́нимум сто рубле́й; **to cut expenditure to the** ~ уре́зать расхо́ды до ми́нимума; *attr* минима́льный; ~ **wage** минима́льная зарпла́та.

mining *n* (*science*) го́рное де́ло; (*process*) разрабо́тка поле́зных ископа́емых; (*industry*) го́рная промы́шленность.

miniskirt, *CQ* **mini** *n* ми́ни-ю́бка.

minister *n* мини́стр; *Rel* свяще́нник, па́стор.

minister *vi*: **to** ~ **to (the needs of) a sick man** уха́живать за больны́м (*impf*).

ministerial *adj*: ~ **duties** обя́занности мини́стра; (*UK*) ~ **changes** измене́ния в соста́ве кабине́та.

ministry *n* **1** министе́рство

2 *Rel* (*clergy*) духове́нство; (*profession*) духо́вный сан.

mink *n* но́рка (*also fur*); *attr*: **a** ~ **coat** но́рковое манто́ (*indecl*).

minnow *n* песка́рь (*m*).

minor *n Law* несовершенноле́тний; *Mus* мино́р.

minor *adj* **1** (*less important*) незначи́тельный, второстепе́нный; (*inessential*) несуще́ственный; **a** ~ **position** незначи́тельный пост; **a** ~ **composer** второстепе́нный компози́тор; **that's a** ~ **detail** э́то несуще́ственная дета́ль; ~ **repairs** ме́лкий ремо́нт (*sing*); *Law* **a** ~ **offence** ме́лкое правонаруше́ние; *Med* ~ **injuries** лёгкие ране́ния

2 *Mus*: **concerto in G-**~ конце́рт соль мино́р; **in a** ~ **key** в мино́рном ключе́; **a** ~ **third** уме́ньшенная те́рция

3 *Law* несовершенноле́тний.

minority *n* меньшинство́; **national**/**racial minorities** национа́льные/ра́совые меньши́нства; **to be in the** ~ быть в меньшинстве́; **I was in a** ~ **of one against** я оди́н/еди́нственный был про́тив; *attr*: ~ **rule** подчине́ние большинства́ меньшинству́.

mint[1] *n Bot* мя́та; (*sweet*) мя́тная конфе́та; *attr* мя́тный.

mint[2] *n* моне́тный двор; *CQ* **he made a** ~ **on the deal** он зарабо́тал на э́том ку́чу де́нег.

mint[2] *vt*: **to** ~ **coins** чека́нить моне́ты (от-, вы́-).

minus *n and prep* ми́нус; **the** ~ **sign** знак ми́нус; **5** ~ **3 leaves 2** пять ми́нус три равно́ двум; **it's** ~ **5° today** сего́дня на у́лице ми́нус пять (гра́дусов); *CQ* **he appeared** ~ **his shirt** он появи́лся без руба́шки; *attr*: ~ **temperatures** ми́нусовая температу́ра (*sing*); *Math* **a** ~ **quantity** отрица́тельная величина́.

minute *n* **1** (*of time, degree*) мину́та; **5** ~**s past 2** пять мину́т тре́тьего; **5** ~**s to 2** без пяти́ два; **it won't take a** ~ э́то и мину́ты не займёт; **at the last** ~ в после́днюю мину́ту; **just a** ~, **wait a** ~ (одну́) мину́точку, подожди́те мину́ту; **I shan't be a** ~ сейча́с, сию́ мину́ту; **it was a matter of** ~**s** э́то бы́ло де́лом одно́й мину́ты (*sing*); **we expect him any** ~ **now** мы ждём его́ с мину́ты на мину́ту; **it's about 10** ~**s walk from here** туда́ идти́ мину́т де́сять; **for a** ~ **I thought that...** на мгнове́ние я поду́мал, что...; **phone me the** ~ **he comes** позвони́ мне, как то́лько он придёт; *attr*: **the** ~ **hand** мину́тная стре́лка

2 (*official record*) коро́ткая за́пись, заме́тка; *pl* (**the** ~**s**) (*of a meeting*) протоко́л (*sing*), (*of several meetings*) протоко́лы (*pl*); **to record smth in the** ~**s** занести́ что-л в протоко́л; **to keep the** ~**s of a meeting** вести́ протоко́л.

minute *adj* (*tiny*) мельча́йший; ~ **particles** мельча́йшие части́цы; **a** ~ **quantity of arsenic can be fatal** да́же ничто́жная до́за мышьяка́ мо́жет уби́ть челове́ка; **a** ~ **examination of the blood sample showed...** тща́тельный ана́лиз кро́ви показа́л...

minutely *adv* (*in detail*) подро́бно; (*carefully, closely*) тща́тельно.

minx *n* коке́тка.

miracle *n* чу́до; *fig*: **to work** ~**s** твори́ть чудеса́; **by some** ~ каки́м-то чу́дом.

miraculous *adj* чуде́сный; **his recovery seemed** ~ его́ выздоровле́ние каза́лось чу́дом.

mirage *n* мира́ж.

mire *n* грязь; **we were knee deep in** ~ мы бы́ли по коле́но в грязи́.

mirror *n* зе́ркало; **hand** ~ зе́ркальце; *Aut* **rear**/**wing** ~ зе́ркало за́днего ви́да, боково́е зе́ркало; **to look at oneself in the** ~ смотре́ться в зе́ркало.

mirror *vt* отра|жа́ть (-зи́ть); **the trees were** ~**ed in the pond** дере́вья отража́лись в пруду́.

mirth *n* весéлье.

misadventure *n* несчáстье, несчáстный слýчай; **death by ~** смерть от несчáстного слýчая.

misapply *vt*: **the word is often misapplied** э́то слóво чáсто непрáвильно употребля́ют.

misapprehend *vt* непрáвильно/преврáтно по|нимáть (-ня́ть).

misapprehension *n* недоразумéние; **there seems to be some ~ here** здесь есть какóе-то недоразумéние; **to be/labour under a ~** быть/пребывáть в заблуждéнии.

misappropriate *vt*: **he was accused of misappropriating the funds** егó обвини́ли в растрáте.

misbehave *vi* плóхо/дýрно вести́ себя́ (*impf*).

miscalculate *vti vt*: **we ~d the distance/the sum needed for repairs** мы ошиблись в подсчёте расстоя́ния/, прики́дывая стóимость ремóнта

vi (*miscount*) просчитáться (*usu pf*).

miscalculation *n* (*in counting*) просчёт, (*error*) оши́бка.

miscarriage *n Med* вы́кидыш; *fig* **a ~ of justice** судéбная оши́бка; *Comm* **~ of goods** недостáвка товáров.

miscarry *vi Med* имéть вы́кидыш; *fig* **the plan miscarried** план лóпнул.

miscast *adj*: **he's ~ in that role** он не годи́тся для э́той рóли.

miscellaneous *adj* рáзный; **~ goods** сáмые рáзные товáры; **a ~ collection of people** пёстрое óбщество; **a ~ collection of stories** *approx* сбóрник расскáзов (рáзных áвторов — *if of several authors*).

mischance *n*: **by some ~** по несчáстной случáйности.

mischief *n* **1** (*used of children*) озорствó, шáлость; **that boy is full of ~/is a little ~** э́тот мальчи́шка — озорни́к/шалýн; **the children are up to some ~ again** дéти опя́ть чтó-то затевáют; **to get into ~** набедокýрить, напрокáзничать; **I let the children watch TV to keep them out of ~** я разрешáю дéтям смотрéть телеви́зор, чтóбы они́ помéньше шали́ли

2 (*harm*) зло; **to do smb a ~** причиня́ть зло комý-л; **he made ~ between the brothers** он поссóрил брáтьев друг с дрýгом.

mischievous *adj* (*of children*) озорнóй, шаловли́вый, прокáзливый; (*doing harm*) злóбный, зловрéдный; **a ~ rumour** злóбные сплéтни (*pl*).

misconceive *vt*: **the plan was ~d from the start** план никудá не годи́лся с сáмого начáла.

misconception *n* заблуждéние; **it's a popular ~ that...** существýет оши́бочное мнéние, что...

misconduct *n* (*at school, etc.*) плохóе поведéние; **professional ~** должностнóе преступлéние.

misconstruction *n*: **your words are open to ~** вáши словá мóжно преврáтно истолковáть.

misconstrue *vt*: **you have ~d my words** вы непрáвильно пóняли мои́ словá, (*if deliberately*) вы искази́ли смысл мои́х слов.

miscount *vti vt*: **I ~ed the pages** я непрáвильно сосчитáл страни́цы

vi обсчитáться (*usu pf*); **I ~ed by 2 roubles** я обсчитáлся на два рубля́.

misdeed *n* простýпок.

misdirect *vt*: **the letter was ~ed** письмó бы́ло адресóвано непрáвильно; **he ~s his energies** он впустýю трáтит свою́ энéргию; **somebody ~ed us** нас послáли не в ту стóрону.

miser *n* скупéц, скря́га (*m and f*).

miserable *adj* (*unhappy*) несчáстный; (*wretched*) жáлкий, убóгий; **what are you so ~ about?** почемý у тебя́ такóй несчáстный вид?; **to feel ~** чýвствовать себя́ несчáстным; **to make smb ~** дéлать когó-л несчáстным; **she looked so ~** у неё был такóй жáлкий вид; **a ~ sum** жáлкая/ми́зерная сýмма; **a ~ hovel** жáлкая/убóгая лачýга; **~ weather** сквéрная погóда; **the play was a ~ failure** пьéса провали́лась.

miserably *adv*: **she's ~ depressed** онá в ужáсно подáвленном состоя́нии; **his wage is ~ inadequate** егó жáлкого зáработка едвá хватáет на жизнь.

miserly *adj* скупóй, скáредный.

misery *n*: **she made his life a ~** онá исковéркала емý жизнь; **her life with him is a ~** ей с ним неслáдко живётся; **do tell me the result and put me out of my ~** скажи́ мне скорéй результáт, а то я мéста себé не нахожý; **we had to put our old dog out of his ~** нам пришлóсь усыпи́ть нáшу стáрую собáку; *CQ* **he's an old ~** он стáрый ворчýн.

misfire *vi*: **the gun ~d** ружьё дáлó осéчку; *fig* **his plans ~d** егó плáны рýхнули; *Aut* **the engine ~s on one cylinder** в однóм цили́ндре нет зажигáния.

misfit *n*: **my dress is a ~** э́то плáтье плóхо на мне сиди́т; *fig* **he's a ~ in that job** он не годи́тся для э́той рабóты.

misfortune *n* бедá; **he met with ~** с ним стрясла́сь бедá; **I had the ~ to be present there** на свою́ бедý я был там.

misgiving *n* опасéние; **not without ~s** не без опасéний; **I have grave ~s about it** э́то вызывáет у меня́ серьёзные опасéния.

mishandle *vt*: **this watch has been ~d** часы́ непрáвильно заводи́ли, с э́тими часáми неумéло обращáлись; *fig* **he ~d the case** он непрáвильно повёл дéло.

mishap *n*: **we arrived home without ~** мы добрали́сь дó дому без вся́ких происшéствий; *CQ* **I've had a ~ in the kitchen** у меня́ на кýхне случи́лось несчáстье.

misinform *vt* дезинформи́ровать (*impf and pf*).

misinterpret *vt* (*a person, words*) невéрно пон|имáть (-я́ть); **he ~ed my words** он не так пóнял мои́ словá.

misjudge *vt*: **I ~d him/the distance** я ошибся в нём, я неверно прикинул расстояние; **I ~d the situation** я неверно оценил ситуацию.

mislay *vt*: **I've mislaid my purse** я куда-то задевал свой кошелёк; **the book's been mislaid** книга куда-то задевалась/запропастилась (*pfs*).

mislead *vt* вводить в заблуждение (ввести); **I fear you have been misled** боюсь, что вас ввели в заблуждение.

misleading *adj*: **a ~ title** вводящее в заблуждение название; **the advertisement is ~** реклама вводит в заблуждение.

mismanage *vt*: **he ~d the affair** он не справился с этим делом.

misnomer *n*: **it's a ~ to call this place a hotel** *CQ* это не гостиница, а чёрт знает что.

misplace *vt*: **that book is ~d** эта книга стоит не на месте; **his confidence in her was ~d** он сделал ошибку, доверившись ей.

misprint *n* опечатка.

misquote *vt* неправильно цитировать (про-); (*deliberately*) **he was ~d in the press** в прессе его слова были искажены.

miss[1] *n* (*of a shot*) промах; *fig* **he didn't win the competition but it was a near ~** он не победил на конкурсе, но был очень близок к победе; *CQ* **I'll give the soup a ~** я не буду есть суп.

miss[1] *vti vt* **1** (*fail to hit*) промахнуться, не попасть в цель (*usu pfs*); **I ~ed the target** я промахнулся, я не попал в цель; **the bullet just ~ed his heart** пуля прошла в одном миллиметре от сердца; **the bullet just ~ed me** пуля чуть не задела меня; **the bus just ~ed the car** автобус чуть не врезался в машину; **he struck at the ball but ~ed it** он хотел ударить по мячу, но промазал

2 (*fail to find, catch, etc.*) *often translated by verbs with prefix* про-: **I ~ed the house I was looking for** я прошёл дом, который искал; **I ~ed that spelling mistake** я пропустил эту орфографическую ошибку; **we ~ed our turning** мы проехали наш поворот; **I ~ed what he said** я прослушал, что он сказал; **to ~ classes** пропус|кать/(*play truant*) прогул|ивать занятия (-тить/-ять); **I wouldn't have ~ed the concert for anything** я ни за что не пропустил бы этот концерт; **you didn't ~ much** ты немного потерял; **he ~ed the ball** он не поймал (*didn't catch*)/пропустил (*in any way*) мяч; **to ~ a train/plane** опаздывать на поезд/на самолёт (опоздать); **he ~ed his footing and fell from the rock** он оступился и упал со скалы; **you've just ~ed him** он только что ушёл; **he's so tall—you can't ~ him** он такой высокий, что его нельзя не заметить; *fig*: **you've ~ed the point** ты не понял, в чём дело; **it's a chance not to be ~ed** эту возможность нельзя упустить; **he's ~ed his vocation** он не нашёл себя/своего призвания; *CQ* **I'm afraid he's ~ed the boat** боюсь, он упустил свой шанс/, его поезд ушёл

3 (*omit*) *also* **~ out: you've ~ed out a word** вы пропустили одно слово; **we'll have to ~ out this paragraph** (нам) придётся опустить этот абзац; **we had to ~ the Hermitage** мы не смогли попасть в Эрмитаж

4 (*note absence of*): **when did you first ~ your wallet?** когда вы обнаружили пропажу бумажника?; **I didn't even ~ the key** я даже не заметил, что ключа не было; **they won't ~ us at the meeting** никто не заметит, что нас нет на собрании; **we're ~ing 5 books** не хватает ещё пяти книг; **I ~ the children terribly** я страшно скучаю по детям

vi (*in shooting*) промах|иваться (-нуться), *also fig*.

miss[2] *n* мисс; *CQ* **she's a proper little ~** она бойкая девчушка.

misshapen *adj* деформированный.

missile *n Mil* ракета; **guided ~** управляемая ракета; *attr*: **~ base** ракетная база.

missing *adj* **1** *attr*: **the ~ pages** недостающие страницы; **the ~ link** недостающее звено; **~ persons** пропавшие без вести

2 *predic*: **one volume is ~** одного тома нет; **6 pages are ~ from the book** в книге не хватает шести страниц; **my wallet is ~** у меня пропал бумажник.

mission *n* миссия, *also Dipl, Rel, fig*; **to go on a ~** отправиться с миссией; **trade ~** торговое представительство, *abbr* торгпредство; **he considers it his ~ in life** он считает это своим призванием.

missionary *n* миссионер.

misspell *vt*: **they've misspelt my name** моя фамилия написана неправильно.

mist *n* туман.

mist *vti*: **the mirror ~ed up/was ~ed up by steam** зеркало запотело (от пара) (*usu pf*).

mistake *n* (*error*) ошибка; **a serious ~** грубая ошибка; **by ~** по ошибке; **he made the ~ of taking me seriously** ему не надо было принимать мои слова всерьёз; **you're making a big ~** вы совершаете большую ошибку; **one learns from one's ~s** на ошибках учатся; **there must be some ~** здесь какая-то ошибка; *CQ*: **it's hot and no ~** очень жарко, ничего не скажешь; **he's guilty, no ~ about it** он виновен, это точно; **my ~!** виноват!

mistake *vt* ошиб|аться в + *P* (-иться); **I mistook the distance** я ошибся в подсчёте расстояния; **I mistook his meaning** я не понял смысла его слов; **I mistook the turning** я свернул не на ту дорогу; **he often gets ~n for his brother** его часто путают с братом; **there's no mistaking him** его нельзя не узнать.

mistaken *adj* ошибочный; **a ~ opinion** ошибочное мнение; **you are ~ about him** вы ошиблись [**NB** *tense*] в нём.

mister, *abbr* **Mr** *n* господин; **Mr Chairman** господин председатель; **give it to Mr Smith** передайте это господину/мистеру Смиту.

mistime *vt*: **we ~d our arrival** мы приéхали не вóвремя (*late or inopportunely*).

mistletoe *n Bot* омéла бéлая.

mistress *n* **1** (*teacher*) учи́тельница; (*of the house*) хозя́йка (дóма); (*lover*) любóвница; *fig*: **she's ~ of the situation** онá хозя́йка положéния; **she's her own ~** онá самá себé хозя́йка

2 *abbr* **Mrs** госпожá; **I said to Mrs Smith** я сказáл госпожé/ми́ссис (*indecl*) Смит.

mistrust *n* недовéрие к + *D*.

mistrust *vt* не доверя́ть + *D* (*impf*).

mistrustful *adj* недовéрчивый.

misty *adj* тумáнный; **~ outlines** тумáнные очертáния; **it's ~ today** сегóдня тумáн; **it's getting ~** поднимáется тумáн.

misunderstand *vt*: **you misunderstood me** вы меня́ не так/непрáвильно пóняли; **don't ~ me** не поймúте меня́ превpáтно.

misunderstanding *n* недоразумéние; **to clear up a ~** устраня́ть недоразумéние.

misuse *n* злоупотреблéние + *I*; **a ~ of public money/power** злоупотреблéние казёнными деньгáми/влáстью.

misuse *vt* непрáвильно употреб|ля́ть (-и́ть); (*abuse*) злоупотреб|ля́ть + *I* (-и́ть); **you're misusing that word** ты непрáвильно употребля́ешь э́то слóво; **he ~d his official position** он злоупотреби́л свои́м служéбным положéнием; **he feels ~d** он считáет, что с ним обошли́сь несправедли́во.

mite *n*: **poor little ~!** бéдная крóшка/малю́тка!

mitigation *n Law*: **he pleaded in ~ that...** в кáчестве смягчáющего обстоя́тельства он привёл...

mitten, *abbr* **mitt** *n* рукави́ца, вáрежка.

mix *n* смесь.

mix *vti vt* **1** смéшивать, мешáть (*pf for both* смешáть) *and other compounds*; **to ~ wine with water** смéшивать винó с водóй; **~ all the ingredients (together)** смешáйте всё/все составны́е чáсти; **she ~ed the sugar and/with the flour** онá добáвила в мукý сáхар и всё как слéдует перемешáла; **you must ~ the dough well** тéсто нáдо как слéдует/хорошéнько вы́месить; **to ~ cement** замéшивать цемéнт; *fig* **to ~ business with pleasure** сочетáть приятное с полéзным

2 (*confuse*): **to ~ up** пýтать (с-, пере-); **I always ~ them up** я вéчно/всегдá их пýтаю; **I ~ him up with his brother** я егó пýтаю с брáтом; **I ~ed up their names** я перепýтал их именá

3 (*be involved*) *only in passive*: **don't get ~ed up in that affair** не впýтывайся в э́то дéло; **he's ~ed up in it somehow** он каки́м-то óбразом замéшан в э́том дéле

vi (*combine*) смéшиваться; сочетáться (*impf and pf*); **oil and water do not ~** мáсло не растворя́ется в водé; **in America many races have ~ed** в Амéрике произошлó смешéние мнóгих национáльностей; (*of people*): **he doesn't ~ well** он плóхо схóдится с людьми́; **they ~ with peculiar people** они́ вóдят дрýжбу с óчень стрáнными людьми́.

mixed *adj* смéшанный; **a ~ marriage** смéшанный брак; **~ doubles** смéшанная пáрная игрá; **~ farming** смéшанное/неспециализи́рованное хозя́йство; **~ sweets** конфéты ассорти́ (*indecl*); **I have ~ feelings about it** я отношýсь к э́тому со смéшанным чýвством; **it's a ~ blessing** в э́том не тóлько блáго.

mixed-up *adj*: **he's all ~** он запýтался; **he's a ~ kid** он трýдный ребёнок/(*teenager*) подрóсток.

mixer *n Cook* мешáлка, ми́ксер; *fig* **he's a good ~** он óчень общи́тельный человéк.

mixture *n* смесь, *also fig*; *Med* микстýра; **the play is a ~ of tragedy and farce** э́та пьéса—смесь трагéдии и фáрса.

mix-up *n* пýтаница; **we got into a ~ over the tickets** у нас былá какáя-то пýтаница/неразбери́ха с билéтами.

moan *n* стон; (*of wind*) завывáние.

moan *vi* стонáть (за-); (*of wind*) завы|вáть (-́ть); **he ~ed with pain** он застонáл от бóли; **the wind ~ed in the chimney** вéтер завывáл в трубé; *CQ* **he's always ~ing about something** он вéчно нóет.

moat *n* ров.

mob *n* толпá; **an angry ~** разъярённая толпá; *CQ* **keep clear of that ~** держи́сь подáльше от э́той компáнии.

mob *vt*: **the speaker was ~bed by angry women** толпá разъярённых жéнщин наброси́лась на орáтора; **the singer was ~bed at the airport** в аэропортý певцá окружи́ла толпá почитáтелей.

mobile *adj* подви́жный; подвижнóй, передвижнóй; **she has a ~ face** у неё подви́жное лицó; **~ library** передвижнáя библиотéка; **~ shop** автолáвка; *Mil* **~ forces** моби́льные войскá; *CQ*: **he's ~ again** (*of invalid*) он снóва на ногáх; **our car's back so we're ~ again** мы получи́ли маши́ну (из ремóнта) и тепéрь опя́ть на колёсах.

mobilize *vti* мобилизовáть(ся) (*impf and pf*).

mocha *n* кóфе мóкко (*indecl*).

mock *n*: **they made a ~ of him** они́ сдéлали из негó посмéшище; *attr*: **~ modesty** притвóрная скрóмность.

mock *vti vt*: **the children ~ed the fat boy** дéти смея́лись над тóлстым мальчи́шкой; **the boys ~ed their teacher** мáльчики передрáзнивали учи́теля

vi: **they ~ed at my efforts to start the car** они́ потешáлись над мои́ми попы́тками завести́ маши́ну.

mockery *n*: **they made a ~ of the ceremony** они́ преврати́ли э́ту церемóнию в фарс; **the trial was a ~ of justice** процéсс был издевáтельством над правосýдием.

mocking *adj* насмéшливый.

mock-up *n* макéт.

modal *adj*: **~ verb** модáльный глагóл.

mod cons *CQ* (*abbr of* **modern conveniences**): **with all ~** со всéми удóбствами.

mode *n* óбраз; (*fashion*) мóда; ~ **of action** óбраз дéйствия; ~ **of life** óбраз/уклáд жúзни; **the latest** ~**s** послéдние мóды.

model *n* **1** модéль; (*architect's*) макéт; (*example*) образéц; **a working** ~ **of an engine** дéйствующая модéль паровóза; **on the** ~ **of smth** по образцý чегó-л; **the latest Paris** ~**s** (*dresses*) новéйшие парúжские модéли; **he's a** ~ **of virtue** он образéц добродéтели; *Aut* **a sports** ~ спортúвная модéль

2 (*person*): (**artist's**) ~ натýрщ|ик, *f* -ица; (**fashion**) ~ манекéнщица.

model *adj* (*exemplary*) образцóвый; **a** ~ **school** образцóвая шкóла; (*of toys*) **a** ~ **aeroplane/train** игрýшечный самолёт/пóезд.

model *vti vt*: **he** ~**led a figure from clay** он вы́лепил фигýрку из глúны; **she** ~**s dresses in a fashion house** онá манекéнщица в дóме модéлей; **to** ~ **oneself on smb** брать примéр с когó-л (взять); **to** ~ **one's conduct on smb** подражáть комý-л в поведéнии (*impf*)

vi: рабóтать натýрщиком (*for artist*)/манекéнщицей (*for fashion house*).

modelling *n* (*making models*) моделúрование; (*of mannequins*) рабóта манекéнщицы; **the children love** ~ **in plasticine** дéти лю́бят лепúть из пластилúна.

moderate *adj* умéренный, *also Polit*; (*average*) срéдний; ~ **prices/winds** умéренные цéны/вéтры; **he is** ~ **in his views/demands** он человéк умéренных взглядов, он умéрен в своúх трéбованиях.

moderate *vti vt* умер|я́ть (-ить); **you'd best** ~ **your enthusiasm** тебé лýчше бы умéрить свой пыл

vi: **the wind is moderating** вéтер стихáет.

moderately *adv*: **a** ~ **large garden** довóльно большóй сад; **he was** ~ **successful** он добúлся нéкоторого успéха.

moderation *n* умéренность; ~ **in eating** умéренность в едé; **wine taken in** ~ **does no harm** úзредка вы́пить рю́мку винá не врéдно.

modern *adj* совремéнный, нóвый; ~ **architecture** совремéнная архитектýра; ~ **languages** нóвые языкú; **in** ~ **times** в нáше врéмя (*sing*), в нáши дни.

modernize *vt* модернизúровать (*impf and pf*).

modest *adj* скрóмный; **a** ~ **house/income/person** скрóмный дом/дохóд/человéк.

modicum *n*: **if she had a** ~ **of common sense** éсли бы у неё былá хоть кáпля здрáвого смы́сла; **with a** ~ **of effort** без осóбого трудá.

modification *n* изменéние, модификáция.

modify *vt* (*change*) модифицúровать (*impf and pf*); *Gram* определя́ть (*only in impf*); **the old models have been considerably modified** стáрые модéли бы́ли значúтельно изменены́/модифицúрованы; (*moderate*) **to** ~ **one's demands** умер|я́ть своú трéбования (-ить).

modish *adj* мóдный.

modulate *vt* модулúровать (*impf*).

mohair *n* мохéр; *attr* мохéровый.

moist *adj* влáжный; **eyes** ~ **with tears** глазá, влáжные от слёз.

moisten *vt* увлажн|я́ть (-úть); **to** ~ **one's lips** облúз|ывать гýбы (-áть).

moisture *n* влáга.

molar *n* моля́р, креннóй зуб.

molasses *npl* мелáсса, чёрная пáтока (*sings*).

Moldavian *n* молдавáнин, молдавáнка.

Moldavian *adj* молдáвский.

mole[1] *n* (*on skin*) родúмое пятнó, рóдинка.

mole[2] *n Zool* крот.

mole[3] *n* (*breakwater*) мол; дáмба.

molecular *adj* молекуля́рный.

molehill *n* кротóвая кóчка; *fig* **to make a mountain out of a** ~ дéлать из мýхи слонá.

molest *vt* приста|вáть к + *D* (-ть).

mollify *vt* смягч|áть (-úть); **he was mollified when I apologized** он смягчúлся пóсле моúх извинéний (*pl*).

mollycoddle *vt* изнéжить (*usu pf*).

molten *adj* расплáвленный.

moment *n* **1** (*of time*) момéнт, миг, минýта; **just a** ~, **wait a** ~ одúн момéнт, однý минýту; **at the present** ~ в настоя́щий момéнт; **at any** ~, **any** ~ **now** в любóй момéнт; **this is not the right** ~ **to...** сейчáс не врéмя + *inf*; **he'll be here in a** ~ он вот-вóт придёт; **come here this** ~ идú сюдá сейчáс же; **he's just this** ~ **left** он тóлько что ушёл; **I don't suspect him for a** ~ я ни на секýнду егó не подозревáю; **from** ~ **to** ~ с минýты на минýту; **that's all for the** ~ покá всё; **at odd** ~**s** уры́вками (*adv*); **at a** ~**'s notice** по пéрвому трéбованию; *as conj*: **I came the** ~ **I knew** я пришёл срáзу, как тóлько узнáл об э́том

2 (*importance*): **matters of** ~ вáжные делá.

momentarily *adv*: ~ **I forget his name** не могý сейчáс вспóмнить егó úмя; (*US*) (*at this moment*) в дáнный момéнт.

momentary *adj* мгновéнный; **a** ~ **flash** мгновéнная вспы́шка; **I had a** ~ **lapse of memory** у меня́ был минýтный провáл пáмяти.

momentous *adj* вáжный; значúтельный; **it was a** ~ **discovery/occasion** э́то бы́ло вáжное откры́тие/собы́тие.

momentum *n Phys* момéнт; *fig* **to gather/lose** ~ нарáщивать/теря́ть скóрость.

monarchy *n* монáрхия.

monastery *n* монасты́рь (*m*).

monastic *adj* монáшеский.

Monday *n* понедéльник.

monetary *adj* валю́тный.

money *n* дéньги (*pl*); **paper/public/ready** ~ бумáжные/общéственные/налúчные дéньги; **we're a bit short of** ~ **just now** мы сейчáс не при деньгáх; **that's worth a lot of** ~ э́то стóит бóльших дéнег; **to put one's** ~ **on smth** стáвить дéньги на что-л; **I wouldn't do it for love or** ~ я не стáну/не бýду э́того дéлать ни за какúе дéньги; **he just throws** ~ **about** он прóсто сорúт деньгáми;

he's made of/rolling in ~ у него́ де́нег ку́ры не клюю́т; **he gets his ~'s worth out of his employees** он зря подчинённым не пла́тит; **you can make good ~ here** здесь мо́жно хорошо́ зарабо́тать; **there's ~ in it** э́то вы́годное де́ло; **we got our ~'s worth at that hotel** в э́той гости́нице зна́ешь, за что пла́тишь; **he has come into ~** он получи́л насле́дство; *attr* де́нежный; **he's just a fool where ~ matters are concerned** он ничего́ не смы́слит в де́нежных дела́х; **the ~ market** де́нежный ры́нок.

moneyed *adj*: **a ~ man** состоя́тельный челове́к.

moneygrubber *n* стяжа́тель (*m*).

moneylender *n* ростовщи́к.

money order *n* де́нежный перево́д.

moneywise *adv*: *CQ* **we're O.K. ~** у нас с деньга́ми всё в поря́дке.

Mongol *n* монго́л, монго́лка.

Mongolian *adj* монго́льский.

mongoose *n* мангу́ста.

mongrel *n* (*dog*) дворня́га, дворня́жка.

monitor *n* (*in school*) ста́роста кла́сса; *TV* (*also* **~-screen**) монито́р; *Radio* контролёр/реда́ктор переда́ч.

monk *n* мона́х.

monkey *n* обезья́на; *fig*: **you little ~** ах ты прока́зник!/озорни́к!/шалуни́шка!; **he made a ~ of me** он вы́ставил меня́ на посме́шище.

monkey *vi*: **the children are ~ing around somewhere** де́ти где́-то но́сятся; **stop ~ing about with the radio!** оста́вь в поко́е приёмник!

monkey nut *n* ара́хис, землян́ой оре́х.

monkey wrench *n* разводно́й га́ечный ключ.

monocle *n* моно́кль (*m*).

monogamy *n* единобра́чие, монога́мия.

monograph *n* моногра́фия.

monopolize *vt Comm* монополизи́ровать (*impf and pf*); *fig* **he ~d the conversation** он не дава́л никому́ сло́ва сказа́ть.

monopoly *n* монопо́лия; **to have the ~ of smth** владе́ть монопо́лией на что-л.

monosyllable *n*: **he answered in ~s** он отвеча́л односло́жно (*adv*).

monotonous *adj* моното́нный, однообра́зный.

monotony *n*: **to break the ~** наруша́ть однообра́зие.

monsoon *n* (*wind*) муссо́н; (*season*) **the ~(s)** сезо́н дожде́й.

monster *n* уро́д; *fig* **he's a ~ of ingratitude** он неблагода́рное чудо́вище; *attr CQ*: **a ~ pumpkin** ты́ква чудо́вищных разме́ров.

monstrosity *n* уро́дство; *CQ* **that building is a ~** э́то не зда́ние, а уро́дство како́е-то.

monstrous *adj* чудо́вищный; **~ crimes** чудо́вищные преступле́ния; *CQ* **the electricity is off again—how ~!** свет опя́ть выключили—како́е безобра́зие!

month *n* ме́сяц; **I'm here for a ~** я здесь на ме́сяц; **it went on for ~s** э́то продолжа́лось месяца́ми; **she arrives next ~** она́ приезжа́ет в сле́дующем ме́сяце; **I'll be back in a ~'s time** я верну́сь че́рез ме́сяц; **once a ~** раз в ме́сяц; **by the ~** поме́сячно (*adv*); **every ~** ка́ждый ме́сяц, ежеме́сячно (*adv*).

monthly *adj* (*lasting a month*) ме́сячный; (*once a month*) ежеме́сячный; *as n*: **a ~** (*magazine*) ежеме́сячник.

monument *n* монуме́нт, па́мятник.

monumental *adj* монумента́льный; *CQ* **~ ignorance** порази́тельное/вопию́щее невежество; **the play was a ~ flop** пье́са с тре́ском провали́лась.

mooch *vi CQ*: **he ~es around** он слоня́ется без де́ла.

mood[1] *n* настрое́ние; **to be in a good/bad ~** быть в хоро́шем/плохо́м настрое́нии; **he's a man of ~s** он челове́к настрое́ния (*sing*); **he's in one of his ~s** он опя́ть не в настрое́нии; **he plays well when he's in the ~** он хорошо́ игра́ет, когда́ он в настрое́нии; **I'm feeling in a generous ~** я сего́дня благоду́шно настро́ен; **I'm in no laughing ~** мне не до сме́ха.

mood[2] *n Gram* наклоне́ние.

moody *adj*: **she's inclined to be ~** у неё ча́сто меня́ется настрое́ние; **he's ~ today** он сего́дня не в настрое́нии.

moon *n* луна́; (*new*) ме́сяц; **at the time of the full/new ~** в полнолу́ние, в новолу́ние; **there was no ~ that night** ночь была́ безлу́нная; *fig*: **there's no use crying for the ~** что то́лку жела́ть невозмо́жного; **once in a blue ~** раз в год по обеща́нию.

moon *vi*: **to ~ about/around** ходи́ть как неприка́янный (*only impf*).

moonbeam *n* луч луны́.

moonlight *n* лу́нный свет; **by ~** при лу́нном све́те, при луне́; *attr*: **a ~ night** лу́нная ночь.

moonlight *vi CQ*: **I want a car so I'm having to do a bit of ~ing** я хочу́ купи́ть маши́ну, поэ́тому прихо́дится подраба́тывать.

moonshine *n CQ* (*nonsense*) чепуха́, чушь; (*US*) (*liquor*) самого́н.

moonstone *n* лу́нный ка́мень.

moor[1] *n approx* ве́ресковая пу́стошь; **let's go for a walk on the ~(s)** дава́й погуля́ем по ве́реску.

moor[2] *vti* швартова́ть(ся) (при-); **his yacht is ~ed near by** его́ я́хта пришварто́вана неподалёку.

mooring *n* (*place*) стоя́нка; *pl* (*ropes, etc.*) шварто́вы.

moorland *n see* **moor**[1].

moose *n* америка́нский лось (*m*).

moot *adj*: **a ~ point** ещё не решённый вопро́с.

moot *vt*: **this question was first ~ed some years ago** э́тот вопро́с был впервы́е по́днят не́сколько лет наза́д.

mop *n* (*for floor*) шва́бра; **a ~ of hair** копна́ воло́с.

mop *vt*: **to ~ the floor** (*wash*) мыть/(*wipe*) про|тира́ть пол шва́брой (вы́-/-тере́ть); **he**

~**ped his brow** он вы́тер лоб; **she ~ped up the spilt milk** она́ вы́терла за́литый молоко́м пол; *Mil* **to ~ up an area** про|чёсывать райо́н (-чеса́ть).

mope *vi* хандри́ть (*impf*).

moped *n* мопе́д.

moral *n* **1** мора́ль; **a story with a ~** расска́з с мора́лью; **to draw a ~ from smth** извлека́ть мора́ль из чего́-л; **to point the ~** подчёркивать мора́ль

2 *pl* (~**s**) мора́ль, нра́вственность (*sings*); **he's got no ~s** у него́ нет никаки́х мора́льных усто́ев.

moral *adj* мора́льный, нра́вственный, эти́ческий; **a ~ victory** мора́льная побе́да; **a ~ man** высоконра́вственный челове́к; ~ **standards** эти́ческие но́рмы; ~ **philosophy** э́тика; **to give smb ~ support** ока́зывать кому́-л мора́льную подде́ржку; *CQ* **it's a ~ certainty** в э́том вы мо́жете быть уве́рены.

morale *n*: **to undermine ~** подрыва́ть мора́льный дух; ~ **is high in the army** в войска́х высо́кий боево́й дух.

moralist *n* морали́ст.

morality *n*: **standards of ~ have gone down** мора́льные усто́и расшата́лись; *attr Theat*: ~ **play** моралите́ (*indecl*).

moralize *vi* морализи́ровать (*impf*); (*preach*) поуча́ть (*impf*); **don't ~** не поуча́й; **to ~ on the failings of the young** критикова́ть нра́вы молодёжи.

morally *adv* мора́льно, нра́вственно; **I'm ~ certain of it** в э́том нет сомне́ния.

morass *n* трясина, топь; *fig* **he got bogged down in a ~ of detail** он завя́з в дета́лях.

moratorium *n* морато́рий.

morbid *adj Med* боле́зненный; *fig*: ~ **curiosity** нездоро́вое любопы́тство; **don't be so ~** не нагоня́й тоски́; **a ~ subject** мра́чная те́ма.

mordant *adj* язви́тельный, ко́лкий.

more *n and pron* бо́льше; **I've got ~ (than you)** у меня́ бо́льше (,чем у тебя́); ~ **(people) came** пришло́ бо́льше наро́ду; **there are 8 or ~ of them** их челове́к во́семь; **no ~ for me** я бо́льше не хочу́; **there's nothing ~ to say** бо́льше не́чего сказа́ть; **say no ~** бо́льше об э́том ни сло́ва; **it'll cost us ~ in the end** в коне́чном ито́ге э́то нам обойдётся доро́же; **I hope to see ~ of you** наде́юсь ча́ще вас ви́деть.

more *adj* бо́льше (*adv*) + *G*, ещё; **he has ~ money/experience than me** у него́ бо́льше де́нег/о́пыта, чем у меня́; **there's ~ sense in it than you'd think** в э́том бо́льше смы́сла, чем мо́жет показа́ться; **I have no ~ stamps** у меня́ бо́льше нет ма́рок; **9 is 3 ~ than 6** де́вять на три бо́льше шести́; **I've bought three ~ pairs** я купи́л ещё три па́ры; **I'm here for two ~ weeks** я здесь пробу́ду ещё две неде́ли; **some ~ tea?** ещё ча́ю?; **could you cut me a little ~ bread?** отре́жьте мне ещё немно́го хле́ба; **it was ~ than I could do to calm her** успоко́ить её бы́ло вы́ше мои́х сил; **no ~ noise** хва́тит шуме́ть; **and what's ~...** и к тому́ же..., бо́лее того́...

more *adv* **1** бо́льше; бо́лее; ещё; **I like this ~** э́то мне бо́льше нра́вится; **he studies much ~ than I do** он занима́ется гора́здо бо́льше, чем я; **he doesn't live here any ~** он здесь бо́льше не живёт; **he got ~ and ~ interested in it** он всё бо́льше и бо́льше э́тим интересова́лся; **the ~ I look at that painting the ~ I like it** чем бо́льше я смотрю́ на э́ту карти́ну, тем бо́льше она́ мне нра́вится; **he was ~ surprised than angry** он был бо́льше удивлён, чем рассе́ржен; **that's ~ than enough** э́то бо́лее чем доста́точно; **that makes me all the ~ ashamed** мне тем бо́лее сты́дно; ~ **or less** бо́лее и́ли ме́нее; **he's bright, but his brother is ~ so** он умён, а его́ брат ещё умне́е; **three days ~** ещё три дня; **once ~** ещё раз; **she is no ~ an actress than I am** она́ така́я же актри́са, как и я

2 *in comparatives of adjs and advs* бо́лее; ~ **significant/naturally** бо́лее значи́тельный/есте́ственно.

moreover *adv* кро́ме того́, бо́лее того́.

morning *n* у́тро; **in the ~s** по утра́м; **this ~** сего́дня у́тром; **early in the ~** ра́но у́тром; **tomorrow/on Wednesday ~** за́втра/в сре́ду у́тром; **at 3/at 4 in the ~** в три часа́ но́чи, в четы́ре часа́ утра́ [**NB** у́тро *used only of hours after* 3 *a.m.*]; **good ~!** до́брое у́тро!, с до́брым у́тром!; *CQ* **he's in a poor way—it's a case of the ~ after** его́ мути́т (*impers*)—должно́ быть, с похме́лья; *attr*: ~ **papers** у́тренние газе́ты.

morocco *n* (*leather*) сафья́н; *attr* сафья́новый.

moron *n* идио́т, крети́н.

morose *adj* мра́чный, угрю́мый.

morphia, morphine *n* мо́рфий.

Morse (code) *n* а́збука Мо́рзе, *CQ* морзя́нка; **in ~** морзя́нкой.

morsel *n* кусо́чек; **a tasty ~** ла́комый кусо́чек.

mortal *n* сме́ртный.

mortal *adj* сме́ртный; (*causing death*) смерте́льный; **a ~ enemy/fear/blow** смерте́льный враг/страх/уда́р.

mortality *n* сме́ртность; **infant ~** де́тская сме́ртность; *attr*: **a high ~ rate** высо́кий проце́нт сме́ртности.

mortar *n* цеме́нтный раство́р.

mortgage *n*: **we've got a ~ from the bank** мы получи́ли в ба́нке ссу́ду на поку́пку до́ма; **we've paid off our ~** мы вы́платили ссу́ду.

mortgage *vt* за|кла́дывать (-ложи́ть); **we had to ~ our house in order to pay our debts** что́бы вы́платить долги́, нам пришло́сь заложи́ть дом.

mortification *n* чу́вство стыда́; **to my ~** к моему́ стыду́.

mortify *vt*: **I was mortified by my son's behaviour/by his rudeness to me** мне бы́ло сты́дно за поведе́ние сы́на, его́ гру́бость бо́льно оби́дела меня́.

mortuary *n* морг.

mosaic *n* моза́ика.

Moslem *adj* мусульма́нский.

mosque *n* мече́ть.

mosquito *n* кома́р; (*tropical*) моски́т; *attr*: **~ bite** комари́ный уку́с.

moss *n* мох.

mossy *adj* мши́стый.

most *n and pron* бо́льшая часть; большинство́; **~ of the team are away** бо́льшая часть/большинство́ кома́нды отсу́тствует (*sing*); **~ of them have gone home** большинство́ из них разъе́халось/мно́гие разъе́хались по дома́м; **~ of the time** бо́льшая часть вре́мени; **that's the ~ I can do** э́то всё, что я могу́ сде́лать; **he's 20 at the ~** ему́ са́мое бо́льшее два́дцать лет; **make the ~ of the opportunity** максима́льно испо́льзуй э́ту возмо́жность; **the press made the ~ they could of the incident** в газе́тах разду́ли э́то собы́тие.

most *adj*: **in ~ cases** в большинстве́ слу́чаев; **for the ~ part** бо́льшей ча́стью; **who scored ~ goals?** кто заби́л бо́льшее коли́чество голо́в?

most *adv* 1 бо́льше всего́; **what pleased me ~ was his equanimity** что бо́льше всего́ мне понра́вилось—э́то его́ вы́держка; **~ probably** вероя́тнее всего́; **~ certainly I'll help** я обяза́тельно помогу́; (*intensively*) **this is ~ odd** э́то в вы́сшей сте́пени стра́нно

2 *in superlatives of adjs and advs* наибо́лее, са́мый; **the ~ interesting discovery** наибо́лее/са́мое интере́сное откры́тие; **the ~ successful method of all** наибо́лее уда́чный ме́тод; **the ~ important thing is to keep calm** са́мое ва́жное—сохраня́ть споко́йствие.

mostly *adv* бо́льшей ча́стью.

mote *n* пыли́нка.

motel *n* моте́ль (*m*).

moth *n* мотылёк; (*in clothes*) моль.

mothballs *npl* нафтали́новые ша́рики.

moth-eaten *adj* изъе́денный мо́лью.

mother *n* мать, ма́ма; **~'s help** ня́ня; *attr*: **~ tongue** родно́й язы́к.

mother-in-law *n* (*wife's mother*) тёща; (*husband's mother*) свекро́вь.

motherland *n* ро́дина.

motherless *adj*: **a ~ child** ребёнок, лишённый ма́тери.

motherly *adj* матери́нский.

mother-of-pearl *n* перламу́тр; *attr* перламу́тровый.

motif *n* моти́в.

motion *n* 1 (*movement*) движе́ние; (*of machine*) ход; **forward/backward ~** движе́ние вперёд/наза́д; **perpetual ~** ве́чное движе́ние; **in ~** в движе́нии, на ходу́; **by/with a ~ of the hand** движе́нием руки́; **the conveyor belt was set in ~** конве́йер был пу́щен в ход; *fig*: **this matter will be set in ~ at once** э́тому де́лу бу́дет сра́зу дан ход; **they don't really clean the office, they just go through the ~s of doing so** они́ не убира́ют как сле́дует в помеще́нии, а то́лько де́лают вид

2 (*proposal*) предложе́ние; **to bring forward a ~** вноси́ть/выдвига́ть предложе́ние; **the ~ was carried** предложе́ние бы́ло при́нято; **let's vote on the ~** дава́йте проголосу́ем за э́то предложе́ние

3 *Med* стул.

motion *vt*: **he ~ed me to a seat** он же́стом пригласи́л меня́ сесть; **he ~ed me to come nearer** он помани́л меня́ к себе́.

motionless *adj* неподви́жный.

motivate *vt* побу|жда́ть (-ди́ть); **what ~d her to do that?** что толкну́ло её на э́то?, что побуди́ло её сде́лать э́то?; **he's ~d by ambition** им дви́жет честолю́бие.

motivation *n* побужде́ние.

motive *n* моти́в; по́вод; побужде́ние; **ulterior ~** скры́тый моти́в; **the ~ for the crime** моти́в преступле́ния; **I was acting from the best ~s** я де́йствовал из лу́чших побужде́ний; *attr Tech*: **~ power** дви́жущая си́ла.

motley *adj* (*variegated*) разноцве́тный, пёстрый.

motor *n* (*engine*) мото́р; дви́гатель (*m*); **electric ~** электромото́р.

motor *vi*: **we ~ed out into the country** мы пое́хали на маши́не за́ город.

motorbike *n CQ see* **motorcycle.**

motorboat *n* мото́рная ло́дка, *CQ* мото́рка.

motorcade *n* автоколо́нна.

motor coach *n* (междугоро́дный) авто́бус.

motorcycle *n* мотоци́кл; *attr*: **a ~ race** мотоцикле́тные го́нки (*pl*), *abbr* мотого́нки (*pl*).

motorcyclist *n* мотоцикли́ст.

motoring school *n* автошко́ла.

motorist *n* автомобили́ст.

motorized *adj*: **~ transport** автотра́нспорт; *Mil* **a ~ division** моторизо́ванная диви́зия.

motor racing *n* автомоби́льные го́нки (*pl*), *abbr* автого́нки (*pl*).

motor rally *n* автомоби́льный пробе́г, *abbr* автопробе́г; мотора́лли (*indecl*).

motor scooter *n* моторо́ллер.

motorway *n* автостра́да.

mottled *adj*: **white ~ with red** бе́лый с кра́сными прожи́лками.

motto *n* деви́з.

mould[1], (*US*) **mold** *n* фо́рма; (*for metal*) лите́йная фо́рма; **jelly ~** фо́рмочка для желе́.

mould[1], (*US*) **mold** *vt* (*in clay, etc.*) лепи́ть (вы́-); *Tech* формова́ть (от-); *fig* формирова́ть (с-); **to ~ smth in/out of clay** лепи́ть что-л в гли́не/из гли́ны; **to ~ smb's character** формирова́ть чей-л хара́ктер.

mould[2], (*US*) **mold** *n* (*fungus*) пле́сень.

mould[3], (*US*) **mold** *n* (*soil*) перегно́й, гу́мус.

moulded, (*US*) **molded** *adj Tech* отли́тый в фо́рме, отформо́ванный; *Archit* **a ~ ceiling** лепно́й потоло́к.

moulder, (*US*) **molder** *vi* рассыпа́ться (в прах) (*only in impf*).

mouldy, (*US*) **moldy** *adj* (*covered with mould*) заплéсневелый; **a ~ smell** зáпах плéсени; **the jam was ~** варéнье покры́лось плéсенью; *CQ* **the food here was ~** здесь парши́во кóрмят.

moult, (*US*) **molt** *vi Orn* линя́ть (вы́-).

mound *n* (*hillock*) хóлмик; (*earthwork*) нá-сыпь; (*pile*) кýча.

mount[1] *n* горá; **M. Everest** горá Эверéст.

mount[2] *n* **1** (*horse*) лóшадь

2 (*of machine*) станúна; (*for gun*) лафéт; (*for picture, etc.*) подлóжка; паспартý (*indecl*); (*for jewel*) опрáва.

mount[2] *vti vt* **1** (*climb*): **to ~ a ladder/steps** взбирáться по лéстнице (взобрáться); (*get on*) **to ~ a horse/bicycle** садúться на лóшадь/на велосипéд (сесть)

2: to ~ a gun устан|áвливать орýдие на лафéт (-овúть); **to ~ photos** наклé|ивать фотогрáфию на картóн/паспартý (-ить); **to ~ a jewel** встав|ля́ть кáмень в опрáву (-ить)

3 (*lay on*): **to ~ an exhibition** устр|áивать вы́ставку (-óить); *Mil*: **to ~ an attack/offensive** под|нимáться в атáку (-ня́ться); **to ~ guard** стоя́ть на часáх (*impf*)

vi **1: they ~ed and rode off** онú вскочú-ли на лошадéй и ускакáли

2 *also* **to ~ up** (*increase*): **the bills are ~ing up** счетá накáпливаются.

mountain *n* горá; *attr* гóрный; **~ pass** гóрный перевáл; **~ rescue team** горноспа-сáтельная грýппа.

mountaineer *n* альпинúст.

mountaineering *n* альпинúзм; *attr*: **~ equipment** гóрное снаряжéние.

mountainous *adj* горúстый; *fig* **~ waves** огрóмные/вздымáющиеся вóлны.

mountainside *n* гóрный склон.

mountebank *n* шарлатáн.

mounted *adj* кóнный; **a ~ policeman** кóн-ный полицéйский.

mourn *vti*: **to ~ smb's death** оплáк|ивать чью-л смерть (-ать); **to ~ for smb** скор-бéть о ком-л.

mournful *adj* печáльный, скóрбный; заунь́ıв-ный.

mourning *n* трáур; **we are in ~ for our father** мы в трáуре по отцý; **to wear ~ for smb** носúть трáур по комý-л; *attr* трáур-ный.

mouse *n* мышь, *dim* мы́шка, мышóнок.

mousehole *n* мышúная норá.

mousetrap *n* мышелóвка.

moustache *n* усы́ (*pl*); **he's got a ~** у негó усы́; **who's the man with a ~?** кто э́тот усáтый мужчúна?

mousy *adj* (*timid*) рóбкий; (*of hair*) мы-шúного цвéта.

mouth *n* рот; (*in phrases and Poet*) устá (*pl*); (*of river*) ýстье; (*of cave, etc.*) вход; (*of bottle*) гóрлышко; **in/out of one's ~** во ртý, изо ртá; **by word of ~** ýстно; **it sounds strange in his ~** э́то стрáнно звучúт в егó устáх; **he's got five ~s to feed** у негó пять человéк на иждивéнии; **it made my ~ water** у меня́ от э́того слю́нки потеклú; *CQ* **keep your ~ shut!** заткнúсь!; *fig*: **to stop smb's ~** затыкáть комý-л рот; **he took the words out of my ~** он слóвно читáл моú мы́сли; **he's putting words into her ~** э́то он ей внушáет; **I'm feeling a bit down in the ~** я немнóго расстрóен.

mouthful *n*: **the invalid couldn't take more than a ~ of soup at a time** больнóй мог есть суп тóлько мáленькими глоткáми; **at one ~** однúм глоткóм; **just a ~ please** мне тóлько небольшóй кусóчек, пожáлуйста; *fig CQ* **his surname is a proper ~** у негó фамúлия — язы́к сломáешь.

mouth organ *n* губнáя гармóника/*CQ* гар-мóшка.

mouthpiece *n Tel* микрофóн; (*of pipe, wind instruments*) мундштýк; *fig* (*spokesman*) рýпор.

mouthwash *n* полоскáние для ртa.

movable *adj* подвижнóй, передвижнóй; *Law* **~ property** двúжимое имýщество.

move *n* **1** (*movement*) движéние; **the army is on the ~** áрмия на мáрше; **it's time we were making a ~** нам порá идтú; **he's always on the ~** он вéчно на колёсах; **get a ~ on!** шевелúсь!

2 *fig* шаг; **it's up to him to make the first ~** пéрвый шаг за ним; **he watches my every ~** он следúт за кáждым моúм шáгом; **they're at last getting a ~ on with the new hospital** наконéц-то онú приступúли к строú-тельству нóвой больнúцы

3 (*in game*) ход; **whose ~ is it?** чей ход?; **to make a ~** дéлать ход; *fig* **he knows all the ~s** он знáет все ходы́

4 (*of house*): **this is our third ~** мы трéтий раз переезжáем.

move *vti vt* **1** (*shift*) дви|гать (-нуть) *and compounds*; *also appropriate verbs with prefix* пере-; **to ~ furniture** (*by hand*) (пере)дви-гáть/(*by lorry*) пере|возúть мéбель (-везтú); **to ~ a chair from its place** сдвúнуть стул с мéста; **I was asked to ~ my car** меня́ попросúли немнóго отъéхать (*only a little*)/перестáвить машúну на другóе мéсто (*some distance away*); **he's been ~d to a new job** егó перевелú на другýю рабóту; **to ~ house** пере|езжáть на нóвую квартúру/в дру-гóй дом (-éхать); **don't ~ anything** ничегó не трóгай; **he ~d his troops south** он пе-ребрóсил своú войскá на юг; *fig* **he won't be ~d on this issue** егó не переубедúть в э́том вопрóсе

2 (*of parts of body*) шевел|úть + *I* (*pfs* пошевелúть *and* -ьнýть); **to ~ one's fingers/lips** шевелúть пáльцами/губáми

3 *fig* (*touch*) трó|гать (-нуть); волновáть (вз-); **I am deeply ~d** я глубокó трóнут; **the film ~d me to tears** фильм растрóгал меня́ до слёз; **he's easily ~d** егó легкó растрóгать; **he was visibly ~d by the news** он был замéтно взволнóван э́тим извéстием; **it ~d her to anger** э́то рассердúло её; (*stim-*

ulate) **what ~d you to change your mind?** что заставило вас изменить мнение?

4 (*propose*): **to ~ a resolution/that...** вносить резолюцию, пред|лагать, чтобы... (внести, -ложить)

vi **1** передвигаться, продвигаться; пере|-ходить (-йти); **the bus wasn't moving** автобус не двигался; **the army ~d 20 miles that day** в этот день армия продвинулась на двадцать миль; **she ~s well** у неё лёгкая походка; **he has ~d to Oxford/to a new job** он переехал в Оксфорд, он перешёл на новую работу

2 (*stir*) двигаться, шевелиться; **don't ~ from your place** не двигайся с места; **I couldn't ~ because of the heat** я не мог пошевелиться из-за жары

3 *fig uses*: **things are moving at last** наконец дело пошло [**NB** *tense*]; **they ~ in artistic circles** они вращаются в артистических кругах (*impf*); *Med* **have your bowels ~d today?** у вас был (сегодня) стул?

4 *Chess, etc.*: **your turn to ~** твой ход; **I can't ~** мне некуда ходить

move about/(a)round *vti*: **she ~d the furniture around** она переставила мебель; **the president ~d around among the guests** президент обходил своих гостей

move along *vti vt*: **the police ~d people along** полицейские расчистили проход

vi продвигаться; **~ along there please!** проходите!

move aside *vti* отодви|гать(ся) (-нуть(ся)); **she ~d aside to let us pass** она отошла, чтобы дать нам пройти

move away *vi*: **the troops ~d away yesterday** войска вчера отступили; **they ~d away from here long ago** они очень давно уехали отсюда

move back *vi*: **to ~ back a step** отойти на шаг; **they've ~d back to Moscow** они вернулись в Москву

move down *vt*: **he's been ~d down a form** его перевели в младший класс

move forward *vti vt*: **the meeting has been ~d forward to the 10th** собрание перенесено на десятое

vi двигаться вперёд

move in/into *vti vt*: **troops have been ~d in** были введены войска

vi: **we've ~d into our new flat** мы въехали в новую квартиру; **Sasha has ~d in with us** Саша переехал к нам

move off *vi* от|ходить (-ойти); (*by car*) отъ|езжать (-ехать); **the train/bus ~d off** поезд тронулся *or* отошёл, автобус ушёл

move out *vti vt*: **we are being ~d out of our flat** нас выселяют из квартиры

vi: **our neighbours have just ~d out** наши соседи недавно съехали с квартиры/выехали; **the factory is moving out to the suburbs** фабрику переводят на окраину (города)

move up *vt*: **she was ~d up to the next form** её перевели в следующий класс; **the general ~d his troops up to the town** генерал подтянул войска к городу.

movement *n* **1** (*motion*) движение; (*from place to place*) передвижение; (*of the body*) телодвижение; **they're keeping an eye on his ~s** они следят за ним; *Med* **bowel ~s** стул (*sing*)

2 *fig, Polit, Art* движение

3 *Tech* (*of clock, etc.*) механизм; *Mus* часть.

movie *n* (*US*) *CQ* (**a ~**) фильм; *pl* (**the ~s**) кино (*indecl*).

movie camera *n* (*US*) кинокамера, киноаппарат.

movie theatre *n* (*US*) кинотеатр.

moving *adj* **1** (*in motion*) движущийся; **a ~ target** движущаяся цель; **~ staircase** эскалатор; *fig* **he's the ~ spirit behind it all** он душа всего дела

2 (*touching*) трогательный, волнующий.

mow *vt* косить (с-); **to ~ the lawn** подстри|гать лужайку/газон (-чь); *fig* **machine-gun fire ~ed down the men** пулемётный огонь косил солдат.

mower *n* (*machine*: *for lawn*) косилка, (*for hay*) сенокосилка.

much *n* многое, много; **~ remains to be done** ещё многое нужно сделать; **~ of what he said is true** многое из того, что он сказал, справедливо; **why did you get so ~?** зачем вы накупили столько/так много?; **how ~ does it cost?** сколько это стоит?; **does it cost ~?** это дорого стоит?; **we don't see ~ of her** мы её редко видим; **I'll do as ~ as I can** я сделаю всё, что смогу; **this ~ is certain** уж это-то точно; **I'll tell you this ~** вот что я вам скажу; **suppose we put aside that ~ every week** предположим, что мы будем откладывать каждую неделю столько-то; **give me as ~ again** дай мне ещё столько же; **that's a bit ~** это уж слишком/чересчур; **I thought as ~** я так и думал; **I expected as ~** именно этого я и ожидал; **there's not ~ to this book** эта книга мало что даёт; **I'm not ~ of a one for reading** я не большой охотник до чтения; **don't make too ~ of this fact** не придавай этому особого значения; **it proved too ~ for him** это оказалось ему не по силам/не под силу; **it was as ~ as I could do not to laugh** я с трудом удержался от смеха; **she's not ~ to look at** она не особенно красива.

much *adj*: **there's not ~ time left** остаётся не много времени; **there's not ~ food in the house** у нас продукты кончаются; **I've got as ~ money as you** у меня столько же денег, сколько у тебя; **it's as ~ my fault as his** это не только его вина, но и моя тоже; **twice as ~ paper** вдвое больше бумаги; *CQ* **take it then and ~ good may it do you** ладно, забирай это, и чёрт с тобой.

much *adv* **1** (*very*) очень; **I'm ~ obliged to you** я вам очень обязан; **~ to my surprise** к моему большому удивлению

2 (*with comparatives*) намнóго; **he's ~ taller than me** он намнóго вы́ше меня́; **I would ~ rather leave** я бы, пожáлуй, ушёл

3 *phrases*: **I've not travelled ~** я мáло где бывáл; **~ as I would like to go** как бы мне ни хотéлось пойти́; **she wanted to slim so ~ that she gave up sugar** онá так хотéла похудéть, что дáже отказáлась от слáдкого; **they're ~ of an age** они́ примéрно одногó вóзраста; **do you agree?—Very ~ so** вы соглáсны?—И óчень дáже/Обéими рукáми за; **it's not so ~ a request as a suggestion** э́то не стóлько прóсьба, скóлько предложéние; **so ~ for your help** и э́то ты называ́ешь пóмощью; **he didn't even smile, ~ less speak** он не тóлько не улыбну́лся, но дáже и разговáривать не стал.

muchness *n*: **they are much of a ~** они́ почти́ одинáковы.

muck *n* (*dung*) навóз; (*dirt*) грязь, *also fig*; (*litter*) му́сор; *CQ*: **I've made a ~ of things** (*arrangements*) я всё перепу́тал; **he's sure to make a ~ of it** он обязáтельно всё напу́тает.

muck *vti vt*: **to ~ out a stable** чи́стить коню́шню (вы́-); *fig CQ*: **he's ~ed up everything** он всё испóртил; **he's ~ed up all my plans** он нару́шил все мои́ плáны

vi CQ: **he's always ~ing about with his motorbike** он вéчно вóзится со свои́м мотоци́клом; **we all ~ed in and finished the job** мы дру́жно взяли́сь за дéло, и скóро всё бы́ло закóнчено.

muckraking *n*: **I can't stand all this ~** не люблю́, когдá вынóсят сор из избы́.

mucky *adj* гря́зный; **my hands/trousers are all ~** у меня́ ру́ки гря́зные/брю́ки в грязи́.

mucous *adj* сли́зистый; *Anat* **~ membrane** сли́зистая оболóчка.

mud *n* грязь, *also fig*; (*slush*) сля́коть; (*on riverbed*) ил; **she was covered in ~** онá вся вы́мазалась в грязи́/перепáчкалась; **the wheels got stuck in the ~** колёса завя́зли в грязи́; *fig*: **to throw ~ at smb** обливáть когó-л гря́зью; **if people hear of this my name will be ~** éсли об э́том услы́шат, моéй репутáции конéц.

mudbath *n* грязевáя вáнна.

muddle *n* (*disorder*) беспоря́док; (*mix-up*) пу́таница, неразбери́ха; **all my papers are in a ~** все мои́ бумáги в беспоря́дке; **there's some ~ at the booking office over the tickets** у них (в кáссе) какáя-то пу́таница/жу́ткая неразбери́ха с билéтами; **things got into a ~** всё так запу́талось; **I was in a terrible ~** я совсéм запу́тался; **I've made a ~ about the date** я перепу́тал дáту.

muddle *vti vt* пу́тать (с-, пере-); **don't ~ up those papers** не перепу́тай э́ти бумáги; **I keep muddling him up with his brother** я вéчно пу́таю егó с брáтом

vi: **we'll ~ through somehow** ну, кáк-нибудь упрáвимся; **he just ~s along** он кóе-кáк справля́ется.

muddle-headed *adj* (*of people*) бестолкóвый.

muddy *adj* гря́зный; **~ boots** гря́зные боти́нки; **a ~ liquid** му́тная жи́дкость.

mudguard *n Aut* крылó.

mudpack *n* космети́ческая мáска.

muff *n* му́фта, *also Tech*.

muff *vt*: *Sport* **to ~ a ball/a catch** пропус|кáть мяч (-ти́ть); *Theat* **to ~ one's lines** пу́тать рéплики (с-).

muffle *vt* заку́т|ывать (-ать); **he was well ~d (up)** он был весь обмóтан шáрфом; **a ~d sound** приглушённый/заглушённый звук.

muffler *n* шарф, кашнé (*indecl*).

mug[1] *n* (*for drinking*) кру́жка.

mug[2] *n sl* (*face*) мóрда, рóжа; (*fool*) простáк, балбéс, дурачóк.

mug[3] *vt*: **she was ~ged yesterday** вчерá на неё напáли хулигáны.

mug[4] *vi*: *CQ* **he's ~ging (up) his history** он зубри́т истóрию.

muggy *adj*: **it's ~ today** сегóдня ду́шно.

mulberry *n* ту́товое дéрево, шелкови́ца; (*berry*) ту́товая я́года.

mule *n* мул; *fig* **as stubborn as a ~** упря́мый как осёл.

mull *vt*: **to ~ wine** дéлать глинтвéйн (с-)

mull over *vt*: **I keep ~ing over my problems** у меня́ в головé всё вéртятся нерешённые проблéмы.

multiple *n Math* крáтное (числó); **lowest common ~** óбщее наимéньшее крáтное.

multiple sclerosis *n Med* рассéянный склерóз.

multiplication *n Biol* размножéние; *Math* умножéние; *attr*: **~ tables** табли́цы умножéния.

multiply *vti vt Math* умнож|áть (-́ить); **to ~ two numbers** перемнóжить два числá; **3 multiplied by 4 is 12** три, умнóженное на четы́ре, равнó двенáдцати

vi Biol размнож|áться (-́иться).

multitude *n* мнóжество, мáсса; **a ~ of people** мнóжество нарóду.

mum[1] *n CQ* мáма, мáмочка.

mum[2] *adj*: **to keep ~ about smth** помáлкивать о чём-л; **~'s the word** об э́том ни гугу́.

mumble *vti* бормотáть (про-); **he was mumbling (something) to himself** он (чтó-то) пробормотáл про себя́; *CQ* **don't ~, speak up** не тяни́ рези́ну, говори́ пря́мо.

mumbo-jumbo *n* тарабáрщина.

mummy *n CQ* мáма, мáмочка.

mumps *n Med* сви́нка; **he's got ~** у негó сви́нка.

munch *vti* (*of ruminants and people*) жевáть (*impf*); (*if hard*) **he was ~ing a biscuit/apple** он грыз печéнье/я́блоко (*impf*).

mundane *adj* банáльный; прозаи́ческий.

municipal *adj* муниципáльный.

munitions *npl* боеприпáсы.

mural *n* стеннáя рóспись, фрéска.

murder *n* уби́йство; **to commit ~** соверши́ть уби́йство; *CQ* **she gets away with ~** ей всё с рук схóдит.

murder *vt* уби|ва́ть (-́ть), *also fig*; *CQ* **the producer simply ~ed the play** режиссёр про́сто изуро́довал пье́су.

murderer *n* уби́йца (*m and f*).

murky *adj*: **a ~ night** глуха́я тёмная ночь; **~ water** му́тная вода́; *fig* **it's a ~ business** э́то де́ло тёмное.

murmur *n*: **a ~ of voices/bees** приглушённый шум голосо́в, жужжа́ние пчёл; **the ~ of a brook** бормота́ние ручья́; **he agreed without a ~** он согласи́лся без зву́ка; *Med* **a heart ~** шу́мы (*pl*) в се́рдце.

murmur *vi* (*whisper*) шеп|та́ть (*semel* -ну́ть); (*mutter*) бормота́ть (про-); (*complain*) **to ~ at high taxation** жа́ловаться на высо́кие нало́ги.

muscle *n* му́скул, мы́шца; **he didn't move a ~** у него́ ни оди́н му́скул не дро́гнул.

Muscovite *n* москви́ч, *f* -ка.

muscular *adj* (*of muscles*) мы́шечный, му́скульный; (*hefty*) му́скулистый.

muse *vi*: **to ~ about/on/over smth** размышля́ть о чём-л (*impf*); заду́м|ываться о чём-л/над чем-л (-аться).

museum *n* музе́й; *attr*: **a ~ piece** музе́йный экспона́т, *fig* музе́йная ре́дкость.

mushroom *n* (*generic*) гриб; (*in UK*) *usu* шампиньо́н.

mushroom *vi*: **we often go ~ing** мы ча́сто хо́дим за гриба́ми.

mushy *adj* (*of food*) кашицеобра́зный; *CQ* (*sentimental*) слаща́во-сентимента́льный.

music *n* му́зыка; **sheet ~** но́ты (*pl*); **to read ~** чита́ть но́ты; **did she play with her ~ or without?** она́ игра́ла с но́тами или без нот?; **to dance to ~** танцева́ть под му́зыку; *fig* **you'll have to face the ~** ты бу́дешь за э́то отвеча́ть, тебе́ за э́то расплачиваться.

musical *n* (**a ~**) мю́зикл.

musical *adj* музыка́льный; **a ~ box** музыка́льная шкату́лка.

music hall *n* мю́зик-хо́лл.

musician *n* музыка́нт.

musicology *n* музыкове́дение.

music school *n* музыка́льное учи́лище.

music stand *n* но́тный пюпи́тр.

muskrat *n* онда́тра.

musquash *n* онда́тра; (*fur*) мех онда́тры.

must *n CQ*: **have you seen the Hermitage? It's a ~** вы бы́ли в Эрмита́же? Обяза́тельно сходи́те.

must *v modal aux* **1** (*of obligation, duty*) до́лжен (должна́, должно́, *pl* должны́) + *inf*; (*of necessity*) на́до, ну́жно; **we ~ help if we can** мы должны́ помо́чь, е́сли мо́жем; **you ~n't do that** ты не до́лжен/тебе́ нельзя́ э́того де́лать; **you simply ~ see this play** вы про́сто обя́заны/должны́ посмотре́ть э́ту пье́су; **I ~ say I was surprised** до́лжен сказа́ть, я был удивлён; **I ~ talk to you** мне на́до с ва́ми поговори́ть; **~ you go so soon?** неуже́ли вам на́до так ра́но уходи́ть?; **do it if you ~** де́лайте, е́сли ну́жно; **I ~ ask you to be quiet** я вы́нужден попроси́ть вас не шуме́ть; *iron* **what ~ I do then but lose the key** и на́до же мне бы́ло и́менно тогда́ потеря́ть ключ

2 (*of surmise*) должно́ быть; **he ~ be there by now** должно́ быть, он уже́ там; **it ~ have been yesterday** э́то бы́ло, должно́ быть, вчера́.

mustard *n* горчи́ца.

mustard plaster *n* горчи́чник.

mustard pot *n* горчи́чница.

muster *n* сбор; *fig* **it'll pass ~** э́то сойдёт.

muster *vti* со|бира́ть(ся) (-бра́ть(ся)); *fig* **to ~ (up) one's courage** собра́ть всё своё му́жество.

musty *adj* за́тхлый; **a ~ atmosphere** за́тхлая атмосфе́ра; **the room looks ~** у ко́мнаты запу́щенный вид; **these books smell ~** от э́тих книг па́хнет (*impers*) пле́сенью.

mute *n* (*person*) немо́й; *Mus* сурди́нка.

mute *adj* (*dumb*) немо́й; **to become ~** онеме́ть.

mutilate *vt* уве́чить (из-); *fig* **a ~d manuscript** ру́копись с больши́м коли́чеством про́пусков.

mutinous *adj* мятéжный, *also fig*; *fig* бунта́рский; **a ~ spirit** мяте́жный/бунта́рский дух.

mutiny *n* бунт, мяте́ж.

mutter *n* бормота́ние; **a ~ of disapproval** недово́льное бормота́ние.

mutter *vti* бормота́ть (про-); (*grumble*) ворча́ть (про-); **to ~ something to oneself** бормота́ть/ворча́ть что́-то себе́ по́д нос.

mutton *n* бара́нина; **a leg of ~** бара́нья нога́.

mutton chop *n* бара́нья отбивна́я; *attr fig CQ*: **~ whiskers** бакенба́рды, ба́чки.

mutual *adj* взаи́мный, обою́дный; о́бщий; **the feeling is ~** э́то взаи́мное чу́вство; **by ~ agreement** по обою́дному согла́сию; **a ~ understanding** взаимопонима́ние; **~ aid** взаимопо́мощь; **thanks to their ~ efforts** благодаря́ их о́бщим уси́лиям; **a ~ friend** наш о́бщий друг.

mutually *adv* взаи́мно, обою́дно; **a ~ beneficial agreement** взаимовы́годное соглаше́ние; **they are ~ dependent** они́ зави́сят друг от дру́га.

muzzle *n* (*snout*) мо́рда, ры́ло; (*of gun*) ду́ло; (*for dog*) намо́рдник.

muzzle *vt*: **to ~ a dog** наде|ва́ть соба́ке намо́рдник (-́ть); *fig* **to ~ smb** заста́вить кого́-л замолча́ть (*usu pf*).

my *poss adj* **1** мой, моя́, моё, *pl* мои́; **that's ~ pen** э́то моя́ ру́чка; **to ~ surprise** к моему́ удивле́нию; **in ~ opinion** по моему́ мне́нию, по-мо́ему [**NB** *stress*]

2 *when the possessor is the subject of the sentence use reflex poss adj* свой; **I've lost ~ key** я потеря́л свой ключ; *omit if ownership obvious*: **I phoned ~ brother** я позвони́л бра́ту; **she phoned ~ brother** она́ позвони́ла моему́ бра́ту

3 *referring to parts of body use* себе́, *or reflex verb*, *or omit translation*: **I cut ~ finger** я поре́зал (себе́) па́лец; **I've had ~ hair cut** я подстри́гся; **~ foot hurts** у меня́ боли́т нога́.

myopic *adj* миопи́ческий, близору́кий.

myrtle *n* мирт.

myself 1 *pron of emphasis* сам (сама́); **I saw her ~** я сам её ви́дел; **I made it all by ~** я всё э́то сде́лал сам; **I like to stroll by ~** я люблю́ броди́ть оди́н

2 *reflex pron* себя́, *etc.*, *or use reflex verb*; **I consider ~ to blame** я счита́ю себя́ винова́тым; **I wasn't thinking of ~** я не ду́мал о себе́; **I don't speak just for ~** я говорю́ не то́лько за себя́; **I am not feeling quite ~ today** мне сего́дня что́-то не по себе́; **I washed ~** я умы́лся; **I've hurt ~** я ушибся.

mysterious *adj* таи́нственный.

mystery *n* та́йна; **wrapped in ~** оку́танный та́йной; **there's no ~ about it** в э́том нет никако́й та́йны; **it's a ~ to me** э́то для меня́ остаётся зага́дкой; *attr*: **a ~ play** мисте́рия.

mystic(al) *adj* мисти́ческий.

mystify *vt* мистифици́ровать (*impf and pf*).

myth *n* миф.

mythical *adj* мифи́ческий.

N

nab *vt CQ* (*arrest*): **the police ~bed him** поли́ция схвати́ла его́.

nag[1] *n* (*horse*) *joc or pejor* кля́ча.

nag[2] *vti vt* (*of woman*) *CQ* пили́ть (*impf*); **she ~s him all day long** она́ пи́лит его́ с утра́ до́ ночи; **his conscience ~ged him** его́ му́чила со́весть

vi: **to ~ at smb** придира́ться к кому́-л; **don't ~!** хва́тит придира́ться!

nagger *n* приди́ра (*m and f*).

nagging *adj*: **a ~ pain** но́ющая боль; **~ anxiety** мучи́тельное беспоко́йство; **a ~ wife** *CQ* «пила́».

nail *n* **1** *Anat* но́готь (*m*); (*animal's*) ко́готь (*m*); **to bite one's ~s** грызть но́гти; **to cut/do one's ~s** стричь но́гти, де́лать маникю́р

2 (*of metal*) гвоздь (*m*); **to drive home a ~** заби́ть гвоздь по са́мую шля́пку; *fig*: **you've hit the ~ on the head** вы попа́ли в то́чку; **to pay on the ~** плати́ть нали́чными.

nail *vt* закол|а́чивать, заби|ва́ть (-оти́ть, -ть) *and other compounds*; **he ~ed down the lid/the lid on to the box** он заколоти́л/заби́л кры́шку (я́щика); **he ~ed a notice board on to the wall/a poster over the door** он приби́л вы́веску к стене́/плака́т над две́рью; **to ~ planks together** сколоти́ть все до́ски вме́сте; **they ~ed up all the windows** они́ заби́ли все о́кна; *fig*: **it's hard to ~ down the exact meaning of the expression** тру́дно переда́ть то́чный смысл э́того выраже́ния; **he ~ed me down in the corridor** он приста́л ко мне в коридо́ре; **I've managed to ~ him down to an appointment tomorrow** мне удало́сь назна́чить с ним встре́чу на за́втра.

nailbrush *n* щёточка для ногте́й.

nailfile *n* пи́лка для ногте́й.

nail polish *n* лак для ногте́й; *attr*: **~ remover** жи́дкость для сня́тия ла́ка.

nail scissors *n* маникю́рные но́жницы.

nail varnish *n see* **nail polish.**

naive *adj* наи́вный, простоду́шный.

naked *adj* го́лый, *also fig*; **a ~ body** го́лое те́ло; **to go about ~** ходи́ть нагишо́м (*adv*); **to strip ~** раздева́ться догола́/донага́ (*advs*); **he was ~ as the day he was born** *CQ* он был в чём мать родила́; *fig*: **a ~ light/bulb** ла́мпочка без абажу́ра; **a ~ wire** го́лый/оголённый про́вод; **a ~ blade** обнажённое ле́звие; **a ~ flame** откры́тое пла́мя; **it's visible to the ~ eye** э́то ви́дно невооружённым гла́зом; **the ~ truth** го́лая пра́вда.

nakedness *n* нагота́.

namby-pamby *adj CQ*: **a ~ child** ню́ня.

name *n* **1** (*of people, pets*): **Christian/first ~** и́мя; **family/second ~** фами́лия; **middle ~** второ́е и́мя, (*SU = patronymic*) о́тчество; **full ~** и́мя и фами́лия, (*SU*) фами́лия, и́мя, о́тчество; **what's your/the cat's ~?** как вас зову́т?, как зову́т ко́шку?; **my ~ is Peter** меня́ зову́т Пётр; **their ~ is Smith** их фами́лия—Смит; **maiden/married ~** де́вичья фами́лия, фами́лия му́жа; **a girl, Anna by ~** де́вушка по и́мени А́нна; **a family Ivanov/Smith by ~** семья́ Ивано́вых/Сми́тов; **I know him only by ~** я зна́ю его́ то́лько по и́мени; **he writes under another ~** он пи́шет под други́м и́менем/под друго́й фами́лией; **the account is in my ~** счёт на моё и́мя; **what ~ shall I say?** (*formal, announcing arrival*) как о вас доложи́ть?; *attr*: **~ day** имени́ны (*pl*); *Theat* **~ part** загла́вная роль

2 (*of things*) назва́ние; **the ~ of a book/river/plant** назва́ние кни́ги/реки́/расте́ния; **what's the ~ of this street?** как называ́ется э́та у́лица?; *Gram* **proper ~** и́мя со́бственное

3 (*reputation*) репута́ция, сла́ва, и́мя; **this hotel has a good ~** у э́той гости́ницы хоро́шая репута́ция; **to get oneself a bad ~** заслужи́ть дурну́ю сла́ву; **he's made a ~ for himself** он сам себе́ сде́лал и́мя; **he originally made his ~ as an actor** снача́ла он был изве́стен как актёр

4 *expressions*: **to speak in smb's ~** говори́ть от чьего́-л и́мени; **in the ~ of freedom** во и́мя свобо́ды; **in the ~ of the law** и́менем зако́на; **he's director only in ~** он лишь номина́льно дире́ктор; **he hasn't a penny to his ~** у него́ ни гроша́ за душо́й; **I put my ~ down as a volunteer** я записа́лся доброво́льцем; **to mention no ~s** не упомина́я имён.

name *vt* **1** (*give name to*) на|зыва́ть + *A and I* (-зва́ть); **the boy was ~d Oleg, they ~d the boy Oleg** ребёнка назва́ли Оле́гом;

a young man ~d Richard took me home какóй-то молодóй человéк, звáли егó Ри́чард, проводи́л меня́ домóй; **the square was ~d in honour of...** плóщадь былá нáзвана в честь + *G*

2 (*list by name*) перечисл|я́ть (поимённо) (-́ить); ~ **all the kings of England** перечи́слите всех англи́йских королéй

3 (*mention*) упом|инáть (-янýть); **he was ~d in the report** о нём упомянýли в доклáде; **the measures ~d above** вышеупомя́нутые мéры

4 (*appoint*) назнач|áть (-́ить); **to ~ a date for a meeting** назначáть день собрáния; ~ **your price** назови́те вáшу цéну.

nameless *adj*: **he wished to remain ~** он пожелáл остáться неизвéстным; **persons who shall remain ~** ли́ца, котóрых мы не бýдем называ́ть.

namely *adv* а и́менно; тó есть.

nameplate *n* (*on door*) табли́чка с фами́лией.

namesake *n* тёзка (*m and f*).

nanny *n* ня́ня, ня́нька.

nap[1] *n*: **he's having a ~** он задремáл [**NB** *tense*].

nap[1] *vi fig*: **to catch smb ~ping** застиг|áть когó-л врасплóх (-́нуть).

nap[2] *n* (*on fabric*) ворс, начёс.

nape *n*: **his hair was so long that it covered the ~ of his neck** вóлосы у негó бы́ли такúе дли́нные, что закрывáли шéю.

naphthalene *n* нафтали́н.

napkin *n* (*table*) салфéтка; (*baby's*) пелёнка.

nappy *n CQ* пелёнка.

narcissus *n Bot* нарци́сс.

narcotic *n* наркóтик; (*person*) наркомáн.

nark *n* (*UK*) *sl* донóсчик, стукáч.

nark *vt* (*UK*) *CQ*: **he was ~ed by the criticism** емý надоéли приди́рки.

narrate *vt* расскáз|ывать о + *P* (-áть); **to ~ one's adventures** расскáзывать о свои́х приключéниях.

narrative *n* (*spoken or written*) расскáз, (*usu written*) повествовáние.

narrator *n* расскáзчик.

narrow *adj* **1** ýзкий, *also fig*; **a ~ street/stripe** ýзкая ýлица/полосá; **this coat is too ~ for me** э́то пальтó мне ýзко; *fig*: **a ~ circle of acquaintances** ýзкий круг знакóмых; **in the ~ sense of the word** в ýзком смы́сле слóва; **a man of ~ views** человéк ýзкого кругозóра/ограни́ченных взгля́дов

2 (*with little margin*): **a ~ majority** незначи́тельное большинствó; **we had a ~ escape** мы едвá спасли́сь.

narrow *vti vt fig*: **the search has been ~ed down to this area** пóиски (*pl*) тепéрь сосредотóчены в э́том райóне

vi сýживаться (сýзиться); *fig* своди́ться (свести́сь); **where the river ~s** где рекá сýживается; *fig* **the argument ~s down to this** весь спор свóдится к э́тому.

narrow-gauge *adj Rail* узкоколéйный.

narrowly *adv*: **he regarded her ~** он при́стально посмотрéл на неё; **he ~ missed being killed** он едвá нé был уби́т.

narrow-minded *adj* ограни́ченный.

narrows *npl* (*of river*) ýзкая часть, (*of sea*) ýзкий проли́в (*sings*).

nasal *adj* носовóй, *also Ling*; (*of intonation*) гнусáвый; **to speak with a ~ twang** гнусáвить.

nastily *adv* (*maliciously*) злóбно, зло.

nasty *adj* проти́вный, (*stronger*) гáдкий, сквéрный; **a ~ smell/taste** проти́вный зáпах, неприя́тный при́вкус; **what ~ weather!** какáя мéрзкая/проти́вная погóда!; **I've got another ~ cold** у меня́ опя́ть э́тот проти́вный нáсморк; **he's got a ~ temper** у негó сквéрный харáктер; **that's a ~ trick!** э́то гáдкий постýпок; **it's a ~ business!** какáя гáдость!; **he kept making ~ remarks** он всё врéмя говори́л гáдости; **things are beginning to look ~ for him** дéло принимáет для негó сквéрный оборóт; **he gave her a ~ look** он зло на неё посмотрéл; **you were very ~ to her** ты ужáсно себя́ с ней вёл; *CQ* **he's a ~ piece of work!** он такóй омерзи́тельный тип!

nation *n* нарóд; нáция; **the American ~** америкáнский нарóд.

national *n*: **foreign ~s** инострáнные пóдданные.

national *adj* национáльный; (*of a state*) госудáрственный; ~ **dress/holiday** национáльный костю́м/прáздник; ~ **debt/anthem** госудáрственный долг/гимн; ~ **flag** национáльный/госудáрственный флаг; ~ **economy** нарóдное хозя́йство; **the ~ press** центрáльная прéсса; ~ **defence** оборóна страны́; (*UK*) ~ **service** вóинская пови́нность; (*SU*) ~ **radio and television** Всесою́зное рáдио и Центрáльное телеви́дение.

nationalist(ic) *adj* националисти́ческий.

nationality *n* **1** граждáнство, пóдданство; **dual ~** двойнóе граждáнство

2 (*SU*: *of ethnic groups*): **the nationalities of the North** нарóдности Сéвера.

nationalize *vt* национализи́ровать (*impf and pf*).

national park *n* заповéдник.

nation-wide *adj* всенарóдный, общенарóдный; (*SU only*) всесою́зный.

native *n* (*by birth, nationality*) урожéн|ец, *f* -ка; (*indigenous*) мéстный жи́тель; **a ~ of London** кореннóй лóндонец; **she speaks Spanish like a ~** испáнский язы́к для неё как роднóй; (*of plants, animals*) **the kangaroo/eucalyptus tree is a ~ of Australia** рóдина кенгурý/эвкали́пта — Австрáлия.

native *adj* **1** (*of one's birth*) роднóй; (*indigenous*) мéстный, кореннóй; ~ **land** рóдина; ~ **language** роднóй язы́к; **the ~ population** мéстное/кореннóе населéние; ~ **flora and fauna** мéстная флóра и фáуна

2 *fig* прирóдный, врождённый; ~ **wit** прирóдный ум; ~ **talent** врождённый талáнт.

nativity *n*: **the N.** рождествó (Христóво).

natter *vi CQ* трепа́ться (*usu impf*).

natural *n* **1** *Mus* бека́р; *also as indecl adj*: **C ~** до бека́р

2 *Med* крети́н

3 *CQ*: **he's a ~ for the part!** он как бу́дто со́здан для э́той ро́ли!

natural *adj* **1** есте́ственный, приро́дный; **a ~ harbour** есте́ственная га́вань; **to study animals in their ~ environment** изуча́ть живо́тных в есте́ственных/приро́дных усло́виях; **death from ~ causes** есте́ственная смерть; **I tried to sound ~** я пыта́лся говори́ть есте́ственным то́ном; **that doesn't sound ~ in Russian** э́то звучи́т не по-ру́сски; **it is ~ that...** есте́ственно, что...; **~ resources** приро́дные ресу́рсы; **~ wool** натура́льная шерсть; **a ~ phenomenon** явле́ние приро́ды; **it's a ~ mistake to make** э́то обы́чная оши́бка

2 (*inborn*): **he has a ~ gift for it** э́то у него́ врождённый дар; **he's a ~ orator** он прирождённый ора́тор

3: a ~ child/son внебра́чный ребёнок, побо́чный сын.

natural history *n* естествозна́ние.

naturalist *n* (*scientist*) естествоиспыта́тель (*m*); (*field or amateur*) натурали́ст.

naturalize *vt*: **to become ~d** (*of people*) получ|а́ть гражда́нство (-и́ть), (*of plants*) прижи|ва́ться (-́ться).

naturally *adv* **1** (*in a natural way*) есте́ственно; **to behave ~** вести́ себя́ есте́ственно; **French comes ~ to him** ему́ легко́ даётся францу́зский

2 (*by nature*): **he's ~ jealous** он от приро́ды ревни́в

3 (*understandably*) есте́ственно, коне́чно; **~ he didn't answer** есте́ственно,/коне́чно, он не отве́тил.

natural science *n* есте́ственные нау́ки (*pl*).

nature *n* **1** приро́да; нату́ра; **the laws of ~** зако́ны приро́ды; **a student of ~** иссле́дователь приро́ды; **to study the ~ of gases** иссле́довать приро́ду га́зов; **he is shy by ~** он ро́бок по нату́ре; **it's not in his ~ to deceive** обма́нывать проти́вно его́ приро́де; **it's all in the ~ of things** э́то в приро́де веще́й; **to draw from ~** рисова́ть с нату́ры; **boasting is second ~ with him** хвастовство́—его́ втора́я нату́ра; **to see lions in a state of ~** наблюда́ть львов в есте́ственном состоя́нии; **that's contrary to ~** э́то противоесте́ственно; *euph* **to answer a call of ~** отправля́ть есте́ственные на́добности (*pl*)

2 (*kind*) род; **coincidences of this ~** совпаде́ния тако́го ро́да; **something of that ~** что́-то в э́том ро́де.

nature study *n* природове́дение.

naughtiness *n* (*disobedience*) непослуша́ние; (*pranks*) озорство́, ша́лости (*pl*).

naughty *adj* **1: a ~ child** шалу́н; **you ~ boy!** ты проти́вный мальчи́шка!; **don't be ~** веди́ себя́ как сле́дует

2: a ~ story пика́нтная исто́рия.

nausea *n* тошнота́.

nauseate *vi fig* тошни́ть (*impf*; *impers*); **the very thought of it ~s me** меня́ тошни́т при/от одно́й то́лько мы́сли об э́том.

nauseating *adj usu fig* тошнотво́рный, отврати́тельный; **his hypocrisy is ~** меня́ тошни́т от его́ лицеме́рия.

nautical *adj* морско́й.

naval *adj* вое́нно-морско́й; **a ~ base** вое́нно-морска́я ба́за; **a ~ battle** морско́й бой; **a ~ power** морска́я держа́ва.

nave *n Archit* неф.

navel *n Anat* пупо́к, пуп.

navigable *adj* судохо́дный.

navigate *vti vt*: **to ~ a ship/plane** (*to plot course of*) про|кла́дывать курс корабля́/самолёта (-ложи́ть), (*steer, etc.*) вести́ кора́бль/самолёт по ку́рсу (*usu impf*)

vi Naut, Aer (*be at the controls*) управля́ть + *I* (*impf*).

navigating officer *n Naut, Aer* шту́рман.

navigation *n* навига́ция; **inland ~** речно́е судохо́дство; *attr* навигацио́нный.

navigator *n* шту́рман; навига́тор.

navvy *n* землеко́п.

navy *n* вое́нно-морско́й флот.

navy(-blue) *adj* тёмно-си́ний.

nazi *n* наци́ст.

NB (*abbr for* **nota bene**) нотабе́не (*indecl*).

near *adj* **1** (*in space, time*) бли́зкий; (*of time*) ско́ро (*adv*); **the station's quite ~** ста́нция совсе́м бли́зко; **holidays are ~** ско́ро кани́кулы; **in the very ~ future** в са́мом ближа́йшем бу́дущем; **what's the ~est way to the bank?** как бли́же всего́ пройти́ к ба́нку?; **on the ~ bank/side** на э́том берегу́, по э́ту сто́рону

2 (*close*) бли́зкий; **a ~ relation** бли́зкий ро́дственник; **one's ~est and dearest** родны́е и бли́зкие; **we worked the cost of the repairs out to the ~est pound** мы вы́числили сто́имость ремо́нта (*sing*) с то́чностью до одного́ фу́нта; **there was no accident but it was a ~ thing** ава́рия не произошла́, но мы едва́ её избежа́ли; **we won but it was a ~ thing** мы вы́играли, но с больши́м трудо́м; **his was a ~ guess** он почти́ угада́л; *fig* **he's ~ with his money** он прижи́мист, он скупова́т.

near *adv* бли́зко; **don't come too ~** не подходи́те сли́шком бли́зко; **a policeman was standing ~** побли́зости стоя́л полице́йский; **the holidays are/spring is getting ~** приближа́ются кани́кулы, бли́зится/ско́ро весна́; **the exams are ~ at hand** ско́ро экза́мены, экза́мены на носу́; **he's ~ on eighty** ему́ ско́ро во́семьдесят (лет); **bring it ~er** подви́нь э́то побли́же; **I searched far and ~ for him** я иска́л его́ всю́ду; **as ~ as I can recall** наско́лько я по́мню; **it's the same thing, or as ~ as makes no difference** э́то то́ же са́мое и́ли почти́ то́ же са́мое; **the theatre's nowhere ~ full** теа́тр далеко́ не по́лон.

near *prep* (*of place*) бли́зко от + *G*, недалеко́ от + *G*; во́зле + *G*, о́коло + *G*; у + *G*; (*place or time*) о́коло + *G*; к + *D*; **~ here**

недалеко́ отсю́да; **come ~er the fire** подойди́те побли́же к ками́ну; **she was ~ (to) despair** она́ была́ близка́ к отча́янию; **the ceremony is ~ its end** церемо́ния приближа́ется к концу́; **~ where he was sitting** недалеко́ от того́ ме́ста, где он сиде́л; **my office is ~ my home** моя́ рабо́та недалеко́ от до́ма; **my house is ~ the station** мой дом во́зле/о́коло ста́нции; **it must be ~ 3** уже́ должно́ быть о́коло трёх (часо́в); **~ the end of the book/the summer** к концу́ кни́ги/ле́та; **I want her to stay ~ me** хочу́, что́бы она́ была́ ря́дом; **she was ~ tears/to crying** она́ чуть не запла́кала; **that cause is very ~ his heart** э́то де́ло до́рого его́ се́рдцу.

near *vt* прибли|жа́ться к + *D* (-зиться); (*in time only*) бли́зиться к + *D* (*impf*); **the ship is ~ing the shore** кора́бль приближа́ется к бе́регу; **construction is ~ing completion** строи́тельство бли́зится к заверше́нию/к концу́; **he's ~ing 40** ему́ ско́ро сту́кнет со́рок.

nearby *adj*: **a ~ house** дом неподалёку (*adv*).

nearby *adv* недалеко́, неподалёку, побли́зости.

Near East *n* (**the ~**) Бли́жний Восто́к.

nearly *adv* **1** (*almost—with numbers, adjs, advs*) почти́; **~ 5 years/3 o'clock** почти́ пять лет/три часа́; **he goes round ~ naked** он хо́дит почти́ нагишо́м; **the theatre was ~ empty** теа́тр был почти́ пусты́м; **she's ~ 90** ей почти́/ско́ро девяно́сто (лет); **it's ~ lunchtime** ско́ро обе́д

2 (*almost—with verbs*) чуть не; **he ~ drowned** он чуть не утону́л

3: not ~ отню́дь не, далеко́ не; **that's not ~ enough!** э́того отню́дь не доста́точно; **he's not ~ as stupid as he looks** он далеко́ не так глуп, как ка́жется

4 (*closely*): **they are ~ related** они́ в бли́зком родстве́; **the two questions are ~ related** э́ти два вопро́са те́сно свя́заны (ме́жду собо́й); **it concerns me ~** э́то каса́ется меня́ непосре́дственно.

near-sighted *adj* близору́кий.

neat *adj* **1** (*of work, appearance*) аккура́тный; (*of appearance*) опря́тный; **his desk is always ~** его́ стол всегда́ в чистоте́ и поря́дке; **she's ~ in her dress** она́ о́чень аккура́тна/опря́тна; **he's ~ in his work** он аккура́тен в рабо́те; **~ handwriting** аккура́тный по́черк; **she's got a ~ figure** у неё стро́йная/ла́дная фигу́рка

2 (*clever*): **a ~ answer/turn of phrase** хи́трый отве́т, уда́чное выраже́ние

3 (*undiluted*) неразба́вленный; **he drinks whisky ~** он пьёт ви́ски, не разбавля́я.

necessary *n* всё необходи́мое; **I'll do the ~** я сде́лаю всё необходи́мое/, что ну́жно.

necessary *adj* необходи́мый; **the ~ formalities** необходи́мые форма́льности; **I'll come back if ~** я верну́сь, е́сли бу́дет необходи́мо/на́до; **it's not ~ for you to come** вам нет необходи́мости приходи́ть; **this made it ~ for us to move (house)** из-за э́того нам пришло́сь перее́хать; **was it ~ for you to be so rude to her?** и заче́м ты нагруби́л ей?; **he does no more than is ~** он де́лает от сих до сих; **a ~ evil** неизбе́жное зло.

necessitate *vt*: **it ~d my immediate return** из-за э́того мне пришло́сь сра́зу же верну́ться.

necessity *n* необходи́мость; **of ~** по необходи́мости; **in case of ~** в слу́чае необходи́мости; **a fridge is a ~ nowadays** в на́ши дни холоди́льник—необходи́мая вещь; **he's under the ~ of appearing in court tomorrow** он обя́зан за́втра яви́ться в суд.

neck *n* **1** *Anat* ше́я; (*of bottle*) го́рлышко; (*of violin*) ше́йка; **to break one's ~** сломать себе́ ше́ю; **she fell on his ~** она́ бро́силась ему́ на ше́ю; *Geog* **a ~ of land** перешеек; *Sport* **the two horses are ~ and ~** две ло́шади иду́т голова́ в го́лову; **to win/lose by a ~** вы́играть/отста́ть на го́лову

2 *fig uses*: **to risk one's ~** рискова́ть свое́й голово́й; *CQ*: **throw him out ~ and crop** гони́те его́ в ше́ю; **I'll wring his ~ for him** я ше́ю ему́ сверну́; **he got it in the ~** он получи́л по ше́е; **he's always ready to stick his ~ out** он всегда́ гото́в пойти́ на риск; **he's a pain in the ~** он как чи́рей на ше́е; **I'm up to my ~ in work** я за́нят по го́рло; **he's in it up to his ~** он завя́з по́ уши в э́том де́ле; **he's got some ~** он про́сто наха́л; **it's ~ or nothing** пан и́ли пропа́л.

necklace *n* ожере́лье (*usu valuable*); (*beads*) бу́сы (*pl*).

neckline *n*: **a dress with a low ~** пла́тье с глубо́ким вы́резом.

necktie *n* га́лстук.

née *adj*: **Anna Smith, ~ Green** А́нна Смит, урождённая Грин.

need *n* **1** (*necessity*) необходи́мость; (*often translated by verbs or predic adjs*); **in case of ~** в слу́чае необходи́мости; **she's in ~ of rest** ей необходи́м о́тдых; **if ~ be** е́сли потре́буется; **the house is badly in ~ of repair** дом на́до сро́чно ремонти́ровать; **I'm in no ~ of his help!** я не нужда́юсь в его́ по́мощи!; **there's no ~ to do that** э́того не на́до/не ну́жно де́лать; **what ~ is there to worry him?** заче́м его́ беспоко́ить?

2 (*requirement*) потре́бность; **my ~s are few** мои́ потре́бности о́чень невелики́; **the ~ to be loved** потре́бность в любви́; **there's a ~ for more hospitals** необходи́мы но́вые больни́цы

3 (*trouble*) беда́; (*want*) нужда́; **he's a good friend in times of ~** он всегда́ помо́жет в тру́дную мину́ту; **to be in ~** нужда́ться.

need *vt* **1** (*with nouns*) нужда́ться в + *P* (*impf*); *impers* ну́жно, на́до; **he ~s support** он нужда́ется в подде́ржке; **it is just what I ~** э́то и́менно то, что мне ну́жно; **the door ~s a coat of paint** ну́жно покра́сить дверь; **a permit is ~ed for this** на э́то ну́жно разреше́ние; **she ~s money** ей нужны́ де́ньги; **he ~ed no second invitation** его́ не на́до бы́ло упра́шивать; **everything that ~ed doing** всё, что на́до бы́ло сде́лать; **the letter ~s no reply** письмо́ не тре́бует отве́та; **I only ~ one more volume to complete the set** у меня́ не хвата́ет одного́ то́ма до по́лного компле́кта

2 (*with inf*) ну́жно, на́до; **you only ~ to ask** вам ну́жно то́лько спроси́ть; **I didn't ~ to be told twice** мне не на́до бы́ло повторя́ть два́жды; **he ~n't be told** заче́м ему́ об э́том говори́ть?

3 *modal verb in questions, neg sentences, etc.*: **nobody ~ ever know** никому́ об э́том не ну́жно знать; **I ~ hardly add that...** вряд ли на́до добавля́ть, что...; **you ~n't worry** вам не́чего беспоко́иться

4 *impers use*: **it ~ed her to do it** то́лько она́ смогла́ бы э́то сде́лать; **it would ~ a miracle to convince him** то́лько чу́до смо́жет убеди́ть его́.

needle *n* иго́лка, игла́; **the ~ of the compass** стре́лка ко́мпаса; **pine ~s** хво́я (*collect*); *fig* **to look for a ~ in a haystack** иска́ть иго́лку в сто́ге се́на; *attr*: **~ case** иго́льник.

needle *vt CQ*: **he kept needling me all evening** он весь ве́чер стара́лся подде́ть меня́.

needless *adj* нену́жный; **~ to say, he was late** разуме́ется, он опозда́л.

needlessly *adv*: **you worry ~** ты волну́ешься по́пусту.

needlewoman *n* швея́, рукоде́льница.

needlework *n* вы́шивка.

needs *adv only in expression* **~ must: if ~ must** е́сли необходи́мо; **if there are no taxis we ~ must walk** поско́льку нет такси́, (нам) придётся идти́ пешко́м.

needy *adj* нужда́ющийся.

negation *n* отрица́ние.

negative *n* отрица́ние, *also Gram*; *Photo* негати́в; *Math, Elec* ми́нус; **he answered in the ~** он отве́тил отрица́тельно; **2 ~s make a positive** ми́нус на ми́нус даёт плюс.

negative *adj* отрица́тельный; *Photo, fig* негати́вный; **a ~ quantity** отрица́тельная величина́; **~ views** негати́вные взгля́ды.

neglect *n* (*carelessness*) пренебреже́ние; **~ of safety regulations** несоблюде́ние пра́вил те́хники безопа́сности; **parental ~** отсу́тствие роди́тельского внима́ния; **the house/garden is in a state of ~** дом/сад в запу́щенном состоя́нии.

neglect *vt* пренебре|га́ть + *I* (-́чь); (*let go*) запус|ка́ть (-ти́ть); **to ~ duties/friends/opportunities** пренебрега́ть обя́занностями/друзья́ми/возмо́жностями; **they ~ed their garden** они́ запусти́ли свой сад; **don't ~ a cold** не запуска́й на́сморк; **she ~s her appearance** она́ совсе́м не следи́т за свое́й вне́шностью; **she ~s herself** (*eats irregularly, etc.*)/**the children** она́ не забо́тится о своём здоро́вье/о свои́х де́тях; **historians have ~ed these facts** исто́рики не при́няли э́ти фа́кты во внима́ние; **I ~ed to check the tyres** я не прове́рил ши́ны.

neglected *adj* (*of house, garden, etc.*) забро́шенный, запу́щенный; **a ~ child** запу́щенный ребёнок; **he looked ~** у него́ был неря́шливый вид; **she felt ~** она́ чу́вствовала себя́ поки́нутой всеми.

neglectful *adj*: **he is ~ of his appearance/duties** он не забо́тится о свое́й вне́шности, он хала́тно отно́сится к свои́м обя́занностям.

negligence *n* (*act*) небре́жность; (*attitude*) хала́тность; **the accident was caused by ~ on the part of the driver** ава́рия произошла́ по/из-за небре́жности води́теля; **the fire was due to the ~ of the watchman** причи́ной пожа́ра послужи́ла хала́тность сто́рожа.

negligent *adj* (*in action*) небре́жный; (*in attitude*) хала́тный; **he was ~ in his work** он хала́тно отно́сится к рабо́те.

negligible *adj* ничто́жный, незначи́тельный; **a ~ quantity** ничто́жное/незначи́тельное коли́чество; **he's by no means a ~ opponent** он проти́вник, с кото́рым прихо́дится счита́ться.

negotiable *adj*: **these points are ~** э́ти пу́нкты мо́жно обсуди́ть; **this track is not ~ for motor vehicles** здесь не прое́хать колёсному тра́нспорту; *Comm* **a ~ cheque** чек с пра́вом переда́чи.

negotiate *vti vt* **1** вести́ перегово́ры, обсужда́ть (*only in impfs*); догов|а́риваться о + *P* (-ори́ться); **they are negotiating/have ~d a peace** они́ веду́т ми́рные перегово́ры, они́ заключи́ли ми́рный догово́р; **to ~ terms/a loan** прийти́ к соглаше́нию об усло́виях/о за́йме

2: **to ~ a bridge** перепра|вля́ться че́рез мост (-́иться); **he ~d the corner at full speed** он поверну́л за́ угол на по́лной ско́рости; **to ~ obstacles** преодоле|ва́ть препя́тствия (-́ть)

vi: **they are negotiating now** сейча́с они́ веду́т перегово́ры.

negotiation *n usu pl* перегово́ры (*pl*); **to enter into ~s with smb** вступи́ть в перегово́ры с кем-л; **the matter is under ~** по э́тому вопро́су веду́тся перегово́ры.

Negro *n* негр, негритя́нка.

Negro *adj* негритя́нский.

neigh *vi* ржать (*impf*).

neighbour, (*US*) neighbor *n* сосе́д, *f* -ка; **our next-door ~s** на́ши ближа́йшие сосе́ди; **he and I were ~s for years** мы с ним мно́го лет жи́ли по сосе́дству; **to love one's ~** люби́ть бли́жнего своего́; **we were ~s at dinner** мы сиде́ли за столо́м ря́дом.

neighbourhood, (*US*) neighborhood *n* (*area*) окру́га, райо́н; **there's no one of that name in this ~** у нас в окру́ге нет никого́ с тако́й фами́лией; **in the ~ of the crime** в райо́не, где совершено́ преступле́ние; *fig* **it costs something in the ~ of £1,000** э́то сто́ит что́-то о́коло ты́сячи фу́нтов.

neighbouring, (*US*) neighboring *adj* сосе́дний.

neighbourly, (*US*) neighborly *adj* добрососе́дский.

neither *pron* никако́й, ни оди́н; **which book do you want?—N.** каку́ю кни́гу вы хоти́те взять?—Никаку́ю; **~ of them knows** ни оди́н из них не зна́ет.

neither *adj*: ~ **question is very important** ни тот, ни другой вопрос большого значения не имеют [**NB** *pl verb*]; **in** ~ **case** ни в том, ни в другом случае.

neither *conj*: **if you don't go,** ~ **will I** если ты не пойдёшь, не пойду и я; **I don't like it.—N. do I** это мне не нравится.—Мне тоже (не нравится); ~ **am I prepared to forget it** и уж конечно я этого не забуду.

neither... nor *adv and conj*: ~ **he nor I went** ни он, ни я не пошли [**NB** *pl verb*]; **he can** ~ **sing nor play the piano** он не умеет ни петь, ни играть на пианино; **I** ~ **know nor care** (я) не знаю и знать не хочу; **that's** ~ **here nor there** это ни к селу ни к городу; **it's** ~ **one thing nor the other** это ни то ни сё.

nemesis *n* возмездие.

neon *adj* неоновый; ~ **light/sign** неоновая лампа/реклама.

nephew *n* племянник.

nerve *n* **1** *Anat* нерв; *fig* **to strain every** ~ **to do smth** напрягать все силы (*pl*), чтобы сделать что-л; *attr* нервный

2 *pl* (~**s**) *fig* нервы; **a fit of** ~**s** нервный припадок; **to be in a state of** ~**s** нервничать; **my** ~**s are all on edge** нервы у меня напряжены до предела; **he's a bundle of** ~**s** он комок нервов; **it/he gets on my** ~**s** это/он действует мне на нервы; **she lives on her** ~**s** она живёт/держится на нервах; **he seems to have no** ~**s** он такой невозмутимый, *CQ* он как истукан

3 *fig* (*courage*): **I hadn't the** ~ **to do it** у меня на это мужества не хватило; **that took some** ~ нужна большая выдержка, чтобы сделать это; **he must have** ~**s of steel** у него, наверное, стальные нервы; **he lost his** ~ у него нервы сдали

4 *fig CQ* (*cheek*) нахальство, наглость; **of all the** ~**!, what a** ~**!, the** ~ **of it!** какое нахальство!; **you've got some/a** ~**!** ну и нахал же вы!; **he had the** ~ **to suggest I pay** у него хватило наглости предложить, чтобы я заплатил.

nerve *vt*: **I** ~**d myself to tell him the truth** я собрался с духом и сказал ему правду.

nerve-racking *adj*: **I found the suspense** ~ эта неопределённость сильно действовала мне на нервы; **I find rush-hour travel quite** ~ для меня езда в часы пик—страшная нервотрёпка (*CQ*).

nervous *adj* **1** нервный; **a** ~ **breakdown** нервный срыв, нервное расстройство

2 (*easily upset, etc.*): **to be** ~ нервничать (*impf*); **to get** ~ разнервничаться; **I feel** ~ **about the exam** я нервничаю перед экзаменом; **that makes me** ~ это действует мне на нервы.

nervousness *n* нервность, нервозность.

nervy *adj CQ* нервный.

nest *n* гнездо; **bird's/wasp's** ~ птичье/осиное гнездо; **to build a** ~ вить гнездо.

nestle *vi*: **to** ~ **against/up to smb** прильнуть к кому-л (*only in pf*), при|жиматься к кому-л (-жаться); **she** ~**d down in a chair** она уютно устроилась в кресле; *fig* **the village** ~**d among the hills** деревенька ютилась среди холмов.

net[1] *n* сеть; сетка; **fishing** ~ рыболовная сеть; **tennis/mosquito** ~ теннисная/москитная сетка.

net[2] *adj Comm* чистый; нетто (*indecl*); ~ **weight** чистый вес, вес нетто; ~ **cost/profit** чистая стоимость/прибыль; **my** ~ **salary** моя зарплата за вычетом всех налогов; **I received £5** ~ на руки мне дали пять фунтов; *fig* **the** ~ **result of it all was that...** конечным результатом всего было то, что...

net[2] *vt Comm*: **he** ~**s 10 thousand a year** он получает в год десять тысяч чистого дохода.

netball *n* нетбол.

netting *n* сеть, сетка; (*fabric*) сетчатый материал; **wire** ~ проволочная сетка.

nettle *n* крапива (*also collect*); *attr*: **he's suffering from** ~ **stings** он обжёгся крапивой.

nettle *vt* раздражать (*usu impf*), сердить (рас-).

nettlerash *n* крапивница.

network *n Tech, Rail, etc.* сеть; **TV** ~ телевизионная сеть; **a** ~ **of roads/spies** дорожная/шпионская сеть.

neuralgia *n* невралгия.

neuritis *n Med* неврит.

neurologist *n* невропатолог.

neurosis *n* невроз.

neurotic *adj Med* невротический; *CQ* нервный.

neuter *adj Gram*: **a** ~ **noun** существительное среднего рода.

neutral *n Aut* нейтральная передача/скорость; **to leave a car in** ~ оставить машину на нейтральной (*CQ*).

neutral *adj* нейтральный, *also Elec, Aut, Chem*; ~ **zone** нейтральная зона; **a** ~ **colour/wire** нейтральный цвет/провод; **they were quarrelling but I remained** ~ они спорили, а я в их споре не принимал участия.

neutrality *n* нейтральность; *Polit* нейтралитет.

neutralize *vt* нейтрализовать (*impf and pf*), *also fig*.

never *adv* **1** никогда; ~ **in all my life** никогда в жизни; **you** ~ **can tell** никогда не знаешь; **I've** ~ **heard that before** первый раз это слышу; **we** ~ **saw him again** мы его больше не видели; ~ **mind** ничего, неважно

2 *as emphatic negative*: ~**!, you** ~ **did!** неужели?; **well I** ~**!** ну и ну!, вот те на!; ~ **a one** ни один; **surely you** ~ **told him about that!** ты не мог ему этого сказать!; **you told him?—I** ~ **did!** это ты ему сказал?—Нет, не я.

never-ending *adj* нескончаемый.

nevermore *adv* никогда больше.

never-never *n CQ*: **to buy smth on the** ~ покупать что-л в рассрочку.

nevertheless *adv and conj* тем не менее, всё же; **we must** ~ **remember that...** и тем не ме́нее нельзя́ забыва́ть, что...; **he came ~** он тем не ме́нее/он всё же пришёл.

never-to-be-forgotten *adj* незабве́нный, незабыва́емый.

new *adj* но́вый; **~ and used furniture** но́вая и поде́ржанная ме́бель; **I'm ~ in these parts** я здесь челове́к но́вый; **in a ~ way** по-но́вому; **he's a ~ boy around here** он у нас но́венький; **a brand ~ car** но́венькая маши́на; **she is still very ~** (*inexperienced*) она́ ещё новичо́к; **~ bread** све́жий хлеб; **~ potatoes** молода́я карто́шка (*collect*); **the ~ moon** молодо́й ме́сяц; **he's become a ~ man** он стал други́м челове́ком; **there's nothing ~ under the sun** ничто́ не но́во под луно́й; *as n*: **the old and the ~** ста́рое и но́вое; *CQ* **what's ~ with you?** что у тебя́ но́вого?

newborn *adj* новорождённый.

newcomer *n* прие́зжий, новоприбы́вший.

new-fangled *adj pejor* новомо́дный.

new-laid *adj*: **a ~ egg** то́лько что снесённое яйцо́.

newly *adv* неда́вно; **they are ~ arrived here** они́ неда́вно сюда́ прие́хали; **the door is ~ painted** дверь то́лько что покра́сили.

newly-weds *npl* новобра́чные, молодожёны.

news *n* но́вость, изве́стие, весть, *all also used in pl*; **good ~** прия́тная но́вость; **no ~ is good ~** отсу́тствие новосте́й—хоро́шая но́вость; **what's your ~?** каки́е у вас но́вости?; **that's ~ to me** э́то для меня́ но́вость; **I've got (a piece of) ~ for you!** у меня́ есть для вас но́вость; **tell me all your ~** расскажи́ мне, что у вас но́венького; **I haven't had ~ of them for ages** я це́лую ве́чность не получа́л от них весте́й; **foreign ~** зарубе́жные но́вости (*pl*); **he's in the ~ again** о нём опя́ть пи́шут в газе́тах; **to break the ~ to smb** сообща́ть кому́-л тяжёлую весть; *Radio* **the ~ follows at 9 o'clock** в де́вять часо́в после́дние изве́стия.

newsagent *n* продаве́ц газе́т.

news editor *n* реда́ктор отде́ла новосте́й.

news flash *n Radio* э́кстренное сообще́ние.

news media *npl* сре́дства информа́ции.

newspaper *n* газе́та; *attr* газе́тный.

newsprint *n* газе́тная бума́га.

newsreel *n* киножурна́л, кинохро́ника.

news stand *n* газе́тный кио́ск.

newsy *adj CQ*: **I got a ~ letter from him** он мне сообщи́л ку́чу новосте́й в письме́.

newt *n Zool* трито́н.

New Testament *n* Но́вый заве́т.

New Year *n* Но́вый год; **Happy ~!** с Но́вым го́дом!; **~'s Eve** кану́н Но́вого го́да; **to see the ~ in** встреча́ть Но́вый год; *attr* новогодний.

New Zealander *n* новозела́ндец, новозела́ндка.

next *adj* **1** (*in order*) сле́дующий; **I'm getting out at the ~ stop** я схожу́ на сле́дующей (остано́вке); **to be continued in our ~ issue** «продолже́ние в сле́дующем но́мере»; **when does the ~ train for Leningrad leave?** когда́ сле́дующий по́езд на Ленингра́д?; **the ~ to come was Anne** сле́дующей пришла́ А́нна; **the ~ turning to the right** пе́рвый поворо́т напра́во; **on the ~ page but one** че́рез одну́ страни́цу; **I'm ~ after this lady** я (стою́) за э́той да́мой; **in the ~ life** на том све́те; **he knows that as well as the ~ man** он э́то зна́ет не ху́же вся́кого друго́го

2 (*in time*) сле́дующий; **until the ~ time** до сле́дующего ра́за; **the ~ time you see him** когда́ вы его́ в сле́дующий раз уви́дите; **(on) the ~ day** на друго́й/на сле́дующий день; **he came back the ~ year** на сле́дующий год он верну́лся; **on Monday ~** в сле́дующий понеде́льник; **~ morning** на друго́е/на сле́дующее у́тро; **we'll be here for the ~ four days** мы здесь пробу́дем ещё четы́ре дня; **the ~ day but one** че́рез день; **by this time ~ year** к э́тому вре́мени на бу́дущий год; **plans for ~ year** пла́ны на бу́дущий год

3 (*neighbouring*) сосе́дний; **in the ~ room/village** в сосе́дней ко́мнате/дере́вне; **they live in the ~ house but one from ours** они́ живу́т че́рез дом от нас.

next *adv* **1** (*in time and place*: *after*) пото́м, зате́м, по́сле того́; **~, add the water** пото́м доба́вьте во́ду; **~ he went to the cupboard** зате́м он подошёл к шка́фу; **what will we do ~?** что нам пото́м/по́сле э́того де́лать?

2 (*in time*: *again*) сно́ва; **when will you see him ~?** когда́ вы сно́ва с ним уви́дитесь?; **until we ~ meet** до сле́дующей встре́чи

3 *with superlative adj*: **the ~ most important fact** сле́дующий по ва́жности факт; **the ~ largest city** второ́й по величине́ го́род; **the ~ smallest size** на разме́р ме́ньше; **the ~ best thing would be to go straight to the dacha** а есть ещё вариа́нт—пое́хать пря́мо на да́чу

4: **what ~!, whatever ~!** ещё чего́!; **what will he say ~?** что он ещё ска́жет?

next *prep* **1** ря́дом с + *I*; у + *G*; **I was sitting ~ to him** я сиде́л ря́дом с ним; **his room is ~ to mine** его́ ко́мната ря́дом с мое́й; **the shop ~ to our house** магази́н ря́дом с на́шим до́мом; **an armchair ~ to the fire** кре́сло у ками́на; **to wear wool ~ to the skin** носи́ть шерсть на го́лое те́ло

2 *fig* почти́; **it cost ~ to nothing** э́то почти́ ничего́ не сто́ило; **there was ~ to nobody there** там почти́ никого́ не́ было.

next-door *adj*: **the ~ neighbours** ближа́йшие сосе́ди.

next door *adv and prep*: **the house ~** сосе́дний дом; **I live ~ to him** мы с ним сосе́ди.

next-of-kin *n* ближа́йший ро́дственник.

nib *n* перо́; **fountain-pen ~** перо́ автору́чки.

nibble *n*: **I took a ~ just to try the apple** я надкуси́л я́блоко; (*fishing*) **I didn't get even a ~ all day** ры́ба не клева́ла весь день; *fig* **have you had an offer for your car?—One or two ~s but nothing serious** есть жела́ющие купи́ть твою́ маши́ну? — Два-три челове́ка интересова́лись, но и то́лько.

nibble *vti vt* обгрыз|а́ть (-ть); **mice have been nibbling (at) the cheese** мы́ши обгры́зли весь сыр; **children, stop nibbling the buns!** де́ти, переста́ньте отщи́пывать от бу́лочек!

vi: **the fish were just nibbling** ры́ба то́лько объе́ла всю нажи́вку; **the invalid just ~d at his dinner** больно́й едва́ притро́нулся к у́жину (*pf*).

nice *adj* **1** (*of people*) ми́лый; сла́вный, симпати́чный; **what a ~ girl!** кака́я ми́лая де́вушка!; **that's very ~ of you** э́то о́чень ми́ло/любе́зно с ва́шей стороны́; **they're ~ people** они́ сла́вные лю́ди; **he's a ~ chap** он сла́вный/симпати́чный па́рень; **you're looking very ~ today** ты сего́дня хорошо́ вы́глядишь; **he was very ~ about it all** (*tactful*) он вёл себя́ о́чень делика́тно в э́том де́ле

2 (*of things*) прия́тный, ми́лый, хоро́ший; **that smells/tastes ~** э́то прия́тно па́хнет, э́то прия́тно на вкус; **it was ~ meeting you** о́чень прия́тно бы́ло с ва́ми познако́миться; **it's very ~ here** здесь о́чень ми́ло; **~ weather** хоро́шая пого́да; **we had a ~ time** мы хорошо́ провели́ вре́мя; **what a ~ day!** како́й чуде́сный день!; **that's a ~ coat!** како́е сла́вное пальти́шко!

3 (*fastidious*) разбо́рчивый; (*subtle*) то́нкий; **he's not too ~ when it comes to methods** он не сли́шком разбо́рчив в сре́дствах; **he has a ~ judgement in these matters** он то́нко су́дит о таки́х веща́х; **he has a ~ eye for detail** он то́нкий наблюда́тель

4 *as intensifier*: **it's ~ and warm in here** здесь о́чень ую́тно; **I'd love a ~ cold drink** я бы с удово́льствием вы́пил чего́-нибудь прохлади́тельного

5 *iron*: **a ~ friend you are!** хоро́ш друг, не́чего сказа́ть!; **a ~ mess you've got us into!** в хоро́шенькую исто́рию ты нас втяну́л!; **that's a ~ thing to say!** ну ты и ска́жешь!

nice-looking *adj* милови́дный, привлека́тельный.

nicely *adv* хорошо́; **he's getting on ~** (*prospering*) он процвета́ет, у него́ дела́ иду́т хорошо́, (*recovering*) он поправля́ется; **she thanked me ~** она́ ми́ло поблагодари́ла меня́; **that will do very ~** э́то вполне́ подойдёт.

nicety *n*: **the niceties of the question** все то́нкости э́того де́ла; **he judged the situation to a ~** он о́чень ве́рно/то́чно оцени́л обстано́вку.

niche *n* ни́ша; *fig* **he found the right ~ for himself** он нашёл своё ме́сто в жи́зни.

nick *n* **1** (*in wood, etc.*) зару́бка, засе́чка; (*cut in skin*) поре́з; *fig* **he arrived in the ~ of time** он пришёл как раз во́время

2 *sl* (*UK*: *prison*): **he's in the ~** он сиди́т (в тюрьме́).

nick *vt* **1** (*cut a notch*) де́лать зару́бку/засе́чку на чём-л (с-); (*cut skin*) поре́зать (*pf*); **I ~ed my chin with the razor** я поре́зал подборо́док бри́твой

2 *sl* (*UK*: *steal*): **my watch has been ~ed** у меня́ стащи́ли часы́; (*UK*: *arrest*): **he got ~ed** его́ схвати́ли.

nickel *n Chem* ни́кель (*m*); (*US*) моне́та в пять це́нтов.

nickname *n* про́звище; кли́чка (*also of animals*).

nickname *vt*: **they ~d him "Fatty"** ему́ да́ли про́звище Толстя́к.

nicotine *n* никоти́н.

niece *n* племя́нница.

niggardly *adj* (*of person*) скупо́й, прижи́мистый; (*of amount*): **a ~ sum** жа́лкая су́мма; **a ~ grant** ску́дная дота́ция.

niggle *vi* мелочи́ться (*impf*); **don't ~** не мелочи́сь; **he ~s over every clause** он придира́ется к ка́ждому пу́нкту.

niggling *adj* (*of person*) ме́лочный; (*of things*): **~ details** несуще́ственные/пустя́чные дета́ли; **a ~ little pain** но́ющая боль.

night *n* ночь [**NB** *until midnight usu translated* ве́чер]; **at/by/in the ~** но́чью; **during the ~** в тече́ние но́чи; **all ~ long** всю ночь напролёт; **every ~** по вечера́м, по ноча́м; **far into the ~** далеко́ за́ полночь; **9 o'clock at ~** де́вять часо́в ве́чера; **we didn't get in till almost 1 at ~** мы верну́лись то́лько о́коло ча́су но́чи; **at dead of ~** глубо́кой но́чью; **tomorrow ~** за́втра ве́чером; **I didn't sleep well last ~, I had a bad ~** я сего́дня/э́ту ночь пло́хо спал; **I had a late ~ last ~** вчера́ я засиде́лся допоздна́ (*adv*); **the ~ before last** позавчера́ ве́чером; **he'd arrived the ~ before the wedding** он прие́хал накану́не сва́дьбы; **good ~!** споко́йной но́чи!; **he spent the ~ at our place** он ночева́л у нас; **the ~ is yet young** ещё не по́здно; *CQ* **we made a ~ of it** мы всю ночь гуля́ли; *Theat* **first ~** премье́ра; *attr*: **~ duty/club** ночно́е дежу́рство, ночно́й клуб.

nightcap *n* ночно́й колпа́к; (*drink*) стака́нчик на́ ночь.

nightdress *n* (же́нская) ночна́я руба́шка/соро́чка.

nightfall *n*: **at ~** в су́мерках (*pl*); **by ~ I was dead tired** к ве́черу я ужа́сно уста́л.

nightgown *n see* **nightdress.**

nightingale *n* солове́й.

night light *n* ночни́к.

nightly *adj* (*of performance*) ежевече́рний.

nightly *adv* по вечера́м, ка́ждый ве́чер; по ноча́м, ка́ждую ночь.

nightmare *n* кошма́р, *also fig*; **he had a ~** он ви́дел стра́шный сон, его́ му́чил кошма́р.

night school *n* вече́рние ку́рсы (*pl*).

nightshade *n Bot*: **deadly ~** чёрный паслён.

nightshift *n* ночна́я сме́на; **I'm on ~** я рабо́таю в ночну́ю сме́ну.

nightshirt *n* (мужска́я) ночна́я руба́шка.

night-time *n* ночно́е вре́мя; **at ~** в ночно́е вре́мя.

night watchman *n* ночно́й сто́рож.

nil *n* нуль (*m*); **they won three — ~** они́ вы́играли со счётом три-ноль (*written* 3 : 0).

nimble *adj* прово́рный, подви́жный; **he's ~ on his feet** он о́чень подви́жен; **~ fingers** (*of craftsmen*) ло́вкие *or* прово́рные/(*of pianists*) подви́жные па́льцы; *fig* **a ~ mind** живо́й/бы́стрый ум.

nimbus *n Meteorol* дождево́е о́блако; *Rel, Art* нимб.

nine *num* де́вять [*see grammatical note under* **five**]; **9 of them came** их пришло́ де́вять челове́к, они́ пришли́ вдевятеро́м; **in 9 cases out of 10** в девяти́ слу́чаях из десяти́; *fig*: **a 9 days' wonder** кратковре́менная сенса́ция; **she was dressed up to the nines** она́ была́ разоде́та в пух и прах.

ninepins *n* ке́гли (*pl*); **to play at ~** игра́ть в ке́гли.

nineteen *num* девятна́дцать [*see* **eleven**]; **there were 19 of us** нас бы́ло девятна́дцать; **does a No 19 (bus) go there?** девятна́дцатый (авто́бус) идёт туда́?; **19 times as much** в девятна́дцать раз бо́льше; **a girl of 19** де́вушка девятна́дцати лет; **1,900** ты́сяча девятьсо́т; **in 1900** в ты́сяча девятисо́том году́; *fig* **she talks ~ to the dozen** она́ треща́т как соро́ка.

nineteenth *adj* **1** девятна́дцатый; **he's in his ~ year** ему́ девятна́дцатый год

2 *as n* (*date*) (**the ~**) девятна́дцатое (число́); **on the ~** девятна́дцатого (числа́); (*fraction*) (**a ~**) одна́ девятна́дцатая; **two ~s** две девятна́дцатых.

ninetieth *adj* **1** девяно́стый; **she's in her ~ year** ей ско́ро девяно́сто лет

2 *as n* (*fraction*) одна́ девяно́стая.

ninety *num* девяно́сто (*in oblique cases* девяно́ста); **90 dollars** девяно́сто до́лларов; **on page 90** на девяно́стой страни́це; **a ~-year old man** девяносто́ле́тний стари́к; **he's well over 90** ему́ далеко́ за девяно́сто; **92%** девяно́сто два проце́нта; **95th anniversary** девяно́сто пя́тая годовщи́на; **more than 98 kilometres** бо́льше девяно́ста восьми́ киломе́тров; **the temperature is in the high nineties** температу́ра о́коло ста гра́дусов; **in the nineties of the last century** в девяно́стых года́х про́шлого ве́ка; **99 people out of 100 would agree** девяно́сто де́вять челове́к из ста согласи́лись бы; **90,000** девяно́сто ты́сяч.

ninny *n* проста́к, простофи́ля (*m and f*).

ninth *adj* **1** девя́тый

2 *as n* (*date*) (**the ~**) девя́тое (число́); **on the ~ of March** девя́того ма́рта; (*fraction*) (**a ~**) одна́ девя́тая; **four ~s** четы́ре девя́тых.

nip *n* щипо́к; **to give smb a ~** ущипну́ть кого́-л; *fig*: **there's a bit of a ~ in the air** в во́здухе лёгкий моро́зец; **a ~ of brandy** (*as restorative*) глото́к коньяка́; **have another ~ before you go** вы́пей ещё рю́мочку пе́ред доро́гой.

nip *vti vt* щипа́ть ((у)щипну́ть); **the crab ~ped my finger** краб ущипну́л/ца́пнул (*only in pf*) меня́ за па́лец; **I ~ped my fingers in the door** я прищеми́л себе́ па́льцы две́рью; **the dog ~ped my leg** соба́ка ца́пнула меня́ за́ ногу; *Hort* **he ~ped off the tomato shoots** он пасынкова́л помидо́ры; **the frost has ~ped all the roses** моро́з поби́л все ро́зы; *fig* **to ~ smth in the bud** пресе|ка́ть что-л в ко́рне (-́чь), подав|ля́ть что-л в заро́дыше (-и́ть)

vi **1**: **crabs ~ with their pincers** кра́бы мо́гут ущипну́ть клешня́ми

2 *CQ* (*hurry*): **I'll just ~ along/down/round to the shop** я то́лько сбе́гаю в магази́н; **I ~ped in to see them on the way** по доро́ге я забежа́л к ним; **she ~ped upstairs for a book** она́ побежа́ла наве́рх за кни́гой; **the cyclist ~ped in and out of the traffic** велосипеди́ст лави́ровал в пото́ке маши́н.

nipper *n* (*on crab, etc.*) клешня́; *pl* (**~s**) (*tool*) клёщи; *CQ* (*boy*) мальчуга́н; **~s** дети́шки.

nipple *n Anat* сосо́к; *Tech* ни́ппель (*m*), па́трубок.

nippy *adj* **1**: **it's a bit ~ this morning** сего́дня лёгкий моро́зец

2 (*of flavour*) о́стрый

3 *CQ*: **look ~!** шевели́сь!, пошеве́ливайся!

nit *n Zool* гни́да; *sl* (*also* **nitwit**) идио́т, крети́н.

nitrate *n Chem* нитра́т.

nitric *adj*: **~ acid** азо́тная кислота́.

nitrogen *n* азо́т.

no *neg particle and n* нет; **~, thank you** нет, спаси́бо; **he won't take ~ for an answer** для него́ «нет» не отве́т; **I couldn't say ~** я не мог отказа́ть; **the ayes and the noes** голоса́ «за» и «про́тив»; **~! you don't say!** не мо́жет быть!, что вы говори́те!

no *adj* **1** никако́й, *or use* нет + *G*; **I have ~ money** у меня́ нет де́нег; **it's of ~ importance at all** э́то не име́ет никако́го значе́ния; **there's ~ alternative** друго́го вы́хода нет; **he made ~ reply** он не отвеча́л; **~ wonder he left** ничего́ удиви́тельного, что он ушёл; *CQ* **it's ~ go, I'm afraid** бою́сь, ничего́ не вы́йдет

2 *understatement, emphatic neg*: **it's ~ easy task** э́то не лёгкое де́ло; **that's ~ mean achievement** э́то всё же достиже́ние; **he is ~ scholar** никако́й он не учёный; **my husband is ~ dancer** мой муж никуды́шный танцо́р

3: **there's ~** + *gerund* нельзя́ + *inf*, *or* не + *2nd pers sing of future tense*; **there's ~ denying that...** нельзя́ отрица́ть, что...; **there's ~ pleasing him** ему́ (ника́к) не угоди́шь; **there's ~ fooling him** его́ не проведёшь.

no *adv* **1**: **whether he comes or ~ we'll have to begin** придёт он и́ли нет, (нам) всё равно́ придётся начина́ть

2 *with comparative adjs and advs*: **he's ~ older than me** он не ста́рше меня́; **they're ~ longer in London** они́ бо́льше не живу́т в Ло́ндоне; **I have ~ more to say** мне бо́льше не́чего сказа́ть.

No (*abbr of* **number** *n*) но́мер (*abbr* №).

nob *n sl* (*person*) ва́жная персо́на, «ши́шка».

Nobel Prize *n* Но́белевская пре́мия.

nobility *n* **1** (*of character*) благоро́дство

2: the ~ дворя́нство, знать; **she married into the ~** она́ вы́шла за́муж за дворяни́на.

noble *adj* благоро́дный; **of ~ birth** благоро́дного/зна́тного происхожде́ния; **how ~ of him!** как благоро́дно с его́ стороны́!

nobleman *n* дворяни́н.

nobody *pron* **1** никто́ (*A*, *G* никого́, *D* никому́, *I* нике́м, *P* ни о ко́м) [**NB** *use with prepositions*]; **~ knows anything about it** никто́ об э́том ничего́ не зна́ет; **tell ~!** никому́ ни сло́ва!; **I saw ~ else** я бо́льше никого́ не ви́дел; **I spoke to ~** я ни с кем не разгова́ривал; **whose book is this?—Nobody's** чья э́то кни́га?—Ничья; **it's ~'s business but mine** э́то никого́, кро́ме меня́, не каса́ется; **I have ~ to advise me** мне не́ с кем посове́товаться; **there's ~ who might help me** никто́ мне не мо́жет помо́чь

2 *as n*: **he's just a ~!** он про́сто пусто́е ме́сто!; **I knew him when he was just a ~** я его́ знал, когда́ он ещё был нике́м.

nocturnal *adj* ночно́й.

nod *n* киво́к; **he gave me a ~/a ~ of approval** он кивну́л мне (в знак одобре́ния).

nod *vti vt* кив|а́ть (-ну́ть); **to ~ one's head** кива́ть голово́й

vi **1: he ~ded as he passed me** проходя́, он кивну́л мне; **the trees were ~ding in the wind** дере́вья кача́лись на ветру́

2 (*doze*): **he sat ~ding in an armchair** он сиде́л в кре́сле и клева́л но́сом.

nodding *adj*: **I have a ~ acquaintance with him** мы с ним о́чень ма́ло знако́мы—так, ша́почное знако́мство.

nodule *n Bot*, *Anat* узело́к.

noise *n* шум; **what's (all) that ~?** что за шум?; **stop making such a ~!** переста́ньте шуме́ть!; **the children made an awful ~** де́ти ужа́сно расшуме́лись; *fig*: **to make a great ~ about smth** поднима́ть шум из-за/по по́воду чего́-л; *CQ* **he's a big ~** он ва́жная ши́шка.

noiseless *adj* бесшу́мный.

noisome *adj* отврати́тельный, проти́вный; (*stinking*) воню́чий.

noisy *adj* (*making noise*) шумли́вый; (*loud, full of noise*) шу́мный; **~ children** шумли́вые де́ти; **it's very ~ here** здесь о́чень шу́мно.

nomad *n* коче́вник.

nomadic *adj* кочево́й, кочу́ющий.

no man's land *n*ániче́йная полоса́.

nominal *adj* номина́льный.

nominate *vt*: **he was ~d chairman** его́ назна́чили председа́телем (*appointed*), его́ вы́двинули на пост председа́теля (*proposed for*).

nomination *n* выдвиже́ние/выставле́ние кандида́тов; **~s to be in by June 1st** кандида́ты должны́ быть наме́чены/вы́двинуты до пе́рвого ию́ня.

nominative *n*, *also* **~ case** *Gram* имени́тельный паде́ж.

nominee *n* кандида́т.

non-aggression pact *n* пакт о ненападе́нии.

non-alcoholic *adj* безалкого́льный.

non-aligned *adj*: *Polit* **~ nations** неприсоедини́вшиеся стра́ны.

non-alignment *n*: **policy of ~** поли́тика неприсоедине́ния.

non-appearance *n Law*, *Sport* нея́вка.

non-attendance *n* (*at meeting, etc.*) нея́вка в + *A or* на + *A*; (*at lectures, etc.*) непосеще́ние + *G*.

nonchalant *adj* беспе́чный.

non-combatant *adj* нестроево́й.

non-committal *adj*: **he gave a ~ answer** он отве́тил укло́нчиво.

non-conductor *n Elec*, *Phys* непроводни́к, изоля́тор.

nondescript *adj* (*of person*) невзра́чный; **a ~ colour** неопределённый цвет; *also as n*: **he's a bit of a ~** он како́й-то невзра́чный.

none *pron* **1** (*person*) никто́, ни оди́н; **~ of them came** никто́ из них не пришёл; **I met ~ of them** я никого́ из них не встре́тил; **can ~ of you help her?** ра́зве никто́ не мо́жет ей помо́чь?; **~ but he knows** никто́, кро́ме него́, не зна́ет; **he knows that, ~ better** э́того никто́ лу́чше него́ не зна́ет; **it was ~ other than the general himself** э́то был не кто ино́й, как сам генера́л; **as a cook, he's second to ~** как по́вару ему́ нет ра́вных

2 (*thing*) ничто́; ни оди́н; **I want ~ of these books** ни одна́ из э́тих книг мне не нужна́; **~ of this is relevant** всё э́то к де́лу не отно́сится; **have you any questions?—N.** у вас есть вопро́сы?—Нет; **bread?—there's ~ left** хле́ба бо́льше нет; **firewood?—we've got next to ~ of that** у нас дрова́ конча́ются; **I want ~ of your advice!** обойду́сь без ва́ших сове́тов (*pl*)!; **~ of that, now!** дово́льно!; **it's ~ of your business** э́то не твоё де́ло.

none *adv* совсе́м не, во́все не; **she was ~ too happy with this** ей э́то совсе́м/во́все не нра́вилось; **he was ~ too polite** он был не о́чень-то ве́жлив; **things are ~ too well with me at the moment** сейча́с дела́ у меня́ иду́т нева́жно; **the doctor arrived ~ too soon** врач едва́ поспе́л; **he was ~ the worse of it** ему́ от э́того ху́же не ста́ло.

nonentity *n* ничто́жество.

nonetheless *adv* тем не ме́нее, всё же.

non-existent *adj* несуществу́ющий.

non-inflammable *adj* невоспламеня́ющийся.

non-intervention *n* невмеша́тельство.

non-iron *adj*: **this material is ~** э́тот материа́л не нужда́ется в гла́жке.

non-member *n*: **open to ~s** откры́то для посторо́нних.

non-party *adj* (*of person*) беспарти́йный; (*of approach*) непарти́йный.

non-payment *n* неплатёж, неупла́та.

nonplus *vt* озада́ч|ивать (-ить); **I was completely ~sed by the question** я был си́льно озада́чен э́тим вопро́сом.

non-political *adj* не свя́занный с поли́тикой.

non-profitmaking *adj*: **it's a ~ organization** э́то не комме́рческая организа́ция.

non-resident *n*: **the hotel restaurant is open to ~s** ресторáн гостúницы откры́т для посторóнней пýблики.

nonsense *n* вздор, бессмы́слица, чушь; **what ~!** какóй вздор!; **to talk ~** нестú вздор/чушь; (*of essay, etc.*) **this is sheer ~** э́то прóсто какáя-то бессмы́слица; **it is ~ to say that...** бессмы́сленно говорúть, что...; **no ~!** хвáтит глýпостей!; **I won't stand any ~ from them** я не позвóлю им шутúть с собóй.

nonsensical *adj* бессмы́сленный; (*absurd*) нелéпый.

non-shrink *adj*: **this is ~ material** э́тот материáл не садúтся.

non-smoker *n* (*person*) некуря́щий; *Rail* купé для некуря́щих.

non-stop *adj* (*uninterrupted*) беспреры́вный; (*Rail, bus*) безостанóвочный; *Aer* **a ~ flight** беспосáдочный перелёт.

non-stop *adv*: **the train goes to Kiev ~** пóезд идёт до Кúева без остановóк; **she talked ~** онá говорúла без ýмолку.

noodle *n* **1** *usu pl* (**~s**) *Cook* лапшá (*collect*); *attr*: **~ soup** суп-лапшá

2 *CQ* (*person*) простофúля (*m and f*).

nook *n*: **to search every ~ and cranny** обшáрить все углы́.

noon *n* пóлдень (*m*); **before ~** до полýдня; **at ~** в пóлдень.

no one *pron see* **nobody.**

noose *n* пéтля; (*lasso*) аркáн; лассó (*indecl*).

nor *conj* ни; и... не; **neither you ~ he** ни ты, ни он; **he can't do it, ~ can I** ни он, ни я не мóжем э́то сдéлать; **~ is it at all likely that he'll come** и он почтú навернякá не придёт.

norm *n* нóрма.

normal *n*: **everything's getting back to ~** всё прихóдит в нóрму; **we soon got back to ~** (нáша) жизнь скóро вошлá в свою́ колею́; **2° above/below ~** два грáдуса вы́ше/нúже нормáльной (температýры).

normal *adj* нормáльный; **a ~ child** нормáльный ребёнок; **it's ~ weather for the time of year** такáя погóда обы́чна для э́того врéмени гóда; *Med CQ* **he's ~ today** сегóдня у негó нормáльная температýра.

normalize *vt* нормализовáть (*impf and pf*); при|водúть в нóрму (-вестú).

normally *adv* нормáльно, обы́чно.

normative *adj* норматúвный.

Norse *n*, *also* **Old ~** древнескандинáвский язы́к.

north *n* сéвер; *Naut* норд; **to the ~** на сéвер, к сéверу; **in the ~** на сéвере; **from the ~** с сéвера; **magnetic ~** сéверный магнúтный пóлюс.

north *adj* сéверный; **a ~ wind** сéверный вéтер, *Naut* норд; **the N. Sea** Сéверное мóре.

north *adv*: **they were heading due ~** онú двигáлись пря́мо на сéвер; **the area ~ of Moscow** райóн к сéверу от Москвы́.

North American *adj* североамерикáнский.

north-east *n* сéверо-востóк; *Naut* норд-óст.

north-east *adj* сéверо-востóчный.

north-east *adv* на сéверо-востóк, к сéверо-востóку.

north-easterly *adj* сéверо-востóчный; **a ~ wind** сéверо-востóчный вéтер, *Naut* норд-óст; **in a ~ direction** в сéверо-востóчном направлéнии.

north-eastern *adj* сéверо-востóчный.

north-eastwards *adv* на сéверо-востóк, к сéверо-востóку.

northerly *adj* сéверный; **in a ~ direction** в сéверном направлéнии.

northern *adj* сéверный.

northerner *n* северя́н|ин, *f* -ка.

northwards *adv* на сéвер, к сéверу.

north-west *n* сéверо-зáпад; *Naut* норд-вéст.

northwest *adj* сéверо-зáпадный.

northwest *adv* на сéверо-зáпад, к сéверо-зáпаду.

north-westerly *adj* сéверо-зáпадный; **a ~ wind** сéверо-зáпадный вéтер, *Naut* норд-вéст.

north-western *adj* сéверо-зáпадный.

north-westwards *adv* на сéверо-зáпад, к сéверо-зáпаду.

Norwegian *n* норвéжец, норвéжка; (*language*) норвéжский язы́к.

Norwegian *adj* норвéжский.

nose *n* **1** нос, *dim* нóсик; **a snub/Roman ~** вздёрнутый/рúмский нос; **to blow one's ~** сморкáться; **to talk through one's ~** говорúть в нос, гнусáвить; **to hold one's ~** зажимáть нос; **stop picking your ~!** перестáнь ковыря́ть в носý!

2 (*sense of smell*): **a dog with a good ~** собáка с хорóшим чутьём; *fig* **he's got a good ~ for scandal** он всегдá все сплéтни узнаёт пéрвым

3 *fig uses*: **it's right under your ~** э́то у тебя́ пря́мо под нóсом; **don't stick your ~ into what doesn't concern you** не суй нос в чужúе делá; **that'll put his ~ out of joint** э́то егó расстрóит; **to turn one's ~ up at smth** воротúть нос от чегó-л; **while he was out I had a good ~ around his study** покá егó нé было, я всё осмотрéл в егó кабинéте; **follow your ~** идú кудá глазá гладя́т; **he keeps my ~ to the grindstone** он меня́ прóсто загнáл [NB *tense*]; **she leads him by the ~** он у неё на поводý; **to look down one's ~ at smb** смотрéть на когó-л свысокá; **we had to pay through the ~ for it** нам пришлóсь заплатúть за э́то бéшеные дéньги.

nose *vti vt* **1** (*of dog, etc.*): **to ~ smth out** учýять что-л (*impf* чýять); *fig* **she ~d out our secret/his whereabouts** онá пронюхала про наш секрéт, онá вы́ведала, где он живёт

2: the ship ~d its way forward сýдно мéдленно двигáлось вперёд

vi: **to ~ about/around for smth** вынюхивать что-л (*usu impf*).

nosebleed *n* кровотечéние из нóса; **I had a ~** у меня́ кровь шла úз носу.

nosey *adj* любопы́тный; **don't be so ~** не будь таки́м любопы́тным; **he's a real ~ parker** он всю́ду суёт свой нос.

nostalgic *adj*: **I was in ~ mood** я был в ностальги́ческом настрое́нии; **he is ~ for the past** он тоску́ет по про́шлому.

nostril *n* ноздря́.

not *adv* **1** *negating verbs* не; **I don't know** я не зна́ю; **he did it ~ thinking of the risk** он сде́лал э́то, не ду́мая о ри́ске; **you're a doctor, aren't you?** вы врач, да?; **he's ~ a doctor, is he?** он ведь не врач?; **surely he's ~ a doctor?** неуже́ли он врач?; **he is ~ at home** его́ нет до́ма; **she hasn't any money** у неё совсе́м нет де́нег; **I couldn't go** я не мог пойти́

2 *negating other parts of speech*: **who'll do it?—Not I** кто э́то сде́лает?—То́лько не я; **he'll never admit it, ~ he** уж о́н-то э́того никогда́ не призна́ет; **~ once did he say thanks** он ни ра́зу не поблагодари́л; **he said it ~ once but many times** он не раз э́то говори́л; **~ too loud, please** поти́ше, пожа́луйста; **~ until he agrees** то́лько по́сле того́, как он согласи́тся

3 *elliptically*: **will he be there?—I fear ~** он там бу́дет?—Бою́сь, что нет; **you'll have to pay whether you like it or ~** придётся плати́ть, ничего́ не поде́лаешь; **why ~?** а почему́ бы и нет?; **~ that I dislike him, but...** я не то, что́бы не люблю́ его́, но...; **~ that that proves anything** коне́чно, э́то ещё ничего́ не дока́зывает; **he was impolite, ~ to say rude** он был о́чень неве́жлив, что́бы не сказа́ть груб; **~ to speak of the expense** не говоря́ уже́ о расхо́дах

4 *emphatic neg*: **certainly ~!, of course ~!** коне́чно, нет!; **~ at all!** (*contradicting*) совсе́м нет!, (*in answer to thanks*) не́ за что!; **she was ~ in the least angry** она́ ничу́ть не рассерди́лась; *CQ*: **was he happy with it?—N. half** он был дово́лен э́тим?—Ещё как!; **will you tell her?—N. likely** ты ей ска́жешь?—Вря́д ли; **~ on your life** ни в ко́ем слу́чае

5 *understatements*: **~ a few** нема́ло; **they were ~ a little surprised** они́ бы́ли весьма́ удивлены́; **~ without reason** не без причи́ны; **in the ~ so distant past** в недалёком про́шлом, не так давно́.

notability *n* (*person*) знамени́тость.

notable *adj* (*of occasions*) знамена́тельный; (*of people*) ви́дный, выдаю́щийся.

notably *adv* в осо́бенности; **in his works and, ~, in his plays** в его́ произведе́ниях, в осо́бенности в его́ пье́сах.

notation *n Mus* нота́ция; *Math* усло́вное обозначе́ние.

notch *n* зару́бка; (*as mark*) ме́тка.

notch *vt* де́лать зару́бки (с-); *Sport CQ* **he ~ed up an impressive score** он сыгра́л с прили́чным счётом.

note *n* **1** *often pl* (*record, memorandum*) заме́тка, за́пись; (*comment*) примеча́ние; **~s for an article** заме́тки для статьи́; **he lectures from ~s** он чита́ет ле́кции по за́писям; **are there ~s in this edition?** есть ли примеча́ния в э́том изда́нии?; **~s of a meeting** протоко́л (*sing*) собра́ния; **to take down ~s of a lecture** запи́сывать ле́кцию; **to make a ~ of smth** запи́сывать что-л; **he spoke without ~s** он говори́л не по бума́жке; *fig* **we compared ~s about the exhibition** мы обме́нивались впечатле́ниями о вы́ставке

2 (*letter*) запи́ска; *Dipl* но́та; **I wrote him a short ~** я черкну́л ему́ не́сколько строк

3 (*notice*): **to take ~ of smth** замеча́ть что-л; **worthy of ~** досто́йный внима́ния, примеча́тельный

4 (*distinction*): **a man of ~** знамени́тость; **a composer of ~** изве́стный компози́тор; **places of ~ in the town** достопримеча́тельности го́рода

5 (*banknote*) банкно́та; **a ten rouble ~** десятирублёвая банкно́та, *CQ* десятирублёвка; *Comm* **a promissory ~** ве́ксель

6 *Mus* но́та; *fig* но́тка, тон; *fig*: **there was a ~ of sadness in her voice** в её го́лосе прозвуча́ла но́тка гру́сти; **to strike the right ~** взять ве́рный тон.

note *vt* заме|ча́ть (-́тить); (*make a mental note of smth*) отме|ча́ть (-́тить); (*in writing*) (*also* **~ down**) запи́с|ывать (-а́ть); *off* **we duly ~ that...** мы соотве́тственно принима́ем к све́дению, что...

notebook *n* записна́я кни́жка; (*exercise book*) тетра́дь.

note-case *n* бума́жник.

noted *adj* изве́стный; **he is ~ for his talent as an actor** он изве́стен как тала́нтливый актёр; **she is ~ for her wit** она́ изве́стна/сла́вится свои́м остроу́мием.

notepaper *n* почто́вая бума́га.

noteworthy *adj* примеча́тельный.

nothing *n* **1** ничего́ (+ не *with verbs*) (*A* ничто́ (*very rare*), *G* ничего́, *D* ничему́, *I* ниче́м, *P* ни о чём) [**NB** *use with prepositions*]; **~ pleases him** ему́ ничего́ не нра́вится; **I need ~** мне ничего́ не ну́жно; **~ would induce me to marry him** ничто́ не заста́вит меня́ вы́йти за него́ за́муж; **it's ~ serious** ничего́ стра́шного; **there was ~ else we could do** ничего́ друго́го нам не остава́лось де́лать; **I see ~ of him** мы с ним совсе́м не ви́димся

2 не́чего + *inf*; **there is ~ to do** де́лать не́чего; **there's ~ more to be said** бо́льше не́чего сказа́ть; **he's got ~ to say for himself** ему́ не́чего сказа́ть; **it's ~ to be proud of** здесь не́чем горди́ться; **I have ~ to write with** мне не́чем писа́ть

3 *with verb "to be"*: **there's ~ in it for us** э́то нам ничего́ не даст; **my worries are ~ to hers** мои́ несча́стья—ничто́ по сравне́нию с её бедо́й; **there's ~ for it but to agree** ничего́ не остаётся, как согласи́ться; **there's ~ of the artist in him** в нём совсе́м нет худо́жественной жи́лки; **it's ~ to her if I go away** ей всё равно́, уйду́ я и́ли нет; **there's ~ in it now** (*of contest*) тепе́рь ша́нсы у всех ра́вные; **it's ~ to do with you** э́то вас не каса́ется; **there's ~ spiteful in him/about him** в нём нет ни ка́пли зло́сти; **there's ~ in/to these rumours** э́то пусты́е слу́хи; **he's ~ if not neat** он в вы́сшей сте́пени аккура́тен; **it's ~!** (*replying to thanks*) не́ за что!, (*replying to apology*) ничего́!, не сто́ит об э́том говори́ть!, пустяки́!; **try it yourself, there's ~ to it** попыта́йся сде́лать сам, э́то о́чень легко́

4 *various*: **they have absolutely ~** (*no money*) у них совсе́м нет де́нег, у них за душо́й ни гроша́; **this has ~ to do with the case** э́то к де́лу не отно́сится; **I can make ~ of it** я в э́том ничего́ не понима́ю/не смы́слю; **he thinks ~ of the risk** риск его́ не страши́т; **he thinks ~ of getting up at 5** ему́ ничего́ не сто́ит встать в пять часо́в утра́; **I want ~ to do with him** я не хочу́ име́ть с ним ничего́ о́бщего; **you get in for ~** вход беспла́тный; **we bought it for next to ~** э́то нам почти́ ничего́ не сто́ило; **it's not for ~ they call him a miser** его́ не зря называ́ют скря́гой; **they live on practically ~** на что они́ живу́т—непоня́тно; **it all came to ~** э́то ни к чему́ не привело́, ничего́ из э́того не вы́шло; **he built up the firm from ~** он созда́л свою́ фи́рму на пусто́м ме́сте; **it's a mere ~** э́то су́щий пустя́к; **to say ~ of the cost** не говоря́ уже́ о сто́имости; **~ of the kind** ничего́ подо́бного; **~ doing** но́мер не пройдёт

5 (*zero*) ноль.

nothing *adv* ниско́лько, совсе́м не; **it's ~ like her** э́то совсе́м/ниско́лько на неё не похо́же; **the book's ~ like as interesting as I'd expected** кни́га совсе́м не так интере́сна, как я ожида́л.

notice *n* 1 (*announcement*) объявле́ние (*also in press*); (*poster*) афи́ша; **to put up a ~** выве́шивать объявле́ние; **to put a ~ in the papers** помести́ть объявле́ние в газе́тах

2 *off* извеще́ние, уведомле́ние; (*warning*) предупрежде́ние; **until further ~** до дальне́йшего уведомле́ния; **~ is hereby given that...** настоя́щим уведомля́ется, что...; **to give/serve smb ~ that...** извеща́ть кого́-л, что...; **I must have ~ of the meeting** пожа́луйста, предупреди́те меня́ о собра́нии зара́нее; **without (prior) ~** без предупрежде́ния; **I'll give you at least a week's ~ of it** я вас предупрежу́ об э́том по кра́йней ме́ре за неде́лю; **at very short ~** в после́днюю мину́ту; **I had to do it at short ~** мне пришло́сь де́лать э́то о́чень бы́стро; **we are ready to leave at a day's ~/at a moment's ~** мы гото́вы отпра́виться че́рез день/в любу́ю мину́ту

3 (*resignation*): **I've given in my ~** я по́дал заявле́ние об ухо́де; (*dismissal*) **I've been given a month's ~** меня́ предупреди́ли, что че́рез ме́сяц я буду́ уво́лен; **he was dismissed without ~** его́ уво́лили без предупрежде́ния

4 *Theat* (*review*) реце́нзия; о́тзыв в печа́ти; **the show has had bad ~s** э́тот спекта́кль получи́л плохи́е о́тзывы в печа́ти

5 (*attention*) внима́ние; **take no ~ of it** не обраща́й на э́то внима́ния; **as soon as she was mentioned, he sat up and took ~** при упомина́нии о ней он встрепену́лся и стал слу́шать; **it's quite beneath one's ~** э́то не заслу́живает внима́ния; **what first attracted your ~ to it?** что впервы́е привлекло́ ва́ше внима́ние к э́тому?; **it has come to our ~ that...** нам ста́ло изве́стно, что...; **it escaped my ~** э́то ускользну́ло от моего́ внима́ния, я не заме́тил, что...; **his absence did not escape ~** его́ отсу́тствие не оста́лось незаме́ченным.

notice *vt* заме|ча́ть (-́тить); **I didn't ~ you** я вас не заме́тил; **I didn't ~ you coming in** я не заме́тил, как вы вошли́; **I didn't particularly ~ what he was wearing** я не обрати́л внима́ния, во что́ он был оде́т; **was she upset?—Not so as you'd ~** она́ расстро́илась?—По ви́ду как бу́дто нет; **it's the first thing you ~** э́то пе́рвое, что броса́ется в глаза́.

noticeable *adj* заме́тный, *CQ* приме́тный; **it's hardly ~** э́то едва́ заме́тно/приме́тно; **there has been a ~ decline in demand** спрос заме́тно уме́ньшился/упа́л.

notifiable *adj*: **~ diseases** инфекцио́нные боле́зни, сообща́ть о кото́рых обяза́тельно.

notification *n* уведомле́ние, (*warning*) предупрежде́ние.

notify *vt* увед|омля́ть (-́омить); изве|ща́ть (-сти́ть); (*report*) заяв|ля́ть + *D* (-и́ть); **we will ~ you of our decision** мы уве́домим вас о на́шем реше́нии; **we notified the police of the loss** мы заяви́ли в поли́цию о пропа́же.

notion *n* иде́я, поня́тие, представле́ние; **she has no ~ of what work means** она́ не име́ет поня́тия о том, что тако́е рабо́та; **I have a ~ of going to see Istanbul** у меня́ есть мысль пое́хать посмотре́ть Стамбу́л; **I have a ~ that it occurs in Hamlet** мне ка́жется, э́то из «Га́млета»; **he comes and goes as the ~ takes him** он прихо́дит и ухо́дит, когда́ ему́ взду́мается; *CQ* **where's my pen?—I haven't the slightest/foggiest ~** где моя́ ру́чка?—Не име́ю ни мале́йшего представле́ния.

notional *adj* теорети́ческий; **it's a purely ~ distinction** э́то чи́сто теорети́ческое разли́чие.

notoriety *n* дурна́я сла́ва; **he positively seems to seek ~** он как бу́дто добива́ется, что́бы о нём пло́хо ду́мали.

notorious *adj* отъя́вленный; **a ~ criminal/liar** он отъя́вленный престу́пник/лгун; **she was ~ for her cruelty** она́ просла́вилась свое́й жесто́костью; **it is ~ that...** общеизве́стно, что...

notoriously *adv*: **he's ~ unreliable** все зна́ют, что на него́ ни в чём положи́ться нельзя́; **it's ~ difficult to prove** всем давно́ изве́стно, что э́то доказа́ть тру́дно.

notwithstanding *adv* тем не ме́нее, всё же.

notwithstanding *prep and conj* несмотря́ на + *A*; вопреки́ + *D*; **~ what you say, I believe him** несмотря́ на всё то, что вы говори́те, я ве́рю ему́; **our advice ~, he refused the post**

вопреки́ на́шим сове́там (*pl*) он отказа́лся от ме́ста.

nought *n* ноль; ~ **point one (0.1)** ноль це́лых, одна́ деся́тая (0,1); ~ **point ~ one (0.01)** ноль це́лых, одна́ со́тая (0,01); **a game of ~s and crosses** игра́ в кре́стики-но́лики.

noun *n* (и́мя) существи́тельное; **proper/common ~** и́мя со́бственное/нарица́тельное.

nourished *adj*: **well ~ children** упи́танные де́ти.

nourishing *adj* пита́тельный.

nourishment *n* пита́ние.

novel *n* рома́н.

novel *adj* но́вый, оригина́льный.

novelist *n* романи́ст.

novelty *n* (*newness*) новизна́; (*of product*) нови́нка; (*of method*) но́вшество; **when the ~ has worn off** когда́ пре́лесть новизны́ прохо́дит; **novelties in footwear/fashion** но́вые моде́ли о́буви, нови́нки мо́ды; **novelties in printing processes** но́вшества в печа́тном де́ле.

November *n* ноя́брь (*m*); *attr* ноя́брьский.

novice *n* нович́ок; *Rel* по́слушни|к, *f* -ца.

now *adv* **1** (*in contrast with past*) тепе́рь; (*at the very moment*) сейча́с; **where do you work ~?** где вы тепе́рь/сейча́с рабо́таете?; **~ everybody has a TV** тепе́рь у ка́ждого есть телеви́зор; **things are different ~** тепе́рь всё измени́лось; **he'll be here right ~** он сейча́с придёт; **he was here just ~** он то́лько что/сейча́с здесь был; **do it right ~** сде́лай э́то сейча́с же; **summer won't be long ~** уже́ ско́ро ле́то; **we see each other every ~ and then** мы ви́димся вре́мя от вре́мени

2 *with preps*: **they must have arrived before/by ~** они́, должно́ быть, уже́ прие́хали; **you should have done that before ~** тебе́ давно́ уже́ сле́довало э́то сде́лать; **by ~ everybody was getting nervous** к э́тому вре́мени все нача́ли не́рвничать; **that's all for ~** пока́ всё; **he's going a month from ~** он уезжа́ет че́рез ме́сяц; **from ~ on** (*in past narrative*) с тех по́р, (*from present time on*) с сего́дняшнего дня, с э́той мину́ты; **until/up till ~** до сих по́р

3: now ... now... то... то...; **~ here ~ there** то здесь, то там

4 (*without reference to time*): **~, what happened was this** так вот, случи́лось сле́дующее; **~ (then), what's wrong?** ну так в чём же де́ло?; **~ stop playing the fool** ла́дно, переста́нь дура́читься; **come ~!** (*expressing disbelief*) да неуже́ли!, да что́ ты!; **~, ~, that'll do** ну, ну, дово́льно!

now *conj*, *also* **~ that: ~ (that) you mention it, I did see that car** тепе́рь, когда́ вы упомяну́ли об э́том, я вспо́мнил, что ви́дел э́ту маши́ну.

nowadays *adv* в на́ши дни; тепе́рь; **everyone can read ~** в на́ше вре́мя все уме́ют чита́ть; **that's very expensive ~** тепе́рь э́то сто́ит о́чень до́рого.

noway(s) *adv* (*US*) *CQ*: **~ will I agree to that** я ни за что́ на э́то не соглашу́сь; **are you coming?—Noway!** ты придёшь?—Ни за что́!

nowhere *adv* **1** (*place*) нигде́; (*direction*) никуда́; **~ have I seen such luxury** я никогда́/нигде́ не ви́дел тако́й ро́скоши; **he was ~ to be seen** его́ нигде́ не́ было ви́дно; **plants of this kind are found ~ else** э́тот вид расте́ний нигде́ бо́льше не встреча́ется; **where are you going?—N.** Ты куда́-нибудь идёшь?—Никуда́ не иду́; **she appeared from ~** она́ появи́лась неизве́стно отку́да; **it's ~ near here** э́то совсе́м не бли́зко

2 не́где; не́куда; **there's ~ to play here** здесь не́где игра́ть; **I've got ~ to go** мне не́куда идти́

3 *fig uses*: **this is getting us ~** э́то ничего́ нам не даёт, э́то ни к чему́ не приведёт [**NB** *tense*]; **he's ~ near as tall as me** он гора́здо/значи́тельно ни́же меня́ (ро́стом); **I came ~ in the competition** я не за́нял никако́го ме́ста в соревнова́нии.

noxious *adj* (*of fumes, etc.*) вре́дный, ядови́тый.

nozzle *n* (*of hose*) наконе́чник; (*detachable; on vacuum cleaner, etc.*) наса́дка.

nuance *n* нюа́нс.

nub *n fig CQ*: **that's the ~ of the question** в э́том суть де́ла.

nuclear *adj* я́дерный; **~ energy** я́дерная эне́ргия.

nucleus *n Phys, Biol* ядро́, *also fig*.

nude *n* **1: in the ~** нагишо́м, голышо́м; **to swim (in the) ~** купа́ться нагишо́м/го́лым

2 *Art* **(a ~)** (*artist's model, live or on canvas*) обнажённая фигу́ра, (*title of painting*) обнажённая; **studies from the ~** этю́ды с обнажённой нату́ры.

nude *adj* обнажённый, го́лый.

nudge *n* толчо́к (ло́ктем); **give him a ~** (под)толкни́те его́.

nudge *vt* под|та́лкивать (-толкну́ть).

nudity *n* нагота́, обнажённость.

nugget *n*: **a gold ~** (золото́й) саморо́док.

nuisance *n*: **what a ~!** кака́я доса́да!; **it's a ~ having to change** (*buses, etc.*) неохо́та де́лать переса́дку; **this zip is a ~** ве́чно возня́ с э́той мо́лнией; **that tap is/the flies are an awful ~** с э́тим кра́ном одно́ муче́ние, от э́тих мух нет никако́го спасе́ния; **what a ~ that child is!** како́й несно́сный ребёнок!; **don't make a ~ of yourself!** не надоеда́й!

null *adj Law*: **the contract is ~ and void** э́то соглаше́ние бо́льше не име́ет си́лы.

nullify *vt* аннули́ровать (*pf and impf*); расторг|а́ть (-́нуть).

numb *adj* онеме́вший; **~ fingers** онеме́вшие па́льцы; **my fingers have gone ~** у меня́ па́льцы занеме́ли; **my leg is ~** (*asleep*) у меня́ нога́ затекла́; *fig* **she was ~ with terror/grief** она́ онеме́ла/оцепене́ла от у́жаса, она́ как бу́дто окамене́ла от го́ря.

number *n* **1** *Math* число́, *also Gram*; (*figure*) ци́фра; **the ~ "7"** ци́фра 7; **a whole ~**

це́лое число́; **in round ~s** в кру́глых ци́фрах, округля́я; **I'm not very good at ~s** я слаб в арифме́тике; *Gram*: **adjectives agree with nouns in ~** прилага́тельные согласу́ются с существи́тельными в числе́; **cardinal/ordinal ~s** коли́чественные/поря́дковые числи́тельные; **superior ~s** цифровы́е и́ндексы

2 (*amount*) число́, коли́чество; **one of their ~** оди́н из их числа́; **they won by force of ~s** они́ победи́ли благодаря́ чи́сленному превосхо́дству; **a ~/quite a ~ of people** како́е-то коли́чество люде́й, дово́льно мно́го наро́ду; **there were a small ~ of exceptions** бы́ло всего́ не́сколько исключе́ний; **there are any ~ of reasons** существу́ет мно́жество причи́н; **I've told him that time without ~** я э́то говори́л ему́ без конца́/миллио́н раз; **in a ~ of cases** в не́которых слу́чаях, в ря́де слу́чаев; **I met her on a ~ of occasions** я встреча́лся с ней не раз; **gulls nest here in great ~s** здесь ча́йки гнездя́тся в большо́м коли́честве; **people came in great ~s** пришло́ мно́го наро́ду; **we were 5 in ~** нас бы́ло пя́теро; **to the ~ of some 200 people** до двухсо́т челове́к

3 (*of house, room, etc.; abbr* **No**) но́мер; **she's in room ~ 6** она́ в ко́мнате но́мер шесть, (*in a hotel*) она́ в шесто́м но́мере; **~ 15 Gorky Street** у́лица Го́рького, дом (но́мер) пятна́дцать; *Tel* **what's your telephone ~?** како́й но́мер ва́шего телефо́на?; **wrong ~** (*in reply*) вы не туда́ попа́ли; (*if caller gets wrong number*) **sorry, wrong ~** извини́те, я не туда́ попа́л; **reference ~** спра́вочный но́мер; **catalogue ~** (*of books*) шифр по катало́гу; *Aut* **registration ~** регистрацио́нный но́мер; *attr*: **he's England's ~ one goalkeeper** он врата́рь но́мер оди́н в А́нглии; **a ~ nine bus** девя́тый авто́бус; *Aut* **~ plate** номерно́й знак

4 (*of journal, etc.*) но́мер; **the current/a back ~ of a journal** после́дний/ста́рый но́мер журна́ла

5 (*item on programme*) но́мер; **for the next ~ the choir will sing ...** сле́дующим но́мером хор испо́лнит...

6 *fig uses, CQ*: **look after ~ one** позабо́титься о со́бственной персо́не; **his ~'s up** его́ пе́сенка спе́та; **he's a bit of a back ~** он немно́го/слегка́ отста́л от жи́зни; **she's a nice little ~** она́ така́я ми́ленькая; **he's my opposite ~ in London** он занима́ет в Ло́ндоне пост, соотве́тствующий моему́.

number *vti vt* **1** (*give number*) нумерова́ть (про-); **to ~ pages** нумерова́ть страни́цы; **the houses on this side are not ~ed** дома́ на э́той стороне́ у́лицы не нумеро́ваны; *fig* **his days are ~ed** его́ дни сочтены́

2 (*amount to*) насчи́тывать (*only in impf*); **the club ~s about 50 members** клуб насчи́тывает о́коло пяти́десяти чле́нов; **we ~ed 50 in all** всего́ нас бы́ло пятьдеся́т челове́к; **the exhibition ~s some 100 items** на вы́ставке предста́влено о́коло ста экспона́тов

3 (*reckon*) счита́ть (*impf*); **I ~ him among my closest friends** я счита́ю его́ одни́м из мои́х бли́зких друзе́й

vi Mil: **to ~ off** рассчита́ться по поря́дку (*only in pf*).

numberless *adj* бесчи́сленный, неисчисли́мый.

numeral *n Gram* числи́тельное; (*figure*) ци́фра; **Arabic/Roman ~s** ара́бские/ри́мские ци́фры.

numerator *n Math* числи́тель (*m*).

numerical *adj* цифрово́й; чи́сленный; **~ data** цифровы́е да́нные; **~ superiority** чи́сленное превосхо́дство.

numerous *adj* многочи́сленный; **in ~ cases** во мно́гих слу́чаях; **the advantages are too ~ to mention** преиму́ществ так мно́го, что их тру́дно перечи́слить.

nun *n* мона́хиня.

nunnery *n* же́нский монасты́рь (*m*).

nurse *n* (*for children*) ня́ня, ня́нька; (*in hospital*) (медици́нская) сестра́, медсестра́; **male ~** *CQ* медбра́т; **district ~** *approx* райо́нный фе́льдшер.

nurse *vti vt*: **to ~ a patient/young plants** уха́живать за больны́м/за са́женцами *or* за молоды́ми побе́гами (*impf*); **to ~ smb back to health** *CQ* вы|ха́живать кого́-л (-ходить); **to ~ a child** (*suckle*) корми́ть ребёнка гру́дью, (*hold*) ня́нчить ребёнка (*impfs*); **he's at home nursing a cold** он до́ма — у него́ си́льный на́сморк; *fig* **to ~ resentment/wrath** затаи́ть оби́ду/зло́бу (*usu pf*)

vi: **she used to ~ in London** ра́ньше она́ рабо́тала медсестро́й в Ло́ндоне.

nursery *n* (*room*) де́тская; *Hort* пито́мник, расса́дник; *attr*: **~ rhyme** де́тский стишо́к; **~ school** де́тский сад; (*skiing*) **~ slopes** склон (*sing*) для начина́ющих слаломи́стов.

nursing *n* (*care*) ухо́д; (*breast feeding*) кормле́ние гру́дью; (*profession*) **she wants to go in for ~** она́ хо́чет стать медсестро́й.

nursing *adj*: **~ mothers** кормя́щие ма́тери; **~ staff** медсёстры.

nursing home *n* (ча́стная) лече́бница.

nut *n* **1** оре́х; *Mech* га́йка; *fig*: **he's a tough ~** он кре́пкий оре́шек; **it's a hard ~ to crack** э́то тру́дная пробле́ма; *attr* оре́ховый

2 *CQ*: **he drives me ~s** он меня́ (про́сто) бе́сит; **~s!** ерунда́!, чушь!; **he's off his ~** он чо́кнутый.

nutcrackers *npl* щипцы́ для оре́хов.

nutmeg *n* муска́тный оре́х.

nutriment *n* пи́ща, еда́.

nutrition *n* пита́ние; (*science*) диете́тика.

nutritional, nutritious, nutritive *adjs* пита́тельный.

nutshell *n* оре́ховая скорлупа́; *fig*: **in a ~** в двух слова́х; **to put it in a ~** коро́че говоря́.

nutty *adj* оре́ховый.

nylon *n* нейло́н; *pl* (**~s**) (*stockings*) нейло́новые чулки́; *attr* нейло́новый.

O

O *n* (*in numbers*) нуль (*m*).

oak *n* дуб; *attr* дубо́вый.

oar *n* весло́; *fig CQ* **who asked you to put your ~ in?** кто проси́л тебя́ лезть не в своё де́ло?

oarsman *n* гребе́ц.

oath *n* **1** (*vow*) кля́тва; прися́га; **under/on ~** под прися́гой; **I swear it on ~** я могу́ в э́том покля́сться; **to break one's ~** наруша́ть кля́тву; **he put me on my ~ not to tell** он заста́вил меня́ покля́сться, что я бу́ду молча́ть об э́том; **to take/swear an ~** (*of allegiance*) дава́ть кля́тву ве́рности, *Mil*, *Hist* принима́ть прися́гу; *Mil*, *Law* **to put smb on ~** приводи́ть кого́-л к прися́ге

2 (*curse*) руга́тельство; **he muttered an ~ under his breath** он тихо́нько вы́ругался про себя́.

oatmeal *n* овся́ная крупа́, *CQ* овся́нка.

oats *n usu pl* овёс (*collect*); *fig* **he's sown his wild ~** он перебеси́лся.

obdurate *adj* упря́мый; **he was ~ in his refusal to...** он упря́мо отка́зывался + *inf*.

obedience *n* повинове́ние, послуша́ние; **to act in ~ to smb's orders** де́йствовать в соотве́тствии с чьи́ми-л приказа́ниями; **to demand total ~ of smb** тре́бовать от кого́-л по́лного/беспрекосло́вного повинове́ния.

obedient *adj* послу́шный.

obese *adj* ту́чный.

obey *vti vt* слу́шаться; повинова́ться + *D* (*usu impf*), подчин|я́ться + *D* (-и́ться); **to ~ one's parents/an officer/the law** слу́шаться роди́телей, подчиня́ться приказа́ниям офице́ра/зако́ну; **he was just ~ing orders** он про́сто выполня́л приказа́ния/прика́з (*sing*)

vi: **they command, we ~** они́ прика́зывают, мы подчиня́емся.

obituary, obituary notice *ns* некроло́г.

object *n* **1** предме́т, объе́кт; **we saw a strange ~** мы ви́дели стра́нный предме́т; **an unidentified flying ~** (*abbr* **UFO**) неопо́знанный лета́ющий объе́кт; **he became an ~ of ridicule** он стал объе́ктом насме́шек (*pl*); *CQ* **a nice ~ you look!** ну и вид у тебя́!

2 (*aim*) цель; **with the ~ of helping them** с це́лью помо́чь им; **what was your ~ in doing that?** с како́й це́лью вы э́то сде́лали?; **to achieve one's ~** дости́чь свое́й це́ли; **cost is no ~** цена́/сто́имость не име́ет значе́ния; **that was the ~ of the exercise** в э́том-то вся и цель

3 *Gram*: **direct/indirect ~** прямо́е/ко́свенное дополне́ние.

object *vti vt* возра|жа́ть (-зи́ть); **to this it will be ~ed that...** на э́то возразя́т, что...

vi: **I ~** я возража́ю, я про́тив; **I ~ most strongly to that remark** я реши́тельно возража́ю про́тив э́того замеча́ния; **do you ~ to my smoking?** вы не возража́ете, е́сли я закурю́?; **I ~ to his coming** я про́тив того́, что́бы он приходи́л; **it's his manner I ~ to** что мне не нра́вится, так э́то его́ мане́ры (*pl*); **I don't ~ to a drink or two** я не про́чь вы́пить стака́нчик-друго́й.

objection *n* возраже́ние; **I see no ~s to the plan** я не ви́жу никаки́х возраже́ний про́тив э́того пла́на; **nobody made any ~s** никто́ не возража́л.

objectionable *adj* о́чень неприя́тный; отврати́тельный; **an ~ man/smell/child** о́чень неприя́тный челове́к, отврати́тельный за́пах, несно́сный ребёнок; **I find his behaviour thoroughly ~** я нахожу́ его́ поведе́ние в вы́сшей сте́пени предосуди́тельным.

objective *n* цель; объе́кт; **with this ~ in view** с э́той це́лью; **the ~ of my research** объе́кт мои́х иссле́дований (*pl*).

objective *adj* объекти́вный.

object lesson *n* нагля́дный приме́р.

obligation *n* обяза́тельство; **to fulfil one's ~s** вы́полнить обяза́тельства; **~s under the contract** обяза́тельства по догово́ру; **to be under an ~ to smb/to do smth** быть обя́занным кому́-л/сде́лать что-л.

obligatory *adj* обяза́тельный; **lectures are ~ for all students** посеще́ние ле́кций обяза́тельно для всех студе́нтов; **driving licences are ~ for all drivers** ка́ждый води́тель обя́зан име́ть води́тельские права́.

oblige *vt* **1** (*require*) обя́з|ывать (-а́ть); **to ~ smb to do smth** обяза́ть кого́-л сде́лать что-л; **you're not ~d to do it** вы не обя́заны э́того де́лать; **we were ~d to sell the house** нам пришло́сь прода́ть дом

2 (*favour*): **I did it to ~ him** я сде́лал э́то в уго́ду ему́; **could you ~ me with a cigarette** сде́лайте одолже́ние, да́йте сигаре́ту; **to ~ a friend** оказа́ть услу́гу дру́гу

3 (*passive—be indebted*): **I'm much ~d to you for the advice** я вам о́чень благода́рен за сове́т; **I don't want to be ~d to him for anything** я не хочу́ ни в чём быть ему́ обя́занным.

obliging *adj* услу́жливый, любе́зный.

oblique *adj* косо́й, *also Math*; *Gram* ко́свенный, *also fig*; **an ~ angle** косо́й у́гол; **an ~ reference to smth** ко́свенная ссы́лка на что-л.

obliterate *vt* уничтож|а́ть (-́ить); стира́ть (стере́ть); **the town was completely ~d** го́род был по́лностью уничто́жен/стёрт с лица́ земли́; **the text is here ~d** текст здесь не сохрани́лся.

oblivion *n* забве́ние.

oblivious *adj*: **~ of her warning, he...** забы́в о её предупрежде́нии, он...; **he walks around the town ~ of his surroundings** он бро́дит по го́роду, ничего́ вокру́г не замеча́я; **she was quite ~ of what was going on** она́ не сознава́ла, что происхо́дит вокру́г.

oblong *adj* продолгова́тый.

obnoxious *adj* (*revolting*) отврати́тельный; (*of people*): **what an ~ child!** како́й несно́сный ребёнок!/проти́вный мальчи́шка!

oboe *n* гобо́й.

obscene *adj* непристóйный.

obscenity *n* (*indecency*) непристóйность; (*foul language*) ругáтельство; **he muttered some ~** он пробормотáл какóе-то ругáтельство.

obscure *adj* тёмный; неясный; малоизвéстный; **an ~ corner** тёмный ýгол; **the meaning is ~** смысл неясен; **an ~ poet** малоизвéстный поэ́т.

obscure *vt* закры|вáть (собóй) (-́ть); (*confuse*) запýт|ывать (-ать); **the moon was ~d by clouds** тýчи закры́ли лунý; **the trees ~d our view** нам бы́ло плóхо ви́дно из-за дерéвьев; **that only ~s the issue** э́то тóлько запýтывает дéло.

obscurity *n fig*: **to live in ~** жить в неизвéстности; **this passage is full of obscurities** в э́том отры́вке мнóго тёмных мест.

obsequious *adj* подобострáстный, угóдливый.

observable *adj* замéтный; ви́димый.

observance *n*: **~ of rules/of an anniversary** соблюдéние прáвил, прáзднование годовщи́ны.

observant *adj* наблюдáтельный.

observation *n* **1** (*watching*) наблюдéние; **the ~ of the habits of mice** наблюдéние за повáдками мышéй; **this escaped ~** э́то ускользнýло от наблюдéния; **he is under police/medical ~** он под наблюдéнием поли́ции/врачá; **powers of ~** наблюдáтельность

2 (*comment*) замечáние

3: ~ of a law соблюдéние закóна.

observatory *n* обсерватóрия.

observe *vt* **1** (*watch, esp scientifically*) наблюдáть (*impf*); **they were observing the behaviour of birds/the progress of the battle** они́ наблюдáли за поведéнием птиц/за хóдом би́твы

2 (*notice*) замe|чáть (-́тить); **the suspect was ~d leaving the house** ви́дели, что подозревáемый вы́шел из дóма; **did you ~ what she was wearing?** вы замéтили, в чём онá былá?

3 (*say, remark*) замечáть

4 (*keep*): **to ~ a rule/custom/silence** соблюдáть прáвило/обы́чай/тишинý (*usu impf*); **to ~ a birthday/an anniversary** отме|чáть день рождéния (-́тить), прáздновать годовщи́ну (от-).

observer *n* наблюдáтель (*m*).

obsess *vt*: **this thought ~ed him** э́та мысль завладéла им; **he's ~ed by that idea/by a feeling of guilt** он одержи́м э́той идéей, егó мýчит чýвство вины́.

obsession *n*: **it's become an ~ with him** э́то стáло у негó навя́зчивой идéей; **he's got an ~ about fresh air** он помéшан на свéжем вóздухе.

obsessive *adj* навя́зчивый.

obsolescent *adj* устаревáющий.

obsolete *adj* (*of attitudes*) устарéлый; (*of words, models, etc.*) устарéвший, вы́шедший из употреблéния.

obstacle *n* препя́тствие, *also Sport*; помéха; **to be an ~ to smth** быть препя́тствием/помéхой чемý-л; **to put ~s in smb's path** чини́ть препя́тствия комý-л; *attr*: **~ race** бег с препя́тствиями.

obstetrician *n* акушёр, *f* акушéрка.

obstetrics *n* акушéрство (*sing*).

obstinacy *n* упря́мство.

obstinate *adj* (*general*) упря́мый; (*in a particular situation*) упóрный; **she was ~ in her refusal** онá упóрно откáзывалась; **they put up an ~ resistance** они́ оказáли упóрное сопротивлéние.

obstreperous *adj*: **an ~ child** сорванéц; **the children are very ~ today** дéти сегóдня óчень расшумéлись.

obstruct *vt* (*block*) загор|áживать (-оди́ть); (*impede*) препя́тствовать + *D* (вос-), мешáть + *D* (по-); **to ~ the road/smb's view** загорáживать дорóгу/комý-л вид; **to ~ traffic** препя́тствовать/мешáть движéнию; *Sport* **to ~ an opponent** блоки́ровать проти́вника (*impf and pf*).

obstruction *n* препя́тствие; *Law* обструкция; **the lorry was causing an ~** грузови́к мешáл движéнию трáнспорта.

obstructive *adj*: **why are you being so ~?** зачéм вы чини́те нам таки́е препя́тствия?

obtain *vti vt* (*receive*) получ|áть (-и́ть); (*get hold of*) достa|вáть (-́ть); **to ~ permission/results** получи́ть разрешéние/результáты; **where can I ~ another copy?** где достáть ещё оди́н экземпля́р?

vi: **this rule no longer ~s** э́то прáвило бóльше не имéет си́лы; **the custom still ~s** э́тот обы́чай ещё существýет; **under the conditions then ~ing** при тогдáшних услóвиях.

obtainable *adj*: **it's ~ at any supermarket** э́то мóжно купи́ть в любóм универсáме; **it's not ~ anywhere** э́то нигдé не достáнешь.

obtrude *vti vt*: **to ~ one's opinions on smb** навя́з|ывать комý-л своё мнéние (*sing*) (-áть)

vi: **as chairman he never lets his personal veiws ~** как председáтель он никогдá не навя́зывает своегó ли́чного мнéния други́м.

obtrusive *adj* навя́зчивый.

obtuse *adj* тупóй, *also Math.*

obverse *n* (**the ~**) лицевáя (*of coin, etc.*)/*fig* оборóтная сторонá.

obverse *adj* лицевóй; *fig* оборóтный.

obviate *vt*: **we will have to ~ this difficulty somehow** нам кáк-то придётся спрáвиться с э́той трýдностью; **this difficulty could have been ~d had we...** э́того затруднéния нé было бы, éсли бы мы...

obvious *adj* я́вный, я́сный, очеви́дный; **his disappointment was ~** он был я́вно разочарóван; **the reason is ~** причи́на яснá; **he's the ~ man for the job** э́та рабóта как раз для негó; *as n*: **you're just stating the ~** вы говори́те очеви́дные и́стины (*pl*).

obviously *adv* я́вно, очеви́дно; **she was ~ upset** онá былá я́вно расстрóена; **~, she was upset** разумéется, онá расстрóилась; **she wasn't ~ upset** по ней нé было ви́дно, что онá расстрóена.

occasion *n* **1** (*time*) слу́чай; раз; **she comes to town on ~** она́ наве́дывается в го́род от слу́чая к слу́чаю; **a dinner on the ~ of the anniversary of...** обе́д по слу́чаю годовщи́ны + *G*; **we've met on two ~s** мы два ра́за встреча́лись; **on that ~** (*of one particular occasion*) в тот раз, (*of one of a succession of occasions*) на э́тот раз; **I did what the ~ demanded** я поступи́л так, как тре́бовали обстоя́тельства; **he rose to the ~** он оказа́лся на высоте́ положе́ния; **this is not the ~ to remind her of it** сейча́с не вре́мя напомина́ть ей об э́том

2 (*reason*) основа́ние; по́вод; **she has no ~ to complain** у неё нет основа́ний (*pl*) жа́ловаться; **this was the ~ for another dispute** э́то послужи́ло по́водом для но́вого спо́ра; **I've already had ~ to warn him about it** мне уже́ приходи́лось предупрежда́ть его́ об э́том

3 (*event*) собы́тие; **it was quite an ~** э́то бы́ло це́лое собы́тие; **he composed the music for the ~** он написа́л му́зыку специа́льно для э́того слу́чая.

occasion *vt* вы|зыва́ть (-́звать), причин|я́ть (-и́ть).

occasional *adj*: **there will be ~ thunderstorms** возмо́жны гро́зы; **she pays us an ~ visit** она́ и́зредка навеща́ет нас; **he writes an/the ~ article** он и́зредка пи́шет статьи́ (*pl*); **~ verses** стихи́, напи́санные на слу́чай.

occasionally *adv* времена́ми, и́зредка.

occult *adj*: **the ~ arts,** *also as n* (**the ~**) окку́льтные нау́ки.

occupant *n* (*of house*) жиле́ц; **the ~s of the car were unhurt** е́хавшие в маши́не не пострада́ли.

occupation *n* **1** (*of dwellings*): **when will the flats be ready for ~?** когда́ мо́жно бу́дет вселя́ться (в кварти́ры?); **I'm already in ~ of the flat** я уже́ въе́хал в кварти́ру

2 *Mil* оккупа́ция; **army of ~** оккупацио́нная а́рмия

3 (*interest, work, profession*) заня́тие; **embroidery was her favourite ~** её люби́мым заня́тием бы́ло вышива́ние; **what's your ~?** чем вы занима́етесь?; **I must find some ~** мне ну́жно найти́ како́е-нибудь заня́тие; **he's an engineer by ~** он по профе́ссии инжене́р.

occupational *adj*: **an ~ disease** профессиона́льное заболева́ние; **~ therapy** трудотерапи́я.

occupier *n* вре́менный жиле́ц.

occupy *vt* за|нима́ть (-ня́ть); *Mil* оккупи́ровать (*impf and pf*); **to ~ a flat/seat/an important post** заня́ть кварти́ру/ме́сто, занима́ть ва́жный пост; **she needs something to ~ her** ей ну́жно че́м-нибудь заня́ть себя́; **~ing forces** оккупацио́нные войска́.

occur *vi* **1** случ|а́ться (-и́ться), про|исходи́ть (-изойти́); **when did this ~?** когда́ э́то произошло́/случи́лось?; **should the opportunity ~** е́сли предста́вится слу́чай/возмо́жность; **if a vacancy ~s** е́сли бу́дет/откро́ется вака́нсия; **it won't ~ again** э́то не повтори́тся

2 (*come to mind*): **it ~s to me that...** мне пришло́ в го́лову, что... [**NB** *tense*]; **it never ~ed to me to invite them** мне и в го́лову не пришло́ пригласи́ть их

3 (*be found*): **this plant ~s throughout Europe** э́то расте́ние растёт/встреча́ется повсю́ду в Евро́пе.

occurence *n* слу́чай, происше́ствие; **a strange ~** стра́нный слу́чай, стра́нное происше́ствие; **the ~ of this disease in children is rare** де́ти заболева́ют э́тим ре́дко; **it's a common enough ~** э́то вполне́ обы́чное явле́ние.

ocean *n* океа́н; *attr* океа́нский; **the ~ bed** дно океа́на.

ochre *n* о́хра; (*colour*) коричнева́то-жёлтый цвет.

o'clock *adv*: **it is now one/four/six ~** сейча́с час/четы́ре часа́/шесть часо́в; **at 7 ~ in the morning/evening** в семь часо́в утра́/ве́чера; **just after 2 ~** в нача́ле тре́тьего, в тре́тьем часу́; **it was just before 9 ~** бы́ло о́коло девяти́ часо́в; **by 5 ~** к пяти́ часа́м.

octagon *n* восьмиуго́льник.

octane *n* окта́н; *attr*: **high ~ petrol** высокоокта́новый бензи́н.

octave *n Mus* окта́ва.

octet *n Mus* окте́т.

October *n* октя́брь (*m*); *attr* октя́брьский.

octopus *n* осьмино́г.

ocular *adj* глазно́й; **~ proof** нагля́дное доказа́тельство.

oculist *n* окули́ст.

odd *adj* **1**: **~ numbers** нечётные чи́сла; **an ~ glove** непа́рная перча́тка; **a few ~ volumes** (*of a set*) не́сколько разро́зненных томо́в; **he's the ~ man out here** он здесь ли́шний; **some 40 ~ books** со́рок с ли́шним книг; **it costs £5 ~** э́то сто́ит пять с ли́шним фу́нтов; **she must be 60 ~** ей, должно́ быть, за шестьдеся́т

2 (*occasional*) случа́йный; **he does ~ jobs now and again** иногда́ ему́ перепада́ет случа́йная рабо́та; **at ~ moments/times** иногда́; **she has the ~ visitor** к ней захо́дит иногда́ кто́-нибудь; **I go to the ~ play** я хожу́ в теа́тр от слу́чая к слу́чаю

3 (*strange*) стра́нный; **he's an ~ sort of chap** он стра́нный па́рень; **the ~ thing about it was that...** стра́нно бы́ло то, что...

oddly *adv* стра́нно; **~ enough** как ни стра́нно; **they're ~ like each other** они́ до стра́нности похо́жи друг на дру́га.

oddment *n* (*remnant*) оста́ток; **the trailer was sold separately, as an ~** прице́п/тре́йлер был про́дан отде́льно.

odds *npl* **1** (*in betting*): **the ~ on this horse are 10 to 1** ста́вки на э́ту ло́шадь—де́сять к одному́; **to lay ~ of two to one on smth** ста́вить два про́тив одного́ на что-л; **what ~ will you give me?** каки́е ста́вки вы мне предлага́ете?

2 (*chances*): **the ~ were in our favour/against us** ша́нсы бы́ли в на́шу по́льзу *or* преиму́щество (*sing*) бы́ло на на́шей стороне́, обстоя́-

тельства сложи́лись про́тив нас; **we must fight, whatever the ~** на́до боро́ться, чего́ бы э́то ни сто́ило/несмотря́ ни на что́; **the ~ are against an agreement** ма́ло ша́нсов на достиже́ние соглаше́ния; **what are the ~ that they'll win?** каки́е у них ша́нсы на побе́ду?

3 (*difference*): **it makes no ~ (to me)** э́то (для меня́) де́ла не меня́ет

4 at ~: they are at ~ over what sort of car to buy они́ расхо́дятся во мне́ниях, каку́ю маши́ну купи́ть; **his actions are at ~ with what he says** у него́ сло́во расхо́дится с де́лом (*sing*)

5: ~ and ends (*remnants*) оста́тки; (*of cloth*) обре́зки; **I brought only a few ~ and ends** я взял с собо́й то́лько ко́е-каки́е ме́лочи.

odds-on *adj*: **this horse is ~ favourite** все ста́вят на э́ту ло́шадь; **he's ~ favourite for the job** у него́ бо́льше ша́нсов получи́ть э́ту рабо́ту.

odious *adj* отврати́тельный; *CQ* **what an ~ woman!** кака́я ужа́сная же́нщина!

odium *n*: **because of this he incurred a great deal of ~** э́то вы́звало всео́бщую не́нависть к нему́.

odour, (*US*) **odor** *n* за́пах.

odourless, (*US*) **odorless** *adj*: **this gas is ~** э́тот газ не име́ет за́паха.

of *prep* **1** (*denoting possession*) *G*; **in the garden ~ the hospital** в саду́ больни́цы; **the love ~ a mother for her child** любо́вь ма́тери к ребёнку

2 (*partitive*) *G*; **a kilo ~ sugar** килогра́мм/*CQ* кило́ са́хару *or* са́хара; **a jar ~ honey** ба́нка мёду/мёда; **a cup ~ tea/~ strong tea** ча́шка ча́ю/кре́пкого ча́я; **a sack ~ flour** мешо́к муки́ (*full of flour*)/с муко́й (*not necessarily full*); **how much ~ the material do you want?** ско́лько вам ну́жно материа́ла?; **I like none ~ the paintings** мне не нра́вится ни одна́ из карти́н; **you ~ all people should know** уж тебе́-то на́до бы знать; **he and I are the best ~ friends** мы с ним лу́чшие друзья́; **all ~ the books** все кни́ги

3 (*descriptive*) *usu G*; **a youth ~ 17** ю́ноша семна́дцати лет; **a man ~ medium height** челове́к сре́днего ро́ста; **the Mayor ~ New York** мэр го́рода Нью-Йо́рка; *but* **NB: the city ~ London** го́род Ло́ндон; **the battle ~ Stalingrad** Сталингра́дская би́тва; **a family ~ four** семья́ из четырёх челове́к; **a writer ~ genius** гениа́льный писа́тель; **it's a gem ~ a house** э́то тако́й преле́стный до́мик

4 (*of cause*) от + *G*, с + *G*, по + *D*; **he died ~ cancer/hunger** он у́мер от ра́ка/с го́лоду *or* от го́лода; **~ his own accord** по со́бственному жела́нию; **~ necessity** по необходи́мости; **it didn't happen ~ itself** э́то не само́ собо́й случи́лось

5 (*of origin*): **it's made ~ plastic** э́то сде́лано из пла́стика; **a bridge ~ wood** деревя́нный мост

6 (*denoting agent*): **how stupid ~ him** как глу́по с его́ стороны́; **it was kind ~ you to come** как ми́ло с ва́шей стороны́, что вы пришли́

7 (*denoting relationship, connection*) *G*; **a cousin ~ my wife** двоюродный брат мое́й жены́; **the leg ~ the table** но́жка стола́; **the poems ~ Blok** стихотворе́ния Бло́ка; **the cause ~ the crash** причи́на ава́рии

8 (*denoting time or place*): **she comes to us ~ a Tuesday** она́ прихо́дит к нам по вто́рникам; **I know him ~ old** я давно́ его́ зна́ю; **I haven't seen her ~ late** я после́днее вре́мя её не ви́дел; **a town north ~ Moscow** го́род к се́веру от Москвы́; **it's within 5 minutes walk ~ the station** э́то в пяти́ мину́тах ходьбы́ от ста́нции; (*US*) **it's a quarter ~ 5** сейча́с без че́тверти пять

9 (*with certain adjs—see also adj entries*): **he's hard ~ hearing** он тугова́т на́ ухо; **I'm short ~ money** у меня́ ту́го с деньга́ми; **it's free ~ tax** с э́того нало́г не беру́т

10 (*with certain verbs—see also verb entries*): **to accuse smb ~ smth** обвиня́ть кого́-л в чём-л; **he's ashamed ~ it** он стыди́тся э́того; **he was beloved ~ everyone** он был всео́бщим люби́мцем; **this cured him ~ the disease** э́то вы́лечило его́; **he was deprived ~ his rights** его́ лиши́ли прав; **I've been robbed ~ everything** у меня́ укра́ли всё, меня́ на́чисто обокра́ли; **it smells ~ damp here** здесь па́хнет сы́ростью; **the soup tasted ~ garlic** суп отдава́л чесноко́м.

off *adj*: **the ~ side of the road** (*UK*) пра́вая/(*SU, US, Europe*) ле́вая сторона́ доро́ги; **the switch must be in the ~ position** переключа́тель до́лжен быть в положе́нии «вы́ключено»; **in the ~ season** во вре́мя мёртвого сезо́на; **I'm ~ today** (*don't work*) сего́дня у меня́ выходно́й (день); *CQ* **it's one of my ~ days** я сего́дня не в фо́рме.

off *adv* **1** (*of distance in space or time*): **that's a long way ~** э́то далеко́ отсю́да; **the village is about five miles ~** до дере́вни приблизи́тельно пять миль; **he's ~ to London** он уе́хал в Ло́ндон; (*in racing*) **they're ~!** (*of runners*) бегу́т!, (*of horses*) ска́чут!; **be ~ with you!** убира́йся!, (*to children*) марш отсю́да!; *Theat* **voices ~** голоса́ за сце́ной

2 (*denoting cancellation*): **the concert/match is ~** конце́рт/матч отменён; **their engagement is ~** их помо́лвка расстро́илась; **the strike is ~** забасто́вка прекращена́ (*has stopped*)/отменена́ (*will not take place*)

3 (*indicating disconnection*): **do you want the radio/light ~?** хо́чешь, я вы́ключу ра́дио?/свет?; **the water has been ~ all day** весь день не́ было воды́; **is the (hand) brake ~?** ты снял с ручно́го то́рмоза?; **fish is ~ (the menu)** ры́бы нет

4 (*indicating absence from work*): **Wednesday is his day ~** у него́ выходно́й по среда́м; **I'll be ~ tomorrow** (*said at home*) за́втра я не рабо́таю, (*said in office*) за́втра я не приду́/меня́ не бу́дет; **we're ~ till Thursday**

мы не рабо́таем до четверга́; **he wants Tuesday ~** он хо́чет взять отгу́л во вто́рник

5 (*of food*): **the meat/milk has gone ~** мя́со испо́ртилось, молоко́ ски́сло; *fig*: **I've gone ~ that idea** я поосты́л к э́той зате́е; *CQ* **I thought his behaviour a bit ~** по-мо́ему, он не совсе́м хорошо́ себя́ вёл

6 *phrases*: **with his coat ~** без пальто́; **~ with those dirty jeans!** сними́ э́ти гря́зные джи́нсы!; **hats ~!** ша́пки доло́й!; **hats ~ to you!** молоде́ц!; **it rained on and ~ all day** дождь шёл весь день с переры́вами; **students get 10% ~** студе́нты получа́ют ски́дку де́сять проце́нтов; **how are they ~?** (*financially*) как у них с деньга́ми?; **he's well ~** он челове́к состоя́тельный; **he doesn't know when he's well ~** (*lucky*) он своего́ сча́стья не зна́ет; **how are you ~ for concerts?/vegetables?** как у вас с конце́ртами?/с овоща́ми?

off *prep* **1** (*from off, down from*) с + *G*; **to take smth ~ a shelf/the lid ~ a jar** снима́ть что-л с по́лки/кры́шку с ба́нки; **the ball rolled ~ the table** мяч скати́лся со стола́; **we ate ~ wooden plates** мы е́ли с деревя́нных таре́лок; **she cut a slice ~ the loaf** она́ отре́зала ломо́ть от бато́на; **she left the phone ~ the hook** она́ забы́ла положи́ть тру́бку; **there are two buttons ~ your coat** у тебя́ не хвата́ет двух пу́говиц на пальто́; **10% ~ all prices** все це́ны сни́жены на де́сять проце́нтов

2 (*away from*) от + *G*; (*near*) у + *G*; **the ship sank 5 miles ~ the cape** кора́бль затону́л в пяти́ ми́лях от мы́са; **we live just ~ the main road** мы живём у са́мого шоссе́; **a rock ~ the coast** скала́ у бе́рега

3 (*with verbs*): **to borrow/buy smth ~ smb** занима́ть/покупа́ть что-л у кого́-л; **we dined ~ cold veal** мы пообе́дали холо́дной теля́тиной; **in summer they live ~ the tourists** ле́том они́ живу́т за счёт тури́стов; *see also verbs* + **"off"**

4 *various*: **he's ~ school with a cold** он не пошёл в шко́лу из-за просту́ды; **she's been ~ her food lately** после́днее вре́мя у неё совсе́м нет аппети́та; **she's ~ drugs** она́ бро́сила принима́ть нарко́тики; **she's ~ her head** *CQ* она́ совсе́м спя́тила/рехну́лась.

offal *n* требуха́ (*no pl*); потроха́ (*pl*); (*butcher's term, also in cookery book*) субпроду́кты (*pl*).

offbeat *adj CQ* необы́чный, эксцентри́чный.

off chance *n*: **it's a bit of an ~** на э́то ма́ло ша́нсов/наде́жды; **I came on the ~ of meeting him** я пришёл туда́ на вся́кий слу́чай — а вдруг он там бу́дет.

off-colour *adj*: **I'm feeling rather ~** мне немно́го нездоро́вится (*impers*).

offence *n* **1** оби́да; **no ~ meant** не в оби́ду будь ска́зано; **to give ~ to smb** обижа́ть кого́-л; **to take ~ at smth** обижа́ться на что-л; **he's quick to take ~** он о́чень оби́дчив

2 *Law* правонаруше́ние; **an ~ against the law** наруше́ние зако́на; **it's his first ~** э́то его́ пе́рвое правонаруше́ние; **it is an ~ to exceed the speed limit** превыше́ние ско́рости явля́ется правонаруше́нием.

offend *vti vt* (*a person*) оби|жа́ть (-́деть); (*feelings*) оскорб|ля́ть (-и́ть); **he didn't ~ me** он не оби́дел меня́; **to be ~ed at** *or* **by smb/smth** обижа́ться на кого́-л/на что-л; **he's too easily ~ed** он о́чень оби́дчив; **it ~s his sense of fair play** э́то оскорбля́ет его́ чу́вство справедли́вости

vi: **to ~ against the law/the proprieties** наруш|а́ть зако́н/прили́чия (-́ить).

offender *n Law* правонаруши́тель (*m*), престу́пник.

offensive *n* наступле́ние, *Mil and fig*; **to be on the ~** вести́ наступле́ние; **to go over to/take the ~** перейти́ в наступле́ние; *attr Mil* наступа́тельный.

offensive *adj* (*insulting*) оби́дный; **his language was most ~** его́ слова́ бы́ли о́чень оби́дны; **there's no need to be so ~ to her** не на́до так обижа́ть её.

offer *n* предложе́ние, *also Comm*; **to make/accept/refuse an ~** де́лать/принима́ть/отклоня́ть предложе́ние; **his ~ of support/to help** его́ предложе́ние оказа́ть подде́ржку/помо́чь; **he made an ~ of £40 for it** он предложи́л за э́то со́рок фу́нтов; **the goods on ~** предлага́емые това́ры; **I'm open to ~s** я гото́в вы́слушать любы́е предложе́ния.

offer *vti vt* пред|лага́ть (-ложи́ть); **to ~ help/one's services** предлага́ть по́мощь/свои́ услу́ги; **I've been ~ed a job in London** мне предложи́ли рабо́ту в Ло́ндоне; **to ~ oneself for a post** предлага́ть свою́ кандидату́ру на пост; **he ~ed me the lot for £5** он предложи́л мне купи́ть всё э́то за пять фу́нтов; **I can ~ no explanation** я не нахожу́ объясне́ния; **to ~ resistance to smb** ока́з|ывать кому́-л сопротивле́ние (-а́ть)

vi: **if (the) opportunity ~s** е́сли предста́вится возмо́жность.

off-hand *adj* бесцеремо́нный; **to treat smb in an ~ manner** бесцеремо́нно вести́ себя́ с кем-л.

off-hand *adv*: **I couldn't tell you the price ~** я сейча́с не по́мню, ско́лько э́то сто́ит.

office *n* **1** (*place of work*) рабо́та, слу́жба; (*accommodation*) конто́ра; кабине́т; **he's gone to the ~** он ушёл на рабо́ту/на слу́жбу; **she's in the ~** она́ в конто́ре; **the papers are in my ~** бума́ги у меня́ в кабине́те; **editorial ~** реда́кция; **I'll get in touch with Head O.** я свяжу́сь с гла́вным управле́нием; **Tourist Information O.** бюро́ информа́ции по тури́зму; *attr*: **in ~ hours** в часы́ рабо́ты; в приёмные часы́; **~ supplies** канцеля́рские това́ры; **for ~ use** для вну́треннего по́льзования

2 (*post*) до́лжность, пост; **he holds some ~ in the ministry** он занима́ет како́й-то пост в министе́рстве; **to run for the ~ of president** выставля́ть свою́ кандидату́ру на пост президе́нта

3 *Polit* власть; **when did this government enter ~?** когда это правительство пришло к власти?; **the party now in ~** правящая партия

4 *used in sing or pl* (*duty*) обязанности (*pl*); **he performed the ~(s) of chairman** он исполнял обязанности председателя

5 *pl* (*services*): **through the good ~s of a friend** благодаря помощи (*sing*) друга.

officer *n Mil* офицер; (*of club, etc.*) член правления; **the society has elected new ~s** общество выбрало новое правление; **administrative ~** административный служащий; **police ~** полицейский (*not SU*).

official *n* (*of government, etc.*) должностное/официальное лицо; **customs ~** таможенник; **trade union ~s** профсоюзные деятели.

official *adj* (*of office*) служебный; (*authorized*) официальный; **~ duties** служебные обязанности; **for ~ use only** только для служебного пользования; **an ~ representative** официальный представитель; **in ~ circles** в официальных кругах; **is the news ~?** это официальное сообщение?

officialese *n pejor* канцелярский стиль.

officiate *vi*: **he ~d as chairman at the meeting** он председательствовал на собрании; **she ~d as hostess at the reception** она была за хозяйку на приёме; *Rel* **the bishop ~d at the service** епископ сам вёл службу/совершал богослужение.

officious *adj* навязчивый, назойливый.

off-peak *adj*: **~ traffic** движение не в часы пик.

offprint *n* отдельный оттиск.

offset *vt*: **our gains this year have more than ~ our losses** наши прибыли в этом году с лихвой возместили наши убытки.

off-shore *adj*: **an ~ breeze** береговой бриз; **~ islands** прибрежные острова.

offside *adv Sport*: **he is ~** он в положении вне игры, он в офсайде.

offspring *n* потомок, *iron* отпрыск; (*animals*) молодняк.

offstage *adv*: **voices ~** голоса за сценой; **she is/went ~** она за кулисами, она ушла за кулисы.

off-the-cuff *adj* импровизированный.

off-the-cuff *adv* экспромтом.

off-the-peg *adj*: **~ clothes** готовая одежда (*collect*).

off-white *adj* сероватo-белый.

often *adv* часто; **how ~ do you go there?** как часто вы туда ходите?; **as ~ as twice a day** не реже двух раз в день; **as ~ as not, more ~ than not** чаще всего; **every so ~** время от времени; **it's not ~ one gets the chance** не так часто выпадает/представляется такая возможность; **it cannot be said too ~ that...** никогда нелишне сказать, что...

oh *interj*: **oh how awful!** ах, какой ужас!; **oh, what a surprise!** ах, какой сюрприз!; **oh, he's coming, is he?** ах, неужели он придёт?; **oh how boring!** ах, как скучно!; **oh, my elbow!** ой, я ушиб локоть!; **oh no!** ну нет!; **oh for a nice cool drink!** вот бы выпить чего-нибудь холодненького!

ohm *n Elec* ом.

oil *n* масло; (*fuel*) нефть; (*paraffin*) керосин; **vegetable/olive/lubricating ~** растительное/оливковое/смазочное масло; **crude ~** нефть-сырец; **cod liver ~** рыбий жир; *Art*: **~s** масляные краски; **to paint in ~(s)** писать маслом; *Aut* **check the ~** проверь масло; *fig*: **he's struck ~** он напал на золотую жилу; **to pour ~ on troubled waters** улаживать дело миром; *attr*: **the ~ industry, an ~ rig/slick/well** нефтяная промышленность/вышка/плёнка/скважина; **an ~ refinery** нефтеперерабатывающий завод; **an ~ lamp/stove** керосиновая лампа/(*for cooking*) плита; (*for heating*) обогреватель, работающий на керосине.

oil *vt* смаз|ывать (-ать).

oilcan *n* маслёнка.

oilcloth *n* клеёнка.

oil-fired *adj*: **~ central heating** центральное отопление, работающее на нефти.

oil gauge *n Aut* указатель (*m*) уровня масла.

oil painting *n* картина, написанная маслом.

oilskin *n* непромокаемый плащ; **~s** непромокаемая одежда (*collect*).

oil tanker *n* (*ship*) танкер; (*lorry*) нефтевоз.

oily *adj* (*of oil*) масляный; (*greasy*) маслянистый; *fig* (*of people*) льстивый, елейный; **~ hair** жирные/сальные волосы; **he got his trousers all ~** у него все брюки были в масле.

ointment *n* мазь, притирание.

O.K., okay *interj CQ* хорошо!, ладно!

O.K., okay *n CQ*: **to give smth the ~** одобрять что-л.

O.K., okay *adj and adv CQ*: **everything's ~** всё в порядке; **it's ~ with/by me** меня это устраивает; **how are you getting on?—O.K.** как дела?—Нормально; **are you feeling ~ again?** ты уже (опять) в норме?

old *n*: **the ~ and the new** старое и новое; **the ~ and the young** старики и молодёжь; **in days of ~** в старину; **he's sure to be late—I know him of ~** я его знаю—он наверняка опоздает.

old *adj* **1** старый; (*ancient*) древний, старинный; былой; **an ~ horse/book** старая лошадь, старинная/старая книга; **an ~ man/woman** старик, старуха; **~ people** старики; **to get/grow ~** стареть; **a very ~ tomb** древнее захоронение; **~ music** старинная музыка; **in the ~ days** в былые времена, в старину; **he's a very ~ friend of mine** он мой старый/старинный друг; *CQ* **that joke is as ~ as the hills** это анекдот с бородой

2 (*expressing age*): **how ~ are you?** сколько вам лет?; **I'm fifteen years ~** мне пятнадцать лет; **she was two/five years ~ yesterday** вчера ей исполнилось два года/пять лет; **she's three years ~er than me** она старше меня на три года; **this building is over 100 years ~** этому зда́нию бо́лее ста лет; **I hope I live to be that ~** наде́юсь, я доживу́ до тако́го во́зраста; **she's ~ enough to know better** она́ уже́ доста́точно взро́слая, должна́ понима́ть; **one's never too ~ to learn** учи́ться никогда́ не по́здно

3 *various*: **the ~ man** (*boss*) шеф, (*father*) «стари́к»; **the ~ boys of the school** бы́вшие ученики́ шко́лы; (*in address*) **good ~ Tom!** дружи́ще/старина́ Том!; **how are you, ~ man?** *CQ* как дела́, стари́к/старина́?; **one sees the same ~ faces** ви́дишь привы́чные/знако́мые ли́ца; **he's an ~ hand at chess/at that game** он о́пытный шахмати́ст, он на э́том соба́ку съел; *CQ* **any ~ thing will do** да что уго́дно, всё подойдёт.

old age *n* ста́рость; *attr*: **~ pension/pensioner** пе́нсия по ста́рости, пенсионе́р.

olden *adj*: **in ~ days** в было́е времена́, в старину́, во вре́мя о́но.

old-fashioned *adj* старомо́дный.

old maid *n* ста́рая де́ва.

old people's home *n* дом для престаре́лых.

Old Testament *n* Ве́тхий заве́т; *attr* ветхозаве́тный.

oligarchy *n* олига́рхия.

olive *n* (*fruit*) масли́на, оли́вка; *attr*: **an ~ tree** оли́вковое де́рево.

olive-green *adj* коричнева́то-зелёный.

olympic *adj*: **the Olympic Games** олимпи́йские и́гры.

omelet(te) *n* омле́т.

omen *n* приме́та, знак, предзнаменова́ние; **a good/bad ~** хоро́шая/плоха́я приме́та.

ominous *adj* злове́щий; **she maintained an ~ silence** она́ храни́ла злове́щее молча́ние; **these clouds look ~** э́ти ту́чи предвеща́ют грозу́.

omission *n* (*error*) про́пуск; (*oversight*) упуще́ние; **there are ~s in the text** в те́ксте есть про́пуски; **it was an ~ on my part** э́то бы́ло упуще́нием с мое́й стороны́; (*deliberate*) **the ~ of important facts** опуще́ние ва́жных фа́ктов.

omit *vt* (*in text, etc.*) пропус|ка́ть, (*on purpose*) опус|ка́ть, (*by oversight*) упус|ка́ть (*pfs* -ти́ть); **we could ~ that word** мо́жно опусти́ть э́то сло́во; **his name was ~ted in error** его́ и́мя не внесли́ в спи́сок по оши́бке; **I ~ted to tell her** я совсе́м забы́л сказа́ть ей об э́том.

omnipotent *adj* всемогу́щий, всеси́льный.

omniscient *adj* всезна́ющий, всеве́дущий.

omnivorous *adj* всея́дный; *fig* **he's an ~ reader** он чита́ет всё подря́д.

on *adj*: **the ~ side of the road** (*UK*) ле́вая/(*SU, US, Europe*) пра́вая сторона́ доро́ги; **the switch must be in the ~ position** переключа́тель до́лжен быть в положе́нии «включено́».

on *adv* **1** (*indicating continuation*): **he went ~ to explain it** зате́м он объясни́л э́то; **read ~** чита́йте да́льше; **we went ~** мы шли да́льше; **I worked ~ till 9** я продолжа́л рабо́тать до девяти́; **she talks ~ and ~** она́ всё говори́т и говори́т; **and so ~** и так да́лее (*abbr* и т. д.)

2 (*in expressions of time*): **from that time ~** с тех пор; **from June ~** начина́я с ию́ня; **later ~** по́зже, поздне́е, пото́м; **well ~ in the year** в конце́ го́да; **time's getting ~** вре́мя идёт; **he's well ~/getting ~ in years** он уже́ немо́лод

3 (*as opposed to* **off**): **the radio is ~** ра́дио включено́; **the light is ~ in the kitchen** в ку́хне гори́т свет; **who left the tap ~?** кто оста́вил кран откры́тым?; **the water is ~ again** вода́ опя́ть идёт; **suddenly the lights went ~** вдруг зажёгся свет; **is the strike still ~?** забасто́вка ещё продолжа́ется? (*continuing*), бу́дет ли забасто́вка? (*will it take place?*); **is the hand brake ~?** (*when moving*) у тебя́ маши́на на ручно́м то́рмозе?, (*when parking*) ты поста́вил (маши́ну) на (ручно́й) то́рмоз?

4 (*expressions with "to be" and "to have"*): **the game is ~** идёт игра́; **what's ~ at the pictures?** что сейча́с идёт в кино́?; **what's ~ TV tonight?** что сего́дня по телеви́зору?; **Macbeth is ~ next week** «Ма́кбет» бу́дет на сле́дующей неде́ле; **the match is ~ after all** игра́ всё-таки состои́тся; **the trip is not ~** пое́здку отмени́ли; **the deal is ~** сде́лка заключена́; **I'm ~ (duty) at six** я начина́ю рабо́ту в шесть; **it's simply not ~** э́то соверше́нно невозмо́жно; **she's always ~ about economizing** она́ ве́чно говори́т о необходи́мости эконо́мии; **I've been ~ at him to get his hair cut** я не отстава́л от него́—тре́бовал, что́бы он подстри́гся; **he had his glasses ~** он был в очка́х; **have you anything ~ tomorrow?** ты за́втра за́нят?

on *prep* **1** (*of position*) на + *P*; **~ the table/shelf/floor** на столе́, на по́лке, на полу́; **~ page three** на тре́тьей страни́це; **to float ~ the water** пла́вать на воде́; **~ foot/horseback** пешко́м, на ло́шади *or* верхо́м; **to drive ~ the left side of the road** е́хать по ле́вой стороне́ доро́ги; **our house is ~ the motorway** наш дом стои́т у шоссе́; **we lunched ~ the plane** мы пообе́дали в самолёте; **the ballet is ~ tour** бале́т на гастро́лях (*pl*)

2 (*with implication of motion*) на + *A*, в + *A*; **he put the book ~ the table/the shelf** он положи́л кни́гу на стол (*flat*), он поста́вил кни́гу на по́лку (*upright*); **we got ~ to a bus** мы се́ли в авто́бус; **I hung my coat ~ a hook** я пове́сил пальто́ на крючо́к; **the parrot flew ~ to the roof** попуга́й взлете́л на кры́шу; **he struck him ~ the neck/the nose** он уда́рил его́ по ше́е/в нос

3 (*in expressions of time*): **~ Wednesdays** по среда́м; **~ Wednesday May the fourth** в сре́ду четвёртого ма́я; **~ May the fifth** пя́того ма́я; **~ or about the tenth** приме́рно деся́того числа́; **~ the evening of the third** тре́тьего ве́чером; **~ the next day** на сле́дующий/на друго́й день; **~ time** во́время (*adv*); **it's just ~ midnight** сейча́с почти́ по́лночь; **~ arrival in Moscow** по прие́зде/по прибы́тии в Москву́; **Christmas is ~ us** рождество́ на носу́; **~ arriving home I...** придя́ домо́й, я...; ~ **seeing me he ran off** уви́дев меня́, он убежа́л; ~ **the occasion of smth** по слу́чаю чего́-л

4 (*indicating basis, cause, etc.*): ~ **principle** из при́нципа; ~ **the grounds that...** на том основа́нии, что...; ~ **whose authority?** по чьему́ прика́зу?; **he was arrested ~ a charge of murder** он был арестова́н по подозре́нию в убийстве; ~ **this account** из-за э́того, по э́той причи́не

5 (*concerning*): **his article ~ bees** его́ статья́ о пчёлах; **I want to see him/he's away ~ business** я хочу́ ви́деть его́ по де́лу, *approx* он в командиро́вке

6 (*with various verbs*): **to congratulate smb ~ smth** поздравля́ть кого́-л с чем-л; **I'm relying ~ him** я полага́юсь на него́; *see also verbs* + **on**

7 *various*: **a tax ~ smth** нало́г на что-л; **my expenditure ~ books** мои́ расхо́ды на кни́ги; **what do they live ~?** на что они́ живу́т?; **he's ~ the staff/committee** он в шта́те, он в коми́ссии; **goods ~ sale** това́ры в прода́же; ~ **average** в сре́днем; ~ **no account** ни в ко́ем слу́чае; **he's ~ a grant** он получа́ет стипе́ндию; **I'm ~ a diet** я на дие́те; ~ **the contrary** наоборо́т, напро́тив; ~ **behalf of smb** от и́мени кого́-л; **she's ~ the phone just now** она́ сейча́с разгова́ривает по телефо́ну; **are they ~ the phone?** у них есть телефо́н?; **who's ~ duty?** кто дежу́рит?; **he's ~ leave** он в о́тпуске; **we're not ~ speaking terms** мы не разгова́риваем; **I've no money ~ me** у меня́ с собо́й нет де́нег

8 *CQ uses*: **the police have nothing ~ him** поли́ция ничего́ про́тив него́ не име́ет; **that's hard luck ~ him** вот бедня́га, как ему́ не повезло́; **their car has nothing ~ ours** их маши́на ниче́м не лу́чше на́шей; **he's ~ to a good thing** (*profitable*) он нашёл вы́годное заня́тие; **you're ~ to something there** (*an idea*) в э́том что́-то есть; **he was ~ to it at once** он сра́зу же по́нял, в чём де́ло; **I'll get ~ to him** я свяжу́сь с ним; **this one's ~ me/the house** я плачу́, хозя́ин угоща́ет; **have a drink ~ me** вы́пей со мной.

once *adv* **1** (*on one occasion*) (оди́н) раз, одна́жды; **he hit me ~** он уда́рил меня́ раз; **I've only ~ been there** я был там то́лько раз; ~ **a week/a day** раз в неде́лю/в день; **I saw him ~** я ви́дел его́ одна́жды; ~ **in a while** вре́мя от вре́мени; **we met ~ before** мы уже́ (оди́н) раз встреча́лись; **for ~ he was wrong** на э́тот раз он оши́бся; **just this ~** хоть (оди́н) раз; ~ **again/more** ещё раз; ~ **or twice** ра́за два(-три); **he's said it more than ~** он не раз э́то говори́л; **he didn't hesitate ~** он ни ра́зу не поколеба́лся; ~ **and for all** раз и навсегда́

2 (*formerly*) когда́-то; одна́жды; не́когда; **he ~ lived in Spain** он когда́-то жил в Испа́нии; ~, **when we were in Spain...** одна́жды, когда́ мы бы́ли в Испа́нии...; **I knew him ~** когда́-то мы с ним бы́ли знако́мы; **the door had ~ been green** э́та дверь была́ когда́-то зелёная/зелёного цве́та; ~ **upon a time** когда́-то, давны́м-давно́, одна́жды, не́когда

3: **at ~** сра́зу (же), то́тчас же, неме́дленно; **do it at ~** сде́лай э́то то́тчас же/неме́дленно; **all at ~ she started to cry** вдруг она́ запла́кала; **he tries to do everything at ~** он хо́чет всё сде́лать сра́зу/за оди́н раз; **everybody cried out at ~** все в оди́н го́лос закрича́ли.

once *conj*: ~ **you understand that, it all becomes clear** сто́ит то́лько поня́ть э́то, и всё стано́вится я́сно; **I'll come ~ I've done the washing-up** я приду́, как то́лько вы́мою посу́ду.

oncoming *adj*: ~ **traffic** встре́чное движе́ние.

one *num* оди́н, одна́, одно́; (*in counting*) ~, **two, three...** раз, два, три...; **the figure 1** едини́ца (*also* = **a "1"**, *lowest school mark*); $\frac{1}{3}$ одна́ тре́тья; **1.5** одна́ це́лая, пять деся́тых (*in Russian written* 1,5); **it costs ~ dollar fifty** э́то сто́ит полтора́ до́ллара/оди́н до́ллар пятьдеся́т це́нтов; **81%** во́семьдесят оди́н проце́нт; ~ **pair of pincers** одни́ щипцы́; **at 1.00 in the morning** в час но́чи; **he's not yet ~** ему́ ещё нет го́да; **the last but ~** предпосле́дний; **the next street but ~** че́рез одну́ у́лицу; **for ~ thing... for another...** во-пе́рвых..., во-вторы́х...; ~ **by ~** по одному́; **in ~s and twos** по одному́ и по́ двое; ~ **after another they all left** оди́н за други́м все ушли́; *Sport* **we're ~ up** мы на очко́ (*point*)/на гол (*goal*) впереди́.

one *pron* **1** *impersonal pron*: ~ **must not forget that...** не сле́дует забыва́ть, что...; **what should ~ take with ~?** что взять с собо́й?; ~ **doesn't pronounce the "k"** здесь "k" не произно́сится; ~ **usually writes it thus** обы́чно пи́шут э́то так; ~ **never knows** никогда́ не зна́ешь; **to offer ~'s services** предлага́ть свои́ услу́ги; **to cut ~'s finger** поре́зать себе́ па́лец

2 *personal pron*: **i) the little ~s** де́ти; **our dear ~s** на́ши дороги́е; **he lay like ~ dead** он лежа́л как мёртвый; **for ~ who has studied history he doesn't know much** для челове́ка, изуча́вшего исто́рию, он зна́ет ма́ло; **he's not the ~ I meant** я не его́ име́л в виду́; **he's the clever ~ of the family** он са́мый у́мный в семье́; **we're at ~ in this** в э́том мы заодно́; **he's chairman and secretary in ~** он и председа́тель и секрета́рь (в одно́м лице́); **each ~** ка́ждый; **never a ~** ни оди́н; ~ **and all** все до одного́; **the ~ and the other** и тот, и друго́й; **ii): one another** друг дру́га, *or use reflex verb*; **we must help ~ another** мы должны́ помога́ть друг дру́гу; **they embraced ~ another** они́ обняли́сь; **iii) one of: he's ~ of the few who are in the secret** он оди́н из немно́гих, посвящённых в та́йну; **any ~ of them** любо́й (из них); **she's like ~ of the family** она́ как член семьи́; ~ **of these days** ка́к-нибудь на днях; **iv)** *CQ*: **that's a good ~!** (*joke*) э́то заба́вно!; **you're the sly ~!** ах ты, хитре́ц како́й!; **you're a fine ~ to talk** тебе́ хорошо́ говори́ть; **he's a great ~**

for reading/the ladies он большóй охóтник до чтéния/до прекрáсного пóла; **he went ~ better** он ещё лýчше сдéлал; **we've time for a quick ~** успéем пропустить по однóй; **have ~ for the road** вы́пей стакáнчик на дорóгу.

one *adj* **1** *indef adj*: **~ day** однáжды; **~ night** однáжды нóчью; **~ summer's day** однáжды в лéтний день/лéтним днём; **he'll do it ~ day** когдá-нибудь он э́то сдéлает; **at ~ time** когдá-то

2 (*single*) еди́нственный; **his ~ talent** егó еди́нственный талáнт; **there's only ~ answer to that** на э́то мóжет быть тóлько оди́н отвéт; **that's the ~ thing I don't need** и́менно э́того мне и не нáдо; **as ~ man** как оди́н человéк; **all in ~ go** одни́м мáхом

3 (*same*): **at ~ and the same time** в однó и тó же врéмя; **we're of ~ opinion about it** мы еди́ного/одногó мнéния на э́тот счёт; **it's all ~ to me** мне всё равнó

4 (*a certain*): **~ Pavlov by name** нéкто Пáвлов.

one-act *adj*: **a ~ play** одноáктная пьéса.

one-armed *adj* однорýкий.

one-eyed *adj* одноглáзый.

one-legged *adj* однонóгий.

onerous *adj* тя́гостный, обремени́тельный.

oneself 1 *pron of emphasis* сам, *f* самá; **one has to do it ~** нáдо самомý э́то сдéлать; (*alone*) **to walk by ~** гуля́ть одномý

2 *reflex pron* себя́, *etc.*, *or use reflex verb*; **to be angry with ~** серди́ться на себя́; **to wash/dress ~** умывáться, одевáться; **to cut ~ on the chin** порéзать себé подборóдок; **to force ~ to do smth** заставля́ть себя́ сдéлать что-л; **to talk to ~** разговáривать с сами́м собóй

3 *phrases*: **to see smth for ~** уви́деть что-л свои́ми глазáми; **not to be ~** быть не в себé; **to keep ~ to ~** сторони́ться людéй, быть зáмкнутым.

one-sided *adj* односторóнний, *also fig*; **a ~ interpretation** односторóннее истолковáние; **it was a ~ contest** э́то былá нерáвная схвáтка.

one-way *adj*: **~ traffic** односторóннее движéние; **a ~ street** ýлица с односторóнним движéнием.

onion *n* лýковица, *pl* (**~s**) лук (*collect*); **spring ~s** зелёный лук; *fig* **he knows his ~s** он знáет в э́том толк; *attr*: **~ soup** лýковый суп.

onlooker *n* зри́тель (*m*), наблюдáтель (*m*).

only *adj* еди́нственный; оди́н; **an ~ child** еди́нственный ребёнок; **it's our ~ chance** э́то наш еди́нственный шанс; **we weren't the ~ ones there** не одни́ мы там бы́ли; **the ~ good thing about it is that it won't last long** еди́нственное утешéние, что э́то скóро кóнчится; **he's the ~ man for the job** тóлько он оди́н подхóдит для э́той рабóты.

only *adv* тóлько; **~ he knows** тóлько он оди́н знáет; **he ~ smiled** он тóлько улыбнýлся; **he's ~ a clerk** он ведь тóлько обы́чный слýжащий; **you ~ have to ask** вам стóит тóлько попроси́ть; **I'll be ~ too glad to help** я бýду тóлько рад вам помóчь; **not ~ ... but also...** не тóлько..., но и...; **we were ~ just speaking about you** мы тóлько что о вас говори́ли; **if ~ we could** éсли бы тóлько мы могли́; **he ~ just made it in time** он едвá успéл; **that's ~ too obvious** э́то сли́шком очеви́дно.

only *conj* тóлько; **I'd gladly do it, ~ I won't be here tomorrow** я бы с рáдостью э́то сдéлал, тóлько меня́ здесь зáвтра не бýдет.

onset *n* (*attack*) нáтиск, при́ступ; (*beginning*) начáло; **the ~ of a disease** начáло заболевáния; **the ~ of winter** наступлéние зимы́.

onslaught *n* нáтиск, нападéние; *fig* **he made a furious ~ on his critics** он я́ростно нападáл на свои́х кри́тиков.

onus *n*: **the ~ of proof is on the prosecution** предоставлéние доказáтельств — дéло обвини́теля.

onward *adj*: **~ movement** движéние вперёд.

onward(s) *adv* вперёд; **from that time ~s** с тех пор.

ooze *vti vt fig*: **he simply ~s confidence** он лóпается от самодовóльства

vi: **pus was oozing from the wound** рáна загнои́лась.

opaque *adj* непрозрáчный; (*of glass*) мáтовый.

open *n*: **(out) in the ~** на откры́том вóздухе; *fig* **he should come out into the ~ about it** он дóлжен откры́то вы́сказаться об э́том.

open *adj* **1** (*not closed*) откры́тый; (*unfolded*) раскры́тый; **with ~ mouth** с откры́тым ртом; **they left the door ~** они́ остáвили дверь откры́той; **he flung ~ the door** он распахнýл дверь; **an ~ vowel** откры́тый глáсный; **the book was ~ at page 12** кни́га былá раскры́та на двенáдцатой страни́це; **his shirt is always ~ at the neck** у негó рубáшка всегдá расстёгнута у вóрота; *Elec* **an ~ circuit** незáмкнутый кóнтур; *fig*: **to keep one's ears ~** прислýшиваться, быть насторожé (*adv*); **he went into it with his eyes ~** он знал, на что шёл

2 (*unenclosed*) откры́тый; **~ country, an ~ car** откры́тая мéстность/маши́на; **in the ~ air** на откры́том вóздухе; **on the ~ sea** в откры́том мóре; **~ to the wind and rain** откры́тый вéтру и дождю́; **an ~ boat** беспáлубное сýдно

3 (*open to the public*) откры́тый; **an ~ competition/ballot/letter** откры́тое состязáние/голосовáние/письмó; **is the post still ~?** э́та дóлжность ещё не занятá?; **it's an ~ secret** э́то ужé ни для когó не секрéт; **she keeps ~ house** у неё дом откры́т для всех

4 (*frank, etc.*) откры́тый, откровéнный; **an ~ face** откры́тое лицó; **he was very ~ about it all** он óчень откровéнно говори́л об э́том; **there's ~ hostility between them** мéжду ни́ми откры́тая враждá

5 *fig uses*: **by this conduct he is laying himself ~ to criticism** такóе поведéние подставля́ет егó под удáр; **the question is ~ to negotiation** вопрóс откры́т для переговóров (*pl*); **what possibilities are ~ to him?** каки́е возмо́жности откры́ты для него́?; **I have an ~ mind about this** я ещё не при́нял никако́го реше́ния относи́тельно э́того; *Comm* **we're ~ to offers** мы ожида́ем предложе́ний.

open *vti vt* **1** откры|ва́ть, (*unfold*) раскры|ва́ть (*pfs* ́-ть); **to ~ a book/umbrella/bottle** открыва́ть кни́гу/зо́нтик/буты́лку; **the road is ~ to traffic** доро́га откры́та для тра́нспорта; **the new hospital was ~ed by the mayor** мэр го́рода откры́л но́вую больни́цу; **they've ~ed (up) a branch in Leeds** они́ откры́ли отделе́ние/филиа́л в Ли́дсе; **to ~ a parcel/letter** вскрыва́ть посы́лку/письмо́; **to ~ (out) a map** раз|вёртывать (-верну́ть) ка́рту; **to ~ an abscess** вскрыть нары́в; *fig*: **to ~ smb's eyes to smth** открыва́ть кому́-л глаза́ на что-л; **this ~s up new possibilities** э́то открыва́ет но́вые возмо́жности

2 (*drive*) проби|ва́ть (́-ть), про|кла́дывать (-ложи́ть); **to ~ a hole in a wall** проби́ть отве́рстие в стене́; **a new road was ~ed through the mountains** в гора́х проложи́ли но́вую доро́гу

3 (*begin*) нач|ина́ть (-а́ть); открыва́ть; **to ~ a conversation/a game** начина́ть разгово́р/игру́; **to ~ a bank account** откры́ть счёт в ба́нке; **to ~ fire** откры́ть ого́нь; *Law* **counsel ~ed the case for the defence** адвока́т на́чал защи́ту подсуди́мого

vi **1** открыва́ться; раскрыва́ться; **the door ~ed** дверь откры́лась; **when do the shops ~?** когда́ открыва́ются магази́ны?; **flowers ~ in the sun** цветы́ раскрыва́ются на со́лнце; *Theat* **the play ~s on Wednesday** премье́ра пье́сы состои́тся в сре́ду

2 (*phrases with preps*): **the sitting room ~s directly into the dining room** дверь гости́ной ведёт в столо́вую; **the door ~s on to a balcony** дверь выхо́дит на балко́н; **a marvellous view ~ed out before us** пе́ред на́ми откры́лся великоле́пный вид.

open-air *adj*: **the ~ life** жизнь на откры́том во́здухе; **an ~ theatre** ле́тний теа́тр.

opener *n*: **(tin) ~** консе́рвный нож, *CQ* открыва́лка (*also for bottle*).

opening *n* **1** (*gap*): **an ~ in a wall** отве́рстие в стене́; **an ~ in the forest** поля́на, прога́лина

2 (*beginning*) нача́ло; (*inauguration*) откры́тие; *Theat* премье́ра; (*chess*) дебю́т; **the ~ of the novel** нача́ло рома́на; **the ~ of an exhibition** откры́тие вы́ставки

3 (*opportunity*, *vacancy*) вака́нсия; **we have an ~ for an engineer** у нас есть вака́нтная до́лжность инжене́ра; **there are many ~s for school leavers in the building trade** строи́тельные профе́ссии предоставля́ют широ́кий вы́бор (*sing*) выпускника́м школ.

opening *adj* нача́льный; **the ~ chapters** нача́льные/пе́рвые главы́; **an ~ address, ~ remarks** вступи́тельное сло́во; **~ ceremony** торже́ственное откры́тие; *Theat* **~ night** премье́ра; *Comm* **~ price** нача́льная цена́.

open-minded *adj* непредубеждённый.

opera *n* о́пера; **I was at the ~ last night** я вчера́ был в о́пере/слу́шал о́перу; *attr*: **~ house** о́перный теа́тр; **~ glasses** театра́льный бино́кль (*m*, *sing*).

operate *vti vt* управля́ть + *I* (*impf*); **to ~ a machine** управля́ть маши́ной; **this company ~s three factories** э́той фи́рме принадлежа́т три заво́да; **the car is ~d electrically** у э́той маши́ны электри́ческий при́вод; **can you ~ this machine?** вы зна́ете, как управля́ть э́тим станко́м?; *Med* **he was ~d on for appendicitis** ему́ вы́резали (*CQ*)/опери́ровали аппендици́т

vi **1** (*work*) рабо́тать (*impf*); (*act*) де́йствовать (*impf*); опери́ровать (*impf*); **the machines ~ on electricity** э́ти маши́ны рабо́тают на электри́честве; **these factors will ~ to his advantage** э́ти фа́кторы бу́дут соде́йствовать его́ успе́ху; **Japanese companies operating in Europe** япо́нские фи́рмы, име́ющие конце́ссии в Евро́пе

2 *Med* опери́ровать (*impf*); **they ~d on his lung** ему́ опери́ровали лёгкое.

operatic *adj* о́перный.

operating *adj*: **~ mechanism** приводно́й механи́зм; *Comm* **~ costs** эксплуатацио́нные расхо́ды; *Med* **~ table/theatre** операцио́нный стол, операцио́нная.

operation *n* **1** (*working*) де́йствие; **the new machines are now in ~** но́вые маши́ны уже́ пу́щены в де́йствие; **when does this law come into ~?** когда́ э́тот зако́н всту́пит в си́лу?

2 (*undertaking*) *Comm*, *Mil* опера́ция; **business/military ~s** комме́рческие/наступа́тельные опера́ции; **he planned the whole ~** он проду́мал всю опера́цию; **mining ~s** го́рные рабо́ты; *attr Mil*: **~s room** кома́ндный пункт

3 *Med* опера́ция; **he's had a major heart ~** он перенёс серьёзную/тяжёлую опера́цию на се́рдце.

operational *adj*: **the new planes will be ~ as from May** самолёты но́вой констру́кции начну́т соверша́ть регуля́рные ре́йсы в ма́е.

operative *n* рабо́чий; (*mechanic*) меха́ник.

operative *adj*: **the regulations become ~ on April 5** э́ти пра́вила всту́пят в си́лу с пя́того апре́ля.

operator *n* меха́ник; (*of electronic machines*, *Tel*) опера́тор; *Comm CQ*: **he's a big time ~** он кру́пный деле́ц *or* вороти́ла (*m*), (*if criminal*) он моше́нник; **he's a slick/smooth ~** он ловка́ч.

ophthalmic *adj* глазно́й; **~ surgeon** глазно́й хиру́рг.

opiate *n* опиа́т, болеутоля́ющее.

opinion *n* мне́ние; **in my ~** по моему́ мне́нию; **what's your ~ of it?/of him?** каково́ ва́ше мне́ние об э́том?/о нём?; **I'm of the ~ that...** я приде́рживаюсь того́ мне́ния, что...; **he's got a good ~ of her/of himself** он о ней/о себе́ высо́кого мне́ния; **to form an ~** соста́вить мне́ние; **to give one's ~** выска́зывать своё мне́ние; **I think we should get another ~** по-мо́ему, нам сле́дует вы́слушать и друго́е мне́ние; **I don't know what his political ~s**

are я не зна́ю его́ полити́ческих взгля́дов; *attr*: ~ **poll** опро́с обще́ственного мне́ния.

opinionated *adj*: **he's very** ~ он упря́мый догма́тик.

opium *n* о́пиум.

opponent *n* проти́вник, *also Sport*; [**NB** оппоне́нт = *official opponent at defence of thesis* (*Univ*)].

opportune *adj* уме́стный; подходя́щий; **an** ~ **remark** уме́стное замеча́ние; **at an** ~ **moment** в подходя́щий моме́нт; **your arrival was most** ~ вы пришли́/прие́хали как раз во́время.

opportunist *n* оппортуни́ст.

opportunity *n* возмо́жность, (удо́бный) слу́чай; **to take the** ~ **to** + *inf* воспо́льзоваться возмо́жностью/удо́бным слу́чаем + *inf*; **I didn't get the** ~ **to** я не име́л возмо́жности + *inf*; **to miss/let slip an** ~ упуска́ть возмо́жность; **to await one's** ~ ждать удо́бного слу́чая.

oppose *vt* проти́виться + *D* (вос-); (*resist*) сопротивля́ться + *D* (*impf*); (*object to*) возра|жа́ть про́тив + *G* (-зи́ть); **he** ~**d the decision** он воспроти́вился э́тому реше́нию; **to** ~ **the enemy** сопротивля́ться врагу́; **he** ~**s the scheme** он (возража́ет) про́тив э́того пла́на; **I** ~ **the motion** я про́тив э́того предложе́ния.

opposed *adj*: **diametrically** ~ **views** диаметра́льно противополо́жные взгля́ды.

opposite *n* противополо́жность; **"fat" is the** ~ **of "thin"** «то́лстый» и «то́нкий» противополо́жны по значе́нию; **that's the exact** ~ **of what I said** э́то пря́мо противополо́жно тому́, что я сказа́л; **I think quite/just the** ~ я ду́маю как раз наоборо́т.

opposite *adj* противополо́жный; **in the** ~ **direction** в противополо́жном направле́нии.

opposite *adv* напро́тив; **he lives (directly)** ~ он живёт (пря́мо) напро́тив.

opposite *prep* напро́тив + *G*, про́тив + *G*; **the house** ~ **ours** дом напро́тив на́шего; **we sat** ~ **each other** мы сиде́ли друг про́тив дру́га.

opposition *n* (*resistance*) противоде́йствие + *D*, сопротивле́ние + *D*; оппози́ция + *D*; **his** ~ **to the plan** его́ противоде́йствие э́тому пла́ну; **to meet with** ~ встреча́ть противоде́йствие/возраже́ния (*pl*); **to offer** ~ **to the enemy** ока́зывать сопротивле́ние врагу́; **to run up against** ~ ната́лкиваться на сопротивле́ние; *Polit* (*UK*) **the O.** оппози́ция; *attr Polit* оппозицио́нный.

oppress *vt* угнета́ть (*impf*), *also fig*; **she was** ~**ed by gloomy thoughts/by the heat** её угнета́ли *or* терза́ли мра́чные мы́сли, жара́ де́йствовала на неё угнета́юще.

oppression *n* (*exploitation*) угнете́ние, гнёт; (*persecution*) притесне́ние, пресле́дование.

oppressive *adj*: **an** ~ **regime** деспоти́ческое правле́ние; ~ **heat** угнета́ющая жара́, зной; ~ **taxes** тяжёлые нало́ги.

oppressor *n* угнета́тель (*m*); притесни́тель (*m*).

opt *vi* предпоч|ита́ть (-е́сть); **my son has** ~**ed for science** мой сын предпочёл то́чные нау́ки (*pl*); **she** ~**ed to wash up, so I dried** она́ ста́ла мыть таре́лки, а я вытира́ть; **she** ~**ed out of the party** она́ реши́ла не ходи́ть на ве́чер.

optic *adj*: *Anat* ~ **nerve** зри́тельный нерв.

optical *adj*: **an** ~ **illusion** опти́ческий обма́н.

optician *n* о́птик; **the** ~**'s** (*shop*) о́птика.

optics *npl* о́птика (*sing*).

optimist *n* оптими́ст.

optimistic *adj* оптимисти́ческий; **what do you think of our chances?—I'm** ~ как вы ду́маете, каки́е у нас ша́нсы?—Я настро́ен оптимисти́чески; **I'm** ~ **that it will be fine tomorrow** я уве́рен, что за́втра бу́дет хоро́шая пого́да.

optimum *adj* оптима́льный.

option *n* вы́бор; **I've no** ~ у меня́ нет вы́бора; **he has the** ~ **of going to Oxford or Cambridge** он мо́жет выбира́ть ме́жду О́ксфордом и Ке́мбриджем; **I'm keeping my** ~**s open** я ещё не сде́лал вы́бора; *Law* **imprisonment without the** ~ **of a fine** заключе́ние без пра́ва заме́ны штра́фом; *Comm* **they bought 40 trucks, with an** ~ **on 100 more** они́ купи́ли со́рок грузовико́в с пра́вом купи́ть ещё сто.

optional *adj*: **that's** ~ э́то по вы́бору; ~ **extras** (*fittings*) дополни́тельные приспособле́ния за отде́льную пла́ту; **French is** ~ **in this school** в э́той шко́ле францу́зский язы́к преподаётся факультати́вно.

opulent *adj* бога́тый; роско́шный.

opus *n Mus* о́пус; **magnum** ~ са́мое кру́пное произведе́ние.

or *conj* **1** и́ли; **either... or** и́ли... и́ли; **black** ~ **white?** чёрный и́ли бе́лый?; **7** ~ **8 people** семь и́ли во́семь/семь-во́семь челове́к; **I'll be there for a day** ~ **two** я там пробу́ду день-два́; **it costs 10p** ~ **so** э́то сто́ит о́коло десяти́ пе́нсов/пе́нсов де́сять [**NB** "*or so*" *indicated by inversion of numeral and noun*]; **have you got a brush** ~ **something?** у вас есть щётка и́ли что́-нибудь в э́том ро́де?

2: **or else** а то; **hurry up** ~ **else we'll be late** поспеши́, а то мы опозда́ем

3 (*with negatives*): **he didn't grumble** ~ **complain** он не ворча́л, не жа́ловался; **without help** ~ **advice from anyone** без сове́та и по́мощи от кого́ бы то ни́ было/от кого́-либо.

oral *n* у́стный экза́мен.

oral *adj* у́стный; *Anat* ротово́й.

orally *adv*: **"not to be taken** ~**"** «не принима́ть вовну́трь».

orange *n* (*fruit*) апельси́н; (*colour*) ора́нжевый цвет; *attr*: ~ **tree** апельси́новое де́рево; ~ **juice** апельси́новый сок.

orange *adj* (*in colour*) ора́нжевый.

orangeade *n* оранжа́д.

orange blossom *n* помера́нцевый цвет.

orbit *n* орби́та; **the** ~ **of the Earth around the Sun** орби́та Земли́ вокру́г Со́лнца; **to**

put a satellite into ~ вы́вести спу́тник на орби́ту; **the rocket is now in ~** раке́та нахо́дится на орби́те.

orbit *vti*: **the spacecraft is ~ing (round) the Moon** косми́ческий кора́бль вы́шел на окололу́нную орби́ту [**NB** *tense*].

orchard *n* фрукто́вый сад; **a cherry ~** вишнёвый сад.

orchestra *n* орке́стр.

orchestral *adj* оркестро́вый; **with ~ accompaniment** в сопровожде́нии орке́стра.

orchestrate *vt* оркестрова́ть (*impf and pf*).

orchid *n* орхиде́я.

ordain *vt*: **what fate has ~ed** что предопределено́ судьбо́й; *Rel* **to be ~ed** быть посвящённым в духо́вный сан.

ordeal *n* испыта́ние.

order *n* **1** (*sequence*) поря́док; **in alphabetical ~** в алфави́тном поря́дке; **in ~ of importance** по сте́пени ва́жности; **to arrange books in ~ according to subject** располага́ть кни́ги по тема́тике; **the natural ~ of things** есте́ственный поря́док веще́й

2 *Mil* строй; **in battle/marching ~** в боево́м/похо́дном строю́

3 (*good order*) поря́док; **he left his affairs in good ~** он оста́вил свои́ дела́ в поря́дке; **is your passport in ~?** ваш па́спорт в поря́дке?; **his liver is out of ~** у него́ больна́я пе́чень; **the car is in good working ~** маши́на на ходу́; **the lift is out of ~** лифт не рабо́тает; **is it in ~ for me to invite her?** ничего́, е́сли я её приглашу́?

4 (*discipline*): **to keep/restore ~** подде́рживать/восстана́вливать поря́док; **he can't keep the children in ~** он не справля́ется с детьми́

5 (*official procedure*): **the ~ of the day** (*agenda*) пове́стка дня; **that question is not in ~** э́тот вопро́с не предусмо́трен пове́сткой дня; **to call smb to ~** призва́ть кого́-л к поря́дку

6 (*command*) прика́з; распоряже́ние; **by ~ of the general** по прика́зу генера́ла; **I'm under ~s to arrest him** мне прика́зано арестова́ть его́; **he gave ~s about provisioning/that he was not to be disturbed** он о́тдал распоряже́ние (*sing*) запасти́сь прови́зией (*sing*), он приказа́л, что́бы его́ не беспоко́или; **I won't take ~s from anyone** я никому́ не позво́лю кома́ндовать собо́й; **an ~ to view** (*a house*) смотрово́й о́рдер; *Law* **an ~ of the court** распоряже́ние суда́; *Mil* **standing ~s** прика́з-инстру́кция (*sing*)

7 *Comm* зака́з; **to place an ~ for smth** сде́лать зака́з на что-л, заказа́ть что-л; **made to ~** (*of clothes, etc.*) сде́ланный на зака́з; **we'll put it on ~ for you** мы зака́жем э́то для вас; *fig* **that's a pretty tall ~** э́то тру́дная зада́ча

8 *Fin*: **banker's/standing ~** постоя́нное распоряже́ние ба́нку; **money/postal ~** де́нежный/почто́вый перево́д

9: in ~ to/that (для того́,) что́бы; **I did it in ~ to help her/that she might rest** я сде́лал э́то, что́бы помо́чь ей/, что́бы она́ смогла́ отдохну́ть

10 (*kind, sort*): **abilities of a high ~** выдаю́щиеся спосо́бности; **they spend something in the ~ of a million a year** они́ тра́тят что́-то о́коло миллио́на в год; *Biol* отря́д

11 (*of knights, monks*) о́рден (*pl* о́рдены); (*decoration*) о́рден (*pl* ордена́); **he was wearing his ~s** он был в ордена́х.

order *vti* **1** (*arrange*) при|води́ть в поря́док (-вести́); **to ~ one's time** распредели́ть своё вре́мя (*usu pf*)

2 (*command*) прика́з|ывать (-а́ть), веле́ть (*impf and pf*); **you must do as you are ~ed** вы должны́ де́лать, как прика́зано; **the doctor ~ed her to stay in bed** врач веле́л ей лежа́ть в посте́ли; **the regiment was ~ed to the front** полк отпра́вили на фронт; **I was ~ed home** меня́ отосла́ли домо́й; **he likes to ~ people around** он лю́бит (все́ми) кома́ндовать; *Sport* **the referee ~ed him off the field** судья́ удали́л его́ с по́ля

3 *Comm* зака́з|ывать (-а́ть); **I've ~ed a new suit** я заказа́л себе́ но́вый костю́м; **~ a taxi/lunch for 2 o'clock** закажи́ такси́/обе́д на два (часа́).

order book *n* кни́га зака́зов.

order form *n* бланк зака́за.

orderly *n Med* санита́р; *Mil* ордина́рец.

orderly *adj* (*of person, clothes*) опря́тный; (*of person, work*) аккура́тный; **his room is always ~** у него́ в ко́мнате всегда́ поря́док; **the crowd was quite ~** пу́блика соблюда́ла поря́док; **an ~ mind** организо́ванный/дисциплини́рованный ум.

ordinal *n*, *also* **~ number** *Gram* поря́дковое числи́тельное.

ordinarily *adv* обы́чно; **she behaved quite ~** она́ вела́ себя́ как обы́чно; **~ I get up at 7** обы́чно я встаю́ в семь утра́; **he was more than ~ polite** он был подчёркнуто ве́жлив.

ordinary *n*: **something out of the ~** не́что из ря́да вон выходя́щее.

ordinary *adj* (*usual*) обыкнове́нный; (*of ways*) обы́чный; (*average*) сре́дний, зауря́дный; **it's his ~ way of talking** э́то его́ обы́чная мане́ра разгова́ривать; **he's no ~ man** он необы́чный (*exceptional*)/необыкнове́нный (*unusually nice*) челове́к; **he's not just an ~ actor** он незауря́дный актёр; **he's an ~ country doctor** он просто́й се́льский врач; **the ~ American** сре́дний америка́нец; **a book for the ~ reader** кни́га, рассчи́танная на сре́днего/рядово́го чита́теля.

ordnance *n Mil* (*supplies*) артиллери́йское снаряже́ние; *attr*: **O. Survey map** ка́рта геодези́ческого управле́ния.

ore *n* руда́.

organ *n* **1** *Anat, Polit, etc.* о́рган; **the reproductive ~s** о́рганы размноже́ния; **the chief ~ of government** гла́вный прави́тельственный о́рган

2 *Mus* орга́н; **to play the ~** игра́ть на орга́не; *attr* орга́нный; **~ stop** реги́стр орга́на.

organic *adj Biol, Chem* органи́ческий.

organism *n* органи́зм.

organist *n* органи́ст.

organization *n* (*act or body*) организа́ция; **international ~s** междунаро́дные организа́ции.

organize *vt* организо́в|ывать (-а́ть); **to ~ deliveries** организова́ть доста́вку (*sing*); **to ~ a conference** подгот|а́вливать созы́в конфере́нции (-о́вить).

organized *adj* организо́ванный; **~ resistance** организо́ванное сопротивле́ние; **a well ~ crime** хорошо́ организо́ванное преступле́ние; *CQ* **it's time you got yourself ~d** пора́ бы тебе́ стать бо́лее организо́ванным/со́бранным.

organizer *n* организа́тор.

Orient *n* (**the ~**) Восто́к.

Oriental *n* жи́тель (*m*) Восто́ка.

oriental *adj* восто́чный.

orientate *vt* ориенти́ровать (*impf and pf*), *also fig*; **to ~ oneself** ориенти́роваться.

orienteering *n Sport* ориенти́рование на ме́стности.

origin *n* происхожде́ние; (*source*) исто́к; (*cause*) причи́на; **the ~ of species/of a word** происхожде́ние ви́дов/сло́ва; **of humble ~** незна́тного происхожде́ния; **the ~s of civilization** исто́ки/ко́рни цивилиза́ции; **the ~s of the dispute** причи́ны э́того спо́ра.

original *n* по́длинник, оригина́л; **the ~ of the painting is lost** по́длинник/оригина́л э́той карти́ны утéрян; **he reads Goethe in the ~** он чита́ет Гёте в оригина́ле; **who was the ~ for this character?** кто послужи́л прообра́зом э́того геро́я?; (*eccentric*) **he's a bit of an ~** он оригина́л.

original *adj* **1** (*first*) пе́рвый; (*earliest*) первонача́льный; **the ~ edition** пе́рвое изда́ние; **the ~ meaning of this word** первонача́льное значе́ние э́того сло́ва; **the ~ inhabitants of the area** дре́вние обита́тели/коренны́е жи́тели э́того райо́на

2 (*not copied*) по́длинный; **this is the ~ document** э́то по́длинный докуме́нт; **in the ~ Greek (text)** в гре́ческом по́длиннике

3 (*creative*) оригина́льный; **it's a highly ~ piece of work** э́то в вы́сшей сте́пени оригина́льная рабо́та; **an ~ artist** самобы́тный худо́жник.

originality *n* оригина́льность, самобы́тность; **his work lacks ~** его́ рабо́те не хвата́ет оригина́льности/самобы́тности.

originate *vti vt* (*introduce*): **she ~d a new fashion** она́ ввела́ но́вую мо́ду

vi возни́к|а́ть (-нуть); **the dispute ~d in/from a misunderstanding** спор возни́к из-за недоразуме́ния; **the plan ~d with my father** отцу́ пе́рвому э́тот план пришёл в го́лову; **where did the fire ~?** где начался́/возни́к пожа́р?

ornament *n* украше́ние, *also fig.*

ornament *vt* укра|ша́ть (-сить).

ornamental *adj* декорати́вный; **this vase is purely ~** э́та ва́за про́сто для украше́ния.

ornamentation *n* украше́ние; *Art, Mus* орна́мент.

ornate *adj* бога́то укра́шенный; (*of style*) цвети́стый, витиева́тый.

ornithology *n* орнитоло́гия.

orphan *n* сирота́ (*m and f*).

orphan *adj* сиро́тский.

orphan *vt*: **to be ~ed** осироте́ть (*pf*); **many children were ~ed by the war** мно́го дете́й осироте́ло во вре́мя войны́; **she was ~ed when she was 4** она́ оста́лась сирото́й в четы́ре го́да.

orphanage *n* де́тский дом.

orthodox *adj* ортодокса́льный; *Rel* правосла́вный; **the O. Church** правосла́вная це́рковь.

orthopaedics, (*US*) **orthopedics** *n* ортопе́дия (*sing*).

oscillate *vi* кача́ться (*impf*); *fig* колеба́ться (*only in impf*); **to ~ between two opinions** колеба́ться ме́жду двумя́ мне́ниями.

osier *n* и́ва.

osprey *n Orn* скопа́.

ossify *vi* костене́ть (о-, *fig* за-).

ostensible *adj*: **his ~ reason was..., but his real reason...** предло́гом бы́ло..., но действи́тельная причи́на...

ostensibly *adv* (*outwardly*) вне́шне; (*implying incredulity*) я́кобы; **he called ~ to deliver a note but really hoping to see her** он пришёл я́кобы зате́м, что́бы переда́ть письмо́, но на са́мом де́ле он наде́ялся уви́деть её.

ostentation *n*: **this is simply ~** э́то всё показно́е.

ostentatious *adj* показно́й; **to behave in an ~ manner** афиши́ровать себя́.

osteopath *n* остеопа́т.

ostrich *n* стра́ус; *attr*: **an ~ feather** стра́усовое перо́.

other *pron* друго́й; **one brother is a doctor, the ~ a lawyer** оди́н брат—врач, друго́й—юри́ст; **I've read those books, haven't you any ~s?** я чита́л э́ти кни́ги, нет ли у вас чего́-нибудь друго́го?; **I can't tell one twin from the ~** я не могу́ отличи́ть одного́ близнеца́ от друго́го; **where are the ~s?** где остальны́е?; **we love/help each ~** мы лю́бим друг дру́га, мы помога́ем друг дру́гу; **she and ~s like her** она́ и подо́бные ей; **how many ~s do you want?** ско́лько вам ещё на́до?; **they and three ~s** они́ и ещё три челове́ка; (*in future time*) **one or ~ of them will do it** кто́-нибудь из них э́то сде́лает; (*in past time*) **someone or ~ told me that** кто́-то сказа́л мне об э́том; **some boy or ~** како́й-то ма́льчик; **I read it in some book or ~** я чита́л э́то в како́й-то кни́ге; **I'll find her somehow or ~** я та́к или ина́че разыщу́ её.

other *adj* друго́й; ино́й; **where are the ~ 40 copies?** где други́е со́рок экземпля́ров?; **come some ~ day/time** приди́ в како́й-нибудь друго́й день, приди́ в друго́й раз; **I wouldn't wish him ~ than he is** я не хоте́л бы, что́бы он стал други́м; **for quite ~ reasons** по соверше́нно ины́м причи́нам; **it was none**

~ **than my uncle** это был не кто иной, как мой дядя; **in ~ words** иными словами; **~ people's property** чужое имущество; **how many ~ children have you got?** сколько у вас ещё детей?; **I need one ~ copy** мне надо ещё один экземпляр; **some ~ guests have come** пришли ещё гости; **the ~ day** на днях; **every ~ day** через день; **write on every ~ line** пишите через строчку; **every ~ person you meet seems to know about it** кажется, это уже известно каждому встречному-поперечному.

other *adv*: **an honourable man could do no ~** порядочный человек не мог поступить иначе; **I could have done no ~** я не мог поступить по-другому; **we haven't discussed it ~ than superficially** мы лишь слегка коснулись этого вопроса.

otherwise *adv* иначе; **he thinks ~** он думает иначе; **I was ~ engaged** я был занят другим делом; **he's stubborn, but ~ a nice chap** он очень упрям, но вообще хороший парень.

otherwise *conj* иначе; а то; **do as you're told ~ I won't take you to the film** делай, как тебе сказали, а то в кино не пойдёшь.

otter *n* выдра.

ought *v modal aux* **1** (*of duty*) *use impers* следует, *past tense* следовало + *inf*; **she ~ to come** ей следует прийти; **you really ~ to tell her** вам действительно следует сказать ей; **he ~ (not) to have agreed** ему следовало согласиться, ему не следовало соглашаться; **you ~ to be more careful** вам следует/(*slightly milder*) следовало бы быть поосторожней; **he ~ to have been a lawyer** ему бы следовало быть адвокатом; **we ~ to be going now** нам пора идти; **you ~ to have seen the look on her face!** надо было видеть выражение её лица!

2 (*of probability*) должен + *inf*; **he ~ to be there by now** он должен уже быть там; **our team ~ to win** наша команда должна выиграть.

ounce *n* унция [= 28,35 граммов]; *fig* **if she had an ~ of common sense** если бы у неё была хоть капля здравого смысла.

our *poss adj* **1** наш; **is this ~ bus?** это наш автобус?; **he'll stay the night at ~ place** он переночует у нас

2: i) *when the possessor is the subject of the sentence or clause, "our" is translated by* свой *or omitted if ownership is obvious*; **we came in ~ own car** мы приехали на своей/нашей машине; **we'll call in for ~ parents** мы зайдём за родителями; **ii)** *using reflex verbs*: **we changed ~ clothes** мы переоделись.

ours *poss pron* наш; **these books are ~** это наши книги; **they're friends of ~** они наши друзья; **they have a nice flat, but I prefer ~** у них хорошая квартира, но мне больше нравится наша; **it's no concern of ~** это не наше дело.

ourselves 1 *pron of emphasis* сами; **we decorated the flat ~** мы сами покрасили всё в квартире; (*alone*) **we were sitting (all) by ~** мы сидели одни

2 *reflex pron* себя, *etc.*, *or use reflex verb*; **we speak only for ~** мы говорим только за себя; **we talked about it among ~** мы говорили об этом между собой; **we dressed ~** мы оделись; **between ~** между нами; **we've no one to blame but ~** нам некого винить кроме самих себя.

out *adv* **1** (*of motion*: *away from, out of*) i): **"Way O."** «Выход»; **~ you go!** вон отсюда!; **on the voyage ~** когда мы плыли туда; **ii)** *with verbs usu translated by prefix* вы-; (*see also under verbs* + **out**): **to go/run ~** выходить, выбегать; **the sun came ~** вышло солнце; **I put the cat ~** я выпустил кошку; **you've left ~ a word** вы пропустили слово

2 (*of position*) в + *P*, на + *P*; **~ at sea** в открытом море; **he lives ~ in the country** он живёт в деревне; **~ in the open (air)** на открытом воздухе; **we're dining ~ again tonight** сегодня мы опять ужинаем не дома; **it's her night ~** сегодня у неё свободный вечер; **let's have a night ~** пойдём сегодня вечером куда-нибудь

3 *uses with verb "to be"* **i)** (*of people*): **he's ~ at the moment** его сейчас нет (*not in his office*), его нет дома (*not at home*); **he's ~ and about again** он опять на ногах; **the dockers are ~** (*on strike*) докеры бастуют; **when the Tories are ~** когда консерваторы не будут у власти; **we were two hours ~ from London when...** мы были в двух часах езды от Лондона, когда...; *CQ* **he's ~** (*of prison*) его выпустили; **ii)** (*of things*): **the sun is ~** вышло солнце; **my new book is ~** вышла моя новая книга; **the miniskirt is ~** мини-юбки (*pl*) вышли из моды; **the tulips are ~** тюльпаны распустились; **the tide is ~** отлив кончился; **the fire is ~** огонь погас; **before the year is ~** до конца года; **the secret is ~** секрет раскрыт; **the exam results are ~** результаты экзаменов объявлены; **the stain is ~** пятно выведено; **iii)** *various*: **you were ~ in you calculations by £5** вы ошиблись в расчётах на пять фунтов; **he's ~ for all he can get** у него на уме только, как бы поживиться; **she's ~ for/to get a husband** она подыскивает себе мужа; *CQ*: **I wasn't all that far ~** я был не очень далёк от истины; **his estimate was miles ~** он намного ошибся в расчётах; **it's the best car ~** это лучшая из существующих марок машин; **he's the biggest crook ~** он мошенник, каких свет не видывал

4 (*combined with other advs*): **I told him straight/right ~ that...** я ему прямо сказал, что...; **he's ~ and away the best student** он, несомненно, лучший студент; *CQ*: **I ran flat ~** я бежал что есть силы; **we're flat ~ at the office** мы будь здоров как выкладываемся на работе.

out-and-out *adj*: **he's an ~ republican/scoundrel** он убеждённый республика́нец, он отъя́вленный негодя́й.

outboard *adj*: **an ~ motor** подвесно́й мото́р.

outbreak *n* вспы́шка; **an ~ of anger/cholera/violence** вспы́шка гне́ва/холе́ры, а́кты (*pl*) наси́лия; **the ~ of hostilities** нача́ло вое́нных де́йствий.

outbuilding *n* (*in yard*) надво́рная постро́йка; (*if attached to house*) пристро́йка; (*shed*) сара́й.

outburst *n* взрыв; **an ~ of anger/indignation/applause** вспы́шка гне́ва, взрыв негодова́ния/аплодисме́нтов (*pl*); **I apologize for my ~** (я) прошу́ проще́ния за мою́ вспы́шку.

outclass *vt* пре|восходи́ть (-взойти́); **he ~ed all the other competitors** он оста́вил позади́/превзошёл всех остальны́х.

outcome *n* результа́т, исхо́д.

outcry *n fig*: **there was a public ~ about it** э́то вы́звало обще́ственный проте́ст; **the press raised an ~ about it** газе́ты по́дняли шум вокру́г э́того.

outdated *adj see* **out-of-date.**

outdistance *vt*: **he ~d all his competitors in the race** в го́нке он обогна́л/перегна́л/оста́вил далеко́ позади́ всех свои́х сопе́рников.

outdo *vt* пре|восходи́ть (-взойти́); *CQ* перещеголя́ть (*pf*); **he outdid them all in generosity** он превзошёл их всех свое́й ще́дростью; **not to be outdone, he upped his offer** не жела́я уступи́ть конкуре́нту, он предложи́л бо́льшую су́мму.

outdoor *adj*: **I love ~ life** я люблю́ быва́ть за́ городом; **an ~ theatre** ле́тний/зелёный теа́тр; **~ clothes** ве́рхняя оде́жда.

outdoors *adv*: **I spend a lot of time ~** я мно́го быва́ю на во́здухе; **it's warm ~** на у́лице тепло́; **she's just gone ~** она́ то́лько что вы́шла (и́з дому).

outer *adj*: **the ~ islands** отдалённые острова́; **~ circle** вне́шний круг; **the ~ suburbs** отдалённые/да́льние окра́ины.

outfit *n* **1** (*equipment*): **camping ~** похо́дное снаряже́ние; **a carpenter's ~** инструме́нты (*pl*) пло́тника; (*clothes*) **my skiing ~** мой лы́жный костю́м

2 *CQ* (*organization*): **he was transferred to another ~** его́ перевели́ на друго́е предприя́тие/в друго́й отде́л (*section*).

outflank *vt*: **to ~ the enemy** обходи́ть врага́ с фла́нга (обойти́).

outflow *n* (*from drain*) сток; *Fin*, *fig* уте́чка.

outgoing *adj* **1**: **the ~ cabinet** уходя́щий в отста́вку кабине́т; **the ~ ambassador** посо́л, покида́ющий свой пост; **the ~ tenants** выезжа́ющие из кварти́ры жильцы́; **~ mail** исходя́щая по́чта

2 (*of character*) общи́тельный.

outgrow *vt*: **to ~ one's clothes** вы|раста́ть из свое́й оде́жды (-́расти); *fig* **she still hasn't outgrown the habit** у неё так и оста́лась э́та привы́чка.

outhouse *n* надво́рная постро́йка, (*if for housing people*) фли́гель (*m*).

outing *n* (за́городная) прогу́лка/экску́рсия; **we went on an ~ to the seaside** мы е́здили к мо́рю.

outlast *vt*: **crêpe soles ~ leather ones** подо́швы из микропо́рки (*CQ*) слу́жат до́льше ко́жаных; **this coat will ~ me** э́то пальто́ меня́ переживёт.

outlay *n* расхо́ды (*pl*); **~ on clothes** расхо́ды на оде́жду.

outlet *n* (*of drain*, *etc.*) сток; *fig*: **she needs an ~ for her emotions/talents** ей на́до с ке́м-то подели́ться свои́ми пережива́ниями, ей на́до найти́ примене́ние свои́м тала́нтам; *Comm* **to find an ~ for goods** найти́ ры́нок сбы́та для това́ров.

outline *n* (*contour*) ко́нтур, очерта́ние; *fig* черта́; **to draw smth in ~** черти́ть ко́нтур чего́-л; *fig*: **in broad/general ~s** в о́бщих черта́х; **"Outlines of Modern Art"** «О́черки о совреме́нном иску́сстве».

outline *vt* **1** (*draw*) черти́ть ко́нтур чего́-л (на-)

2 (*summarize*) обрисова́ть (*usu pf*); **he ~d his views to me** он обрисова́л мне в о́бщих черта́х свои́ взгля́ды.

outlive *vt* пережи|ва́ть (-́ть), *also fig*; **she ~d her husband/the disgrace** она́ пережила́ му́жа/э́тот позо́р.

outlook *n* **1** (*vista*) вид; *fig* перспекти́вы (*pl*); **the ~ for the harvest is bright** ви́ды (*pl*) на урожа́й хоро́шие; *Meteorol* **~ for Wednesday** прогно́з пого́ды на сре́ду

2 (*mental horizon*) взгля́ды (*usu pl*); **he has a pessimistic ~ on life** у него́ пессимисти́ческий взгляд (*sing*) на ве́щи.

outlying *adj* да́льний, удалённый, отдалённый.

outmoded *adj* старомо́дный.

outnumber *vt*: **they were ~ed** враг превосходи́л их в чи́сленности; **we were ~ed 10 to 1** нас бы́ло оди́н про́тив десяти́.

out of *prep* **1** (*outside*): **i)** (*of position*, *away from*): **he's ~ town/~ the office today/~ prison again** он не в го́роде, его́ сего́дня нет на рабо́те, он опя́ть на свобо́де; **the airport is 7 miles ~ the city** аэропо́рт в семи́ ми́лях от го́рода; **when we were 3 days ~ port** на тре́тий день пла́вания; **~ sight/earshot** вне по́ля зре́ния, вне преде́лов слы́шимости; **fish can't live ~ water** ры́ба не мо́жет жить на су́ше; **nothing was ~ place** всё бы́ло на своём ме́сте; **ii)** (*of movement from a place*) из + *G*, с + *G*; **he went ~ the room** он вы́шел из ко́мнаты; **he jumped ~ bed** он вскочи́л с посте́ли; **he got ~ his chair** он встал с кре́сла; **she looked ~ the window** она́ вы́глянула из окна́/в окно́; **I threw the ball ~ the window** я вы́бросил мяч в окно́; **get ~ my sight!** уйди́ с глаз мои́х!; **he ran ~ the door** он вы́бежал за дверь; **when I get ~ here** когда́ я отсю́да вы́берусь; **iii)** *fig*: **the remark was ~ place** э́то замеча́ние бы́ло не к ме́сту; (*of a patient*) **she's ~ danger** ей сейча́с не угрожа́ет опа́сность; **strawberries**

are ~ season сейча́с для клубни́ки не сезо́н; **that's quite ~ the question** об э́том не мо́жет быть и ре́чи; **he's just ~ school** он то́лько что ко́нчил шко́лу; *CQ*: **we're well ~ that** хорошо́, что мы вы́путались из э́той исто́рии; **I felt a bit ~ it** я чу́вствовал себя́ не в свое́й таре́лке

2 (*of origin, source*) из + *G*; **we drank ~ glasses** мы пи́ли из стака́нов; **he took the key ~ his pocket** он вы́нул ключ из карма́на; **she made a skirt ~ the silk** она́ сши́ла ю́бку из э́того шёлка; **they'll never make an actor ~ him** он никогда́ не ста́нет актёром; **I get a lot ~ his lectures** мне его́ ле́кции мно́го даю́т; **he made a lot ~ it** он зарабо́тал на э́том хоро́шие де́ньги; **it was like something ~ a fairy story** э́то бы́ло как в ска́зке

3 (*of cause, motive*) из + *G*, от + *G*, с + *G*; **~ respect for you** из уваже́ния к вам; **~ joy/grief/shame** от ра́дости, с го́ря, со стыда́; **she did it ~ fear/spite** она́ сде́лала э́то от стра́ха *or* со стра́ху/назло́ (*adv*)

4 (*from among*) из + *G*; **in 9 cases ~ 10** в девяти́ слу́чаях из десяти́; **times ~ number** бессчётное число́ раз

5 (*without*): **we're ~ bread** у нас ко́нчился хлеб; **we ran ~ petrol** у нас ко́нчился бензи́н; **it's ~ stock** э́то всё распро́дано; **I'm ~ breath** я запыха́лся; **you're ~ luck** тебе́ не повезло́; **he's ~ a job** он сейча́с без рабо́ты.

out-of-date *adj* (*of ideas*) устаре́лый; (*of cars, clothes, etc.*) устаре́вший, (*of clothes*) вы́шедший из мо́ды.

out-of-doors *adv see* **outdoors**.

out-of-the-way *adj*: **an ~ farm** отдалённая фе́рма; *CQ* **I noticed nothing ~** я не заме́тил ничего́ необы́чного/из ря́да вон выходя́щего.

outpatient *n* амбулато́рный больно́й; *attr*: **O. Department** *approx* поликли́ника при больни́це.

outpost *n Mil* аванпо́ст, *also fig*; *fig* **an ~ of civilization** аванпо́ст цивилиза́ции.

output *n* вы́пуск, проду́кция; **the ~ of new goods** вы́пуск но́вых това́ров; **the factory's ~ for the year** проду́кция заво́да за́ год.

outrage *n*: **an ~ against humanity** преступле́ние про́тив челове́чества; **feelings of ~** чу́вство (*sing*) негодова́ния; *CQ* **it's an ~!** э́то возмути́тельно!

outrage *vt* (*scandalize*) возму|ща́ть (-ти́ть); (*offend*) оскорб|ля́ть (-и́ть); **public opinion/my sense of justice was ~d** обще́ственное мне́ние бы́ло возмущено́, во мне бы́ло оскорблено́ чу́вство справедли́вости.

outrageous *adj* (*of conduct, etc.*) возмути́тельный; **it's an ~ price** э́то неслы́ханная цена́.

outright *adj* (*frank*) откры́тый, прямо́й; (*definite*) реши́тельный; **an ~ manner** откры́тая мане́ра; **an ~ refusal/lie** реши́тельный отка́з, открове́нная/на́глая ложь.

outright *adv* откры́то, пря́мо, реши́тельно; **I'll tell him so ~** я ему́ пря́мо так и скажу́; **he laughed at it ~** он откры́то смея́лся над э́тим; **he won the contest ~** он одержа́л реши́тельную побе́ду; **he rejected the offer ~** он наотре́з отказа́лся от э́того предложе́ния; **he was killed ~** он был уби́т напова́л; **to buy a house ~** купи́ть дом, уплати́в всю су́мму сра́зу.

outset *n*: **at the ~** внача́ле (*adv*); **from the very ~** с са́мого нача́ла.

outshine *vt fig* затм|ева́ть (-и́ть).

outside *n* **1** нару́жность; **judging from the ~** су́дя по нару́жности/по вне́шнему ви́ду; **the window opens to the ~** окно́ открыва́ется нару́жу; **to lock a door on the ~** запира́ть дверь снару́жи; **repairs to the ~** (*of a building*) нару́жный ремо́нт

2: **at the ~** са́мое бо́льшее; **it will take an hour at the ~** э́то займёт са́мое бо́льшее час; **it will cost £100 at the ~** э́то сто́ит са́мое бо́льшее сто фу́нтов.

outside *adj* вне́шний; нару́жный; **the ~ world** вне́шний мир; **the ~ edge of smth** вне́шний край чего́-л; **~ appearance** нару́жность, вне́шность, вне́шний вид; **in the ~ lane** *Aut* во вне́шнем ряду́, *Sport* по вне́шней доро́жке; **an ~ seat** (*on bus, plane*) ме́сто у окна́; **he gave us an ~ estimate of £100 for the repairs** он сказа́л, что ремо́нт бу́дет сто́ить са́мое бо́льшее сто фу́нтов; **without ~ help** без посторо́нней по́мощи; **let's get an ~ opinion on this** дава́йте спро́сим кого́-нибудь друго́го об э́том; *Sport*: **he's got an ~ chance of winning** у него́ ничто́жный шанс на побе́ду; **~ left** ле́вый кра́йний.

outside *adv* (*on the outside*) нару́жу; (*from the outside*) снару́жи; (*outdoors*) на у́лице, на дворе́, (*of movement*) на у́лицу, во двор; **the shed is painted red ~** снару́жи сара́й покра́шен в кра́сный цвет; **he went ~** он вы́шел и́з дому/на у́лицу; **the toilet is ~** убо́рная во дворе́; **it's cold ~** на у́лице хо́лодно; **to work ~** рабо́тать на откры́том во́здухе.

outside *prep* **1** (*at, near*) у + *G*, ря́дом с + *I*, *etc.*; **he was waiting ~ the door** он ждал у две́ри; **we met her ~ the cinema** мы встре́тились с ней у вхо́да в кинотеа́тр; **there's a bus stop ~ our house** ря́дом с на́шим до́мом есть авто́бусная остано́вка; **someone was talking ~ the window** под о́кнами (*pl*) кто́-то разгова́ривал; **a village 7 kilometers ~ Kiev** дере́вня в семи́ киломе́трах от Ки́ева

2 (*beyond*): **~ working hours** в нерабо́чее вре́мя, в нерабо́чие часы́, не на рабо́те; **they live ~ the area** они́ живу́т не в э́том райо́не; **it's ~ my experience** у меня́ нет о́пыта в э́том де́ле; **he's famous ~ his own country** он изве́стен за преде́лами свое́й страны́; **this species isn't found ~ Africa** э́тот вид встреча́ется то́лько в А́фрике.

outsider *n* посторо́нний, чужо́й; *CQ* **he's looked on as an ~** на него́ смо́трят как на чужо́го.

outsize *adj*: ~ **clothes** одéжда больши́х/нестандáртных размéров.

outskirts *npl* окрáина, (*of wood*) опу́шка (*sings*); **on the ~ of Moscow** на окрáине Москвы́.

outspoken *adj* откровéнный.

outspread *adj*: **with ~ wings** с распростёртыми кры́льями.

outstanding *adj* (*exceptional*) выдаю́щийся, знамени́тый; *Comm*: ~ **bills** неоплáченные счетá; **business still ~** незакóнченная рабóта.

outstay *vt*: **she ~ed the other guests** онá пересидéла всех гостéй; *pejor* **to ~ one's welcome** злоупотребля́ть чьим-л. гостеприи́мством.

outstretched *adj* протя́нутый; **an ~ hand/arm** протя́нутая рукá; **with ~ arms** с распростёртыми объя́тиями.

outstrip *vt* об|гоня́ть (-огнáть); опере|жáть (-ди́ть).

out-tray *n* я́щик для исходя́щих бумáг/пи́сем.

outward *adj* вне́шний; **judging by ~ appearances** су́дя по вне́шнему ви́ду (*sing*); *Naut, etc.* **on the ~ voyage to Sydney** во врéмя плáвания в Си́дней.

outward *adv*: **ships ~ bound from London** корабли́, отплывáющие из лóндонского пóрта.

outwardly *adv* вне́шне; **she remained ~ calm** вне́шне онá оставáлась спокóйной.

outwards *adv*: **turn it ~** вы́верни э́то нару́жу.

outweigh *vt* перевé|шивать (-сить), *also fig*; **this ~ed all other considerations** э́то перевéсило все остальны́е соображéния.

outwit *vt* перехитри́ть (*pf*).

outworn *adj* изнóшенный, *also fig*; *fig* изби́тый.

oval *n* овáл; *attr* овáльный.

ovary *n Anat* яи́чник; *Bot* зáвязь.

ovation *n* овáция; **to give smb an ~** устрáивать кому́-л овáцию; **she got a standing ~** её встрéтили бу́рной овáцией.

oven *n* духóвка; (*kiln*) печь.

ovenproof *adj* жаростóйкий, жаропрóчный, жароупóрный.

ovenware *n* огнеупóрная/жаропрóчная посу́да.

over *adv* **1** (*of place*) **i)**: ~ **here/there** здесь, там; **she's ~ in Sweden** онá сейчáс в Швéции; **they're ~ from Canada** они́ приéхали из Канáды; **put your bike ~ against the shed** постáвь велосипéд там, у сарáя; **ii)**: **all ~** повсю́ду; **the world ~** во всём ми́ре; **they searched the whole country ~** они́ искáли по всей странé; **I ache all ~** у меня́ всё боли́т; **she was shaking all ~** онá вся дрожáла; **the wall was covered all ~ with notices** вся стенá былá заклéена объявлéниями; *CQ* **that's him all ~** э́то так похóже на негó; **iii)** *fig*: **children aged 13 and ~** дéти тринáдцати лет и стáрше

2 (*of motion*): **come ~ here** иди́ сюдá; **we drove ~ there/~ to see them** мы éздили тудá/к ним; **he went ~ to the fireplace** он подошёл кками́ну; **this strap goes ~ and this one under** э́тот ремéнь дóлжен быть свéрху, а э́тот сни́зу; *fig* **when we went ~ to decimal currency** когдá мы перешли́ на десяти́чную монéтную систéму

3 *with verbs—see also verb entries*: **i)**: **the milk has boiled ~** молокó убежáло/сплы́ло; **to fall ~** опроки́нуться; **to knock smth ~** опроки́нуть что-л; **to hand smth ~ to smb** передавáть что-л кому́-л; **to look smth ~** осмáтривать что-л; **have you talked it ~ with her?** вы э́то с ней обговори́ли?; **ii) over again**: **I had to do it all ~ again** мне пришлóсь всё передéлать; **I counted the money ~ again** я пересчитáл дéньги ещё раз; **she repeated it ~ and ~ again** онá снóва и снóва повторя́ла э́то

4 (*remaining*): **4 and 1 ~** четы́ре и оди́н в остáтке; **I had £5 ~** у меня́ остáлось пять фу́нтов; **I bought a book with what I had ~** на остáвшиеся дéньги я купи́л кни́гу

5 (*excessively*) чересчу́р, сли́шком; **she's ~ particular** онá чересчу́р привередлива; **he wasn't ~ polite** он был не сли́шком вéжлив

6 (*finished*): **the lecture is ~** лéкция окóнчена; **as soon as the war was ~** как тóлько окóнчилась войнá; **it's all ~ between them** мéжду ни́ми всё кóнчено; **the storm will soon be ~** грозá скóро пройдёт.

over *prep* **1** (*of place*) **i)** (*on*) на + *P*; **he had a patch ~ one eye** у негó на глазу́ былá повя́зка; **she spread a blanket ~ the floor** онá расстели́ла одея́ло на полу́; **she put an apron ~ her dress** онá надéла повéрх плáтья фáртук; **to trip ~ smth** спотыкáться обо что-л; **ii)** (*above*) над + *I*; (*over the top of*) чéрез + *A*; повéрх + *G*; **the plane was now ~ the aerodrome** тепéрь самолёт был над аэродрóмом; **she leaned ~ me/the table** онá наклони́лась надо мнóй/над столóм; **he looked ~ the wall/~ his spectacles** он посмотрéл чéрез забóр/повéрх очкóв; **to sit ~ the fire** сидéть у ками́на; **iii)** (*across*) чéрез + *A*; за + *I*; по + *D*; **they live ~ the road** они́ живу́т за дорóгой; **~ the border in Spain** за грани́цей в Испáнии; **the birds flew away ~ the hills** пти́цы улетéли за гóры; **we walked ~ the fields** мы шли по поля́м; **he ran his hand ~ the surface** он провёл рукóй по повéрхности; **iv)** (*down from*) с + *G*; **to fall ~ a cliff** упáсть со скалы́; **v)** (*everywhere, all over*): **all ~ the country** по всей странé; **I spilt fat all ~ the floor** я разбры́згал жир по всему́ пóлу; **he's been all ~ the Highlands** он объéздил весь Хáйленд (*sing*); *CQ* **they were all ~ her** они́ так носи́лись с ней

2 *with verbs—see also particular verbs*: **to worry ~ smth** беспокóиться о чём-л; **to quarrel ~ smth** ссóриться из-за чегó-л; **he had control ~ the whole department** он руководи́л всем отдéлом; **to win an advantage ~ smb** доби́ться преиму́щества над кем-л

3 (*of time*) за + *A*, в течéние + *G*; ~ **the whole period** за весь э́тот перйод; **the school was done up ~ the holidays** за лéто шкóлу отремонтйровали; ~ **many years** в течéние мнóгих лет, мнóгие гóды; **we stayed with her ~ the weekend** мы остáлись у неё на суббóту и воскресéнье; **how long did you take ~ the job?** скóлько врéмени ушлó у вас на э́ту рабóту?; **the payments are spread ~ 6 months** платежй рассчйтаны на полгóда/на шесть мéсяцев

4 (*more than*) свы́ше + *G*, бóльше + *G*; **well ~ 40%** намнóго вы́ше/бóльше сорокá процéнтов; **we paid £100 ~ and above the asking price** мы заплатйли на сто фýнтов бóльше назнáченной цены́; **he's ~ 90** емý за девянóсто

5 *various*: **let's discuss it ~ a drink** давáйте обсýдим э́то за бокáлом винá; **he sits up all night ~ his books** он всю ночь сидйт над кнйгами; **we've been ~ all this before** мы ужé об э́том говорйли; **what's come ~ you?** что на тебя́ нашлó?; **I heard it ~ the radio** я слы́шал об э́том по рáдио.

overact *vi* переигр|ывать (-áть).

overall *n* халáт; *pl* (~**s**) (*industrial*) комбинезóн (*sing*).

overall *adj* óбщий; **an ~ survey of the situation** óбщий обзóр собы́тий (*pl*); **the ~ result** óбщий результáт; **the ~ measurements** *Tech* габарйтные размéры.

overawe *vt*: **he was quite ~d by his teacher/by the splendour of the ceremony** он óчень боя́лся своегó учйтеля, великолéпие церемóнии поразйло егó.

overbalance *vti vt*: **don't ~ the canoe** не переверні́ канóэ

vi теря́ть равновéсие (по-).

overbearing *adj* влáстный, деспотйчный.

overboard *adv*: **man ~!** человéк за бóртом!; **to throw smth ~** выбрáсывать что-л зá борт, *also fig*.

overburden *vt* перегру|жáть (-зйть), *also fig*.

overcast *adj* пáсмурный; **it became ~** нéбо покры́лось тýчами.

overcharge *vt*: **they've ~d me for it** с меня́ взя́ли слйшком мнóго за э́то; *Elec* переза-ря|жáть (-дйть).

overcoat *n* пальтó (*indecl*).

overcome *vt* (*defeat*) поборóть (*pf*); (*surmount*) преодоле|вáть (́-ть); **to ~ difficulties** преодолевáть трýдности; **he was ~ by grief** он был убйт гóрем.

overconfident *adj* самоувéренный, самонадéянный.

overcook *vt* (*roast*) пережáр|ивать (-ить); (*boil*) перевáр|ивать (-йть).

overcrowded *adj* переполненный.

overcrowding *n* перенаселённость.

overdo *vt* (*exaggerate*): **he overdid the apologies** он слйшком дóлго извиня́лся; **the actor overdid the part** актёр здесь переигрывал; *CQ* **he's been ~ing it/things lately** послéднее врéмя он слйшком перегружáл себя́.

overdone *adj* (*exaggerated*) преувелйченный, утрйрованный; *Cook* пережáренный; переварéнный; (*tired*) переутомлённый.

overdose *n*: **he took an ~** он прйнял слйшком большýю дóзу.

overdraft *n*: **I've got a huge ~ at the bank** я намнóго превы́сил кредйт в бáнке.

overdraw *vt*: **to ~ one's account** превы|шáть кредйт в бáнке (́-сить).

overdress *vti*: **it's very hot—I'm ~ed** óчень жáрко, а я слйшком теплó одéт; **she was ~ed for the occasion** онá нарядйлась по э́тому слýчаю.

overdue *adj*: **the train is half an hour ~** пóезд опáздывает на полчасá; **she is a week ~** (*her baby*) *CQ* онá ужé недéлю перехáживает; **the change was long ~** э́тих изменéний (*pl*) давнó ждáли; *Comm* **these bills are ~** э́ти счетá просрóчены.

overeat *vi* пере|едáть (-éсть).

overestimate *vt* переоцéни|вать (́-ть).

overexcited *adj*: **the children were ~** дéти бы́ли возбуждены́; **my father became ~** мой отéц óчень разволновáлся.

overexert *vt*: **to ~ oneself** перенапря|гáться (́-чься).

overexpose *vt Photo* передéрж|ивать (-áть).

overflow *n*: **there is an ~ from the cistern** цистéрна переполнена; *fig* **population ~** избы́точное населéние, перенаселéние; *attr*: ~ **pipe** сливнáя трубá.

overflow *vi* (*of rivers*) разли|вáться (́-ться); **to fill a cup to ~ing** нали|вáть в чáшку до краёв (́-ть); **the barrel is ~ing** из бóчки водá переливáется чéрез край; *fig* **the crowd ~ed into the street** толпá вы́плеснулась на ýлицу.

overfull *adj* перепóлненный.

overgrown *adj*: **an ~ schoolboy** переростóк; **a path ~ with weeds** тропйнка, зарóсшая сорнякáми.

overhanging *adj* нависáющий.

overhaul *n* (*check*) осмóтр; (*repair*) ремóнт; **the engine needs an ~** мотóр нуждáется в ремóнте; *CQ* **the doctor gave me a thorough ~** врач внимáтельно меня́ осмотрéл.

overhaul *vt* (*check*) осмáтривать (осмотрéть); (*repair*) ремонтйровать (от-).

overhead *adj* **1**: ~ **wires** воздýшная лйния (*sing*); **an ~ railway** надзéмная желéзная дорóга

2 *Comm*: ~ **costs/expenses,** *also as n* (~**s**) накладнúе расхóды.

overhead *adv*: **the eagle was circling ~** орёл кружйл над головóй; **in the room ~** в кóмнате наверхý.

overhear *vt*: **I couldn't help ~ing them** я не мог не слы́шать их; **she was ~d to say that...** слы́шали, как онá сказáла, что...

overheat *vti vt* перегре|вáть (́-ть)

vi: **the engine should not ~** мотóр не дóлжен перегревáться.

overindulge *vti vt*: **you ~ your child** ты слйшком балýешь ребёнка; **she ~s her passion**

for sweet things она́ позволя́ет себе́ сли́шком мно́го сла́дкого

vi: **I ~d last night** вчера́ ве́чером я в гостя́х переéл и вы́пил ли́шнее.

overindulgent *adj*: **~ parents** сли́шком снисходи́тельные роди́тели; **he is ~ towards her extravagance** он сли́шком снисходи́тельно отно́сится к её расточи́тельности.

overjoyed *adj*: **he'll be ~ to see her** он бу́дет о́чень рад уви́деть её; **we were ~ about the news** мы о́чень ра́довались э́тому изве́стию.

overland *adj*: **an ~ route** сухопу́тный маршру́т.

overland *adv* по су́ше; **to travel ~** путеше́ствовать по су́ше.

overlap *n Tech* перекры́тие; *Sew* **leave a good ~** оста́вьте побо́льше для запа́ха.

overlap *vi*: **the planks must ~** до́ски должны́ заходи́ть одна́ за другу́ю; **the pleats ~** скла́дки нахо́дят одна́ на другу́ю; **our duties ~** на́ши обя́занности части́чно совпада́ют.

overleaf *adv*: **see ~** смотри́ на оборо́те.

overload *vt* перегру|жа́ть (-зи́ть); *Elec* перезаря|жа́ть (-ди́ть).

overlook *vt* **1** (*of view*): **the window ~s the bay** окно́ выхо́дит на зали́в; **a house ~ing the sea** дом с ви́дом на мо́ре; **from my window I ~ the Zoo** из моего́ окна́ ви́ден зоопа́рк

2 (*omit*) пропус|ка́ть (-ти́ть); упус|ка́ть из ви́ду (-ти́ть); про|сма́тривать (-смотре́ть); **I ~ed that possibility/her name on the list** я упусти́л из ви́ду э́ту возмо́жность, я наве́рно просмотре́л её и́мя в спи́ске; **to ~ smb's faults** смотре́ть сквозь па́льцы на чьи-л недоста́тки; **I'll ~ it this time** на сей раз я закро́ю на э́то глаза́.

overmuch *adv* чрезме́рно, сли́шком.

overnight *adj*: **an ~ journey** ночно́е путеше́ствие; **we had an ~ stay in Novgorod** мы останови́лись на ночлéг в Но́вгороде; **an ~ bag** саквоя́ж.

overnight *adv*: **we drove there ~** мы е́хали туда́ одну́ ночь; **the weather changed ~** пого́да за́ ночь измени́лась; **I stayed with them ~** я оста́лся у них на́ ночь.

overpass *n* путепрово́д.

overpayment *n* перепла́та.

overpopulated *adj* перенаселённый.

overpower *vt* одоле|ва́ть (-́ть), переси́л|ивать (-ить); **to ~ an opponent** одоле́ть/переси́лить проти́вника; *fig* **she was ~ed by the heat** её угнета́ла жара́.

overproduction *n* перепроизво́дство.

overrate *vt* переоце́ни|вать (-́ть).

overreach *vt*: **he ~ed himself that time** *CQ* на э́тот раз он зарва́лся.

overripe *adj* перезре́лый.

overrule *vt* отклон|я́ть, отмен|я́ть (*pfs* -и́ть); **he ~d all objections** он отклони́л все возраже́ния; **to ~ a decision** отменя́ть реше́ние; **we were ~d by the majority** большинство́ голосова́ло про́тив нас.

overrun *vt*: **rabbits have ~ the whole island** кро́лики рассели́лись по всему́ о́строву; **the house is ~ with cockroaches** дом киши́т тарака́нами; **the town was ~ with tourists** го́род наводни́ли тури́сты; **a garden ~ with weeds** сад, заро́сший сорняка́ми; **the programme overran its time by 5 minutes** переда́ча шла до́льше поло́женного вре́мени на пять мину́т.

overscrupulous *adj*: **one needn't/can't be ~ in such matters** в таки́х вопро́сах нельзя́ быть чересчу́р щепети́льным.

overseas *adj* иностра́нный; **~ tourists** иностра́нные тури́сты; **~ territories** замо́рские террито́рии; **~ trade** вне́шняя торго́вля.

overseas *adv* за грани́цей; **she studied ~** она́ учи́лась за грани́цей; **he went ~** он уе́хал за грани́цу; **visitors from ~** го́сти из-за рубежа́.

overseer *n* (*warden*) надзира́тель (*m*); (*foreman*) ма́стер; контролёр.

overshoe *n* гало́ша.

overshoot *vt*: **to ~ the runway** пролете́ть поса́дочную площа́дку (*usu pf*); *fig* **to ~ the mark** зайти́ сли́шком далеко́.

oversight *n* недосмо́тр, упуще́ние; **by an ~** по недосмо́тру; **it was an ~ on my part** э́то бы́ло упуще́нием с мое́й стороны́.

oversleep *vi* про|сыпа́ть (-спа́ть).

overspend *vti*: **I overspent my allowance by 5 dollars** я истра́тил на пять до́лларов бо́льше поло́женного; **we've overspent by £100** мы истра́тили ли́шних сто фу́нтов.

overspill *n* (*excess population*) избы́точное населе́ние; *attr*: **an ~ town** го́род-спу́тник

overstaff *vt*: **this department is ~ed** в э́том отде́ле разду́ты шта́ты.

overstate *vt* преувели́ч|ивать (-ить).

overstock *vt*: **to ~ a shop with goods** затова́ри|ваться (-ться); **our farm is ~ed** у нас на фе́рме бо́льше скота́, чем мы мо́жем прокорми́ть.

overstrung *adj* перенапряжённый.

overt *adj* откры́тый, я́вный.

overtake *vt*: **to ~ a car** об|гоня́ть маши́ну (-огна́ть); **Canada has ~n the USA in grain exports** Кана́да обогнала́ США в э́кспорте зерна́; **he was ~n by events** собы́тия заста́ли его́ врасплóх.

overtaking *n*: **"No O."** «обго́н запрещён».

overtax *vt*: **the country is ~ed** страна́ несёт непоси́льное бре́мя нало́гов; *fig*: **to ~ oneself** перенапря|га́ться (-́чься); **don't ~ my patience** не испы́тывай моё терпе́ние.

overthrow *vt* сверг|а́ть (-́нуть).

overtime *n* сверхуро́чная рабо́та; **to do/work/be on ~** рабо́тать сверхуро́чно (*adv*); *attr*: **~ pay** сверхуро́чная опла́та, сверхуро́чные (*pl*).

overtone *n Mus* оберто́н; *fig*: **his words had sinister ~s** в его́ слова́х таи́лся злове́щий намёк (*sing*); **this word has subtle ~s** э́то сло́во неоднозна́чно.

overture *n Mus* увертю́ра; *fig* **to make peace ~s** де́лать ми́рные предложе́ния.

overturn *vti* опроки́|дывать(ся) (-нуть(ся)).

overweening *adj* чрезме́рный; ~ **ambition** чрезме́рное честолю́бие.

overweight *adj*: **he's** ~ **for his height** он сли́шком мно́го ве́сит для своего́ ро́ста; **I'm 4 kilos** ~ я ве́шу на четы́ре килогра́мма бо́льше но́рмы; **this parcel is** ~ э́та посы́лка сли́шком тяжела́; ~ **luggage** изли́шек багажа́.

overwhelm *vt* одоле|ва́ть (-́ть); **to** ~ **an opponent** одоле́ть проти́вника; **he was** ~**ed by/with grief** он был уби́т го́рем; **your kindness has** ~**ed me** ва́ша доброта́ ошеломи́ла меня́.

overwhelming *adj*: **an** ~ **majority** подавля́ющее большинство́; **an** ~ **defeat** по́лное пораже́ние.

overwind *vt*: **to** ~ **a watch** перекрути́ть пружи́ну часо́в (*usu pf*).

overwork *vti vt*: **to** ~ **oneself** переутом|ля́ться (-и́ться); **to** ~ **a horse** заезди́ть ло́шадь (*pf*); **to** ~ **smb** перегру|жа́ть кого́-л рабо́той (-зи́ть)

vi: **he's been** ~**ing** он переутоми́лся.

overwrought *adj* перевозбуждённый.

owe *vt*: **he** ~**s me £5** он до́лжен мне пять фу́нтов; **I'll** ~ **it to you** я бу́ду тебе́ до́лжен; **he** ~**s everything to his mother** он всем обя́зан свое́й ма́тери; **he** ~**s his success to good luck** свои́м успе́хом он обя́зан счастли́вому слу́чаю; **to** ~ **smb a grudge** име́ть зуб про́тив кого́-л; **you** ~ **it to her to be present** вы должны́ там прису́тствовать ра́ди неё; **you** ~ **it to yourself to accept the offer** вам необходи́мо приня́ть э́то предложе́ние ра́ди своего́ же бла́га.

owing *adj* **1**: **the amount still** ~ **on the house** су́мма, ещё не вы́плаченная за дом; **there's still £5** ~ **to me** мне ещё должны́ пять фу́нтов

2: **owing to** *prep* из-за + *G*; ~ **to illness** из-за боле́зни; **the game was cancelled** ~ **to bad weather** игра́ была́ отменена́ из-за плохо́й пого́ды.

owl *n* сова́.

own *pron* **1** *translated by poss adjs*; *where it refers to subject of sentence by* свой, *etc.*; **he was carrying my case as well as his** ~ он нёс и мой и свой чемода́ны; **she likes this bag better than her** ~ э́та су́мка ей нра́вится бо́льше, чем своя́; **I have a copy of my** ~ у меня́ есть свой экземпля́р; **she has money of her** ~ у неё есть свои́ де́ньги; **I want a flat of my** ~ я хочу́ име́ть свою́ кварти́ру; **for reasons of his** ~ по изве́стным то́лько ему́ причи́нам

2 (*by oneself*, *alone*) оди́н, сам; **I'm (all) on my** ~ **now** я сейча́с оди́н; **they left her on her** ~ они́ оста́вили её одну́; **she does all the cooking on her** ~ она́ всё гото́вит сама́; **the children did it all on their** ~ де́ти са́ми всё э́то сде́лали

3 *phrases*: **oranges have a flavour (all) of their** ~ у апельси́нов свой осо́бенный вкус; *fig*: **to get one's** ~ **back on smb** рассчита́ться с кем-л; **he can hold his** ~ **with anybody** он себя́ в оби́ду не даст; **the patient is holding his** ~ больно́й де́ржится; **he came into his** ~ **in the army** в а́рмии он был в свое́й стихи́и.

own *adj* **1** *attr* со́бственный; **they've got their** ~ **problems** у них есть свои́ (со́бственные) пробле́мы; **his** ~ **brother told me** э́то сказа́л мне его́ брат; **to be master in one's** ~ **house** быть хозя́ином в со́бственном до́ме; **I'm my** ~ **master** я сам себе́ хозя́ин; **she makes all her** ~ **clothes** она́ всё шьёт себе́ сама́; **with one's** ~ **eyes** свои́ми со́бственными глаза́ми

2 *predic*: **is the flat your** ~? э́то ва́ша кварти́ра?; **the work was all his** ~ э́то была́ целико́м его́ рабо́та; **the decision was my** ~ э́то бы́ло моё со́бственное реше́ние; **my time is my** ~ я распоряжа́юсь/я могу́ распоряжа́ться свои́м вре́менем, как хочу́.

own *vti vt* **1** (*possess*) владе́ть + *I* (*impf*); **to** ~ **property** владе́ть иму́ществом; **he** ~**s his own house** у него́ свой дом; **who** ~**s this car?** чья э́та маши́на?; **the factory is** ~**ed by a French company** заво́д принадлежи́т францу́зской компа́нии; **he acts as though he** ~**ed the place** он ведёт себя́ как бу́дто он здесь хозя́ин

2 (*confess*) призна|ва́ть (-́ть); **I** ~ **I was surprised** признаю́сь, я был удивлён; **he would not** ~ **himself in the wrong** он не хоте́л призна́ть, что был не прав

vi: **to** ~ **up to smth** призна|ва́ться/созна|ва́ться в чём-л (*pfs* -́ться); **she** ~**ed to telling lies** она́ призна́лась, что солгала́/сказа́ла непра́вду; **he** ~**ed up to the theft** он созна́лся в кра́же.

owner *n* владе́лец, хозя́ин; **the** ~ **of a house/a dog** владе́лец *or* хозя́ин до́ма/соба́ки.

ox *n* вол.

oxide *n Chem* о́кись.

oxygen *n* кислоро́д; *attr*: ~ **tent** кислоро́дная пала́тка.

oyster *n* у́стрица; *attr*: ~ **bed** у́стричный садо́к.

ozone *n* озо́н.

P

P: **you'd better mind your P's and Q's with him** смотри́, веди́ себя́ при нём как сле́дует.

pace *n* **1** (*step*) шаг; **take one** ~ **forward!** (оди́н) шаг вперёд!; **the gate was about 6** ~**s away** кали́тка была́ в шести́ шага́х; *fig* **to put smb through his** ~**s** прове́рить кого́-л на де́ле

2 (*speed*) темп, ско́рость, ход; шаг; **to set the** ~ **for smb/smth** задава́ть темп кому́-л/чему́-л; **the** ~ **of development** те́мпы разви́тия; **to quicken one's** ~ убыстря́ть шаг, прибавля́ть хо́д(у); **at a snail's** ~ черепа́шьим ша́гом; **I found it hard to keep** ~ **with him** я с трудо́м поспева́л за ним.

pace *vti vt*: **to** ~ **a room** ходи́ть по ко́мнате (*only in impf*); **to** ~ **off a distance** измер|ять расстоя́ние шага́ми (́-ить); **he ~d out the room** он изме́рил ко́мнату шага́ми

vi: **to ~ up and down** ходи́ть взад и вперёд.

pacific *adj* ми́рный; **the P.** Ти́хий океа́н.

pacifist *n* пацифи́ст.

pacify *vt* (*country in rebellion*) усмир|я́ть (-и́ть); (*people*) умиротвор|я́ть (-и́ть), мири́ть (по-), успок|а́ивать (-о́ить); **I managed to ~ the quarrelling sisters/the sobbing child/my creditors** я суме́л помири́ть ссо́рящихся сестёр, я успоко́ил пла́чущего ребёнка, мне удало́сь уми́лостивить кредито́ров.

pack *n* (*rucksack*) рюкза́к; *Mil* ра́нец; (*on mule*) тюк, вьюк; **a ~ of cards** коло́да карт; **a ~ of hounds/wolves** сво́ра го́нчих, стая волко́в; *CQ*: **a ~ of thieves/idiots** ша́йка воро́в, сбо́рище идио́тов; **it's a ~ of lies** э́то сплошна́я ложь (*sing*).

pack *vti vt* **1** пакова́ть (у-), укла́дывать (уложи́ть); **I've ~ed my things/case** я упакова́л *or* уложи́л свои́ ве́щи, я собра́л *or* уложи́л чемода́н; **the meat comes ~ed in polythene bags** мя́со поступа́ет расфасо́ванным в полиэтиле́новые паке́ты; **the glasses were ~ed in shavings** стака́ны бы́ли перело́жены стру́жкой; **we took with us a ~ed lunch** мы взя́ли с собо́й за́втрак

2 (*crowd*): **the cinema was ~ed with children** кинотеа́тр был запо́лнен детьми́; **the bus was ~ed** авто́бус был битко́м наби́т; **we were ~ed in like sardines** нас наби́лось, как сельде́й в бо́чку; (*press down*) **I ~ed soil round the plant** я утрамбова́л зе́млю вокру́г расте́ния

3 *CQ*: **she ~ed the children off to bed** она́ отпра́вила дете́й спать; **she sent him ~ing** она́ прогнала́ его́; **it's time we ~ed it in** пора́ поко́нчить с э́тим

vi: **I'm going to ~ now** я иду́ укла́дывать ве́щи; **it began to rain and people ~ed into the cafe** начался́ дождь, и лю́ди наби́лись в кафе́; **the snow had ~ed hard** снег слежа́лся; *CQ*: **let's ~ up** (*stop work*) дава́йте зака́нчивать (рабо́ту); **the engine ~ed up on us** нас подвёл мото́р.

package *n* (*parcel*) паке́т, свёрток; *attr*: **a ~ deal** *Dipl* ко́мплексное соглаше́ние, *Comm* ко́мплексная сде́лка; **a ~ tour** *approx* организо́ванная туристи́ческая пое́здка, ко́мплексное турне́ (*indecl*).

packer *n* упако́вщик.

packet *n* (*tied with string*) свя́зка; (*parcel, envelope*) паке́т; (*small carton or bundle*) па́чка; **a ~ of books** свя́зка/па́чка книг; **a ~ of cigarettes/letters** па́чка сигаре́т/пи́сем; **a ~ of sweets** паке́тик/кулёк с конфе́тами; *CQ*: **he's made a ~** он сорва́л куш; **it cost him a ~** э́то ему́ влете́ло в копе́ечку.

pack ice *n* па́ковый лёд, пак.

packing *n* (*process or material*) упако́вка; **she's busy with her ~** она́ занята́ упако́вкой; **I've done all my ~** я всё своё уложи́л/упакова́л; *attr*: **~ material** упако́вка, наби́вка, упако́вочный материа́л; **a ~ case** упако́вочный я́щик, та́ра.

pact *n off* пакт; **to make a ~** заключи́ть пакт; (*privately*) **we made a ~ not to tell her about it** мы договори́лись ничего́ не говори́ть ей об э́том.

pad *n* (*soft material*) наби́вка; (*on paw of dog, etc.*) поду́шечка; (*of fox*) ла́па; **writing ~** блокно́т; (*for rocket, etc.*) **launching ~** пускова́я площа́дка.

pad *vt* (*stuff*) подби|ва́ть (́-ть); (*clothing*) под|кла́дывать (-ложи́ть); **a jacket with ~ded shoulders** пиджа́к с подкладны́ми плеча́ми; **a ~ded quilt** ва́тное одея́ло.

paddle *n* (*oar*) весло́; (*of paddle-wheel*) ло́пасть.

paddle *vti*: **to ~ (a boat)** грести́ (*impf*); **ducks/children were paddling in the pond** у́тки пла́вали/де́ти плеска́лись в пруду́.

paddle-steamer *n* колёсный парохо́д.

paddling-pool *n CQ* лягуша́тник.

paddock *n* вы́гон.

padlock *n* вися́чий замо́к.

padlock *vt*: **the door was ~ed** на две́ри висе́л замо́к.

paediatrician, (*US*) **pediatrician** *n* педиа́тр.

pagan *n* язы́чник; *attr* язы́ческий.

page[1] *n* страни́ца; **on ~ 12** на двена́дцатой страни́це (*abbr* **on p. 12** на стр. 12).

page[2] *n* (*in hotels, etc.*; *also* **~ boy**) ма́льчик-слуга́; *Hist* паж.

page[2] *vt* (*in hotel, etc.*): **to ~ smb** вы|зыва́ть кого́-л (́-звать).

pail *n* ведро́.

pain *n* **1** боль; **a sharp/dull ~** о́страя/тупа́я боль; **he felt a ~ in his back** он почу́вствовал боль в спине́; **he's in great ~** у него́ си́льная боль; **I've got a ~ in my leg/stomach** у меня́ боли́т нога́/живо́т; **her words caused me great ~** её слова́ огорчи́ли/оби́дели меня́.

2 *Law*: **on ~ of death** под стра́хом сме́рти

3 *pl* (*trouble*): **she took great ~s over the dinner** она́ уж так стара́лась пригото́вить обе́д повкусне́е; **he was at great ~s to convince us** он изо всех си́л стара́лся убеди́ть нас; **that was all he got for his ~s** э́то всё, что он получи́л за свои́ труды́.

pain *vt* (*physically*) боле́ть (*impf*); (*mentally*) огорч|а́ть (-и́ть); **does your foot ~ you?** у тебя́ боли́т нога́?; **your behaviour ~s me** твоё поведе́ние огорча́ет меня́; **however much it ~s me to say so...** как мне ни бо́льно говори́ть об э́том...

pained *adj*: **a ~ expression** огорчённое выраже́ние (лица́); **she looked ~** у неё был оби́женный вид.

painful *adj* (*physically*) боле́зненный; (*physically or mentally*) мучи́тельный; **a ~ sting** боле́зненный уку́с; **a ~ disease** тяжёлая/мучи́тельная боле́знь; **my arm is ~** у меня́ боли́т рука́; **do you find it ~ to walk?** вам не бо́льно ходи́ть?

painfully *adv usu fig*: **he's ~ shy** он боле́зненно ро́бок; **it was ~ obvious that...** броса́лось в глаза, что...

painkiller *n* болеутоля́ющее (сре́дство).

painless *adj* безболе́зненный.

painstaking *adj* стара́тельный.

paint *n* кра́ска; **a box of ~s** коро́бка с кра́сками; **"Wet P."** «Осторо́жно, окра́шено»; (*pejor of make-up*): **she's got too much ~ on** она́ чересчу́р накра́шена.

paint *vti vt* **1** (*walls, etc.*) кра́сить (по-), раскра́|шивать (-сить) *and other compounds*; **to ~ a door** кра́сить дверь; **we ~ed the walls yellow** мы вы́красили сте́ны в жёлтый цвет, мы покра́сили сте́ны жёлтым; **to ~ smth out** закра́шивать что-л; **to ~ one's face** кра́ситься (на-); *fig* **they ~ed the town red yesterday** вчера́ они́ покути́ли/погуля́ли

2 *Art* рисова́ть, писа́ть (*pfs* на-); **to ~ a picture** писа́ть карти́ну (на-); **the monks used to ~ frescoes on the walls** мона́хи расписы-вали сте́ны фре́сками; *fig* **he's not as black as he's ~ed** он не тако́й плохо́й челове́к, каки́м его́ представля́ют/изобража́ют

vi: **he usually ~s in oils** он обы́чно пи́шет ма́слом (*sing*).

paintbrush *n* кисть.

painter *n* (*artist*) худо́жник, живопи́сец; (*decorator*) маля́р.

painting *n* (*process*) жи́вопись; рисова́ние; (*picture*) карти́на; **I love ~** я люблю́ рисова́ть.

pair *n* па́ра; **a ~ of gloves/shoes** па́ра перча́ток/ту́фель; **a ~ of trousers/tights** брю́ки, колго́тки; **a ~ of scales/scissors/tongs** весы́, но́жницы, щипцы́; **2 ~s of scissors** дво́е но́жниц; *CQ* **I've only got one ~ of hands** у меня́ всего́ две руки́.

pair off *vi*: **we all ~ed off** мы раздели́лись на па́ры; *Biol* спа́ри|ваться (-ться).

Pakistani *n* пакиста́нец, пакиста́нка.

Pakistani *adj* пакиста́нский.

pal *n CQ* друг, прия́тель (*m*).

pal *vi*: **to ~ up with smb** подружи́ться с кем-л (*pf*).

palace *n* дворе́ц; *attr* дворцо́вый.

palate *n Anat* нёбо; *fig* **a fine ~** то́нкий вкус.

palatial *adj usu iron*: **their house is ~** у них не дом, а дворе́ц.

palaver *n CQ*: **they had a long ~ about it** таку́ю устро́или говори́льню на э́ту те́му; **what a ~ we had to go through to get permission!** и с како́й же волоки́той мы столкну́лись, что́бы получи́ть (э́то) разреше́ние!; **why make such a ~ about it?** к чему́ весь э́тот шум?/вся э́та пуста́я болтовня́?

pale *adj* бле́дный; **~ yellow** бле́дно-жёлтый; **~ blue** голубо́й; **to turn ~** побледне́ть.

palette *n* пали́тра; *attr*: **~ knife** *Art* мастихи́н, *Cook* лопа́точка.

paling *n* (*fence*) частоко́л.

pall[1] *n* (*on coffin*) покро́в; *fig*: **under a ~ of snow** под сне́жным покро́вом; **a ~ of smoke** о́блако ды́ма.

pall[2] *vi* при|еда́ться (-е́сться); **after the third hearing his stories begin to ~** он со свои́ми исто́риями надое́л до чёртиков — тре́тий раз его́ слу́шаю.

palliate *vt* облегч|а́ть (-и́ть).

pallor *n* бле́дность.

pally *adj CQ*: **he's very ~ with them** он с ни́ми в дру́жбе, они́ с ним больши́е друзья́; **to get ~ with smb** подружи́ться с кем-л.

palm[1] *n Anat* ладо́нь.

palm[1] *vt*: **to ~ smth off on smb,** *also* **to ~ smb off with smth** под|со́вывать что-л кому́-л (-су́нуть), всу́ч|ивать что-л кому́-л (-и́ть).

palm[2] *n Bot* па́льма; *attr*: **~ oil** па́льмовое ма́сло; *Rel* **P. Sunday** ве́рбное воскресе́нье.

palmist *n* хирома́нт.

palpable *adj* осяза́емый; ощути́мый; *fig* **a ~ error** я́вная оши́бка.

palpably *adv fig*: **that's ~ untrue** э́то я́вная ложь.

palpate *vt Med* ощу́п|ывать, прощу́п|ывать (*pfs* -ать).

palpitate *vi* (*of heart*) си́льно би́ться (*only in impf*); **I was palpitating with fear** у меня́ се́рдце колоти́лось от стра́ха.

palpitation *n often pl* си́льное сердцебие́ние (*only sing*).

paltry *adj* пустяко́вый.

pamper *vt* (*spoil*) балова́ть, не́жить (*only in impfs*).

pamphlet *n* памфле́т.

pan *n* (*saucepan*) кастрю́ля; (*of scales*) ча́шка; **frying ~** сковоро́дка; **lavatory ~** унита́з.

panacea *n* панаце́я.

panama (hat) *n* пана́ма.

pan-American *adj* панамерика́нский.

pancake *n* блин; (*stuffed*) бли́нчик (с начи́нкой); **as flat as a ~** пло́ский как блин.

pandemonium *n*: **this caused ~** э́то вы́звало столпотворе́ние.

pander *vi*: **that magazine ~s to low tastes** э́тот журна́л угожда́ет ни́зменным вку́сам.

pane *n*: **a ~ of glass, a window ~** око́нное стекло́.

panel *n* **1** (*of wall, etc.*) пане́ль, *Sew* вста́вка; *Tech* **control ~** пульт/пане́ль (управле́ния); **instrument ~** *Aer* прибо́рный щит, прибо́рная пане́ль, *Aut* прибо́рная доска́

2 (*of people*): **a ~ of jurors** спи́сок прися́жных (заседа́телей); **a ~ of experts** гру́ппа специали́стов; **to be on a doctor's ~** быть пацие́нтом врача́; *Radio, TV* **the ~ of a quiz-show** уча́стники ра́дио-/телевиктори́ны.

panelled, (*US*) **paneled** *adj* оби́тый пане́лями.

pang *n* о́страя боль; **she felt a sharp ~ in her side** у неё си́льно кольну́ло в боку́; **~s of hunger** му́ки го́лода; **to feel a ~/~s of conscience** испы́тывать угрызе́ния (*pl*) со́вести.

panic *n* па́ника; **it threw them into a ~** их охвати́ла па́ника; **in ~** в па́нике.

panic *vi* впа|да́ть в па́нику (-сть); паникова́ть (*impf*).

panicky *adj CQ*: **to be ~** паникова́ть.

panic-stricken *adj*: **they were ~** их обуя́л страх, их охвати́л у́жас.

pan out *vi fig*: **it all ~ned out quite well** де́ло пошло́ на лад; **how did it all ~ out?** чем всё э́то ко́нчилось?

pansy *n Bot* аню́тины гла́зки (*no sing*); *fig CQ* педера́ст.

pant *vi* тяжело́ дыша́ть (*impf*); (*puff*) пыхте́ть (*impf*); **the runner/fat man was ~ing** бегу́н/толстя́к тяжело́ дыша́л; **we were ~ing from the effort** мы про́сто пыхте́ли—так э́то бы́ло тяжело́.

pantechnicon *n* ме́бельный фурго́н.

panther *n* панте́ра.

panties *npl CQ* (же́нские) тру́сики.

pantry *n* кладова́я, *CQ* кладо́вка.

pants *n* (*underpants*: *long*) кальсо́ны, (*short*) трусы́; (*US*) (*trousers*) брю́ки.

papa, *also* **pa** *n CQ* па́па.

papacy *n* па́пство.

papal *adj* па́пский.

paper *n* **1** бума́га; (*for pulp*) макулату́ра; **brown/wrapping ~** обёрточная бума́га; **lined/blank ~** лино́ванная/чи́стая бума́га; **a piece/sheet of ~** лист бума́ги; **wall ~** обо́и (*pl*); **to put smth on ~** записа́ть что-л; **the plan looks O.K. on ~** на бума́ге план вы́глядит непло́хо; **identity ~s** ли́чные бума́ги/докуме́нты; **ship's ~s** судовы́е бума́ги/докуме́нты

2 (*academic*: *written*) сочине́ние; (*to be read out*) докла́д; **he wrote a ~** он написа́л сочине́ние/докла́д; **he read a ~ at the seminar** он сде́лал докла́д на семина́ре; **I'm correcting/setting exam ~s** я проверя́ю экзаменацио́нные рабо́ты, *approx* я составля́ю экзаменацио́нные биле́ты (*i.e. questions which are picked by candidate at oral exam*)

3 (*newspaper*) газе́та.

paper *adj* бума́жный; **~ money/handkerchiefs** бума́жные де́ньги/носовы́е платки́.

paper *vt*: **to ~ a room** окле́|ивать ко́мнату обо́ями (*pl*) (-ить).

paperback *n* кни́га в мя́гком/бума́жном переплёте.

paper clip *n* скре́пка.

paper knife *n* нож для разреза́ния бума́ги.

paper mill *n* бума́жная фа́брика.

paperweight *n* пресс-папье́ (*indecl*).

paper work *n* канцеля́рская рабо́та.

paprika *n* па́прика.

par *n* **1**: **I would put him on a ~ with Gogol** я бы поста́вил его́ ря́дом/наравне́ с Го́голем

2 *Comm* номина́л, номина́льная цена́; **above/under/at ~** вы́ше/ни́же номина́ла, по номина́лу; *fig* **he's feeling a bit under ~** он нева́жно чу́вствует себя́.

parable *n* при́тча.

parachute *n* парашю́т; *attr*: **~ landing** парашю́тный деса́нт.

parachute *vti vt* сбра́сывать с парашю́том (сбро́сить)

vi пры́г|ать с парашю́том (-нуть).

parachutist *n* парашюти́ст.

parade *n* пара́д; **the May Day ~** первома́йский пара́д; **a mannequin ~** демонстра́ция/пока́з мод.

parade *vti vt*: *fig* **to ~ one's learning** щеголя́ть свое́й учёностью (*usu impf*)

vi Mil (*march*) идти́ стро́ем (пройти́); (*drill*) стро́иться (по-).

parade ground *n* (уче́бный) плац.

paradise *n* рай; *CQ* **it's ~ here!** здесь про́сто рай!

paradoxical *adj* парадокса́льный.

paraffin *n* кероси́н; *Med* **liquid ~** парафи́новое ма́сло; *attr*: **~ lamp** кероси́новая ла́мпа.

paragon *n*: **a ~ of virtue** образе́ц доброде́тели.

paragraph *n* абза́ц; (*in newspaper*) **there was a ~ in the paper about him** о нём была́ заме́тка в газе́те; (*in dictating*) **"new ~"** кра́сная строка́, абза́ц.

parallel *n Math*, *Geog* паралле́ль, *also fig*; **to draw a ~ between two events** проводи́ть паралле́ль ме́жду двумя́ собы́тиями; **it is something without ~ in our time** э́тому нет паралле́ли в на́ши дни.

parallel *adj* паралле́льный; **~ lines/bars** паралле́льные ли́нии/бру́сья; **the road runs ~ to** *or* **with the railway** шоссе́ идёт/прохо́дит паралле́льно желе́зной доро́ге; **this is not a ~ case** э́то не аналоги́чный слу́чай.

paralysis *n* парали́ч; *fig* **the traffic was in a state of ~** движе́ние бы́ло парализо́вано.

paralytic *adj* паралити́ческий; *CQ* (*drunk*) мертве́цки пья́ный.

paralyze *vt* парализова́ть (*impf and pf*), *also fig*; **he is ~d** он парализо́ван, его́ разби́л парали́ч, его́ парализова́ло (*impers*); **she was ~d with terror** страх парализова́л её.

paramount *adj*: **of ~ importance** первостепе́нной ва́жности.

parapet *n* парапе́т.

paraphernalia *npl* ве́щи.

paraphrase *vt* переска́з|ывать (-а́ть).

parasite *n* парази́т, *also fig*; *fig* тунея́дец.

parasol *n* зо́нтик от со́лнца.

paratroops *npl* парашю́тно-деса́нтные во́йска́; парашюти́сты.

parboil *vt* слегка́ отвари́ть (*usu pf*).

parcel *n* свёрток; (*for posting*) посы́лка; **I'll make a ~ of it** я заверну́ э́то; *attr*: **to send smth by ~ post** отправля́ть что-л посы́лкой.

parcel *vt*: **to ~ smth out** дели́ть что-л на ча́сти (раз-); **to ~ smth up** за|вёртывать что-л (-верну́ть).

parched *adj*: **my throat is ~** у меня́ в го́рле пересо́хло (*impers*); **I'm ~** я умира́ю от жа́жды; **the ground is ~** по́чва пересо́хла.

parchment *n* перга́мент.

pardon *n* проще́ние, извине́ние; *Law* поми́лование; **(I beg your) ~!** (*excuse me*) прошу́ проще́ния!, прости́те!, (*please repeat*) прости́те, не расслы́шал; **to grant smb a ~** поми́ловать кого́-л.

pardon *vt* про|щáть (-стúть); извин|я́ть (-úть); *Law* помúловать (*pf*); ~ **me, do you have the right time?** простúте, скóлько сейчáс врéмени?; ~ **me for mentioning it** извинúте, что я упоминáю об э́том; **to ~ smb (for) smth** прощáть что-л комý-л.

pardonable *adj* простúтельный.

pare *vt* (*cut*) стричь (под-, о-); (*peel*) чúстить (о-, по-); **to ~ one's nails** стричь себé нóгти; **to ~ potatoes** чúстить картóфель (*collect*); **to ~ an apple** срезáть кожурý с я́блока; *fig* **expenses have been ~d to the minimum** расхóды сокращены́ до мúнимума.

parent *n* родúтель (*m*); **my ~s-in-law** родúтели моéй жены́/моегó мýжа; *attr*: *Comm* **the ~ company** компáния-учредúтель (*m*).

parentage *n approx* происхождéние.

parental *adj* родúтельский.

parenthesis *n* (*bracket*) скóбка; *Gram* (*of a clause*) ввóдное предложéние; **in ~, in parentheses** в скóбках, *also fig*.

parenthood *n* (*of father*) отцóвство; (*of mother*) матерúнство.

par excellence *adv*: **Hamlet is the tragic hero ~** Гáмлет—классúческий образéц трагúческого герóя.

parings *npl* (*of fruit, vegetables*) очúстки; (*peel*) кожурá (*collect*); (*of fingernails*) обрéзки.

parish *n* церкóвный прихóд; *attr* прихóдский.

parity *n* рáвенство; *Fin* паритéт.

park *n* парк; **game ~** заповéдник; **car ~** (*outside*) стоя́нка (автомобúлей), (*in building*) гарáж.

park *vti vt Aut*: **to ~ a car** стáвить машúну на стоя́нку (по-), *CQ* парковáть (при-); *CQ*: **where can I ~ my case?** кудá мне постáвить чемодáн?; **~ yourself in the study till I'm ready** подождúте в кабинéте, покá я собирáюсь

vi Aut: **where are/have you ~ed?** где вы постáвили машúну/*CQ* припарковáлись?

parking *n*: **"No P."** «стоя́нка запрещенá»; *attr*: **~ lights** стоя́ночные фонарú; **~ metre** счётчик врéмени стоя́нки; **~ ticket** *approx* штраф за нарушéние прáвил стоя́нки.

parky *adj CQ*: **it's a bit ~ today** сегóдня прохлáдно.

parlance *n*: **in common ~** в обихóдной рéчи; **in legal ~** на юридúческом языкé.

parliament *n* парлáмент; **an act/member of P.** парлáментский акт, член парлáмента.

parliamentary *adj* парлáментский.

parlour, (*US*) parlor *n approx* гостúная; *attr*: **~ games** кóмнатные úгры.

parody *n* парóдия; **a ~ of justice** парóдия на правосýдие.

parody *vt* пароди́ровать (*impf and pf*).

parole *n*: **to release a prisoner on ~** освободúть заключённого под чéстное слóво.

parquet *n* паркéт; *attr* паркéтный.

parrot *n* попугáй; *attr*: **he repeats everything she says (in) ~ fashion** он повторя́ет как попугáй всё, что онá говорúт.

parry *vt* (*in fencing*) парúровать (*impf and pf*), *also fig*; **to ~ a blow/a question** парúровать удáр/вопрóс.

parse *vt Gram*: **to ~ a sentence** раз|бирáть предложéние (-обрáть).

parsimonious *adj* скупóй.

parsley *n Bot* петрýшка.

parsnip *n Bot* пастернáк.

parson *n CQ* свящéнник, пáстор.

part *n* **1** (*portion*) часть; **a novel in 6 ~s** ромáн в шестú частя́х; **2 ~s vinegar to 5 ~s oil** две чáсти ýксуса на пять частéй мáсла; **that's an integral ~/*CQ* ~ and parcel of the plan** э́то неотъéмлемая часть плáна; **our success was in great ~ due to him** своúм успéхом мы в основнóм обя́заны емý; **in the early/latter ~ of the week** в начáле/к концý недéли; **I agree with that in ~** я отчáсти/ частúчно (*advs*) с э́тим соглáсен; **the book is interesting in ~s** кнúга интерéсна местáми; *Mech* **spare ~s** запасны́е чáсти, *CQ* запчáсти; *Gram* **~s of speech** чáсти рéчи; **principal ~s of a verb** основны́е фóрмы глагóла

2 (*share*) учáстие; **he had/took no ~ in the affair** он в э́том дéле не принимáл учáстия/ не учáствовал

3 (*side*) сторонá; **to take smb's ~ in a quarrel** брать чью-л стóрону в спóре, вставáть на чью-л стóрону; **for my ~** с моéй стороны́, что касáется меня́; **he took it all in good ~** он э́то хорошó воспринял

4 *Theat* роль, *also fig*; **she plays the ~ of the Queen** онá игрáет роль королéвы; **he didn't know his ~** он не знал своéй рóли; **she certainly looked the ~** онá óчень/вполнé подходúла для э́той рóли; *fig* **he's just playing a ~** он тóлько притворя́ется, он прóсто прикúдывается

5 *Mus* пáртия; **the violin ~** пáртия скрúпки

6 (*region*) мéсто, край; **in these ~s** в э́тих местáх/края́х; **in foreign ~s** в чужúх края́х; **it's a lovely ~ of the country** э́то живопúсное мéсто; **are you from these ~s?** вы из э́тих мест?, *CQ* вы здéшний?

part *adv*: **the house is ~ brick, ~ wood** дом напоповúну кирпúчный, наполовúну деревя́нный; **he's ~ poet, ~ philosopher** он отчáсти поэ́т, отчáсти филóсоф.

part *vti vt* (*several things*) раздел|я́ть, (*two things*) отдел|я́ть (*pfs* -úть); (*of people*) разлуч|áть (-úть); **our garden is ~ed from theirs by a low fence** наш сад отделён от их сáда нúзким забóром; **the war ~ed them from their families** войнá разлучúла их с сéмьями; **I ~ed the fighting dogs** я разня́л сцепúвшихся собáк; **he can't bear to be ~ed from her** он не мóжет жить с ней в разлýке; **to ~ one's hair** дéлать пробóр (с-); **to ~ company with smb** расста|вáться с кем-л (´-ться); *fig* **that's where I ~ company with you** здесь мы с вáми расхóдимся

vi расста|вáться (´-ться); расходúться (разойтúсь); **we ~ed on the quay** мы расстáлись/прощáлись на при́стани; **we ~ed the best of friends** мы расстáлись лу́чшими друзья́ми; **he doesn't like ~ing with his money** он не óчень-то лю́бит расставáться со свои́ми деньгáми; **here the roads ~** здесь дорóги расхóдятся; **he ~ed from his wife a year ago** он год назáд разошёлся с женóй; **the rope ~ed under the strain** верёвка лóпнула от напряжéния; **the curtain ~ed** зáнавес раздви́нулся.

part exchange *n*: **in ~** в счёт оплáты (нóвой вéщи).

partial *adj* **1** (*in part*) части́чный; **a ~ success** части́чный успéх

2: I'm ~ to grapes/blondes я люблю́ виногрáд/блонди́нок.

partially *adv* части́чно, отчáсти.

participant *n* учáстник.

participate *vi*: **to ~ in smth** учáствовать в чём-л (*impf*).

participation *n* учáстие.

participle *n Gram* причáстие; **present/past ~** причáстие настоя́щего/прошéдшего врéмени.

particle *n Phys, Gram* части́ца; **a ~ of dust** пыли́нка.

parti-coloured, (*US*) **parti-colored** *adj* разноцвéтный, пёстрый.

particular *n* **1** (*detail*) подрóбность, детáль; **the ~s of the case** подрóбности э́того дéла; **to go into ~s** вдавáться в подрóбности/в детáли; **I'd like further ~s of the job** я хотéл бы узнáть поподрóбнее об э́той рабóте; **personal ~s** ли́чные дáнные

2 in ~ (= *special*): **I meant nobody in ~** я никогó конкрéтно не имéл в виду́; **I remember one of them in ~** я осóбенно пóмню одногó из них; **have you anything ~ in mind?** вы чтó-нибудь определённое имéете в виду́?

particular *adj* **1** (*distinct from others*): **this refers only to ~ cases** э́то относи́тся тóлько к вполнé определённым слу́чаям; **in this ~ case** в дáнном слу́чае; **I can't tell her that at this ~ time** я не могу́ ей э́то сказáть в такóй момéнт; **I need that ~ book** и́менно э́та кни́га мне нужнá

2 (*special*) осóбый, осóбенный; **I read it with ~ interest** я читáл э́то с осóбым интерéсом; **for no ~ reason** без осóбой причи́ны; **nothing ~ happened** ничегó осóбенного не случи́лось

3 (*fastidious*) разбóрчивый; щепети́льный; **she is very ~ about her food/company/money matters** онá óчень разбóрчива в едé/в друзья́х, онá óчень щепети́льна в дéнежных вопрóсах; **he's most ~ about his appearance** он большóй педáнт в вопрóсах одéжды; **the cleaning lady isn't over ~** убóрщица не сли́шком-то старáется.

particularize *vi* вдавáться в подрóбности (*usu impf*).

particularly *adv* осóбенно; **some of the children, ~ the youngest** нéкоторые дéти, осóбенно млáдшие; **she ~ said we weren't to go there** онá осóбенно настáивала (на том), чтóбы мы тудá не ходи́ли.

parting *n* (*separation*) разлу́ка, расставáние; (*farewell*) прощáние; (*in hair*) пробóр; **on ~ she said...** прощáясь, онá сказáла...; **at the ~ of the ways** на перекрёстке дорóг, *fig* на распу́тье; *attr*: **a ~ gift** прощáльный подáрок.

partisan *n* (*supporter*) сторóнник, привéрженец; *Mil* партизáн.

partition *n* (*dividing*) разделéние, раздéл; (*wall*) перегорóдка.

partition *vt* раздел|я́ть, отдел|я́ть (*pfs* -и́ть); **to ~ off a corner of a room** отдели́ть у́гол кóмнаты перегорóдкой.

partly *adv* (*physically*) части́чно, чáстью; (*abstractly*) отчáсти; **the house was ~ destroyed** дом был части́чно разру́шен; **a ~ opened door** полуоткры́тая дверь; **he was ~ hurt, ~ angry** он отчáсти оби́делся, отчáсти рассерди́лся.

partner *n* соучáстник; *Sport, Cards, in dancing* партнёр, *f* -ша; *Comm* компаньóн, партнёр; **~s in crime** соучáстники преступлéния.

partner *vt*: **he ~ed her** он был её партнёром.

partnership *n Comm* компáния, товáрищество; **to go into ~ with smb** станови́ться чьим-л партнёром; **they are in ~** они́ компаньóны; **they offered him a ~ in the firm** ему́ предложи́ли стать компаньóном в фи́рме.

part owner *n* совладéлец.

part payment *n*: **in ~** в счёт оплáты (нóвой вéщи).

partridge *n* куропáтка.

part-time *adj*: **I've got ~ work, I'm ~** я рабóтаю на полстáвки/непóлный рабóчий день; **~ teachers** преподавáтели на полстáвки.

party *n* **1** *Polit* пáртия; **to join a ~** вступáть в пáртию; **a member of the ~** член пáртии; *attr* парти́йный; **~ spirit** парти́йный дух, парти́йность; **to follow the ~ line** придéрживаться ли́нии пáртии

2 (*group*) пáртия, гру́ппа; (*team*) отря́д, *also Mil*; **a ~ of geologists/tourists** геологи́ческая пáртия, тури́стская гру́ппа; **the working ~ of a committee** рабóчая гру́ппа при коми́ссии; **a rescue ~** спасáтельный отря́д; **a small ~ had gathered** собралáсь небольшáя компáния; **the Presidential ~** президéнт и сопровождáющие егó ли́ца

3 (*entertainment*): **to give/throw a ~** устрáивать вéчер; **they gave a dinner ~ for us** они́ устрóили обéд в нáшу честь; **a children's ~** дéтский у́тренник; **a fancy-dress ~** маскарáд; **he invited me to his birthday ~** он пригласи́л меня́ на свой день рождéния; *attr*: **a ~ frock** наря́дное плáтье

4 *Law, etc.* сторонá; **the parties in a dispute** стóроны в спóре; **the injured ~** пострадáвшая сторонá; **he was a ~ to the conspiracy** он был учáстником зáговора

5 *CQ joc*: **who's that stout ~ by the door?** кто э́та по́лная осо́ба у две́ри?

party line *n Tel* спа́ренный телефо́н.

pass *n* **1** (*permit*) про́пуск; *Mil* (*for leave*) увольни́тельная; *Rail, etc.* **a free ~** беспла́тный биле́т; **"All ~es must be shown"** «Предъявля́йте про́пуск» (*sing*)

2 *Univ*: **she got a ~ in English** она́ сдала́ англи́йский; *attr*: **~ mark** посре́дственная оце́нка, проходно́й балл, (*SU only*) тро́йка

3 *Geog* перева́л; **a ~ through/over the Alps** перева́л че́рез А́льпы

4 *Sport* пас, переда́ча

5 *fig CQ*: **he made a ~/~es at her** он за ней приударя́л; **things have come to a pretty ~** да́льше уж не́куда.

pass *vti vt* **1** (*go past*: *on foot*) про|ходи́ть ми́мо + *G* (-йти́); (*in vehicle*) про|езжа́ть + *A or* ми́мо + *G* (-е́хать); (*meet and pass*) встре|ча́ться с + *I* (-́титься); **he ~ed me without speaking** он прошёл ми́мо меня́, ничего́ не сказа́в; **we've ~ed our turning/the cathedral** мы прое́хали наш поворо́т (*overshot it*)/ми́мо собо́ра (*went past*); **I just ~ed her in the street** я то́лько что встре́тил её на у́лице; **we ~ed each other on the way** мы встре́тились по доро́ге; *Aut* **we ~ed their car** мы обогна́ли (*overtook*)/ви́дели (*met*) их маши́ну

2 (*move*): **he ~ed his hand over the surface** он провёл руко́й по пове́рхности; **to ~ a rope round a barrel** обвя́з|ывать бо́чку верёвкой (-а́ть)

3 (*hand over*) переда|ва́ть (-́ть); **~ her the letter** переда́й ей письмо́; *Sport* **to ~ the ball to smb** передава́ть/пасова́ть мяч кому́-л (*impf and pf*)

4 (*spend time*) про|води́ть (-вести́); **we ~ed the time playing cards** мы провели́ вре́мя за ка́ртами; **where did you ~ the summer?** где вы провели́ ле́то?; *CQ* **I stopped to ~ the time of day with her** я останови́лся поболта́ть с ней

5 (*get through*) проходи́ть; **he ~ed his medical** он прошёл медици́нский осмо́тр; **the film ~ed the censors** фильм прошёл цензу́ру; **to ~ an exam** сдать экза́мен (*only in pf*)

6 (*approve*): **to ~ a law/a resolution** при|нима́ть зако́н/резолю́цию (-ня́ть); **the censor ~ed the play** цензу́ра пропусти́ла пье́су; **the doctor ~ed him (as) fit** врач призна́л его́ го́дным

7 (*pronounce*): **to ~ a remark** де́лать замеча́ние (с-); **I don't want to ~ an opinion on it** я не хочу́ выска́зывать своего́ мне́ния по э́тому вопро́су; **the judge ~ed sentence on him** судья́ вы́нес ему́ пригово́р

8 (*surpass*): **it ~es belief** э́то невероя́тно; **it ~es my comprehension** э́то вы́ше моего́ понима́ния

vi **1** (*come, go*) проходи́ть, проезжа́ть (ми́мо); **I heard someone ~ing** я слы́шал, как кто́-то прошёл ми́мо; **~ along there please!** проходи́те, пожа́луйста!; **the road ~es near the lake** доро́га прохо́дит недалеко́ от о́зера; **we were now ~ing through a forest** мы тепе́рь е́хали ле́сом/проезжа́ли че́рез лес; **the estate ~ed to the daughter** име́ние перешло́ к до́чери; **letters ~ed between them** они́ обменя́лись пи́сьмами; *fig*: **she ~ed from rage to despair** она́ переходи́ла от гне́ва к отча́янию; **words ~ed between them** они́ поспо́рили; **I don't know what ~ed between them** (я) не зна́ю, что произошло́ ме́жду ни́ми; **we can't let that ~** мы не мо́жем э́того допусти́ть; **I couldn't let his words ~ without comment** я не мог оста́вить без отве́та его́ слова́

2 (*of time*) проходи́ть; **two months ~ed** прошло́ два ме́сяца; **the pain/storm will soon ~** боль/гроза́ ско́ро пройдёт; **in the garden I don't notice time ~ing** рабо́тая в саду́, я не замеча́ю, как идёт вре́мя

3 *Univ*: **he didn't ~ in geography** он не сдал геогра́фию

4 *Sport, Cards* пасова́ть (*impf and pf*)

pass down *vt*: **the tradition was ~ed down from father to son** тради́ция передава́лась от отца́ к сы́ну

pass for *vi*: **he can easily ~ for a Frenchman** его́ легко́ мо́жно приня́ть за францу́за; **she's 40, but might ~ for less** ей со́рок, но она́ вы́глядит моло́же; **what ~es for art nowadays** то, что сего́дня называ́ется иску́сством/схо́дит за произведе́ние иску́сства

pass off *vti vt*: **he tried to ~ it off as a joke** он пыта́лся вы́дать э́то за шу́тку; **he ~ed her off as his wife** он выдава́л её за свою́ жену́

vi: **the effect of the medicine soon ~es off** де́йствие лека́рства дли́тся недо́лго; **the meeting ~ed off without incident** собра́ние прошло́ споко́йно

pass on *vi*: **he shook my hand and ~ed on** он пожа́л мне ру́ку и пошёл да́льше; **let us ~ on to the next subject** дава́йте перейдём к сле́дующему вопро́су

pass out *vi Mil*: **he ~ed out of Military College** он око́нчил вое́нное учи́лище; *CQ* (*faint*) теря́ть созна́ние (по-)

pass over *vt*: **I will ~ over these events in silence** я обойду́ э́ти собы́тия молча́нием, я умолчу́ об э́тих собы́тиях; **they ~ed him over for promotion** его́ обошли́ при повыше́нии

pass round *vt*: **do ~ round the cakes** обнеси́ всех пиро́жными; *fig* **they ~ed the hat round** они́ пусти́ли ша́пку по кру́гу

pass through *vi*: **I ~ed through Oxford** я пое́хал че́рез О́ксфорд; **my son is ~ing through a difficult stage** у моего́ сы́на сейча́с тру́дный во́зраст

pass up *vt CQ*: **to ~ up an opportunity** упус|ка́ть возмо́жность (-ти́ть).

passable *adj* **1** (*of roads*) проходи́мый; **is the road to Bristol ~ just now?** в Бристо́ль сейча́с мо́жно прое́хать?

2 (*fair*): **his essay is ~ though far from good** его́ сочине́ние в о́бщем вполне́ прили́чно написано, но, конечно, блестящим его не назовёшь.

passage *n* **1** *Aer* перелёт; *Naut* плавание; **we had a rough ~** это плавание было трудным; **he paid his own ~** он сам платил за дорогу; *fig*: **the bill had a rough ~ through Parliament** законопроект с трудом прошёл через парламент; **with the ~ of time it will all be forgotten** со временем всё это забудется

2 (*corridor*) коридор; (*in the open*) проход, *also Anat*

3 (*extract*) отрывок; *Mus* пассаж; **there are some brilliant ~s in the book** в книге есть блестящие места.

passenger *n* пассажир; *attr*: **~ trains** пассажирские поезда.

passer-by *n* прохожий.

passing *n*: **in ~** мимоходом; **with the ~ of the last generation** с уходом старого поколения.

passing *adj*: **a ~ car** проходящая/(*if coming towards one*) встречная *or* мимо идущая машина; **a ~ fancy** мимолётная прихоть; **a ~ glance** беглый взгляд; **a ~ remark** беглое замечание.

passion *n* страсть; **he spoke with ~** он говорил с жаром; **she flew into a ~** она вспылила; *CQ* **I have a ~ for strawberries/opera** я обожаю клубнику/оперу.

passionate *adj* страстный.

passive *adj* пассивный; **~ resistance** пассивное сопротивление; *Gram* **the ~ voice** (*also as n* **the ~**) страдательный залог.

passport *n* паспорт; (*SU*: *for overseas travel*) заграничный паспорт.

password *n* пароль (*m*).

past *n* (**the ~**) прошлое, минувшее; **in the ~** в прошлом; **it's a thing of the ~** это дело прошлое.

past *adj* прошлый, минувший; **in the ~ week** на прошлой/минувшей неделе; **for some time ~** (за) последнее время; **in times ~** в прошлом; **~ generations** минувшие поколения; **all that is ~** всё это теперь в прошлом; *Gram* **the ~ tense** прошедшее время; *fig* **he's a ~ master at that game** в этой игре ему нет равных.

past *adv* мимо; **she walked ~ without recognizing me** она прошла мимо, не узнав меня; **the years have flown ~** годы пролетели.

past *prep* **1** (*of place*: *by*) мимо + *G*; (*beyond*) за + *I*; **she walked ~ us** она прошла мимо нас; **buses go ~ here quite often** автобусы здесь ходят довольно часто; **the station is just ~ the post office** станция (находится) сразу за почтой

2 (*of time*): **at half ~ 3** в половине четвёртого; **20 ~ 7** двадцать минут восьмого; **it's already ~ eleven** уже двенадцатый час; **it's well ~ midnight** уже далеко за полночь; **he's ~ 60** ему за шестьдесят

3 *fig* (*beyond*): **that's ~ belief** это невероятно; **the epidemic is ~ its worst** эпидемия уже утихает; **he's ~ his best/prime** он уже немолод; **I'm ~ caring about it** мне это уже всё равно/безразлично; **I wouldn't put it ~ him** по-моему, он вполне способен на это.

paste *n* (*glue*) клей, клейстер; **tooth ~** зубная паста; **fish ~** рыбный паштет.

paste *vt* (*glue*) клеить (с-) *and compounds*; **to ~ a notice on the wall** наклеи|вать объявление на стену (-ть); **to ~ together** склеи|вать (-ть).

pastel *n Art* пастель; *attr* пастельный.

pasteurize *vt* пастеризовать (*impf and pf*).

pastime *n* время(пре)провождение; занятие; (*less serious*) развлечение; **reading/water-skiing is his favourite ~** чтение — его любимое время(пре)провождение/занятие, водные лыжи (*pl*) — его любимое развлечение.

pastor *n* пастор.

pastoral *n Lit, Mus* пастораль.

pastoral *adj Lit, Mus* пасторальный.

pastry *n* (*dough*) тесто; **short/flaky ~** песочное/слоёное тесто; *pl* **pastries** пирожные.

pasture *n* пастбище.

pasty *n* пирожок.

pasty *adj* (*in texture*) тестообразный; (*in colour*) бледный.

pat[1] *vt* хлопать, похлопывать (*pf for both* похлопать); **to ~ a dog** гладить собаку (по-); **to ~ smb on the back** похлопать/(*to stop a cough*) стукнуть кого-л по спине (*usu pf*), *fig* гладить кого-л по головке.

pat[2] *adv*: **he always has his excuse ~** у него всегда наготове благовидный предлог; **he knows it all off ~** он всё это знает назубок; **I'm standing ~ on this** от этого я не отступлюсь [**NB** *tense*].

patch *n* (*on cloth*) заплата; (*stain, spot*) пятно; **trousers with ~es on them** брюки в заплатах; **a damp ~ on the wall** сырое пятно на стене; **a dog with a white ~ on his forehead** собака с белым пятном на лбу; **an eye ~** повязка на глазу; **a ~ of blue sky** клочок синего неба; **a vegetable ~** огород; **a bad ~ of road** плохой участок дороги; **the play is good in ~es** пьеса хороша местами; *fig*: **we're going through/have struck a bad ~ at the moment** сейчас мы попали в полосу невезения; **the new conductor isn't a ~ on the old one** новый дирижёр не идёт ни в какое сравнение со старым.

patch *vt*: **to ~ a pair of trousers** латать брюки (за-), ставить заплаты на брюки (по-); **he ~ed up an old bike for me** он починил мне старый велосипед; *fig* **to ~ up a quarrel** ула|живать ссору (-дить).

patchwork *n* шитьё из лоскутов; *attr*: **a ~ quilt** лоскутное одеяло.

pâté *n* паштет; **~ de foie gras** паштет из гусиной печёнки.

patent *n* патент; **to take out a ~ for smth** брать патент на что-л; *attr* патентный; **~ law** патентное право; **P. Office** бюро патентов; **~ medicines** патентованные лекарства.

patent *adj* (*obvious*) очевидный.

patent *vt* патентовать (за-).

patent leather *n* лакиро́ванная ко́жа; *attr*: ~ **shoes** лакиро́ванные ту́фли.

paternal *adj* (*of one's father*) отцо́вский; (*fatherly*) оте́ческий; **my ~ grandmother** моя́ ба́бушка по отцу́.

path *n* доро́жка; (*unpaved*) тропи́нка; *fig* путь; **a ~ through the woods** лесна́я тропи́нка; *fig* **our ~s never crossed again** на́ши пути́ бо́льше не пересека́лись.

pathetic *adj* жа́лкий; жа́лостный; **what a ~ excuse!** како́й жа́лкий предло́г!; **she's a ~ creature** она́ несча́стное созда́ние; **in a ~ voice** жа́лобным то́ном.

pathological *adj* патологи́ческий.

patience *n* терпе́ние; **to have ~** име́ть терпе́ние; **I've got no ~ with him** он меня́ выво́дит из терпе́ния; **he's got the ~ of Job** у него́ а́нгельское терпе́ние; **my ~ is exhausted** моё терпе́ние ло́пнуло; **she tries/taxes everybody's ~** она́ так надое́длива.

patient *n* больн|о́й, *f* -а́я; пацие́нт, *f* -ка.

patient *adj* терпели́вый; **be ~ with her** будь с ней терпели́в.

patriarch *n* патриа́рх, *also Rel*.

patriotic *adj* патриоти́ческий.

patrol *n* патру́ль (*m*); **on ~** в дозо́ре; *attr* патру́льный.

patrol *vt* патрули́ровать (*impf*); **soldiers ~led the streets** солда́ты патрули́ровали на у́лицах.

patrolman *n* (*US*) полице́йский.

patron *n* (*protector*) покрови́тель (*m*); (*customer*) постоя́нный покупа́тель (*m*)/клие́нт; **a ~ of the arts** мецена́т.

patronage *n* покрови́тельство.

patronize *vt* (*protect*) покрови́тельствовать (*impf and pf*); *pejor* (*condescend to*) относи́ться свысока́/снисходи́тельно к + *D*; **a pub ~d largely by journalists** бар, посеща́емый в основно́м журнали́стами.

patronizing *adj* покрови́тельственный, *also pejor*; *pejor* снисходи́тельный.

patronymic *n* о́тчество.

patter[1] *n* (*of comedian*) скорогово́рка; (*talk*) разгово́р; **he has got the salesman's/conjuror's ~ off perfectly** он блестя́ще подража́ет разгово́ру продавцо́в/фо́кусников.

patter[2] *vi* посту́кивать, бараба́нить (*impfs*); **the rain ~ed on the windows** дождь бараба́нил в о́кна.

pattern *n* (*way*) о́браз; (*model*) образе́ц, *also fig*; (*sample*) обра́зчик; (*design*) узо́р; *Sew* (*for cutting out*) вы́кройка; **on/following the ~ of** по образцу́ + *G*; **~s of tweed** обра́зчики тви́да.

paunch *n* брюшко́, пу́зо (*both CQ*); **he's getting quite a ~** у него́ уже́ прили́чное брюшко́.

pauper *n* ни́щий.

pause *n* па́уза, *also Mus*; переры́в.

pause де́лать па́узу (с-); **he delivered his speech without pausing once** он произнёс речь, не сде́лав ни еди́ной па́узы.

pave *vt* мости́ть (вы́-); *fig* **to ~ the way for smth** про|кла́дывать путь чему́-л (-ложи́ть).

paved *adj* мощёный; **a ~ road** (*in city*) мостова́я.

pavement *n* тротуа́р.

paving-stone *n* плита́; (*smaller, only for street*) брусча́тка.

paw *n* ла́па.

pawn[1] *n Chess* пе́шка, *also fig*.

pawn[2] *n*: **in ~** в закла́де; **to put smth in ~** отдава́ть что-л в закла́д/в ломба́рд; *attr*: **~ ticket** ломба́рдная квита́нция.

pawn[2] *vt* за|кла́дывать (-ложи́ть).

pawnbroker *n* хозя́ин ломба́рда.

pawnshop *n* ломба́рд.

pay *n* опла́та; (*wages*) за́работная пла́та, *CQ* зарпла́та; (*earnings*) за́работок; **basic rate of ~** основна́я но́рма опла́ты; **take-home ~** чи́стый за́работок; **to draw one's ~** получа́ть зарпла́ту; **what's the ~ like here?** как/ско́лько здесь пла́тят?; *attr*: **~ freeze** замора́живание за́работной пла́ты.

pay *vti vt* **1** плати́ть (за-) *and compounds*; **do you get paid for doing it?** вам за э́то пла́тят?; **she always ~s for herself** она́ всегда́ пла́тит сама́ за себя́; **he had to ~ an extra five roubles** ему́ на́до бы́ло доплати́ть пять рубле́й; **it's a badly paid job** э́то низкоопла́чиваемая до́лжность; **when do you get paid?** когда́ вы получа́ете зарпла́ту?, *CQ* когда́ у вас полу́чка?; **to ~ a subscription** уплати́ть взнос

2 (*settle*) упла́|чивать (-ти́ть), распла́чиваться с + *I*; **to ~ a bill** плати́ть по счёту, опла́чивать счёт; **"paid"** (*on bill*) «упла́чено»; **to ~ one's debts** распла́чиваться с долга́ми, выпла́чивать долги́; **to ~ one's creditors** распла́чиваться с кредито́рами; **to ~ damages/compensation** опла́чивать убы́тки, возмеща́ть убы́тки

3 (*be profitable*): **does it ~ them to employ such a large staff?** вы́годно ли им име́ть тако́й большо́й штат?

4 *fig uses*: **it would ~ you to be more careful** вам не меша́ло бы быть поосторо́жней; **to ~ one's respects to smb** засвиде́тельствовать своё почте́ние кому́-л (*pf*); **to ~ a call on smb** на|носи́ть визи́т кому́-л (-нести́); **to ~ a visit to** посе|ща́ть + *A* (-ти́ть)

vi **1** плати́ть (за-); **who's ~ing?** кто пла́тит?; **~ as you go in** плати́ть при вхо́де; **to ~ (in) cash/in kind** плати́ть нали́чными/нату́рой; **to ~ in advance/in full/in instalments** плати́ть вперёд/по́лностью/в рассро́чку; *fig CQ* **that puts paid to our plans** на́шим пла́нам коне́ц/кры́шка

2 (*be profitable*) окуп|а́ться (-и́ться); **it ~s to advertise** рекла́ма всегда́ окупа́ется; **does the business ~?** э́то де́ло рента́бельно?; *fig* **it ~s to be careful** не меша́ет быть осторо́жным

pay back *vt*: **to ~ back a debt** отда́ть долг; **I paid him back the money** я расплати́лся с ним; *fig*: **he paid me back in my own coin** он отплати́л мне той же моне́той; **I'll ~ you back for that** я тебе́ за э́то отплачу́

pay for *vi*: **the state ~s for everything** за всё пла́тит госуда́рство; **the new machines will soon ~ for themselves** но́вые маши́ны бы́стро оку́пятся; *fig* **he'll ~ for this** он за э́то попла́тится

pay into *vi*: **I've been ~ing into the fund for 10 years** я де́сять лет плачу́ взно́сы в э́тот фонд; **to ~ money/a cheque into a bank** класть де́ньги (положи́ть)/по|сыла́ть чек (-сла́ть) в банк

pay off *vti vt*: **to ~ off a debt** вы́платить долг; **we're still ~ing off the mortgage** мы всё ещё выпла́чиваем ссу́ду; **all the workmen were paid off** все рабо́чие получи́ли расчёт; *fig* **to ~ off old scores** распла́чиваться по ста́рым счета́м

vi: **the trouble we took/the investment paid off** на́ши труды́ не прошли́ да́ром, капиталовложе́ния (*pl*) окупи́лись

pay out *vt* **1: to ~ out a huge sum** вы́платить огро́мную су́мму

2: to ~ out rope трави́ть кана́т (*impf*)

pay up *vi*: **there was nothing for it but to ~ up** ничего́ не остава́лось, как заплати́ть.

payable *adj*: **total amount ~** су́мма, подлежа́щая вы́плате; **to make a cheque ~ to smb** выпи́сывать чек на чьё-л и́мя.

payday *n*: **when is your ~?** когда́ у вас зарпла́та?

paydesk *n* ка́сса.

payee *n* (*of cheque*) предъяви́тель (*m*) че́ка.

paying *adj* вы́годный, рента́бельный; **it's not a ~ proposition** э́то невы́годное/нерента́бельное де́ло.

payment *n* упла́та; (*remuneration*) опла́та, пла́та; платёж; (*of debts*) вы́плата; **~ by the hour** почасова́я опла́та; **~ on delivery** нало́женным платежо́м; **to defer ~** откла́дывать срок платежа́; **~ by instalments** пла́та/вы́плата в рассро́чку; **~ of an instalment** вы́плата очередно́го взно́са; **~ of a debt** (*by an organization*) вы́плата/(*by individual*) отда́ча до́лга; **to make a down ~ on smth** де́лать пе́рвый взнос за что-л.

payoff *n CQ*: **we made a lot of improvements and are already beginning to see the ~** мы ввели́ не́которые усоверше́нствования, и уже́ видны́ результа́ты.

pay packet *n* зарпла́та, *CQ* полу́чка.

payphone *n* (*US*) телефо́н-автома́т.

payroll *n* платёжная ве́домость; **we have 100 men on the ~** у нас в ве́домости чи́слится сто челове́к.

pea *n Bot* горо́х, *also collect as food*; **a ~** горо́шинка; **green/garden ~s** зелёный горо́шек (*collect*); **split ~s** лущёный горо́х; **sweet ~s** души́стый горо́шек; **they're as like as two ~s** они́ похо́жи друг на дру́га как две ка́пли воды́; *attr*: **~ soup** горо́ховый суп.

peace *n* **1** (*not war*) мир; **world ~** всео́бщий мир, мир во всём ми́ре; **a ~ was signed** ми́рный догово́р был подпи́сан; *fig* **I made my ~ with him** я помири́лся с ним; *attr*: **~ talks** ми́рные перегово́ры

2 (*civil order*) поря́док; **to keep/break the ~** соблюда́ть/наруша́ть обще́ственный поря́док; **troops were brought in to maintain the ~** для подде́ржания поря́дка бы́ли введены́ войска́

3 (*calm*: *of people*) поко́й; (*of countryside*) тишина́; **~ of mind** душе́вный поко́й; **I did it for my own ~ of mind** я сде́лал э́то ра́ди со́бственного споко́йствия; **he feels at ~ with himself** у него́ споко́йно на душе́; **he gave me no ~** он не дава́л мне поко́я; **I never get a moment's ~** у меня́ ни мину́ты поко́я.

peaceable *adj* (*of people*) споко́йный, ми́рный.

peaceful *adj* ми́рный; (*calm*) споко́йный, ти́хий; **a ~ demonstration** ми́рная демонстра́ция; **a ~ summer day** ти́хий ле́тний день.

peace-keeping *adj*: **a UN ~ force** войска́ ООН (*pl*).

peach *n* пе́рсик (*fruit or tree*); *fig CQ* **she's a ~!** да она́ про́сто красо́тка!; *attr* пе́рсиковый (*also of colour*).

peacock *n* павли́н.

peak *n* (*of mountain*) пик, верши́на, *both also fig*; (*of cap*) козырёк; *fig* разга́р; **mountain ~s** верши́ны гор; *fig*: **traffic is at its ~ between 5 and 6** у́личное движе́ние достига́ет пи́ка ме́жду пятью́ и шестью́ часа́ми ве́чера; **he was at the ~ of his fame** он был на верши́не сла́вы; **tourism is at its ~ in summer** разга́р тури́стского сезо́на прихо́дится на ле́то; *attr*: **~ load** максима́льная нагру́зка.

peaked *adj*: **a ~ cap** фура́жка (*of officer*).

peaky *adj*: **she's looking ~** она́ вы́глядит измождённой.

peal *n*: **~ of bells** перезво́н (*sound*)/набо́р (*set*) колоколо́в; **there was a ~ of laughter** разда́лся взрыв сме́ха; **a ~ of thunder** раска́т гро́ма.

peal *vi*: **the bells ~ed out** зазвони́ли колокола́.

peanut *n* земляно́й оре́х, ара́хис, *also collect*; *fig CQ* **his pay is just ~s** ему́ пла́тят гроши́.

pear *n* гру́ша (*fruit or tree*); *attr* гру́шевый.

pearl *n* же́мчуг, *also collect*; **a ~** жемчу́жина; **cultivated ~s** культиви́рованный же́мчуг; *attr*: **a ~ necklace** жемчу́жные бу́сы (*pl*).

pearl barley *n* перло́вая крупа́, *CQ* перло́вка.

peasant *n* крестья́нин, крестья́нка; *attr* крестья́нский.

peat *n* торф; *attr* торфяно́й; **~ bog** торфяно́е боло́то, торфяни́к.

pebble *n* га́лька, *also collect*; *fig* **you're not the only ~ on the beach** на тебе́ свет кли́ном не сошёлся; *attr* га́лечный.

peccadillo *n* грешо́к.

peck *vti vt* клева́ть (клю́нуть); **the parrot ~ed my finger** попуга́й клю́нул меня́ в па́лец; **the hens ~ed a hole in the sack** ку́ры проклева́ли ды́рку в мешке́

vi: **the hens ~ed at the grain** ку́ры клева́ли зёрна; *fig* **she just ~ed at her food** она́ то́лько поковыря́ла ви́лкой в таре́лке.

peckish *adj CQ*: **I'm feeling a bit ~** я не прочь чего-нибудь пожева́ть.

peculiar *adj* **1** (*exclusive to*) сво́йственный + *D*; своеобра́зный; (*distinctive*) характе́рный; **the humour ~ to the English** сво́йственный англича́нам ю́мор; **he has his own ~ style** у него́ своеобра́зный стиль; **a plant ~ to Europe** расте́ние, характе́рное для Евро́пы

2 (*strange*) стра́нный; **a ~ sort of chap** стра́нный па́рень

3 (*special*) осо́бый; **a matter of ~ interest to us** де́ло, представля́ющее для нас осо́бый интере́с.

peculiarity *n* осо́бенность; (*strangeness*) стра́нность; **the peculiarities of the French language** осо́бенности францу́зского языка́; **we all have our peculiarities** у ка́ждого есть свои́ стра́нности.

pecuniary *adj* де́нежный.

pedal *n* педа́ль, *also Mus*; *Mus* **loud/soft ~** пра́вая/ле́вая педа́ль; *Aut* **brake ~** педа́ль ножно́го то́рмоза.

pedantic *adj* педанти́чный.

pedestal *n* пьедеста́л, основа́ние, постаме́нт; *fig* **he puts her on a ~** он возно́сит её на пьедеста́л, он её превозно́сит.

pedestrian *n* пешехо́д.

pedestrian *adj* **1**: **a ~ crossing** пешехо́дный перехо́д

2 (*dull*) ску́чный, прозаи́чный; **a ~ article** ску́чная статья́; **he is very ~** он како́й-то бескры́лый.

pedigree *n* родосло́вная; **he's proud of his (long) ~** он горди́тся свое́й родосло́вной; **does your dog have a ~?** у ва́шей соба́ки есть родосло́вная?; *attr*: **~ cattle** поро́дистый скот.

pediment *n Archit* фронто́н.

pedlar *n* у́личный торго́вец.

pedometer *n* шагоме́р.

pee *vi CQ euph* де́лать пи-пи́/по-ма́ленькому (с-).

peek *n and vi CQ see* **peep**[1] *n and vi*.

peel *n* (*thin*: *of apples, etc.*) кожура́; (*of apples, potatoes when peeled*) очи́стки (*pl*); (*of citrus fruit*) ко́рка; **I keep the orange ~ for marmalade** я храню́ апельси́новые ко́рки (*pl*) для варе́нья; **candied ~** цука́т.

peel *vti vt* (*fruit, vegetables*) чи́стить (по-, о-); *CQ* **we ~ed off our clothes and plunged into the water** мы сбро́сили с себя́ оде́жду и ки́нулись в во́ду

vi (*of skin*) лупи́ться (об-); **my back is beginning to ~** у меня́ лу́пится спина́; **the plaster is ~ing** штукату́рка сы́плется; **the paint is ~ing off the wall** кра́ска схо́дит со стены́; **the wallpaper is beginning to ~** обо́и (*pl*) начина́ют отстава́ть.

peelings *npl* (*of vegetables, etc.*) очи́стки.

peep[1] *n*: **do you want to have a ~ at the Christmas tree?** хо́чешь взгляну́ть на ёлку?; **I only got a ~ of her** я то́лько ме́льком её ви́дел; **let me have a ~, Mummy** ма́ма, дай мне посмотре́ть/*CQ* гля́нуть.

peep[1] *vi* взгляну́ть (*pf*); **to ~ at smth** взгляну́ть на что-л; **she ~ed into the room/round the door** она́ загляну́ла в ко́мнату, она́ вы́глянула за́ дверь; *fig* **the moon ~ed out from behind the clouds** луна́ вы́глянула из-за облако́в.

peep[2] *n* (*sound*) писк; *CQ*: **one ~ out of you!** попро́буй то́лько пи́кнуть!; **the car gave a ~ of its horn** маши́на просигна́лила; (*child playing cars*) **~, ~!** би-би́!

peephole *n* глазо́к (в две́ри).

peer[1] *n* **1** (*equal*) ро́вня, ра́вный; (*contemporary*) рове́сник

2 (*lord*) пэр; **he was made a ~** его́ возвели́ в пэ́ры; **a life ~** пожи́зненный пэр.

peer[2] *vi*: **she took off her glasses and ~ed at him** она́ сняла́ очки́ и, близору́ко щу́рясь, посмотре́ла на него́; **he ~ed through the keyhole** он подсма́тривал в замо́чную сква́жину.

peeved *adj CQ*: **he was ~ at the delay/with me** он был раздражён отсро́чкой, он был недово́лен мной.

peevish *adj CQ* капри́зный.

peg *n* (*in ground, for tent, etc.*) ко́лышек; (*on wall, etc.*) крючо́к; **he hung his coat on a ~** он пове́сил пальто́ на крючо́к; **a row of coat ~s** ве́шалка; **clothes ~** (бельева́я) прище́пка; *fig*: **to buy clothes off the ~** покупа́ть гото́вую оде́жду; **he's a square ~ in a round hole** он для э́того соверше́нно не годи́тся/не подхо́дит; **to take smb down a ~ (or two)** сбить спесь с кого́-л.

peg *vti vt*: **to ~ out an area** разме|ча́ть площа́дку ко́лышками (-́тить); **we must ~ down the tent more securely** на́до вбить бо́льше ко́лышков, на́до прочне́е закрепи́ть пала́тку; **to ~ out/up the washing** вы|ве́шивать бельё (-́весить); *fig* **to ~ prices/wages** замор|а́живать це́ны/зарпла́ту (-о́зить)

vi fig CQ: **he's been ~ging away at his thesis for two years** он уже́ два го́да корпи́т над свое́й диссерта́цией.

pejorative *adj* уничижи́тельный.

pekinese, *abbr CQ* **peke** *n* кита́йский мопс.

pellet *n* (*pill*) пилю́ля; (*small shot*) дроби́на, *pl* (**~s**) дробь (*collect*); **a ~ of bread** ша́рик из хле́бного мя́киша.

pell-mell *adv* (*in confusion*) впереме́шку, как попа́ло.

pelmet *n* ламбреке́н.

pelt[1] *n* шку́ра, ко́жа.

pelt[2] *n*: **at full ~** со всех ног.

pelt[2] *vti vt*: **to ~ smb with stones/tomatoes** за|бра́сывать кого́-л камня́ми/помидо́рами (-броса́ть)

vi: **the rain was ~ing down, it was ~ing (with rain)** дождь лил как из ведра́; *CQ* **he ~ed past me** он пронёсся ми́мо меня́.

pelvis *n Anat* таз.

pen[1] *n* ру́чка; **fountain ~** авторучка; **ball-point ~** ша́риковая ру́чка; **to put ~ to paper** взя́ться за перо́.

pen[1] *vt* писа́ть (на-); **he ~ned her a note** он черкну́л ей запи́ску.

pen[2] *n Agric* заго́н (для скота́).

pen[2] *vt*: **to ~ sheep** за|гоня́ть ове́ц (-гна́ть); *fig* **I feel ~ned in there** я чу́вствую себя́ там как в тюрьме́.

penal *adj*: **a ~ offence** наказу́емое правонаруше́ние; **the P. Code** уголо́вный ко́декс; **~ servitude** ка́торжные рабо́ты (*pl*).

penalize *vt* (*punish*) нака́з|ывать (-а́ть); *Sport* штрафова́ть (о-); *fig* **such prices ~ the less well-off** таки́е це́ны бьют по малообеспе́ченным слоя́м населе́ния.

penalty *n* (*punishment*) наказа́ние; (*fine*) штраф, *also Sport*; **what's the ~ for this?** како́е за э́то сле́дует наказа́ние?; *fig* **we are paying the ~ for our mistakes** мы распла́чиваемся за свои́ оши́бки; *attr*: *Law* **~ clause** пункт о штра́фе за невыполне́ние догово́ра; *Sport* **~ area** штрафна́я площа́дка; **~ kick** штрафно́й уда́р, пена́льти (*indecl*).

penance *n Rel*, *also semi-joc*: **to do ~ for one's sins** искуп|а́ть свои́ грехи́ (-и́ть).

pen-and-ink *adj*: **~ drawings** рису́нки перо́м.

pence *n see* **penny.**

pencil *n* каранда́ш; **in ~** карандашо́м; **a propelling ~** автомати́ческий каранда́ш; **an eyebrow ~** каранда́ш для брове́й; *attr*: **~ drawing** каранда́шный рису́нок; **~ case/sharpener** пена́л, точи́лка для карандаше́й.

pencil *vt* (*write*) писа́ть/(*draw*) черти́ть карандашо́м (*pfs* на-); **finely ~led eyebrows** то́нко подведённые бро́ви.

pendant *n* кулóн, подве́ска; (*charm*) брело́к.

pending *adj*: **the judgement was then still ~** тогда́ ещё суде́бный проце́сс не ко́нчился; **an agreement on this is still ~** соглаше́ние об э́том ещё не заключено́; **"patent ~"** «пате́нт зая́влен»; **it's in the ~ tray** э́то (нахо́дится) в па́пке (*folder*) «К рассмотре́нию».

pending *prep* до + *G*; **~ their arrival, nothing can be done** до их прихо́да/пока́ их нет,/ пока́ они́ не пришли́, ничего́ нельзя́ сде́лать.

pendulum *n* ма́ятник.

penetrate *vti vt* проник|а́ть в + *A* (-́нуть); **such a light shower won't ~ the soil** тако́й лёгкий дождь не прони́кнет глубоко́ в по́чву; **a ray of light ~d the room/the darkness** луч све́та прони́к в ко́мнату/прониза́л темноту́; **to ~ a mystery** проника́ть в та́йну; **the needle ~d my skin** иго́лка вонзи́лась мне в те́ло; *Mil* **our troops ~d the enemy's lines** на́ши ча́сти прорва́ли оборо́ну проти́вника

vi CQ: **he's so dumb I doubt if your words will ~** бою́сь, ва́ши слова́ до него́ не дойду́т—так он туп.

penetrating *adj* (*acute*) проница́тельный; (*of look, sound*) пронзи́тельный.

pen-friend *n* знако́мый по перепи́ске.

penguin *n* пингви́н.

penicillin *n* пеницилли́н; *attr* пеницилли́новый.

peninsula *n* полуо́стров.

peninsular *adj* полуострово́й.

penis *n Anat* мужско́й полово́й член, пе́нис.

penitence *n* раска́яние; *Rel* покая́ние.

penitent *adj* ка́ющийся.

penknife *n* перочи́нный нож.

pen name *n* псевдони́м.

pennant *n* вы́мпел.

penniless *adj*: **she was left ~** она́ оста́лась без гроша́; **he's quite ~** у него́ нет ни гроша́ за душо́й.

pennon *n* флажо́к.

penny, *abbr* **p** *n* пе́нни (*indecl*), пенс; *pl* **pennies** *or* **pence** пе́нсы; **a ~** одно́ пе́нни; **a new ~** оди́н но́вый пенс; *fig*: **I haven't a ~ to my name** у меня́ нет ни гроша́ в карма́не; **it cost him a pretty ~** э́то ему́ влете́ло в копе́ечку; **to earn/turn an honest ~** подраба́тывать; *CQ* **at last the ~ dropped and he laughed** наконе́ц до него́ дошло́ и он засмея́лся.

penny-pinching *adj* скупо́й, ска́редный.

pension[1] *n* пе́нсия; **old age/disability ~** пе́нсия по ста́рости/по инвали́дности; **to retire on a ~** уходи́ть на пе́нсию; **to draw a ~** получа́ть пе́нсию.

pension[1] *vt*: **he has been ~ed off** его́ отпра́вили на пе́нсию.

pension[2] *n* (*boarding house*) пансио́н; (*board*) **terms with full ~** сто́имость содержа́ния с по́лным пансио́ном.

pensioner *n*, *also* **old age ~** пенсионе́р, *f* -ка.

pensive *adj* заду́мчивый.

pentagon *n* пятиуго́льник; (*US*) **the P.** Пентаго́н.

pentathlon *n* пятибо́рье.

penthouse *n*, *also* **~ flat** *approx* фешене́бельная кварти́ра на кры́ше.

pent-up *adj*: **~ fury** сде́рживаемый гнев; **he is all ~** он взви́нчен до преде́ла.

penultimate *adj* предпосле́дний.

penury *n* нужда́, бе́дность.

peony *n* пио́н.

people *n* **1** *collect* (*persons*) лю́ди [**NB** *G pl after numerals* челове́к; *after* мно́го, ма́ло *use* наро́ду]; **most ~** большинство́ люде́й; **whatever will ~ think?** что лю́ди поду́мают?; **many/some ~ think that...** мно́гие/не́которые ду́мают, что...; **how many ~ were there?** ско́лько там бы́ло люде́й/наро́ду?; **there were a lot of ~/6 ~ there** там бы́ло мно́го наро́ду/шесть челове́к; (*impersonal*): **~ say that...** говоря́т, что...; **country ~** дереве́нские/се́льские жи́тели; **all the best ~ go there** там быва́ют сли́вки о́бщества; **young ~** молодёжь; (*SU*) **P.'s Courts** наро́дные суды́

2 *sing* (*race*) наро́д; **the Scots are a proud ~** шотла́ндцы—го́рдый наро́д; **the English-speaking ~s** англоязы́чные наро́ды

3 *CQ* (*family*): **have you met her ~?** вы знако́мы с её родны́ми?

people *vt* насел|я́ть, засел|я́ть (*pfs* -и́ть); **a region ~d by primitive tribes** райо́н, населённый первобы́тными племена́ми.

pep *n CQ* жи́вость; **put some ~ into it!** поживе́е!; *attr*: **~ pills** стимули́рующие табле́тки.

pepper *n* пе́рец, *also Bot*; **I put too much ~ in the stew** я перепе́рчила жарко́е.

pepper *vt Cook* пе́рчить (на-); *fig*: **to ~ smb with questions** за|бра́сывать кого́-л вопро́сами (-броса́ть); **an article ~ed with quotations** статья́ пестри́т цита́тами.

peppercorn *n* перчи́нка.

pepper mill *n* ме́льница для пе́рца.

peppermint *n Bot* мя́та пе́речная; (*sweet*) мя́тная конфе́та.

pepperpot *n* пе́речница.

peppery *adj* (*of taste*) напе́рченный; (*hot*) о́стрый; *fig* **a ~ old man** жёлчный/раздражи́тельный стари́к.

peptalk *n*: **our teacher gave us a ~** *CQ* учи́тель стара́лся расшевели́ть нас.

per *prep*: **£1,000 ~ annum/~ year** ты́сяча фу́нтов в год; **30 miles ~ hour** три́дцать миль в час; **how much do you get ~ day?** ско́лько вы получа́ете в день?; **50p ~ kilo** пятьдеся́т пе́нсов (за) кило(гра́мм); **how many kilometres ~ litre will your car do?** на ско́лько киломе́тров хвата́ет ли́тра бензи́на ва́шей маши́не?; **cost ~ head** *see* **head** *n*; **~ capita income** (*nationally*) дохо́д на ду́шу населе́ния; **as ~ instructions** согла́сно инстру́кциям; *CQ* **as ~ usual** по обыкнове́нию.

perambulator, *abbr* **pram** *n* де́тская коля́ска.

perceive *vt* (*visually*) различ|а́ть (-и́ть); заме|ча́ть (-́тить); (*mentally*) пон|има́ть (-я́ть), осозна|ва́ть (-́ть); **I ~d a figure in the distance** я заме́тил вдали́ каку́ю-то фигу́ру; **she ~d at once what he was getting at** она́ сра́зу поняла́, куда́ он кло́нит; **I soon ~d my mistake** я ско́ро осозна́л свою́ оши́бку.

per cent *n* проце́нт; **the price has risen by 10%** цена́ повы́силась на де́сять проце́нтов; **in 10% of such cases** в десяти́ проце́нтах подо́бных слу́чаев; **a discount of 5%** пятипроце́нтная ски́дка.

percentage *n* проце́нт; **what ~ of wool is there in this material?** ско́лько проце́нтов (*pl*) ше́рсти в э́той тка́ни?; **a figure expressed as a ~** число́, вы́раженное в проце́нтах: **what ~ of the profits goes in tax?** како́й проце́нт при́были идёт на упла́ту нало́гов?; **a high ~ of our students** большо́й проце́нт на́ших студе́нтов.

perceptible *adj* различи́мый, ощути́мый; **the sound was scarcely ~** звук был едва́ различи́м; **there's been a ~ improvement in the patient's condition** состоя́ние больно́го заме́тно улу́чшилось.

perception *n* восприя́тие.

perceptive *adj* восприи́мчивый.

perch[1] *n* (*fish*) о́кунь.

perch[2] *n* насе́ст; *fig* **to knock smb off his ~** осади́ть кого́-л.

perch[2] *vti vt*: **a castle ~ed on top of a cliff** за́мок на верши́не скалы́; **he was ~ed on a high stool** он усе́лся на высо́кую табуре́тку

vi уса́живаться (усе́сться); **the birds ~ed on the wires** пти́цы усе́лись на провода́.

percolate *vti vt*: **to ~ coffee** вари́ть ко́фе в перколя́торе (с-)

vi (*filter*): **water ~s through limestone** вода́ про|са́чивается сквозь известня́к (-сочи́ться).

percolator *n* (*for coffee*) перколя́тор.

percussion *n Mus collect* (**the ~**) уда́рные инструме́нты; *attr*: **~ player** уда́рник.

peremptory *adj* (*of command, tone, etc.*) вла́стный, категори́чный.

perennial *adj Bot* многоле́тний; *fig* ве́чный; **it's a ~ subject of debate** э́то ве́чный предме́т спо́ров; *as n Bot* многоле́тнее расте́ние.

perfect *adj* **1** соверше́нный; безупре́чный, идеа́льный; **he's a ~ stranger to me** он мне соверше́нно незнако́м; **he speaks ~ French** он говори́т по-францу́зски безупре́чно; **she's the ~ wife for him** она́ для него́ идеа́льная жена́; **he's ~ for the role** он идеа́льно подхо́дит для э́той ро́ли; **a ~ copy** то́чная ко́пия; *CQ*: **the weather was ~** пого́да была́ прекра́сная; **we had a ~ day** мы чуде́сно провели́ день; **what ~ nonsense!** э́то абсолю́тнейшая чепуха́!

2 *Gram*: **the ~ tense** (*also as n* **the ~**) перфе́кт.

perfect *vt* соверше́нствовать (у-); **I am trying to ~ my French** я соверше́нствую свой францу́зский.

perfection *n* соверше́нство; **she plays the part to ~** она́ прекра́сно исполня́ет э́ту роль; **the meat's done to ~** мя́со пригото́влено бесподо́бно.

perfective *adj Gram*: **the ~ aspect** (*also as n* **the ~**) соверше́нный вид (глаго́ла).

perforate *vt* перфори́ровать (*impf and pf*); *Med* **a ~d ulcer** прободна́я я́зва желу́дка.

perforation *n* перфора́ция.

perforce *adv* по необходи́мости, во́лей-нево́лей.

perform *vti vt* **1** исполн|я́ть (-́ить), вы|полня́ть (-́полнить); де́лать (с-); **he ~ed his task well** он хорошо́ вы́полнил зада́ние; **to ~ an experiment** про|води́ть экспериме́нт (-вести́); *Med* **to ~ an operation** де́лать опера́цию

2 *Theat, Mus, etc.* игра́ть (сыгра́ть), исполня́ть; **they're ~ing Hamlet tomorrow** за́втра у них идёт «Га́млет»; **the orchestra is ~ing a new symphony tonight** сего́дня орке́стр исполня́ет но́вую симфо́нию; *fig* **she ~ed her part very well** она́ хорошо́ сыгра́ла свою́ роль

vi игра́ть, вы|ступа́ть (-́ступить); **the actor ~ed well tonight** актёр хорошо́ игра́л сего́дня; **he's ~ing in Paris tomorrow** за́втра он выступа́ет в Пари́же; **he has ~ed all over the country** он объе́здил с конце́ртами всю страну́; **how did the team ~?** как игра́ла кома́нда?; **how are the new machines ~ing?** как рабо́тают но́вые маши́ны?

performance *n* исполне́ние, выполне́ние; *Theat* спекта́кль (*m*), представле́ние; **the first**

~ **of a symphony** пéрвое исполнéние симфóнии; **the play had its first ~ in March** пéрвое представлéние э́той пьéсы состоя́лось в мáрте; **tonight's ~ begins at 7 o'clock** *Theat* вечéрний спектáкль/*Cine* вечéрний сеáнс/*Mus* концéрт начинáется сегóдня в семь часóв; **no ~ tonight** сегóдня спектáкля нет; **they gave a ~ of Hamlet** они́ постáвили/сыгрáли «Гáмлета»; **I liked his ~ of Lear/of the sonata** мне понрáвилось, как он сыгрáл Ли́ра/как он испóлнил сонáту; **the show had 100 ~s** спектáкль вы́держал сто представлéний; **are you satisfied with the car's ~?** вы довóльны своéй маши́ной?; *CQ* **the team put up a good ~** комáнда показáла хорóшую игру́.

performer *n* исполни́тель (*m*); **the ~s were exhausted** актёры/музыкáнты устáли; *CQ pejor* **I find him a bit of a ~** мне кáжется, он позёр.

performing *adj*: **~ animals** дрессирóванные живóтные.

perfume *n* (*bottled*) духи́ (*pl*); (*smell*) аромáт; **a bottle of ~** флакóн духóв; **the ~ of lilac** зáпах/аромáт сирéни.

perfunctory *adj* (*careless*) небрéжный, невнимáтельный; (*superficial*)повéрхностный.

perhaps *adv* мóжет быть; возмóжно; пожáлуй; **~ so** мóжет быть; **~ he'll come** возмóжно,/мóжет быть,/пожáлуй, он придёт.

peril *n* опáсность; **in ~** в опáсности.

perilous *adj* опáсный.

perimeter *n* пери́метр.

period *n* **1** (*of time*) пери́од; (*term*) срок; **the postwar ~** послевоéнный пери́од; **a painting of his early ~** карти́на рáннего пери́ода егó твóрчества; **for a ~ of 6 months the new firm had a lot of troubles** полгóда нóвая фи́рма переживáла значи́тельные тру́дности; **within a ~ of two days the weather had completely changed** за два дня погóда совершéнно перемени́лась; **for a short/trial ~** на корóткий/испытáтельный срок; **~ of validity** срок дéйствия; *attr*: **~ furniture** сти́льная мéбель

2 (*special uses*) *School* урóк; *Gram* (*sentence*) пери́од; (*full stop*) тóчка; *Med* менструáция, мéсячные (*pl*).

periodic *adj* периоди́ческий.

periodical *n* периоди́ческое издáние.

peripheral *adj* перифери́йный.

periscope *n* перискóп.

perish *vti vt*: *CQ* **we were ~ed with cold** мы погибáли от хóлода

vi **1** (*of people*) погиб|áть (-нуть); **thousands ~ed in the earthquake** ты́сячи людéй поги́бли во врéмя землетрясéния; *fig joc* **~ the thought!** бóже упаси́!

2 (*of material*): **the tread of the tyre has ~ed** ши́на протёрлась; **the silk had ~ed** шёлк изорвáлся.

perishable *adj* (*of food*) скоропóртящийся.

perishing *adj CQ*: **it's ~ here!** здесь áдски хóлодно!; **I'm ~** я совсéм окоченéл [**NB** *tense*].

peritonitis *n Med* перитони́т.

perjure *vt*: **to ~ oneself** лжесвидéтельствовать (*impf and pf*), да|вáть лóжные показáния (-ть).

perk *n see* **perquisite.**

perk up *vi* оживл|я́ться (-и́ться); **she ~ed up when she saw us** онá оживи́лась при ви́де нас; **business is ~ing up** делá пошли́ в гóру [**NB** *tense*].

perky *adj* оживлённый, бóйкий.

perm *n CQ* перманéнт; **to have a ~** дéлать перманéнт.

permafrost *n* вéчная мерзлотá.

permanent *adj* постоя́нный; **a ~ job** постоя́нная рабóта; **~ address** постоя́нное местожи́тельство; **a ~ solution of the problem** окончáтельное решéние вопрóса; **a ~ wave** зави́вка перманéнт.

permanently *adv* постоя́нно; **we live here ~** мы живём здесь постоя́нно; **I don't want to stay here ~** я не хочу́ оставáться здесь навсегдá; **he's ~ drunk** он вéчно пьян.

permeable *adj* водопроницáемый.

permeate *vt* (*of fluids*) пропи́т|ывать (-áть); (*of smells, ideas*) распростран|я́ться (-и́ться); **water quickly ~s sand** песóк бы́стро впи́тывает вóду; **the smell of burnt meat ~d the flat** зáпах подгорéвшего мя́са распространи́лся по всей квати́ре.

permissible *adj* допусти́мый, позволи́тельный; **such conduct is not ~** подóбное поведéние недопусти́мо; **if it is ~ to ask** éсли позволи́тельно спроси́ть.

permission *n* разрешéние; **you need written ~ for that** на э́то ну́жно пи́сьменное разрешéние; **with your ~** с вáшего разрешéния/позволéния.

permissive *adj*: **modern society is very ~** в совремéнном óбществе нрáвы горáздо мéнее стрóгие.

permit *n* разрешéние; (*pass*) прóпуск; **an import ~** разрешéние на и́мпорт; **they won't let one enter without a ~** без прóпуска тудá не пу́стят.

permit *vti vt* (*give permission*) разреш|áть (-и́ть); (*allow*) позвол|я́ть (-и́ть); допус|кáть (-ти́ть); **the doctor won't ~ him to go out yet** дóктор ещё не разрешáет ему́ выходи́ть; **smoking is now ~ted** сейчáс мóжно кури́ть; **if I might be ~ted to say so** éсли мне позвóлят так вы́разиться; **she won't ~ any familiarity** онá не позволя́ет/не допускáет никакóй фамилья́рности; **sometimes I ~ myself the luxury of a bottle of good wine** иногдá я позволя́ю себé рóскошь вы́пить буты́лку хорóшего винá; **the public is not ~ted beyond this point** дáльше пу́блика не допускáется, посторóнним вход запрещён

vi: **weather ~ting** éсли погóда позвóлит; **the situation ~s of no delay** обстанóвка трéбует дéйствовать безотлагáтельно/без промедлéния.

permutation *n Math* перестанóвка.

pernicious *adj* пáгубный, врéдный; **a ~ habit** врéдная привы́чка; **he has a ~ influence**

on the students он ока́зывает па́губное влия́ние на студе́нтов; *Med* ~ **anaemia** злока́чественное малокро́вие.

pernickety *adj* привере́дливый; **she's very ~ about her food/about what she wears** она́ о́чень привере́длива в еде́/в оде́жде.

peroxide *n Chem* пе́рекись; (*for hair*) пе́рекись водоро́да; *attr CQ*: **a ~ blonde** хими́ческая блонди́нка.

perpendicular *n* (*line*) перпендикуля́р; **the wall is out of the ~** э́та стена́ име́ет небольшо́й накло́н.

perpendicular *adj* перпендикуля́рный.

perpetrate *vt* соверш|а́ть (-и́ть); **to ~ a crime/a blunder** соверши́ть преступле́ние/оши́бку.

perpetual *adj* ве́чный, бесконе́чный; **~ motion** ве́чное движе́ние; **this ~ bickering gets me down** э́та бесконе́чная перепа́лка мне надое́ла [**NB** *tense*]; **~ anxiety** постоя́нная трево́га.

perpetually *adv* постоя́нно, всё вре́мя, ве́чно; **they're ~ quarrelling** они́ постоя́нно/всё вре́мя/ве́чно ссо́рятся.

perpetuate *vt* увекове́ч|ивать (-ить).

perpetuity *n Law*: **right of ownership in ~** пра́во на ве́чное по́льзование.

perplex *vt* озада́ч|ивать (-ить); **I'm thoroughly ~ed—I don't know what to do** я си́льно озада́чен—про́сто не зна́ю, что де́лать.

perplexing *adj*: **it's all very ~** э́то всё о́чень озада́чивает, над э́тим придётся полома́ть го́лову.

perplexity *n* недоуме́ние, озада́ченность; **we're in some ~** мы в не́котором недоуме́нии; **she looked at me in ~** она́ озада́ченно посмотре́ла на меня́.

perquisite, *CQ* **perk** *n* преиму́щество; **meal vouchers are one of the perks of the job** беспла́тный обе́д—одно́ из преиму́ществ э́той рабо́ты.

persecute *vt* пресле́довать (*impf*).

persecution *n* пресле́дование, гоне́ние; *attr*: **~ mania/complex** ма́ния пресле́дования.

perseverance *n* упо́рство, насто́йчивость.

persevere *vi* (насто́йчиво) продолжа́ть (*impf*), *see also* **persist; it's very boring but we'll just have to ~** э́то о́чень ску́чно, но дева́ться не́куда—ну́жно продолжа́ть.

persevering *adj* (*of person, effort, etc.*) упо́рный, насто́йчивый.

persist *vi* упо́рствовать (*impf*); продолжа́ть(ся) (*usu impf*); **if you ~ in doing this, you will regret it** е́сли ты бу́дешь в э́том упо́рствовать, то пожале́ешь; **they ~ed in their efforts to convince him** они́ все продолжа́ли убежда́ть его́; **he will ~ in smoking in spite of the doctor's warning** он продолжа́ет кури́ть, несмотря́ на предупрежде́ние врача́; **if the fog/rain ~s** е́сли тума́н не рассе́ется, е́сли дождь не прекрати́тся.

persistence *n* упо́рство; **he shows great ~ in his work** он проявля́ет большо́е упо́рство в рабо́те.

persistent *adj* (*dogged*) насто́йчивый, упо́рный; (*unceasing*) беспреста́нный, непреры́вный; **he's very ~** он о́чень насто́йчив; **~ demands** насто́йчивые тре́бования; **there was ~ rain all day** весь день непреры́вно шёл дождь; **a ~ pain/cough** непрекраща́ющаяся боль, упо́рный ка́шель.

person *n* челове́к; *off* лицо́, *also Gram*; (*personage*) персо́на, осо́ба; *pejor* тип; **she's a lovely ~** она́ о́чень ми́лый челове́к; **a very important ~** (*abbr* **VIP**) ва́жная осо́ба, ва́жное лицо́; **my uncle is an important ~ in the ministry** мой дя́дя занима́ет ва́жный пост в министе́рстве; **I'll be there in ~** я ли́чно там бу́ду; **he found a supporter in the ~ of his brother** он нашёл сторо́нника в лице́ бра́та; **who is this ~?** кто э́тот тип?; **he's always neat in his ~** он всегда́ опря́тно вы́глядит.

persona *n*: *Dipl* **~ non grata** персо́на нон гра́та; *Theat* **dramatis ~e** де́йствующие ли́ца.

personable *adj* представи́тельный, ви́дный.

personage *n* персо́на, осо́ба.

personal *adj* ли́чный, *also Gram*; (*assigned to one particular person*) персона́льный; **I know it from ~ experience** я зна́ю э́то по ли́чному о́пыту; **I'll give it my ~ attention** я ли́чно займу́сь э́тим вопро́сом; **could I see you for a minute on a ~ matter?** могу́ я с ва́ми поговори́ть по ли́чному вопро́су?; **don't make ~ remarks** не переходи́ на ли́чности; **he's a ~ friend of mine** он мой бли́зкий друг; **it's the minister's ~ car** э́то персона́льная маши́на мини́стра; *Tel* **to make a ~ call** заказа́ть телефо́нный разгово́р с указа́нием вызыва́емого лица́.

personality *n* ли́чность; индивидуа́льность; **he has a striking ~** он интере́сная ли́чность; **his ~ emerges clearly in his paintings** в его́ карти́нах я́рко проявля́ется его́ индивидуа́льность; **let's not bring personalities into it** дава́йте не переходи́ть на ли́чности; *Psych* **he has a split ~** у него́ раздвое́ние ли́чности.

personally *adv* ли́чно; **~, I think he's wrong** я ли́чно счита́ю, что он не прав; **don't take this ~** не принима́й э́то на свой счёт.

personify *vt*: **these characters ~ various vices** э́ти персона́жи олицетворя́ют ра́зные поро́ки; **she's good nature/meanness personified** она́ само́ раду́шие, она́ олицетворе́ние ску́пости.

personnel *n* персона́л, штат; *attr*: **~ department** отде́л ка́дров; **~ manager** нача́льник отде́ла ка́дров.

perspective *n* перспекти́ва; **the drawing is out of ~** в рису́нке нару́шена перспекти́ва; *fig* **let's get this into ~** дава́йте посмо́трим на э́то в и́стинном све́те; *attr*: **~ drawing** рису́нок в перспекти́ве.

perspex *n* плексигла́с; *attr* плексигла́совый.

perspicacious *adj* проница́тельный.

perspiration *n* (*sweating*) поте́ние; (*sweat*) пот; **I'm dripping with ~** я весь в поту́.

perspire *vi* поте́ть (вс-).

persuade *vt* убе|жда́ть (-ди́ть); угов|а́ривать (-ори́ть); **he ~d me to come** он убеди́л/уговори́л меня́ прийти́; **how can I ~ you of my sincerity?** как мне убеди́ть вас в мое́й и́скренности?; **I am ~d that...** я убеждён, что...

persuasion *n* **1** убежде́ние; **he needed a lot of ~** его́ нелегко́ бы́ло убеди́ть; **by means of ~** путём убежде́ния

2 (*belief*) убежде́ние; **I myself am not of that ~** я сам не разделя́ю э́то убежде́ние.

persuasive *adj* убеди́тельный; **~ arguments** убеди́тельные до́воды/аргуме́нты; **she was very ~** она́ о́чень убеди́тельно говори́ла.

pert *adj* де́рзкий.

pertain *vi* (*have reference to*) относи́ться к + *D* (*only in impf*); **the documents that ~ to this case/period** докуме́нты, относя́щиеся к э́тому де́лу/пери́оду; *Law* **the house and the land ~ing to it** дом с относя́щимся к нему́ земе́льным уча́стком.

pertinacious *adj* упо́рный, насто́йчивый.

pertinent *adj* уме́стный; **a ~ remark** уме́стное замеча́ние; **that's scarcely ~ to the matter in hand** э́то вряд ли отно́сится к де́лу.

perturb *vt* беспоко́ить (о-), волнова́ть (вз-), трево́жить (вс-); **no need to get ~ed** не на́до беспоко́иться/волнова́ться.

perusal *n* (*formal*): **on ~ of this letter** прочита́в э́то письмо́; **I enclose for your ~** прилага́ю для ва́шего прочте́ния.

pervade *vt*: **a strange smell ~d the flat** по кварти́ре распространи́лся како́й-то стра́нный за́пах; **the influence of Pushkin ~s Russian literature** тво́рчество Пу́шкина оказа́ло большо́е влия́ние на всю ру́сскую литерату́ру.

perverse *adj* (*stubborn*) упря́мый; (*contrary*) своенра́вный; **you're just being ~—you know quite well what I mean** ты про́сто упря́мишься, ведь хорошо́ понима́ешь, что я име́ю в виду́.

perversion *n* извраще́ние; **a ~ of the truth** извраще́ние и́стины; **sexual ~** полово́е извраще́ние.

perverted *adj* развращённый; извращённый.

pessimistic *adj* пессимисти́ческий, пессимисти́чный.

pest *n Zool* вреди́тель (*m*); **garden ~s** садо́вые вреди́тели; *CQ*: **the flies are a ~ here** здесь от мух нет житья́; **what a ~ that boy is!** что за наказа́ние/надое́да э́тот мальчи́шка!

pester *vt* пристава́ть к + *D* (*impf*); **to ~ smb with questions** пристава́ть к кому́-л с вопро́сами; **we were ~ed with mosquitoes** нас изводи́ли/му́чили комары́.

pesticide *n* пестици́д.

pet[1] *n* **1** (*tame animal*): **they keep lots of ~s** у них в до́ме мно́го живо́тных; **he keeps white mice as ~s** у него́ до́ма живу́т бе́лые мы́ши; *attr*: **a ~ magpie/monkey** ручна́я соро́ка/обезья́на

2 (*favourite*) люби́мец, *dim* люби́мчик; **she's teacher's/such a ~** она́ люби́мица учи́теля, она́ така́я ми́лая; **yes, my ~** да, моя́ ми́лая/*CQ* ла́почка; *attr*: **he's on his ~ subject again** он опя́ть сел на своего́ конька́; **a ~ name** ласка́тельное и́мя; **she's my ~ aversion** она́ мне осо́бенно не нра́вится.

pet[1] *vti vt* ласка́ть (*impf*)

vi не́жничать (*impf*).

pet[2] *n*: **she's in a ~ again** она́ опя́ть не в ду́хе.

petal *n* лепесто́к.

peter *vi*: **our supplies are ~ing out** на́ши запа́сы иссяка́ют; **the path just ~s out** тропи́нка незаме́тно исчеза́ет/теря́ется в траве́; **his enthusiasm soon ~ed out** его́ энтузиа́зм бы́стро испари́лся.

petition *n* пети́ция, хода́тайство; заявле́ние; **to present a ~ to smb** пода́ть кому́-л пети́цию; *Law* **a ~ for mercy** хода́тайство о поми́ловании; **to file a ~ for divorce** пода́ть заявле́ние о разво́де.

petition *vt*: **to ~ a Minister/Parliament for smth** обра|ща́ться к мини́стру/в парла́мент с пети́цией о чём-л (-ти́ться); *Law* **to ~ the court for smth** хода́тайствовать пе́ред судо́м о чём-л (*impf*).

petitioner *n* проси́тель (*m*); *Law* исте́ц.

petrify *vti vt fig* окамене́ть, оцепене́ть, остолбене́ть (*usu pfs*); **I was petrified** я оцепене́л, я остолбене́л

vi (*turn to stone*) камене́ть (о-).

petrochemicals *n* нефтехими́ческие проду́кты.

petrol *n* бензи́н.

petroleum *n* нефть; *attr*: **~ jelly** вазели́н.

petrol gauge *n* указа́тель (*m*) у́ровня бензи́на, бензиноме́р.

petrol pump *n* (*at filling station*) бензоколо́нка; (*in engine*) бензонасо́с, бензопо́мпа.

petrol tank *n* бензоба́к.

petrol tanker *n* (*lorry*) бензово́з.

petticoat *n* (*full length*) комбина́ция; (*waist slip*) ни́жняя ю́бка.

pettiness *n* ме́лочность.

petty *adj* **1** (*trivial, on a small scale*) ме́лкий; **~ details/officials** ме́лкие дета́ли/чино́вники; **~ cash** де́ньги на ме́лкие расхо́ды; *Law* **~ larceny** ме́лкая кра́жа

2 (*small-minded*) ме́лочный; **a ~ person** ме́лочный челове́к.

petty officer *n Naut* старшина́.

petulant *adj* капри́зный; вздо́рный; **a ~ child/old man** капри́зный ребёнок, ворчли́вый стари́к.

pewter *adj* оловя́нный.

phantom *n* при́зрак, фанто́м; *attr* при́зрачный.

pharmacist *n* фармаце́вт.

pharmacology *n* фармаколо́гия.

phase *n* фа́за, *also Astron*; ста́дия; **a new ~ of history** но́вая фа́за в исто́рии; **the ~s of an illness** ста́дии боле́зни; **it's just a ~ he's going through** у него́ сейча́с тако́й во́зраст.

phase *vt*: **to ~ the increase in rail fares** постепе́нно увели́чивать пла́ту за прое́зд по желе́зной доро́ге; **these planes are being ~d**

out эти самолёты постепе́нно снима́ются с авиали́ний.

pheasant *n* фаза́н.

phenomenal *adj* феномена́льный, *also CQ*.

phenomenon *n* явле́ние, фено́мен; **natural phenomena** явле́ния приро́ды; **rain is a rare ~ in the desert** дождь в пусты́не—явле́ние необы́чное.

phew *interj* (*expressing surprise*) ну и ну́!; (*relief*) уф!; **~, it's hot!** ну и жара́!

philanderer *n* волоки́та, донжуа́н.

philharmonic *adj* филармони́ческий; *as n*: **the London P.** Ло́ндонский филармони́ческий орке́стр.

philistine *n* обыва́тель (*m*).

philology *n* филоло́гия.

philosopher *n* фило́соф.

philosophical *adj* филосо́фский; *CQ* **she was quite ~ about her failure** она́ дово́льно филосо́фски отнесла́сь к свое́й неуда́че.

philosophy *n* филосо́фия.

phlegm *n Med* мокро́та, слизь.

phobia *n Med* фо́бия; *fig* **she has a ~ about rats** она́ пани́чески бои́тся крыс.

phone *n* (*abbr of* **telephone**) телефо́н.

phone *vti* звони́ть (по телефо́ну) + *D* (по-); **I'll keep on phoning till I get her** я бу́ду звони́ть, пока́ её не заста́ну, я дозвоню́сь до неё.

phonetics *n* фоне́тика (*sing*).

phoney *adj CQ* стра́нный; фальши́вый, неесте́ственный, подде́льный; **there's something ~ about him** в нём есть кака́я-то фальшь; **his sympathy seemed a bit ~** его́ сочу́вствие каза́лось мне нейскренним.

phonograph *n* (*US*) прои́грыватель (*m*).

phosphorescent *adj* фосфоресци́рующий.

photocopy *n* фотоко́пия, ксероко́пия.

photocopy *vt* фотокопи́ровать, ксерокопи́ровать (*both impf and pf*).

photocopying machine *n* копирова́льная маши́на.

photo-finish *n Sport* фотофи́ниш.

photograph, *abbr* **photo** *n* фотогра́фия, *abbr* фо́то; сни́мок; **to get one's ~ taken** сфотографи́роваться.

photograph *vti* фотографи́ровать (с-); снима́ть (снять), *also Cine*; **I don't ~ well** я пло́хо выхожу́ на фотогра́фиях/на сни́мках.

photographic *adj* фотографи́ческий; **a ~ print** фотосни́мок; **a ~ memory** фотографи́ческая па́мять.

photography *n* фотогра́фия; **colour/aerial ~** цветна́я фотогра́фия, аэрофотосъёмка; *Cine* **the ~ in the film is first class** в фи́льме великоле́пные съёмки (*pl*).

photostat *n and vt see* **photocopy** *n and vt*.

phrase *n* фра́за, *also Mus*; выраже́ние; **an empty ~** пуста́я фра́за; **a neat turn of ~** уда́чное выраже́ние; **as the ~ goes** как говоря́т/говори́тся; *Gram* **a prepositional ~** предло́жный оборо́т.

phrase *vt* вы|ража́ть (́-разить); формули́ровать (с-); **I would have ~d that differently** я бы не так э́то вы́разил; **his request was well ~d** его́ заявле́ние бы́ло хорошо́ сформули́ровано.

phrasebook *n* разгово́рник.

phrasing *n* (*of ideas, letters, etc.*) формулиро́вка; *Mus* фразиро́вка.

phrenetic *adj* исступлённый, неи́стовый.

physical *adj* физи́ческий; **~ force/fitness** физи́ческая си́ла/подгото́вленность; *Philos* **the ~ world** материа́льный мир.

physical training, *abbr* **P.T.** *n* физи́ческое воспита́ние, физкульту́ра.

physician *n* терапе́вт.

physicist *n* фи́зик.

physics *n* фи́зика (*sing*).

physiotherapy *n* физиотерапи́я.

physique *n* телосложе́ние.

pianist *n* пиани́ст.

piano *n* фортепья́но (*indecl*); **grand ~** роя́ль (*m*); **upright ~** пиани́но (*indecl*); **to play the ~** игра́ть на пиани́но/на роя́ле; *attr*: **~ stool** стул для роя́ля; **~ concerto** фортепья́нный конце́рт.

piano tuner *n* настро́йщик роя́лей.

pick *n* **1** (*pickaxe*) кирка́; **ice ~** ледору́б; **tooth ~** зубочи́стка

2 (*choice*) вы́бор; **take your ~** выбира́й; **he's the ~ of the bunch** он среди́ них/из них са́мый лу́чший.

pick *vti vt* **1** (*pluck*) рвать (*impf*) *and compounds*; со|бира́ть (-бра́ть); **to ~ a rose/an apple** срыва́ть ро́зу/я́блоко (сорва́ть); **to ~ flowers/fruit** собира́ть цветы́/фру́кты; **he ~ed a hair off his jacket** он снял во́лос с пиджака́; **I ~ed this button off the floor—is it yours?** э́то твоя́ пу́говица? Я нашёл её на полу́

2 (*choose*) вы|бира́ть (́-брать); (*select for a purpose*) под|бира́ть (-обра́ть); **these apples are mostly rotten—just ~ the best** э́ти я́блоки почти́ все гнилы́е, ты вы́бери что полу́чше; **I ~ed a tie to go with this shirt** я подобра́л га́лстук к э́той руба́шке; **he ~ed himself an able assistant** он подобра́л себе́ спосо́бного помо́щника; **she ~ed her way through the puddles** она́ осторо́жно обходи́ла лу́жи; *Sport*: **to ~ sides** вы́брать кома́нду (*sing*); **to ~ a winner** поста́вить на победи́теля

3 (*pick at, remove*) ковыря́ть в + *P* (*usu impf*); **to ~ one's nose** ковыря́ть в носу́; **he ~ed his teeth with a toothpick** он ковыря́л в зуба́х зубочи́сткой; **to ~ a lock** откры|ва́ть замо́к отмы́чкой (́-ть); **to ~ smb's pocket** залез|а́ть к кому́-л в карма́н (́-ть); **the dog ~ed the bone clean** соба́ка обглода́ла кость до́чиста; *fig*: **can I ~ your brains on this matter?** что ты мне посове́туешь в э́том де́ле?

vi: **to ~ and choose** выбира́ть

pick at *vt*: **to ~ at a scab** сковы́р|ивать боля́чку (-ну́ть); **she just ~ed at her food** она́ то́лько поковыря́ла еду́ (ви́лкой) (*pf*)

pick off *vt*: **to ~ off dead heads** срыва́ть засо́хшие голо́вки цвето́в; **I ~ed off a branch** я отломи́л ве́тку; **to ~ off flakes of paint**

сковыривать краску; (*shoot*) **he ~ed off both sentries** он убрал/снял обоих часовых

pick on *vt CQ*: **why ~ on me every time?** что ты всё время ко мне цепляешься?

pick out *vt*: **she ~ed out three names from the list** она отобрала три фамилии из списка; **it's hard to ~ her out in the crowd** трудно отличить её в толпе; **to ~ out a tune on the piano** подбирать мелодию на рояле; **the inscription was ~ed out in gold** надпись была сделана золотом

pick over *vt*: **to ~ over strawberries** пере|-бирать клубнику (*collect*) (-брать)

pick up *vti vt* **1** (*lift*) под|нимать (-нять); **I ~ed up the book from the floor/the receiver** я поднял книгу с пола, я взял трубку (телефона); **he ~ed himself up** он поднялся; **she ~ed up the fallen pages** она подобрала упавшие листы бумаги; **the lifeboat ~ed up the survivors** спасательная лодка подобрала уцелевших

2 (*collect*): **I'll ~ you up** я зайду/я заеду (*in car*) за тобой; **~ up a paper for me when you go out** купи мне газету, когда выйдешь; *Aut* **I ~ed up a student when driving to Oxford** я подобрал по дороге студента, когда ехал в Оксфорд

3 (*arrest*): **the police ~ed him up at the airport** полиция задержала его в аэропорту

4 *pejor CQ*: **he ~ed her up at some café** он подцепил её где-то в кафе

5 (*obtain, find*) доста|вать (-ть); **where did you ~ up that book?** где ты достал эту книгу?; **students ~ up a lot of money in summer jobs** студенты хорошо подрабатывают на летних работах

6 (*learn, acquire*): **he ~ed up that expression from his father** он перенял это выражение у отца; **I probably ~ed up flu from them** *CQ* я, наверное, у них подхватил грипп; **he ~ed up a smattering of French** он нахватался французских фраз (*G*) (*pf*); **he ~s things up very quickly** он всё схватывает на лету; **where did you ~ up that habit?** откуда у тебя эта привычка?

7 *Radio*: **we ~ed up Paris** мы поймали Париж

8 *CQ* (*correct*): **he ~ed me up for careless punctuation** он отчитал меня/сделал мне замечание за невнимание к знакам препинания

vi **1** (*improve*): **the patient/business is beginning to ~ up** больной начинает поправляться, дела (*pl*) налаживаются

2 (*take up again*): **I ~ed up with him again after many years** я возобновил с ним знакомство после многих лет.

pickaback *n and adv*: **give me a ~, Daddy** папа, посади меня на плечи; **he carried his son ~** он нёс сына на плечах.

pickaxe *n* кирка.

picked *adj* (*gathered*) собранный; (*selected*) отобранный; (*select*) отборный.

picket *n* (*stake*) кол; (*group of strikers*) пикет; (*single striker*) пикетчик; *Mil* пост; *attr*: **~ line** заслон пикетчиков.

picket *vt*: **to ~ a factory** пикетировать завод (*impf*).

picking *n* **1** (*of fruit*) сбор

2 *pl CQ*: **he took the best bits and left us the ~s** он выбрал себе самое лучшее, а нам—что осталось/остатки; **the ~s on that deal were considerable** они/мы прилично заработали на этой сделке.

pickle *n* (*solution*) рассол, маринад; *pl* (**~s**) (*of gherkins, cucumbers, etc.*) соленья (*collect*); *fig CQ*: **I'm in a bit of a ~** я влип; **that child is a little ~** с этим ребёнком никакого сладу нет.

pickle *vt* солить, мариновать (*pfs* за-).

pickled *adj* солёный; маринованный; *CQ* (*drunk*) подвыпивший.

pick-me-up *n CQ*: **let's have a ~** давай выпьем по маленькой.

pick-pocket *n* вор-карманник.

pickup *n* **1** (*of gramophone*) звукосниматель (*m*), адаптер

2 *Aut* (*also* **~ van**) пикап.

picnic *n* пикник; **to go for a ~** устроить пикник; *CQ* **the job's no ~** эта работа не такая уж лёгкая; *attr*: **~ basket** корзина с едой.

pictorial *adj*: **~ art** изобразительное искусство; **a ~ magazine** иллюстрированный журнал.

picture *n* **1** картина; *Cine* (кино)картина, (кино)фильм; (*illustration*) рисунок, картинка; **there was a ~ of him in the paper** в газете была его фотография; **we get a good ~ on our TV** наш телевизор даёт хорошее изображение; *attr*: **~ book/frame/gallery/postcard** книжка с картинками, рама для картины, картинная галерея, видовая открытка

2 *fig uses*: **he painted a gloomy ~ of the future** он нарисовал мрачную картину будущего; **this will give you the general ~** это даст вам общую картину; **our garden is a ~ in spring** весной наш сад—просто картинка; **he's the (very) ~ of health** он воплощение здоровья; **there is another side to the ~** в этом (деле) есть и оборотная сторона; **he doesn't come into the ~** он здесь ни при чём; **put me in the ~** введи меня в курс дела

3 *pl* (**the ~s**) *Cine* кино; **what's on at the ~s?** что идёт в кино?

picture *vt* представ|лять (-ить); **~ (to yourself) the scene** представь себе эту сцену.

picturesque *adj* живописный.

piddle *vi CQ* (*of baby*) *euph* делать по-маленькому (с-); (*of puppy, etc.*) сделать лужу (*usu pf*).

piddling *adj CQ* пустячный.

pie *n* (*large*) пирог, (*small*) пирожок; **a meat/an apple ~** пирог с мясом/с яблоками *or* мясной/яблочный пирог.

piebald *adj* пе́гий.

piece *n* **1** (*bit*) кусо́к, кусо́чек; **a ~ of cheese/material/paper** кусо́к сы́ра/тка́ни, лист(о́к) бума́ги; **a ~ of land** кусо́к/уча́сток земли́; **a ~ (*length*) of tweed for a suit** отре́з тви́да на костю́м; **I got the vase home all in one ~** я принёс ва́зу домо́й в це́лости и сохра́нности

2 *pl* (**~s**) кусо́чки; (*of wood, stone, wreckage*) обло́мки; (*of glass, china*) оско́лки; **the vase/boat broke in ~s** ва́за/ло́дка разби́лась вдре́безги (*adv*); **pick up the ~s** подбери́ оско́лки; **does this model come to ~s?** э́та моде́ль разбо́рная?/разбира́ется?; **this shirt is falling to ~s** руба́шка вся изорвала́сь; **I tore the old sheet in ~s** я разорвала́ ста́рую простыню́ на тря́пки

3 (*single item*) вещь; шту́ка; предме́т; **what a lovely ~ of furniture!** кака́я краси́вая вещь! [**NB** *otherwise be specific, use* стол, стул, *etc.*]; **a valuable ~ of silver/china** це́нная серебря́ная/фарфо́ровая вещь; **the Monet is the best ~ in the collection** э́та карти́на Моне́—лу́чшее, что есть в колле́кции; **how many ~s in the dinner service?** ско́лько предме́тов в серви́зе?; **I have two ~s of luggage** у меня́ два ме́ста багажа́; **a chess ~** ша́хматная фигу́ра; **I wrote a ~ for the journal** я написа́л статью́ для журна́ла; **a 50p ~** моне́та в пятьдеся́т пе́нсов; **a five-kopeck ~** пятикопе́ечная моне́та, *CQ* пята́к; **it's a good ~ of work** э́то хоро́шая рабо́та; **I get paid by the ~** я получа́ю сде́льно; **to sell by the ~** продава́ть пошту́чно; *CQ* **a two/three ~ suit** пиджа́к и брю́ки, костю́м-тро́йка

4 *fig uses*: **that's all of a ~ with what I've heard of him** э́то всё схо́дится с тем, что я о нём слы́шал; **by an incredible ~ of luck** благодаря́ неслы́ханному везе́нию; **he got back all in one ~** он верну́лся цел и невреди́м; **the critics tore the play to ~s** кри́тики разнесли́ пье́су в пух и прах; **her health has/nerves have gone to ~s** здоро́вье у неё пошатну́лось, у неё совсе́м расшата́лись не́рвы; **our team went to ~s in the second half** во второ́м та́йме на́ша кома́нда совсе́м вы́дохлась; *CQ*: **he's a nasty ~ of work** он проти́вный тип; **it's a ~ of cake!** э́то про́ще просто́го!; **I'll give him a ~ of my mind** я ему́ покажу́!/зада́м!

piece *vt*: **he ~d the clock together** он собра́л часы́; **I ~d the cup together** я скле́ил (*glued*) ча́шку; *fig* **in the end we ~d the story together** в конце́ концо́в мы разобрали́сь в э́той исто́рии.

piece goods *npl* шту́чный това́р (*collect*).

piecemeal *adj and adv* (*in bits*) по частя́м; **the work has been done ~** э́то всё бы́ло сде́лано по частя́м.

piecework *n* сде́льная рабо́та; *CQ* сде́льщина; **I'm on ~** я на сде́льщине.

pieceworker *n* сде́льщик.

piecrust *n* ко́рочка пирога́.

pied *adj* (*of birds*) чёрно-бе́лый.

pier *n Naut* пирс; *Archit* (*of bridge*) бык/усто́й (моста́).

pierce *vt* про|тыка́ть (-ткну́ть); прон|зыва́ть (-зи́ть); про|ка́лывать (-коло́ть); **the nail ~d the tyre** гвоздь проткну́л/проколо́л ши́ну; **to have one's ears ~d** прока́лывать себе́ у́ши; **a ray of light ~d the darkness** луч све́та пронзи́л темноту́; **the bullet ~d his shoulder** пу́ля проби́ла ему́ плечо́.

piercing *adj* (*of cry, look*) пронзи́тельный; **a ~ wind/cold** прони́зывающий ве́тер/хо́лод.

piety *n* на́божность, благоче́стие.

piffle *n CQ* вздор, чепуха́.

piffling *adj* ничто́жный, пустяко́вый.

pig *n* свинья́, *also fig*; *fig* **to make a ~ of oneself** обжира́ться; *attr*: **~ breeding** свиново́дство.

pig *vt CQ*: **we rather ~ it in the country** у нас на да́че так всё неустро́енно/всё по-похо́дному.

pigeon *n* го́лубь (*m*); **carrier ~** почто́вый го́лубь.

pigeon-fancier *n* голубя́тник.

pigeonhole *n*: **leave the letter in my ~** оста́вьте письмо́ в моём я́щике.

pigheaded *adj* упря́мый.

piglet *n* поросёнок.

pigskin *n* свина́я ко́жа; *attr* из свино́й ко́жи.

pigsty *n* свина́рник, *also fig*.

pigswill *n* по́йло (для свине́й), *also fig*.

pigtail *n* коса́, коси́ца; **she wears her hair in a ~** у неё коса́.

pike *n* щу́ка.

pilaff *n Cook* плов.

pile[1] *n* (*in building*) сва́я.

pile[2] *n* (*heap*) ку́ча, (*larger*) гру́да; (*stack*) сто́пка; **a ~ of sand/rubbish** ку́ча песка́/му́сора; **a large ~ of stones** гру́да камне́й; **a ~ of plates/of books** сто́пка таре́лок/книг; **a ~ of planks** (*stacked*) шта́бель досо́к; *Phys* **atomic ~** я́дерный реа́ктор; *CQ*: **he made his ~ in wool** он нажи́лся на торго́вле ше́рстью; **he made a tidy ~** он сорва́л большо́й куш.

pile[2] *vti vt* вали́ть (с-) (в ку́чу) *and compounds*; (*of smth heavy and fig*) громозди́ть, нагроможда́ть (*pf for both* нагромозди́ть); **~ it all in a heap** сва́ливайте всё в ку́чу; **we ~d the cases into the boot** мы свали́ли чемода́ны в бага́жник; **to ~ a table with books/plates** зава́ли|вать стол кни́гами (-ть), застав|ля́ть стол таре́лками (-ить); **he ~d the boxes one on top of the other** он нагромозди́л я́щики оди́н на друго́й; *fig*: **he ~d it on a bit** он немно́го переборщи́л; **she ~d on the agony** она́ наговори́ла вся́ких у́жасов; **to ~ up evidence** на|ка́пливать доказа́тельства (*pl*) (-копи́ть); *CQ* **he ~d up his car yesterday** вчера́ он разби́л свою́ маши́ну

vi: **the ship ~d up on the rocks** кора́бль разби́лся о ска́лы; **we all ~d into his car** мы все наби́лись в его́ маши́ну; **my work keeps ~ing up** рабо́та у меня́ всё накапливается; **the cars ~d up behind the traffic lights** машины скопились у светофора.

pile[3] *n* (*of carpet*) ворс.

pile-driver *n Tech* копёр.

piles *npl Med* геморрой (*sing*).

pileup *n Aut* (*in traffic jam*) пробка, скопление машин; **there was a 10-car ~ on the motorway** в автомобильной аварии наехали друг на друга десять машин.

pilfer *vt* стянуть (*CQ*) (*only in pf*).

pilferer *n* воришка.

pilfering *n* мелкое воровство.

pilgrim *n* паломник, пилигрим.

pill *n* пилюля; *fig* **it was a bitter ~ (to swallow)** это было горькой пилюлей.

pillage *vt* грабить (о-).

pillar *n* столб; *fig*: **a ~ of smoke** столб дыма; **he's ~ of strength to her** он ей надёжная опора.

pillar box *n* (*UK*) *approx* почтовый ящик.

pillion *n*: (*on motorcycle*) **to ride ~** ехать на заднем сиденье мотоцикла.

pillow *n* подушка; *attr*: **the children are having a ~ fight** дети кидаются друг в друга подушками.

pillowcase, pillow slip *ns* наволочка.

pilot *n Naut* лоцман; *Aer* пилот, лётчик; *attr Naut*: **~ boat** лоцманский катер.

pilot *adj* (*experimental*): **a ~ plant** опытный завод.

pilot *vt*: **to ~ a vessel through a strait** *Naut*/**a bill through parliament** *Law* про|водить судно через пролив/законопроект через парламент (-вести).

pilot officer *n* лейтенант авиации.

pimento *n* перец душистый/гвоздичный.

pimple *n* прыщ, *dim* прыщик; **he came out in ~s** у него появились прыщи.

pimply *adj* прыщавый.

pin *n Sew* булавка; (*for hat, hair*; *Tech*) шпилька; *Elec* (*of plug*) штырь (*m*); **drawing ~** кнопка; *fig*: **she's as neat as a new ~** она всегда такая опрятная; **you could have heard a ~ drop** слышно было, как муха пролетит; **I've got ~s and needles in my foot** у меня нога затекла.

pin *vt* **1** при|калывать (-колоть) *and other compounds*; **to ~ a notice to a board** приколоть объявление к доске; **she ~ned a medal on him** она приколола ему медаль; **to ~ papers together** скреп|лять бумаги (-ить); **she ~ned up the nappy/her hair** она заколола пелёнку булавкой/волосы шпилькой; **to ~ up a hem** подколоть подол булавками

2 *fig uses*: **he was ~ned under the beam** его придавило (*impers*) балкой; **to ~ one's hopes on smb/smth** воз|лагать надежды на кого-л/на что-л (-ложить); **he's difficult to ~ down** его трудно припереть к стене, он умеет увильнуть от ответа; **they wouldn't ~ themselves down to a definite date** они не хотели связывать себя определённой датой; **to ~ the blame on smb** свалить всю вину на кого-либо.

pinafore *n* (*apron*) передник; фартук; *attr*: **~ dress** *approx* сарафан.

pince-nez *n* пенсне (*indecl*).

pincers *npl*, *also* **a pair of ~** (*tool*) клещи (*no sing*); (*smaller*) пинцет (*sing*); (*of crab*) клешни.

pinch *n* (*with fingers*) щипок; **a ~ of salt** щепотка соли; **a ~ of snuff** понюшка табаку; *fig*: **take that with a ~ of salt** не очень-то верь этому; **they're beginning to feel the ~** вот теперь их прижало (*impers*); *CQ* **at a ~** в крайнем случае.

pinch *vti vt* **1** (*tweak*) щипать (ущипнуть); (*in door, etc.*) прищем|лять (-ить); (*of shoes*) жать (*impf*); **he ~ed her cheek** он ущипнул её за щёку; **I ~ed my finger in the door** я прищемил палец дверью; **his boots were ~ing him** сапоги ему жали; *Hort* **to ~ off buds** отщипывать почки (*usu impf*)

2 *fig uses*: **she looked ~ed with cold** она вся съёжилась от холода; **I'm ~ed for money** у меня туго с деньгами; *CQ* (*steal*): **somebody has ~ed my pen** кто-то стащил у меня ручку; **he ~es other people's ideas** он присваивает себе чужие идеи

vi: **my shoes ~** мои ботинки жмут; *fig*: **that's where the shoe ~es** вот в чём загвоздка; **to ~ and scrape** экономить на всём (*impf*).

pincushion *n* подушечка для булавок.

pine[1] *n*, *also* **~ tree** сосна.

pine[2] *vi*, *also* **to ~ away** чахнуть (за-); **to ~ for smb/smth** тосковать по кому-л/по чему-л (*impf*).

pineapple *n* ананас; *attr* ананасовый.

pinecone *n* сосновая шишка.

pine needle *n* сосновая иголка; (**~s**) хвоя (*collect*).

ping-pong *n* пинг-понг.

pinion *n Orn* оконечность крыла; *Mech* шестерня.

pink *n* (*colour*) розовый цвет; *Bot* гвоздика; *CQ* **how are you?—I'm in the ~** как вы поживаете?—Прекрасно; *Sport* **he's in the ~ of condition** он в прекрасной форме.

pink *adj* розовый; **she turned ~ with embarrassment** она залилась румянцем от смущения; *CQ* **she was tickled ~ to be invited too** она была очень польщена, когда её тоже пригласили.

pin money *n* деньги «на булавки», деньги на мелкие расходы.

pinnacle *n Archit* шпиц; (*rock*) остроконечная скала; (*peak*) пик.

pinpoint *vt* (*define*) точно определ|ять (-ить); (*point out on map*) точно указ|ывать (-ать).

pinprick *n* булавочный укол; *fig* **I get constant little ~s from her** она всё время подпускает мне шпильки/подкалывает меня.

pinstripe *adj*: **a ~ suit** костюм в тонкую полоску.

pin-up *n CQ* фотография журнальной красотки; *attr*: **she's my ~ girl** *joc* она мой идеал.

pioneer *n* **1** (*discoverer*) первооткрыва́тель (*m*), пионе́р; (*settler*) пе́рвый поселе́нец; **he was a ~ in atomic studies** он был пе́рвым иссле́дователем строе́ния а́томного ядра́

2 (*SU*: *member of youth organization, age 8–14*) пионе́р.

pioneer *vt*: **to ~ new methods** примен|я́ть но́вые ме́тоды (-и́ть).

pious *adj* на́божный, благочести́вый.

pip[1] *n Bot* (*in orange, grape, etc.*) зёрнышко; (*in melon, apple, pear*) се́мечко; (*on dice*) очко́; *Mil CQ* (*on uniform*) звёздочка.

pip[2] *n CQ*: **he/it gives me the ~** он/э́то на меня́ тоску́ нагоня́ет.

pip[3] *n Tel, Radio* коро́ткий гудо́к/сигна́л.

pip[3] *vt fig CQ*: **he just ~ped me at the post** он обошёл меня́ на са́мом фи́нише.

pipe *n* **1** труба́; **gas ~** газопрово́д; **organ ~** труба́ орга́на

2 (*smoker's*) тру́бка; *attr*: **~ tobacco** тру́бочный таба́к.

pipe *vti vt*: **oil is ~d across the desert** нефть перека́чивается по тру́бам че́рез пусты́ню; **we've got ~d water in the garden** у нас в саду́ проведён водопрово́д

vi (*of birds*) петь (*usu impf*); *Mus* труби́ть (*impf*); *CQ*: **a little voice ~d up** послы́шался то́ненький голосо́к; **~ down!** замолчи́!

pipe cleaner *n* ёршик для тру́бки.

pipe dream *n* несбы́точная мечта́.

pipeline *n* трубопрово́д; (*for gas, oil, water*) газо-/нефте-/водопрово́д; *fig* **the new regulations are in the ~** сейча́с выраба́тываются но́вые пра́вила.

piping *n* **1** (*pipes*) трубопрово́д, тру́бы (*pl*); систе́ма труб

2 *Sew* кант.

piping *adv*: **the soup is ~ hot** суп о́чень горя́чий.

piquant *adj* пика́нтный, *also fig*.

pique *n*: **she left the room in a fit of ~** она́ ушла́ раздоса́дованная.

pique *vt* заде|ва́ть самолю́бие (-́ть); **she was ~d at that** э́то заде́ло её (самолю́бие).

pirate *n* пира́т; *attr*: **a ~ radio station** радиоста́нция, рабо́тающая на чужо́й волне́.

pirate *vt fig*: **to ~ a book** незако́нно переизда|ва́ть кни́гу (-́ть); **to ~ smb's ideas/inventions** присв|а́ивать чьи-л иде́и/изобрете́ния (-о́ить).

pistachio (nut) *n* фиста́шка.

pistol *n* пистоле́т; *fig* **I only did it because he held a ~ to my head** я сде́лал э́то под его́ нажи́мом.

piston *n* по́ршень (*m*); *attr*: **~ stroke/rod** ход по́ршня, поршнево́й шток.

pit[1] *n* **1** (*hole*) я́ма, *dim* я́мка; *Theat* (*UK*) за́дние ряды́ парте́ра; *Aut* **inspection ~** я́ма; **orchestra ~** оркестро́вая я́ма; **a potato ~** я́ма для хране́ния карто́феля; **I've a sinking feeling in the ~ of my stomach** у меня́ но́ет под ло́жечкой

2 (*in mining*: *general*) ша́хта; **to go down a ~** спусти́ться в забо́й; *attr*: **~ face** забо́й.

pit[1] *vt*: **the moon is ~ted with craters** луна́ испещрена́ кра́терами; **his face is ~ted by smallpox** его́ лицо́ изры́то о́спой; *fig* **to ~ one's wits/strength against smb** ме́риться умо́м/си́лами с кем-л (по-).

pit[2] *n* (*US*: *fruit stone*) ко́сточка.

pit[2] *vt* (*US*): **to ~ cherries** вы|нима́ть ко́сточки из ви́шен (-́нуть).

pitch[1] *n* **1** *Sport* (*for football*) по́ле; (*for volleyball, ice hockey*) площа́дка

2 *Mus*: **the ~ of this piano is too low** э́то пиани́но сли́шком ни́зко настро́ено; **the ~ of a voice** высота́ го́лоса; **she has perfect ~** у неё абсолю́тный слух; **she sang off ~** она́ фальши́вила; **to give the ~** дава́ть тон; *fig*: **excitement rose to fever ~** всех охвати́ло лихора́дочное возбужде́ние; **matters reached such a ~ that...** де́ло дошло́ до того́, что...

3 (*of roof*) накло́н, скат.

pitch[1] *vti vt* **1** (*throw*) брос|а́ть (-́ить), кида́ть (ки́нуть) *and compounds*; пода|ва́ть (-́ть); **~ the ball higher** (под)ки́нь/пода́й мяч вы́ше; **to ~ hay on to a stack** подава́ть се́но на стог; **he was ~ed out of the car** его́ вы́бросило (*impers*) из маши́ны

2: **to ~ a tent/camp** ста́вить пала́тку (по-), разби|ва́ть ла́герь (-́ть)

3 *Mus*: **to ~ one's voice higher** повы|ша́ть го́лос (-́сить); **the part is ~ed too high for her** э́та па́ртия сли́шком высока́ для её го́лоса; *fig*: **he ~ed his hopes too high** он сли́шком высоко́ ме́тил; *CQ* **he's ~ing it a bit strong** он я́вно преувели́чивает

vi **1** па́дать (упа́сть); брос|а́ться (-́иться); **the plane ~ed into the sea** самолёт упа́л в мо́ре; **the train stopped with a jerk and he ~ed forward** по́езд ре́зко останови́лся, и его́ бро́сило (*impers*) вперёд; **he ~ed over the handlebars** его́ перебро́сило (*impers*) че́рез руль

2 *Naut*: **the ship was ~ing badly** кора́бль попа́л в си́льную килеву́ю ка́чку

3 *fig CQ*: **I am not to blame—why ~ into me?** я не винова́т—почему́ ты на меня́ набра́сываешься?

pitch[2] *n* (*tar*) смола́, дёготь (*m*); **as black as ~** чёрный как смоль.

pitcher[1] *n* кувши́н.

pitcher[2] *n Sport* (*baseball*) пи́тчер, подаю́щий.

pitchfork *n* ви́лы (*pl*).

pitching *n Naut* килева́я ка́чка; **I prefer ~ to rolling** я переношу́ килеву́ю ка́чку лу́чше, чем бортову́ю.

pith *n Bot* сердцеви́на, *also fig*; *fig* суть.

pithead *n* (надша́хтный) копёр.

pitiful *adj* жа́лкий; **a ~ sight** жа́лкое зре́лище.

pitifully *adv*: **she sobbed ~** она́ жа́лобно всхли́пывала; **a ~ inadequate sum** жа́лкая су́мма.

pitiless *adj* безжа́лостный.

pittance *n*: **he gets paid a ~** он получа́ет гроши́.

pity *n* **1** (*compassion*) жáлость; сожалéние; **out of ~ for her** из жáлости к ней; **I felt ~ for her** мне бы́ло её жáлко; **to take ~ on smb** пожалéть когó-л, сжáлиться над кем-л

2 (*misfortune*): **it's a thousand pities that...** óчень, óчень жаль, что...; **what a ~!** как жаль!, как жáлко!; **the more's the ~** тем хýже; *CQ* **for ~'s sake!** рáди бóга!, умоляю (вас)!

pity *vt* жалéть (по-); **I ~ her** я жалéю её, мне жаль её.

pivot *n* тóчка вращéния; *Tech* стéржень (*m*), ось.

pivot *vi* вращáться (*impf*).

placard *n* плакáт.

placate *vt* умиротвор|я́ть (-и́ть).

place *n* **1** мéсто; **this is a good ~ for a picnic/for catching trout** э́то хорóшее мéсто для пикникá, в э́том мéсте хорошó лóвится форéль; **to move from ~ to ~** переходи́ть/переезжáть с мéста на мéсто; **I can't be in two ~s at once** я не могý быть в двух местáх срáзу; **there were papers all over the ~** вездé бы́ли разбрóсаны бумáги; (*US*) **I can't find it any ~** я нигдé не могý э́то найти́; (*US*) **I've seen her before some ~** я её ужé гдé-то ви́дел; **we must find a stopping ~** нáдо вы́брать, где останови́ться; (*in book*) **I've lost my ~** я потеря́л то мéсто, где читáл

2 (*spot, district, area*) мéсто; **~ of birth/work** мéсто рождéния, мéсто рабóты; **he bought a ~ in the country** он купи́л дом за гóродом (*house*)/имéние (*country estate*); **our village isn't much of a ~** нáша дерéвня ничегó осóбенного — дерéвня как дерéвня; **come round to my ~** заходи́те ко мне; **we were at my ~ when...** мы бы́ли у меня́, когдá...

3 (*seat*) мéсто; **keep me a ~** займи́ мне мéсто; **I've booked a ~ on the excursion** я записáлся на экскýрсию; **we changed ~s** мы поменя́лись местáми; (*at table*) **she set a ~ for me** онá постáвила мне прибóр

4 (*post*) рабóта, мéсто, дóлжность; **he's got a ~ in a publishing house/in the Ministry** он стал рабóтать в издáтельстве, он получи́л дóлжность в министéрстве; (*of student*) **he's got a ~ at Cambridge** он поступи́л в Кéмбриджский университéт/в Кéмбридж; *Sport* **he lost his ~ in the team** он потеря́л мéсто в комáнде; *fig*: **he's going ~s** емý сопýтствует успéх; **he has friends in high ~s** у негó есть влия́тельные друзья́

5 (*position, proper place*) мéсто; **everything has its ~** всемý своё мéсто; **the picture looks out of ~ here** э́та карти́на здесь не на мéсте; **I gave up my ~ in the queue to an old lady** я уступи́л старýшке свою́ óчередь; *fig*: **to know one's ~** знать своё мéсто; **he put her in her ~** он постáвил её на мéсто; **in your ~ I would complain** на вáшем мéсте я бы пожáловался; **that remark is out of ~** э́то замечáние неумéстно/не к мéсту; **it's not my ~ to interfere** не моё дéло вмéшиваться; **oil has taken the ~ of coal** нефть пришлá на смéну ýглю; **when did it take ~?** когдá э́то случи́лось?; **the wedding will not take ~** свáдьба не состои́тся

6 (*place in series*) мéсто; **he's now in the second ~** он сейчáс на вторóм мéсте; **he took the third ~** он зáнял трéтье мéсто; **in the first/second ~** во-пéрвых, во-вторы́х; *Math*: **decimal ~** десяти́чный разря́д/знак; **to work smth out to three decimal ~s** вычисля́ть что-л до трéтьего знáка; *fig* **why did you go there in the first ~?** и вообщé, зачéм ты тудá пошёл?

place *vt* **1** (*put*) класть (положи́ть), стáвить (по-); поме|щáть (-сти́ть); **he ~d the book on the shelf** он положи́л (*if flat*)/постáвил (*if upright*) кни́гу на пóлку; **to ~ a notice in a paper** помещáть объявлéние в газéте; **the town is well ~d as regards communications** гóрод удáчно располóжен в смы́сле сообщéния (*sing*); *fig*: **he has ~d his flat at my disposal** он предостáвил свою́ кварти́ру в моё распоряжéние; **the child was ~d in his uncle's care** ребёнка отдáли на попечéние дя́ди; **I would ~ him among the best modern writers** я бы постáвил егó в ряд̆ý лýчших совремéнных писáтелей; **I've ~d an order with my wine merchant/with him for two dozen champagne** я заказáл в магази́не/у негó две дю́жины буты́лок шампáнского; **I've ~d the matter in the hands of my solicitor** я передáл дéло моемý адвокáту; **I've managed to ~ my book with a publisher** я нашёл издáтеля для моéй кни́ги; *CQ* **I don't know how he's ~d** (*financially*)/**how he's ~d on Tuesday** (*what he's doing*) я не знáю, как у негó с дéньгáми/, что он дéлает во втóрник

2 (*appoint in job*): **they ~d him in charge of the department/in the treasury** егó назнáчили начáльником отдéла, он получи́л мéсто в казначéйстве; **we are trying to ~ him** мы старáемся подыскáть емý мéсто/рабóту

3 (*remember, identify*): **I know her face, but I can't ~ her** её лицó мне знакóмо, но я не могý вспóмнить, где я её ви́дел; **it's hard to ~ her accent** трýдно определи́ть, какóй у неё акцéнт.

place mat *n* (*hard*) подстáвка; (*of lace, etc.*) салфéтка.

place-name *n* географи́ческое назвáние; **I'm writing a thesis on the ~s of Wales** я пишý диссертáцию по топони́мике (*sing*) Уэ́льса.

placenta *n Anat* плацéнта.

placid *adj* спокóйный.

plagiarism *n* плагиáт.

plagiarize *vt*: **he has ~d my ideas** он укрáл мои́ идéи.

plague *n* чумá; *CQ* **I avoid him like the ~** я бегý от негó как от чумы́.

plague *vt* мýчить (за-, из-), из|води́ть (-вести́); **that child ~s the life out of me** э́тот ребёнок меня́ изведёт/в моги́лу вгóнит [**NB** *tense*]; **to ~ smb with questions** изводи́ть когó-л вопрóсами.

plaice *n* ка́мбала.

plain *n* равни́на.

plain *adj* **1** (*clear*) я́сный, поня́тный; **the sense is ~** смысл я́сен; **I made it quite ~ that...** я я́сно дал поня́ть, что...; **I made myself ~** я я́сно вы́разился; *fig* **after that it was ~ sailing** по́сле э́того всё пошло́ как по ма́слу

2 (*simple*, *unadorned*) просто́й; **I like ~ food** я люблю́ просту́ю пи́щу; **can I have just ~ water?** мо́жно мне про́сто воды́?; **it's a pity she's so ~** жаль, что она́ така́я просту́шка; **a ~ fabric/skirt** одноцве́тная ткань/юбка

3 (*frank*) прямо́й, открове́нный; **let me be ~ with you** я тебе́ пря́мо скажу́; **I believe in ~ dealing** *or* **speaking** я люблю́ прямоту́/открове́нность.

plain *adv* (*US*): **that's ~ silly** э́то про́сто глу́по.

plain-clothes *adj*: **there were a number of ~ men in the crowd** в толпе́ бы́ли переоде́тые полице́йские/(*SU*) рабо́тники уголо́вного ро́зыска.

plain-spoken *adj* прямо́й.

plaintiff *n* исте́ц.

plaintive *adj* жа́лобный.

plait *n* коса́; (*if short*) коси́чка; **she wears her hair in a ~/in ~s** у неё коса́/ко́сы.

plait *vt* запле|та́ть (-сти́).

plan *n* план; прое́кт, *also Archit*; **to draw up a ~** составля́ть план; **if everything goes according to ~** е́сли всё пойдёт по пла́ну; **we're making ~s for the summer holidays** мы плани́руем ле́тний о́тпуск (*sing*); **the best ~ would be to phone him** са́мое лу́чшее—позвони́ть ему́; **a ~ of the building** (*guide*) план зда́ния; **to make a ~ of a** (*new*) **building** проекти́ровать зда́ние; **have you seen the ~s for the new hospital?** вы ви́дели прое́кт (*sing*) но́вой больни́цы?

plan *vti* плани́ровать + *A or* + *inf* (*impf and pf*; *pf also* за-, рас-); **they ~ to build the school next year** они́ плани́руют/заплани́ровали [NB *tense*] постро́йку шко́лы на сле́дующий год; **we have ~ned a holiday/to holiday in the Crimea** мы плани́руем *or* ду́маем [NB *tenses*] провести́ о́тпуск в Крыму́; **the garden has been well ~ned** сад хорошо́ распланн́рован.

plane[1] *n* (*tool*) руба́нок.

plane[1] *vt*: **to ~ a board** строга́ть до́ску (вы́-).

plane[2] *n Math* пло́скость; *fig* **his thesis is on a very high ~** его́ диссерта́ция о́чень высо́кого у́ровня.

plane[2] *adj* пло́ский; **a ~ surface** пло́ская пове́рхность; **~ geometry** планиме́трия.

plane[3] *n* самолёт; **to go by ~** лете́ть самолётом/на самолёте.

planet *n* плане́та.

planetarium *n* планета́рий.

plane tree *n* плата́н.

plank *n* доска́; *fig Polit* пункт програ́ммы.

planned *adj* пла́новый; **a ~ economy** пла́новое хозя́йство.

planner *n* планови́к.

planning *n* плани́рование; **town/family ~** городско́е плани́рование, регули́рование рожда́емости; *attr*: **~ commission** пла́новая коми́ссия.

plant *n* **1** *Bot* расте́ние

2 (*factory*) заво́д; (*machinery*) маши́ны (*pl*); (*equipment*) обору́дование

3 (*hoax*) *CQ*: **it's a ~** э́то всё подстро́ено.

plant *vt* **1** *Agric*, *Hort* сажа́ть (посади́ть); засе́|ивать (-ять); заса́|живать (-ди́ть); **to ~ a tree/potatoes** сажа́ть де́рево/карто́фель (*collect*); **to ~ a field with barley** засе́ивать по́ле ячменём; **to ~ a garden with turnips/apple trees** посе́ять ре́пу в огоро́де, сажа́ть в саду́ я́блони

2 (*place*): **they ~ed a stick in the ground to mark the boundary** они́ воткну́ли в зе́млю кол, что́бы отме́тить грани́цу; **she ~ed herself in an armchair** она́ опусти́лась в кре́сло; *fig*: **to ~ an idea in smb's head** внуш|а́ть кому́-л мысль (-и́ть); **he has his feet firmly ~ed on the ground** он твёрдо стои́т на земле́; **to ~ stolen goods on smb** подбр|а́сывать кому́-л кра́деное (-о́сить).

plantation *n* планта́ция.

plaque *n* (*on door*, *etc.*) доще́чка, табли́чка; **a memorial ~** мемориа́льная доска́.

plaster *n* **1** (*for building*) штукату́рка

2 *Med* (**sticking**) **~** (ли́пкий) пла́стырь (*m*); **~ of Paris** гипс; **I put ~ on my finger** я накле́ил пла́стырь на па́лец; **his arm is in ~** у него́ рука́ в ги́псе.

plaster *vt*: **to ~ a wall** штукату́рить сте́ну (о-, от-); **to ~ over a hole** заштукату́р|ивать ды́рку (-ить); **to ~ a wall with posters** окле́ивать сте́ну плака́тами; **I was ~ed with mud** я был весь в грязи́; **he ~ed (down) his hair with oil** он сма́зал во́лосы брилья́нти́ном; *CQ* **he was absolutely ~ed** он был вдре́безги пьян.

plaster cast *n* ги́псовый сле́пок; *Med* ги́псовая повя́зка.

plasterer *n* штукату́р.

plastic *n* пластма́сса, пла́стик.

plastic *adj* (*made of plastic*) пластма́ссовый, пла́стиковый; (*pliant*) пласти́чный; **the ~ arts** пласти́ческие иску́сства.

plasticine *n* пластили́н.

plastic surgery *n* пласти́ческая хирурги́я.

plate *n* **1** (*dish*) таре́лка; **a soup/dinner ~** глубо́кая/ме́лкая таре́лка; *fig*: **he wants everything handed to him on a ~** он хо́чет, что́бы ему́ всё подава́ли на таре́лочке; *CQ* **I've a lot on my ~ just now** сейча́с у меня́ дел по го́рло

2 (*of silver*, *gold*, *etc.*): **he's got some beautiful silver/gold ~** у него́ краси́вая серébряная/золота́я посу́да

3 *special uses*: (*on door*) доще́чка; табли́чка; *Photo* (фото)пласти́нка; (*illustration in book*) иллюстра́ция; *Tech* (*of metal*) пласти́на, (*larger*) лист; **dental ~** (вставна́я) че́люсть.

plate *vt*: **to ~ smth with gold/silver** покры|ва́ть что-л серебро́м/зо́лотом (-́ть).

plateau *n* плато́ (*indecl*).

plateful *n*: **a ~ of porridge** таре́лка ка́ши.

plate glass *n* зерка́льное стекло́; *attr* из зерка́льного стекла́; **a ~ window** зерка́льное окно́.

platelayer *n Rail* путево́й рабо́чий.

plate rack *n* суши́лка для посу́ды.

platform *n* **1** *Rail* платфо́рма; (*double platform with rails each side*) перро́н; **the train is standing at/will depart from ~ 6** по́езд стои́т у/отправля́ется от шесто́й платфо́рмы

2 (*at concert, etc.*) сце́на; (*for speakers, at parades*) трибу́на; (*on bus*) площа́дка; (*in open air, or in lecture room, or dais for cello*) помо́ст; **the conductor is coming on to the ~** дирижёр выхо́дит на сце́ну; **the chairman read his address from the ~** председа́тель произнёс речь с трибу́ны

3 *fig Polit* полити́ческая платфо́рма.

platinum *n* пла́тина; *attr* пла́тиновый; *fig* **a ~ blonde** пла́тиновая/о́чень све́тлая блонди́нка.

platitude *n* бана́льность, изби́тая фра́за.

platitudinous *adj* изби́тый, бана́льный, по́шлый.

platoon *n* взвод.

plausible *adj* правдоподо́бный; благови́дный; **a ~ story/excuse** правдоподо́бный расска́з, благови́дный предло́г; **he's a ~ liar** он врёт (*CQ*) так убеди́тельно.

play *n* **1** (*game, etc.*) игра́; **a ~ on words** игра́ слов; **he only said it in ~** он э́то сказа́л то́лько шу́тки ра́ди

2 *Sport* игра́; **rough ~** гру́бая игра́; **at the start of ~** в нача́ле игры́; **the ball is in/out of ~** мяч в игре́/вне игры́; **that's a nice bit of ~** (э́то) хоро́шая игра́; **fair/foul ~** игра́ (не) по пра́вилам, (не)че́стная игра́; *Cards* **he lost heavily in last night's ~** он мно́го проигра́л вчера́ в ка́рты

3 *Theat* пье́са; **she's gone to the ~** она́ пошла́ в теа́тр

4 *fig uses*: **the ~ of light on water** игра́ све́та на воде́; **I'll see he gets fair ~** я прослежу́, что́бы его́ не наду́ли; **foul ~** злоде́йство; **the police suspect foul ~** поли́ция подозрева́ет, что совершено́ уби́йство; **give the rope more ~** осла́бь верёвку; **to give free ~ to one's imagination** дать во́лю воображе́нию; **here other factors come into ~** здесь начина́ют де́йствовать други́е фа́кторы.

play *vti vt* **1** (*children's games, also Cards, Sport*) игра́ть в + *A* (сыгра́ть); **the children were ~ing a noisy game** де́ти игра́ли в каку́ю-то шу́мную игру́; **to ~ tennis/cards** игра́ть в те́ннис/в ка́рты; **the match is to be ~ed on Tuesday** матч состои́тся во вто́рник; **France ~s Spain in the final** *CQ* в фина́ле францу́зы игра́ют с испа́нской кома́ндой; **England is ~ing three substitutes** англи́йская кома́нда вы́ставила трёх запасны́х; *Cards* **he first/next ~ed the ace of diamonds** он пошёл бубно́вым тузо́м; *fig* **if he ~s his cards well** е́сли он не сде́лает оши́бки

2 (*jokes, tricks*): **he ~ed a (dirty) trick on me** он сыгра́л со мной (злу́ю) шу́тку; **to ~ a joke on smb** подшу́|чивать над кем-л (-ти́ть)

3 *Theat* игра́ть + *A*; **they are/he is ~ing Macbeth** они́ поста́вили «Ма́кбета», он игра́ет Ма́кбета; *fig*: **he ~ed a major role in negotiations** он сыгра́л ва́жную роль в перегово́рах; **don't ~ the fool** не валя́й дурака́; **let's ~ it by ear** поживём — увиди́м

4 *Mus* игра́ть на + *P*, исполн|я́ть + *A*(-́ить); **she ~s the piano/violin** она́ игра́ет на роя́ле/на скри́пке; **the orchestra will ~ Beethoven's fifth symphony** орке́стр испо́лнит пя́тую симфо́нию Бетхо́вена; **I want to ~ you this record** я хочу́ проигра́ть тебе́ э́ту пласти́нку; **to ~ the gramophone** ста́вить пласти́нки (*usu impf*)

5 (*direct*) направ|ля́ть (-́ить); **he ~ed the hose on the flames** он напра́вил шланг на ого́нь; **to ~ a searchlight on smth** направля́ть проже́ктор на что-л

vi **1** игра́ть (*usu impf*), *also Sport, Cards*; **they were ~ing at pirates/with toys/with the kitten** они́ игра́ли в пира́тов/в игру́шки/с котёнком; **let's go out and ~** пойдём поигра́ем; **fountains were ~ing** би́ли фонта́ны; *Sport* **we're ~ing away this week** на э́той неде́ле мы игра́ем на чужо́м по́ле; *Cards* **to ~ for money** игра́ть на де́ньги; *fig*: **to ~ with fire** игра́ть с огнём; **he ~ed into their hands** он сыгра́л им на́ руку (*sing*); *CQ* **what do you think you're ~ing at?** ты хоть понима́ешь, с чем ты игра́ешь?

2 *Theat* игра́ть; **who's ~ing in the film?** кто игра́ет в э́том фи́льме?; **what films are ~ing just now?** каки́е сейча́с иду́т фи́льмы?; *fig* **to ~ to the gallery** игра́ть на пу́блику

3 *Mus* игра́ть; **an organ was ~ing/began to ~** игра́л/заигра́л орга́н

play along *vi fig*: **I'll ~ along with you that far** до э́того ме́ста я с ва́ми согла́сен

play around *vi*: **it's time you stopped ~ing around (with her)** пора́ бы тебе́ стать серьёзнее/переста́ть моро́чить ей го́лову

play back *vt*: **after recording they ~ed back the tape** сде́лав за́пись, они́ ста́ли прослу́шивать плёнку

play down *vt*: **he ~ed down his part in the affair** он преуменьша́л свою́ роль в э́том де́ле

play off *vt*: **he ~ed them off against each other** он натра́вливал их друг на дру́га

play on/upon *vt*: **to ~ on words** игра́ть слова́ми; **he ~ed upon her fears/credulity** он сыгра́л на её стра́хах/на её дове́рчивости

play through *vt*: **he ~ed the sonata through to the end** он доигра́л сона́ту до конца́

play up *vti vt*: **he ~ed up his part in the affair** он преувели́чил свою́ роль в э́том де́ле *vi*: **the children/my brakes are ~ing up** дети шалят, у меня что-то с тормозами; **my back is ~ing up** у меня спина побаливает; **he ~s up to the professor** он подлизывается к профессору.

playbill *n* (театральная) афиша.

playboy *n* жуир, повеса.

player *n Sport* игрок; *Theat* актёр; *Mus* музыкант; **viola ~** альтист.

playful *adj* игривый.

playground *n* детская площадка.

playing card *n* игральная карта.

playing field *n* игровое поле.

play-off *n* решающая игра.

playpen *n* детский манеж.

playwright *n* драматург.

plea *n* **1** мольба; **a ~ for help** мольба/просьба о помощи; *Law*: **a ~ for mercy** прошение о помиловании; **he entered a ~ of "not guilty"** он не признавал себя виновным

2 (*excuse*): **he didn't come on the ~ that he was ill** он не пришёл, сославшись на болезнь/на недомогание.

plead *vti vt*: **I can only ~ ignorance of the matter** я могу только привести в оправдание незнание дела; *Law*: **to ~ smb's case** защищать кого-л на суде (*only in impf*); **to ~ insanity** ссылаться на невменяемость (подзащитного) (сослаться)

vi: **I ~ed with her not to go there** я умолял её не ходить туда; **he ~ed for more time to pay** он упрашивал отсрочить платёж; *Law* **he ~ed guilty/not guilty** он (не) признал себя виновным.

pleasant *adj* приятный; **it makes a ~ change to be in the country** как приятно после городской суеты оказаться в деревне; **he made himself very ~ to us** он был очень любезен/мил с нами.

please *vti vt* уго|ждать + *D or* на + *A* (-дить); **you can't ~ everyone** всем/на всех не угодишь; **she's easily ~d** ей легко угодить; **~ yourself** как тебе угодно; **she ~s herself about whom she invites/what she wears** она приглашает только того *or* тех, кто ей приятен [**NB** кто *after sing or pl antecedent*], что ей нравится, то она и носит; **your article ~d me** мне понравилась ваша статья

vi: **come in,/be quiet, ~** войдите,/потише, пожалуйста; **she's anxious to ~** она старается угодить; **listen to me, if you ~** будьте добры, выслушайте меня; **he charged me £5, if you ~** он взял с меня пять фунтов, представь себе; **I will do as I ~** я сделаю как мне будет угодно; **take as many as you ~** бери сколько хочешь.

pleased *adj* довольный; рад (*short form only*); **they are very ~ with the results/with themselves** они очень довольны результатами/собой; **I'm very ~ for you** я очень рад за вас; **(I'm) ~ to meet you** очень приятно/очень рад(а) (с вами познакомиться); **we are ~ to announce that...** нам приятно сообщить, что...

pleasing, pleasurable *adjs* приятный.

pleasure *n* удовольствие; (*replying to thanks*) **it's a/my ~** это для меня удовольствие; **it gives me great ~ to announce that...** я с большим удовольствием сообщаю, что...; **the ~s of youth** развлечения молодости; **the minister requests the ~ of the company of Mr X at dinner on June the 2nd** министр приглашает господина X на (торжественный) обед второго июня.

pleasure craft *n* (*boat*) прогулочный катер.

pleat *n* (*single pleat*) складка; **a skirt with ~s** юбка в складку (*sing*)/(*if very small*) плиссе (*indecl*); **accordion ~s** гофре (*indecl*).

pleat *vt* (*with flat pleats*) плиссировать, (*with accordion pleats*) гофрировать (*impfs*).

pledge *n* **1** (*as security, or in pawnshop, fig as token*) залог; **to leave in ~** оставлять в залог; *fig* **as a ~ of my intentions** как залог моих намерений

2 (*promise*) обещание.

pledge *vt* (*promise*) обещать (*impf and pf*); (*vow*) клясться (по-); **he ~d his help** он обещал помочь; **we are ~d to secrecy** мы поклялись молчать.

plenary *adj* (*of meeting*) пленарный.

plenipotentiary *n* полномочный представитель (*m*).

plentiful *adj* обильный; **apples are ~ this year** в этом году обильный урожай яблок; **fruit is ~ just now** сейчас фрукты в изобилии; **a ~ supply** большой запас.

plenty *n* **1** (*abundance*) изобилие; **in ~** в изобилии

2 (*sufficiency*) достаточно + *G*, полно + *G*; **there's ~ of time** времени ещё достаточно; **£5 is ~** пяти фунтов достаточно; **we've got ~ to live on** на жизнь нам вполне хватает; **we got there in ~ of time** мы пришли туда пораньше/заранее.

plenty *adv CQ* довольно, достаточно; **the flat is ~ big enough** квартира довольно большая; **he's ~ rich enough to afford that** он достаточно богат, может позволить себе это.

pleurisy *n Med* плеврит.

pliable, pliant *adjs* податливый, *also fig*.

pliers *npl* плоскогубцы; **two pairs of ~** двое плоскогубцев.

plight *n* состояние.

Plimsoll line/mark *n Naut* грузовая марка.

plimsolls *npl* спортивные тапочки.

plod *vti* плестись (*impf*); **he ~ded his weary way home** он устало плёлся домой; *fig* **he's still ~ding at his home work** он всё ещё корпит над домашним заданием.

plonk[1] *vti CQ*: **he ~ed the book down on the table** он швырнул книгу на стол; **he ~ed himself down on the divan** он плюхнулся/бухнулся на диван.

plonk[2] *n CQ* дешёвое вино.

plop *n*: **the stone fell with a ~/(*as adv*) fell ~ into the water** камень бултыхнулся в воду.

plot[1] *n* участок земли́; **a vegetable ~** огоро́дный уча́сток, огоро́д; **a building ~** строи́тельный уча́сток.

plot[2] *n* (*conspiracy*) интри́га, *Polit* за́говор; *Lit* сюже́т.

plot[2] *vti vt* **1: to ~ smth on a graph** черти́ть гра́фик чего́-л (на-); *Naut*, *Aer* **to ~ a course** про|кла́дывать курс (-ложи́ть)

2 (*plan*): **to ~ a murder** замы|шля́ть уби́йство (-́слить)

vi: **they are ~ting against me/to overthrow the government** они́ что́-то замышля́ют про́тив меня́, они́ замышля́ют све́ргнуть прави́тельство.

plough, (*US*) **plow** *n* плуг; *Astron* **the P.** Больша́я Медве́дица.

plough, (*US*) **plow** *vti vt* паха́ть, вспа́хивать (*pf for both* вспаха́ть); **to ~ (up) a field** вспаха́ть по́ле; **the tanks ~ed up the road** та́нки разворoти́ли всю доро́гу; *fig*: **we ~ed our way through the mud** мы меси́ли грязь; *Comm* **to ~ back profits** пус|ка́ть при́были в оборо́т (-ти́ть); *Univ sl*: **they ~ed me in physics** меня́ провали́ли по фи́зике; **I ~ed the exam** я завали́л экза́мен

vi паха́ть; *fig* **I found the book heavy going, but I did ~ through to the end** кни́га тяжело́ чита́ется, но я всё же её оси́лил.

ploughland, (*US*) **plowland** *n* па́шня.

ploughman, (*US*) **plowman** *n* па́харь (*m*).

plover *n* ржа́нка.

ploy *n*: **I must think up some ~ to occupy the children** мне на́до что́-то приду́мать, что́бы заня́ть дете́й.

pluck *vti vt*: **to ~ a flower/an apple** срыва́ть цвето́к/я́блоко (сорва́ть); **to ~ a bird** ощи́п|ывать пти́цу (-а́ть); **to ~ one's eyebrows** вы|щи́пывать бро́ви (-́щипать); *Mus* **to ~ strings** перебира́ть стру́ны (*impf*); *fig* **to ~ up courage to** со|бира́ться с ду́хом + *inf* (-бра́ться)

vi: **she ~ed at his sleeve** она́ дёрнула его́ за рука́в.

plucky *adj* сме́лый, хра́брый.

plug *n* (*in sink, etc.*) про́бка, *CQ* заты́чка; (*in barrel*) заты́чка; (*of tobacco*) пли́тка; *Elec* ште́псельная ви́лка; **a 3-point ~** трёхфа́зовая ште́псельная ви́лка; **where's the socket for the ~?** где розе́тка для ште́пселя?; (*in W.C.*) **to pull the ~** спуска́ть во́ду в туале́те.

plug *vti vt* **1** (*a hole, leak*) за|тыка́ть (-ткну́ть); **to ~ in a radio/a lamp** включ|а́ть приёмник/ла́мпу в сеть (-и́ть)

2 *Comm sl*: **to ~ a new product** реклами́ровать но́вый това́р (*impf and pf*)

vi: *CQ* **to ~ away at smth** корпе́ть над чем-л (*impf*).

plughole *n* отве́рстие в ра́ковине *or* в ва́нне.

plum *n* (*tree or fruit*) сли́ва; *attr*: **~ jam** сли́вовый джем; *fig* **he has a ~ job** у него́ тёпленькое месте́чко.

plumage *n* опере́ние.

plumb *adv* пря́мо, как раз; **~ in the middle of the road** пря́мо посереди́не доро́ги; *CQ*: **she rang ~ in the middle of dinner** она́ позвони́ла, как раз когда́ мы обе́дали; (*US*) **she's ~ crazy** она́ совсе́м спя́тила.

plumber *n* сле́сарь(-водопрово́дчик).

plumbing *n* (**the ~**) (*pipes, etc. in house*) водопрово́д и канализа́ция.

plumbline *n* отве́с.

plummet *n* отве́с.

plummet *vi* ре́зко па́дать (упа́сть); **the plane ~ed into the sea** самолёт упа́л в мо́ре; **prices have ~ed** це́ны ре́зко упа́ли.

plump[1] *adj* (*chubby*) пу́хлый; (*of adult*) по́лный; **a ~ baby** пу́хленький младе́нец; **a ~ bird** жи́рная пти́ца.

plump[2] *vti see* **plonk**[1] *vti*.

plunder *n* (*act*) грабёж; (*loot*) награ́бленное (добро́), добы́ча.

plunder *vt* гра́бить (раз-).

plunge *n*: **I'm going for a quick ~** пойду́ нырну́ разо́к; *fig* **I hesitated a long time but finally took the ~** я до́лго колеба́лся, но наконе́ц реши́лся/отва́жился.

plunge *vti vt*: **he ~d his hand into the hole/the water** он просу́нул ру́ку в ды́рку, он опусти́л *or* окуну́л ру́ку в во́ду; *fig*: **the city was ~d into darkness** го́род был погружён в темноту́; **we were ~d into gloom by the news** э́та но́вость пове́рг|ла нас в уны́ние (-нуть)

vi: **he ~d into the water** он бро́сился в во́ду; **the path here ~s into the valley** здесь тропи́нка кру́то спуска́ется в доли́ну.

plunger *n* (*for stopped-up sink*) плу́нжер.

plural *n Gram* мно́жественное число́; **in the ~** во мно́жественном числе́.

plus *n* плюс; *CQ*: **his experience is a big ~** его́ о́пыт—большо́й плюс; **I'd put her age at 30 ~** я бы дал ей три́дцать с хвостико́м; *attr*: **a ~ quantity** положи́тельная величина́; **the ~ sign** знак плюс; *as prep* **3 + 4 = 7** три плюс четы́ре—семь/равня́ется семи́; **he paid the sum ~ interest** он вы́платил су́мму плюс проце́нты.

ply *n attr*: **three-~ wood** трёхсло́йная фане́ра; **I'm using three-~ wool** я вяжу́ в три ни́тки.

plywood *n* фане́ра; *attr* фане́рный.

pneumatic *adj* пневмати́ческий.

pneumonia *n* пневмони́я, воспале́ние лёгких.

poach[1] *vt Cook*: **to ~ eggs** вари́ть яйцо́-пашо́т (с-); **to ~ fish in milk** туши́ть ры́бу в молоке́ (по-).

poach[2] *vti vt* (*deer, etc.*) незако́нно охо́титься на + *A*, (*fish*) незако́нно лови́ть ры́бу (*usu impfs*)

vi браконье́рствовать (*impf*); *fig* **don't ~ on my preserves** не посяга́й на мои́ права́; *Sport* (*tennis*) **don't ~** не заходи́ на мою́ сто́рону.

poacher *n* браконье́р.

pocket *n* карма́н; (*on billiard table*) лу́за; *fig*: **~s of resistance** оча́ги сопротивле́ния; **he's £5 in ~/out of ~** он положи́л в карма́н/он потеря́л пять фу́нтов; **he paid for it out of his own ~** он заплати́л за э́то из своего́ карма́на; **he had to dip into his ~** ему́ пришло́сь раскоше́литься; **to line one's ~** набива́ть карма́н; *attr*: **~ knife/money** карма́нный нож, карма́нные де́ньги (*pl*).

pocket *vt*: **he ~ed the change** он положи́л сда́чу в карма́н; *fig*: *pejor* **he ~ed all the money himself** он прикарма́нил все де́ньги; **to ~ one's pride** спря́тать свою́ го́рдость в карма́н (*usu pf*).

pocketbook *n* (*wallet*) бума́жник.

pockmark *n* о́спина, ряби́на.

pockmarked *adj* рябо́й.

pod *vt*: **to ~ peas** лущи́ть горо́х (*impf*).

podgy *adj* ни́зенький и то́лстый.

poem *n* (*short*) стихотворе́ние; (*long*) поэ́ма.

poet *n* поэ́т.

poetic(al) *adj* поэти́ческий; поэти́чный; **poetic licence** поэти́ческая во́льность; **the poetical works of Keats** поэ́зия Ки́тса.

poetry *n* поэ́зия; стихи́ (*pl*); **Russian ~** ру́сская поэ́зия; **he writes ~** он пи́шет стихи́.

poignant *adj* тро́гательный.

point *n* **1** (*tip*) коне́ц; (*sharp end*) остриё; *Geog* мыс; (*in ballet*) пуа́нт; **the stick has a sharp ~** у па́лки о́стрый коне́ц; **the ~ of a needle/pencil** остриё иго́лки/карандаша́; **a star with five ~s** пятиконе́чная звезда́; *fig* **not to put too fine a ~ on it** по́просту говоря́

2 *Geom* то́чка; *Math* **decimal ~** *equiv* запята́я в десяти́чной дро́би; **five ~ seven/~ nought seven (5.7, 5.07)** пять це́лых, семь деся́тых/семь со́тых (5,7, 5,07)

3 (*counting unit*): **the temperature went up two ~s** температу́ра подняла́сь на два гра́дуса; **shares have gone down two ~s** а́кции пони́зились на два пу́нкта; **boiling ~** то́чка кипе́ния; *Sport* (*of score*) очко́

4 (*place, juncture*) пункт, то́чка, ме́сто; **passengers for all ~s south of London** пассажи́ры, е́дущие во все пу́нкты к ю́гу от Ло́ндона; **~ of departure** пункт отправле́ния; **it's a turning ~ in his career** э́то поворо́тный пункт в его́ карье́ре; **the highest ~ in Wales** вы́сшая то́чка в Уэ́льсе; **from his/my ~ of view** с его́/мое́й то́чки зре́ния; **at the ~ where the river narrows** в ме́сте, где река́ сужа́ется; **at this ~** (*in time*) в э́тот моме́нт, (*in space*) на э́том ме́сте; **at any ~** (*in time*) в любо́й моме́нт, (*in space*) в любо́м ме́сте; **up to a ~** до изве́стной сте́пени; **matters have reached the ~ where...** дела́ при́няли тако́й оборо́т, что...; **it all depends on one's ~ of view** всё зави́сит от того́, как на э́то посмотре́ть; **the ~s of the compass** стра́ны све́та; **at the ~ of death** при́ смерти; **when it came to the ~, he couldn't face it** когда́ дошло́ до де́ла, он испуга́лся; **he's economical to the ~ of meanness** он эконо́мен до ску́пости; **she's on the ~ of leaving** она́ собира́ется уйти́

5 (*matter*) де́ло, вопро́с; (*item*) пункт; **in ~ of fact** в са́мом де́ле, факти́чески; **his remark was very much to the ~** его́ замеча́ние бы́ло о́чень де́льным; **keep to the ~** бли́же к де́лу, говори́ по существу́; **a ~ of honour** вопро́с че́сти; **that's a sore ~** э́то больно́й вопро́с; **the main ~s of a speech** гла́вные пу́нкты докла́да; **let's go over it ~ by ~** дава́й разло́жим э́то по пу́нктам; **we agree on that ~** по э́тому пу́нкту мы согла́сны; **he made several important ~s** он вы́делил не́сколько ва́жных моме́нтов; **he made the ~ that...** он отме́тил, что...; **I made my ~ clear** я вы́сказался; **to press one's ~** наста́ивать на своём; **no need to labour the ~** не на́до остана́вливаться на э́том; **I'll stretch a ~ for you/in this case** так и быть, пойду́ тебе́ на усту́пку, в э́том слу́чае я сде́лаю посла́жку

6 (*significant part*) смысл, де́ло; **that's not/just the ~** де́ло не в э́том, в э́том-то всё и де́ло; **I don't get the ~** я не понима́ю, в чём смысл; **he missed the whole ~ of the story** до него́ не дошёл смысл расска́за; **I take your ~** я тебя́ по́нял [**NB** *tense*]; **he's got a ~ there** в том, что он говори́т, есть смысл; **the ~ is that...** де́ло в том, что...; **that's beside the ~** тут э́то ни при чём; **the interesting ~ is that...** са́мое интере́сное, что...; **the ~ of the joke is that...** соль шу́тки в том, что...

7 (*characteristic*) черта́; **what ~s do you look for in a footballer?** каки́е черты́ вы це́ните в футболи́сте?; **he has his ~s** он не лишён досто́инств; **music was never my strong ~** я никогда́ не́ был силён в му́зыке; **that's my weak ~** э́то моё сла́бое ме́сто

8 *Tech uses*: (*UK*) *Elec* (ште́псельная) розе́тка; *pl* (**the ~s**) *Rail* стре́лка (*sing*); **to switch the ~s over** переводи́ть стре́лку.

point *vti vt* **1** (*direct*) направ|ля́ть (-́ить); на|води́ть (-вести́); **to ~ a gun at smb** направля́ть пистоле́т на кого́-л; **to ~ a telescope at smth** наводи́ть телеско́п на что-л; **to ~ one's finger at smb** пока́з|ывать на кого́-л па́льцем (-а́ть)

2 (*indicate*): **to ~ (out)** ука́з|ывать (на + *A*) (-а́ть); **arrows ~ the way** путь ука́зывают стре́лки; **he ~ed her out to me** он указа́л мне на неё; **to ~ out smb's faults** ука́зывать на чьи-л недоста́тки; **he ~ed out that...** он указа́л, что...; **to ~ a moral/a contrast** под|чёркивать мора́ль/контра́ст (-черкну́ть)

vi пока́з|ывать, ука́з|ывать (*pfs* -а́ть); *Sport* (*of dog*) де́лать сто́йку (с-); **it's rude to ~** пока́зывать па́льцем неве́жливо; *fig* **this/everything ~s to the conclusion that...** всё говори́т о том, что...

point-blank *adj*: **to fire at ~ range** стреля́ть в упо́р; **a ~ refusal** категори́ческий отка́з.

point-blank *adv*: **I asked him ~** я спроси́л его́ в упо́р; **he refused ~** он категори́чески отказа́лся.

point duty *n*: **a policeman on ~** регулиро́вщик на посту́.

pointed *adj* заострённый; *Archit* стре́льчатый; **a ~ nose** заострённый нос; **shoes with**

~ toes остроно́сые ту́фли/боти́нки; *fig* **a ~ remark** ко́лкое замеча́ние, ко́лкость.

pointedly *adv*: **...he asked ~** ...спроси́л он со значе́нием.

pointer *n* (*needle*) стре́лка; (*of lecturer*) ука́зка; (*dog*) по́йнтер; (*clue*) показа́тель (*m*); (*hint*) намёк.

pointless *adj* бессмы́сленный; **a ~ existence** бессмы́сленное существова́ние; **it's ~ talking about it** бессмы́сленно говори́ть об э́том.

poise *n* (*balance*) равнове́сие, *also fig*; (*of posture*) оса́нка.

poise *vti* баланси́ровать (*impf*); **he held his pen ~d** он держа́л ру́чку нагото́ве; **the tiger (was) ~d ready to jump** тигр присе́л пе́ред прыжко́м.

poison *n* яд, отра́ва; **to put rat ~ down** положи́ть яд для крыс; *fig* **she hates him like ~** она́ его́ смерте́льно ненави́дит; *attr*: **~ gas** отравля́ющий/ядови́тый газ.

poison *vt* отрав|ля́ть (-и́ть), *also fig*; **she ~ed herself** она́ отрави́лась; **she has a ~ed finger** у неё гно́ится па́лец.

poisonous *adj* ядови́тый, *also fig*; *fig* зло́й; **a ~ snake** ядови́тая змея́; *fig*: **a ~ remark** ядови́тое замеча́ние; **a ~ tongue** злой язы́к.

poke *vt* ты́кать (ткнуть); сова́ть (су́нуть) *and compounds*; **to ~ smth with a stick** ты́кать что-л па́лкой; **he ~d me in the ribs/with his elbow** он ткнул меня́ в бок/ло́ктем; **don't ~ your umbrella through the bars** не просо́вывайте зо́нтик сквозь пру́тья; **to ~ the fire** меша́ть кочерго́й у́гли в ками́не (по-); **she ~d her head out of the window** она́ вы́сунула го́лову из окна́; *fig*: **to ~ one's nose into other people's business** сова́ть свой нос в чужи́е дела́; **to ~ fun at smb** подшу́чивать над кем-л.

poker[1] *n approx* кочерга́.

poker[2] *n Cards* по́кер.

poker-faced *adj* с бесстра́стным/ка́менным лицо́м.

poky *adj*: **a ~ flat** те́сная кварти́рка.

polar *adj* поля́рный; **a ~ bear** бе́лый/поля́рный медве́дь.

Pole *n* поля́к, по́лька.

pole[1] *n Geog, Phys* по́люс; **the North P.** се́верный по́люс; **the ~s of a magnet** по́люсы магни́та; *fig* **they're ~s apart** они́ как два по́люса, они́ поля́рно противополо́жны друг дру́гу.

pole[2] *n* (*staff*) шест, *also Sport*; (*stake*) кол; **tent ~** кол для пала́тки; **telegraph ~** телегра́фный столб.

pole star *n* Поля́рная звезда́.

pole vault(ing) *n* прыжо́к с шесто́м.

police *n*, *also* **the ~ force** поли́ция; [*for SU see* **militia**]; **the traffic ~** автоинспе́кция; **the ~ have made five arrests** поли́ция арестова́ла пятеры́х; *attr*: **a ~ dog** полице́йская соба́ка.

police *vt*: **the army is policing the border** а́рмия охраня́ет грани́цу.

policeman *n* полице́йский; [*for SU see* **militiaman**].

police station *n* полице́йский уча́сток.

policy[1] *n* поли́тика (*no pl*); **foreign ~** вне́шняя поли́тика прави́тельства; **it's my ~ not to interfere** моё пра́вило—не вме́шиваться.

policy[2] *n*: **an insurance ~** страхово́й по́лис; **to take out a life ~** застрахова́ть свою́ жизнь.

poliomyelitis, *abbr* **polio** *n* полиомиели́т.

Polish *n* по́льский язы́к.

Polish *adj* по́льский.

polish *n* **1** (*substance*): **furniture ~** соста́в для полиро́вки ме́бели; **floor ~** масти́ка для по́ла; **shoe ~** крем для о́буви; **nail ~** лак для ногте́й

2 (*shine*) блеск, *also fig*; лоск, *usu fig*; **he brushed his shoes to a high ~** он начи́стил боти́нки до бле́ска; **the floor has lost its ~** пол потеря́л блеск; *fig* **he/his style lacks ~** ему́ не хвата́ет ло́ска, его́ стиль недоста́точно отшлифо́ван/отто́чен.

polish *vt* полирова́ть (от-); *Tech* (*stones, metal*) шлифова́ть (от-), *also fig*; **to ~ the furniture/floor/silver/shoes** полирова́ть ме́бель, на|тира́ть пол (-тере́ть), чи́стить серебро́/боти́нки (на-, по-); *fig*: **to ~ one's manners/one's style** шлифова́ть мане́ры/стиль; **I need to ~ up my German** мне на́до подучи́ть не́мецкий; *CQ* **the children ~ed off everything/the pie** де́ти всё подчи́стили/съе́ли весь пиро́г; **we'll soon ~ off the work** мы ско́ро поко́нчим с э́той рабо́той.

polished *adj*: **a ~ table** полиро́ванный стол; *fig* **~ manners** изы́сканные мане́ры.

polite *adj* ве́жливый.

politic *adj*: **it was a ~ move** э́то был то́нкий манёвр; **it would not be ~ to intervene** вме́шиваться бы́ло бы неполити́чно.

political *adj* полити́ческий.

politician *n* поли́тик, полити́ческий де́ятель, *pejor* политика́н.

politics *npl* поли́тика (*sing*); **party/local ~** поли́тика па́ртии, *approx* поли́тика на места́х.

polka *n* (*dance*) по́лька; *attr*: **~ dot scarf** шарф в горо́шек.

poll *n* **1** (*voting*) голосова́ние; (*elections*) вы́боры; **the result of the ~s** результа́т голосова́ния; **to go to the ~s** (*vote*) голосова́ть; **the government decided to go to the ~s** прави́тельство реши́ло провести́ вы́боры; **there was a heavy ~** в вы́борах уча́ствовал высо́кий проце́нт избира́телей; **our candidate is heading the ~** наш кандида́т лиди́рует

2 опро́с (населе́ния); **to conduct a ~ about smth** проводи́ть опро́с обще́ственного мне́ния в связи́ с чем-л.

poll *vt*: **he ~ed 500 votes** он получи́л пятьсо́т голосо́в.

pollinate *vt* опыл|я́ть (-и́ть).

polling *n* голосова́ние; **~ has been light** проголосова́ло ма́ло наро́ду; *attr*: **~ day** день вы́боров.

polling booth *n* каби́на для голосова́ния.

polling station *n* избира́тельный уча́сток.

pollute *vt* загрязн|я́ть (-и́ть).

pollution *n* загрязне́ние; ~ **of the environment** загрязне́ние окружа́ющей среды́.

polo *n* по́ло (*indecl*).

poloneck *n attr*: **a** ~ **sweater** водола́зка.

polygamy *n* многобра́чие, полига́мия.

polygon *n* многоуго́льник.

polytechnic *n* политехни́ческий институ́т.

polythene *n* полиэтиле́н; *attr*: **a** ~ **bag** полиэтиле́новый паке́т.

pomegranate *n* (*tree or fruit*) грана́т.

pompous *adj* напы́щенный, помпе́зный.

pond *n* пруд.

ponder *vti vt*: **to** ~ **a question** обду́м|ывать вопро́с (-ать)

vi размышля́ть (*only in impf*); **to** ~ **on/about smth** размышля́ть над чем-л/о чём-л.

ponderous *adj* тяжёлый; *fig* **a** ~ **style** тяжелове́сный стиль.

pontificate *vi* разглаго́льствовать (*impf*); **to** ~ **about smth** говори́ть о чём-л (*usu impf*).

pony *n* по́ни (*m, indecl*).

ponytail *n*: **she wears her hair in a** ~ она́ но́сит приче́ску «ко́нский хвост».

poodle *n* пу́дель (*m*).

pooh-pooh *vt*: **he** ~**ed the idea** он отмахну́лся от э́той иде́и.

pool[1] *n* (*pond*) пруд; (*puddle of spilt liquid*) лу́жа; (*on river*) за́водь; **swimming** ~ бассе́йн.

pool[2] *n* **1**: **transport** ~ тра́нспортный отде́л; **typing** ~ машинопи́сное бюро́; *Comm* (*cartel*) пул, объедине́ние; *Fin* фонд

2 *Cards* банк, пу́лька; (*UK*): **the (football)** ~**s** *approx* спорти́вная лотере́я.

pool[2] *vt* (*unite*) объедин|я́ть (-и́ть); (*share*) дели́ться + *I* (по-); **they** ~**ed their resources/information** они́ объедини́ли ресу́рсы, они́ подели́лись информа́цией; **they** ~**ed their money and bought a car** они́ купи́ли маши́ну на пая́х.

poor *adj* **1** (*not rich*) бе́дный, *also fig*; **a** ~ **man** бедня́к; *fig*: ~ **mother isn't feeling well** бе́дная моя́ ма́ма пло́хо себя́ чу́вствует; *CQ* ~ **you!** ах ты, бедня́га!/бедола́га!

2 (*bad*) плохо́й; (*miserable*) жа́лкий; ~ **health** плохо́е здоро́вье; **of** ~ **quality** плохо́го/ни́зкого ка́чества; **he has a** ~ **opinion of me** он обо мне плохо́го/невысо́кого мне́ния; **a** ~ **excuse** жа́лкий предло́г; **a** ~ **harvest** плохо́й/ни́зкий урожа́й; ~ **soil** ску́дная/бе́дная по́чва; **the pay here is** ~ здесь ма́ло пла́тят.

poorly *adj* нева́жный; **she's looking/feeling** ~ она́ нева́жно вы́глядит/себя́ чу́вствует.

pop[1] *n* (*of cork*) хлопо́к; **the cork came out with a** ~ про́бка хло́пнула/вы́стрелила.

pop[1] *vti vt* (*put*) брос|а́ть (́-ить), сова́ть (су́нуть) *and compounds*; **I'll** ~ **the letter in the post** я бро́шу письмо́ в (почто́вый) я́щик; ~ **the bottle into the cupboard** сунь буты́лку в шкаф; **he** ~**ped his head out of the window** он вы́сунул го́лову из окна́; *CQ* (*propose marriage*) **to** ~ **the question** де́лать предложе́ние (с-); *sl* **he** ~**ped his watch** он заложи́л часы́

vi **1**: **corks were** ~**ping** хло́пали про́бки

2 *fig uses*: **I'm just going to** ~ **across to the shop** я то́лько схожу́/сбе́гаю в магази́н; **I'll** ~ **in to say goodbye** я забегу́ попроща́ться с тобо́й; **she's** ~**ped out for a paper** она́ вы́бежала за газе́той; **his eyes were** ~**ping out of his head** он вы́таращил глаза́; **he** ~**s up where you least expect him** он появля́ется там, где его́ ме́ньше всего́ ожида́ешь.

pop[2] *n* (*esp. US*) *CQ* па́па.

pop[3] *adj*: ~ **art/music** поп-а́рт, поп-му́зыка.

popcorn *n* возду́шная кукуру́за.

pope *n*: **the P.** па́па ри́мский.

popgun *n* пуга́ч.

poplar *n* то́поль (*m*).

poppet *n CQ* кро́шка, ла́почка.

poppy *n* мак.

populace *n* населе́ние, наро́д.

popular *adj* **1** наро́дный; ~ **front** Наро́дный фронт

2 (*well-liked*) популя́рный; ~ **literature** популя́рная литерату́ра; **the film/he is very** ~ фильм/он по́льзуется большо́й популя́рностью; *iron* **I wasn't very** ~ **with him after that** по́сле э́того он стал не о́чень-то меня́ жа́ловать; **at** ~ **prices** по общедосту́пным це́нам.

popularity *n* популя́рность.

popularly *adv*: **he's** ~ **believed to be rich** его́ счита́ют о́чень бога́тым; (*of omens, etc.*) **it's** ~ **supposed...** в наро́де говоря́т...

populated *adj*: ~ **by** населённый + *I*.

population *n* населе́ние; **the town has a** ~ **of 10,000** населе́ние го́рода—де́сять ты́сяч челове́к; **per head of** ~ на ду́шу населе́ния; *attr*: ~ **explosion** демографи́ческий взрыв.

populous *adj* густонаселённый.

porcelain *n* фарфо́р (*substance or, collect, pieces of porcelain*).

porch *n* (*roofed, but open-sided*) крыльцо́; (*inside house*) прихо́жая; (*US*) вера́нда.

porcupine *n* дикобра́з.

pore[1] *n* по́ра.

pore[2] *vi*: **to** ~ **over a book/one's books** склон|я́ться над кни́гой (-и́ться), сиде́ть над кни́гами (*impf*); **to** ~ **over a problem** размышля́ть над пробле́мой (*impf*).

pork *n* свини́на; *attr*: **a** ~ **chop** свина́я отбивна́я; **a** ~ **pie** пиро́г со свини́ной.

pornography, *CQ* **porn** *n* порногра́фия.

porous *adj*: **a sponge is** ~ гу́бка по́ристая; ~ **limestone** ноздрева́тый/по́ристый известня́к.

porpoise *n* морска́я сви́нка.

porridge *n* овся́ная ка́ша.

port[1] *n* (*harbour*) порт; ~ **of registration** порт припи́ски; *attr* порто́вый; ~ **authority** порто́вая администра́ция.

port[2] *n Naut* (*left side*) ле́вый борт; **land to** ~! сле́ва по бо́рту—земля́!; *attr*: **on the** ~ **bow** сле́ва по но́су.

port[3] *n* (*wine*) портве́йн.

portable *adj* переносный, портативный; **a ~ lamp/TV** переносная лампа, портативный телевизор.

portend *vt* предвещать (*impf*).

portent *n* предзнаменование, предвестник.

porter *n* (*doorman*: *at office*, *etc.*) вахтёр; (*at hotels*) швейцар; (*Rail*, *etc.*) носильщик; (*US*) (*attendant on train*) проводник.

porthole *n* иллюминатор.

portion *n* (*part*) часть; (*helping*) порция; **a ~ of the population** часть населения; **this ~** (*of ticket*, *etc.*) **to be retained** эта часть билета сохраняется; **a half ~ of soup** полпорции (*f*) супа.

portly *adj* дородный.

portrait *n* портрет; **full-/half-length ~** портрет в полный рост, поясной портрет; **to sit for one's ~** позировать для портрета.

portrait painter *n* портретист.

portray *vt* (*of writer or artist*) изобра|жать + *A* (-зить), рисовать портрет + *G* (на-); (*of writer or actor*) созда|вать образ + *G* (-ть).

Portuguese *n* португалец, португалка.

Portuguese *adj* португальский.

pose *n* поза, *also fig*; **to strike a ~** принимать позу; **that's just a ~ with him** это он просто встал в позу.

pose *vti vt*: **to ~ a question** зада|вать вопрос (-ть); **this ~d certain problems** это создало некоторые проблемы

vi: **to ~ for an artist/one's portrait** позировать для художника/для портрета (*impf*); *fig*: **he's always posing** он вечно рисуется; **he ~s as a historian** он считает себя специалистом по истории.

poser *n*: *CQ* **that's a ~** вот головоломка!

posh *adj CQ* шикарный.

position *n* **1** положение, поза; расположение; (*in ballet*, *Mil*) позиция; **the ~ of the corpse/of a town** положение трупа, расположение города; **I slept in an awkward ~** я спал в неудобной позе; *Naut*, *Aer* **to fix one's ~** определять положение; *fig*: **the country's economic ~** экономическое положение страны; **this puts me in a false ~** это ставит меня в ложное положение; **he's in no ~ to criticize** ему не следовало бы критиковать; **put yourself in my ~** поставьте себя на моё место; **he's in the best ~ to judge** ему лучше всего судить (об этом), ему всего виднее

2 (*job*) место, должность.

position *vt* распол|агать (-ожить), *also Mil*; **I ~ed myself on the roof to see the parade** я устроился на крыше, чтобы лучше видеть парад.

positive *n Photo* позитив; *attr* позитивный.

positive *adj* **1** (*affirmative*) положительный, *also Elec*, *Gram*, *Math*; **~ criticism** конструктивная критика

2 (*definite*) определённый; **that's proof ~** это вполне определённое доказательство; *CQ*: **he's a ~ danger** он представляет определённую опасность; **it's a ~ disgrace** это просто позор

3 (*sure*): **I'm ~ about it/that...** я уверен в этом/, что...

possess *vt* (*things*) владеть + *I*, (*qualities*) обладать + *I* (*impfs*); **he ~es property in London/great ability** он владеет недвижимостью в Лондоне, он обладает большими способностями (*pl*); **you'll have to ~ your soul in patience** тебе придётся потерпеть; **he is ~ed by the idea that...** он одержим идеей, что...; *CQ* **what ~ed you to do that?** что тебя дёрнуло сделать это?

possession *n* **1** (*ownership*) владение; **we took ~ of the house on the first of May** мы вступили во владение домом первого мая; **the painting is in the ~ of the artist's son** картиной теперь владеет сын художника; **he's in ~ of valuable information** он располагает ценными сведениями (*pl*); **he's in full ~ of his faculties** он в здравом уме и полной памяти; *CQ* **he's taken ~ of my car for two days** он взял у меня машину на два дня

2 (*property*) имущество; (*territory*) владение; **he lost all his ~s in the fire** он потерял всё своё имущество (*sing*) во время пожара; **overseas ~s** заморские владения; **personal ~s** личные вещи.

possessive *adj*: **she's very ~ about her children** она не отпускает детей от себя; **my mother-in-law is very ~ about my husband** моя свекровь очень ревнует сына ко мне; *Gram* **the ~ pronoun** притяжательное местоимение.

possessor *n* владелец; обладатель (*m*); **I've become the proud ~ of a car** я стал счастливым обладателем автомобиля.

possibility *n* возможность; **the plan has great possibilities** этот план открывает большие возможности; **there's no ~ of his agreeing** он никогда не согласится.

possible *adj* возможный; **I'll do everything ~ to help you** я сделаю всё возможное, чтобы помочь вам; **that's not ~** это невозможно; **as often as ~** как можно чаще; **as much/far as ~** насколько возможно, по возможности.

possibly *adv* возможно, может быть; **will he come?—P.** он придёт?—Возможно/Может быть; **as soon as I ~ can** как только смогу.

post[1] *n* **1** (*job*) должность, место; (*usu of a high position*) пост; **to apply for a ~** подавать заявление о приёме на работу; **he got a lecturing ~** он получил место/должность преподавателя

2 *Mil* (*station*) пост; **a sentry died at his ~** часовой погиб на посту.

post[1] *vt* **1** (*place*): **to ~ sentries** вы|ставлять часовых (-ставить)

2 (*appoint*) назнач|ать (-ить); **he was ~ed to the Paris embassy/to a regiment** его назначили в посольство в Париже/в полк.

post[2] *n* (*mail*) почта; **has the ~ come yet?** почта уже была?, почта пришла?; **by ~** по почте; **by return of ~** с обратной почтой; **by registered ~** заказным письмом.

post[2] *vt* **1** отправ|ля́ть/по|сыла́ть по по́чте (-́ить/-сла́ть); **this letter was ~ed yesterday** э́то письмо́ бы́ло отпра́влено/по́слано вчера́

2: I'll keep you ~ed я бу́ду держа́ть тебя́ в ку́рсе де́ла (*impf*).

post[3] *n* (*pole*) столб; **gate/lamp ~** столб воро́т, фона́рный столб; *Sport* **he was left at the ~** его́ обошли́ на ста́рте.

post[3] *vt*: **to ~ up an announcement** вы|ве́шивать объявле́ние (-́весить); **he was ~ed as missing** его́ объяви́ли пропа́вшим бе́з вести.

postage *n* (*expenditure on postage*) почто́вые расхо́ды (*pl*); **what is the ~ to India?** (*for parcels*) ско́лько бу́дет сто́ить посы́лка в И́ндию?, (*for letter*) ско́лько сто́ит ма́рка, что́бы посла́ть письмо́ в И́ндию?

postage stamp *n* почто́вая ма́рка.

postal *adj* почто́вый; **~ code** почто́вый и́ндекс.

postal order *n* де́нежный/почто́вый перево́д.

postbox *n* почто́вый я́щик.

postcard *n* почто́вая откры́тка.

postdate *vt* дати́ровать бо́лее по́здним число́м (*impf and pf*).

poster *n* афи́ша, объявле́ние.

poste restante *adv* до востре́бования.

posterity *n* (*descendants*) пото́мство.

postgraduate *n* аспира́нт, *f* -ка; (*if not working for a special degree*) стажёр; *attr* аспира́нтский; **~ study** аспиранту́ра.

posthaste *adv* поспе́шно.

posthumous *adj* посме́ртный.

posthumously *adv*: **he was born ~** он роди́лся по́сле сме́рти отца́; **the novel was published ~** рома́н был опублико́ван по́сле сме́рти а́втора.

postman *n* почтальо́н.

postmark *n* почто́вый ште́мпель (*m*).

postmark *vt*: **the letter was ~ed Moscow** на письме́ стоя́л моско́вский ште́мпель.

postmaster *n* нача́льник почто́вого отделе́ния/по́чты.

post meridiem, *abbr* **p.m.** *adv*: **1 p.m.** час дня, трина́дцать часо́в; **at 6 p.m.** в шесть ве́чера, в восемна́дцать часо́в.

post-mortem *n* вскры́тие тру́па, аутопси́я.

postnatal *adj*: **~ care** послеродово́й ухо́д.

post office *n* по́чта, почто́вое отделе́ние, *off* отделе́ние свя́зи; **general ~** (гла́вный) почта́мт.

post-paid *adj* с опла́ченными почто́выми расхо́дами.

postpone *vt* от|кла́дывать (-ложи́ть); **to ~ the wedding** отложи́ть сва́дьбу; **to ~ payment** отсро́ч|ивать платёж (-ить); **the meeting has been ~d until the 10th of June** заседа́ние перенесли́ на деся́тое ию́ня.

postponement *n* отсро́чка; перено́с.

postscript *n* (*abbr* **P.S.**) постскри́птум (*abbr* **P.S.**).

posture *n* оса́нка.

postwar *adj* послевое́нный.

posy *n* буке́тик.

pot *n* **1** котело́к; (*earthenware*) горшо́к; **~s and pans** ку́хонная посу́да (*collect*); **flower ~** цвето́чный горшо́к; **chamber ~** (ночно́й) горшо́к; **a ~ of jam** ба́нка варе́нья; *CQ*: **they've got ~s of money** у них ку́ча де́нег; **the firm/discipline has gone to ~** фи́рма разори́лась, дисципли́на расшата́лась; **he writes detective stories only to keep the ~ boiling** он пи́шет детекти́вные рома́ны то́лько ра́ди за́работка

2 *sl* марихуа́на.

pot *vt* **1**: **to ~ a plant** сажа́ть расте́ние в горшо́к (посади́ть); **to ~ jam** разли|ва́ть варе́нье в ба́нки (-́ть)

2 *CQ* (*shoot*) подстре́ли|вать (-́ть).

potassium *n* ка́лий.

potato *n* карто́фель (*m*), *CQ* карто́шка (*collects*); **a ~** карто́фелина; **new ~es** молодо́й карто́фель; **baked/boiled/fried ~es** печёная/варёная/жа́реная карто́шка; **mashed ~es** карто́фельное пюре́ (*indecl*).

potbellied *adj CQ* пуза́тый, толстопу́зый.

potboiler *n CQ* халту́ра (*collect*).

potency *n* (*of medicine, etc.*) эффекти́вность, де́йственность; (*of drink*) кре́пость.

potent *adj* (*of medicine, etc.*) эффекти́вный; (*of drink*) кре́пкий; (*of reasons*) убеди́тельный.

potential *adj* потенциа́льный.

pothole *n* (*in road*) ры́твина, вы́боина; (*underground*) я́мы в подзе́мных пеще́рах.

potion *n* (*magic or iron Med*) зе́лье; **a love ~** приворо́тное зе́лье; **a herbal ~** насто́йка из трав.

potluck *n*: **come and take ~ with us** пойдём ко мне, пообе́даем чем бог посла́л.

pot plant *n* ко́мнатное расте́ние.

potted *adj*: **~ meat** *approx* мясно́й паште́т; **~ shrimps** консерви́рованные креве́тки; *fig* **a ~ biography** кра́ткая биогра́фия.

potter[1] *n* гонча́р; **a ~'s wheel** гонча́рный круг.

potter[2] *vi*: **to ~ about in the garden/with an engine** вози́ться в саду́/с мото́ром (*impf*).

pottery *n* (*place*) гонча́рная мастерска́я; (*craft*) гонча́рное де́ло; (*pots*) гонча́рные изде́лия.

potty[1] *n CQ* (*baby's*) горшо́чек.

potty[2] *adj CQ*: **he's ~** он чо́кнутый; **he's ~ about her/about it** он с ума́ схо́дит по ней, он без ума́ от э́того; **~ little details** ме́лкие/несуще́ственные подро́бности.

pouch *n* су́мка, *also Zool*; мешо́чек; (*for papers*) портфе́ль (*m*); **tobacco ~** кисе́т.

poultice *n* припа́рка.

poultry *n* дома́шняя пти́ца; *attr*: **~ breeding** птицево́дство.

pound[1] *n* (*weight or money*) фунт; **~s, shillings and pence,** *abbr* **£SD** фу́нты, ши́ллинги, пе́нсы, *CQ* де́ньги; *attr*: **a ~ note** (банкно́т в) оди́н фунт; **£1 sterling** фунт сте́рлингов.

pound[2] *vti vt* (*strike*) колоти́ть, бить (*only in impfs*); (*crush*) толо́чь (рас-, ис-); **he ~ed the table with his fist** он колоти́л по́ столу кулако́м; **the ship was ~ed to pieces/was ~ed on the rocks** кора́бль разби́лся/би́ло (*impers*) о ска́лы; **to ~ something in a mortar** толо́чь что-л в сту́пке *vi*: **her heart was ~ing** у неё колоти́лось се́рдце; **he was ~ing at the door** он колоти́л в дверь; **someone was ~ing away at the piano** кто́-то бараба́нил по кла́вишам; **the sea ~ed against the rocks** мо́ре би́лось о ска́лы.

pour *vti vt* **1** (*of liquids*) лить (*impf*), нали|ва́ть (-́ть) *and other compounds*; **can I ~ you some coffee?** вам нали́ть ко́фе?; **~ yourself some brandy** нале́й себе́ коньяку́; **he ~ed the milk from the bottle into a jug** он вы́лил/перели́л молоко́ из буты́лки в кувши́н; **~ off a little of the liquid** отле́йте/сле́йте немно́го жи́дкости; **~ water on the bonfire** зале́й костёр (водо́й)

2 (*of dry substances*) сы́пать (*impf*) *and compounds*; **to ~ sand on a bonfire** засыпа́ть костёр песко́м

3 *fig uses*: **to ~ in reinforcements** влива́ть но́вое пополне́ние; **he ~ed scorn/** *CQ* **cold water on my idea** он презри́тельно отнёсся к мое́й иде́е; **she is good at ~ing oil on troubled waters** она́ уме́ет успоко́ить/утихоми́рить разбушева́вшиеся стра́сти; **she ~ed it all out to me** она́ излила́ мне (свою́) ду́шу

vi **1** (*of liquids*) ли́ть(ся), течь (*impfs*) *and compounds*; **sweat was ~ing off him** с него́ гра́дом лил пот; **water is ~ing out of the tap** вода́ льётся из кра́на; **blood was ~ing from the wound** кровь лила́сь/си́льно текла́ из ра́ны; **it was ~ing (with rain)** лил дождь

2 (*of dry substances*) сы́паться (*impf*) *and compounds*; **salt ~ed out of the bag** соль сы́палась из мешка́

3 *fig uses*: **sunlight ~ed into the room** со́лнечный свет залива́л ко́мнату; **protests started to ~ in** посы́пались проте́сты; **people used to ~ in to hear him play** пу́блика вало́м вали́ла на его́ конце́рты; **we couldn't get a taxi as people were ~ing out of the cinema** наро́д как раз выходи́л из кино́ то́лпами, и мы не могли́ пойма́ть такси́.

pouring *adj*: **~ rain** проливно́й дождь.

pout *n*: **...she said with a ~** ...сказа́ла она́, наду́вшись.

pout *vti vt*: **to ~ one's lips** наду|ва́ть гу́бы (-́ть)

vi ду́ться (на-).

poverty *n* бе́дность, нищета́; **to live in ~** жить в бе́дности/в нищете́; *fig* **his thesis shows a ~ of ideas** его́ диссерта́ция бедна́ иде́ями.

poverty-stricken *adj* обнища́вший, обнища́лый.

powder *n* порошо́к; (*for face*) пу́дра; **gun ~** по́рох; *attr*: **~ magazine** порохово́й по́греб; **~ compact** пу́дреница; **~ puff** пухо́вка; **~ room** да́мская ко́мната.

powder *vt*: **to ~ one's face/nose** пу́дрить лицо́/нос (на-); **to ~ oneself** пу́дриться.

powdered *adj*: **~ milk** порошко́вое молоко́.

powdery *adj* порошкообра́зный; **a light ~ snow was falling** сы́пал ме́лкий снежо́к.

power *n* **1** (*capability*) спосо́бность; си́лы (*pl*); **mental ~s** у́мственные спосо́бности; **his ~s are failing** его́ си́лы убыва́ют; **after his stroke he lost the ~ of speech** по́сле инсу́льта он потеря́л речь; **I'll do everything in my ~** я сде́лаю всё, что в мои́х си́лах; **it's not in my ~ to do more** я не в си́лах сде́лать бо́льше; **that's beyond his ~** э́то ему́ не по си́лам

2 (*strength, force*) си́ла; (*might*) мощь; **the ~ of a blow/of love** си́ла уда́ра/любви́; **~s of persuasion/imagination** си́ла (*sing*) убежде́ния/воображе́ния; **the military ~ of a country** вое́нная мощь страны́; **the ~ of a country** могу́щество страны́; **the ~ of an explosion** мо́щность взры́ва

3 *Mech, Phys, etc.* эне́ргия, си́ла; (*rating*) мо́щность; **nuclear/electric ~** а́томная эне́ргия, электроэне́ргия; **horse ~** лошади́ная си́ла; **the engine is working at half ~** дви́гатель рабо́тает в полси́лы; **the ~ of an engine** мо́щность мото́ра; **the ship was moving under her own ~** су́дно дви́галось свои́м хо́дом; **the ~ has been cut off** электри́чество отключи́ли

4 (*authority*) власть, *off* полномо́чие; **to come to ~** прийти́ к вла́сти; **to seize ~** захвати́ть власть; **the ~s of parliament/of the president** полномо́чия парла́мента/президе́нта; **emergency ~s** чрезвыча́йные полномо́чия; **the ~ of veto** пра́во ве́то; *Law* **I gave him ~ of attorney** я назна́чил его́ свои́м пове́ренным

5 (*nation*): **the great ~s** вели́кие держа́вы

6 *Math* сте́пень; **to raise 4 to the power of 6** возвести́ четы́ре в шесту́ю сте́пень

7 *fig* си́ла, власть; **the ~s that be** вла́сти, *iron* вла́сти предержа́щие; **the ~ behind the throne** власть, стоя́щая за тро́ном; **he's a ~ in the land** он по́льзуется влия́нием в стране́; *CQ* **the rest did him a ~ of good** о́тдых принёс ему́ большу́ю по́льзу.

power cable *n* электрока́бель (*m*).

power cut *n*: **there will be a ~ from 1 till 3** электри́чество бу́дет отключено́ с ча́су до трёх; **due to the thunderstorm we had a 4-hour ~** из-за грозы́ у нас четы́ре часа́ не́ было электри́чества.

powered *adj*: **the plane is ~ by 4 jet engines** у э́того самолёта четы́ре реакти́вных дви́гателя; **the turbine is ~ by steam** турби́на рабо́тает на па́ре.

powerful *adj* си́льный, могу́чий; мо́щный; **a ~ man** си́льный челове́к; **~ shoulders** могу́чие пле́чи; **a ~ blow** си́льный/мо́щный уда́р; **a ~ machine** мо́щная маши́на; **a ~ state** могу́щественное госуда́рство; **a ~ drug** сильноде́йствующий нарко́тик; *fig*: **a ~ novel** си́льно напи́санная кни́га; **~ emotions** си́льные эмо́ции.

powerless *adj* бесси́льный; **I'm ~ to help** я бесси́лен помо́чь.

power point *n* (ште́псельная) розе́тка.

power station *n* электроста́нция.

practicable *adj* (*of plan, etc.*) реа́льный.

practical *adj* практи́ческий; практи́чный; **~ training/measures** практи́ческие заня́тия, де́йственные мéры; ~ **experience** практи́ческий óпыт; **a ~ mind/plan** практи́чный ум, реáльный план; **a ~ wife/kitchen** практи́чная хозя́йка, удóбная кýхня; **these shoes are not ~ for the mountains** э́ти боти́нки не годя́тся для гор; **a ~ joke** рóзыгрыш.

practically *adv* факти́чески; *CQ* практи́чески; **we've had ~ no summer this year** факти́чески/по существý у нас в э́том годý нé было лéта; **~ everybody** практи́чески все.

practice *n* **1** (*usage*) прáктика; **in ~** на прáктике; **to put a theory into ~** применя́ть теóрию на прáктике

2 (*custom*) привы́чка, обы́чай; **it was his ~ to go walking every evening** у негó вошлó в привы́чку/в обы́чай гуля́ть кáждый вéчер; **the old ~ of seeing in the New Year** стáрый обы́чай встречáть Нóвый год; **in accordance with the usual ~** как обы́чно; **it is not our ~ to advertise** обы́чно мы не даём реклáмы; **sharp ~** мошéнничество; **corrupt ~s** взя́точничество (*sing*)

3 (*training*) прáктика; тренирóвка; **conversational ~** разговóрная прáктика; **she does an hour's ~ (on the piano) every day** кáждый день онá игрáет час на роя́ле; **I'm out of ~ at tennis** я давнó не игрáл в тéннис; **basketball ~** баскетбóльная тренирóвка; *attr*: **a ~ match** тренирóвочная игрá

4 *Law, Med* прáктика; **he has a large ~** у негó большáя прáктика; **he set up in ~ in London** он заня́лся́ чáстной прáктикой в Лóндоне.

practise, (*US*) **practice** *vti vt* **1** (*put into practice*): **to ~ restraint/deceit/a new method** быть воздéржанным, обмáнывать, применя́ть нóвый мéтод; **to ~ medicine/law** занимáться врачéбной/адвокáтской прáктикой (*only in impf*); **he doesn't ~ what he preaches** у негó на словáх однó, а на дéле другóе

2 (*work at*) практиковáться в + *P*, упражня́ться в + *P* or на + *P* (*usu impfs*); *Sport* тренировáть (*impf*); **I must ~ my French** мне нáдо практиковáться во францýзском; **to ~ shooting** упражня́ться в стрельбé; **to ~ scales** игрáть гáммы; (*in tennis*) **to ~ one's backhand** тренировáть удáр закры́той ракéткой

vi занимáться (прáктикой); *Mus* занимáться; *Sport* тренировáться; **to ~ as a doctor/lawyer** занимáться врачéбной/адвокáтской прáктикой; **the team ~s on Wednesdays** комáнда тренирýется по средáм.

practised, (*US*) **practiced** *adj*: **a ~ player** óпытный игрóк; **a ~ eye/movement** намётанный глаз, заýченное движéние.

practising, (*US*) **practicing** *adj*: **a ~ doctor/catholic** практикýющий врач, вéрующий католи́к.

practitioner *n Med*: **general ~** врач óбщей прáктики.

pragmatic *adj* прагмати́ческий.

prairie *n usu pl* (**the ~s**) прéрия (*sing*).

praise *n* похвалá; **beyond ~** вы́ше вся́ких похвáл (*pl*); **to heap ~ on smb** осыпáть когó-л похвалáми; **she's always singing his ~s** онá вéчно поёт емý дифирáмбы.

praise *vt* хвали́ть (по-); **to ~ smb to the skies** воз|носи́ть когó-л до небéс (-нести́).

praiseworthy *adj* похвáльный, достóйный похвалы́.

pram *n* дéтская коля́ска.

prance *vi* (*of horse*) гарцевáть (*impf*); **the children were prancing about on the grass** дéти пры́гали/скакáли по травé.

prank *n* (*practical joke*) продéлка; (*escapade*): **childish ~s** дéтские прокáзы.

prattle *vi* (*of child*) лепетáть, (*of adults*) болтáть (*impfs*).

prawn *n* кревéтка.

pray *vi* моли́ться (по-); **to ~ (to God) for smth/for smb** моли́ться (бóгу) о чём-л/за когó-л; *fig*: **she ~ed it wouldn't happen** онá моли́ла бóга, чтóбы (тóлько) э́того не случи́лось; **~ be seated** прошý сади́ться; *iron* **and what good will that do, ~?** и какáя от э́того пóльза, скажи́те пожáлуйста?/на ми́лость?

prayer *n* моли́тва; **to say one's ~s** читáть моли́твы, моли́ться; **her ~s were answered** её моли́твы/мольбы́ бы́ли услы́шаны; *attr*: **a ~ meeting** моли́твенное собрáние; **a ~ book** моли́твенник.

preach *vti vt* проповéдовать (*impf*); **to ~ the Gospel/tolerance** проповéдовать евáнгелие/терпи́мость; **to ~ a sermon** читáть прóповедь (*usu impf*)

vi проповéдовать, *also fig and pejor*.

prearranged *adj*: **at a ~ time** в зарáнее назнáченное врéмя; **their meeting was ~** они́ услóвились о встрéче зарáнее.

precarious *adj* ненадёжный.

precariously *adv*: **he balanced his glass ~ on the arm of his chair** он постáвил стакáн на рýчку крéсла—вот-вот упадёт.

precaution *n* предосторóжность; **to take ~s against smth** принимáть мéры предосторóжности прóтив чегó-л.

precede *vt* предшéствовать + *D* (*impf*); **a period of prosperity ~d the war** войнé предшéствовал перúод процветáния; **the text is ~d by a short introduction** тéксту предшéствует крáткое вступлéние; **in the week preceding the elections** на недéле, предшéствовавшей вы́борам.

precedence *n*: **order of ~** поря́док старшинствá; **these matters are urgent and must take ~ over all others** э́то срóчные делá, и и́ми нáдо заня́ться в пéрвую óчередь.

precedent *n* прецедéнт; **to create a ~** создавáть прецедéнт; **there's no ~ for this** э́то беспрецедéнтно.

preceding *adj* предыдýщий, предшéствующий.

precept *n* наставлéние.

precinct *n*: **within the ~s of the cathedral/city** во дворé (*sing*) собóра, в предéлах гóрода; **a shopping ~** торгóвый центр; (*US*) **electoral ~** избирáтельный учáсток.

precious *adj* **1**: **a ~ stone** драгоце́нный ка́мень; **~ metals** благоро́дные мета́ллы; **her friendship is very ~ to me** мне о́чень дорога́ её дру́жба; *as n*: **no, my ~** нет, моя́ пре́лесть/ми́лочка

2 (*affected*) мане́рный.

precious *adv CQ*: **there's ~ little left** чёрта с два там оста́лось; **she thinks ~ little of him** она́ его́ ни в грош не ста́вит.

precipice *n* обры́в.

precipitate *n Chem* оса́док.

precipitate *adj* (*hasty*) поспе́шный; (*rash*) опроме́тчивый.

precipitate *vt fig*: **these events ~d the crisis/the country into war** э́ти собы́тия уско́рили кри́зис/вве́ргли страну́ в войну́.

precipitous *adj* (*steep*) обры́вистый.

précis *n* кра́ткое изложе́ние.

precise *adj* то́чный; **~ measurements** то́чные разме́ры; **at that ~ moment** как раз в э́тот моме́нт.

precision *n* то́чность; *attr*: **~ instruments** то́чные прибо́ры.

preclude *vt*: **this will ~ me from joining you at dinner** э́то помеша́ет мне пообе́дать/поу́жинать с ва́ми; **this ~s all doubt** э́то устраня́ет вся́кие сомне́ния (*pl*).

precocious *adj*: **a ~ child** не по года́м/лета́м разви́той ребёнок.

preconceived *adj*: **a ~ idea** предвзя́тое мне́ние.

precondition *n* непреме́нное усло́вие.

predatory *adj Zool* хи́щный; *fig* **~ instincts/habits** хи́щнические инсти́нкты/пова́дки.

predecease *vt*: **he ~d his wife** он у́мер ра́ньше жены́.

predecessor *n* предше́ственник.

predestined *adj*: **he seemed ~ to succeed in life** ему́ бы́ло предопределено́/предназна́чено судьбо́й доби́ться успе́ха *or* преуспе́ть в жи́зни.

predetermine *vt* предопредел|я́ть, предреш|а́ть (*pfs* -и́ть).

predicament *n*: **I'm in a ~** я в нело́вком положе́нии.

predicate *n Gram* сказу́емое, предика́т.

predicative *adj Gram* предикати́вный.

predict *vt* предска́з|ывать (-а́ть).

predictable *adj* предсказу́емый.

predispose *vt* предраспо|лага́ть (-ложи́ть).

predominant *adj*: **~ characteristics/features** преоблада́ющие черты́.

predominantly *adv* преиму́щественно.

pre-eminent *adj* выдаю́щийся.

prefabricated *adj*: **a ~ house** (*CQ* **prefab**) сбо́рный дом.

preface *n* предисло́вие.

preface *vt*: **he ~d his speech with a quotation from Shakespeare** он на́чал свою́ речь цита́той из Шекспи́ра.

prefatory *adj* вступи́тельный.

prefer *vt* **1** предпо|чита́ть (-че́сть); **I ~ coffee to tea** я предпочита́ю ко́фе ча́ю; **I'd ~ to remain silent** я предпочёл бы промолча́ть; **which dress do you ~?** како́е пла́тье тебе́ бо́льше нра́вится?

2 *Law*: **to ~ charges against smb** вы|двига́ть обвине́ние (*sing*) про́тив кого́-л (-дви́нуть).

preferable *adj* предпочти́тельный.

preference *n* предпочте́ние; **I'll have beer in ~ to vodka/for ~** я предпочёл бы (во́дке) пи́во; **they gave him ~ over the other candidates** ему́ бы́ло о́тдано предпочте́ние пе́ред други́ми претенде́нтами; **I've no particular ~** мне всё равно́

preferential *adj*: **she gets ~ treatment from him** он ока́зывает ей предпочте́ние; *Comm, Econ* льго́тный; **to buy on ~ terms** покупа́ть на льго́тных усло́виях.

preferment *n* повыше́ние по слу́жбе.

prefix *n* приста́вка, пре́фикс.

pregnancy *n* бере́менность.

pregnant *adj* бере́менная; *fig*: **a ~ silence** многозначи́тельное молча́ние; **words ~ with meaning** слова́, по́лные смы́сла.

preheat *vt* предвари́тельно нагре|ва́ть (-ть).

prehistoric *adj* доистори́ческий.

prejudge *vt*: **to ~ the issue** предреш|а́ть вопро́с (-и́ть).

prejudice *n* **1** (*bias*) предубежде́ние, предвзя́тость; (*ignorant hostility*) предрассу́док; **that's sheer ~ on his part** э́то в нём говори́т чи́стое предубежде́ние; **to consider a case without ~** беспристра́стно/непредвзя́то рассма́тривать де́ло; **racial ~** ра́совые предрассу́дки (*pl*); **steeped in ~** по́лный предрассу́дков

2 *Law*: **to the ~ of smb** в уще́рб кому́-л; **without ~ to one's own rights** без ущемле́ния свои́х со́бственных прав.

prejudice *vt* **1** (*bias*): **to ~ smb against smb/smth** настр|а́ивать кого́-л про́тив кого́-л/чего́-л (-о́ить); **to ~ smb in favour of smth** распо|лага́ть кого́-л в по́льзу чего́-л (-ложи́ть); **she's ~d against me** она́ настро́ена про́тив меня́

2 (*harm*) вреди́ть + *D* (по-); **this will ~ his interests/chances of success** э́то повреди́т его́ интере́сам, э́то уме́ньшит его́ ша́нсы на успе́х.

prejudiced *adj* предубеждённый, предвзя́тый.

prejudicial *adj*: **this will be ~ to his interests** э́то нанесёт/бу́дет в уще́рб его́ интере́сам.

preliminary *adj* предвари́тельный.

premarital *adj* добра́чный.

premature *adj* преждевре́менный; **~ death/baldness** преждевре́менная смерть, преждевре́менное облысе́ние; **his optimism was ~** его́ оптими́зм оказа́лся преждевре́менным; **a ~ baby** недоно́шенный ребёнок.

prematurely *adv* преждевре́менно; **the child was born ~** ребёнок роди́лся недоно́шенным; **she looked ~ old** она́ вы́глядела ста́рше свои́х лет.

premeditated *adj* преднаме́ренный, предумы́шленный, *also Law*.

première *n* премье́ра.

premise *n* **1** (*also* **premiss**) предпосы́лка

2 *pl* (**~s**) помеще́ние (*sing*); **business ~s**

служе́бное помеще́ние; **to be consumed on the ∼s** продаётся в ро́злив/распи́вочно.

premium *n* пре́мия; **insurance ∼** страхова́я пре́мия; *fig* **flats in the centre of the town are at a ∼** сейча́с на кварти́ры в це́нтре большо́й спрос; *attr*: **∼ bond** *approx* лотере́йный биле́т.

premonition *n* предчу́вствие; **I had a ∼ it would happen** у меня́ бы́ло тако́е предчу́вствие, что э́то случи́тся; **he had a ∼ of disaster** он предчу́вствовал беду́.

prenatal *adj* предродово́й.

preoccupation *n* озабо́ченность; **in my ∼ I forgot to buy bread** я был так погружён в свои́ мы́сли, что забы́л купи́ть хле́ба; **my chief ∼ is to find money for the rent** моя́ гла́вная забо́та—найти́ де́ньги, что́бы заплати́ть за кварти́ру.

preoccupy *vt* озабо́|чивать (-тить); за|нима́ться (-ня́ться); **she is preoccupied with family troubles** она́ озабо́чена семе́йными неуря́дицами; **I am entirely preoccupied with proofreading** у меня́ сейча́с нет свобо́дной мину́ты—чита́ю корректу́ру.

prep *n School CQ*: **he's doing his ∼** он де́лает уро́ки (*pl*); **have you any ∼ today?** у тебя́ сего́дня есть зада́ние на́ дом?

prepackaged, prepacked *adjs* фасо́ванный.

prepaid *adj*: **carriage/reply ∼** доста́вка опла́чена, с опла́ченным отве́том.

preparation *n* (*act*) подгото́вка; приготовле́ние; *Chem* препара́т; **without ∼** без подгото́вки; **a new edition is in ∼** идёт подгото́вка но́вого изда́ния; **∼ for an exam** подгото́вка к экза́мену; **the ∼ of a medicine** приготовле́ние лека́рства; **∼s for a party** приготовле́ния (*pl*) к приёму госте́й; **∼s are complete** приготовле́ния зако́нчены; **we are making ∼s for our holiday** мы гото́вимся к о́тпуску, мы собира́емся в о́тпуск.

preparatory *adj* подготови́тельный; (*UK*) **∼**/(*abbr*) **prep school** подготови́тельная шко́ла; *as prep*: **he is tidying up ∼ to going on holiday** он наво́дит поря́док в дела́х (*at office*)/в кварти́ре (*at home*) пе́ред о́тпуском.

prepare *vti vt* гото́вить (*impf*); пригот|а́вливать, подгот|а́вливать (*pfs* -о́вить); **to ∼ food/dinner** гото́вить еду́/обе́д; **I ∼d the soup yesterday** я вчера́ свари́ла суп; **to ∼ a lesson** (*of teacher*) гото́виться к уро́ку, (*of pupil*) гото́вить уро́к; **to ∼ smb for an exam/for university** гото́вить *or* подгота́вливать кого́-л к экза́мену/в университе́т; **to ∼ oneself for an exam** гото́виться к экза́мену; **to ∼ a book for publication** гото́вить кни́гу для изда́ния; **to ∼ a surprise for smb** пригото́вить сюрпри́з кому́-л; **I'll mention it to him to ∼ the way** я упомяну́ об э́том при нём, что́бы подгото́вить по́чву; **to ∼ smb for bad news** подгота́вливать кого́-л к неприя́тной но́вости

vi: **he's preparing for an exam/to leave** он гото́вится к экза́мену/к отъе́зду.

prepared *adj* гото́вый; **I'm ∼ to help her** я гото́в помо́чь ей; **I wasn't ∼ for that** я не́ был к э́тому гото́в.

preponderance *n*: **there was a ∼ of students in the audience** в за́ле бы́ли в основно́м студе́нты.

preponderantly *adv*: **the population of the town is ∼ Polish** в го́роде живу́т преиму́щественно поля́ки.

preposition *n Gram* предло́г.

prepositional *adj Gram* предло́жный.

prepossessing *adj* привлека́тельный; **she is not very ∼** она́ не о́чень располага́ет к себе́.

preposterous *adj* неле́пый.

prerequisite *n* непреме́нное усло́вие.

pre-revolutionary *adj* дореволюцио́нный.

presage *vt* предвеща́ть (*impf*).

pre-school *adj*: **children of ∼ age** де́ти дошко́льного во́зраста.

prescribe *vt* (*of diet*) предпи́с|ывать, (*of medicine*) пропи́с|ывать (*pfs* -а́ть); **to ∼ a course of treatment** назнач|а́ть (-́ить)/предпи́сывать курс лече́ния; **what did the doctor ∼ for her arthritis?** что врач прописа́л ей про́тив/от артри́та?; **the ∼d textbooks for a course** обяза́тельные уче́бники по ку́рсу.

prescription *n Med* реце́пт; **to make up a ∼** приготовля́ть лека́рство по реце́пту.

presence *n* прису́тствие; **in his ∼** в его́ прису́тствии; **your ∼ at the meeting is essential** ва́ше прису́тствие на собра́нии необходи́мо; **to make one's ∼ felt** сообща́ть о своём прису́тствии; **∼ of mind** прису́тствие ду́ха.

present[1] *n* (**the ∼**) настоя́щее вре́мя, *also Gram*; **up to the ∼** до настоя́щего вре́мени; **for the ∼ I'll say nothing** пока́ я ничего́ не скажу́.

present[1] *adj* **1** (*in attendance*): **those ∼** прису́тствующие; **to be ∼ at a meeting** прису́тствовать на собра́нии; **she must know—she was ∼ when I said it** она́ должна́ знать—она́ там была́, когда́ я э́то сказа́л

2 (*of time*) настоя́щий; **in the ∼ case** в да́нном слу́чае; **the ∼ government** ны́нешнее прави́тельство; *Gram* **the ∼ participle** прича́стие настоя́щего вре́мени.

present[2] *n* (*gift*) пода́рок; **I got it as a birthday ∼** мне э́то подари́ли на день рожде́ния; **I'll make you a ∼ of this book** я подарю́ вам э́ту кни́гу.

present[2] *vt* **1** (*give*) дари́ть (по-); (*ceremoniously*) препод|носи́ть (-нести́), вруч|а́ть (-и́ть); **he ∼ed me with a book/a book to me** он подари́л мне кни́гу; **to ∼ a bouquet to smb** преподноси́ть кому́-л буке́т; **to ∼ a prize/a cup to smb** вруча́ть приз/ку́бок кому́-л

2 (*introduce*) представ|ля́ть (-́ить); **may I ∼ my brother?** разреши́те предста́вить моего́ бра́та

3 (*put forward*) представля́ть; **to ∼ a report to a committee/a thesis** предста́вить докла́д комите́ту/диссерта́цию; **to ∼ smb as a hero/in a favourable light** предста́вить кого́-л геро́ем/в вы́годном све́те; **that ∼ed a problem for us** э́то представля́ло для нас пробле́му; **to**

~ evidence предста́вить доказа́тельства (*pl*); **the case ~s some interesting points** в э́том де́ле есть не́сколько любопы́тных моме́нтов; **to ~ one's ideas/a programme** из|лага́ть свои́ мы́сли/програ́мму (-ложи́ть); **the ceremony ~ed a magnificent spectacle** церемо́ния явля́ла собо́й великоле́пное зре́лище

4 (*submit*) предъяв|ля́ть (-и́ть); **to ~ one's passport/tickets** предъявля́ть па́спорт/биле́ты; **to ~ a cheque for payment** предъяви́ть чек к опла́те; **to ~ a petition** подава́ть пети́цию; **to ~ oneself at a meeting/for an exam** яв|ля́ться на собра́ние/на экза́мен (-и́ться).

presentable *adj* прили́чный, *iron* презента́бельный; **I'll just make myself ~** я то́лько приведу́ себя́ в поря́док/в прили́чный вид; **he looks quite ~ in that suit** в э́том костю́ме он вы́глядит дово́льно презента́бельно.

presentation *n* 1 (*giving*): **the ~ of prizes** вруче́ние призо́в; **they made him a ~ of a clock** ему́ преподнесли́ часы́

2 (*submission*): **on ~ of this cheque** по предъявле́нии э́того че́ка

3 (*exposition*) изложе́ние; **the ~ of a case/one's ideas** изложе́ние де́ла/свои́х мы́слей; **the ~ of evidence** представле́ние доказа́тельств; **the ~ of food** оформле́ние блюд.

present-day *adj* ны́нешний, совреме́нный.

presentiment *n* предчу́вствие; **I had a ~ that...** у меня́ бы́ло предчу́вствие, что...

presently *adv* 1 ско́ро, сейча́с; (*in narration*) вско́ре

2 (*US*: *at present*) в настоя́щее вре́мя, тепе́рь, сейча́с.

preservation *n* сохране́ние; охра́на; **the ~ of historic buildings** сохране́ние/охра́на па́мятников архитекту́ры; **the ~ of wild life** охра́на приро́ды; **a building in a good state of ~** хорошо́ сохрани́вшееся зда́ние.

preservative *n* сре́дство для консерви́рования/презерви́рования.

preserve *n* 1 *usu pl* (**~s**) *Cook* варе́нье (*usu sing*)

2: a game ~ охо́тничий запове́дник.

preserve *vt* 1 сохран|я́ть (-и́ть); охраня́ть (*impf*); **she is well ~d** она́ хорошо́ сохрани́лась; **all his paintings have been ~d** все его́ карти́ны бы́ли сохранены́; **to ~ an old building/one's sanity** бере́чь стари́нное зда́ние, сохраня́ть я́сность ума́; **God ~ us!** бо́же упаси́!; **to ~ smb from harm** оберега́ть кого́-л от беды́ (**NB** *pf* убере́чь)

2 *Cook* консерви́ровать (за-).

preside *vi* председа́тельствовать (*impf*).

president *n* президе́нт; (*in some administrative bodies*) председа́тель (*m*); (*US*) *Univ* ре́ктор; **P. of the Academy of Sciences/of the Council of Ministers of the USSR** президе́нт Акаде́мии нау́к СССР, Председа́тель Сове́та Мини́стров СССР; (*UK*) **P. of the Board of Trade** мини́стр торго́вли.

presidential *adj*: **~ elections** президе́нтские вы́боры; **a ~ candidate** кандида́т на пост президе́нта.

press *n* 1 (*squash*, *crush*, *throng*) толчея́, да́вка; **there was such a ~ at the entrance, I just went away** у вхо́да была́ така́я да́вка, что я про́сто ушёл отту́да; **I got lost in the ~** я затеря́лся в толпе́

2: I gave your trousers a ~ я вы́гладил твои́ брю́ки; *fig* **in the ~ of business I forgot the tickets** за дела́ми я забы́л про биле́ты

3 (*machine*) пресс; **hydraulic/wine ~** гидравли́ческий/виногра́дный пресс; **printing ~** печа́тный стано́к

4 (*cupboard*) шкаф; **linen ~** шкаф для белья́

5 **(the P.)** печа́ть; пре́сса; **the freedom of the ~** свобо́да печа́ти; **the gutter ~** бульва́рная пре́сса; **the ~ will be at the airport** в аэропорту́ бу́дут представи́тели пре́ссы/журнали́сты; **the match was reported in the ~** газе́ты писа́ли об э́том ма́тче; **it was reported in the ~ that...** в печа́ти сообща́лось, что...

6 (*printing*) печа́ть, печа́тание; **my book is now in the ~** моя́ кни́га печа́тается; **when does the paper go to ~?** когда́ но́мер (газе́ты) идёт в печа́ть?; **Cambridge University P.** изда́тельство Ке́мбриджского университе́та; *fig* **my book had a good ~** моя́ кни́га была́ хорошо́ встре́чена кри́тикой; *attr*: **~ agency/box/cutting** аге́нтство печа́ти, ло́жа пре́ссы, газе́тная вы́резка.

press *vti vt* 1 жать (*impf*) *and compounds*; надав|ливать (-и́ть); **he ~ed the button/the trigger/(down) the accelerator** он нажа́л на кно́пку/на куро́к/на акселера́тор; **he ~ed her to his breast** он прижа́л её к груди́; **she ~ed his hand** она́ сжа́ла ему́ ру́ку; **I ~ed myself against the wall** я прижа́лся к стене́; **to ~ a cork into a bottle** за|тыка́ть про́бкой буты́лку (-ткну́ть)

2 (*using implements or machines*): **to ~ juice out of a lemon** вы|жима́ть лимо́н (-́жать); **to ~ flowers/***Tech* **cotton** засу́ши|вать цветы́ для герба́рия (-́ть), прессова́ть хло́пок (с-); **to ~ grapes/olives** дави́ть виногра́д/оли́вки (*impf*); **to ~ trousers** гла́дить брю́ки (по-, вы-)

3 *fig uses*: **they are ~ing (us) for an answer** они́ торо́пят (нас) с отве́том; **to ~ one's claims** наста́ивать на свои́х тре́бованиях; **they are ~ing us to come on Sunday** они́ о́чень про́сят, что́бы мы прие́хали (к ним) на воскресе́нье; **they ~ed the money on me** они́ заста́вили меня́ взять э́ти де́ньги; **he is being ~ed by his creditors** на него́ наседа́ют кредито́ры; **we're hard ~ed for money/time** у нас ту́го с деньга́ми, у нас де́нег/вре́мени в обре́з; *Mil*, *Sport*: **they ~ed the enemy** они́ тесни́ли проти́вника; **the enemy/our opponents were hard ~ed** проти́вник был/на́ши сопе́рники бы́ли в тру́дном положе́нии

vi 1 дави́ть; прижима́ть; **the weight of the beam was ~ing on my foot** ба́лка придави́ла мне но́гу; **the shoe is ~ing on my toes** боти́нок жмёт (мне) вноске́; **the boy ~ed close to his father** ма́льчик прижа́лся к отцу́; **the crowd ~ed round them** толпа́ сдави́ла их

2 *fig uses*: **the students are ~ing for higher allowances** студе́нты насто́йчиво тре́буют повыше́ния стипе́ндий; **time ~es** вре́мя не те́рпит/не ждёт; **his responsibilities ~ heavily on him** бре́мя отве́тственности (*sing*) тяготи́т его́; **we decided to ~ on** мы реши́ли дви́гаться да́льше (*with the journey*)/продолжа́ть рабо́ту (*with the job*).

pressing *adj* (*urgent*) сро́чный, неотло́жный; (*insistent*) настоя́тельный; **~ debts** сро́чные долги́; **~ business** неотло́жное де́ло; **a ~ need for more housing** настоя́тельная потре́бность в жилье́; **he was very ~—I couldn't refuse** он о́чень наста́ивал—я не мог отказа́ться.

pressman *n* репортёр, журнали́ст.

pressure *n* **1** давле́ние; **atmospheric/blood ~** атмосфе́рное/кровяно́е давле́ние; **tyre ~** давле́ние в ши́нах

2 *fig* (*influence*) давле́ние, нажи́м; (*strain*) напряже́ние; **to bring ~ to bear on smb** ока́зывать давле́ние на кого́-л; **I did it under ~** я сде́лал э́то под нажи́мом; **the ~s of modern life** напряже́ние (*sing*)/перегру́зки совре́менной жи́зни; **we are working under ~** мы о́чень напряжённо рабо́таем.

pressure cooker *n* скорова́рка.

pressure gauge *n* мано́метр.

pressure group *n approx* инициати́вная гру́ппа.

pressurize *vt Tech* герметизи́ровать (за-); *fig* **I don't like to be ~d** не люблю́, когда́ на меня́ да́вят.

prestige *n* прести́ж.

prestigious *adj* прести́жный.

presumably *adv* вероя́тно, наве́рно(е).

presume *vti vt* (*suppose*) полага́ть (*impf*), предпол|ага́ть (-ожи́ть); **I ~ you've told him everything** полага́ю, вы ему́ всё рассказа́ли; **let us ~ that...** (пред)поло́жим...; **he was missing, ~d dead** он пропа́л бе́з вести и счита́лся поги́бшим

vi: **I wouldn't ~ to advise you** я не осме́лился бы/я не взял бы на себя́ сме́лость сове́товать вам; **he just ~s on her good nature** он про́сто по́льзуется её доброто́й; **I hope I'm not presuming** наде́юсь, я не сли́шком навя́зчив; **you ~ too much** ты сли́шком мно́го себе́ позволя́ешь.

presumption *n* **1** предположе́ние; **on the ~ that...** предполага́я, что...

2: **excuse my ~** извини́те меня́ за сме́лость; *pejor* **he took your car? What ~!** он взял твою́ маши́ну? Как он осме́лился!

presumptuous *adj* (*overbold*) наха́льный; **that would be ~ of me** бы́ло бы наха́льством с мое́й стороны́.

presuppose *vt* предпо|лага́ть (-ложи́ть).

presupposition *n* (*assumption*) предположе́ние; (*premiss*) предпосы́лка.

pretence, (*US*) **pretense** *n* (*sham*) притво́рство; (*appearance*) вид; (*pretext*) предло́г, отгово́рка; **his friendliness is just a ~** его́ дру́жеское расположе́ние—одно́ притво́рство; **under the ~ of friendship/helping/of being tired** под ви́дом дру́жбы/по́мощи, под предло́гом уста́лости; **they got the loan under false ~s** они́ получи́ли ссу́ду обма́нным путём (*sing*); **he makes a ~ of being interested in art** он де́лает вид, что интересу́ется иску́сством; **I make no ~ to learning** я не претенду́ю на учёность.

pretend *vti vt* **1** притвор|я́ться (-и́ться); де́лать вид (с-); **he is ~ing to be ill/asleep/a tiger** он притворя́ется больны́м/спя́щим, он игра́ет в ти́гра; **he ~ed ignorance/to be ignorant of the matter** он притвори́лся/сде́лал вид, что ничего́ не зна́ет об э́том

2 (*claim*) претендова́ть (*impf*); **I don't ~ to understand music** я не претенду́ю на серьёзное понима́ние му́зыки

vi притворя́ться; де́лать вид; **let's not ~ to each other** дава́й не бу́дем притворя́ться друг пе́ред дру́гом; **Mummy, he's not really hurting me—he's just ~ing** ма́ма, не бо́йся, он меня́ не бьёт, мы про́сто игра́ем.

pretended *adj* притво́рный; мни́мый.

pretension *n* прете́нзия (*usu pl*); **she has no ~s to learning** она́ не претенду́ет на учёность; **he is completely without ~** он челове́к без вся́ких прете́нзий.

pretentious *adj* претенцио́зный.

preternatural *adj* сверхъесте́ственный.

pretext *n* предло́г, отгово́рка; **he called on the ~ of borrowing some music** он пришёл под предло́гом взять у меня́ но́ты.

pretty *adj* **1** (*of people*) хоро́шенький, привлека́тельный; симпати́чный (*also of things*); **~ girls** хоро́шенькие/привлека́тельные/симпати́чные де́вушки; **what a ~ ring!/dress!** како́е краси́вое коле́чко!/пла́тье!

2 *CQ*: **he's got us into a ~ mess!** в хоро́шенькую исто́рию он нас втяну́л!; **this is a ~ state of affairs!** ничего́ себе́ положе́ньице!

pretty *adv CQ*: **that's ~ good** э́то вполне́ прили́чно, э́то совсе́м непло́хо; **how are you?—P. well, thanks** как пожива́ете?—Ничего́, непло́хо, спаси́бо; **I'm ~ tired** я дово́льно-таки уста́л; **he did ~ well in his exam** он дово́льно прили́чно сдал экза́мен; **that's ~ much/well the same thing** э́то почти́ одно́ и то́ же.

prevail *vi* **1** (*get upper hand*) одоле|ва́ть (́-ть); **they ~ed over their enemies** они́ одоле́ли свои́х враго́в; **at last common sense ~ed** наконе́ц здра́вый смысл восторжествова́л (*pf*)

2 (*persuade*) уговори́ть (*usu pf*); **we ~ed upon him to come with us** мы уговори́ли его́ пойти́ с на́ми

3 (*be widespread*): **here easterly winds ~** здесь преоблада́ют восто́чные ве́тры; **the use of opium still ~s in the East** куре́ние о́пиума всё ещё распространено́ на Восто́ке; **the conditions then ~ing** существова́вшие тогда́ усло́вия; **the fashions that then ~ed** госпо́дствовавшие тогда́ мо́ды.

prevalent *adj* распространённый; (*generally accepted*) общепри́нятый.

prevaricate *vi* увиливать, извора́чиваться (*only in impfs*).

prevent *vt* предотвра|щать (-тить), преду-пре|ждать (-дить); **to ~ a war/a catastrophe/accidents** предотвращать войну/катастрофу/несчастные случаи; **to ~ crime** предупреждать преступность; **the rain ~ed us from coming** дождь помешал нам прийти; **a sense of delicacy ~ed me from speaking my mind** я из деликатности не мог высказаться откровенно.

preventive *adj* предупредительный; **~ measures** предупредительные меры; **~ medicine** профилактическая медицина, профилактика заболеваний.

preview *n* предварительный (закрытый) просмотр.

previous *adj* **1** предыдущий; **on the ~ page** на предыдущей странице; **in ~ years** в прошлые годы; **as all ~ experience has shown** как показал весь прошлый опыт; **she had a ~ engagement** у неё уже было что-то назначено на это время; **has he any ~ convictions?** у него были в прошлом судимости?; **what is the ~ history of this movement?** какова предыстория этого движения?; *Med* **what is his ~ case history?** какова история его болезни?

2 (*premature*) преждевременный; **you are a bit ~ in deciding that...** ты несколько преждевременно решил, что...

3: ~ to *as prep* перед + *I*; **~ to his death he rewrote his will** перед смертью он переписал своё завещание; **~ to going on holiday I have to find myself a deputy** прежде чем/перед тем как уйти в отпуск, я должен найти себе заместителя.

previously *adv* прежде, ранее, раньше; (*already*) уже; (*as a preliminary*) предварительно.

prewar *adj* (*of the last war*) довоенный; (*of earlier wars*) предвоенный.

prey *n*: **birds of ~** хищные птицы; *fig* **she is a ~ to anxiety** её терзают заботы.

prey *vi* охотиться на + *A* (*impf*); **hawks ~ on small animals** ястребы охотятся на мелких животных; *fig* **this thought kept ~ing on his mind** эта мысль преследовала его.

price *n* цена, *also fig*; **gold has risen in ~** золото поднялось в цене; **at reduced ~s** по сниженным ценам; **this is beyond ~** этому цены нет; **what's the ~ of this?** сколько это стоит?; **you can buy it, but at a ~** это можно достать, но стоить будет дорого; *fig*: **he paid a high ~ for his success** успех достался ему дорогой ценой; **we must prevent it at any ~** это надо предотвратить любой ценой; *attr*: **~ control** контроль над ценами; **that's not in my ~ range** это мне не по карману.

price *vt*: **to ~ goods** (*evaluate*) оцени|вать товары (-ть), (*mark price on*) ставить цену на товарах (по-); (*ask price of*) **I ~d the vase** я приценялся к этой вазе; **they have ~d that book out of the market** эта книга сейчас мало кому по карману.

priceless *adj* (*of things*) бесценный; (*of qualities*) неоценимый; *CQ* (*funny*) **it was ~** это было очень забавно.

price list *n* прейскурант.

pricey *adj CQ*: **it's a bit ~** это немного дороговато.

prick *n* укол; **the ~ of a needle** укол иглы; *fig* **a ~ of conscience** укор совести.

prick *vt* колоть (*pfs* кольнуть, уколоть); **I ~ed my finger with a pin** я уколол себе палец булавкой; **I ~ed myself on the brambles** я укололся о колючки ежевики (*collect*); **to ~ a bubble** про|калывать пузырь (-колоть); *Hort* **to ~ out plants** вы|саживать растения (-садить); *fig* **his conscience ~ed him** его мучили угрызения совести.

prickle *n Bot* шип; колючка; (*of hedgehog*) иголка.

prickle *vi* покалывать (*impf*).

prickly *adj* колючий; **a ~ beard** колючая борода; **a ~ sensation** покалывание; **these are ~ roses** эти розы очень колючие; *fig* **he's very ~ on that subject** это для него больной вопрос.

pride *n* гордость; *pejor* спесь; **he's the ~ of his family** он гордость семьи; **he pocketed his ~ and apologized** он поборол свою гордость и извинился; **he takes (a) ~ in his garden** он гордится своим садом; **he has no (proper) ~** у него нет никакой гордости; **she takes no ~/a ~ in her appearance** она (не) очень заботится о своей внешности; *pejor* **his ~ is insufferable** он уж слишком спесив.

pride *vt*: **he ~s himself on his French** он гордится своим знанием французского языка (*impf*).

priest *n* священник.

prig *n CQ* цаца (*m and f*).

prim *adj*: **~ and proper** чопорный.

prima facie *adv* на первый взгляд.

primarily *adv* (*basically*) главным образом, в основном; (*originally*) первоначально.

primary *n* (*US*) *Polit* предварительные выборы (*pl*).

primary *adj* основной; первоначальный; первоочередной; первостепенный; *Geol* первичный; **~ cause** основная причина, первопричина; **the ~ meaning of the word** первоначальное значение слова; **our ~ concern** наша первоочередная задача; **of ~ importance** первостепенной важности; **~ education** начальное образование; **~ colours** основные цвета.

primary school *n* начальная школа.

prime *n*: **in the ~ of life, in one's ~** в расцвете сил.

prime *adj* **1** (*principle*) главный, основной; **the ~ reason** главная/основная причина; **a ~ advantage** главное/основное преимущество; **of ~ importance** первостепенной важности; *Math* **~ number** простое число

2 (*best*): **~ beef** говядина высшего сорта; **a ~ example** яркий пример; **in ~ condition** в превосходном состоянии.

prime *vt* (*with paint*): **to ~ walls/*Art* canvas** грунтовать стены/холст (за-); *fig*: **he came to the meeting well ~d** он хорошо был подготовлен к разговóру; **he was well ~ed** он был ужé пья́ный (*in liquor*); **to ~ smb with drink** спáивать когó-л (*usu impf*).

prime minister *n* премьéр-минúстр.

primer *n* (*textbook*) букварь (*m*); (*paint*) грунтóвка, грунт.

primeval *adj* первобы́тный.

primitive *adj*: **~ tools** примитúвные орýдия; **~ tribes** первобы́тные племенá; *fig* **our dacha is a bit ~** у нас на дáче всё прóсто.

primrose *n* первоцвéт.

primula *n* прúмула.

primus (stove) *n* прúмус.

prince *n* принц; (*Russian Hist*) князь; **the P. of Wales** принц Уэ́льский.

princely *adj usu iron*: **he lives in ~ style** он живёт по-цáрски; **a ~ sum** огрóмная сýмма.

princess *n* принцéсса; (*Russian Hist*) (*wife of* князь) княгúня, (*daughter*) княжнá.

principal *n* (*of school*) дирéктор; *Univ* рéктор: *Theat* (**the ~s**) ведýщие актёры; *Comm* (*capital*) óбщая сýмма, капитáл; *Law* глáвный престýпник/винóвник.

principal *adj* глáвный, основнóй.

principally *adv* глáвным óбразом; в основнóм.

principle *n* прúнцип; **a matter of ~** дéло прúнципа; **a man of ~** принципиáльный человéк; **I did it as a matter of ~** я сдéлал э́то из прúнципа; **I disagree with you on ~** я принципиáльно с вáми не соглáсен; **in ~ I agree with you** в прúнципе я с вáми соглáсен; **this machine works on the same ~** э́та машúна рабóтает по томý же прúнципу; **I make it a ~ never to lend money** я взял за прáвило никомý не давáть взаймы́; **the first ~s of geometry** оснóвы геомéтрии.

print *n* **1** (*imprint*) след, отпечáток

2 *Typ* (*type*) шрифт; (*process*) печáть; **in bold/small ~** крýпным/мéлким шрúфтом; **he likes to see his name in ~** емý прия́тно вúдеть своё úмя напечáтанным; **is this book still in ~?** (*being printed*) э́та кнúга ещё печáтается?; **the book is no longer in ~** тирáж э́той кнúги распрóдан; **this mustn't get into ~** э́то не должнó попáсть в печáть

3 *Art* эстáмп; *Photo* отпечáток.

print *vti vt* печáтать (на-, от-), *also Photo*; *Text* наби|вáть (ʹ-ть); **how many copies of the book were ~ed?** какóй был тирáж э́той кнúги?; (*write in capitals*) **to ~ one's name** написáть своё úмя печáтными бýквами; *fig* **the scene was ~ed indelibly on her memory** э́та сцéна навсегдá запечатлéлась в её пáмяти

vi: **the book is ~ing now** кнúга печáтается.

printed *adj*: **~ cotton** сúтец; **~ matter** печáтный материáл.

printer *n* печáтник, типóграф; **to send smth to the ~'s** отправля́ть что-л в типогрáфию/в печáть; **~'s ink** печáтная крáска.

printing *n* (*craft*) печáтное дéло; (*process*) печáтание, печáть; (*quantity*): **a ~ of 1,000 copies** тирáж в ты́сячу экземпля́ров.

printing office, printing works *ns* типогрáфия.

prior *adj* **1: I have a ~ commitment** я ужé связáл себя́ обязáтельством; **to have a ~ claim to smth** имéть преимýщественное прáво на что-л; **without ~ warning** без предупреждéния; **to have ~ knowledge of smth** знать о чём-л зарáнее

2 *as prep*: **~ to the revolution** до революции; **~ to the introduction of ball-point pens** до появлéния шáриковых рýчек; **~ to making a decision** прéжде чем приня́ть решéние.

priority *n* поря́док очерёдности; **let's discuss the items in order of ~** давáйте обсýдим вопрóсы в поря́дке очерёдности; **we must get our priorities right** мы должны́ установúть поря́док очерёдности; **we must give top ~ to housing** мы должны́ в пéрвую óчередь решúть жилúщную проблéму; *CQ* **he's got his priorities right** он знáет что к чемý.

prise *vt*: **to ~ the top off a bottle** (с трудóм) откры|вáть буты́лку (ʹ-ть); **to ~ open a box** взлáмывать кры́шку я́щика (взломáть); **to ~ planks apart** раско|лáчивать дóски (-лотúть).

prism *n* прúзма.

prison *n* тюрьмá; **to put smb in ~** сажáть когó-л в тюрьмý (посадúть); **he's in ~** он сидúт в тюрьмé, *CQ* он сидúт; **he was put in ~** *CQ* егó посадúли; *attr*: **~ camp** лáгерь для заключённых.

prisoner *n* (*in jail*) заключённый; *Mil* **~s of war** (военно)плéнные; **~ at the bar** подсудúмый; **political ~** политзаключённый; *Mil*: **to take smb ~** взять когó-л в плен; **he was taken/held ~** он попáл в плен, он находúлся в пленý.

privacy *n* уединéние; **in the ~ of my own house** у себя́ дóма; **to invade smb's ~** нарушáть чьё-л уединéние; **there is no ~ in a hostel** в общежúтии трýдно жить своéй жúзнью.

private *n* **1** *Mil* (*also* **~ soldier**) рядовóй

2: I was told it in ~ мне э́то сказáли по секрéту/конфиденциáльно; **the meeting was held in ~** собрáние бы́ло закры́тым; **can I speak to you in ~?** могý я с тобóй поговорúть наединé?

private *adj* (*personal*) лúчный; (*non-public*) чáстный; **my ~ opinion** моё лúчное мнéние; **~ property** чáстная сóбственность; **this matter is strictly ~** э́то сугýбо лúчное дéло; **a ~ secretary** лúчный секретáрь; **to keep smth ~** держáть что-л в тáйне; **"P. and Confidential"** (*on letter*) «лúчно», «в сóбственные рýки»; **we're not ~ here** мы здесь не однú; **a ~ school** чáстная шкóла; **a ~ detective** чáстный детектúв; **in ~ life** в чáстной жúзни; **speaking as a ~ individual** говоря́ как чáстное лицó; **a ~ viewing** закры́тый просмóтр.

privately *adv* лúчно; чáстным óбразом; **~, I think that...** я лúчно дýмаю, что...; **he was educated ~** он учúлся в чáстной шкóле; **I spoke to him ~ about it** я с ним говорúл об э́том конфиденциáльно; **he published the book ~** он опубликовáл кни́гу за свой счёт.

privation *n* лишéние.

privilege *n* привилéгия; **diplomatic ~** дипломати́ческие привилéгии (*pl*); **it is my ~ to** + *inf* я имéю честь + *inf*.

privy *adj*: **to be ~ to smth** быть причáстным к чемý-л; **the P. Council** тáйный совéт.

prize *n* прéмия, приз; **the Lenin ~** Лéнинская прéмия; **a Nobel ~** Нóбелевская прéмия; **a cash ~** дéнежная прéмия; **he won first ~ in the competition** он получи́л пéрвую прéмию/пéрвый приз на кóнкурсе; *attr* призовóй; *Agric* **a ~ bull** бык-рекорди́ст; *CQ* **he's a ~ idiot** он идиóт каки́х мáло.

prize *vt* высокó цени́ть (*impf*).

prize fighter *n* боксёр-профессионáл.

prize giving *n* вручéние призóв.

prizewinner *n Sport* призёр; (*SU*: *in school*) медали́ст; (*in music competitions*) лауреáт; (*in magazine competitions, etc.*) победи́тель (*m*); (*in lottery*) обладáтель (*m*) вы́игрышного билéта; **Nobel P.** нóбелевский лауреáт.

pro[1] *n Sport CQ* профессионáл.

pro[2] *n*: **we must weigh up the ~s and cons** нáдо взвéсить все «за» и «прóтив».

pro[2] *prep*: **he's ~ the Common Market** он сторóнник Óбщего ры́нка; **I'm ~ going** я за то, чтóбы поéхать.

pro- *pref*: **he's ~-French** он настрóен профранцýзски; **the ~-Rector** прорéктор.

probability *n* вероя́тность; **in all ~** по всей вероя́тности; **the ~ is that...** вполнé вероя́тно, что...

probable *adj* вероя́тный; **the ~ outcome of smth** вероя́тный исхóд чегó-л; **it seems ~ that...** по всей вероя́тности..., скорée всегó...

probation *n* (*in a job*) испытáтельный срок, стажирóвка; **he's still on ~** егó испытáтельный срок ещё не кóнчился; *Law* **he was put on ~ for a year** емý дáли год услóвно.

probe *n* зонд, *also Med*; *fig* (*investigation*) расслéдование; **a space ~** косми́ческая исслéдовательская ракéта.

probe *vti vt Med* зонди́ровать (*usu impf*) *vi fig*: **we'll have to ~ into this matter more deeply** нáдо поглýбже рассмотрéть э́тот вопрóс (*impf* рассмáтривать).

problem *n* проблéма, вопрóс; задáча, *also Math*; **the housing ~** жили́щная проблéма; **the ~s facing us** проблéмы/вопрóсы, стоя́щие пéред нáми; **money's no ~ for them** дéньги для них не проблéма; *attr*: **~ children** трýдные дéти.

problematic *adj* проблемати́чный.

procedure *n* процедýра; **legal/the usual ~** судéбная/обы́чная процедýра.

proceed *vi* (*go on*) продолж|áть (-и́ть); **to ~ on one's way/with one's work** продолжáть путь/рабóту; **from there we ~ed on foot** оттýда мы пошли́/дви́нулись дáльше пешкóм; **before we ~ any further** прéжде чем продóлжить; **the traffic ~ed slowly** маши́ны продвигáлись мéдленно; **passengers for Kiev should ~ to platform 6** пассажи́ров на Ки́ев прóсят пройти́ к платфóрме нóмер шесть; **everything is ~ing according to plan** всё идёт по плáну; **let us ~ to the next point** перейдём к слéдующему вопрóсу/пýнкту; **she ~ed to explain her views** онá стáла излагáть свои́ взгля́ды; **how should we ~ in this matter?** как нам поступи́ть в э́том вопрóсе?

proceeding *n* **1** (*course of action*): **that was a strange ~ on his part** э́то был стрáнный постýпок с егó стороны́; **a rather doubtful ~** довóльно сомни́тельное дéло/сомни́тельный постýпок

2 *pl* (**~s**): **I took no part in the ~s** я не принимáл учáстия в происходя́щем (*sing*); (*of a meeting*) **~s began at 3 o'clock** собрáние началóсь в три часá; (*publication*) **the ~s of a society** труды́/запи́ски (наýчного) óбщества

3 *pl Law*: **legal ~s** судопроизвóдство (*sing*); **to take/drop ~s against smb** возбуждáть/прекращáть дéло прóтив когó-л.

proceeds *npl* вы́ручка (*sing*); **I sold my watch and bought a bicycle with the ~** я прóдал свои́ часы́ и купи́л на э́ти дéньги велосипéд.

process *n* процéсс; *Law* судéбный процéсс; **in ~ of construction** в процéссе строи́тельства; **we're in the ~ of redecorating the flat** мы кóе-что передéлываем в кварти́ре.

process *vt* обраб|áтывать (-óтать); **to ~ leather/information/a film** обрабáтывать кóжу/информáцию/плёнку *or* проя́в|ля́ть плёнку (-и́ть).

processed *adj* обрабóтанный; **~ cheese** плáвленый сыр.

procession *n* процéссия, шéствие; **funeral ~** похорóнная процéссия; **they walked in ~ to the palace** они́ дви́нулись процéссией ко дворцý; **torchlight ~** фáкельное шéствие.

proclaim *vt* провозгла|шáть (-си́ть); объяв|ля́ть (-и́ть); **he was ~ed king** егó провозгласи́ли королём; **they ~ed a republic** они́ провозгласи́ли респýблику; **to ~ a holiday** объяви́ть прáздник.

proclamation *n* провозглашéние, объявлéние.

procrastinate *vi* тянýть (*only in impf*), оття́|гивать (-нýть).

procure *vt* доста|вáть (-́ть), добы|вáть (-́ть).

prod *vti* ты́кать (ткнуть); **to ~ smb in the ribs** ткнуть когó-л под ребрó; **he ~ded at the rubbish with his stick** он ты́кал/стал ты́кать в мýсор пáлкой; *fig* **he ~ded me into visiting the exhibition** э́то из-за негó я пошёл на э́ту вы́ставку.

prodigious *adj* (*amazing*) удиви́тельный, изуми́тельный; (*huge*) огрóмный, громáдный.

prodigy *n* чýдо; **an infant/child ~** вундерки́нд.

produce *n* продýкты (*pl*).

produce *vt* **1** (*manufacture*) произ|води́ть (-вести́), *also fig*; изготов|ля́ть (-́ить), вы|пускáть (-́пустить); (*yield*) давáть (дать); **this factory ~s tractors** э́тот завóд произвóдит/выпускáет трáкторы; **they ~ children's books** они́ выпускáют/издаю́т дéтские кни́ги; **the mine ~s very little coal** шáхта даёт óчень мáло ýгля;

this field ~d a good crop э́то по́ле да́ло хоро́ший урожа́й

2 (*cause*): to ~ results/sparks да|ва́ть результа́ты (-ть), искри́ть (*impf*)

3 (*present*) предъяв|ля́ть (-и́ть); to ~ one's passport/a proof of smth предъявля́ть па́спорт, приводи́ть что-л как доказа́тельство; he ~d a pen from his pocket он извлёк ру́чку из карма́на

4 *Theat*: to ~ a play ста́вить пье́су (по-).

producer *n Comm* производи́тель (*m*), изготови́тель (*m*); *Theat, Cine* режиссёр, постано́вщик; *Cine* продю́сер.

product *n Econ* проду́кт, *also fig*; изде́лие; *Math* произведе́ние; **food ~s** проду́кты; **dairy ~s** моло́чные проду́кты; **the finished ~** гото́вое изде́лие; **the gross national ~** вало́вой проду́кт страны́.

production *n* 1 (*emphasis on output*) произво́дство; (*emphasis on manufacture*) изготовле́ние; (*output*) проду́кция; (*in mining, etc.*) добы́ча; **car ~** произво́дство автомоби́лей; **mass ~** ма́ссовое/сери́йное произво́дство; **the new plane is now in ~** на́чато сери́йное произво́дство самолёта но́вой констру́кции; **the new factory is in full ~** но́вый заво́д рабо́тает на по́лную мо́щность; **the annual ~ of a factory** годова́я проду́кция заво́да; *attr*: **~ costs** изде́ржки произво́дства; **~ line** пото́чная ли́ния

2 (*presentation*) предъявле́ние; **on ~ of one's pass** по предъявле́нии про́пуска; **the ~ of new evidence decided the case** бы́ли предъя́влены но́вые доказа́тельства, что и реши́ло исхо́д де́ла

3 *Theat, Cine* постано́вка.

productive *adj* (*industrial*) производи́тельный; (*fertile*) плодоро́дный; *fig* продукти́вный; **our meeting was very ~** на́ша встре́ча была́ о́чень поле́зной/продукти́вной.

productivity *n* производи́тельность.

profane *vt* оскверн|я́ть (-и́ть).

profess *vt* (*declare*) заяв|ля́ть, (*show*) проявл|ля́ть (*pfs* -и́ть); (*a religion*) призна|ва́ть (-́ть); **he ~ed himself satisfied with it** он заяви́л,/утвержда́л, что дово́лен э́тим; **he ~ed an interest in it** он прояви́л интере́с к э́тому; **he ~es to know nothing about it** он утвержда́ет,/(*feigns*) де́лает вид, что ничего́ не зна́ет об э́том; **I do not ~ to be an expert** я не счита́ю себя́ (таки́м уж больши́м) специали́стом; **to ~ a faith** признава́ть/испове́довать (*impf*) ве́ру.

professed *adj*: **he's a ~ liberal** он изве́стен свои́ми либера́льными взгля́дами; *pejor* **for all his ~ liberalism** несмотря́ на весь его́ показно́й либерали́зм.

profession *n* 1: **~ of friendship/faith/love** завере́ния (*pl*) в дру́жбе, вероисповеда́ние, объясне́ние в любви́

2 (*occupation*) профе́ссия, специа́льность; **he's a doctor by ~** он по профе́ссии врач; **the legal/medical ~** юри́сты, врачи́ (*pls*).

professional *n* профессиона́л.

professional *adj* профессиона́льный; **they gave a highly ~ performance** они́ показа́ли высокопрофессиона́льную игру́; **to seek ~ advice** обраща́ться к специали́сту за консульта́цией/за сове́том; **a ~ footballer/writer** футболи́ст--профессиона́л, профессиона́льный писа́тель; **~ people/the ~ classes** интеллиге́нция; *Sport* **he turned ~** он стал профессиона́лом.

professionally *adv* профессиона́льно; **I know him only ~** я зна́ю его́ то́лько по рабо́те.

professor, *abbr* **prof.** *n* профе́ссор (*abbr* проф.); (*US*) (*lecturer*) преподава́тель (*m*); **P. of History** профе́ссор исто́рии.

professorial *adj* профе́ссорский.

professorship *n* профе́ссорство.

proffer *vt* пред|лага́ть (-ложи́ть); **to ~ help** предложи́ть по́мощь.

proficient *adj* (*of craftsman*) уме́лый, иску́сный; **he's a ~ carpenter** он иску́сный столя́р; **she's a ~ typist** она́ хоро́шая машини́стка; **are you ~ in French?** вы хорошо́ зна́ете францу́зский (язы́к)?

profile *n* про́филь (*m*); **a fine ~** то́нкий про́филь.

profit *n Fin* при́быль, дохо́д; *fig* по́льза, вы́года; **gross/net ~** вало́вой дохо́д, чи́стая при́быль; **~ and loss** при́были и убы́тки (*pls*); **he made a ~ of £50** он получи́л пятьдеся́т фу́нтов при́были; **it yielded a 40% ~** э́то да́ло/принесло́ со́рок проце́нтов при́были; **to sell smth at a ~** вы́годно прода́ть что-л; *fig* **it would be to your ~ to read some Plato** ты почита́ешь Плато́на не без по́льзы для себя́; *attr*: **~ margins** разме́р (*sing*) при́были.

profit *vti* быть поле́зным, приноси́ть по́льзу; **he ~ed by my mistake/from the change of air** моя́ оши́бка/переме́на кли́мата пошла́ ему́ на по́льзу; **I ~ed a lot from your book** мне бы́ло о́чень поле́зно почита́ть ва́шу кни́гу; **what will it ~ him?** кака́я ему́ от э́того по́льза?

profitable *adj Fin* при́быльный, вы́годный, рента́бельный, дохо́дный; *fig* поле́зный.

profiteer *n* спекуля́нт.

profligate *adj* распу́тный, развра́тный.

profound *adj* глубо́кий; **a ~ thinker/thought** глубо́кий мысли́тель, глубо́кая мысль; **with ~ regret** с глубо́ким сожале́нием; **his ignorance is ~** он на ре́дкость невéжественный челове́к.

profuse *adj* оби́льный, ще́дрый; **a ~ growth** оби́льная расти́тельность; **he was ~ in his apologies/his praise** его́ извине́ниям не́ было конца́, он был щедр на похвалы́.

progeny *n* пото́мство. *also CQ joc*; **she's coming with all her ~** она́ придёт со всем свои́м пото́мством.

prognostication *n* прогнози́рование; прогно́з; **my ~ is that there'll be an autumn election** по мои́м прогно́зам (*pl*) о́сенью бу́дут внеочередны́е вы́боры.

programme, (*US*) **program** *n* програ́мма; *Radio, TV* переда́ча; **a theatre/study ~** театра́льная/уче́бная програ́мма; **the next item on the ~**

сле́дующий но́мер на́шей програ́ммы; **a computer ~** програ́мма для компью́тера; **a radio/TV ~** радиопереда́ча, телепереда́ча; **what's our ~ for today?** кака́я у нас програ́мма на сего́дня?

programme, (*US*) **program** *vt* (*computers, etc.*) программи́ровать (за-); (*plan events*) плани́ровать (за-); **the meeting is ~d for tomorrow** собра́ние назна́чено на за́втра.

progress *n* продвиже́ние, *also fig*; *fig* прогре́сс; **we watched his slow ~ up the cliff** мы наблюда́ли, как он ме́дленно кара́бкался вверх по скале́; *fig*: **the ~ of science** прогре́сс нау́ки; **he is making ~ in his maths** он де́лает успе́хи в матема́тике (*sing*); **the patient is beginning to make ~** больно́й пошёл на попра́вку; **the exam/match is now in ~** сейча́с идёт экза́мен/матч; **negotiations are in ~** веду́тся перегово́ры.

progress *vi* (*move*) продви|га́ться (-́нуться), *also fig*; *fig* (*develop*) разви|ва́ться (-́ться); де́лать успе́хи (с-); **the procession ~ed towards the cathedral** проце́ссия дви́галась к собо́ру; **matters are ~ing slowly** дела́ продвига́ются ме́дленно; **as the play ~es** по хо́ду де́йствия/пье́сы; **the plot ~es slowly** сюже́т развива́ется ме́дленно; **he has ~ed well in his studies** он сде́лал больши́е успе́хи в учёбе; **the patient is ~ing** больно́й поправля́ется.

progressive *adj* прогресси́вный; **~ taxation** прогресси́вное налогообложе́ние; *Med* **~ paralysis** прогресси́вный парали́ч.

progressively *adv*: **the situation got ~ worse** положе́ние всё ухудша́лось; **the standard of living is getting ~ higher** у́ровень жи́зни всё повыша́ется.

prohibit *vt* запре|ща́ть, воспре|ща́ть (*pfs* -ти́ть); **we were ~ed from bathing in the river** нам запрети́ли/нам бы́ло запрещено́ купа́ться в реке́; **smoking is ~ed** кури́ть воспреща́ется.

prohibition *n* запреще́ние, воспреще́ние; (*US*) **P.** сухо́й зако́н.

prohibitive *adj* (*of taxes, etc.*) запрети́тельный; *CQ* **prices are ~** це́ны недосту́пные/про́сто бе́шеные.

project *n* (*plan*) прое́кт, *also Archit, Univ.*

project *vi* (*jut out*): **the balcony ~s over the street** балко́н нависа́ет над тротуа́ром.

projectile *n* снаря́д.

projector *n Cine* кинопрое́ктор.

prolapse *n Med* выпаде́ние, прола́пс.

proletarian *adj* пролета́рский.

proletariat *n* пролетариа́т.

proliferate *vi* (*multiply*) размнож|а́ться (-́иться), (*spread*) распростран|я́ться (-и́ться).

proliferation *n* размноже́ние, *also Biol*; (*spread*) распростране́ние; **the ~ of nuclear weapons** распростране́ние я́дерного ору́жия (*collect*).

prolific *adj* плодови́тый, *also fig*.

prolix *adj* многосло́вный.

prolong *vt* продл|ева́ть (-и́ть); **to ~ a line/a visit/***CQ* **the agony** продлева́ть ли́нию/визи́т/муче́ние.

prolonged *adj* продолжи́тельный; **~ applause** продолжи́тельные аплодисме́нты (*pl*).

promenade *n* **1** (*stroll*) прогу́лка

2 (*place: by sea front*) на́бережная; (*in park*) алле́я

3 (*US*) (*dance*): **a high-school ~** шко́льный бал.

promenade *vi* прогу́л|иваться (-я́ться).

prominent *adj* ви́дный, заме́тный; **put it in a ~ position** поста́вь э́то на ви́дное ме́сто; **~ teeth/cheekbones** выступа́ющие вперёд зу́бы, высо́кие ску́лы; **~ features of a landscape** географи́ческие осо́бенности; *fig*: **a ~ scientist** ви́дный/выдаю́щийся учёный; **he occupies a ~ position in the ministry** он занима́ет ви́дный пост в министе́рстве.

promiscuous *adj* сексуа́льно распу́щенный; распу́тный; **the older boy has a steady but the younger one is a bit ~** у ста́ршего бра́та постоя́нная де́вушка, а у мла́дшего они́ меня́ются ка́ждый день.

promise *n* обеща́ние; **a ~ of help** обеща́ние помо́чь; **to give/make a ~** дава́ть обеща́ние, обеща́ть; **you should hold him to his ~** заста́вь его́ вы́полнить своё обеща́ние; *fig*: **a young man of ~** многообеща́ющий ю́ноша; **she shows ~** она́ подаёт наде́жды.

promise *vti vt* обеща́ть (*impf and pf*); **I ~d to ring them** я обеща́л им позвони́ть; **it ~s to be a good harvest** урожа́й обеща́ет быть хоро́шим; **I've ~d myself a new dress** я давно́ собира́юсь купи́ть себе́ но́вое пла́тье; **I don't mind, I ~ you** че́стное сло́во, я не возража́ю

vi: **but you ~d** но ты же обеща́л.

promising *adj* многообеща́ющий; **a ~ start** многообеща́ющее нача́ло; **a ~ student** студе́нт, подаю́щий наде́жды; **the weather doesn't look very ~** пого́да не предвеща́ет/не обеща́ет ничего́ хоро́шего.

promontory *n Geog* мыс.

promote *vt* **1** (*in rank*) повы|ша́ть (-́сить); **he was ~d manager/colonel** его́ назна́чили заве́дующим, ему́ присво́или зва́ние полко́вника

2 (*further*) соде́йствовать + *D*, спосо́бствовать + *D* (*usu impfs*); **to ~ trade/friendship between nations** спосо́бствовать разви́тию торго́вли, крепи́ть дру́жбу ме́жду наро́дами; **to ~ a new company/campaign** учре|жда́ть но́вую компа́нию (-ди́ть), нач|ина́ть но́вую кампа́нию (-а́ть); **to ~ a new product** реклами́ровать но́вый това́р (*impf and pf*).

promoter *n Comm* (*founder*) учреди́тель (*m*); (*entrepreneur*) предпринима́тель (*m*); *Theat* антрепренёр.

promotion *n* (*in rank*) повыше́ние, продвиже́ние по слу́жбе; **I have no hope of ~** у меня́ нет наде́жды на повыше́ние/продвиже́ние по слу́жбе.

prompt[1] *adj* бы́стрый; неме́дленный; **the service here is very ~** здесь бы́стро обслу́живают; **a ~ reply** незамедли́тельный отве́т.

prompt[1] *adv* ро́вно, то́чно; **at 9 o'clock ~** в де́вять часо́в ро́вно, ро́вно/то́чно в де́вять.

prompt[2] *vt* (*spur*) побу|жда́ть (-ди́ть); (*suggest, help out*) подска́з|ывать (-а́ть); *Theat* суфли́ровать (*impf*); **what ~ed you to do that?** что побуди́ло тебя́ сде́лать э́то?; **this ~s the thought/feeling that...** э́то внуша́ет мысль,/чу́вство, что...

prompt box *n* суфлёрская бу́дка.

prompter *n Theat* суфлёр.

prompting *n* подска́зка; **at his ~** по его́ подска́зке; **without any ~** без подска́зки; **the ~s of conscience** го́лос (*sing*) со́вести; (*at school*) **no ~ now!** не подска́зывайте!

promptly *adv* (*quickly*) бы́стро, неме́дленно; (*punctually*) во́время.

prone *adj* **1** (*flat*): **to lie/fall ~** лежа́ть/упа́сть ничко́м

2 (*liable*): **I'm ~ to colds in winter/to put on weight** зимо́й у меня́ ча́сто быва́ет на́сморк, я скло́нен к полноте́.

prong *n* (*of fork*) зубе́ц.

pronoun *n Gram* местоиме́ние.

pronounce *vti vt* **1** (*declare*) объяв|ля́ть, заяв|ля́ть (*pfs* -и́ть); **he ~d the wine excellent** он заяви́л, что вино́ превосхо́дно; **he was ~d unfit for active service** его́ призна́ли него́дным к действи́тельной слу́жбе; *Law* **to ~ sentence on smb** объявля́ть пригово́р кому́-либо

2 произ|носи́ть (-нести́); **how is that word ~d?** как произно́сится э́то сло́во?

vi: *Law* **to ~ for/against smb** вы|носи́ть реше́ние (не) в чью-л по́льзу (´-нести).

pronounced *adj*: **he has a ~ limp/accent** он си́льно хрома́ет, он говори́т с си́льным акце́нтом; **he has ~ views on this subject** у него́ определённые взгля́ды по э́тому вопро́су.

pronto *adv CQ* бы́стро, ско́ро.

pronunciation *n* произноше́ние.

proof *n* **1** (*evidence*) доказа́тельство, *also Law, Math*; **as/in ~ of his statement** в доказа́тельство своего́ утвержде́ния/свои́х слов; **as ~ of his regard** в знак своего́ уваже́ния; **is there any ~ that he killed her?** есть ли доказа́тельства (*pl*), что он уби́л её?

2 (*test*) прове́рка; **to put a theory to the ~** прове́рить тео́рию

3 *Typ* корректу́ра (*collect*); *Photo* про́бный отпеча́ток; **galley ~s** гра́нки; **page ~s** вёрстка (*collect*); **have you seen the ~s?** вы ви́дели корректу́ру?; **to read smth in ~** чита́ть что-л в корректу́ре; *attr*: **~ sheets** листы́ корректу́ры

4 (*of alcohol*) кре́пость; **40° ~** кре́пость со́рок гра́дусов.

proof *adj*: **this material is ~ against water** э́то водоотта́лкивающий материа́л; **he was ~ against temptation** он не подда́лся собла́зну; **he remained ~ against her entreaties** его́ не тро́нули её мольбы́.

proofreader *n* корре́ктор.

proofreading *n* чте́ние корректу́ры.

prop[1] *n* подпо́рка; *fig* (*person*) опо́ра; **clothes ~** подпо́рка для бельево́й верёвки.

prop[1] *vt* (*support*) под|пира́ть (-пере́ть); (*lean*) прислон|я́ть (-и́ть); **to ~ a roof up with supports** подпира́ть кры́шу сто́йками; **the wall had to be ~ped up** сте́ну пришло́сь подпере́ть; **he ~ped his chin on his hand** он подпёр руко́й подборо́док; **he ~ped the bicycle against the wall** он прислони́л велосипе́д к стене́.

prop[2] *n Theat* (*abbr of* **property**), *also pl* (**~s**) реквизи́т (*sing*).

propel *vt*: **a plane ~led by jet engines** самолёт с реакти́вным дви́гателем (*sing*); **a fish is ~led through the water by its fins** ры́ба дви́жется в воде́ с по́мощью плавнико́в; **he ~led me towards the door** он подтолкну́л меня́ к две́ри.

propeller *n Aer* пропе́ллер; *Aer* возду́шный/*Naut* гребно́й винт; *attr*: **~ blade** ло́пасть возду́шного винта́.

proper *adj* **1** (*correct*) пра́вильный; (*fitting*) надлежа́щий, до́лжный; **the ~ pronunciation of a word** пра́вильное произноше́ние сло́ва; **to put smth to its ~ use** испо́льзовать что-л надлежа́щим о́бразом; **with ~ respect** с до́лжным уваже́нием; **at the ~ time** в до́лжное вре́мя, когда́ на́до; **in the ~ way** надлежа́щим/до́лжным о́бразом; **the ~ clothes for a given occasion** оде́жда, соотве́тствующая да́нному слу́чаю; **everything should be in its ~ place** всё должно́ быть на своём ме́сте; **in the ~ sense of the word** в по́лном смы́сле э́того сло́ва; **that's not the ~ word** э́то не то сло́во; **do as you think ~** поступа́йте, как счита́ете ну́жным

2 (*following noun*): **linguistics ~ doesn't interest him** лингви́стика (*sing*) как такова́я его́ не интересу́ет; **the war ~ began two months later** настоя́щая война́ начала́сь два ме́сяца спустя́

3: *Gram* **a ~ noun** и́мя со́бственное; *Math* **a ~ fraction** пра́вильная дробь

4 *CQ*: **he made a ~ fool of himself over this** он вёл себя́ в э́том де́ле как после́дний дура́к/о́чень глу́по; **he's a ~ rogue** он зако́нченный негодя́й; **we're in a ~ mess** мы по-настоя́щему вли́пли.

properly *adv* (*correctly*) пра́вильно, как сле́дует, до́лжным о́бразом, как полага́ется; **to use a word ~** пра́вильно употребля́ть сло́во; **to treat smb ~** обраща́ться с кем-л до́лжным о́бразом/как полага́ется; **~ speaking** со́бственно говоря́; **she very ~ protested at this** она́ весьма́ справедли́во возрази́ла на э́то; *CQ* **our team was ~ beaten** на́шей кома́нде доста́лось, на́шу кома́нду отде́лали будь здоро́в.

propertied *adj*: **the ~ classes** иму́щие кла́ссы.

property *n* **1** (*possession*) со́бственность, (дви́жимое) иму́щество; (*estate*) име́ние; (*real estate*) недви́жимое иму́щество; **he left her all his ~** он оста́вил ей всё своё иму́щество (*belongings*)/всю свою́ со́бственность (*land, house, factory, etc.*); **public ~** обще́ственная со́бственность, обще́ственное достоя́ние; **per-**

sonal ~ ли́чное иму́щество, ли́чные ве́щи; **he owns several properties in London which he lets** в Ло́ндоне ему́ принадлежи́т не́сколько домо́в, кото́рые он сдаёт; *fig* **that news is already common** ~ э́та но́вость уже́ всем изве́стна; *attr*: ~ **tax** нало́г на недви́жимое иму́щество; **lost** ~ **office** бюро́ нахо́док

2 *Chem*, *etc*. (*quality*) сво́йство; **the medicinal properties of plants** целе́бные сво́йства расте́ний

3 *pl* (**properties**) *Theat* реквизи́т (*sing*).

prophesy *vt* проро́чить (на-); (*foretell*) предска́з|ывать (-а́ть).

prophet *n* проро́к.

prophetic *adj* проро́ческий.

prophylactic *adj* профилакти́ческий.

propitiate *vt* успок|а́ивать (-о́ить), умиротвор|я́ть (-и́ть).

propitious *adj* благоприя́тный; **the weather was** ~ **for our expedition** пого́да благоприя́тствовала на́шей экспеди́ции.

proportion *n* **1** (*ratio*) пропо́рция; соотноше́ние; **in the** ~ **of 3:1** в пропо́рции/в соотноше́нии три к одному́; **the** ~ **of men to women** соотноше́ние числа́ мужчи́н и же́нщин; **the room is high in** ~ **to its width** потоло́к несоразме́рно высо́кий для ко́мнаты тако́й ширины́; **his head is (too) large in** ~ **to his body** у него́ непропорциона́льно больша́я голова́; **the price of the vase is out of all** ~ **to its value** цена́ ва́зы соверше́нно не соотве́тствует её реа́льной це́нности; **in** ~ **as...** по ме́ре того́, как...; *fig* **don't get things out of** ~, **don't lose your sense of** ~ не теря́й чу́вства ме́ры

2 *pl* (~**s**) (*size*) разме́ры; **a ship of perfect/vast** ~**s** кора́бль идеа́льных пропо́рций/внуши́тельных разме́ров

3 (*part*, *amount*) пропо́рция, часть; **mix milk and water in equal** ~**s** смеша́йте молоко́ и во́ду в ра́вной пропо́рции (*sing*); **a large** ~ **of the audience** большинство́/значи́тельная часть зри́телей.

proportional, *also more off* **proportionate** *adjs* пропорциона́льный, соразме́рный; **the pay is** ~ **to the work done** пла́та соотве́тствует/пропорциона́льна вы́полненной рабо́те.

proposal *n* предложе́ние; **peace** ~**s** ми́рные предложе́ния; **he made her a** ~ он сде́лал ей предложе́ние.

propose *vti vt* пред|лага́ть (-ложи́ть); **to** ~ **a toast** предлага́ть тост; **what do you** ~ **to do?/doing?** что ты предлага́ешь (де́лать)?; **I** ~ **(that) we stop and have a drink** предлага́ю останови́ться и чего́-нибудь вы́пить; **he** ~**d me for the job** он предложи́л мою́ кандидату́ру на э́ту до́лжность; **he was** ~**d as chairman** его́ вы́двинули на пост председа́теля; *off* **to** ~ **a motion** вноси́ть предложе́ние (внести́)

vi: **he** ~**d to her** он сде́лал ей предложе́ние.

proposition *n* (*offer*) предложе́ние; (*statement*) утвержде́ние, *also Philos*, *Math*; *CQ*: **it's a paying/tough** ~ э́то вы́годное/тру́дное де́ло; **that's quite a different** ~ э́то совсе́м друго́е де́ло.

propound *vt*: **to** ~ **a theory** вы|двига́ть тео́рию (-´двинуть).

proprietary *adj*: ~ **rights** права́ со́бственности; **he has a** ~ **interest in this** у него́ в э́том де́ле заинтересо́ванность совладе́льца, (*more casually*) у него́ в э́том де́ле есть свой интере́с; *Comm*: **a** ~ **name/brand** фи́рменное назва́ние, фабри́чная ма́рка; ~ **medicines** патенто́ванные лека́рства.

proprietor *n* владе́лец, хозя́ин.

propriety *n* прили́чие; **a breach of** ~ наруше́ние прили́чий (*pl*); **to observe the proprieties** соблюда́ть прили́чия.

pro rata *adv* пропорциона́льно.

prosaic *adj* прозаи́чный.

prose *n* про́за; **in** ~ в про́зе; *attr*: ~ **works** прозаи́ческие произведе́ния; **a** ~ **writer** прозаи́к.

prosecute *vt Law*: **I'm going to** ~ **him** я ему́ предъявля́ю иск, *CQ* я на него́ пода́м в суд; **he was** ~**d for theft** его́ суди́ли за кра́жу.

prosecution *n Law* (*proceedings*) суде́бное пресле́дование; **the** ~ обвине́ние; **if you exceed the speed limit you are liable to** ~ превыше́ние ско́рости наказу́емо зако́ном; **counsel/witness for the** ~ обвини́тель, свиде́тель обвине́ния; **he appeared for the** ~ он представля́л обвине́ние.

prosecutor *n Law* обвини́тель (*m*); (*UK*) **Public P.** госуда́рственный обвини́тель, прокуро́р.

prospect[1] *n* **1** (*view*) вид, *also fig*; **from the house there is a fine** ~ **of the sea** из о́кон до́ма открыва́ется чуде́сный вид на мо́ре

2 *often pl fig* (*expectations*) перспекти́ва, ви́ды (*pl*); наде́жда; **what are your** ~**s?** каки́е у вас перспекти́вы?; **what are the** ~**s for the harvest?** каковы́ ви́ды на урожа́й?; **a young man with good** ~**s** перспекти́вный молодо́й челове́к; **he has no** ~**s** у него́ нет никаки́х перспекти́в; **he was utterly dismayed at the** ~ **of unemployment** перспекти́ва безрабо́тицы пове́ргла его́ в отча́яние; **I can't see much** ~ **of success** я не о́чень наде́юсь на успе́х; **there is little** ~ **of his agreeing** ма́ло наде́жды, что он согласи́тся; **we are faced with the** ~ **of a long winter** нас ожида́ет до́лгая зима́

3 (*of person*): **as a client, he's a good** ~ он бу́дет вы́годным клие́нтом.

prospect[2] *vi*: **to** ~ **for gold** иска́ть зо́лото (*impf*).

prospective *adj*: **a** ~ **customer** возмо́жный покупа́тель; **her** ~ **husband** её бу́дущий муж.

prospectus *n* (*of book*, *business*, *school*, *etc*.) проспе́кт.

prosper *vi* процвета́ть (*impf*), преуспе|ва́ть (-´ть); **the business/he is** ~**ing** предприя́тие процвета́ет, он преуспева́ет.

prosperous *adj* (*thriving*) процвета́ющий, преуспева́ющий; (*of people*: *well-off*) состоя́тельный.

prostate (gland) *n Anat* проста́та, предста́тельная железа́.

prostitute *n* проститу́тка.

prostrate *adj* (*prone*) распростёртый; *fig* ~ **with grief** сло́мленный го́рем.

protect *vt* защи|ща́ть (-ти́ть); **the fence** ~**s the roses from the wind** забо́р защища́ет ро́зы от ве́тра; **he was** ~**ed by a bodyguard** его́ сопровожда́л телохрани́тель; **you should insure to** ~ **yourself in case of fire** вам ну́жно застрахова́ться на слу́чай пожа́ра.

protection *n* защи́та, охра́на; (*patronage*) покрови́тельство; *Econ* протекциони́зм.

protective *adj* защи́тный; ~ **clothing/colouring** защи́тная оде́жда/окра́ска; **men feel** ~ **towards her** мужчи́н тро́гает её беззащи́тность; *Econ* ~ **tariffs** покрови́тельственные/протекцио́нные тари́фы.

protector *n* (*defender*) защи́тник; (*patron*) покрови́тель (*m*).

protein *n* бело́к, протеи́н.

pro tem *adv CQ* (*abbr of* **pro tempore**) пока́; **I can't answer** ~ я пока́ не могу́ отве́тить.

protest *n* проте́ст; **to make a** ~ протестова́ть; **to lodge a** ~ **about smth** заявля́ть проте́ст про́тив чего́-л; **my husband came but only under** ~ мой муж пришёл, но о́чень неохо́тно.

protest *vti vt* (*declare*) заяв|ля́ть (-и́ть), утвержда́ть (*usu impf*); **to** ~ **one's innocence** заявля́ть о свое́й невино́вности; **I** ~**ed that...** я утвержда́л, что...

vi протестова́ть; **they** ~**ed loudly** они́ гро́мко (за)протестова́ли.

Protestant *n* протеста́нт, *f* -ка.

protestation *n usu pl*: ~**s of friendship** заве́рения в дру́жбе.

protocol *n off* (*draft*) протоко́л, *also Dipl*; **we were seated according to** ~ мы сиде́ли согла́сно протоко́лу; *attr*: **the** ~ **department** протоко́льный отде́л.

protract *vt usu pass*: **the meeting was** ~**ed for another hour** собра́ние затяну́лось ещё на час.

protracted *adj*: **a** ~ **argument/visit** затяну́вшийся спор/визи́т.

protractor *n Geom* транспорти́р.

protrude *vi* выступа́ть, выдава́ться (*usu impfs*), торча́ть (*impf*); **his lower jaw** ~**s** у него́ выступа́ющая ни́жняя че́люсть; **his teeth/eyes** ~ у него́ торча́т зу́бы/глаза́ навы́кате (*adv*).

protuberance *n* (*bulge*) вы́пуклость.

proud *adj* го́рдый; *pejor* (*arrogant*) спеси́вый, надме́нный; **a** ~ **father** го́рдый оте́ц; **I am** ~ **to work with him** я горд, что рабо́таю с ним; **to be** ~ **of smb/smth** горди́ться кем-л/чем-л; **it was a** ~ **day for us** э́то был для нас тако́й торже́ственный день; *as adv CQ*: **he did us** ~ **and ordered champagne** он расще́дрился и заказа́л шампа́нское.

prove *vti vt* дока́з|ывать (-а́ть); **you can't** ~ **anything against me** ты не мо́жешь привести́ про́тив меня́ никаки́х улича́ющих доказа́тельств; **that remains to be** ~**d** э́то ещё на́до доказа́ть; **to** ~ **one's identity** удостовер|я́ть ли́чность (-́ить); **he was** ~**d innocent of the theft** бы́ло дока́зано, что он невино́вен в кра́же; **the exception that** ~**s the rule** исключе́ние, подтвержда́ющее пра́вило; **he** ~**d himself to be a good worker** он прояви́л себя́ хоро́шим рабо́тником

vi ока́з|ываться (-а́ться); **it** ~**d useless** э́то оказа́лось бесполе́зным; **our stocks are proving insufficient** на́ши запа́сы оказа́лись [**NB** *tense*] недоста́точными.

proverb *n* посло́вица.

proverbial *adj*: **the magpie's curiosity is** ~ любопы́тство соро́ки вошло́ в погово́рку.

provide *vti vt* **1** снаб|жа́ть (-ди́ть); обеспе́ч|ивать (-ить); предостав|ля́ть (-́ить); **we** ~**d them with money** мы снабди́ли их деньга́ми; **you have to** ~ **your own transport** вы должны́ са́ми себя́ обеспе́чить тра́нспортом; **the government** ~**s the money** сре́дства предоставля́ет прави́тельство; **all the flats are** ~**d with fridges** во всех кварти́рах устано́влены холоди́льники; **I** ~**d myself with a toothbrush and left for the country** я запа́сся зубно́й щёткой и отпра́вился за́ город; **my job** ~**s me with the opportunity to travel** моя́ рабо́та даёт мне возмо́жность е́здить

2 (*stipulate*): **this clause** ~**s that...** э́тот пункт предусма́тривает, что...

vi **1**: **to** ~ **for one's family** обеспе́чивать семью́

2: **the contract** ~**s for that possibility** контра́кт предусма́тривает э́ту возмо́жность.

provided *conj*, *also* ~ **that** при усло́вии, что...; **I'll do it** ~ **(that) they pay me** я сде́лаю э́то при усло́вии, что мне запла́тят.

providence *n* провиде́ние.

provident *adj* предусмотри́тельный.

providential *adj*: **a** ~ **escape** счастли́вое избавле́ние.

province *n* прови́нция; о́бласть, *also fig*; **in the** ~**s** в прови́нции (*sing*); *fig* **that's outside my** ~ э́то не вхо́дит в мою́ компете́нцию.

provincial *adj* провинциа́льный.

provision *n* **1** снабже́ние, обеспе́чение; **the** ~ **of food supplies** снабже́ние продово́льствием (*collect*); **the** ~ **of housing** обеспе́чение жильём, предоставле́ние жилья́; **the** ~ **of essential services** предоставле́ние необходи́мых услу́г; **to make** ~**s for one's future** обеспе́чивать своё бу́дущее; **he's made** ~ **for her family in his will** он не обошёл в своём завеща́нии её семью́

2 *pl* (~**s**) (*foodstuffs*: *on domestic scale*) проду́кты, (*on large scale*) продово́льствие, прови́зия (*collects*)

3 (*in document*) положе́ние, усло́вие; **the** ~**s of the agreement** положе́ния/усло́вия догово́ра; **the law has made** ~ **for that** э́то предусмо́трено зако́ном.

provision *vt* снаб|жа́ть продово́льствием (-ди́ть).

provisional *adj*: **a ~ government** вре́менное прави́тельство; **a ~ date** предвари́тельная да́та.

provisionally *adv* предвари́тельно; **let's ~ say we'll meet on Thursday** дава́й предвари́тельно назна́чим встре́чу на четве́рг.

proviso *n* усло́вие, огово́рка; **with the ~ that...** с усло́вием/с огово́ркой, что...

provocation *n* провока́ция; **acts of ~** провокацио́нные де́йствия; **she flares up at the slightest ~** она́ вспы́хивает по мале́йшему по́воду; **he said it only under extreme ~** он бы никогда́ э́того не сказа́л, е́сли бы его́ не довели́; **he hit his sister but only under ~** он уда́рил сестру́, но ведь она́ вы́вела его́ из себя́.

provocative *adj* провокацио́нный; вызыва́ющий; (*seductive*) соблазни́тельный; **~ remarks** провокацио́нные замеча́ния; **he was deliberately ~ in order to annoy me** он вёл себя́ вызыва́юще, специа́льно что́бы позли́ть меня́; **a ~ smile/skirt** маня́щая улы́бка, вызыва́юще коро́ткая ю́бка.

provoke *vt* провоци́ровать (с-); (*rouse*) вы|зыва́ть (-звать); (*annoy*) раздража́ть (*only in impf*); **he ~d a quarrel** он спровоци́ровал сканда́л; **they ~d the troops to revolt** они́ спровоци́ровали в войска́х мятёж; **children, don't ~ your grandfather** де́ти, не серди́те де́душку; **don't ~ the dog** не дразни́те соба́ку.

provoking *adj*: **how ~ of them to be so late** как доса́дно/неприя́тно, что они́ опозда́ли.

provost *n Univ* (*Oxford or Cambridge*) глава́ колле́джа; *Scot* мэр; **~ marshal** нача́льник вое́нной поли́ции.

prow *n Naut* нос.

prowl *vti* ры́скать (*impf*); **wild beasts ~ about in these forests** в э́тих леса́х ры́щут ди́кие зве́ри; **hooligans are ~ing about the streets** ша́йки хулига́нов ры́щут по у́лицам.

proximity *n* бли́зость; **in close ~ to smth** вблизи́ чего́-л, побли́зости от чего́-л.

proximo, *abbr* **prox** *n Comm*: **on the 10th ~** деся́того числа́ сле́дующего ме́сяца.

proxy *n*: **to vote by ~** голосова́ть по дове́ренности; **to stand ~ for smb** быть чьим-л дове́ренным лицо́м.

prudent *adj* благоразу́мный; **a ~ housekeeper** расчётливая/бережли́вая хозя́йка.

prudish *adj* ха́нжеский; **he/she is ~** он/она́ ханжа́.

prune[1] *n* чернosли́в (*collect*).

prune[2] *vt Hort* подрез|а́ть, обрез|а́ть (*pfs* -ать); *fig* **to ~ costs** уреза́ть расхо́ды.

pruning *n* подре́зка; *attr*: **~ shears** садо́вые но́жницы.

prussic acid *n Chem* сини́льная кислота́.

pry[1] *vi*: **to ~ into other people's affairs** сова́ть нос/лезть в чужи́е дела́ (*usu impfs*); **I don't mean to ~ but...** я не хочу́ вме́шиваться/сова́ть нос в твои́ дела́, но...

pry[2] *vt* (*US*) *see* **prise.**

prying *adj*: **nothing escaped her ~ eyes** ничего́ не укры́лось от её любопы́тных глаз.

psalm *n* псало́м.

pseudo *adj CQ*: **he's a bit ~** он како́й-то весь фальши́вый.

pseudo- *pref*: **he's a ~-scientist/-artist** он псевдоучёный, он го́ре-худо́жник *or* како́й он худо́жник!

pseudonym *n* псевдони́м.

pshaw *interj* тьфу!, фи!, фу!

psyche *n* пси́хика.

psychiatric *adj* психиатри́ческий.

psychiatrist *n* психиа́тр.

psychic(al) *adj* (*clairvoyant*) ясновидящий; (*telepathic*) телепати́ческий; **she must be ~** она́, должно́ быть, ясновидящая; **~ phenomena** сверхъесте́ственные явле́ния.

psychoanalysis *n* психоана́лиз.

psychological *adj* психологи́ческий.

psychologist *n* психо́лог.

psychology *n* психоло́гия.

psychopath *n* психопа́т.

psychosomatic *adj* психосомати́ческий.

pub *n CQ* (*abbr of* **public house**) паб, *approx* пивна́я; *attr*: **to go on a ~ crawl** пройти́сь по пивны́м.

puberty *n* полова́я зре́лость.

public *n* пу́блика; обще́ственность; **the general ~** широ́кая пу́блика; **the British ~** брита́нская обще́ственность; **the theatre-going ~** театра́льная пу́блика, театра́лы (*pl*); **in ~** публи́чно (*adv*).

public *adj* обще́ственный; публи́чный; (*of industry*) национализи́рованный; (*of the state*) госуда́рственный; **~ buildings/toilets** обще́ственные зда́ния/туале́ты; **~ holidays** общенаро́дные пра́здники; **~ opinion** обще́ственное мне́ние; **a ~ figure** обще́ственный де́ятель; **he shows no ~ spirit** он не проявля́ет гражда́нских чувств (*pl*); **~ library/debate** публи́чная библиоте́ка, откры́тая диску́ссия; **~ and private sectors of industry** национализи́рованный и ча́стный се́кторы промы́шленности; **~ servants** госуда́рственные слу́жащие; **~ transport** городско́й тра́нспорт; **to make smth ~** *off* оглаша́ть/опублико́вывать что-либо.

publication *n* (*act*) опубликова́ние, изда́ние; (*thing published*) публика́ция; *pl* (**~s**) опублико́ванные рабо́ты.

publicity *n* (*fame*) гла́сность; (*advertising*) рекла́ма; **to seek/avoid ~** добива́ться/избега́ть гла́сности; **it will be good ~ for us** э́то бу́дет для нас хоро́шей рекла́мой; **to give a film ~** реклами́ровать фильм; **the visit got a lot of ~** об э́том визи́те мно́го писа́ли.

publicize *vt* (*advertise*) реклами́ровать (*impf and pf*); (*make public*) публикова́ть (о-).

public relations *npl*: **the firm/government pays too little attention to ~** у руково́дства фи́рмы сла́бый конта́кт со свои́ми слу́жащими, прави́тельство не счита́ется с обще́ственным мне́нием (*sing*); *attr*: **~ department** отде́л информа́ции.

public school *n* (*UK*) ча́стная шко́ла.

publish *vt* **1** (*a book, an article*) публикова́ть (о-), (*a book*) изда|ва́ть (-́ть); **the newspaper was not ~ed today** сего́дня газе́та не вы́шла; **the book was ~ed this year** кни́га вы́шла в э́том году́

2 (*make known*): **there's no need to ~ the fact that...** нет на́добности говори́ть о том, что...

publisher *n* изда́тель (*m*).

publishing *n* (*business*) изда́тельское де́ло; (*publication*) изда́ние.

publishing firm, publishing house *ns* изда́тельство.

puck *n Sport* ша́йба.

pucker *vti vt*: **to ~ one's brow** насу́пить бро́ви, насу́питься, намо́рщить лоб (*usu pfs*)

vi: **your jacket ~s under the arm** твой пиджа́к морщи́т под мы́шкой.

puckish *adj* прока́зливый, шаловли́вый.

pudding *n* запека́нка, пу́динг; **black ~** кровяна́я колбаса́.

puddle *n* лу́жа.

puerile *adj* ребя́ческий.

puerperal fever *n* роди́льная горя́чка.

puff *n* **1**: **there's hardly a ~ of wind today** сего́дня нет ни ветерка́; **a ~ of smoke** клуб ды́ма; **he took a few ~s at his pipe** он попы́хивал тру́бкой; **I'm quite out of ~** я совсе́м запыха́лся

2 *CQ*: **his book got a good ~ in the paper** о его́ кни́ге была́ прекра́сная реце́нзия в печа́ти

3: *Cook* **jam ~** сло́йка с варе́ньем; *attr Sew*: **~ sleeves** бу́фы на рукава́х.

puff *vti vt, usu* **to ~ out** наду|ва́ть (-ть) *and other compounds*; **he ~ed out his cheeks** он наду́л щёки; **to ~ out smoke** пуска́ть дым (*usu impf*); **I was ~ed** я запыха́лся; **her eye was all ~ed up** у неё глаз весь опу́х; *fig* **he's ~ed up with conceit/pride** его́ распира́ет от самодово́льства/от го́рдости

vi пыхте́ть (*impf*); **he was ~ing and panting** он пыхте́л и отдува́лся; **the train ~ed out of the station** по́езд, пыхтя́, отошёл от ста́нции; **to ~ (away) at a pipe** попы́хивать тру́бкой (*impf*).

puffball *n* гриб-дождеви́к.

puff pastry/(*US*) paste *n* слоёное те́сто.

puffy *adj* опу́хший.

pug *n* мопс.

pugnacious *adj* драчли́вый.

pug-nosed *adj* с приплю́снутым но́сом.

puke *vi* рвать (вы́-) (*impers*); **he ~d** его́ вы́рвало.

pull *n* тя́га, *usu fig*; (*of magnet, gravity*) притяже́ние; **he gave the rope a ~/a ~ at the rope** он потяну́л (за) верёвку; **to take a ~ at a cigarette** затяну́ться сигаре́той, сде́лать затя́жку; **he took a ~ at the bottle** он отпи́л глото́к из буты́лки; **it was a hard ~ uphill** э́то был тру́дный подъём; *fig*: **the ~ of a big city** притяга́тельная си́ла большо́го го́рода; *CQ*: **you've got to have ~ to get a job like that** на таку́ю рабо́ту мо́жно устро́иться то́лько по знако́мству/по бла́ту; **he's got plenty of ~ with the head office** у него́ больши́е свя́зи в управле́нии.

pull *vti vt* тяну́ть (*impf*) *and compounds*; (*tug*) дёр|гать (-нуть); **to ~ a rope/a bell** тяну́ть (за) верёвку, дёргать (за) шнуро́к звонка́; **to ~ smb's sleeve/hair** тяну́ть *or* дёргать кого́-л за рука́в, дёргать кого́-л за во́лосы; **the engine is ~ing ten coaches** парово́з тя́нет де́сять ваго́нов; **he ~ed her towards him** он потяну́л её к себе́ (*pf*); **to ~ a thread** зацепи́ть ни́тку (*usu pf*); **to ~ a muscle** растя́|гивать мы́шцу (-ну́ть); **to ~ the curtains** отдёргивать (*open*)/задёргивать (*shut*) занаве́ски; **he ~ed the door to** он закры́л дверь; **to ~ a tooth/cork** тащи́ть зуб/про́бку (вы́-); **to ~ a trigger** наж|има́ть на куро́к (-а́ть); **to ~ a face/faces** грима́сничать (*impf*), стро́ить ро́жи (со-); **to ~ smth to pieces** (*for reassembling*) раз|бира́ть что-л на ча́сти (-обра́ть), (*destructively*) раз|рыва́ть что-л (-орва́ть); *fig*: **to ~ smb's leg** води́ть кого́-л за́ нос (*usu impf*); **he's not ~ing his weight** он де́лает ме́ньше, чем на́до, он рабо́тает не в по́лную си́лу; *CQ* **he ~ed a fast one on you** он тебя́ здо́рово облапо́шил

vi тяну́ть; **he pushed and I ~ed** он толка́л, а я тяну́л; (*on door*) **"P."** «К себе́»; **the bus ~ed slowly up hill** авто́бус ме́дленно тащи́лся в го́ру; **he ~ed ahead of his pursuers** он оторва́лся от пресле́дователей; **we ~ed ahead of the lorry** (*overtook it*) мы обогна́ли грузови́к; (*rowing*) **we ~ed for the shore** мы гребли́ к бе́регу

pull apart *vti vt* (*take to pieces*) раз|бира́ть (-обра́ть); **I ~ed the boys apart** я разня́л ма́льчиков

vi: **this table ~s apart** э́тот стол раздвига́ется

pull away *vti vt* оття́|гивать (-ну́ть), отта́|скивать (-щи́ть); (*snatch*) вы|рыва́ть (-́рвать); **he ~ed her away from the window/from the burning car** он оттащи́л её от окна́/от горя́щей маши́ны; **he ~ed the doll away from her** он вы́хватил/вы́рвал у неё ку́клу из рук, он отня́л у неё ку́клу

vi: **he ~ed away from the kerb** он отъе́хал от тротуа́ра

pull down *vt*: **he ~ed his hat down over his eyes** он надви́нул шля́пу на глаза́; **I ~ed the sweater down from the shelf** я стяну́л сви́тер с по́лки; **to ~ down the blinds** опус|ка́ть што́ры (-ти́ть); **they've ~ed down our old house** наш ста́рый дом снесли́; *fig*: **the flu ~ed me down a lot** я по́сле гри́ппа о́чень осла́б; **her history mark(s) ~ed her down** её подвела́ оце́нка по исто́рии

pull in *vt*: **I ~ed in my (*fishing*) line** я вы́тащил ле́ску; *fig* **the new show is ~ing in the crowds** но́вый спекта́кль де́лает больши́е сбо́ры

pull into *vi*: **the train ~ed into the station** по́езд подошёл к ста́нции; *Aut*: **we ~ed into the kerb** мы останови́лись у тротуа́ра; ~

16*

into the side of the road and stop съезжа́й на обо́чину и останови́сь

pull off *vti vt*: **to ~ off one's clothes/shoes** стя́|гивать с себя́ оде́жду/боти́нки (-ну́ть); *fig* **we've ~ed it off** нам э́то удало́сь

vi: **the bus ~ed off the motor way** авто́бус съе́хал на обо́чину

pull on *vt* (*clothes*) натя́|гивать (-ну́ть)

pull out *vti vt* вы|тя́гивать (-́тянуть), вы|та́скивать (-́тащить); **to ~ out a cork/a handkerchief** вы́тащить про́бку/носово́й плато́к; **I ~ed the cat out of the water** я вы́тащил ко́шку из воды́; **to ~ out a drawer** вы|двига́ть я́щик (-́двинуть); *Elec* **to ~ a plug out of a socket** вы|нима́ть ште́псель из розе́тки (-́нуть); *Mil* **the general ~ed the troops out of the area** генера́л вы́вел войска́ из э́того райо́на

vi: **the train ~ed out (of the station)** по́езд отошёл (от ста́нции); **we ~ed out to overtake the bus** мы вы́ехали на ле́вую/(*UK*) пра́вую по́лосу, что́бы обогна́ть авто́бус; *Mil* **to ~ out of an area** остав|ля́ть райо́н (-́ить); *CQ*: **he ~ed out of the deal at the last moment** он вы́шел из игры́ в са́мый после́дний моме́нт; **he's in one of his moods, but he'll ~ out of it** он не в ду́хе, но э́то ско́ро пройдёт

pull over *vi*: **the lorry ~ed over to let us pass** грузови́к прижа́лся к обо́чине, уступа́я нам доро́гу

pull round *vi* (*recover*) поправ|ля́ться (-́иться); (*regain consciousness*) прийти́ в созна́ние (*usu pf*)

pull together *vti vt*: **the crisis ~ed the family together** тяжёлые испыта́ния (*pl*) сплоти́ли семью́; **~ yourself together!** возьми́ себя́ в ру́ки!

vi: **we must all ~ together** мы должны́ сплоти́ться/объедини́ться

pull up *vti vt*: **to ~ up a bucket on a rope** подтяну́ть/подня́ть ведро́ на верёвке; **he ~ed up his trousers** он подтяну́л брю́ки; **he ~ed his chair up to the fire** он пододви́нул стул кками́ну; **I ~ed the plant up by the roots** я вы́рвал/вы́тащил расте́ние с ко́рнем (*sing*); **~ me up if I go on too long** останови́те меня́, е́сли я бу́ду сли́шком до́лго говори́ть; **he ~ed me up for being late** он сде́лал мне вы́говор за опозда́ние

vi: **to ~ up sharp** ре́зко затормози́ть (*usu pf*); **the car ~ed up at the traffic lights/the door** маши́на останови́лась у светофо́ра/у подъе́зда; *Sport* **he ~ed up with the other runners** он догна́л други́х бегуно́в.

pulley *n Tech* блок.

pull-in *n* (**a ~**): (*lay-by*) придоро́жная стоя́нка; (*café*) придоро́жное кафе́.

pullover *n* пуло́вер.

pulmonary *adj* лёгочный.

pulp *n* (*of fruit*) мя́коть; **wood ~** древе́сная ма́сса; **his leg was crushed to ~ in the accident** ему́ раздроби́ло (*impers*) но́гу в ава́рии; *fig* **the heat reduced me to ~** от жары́ я преврати́лся в кисе́ль.

pulsate *vi* пульси́ровать (*impf*).

pulse[1] *n Anat* пульс; **to feel/take smb's ~** щу́пать пульс у кого́-л.

pulse[2] *n Bot, collect or in pl* бобо́вые (*no sing*).

pumice (stone) *n* пе́мза.

pummel *vt* колоти́ть (по-), тузи́ть (*impf*).

pump[1] *n* насо́с, по́мпа; **petrol ~** (*in car*) бензопо́мпа, (*at garage*) бензоколо́нка.

pump[1] *vt*: **to ~ water out of a basement** вы|ка́чивать во́ду из подва́ла (-́качать); **to ~ water into a tank** нака́ч|ивать во́ду в бак (-а́ть); **to ~ up a tyre** нака́чивать ши́ну; *fig* **it's no use ~ing me—I know nothing about it** меня́ бесполе́зно выспра́шивать—я ничего́ не зна́ю.

pump[2] *n usu pl* (**~s**) (*for dancing*) ба́льные ту́фли.

pumping station *n* насо́сная ста́нция.

pumpkin *n* ты́ква.

pun *n* каламбу́р, игра́ слов.

pun *vi* каламбу́рить (с-).

punch[1] *n* (*blow*) уда́р (кулако́м); **to give smb a ~ on the nose** уда́рить кого́-л по́ носу; *CQ* **he packs quite a ~** у него́ кре́пкий кула́к; *fig*: **he doesn't pull his ~es** он не выбира́ет выраже́ний; **he lacks ~** ему́ не хвата́ет эне́ргии.

punch[1] *vt*: **I ~ed him on the jaw** я дал ему́ в че́люсть.

punch[2] *n* (*for tickets*) компо́стер; *Tech* пробо́йник.

punch[2] *vt* проби|ва́ть (-́ть); **to ~ a hole in smth** пробива́ть ды́рку/отве́рстие в чём-л; **to ~ out computer cards** пробива́ть перфока́рты; **to ~ a ticket** компости́ровать биле́т (про-, за-).

punch[3] *n* (*drink*) пунш.

punchball *n* (*in boxing*) подвесна́я гру́ша.

punch-line *n*: **the ~ of a story** *approx* соль анекдо́та.

punch-up *n CQ* потасо́вка.

punctilious *adj* скрупулёзный.

punctual *adj* пунктуа́льный, то́чный; **he's always ~ in paying his bills** он всегда́ пунктуа́льно опла́чивает счета́; **please be ~** пожа́луйста, не опа́здывай.

punctually *adv*: **at 7 o'clock ~** ро́вно/то́чно в семь часо́в; **I'll try to come ~** я постара́юсь прийти́ во́время.

punctuate *vt*: **to ~ a sentence** ста́вить зна́ки препина́ния в предложе́нии (рас-); *fig* **a speech ~d by bursts of applause/by quotations** речь, прерыва́емая взры́вами аплодисме́нтов/, пересы́панная цита́тами.

punctuation *n* пунктуа́ция; *attr*: **~ marks** зна́ки препина́ния.

puncture *n Aut* проко́л; *Med* пу́нкция; **I've got a ~** у меня́ проко́л.

puncture *vti* про|ка́лывать (-коло́ть); проби|ва́ть (-́ть); **to ~ a tyre** проколо́ть ши́ну; **my tyre has ~d** у меня́ проко́л ши́ны.

pundit *n iron*: **the ~s say...** знатоки́ говоря́т...

pungent *adj* о́стрый, е́дкий, *also fig*; **a ~ smell** е́дкий за́пах; **~ sarcasm** е́дкий сарка́зм.

punish *vt* нака́з|ывать (-а́ть); **he was ~ed for being late** за опозда́ние он был нака́зан; *fig CQ*: **he really ~es that car** он э́ту маши́ну не щади́т; **the boys have fairly ~ed the beef** ма́льчики бы́стро разде́лались с мя́сом.

punishable *adj* наказу́емый; **that is ~ by a fine** за э́то полага́ется штраф.

punishment *n* наказа́ние; **corporal ~** теле́сное наказа́ние; **to take one's ~ like a man** му́жественно переноси́ть наказа́ние; **capital ~** сме́ртная казнь; *fig* **his opponent took a lot of ~** его́ проти́внику здо́рово доста́лось.

punitive *adj* кара́тельный.

punt *n* (*boat*) плоскодо́нка; *attr*: **~ pole** шест.

puny *adj*: **a ~ child/youth** сла́бый ребёнок, тщеду́шный ю́ноша (*m*); **~ muscles** жи́дкие му́скулы; *iron* **our ~ efforts** на́ши жа́лкие уси́лия.

pup *n* щено́к; *fig* **he's a conceited young ~** он про́сто самонаде́янный щено́к.

pupa *n* ку́колка (насеко́мого).

pupil[1] *n* учени́|к, *f* -ца.

pupil[2] *n Anat* зрачо́к.

puppet *n* ку́кла; марионе́тка, *also fig*; *attr* ку́кольный; *fig* **a ~ government** марионе́точное прави́тельство.

puppeteer *n* ку́кольник.

puppy *n* щено́к.

purchase *n* **1** (*act or item*) поку́пка; *attr*: **~ tax** нало́г на поку́пку

2 *Tech* (*leverage*) де́йствие рычага́; упо́р; **I can't get enough ~ on it** мне не хвата́ет упо́ра.

purchase *vt* покупа́ть (купи́ть).

purchaser *n* покупа́тель (*m*).

purchasing power *n* покупа́тельная спосо́бность.

pure *adj* (*in all senses*) чи́стый; **~ air/alcohol** чи́стый во́здух/спирт; *CQ*: **by ~ chance** по чи́стой случа́йности; **that's ~ nonsense** э́то чисте́йший вздор.

purebred *adj* чистокро́вный, поро́дистый.

purée *n* пюре́ (*indecl*).

purge *n Med* слаби́тельное.

purge *vt* очи|ща́ть (-́стить), *also Med*; *Polit* про|води́ть чи́стку (-вести́).

purify *vt* очи|ща́ть (-́стить).

puritanical *adj* пурита́нский.

purl *vt* (*in knitting*) вяза́ть изна́ночной пе́тлей.

purple *adj* фиоле́товый, лило́вый; **he went ~ with rage** он побагрове́л от зло́сти.

purport *n* (*meaning*) смысл.

purport *vt*: **he ~s to be a poet** он счита́ет себя́ поэ́том, он выдаёт себя́ за поэ́та; **this document ~s to be the original** э́тот докуме́нт при́нято счита́ть оригина́лом.

purpose *n* **1** (*aim*) цель; **this tool can be used for various ~s** э́тот инструме́нт мо́жет быть испо́льзован для ра́зных це́лей; **he is using you for his own ~s** он испо́льзует тебя́ в свои́х це́лях; **what was his ~ in doing that?** с како́й це́лью он э́то сде́лал?; **it is not my ~ to justify this** я не ста́влю себе́ це́лью/в мои́ це́ли не вхо́дит опра́вдывать э́то; **to pursue/achieve one's ~** добива́ться/доби́ться свое́й це́ли; **for all practical ~s** факти́чески (*adv*), по существу́; **for the ~s of this lecture** в соотве́тствии с те́мой ле́кции; **this knife will answer the ~** э́тот нож подойдёт; **these prolonged discussions are serving no useful ~** э́ти до́лгие диску́ссии ни к чему́ не приведу́т [**NB** *tense*]

2 *phrases*: **on ~** наро́чно; **he spent his six months in France to some/good ~** он провёл полго́да во Фра́нции с большо́й по́льзой для себя́; **I spent a whole hour talking to him but to no/little ~** я говори́л с ним би́тый час, но всё безрезульта́тно

3 (*determination*) реши́тельность; **he has great strength of ~** он целеустремлённый челове́к; **he lacks all sense of ~** ему́ не хвата́ет целеустремлённости.

purpose *vt* намерева́ться (*impf*).

purposeful *adj* целеустремлённый.

purposeless *adj* бесце́льный.

purposely *adv* наро́чно, с це́лью.

purr *vi* мурлы́кать, (*of engine*) урча́ть (*impfs*).

purse *n* кошелёк; (*US*) (*handbag*) су́мочка.

purse *vt*: **to ~ one's lips** под|жима́ть гу́бы (-жа́ть).

purse strings *n fig*: **she holds the ~** деньга́ми распоряжа́ется она́.

pursuance *n*: **in ~ of one's duties** при исполне́нии свои́х обя́занностей.

pursue *vt* **1** (*follow*) пресле́довать (*impf*); гна́ться за + *I* (*det impf*); **the hounds ~d the hare** соба́ки гнали́сь за за́йцем; **the police ~d the thief** полице́йские (*pl*) пресле́довали во́ра/гнали́сь за во́ром; *fig*: **tragedy ~d her all her life** несча́стья (*pl*) всю жизнь пресле́довали её; **to ~ an objective** пресле́довать цель; **to ~ fame** гна́ться за сла́вой

2 (*go on with*): **to ~ a policy/an inquiry** вести́ *or* проводи́ть поли́тику/рассле́дование (*only in impfs*); **I won't ~ the matter further** я не бу́ду бо́льше об э́том говори́ть; **he ~d his studies after leaving college** по́сле оконча́ния колле́джа он продо́лжил свои́ заня́тия нау́кой.

pursuer *n* пресле́дователь (*m*).

pursuit *n* **1** (*chase*) пресле́дование, пого́ня; **he ran off in ~ of the burglar** он бро́сился в пого́ню за во́ром/догоня́ть во́ра; **the dog ran off in ~ of the deer** соба́ка погнала́сь за оле́нем; **he ran off with a policeman in hot ~** он убежа́л, пресле́дуемый по пята́м полице́йским; *fig* **in ~ of pleasure** в по́исках удово́льствий (*pl*)

2 (*occupation*) заня́тие; **his leisure ~s are reading and fishing** его́ люби́мые заня́тия на досу́ге—чте́ние и ры́бная ло́вля.

pus *n* гной.

push *n* (*shove*) толчо́к; *fig* напо́ристость; **to give smb/smth a ~** толкну́ть кого́-л/что-л; **the door needs a good ~** дверь ну́жно хороше́нько толкну́ть; *fig*: *CQ* **he's got ~** он пробивно́й; **he's got no ~** у него́ не хвата́ет напо́ристости; **we could do it at a ~** э́то сде́лать нелегко́, но éсли нáдо, то сдéлаем; **when it came to the ~ he couldn't tell her** когдá дошлó до дéла, он не реши́лся сказáть ей об э́том; **he's got the ~** егó вы́гнали с рабóты.

push *vti vt* **1** (*shove*) толк|áть (-нýть) *and compounds*; (*press*) наж|имáть (-áть); **someone ~ed me** ктó-то толкнýл меня́; **he ~ed the door shut** он толчкóм закры́л дверь; **to ~ a wheelbarrow/a pram** кати́ть тáчку/коля́ску; **~ the table nearer (to)/against the wall** придви́нь стол к стенé; **to ~ a button** нажáть (на) кнóпку; *fig*: **his parents ~ him too hard** роди́тели сли́шком на негó дáвят; **to ~ a product** реклами́ровать товáр (*impf and pf*); **to ~ drugs** торговáть наркóтиками (*impf*); *CQ* **don't ~ your luck** не испы́тывай судьбý

2 (*put pressure on*): **I was ~ed into medicine by my father** отéц застáвил меня́ заня́ться медици́ной; **they're ~ing him for payment/for an answer** они́ настáивают, чтóбы он уплати́л/отвéтил; **you have to ~ yourself if you want to get on** нýжно быть пробивны́м, чтóбы доби́ться чегó-нибудь в жи́зни; **he's ~ed for money/for time** у негó тýго с деньгáми, у негó óчень мáло врéмени

vi толкáть; **don't ~** не толкáйтесь; (*on door*) **"P."** «От себя́»

push ahead *vi*: **let's ~ ahead while it's still light** бýдем продолжáть, покá светлó

push along *vi CQ*: **we must be ~ing along** нам порá (идти́)

push around *vt CQ*: **to ~ smb around** (*bully*) задирáть когó-л (*usu impf*), (*order about*) помыкáть кем-л (*impf*)

push aside/away *vt* от|тáлкивать (-толкнýть); *fig* (*of objections, suggestions*) отме|тáть (-сти́)

push back *vt* (*a person*) оттáлкивать, (*a crowd, the enemy*) оттес|ня́ть (-ни́ть); **to ~ one's chair back from the fire** отодви|гáть стул от огня́ (-́нуть); **to ~ back one's hair** отки́|дывать вóлосы со лбá (-нуть)

push down *vt* надáв|ливать (-и́ть) на + *A*; **~ down the lid and lock the box** надави́ на кры́шку и запри́ я́щик

push forward *vt*: **they ~ed me forward as their spokesman** они́ подтáлкивали меня́ вперёд, чтóбы я вы́ступил; **to ~ oneself forward** протáлкиваться вперёд, *fig* пробивáться (в жи́зни)

push into *vti*: **she ~ed him into the water** онá толкнýла егó в вóду; **he ~ed (himself) into the queue** *CQ* он влез без óчереди

push off *vti vt*: **to ~ a boat off** оттáлкивать лóдку (от бéрега); **he ~ed her off the ladder** он столкнýл её с лéстницы

vi: **~ off!** убирáйся!

push on *vi*: **we must ~ on** нам нáдо дви́гаться дáльше (*with journey*)/продолжáть (*with a job*)

push out *vt* (*a boat, etc.*) оттáлкивать; **she ~ed him out of the room** онá вы́толкала егó из кóмнаты

push over *vt* (*topple*: *an object*) опрокі́|дывать (-нýть), (*a person*) вали́ть (по-); **we ~ed the old car over the cliff** мы столкнýли стáрую маши́ну в прóпасть

push through *vti vt*: **he ~ed his head through the window** он вы́сунул гóлову в окнó; *fig* **to ~ a proposal through a committee** протолкнýть предложéние чéрез коми́ссию

vi: **to ~ through a crowd** протáлкиваться сквозь толпý

push up *vt fig*: **it ~ed up demand** э́то увели́чило/повы́сило спрос; **the new tax ~ed up prices** нóвый налóг повлёк за собóй повышéние цен.

push-bike *n CQ* велосипéд.

push-button *n* кнóпка; *attr*: **~ control** кнóпочное управлéние.

pushcart *n* тáчка, ручнáя телéжка.

push chair *n* (*for child*) дéтская прогýлочная коля́ска; (*for invalid*) инвали́дное крéсло.

pusher *n CQ*: **he's a real ~** он óчень пробивнóй.

pushover *n CQ*: **the next match should be a ~** слéдующий матч дóлжен быть лёгким.

pusillanimous *adj* малодýшный.

puss, pussy(-cat) *n CQ* ки́ска; *as interj*: **~,~!** кис-кис!

pussy willow *n* вéрба.

put *vti vt* **1** (*put horizontally*) класть (положи́ть), (*put standing*) стáвить (по-), (*put in sitting position*) сажáть (посади́ть); **to ~ a book on a shelf** положи́ть (*if flat*)/постáвить (*if upright*) кни́гу на пóлку; **to ~ a letter/a bottle on a table** положи́ть письмó/постáвить буты́лку на стол; **I have ~ my clothes into the case** я положи́л вéщи в чемодáн; **to ~ flowers in water** постáвить цветы́ в вóду; **~ the baby in her chair** посади́ ребёнка на стýльчик; **to ~ a bird in a cage** посади́ть пти́цу в клéтку; **he's been ~ in prison** егó посади́ли в тюрьмý

2 (*without reference to position*) класть, стáвить; **he ~ the key in his pocket** он положи́л ключ в кармáн; **have you ~ sugar in my tea?** ты мне положи́л сáхару в чай?; **to ~ money in the bank** класть дéньги в банк; **~ the stress on the last syllable** постáвьте ударéние на послéднем слóге; **to ~ a patch on one's sleeve** стáвить заплáту на рукáв; **to ~ one's signature to a document** постáвить пóдпись под докумéнтом; **~ a cross against the name of your candidate** постáвьте крéстик прóтив и́мени вáшего кандидáта; *fig*: **we'll ~ the guest in our son's bedroom** мы постéлем гóстю в спáльне нáшего сы́на; **to ~ money on a horse** стáвить на лóшадь; **to ~ smb in a difficult position/in charge of an expedition** постáвить когó-л в затрудни́тельное положéние, назнáчить когó-л начáльником экспеди́ции; **to ~ a resolution to the vote** стáвить резолю́цию на голосовáние; **I ~ him in his place** я постáвил егó на мéсто; **~ yourself in my place** постáвь себя́ на моё мéсто; **I would ~ Picasso above Dali** я бы постáвил Пикассó вы́ше Дали́

3 *compound verbs with pf* -ложи́ть [**NB** *impfs usu* -клáдывать *in direct uses and* -лагáть *in fig uses*]: **to ~ a letter in an envelope** вклáдывать письмó в конвéрт; **to ~ one's hand to one's head** приклáдывать рýку ко лбý; **to ~ a**

bandage/compress on one's knee накла́дывать повя́зку/компре́сс на коле́но; **to ~ a child to bed** укла́дывать ребёнка в посте́ль/спать; *fig*: **to ~ smth on paper/in writing** излага́ть что-л на бума́ге/в пи́сьменной фо́рме; **he ~ it very well** он я́сно изложи́л суть де́ла; **to ~ smb under an obligation** налага́ть обяза́тельство на кого́-л; **to ~ a veto on smth** налага́ть ве́то/запре́т на что-л; **to ~ a tax on imports** облага́ть и́мпортные това́ры нало́гом; **~ the names in alphabetical order** напиши́ фами́лии по алфави́ту

4 *uses with other verbs*: **he ~ his hands in his pockets** он су́нул ру́ки в карма́ны; **I ~ the glass to my lips** я поднёс стака́н к губа́м; **~ your dress in the cupboard** пове́сь пла́тье в шкаф; **where can I have ~ the ticket?** куда́ я положи́л/задева́л биле́т?; **I've ~ milk in your tea/salt in the soup** я вам нали́л молока́ в чай, я посоли́л суп; **I ~ some brandy in the punch** я подли́л бре́нди в пунш; **to ~ an advertisement in the paper** поме|ща́ть объявле́ние в газе́те (-сти́ть); **they ~ us (up) in a hotel** нас помести́ли в гости́нице; **to ~ goods on the market** вы|пуска́ть това́ры (в прода́жу) (-пустить); *fig*: **I'll ~ the matter in the hands of my lawyer** я переда́м де́ло адвока́ту; **to ~ the blame on smb** свали́ть вину́ на кого́-л; **to ~ smth out of harm's way** пря́тать что-л от греха́ пода́льше (с-); **he's always ready to ~ his hand into his pocket** он всегда́ гото́в раскоше́литься; **if you had stayed ~, we should have found you much sooner** е́сли бы ты остава́лся на ме́сте, мы бы скоре́е тебя́ нашли́; **stay ~!** ни с ме́ста!; **he's hard ~ to it to pay his debts** ему́ тру́дно распла́чиваться с долга́ми

5 (*causal*): **to ~ smb to expense/inconvenience** вводи́ть кого́-л в расхо́ды (ввести́), причин|я́ть кому́-л неудо́бство (-и́ть); **it ~ me in a bad mood** э́то испо́ртило мне настрое́ние; **the doctor ~ her on a course of injections/on a diet** врач прописа́л ей курс инъе́кций/посади́л её на дие́ту; **he ~ me to work peeling potatoes** он посади́л меня́ чи́стить карто́шку; **~ an end to this nonsense** конча́й с э́той ерундо́й

6 (*estimate*): **I would ~ (the price of) the vase at £100** я бы оцени́л э́ту ва́зу в сто фу́нтов; **I'd ~ her at about 50** я бы дал ей (лет) пятьдеся́т

7 (*submit*): **he ~ it to them that...** он сказа́л им, что..., *Law* он предложи́л, что́бы...; **now let me ~ my side of the case** тепе́рь позво́льте мне изложи́ть мою́ то́чку зре́ния; **to ~ the arguments for and against** изложи́ть/привести́ до́воды за и про́тив

vi Naut: **to ~ to sea** выходи́ть в мо́ре (вы́йти); **the ship ~ in at/out from Odessa** су́дно шло в Оде́ссу/отплы́ло из Оде́ссы

put about *vti*: **our rivals are ~ting it about that we are bankrupt** на́ши конкуре́нты распространя́ют слух, что мы обанкро́тились; **to ~ about** де́лать поворо́т (с-)

put across *vt*: **to ~ smb across a river** пере|вози́ть кого́-л че́рез ре́ку (-везти́); *fig* **I tried to ~ my point of view across to him** я про́бовал объясни́ть ему́ мою́ то́чку зре́ния; *CQ* **you can't ~ that across me** тут уж ты меня́ не проведёшь

put aside *vt*: **to ~ money aside to buy a car** откла́дывать де́ньги на маши́ну; **I'll ~ the book aside for you** я отложу́ для тебя́ э́ту кни́гу; **she ~ aside her knitting and got up** она́ отложи́ла вяза́нье и вста́ла

put away *vt* убира́ть (убра́ть); **~ your toys away in the cupboard** убери́ игру́шки в шкаф; **~ the matches away out of reach of the children** спрячь спи́чки пода́льше от дете́й; **I'll just ~ the car away** я то́лько поста́влю маши́ну; **I've had to ~ away all thoughts of an American trip** мне пришло́сь отказа́ться от мы́сли пое́хать в Аме́рику; *CQ* **he could ~ away four steaks at one sitting** он мог съесть/*low CQ* умя́ть четы́ре бифште́кса за оди́н присе́ст

put back *vt* **1** (*replace*) положи́ть/поста́вить обра́тно; **~ the book back where you found it/in the cupboard** положи́ кни́гу туда́, где ты её взял/обра́тно в шкаф *or* поста́вь кни́гу в шкаф

2 (*retard*): **the meeting was ~ back for a week** заседа́ние отложи́ли на неде́лю; **the puncture ~ us back a whole hour** проко́л задержа́л нас на це́лый час; **to ~ the clock back an hour** перевести́ часы́ на час наза́д; *fig* **one can't ~ the clock back** вре́мя нельзя́ поверну́ть наза́д

put by *vt*: **to ~ by money** откла́дывать/копи́ть де́ньги (отложи́ть/на-)

put down *vt* **1** (*set down*): **he ~ down his rucksack/his suitcase** он положи́л рюкза́к, он поста́вил чемода́н; **the book was so thrilling I couldn't ~ it down** кни́га захва́тывающе интере́сна, я про́сто не мог оторва́ться от неё; **we're buying a flat and have to ~ down a deposit** мы покупа́ем кварти́ру и должны́ внести́ зада́ток; **the bus stopped to ~ down passengers** авто́бус останови́лся, что́бы вы́садить пассажи́ров

2 (*write down*) запи́с|ывать (-а́ть); **~ it down in your diary** запиши́ э́то себе́ в календа́рь; **~ it down to my account** запиши́ э́то на мой счёт; **you should get it ~ down in writing** вам на́до бы име́ть э́то в пи́сьменной фо́рме

3 (*attribute*) объясн|я́ть + *I* (-и́ть); **we ~ down her behaviour to nervousness** мы объясни́ли её поведе́ние расстро́енными не́рвами; **the bad harvest can be ~ down to the dry summer** неурожа́й мо́жно объясни́ть тем, что ле́то бы́ло о́чень засу́шливое

4 (*suppress*): **to ~ down a rebellion** подав|ля́ть восста́ние (-и́ть)

5 *Agric*: **to ~ down roots** пус|ка́ть ко́рни (-ти́ть), *also fig*; **to ~ a field down to wheat** от|води́ть по́ле под пшени́цу (-вести́)

6 *euph*: **to ~ down a dog** усып|ля́ть соба́ку (-и́ть)

put forward *vt* вы|двига́ть (-двинуть); **to ~ forward a theory/proofs** выдвига́ть тео́рию/доказа́тельства; **to ~ smb/oneself forward as a candidate** выдвига́ть чью-л/свою́ кандидату́ру; **to ~ smb's name forward for an award** представ|ля́ть кого́-л к награ́де (-ить); **to**

PUT

~ the clock forward two hours пере|водить часы на два часа вперёд (-вести); **they've ~ the wedding forward to June 3rd** свадьбу перенесли на третье июня

put in *vti vt* 1 (*insert*) вкладывать (вложить); встав|лять (-ить); **I ~ a cheque in with my letter** я вложил чек в письмо; **did you ~ the swimsuits in?** ты положил купальные костюмы?; **to ~ a key in a lock** вставить ключ в замок; **to ~ in a window pane** вставить оконное стекло; **to ~ coins in a slot machine** опус|кать монеты в автомат (-тить); **they've just ~ in our telephone** нам только что поставили телефон; *fig*: **to ~ in a remark** вставить замечание; **he ~ in a good word for me with the director** он замолвил за меня словечко перед директором; **she ~ in a brief appearance at our party** она недолго побыла у нас на вечере; *CQ* **I ~ my foot in it** я сплоховал, я дал маху

2 (*of time*): **she ~ in an hour's practice on the violin before breakfast** она успела до завтрака час поиграть на скрипке; **he has ~ in a lot of time on the plans** он много времени потратил на составление планов

3 (*submit*): **to ~ in a claim for damages** предъяв|лять иск об убытках (-ить); **to ~ in an order/an application for smth** заказ|ывать что-л *or* пода|вать заявку на что-л(-ать, -ть), подавать заявление о чём-л

vi: **to ~ in for a job/for a transfer** подать заявление о приёме на работу/о переводе

put into *vt* вкладывать (вложить); *fig*: **to ~ an order into effect** испол|нять/вы|полнять приказ (-нить/-полнить); **to ~ a satellite into orbit** вы|водить спутник на орбиту (-вести); **to ~ smth into production/circulation** пус|кать что-л в производство/в обращение (-тить); **to ~ smth into Russian** пере|водить что-л на русский язык (-вести); **to ~ one's money into property** вложить деньги в собственность; **he ~ a lot of work into that article** он много трудился над этой статьёй

put off *vt* 1 (*defer*) от|кладывать (-ложить); **the match has been ~ off till Tuesday** матч отложили на вторник; **he wants to ~ off paying me till next week** он попросил меня подождать с деньгами до следующей недели; **unfortunately I'll have to ~ you off** к сожалению, я не могу вас принять; **he always ~s me off with promises** он вечно кормит меня обещаниями

2 (*distract*): *CQ* **stop watching me, you're ~ting me off** не смотри на меня, ты меня смущаешь; **don't be ~ off by his manner** пусть вас не смущают его манеры (*pl*); **I tried to ~ him off the idea** я всячески старался отвлечь его от этой мысли; (*repel*): **his manner ~s me off** мне неприятна его манера вести себя; **it ~ me off my food** это испортило мне аппетит

3 (*switch off*) вы|ключать (-ключить)

put on *vt* 1 (*of garments*) наде|вать (-ть); **~ your coat on** надень пальто; **he ~ his clothes on** он оделся

2 (*add*) прибав|лять (-ить); **to ~ on weight/speed** прибавлять вес *or* в весе/ходу (*G*); **they ~ on another two goals in the second half** они забили ещё два гола во втором тайме

3 (*pretend*): **she's not offended, she's just ~ting it on** она не обиделась — (она) просто делает вид/притворяется, что обижена; **his illness is ~ on** его болезнь — одно притворство; **her modesty is just ~ on** её скромность напускная; **to ~ on airs** важничать (*impf*); **to ~ on an act** (*a brave face*) делать вид (с-), *pejor* ломаться, манерничать (*usu impfs*)

4 (*switch on*) включ|ать (-ить); **~ on the lights/kettle/potatoes** включи свет, поставь чайник/картошку (*collect*); **to ~ on a record** ставить пластинку (по-); **to ~ on the brakes** тормозить (за-)

5 (*organize, etc.*): **to ~ on a play/display** ставить пьесу, организо|вывать показ (-вать); **to ~ on an extra train** да|вать дополнительный поезд (-ть); **they ~ on a special bus for us** они нам дали автобус

6 (*inform*): **he ~ me on to a good doctor** он связал меня с хорошим врачом; **who/what ~ you on to that?** кто тебе это сказал?, что тебя навело на эту мысль?

7 *Tel*: **I was ~ on to him at once** меня сразу же соединили с ним

put out *vt* 1 (*put outside*): **to ~ out the rubbish** вы|носить мусор (-нести); **~ the dog out for five minutes** выпусти собаку на пять минут; **to ~ out the washing/flags** разве|шивать бельё (-сить), вы|вешивать флаги (-весить); **to ~ a horse out to grass** пускать лошадь пастись; *fig* **he should ~ that/all thought of that out of his head** пусть он выбросит это/всякую мысль об этом из головы

2 (*extend*): **to ~ out one's hand** (*in greeting, for money*) протя|гивать руку (-нуть), (*as signal*) подн|имать руку (-ять), *Aut* вы|ставлять руку (-ставить); **to ~ one's head out of the window** высунуть голову в окно; **to ~ out one's tongue** высунуть/показать язык; *Bot* **to ~ out shoots** пускать ростки

3 (*dislocate*): **to ~ one's knee out** вы|вихивать себе колено (-вихнуть)

4 (*extinguish*): **to ~ out the light** гасить/тушить/выключать свет (по-/по-/выключить); **to ~ out a fire** тушить пожар (за-); **he ~ out his cigarette** он погасил сигарету

5 (*issue*): **to ~ out a rumour** пустить слух; **the government ~ out a statement** правительство выступило с заявлением

6 (*displease*): **he was obviously ~ out about it** он был явно этим недоволен; **nothing ever ~s her out** её невозможно вывести из себя

7 (*inconvenience*): **I don't want to ~ you out** я не хочу вас затруднять; **don't ~ yourself out** не беспокойтесь; **he ~ himself out to help me** он так старался мне помочь

put over *vt see* **put across**

put through *vt Tel*: **to ~ smb through to smb** соедин|ять кого-л с кем-л (-ить)

put together *vt* 1 со|бирать (-брать); **~ the papers together in this drawer** собери/сложи бумаги в э́тот я́щик; ~ **the chairs together in the corner** соста́вь сту́лья в у́гол; **the new boys were ~ together in one dormitory** но́вых ма́льчиков/новичко́в помести́ли вме́сте в одно́й спа́льне; **I hope they don't ~ us together at table** я наде́юсь, нас не поса́дят за стол ря́дом; **he has more sense than all the rest ~ together** у него́ бо́льше здра́вого смы́сла, чем у всех остальны́х вме́сте взя́тых

2 (*assemble*) собира́ть; состав|ля́ть (-́ить); **to ~ together a bookcase** собира́ть кни́жный шкаф; **the programme/exhibition is well ~ together** програ́мма хорошо́ соста́влена, экспози́ция вы́ставки хорошо́ проду́мана

put up *vti vt* **1** (*raise*) под|нима́ть (-ня́ть); **to ~ up sail(s)** подня́ть паруса́ (*pl*); (*in class or to vote*) **he ~ up his hand** он по́днял ру́ку; **to ~ up a notice** вы́весить объявле́ние; **to ~ up a picture/wallpaper** пове́сить карти́ну, окле́|ивать сте́ны обо́ями (-ить); **to ~ up a tent/a building** ста́вить пала́тку, стро́ить зда́ние (*pfs* по-); **to ~ up a memorial to smb** воздвига́ть/ста́вить кому́-л па́мятник; **she ~ up her hair** она́ подобрала́ во́лосы, она́ забрала́ во́лосы вверх; *CQ* **~ them up!** ру́ки вверх!

2 (*increase*): **to ~ up prices** повы|ша́ть це́ны (-́сить)

3 *fig uses*: **the house has been ~ up for sale** дом продаётся; **the painting has been ~ up for sale/auction** карти́на вы́ставлена на прода́жу/на аукцио́не; **the government ~ up the money for the project** прави́тельство финанси́ровало э́тот прое́кт; **my father ~ up the money for my car** оте́ц дал мне де́ньги на маши́ну; **I can ~ you up for the night** я могу́ приюти́ть вас на́ ночь; *CQ* **to ~ smb up to smth** подстрека́ть кого́-л к чему́-л, толка́ть кого́-л на что-л

vi: **we ~ up in a hotel/with my aunt** мы останови́лись в гости́нице/у моёй тётки; **I won't ~ up with that** я э́того не потерплю́, я с э́тим не примирю́сь.

putative *adj* предполага́емый.

putrefy *vi* гнить (с-), раз|лага́ться (-ложи́ться).

putrid *adj* гнило́й.

putty *n* зама́зка.

put-up *adj CQ*: **it's a ~ job** э́то всё подстро́ено.

puzzle *n* (*riddle*) зага́дка, головоло́мка, *also fig*; (*jigsaw*) карти́нка-зага́дка; **a crossword ~** кроссво́рд; **his behaviour is a ~ to me** его́ поведе́ние для меня́ зага́дка/меня́ озада́чивает.

puzzle *vti vt* озада́чи|вать (-ть); **it ~d everyone** э́то всех озада́чило; **I am ~d as to what to do** не зна́ю, что и де́лать; **I'm trying to ~ out his handwriting/why he did it** я пыта́юсь *or* си́люсь разобра́ть его́ по́черк/поня́ть, почему́ он э́то сде́лал

vi: **to ~ over smth** лома́ть го́лову над чем-л (*only in impf*).

puzzler *n CQ* головоло́мка.

pyjama *n usu pl* (~**s**) пижа́ма (*sing*); *attr*: ~ **trousers** пижа́мные штаны́.

Q

quack[1] *vi* (*of duck*) кря́к|ать (*semel* -нуть).

quack[2] *n* (*of doctor*) *pejor* зна́харь (*m*); шарлата́н; *attr*: **a ~ remedy** зна́харское зе́лье.

quadrangle *n Geom* четырёхуго́льник; (*court esp. of Oxford college, abbr* **quad**) двор.

quadrant *n Math* че́тверть кру́га; (*instrument*) квадра́нт.

quadratic *adj*: ~ **equation** квадра́тное уравне́ние.

quadrilateral *adj* четырёхсторо́нний

quadruped *n* четвероно́гое (живо́тное).

quadruple *adj*: ~ **alliance** четырёхсторо́нний сою́з.

quadruplets, *abbr CQ* **quads** *npl* че́тверо близнецо́в (*collect*).

quadruplicate *n*: **in ~** в четырёх экземпля́рах.

quagmire *n* трясина.

quail[1] *n Orn* пе́ре|пел, *f* -пёлка.

quail[2] *vi*: **my heart ~ed** меня́ охвати́л страх; **he ~ed at the very thought of it** он дрожа́л при одно́й мы́сли об э́том.

quaint *adj* причу́дливый; *CQ* чудно́й; **Americans love our ~ old villages** америка́нцам о́чень нра́вится причу́дливая архитекту́ра на́ших ста́рых дереву́шек; **they have ~ customs here** здесь обы́чаи каки́е-то чудны́е; **she's a ~ child** она́ стра́нный ребёнок.

quake *vi* содрог|а́ться (-ну́ться); (*less strong*) трясти́сь, дрожа́ть (*pfs* за-); **the ground ~d** земля́ содрогну́лась; **to ~ with fright** трясти́сь/дрожа́ть от стра́ха.

Quaker *n* ква́кер.

qualification *n* **1** (*particulars asked for on application form, education, degrees, specialized experience; usu pl*) (~**s**) квалифика́ция (*sing*); (*if including previous jobs, general experience*) да́нные; [**NB** квалифика́ция *in singular does not = diploma, certificate, but rather = level of skill*]; **what are the ~s needed for that job?** каки́е да́нные нужны́ для э́той рабо́ты?; **I haven't the necessary ~s for such a job** у меня́ недоста́точная квалифика́ция, что́бы получи́ть э́то ме́сто, у меня́ нет о́пыта рабо́ты в э́той о́бласти; **he has the better ~s** у него́ бо́льше да́нных, его́ квалифика́ция вы́ше; **paper ~s are not enough—you need experience** одного́ дипло́ма ма́ло/недоста́точно—ну́жен о́пыт; **you can't get a decent job without ~s** не име́я дипло́ма, хоро́шей рабо́ты не найти́; **I'm attending evening classes to get some more ~s** я хожу́ на вече́рние ку́рсы, что́бы повы́сить (свою́) квалифика́цию; **she has all the ~s needed to make a good nurse** у неё есть всё, что́бы стать хоро́шей медсестро́й

2 ценз; **there's an age ~ for voters** существу́ет возрастно́й ценз для избира́телей

3 (*reservation*) огово́рка; **they accepted my proposal without ~/with certain ~s** они́ при́няли моё предложе́ние безогово́рочно (*adv*)/с не́которыми огово́рками.

qualified *adj* **1** (высоко)квалифици́рованный (*usu of skilled workmen*); **he is a highly ~ engineer/specialist** он высококвалифици́рованный инжене́р, он о́чень кру́пный специали́ст; **he's a ~ teacher/electrician** он дипломи́рованный педаго́г, он квалифици́рованный электромонтёр; **is he ~ to assemble this mechanism?** доста́точная ли у него́ квалифика́ция, что́бы рабо́тать на сбо́рке э́того механи́зма?; **I'm not ~ to judge** не мне об э́том суди́ть; **are you ~ to vote?** име́ете ли вы пра́во голосова́ть?

2 (*limited*): **the play was only a ~ success** пье́са не име́ла осо́бого успе́ха; **the plan has his ~ approval** он одо́брил э́тот план с не́которыми огово́рками.

qualify *vti vt* **1**: **a year's training will ~ you for the post** поу́читесь год на ку́рсах и смо́жете заня́ть э́ту до́лжность; **that doesn't ~ you to lecture on topography** э́то ещё не даёт вам пра́ва выступа́ть с ле́кциями по топогра́фии

2 (*modify*) уточн|я́ть (-и́ть), огов|а́ривать (-ори́ть); *Gram* определя́ть (*only in impf*); **I'd like to ~ that statement** я хоте́л бы не́сколько уточни́ть э́ту мысль; **he qualified his criticism** он смягчи́л свою́ кри́тику

vi: **to ~ as an engineer/a teacher/a doctor** получ|а́ть дипло́м инжене́ра/педаго́га/врача́ (-и́ть); **I qualified last year** я получи́л дипло́м в про́шлом году́; **this book hardly qualifies as a work of art** э́ту кни́гу вряд ли назовёшь произведе́нием иску́сства; *Sport*: **to ~ for the final** вы́йти в фина́л; **does he ~ as a lightweight?** он выступа́ет в лёгком ве́се?

qualifying *adj Sport* отбо́рочный; **~ rounds** отбо́рочные соревнова́ния, (*for competition*) предвари́тельные выступле́ния.

qualitative *adj* ка́чественный.

quality *n* **1** ка́чество; **she has many good qualities** у неё мно́го хоро́ших ка́честв; *attr Comm*: **high/low ~ goods** това́ры высо́кого/ни́зкого ка́чества; **good/high ~ cloth** добро́тная/высокока́чественная ткань

2 (*property*) сво́йство; **one of the qualities of gold is malleability** одно́ из свойств зо́лота — ко́вкость.

qualm *n* сомне́ние; **I had ~s about leaving her alone** я сомнева́лся, оставля́ть ли её одну́; **he has no ~s about borrowing money from his parents** он без зазре́ния со́вести берёт де́ньги у роди́телей.

quandary *n* недоуме́ние; **he is in a ~** он в недоуме́нии; **help me out of a ~** помоги́те мне, я в не́котором затрудне́нии.

quantitative *adj* коли́чественный.

quantity *n* коли́чество; *Math* величина́; *Ling* долгота́; **in large quantities** в большо́м коли́честве (*sing*); **a known/an unknown ~** да́нная величина́, неизве́стное; **the ~ of a syllable** долгота́ сло́га; *fig* **he is a bit of an unknown ~** неизве́стно, что он за челове́к.

quantum *n Phys* квант; *attr*: **~ theory** ква́нтовая тео́рия.

quarantine *n* каранти́н; **to put smb in ~** посади́ть кого́-л на каранти́н; **to be/keep smb in ~** быть/держа́ть кого́-л на каранти́не.

quarrel *n* ссо́ра; **I had a ~ with my sister** я поссо́рился с сестро́й; **we had a slight ~** у нас была́ небольша́я размо́лвка; **I have no ~ with you/that statement** я ничего́ про́тив вас не име́ю, я не оспа́риваю э́то утвержде́ние; *CQ* **to pick a ~** зате́ять ссо́ру.

quarrel *vi* ссо́риться (по-); (*argue*) спо́рить (по-); **to ~ about/over money** ссо́риться из-за де́нег; **we shouldn't ~ among ourselves** мы не должны́ ссо́риться ме́жду собо́й; **we ~led about which way to go** мы поспо́рили, како́й доро́гой лу́чше е́хать туда́.

quarrelling, (*US*) **quarreling** *n*: **there was constant ~ in their house** у них в до́ме бы́ли постоя́нные ссо́ры.

quarrelsome *adj* сварли́вый; **the children are very ~** де́ти всегда́ ссо́рятся.

quarry *n* карье́р; (*stone quarry*) каменоло́мня.

quarry *vti vt* добы|ва́ть (-́ть); **to ~ marble** добыва́ть мра́мор

vi разраб|а́тывать карье́р (-о́тать).

quart *n* ква́рта (*UK* = 1.14/*US* = 0.95 *litres*).

quarter *n* **1** че́тверть, четвёртая часть; **for a ~ of the price** за че́тверть цены́; **a mile and a ~** ми́ля с че́твертью; **this room is a ~ the size of yours** э́та ко́мната в четы́ре ра́за ме́ньше твое́й; **to divide smth into ~s** дели́ть что-л на четы́ре ча́сти

2 (*of time*): **a ~ of an hour/of a year** че́тверть ча́са, кварта́л го́да; **a ~ to 5/(*US*) of 5** без че́тверти пять; **a ~ past 5/(*US*) after 5** че́тверть шесто́го; **he pays every ~** он пла́тит поквarта́льно; **the moon is in its last ~** луна́ в после́дней че́тверти

3 (*of town*) кварта́л; **the German/business ~** неме́цкий/делово́й кварта́л

4 (*direction*): **from every ~** со всех сторо́н, отовсю́ду; **when I saw her at close ~s** когда́ я уви́дел её вблизи́; **we can only go sailing if the wind's in the right ~** на ло́дке мо́жно ката́ться, то́лько когда́ ду́ет благоприя́тный ве́тер; *fig*: **to apply to the right ~** обраща́ться куда́ на́до; **you're complaining to the wrong ~** вы не туда́ жа́луетесь; **you'll get no sympathy from that ~** вы не найдёте там сочу́вствия; **in the highest ~s** в вы́сших круга́х, в вы́сших сфе́рах.

5 *pl* (**~s**) (*accommodation*): **I'm moving to new ~s soon** я ско́ро переезжа́ю на но́вую кварти́ру; **to live in cramped ~s** жить в тесноте́; *Mil* **winter ~s** зи́мние кварти́ры

6: **to give no ~** не дава́ть поща́ды.

quarter *vt* (*divide*) дели́ть на четы́ре ча́сти (раз-); *Mil*: **to ~ the troops in the town** расквартиро́в|ывать войска́ в го́роде (-а́ть); **to ~ soldiers on smb** ста́вить солда́т на посто́й к кому́-л (по-).

quarter final *n*: **to reach the ~(s)** вы́йти в четвертьфина́л (*sing*).

quarterly *adj* кварта́льный; **a ~ magazine** ежекварта́льный журна́л.

quarterly *adv*: **I pay my rent ~** я вношу́ квартпла́ту поквarта́льно.

quartermaster *n Mil* квартирме́йстер, нача́льник хозя́йственной ча́сти.

quartet *n Mus* кварте́т.

quartz *n* кварц; *attr* ква́рцевый.

quash *vt Law*: **to ~ a verdict** аннули́ровать/отмен|я́ть пригово́р (*impf and pf*/-и́ть).

quaver *n* (*in voice*) дрожа́ние го́лоса; *Mus* восьма́я.

quay *n* при́стань; **alongside the ~** на при́стани.

queasiness *n* тошнота́, дурнота́.

queasy *adj*: **I feel ~** меня́ тошни́т (*impers*), мне ду́рно.

queen *n* короле́ва; (*in folklore*) цари́ца; (*of insects*) ма́тка; *Chess* ферзь, короле́ва; *Cards* да́ма.

queer *n CQ* педера́ст.

queer *adj* стра́нный; **she wears ~ clothes** она́ стра́нно одева́ется; **a ~ person/*CQ* fish** чуда́к; **he is ~ in the head** у него́ не все до́ма/мозги́ набекре́нь; **it's a ~ sort of business** э́то де́ло подозри́тельное.

quell *vt* подав|ля́ть (-и́ть).

quench *vt* (*flames, etc.*) туши́ть, гаси́ть (*pfs* по-); **the fire was ~ed** пожа́р был поту́шен; **to ~ one's thirst** утол|я́ть жа́жду (-и́ть); *fig* **that should ~ his ardour** э́то должно́ охлади́ть его́ пыл.

querulous *adj* капри́зный; раздражи́тельный; **a ~ old man/child** капри́зный/раздражи́тельный стари́к, капри́зный ребёнок.

query *n* (*question*) вопро́с; (*doubt*) сомне́ние; **put a ~ against it in the margin** поста́вь вопро́с про́тив э́того на поля́х; **there is a ~ as to the validity of his claim** есть сомне́ния (*pl*) в обосно́ванности его́ притяза́ний (*pl*); **they've raised a ~ about my travelling expenses** они́ поста́вили под вопро́с пра́вильность су́ммы мои́х путевы́х расхо́дов.

query *vt* сомнева́ться (*impf*), усомни́ться (*pf*); **I ~ his honesty** я сомнева́юсь в его́ че́стности/поря́дочности; **I queried the bill/the instructions** я усомни́лся в пра́вильности счёта/да́нных мне инстру́кций.

question *n* **1** вопро́с; **to ask smb a ~** зада́ть кому́-л вопро́с; **to answer ~s** отвеча́ть на вопро́сы; **a leading ~** наводя́щий вопро́с

2 (*problem*) вопро́с, пробле́ма; **a topical ~** актуа́льный/(*pressing*) злободне́вный вопро́с; **to bring up the ~ of smth** поднима́ть вопро́с о чём-л; **it's the ~ of money which is holding us up** всё упира́ется в де́ньги; **that's the ~** вот в чём вопро́с; **there was no ~ of my being invited** о моём приглаше́нии да́же вопро́са не́ было; **it is out of the ~** об э́том не мо́жет быть и ре́чи; **to call smth in ~** поста́вить что-л под вопро́с; **that is no longer in ~** вопро́с об э́том бо́льше не сто́ит.

question *vt* **1** (*people*) расспр|а́шивать, опр|а́шивать, *Law* допр|а́шивать (*pfs* -оси́ть); **he ~ed me closely about what I had seen** он подро́бно расспроси́л меня́ о том, что я ви́дел; **they were ~ing passers-by** они́ опра́шивали прохо́жих; **to ~ a witness** допроси́ть свиде́теля

2 (*doubt*) сомнева́ться; **to ~ the truth of smth** сомнева́ться в и́стинности чего́-л; **I ~ whether it is worth the expense** я сомнева́юсь, сто́ит ли э́то таки́х затра́т (*pl*).

questionable *adj* сомни́тельный; **it is ~ whether he has enough experience** весьма́ сомни́тельно, что́бы у него́ бы́ло доста́точно о́пыта; **that remark is in ~ taste** э́то замеча́ние весьма́ сомни́тельного сво́йства.

questioning *n*: **the police called them in for ~** их вызыва́ли в поли́цию на допро́с.

question mark *n* вопроси́тельный знак.

questionnaire *n* (*official form*) анке́та; (*for polls, etc.*) вопро́сник.

queue *n* о́чередь; **a ~ for apples** о́чередь за я́блоками; **I joined/jumped the ~** я встал в о́чередь, я прошёл/*CQ* влез без о́череди; **I lost my place in the ~** я потеря́л о́чередь.

queue *vi* стоя́ть в о́череди (*impf*).

quibble *n* софи́зм, увёртка.

quibble *vi*: **don't ~** не спорь из-за пустяко́в; **it's not worth quibbling about** об э́том не сто́ит спо́рить.

quick *n*: **to bite one's nails to the ~** грызть но́гти до кро́ви; *fig* **to cut smb to the ~** заде́ть кого́-л за живо́е.

quick *adj* **1** (*fast*) бы́стрый; **at a ~ pace** бы́стрым ша́гом; **~ service** бы́строе обслу́живание; **be ~ about it!** побыстре́е!; **~ as a flash** молниено́сно; **three times in ~ succession** три ра́за подря́д; *CQ* **let's have a ~ one** (*drink*) дава́й пропу́стим по ма́ленькой

2 *fig uses*: **a ~ eye/ear** зо́ркий глаз, то́нкий слух; **he has a ~ wit** он остроу́мный челове́к; **she is ~ with her hands** у неё прово́рные ру́ки; **~ to anger/to take offence** вспы́льчивый, оби́дчивый; **you are too ~ for me** (*in speech*) вы говори́те сли́шком бы́стро, (*clever*) *CQ* ишь ты, како́й бы́стрый/шу́стрый; **he was too ~ for me and got away** он был куда́ прово́рнее меня́ и убежа́л; *CQ* **he's ~ off the mark** он лёгок на подъём.

quick-acting *adj* быстроде́йствующий.

quicken *vti* ускор|я́ть(ся) (-ить(ся)); **we ~ed our pace** мы уско́рили шаг; **the pace ~ed** темп уско́рился.

quickie *n CQ*: **there is time for a ~ before you go** (*drink*) мы успе́ем вы́пить по рю́мочке до ва́шего ухо́да.

quicklime *n* негашёная и́звесть.

quickly *adv* бы́стро, ско́ро; **be as ~ as you can** приходи́ как мо́жно скоре́е.

quickness *n* быстрота́; *fig* **he's remarkable for his ~ of mind** он отлича́ется замеча́тельной жи́востью ума́.

quicksand *n* зыбу́чий песо́к, плыву́н.

quicksilver *n* ртуть; *attr* рту́тный.

quickstep *n* (*dance*) куик-сте́п; *Mil* ско́рый шаг.

quick-tempered *adj* вспы́льчивый.

quick-witted *adj* сообрази́тельный, смышлёный; (*witty*) остроу́мный.

quid *n CQ*: **can you lend me a ~?/20 ~?** (*collect*) ты мо́жешь одолжи́ть мне фунт?/два́дцать фу́нтов?

quiet *n* (*silence*) тишина́; (*peace*) поко́й, споко́йствие; **I'm longing for some peace and ~** мне так хо́чется тишины́ и поко́я; **the ~ of the night/countryside** ночно́й поко́й, безмяте́жность се́льского пейза́жа; *CQ* **he did it on the ~** он сде́лал э́то тайко́м.

quiet *adj* **1** (*silent*) ти́хий; (*calm*) споко́йный; (*of child, animal = well-behaved*) сми́рный; **a ~ town/temperament** ти́хий *or* споко́йный городо́к/нрав; **a ~ corner** ти́хий уголо́к; **a ~ horse** сми́рная ло́шадь; **anything for a ~ life!** всё отда́л бы, что́бы пожи́ть споко́йно!; **everything is ~ after midnight** всё затиха́ет/замира́ет по́сле полу́ночи; **(be) ~!** ти́хо!, замолчи́те!, не шуми́те!; **isn't it ~?** кака́я тишина́!; **she dresses in ~ colours** она́ но́сит споко́йные цвета́; **a ~ wedding** скро́мная сва́дьба; **with ~ irony** с мя́гкой иро́нией; **business is ~** в дела́х зати́шье, дела́ иду́т ни ша́тко ни ва́лко

2 (*secret*): **they kept ~ about it** они́ умолча́ли об э́том; **they paid £100 to keep him ~** они́ да́ли ему́ сто фу́нтов, что́бы он молча́л.

quiet, quieten *vti vt*: **to ~ a child** успок|а́ивать/унима́ть ребёнка (-о́ить/уня́ть); **he ~ed our fears** он рассе́ял на́ши опасе́ния

vi: **the child eventually ~ed down** в конце́ концо́в ребёнок успоко́ился/угомони́лся; **his anger ~ed down** его́ гнев ути́х; **the wind ~ed down** ве́тер уня́лся/ути́х.

quietly *adv* ти́хо, споко́йно; сми́рно; **he entered ~** он ти́хо вошёл; **sit ~!** сиди́ споко́йно!/сми́рно!; **she dresses ~** она́ одева́ется про́сто; **we dined ~** мы споко́йно пообе́дали.

quill *n* (*feather*) пти́чье перо́; (*pen*) перо́; (*of porcupine*) игла́.

quilt *n* (*UK*) пери́нка; (*of duvet size*) стёганое одея́ло.

quilted *adj* стёганый; **~ jacket** *CQ* стёганка.

quince *n* (*fruit and tree*) айва́; *attr* айво́вый.

quincentenary *n* пятисотле́тие.

quinine *n* хини́н.

quinsy *n* анги́на.

quintet *n Mus*: **a piano ~** фортепья́нный квинте́т.

quintuple *adj* (*5-fold*) пятикра́тный; (*of 5 parts*) из пяти́ часте́й.

quintuplets, *abbr CQ* **quins** *npl* пя́теро близнецо́в (*collect*).

quip *n* остро́та.

quirk *n* причу́да; **he has his ~s** у него́ есть свои́ причу́ды/*CQ* бзи́ки; **by some ~ of fate** по при́хоти судьбы́.

quit *adj*: **we are well ~ of him** хорошо́, что мы от него́ отде́лались.

quit *vti vt* (*leave*) остав|ля́ть (-́ить); поки|да́ть (-́нуть); (*stop*) кон|ча́ть (-́чить), прекра|ща́ть (-ти́ть); **he ~ted Paris/his job** он поки́нул Пари́ж, он бро́сил рабо́ту *or* он ушёл с рабо́ты; **we ~ work at 6** мы ухо́дим с рабо́ты в шесть; **~ fooling!** переста́нь дура́читься!, конча́й дурака́ валя́ть!

vi: **they have given us notice to ~** нас предупреди́ли, что́бы мы съе́хали с кварти́ры.

quite *adv* **1** (*completely*) совсе́м, соверше́нно; (*fully*) вполне́; **~ new** совсе́м но́вый; **~ right!** соверше́нно ве́рно!; **I ~ agree** я вполне́ согла́сен; **that is ~ enough** э́того вполне́ доста́точно; **that's ~ another matter** э́то совсе́м друго́е де́ло; **~ so!** вот и́менно!, то́чно!; **I don't ~ know** я то́чно не зна́ю, я не совсе́м уве́рен; **I'm ~ sure** я вполне́ уве́рен; **I'm sorry I was cross.—That's ~ all right** Прости́те, я погорячи́лся.—Ничего́, пустяки́

2 (*rather*) дово́льно: **it's ~ late** уже́ дово́льно по́здно

3 (*emphatic*): **he's ~ a lad!** вот э́то па́рень!; **that was ~ a party!** вот э́то был ве́чер!

quits *predic adj*: **now we're ~ with him** тепе́рь мы с ним квиты/в расчёте.

quiver *vi* дрожа́ть (за-); **he was ~ing with indignation** он весь дрожа́л от негодова́ния.

quixotic *adj* донкихо́тский.

quiz *n* виктори́на; *Radio, TV* **~ program(me)** радиовиктори́на, телевиктори́на.

quiz *vt* рассп р|а́шивать (-оси́ть); **I ~zed him about his work** я расспроси́л его́ о его́ рабо́те.

quizzical *adj*: **a ~ look** насме́шливый взгляд.

quoit *n* мета́тельное кольцо́; **to play ~s** мета́ть ко́льца.

quorum *n* кво́рум; **have we a ~?** есть ли кво́рум?; **what number constitutes a ~?** ско́лько челове́к составля́ют кво́рум?

quota *n* **1** квота; **the ~ of imports** и́мпортная кво́та

2 (*share*) но́рма; **to fulfil one's ~** выполня́ть но́рму.

quotation *n* цита́та; *Comm* цена́; (*Stock Exchange*) котиро́вка, курс; **a ~ from Byron** цита́та из Ба́йрона; **can you give me a ~ for painting the house?** вы мне не ска́жете, ско́лько сто́ит покра́сить дом?

quotation marks *npl* кавы́чки; **put that phrase in ~** поста́вь э́ту фра́зу в кавы́чки.

quote *n* цита́та: *pl* (**~s**) (*in punctuation*) кавы́чки; **start of ~s** откро́йте кавы́чки; **end of ~s** закро́йте кавы́чки.

quote *vti vt* цити́ровать (про-); *Comm* назна|ча́ть це́ну (-́чить); (*Stock Exchange*) коти́ровать (*impf and pf*); **to ~ Shakespeare** цити́ровать Шекспи́ра; **he ~d the example of Napoleon** он привёл в приме́р Наполео́на; **in reply please ~ the reference number** в отве́те укажи́те, пожа́луйста, спра́вочный но́мер; **he ~d me a price for doing up my flat** он сказа́л, ско́лько бу́дет сто́ить ремо́нт мое́й кварти́ры; **tobacco shares are ~d at £10** курс таба́чных а́кций—де́сять фу́нтов

vi: **to ~ from Pushkin** цити́ровать Пу́шкина.

quotient *n* **1** *Math* ча́стное

2: **intelligence ~,** *abbr* **I. Q.** коэффицие́нт у́мственного разви́тия.

R

rabbit *n* кро́лик; *attr*: ~ **burrow/hutch** кро́личья нора́, крольча́тник.

rabble *n* сброд, чернь.

rabid *adj* бе́шеный, взбеси́вшийся.

rabies *n Med* бе́шенство.

race[1] *n* **1** *Sport* (*running*) забе́г; (*swimming*) заплы́в; (*on skis, in boats, Aut*) го́нка, го́нки (*pl*); **horse** ~(**s**) ска́чки (*pl*); **he's in for the 100 metres** ~ он уча́ствует в бе́ге/в заплы́ве на сто ме́тров; **relay** ~ эстафе́та; **a bicycle** ~ велосипе́дные го́нки; **a boat** (*rowing*)/**dinghy** (*sailing*) ~ гребны́е/ло́дочные го́нки; **I saw him at the** ~**s** я его́ ви́дел на го́нках/на ска́чках; *attr*: **a** ~ **meeting** ска́чки

2 *fig* го́нка; **the arms** ~ го́нка вооруже́ний; **we had a** ~ **to get finished/for the train** мы в спе́шке зака́нчивали рабо́ту, мы бежа́ли бего́м, что́бы успе́ть на по́езд

3 (*swift current*) бы́строе тече́ние.

race[1] *vti vt*: **I'm racing my horse in the Derby/at Ascot** я записа́л мою́ ло́шадь для уча́стия в де́рби/в ска́чках в Э́скоте; **I'll** ~ **you home** дава́й побежи́м наперегонки́ (*adv*) до до́ма; **the car was racing the train** маши́на шла наперегонки́ (*adv*) с по́ездом; *Aut* **to** ~ **the engine** увели́чи|вать оборо́ты (-ть)

vi **1** (*in contest*): **I used to** ~ **a lot** я ча́сто уча́ствовал в забе́гах (*athletics*)/в го́нках (*Aut, etc.*)/в ска́чках (*on horse*)

2 (*rush*) мча́ться (по-); **we** ~**d home/to the scene of the accident** мы помча́лись домо́й, мы побежа́ли к ме́сту происше́ствия.

race[2] *n* (*in reference to colour of skin*) ра́са; (*tribe*) род, пле́мя; **the human** ~ род челове́ческий; **the different African** ~**s** разли́чные африка́нские племена́; *attr* ра́совый.

racecourse *n* ипподро́м.

racehorse *n* скакова́я ло́шадь, скаку́н.

racetrack *n* (*for people*) бегова́я доро́жка; (*for cars*) трек, (*for horses*) скакова́я диста́нция.

racialist *n* раси́ст; *attr* раси́стский.

racing *n*: **motor** ~ автомоби́льные го́нки (*pl*); *attr*: **a** ~ **car/yacht/driver** го́ночный автомоби́ль, го́ночная я́хта, го́нщик.

rack[1] *n* (*for coats, hats*) ве́шалка; (*for drying dishes*) суши́лка; (*set of shelves for tools, wine*) стелла́ж; (*for hay, etc.*) корму́шка; **luggage** ~ бага́жная по́лка.

rack[2] *vt*: **he was** ~**ed by remorse/pain** его́ му́чило раска́яние, его́ му́чила боль; **he** ~**ed his brains over the problem** он лома́л го́лову над э́той пробле́мой.

rack[3] *n*: **to go to** ~ **and ruin** (*of building*) ветша́ть, (*of country*) идти́ к разоре́нию (*financially*).

racket[1] *n Sport* раке́тка.

racket[2] *n* **1** шум; (*of voices*) *CQ* гам, галдёж; **to make a terrible** ~ подня́ть стра́шный шум; **the** ~ **of city life** су́толока городско́й жи́зни

2 *CQ* (*swindle*) моше́нничество; (*in business*) афе́ра; **it's a** ~! э́то моше́нничество!, э́то (чи́стый) грабёж!, э́то про́сто афе́ра!; **the drug** ~ торго́вля нарко́тиками.

racketeer *n* афери́ст, моше́нник.

raconteur *n* (уме́лый) расска́зчик.

racy *adj*: **a** ~ **style/story** колори́тная мане́ра, пика́нтная исто́рия.

radar *n* рада́р, радиолока́тор: *attr*: ~ **operator** опера́тор радиолока́тора; ~ **screen** рада́рный экра́н; ~ **station** радиолокацио́нная ста́нция.

radiant *adj* сия́ющий, *also fig*; (*of colour*) я́ркий; **a** ~ **smile** сия́ющая улы́бка; **his face was** ~ **with happiness** его́ лицо́ сия́ло от сча́стья; **the bride was** ~ неве́ста вся свети́лась; *Phys* ~ **heat** лучи́стое тепло́.

radiate *vti vt* излуча́ть (*impf*), *also fig*; **to** ~ **light/heat/health/enthusiasm** излуча́ть свет/тепло́/здоро́вье, зара́жать энтузиа́змом

vi излуча́ться; **heat** ~**s from the stove** пе́чка даёт тепло́; *fig* **streets** ~ **from the square** у́лицы радиа́льно расхо́дятся от пло́щади.

radiation *n* (*of light, heat*) излуче́ние; (*radioactivity*) радиа́ция, радиоакти́вное излуче́ние; **atomic/solar** ~ я́дерное излуче́ние, со́лнечная радиа́ция; *attr*: ~ **sickness** лучева́я боле́знь.

radiator *n* (*for heating*) батаре́я, радиа́тор; *Aut* радиа́тор.

radical *n Polit* радика́л; *Math* ко́рень числа́.

radical *adj* радика́льный.

radio *n* ра́дио (*indecl*); (*set*) (радио)приёмник; **by** ~, **on the** ~ по ра́дио.

radio *vti*: **to** ~ **a message** переда|ва́ть сообще́ние по ра́дио (-́ть); **to** ~ **for help** ради́ровать о по́мощи (*impf and pf*).

radioactive *adj* радиоакти́вный.

radiogram *n* (*message*) радиогра́мма; (*UK*) радио́ла, прои́грыватель (*m*).

radiograph *n* рентгеногра́мма.

radiologist *n* радио́лог, рентгено́лог.

radio operator *n* ради́ст.

radio station *n* радиоста́нция.

radio therapy *n* радиотерапи́я, рентгенотерапи́я.

radish *n* реди́ска; *pl* (~**es**) реди́с (*collect*).

radium *n* ра́дий; *attr* ра́диевый.

radius *n Math* ра́диус; **within a** ~ **of** в ра́диусе + *G*.

raffle *n* (вещева́я) лотере́я; **to hold a** ~ провести́ лотере́ю.

raffle *vt*: **to** ~ **a doll** разы́гр|ывать ку́клу в лотере́е (-а́ть).

raft *n* плот.

rafter *n* стропи́ло.

rag[1] *n* **1** тря́пка, *also fig*; *CQ* **what's that** ~ **you're wearing?** что э́то за тря́пку ты наце́пила?; **I feel like a wet** ~ я чу́вствую себя́ как вы́жатый лимо́н; **he/his jacket was in** ~**s** он был в лохмо́тьях *or* в отре́пьях, его́ пиджа́к обтрепа́лся; *CQ* **she was in her glad** ~**s** она́ была́ в своём лу́чшем наря́де; *attr*: ~ **doll** тряпи́чная ку́кла

2 (*newspaper*) *CQ pejor* газетёнка.

rag[2] *n CQ*: **a student** ~ студе́нческие проде́лки (*pl*); **for a** ~ для заба́вы.

rag[2] *vt CQ* (*tease*) дразни́ть (*impf*); (*by practical joke*) разы́гр|ывать (-а́ть); **they ~ged him about his accent** они́ подшу́чивали над его́ акце́нтом.

ragamuffin *n* обо́рвыш, оборва́нец.

rage *n* (*anger*) гнев, я́рость, бе́шенство; **he was in a blind ~** он был в слепо́й я́рости; **to be in a ~ about smth** быть в я́рости/в бе́шенстве от чего́-л, неи́стовствовать по по́воду чего́-л; *fig CQ* **jeans are all the ~** все помеша́лись на джи́нсах.

rage *vi* (*of fire, sea, wind*; *fig of person*) бушева́ть, (*of storm, person*) неи́стовствовать, (*of famine, disease*) свире́пствовать (*impfs*); **he ~d and fumed** он разбушева́лся; **to ~ against smb** разозли́ться на кого́-л.

ragged *adj* (*of clothes*) обо́рванный, потрёпанный, *CQ* дра́ный, изо́дранный; **a ~ tramp/urchin** обо́рванный бродя́га, ма́ленький обо́рвыш; **a ~ edge/coastline** зазу́бренный край, изре́занные берега́ (*pl*).

raging *adj*: **a ~ sea/storm** бушу́ющее мо́ре, неи́стовая бу́ря.

raglan *adj*: **a ~ coat/sleeve** пальто́/рука́в регла́н.

ragout *n* рагу́ (*indecl*).

raid *n Mil* рейд, налёт; **an air/bank ~** возду́шный налёт, налёт на банк; **a police ~** полице́йская обла́ва.

raid *vt Mil, etc.* соверш|а́ть рейд/налёт (-и́ть); **the police ~ed the casino** поли́ция нагря́нула в казино́.

rail[1] *n* **1** (*handrail*) по́ручень (*m*), пери́ла (*pl*); **towel ~** ве́шалка для полоте́нца

2 *Rail* рельс; **to go off the ~s** сойти́ с ре́льсов, *fig* сби́ться с пути́; **to send by ~** отправля́ть по желе́зной доро́ге.

rail[2] *vi*: **to ~ against** *or* **at smb/smth** руга́ть *or* брани́ть кого́-л/что-л (*impfs*).

railing *n often pl* (*on stairs, bridge, etc.*) пери́ла (*pl*); (*fence*) огра́да; (*of wrought iron*) решётка.

railway *n* желе́зная доро́га; *attr*: **~ carriage/line** железнодоро́жный ваго́н/путь; **~ station/timetable** (*large*) вокза́л *or* (*usu of smaller, intermediate stations*) железнодоро́жная ста́нция, расписа́ние поездо́в.

rain *n* дождь (*m*); **in the ~** в дождь, под дождём; **if the ~ keeps off** е́сли не бу́дет дождя́; **come ~ or shine, we'll be there** дождь и́ли хоро́шая пого́да, а мы всё равно́ придём: **we usually get 40 cm of ~ a year** у нас обы́чно выпада́ет со́рок сантиме́тров годовы́х оса́дков; *attr* дождево́й.

rain *vti vt*: **it is ~ing cats and dogs/buckets** дождь льёт как из ведра́; *fig* **to ~ blows/gifts on smb** осып|а́ть кого́-л уда́рами, засып|а́ть кого́-л пода́рками (*pfs* ́-ать)

vi: **it is ~ing** идёт дождь; **it ~ed a lot last summer** про́шлым ле́том бы́ло мно́го дожде́й (*pl*); *fig*: **bombs ~ed down on the town** бо́мбы сы́пались на го́род; **it never ~s but it pours** беда́ никогда́ не прихо́дит одна́.

rainbow *n* ра́дуга.

raincoat *n* дождеви́к.

rainfall *n* оса́дки (*pl*).

rainstorm *n* ли́вень (*m*); **there was a sudden ~** хлы́нул ли́вень.

rainy *adj* дождли́вый; **the ~ season** перио́д/сезо́н дожде́й; *fig* **for/against a ~ day** на чёрный день.

raise *vt* **1** (*lift*) под|нима́ть, (*slightly*) приподнима́ть (*pfs* -ня́ть); **to ~ one's hand/hat to smb** подня́ть ру́ку,/шля́пу, приве́тствуя кого́-л; **to ~ one's glass to smb** подня́ть бока́л за кого́-л; **he ~d the blinds a little** он приподня́л жалюзи́; **he ~d himself on his elbow** он приподня́лся на ло́кте; **to ~ a flag/a cloud of dust** подня́ть флаг/о́блако пы́ли: *fig*: **he ~d the people to rebellion** он по́днял наро́д на восста́ние; **to ~ smb to power** привести́ кого́-л к вла́сти (*usu pf*); **to ~ smb's hopes** обнадёжи|вать кого́-л (-ть); **eyebrows were ~d at the proposal** предложе́ние бы́ло встре́чено с не́которым удивле́нием (*surprise*)/ неодобре́нием (*disapproval*)

2 (*erect*): **they ~d statue to him** они́ воздви́гли ему́ па́мятник

3 (*increase*) повы|ша́ть (́-сить); **to ~ prices/production/smb's salary/standards** повы́сить це́ны/производи́тельность/чью-л зарпла́ту/станда́рты; **he ~d his voice** он повы́сил го́лос

4 (*rear*): **to ~ children/sheep/vegetables** расти́ть дете́й (*impf*), раз|води́ть ове́ц (-вести́), выра́щивать о́вощи (*usu impf*); **I was ~d in the country** я вы́рос в дере́вне

5 (*produce*): **to ~ doubts/a laugh** вы|зыва́ть сомне́ния/смех (́-звать); **can't you ~ a smile?** хоть улыбну́лся бы!

6 (*bring up for discussion*): **to ~ a question/problem/objections** поднима́ть вопро́с/пробле́му, вы|двига́ть возраже́ния (́-двинуть)

7 (*collect*): **to ~ taxes** взима́ть нало́ги (*impf*); **to ~ a loan** стара́ться получи́ть ссу́ду/заём; **to ~ money** со|бира́ть/добы|ва́ть де́ньги (-бра́ть/́-ть); **to ~ an army** собра́ть а́рмию.

raisin *n* изю́минка; *pl* изю́м (*collect*).

rake[1] *n* гра́бли (*no sing*); *fig* **as thin as a ~** худо́й как ще́пка.

rake[1] *vti vt* грести́ (*impf*) *and compounds*; **to ~ hay/dead leaves** сгре|ба́ть се́но/сухи́е ли́стья (-сти́); **to ~ the fire/the ashes** вы|греба́ть золу́ (́-грести); **he ~d the soil even** он заровня́л по́чву гра́блями; **the croupier ~d in the money** крупье́ сгрёб лопа́точкой де́ньги; *fig*: **they managed to ~ together a team** им всё-таки удало́сь сколоти́ть кома́нду; **he ~d together enough money to buy a bike** он наскрёб де́нег на велосипе́д; **to ~ up old memories** вороши́ть ста́рое; **why did you have to ~ up that incident?** заче́м тебе́ ну́жно бы́ло вспомина́ть э́тот слу́чай?; *CQ*: **he's raking it in** он гребёт де́ньги лопа́той; **he ~s in £100 on every deal** он загреба́ет по сто фу́нтов на ка́ждой сде́лке

vi ры́ться (по-); **I'll ~ around in the attic/through my drawers** я поро́юсь на чердаке́/в я́щиках.

rake[2] *n* (*person*) пове́са (*m*).

rake-off *n CQ*: **what ~ do I get?** ско́лько придётся на мою́ до́лю?; **he gets a ~ of 10% on every deal** он зараба́тывает де́сять проце́нтов на ка́ждой сде́лке.

rally *n* сбор; (*of scouts, etc.*) слёт; *Polit* ми́тинг; *Aut* авторалли (*indecl*).

rally *vti vt* со|бира́ть (-бра́ть); **he rallied his troops for a fresh attack** он собра́л войска́ для но́вого наступле́ния; **he rallied his party** он сплоти́л свою́ па́ртию (*usu pf*)

vi **1: they rallied round him/to his support** они́ сплоти́лись вокру́г него́; **if everyone rallies round we'll soon finish** е́сли все вме́сте возьму́тся за де́ло, мы ско́ро зако́нчим

2 (*get stronger*): **he rallied for a few days, but then relapsed** не́сколько дней ему́ бы́ло лу́чше, но пото́м состоя́ние опя́ть уху́дшилось; *Comm* **the market rallied** торго́вля оживи́лась.

ram *n* бара́н; *Astron* Ове́н.

ram *vt* (*push down*) заби|ва́ть (-́ть); **to ~ in a pile/a charge into a gun** заби́ть сва́ю/заря́д в пу́шку; *CQ* **he ~med his hat on/his things into a case** он нахлобу́чил шля́пу, он запихну́л ве́щи в чемода́н; **the lorry ~med the bus** грузови́к вре́зался в авто́бус; *fig CQ*: **I tried to ~ the point home/some sense into him** я стара́лся вдолби́ть ему́ э́то в го́лову/вразуми́ть его́; **he's always ~ming it down my throat/into my head that...** он ве́чно втолко́вывает мне,/вдалбливает мне в го́лову, что...

ramble *vi*: **to ~ through the woods** броди́ть по ле́су; **I'm going rambling tomorrow** за́втра я собира́юсь за́ город поброди́ть; *fig* **he ~d on for an hour** он це́лый час болта́л.

rambling *adj* (*of climbing plants*) вью́щийся; **a ~ old town** ста́рый беспоря́дочно раски́нувшийся го́род; **~ buildings** разбро́санные в беспоря́дке дома́; **he made a long ~ speech** он вы́ступил с дли́нной запу́танной ре́чью.

ramp *n* (*for wheelchairs, etc.*) скат, укло́н; (*on roads*) подъём; (*into garage*) накло́нный въезд. па́ндус.

rampage *vi*: **the children are rampaging all over the house** де́ти но́сятся по всему́ до́му.

rampant *adj* (*of plants*) бу́йный, пы́шный; **flu is ~ just now** сейча́с свире́пствует грипп.

ramshackle *adj* ве́тхий, разби́тый.

ranch *n* (*US*) ра́нчо (*indecl*).

rancid *adj*: **to go ~** проту́хнуть; **the butter tastes/smells ~** у ма́сла прого́рклый вкус, ма́сло проту́хло.

rancorous *adj* зло́бный, озло́бленный.

random *n*: **to choose smth at ~** вы́брать что-л наобу́м/науга́д/науда́чу; **he hit out at ~** он бил куда́ придётся.

random *adj* вы́бранный науга́д; случа́йный; **a ~ sample of the population** вы́бранная науга́д гру́ппа населе́ния; **~ remarks** случа́йные замеча́ния; **he fired a ~ shot** он вы́стрелил науга́д; **I chose a ~ selection of records** я вы́брал науга́д не́сколько пласти́нок, я взял пе́рвые попа́вшиеся пласти́нки.

range *n* **1** (*row*) ряд; **a mountain ~** го́рный хребе́т, го́рная цепь

2 (*US*) (*area of pasture*) па́стбища (*pl*)

3 *Biol* (*of animal*) райо́н обита́ния; (*of plant*) о́бласть распростране́ния

4: artillery ~ полиго́н; **rifle ~** (*in open*) стре́льбище, (*covered, or at fair*) тир

5 (*distance attainable*): **~ of vision** по́ле зре́ния; **out of ~ of hearing/of our weapons** вне преде́лов слы́шимости, вне ра́диуса де́йствия на́ших ору́дий; **the ~ of a plane/missile** да́льность полёта самолёта/снаря́да; **this gun has a ~ of 5 km** прице́льная да́льность э́той пу́шки—пять киломе́тров; **at a ~ of 3 km** на расстоя́нии трёх киломе́тров; **at close/point-blank ~** на бли́зком расстоя́нии, в упо́р; **wait till they come within ~** подпусти́ их на расстоя́ние вы́стрела; *fig* **economics is outside my ~** эконо́мика не по мое́й ча́сти

6 (*extent, compass*) диапазо́н, *also Mus*; *Radio* **frequency ~** часто́тный диапазо́н; **a wide ~ of goods** большо́й вы́бор/ассортиме́нт това́ров; **we have the full ~ of sizes in a wide ~ of prices** у нас име́ются все разме́ры по любо́й цене́; **a new ~ of cars** но́вая се́рия маши́н; **a wide ~ of colours** широ́кая цветова́я га́мма; **he has a wide ~ of interests/knowledge** круг его́ интере́сов о́чень широ́к, у него́ широ́кий диапазо́н зна́ний; **a wide ~ of activities** широ́кий разма́х де́ятельности; **we covered a wide ~ of subjects** мы охвати́ли весь круг вопро́сов

7 (*for cooking*) ку́хонная плита́.

range *vti vt* **1** (*arrange*) распо|лага́ть (-ложи́ть); **spectators were ~d along the route** зри́тели расположи́лись вдоль пути́ сле́дования; **two divisions were ~d against us** про́тив нас вы́ставлены две диви́зии; **finally he ~d himself on our side** в конце́ концо́в он примкну́л к нам

2 (*roam over*): **to ~ the hills** броди́ть по гора́м (*impf*); **his eyes ~d the horizon** он обвёл глаза́ми горизо́нт

vi **1** (*extend*): **fields ~ for miles along the river** поля́ простира́ются на ми́ли вдоль реки́; **the children ~ in age from 3 to 10** де́ти в во́зрасте от трёх до десяти́ лет; **the price of coats ~s from £20 to £200** це́ны на пальто́ в преде́лах от двадцати́ фу́нтов до двухсо́т; **temperature ~s from —5° to —30°** температу́ра коле́блется от ми́нус пяти́ гра́дусов до ми́нус тридцати́; **his research ~s over a wide area** его́ иссле́дования охва́тывают широ́кую о́бласть; **his interests ~ from beekeeping to stamp collecting** его́ интере́сы о́чень разнообра́зны—от пчелово́дства до коллекциони́рования ма́рок

2 (*roam over*): **troops ~d over the whole area** войска́ рассредото́чились по всему́ райо́ну; **he allowed his imagination to ~ freely** он дал во́лю (своему́) воображе́нию.

rank[1] *n* **1** (*row*) ряд; *Mil* шере́нга; *Mil* (**~s**) строй (*sing*); **in the first ~s** в пе́рвых ряда́х; **a taxi ~** стоя́нка такси́; **he joined our ~s** он примкну́л к на́шим ряда́м; **in serried ~s** в со́мкнутом строю́ (*sing*), со́мкнутыми ряда́ми; **to break ~** вы́йти из строя

2 *Mil* (*soldiers*): **the ~s, the ~ and file, other ~s** рядовой состав; **to reduce smb to the ~s** разжаловать кого-л в рядовые; *attr fig*: **~ and file members** рядовые члены

3 (*status*) *Mil* звание, чин, ранг, *also fig*; **the highest in ~** самый высокий по званию/по чину; **of high ~** высокого ранга; **the ~ of captain** капитанский чин, звание капитана; **a writer of the first ~** первоклассный писатель.

rank[1] *vti vt*: **I ~ Tolstoy/Tolstoy is ~ed among the world's greatest writers** я считаю Толстого/Толстой считается одним из величайших писателей мира; **I ~ Tolstoy with/higher than Pushkin** я ставлю Толстого в один ряд с Пушкиным/выше Пушкина

vi: **a general ~s above a major** генерал по званию выше майора; **as a playwright he ~s second to none** как драматургу ему нет равных.

rank[2] *adj* **1** *Bot* буйный; **~ vegetation** буйная растительность; **a garden ~ with weeds** сад, заросший сорняками

2 (*of smell*) прогорклый; **~ tobacco** вонючая махорка

3 *fig*: **~ injustice/cowardice/treason** вопиющая несправедливость, подлая трусость, гнусная измена.

rankle *vt*: **the insult still ~d in his mind** его всё ещё жгло воспоминание об этом оскорблении.

ransack *vt* **1** (*search*) рыться в + *P* (*impf*); шарить в + *P* (*impf*), обшар|ивать (-ить); **to ~ a drawer/one's pockets** рыться в ящике, шарить в карманах; **he ~ed every corner of the room** он обшарил все углы в комнате; **he ~ed the cupboard** он перерыл всё в шкафу

2 (*rob*): **they ~ed the house** они разграбили дом (*pf*).

ransom *n* выкуп; **to hold smb to ~** держать кого-л в заложниках, требовать выкуп за кого-л.

rant *vi* (*of orator*) разглагольствовать (*impf*); **to ~ and rave** рвать и метать.

rap *n* стук; **a ~ on the door** стук в дверь; *CQ*: **I had to take the ~ for her mistake** мне пришлось отвечать за её ошибку; **I don't care a ~** мне наплевать.

rap *vti vt*: **to ~ the table** стучать по столу (по-, *semel* стукнуть); **to ~ smb over the knuckles** дать кому-л по рукам/*fig* нагоняй

vi: **to ~ at the door** стучать в дверь.

rapacious *adj* (*greedy*) жадный; (*predatory*) хищный.

rape *vt* насиловать (из-).

rapid *n usu pl* быстрина, речной порог.

rapid *adj* быстрый; **~ movements** быстрые движения; **a ~ descent** крутой спуск; *Mil* **~ fire** беглый огонь.

rapport *n*: **he soon established a ~ with his pupils** между ним и учениками быстро возникло взаимопонимание.

rapture *n* восторг, восхищение; **to be in ~s over/about smth** быть в восторге от чего-л; **to go into ~s over/about smth** восторгаться/восхищаться чем-л, прийти в восторг от чего-л.

rapturous *adj* восторженный, восхищённый.

rare[1] *adj* **1** редкий; редкостный; (*of air*) разрежённый; **a ~ book** редкая книга; **an object of ~ beauty** вещь редкостной красоты; **this plant is ~ in Scotland** это растение редко встречается в Шотландии; **at ~ intervals** редко.

rare[2] *adj*: **~ meat** мясо с кровью.

rascal *n* негодяй, плут; (*child*) плутишка.

rash[1] *n Med* сыпь; **he came out in a ~** у него выступила сыпь.

rash[2] *adj* (*ill-considered*) необдуманный; (*hasty*) опрометчивый; **a ~ promise** опрометчивое обещание; **a ~ decision** опрометчивое/необдуманное решение; **a ~ judgement** поспешное суждение; **that was ~ of you** вы поступили опрометчиво.

rasher *n*: **a ~ of bacon** ломтик бекона.

raspberry *n* малина (*collect*).

raspberry bush, raspberry cane *n* куст малины; *pl* малинник (*collect*).

rasping *adj*: **a ~ voice** скрипучий голос; **a ~ sound** скрежещущий звук.

rat *n* крыса, *also fig pejor*; *fig pejor* доносчик, *CQ* стукач; *fig* **he smelt a ~** он почуял неладное; *CQ* **~s!** ерунда!; *attr*: **~ poison** крысиный яд; *fig* **the ~ race** погоня за богатством/за чинами.

rat *vi*: **to ~ on smb** под|водить кого-л (-вести).

ratcatcher *n* крысолов.

rate *n* **1** (*ratio, proportion*) норма; размер; **~ of output/profit** норма выработки/прибыли; **discount at a ~ of 10p in the pound** сбавка в размере десяти пенсов на один фунт; **birth ~** рождаемость; **the failure ~** (*in exams*) **was 20%** количество провалившихся на экзаменах достигло двадцати процентов; **they arrived at the ~ of five a day** каждый день прибывало пять человек; *fig*: **at any ~** во всяком случае; **at that ~** в таком случае; **if he goes on at that ~ he'll kill himself** если он будет так продолжать дальше, он погубит себя

2 (*price*): **what is the ~ for this job?** какая ставка на этой работе?; **the hotel offers cheap ~s in winter** зимой в этом отеле низкие цены; **what are your ~s for a single room?** сколько стоит номер на одного?

3 *Fin*: **the dollar ~** курс доллара; **~ of exchange** валютный курс; **to borrow at a high ~ of interest** занять деньги под высокий процент

4 *pl* (*local tax*) местные сборы, муниципальные налоги

5 (*speed*) темп, скорость; **~ of growth** темпы (*pl*) роста; **work is progressing at a great ~** работа ведётся ударными темпами; **~ of flow** скорость потока; **pulse ~** частота пульса; *Aer* **~ of climb** скороподъёмность.

rate *vti vt* **1** оцен|ивать (-ить); считать (*only in impf*); **the critic ~d the book highly** критик высоко оценил книгу; **how do you ~ my chances?/her?** как вы оцениваете мои шансы?, что вы ду́маете о ней?; **I ~ him highly / among my best pupils** я его́ о́чень ценю́, я счита́ю его́ одни́м из мои́х лу́чших ученико́в

2 *Fin*: **our house is ~d at £100 per annum** наш дом облага́ется нало́гом (в) сто фу́нтов в год

vi: **he ~s as a colonel** он по чи́ну ра́вен полко́внику.

rather *adv* **1** (*more accurately*): **~ it is a question of money** де́ло скоре́е в деньга́х; **late last night or, ~, early this morning** вчера́ по́здно но́чью, и́ли, верне́е/точне́е сказа́ть, сего́дня ра́но у́тром

2 (*somewhat*) немно́го, не́сколько; **I'm ~ tired** я немно́го уста́л; **it's ~ difficult** э́то труднова́то/дово́льно тру́дно; **~ more serious** не́сколько бо́лее серьёзный; **I ~ think he won't come** я ду́маю, что, пожа́луй, он не придёт; **I ~ expected that of him** я в о́бщем-то э́того от него́ ожида́л; **is he handsome?—Yes, he is ~** он краси́вый?—Пожа́луй, что да; **I ~ like her** она́ мне в о́бщем нра́вится

3 (*used of preference*): **I'd ~ drink whisky than gin** мне бы лу́чше ви́ски, а не джин; **I'd ~ do the dishes than play chess** я уж лу́чше посу́ду помо́ю, чем в ша́хматы игра́ть; **I'd ~ have tea please** мне бы лу́чше ча́ю, е́сли мо́жно; **have a drink!—I'd ~ not** тебе́ нали́ть?—Пожа́луй, не на́до.

rather *interj* ещё бы!

ratify *vt* ратифици́ровать (*impf and pf*).

rating *n* **1** оце́нка; **credit ~** оце́нка кредитоспосо́бности

2: *Naut* **officers and ~s** офице́ры и матро́сы.

ratio *n* пропо́рция; соотноше́ние; **in direct ~ to** в прямо́й пропо́рции с + *I*; **teacher—pupil ~** соотноше́ние коли́чества учителе́й и уча́щихся; **in the ~ of 5 to 1** в отноше́нии пять к одному́.

ration *n* рацио́н; *pl* (**~s**) паёк (*sing*); **daily ~ of bread** су́точный рацио́н хле́ба; **they were put on reduced ~s** их посади́ли на уме́ньшенный паёк; **emergency / iron ~** неприкоснове́нный запа́с.

ration *vt*: **food was ~ed in the war** во вре́мя войны́ продукты продава́лись по ка́рточкам; **they are ~ed to a kilo of bread a day** им выдаётся по килогра́мму хле́ба в день; **I ~ myself to 5 cigarettes a day** я ограни́чиваю себя́ пятью́ сигаре́тами в день; **we ~ed out our provisions to last a week** мы распредели́ли продово́льствие на неде́лю.

rational *adj* рациона́льный, *also Math*; (*of people*) разу́мный; **~ use of resources** рациона́льное испо́льзование ресу́рсов; **let's be ~ about this** дава́й отнесёмся к э́тому разу́мно.

rationale *n* логи́ческое обоснова́ние.

rationalize *vt* (*explain*) объясн|я́ть (-и́ть); **to ~ one's fears** (стара́ться) объясни́ть свои́ стра́хи; (*organize*) **to ~ production** рационализи́ровать произво́дство (*impf and pf*).

rationing *n*: **to introduce ~** ввести́ ка́рточки на проду́кты; **during ~** во вре́мя ка́рточной систе́мы.

rat-tat-tat *interj* тук-тук-ту́к.

rattle *n* **1** трещо́тка; (*toy*) погрему́шка

2 (*noise*: *of machine gun*) пулемётная о́чередь, дробь; (*of crockery, window*) дребезжа́ние; (*of cart, etc.*) громыха́ние; (*of cans*) стук; **death ~** предсме́ртный хрип.

rattle *vti vt*: **he ~d the cups** он греме́л ча́шками; *fig* **he ~d off a list of names** он отбараба́нил спи́сок имён; *CQ*: **he never gets ~d** он никогда́ не теря́ет споко́йствия; **that got him ~d** э́то заста́вило его́ поне́рвничать

vi: **the doors / windows ~d** две́ри хло́пали, о́кна дребезжа́ли; **the cups / coins ~d** ча́шки стуча́ли, моне́ты бренча́ли; **hail ~d on the roof** град бараба́нил по кры́ше; **the cart ~d over the cobbles** теле́жка громыха́ла по булы́жной мостово́й; **the train ~d past** по́езд прогромыха́л ми́мо; *fig* **he ~d on about his trip** он нам всем у́ши прожужжа́л о свое́й пое́здке.

rattlesnake *n* грему́чая змея́.

raucous *adj*: **a ~ laugh / voice** ре́зкий смех/го́лос; **the ~ croak of a raven** хри́плый крик во́рона.

ravage *vt* опустош|а́ть (-и́ть), разор|я́ть (-и́ть); **a country ~d by war** страна́, разорённая войно́й; **forests ~d by fire** леса́, опустошённые пожа́ром.

rave *adj*: **~ reviews** восто́рженные о́тзывы/реце́нзии.

rave *vi* (*be delirious*) бре́дить (*impf*), *also fig*, быть в бреду́; (*in fury*) бесноваться (*impf*); *fig* **he ~s about jazz / about her beauty** он про́сто бре́дит джа́зом/её красото́й.

raven *n* во́рон.

ravenous *adj*: **I am ~** я го́лоден как волк; **a ~ appetite** во́лчий аппети́т.

ravine *n* уще́лье.

raving *adj usu fig*: **he's ~ mad** он совсе́м спя́тил.

raw *n fig*: **to touch smb on the ~** заде́ть кого́-л за живо́е.

raw *adj* **1** (*unprocessed*) сыро́й; **~ materials** сырьё (*collect*); **~ cotton / silk / sugar** хло́пок-/шёлк-сыре́ц, нерафини́рованный са́хар; **~ meat** сыро́е мя́со; **a ~ morning** сыро́е у́тро; **~ spirit** чи́стый спирт; *fig* **a ~ youth** зелёный юне́ц

2 (*sore*): **a ~ wound** откры́тая ра́на; **these boots rubbed my skin ~** э́ти боти́нки натёрли мне но́ги до кро́ви; *CQ* **he got a ~ deal** с ним пло́хо обошли́сь.

ray *n* луч, *also fig*; **a ~ of hope** про́блеск наде́жды.

raze *vt*, *also* **to ~ to the ground** разруш|а́ть до основа́ния (-́ить), сноси́ть с лица́ земли́ (снести́).

razor *n* бри́тва; **safety / electric ~** безопа́сная бри́тва, электробри́тва; *attr*: **~ blade** ле́звие бри́твы.

re[1] *prep*, *also* **in re** *Comm*, *Law* относи́тельно + *G*.

re[2] *n Mus* ре.

re- *pref usu translated by Russian pref* пере-.

reach *n* **1: he has a long ~** у него́ дли́нные ру́ки; **my books are all within (easy) ~** у меня́ все кни́ги под руко́й; **the house is within (easy) ~ of the station** дом (нахо́дится) недалеко́ от ста́нции; **the school is within easy ~ by bus** до шко́лы удо́бно добира́ться авто́бусом; **put those bottles out of ~ of the children** убери́ э́ти буты́лки пода́льше от дете́й; **the flowers are out of my ~** я не могу́ дотяну́ться до цвето́в; *fig* **these cars are within ~ of most people** (*financially*) э́ти маши́ны продаю́тся по досту́пной цене́

2 (*of river*): **the upper/lower ~es** верхо́вье/низо́вье реки́ (*may be sing or pl*); **one of the prettiest ~es of the Thames** одно́ из краси́вейших мест на Те́мзе.

reach *vti vt* **1** (*stretch out*): **to ~ a hand out for smth** протя́|гивать ру́ку за чем-л (-ну́ть)

2 (*get and pass*): **can you ~ me (over) the salt/down my case?** переда́йте, пожа́луйста, соль, вы не могли́ бы доста́ть мне чемода́н с по́лки?

3 (*get as far as*) доста|ва́ть до + *G* (-́ть); дости|га́ть + *G* (-́чь); **can you ~ that branch?** ты мо́жешь доста́ть/дотяну́ться до э́той ве́тки?; **he hardly ~ed my shoulders** он едва́ достава́л мне до плеч; **the stick doesn't ~ the bottom** па́лка не достаёт до дна; **when we ~ed the bridge** когда́ мы дости́гли моста́; **your letter ~ed me today** ва́ше письмо́ пришло́ сего́дня; **to ~ the summit** до|бира́ться до верши́ны (-бра́ться); **the train ~ed London at 6 o'clock** по́езд при́был в Ло́ндон в шесть часо́в; **he ~ed a ripe old age** он до́жил до глубо́кой ста́рости; **where can I ~ you?** где вас мо́жно найти́?, (*by phone*) как с ва́ми мо́жно связа́ться?; **to ~ an agreement/a conclusion/a compromise** при|ходи́ть к соглаше́нию/к заключе́нию (-йти́), на|ходи́ть компроми́сс (-йти́)

vi до|ходи́ть до + *G* (-йти́); достава́ть; **I can't ~** я не доста́ну, мне не доста́ть; **the garden ~es to the river** сад тя́нется до са́мой реки́; **his voice doesn't ~ to the back of the hall** его́ не слы́шно в за́дних ряда́х; **her coat ~es to the floor** пальто́ у неё до́ полу; **he ~ed for the phone/the cream** он протяну́л ру́ку к телефо́ну, он потяну́лся за сли́вками; **as far as the eye can ~** наско́лько хвата́ет глаз.

react *vi* реаги́ровать (*impf*), *also Chem*; **how did he ~ to the idea?** как он отнёсся к э́той иде́е?; **he ~ed strongly against the idea/his upbringing** он реши́тельно возража́л про́тив э́той иде́и, он бро́сил вы́зов свое́й среде́.

reaction *n* реа́кция, *also Chem, Med*; **what was his ~ to your suggestion?** как он реаги́ровал на ва́ше предложе́ние?; **a ~ set in** наступи́ла реа́кция; **the forces of ~** си́лы реа́кции.

reactionary *adj* реакцио́нный.

reactor *n*: **nuclear ~** а́томный реа́ктор.

read *vti vt* **1** чита́ть (про-, проче́сть) *and compounds*; **to ~ smth aloud/to oneself** чита́ть что-л вслух/про себя́; **he can ~ (*written*) music/several languages** он чита́ет но́ты/на не́скольких языка́х; **to ~ a will** зачи́т|ывать завеща́ние (-а́ть); **to finish ~ing smth** дочита́ть что-л; **instead of "nose" ~ "rose"** вме́сто **nose** сле́дует чита́ть **rose**; **I read her to sleep** я чита́л, пока́ она́ не засну́ла; **the minutes were taken as read** протоко́л был утверждён без зачи́тывания; **he read off/out the list of names** он зачита́л спи́сок имён; **he read over his essay/through the letter** он перечита́л своё сочине́ние, он прочита́л письмо́; *fig*: **we can take it as read that...** само́ собо́й разуме́ется, что...; **you are ~ing too much into that sentence** ты ви́дишь в э́той фра́зе бо́льше того́, что в ней есть.

2 (*interpret*): **to ~ smb's palm** гада́ть кому́-л по руке́ (по-); **to ~ smb's fortune/the future** предска́з|ывать чью-л судьбу́/бу́дущее (-а́ть); **I ~ it differently** я не так э́то понима́ю; **this article can be read in different ways** э́ту статью́ мо́жно толкова́ть по-ра́зному; **to ~ smb's thoughts** чита́ть чьи-л мы́сли; **she can ~ him like a book** она́ его́ насквозь ви́дит

3 (*of instruments*): **to ~ a meter** снима́ть показа́ния счётчика (снять); **the speedometer ~s 90** спидо́метр пока́зывает девяно́сто

4 *Univ*: **he is ~ing Spanish/music** он изуча́ет испа́нский язы́к/тео́рию му́зыки

vi: **to ~ between the lines/for an examination** чита́ть ме́жду строк, гото́виться к экза́мену; **he read far into the night** он чита́л/зачита́лся далеко́ за́ полночь; **I have read up to page 20** я дочита́л до двадца́той страни́цы; **the letter ~s as follows** в письме́ говори́тся так; **how does this phrase ~ now?** как тепе́рь звучи́т э́та фра́за?

reader *n* чита́тель (*m*); (*schoolbook*) кни́га для чте́ния; *Univ* ле́ктор, (*if senior*) доце́нт; (*professional reciter*) чтец; **he's an avid ~** он глота́ет кни́ги.

readership *n Univ* доценту́ра.

readily *adv* охо́тно; **he ~ agreed** он охо́тно/с гото́вностью согласи́лся; **he is not ~ dissuaded** его́ нелегко́ отговори́ть.

readiness *n*: **to show a ~ for smth/to do smth** прояви́ть гото́вность к чему́-л/сде́лать что-л; **everything is in ~** всё гото́во; **they are holding themselves in ~** они́ нагото́ве (*adv*).

reading *n* чте́ние; **he enjoys ~** он лю́бит чита́ть; **a series of ~s from Chekhov** програ́мма че́ховских чте́ний; **there's very little ~ in this magazine** в э́том журна́ле почти́ не́чего чита́ть; **the first ~ of the play** пе́рвая чи́тка пье́сы; **what is your ~ of the facts?** как вы понима́ете/толку́ете э́ти фа́кты?; **the ~ on a thermometer** показа́ние термо́метра.

reading lamp *n* насто́льная ла́мпа.

reading room *n* чита́льный зал, чита́льня; *Univ CQ* чита́лка.

readjust *vt* (*instruments, etc.*) перестр|а́ивать (-о́ить); (*machines*) отрегули́ровать (*pf*); (*salary, etc.*) пере|сма́тривать (-смотре́ть).

ready *adj* **1** гото́вый; **are you ~?** ты гото́в?; **~ to hand** под руко́й; **he is ~ for anything** он гото́в ко всему́; **to get lunch ~** пригото́вить обе́д; **I must get ~ for the journey** мне на́до собра́ться в доро́гу/пригото́виться к пое́здке; **she got the children ~ for a walk** она́ собрала́ дете́й на прогу́лку; **I was ~ to cry** я был гото́в распла́каться; **~, steady, go!** на старт—внима́ние—марш!

2 (*willing*): **he is a ~ helper** он охо́тно помо́жет; **he gave a ~ assent** он охо́тно согласи́лся

3 (*prompt*): **a ~ wit** бы́стрый ум; **he has a ~ tongue** язы́к у него́ хорошо́ подве́шен; **the goods found a ~ sale** това́ры хорошо́ шли/распродава́лись/по́льзовались больши́м спро́сом.

ready-cooked *adj*: **~ foods** кулина́рные изде́лия; **a ~ chicken** гото́вый цыплёнок.

ready-made *adj*: **~ clothes** гото́вая оде́жда.

ready reckoner *n* арифмети́ческие табли́цы (*pl*) гото́вых расчётов.

real *n CQ*: **they're not bluffing—it's for ~** они́ не шу́тят—э́то вполне́ серьёзно.

real *adj* настоя́щий; действи́тельный; реа́льный; **~ gold** настоя́щее зо́лото; **a ~ friend/idiot** настоя́щий друг, кру́глый идио́т; **a ~ danger** действи́тельная/реа́льная опа́сность; **~ coffee** натура́льный ко́фе; **the ~ power is in her hands** по́длинная/реа́льная власть—в её рука́х; **in ~ life** в жи́зни.

realistic *adj* реа́льный; *usu Art* реалисти́ческий; **a ~ plan** реа́льный план; **a ~ portrayal** реалисти́ческое изображе́ние; **let's be ~** дава́йте бу́дем смотре́ть на ве́щи реа́льно.

reality *n* (*actuality*) действи́тельность, реа́льность; **harsh realities** суро́вая действи́тельность (*sing*); **he doesn't understand the realities of the situation** он не понима́ет действи́тельного положе́ния веще́й; **in ~** на са́мом де́ле; **let's get back to ~** дава́й спу́стимся с небе́с на зе́млю.

realization *n* **1** (*awareness*) осозна́ние

2 (*implementation*) осуществле́ние, реализа́ция.

realize *vt* **1** (*be aware of*) осозна|ва́ть (´-ть); понима́ть (поня́ть); представ|ля́ть себе́ (´-ить); **I at once ~d what I had said** я сра́зу же осозна́л/по́нял, что я сказа́л; **he doesn't ~ the problems** он не понима́ет/не ви́дит стоя́щих пе́ред на́ми пробле́м; **I didn't ~ you had moved** я не знал, что вы перее́хали

2 (*plans*) реализова́ть (*impf and pf*), *also Fin*; осуществ|ля́ть (-и́ть); **our hopes have been ~d** сбыли́сь на́ши наде́жды.

really *adv* **1** (*used alone*): **~?** пра́вда?, вот как!; вот что!; **not ~?** неуже́ли?; **~, you're impossible!** в са́мом де́ле, ты про́сто невыноси́м!; **he's not bad-looking ~** он во́все не так безобра́зен; **are you hungry?—Not ~** ты го́лоден?—Не осо́бенно

2 (*with adj or verb*): **it was ~ cold** бы́ло о́чень хо́лодно; **has he ~ gone?** он действи́тельно уе́хал?; **he was ~ very angry** он действи́тельно о́чень рассерди́лся; **now tell me what you ~ think** тепе́рь скажи́, что ты на са́мом де́ле ду́маешь; **I don't ~ believe him** я не о́чень-то ему́ ве́рю; **you don't ~ believe him?** неуже́ли ты ве́ришь ему́?; **is it ~ possible to do that?** ра́зве э́то возмо́жно сде́лать?; **I don't ~ know** я про́сто не зна́ю; **you ~ must come with me next time** сле́дующий раз ты обяза́тельно до́лжен пойти́ со мной.

reap *vti* жать (с-); *fig* по|жина́ть (-жа́ть); *fig*: **who ~s the rewards?** кто бу́дет пожина́ть ла́вры?; **to ~ what one has sown** что посе́ешь, то и пожнёшь.

reaper *n* (*person*) жнец; (*machine*) жа́тка, жне́йка.

reappear *vi* сно́ва появ|ля́ться (-и́ться).

reappraisal *n* переоце́нка.

rear *n* за́дняя часть; *Mil* тыл; **in the ~** позади́, *Mil* в тылу́; **at/to the ~ of the building** позади́ зда́ния; **the ~ of the train** за́дние ваго́ны по́езда; **the fifth coach/the view from the ~** пя́тый ваго́н от конца́, вид сза́ди.

rear *adj* за́дний; *Mil* тылово́й; **~ axle** за́дняя ось.

rear *vti vt* **1** (*livestock*) раз|води́ть (-вести́); (*children*) расти́ть (вы́-); **I was ~ed in Siberia** я рос в Сиби́ри

2: the snake ~ed its head змея́ подняла́ го́лову

vi (*of horse*) станови́ться на дыбы (стать).

rear admiral *n* контр-адмира́л.

rearguard *n Mil* арьерга́рд; *attr*: **~ action** арьерга́рдный бой.

rearmament *n* перевооруже́ние.

rearrange *vt*: **to ~ a programme/exhibits/the timetable** переставля́ть номера́ в програ́мме, по-но́вому размеща́ть экспона́ты, измен|я́ть *or* переде́л|ывать расписа́ние (-и́ть, -ать).

rear-view mirror *n Aut* зе́ркало за́днего ви́да.

reason *n* **1** (*motive, cause*) причи́на; **the ~ is that...** причи́на в том, что...; **by ~ of his age** по причи́не во́зраста; **for ~s best known to himself** по одному́ ему́ изве́стным причи́нам; **for one ~ or another** по той и́ли ино́й причи́не; **for no good ~, for no ~ at all** без вся́кой причи́ны; **for ~s of my own** по ли́чным моти́вам; **with good ~, not without ~** не без причи́ны; **that is the ~ why...** вот по како́й причи́не..., вот почему́...; **that's the real ~ why he left** вот настоя́щая причи́на его́ отъе́зда, вот почему́ он уе́хал; **we had ~ to suspect** у нас бы́ли причи́ны (*pl*) подозрева́ть; **all the more ~ why you should go/for you to go** тем бо́лее тебе́ сле́дует идти́; **there is every ~ to suppose that...** есть все основа́ния предполага́ть, что...

2 (*faculty*) рассу́док, ра́зум; **to lose one's ~** лиши́ться рассу́дка

3 (*sense*) смысл; **there is ~ in what he says** в том, что он говори́т, есть смысл; **he won't listen to ~** он не прислу́шивается к го́лосу рассу́дка; **I'll do anything within ~** я сде́лаю всё, что в разу́мных преде́лах; **his demands are**

beyond all ~ его́ тре́бования неразу́мны; **it stands to** ~ **that...** разуме́ется, что...

reason *vti vt* (*think out*) рассу|жда́ть (-ди́ть), проду́м|ывать (-ать); (*persuade*) уго|ва́ривать (-вори́ть); **he** ~**ed that...** (*to himself*) он рассуди́л,/(*to smb else*) он говори́л, что...; **to** ~ **out a problem/the consequences** проду́мать вопро́с/возмо́жные после́дствия; **a well** ~**ed argument** хорошо́ обосно́ванный аргуме́нт; **he** ~**ed her into/out of agreeing** он уговори́л её согласи́ться/не соглаша́ться

vi: **I** ~**ed about it thus** я рассужда́л об э́том сле́дующим о́бразом; **we tried to** ~ **with him** мы пыта́лись убеди́ть его́.

reasonable *adj* разу́мный; **be** ~**!** будь благоразу́мным!; **let's be** ~ **about this** дава́й подойдём к э́тому разу́мно; **beyond any** ~ **doubt** вне вся́ких сомне́ний; ~ **prices** уме́ренные це́ны.

reasonably *adv* (*sensibly*) разу́мно; (*quite*) дово́льно.

reasoning *n* рассужде́ние; **I don't follow your** ~ я не ула́вливаю ло́гики ва́ших рассужде́ний (*pl*).

reassemble *vti vt* (сно́ва) со|бира́ть (-бра́ть), *also Tech*

vi (сно́ва) собира́ться.

reassess *vt* переоце́ни|вать (-́ть).

reassurance *n*: **he needs** ~ **that he made the right decision** ему́ не меша́ет ли́шний раз услы́шать, что он при́нял пра́вильное реше́ние; **his words were a great** ~ **to me** его́ слова́ бы́ли для меня́ большо́й подде́ржкой.

reassure *vt*: **I was greatly** ~**d after speaking to the doctor** разгово́р с врачо́м успоко́ил меня́; **I felt greatly** ~**d on hearing that...** у меня́ отлегло́ от се́рдца, когда́ я узна́л, что...

reassuring *adj*: **she found his presence/promise** ~ его́ прису́тствие/обеща́ние ободри́ло её; **it is** ~ **that he is now eating** он стал есть — э́то обнадёживает.

rebel *n* (*insurgent*) повста́нец; (*mutineer*) мяте́жник, бунтовщи́к; *fig* бунта́рь (*m*); *attr*: **the** ~ **troops/students** восста́вшие/(*mutinous*) мяте́жные войска́, бунту́ющие студе́нты.

rebel *vi* восста|ва́ть (-́ть), *also fig*; (*if chaotic*) бунтова́ть (взбунтова́ться); **to** ~ **against smth** восста́ть про́тив чего́-л; *fig* **the children** ~**led against the strict discipline** де́ти взбунтова́лись про́тив стро́гой дисципли́ны.

rebellion *n* восста́ние; (*riot*) бунт.

rebellious *adj*: **a** ~ **speech/spirit** бунта́рская речь, бунта́рский дух; **the troops were** ~ в войска́х зре́ло недово́льство; ~ **students** недово́льные студе́нты; **a** ~ **child** непослу́шный ребёнок.

rebound *n* отско́к; **to hit the ball on the** ~ бить по мячу́ с отско́ка; *fig* **she quarrelled with her boyfriend and married my son on the** ~ она́ поссо́рилась со свои́м возлю́бленным и в пи́ку ему́ вы́шла за́муж за моего́ сы́на.

rebound *vi* отск|а́кивать (-очи́ть); **the ball** ~**ed from the wall** мяч отскочи́л от стены́; *fig* **the wrong he did** ~**ed on himself** зло, кото́рое он причини́л, оберну́лось про́тив него́.

rebuff *n* отпо́р; **to meet with a** ~ встре́тить отпо́р.

rebuild *vt* перестр|а́ивать (-о́ить).

rebuke *n* упрёк; **to administer a** ~ **to smb** сде́лать кому́-л вы́говор.

rebuke *vt* упрек|а́ть (-ну́ть).

recalcitrant *adj* (*disobedient*) непоко́рный; (*obstinate*) упря́мый.

recall *n*: **beyond** ~ безвозвра́тно, бесповоро́тно (*advs*); **the chance is gone beyond** ~ возмо́жность безвозвра́тно упу́щена; *Dipl* отозва́ние, отзы́в; **letters of** ~ отзывны́е гра́моты.

recall *vt* **1** *Dipl, Mil* от|зыва́ть (-озва́ть); **he was** ~**ed from holiday** он был вы́зван из о́тпуска

2 (*call to mind*) припом|ина́ть (-нить); **I cannot** ~ **where I met him** я не могу́ припо́мнить, где я его́ ви́дел; *fig* **it** ~**s to me the day when...** э́то напо́мнило [**NB** *tense*] мне тот день, когда́...

recapitulate, *abbr CQ* **recap** *vti* резюми́ровать (*impf and pf*).

recapitulation, *abbr CQ* **recap** *n* резюме́ (*indecl*).

recapture *vt*: **the runaway was** ~**d** беглеца́ пойма́ли; **the author** ~**s the atmosphere of the twenties** а́втор воссоздаёт атмосфе́ру двадца́тых годо́в.

recede *vi* отступ|а́ть (-и́ть); **the floods** ~**d/are receding** наводне́ние (*sing*) отступи́ло/убыва́ет *or* спада́ет; **we watched the coastline slowly** ~ мы смотре́ли на постепе́нно удаля́ющийся бе́рег; **his hair is receding** он лысе́ет; **our hopes** ~**d** на́ши наде́жды та́яли.

receding *adj*: **a** ~ **chin/forehead** сре́занный подборо́док, пока́тый лоб.

receipt *n* **1** получе́ние; **on** ~ **of the letter/goods** по получе́нии письма́/това́ра (*collect*); *Comm* **I am in** ~ **of your letter** я получи́л ва́ше письмо́

2 (*document*) квита́нция; **a** ~ **for 10 roubles** квита́нция/распи́ска в получе́нии десяти́ рубле́й; *attr*: ~ **book** квитанцио́нная кни́жка

3 *pl* (~**s**) *Comm* (*takings*) прихо́д

4 *Cook* реце́пт.

receive *vt* получ|а́ть (-и́ть); при|нима́ть (-ня́ть); **to** ~ **information/a refusal/a wound/a shock** получи́ть све́дения (*pl*)/отка́з/ра́ну/шок; **he** ~**d the news in silence** он при́нял/встре́тил э́ту но́вость мо́лча; **to** ~ **guests** принима́ть госте́й; **we were warmly** ~**d** нас тепло́ при́няли; **the idea/book was well** ~**d** э́та иде́я была́ хорошо́ воспри́нята, кни́га получи́ла хоро́шие о́тзывы; **I** ~**d no sympathy from him** я не нашёл в нём никако́го сочу́вствия.

receiver *n* получа́тель (*m*); *Radio* (радио-) приёмник; *Tel* (телефо́нная) тру́бка; **a** ~ **of stolen goods** ску́пщик кра́деного.

recent *adj* неда́вний; ~ **discoveries/events** неда́вние откры́тия/собы́тия; **in the** ~ **past** в неда́внем про́шлом; **within** ~ **memory** на на́шей па́мяти; **in** ~ **years** за после́дние го́ды; ~ **experiments have shown...** после́дние экспериме́нты показа́ли...

recently *adv* недáвно; **we lived here until very ~** мы жи́ли здесь до недáвнего врéмени; **as ~ as last week** ещё на прóшлой недéле.

receptacle *n* сосýд; (*dish*) посýда (*collect*).

reception *n* **1** (*party*) приём; **to hold a ~** дать приём

2 (*welcome*): **we got a friendly ~** нас встрéтили привéтливо; **the play met with a favourable ~** пьéса былá хорошó принятá/встрéчена

3 (*in hotel, hospital*) (*also* **~ desk**) регистратýра

4 *Radio, TV* приём; **~ is very bad here** здесь приём óчень плохóй.

receptionist *n* (*of doctor, in hotel, etc.*) регистрáтор.

receptive *adj*: **~ (to)** восприи́мчивый (к + *D*).

recess *n* **1**: **Parliament is in ~** парлáмент распýщен на кани́кулы

2 *Archit* ни́ша; (*for bed*) алькóв; (*for window*) амбразýра

3 *pl*: **in the ~es of the cave/mind** в глуби́нах пещéры/сознáния.

recession *n Econ* спад.

recharge *vt* (*battery, gun*) перезаря|жáть (-ди́ть).

recipe *n* рецéпт; **a ~ for soup**/*fig* **for success** рецéпт для сýпа, рецéпт успéха; *attr*: **~ book** кулинáрная кни́га.

recipient *n* получáтель (*m*).

reciprocal *adj* взаи́мный, обою́дный.

reciprocate *vi*: **they have been very kind and it is up to us to ~** они́ бы́ли óчень добры́, и мы должны́ отвéтить им тем же; **he ~d by giving her his book** в отвéт он подари́л ей свою́ кни́гу.

recital *n* **1** (*account*) расскáз; **the ~ of his adventures** расскáз о егó приключéниях

2 *Mus* сóльный концéрт; **a poetry ~** вéчер поэ́зии.

recitation *n* (*of poetry*) декламáция; **he will give a ~ of poems by Blok** он прочтёт стихи́ Блóка.

recite *vti vt*: **to ~ poetry** читáть/(*more formally*) деклами́ровать стихи́ (про- *or* прочéсть/*usu impf*); (*list*) **he ~d all the details** он перечи́слил все детáли

vi деклами́ровать.

reckless *adj* (*of person, behaviour*) безрассýдный, опромéтчивый; **~ of the danger/consequences** пренебрегáя опáсностью, не дýмая о послéдствиях; **~ driving** неосторóжная ездá.

reckon *vti vt* **1** (*calculate*) считáть (*impf*) *and compounds*; **the waiter ~ed up the bill** официáнт всё подсчитáл; **the charge is ~ed from the date of hire** плáта взимáется со дня нáйма

2 (*consider*) считáть, дýмать, полагáть (*only in impfs*); **I ~ him (to be)/that he is a genius** я считáю егó гéнием/, что он гéний; **he'll come, I ~** дýмаю, что он придёт

vi считáть; рассчи́тывать (*usu impf*); **~ing from today** считáя с сегóдняшнего дня; **he ~ed on spending £100/on another ten guests** он рассчи́тывал потрáтить сто фýнтов/приня́ть ещё дéсять гостéй; **let me ~ up with you** давáйте я с вáми рассчитáюсь; **they had ~ed without the weather** они́ не учли́ погóду; **he is a man to be ~ed with** он человéк, с котóрым прихóдится считáться.

reckoning *n* (*bill*) счёт; (*calculation*) подсчёт, расчёт, *also fig*; **by my ~** по мои́м подсчётам/расчётам/*fig only* соображéниям (*pls*); **he was a long way out in his ~** он крýпно оши́бся в расчётах, *fig* он просчитáлся; *fig*: **by any ~ he's a rogue** что ни говори́те, он плут; **the day of ~** час расплáты.

reclaim *vt*: **to ~ one's belongings** за|бирáть свои́ вéщи (-брáть); **to ~ land** (*neglected or virgin*) освáивать нóвые зéмли (*pl*) (освóить); **to ~ land from the sea** отвоёв|ывать зéмлю у мóря (-áть).

recline *vi*: **he was reclining on the grass/sofa** он прилёг на травé, он устрóился на дивáне полулёжа.

recluse *n* затвóрник.

recognition *n* (*awareness*) сознáние; (*realization*) осознáние; (*acknowledgement*) признáние; **to win general ~** получи́ть всеóбщее признáние; **in ~ of your services** признавáя вáши заслýги; (*identification*): **to avoid ~ he...** чтóбы егó не узнáли, он...; **he gave her a smile of ~** он её узнáл, и лицó егó расплылóсь в улы́бке; **he has changed beyond ~** он изменился до неузнавáемости.

recognizable *adj*: **he is scarcely ~** егó с трудóм мóжно узнáть; **it is immediately ~ as the work of a genius** срáзу ви́дно рýку гéния.

recognize *vt* (*realize*) сознавáть (*impf*), осозн|авáть (-áть); (*identify*) узна|вáть (-́ть); (*acknowledge*) призна|вáть (-́ть); **to ~ a new government** признáть нóвое прави́тельство.

recoil *n* (*of gun*) отдáча; (*of big gun*) откáт.

recoil *vi* **1** (*draw back*): **she ~ed in horror from him/at the sight of him** онá в ýжасе отшатнýлась *or* отпря́нула от негó/при ви́де егó

2 (*of gun*) отда|вáть (-́ть); (*of big gun*) откáт|ываться (-и́ться); *fig* **his meanness ~ed on his own head** егó пóдлость рикошéтом удáрила по немý самомý.

recollect *vt* припом|инáть (-́нить); **as far as I ~** наскóлько я припоминáю/я пóмню; **I don't ~ having said that** не припоминáю, чтóбы я говори́л э́то.

recollection *n*: **~s of the past** воспоминáния прóшлого/о прóшлом; **to the best of my ~** наскóлько я пóмню.

recommence *vti* возобнов|ля́ть(-ся) (-и́ть(ся)).

recommend *vt* рекомендовáть (*impf and pf, pf also* по-); (*advise*) совéтовать (по-); **this method is not to be ~ed** э́тот мéтод не нáдо рекомендовáть; **to ~ smb for a post/a decoration** рекомендовáть когó-л на пост, представ|ля́ть когó-л к óрдену (-́ить); **I ~ you to take a holiday** я вам рекомендýю/совéтую взять óтпуск; **a list of ~ed books** рекомендáтельный спи́сок книг.

recommendation *n* рекомендáция; предложéние; (*advice*) совéт; **on her ~** по её рекомендáции; **the ~s of the report** предложéния в доклáде; **to make ~s** дать рекомендáции/предложéния; **a letter of ~** рекомендáтельное письмó.

recompense *n* компенсáция.

recompense *vt*: **to ~ smb for a loss** компенсúровать/возме|щáть комý-л убы́тки (*pl*) (*impf and pf*/-стúть).

reconcile *vt*: **to ~ two people/smb with smb** мирúть двух людéй/когó-л с кем-л (по-); **they became ~d** онú помирúлись; **to ~ oneself to smth** мирúться с чем-л (при-); **it's impossible to ~ the two theories** невозмóжно увязáть э́ти две теóрии вмéсте.

reconnaissance *n* развéдка, рекогносцирóвка; *attr*: **a ~ patrol** развéдывательный дозóр.

reconnoitre, (*US*) reconnoiter *vti* произ|водúть развéдку/рекогносцирóвку (-вестú).

reconsider *vti vt* пересм|áтривать (-отрéть) *vi* передýм|ывать (-ать).

reconstruct *vt* реконструúровать (*impf and pf*); (*completely rebuild*) перестр|áивать (-óить); *fig* **to ~ events/a crime** воссозда|вáть *or* восстан|áвливать собы́тия/картúну преступлéния (-́ть, -овúть).

reconstruction *n* реконструкция; перестрóйка; *fig* воссоздáние.

record *n* **1** (*note*) зáпись; (*of meetings*) протокóл; *pl* (*archives*) архúвы; **we keep a ~ of everyone who comes in** мы ведём зáпись всех приходя́щих; **he left no ~ of his transactions** он не остáвил никакúх зáписей (*pl*) (своúх) торгóвых операций; **I have no ~ of your application** вáше заявлéние у меня́ не зарегистрúровано; **the highest temperature on ~** сáмая высóкая зарегистрúрованная температýра; **a ~ of attendance** спúсок/регистрáция присýтствующих; **a ~ of proceedings** протокóл; **he is on ~ as saying...** как я́вствует из протокóла, он сказáл...; **to enter smth in the ~** занестú что-л в протокóл; (*to journalists*) **speaking off the ~** говоря́ неофициáльно/не для протокóла; **his diary gives a good ~ of the trip** егó дневнúк даёт прекрáсное описáние поéздки

2 (*personal history*): **he has a criminal ~** у негó есть судúмость; **he has a ~ of mental illness** у негó бы́ло психúческое расстрóйство/заболевáние; **he has an excellent (work) ~** у негó великолéпный послужнóй спúсок; **his ~ of attendance is bad** у негó плохáя посещáемость; **her past ~ shows...** её прóшлое покáзывает...

3 *Sport* рекóрд; **to break/beat the ~ (for the 100m)** побúть рекóрд (на сто мéтров); **he holds/has established the ~ for the high jump** емý принадлежúт/он установúл рекóрд в прыжкáх в высотý

4 *Mus* пластúнка; **a long-playing ~** долгоигрáющая пластúнка; **to make a ~** записáть на пластúнку; *attr*: **a ~ library/player** фонотéка, проúгрыватель.

record *adj* рекóрдный; **with a ~ time of 12 secs** с рекóрдным врéменем двенáдцать секýнд; *fig* **in ~ time** в рекóрдно корóткий срок.

record *vti vt* **1** (*set down*) запúс|ывать (-áть), *also Mus*; (*enter*) за|носúть (-нестú); **to ~ smth in one's diary/a song on tape** записáть *or* занестú что-л в дневнúк, записáть пéсню на магнитофóн

2 (*of instruments*) регистрúровать (за-); покáз|ывать (-áть); **the thermometer ~ed 40°** термóметр покáзывал сóрок грáдусов

vi: **he's ~ing just now** у негó сейчáс зáпись; **her voice does not ~ well** её гóлос плóхо запúсывается.

recording *n* зáпись, *also Mus*.

recount *vt* расскáз|ывать (-áть).

re-count *vt* пересчúт|ывать (-áть).

recourse *n*: **to have ~ to the law** обращáться в суд.

recover *vti vt*: **he ~ed his luggage a week later** он получúл свой багáж обрáтно чéрез недéлю; **to ~ debts from smb** взыскáть долгú с когó-л (*only in pf*); **he ~ed his bicycle from the river** он вы́тащил велосипéд из рекú; **to ~ one's balance/breath** восстан|áвливать равновéсие (-овúть), отдышáться (*pf*); **to ~ consciousness** при|ходúть в сознáние (-йтú); **he ~ed his health/sight** к немý вернýлось здорóвье/зрéние; **he ~ed his losses** емý возместúли убы́тки, *Cards* он отыгрáлся; **to ~ oneself** опóмниться (*pf*)

vi Med вы|здорáвливать (-́здороветь), поправ|ля́ться (-́иться); **to ~ from an illness/a shock** вы́здороветь, прийтú в себя́ (*usu pf*) от шóка; **business is ~ing** торгóвля налáживается.

recoverable *adj*: **~ losses/expenses** возместúмые потéри/расхóды.

recovery *n Med* выздоровлéние; **the ~ of his wallet** обнарýжéние (*if lost*)/возвращéние (*if stolen*) егó бумáжника; *Econ* **economic ~** восстановлéние нарóдного хозя́йства; *Law* **~ of damages** возмещéние убы́тков.

recreation *n* развлечéние; **facilities for ~** увеселúтельные сооружéния, аттракциóны; *attr*: **~ ground** площáдка для игр.

recrimination *n*: **don't indulge in ~s** не обвиня́йте/не упрекáйте друг дрýга.

recruit *n Mil* новобрáнец; (*to club*) **a new ~** нóвый член.

recruit *vt Mil* (*also of work force*) вербовáть (за-); **he was ~ed into the army** егó завербовáли в áрмию; **to ~ new players/a new goalkeeper** набирáть нóвых игрокóв, найтú нóвого вратаря́; **he ~ed me to help** он привлёк меня́ на пóмощь.

rectangle *n* прямоугóльник.

rectify *vt* исправ|ля́ть (-́ить).

rectilinear *adj* прямолинéйный.

rector *n Univ* рéктор.

rectum *n Anat* прямáя кишкá.

recumbent *adj*: **a ~ position** лежáчая позúция; **there she is, ~ on the sofa** вот онá—

лежи́т на дива́не; *Art* **a ~ figure** лежа́щая фигу́ра.

recuperate *vi* вы|здора́вливать (-здороветь), поправ|ля́ться (-иться).

recur *vi* повтор|я́ться (-и́ться); **I hope the illness will not ~** наде́юсь, (что) э́та боле́знь не повтори́тся; **the memory of it often ~s to me** мне э́то ча́сто прихо́дит на па́мять.

recurrence *n* повторе́ние, возвра́т; **there has been no ~ of the symptoms** симпто́мы не повтори́лись/не возобнови́лись.

recurrent *adj*: **a ~ illness** рецидиви́рующая боле́знь; **~ outbreaks of violence** периоди́ческие вспы́шки наси́лия; **~ expenses** теку́щие расхо́ды.

recurring *adj*: **a ~ dream** повторя́ющийся сон; *Math* **a ~ decimal** периоди́ческая дробь.

red *n* кра́сный цвет; *Polit* (**a ~**) «кра́сный»; *fig CQ*: **he is £100 in the ~** у него́ сто фу́нтов до́лгу; **we're in the ~ just now** мы сейча́с в долга́х; **I saw ~** я пришёл в я́рость, я озвере́л.

red *adj* кра́сный; **to be/go/turn ~** покрасне́ть; **her eyes were ~ with weeping** её глаза́ покрасне́ли/бы́ли кра́сными от слёз; **~ cheeks** (*rosy*) румя́ные щёки; **~ hair** ры́жие во́лосы.

Red Cross *n* Кра́сный Крест.

red currant *n* кра́сная сморо́дина (*bush or fruit*; *collect*).

redecorate *vt* (*repaint*) перекра́|шивать (-сить); **to ~ a house/room** де́лать ремо́нт до́ма/ко́мнаты (с-).

redeem *vt* (*by payment*) вы|купа́ть (-купить); *Rel*, *fig* искуп|а́ть (-и́ть); **to ~ smth from pawn** вы́купить что-л из зало́га; **to ~ oneself** искупи́ть свою́ вину́; **to ~ a promise** вы|полня́ть обеща́ние (-полнить).

red-haired *adj* ры́жий, рыжеволо́сый.

red-handed *adj*: **to catch smb ~** пойма́ть кого́-л с поли́чным.

red-hot *adj*: **~ metal** мета́лл, раскалённый до́красна́; *fig* **~ plates/news** горя́чие таре́лки, све́жие но́вости.

redirect *vt* переадресо́в|ывать (-а́ть).

redistribute *vt* перераспредел|я́ть (-и́ть).

redo *vt* переде́л|ывать (-ать); перераб|а́тывать (-о́тать).

redouble *vti* удв|а́ивать(ся) (-о́ить(ся)).

redraft *vt*: **to ~ an agreement** переде́л|ывать соглаше́ние (-ать).

redress *n* возмеще́ние; **to seek ~ for smth** тре́бовать возмеще́ния за что-л; **you have no ~** вы не полу́чите возмеще́ния.

red tape *n* волоки́та, бюрократи́зм.

reduce *vti vt* **1** (*cut*) пони|жа́ть, сни|жа́ть (*pfs* -зить); (*lessen*) уменьш|а́ть (-ить); (*shorten*) сокра|ща́ть (-ти́ть); **to ~ prices** сни́зить це́ны; **to ~ the price of smth by £5** сни́зить це́ну на что-л на пять фу́нтов; **to ~ taxation/wages** сни́зить нало́ги (*pl*)/зарпла́ту (*sing*); **to ~ pressure/temperature** пони́зить давле́ние/температу́ру; **to ~ pain** уме́ньшить боль; **to ~ speed/pace/smb's chances** уме́ньшить *or* сба́вить ско́рость, уба́вить шаг, уме́ньшить чьи-л ша́нсы; **to ~ expenditure** сократи́ть/уме́ньшить расхо́ды; **you must ~ this chapter by half** вам на́до сократи́ть э́ту главу́ наполови́ну; **to ~ production/staff/smb's sentence** сократи́ть произво́дство/шта́ты (*pl*)/кому́-л срок заключе́ния; **boil until the liquid is ~d by half** да́йте полови́не жи́дкости вы́кипеть

2 (*bring*): **to ~ smb to despair/tears/poverty** до|води́ть кого́-л до отча́яния/слёз/нищеты́ (-вести́); **to ~ smth to basic principles** своди́ть что-л к основны́м при́нципам (свести́); **to ~ smb to submission** прину|жда́ть кого́-л к повинове́нию (-дить); **he was ~d to stealing** он был вы́нужден ворова́ть; **she was ~d to a shadow** она́ преврати́лась в тень; **the question/his look ~d them to silence** э́тот вопро́с пове́рг их в молча́ние, его́ взгляд заста́вил их замолча́ть; **to ~ smth to ashes** сжига́ть что-л дотла́ (сжечь)

vi (*slim*) худе́ть (по-).

reduced *adj*: **at ~ prices** по сни́женным це́нам; **they offer ~ fares for children** на де́тские биле́ты ски́дка; **she is living in ~ circumstances** она́ сейча́с в стеснённых обстоя́тельствах; **on a ~ scale** в уме́ньшенном масшта́бе.

reduction *n* пониже́ние; сниже́ние; сокраще́ние; уменьше́ние; **a ~ in speed** сниже́ние/уменьше́ние ско́рости; **a ~ in demand/in the level of unemployment** сниже́ние спро́са/у́ровня безрабо́тицы; **a ~ in sales/arms production** сокраще́ние сбы́та/произво́дства ору́жия; **to get a ~ of 10%** получи́ть ски́дку де́сять проце́нтов; **"big ~s"** «це́ны с большо́й ски́дкой».

redundancy *n*: **it caused a lot of ~/redundancies at the factory** э́то вы́звало большо́е сокраще́ние шта́тов на фа́брике.

redundant *adj* ли́шний; **there wasn't a ~ word/example in the article** в статье́ не́ было ни одного́ ли́шнего сло́ва/приме́ра; (*in industry*): **he was made ~** он был уво́лен по сокраще́нию шта́тов; **this has made some workers ~** э́то привело́ к увольне́нию не́которого числа́ рабо́чих.

reed *n* камы́ш, тростни́к (*collects*); *Mus* язычо́к.

re-educate *vt* перевоспи́т|ывать (-а́ть).

reef *n Geog*, *Naut* риф.

reefer *n sl* сигаре́та с марихуа́ной.

reef knot *n Naut* ри́фовый у́зел.

reek *n* вонь.

reek *vi*: **he ~s of garlic** от него́ па́хнет (*impers*) чесноко́м; **his clothes ~ of smoke** его́ оде́жда вся провоня́ла ды́мом (*pf*).

reel *n* **1** *Sew*, *in fishing* кату́шка; (*for film, tape*) боби́на

2 (*dance*) рил.

reel *vti vt*: **he ~ed in his line** он смота́л ле́ску; *fig* **to ~ off a list of names** отбараба́нить спи́сок имён (*pf*)

vi (*go round*) кружи́ться, (*stagger*) шата́ться, кача́ться (*pfs* за-); **my head was ~ing** у меня́ кружи́лась голова́; **the drunk ~ed down the**

street пья́ный шёл по у́лице шата́ясь; **the blow sent him ~ing** он зашата́лся от уда́ра.

re-elect *vt* переиз|бира́ть (-бра́ть).

re-examine *vt* (*of evidence*) пересм|а́тривать, повто́рно рассм|а́тривать (*pfs* -отре́ть); (*of witness*) повто́рно опр|а́шивать (-оси́ть); *School* переэкзамено́в|ывать (-а́ть).

refectory *n Univ, etc.* столо́вая; (*in monastery*) тра́пезная.

refer *vti vt* от|сыла́ть (-осла́ть), направ|ля́ть (-́ить); **I ~red him/the matter to the manager** я отосла́л *or* напра́вил его́/э́то де́ло к управля́ющему; **the matter was ~red back to the committee** де́ло бы́ло о́тослано обра́тно/возвращено́ в коми́ссию; **the matter was ~red to the UN** вопро́с был напра́влен в ООН; **the patient was ~red to a specialist** больно́го напра́вили к специали́сту

vi (*allude to*) ссыла́ться на + *A* (сосла́ться); (*consult*) обра|ща́ться к + *D* (-ти́ться); **please do not ~ to this again** прошу́ вас бо́льше не ссыла́ться на э́то; *Comm* **~ring to your letter...** ссыла́ясь на ва́ше письмо́...; **to ~ to the original/to the minutes** обрати́ться к оригина́лу/к протоко́лу (*sing*); **he often ~red to his notes** он ча́сто обраща́лся к свои́м запи́скам; **to whom are you ~ring?** о ком вы говори́те?, кого́ вы име́ете в виду́?; **this ~s to you all** э́то отно́сится ко всем вам.

referee *n* **1** *Sport* судья́; (*in football*) арби́тр, *also fig*; (*in boxing*) рефери́ (*indecl*)

2 (*for job*): **he was my ~** он дал мне рекоменда́цию.

referee *vti Sport* суди́ть (*impf*).

reference *n* **1** (*act of referring*): **they did it without ~ to me** они́ э́то сде́лали, не спроси́в меня́; **that is outside the terms of ~ of our commission** э́то не вхо́дит в компете́нцию на́шей коми́ссии; **to keep to/within the terms of ~** не выходи́ть за ра́мки полномо́чий

2 (*allusion*) ссы́лка; упомина́ние; **he spoke without any ~ to the past** он говори́л, не каса́ясь про́шлого/, не упомина́я о про́шлом; **with ~ to your letter** в связи́ с ва́шим письмо́м, ссыла́ясь на ва́ше письмо́; *Comm* **please quote this ~ in reply** в отве́те сошли́тесь на э́тот спра́вочный но́мер

3 (*in book*) ссы́лка; (*footnote*) сно́ска; **cross ~** перекрёстная ссы́лка

4 (*testimonial*): **a ~ from one's last job** характери́стика/спра́вка с ме́ста пре́жней рабо́ты; **he has good ~s** у него́ хоро́шие рекоменда́ции; *Comm* **a bank ~** ба́нковская рекоменда́ция

5 *attr*: **a ~ library** спра́вочная библиоте́ка; **a ~ mark** знак сно́ски; *Comm, etc.* **a ~ number** спра́вочный но́мер.

referendum *n* рефере́ндум.

refill *n* (*for pen, etc.*) запасно́й сте́ржень (*m*).

refill *vt*: **to ~ a fountain pen** заправ|ля́ть автору́чку (-́ить); **let me ~ your glass** дава́й я тебе́ налью́ ещё.

refine *vt* утонч|а́ть (-и́ть); *Tech* (*of sugar*) рафини́ровать (*impf and pf*), (*of oil*) очи|ща́ть (-́стить).

refined *adj* (*of person*) рафини́рованный; (*of style, taste*) утончённый, изы́сканный; (*of oil*) очи́щенный; **~ cruelty** утончённая жесто́кость.

refinery *n* (*of sugar*) са́харорафина́дный/(*of oil*) нефтеочисти́тельный заво́д.

refit *vt Naut* переобору́довать (су́дно) (*pf*).

reflect *vti vt* отра|жа́ть (-зи́ть), *also fig*; **the swan was ~ed in the water** ле́бедь отража́лся в воде́; *fig* **his work ~s credit on him** э́та его́ рабо́та де́лает ему́ честь

vi **1** (*ponder*) размышля́ть (*usu impf*); (*think*) ду́мать (по-); **I need time to ~ (on it)** мне ну́жно вре́мя, что́бы поразмы́слить над э́тим

2 (*discredit*): **his behaviour ~s upon us all** его́ поведе́ние отража́ется на всех нас.

reflection *n* **1** отраже́ние; *fig* (*aspersion*): **this is no ~ on your honesty** я не ста́влю под сомне́ние ва́шу че́стность

2 (*thought*) размышле́ние; **it gave me cause for ~** э́то да́ло мне по́вод для размышле́ния; **without due ~** не проду́мав как сле́дует; **I think, on ~, that...** поду́мав, я пришёл к вы́воду, что...

reflectively *adv* вду́мчиво, заду́мчиво.

reflector *n Tech* рефле́ктор, отража́тель (*m*).

reflex *n* рефле́кс; *attr* рефлекто́рный.

reflexive *adj Gram* возвра́тный.

reform *n* рефо́рма.

reform *vti vt* (*institutions, etc.*) реорганизо́в|ывать (-а́ть); (*people*) исправ|ля́ть (-́ить); **he's a ~ed character now** он тепе́рь испра́вился

vi исправля́ться.

reformation *n Hist* (**the R.**) Реформа́ция.

refraction *n Phys* преломле́ние, рефра́кция.

refrain[1] *n* (*in song*) припе́в; (*in poem*) рефре́н.

refrain[2] *vi* возде́рж|иваться, удерж|иваться от + *G* (*pfs* -а́ться); **he ~ed from comment** он воздержа́лся от коммента́риев (*pl*); **I couldn't ~ from smiling** я не мог сдержа́ть улы́бки.

refresh *vt* освеж|а́ть (-и́ть); **will you ~ my memory about that?** не мо́жете ли вы освежи́ть э́то в мое́й па́мяти?; **we ~ed ourselves with a swim/a glass of beer** мы освежи́лись купа́нием/стака́ном пи́ва.

refresher course *n*: **to take a ~** пройти́ курс повыше́ния квалифика́ции.

refreshing *adj*: **a ~ breeze/sleep** освежа́ющий ве́тер/сон; **his sincerity is most ~** прия́тно встре́тить тако́го и́скреннего челове́ка.

refreshment *n*: **we stopped at a café for some light ~** мы зашли́ в кафе́ перекуси́ть; **~s will be served during the flight** еда́ бу́дет по́дана во вре́мя полёта.

refrigerate *vt* (*cool*) охла|жда́ть (-ди́ть); (*freeze*) замор|а́живать (-о́зить).

refrigeration *n* охлажде́ние; (*in deep freeze*) замора́живание.

refrigerator *n* холоди́льник.

refuel *vti* заправ|ля́ть(ся) (-́ить(ся)).

refuelling *n* запра́вка.

refuge *n* убе́жище; *fig* прибе́жище; **a mountain ~** убе́жище в гора́х; **he took ~ in a cave** он укры́лся в пеще́ре.

refugee *n* бе́женец; *attr*: **a ~ camp** ла́герь бе́женцев.

refund *n* возмеще́ние; **to demand a ~** тре́бовать возмеще́ния; **the ~ of a deposit** вы́плата вкла́да.

refund *vt* возме|ща́ть (-сти́ть); **I will ~ you the full amount** я вам возмещу́ сто́имость в по́лном разме́ре.

refusal *n* отка́з; **to meet with a blank ~** получи́ть категори́ческий отка́з.

refuse[1] *n* отбро́сы (*pl*), му́сор; *attr*: **~ bin** (*inside*) ведро́ для му́сора, (*outside*) му́сорный я́щик; **~ dump/tip** сва́лка.

refuse[2] *vt* (*deny*) отка́з|ывать + *D and* в + *P* (-а́ть); (*decline*) отка́зываться от + *G or* + *inf*; **they ~ me nothing** они́ мне ни в чём не отка́зывают; **I ~d his offer/to do it** я отказа́лся от его́ предложе́ния/сде́лать э́то.

refutation *n* опроверже́ние.

refute *vt* опроверг|а́ть (-́нуть).

regain *vt*: **she ~ed her good looks/confidence/popularity** к ней верну́лась красота́/уве́ренность в себе́, она́ опя́ть по́льзуется популя́рностью; **he ~ed his balance** он восстанови́л равнове́сие; **to ~ consciousness** приходи́ть в созна́ние (прийти́); **to ~ one's former position** верну́ть себе́ пре́жние пози́ции (*pl*) (*only in pf*).

regal *adj fig* ца́рственный, вели́чественный.

regale *vt*: **to ~ smb with oysters/anecdotes** уго|ща́ть кого́-л у́стрицами (-сти́ть), развле|ка́ть кого́-л анекдо́тами (-́чь).

regard *n* **1** (*respect*) отноше́ние; **in this ~** в э́том отноше́нии; **with ~ to your application** относи́тельно/что каса́ется ва́шего заявле́ния

2 (*attention*) внима́ние; **he writes with no ~ for accuracy** он пи́шет, совсе́м не обраща́я внима́ния на то́чность изложе́ния

3 (*esteem*) уваже́ние; **out of ~ for his age** из уваже́ния к его́ во́зрасту; **I hold his work in high ~** я с больши́м уваже́нием отношу́сь к его́ рабо́те; **I have a high ~ for his ability** я высоко́ ценю́ его́ спосо́бности (*pl*)

4 *pl* (*greetings*) приве́т (*sing*); **give my ~s to Tom** переда́йте от меня́ приве́т То́му; (*in letter*) **with kind ~s** с уваже́нием.

regard *vt* **1** (*look at*) смотре́ть на + *A* (по-), *also fig*; **he has always ~ed her/the matter with contempt** он всегда́ смотре́л на неё/на э́то с презре́нием

2 (*consider*) счита́ть (*impf*); **I ~ it as essential** я счита́ю э́то необходи́мым

3 (*concern*) каса́ться + *G* (*only in impf*); **as ~s his brother** что каса́ется его́ бра́та.

regarding *prep* относи́тельно + *G*; **~ your offer** относи́тельно/что каса́ется ва́шего предложе́ния; **what are the arrangements ~ the meeting?** когда́ и где бу́дет собра́ние?; **and other matters ~ the wedding** и други́е дела́, свя́занные со сва́дьбой.

regardless *adj*: **he buys things quite ~ of expense** он де́лает поку́пки, не счита́ясь с расхо́дами; **I shall buy it ~ of the cost** я куплю́ э́то за любу́ю це́ну.

regardless *adv*: **I warned him but he carried on ~** я его́ предупрежда́л, но он продолжа́л своё, как бы не слы́ша.

regime *n* режи́м.

regiment *n* полк.

regimental *adj* полково́й.

region *n* райо́н, о́бласть; (*of very large areas*) край; (*in administration*) о́бласть; **forest ~s** лесны́е райо́ны/о́бласти; **Arctic ~s** аркти́ческий райо́н (*sing*); **a fertile ~** плодоро́дный край; **he has a pain in the ~ of the kidneys** у него́ боль в поясни́це; *fig* **he owes me something in the ~ of £1,000** он мне до́лжен что́-то о́коло ты́сячи фу́нтов.

regional *adj* областно́й; райо́нный; региона́льный; **~ offices** райо́нные/ме́стные отделе́ния.

register *n* за́пись; *Mus*, *Tech*, *Typ* реги́стр; **~ of births/deaths/marriages** за́пись рожде́ний/смерте́й/бра́ков; **~ of voters** спи́сок избира́телей.

register *vti vt* **1** (*record*) регистри́ровать (за-); **to ~ a birth** регистри́ровать рожде́ние ребёнка

2 (*show*) регистри́ровать, пока́з|ывать (-а́ть); **the thermometer ~s 40°** термо́метр пока́зывает со́рок гра́дусов; **he ~ed no surprise** он не вы́казал никако́го удивле́ния

3 (*of mail*): **I want to ~ this letter** я хочу́ отпра́вить э́то письмо́ заказны́м

vi **1**: **to ~ at a hotel/with the police** зарегистри́роваться в гости́нице, отме|ча́ться в поли́ции (-́титься); **to ~ with a doctor** стать клие́нтом врача́ (*only in pf*)

2: *CQ* **I told her twice but it didn't ~** я повтори́л два ра́за, но до неё всё равно́ не дошло́.

registered *adj*: **a ~ letter** заказно́е письмо́; **a ~ trademark** зарегистри́рованный това́рный знак.

registrar *n* регистра́тор.

registration *n* регистра́ция; *attr*: **~ fee** пла́та за посы́лку багажа́, заказно́го письма́, *etc.*; *Aut* **~ number** номерно́й знак.

registry *n* регистрату́ра.

registry office *n*: **we were married in a ~** мы зарегистри́ровали брак в муниципалите́те, (*SU*) мы расписа́лись в за́гсе.

regressive *adj* регресси́вный.

regret *n* сожале́ние; **to my ~** к моему́ сожале́нию; **to feel ~** испы́тывать сожале́ние; **he refused with many ~s** он отказа́лся, вы́разив сожале́ние (*sing*); (*formal*) **he sent his ~s for not being able to come** он присла́л свои́ извине́ния по по́воду того́, что не мог прийти́.

regret *vt* сожале́ть о + *P* (*impf*); **I ~ my decision/that I came** я сожале́ю о своём реше́нии/, что пришёл; **we ~ to inform you that...** мы с сожале́нием сообща́ем вам, что...

regretfully *adv* к сожале́нию.

regrettable *adj* прискóрбный; **a ~ state of affairs** óчень прискóрбное положе́ние дел; **it is most ~ that** óчень прискóрбно, что...

regrouping *n* перегруппирóвка.

regular *n Mil* солда́т регуля́рной а́рмии: (*in café*) **he's a ~ here** он завсегда́тай кафе́.

regular *adj* **1** (*symmetrical*) пра́вильный; **a ~ shape** пра́вильная фóрма; **~ features/teeth** пра́вильные черты́ лица́, рóвные зу́бы; *Gram* **a ~ verb** пра́вильный глагóл

2 (*recurring at even intervals*) постоя́нный, регуля́рный; рóвный; **a ~ visitor/customer** постоя́нный посети́тель/клие́нт; **he makes ~ use of the library** он постоя́нно пóльзуется библиоте́кой; **~ use of this medicine** регуля́рный приём э́того лека́рства; **~ breathing** рóвное дыха́ние; **a ~ pulse** рóвный пульс; **he comes at 7 every day, as ~ as clockwork** (ка́ждый день) он прихóдит рóвно в семь как часы́; **~ steps** разме́ренные шаги́; **he keeps ~ hours** он ведёт разме́ренный óбраз жи́зни, он соблюда́ет режи́м

3 (*habitual*) обы́чный; **~ passengers on this train** обы́чные для э́того пóезда пассажи́ры; **is it the ~ procedure?** э́то обы́чная процеду́ра?

4 (*permissible*): **it is quite ~ to wait inside** так уж при́нято ждать внутри́

5 (*full-time, professional*): **the ~ staff** основны́е/постоя́нные шта́ты (*pl*); *Mil* **the ~ army** регуля́рная а́рмия

6 *CQ*: **he's a ~ hero** он настоя́щий герóй.

regularity *n* регуля́рность; пра́вильность; рóвность (*see adj* **regular**); **with great ~** óчень регуля́рно.

regularly *adv* регуля́рно; *Gram* **to decline ~** склоня́ться по пра́вилам.

regulate *vt* регули́ровать (у-, от-), *also Tech*; контроли́ровать (про-); **to ~ prices** регули́ровать/контроли́ровать це́ны; **to ~ a watch/traffic** отрегули́ровать часы́ (*no sing*), регули́ровать у́личное движе́ние; **to ~ one's own/the firm's expenditure** следи́ть за свои́ми расхóдами (*pl*), вести́ учёт расхóдов фи́рмы (*usu impfs*).

regulation *n* (*act*) регули́рование; (*rule*) пра́вило; **safety ~s** пра́вила безопа́сности; *attr*: *Mil* **~ dress** фóрменная оде́жда.

rehash *n CQ*: **it was a ~ of last year's lectures** э́то бы́ли немнóго переде́ланные прошлогóдние ле́кции.

rehearsal *n* репети́ция, *also fig*; **dress ~** генера́льная репети́ция.

rehearse *vti* репети́ровать (*usu impf*); **to ~ a role/an actor** репети́ровать роль/с актёром.

rehouse *vt* пересел|я́ть (-и́ть); **the families were ~d** се́мьи бы́ли переселены́ в нóвый дом; **we've ~d the tractor in the old barn** мы поста́вили/перевезли́ тра́ктор в ста́рый сара́й.

reign *n* ца́рствование; **in the ~ of Queen Elizabeth** в ца́рствование королéвы Елизаве́ты, при королéве Елизаве́те; *fig*: **a ~ of terror** разгу́л террóра.

reign *vi* ца́рствовать (*impf*), *also fig*; *fig* цари́ть (*impf*).

reimburse *vt* возвра|ща́ть (-ти́ть *and* верну́ть); возме|ща́ть (-сти́ть); **I shall ~ you the cost of your ticket** я верну́ вам стóимость биле́та.

rein *n* вожжа́, пóвод; *fig* узда́; **to keep a tight ~ on smb/on expenditure** держа́ть когó-л в узде́, стрóго следи́ть за расхóдами; **to give ~ to one's imagination** дать вóлю воображе́нию.

reindeer *n* се́верный оле́нь.

reinforce *vt* подкреп|ля́ть, укреп|ля́ть (*pfs* -и́ть), *both also fig*; **to ~ a bridge/wall** укрепи́ть мост/сте́ну; **to ~ the troops at the front** при|сыла́ть подкрепле́ние войска́м на фрóнте (-сла́ть); **to ~ one's argument** подкрепи́ть свои́ дóводы (*pl*); **to ~ concrete** арми́ровать бетóн (*impf and pf*).

reinforcement *n Mil* подкрепле́ние, укрепле́ние, *both also fig*.

reinstate *vt* восстан|а́вливать (-ови́ть); **the employee was ~d** слу́жащего восстанови́ли в дóлжности; **the passage was ~d in the text** отры́вок был восстанóвлен в те́ксте.

reissue *n* (*of book*) переизда́ние; (*of films, stamps*) повтóрный вы́пуск.

reissue *vt* (*of book*) переизда|ва́ть (-́ть); (*of films, stamps*) повтóрно вы|пуска́ть (-́пустить).

reiterate *vt* повтор|я́ть (-и́ть).

reject *n* (*of goods*) (**a ~, ~s**) брак, бракóванный това́р (*collects*).

reject *vt* отверг|а́ть (-́нуть), отклон|я́ть (-и́ть), отка́з|ывать (-а́ть); **to ~ an idea** отве́ргнуть иде́ю; **he felt ~ed by society** он чу́вствовал себя́ отве́ргнутым óбществом; **to ~ a suitor** отказа́ть жениху́; **I was ~ed for that job** меня́ не взя́ли на э́ту рабóту; **to ~ faulty goods** бракова́ть негóдные това́ры.

rejection *n* отка́з; (*of faulty goods*) бракóвка.

rejoice *vti vt*: **it ~d my heart** э́то меня́ óчень порáдовало

vi ра́доваться (по-); **to ~ about/in/over smth** ра́доваться чему́-л; **I ~ to hear that...** я сча́стлив слы́шать, что...; *iron* **she ~s in the name of Mrs Bloggs** её велича́ют ми́ссис Блоггс.

rejoicings *npl* весе́лье (*sing*).

rejoin *vt*: **to ~ one's regiment** возвраща́ться в свой полк (верну́ться); **he will ~ us later** он пóзже присоедини́тся к нам.

rejoinder *n* отве́т; (*retort*) возраже́ние.

rejuvenate *vti* омол|а́живать(ся) (-оди́ть(ся)).

relapse *n*: **the patient had a ~** у больнóго был рециди́в боле́зни.

relapse *vi*: **he ~d into his old ways** он верну́лся к ста́рым привы́чкам; **he ~d into silence** он умóлк.

relate *vti vt* **1** (*tell*) расска́з|ывать (-а́ть); **he ~d a story/his adventures to us** он рассказáл нам истóрию/о своúх приключéниях; **strange to** ~ стрáнно сказáть, но...

2 (*connect*): **it is difficult to** ~ **these events** трýдно установúть связь мéжду éтими событиями; **his illness is obviously** ~**d to his worries** егó болéзнь, по-вúдимому, свя́зана с переживáниями

vi: **this** ~**s to what I said yesterday** éто имéет прямóе отношéние к томý, что я сказáл вчерá.

related *adj* 1 (*of subjects, etc.*) свя́занный; **geography and other** ~ **subjects** геогрáфия и другúе свя́занные с ней предмéты; **these questions are not** ~ éти вопрóсы не свя́заны мéжду собóй

2 (*of people*): **we are distantly** ~ мы дáльние рóдственники; **she is** ~ **to him by marriage** онá емý рóдственница по мýжу; **how are they** ~**?** в какóм онú родствé?

relation *n* 1 (*of story, etc.*) расскáз

2 (*connection*) отношéние; **Gogol in** ~ **to the Russian novel** Гóголь и егó влия́ние на рýсский ромáн; **it bears no** ~ **to the facts** éто не имéет никакóго отношéния к фáктам

3 *pl* (*dealings*) отношéния; ~**s are somewhat strained** отношéния нéсколько натя́нуты; **to enter into/break off** ~**s with smb** завязáть/порвáть отношéния с кем-л; **to have sexual** ~**s with smb** быть в интúмных отношéниях с кем-л

4 (*relative*) рóдственн|ик, *f* -ица; **a near/distant** ~ блúзкий/дáльний рóдственник; **what** ~ **is he to you?** в какóм вы с ним родствé?; **she is a** ~ **on my father's side** онá мне рóдственница со стороны́ отцá/по отцóвской лúнии.

relationship *n* (*connection*) отношéние; связь; (*kinship*) родствó; **the** ~ **between smoking and lung cancer is well established** связь мéжду курéнием и рáком лёгких давнó установлена; **she has a good** ~ **with her children** у неё хорóшие отношéния с детьмú; **blood** ~ крóвное родствó.

relative *n* рóдственн|ик, *f* -ица.

relative *adj* относúтельный, *also Gram*; **happiness is** ~ счáстье—поня́тие относúтельное; **what are the** ~ **advantages of the two plans?** каковы́ относúтельные преимýщества кáждого из éтих двух плáнов?; **with** ~ **calm** с относúтельным спокóйствием; **the papers** ~ **to this case** бумáги, относя́щиеся к éтому дéлу.

relativity *n* относúтельность.

relax *vti vt* ослаб|ля́ть, расслаб|ля́ть (*pfs* -ить); **to** ~ **one's attention/grip/efforts** ослабля́ть внимáние/хвáтку/(свои) усúлия; **to** ~ **one's muscles** расслабля́ть мы́шцы

vi слáбнуть (о-); расслабля́ться; **his grip** ~**ed** егó хвáтка ослáбла; **the tension** ~**ed** напряжéние ослáбло; **try to** ~ постарáйся расслáбиться; **I** ~ **for an hour after lunch** я отдохнý часóк пóсле обéда; **she never** ~**es** онá всегдá скóвана, онá всегдá в напряжéнии.

relaxation *n* 1 (*loosening*) ослаблéние; расслаблéние

2 (*recreation*) óтдых; **my favourite** ~ мой любúмый вид óтдыха; **I find reading a great** ~ я нахожý, что чтéние—замечáтельный óтдых; **it's time you had some** ~ тебé порá отдохнýть.

relaxed *adj*: **he always looks so** ~ у негó всегдá такóй безмятéжный вид; **you should be more** ~ **in your work** тебé слéдует бóлее спокóйно относúться к рабóте.

relay *n* (*of workmen, etc.*) смéна; *Elec* релé (*indecl*); *Radio, TV* ретрансля́ция; **they worked in** ~**s** онú рабóтали посмéнно; *attr*: *Sport* ~ **race** эстафéта, эстафéтный бег; *Radio, TV* ~ **station** ретрансляциóнная стáнция.

relay *vt Radio, TV* ретранслúровать (*impf and pf*).

release *n* 1 освобождéние; **on his** ~ **from prison** по освобождéнии из тюрьмы́; **death was a merciful** ~ **for him** смерть былá для негó избавлéнием

2 (*of mechanism, spring*) спуск

3 (*issue*) вы́пуск; **this record is a new** ~ éта пластúнка вы́шла недáвно; **a press** ~ сообщéние для прéссы.

release *vt* 1 (*set free*) освобо|ждáть (-дúть), вы|пускáть (-пустить); **to** ~ **smb from prison** освободúть/вы́пустить когó-л из тюрьмы́; **to** ~ **a rabbit from a trap** вы́пустить крóлика из капкáна; **to** ~ **smb from a debt/duty** простúть комý-л долг, освободúть когó-л от обя́занности; **the firm** ~**s him two days a week for study** фúрма предоставля́ет емý два дня в недéлю для учёбы

2 (*let go*) отпус|кáть (-тúть) *and other compounds*; **he** ~**d her hand/his grip on the rope** он отпустúл её рýку, он вы́пустил верёвку из рук; **to** ~ **the brake/trigger** отпустúть тóрмоз, спустúть курóк; **the mechanism is** ~**d by pressing a switch** механúзм пускáется в ход нажáтием кнóпки

3 (*issue*) вы́пустить; **to** ~ **a new book/film** вы́пустить нóвую кнúгу/нóвый фильм; **to** ~ **a text to the press** передáть текст для опубликовáния.

relegate *vt*: **he was** ~**d to the position of clerk** егó понúзили, он тепéрь простóй клерк; **that old chair has been** ~**d to the attic** éтот стáрый стул отпрáвили на чердáк; *Sport* **to** ~ **a team to the second division** пере|водúть комáнду во вторýю грýппу (-вестú).

relent *vi* смягч|áться (-úться).

relentless *adj* (*implacable*) неумолúмый; (*pitiless*) безжáлостный.

relevance *n*: **I don't see the** ~ **of that question** мне кáжется, éтот вопрóс не отнóсится к дéлу; **it is a matter of great** ~ **to our society** éто óчень вáжный/актуáльный вопрóс для нáшего óбщества.

relevant *adj*: **your question is very** ~ ваш вопрóс по существý; **this question is very** ~ **today** éтот вопрóс óчень актуáлен; **the papers** ~ **to the case** бумáги, относя́щиеся к дéлу; **refer to the** ~ **clause** обратúтесь к соответствующему пýнкту.

reliable *adj* надёжный; **from a ~ source** из надёжного источника; **their guarantee is entirely ~** на их гарантию вполне можно положиться.

reliably *adv*: **I am ~ informed that...** у меня надёжная информация о том, что...

relic *n Archaeol* след, остаток, реликт.

relief *n* **1** (*from pain, etc.*) облегчение; **to heave a sigh of ~** вздохнуть с облегчением; **it was a ~ to him that...** для него было большим облегчением, что...

2 (*from monotony, etc.*): **to provide some light ~** вносить некоторое оживление; **a black dress without any ~** чёрное платье без всяких украшений

3 (*assistance*) помощь; **the government are providing for famine ~** правительство оказывает (денежную) помощь голодающим; **to come to smb's ~** прийти кому-л на помощь/на выручку; *Mil* **the ~ of a city** освобождение города

4 (*in shiftwork*) смена, *also Mil*; **my ~ comes on at 6** моя смена приходит/меня сменяют в шесть

5 *Art, Geog* рельеф; **high/low ~** горельеф, барельеф; **done in ~** сделанный рельефно; **the house stands out in ~ against the sky** дом рельефно выделяется на фоне неба

6 *attr*: **a ~ fund** фонд помощи голодающим, *etc.*; **a ~ train** разгрузочный поезд; **a ~ pilot** сменный пилот.

relieve *vt* **1** (*alleviate*) облегч|ать (-ить); (*soften*) смягч|ать (-ить); (*help*) помо|гать (-чь); **to ~ smb's mind/sufferings** облегчить кому-л душу/чьи-л страдания; **this will ~ your cough** это смягчит твой кашель; **the trees ~ the bare landscape** деревья скрашивают голый пейзаж; **I am so ~d to see you** я так рад наконец видеть вас; **to ~ boredom** разогнать скуку

2 (*free*) освобо|ждать (-дить); **to ~ smb of an unpleasant duty** освободить кого-л от неприятной обязанности; **this ~s us of financial worries** это освобождает нас от денежных забот; **he was ~d of his command** его отстранили от командования; **let me ~ you of your coat/case** давайте я возьму ваше пальто/ваш чемодан; *Mil* **to ~ a town** освободить город

3 (*on shift*): **to ~ smb** смен|ять кого-л (-ить); **I was ~d at six** я сменился с дежурства в шесть часов

4: *CQ euph* **to ~ oneself** облегчиться.

religion *n* религия.

religious *adj* религиозный.

relinquish *vt* (*quit*) остав|лять (-ить); **to ~ a hope/plan/one's post** оставить надежду/план/свой пост; **to ~ one's rights to smb** уступ|ать кому-л права (-ить).

relish *n*: **to eat with ~** есть с аппетитом; **he told the story with evident ~** он рассказывал это со смаком.

relish *vt*: **he ~ed every mouthful** он смаковал каждый кусочек; **I would ~ some caviare** я бы полакомился чёрной икрой; **I don't ~ the thought of getting up so early** мне не улыбается так рано встать.

reluctance *n* неохота, нежелание; **with ~** неохотно, с неохотой; **to show ~** проявить нежелание.

reluctant *adj* неохотный.

rely *vi*: **to ~ on** по|лагаться на + *A* (-ложиться); (*depend on*) зависеть от + *G* (*impf*); **I ~ on you/on his word** я полагаюсь на тебя/на его слово; **he relies too much on his mother** он слишком зависит от матери; **he's not to be relied on** на него нельзя положиться; **~ upon it** будь уверен, уверяю тебя.

remain *vi* оста|ваться (-ться); **he ~ed behind** он остался; **nothing ~s for me but to...** мне ничего не остаётся, как...; **it only ~s for me to thank you** мне остаётся только поблагодарить вас; **the room still ~s to be painted** ещё остаётся покрасить комнату; **that ~s to be seen** остаётся увидеть это своими глазами; (*in letter*) **I ~ yours faithfully** остаюсь преданный вам; **he ~ed seated when I entered** он не встал, когда я вошёл; **if the weather ~s fine** если погода не испортится, (*over a period*) если продержится погода; **he ~ed standing/silent throughout the evening** он простоял/(про)молчал весь вечер.

remainder *n* остаток, *also Math*; (*of people*) остальные (*pl*).

remains *npl* остатки; **give the cat the ~** отдай кошке остатки; **human ~** останки; **the ~ of an old castle/of an ancient vase** развалины *or* руины старого замка, осколки античной вазы.

remake *vt* передел|ывать (-ать).

remark *n* **1** (*comment*) замечание; **introductory ~s** вступительные замечания; **to make/pass a ~** сделать замечание; **he made no ~** он ничего не сказал

2 (*notice*): **worthy of ~** достойный внимания.

remark *vti vt* (*say or notice*) заме|чать (-тить)

vi: **he ~ed on your absence** он отметил ваше отсутствие.

remarkable *adj* замечательный; **he is ~ for his bravery** он человек замечательной храбрости.

remarry *vi* вступ|ать в новый брак (-ить); (*of man*) вновь жениться (*pf*), (*of woman*) вновь выходить замуж (выйти).

remedial *adj*: *Med* **~ exercises** лечебная гимнастика (*sing*).

remedy *n* средство; **a ~ for a cold** средство от простуды; **there's no ~ for that disease** нет средства от этой болезни; **the situation is past ~** ситуация безнадёжна; **the ~ for boredom is work** работа — лучшее лекарство от скуки.

remedy *vt* исправ|лять (-ить); **that can soon be remedied** это дело поправимое.

remember *vti vt* помнить (*impf*); (*recall*) вспом|инать, припом|инать (*pfs* -нить); **I ~ him/having seen him/what he said** я помню его/, что видел его/, что он сказал; **I don't ~ your name** я не помню/не припомню ваше имя; **I**

suddenly ~ed about the meeting я вдруг вспо́мнил о собра́нии; **he ~ed her in his will** он не забы́л её в завеща́нии; **he asked to be ~ed to you** он проси́л переда́ть вам приве́т

vi по́мнить, вспомина́ть; **as far as I ~** наско́лько мне по́мнится (*impers*)/я по́мню.

remembrance *n*: **here is a small ~ of me** вот ма́ленький пода́рок на па́мять (обо мне́).

remind *vt* напом|ина́ть (-́нить); **you ~ me of my mother** вы мне напомина́ете мою́ мать; **he ~ed me about** *or* **of our plan/to buy petrol** он мне напо́мнил о на́шем пла́не/, что на́до купи́ть бензи́на.

reminder *n* напомина́ние; (*souvenir*) сувени́р; **they haven't sent me the money yet, I must send them a (gentle) ~** они́ не верну́ли мне де́ньги, и мне придётся (ве́жливо) напо́мнить им об э́том.

reminisce *vi* вспомина́ть о + *P* (*usu impf*).

reminiscence *n* воспомина́ние.

reminiscent *adj*: **he was in a ~ mood** он был настро́ен на воспомина́ния; **that phrase is ~ of Mozart** э́то ме́сто звучи́т как у Мо́царта.

remiss *adj* неради́вый, невнима́тельный; **I have been very ~ about writing** извини́те, что до́лго не писа́л вам; **that was ~ of you** ты прояви́л невнима́тельность.

remit *vt* **1: his debts/three months of his sentence were ~ted** ему́ прости́ли его́ долги́, его́ освободи́ли на три ме́сяца ра́ньше сро́ка

2 (*send, esp. of money*) от|сыла́ть (-осла́ть), пере|сыла́ть (-сла́ть).

remittance *n* (*sending*) отсы́лка/пересы́лка де́нег; (*money sent*) де́нежный перево́д.

remnant *n* (*trace*) след; (*of material*) оста́ток, отре́зок; *pl* (*of food*) оста́тки.

remonstrate *vi*: **I ~d with him about his rudeness** я сде́лал ему́ замеча́ние за гру́бость.

remorse *n* угрызе́ния (*pl*) со́вести; **he was overcome with ~** его́ му́чили угрызе́ния со́вести; **without any ~** без зазре́ния со́вести (*without prick of conscience*), безжа́лостно (*adv*) (*without pity*).

remorseful *adj*: **to be ~** чу́вствовать угрызе́ния со́вести.

remorseless *adj* безжа́лостный.

remote *adj* отдалённый, *also fig*; **a ~ village/spot** отдалённая *or* глуха́я дере́вня, медве́жий у́гол *or* глухома́нь; **in the ~ parts of Africa** в дебря́х А́фрики; **the house is ~ from any main road** дом нахо́дится вдалеке́/вдали́ от больши́х доро́г; *fig*: **a ~ resemblance** отдалённое схо́дство; **he's a ~ relation of mine** он мой да́льний ро́дственник; **a ~ possibility** маловероя́тная/ма́ленькая возмо́жность; **in the ~ past/future** в далёком про́шлом, в отдалённом бу́дущем; **he is a ~ figure** с ним не так легко́ сойти́сь.

remote control *n* телеуправле́ние, дистанцио́нное управле́ние.

removal *n* (*of furniture, etc.*) перево́зка; (*of people to new house*) перее́зд; (*to new office*) перемеще́ние; **~ of a threat** устране́ние угро́зы; *attr*: **~ van** фурго́н для перево́зки ме́бели; **~ firm** тра́нспортное аге́нтство.

remove *n*: **this is but one ~ from disaster** от э́того оди́н шаг до беды́.

remove *vti vt* **1** (*take off*) снима́ть (снять); (*take away*) убира́ть (убра́ть); **to ~ one's coat/the lid** снять пальто́, под|нима́ть кры́шку (-ня́ть); **to ~ a tax** отмен|я́ть нало́г (-и́ть); **he ~d the carpet/the plates from the table/her name from the list** он убра́л ковёр/таре́лки со стола́, он вы́черкнул её и́мя из спи́ска; **to ~ obstacles** устраня́ть препя́тствия; **to ~ stains** вы|води́ть пя́тна (-́вести); **to ~ smb from a post** сме|ща́ть кого́-л с до́лжности (-сти́ть); **she ~d him from that school** она́ забрала́ его́ из э́той шко́лы

2 (*transfer*): **to ~ smth from one place to another** (*carrying*) пере|носи́ть/(*by lorry*) пере|вози́ть что-л с одного́ ме́ста на друго́е (-нести́/-везти́)

vi (*to new house*) пере|езжа́ть (-е́хать); (*to new premises*) переме|ща́ться (-сти́ться).

remunerate *vt* вознагра|жда́ть (-ди́ть).

remunerative *adj* вы́годный.

Renaissance *n* эпо́ха Возрожде́ния, Ренесса́нс.

rename *vt* переименов|ывать (-а́ть).

render *vt* **1** (*formal: give*): **to ~ homage/tribute/thanks** ока́з|ывать уваже́ние (-а́ть), отда|ва́ть дань (-́ть), при|носи́ть благода́рность (*sing*) (-нести́); **to ~ assistance/a service** оказа́ть по́мощь/услу́гу; *Comm*: **to ~ an account** представ|ля́ть счёт (-́ить)

2 *Cook*: **to ~ (down) fat** топи́ть са́ло (рас-).

rendering *n Mus* исполне́ние; *Lit* перево́д.

rendez-vous *n* (*meeting*) свида́ние; (*place*) **a favourite ~** излю́бленное ме́сто встре́чи; **a ~ in space** сты́ковка в косми́ческом простра́нстве.

renew *vt* возобнов|ля́ть (-и́ть); **to ~ an acquaintance/an attack/one's efforts/a subscription** возобнови́ть знако́мство/ата́ку/уси́лия/подпи́ску; **to ~ a lease/contract** про|длева́ть срок аре́нды/контра́кт (-дли́ть); **I must ~ my library book** мне на́до продли́ть э́ту кни́гу; **he ~ed his invitation** он повтори́л приглаше́ние; **with ~ed strength/hope** с но́вой си́лой/наде́ждой.

renounce *vt* отре|ка́ться от + *G* (-́чься).

renovate *vt*: **to ~ a flat** за́ново отремонти́ровать кварти́ру (*usu pf*).

renown *n* сла́ва, изве́стность.

renowned *adj* изве́стный, знамени́тый; **London is ~ for its parks** Ло́ндон изве́стен/сла́вится свои́ми па́рками.

rent[1] *n* (*tear in cloth*) проре́ха.

rent[2] *n* аре́ндная/(*for flat*) кварти́рная пла́та, (*abbr in SU*) квартпла́та; **we pay a big ~ for our flat** мы мно́го пла́тим за кварти́ру; **we owe 2 months' ~** мы не плати́ли за кварти́ру два ме́сяца; (*US*) **his house is for ~** его́ дом сдаётся

rent[2] *vt*: **to ~ a flat/an office from smb** снима́ть у кого́-л кварти́ру (снять), арендова́ть у кого́-л помеще́ние для конто́ры (*impf and* *pf*); **to ~ a flat (out) to smb** сда|ва́ть кому́-л кварти́ру (-ть); **to ~ a TV** брать телеви́зор напрока́т (*adv*) (взять).

reopen *vti vt*: **to ~ negotiations**/*Law* **a case** возобнов|ля́ть перегово́ры/де́ло (-и́ть)

vi (вновь) открыва́ться; **the library/wound has ~ed** библиоте́ка вновь откры́та, ра́на сно́ва *or* опя́ть откры́лась.

reorganize *vt* реорганизова́ть (*impf and pf*).

repair *n* ремо́нт (*no pl*), (*of small things*) почи́нка; **under ~** в ремо́нте; **"closed for ~s"** «закры́то на ремо́нт»; **major/running ~s** капита́льный/теку́щий ремо́нт; **shoe/watch ~s** ремо́нт *or* почи́нка о́буви, ремо́нт часо́в; **the building is in good/is beyond ~** дом в хоро́шем/в безнадёжном состоя́нии; **the car is damaged beyond ~** маши́на разби́лась, и никако́й ремо́нт не помо́жет.

repair *vt* (*of large things*) ремонти́ровать (от-), (*of small things*) чини́ть, починя́ть (*pf for both* почини́ть); **to ~ a puncture** закле́|ивать проко́л (-ить).

reparation *n* возмеще́ние; *Mil* репара́ция; **he's doing it to make ~s for his carelessness** он де́лает э́то, что́бы загла́дить свою́ оплошность.

repartee *n*: **witty ~** остро́ты (*pl*); **there's some brilliant ~ in the play** в пье́се мно́го о́стрых диало́гов (*pl*).

repast *n*: **a light ~** лёгкая заку́ска.

repatriate *vt* репатрии́ровать (*impf and pf*).

repay *vt*: **how can I ever ~ you?** как мне вас отблагодари́ть?; **to ~ a debt** вы́платить долг (*pf*); **the article will ~ careful reading** э́ту статью́ сто́ит внима́тельно проче́сть.

repayment *n* (*of debt*) вы́плата; **as ~ for your kindness** в отве́т на ва́шу доброту́.

repeal *vt* отмен|я́ть (-и́ть).

repeat *n* повторе́ние; *attr* повто́рный.

repeat *vti vt* повтор|я́ть (-и́ть); **~ after me** повторя́й за мной; **to ~ oneself** повторя́ться; **don't ~ it** никому́ э́того не говори́; **she ~s everything to the boss** она́ всё расска́зывает своему́ нача́льнику

vi повторя́ться; **onions ~ on me** от лу́ка у меня́ отры́жка.

repeated *adj*: **after ~ efforts/requests** по́сле неоднокра́тных уси́лий, по́сле повто́рных про́сьб.

repel *vt* отби|ва́ть (-́ть), отра|жа́ть (-зи́ть); **to ~ an attack/the enemy** отби́ть/отрази́ть ата́ку, отби́ть проти́вника; *fig* **he ~s me** я чу́вствую к нему́ неприя́знь.

repellent *n*: **an insect ~** сре́дство от насеко́мых.

repent *vti* ка́яться, раска́иваться (*pf for both* раска́яться); **he ~ed bitterly of his folly/of what he had done/that...** он го́рько раска́ивался в свое́й глу́пости/в том, что он сде́лал/, что...; **I ~ having sold my car** я о́чень жале́ю, что прода́л маши́ну.

repentance *n* раска́яние.

repentant *adj* раска́ивающийся; **he was ~** он раска́ивался.

repercussion *n fig* после́дствие; **his assassination had far-reaching ~s** его́ уби́йство существенно измени́ло ход собы́тий; **he felt the ~s of the scandal** после́дствия э́того сканда́ла косну́лись и его́; **the rise in the cost of imports will have ~s on prices** увеличе́ние сто́имости и́мпорта (*sing*) отрази́тся на це́нах.

repertoire *n* репертуа́р; **a wide ~** обши́рный репертуа́р; **a large ~ of funny stories** большо́й запа́с анекдо́тов.

repertory company, repertory theatre (*abbr* **rep**) *n approx* провинциа́льный теа́тр.

repetition *n* повторе́ние.

repetitive *adj*: **the article/he is very ~** в э́той статье́ а́втор/он всё вре́мя повторя́ется.

replace *vt* **1**: **he ~d the book on the shelf** он поста́вил кни́гу обра́тно на по́лку; **to ~ the receiver** положи́ть тру́бку

2 (*substitute*) замен|я́ть (-и́ть); **it is impossible to ~ him/those cups** невозмо́жно замени́ть его́/э́ти ча́шки; **I ~d the nails with screws** я замени́л гво́зди винта́ми; **he ~d his father as the head of the company** он стал вме́сто отца́ главо́й компа́нии.

replacement *n* заме́на; **he is my ~** он моя́ заме́на.

replay *n Sport* (**a ~**) переигро́вка; **there will be a ~** они́ бу́дут игра́ть повто́рно.

replenish *vt* пополн|я́ть (-́ить).

replete *adj*: **I am ~** я сыт, я нае́лся.

replica *n* то́чная ко́пия.

reply *n* отве́т; **in ~ to his question** в отве́т на его́ вопро́с.

reply *vi* отве|ча́ть (-́тить); **to ~ to smb/to a letter** отвеча́ть кому́-л/на письмо́.

report *n* **1** (*official, usu read out*) докла́д; (*by an individual on departmental business, etc.*) отчёт; *Mil* донесе́ние; **to present a ~ on/about smth** предста́вить докла́д о чём-л; **an annual ~** ежего́дный отчёт; **intelligence ~s** донесе́ния разве́дки; **to make a ~ on a business trip** написа́ть отчёт о командиро́вке; **to send in personal ~s on staff** предста́вить характери́стики на сотру́дников; **the policeman wrote his ~** полице́йский соста́вил протоко́л; (*in newspapers*) **according to the latest ~s** согла́сно после́дним сообще́ниям; **a weather ~** сво́дка пого́ды; **a school ~** та́бель; **we received a good ~ about him** мы получи́ли хоро́ший о́тзыв о нём; **I know of it only by ~** я зна́ю об э́том то́лько понаслы́шке (*adv*)

2 (*bang*): **a rifle went off with a loud ~** разда́лся гро́мкий винто́вочный вы́стрел.

report *vti vt* сообщ|а́ть (-и́ть); **the incident was ~ed in the newspaper** о происше́ствии бы́ло напеча́тано в газе́те; **the paper ~ed the talks in detail** газе́та подро́бно писа́ла о перегово́рах; **it is ~ed from Rome that...** из Ри́ма сообща́ют, что...; **he was ~ed missing** бы́ло объя́влено, что он бе́з вести пропа́л; **to ~ a theft to the police** заяви́ть/сообщи́ть в поли́цию о кра́же; **she ~ed Tom to the headmaster for rudeness** она́ пожа́ловалась дире́ктору на гру́бость То́ма; **he ~ed (on) his findings to the**

committee он сде́лал докла́д/доложи́л о свои́х вы́водах коми́ссии

vi **1** (*give report*): **he used to ~ for the Times** он рабо́тал репортёром в «Таймс»; **they ~ed well of you** они́ хорошо́ отзыва́лись о вас

2 (*present oneself*): **to ~ to the director/to the director's office/for duty** явля́ться к дире́ктору/в дире́кцию/на слу́жбу (яви́ться); **~ back to me in a week** яви́тесь ко мне че́рез неде́лю; **to ~ sick** сказа́ть, что заболе́л.

reporter *n* репортёр.

repose *n* о́тдых.

repose *vi*: **his head ~d on a cushion** его́ голова́ поко́илась на поду́шке; **he was reposing on the sofa** он лежа́л на дива́не.

repository *n* склад.

represent *vt* **1** (*depict*) представ|ля́ть (-́ить), изобража́ть (*impf*); **sounds are ~ed by symbols** зву́ки на письме́ изобража́ются зна́ками; **the facts are not as he ~ed them** фа́кты на са́мом де́ле не таки́е, как он их предста́вил; **we ~ed to him the need for financial support** мы указа́ли ему́ на необходи́мость фина́нсовой подде́ржки

2 (*act for*) представля́ть, *also Law*, *Sport*, *Comm*; **to ~ smb/smb's interests** представля́ть кого́-л/чьи-л интере́сы.

representation *n* **1**: **~ in Parliament** представи́тельство в парла́менте; **proportional ~** пропорциона́льное представи́тельство; **there was no diplomatic/commercial ~ at the conference** на конфере́нции не́ было дипломати́ческих/торго́вых представи́телей

2: **the ambassador made ~s to the government** посо́л заяви́л проте́ст прави́тельству.

representative *n* представи́тель (*m*), *also Comm* (*abbr* **rep**).

representative *adj* представи́тельный, *also Polit*; (*typical*) характе́рный; **a ~ group of students** представи́тельная гру́ппа студе́нтов; **these cases are not ~** э́ти слу́чаи не характе́рны.

repress *vt* подав|ля́ть (-и́ть), *also Psych*; *Polit* репресси́ровать (*impf and pf*); **with difficulty I ~ed my tears** я с трудо́м подави́л слёзы; **a ~ed type** челове́к с пода́вленной пси́хикой.

repressive *adj*: **~ measures** репресси́вные ме́ры.

reprieve *n* отсро́чка, *also fig*; **to grant smb a ~** дать кому́-л отсро́чку; *fig* **I've had a ~ and don't start my military service for another two months** я получи́л отсро́чку от вое́нной слу́жбы на два ме́сяца.

reprimand *n* вы́говор; **to give/receive a ~** дать/получи́ть вы́говор.

reprint *n* перепеча́тка.

reprint *vt* перепеча́т|ывать (-ать).

reprisal *n*: **the attack was by way of ~** э́то была́ отве́тная ата́ка; **they threatened to take ~s** они́ пригрози́ли отве́тными де́йствиями.

reproach *n* упрёк; уко́р; **beyond ~** безупре́чный, безукори́зненный.

reproach *vt*: **to ~ smb for/with smth** упрек|а́ть/укор|я́ть кого́-л за что-л *or* в чём-л (-ну́ть/-и́ть); **we have nothing to ~ ourselves with** нам не́ в чем упрекну́ть себя́.

reproachful *adj* укори́зненный.

reprobate *n* развра́тник, распу́тник.

reproduce *vti vt* воспроиз|води́ть (-вести́); *Tech* репродуци́ровать (*impf and pf*); **to ~ a voice on tape** воспроизвести́ го́лос на плёнке; **to ~ 1,000 copies of a painting** напеча́тать ты́сячу репроду́кций карти́ны

vi Biol размнож|а́ться (-́иться).

reproduction *n* воспроизведе́ние, *also Biol*; *Biol* размноже́ние; *Art*, *Tech* репроду́кция.

reprove *vt*: **to ~ smb for smth** де́лать кому́-л вы́говор за что-л (с-).

reptile *n* пресмыка́ющееся, репти́лия.

republic *n* респу́блика.

republican *adj* республика́нский.

republish *vt* переизда|ва́ть (-́ть).

repudiate *vt* (*reject*) отверг|а́ть (-́нуть); (*disown*) отре|ка́ться от + *G* (-́чься); отка́з|ываться от + *G* (-а́ться); **he ~d the accusation/his son/the debt** он отве́рг обвине́ние, он отрёкся от сы́на, он отказа́лся плати́ть долг; **the government ~d the debts/the treaty** прави́тельство отказа́лось призна́ть долги́/аннули́ровало догово́р.

repugnant *adj* отврати́тельный.

repulse *vt* (*repel*) отра|жа́ть (-зи́ть); отби|ва́ть (-́ть), *also Mil*; *fig* **to ~ smb/smb's advances** дать кому́-л отпо́р.

repulsion *n* (*disgust*) отвраще́ние; *Phys* отта́лкивание.

repulsive *adj* отврати́тельный, омерзи́тельный, отта́лкивающий.

reputable *adj* (*of person*) уважа́емый; (*of goods, etc.*) изве́стный, надёжный; **a ~ firm** изве́стная/соли́дная фи́рма.

reputation *n* репута́ция; **you'll ruin my ~!** вы погу́бите мою́ репута́цию!; **he sets store by his ~** он дорожи́т свое́й репута́цией; **he has a ~ for meanness/wit** его́ ску́пость всем изве́стна, он изве́стен свои́м остроу́мием; **this restaurant has a good ~/a ~ for good food** э́тот рестора́н изве́стен/сла́вится свое́й ку́хней; **he earned the ~ of a good teacher** он зарекомендова́л себя́ хоро́шим педаго́гом.

repute *n* репута́ция, сла́ва; **a firm of good ~** соли́дная фи́рма; **I know him by ~** я о нём зна́ю понаслы́шке (*adv*).

reputed *adj* предполага́емый; **he is ~ to be rich** он слывёт богачо́м.

request *n* про́сьба; **at my ~** по мое́й про́сьбе; **a ~ for help** про́сьба о по́мощи; *off* **to put in a ~ for stationery** де́лать зая́вку на бума́гу.

request *vt* проси́ть (по-); **to ~ smb to do smth** попроси́ть кого́-л сде́лать что-л; **to ~ permission from smb** спроси́ть у кого́-л разреше́ния; **"You are ~ed not to smoke"** «про́сьба не кури́ть»; **your help is ~ed** тре́буется ва́ша по́мощь.

requiem *n* ре́квием.

require *vt* **1** (*need*) тре́боваться (по-); *or use* ну́жно (*impers*); **if you ~ anything** е́сли вам что́-нибудь потре́буется; **we ~ help** нам тре́буется/нужна́ по́мощь; **do you ~ anything else?** вам ну́жно ещё что́-нибудь?; **this plant ~s**

frequent watering цветóк нáдо чáсто поливáть; **the lock ~s attention** замóк нáдо чинѝть

2 (*formal*: *demand*) трéбоваться; **he did everything that was ~d of him** он сдéлал всё, что от негó трéбовалось; **you are ~d to be there by 9 o'clock** нýжно, чтóбы вы бы́ли там в дéвять часóв утрá.

required *adj* необходѝмый; обязáтельный; трéбуемый; **does he have the ~ qualifications?** есть ли у негó необходѝмая квалификáция (*sing*)?; **a pipe of the ~ length** трýбка трéбуемой/необходѝмой длины́; **within the ~ time** за дáнный промежýток врéмени; **by the ~ date** к устанóвленному срóку.

requirement *n* (*demand*) трéбование; (*need*) потрéбность; **to meet all the ~s** отвечáть всем трéбованиям; **what are the ~s?** какѝе предъявля́ются трéбования?; **maths is a ~ for the course** для э́того кýрса трéбуется знáние матемáтики.

requisite *n*: **all the ~s** всё необходѝмое; **toilet ~s** туалéтные принадлéжности.

requisition *n* реквизѝция; (*for stationery*, *etc.*) зая́вка, трéбование.

rescind *vt* аннулѝровать (*impf and pf*), отмен|я́ть (-ѝть).

rescue *n* (*being rescued*) спасéние; **after his ~** пóсле егó спасéния; (*act*) **a daring ~** смéлая спасáтельная оперáция; **to go to the/smb's ~** идтѝ на пóмощь (комý-л); *attr*: **~ boat/party** спасáтельная лóдка/комáнда.

rescue *vt* спасáть (спастѝ); освобо|ждáть (-дѝть); **to ~ smb from drowning** спастѝ утопáющего; **they waited three days to be ~d** онѝ ждáли пóмощи три дня; **you ~d me from an awkward situation** вы вы́ручили меня́ из нелóвкого положéния.

rescuer *n* спасѝтель (*m*).

research *n* исслéдования, изыскáния (*pls*); **to carry out ~ in the field of genetics** проводѝть исслéдования/изыскáния в óбласти генéтики; **a piece of ~** исслéдование; *attr*: **~ work** наýчно-исслéдовательская рабóта.

research *vi*: **to ~ into smth** исслéдовать что-л (*impf and pf*).

researcher *n* исслéдователь (*m*).

resemblance *n* схóдство; **the ~ between them** схóдство мéжду нѝми; **he bears a strong ~ to his father** он óчень похóж на отцá.

resemble *vt* быть похóжим на + *A*; походѝть на + *A* (*impf*); **she ~s her mother** онá похóжа/похóдит на мать.

resent *vt*: **he ~ed my saying that** егó обѝдели/задéли моѝ словá; **I ~ that!** мне э́то óчень обѝдно!; **he ~s my success** он завѝдует моемý успéху; **I ~ the way he treats me** меня́ возмущáет, как он ко мне отнóсится.

resentful *adj* обѝженный; **a ~ tone** обѝженный тон; **he feels ~ about his dismissal** он возмущён тем, что егó увóлили.

resentment *n* (сѝльная) обѝда; **a feeling of ~** чýвство обѝды; **to harbour ~ against smb** затáивать обѝду на когó-л.

reservation *n* **1** (*reserved place*) зарáнее заказáнное мéсто; (*US*: *for Indians*, *etc.*) резервáция; **did you make the ~s?** ты заказáл местá?

2 (*proviso*) оговóрка; **with certain ~s** с нéкоторыми оговóрками; **without ~** без оговóрок, безоговóрочно (*adv*); **I have ~s about the trip** у меня́ есть сомнéния насчёт э́той поéздки.

reserve *n* **1** (*of money*, *resources*) запáс, резéрв; *Mil* (**~s**) резéрвы; *Sport* запаснóй (игрóк); **mineral ~s** запáсы полéзных ископáемых; **we are holding him in ~** мы дéржим егó в запáсе/в резéрве, *also Sport*; *attr*: **a ~ fund** резéрвный фонд; **~ supplies** запáсы

2 (*restriction*): **without ~** без оговóрок, безоговóрочно

3 (*land*) заповéдник; **nature/game/forest ~** заповéдник, закáзник, заповéдный лес

4 (*of manner*) сдéржанность; **he treated me with some ~** он относѝлся ко мне с нéкоторой сдéржанностью.

reserve *vt* **1** (*keep*) берéчь (*impf*), сбере|гáть (-́чь); **I am reserving this wine for winter/for Christmas** я берегý э́то винó нá зиму/к рождествý; **I am reserving my strength for tomorrow** я берегý/сберегáю (своѝ) сѝлы (*pl*) на зáвтра; **to ~ judgment on smth** воздéрживаться от суждéния по какóму-л вопрóсу; **he ~d the right to withdraw from the trip** он сохранѝл за собóй прáво отказáться от поéздки

2 (*book*) закáз|ывать (-áть); бронѝровать (за-).

reserved *adj* **1** (*of a person*) сдéржанный; **he was very ~ on the subject** он был óчень сдéржан в э́том вопрóсе

2: **~ seats** зарáнее закáзанные местá.

reservoir *n* (*natural or artificial*) водоём; (*artificial*) водохранѝлище; (*smaller*) резервуáр; (*in fountain pen*, *lamp*) баллóн.

resettlement *n* переселéние.

reshuffle *n* (*in government*, *etc.*) перестанóвка; *Cards* перетасóвка.

reshuffle *vt*: **to ~ the Cabinet** произ|водѝть перестанóвку в кабинéте минѝстров (-вестѝ); *Cards* перетасóв|ывать (-áть).

reside *vi* (*live*) жить (*impf*).

residence *n* **1**: **place of ~** местожѝтельство; **during my ~ abroad** когдá я жил за границéй; **to take up one's ~ somewhere** поселѝться где-л; *attr*: **~ permit** разрешéние на прáво жѝтельства

2 (*house*, *etc.*) дом, жилѝще; (*large*, *official*) резидéнция; *Univ* **hall of ~** общежѝтие.

resident *n* (*of area*) (постоя́нный) жѝтель (*m*); (*of flats*) жилéц; (*in hotel*) постоя́лец.

resident *adj*: **the ~ population** постоя́нное населéние; **a ~ doctor** врач, живýщий при больнѝце; **he is at present ~ in Leeds** в настоя́щее врéмя он живёт/*off* проживáет в Лѝдсе.

residential *adj*: **a ~ area** жилóй райóн.

residual *adj* остáточный.

residue *n* остáток, остáтки (*pl*); (*sediment*) осáдок.

resign *vti vt* **1**: **to ~ one's right to smth** откáз|ываться от своегó прáва на что-л (-áться); **he ~ed his job in the bank/his commission** он оставил работу в банке, он подал в отставку

2: to ~ oneself to one's fate покор|яться (своей) судьбе (-иться), смириться со своей участью (*usu pf*); **he ~ed himself to the idea** он смирился с этой мыслью

vi Mil, Polit пода|вать в отставку (-ть); **to ~ from work** подавать заявление об уходе (с работы); **I ~ed from that job** я ушёл с этой работы; **he was asked to ~ from his job/from the committee** ему предложили подать заявление об уходе/выйти из членов *or* состава комиссии; **he ~ed in favour of a younger man** он отказался от своего поста в пользу более молодого работника.

resignation *n* **1** уход (с работы); отставка; **to hand in/submit one's ~** подать заявление об уходе, *Mil, Polit* подать в отставку

2 (*state*) смирение.

resilient *adj* (*physically*) упругий; (*mentally*) жизнестойкий; неунывающий.

resin *n* смола.

resinous *adj* смолистый.

resist *vti vt* (*oppose*) сопротивляться + *D*, (*withstand*) противостоять + *D* (*impfs*); (*keep from*) удерж|иваться от + *G* (-аться); **I couldn't ~ the temptation** я не мог противостоять искушению; **she couldn't ~ buying the bag/another cake** она не удержалась и купила сумку/и съела ещё одно пирожное; **to ~ an attack/changes** сдерж|ивать атаку (-ать), противиться изменениям (вос-)

vi сопротивляться; противостоять; удерживаться.

resistance *n* сопротивление, *also Elec, Polit*; **I shall take the line of least ~** я пойду по линии наименьшего сопротивления; **the body's ~ is low in winter** зимой сопротивляемость организма низка; *attr*: **the R. movement** движение сопротивления.

resistant *adj*: **rats are becoming ~ to poison** у крыс вырабатывается невосприимчивость к яду; **he is ~ to pressure** он не поддаётся нажиму.

re-sit *vt*: **to ~ an exam** пересдавать экзамен (*only in impf*).

resolute *adj* решительный; **a ~ man/tone** решительный человек/тон; **he is ~ in his decision** его решение бесповоротно.

resolution *n* **1** (*firmness*) решительность, решимость

2 (*solving*) разрешение, *also Mus*

3 (*motion*) резолюция; **to pass a ~ in favour of smth/against smth** вынести *or* принять резолюцию в пользу/против чего-л

4 (*resolve*): **he made a ~ to give up smoking** он решил бросить курить.

resolve *n* **1** (*decision*) решение; **to make a ~ to do smth** принять решение/решить сделать что-л

2 (*resoluteness*) решительность.

resolve *vti vt* **1** реш|ать (-ить), разрешить (*only in pf*); **the problem was ~d by a vote/only by his death** вопрос решился голосованием, только его смерть разрешила эту проблему; **it will all ~ itself in the end** в конце концов всё как-нибудь разрешится/уладится; **his assurances ~d their doubts** его заверения рассеяли их сомнения

2: to ~ smth into its separate elements раз|лагать что-л на составные части (-ложить)

vi **1** решить(ся) + *inf* (*usu pf*); **we ~d on a trip to Ireland** мы решили(сь) поехать в Ирландию; **we ~d to make a stand** мы решили стоять на своём

2: the question ~s into three parts вопрос распадается на три пункта.

resonance *n* резонанс.

resonant *adj* (*of voice, sound*) звучный; (*of acoustics*) **a ~ hall** зал с хорошей акустикой.

resort *n* **1: he turned to her as a last ~** он обратился к ней как к последней надежде; **in the last ~ you can always ring me** в крайнем случае ты всегда можешь позвонить мне

2: a holiday ~ курорт.

resort *vi*: **to ~ to smth/to smb** прибег|ать к чему-л (-нуть), обра|щаться к кому-л (-титься).

resound *vi* (*of noise*) разда|ваться (-ться); (*of place*) огла|шаться (-ситься); **a shot ~ed** раздался выстрел; **the cave ~ed with the echo** пещера огласилась эхом.

resounding *adj* (*sonorous*) звучный; *fig*: **the play was a ~ success in London** пьеса пользовалась шумным успехом/нашумела в Лондоне; **a ~ defeat** полное поражение.

resource *n* **1** (*quality*) находчивость

2 *pl* (**~s**) ресурсы, запасы; **financial/natural ~s** денежные/природные ресурсы; **~s of men and materials** людские ресурсы и запасы продовольствия; **they pooled their ~s to buy a car** они сложились, чтобы купить машину; **he has great ~s of energy** в нём большой заряд (*sing*) энергии; *fig* **he was left to his own ~s** он был предоставлен самому себе.

resourceful *adj* находчивый.

respect *n* **1** отношение; **in every ~** во всех отношениях (*pl*); **in ~ of smth** в отношении чего-л, относительно чего-л; **without ~ of persons** невзирая на лица

2 (*esteem*) уважение, почтение; **out of ~ for smb/smth** из уважения к кому-л/к чему-л; **to command ~** пользоваться уважением; **to win smb's ~** завоевать чьё-л уважение; **with due ~** с должным уважением/почтением; **with all ~, I disagree** при всём уважении к вам, я не согласен

3 *pl* (**~s**): **he sends you his ~s** он передаёт вам привет (*sing*); **I must pay my ~s to the Minister** я должен нанести визит министру.

respect *vt* уважать, почитать (*impfs*); **we must ~ his wishes** мы должны считаться с его желаниями (*usu impf*).

respectability *n* респектабельность.

respectable *adj* (*socially acceptable*) прили́чный, респекта́бельный; (*of some size*) значи́тельный, поря́дочный; **~ motives** благоро́дные побужде́ния; **he is outwardly ~ but...** вид у него́ тако́й респекта́бельный, одна́ко...; **a ~ hotel** о́чень прили́чная/респекта́бельная гости́ница; **in ~ society** в прили́чном о́бществе; **do I look ~?** я прили́чно вы́гляжу?; **a ~ sum** прили́чная/значи́тельная су́мма; **at a ~ distance from here** на поря́дочном/прили́чном расстоя́нии отсю́да.

respected *adj* уважа́емый, почита́емый.

respecter *n*: **he is no ~ of persons** для него́ все равны́, он челове́к нелицеприя́тный.

respectful *adj* почти́тельный; **he kept at a ~ distance** он держа́лся на почти́тельном расстоя́нии; **he is ~ towards his elders** он уважа́ет ста́рших.

respecting *prep* относи́тельно + *G*.

respective *adj*: **we went off to our ~ rooms** мы разошли́сь по свои́м ко́мнатам; **according to their ~ needs** в соотве́тствии с потре́бностями ка́ждого.

respectively *adv*: **they got first and second prizes ~** они́ получи́ли соотве́тственно пе́рвый и второ́й приз.

respiratory *adj Med* дыха́тельный; респирато́рный.

respite *n* передышка; *Law* отсро́чка; **without ~** без переды́шки; **we got no ~ from the heat** от жары́ не́ было никако́го спасе́ния.

respond *vi* (*answer*) отве|ча́ть (-́тить); (*react*) отзыва́ться (отозва́ться), реаги́ровать (про-); **he ~ed to my suggestion with a laugh** он отве́тил на моё предложе́ние сме́хом; **to ~ to an appeal/a suggestion** отозва́ться на призы́в/на предложе́ние; **the cat ~s to kindness** ко́шка отвеча́ет на ла́ску; **plants ~ to light** расте́ния реаги́руют на свет; **the patient is ~ing to treatment** больно́му помога́ет э́то лече́ние; **how did he ~?** как он отве́тил (*answer*)/прореаги́ровал (*react*)?; **the plane ~s well to the controls** самолёт послу́шен в управле́нии; **the brakes did not ~** тормоза́ не слу́шались.

response *n* (*answer*) отве́т; (*reaction*) реа́кция; (*positive reaction*) о́тзыв, о́тклик; **in ~ to many requests** в отве́т на мно́гие про́сьбы; **his only ~ was a yawn** в отве́т он то́лько зевну́л; **we had hoped for a bigger ~ to our appeal** мы ожида́ли бо́льшего о́тклика на наш призы́в.

responsibility *n* отве́тственность; **to accept/take ~ for smth** взять на себя́ отве́тственность за что-л; **it/she is your ~** э́то на ва́шей отве́тственности, ты за неё отвеча́ешь/в отве́те; **it is my ~ to decide** я отвеча́ю за приня́тие реше́ния; **he has no sense of ~** у него́ нет чу́вства отве́тственности.

responsible *adj* отве́тственный; **a ~ post/worker** отве́тственный пост/рабо́тник; **I hold you ~ for the crash** я счита́ю вас отве́тственным за ава́рию; **he is not ~ for his actions** он не отвеча́ет за свои́ посту́пки; **I am ~ for you to your parents** я отвеча́ю за тебя́ пе́ред твои́ми роди́телями; **those ~ will be punished** вино́вные бу́дут нака́заны.

responsibly *adv* со всей отве́тственностью.

responsive *adj*: **he is ~ to affection** он отвеча́ет/он отзы́вчив на ла́ску/на любо́вь; **a ~ audience** чу́ткая пу́блика.

rest[1] *n* **1** о́тдых, поко́й; **she never has a moment's ~** у неё никогда́ не быва́ет/она́ не зна́ет ни мину́ты поко́я; **we took a short ~** мы передохну́ли/немно́го отдохну́ли; **to come to ~** (*stop moving*) останови́ться; **to set smb's mind at ~** успока́ивать кого́-л; **you can set your mind at ~** мо́жешь успоко́иться; **I had a good night's ~** я хорошо́ вы́спался

2 *Mus* па́уза

3 (*stand*) подста́вка; *Tech* упо́р.

rest[1] *vti vt* **1**: **to ~ one's men/horses** да|ва́ть отдохну́ть свои́м войска́м/лошадя́м (-ть); **I feel quite ~ed** я чу́вствую себя́ отдохну́вшим; **these dark glasses ~ my eyes** в э́тих тёмных очка́х у меня́ отдыха́ют глаза́

2 (*lean, place*): **to ~ one's eyes on** останови́ть взгляд на + *P*; **to ~ a ladder against a tree** прислон|я́ть ле́стницу к де́реву (-и́ть); **he ~ed his head on his arms/his elbows on the table** он положи́л го́лову на́ руки, он облокоти́лся на стол

vi **1** (*repose*) отдыха́ть (отдохну́ть); **to ~ from one's exertions** отдохну́ть от трудо́в; *fig*: **may he ~ in peace** мир пра́ху его́; **we will not ~ until the matter is settled** мы не успоко́имся, пока́ де́ло не бу́дет решено́

2 (*remain*) оста|ва́ться (-́ться); **and there the matter ~s** тем де́ло и ко́нчилось; **we cannot let the matter ~ there** мы не мо́жем оста́вить де́ло так; **you can ~ assured that...** (вы) мо́жете быть уве́рены, что...

3 (*lean, be supported*): **he ~ed on his spade** он опира́лся на лопа́ту; **the roof ~s on six columns** шесть коло́нн подпира́ют кры́шу; *fig*: **the case ~s on the following facts** в осно́ву э́того де́ла поло́жены сле́дующие фа́кты; **responsibility ~s with him** отве́тственность лежи́т на нём; **it does not ~ with me to decide** не мне реша́ть.

rest[2] *n* оста́ток, оста́тки; остально́е; (*of people*) (**the ~**) остальны́е (*pl*); **we spent the ~ of the day here** мы провели́ здесь оста́ток дня; **what happened to the ~ of the cake?** а где оста́тки то́рта?; **I gave the ~ to him** остально́е я о́тдал ему́; **the ~ of the boys** остальны́е ребя́та.

restaurant *n* рестора́н; *attr*: **~ car** ваго́н-рестора́н.

restful *adj* (*of a person, occupation*) споко́йный; **she is a ~ companion** с ней так споко́йно.

rest home *n* дом о́тдыха.

restitution *n*: **to make ~ to smb (of smth)** верну́ть кому́-л (како́е-л иму́щество).

restive *adj* (*of horse*) норови́стый; (*of person*) беспоко́йный; **the crowd got ~** толпа́ заволнова́лась; **he gets ~ if he has nothing to do** ему́ без де́ла не сиди́тся.

restless *adj* (*fidgety*) беспоко́йный; непосе́дливый; **a ~ child** беспоко́йный/непосе́дливый ребёнок; **I had a ~ night** у меня́ была́ беспоко́йная ночь; **the audience is getting ~** пу́блика начина́ет проявля́ть нетерпе́ние; **the troops are getting ~** в войска́х начина́ется броже́ние.

restoration *n* восстановле́ние; *Art*, *Archit*, *Hist* реставра́ция.

restore *vt* восстан|а́вливать (-ови́ть); *Art*, *Archit*, *Hist* реставри́ровать (*impf and pf*); **to ~ order/smb's health/smb's sight** восстанови́ть поря́док/чьё-л здоро́вье/чьё-л зре́ние; **to ~ the monarchy/a painting** реставри́ровать мона́рхию/карти́ну; **the painting was ~d to its rightful owner/previous position** карти́на была́ возвращена́ зако́нному владе́льцу/на пре́жнее ме́сто.

restrain *vt* уде́рж|ивать, сде́рж|ивать (*pfs* -а́ть); **you must ~ him from doing that** ты до́лжен удержа́ть его́ от э́того; **he barely ~ed himself from laughing** он е́ле удержа́лся от сме́ха; **he ~ed his anger** он сдержа́л гнев.

restraint *n* сде́ржанность; (*restriction*) ограниче́ние; **with ~** сде́ржанно; **we can speak here without ~** здесь мы мо́жем говори́ть не стесня́ясь; **she wept without ~** она́ рыда́ла взахлёб (*adv*); **to impose ~s on the import of...** наложи́ть ограниче́ния на и́мпорт + *G*.

restrict *vt* ограни́ч|ивать (-ить); **sale of alcohol is ~ed by law** прода́жа алкого́льных напи́тков ограни́чена зако́ном; **I ~ myself to five cigarettes a day** я ограни́чиваюсь пятью́ сигаре́тами в день; **those trees ~ the view** э́ти дере́вья загора́живают вид; *Mil* **a ~ed area** запре́тная зо́на.

restriction *n* ограниче́ние.

restrictive *adj* ограничи́тельный.

result *n* результа́т; (*consequence*) после́дствие; **his limp is the ~ of a fall** его́ хромота́—результа́т паде́ния; **his trip had some strange ~s** его́ пое́здка име́ла стра́нные после́дствия; **as a ~ of smth** из-за чего́-л; **as a ~ we quarrelled** в результа́те мы поссо́рились; **without ~** безрезульта́тно; **the net ~ was...** в коне́чном ито́ге...; **what will be the ~ of all this?** к чему́ всё э́то приведёт?

result *vi* **1** (*follow*): **the idea ~ed from our talks yesterday** э́та иде́я родила́сь в результа́те на́ших вчера́шних разгово́ров; **nothing ~ed from my efforts** мои́ уси́лия ни к чему́ не привели́/бы́ли безрезульта́тны

2 (*end in*): **to ~ in** (*end in*) конч|а́ться + *I* (-́иться); (*lead to*) при|води́ть к + *D* (-вести́); **it ~ed in a quarrel** э́то ко́нчилось ссо́рой, э́то привело́ к ссо́ре; *Sport* **the game ~ed in a draw** игра́ зако́нчилась вничью́ (*adv*).

resume *vti vt* (*continue*) продолж|а́ть (-́ить); (*renew*) возобнов|ля́ть (-и́ть); **he ~d his story** он продолжа́л свой расска́з; **they ~d the game after the shower** они́ продо́лжили/возобнови́ли игру́ по́сле ли́вня; **he ~d work** он верну́лся на рабо́ту; **he ~d his seat** он (сно́ва) сел

vi: **classes have ~d** заня́тия возобнови́лись.

resumé *n* резюме́ (*indecl*); **to give a ~ of smth** резюми́ровать что-л, де́лать резюме́.

resurface *vti vt*: **to ~ a road** меня́ть покры́тие доро́ги (смени́ть)

vi (*of submarine*) вновь всплы|ва́ть на пове́рхность (-ть).

resurrect *vt* воскре|ша́ть (-си́ть), *also fig*; *CQ* **I've ~ed my old bicycle** я извлёк на свет бо́жий мой ста́рый велосипе́д.

resurrection *n Rel* (**the R.**) воскресе́ние.

resuscitate *vt Med* при|води́ть в созна́ние (-вести́).

retail *n usu attr*: **~ price/trade** ро́зничная цена́/торго́вля.

retail *adv* в ро́зницу.

retain *vt* (*preserve*) сохран|я́ть (-и́ть); (*hold, hold on to*) уде́рж|ивать (-а́ть); **the streets ~ their old names** у́лицы сохраня́ют свои́ ста́рые назва́ния; **he has ~ed all his faculties** он сохрани́л все свои́ спосо́бности; **he ~s his place in the team** он уде́рживает своё ме́сто в кома́нде; **a sponge ~s water** гу́бка уде́рживает во́ду.

retainer *n* (*servant*) слуга́ (*m*); *Law* предвари́тельный гонора́р; *Comm* зада́ток; **I paid a ~ for my room** я заплати́л зада́ток за ко́мнату.

retaliate *vi*: **they ~d by killing the prisoners/with a storm of abuse** они́ отомсти́ли, уби́в пле́нных, они́ отве́тили пото́ком оскорбле́ний; **they threatened to ~** они́ пригрози́ли отве́тными ме́рами.

retaliation *n*: **in ~ for smth** в отве́т на что-л; **for fear of ~** из стра́ха пе́ред отве́тным уда́ром.

retaliatory *adj* отве́тный.

retard *vt* замедл|я́ть (-́ить).

retarded *adj*: **a (mentally) ~ child** у́мственно отста́лый ребёнок.

retch *vi*: **he ~ed** его́ подта́шнивало (*impers*).

retentive *adj*: **a ~ mind** це́пкий ум.

rethink *vti*: **they will have to ~ their policy/to do a lot of ~ing on this question** им придётся пересмотре́ть свою́ поли́тику/мно́гое обду́мать в э́том вопро́се за́ново.

reticent *adj*: **he is naturally ~** он по нату́ре челове́к скры́тный; **she is ~ about her personal affairs** она́ никому́ о себе́ ничего́ не расска́зывает.

retina *n Anat* сетча́тка гла́за.

retinue *n* сви́та, эско́рт.

retire *vti vt*: **to ~ smb** увол|ьня́ть кого́-л со слу́жбы (-́ить)

vi (*from work*) вы|ходи́ть в отста́вку (-́йти); *Mil* (*retreat*) от|ходи́ть (-ойти́), *also fig*; **they hope to ~ into the country** они́ наде́ются уе́хать в дере́вню, когда́ уйду́т на пе́нсию; **to ~ for the night** ложи́ться спать; *Sport* **he had to ~ in the 5th lap** ему́ пришло́сь сойти́ на пя́том кру́ге.

retired *adj attr* отставно́й; *predic*: **he is ~** он в отста́вке.

retirement *n* отста́вка; **on his ~** когда́ он уходи́л в отста́вку; **how will you spend your**

~? что вы бу́дете де́лать, уйдя́ на пе́нсию?; *attr*: ~ **age** пенсио́нный во́зраст.

retiring *adj* (*shy*) скро́мный, засте́нчивый; **the ~ members of the committee** чле́ны, выходя́щие из соста́ва комите́та.

retort *vt* отве|ча́ть (-́тить); (*in contradiction*) возра|жа́ть (-зи́ть).

retrace *vt*: **he ~d his steps** он возврати́лся то́й же доро́гой; **we are trying to ~ his movements of last week** мы стара́емся вы́яснить, что он де́лал на про́шлой неде́ле.

retract *vti*: **to ~ a promise** отре́чься от обеща́ния; *Aer* **the undercarriage failed to ~** шасси́ ника́к не убира́лось.

retraining *n* переподгото́вка.

retreat *n* **1** (*place*) убе́жище

2 *Mil* отступле́ние; **Napoleon's ~ from Moscow** отступле́ние Наполео́на из Москвы́; **to beat the**/*fig* **a ~** дава́ть отбо́й, *also fig*; *fig* **he went into ~ for a year** он отошёл от дел на́ год.

retreat *vi* отступ|а́ть (-и́ть), *also Mil*, *fig*; **he ~ed a step/to his room** он отступи́л на шаг, он ушёл к себе́.

retrench *vi* эконо́мить (с-), соблюда́ть эконо́мию (*only in impf*).

retrial *n Law* повто́рное слу́шание де́ла.

retribution *n* возме́здие, ка́ра.

retributive *adj* кара́тельный.

retrieve *vt*: **I have ~d/have come to ~ my suitcase** я получи́л обра́тно/я пришёл забра́ть свой чемода́н; **he ~d his papers from the burning house** он вы́нес бума́ги из горя́щего до́ма; **the dog ~d the duck** соба́ка принесла́ подстре́ленную у́тку; **to ~ a mistake/a situation** исправ|ля́ть оши́бку (-́ить), спас|а́ть положе́ние (-ти́).

retrograde *adj fig*: **a ~ policy** реакцио́нная поли́тика.

retrospect *n*: **in ~** вспомина́я об э́том сего́дня, огляну́вшись наза́д.

retrospective *adj*: **~ legislation** зако́ны, име́ющие обра́тную си́лу; **the pay rise will be ~ to August the 1st** ра́зница в зарпла́те бу́дет выпла́чиваться с пе́рвого а́вгуста.

return *n* **1** возвраще́ние; возвра́т; **he demanded the ~ of his money** он тре́бовал возвра́та (свои́х) де́нег; **telephone at once on your ~** позвони́, как то́лько вернёшься; **on my ~ to England I...** возврати́вшись в А́нглию, я...; **by ~ (of post)** обра́тной по́чтой; (*in tennis*) **~ of service** приём пода́чи; *fig*: **in ~ for** в отве́т/в обме́н на + *A*; **in ~ I promised to help him** взаме́н я обеща́л помо́чь ему́; **they had reached the point of no ~** тепе́рь им не́ было ино́го вы́хода; **many happy ~s!** с днём рожде́ния!

2 *Comm* при́быль; **it brings in a good ~** э́то прино́сит хоро́шую при́быль; **the ~ on my shares is 5%** при́быль от мои́х а́кций — пять проце́нтов; **you'll get a quick ~ from this (investment)** э́то даст вам бы́стрый оборо́т

3 *special uses*: **tax ~** нало́говая деклара́ция; **the census ~s show that...** результа́ты пе́реписи (населе́ния) пока́зывают, что...

4 *attr*: **a ~ match/visit** отве́тный матч/визи́т; **on the ~ journey** на обра́тном пути́; **a ~ (ticket) to London** обра́тный биле́т до Ло́ндона.

return *vti vt* возвра|ща́ть (*pfs* -ти́ть *or* верну́ть); **she ~ed the ring to him** она́ верну́ла ему́ кольцо́; **he ~ed the book to the shelf/library** он поста́вил кни́гу обра́тно на по́лку, он возврати́л кни́гу в библиоте́ку; **to ~ a ball** верну́ть мяч; **to ~ smb's love** отвеча́ть кому́-л взаи́мностью; **he ~ed my visit** он нанёс мне отве́тный визи́т; **I should like to ~ his kindness** я хоте́л бы отблагодари́ть [NB *prefix*] его́ за (его́) доброту́; **he was ~ed to Parliament** он был и́збран в парла́мент; *Law* **they ~ed a verdict of guilty** его́ призна́ли вино́вным

vi возвраща́ться; **to ~ home/from France** верну́ться/возврати́ться домо́й/из Фра́нции; **he ~ed to his books** он верну́лся к свои́м кни́гам.

returnable *adj*: **the deposit is not ~** зало́г не возвраща́ется; **this book is ~ on the 5th** э́ту кни́гу ну́жно верну́ть/возврати́ть пя́того числа́.

reunion *n*: **a touching ~** тро́гательная встре́ча; **to arrange a family ~** устро́ить встре́чу всей семьи́; **an annual college ~** ежего́дная встре́ча выпускнико́в ко́лледжа.

reunite *vti vt*: **at last the family were ~d** наконе́ц вся семья́ собрала́сь вме́сте; **she was ~d with her husband after two years** че́рез два го́да она́ верну́лась к му́жу/муж верну́лся к ней

vi воссоедин|я́ться (-и́ться).

rev *vti*, *also* **to rev up** *CQ vt*: **don't ~ up (the engine) needlessly** не увели́чивай оборо́ты, е́сли нет необходи́мости.

revalue *vt* переоце́ни|вать (-́ть).

reveal *vt* откры|ва́ть (-́ть); обнару́жи|вать (-ть); **to ~ a secret to smb** открыва́ть кому́-л секре́т; **he ~ed to us that...** он нам сообщи́л, что...; **one day the truth will be ~ed** когда́-нибудь пра́вда вы́плывет нару́жу; **his poetry ~s a new side to his character** в стиха́х раскрыва́ются но́вые сто́роны (*pl*) его́ ли́чности.

revealing *adj*: **despite the omissions it was a ~ statement** несмотря́ на недомо́лвки, э́то бы́ло весьма́ открове́нное заявле́ние.

revel *vi* наслажда́ться (*impf*); (*carouse*) кути́ть (*impf*); **he ~led in his new found freedom** он наслажда́лся вновь обретённой свобо́дой.

revelation *n* открове́ние; (*headline*) **Startling ~s!** «Потряса́ющее разоблаче́ние!» (*sing*).

reveller *n* гуля́ка (*m*), кути́ла (*m*).

revelry *n*, **revels** *npl* весе́лье, пиру́шка, (*binge*) кутёж (*sings*).

revenge *n* месть, мще́ние; *Sport*, *Mil* рева́нш; **to take ~ on smb for smth** мстить кому́-л за что-л; **in ~ for** в отме́стку за + *A*; **we**

had our ~ on them мы отомсти́ли им, *Sport* мы взя́ли у них рева́нш.

revenge *vt* мстить (ото́-); **to ~ an insult/a friend** мстить за оби́ду/за дру́га; **to be ~d/to ~ oneself on smb for smth** отомсти́ть кому́-л за что-л.

revengeful *adj* мсти́тельный.

revenue *n* дохо́д; (*UK*) **Inland**/(*US*) **Internal R.** департа́мент нало́гов и сбо́ров.

reverberate *vi* (*of sound*) отра|жа́ться э́хом (-зи́ться), *also Phys*; **the sound ~d in the valley, the valley ~d with the sound** звук отрази́лся в доли́не/разнёсся э́хом по всей доли́не.

revere *vt* глубоко́ уважа́ть, почита́ть, благогове́ть (*impfs*).

reverent *adj* почти́тельный; благогове́йный.

reverie *n* мечта́ние; *Mus* фанта́зия; **she was lost in ~** она́ замечта́лась, она́ погрузи́лась в мечты́/в мечта́ния (*pls*).

revers *n Sew* отворо́т, ла́цкан.

reversal *n*: **~ of a judgment** отме́на суде́бного реше́ния; **a ~ of policy** круто́й поворо́т в поли́тике.

reverse *n* (*of coin, etc.*) обра́тная сторона́; (*of paper*) оборо́т, оборо́тная сторона́, *also fig*; **quite the ~** как раз наоборо́т (*adv*); **but it turned out just the ~** но вы́шло как раз наоборо́т; **in fact the ~ is true** в действи́тельности и́стина заключа́ется в противополо́жном; **our forces suffered a ~** на́ши войска́ потерпе́ли неуда́чу; *Aut* **to put the car into ~** включи́ть за́днюю переда́чу.

reverse *adj*: **on the ~ side** на обра́тной/оборо́тной стороне́; **in the ~ direction** в обра́тную сто́рону; **a ~ turn** обра́тный поворо́т; *Aut* **~ gear** за́дняя переда́ча.

reverse *vti vt* **1**: **he ~d his opinion/policy** он кру́то измени́л своё мне́ние/свою́ поли́тику; **he ~d his decision** он переду́мал, он измени́л своё реше́ние; **their roles are now ~d** тепе́рь они́ поменя́лись роля́ми; *Law* **to ~ a decision** отмен|я́ть реше́ние суда́ (-и́ть)

2 *Aut*: **he ~d the car into the garage/into a tree** он въе́хал за́дним хо́дом в гара́ж, он вре́зался в де́рево на за́днем ходу́

vi Aut: **the car ~d down the road** маши́на е́хала по доро́ге за́дним хо́дом; **I ~d into a van** я вре́зался за́дом в грузови́к.

reversible *adj* обрати́мый; **a ~ decision/process** обрати́мое реше́ние, обрати́мый проце́сс; **~ cloth** двусторо́нняя/двухлицева́я ткань.

revert *vi* возвраща́ться (верну́ться); **on his death the property ~s to the state** по́сле его́ сме́рти иму́щество перейдёт к госуда́рству; **I'll ~ to this later** я верну́сь к э́тому по́зже.

review *n* **1** (*consideration*) рассмотре́ние; *Law* пересмо́тр (де́ла); **my application is under ~** моё заявле́ние рассма́тривается; **his case is under ~** его́ де́ло пересма́тривается

2 (*survey*) обзо́р; **a ~ of the year's events** обзо́р собы́тий э́того го́да

3 *Mil* смотр, пара́д

4 (*of book*) реце́нзия; **a ~ of his book** реце́нзия на его́ кни́гу

5 (*journal*): **a literary ~** литерату́рно-крити́ческий журна́л.

review *vti vt* пересм|а́тривать, *also Law*, рассм|а́тривать (*pfs* -отре́ть); *Mil* **to ~ the troops** произ|води́ть смотр войска́м (-вести́); *Lit* **to ~ a book** рецензи́ровать кни́гу (*usu impf*)

vi: **he ~s for the Times** он пи́шет реце́нзии в «Таймс».

reviewer *n* рецензе́нт.

revile *vti* (*a person*) оскорб|ля́ть (-и́ть); **to ~ at/against smth** руга́ть, поноси́ть что-л (*impfs*).

revise *vti vt*: **to ~ one's opinion** пересм|а́тривать своё мне́ние (-отре́ть); (*correct, amend*) **to ~ a document** исправ|ля́ть докуме́нт (-́ить); **to ~ a text** перераб|а́тывать текст (-о́тать); **a ~d edition** (*corrected*) испра́вленное/(*worked anew*) перерабо́танное изда́ние

vi: **to ~ for exams** гото́виться к экза́менам (под-).

revision *n* (*correction*) пересмо́тр, исправле́ние; (*reworking*) перерабо́тка; **the ~ of his plans** пересмо́тр его́ пла́нов; **the ~ of a document** исправле́ние докуме́нта; **his ~ of the text** его́ перерабо́тка те́кста; *School* **I have two weeks for ~** у меня́ две неде́ли на подгото́вку.

revival *n* (*of person, trade, interest*) оживле́ние; (*of tradition*) возрожде́ние; **~ of an old film** возобновле́ние пока́за ста́рого фи́льма.

revive *vti vt*: **he ~d her with a sip of brandy** он привёл её в чу́вство глотко́м коньяка́; *fig*: **have a drink, it will ~ you** вы́пей, э́то тебя́ подбодри́т; **the rest ~d me** о́тдых восстанови́л мои́ си́лы; **the photos ~d many memories** э́ти фотогра́фии пробуди́ли мно́го воспомина́ний; **to ~ suspicions** сно́ва возбуди́ть подозре́ния; **to ~ an old custom** возроди́ть/воскреси́ть ста́рый обы́чай; **to ~ a play** возобнов|ля́ть постано́вку пье́сы (-и́ть)

vi ожив|ля́ться (-и́ться); **he/the flowers ~d** он оживи́лся *or* о́жил, цветы́ (в воде́) ско́ро о́жили *or* отошли́; **his hopes/strength ~d** в нём возроди́лись наде́жды/си́лы; **his spirits ~d** он воспря́нул ду́хом.

revoke *vt* (*of laws*) отмен|я́ть (-и́ть); (*of promise*) брать наза́д (взять).

revolt *n* (*organized*) восста́ние; (*disorganized*) бунт.

revolt *vti vt*: **the film/that kind of behaviour ~s me** меня́ воро́тит от э́того фи́льма, тако́е поведе́ние мне прети́т *or* мне отврати́тельно

vi восста|ва́ть (-́ть); бунтова́ть (*impf*); *fig* **his nature ~ed against it** всё в нём восстава́ло про́тив э́того.

revolting *adj* отврати́тельный.

revolution *n* (*turn*) оборо́т; *Polit* револю́ция.

revolutionary *adj* революцио́нный.

revolve *vti* враща́ть(ся), верте́ть(ся) (*impfs*); **the earth ~s on its axis** земля́ враща́ется вокру́г свое́й оси́; **a revolving door** враща́ющаяся дверь; *fig* **her life ~s around her son** вся её жизнь в сы́не.

revolver *n* револьве́р.

revue *n* ревю́ (*indecl*); **a students' ~** студе́нческий капу́стник.

reward *n* вознагражде́ние, *also fig*; **a ~ of £50 is offered for...** предлага́ется вознагражде́ние в пятьдеся́т фу́нтов за + *A*; *fig* **the ~ of patience** вознагражде́ние за терпе́ние.

reward *vt* вознагра|жда́ть (-ди́ть); **our efforts were ~ed** на́ши уси́лия бы́ли вознаграждены́.

rewarding *adj*: **a ~ book** сто́ящая кни́га; **it is most ~ work** э́то благода́рная рабо́та; **it is financially ~ work** э́то хорошо́ опла́чиваемая рабо́та.

rhapsody *n Mus* рапсо́дия; *fig* **to be in/to go into rhapsodies about smth** быть в восто́рге (*sing*) от чего́-л, восторга́ться *or* восхища́ться чем-л, приходи́ть в восто́рг от чего́-л.

rhetoric *n* рито́рика.

rheumatic *adj* ревмати́ческий.

rheumatism *n* ревмати́зм.

rhinoceros, *CQ* **rhino** *n* носоро́г.

rhododendron *n* рододе́ндрон.

rhombus *n* ромб.

rhubarb *n* реве́нь (*m*).

rhyme *n* ри́фма; **nursery ~s** де́тские стишки́; **in ~** в стиха́х; *fig*: **there is neither ~ nor reason to it** в э́том нет ни скла́ду ни ла́ду; **he did it without ~ or reason** он э́то сде́лал ни с того́ ни с сего́.

rhythm *n* ритм, ритми́чность.

rhythmic *adj*: **~ prose** ритми́ческая про́за; **~ movement** ритми́чное движе́ние.

rib *n Anat* ребро́; (*on material*) ру́бчик; *Bot* жи́лка.

ribald *adj* (*of jokes, etc.*) скабрёзный, непристо́йный; (*of person*) гру́бый.

ribbed *adj* (*in appearance*) ребри́стый; (*of material*) ру́бчатый; (*striped*) полоса́тый.

ribbon *n* ле́нта, *dim* ле́нточка; *Mil* о́рденская ле́нта; **type-writer ~** ле́нта для пи́шущей маши́нки; **torn to ~s** изо́рванный в кло́чья; *attr*: (*in building*) **~ development** ле́нточная застро́йка.

rice *n* рис; *attr* ри́совый.

rich *adj* бога́тый, *also fig*; **a ~ experience/harvest** бога́тый о́пыт/урожа́й; **the earth is ~ in minerals** земля́ бога́та минера́лами; **~ soil** ту́чная/жи́рная по́чва; **~ food** жи́рная пи́ща; **~ colours** я́ркие цвета́; **to get ~** разбогате́ть.

riches *npl* бога́тство (*sing*).

richly *adv* бога́то; (*fully*) **he ~ deserves punishment** он в по́лной ме́ре заслу́живает наказа́ния.

rick[1] *n* (*of hay*) скирда́, стог.

rick[2] *vt*: **to ~ one's ankle** вы́вихнуть/растяну́ть лоды́жку (*usu pfs*).

rickets *n Med* рахи́т.

rickety *adj* (*unsteady*) расша́танный, ша́ткий, (*of furniture only*) колчено́гий.

rid *vt* избав|ля́ть (-́ить); **the medicine ~ me of my cough** лека́рство изба́вило меня́ от ка́шля; **how can we get ~ of the rats?** как нам вы́вести крыс?; **I couldn't get ~ of him** я не мог от него́ отде́латься; **we had to get ~ of the car** нам пришло́сь прода́ть маши́ну.

riddance *n*: **good ~!** ска́тертью доро́га!

riddle[1] *n* (*conundrum*) зага́дка, *also fig*; **to ask smb a ~** загада́ть кому́-л зага́дку; **to solve a ~** отгада́ть зага́дку.

riddle[2] *n* (*sieve*) си́то, решето́; *Agric* гро́хот.

riddle[2] *vt*: **to ~ soil/coal** просе́|ивать зе́млю/у́голь (-ять); **to ~ a door with bullets** изрешети́ть дверь пу́лями (*usu pf*).

ride *n* (*on horse, bicycle, in car*) пое́здка; (*for pleasure only*) прогу́лка; (*of distance*) езда́; **I'm going for a ~ on my pony** пойду́ поката́юсь на по́ни; **we went for a ~ in the mountains** (*on horse*) мы пое́хали верхо́м в го́ры; **a bicycle ~** велосипе́дная прогу́лка; **we had a rough ~ on the bus** в авто́бусе нас растрясло́ (*impers*); **we went for/he gave us a ~ in the car** мы поката́лись/он нас поката́л на маши́не; **we had a ~ on the roundabout** мы поката́лись на карусе́ли; **our house is a ten minute ~ from the station** до на́шего до́ма от ста́нции де́сять мину́т езды́; **he gave her a ~ into town/on his back** он подвёз её в го́род, он понёс её на спине́; *CQ* **to take smb for a ~** обману́ть кого́-л.

ride *vti vt* е́здить на + *P* (*indet impf, pf* по- = *to ride round a while*), е́хать (*det impf, pf* по- = *to start to ride*) [**NB** *the true pf of completed action requires a compound formed with a prefix, e.g.* прое́хать]; (*go for a ride on*) ката́ться на + *P* (по-); **can you ~ a bicycle?** ты уме́ешь е́здить на велосипе́де?; **to ~ a horse/a camel** е́здить верхо́м/на верблю́де; **this horse has never been ridden** на э́той ло́шади никогда́ не е́здили верхо́м; **I have never ridden that horse** я никогда́ не е́здил верхо́м на э́той ло́шади; **he rode his horse hard/in two races** он загна́л свою́ ло́шадь, он уча́ствовал в двух забе́гах на свое́й ло́шади; **we rode 70 km in 5 hours** мы прое́хали се́мьдесят киломе́тров за пять часо́в; *fig* **to ~ out the storm** вы́держать шторм

vi е́здить, е́хать; ката́ться; **do you ~?** ты е́здишь верхо́м?; **he rode like the wind** он мча́лся как ве́тер; **they rode into town** (*one way*) они́ е́хали в го́род, (*and back*) они́ съе́здили в го́род; **he often ~s around in his car** он ча́сто ката́ется на маши́не; **we'll ~ over to see you** мы прие́дем к вам; *fig*: **the moon is riding high in the sky** луна́ плывёт высоко́ в не́бе; **I'll let the matter ~ for a few weeks** я отложу́ э́то де́ло на па́ру неде́ль; **we'll have to let things ~** пусть бу́дет, что бу́дет

ride at *vi*: **he rode straight at the fence** он е́хал пря́мо на барье́р; **he rode at the enemy** он мча́лся на врага́

ride away *vi* отъ|езжáть, у|езжáть (*pfs* -éхать); **they rode away in different directions** они́ разъéхались в рáзные стóроны

ride back *vi*: **he rode back to town** он éхал обрáтно в гóрод

ride into *vi* въезжáть (въéхать); **he rode straight into a lamppost** он наéхал прямо на фонáрный столб

ride past *vi* про|езжáть ми́мо + *G* (-éхать)

ride round *vi*: **he ~s round his estate each day** кáждый день он объезжáет верхóм на лóшади своё имéние

ride up *vi* (*of clothing*) за|дирáться (-дрáться)

ride up to *vi* подъ|езжáть к + *D* (-éхать).

rider *n* (*on horse*) всáдник, наéздник; (*on cycle*) велосипеди́ст; (*in document*, *etc.*) дополнéние; **I must add the ~ that...** в дополнéние я дóлжен сказáть, что...

ridge *n* **1** (*of hills*) (гóрная) грядá, (гóрный) хребéт; (*on material*) рýбчик; **the ~ of a roof** конёк кры́ши

2 *Meteorol*: **a ~ of high pressure** óбласть высóкого давлéния.

ridicule *n*: **an object of ~** предмéт насмéшек (*pl*), посмéшище; **to hold smb up to ~** подня́ть когó-л нá смех.

ridicule *vt* вы|смéивать (-смеять), осмé|ивать (-ять), насмехáться над + *I* (*impf*).

ridiculous *adj* нелéпый; **a ~ hat** нелéпая шля́па; **he looks ~** он вы́глядит нелéпо/смешнó (*advs*); **to make oneself ~** постáвить себя́ в нелéпое положéние; **it is ~ to expect me to do that** смешнó ожидáть, что я э́то сдéлаю.

ridiculously *adv*: **it was ~ easy** э́то бы́ло до смешнóго легкó.

riding *n* верховáя ездá; **she loves ~** онá óчень лю́бит éздить/катáться верхóм; *attr*: **~ boots/breeches** сапоги́/бри́джи для верховóй езды́.

rife *adj*: **famine/superstition was ~** гóлод свирéпствовал, суевéрие бы́ло широкó распространенó.

riffraff *n* подóнки (*pl*) óбщества.

rifle *n Mil* винтóвка; (*for hunting*) ружьё; *pl* (**the Rifles**) (*regiment*) стрелки́; *attr*: **a ~ battalion** стрелкóвый батальóн; **~ range** стрéльбище.

rift *n* (*crack*) трéщина, рассéлина, щель; (*in clouds*) просвéт; *fig* разры́в.

rig[1] *n* **1** *Naut* пáрусное вооружéние

2: **an oil ~** буровáя вы́шка (*on land or sea*).

rig[1] *vt Naut* осна|щáть (-сти́ть), *also fig*; *fig*: **to ~ smth/smb out with the latest equipment** оснасти́ть что-л новéйшим обору́дованием, снабди́ть когó-л новéйшим снаряжéнием (*usu pf*); **they ~ged up a shelter out of branches** они́ нáскоро сооруди́ли убéжище из вéток; *CQ* **she was ~ged out in her new dress** онá наряди́лась в нóвое плáтье.

rig[2] *vt* (*manage fraudulently*) подстр|áивать (-óить); **it's been ~ged!** э́то всё подстрóено!; **to ~ an election** фальсифици́ровать/подтасóв|ывать результáты вы́боров (*impf and pf*/-áть).

rigging *n Naut* такелáж, оснáстка.

right *n* **1** прáвда; **he has ~ on his side** прáвда за ним; **to know ~ from wrong** знать, что прáвильно и что нет; **he is in the ~** он прав; **I don't know the ~s and wrongs of the matter** я не знáю, что здесь прáвда, а что ложь

2 (*entitlement*) прáво; **human/civil ~s** правá человéка, граждáнские правá; **the ~ of veto** прáво вéто (*indecl*); **by ~ of smth** по прáву чегó-л; **I have a ~ to the money** я имéю прáво на э́ти дéньги; **you have no ~ to ask** ты не имéешь прáва проси́ть, ты не впрáве (*adv*) проси́ть; **to exercise one's ~ to vote** воспóльзоваться свои́м прáвом гóлоса; **film ~s** прáво (*sing*) на экранизáцию; **she is a good painter in her own ~** онá и самá хорошó рису́ет

3 *pl* (*order*): **she quickly set the room to ~s** онá бы́стро навелá в кóмнате поря́док/привелá кóмнату в поря́док

4 (*not left*): **keep to the ~** держи́тесь прáвой сторонь́і; **to the ~ of the door** напрáво/спрáва (*advs*) от двéри; **from left to ~** слéва напрáво; **parties of the ~** прáвые пáртии; **he is further to the ~ than I am** он бóлее прáвый, чем я [**NB** *Polit always long form of adj*].

right *adj* **1** (*just*) прáвильный, справедли́вый; **I think it ~ that he is here** я считáю прáвильным/справедли́вым то, что он здесь; **I thought it ~ to warn you** я счёл свои́м дóлгом предупреди́ть вас; **is it ~ for me to ask him?** я прáвильно сдéлаю, éсли спрошу́ у негó?; **it's not ~** э́то непрáвильно; **to do the ~ thing by smb** чéстно поступи́ть с кем-либо

2 (*correct*) прáвильный; вéрный; прав (*only in short form*); **the ~ answer** прáвильный отвéт; **you're quite ~** вы совершéнно правы́; **~!** прáвильно!; **quite ~!** совершéнно вéрно!; **am I ~ in thinking that..?** прав ли я, дýмая, что..?; **is it ~ that you're not coming?** э́то прáвда, что ты не придёшь?; **you were ~ to come** вы прáвильно сдéлали, что пришли́; **am I ~/on the ~ road for the station?** я прáвильно идý к вокзáлу?; **have I got that ~?** я прáвильно пóнял?; **is your watch ~?** у вас вéрные часы́?; **what is the ~ time?** скажи́те мне тóчное врéмя; **it's not the ~ size** э́то не тот размéр; **to put a mistake ~** испрáвить оши́бку; **we'll soon put that ~** мы скóро э́то вы́ясним (*clear up*)/попрáвим (*mend*); **put me ~ if I am mistaken** попрáвь меня́, éсли я ошибу́сь; **ask him, he'll put you ~** спроси́ егó, он тебé скáжет; **stand the box ~ side up** постáвь я́щик кры́шкой квéрху; **the ~ side** (*of cloth*) лицевáя сторонá; *CQ* **are you in your ~ mind?** да ты в своём ли умé?

3 (*suitable*) подходя́щий; (*needful*) нýжный; **that dress isn't ~ for you** э́то плáтье тебé не подхóдит; **you have to choose the ~ moment**

нужно выбрать подходящий момент; **he arrived at the ~ time** он пришёл в нужный момент; **it is not ~ for you to go there alone** тебе не надо идти туда одному; **he's on the ~ side of 40** ему под сорок

4 (*well*): **this medicine will soon put you ~** от этого лекарства вы скоро поправитесь; **it all came ~ in the end** в конце концов всё обошлось/вышло/получилось хорошо; **everything will come ~** всё уладится; *CQ* **he'll be as ~ as rain tomorrow** завтра он будет вполне здоров

5 (*not left*) правый, *also Polit*

6 *CQ expressions*: **~ you are!/~ oh! I'm coming** хорошо, хорошо, я иду; **he's the ~ sort** он настоящий парень.

right *adv* **1** (*rightly*) правильно; **you did ~ to wait** вы правильно сделали, что подождали; **if I remember ~** если я правильно помню; **he guessed ~** он догадался; **to do smth ~** делать что-л как следует; **nothing goes ~ for them** у них всё идёт не так; **it serves him ~** поделом (*adv*) ему, так ему и надо; **it was him ~ enough** это был, конечно, он

2 (*exactly, directly*) прямо; как раз; **~ in the middle** в самой середине, прямо посередине; **~ on the nose** прямо в нос; **~ opposite** как раз/прямо напротив; **it happened ~ here** это случилось как раз/именно здесь; **~ to the end** вплоть до самого конца; **go away ~ now** иди сейчас же; **he went ~ on talking** он всё продолжал говорить

3 (*not left*) направо; **~ turn!** направо!; *CQ* **they owe money ~, left and centre** они кругом в долгах.

right *vt* (*correct*) исправ|лять (-ить); **it will ~ itself** это само собой образуется; **to ~ a wrong** устран|ять несправедливость (-ить); (*straighten*) **the boat ~ed itself** лодка выровнялась.

right-angled *adj* прямоугольный.

righteous *adj* (*of people*) праведный; **don't be so ~** не будь таким праведником; **~ indignation** справедливое негодование.

rightful *adj*: **the ~ heir/owner** законный наследник/владелец.

right-hand *adj* правый; **on the ~ side** по правой стороне; **a ~ turn** поворот направо (*adv*); *fig* **he's my ~ man** он моя правая рука.

right-handed *adj*: **he is ~** он не левша; **a ~ blow** удар справа (*adv*).

rightly *adv* (*correctly*) правильно; (*justly*) справедливо; **you acted ~** вы поступили правильно; **and ~ so** и правильно; **as he ~ believed** как он справедливо полагал; **~ or wrongly, I told him** как бы там ни было, я ему это сказал.

right-wing *adj Polit* правый.

rigid *adj* жёсткий, *also fig*; *fig* (*of person*) негибкий; **a ~ board/rule** жёсткая доска, жёсткое правило; **he has ~ views** он не гибок в своих взглядах.

rigidly *adv*, *usu fig*: **he stood ~ at attention** он стоял, застыв по стойке смирно; **he is ~ opposed to the idea** он упорно не соглашается с этой идеей.

rigmarole *n*: **he told me some long ~ about...** он рассказал мне какую-то длинную историю о...; **they go through the same ~ every time** с ними вечно одна и та же история.

rigorous *adj* (*of discipline, control, measures*) строгий; **a ~ climate** суровый климат; **a ~ search** тщательные поиски (*pl*).

rile *vt* раздражать (*usu impf*).

rim *n* (*of cup, etc.*) ободок; (*of specs*) оправа; (*of wheel*) обод.

rind *n* (*of fruit*) кожура, *CQ* шкурка; (*of cheese, bacon*) корка.

ring[1] *n* **1** кольцо; **engagement/wedding ~** обручальное кольцо; **curtain ~** кольцо для портьер; **~s under the eyes** круги под глазами

2 (*of people*): **to form a ~** стать в круг; **there was a ~ of admirers round her** её обступила толпа поклонников; **a spy ~** шпионская сеть

3 (*at circus, Sport*) арена; (*boxing*) ринг.

ring[2] *n* (*noise*) звон; (*of door, Tel*) звонок; **there was a loud ~** раздался громкий звонок; **there was a ~ at the door** позвонили в дверь; **give me a ~** позвони мне; **there was a ~ of irony in his voice** в его голосе звучала ирония.

ring[2] *vti vt*: **to ~ the bell** звонить в звонок/(*door bell*) в дверь/(*church bell*) в колокол (по-); **he rang me up** он позвонил мне; *fig* **that ~s a bell with me** это мне о чём-то напоминает

vi (*of telephone, electric, large bells*) звонить (по-); (*jingle, of small bells, etc.*) звенеть (*impf*); **to begin to ~** зазвонить, зазвенеть (*pfs*); **the phone stopped ~ing** телефон перестал звонить/замолчал; **he rang off** он повесил трубку; **I'll ~ for some milk** я позвоню, чтобы принесли молока; **to ~ for the lift** вызывать лифт; **her voice was ~ing in my ears** её голос звучал/звенел у меня в ушах; **the house rang with their laughter** дом оглашался их смехом; **a cry/shot rang out** раздался крик/выстрел; **his story ~s true** его рассказ звучит правдиво.

ringing *n* звон; **there was a ~ in her ears** у неё звенело в ушах.

ringing *adj* (*of voice, laugh*) звонкий, звучный; (*tinkling*) звенящий; *Tel* **the ~ tone** длинные гудки.

ringleader *n* зачинщик, главарь (*m*).

ringlet *n* локон, завиток.

ring road *n* кольцевая дорога.

rinse *n* (*for hair*) краска для волос; **to give one's mouth a ~** прополоскать рот; **he gave the clothes/dishes a ~** он выполоскал одежду, он сполоснул посуду.

rinse *vt* полоскать (вы-, про- (*of clothes*), сполоснуть (*of dishes*), про- (*of mouth, hair*)); (*of hair, with dye*) красить (по-).

riot *n* волнения (*pl*); **there were ~s in the streets** на улицах были волнения; **the crowd ran ~** толпа пришла в волнение; *fig*: **the weeds have run ~** сорняки буйно разрослись;

the party was a ~! ну и повеселились мы!; **he let/lets his imagination run ~** он дал волю (своему) воображению, у него слишком буйное воображение.

riot *vi* бунтовать, *CQ* буйствовать (*impfs*).

rioter *n* бунтовщик.

riotous *adj* буйный; **~ behaviour** буйное поведение; **~ growth** буйный рост; **a ~ party** буйная пирушка; *CQ*: **we had a ~ time** мы от души повеселились; (*funny*) **it was a ~ meeting** собрание было очень забавным.

rip[1] *n* (*tear*) прореха.

rip[1] *vti vt* рвать (по-, изо-), драть (изо-); **to ~ down a poster/off buttons** сорвать афишу, оторвать пуговицы; **to ~ pages out of a book** вырывать/выдирать страницы из книги; **she ~ped the seam/the envelope open** она распорола шов, она вскрыла конверт; **to ~ up a document** разорвать документ; *fig*: **he let ~ a few oaths** он разразился ругательствами/бранью; **he really let ~** (*singing*) он пел от всей души, (*in anger*) он вышел из себя

vi рваться *and compounds*; **my trousers ~ped on the wire** я разодрал себе брюки о проволоку; *CQ Aut* **let her ~** прибавь ходу.

rip[2] *n CQ*: **he's an old ~** он просто старый распутник.

ripe *adj* спелый; зрелый, *also fig*; **to grow ~** поспеть, созреть; **the plums are ~ for picking** сливы созрели для сбора; *fig*: **to live to a ~ old age** достичь преклонного возраста; **~ judgment** зрелое суждение; **they are ~ for revolt** они готовы восстать; **when the time is ~** когда придёт время.

ripen *vti vt*: **how can I ~ these tomatoes?** что мне сделать, чтобы эти помидоры созрели?; **the sun will soon ~ them** они скоро созреют на солнце

vi зреть (со-), созре|вать (-ть), спеть (по-).

ripping *adj CQ* потрясающий.

ripple *n* (*on water*) рябь, зыбь (*no pls*); **~s on the sand** рябь на песке; *fig* **a ~ of excitement/applause went round the hall** волна возбуждения/аплодисментов прокатилась по залу.

ripple *vti vt*: **the wind ~d the surface of the water** вода под ветром подёрнулась рябью

vi покры|ваться/подёр|гиваться рябью (-ться/-нуться).

rise *n* **1** подъём; (*of sun, moon*) восход; **a ~ in the road/in the river** подъём дороги/уровня воды в реке; (*of fishing*) **there should be a good ~ tonight** вечером должен быть клёв; *fig*: **the ~ and fall of the Roman Empire** возвышение и гибель Римской империи; **Napoleon's ~ to power** приход Наполеона к власти; **the ~ of socialism** возникновение социализма; *CQ* **I got a ~ out of her** я её разыграл

2 (*increase*) повышение; увеличение; **a ~ in prices/salary/temperature/living standards** повышение цен/зарплаты/температуры/уровня жизни; **a ~ in production/crime** увеличение продукции, рост преступности; **to ask for a ~** просить о повышении зарплаты/*CQ* о прибавке; **to get a ~ of £10** получить прибавку в десять фунтов

3 (*high ground*): **he stood on a ~** он стоял на возвышении

4 (*source*): **the river has its ~ in the hills** река берёт начало в горах; *fig*: **this gave ~ to many problems** это породило много проблем; **it gave ~ to suspicion/many jokes** это дало повод к подозрению/ко многим шуткам.

rise *vi* **1** (*get up*) подн|иматься (-яться), вста|вать (-ть); **to ~ from the table** подняться/встать из-за стола; **to ~ to one's feet/from one's knees** подняться *or* встать на ноги/с колен; **the meeting rose at six** собрание закончилось в шесть (часов)

2: **to ~ (in revolt) against smth** подниматься/восставать против чего-л, *also fig*

3 (*go up*) подняться; повы|шаться (-ситься); (*of sun, moon*) всходить (взойти); (*of fish*) клевать (клюнуть); **the barometer is rising** барометр поднимается; **the river rose two metres** вода в реке поднялась на два метра; **the ground ~s slightly here** тут начинается небольшой подъём; **to ~ to the surface** всплы|вать на поверхность (-ть); **his temperature rose** у него поднялась/повысилась температура; **her voice rose** она повысила голос; *fig*: **our spirits rose** у нас поднялось настроение; **to ~ in smb's estimation** подняться в чьём-л мнении, вырасти в чьих-л глазах; **to ~ to the occasion** оказ|ываться на высоте положения (-аться)

4 (*increase*) увеличиваться; повышаться; расти; **prices are rising** цены повышаются/растут; **the price of bread rose by 2p** хлеб стал дороже/хлеб подорожал на два пенса; **the tide/the wind/tension is rising** идёт прилив, ветер усиливается, напряжение растёт; **her colour rose** она покраснела

5 (*in rank, society*): **he rose from the ranks/to (the rank) of colonel** он начинал с рядового, он дослужился до (чина) полковника; **he rose in the firm to become director** он успешно продвигался по службе и стал директором; **he has ~n in the world** он преуспел в жизни

6 (*begin*): **the river ~s from a lake** река берёт начало из озера; **the quarrel rose from a misunderstanding** ссора возникла/вспыхнула из-за недоразумения.

riser *n*: **he is an early/late ~** он рано/поздно встаёт.

rising *n* повышение; подъём; (*rebellion*) восстание; (*of sun, moon*) восход.

rising *adj*: **~ ground** возвышенная местность; **the ~ tide** нарастающий прилив; **~ excitement/numbers** возрастающее волнение/количество (*sing*); **the ~ generation** подрастающее поколение; **a ~ young lawyer** подающий надежды молодой адвокат; **he is ~ five** ему скоро пять лет.

risk *n* риск, опасность; **an occupational ~** профессиональный риск, *also fig*; **at one's own ~** на свой (страх и) риск; **at ~ of one's life/of offending him** с риском для жизни, рискýя обúдеть егó; **it's not worth the ~** не стóит рисковáть; **you are running the ~ of losing your job** вы рискýете потерять рабóту; **I'll take the ~** я рискнý; **he takes too many ~s** он слúшком чáсто рискýет/идёт на риск; **it's only a small ~** риск невелúк; **there is a ~ of fire/of him seeing you** есть опáсность пожáра/, что он вас увúдит; **he is a security ~** емý нельзя доверять, он ненадёжный человéк.

risk *vt* (*put at risk*) рисковáть + *I* (*impf*); (*venture to*) рискнýть + *inf* (*pf*); **to ~ one's life/neck** рисковáть жúзнью/головóй; **I ~ed his disapproval** я рисковáл вы́звать егó неодобрéние; **I can't ~ failure** я не могý рисковáть всем.

risky *adj* рискóванный.

risqué *adj* (*of joke, etc.*) сомнúтельный.

rissole *n* битóк, котлéта.

rite *n* обряд; **last ~s** послéднее причáстие (*sing*).

rival *n* сопéрник; (*competitor*) конкурéнт.

rival *adj*: **a ~ firm** конкурúрующая фúрма; **the ~ team** комáнда-сопéрник.

rival *vt* сопéрничать с + *I* (*impf*); **nobody can ~ his strength** никтó не мóжет сравнúться с ним сúлой.

rivalry *n* сопéрничество.

river *n* рекá; **up/down ~** вверх/вниз по рекé; *attr* речнóй.

riverbank *n* бéрег рекú.

riverbed *n* рýсло рекú.

rivermouth *n* ýстье рекú.

riverside *n* бéрег рекú; *attr* прибрéжный.

rivet *n* заклёпка.

rivet *vt* *Tech* (*one thing to another*) приклёп|ывать, (*two things together*) склёп|ывать (*pfs* -áть); *fig* **all eyes were ~ed on him** все взóры бы́ли прикóваны к немý.

rivulet *n* ручеёк.

roach *n* (*fish*) плотвá; (*US*: *cockroach*) таракáн.

road *n* дорóга, путь, *both also fig*; **an arterial/trunk/main ~** (автодорóжная) магистрáль; **a dirt ~** грунтовáя дорóга; **to send goods by ~** перевозúть товáры по шоссé; **we went by ~** мы éхали по дорóге; **to cross the ~** перейтú дорóгу/ýлицу; **he lives across the ~ (from us)** он живёт (от нас) чéрез дорóгу; **he took the ~ to Bristol** он поéхал по дорóге на Бристóль; **to be on the ~** (*travelling*) быть в путú, (*be a tramp*) бродяжничать, *Theat* быть на гастрóлях, *Comm* разъезжáть; **the car holds the ~ well** машúна устóйчива на дорóге; **"~ up"** «Путь закры́т»; **are we on the right ~?** мы прáвильно идём?; *fig*: **to be on the right ~** быть на прáвильном путú; **he is on the ~ to fame/recovery** он на путú к слáве/к выздоровлéнию; **my car is off the ~** я сейчáс без машúны; **let's have one for the ~** давáй вы́пьем на дорóгу; **he's a menace on the ~** он опáсный лихáч; **get out of the ~!** прочь с дорóги!; *attr*: **a ~ accident** дорóжная авáрия.

roadblock *n* дорóжное заграждéние.

roadmap *n* дорóжная кáрта.

road metal *n* щéбень (*m*).

road sense *n* чýвство дорóги.

roadside *n* обóчина; *attr*: **a ~ café** придорóжное кафé.

roadsign *n* дорóжный знак.

roadworks *npl* дорóжные рабóты.

roam *vti* бродúть (*impf*); (*of eyes*) бéгать (*impf*).

roan *n* чáлая лóшадь.

roar *n* (*of animal*) рёв, *also fig*; (*ferocious*) рык; (*of sea*) рóкот; (*of guns*) грóхот орýдий; **the ~ of the river/wind/engines** шум рекú/вéтра, рёв motóров; **the distant ~ of traffic** отдалённый гул ýличного движéния.

roar *vi* ревéть (вз-); (*of sea*) рокотáть (*impf*); (*of guns, thunder, traffic*) грохотáть (про-); **the engine ~ed** motóр взревéл; **the wind ~ed in the chimney** вéтер ревéл/выл в трубé; **a lorry ~ed past** мúмо с рёвом пронёсся грузовúк; **to ~ oneself hoarse** кричáть до хрипоты́; **to ~ with laughter** покáтываться сó смеху, хохотáть (*impfs*).

roaring *adj*: **by a ~ fire** у я́рко пылáющего огня́; *CQ*: **they do a ~ trade in bicycles** онú бóйко торгýют велосипéдами; **the play was a ~ success** пьéса имéла шýмный успéх; **~ drunk** вдрызг пья́ный.

roast *n* жáреное мя́со, жаркóе.

roast *adj* жáреный; **~ beef** рóстбиф.

roast *vti vt* жáрить (за-, по-, из-); **to ~ coffee** жáрить кóфе; *fig* **to ~ oneself/one's feet by the fire** грéться/греть нóги у огня́ (*impf*)

vi жáриться, *also fig CQ*.

rob *vt* красть (у-); (*usu a person*) обкрáдывать (обокрáсть); (*bank, etc.*) грáбить (о-); **they ~bed him of his watch** у негó укрáли часы́; *fig* **to ~ smb of his inheritance** лиш|áть когó-л наслéдства (-úть).

robber *n* грабúтель (*m*), вор.

robbery *n* грабёж; **~ with violence** грабёж с применéнием насúлия; *fig* **it's sheer/daylight ~!** э́то прóсто грабёж!, (э́то) грабёж средь бéла дня!

robe *n* (*dress*) плáтье; (*oriental robe, bath robe*) халáт; (*ceremonial, usu pl*) мáнтия (*sing*); **the mayor's ~s** мáнтия мэ́ра.

robin (redbreast) *n* малúновка.

robust *adj* здорóвый, крéпкий.

rock *n* (*crag, reef*) скалá; *Geol* порóда; **a house built on ~** дом, пострóенный на скалé; **the ship was smashed on the ~s** корáбль разбúлся о скáлы; *fig* **as firm as a ~** твёрдый как скалá; *CQ*: **he/their marriage is on the ~s** он на мелú (*broke*), онú вот-вóт разведýтся; (*US*) **whisky on the ~s** вúски со льдом.

rock *vti vt* кач|áть (*semel* -нýть); (*violently*) шатáть (пошатнýть); **she ~ed the cradle/the child to sleep** онá качáла колыбéль, онá укáчивала ребёнка; **the waves ~ed the boat** лóдка качáлась на волнáх; **the explosion ~ed the**

house дом закача́лся/зашата́лся от взры́ва

vi кача́ться; **the carriage ~ed violently from side to side** ваго́н си́льно кача́ло; *fig* **the audience ~ed with laughter** зри́тели (*pl*) па́дали от сме́ха.

rock-bottom *n CQ*: **prices are at ~** це́ны сейча́с—ни́же не́куда; **he has reached ~** он дошёл до ру́чки.

rock-climber *n* скалола́з.

rock crystal *n* го́рный хруста́ль (*m*).

rockery *n* альпи́йский сад.

rocket *n* раке́та; **a distress ~** сигна́льная раке́та; *fig CQ* **to get/give smb a ~** получи́ть/зада́ть кому́-л взбу́чку; *attr*: **~ base/range** раке́тная ба́за, раке́тный полиго́н.

rocket *vi CQ*: **prices have ~ed** це́ны подскочи́ли.

rock fall *n* камнепа́д.

rock garden *n* альпи́йский сад.

rocking chair *n* (кре́сло-) кача́лка.

rocking horse *n* ко́нь-кача́лка.

rock plant *n* альпи́йское расте́ние.

rock salt *n* ка́менная соль.

rocky *adj* (*of area*) скали́стый; (*stony*) камени́стый.

rococo *n* рококо́ (*indecl*); *attr* в сти́ле рококо́.

rod *n* (*of metal*) прут; (*for punishment*) ро́зга; (*symbol of authority*) жезл; *Tech* сте́ржень (*m*); (*for fishing*) у́дочка; *fig* **he rules the country with a ~ of iron** он пра́вит желе́зной руко́й.

rodent *n* грызу́н.

rodeo *n* (*US*) роде́о (*indecl*).

roe *n* (*of fish*: *hard*) икра́, (*soft*) моло́ки (*pl*).

roe (deer) *n Zool* косу́ля.

rogue *n* моше́нник, плут, *also joc.*

roguish *adj* плутова́тый; **with a ~ smile** с плутова́той улы́бкой.

role *n Theat* роль, *also fig*; **leading/supporting/title ~** гла́вная/второстепе́нная/загла́вная роль; **to play the ~ of Hamlet** игра́ть/исполня́ть роль Га́млета.

roll *n* **1** (*of paper, cloth*) руло́н; (*scroll*) сви́ток; **a ~ of wallpaper/linoleum** руло́н обо́ев/лино́леума; **a ~ of film** мото́к плёнки; **~s of fat** жировы́е скла́дки

2 (*of bread*) бу́лочка

3 (*list*) спи́сок; **electoral ~** избира́тельный спи́сок; **the school has 1,000 pupils on its ~** в шко́ле ты́сяча ученико́в; **to call the ~** де́лать перекли́чку

4 (*noise*): **a ~ of thunder** раска́т гро́ма; **to give a ~ on the drums** дать бараба́нную дробь

5 (*action*): **the ~ of a ship** бортова́я ка́чка; **the dog had a ~ on the grass** соба́ка поката́лась по траве́.

roll *vti vt* **1** (*move by rolling*) ката́ть (*indet impf*), кати́ть (*det impf*) *and compounds* [**NB** *pf* покати́ть *means* "*to begin to roll*"; *for true pfs use a compound, e.g.* откати́ть, *etc.*]; **to ~ a ball between one's palms/along the street** ката́ть ша́рик в ладо́нях, кати́ть мяч по у́лице; **we ~ed the wheel to the side of the road** мы откати́ли колесо́ к обо́чине; **to ~ pastry** раска́т|ывать те́сто (-а́ть); **to ~ metal** прока́т|ывать мета́лл (-а́ть); **to ~ a road/lawn** утрамбо́вывать доро́гу катко́м, ука́тывать лу́жайку (*usu impfs*)

2 (*fold up by rolling*): **to ~ a cigarette** свёртывать/скру́|чивать сигаре́ту (сверну́ть/-ти́ть); **to ~ an umbrella** сложи́ть зо́нтик (*usu pf*)

vi **1** ката́ться; кати́ться; (*wallow*) валя́ться; **to ~ on the grass** ката́ться по траве́; **the coin ~ed along the ground** моне́та кати́лась по земле́; **the pig ~ed in the mud** свинья́ валя́лась в гря́зи

2 (*of ship*) пока́чиваться (*impf*); **he ~s from side to side as he walks** он хо́дит вперева́лку (*adv*)

3 (*of thunder*) греме́ть, грохота́ть (*impfs*)

roll away *vti vt* отка́т|ывать (-и́ть)

vi откати́ться; **the stone/clouds ~ed away** ка́мень откати́лся, облака́ разошли́сь

roll back *vt*: **we ~ed the carpet/armchair back** мы отверну́ли ковёр, мы откати́ли кре́сло; **to ~ one's sleeves back/up** заверну́ть рукава́

roll down *vti vt*: **to ~ a stone down a hill** скати́ть ка́мень с горы́

vi скати́ться; **tears ~ed down her cheeks** слёзы кати́лись по её щека́м; **mist ~ed down over the valley** тума́н опусти́лся на доли́ну

roll in *vti vt*: **he ~ed the child/himself in a blanket** он уку́тал ребёнка/уку́тался в одея́ло

vi CQ: **he ~ed in at 1 a.m.** он прикати́л в час но́чи; **orders/invitations ~ed in from all sides** зака́зы/приглаше́ния сы́пались со всех сторо́н

roll into *vt*: **to ~ string into a ball** сма́тывать бечёвку в клубо́к (смота́ть); **the hedgehog ~ed itself into a ball** ёжик сверну́лся в клубо́к/клубко́м

roll off *vi* скати́ть с + *G*

roll out *vti vt* вы́катить из + *G*; (*of pastry*) раската́ть

vi: **to ~ out of bed** скати́ться с крова́ти; **they ~ed out of the bar** они́ вы́шли из ба́ра поша́тываясь

roll over *vi*: **the car/cat ~ed over on its side** маши́на переверну́лась на́ бок, ко́шка улегла́сь на́ бок; **he ~ed over and went to sleep** он поверну́лся на́ бок и засну́л; **the puppy ~ed over and over on the grass** щено́к кувырка́лся на траве́

roll under *vi*: **the coin ~ed under a chair** моне́та закати́лась под стул

roll up *vti vt* (*of map, rug*) сверну́ть; (*of sleeves*) заверну́ть

vi: **a car ~ed up to the door** маши́на подкати́ла к две́ри; **look who's just ~ed up** смотри́, кто прие́хал!

roll call *n* перекли́чка; **to take the ~** де́лать перекли́чку.

rolled *adj*: **a ~ umbrella** свёрнутый/сло́женный зо́нтик; **~ gold** накладно́е зо́лото; **~ oats** овся́ные хло́пья.

roller *n Tech* като́к; (*castor*) ро́лик, колёсико; (*wave*) вал; (*for hair*) бигуди́ (*pl, indecl*).

roller-skate *vi*, *also* **to go roller-skating** ката́ться на ро́ликовых конька́х (по-).

roller towel *n* полоте́нце на ро́лике.

rolling *adj*: ~ **countryside** волни́стый релье́ф ме́стности; ~ **pin** ска́лка; *Rail* ~ **stock** подвижно́й соста́в; *fig* **a** ~ **stone** (*person*) перекати́-по́ле.

Roman *n* ри́млянин.

Roman *adj* ри́мский; **a** ~ **nose** ри́мский нос.

Roman Catholic *n* като́лик; *attr* ри́мско-католи́ческий.

romance *n* **1** (*tale*) рома́н; (*sentimental*) романти́ческая по́весть; (*medieval*) ры́царский рома́н; *Mus* рома́нс; (*fabrication*) фанта́зия; **a historical** ~ истори́ческий рома́н

2 *CQ* (*love affair*) рома́н; **they are having a** ~ у них рома́н

3 (*abstract*) рома́нтика; **to travel in search of** ~ путеше́ствовать в по́исках рома́нтики; **the castle has an air of** ~ за́мок вы́глядит романти́чески.

romance *adj*: ~ **languages** рома́нские языки́.

romance *vi*: *CQ* **he's just romancing!** он про́сто фантази́рует!

romantic *adj*: ~ **literature** романти́ческая литерату́ра; **a** ~ **setting/girl** романти́чная обстано́вка/де́вушка.

Romany *n* цыга́н, цыга́нка; (*language*) цыга́нский язы́к.

romp *vi* (*of children, animals*) пры́гать (по-); резви́ться (*impf*); *fig*: **he** ~**ed through his driving test** он шутя́ сдал экза́мен на води́тельские права́; **his horse** ~**ed home** его́ ло́шадь легко́ победи́ла в зае́зде.

rompers *npl* де́тский комбинезо́н (*sing*).

roof *n* кры́ша; **the** ~ **of the mouth** нёбо; (*of car*) **a sliding/sunshine** ~ откидна́я кры́ша; *fig CQ*: **their singing raised the** ~ (*was loud*) от их пе́ния дрожа́ли сте́ны, (*was well-received*) их пе́ние име́ло бе́шеный успе́х у пу́блики; **father raised the** ~ **when he found out** узна́в об э́том, оте́ц пришёл в я́рость.

roofing *n* кро́вельный материа́л.

rook[1] *n* (*bird*) грач.

rook[1] *vt CQ* (*fleece*) обдира́ть (ободра́ть); (*by giving wrong change*) обсчи́т|ывать (-а́ть); **he** ~**ed me of 2 roubles (change)** он обсчита́л меня́ на два рубля́.

rook[2] *n Chess* ладья́, тура́.

room *n* **1** ко́мната; (*in hotel*) но́мер; **a furnished** ~ меблиро́ванная ко́мната; **a single/double** ~ но́мер на одного́/на двои́х; **waiting** ~ (*at doctor's*) приёмная врача́, (*at station*) зал ожида́ния; **the doctor's consulting** ~ кабине́т врача́; *euph* **ladies'/men's** ~ же́нский/мужско́й туале́т; **he stayed in his** ~ он оста́лся у себя́ в ко́мнате

2 (*space*) ме́сто; **there is no** ~ **for anything else** здесь бо́льше ничего́ не поме́стится; **they moved up to make** ~ **for her** они́ подви́нулись, что́бы дать ей ме́сто; **it takes up too much** ~ э́то занима́ет сли́шком мно́го ме́ста; **there isn't** ~ **to move here** тут не́где поверну́ться; *fig* **there is still** ~ **for doubt/for improvement** ещё есть основа́ния сомнева́ться, ещё мо́жно ко́е-что́ улу́чшить.

-roomed *adj*: **a five-**~ **flat** пятико́мнатная кварти́ра.

roommate *n* сосе́д/сосе́дка по ко́мнате.

room service *n* обслу́живание в номера́х.

roomy *adj*: **a** ~ **handbag/flat** вмести́тельная су́мка, просто́рная кварти́ра.

roost *vi*: **the hens are already** ~**ing** ку́ры уже́ се́ли на насе́ст; **birds** ~ **in that tree** пти́цы сидя́т на э́том де́реве.

root *n* ко́рень (*m*), *also Math, Ling, fig*; **to strike/take** ~ пуска́ть ко́рни, укореня́ться, *also fig*; **to pull up smth by the** ~**s** вы́рвать что-л с ко́рнем (*sing*); *Math* **square** ~ квадра́тный ко́рень; *fig*: **to blush to the** ~**s of one's hair** покрасне́ть до корне́й воло́с; **money is the** ~ **of all evil** де́ньги—ко́рень всех зол; **my** ~**s are in Scotland** я ро́дом из Шотла́ндии; **to get to the** ~ **of the matter** добра́ться до су́ти (де́ла); *attr*: ~ **vegetables** корнепло́ды; ~ **cause** основна́я причи́на.

root *vti vt*: **to** ~ **smth out/up** вы|рыва́ть что-л с ко́рнем (-рвать), *also fig*, *fig* (*remove*) искорен|я́ть что-л (-и́ть); *fig*: **a deeply** ~**ed prejudice** глубоко́ укорени́вшийся предрассу́док; **I've** ~**ed out these old photos from the cupboard** я разыска́л э́ти ста́рые фотогра́фии в шкафу́; **he stood** ~**ed to the ground** он стоя́л как вко́панный, он как в зе́млю врос

vi Bot пус|ка́ть ко́рни (-ти́ть); (*of pig, also fig*) ры́ться (*impf*); **the cuttings are beginning to** ~/**have** ~**ed well** черенки́ пуска́ют ко́рни/хорошо́ прижили́сь; **to** ~ **around (for smth) in a drawer** ры́ться в я́щике (,ища́ что-л).

rootless *adj* без корне́й, *also fig*.

rope *n* верёвка (*also for mountaineering*); (*thick, also in circus*) кана́т; *Naut* трос; **a** ~ **of pearls/onions** ни́тка же́мчуга, вя́зка лу́ка; *fig*: **if only he would give me more** ~ е́сли бы то́лько он дал мне бо́льше свобо́ды; **he will show you the** ~**s** он введёт тебя́ в курс де́ла; *attr*: ~ **ladder** верёвочная ле́стница.

rope *vt* свя́з|ывать что-л верёвкой (-а́ть) *and other compounds*; **I** ~**d the two sacks together** я связа́л э́ти два мешка́ вме́сте; **to** ~ **a box on to the roof of a car/smth to a tree** привяза́ть я́щик на кры́ше маши́ны/что-л к де́реву; **the climbers were** ~**d** альпини́сты шли в свя́зке; **to** ~ **off a square** отгор|а́живать площа́дку верёвкой/кана́том (-оди́ть); *fig CQ* **I've been** ~**d in to help with the packing** меня́ подключи́ли к упако́вке веще́й.

ropey *adj CQ* ста́рый, него́дный.

rose *n Bot* ро́за; (*bush*) ро́зовый куст; (*colour*) ро́зовый цвет; (*on sprinkler*) наса́дка; **wild** ~ (*flower*) ди́кая ро́за, (*tree*) шипо́вник; *fig* **life is not a bed of** ~**s** жизнь прожи́ть—не по́ле перейти́; *attr* ро́зовый; **a** ~ **garden** роза́рий.

rosé *n* ро́зовое вино́.

rose-coloured *adj*: *fig* **he sees everything through ~ spectacles** он на всё смо́трит сквозь ро́зовые очки́.

rosemary *n* розмари́н.

rosin *n* канифо́ль.

roster *n* расписа́ние дежу́рств/*Mil* наря́дов.

rostrum *n* ка́федра, трибу́на; *Mus* помо́ст.

rosy *adj* ро́зовый; ~ **cheeks** румя́ные щёки; *fig* **the future looks ~ for us** бу́дущее представля́ется нам в ро́зовом цве́те.

rot *n* (*process*) гние́ние; (*result*) гниль; **dry ~** сухо́е гние́ние; ~ **has set in to the tree/flooring** де́рево ста́ло гнить, полови́цы подгни́ли; *fig* **to stop the ~** навести́ поря́док; *CQ* **what ~!** кака́я чушь!

rot *vti vt*: **damp ~s wood** де́рево гниёт от сы́рости

vi гнить (с-); *fig* раз|лага́ться (-ложи́ться); **to begin to ~** загни|ва́ть (-́ть); **to let ~** гнои́ть (с-); **the corn was ~ting in fields** зерно́ (*collect*) гни́ло на корню́; ~**ting apples/corpses** гнию́щие я́блоки, разлага́ющиеся тру́пы.

rota *n see* **roster.**

rotary *adj* враща́тельный.

rotate *vti vt* (*turn*) враща́ть (*impf*); (*alternate*) чередова́ть (*impf*); **to ~ crops** чередова́ть культу́ры, примен|я́ть севооборо́т (-и́ть)

vi враща́ться; чередова́ться, сменя́ться.

rotation *n* (*turning*) враще́ние; (*turn*) оборо́т; (*succession*) очерёдность; *Agr* севооборо́т, рота́ция; **orders are dealt with in strict ~** зака́зы исполня́ются в поря́дке стро́гой очерёдности.

rote *n*: **to learn smth by ~** зазубри́ть что-л.

rotten *adj* **1** (*of wood, crops, etc.*) гнило́й; (*of meat, eggs, etc.*) ту́хлый; **the wood smells ~** де́рево па́хнет гнилью

2 *fig uses*: **a ~ administration** прода́жная верху́шка; *CQ*: **I feel ~** я ужа́сно/ме́рзко себя́ чу́вствую; **they played a ~ trick on you** с тобо́й сыгра́ли ме́рзкую шу́тку; **a ~ film** дрянно́й фильм; **what ~ luck!** прокля́тое невезе́ние!

rotter *n CQ* мерза́вец, подле́ц.

rotund *adj* (*of figure*) по́лный; (*of face*) кру́глый.

rouble, (*US*) **ruble** *n* рубль (*m*).

rouge *n* румя́на (*pl*).

rough *n*: **to do smth in ~** сде́лать что-л вчерне́ (*adv*); **you have to take the ~ with the smooth** лю́бишь ката́ться, люби́ и са́ночки вози́ть.

rough *adj* **1** (*uneven*) неро́вный; (*to touch*) шерохова́тый, верша́вый; (*harsh*) жёсткий; ~ **ground, a ~ edge** неро́вный грунт/край; **a ~ surface** неро́вная/шерохова́тая пове́рхность; ~ **skin** шерша́вая/жёсткая ко́жа; ~ **hands** шерша́вые ру́ки; ~ **cloth** гру́бое сукно́; *fig* **he's a ~ diamond** он неотёсанный, но па́рень неплохо́й

2 (*in work, play, etc.*) гру́бый; **a ~ game, ~ play** гру́бая игра́; ~ **workmanship** гру́бая рабо́та; **they are ~ boys** они́ грубия́ны; **a ~ wine** те́рпкое вино́; **he was very ~ with me** он был о́чень груб/ре́зок со мной; **road-building is ~ work** прокла́дка доро́г—трудоёмкая рабо́та; *CQ*: **we had a ~ time of it last year** нам ту́го пришло́сь в про́шлом году́; **it's ~ luck on her** ей нелегко́ прихо́дится

3 (*of sea, etc.*): **a ~ crossing** бу́рная перепра́ва; **the sea got ~** мо́ре разбушева́лось; ~ **weather/climate** нена́стная пого́да, суро́вый кли́мат

4 (*unfinished*): **a ~ translation** чернови́й перево́д; **a ~ draft/sketch** чернови́к, эски́з; **in ~ outline** в о́бщих черта́х; **to give you a ~ idea** что́бы дать вам приблизи́тельное представле́ние; *Comm* **a ~ estimate** приблизи́тельная сме́та.

rough *vt*: **he ~ed out a plan** он наброса́л план (вчерне́); **we decided to ~ it and sleep out** мы реши́ли плю́нуть на удо́бства и спать под откры́тым не́бом.

rough-and-ready *adj*: **to do everything in a ~ manner** де́лать всё на ско́рую ру́ку/ко́е-ка́к; ~ **methods** гру́бые приёмы.

roughcast *adj*: **a ~ wall** стена́, отде́ланная га́лечной штукату́ркой.

roughen *vt*: ~ **the surface before applying the glue** сде́лайте пове́рхность шерохова́той пе́ред тем, как нама́зать клей.

roughly *adv* гру́бо; (*approximately*) приблизи́тельно; ~ **speaking** гру́бо говоря́.

roughneck *n CQ* хулига́н.

roughshod *adv*: **he rides ~ over us** он не счита́ется с на́ми.

rough-spoken *adj*: **he is ~** он о́чень груб.

roulette *n* руле́тка.

round *n* **1** (*circle*) круг; (*slice*) **a ~ of beef/bread** ло́мтик говя́дины/хле́ба; **he fired six ~s of ammunition** он расстреля́л шесть патро́нов; (*of drinks*): **they ordered another ~** они́ заказа́ли ещё по одно́й; **whose ~ is it?** кому́/чья о́чередь плати́ть?

2 (*of doctor, watchman*) обхо́д; (*of postman, milkman*) маршру́т; (*of talks*) эта́п, тур; **the doctor is out on his ~s** врач сейча́с на обхо́де (*sing*); **the watchman is making his ~s** сто́рож де́лает обхо́д; **the first ~ of negotiations** пе́рвый эта́п/тур перегово́ров; **the next ~ of the elections** сле́дующий эта́п вы́боров; **he went the ~s of the publishers with his novel** он обошёл все изда́тельства со свои́м рома́ном; **the story went the ~s** э́та исто́рия обошла́ весь го́род; **a ~ of applause** взрыв аплодисме́нтов; **for him life is one long ~ of pleasures** для него́ жизнь—сплошны́е удово́льствия

3 *Sport*: (*in boxing*) ра́унд; (*of golf*) па́ртия; (*lap*) эта́п; (*stage*) тур; **we had a ~ of golf** мы сыгра́ли па́ртию в гольф; **our team is through to the second ~** на́ша кома́нда прошла́ на второ́й тур; **he had a clear ~** он чи́сто прошёл диста́нцию.

round *adj* кру́глый; **a ~ table** кру́глый стол; *fig*: **a ~ figure** це́лое число́; **at a ~ pace** бы́стро; **he told me in ~ terms ...** он открове́нно сказа́л мне...; **a ~ trip** тури́стская поездка, тур; **a ~ ticket** *approx* туристская путёвка.

round *adv* **1** кругом, вокруг; **a crowd gathered ~** вокруг собралась толпа; **~ about all was still** кругом всё было тихо; **taken all ~** в общем, в целом; **all the year ~** круглый год; **do you live ~ here?** ты живёшь здесь поблизости?; **he lives somewhere ~ here** он живёт где-то здесь рядом/недалеко; **the taxi brought us a long way ~** такси везло нас кружным путём; **we came ~ by the castle** мы прошли/проехали мимо замка, (*out of our way*) мы пошли в обход/поехали в объезд (мимо) замка

2 *not translated*: **is there enough wine to go ~?** хватит ли вина на всех?; **we shall be ~ at the pub** вы найдёте нас в пабе; **come ~ and see me** заходите ко мне

3 *translated by verbal prefix*: **he turned ~** он обернулся; **to hand ~ cups of tea/books** передавать чашки чая, раздавать книги; *see also under verb entries.*

round *prep* (*of place, etc.*) вокруг + *G*; **a fence ~ the house** забор вокруг дома; **a trip ~ the world** путешествие вокруг света; **a crowd gathered ~ them** вокруг них собралась толпа; **we walked ~ the museum** мы ходили по музею; **we sat ~ the table/fire/the campfire** мы сидели вокруг стола/у камина/у костра; **it's just ~ the corner** это как раз за углом; **to work ~ the clock** работать круглые сутки/(*of factory, etc.*) круглосуточно (*adv*); **she is 60 cm ~ the waist** объём её талии шестьдесят сантиметров; **he looked ~ the room** (*inspected*) он осмотрел комнату, (*glanced*) он обвёл комнату глазами; **he walked ~ the statue** он обошёл статую кругом; *fig*: **it's ~ 2 o'clock** сейчас часа два; **he is ~ 40** ему лет сорок.

round *vt*: **to ~ one's lips** округл|ять губы (-ить); **to ~ a corner** по|ворачивать за угол (-вернуть); **the ship ~ed the headland** корабль обогнул мыс

round off *vt*: **to ~ off a sentence** закругл|ять фразу (-ить); **to ~ off/up an amount** округлить сумму; **to ~ off the day/programme** чтобы завершить день/программу (*only in pf*)

round on *vi*: **to ~ on smb** набр|асываться на кого-л (-оситься)

round up *vt*: **to ~ up cattle/tourists** сгонять скот (согнать), со|бирать туристов (-брать); **the police ~ed up the gang** полиция захватила всю шайку.

roundabout *n* (*at fair*) карусель; *Aut* кольцевая транспортная развязка с односторонним движением, (*as roadsign*) круговое движение.

roundabout *adj* кружный, обходной; окольный, *also fig*; **we came by a ~ way** мы приехали кружным/окольным путём; **I learnt about it in a ~ way** я узнал об этом окольным путём.

rounded *adj* закруглённый, округлённый; **a ~ sentence** закруглённая фраза.

roundly *adv*: **to scold smb ~** ругать кого-л на чём свет стоит; **I told her ~ that...** я сказал ей без обиняков, что...

round-shouldered *adj* сутулый.

round-up *n* (*of cattle*) загон скота; (*of criminals*) облава.

rouse *vt* будить (раз-, *fig* про-); *fig* побу|ждать, возбу|ждать (*pfs* -дить); **to ~ smb from sleep** разбудить кого-л; **we had to ~ the doctor during the night** нам пришлось разбудить врача среди ночи; **to ~ smb to action** побудить кого-л к действию; **to ~ smb's interest** возбудить в ком-л интерес; **it's time you ~d yourself** тебе пора встряхнуться; **he's frightening when he's ~d** он страшен, когда разойдётся.

rousing *adj*: **a ~ speech/song** воодушевляющая речь/песня; **~ cheers** бурные приветствия.

rout *vt Mil* громить (раз-).

route *n* (*itinerary*) маршрут; **to plan one's ~** наметить маршрут; **bus ~** автобусный маршрут; **shipping ~s** морские пути/линии; *attr*: **~ map** маршрутная карта.

routine *n* режим, порядок; (*wearisome routine*) рутина, шаблон; **hospital ~** больничный режим; **what is your ~ for issuing books/your daily ~?** какой у вас порядок выдачи книг?/распорядок дня?; **we check the price labels as a matter of ~** у нас принято проверять ценники на товарах; **there is a lot of ~ in every job** в каждой работе есть доля рутины; **he's a slave to ~** он рутинёр, он всё делает по шаблону.

routine *adj*: **a ~ job** работа по шаблону; **the police are making ~ inquiries/a ~ check** полиция ведёт обычное следствие (*sing*)/обычную проверку.

rove *vi* бродить, скитаться (*impfs*).

roving *adj* (*wandering*) бродячий; **a ~ correspondent** разъездной корреспондент; **a ~ ambassador** посол по особым поручениям; *CQ* **he has a ~ eye** он любит приударить за девочками.

row[1] *n* (*line*) ряд, *also Theat*; **in the front/back ~** в первом/последнем ряду; **~ upon ~** ряд за рядом; **they sat in a ~** они сидели в ряд; **three days in a ~** три дня подряд (*adv*).

row[2] *vti vt*: **to ~ a boat** грести на лодке (*impf*); **he ~ed the boat out to sea** он выгреб в море; **to ~ smb across a river/out to a yacht** пере|возить кого-л через реку (-везти), переправ|лять кого-л на яхту лодкой (-ить)

vi грести (*impf*); **he ~ed for the shore/against the current** он грёб к берегу/против течения; **we ~ed round the bay** мы обошли бухту, мы покатались на лодке по бухте; **he ~s for Cambridge** он принимает участие в гребных гонках за команду Кембриджжа.

row[3] *n* **1** (*noise*) шум; **how can I work with that ~ going on?** разве я могу работать при таком шуме?; *CQ*: **to kick up a ~** поднять шум; **they were making a devil of a ~** они́ ужа́сно расшуме́лись

2 *CQ* (*quarrel*) сканда́л; **they had a dreadful ~** у них был ужа́сный сканда́л; **we had a ~ about who should pay** мы ста́ли спо́рить, кому́ плати́ть

3 *CQ* (*scolding*): **I got into a ~ for disobeying him** мне доста́лось за то, что не послу́шался его́; **he gave me a ~ for being late** он отруга́л меня́ за опозда́ние.

rowan *n* (*tree*) ряби́на (*also collect of berries*).

rowdy *adj* шу́мный; бу́йный; **a ~ meeting/party** шу́мное собра́ние, бу́йное засто́лье; **to be ~** расшуме́ться.

royal *adj* короле́вский; **R. Academy** Короле́вская акаде́мия; **R. Air Force** брита́нские вое́нно-возду́шные си́лы; *fig* **a ~ welcome** ца́рский приём.

royal blue *n* я́рко-си́ний цвет.

royally *adv fig*: **we were ~ entertained** нас при́няли пря́мо по-ца́рски.

royalty *n* **1** (*persons*) чле́ны короле́вской семьи́; (*power*) короле́вская власть

2 *pl* (**royalties**) (а́вторский) гонора́р (*sing*).

rub *vti vt* тере́ть (по-) *and compounds*; (*massage*) рас|тира́ть (-тере́ть); **he ~bed his nose** он потёр себе́ нос; **he kept ~bing his hands in glee** он потира́л ру́ки от ра́дости; **the cat ~bed itself against the table** ко́шка тёрлась о стол; **~ your chest with this ointment** натри́ себе́ грудь э́той ма́зью; **he ~bed the table till it shone** он отполирова́л стол до бле́ска; *fig* **in my job I ~ shoulders with all sorts of people** по рабо́те я встреча́юсь с са́мыми ра́зными людьми́

vi тере́ть; **my shoes ~** мои́ боти́нки трут

rub along *vi CQ*: **he ~s along in Russian** он мо́жет объясни́ться по-ру́сски; **they ~ along together** они́ ла́дят друг с дру́гом

rub away *vt*: **the paint had been all ~bed away** кра́ска вся стёрлась; **she ~bed away her tears** она́ отёрла/смахну́ла слёзы

rub down *vti*: **he ~bed (himself) down** он обтёрся; **to ~ down a horse** обтира́ть ло́шадь

rub dry *vt* вы|тира́ть (-́тереть); **he ~bed his hair/the dog dry** он вы́тер во́лосы/соба́ку до́суха (*adv*)

rub in/into *vt* втира́ть (втере́ть); **~ the cream in well** хорошо́ вотри́ крем; *fig CQ*: **I know you're right, there's no need to ~ it in** хва́тит повторя́ть одно́ и то́ же, я и так зна́ю, что ты прав; **don't ~ salt into the wound** не растравля́йте ра́ну

rub off/out *vti* стира́ть(ся) (стере́ть(ся)); **I've ~bed it out** я э́то стёр; **the stain won't ~ out** пятно́ не сотрётся/не стира́ется; *fig* **some of his opinions ~bed off on her** она́ восприняла́ не́которые его́ взгля́ды

rub through *vt*: **to ~ smth through a sieve** про|тира́ть что-л сквозь/че́рез си́то (-тере́ть)

rub up *vt* (*polish*) начи|ща́ть (-́стить); *fig*: **he ~s me up the wrong way** он меня́ раздража́ет; **I must ~ up my French** мне на́до подучи́ть францу́зский.

rubber *n* (*raw material*) каучу́к; (*product*) рези́на; (*eraser*) рези́нка, ла́стик; *pl* (*US*) гало́ши; *attr*: **a ~ band** рези́новая тесьма́, рези́нка; **a ~ plantation** каучу́ковая планта́ция; **a ~ stamp** штамп.

rubberized *adj* прорези́ненный.

rubber-soled *adj*: **~ shoes** ту́фли на каучу́ковой подо́шве.

rubbish *n* (*general word*) му́сор, сор, (*leftovers, etc.*) отбро́сы (*pl*); (*old clothes, etc.*) хлам, старьё; *fig* дрянь, (*spoken*) ерунда́, чепуха́, чушь; **this shop sells nothing but ~** э́тот магази́н продаёт дрянно́й това́р; **this film is ~** э́то дрянно́й фильм; **he talks a lot of ~** он ерунду́/чепуху́ говори́т, он несёт чушь; *attr* му́сорный; **~ dump** сва́лка.

rubbishy *adj CQ* дрянно́й, никуда́ не го́дный.

rubble *n* (*as basis for building, etc.*) бут; (*debris*) обло́мки.

rubric *n* ру́брика.

ruby *n* руби́н; *attr*: **~ lips** а́лые гу́бы

ruck *vti*, *also* **~ up** (*crease*) мять (с-).

rucksack *n* рюкза́к.

ructions *npl CQ*: **there'll be ~ if the government goes on with that policy** така́я поли́тика прави́тельства вы́зовет возмуще́ние/проте́ст (*sings*).

rudder *n* руль (*m*).

ruddy *adj* румя́ный; *CQ euph* прокля́тый.

rude *adj* **1** (*coarse*) гру́бый; (*impolite*) неве́жливый; (*indecent*) неприли́чный, непристо́йный; **~ remarks** гру́бые замеча́ния; **don't be ~ to your elders** не груби́ ста́ршим; **you were very ~ to him** ты был с ним о́чень груб; **a ~ question** неве́жливый вопро́с; **it's ~ to interrupt** прерыва́ть неве́жливо; **a ~ song/story** непристо́йная пе́сенка, неприли́чный анекдо́т

2 (*sudden*): **a ~ shock** внеза́пное потрясе́ние; **it was a ~ awakening for him** э́то бы́ло для него́ неприя́тным откры́тием

3: he is in ~ health он здоро́в как бык, у него́ кре́пкое здоро́вье.

rudiment *n Biol* рудиме́нт; *fig* **the ~s of physics** осно́вы фи́зики (*sing*).

rudimentary *adj Biol*: **a ~ tail** рудимента́рный хвост; *fig* **a ~ knowledge of** элемента́рные зна́ния + *G* (*pl*).

rue *vt* сожале́ть о + *P* (*impf*); **I ~ the day when...** (*curse*) я проклина́ю тот день, /(*regret*) я го́рько сожале́ю о том дне, когда́...

ruffian *n* хулига́н, банди́т; (*in old times or joc*) разбо́йник.

ruffle *n Sew* (*frill*) обо́рка; (*gather*) сбо́рка.

ruffle *vt* (*of hair, feathers, etc.*) еро́шить (взъ-); (*of water*) ряби́ть (*impf*); (*annoy*) раздража́ть (*usu impf*); (*worry*) беспоко́ить (о-); (*upset*) расстр|а́ивать (-о́ить); **nothing ~s him** его́ ничто́ не тро́гает.

rug *n* (*for floor*) ковёр, (*small*) ко́врик; (*woollen cover*) плед.

rugged *adj*: ~ **country** пересечённая мéстность; **a** ~ **coast** изрéзанный бéрег; **the** ~ **outline of the hills** зубчáтые/нерóвные очертáния гор; ~ **manners/features** неотёсанность, грýбые чéрты́ лицá; **with** ~ **determination** с непреклóнной решимостью.

ruin *n* (*state*) разрушéние, гибель, разорéние; (*thing*) развáлины; руины (*pls*); **the castle is now a** ~ от зáмка остáлись одни развáлины/руины; *fig*: **it was the** ~ **of his hopes/career** это было для негó крушéнием надéжд, это погубило егó карьéру; **his life was in** ~**s** егó жизнь былá загýблена; **drink was the** ~ **of him** егó погубило пьянство; *CQ* **you will be the** ~ **of me** ты меня погýбишь.

ruin *vt* губить (по-), *also fig*; (*financially*) разор|ять (-ить); **the rain** ~**ed the roses** дождь погубил рóзы; **he** ~**ed my new car** он разбил мою нóвую машину; (*because of a spill*) **the carpet is** ~**ed** ковру конéц; **he** ~**ed himself through speculation** он разорился на спекуляциях (*pl*); **she is** ~**ing her health by smoking/her grandchildren** онá разрушáет себé здорóвье курéнием, онá óчень бáлует своих внучáт.

ruinous *adj* губительный, пáгубный; (*financially*) разорительный; *CQ* **it's a** ~ **price** это неслыханно дóрого.

rule *n* **1** (*regulation, guiding principle*) прáвило; **against the** ~**s** прóтив прáвил; **as a (general)** ~ как прáвило; **the golden** ~ **is...** золотóе прáвило гласит...; **there is no hard-and-fast** ~ **about that** относительно этого нет установленных прáвил (*pl*); **I make it a** ~ **never to drive without my safety belt** я взял за прáвило никогдá не éздить без привязных ремнéй; **the exception proves the** ~ исключéние подтверждáет прáвило

2 (*measure*) линéйка; **slide** ~ логарифмическая линéйка; **folding** ~ складнóй метр; **to work by** ~ **of thumb** дéлать на глазóк/без тóчных расчётов

3 (*authority*): **the** ~ **of the majority** власть большинствá; **the island is under British** ~ этот óстров нахóдится под британским контрóлем; **under the** ~ **of Ivan the Terrible** при Ивáне Грóзном; **home** ~ **for Ireland** автонóмия/гóмруль для Ирлáндии.

rule *vti vt* **1** (*govern*) прáвить + *I*; (*of institutions*) руководить; (*have dominion over*) господствовать, влáствовать (*all impfs*); **to** ~ **an empire** прáвить импéрией; **they** ~**d the country for ten years** они прáвили/влáствовали в странé дéсять лет; **to** ~ **the seas** господствовать на мóре (*sing*); **you had best be** ~**d by my advice** вам лýчше послéдовать моемý совéту; **he is** ~**d by his wife in everything he does** он во всём слýшается женý

2 *Law* постанов|лять (-ить); **the court** ~**d that** суд постановил, что...; **the judge** ~**d the question out of order** судья признáл вопрóс не относящимся к дéлу

3 (*on paper, etc.*): **to** ~ **a line** линовáть (про-); ~**d paper** линóванная бумáга; **to** ~ **off a column of figures/a margin** отдел|ять колóнку цифр/пóле чертóй (-ить)

4 (*exclude*): **to** ~ **out** исключ|áть (-ить); **we can't** ~ **him/that possibility out** мы не мóжем исключить егó/эту возмóжность

vi **1** (*reign*) цáрствовать

2: **the committee** ~**d in favour of/against the motion** комитéт постановил принять/не принимáть предложéние; **the court** ~**d against him/in his favour** суд вынес решéние (не) в егó пóльзу.

ruler *n* правитель (*m*); *Math* линéйка.

ruling *n* постановлéние; **the judge gave a** ~ **against him** судья вынес постановлéние не в егó пóльзу.

rum[1] *n* ром.

rum[2] *adj CQ* стрáнный.

Rumanian *n* (*person*) румын, румынка.

Rumanian *adj* румынский.

rumble *n* (*of earthquake, guns*) гул; (*of carts*) грóхот, громыхáние; (*in stomach*) урчáние; **the** ~ **of distant thunder** далёкие раскáты грóма.

rumble *vi* грохотáть, громыхáть (*impfs*); (*of stomach*) урчáть (*impf*); **the train** ~**d past** пóезд прогромыхáл мимо; **thunder was rumbling in the hills** в горáх грохотáл гром.

rumbustious *adj* шумливый.

ruminate *vi* жевáть жвáчку (*impf*); *fig* раздýмывать, размышлять (*impfs*).

ruminative *adj fig* задýмчивый.

rummage *vi* рыться; копáться (*impfs*); **to** ~ **(about) in a drawer/amongst papers** рыться в ящике/в бумáгах.

rumour, (*US*) **rumor** *n* слух.

rumour, (*US*) **rumor** *vt*: **it is** ~**ed that...** хóдит слух, говорят, что...

rump *n* (*of animal*) крестéц; *Cook* огýзок; *attr*: ~ **steak** ромштéкс.

rumple *vt* (*of clothes, paper*) мять (с-); (*of hair*) ерóшить (взъ-), растрепáть (*pf*).

rumpus *n CQ* шум, гам; **to kick up a** ~ поднять шум/гам.

run *n* **1** бег; **at a** ~ бегóм; **to break into a** ~ брóситься бежáть; **he set off at a** ~ он побежáл; **we gave the dog a** ~ **in the park** мы пустили собáку побéгать в пáрке; **I go for a** ~ **every morning** кáждое ýтро я дéлаю пробéжку; **we made a** ~ **for it and got away** мы спаслись бéгством; **he is on the** ~ **from the police** он скрывáется от полиции; **she kept me on the** ~ **all day** онá застáвила меня бéгать цéлый день

2 (*outing*) прогýлка; **we had a** ~ **in the car/down to the coast** мы покатáлись в машине, мы прокатились к мóрю; **I took the car for a trial** ~ я проéхался на машине, чтóбы провéрить её на ходý

3 (*distance*): **it's a 2 hour** ~ **from here to the coast** отсюда до мóря два часá езды; (*of ship*) **the day's** ~ расстояние, прóйденное зá день

4 (*sequence*): **a** ~ **of luck/bad luck/bad weather** полосá везéния/неудáч (*pl*)/ненáстья;

the play had a long ~ пье́са шла до́лго; **the Conservatives had a long ~ in office** консерва́торы до́лго бы́ли у вла́сти; **to follow the ~ of events/of the game** следи́ть за хо́дом собы́тий/игры́; **in the long ~** в коне́чном счёте; *Typ* **a ~ of 5,000 copies** тира́ж пять ты́сяч экземпля́ров; *Mus* пасса́ж; *fig*: **the common ~ of people** зауря́дные лю́ди; **he/the hotel is out of the common ~** он незауря́дный челове́к, таку́ю гости́ницу ре́дко найдёшь

5 *special uses*: (*route of ship, bus*) маршру́т; (*animal enclosure*) заго́н, (*for hens*) куря́тник; **ski ~** (*in mountains*) лы́жный спуск, (*in woods, etc.*) лыжня́; *Comm*: **there was a ~ on candles** был большо́й спрос на све́чи; **there was a ~ on the banks when the news was announced** когда́ но́вость ста́ла изве́стна, лю́ди ста́ли изыма́ть свои́ вкла́ды из ба́нков; *fig* **he gave us the ~ of his library** он предоста́вил свою́ библиоте́ку в на́ше распоряже́ние.

run *vti vt* **1** (*general*) бе́гать (*see vi*); **he ran 5 miles** он пробежа́л пять миль; **he ran a good race** он хорошо́ прошёл диста́нцию/пробежа́л; **he ran himself to a standstill** он забе́гался; **the race is run over a 3 mile course** диста́нция забе́га (*on foot*)/зае́зда (*on horse, etc.*)—три ми́ли; **I want you to ~ an errand** я хочу́ посла́ть тебя́ с поруче́нием; *fig*: **he is ~ning a high temperature** у него́ высо́кая температу́ра; **the illness must ~ its course** боле́знь должна́ идти́ свои́м хо́дом; *CQ* **when he starts talking about his hobby, I ~ a mile** я бегу́ от него́ за версту́, когда́ он начина́ет говори́ть о своём хо́бби

2 (*hunt, put in for race, etc.*): **I am ~ning a horse in the Derby** я выставля́ю ло́шадь на де́рби; *Polit* **the Liberals are not ~ning a candidate this year** в э́том году́ либера́лы не выставля́ют кандида́та; *fig*: **I ran him to earth in the library** я отыска́л/разыска́л его́ в библиоте́ке; **the children/he ran her off her feet** она́ сби́лась с ног с детьми́, он её соверше́нно загоня́л; **I was ~ off my feet all day** я набе́гался за́ день; **that will ~ you into trouble/expense** у тебя́ бу́дут из-за э́того неприя́тности (*pl*), э́то влети́т тебе́ в копе́ечку

3 (*transport*) *compounds of* вози́ть (везти́); **I'll ~ you to the station** я вас отвезу́ на вокза́л; **I'll ~ you home** (*on my way*) я вас подвезу́ домо́й; **to ~ whisky/guns across a frontier** про|вози́ть ви́ски/ору́жие че́рез грани́цу (-везти́)

4 (*organize, manage*) води́ть (вести́); (*direct*) управля́ть (*impf*); **she ~s the house/a small business** она́ ведёт хозя́йство, она́ возглавля́ет небольшу́ю фи́рму; **the scheme is ~ on a commercial basis** э́то де́ло ведётся на комме́рческой осно́ве; **he ~s the factory** он управля́ющий на фа́брике; **the school is run by a committee** шко́ла управля́ется сове́том; **to ~ a campaign/series of experiments** про|води́ть кампа́нию/се́рию о́пытов (-вести́); **the magazine is ~ning a series of articles on penguins** в журна́ле печа́тается се́рия стате́й о пингви́нах; **the cinema is ~ning a series of Italian films** в э́том кинотеа́тре идёт пока́з италья́нских фи́льмов; **they ~ extra trains in the rush hours** они́ пуска́ют в часы́ пик дополни́тельные поезда́

5 (*operate*): **I can't afford to ~ a car** я не могу́ содержа́ть маши́ну; **he ~s a Rolls Royce** у него́ «Роллс-Ро́йс»; **this car is cheap to ~** э́та маши́на потребля́ет ма́ло бензи́на; **to ~ a boat aground** посади́ть кора́бль на мель (*usu pf*)

6 (*of water*): **to ~ a bath** напо́лнить ва́нну; **you have to ~ the water for a few minutes till it gets hot** ну́жно не́сколько мину́т спуска́ть во́ду из кра́на, пока́ не пойдёт горя́чая

vi **1** бе́гать (*indet impf, pf* по- = *to run around for a while*), бежа́ть (*det impf, pf* по- = *to begin to run*) *and compounds* [**NB** *for the true pf of completed action the pf of a compound is used*]; **he ran up and down the street** он бе́гал взад и вперёд по у́лице; **~ after her!** беги́ за ней!; **I must ~** я до́лжен бежа́ть; **he ran to his mother** он побежа́л к ма́тери; **I ran for all I was worth to catch the bus** я бежа́л со всех ног, что́бы успе́ть на авто́бус; **he ran upstairs/downstairs** он взбежа́л по ле́стнице, он сбежа́л с ле́стницы; **we ran for/to fetch the doctor** мы сбе́гали за врачо́м (*pf*); **we ran to him for help** мы побежа́ли к нему́ за по́мощью; **he ran to help us** он прибежа́л нам на по́мощь; **the children ran to their places** де́ти разбежа́лись по свои́м места́м; **we'll have to ~ for it** нам придётся бежа́ть; **~ for your lives!** спаса́йся кто мо́жет!; **they ran for their lives when they saw us** уви́дев нас, они́ бро́сились наутёк

2 *fig uses*: **the text ~s like this...** текст (идёт) тако́й...; **so the story ~s** так расска́зывают; **a shiver ran down his spine** дрожь пробежа́ла у него́ по те́лу; **her blood ran cold** у неё кровь засты́ла в жи́лах; **red hair ~s in their family** у них в роду́ мно́го ры́жих; **to ~ for President/for election** выставля́ть свою́ кандидату́ру на пост президе́нта/на вы́борах

3 (*function, move: of cars, etc.*) рабо́тать (*impf*); ходи́ть, идти́ (*only in impfs*); **the lift isn't ~ning** лифт не рабо́тает; **the lawnmower ~s on petrol** газонокоси́лка рабо́тает на бензи́не; **the television ~s off the mains** телеви́зор рабо́тает от се́ти; **the car ~s smoothly** маши́на идёт ро́вно; *fig* **everything is ~ning smoothly** всё идёт норма́льно; *Naut* **to ~ before the wind/aground** идти́ по ве́тру, сади́ться на мель (сесть)

4 (*function: of services*) ходи́ть (*only in impf*); **there are no buses ~ning today** сего́дня авто́бусы не хо́дят; **steamers ~ every hour** парохо́ды отхо́дят ка́ждый час; **ships ~ning between London and Leningrad** корабли́, курси́рующие ме́жду Ло́ндоном и Ленингра́дом

5 (*flow*) течь *and compounds*; **the river ~s fast here** здесь река́ течёт бы́стро; **the river ~s for 200 miles/into the lake** протяжённость реки́ — две́сти миль, река́ впада́ет в о́зеро; **the river/well ran dry** река́ вы́сохла/пересо́хла, исто́чник исся́к; **my nose is ~ning** у меня́ течёт (*impers*) и́з носу; **the milk ran all over the table** молоко́ растекло́сь по всему́ столу́; **melted wax ran down the candle** расто́пленный воск стека́л по свече́; **who left the tap ~ning?** кто оста́вил кран откры́тым?; **tears ran down her cheeks** слёзы кати́лись по её щека́м; **the streets are ~ning with water** у́лицы за́литы водо́й; **the street ~s off/into the square** у́лица начина́ется от пло́щади/ведёт к пло́щади; **wash this towel separately — the dye ~s** стира́й э́то полоте́нце отде́льно — оно́ линя́ет; **the colours ran in the wash** кра́ска (*sing*) полиня́ла от сти́рки; *fig* **feelings were ~ning high** стра́сти разгора́лись

6 (*continue, extend*): **the play ran for 3 months/for 40 performances** пье́са шла три ме́сяца/вы́держала со́рок представле́ний; **the book ran to 500 pages/5 editions** в кни́ге набрало́сь пятьсо́т страни́ц, кни́га вы́держала пять изда́ний; **there is a good film ~ning this week** на э́той неде́ле идёт хоро́ший фильм; **the contract ~s for 3 years** контра́кт действи́телен три го́да; **the road ~s beside the river/from London to the coast** доро́га прохо́дит вдоль реки́, шоссе́ идёт от Ло́ндона до побере́жья; *CQ* **I can't ~ to a new car** я не потяну́ на но́вую маши́ну

7: my stocking has ~ у меня́ на чулке́ спусти́лась петля

run across *vi*: **to ~ across the road** перебе|га́ть (че́рез) у́лицу (-жа́ть); *fig* **to ~ across an old friend/a rare book** случа́йно встре́тить ста́рого прия́теля, натолкну́ться на ре́дкую кни́гу (*usu pfs*)

run away *vi* убе|га́ть (-жа́ть); **she ran away from school/with her lover** она́ убежа́ла из шко́лы/с возлю́бленным; **don't ~ away from difficulties/with the idea that...** не бо́йся тру́дностей, вы́броси из головы́ мысль, что...

run back *vti vt*: **I'll ~ the film back to the beginning** я перемота́ю плёнку наза́д до са́мого нача́ла

vi: **they ran back to the house** они́ побежа́ли обра́тно в дом, они́ бего́м верну́лись в дом; **his mind ran back to the events of last week** он мы́сленно верну́лся к собы́тиям про́шлой неде́ли

run behind *vi*: **programmes are ~ning 15 minutes behind schedule** сего́дня на́ши програ́ммы запа́здывают на пятна́дцать мину́т

run down *vti vt*: **she was run down by a lorry** её сбил грузови́к; *fig*: **to ~ smb down** критикова́ть кого́-л; **you look ~ down** ты вы́глядишь о́чень утомлённым; **you'll ~ the battery down if you...** аккумуля́тор ся́дет, е́сли ты...

vi: **our garden ~s down to the river** наш сад спуска́ется к реке́; *Aut* **the battery has ~ down** аккумуля́тор сел

run in *vti vt*: **to ~ a new car in** обка́т|ывать но́вую маши́ну (-а́ть); **he was ~ in for dangerous driving** его́ задержа́ли за наруше́ние пра́вил доро́жного движе́ния

vi: **he ran in** он вбежа́л

run into *vti*: **to ~ into a room** вбе|га́ть в ко́мнату (-жа́ть); **I ran (the car) into a wall/the garage** я вре́зался в стену, я поста́вил *or CQ* загна́л маши́ну в гара́ж; **I ran into your brother in the street today** я сего́дня столкну́лся на у́лице с твои́м бра́том; **we ran into fog** мы въе́хали в полосу́ тума́на; **the ship ran into a storm** кора́бль был засти́гнут што́рмом; **to ~ into difficulties** столкну́ться/встре́титься с тру́дностями; **to ~ into debt** залез|а́ть в долги́ (-́ть); **his debt ~s into thousands** его́ долг достига́ет не́скольких ты́сяч

run off *vti vt*: **she ran off all the hot water** она́ истра́тила всю горя́чую во́ду; **~ me off a few copies of this text** сде́лайте мне не́сколько ко́пий э́того те́кста; **the heats are being ~ off tomorrow** забе́ги бу́дут проводи́ться за́втра

vi: **he ran off with another woman** он ушёл к друго́й же́нщине [**NB** *prep*]; **someone has ~ off with my papers** кто́-то взял мои́ бума́ги; **the car ran off the road** маши́на сверну́ла с доро́ги

run on *vti vt*: **he ran the ship on to a reef** он завёл кора́бль на ри́фы (*pl*)

vi: **she ran on for hours about her grandson** она́ часа́ми говори́ла о своём вну́ке; **the conversation ran on wine/on familiar lines** разгово́р зашёл о вине́, бесе́ду вели́ на привы́чные те́мы

run out *vi* вы|бега́ть (-́бежать); (*come to an end*): **we are ~ning out of sugar/petrol/time** у нас конча́ется са́хар/бензи́н/вре́мя; **supplies ran out** запа́сы исся́кли; **the lease ~s out tomorrow** срок аре́нды истека́ет за́втра

run over *vti vt*: **the child was run over by a tram** ребёнок попа́л под трамва́й; **I'll just ~ the iron over this dress/the vacuum over the carpet** я то́лько разо́к проведу́ утюго́м по э́тому пла́тью/пылесо́сом по ковру́; **~ your eye over this** просмотри́ э́то бы́стренько; **he ran his eye over the text** он бы́стро пробежа́л глаза́ми текст; **he ran over in his mind what he was going to say** он повтори́л про себя́ то, что собира́лся сказа́ть

vi: **the wine ran over on to the floor** вино́ пролило́сь на́ пол

run round *vi*: **the children were ~ning round the garden** де́ти бе́гали по са́ду; *fig* **to ~ round in small circles** крути́ться как бе́лка в колесе́

run through *vti vt*: **I'll ~ the first part of the film through again** я прокручу́ ещё раз пе́рвую часть фи́льма; **he ran a comb/his fingers through his hair** он провёл расчёской/па́льцами по волоса́м; **to ~ elastic through**

the waist of skirt продёргивать рези́нку в по́яс ю́бки

vi: **he ran through the wood** он пробежа́л че́рез ро́щу; **a murmur ran through the audience** ро́пот пробежа́л по за́лу; **the tune keeps ~ning through my head** э́та мело́дия ве́ртится у меня́ в голове́; **he ~s through money quickly** у него́ де́ньги не заде́рживаются; **we ~ through a lot of sugar in a week** мы расхо́дуем в неде́лю мно́го са́хара; **I'll ~ through the main points again** я опя́ть повторю́ гла́вные пу́нкты; **we'll ~ through the first act now** мы сейча́с порепети́руем пе́рвый акт

run up *vti vt*: **he ran up a large bill/a lot of debts** у него́ набежа́л большо́й счёт, он накопи́л мно́го долго́в; *CQ* **to ~ up a dress** смета́ть пла́тье

vi: **he ran up to me/up the hill** он подбежа́л ко мне, он взбежа́л на́ гору; **we ran up against some opposition/problems** мы натолкну́лись на сопротивле́ние, мы столкну́лись с пробле́мами.

rung *n* ступе́нька стремя́нки.

runner *n* (*athlete*) бегу́н; (*messenger*) посы́льный; (*of sledge, etc.*) по́лоз (сане́й).

runner-up *n*: *Sport* **he was ~** он пришёл вторы́м.

running *n* (*management*) веде́ние; *Sport* бег: **the ~ of the house/the school was left to her** веде́ние хозя́йства/руково́дство шко́лой бы́ло возло́жено на неё; **he's good at ~** он хорошо́ бе́гает; *fig*: **he is in the ~ for promotion/the job** он кандида́т на повыше́ние/на э́ту до́лжность; *Sport* **he is still in the ~** он ещё име́ет ша́нсы на вы́игрыш.

running *adj*: **a ~ track** бегова́я доро́жка; **a ~ jump** прыжо́к с разбе́га; **he took a ~ jump** он разбежа́лся и пры́гнул; **the sound of ~ water** (*from tap*) звук лью́щейся воды́, (*in stream*) журча́нье ручья́; **does your dacha have ~ water?** у вас на да́че есть водопрово́д?; **a ~ sore** гноя́щаяся боля́чка; **a ~ knot** затяжно́й у́зел, уда́вка; **to keep up a ~ commentary on smth** вести́ репорта́ж о чём-л; **three times ~** три ра́за подря́д.

running board *n Aut* подно́жка.

running-in *n Aut* обка́тка.

runny *adj* (*of jam, etc.*) жи́дкий; *CQ* **a ~ nose** сопли́вый нос.

runway *n Aer* взлётно-поса́дочная полоса́.

rupture *n* разры́в; *Med* гры́жа.

rupture *vt* раз|рыва́ть(ся) (-орва́ть(ся)), про|рыва́ть(ся) (-рва́ть(ся)); **to ~ oneself** надорва́ться (*usu pf*).

rural *adj* се́льский.

ruse *n* уло́вка, хи́трость.

rush[1] *n* **1** (*haste*) спе́шка; **why all this ~?** к чему́ вся э́та спе́шка?; **the ~ of city life** спе́шка городско́й жи́зни; **the pre-Christmas ~** *approx* предпра́здничная сумато́ха; **we lost each other in the ~ for our coats** мы в спе́шке ри́нулись в раздева́лку и потеря́ли друг дру́га; **there was a ~ to the door/for shelter** все бро́сились к две́ри/в укры́тие; *CQ* **we had a ~ to get everything in time** нам пришло́сь поспеши́ть, чтобы всё успе́ть к сро́ку

2 *Comm*: **there has been a ~ on candles** был большо́й спрос на све́чи; **there was a ~ on that model** эту моде́ль бы́стро раскупи́ли

3 (*stream*) пото́к, *also fig*; **a ~ of air/water/people/words** пото́к во́здуха/воды́/люде́й/слов; **a ~ of orders** наплы́в зака́зов; **a ~ of blood to the head** прили́в кро́ви к голове́

4 *attr*: **in the ~ hour(s)** в час(ы́) пик; **a ~ order** спе́шный зака́з; **it's been a ~ job** э́та рабо́та сде́лана на́спех (*adv*)/на ско́рую ру́ку.

rush[1] *vti vt* **1** (*hurry*: *a person*) торопи́ть (по-); **I hate being ~ed** я о́чень не люблю́, когда́ меня́ торо́пят/подгоня́ют; **you ~ed that work** вы сде́лали э́ту рабо́ту на́спех (*adv*); **I was ~ed off my feet/to hospital** я сби́лся с ног, меня́ сро́чно увезли́ в больни́цу; **can you ~ this order through for me?** не могли́ бы вы поскоре́е вы́полнить мой зака́з?

2 (*charge*) бро́ситься (*usu pf*)

3 *sl*: **how much did they ~ you?** ско́лько с тебя́ содра́ли?

vi (*hurry*) торопи́ться, *CQ* гнать (*only in det impf*); бежа́ть *and compounds*; мча́ться (*impf*); *with preps often translated by* бро́ситься (*usu pf*); **don't ~(off)** не торопи́сь *or CQ* не гони́, не убега́й; **cheerio, I must ~ now** ну пока́, мне на́до бежа́ть; **he ~ed downstairs/up to me** он сбежа́л с ле́стницы, он подбежа́л *or* бро́сился ко мне; **he ~ed past** он промча́лся ми́мо; **the blood ~ed to her face** кровь бро́силась ей в лицо́; **they ~ed through the gates** они́ метну́лись в воро́та.

rush[2] *n Bot* камы́ш, *also collect*; *attr*: **a ~ mat** цино́вка.

rusk *n* суха́рь (*m*).

russet *n* желтова́то-кори́чневый цвет.

Russian *n* (*person*) ру́сский, ру́сская; (*language*) ру́сский язы́к.

Russian *adj* ру́сский.

rust *n* ржа́вчина.

rust *vi* ржа́веть (за-).

rustic *adj* дереве́нский, крестья́нский.

rustle *n* (*of pages, silk*) ше́лест; (*of papers, fallen leaves*) шурша́ние; (*of leaves on tree*) шо́рох.

rustle *vti* шелесте́ть + *I*, шурша́ть + *I* (*impfs*).

rustproof, rust-resistant *adjs* нержаве́ющий, коррозиесто́йкий.

rusty *adj* ржа́вый, заржа́вленный; *CQ* **my French is a bit ~** я немно́го подзабы́л францу́зский.

rut *n* колея́; *fig*: **you're in a ~** тебя́ засоса́ла рути́на; **to get out of a ~** сойти́ с проторённой доро́жки.

ruthless *adj* безжа́лостный.

rye *n* рожь; *attr*: **~ bread** ржано́й хлеб.

S

sabbatical *adj*: *Univ* **to take a ~ year** брать академи́ческий о́тпуск на́ год.

sable *n* со́боль (*m*); (*fur*) собо́лий мех.

sabotage *n Mil* диве́рсия; (*in industry, etc.*) сабота́ж.

sabotage *vt*: *fig* **to ~ talks** саботи́ровать перегово́ры (*impf and pf*).

sack[1] *vt* (*pillage*) гра́бить (раз-).

sack[2] *n* мешо́к; **a ~ of flour** мешо́к муки́/с муко́й; **a flour ~** мешо́к из-под муки́; *CQ* **to give smb the ~** уво́лить кого́-л.

sack[2] *vt CQ* (*dismiss*) увол|ьня́ть (-́ить).

sacrament *n Rel* прича́стие.

sacred *adj* свяще́нный, свято́й; (*on tombstone*) **~ to the memory of** све́тлой па́мяти + *G*; **nothing is ~ to him** для него́ нет ничего́ свято́го; **~ music** духо́вная му́зыка.

sacrifice *n* (*fig*: *act or object*) же́ртва; *fig* **she is making these ~s for the sake of her children** она́ гото́ва идти́ на э́ти же́ртвы ра́ди свои́х дете́й.

sacrifice *vt Rel* при|носи́ть в же́ртву (-нести́); же́ртвовать + *A*/*fig* + *I* (по-); *fig*: **to ~ oneself** же́ртвовать собо́й; **he ~d his holiday in order to look after his sick mother** он не пое́хал в о́тпуск, оста́лся, что́бы уха́живать за больно́й ма́терью.

sad *adj* печа́льный; гру́стный; **it was a ~ mistake to...** печа́льно, что...; **I feel/am ~** мне гру́стно; **he was ~** ему́ взгрустну́лось (*impers*); **why does she look so ~?** почему́ у неё тако́й гру́стный вид?; **a ~ state of affairs** плаче́вное состоя́ние дел.

saddle *n* (*for horse, bicycle*) седло́; (*of hill*) седлови́на; **~ of mutton** бара́нье седло́.

saddle *vt* седла́ть (о-); *fig CQ* **we got ~d with (looking after) the children** на нас взвали́ли забо́ту о де́тях.

sadistic *adj* сади́стский.

safe *n* сейф; (*for food*) кладо́вка.

safe *adj* **1** (*unharmed*) благополу́чный; (*without risk*) безопа́сный; (*reliable*) надёжный; **are these toys ~ for children?** э́ти игру́шки безопа́сны для дете́й?; **to keep smth ~** храни́ть что-л в безопа́сном ме́сте; **he is now ~ from danger** ему́ бо́льше не грози́т опа́сность; **in ~ hands** в надёжных рука́х; **~ and sound** цел и невреди́м; **he's in a ~ job** на э́той рабо́те ему́ не грози́т увольне́ние; *CQ* **we're ~ as houses here** мы здесь как за ка́менной стено́й

2 (*cautious*): **a ~ driver/policy** осторо́жный води́тель, осторо́жная поли́тика; **to be on the ~ side** для бо́льшей надёжности, что́бы подстрахова́ться; **I'll take my umbrella just to be ~** на вся́кий слу́чай возьму́ с собо́й зо́нтик; *CQ* **to play it ~** игра́ть наверняка́.

safe-conduct *n* охра́нная гра́мота; **under ~** имея́ охра́нную гра́моту.

safeguard *n*: **a ~ against** гара́нтия про́тив + *G*.

safeguard *vt* охраня́ть (*usu impf*); гаранти́ровать (*impf and pf*); **to ~ smb's interests** охраня́ть чьи-л интере́сы.

safekeeping *n*: **I left it at the bank for ~** я оста́вил э́то на хране́ние в ба́нке.

safely *adv*: **he arrived ~** он дое́хал благополу́чно; **put it away ~** спрячь э́то в надёжном ме́сте; **one can ~ say** мо́жно с уве́ренностью сказа́ть.

safety *n* безопа́сность; **regulations for road ~** пра́вила доро́жной безопа́сности; **there is ~ in numbers** чем бо́льше, тем надёжнее.

safety belt *n Aut* привязно́й реме́нь.

safety catch *n* защёлка предохрани́теля.

safety curtain *n Theat* противопожа́рный за́навес.

safety measures *npl* ме́ры предосторо́жности.

safety pin *n* англи́йская була́вка.

safety valve *n* предохрани́тельный кла́пан.

sag *vi* про|гиба́ться (-гну́ться), провис|а́ть (-́нуть); **the ceiling ~ged** потоло́к прогну́лся/прови́с; *fig* **his spirits ~ged** он упа́л ду́хом.

sage[1] *adj* му́дрый.

sage[2] *n Bot* шалфе́й.

sail *n* па́рус; **to be under full ~** идти́/плыть на всех паруса́х (*pl*); **to set/lower the ~s** подня́ть/спусти́ть паруса́; **to set ~** отплыва́ть, отправля́ться в пла́вание; **let's go for a ~** пое́хали ката́ться на ло́дке; *fig* **that took the wind out of his ~s** его́ опереди́ли.

sail *vti vt* пра́вить + *I* (*impf*), води́ть (вести́); **he ~s his yacht magnificently** он великоле́пно пра́вит я́хтой; **to ~ the Atlantic** перепл|ыва́ть че́рез Атланти́ческий океа́н (-́ть)

vi **1** (*of boat*) пла́вать (*indet impf*), плыть (*det impf*), идти́ (*det impf*) *and compounds*; **the ship ~ed into harbour/round the cape/down river** кора́бль вошёл в га́вань/обогну́л мыс/плыл *or* шёл вниз по реке́; **the ship ~s at 3 o'clock** кора́бль отплыва́ет/отхо́дит в три часа́

2 (*of person*): **he has ~ed round the world/for Odessa** он пла́вал вокру́г све́та, он отплы́л/отпра́вился в Оде́ссу; **let's go ~ing** дава́й поката́емся на ло́дке; *fig* **he ~s very near the wind** *CQ* он конъюнкту́рщик.

sailcloth *n* паруси́на.

sailing *n* пла́вание; (*navigation*) навига́ция, кораблевожде́ние; **daily ~s to Dover** ежедне́вные ре́йсы в Дувр; **the time of ~ has not been announced yet** вре́мя отплы́тия ещё не объявля́ли; **I love ~** я люблю́ ката́ться на ло́дке; *fig* **it's not exactly plain ~** э́то не просто́е де́ло, э́то не так про́сто.

sailing boat, (*US*) **sailboat** *n* па́русная ло́дка, па́русник.

sailor *n* моря́к, матро́с; **to be a good/bad ~** хорошо́/пло́хо переноси́ть ка́чку на мо́ре.

saint *n* свято́й; *CQ* **she's really a ~** она́ пря́мо как свята́я.

sake *n*: **for the ~ of** ра́ди + *G*, для + *G*; **for God's ~** ра́ди бо́га; **for your own ~** для твое́й же по́льзы; **he goes there every summer for the ~ of his health** он е́здит туда́ ка́ждое ле́то ра́ди своего́ здоро́вья; **he argues just for the ~ of it** он спо́рит ра́ди интере́са; **art for art's ~** иску́сство для иску́сства.

salad *n* сала́т; **vegetable ~** овощно́й сала́т, (*with pickles*) *approx* винегре́т; **(fresh) fruit ~** фрукто́вый сала́т; *attr*: **~ dressing** запра́вка к сала́ту.

salami *n* колбаса́ саля́ми (саля́ми *indecl*).

salaried *adj* шта́тный; **a ~ post** шта́тная до́лжность; **~ teachers** учителя́ на твёрдом окла́де.

salary *n* жа́лованье, за́работная пла́та, *CQ* зарпла́та; **to be paid a fixed ~** получа́ть твёрдый окла́д.

sale *n* прода́жа; **these goods have just come on ~** э́ти това́ры то́лько что поступи́ли в прода́жу; **is this car for ~?** э́та маши́на продаётся?; **auction ~** прода́жа с аукцио́на/с торго́в; **clearance ~** распрода́жа.

salesman *n* (*in shop*) продаве́ц; **travelling ~** коммивояжёр.

salesmanship *n*: **he knows all there is to know about ~** он зна́ет назубо́к все зако́ны ку́пли-прода́жи.

saline *adj*: **a ~ solution** солево́й раство́р; **a ~ spring** соляно́й исто́чник.

saliva *n* слюна́.

salivate *vi* вы|деля́ть слюну́ (-делить).

sallow *adj*: **a ~ complexion** лицо́ желтова́того цве́та.

salmon *n* сёмга, лосо́сь (*m*); (*as food*) сёмга, лососи́на.

salmon trout *n* лосо́сь-таймéнь (*m*), ку́мжа.

salon *n*: **a beauty ~** космети́ческий сало́н.

saloon *n* зал; *Naut* каю́т-компа́ния, сало́н; (*US*) каба́к, таве́рна, бар; *attr*: **~ bar** пивно́й бар; **~ car** автомоби́ль-седа́н.

salt *n* соль; **table/cooking/rock ~** столо́вая/пова́ренная/ка́менная соль; **smelling/Epsom ~s** ню́хательная/англи́йская соль (*sings*); *fig*: **such people are the ~ of the earth** таки́е лю́ди—соль земли́; **an old ~** быва́лый моря́к, «морско́й волк»; **I took it with a pinch/grain of ~** я э́тому не о́чень пове́рил.

salt *adj* (*of food*) солёный; **~ spring** солёный исто́чник; **the soup is too ~ for my taste** на мой вкус суп пересо́лен.

salt *vt* соли́ть (по-); (*cure*) *also* **~ down** за|са́ливать (-соли́ть); *fig* **to ~ away one's money in Switzerland** вкла́дывать де́ньги в швейца́рские ба́нки (вложи́ть).

saltcellar *n* соло́нка.

salt-free *adj*: **a ~ diet** бессолева́я дие́та.

salt marsh *n* солонча́к.

salt mine *n* соляны́е ко́пи (*pl*).

saltwater *adj*: **~ fish** морска́я ры́ба.

salutary *adj* благотво́рный; **a ~ influence** благотво́рное влия́ние.

salute *n Mil, Naut* (*with guns, etc.*) салю́т.

salute *vti* (*greet*) приве́тствовать (*CQ* по-); *Mil* **to ~ (smb)** отда|ва́ть честь (кому́-л) (-ть).

salvage *n Naut* (*act*) спасе́ние; (*objects*) спасённое иму́щество, спасённый груз; (*scrap*)ути́ль (*m*); **to collect paper for ~** собира́ть макулату́ру.

salvage *vt* спас|а́ть (-ти́); **the wreck can't be ~d but the gear can be** кора́бль уже не спасёшь, но ко́е-како́е обору́дование ещё мо́жно испо́льзовать; **to ~ scrap** со|бира́ть ути́ль (-бра́ть); *fig* **I ~d the old books he was throwing out** я спас ста́рые кни́ги, кото́рые он выбра́сывал.

salve *vt fig*: **to ~ one's conscience** успо-к|а́ивать со́весть (-о́ить).

same *pron* **1: they always say the ~** они́ всегда́ говоря́т одно́ и то́ же; **have a nice time!—S. to you!** жела́ю тебе́ хорошо́ провести́ вре́мя!—И тебе́ то́же!; **it's all the ~ to him** ему́ э́то всё равно́; *Comm* (*on a bill*) **to cleaning of man's suit £2, to repair of ~ £1** за чи́стку мужско́го костю́ма—два фу́нта, за почи́нку—оди́н фунт

2 *adverbial uses*: **they feel the ~ about this question as I do** они́ отно́сятся к э́тому вопро́су так же, как (и) я; **although she looks better, she feels much the ~** хотя́ она́ и лу́чше вы́глядит, чу́вствует она́ себя́ всё так же; **just the ~, all the ~** тем не ме́нее, всё-таки; **the snapshots all look the ~ to me** э́ти сни́мки мне ка́жутся одина́ковыми.

same *adj* тако́й же, то́т же са́мый, оди́н и то́т же; (*identical*) одина́ковый; **he has the ~ make of car as I do** у него́ та́ же моде́ль маши́ны, что и у меня́, у нас одина́ковые (моде́ли) маши́ны; **the very ~ day** в то́т же са́мый день; **they all arrived at the ~ time** все прие́хали одновреме́нно; **she is the ~ age as me** мы с ней одного́ во́зраста; **we went to the ~ school** мы учи́лись в одно́й шко́ле; **she still wears the ~ old hat** она́ по-пре́жнему но́сит ту́ же са́мую ста́рую шля́пу; **these programmes are too much the ~** э́ти програ́ммы уж сли́шком однообра́зны.

sample *n* образе́ц, обра́зчик, про́ба; *fig* образе́ц, приме́р; **a book of ~s** альбо́м образцо́в; **~s of silks and satins** обра́зчики шёлка и атла́са; **to take a blood ~** взять кровь для ана́лиза.

sample *vt* про́бовать (по-); **to ~ wine** дегусти́ровать ви́на (*pl*) (*impf and pf*).

sanatorium (*US also* **sanitarium**) *n* больни́ца санато́рного ти́па; **school ~** *approx* шко́льный изоля́тор.

sanction *n* (*permission*) согла́сие, разреше́ние; (*official*) са́нкция; **without his ~** без его́ согла́сия, без его́ разреше́ния; **to apply ~s against** применя́ть са́нкции про́тив + *G*.

sanction *vt* (*permit*) разреш|а́ть (-и́ть); **our plan has been ~ed** наш план был утверждён/одо́брен.

sanctuary *n Rel* святи́лище; (*place of refuge*) прию́т, убе́жище; **a bird ~** пти́чий запове́дник.

sand *n* песо́к; **a grain of ~** песчи́нка; *pl* (**~s**) (*beach*) пляж (*sing*); *attr*: **a ~ dune** песча́ная дю́на.

sandal *n* санда́лия, *CQ* босоно́жка.

sandbank *n* песча́ная о́тмель, мель, ба́нка.

sandpaper *n* наждáчная бумáга, «шкýрка».
sandpaper *vt* зачи|щáть/шлифовáть «шкýркой» (-́стить/от-).
sandpit *n* песчáный карьéр; (*children's*) песóчница.
sand shoes *npl approx* кéды.
sandstone *n* песчáник.
sandstorm *n* песчáная бýря, самýм.
sandwich *n* бутербрóд; **a ham ~** бутербрóд с ветчинóй.
sandwich *vt*: **to ~ between** втúс|кивать мéжду + *I* (-нуть); **the child was ~ed between two fat ladies** ребёнка втúснули мéжду двумя́ тóлстыми дáмами.
sandy *adj* песчáный; (*of colour*) желтовáтый; **~ soil** песчáная пóчва.
sane *adj* (*of person*) в здрáвом умé, здравомы́слящий, разýмный; (*balanced*) уравновéшенный; (*of policy*) здрáвый, разýмный.
sanguine *adj* (*of temperament*) жизнерáдостный, сангвинúческий; **I'm fairly ~ about our chances of success** по-мóему у нас есть шáнсы на успéх.
sanitary *adj* санитáрный.
sanitary towel *n* гигиенúческая повя́зка.
sanitation *n* канализáция.
sanity *n* здрáвый ум, рáзум; (*of judgement, etc.*) разýмность; **one begins to question his ~** начинáешь сомневáться в егó здрáвом умé/здравомы́слии.
sap[1] *vt fig*: **that ~ped his confidence** э́то подорвáло егó увéренность в себé.
sap[2] *n Bot* сок.
sapling *n* молодóе дéревце.
sapper *n* сапёр.
sapphire *n* сапфúр; *attr* сапфúровый.
sarcastic *adj* саркастúческий.
sardine *n* сардúна, сардúнка; **packed like ~s** (наби́ты) как сéльди в бóчке.
sash[1] *n* кушáк.
sash[2] *n attr*: **~ window** подъёмное окнó; **~ cord** шнур подъёмного окнá.
Satan *n* сатанá, дьявол.
satchel *n* рáнец.
satellite *n*: **space ~** спýтник, *also Astron*; **communications ~** спýтник свя́зи; *attr fig*: **~ town/state** гóрод-спýтник, госудáрство-сателлúт.
satiated *adj* сы́тый; **we ate till we were ~** мы éли и пúли дóсыта/до отвáла (*advs*).
satin *n* атлáс; *attr* атлáсный.
satiric *adj* сатирúческий.
satirize *vt*: **the author ~d/the play ~s modern morals** áвтор написáл сатúру/э́та пьéса — сатúра на совремéнную морáль (*sing*).
satisfaction *n* удовлетворéние; удовлетворённость; *Law* компенсáция; **the job gave me great ~/a feeling of great ~** рабóта достáвила мне огрóмное удовлетворéние; **he is giving ~ in his work** он рабóтает вполнé удовлетворúтельно.
satisfactory *adj* удовлетворúтельный; **there is no ~ explanation** нет удовлетворúтельного/убедúтельного объяснéния; **the visit was highly ~** визúт прошёл весьмá удовлетворúтельно.
satisfy *vt* **1** удовлетвор|я́ть (-úть); **to ~ requirements/conditions** удовлетворя́ть *or* отвечáть трéбованиям/услóвиям (*usu impf*); **he is satisfied with his job** он довóлен своéй рабóтой; **you can rest satisfied that...** мóжете быть увéренными, что...; **to ~ one's hunger** утол|я́ть гóлод (-úть); **nothing satisfies him** всё емý не так
2 (*convince*) убе|ждáть (-дúть); **I am satisfied** *or* **I have satisfied myself as to the truth of his testimony/that he can do the work** я убедúлся в правдúвости егó показáний (*pl*)/в том, что он мóжет спрáвиться с рабóтой; **I'm satisfied that we've done all we can** я убеждён, мы сдéлали всё, что моглú.
satisfying *adj* удовлетворя́ющий; (*of food*) **a ~ lunch** сы́тный обéд.
saturate *vt*: **to ~ with** пропúт|ывать + *I* (-áть); *Chem* насы|щáть + *I* (-́тить); **to be ~d** (*wet*) намок|áть (-́нуть); **the wick is ~d with oil** фитúль пропúтан мáслом/керосúном; **my shoes are ~d** у меня́ промóкли ботúнки; **the ground is ~d** земля́ óчень сырáя; **the market for cars is ~d** ры́нок наводнён автомобúлями.
Saturday *n* суббóта.
saturnine *adj* угрю́мый, мрáчный.
sauce *n* сóус; (*thinner*) подлúвка; *fig* **what ~!** какáя дéрзость!, какóе нахáльство!
sauceboat *n* сóусница.
saucepan *n* кастрю́ля.
saucer *n* (чáйное) блю́дце; *fig* **flying ~s** «летáющие тарéлки».
saucy *adj*: **1** (*impudent*): **a ~ little girl** дéрзкая девчóнка; **don't be ~!** не дерзú!; **a ~ little hat** кокéтливая шля́пка
2 *CQ* (*choosy*) привирéдливый в + *P*.
sauerkraut *n* кúслая капýста.
sauna *n* фúнская бáня, сáуна.
saunter *vi*: **to ~ up and down the street** прогýливаться по ýлице.
sausage *n* (*salami*) колбасá; (*frankfurter*) сосúска; (*fat and short*) сардéлька; *attr*: **~ meat** колбáсный фарш; **~ roll** пирожóк с сосúской.
savage *n* дикáрь (*m*).
savage *adj* (*wild*) дúкий; (*ferocious*) свирéпый; **~ tribes** дúкие племенá; **a ~ dog** злáя собáка; **he got ~** он рассвирепéл (*also of animal*).
savage *vt* (*maul*) изувéч|ивать (-ить); *fig* **his book was ~d by the critics** крúтики я́ростно набрóсились на егó кнúгу.
save *n*: *Sport* **that was a great ~!** он великолéпно/мастерскú взял мяч!
save *vti vt* **1** (*rescue*) спас|áть (-тú); **to ~ smb from death/danger** спастú когó-л от смéрти, уберéчь когó-л от опáсности; **to ~ the situation** спастú положéние
2 (*put by*) от|клáдывать (-ложúть); **she has ~d £40** онá отложúла сóрок фýнтов; **I ~d this copy of the magazine for you** я отложúл/сохранúл э́тот нóмер журнáла для тебя́; **~**

me a seat займи́ мне ме́сто; ~ **the meat for tomorrow's lunch** оста́вим э́то мя́со на за́втра на обе́д

3 (*relieve from using*) сбере|га́ть (-́чь), эконо́мить (с-); **it could ~ you a lot of money** так вы мо́жете сбере́чь мно́го де́нег; **that will ~ a lot of time** э́то сэконо́мит мно́го вре́мени; **the new model ~s petrol** но́вая моде́ль эконо́мит бензи́н; **he is saving himself/his strength for tomorrow's match** он бережёт себя́/свои́ си́лы для за́втрашнего ма́тча; **it ~d them a lot of bother** э́то изба́вило их от мно́гих хлопо́т

vi: **he has ~d up for a summer holiday** он отложи́л де́ньги/он накопи́л/он скопи́л де́нег на ле́тний о́тпуск *or* на ле́то.

save for, save that *preps* кро́ме + *G*.

saving *n*: **bulk buying means a ~ of 20% for us** покупа́я о́птом, мы эконо́мим два́дцать проце́нтов; **a considerable ~ of time/in money** значи́тельный вы́игрыш во вре́мени, значи́тельная эконо́мия де́нег; **she keeps her ~s in the bank** она́ храни́т свои́ сбереже́ния в ба́нке; **we all have to make ~s** нам всем прихо́дится эконо́мить; *attr*: **~s bank** сберега́тельный банк, (*SU*) сберега́тельная ка́сса, *abbr* сберка́сса.

saving *adj*: **generosity in his ~ grace** ще́дрость—черта́, кото́рая в нём подкупа́ет.

savour, (*US*) **savor** *vti vt*: **I ~ed every mouthful** я смакова́л ка́ждый кусо́к (*impf*)

vi: *fig* **that remark ~s of jealousy** в э́тих слова́х сквози́т ре́вность.

savoury *adj* (*appetizing*) вку́сный, аппети́тный; (*not sweet*) о́стрый, солёный.

saw *n* пила́; **circular ~** циркуля́рная пила́.

saw *vti* пили́ть (*impf*) *and compounds*; **to ~ off/up** отпи́л|ивать, распи́л|ивать (*pfs* -и́ть).

sawdust *n* (древе́сные) опи́лки (*pl*).

saw-edged *adj*: **a ~ knife** зазу́бренный нож.

sawmill *n* лесопи́лка.

saxophone *n* саксофо́н.

say *n*: **you have had your ~** ты своё (сло́во) сказа́л; **I had the final ~ in this matter** в э́том де́ле реша́ющее сло́во бы́ло за мной.

say *vti* **1** говори́ть (сказа́ть); **I have nothing to ~** мне не́чего сказа́ть; **everybody ~s that...** все говоря́т, что...; **as our friend used to ~** как гова́ривал наш друг; **if I may ~ so** е́сли мне позволи́тельно бу́дет заме́тить; **he didn't ~ a word** он не сказа́л/не вы́молвил ни сло́ва; **he said yes to the proposal** он вы́сказался за э́то предложе́ние; **I wouldn't ~ no to some tea** я бы не отказа́лся от ча́я; **the law ~s** зако́н гласи́т; **this clock ~s ten o'clock** на э́тих часа́х де́сять (часо́в)

2 (*in exclamation*): **I ~!**, (*US*) **~!** (*calling attention*) послу́шай!, (*in surprise*) поду́мать то́лько!; **you don't ~!** что вы говори́те!; **you can ~ that again!** и не говори́!; **I should ~ so!** ещё бы!; **~ no more!** всё я́сно!/поня́тно!; **I dare ~** (вполне́) возмо́жно

3 *expressions*: **what do you ~ to this?** что ты на э́то ска́жешь?; **that doesn't ~ much for his good intentions** э́то не говори́т о его́ до́брых наме́рениях; **to ~ nothing of the rest of them** не говоря́ уже́ об остальны́х; **she hasn't much to ~ for herself** она́ неразгово́рчива; **he has plenty to ~ for himself** он лю́бит поговори́ть; **it goes without ~ing that...** само́ собо́й разуме́ется, что...

4 *phrases with ppp* **said**: **he is said to be a good driver** говоря́т, что он хоро́ший води́тель; **there's something to be said for that** есть что сказа́ть в по́льзу э́того; **when all is said and done** в коне́чном счёте; **the less said the better** чем ме́ньше слов, тем лу́чше

5 (*suppose*): **~ he refuses to come, what then?** предполо́жим, он отка́жется прийти́, тогда́ что?; **let's meet, ~, on Wednesday** встре́тимся, ну ска́жем, хотя́ бы в сре́ду.

saying *n* погово́рка; **as the ~ goes** как говори́тся.

scabies *n* чесо́тка.

scaffolding *n* (строи́тельные) леса́ (*pl*).

scald *n* ожо́г; *attr*: **~ marks** следы́ от ожо́гов.

scald *vt* (*and burn*) обва́р|ивать (-и́ть), ошпа́р|ивать (-ить); (*to sterilize dishes or scald vegetables*) ошпа́ривать кипятко́м; (*milk*) кипяти́ть (вс-); **to ~ oneself/one's hand** обвари́ться кипятко́м *or* ошпа́риться, обвари́ть себе́ ру́ку.

scalding *adj*: **~ (hot)** о́чень горя́чий.

scale[1] *n Zool* (*single scale, or flaked skin*) чешу́йка; **~s** чешуя́, (*on kettle*) на́кипь, (*tartar*) зубно́й ка́мень (*collects*).

scale[1] *vti vt*: **to ~ teeth** счи|ща́ть зубно́й ка́мень (-́стить)

vi: **to ~ off** (*of paint, plaster, skin*) лупи́ться (об-).

scale[2] *n* **1** (*in measuring*) шкала́; **decimal ~** десятичн... десима́льная шкала́; **what is the ~ of this thermometer?—Celsius** кака́я шкала́ на э́том термо́метре?—По Це́льсию; **the ~ of the ruler is in centimetres** на э́той лине́йке сантиме́тровые деле́ния; **the ~ of wages/of payments** шкала́ за́работной пла́ты, та́кса опла́ты

2 (*relative size*) масшта́б; *fig* разма́х; **this map is drawn to ~/to a ~ of one to ten** э́то масшта́бная ка́рта, масшта́б э́той ка́рты оди́н к десяти́; **I was impressed by the ~ of their planning** на меня́ произвёл впечатле́ние разма́х их плани́рования; *attr*: **it's a large ~ work** э́то рабо́та большо́го масшта́ба

3 *Mus* га́мма; **~ of F major** га́мма фа мажо́р.

scale[3] *n* (*balance*) ча́ша/ча́шка весо́в; **a pair of ~s** весы́ (*pl*); **kitchen ~s** ку́хонные весы́; **he tips the ~(s) at 70 kgs** он ве́сит се́мьдесят килогра́мм.

scale[4] *vt* (*climb*) взбира́ться на + *A* (взобра́ться).

scalp *n* скальп; **I have an itchy ~** у меня́ голова́ че́шется.

scalpel *n Med* ска́льпель (*m*).

scamp *vt CQ*: **he ~s his work** он рабо́тает спустя́ рукава́ (*impf*).

scamper *vi* носи́ться (*impf*), резви́ться (по-); **to ~ away/off** удира́ть (удра́ть), улепётывать (*usu impf*); **to ~ past** про|бега́ть (-бежа́ть); **the children/rabbit ~ed off** де́ти разбежа́лись, кро́лик удра́л.

scan *vti vt*: **he ~ned the horizon** он обвёл глаза́ми горизо́нт; *Tech* (*by radar*) скани́ровать (*impf and pf*)

vi (*of verse*): **this line does not ~** э́та стро́чка не сканди́руется.

scandal *n* **1** сканда́л; **a political ~** полити́ческий сканда́л; **to create/hush up a ~** вы́звать/замя́ть сканда́л; **what a ~ that...** возмути́тельно, что...

2 (*gossip*): **have you heard the latest ~?** вы слы́шали после́днюю спле́тню?; **one hears a lot of ~ about his wife** о его́ жене́ чего́ то́лько не говоря́т.

scandalize *vt* шоки́ровать (*impf*); возму|ща́ть (-ти́ть); **she was ~d** она́ была́ шоки́рована; **he ~d the neighbours by his behaviour** сосе́ди бы́ли возмущены́ его́ поведе́нием.

scandalous *adj*: **~ rumours** сканда́льные слу́хи; **conditions at that hospital are quite ~** усло́вия в э́той больни́це про́сто ужа́сные/*CQ*— про́сто ни в каки́е воро́та не ле́зет.

scanner *n* (*in radar*) лока́торная анте́нна.

scant, scanty *adjs* ску́дный; **~ vegetation** ску́дная расти́тельность; **her attire was ~ in the extreme** она́ была́ чуть ли не го́лая; *CQ* **a scanty bikini** малю́сенькое бики́ни.

scapegoat *n* козёл отпуще́ния.

scar *n* шрам, рубе́ц.

scar *vt*: **his face is badly ~red** у него́ всё лицо́ в шра́мах.

scarce *adj*: **a ~ commodity** дефици́тный това́р; **eggs are ~ just now** я́йца тепе́рь тру́дно доста́ть; **after the war food was ~** по́сле войны́ бы́ло пло́хо с проду́ктами; **such opportunities are ~** таки́е возмо́жности быва́ют неча́сто; *CQ* **I made myself ~** я улизну́л, я смы́лся.

scarcely *adv* едва́, почти́ не, е́ле; **I ~ know him** я его́ почти́ не зна́ю; **I can ~ walk** я е́ле хожу́; **~ had he gone when the phone rang** то́лько он ушёл, как зазвони́л телефо́н.

scarcity *n* недоста́ток, нехва́тка; **there is a ~ of eggs** сейча́с яи́ц не доста́нешь; **times of great ~** вре́мя (*sing*) большо́й нужды́ и лише́ний.

scare *n* страх; па́ника; **you gave me such a ~!** ты меня́ так испуга́л/напуга́л.

scare *vt* пуга́ть (ис-, на-, пере-); **she was ~d by the scream** её испуга́л э́тот крик; **she was ~d and ran away** она́ испуга́лась/перепуга́лась и убежа́ла; **our dog ~d away/off the burglar** на́ша соба́ка испуга́ла во́ра, и он убежа́л; **he was ~d stiff of spiders/his teacher** он ужа́сно боя́лся пауко́в/учи́теля.

scarecrow *n* пу́гало, *also fig.*

scaremonger *n* пани́кёр.

scarf *n* шарф; **head ~** плато́к, (*triangular*) косы́нка.

scarlet *adj* а́лый.

scathing *adj*: **a ~ glance** испепеля́ющий/уничтожа́ющий взгляд; **a ~ remark** е́дкое/язви́тельное замеча́ние; **he was ~ about the standard of the work** он язви́л насчёт того́, как сде́лана э́та рабо́та.

scatter *vti vt* раз|бра́сывать (-броса́ть), раски́д|ывать (-а́ть), рассе́|ивать (-ять), рассып|а́ть (-́ать); **to ~ seed** разбра́сывать семена́; **on the island the population is thinly ~ed** населе́ние о́строва живёт в ре́дко разбро́санных небольши́х селе́ниях; **he ~s his belongings all over the house** он разбра́сывает/раски́дывает свои́ ве́щи по всему́ до́му; **my schoolmates are ~ed all over the world** мои́ одноклáссники разъе́хались по всему́ све́ту; **to ~ crumbs for the birds** рассы́пать кро́шки для птиц; **the troops ~ed the crowd** солда́ты разогна́ли толпу́

vi рассе́иваться; **the crowd ~ed (in all directions)** толпа́ рассе́ялась, лю́ди разбежа́лись в ра́зные сто́роны; **the birds ~ed** пти́цы разлете́лись.

scatterbrained *adj* ве́треный, легкомы́сленный.

scatty *adj CQ* смурно́й.

scavenge *vi*: **to ~ in the dustbins** ры́ться в му́сорных я́щиках (*impf*).

scenario *n* (кино)сцена́рий.

scene *n* **1** *Theat* сце́на; *pl* (**~s**) (*scenery*) декора́ции; **act one, ~ two** де́йствие пе́рвое, сце́на втора́я; **the opening ~ is in the palace** де́йствие открыва́ется сце́ной во дворце́ короля́; **they change the ~s during the interval** декора́ции меня́ют во вре́мя антра́кта; **behind the ~s** за кули́сами, *also fig*; *attr*: **a ~ painter/shifter** худо́жник-декора́тор, рабо́чий сце́ны

2 (*place in general*) ме́сто; *fig* обстано́вка; **at the ~ of the crime** на ме́сте преступле́ния; **the political ~ in India** полити́ческая обстано́вка в И́ндии; **he needs a change of ~** ему́ ну́жно перемени́ть обстано́вку

3 (*sight, picture*) сце́на, карти́на; **a typical ~ of English life** типи́чная карти́на англи́йской жи́зни; **what terrible ~s there were during the earthquake** каки́е стра́шные карти́ны мо́жно бы́ло наблюда́ть во вре́мя землетрясе́ния

4 (*fuss*) сканда́л, сце́на; **she made a ~ at the wedding** она́ закати́ла тако́й сканда́л/она́ устро́ила таку́ю сце́ну на сва́дьбе; **I do hate ~s** я не терплю́ сцен.

scenery *n* пейза́ж; *Theat* декора́ции (*pl*); **beautiful mountain ~** краси́вый го́рный пейза́ж.

scenic *adj* (*picturesque*) живопи́сный; *Theat* **~ effects** сцени́ческие эффе́кты.

scent *n* **1**: **a ~ of lavender** арома́т лава́нды; **this rose has no ~** у э́той ро́зы нет за́паха

2 (*perfume*) духи́ (*no sing*); **she uses too much ~** она́ чересчу́р си́льно ду́шится

3 (*in hunting*) след; **to pick up/lose the ~** напа́сть на след, потеря́ть след; **dogs hunt by ~** соба́ки охо́тятся по ню́ху; *fig* **he was on a false ~** он шёл по ло́жному сле́ду.

scent *vt* (*perfume*) души́ть (на-); *fig* **to ~ danger** чу́ять опа́сность.

scented *adj*: **a ~ handkerchief** наду́шенный плато́к; **~ soap** арома́тное мы́ло.

sceptical, (*US*) **skeptical** *adj* скепти́ческий; **he is very ~ about it** он отно́сится к э́тому о́чень скепти́чески.

schedule *n* (*timetable*) расписа́ние; (*of events, etc.*) програ́мма; (*of planned work, etc.*) план, гра́фик; **the plane will arrive according to/on ~** самолёт прилета́ет то́чно по расписа́нию; **our ~ includes a visit to the zoo** на́ша програ́мма включа́ет посеще́ние зоопа́рка; **the work is on ~** рабо́та идёт по пла́ну/по гра́фику.

schedule *vt usu pass*: **the train is ~d to arrive at 8.00 a.m.** по расписа́нию по́езд прибыва́ет в во́семь утра́; **three new productions are ~d for this season** в э́том сезо́не наме́чены три но́вых постано́вки.

schematic *adj* схемати́чный, схемати́ческий.

scheme *n* **1** (*plan, etc.*): **they developed a ~ for a new road system** они́ разрабо́тали план но́вой систе́мы доро́г; **they are working on/out a ~ for widows' pensions** они́ разраба́тывают програ́мму пе́нсий и посо́бий вдо́вам; **the ~ of a fugue** построе́ние/структу́ра фу́ги; **colour ~** сочета́ние цвето́в; **he's got this crazy ~ to open a shop** ему́ вдруг взбрело́ (*impers*) в го́лову откры́ть магази́н

2 (*plot*) интри́га.

scheme *vi* (*usu pejor*): **they are scheming to get rid of him** они́ плету́т интри́ги, что́бы изба́виться от него́.

scheming *n pejor* интри́ги, махина́ции (*pls*).

schizophrenic *n* шизофре́ник.

scholar *n* **1** (*expert*) учёный; **a Pushkin ~** пушкини́ст, иссле́дователь тво́рчества Пу́шкина; *CQ* **I'm not much of a ~** в нау́ке я не силён

2 (*holder of scholarship*) стипендиа́т.

scholarly *adj* учёный; нау́чный; **he's a ~ type** он учёный челове́к; **a ~ approach** нау́чный подхо́д.

scholarship *n* **1** (*learning*) учёность, образо́ванность

2 (*award*) стипе́ндия; **he has won a ~ to Cambridge** он получи́л стипе́ндию в Ке́мбридже.

school[1] *n* **1** (*in general*) шко́ла; **preparatory/primary ~** нача́льная шко́ла (*UK*: *age* 5—11, *US*: 6—11, *SU*: 7—9); **secondary/high ~** сре́дняя шко́ла (*UK*, *US*: *age* 12—17, *SU*: 10—17); **a private/state ~** ча́стная/госуда́рственная шко́ла; **ballet ~** бале́тная шко́ла, бале́тное учи́лище

2 (*uses without article*) шко́ла; (*lessons*) уро́ки, заня́тия (*usu pls*); **where did you go to ~?, where were you at ~?** в како́й шко́ле вы учи́лись?; **I have two sons at ~** у меня́ два сы́на у́чатся в шко́ле; **he left ~ to earn his living** он бро́сил/оста́вил шко́лу и пошёл рабо́тать; **he left ~ and went to university** он око́нчил шко́лу и поступи́л в университе́т; **~ starts at 9.00** заня́тия/уро́ки начина́ются в де́вять часо́в; **there is no ~ tomorrow** за́втра заня́тий/уро́ков не бу́дет

3 (*with def article*): **the whole ~ went to the match** вся шко́ла пошла́ на матч

4 *Univ*: **medical/law ~** медици́нский/юриди́ческий факульте́т (*as part of Univ*) *or* институ́т (*separate institution*)

5 *Art*, *Philos* шко́ла; **the Flemish/Hegelian ~** флама́ндская/гегелья́нская шко́ла

6 *attr*: **~ age** шко́льный во́зраст; **~ year** уче́бный год; **~ book** уче́бник; **~ leaver** выпускни́к (шко́лы).

school[1] *vt* приуч|а́ть (-и́ть); учи́ть (на-); (*a horse*) тренирова́ть (на-); **they have been ~ed to discipline/to hardship** они́ приу́чены к дисципли́не/к тру́дностям; **he ~ed himself to be punctual** он научи́лся быть пунктуа́льным; **they have been well ~ed in etiquette** их хорошо́ обучи́ли этике́ту.

school[2] *n* (*of fish*) сея́к (ры́бы).

schoolboy *n* шко́льник.

schooldays *npl* шко́льные го́ды.

schoolfellow *n* одноклáссник.

schoolgirl *n* шко́льница.

schooling *n* образова́ние, обуче́ние; **we get free ~** у нас образова́ние беспла́тное, у нас шко́лы беспла́тные.

schoolmaster *n* учи́тель (*m*), преподава́тель (*m*), педаго́г.

schoolmistress *n* учи́тельница, преподава́тельница, педаго́г.

schoolroom *n* класс, кла́ссная ко́мната.

sciatica *n Med* и́шиас.

science *n* нау́ка; **natural/applied/social ~s** есте́ственные/прикладны́е/обще́ственные нау́ки; *attr*: **~ fiction** нау́чная фанта́стика.

scientific *adj* нау́чный.

scientist *n* учёный.

scintillating *adj fig*: **a ~ wit** блестя́щий ум.

scissors *npl*, *also* **a pair of ~** но́жницы (*pl*).

sclerosis *n Med* склеро́з; **multiple ~** рассе́янный склеро́з.

scoff *vi*: **to ~ at danger** смея́ться над опа́сностью (*usu impf*).

scoffing *adj* насме́шливый, (*stronger*) издева́тельский.

scold *vti vt* брани́ть (вы́-), руга́ть (вы́-, от-); **to ~ smb for doing smth** брани́ть/руга́ть кого́-л за что-л

vi брани́ться, ворча́ть.

scolding *n* вы́говор, нагоня́й; **she gave him a ~** она́ отруга́ла/вы́ругала его́, она́ дала́ ему́ нагоня́й.

scoop *n* **1** (*for grain, sugar, etc.*) сово́к, *dim* сово́чек; (*for liquids*) черпа́к, ковш, *dim* ко́вшик

2 *CQ*: *Comm* **this deal**/(*press*) **this news was a real ~ for us** заключи́в э́ту сде́лку,/

напечáтав э́то сообщéние, мы остáвили позади́ нáших конкурéнтов.

scoop *vt* (*excavate, hollow*), *also* ~ **out** вы|кáпывать (́-копать), (*of wood, frozen ground*) вы|дáлбливать (́-долбить); (*of liquid, grain, etc.*), *also* ~ **up** чéрпать (зачерпну́ть), (*until empty*) вы|чéрпывать (́-черпать).

scooter *n* (*child's*) самокáт; (**motor**) ~ моторóллер.

scope *n*: **the** ~ **of government activity** размáх / сфéра дéятельности прави́тельства; **the** ~ **of his influence** масштáбы (*pl*) его́ влия́ния; **it is beyond my** ~ э́то не вхóдит в мою́ компетéнцию; **this job gives him** ~ **for his abilities** э́та рабóта даёт ему́ возмóжность разверну́ться.

scorch *n attr*: ~ **marks** следы́ от утюгá.

scorch *vti vt* (*of sun, heat*) пали́ть (с-, о-); (*by ironing*) жечь (с-); (*singe*) подпáл|ивать (-и́ть); **the heat** ~**ed the grass** жарá иссуши́ла травý; **I** ~**ed my dress while ironing it** я сожглá плáтье утюгóм; **I** ~**ed my hair** я подпали́ла вóлосы

vi Aut CQ: **he** ~**ed past us** он промчáлся ми́мо нас.

scorcher *n CQ*: **today has been a** ~ сегóдня стрáшная жарá.

scorching *adj*: **the sun is** ~ **today** сегóдня сóлнце пали́т нещáдно; *CQ as adv*: **it is** ~ **hot in the afternoon** пóсле обéда невыноси́мо жáрко.

score *n* **1** (*made by a cut*) рубéц; (*notch*) зару́бка

2 (*account*) счёт, *also fig*; **to run up a** ~ дéлать долги́; *fig*: **to settle old** ~**s** расплáчиваться по стáрым счетáм; **I have an old** ~ **to settle with him** у меня́ с ним стáрые счёты (*pl*); **you need have no worries on that** ~ на э́тот счёт вам нéчего беспокóиться

3 *Sport* счёт; **the** ~ **was 2-3** счёт был 2 : 3; **to keep the** ~ вести́ счёт, *Cards* подсчи́тывать очки́

4 *Mus* партиту́ра; **piano** ~ клави́р; **a film** ~ му́зыка к фи́льму.

score *vti vt* **1** (*scratch*) царáпать (о-, *semel* царáпнуть); **to** ~ **out, to** ~ **through** вы|чёркивать (́-черкнуть), за|чёркивать (-черкну́ть); **his manuscript is heavily** ~**d** его́ ру́копись вся исчёркана

2 (*in exams*): **he** ~**d 70% in maths** он получи́л (*SU approx*) четвёрку по математи́ке; *Sport*: **to** ~ **a goal** заби|вáть гол (*soccer, etc.*) / шáйбу (*ice-hockey*) (́-ть), за|брáсывать мяч в корзи́ну (*basketball*) (-брóсить); **to** ~ **points** (*tennis, basketball*) получ|áть / (*boxing, athletics, etc.*) на|бирáть очки́ (-и́ть / -брáть); *Cards* **we** ~**d five tricks** у нас бы́ло пять взя́ток; *fig*: **to** ~ **an advantage over smb** доби|вáться преиму́щества (*G*) над кем-л (́-ться); **she** ~**d an enormous hit with her performance** её выступлéние имéло огрóмный успéх

3 *Mus*: **to** ~ **a symphony** оркестровáть симфóнию (*impf and pf*); **this work is** ~**d for a small group** э́то произведéние напи́сано для мáлого состáва инструмéнтов

vi Sport (*keep score*) вести́ счёт, подсчи́т|ывать очки́ (-áть); **no one has** ~**d so far** счёт ещё не откры́т; **he** ~**d within the first five minutes** в пéрвые пять мину́т он заби́л гол.

scoreboard *n Sport* таблó (*indecl*).

scorecard *n Sport* кáрточка учáстника соревновáний.

scorn *n* презрéние.

scorn *vt*: **to** ~ **smb / danger** презирáть когó-л / опáсность (*impf*); **to** ~ **smb's advice** пренебре|гáть чьим-л совéтом (́-чь); **I would** ~ **to do such a thing** я бы до э́того не опусти́лся.

scornful *adj* презри́тельный; **she was** ~ **of our efforts** онá весьмá скепти́чески отнеслáсь к нáшим попы́ткам.

Scot *n* шотлáндец, шотлáндка.

Scotch *n* **1**: **he talks broad** ~ он говори́т с си́льным шотлáндским акцéнтом

2 *CQ* (шотлáндское) ви́ски (*indecl*).

scot-free *adj* безнакáзанный; **he got off** ~ ему́ сошлó с рук.

Scotsman *n see* **Scot.**

Scottish *adj* шотлáндский.

scoundrel *n* подлéц.

scour[1] *vt* (*scrub*) от|скáбливать (-скобли́ть), скрести́ (со-, от-); **to** ~ **the frying pan** отскобли́ть сковорóдку.

scour[2] *vt*: **the police** ~**ed the district for the murderer** поли́ция про|чёсывала райóн в пóисках уби́йцы (-чесáть).

scourer *n* металли́ческая мочáлка.

scout *n Mil* развéдчик; **boy** ~ бойскáут; **a talent** ~ и́щущий талáнты.

scout *vi*: **to** ~ **about / around for smb / smth** искáть когó-л / что-л (по-); *Mil* вести́ развéдку (*usu impf*).

scowl *vi* серди́то хму́риться (на-); **he** ~**ed at me** он хму́ро / зло посмотрéл на меня́.

scrag end *n Cook* барáнья шéя.

scraggy *adj* тóщий.

scram *vi CQ*: ~! пошёл вон!, убирáйся!; **we** ~**med** мы удрáли.

scramble *n* (*climbing*) карáбканье; **the last part of the ascent was a** ~ на послéднем учáстке / послéдние мéтры подъёма пришлóсь карáбкаться; **there was a** ~ **for places in the bus** в автóбусе все брóсились занимáть местá.

scramble *vti vt*: **to** ~ **eggs** *approx* дéлать яи́чницу-болту́нью; (*of message*) зашифрóв|ывать (-áть)

vi (*climb up*) карáбкаться (вс-); **we** ~**d up the cliff / over the rocks** мы вскарáбкались на верши́ну скалы́, мы карáбкались по скалáм; **he** ~**d up on to / over the wall** он влез на / перелéз чéрез забóр; **he** ~**d through the bushes** он продирáлся сквозь кусты́.

scrap[1] *n* **1** (*fragment*) клочóк; **a** ~ **of paper** клочóк бумáги; *fig*: **there is not a** ~ **of truth in it** в э́том нет и дóли прáвды; ~**s**

of news обры́вки новосте́й; *attr*: ~ **album/book** альбо́м с вы́резками, откры́тками *и т.п.*

2 (*left-overs*) *usu pl* (*of food*) объе́дки; (*of cloth*) обре́зки

3 (*waste, salvage*) ути́ль (*m*); **is it worth anything as ~?** э́то возьму́т в ути́ль?; **we sold the car for ~** мы про́дали маши́ну на металлоло́м; *attr*: ~ **dealer** ути́льщик, (*for iron*) сбо́рщик металлоло́ма; ~ **heap** сва́лка; ~ **iron** металлоло́м; ~ **paper** (*for making notes*) бума́га для заме́ток, (*for pulp*) макулату́ра.

scrap[1] *vt*: **I shall ~ the old bicycle** я вы́брошу ста́рый велосипе́д; **you'll have to ~ your plans/that idea** тебе́ придётся отказа́ться от э́тих пла́нов/оста́вить э́ту иде́ю.

scrap[2] *n CQ* (*fight*) потасо́вка.

scrap[2] *vi* (*physically*) дра́ться (по-); (*verbally*) повздо́рить (*pf*), ссо́риться (по-).

scrape *n* (*noise*) скрип; (*action*) **the frying pan needs a good ~** ну́жно как сле́дует отскрести́ сковоро́дку; *fig*: **he is always getting into silly ~s** он ве́чно попада́ет/*CQ* влипа́ет в глу́пые исто́рии; **to get smb out of a ~** вы́зволить кого́-л из беды́.

scrape *vti vt* **1** скрести́, скобли́ть (*impfs*) *and compounds*; **to ~ away/down/off** соск|а́бливать (-обли́ть), соскре|ба́ть (-сти́); (*skin, etc.*) об|дира́ть, с|дира́ть (*pfs* -одра́ть); **I ~d the pan** я скобли́л кастрю́лю; **to ~ down paint** соскобли́ть/соскрести́ кра́ску; **to ~ mud off one's shoes** соскрести́ грязь с боти́нок; **to ~ carrots/potatoes** чи́стить морко́вку/карто́шку (*collects*); **the boat ~d the bottom** ло́дка чи́ркнула дном; **I ~d my knee/the skin off my elbow** я ободра́л коле́но/ло́коть; *Aut*: **the car ~d the wall** маши́на заде́ла за сте́ну; **I ~d the paint on the wing** я поцара́пал крыло́, я ободра́л кра́ску на крыле́ (*pfs*)

2 *fig uses*: **to ~ some money together** наскрести́ де́нег (*usu pf*); **we managed to ~ together/up an audience for the concert** нам удало́сь собра́ть ко́е-каку́ю пу́блику на конце́рт; **to ~ a living** своди́ть концы́ с конца́ми

vi fig: **there's room to ~ by/past** (*in car*) здесь мо́жно разъе́хаться; (*in exam*) **I just ~d through!** я е́ле сдал!/прошёл!; **to ~ and save** откла́дывать по копе́йке (*only in impf*); **he can ~ along/by in Russian** он мо́жет ко́е-ка́к объясни́ться по-ру́сски; **he ~s away at/on his fiddle** он всё пили́кает на свое́й скри́пке.

scraper *n* (*tool, also at door*) скребо́к.

scrappy *adj* обры́вочный; ~ **knowledge** обры́вочные зна́ния (*pl*); **a ~ conversation** несвя́зный разгово́р.

scratch *n* **1** (*wound*) цара́пина; **he escaped without a ~** он не получи́л ни еди́ной цара́пины; **her hands are covered with ~es** у неё все ру́ки исцара́паны

2 (*sound*) скрип

3 *Sport* (*sing only*) ста́ртовая черта́; *fig CQ*: **to start from ~** начина́ть всё снача́ла; **he didn't come up to ~** он оказа́лся не на высоте́/у́ровне; *attr*: **we are a ~ team** *CQ* на́ша кома́нда—сбо́рная соля́нка.

scratch *vti vt* **1** (*with nail, etc.*) цара́п|ать (-нуть, по-, о-), (*if itchy*) чеса́ть (по-); **I ~ed my hand on the wire** я поцара́пал ру́ку о про́волоку; **we ~ed our names on the wall** мы нацара́пали на́ши имена́ на стене́; **he ~ed his head/the cat's back** он почеса́л го́лову/ко́шке спи́нку; **don't ~ yourself!** не чеши́сь!

2 (*scrape*) скрести́ (*impf*) *and compounds*; **the dog is ~ing the ground/a hole** соба́ка скребёт зе́млю/выскреба́ет я́му; **to ~ paint off** соскрести́ кра́ску; ~ **that item off the list** вы́черкни э́тот пункт из спи́ска

3 *Sport*: **that horse has been ~ed from the race** э́ту ло́шадь сня́ли со ска́чек; **the match has been ~ed** матч отмени́ли

vi **1** цара́паться; (*from itch*) чеса́ться; **the dog ~ed at the door** соба́ка скребла́сь в дверь; **the hens are ~ing about in the yard** ку́ры ро́ются во дворе́

2 *Sport*: **he ~ed at the last minute** в после́дний моме́нт он отказа́лся (от уча́стия в соревнова́ниях).

scrawl *n*: **I can't make out this untidy ~** я не могу́ разобра́ть э́ти кара́кули (*pl*); **his signature is just a ~** у него́ не по́дпись, а закорю́чка кака́я-то.

scrawl *vti vt CQ*: **I ~ed a few words to him** я черкну́л ему́ па́ру строк

vi: **who has ~ed all over the blackboard?** кто исчерка́л всю до́ску?

scream *n* крик; вопль (*m*); **a ~ of terror** крик у́жаса; **we heard ~s of delight from the children** мы слы́шали восто́рженные кри́ки дете́й; **there were ~s of laughter** раздава́лись взры́вы сме́ха; *CQ* **he's a perfect ~** он про́сто умо́ра/умори́телен.

scream *vi* крича́ть (*pfs* кри́кнуть, *fig* (*shout at*) на-); **she ~ed in terror/in pain/for help/at him** она́ вскри́кнула от стра́ха, она́ крича́ла от бо́ли, она́ звала́ на по́мощь, она́ накрича́ла на него́.

screech *n* крик; визг; **the ~ of an owl/of brakes** крик совы́, визг тормозо́в; **she let out a ~** она́ взвизгнула.

screed *n CQ*: **I got the usual ~ from mother today** сего́дня я вы́слушал от ма́тери её обы́чную дли́нную тира́ду; **he wrote ~s** он исписа́л то́нны бума́ги.

screen *n* экра́н, *also Cine*; *Tech* си́то, гро́хот; **a ~ for the fireplace** ками́нный экра́н; **a folding ~** складна́я ши́рма; **a smoke ~** дымова́я заве́са; *attr Cine*: **a ~ test** экра́нная про́ба; **a ~ adaptation** экраниза́ция.

screen *vt* (*shelter, protect*) загор|а́живать (-оди́ть); заслон|я́ть (-и́ть); защи|ща́ть (-ти́ть); (*sift*) просе́|ивать (-ять); (*investigate*) провер|я́ть (-ить); **the hills ~ the house from the wind** холмы́ загора́живают/защища́ют дом от ве́тра; **you should ~ your lens from direct light** ну́жно заслони́ть объекти́в от прямы́х луче́й; **to ~ off a part of the room** отгор|а́живать часть ко́мнаты (-оди́ть); **the company**

~s all its employees компа́ния проверя́ет/подверга́ет прове́рке всех рабо́тников.

screw *n* (*of metal*) винт; шуру́п; *fig CQ*: **he's got a ~ loose** у него́ ви́нтика в голове́ не хвата́ет; **to put the ~(s) on smb** ока́зывать нажи́м на кого́-л.

screw *vt*: **to ~ up (tight)** зави́н|чивать (-ти́ть); **to ~ off** отви́нчивать; **the lid is loose, ~ it down a bit** кры́шка осла́бла, подвинти́ её; **I ~ed the letter up into a ball** я смял письмо́; *fig*: **to ~ money out of smb** вымога́ть у кого́-л де́ньги; **he's got his head ~ed on** он толко́вый челове́к; **I am ~ing up my courage to ask him** я собира́юсь с ду́хом, что́бы зада́ть ему́ э́тот вопро́с.

screwdriver *n* отвёртка.

scribble *n* кара́кули (*usu pl*).

scribble *vti vt*: **I ~d a few lines/my signature** я нацара́пал не́сколько строк/свою́ по́дпись *vi*: **the child ~d all over the paper** ребёнок исчерка́л всю бума́гу (*usu pf*); **he's still scribbling away at his novel** он всё ника́к не зако́нчит свой рома́н.

scribbling pad *n* блокно́т.

scrimmage *n* сва́лка, потасо́вка; *Sport* схва́тка.

scrimp *vi*: *CQ* **mother ~ed and saved to send me to college** моя́ мать на всём эконо́мила (*usu impf*), что́бы посла́ть меня́ учи́ться в колле́дж.

script *n* (*of play*) текст; (*of film, TV*) сцена́рий; **Gothic ~** готи́ческий шрифт; *attr*: **~ writer** сценари́ст.

Scripture *n*, *also* **Holy ~** свяще́нное писа́ние (*also as school subject*).

scrofula *n Med* золоту́ха, скрофулёз.

scroll *n*: **a Chinese ~** кита́йский сви́ток; **the Dead Sea ~s** ру́кописи Мёртвого мо́ря.

scrounge *vti vt CQ*: **I ~d a cigarette off him** я стрельну́л у него́ сигаре́ту; **he ~d five roubles/a meal off me** он вы́клянчил у меня́ пятёрку, он напроси́лся на обе́д *vi*: **he is always scrounging off people** ве́чно он попроша́йничает.

scrounger *n* попроша́йка (*m and f*).

scrub *vt* скрести́ (*impf*) *and compounds*; **to ~ the floor/a pan/one's hands** скрести́ пол, чи́стить кастрю́лю, хороше́нько отмы́ть ру́ки; *CQ* **let's ~ the whole idea** брось всё э́то.

scrubbing brush *n* щётка (для по́ла).

scruff *n*: **he picked the cat up by the ~ of its neck** он схвати́л ко́шку за шки́рку.

scruffy *adj* неопря́тный.

scrum *n fig*: **there was a fearful ~ at the bar** в ба́ре была́ стра́шная толку́чка.

scrumptious *adj CQ*: **what ~ food!** как вку́сно!, про́сто объеде́ние!

scruple *n* **1** (*measure*) скру́пул

2: she has no ~s about making use of her friends она́ без зазре́ния со́вести испо́льзует свои́х друзе́й.

scrupulous *adj* (*thorough*) скрупулёзный, то́чный; **he is most ~ about doing his share of the work/about money matters** он скрупулёзно выполня́ет свою́ часть рабо́ты, он то́чен *or* аккура́тен в де́нежных расчётах; **~ honesty/cleanliness** безупре́чная че́стность/чистота́; **he pays ~ attention to detail** он о́чень внима́телен к деталя́м.

scrutinize *vt* тща́тельно рассм|а́тривать/изуч|а́ть (-отре́ть/-и́ть); **he ~d the contract carefully** он тща́тельно/внима́тельно изучи́л контра́кт.

scrutiny *n*: **his evidence won't bear ~** его́ показа́ния (*pl*) не вы́держивают кри́тики при ближа́йшем рассмотре́нии.

scud *vi* нести́сь (*only in impf*); **clouds ~ded across the sky** облака́ несли́сь по не́бу; **the yacht ~ded (along) before the wind** я́хта несла́сь, подгоня́емая попу́тным ве́тром.

scuffle *n* потасо́вка, сва́лка.

scullery *n* судомо́йня.

sculpt *vti vt* ва́ять (из-), (*chisel*) вы|сека́ть (-сечь); (*mould*) лепи́ть (вы́-); **he ~ed a figure from marble** он вы́сек фигу́ру из мра́мора *vi*: **he ~s in wood** он ску́льптор по де́реву.

sculpture *n* скульпту́ра.

scum *n* пе́на; (*on soup, stew*) на́кипь; (*on jam*) пе́нки (*pl*); *fig* **the ~ of the earth** подо́нки (*pl*) о́бщества, вся́кий сброд.

scurf *n* пе́рхоть.

scurrilous *adj* бра́нный, непристо́йный.

scurry *vi*: **the mouse scurried off into its hole** мышь юркну́ла в свою́ но́рку; **we scurried for shelter/for the bar** мы ки́нулись под наве́с/в буфе́т.

scurvy *n Med* цинга́.

scuttle *n*: **coal ~** ведёрко для у́гля.

scythe *n* коса́.

sea *n* **1** мо́ре; **Baku is on the Caspian ~** Баку́ нахо́дится на Каспи́йском мо́ре; **right by the ~** у са́мого мо́ря; **we came here by ~** мы приплы́ли сюда́ мо́рем; **on the high ~s** в откры́том мо́ре (*sing*); **he spent three weeks at ~** он провёл три неде́ли в мо́ре; **he went to ~** он стал моряко́м; (*of boat*) **to go/put to ~** вы́йти в мо́ре; **to swim in the ~** пла́вать в мо́ре; **heavy ~s are forecast** *approx* ожида́ется шторм

2 *fig uses*: **a ~ of faces/of flame** мо́ре лиц, мо́ре огня́; **I'm completely at ~** я в по́лном недоуме́нии; *CQ* **he is half ~s over** (*drunk*) тепе́рь ему́ мо́ре по коле́но

3 *attr* морско́й; **~ air/transport** морско́й во́здух/тра́нспорт.

sea anemone *n Zool* акти́ния.

seafaring *adj*: **~ man** морепла́ватель (*m*).

sea front *n* примо́рье.

seagoing *adj*: **a ~ ship** океа́нское су́дно.

seagull *n* ча́йка.

seal[1] *n Zool* тюле́нь (*m*).

seal[2] *n* печа́ть; **wax ~** сургу́чная печа́ть; **lead ~** (*on package, etc.*) пло́мба.

seal[2] *vt* (*of document*) ста́вить печа́ть на + *A* (по-), скреп|ля́ть печа́тью (-и́ть), (*of letter, envelope*) запеча́т|ывать (-ать), закле́|ивать (-ить); **to ~ (up) a package** запеча́тать паке́т; **to ~ up a room** опеча́т|ывать ко́мнату

(-ать); **the police have ~ed off the area** полиция оцепила этот район.

sea legs *npl CQ*: **I've already got my ~** я уже привык к качке.

sea level *n* уровень (*m*) моря; **500 m above/below ~** пятьсот метров над уровнем моря/ниже уровня моря.

sealing wax *n* сургуч.

sealskin *n* тюленья кожа; (*of high quality*) котиковый мех; *attr*: **~ cap** котиковая шапка.

seam *n* шов, *also Naut*; *Geol* прослоек, пласт; **to split at the ~s** лопнуть по швам.

seaman *n* моряк; **able-bodied ~** матрос первого класса; **ordinary ~** простой/рядовой матрос.

seamy *adj fig*: **the ~ side of life** неприглядная/тёмная сторона жизни.

seaplane *n* гидросамолёт.

search *n* поиски (*pl*); (*by police, etc.*) обыск; **in his ~ for truth/happiness** в поисках истины/счастья; **I had a thorough ~ for the book** я долго искал эту книгу; *attr*: **to issue a ~ warrant** выдать ордер на обыск; **~ party** поисковая группа, *Mil* поисковый отряд.

search *vti vt* искать (*impf*) *and compounds*; **we ~ed the woods for mushrooms** мы искали в лесу грибы; **the guard ~ed the prisoner** надзиратель обыскал заключённого; **the police ~ed the house for drugs** полиция обыскала весь дом в поисках наркотиков; **the child ~ed his pockets/the shelves for some sweets** ребёнок обшарил все карманы/шарил по полкам—нет ли где конфет; **I ~ed my memory but couldn't remember the name** я напрягал память, но не мог вспомнить имя; *CQ* **do you know where the keys are?—S. me!** не знаешь, где ключи?—Понятия не имею

vi: **I ~ed through the book for the answer** я перелистал всю книгу, чтобы ответить на этот вопрос; **I ~ed through my cupboards for a sweater** я перерыл все шкафы в поисках свитера; **he ~ed out his friend** он разыскал/отыскал своего друга; **the police are ~ing for the criminal** полиция разыскивает преступника.

searching *adj*: **a ~ look** ищущий взгляд; **they asked him some ~ questions** они подробно расспросили его.

searchlight *n* прожектор.

seascape *n* морской пейзаж.

seashore *n* морской берег, морское побережье.

seasick *adj*: **I always get ~** меня на море всегда укачивает; **I feel ~** меня укачало (*impers*) [**NB** *tense*]; **he was ~ right through the voyage** его тошнило (*impers*) всю дорогу.

seasickness *n* морская болезнь.

seaside *n*: **we went to the ~** мы съездили к морю; **the children love (being at) the ~** дети очень любят море; *attr*: **to have a ~ holiday** отдохнуть у моря.

season *n* (*of year*) время года; (*social, sporting, etc.*) сезон; **the football/concert/rainy ~** футбольный/концертный сезон, сезон дождей; **in the holiday ~** в период отпусков, на каникулах; **strawberries are now in ~** сейчас поспела клубника; **a word in ~** слово, сказанное вовремя; *attr*: **a ~ ticket** *Rail* сезонный билет, (*for concerts*) концертный абонемент.

season *vt*: **to ~ a dish with** приправ|лять блюдо + *I* (-ить).

seasonable *adj* (*of advice, gifts, etc.*) своевременный, уместный; **it's ~ weather for October** погода, обычная для октября.

seasonal *adj*: **~ work** сезонная работа.

seasoned *adj* (*of wood*) высушенный, выдержанный; (*of food*) приправленный; **highly ~ dishes** очень острые блюда.

seasoning *n Cook* приправа.

seat *n* **1** (*place*) место; **an empty ~** свободное место; **keep me a ~ by the window** займи мне место у окна; **take your ~s for the performance** занимайте места, спектакль начинается; **all ~s are sold** все билеты проданы

2: the ~ of a chair/bicycle сиденье стула/велосипеда; **the ~ of one's trousers** зад брюк; *CQ* (*of person*) зад; *Aut* **the driver's/the back ~** место водителя, заднее сиденье; *Rail* **hard ~s** жёсткие места

3: a ~ in Parliament место в парламенте; **he kept his ~** он снова был выбран

4: Washington is the ~ of government Вашингтон—местопребывание американского правительства; **he lives at his country ~** он живёт в своём поместье

5 (*of rider*): **she has a good ~** она хорошо держится в седле.

seat *vt* **1** (*of people*) сажать (посадить), уса|живать (-дить); **to ~ oneself** садиться (сесть); **please be ~ed** присаживайтесь,/садитесь, пожалуйста; **where shall we ~ the headmaster?/the children?** куда посадим директора?/усадим детей?; **when you are comfortably ~ed, let us proceed** когда вы усядетесь, давайте начнём; **please remain ~ed** пожалуйста, оставайтесь на своих местах

2 (*hold*) поме|щать (-стить); **our car/table ~s six** в нашей машине помещается/за нашим столом усядутся шесть человек; **the theatre ~s 1,000** театр вмещает тысячу зрителей.

seat belt *n* привязной ремень (*m*).

seating *n*: **there is ~ for 100 people** есть сто сидячих мест; *attr*: **~ capacity** число мест; **what is the ~ capacity of the auditorium?** сколько мест в этой аудитории?

sea urchin *n* морской ёж.

sea wall *n* каменная стенка набережной.

seaweed *n usu collect* морские водоросли (*pl*).

secateurs *npl*, *also* **a pair of ~** садовые ножницы, секатор (*sing*).

secede *vi*: **to ~ (from)** отдел|яться (от + *G*) (-иться).

secluded *adj* (*of life, house, etc.*) уединённый; изолированный.

seclusion *n*: **to live in ~** жить в уединéнии/вдали́ от óбщества.

second[1] *n* секýнда, *also Mus, Math, Geog*; **I'm coming this very ~** я придý сию́ же секýнду; **just a ~** (однý) секýнду/секýндочку; **to a split ~** тóчно минýта в минýту; **in a split ~** в считанные секýнды, в считанные дóли секýнды (*G*); *attr*: **~ hand** (*on watch*) секýндная стрéлка.

second[2] *n*: *Univ* **he got a ~ in his finals** он закóнчил университéт с диплóмом вторóй стéпени; *Comm* **the cups are slightly damaged, that's why they are being sold as ~s** э́ти чáшки с небольши́м брáком, поэ́тому они́ продаю́тся по сни́женной ценé.

second[2] *adj* вторóй; **he came in ~** он пришёл вторы́м; **he is ~ in command** он вторóй по звáнию/по чи́ну; **every ~ car was a Moskvich** кáждый вторóй автомоби́ль был «Москви́ч»; **the ~ largest city** вторóй по вели́чине гóрод; **I always travel ~ class** я всегдá éзжу вторы́м клáссом; **take a ~ pair of shoes with you** возьми́ с собóй запаснýю пáру тýфель; **he won't get a ~ chance** у негó не бýдет другóй такóй возмóжности; **will you have a ~ cup of tea?** вам ещё чáшку чáя?; **on ~ thoughts better not tell him** éсли подýмать, то, пожáлуй, лýчше не говори́ть емý об э́том.

second[2] *vt*: **to ~ a motion** поддéрж|ивать предложéние (-áть).

secondary *adj* второстепéнный; втори́чный; **that question is of ~ importance** э́тот вопрóс второстепéнной вáжности; **~ shoots** втори́чные отрóстки; **~ education** срéднее образовáние.

second-class *adj* вторóго клáсса/сóрта; **a ~ passenger/hotel** пассажи́р вторóго клáсса, дешёвая гости́ница; *fig* **they are treated like ~ citizens** с ни́ми обращáются, как с людьми́ вторóго сóрта.

secondhand *adj* подéржанный; **a ~ camera** подéржанный фотоаппарáт; **a ~ shop/bookshop** комиссиóнный/букинисти́ческий магази́н; **a ~ bookseller** букини́ст; **~ ideas** заи́мствованные идéи.

secondhand *adv*: **I heard it (at) ~** я э́то узнáл из вторы́х рук.

secondly *adv* во-вторы́х.

second-rate *adj usu pejor*: **a ~ hotel** второразря́дная гости́ница; **he sells ~ goods** он продаёт низкосóртный товáр (*collect*); **a ~ artist** посрéдственный худóжник.

secrecy *n*: **it was done in great ~** э́то бы́ло сдéлано в глубóкой тáйне; **he swore me to ~** он взял с меня́ слóво храни́ть тáйну.

secret *n* секрéт, тáйна; **I was told this in ~** мне э́то сказáли по секрéту; **the deal was concluded in ~** сдéлку заключи́ли тайкóм (*adv*); **to keep a ~** храни́ть тáйну; **she is in on the ~** онá посвященá в э́ту тáйну; **he made no ~ of his feelings** он не скрывáл свои́х чувств; **an open ~** секрéт полишинéля.

secret *adj* секрéтный, тáйный; **the papers are marked "top ~"** докумéнты с гри́фом «совершéнно секрéтно»; **to keep smth ~** держáть что-л в секрéте; **a ~ agent/marriage/door** секрéтный *or* тáйный агéнт, тáйный брак, потайнáя дверь.

secretarial *adj* секретáрский.

secretariat *n* секретариáт.

secretary *n* секретáрь (*m*) (*also of women*), *f CQ* секретáрша; **private ~** ли́чный секретáрь; (*UK*) **S. of State for** мини́стр + *G*; (*US*) **S. of State** госудáрственный секретáрь, мини́стр инострáнных дел.

secretary-general *n* генерáльный секретáрь (*m*).

secrete *vt* (*hide*) укры|вáть (´-ть), пря́тать (с-); *Med* вы|деля́ть (´-делить).

secretive *adj* (*of people*) скры́тный; **he is being ~ about his plans** он скрывáет свои́ плáны; **with a ~ air** с таи́нственным ви́дом.

sect *n* сéкта.

section *n* (*part*) часть; сéкция; отрéзок; (*of orange*) дóлька; (*cut*) сечéние, разрéз; *Comm* отдéл; *Law* парáграф, раздéл, пункт; **to cut into ~s** разрéзать на чáсти; **the unfinished ~ of the road/building** неокóнченный отрéзок пути́, недострóенная часть *or* сéкция здáния; **a ~ of pipeline** отрéзок трубопровóда; **it/the bookcase is built in ~s** э́то стрóится сбóрным мéтодом, э́то разбóрный шкаф; **longitudinal/vertical/conical ~** продóльный/вертикáльный разрéз, кони́ческое сечéние; **a ~ of muscle** сечéние мы́шцы; (*in press*) **sports ~** отдéл спóрта в газéте; **the first ~ of the article/document** пéрвый раздéл статьи́, пéрвый парáграф докумéнта.

sectional *adj* (*made in parts, e.g. bookcase*) секциóнный, разбóрный; **~ view** вид в разрéзе; *fig* **~ interests** группови́е интерéсы.

sector *n* сéктор, *also Math*; **public and private ~s of industry** национализи́рованный и чáстный сéкторы промы́шленности.

secular *adj* свéтский, мирскóй.

secure *adj* (*firm, safe*) надёжный; прóчный; (*ensured*) обеспéченный; **is the ladder/door ~?** э́та лéстница прóчная?/вы́держит?, дверь плóтно прикры́та?; **a ~ foothold** надёжная опóра, *also fig*; **he made the boat ~** он нáкрепко привязáл лóдку; **he has a ~ job** у негó гаранти́рованная рабóта, он не подлежи́т увольнéнию; **he has a ~ financial position** у негó обеспéченное финáнсовое положéние; **she feels ~ about her future** онá увéрена в своём бýдущем; **are we ~ from interruptions here?** нам здесь не помешáют?

secure *vt* **1** надёжно защи|щáть (-ти́ть); **the building is ~d against flooding** здáние надёжно защищенó от наводнéния; **I ~d all the windows and doors/the rope** я плóтно закры́л все óкна и двéри, я хорошó закрепи́л верёвку

2 (*get*) достa|вáть (´-ть); **I ~d tickets for the play/the services of an expert** я достáл билéты на спектáкль, я нашёл специали́ста.

security *n* **1** безопа́сность; **children need the ~ of a stable home** де́тям нужна́ споко́йная дома́шняя обстано́вка; **~ of tenure** (*of leasehold*) гаранти́рованное пра́во на аре́нду, (*of job*) гаранти́рованная рабо́та; *attr*: **~ check** прове́рка лоя́льности; **he is a ~ risk** он ненадёжен; **S. Council** Сове́т Безопа́сности

2 (*guarantee*): **to lend money on ~** ссужа́ть де́ньги под зало́г; **to stand ~ for smb** дава́ть поручи́тельство за кого́-л, *fig* руча́ться за кого́-л

3 *pl* (**securities**) *Fin* це́нные бума́ги.

sedate *adj* степе́нный.

sedative *n Med* успока́ивающее сре́дство.

sedge *n Bot* осо́ка.

sediment *n* оса́док, отсто́й; *Geol* отложе́ние, оса́дочная поро́да.

seditious *adj* подстрека́тельский.

seduce *vt* соблазн|я́ть (-и́ть), совра|ща́ть (-ти́ть), *both also fig*.

seducer *n* соблазни́тель (*m*), обольсти́тель (*m*).

seductive *adj* соблазни́тельный.

see[1] *vti vt* **1** (*general*) ви́деть (у-); (*look at*) смотре́ть (по-); **I can't ~ things at a distance** я не ви́жу на расстоя́нии; **he was ~n at the post office** его́ ви́дели на по́чте; **I saw her go out just now** я ви́дел, как она́ то́лько что ушла́; **you can ~ the mountains from here** отсю́да видны́ го́ры; **have you ~n Venice?** ты ви́дел Вене́цию?; **did you ~ the exhibition?** ты был на вы́ставке?; **I went to ~ the exhibition** я пошёл посмотре́ть вы́ставку; **~ page one** смотри́ пе́рвую страни́цу; **~ who's at the door** посмотри́, кто пришёл; **you're not fit to be ~n in public** в тако́м ви́де тебе́ нельзя́ пока́зываться на лю́дях; *fig*: **I don't ~ any point in it** я не ви́жу в э́том смы́сла; **I ~ it this way** я э́то ви́жу так; **I'm glad to ~ the last/the back of her** я рад, что мы изба́вились от неё; **I don't ~ how I'll find time for that** я не зна́ю, смогу́ ли я вы́кроить вре́мя для э́того; **he never ~s the joke** он никогда́ не понима́ет шу́ток (*pl*); **I fail to ~ why** я не понима́ю, почему́; **we saw it was useless to insist** мы по́няли, что бесполе́зно наста́ивать; **I can't ~ him as a teacher** я не могу́ предста́вить его́ педаго́гом; **I saw from the paper that...** я чита́л в газе́те, что...; **what does she ~ in him?** что она́ в нём нашла́? [**NB** *tense*]; *CQ* **I can't ~ them stuck for money** они́ ве́чно без де́нег—я не могу́ на э́то споко́йно смотре́ть

2 (*meet, visit*) ви́деть(ся); **I don't ~ him often** я ре́дко ви́жу его́/ви́жусь с ним; **you ought to ~ the doctor** тебе́ ну́жно показа́ться врачу́; **he's too busy to ~ us today** он сли́шком за́нят, что́бы сего́дня приня́ть нас; *CQ* **~ you soon!, be ~ing you!** пока́!, уви́димся!

3 (*experience*) ви́деть; вида́ть (по-); **have you ever ~n the like?** ты ви́дел что́-нибудь подо́бное?; **we'll never ~ his like again** мы таки́х, как он, бо́льше не встре́тим; **he has ~n the world** он повида́л свет; **this car has ~n better days** э́та маши́на знава́ла лу́чшие времена́

4 (*accompany*) прово|жа́ть (-ди́ть); **I'll ~ you home** (дава́й) я провожу́ тебя́ домо́й

5 (*ensure*) просле́|живать (-ди́ть); **~ (to it) that the light is switched off** проследи́, что́бы свет был вы́ключен; **~ that he has what he needs** проследи́, что́бы у него́ бы́ло всё, что ну́жно; **I'll ~ to this myself** я за э́тим сам прослежу́, я сам э́тим займу́сь; **~ that you are not late again** смотри́, бо́льше не опа́здывай

vi **1** ви́деть; **cats can ~ in the dark** ко́шки ви́дят в темноте́; **he can't ~ to read** ему́ тру́дно чита́ть; **I don't understand.—So I ~!** я не понима́ю.—Э́то ви́дно!

2 (*look*) смотре́ть; **go and ~ if lunch is ready** иди́ посмотри́, гото́в ли обе́д; **~ for yourself** (по)смотри́ сам; **let's wait and ~ if he has forgotten** посмо́трим, забы́л он и́ли нет

3 (*understand*) понима́ть; **as far as I can ~** наско́лько я понима́ю; **I ~!** поня́тно!; **it wasn't easy, you ~, to leave** ви́дите ли, уе́хать бы́ло не так про́сто

4 (*think*): **now let me ~, have I posted the letter?** дай поду́мать, отпра́вил ли я письмо́?; **let me ~, it should be on the first page** посто́й, посто́й, э́то должно́ быть на пе́рвой страни́це

see about *vt* (*deal with*) зан|има́ться + *I* (-я́ться); **I'll ~ about it** я э́тим займу́сь (*do it*), я поду́маю (*think it over*); **can you ~ about the tickets?** ты мо́жешь заня́ться биле́тами?; **he came to ~ about the car** он пришёл насчёт маши́ны

see in *vt*: **~ him in** введи́те его́; **to ~ the New Year in** встре|ча́ть Но́вый год (-тить)

see off *vt*: **my mother came to ~ me off at the airport** ма́ма прие́хала в аэропо́рт проводи́ть меня́

see out *vt* **1**: **please ~ him out** пожа́луйста, проводи́те его́; **I'll ~ myself out** я сам вы́йду

2 (*last*): **will he ~ the week out?** дотя́нет ли он до конца́ неде́ли?

see over *vt*: **he wants to ~ over the school/garden** он хо́чет осмотре́ть шко́лу/сад

see through *vt*: **I can ~ through his tricks/him** я все его́ трю́ки/его́ насквозь ви́жу; **they saw me through my troubles** они́ подде́рживали меня́ в тяжёлую мину́ту; **£20 should ~ me through till Monday** мне хва́тит двадцати́ фу́нтов до понеде́льника

see to *vt*: **I'll ~ to it/to the car** я э́тим займу́сь, я займу́сь маши́ной; **she ~s to everything in the house** она́ за всем смо́трит в до́ме.

see[2] *n*: **the Holy S.** па́пский престо́л.

seed *n* се́мя, *also fig*; *collect* (*of grain*) зерно́ (*collect*); (*of sunflower, pumpkin, melon*) се́мечко, (*of orange, pomegranate*) зёрнышко; **mustard/poppy/caraway ~** зёрна горчи́цы/ма́ка/тми́на; **to run/go to ~** пойти́ в семена́; *fig*: **he has gone to ~** он опусти́лся; **to**

sow the ~s of doubt in smb's mind посе́ять сомне́ния в чьей-л душе́; *attr*: ~ **drill/potatoes** рядова́я се́ялка, семенно́й карто́фель (*collect*).

seedbed *n* расса́дочная гря́дка, гря́дка для расса́ды.

seedling *n* се́янец; расса́да (*collect*); (*of bushes, tree*) са́женец.

seedy *adj* (*shabby*): **he looks** ~ у него́ потрёпанный вид; *CQ* **I feel a bit** ~ я нева́жно себя́ чу́вствую.

seeing (that) *conj*: ~ **you aren't ready, I'll go by myself** поско́льку/так как вы ещё не гото́вы, я пойду́ оди́н.

seek *vt* (*look for*) иска́ть + *A* (*smth specific*) *or* + *G* (*non-specific*) (*impf*); **he is ~ing employment/information/my help in the matter** он и́щет рабо́ту/информа́цию, он ждёт от меня́ по́мощи в э́том де́ле; **we sought shelter from the storm** мы иска́ли, где бы пережда́ть бу́рю; **I am ~ing advice upon...** мне ну́жен сове́т/мне ну́жно посове́товаться относи́тельно + *G*; **I will** ~ **my lawyer's advice** я обращу́сь к адвока́ту за сове́том

seek after *vt*: **he is much sought after as a speaker** его́ ча́сто приглаша́ют как ле́ктора; **holiday houses are much sought after in August** в а́вгусте на да́чи большо́й спрос; **this edition is greatly sought after** за э́тим изда́нием охо́тятся

seek out *vt* разы́ск|ивать, оты́ск|ивать (*pfs* -а́ть = *seek and find*).

seem *vi* каза́ться (по-), *often impers*; **it ~s that she is really ill** ка́жется, что она́ на са́мом де́ле больна́; **he ~s honest to me** он мне ка́жется поря́дочным челове́ком; **they** ~ **to enjoy the lessons** они́ как бу́дто получа́ют удово́льствие от э́тих заня́тий; **it's not as easy as it ~s** э́то не так про́сто, как ка́жется; **he ~ed to me to have aged a lot** мне показа́лось, что он си́льно постаре́л; **it would** ~ **that he knows best** каза́лось бы, ему́ лу́чше знать; **he likes good food.—So it ~s!** он лю́бит хорошо́ пое́сть.—Не сомнева́юсь!/Э́то ви́дно!

seemingly *adv* по-ви́димому.

seep *vi* про|са́чиваться (-сочи́ться).

seesaw *n* доска́-каче́ли (*no sing*); **to play on a** ~ кача́ться на доске́.

seethe *vi* (*of sea*) бурли́ть (*impf*); *fig* кипе́ть (вс-); **he was seething with indignation** он кипе́л от возмуще́ния; **the square was seething with people** пло́щадь была́ запру́жена людьми́.

segment *n* часть, кусо́к; (*of orange*) до́лька; *Math* сегме́нт, отре́зок.

segregate *vt* отдел|я́ть (-и́ть); **the cholera patient was ~d from the rest** больно́й холе́рой был отделён/изоли́рован от други́х; **in our school the sexes are ~d** в на́шей шко́ле разде́льное обуче́ние.

seize *vti vt* хвата́ть (схвати́ть); *fig* охва́т|ывать (-и́ть), ухвати́ться за + *A* (*pf*); *Law* конфискова́ть (*impf and pf*); **he ~d me by the arm** он схвати́л меня́ за́ руку; **I was ~d by a longing to see him** меня́ охвати́ло жела́ние уви́деть его́; **he was ~d by a fit of yawning/coughing** на него́ напа́ла зево́та/напа́л ка́шель; **to** ~ **power** захва́т|ывать власть (-и́ть); **he ~d the opportunity with both hands** он ухвати́лся за э́ту возмо́жность обе́ими рука́ми

vi: *fig* **the engine ~d up** мото́р заклини́ло (*impers*).

seldom *adv* ре́дко.

select *adj* и́збранный; отбо́рный; **their wedding was a very** ~ **gathering** у них на сва́дьбе собрало́сь са́мое и́збранное о́бщество; **with a** ~ **group of friends** с не́сколькими бли́зкими друзья́ми; **a** ~ **blend of tobaccos** таба́к отбо́рных сорто́в; (*in Parliament*) ~ **committee** специа́льная коми́ссия.

select *vt* вы|бира́ть (´-брать); под|бира́ть, от|бира́ть (*pfs* -обра́ть); **I ~ed a gift for her** я вы́брал ей пода́рок; **I ~ed this tie to match the shirt** я подобра́л э́тот га́лстук к руба́шке; **he ~ed the books he needed from the shelf** он отобра́л ну́жные кни́ги с по́лки; **he was ~ed for the Olympic team** его́ взя́ли в олимпи́йскую кома́нду; **~ed works** и́збранные произведе́ния.

selection *n* вы́бор; подбо́р; отбо́р; **they have a good** ~ **of paintings** у них хоро́ший вы́бор карти́н; **he bought an interesting** ~ **of books** он купи́л о́чень интере́сную подбо́рку книг; **they still have to make the ~s for the contest** они́ ещё не отобра́ли уча́стников ко́нкурса; **natural** ~ есте́ственный отбо́р; *attr*: ~ **committee** отбо́рочная коми́ссия.

selective *adj*: ~ **breeding** селекти́вное разведе́ние; **he is not very** ~ **about what he reads** он чита́ет, что попа́ло.

self *n*: **he has no thought of** ~ он никогда́ не ду́мает о себе́; **the conscious** ~ созна́ние; **she is her old** ~ **again** она́ опя́ть така́я, как была́ пре́жде; **be your own sweet** ~ будь сами́м собо́й; **my better** ~ **prompted me to give up my seat to the old lady** со́весть во мне заговори́ла, и я уступи́л ме́сто стару́шке; **please reserve a room for wife and** ~ пожа́луйста, зарезерви́руйте ко́мнату для меня́ и мое́й жены́.

self-assurance *n* самоуве́ренность.

self-assured *adj*: **a** ~ **manner/young man** уве́ренные мане́ры (*pl*), уве́ренный в себе́ молодо́й челове́к.

self-centred, (*US*) **-centered** *adj* эгоцентри́чный.

self-confident *adj* уве́ренный в себе́.

self-conscious *adj*: **I felt** ~ **wearing that hat** я о́чень стесня́лся носи́ть э́ту ша́пку; **her remark made me feel** ~ её замеча́ние смути́ло меня́; **I find his style** ~ его́ стиль ка́жется мне неесте́ственным/вы́мученным.

self-contained *adj* **1** (*of person*) *see* **self-sufficient**

2: **a** ~ **flat** отде́льная кварти́ра.

self-control *n* самооблада́ние; **to lose one's** ~ потеря́ть контро́ль над собо́й; **he exercised**

great ~ он проявил большое самообладание.

self-deception *n* самообман.

self-defence *n* самозащита, самооборона; **he acted in ~** он действовал в целях самообороны.

self-determination *n Polit* самоопределение.

self-effacing *adj*: **she is so ~** она старается держаться в тени.

self-esteem *n*: **any failure is damaging to his ~** любая неудача подрывает в нём уверенность в себе.

self-evident *adj* очевидный.

self-explanatory *adj*: **his answer is ~** его ответ предельно ясен.

self-expression *n* самовыражение.

self-government *n* самоуправление.

self-importance *n*: **he is full of ~** он полон сознания собственной важности, у него большое самомнение, *CQ* он очень важничает.

self-imposed *adj*: **for me it was a ~ task/duty** я сам взвалил на себя эту обязанность.

self-indulgent *adj*: **he is ~** он не отказывает себе в удовольствиях, он во всём себе потакает.

self-inflicted *adj*: **a ~ wound** самострел.

self-interest *n*: **he acted out of ~** он действовал в своих личных интересах.

selfish *adj* (*of action, motive*) эгоистический; (*of person*) эгоистичный; **he is very ~** он большой эгоист.

selfless *adj* (*of people*) самоотверженный; (*of actions, etc.*) бескорыстный.

self-made *adj*: **he is a ~ man** он всего в жизни добился сам.

self-pity *n* жалость к себе.

self-portrait *n* автопортрет.

self-possessed *adj*: **she is very ~** у неё большая выдержка, у неё большое самообладание.

self-preservation *n*: **the instinct of ~** инстинкт самосохранения.

self-raising *n*: **~ flour** мука с разрыхлителем.

self-reliant *adj*: **he is ~** он во всём полагается только на самого себя.

self-reproach *n* самопорицание.

self-respect *n*: **he's got no ~** у него нет чувства собственного достоинства.

self-respecting *adj*: *usu joc* **no ~ man would be seen in that tie** ни один уважающий себя человек не наденет такого галстука.

self-righteous *adj pejor*: **he is so ~** он такой правильный, что противно.

self-sacrifice *n* самопожертвование.

self-satisfied *adj* самодовольный.

self-seeking *adj* своекорыстный.

self-service *n* самообслуживание; *attr*: **a ~ shop** магазин самообслуживания.

self-starter *n Aut* автоматический стартер.

self-sufficient *adj*: **he is quite ~ with his books and his records** дайте ему книги и пластинки—и ему больше ничего в жизни не надо; **the country is ~ in fuel** страна полностью обеспечивает себя топливом.

self-supporting *adj*: **my daughter is ~ now** дочка теперь сама зарабатывает на жизнь.

self-taught *adj*: **he is ~** он самоучка.

self-willed *adj* своевольный, своенравный, упрямый.

sell *vti vt* **1** про|давать (-дать); **they ~ apples at 30p a pound** яблоки продают по тридцать пенсов за фунт; **he sold the car at a good price/at a loss** он продал машину за хорошую цену/с убытком; **how much are oranges ~ing for today?** почём сегодня апельсины?

2 *fig uses*: **to ~ one's life dearly** дорого продать свою жизнь; **he knows how to ~ himself/his ideas** он знает, как подать себя/свои идеи; *CQ* **I'm still not sold on the idea** я пока ещё не в восторге от этой идеи

vi продаваться; **his book is ~ing well** его книга хорошо расходится; *fig* **this idea won't ~** это не пройдёт

sell off *vt* распрода|вать (-ть)

sell out *vt*: **he sold out his share of the business** он продал свою долю/свой пай в деле; **this item is sold out** этот товар распродан; **the shop is sold out of tomatoes** в магазине кончились помидоры; *Theat* **the concert is sold out** на концерт все билеты проданы

sell up *vti*: **he went bankrupt and was sold up** он обанкротился, и его имущество пошло с молотка; **he sold up and moved away** он продал всё и уехал.

seller *n* (*in shop*) продавец; **this model is a good ~** эта модель хорошо раскупается/расходится; **it's not easy to buy a house now—it's a ~'s market** сейчас трудно купить дом—на них большой спрос.

selling price *n* рыночная/продажная цена.

sellotape *n* скотч.

selvage, selvedge *n* кромка.

semaphore *n* семафор.

semblance *n* подобие; **a ~ of justice** подобие справедливости; **she was without a ~ of fear** она ничуть не испугалась; **he put on a ~ of gaiety** он только притворялся весёлым.

semen *n* семя, сперма.

semester *n* семестр.

semibasement *n* полуподвал.

semicircle *n* полукруг.

semicolon *n* точка с запятой.

semidarkness *n* полутьма.

semidetached *adj*: **their house is ~** их дом примыкает к соседнему.

semifinal *n* полуфинал.

seminar *n* семинар.

semiprecious *adj*: **a ~ stone** полудрагоценный камень (*m*), самоцвет.

Semitic *adj* семитский.

semolina *n* манная крупа, (*when cooked*) манная каша.

senate *n* сенат; *Univ* учёный совет.

senator *n* (*US*) сенатор.

send *vti vt* **1** по|сылать (-слать) *and other compounds*; отправ|лять (-ить); **I sent the luggage by train** я послал багаж поездом; **he sent the letter/goods yesterday** он послал *or* отпра́вил письмо́/това́ры вчера́; **the children were sent to bed/into another room** дете́й посла́ли спать/отосла́ли в другу́ю ко́мнату; **he was sent to Kiev** его́ посла́ли в Ки́ев; **he was sent to hospital/to prison/home from school** его́ отпра́вили в больни́цу/в тюрьму́/домо́й с уро́ков; **they ~ their children to the local school** они́ отдаю́т свои́х дете́й в ме́стную шко́лу; **she ~s greetings/her love** она́ передаёт приве́т; **I have sent my suit to the cleaner's** я отда́л свой костю́м в химчи́стку; **~ me word/news of your results** сообщи́те мне о (ва́ших) результа́тах: *CQ* **I sent him packing/about his business** я его́ прогна́л

2 (*causative*): **a gust of wind sent the balloon over the fence** возду́шный шар поры́вом ве́тра унесло́ (*impers*) за забо́р; **his lecture sent me to sleep** я засну́л на его́ ле́кции; **this noise is ~ing me crazy** э́тот шум меня́ сведёт с ума́

vi: **he sent to say that...** он веле́л сказа́ть,/переда́ть, что...

send away *vti vt*: **~ him away!** вели́ ему́ уходи́ть!; **I was sent away to my aunt** меня́ отпра́вили к тётке

vi: **I sent away for an application form** я посла́л за бла́нком заявле́ния

send back *vt*: **~ her back at once** неме́дленно пошли́ её обра́тно; **when I've read it I'll ~ it back to you** я верну́ э́то, когда́ прочту́; **I'll ~ your book back with Tom** я пошлю́ твою́ кни́гу с То́мом

send down *vt*: *Univ* **he was sent down** его́ исключи́ли (из университе́та)

send for *vt*: **did you ~ for me?** вы посыла́ли за мной?; **I'll ~ for a taxi/a doctor** я вы́зову такси́/врача́; **I'll ~ away for tickets** я закажу́ биле́ты по по́чте

send in *vt*: **~ him in!** пусть он войдёт; **he had his card/name sent in** он проси́л доложи́ть о себе́; **he sent in his resignation/application for the contest** он по́дал заявле́ние об ухо́де/на уча́стие в ко́нкурсе

send on *vt*: **I'll ~ on the invitation** я пришлю́ приглаше́ние; **have my post sent on** перешли́те мне мою́ по́чту; **I was sent on an errand/a language course** меня́ посла́ли с поруче́нием/на языковы́е ку́рсы (*pl*)

send out *vt*: **to ~ out a signal** посла́ть сигна́л; **a search party was sent out** вы́слали поиско́вую па́ртию; **the pupils were sent out for misbehaving** ученико́в вы́гнали из кла́сса за плохо́е поведе́ние; **I sent her out for some fresh air** я посла́л её подыша́ть во́здухом; **I sent out the invitations yesterday** я вчера́ разосла́л приглаше́ния

send over/round *vt*: **I'll send the car over/round for you** я пришлю́ маши́ну за ва́ми

send up *vt*: **~ him up** проси́те его́ наве́рх; **~ up the letters** пришли́те по́чту (к нам) наве́рх; **to ~ up a balloon/rocket** пус|ка́ть ша́рик/раке́ту (-ти́ть).

sender *n* отправи́тель (*m*).

send-off *n*: *CQ* **we gave him a terrific ~** мы устро́или ему́ пы́шные про́воды.

senile *adj* ста́рческий.

senior *n* ста́рший; (*US Univ*) студе́нты после́днего ку́рса.

senior *adj* ста́рший; **John Smith ~** Джон Смит ста́рший; **the ~ partner** ста́рший партнёр; **he is ~ to me** (*in age*, *at school*, *Univ*) он ста́рше меня́, (*in rank*, *job*) он вы́ше меня́ (по зва́нию, по до́лжности); **he holds a ~ position in the Ministry** он занима́ет высо́кий пост в министе́рстве; **a ~ official** высо́кий чин; **a ~ citizen** *euph approx* пенсионе́р.

sensation *n* **1** (*feeling*) ощуще́ние; чу́вство; **a ~ of warmth** ощуще́ние тепла́; **I have lost all ~ in my left arm** моя́ ле́вая рука́ потеря́ла вся́кую чувстви́тельность

2 (*excitement*): **she/the news caused a ~** она́/э́та но́вость вы́звала сенса́цию.

sensational *adj* сенсацио́нный; *CQ* потряса́ющий.

sense *n* **1** (*faculty*) ощуще́ние, чу́вство; **the five ~s** пять чувств; **~ of taste/pain** вкусово́е/болево́е ощуще́ние; **a keen ~ of smell** о́строе обоня́ние; **sixth ~** шесто́е чу́вство; **to bring smb to his ~s** привести́ кого́-л в чу́вство (*sing*), *also fig*; *fig CQ* **it's time he came to his ~s** пора́ бы ему́ образу́миться/оду́маться

2 (*feeling*) чу́вство; **a ~ of pleasure/shame/humour/proportion** чу́вство удово́льствия/стыда́/ю́мора/ме́ры; **he acted out of a ~ of duty** он поступа́л из чу́вства/по веле́нию до́лга; **he has a great ~ of his own importance** его́ распира́ет чу́вство со́бственной значи́мости; **he has a good business ~** у него́ есть делово́е чутьё; **he has a bad ~ of direction** он пло́хо ориенти́руется

3 (*wisdom*, *reasonableness*): **good/sound/common ~** здра́вый смысл; **there is no ~ in continuing** нет смы́сла продолжа́ть; **there's a lot of ~ in what he says** в его́ слова́х мно́го пра́вды; **it makes no ~ to me** я не ви́жу в э́том никако́го смы́сла; **she had enough ~ to refuse** у неё хвати́ло ума́ отказа́ться; **now you are talking ~** тепе́рь ты говори́шь де́ло; **can you make ~ of this letter?** ты мо́жешь поня́ть, о чём э́то письмо́?

4 (*meaning*) смысл, значе́ние; **in which ~?** в како́м смы́сле?; **in the strict/literal ~** в буква́льном смы́сле; **in the full ~ of the word** в по́лном смы́сле э́того сло́ва; **in a certain ~ you are right** в како́й-то сте́пени вы пра́вы

5 (*opinion*): **the ~ of the meeting** о́бщий настро́й собра́ния

6 *pl* (**~s**) *fig*: **he has taken leave/is out of his ~s** он совсе́м потеря́л рассу́док, *CQ* он не в своём уме́, он про́сто рехну́лся; **she is frightened out of her ~s** она́ напу́гана до́ смерти.

sense *vt* чу́вствовать (по-); **he ~d the danger/that there was no use waiting** он почу́вствовал опа́сность, он по́нял, что ждать бесполе́зно.

senseless *adj* **1: it's ~ to do that** э́то абсолю́тно бессмы́сленный посту́пок; **~ talk** бессмы́слица, чушь

2: to fall ~ упа́сть без чувств; **to knock smb ~** оглуши́ть кого́-л (уда́ром); **he was knocked ~** от уда́ра он потеря́л созна́ние.

sensible *adj* **1** (*perceptible*) ощути́мый; **a ~ rise in temperature** ощути́мое повыше́ние температу́ры; (*aware*) **I am ~ of your kindness** я чу́вствую ва́шу доброту́

2 (*reasonable*) разу́мный; **a ~ woman/idea** у́мная же́нщина, разу́мная мысль; **the ~ thing to do would be + *inf*** са́мое разу́мное бы́ло бы + *inf*; **wear ~ shoes/clothes** наде́нь подходя́щие боти́нки, оде́нься как сле́дует.

sensitive *adj* чувстви́тельный; (*of person*) восприи́мчивый; **a ~ skin** чувстви́тельная ко́жа; **~ to light/criticism** чувстви́тельный к све́ту/к кри́тике; **he has a ~ nature** у него́ восприи́мчивая/то́нкая нату́ра; **he is a ~ artist** он то́нко чу́вствующий худо́жник; **he is very ~ about his bald patch** он о́чень страда́ет из-за свое́й лы́сины; *Photo* **~ paper** светочувстви́тельная бума́га; *fig* **that is a ~ spot** э́то уязви́мое ме́сто.

sensitivity *n* чувстви́тельность.

sensory *adj*: **~ organs** о́рганы чувств; **~ perception** чу́вственное восприя́тие.

sensual *adj* чу́вственный.

sentence *n* **1** *Gram* предложе́ние; **compound/complex/simple ~** сложносочинённое/сложноподчинённое/просто́е предложе́ние; **he writes such long ~s** он пи́шет таки́ми дли́нными предложе́ниями

2 *Law* пригово́р; **death ~** сме́ртный пригово́р; **to pass ~ on smb** вы́нести кому́-л пригово́р; **he served his ~** он отсиде́л/о́тбыл свой срок.

sentence *vt Law* пригов|а́ривать (-ори́ть); **he was ~d to death/to life imprisonment/to three years' imprisonment** его́ приговори́ли *or* он был приговорён к сме́ртной ка́зни/к пожи́зненному заключе́нию/к трём года́м заключе́ния.

sententious *adj* (*of speech, etc.*) нравоучи́тельный.

sentient *adj* чу́вствующий, ощуща́ющий.

sentiment *n* **1** (*feeling*) чу́вство; (*opinion*) мне́ние; **the ~ of pity** чу́вство жа́лости; **these are my ~s** вот вам моё мне́ние (*sing*)

2: there is no place for ~ in a war на войне́ нет ме́ста для сантиме́нтов (*no sing*).

sentimental *adj* сентимента́льный.

sentimentality *n* сентимента́льность, *iron* сантиме́нты (*no sing*).

sentry *n* часово́й; *attr*: **to be on ~ duty** нести́ карау́льную слу́жбу; **~ box** карау́льная бу́дка.

separate *adj* отде́льный; **on a ~ piece of paper** на отде́льном листке́; **keep the pills ~** храни́те табле́тки отде́льно; **a ~ peace treaty** сепара́тный ми́рный догово́р

separate *vti vt* (*one thing from another*) отдел|я́ть (-и́ть); **the river ~s the old town from the new** река́ отделя́ет ста́рый го́род от но́вого; **he tried to ~ the dogs** он стара́лся разня́ть соба́к; **he got ~d from the group** он отдели́лся от гру́ппы

vi отделя́ться; расходи́ться (разойти́сь); расст|ава́ться (-а́ться); **he has ~d from his wife** он ушёл от жены́, они́ с жено́й разошли́сь.

separation *n* отделе́ние; (*of people*) разлу́ка, расстава́ние; **~ of Church and State** отделе́ние це́ркви от госуда́рства; **I find ~ from my children very hard to bear** для меня́ разлу́ка с детьми́ о́чень тяжела́; *attr*: **~ allowance** (*alimony*) алиме́нты (*pl*), *Mil* посо́бие жене́.

separatist *n* сепарати́ст.

sepsis *n* загное́ние.

September *n* сентя́брь (*m*); *attr* сентя́брьский.

septic *adj Med* септи́ческий; (*infected*) заражённый; **a ~ wound** заражённая ра́на; **my finger has gone ~** у меня́ воспали́лся па́лец; **a ~ tank** выгребна́я я́ма.

septicaemia, (*US*) **septicemia** *n Med* о́бщее зараже́ние кро́ви, се́псис.

sepulchre, (*US*) **sepulcher** *n* гробни́ца; **the Holy S.** гроб госпо́день.

sequel *n* после́дствие; (*of story, film*) продолже́ние.

sequence *n* после́довательность; *Mus* секве́нция; *Cine* эпизо́д; **in strict/natural ~** в стро́гой/логи́чной после́довательности; **~ of events** ход собы́тий; **we had a ~ of bad harvests** у нас бы́ло не́сколько неурожа́ев подря́д; *Cards* **a ~ in hearts** после́довательность/поря́док черве́й; *Gram* **~ of tenses** согласова́ние времён.

Serbo-Croat *n* сербскохорва́тский язы́к.

serene *adj* безмяте́жный, споко́йный, умиротворённый.

serf *n* крепостно́й.

serge *n* са́ржа; *attr* са́ржевый.

sergeant *n* сержа́нт.

sergeant-major *n* (*SU equiv*) ста́рший сержа́нт.

serial *adj*: **a ~ story/film** по́весть, печа́тающаяся с продолже́нием, многосери́йный телефи́льм.

series *n* (*set*) се́рия; (*number*) ряд; **a new ~ of stamps/lectures** но́вая се́рия ма́рок, но́вый цикл ле́кций; **there was a whole ~ of thefts** был це́лый ряд краж.

serious *adj* серьёзный; **a ~ wound/illness** серьёзная ра́на, тяжёлая боле́знь; **she is not ~ about her work** она́ несерьёзно отно́сится к свое́й рабо́те; **let's be ~** дава́й поговори́м всерьёз (*adv*); **you can't be ~?** (э́то) ты серьёзно?

sermon *n* про́поведь.

serpent *n* змея́.

serpentine *adj*: **a ~ road** изви́листая доро́га, серпанти́н.

serum *n* сы́воротка.

servant *n* **1** слугá (*m*), *f* служáнка; прислýга (*collect*); **to keep ~s** держáть слуг/прислýгу; *usu iron* **your humble ~** ваш покóрный слугá
2: a public/civil ~ госудáрственный слýжащий.

serve *n* (*in tennis*) подáча (мячá).

serve *vti vt* **1** (*work for*) служи́ть + *D or* в + *P* (по-); **to ~ one's country** служи́ть рóдине
2 (*work out time*): **to ~ one's sentence/time** от|бывáть/отси́|живать свой срок (-бы́ть/-дéть); **he ~d his apprenticeship with a watchmaker** он был ученикóм у часовщикá; *Mil* **to ~ one's time** отслýж|ивать срок (-и́ть)
3 (*supply*) обслýж|ивать (-и́ть); **the bus ~s remote areas** автóбус обслýживает отдалённые райóны; **are you being ~d?** (*in shop, restaurant*) вас ужé обслýживают?; **to ~ dinner/coffee** пода|вáть обéд/кóфе (-́ть); **these meatballs should be ~d with tomato sauce** с э́тими битóчками подаю́т/подаётся томáтный сóус; **this recipe ~s six** э́тот рецéпт рассчи́тан на шесть пóрций; **shall I ~ the soup?/pudding?** разливáть суп?, наклáдывать пýдинг?; **to ~ at table/dinner** прислýживать за столóм/за обéдом; **rations were ~d out to the troops** солдáтам раздáли паёк (*sing*); *fig*: **if my memory ~s me** éсли мне не изменя́ет пáмять; **it ~d him right for being so obstinate** так емý и нáдо—/и поделóм емý—впредь не бýдет упря́миться
4 *Law*: **they ~d a writ/summons on him** емý прислáли повéстку в суд
vi **1** (*of person, work*) служи́ть (по-); **he ~d as a clerk/in the army/under General Eisenhower** он служи́л клéрком/в áрмии/у генерáла Эйзенхáуэра; **he ~d three years in the ranks** он прослужи́л три гóда рядовы́м (*pf*); **he is serving on the board of directors/the jury** он заседáет в правлéнии/в жюри́
2 (*be used*): **the box can ~ as a seat** э́тот я́щик мóжет служи́ть стýлом; **it will ~ for this occasion** на э́тот раз сойдёт; **it ~d as evidence against him** э́то свидéтельствовало прóтив негó
3 (*in tennis*) пода|вáть (-́ть)

serve up *vt*: **he ~d up a delicious supper** он приготóвил вкýсный ýжин; **they always ~ up the same old dishes**/*fig* **programmes** у них всегдá подаю́т одни́ и тé же блю́да, они́ покáзывают одни́ и те же стáрые прогрáммы.

service *n* **1** слýжба; **he's in the Civil/Diplomatic S.** он на госудáрственной/дипломати́ческой слýжбе; **military ~** воéнная слýжба; **he saw long ~ in the navy** он дóлго служи́л во флóте; **the (armed) Services** вооружённые си́лы; **the Health S.** медици́нское обслýживание
2 (*domestic*): **to go into ~** пойти́ в прислýги (*pl*); **she was in ~ with them for 20 years** онá двáдцать лет жилá у них в прислýгах
3 (*in hotel, etc.*) **prompt ~** бы́строе обслýживание; **the ~ here is poor** здесь плóхо обслýживают
4 (*of services provided*): **postal ~** почтóвая связь; **there is a good train ~ between Moscow and Leningrad** мéжду Москвóй и Ленингрáдом хорóшее железнодорóжное сообщéние; **they are taking off the no. 6 bus ~** шестóй маршрýт автóбуса отменя́ется
5 (*act of help*) заслýга; услýга; **he was rewarded for his ~s to the state/to education** егó награди́ли за заслýги пéред госудáрством/за большóй вклад в дéло нарóдного образовáния; **I am/my library is at your ~** я/моя́ библиотéка в вáшем распоряжéнии *or* к вáшим услýгам; **he needs the ~s of a lawyer** он нуждáется в услýгах адвокáта; **he did us a great ~** он нам сослужи́л большýю слýжбу
6 *Tech*: **the car needs a ~** маши́на нуждáется в техобслýживании
7 (*in church*) слýжба
8 (*in tennis*) подáча
9 (*set*): **dinner/tea ~** обéденный/чáйный серви́з
10 *attr*: **~ charge** плáта за обслýживание; **~ flat** кварти́ра с гости́ничным обслýживанием; **~ lift** грузовóй лифт; **~ station** стáнция техни́ческого обслýживания, (*for petrol only*) бензоколóнка; (*in tennis*) **~ line** ли́ния подáчи.

service *vt Tech* обслýж|ивать (-и́ть).

serviceable *adj* (*practical*) практи́чный; (*durable*) прóчный.

serviceman *n* военнослýжащий.

serviette *n* салфéтка.

servile *adj* подобострáстный.

servitude *n* рáбство; **penal ~** кáторга, кáторжные рабóты (*pl*).

sesame *n Bot* кунжýт.

session *n* (*of committee, also Law*) заседáние; **the court is in ~** суд на заседáнии; **a ~ of Parliament** сéссия парлáмента; **to go into secret ~** удали́ться на закры́тое совещáние; (*general*) **at our next ~** при слéдующей встрéче; *CQ* **I have another ~ with the dentist tomorrow** зáвтра я снóва идý к зубнóму врачý; *Mus* **a recording ~** зáпись.

set *n* **1** (*of things*) набóр; **a ~ of rackets/stamps** комплéкт ракéток, набóр мáрок; **a tea/dinner/cutlery ~** чáйный/обéденный серви́з, набóр ножéй, лóжек и ви́лок; **a ~ of teeth** вставны́е зýбы; **a complete ~ of Dickens** пóлное собрáние сочинéний Ди́ккенса
2 (*of people*) óбщество, круг; **the smart/literary/gambling ~** фешенéбельное óбщество, литератýрные круги́ (*pl*), компáния картёжников; **he doesn't belong to their ~** он не принадлежи́т к их крýгу
3 (*position, direction*): **the ~ of the head/shoulders** посáдка головы́, разворóт плеч; *CQ* **he made a dead ~ at the stewardess** он приставáл к стюардéссе
4 *special uses*: (*scenery*) декорáции (*pl*); *Cine* съёмочная площáдка; *Radio* приёмник; *TV* телеви́зор; (*in tennis*) сет.

set *adj* **1** (*of expression*): **a ~ smile** засты́вшая улы́бка; **he came in, his face ~** он вошёл с ка́менным лицо́м

2 (*ready*): **we're all ~ to begin** мы гото́вы нача́ть; **all ~?** все гото́вы?; **I was all ~ to leave when it started to snow** я как раз собира́лся идти́, как вдруг пошёл снег

3 (*fixed*): **a ~ time/task** определённое вре́мя/зада́ние; **~ rules/limits** устано́вленные пра́вила/грани́цы; **a ~ lunch** ко́мплексный обе́д; **she is ~ in her ways** у неё устоя́вшиеся привы́чки; **the weather is ~ fair** установи́лась/стои́т хоро́шая пого́да; **the wind is ~ in the south** ве́тер постоя́нно ду́ет с ю́га; *Univ* **~ books** обяза́тельная литерату́ра (*sing*)

4 (*resolved*): **I am ~ in my purpose** я утверди́лся в своём наме́рении; **I am dead ~ against it** я категори́чески про́тив (э́того).

set *vti vt* **1** (*place, put*) ста́вить (по-); **he ~ the plates on the table/food before us** он поста́вил таре́лки на стол/пе́ред на́ми еду́; **to ~ the table for six** накры|ва́ть (на) стол на шестеры́х (-́ть); **I'll ~ another place for him** я поста́влю ещё оди́н прибо́р для него́; *fig*: **he ~ his hopes on getting that post/on his youngest son** он так наде́ялся получи́ть э́ту до́лжность, он возлага́л наде́жды на мла́дшего сы́на; **the story is ~ in Rome** де́йствие расска́за происхо́дит в Ри́ме

2 (*adjust, apply*): **I always ~ my watch by the radio** я всегда́ ста́влю часы́ по ра́дио; **he ~ the alarm for six o'clock** он поста́вил буди́льник на шесть часо́в; **he ~ a match to the fire** он поднёс спи́чку к дрова́м; **to ~ one's hair** укла́дывать во́лосы (уложи́ть); *Med* **to ~ a bone** вправ|ля́ть кость (-́ить)

3 (*fix, assign*) назнач|а́ть (-́ить); устан|а́вливать (-ови́ть); **there was no time ~ for the next meeting** сле́дующее собра́ние ещё не назна́чено; **to ~ limits to one's expenditure** установи́ть преде́л для расхо́дов; **to ~ oneself a task** ста́вить пе́ред собо́й зада́чу; **the teacher ~s them too much homework** учи́тель задаёт им сли́шком мно́го уро́ков; **that ~s a precedent** э́то создаёт прецеде́нт; **to ~ an example** пода|ва́ть приме́р (-́ть); **to ~ an exam paper** состав|ля́ть вопро́сы для экза́мена (-́ить); *Sport*: **he ~ a new record** он установи́л но́вый реко́рд; **he ~ the pace** он за́дал темп, *also fig*; *Naut, Aer* **to ~ (a) course for** про|кла́дывать курс на + *A* (-ложи́ть)

4 (*cause to do*) *CQ* засади́ть за + *A or* + *inf* (*usu pf*); застав|ля́ть (-́ить); **we were ~ to work** нас тут же засади́ли за рабо́ту; **that ~ me thinking** э́то заста́вило меня́ призаду́маться; **he ~ himself to study the problem** он взя́лся за изуче́ние э́той пробле́мы; **he ~ everyone laughing** от его́ шу́тки все покати́лись со́ смеху; **the noise ~ the dog barking** соба́ка зала́яла, услыха́в шум

vi **1** (*of sun, moon*) за|ходи́ть (-йти́), сади́ться (сесть)

2: **the jelly/cement has ~** желе́ засты́ло, цеме́нт затверде́л

set against *vt*: **he ~ her against me** он восстанови́л/настро́ил её про́тив меня́

set aside *vt*: **I've ~ aside some books for you** я отложи́л для тебя́ кни́ги; *Law* **to ~ aside a verdict** отмен|я́ть/аннули́ровать пригово́р (-и́ть/*impf and pf*)

set back *vt*: **the shed is ~ back from the road** сара́й стои́т в стороне́ от доро́ги; **~ your watches back one hour** переведи́те часы́ на час наза́д; **material shortages ~ back the building programme** из-за нехва́тки материа́лов задержа́лось строи́тельство; *CQ* **the dinner ~ me back £10** обе́д мне обошёлся в де́сять фу́нтов

set down *vt*: **the lorry ~ down its load** грузови́к разгрузи́ли; **the taxi ~ us down right at the door** такси́ст вы́садил нас у са́мой две́ри; **we ~ it down to his poor health** мы отнесли́ э́то за счёт его́ нездоро́вья

set in *vi*: **winter ~s in early in Moscow** в Москве́ зима́ наступа́ет ра́но; **the rain has ~ in for the night** похо́же, дождь заряди́л на всю ночь (*pf*); *fig* **reaction ~ in** начала́сь реа́кция

set off *vti vt*: **a gas leak ~ off an explosion** уте́чка га́за привела́ к взры́ву; **the docker's action ~ off many strikes in sympathy** забасто́вку до́керов поддержа́ли рабо́чие други́х предприя́тий; **don't ~ her off (laughing) again** бо́льше не смеши́ её

vi: **we ~ off for the theatre/towards the river** мы отпра́вились в теа́тр, мы напра́вились к реке́

set on *vt*: **the dog ~ on the cat** соба́ка набро́силась на ко́шку

set out *vti vt*: **she ~ out her best china for us** она́ поста́вила/вы́ставила для нас лу́чший серви́з; **he ~ out the chessmen/chairs** он расста́вил ша́хматы/сту́лья; (*expound*) **to ~ out rules/conditions/one's ideas** излага́ть пра́вила/усло́вия/свои́ мы́сли

vi: **we ~ out in search of him/for the north** мы отпра́вились его́ иска́ть, мы дви́нулись на се́вер; **he ~ out to become a writer** он хоте́л стать писа́телем; **his book ~s out to prove that...** в свое́й кни́ге он стара́ется доказа́ть, что...

set right *vt*: **I thought that... but he soon ~ me right** я ду́мал, что..., но он указа́л мне на мою́ оши́бку

set straight *vt*: **to ~ things straight** привести́ все дела́ в поря́док

set to *vi*: **they ~ to ravenously/with their fists** они́ набро́сились на еду́/друг на дру́га с кулака́ми; **they ~ to to clean up the room** они́ приняли́сь/взяли́сь за убо́рку ко́мнаты

set up *vti vt*: **to ~ up a monument to** воздви́гнуть па́мятник + *D*; **the smoke ~ up an irritation in my throat** от ды́ма у меня́ заперши́ло (*impers*) в го́рле; **to ~ up a new government/a committee** формирова́ть но́вое прави́тельство (с-), созда|ва́ть коми́ссию (-́ть);

his father ~ him up in business оте́ц помо́г ему́ нача́ть своё де́ло; **the holiday ~ her up** о́тпуск ей помо́г, в о́тпуске она́ набрала́сь сил; *Typ* **to ~ up type** на|бира́ть шрифт (-бра́ть)

vi: **to ~ up in business** откры|ва́ть де́ло (-́ть); **she ~ up as a photographer** она́ устро́илась рабо́тать фото́графом.

setback *n*: **some ~s** ряд неуда́ч; **production suffered a ~** в произво́дстве произошёл спад; **he had a bit of a ~ after the operation** по́сле опера́ции у него́ бы́ло не́которое ухудше́ние.

set square *n* уго́льник.

settee *n*, *also* **~ bed** куше́тка, канапе́.

setter *n* (*dog*) се́ттер; *Typ* набо́рщик.

setting *n* (*of sun*) захо́д, зака́т; (*of jewel*) опра́ва; *Typ* набо́р; *Med* вправле́ние; **the house stands in a superb ~** дом стои́т в о́чень краси́вом ме́сте; **the ruined castle makes a marvellous ~ for the play** руи́ны за́мка — прекра́сная декора́ция для э́той пье́сы; *Mus* **do you like Tchaikovsky's ~ of the poem?** тебе́ нра́вится му́зыка Чайко́вского к э́тим стиха́м?

settle *vti vt* **1** (*colonize*) посел|я́ть (-и́ть); **who first ~d Australia?** кто бы́ли пе́рвые поселе́нцы в Австра́лии?

2 (*place*): **she ~d him (down) in front of the fire** она́ усади́ла его́ пе́ред ками́ном; **he ~d himself at the table/in the armchair** он усе́лся за стол, он устро́ился в кре́сле

3 (*stabilize*) успок|а́ивать (-о́ить); **these pills will ~ your nerves/stomach** э́ти табле́тки успоко́ят ва́ши не́рвы/сни́мут боль в желу́дке; **to ~ smb's fears/doubts** рассе́|ивать чьи-л стра́хи/сомне́ния (-ять); **the thunder should ~ the weather** по́сле грозы́ пого́да должна́ установи́ться; **the rain has ~d the dust** дождь приби́л пыль

4 (*of money, etc.*): **he ~d the bill** он оплати́л счёт, он расплати́лся по счёту; **he ~d his debts** он рассчита́лся с долга́ми; *fig* **he ~d his account with her** он свёл счёты/рассчита́лся с ней

5 (*arrange*) ула́|живать (-дить), разреш|а́ть (-и́ть); **they ~d the dispute/their differences** они́ ула́дили/разреши́ли спор, они́ ула́дили/урегули́ровали разногла́сия; **~ it among yourselves** ула́дьте э́то ме́жду собо́й; **we must ~ these points/the price of the table** нам ну́жно договори́ться по э́тим пу́нктам/о цене́ на стол; **the terms are ~d** усло́вия определены́; **to ~ the date for delivery of the manuscript** устан|а́вливать срок пода́чи а́вторского материа́ла (-ови́ть); *fig CQ*: **that'll ~ her all right** э́то ей нау́ка/уро́к; **I'll soon ~ him** погоди́, я ему́ покажу́

vi **1**: **the bird ~d on the roof** пти́ца усе́лась на кры́шу; **the cold has now ~d on my chest** тепе́рь у меня́ грудь заложи́ло (*impers*); **the weather has ~d** пого́да установи́лась; **when the building/the road bed has ~d** когда́ фунда́мент зда́ния осе́л, когда́ полотно́ доро́ги осе́ло; **wait till the grounds ~** подожди́, пока́ гу́ща ося́дет

2 (*agree*): **to ~ for a compromise** пойти́ на компроми́сс; **I would ~ for £400** меня́ устро́ят четы́реста фу́нтов; **let's ~ on a time to meet/a plan of action** дава́й усло́вимся *or* договори́мся о вре́мени встре́чи/вы́работаем план де́йствий

3 (*go to live*) посел|я́ться (-и́ться)

settle down *vi*: **when the excitement ~d down** когда́ возбужде́ние улегло́сь; **he has married and ~d down** он жени́лся и остепени́лся; **he can't ~ down anywhere** он нигде́ не мо́жет осе́сть; **I can't ~ down to work** я ника́к не могу́ споко́йно сесть за рабо́ту; **he is settling down in the new job** он осва́ивается на но́вой рабо́те; **things seem to be settling down** похо́же, что дела́ нала́живаются

settle in *vi*: **come round when we have ~d in** приходи́ к нам, когда́ мы устро́имся

settle up *vi*: **to ~ up (with)** рассчи́т|ываться (с + *I*) (-а́ться), *also fig*.

settlement *n* **1** (*colony*) поселе́ние

2 (*act of agreeing*): **the ~ of a difference/quarrel** урегули́рование спо́рного вопро́са, разреше́ние спо́ра; **I enclose a cheque in ~ of your account/of the claim** я прилага́ю чек для опла́ты ва́шего счёта/для возмеще́ния уще́рба

3 (*agreement*) соглаше́ние; **to reach a ~ on** прийти́ к соглаше́нию по вопро́су о + *P*; **a negotiated ~** урегули́рование путём перегово́ров; *Law*: **to draw up a marriage ~** соста́вить бра́чный контра́кт; **to make a ~ on smb** распоря|жа́ться иму́ществом/деньга́ми в по́льзу кого́-л (-ди́ться)

4 (*subsidence*) оседа́ние, оса́дка.

settler *n* поселе́нец.

set-to *n CQ* (*fight*) потасо́вка; (*verbal*) перебра́нка.

setup *n CQ*: **it's a weird ~** э́то како́е-то стра́нное положе́ние дел.

seven *num* семь (*G, D, P* семи́, *I* семью́); *collect* се́меро; **a "7"** семёрка; [*see grammatical notes under* **four** *and* **five**].

sevenfold *adv* в семикра́тном разме́ре.

seventeen *num* семна́дцать [*see* **eleven**].

seventeenth *adj* семна́дцатый.

seventh *adj* седьмо́й; *as n* седьма́я часть, одна́ седьма́я.

seventieth *adj* семидеся́тый.

seventy *num* се́мьдесят (*G, D, P* семи́десяти, *I* семью́десятью).

sever *vti vt* разрез|а́ть (-́ать); *fig* **to ~ a connection** по|рыва́ть связь (-рва́ть)

vi: **the rope ~d** кана́т ло́пнул.

several *pron*: **~ of us wore coats** не́которые из нас бы́ли в пальто́; **~ were found dead** не́сколько челове́к бы́ли на́йдены/бы́ло на́йдено мёртвыми; [**NB** не́которые *implies contradistinction with others of a group*, не́сколько *is purely numerical*].

several *adj* **1** (*of number*) не́сколько (*declines in oblique cases*); **I went there ~ times** я не́сколько раз туда́ ходи́л; **with ~ mistakes**

с нéсколькими ошúбками; **this model comes in ~ colours** эта модéль имéется в нéскольких цветáх

2 (*respective*): **we went our ~ ways** мы пошлú рáзными дорóгами; *Law* **joint and ~ liability** óбщая и лúчная ответственность.

severally *adv* по отдéльности.

severance *n* (*of relations, communications*) разрыв; *attr*: **~ pay** выходнóе пособие.

severe *adj* стрóгий, сурóвый; жестóкий; тяжёлый; **a ~ reprimand** стрóгий вы́говор; **~ discipline/criticism** стрóгая *or* сурóвая дисциплúна/крúтика; **~ restrictions/measures** стрóгие *or* сурóвые ограничéния/мéры; **a ~ winter/frost** сурóвая зимá, сúльный *or* трескýчий морóз; **a ~ attack of migraine** жестóкий/сúльный прúступ мигрéни; **it is a ~ blow to him** э́то для негó тяжёлый удáр; **there was ~ fighting** шли ожесточённые бои (*pl*); **a ~ loss** тяжёлая утрáта (*bereavement*).

sew *vti vt* шить (с-) *and compounds*; **she ~s her own dresses** онá самá себé шьёт (плáтья); **the blouse is hand ~n** э́та блýзка ручнóй рабóты; **to ~ in a zip** приши|вáть мóлнию (-́ть); **to ~ on a button/sequins** пришúть пýговицу/блёстки на + *A*; **to ~ up a wound** зашивáть рáну

vi шить.

sewage *n* стóчные вóды (*pl*); *attr*: **~ disposal** отвóд стóчных вод; **~ farm/works** пóле орошéния; **~ system** канализáция.

sewer *n* канализациóнная трубá.

sewing *n* шитьё; *attr*: **~ machine/thread** швéйная машúна/нúтка.

sex *n* пол; **the fair ~** прекрáсный пол; *attr*: **~ appeal** (*abbr* **S.A.**) сексуáльная привлекáтельность.

sextant *n* секстáнт.

sextet *n* секстéт.

sexual *adj* сексуáльный, половóй; **~ intercourse** половóй акт.

sexy *adj CQ* сексуáльный.

sh *interj* тс!, шш!

shabby *adj* **1** (*of things*) убóгий; **the buildings look so ~** у э́тих здáний такóй убóгий вид

2 (*of people, behaviour*): **~ tricks** пóдлые трю́ки; **~ behaviour** гнýсное поведéние; **a ~ excuse** жáлкая отговóрка.

shack *n* лачýга, хибáра.

shack up *vi*: *sl* **to ~ (with)** сожúтельствовать (с + *I*) (*impf*).

shade *n* **1** тень; **in the ~** в тенú; *Art* **light and ~** свет и тéни (*pl*); *fig* **his performance put everyone in the ~** он своúм исполнéнием затмúл всех

2 (*for lamp*) абажýр; (*US*) (*blind*) штóра; **eye ~** козырёк; (*US*) *pl* (**~s**) *CQ* (*sunglasses*) тёмные очкú

3 (*hue*) оттéнок, *also fig*; **subtle ~s of blue**/*fig* **of meaning** оттéнки голубóго/значéния; **it is difficult to represent all ~s of opinion** трýдно передáть всё разнообрáзие мнéний (*pl*)

4 *CQ*: **he feels a ~ better today** сегóдня он чуть лýчше себя́ чýвствует; **it is a ~ awkward for us** нам немнóго нелóвко

5 (*ghost*) привидéние, прúзрак.

shade *vti vt* **1** заслон|я́ть (-úть); затен|я́ть (-úть); **he ~d his eyes with his hand** он заслонúл глазá рукóй; **her hat ~s her face from the sun** шля́па закрывáет её лицó от сóлнца

2 *Art* класть тéни (положúть); (*with crayon*) тушевáть (за-); **to ~ off colours** затушёвывать крáски (*usu impf*)

vi: **the blue ~s away/off into a light grey** голубóй цвет постепéнно перехóдит в серовáтый.

shading *n Art* штрихóвка, растушёвка.

shadow *n* тень, *also fig*; **her face was in deep ~** её лицó бы́ло в глубóкой тенú; **he followed her like a ~** он ходúл за ней как тень; **he has ~s under his eyes** у негó тёмные кругú под глазáми; *fig*: **she is worn to a ~** от неё однá тень остáлась; **he is a ~ of his former self** он преврати́лся в сóбственную тень; **without a ~ of doubt** вне вся́кого сомнéния; **his illness cast a ~ over the wedding party** егó болéзнь омрачúла свáдебное торжествó; *attr*: **~ boxing** «бой с тéнью».

shadow *vt*: **he was ~ed** за ним былá слéжка.

shadowy *adj*: **~ outlines** нея́сные/смýтные очертáния.

shady *adj* (*in shade*) тенúстый; *fig* тёмный; **a ~ affair** тёмное дéло.

shaft *n* **1** (*of tool*) рукоя́тка, черенóк; (*of axe*) топорúще; (*of cart*) оглóбля; *Tech, Aut* (*of steering wheel, piston*) стéржень (*m*); **driving ~** приводнóй вал; *fig* **a ~ of light** сноп свéта

2 (*mine, lift*) шáхта, шáхтный ствол; **ventilation ~** вентиляциóнная шáхта.

shaggy *adj*: **a ~ mane** космáтая/лохмáтая грúва; **~ eyebrows** космáтые/мохнáтые брóви.

shake *n*: **I gave the carpet a good ~** я хорошéнько вы́тряс ковёр; **a milk ~** молóчный коктéйль; *fig*: *CQ* **he's no great ~s as a singer** как певéц он ничегó осóбенного собóй не представля́ет; *sl* **in two ~s** в два счёта.

shake *vti vt* **1** трясти́ (по-) *and compounds*; встря́х|ивать (-нýть); **to ~ a rug** трясти́/вытря́хивать кóврик; **to ~ smb by the shoulders** трясти́ когó-л за плéчи; **the explosion shook the building** взрыв потря́с здáние; **to ~ dice** встря́хивать кóсти; **to ~ hands with smb** пожáть/(*energetically*) трясти́ комý-л рýку (*sing*); **the dog shook itself** собáка отряхнýлась; **to ~ one's head** (*in negation*) покачáть головóй; **the wind shook the trees** вéтер раскáчивал дерéвья; **he shook his fist at her** он ей погрозúл кулакóм; **"~ the bottle before using"** «пéред употреблéнием взб|áлтывать» (-олтáть)

2 *fig uses*: **I was ~n by the news** я был потрясён э́той нóвостью; **I would like to ~ him out of his complacency** он такóй самодовóльный, так и хóчется сбить с негó спесь;

to ~ smb's faith/resolve поколеба́ть чью-л ве́ру/реши́мость; **the prosecution was unable to ~ the witness** обвини́телю не удало́сь запу́тать свиде́теля

vi дрожа́ть (*impf*); трясти́сь, сотряса́ться (*usu impfs*); **to ~ with cold/fear** дрожа́ть от хо́лода/от стра́ха; **his hands/head shook** у него́ ру́ки дрожа́ли/голова́ трясла́сь; **I was shaking all over** я весь дрожа́л; **her voice shook with emotion** её го́лос дрожа́л/прерыва́лся от волне́ния; **she was shaking with laughter/with sobs** она́ вся трясла́сь от сме́ха, её сотряса́ли рыда́ния; **the house shook from the explosions** дом сотряса́лся от взры́вов; *CQ*: **he was shaking in his shoes** у него́ се́рдце в пя́тки ушло́; **let's ~ on it** по рука́м

shake down *vti vt*: **to ~ down apples** трясти́ я́блоню

vi: **to ~ down for the night** устро́иться на́ ночь

shake off *vt*: **he shook the snow off his collar/coat** он стряхну́л снег с воротника́, он отряхну́л снег с пальто́; *fig*: **you must try to ~ off your depression** тебе́ на́до встряхну́ться; **I can't ~ off my cold** я ника́к не могу́ изба́виться от на́сморка; **he shook off his pursuers** он ушёл от свои́х пресле́дователей

shake out *vt* (*unfurl*) раз|вёртывать (-верну́ть); **I shook out the rugs/the sand out of my shoes** я вы́тряхнул ковры́/песо́к из боти́нок

shake up *vt* (*bottle, liquids, etc.*) взб|а́лтывать (-олта́ть); **to ~ up a pillow** взби|ва́ть поду́шку (-́ть); **he was badly ~n up by the rough flight** его́ си́льно укача́ло/растрясло́ (*impers*) в самолёте.

Shakespearian *adj* шекспи́ровский; **a ~ scholar** шекспирове́д.

shake-up *n*: **he needs a good ~** ему́ ну́жно хороше́нько встряхну́ться.

shakily *adv*: **he got ~ to his feet** он, шата́ясь, подня́лся на́ ноги.

shaky *adj*: **~ hands** трясу́щиеся/дрожа́щие ру́ки; **~ writing, a ~ voice** дрожа́щий по́черк/го́лос; **he is ~ on his legs** он нетвёрдо де́ржится на нога́х; **a ~ table** ша́ткий стол; *fig*: **he was in ~ health last year** в про́шлом году́ у него́ поша́ливало здоро́вье; **my Russian is ~** я подзабы́л ру́сский [**NB** *tense*]; **my memory is ~** меня́ ча́сто подво́дит па́мять.

shale *n* сла́нец; *attr* сла́нцевый.

shall *v aux* **1** (*forming future tense of first person*) **i)** (*of continuous or repeated action*) *future of impf aspect*: **I ~ love you for ever** я тебя́ бу́ду люби́ть всегда́; **I ~ go to the theatre regularly** я тепе́рь бу́ду ча́сто ходи́ть в теа́тр; **ii)** (*of single action*) *future of pf aspect*: **we ~ arrive late tonight** мы прие́дем сего́дня по́здно; **I ~ not/shan't go** я не пойду́

2 (*in questions*): **~ I come in or ~ I wait outside?** мне войти́ и́ли подожда́ть на у́лице?; **I'll open the door, ~ I?** я откро́ю дверь, хорошо́?

3 (*in commands, for emphasis, etc.*): **you ~ not/shan't have another piece** ты не полу́чишь бо́льше ни кусо́чка; **he ~ pay for this** он за э́то запла́тит.

shallow *adj* (*of water, dish; fig of person, mind, etc.*) ме́лкий, неглубо́кий; **a ~ pond** ме́лкий/неглубо́кий пруд; **~ breathing**/*fig* **knowledge** пове́рхностное дыха́ние, пове́рхностные *or* неглубо́кие зна́ния (*pl*).

shallows *npl* мелково́дье (*sing*).

sham *n*: **the announcement is a ~** э́то заявле́ние—про́сто фи́кция; **he's not ill, he's just a ~** он не бо́лен, он про́сто притворя́ется.

sham *adj* притво́рный; мни́мый; подде́льный; фальши́вый; **~ piety/illness** притво́рная на́божность, мни́мая боле́знь; **a ~ diamond** подде́льный брилья́нт; **it was only a ~ fight** они́ то́лько де́лали вид, что деру́тся.

sham *vti vt* симули́ровать (*impf and pf*); притвор|я́ться + *I*(-и́ться); **he was ~ming illness** он симули́ровал боле́знь, он притворя́лся больны́м

vi: **the dog ~med dead** соба́ка притвори́лась мёртвой.

shamble *vi*: **the old man ~d off** стари́к шёл, волоча́ но́ги; **he ~d into the room/up to the bar** он ввали́лся в ко́мнату, он вразва́лку подошёл к ба́ру.

shambles *n* (*no pl*) *CQ* беспоря́док, хао́с; **his flat is a complete ~** у него́ в кварти́ре ужа́сный беспоря́док/каварда́к; **the match ended as a complete ~** матч зако́нчился всео́бщей сва́лкой.

shame *n* стыд; **to my ~** к моему́ стыду́; **he has lost all sense of ~** он потеря́л вся́кий стыд; **his appearance put me to ~** он был тако́й наря́дный, что я устыди́лся своего́ ви́да; **you work so hard you put me to ~** гля́дя, как ты рабо́таешь, я устыди́лся свое́й ле́ни; **what a dreadful ~ to cheat the old woman!** как не сты́дно обма́нывать ста́рую же́нщину!; **~ on you!** как тебе́ не сты́дно!; **for ~!** како́й стыд!/срам!; **what a ~ that I can't be with you** как жаль, что я не смогу́ быть с ва́ми.

shame *vt* стыди́ть (при-); **he ~d me into doing it** я сде́лал э́то, потому́ что он пристыди́л меня́; **he was ~d into apologizing** ему́ ста́ло сты́дно, и он извини́лся.

shamefaced *adj*: **he made a rather ~ apology** он попроси́л проще́ния с винова́тым ви́дом.

shameful *adj* посты́дный, позо́рный.

shamefully *adv*: **he was ~ drunk** он был до неприли́чия пьян; **I am ~ ignorant about that** я кра́йне неве́жествен в э́том вопро́се.

shameless *adj* бессты́дный; **she's quite ~** у неё про́сто стыда́ нет; **you ~ little boy!** вот бессты́дник!; **are you completely ~?** ты совсе́м потеря́л стыд?

shaming *adj* позо́рящий; **how ~!** како́й стыд!/срам!/позо́р!

shampoo *n* (*liquid, powder*) шампу́нь (*m*); (*process*) **a ~ and set** мытьё и укла́дка воло́с.

shampoo *vt*: **to ~ one's hair** мыть го́лову (шампу́нем) (вы́-).

shamrock *n Bot* трили́стник.

shape *n* фо́рма; *Cook* фо́рмочка; **in the ~ of a crescent** в фо́рме полуме́сяца; **toys of all ~s and sizes** са́мые разнообра́зные игру́шки; **to take ~** вырисо́вываться, *also fig*; *fig*: **we need help in any ~ or form** нам нужна́ по́мощь в любо́м ви́де; *CQ*: **I'm/my affairs are in good ~** сейча́с я в фо́рме, у меня́ всё в поря́дке; **to knock/lick smb into ~** привести́ кого́-л в надлежа́щий вид.

shape *vti vt* прида|ва́ть фо́рму (-́ть); (*mould*) лепи́ть (вы́-, с-); *fig* формирова́ть (с-); **it is ~d like an egg** э́то сде́лано в фо́рме яйца́, э́то име́ет яйцеви́дную фо́рму; **to ~ a pot from clay** вы́лепить горшо́к из гли́ны; *fig*: **to ~ plans** формирова́ть пла́ны; **economic factors ~d the course of events** экономи́ческие фа́кторы повлия́ли на ход собы́тий

vi: **the boy is shaping satisfactorily** ма́льчик развива́ется норма́льно; **he is shaping well as a runner** из него́ полу́чится [**NB** *tense*] хоро́ший бегу́н; **things aren't shaping (up) too well** дела́ скла́дываются не о́чень уда́чно.

shapeless *adj* бесфо́рменный.

shapely *adj* стро́йный, хорошо́ сложённый.

share *n* **1** часть, до́ля; **we will all have a ~ in the profits** ка́ждый из нас полу́чит часть/до́лю при́былей; **everyone must pay his ~** ка́ждый пла́тит за себя́; **he got the lion's ~** ему́ доста́лась льви́ная до́ля; **let's go ~s** дава́й заплати́м попола́м; **fair ~s for all** всем по́ровну; **you must take your ~ of the blame/of the housework** ты то́же до́лжен нести́ отве́тственность/помога́ть по хозя́йству; **she has had more than her ~ of trouble** ей довело́сь испыта́ть нема́ло бед

2 *Fin* а́кция; *attr*: **~ index** и́ндекс а́кций.

share *vti vt* дели́ть (по-, раз-); **to ~ smth with smb** подели́ться чем-л с кем-л; **he ~d (out) £100 equally among five** он по́ровну подели́л сто фу́нтов на пятеры́х/на пять челове́к; **to ~ blame/responsibility** раздел|я́ть вину́/отве́тственность (-и́ть); **he ~s my opinion** он разделя́ет моё мне́ние; **he ~d the same fate** его́ пости́гла та́ же у́часть; **we ~ everything** у нас всё по́ровну; **we ~d a room in the hostel** мы жи́ли в одно́й ко́мнате в общежи́тии; **I have to ~ the kitchen** мы с сосе́дями гото́вим в одно́й ку́хне

vi: **as children we have to learn to ~** с де́тства на́до учи́ться дели́ться с дру́гом/това́рищем; **he ~s in all my troubles and joys** он де́лит со мной и го́ре (*sing*) и ра́дости; **I will ~ in the cost** я возьму́ часть расхо́дов на себя́.

shareholder *n Fin* акционе́р.

share-out *n CQ* делёж.

shark *n* аку́ла, *also fig*.

sharp *n Mus* дие́з.

sharp *adj* **1** (*keen*) о́стрый, *also fig*; **a ~ knife/mind/sauce** о́стрый нож/ум/со́ус; **she has ~ eyes/hearing/a ~ pain** у неё о́строе зре́ние/о́стрый слух/о́страя боль; **a stick with a ~ point** па́лка с заострённым концо́м; **a ~ pencil** о́стро отто́ченный каранда́ш; **she has a ~ tongue** у неё о́стрый язычо́к; **~ frost** си́льный моро́з; **a ~ outline** отчётливый ко́нтур; **keep a ~ look-out** смотри́ в о́ба; *Photo* **a ~ image** ре́зкое изображе́ние

2 (*abrupt*) ре́зкий, *also fig*; (*steep*) круто́й; *fig pejor* ло́вкий, хи́трый; **a ~ cry/wind/contrast/rebuke** ре́зкий крик/ве́тер/контра́ст/упрёк; **they exchanged ~ words** они́ обменя́лись ре́зкими замеча́ниями; **there's been a ~ fall in prices** це́ны ре́зко сни́зились; **a ~ descent/corner** (*of road*) круто́й спуск/поворо́т; **a ~ lawyer** ло́вкий адвока́т; **he's too ~ for me** он для меня́ сли́шком хитёр.

sharp *adv* (*punctually*) то́чно; (*abruptly*) ре́зко, кру́то; **at 7 o'clock ~** то́чно/ро́вно в семь часо́в; **the train left ~ on time** по́езд отошёл то́чно по расписа́нию; **the road turns ~ left** доро́га кру́то повора́чивает вле́во; *CQ* **do it and look ~ about it** сде́лай э́то, да поживе́е; *Mus* **she sings ~** она́ берёт сли́шком высо́кие но́ты.

sharpen *vt* точи́ть (на-), отт|а́чивать (-очи́ть), заостр|я́ть (-и́ть); **to ~ a knife/pencil/an axe** точи́ть нож/каранда́ш/топо́р; **to ~ a stake/*fig* one's wits** заостря́ть кол, отта́чивать ум (*sing*).

sharpener *n*точи́лка.

sharply *adv* ре́зко; **to speak/brake ~** ре́зко говори́ть/затормози́ть.

sharp-witted *adj* сообрази́тельный.

shatter *vti vt* (*glass, etc.*) разби|ва́ть (-́ть); **the window was ~ed** окно́ разби́лось (вдре́безги); **the explosion ~ed the windows** взры́вом вы́било (*impers*) о́кна; *fig*: **I feel ~ed** я чу́вствую себя́ разби́тым; **my hopes/illusions were ~ed** мои́ наде́жды ру́хнули, мои́ иллю́зии развея́лись; **he was ~ed by the news** он был потрясён э́той но́востью

vi разби́ться.

shattering *adj* сокруши́тельный; сокруша́ющий; (*of noise*) оглуши́тельный; **a ~ blow/defeat** сокруши́тельный уда́р, сокруши́тельное пораже́ние; **~ news** ошеломля́ющая но́вость.

shave *n* бритьё; **he needs a ~** ему́ ну́жно побри́ться; *fig* **that was a close/narrow ~!** мы едва́ спасли́сь!

shave *vti vt* брить (по-́, с-); **to ~ smb** брить кого́-л; **to ~ smb's head** (*in army, prison*) обри|ва́ть кому́-л го́лову (-́ть); **he ~d off his beard** он сбрил бо́роду; **he ~d a thin strip off the plank** он слегка́ обструга́л до́ску; *fig* **the car only just ~d past me** маши́на промча́лась буква́льно в миллиме́тре от меня́

vi бри́ться (по-).

shaven *adj*: **he is clean ~** он гла́дко вы́брит.

shaving *n* **1** бритьё; *attr*: **~ brush/cream** ки́сточка/крем для бритья́; **~ accessories** бри́твенные принадле́жности

2 *pl* (**~s**) (*of wood*) стру́жки.

shawl *n* шаль, платóк.

she *pers pron* онá; *see also* **her.**

sheaf *n* (*of paper*) свя́зка, пáчка; (*of corn*) сноп.

shear *vt* (*of sheep*) стричь (о-́).

shears *npl, also* **pair of** ~ нóжницы; **garden** ~ садóвые нóжницы.

sheath *n* (*case*) футля́р; (*contraceptive*) презервати́в; *Bot* оболóчка; *attr*: ~ **knife** фи́нка, охóтничий нож.

shed[1] *n* сарáй.

shed[2] *vt* (*of tears, leaves*) роня́ть (*usu impf*); (*of tears*) лить (*impf*); (*of blood, fig of light*) проли|вáть (-́ть); (*of clothes, etc.*) сбр|áсывать (-óсить); **the snake** ~**s its skin** змея́ сбрáсывает кóжу/линя́ет; **the cat is** ~**ding its hair** у кóшки лéзет шерсть; *fig* **that** ~**s a new light on events** э́то проливáет нóвый свет на случи́вшееся.

sheen *n* блеск.

sheep *n* овцá, *m* барáн; *fig*: **a wolf in** ~**'s clothing** волк в овéчьей шкýре; **a lost** ~ заблýдшая овцá; **he is the black** ~ **of the family** он в семьé «парши́вая овцá»; *attr*: ~ **farming** овцевóдство.

sheepdog *n* овчáрка.

sheepish *adj*: **he looked rather** ~ у негó был довóльно-таки глýпый вид.

sheepskin *n* овчи́на; *attr*: **a** ~ **coat/jacket** дублёнка, корóткая дублёнка *or* (*peasant's*) кожýх.

sheer *adj* **1: a** ~ **rock** отвéсная скалá; **a** ~ **drop of 100m** обры́в высотóй в сто мéтров

2 (*utter*): **by** ~ **chance** по чи́стой случáйности; **it was a** ~ **waste of time**/~ **nonsense** э́то былá чистéйшая потéря врéмени/глýпость; **out of** ~ **desperation** прóсто от/с отчáяния

3 (*of fabric, etc.*) прозрáчный; ~ **stockings** тóнкие чулки́.

sheer *adv* (*steeply*) отвéсно.

sheet *n* (*for bed*) простыня́; (*of paper, metal*) лист; *Naut* шкот; **to put clean** ~**s on a bed** постели́ть чи́стые прóстыни; **the furniture is covered in dust** ~**s** мéбель в чехлáх; **white as a** ~ бéлый/блéдный как полотнó; *fig*: **a** ~ **of water/snow** вóдное прострáнство, снéжный покрóв; **the rain came down in** ~**s** дождь лил потóками; *attr*: ~ **glass/steel** листовóе стеклó, листовáя сталь; ~ **music** нóты (*pl*).

shelf *n* пóлка; (*of rock*) вы́ступ, устýп; *fig* **she is on the** ~ онá остáлась в деви́цах.

shell *n* **1** (*of mollusc*) рáковина, *also fig*; *dim* ракýшка; (*of egg, nut*) скорлупá, шелухá; (*of tortoise, lobster*) пáнцирь (*m*); *fig*: **to come out of one's** ~ вы́йти из своéй скорлупы́; **he retired into his** ~ он замкнýлся в себé

2 *Mil* снаря́д

3 *Tech* (*framework*) кóрпус; (*of building, after fire, etc.*) óстов, каркáс; (*casing*) оболóчка, кожýх.

shell *vt* **1** (*of eggs, nuts*) очи|щáть от скорлупы́ (-́стить); **to** ~ **peas** лущи́ть горóх (*usu impf*); *fig CQ* **I** ~**ed out 10 roubles for the tickets** я вы́ложил дéсять рублéй за билéты

2 *Mil* обстрéл|ивать (-я́ть).

shellfish *n Zool* моллю́ск, *also as food.*

shell-shocked *adj* контýженный.

shelter *n* (*refuge*) убéжище, прию́т, *also fig*; (*from rain, etc., Mil*) укры́тие; **to give** ~ **to smb** приюти́ть когó-л, (*to fugitive*) предостáвить комý-л убéжище; **air-raid** ~ бомбоубéжище; **mountain** ~ пристáнище в горáх; **we ran for** ~ мы брóсились под навéс; **we took** ~ **from the rain under the trees** мы укры́лись от дождя́ под дерéвьями.

shelter *vti vt* укры|вáть (-́ть); приюти́ть (*pf*); (*protect*) защи|щáть (-ти́ть); **to** ~ **a criminal/an orphan** укрывáть престýпника, приюти́ть сиротý; **the trees** ~ **the house from the winds** дерéвья защищáют дом от ветрóв

vi укрывáться.

shelve[1] *vt*: *fig* **to** ~ **a problem** класть дéло под сукнó (положи́ть), от|клáдывать дéло в дóлгий я́щик (-ложи́ть).

shelve[2] *vi* отлóго спускáться (*only in impf*).

shelving *n* стеллáж.

shepherd *n* пастýх.

sheriff *n* (*US*) шери́ф.

sherry *n* хéрес.

shield *vt* (*protect*) защи|щáть (-ти́ть); (*shade*) заслон|я́ть (-и́ть); **to** ~ **one's eyes from the sun** защищáть глазá от сóлнца; *fig* **he** ~**ed me from their questions** он огради́л меня́ от их вопрóсов.

shift *n* **1** (*change*) изменéние; **a** ~ **of wind/of attitude/in policy** перемéна вéтра/пози́ции, перемéны *or* изменéния (*pls*) в поли́тике; *Ling* ~ **of consonant/accent** чередовáние соглáсных, изменéние ударéния

2 (*at work*) смéна; **a night/eight-hour** ~ ночнáя/восьмичасовáя смéна; **to work in** ~**s** рабóтать посмéнно; *attr*: ~ **work/worker** (по-) смéнная рабóта, смéнный рабóчий; **we have a three** ~ **system** мы рабóтаем в три смéны

3 (*expedient*): **we must make** ~ **with this sum/without heating** нáдо уложи́ться в э́ту сýмму, кáк-нибудь обойдёмся без отоплéния

4 (*dress*) прямóе/неотрезнóе плáтье; (*petticoat*) комбинáция

5 *Aut*: **manual (gear)** ~ ручнóе переключéние.

shift *vti vt* дви́|гать (-нуть) *and compounds*; **I** ~**ed the books out of the way** я отодви́нул кни́ги в стóрону; **to** ~ **furniture (around)** передвигáть/переставля́ть мéбель; **he was** ~**ed around from job to job** егó переводи́ли с однóй рабóты на другýю; ~ **the bag to your other hand** возьми́ сýмку в другýю рýку; *fig*: **you can't** ~ **him** егó не сдви́нешь с мéста; **to** ~ **one's ground** меня́ть пози́цию (по-)

vi: **they haven't** ~**ed from their original position** они́ не сдви́нулись с первоначáльной пози́ции, *also fig*; **to** ~ **from one foot**

to another переступ|áть с ногú нá ногу (-úть); **the wind has ~ed** вéтер переменúл направлéние/переменúлся; **the scene ~s to Moscow** дéйствие перенóсится в Москвý.

shifty *adj*: **a ~ answer** уклóнчивый отвéт; **a ~ customer** изворóтливый тип; **he has a ~ expression/~ eyes** у негó бéгающие глáзки.

shilly-shally *vi* колебáться (*only in impf*).

shimmer *vi* мерцáть, поблёскивать (*impfs*).

shin *n Anat* гóлень.

shin *vi*: **to ~ up a tree/over a wall** взбирáться/карáбкаться на дéрево (взобрáться/вс-), перелез|áть чéрез úзгородь (-́ть).

shindy *n CQ* скандáл, шум; **to kick up a ~** устрóить скандáл, поднять шум.

shine *n* блеск; **to give one's shoes a good ~** начúстить ботúнки до блéска; **we'll go, (come) rain or ~** мы пойдём, какáя бы ни былá погóда.

shine *vti vt*: **to ~ a torch** светúть фонáриком (по-); **to ~ a light on smth** осветúть что-л (*usu pf*)

vi блестéть, *also fig*, сиять (*impfs*); **the metal ~s in the sun** метáлл блестúт на сóлнце; **the sun is shining** сияет сóлнце; **her eyes shone** её глазá блестéли; *fig* **he does not ~ in conversation** он не блéщет в разговóре.

shingle[1] *n* (*pebbles*) гáлька; *attr*: **a ~ beach** пляж, покрытый гáлькой.

shingle[2] *n* (*hairstyle*) корóткая стрúжка.

shingles *n Med* опоясывающий лишáй.

shiny *adj*: **~ boots** (*patent, etc.*) лакиро́ванные ботúнки, (*polished*) ботúнки, начúщенные до блéска; **a ~ surface** блестящая повéрхность; **my trousers are ~** (*worn*) моú брюки лоснятся.

ship *n* сýдно;. корáбль (*m*); **a war/merchant ~** воéнное/торгóвое сýдно; **on board ~** на бортý корабля; **the ~'s company** экипáж корабля; **~'s doctor/chandler** судовóй врач/ поставщúк; **the ~'s papers** судовые докумéнты; *attr*: **~ canal** судохóдный канáл.

ship *vti vt* (*transport*) пере|возúть по водé (-везтú); (*load*) грузúть на сýдно (по-); **the goods were ~ped at Riga/to Riga** товáр был прúнят нá борт *or* погрýжен в Рúге, товáр был отпрáвлен мóрем в Рúгу; **to ~ oars** поднять вёсла и положúть в лóдку; **the boat ~ped water** лóдка зачерпнýла вóду

vi: **he ~ped as a steward on the liner** он нанялся официáнтом на сýдно.

shipbuilding *n* судостроéние, кораблестроéние.

shipment *n*: **a ~ of coal/lorries** груз ýгля, пáртия грузовикóв; **~ in bulk** погрýзка без упакóвки *or* нáсыпью/внавáлку (*advs*).

shipowner *n* судовладéлец.

shipping *n* (*traffic*) судохóдство; (*ships*) судá (*pl*); (*loading*) погрýзка, перевóзка; **the canal is again open to ~** канáл вновь открыт для судохóдства; *attr*: **~ company** судохóдная компáния; **~ intelligence** свéдения (*pl*) о движéнии судóв.

shipshape *adv*: **everything is ~** всё в пóлном порядке.

shipwreck *vt*: **to be ~ed** терпéть (корабле-) крушéние (по-); **~ed sailors** морякú, потерпéвшие крушéние.

shipyard *n* верфь, судостроúтельный завóд.

shirk *vti vt* увú|ливать от + *G* (-льнýть); уклон|яться от + *G* (-úться); (*work or school*) прогýл|ивать (-ять); **he ~ed the issue** он увильнýл от вопрóса; **he ~ed his duty/the excursion** он уклонúлся от исполнéния своегó дóлга/от э́той поéздки; **to ~ difficulties** избе|гáть трýдностей (-жáть); **he ~ed school** он прогулял урóки (*pl*)

vi: **he is ~ing** (*hasn't turned up*) он прогýливает, (*when on a job*) он увúливает от рабóты.

shirt *n* рубáшка; **dress/starched ~** наря́дная/ крахмáльная рубáшка; *attr*: **~ collar/front** воротнúк рубáшки, манúшка; **in ~ sleeves** без пиджакá.

shirty *adj CQ*: **he was very ~ with her** он говорúл с ней óчень раздражённым/рéзким тóном; **to get ~** раздражáться, сердúться.

shiver *n* дрожь; **he gives me the ~s** меня́ от негó в дрожь бросáет (*impers*); **it sends ~s down my spine** у меня от э́того мурáшки по спинé бéгают.

shiver *vi* дрожáть (*impf*), ёжиться (съ-); **she is ~ing all over with cold** онá ёжится/вся дрожúт от хóлода; **he started ~ing** он задрожáл.

shivery *adj*: **I feel ~** меня знобúт (*impers*).

shoal[1] *n* (*shallows*) мелковóдье; (*sandbank*) мель.

shoal[2] *n* (*of fish*) косяк.

shock[1] *n* сотрясéние; *fig* потрясéние, удáр; *Med* шок; **we felt the ~ of the earthquake** мы почýвствовали подзéмный толчóк; **it came as a ~ to hear that...** мы были потрясены́, услышав, что...; **the ~ killed him** он не пережúл э́того потрясéния/удáра; **what a ~ you gave me!** ты меня напугáл!; **he is suffering from ~, he is in ~** он в шóке, он в шóковом состоянии; *Elec* **don't touch that wire—it'll give you a ~** не трóгай э́тот прóвод—удáрит тóком; *attr*: *Mil* **~ tactics** тáктика сокрушúтельных удáров; **~ troops** удáрные чáсти; *Med* **~ treatment/therapy** шокотерапúя; *Aut* **~ absorber** амортизáтор.

shock[1] *vt* (*by bad news, etc.*) потряс|áть (-тú); (*by bad behaviour, etc.*) шокúровать (*impf*); **I was ~ed by the price/by their behaviour** я был потрясён, услышав цéну, я был шокúрован их поведéнием; **nothing can ~ her** её ничéм не удивúшь; *fig* **he needs to be ~ed out of his complacency** нáдо сбить с негó спесь.

shock[2] *n* (*of corn, fig of hair*) копнá.

shocker *n CQ*: **that mistake was a ~** такáя ошúбка—прóсто позóр; **that boy is a real ~** э́тот мальчúшка—настоящий хулигáн; **have you any ~s for me to read?** у тебя нет какóго-нибудь детектúвчика почитáть?

shock-headed *adj*: **a ~ boy** мальчик с копной непокорных волос.

shocking *adj* ужасающий; возмутительный; **it was a ~ sight** это было ужасающее зрелище; **how simply ~!** это ни в какие ворота не лезет!; **~ behaviour/weather** возмутительное поведение, отвратительная погода; **~ handwriting** ужасный почерк; **some parts of the film are ~** фильм местами шокирует.

shoddy *adj* дрянной; **~ cloth/work** дрянная ткань, плохая работа.

shoe *n* (*light, man's or woman's*) туфля, (*heavy*) башмак; (*covering ankle*) ботинок; (*horse's*) подкова; *Tech* колодка; **a pair of ~s** пара туфель; **strong ~s** крепкие башмаки; **lace-up ~s** туфли со шнурками; **~s are expensive now** обувь (*no pl*) сейчас дорогая; *fig*: **I wouldn't like to be in his ~s** я бы не хотел быть в его шкуре; **to step into smb's ~s** занять чьё-л место; *attr*: **~ repair** ремонт обуви.

shoe *vt* обу|вать (´-ть); (*of horses*) подков|ывать (-ать); **she is well shod** она хорошо обута.

shoebrush *n* сапожная щётка.

shoehorn *n* рожок (для обуви).

shoelace *n* шнурок (для ботинок); **to do up one's ~s** завязать шнурки.

shoemaker *n* сапожник.

shoeshop *n* обувной магазин.

shoestring *n* (*US*) шнурок; *fig* **they live on a ~** они живут просто на гроши.

shoetree *n* (сапожная) колодка.

shoo *interj* брысь!, пошёл вон!

shoo *vt*, *also* **to ~ away/off** про|гонять (-гнать).

shoot *n* **1** *Bot* побег, росток; **to put out ~s** пустить побеги/ростки

2 (*hunt*) (**a ~**) охота; (*area*) охотничье угодье.

shoot *vti vt* **1** стрелять (*impf*) *and compounds*; **he shot** (*and killed*) **his wife/himself** он застрелил жену, он застрелился; **he shot her/himself in the arm** он выстрелил ей/себе в руку; **he was shot as a traitor** его расстреляли как предателя; **he was sentenced to be shot** его приговорили к расстрелу; **he was shot in the head/through the heart** пуля попала ему в голову/пробила ему сердце; **to ~ game** охотиться (*usu impf*); **he shot a rabbit/a snipe on the wing** он подстрелил кролика, он сбил бекаса на лету

2: *Cine* **to ~ a film** снимать фильм (снять)

3 *fig uses*: **to ~ the rapids** плыть через пороги; *CQ*: **he shot lots of questions at me** он забросал меня вопросами; **he has shot his bolt** он истратил весь порох; **I'll be shot if I'm late** я пропал, если опоздаю; **he was ~ing a line about his success on the stage** он всем растрезвонил о своём успехе на сцене

vi **1** стрелять; (*if hunting*) охотиться (*usu impf*); **he/this gun ~s well** он хорошо стреляет, это ружьё хорошо бьёт; **he ~s to kill** он стреляет с намерением убить; **he shot wide of the mark** он промахнулся, *also fig*; *fig* **I have a ~ing pain in my ear/side/tooth** у меня стреляет (*impers*) в ухе, у меня колет (*impers*) в боку, у меня острая боль в зубе

2 (*move quickly*) мет|аться (-нуться); рвануться (*pf*); нестись, мчаться (*for true pfs use* про-, *pf* по- *has sense of "to begin to move"*); **the meteor shot across the sky** метеор пронёсся по небу; **he shot across the road** он метнулся через дорогу; **he shot ahead** (*in race or class*) он сделал рывок вперёд; **he shot by/past in his old banger** он пронёсся/промчался мимо в своём (старом) драндулете; **sparks shot out of the burning log** горящее полено стреляло искрами; **he shot over the horse's head** он перелетел через голову лошади

shoot at *vi*: **he ~ at a pheasant** он выстрелил в фазана; **to ~ at the crowd** стрелять по толпе/в толпу; *Sport* **to ~ at goal** бить по воротам

shoot down *vt*: **to ~ down a plane** сби|вать самолёт (-ть)

shoot up *vi* (*of prices, temperature*) подск|акивать (-очить); *CQ* **goodness, how you've shot up!** боже мой, как ты вырос!

shooting *n* **1: the ~ was continuous through the night** стрельба/пальба продолжалась всю ночь

2 (*hunting*): **to go ~** пойти на охоту; **there is good ~ on his estate** в его имении хорошо охотиться

3 *Cine* съёмка; **~ has started** начались съёмки (*pl*)

4 *attr*: **~ gallery/range** тир, стрельбище; **~ season** охотничий сезон; **~ star** падающая звезда.

shop *n* магазин; (*small*) лавка; (*in factory*) цех; **butcher's/grocer's ~** мясной/бакалейный магазин; **a tobacconist's ~** табачная лавка; **he keeps a ~** он держит магазинчик/лавку; **tool ~** инструментальный цех; **it's a closed ~ here** здесь работают только члены профсоюза; *fig*: **he's shut up ~** он ушёл от дел; **you've come to the wrong ~** ты обратился не по адресу; **to talk ~** говорить о работе; *attr*: **on the ~ floor** в цехе; **~ window** витрина.

shop *vti*: **I am going ~ping** я иду за продуктами; **I always ~ at the local stores** я всегда/всё покупаю в местных магазинах; *CQ* **to ~ smb** до|носить на кого-л (-нести)

shop around *vi*: **you should ~ around before deciding** нужно присмотреться, прежде чем покупать.

shop assistant *n* продав|éц, *f* -щица.

shopkeeper *n* лавочник.

shoplifter *n* магазинный вор.

shopper *n* покупатель (*m*).

shopping *n*: **I do the ~ on Fridays** я закупаю продукты по пятницам; **I did all the ~ yesterday** я вчера сделал все покупки; **I am**

going out to do the ~ я иду́ в магази́н; *attr*: ~ **bag** хозя́йственная су́мка; ~ **centre** торго́вый центр.

shore *n* бе́рег; **on the** ~ **of the lake** на берегу́ о́зера; **to go on** ~ сходи́ть на бе́рег; *attr*: ~ **leave** увольне́ние на бе́рег.

short *adj* **1** (*of distance, etc.*) коро́ткий, кра́ткий; **a** ~ **stick**/**memory** коро́ткая па́лка/па́мять; **she has** ~ **hair** у неё коро́ткая стри́жка/коро́ткие во́лосы; **the jacket is** ~ **in the sleeve** рукава́ э́того пиджака́ ко́ротки; **her explanation was** ~ **and to the point** её объясне́ние бы́ло толко́вым и кра́тким; ~ **grass** ни́зкая трава́; **he is quite** ~ он ма́ленького ро́ста; **call me Tim for** ~ зови́ меня́ про́сто Тим; **Tim is** ~ **for Timothy** Тим—уменьши́тельное и́мя от Ти́моти; **the** ~**est distance from A to B** кратча́йшее расстоя́ние от А до В; **a** ~ **way off** недалеко́; **a** ~ **distance from my house** неподалёку от моего́ до́ма; **I took a** ~ **cut through the field** я пошёл напрями́к че́рез по́ле; **there is a** ~ **cut down that side street** э́тим переу́лком идти́ гора́здо бли́же; *fig*: **you must practise hard—there are no** ~ **cuts** на́до мно́го занима́ться—лёгких путе́й нет; **nothing** ~ **of a miracle can help us** то́лько чу́до нам помо́жет; **it is little** ~ **of madness** э́то чуть ли не безу́мие; **the factory fell** ~ **of its target** заво́д не вы́полнил зада́ния

2 (*of time*) коро́ткий, кра́ткий, недо́лгий; **the days are getting** ~**er** дни стано́вятся коро́че; **to cut a long story** ~ коро́че говоря́; **I can't come at such** ~ **notice** я не могу́ прие́хать так сра́зу—на́до бы́ло предупреди́ть зара́нее; **he stayed with us for a** ~ **time** он был у нас недо́лго; **a** ~ **time ago** неда́вно; **I took a** ~ **holiday from work** я сде́лал себе́ небольшо́й переры́в в рабо́те; **time is getting** ~ остаётся ма́ло вре́мени; **the factory is on** ~ **time**/**hours** фа́брика переведена́ на непо́лный рабо́чий день

3 (*abrupt*) ре́зкий; **he was** ~ **with her** он был ре́зок с ней; **he has a** ~ **temper** он вспы́льчив

4 (*insufficient*) *often translated by impers* не хвата́ет + *G*; **I am** ~ **of time**/**money** мне не хвата́ет вре́мени/де́нег; **it is 3 kilos** ~ тут не хвата́ет трёх кило́; **the fund is $100** ~ **of its target** фо́нду не хвата́ет ста до́лларов до необходи́мой су́ммы; **we are** ~ **of flour**/**bread** у нас конча́ется мука́/нет хле́ба; **at that time goods were in** ~ **supply** в то вре́мя не хвата́ло мно́гих това́ров; ~ **weight**/**measure** недове́с, недоме́р; **he gave me** ~ **weight**/**change**/**measure** он обве́сил/обсчита́л меня́, он непра́вильно отме́рил мне; **he was** ~ **of breath** он задыха́лся, он запыха́лся.

short *adv* **1** (*abruptly*) ре́зко; **to stop** ~ ре́зко останови́ться; **to pull up** ~ (*of car*) ре́зко останови́ться; **to cut smb** ~ оборва́ть/прерва́ть кого́-л; **to cut a meeting**/**trip** ~ прерва́ть собра́ние/пое́здку; *fig* **to sell smb** ~ наду́ть кого́-л; *CQ* **he was taken** ~ **in the bus** у него́ живо́т схвати́ло (*impers*) в авто́бусе

2: to fall/**go**/**run** ~ *etc.*: **during the war we all went** ~ во вре́мя войны́ мы ощуща́ли нехва́тку во всём; **the children often went** ~ **of food** де́ти ча́сто ходи́ли голо́дные; **we are running** ~ **of petrol** у нас конча́ется бензи́н; **to fall** ~ **of expectations** не оправда́ть ожида́ний; **production fell** ~ **of target** произво́дственный план не́ был вы́полнен; *CQ*: ~ **of murder he'd do anything** он ни перед че́м не остано́вится; ~ **of doing it yourself, you won't get it done** е́сли сам не сде́лаешь, никто́ не сде́лает.

shortage *n* нехва́тка, недоста́ток; **the housing**/**food** ~ нехва́тка жилья́/продово́льствия; **there is a** ~ **of potatoes** карто́шки в э́том году́ ма́ло; **there was no** ~ **of information** в информа́ции недоста́тка не́ было.

short-circuit *n Elec* коро́ткое замыка́ние.

shortcoming *n* недоста́ток.

shorten *vt* укор|а́чивать (-оти́ть); сокра|ща́ть (-ти́ть); **to** ~ **a journey**/**an essay** сократи́ть пое́здку/о́черк; **I** ~**ed the sleeves** я укороти́л/подкороти́л рукава́.

shorthand *n* стеногра́фия; **to take down in** ~ стенографи́ровать; *attr*: ~ **notes** стенографи́ческая за́пись (*sing*); ~ **typist** машини́стка-стенографи́стка.

short-handed *adj*: **we were** ~ нам не хвата́ло (*impers*) рабо́чей си́лы.

short-list *vt*: **we've** ~**ed ten applicants** мы отобра́ли де́сять кандида́тов; **he was** ~**ed** он был в числе́/в спи́ске ото́бранных кандида́тов.

short-lived *adj fig* недо́лгий.

shortly *adv* **1** (*soon*) ско́ро; вско́ре; **he is coming** ~ он ско́ро придёт; ~ **before**/**after his graduation** незадо́лго до/вско́ре по́сле его́ оконча́ния

2 (*briefly*) кра́тко

3 (*abruptly*) ре́зко.

shorts *npl* (*for children*) коро́ткие штани́шки, (*for adults*) шо́рты; (*US*: *men's underpants*) трусы́.

short-sighted *adj* близору́кий, *also fig*; *fig* недальнови́дный.

short-tempered *adj* раздражи́тельный, вспы́льчивый.

short-term *adj*: **a** ~ **loan**/**lease** краткосро́чная ссу́да/аре́нда; **the** ~ **advantages of the plan** непосре́дственные преиму́щества э́того пла́на; **the** ~ **weather forecast** сво́дка пого́ды на ближа́йшие дни.

shortwave *adj Radio* коротково́лновый.

shot *n* **1** (*sound of*) вы́стрел; (*pellets, also* **small** ~) дробь; **we heard** ~**s** мы слы́шали вы́стрелы; **without firing a** ~ без еди́ного вы́стрела; **he fired a** ~ **at the deer** он вы́стрелил/пальну́л в оле́ня; **a random** ~ вы́стрел науга́д (*adv*); **a space** ~ косми́ческий полёт

2 *fig uses, usu CQ*: **he was off like a** ~ он вы́летел пу́лей; **I'd do it like a** ~ **if...** я бы ту́т же э́то сде́лал, е́сли бы...; **his**

parting ~ его́ замеча́ние под за́навес; **it's just a ~ in the dark** я сказа́л э́то про́сто науга́д; **it's a long ~, but perhaps he might know** э́то маловероя́тно, но, мо́жет быть, он и зна́ет (об э́том); **I had a ~ at skiing** я попро́бовал встать на лы́жи

3 (*of person*) стрело́к; **he is a crack ~** он отли́чный стрело́к, он бьёт без про́маха; *fig CQ* **a big ~** ва́жная ши́шка

4 *Sport*: **putting the ~** толка́ние ядра́; **he had a ~ at goal** (*football, hockey*) он уда́рил по воро́там; **good ~!** (*football, tennis*) хоро́ший уда́р!

5 (*injection*) уко́л; **he gave me a ~ of penicillin/in the arm** он сде́лал мне уко́л пеницилли́на/в ру́ку

6 *Photo* сни́мок; *Cine* кадр.

shotgun *n* дробови́к.

should *v aux* (*see* **shall**) **1** (*conditional*): **~ he ask, tell him that...** е́сли он спро́сит, скажи́ ему́, что...; **had I been warned I ~ have stayed at home** е́сли бы меня́ предупреди́ли, я бы оста́лся до́ма; **I ~n't be surprised if...** меня́ не удиви́т, е́сли...; **I ~ have thought/said that...** я бы мог поду́мать, что..., я бы сказа́л, что...; **he said he'd write.—I ~ hope so!** он сказа́л, что напи́шет.—Я наде́юсь!; **I ~ say so!** ещё бы!

2 (*subjunctive*): **it is vital that we ~ be there** нам необходи́мо быть там; **we took a taxi so that we ~n't be late** мы взя́ли такси́, что́бы не опозда́ть; **I am worried lest he ~ fall** я бою́сь, как бы он не упа́л; **I didn't think I ~ see him again** я не ду́мал, что уви́жу его́ сно́ва; **I'm surprised that he ~ be so careless** меня́ удивля́ет така́я его́ небре́жность

3 (*obligation, advisability, need*): **we ~ leave right now** мы должны́ сейча́с же уйти́; **he ~ have rung me at six** он до́лжен был мне звони́ть в шесть (часо́в); **he ~ have rung/~ ring her himself** он до́лжен был/он до́лжен бы сам ей позвони́ть; **you ~ go to the doctor** тебе́ на́до бы сходи́ть к врачу́; **he ~ have thought about it earlier** ему́ бы на́до бы́ло поду́мать об э́том ра́ньше; **you ~ be more tactful with your colleagues** тебе́ сле́довало бы/сле́дует быть потакти́чнее с сотру́дниками; **how ~ I know?** отку́да мне знать?; **it is he who ~ be worried, not you** э́то ему́ на́до беспоко́иться, а не тебе́; **I'm not sure whether I ~ write or phone** не зна́ю, что де́лать—написа́ть и́ли позвони́ть; **~ I wait outside?** мне подожда́ть на у́лице?; **~n't you have told him?** а мо́жет сле́довало бы ему́ сказа́ть?; **I think I ~ tell you that...** счита́ю ну́жным сообщи́ть вам, что...

4 (*probability*): **it ~ be fun** э́то должно́ быть заба́вно; **he ~ be there now** он должно́ быть уже́ там; **the film ~ be ending soon** фильм до́лжен ско́ро ко́нчиться.

shoulder *n* плечо́; (*of meat*) лопа́тка; (*of hill*) плечо́ горы́; **hard ~** (*of road*) асфа́льтовая обо́чина доро́ги; **to carry on one's ~(s)** нести́ на плеча́х; **the coat is too tight across the ~(s)** пальто́ у́зко в плеча́х; **~ to ~** плечо́м к плечу́; *fig*: **his colleagues gave him the cold ~** колле́ги встре́тили его́ хо́лодно; *attr*: *Anat* **~ blade** лопа́тка; **~ strap** брете́лька, ля́мка, *Mil* пого́н.

shout *n* крик; **~s of applause/protest** восто́рженные кри́ки, во́згласы проте́ста; **~s of joy/laughter** ра́достные во́згласы *or* кри́ки, взры́вы сме́ха; *CQ* **give me a ~ when you're ready** кри́кни мне, когда́ бу́дешь гото́в.

shout *vti vt* кри|ча́ть (-кнуть); **the demonstrators ~ed slogans** демонстра́нты выкри́кивали ло́зунги; **the crowd ~ed him down** толпа́ заглуши́ла его́ го́лос кри́ками

vi: **don't ~ at me** не кричи́ на меня́; **the teacher ~ed at the class** учи́тель прикри́кнул на ученико́в; **I ~ed to him in the street/to bring my coat** я окли́кнул его́ на у́лице, я кри́кнул ему́, что́бы он принёс мне пальто́; **he ~ed for help** он звал на по́мощь.

shove *n*: **one more ~ and the boat's in the water** ещё разо́к толкнём, и ло́дка бу́дет в воде́.

shove *vti vt* (*push*) толк|а́ть, (*roughly*) пих|а́ть (*pfs* -ну́ть) *and compounds*; (*put*) сова́ть (су́нуть) *and compounds*; **he ~d me aside** он меня́ оттолкну́л/отпихну́л; **they ~d her forward** её подтолкну́ли вперёд; **he ~d a packet into my hand** он су́нул паке́т мне в ру́ку; **I ~d the stew into the oven** я засу́нул жарко́е в духо́вку; **he ~d his head out of the window** он вы́сунул го́лову в окно́/из окна́

vi толка́ться, пиха́ться; **don't ~** не толка́йся, не пиха́йся

shove back *vt*: (*move backwards*) **I ~d back the table** я отодви́нул стол; *CQ* **~ the knife back in the drawer** положи́ нож обра́тно/наза́д в я́щик

shove off *vti vt*: **we ~d the car off the road** мы столкну́ли маши́ну с доро́ги; **I was ~d off the pavement** меня́ столкну́ли с тротуа́ра; **to ~ a boat off** от|та́лкивать ло́дку от бе́рега (-толкну́ть)

vi Naut отта́лкиваться; *CQ* **~ off!** прова́ливай!, кати́сь!

shovel *n* (*for ashes*) сово́к; (*for snow* = *spade*) лопа́та.

shovel *vt*: **he ~led snow off the path** он расчи́стил доро́жку от сне́га; **to ~ coal on to the fire** под|бра́сывать у́голь в ого́нь (-бро́сить).

show *n* **1** (*showing*): **a ~ of force** демонстра́ция си́лы; **voting by a ~ of hands** голосова́ние подня́тием руки́ (*sing*); **what a splendid ~ of roses!** каки́е роско́шные ро́зы!

2 (*outward appearance*) вид, ви́димость; *CQ pejor* показу́ха; **he made a ~ of sympathy** он сде́лал вид, что сочу́вствует; **she offered a ~ of resistance** она́ для ви́да посопротивля́лась; *CQ pejor* **it's all just a ~** э́то сплошна́я показу́ха

3 (*exhibition*) вы́ставка; **the motor ~** вы́ставка маши́н; **the jewels were on ~ at the**

museum драгоце́нности бы́ли вы́ставлены в музе́е

4 *Theat*, *Cine*: **have you seen any good ~s lately?** ты за после́днее вре́мя ви́дел что́-нибудь интере́сное в теа́тре?/в кино́?

5 *CQ uses*: **who's in charge of this ~?** кто здесь гла́вный?; **she runs the ~ here** она́ здесь кома́ндует; **he giggled and gave the whole ~ away** он хихи́кнул, и ро́зыгрыш не уда́лся; **she stole the ~** она́ затми́ла всех; **he put up a good ~** он хорошо́ себя́ показа́л; **it was a pretty poor ~ that he didn't even apologize** как э́то некраси́во—он да́же не извини́лся.

show *vti vt* **1** пока́|зывать (-за́ть); **I was ~n the way/over the house/how to do it** мне показа́ли доро́гу/дом/, как э́то сде́лать; **as ~n in the diagram** как пока́зано на рису́нке; **he ~ed me to my place** он провёл меня́ к моему́ ме́сту; **the roads are ~n in red** доро́ги обозна́чены кра́сным; **you must ~ your passport** ну́жно предъяви́ть па́спорт; *Theat*, *etc.* **what film is ~ing at the club?** како́й фильм идёт в клу́бе?; *Comm* **the figures ~ a loss for last year** ци́фры за про́шлый год говоря́т об убы́тках (*pl*)

2 (*exhibit*) вы|ставля́ть (-ставить); **he's ~ing five paintings/his dogs** он выставля́ет пять карти́н/свои́х соба́к

3 (*indicate*, *demonstrate*) пока́зывать, *also Math*; ока́з|ывать (-а́ть) (*of inner qualities*) прояв|ля́ть (-и́ть); (*in deductions*) говори́ть о + *P*, свиде́тельствовать о + *P* (*impfs*); **the speedometer ~s 100 miles per hour** спидо́метр пока́зывает сто миль в час; **he ~ed himself to be unreliable** он показа́л себя́ ненадёжным челове́ком; **he has ~n the story is not true** он доказа́л, что э́то непра́вда; **to ~ consideration/preference to smb** оказа́ть кому́-л внима́ние, отда|ва́ть кому́-л предпочте́ние (-́ть); **to ~ courage/intelligence** прояви́ть хра́брость/ум; **that ~s (that) he knows nothing** э́то говори́т о том, что он ничего́ не зна́ет; **his edginess ~s a lack of self-confidence** его́ нерво́зность говори́т о неуве́ренности в себе́; **he ~ed no sign of life** он не подава́л никаки́х при́знаков жи́зни

4 *fig uses*: **he doesn't ~ his face at the club** он не пока́зывается в клу́бе; **to ~ one's hand/cards** раскры́ть ка́рты (*usu pf*); **to ~ a clean pair of heels** дать тя́гу, зада́ть стрекача́ (*usu pf*); *CQ* **I could ~ him a thing or two** я могу́ ему́ ко́е-что показа́ть

vi: **the scar still ~s** шрам ещё заме́тен; **your straps are ~ing** у тебя́ брете́льки видны́; **where is the film ~ing?** где идёт э́тот фильм?

show in *vi*: **~ him in** введи́те его́; **I was ~n into the study** меня́ провели́ в кабине́т

show off *vti vt*: **the dress ~s off her figure** э́то пла́тье вы́годно обрисо́вывает её фигу́ру; **he likes to ~ off his knowledge** он лю́бит блесну́ть свои́ми зна́ниями (*pl*)

vi: **he's only ~ing off** он то́лько рису́ется

show out *vt*: **~ him out** вы́ведите его́

show through *vi*: **the scratch ~s through the paint** под сло́ем кра́ски видна́ цара́пина

show up *vti vt*: **~ her up to her room** проводи́те её наве́рх в её ко́мнату; **this lighting ~s up all my wrinkles** при э́том све́те видны́ все мои́ морщи́ны; **he was shown up as a fraud** он оказа́лся моше́нником

vi CQ: **he didn't ~ up at the lecture** он так и не появи́лся на ле́кции.

showcase *n* витри́на.

showdown *n*: **if it comes to a ~** е́сли придётся раскры́ть ка́рты; **I had a ~ with my boss** у меня́ был кру́пный разгово́р с ше́фом.

shower *n* **1** (*of rain*): **a light/heavy ~** до́ждик, ли́вень (*m*); **we were caught in a ~** мы попа́ли под дождь; **~s with sunny intervals** кратковре́менные дожди́ с проясне́ниями

2 душ; **to take/have a ~** принима́ть душ

3 *fig* (*of arrows*, *blows*, *stones*) град; **a ~ of sparks/insults** сноп искр, пото́к оскорбле́ний.

shower *vt* осып|а́ть (-ать); **to ~ blows/honours on smb** осы́пать кого́-л уда́рами/по́честями; **he was ~ed with gifts/invitations/questions** его́ засы́пали пода́рками/приглаше́ниями/вопро́сами.

showerproof *adj*: **a ~ coat** непромока́емый плащ.

showery *adj*: **~ weather** дождли́вая пого́да; **it looks ~** похо́же, бу́дет дождь.

showing *n* (*exhibition*) вы́ставка; *Cine* пока́з, (кино)сеа́нс; **the last ~ starts at 10** после́дний сеа́нс начина́ется в де́сять; **he made a good ~** он хорошо́ себя́ прояви́л/показа́л; **on his own ~** по его́ со́бственному призна́нию.

show jumping *n Sport* конку́р-иппи́к.

showman *n*: *CQ* **he's a real ~** он уме́ет показа́ть себя́.

show-off *n CQ* позёр, хвасту́н.

showpiece *n*: **the ~ of the museum is the Rubens** го́рдость музе́я—карти́на Ру́бенса.

showroom *n* вы́ставочный/демонстрацио́нный зал.

showy *adj* (*of dress*, *colour*) крича́щий, бро́ский; (*of behaviour*) показно́й.

shred *n* клочо́к; клок (*pl* кло́чья, клоки́); **he tore the letter to ~s** он разорва́л письмо́ на клочки́; **my coat was ripped to ~s** моё пальто́ бы́ло изо́драно в кло́чья; *fig* **there's not a ~ of evidence against him** про́тив него́ нет никаки́х ули́к (*pl*).

shred *vt Cook* шинкова́ть (на-).

shrew *n Zool* землеро́йка; *fig* меге́ра.

shrewd *adj* (*in business*) тре́звый, расчётливый в дела́х; (*intelligent*) проница́тельный; **he's very ~** он о́чень расчётлив/проница́телен; **~ reasoning** тре́звое сужде́ние; **a ~ remark/observer** ме́ткое замеча́ние, то́нкий наблюда́тель; **I can make a ~ guess at what he'll say** я могу́ дово́льно то́чно предугада́ть, что он ска́жет.

shriek *n* визг, вопль (*m*); **the children's excited ~s** восторженные вопли детей; **a ~ of pain** крик боли; **~s of laughter** взрывы смеха.

shriek *vi* визжать, вопить (*usu impfs*); **to ~ with pain/laughter** вопить от боли, визжать от смеха.

shrill *adj* пронзительный, визгливый; резкий; **a ~ voice/whistle** пронзительный *or* визгливый голос, резкий свист.

shrimp *n Zool* мелкая креветка; *fig* (*of a child*) крошка.

shrink *vi* **1** (*of cloth*) садиться (сесть); (*contract*) сжиматься (сжаться); **to ~ in the wash** садиться при стирке; **metals ~ when cooled** металлы сжимаются при остывании; *fig* **my income has shrunk** мои доходы уменьшились

2 *fig uses*: **he has shrunk away to nothing** он как-то весь усох; **she ~s from meeting strangers** она избегает встреч с незнакомыми людьми.

shrivel *vi* ссыхаться (ссохнуться).

shroud *n* саван; *fig* **a ~ of mist/snow** пелена тумана, снежный покров.

shroud *vt fig*: **the valley was ~ed in mist** долину окутал туман; **the affair is ~ed in mystery** эта история окутана/покрыта тайной.

Shrovetide *n* масленица.

shrub *n* куст.

shrubbery *n* кустарник; кусты (*pl*).

shrug *vt*: **in reply he ~ged his shoulders** в ответ он пожал плечами

shrug off *vt fig*: **she just ~s off criticism** она на замечания только плечами пожимает; **you can't ~ that off so lightly** от этого так легко не отделаешься/отмахнёшься.

shuck (*US*) *vt see* **pod.**

shudder *vi* содрог|аться (-нуться); **I ~ to think of it** я содрогаюсь при одной мысли об этом; **to ~ with cold** дрожать от холода (*only in impf*).

shuffle *n* (*of feet*) шарканье; *Cards* перетасовка; **give the cards a good ~** перетасуй карты как следует; *fig* **a cabinet ~** перетасовка членов кабинета.

shuffle *vti vt Cards* тасовать (пере-); *fig* **he was shuffling his papers around** он перебирал свои бумаги

vi: **he ~d across to the bar** он пошёл шаркающей походкой к бару.

shun *vt*: **to ~ society/temptation** избе|гать общества/соблазнов (*pl*) (-жать); **he is ~ned by all decent people** порядочные люди сторонятся его (*only in impf*).

shunting *n Rail* маневрирование; *attr*: **a ~ engine/yard** маневровый паровоз/парк.

shut *vti vt* закры|вать (-ть), затвор|ять (-ить); **~ the window** закрой/затвори окно; **he had the door ~ in his face** у него перед носом захлопнули дверь; **I ~ my finger in the door** я прищемил себе палец дверью; *fig*: **he ~ his eyes to all her faults** он закрыл глаза на все её недостатки; **he ~ his ears to all our appeals** он был глух ко всем нашим призывам

vi закрываться, затворяться

shut down *vt*: **they are ~ting down the factory** завод закрывают/закрывается

shut in *vt* закрывать; *fig*: **the village is ~ in by mountains** деревню со всех сторон загораживают горы; **in a big city I feel ~ in** в большом городе у меня начинается клаустрофобия

shut out *vt*: **the cat was ~ out last night** (*by mistake*) сегодня ночью кошка осталась на дворе; **to ~ out noise** заглуш|ать шум (-ить); **the trees ~ out the view** деревья заслоняют вид

shut up *vti vt*: **he ~ himself up in his room** он закрылся в своей комнате; **he was ~ up in a lunatic asylum** его положили в психиатрическую больницу

vi CQ: **~ up!** замолчи!, заткнись!

shutdown *n* закрытие; *Radio* (*for the day*) окончание передач.

shutter *n* ставень (*m*); *Photo* (*of lense*) затвор объектива.

shuttle *n* челнок; *attr fig Rail, etc.*: **~ service** челночное сообщение/движение.

shuttle *vti*: **the ferry ~s between the ports** паром курсирует между портами.

shuttlecock *n* волан.

shy *adj* робкий, застенчивый; (*of animals*) пугливый; **he's ~ with women** он робок/застенчив с женщинами; **he makes her feel ~** она робеет/смущается в его присутствии; **he is/***CQ* **fights ~ of meeting other writers** он избегает встреч с коллегами по перу; **she felt ~ about telling the full story** она стеснялась рассказать все подробности.

shy *vi*: **the mare shied at the haystack** кобыла отскочила, испугавшись стога сена; *fig* **she shied away from the very idea of meeting the examiner** у неё сердце ёкало при одной мысли о беседе с экзаменатором.

Siamese *adj*: **~ twins** сиамские близнецы.

Siberian *adj* сибирский.

sibilant *n Ling* шипящий звук, сибилянт.

sick *adj* **1** (*ill*) больной; *as collect n* (**the ~**) больные (*pl*); **I was ~** (*ill*) я болел, (*vomited*) меня стошнило/вырвало (*impers*); **to fall ~** заболеть; **he has been ~ for two weeks** он болен уже две недели; **I feel ~** меня тошнит/мутит (*impers*); **it makes me ~** меня от этого тошнит

2 *fig uses*: **it makes me ~ to think of how she is treated** я возмущена тем, как с ней обращаются; **he was ~ at not getting into college** он очень переживал, что не поступил в колледж; *CQ*: **you make me ~** ты мне надоел [**NB** *tense*]; **I'm ~ and tired/~ to death of his stories** мне до смерти надоели эти его истории; **I'm ~ of him** он мне осточертел [**NB** *tense*]; **~ jokes** жестокие шутки; **~ humour** мрачный юмор.

sick bay *n Naut* лазарет; *School* изолятор.

sicken *vti vt*: **cruelty ~s me** жестокость мне отвратительна *vi* заболева́ть (*only in impf*); **he's ~ing for measles** у него́ начина́ется корь; *fig* **eventually he ~ed of their methods** посте-пе́нно их поведе́ние опроти́вело ему́.

sickening *adj fig CQ*: **it's ~ to see money thrown away** э́то про́сто возмути́тельно, как де́ньги выбра́сываются на ве́тер.

sickle *n* серп.

sick leave *n*: **he is on ~** он на бюллете́не, *CQ* он бюллете́нит.

sickly *adj* (*person*) боле́зненный, *also fig*; (*puny*) хи́лый; (*of taste, smell*) тошнотво́рный; **a ~ plant** хи́лое расте́ние; **a ~ smile** бо-ле́зненная улы́бка; **a ~ green** ядови́то-зелё-ный цвет.

sickness *n* боле́знь, заболева́ние; (*vomiting*) рво́та, тошнота́; **there is ~ in the village** в дере́вне есть слу́чаи заболева́ния; **he was absent because of ~** он отсу́тствовал по бо-ле́зни; **to what does the doctor ascribe his ~?** чем врач объясня́ет то, что его́ ча́сто тош-ни́т?; *attr*: **~ benefit** посо́бие по боле́з-ни.

sick pay *n* вы́плата по бюллете́ню.

side *n* **1** бок; **a ~ of beef** говя́жий бок; **I sleep on my ~** я сплю на боку́; **he tossed from ~ to ~** он воро́чался с бо́ку на́ бок; **he was wounded in the ~** его́ ра́нило (*impers*) в бок; **we sat ~ by ~** мы сиде́ли бок о́ бок; **come and sit by my ~** иди́, сядь ря́дом со мной

2 (*as opposed to top, bottom*): **the address was painted on the ~ of the box** на боково́й сте́нке я́щика был напи́сан а́дрес; **put the box on it's ~** поста́вь я́щик на́ бок; **the lorry lay on its ~** грузови́к лежа́л на боку́: **from the ~ the house looks small** сбо́ку (*adv*) дом вы́глядит небольши́м; **by the ~ of the building stood a shed** ря́дом со зда́нием был сара́й; **she went round the ~ of the house** она́ обошла́ дом вокру́г (*adv*); **the ~ of a ship** борт корабля́; **the ~s of a mountain** скло́ны горы́; *Aut* **on the near/off ~ of the car** (*UK*) с ле́вой/с пра́вой стороны́ маши́ны, (*US, SU, etc.*) с пра́вой/с ле́вой стороны́ маши́ны

3 (*edge*) край; **at the ~ of the road** на краю́/на обо́чине доро́ги; **the ~ of a lake/river** бе́рег о́зера/реки́

4 (*surface or lateral part*) сторона́; **what's on the other ~ of the record?** что на друго́й стороне́ пласти́нки?; **write on both ~s of the paper** пиши́те на обе́их сторона́х листа́; **the right/wrong ~ of cloth** лицева́я сторона́ тка́ни, изна́нка тка́ни; **the six ~s of a cube** шесть пове́рхностей ку́ба; (*on label*) **"This ~ up"** «верх»; **on both/all ~s** с обе́их/со всех сторо́н; **on one ~ of the room** вдоль одно́й стены́ ко́мнаты; **he took me on one ~** он отвёл меня́ в сто́рону; **he moved to one ~** он посторони́лся; **he lives (on) the other ~ of London** он живёт на друго́м конце́ Ло́ндона; **she crossed to the far ~ of the room** она́ пошла́ в да́льний коне́ц ко́мнаты; **I'll put it on one ~ for yòu** я оста́влю/отложу́ э́то для тебя́

5 (*party*) сторона́; *Sport* кома́нда; **our ~** на́ша сторона́; **to take smb's ~** принима́ть чью-л сто́рону; **to let the ~ down** подвести́ свои́х; **the home ~** хозя́ева по́ля; **which ~ do you support?** за кого́ ты боле́ешь?; **there are faults on both ~s** они́ о́ба винова́ты

6 *fig uses*: **there are some good ~s to his character** в его́ хара́ктере есть и хоро́шие сто́роны; **there's a bright ~ to all this** в э́том есть своя́ положи́тельная сторона́; **the other ~ of the picture** оборо́тная/обра́тная сторона́ меда́ли; **there are several ~s to the story** на э́ту исто́рию мо́жно взгляну́ть с не́сколь-ких сторо́н; **let's discuss all ~s of the question** дава́йте обсу́дим вопро́с всесторо́нне (*adv*); **an aunt on my father's ~** тётя со стороны́ отца́; **he got on the wrong ~ of his boss** он не угоди́л ше́фу; **the dress is on the small ~** э́то пла́тье мне мало́; *CQ* **he makes a bit on the ~** он подраба́тывает на стороне́

7 *CQ* (*UK*): **he's completely without ~** он нниско́лько не зазнаётся, он не зазна́йка

8 *attr*: **a ~ door/street** бокова́я дверь/ у́лочка; **a ~ issue/effect** второстепе́нный вопро́с, побо́чный эффе́кт.

side *vi*: **to ~ with smb** вста|ва́ть на чью-л сто́рону (-ть), прин|има́ть чью-л сто́рону (-я́ть).

sideboard *n* буфе́т, серва́нт.

sidecar *n* коля́ска (мотоци́кла).

side face *adv* в про́филь.

sidelight *n* подфа́рник.

sideline *n* **1** *Sport* бокова́я ли́ния; *Rail* бокова́я ве́тка

2: he does photography as a ~ фотогра́-фия—его́ побо́чный за́работок; **the foodshop sells tights as a ~** вообще́ э́то продукто́вый магази́н, но там мо́жно купи́ть и колго́тки.

sidelong *adj*: **a ~ glance** взгляд и́скоса (*adv*).

sidetrack *vti fig*: **he keeps ~ing/getting ~ed** он всё вре́мя отвлека́ется.

side whiskers *npl* бакенба́рды, ба́ки, ба́чки.

siding *n Rail* запа́сный путь.

siege *n* оса́да; **a state of ~** оса́дное поло-же́ние; **to lay ~ to** осади́ть + *A*; **to raise a ~** снять оса́ду.

sieve *n* решето́, си́то; *CQ* **my memory is like a ~** у меня́ па́мять как решето́.

sieve *vt see* **sift.**

sift *vt* (*sugar, flour, sand, wheat*) просе́|ивать (-ять); (*coal, gravel*) грохоти́ть (*usu impf*); *fig* **to ~ evidence** тща́тельно анализи́ровать по-каза́ния (*pl*) (про-).

sigh *n* вздох; **I breathed a ~ of relief** я облегчённо вздохну́л.

sigh *vi* взд|ыха́ть (-охну́ть); (*of wind*) по-ду́ть (*pf*).

sight *n* **1** (*faculty*) зре́ние; (*act of seeing*) вид; взгляд; **he regained his ~** к нему́ возвра-ти́лось зре́ние; **he has long/short ~** он даль-нозо́ркий, он близору́кий; **at the ~ of his face** при ви́де его́ лица́; **the mere ~ of him makes**

me ill меня́ от одного́ его́ ви́да воро́тит (*impers*); **I hate the ~ of her** я ви́деть её не могу́; **I can't bear the ~ of her crying** я не могу́ ви́деть, как она́ пла́чет; **love at first ~** любо́вь с пе́рвого взгля́да; **at first ~ it seemed that...** на пе́рвый взгляд каза́лось, что...; **I caught ~ of her at the theatre** я ме́льком ви́дел её в теа́тре; **if I catch ~ of him again** если́ он мне ещё раз попадётся на глаза́; **I know him by ~** я его́ зна́ю в лицо́; **to play music/translate at ~** чита́ть но́ты/переводи́ть с листа́; **to shoot at/on ~** стреля́ть без предупрежде́ния; *Comm* **payable at ~** с опла́той по предъявле́нии

2 (*range of vision*) по́ле зре́ния; **the boat remained in ~ for a long time** кора́бль до́лго был в по́ле зре́ния; **to come into ~** появи́ться в по́ле зре́ния; **we are in ~ of the end** коне́ц на́шей рабо́ты уже́ ви́ден; **don't let her out of your ~** не упуска́й её и́з виду; **keep out of my ~** не попада́йся, не пока́зывайся мне на глаза́; **out of ~, out of mind** с глаз доло́й, из се́рдца вон

3 (*spectacle*) вид, зре́лище; **have you seen the ~s of Leningrad?** ты ви́дел Ленингра́д?; **the cherry blossom is a wonderful ~** цвету́щая ви́шня—прекра́сное зре́лище; **it's a ~ for sore eyes** э́то отра́да для глаз; **it's a ~ worth seeing** на э́то сто́ит взгляну́ть; *CQ* **what a ~ you are in these old boots!** ну и вид у тебя́ в э́тих ста́рых сапога́х!

4 (*on gun, etc.*) прице́л; *Naut* **to take a ~ on smth** визи́ровать что-л; *fig* **he has set his ~s on being elected** он поста́вил себе́ цель победи́ть на вы́борах

5 *adv use CQ*: **it's a long ~ better than I expected** э́то намно́го лу́чше, чем я ожида́л; **he's a ~ too clever for me** он сли́шком уж умён.

sight *vt*: **to ~ land** уви́деть зе́млю (*pf*).

sightseer *n* тури́ст.

sign *n* **1** (*symbol*) знак; **plus/minus ~** знак плюс/ми́нус; **~s of the Zodiac** зна́ки зодиа́ка

2 (*with hand, head, etc.*) знак; **he nodded in ~ of agreement** он кивну́л голово́й в знак согла́сия; **to make the ~ of the cross** перекрести́ться; **he made a ~ to her that he wanted to leave** он сде́лал/по́дал ей знак, что хо́чет уйти́; *attr*: **~ language** язы́к же́стов, (*for deaf and dumb*) а́збука глухонемы́х

3 (*indication*) при́знак; **a clear sky at night is a ~ of frost** я́сное ночно́е не́бо—при́знак моро́за/к моро́зу; **as a ~ of respect** в знак уваже́ния; **there's still no ~ of my luggage/of them reaching a settlement** моего́ багажа́ всё ещё нет, пока́ никаки́х при́знаков (*pl*), что они́ ско́ро приду́т к соглаше́нию; **there is no ~ of her anywhere** её нигде́ не ви́дно; **he shows ~s of age** у него́ появля́ются при́знаки ста́рости; **a ~ of the times** зна́мение вре́мени (*sing*); **a black cat is said to be an unlucky ~** чёрная ко́шка счита́ется дурно́й приме́той

4 (*on signboard*) вы́веска; (*notice*) объявле́ние; **traffic ~** доро́жный знак.

sign *vti vt* подпи́с|ывать (-а́ть); **he ~ed the letter/his name** он подписа́л письмо́, он подписа́лся; **we ~ed the petition** мы подписа́лись под пети́цией; **the agreement is ~ed** догово́р подпи́сан; **he gave me a ~ed photo of himself** он подари́л мне свою́ фотогра́фию с на́дписью

vi **1**: **~ on this line** подпиши́тесь над э́той ли́нией

2 (*signal*): **he ~ed to me to leave the room** он сде́лал/по́дал мне знак вы́йти из ко́мнаты

sign in *vi*: **we ~ed in at the hotel** мы зарегистри́ровались в гости́нице; **the workers ~ in at 8 o'clock** рабо́чие отмеча́ются в та́беле в во́семь часо́в (утра́)

sign on *vt*: **to ~ on new workers** на|нима́ть но́вых рабо́чих (-ня́ть); **he was ~ed on/up** с ним подписа́ли контра́кт; **the club ~ed on/up some new players** клуб подписа́л контра́кты с не́сколькими но́выми игрока́ми

sign out *vi*: **we ~ed out (of the hotel)** мы вы́писались из гости́ницы.

signal *n* сигна́л; **he gave the ~ to/for retreat** он дал сигна́л отступи́ть/к отступле́нию; **distress/***Tel* **engaged ~** сигна́л бе́дствия/«за́нято»; **traffic ~s** светофо́р (*sing*); *attr*: **~ box/lamp** сигна́льная бу́дка/ла́мпа.

signal *vti vt* (по)да|ва́ть сигна́л (-́ть); сигна́лить (по-, про-); **he ~led that he was turning left** он просигна́лил ле́вый поворо́т; *Mil* **he ~led a message to headquarters** он переда́л донесе́ние в штаб

vi: **he ~led to the waiter to bring the menu** он по́дал знак официа́нту принести́ меню́; **~ before stopping** дай сигна́л пе́ред остано́вкой; **the vessel ~led with flares** су́дно подава́ло сигна́лы вспы́шками.

signalman *n* сигна́льщик.

signatory *n* подписа́вшаяся сторона́; *attr*: **~ powers** госуда́рства, подписа́вшие догово́р.

signature *n* по́дпись; **to put one's ~ to a document** поста́вить по́дпись под докуме́нтом; *Mus* **key ~** знак при ключе́; *attr*: **~ tune** позывны́е (*pl*).

signet *n* печа́тка; *attr*: **~ ring** кольцо́ с печа́ткой.

significance *n* значе́ние; смысл; **a matter of great ~** де́ло огро́много значе́ния.

significant *adj*: **a ~ sum** значи́тельная су́мма; **a ~ look** многозначи́тельный взгляд; **it is ~ that...** показа́тельно то, что...

signify *vti vt* (*mean*) означа́ть (*impf*); (*show*) вы|ража́ть (-́разить); **what does this phrase ~?** что означа́ет э́та фра́за?; **he signified his approval** он вы́разил своё одобре́ние

vi: **in this case it does not ~** в э́том слу́чае э́то не име́ет значе́ния.

signpost *n* указа́тель (*m*), указа́тельный столб.

silage *n* си́лос; *attr* си́лосный.

silence *n* (*state*) тишина́, безмо́лвие; (*not speaking*) молча́ние; **dead ~** мёртвая тишина́;

the ~ was broken by a clap of thunder тишину́ нару́шил уда́р/раска́т гро́ма; **there was a sudden ~** вдруг наступи́ла тишина́/(*of people*) все замолча́ли; **~ gives consent** молча́ние—знак согла́сия; **to suffer in ~** страда́ть мо́лча; **we cannot pass over this in ~** мы не мо́жем обойти́ э́то молча́нием/умолча́ть об э́том.

silence *vt*: **to ~ one's critics/the enemy's guns** заста́вить замолча́ть свои́х кри́тиков/вра́жеские пу́шки.

silencer *n Tech* глуши́тель (*m*).

silent *adj* (*of person*) молчали́вый; (*of night, etc.*) ти́хий, безмо́лвный; **to remain/keep ~** молча́ть, (*withholding information*) промолча́ть, (*evading answer*) отма́лчиваться; **he was ~ on this matter** он обходи́л молча́нием э́тот вопро́с; **to fall ~** замолча́ть; **a ~ film/prayer** немо́й фильм, молчали́вая моли́тва; **it was ~ as the grave** была́ гробова́я/мёртвая тишина́.

silhouette *n* силуэ́т.

silhouette *vt*: **he was ~d against the sky** его́ силуэ́т вырисо́вывался на фо́не не́ба.

silicon *n* кре́мний; *attr*: **~ chip** кре́мниевый чип.

silk *n* шёлк; **~s** шелка́; *attr*: **~ stockings** шёлковые чулки́; **~ moth** шелкопря́д.

silkworm *n* шелкови́чный червь, ту́товый шелкопря́д.

sill *n* (*of window*) подоко́нник.

silly *adj* глу́пый; **don't be ~** не на́до глупи́ть; **that was a ~ thing to do** э́то была́ глу́пость; **to make smb look ~** де́лать из кого́-л дурака́; *CQ* **how ~ can you get!** кака́я глу́пость!

silo *n* си́лосная я́ма.

silt *n* ил.

silt up *vti*: **the mouth of the river is/has ~ed up** у́стье реки́ заби́то и́лом.

silver *n* серебро́ (*also collect and of coins*); **to clean the ~** чи́стить серебро́; *attr*: **~ foil/wedding** сере́бряная фо́льга/сва́дьба; **~ fox** черно-бу́рая лиси́ца/(*fur*) лиса́; **~ gilt** позоло́ченное серебро́.

silver-plated *adj* покры́тый серебро́м.

silvery *adj* серебри́стый.

similar *adj* схо́дный; похо́жий; подо́бный; аналоги́чный; **we have ~ tastes** у нас схо́дные вку́сы; **a ~ system** подо́бная/аналоги́чная систе́ма; **the two houses are very ~** э́ти дома́ о́чень похо́жи; **I had a ~ experience** со мной случи́лось не́что подо́бное.

similarity *n* схо́дство, подо́бие; **there are points of ~ between...** существу́ет не́которое схо́дство ме́жду + *I*.

similarly *adv* подо́бным о́бразом.

simile *n* сравне́ние.

simmer *vti vt* держа́ть на ма́леньком огне́ (*usu impf*)

vi кипе́ть на ма́леньком огне́ (*usu impf*); *fig*: **to ~ with rage/indignation** кипе́ть от я́рости/негодова́ния; **give him time to ~ down** дай ему́ осты́ть/успоко́иться.

simple *adj* **1** (*easy*) просто́й, *also Gram*; **it's very ~** э́то о́чень про́сто; **a ~ village girl/problem** проста́я дереве́нская де́вушка, несло́жная пробле́ма; **written in ~ language** напи́сано просты́м, поня́тным языко́м; **the ~ life** просто́й о́браз жи́зни; **the ~ truth is that...** про́сто всё де́ло в том, что...; **he's a genius pure and ~** он про́сто ге́ний; *Math*: **~ fraction** проста́я дробь; **~ equation** уравне́ние пе́рвой сте́пени; *Comm* **~ interest** просты́е проце́нты (*pl*)

2 (*naive*): **he's a bit ~** он немно́го простова́т; **a ~ soul** простоду́шный челове́к, проста́я душа́; **she's not so ~ as would appear** она́ не так проста́, как ка́жется; **you must be ~ to believe that** ты наи́вный челове́к, е́сли э́тому ве́ришь.

simple-minded *adj*: **he's ~** он простова́т; **I'm not so ~ as to believe him** я не тако́й уж проста́к, что́бы ему́ пове́рить.

simpleton *n* проста́к, простофи́ля.

simplification *n* упроще́ние.

simplify *vt* упро|ща́ть (-сти́ть).

simulate *vt* (*sham*) симули́ровать (*impf and pf*); притвор|я́ться (-и́ться); **to ~ illness** симули́ровать боле́знь, притворя́ться больны́м; **he ~d sympathy** он вы́разил притво́рное сочу́вствие.

simultaneous *adj* одновреме́нный.

sin *n* грех; **original ~** первоаро́дный грех; **they live in ~** они́ любо́вники; *fig*: **it's a ~ to sit indoors on a day like this** грех сиде́ть до́ма в тако́й день; **it would be a ~ to cut the manuscript heavily** бы́ло бы грешно́ так искромса́ть ру́копись; *joc* **for my ~s, I'll have to...** ви́дно за мои́ грехи́ мне прихо́дится...

sin *vi* греши́ть (со-); **to ~ against smth** греши́ть про́тив чего́-л (по-); **he's more ~ned against than ~ning** он скоре́е же́ртва, чем злоде́й.

since *adv* с тех по́р; **he has lived here ever ~** с тех по́р он здесь и живёт [**NB** *tense*]; **she's never been heard of ~** с тех по́р о ней ничего́ неизве́стно; **not long ~** неда́вно.

since *prep* с + *G*; по́сле + *G*; **he has been waiting ~ 10 o'clock/~ yesterday** он с десяти́ часо́в/со вчера́шнего дня ждёт [**NB** *tense*]; **~ talking to you/~ our talk, I've decided what to do** по́сле на́шего разгово́ра я по́нял, что на́до де́лать

since *conj* **1** (*of time*) с тех по́р как...; **where have you been ~ we parted?** где ты был, с тех по́р как мы расста́лись?

2 (*causal*) так как, поско́льку; **~ he doesn't know Russian, he can't do the job** так как/поско́льку он не зна́ет ру́сского, он не мо́жет де́лать э́ту рабо́ту.

sincere *adj* и́скренний.

sincerely *adv* и́скренне; (*in letters*) **Yours ~** и́скренне Ваш/Ва́ша.

sincerity *n* и́скренность; **in all ~ I thought it was for the best** я действи́тельно счита́л, что э́то к лу́чшему.

sine *n Math* си́нус.

sinew *n Anat* сухожи́лие.

sinewy *adj* жи́листый.

sinful *adj* гре́шный, грехо́вный.

sing *vti vt* петь (про-, с-) *and compounds*; **these songs are rarely sung** э́ти пе́сни ре́дко пою́тся; **let's ~ the piece through** дава́йте э́то споём/пропоём; **to ~ a child to sleep** баю́кать ребёнка (у-); *fig*: **to ~ smb's praises** петь кому́-л дифира́мбы; *CQ* **he'll ~ another tune** он запоёт по-друго́му

vi петь; **to ~ in/out of tune** петь чи́сто/фальши́во; **let's ~** дава́йте споём; **he started ~ing** он запе́л; **he couldn't ~ to the end** он не смог допе́ть до конца́; **just listen to the birds ~ing away** послу́шай, как пти́цы распе́лись; **the kettle is ~ing** ча́йник заки-па́ет

sing out *vi*: **~ out, basses, you can't be heard** басы́, гро́мче, вас не слы́шно; *fig CQ* **~ out if you need anything** кри́кни, е́сли что́-нибудь бу́дет ну́жно.

singe *vt* пали́ть (о-, с-); **the iron ~d the cloth** утю́г спали́л ткань; **the moth ~d its wings** мотылёк опали́л себе́ кры́лья.

singer *n* пев́ец, певи́ца.

singing *n* пе́ние.

single *adj* (*sole*) оди́н, еди́ный; (*alone*) одино́кий; (*separate*) отде́льный; **there isn't a ~ ticket left** не оста́лось ни одного́/ни еди́ного биле́та; **there wasn't a ~ soul there** там не́ было ни души́; **not a ~ person dared to speak out** ни оди́н не осме́лился вы́ступить; **the ~ life** одино́кая жизнь; **he is ~** он не жена́т; **they have a ~ aim** у них еди́ная цель; **two ~ rooms** два отде́льных но́мера; **a ~ sock** непа́рный носо́к; (*emphatic*): **every ~ day** ка́ждый день; **every ~ book I looked at cost more than £5** все кни́ги, что я смотре́л, сто́или бо́льше пяти́ фу́нтов ка́ждая.

single out *vt*: **he was ~d out to represent the school** его́ вы́брали представля́ть шко́лу; **they ~d him out as an example** его́ поста́вили в приме́р.

single-breasted *adj* одноб́ортный.

single-handed *adj*: **his ~ efforts** его́ односторо́нние уси́лия.

single-handed *adv*: **he sailed the boat ~** он оди́н управля́л ло́дкой.

single-lane *adj*: **~ traffic** одноря́дное движе́ние.

single-minded *adj* целенапра́вленный.

singles *npl Sport*: **ladies' ~** же́нские одино́чные соревнова́ния.

single-seater *n* (*car, plane*) одноме́стный автомоби́ль/самолёт.

single-track *adj Rail* одноколе́йный.

singly *adv* по отде́льности; **he interviewed us ~** он нас при́нял ка́ждого по отде́льности.

singular *n Gram* еди́нственное число́.

singular *adj* **1** *Gram* в еди́нственном числе́

2 (*exceptional*) исключи́тельный; (*odd*) стра́нный.

singularly *adv*: **that was a ~ inappropriate remark** э́то бы́ло ска́зано совсе́м не к ме́сту, э́то бы́ло в вы́сшей сте́пени неуме́стное замеча́ние.

sinister *adj* (*ominous*) злове́щий; (*malicious*) злой.

sink *n* (ку́хонная) ра́ковина; **I spend half my life at the (kitchen) ~** *equiv* я полжи́зни провожу́ у плиты́.

sink *vti vt* **1** (*a ship*) (*scuttle*) затоп|ля́ть (-и́ть); (*by torpedo, etc.*) топи́ть (по-); *fig*: **he was sunk in thought** он был погружён в размышле́ния (*pl*); *CQ* **if she hears about it, I'm sunk** е́сли она́ узна́ет об э́том, я поги́б/я пропа́л

2 (*by digging*): **to ~ a mine/a well/a hole** рыть ша́хту/коло́дец/я́му (вы-); **to ~ a post into the ground** врыть столб в зе́млю (*usu pf*); *fig* **he sank a lot of money in this venture** он ухло́пал у́йму де́нег в э́то предприя́тие

vi **1** тону́ть (за- (*of ship*), у- (*of person*)); **wood doesn't ~** де́рево в воде́ не то́нет; **the box sank to the bottom like a stone** я́щик пошёл ка́мнем ко дну

2 (*fall*) опус|ка́ться (-ти́ться); *fig* па́дать (упа́сть); **he sank to his knees/into a chair** он опусти́лся на коле́ни/в кре́сло; **the sun sank behind the horizon** со́лнце опусти́лось за горизо́нт; **he sank to his waist in snow** он провали́лся в снег по по́яс; *fig*: **my heart sank at the thought** у меня́ се́рдце упа́ло при э́той мы́сли; **he has sunk in my estimation** он упа́л в мои́х глаза́х; **to ~ into poverty/debt** впасть в нищету́, увя́знуть в долга́х; **he sank into a heavy sleep/deep depression** он погрузи́лся в тяжёлый сон, он впал в меланхо́лию; **his courage sank to his boots** у него́ се́рдце в пя́тки ушло́; **the pound has sunk to a new low** фунт обесце́нился как никогда́ ра́ньше; **his voice sank to a whisper** он перешёл на шёпот; *CQ* **I wanted to ~ through the floor** я гото́в был сквозь зе́млю провали́ться

3 (*subside*) осе|да́ть (-́сть); **the foundations have sunk** фунда́мент (*sing*) осе́л

sink in *vi* впит|ываться в + *A* (-а́ться); **the paint will ~ in over night** за́ ночь кра́ска впита́ется; *fig* **it looks as if our warnings have sunk in** похо́же, они́ вня́ли на́шим предостереже́ниям.

sinker *n* грузи́ло.

sinus *n Anat* га́йморова по́лость.

sip *vt*: **she ~ped her coffee** она́ пила́ ко́фе ма́ленькими глотка́ми; **to ~ wine** потя́гивать вино́.

siphon *vt, also* **to ~ off** отка́ч|ивать (-а́ть); **he ~ed (off) some petrol from the tank** он откача́л бензи́н из ба́ка.

sir *n* (*English title*) сэр; **yes, ~** да, сэр, *Mil* так то́чно; **Dear S.** (*in letters*) уважа́емый господи́н.

sire *vt Agric*: **this stallion ~d twenty champions** э́тот жеребе́ц—оте́ц двадцати́ чемпио́нов.

siren *n* сирéна (*in all senses*).

sissy *n CQ* нéженка, мáменькин сынóк.

sister *n* сестрá, *also Rel*; *Med* стáршая медици́нская сестрá, *abbr* медсестрá; **little/younger** ~ млáдшая сестрá *or* (*affectionate*) сестрёнка; *attr*: ~ **ship** однотúпное сýдно.

sister-in-law *n* (*wife's sister*) своя́ченица; (*husband's sister*) золóвка; (*brother's wife*) невéстка.

sit *vti vt* **1** сажáть (посади́ть), усá|живать (-ди́ть); **she sat the baby on her knees** онá посади́ла ребёнка на колéни; **to ~ a child at table/in a pram** усади́ть ребёнка за стол/в коля́ску; **he sat her in a chair/an armchair** он усади́л её на стул/в крéсло; **he ~s his horse well** он краси́во сиди́т на лóшади

2 *Univ*: **to ~ an examination** сдавáть экзáмен (*only in impf*)

vi **1** сидéть (по-); (*of motion*) сади́ться (сесть) *see* **sit down; the bird sat on the branch singing** пти́ца сидéла на вéтке и пéла; **the hen is ~ting** (*on eggs*) кýрица сиди́т на яйцáх; **to ~ on a chair/at a table/on a horse** сидéть на стýле/за столóм/на лóшади; **come and ~ by/with me** иди́ посиди́ со мной; **he ~s in Parliament/Congress** он член парлáмента/конгрéсса; *fig*: **the coat ~s badly** пальтó плóхо сиди́т; **cheese ~s heavy on the stomach** сыр тяжёл для желýдка

2 (*of assembly, etc.*) заседáть (*impf*); **the committee ~s tomorrow** коми́ссия заседáет зáвтра

sit about/around *vi*: **I sat about all day waiting** я цéлый день просидéл, дожидáясь; **he ~s about/around in bars drinking** он провóдит дни в бáрах и пьёт

sit back *vi*: **he sat back and did nothing** он прóсто сидéл и ничегó не дéлал

sit down *vti vt*: **~ the guests down** усáживай гостéй; **~ yourself down** сади́сь, усáживайся, присáживайся

vi сади́ться (сесть); **we were ~ting down (to dinner) when...** мы как раз сади́лись за стол, когдá...; **we sat down to a game of cards** мы усéлись за кáрты; **he came and sat down with me** он подсéл ко мне

sit for *vi*: **to ~ for one's portrait** пози́ровать худóжнику (*impf*)

sit in *vi*: **he sat in on the talks (as an observer)** он присýтствовал на переговóрах (в кáчестве наблюдáтеля)

sit on *vi*: **he ~s on our committee** он заседáет в нáшей коми́ссии; *fig*: **they sat on the report** они́ положи́ли доклáд под сукнó; **they sat on my application for ages** они́ дóлго тянýли с отвéтом; *CQ* **he needs to be sat on** егó нáдо постáвить на своё мéсто

sit through *vt*: **I sat through the whole meeting** я вы́сидел всё заседáние до концá

sit up *vi*: **we let the child ~ up a little** мы разреши́ли ребёнку немнóго посидéть; **to ~ up in bed** сидéть в постéли; **~ up straight** сиди́ пря́мо; **we sat up all night with the baby** мы просидéли всю ночь с ребёнком; **I sat up late** я засидéлся допоздна́ (*adv*); **don't ~ up for me, I'll be very late** не жди меня́, я придý óчень пóздно.

sit-down *adj*: **a ~ strike** сидя́чая забастóвка.

site *n* мéсто; **this is the ~ of Caesar's palace** на э́том мéсте стоя́л дворéц Цéзаря; **a building ~** строи́тельный объéкт.

sit-in *n*: **the students have organized a ~** студéнты устрóили сидя́чую демонстрáцию.

sitting *n* (*meeting, etc.*) заседáние; *Art* сеáнс; **second ~ for lunch** вторáя смéна на обéд.

sitting *adj*: **there's ~ room** есть сидя́чие местá (*pl*); **a ~ target** неподви́жная мишéнь, *fig* лёгкая добы́ча.

sitting room *n* гости́ная.

situated *adj* располóженный; **the house is ~ near the sea** дом стои́т на берегý мóря; **I'm awkwardly ~** я в нелóвком положéнии.

situation *n* **1** ситуáция, положéние; **to be in a difficult ~** быть в трýдном положéнии; **the ~ is that...** ситуáция таковá, что...

2 (*job*) мéсто; **"S. vacant/wanted for typist"** «трéбуется машини́стка», «ищý мéсто машини́стки».

six *num* шесть (*G, D, P* шести́, *I* шестью́); *collect* шéстеро; **a "6"** шестёрка [*see grammatical notes under* **four** *and* **five**].

sixteen *num* шестнáдцать [*see* **eleven**].

sixteenth *adj* шестнáдцатый.

sixth *n* шестáя (часть); **5 ~s** пять шесты́х.

sixth *adj* шестóй.

sixtieth *adj* шестидеся́тый.

sixty *num* шестьдеся́т (*G, D, P* шести́десяти, *I* шестью́десятью).

size *n* (*of dimensions*) размéр; (*magnitude*) величинá; **a building of vast ~** здáние огрóмных размéров (*pl*); **he's about your ~** у негó тот же размéр, что и у тебя́; **what ~ are you?, what ~ do you take?** (*for clothes, etc.*) какóй у тебя́ размéр?; **I take ~ 41 shoes** я ношý сóрок пéрвый размéр óбуви; **the coat is a ~ too big for me** э́то пальтó мне великó на размéр; **to cut a board to ~** обрéзать дóску соглáсно размéрам чегó-л; **it's about the ~ of an egg** э́то величинóй с яйцó; **it's drawn to life ~** э́то нарисóвано в натурáльную величинý; **the ~ of the problem** масштáбы (*pl*) проблéмы; *fig* **he cut us down to ~** он постáвил нас на мéсто.

size up *vt*: *fig* **he ~d up the situation** он оцени́л ситуáцию; **I soon ~d him up** я бы́стро пóнял, что он за человéк.

sizeable *adj*: **a ~ sum of money/school** довóльно крýпная сýмма дéнег, большáя шкóла.

sizzle *vi* шипéть (при жáренье) (*impf*).

skate[1] *n Zool* скат.

skate[2] *n* конёк; **(a pair of) ~s** коньки́.

skate[2] *vi* катáться/(*racing*) бéгать на конькáх (*pfs* по-); *fig* **he ~d over/round the issue** он обошёл э́ту проблéму.

skating *n* катáние/(*racing*) бег на конькáх; **free/figure ~** произвóльное/фигýрное катáние.

skein *n* мотóк.

skeleton *n Anat* скелéт, *also fig*; *Tech* каркáс, óстов; **the ~ of a building** каркáс здáния; *fig*: **he is reduced to a ~** он преврати́лся в скелéт; **the family ~, the ~ in the cupboard** семéйная тáйна; *attr*: **~ staff** минимáльный персонáл; **a ~ key** отмы́чка; **a ~ plan/outline** набрóсок плáна, эски́з.

sketch *n Art* зарисóвка, эски́з, набрóсок; *Mus* этю́д; *Theat* скетч; **he made a ~ of the castle** он сдéлал набрóсок зáмка; **a ~ for costumes** эски́з костю́мов; **he gave me a rough ~ of his project** он обрисовáл/набросáл мне свой проéкт в óбщих чертáх.

sketch *vt* дéлать зарисóвку/эски́з/набрóсок (с-); зарисóв|ывать (-áть); (*outline*) набр|áсывать (-осáть).

sketchbook *n* альбóм (для зарисóвок).

sketchy *adj* повéрхностный.

skewer *n* (*for roast*) вéртел; (*for kebabs*) шампу́р.

ski *n* лы́жа; *attr* лы́жный; **~ suit/slopes** лы́жный костю́м/склон (*sing*).

ski *vi* ходи́ть/катáться/(*cross-country racing*) бéгать на лы́жах (*pfs* по-).

skid *n Aut* занóс, юз; (*of wheels spinning in mud*) буксовáние; **how do you correct a ~?** как вы́йти из занóса/ю́за?

skid *vi Aut* за|носи́ть (-нести́) *used impers*, идти́ ю́зом (пойти́); (*of person*) скользи́ть (*impf*); **the car ~ded into a wall** маши́ну занеслó, и онá врéзалась в стéну; **the dog ~ded on the polished floor** собáка скользи́ла по натёртому пóлу.

skier *n* лы́жник; (*cross-country racer*) (лы́жник-)гóнщик.

skiing *n* (*as pastime*) катáние/ходьбá на лы́жах; *Sport* лы́жный спорт.

skijumping *n* прыжки́ (*pl*) на лы́жах с трампли́на.

skilful *adj* умéлый; искýсный; **~ guidance** умéлое руковóдство; **a ~ craftsman/artist** умéлец, искýсный мáстер *or* худóжник.

skilift *n* канáтная дорóга.

skill *n* мастерствó; **a surgeon's ~** мастерствó хиру́рга; **his ~ as a boxer** егó боксёрское мастерствó; **he shows great ~ as a negotiator** он умéло ведёт переговóры.

skilled *adj* óпытный, искýсный; **he is a ~ business man** он óпытен в делáх; **he is ~ in diplomacy** он óпытный/искýсный дипломáт; **a ~ workman** (*as a category*) квалифици́рованный рабóчий; **~ labour** квалифици́рованная рабóчая си́ла.

skim *vti vt* снимáть (снять); **to ~ milk** снять сли́вки с молокá; **to ~ grease off the soup** снять жир с сýпа

vi: **the swallow ~med (over) the water** лáсточка скользи́ла над сáмой водóй; *fig* **I'll just ~ through my notes** я тóлько пробегý мои́ зáписи.

skimp *vti vt*: **don't ~ material/the sugar** не жалéй материáла/сáхара

vi скупи́ться (по-); эконóмить (*only in impf*).

skimpy *adj* скýдный; **a ~ supper** скýдный ýжин; **a ~ dress** узковáтое плáтье.

skin *n* **1** кóжа; (*fur of large animal*) шкýра, *also fig*, (*of small*) шкýрка; **he's only ~ and bones** от негó остáлись кóжа да кóсти; **I can't wear wool next to the ~** я не могý носи́ть шерсть на гóлое тéло; **we got wet to the ~** мы промóкли до ни́тки; **a bear ~** медвéжья шкýра; *fig* **to save one's ~** спасáть свою́ шкýру; *CQ*: **we made it by the ~ of our teeth** мы чýдом тудá добрали́сь; **he gets under my ~** он мне дéйствует на нéрвы.

2 (*for water, wine*) бурдю́к, мех

3 (*of apple, banana, lemon, potato*) кожурá; (*of grape, tomato*) кóжица; (*on boiled milk, etc.*) плёнка, пéнка.

skin *vt* (*animals*) снимáть шкýру с + *G* (снять); (*to skin and clean*) свежевáть (о-); **to ~ a rabbit** свежевáть крóлика; **I ~ned my knee** я ободрáл себé колéно; *fig CQ* **keep your eyes ~ned** смотри́ в óба.

skin-deep *adj fig* повéрхностный, неглубóкий.

skin diver *n* аквалангúст.

skinflint *n* скря́га.

skinny *adj* тóщий.

skintight *adj*: **her jeans are ~** на ней джи́нсы в обтя́жку.

skip *n* прыжóк, скачóк; **with a hop, ~ and a jump** подпры́гивая.

skip *vti vt* (*miss*) пропус|кáть (-ти́ть); **let's ~ the next chapter** давáй пропýстим слéдующую главý; **to ~ school** прогуля́ть урóки (*pl*); **I ~ped lunch today** сегóдня я не обéдал; **I ~ped a grade/class at school** я перескочи́л чéрез класс

vi пры́г|ать (-нуть), скакáть (*impf*); (*with rope*) пры́гать со скакáлкой (*only in impf*); (*frolic: of lambs, children*) резви́ться (*impf*); *fig* **he ~ped from one subject to another** он перескáкивал с однóй тéмы на другýю.

skipper *n Naut* шки́пер; *Sport* капитáн; *CQ* хозя́ин, начáльник.

skipping rope *n* скакáлка.

skirmish *n* сты́чка, *also fig*.

skirt *n* ю́бка; (*of coat*) полá; (*of dress*) подóл; **the boy clung to her ~s** мáльчик держáлся за её подóл (*sing*).

skirt *vt* об|ходи́ть (-ойти́); объ|езжáть (-éхать); **we ~ed the town to the south** мы объéхали гóрод с ю́га; **the path ~s the forest** тропи́нка идёт вдоль опýшки.

skirting (board) *n* пли́нтус.

ski run *n* лыжня́.

skit *n* парóдия; **a ~ on Hamlet** парóдия на Гáмлета; **a student's ~** (студéнческий) капýстник.

skittle *n* кéгля; **to play ~s** игрáть в кéгли; *attr*: **~ alley** кегельбáн.

skulk *vi* крáсться (*impf*); **he ~ed around the house** он крáлся по дóму; **the thief ~ed about, waiting his moment** вор притаи́лся, выжидáя удóбный *or* подходя́щий момéнт/и ждал своегó чáса.

skull *n* чéреп; ~ **and crossbones** чéреп и кóсти.

skunk *n Zool* вонючка, скунс; *sl* подлéц, дрянь.

sky *n* нéбо; **sunny skies** сóлнечное нéбо (*sing*); *fig* **to praise smb to the skies** превозноси́ть когó-л до небéс.

sky-blue *adj* лазýрный.

sky-high *adv*: **prices rose** ~ цéны рéзко подскочи́ли.

skylark *n* (полевóй) жáворонок.

skylight *n* световóй люк.

skyline *n* ли́ния горизóнта; (*of building, city*) кóнтур, очертáния (*pl*).

skyscraper *n* (*UK, US, etc.*) небоскрёб; (*SU*) высóтное здáние, высóтный дом.

slab *n*: **a marble/stone** ~ мрáморная/кáменная плитá; **a great** ~ **of meat/chocolate** большóй кусóк мя́са, большáя пли́тка шоколáда.

slack *n* **1**: **to haul in/take up the** ~ (**of a rope**) натянýть полýчше верёвку
2 *pl* (~**s**) брю́ки.

slack *adj* (*not taut*) слáбый; (*without energy*) вя́лый; (*of person, behaviour*) расхля́банный; ~ **muscles** вя́лые мы́шцы; **trade is** ~ **today** торгóвля сегóдня идёт вя́ло; **a** ~ **rope** плóхо натя́нутая верёвка; ~ **discipline** слáбая дисципли́на; **they are** ~ **about their work** они́ рабóтают кóе-кáк.

slack *vi*: **he's been** ~**ing of late** послéднее врéмя он стал мéньше старáться/чтó-то лени́ться.

slacken *vti vt*, *also* **to** ~ **off** ослаб|ля́ть (-́ить); **to** ~ (**off**) **a rope/pressure/tension** ослáбить канáт/нажи́м/напряжéние; **to** ~ **pace** (*of person*) замедл|я́ть ход/(*of car, boat, etc.*) сбав|ля́ть скóрость *or* ход (*pfs* -́ить)
vi: **the rope** ~**ed** верёвка ослáбла; **the wind/tension** ~**ed** вéтер стих, напряжéние спáло; **demand for this** ~**s over the summer** в лéтний перúод спрос (на э́то) пáдает.

slacker *n* лóдырь (*m*).

slag *n* шлак, окáлина; *attr*: ~ **heap** шлáковая горá.

slake *vt*: **to** ~ **one's thirst** утол|я́ть жáжду (-и́ть).

slam *vti vt* хлóп|ать + *I* (-нуть), захлóп|ывать (-нуть); **he** ~**med the door** (**in my face**) он хлóпнул двéрью, он захлóпнул дверь у меня́ пéред нóсом; **she** ~**med the plate down on the table** онá швырнýла тарéлку на стол; **he** ~**med down the receiver** он брóсил трýбку; **I** ~**med on the brakes** я рéзко затормози́л
vi захлóпываться; **the door** ~**med** (**shut/to**) дверь захлóпнулась; **doors were** ~**ming in the wind** двéри хлóпали от вéтра.

slander *n* клеветá.

slander *vt* клеветáть на + *A* (на-).

slanderous *adj* клеветни́ческий.

slang *n* жаргóн; сленг; **army** ~ армéйский жаргóн/сленг; **to use** ~ говори́ть на жаргóне; *attr* жаргóнный.

slanging *adj*: **a** ~ **match** перебрáнка.

slant *n* наклóн; уклóн, *also fig*; **the** ~ **of the road** уклóн дорóги; **the steep** ~ **of the roof** скат кры́ши; **the gentle** ~ **of the hill** отлóгий склон холмá; *fig*: **the school has a** ~ **towards science** э́та шкóла с наýчным уклóном; **his mind has a curious** ~ у негó необы́чный склад умá.

slanted *adj* (*of news, etc.*) тенденциóзный.

slant-eyed *adj* с раскóсыми глазáми.

slanting *adj* косóй; ~ **rain** косóй дождь; **a** ~ **desk/roof** наклóнная пáрта/кры́ша.

slantwise *adv* наклóнно, кóсо.

slap *n* шлепóк; **to give smb a** ~ **in the face** дать комý-л пощёчину, *CQ* влепи́ть комý-л оплеýху; *fig* **that was a** ~ **in the face for me** э́то бы́ло мне как пощёчина.

slap *adv CQ* пря́мо, тóчно; ~ **into the middle** пря́мо/тóчно в середи́ну.

slap *vt* шлёп|ать (-нуть), хлóп|ать (-нуть); **he** ~**ped his hand** он хлóпнул егó по рукé

slap down *vt*: **he** ~**ped the book down on the table** он швырнýл кни́гу на стол; *fig* **if you speak out of turn, you'll be** ~**ped down** éсли бýдешь всё врéмя вылезáть, тебя́ осáдят

slap on *vt CQ*: **to** ~ **paint on the walls** заля́пать стéны крáской; **they've** ~**ped on a surcharge to** они́ ввели́ дополни́тельную плáту за + *A*.

slapdash *adj*: **she's a** ~ **worker** онá небрéжна в рабóте; **it's a** ~ **job** э́то сдéлано кóе-кáк/на авóсь.

slapstick comedy *n* фарс, балагáн.

slap-up *adj CQ*: **he gave us a** ~ **dinner** он угости́л нас шикáрным обéдом.

slash *vt* (*with knife, whip*) полосовáть (ис-); (*with whip*) хлест|áть (-нýть); *Sew* дéлать разрéзы (с-); **he** ~**ed my shoulder with a knife** он полоснýл меня́ ножóм по плечý; *fig*: **to** ~ **prices/salaries** си́льно сни|жáть цéны (-́зить), урез|áть зарплáту (-́ать); **to** ~ **the text of a speech** си́льно сокра|щáть текст рéчи (-ти́ть); **the critics** ~**ed his book** кри́тики разнесли́ егó кни́гу.

slat *n* плáнка, филёнка.

slate *n* **1** *Geol* слáнец; (*for roof*) ши́фер; **a** ~ ши́ферная пли́тка; (*in school*) гри́фельная доскá; *fig* **let's wipe the** ~ **clean** давáй забýдем прóшлое; *attr* слáнцевый; ши́ферный
2 (*colour*) цвет слáнца, гри́фельный цвет.

slate *vt CQ* (*criticize*): **the play was** ~**d in the press** пьéсу раскритиковáли в печáти в пух и прах; (*US*) **Smith has been** ~**d for mayor** Сми́та выдвигáют на пост мэ́ра.

slaughter *n* (*of people*) резня́, бóйня; (*of animals*) убóй; ~ **on the roads** смéртность на дорóгах.

slaughter *vt* (*animals*) заби|вáть (-́ть), рéзать (за-); **all the villagers were** ~**ed** всех жи́телей дерéвни уби́ли.

slaughterhouse *n* (ското)бóйня.

Slav *n* славяни́н, славя́нка.

Slav *adj* славя́нский.

slave *n* раб, *also fig*; *fig* **she is the ~ of habit/of fashion** она́ раб привы́чки, она́ ра́бски сле́дует мо́де; *attr*: **~ driver** надсмо́трщик.

slave *vti CQ* рабо́тать как про́клятый; **to ~ away at the accounts** погиба́ть над счета́ми.

Slavonic *adj* славя́нский; *as n* **Old/Church ~** старославя́нский/церковнославя́нский язы́к.

slaw *n* (*US*) сала́т из све́жей капу́сты.

sled, sledge *n* (*for transport*) са́ни (*no sing*), (*for children*) са́нки, сала́зки (*no sings*).

sledgehammer *n* кува́лда.

sleek *adj* (*of hair, fur*) лосня́щийся; **a ~ cat/horse** хо́леная ко́шка/ло́шадь.

sleep *n* сон; *Zool* **winter ~** зи́мняя спя́чка; **a dead/deep/heavy ~** мёртвый/кре́пкий/тяжё-лый сон; **to go to ~** засну́ть; **I had a broken ~** я спал уры́вками; **I had a good/bad night's ~** я хорошо́ вы́спался, я пло́хо спал; **she walked in her ~ last night** сего́дня [NB] но́чью она́ ходи́ла во сне; **he talks in his ~** он разгова́ривает во сне; **this pill will put you to ~** от э́той табле́тки ты уснёшь; *fig*: **my leg has gone to ~** у меня́ нога́ затекла́; *euph* **to put a cat to ~** усыпи́ть ко́шку.

sleep *vi* спать (по-); **I slept lightly/like a log** я спал чу́тко, я спал как уби́тый; **I slept for 8 hours/the clock round** я спал во́семь часо́в, я проспа́л двена́дцать часо́в кря́ду; **I didn't ~ a wink** я глаз не сомкну́л; **I slept at their place** я у них переночева́л; *euph*: **they ~ together** они́ любо́вники; **she ~s around** она́ гуля́ет с кем попа́ло

sleep in *vi*: **does the cook ~ in?** по́вар у них живёт?; **I slept in this morning** я сего́дня проспа́л (*overslept*)/отсыпа́лся (*had a long lie*)

sleep off *vi*: **she's ~ing off the anaesthetic** она́ ещё спит по́сле нарко́за; **I slept off my headache** я поспа́л, и голова́ переста́ла боле́ть

sleep on *vi*: **don't decide now, ~ on it** не реша́й сейча́с, у́тро ве́чера мудрене́е

sleep out *vi*: **he's ~ing out just now** сейча́с он не ночу́ет до́ма (*i.e. away from home*)/ он спит на откры́том во́здухе (*outside*)

sleep through *vt*: **I slept through the alarm** я не услы́шал буди́льника; **I can ~ through any amount of noise** мне шум не меша́ет спать.

sleeper *n Rail* (*on track*) шпа́ла; (*berth*) спа́льное ме́сто.

sleepiness *n* сонли́вость.

sleeping *adj*: **~ bag/car/pill** спа́льный мешо́к/ваго́н, снотво́рное *or* снотво́рная табле́тка.

sleepless *adj* бессо́нный; **I had a ~ night** я провёл бессо́нную ночь.

sleepwalker *n* сомна́мбула, луна́тик (*of man or woman*).

sleepy *adj* со́нный, *also fig*; сонли́вый; **a ~ little town** со́нный городо́к.

sleepyhead *n CQ* со́ня.

sleet *n* мо́крый снег.

sleeve *n* рука́в; (*of record*) конве́рт; *fig* **I've something up my ~** у меня́ есть ко́е-что про запа́с.

slender *adj* то́нкий; **a ~ waist/girl/figure** то́нкая та́лия, то́ненькая де́вушка, стро́йная фигу́ра; *fig*: **~ resources/means** ску́дные запа́сы/сре́дства; **a ~ chance** маловероя́тная возмо́жность; **a ~ excuse/hope** сла́бая отгово́рка/наде́жда.

sleuth *n CQ* сы́щик, детекти́в.

slice *n* ломо́ть (*m*), ло́мтик; *Cook* лопа́точка; **thin ~s of bread/lemon** то́нкие ло́мтики хле́ба/лимо́на; *fig CQ*: **he took a good ~ of the profit** он сорва́л хоро́ший куш; **a ~ of luck** полоса́ уда́ч.

slice *vt* нарез|а́ть (ло́мтиками) (-́ать); **he ~d the loaf in two** он разре́зал бато́н попола́м (*adv*); **he ~d off a piece of meat** он отре́зал кусо́к мя́са; **to ~ up a cake/sausage** наре́зать торт/колбасу́; **~d bread** наре́занный хлеб; *Sport* **to ~ a ball** сре́зать мяч (*usu pf*).

slicer *n* ломтере́зка.

slick *n*: **an oil ~** плёнка не́фти.

slick *adj pejor* ло́вкий; ско́льзкий; **a ~ salesman/answer** ло́вкий продаве́ц, бо́йкий отве́т; **he's the ~ type** он ско́льзкий тип.

slicker *n*: **a city ~** пижо́н.

slide *n* (*in playground*) де́тская го́рка; *Photo* диапозити́в, слайд; (*for microscope*) предме́тное стекло́.

slide *vti vt*: *Aut* **~ the seat forward** вы́двинь сиде́нье вперёд; **~ the drawer back** задви́нь я́щик; *fig* **they've let things ~ in the office** в конто́ре все дела́ запу́щены

vi скольз|и́ть (-ну́ть) *and compounds*; **the children are sliding on the ice** де́ти ката́ются по льду; **I slid on the ice and fell** я поскользну́лся на льду и упа́л; **the music slid off the piano** но́ты соскользну́ли с роя́ля; **he slid down the banisters/the sand dune/from the tree** он съе́хал вниз по пери́лам/с дю́ны, он слез с де́рева; **the drawers ~ in and out easily** я́щики хорошо́ задвига́ются и выдвига́ются.

slide rule *n* логарифми́ческая лине́йка.

sliding *adj*: **a ~ scale** скользя́щая шкала́; **a ~ door/***Aut* **seat** задвижна́я дверь, подвижно́е сиде́нье.

slight *n* униже́ние; **it was a ~ on all of us** э́то бы́ло унизи́тельно для всех нас.

slight *adj* (*small*) небольшо́й; (*unimportant*) незначи́тельный; лёгкий; (*slim*) то́нкий; **a ~ mistake** небольша́я оши́бка; **I have a ~ cold** у меня́ лёгкая просту́да; **a ~ figure** то́ненькая фигу́рка; **this knife is not the ~est use** э́тот нож совсе́м не ре́жет; **it's not the ~est use grumbling** что то́лку ворча́ть; **he wasn't in the ~est offended** он ни ка́пельки не оби́делся.

slight *vt* оби|жа́ть (-́деть), (*stronger*) уни|жа́ть (-́зить).

slighting *adj* оби́дный, оскорби́тельный.

slightly *adv* **1: I know him ~/only ~** я его́ немно́го зна́ю, я его́ почти́ не зна́ю

2: she's ~ built она́ хру́пкого сложе́ния.

slim *adj* (*slender*) то́нкий, стро́йный; **she's got ~mer** она́ ста́ла стройне́е; **a ~ volume**

of poems то́ненькая кни́жка стихо́в; *fig*: **he was convicted on the ~mest of evidence** его́ призна́ли вино́вным, хотя́ ули́к почти́ не́ было; **his chances of success are very ~** у него́ ма́ло ша́нсов на успе́х.

slim *vi* худе́ть (по-).

slime *n* ил; (*of snail*) слизь.

slimming *adj*: **a ~ diet/exercises** дие́та для похуде́ния, упражне́ния, что́бы похуде́ть; **your skirt is ~** э́та ю́бка тебя́ худи́т.

slimy *adj* ско́льзкий и ли́пкий.

sling *n Med* повя́зка; **he has his arm in a ~** у него́ рука́ на пе́ревязи.

sling *vt* (*throw*) швыр|я́ть (-ну́ть); **the boys were ~ing stones at a tin** ма́льчики швыря́ли камня́ми по ба́нке; **he slung his rifle over his shoulder** он наде́л винто́вку на плечо́; **to ~ up a hammock** подве́|шивать гама́к (-сить); *CQ* **he was slung out of the pub** его́ вы́швырнули из пивно́й.

slink *vt*: **to ~ away/off** ускольз|а́ть (-ну́ть), улизну́ть (*pf*); **to ~ in/out** проскользну́ть, вы́скользнуть (*pfs*); **he slunk about the house** он кра́лся по до́му.

slip *n* **1**: *CQ* **he gave me the ~** он улизну́л от меня́

2 (*error*) про́мах, оши́бка; **he made a ~** он оши́бся; **it was a silly ~** э́то был оби́дный про́мах; **a ~ of the tongue/pen** обмо́лвка, опи́ска

3 (*for pillow*) на́волочка; (*petticoat*) комбина́ция

4: **a ~ of paper** поло́ска бума́ги.

slip *vti vt* скольз|и́ть (-ну́ть) *and compounds*; **he ~ped his arm round my waist/through mine** он о́бнял меня́ за та́лию, он взял меня́ по́д руку; **I ~ped him a fiver** я су́нул ему́ пять фу́нтов; **it ~ped my memory** э́то вы́скользнуло у меня́ из па́мяти, у меня́ вы́летело э́то из головы́; **it ~ped his attention** э́то ускользну́ло от его́ внима́ния; **to ~ a stitch** снима́ть пе́тлю (снять)

vi скользи́ть; поскользну́ться (*pf*); **the ring ~s along the rope** кольцо́ скользи́т по верёвке; **the clutch ~ped** сцепле́ние пробуксова́ло; **he ~ped on the stairs** он поскользну́лся на ле́стнице; **don't let this chance ~** не упуска́й э́той возмо́жности; **he let ~ that...** он проговори́лся, что...

slip away *vi*: **I'll ~ away early** я уйду́ незаме́тно пора́ньше; **they ~ped away while I was in the kitchen** они́ улизну́ли, пока́ я был на ку́хне

slip in/into *vti vt*: **I ~ped the letter into her hand** я отда́л письмо́ ей в ру́ки (*pl*); **I ~ped in a good word for him** я замо́лвил за него́ слове́чко

vi: **he ~ped into Russian** он незаме́тно перешёл на ру́сский; **many errors have ~ped into the text** в текст вкра́лось мно́го оши́бок

slip off *vi*: **the shawl ~ped off her shoulders** шаль соскользну́ла у неё с плеч

slip out *vi*: **the knife ~ped out of my hand** нож вы́скользнул у меня́ из рук; **I'll ~ out for some bread** я сбе́гаю за хле́бом; **I let it ~ out without thinking** у меня́ э́то вы́летело нечая́нно

slip over *vt*: **~ a shawl over your shoulders** наки́нь на пле́чи шаль; **~ the life jacket over your head** наде́нь спаса́тельный по́яс че́рез го́лову

slip up *vi*: **he sometimes ~s up on grammar** он иногда́ де́лает граммати́ческие оши́бки; *CQ* **he ~ped up badly on this one** тут он сде́лал серьёзную прома́шку.

slipknot *n*: **to tie with a ~** завяза́ть скользя́щим узло́м.

slipper *n* ко́мнатная ту́фля/та́почка.

slippery *adj* ско́льзкий, *also fig*; *fig*: **we're on ~ ground** мы вступи́ли на ско́льзкий путь; *CQ* **he's a ~ customer** он ско́льзкий тип.

slipshod *adj* неря́шливый; небре́жный.

slipstream *n Aer* возду́шный пото́к.

slip-up *n CQ*: **there's been a ~ somewhere** здесь где́-то оши́бка.

slit *n* (*chink*) щель; **the ~ of a letter box** щель почто́вого я́щика; **her eyes are like ~s** у неё глаза́ как щёлочки; **a skirt with ~s** ю́бка с разре́зами.

slit *vt* разрез|а́ть (-́ать); **to ~ an envelope open** разреза́ть конве́рт.

slither *vi* скользи́ть (*usu impf*); **I ~ed on the mud** я скользи́л по гря́зи; **the fish ~ed back into the water/out of my hands** ры́ба скользну́ла обра́тно в во́ду/вы́скользнула у меня́ из рук.

sliver *n* (*of wood*) ще́пка, лучи́на; (*of metal, glass*) оско́лок; (*of meat*) кусо́чек.

slobber *vi* пус|ка́ть слю́ни (-ти́ть); слюня́вить (*usu impf*).

sloe *n* ди́кая сли́ва; *attr*: **~ gin** сливя́нка.

slog *vi CQ*: **we'll have to ~ to get finished in time** (нам) на́до поднажа́ть, что́бы во́время зако́нчить; **I ~ged away at German/in the garden all morning** я всё у́тро зубри́л неме́цкий/труди́лся в саду́.

slogan *n* ло́зунг.

slop *vti vt*: **he ~ped paint all over the floor** он заля́пал кра́ской весь пол

vi вы|плёскиваться (-́плеснуться); **the tea ~ped over into the saucer** чай вы́плеснулся на блю́дечко; *fig* **she ~s around the house in an old dressing gown** она́ слоня́ется по до́му в ста́ром хала́те.

slope *n* (*down*) склон, укло́н; отко́с, спуск; **the ~ of a roof** скат кры́ши; **the angle of ~** у́гол пока́тости; **the car got stuck on the ~** (*going up*) маши́на застря́ла на подъёме.

slope *vi*: **his handwriting ~s backwards** он пи́шет с накло́ном вле́во; **the garden ~s down to the river** сад спуска́ется к реке́; **the roof/road ~s steeply** кры́ша име́ет круто́й скат, доро́га кру́то спуска́ется; *CQ* **to ~ off** смы|ва́ться (-́ться).

sloping *adj* (*of roof, shoulder, etc.*) пока́тый; **a ~ garden** сад, располо́женный на скло́не; **~ writing** накло́нный по́черк.

slop pail *n* помо́йное ведро́.

sloppy *adj* (*slovenly*) неряшливый, небрежный; *fig* (*sentimental*) сентиментальный.

slops *npl* (*food*) пойло (*sing*); (*dirty water*) помои.

slosh *vt CQ*: **he ~ed water over the steps/paint on the door** он выплеснул воду на крыльцо, он заляпал краской дверь (*usu pfs*).

sloshed *adj CQ*: **to get ~** напиться, надраться.

slot *n* (*of machine*) щель (автомата); *fig CQ* **we must find a ~ in the programme for...** надо найти место в программе для + *G*; *attr*: **~ machine** (*for cigarettes, etc.*) (торговый)/(*at fair*) игральный автомат.

slouch *vi* (*standing*) сутулиться, (*sitting*) горбиться (*pfs* с-); **to ~ about/around** болтаться/слоняться без дела (*impfs*).

slovenly *adj* неряшливый.

slow *adj* **1** (*in moving, working*) медленный, небыстрый; **his progress is ~** его работа продвигается медленно; **it's ~ going** (*of walking*) здесь тяжело идти, (*of work*) дело идёт медленно; **to walk/work at a ~ pace** ходить медленным шагом, работать в замедленном темпе; **a ~ pulse** замедленный пульс; **a ~ oven** медленный огонь (в духовке); **to cook on a ~ flame** варить на медленном/слабом огне; **a ~ poison** медленно действующий яд; **a ~ train** поезд со всеми остановками; *Sport* **it was a ~ game** игра была вялая; *Photo* **a ~ film** малочувствительная плёнка; *fig* **business is ~** дела идут неважно

2 (*not prompt, backward*) медленный, медлительный; **he's very ~** (*physically*) он очень медлительный, (*mentally*) он медленно/туго соображает; **he's a ~ developer** у него замедленное развитие; **he is ~ of speech/to anger** он говорит не торопясь, его нелегко вывести из себя; **he was ~ to answer/in getting the tickets** он медлил с ответом/с покупкой билетов; **he was not ~ to notice** он тут же/*CQ* с ходу заметил; *fig*: **my watch is ~** мои часы отстают; **the clock was 5 minutes ~** часы отставали на пять минут.

slow *adv*: **after her illness she'll have to go ~** после болезни ей надо меньше двигаться; **go ~ with your decision** не торопись с решением; (*in industry*) **to go ~** снизить темп работы.

slow *vti vt*, *also* **to ~ down/up** замедл|ять (-ить); задерж|ивать (-ать); **to ~ down one's pace** замедлить/сбавить ход/шаг; **the roadworks ~ed down the traffic** дорожные работы замедлили движение транспорта

vi замедляться; (*of car, train, etc.*) сбав|лять ход/скорость (-ить); **the traffic ~ed down** движение замедлилось; **the train ~ed to a halt** поезд замедлил ход и остановился; **he ~ed down/up before the turning** он сбавил скорость перед поворотом; **he'll have to ~ up** ему придётся сбавить темп.

slowcoach *n* копуша (*m and f*).

slowmotion *n Cine* замедленная съёмка.

slow-witted *adj* туповатый.

slug *n Zool* слизняк; (*bullet*) пуля; *CQ* **a ~ of whisky** глоток виски.

sluggard *n* лентяй, лежебока (*m and f*).

sluggish *adj* (*of person*) медлительный; (*of person, mind*) неповоротливый; (*of character, reactions, business, pulse*) вялый; **a ~ river** медленно текущая река; **~ circulation** замедленная циркуляция; **the engine is ~** *CQ* мотор не тянет.

sluice *n* **1** шлюз; *attr*: **~ gates** шлюзные ворота

2 (*in hospital*) мойка.

sluice *vt*, *also* **to ~ down/out**: **I ~d out the drain with boiling water** я промыл слив кипятком; **he ~d down the decks** он окатил палубу водой.

slum *n* трущоба; *attr*: **~ clearance** снос трущоб.

slumber *n* сон, дремота (*only in sings*).

slumber *vi* спать (по-); дремать (за-).

slump *n* резкое падение, спад; **a ~ in oil production/prices** резкий спад добычи нефти, резкое падение цен на нефть; **a ~ in shares** падение акций.

slump *vi* **1** (*of prices, etc.*) резко падать (упасть)

2 (*fall heavily*): **he ~ed into a chair** он повалился в кресло.

slur *n* (*on reputation*) пятно; *Mus* лига; **to cast a ~ on smb** порочить кого-л.

slur *vt*: **his speech is ~red** у него невнятная речь

slur over *vt* (*try to conceal*): **he ~red over the painful subject** он обошёл молчанием этот наболевший вопрос.

slush *n* слякоть; *fig CQ* сентиментальный вздор.

slushy *adj* слякотный; **it's ~ today** сегодня слякоть.

slut *n* неряха, грязнуля (*both m and f*).

sluttish *adj* неряшливый.

sly *n*: **on the ~** украдкой, потихоньку (*advs*).

sly *adj* хитрый; *CQ* **he's a ~ dog** он хитрая/продувная бестия.

smack[1] *n* (*slap*) шлепок, хлопок; **he gave the ball a hard ~** он сильно ударил по мячу; *fig CQ* **it was a ~ in the eye for them** для них это было как пощёчина.

smack[1] *adv* прямо; **~ in the middle** прямо в середине; **he kissed her ~ on the lips** он её поцеловал прямо в губы; **he ran ~ into the wall** он врезался в стену.

smack[1] *vt* шлёп|ать, хлоп|ать (*pfs* -нуть); **he ~ed the paper down on the table** он швырнул газету на стол; **she ~ed his face/the child's bottom** она дала ему пощёчину, она отшлёпала ребёнка; **to ~ one's lips** чмок|ать губами (-нуть).

smack[2] *n*: **a ~ of garlic** привкус чеснока.

smack[2] *vi*: **to ~ of** (*of taste*) иметь привкус + *G*, *fig* отдавать + *I* (*only in impf*).

smack[3] *n*, *also* **fishing ~** смэк, небольшое рыбачье судно.

smacking *n*: **he needs a good ~** его́ ну́жно хороше́нько отшлёпать.

small *n*: **the ~ of the back** поясни́ца; *CQ pl* (**~s**) (*underclothes*) (ни́жнее) бельё.

small *adj* ма́ленький, небольшо́й; (*small-scale*) ме́лкий; (*petty*) ме́лочный; **a ~ girl** (ма́ленькая) де́вочка; **a ~ house** ма́ленький дом, до́мик; **a ~ town** небольшо́й го́род, городо́к; **a ~ dose** ма́лая до́за; **on a ~ scale** в ма́лом масшта́бе; **the jacket is too ~/on the ~ side for me** пиджа́к мне мал/малова́т; **~ farmers** ме́лкие фе́рмеры; **a ~ business** небольшо́е де́ло, ме́лкое предприя́тие; **~ print** ме́лкий шрифт; *fig*: **it's a ~ matter of money** э́то лишь вопро́с де́нег; **be thankful for ~ mercies** благодари́ судьбу́ за ма́ленькие ра́дости жи́зни; **he's a ~ eater** он ма́ло ест; **write it in ~ letters** пиши́ э́то строчны́ми бу́квами; **~ wonder that...** не удиви́тельно, что...; **in my ~ way, I am a poet** како́й уж ни на есть, а всё-таки я поэ́т; **he made me feel/look ~** он меня́ уни́зил.

small-arms *npl* стрелко́вое ору́жие (*collect*).

small hours *npl* (**the ~**) предрассве́тные часы́.

small-minded *adj* ме́лочный, ограни́ченный.

smallpox *n* о́спа.

small-scale *adj* в ма́лом масшта́бе.

small-time *adj CQ*: **a ~ thief** ме́лкий вори́шка.

small-town *adj* провинциа́льный.

smarmy *adj CQ* еле́йный, подобостра́стный.

smart *adj* **1** наря́дный, элега́нтный; мо́дный; фешене́бельный; *CQ* шика́рный; **a ~ coat** мо́дное пальто́; **should I wear something ~?** мне наде́ть что́-нибудь понаря́днее?; **you do look ~ today** ты сего́дня так элега́нтен; **what a ~ car!/house!** кака́я шика́рная маши́на!/ви́лла!; **they live in a ~ neighbourhood** они́ живу́т в фешене́бельном/аристократи́ческом райо́не; **the ~ set** фешене́бельное о́бщество

2 (*clever, cunning*) толко́вый, у́мный; **a ~ answer** толко́вый отве́т; **he thinks it ~ to do that** он ду́мает, что э́то о́чень у́мно́; **he's a ~ chap/(***US***) guy** он толко́вый па́рень; **he's too ~ for me** он для меня́ сли́шком умён; *CQ pejor*: **he's a ~ one** хи́трый чёрт; **a ~ trick** хи́трый/ло́вкий трюк

3 (*prompt*): **and look ~ about it!** и побыстре́й!; **that was ~ work** всё бы́ло ло́вко (*clever*)/бы́стро (*prompt*) сде́лано; **he gave him a ~ box on the ear** он дал ему́ по физионо́мии.

smart *vi* са́днить, щипа́ть (*impfs*); **the wound is ~ing** ра́на са́днит; **my eyes are ~ing** глаза́ щи́плет (*impers*); **the iodine makes the cut ~** ра́ну жжёт/щи́плет (*impers*) от йо́да; *fig* **he was ~ing under her taunts** его́ жгли её насме́шки.

smart-alec(k) *n CQ* у́мник.

smarten up *vi*: **he has ~ed up a lot** он тепе́рь поприли́чнее вы́глядит; **to ~ up for dinner** приоде́ться к у́жину.

smash *n* катастро́фа; (*on road*) ава́рия; *Fin* крах, банкро́тство; (*in tennis*) смэш; (*noise*) гро́хот; **he was killed in a car ~** он поги́б в автомоби́льной катастро́фе/ава́рии.

smash *vti vt* (*break*) разби|ва́ть (-́ть); **he ~ed the bottle against the wall** он разби́л буты́лку о сте́ну; **the waves ~ed the dinghy against the rocks** во́лны разби́ли ло́дку о ска́лы; **the thieves ~ed open the door** во́ры взлома́ли дверь; **to ~ the enemy** разби́ть/сокруши́ть врага́; *Sport* **he ~ed the ball into the net** он погаси́л мяч о се́тку

vi (*break*) разбива́ться; (*collide*) врез|а́ться (-́аться), ста́лкиваться (столкну́ться); *Fin* разор|я́ться (-и́ться); **the plates ~ed on the floor** таре́лки упа́ли на́ пол и разби́лись; **the car ~ed into the lamppost** маши́на вре́залась в фона́рный столб; **the cars ~ed into each other** маши́ны столкну́лись

smash up *vt*: **they ~ed up the café** они́ разгроми́ли кафе́; **he was badly ~ed up in the car crash** он си́льно пострада́л в автомоби́льной ава́рии.

smash-and-grab (raid) *n* граби́тельский налёт (на магази́н).

smashing *adj CQ* потряса́ющий; **we had a ~ time** мы потряса́юще провели́ вре́мя; **she's ~!** сногсшиба́тельная красо́тка!

smattering *n*: **I have a ~ of Chinese** я зна́ю по-кита́йски два-три сло́ва.

smear *n* мазо́к, *also Med*; **a ~ of paint/blood** мазо́к кра́ски/кро́ви; *fig* **a ~ on his reputation** пятно́ на его́ репута́ции; *attr*: *Med* **a ~ test** мазо́к для иссле́дования; *fig* **a ~ campaign** клеветни́ческая кампа́ния.

smear *vt* ма́зать (с-, по-) *and compounds*; **to ~ paint on/all over the walls** вы́мазать сте́ны кра́ской; **he got his hands ~ed with grease** он изма́зал ру́ки в ма́сле.

smell *n* (*sense of smell*) обоня́ние; (*odour*) за́пах; **he/the dog has a keen sense of ~** у него́ то́нкое обоня́ние, у соба́ки то́нкий нюх; **there's a ~ of baking/burning** па́хнет че́м-то печёным/палёным *or* подгоре́вшим; **take/have a ~ and tell me if this milk is sour** поню́хай и скажи́, не ки́сло ли молоко́.

smell *vti vt* (*sense*) чу́вствовать за́пах (по-); (*sniff at*) ню́хать (по-); (*usu of animals*) чу́ять (за́пах) (по-); **can you ~ gas?/burning?** ты чу́вствуешь за́пах га́за?/, что па́хнет палёным?; **animals can ~ danger** живо́тные чу́ют опа́сность; **to ~ a rose** ню́хать ро́зу; **dogs like to ~ each other** соба́ки лю́бят обню́хивать друг дру́га; *fig* **to ~ a rat** чу́ять нела́дное

vi па́хнуть + *I*; **it ~s damp here** здесь па́хнет (*impers*) сы́ростью; **he ~s of garlic** от него́ па́хнет (*impers*) чесноко́м; **this rose ~s sweet** у э́той ро́зы си́льный за́пах; *CQ* **this cheese ~s to high heaven** у э́того сы́ра о́чень о́стрый за́пах; *fig* **it ~s of treachery** тут па́хнет изме́ной.

smelling salts *npl* ню́хательная соль (*sing*).

smelly *adj CQ* воню́чий.

smile *n* улы́бка; **on hearing that, he was all ~s** он услы́шал об э́том, и его́ лицо́ засия́ло улы́бкой; **he broke into a ~** его́ лицо́ расплыло́сь в улы́бке; **that raised a ~ with the audience** э́то вы́звало улы́бку пу́блики.

smile *vti vt*: **he ~d his approval** он улыбну́лся в знак одобре́ния

vi улыб|а́ться (-ну́ться); **he ~d at me/at the thought** он мне улыбну́лся, он улыбну́лся при э́той мы́сли; **keep smiling!** не ве́шай но́са!

smirk *vi* ухмы|ля́ться (-льну́ться).

smithereens *npl*: **to break to/in ~** разби́ть(ся) вдре́безги (*adv*).

smithy *n* ку́зница.

smitten *adj fig*: **he was ~ with remorse** его́ му́чила со́весть; *CQ* **he's badly ~ with her** он от неё без ума́.

smock *n* (*artist's*) блу́за; (*child's*) де́тское пла́тьице в сбо́рочку; (*expectant mother's*) пла́тье для бере́менной.

smog *n* смог.

smoke *n* **1** (*vapour*) дым; **cigar ~** сига́рный дым; **the room is full of tobacco ~** в ко́мнате наку́рено; **there's no ~ without fire** нет ды́ма без огня́; **to go up in ~** (*of a building*) сгоре́ть, *fig* (*in anger*) *CQ* вспыли́ть

2 (*act*): **he likes a ~ after lunch** он лю́бит покури́ть по́сле обе́да; **I'm dying for a ~** умира́ю хочу́ кури́ть; **they're having a break for a ~** у них сейча́с переку́р; *CQ* **I haven't got a ~** у меня́ нет ку́рева.

smoke *vti vt* (*cigars, etc.*) кури́ть (по-, вы́-); (*fish, bacon, glass*) копти́ть (за-); **he ~s cigars/a pipe** он ку́рит сига́ры/тру́бку

vi **1** (*of person*) кури́ть; **do you ~?** ты ку́ришь?; **do you mind if I ~?** вы не возража́ете, е́сли я закурю́?; **he ~s like a chimney** он дыми́т как парово́з

2 (*of fire*) дыми́ть (на-), дыми́ться (*impf*); **the stove ~s badly** печь си́льно дыми́т.

smoked *adj* (*of fish, etc.*) копчёный; **~ glass** ды́мчатое стекло́.

smokeless *adj* безды́мный; **~ fuel** безды́мное то́пливо.

smoker *n* (*person*) кури́льщик, куря́щий; *Rail* ваго́н для куря́щих; **he's a heavy ~** он зая́длый кури́льщик.

smoke screen *n* дымова́я заве́са, *also fig*; **to put up a ~** устро́ить дымову́ю заве́су.

smoke signal *n* дымово́й сигна́л.

smoking *n* **1** куре́ние; **"no ~"** «не кури́ть», «кури́ть воспреща́ется»; *attr*: **~ car/compartment** ваго́н/купе́ для куря́щих

2 (*curing*) копче́ние.

smoky *adj*: **a ~ atmosphere** задымлённая атмосфе́ра; **~ grey** ды́мчато-се́рый; **this whisky has a ~ flavour** ви́ски отдаёт дымко́м.

smooth *adj* **1** (*of surfaces*) гла́дкий; (*of sea*) споко́йный; **a ~ stone** гла́дкий ка́мень; **a ~ face/chin** гла́дкое лицо́, гла́дкий подборо́док; **the ~ surface of the lake** гла́дкая/зерка́льная пове́рхность о́зера; **a ~ road** ро́вная доро́га; **we had a ~ crossing** перее́зд по́ морю прошёл споко́йно; **a ~ sauce** протёртый со́ус; **this tyre has worn ~** *CQ* ши́на совсе́м лы́сая; *Aer* **a ~ descent/take-off** пла́вный спуск/взлёт; *fig* **the bill had a ~ passage** законопрое́кт прошёл гла́дко

2 (*of people, usu pejor*): **~ manners** вкра́дчивые мане́ры; **he has a ~ tongue** он красноба́й; **I don't like these ~ types** я не люблю́ э́тих прили́занных ти́пов.

smooth *vt* пригла́|живать (-дить); **to ~ one's hair** пригла́дить во́лосы; **to ~ a plank with sandpaper** шку́рить до́ску (про-); *fig* **to ~ the way for smb** расчи|ща́ть кому́-л путь (-стить)

smooth out *vt*: **to ~ out creases** разгла́живать скла́дки

smooth over *vt fig*: **to ~ over differences/difficulties** устран|я́ть разногла́сия/тру́дности (-и́ть).

smoothly *adv* гла́дко, споко́йно; **the journey went ~** путеше́ствие прошло́ споко́йно/гла́дко; **everything is going ~** всё идёт гла́дко/как по ма́слу; **the engine is running ~** мото́р рабо́тает ро́вно.

smother *vt* (*asphyxiate*) души́ть (за-); **he ~ed a yawn/his anger** он подави́л зево́к/гнев; **he ~ed the flames with a blanket** он затуши́л ого́нь одея́лом.

smoulder, (*US*) **smolder** *vi* тлеть (*impf*); **the logs were ~ing** брёвна тле́ли; *fig* **her resentment ~ed** в ней зре́ло негодова́ние.

smudge *n* мазо́к; кля́кса.

smudge *vt* сма́з|ывать (-ать); **the address is ~d** а́дрес на письме́ сма́зан; **the rain ~d her eye-shadow** от дождя́ у неё смы́лась кра́ска с ресни́ц.

smug *adj* самодово́льный.

smuggle *vti vt* про|вози́ть что-л контраба́ндой (-везти́); **to ~ goods into a country** провози́ть контраба́нду в страну́; *fig* **he was ~d out of the country** его́ та́йно вы́везли из страны́

vi занима́ться контраба́ндой (*only in impf*).

smuggled *adj*: **~ goods** контраба́нда, контраба́ндный това́р (*collect*).

smuggler *n* контрабанди́ст.

smut *n* са́жа, ко́поть; **you've got a ~ on your nose** у тебя́ на носу́ са́жа; *fig CQ* **don't talk ~** хва́тит э́той поха́бщины.

snack *n*: **I had a quick ~ in the canteen** я перекуси́л в столо́вой; **I brought a ~ to work** я принёс с собо́й за́втрак на рабо́ту; *pl* (**~s**) *approx* заку́ски.

snag *n* (*in stocking*) затя́жка; *fig*: **that's the ~** вот в чём загво́здка; **there's only one ~** тут есть одно́ препя́тствие.

snail *n* ули́тка; *fig* **he walks/does everything at a ~'s pace** он та́щится как черепа́ха, он всё де́лает стра́шно ме́дленно.

snake *n* змея́; *fig CQ* **he's a ~ in the grass** он змея́ подколо́дная.

snakebite *n* уку́с змеи́, змеи́ный уку́с.

snap *n* **1** (*of twig: sound*) треск; (*of finger: sound or act*) щелчо́к; **the stick broke with a ~** па́лка с тре́ском переломи́лась; **with a ~ of his fingers** щёлкнув па́льцами

2 *Meteorol*: **a cold ~** внезáпное/рéзкое похолодáние

3 *Photo CQ* снúмок; **I'll take a ~ of you** давáй я тебя сниму́/*CQ* щёлкну.

snap *adj*: **I made a ~ decision** я мгновéнно прúнял решéние; **a ~ election** внеочереднúе вы́боры (*pl*) (на ближáйший срок).

snap *adv*: **the branch went ~** вéтка с трéском переломúлась; **the rubber band went ~** резúнка лóпнула.

snap *vti vt* **1** (*break*) ломáть (с-); (*snap shut*) защёлк|ивать (-нуть); (*a whip, one's fingers*) щёлк|ать + *I* (-нуть); **he ~ped the stick in two** он сломáл пáлку пополáм; **she ~ped her bag shut** онá защёлкнула сýмку

2 *Photo CQ* снимáть (снять), щёлкать + *A*

vi **1** (*break*) лóп|аться (-нуть); защёлкиваться; (*break or make sound*) трéс|каться (-нуть); **the branch/rope ~ped** вéтка трéснула, канáт лóпнул; **the lid ~ped shut** кры́шка защёлкнулась

2: to ~ at smb (*of person or of a dog*) огрыз|áться на + *A* (-нýться); **the dog ~ped at the bee/at my heels** собáка щёлкнула зубáми на пчелý/пытáлась цáпнуть меня́ за пя́тки

snap off *vt* (*break*) от|лáмывать (-ломáть/-ломúть); **I ~ped off a twig** я отломúл вéтку; *fig* **he ~ped my head off** он на меня́ как набрóсится [**NB** *tense*]

snap out *vi*: **to ~ out of a depression** стряхнýть с себя́ меланхóлию/хандрý; *CQ* **~ out of it** перестáнь ворчáть

snap up *vt* расхвáт|ывать (-áть); (*buy up*) раскуп|áть (-úть); **all the mohair scarves were ~ped up** мохéровые шáрфы бы́стро раскупúли/расхватáли.

snapdragon *n Bot* львúный зев.

snap fastener *n* кнóпка.

snappy *adj CQ*: **a ~ answer** бóйкий отвéт; **look ~!, be ~ about it!, make it ~!** давáй побыстрéй!/поживéй!

snapshot *n* снúмок.

snare *n* (*noose*) силóк; **to be caught in a ~** попáсться в силкú (*pl*); *fig* **a ~ and a delusion** сплошнóй обмáн.

snare *vt* ловúть силкáми (*pl*) (поймáть).

snarl *vi* рычáть на + *A* (*impf*), *also fig*; **the dog started to ~ at him** собáка зарычáла на негó

snarl up *vt*: **he ~ed up the rope** он смотáл/свернýл верёвку в клубóк (*usu pf*); *fig* **the heavy traffic ~s up the approach to the bridge** к мостý проéхать трýдно из-за большóго движéния.

snatch *n usu pl* (**~es**) (*fragments*) отры́вки; обры́вки; **he whistled ~es of Carmen** он насвúстывал отры́вки из «Кармéн»; **I heard ~es of their conversation** я услы́шал обры́вки их разговóра; **I work/sleep in ~es** я рабóтаю/сплю уры́вками (*adv*).

snatch *vt* (*seize*) хватáть (схватúть); (*from smb*) вы|рывáть (-рвать), вы|хвáтывать (-хватить); **he ~ed the pen from my hand/the book from under my nose** он вы́рвал рýчку у меня́ из рук (*pl*), он вы́хватил *or* вы́рвал кнúгу у меня́ из-под нóса; **I ~ed an hour's sleep** *CQ* я урвáл часóчек для сна.

snatch at *vi*: **to ~ at** хватáться за + *A*, ухватúться за + *A*; **he ~ed at the rope** он схватúлся/ухватúлся за верёвку; *fig*: **to ~ at a straw/at any excuse** хватáться за солóминку/за лю́бые отговóрки (*pl*)

snatch up *vt*: **she ~ed up her child/her handbag** онá подхватúла ребёнка, онá схватúла сýмку.

snazzy *adj CQ* пижóнский.

sneak *n* я́беда (*m and f*).

sneak *vi CQ* **1** (*move stealthily*): **to ~ about/around** крáсться (*impf*); **to ~ in** прокрá|дываться (-сться); **to ~ off** вы|скáльзывать (-скользнуть), ускольз|áть (-нýть), улизнýть (*pf*); **he ~ed up from behind** он подкрáлся сзáди

2 *School CQ*: **to ~ on smb** я́бедничать на когó-л (на-).

sneakers *npl CQ* кéды.

sneaking *adj*: **I have a ~ sympathy for him** я в душé емý сочýвствую; **I have a ~ suspicion that...** у меня́ есть нéкоторое подозрéние, что...

sneer *n* (*facial expression*) ухмы́лка, усмéшка; (*jeer, remark*) насмéшка.

sneer *vi* ухмы|ля́ться (-льнýться), умех|áться (-нýться); **to ~ at smb/smth** насмехáться над кем-л/над чем-л.

sneering *adj* насмéшливый.

sneeze *n*: **a loud ~** грóмкое чихáнье.

sneeze *vi* чих|áть (-нýть); *fig* **that's an offer not to be ~d at** *CQ* такúе предложéния на дорóге не валя́ются.

snide *adj*: **a ~ remark** ехúдное замечáние.

sniff *vti vt* нюхать (по-); **she ~ed the rose** онá понюхала рóзу; **can you ~ gas?/smoke?** ты чýвствуешь зáпах гáза?/ды́ма?; **the dog ~ed out a rat** собáка почýяла кры́су

vi (*of person*) шмы́г|ать нóсом (-нýть); (*of animals*) нюхать; **to ~ at** обнюх|ивать (-ать); **use your handkerchief, don't ~** возьмú платóк, вы́сморкайся, не шмы́гай нóсом; **the dog ~ed at/around the lamppost** собáка обнюхала столб; *fig CQ* **that's a sum not to be ~ed at** такúми деньгáми не бросáются.

sniffle *vi* посáпывать (*impf*).

snigger *vi* хихúк|ать (-нуть); **to ~ about/at smth** посмéиваться над чем-л (*impf*).

snip *n*: **I cut off a ~ of the material** я отрéзал кусóчек э́той ткáни; *fig CQ* **it only costs 50p—it's a ~** э́то стóит всегó пятьдеся́т пéнсов—дешéвле (уж) нéкуда!

snip *vt* рéзать (*impf*) *and compounds*; **I ~ped the ends off the ribbon** я отрéзал/*CQ* отхватúл концы́ лéнты.

snipe *n Orn* бекáс.

snipe *vi*: *fig* **to ~ at smb** ехúдничать по пóводу когó-л (*impf*).

snivel *vi* (*whimper*) хны́кать (*impf*); (*after crying*) всхлúп|ывать (-нуть).

snob *n* сноб.

snobbery *n* снобизм.

snood *n* лента для волос.

snook *n CQ*: **to cock a ~ at smb** показывать кому-л (длинный) нос.

snooker *n* (*game*) снукер.

snoop *vi*: **he was ~ing round my study** он как будто что-то искал в моём кабинете; **he's always ~ing into other people's affairs** он вечно суёт нос в чужие дела.

snooty *adj CQ*: **she's very ~** она страшный сноб.

snooze *vi* дремать (по-, вздремнуть); **I left him snoozing in the garden/in the sun** когда я уходил, он дремал в саду/на солнце.

snore *n* храп; **I was woken by his loud ~s** я проснулся от его громкого храпа (*sing*).

snore *vi* храпеть (*impf*); **to ~ a little** похрапывать (*impf*).

snorkel *n* (*for swimmer*) трубка акваланга; (*of submarine*) шноркель (*m*).

snort *vi* (*of person or horse*) фырк|ать (-нуть).

snorter *n CQ*: **that's a ~ of a gale/problem** какая ужасная буря!, над этим придётся голову поломать.

snout *n* (*of pig, etc.*) рыло, *CQ* пятачок; (*of dog, etc.*) морда.

snow *n* снег; **a heavy fall of ~** снегопад; *attr* снежный; **~ bank/fence/line** сугроб, снегозащитное заграждение, снеговая граница *or* линия.

snow *vi*: **it's ~ing** идёт снег; **it's started ~ing** пошёл снег; **it ~ed all day** целый день шёл снег

snow off *vt*: **the match was ~ed off** матч был отменён из-за сильного снегопада

snow under *vt fig*: **the editor was ~ed under with complaints** редактор был завален жалобами

snow up *vt*: **we were ~ed up for three days** мы застряли на три дня из-за снежных заносов (*drifts*); **the road is ~ed up** дорогу занесло (*impers*) снегом.

snowball *n* снежок; снежный ком.

snowball *vti vt*: **the boys were ~ing each other** мальчики кидались друг в друга снежками

vi играть в снежки (по-); *fig CQ* **opposition to the proposal ~ed** недовольство этим предложением росло как снежный ком.

snow-blind *adj*: **after two days in the mountains he was ~** после двух дней в горах у него началась снежная слепота.

snowbound *adj*: **we were ~ for two days** мы на два дня застряли из-за снежных заносов.

snowdrift *n* занос.

snowdrop *n* подснежник.

snowfall *n* снегопад.

snowfield *n* снежная равнина.

snowflake *n* снежинка.

snowman *n* снежная баба, снеговик.

snowplough, (*US*) **snowplow** *n* снегоочиститель (*m*).

snowshoe *n* снегоступ.

snowstorm *n* метель; вьюга, буран; снежная буря.

snow-white *adj* белоснежный.

snowy *adj* снежный; **a ~ winter/roof** снежная зима, крыша, покрытая снегом.

snub *n*: **it was intended as a ~ to me** этим хотели поставить меня на место.

snub *vt* оса|живать (-дить).

snub-nosed *adj* курносый, со вздёрнутым носом.

snuff *n* нюхательный табак; **a pinch of ~** понюшка; **to take ~** нюхать табак.

snuff *vt*: **to ~/~ out a candle** снимать нагар (со свечи) (снять), заду|вать свечу (-ть).

snug *adj* (*cosy*) уютный; (*of income*) приличный; **a ~ little room** уютная комнатка; *fig* **the coat is a ~ fit** это пальто хорошо сидит.

snuggle *vi*: **the child ~d up to its mother/down in bed** ребёнок прижался к матери/свернулся калачиком (*adv = curled up*) в кровати.

so *adv* **1** (*of degree*) *before short form of adj or adv* так, *before long form of adj* такой; **I'm ~ glad** я так рад; **she's ~ happy** она так счастлива/такая счастливая; **I'm ~ bored** мне так скучно; **he's not ~ strong as he appears** он не так силён/не такой сильный, как кажется; **he's not ~ good a student as his sister** он не так хорошо успевает, как его сестра; **I love you ~ much** я так люблю тебя; **there's ~ little time and ~ much to do** времени так мало, а сделать нужно так много; **I'm not ~ sure** я не очень-то уверен; **that's ever ~ much better** это намного лучше; **he left without ~ much as a thank you** он уехал, даже не сказав спасибо; **he's not ~ much stupid as ignorant** он не столько глуп, сколько невежествен; **he's not angry ~ much as upset** он скорее огорчён, чем рассержен; **~ much the better** тем лучше; **~ much for them, let's talk about us** довольно о них, поговорим лучше о нас; **~ far, ~ good** пока всё хорошо; **~ far no one has phoned** пока что никто не звонил; **~ far as I can tell** насколько я могу судить; **~ long as you make no noise, you can stay** ты можешь остаться, если не будешь шуметь

2 (*of manner*) так; **is that ~?—I can scarcely believe it, but it is ~** неужели?—Мне трудно поверить, но так оно и есть; **~ be it** пусть так и будет; **it's not ~** это не так; **why ~?** а почему так?; **if ~, why?** если так, то почему?; **did the train leave?—I think ~** поезд ушёл?—Думаю, что да; **~ to speak** так сказать; **~ saying, he opened the door** с этими словами он открыл дверь; **he said he'd phone, but he hasn't done ~** он сказал, что позвонит, но так и не позвонил; **he likes things just ~** ему нравится, чтобы всё было именно так; **as A is to B, ~ X is to Y** X относится к Y, как A к B; **and ~ on and ~ forth** и так далее и тому подобное (*abbr* и т.д., и т.п.)

3 (*in affirmation*): **you look tired.—And ~ I am** у тебя́ уста́лый вид.—Я и в са́мом де́ле уста́л; **I thought he was an Italian.—And ~ he is** я ду́мал, он италья́нец.—А так оно́ и есть; **it was hot this morning.—So it was** сего́дня у́тром бы́ло жа́рко.—Да, жа́рко

4 (= *also*) и, то́же; **I was at the theatre yesterday.—So was I** я был вчера́ в теа́тре.—И я то́же был; **I am wrong, and ~ are you** и я не пра́в, и ты то́же (не пра́в); **he was late, but ~ were most of us** он опозда́л, но ведь большинство́ из нас то́же опозда́ли

5 (*expressing purpose*): **so that, so as to** что́бы + *inf*, *or if subject of subordinate clause is different from subject of main clause*, что́бы + *past tense*; **I'm leaving early ~ as to collect the tickets** я ухожу́ ра́ньше, что́бы зайти́ за биле́тами; **I'll give you the key ~ that you can get in** я дам тебе́ ключ, что́бы ты смог попа́сть в кварти́ру

6 (*expressing result*) что + *present or past tense*; **he was ~ weak he couldn't stand up** он был так слаб/он так ослабе́л, что не мог стоя́ть на нога́х; **he's deaf—~ much ~, that he can't hear a word** он тако́й глухо́й, что ни сло́ва не слы́шит; **snow blocked the road, ~ that all traffic was diverted** доро́гу занесло́ (*impers*) так, что движе́ние пусти́ли в объе́зд

7 *various*: **you need ~ much butter, ~ many eggs** ну́жно сто́лько-то ма́сла, сто́лько-то яи́ц; **he gave me ~ much money and no more** он мне дал и́менно сто́лько де́нег и не бо́льше; **he is 30 or ~** ему́ лет три́дцать [*"or so" conveyed by inversion of noun and numeral*].

so *conj*: **(and) ~** по́этому, та́к что; **it was raining (and) ~ we stayed at home** шёл дождь, по́этому мы оста́лись до́ма; **he said we shouldn't come, ~ we didn't** он сказа́л, что́бы мы не приходи́ли, ну мы и не пришли́.

so *interj* ну; так; **~ what?** ну и что́?; **~ that's that** ну вот и всё; **and ~ you finally made it** так, зна́чит, ты всё-таки успе́л.

soak *n*: **give the sheets a good ~** про́стыни ну́жно хорошо́ замочи́ть; *CQ* (*person*) пьяни́ца.

soak *vti vt* **1** на|ма́чивать (-мочи́ть) *and other compounds*; **to get ~ed** промок|а́ть (-́нуть); **to ~ bread in milk** намочи́ть хлеб в молоке́; **to ~ cloth in dye** замочи́ть ткань в кра́ске; **his shirt was ~ed in sweat** его́ руба́шка была́ мо́края от по́та; **we got ~ed to the skin** мы промо́кли/вы́мокли насквозь (*adv*) *or* до ни́тки

2: *CQ* **he ~s his rich clients** он выка́чивает де́ньги у свои́х бога́тых клие́нтов (*usu impf*)

vi: **I've left the pan to ~** я зали́л сковоро́дку водо́й, что́бы отмо́кла

soak in *vti vt fig*: **to ~ oneself in classical poetry** с голово́й уйти́ в класси́ческую поэ́зию (*only in pf*)

vi впи́тываться; **stand the geranium in water and let it ~ in** поста́вь горшо́к с гера́нью в таз с водо́й, что́бы земля́ пропита́лась вла́гой

soak up *vt* впи́т|ывать (-а́ть); **a sponge ~s up water** гу́бка впи́тывает во́ду.

soaking *adj*: **my coat is ~ wet** моё пальто́ насквозь промо́кло; **it's a ~ wet day** сего́дня весь день льёт.

so-and-so *n* **1: Mr ~** господи́н тако́й-то

2 *euph* тако́й-сяко́й, тако́й-растако́й; **don't worry about what the old ~ said** он, тако́й-сяко́й, наговори́л тебе́ всего́, а ты обраща́ешь внима́ние.

soap *n* мы́ло; *attr*: **~ powder** стира́льный порошо́к.

soap *vt* мы́лить (на-); **to ~ oneself** намы́литься.

soapdish *n* мы́льница.

soapflakes *npl* мы́льная стру́жка (*collect*).

soapsuds *npl* мы́льная пе́на (*sing*).

soapy *adj* мы́льный; **~ water** мы́льная вода́; **~ hands** намы́ленные ру́ки.

soar *vi* (*of a bird*) взмы|ва́ть (-ть), пари́ть (*impf*); *fig* **prices/our hopes ~ed** це́ны подскочи́ли, на́ши наде́жды возроди́лись с но́вой си́лой.

sob *n* рыда́ние; *attr CQ*: **~ stuff** сентимента́льщина.

sob *vti vt*: **to ~ one's heart out** рыда́ть (*impf*) навзры́д (*adv*); **she ~bed herself to sleep** она́ всё пла́кала, пока́ не засну́ла

vi рыда́ть; **to start to ~** зарыда́ть.

sober *adj* тре́звый, *also fig*; **he's stone ~** он трезв как стёклышко, у него́ ни в одно́м глазу́; *fig* **a ~ critic/judgement** объекти́вный кри́тик, тре́звое сужде́ние.

sober *vti vt*: **to ~ smb up** отрезв|ля́ть кого́-л (-и́ть); *fig* **the news ~ed him down** но́вость отрезви́ла его́

vi: **to ~ up/down** протрезв|ля́ться, отрезв|ля́ться (*pfs* -и́ться); *fig* **with age he has ~ed down** с года́ми он остепени́лся.

soberly *adv* тре́зво; **he dresses ~** он одева́ется скро́мно.

so-called *adj* так называ́емый.

soccer *n* футбо́л.

sociable *adj* общи́тельный, *CQ* компане́йский; **I'm not feeling ~ today** мне сего́дня никого́ не хо́чется ви́деть.

social *adj* (*of group, society, company*) обще́ственный, социа́льный; **~ sciences** обще́ственные нау́ки; **~ work** обще́ственная рабо́та; **~ changes** социа́льные измене́ния; **~ security** социа́льное обеспе́чение (*system*), посо́бие (*payment*); **they belong to different ~ circles** они́ принадлежа́т к ра́зным слоя́м о́бщества; **he leads a very ~ life** он ча́сто быва́ет в о́бществе; *fig* **he's a ~ climber** он вы́скочка.

socialism *n* социали́зм.

socially *adv*: **I met him ~** я встреча́л его́ в гостя́х.

society *n* о́бщество; **high ~** вы́сшее о́бщество, вы́сший свет; **a learned ~** учёное о́бщество; **a dramatic ~** драмати́ческий кружо́к; *attr*: **a ~ woman** све́тская да́ма.

sociology *n* социоло́гия.

sock[1] *n* носо́к; (*in sole*) сте́лька; **knee-length ~s** го́льфы; *fig CQ* **you must pull up your ~s** тебе́ на́до подтяну́ться.

sock[2] *n sl*: **he gave me a ~ on the jaw** он съе́здил мне по физионо́мии; **he got a ~ in the eye** ему́ да́ли в глаз.

socket *n* (*of eye*) глазна́я впа́дина; *Elec* (*wall socket*) розе́тка, (*for bulb*) патро́н; **he wrenched my arm almost out of its ~** он чуть не вы́вихнул мне ру́ку.

sod *n* (*turf*) дёрн.

soda *n* (*drink*) со́довая/газиро́ванная вода́; *Chem* **bicarbonate of ~** углеки́слый на́трий; **whisky and ~** ви́ски с со́довой; **washing/baking ~** стира́льная/пищева́я со́да.

sodden *adj* (*of clothes*) намо́кший; (*of ground*) мо́крый, сыро́й.

sodium *n Chem* на́трий; *attr* на́триевый.

sofa *n* дива́н.

soft *adj* **1** (*not firm*) мя́гкий, *also fig*; **a ~ cheese/mattress** мя́гкий сыр/матра́ц; **~ fruit** я́годы (*pl*); **the bananas/biscuits have gone ~** бана́ны ста́ли по́ртиться, пече́нье ста́ло мя́гким; **his muscles have grown ~** у него́ мы́шцы ста́ли дря́блыми; *Gram* **the ~ sign** мя́гкий знак; *fig* **he's ~ with the staff** он сли́шком мя́гок с подчинёнными

2 (*of climate, colour, wind*) мя́гкий; (*of sound, voice*) ти́хий; **~ water** мя́гкая вода́; **~ words** не́жные слова́; **~ drinks** безалкого́льные напи́тки; *Aer* **a ~ landing** мя́гкая поса́дка; *Fin* **~ currency** неконверти́руемая валю́та; *fig*: **a ~ option/job** лёгкий вы́бор, лёгкая рабо́та; *CQ* **he's ~ in the head** у него́ не все до́ма.

soften *vti vt* смягч|а́ть, размягч|а́ть (*pfs* -и́ть); **to ~ water** смягча́ть во́ду; **rain ~ed the pitch** по́сле дождя́ по́ле ста́ло мя́гче; *fig* **to ~ smb up/an effect** (*by cajoling*) разжа́лобить кого́-л (*pf*), (*by bullying*) припугну́ть кого́-л (*usu pf*), смягча́ть эффе́кт

vi: **the leather is ~ing (up)** ко́жа стано́вится мя́гче; *fig* **his expression ~ed at the thought of her** он поду́мал о ней, и у него́ сра́зу смягчи́лось выраже́ние лица́.

softener *n*: **water ~** смягча́ющее сре́дство для воды́.

soft-hearted *adj* мягкосерде́чный.

softly *adv* (*quietly*) ти́хо; (*mildly*) мя́гко; (*lightly*) легко́.

soft pedal *n Mus* ле́вая педа́ль.

soft-pedal *vti*: *fig* **better ~ that statement** лу́чше смягчи́ть формулиро́вку; *Mus* брать ле́вую педа́ль (взять).

soft-soap *vt fig pejor*: **to ~ smb** подли́з|ываться к кому́-л (-а́ться).

soggy *adj* (*of bread*) сыро́й; (*of ground*) боло́тистый, то́пкий.

soil *n* по́чва; земля́; *fig* **on foreign/one's native ~** на чужо́й/на родно́й земле́.

soil *vti* па́чкать(ся) (за-, ис-); грязни́ть(ся) (за-); **to ~ one's hands** испа́чкать ру́ки.

soiled *adj*: **a ~ nappy** зама́ранная пелёнка; **~ linen** гря́зное бельё.

solace *n* утеше́ние; **to seek/find ~** иска́ть/найти́ утеше́ние.

solar *adj Astron* со́лнечный.

solder *n Tech* припо́й.

solder *vt* пая́ть (при-, с-); **to ~ together** спа́|ивать (-я́ть).

soldier *n* солда́т; вое́нный; **~s and civilians** вое́нные и шта́тские; **a toy ~** солда́тик; **to play at ~s** игра́ть в солда́тики.

soldier *vi* служи́ть в а́рмии (про-); **after 3 years of ~ing** по́сле трёх лет солда́тской слу́жбы

soldier on *vi fig* труди́ться (*impf*); **I'll have to ~ on for another year in this job** мне придётся ещё год тяну́ть э́ту ля́мку.

sole[1] *n Anat* ступня́, подо́шва; (*of shoe*) подо́шва, подмётка.

sole[1] *vt*: **these shoes need soling** на э́ти боти́нки на́до поста́вить но́вые подмётки.

sole[2] *n Zool approx* ка́мбала (*generic term for flat fish*).

sole[3] *adj* (*only*) еди́нственный; (*exclusive*) единоли́чный; **the ~ cause of their quarrel** еди́нственная причи́на их ссо́ры; **the ~ right to smth** единоли́чное пра́во на что-л.

solely *adv* еди́нственно; **I got the job ~ due to her efforts** я получи́л э́то ме́сто еди́нственно благодаря́ её хло́потам.

solemn *adj* (*of occasion, etc.*) торже́ственный; (*serious*) серьёзный; **a ~ ceremony/oath** торже́ственная церемо́ния/кля́тва; **~ faces** серьёзные ли́ца.

solenoid *n Elec* солено́ид.

sol-fa *n Mus* сольфе́джио (*indecl*).

solicit *vi* (*of prostitute*) пристава́ть к мужчи́нам (*only in impf*).

solicitor *n* (*UK*) пове́ренный, соли́ситор; (*US*) *approx* хода́тай.

solicitous *adj* забо́тливый.

solicitude *n* забо́тливость; **he showed ~ for her comfort** он прояви́л забо́ту/забо́тился о её удо́бствах (*pl*).

solid *adj* твёрдый; (*not hollow*) сплошно́й; (*solidly constructed*) соли́дный, про́чный; (*close-knit*) пло́тный; *fig* (*united*) солида́рный; (*weighty*) ве́ский; **~ fuel** твёрдое то́пливо; **a ~ ball/tyre** сплошно́й шар, сплошна́я ши́на; **to build on ~ foundations** стро́ить на соли́дном/про́чном фунда́менте (*sing*); **a ~ house** добро́тно постро́енный дом; **a man of ~ build** челове́к пло́тного сложе́ния; **to eat a ~ meal** пло́тно пое́сть; **~ gold** чи́стое зо́лото; **the pond has frozen ~** пруд промёрз до дна; *fig*: **here we're on ~ ground** здесь мы стои́м на твёрдой по́чве; **he has ~ grounds for thinking so** у него́ есть ве́ские основа́ния так ду́мать; **there's ~ sense in that** в э́том есть большо́й смысл; **they are ~ on this issue** они́ солида́рны в э́том вопро́се; *CQ*: **I slept 10 hours ~** я проспа́л це́лых де́сять часо́в; **we waited a ~ hour** мы прожда́ли там би́тый час.

solidarity *n* солида́рность; *attr*: **a ~ strike** забасто́вка солида́рности.

solidly *adv* соли́дно, про́чно; пло́тно (*see adj*); *fig*: **they voted ~ for him** они́ все как оди́н проголосова́ли за него́; **they are ~ behind him** они́ сплоти́лись вокру́г него́.

soliloquy *n* моноло́г.

solitary *adj* (*of person*) одино́кий; (*of place*) уединённый; (*sole*) едини́чный; **I feel so ~** я чу́вствую себя́ таки́м одино́ким; **he is a ~ person** он необщи́тельный челове́к; **I took a ~ walk** я гуля́л оди́н/в одино́честве; **a ~ instance** едини́чный слу́чай; **~ confinement** одино́чное заключе́ние.

solo *n Mus* со́ло (*indecl*); **a tenor ~** со́ло для те́нора; *attr*: **a ~ recital/violin** со́льный конце́рт, скри́пка-со́ло; **a ~ flight** одино́чный полёт.

soloist *n* соли́ст, *f* -ка.

solstice *n* солнцестоя́ние.

soluble *adj* (*of substances*) раствори́мый; (*of problem, riddle*) разреши́мый; **this powder is ~ in water** э́тот порошо́к растворя́ется в воде́.

solution *n* (*to problems*) реше́ние; (*to riddle*) разга́дка; *Chem* раство́р.

solve *vt* (*problems*) (раз)реш|а́ть (-и́ть); **to ~ a riddle** разга́д|ывать зага́дку (-а́ть).

solvency *n* платёжеспосо́бность.

solvent *adj Fin* платёжеспосо́бный; кредитоспосо́бный.

sombre, (*US*) **somber** *adj*: **a ~ sky** хму́рое не́бо; **a ~ day** па́смурный день; **~ clothes** тёмные оде́жды.

some *pron* **1** (*a few*) не́которые (*pl*), не́сколько; (*less vague*) ко́е-кто́; ко́е-что́; **I like ~ of the pictures** мне нра́вятся не́которые карти́ны, мне нра́вится не́сколько карти́н; **~ of us know Russian/want to stay** не́которые из нас зна́ют ру́сский, ко́е-кто́ из нас хо́чет оста́ться; **I need ~ of these things** мне ну́жно ко́е-что́ из э́тих веще́й

2 (*part of a whole*) часть; **~ of the lecture was interesting** часть ле́кции была́ интере́сной

3: some... some не́которые..., а не́которые, кто..., а кто; **some... others...** одни́..., а други́е...; **~ like tea, ~ like coffee** не́которые/одни́ лю́бят чай, а не́которые/други́е ко́фе, кто лю́бит чай, а кто ко́фе.

some *adj* **1** (*as indefinite numeral = a few*) не́сколько [**NB** *it is declined in oblique cases*]; **~ years ago** не́сколько лет наза́д; **in ~ towns** в не́скольких города́х

2 (*in contrast to others*) не́которые (*usu pl*); **~ teachers believe in it** не́которые педаго́ги в э́то ве́рят; **~ people just don't care** не́которым про́сто безразли́чно

3 (*unspecified*) како́й-то; (*more vaguely and usu referring to future*) како́й-нибудь, (*off and even vaguer*) како́й-либо; [**NB** *the suffixes* -то, -нибудь, -либо *can be added to* кто, где, когда́, *etc., with similar implications*]; **there's ~ man asking for you** како́й-то челове́к/кто́-то (*pron*) спра́шивает тебя́; **~ idiot of a driver** како́й-то идио́т-води́тель; **there must be ~ solution** должно́ же быть како́е-то реше́ние; **for ~ reason or other** по той и́ли ино́й/по како́й-то причи́не, почему́-то; **she lives ~ place in Belgium** она́ живёт где́-то в Бе́льгии; **I saw her ~ time or other** я её ви́дел когда́-то; **I'll write to you ~ day** я вам ка́к-нибудь напишу́; **I'll see her ~ day soon** я её вско́ре уви́жу; **come ~ day next week** приходи́ ка́к-нибудь на той неде́ле

4 (*a certain amount/number of*) немно́го, не́сколько, *also often translated by partitive genitive*; **give me ~ bread** дай мне (немно́го) хле́ба; **do you want ~ tea?** ча́ю хоти́те?; **have ~ more (cake)** бери́/возьми́ ещё (то́рта); **have you got ~ stamps?/money on you?** у тебя́ есть с собо́й (каки́е-нибудь) ма́рки?/де́ньги?; **there are ~ eggs in the fridge** в холоди́льнике есть немно́го яи́ц

5 (*a considerable amount*): **he spoke at ~ length** он дово́льно до́лго говори́л; **we had ~ difficulty in finding the hotel** (нам) бы́ло дово́льно тру́дно найти́ гости́ницу; **that happened ~ time ago** э́то случи́лось дово́льно давно́; **it took ~ courage to do that** на́до име́ть му́жество, что́бы так поступи́ть

6 (*emphatic*) хоть како́й-то; **do have ~ consideration** прояви́ хоть како́е-то внима́ние; **at least that's ~ proof** по кра́йней ме́ре э́то хоть како́е-то доказа́тельство

7 (*intensive*): **that was ~ fish you caught!** ну и ры́бу ты пойма́л!; **it was ~ match!** вот э́то был матч!; **she's ~ girl!** она́ де́вочка что на́до!; *iron* **you're ~ electrician!** ну ты и эле́ктрик!

some *adv* **1** (*approximately*) *translated by inversion of numeral and noun*: **I waited ~ 40 minutes** я прожда́л мину́т со́рок

2 (*US*) *CQ* немно́го; **it hindered us ~** э́то нам немно́го помеша́ло.

somebody *pron* **1** кто́-то; ко́е-кто́ (*suggests speaker knows who*); (*unspecified, and esp. with future tense*) кто́-нибудь; **there's ~ in the kitchen** на ку́хне кто́-то есть; **a certain ~ told me this** кто́-то мне э́то сказа́л; **he's ~ from my class** он из моего́ кла́сса; **~ else will do it** кто́-нибудь друго́й э́то сде́лает; **~ will help you** кто́-нибудь тебе́ помо́жет; **but ~ must have been there** но кто́-то до́лжен был там быть

2: he thinks he's (a) ~ он счита́ет себя́ ва́жной персо́ной.

somehow *adv* ка́к-то; (*with future tense*) ка́к-нибудь; **it's ~ odd** э́то ка́к-то стра́нно; **I ~ don't trust him** я ему́ не о́чень-то доверя́ю; **I'll get the money ~** я ка́к-нибудь доста́ну де́нег; **~ or other** так и́ли ина́че.

someone *pron see* **somebody 1.**

someplace *adv* (*US*) *see* **somewhere.**

somersault *n* (*in the air*) са́льто (*indecl*); (*on the ground*) кувыро́к.

somersault *vi* де́лать са́льто (с-); кувырк|а́ться (-ну́ться).

something *pron* что́-то; ко́е-что́ (*suggests speaker knows what*); (*unspecified*) что́-нибудь; **is ~ the matter?** что́-то/что́-нибудь не в поря́дке?; **there's ~ wrong here** здесь что́-то не так; **~ is missing** чегó-то / кóе-чегó не хватáет; **she has a certain ~ / that extra ~** в ней есть чтó-то / изю́минка; **it's not what you think — it's ~ else** это не то, что ты дýмаешь,— это совсéм другóе; **I've ~ else for you** у меня́ есть для вас кóе-что ещё; **I gave him ~ for himself** я емý дал немнóго за услýги; **you should take ~ for your headache** тебé нýжно приня́ть чтó-нибудь от головнóй бóли; **have ~ to eat** поéшь чтó-нибудь; **her private lessons give her ~ to live on** чáстные урóки даю́т ей кóе-какóй зáработок; **I have ~ to aim for** у меня́ есть к чемý стреми́ться; **he's called Sasha ~ (or other)** егó зовýт Сáша, фами́лию не пóмню; **he's a physicist or ~ of the kind** он фи́зик и́ли чтó-то в э́том рóде; **he's ~ of a singer** он неплохóй певéц; **we'll see ~ of him now** мы тепéрь егó чáще бýдем ви́деть; (*emphatic*) **he swam the Channel, and that's ~** он переплы́л Ла-Мáнш, а э́то чтó-нибудь да знáчит.

something *adv* 1 (*approximately*): **he collected ~ like £100** он собрáл чтó-то óколо ста фýнтов; **it sounds ~ like Brahms** э́то, кáжется, Брамс, (*comparing*) э́то óчень похóже на Брáмса; **that's better — that's ~ like it** э́то лýчше — э́то ужé на чтó-то похóже

2 *CQ*: **the weather was ~ awful** погóда былá прóсто ужáсная; **it's ~ shocking** э́то какóе-то безобрáзие.

sometime *adv* когдá-то; (*unspecific*) когдá-нибудь, кáк-нибудь; **~ next week** кáк-нибудь на той недéле; **~ before lunch** *CQ* гдé-нибудь пéред обéдом; **come and see us ~ or other** приходи́ к нам кáк-нибудь; **he'll arrive ~ tomorrow** он приезжáет зáвтра, когдá тóчно — не знáю.

sometimes *adv* иногдá.

somewhat *adv* нéсколько; **I was ~ surprised** я был нéсколько удивлён.

somewhere *adv* гдé-то, (*even vaguer*) гдé-нибудь; (*of motion*) кудá-то, кудá-нибудь; **~ near Moscow** гдé-то недалекó от Москвы́; **~ near here** гдé-то побли́зости; **I'm looking for ~ to live** я ищý кварти́ру; **he was sent to Africa ~** егó послáли кудá-то в Áфрику; **I'd like to go ~ hot** мне хóчется поéхать кудá-нибудь, где жáрко; *fig CQ* **I paid ~ round £10** я заплати́л чтó-то óколо десяти́ фýнтов.

son *n* сын, *dim* сынóк.

sonata *n* сонáта.

song *n* пéсня, *dim* пéсенка; *Lit* песнь; **a drinking ~** застóльная (пéсня); **give us a ~** спой нам (пéсню); *fig*: **I bought it for a ~** я купи́л э́то за бесцéнок; **what a ~ and dance about nothing!** скóлько шýму, и бы́ло бы из-за чегó!; *attr*: **~ cycle** цикл пéсен; **~ writer** (*of music*) композúтор, (*of words*) поэ́т-пéсенник.

songbird *n* пéвчая пти́ца.

sonic *adj* звуковóй.

son-in-law *n* зять (*m*).

soon *adv* 1 скóро, вскóре; рáно; **must you leave so ~?** ты так скóро дóлжен уходи́ть?; **~ after lunch / afterwards** вскóре пóсле обéда / пóсле э́того; **see you ~** скóро / вскóре увиди́мся; **come ~** иди́ скорéе; **come and see us ~** приходи́ к нам поскорéе; **come back ~** возвращáйся побыстрéй; **Friday is too ~** пя́тница — (э́то) сли́шком рáно; **we arrived an hour / none too ~** мы приéхали на час рáньше / как раз вóвремя; **you'd ~ get lost there** ты там бы́стро заблýдишься; **you spoke too ~** ты сли́шком поторопи́лся с предсказáниями

2: **as ~ as** как тóлько; **as ~ as possible** как мóжно скорéе; **as ~ as you are ready** как тóлько ты бýдешь готóв; **we couldn't arrive as / so ~ as we'd hoped** мы не могли́ приéхать тудá рáньше, как нам тогó хотéлось.

sooner *adv* 1 (*of time*) скорéе, рáньше; **the ~ the better** чем скорéе, тем лýчше; **the ~ you start, the ~ you'll finish** чем рáньше начнёшь, тем скорéе закóнчишь; **~ or later** рáно и́ли пóздно; **no ~ said than done** скáзано — сдéлано

2 (*of preference*): **~ you than me!** скорéе ты, чем я!; **he would resign ~ than sign this document** он скорéе уйдёт с рабóты, чем подпи́шет э́тот докумéнт; **I'd ~ you came to me** лýчше бýдет, éсли ты ко мне придёшь; **I'd ~ stay** я лýчше остáнусь.

soot *n* (*in chimney*) сáжа; (*on surface*) кóпоть.

soothe *vt* успок|áивать (-óить), *also fig.*

sooty *adj* закопчённый, покры́тый сáжей.

sop *n*: **as a ~ to my conscience** чтóбы успокóить сóвесть.

sophisticated *adj* изы́сканный, утончённый, изощрённый; (*of people*) свéтский, искушённый; **~ taste** изы́сканный / утончённый вкус; **a ~ argument** изощрённый аргумéнт; **a ~ woman / outfit** свéтская дáма, мóдные наря́ды (*pl*); **a ~ audience** искушённая пýблика; **~ technology** усложнённая технолóгия.

sophomore *n* (*US*) второкýрсник.

soprano *n* (*voice*) сопрáно (*indecl*); **she's a ~** у неё сопрáно; *attr*: **the ~ part** пáртия сопрáно.

sordid *adj* (*squalid*) убóгий, жáлкий; (*of behaviour, details, etc.*) гнýсный; **what a ~ business!** какáя гнýсность!

sore *n Med* боля́чка, рáна; (*caused by rubbing*) натёртое мéсто; **a running ~** я́зва.

sore *adj* больнóй; **a ~ knee** больнóе колéно; **my eyes are ~** у меня́ боля́т глазá; **I've a ~ throat** у меня́ боли́т гóрло; *fig*: **it's a sight for ~ eyes** э́то рáдует глаз; **you touched him on a ~ point** ты егó задéл за живóе; *CQ* **he feels ~ he wasn't invited** емý оби́дно, что егó не пригласи́ли.

sorely *adv*: **her patience has been ~ tried by him** он испы́тывал её терпéние; **I feel ~ tempted to shirk work today** мне сегóдня так не хóчется идти́ на рабóту.

sorrel *n Bot* щавéль (*m*); *attr*: **~ soup** щавéлевые щи (*no sing*).

sorrow *n* печáль, гóре; (*regret*) сожалéние; **what are my ~s to them?** что им до мои́х печáлей?; **to my great ~, it is a great ~ to me (that)** к моемý велúкому сожалéнию, мне óчень жаль (, что); **~ has aged him** гóре состáрило егó; **more in ~ than in anger** скорéе с гóречью, чем со злóбой; *fig* **to drown one's ~s in drink** топúть гóре (*sing*) в винé.

sorry *adj* 1 *attr* жáлкий; **a ~ excuse** жáлкая отговóрка; **he cut a ~ figure** он являл собóй жáлкую фигýру

2 *predic*: **(I'm) ~!** виновáт!, простúте!, извинúте!; **I feel ~ for her** мне её жáлко/жаль; **there's no need to be ~ for her/for yourself** нéчего её жалéть/жалéть себя; **I'm so ~ that** я так жалéю, что...; **I would be ~ if...** мне бы́ло бы жаль, éсли бы...; **you'll be ~ for this** ты ещё об э́том пожалéешь; **he'll never say he's ~** от негó не дождёшься извинéний; **I'm ~ about the mess/to be so late** извинú за беспоря́док, простúте, что я так опоздáл; **~, I'm busy** извинú, но я зáнят; **~ about the broken cup** óчень сожалéю, что чáшка разбúлась; **tell Mummy you're ~** попросú у мáмы прощéния; **we are ~ to inform you** с сожалéнием сообщáем вам; **I'm ~ to hear about her death** я с прискóрбием узнáл о её смéрти.

sort *n* 1 (*type, kind*) сорт, род; (*strain*) вид; (*breed*) порóда; *usu pejor* тип; **what ~ of tobacco/rose/dog is that?** какóй э́то сорт табакá?/вид рóзы?, какóй порóды э́та собáка?; **it's perfect of its ~** э́то в своём рóде совершéнство; **I know his ~** я знáю/мне хорошó знакóм э́тот тип людéй; **what ~ of car do you have?** какóй мáрки у вас/вáша машúна?, какáя у вас машúна?; **he's an old-fashioned ~ of person** он нéсколько старомóден; **what ~ of theatre interests you?** какóй теáтр вам нрáвится?; **I hate that ~ of film** я терпéть не могý такúе фúльмы (*pl*); **he's not that ~ of person** он не такóй человéк; **I'm not that ~ of girl** я не такáя; **what ~ of answer is that?** что э́то за отвéт?; **this is your ~ of book** э́та кнúга в твоём вкýсе; **you know the ~ of thing I mean** ты знáешь, что я имéю в видý; *CQ* **he's a good ~** он слáвный мáлый

2 *phrases, usu CQ*: **something of the ~** чтó-то в э́том рóде; **after a ~** в нéкотором рóде, нéкоторым óбразом; **he's a lawyer of ~s/a ~ of lawyer** он чтó-то врóде адвокáта; **it tastes like tea of a ~/of ~s** э́то по вкýсу похóже на чай; **I ~ of knew it would happen** я как знал, что э́то случúтся; **it's ~ of green** цвет зеленовáтый; **are you happy?—S. of** ты счáстлив?—Врóде бы да; **it's ~ of funny** э́то немнóго смешнó; **I'll say nothing of the ~** я ничегó подóбного не скажý; **he feels out of ~s** емý (чтó-то) не по себé; **it takes all ~s to make a world** чегó тóлько нет на свéте.

sort *vt* сортировáть (*impf*); раз|бирáть (-обрáть); **to ~ things according to size** сортировáть вéщи по размéрам; **to ~ clothes into clean and dirty piles** сортировáть/разбирáть бельё на чúстое и гря́зное; *Cards* **to ~ one's hand/cards** разбирáть кáрты; *CQ* **I'm going to ~ my desk** я наведý поря́док у себя́ на столé

sort out *vt* раз|бирáть, от|бирáть (*pfs* -обрáть); рассортирóв|ывать (-áть); **can you ~ out the unsigned letters?** ты мóжешь отобрáть неподпúсанные пúсьма?; *fig*: **we'll soon ~ out this problem** мы скóро разберёмся в э́том вопрóсе; **things will ~ themselves out** всё кáк-нибудь улáдится.

so-so *adv CQ* так себé, ничегó.

soufflé *n Cook* суфлé (*indecl*).

soul *n* 1 душá, *also fig*; *fig*: **he put his heart and ~ into the work** он вложúл всю дýшу в рабóту; **she was the life and ~ of the party** онá былá душóй óбщества; **he hardly has enough to keep body and ~ together** емý едвá хватáет на жизнь; **he couldn't call his ~ his own** он себé не принадлежáл

2 *fig* (*person*) человéк, душá; **there wasn't a ~ to be seen** нé было вúдно ни душú; **he's a good ~** он дóбрая душá; **don't tell a ~** никомý ни словá.

sound[1] *n* звук; (*quality of tone*) звучáние; (*noise*) шум; **the speed of ~** скóрость звýка; **not a ~ was heard** нé было слы́шно ни звýка; **the ~ of rain/the sea/the wind/the surf** шум дождя́/мóря/вéтра/прибóя; **we heard the ~ of singing/of voices** мы слы́шали пéние/звук голосóв; **without a ~** беззвýчно (*adv*); **I don't like the ~ of the engine/this cello** мне не нрáвится, как рабóтает мотóр/, как звучúт э́та виолончéль; *CQ* **is that O.K. for ~?** звук хорóший?; *attr* звуковóй.

sound[1] *vti vt*: **the driver ~ed his horn** водúтель просигнáлил/дал сигнáл; **you do not ~ the letter "n" in "hymn"** в слóве **hymn** бýква **n** не произнóсится

vi 1 звучáть (про-); (*of bell, alarm*) звенéть (*impf*); **does it ~ loud enough?** достáточно ли грóмко (э́то) звучúт?; **footsteps ~ed in the distance** вдалú послы́шались шагú

2 (*suggest by sound*): **this wall ~s hollow** у э́той стены́ пóлый звук; **the box ~s empty** на звук я́щик пустóй; **it ~s as if it's raining** сýдя по звýку, идёт дóждь; **he ~s Georgian** сýдя по акцéнту, он грузúн; **that ~s like the postman** похóже, что пришёл почтальóн; *fig*: **that ~s very odd/like an excuse** э́то звучúт óчень стрáнно/как отговóрка; **from what you've said he doesn't ~ like the right candidate** сýдя по вáшим словáм, он не óчень-то подходя́щий кандидáт.

sound[2] *adj* 1 (*healthy*) здорóвый; **~ in mind and body** здорóвый тéлом и душóй; **~ teeth** хорóшие зýбы; **a ~ horse/tree** здорóвая *or* крéпкая лóшадь, крéпкое дéрево; **a ~ sleep** крéпкий сон

2 (*sensible*) здрáвый; **~ advice/sense, a ~ move** здрáвый совéт/смысл, разýмный шаг; **he's ~ on theory** он силён в теóрии; **a ~ scholar/argument** настоя́щий учёный, убедú-

тельный до́вод; *Comm* **a ~ investment** надёжное капиталовложе́ние.

sound[3] *vt*: *Med* **to ~ smb's chest** просту́к|ивать кому́-л грудну́ю кле́тку (-ать); *fig* **I'll ~ him out (about your fee)** попро́бую узна́ть у него́ (насчёт ва́шего гонора́ра).

sound[4] *n Geog* проли́в.

sounding *n Naut*: **to take a ~** промер|я́ть глубину́ воды́ (ʹ-ить).

soundly *adv* (*of defeat, thrashing*) как сле́дует; **to sleep ~** кре́пко спать.

soundproof *adj* звуконепроница́емый.

soundproofing *n* звукоизоля́ция.

soup *n* суп (*usu thick*); **clear ~** бульо́н; **vegetable/cabbage ~** овощно́й суп, щи (*pl*); **fish ~** ры́бный суп, уха́; *fig CQ* **he's really in the ~!** ну и попа́л же он в переде́лку!/ переплёт!; *attr*: **~ plate** глубо́кая таре́лка; **~ tureen** су́пница.

sour *adj* ки́слый, *also fig*; (*of milk, etc.*) проки́сший; **~ cream** смета́на; **what a ~ taste!** кака́я кисля́тина!; **to turn ~** ки́снуть (*impf*), закис|а́ть, скис|а́ть, прокис|а́ть (*pfs* ʹ-нуть); *fig* **a ~ face/remark** ки́слая ми́на, жёлчное замеча́ние.

source *n* исто́к; исто́чник; **where does the Volga have its ~?** где Во́лга берёт (своё) нача́ло?; **a ~ of energy/infection/information** исто́чник эне́ргии/инфе́кции/информа́ции; **historical/primary ~s** истори́ческие исто́чники, первоисто́чники.

souse *vt* **1** (*throw water over*) окати́ть (водо́й) (*usu pf*); (*soak*) зам|а́чивать (-очи́ть); *sl* **to get ~d** набра́ться, наліза́ться

2 (*pickle: with salt*) зас|а́ливать (-оли́ть), соли́ть (по-); (*with vinegar*) маринова́ть (за-); **~d herring** марино́ванная селёдка.

south *n* юг; *Naut* зюйд; **the wind is from the ~** ве́тер ю́жный/с ю́га.

south *adj* ю́жный; *Naut* зю́йдовый.

south *adv* на юг, к ю́гу; **the house faces ~** о́кна до́ма выхо́дят на юг; **Kiev lies ~ of Moscow** Ки́ев располо́жен к ю́гу от Москвы́.

south-east *n* ю́го-восто́к; *Naut* зюйд-о́ст; *attr* ю́го-восто́чный.

south-easter *n* (*wind*) ю́го-восто́чный ве́тер; *Naut* зюйд-о́ст.

southerly, southern *adjs* ю́жный.

southerner *n* южа́нин, южа́нка.

southwards *adv* на юг, в ю́жном направле́нии.

south-west *n* ю́го-за́пад; *Naut* зюйд-ве́ст; *attr* ю́го-за́падный.

southwester, *CQ* **sou'wester** *n* (*wind*) ю́го-за́падный ве́тер; *Naut* зюйд-ве́ст; (*hat*) зюйдве́стка.

souvenir *n* сувени́р.

sovereign *n* мона́рх, сувере́н; (*coin*) сoveréн.

sovereignty *n Polit, Law* суверените́т.

Soviet *n*: **the Supreme S. of the USSR** Верхо́вный Сове́т СССР; **Soviets of People's Deputies** сове́ты наро́дных депута́тов; *attr* сове́тский; **the S. Union** Сове́тский Сою́з.

sow[1] *n* свинома́тка.

sow[2] *vti vt* се́ять (по-); **to ~ grass** се́ять траву́; **to ~ a field with wheat** засе́ять по́ле пшени́цей; *fig* **to ~ doubt in smb's mind** се́ять сомне́ние в чьей-л душе́

vi се́ять.

sowing *n* сев, посе́в; *attr*: **~ machine** се́ялка.

soya *n Bot* со́я; *attr* со́евый.

sozzled *adj sl*: **he's usually ~** он ве́чно пьян, он никогда́ не просыха́ет; **he got ~** он вдрызг пьян.

spa *n* куро́рт (с минера́льными исто́чниками); **to take a cure at a ~** лечи́ться на во́дах (*pl*).

space *n* **1** простра́нство; **outer ~** косми́ческое простра́нство, ко́смос; **to stare into ~** уста́виться в простра́нство; *attr* косми́ческий; **a ~ flight/shot** косми́ческий полёт, за́пуск косми́ческой раке́ты

2 (*place, room*) ме́сто; простра́нство; **leave a ~ for signature** оста́вь ме́сто для по́дписи; **in an enclosed ~** в огоро́женном ме́сте/ простра́нстве; **I have a ~ in my timetable** *CQ* у меня́ окно́ в расписа́нии

3 (*distance, interval*): **a ~ between the lines** простра́нство ме́жду стро́чками; **there's a ~ of 30 metres between the houses** расстоя́ние ме́жду дома́ми три́дцать ме́тров; **the rows are separated by a ~ of two feet** ме́жду ряда́ми промежу́ток в два фу́та

4 (*of time*) пери́од; **within the ~ of 10 years/an hour** за десятиле́тний пери́од, за час.

space *vt*, *also* **to ~ out: ~ the plants further apart** расса́ди́ э́ти расте́ния пода́льше друг от дру́га; **the posts are ~d out evenly** столбы́ стоя́т на ра́вном расстоя́нии друг от дру́га; **we ~d out the payments over 5 years** э́ту су́мму мы бу́дем выпла́чивать пять лет [**NB** *tense*].

spacecraft *n* косми́ческий кора́бль (*m*).

spacing *n* (*in typing*) интерва́л, промежу́ток; **with double ~** с двойны́м интерва́лом.

spacious *adj* просто́рный.

spade *n* лопа́та, (*child's*) лопа́тка; *fig* **to call a ~ a ~** называ́ть ве́щи свои́ми имена́ми.

spaghetti *n* спаге́тти (*indecl*).

span *n* (*of time*) промежу́ток, пери́од; (*of bridge, arch*) пролёт; (*of hand, wings*) разма́х; **a brief ~** коро́ткий промежу́ток/пери́од; **the average ~ of life** сре́дняя продолжи́тельность жи́зни; **a single ~/5 ~ bridge** однопролётный мост, мост с пятью́ пролётами.

span *vt*: **the Thames is ~ned by many bridges** че́рез Те́мзу переки́нуто мно́го мосто́в.

spangled *adj* покры́тый блёстками, в блёстках.

Spaniard *n* испа́нец, испа́нка.

Spanish *n* (*language*) испа́нский язы́к; **the ~** испа́нцы (*pl*).

Spanish *adj* испа́нский.

Spanish-American *adj* латиноамерика́нский.

spank *vt* шлёп|ать (-нуть) *and compounds.*

spanking *adj CQ*: **a ~ breeze** свéжий бриз; **at a ~ pace** бы́стро.

spanner *n* гáечный ключ; *fig* **to put a ~ into the works** вставля́ть пáлки (*pl*) в колёса.

spare *n*: **do you stock ~s?** у вас есть запасны́е чáсти/*abbr* запчáсти?

spare *adj* **1** (*reserve*) запаснóй; (*surplus*) ли́шний; **take a ~ pair of socks** возьми́ запасну́ю пáру носкóв; **I've got a ~ pair** у меня́ есть ли́шняя пáра; **I've two ~ tickets** у меня́ два ли́шних билéта; **a ~ bed/room** свобóдная кровáть, кóмната для гостéй; **in my ~ time I go swimming** в свобóдное врéмя я плáваю

2 (*thin*): **a tall ~ man** высóкий худощáвый человéк; (*meagre*): **a ~ meal/diet** скýдный обéд, стрóгая диéта.

spare *vt* **1** (*grudge*) жалéть + *G* (по-), щади́ть (по-); **he ~d no trouble** он не жалéл сил/трудóв (*pls*); **he doesn't ~ himself** он не жалéет/не щади́т себя́; **no expenses ~d** не жалéя затрáт; **he ~d no pains in helping me** он мне помогáл, не щадя́ сил

2 (*do without*): **we can't ~ him at present** сейчáс мы без негó не мóжем обойти́сь; **can you ~ a hand?/me a moment?/£5?** ты мóжешь мне помóчь?/удели́ть мне минýтку?/одолжи́ть мне пять фýнтов?

3 (*have extra*): **I have no milk to ~** у меня́ нет ли́шнего молокá; **we arrived with 5 minutes to ~** мы приéхали за пять минýт; **I have time and to ~** врéмени у меня́ бóлее чем достáточно; **we've enough and to ~** у нас всегó предостáточно

4 (*show mercy*) щади́ть (по-); **he ~d the life of his enemy** он пощади́л своегó врагá; **you should have ~d her feelings** ты бы пощади́л её чýвства; **you could have ~d me all this trouble if...** ты бы избáвил меня́ от всех э́тих хлопóт, éсли бы...; **if we're ~d and well** éсли бýдем жи́вы-здорóвы.

spare ribs *n Cook* свины́е рёбрышки.

sparing *adj* скупóй; эконóмный; **he is ~ of words/praise/with the wine** он скуп на словá/на похвалы́, емý жáлко винá для гостéй.

spark *n* и́скра, *also fig*; *fig*: **a ~ of talent/interest** и́скра талáнта, и́скорка интерéса; **he hasn't a ~ of humour in him** у негó нет ни кáпли юмора; *CQ* **a bright young ~** блестя́щий франт.

spark *vti vt*, *usu* **to ~ off: the fire was ~ed off by a cigarette stub** пожáр начался́ с брóшенного окýрка; *fig* **the announcement ~ed off many complaints** э́то заявлéние вы́звало мнóго протéстов

vi искри́ть (*impf*), да|вáть и́скру (-ть).

sparking plug *n Aut* свечá зажигáния.

sparkle *n* (*of eyes*, *stars*, *silver*) блеск, сверкáние; **this champagne has lost its ~** шампáнское потеря́ло игри́стость/вы́дохлось.

sparkle *vi* и́скри́ться, блестéть, сверкáть (*usu impfs*); (*of wine*, *etc.*) игрáть (*impf*); **the snow ~s in the sunshine** снег искри́тся на сóлнце; **her eyes ~d with excitement/anger** глазá у неё блестéли от возбуждéния/сверкáли гнéвом; **she doesn't exactly ~** онá умóм осóбенно не блéщет.

sparkling *adj* искри́стый; искря́щийся, *also fig*; (*of wine*, *etc.*) игри́стый, пéнящийся; *fig* **~ conversation** блестя́щая бесéда.

sparrow *n* воробéй.

sparse *adj* рéдкий; **~ population** рéдкое населéние; **a ~ beard** рéденькая борóдка; **his hair is getting ~** у негó вóлосы редéют; **~ furnishings** скрóмная обстанóвка (*sing*).

spasm *n Med* сýдорога, спазм; при́ступ; *fig* поры́в; **his leg is in ~** у негó сýдорогой свóдит (*impers*) нóгу; **a ~ of coughing/asthma** при́ступ кáшля/áстмы; *fig* **in a ~ of grief** в поры́ве гóря.

spasmodically *adv* уры́вками.

spastic *adj Med* спасти́ческий, сýдорожный.

spate *n*: **the river is in ~** рекá вздýлась; *fig* **a ~ of words** потóк слов.

spatter *n* бры́зги (*no sing*); **a ~ of blood on the wall** бры́зги крóви на стенé; **there was a ~ of rain** бры́знул дóждик.

spatter *vt* бры́з|гать + *I* (-нуть) *and compounds*; **my coat is ~ed with paint** моё пальтó забры́згано крáской; **the bus ~ed us with mud** автóбус обры́згал/забры́згал нас грязью.

spatula *n* шпáтель (*m*), лопáточка.

spawn *n* (*of fish*, *frog*) икрá; (*of fungi*) грибни́ца.

spay *vt*: **to ~ a cat** удал|я́ть у кóшки яи́чники (-и́ть).

speak *vti vt* **1** говори́ть (сказáть); **no one spoke a word** никтó (и) слóва не сказáл; **to ~ one's mind** вы|скáзываться (-сказаться); *Theat* **to ~ one's lines** произноси́ть свои́ рéплики

2 (*of languages*): **he ~s several languages/fluent German/an excellent Russian** он говори́т на нéскольких языкáх/свобóдно по-немéцки, он прекрáсно говори́т по-рýсски

vi **1** (*talk*) говори́ть; (*converse*) разговáривать (*impf*); (*have a talk*) поговори́ть (*pf*); **to begin to ~** заговори́ть (*pf*); **~ more slowly/to the point** говори́ мéдленнее/по дéлу; **did you ~?** ты чтó-то сказáл?; **don't ~ until spoken to** молчи́, покá к тебé не обратя́тся; **~ing personally/as a trade union member...** выражáя (своё) сóбственное мнéние, как член профсою́за, я...; **properly ~ing** вообщé говоря́; **I haven't spoken to her yet about it** я ещё не говори́л с ней об э́том; **she was late again, I'll have to ~ to her** онá опя́ть опоздáла, мне нáдо с ней поговори́ть; **I know him to ~ to** у меня́ с ним шáпочное знакóмство; *Tel* **(this is) Dr Smith ~ing** (с Вáми) говори́т дóктор Смит; **can I ~ to Tim?—Speaking** мóжно Ти́ма к телефóну? *or* позови́те, пожáлуйста, Ти́ма.—Я у телефóна *or* Э́то я

2 (*make a speech*): **to ~ in public/at a debate** вы|ступáть публи́чно *or* с рéчью/в дебáтах (*no sing*) (-ступить); (*at a meeting*) **may I ~?** (я) прошý слóва; **Mrs Green will now ~ about**

her trip to Africa тепéрь госпожá Грин расскáжет о своéй поéздке в Áфрику

3 *various*: ~ **for yourself!** говорú (сам) за себя́!; ~**ing for myself/of poetry** что касáется меня́, говоря́ о поэ́зии; **the facts ~ for themselves** фáкты говоря́т сáми за себя́; **that ~s well for him** э́то хорошó о нём говорит; **she's highly spoken of** о ней хорошó отзывáются; **she has no money to ~ of** бóльших дéнег у неё нет; **there are no shops to ~ of here** здесь и магазúнов-то настоя́щих нет

speak up *vi*: ~ **up please** говорú грóмче (*louder*)/отчётливее (*more clearly*); *fig* **he's not afraid to ~ up for his friends** *or* **principles/against...** он готóв постоя́ть за своúх друзéй *or* за свой прúнципы/вы́сказаться прóтив + *G*.

speaker *n* **1** (*at meeting, etc.*) выступáющий, доклáдчик; (*at lecture*) лéктор; (*in debate*) орáтор; (*UK*: *in Parliament*) (**the S.**) спúкер

2 (*of languages*): **how many Russian ~s are there here?** скóлько человéк здесь говоря́т по-рýсски?; **he is a native Welsh ~** егó роднóй язы́к—валлúйский .

3 *pl* (~**s**) *Radio* (*on stereo, etc.*) динáмики; (*in public places*) репродýкторы, громкоговорúтели.

speaking *adj*: **we aren't on ~ terms** мы не разговáриваем (друг с дрýгом); **within ~ distance** в предéлах слы́шимости; *fig* **the portrait is a ~ likeness of her** на э́том портрéте онá пря́мо как живáя.

special *adj* **1** (*particular*) осóбый; специáльный; **he did it as a ~ favour to me** он э́то сдéлал для меня́ в вúде осóбого одолжéния; **why does he get ~ treatment?** почемý к немý осóбое отношéние?; **a ~ order** специáльный закáз; **chemistry is his ~ subject** егó специáльный предмéт—хúмия; **is there any ~ day you'd prefer?** какóй день вам бóльше всегó подхóдит?

2 (*exceptional*) осóбенный; **it's a ~ day for me** сегóдня для меня́ осóбенный день; **my ~ friend** мой большóй друг; **take ~ care of yourself/of it** будь осóбенно осторóжен, будь поосторóжнее с э́тим

3 (*in combinations*): ~ **correspondent/edition** специáльный корреспондéнт/вы́пуск; **a ~ train** специáльный пóезд; ~ **delivery** срóчная достáвка; **by ~ messenger** с нáрочным; *Comm* **a ~ agent** специáльный представúтель; *Polit* ~ **powers** осóбые/чрезвычáйные полномóчия.

specialist *n* специалúст; **an eye/heart ~** специалúст по глазны́м/сердéчным болéзням; **he's a ~ on Tolstoy** он специалúст по Толстóму.

speciality *n* специáльность; **her ~ is Greek tragedy** тéма её исслéдования—грéческая трагéдия; **the firm's ~ is rocking chairs** фúрма специализúруется на изготовлéнии крéсел-качáлок; **this dish is her ~** э́то её фúрменное блю́до.

specialize *vi*: **to ~ in** специализúроваться в + *P* *or* по + *D* (*impf and pf*); **he ~s in Chinese history** он специализúруется по истóрии Китáя.

specially *adv* осóбенно; специáльно; **I'm ~ glad to see you** я осóбенно рад вúдеть тебя́; **but I ~ asked for trout** я ведь закáзывал форéль; **his suits are ~ tailored** егó костю́мы сшúты по осóбому закáзу; **it was ~ made for me** э́то сдéлано специáльно для меня́.

species *n* (*sing or pl*) (*of plant, animal*) вид, род; порóда; **the origin of ~** происхождéние вúдов; **the human ~** человéческий род; *fig* **that's a ~ of blackmail** э́то разновúдность шантажá.

specific *adj* специфúческий, осóбый; определённый; **a ~ remedy** специфúческое срéдство; **I brought this book for a ~ purpose** я принёс э́ту кнúгу с осóбой/определённой цéлью; *Phys* ~ **gravity** удéльный вес.

specification *n* спецификáция; ~**s for a yacht** спецификáция (*sing*) для я́хты.

specify *vti* уточн|я́ть (-úть); определ|я́ть (-úть); (*stipulate*) предусм|áтривать (-отрéть), обуслóв|ливать (-ить); **the contract specifies payment in cash** в контрáкте предусмóтрена вы́плата налúчными (*pl*); **you didn't ~ the colour** ты не указáл, какóй цвет.

specimen *n* образéц, обрáзчик; экземпля́р; ~**s of minerals** образцы́ минерáлов; **this beetle is a good ~ of its kind** э́тот жук—типúчный экземпля́р своегó вúда; *Med* **a blood/urine ~** прóба крóви/мочú; *attr*: ~ **copy** сигнáльный экземпля́р; ~ **page/signature** образéц рýкописи/пóдписи.

specious *adj* благовúдный.

speck *n* пя́тнышко, крáпинка; **there wasn't a ~ of dirt anywhere** нигдé нé было ни сорúнки; **a ~ of dust** пылúнка.

speckled *adj*: **a ~ hen** ряба́я/пёстрая кýрица, пестрýшка; ~ **tweed** твид в крáпинку.

spectacle *n* **1** зрéлище, *also Theat, Cine*

2 *pl* (~**s**) *CQ abbr* **specs,** *also* **a pair of ~s** очкú (*no sing*); *fig* **to see things through rose-coloured ~s** смотрéть на всё сквозь рóзовые очкú; *attr*: ~ **case** футля́р для очкóв.

spectacular *adj* эффéктный; *CQ* потрясáющий; **a ~ occasion/***CQ* **success** эффéктное зрéлище, потрясáющий успéх.

spectator *n* зрúтель (*m*).

spectrum *n* спектр.

speculate *vi* **1** (*ponder*) размышля́ть, раздýмывать (*impfs*); **to ~ about/upon the future** размышля́ть о бýдущем

2 *Fin*: **to ~ in shares/currency** спекулúровать áкциями/валю́той (*impf*).

speculation, *CQ abbr* **spec** *n* **1** (*thought*) размышлéние, раздýмье; (*supposition*) предположéние; (*guess*) догáдка; **it's pure ~** э́то всегó лишь предположéние, э́то чúстая догáдка; *CQ* **I bought it/I went along on spec** я э́то купúл/я пошёл тудá наугáд (*adv*)

2 *Fin* спекуля́ция; ~ **in gold** спекуля́ция зóлотом.

speculator *n* биржевóй делéц; *pejor* спекуля́нт.

speech *n* **1** (*faculty or manner of speech*) речь; **freedom of ~** свобо́да сло́ва; **by his ~ I'd say he's from the Ukraine** по его́ ре́чи/вы́говору я бы сказа́л, что он отку́да-то с Украи́ны

2 (*formal address*) речь; **to make/deliver a ~** произноси́ть речь, выступа́ть с ре́чью.

speechify *vi pejor* разглаго́льствовать (*impf*).

speechless *adj*: **we were left ~** мы потеря́ли дар ре́чи; **I was ~ with fury** я задохну́лся от я́рости.

speed *n* **1** ско́рость; быстрота́; **the ~ of light/sound** ско́рость све́та/зву́ка; **I drove at an average ~ of 40 km per hour** я е́хал в сре́днем со ско́ростью со́рок киломе́тров в час; **at full/lightning ~** на по́лной ско́рости, с быстрото́й мо́лнии; *attr*: **to exceed the ~ limit** превыша́ть преде́льную ско́рость

2 *Photo* (*of film*) светочувстви́тельность; (*length of exposure*) вы́держка.

speed *vi* нести́сь, мча́ться (*impfs*); **he/the train sped past** он/по́езд промча́лся ми́мо; **how the years ~ by** как бы́стро летя́т го́ды; *Aut CQ* **he was ~ing** он превы́сил преде́льную ско́рость

speed up *vti vt* ускор|я́ть (-́ить); **to ~ up production/the work** ускоря́ть вы́пуск проду́кции/темп рабо́ты

vi: **the train is ~ing up** по́езд набира́ет/увели́чивает ско́рость/ход.

speedboat *n* быстрохо́дный ка́тер.

speeding *n Aut* превыше́ние ско́рости.

speed merchant *n CQ* (*of driver*) лиха́ч.

speedometer *n* спидо́метр.

speedy *adj* бы́стрый, ско́рый; **a ~ recovery/service** бы́строе выздоровле́ние/обслу́живание; **a ~ answer** незамедли́тельный отве́т.

spell[1] *n* (*in words*) за́говор, заклина́ние; (*fascination*) ча́ры (*no sing*), *also fig*; *fig*: **he was under the ~ of her beauty/of the music** он был очаро́ван *or* околдо́ван её красото́й, его́ плени́ла му́зыка; **to break the ~** наруша́ть очарова́ние.

spell[2] *n* **1** (*turn*; *of work, etc.*): **we took ~s at digging** мы копа́ли по о́череди; **let me take a ~ at the wheel** тепе́рь я поведу́ маши́ну; **a ~ of duty** дежу́рство

2 (*period*) пери́од, срок; **by/in ~s** пери́одами; **he's done his ~ in prison** он о́тбыл срок/отсиде́л своё в тюрьме́; **they are going through a bad ~** сейча́с у них тяжёлый пери́од; **a ~ of cold weather** пери́од холодо́в; **I did a ~ as a travelling salesman** я како́е-то вре́мя был коммивояжёром.

spell[3] *vti vt*: **how do you ~ your name?** как пи́шется ва́ша фами́лия?; **he can't even ~ his name correctly** он не уме́ет да́же пра́вильно написа́ть своё и́мя; **~ it for me** скажи́ мне по бу́квам; *fig* **it ~s disaster/ruin for us** э́то сули́т нам беду́, э́то для нас означа́ет разоре́ние (*financial*)

vi: **he can't ~** он пи́шет негра́мотно/с оши́бками

spell out *vt* (*read letter by letter*) раз|бира́ть по бу́квам (-обра́ть); (*decipher*) расшифро́в|ывать (-а́ть); *fig* **no need to ~ out the problem for you** я тебе́ не собира́юсь разжёвывать э́тот вопро́с.

spellbound *adj* очаро́ванный, околдо́ванный; **he held his audience ~** он околдова́л слу́шателей.

spelling *n* (*subject*) орфогра́фия; **this is the American ~** так америка́нцы пи́шут э́то сло́во; **what is the correct ~ of this word?** как пра́вильно пи́шется э́то сло́во?; *attr* орфографи́ческий.

spend *vti vt* **1** тра́тить (ис-, по-); расхо́довать (из-); затра́|чивать (-тить); **to ~ money on smth** тра́тить де́ньги (*pl*) на что-л, *CQ* тра́титься на что-л; **to ~ a fortune** истра́тить ку́чу де́нег/це́лое состоя́ние; **he didn't ~ a single penny** он не потра́тил ни копе́йки; **he ~s money like water** он сори́т деньга́ми; *euph* (*UK*) **to ~ a penny** пойти́ в туале́т

2 (*energy*) истра́тить, затра́тить; (*time*) про|води́ть (-вести́); **I spent a lot of energy in getting the spare parts** мне сто́ило таки́х уси́лий (*pl*) раздобы́ть запасны́е ча́сти; **he ~s his spare time reading** всё свобо́дное вре́мя он чита́ет; **I spent a week in Paris** я провёл неде́лю в Пари́же

3 (*in passive* = **used up**): **our ammunition is spent** на́ши боеприпа́сы (*pl*) ко́нчились

vi: **he's always ~ing** он ве́чно тра́тит де́ньги.

spending *n*: **government ~** прави́тельственные расхо́ды (*pl*).

spendthrift *n* расточи́тель (*m*), *f* -ница; мот, *f* -о́вка.

sperm *n* спе́рма.

sphere *n* сфе́ра, *also fig*; *fig* **~ of activity/influence** сфе́ра де́ятельности/влия́ния.

spherical *adj* сфери́ческий.

spice *n* спе́ция, пря́ность, припра́ва; *fig* пика́нтность; **to add ~ to the story** придава́ть пика́нтность расска́зу.

spice *vt*: **to ~ with** приправ|ля́ть + *I* (-́ить); сда́бривать + *I* (сдо́брить); *fig* **his account was highly ~d** его́ расска́з был по́лон пика́нтных подро́бностей.

spick-and-span *adj*: **she keeps the house ~** у неё в до́ме всё блести́т; **she is always ~** она́ всегда́ опря́тно оде́та.

spicy *adj* о́стрый, пря́ный; *fig* пика́нтный.

spider *n* пау́к.

spike *n* (*sharp point*) остриё; (*on railings*) зубе́ц; (*on shoe*) шип; (*to hold letters, bills*) нако́лка; (*of corn*) ко́лос; (*of cello*) шпиль (*m*).

spike *vt* пронз|а́ть (-и́ть), про|ка́лывать (-коло́ть); **~d shoes** башмаки́ с шипа́ми; *fig* **we ~d his guns for him** мы ста́вили ему́ па́лки в колёса.

spill *n*: **he had a nasty ~ from/out of...** он упа́л с + *G* (и си́льно ушибся).

spill *vti vt* **1** (*liquids*) проли|ва́ть, разли|ва́ть (*pfs* -́ть); (*sand, salt*) просып|а́ть, рассып|а́ть (*pfs* -́ать); (*objects*) вы|ва́ливать (-́валить); **she spilt wine down her dress** она пролила́ вино́ себе́ на пла́тье; **I spilt milk/salt all over the table** я проли́л *or* разли́л молоко́, я рассы́пал соль по всему́ столу́; **when the box opened, it spilt its contents on to the floor** когда́ я́щик откры́лся, из него́ вы́валилось всё содержи́мое; *fig* **there's no use crying over spilt milk** потéрянного не вернёшь

2: the boat capsized and we were spilt into the water ло́дка опроки́нулась, и мы свали́лись в во́ду

vi (*of liquids*) пролива́ться, разлива́ться; (*of sand, etc.*) просыпа́ться, рассыпа́ться; (*of objects*) выва́ливаться.

spin *n* (*rotation*) круже́ние, враще́ние; (*instructions on washing machine*) **long/short ~** (не)продолжи́тельный отжи́м; *Aer* **to go into/to get out of a ~** войти́ в што́пор, вы́йти из што́пора; *Sport*: **to put ~ on a ball** закрути́ть мяч; (*in tennis*) **top ~** то́пспин; *fig CQ*: **to go for a ~ in the car/on a bike** прокати́ться на маши́не/на велосипе́де; **I got into a (flat) ~** я впал в па́нику.

spin *vti vt* **1** (*thread, yarn*) прясть (с-); **to ~ a web** плести́ паути́ну (с-); *fig CQ* **to ~ a yarn** плести́ небыли́цы (*pl*)

2: to ~ a wheel враща́ть/верте́ть колесо́ (*usu impfs*); **to ~ a coin/a top** пус|ка́ть моне́ту волчко́м/волчо́к (-ти́ть)

vi **1** (*of spinner*) прясть; (*of spider*) плести́

2 *also* **to ~ round** крути́ться, кружи́ться, верте́ться, враща́ться (*impfs*); **the earth ~s on its axis** земля́ враща́ется/ве́ртится вокру́г свое́й оси́; **the record/wheel is ~ning (round)** пласти́нка ве́ртится, колесо́ кру́тится; **the dancers were ~ning faster and faster** танцо́ры кружи́лись всё быстре́е и быстре́е; **my head is ~ning** у меня́ голова́ кру́жится; **he spun round on his heel** он ре́зко поверну́лся на каблука́х

3 *Sport*: **to ~ for fish** лови́ть ры́бу (со) спи́ннингом

spin out *vt* растя́|гивать (-ну́ть); **he spun out the work over a month/his story** он растяну́л рабо́ту на ме́сяц, он не́сколько затяну́л расска́з; **I'll have to ~ out the money till pay day** мне придётся растяну́ть э́ти де́ньги до зарпла́ты.

spinach *n* шпина́т.

spinal *adj*: **~ cord/column** спинно́й мозг, спинно́й хребе́т *or* позвоно́чный столб.

spin-drier *n* суши́льный бараба́н.

spindrift *n* морска́я пе́на.

spine *n Anat* позвоно́чник; *Zool* (*of hedgehog, etc.*) игла́; *Bot* шип, колю́чка; (*of book*) корешо́к.

spineless *adj Zool* беспозвоно́чный; *fig* бесхребе́тный.

spinning *n* пряде́ние; *attr*: **~ machine** пряди́льный стано́к; **~ wheel** пря́лка; **~ top** волчо́к; (*for fishing*): **~ rod** спи́ннинг; **~ reel** кату́шка спи́ннинга.

spinster *n* незаму́жняя же́нщина; *CQ* ста́рая де́ва.

spiral *n* спира́ль; **in a ~** по спира́ли; *attr* спира́льный; **a ~ staircase** винтова́я ле́стница.

spire *n* шпиль (*m*).

spirit *n* **1** (*soul*) дух, душа́; **the life of the ~** духо́вная жизнь; **I shall be with you in ~** мы́слями/се́рдцем бу́ду с тобо́й

2 (*supernatural being*) дух

3 (*person*) душа́; **kindred ~s** ро́дственные ду́ши; **he was the leading ~ of the movement** он был душо́й э́того движе́ния

4 (*vitality, courage*): **he has great ~** он си́льный ду́хом челове́к; **he lacks ~** ему́ не хвата́ет жи́зненной си́лы; **he sang with great ~** он пел с больши́м чу́вством

5 (*mood, attitude*) дух; **fighting ~** боево́й дух; **in a ~ of forgiveness** в ду́хе проще́ния; **the ~, not the letter of the law** дух, а не бу́ква зако́на; **to enter into the ~ of things** осво́иться с обстано́вкой; **he took it in the wrong ~** он не так э́то по́нял

6 *pl* (**~s**) (*frame of mind*) дух, настрое́ние (*sings*); **he kept his ~s up by singing** он пел для бо́дрости ду́ха; **keep your ~s up** не па́дай ду́хом, не уныва́й; **he is in excellent/high/poor ~s** он в отли́чном/припо́днятом/пода́вленном настрое́нии

7 *Chem* спирт; (*alcohol*) (**~s**) спиртны́е напи́тки; **raw ~** чи́стый спирт; **I don't drink ~s** я не пью спиртно́го (*sing*); *attr*: **~ lamp/stove** спирто́вка; **~ level** ватерпа́с.

spirited *adj* (*of person, horse, etc.*) живо́й; **a ~ argument** горя́чий спор; **a ~ performance** вдохнове́нное исполне́ние.

spiritual *n*: **a (negro) ~** спи́ричуал.

spiritual *adj* духо́вный; *fig* **he was the ~ heir of Herzen** он был духо́вный насле́дник Ге́рцена.

spiritualism *n* спирити́зм.

spiritualist *n* спири́т.

spit[1] *n Geog* коса́, о́тмель, стре́лка; *Cook* ве́ртел.

spit[2] *n* (*spittle*) слю́ни (*no sing*); плево́к; (*saliva*) слюна́; *fig* **he is the dead ~ of his uncle** он вы́литый дя́дя.

spit[2] *vti vt, also* **~ out/up** вы|плёвывать (-плюнуть); **to ~ blood** плева́ть/ха́ркать кро́вью (*usu impfs*); **I spat out the plum stone** я вы́плюнул сли́вовую ко́сточку; *fig* **it was ~ting rain** накра́пывал до́ждик, (*under a sunny sky*) шёл грибно́й дождь

vi плева́ть (плю́нуть), *CQ* плева́ться (*impf*); (*of fat, etc.*) бры́з|гать (-нуть), бры́згаться (*impf*); **he spat in my face** он плю́нул мне в лицо́; **the bacon is ~ting in the pan** беко́н шипи́т на сковоро́дке; **the cat spat at the dog** ко́шка шипе́ла на соба́ку; **it began to ~** (*rain*) ста́ло накра́пывать.

spite *n* **1** зло́ба; **out of ~** по зло́бе, назло́ (*adv*)

2: in ~ of *as prep* несмотря́ на + *A*; **in ~ of the fact that I was late** несмотря́ на то, что я опозда́л; **I'll do it in ~ of everyone** я сде́лаю э́то наперекор всем.

spite *vt*: **he said it to ~ me** он э́то сказа́л мне назло́.

spiteful *adj* зло́бный.

spittle *n* слю́ни (*pl*); плево́к.

spittoon *n* плева́тельница.

spiv *n* (*UK*) *sl* спекуля́нт.

splash *n* всплеск; **the bottle fell into the water with a ~** буты́лка с всплёском упа́ла в во́ду; **a ~ of colour** цветово́е пятно́; *fig* **the news made a ~** э́ти но́вости (*pl*) наде́лали мно́го шу́му/шу́ма.

splash *vti vt* плес|ка́ть (-ну́ть) *and compounds*; **he ~ed water at me** он плесну́л на меня́ водо́й; **I ~ed ink all over the book/milk on the floor** я зака́пал всю кни́гу черни́лами, я расплеска́л молоко́ на́ пол; **don't ~ me!** не бры́згайся!; **he ~ed his face with water** он ополосну́л лицо́ водо́й; **your coat is ~ed with mud** у тебя́ пальто́ забры́згано гря́зью; **be careful the hot fat doesn't ~ you** осторо́жно, что́бы на тебя́ не бры́знуло (*impers*) горя́чим жи́ром; *fig*: **the news was ~ed all over the front page** э́той но́вости была́ посвящена́ вся пе́рвая страни́ца газе́ты; **they ~ money about** они́ броса́ют де́ньги на ве́тер

vi плеска́ться; **she/a fish was ~ing about in the water** она́/ры́ба плеска́лась в воде́; **the dog loves ~ing in puddles** соба́ка лю́бит бе́гать по лу́жам и бры́згаться; **milk ~ed out of the jug** молоко́ вы́плеснулось из кувши́на

splash down *vi* (*of spacecraft*) приводн|я́ться (-и́ться).

spleen *n Anat* селезёнка; *fig*: **a fit of ~** при́ступ хандры́; **to vent one's ~ on smb** сорва́ть зло́бу на ком-л.

splendid *adj* великоле́пный, *also CQ*.

splice *vt* (*of rope*) сра́|щивать (-сти́ть); (*of film*, *tape*) скле́и|вать (-ть).

splint *n Med* ши́на; **they put my arm in a ~** мне на́ руку наложи́ли ши́ну.

splinter *n* (*of wood*) лучи́на, ще́пка; (*of glass*, *bone*, *shell*, *stone*, *etc*.) оско́лок; (*in finger*) зано́за; *attr fig*: **~ group** отколо́вшаяся группиро́вка.

splinter *vti* (*of wood*, *bone*) расщеп|ля́ть(ся) (-и́ть(ся)); (*of glass*, *etc*.) раск|а́лывать(ся) (-оло́ть(ся)).

splinterproof *adj* безоско́лочный.

split *vti vt* **1** (*of wood*) коло́ть, раска́лывать (*pfs* расколо́ть); (*of fabric*, *seam*, *etc*.) раз|рыва́ть (-орва́ть); (*of fission*) расщеп|ля́ть (-и́ть); **he ~ the log in two** он расколо́л бревно́ попола́м (*adv*); **he/the blow ~ his head open** он раскрои́л себе́/уда́р раскрои́л ему́ че́реп; **the lightning ~ the tree** мо́лния расщепи́ла де́рево; *Phys* **to ~ the atom** расщепи́ть а́томное ядро́; *Polit* **this issue ~ the party** э́тот вопро́с вы́звал раско́л в па́ртии; *fig* **let's not ~ hairs** не бу́дем копа́ться в мелоча́х; **I ~ my sides laughing** я чуть со́ смеху не ло́пнул

2 (*divide*, *share*) дели́ть (по-), раздел|я́ть (-и́ть); **shall we ~ the difference?** дава́й поде́лим ра́зницу ме́жду собо́й; **we ~ the money three ways** мы раздели́ли де́ньги на три ча́сти

vi **1** (*of wood*, *etc*.) раска́лываться; (*of fabric*, *etc*.) разрыва́ться; (*of earth*, *rocks*, *skin*) тре́с|каться (-нуть); **my trousers have ~ at the seams** у меня́ брю́ки ло́пнули по швам; **the bag ~ open** мешо́к ло́пнул

2 (*divide*): **we ~ into three groups** мы раздели́лись (*by agreement*)/расколо́лись (*through conflict*) на три гру́ппы

3 *CQ*: **don't ~ on me** не выдава́й меня́

split off *vti* (*of wood*, *branch*) от|ка́лывать(ся) (-коло́ть(ся)), (*separate*) отдел|я́ть(ся) (-и́ть(ся)), *both also fig*

split up *vti vt* дели́ть (раз-, по-); **I ~ the work up between three of the students** яподели́л э́ту рабо́ту ме́жду тремя́ студе́нтами

vi (*of people*) расходи́ться (разойти́сь); **the crowd ~ up** толпа́ разошла́сь; **they ~ up after ten years of marriage** они́ разошли́сь, прожи́в вме́сте де́сять лет.

split-level *adj*: **a ~ house** дом, постро́енный на ра́зных у́ровнях.

splitting *adj CQ*: **I've got a ~ headache** у меня́ голова́ раска́лывается.

splodge *n* (*of colour*, *dirt*) пятно́; (*of ink*) кля́кса.

splutter *vi* (*of candle*, *fat*, *fire*) потре́скивать (*impf*); (*of engine*) треща́ть (*impf*); *fig* **he was ~ing with rage** он бры́згал слюно́й от я́рости.

spoil *n usu pl* добы́ча (*sing*); *Comm joc* при́быль.

spoil *vti vt* **1** (*damage*) по́ртить (ис-); **the building ~s the view** э́то зда́ние по́ртит вид; **it will ~ your appetite** э́то испо́ртит тебе́ аппети́т; **our holidays were ~t by bad weather** плоха́я пого́да испо́ртила нам весь о́тпуск (*sing*); **the effect is quite ~t** всё впечатле́ние испо́рчено; **a ~t ballot paper** недействи́тельный избира́тельный бюллете́нь

2 (*pamper*) балова́ть (из-)

vi по́ртиться; *CQ* **he is ~ing for a fight** он ле́зет в дра́ку.

spoilsport *n*: **he's such a ~** он всегда́ всё по́ртит.

spoke *n* (*of wheel*) спи́ца; (*of ladder*) перекла́дина, ступе́нька; *fig* **to put a ~ in smb's wheel** вставля́ть кому́-л па́лки в колёса (*pls*).

spoken *adj*: **a ~ promise** у́стное обеща́ние; **the ~ language** разгово́рный язы́к.

spokesman *n*: **a government ~ said...** представи́тель (*m*) прави́тельства заяви́л...

sponge *n* **1** гу́бка; (*a wash*) **to give smb a ~** вы́мыть кого́-л; *fig* **to throw up the ~** сда́ться; *attr*: **~ bag** су́мочка для туале́тных принадле́жностей

2 *Cook* бискви́тный торт.

sponge *vti vt* **1** *also* **to ~ down** тере́ть/мыть гу́бкой (*impfs*) *and compounds*; **she ~d his face/down the invalid** она́ вы́терла ему́ лицо́ гу́бкой, она́ обтёрла больно́го гу́бкой; **to ~ a carpet** чи́стить/про|тира́ть ковёр (вы́-/-тере́ть)

2 *CQ*: **he ~d a fiver off me** он вы́удил у меня́ пять фу́нтов

vi CQ: **he is always sponging (on/off his friends)** он ве́чно угоща́ется за счёт друзе́й.

sponger *n* прижива́л, *f* -ка.

sponsor *n* (*guarantor*) поручи́тель (*m*); (*UN*) **~ of a resolution** а́втор прое́кта резолю́ции; **to stand ~ for smb** руча́ться за кого́-л; *TV*, *Radio*, *Sport* **their firm is the ~ of the programme** програ́мма финанси́ровалась их фи́рмой.

sponsor *vt*: (*UN*) **to ~ a resolution** вноси́ть прое́кт резолю́ции (внести́); **to ~ a new member** (*of club*) рекомендова́ть но́вого чле́на; *Sport* **to ~ a team/competition** финанси́ровать кома́нду/соревнова́ния (*pl*); *TV*, *Radio* **the programme is ~ed by** програ́мма финанси́руется + *I*.

spontaneous *adj* (*of one's own accord*) самопроизво́льный; (*of character*, *talk*, *etc.*) непринуждённый, непосре́дственный; **~ combustion** самовоспламене́ние, самовозгора́ние; **a ~ demonstration** стихи́йная демонстра́ция; **his offer was ~** он предложи́л э́то с хо́ду.

spooky *adj CQ* жу́ткий; **a ~ film** фильм у́жасов; **it's really ~ in that cellar** в э́том по́гребе действи́тельно жуткова́то.

spool *n* (*of film*, *camera*, *fishing rod*) кату́шка; (*of sewing machine*) шпу́ля, шпу́лька; (*of tape-recorder*) боби́на.

spoon *n* ло́жка; **dessert/table/tea ~** десе́ртная/столо́вая/ча́йная ло́жка; *fig* **to be born with a silver ~ in one's mouth** роди́ться в руба́шке.

spoonfeed *vt* (*of child*, *etc.*) корми́ть с ло́жечки (на-); *fig* **teachers shouldn't ~ their pupils** учителя́ не должны́ всё разжёвывать/преподноси́ть ученика́м всё на блю́дечке.

spoonful *n*: **one ~ of honey** ло́жка мёда.

spoor *n* след, следы́ (*pl*).

sporadically *adv* споради́чески, уры́вками.

spore *n Biol* спо́ра.

sport *n* **1** спорт (*no pl*), спорти́вные и́гры; **outdoor/indoor ~s** и́гры на откры́том во́здухе/в закры́том помеще́нии; **he is good at ~/at several ~s** он хоро́ший спортсме́н, он выступа́ет в не́скольких ви́дах спо́рта; **school ~s** шко́льные соревнова́ния

2: **we had some good ~** (*fun*) мы хорошо́ повесели́лись/(*when hunting*) поохо́тились; **it was great ~** бы́ло о́чень заба́вно; *CQ* (*person*): **he's a good ~** он па́рень что на́до, он свой в доску; **come on, be a ~!** ну-ну́, подбодри́сь!

3 *Biol* мута́ция.

sport *vt*: **he was ~ing a flashy tie** он ходи́л, вы́ставив напока́з свой мо́дный га́лстук.

sporting *adj* **1** (*of dog*, *gun*) охо́тничий

2 *fig CQ*: **he's very ~** он па́рень что на́до; **give him a ~ chance** отнеси́сь к нему́ по-ры́царски; **there's a ~ chance he'll succeed** есть всё-таки наде́жда, что э́то ему́ уда́стся; **that's a ~ offer on his part** э́то великоду́шно с его́ стороны́.

sports *adj attr* спорти́вный; **~ ground/page/wear** спорти́вная площа́дка/страни́ца/оде́жда; **~ commentator** спорти́вный коммента́тор.

sportsman *n* спортсме́н; (*hunter*) охо́тник.

spot *n* **1** (*mark*) пятно́ (*also on animals*), *dim* пя́тнышко; (*as pattern*) кра́пинка; (*pimple*) прыщ(ик); *pl* (*rash*) сыпь; **a ~ of blood/dirt/red** крова́вое/гря́зное/кра́сное пятно́; **the wax made a dark ~ on the cloth** от во́ска на ска́терти оста́лось тёмное пятно́; **a dress with red ~s** пла́тье в кра́сный горо́шек (*collect*); **I felt a ~ of rain** на меня́ упа́ла ка́пля дождя́; **I came out in ~s** у меня́ вы́сыпала сыпь; *Astron* **sun ~s** пя́тна на со́лнце; *fig CQ* **he can knock ~s off his brother every time** он во всём опережа́ет своего́ бра́та

2 *CQ* (*esp. UK*) (*small amount*): **just a ~ of milk in my tea** нале́йте мне в чай немно́го молока́; **just a ~ of whisky please** мне, пожа́луйста, немно́го ви́ски; **will you have some more?—Just a ~** ещё доба́вить?—Чуть-чу́ть; **we had a ~ of lunch before we left** мы перекуси́ли пе́ред отъе́здом; **he is having a ~ of bother with his car** у него́ кака́я-то непола́дка в маши́не

3 (*place*) ме́сто; **a lovely ~** краси́вое ме́сто; **there's a tender ~ on my leg** у меня́ на ноге́ есть больно́е ме́сто; **he's our man on the ~** он там наш представи́тель; **I decided on the ~...** я на ме́сте/тут же реши́л...; *Aut*: **a blind ~** слепо́й се́ктор; **an accident/black ~** опа́сный уча́сток доро́ги; *fig*: **I know his weak ~s** я зна́ю его́ сла́бые сто́роны; **I've got a soft ~ for her** я пита́ю к ней сла́бость; **he's in a tight ~** сейча́с ему́ прихо́дится ту́го; **you've put me on the ~—I don't know what to say** тут вы меня́ озада́чили, не зна́ю что и отве́тить

4 *attr*: **~ remover** пятновыводи́тель (*m*); **~ check** вы́борочная прове́рка; *Radio* **~ announcement** э́кстренное сообще́ние.

spot *vti vt* **1** (*mark*) па́чкать (за-, пере-), зака́пать (*usu pf*); **a dress all ~ted with fat** пла́тье всё в жи́рных пя́тнах; **a page ~ted with ink stains** страни́ца, зака́панная черни́лами

2 (*notice*) заме|ча́ть (-тить); обнару́живать (-ть); разгляде́ть (*pf*); опозна|ва́ть (-ть); **he ~ted the mistake at once** он сра́зу заме́тил/обнару́жил оши́бку; **his deafness wasn't ~ted immediately** его́ глухоту́ не сра́зу обнару́жили/заме́тили; **I ~ted a flaw in the material** я разгляде́л дефе́кт на тка́ни; **I ~ted the winner** (*in horse race*)/**a French plane** я определи́л победи́теля ещё до нача́ла ска́чек, я опозна́л францу́зский самолёт

vi: **it is ~ting with rain** накра́пывает дождь.

spotless *adj*: **the floor is ~** пол чи́стый-пречи́стый; **he was in a ~ white shirt** он был в белосне́жной руба́шке.

spotlight *n Theat* проже́ктор.

spotlight *vt* осве|ща́ть (проже́ктором) (-ти́ть).

spot-on *adj CQ*: **what he said was ~** он попа́л как раз в то́чку.

spotted *adj* (*of animal*) пятни́стый; (*of fabric*) в горо́шек; **a ~ tie** га́лстук в горо́шек; *Med* **~ fever** сыпно́й тиф.

spotty *adj* (*of skin*) прыщева́тый; (*dirty*) в пя́тнах; **my apron is ~** у меня́ фа́ртук в пя́тнах.

spouse *n* супру́г, супру́га.

spout *n* (*of teapot, pump, etc.*) но́сик; (*jet of liquid*) струя́.

spout *vti vt*: **the fountain ~ed water** из фонта́на би́ла струя́ воды́

vi (*of water*) бить струёй, (*gush*) хлеста́ть (*only in impfs*); **water was ~ing from the pipe** вода́ би́ла струёй из трубы́; **blood was ~ing from the wound** из ра́ны хлеста́ла кровь; *fig CQ* **he could go on ~ing for hours** он мог часа́ми разглаго́льствовать.

sprain *n Med* растяже́ние.

sprain *vt* растя́|гивать (-ну́ть); **I ~ed a ligament/my ankle** я растяну́л себе́ свя́зку/лоды́жку.

sprat *n* ки́лька, шпрот.

sprawl *vi* (*of person*) растя́|гиваться (-ну́ться), *CQ* разва́ли|ваться (-́ться); **he was ~ing on the sofa** он растяну́лся/развали́лся на дива́не; **the blow sent him ~ing** уда́р сбил его́ с ног; **the suburbs ~ nearly to the edge of the forest** при́городы тя́нутся почти́ до ле́са.

spray[1] *n* гроздь, кисть; **a ~ of lilac** гроздь сире́ни.

spray[2] *n* **1** (*of waves, etc.*) бры́зги (*no sing*); (*from hose-nozzle, atomizer, etc.*) водяна́я пыль; **the ~ of a waterfall** бры́зги водопа́да; **hair ~** лак-аэрозо́ль для воло́с; **insecticide ~** ядохимика́т для опры́скивания

2 (*instrument: for water, insecticide*) распыли́тель (*m*), опры́скиватель (*m*); (*for scent, paint*) пульвериза́тор; (*for hair, etc.*) аэрозо́ль (*m*); *attr*: **~ attachment/nozzle** распыля́ющая наса́дка, распыля́ющее сопло́.

spray[2] *vt* опры́ск|ивать (-ать), *also Agric*; **the oil slick was ~ed with chemicals** нефтяна́я плёнка была́ опры́скана химика́лиями; **to ~ plants with insecticide** опры́скивать расте́ния ядохимика́тами (*pl*); **he ~ed some paint on the surface** он нанёс пульвериза́тором немно́го кра́ски на пове́рхность; **she ~ed herself with scent** она́ попры́скала себя́ духа́ми; **to ~ foam on flames** гаси́ть ого́нь пе́ной.

spread *n* **1** (*of fire, disease, knowledge*) распростране́ние; **to stop the ~ of nuclear weapons** останови́ть распростране́ние я́дерного ору́жия (*collect*)

2 (*span of wings, sail, etc.*) разма́х; *fig CQ joc* **middle-aged ~** возрастно́й жиро́к

3 *Cook* паште́т; **cheese ~** пла́вленый сыр(о́к); *fig CQ* **there was a marvellous ~ on the table** стол ломи́лся от яств.

spread *vti vt* **1** (*of sails, banner, newspapers*) раз|вёртывать (-верну́ть); (*of map, cards*) раскла́дывать (разложи́ть); (*of sheets, rugs*) расстила́ть (разостла́ть, расстели́ть); **he ~ the cards on the table** он разложи́л ка́рты на столе́; **to ~ a cloth on the table/a rug on the floor** постели́ть ска́терть на стол/ковёр на́ пол; **to ~ manure on the garden** разбр|а́сывать наво́з в огоро́де (-оса́ть); **to ~ one's hands** растопы́рить па́льцы (*usu pf*); **I ~ myself in front of the fire** я растяну́лся у огня́; **to ~ one's wings** расправ|ля́ть кры́лья (-́ить), *also fig*

2 (*of butter, bread, etc.*) ма́зать (на-, по-); (*smear*) разма́з|ывать (-ать); **to ~ butter on bread/bread with butter** нама́зать ма́сло на хлеб/хлеб ма́слом; **the child ~ jam all over his face** ребёнок вы́мазал лицо́ варе́ньем

3 (*distribute*) распростран|я́ть (-и́ть); (*carry*) раз|носи́ть (-нести́); **to ~ knowledge/news** распространя́ть зна́ния (*pl*)/но́вости (*pl*); **to ~ gossip/rumours** распространя́ть *or* распус|ка́ть спле́тни (*pl*)/слу́хи (-ти́ть); **the wind ~ the flames** ве́тер перебро́сил/разнёс пла́мя (*sing*); **flies ~ disease** му́хи разно́сят боле́зни (*pl*); **to ~ panic** се́five па́нику (*impf*); **to ~ (out) payments over two years** растяну́ть вы́плату на два го́да

vi **1**: **the desert ~s for hundreds of miles** пусты́ня простира́ется/тя́нется на со́тни миль

2 (*extend further*) распространя́ться, разноси́ться; **the fire/oil slick is ~ing** ого́нь/нефтяна́я плёнка распространя́ется всё да́льше и да́льше; **the news ~ quickly** э́та но́вость разнесла́сь о́чень бы́стро; **weeds have ~ all over the garden** сорняки́ заполони́ли весь сад

3 (*of butter, etc.*) нама́зываться.

spree *n*: **he is out on a ~** он загуля́л [**NB** *tense*]; **we had a wonderful ~** мы хорошо́ погуля́ли; **we went on a shopping ~** мы прошли́сь по магази́нам и чего́ то́лько не накупи́ли.

sprig *n* ве́точка.

sprightly *adj* живо́й, оживлённый, бо́дрый; **with a ~ step** бо́дрой похо́дкой.

spring[1] *n* **1** (*leap*) прыжо́к, скачо́к

2 (*of water*) исто́чник, родни́к, ключ; **hot/mineral ~s** горя́чие/минера́льные исто́чники; *attr*: **~ water** ключева́я вода́, вода́ из родника́

3 (*resilience*) упру́гость, эласти́чность

4 *Mech* пружи́на; (*of vehicle*) рессо́ра; **coil ~** пружи́нная рессо́ра; *attr*: **a ~ mattress** пружи́нный матра́ц.

spring[1] *vti vt* (*cause to go off, etc.*): **to ~ a mine/a trap** взрыва́ть ми́ну (взорва́ть), захло́п|ывать капка́н (-нуть); **the ship sprung a leak** кора́бль дал течь; *fig* **I wish you wouldn't ~ these surprises on me** хва́тит с меня́ э́тих сюрпри́зов; **he sprang the news on me without warning** он огоро́шил меня́ э́той но́востью

vi **1** (*leap*) пры́г|ать (-нуть), скака́ть (*impf*) *and compounds*; **he sprang across the fence/forward** он перепры́гнул че́рез забо́р, он бро́сился вперёд; **I managed to ~ aside** я успе́л отскочи́ть в сто́рону; **the dog sprang at him** соба́ка бро́силась на него́; **he sprang into the saddle/to his feet/out of the bushes** он вскочи́л в седло́/на́ ноги, он вы́скочил из кусто́в; **the cat sprang in through the window** ко́шка прыгнула в комнату через окно; **tears sprang to her eyes** у неё на глаза навернулись слёзы; **weeds are ~ing up everywhere** сорняки повсюду пошли в рост; **a breeze sprang up** поднялся ветерок

2 (*of timbers*: *begin to split*) трескаться (по-); (*split open*) лоп|аться (-нуть)

3 (*originate from*): **trees ~ from small seeds** деревья вырастают из маленьких семян; **his actions ~ from a desire to please** он так ведёт себя, желая понравиться

4 *fig uses*: **doubts ~ to mind** возникают сомнения; **a friendship sprang up between them** между ними завязалась дружба; **buildings are ~ing up like mushrooms** дома растут как грибы.

spring[2] *n* (*season*) весна; **in ~** весной; **~ is in the air** в воздухе пахнет весной; *attr* весенний.

springboard *n* трамплин.

spring tide *n Naut* сизигийный прилив.

sprinkle *vt* (*of liquids*) брыз|гать (-нуть); обрызг|ивать, опрыск|ивать (*pfs* -ать); (*of powders*) посып|ать (-ать); **to ~ the lawn** опрыскивать газон; **she ~d sugar over the strawberries** она посыпала клубнику (*collect*) сахаром; **to ~ sand on the roads** посыпать дороги песком; *fig* **the lawn is ~d with daisies** газон усеян/усыпан маргаритками.

sprinkler *n* (*for fire-fighting*) тушитель (*m*), спринклер; (*for lawn*) опрыскиватель (*m*); *Tech* пульверизатор.

sprint *n Sport* спринт; *fig* **he made a final ~** он сделал рывок на финише.

sprint *vi Sport* спринтовать; *fig* **I ~ed down the road/for the bus** я бросился бежать по улице/к автобусу.

sprout *n Bot* отросток, росток; **Brussels ~s** брюссельская капуста (*sing*).

sprout *vti vt*: **to ~ new shoots** пус|кать новые ростки (-тить)

vi прорас|тать (-ти); **mushrooms/weeds are ~ing (up) everywhere** пошли грибы, всюду вылезли сорняки [**NB** *tense*]; *fig* **skyscrapers are ~ing up in the suburbs** в пригородах вырастают небоскрёбы.

spruce[1] *n Bot* ель.

spruce[2] *adj* опрятный, чистенький.

spry *adj* проворный; живой; бодрый.

spunk *n CQ*: **he has no ~** он «тряпка».

spur *n* (*of rider, on cock*) шпора; **a mountain ~** отрог; **to set ~s to one's horse** пришпорить коня; *fig*: **it acted as a ~ to his ambition** это подстегнуло его самолюбие; **I invited them on the ~ of the moment** я их сразу же/тут же пригласил.

spur *vt*, *also* **to ~ on** пришпори|вать (-ть), *fig* под|стёгивать (-стегнуть); **this triumph ~red him on to yet greater efforts** эта победа вдохнула в него новые силы.

spurious *adj* поддельный.

spurn *vt* пренебре|гать + *I* (-чь).

spurt *n*: **a ~ of flame/water** вспышка пламени, струя воды; *Sport* спурт; **to put on a ~** сделать рывок, *also fig*; *fig* **a ~ of energy** прилив энергии.

spurt *vi* (*of water, blood, etc.*): **to ~ from** хлынуть/забить из + *G* (*pfs*).

spy *n* шпион.

spy *vti vt* (*notice*) заметить, подметить (*usu pfs*); **I spied him leaving the house** я заметил, как он вышел из дома; *fig* **to ~ out the land** зондировать почву (по-)

vi: **to ~ on the enemy/on smb's movements** выслеживать врага, следить за чьими-л действиями (*impfs*).

spying *n* шпионаж.

squabble *n* перепалка, перебранка.

squabble *vi* пререкаться (*impf*); вздорить (по-).

squad *n* отряд, *also Mil*; группа, команда, *also Sport*; **the flying/drug ~** летучий полицейский отряд, группа по борьбе с наркоманией.

squadron *n Mil* эскадрон; *Naut* эскадра; *Aer* эскадрилья; *attr*: **~ leader** командир эскадрильи.

squalid *adj* убогий; **to live in ~ conditions** жить в очень плохих условиях; **it's a ~ business** это гнусное занятие.

squall *n* **1** (*cry*) вопль, визг

2 *Meteorol* шквал; *fig* **there are ~s ahead** нас ожидают неприятности.

squall *vi* вопить (*impf*), визжать (взвизгнуть); орать (*impf*).

squally *adj* шквалистый.

squalor *n* запустение, убожество.

squander *vt* про|матывать (-мотать), растра|чивать (-тить), транжирить (рас-); **he ~ed his fortune** он промотал своё состояние; **he ~s his energy on trivialities** он растрачивает свою энергию по пустякам.

square *n* **1** *Geom, etc.* квадрат; (*of chessboard, crossword*) клетка, поле; **a ~ of cloth/paper** квадратный кусок ткани/бумаги; **a floor with black and white ~s** пол в чёрных и белых квадратах; **fold the paper into a ~** сложи бумагу, чтобы получился квадрат; *fig CQ* **now we're back to ~ one** теперь нам опять танцевать от печки

2 (*in town*) площадь

3 *Math* квадрат; **the ~ of 3 is 9** три в квадрате равно девяти, девять есть квадрат трёх

4 (*drawing instrument*: *T-square*) рейсшина; (*set square*) угольник; **it is on/out of the ~** это под прямым/косым углом; *fig*: **this deal is not on the ~** это нечестная сделка; *CQ pejor* **he's a ~** у него допотопные взгляды.

square *adj* **1** квадратный, *also Math*; (*right-angled*) прямой; **~ brackets** квадратные скобки; **he has ~ shoulders** у него прямые плечи, он широкоплечий; **a ~ corner/sail** прямой угол/парус; *Math* **a ~ root/kilometre** квадратный корень/километр; **the lawn is three metres ~** газон площадью (в) три квадратных метра

2 *fig* (*honest*) честный; (*upright*) прямой; **a ~ deal** честная сделка; **he was given a ~**

deal с ним поступи́ли че́стно; **we had a ~ meal** мы сы́тно/пло́тно пое́ли; **now we are all ~** мы тепе́рь в расчёте *or* мы тепе́рь кви́ты; **I'll get ~ with him** я с ним рассчита́юсь.

square *adv* пря́мо; **she looked me ~ in the face** она́ смотре́ла мне пря́мо в лицо́; **the house stands ~ with/to the church** дом стои́т под прямы́м угло́м к це́ркви.

square *vt* (*settle*): **to ~ one's accounts** при|води́ть в поря́док счета́ (-вести́); *fig*: **I'll ~ the porter so that we can get in late** я договорю́сь со швейца́ром, что́бы мы могли́ верну́ться по́здно; **I can't ~ that with my conscience/with what he told us** мне со́весть не позволя́ет с э́тим примири́ться, э́то ника́к не согласу́ется с тем, что он нам говори́л ра́ньше

vi: *fig* **that doesn't ~ with the facts** э́то не увя́зывается с фа́ктами.

squared *adj Math* в квадра́те; *School*: **a ~ exercise book, ~ paper** тетра́дь/бума́га в кле́точку.

square dance *n* (*country dancing, esp. US*) пля́ска, наро́дный та́нец.

squash *n* **1** (*crowd*) да́вка, толку́чка; **there was a ~ in the bus/at the bar** в авто́бусе была́ да́вка, о́коло сто́йки толпи́лся наро́д

2 (*UK*: *drink*): **lemon ~** концентри́рованный лимо́нный сок

3 (*US*: *vegetable*) ты́ква.

squash *vti vt* **1** (*press flat*) разда́в|ливать (-и́ть), *also fig*; **to ~ a fly** раздави́ть му́ху; **the child got ~ed in the throng** ребёнка чуть не задави́ли в толпе́; **the parcel got ~ed in the post** посы́лка вся была́ сплю́щена при пересы́лке; **he ~ed his nose against the glass** он прижа́л нос к стеклу́; *fig* **I felt completely ~ed** я чу́вствовал себя́ соверше́нно уничто́женным

2 (*squeeze*) вти́с|кивать (-нуть), запи́х|ивать (-ну́ть); **we can ~ in one more** мы мо́жем взять/вти́снуть ещё одного́ челове́ка; **to ~ smth into a case** запихну́ть что-л в чемода́н

vi вти́с|киваться, проти́с|киваться (*pfs* -нуться); сжима́ться (сжа́ться); тесни́ться (по-); **we ~ed through the gates** мы проти́снулись в воро́та; **if you ~ together/up there will be room for me** е́сли вы потесни́тесь, бу́дет ме́сто и для меня́; **we can all ~ into the car** мы мо́жем все умести́ться в маши́не.

squashy *adj* (*of fruit*) мяси́стый; (*of ground*) то́пкий, вя́зкий.

squat *adj* (*of person*) корена́стый, (*also of thing*) призе́мистый.

squat *vi* **1** *also* **to ~ down** сиде́ть на ко́рточках (*be down*), сесть/присе́сть на ко́рточки (*process of going down*)

2 (*occupy illegally*): **they are ~ting in the empty house** они́ всели́лись в/за́няли пусту́ющий дом.

squawk *vi* (*of bird*) крича́ть (кри́кнуть); (*of people*) визжа́ть (взви́згнуть).

squeak *n* (*of wheel, pen, hinge, shoes, etc.*) скрип; (*of mouse, person, etc.*) писк; *CQ* **one more ~ from you!** смотри́, то́лько пи́кни у меня́!

squeak *vi* (*of wheel, etc.*) скрип|е́ть (*-*нуть); (*of mouse, person, etc.*) пища́ть (пи́скнуть).

squeaky *adj* скрипу́чий; (*of voice*) пискли́вый.

squeal *vi* **1** (*of person, animal, brakes*) визжа́ть (взви́згнуть); **I'll make him ~!** он у меня́ попля́шет!

2 *CQ* (*inform*) я́бедничать (на-).

squeamish *adj* (*fastidious*) привере́дливый, брезгли́вый; **don't be so ~** не будь таки́м привере́дой; **I'm ~ about gutting fish** я бре́згую потроши́ть ры́бу; (*queasy*) **I feel ~** меня́ тошни́т (*impers*).

squeeze *n*: **he gave my hand a ~** он сжал/(*tightly*) сти́снул мне ру́ку; **she gave him a hug and a ~** она́ обняла́ и прижа́ла его́ к себе́; **I like a ~ of lemon in my tea** я люблю́ чай с лимо́ном; **it was a tight ~ but we all got in/got past the lorry** бы́ло о́чень те́сно, но мы все помести́лись в маши́не, грузови́к прое́хал ми́мо, едва́ не заде́в нас.

squeeze *vti vt* **1** (*press*) сжима́ть (сжать); (*more tightly*) сти́с|кивать (-нуть), сда́в|ливать (-и́ть); вы|жима́ть (*-*жать); **I ~d my fingers in the door** я прищеми́л себе́ па́льцы две́рью; **to ~ a lemon/a sponge** вы́жать лимо́н/гу́бку; **to ~ water out of a towel/cream from a tube** вы́жать полоте́нце/крем из тю́бика; *fig* **to ~ money out of smb** вымога́ть де́ньги у кого́-л (*impf*)

2 (*pack in*) вти́с|кивать (-нуть); впи́х|ивать (-ну́ть); **I ~d everything into my bag** я запихну́л всё в су́мку; **we can ~ you into the car** мы мо́жем вти́снуть тебя́ в маши́ну; **the dentist ~d me in during the morning** зубно́й врач вы́кроил для меня́ вре́мя у́тром

vi вти́скиваться, проти́скиваться; **he ~ed into the car/under the fence** он с трудо́м вти́снулся в маши́ну/проле́з под забо́ром; **the four of us can ~ on to the sofa** мы вчетверо́м помести́мся на дива́не; **I could hardly ~ past** я едва́ мог проти́снуться.

squeezer *n* соковыжима́лка.

squelch *vi*: **they ~ed through the mud** они́ хлю́пали по гря́зи (*impf*).

squiggle *n* закорю́чка, загогу́лина, кара́кули (*pl*).

squint *n*: **he has a ~** у него́ косогла́зие, *CQ* он коси́т; *CQ*: **I had a ~ at the paper** я и́скоса взгляну́л на докуме́нт; **let's have a ~** да́й-ка взгляну́ть.

squirm *vi* извива́ться, ко́рчиться (*impfs*); **the worm was ~ing** червя́к извива́лся; **I ~ed with shame** я ко́рчился от стыда́.

squirrel *n* бе́лка.

squirt *vti vt* брыз|гать (-нуть); **he ~ed water at me** он бры́знул на меня́ водо́й; **he ~ed soda water into the glass** он плесну́л со́довой в стака́н

vi: **the juice ~ed into my eye/out of the tin** мне со́ком бры́знуло (*impers*) в глаз, сок бры́знул из ба́нки.

stab *n* **1** (*wound*) ко́лотая ра́на; (*blow*) уда́р (ножо́м); *fig*: **I felt a ~ of pain in my side** у меня́ кольну́ло/стрельну́ло (*impers*) в боку́; **a ~ of conscience** уко́р со́вести

2 *CQ* (*attempt*): **I'll have a ~ at it** я попыта́юсь; **she'll have a ~ at anything** она́ гото́ва взя́ться за что уго́дно.

stab *vti vt* ко|ло́ть (*semel* -льну́ть); (*and kill*) за|ка́лывать (-коло́ть); **he was ~bed in the leg/through the heart** его́ уда́рили ножо́м по ноге́/в се́рдце; **to ~ smb in the back** всади́ть кому́-л нож в спи́ну, *also fig*

vi ты́кать (ткнуть); **he ~bed at the adder with his stick** он ткнул гадю́ку па́лкой.

stabilize *vt* стабилизи́ровать (*impf and pf*).

stabilizer *n Naut, Aer* стабилиза́тор.

stable[1] *n* (*building or horses*) коню́шня; **he keeps a large ~** у него́ больша́я коню́шня.

stable[2] *adj* усто́йчивый, *also Chem, Phys*; (*of prices, situation*) стаби́льный; **a ~ currency/ladder/dinghy** усто́йчивая валю́та/ле́стница/ло́дка; **he is not very ~** у него́ не о́чень усто́йчивая пси́хика; **a ~ marriage** про́чный брак.

stack *n* **1** *Agric* (*of hay*) стог, скирда́; **a ~ of straw/logs** омёт соло́мы, шта́бель дров *or* поле́нница; **a ~ of books/papers/plates** ку́ча *or* гру́да книг/бума́г, гру́да таре́лок; *fig CQ* (*pl*) **~s of money/time** ку́ча (*sing*) де́нег, у́йма (*sing*) вре́мени

2 (*of chimney*) дымова́я труба́

3 (*in library, bookshop*) стелла́ж.

stack *vt*: **to ~ books/plates/wood** скла́дывать кни́ги/таре́лки в ку́чу, скла́дывать дрова́ в поле́нницу (сложи́ть); **to ~ hay** копни́ть се́но (с-); *fig* **the cards were ~ed against him** всё бы́ло про́тив него́.

stadium *n* стадио́н.

staff *n* (*of school, office, etc.*) персона́л; штат, шта́ты (*pl*); **the office ~** персона́л конто́ры; **to be on the ~** быть в шта́те; **to take smb on the ~** зачи́слить кого́-л в штат; **the teaching/editorial ~** преподава́тельский соста́в, сотру́дники реда́кции; **the professor and his ~** профе́ссор и его́ помо́щники/ассисте́нты; **he left/joined our ~** он ушёл от нас, он поступи́л к нам (на рабо́ту); **they keep a ~ of three** (*servants*) у них штат прислу́ги—три челове́ка; *attr*: **a ~ meeting** собра́ние сотру́дников/*School* учителе́й, *SU equiv* педсове́т; *Mil* **~ officer** офице́р шта́ба.

staff *vt*: **a well ~ed hospital** больни́ца, хорошо́ обеспе́ченная персона́лом; **they haven't ~ed the new college yet** в но́вом колле́дже ещё не укомплекто́ваны шта́ты.

stag *n* оле́нь-саме́ц (*m*); *fig CQ* **a ~ party** холостя́цкая вечери́нка, мальчи́шник.

stag beetle *n* жук-рога́ч.

stage *n* **1** *Theat* (*general*) сце́на; **to go on ~/(*as career*) the ~** вы́йти на сце́ну *or* эстра́ду, стать актёром; *attr*: **~ direction/door/fright** (сцени́ческая) рема́рка, служе́бный вход в теа́тр, волне́ние пе́ред вы́ходом на сце́ну

2 (*platform*) сце́на; помо́ст; подмо́стки (*pl, also in scaffolding*); **landing ~** при́стань

3 (*point, section*) ста́дия, эта́п; **in the early ~s of history/of his career** на ра́ннем эта́пе (*sing*) разви́тия/его́ карье́ры; **what ~ has the work reached?** на како́й ста́дии сейча́с рабо́та?; **we travelled by easy ~s** мы де́лали коро́ткие перее́зды; (*of work*) **take it in easy ~s** де́лай не всё сра́зу/э́то потихо́ньку.

stage *vt Theat* ста́вить (по-); *fig* **to ~ a demonstration** организо́в|ывать демонстра́цию (-а́ть).

stagehand *n* рабо́чий сце́ны.

stage manager *n* режиссёр.

stage whisper *n fig* гро́мкий шёпот.

stagger *vti vt* **1** потряс|а́ть (-ти́); **I was ~ed to hear of...** я был потрясён, узна́в о + *P*; **you ~ me** (*often iron*) ты меня́ поража́ешь

2 (*hours, etc.*): **the management have ~ed working hours** администра́ция распредели́ла часы́ рабо́ты

vi шата́ться (пошатну́ться); **he ~ed and fell** он пошатну́лся (*when standing*)/оступи́лся (*when walking*) и упа́л; **he ~ed from the blow/under the load** он пошатну́лся от уда́ра/под тя́жестью гру́за; **the drunk ~ed about/home** у пья́ного заплета́лись но́ги, пья́ный е́ле приплёлся домо́й.

staggering *adj fig CQ* потряса́ющий.

staging *n* (*production*) постано́вка.

stagnant *adj* стоя́чий; **a ~ pond** стоя́чий пруд; **there was ~ water in the ditches** вода́ застоя́лась в кана́вах; *fig* **production/trade is ~** в произво́дстве/в торго́вле засто́й.

stagnate *vi fig* (*of business, etc.*) быть в засто́е; **I don't want to ~ in this job** я не хочу́ до́лго заси́живаться на э́той рабо́те—от неё про́сто отупе́ешь.

staid *adj* (*of person*) степе́нный.

stain *n* (*mark*) пятно́, *also fig*.

stain *vti vt* пятна́ть (за-), *also fig*; **the juice has ~ed the cloth** сок оста́вил пя́тна на ска́терти; **to ~ floors/wood** пропи́т|ывать полы́ (-а́ть), мори́ть де́рево (про-)

vi оставля́ть пя́тна (*usu impf*); **that ink will ~** от э́тих черни́л пя́тна не смыва́ются.

stained-glass *adj*: **a ~ window** витра́ж.

stainless steel *n* нержаве́ющая сталь.

stair *n* (*one step*) ступе́нь(ка); *pl* (**~s**) ле́стница (*sing*); **he ran up/down the ~s** он взбежа́л/сбежа́л по ле́стнице; *attr*: **~ carpet** ле́стничный ковёр.

stake *n* **1** (*post*) кол

2 (*bet*) ста́вка; **high ~s** высо́кие ста́вки; **they played for high/low ~s** они́ игра́ли по большо́й/по ма́ленькой; *Sport* (*horse-race*) **Newmarket ~s** ска́чки в Ньюма́ркете; *fig*: **his honour was at ~** его́ честь была́ поста́влена на ка́рту; **he has a ~ in the company** он име́ет пай/владе́ет па́ем в э́той компа́нии.

stake *vt* **1**: **to ~ a plant** под|пира́ть расте́ние (-пере́ть); *fig* **to ~ a claim to** заяв|ля́ть свои́ права́ на + *A* (-и́ть)

2 (*bet*) де́лать ста́вку (с-); ста́вить (по-), *also fig*; **he ~d money on that horse**/*fig* **his all on the venture** он поста́вил на э́ту ло́шадь, он вложи́л всё в э́то предприя́тие.

stale *adj* (*food*) несве́жий; (*bread*) чёрствый; (*air*) спёртый; *fig*: **~ news** устаре́вшие но́вости (*pl*); (*of actor*) **he is growing ~** в его́ игре́ нет уже́ той све́жести исполне́ния; **he worked himself ~ before the exam** к экза́мену он совсе́м вы́дохся.

stalemate *n Chess* пат; *fig* тупи́к; **to reach a ~** зайти́ в тупи́к; **the ~ has been broken** вы́ход из тупика́ на́йден.

stalk[1] *n* (*of flower*) сте́бель (*m*); (*of fruit*, *leaf*) черено́к.

stalk[2] *vti vt* (*creep up on*) подкра́|дываться к + *D* (-сться); (*locate and follow*) вы|сле́живать (-следить); **he ~ed a large stag and shot/photographed it** он подкра́лся к большо́му оле́ню и уби́л его́/и сфотографи́ровал его́; **the Red Indians ~ed their foes in the forest** инде́йцы вы́следили враго́в в лесу́

vi: **he ~ed in as if he owned the place** он вошёл в дом хозя́йским ша́гом; **he ~ed out in a huff** он в гне́ве вы́шел из ко́мнаты.

stall *n* (*in stable*, *etc.*) сто́йло; (*vendor's*) ларёк, лото́к; (*for papers*, *etc.*) кио́ск; *pl* (~s) *Theat* парте́р (*sing*); **a book ~** кни́жный кио́ск.

stall *vti vt Aut*: **don't ~ the engine** смотри́, что́бы не загло́х мото́р

vi Aut, *Aer*: **the engine ~ed** мото́р загло́х; *fig* **they wouldn't answer definitely, but just ~ed** они всё тяну́ли с отве́том.

stallion *n* жеребе́ц.

stalwart *adj* (*strong*) кре́пкий, дю́жий; (*resolute*) сто́йкий, ве́рный; **a ~ Labour supporter** сто́йкий приве́рженец лейбори́стов.

stamina *n* сто́йкость, выно́сливость; **the athlete has no ~** у э́того спортсме́на не хвата́ет выно́сливости; **has he the intellectual ~ to do research?** хва́тит ли у него́ терпе́ния довести́ до конца́ иссле́дование?

stammer *n* заика́ние; **he speaks with/has a bad ~** он си́льно заика́ется; **they cured his ~** его́ вы́лечили от заика́ния.

stammer *vti vt*: **he ~ed out an apology** он, заика́ясь, пробормота́л извине́ния (*pl*)

vi заика́ться (*impf*).

stamp *n* **1** (*implement or impress*) печа́ть, штамп, ште́мпель (*m*); **a rubber ~ with the date** рези́новый ште́мпель (*m*) с ци́фрой да́ты; **a metal/wooden ~** печа́ть *or* чека́н, деревя́нная печа́ть

2 (*postage*, *etc.*) ма́рка; **(un)used ~s** (не)гашёные ма́рки; **insurance ~s** ма́рки для страхово́го свиде́тельства; *attr*: **~ album/collection/collector** альбо́м для ма́рок, колле́кция ма́рок, филатели́ст

3 *fig* печа́ть; отпеча́ток; **his work has the ~ of genius** его́ рабо́та отме́чена печа́тью ге́ния; **that school sets its ~ on its pupils** э́та шко́ла накла́дывает отпеча́ток на свои́х воспи́танников; **a man of his ~** челове́к тако́го скла́да.

stamp *vti vt* **1** (*foot*) то́п|ать (-нуть); **he ~ed his foot with rage** он я́ростно то́пнул ного́й; **we ~ed a trail in the snow** мы протопта́ли тропи́нку в снегу́; **he ~ed to shake the snow off his boots** он прито́пнул, отря́хивая снег с башмако́в

2 (*mark*, *impress*) ста́вить штамп/ште́мпель/печа́ть (по-), штампова́ть (про-); **an official ~ed the documents** чино́вник проштампова́л докуме́нты; **his briefcase was ~ed with his initials** на портфе́ле бы́ли вы́биты его́ инициа́лы; *fig* **his features are ~ed on my memory** его́ черты́ лица́ мне хорошо́ запо́мнились

3 (*postage*): **to ~ a letter** накле́и|вать ма́рку на письмо́/на конве́рт (-ть); **the letter is insufficiently ~ed** на письме́ накле́ено ма́ло ма́рок

vi то́п|ать (*semel* -нуть); (*of animal*) бить копы́том (*impf*); **he ~ed on my foot/on the spider** он наступи́л мне на́ ногу, он раздави́л паука́ ного́й

stamp out *vt*: **they ~ed out the rhythm** они́ отбива́ли такт нога́ми; **he ~ed out his cigarette** он затопта́л оку́рок; *fig* (*disease*, *corruption*) искорен|я́ть (-и́ть); (*resistance*) подав|ля́ть (-и́ть).

stampede *n*: **the procession turned into a ~** уча́стники проце́ссии обрати́лись в пани́ческое бе́гство.

stampede *vi*: **the horses ~d** ло́шади понесли́.

stand *n* **1** (*position*) ме́сто; *fig* пози́ция; *Mil* (*resistance*) сопротивле́ние, *also fig*; **he took up his ~ beside her** он за́нял ме́сто ря́дом с ней; *fig*: **he took a strong ~ on that point** он за́нял твёрдую пози́цию в э́том вопро́се; **the government made a ~ for its right to** пра́вительство отста́ивало пра́во свое́й страны́ + *inf*; *Mil* **the regiment made a heroic ~** полк герои́чески сопротивля́лся

2 (*supporting structure*) (*for parades*, *sport*, *etc.*) трибу́на; (*for vase*, *plant*, *etc.*) подста́вка; (*for coats*) ве́шалка; (*for camera*) штати́в; (*for music*) пюпи́тр; (*for newspapers*) кио́ск; (*in market*) лото́к; (*at exhibition*) стенд.

stand *vti vt* **1** (*place*) ста́вить (по-); **he stood the bottle on the table/the ladder against the wall** он поста́вил буты́лку на стол, он прислони́л/приста́вил ле́стницу к стене́

2 (*endure*) вы|носи́ть (-нести); терпе́ть (вы́-), вы|де́рживать (-держать); **I can't ~ this heat/heat** я не вы́держу э́той жары́, я не выношу́ жару́; **I can't ~ the thought of leaving** мне невыноси́ма са́мая мысль об отъе́зде; **I can ~ anything but that** я всё что уго́дно могу́ вы́нести/вы́терпеть, но то́лько не э́то; **I can't ~ being kept waiting** я терпе́ть не могу́, когда́ меня́ заставля́ют ждать; **his heart won't ~ the strain** его́ се́рдце не вы́держит тако́го напряже́ния; **she stood the shock well** она́ му́жественно перенесла́ э́тот уда́р

3 (*treat*): **he'll ~ us lunch/us each a vodka** он угости́т нас обе́дом, он нам поста́вит по рю́мке во́дки

4 *phrases*: **they stood their ground under attack/criticism** они́ отби́ли ата́ку, они́ не испуга́лись кри́тики; **he'll have to ~ trial** он до́лжен предста́ть пе́ред судо́м; **he ~s a fair chance of getting the job** у него́ есть шанс получи́ть э́то ме́сто

vi **1** (*be upright*) стоя́ть (*impf*) *and compounds*; **don't just ~ there, do something!** что же ты стои́шь, сде́лай что́-нибудь!; **we stood waiting for an hour** мы простоя́ли час в ожида́нии; **we had to ~ all the way** мы простоя́ли всю доро́гу; **he stood on my foot/on the beetle** он наступи́л мне на́ ногу/на жука́; (*in measurement*): **he ~s a good two metres** он ро́стом до́брых два ме́тра; **the tree ~s thirty metres high** высота́ де́рева достига́ет тридцати́ ме́тров; *fig*: **it's time to ~ on your own feet** пора́ тебе́ быть самостоя́тельным; **time seemed to ~ still** каза́лось, что вре́мя не дви́жется; **she stood in mortal fear of him** она́ смерте́льно его́ боя́лась; **he doesn't ~ on ceremony/on his dignity** он не церемо́нится/не ва́жничает

2 (*rise up*) вста|ва́ть (-ть); **all ~!** всем встать!; **his hair stood on end** у него́ во́лосы вста́ли ды́бом

3 (*be situated*) стоя́ть; **the house ~s on a hill** дом стои́т на холме́; **the truck stood in their way** грузови́к загора́живал им доро́гу; *fig*: **nothing now ~s in our way** ничто́ бо́льше нам не меша́ет; **where does he ~ in the firm?** како́й пост он занима́ет в э́той фи́рме?; **how do things ~?** как обстоя́т дела́?; **as things ~ we've no choice** положе́ние таково́, что у нас нет вы́бора; **where do you ~ with him?** каки́е у вас с ним отноше́ния?; **where do you ~ on that question?** каку́ю пози́цию ты занима́ешь в э́том вопро́се?

4 (*let remain unchanged*) оста|ва́ться (в си́ле) (-́ться); **the order/agreement ~s** прика́з/соглаше́ние остаётся в си́ле; **leave the text as it ~s** оста́вь текст как есть; **we'll let matters ~** мы оста́вим всё как есть; **the thermometer ~s at zero** термо́метр пока́зывает ноль гра́дусов; *Sport* **the record ~s at ten minutes** реко́рд по-пре́жнему ра́вен десяти́ мину́там

5 *various*: **we ~ to lose/gain a lot** мы мо́жем мно́гое потеря́ть/вы́играть; **to ~ as a candidate** быть кандида́том; **he stood for election** он баллоти́ровался на вы́борах; **he stood godfather to me** он мой крёстный (оте́ц) [**NB** *tense*]; **it ~s to reason that...** само́ собо́й разуме́ется, что...

stand about/around *vi*: **they stood about** *or* **around doing nothing/smoking** они стоя́ли без де́ла, они́ стоя́ли и кури́ли

stand back *vi*: **~ back or you'll be crushed** посторони́сь, а то зада́вят; **~ back from the barrier** отойди́ от барье́ра; **you need to ~ well back to see the picture** на э́ту карти́ну лу́чше смотре́ть, немно́го отступя́

stand by *vti vt*: **he ~s by his principles/word** он приде́рживается свои́х при́нципов, он де́ржит своё сло́во; **he stood by me** он меня́ подде́рж|ивал (-а́ть); **I ~ by all I said then** я ве́рен тому́, что тогда́ сказа́л

vi: (*idly*) **he stood by helplessly** он беспо́мощно стоя́л в стороне́; (*in readiness*) **~ by to welcome them** подгото́вьтесь к их встре́че; **troops are ~ing by** войска́ в боево́й гото́вности

stand down *vi* (*withdraw*): **to ~ down in smb's favour** уступ|а́ть своё ме́сто кому́-л (-и́ть), да|ва́ть кому́-л доро́гу (-ть)

stand for *vt fig*: **"K" ~s for kitten** «К» означа́ет «котёнок»; **I dislike him and all he ~s for** я не люблю́ его́ и всё, что с ним свя́зано

stand in *vi*: **he will ~ in for me at the meeting** он бу́дет на собра́нии вме́сто меня́

stand off *vti vt*: **to ~ workers off** отстра|ня́ть рабо́чих от рабо́ты (-и́ть)

vi: **the ships were ~ing off** суда́ удаля́лись от бе́рега

stand out *vi*: **he ~s out from the rest of the students** он выделя́ется среди́ студе́нтов; **it ~s out a mile that...** так и броса́ется в глаза́, что...; **he is ~ing out for his rights/against the proposal** он наста́ивает на свои́х права́х, он бо́рется про́тив э́того предложе́ния; *Naut* **the ship stood out to sea** кора́бль ушёл в мо́ре

stand over *vt*: **he stood over me all the time I was working** он всё вре́мя стоя́л у меня́ над душо́й, пока́ я рабо́тал

stand up *vti vt*: **~ the box up on end/against the wall** поста́вь я́щик стоймя́ *or CQ* на попа́/к сте́нке

vi: **when he ~s up properly, he's taller than you** когда́ он стои́т вы́прямившись, он вы́ше тебя́; **he owns nothing but the clothes he ~s up in** он гол как соко́л; *fig* **that story won't ~ up in court** э́та исто́рия прозвучи́т на суде́ неубеди́тельно

stand up for *vt* (*defend*): **she stood up for me/for herself** она́ за меня́ заступи́лась, она́ за себя́ постоя́ла; **~ up for what you think right** стой на том, что счита́ешь пра́вильным

stand up to *vt* (*resist*, *endure*): **his statement won't ~ up to close examination** его́ утвержде́ние не выде́рживает кри́тики; **no car could ~ up to that kind of treatment** тако́го обраще́ния ни одна́ маши́на не вы́держит.

standard *n* **1** (*flag*) зна́мя, флаг, *also fig*; (*royal*, *regimental*) штанда́рт

2 (*measure*, *degree*, *norm*) станда́рт, у́ровень (*m*), ме́рка, но́рма; **the gold ~** золото́й станда́рт; **this model is not up to ~** э́та моде́ль не соотве́тствует при́нятому станда́рту; **~ of living** жи́зненный у́ровень; **~s of education are falling** у́ровень (*sing*) образова́ния па́дает; **his work is of university ~** его́ рабо́та—на университе́тском у́ровне; **I'll never live up to those ~s** мне никогда́ не подня́ться до э́того у́ровня; (*moral*) **they can't be judged by our ~s** их нельзя́ суди́ть по на́шим ме́ркам, к ним не подхо́дят на́ши ме́рки; **you're applying a double ~ on this question** ты к э́тому вопро́су подхо́дишь с двойно́й ме́ркой; **~s have changed of late** за после́днее вре́мя но́рмы поведе́ния заме́тно измени́лись; **moral ~s** мора́льные при́нципы; **this work is of a high/low ~** э́та рабо́та высо́кого/ни́зкого ка́чества.

standard *adj* **1** станда́ртный, устано́вленный, типово́й; **~ weights and measures** станда́ртные ме́ры ве́са и длины́; **the ~ price** станда́ртная/устано́вленная цена́; **a ~ model** типово́й образе́ц; **~ English** литерату́рный/пра́вильный англи́йский язы́к; **~ pronunciation** при́нятое произноше́ние; **it is ~ practice to +** *inf* так при́нято,/повело́сь, что...; **a ~ work of reference** авторите́тный спра́вочник

2 (*upright*): **~ roses** шта́мбовые ро́зы; **~ lamp** торше́р.

standardize *vt* стандартизи́ровать (*impf and pf*).

stand-by *n*: **troops are on 24-hour ~** войска́ в положе́нии боеготовности; **he's a great ~ in a crisis** в тру́дном положе́нии на него́ всегда́ мо́жно положи́ться; **the freezer is a great ~** холоди́льник — больша́я по́мощь в хозя́йстве; **I always have tins as a ~** у меня́ всегда́ есть консе́рвы на вся́кий слу́чай.

stand-in *n* заме́на; *Theat, Cine* дублёр.

standing *n* **1** (*duration*): **a tradition of long ~** стари́нная тради́ция; **I'm a resident of 10 years ~** я здесь живу́ уже́ де́сять лет

2 (*rank, reputation*): **what is his ~ in the organization?** кем он явля́ется в э́той организа́ции?; **he has a high professional ~** у него́ высо́кие профессиона́льные ка́чества (*pl*).

standing *adj* (*continuous*) постоя́нный; **~ committee** постоя́нный комите́т; **we have a ~ order for that journal** на э́тот журна́л у нас постоя́нная подпи́ска; *fig* **it's a ~ joke** э́то постоя́нный предме́т для шу́ток.

standing room *n*: **~ only** есть то́лько стоя́чие места́ (*pl*).

stand-offish *adj* чо́порный.

standpipe *n* стоя́к.

standpoint *n*: **from the ~ of the consumer** с то́чки зре́ния потреби́теля.

standstill *n*: **wait till the bus has come to a ~** не выходи́те, пока́ авто́бус не остано́вится; *fig*: **the factory is at a ~** фа́брика проста́ивает; **the business was at a ~ for months** застой в дела́х дли́лся месяца́ми; **he worked himself to a ~** он заму́чил себя́ рабо́той.

stanza *n* строфа́.

staple[1] *n* (*for fixing wire, etc.*) скоба́; (*for papers*) скре́пка.

staple[1] *vt* (*wire, etc.*) прикреп|ля́ть скоба́ми к + *D* (-и́ть); **to ~ papers together** скрепля́ть бума́ги.

staple[2] *adj* основно́й; **~ products** основны́е това́ры; **rice is their ~ diet** рис — их основно́й проду́кт пита́ния.

star *n* звезда́ (*also for merit, Theat, Cine*); (*asterisk, star on epaulette, etc.*) звёздочка; (*on dog, etc.*) звёздочка, пятно́; *fig*: **to be born under a lucky ~** роди́ться под счастли́вой звездо́й; **you can thank your lucky ~s for that** благодари́ свою́ судьбу́/счастли́вую звезду́ (*sings*) за э́то; **he was the ~ of the match** он был геро́ем ма́тча.

star *vti*: **the film ~s Valentino, Valentino ~s in that film** в э́том фи́льме Валенти́но игра́ет гла́вную роль.

starboard *n Naut* пра́вый борт; **to ~** напра́во; **helm to ~!** пра́во руля́!; *attr*: **on the ~ side** с пра́вого бо́рта, по пра́вому бо́рту.

starch *n* крахма́л; **they eat a lot of ~** *approx* они́ едя́т мно́го мучно́го.

starch *vt* крахма́лить (на-); **stiffly ~ed collars** жёстко накрахма́ленные воротнички́.

stare *n* при́стальный взгляд; **a vacant ~** пусто́й взгляд.

stare *vti vt*: **he ~d the stranger up and down** он сме́рил незнако́мца при́стальным взгля́дом; *fig*: **disaster ~s us in the face** над на́ми нави́сла [**NB** *tense*] неминуе́мая беда́; *CQ* **your spectacles are staring you in the face!** да вот же твои́ очки́, пря́мо на тебя́ смо́трят!

vi при́стально смотре́ть на + *A* (по-), уста́виться на + *A* (*pf*), *CQ* пя́лить глаза́ на + *A* (*impf*); **she ~d at him/into his eyes** она́ при́стально посмотре́ла на него́/ему́ в глаза́; **she ~d at him in amazement** она́ уста́вилась на него́ в изумле́нии; **he ~d into the distance/up at the windows** он всма́тривался вдаль, он загля́дывал в о́кна; **it's rude to ~ like that** неве́жливо так пя́лить глаза́.

starfish *n Zool* морска́я звезда́.

stark *adv*: **~ naked** соверше́нно го́лый; **the children ran around ~ naked** де́ти бе́гали нагишо́м; *fig CQ* **are you ~ staring mad?** ты что, совсе́м уж спя́тил?

starling *n* скворе́ц.

starlit *adj*: **a ~ night** звёздная ночь; **~ landscape** пейза́ж под звёздным не́бом.

starry *adj* звёздный.

start *n* **1** (*beginning*) нача́ло; *Sport* старт; **at the ~ of the century** в нача́ле ве́ка; **for a ~ we must...** для нача́ла на́до + *inf*; **from ~ to finish** с нача́ла до конца́; **from the very ~** с са́мого нача́ла; **he gave his sons/he had a good ~ in life** он о́чень помо́г свои́м сыновья́м в нача́ле их жи́зненного пути́, ему́ о́чень повезло́ в са́мом нача́ле; **we'll make an early ~** мы ра́но отпра́вимся; *Sport*: **a false ~** фальста́рт; **the small boys had a ~ of two metres** ма́леньким ма́льчикам да́ли фо́ру два ме́тра; *fig* **after a few false ~s the business got going** по́сле не́скольких неуда́чных попы́ток де́ло наконе́ц дви́нулось/пошло́

2 (*sudden movements, fright*): **he sprang up with a ~** он вскочи́л с ме́ста, как пружи́ной подбро́шенный; **I got/you gave me quite a ~** я си́льно перепуга́лся, ну ты меня́ и напуга́л!

start *vti vt* **1** (*begin*) нач|ина́ть (-а́ть); **he ~s (off) the lesson with questions** он начина́ет уро́к с вопро́сов; **they have ~ed negotiations** они́ на́чали перегово́ры; **did you ~ (on) the bottle?** ты уже́ откры́л э́ту буты́лку?; **I ~ed "The Idiot"** я на́чал (чита́ть) «Идио́та»; **when do you ~ your new job?** когда́ ты приступа́ешь к но́вой рабо́те?; **I ~ this project tomorrow** я беру́сь за э́тот прое́кт за́втра; *Sport* (*of starter*) **to ~ a race** да|ва́ть старт (-ть); **he ~ed the horse at a gallop** он пусти́л ло́шадь гало́пом; **the dog ~ed a hare** соба́ка подняла́ за́йца

2 (*initiate, originate*) вы|зыва́ть (-звать); зате|ва́ть (-я́ть); **yeast ~s fermentation** дро́жжи вызыва́ют броже́ние; **his remark ~ed a quarrel** его́ замеча́ние вы́звало ссо́ру; **to ~ a fight/quarrel** нача́ть дра́ку, затя́ть ссо́ру; **new factories have been ~ed up** вошли́ в строй но́вые фа́брики; **I need capital to ~ me (off)** мне нужна́ прили́чная су́мма де́нег, что́бы нача́ть де́ло; **he ~ed life as an errand boy** снача́ла он был ма́льчиком на побегу́шках; **they ~ed the fashion/a shop** они́ ввели́ э́ту мо́ду, они́ откры́ли магази́н; **the forest fire was ~ed by vandals/lightning** лес подожгли́ хулига́ны, лесно́й пожа́р начался́ от мо́лнии; **he ~ed the bonfire with paraffin** он развёл костёр, плесну́в немно́го кероси́на; **who ~ed this rumour?** кто пусти́л э́тот слух?; **the wine ~ed him talking** от вина́ он разговори́лся; *CQ* **just look (at) what you've ~ed!** ви́дишь, каку́ю ты ка́шу завари́л!

3 *Mech*: **I can't ~ the car** у меня́ маши́на не заво́дится; **~ the car in first** тро́гай маши́ну с ме́ста на пе́рвой ско́рости

vi **1** нач|ина́ть(ся) (-а́ть(ся)); **it's time to ~** пора́ начина́ть (*begin*)/идти́ (*set out*); **it all ~ed when...** э́то всё начало́сь, когда́...; **we were late ~ing** мы по́здно вы́шли; **school ~s on Monday** заня́тия (*pl*) начина́ются в понеде́льник; **~ing on/from Tuesday** начина́я со вто́рника; **how did the rumour ~?** отку́да взя́лся/пошёл э́тот слух?; **the river ~s in the high Alps** река́ берёт нача́ло высоко́ в А́льпах; **the train had just ~ed when...** по́езд то́лько отошёл, когда́...; **he ~ed by telling me...** он на́чал с того́, что сказа́л мне...; **he ~ed (off) as an actor** снача́ла он был актёром; **the business ~ed (off) well/badly** у них с са́мого нача́ла де́ло пошло́/не зала́дилось; **~ on a new page** начни́те с но́вой страни́цы; **the play ~s with a prologue** пье́са начина́ется с проло́га; **let's ~ on a new chapter** начнём но́вую главу́; **he ~ed on a long explanation** он пусти́лся в дли́нные объясне́ния (*pl*); **we'll ~ with soup** начнём с су́па; **to ~ with, they had no money** во-пе́рвых, у них не́ было де́нег

2 (*with inf or gerund*) начина́ть(ся); станови́ть(ся) (стать); **he ~ed to write a book** он на́чал писа́ть кни́гу; **it is ~ing to get warmer** стано́вится тепле́е; **he ~ed to treat me with respect** он стал относи́ться ко мне с уваже́нием; **before it ~s to snow** пока́ не пошёл снег; **it will soon ~ thawing** ско́ро начнёт та́ять; **he ~ed speaking/shouting** он на́чал говори́ть *or* он заговори́л, он стал крича́ть *or* он раскрича́лся; **it ~ed raining** пошёл дождь; **the music ~ed up again** сно́ва заигра́ла/зазвуча́ла му́зыка; **we'd better ~ going now** нам лу́чше пойти́ сейча́с; **I ~ed out to say...** я хоте́л бы́ло сказа́ть...; **don't ~ crying!** не плачь!

3 (*jump*) вздр|а́гивать (-о́гнуть); **she ~ed at every sound** она́ вздра́гивала при ка́ждом зву́ке; **the bell made me ~** я вздро́гнул от звонка́; **he ~ed back in fear** он в у́жасе отшатну́лся

4 *Mech*: **the car wouldn't ~** мото́р не заводи́лся; **this clock keeps ~ing and stopping** э́ти часы́ (*pl*) то хо́дят, то стоя́т.

starter *n Sport* (*who signals start*) стартёр, (*participant*) уча́стник забе́га; *Aut* ста́ртер; **they are under ~'s orders** они́ уже́ вы́шли на старт; *fig*: **he's an early ~** он ра́нняя пта́шка; *Cook* **what's for ~s?** что на заку́ску? (*sing*).

starting handle *n Tech* пускова́я рукоя́тка.

starting point *n*: **the ~ of a trip/an argument** нача́льный пункт путеше́ствия, отправна́я то́чка аргуме́нтов/до́водов (*pls*).

starting post *n Sport* ста́ртовый столб, ста́ртовая отме́тка.

starting price *n Comm* нача́льная цена́; (*in betting*) первонача́льная ста́вка.

startle *vt* пуга́ть (на-, ис-); **his cry/you ~d me** его́ крик/ты напуга́л меня́; **we ~d a flock of sheep** мы вспугну́ли ста́до ове́ц; **I was ~d to see so many people/to hear that** я был поражён, увидев сто́лько люде́й/, услы́шав э́то.

startling *adj* порази́тельный.

starvation *n* го́лод; голода́ние; **they died of ~** они́ у́мерли с го́лоду; **oxygen ~** кислоро́дное голода́ние; *attr*: **they live on ~ wages/rations** они́ живу́т на ни́щенскую зарпла́ту (*sing*)/на голо́дном пайке́ (*sing*); **a ~ diet** голо́дная дие́та.

starve *vti vt*: **they ~d the animals/prisoners** живо́тных/пле́нных мори́ли го́лодом (за-); **she ~d herself to feed the children** она́ сама́ голода́ла, что́бы прокорми́ть дете́й; **these tomato plants are ~d of nitrogen** э́ти помидо́ры ча́хнут без азо́тной подко́рмки; *fig* **the children were ~d of affection** де́ти стоскова́лись по ла́ске

vi голода́ть (*impf*), умира́ть от го́лода (*usu impf*); **the troops were starving** войска́ голода́ли; *fig CQ* **I'm starving** я умира́ю от/с го́лода, умира́ю есть хочу́.

state *n* **1** (*condition*) состоя́ние; положе́ние; **in a good ~ of repair** в хоро́шем состоя́нии; **in a ~ of war/weightlessness** в состоя́нии войны́/невесо́мости; **in an advanced ~ of decay** в разложи́вшемся состоя́нии; **his ~ of health/of mind** состоя́ние его́ здоро́вья, его́ душе́вное состоя́ние; **he's not in a fit ~ to go** он не в состоя́нии е́хать; **that was the ~ of affairs** таково́ бы́ло положе́ние дел; *iron* **a fine/nice ~ of affairs!** ничего́ себе́ положе́ньице!; **you can't leave the kitchen in that ~** нельзя́ оставля́ть ку́хню в тако́м ви́де; **what a ~ you/your clothes are in!** в како́м ты ви́де!, в како́м ви́де у тебя́ оде́жда!; **what**

is the ~ of play? каково́ положе́ние (*Sport*) игры́?/*fig* дел?; *CQ* **don't work yourself into a ~** не взви́нчивай/не доводи́ себя́

2 (*high style, pomp*): **they dined in ~** у них был торже́ственный обе́д; **he received them in ~** он их при́нял по всей фо́рме; **his body lay in ~** его́ те́ло бы́ло вы́ставлено для после́днего проща́ния; *attr*: **a ~ visit** официа́льный визи́т; **~ carriage/coach** (*UK*) короле́вская каре́та; **~ apartments** пара́дные поко́и

3 (*country*) госуда́рство; (*US, India, etc.*) штат; **the powers of the ~** госуда́рственная власть (*sing*); **affairs of ~** госуда́рственные дела́; **the member ~s of the UN** госуда́рства-чле́ны ООН; **the welfare ~** госуда́рство с ра́звитой систе́мой социа́льного обеспе́чения; (*UK*) **the Secretary of S. for Health** мини́стр здравоохране́ния; **the S. of Texas/Kerala** штат Теха́с/Кера́ла; *attr* госуда́рственный; **~ papers/forests** госуда́рственные докуме́нты/зака́зники; **~ property** казённое иму́щество; (*US*) **the S. Department** госуда́рственный департа́мент, министе́рство иностра́нных дел; (*US*) **S. law** зако́н шта́та.

state *vt* (*declare*) утвержда́ть (*impf*); заяв|ля́ть (-и́ть); **he ~s that he was present** он утвержда́ет, что был там; **it is now ~d that the figures were wrong** тепе́рь утвержда́ют, что ци́фры бы́ли неверны́; **the letter ~s that** в письме́ сообща́ется, что...; **he ~d his opinion/position/the reason** он изложи́л своё мне́ние/свою́ пози́цию, он объясни́л причи́ну; **it must be ~d at the outset that...** с са́мого нача́ла необходи́мо заяви́ть, что...; *Law* **to ~ a case** изложи́ть де́ло; (*official*): **it is nowhere/expressly ~d that...** нигде́ не ска́зано,/осо́бо ука́зано, что...; **~ your name/business/requirements in the space below** укажи́те ни́же своё и́мя/род заня́тий, изложи́те свои́ тре́бования.

state-aided *adj*: **the institute is ~** институ́т получа́ет субси́дию от госуда́рства.

stated *adj* устано́вленный; **on ~ days** в устано́вленные дни; **at the ~ time** в устано́вленный срок; **within ~ limits** в устано́вленных преде́лах; **the ~ sum** ука́занная су́мма.

stateless *adj Law*: **a ~ person** апатри́д.

stately *adj*: **a ~ bow** велича́вый покло́н; **~ bearing** вели́чественная оса́нка.

statement *n* (*assertion*) утвержде́ние; (*usu official*) заявле́ние; **according to his own ~** по его́ со́бственному утвержде́нию; **to make a ~ to the press** сде́лать заявле́ние в пре́ссе; **to make unfounded ~s** необосно́ванно утвержда́ть, де́лать необосно́ванные заявле́ния; *Law*: **a written ~** пи́сьменное заявле́ние; **~ for the defence/prosecution** изложе́ние де́ла защи́той/прокуро́ром; *Comm*: **bank ~** вы́писка из ба́нковского счёта; **the shop sends a monthly ~** магази́н присыла́ет ежеме́сячную вы́писку из счёта.

statesman *n* госуда́рственный де́ятель (*m*).

statesmanlike *adj*: **he dealt with the problem in a ~ manner** он прояви́л госуда́рственный подхо́д к реше́нию э́той пробле́мы; **the president's behaviour was not exactly ~** президе́нт вёл себя́ не совсе́м так, как подоба́ет госуда́рственному де́ятелю.

static *adj*: **business has been ~ for weeks** де́ло стои́т уже́ не́сколько неде́ль; **~ electricity** стати́ческое электри́чество; *Tech* **~ friction** тре́ние поко́я.

statics *npl Phys, Tech* ста́тика (*sing*); *Radio* (*atmospherics*) атмосфе́рные поме́хи.

station *n* **1** (*Rail, metro, bus*) ста́нция; (*larger, or station building*) вокза́л; (*lifeboat, meteorological, etc.*) ста́нция; **fire ~** пожа́рное депо́ (*indecl*); **hydroelectric/radio ~** гидроэлектроста́нция, радиоста́нция; *Aut* **service ~** ста́нция техобслу́живания; *Naut* **naval ~** вое́нно-морска́я ба́за; *Mil* **action ~s** боевы́е пози́ции; **coastguard ~** пост берегово́й охра́ны; *attr*: **~ master** нача́льник ста́нции/вокза́ла; *Aut* **~ wagon** «универса́л»

2 (*position in life*): **people of all ~s** лю́ди всех ра́нгов и зва́ний; **you're getting ideas above your ~** ты сли́шком высоко́ зама́хиваешься.

station *vt* разме|ща́ть (-сти́ть); **they ~ed troops at the frontier** войска́ бы́ли размещены́ на грани́це; **he/the fleet was ~ed at Malta** его́ назна́чили на Ма́льту, флот стоя́л у берего́в Ма́льты; **he ~ed himself on the roof** он за́нял пози́цию/устро́ился на кры́ше.

stationary *adj* неподви́жный; стоя́щий; (*of machinery*) стациона́рный; **a ~ target** неподви́жная мише́нь; **he ran into a ~ car** он вре́зался в стоя́щую маши́ну; **the train is ~** по́езд стои́т; **do not alight until the train is ~** не выходи́ть до по́лной остано́вки по́езда.

stationery *n* (*for office*) канцеля́рские принадле́жности; (*writing paper, etc.*) **a set of ~** почто́вый набо́р.

statistical *adj* статисти́ческий.

statistics *npl* (*subject*) стати́стика (*sing*); (*figures*) статисти́ческие да́нные; **~ indicate that women smoke more than men** по стати́стике же́нщины ку́рят бо́льше, чем мужчи́ны.

statue *n* ста́туя.

stature *n* рост; **of short ~** ни́зкого ро́ста; *fig* **he's a man of remarkable moral ~** он челове́к высо́ких мора́льных ка́честв.

status *n* ста́тус, положе́ние; **civil/marital/social ~** гражда́нский ста́тус, семе́йное/социа́льное положе́ние; **without any official ~** не занима́я никако́го официа́льного поста́; **the ~ of the coloured population** положе́ние темноко́жего населе́ния; *attr*: **a big car is a ~ symbol** большо́й автомоби́ль—при́знак положе́ния в о́бществе.

status quo *n* существу́ющее положе́ние; ста́тус-кво́ (*indecl*).

statute *n* (*act*) законода́тельный акт; **company/university ~s** уста́в (*sing*) компа́нии/университе́та; *attr*: **~ book** свод зако́нов.

statutory *adj*: **~ price control** устано́вленный зако́ном контро́ль над це́нами.

staunch[1] *adj*: **a ~ supporter** ве́рный сторо́нник; **~ loyalty** непоколеби́мая ве́рность.

staunch[2] *vt*: **to ~ blood** остан|áвливать кровотечéние (-ови́ть).

stave *n* (*on barrel*) клёпка; *Mus* нóтный стан.

stave in *vti*: **in the collision the crane ~d** (*also* **stove**) **in the car door** при авáрии кран помя́л дверь маши́ны; **the hull was ~d** (*also* **stove**) **in when the boat struck the rock** лóдка получи́ла пробóину, удáрившись о скалу́.

stave off *vt*: **they ~d off the danger/the epidemic** они́ предотврати́ли опáсность/эпидéмию; **thanks to the loan we ~d off bankruptcy** éсли бы не заём, мы обанкрóтились бы; **to ~ off our hunger** чтóбы утоли́ть гóлод.

stay *n* **1** пребывáние; визи́т; **I had a short ~ there/a busy ~ in Paris** моё пребывáние там дли́лось недóлго, у меня́ бы́ло мнóго вся́ких дел в Пари́же; **he enjoyed his ~ with his uncle** ему́ понрáвилось гости́ть у дя́ди; **you made our ~ delightful** мы у вас чудéсно провели́ врéмя; **their ~ was a success** их визи́т прошёл успéшно; **come for a longer ~** приезжáйте к нам погости́ть подóльше

2 *Law*: **~ of execution** отсрóчка в исполнéнии решéния.

stay *vti vt* **1** (*check*): *Law* **to ~ proceedings** приостан|áвливать судопроизвóдство (-ови́ть)

2 (*last out*): **he'll never ~ the course** ему́ ни за что́ не вы́держать до концá

vi **1** (*remain*) остa|вáться (-́ться); **~ where you are** оставáйся на мéсте; **I ~ed in town/to listen** я остáлся в гóроде/послу́шать; **do ~ for/to dinner** оставáйся обéдать; **I shan't ~ long** я не надóлго; **he ~ed calm** он оставáлся спокóйным; **the floor doesn't ~ clean (for) long** пол недóлго остаётся чи́стым; **he's ~ing at home/in bed** он сиди́т дóма, он лежи́т (в постéли); **will the bread ~ fresh till tomorrow?** хлеб не зачерствéет до зáвтра?; **if the weather ~s fine** éсли сохрани́тся/продéржится хорóшая погóда; **computers are here to ~** вычисли́тельные маши́ны прóчно вошли́ в жизнь; *CQ*: **the lampshade won't ~ put** абажу́р не дéржится; **we're ~ing put this year** мы никудá не éдем в э́том году́

2 (*spend night, visit as guest*) остан|áвливаться (-ови́ться); гости́ть (по-); **are you ~ing with friends or in a hotel?** ты останови́лся [**NB** *tense*] у друзéй и́ли в гости́нице?; **he owns the house, I'm just ~ing** он хозя́ин (дóма), а я здесь в гостя́х; **he ~ed with us for a week/a year** он гости́л у нас недéлю, он жил у нас год; **he came for a week and ~ed a year** он приéхал погости́ть на недéлю, а прóжил цéлый год

stay away *vi*: **he ~ed away in protest** он демонстрати́вно отсу́тствовал; **tell them all to ~ away** скажи́ им, чтóбы никтó не приходи́л; **he often ~s away from school/rehearsals** он чáсто пропускáет шкóлу/репети́ции

stay in *vi*: **the doctor says I must ~ in for another day** дóктор говори́т, что я ещё день дóлжен быть/сидéть дóма; **the cork won't ~ in** прóбка не дéржится в гóрлышке; **he was made to ~ in (after school)** егó остáвили пóсле урóков

stay off *vi*: **he ~ed off work** он не выходи́л на рабóту; **the electricity won't ~ off long** электри́чество скóро включáт

stay out *vi*: **we haven't a garage, so the car has to ~ out** у нас нет гаражá, поэ́тому маши́на стои́т на у́лице; **don't ~ out late** пóздно не возвращáйся; **try and ~ out of trouble/debt** не лезь на рожóн, постарáйся не влезáть в долги́; **they ~ed out** (*on strike*) они забастовáли

stay up *vi*: **the kite ~ed up** возду́шный змей всё летéл; (*of swimmer*) **he managed to ~ up** ему́ удалóсь удержáться наповéрхности; **I ~ed up all night** я не ложи́лся всю ночь; **don't ~ up for me** не жди меня́, ложи́сь; **you shouldn't ~ up so late** тебé не слéдует так пóздно заси́живаться; **we ~ed up talking** мы заговори́лись допозднá.

stay-at-home *n* домосéд.

staying power *n* вы́держка.

stead *n*: **I went in his ~** я поéхал вмéсто негó; **your gift stood him in good ~** твой подáрок пришёлся емý óчень кстáти (*adv*).

steadfast *adj*: **a ~ gaze** упóрный взгляд; **he remained ~ in his loyalty** он оставáлся таки́м же вéрным/прéданным.

steadily *adv*: **we'd been going ~ for an hour** (*on foot*) мы шли без останóвки ужé час; **the water/excitement rose ~** у́ровень воды́ неуклóнно поднимáлся, возбуждéние всё рослó.

steady *n CQ*: **she's his ~** онá егó дéвушка, он с ней встречáется.

steady *adj* **1** (*stable, unmoving*) устóйчивый, твёрдый, рóвный; **he has a ~ hand** у негó твёрдая рукá, у негó рукá не дрожи́т; **keep your hand/the camera ~** держи́ ру́ку рóвно/аппарáт неподви́жно; **a ~ voice** рóвный гóлос; **under his ~ gaze** под егó при́стальным взгля́дом; **~ nerves** крéпкие нéрвы; **the chair/table is not ~** э́тот стул/стол шатáется; **I'm not yet ~ on my bicycle** я ещё неувéренно éзжу на велосипéде; (*of character, etc.*): **a ~ worker** надёжный рабóтник; **a ~ young man** уравновéшенный молодóй человéк; **a ~ faith** твёрдая вéра

2 (*regular, constant*) рóвный, равномéрный; постоя́нный; **a ~ pulse** рóвный пульс; **a ~ flame** рóвное плáмя; **we walked at a ~ pace** мы шли рóвным шáгом; **we drove at a ~ 70 kilometres per hour** мы éхали с постоя́нной скóростью сéмьдесят киломéтров в час; **a ~ drizzle/downpour** непрекращáющийся дождь/ли́вень; **he has a ~ job** у негó постоя́нная рабóта; **the boy made ~ progress** мáльчик дéлал всё бóльшие и бóльшие успéхи; *Mil* **~ fire** непреры́вный огóнь; *Comm*: **~ prices** устóйчивые цéны; **~ demand** постоя́нный спрос.

steady *adv*: **~!** осторóжно!; **~ on!** (*of movement*) ти́хо!, (*of emotion*) успокóйся!, ты лу́чше помолчи́!; *CQ* **they are going ~** они́ постоя́нно вме́сте/ви́дятся.

steady *vt*: **he put a wedge under the table to ~ it** он подложи́л деревя́шку под но́жку стола́ для усто́йчивости; **to ~ himself he held on to the rail** что́бы не упа́сть, он ухвати́лся за пери́ла (*pl*); **I tried to ~ the boat/my nerves** я попыта́лся вы́ровнять ло́дку/успоко́иться.

steak *n* (*for frying*) кусо́к мя́са, *approx* ланге́т, бифште́кс; **stewing ~** духово́е мя́со; *attr*: **~ and kidney pie** пиро́г с говя́диной и по́чками.

steal *vti vt* красть (у-); ворова́ть (с-); **my watch has been stolen** у меня́ укра́ли часы́ (*no sing*); *fig*: **I stole a few hour's sleep** я урва́л не́сколько часо́в, что́бы поспа́ть; **I stole a glance at them** я укра́дкой взгляну́л на них; **to ~ a march on smb** опере|жа́ть кого́-л (-ди́ть); **he stole the show** он затми́л всех

vi: **he stole across the room** он прошёл на цы́почках/он кра́лся (*impf*) по ко́мнате; **to ~ away** улизну́ть (*pf*), ускольз|а́ть (-ну́ть); **he stole into/out of** он тихо́нько прокра́лся в + *A*, он вы́скользнул из + *G*.

stealth *n*: **by ~** укра́дкой (*adv*).

stealthy *adj*: **~ steps** кра́дущиеся шаги́; **a ~ manoeuvre** хи́трая уло́вка.

steam *n* пар; **to get up ~** разводи́ть пары́ (*pl*); **to let off ~** выпуска́ть пар; **at/under full ~** на по́лных пара́х (*pl*); **full ~ ahead** по́лным хо́дом; *fig CQ*: **I fairly let off ~** я дал во́лю свои́м чу́вствам; **I'll go/finish under my own ~** я сам пое́ду/зако́нчу.

steam *vti vt Cook* вари́ть на пару́ (с-), па́рить (*impf*); **~ed fish** ры́ба, пригото́вленная на пару́; **I ~ed the envelope open/the stamp off** я вскрыл конве́рт/откле́ил ма́рку над па́ром; **the window was ~ed up** окно́ запоте́ло; *fig CQ* **to get ~ed up about smth** волнова́ться по по́воду чего́-л

vi: **a ~ing hot bath** горя́чая ва́нна; **the horses ~ed with sweat** от разгорячённых лошаде́й шёл пар.

steam boiler *n* парово́й котёл.

steam engine *n Rail* парово́з.

steamer *n Naut* парохо́д; *Cook* парова́рка, скорова́рка.

steamroller *n* парово́й като́к.

steamy *adj* (*of atmosphere*) напо́лненный па́ром; (*of glass*) запоте́вший.

steel *n* сталь; *fig* **nerves of ~** стальны́е не́рвы; *attr*: **~ blue/grey** синева́то-стально́й, стально́го цве́та.

steel *vt fig*: **I ~ed myself to tell him the truth** я собра́л всё своё му́жество, что́бы сказа́ть ему́ пра́вду.

steel engraving *n* (*technique*) гравирова́ние на ста́ли; (*object*) гравю́ра на ста́ли.

steel-plated *adj* (*armoured*) брониро́ванный.

steel wool *n* то́нкая стальна́я стру́жка.

steelworks *npl* сталелите́йный заво́д (*sing*).

steep[1] *adj* (*of gradient*) круто́й; *fig CQ*: **the price is pretty ~** ну и це́ну же заломи́ли!; **his stories are a bit ~** он тако́е накру́чивает в свои́х исто́риях!

steep[2] *vt* (*in liquid*) вы|ма́чивать (-мочить); *fig* **~ed in prejudice** по́лный предрассу́дков.

steeple *n* шпиль (*m*); (*with bell*) колоко́льня.

steeplechase *n* ска́чки (*pl*) с препя́тствиями.

steer[1] *vti vt* направ|ля́ть (-ить); пра́вить + *I*, управля́ть + *I* (*impfs*); **I ~ed the boat towards the harbour** я напра́вил ло́дку к при́стани; **can you ~ a boat?** ты уме́ешь пра́вить ло́дкой?; **you nearly ~ed us into the ditch** ты чуть не завёз нас в кана́ву; **I ~ed him away from the bar** я увёл его́ пода́льше от ба́ра; **I ~ed my way past piles of rubbish** я пробира́лся ме́жду му́сорными ку́чами; **he ~s the committee well** он хорошо́ руково́дит коми́ссией

vi пра́вить (рулём); **~ north/for the buoy** правь на се́вер/на ба́кен; **we ~ed by the stars/by the chart** мы держа́ли курс по звёздам/по ка́рте; **the boat ~s well** э́той ло́дкой легко́ управля́ть; **~ clear of the rocks** держи́сь пода́льше от скал; *fig* **he tried to ~ clear of trouble** он стара́лся избега́ть непри́ятностей.

steer[2] *n* молодо́й вол.

steering *n Aut, Naut* (*act and system*) рулево́е управле́ние; *attr*: **~ wheel** *Naut* штурва́л, *Aut* руль; **~ column** рулева́я коло́нка.

stem[1] *n* (*of flower*) сте́бель (*m*); (*of fruit, leaf*) черешо́к; (*of tobacco pipe, knife*) черено́к; (*of glass*) но́жка; (*of word*) осно́ва; *Naut* **from ~ to stern** он но́са до кормы́.

stem[1] *vi*: **it all ~s from the fact that...** а всё (происхо́дит) оттого́, что...

stem[2] *vt* (*a flood, current*) запру́живать (*usu impf*), перегор|а́живать (-оди́ть); (*flow of blood, spread of disease*) остан|а́вливать (-ови́ть).

stench *n* вонь, смрад.

stencil *n* трафаре́т; **to cut a ~** вы́резать трафаре́т.

stencil *vt* (*of pattern, lettering*) на|носи́ть узо́р/де́лать на́дпись по трафаре́ту (-нести́/с-); **to ~ 100 copies** сде́лать сто ко́пий по трафаре́ту.

stenographer *n* стенографи́стка.

step *n* **1** шаг, *also fig*; (*dancing*) па (*indecl*); **with brisk ~s** бы́стрыми шага́ми; **waltz ~** па ва́льса; **it's only a ~/a good ~** *or* **quite a ~ from here to the village** отсю́да до дере́вни руко́й пода́ть/дово́льно далеко́; **he turned his ~s towards home** он напра́вил свои́ стопы́ к до́му; **we retraced our ~s** мы верну́лись; **I can't go a ~ further** я шагу не могу́ ступи́ть да́льше; **they kept in/broke ~** они́ шли в но́гу, они́ пошли́ не в но́гу; **at every ~** при ка́ждом шаге, *fig* на ка́ждом шагу́; **watch your ~, it's slippery** осторо́жно, здесь ско́льзко, *fig* будь (по)осторо́жнее; *fig*: **the next ~** сле́дующий шаг; **that's a ~ in the right direction** э́то шаг в пра́вильном направле́нии; **it's a difficult ~ for**

her to take для неё э́то тру́дный шаг; **the first ~s in his career** пе́рвые шаги́ на слу́жбе/в его́ карье́ре; **that is a ~ up in his profession** э́то шаг к повыше́нию; **the first ~ is to tell them** пе́рвым де́лом на́до им сказа́ть; **he took ~s to clarify the matter** он предпри́нял шаги́ для рассле́дования э́того де́ла; **he is out of ~ with modern life** он идёт не в но́гу с ве́ком

2 (*of stairs, etc.*) ступе́нь(ка); **mind the ~** осторо́жно, ступе́нька; **he cut ~s in the ice** он проруби́л ступе́ньки во льду́; **a flight of ~s** пролёт (ле́стницы).

step *vi* шаг|а́ть (-ну́ть), ступ|а́ть (-и́ть); **he ~ped carefully past the dogs** он осторо́жно прошёл ми́мо соба́к

step across *vt*: **he ~ped across the stream/street** он перешагну́л че́рез руче́й, он перешёл у́лицу

step aside *vi*: **I ~ped aside to let him pass** я посторони́лся, что́бы пропусти́ть его́/дать ему́ пройти́

step back *vt*: **I ~ped back from the door/to look** я отошёл от две́ри, я отступи́л наза́д, что́бы взгляну́ть; **~ back there!** посторони́сь!

step down *vi*: **I ~ped down from the bus** я сошёл с авто́буса; *fig* **he ~ped down in favour of his brother** он уступи́л в по́льзу бра́та

step forward *vi*: **he ~ped forward to greet me** он шагну́л/вы́шел вперёд, что́бы приве́тствовать меня́

step in/into *vi*: **~ in!** входи́те!; **I ~ped into a puddle** я ступи́л в лу́жу; *fig*: **I ~ped into his shoes** я за́нял его́ ме́сто; **the authorities ~ped in** вмеша́лись вла́сти

step off *vi* сходи́ть (сойти́) с + *G*

step on *vi*: **I ~ped on his toe/***fig* **toes** я наступи́л ему́ на́ ногу/*fig* на люби́мую мозо́ль (*sing*); **I ~ped on the accelerator/gas** я нажа́л на газ

step out *vti vt* (*measure*): **they ~ped out the 10 metres** они́ отме́рили шага́ми де́сять ме́тров

vi: **~ out or we'll be late** приба́вь ша́гу, а то мы опозда́ем

step up *vti vt* (*demands, production*) повы|ша́ть (-́сить), (*a campaign*) усили|вать (-ть); *Elec* **to ~ up the current** повыша́ть напряже́ние

vi: **he ~ped up to me/to receive the prize** он подошёл ко мне/, что́бы получи́ть приз.

stepbrother *n* сво́дный брат.

stepchild *n* (*boy*) па́сынок, (*girl*) па́дчерица.

stepfather *n* о́тчим.

stepmother *n* ма́чеха.

steppe *n* степь.

stepping stone *n*: **we crossed the stream on ~s** мы перешли́ руче́й по ка́мешкам; *fig* **this job is a ~ to promotion** э́то ме́сто—ступе́нька к повыше́нию.

stepsister *n* сво́дная сестра́.

stereo *n* (*abbr of* **stereophonic record player**) стереофони́ческий прои́грыватель (*m*).

stereotype *n* стереоти́п.

stereotyped *adj fig* стереоти́пный.

sterile *adj* (*infertile*) беспло́дный; (*aseptic*) стери́льный.

sterilize *vt* стерилизова́ть (*impf and pf*).

sterling *n Fin* сте́рлинги, фу́нты сте́рлингов (*pls*); **the fare is payable in ~** прое́зд опла́чивается в фу́нтах (сте́рлингов).

sterling *adj Fin*: **the pound ~** фунт сте́рлингов; **the ~ area** сте́рлинговая зо́на; **~ silver** серебро́ устано́вленной про́бы; *fig* **a man of ~ qualities/sense** челове́к безупре́чно че́стный, здравомы́слящий челове́к; **he's a ~ fellow** он благоро́дный челове́к.

stern[1] *n Naut* корма́; **~ foremost** кормо́й вперёд; *attr* кормово́й.

stern[2] *adj* стро́гий, суро́вый; **~ discipline** стро́гая дисципли́на.

stertorous *adj*: **~ breathing** хри́плое/тяжёлое дыха́ние.

stet *vi*: *Typ* **~** оста́вить как бы́ло *or* не пра́вить!

stethoscope *n Med* стетоско́п.

stevedore *n* стивидо́р, порто́вый гру́зчик.

stew *n* тушёное мя́со; *fig CQ* **to be in a ~** волнова́ться, не́рвничать.

stew *vti vt* туши́ть (по-); **~ing meat** мя́со для туше́ния; **~ed apples** печёные я́блоки

vi: **allow to ~ slowly** туши́ть на ме́дленном огне́.

steward *n* (*barman*) буфе́тчик; (*on estate*) управля́ющий; (*of club, college*) заве́дующий хозя́йством; *Naut, Aer* стю́ард; *Sport* (*at race meeting*) распоряди́тель (*m*).

stewardess *n* стюарде́сса.

stick *n* (*for walking, also cane in school*) па́лка; (*of chalk, sealing wax, for lollipops*) па́лочка; (*for supporting peas, etc.*) подпо́рка; (*of celery, rhubarb*) сте́бель (*m*); *pl* (**~s**) (*kindlings*) хво́рост (*sing*); *Sport* (*in steeplechase*) *pl* (**the ~s**) препя́тствия; **a ~ of chewing gum** пли́точка жева́тельной рези́нки; *fig*: **he got hold of the wrong end of the ~** он всё совсе́м не так по́нял; **he has us in a cleft ~** он загна́л нас в у́гол; **a funny old ~** ста́рый хрыч.

stick *vti vt* **1** (*thrust, stab*) втыка́ть (воткну́ть); вонз|а́ть (-и́ть), вса́|живать (-ди́ть); **I stuck a flag into the map/a spade into the ground/a nail into the door** я воткну́л флажо́к в ка́рту/лопа́ту в зе́млю, я вбил гвоздь в дверь; **to ~ a knife in smb's back** вонзи́ть/всади́ть нож кому́-л в спи́ну; **to ~ meat on skewers** насади́ть мя́со на шампу́ры; **~ a fork into the meat to see if it's ready** поты́кай мя́со ви́лкой, гото́во ли оно́; *fig* **they'd ~ a knife into you for tuppence** они тебя́ за копе́йку заре́жут

2 (*with glue*) кле́ить *and compounds* (*impf*); **he stuck the stamps on the envelope/into the album** он накле́ил ма́рки на конве́рт/в альбо́м; **I stuck the page into the book** я вкле́ил страни́цу в кни́гу; **to ~ (up) posters on the walls** раскле́ивать афи́ши по сте́нам, окле́ивать сте́ны афи́шами; **I stuck the pieces together with sellotape** я скле́ил обры́вки ско́тчем

3 *CQ* (*put*) сова́ть (су́нуть) *and compounds*; **he stuck his hands in his pockets/the book into the drawer** он су́нул ру́ки в карма́ны/кни́жку в я́щик; **he stuck his hat on his head** он нахлобу́чил шля́пу; *CQ*: **~ it back on the table** поста́вь э́то обра́тно на стол; **they stuck a fiver on the price** они наба́вили ещё пять фу́нтов; **they stuck him on the jury** его́ посади́ли в жюри́

4 *passive only*: **to be stuck** застр|ева́ть (-я́ть) (*see also vi*); **the car was stuck in the mud** маши́на застря́ла в грязи́; **a bone got stuck in my throat** у меня́ застря́ла ко́сточка в го́рле; *CQ*: **I was stuck in London all summer** я на всё ле́то застря́л в Ло́ндоне; **I got stuck on the first chapter** я застря́л на пе́рвой главе́; **I was stuck for an answer** я заме́шкался с отве́том; **I was stuck with the job of cleaning up afterwards** и всю убо́рку свали́ли на меня́; **I was stuck with him all morning** я всё у́тро с ним провози́лся; **if you're stuck I'll help** е́сли у тебя́ де́ло не ла́дится, я помогу́; **now we're stuck with his debts** тепе́рь нам плати́ть его́ долги́

5 *CQ* (*tolerate*): **I can't ~ him/this climate for long** я его́ не выношу́, мне в э́том кли́мате до́лго не вы́держать

vi **1** (*embed itself*) втыка́ться; (*stick up/out*) торча́ть (*impf*); **the needle stuck in my finger** иго́лка воткну́лась мне в па́лец; **the pins are ~ing in the cushion** була́вки торча́т из поду́шки

2 (*adhere to*) прикле́и|ваться (-ться); прилип|а́ть (-нуть) *and other compounds*; **the glue/stamp/envelope won't ~** клей не кле́ит, ма́рка не прикле́ивается, конве́рт не закле́ивается; **the stamps have stuck together** ма́рки скле́ились/сли́плись; **the plate stuck to the table** таре́лка прили́пла к столу́; **the porridge has stuck to the pan** ка́ша приста́ла к кастрю́ле; *fig*: **that nickname will ~** э́то про́звище приста́нет/прили́пнет к нему́; **he stuck to his story/***CQ* **his guns** он стоя́л на своём; **~ to the point** приде́рживайтесь су́ти

3 *CQ* (*remain, stay*): **the dog stuck at my heels** соба́ка увяза́лась за мной; **he stuck to me like a limpet** он приста́л ко мне как ба́нный лист; **he stuck by her (side)/***fig* **through thick and thin** он оста́лся с ней, он был ря́дом с ней во всех её злоключе́ниях

4 (*of moving parts, etc. to jam*) застр|ева́ть (-я́ть); за|еда́ть (-е́сть); **the car stuck in the gate** маши́на застря́ла в воро́тах; **the key stuck in the lock** ключ застря́л в замке́; **the drawer/lift/lid often ~s** я́щик/лифт ча́сто застрева́ет, кры́шка пло́хо открыва́ется; **the lock/door/window ~s** замо́к/дверь/окно́ заеда́ет; **we stuck fast in the mud/snow** мы завя́зли в грязи́/застря́ли в снегу́; *fig* **the words stuck in my throat** слова́ застря́ли у меня́ в го́рле

5 (*jib at*): **he'll ~ at nothing** он ни пе́ред че́м не остано́вится; **I think they'll ~ at this clause** я ду́маю, они́ придеру́тся к э́тому пу́нкту

stick down *vt*: *CQ* **I'll ~ down the dates in my diary** я запишу́ э́ти да́ты в свою́ записну́ю кни́жку/в свой календа́рь

stick in *vt CQ* встав|ля́ть (-́ить); **he stuck in a few quotations** он вста́вил не́сколько цита́т; *Cook* **I'll ~ in some herbs** я доба́влю тра́вки

stick out *vti vt*: **he stuck out his tongue** он показа́л (*for doctor*)/вы́сунул (*rudely*) язы́к; **don't ~ your head out of the window** не высо́вывайся из окна́; *fig CQ*: **I'll ~ my neck out and speak to the director** я рискну́ и поговорю́ с дире́ктором; **we'll have to ~ it out** нам придётся э́то вы́терпеть

vi торча́ть (*impf*); **his ears/teeth ~ out** у него́ у́ши/зу́бы торча́т; **his shirt was ~ing out** у него́ руба́шка вы́лезла из брюк; *fig*: **it ~s out a mile that...** за версту́ ви́дно, что...; **to ~ out for better terms** от|ста́ивать лу́чшие усло́вия (-стоя́ть)

stick up *vti vt*: **to ~ up a notice** вы́весить объявле́ние; **he stuck up his hand** он вы́ставил ру́ку; **~ your hands up!/***sl* **~ 'em up!** ру́ки вверх!

vi **1** торча́ть (*impf*); **the rock ~s up out of the water** скала́ торчи́т из воды́

2: to ~ up for smb заступи́ться за кого́-л; **~ up for your rights** отста́ивай/защища́й свои́ права́.

sticker *n* ли́пкая накле́йка.

sticking plaster *n* ли́пкий пла́стырь (*m*), лейкопла́стырь (*m*).

stickler *n*: **he is a ~ for punctuality** он поме́шан на пунктуа́льности.

sticky *adj* кле́йкий, ли́пкий; **a ~ label** ли́пкая накле́йка; **~ fingers/sweets** ли́пкие па́льцы/конфе́тки; **~ hands** (*sweaty*) ли́пкие/вспоте́вшие ру́ки; **after the rain the road is ~** по́сле дождя́ доро́гу развезло́ (*impers*); **~ heat** вла́жная жара́; **it is very ~ today** сего́дня па́рит как в ба́не; *fig* **he came to a ~ end** он пло́хо ко́нчил.

stiff *adj* **1** жёсткий; твёрдый; (*of door, lock*) туго́й; **~ cardboard** жёсткий/твёрдый карто́н; **a ~ collar** жёсткий воротни́к; **~ joints** негну́щиеся суста́вы; **a ~ shirt front** накрахма́ленная мани́шка; **the lock is ~** замо́к ту́го открыва́ется; **I have a ~ neck/back** у меня́ ше́я не повора́чивается/спина́ не гнётся; **after the walk I felt ~** по́сле прогу́лки у меня́ но́ги е́ле дви́гались; **I was ~ with cold/terror** я окочене́л от хо́лода, я засты́л от у́жаса; *Cook*: **~ dough** густо́е те́сто; **mix to a ~ paste** меша́йте до загусте́ния; *fig* **to keep a ~ upper lip** сохраня́ть хладнокро́вие

2 *fig uses*: **he has a ~ manner** он ведёт себя́ о́чень официа́льно (*is formal*), он де́ржится чо́порно (*is stand-offish*); **this article is ~ reading** э́та статья́ тру́дно чита́ется; **a ~ climb/exam** тяжёлый подъём/экза́мен; **~ resistance** упо́рное сопротивле́ние; **a ~**

price высо́кая цена́; **I need a ~ drink** мне ну́жно что́-нибудь покре́пче.

stiff *adv CQ*: **I was bored/scared ~** мне бы́ло смерте́льно ску́чно, я испуга́лся до́ смерти.

stiffen *vi*: **the breeze/*fig* resistance ~ed** ве́тер свеже́л, сопротивле́ние росло́; **the starch/paste ~ed** крахма́л/клей загусте́л.

stiffly *adv*: **he moves ~** он дви́гается тяжело́; **he bowed ~** он (*formally*) церемо́нно/(*coldly*) хо́лодно поклони́лся; **they stood ~ to attention** они́ засты́ли по сто́йке сми́рно.

stiffness *n* (*of paper, cloth*) жёсткость; (*of consistency*) густота́; *fig* (*of behaviour, etc.*) чо́порность; **~ in the joints** неподви́жность в суста́вах.

stifle *vt*: **he was ~d by the fumes/the heat** он задыха́лся от испаре́ний/от жары́; **to ~ a laugh/a yawn/opposition/a sneeze** подав|ля́ть смешо́к/зево́к/сопротивле́ние (-и́ть), стара́ться не чихну́ть.

stifling *adj*: **~ heat** уду́шливая жара́; **it is ~ in here** здесь ду́шно.

stigma *n Bot* ры́льце; *fig* клеймо́; **the ~ of illegitimacy** клеймо́ незаконнорождённости.

stile *n* переля́з.

stiletto *adj*: **~ heels** гво́здики, шпи́льки.

still[1] *n* **1** тишина́, тишь

2 *Cine*: **~s from a film** ка́дры из фи́льма.

still[1] *adj*: **the ~ surface of the lake** неподви́жная/споко́йная гладь о́зера; **a ~ night** ти́хая ночь; (*not fizzy*) **~ lemonade** негазиро́ванный лимона́д.

still[1] *adv* неподви́жно, споко́йно, ти́хо; **stand ~!** стой споко́йно!/сми́рно!; **keep ~!** не дви́гайся!, не верти́сь!; **he lay perfectly ~** он лежа́л соверше́нно неподви́жно; **my heart stood ~** у меня́ се́рдце за́мерло.

still[2] *adv* ещё, (*emphatic*) всё ещё; **he ~ hasn't come** он (всё) ещё не пришёл; **I ~ play a bit** я ещё игра́ю иногда́; **it would be ~ better if...** бы́ло бы ещё лу́чше, е́сли...; **even when it rains he ~ goes out for a walk** да́же в дождь он хо́дит гуля́ть.

still[2] *conj* всё же; тем не ме́нее; **he may be stupid, but ~ he's my brother** пусть он не тако́й у́мный, а ведь всё же он мой брат; **I paid dearly for my fun, ~ I don't regret it** я до́рого заплати́л за э́то удово́льствие, но тем не ме́нее ниско́лько не жале́ю об э́том.

stillborn *adj* мертворождённый, *also fig*.

still life *n* натюрмо́рт.

stilt *n* ходу́ля; **to walk on ~s** ходи́ть на ходу́лях.

stilted *adj* ходу́льный.

stimulant *n* стимули́рующее/возбужда́ющее сре́дство; *fig* сти́мул.

stimulate *vt* стимули́ровать (*impf and pf*), *also Med*; побу|жда́ть, возбу|жда́ть (*pfs* -ди́ть); **his encouragement ~d me to try again** его́ подде́ржка была́ мне как бы сти́мулом, что́бы ещё раз попыта́ться; **this aperitif ~s the appetite** э́тот напи́ток возбужда́ет аппети́т.

stimulating *adj*: **a ~ drink** стимули́рующий напи́ток; **I found her/her lecture very ~** она́/её ле́кция меня́ о́чень вдохнови́ла.

stimulus *n* сти́мул.

sting *n* (*organ of insect, snake*) жа́ло, *also fig*; (*wound, bite*) уку́с, *also fig*; **the ~ of a nettle/iodine** ожо́г крапи́вой/йо́дом; *fig* **the ~ of sarcasm** жа́ло сарка́зма.

sting *vti vt* (*of insect, snake, scorpion*) жа́лить (у-), *also fig*; (*of nettle, ointment, whip*) жечь (об-); **the wasp stung me in the finger** оса́ ужа́лила меня́ в па́лец; **I was badly stung by nettles** я си́льно обжёгся крапи́вой (*collect*); **the hail/rain stung my face** град бил/дождь хлеста́л мне в лицо́; **the salt water stung my eyes** глаза́ мои́ щипа́ло (*impers*) от солёной воды́; *fig* **I was stung by remorse** меня́ жгло раска́яние; *CQ* **how much did they ~ you for it?** ско́лько с тебя́ за э́то содра́ли?

vi (*of insects*) жа́лить; (*of nettle, ointment, etc.*) жечь; (*smart*) садни́ть (*impf*); **some insects/nettles don't ~** не́которые насеко́мые не жа́лят, не вся́кая крапи́ва жжётся; **the iodine will ~** йод щи́плет; **this bite/burn ~s** уку́с жжёт, ожо́г боли́т; **my eyes ~ from the smoke** глаза́ ест (*impers*) от ды́ма.

stinging *adj*: **a ~ nettle/cut/remark** жгу́чая крапи́ва, садня́щая ра́на, язви́тельное/ко́лкое замеча́ние.

stingy *adj* (*of person*) ска́редный, скупо́й; (*of portion*) жа́лкий, мизе́рный; **don't be so ~ with the butter** не жале́й ма́сла; **he is ~ with money** он скупова́т/прижи́мист.

stink *n* вонь, злово́ние; **there is a ~ of burning rubber here** здесь воня́ет горе́лой рези́ной; *fig CQ* **there was a ~ about the money** из-за э́тих де́нег был сканда́л.

stink *vti vt*: **the cigar smoke stunk out the whole room** вся ко́мната пропа́хла сига́рным ды́мом

vi воня́ть + *I* (*impf*); **it ~s of fish in here** здесь воня́ет (*impers*) ры́бой; **his breath ~s of garlic** от него́ рази́т (*impers*) чесноко́м; *fig* **the whole business ~s** э́то гря́зные дела́.

stinker *n CQ* (*person*) мерза́вец; **he wrote me a ~** он написа́л мне про́сто безобра́зное письмо́; **the exam was a ~** э́то был ужа́сный экза́мен.

stinking *adj* воню́чий, смра́дный; *fig CQ*: **I've got a ~ cold** у меня́ ужа́сный на́сморк; *as adv* **they are ~ rich** они́ невероя́тно бога́ты.

stint *n* **1** *CQ* но́рма; **I've done my ~ at the wheel** я уже́ свою́ но́рму отъе́здил; **he does a daily ~ at the hospital** он ка́ждый день отраба́тывает свои́ часы́ (*pl*) в больни́це

2: **without ~** не жале́я, не скупя́сь.

stint *vti vt*: **he doesn't ~ himself/his praise** он ни в чём не отка́зывает себе́, он не скупи́тся на похвалы́

vi: **he ~s on drink** он жале́ет де́ньги на вы́пивку.

stipulate *vti vt* преду|сма́тривать (-смотре́ть); **the contract ~s that delivery should be within**

two weeks контра́кт предусма́тривает двухнеде́льный срок доста́вки това́ра; **the ~d sum** обусло́вленная су́мма

vi: **he ~d for the best materials to be used** (*for building*) он поста́вил усло́вием, чтобы ему́ был предоста́влен са́мый лу́чший строи́тельный материа́л (*collect*).

stipulation *n* усло́вие; **on the ~ that...** при усло́вии, что...

stir *n*: *fig* **the news caused quite a ~** но́вости (*pl*) наде́лали мно́го шу́му/шу́ма.

stir *vti vt* **1** (*mix*) меша́ть (по-) *and compounds*; **I ~red my tea** я помеша́л чай; **I ~red sugar into my tea** я размеша́л са́хар в ча́е; **I ~red the cream into the soup** я влил сли́вки в суп и размеша́л; **keep ~ring the soup till it boils** поме́шивайте суп, пока́ не закипи́т

2 (*move*) шеве|ли́ть (по-, *semel* -льну́ть); **the breeze ~red the leaves** ветеро́к шевели́л ли́стья; **you'd better ~ yourself** тебе́ пора́ встряхну́ться

3 *fig* будора́жить, волнова́ть (*pfs* вз-); **my imagination was ~red by the film** фильм меня́ взбудора́жил; **we were all ~red by his speech** мы все бы́ли взволно́ваны его́ ре́чью; **the sight ~red her to pity** э́то зре́лище разжа́лобило её; **to ~ a nation to revolt** подня́ть наро́д на восста́ние; **to ~ up trouble/passions** устра́ивать неприя́тности (*pl*), разжига́ть стра́сти (*usu impfs*); **he needs ~ring up** его́ ну́жно расшевели́ть

vi шевели́ться; **she ~red in her sleep** она пошевели́лась во сне; **I haven't ~red all day/from my chair all day** я це́лый день сижу́ без движе́ния, я не встава́л со сту́ла це́лый день; **at that early hour nobody was ~ring** в э́тот ра́нний час все ещё спа́ли.

stirring *adj*: **a ~ tale** приключе́нческий расска́з; **these were ~ times** э́то была́ романти́ческая эпо́ха (*sing*).

stirrup *n* стре́мя.

stitch *n Sew* стежо́к; (*knitting*) пе́тля; *Med* шов; **what ~ is that?** *Sew* каки́м стежко́м ты шьёшь?/вышива́ешь?, (*knitting*) кака́я э́то пе́тля?; **to drop/pick up a ~** спусти́ть/подня́ть пе́тлю; *fig CQ*: **I've got a ~** у меня́ заколо́ло (*impers*) в боку́; **he hadn't a ~ on** он был в чём мать родила́; **we were all in ~es listening to his jokes** мы ката́лись со́ смеху, слу́шая его́ анекдо́ты.

stitch *vt* шить (с-) *and compounds*; **I'll just ~ the hem up** я то́лько подошью́ подо́л; **to ~ leather** проши|ва́ть ко́жу (-́ть); **to ~ a button/a patch on to a shirt** приши́ть пу́говицу к руба́шке, наши́ть запла́ту на руба́шку; *Med* **to ~ a wound** на|кла́дывать швы на ра́ну (-ложи́ть).

stoat *n* горноста́й.

stock *n* **1** (*supply*) запа́с, *also fig*; **~ in hand** нали́чный запа́с; **coal ~s are low** запа́сы у́гля конча́ются; **to lay in ~s of fuel for the winter** запаса́ться то́пливом на́ зиму; **surplus ~** изли́шек това́ров; **~ of spares** склад запчасте́й; **this book is out of ~** э́той кни́ги нет на скла́де; **to take ~** проводи́ть инвентариза́цию; *fig* **we stopped to take ~ of our situation** мы огляну́лись на про́йденное, что́бы оцени́ть обстано́вку

2 *Fin* а́кция; **he has £10,000 in ~s** у него́ де́сять ты́сяч фу́нтов а́кциями/вло́жено в а́кции; **his ~s are going up** его́ а́кции расту́т/повыша́ются, *also fig*

3 *various*: *Cook* бульо́н; (*of gun*) ло́же; (*of anchor*) шток; *Agric* **live ~** скот, поголо́вье скота́; *Rail* **rolling ~** подвижно́й соста́в; (*origin*) **he is of Irish ~** он ирла́ндец по происхожде́нию.

stock *adj* станда́ртный; **she is ~ size** у неё станда́ртная фигу́ра; *Theat* **~ repertoire** обы́чный репертуа́р; *fig* **a ~ phrase** шабло́нная фра́за.

stock *vti vt* (*supply*) запас|а́ть (-ти́); (*equip*) снаб|жа́ть (-ди́ть), обору́довать (*impf and pf*); **to ~ the larder with provisions** пополн|я́ть кладову́ю запа́сами продово́льствия (-́ить); **the bookshop is well ~ed** в кни́жном магази́не хоро́ший вы́бор книг; **do you ~ large sizes?** у вас име́ются (в прода́же) больши́е разме́ры?; **we don't ~ that brand of tobacco** у нас нет э́того со́рта табака́

vi: **to ~ up with sugar** запас|а́ться са́харом (-ти́сь).

stockbreeder *n* животново́д.

stockbroker *n* (биржево́й) ма́клер.

stock exchange *n* (фо́ндовая) би́ржа; **prices on the ~** у́ровень цен на би́рже.

stockholder *n* акционе́р.

stocking *n* чуло́к; **a pair of ~s** па́ра чуло́к; *attr*: **in one's ~ feet** в одни́х чулка́х.

stock-still *adv*: **he stood ~** он стоя́л неподви́жно/как вко́панный.

stocktaking *n* инвентариза́ция, учёт.

stocky *adj* корена́стый, призе́мистый.

stodgy *adj CQ* (*of food*) тяжёлый, трудноперева́риваемый (*also fig of books*); (*of person*) ску́чный, зану́дливый.

stoic(al) *adj* стои́ческий.

stoke *vt*: **he ~s the boilers** он то́пит котлы́; **we ~d up the stove** мы подложи́ли дров (*with wood*)/подбро́сили у́гля (*with coal*) в печь.

stoker *n* кочега́р, истопни́к.

stolid *adj* уравнове́шенный.

stomach *n* желу́док, *CQ* живо́т; **on an empty ~** на голо́дный желу́док; **he lay on his ~** он лежа́л на животе́; **I have a pain in my ~** у меня́ боли́т живо́т; **it turns my ~** меня́ от э́того тошни́т/воро́тит (*impers*), *also fig*; *attr*: **~ ache** боль в желу́дке; **~ pump** желу́дочный зонд; **~ upset** расстро́йство желу́дка.

stomach *vt*: **I can't ~ cruelty** мне прети́т жесто́кость.

stone *n* **1** ка́мень (*m*), *also Med*; (*pebble*) ка́мешек, (*on beach*) га́лька; (*in fruit*) ко́сточка; **precious ~** драгоце́нный ка́мень; **hail ~** гра́дина; *attr*: **the S. Age** ка́менный век; **~ quarry** ка́менный карье́р, каменоло́мня

2 *fig uses*: **a heart of ~** ка́менное се́рдце; **he turned to ~** он как окамене́л; **I live within a ~'s throw of the school** я живу́ в двух шага́х от шко́лы, от моего́ до́ма до шко́лы руко́й пода́ть; **I left no ~ unturned in my efforts to find the paper** я всё переверну́л в по́исках э́того докуме́нта; **to kill two birds with one ~** уби́ть двух за́йцев (одни́м вы́стрелом)

3 (*measure*) сто́ун (6.348 *kg*).

stone *vt* **1** кида́ть ка́мни в кого́-л (*usu impf*); **he was ~d to death** его́ заби́ли камня́ми на́смерть

2: to ~ plums вы|нима́ть ко́сточки из слив (-́нуть); **~d cherries** ви́шни без ко́сточек.

stone-deaf *adj CQ* глухо́й как пень.

stonemason *n* каменотёс.

stony *adj* камени́стый; *fig* ледяно́й, холо́дный.

stool *n* табуре́т(ка); *Med* стул; **folding ~** складно́й табуре́т; **piano ~** (враща́ющийся) табуре́т у роя́ля; *fig* **it falls/he fell between two ~s** э́то ни к селу́ ни к го́роду, он сиде́л ме́жду двух сту́льев.

stool pigeon *n CQ* провока́тор; (*informer*) осведоми́тель (*m*), *CQ* стука́ч.

stoop *vi* суту́литься (с-), го́рбиться (с-); **don't ~** не суту́лься, не го́рбись; **I ~ed down to pick up the pen** я наклони́лся/нагну́лся, что́бы подня́ть ру́чку; **he had to ~ to get into the car** ему́ пришло́сь нагну́ться, что́бы влезть в маши́ну; *fig* **I would never ~ to that** я до э́того не уни́жусь.

stooping *adj* суту́лый.

stop *n* **1** остано́вка; (*break*) переры́в; (*end*) коне́ц; **he spoke for two hours without a ~** он говори́л два часа́ без остано́вки/без переры́ва; **we had a 3-hour ~ in Warsaw** мы сде́лали трёхчасову́ю остано́вку в Варша́ве; **we made a ~ of 3 days in Paris** мы останови́лись на три дня в Пари́же; **the train to Leningrad has only three ~s** по́езд, иду́щий в Ленингра́д, де́лает то́лько три остано́вки; **the blizzard brought traffic to a ~** движе́ние останови́лось из-за мете́ли; **production was brought to a ~ by the strike** произво́дство засто́порилось из-за забасто́вки; **to put a ~ to smth** положи́ть коне́ц чему́-л; **I've come to a ~ in my work** сейча́с у меня́ рабо́та приостанови́лась/засто́порилась

2 (*stopping place*) остано́вка; **the bus ~, a request ~** остано́вка авто́буса/по тре́бованию

3 *Mus* (*on wind instrument*) кла́пан; (*on organ*) реги́стр; (*on stringed instruments*) мензу́ра; *fig* **we'll have to pull out all the ~s** на́до нажа́ть на все педа́ли

4 *other specialized uses*: (*in punctuation, telegrams*) то́чка; *Photo* регуля́тор диафра́гмы; *Ling* взрывно́й согла́сный звук; (*on typewriter, window*) упо́р.

stop *vti vt* **1** (*block*) заде́л|ывать (-ать), за|тыка́ть (-ткну́ть); **to ~ a hole** заде́лать/заткну́ть отве́рстие; **to ~ one's ears (to smth)** затыка́ть у́ши (и не слу́шать что-л), *fig* быть глухи́м (к чему́-л); **to ~ a tooth/a gap** запломбирова́ть зуб, запо́лнить пробе́л, *also fig*; **the drain is ~ped with leaves** сток заби́ло (*impers*) ли́стьями

2 (*prevent*) остан|а́вливать (-ови́ть), уде́рж|ивать (-а́ть); **there's no ~ping him** его́ не остано́вишь/не уде́ржишь; **I can't ~ myself from overeating** я не могу́ удержа́ться, что́бы не съесть ли́шнего; **he ~ped it happening/us from going to the theatre** он не дал э́тому случи́ться, он не дал нам пойти́ в теа́тр; **you can't ~ it from happening** ты не мо́жешь э́то предотврати́ть

3 (*halt*) остана́вливать; **to ~ an engine/progress/traffic** останови́ть мото́р/прогре́сс/движе́ние; **this will ~ the pain** э́то сни́мет боль; **he ~ped me short** он меня́ останови́л, *fig* он оборва́л/прерва́л меня́; **the walls ~ most of the noise** сте́ны почти́ не пропуска́ют зву́ка

4 (*cease*) переста|ва́ть (-́ть) (*used only with verbs*); прекра|ща́ть (-ти́ть) (*used with verbs or nouns*); **~ biting your nails!** переста́нь/прекрати́ грызть но́гти!; **~ it at once!** переста́нь/прекрати́ неме́дленно!; **~ that noise!** прекрати́ э́тот шум!; **we ~ped work at six** мы зако́нчили рабо́ту в шесть; **they ~ped work in protest** в знак проте́ста они́ прекрати́ли рабо́ту

5 (*interrupt, cut short*) прекра|ща́ть (-ти́ть); (*for short time*) приостан|а́вливать (-ови́ть); **building was ~ped because of the snow/because the firm went bankrupt** строи́тельство бы́ло приостано́влено из-за си́льного снегопа́да/прекращено́ из-за банкро́тства фи́рмы; **to ~ smb's salary/payments/one's subscription** прекрати́ть вы́плату зарпла́ты/платежи́/подпи́ску; **rain ~ped play** игра́ прекрати́лась из-за дождя́; **to ~ a cheque** заде́рж|ивать опла́ту че́ка (-а́ть); **they ~ped £6 out of his wages** у него́ удержа́ли шесть фу́нтов из зарпла́ты; **my leave has been ~ped** мне не да́ли сейча́с о́тпуска; **his scholarship was ~ped** его́ лиши́ли стипе́ндии; **I ~ped the papers for two weeks** я попроси́л не доставля́ть газе́ты две неде́ли

vi **1** (*cease motion or action*) остана́вливаться; (*discontinue*) перестава́ть, прекраща́ться; **the car/he ~ped** автомоби́ль/он останови́лся; **the clock has ~ped** часы́ стоя́т [**NB** *tense*]/останови́лись; **how long does the train ~ at Kiev?** ско́лько по́езд стои́т в Ки́еве?; **he never ~s complaining** он не перестаёт жа́ловаться; **it didn't ~ raining all day** дождь не перестава́л весь день; **has it ~ped raining?** дождь переста́л?/прошёл?/ко́нчился?; **the noise ~ped** шум прекрати́лся; **has the pain ~ped?** боль прошла́?; **we ~ped for lunch** (*at a meeting, etc.*) мы сде́лали переры́в на обе́д, (*on journey, etc.*) мы останови́лись пообе́дать

2 (*finish*) конч|а́ться (-́иться); (*be cut short*) прекраща́ться; (*temporarily*) приостана́вли-

ваться; **work has ~ped for today/for the winter** на сегóдня рабóта кóнчена, рабóты (*pl*) приостановúлись нá зиму; **work ~ped when the money ran out** рабóта прекратúлась, когдá дéньги кóнчились

3 (*stay*): **I'm ~ping at a hotel/with my aunt** я остановúлся в гостúнице/у тётки [**NB** *tense*]; **I'm ~ping at home tonight** сегóдня вéчером я остáнусь дóма

stop behind *vi*: **I ~ped behind to talk to him** я остáлся поговорúть с ним; **Tom was made to ~ behind after school** Тóма оставúли пóсле урóков

stop by *vi*: **I'll ~ by on my way home** я зайдý/заéду по дорóге домóй

stop up *vti vt*: **to ~ up a hole/gap/bottle** задéлать дырý, запóлнить пробéл, закýпорить бутылку; **the crack was ~ped up with dirt** щель былá забúта грязью; **my nose is ~ped up** у меня нос залóжен

vi CQ: **don't ~ up for me—I'll be late** ложúсь, не жди меня—я пóздно придý.

stopcock *n Tech* запóрный кран.

stopgap *n* врéменная замéна; *attr* врéменный.

stopover *n* остано́вка.

stoppage *n* (*in game, work*) остано́вка; (*blockage, also of traffic*) прóбка; *Med* засорéние; **~ of pay/payments** прекращéние выплаты платежéй.

stopper *n* (*of bottle, in basin*) прóбка; (*plug for barrel, etc.*) затычка; *fig CQ* **to put a ~ on smth** положúть конéц чемý-л.

stopping *n* (*dental*) плóмба; *Mus* **double ~** двойные нóты (*pl*).

stop-press (*news*) *n* экстренное сообщéние.

stopwatch *n* секундомéр.

storage *n*: **to put smth into ~** сдать вéщи на хранéние.

store *n* **1** (*stock, supply, reserve*) запáс; **to keep smth in ~** (*reserve*) держáть что-л про запáс; **~s of food** запáсы пúщи, съестные припáсы (*no sing*); **we laid in ~s of tinned food** мы запаслúсь консéрвами; *fig*: **he sets great ~ by her opinion** он óчень считáется с её мнéнием; **what does the future hold in ~ for us?** что нам сулúт бýдущее?, что нас ждёт в бýдущем?

2 (*depot*) склад

3 (*shop, esp. US*) магазúн; лáвка; **the village ~** сéльская лáвка; **general ~(s)** универмáг (*sing*).

store *vti vt, also* **to ~ away** хранúть (*impf*); **the boat is ~d in the garage** лóдку хранят в гаражé; **the wine is ~d in the cellar** винó хранúтся в подвáле; **to ~ one's furniture** хранúть мéбель на склáде; **squirrels ~ up nuts for the winter** бéлки запасáются орéхами нá зиму

vi: **these apples ~ well** эти яблоки хорошó хранятся.

storehouse *n* склад; хранúлище.

storekeeper *n* кладовщúк; (*US*) лáвочник.

storeroom *n* кладовáя.

storey, (*US*) **story** *n* этáж; **a 2-/5-~ house** двухэтáжный/пятиэтáжный дом; **on the third ~** на четвёртом этажé [**NB** *Russians count ground floor as first storey*].

stork *n Orn* áист.

storm *n* **1** бýря, *also fig*; *Naut* шторм; **snow ~** вьюга, метéль; **I was caught in/by a thunder ~** меня захватúла грозá; *fig*: **a ~ of applause/protest** бýря аплодисмéнтов/протéстов (*pls*); **his speech raised a ~ of indignation** егó речь вызвала бýрю/взрыв негодовáния; **a ~ in a teacup** бýря в стакáне воды

2 *Mil*: **to take by ~** взять штýрмом/прúступом; *attr*: **~ troops** штурмовые отряды.

storm *vti vt Mil* штурмовáть (*impf*), *also fig*; *fig* **the demonstrators ~ed the embassy** демонстрáнты штурмовáли посóльство

vi fig: **to ~ at smb** кричáть на когó-л (*usu impf*); **he ~ed out of the room** он в ярости брóсился вон из кóмнаты.

stormbound *adj*: *Naut* **we were ~ for 2 days** из-за штóрма мы два дня не моглú отплыть.

stormy *adj* бýрный, *also fig*; *Naut* штормовóй; **a ~ crossing** бýрный перехóд; **a ~ sky** грозовóе/(*at sea*) штормовóе нéбо; *fig* **a ~ discussion/meeting** бýрное обсуждéние/собрáние.

story *n* **1** (*account*) истóрия, расскáз; **I've heard his ~** я слышал егó истóрию (*account or personal history*); **according to her ~ it appears that...** по её словáм выхóдит, что...; *fig*: **it's always the same old ~** вéчно однá и тá же истóрия; **that's quite another ~** это совсéм другóй вопрóс; **these scars tell their own ~** эти шрáмы говорят за себя; *pejor* (*fib*) **stop telling stories** не сочиняй, не выдýмывай, не расскáзывай скáзки

2 *Lit* (*short*) расскáз, (*longer*) пóвесть; **fairy ~** скáзка; **she told the children a ~** онá рассказáла дéтям скáзку; **a detective/ghost/funny ~** детектúвный ромáн, расскáз с привидéниями, анекдóт; **a dirty ~** грýбый/неприлúчный анекдóт; **it's a true ~** это было на сáмом дéле; *Theat, Cine*: **the ~ of the film** сюжéт фúльма

3 (*in newspaper, etc.*) статья; репортáж; **he's done some good stories for the Times** он написáл нéсколько хорóших статéй для «Таймс»; **he's covering the ~ of the space flight** он ведёт репортáжи (*pl*) о космúческом полёте.

storybook *n* сбóрник расскáзов/скáзок.

stout *adj* (*of person*: *fat*) пóлный, дорóдный; (*sturdy*) плóтный, дюжий; (*of things*) прóчный, крéпкий; **to get/grow ~** располнéть; **of ~ build** крéпкого сложéния; **~ shoes** прóчные тýфли; **a ~ stick/coat** крéпкая трость, тяжёлое пальтó; **a ~ rope** тóлстый трос; *fig*: **he's a ~ fellow** он брáвый мáлый; **~ resistance/denial** упóрное сопротивлéние/отрицáние.

stove *n* (*cooker*) плитá; (*for heating*) печь, пéчка.

stow *vti vt* (*pack*) у|кла́дывать, с|кла́дывать (*pfs* -ложи́ть); **to ~ clothes in a trunk**/*Naut* **a locker** сложи́ть оде́жду в сунду́к/в рунду́к; **I've ~ed the boxes (away) in the attic**/*Naut* **the hold** я унёс я́щики на черда́к, я уложи́л я́щики в трю́ме

vi (*on ship, plane*): **to ~ away** е́хать без биле́та/*CQ* за́йцем.

stowaway *n* безбиле́тный пассажи́р, *CQ* за́яц.

straggle *vi* **1** (*of things*) раски́|дываться (-нуться); **the village ~s along the river** дере́вня раски́нулась [**NB** *tense*] вдоль реки́; **straggling branches/vines** раски́нувшиеся ве́тви, разро́сшиеся ло́зы; **ivy ~s along/over the wall** плющ оплёл сте́ну

2 (*of people*): **the children ~d out/behind** де́ти уходи́ли по́рознь (*adv*)/тащи́лись позади́.

straggler *n* отста́вший.

straight *n*: **to cut cloth on the ~** ре́зать материа́л по прямо́й; **that wall is out of the ~** э́та стена́ неро́вная; (*in racing*) **the horses are coming into the ~ now** ло́шади вы́шли на пряму́ю [**NB** *tense*].

straight *adj* **1** (*not curved*) прямо́й; **~ hair** прямы́е во́лосы; **is my tie ~?** у меня́ га́лстук повя́зан ро́вно?/пра́вильно?; **he put his tie ~** он попра́вил га́лстук; **the picture isn't ~** карти́на виси́т ко́со/кри́во; *fig* **I could hardly keep a ~ face** я едва́ мог удержа́ться от сме́ха

2 (*direct, frank, honest*) прямо́й; че́стный; **a ~ answer/refusal** прямо́й отве́т/отка́з; **he's ~ in his dealings** он че́стно ведёт дела́; **I'll be ~ with you** я бу́ду с ва́ми открове́нен

3 (*tidy*): **to put a room/one's affairs ~** привести́ ко́мнату/свои́ дела́ в поря́док; **I'll put my papers ~** я наведу́ поря́док в свои́х бума́гах

4 (*plain*): **a ~ whisky** неразба́вленное ви́ски; *Theat* **a ~ part** обы́чная роль; (*in an election*) **it was a ~ fight** бы́ло то́лько два кандида́та.

straight *adv* **1** пря́мо; **to walk/stand ~** ходи́ть/стоя́ть пря́мо; **drive ~ on for two miles** езжа́й две ми́ли, не свора́чивая; **~ opposite the school** пря́мо напро́тив шко́лы; **he looked ~ at me** он посмотре́л на меня́ в упо́р; **he shoots ~** он ме́тко стреля́ет

2 (*directly*) пря́мо, (*without delay*) *also* **~ away** сра́зу; **go ~ home** иди́ пря́мо/сра́зу домо́й; **he came ~ to the point** он перешёл пря́мо к су́ти де́ла; **I went ~ to bed** я сра́зу же лёг спать; **I'll come back ~ away** я сейча́с же верну́сь; **I told him ~ out he was a fool** я ему́ пря́мо сказа́л, что он дура́к

3 *various*: **I'll have my whisky ~** мне ви́ски неразба́вленное; **since he's been out** (*of prison*) **he's been going ~** вы́йдя из тюрьмы́, он стал вести́ че́стную жизнь.

straighten *vt* вы|прямля́ть (-́прямить); (*adjust*) поправ|ля́ть (-́ить); **to ~ a piece of wire/road** выпрямля́ть кусо́к про́волоки/шоссе́; **he ~ed his tie/glasses** он попра́вил га́лстук/очки́; **you should ~ the picture** ну́жно попра́вить/вы́ровнять карти́ну; **he ~ed his back/himself** он распра́вил спи́ну, он вы́прямился *or* он встал во весь рост

straighten out *vt fig*: **to ~ out one's ideas/a timetable/a misunderstanding** разобра́ться в свои́х мы́слях/с расписа́нием, устрани́ть недоразуме́ние.

straightforward *adj* прямо́й; **he is a ~ man** он прямо́й челове́к; **a ~ answer** прямо́й отве́т; **it's quite ~** э́то о́чень про́сто.

strain[1] *n* **1** *Tech* (*of pull*) натяже́ние; (*of weight*) нагру́зка; **the ~ on a rope** натяже́ние верёвки; **it will put a great ~ on the beam** на ба́лку бу́дет сли́шком больша́я нагру́зка

2 (*on nerves, heart, Psych*) напряже́ние; (*overstrain*) перегру́зка; **mental ~** у́мственное напряже́ние; **he broke under the ~** он не вы́держал напряже́ния; **it is a ~ on his heart/nerves** э́то ему́ нагру́зка на се́рдце/перегру́зка для не́рвов; **he is under severe ~** он перегру́жен; **it was a great ~ on their meagre resources** э́то си́льно уда́рило по их скро́мным ресу́рсам

3 (*muscular, etc.*) растяже́ние.

strain[1] *vti vt* **1** (*stretch*) натя́|гивать, *Med* растя́|гивать (*pfs* -ну́ть); переутом|ля́ть (-и́ть); **to ~ a rope to breaking point** натяну́ть верёвку до преде́ла; *Med*: **he ~ed his shoulder/a muscle in his foot/his heart** он растяну́л себе́ плечо́/ножну́ю мы́шцу, у него́ переутомле́ние се́рдца; **to ~ one's eyes** напря|га́ть зре́ние (-́чь)

2 *fig* напря|га́ть (-́чь); **to ~ oneself** напря́чься; **he ~ed every nerve to reach the other bank** он напряга́л все си́лы, что́бы доплы́ть до друго́го бе́рега; **he ~ed our patience/credulity** он испы́тывал на́ше терпе́ние, он злоупотребля́л на́шим дове́рием

3 (*filter*) проце́|живать (-ди́ть); **to ~ soup through a sieve** процеди́ть суп (че́рез си́течко); **~ the water from the potatoes** слей во́ду с карто́шки (*collect*)

vi напряга́ться; **to ~ under the weight of smth** напряга́ться под тя́жестью чего́-л; **the dog ~ed at the leach** соба́ка тяну́ла за поводо́к.

strain[2] *n* (*breed*) поро́да, род; вид; **a new ~ of virus** но́вый вид ви́руса; **a good ~ of Alsatian** хоро́шая поро́да овча́рок; *fig*: **there's a ~ of madness in the family** у них в семье́ бы́ли слу́чаи психи́ческих заболева́ний; **and a lot more was said in the same ~** и мно́го ещё бы́ло ска́зано в том же ду́хе.

strained *adj* **1** *Med* растя́нутый; (*nerves, relations, etc.*) натя́нутый; **he has a ~ shoulder** у него́ растяже́ние плеча́; **a ~ atmosphere** натя́нутая атмосфе́ра

2 (*filtered*) проце́женный.

strainer *n Cook* си́то, си́течко.

strait *n* **1** *also* **~s** *Geog* проли́в (*sing*); **the Straits of Dover** Ду́врский проли́в, Па-де-Кале́ (*indecl*)

2 *pl* (~**s**): **he is in financial ~s** он в бе́дственном фина́нсовом положе́нии.

straitened *adj*: **to be in ~ circumstances** быть/находи́ться в стеснённых обстоя́тельствах.

strand[1] *n* (*by sea*) бе́рег; прибре́жная полоса́.

strand[1] *vt*: *fig* **I was left ~ed without a penny** я оста́лся на мели́/без копе́йки.

strand[2] *n* (*of wool, etc.*) прядь; ни́тка; **a ~ of rope/hair** прядь кана́та/воло́с (*pl*); **a ~ of a cable** жи́ла ка́беля.

strange *adj* **1** (*alien, unknown*) чужо́й; **a ~ country** чужа́я страна́; **don't speak to ~ men** не разгова́ривай с незнако́мыми мужчи́нами; **there were some ~ faces at the meeting** на собра́нии бы́ло не́сколько незнако́мых лиц

2 (*odd*) стра́нный, чудно́й; **he was behaving in a ~ manner** он о́чень стра́нно вёл себя́; **~ to say** стра́нно сказа́ть; **~ as it may seem, he's a specialist** как э́то ни стра́нно, но ведь он специали́ст; **she wears ~ clothes** она́ ка́к-то стра́нно/о́чень чудно́ одева́ется

3 (*unusual*) необы́чный, непривы́чный; **at first it tastes ~** снача́ла вкус ка́жется необы́чным; **he is ~ to city life** он не привы́к к городско́й жи́зни; **everything was ~ to him** всё ему́ бы́ло непривы́чно/стра́нно; **I am ~ to this job** мне э́та рабо́та незнако́ма.

stranger *n* незнако́мец, незнако́мый; чужо́й; посторо́нний; **he's a perfect ~ to me/to politics** я его́ совсе́м не зна́ю, он в поли́тике новичо́к; **the dog barks at ~s** соба́ка ла́ет на чужи́х; **I am a ~ to London/to these parts** я не зна́ю Ло́ндона, я не зде́шний; *fig CQ* **why, you're quite a ~ these days!** ты что́-то совсе́м (за)пропа́л!

strangle *vt* души́ть (за-), удави́ть (*pf*); **this collar is strangling me** э́тот воротни́к ду́шит меня́.

strangulate *vt Med* ущем|ля́ть (-и́ть).

strap *n* (*on watch, shoe, suitcase, harness*) ремешо́к; (*under foot on ski trousers*) штри́пка; (*shoulder strap on underclothes*) брете́лька; *Mil* пого́н.

strap *vt* (*tie up*) свя́з|ывать (-а́ть), перетя́|гивать (-ну́ть) *and other compounds*; **to ~ a case to the roof of a car** привяза́ть чемода́н к кры́ше маши́ны; **to ~ up a suitcase** перетяну́ть чемода́н ремнём; **to ~ a baby in a chair** при|стёгивать ребёнка к сту́лу (-стегну́ть); **she ~ped on her watch** она́ застегну́ла ремешо́к часо́в; **he ~ped up the cut with plaster** он закле́ил поре́з пла́стырем.

strapless *adj*: **a ~ dress** откры́тое пла́тье без брете́лек.

stratagem *n* уло́вка, хи́трость.

strategy *n* страте́гия.

stratosphere *n* стратосфе́ра.

stratum *n Geol* слой; пласт.

straw *n* соло́ма (*collect*); **a piece of ~** соло́минка; **to drink through a ~** пить че́рез соло́минку; *fig*: **to clutch at a ~** хвата́ться за соло́минку; **it's a ~ in the wind** э́то хоть како́й-то намёк; **it's the last ~** э́то после́дняя ка́пля; *attr* соло́менный.

strawberry *n* (*wild*) земляни́ка, (*cultivated*) клубни́ка (*collects*); *attr* земляни́чный, клубни́чный; **~ bed** клубни́чная гря́дка.

straw-coloured *adj* соло́менного цве́та.

stray *adj*: **a ~ cat/dog** бездо́мная *or* бродя́чая ко́шка/соба́ка; *fig*: **a ~ bullet** шальна́я пу́ля; **a few ~ taxis/houses** не́сколько случа́йных такси́/разбро́санных домо́в; **~ thoughts/ideas** случа́йные/несвя́зные мы́сли.

stray *vi* забрести́ (*pf*); **the cattle ~ed through the open gate** скот забрёл в откры́тые воро́та (*pl*); **we ~ed from the path** мы уклони́лись дово́льно далеко́ от тропи́нки; **the child ~ed from home** ребёнок ушёл от до́ма и потеря́лся; *fig*: **my thoughts ~ed** мои́ мы́сли блужда́ли; **he ~ed from the point** он отклони́лся от су́ти/от те́мы.

streak *n* полоса́, поло́ска; жи́лка, прожи́лка; **a blond ~ in hair** све́тлая прядь в волоса́х; **her hair has ~s of grey in it** у неё во́лосы с про́седью; **a ~ of paint/light** поло́ска кра́ски/све́та; **~s of quartz** (*in rocks*) прожи́лки ква́рца; **a ~ of lightning** вспы́шка мо́лнии; *fig*: **he has a mean ~** он скупова́т; **she has a ~ of German blood** в ней есть при́месь неме́цкой кро́ви.

streaky *adj* полоса́тый; **~ bacon** беко́н с прожи́лками жи́ра.

stream *n* (*brook*) ре́чка, руче́й, ручеёк; (*flow*) пото́к, *also fig*; (*jet*) струя́; (*current*) тече́ние; **a ~ of blood/light** пото́к кро́ви/све́та; **a ~ of oil/cold air** струя́ не́фти/холо́дного во́здуха; **to go with/against the ~** плыть по тече́нию/про́тив тече́ния, *also fig*; *fig* **a ~ of people/cars/curses** пото́к люде́й/маши́н/руга́тельств; *Psych* **the ~ of consciousness** пото́к созна́ния.

stream *vti vt* **1: his face ~ed blood** по его́ лицу́ текла́ кровь

2: they ~ the pupils for French для заня́тий францу́зским языко́м ученико́в де́лят на гру́ппы

vi течь, ли́ться (*impfs*) *and compounds*; струи́ться (*impf*); **the smoke made my eyes ~** от ды́ма у меня́ слези́лись глаза́; **her eyes were ~ing with tears** она облива́лась слеза́ми; **the sunlight ~ed through the window** со́лнце я́рко свети́ло в окно́; **sweat ~ed down his face** пот кати́лся гра́дом/струи́лся по его́ лицу́; **the flag ~ed in the wind** флаг развева́лся на ветру́; **children were ~ing out of the cinema** из двере́й кинотеа́тра хлы́нул пото́к дете́й.

streamlined *adj*: **~ cars** автомоби́ли обтека́емой фо́рмы; *fig* **~ methods** *approx* рациона́льные ме́тоды.

street *n* у́лица; **main/back ~** гла́вная у́лица, переу́лок; **I live in this ~** я живу́ на э́той у́лице; *fig CQ*: **that's right up his ~** э́то по его́ ча́сти; **they are ~s ahead of us in technology** они́ намно́го опережа́ют нас в техноло́гии; **he's not in the same ~ as you**

ты себя́ с ним не равня́й; **the man in the ~** зауря́дный/обыкнове́нный челове́к; *attr* ули́чный; **~ lighting** ули́чное освеще́ние; **~ map** план у́лиц; **at ~ level** на у́ровне земли́.

streetcar *n* (*US*) трамва́й.

strength *n* **1** (*of person*) си́ла; (*of rope, building, etc.*) про́чность; (*of tea, alcohol, solution*) кре́пость; (*of colour, smell*) интенси́вность; **by sheer ~** одно́й то́лько си́лой; **he has the ~ of an ox** он силён как бык; **~ of character/will** си́ла хара́ктера/во́ли; **the ~ of his position** си́ла его́ пози́ции; **it's beyond my ~** э́то мне не по си́лам (*pl*); **~ of alcohol/of a solution** кре́пость спи́рта/раство́ра; *Fin* **the pound has lost/gained in ~** досто́инство фу́нта пони́зилось/повы́силось; *fig* **I took him on the ~ of your recommendation** я взял его́ на рабо́ту по ва́шей рекоменда́ции

2 *Mil*: **fighting ~** боево́й/боеспосо́бный соста́в; **the division was brought up to ~** диви́зия была́ укомплекто́вана по́лностью; **in ~** в по́лном соста́ве; *fig* **the class turned out at the match in ~** на э́тот матч пошёл весь класс.

strengthen *vti vt* укреп|ля́ть, упрочн|я́ть (*pfs* -и́ть), крепи́ть (*impf*); **to ~ one's muscles** укрепля́ть/развива́ть мы́шцы (*usu impfs*); **to ~ walls/a building/one's position** укрепля́ть сте́ны/всё зда́ние/своё положе́ние; **to ~ defences** крепи́ть оборо́ну (*sing*)

vi (*of muscles, limbs*) укрепля́ться; (*of desire, influence*) расти́ (*usu impf*); (*of wind*) уси́ли|ваться (-ться).

strenuous *adj*: **a ~ day** напряжённый день; **~ work** (*mental or physical*) тяжёлая рабо́та; **he made ~ efforts to** он напря́г все свои́ си́лы, что́бы + *inf*; **the walk/game was too ~ for me** прогу́лка/э́та па́ртия была́ сли́шком утоми́тельной (для меня́).

stress *n* **1** напряже́ние, *also Tech*; **mental/nervous ~** у́мственное/не́рвное напряже́ние; **he's under great ~ just now** *CQ* на него́ сейча́с сто́лько всего́ навали́лось

2 (*accent, emphasis*) ударе́ние; *fig* значе́ние; **the ~ is/put the ~ on the second syllable** ударе́ние па́дает/поста́вь ударе́ние на второ́й слог; *fig*: **they lay great ~ on physics** они́ придаю́т большо́е значе́ние изуче́нию фи́зики; **he lays great ~ on accuracy** он осо́бо подчёркивает, что рабо́та тре́бует большо́й то́чности.

stress *vt* (*a syllable*) ста́вить ударе́ние на + *A* (*no-*); *fig*: **he ~ed that...** он подчеркну́л, что...; **they ~ the practical side of the subject** они́ придаю́т осо́бое значе́ние практи́ческой стороне́ де́ла.

stretch *n* **1** (*of elastic, etc.*): **this elastic has lost its ~** э́та рези́нка потеря́ла эласти́чность; **this material has a lot of ~** э́та ткань легко́ растя́гивается; **to give shoes a ~** растяну́ть ту́фли; *fig*: (*of factory, person, etc.*) **to work at full ~** рабо́тать на по́лную мо́щность; **even by a great ~ of the imagination...** да́же при са́мом большо́м воображе́нии...; **it might be allowed at a ~** э́то мо́жно допусти́ть с натя́жкой

2 (*of time*): **for hours at a ~** часа́ми; **I read the book at one ~** я прочёл кни́гу в оди́н присе́ст; **to work two hours at a ~** рабо́тать подря́д (*adv*) два часа́; *sl*: **he did a 3 year ~** (*in prison*) он о́тбыл трёхле́тний срок; **he's doing another ~** он опя́ть сиди́т

3 (*distance*) протяже́ние; **for a long ~ the road runs by the river** доро́га на большо́м протяже́нии идёт вдоль реки́; **that ~ of road is under repair** на э́том уча́стке доро́ги иду́т ремо́нтные рабо́ты; **in that ~ of the river the fishing is excellent** в э́той ча́сти реки́ отли́чный клёв; **a beautiful ~ of country** краси́вое ме́сто; *Sport* **the home ~** фи́нишная пряма́я.

stretch *vti vt* **1** (*make longer, wider*) тяну́ть *and compounds*; **to ~ rope/elastic/gloves** рас-тя́|гивать верёвку/рези́нку/перча́тки (-ну́ть); **to ~ a rope tight** ту́го натяну́ть верёвку; *fig*: **we might ~ a point and give him a three** мо́жно с натя́жкой поста́вить ему́ тро́йку; **that's ~ing things too far!** э́то уже́ сли́шком!

2 (*extend*) протя́|гивать (-ну́ть) *and other compounds*; **he ~ed a rope between two trees** он протяну́л верёвку ме́жду двумя́ дере́вьями; **I ~ed out my hand to turn on the light** я протяну́л ру́ку и включи́л свет; **I ~ed out my leg to ease the cramp** что́бы су́дорога прошла́, я вы́тянул но́гу; **the cat ~ed herself** ко́шка потяну́лась; **I'm going to ~ my legs before supper** пойду́ прогуля́юсь пе́ред у́жином; *fig*: **the engine/he is fully ~ed** мото́р рабо́тает на по́лную мо́щность, он рабо́тает с по́лной отда́чей; **the course doesn't ~ him enough** э́ти заня́тия (*pl*) не тре́буют от него́ больши́х уси́лий

vi тяну́ться (*impf*) *and compounds*; **the elastic has ~ed/won't ~ any more** рези́нка натяну́лась/бо́льше не растя́гивается; **he ~ed and yawned** он потяну́лся и зевну́л; **he ~ed out on the sofa** он растяну́лся на дива́не; **the queue ~ed to the corner** о́чередь протяну́лась/растяну́лась до угла́; **he ~ed for his glass** он потяну́лся за стака́ном; **the road ~ed away across the steppe** доро́га шла сте́пью; **if you ~ up you'll reach the book** ты дотя́нешься до э́той кни́ги, постара́йся; *fig* **the money won't ~ to a new TV** э́тих де́нег не хва́тит на но́вый телеви́зор.

stretcher *n Med* носи́лки (*no sing*); *Art* (*for canvas*) подра́мник.

stretcher-bearer *n* санита́р-носи́льщик.

strew *vt* разбр|а́сывать (-оса́ть); посып|а́ть (-́ать) *and other compounds*; **the floor was ~n with sawdust/with his shirts** пол был усы́пан древе́сными опи́лками (*pl*), его́ руба́шки валя́лись на полу́; **the wreckage was ~n over a wide area** обло́мки самолёта разброса́ло (*impers*) на большо́й пло́щади.

stricken *adj* **1** *attr* поражённый; **the ~ city** пострада́вший го́род

2 *predic*: *fig* **he was ~ with grief/remorse/terror** он был убит горем/полон раскаяния/охвачен *or* объят ужасом.

strict *adj* **1** (*severe*) строгий; **a ~ diet** строгая диета; **he is ~ with his children** он строг со своими детьми

2 (*precise*) точный, строгий; **a ~ meaning/translation** точный смысл/перевод; **I was told in ~ confidence/secrecy** мне сообщили строго конфиденциально/совершенно секретно; **in the ~ sense of the word** строго говоря; **we're working to a ~ time limit** мы работаем в жёстком графике.

stride *n* (большой) шаг; **in a few ~s he reached the door** он достиг двери в два-три шага; *fig*: **it took him time to get into his ~** он не сразу вошёл в нужный ритм; **he has made great ~s in his studies** он сделал большие успехи в учёбе; **she takes it all in her ~** она ни из чего не делает проблемы.

stride *vi* шагать (*impf*) *and compounds*; **he strode along the beach** он шагал по пляжу; **he strode off/on** он зашагал дальше.

strident *adj* пронзительный, резкий.

strife *n* конфликт, борьба; (*discord*) раздор; **industrial/domestic ~** производственный конфликт, домашние дрязги (*no sing*).

strike *n* **1** (*act*) удар, *also Mil*, *Sport*; (*of clock*) удар, бой

2 (*in industry*) забастовка; стачка; **hunger ~** голодовка; **a sympathy ~** забастовка солидарности; **to come out on ~** объявить забастовку; **to go/be on ~** (за)бастовать; *attr*: **~ pay** пособие забастовщикам

3 (*in mining*): **a big oil ~** открытие крупного месторождения нефти.

strike *vti vt* **1** (*hit*) удар|ять (-ить); на|носить удар (-нести); бить (*impf*) *and other compounds*; (*knock*) стук|ать (-нуть); **he struck the table with his fist** он ударил/стукнул кулаком по столу; **I struck the nail with a hammer** я ударил молотком по гвоздю; **I struck him a blow on the chest** я нанёс ему удар в грудь; **the bullet struck his chest/the rock** пуля попала ему в грудь/в скалу; **to ~ a ball** ударить по мячу; **the tree was struck by lightning** молния ударила в дерево; **never ~ a child/a man when he's down** никогда не бей ребёнка, лежачего не бьют; **the knife was struck out of his hand** нож выбили у него из рук

2 *fig* (*hit*): **paralysis struck him** его разбил паралич; **he was struck blind/deaf/dumb with horror** он ослеп/оглох/онемел от ужаса; **the bombs struck terror into everyone** эти бомбы вселяли ужас во всех

3 (*knock against*) ударяться о + *A*; **the ship struck a reef** корабль ударился о риф; **the spade struck rock** лопата ударила о камень; **they struck gold/oil** они напали на золотую жилу, они обнаружили нефть; *fig* **we struck lucky** нам повезло (*impers*)

4 (*make, produce*): **to ~ a coin/a medal** чеканить монету (вы-), выбить медаль (*usu pf*); **to ~ a match** заж|игать спичку (-ечь), чирк|ать спичкой (-нуть); *Bot* **to ~ roots** пус|кать корни (-тить); **parents must ~ a balance between indulgence and severity** родители не должны быть ни слишком снисходительны, ни слишком строги к детям

5 (*of clocks, Mus*): **the clock/it struck 3** часы (*no sing*) пробили три, пробило (*impers*) три (часа)

6: **to ~ camp** сниматься с лагеря

7 (*make an impression on*): **it ~s me he's lying** мне кажется, что он лжёт; **it suddenly struck me that...** меня вдруг осенило (*impers*), что...; **I was struck by her patience** я был поражён её терпением; **how does he ~ you?** как он тебе показался? [**NB** *tense*]

vi **1** (*attack*) ударять, напа|дать (-сть); (*knock against*) ударяться; **the enemy struck at dawn** враг напал на рассвете; **his foot struck against a rock** он ударился ногой о выступ скалы; *fig*: **~ while the iron is hot** куй железо, пока горячо; **the remark struck home** замечание попало в точку/в цель

2 (*of clocks*): **the clock is striking** бьют часы; **has 5 o'clock struck?** пять часов уже пробило (*impers*)?

3 (*in industry*) бастовать (за-)

strike back *vt* на|носить ответный удар (-нести), *also Mil*

strike down *vt*: **he struck him down** он ударом свалил его на землю; **she was struck down with flu** её свалил грипп

strike off *vti vt*: **the doctor was struck off the register** врача лишили права практиковать; **I struck her name off the list** я вычеркнул её имя из списка

vi: **he struck off down the track/across the beach** он пошёл по дорожке, он пошёл через пляж

strike on *vi*: **I struck on the ideal solution** я нашёл идеальное решение

strike out *vti vt* (*delete*) вы|чёркивать (-черкнуть)

vi (*of swimmer*): **he struck out for the shore** он поплыл к берегу; *fig* **he struck out on his own** он завёл собственное дело

strike up *vti*: **to ~ up an acquaintance/conversation** завести знакомство/разговор; **the band struck up (a march)** оркестр заиграл (марш).

strikebreaker *n* штрейкбрехер.

striker *n* забастовщик.

striking *adj* **1**: **a ~ contrast** разительный контраст; **a woman of ~ beauty** женщина поразительной красоты

2 *Mil*: **a ~ force** ударная группа; **within ~ range** в пределах досягаемости

3: **a ~ clock** часы с боем.

string *n* **1** (*for parcels, etc.*) бечёвка; (*for puppet*) верёвочка; (*for violin, piano, for tennis racket*) струна; (*for apron*) завязка; (*for anorak*) шнурок; *Bot* (*fibre*) волокно; **a piece/ball of ~** кусок/клубок бечёвки; *Mus* **the ~s** струнные инструменты; *fig*: **he is tied to his mother's**

apron ~s он де́ржится за ма́мину ю́бку; **a deal with no ~s attached** сде́лка без вся́ких дополни́тельных усло́вий; **his father will pull ~s** его́ оте́ц испо́льзует свя́зи; *attr*: *Mus* **a ~ quartet** стру́нный кварте́т

2: a ~ of pearls/beads нить же́мчуга, бу́сы; **a ~ of onions** свя́зка лу́ка; *fig*: **a ~ of cars** верени́ца маши́н; **a ~ of questions** ряд вопро́сов.

string *vt*: **to ~ beads** нани́з|ывать бу́сы на ни́тку (-а́ть); **to ~ beans** чи́стить стручки́ фасо́ли (*usu impf*); **to ~ a violin/a racket** натя́|гивать стру́ны на скри́пку/на раке́тку (-ну́ть); **the cars were strung out along the road** маши́ны вы́строились верени́цей вдоль доро́ги.

string bean *n Bot* фасо́ль волокни́стая.

stringed *adj Mus* стру́нный.

stringent *adj* стро́гий; **~ measures** стро́гие ме́ры; **~ necessity** суро́вая необходи́мость.

stringy *adj* волокни́стый; (*of meat*) жи́листый.

strip *n* полоса́, поло́ска; **landing ~** поса́дочная полоса́; **a ~ of land** поло́ска земли́; *fig CQ* **to tear a ~ off smb** снять стру́жку с кого́-л.

strip *vti vt*: **they ~ped him naked** его́ разде́ли догола́ (*adv*); **he ~ped off his shirt** он снял руба́шку; **the wind ~ped the trees of their leaves** ве́тер срыва́л ли́стья с дере́вьев; **he ~ped some bark off the tree** он ободра́л кору́ с де́рева; **to ~ (down) walls/off wallpaper** ободра́ть сте́ны, содра́ть обо́и; **to ~ a bed** снима́ть посте́льное бельё (снять); **burglars ~ped the flat** во́ры обчи́стили (*CQ*) кварти́ру; **he was ~ped of everything/of his honours** его́ лиши́ли всего́ *or* у него́ всё о́тняли, у него́ отобра́ли награ́ды; **to ~ down an engine** раз|бира́ть мото́р (-обра́ть)

vi разде|ва́ться (-́ться); **he ~ped off** *or* **to the skin/to the waist** он разде́лся догола́ *or* донага́/до по́яса.

strip cartoon *n* расска́з в карти́нках.

stripe *n* полоса́; (*weal*) рубе́ц; *Mil* наши́вка; **a black dress with white ~s** чёрное пла́тье в бе́лую поло́ску; *Mil* **to get one's ~s** получи́ть наши́вку.

striped *adj* полоса́тый.

strip lighting *n* ла́мпы дневно́го освеще́ния.

striptease *n* стрипти́з.

strive *vi*: **to ~ for/after smth** стреми́ться к чему́-л (*impf*); **he is striving for effect** он стреми́тся произвести́ эффе́кт; **to ~ against smth** боро́ться про́тив чего́-л (*impf*); **he strove to conceal his anxiety** он стара́лся скрыть своё беспоко́йство.

stroke *n* **1** (*blow*) уда́р, *also Med*; **sun ~** со́лнечный уда́р; **breast ~** брасс; **to put smb off his ~** *Sport* сбить кого́-л с ри́тма/*fig* с то́лку

2 *fig uses*: **at a/one ~** одни́м ма́хом/уда́ром, с одного́ уда́ра; **that was a ~ of genius** э́то бы́ло гениа́льно; **a master ~** ма́стерский приём; **we had a ~ of luck** нам повезло́ (*impers*); **he arrived on the ~ of three** он прие́хал то́чно в три (часа́); *CQ*: **he doesn't do a ~** он па́лец о па́лец не уда́рит; **I haven't done a ~ today** я сего́дня к рабо́те не притро́нулся

3 *Art* (*with pencil, charcoal*) штрих, мазо́к; **with a few ~s** не́сколькими штриха́ми; **he paints with delicate ~s** он пи́шет лёгкими мазка́ми; *Mus* **a ~ of the bow** взмах смычка́.

stroke *vt* гла́дить (по-); (*several times*) погла́живать.

stroll *n* прогу́лка.

stroll *vi* гуля́ть (по-); прогу́л|иваться (-я́ться); **he ~ed along the beach/up and down the terrace** он гуля́л по пля́жу, он прогу́ливался по терра́се; **he ~ed into the garden/up to me** он зашёл в сад, он подошёл ко мне.

strong *adj* **1** кре́пкий; си́льный; (*of furniture, buildings*) про́чный; **a ~ stick/constitution/heart/nerves** кре́пкая па́лка, кре́пкое сложе́ние, здоро́вое се́рдце, кре́пкие не́рвы; **he is not very ~** у него́ не о́чень кре́пкое здоро́вье; **he is as ~ as a horse** он силён как бу́йвол; **to grow ~** (*of person*) кре́пнуть, (*of wind, etc.*) уси́ливаться; **she is getting ~er every day** она́ с ка́ждым днём набира́ется сил; **a ~ arm** кре́пкая/си́льная рука́; **a ~ lens** си́льная ли́нза; **a ~ magnet/wind** си́льный магни́т/ве́тер; **you must be ~** (*courageous*) ну́жно быть си́льным; **he is ~ in maths** он силён в матема́тике (*sing*); **a ~ table/wall** про́чный стол, про́чная стена́; **you'll need ~ shoes** тебе́ нужны́ кре́пкие/про́чные боти́нки; **he is a ~ candidate** у него́ мно́го ша́нсов

2 *fig* си́льный; **~ emotions** си́льные эмо́ции; **a ~ accent/protest** си́льный акце́нт/проте́ст; **a ~ personality/will** си́льная ли́чность/во́ля; **a ~ imagination/resemblance** большо́е воображе́ние/схо́дство; **he expressed himself in ~ terms/language** он вы́разился кре́пко; **that is his ~ point** э́то его́ си́льная сторона́; **it is my ~ belief that...** я твёрдо ве́рю/убеждён, что...; **a ~ interest** живо́й интере́с; **he is a ~ supporter of the theory** он я́рый сторо́нник э́той тео́рии; **~ measures** стро́гие/круты́е ме́ры; **there are ~ indications that...** есть я́вные при́знаки того́, что...; *Fin*: **a ~ currency** усто́йчивая валю́та; **the pound is ~ just now** фунт сейча́с усто́йчивая валю́та

3 (*of drink, flavour, etc.*) кре́пкий; си́льный; **~ tea** кре́пкий чай; **I want a ~ drink** мне чего́-нибудь покре́пче; **there was a ~ smell of fish** си́льно па́хло ры́бой; **~ cheese** о́стрый сыр

4 (*in numbers*): **a group 20 ~** гру́ппа из двадцати́ челове́к.

strong *adv*: **he is eighty and still going ~** ему́ во́семьдесят, а он ещё в по́лной си́ле.

strongly *adv* си́льно; кре́пко; про́чно (*see adj usage*); **a ~ worded letter** письмо́, напи́санное в ре́зких выраже́ниях; **he is ~ against her coming** он реши́тельно настро́ен про́тив её прие́зда; **they reacted ~** они́ бу́рно реаги́ровали (*emotionally*); **I ~ advise you to** я вам о́чень/настоя́тельно сове́тую + *inf*; **I can't emphasize ~ enough...** я до́лжен ещё и ещё раз подчеркну́ть...; **he feels very ~ about it** у него́ твёрдое/определённое мне́ние на э́тот счёт.

strong-willed *adj* волево́й.

strop *vt*: **to ~ a razor** пра́вить бри́тву (*impf*).

structural *adj* конструкти́вный; *Phys*, *Ling*, *etc.* структу́рный; **~ alterations** измене́ния в констру́кции; **~ engineering** строи́тельная те́хника.

structure *n* строе́ние, констру́кция; структу́ра; **the ~ of the human body** строе́ние те́ла челове́ка; **molecular ~** молекуля́рное строе́ние; **the ~ of the house is weak** у до́ма ненадёжная констру́кция; **social ~** обще́ственный строй, социа́льная структу́ра; *Ling* **the ~ of (a) language/sentence** строй языка́/предложе́ния.

struggle *n* борьба́; (*resistance*) сопротивле́ние; (*scuffle*) схва́тка, дра́ка; **the ~ for existence/against injustice** борьба́ за существова́ние/про́тив несправедли́вости; **he put up a ~** он оказа́л сопротивле́ние, *also fig*; **he lost his glasses in the ~** он потеря́л очки́ в дра́ке; **it is a ~ for her to make ends meet** ей сто́ит больши́х трудо́в своди́ть концы́ с конца́ми.

struggle *vi* сопротивля́ться, боро́ться (*impfs*); **he ~d with the policeman** он оказа́л сопротивле́ние полице́йскому; **he kicked and ~d** он отбива́лся рука́ми и нога́ми; **she ~d with her suitcase** она́ с трудо́м тащи́ла чемода́н; **he ~d to his feet** он с трудо́м подня́лся на́ ноги; **I ~ along somehow** я ко́е-ка́к перебива́юсь; **they were struggling for better conditions/against difficulties** они́ боро́лись за лу́чшие усло́вия/с тру́дностями.

strum *vti*: **to ~ a guitar/on the piano** бренча́ть на гита́ре/на роя́ле (*impf*).

strung *adj fig*: **he is highly ~** он тако́й не́рвный/взви́нченный.

strut *n Tech* распо́рка; сто́йка.

strychnine *n* стрихни́н.

stub *n* (*of tail*) обру́бок; (*of pencil*) огры́зок; (*of cigarette*) оку́рок; (*counterfoil*) корешо́к.

stub *vt*: **to ~ one's toe against smth** споткну́ться обо что-л (*usu pf*); **to ~ out a cigarette** гаси́ть оку́рок (по-).

stubble *n* (*in field*: *also* **a field of ~**) стерня́, жнивьё; (*on chin*) щети́на.

stubborn *adj* (*of person*) упря́мый; (*of resistance*, *refusal*, *denial*) упо́рный.

stubby *adj*: **~ fingers** коро́ткие то́лстые па́льцы; **a ~ pencil** коро́ткий каранда́ш; **a ~ tail** хвост как обру́бок.

stucco *n* штукату́рная/(*if moulded*) лепна́я рабо́та.

stuck-up *adj CQ*: **he's so ~** он тако́й задава́ла (*m and f*).

stud[1] *n* (*on collar*) за́понка; (*press-stud*) кно́пка; (*on door*, *boots*, *road*) шип; (*for upholstery*, *etc.*) гвоздь с большо́й шля́пкой.

stud[2] *n*, *also* **~ farm, racing ~** ко́нный заво́д; *attr*: **~ mare** племенна́я кобы́ла.

student *n* студе́нт, *f* -ка; **a medical/law ~** студе́нт-ме́дик/-юри́ст, студе́нт медици́нского/юриди́ческого факульте́та; *attr* студе́нческий.

studied *adj*: **a ~ insult** умы́шленное оскорбле́ние; **a ~ calm** напускно́е споко́йствие.

studio *n* сту́дия, *also Art*; *Art* ателье́ (*indecl*), мастерска́я; **radio/television/film ~** радиосту́дия, телесту́дия, киносту́дия.

studious *adj* (*of person*) приле́жный, усе́рдный, стара́тельный; **with ~ attention** с больши́м внима́нием.

study *n* (*room*) кабине́т; (*of subject*) изуче́ние, иссле́дование; *Mus* этю́д; *Art* этю́д, (*practice sketch*) эски́з; **my studies show that...** мои́ иссле́дования пока́зывают, что...; **he is fond of ~** он лю́бит нау́чные заня́тия (*pl*); **humane studies** гуманита́рные нау́ки; **after a careful ~ of the matter** тща́тельно изучи́в/рассмотре́в э́тот вопро́с; *fig*: **he was in a brown ~** он был погружён в глубо́кое разду́мье; **his face was a real ~** на его́ лице́ сто́ило посмотре́ть.

study *vti vt* изуч|а́ть (-и́ть); **to ~ physics/a text** изуча́ть фи́зику/текст; **I studied the map/his proposals carefully** я тща́тельно изучи́л ка́рту/его́ предложе́ния; **he is ~ing the effects of radiation on plants** он изуча́ет/иссле́дует де́йствие радиа́ции на расте́ния; **I studied his reactions/his face** я наблюда́л за его́ реа́кцией (*sing*)/лицо́м

vi учи́ться (*impf*); занима́ться (*only in impf*); **I ~ with/under Professor S.** я занима́юсь у профе́ссора С.; **he is ~ing to be a doctor/for exams** он у́чится на врача́, он гото́вится к экза́менам; **he studies hard** он мно́го занима́ется.

study group *n* кружо́к.

stuff *n* **1** (*cloth*) мате́рия, ткань

2 (*material*, *substance*): **this chemical is dangerous ~** э́тот химика́т опа́сен; **his article is really good ~** его́ статья́ действи́тельно о́чень интере́сна; *CQ*: **he knows his ~** он своё де́ло зна́ет; **do your ~** де́лай своё де́ло; **what's that ~ you're eating?** что э́то ты ешь?; **do you call this ~ wine?** и э́то по́йло ты называ́ешь вино́м?; **all that ~ about eternal love** вся э́та болтовня́ про ве́чную любо́вь; **~ and nonsense!** чушь!, ерунда́!; **this whisky is the ~!** э́то ви́ски что на́до!

3 *CQ* (*things*) ве́щи (*pl*); **he scatters his ~ all over the place** он разбра́сывает свои́ ве́щи повсю́ду; **I moved the ~ off the table** я убра́л всё со стола́; **he brought back lots of ~ from Spain** он привёз мно́го чего́/всего́/вся́ких веще́й из Испа́нии.

stuff *vt* (*fill*) наби|ва́ть (-́ть); (*cram*) запи́х|ивать (-ну́ть); заби|ва́ть (-́ть); *Cook* фарширова́ть (на-), начин|я́ть (-и́ть); **to ~ a cushion with feathers** наби́ть поду́шку пе́рьями; **he ~ed himself/his mouth with chocolate** он объе́лся шокола́дом, он наби́л себе́ рот шокола́дом;

my head is ~ed with useless facts у меня́ голова́ заби́та вся́кими нену́жными све́дениями; **I ~ed another shirt into the suitcase** я су́нул ещё одну́ руба́шку в чемода́н; **he ~ed cotton wool into his ears** он заткну́л у́ши ва́той; **he ~ed the hole with cement** он зама́зал дыру́ цеме́нтом; **he ~ed the child with sweets** он напи́чкал ребёнка конфе́тами; **I am completely ~ed** я нае́лся до отва́ла; **I'm ~ed up with a cold** у меня́ совсе́м нос зало́жен.

stuffing *n* наби́вка; *Cook* фарш, начи́нка; *fig CQ* **he had the ~ knocked out of him** с него́ сби́ли спесь.

stuffy *adj* (*of air*) ду́шный, спёртый; (*of smell*) за́тхлый; **it's ~ in here** здесь ду́шно; *CQ* **she's a ~ old thing** она́ така́я чо́порная.

stumble *vi* **1** спот|ыка́ться (-кну́ться); осту-п|а́ться (-и́ться); **the horse/she ~d and fell** ло́шадь/она́ споткну́лась *or* оступи́лась и упа́ла; **I ~d on a stone** я споткну́лся о ка́мень

2 (*in speech*) за|пина́ться (-пну́ться); **he ~d over his words** он запина́лся на ка́ждом сло́ве; **he ~d through the speech** он произнёс свою́ речь, запина́ясь; **he recited the poem without stumbling** он прочёл стихи́ без запи́нки.

stumbling block *n* ка́мень преткнове́ния.

stump *n* (*of tree*) пень; (*of tooth*) пенёк зу́ба; (*of cigar*) оку́рок; (*of pencil*) огры́зок; (*of maimed limb*) обру́бок, культя́; **a ~ of a tail** обру́бок хвоста́.

stump *vti vt* **1** *CQ* озада́чи|вать (-ть); **he was ~ed by the problem** его́ озада́чила э́та пробле́ма; **I ~ed him with that question** я его́ огоро́шил э́тим вопро́сом

2 *CQ*: **he ~ed up the cash** он вы́ложил де́нежки

vi ковыля́ть, то́пать (*impfs*) *and compounds*; **he ~ed along tapping with his stick** он заковыля́л да́льше, посту́кивая па́лкой; **he ~ed out of the room** тяжело́ ступа́я, он вы́шел из ко́мнаты; *CQ* **you'll have to ~ up for the dinner** тебе́ придётся распла́чиваться за у́жин.

stumpy *adj* (*of object*) коро́тенький; (*of person*) корена́стый, призе́мистый.

stun *vt* оглуш|а́ть (-и́ть); *fig* ошелом|ля́ть (-и́ть); **he was ~ned by the blow**/*fig* **by the news** он был оглушён уда́ром, его́ ошеломи́ла э́та но́вость.

stunning *adj* ошеломля́ющий, *CQ* сногсшиба́тельный, потряса́ющий.

stunt *n* трюк; (*students'*) проде́лка; *Aer* фигу́ра вы́сшего пилота́жа; **a publicity ~** рекла́мный трюк.

stunted *adj* (*of person, plant*) низкоро́слый; (*of plant*) ча́хлый.

stupefaction *n* си́льное изумле́ние; остолбене́ние.

stupefied *ppp*: **to be ~** быть потрясённым/ошеломлённым (*by news, etc.*)/одурма́ненным (*by alcohol, drugs, etc.*).

stupendous *adj CQ* потряса́ющий, колосса́льный.

stupid *adj* глу́пый; **don't be ~!** не глупи́!; **I've done something ~** я сде́лал глу́пость; **what a ~ thing to do!** кака́я глу́пость!

stupidity *n* глу́пость.

stupor *n*: **he drunk himself into a ~** он напи́лся до бесчу́вствия.

sturdy *adj* (*of person*) здоро́вый, кре́пкий, си́льный; (*of thing*) **a ~ chair/bicycle** про́чный стул, надёжный велосипе́д.

sturgeon *n Zool* осётр; (*as food*) осетри́на.

stutter *n* заика́ние; **he has a bad ~** он си́льно заика́ется, он за́ика (*m and f*); **he answered with a ~** он отве́тил заика́ясь.

stutter *vti* заика́ться (*impf*); **he ~ed out an apology** он, заика́ясь, пробормота́л извине́ние.

sty *n* свина́рник; хлев.

sty(e) *n Med* ячме́нь (*m*) (на глазу́).

style *n* **1** (*general: Art, Lit, Mus, Sport*) стиль (*m*); **in baroque ~** в сти́ле баро́кко (*indecl*); **March 3rd old ~** тре́тье ма́рта по ста́рому сти́лю; **I don't like his ~ of acting/speaking** мне не нра́вится стиль его́ игры́/его́ мане́ра говори́ть; **written in an elegant ~** напи́санный изя́щным сло́гом; **their ~ of life** их о́браз жи́зни; *Sport* **free ~ (of swimming)** во́льный стиль; *fig* **this is not my ~** э́то не мой стиль

2 (*elegance*) стиль; **there's no ~ about him** у него́ простова́тые мане́ры, (*of dress*) он не уме́ет одева́ться; **to travel/live in ~** путеше́ствовать с ши́ком, жить на широ́кую но́гу

3 (*fashion*) фасо́н; **the latest Paris ~s** после́дние пари́жские фасо́ны/мо́ды; **I like that ~ of car** мне нра́вятся таки́е маши́ны (*pl*); **a new hair ~** но́вая причёска.

style *vt* **1** (*call*) именова́ть (*impf*); **how should he be ~d correctly?** как пра́вильно именова́ть его́?; **he ~s himself "director"** он имену́ет себя́ «дире́ктор»

2 (*design*): **to ~ a dress/smb's hair** созда|ва́ть но́вый фасо́н пла́тья (-ть), де́лать кому́-л мо́дную причёску (с-); **this model** (*of car*) **is ~d for maximum comfort** э́та моде́ль предусма́тривает максима́льные удо́бства (*pl*).

stylish *adj* (*of dress*) мо́дный, *CQ* сти́льный, шика́рный.

stylized *adj* стилизо́ванный.

stylus *n* граммофо́нная иго́лка.

suave *adj* (*polite*) учти́вый; *pejor* **he's a really ~ type** он так льстив; **~ phrases** льсти́вые фра́зы.

subaltern *n Mil* мла́дший офице́р.

subcommittee *n* подкоми́ссия; подкомите́т.

subconscious *n* (**the ~**) подсозна́ние.

subconscious *adj* подсозна́тельный.

subcontract *n* субдогово́р.

subdivide *vt* подраздел|я́ть (-и́ть).

subdivision *n* (*act*) подразделе́ние; (*group*) се́кция, подотде́л, подразделе́ние.

subdue *vt* (*people, country*) покор|я́ть, подчин|я́ть (*pfs* -и́ть).

subdued *adj fig* пода́вленный; **she was a bit ~** она́ была́ че́м-то пода́влена; **a ~ atmosphere** атмосфе́ра пода́вленности; **in a ~ voice/**

light приглушённым го́лосом, в приглушённом све́те.

sub-editor *n* помо́щник реда́ктора в газе́те.

subheading *n* подзаголо́вок.

subject *n* **1** *Polit* по́дданный

2 (*theme*) те́ма, предме́т (*also in school*); **~ of a novel/of research** сюже́т рома́на, те́ма иссле́дования; **let's keep to/change/drop the ~** не бу́дем отклоня́ться от те́мы *or* от предме́та, переведём разгово́р на другу́ю те́му, забу́дем об э́том; **while we're on the ~** поско́льку/раз мы уже́ об э́том заговори́ли; *attr*: **~ heading/index** предме́тный заголо́вок/указа́тель; **~ matter** те́ма, предме́т

3 (*in science, art*) объе́кт; **the ~ of an experiment** объе́кт о́пыта/экспериме́нта; **he'd be a good ~ for psychoanalysis** он был бы прекра́сным объе́ктом для психоана́лиза; **it would make a good ~ for a painting** э́то так и про́сится на карти́ну

4 *Gram* подлежа́щее.

subject *adj* **1** *Polit*: **a territory ~ to** террито́рия, подвла́стная + *D*

2 (*liable to*): **all prices are ~ to alteration** все це́ны подлежа́т измене́нию; **he is ~ to attacks of bronchitis** он подве́ржен бронхи́ту

3 (*conditional upon*): **the plan will be operative at once ~ to the director's approval** план сра́зу бу́дет осуществля́ться, е́сли дире́ктор его́ одо́брит; **you will get your visa quickly ~ to producing the necessary papers** вы бы́стро полу́чите ви́зу при усло́вии предоставле́ния необходи́мых докуме́нтов.

subject *vt* **1** *see* **subjugate**

2 (*expose to*) подверг|а́ть (-́нуть); **he was ~ed to great hardship/to severe criticism** он испы́тывал огро́мные лише́ния (*pl*), он подве́ргся суро́вой кри́тике.

subjective *adj* субъекти́вный; **~ judgement/impression** субъекти́вное сужде́ние, ли́чное впечатле́ние.

subjugate *vt* поко́р|я́ть, подчин|я́ть (*pfs* -и́ть).

subjunctive *n*, *also* **the ~ mood** *Gram* сослага́тельное наклоне́ние.

sublease *n* субаре́нда.

sublet *vt* сда|ва́ть в поднаём (-ть).

sublimate *vt Chem, Psych* сублими́ровать (*impf and pf*).

sublime *adj* возвы́шенный, благоро́дный; (*extreme*) **with ~ indifference** с надме́нным/холо́дным безразли́чием; *as n*: **from the ~ to the ridiculous** от вели́кого до смешно́го (оди́н шаг).

subliminal *adj Psych* подсозна́тельный.

submarine *n* подво́дная ло́дка, подло́дка.

submerge *vti vt* погру|жа́ть (-зи́ть); **the wreck is ~d at high tide** о́стов разби́того су́дна затопля́ется во вре́мя прили́ва; *fig* **I'm completely ~d by papers** я про́сто зава́лен бума́гами

vi погружа́ться.

submission *n* **1** (*submissiveness*) повинове́ние, подчине́ние; (*obedience*) поко́рность; **the tribes were reduced to total ~** племена́ по́лностью покори́лись

2 *Law* заявле́ние; **the defendant's ~ was that...** подсуди́мый заяви́л, что...

submissive *adj* поко́рный.

submit *vti vt*: **this problem will be ~ted to the committee** э́тот вопро́с бу́дет предста́влен на рассмотре́ние коми́ссии; *Law* **we ~ that...** мы заявля́ем, что...

vi (*yield*) покор|я́ться (-и́ться).

subnormal *adj* (*of person*) недора́звитый; **his temperature is ~** у него́ температу́ра ни́же норма́льной.

subordinate *n* подчинённый.

subordinate *adj* (*in rank*) подчинённый (+ *D*); *Gram* **a ~ clause** прида́точное предложе́ние.

subplot *n* побо́чная сюже́тная ли́ния.

subscribe *vti vt* же́ртвовать (по-); **he ~d £20 to the fund** он поже́ртвовал два́дцать фу́нтов в фонд

vi подпи́с|ываться (-а́ться); **I ~ to several journals** я подпи́сываюсь на/я выпи́сываю не́сколько журна́лов; **he ~s liberally to charity** он мно́го же́ртвует на благотвори́тельные це́ли; *fig* **I don't ~ to that idea** я э́ту иде́ю не подде́рживаю.

subscriber *n* (*to journal*) подпи́счик; (*to concert series, telephone*) абоне́нт; (*to appeal, charity*) же́ртвователь (*m*).

subscription *n* (*to journal*) подпи́ска; (*to club*) взнос; (*to concerts, etc.*) абонеме́нт; (*to charity*) поже́ртвование; **he took out a ~ to Novy Mir** он подписа́лся на (журна́л) «Но́вый мир»; **to pay a ~ to a club** плати́ть чле́нские взно́сы (*pl*) в клуб; **all ~s welcome however small** принима́ются любы́е поже́ртвования, да́же са́мые незначи́тельные/ма́ленькие; *attr*: **~ concert** абонеме́нтный конце́рт; **~ rate** подписна́я цена́.

subsection *n* (*of department, etc.*) подсе́кция, подотде́л; (*of document*) пара́граф, пункт, подразде́л.

subsequent *adj* после́дующий; **on a ~ visit** во вре́мя после́дующего визи́та.

subsequently *adv* впосле́дствии, зате́м.

subservient *adj* подобостра́стный.

subside *vi* (*of land, building*) осе|да́ть (-́сть); (*of floods, etc.*) спа|да́ть (-сть), убы|ва́ть (-́ть); *fig*: **he ~d into a chair** он упа́л в кре́сло; **let's wait till the fuss ~s** подождём, пока́ сумато́ха уля́жется.

subsidence *n* (*of ground*) оседа́ние.

subsidiary *n* (*company*) отделе́ние, филиа́л.

subsidiary *adj*: **a ~ enterprise** филиа́л, доче́рнее предприя́тие; **a ~ branch** (*of bank*) филиа́л ба́нка; **~ means of income** дополни́тельные исто́чники дохо́да; **a ~ reason** дополни́тельная причи́на.

subsidize *vt* субсиди́ровать (*impf and pf*).

subsidy *n* субси́дия.

subsist *vi*: **he ~s on 40 dollars a week/entirely on vegetables** он живёт на со́рок до́лларов в неде́лю, он пита́ется одни́ми овоща́ми.

subsistence *n*: **means of** ~ сре́дства к существова́нию; *attr*: **a** ~ **wage** прожи́точный ми́нимум; **they live on a** ~ **diet/on** ~ **level** они́ живу́т на голо́дном рацио́не, *CQ* им де́нег то́лько-то́лько хвата́ет.

subsoil *n* подпо́чва.

subspecies *n* подви́д, разнови́дность.

substance *n* **1** (*matter*, *material*) вещество́; *Philos* субста́нция, мате́рия; (*content*) су́щность, суть; **I agree in** ~ **with his proposition** я в су́щности/по су́ти согла́сен с его́ предложе́нием; **the** ~ **of his argument/plan** вся суть его́ до́водов (*pl*)/пла́на; **his claim/the book lacks** ~ его́ прете́нзии (*pl*) легкове́сны, в кни́ге нет са́мого основно́го.

substandard *adj* нека́чественный.

substantial *adj* **1** соли́дный, про́чный; **a** ~ **meal** пло́тный обе́д; *fig* **we have** ~ **proof** у нас есть ве́ские доказа́тельства (*pl*)

2 (*essential*): **we're in** ~ **agreement** в су́щности/по существу́ мы согла́сны

3 (*considerable*) суще́ственный, значи́тельный; **a** ~ **contribution/**~ **part,** ~ **progress** суще́ственный вклад, значи́тельная часть, значи́тельные успе́хи (*pl*).

substantially *adv*: **a** ~ **built house** основа́тельно постро́енный дом; **it's not** ~ **different from the first article** э́то о́чень немно́гим отлича́ется от пе́рвой статьи́.

substantiate *vt*: **to** ~ **a statement/charge** обосно́в|ывать утвержде́ние/обвине́ние (-а́ть).

substantive *n Gram* и́мя существи́тельное.

substitute *n* заме́на, (*only of things*) замени́тель (*m*), суррога́т; **the actor had to find a** ~ актёр до́лжен был найти́ себе́ заме́ну; **saccharine is a** ~ **for sugar** сахари́н—замени́тель/суррога́т са́хара; **there's no** ~ **for wool** у ше́рсти нет замени́телей (*pl*); *Comm* **Beware of substitutes!** «Остерега́йтесь суррога́тов!»; *Sport*: **he's playing as** ~ **for X** он сейча́с заменя́ет X; **our team are playing one** ~ в на́шей кома́нде игра́ет оди́н запасно́й.

substitute *vti vt* замен|я́ть, *pejor* подмен|я́ть (*pfs* -и́ть); **to** ~ **tea for coffee** заменя́ть ко́фе ча́ем; **he** ~**d fake documents** он подмени́л докуме́нты; *Math* **to** ~ **x for...** подстав|ля́ть x вме́сто + *G* (-́ить)

vi: **to** ~ **for smb** заменя́ть кого́-л.

substitution *n* заме́на; замеще́ние, *Math* подстано́вка.

substratum *n Geol* (*of soil*) подпо́чва; (*of rock*) ни́жний слой.

subtenant *n Law* субарендатор, поднанима́тель (*m*).

subterfuge *n* уло́вка, увёртка; **to resort to** ~ прибега́ть к уло́вке.

subterranean *adj* подзе́мный.

subtitle *n* подзаголо́вок; *Cine* субти́тр.

subtle *adj* то́нкий, утончённый; **a** ~ **mind/perfume/hint** то́нкий ум/арома́т/намёк; ~ **charm** неулови́мое очарова́ние.

subtract *vt Math* вы|чита́ть (-́честь).

subtraction *n Math* вычита́ние.

subtropical *adj* субтропи́ческий.

suburb *n* окра́ина; (*usu further out and residential*) при́город.

suburban *adj* при́городный; *fig* **he's a** ~ **type** *approx* он тако́й мещани́н.

subvention *n* субси́дия, дота́ция.

subversive *adj* подрывно́й.

subway *n* (*UK*: *underpass*) подзе́мный перехо́д; (*US*: *metro*) метро́ (*indecl*).

sub-zero *adj*: ~ **temperatures** ми́нусовые температу́ры.

succeed *vti vt*: **he** ~**ed his father on the throne** он смени́л отца́ на тро́не; **he was** ~**ed as chairman by Smith** по́сле него́ председа́телем стал Смит; **year** ~**ed year, but there was no change** го́ды шли, а переме́н никаки́х не́ было

vi **1** (*follow*): **to** ~ **to** насле́довать + *A* (у-)

2 (*prosper*) преуспе|ва́ть (-́ть); **he** ~**ed as a playwright/in business/in his career** он преуспе́л как драмату́рг/в дела́х. он сде́лал хоро́шую карье́ру

3 (*come off*) уда|ва́ться (-́ться); **the attempt** ~**ed** попы́тка удала́сь; **he** ~**ed in finishing his thesis/***iron* **in cutting his finger** ему́ удало́сь (*impers*) зако́нчить диссерта́цию, он умудри́лся поре́зать себе́ па́лец.

succeeding *adj* после́дующий.

success *n* успе́х, уда́ча; ~ **will increase his confidence** успе́х/уда́ча приба́вит ему́ уве́ренности в себе́; **I wish you (every)** ~ жела́ю (вам) успе́ха/вся́ческих успе́хов (*pl*); **the project met with no** ~ прое́кт не име́л успе́ха; **I tried to phone you without** ~ я безуспе́шно пыта́лся дозвони́ться до тебя́; **the experiment was a** ~ о́пыт прошёл уда́чно, о́пыт уда́лся; **he was a great** ~ **in business/as Macbeth** он преуспе́л в дела́х, он име́л большо́й успе́х в ро́ли Ма́кбета; **she made a** ~ **of the shop** её магази́н процвета́л.

successful *adj* уда́чный, успе́шный; **a** ~ **attempt/businessman** уда́чная попы́тка, преуспева́ющий бизнесме́н; **he was** ~ **in life** он доби́лся успе́ха в жи́зни; **the business was** ~ дела́ (*pl*) шли успе́шно.

succession *n* **1**: **he took over the business in** ~ **to his father** он унасле́довал де́ло своего́ отца́; **after his** ~ по́сле его́ вступле́ния на престо́л; **he is third in** ~ **to the throne** он тре́тий по счёту претенде́нт на престо́л

2 (*series*) ряд; **a** ~ **of accidents** ряд ава́рий; **there were two accidents in (close)** ~ бы́ло две ава́рии подря́д/одна́ за друго́й.

successive *adj*: **with each** ~ **day** с ка́ждым (после́дующим) днём; **he made three** ~ **attempts** он сде́лал три попы́тки подря́д; **at each** ~ **attempt** при ка́ждой сле́дующей попы́тке.

successor *n* (*to throne*) насле́дник, пре́емник; (*in a job*) пре́емник.

succinct *adj* (*of style, etc.*) кра́ткий, сжа́тый.

succulent *adj* со́чный; ~ **meat/grass** со́чное мя́со, со́чная трава́.

succumb *vi*: **he** ~**ed to temptation** он подда́лся искуше́нию; (*die*) **he** ~**ed to typhus** он у́мер от ти́фа.

such *adj and adv* **1** такóй, подóбный; **~ people should be punished** такúх людéй нáдо накáзывать; **there was just ~ a case last year** в прóшлом годý был тóчно такóй (же) слýчай; **I said no ~ thing** я ничегó такóго/подóбного не говорúл; **I've never heard ~ nonsense** в жúзни не слы́шал подóбной чепухú; **~ is life** таковá жизнь; **he replied in ~ a way, that I had to laugh** он так отвéтил, что я не мог не засмея́ться; **we've ~ a lot to talk about** нам о стóльком нáдо поговорúть; **it's ~ a pity** как жаль

2 *with* **as:** (*e.g.*) **~ as** как напримéр; **~ a writer as Tolstoy** такóй писáтель, как Толстóй; **his health is not ~ as to cause concern** егó здорóвье не в такóм состоя́нии, чтóбы вызывáть беспокóйство; **he's not ~ a fool as he seems** не такóй он дурáк, как кáжется; **use my suitcase ~ as it is** возьмú мой чемодáн, он хоть и стáрый, но ещё годúтся.

such *pron*: **all ~ should report at once** всем таковы́м надлежúт немéдленно явúться; **he was a genius, but not recognized as ~ in his lifetime** он был гéнием, но при жúзни егó таковы́м не считáли; **have you any plates?—I'll lend you ~ as I have** у тебя́ есть тарéлки?—*Я* тебé дам какúе уж у меня́ есть.

such-and-such *adj* такóй-то; **on ~ a day last month** такóго-то числá прóшлого мéсяца.

suchlike *pron*: **flies, mosquitoes and ~** мýхи, комары́ и томý подóбное.

suck *vt* сосáть (по-); **the calf was ~ing its mother** телёнок сосáл своЮ мать; **the child was ~ing his thumb/a dummy teat** ребёнок сосáл пáлец/сóску; **he was ~ing (at) his pipe** он посáсывал трýбку; **he ~ed the orange dry** он вы́сосал из апельсúна весь сок

suck down *vt* (*of quicksands*) за|сáсывать (-сосáть)

suck up *vti* (*absorb*) всáсывать (всосáть); *CQ* **to ~ up to smb** под|лúзываться к комý-л (-лизáться).

sucker *n Biol*, *Zool* присóска; *CQ* **he's a ~ for flattery** он пáдок на лесть.

suckle *vt* (*a child*) кормúть грýдью (по-), да|вáть грудь (-ть); (*animal*) давáть сосáть.

suction *n* присáсывание; *Tech* всáсывание: *attr*: **~ pump/valve** всáсывающий насóс, впускнóй клáпан.

sudden *adj* внезáпный; **a ~ decision** внезáпное решéние; **a ~ change** внезáпная перемéна; **~ death** внезáпная/скоропостúжная смерть; **this is so ~** э́то так неожúданно; **all of a ~** вдруг.

suddenly *adv* внезáпно, вдруг.

suds *npl* мы́льная пéна (*no pl*).

sue *vti vt*: **to ~ smb for damages/libel** предъяв|ля́ть комý-л иск о возмещéнии убы́тков (-úть), возбу|ждáть прóтив когó-л дéло о клеветé (-дúть)

vi: **to ~ for mercy** молúть о пощáде (*impf*); *Law* **my client will ~** мой клиéнт подáст в суд; **she is suing for divorce** онá возбуждáет дéло о развóде.

suede *n* зáмша; *attr* зáмшевый.

suet *n* околопóчечный жир.

suffer *vti vt* **1** (*undergo*) испы́т|ывать (-áть); (*endure*) терпéть (вы́-), пережи|вáть (-́ть), пере|носúть (-нестú); **he ~ed great pain** он испы́тывал ужáсную боль; **they ~ed a severe setback/defeat/losses** онú пережúли серьёзный спад, онú потерпéли тяжёлое поражéние, онú понеслú большúе убы́тки; **she ~ed a great shock** онá перенеслá тяжёлый удáр

2 (*tolerate*) терпéть (с-); **he doesn't ~ fools gladly** он не тéрпит дуракóв

vi страдáть (по-); **to ~ from insomnia** страдáть бессóнницей; **the children ~ed from having no friends** дéти страдáли от отсýтствия друзéй; **your reputation will ~** вáша репутáция пострадáет; **she ~ed badly from headaches** её мýчили головны́е бóли; **he ~s from a limp** он хромáет; **the car ~ed from lack of maintenance** за машúной нé было дóлжного ухóда; *CQ* **you'll ~ for this later!** ты бýдешь потóм за э́то расплáчиваться!

sufferance *n*: **he's here on ~** егó здесь тéрпят из мúлости.

sufferer *n* страдáлец, мýченик; **he's another ~ from arthritis** он ещё однá жéртва артрúта; **fellow ~s** товáрищи по несчáстью.

suffering *n* страдáние.

suffice *vti vt* хват|áть (-úть); **ten pounds should ~ him** емý должнó хватúть десятú фýнтов

vi: **his word will ~** егó слóва бýдет достáточно; **that will ~** достáточно, хвáтит; **~ it to say, that...** достáточно сказáть, что...

sufficient *adj* достáточный; **we have ~ food for a week** у нас достáточно еды́ на недéлю; **I wasn't given ~ warning** меня́ зарáнее не предупредúли.

suffocate *vti vt* душúть (за-), удуш|áть (-úть); *fig* **I felt ~ed in that atmosphere** я задыхáлся в э́той атмосфéре

vi за|дыхáться (-дохнýться), *also fig*.

suffocating *adj CQ*: **it's ~ here** здесь мóжно задохнýться; *fig* **a ~ atmosphere** удýшливая атмосфéра.

suffocation *n* удýшье; (*murder*) удушéние.

suffrage *n* прáво гóлоса; избирáтельное прáво; **women's ~** избирáтельное прáво для жéнщин.

sugar *n* сáхар; **granulated/lump** *or* **cube ~** сáхарный песóк, (сáхар-) рафинáд; **a lump of ~** кусóк сáхара; *attr*: **~ basin/bowl** сáхарница; **~ beet** сáхарная свёкла; **~ refinery** рафинáдный завóд.

sugar *vt*: **to ~ tea**/*fig* **the pill** положúть сáхар в чай, *fig* подсластúть пилЮлю; **~ed almonds** засáхаренный миндáль (*collect*).

suggest *vt* **1** (*propose*) предл|агáть + *inf* (-ожúть); **I ~ (that) we leave/leaving at once** я предлагáю тут же уéхать; **it is ~ed that...** предполагáется, что...

2 (*indicate*, *imply*): **what does that sound ~ to you?** что тебé напоминáет э́тот звук?; **it hardly ~s a peaceful family scene** э́то вряд ли похóже на мúрную семéйную сцéну; **what**

are you ~ing by that (remark)? что ты хо́чешь э́тим сказа́ть?

suggestion *n* (*proposal*) предложе́ние; (*trace*) намёк; **to make a ~** сде́лать предложе́ние; **I have a ~ (to make)** у меня́ есть предложе́ние; **I have no ~ to offer** мне не́чего предложи́ть; **at her ~** по её предложе́нию; **there was no ~ of corruption** не́ было и намёка на то, что име́ли ме́сто слу́чаи взя́точничества; *Psych* **the power of ~** си́ла внуше́ния.

suggestive *adj*: **it is a ~ article** э́та статья́ заставля́ет заду́маться; *pejor* **a ~ joke** шу́тка с намёком.

suicidal *adj*: **that would be ~** э́то бы́ло бы самоуби́йством; *CQ* **his driving is ~** так то́лько самоуби́йцы во́дят маши́ну; **I feel ~ today** сего́дня я чу́вствую себя́ о́чень скве́рно.

suicide *n* самоуби́йство; **to commit ~** соверши́ть самоуби́йство, поко́нчить с собо́й; **attempted ~** попы́тка самоуби́йства/поко́нчить с собо́й; *fig* **political ~** полити́ческое самоуби́йство; *attr*: **the ~ rate** число́ самоуби́йств.

suit *n* **1** (*of clothes*) костю́м; **a summer/trouser ~** ле́тний/брю́чный костю́м

2 *Law* иск, суде́бное де́ло; **to bring a ~ against smb** возбужда́ть иск про́тив кого́-л; **criminal ~** уголо́вное де́ло

3 *Cards* масть; **to follow ~** ходи́ть в масть, *fig* сле́довать приме́ру.

suit *vti vt* **1** (*adapt*) приспос|а́бливать (-о́бить); **he ~ed his style to his audience** он приспосо́бил свой стиль ко вку́сам пу́блики; **he ~ed the action to the word** он подкрепи́л сло́во де́лом

2 (*be appropriate to*) под|ходи́ть + *D* (-ойти́); **this job/part/weather doesn't ~ him** э́та рабо́та/роль/пого́да ему́ не подхо́дит; **they are well ~ed** они́ подхо́дят друг дру́гу; **he is not ~ed to teaching** он как педаго́г никуда́ не годи́тся; **the dress ~s her perfectly** пла́тье о́чень ей идёт

3 (*be convenient*) подходи́ть; устр|а́ивать (-о́ить); **it doesn't ~ me to come this evening** мне неудо́бно прийти́ сего́дня ве́чером; **~ yourself** как тебе́ удо́бно

vi (*be appropriate, convenient*) подходи́ть, устра́ивать; **will tomorrow/the proposal ~?** тебя́ устра́ивает за́втра/э́то предложе́ние?

suitability *n* го́дность, приго́дность.

suitable *adj* подходя́щий, приго́дный; **she's the most ~ person for the job** она́ са́мый подходя́щий челове́к/бо́льше всех подхо́дит на э́то ме́сто; **what dress would be ~ for this occasion/weather?** кака́я оде́жда подойдёт для э́того слу́чая/нужна́ для тако́й пого́ды?; **the hall is ~ for concerts** э́тот зал для конце́ртов вполне́ подхо́дит; **the film is not ~ for children** э́тот фильм не для дете́й.

suitably *adv*: **he's not at all ~ dressed** он оде́т неподходя́ще к слу́чаю.

suitcase *n* чемода́н.

suite *n* (*retinue*) сви́та; (*rooms*) но́мер-люкс; (*furniture*) ме́бельный гарниту́р; *Mus* сюи́та; **a complete bedroom/dining room ~** по́лный спа́льный/столо́вый гарниту́р.

suitor *n* покло́нник, *CQ* ухажёр.

sulk *vi* ду́ться (на-).

sulkily *adv*: **she answered ~** она́ отве́тила недово́льным то́ном.

sulky *adj* наду́тый; **he looked ~** у него́ был наду́тый вид.

sullen *adj* угрю́мый; мра́чный; **a ~ look/sky** угрю́мый *or* мра́чный взгляд, па́смурное не́бо.

sulphate *n* сульфа́т.

sulphur *n* се́ра; *attr*: **~ dioxide** серни́стый ангидри́д; **a ~ spring** се́рный исто́чник.

sulphuric *adj*: **~ acid** се́рная кислота́.

sultana *n* (*dried fruit*) кишми́ш (*collect*).

sultry *adj* (*of weather*) зно́йный.

sum *n* **1** (*amount*) су́мма

2 *Math, School*: **the ~ of 3 and 2 is 5** три плюс два равня́ется пяти́; **I can do that ~ in my head** я могу́ э́то сложи́ть в уме́

3 (*summary, substance*): **the ~ of our experience** весь наш о́пыт; **the ~ of what he said** суть того́, что он сказа́л; *attr*: **the ~ total of the bill** о́бщая су́мма счёта; **the ~ total of all these arguments is...** все аргуме́нты сво́дятся к тому́, что...

sum up *vti vt* (*summarize*) под|води́ть ито́г (-вести́); подыто́|живать (-жить); сумми́ровать (*impf*); **I will ~ up what has been said** я подыто́жу всё ска́занное; **her remark exactly ~s up what I think** её замеча́ние выража́ет са́мую суть мои́х мы́слей; *Law* **the judge ~med up the proceedings** судья́ подыто́жил результа́ты (суде́бного) сле́дствия

vi: **let me ~ up by saying that...** позво́льте мне подвести́ ито́г..., я счита́ю, что...

summarize *vt* под|води́ть ито́г (-вести́); подыто́|живать (-жить); сумми́ровать, резюми́ровать (*impfs and pfs*).

summary *n* кра́ткое изложе́ние; **news ~** сво́дка новосте́й; **a ~ of proceedings** резюме́ (*indecl*).

summary *adj* (*abbreviated*) сумма́рный; кра́ткий; **a ~ version** кра́ткое изложе́ние; (*abrupt*) **he received a ~ order to leave** он получи́л прика́з неме́дленно вы́ехать.

summer *n* ле́то; **in ~** ле́том; **high ~** разга́р ле́та; **Indian ~** ба́бье ле́то; **last ~ I was in France** про́шлым ле́том я был во Фра́нции; *attr* ле́тний; **~ camp/resort** ле́тний ла́герь/куро́рт; **~ time** вре́мя, при́нятое в ле́тние ме́сяцы, ле́тнее вре́мя.

summerhouse *n* бесе́дка.

summery *adj* ле́тний.

summit *n* (*peak*) верши́на, *also fig*; **the ~ of my ambition** преде́л мои́х честолюби́вых мечта́ний; *attr*: **a ~ conference** совеща́ние в верха́х; **~ talks** перегово́ры на вы́сшем у́ровне.

summon *vt* звать (по-́); *off, Mil* вы|зыва́ть (-́звать); **they ~ed him into the room** его́ позва́ли в ко́мнату; **to ~ a servant/the police** звать слугу́, вызыва́ть поли́цию; **I was ~ed to the director** меня́ вы́звали к дире́ктору;

Polit (*UK*) **to ~ parliament** созывáть парлáмент; *Law* **to ~ a witness/a jury** вызывáть свидéтеля, созывáть присяжных заседáтелей

summon up *vt*: **I ~ed up my courage to go to the dentist** я собрáлся с дýхом и пошёл к зубнóму врачý; **I tried to ~ up a bit more enthusiasm** я постарáлся проявить побóльше энтузиáзма.

summons *n Law*: **he got a ~ for careless driving** он получил повéстку явиться в суд за неосторóжную ездý; **to serve a ~ on smb** вызывáть когó-л повéсткой в суд.

sump *n Aut* поддóн кáртера; маслосбóрник.

sumptuous *adj* роскóшный; пышный; **what a ~ meal!** какóй роскóшный обéд!

sun *n* сóлнце; **the ~ is in my eyes** сóлнце свéтит в глазá; **the ~ is behind us/the hill** сóлнце у нас за спинóй/за холмóм; **the table is right in/out of the ~** стол стóит на сáмом сóлнце/в тени; *fig*: **everything under the ~** всё в э́том мире; **a place in the ~** мéсто под сóлнцем; *attr*: **~ hat/helmet** шляпа/шлем от сóлнца; **~ lamp** квáрцевая лáмпа; *Aut* **~ roof** откиднáя крыша, откиднóй верх.

sun *vt*: **to ~ oneself** грéться на сóлнышке (*usu impf*).

sunbaked *adj*: **~ earth** выжженная сóлнцем земля́.

sunbathe *vi* загорáть (*only in impf*).

sunburn *n* (*tan*) загáр; (*from overexposure*) сóлнечный ожóг.

sunburnt *adj*: **his ~ face** егó (*tanned*) загорéлое/(*burnt*) опалённое *or* обожжённое сóлнцем лицó; **he got ~** он загорéл.

sundae *n* пломбир; **peach ~** пéрсиковый пломбир.

Sunday *n* воскресéнье; *fig* **never in a month of ~s will you make him...** в жизни не застáвишь егó + *inf*; *attr* воскрéсный; **~ concerts/editions** воскрéсные концéрты/выпуски газéт; **on ~ mornings** по воскресéньям ýтром; **he was in his ~ best/clothes** он был в своём выходнóм костюме.

sundial *n* сóлнечные часы́.

sundries *npl* вся́кая вся́чина, рáзное (*sings*).

sundry *adj* рáзный; **they have invited all and ~** они пригласили всех до одногó/без исключéния.

sunflower *n* подсóлнечник; *attr*: **~ oil/seeds** подсóлнечное мáсло, сéмечки (подсóлнуха).

sunglasses *n* тёмные очки́.

sunlight *n* сóлнечный свет.

sunlit *adj*: **a ~ landscape** зáлитый сóлнцем пейзáж.

sunny *adj* сóлнечный; **a ~ day** сóлнечный день; *Meteorol* **there will be ~ intervals** бýдут периóды прояснéния; *fig*: **let's look on the ~ side of things** бýдем смотрéть на вéщи оптимисти́чно; **a ~ smile/disposition** сияющая улыбка, жизнерáдостный харáктер.

sunray *n* сóлнечный луч; *attr*: **~ treatment** лечéние сóлнечными лучáми, гелиотерапи́я.

sunrise *n* восхóд (сóлнца); **I get up at ~** я встаю с восхóдом сóлнца/на зарé.

sunset *n* захóд сóлнца, закáт.

sunshade *n* (*awning of shop, etc.*) навéс, тент; (*parasol*) зóнтик от сóлнца.

sunshine *n* сóлнечный свет; **to sit out in the ~** сидéть/грéться на сóлнце; **yesterday there were three hours of ~** вчерá сóлнце светило три часá; *fig* (*sometimes iron*) **you're a real ray of ~!** ты моё сóлнышко!

sunstroke *n*: **I got ~** у меня́ был сóлнечный удáр.

suntan *n* загáр; **she has a lovely ~** у неё красивый загáр; *attr*: **~ lotion/oil** лосьóн/мáсло для загáра.

suntrap *n*: **cats always search out ~s** кóшки лю́бят погрéться на солнцепёке (*sing*); **the verandah is a positive ~** на верáнде мнóго сóлнца/*pejor* изжáриться мóжно.

sup *vi* ýжинать (по-); **I ~ped on cheese and fruit** я поýжинал сыром и фрýктами.

super *adj sl* потрясáющий, колоссáльный.

superabundant *adj attr* изоби́льный; *predic* в изоби́лии, в избытке.

superannuate *vt* (*dismiss*) увол|ьня́ть по стáрости (-ить); (*out of date*): **a ~d model** устарéвшая модéль.

superannuation *n* (*dismissal*) увольнéние/(*pension*) пéнсия по стáрости; *attr*: **~ contribution** пенсиóнный взнос; **~ fund** пенсиóнный фонд.

superb *adj* великолéпный; превосхóдный.

supercilious *adj* высокомéрный; надмéнный.

superficial *adj* неглубóкий; повéрхностный, *also fig*; **a ~ wound** неглубóкая рáна; *fig*: **a ~ knowledge/resemblance** повéрхностные знáния (*pl*), кáжущееся схóдство.

superfluity *n* изоби́лие, оби́лие; **there was a ~ of food and drink at the party** на вéчере бы́ло оби́лие вся́ких угощéний.

superfluous *adj* (*of quantity*) изоби́льный, оби́льный; (*unneeded, unnecessary*) ли́шний, изли́шний, ненýжный; **he felt ~ in their company** он чýвствовал себя́ ли́шним в их компáнии; **a ~ remark** изли́шнее/ненýжное замечáние.

superhuman *adj* сверхчеловéческий.

superimpose *vt*: **to ~ smth on to smth** на|клáдывать что-л на что-л (-ложи́ть).

superintend *vt* (*manage*) управля́ть + *I*, (*direct*) руководи́ть + *I*, (*watch*) надзирáть за + *I* (*impfs*); **to ~ production/the work** руководи́ть произвóдством/рабóтой.

superintendent *n* управля́ющий; руководи́тель (*m*); (*at swimming pool, etc.*) наблюдáющий; (*of police*) стáрший офицéр.

superior *n* стáрший, начáльник; **I've passed your application on to my ~/~s** я передáл вáше заявлéние моемý начáльнику/начáльству; *Rel* **the Father/Mother S.** игýмен, игýменья.

superior *adj* (*in quality*) превосхóдный, высóкого кáчества; (*in numbers*) превосходя́щий; (*in rank*) стáрший, высший; **this is a ~ cloth/brand of tobacco** э́то превосхóдное сукнó, э́то табáк высшего кáчества; **this cigar is ~ to the other ones** э́та сигáра превосхóдит все остальные по кáчеству; **he is ~ to me**

in rank он ста́рше/вы́ше меня́ по чи́ну, он меня́ ра́нгом вы́ше; **she is a ~ woman** она́ незауря́дная же́нщина; *pejor* **his manner is so ~** он так высокоме́рен/зано́счив; **a ~ smile** надме́нная улы́бка.

superiority *n* старшинство́; превосхо́дство; *Mil* **air ~** превосхо́дство в во́здухе.

superlative *adj* (*of condition, quality*) превосхо́дный; высоча́йший, велича́йший; **a ~ performance** великоле́пное исполне́ние; *Gram* **the ~ degree** превосхо́дная сте́пень.

supermarket *n* универса́м.

supernatural *adj* сверхъесте́ственный.

supersede *vt* (*replace*) заме́н|я́ть (-и́ть); вы|тесня́ть (-́теснить); **the car has ~d the horse** автомоби́ль замени́л/вы́теснил ло́шадь; **this model has been ~d** э́та моде́ль заменена́.

supersonic *adj* ультразвуково́й; (*of plane*) сверхзвуково́й.

superstition *n* суеве́рие.

superstitious *adj* суеве́рный; **~ beliefs** суеве́рия.

superstructure *n* надстро́йка.

supervene *vi*: **new conditions ~d** возни́кли но́вые обстоя́тельства.

supervise *vt* (*department, research*) руководи́ть + *I* (*impf*); (*work*) контроли́ровать (про-); (*exam, etc.*) смотре́ть/наблюда́ть за + *I* (*impfs*); **I must ~ the packing** я до́лжен наблюда́ть за упако́вкой.

supervision *n* надзо́р, контро́ль (*m*); **under strict ~** под стро́гим надзо́ром; **the project will need ~** за осуществле́нием прое́кта бу́дет ну́жен контро́ль.

supervisor *n* (*in factories, etc.*) инспе́ктор, контролёр; *Univ approx* нау́чный руководи́тель; (*at exam*) ассисте́нт экзамена́тора.

supine *adj*: **a ~ position** лежа́чее положе́ние; **he lay ~** он лежа́л на спине́.

supper *n* у́жин; **to have ~** у́жинать; **we'll discuss it at/over ~** мы обсу́дим э́то за у́жином; *Rel* **the Last S.** та́йная ве́черя.

supplant *vt* вы|тесня́ть (-́теснить); **she was ~ed in his affections by her sister** её сестра́ вы́теснила её из его́ се́рдца.

supple *adj* ги́бкий, *also fig*.

supplement *n* (*addition*) дополне́ние к + *D*; **cost of living ~** надба́вка на рост сто́имости жи́зни; (*to newspaper*) **colour ~** цветно́е приложе́ние.

supplement *vt* допол|ня́ть (-́нить), добав|ля́ть (-́ить); **to ~ one's knowledge** пополня́ть свои́ зна́ния (*pl*); **I do translations to ~ my income** я де́лаю перево́ды ра́ди при́работка.

supplementary *adj* дополни́тельный; **~ benefits** дополни́тельные посо́бия.

supplier *n* поставщи́к.

supply *n* **1** (*action*) снабже́ние, поста́вка; **the ~ of fuel to the villages** снабже́ние дереве́нь то́пливом, поста́вка то́плива деревня́м; *Econ* **~ and demand** спрос и предложе́ние

2 (*stocks, reserves*) запа́с; **supplies of food** све́жие запа́сы продово́льствия, (*for expedition*) съестны́е припа́сы; **oil is in short ~** не́фти не хвата́ет; **supplies of ammunition** боеприпа́сы; *attr*: **a ~ ship/train** су́дно/тра́нспорт *or* по́езд снабже́ния; (*UK*) **a ~ teacher** вре́менно замеща́ющий педаго́г.

supply *vt* (*provide, equip*) снаб|жа́ть (-ди́ть); обеспе́чи|вать (-ть); постав|ля́ть (-́ить); (*furnish*) предостав|ля́ть (-́ить); **batteries are supplied with the torch** фона́рик снабжён батаре́йками; **they keep us supplied with milk** они́ снабжа́ют/обеспе́чивают нас молоко́м; **the office will ~ all necessary information** конто́ра предоста́вит всю необходи́мую информа́цию.

support *n* **1** (*physical*) опо́ра, подде́ржка, *both also fig*; **~s of a bridge** опо́ры моста́; **he leaned on me for ~** он привали́лся ко мне, что́бы не упа́сть; *fig*: **he is the family's chief ~** он гла́вная опо́ра семьи́; **he spoke in ~ of the motion** он вы́ступил в подде́ржку э́того предложе́ния; **the miners went on strike in ~ of the dockers** шахтёры забастова́ли в подде́ржку тре́бований до́керов

2 (*financial*): **he receives ~ from his parents** роди́тели ока́зывают ему́ материа́льную подде́ржку; **he has no obvious means of ~** у него́ нет постоя́нного за́работка/дохо́да; *attr Mil*: **~ troops** си́лы подде́ржки.

support *vt* **1** (*physical*) подде́рж|ивать (-а́ть), *also fig*; **the roof was ~ed by eight pillars** кры́шу подде́рживали во́семь коло́нн; *fig*: **to ~ a candidate/application/motion** подде́ржа́ть кандида́та/заявле́ние/предложе́ние; **the facts ~ your theory** фа́кты подтвержда́ют твою́ тео́рию; **which side/team do you ~?** ты чью сто́рону де́ржишь?, ты за каку́ю кома́нду боле́ешь?

2 (*financial*): **he has a family to ~** он до́лжен содержа́ть семью́; **the Academy is ~ed by a government grant** госуда́рство ока́зывает Акаде́мии фина́нсовую подде́ржку.

supporter *n* сторо́нник; *Sport* боле́льщик.

supporting *adj Tech* опо́рный, несу́щий; **a ~ wall** опо́рная/несу́щая стена́; *Theat* **~ role** второстепе́нная роль.

suppose *vti vt* **1** (*imagine, believe, assume*) полага́ть (*impf*), предпол|ага́ть (-ожи́ть); **I ~ he's right** (я) полага́ю, что он прав; **I never ~d him to be married** вот никогда́ не предполага́л/не ду́мал, что он жена́т; **I don't ~ he'll come** я полага́ю, что он не придёт; **she's ~d to be pretty** она́ счита́ется хоро́шенькой; **what do you ~ he's trying to say?** что, по-тво́ему, он хо́чет сказа́ть?; **~ that...** предполо́жим, что...; **even supposing that...** да́же е́сли предположи́ть, что...; **and supposing he refuses to speak to me?** а е́сли/а вдруг он отка́жется говори́ть со мной?; **but supposing it rains?** ну а е́сли пойдёт дождь?

2 (*ought to*): **he's ~d to leave today** он до́лжен уе́хать сего́дня; **this key is ~d to fit the lock** э́тот ключ до́лжен подходи́ть к замку́; **did you know you're not ~d to smoke during the lecture?** ты ра́зве не зна́ешь, что нельзя́ кури́ть во вре́мя ле́кции?

vi: **will he stay to supper?—I ~ so** он остáнется ýжинать?—Я дýмаю, да; **you'll be there, I ~?** я надéюсь, ты там бýдешь?

supposed *adj* предполагáемый.

supposedly *adv*: **he had ~ left a week ago** предполагáлось, что он уéхал недéлю назáд.

supposition *n* предположéние; **on the ~ that he'll come, let's...** в слýчае, éсли он приéдет, давáйте...; **will he come?—That's the ~** он придёт?—Предполагáется, что да.

suppress *vt* (*of revolt, yawn, emotion, cough*) подав|лять (-йть); (*of anger, tears, feelings*) сдéрж|ивать (-áть); **to ~ a scandal** замять скандáл; **to ~ facts/truth** замáлчивать фáкты/прáвду (*usu impf*); **to ~ a book** запретить книгу.

supremacy *n*: **naval/air ~** превосхóдство на мóре/в вóздухе.

supreme *adj off* верхóвный; *CQ* **it's a ~ example of egotism** это ярчáйший образéц эгоизма.

surcharge *n*: **to put a ~ on alcohol** взимáть дополнительную плáту/брать надбáвку за спиртные напитки; **you must pay a ~ on this letter** вам нýжно доплатить за это письмó.

sure *adj* (*reliable*) вéрный; (*certain*) увéренный; **a ~ method/remedy** вéрный спóсоб, вéрное срéдство; **it's a ~ bet/thing** это вéрная стáвка, дéло вéрное; **you can't be ~ of him** в нём нельзя быть увéренным; **to be ~ of oneself/of success** быть увéренным в себé/в успéхе; **I'm not ~ of his ability to translate** я не увéрен, что он смóжет переводить; **I'm ~ you'll like the play** я увéрен, что тебé понрáвится пьéса; **he says he'll come, but I'm not so ~** он говорит, что придёт, но я не óчень увéрен в этом; **be ~ to tell me about it** обязáтельно/непремéнно скажи мне об этом; **he's ~ to win** он навернякá/непремéнно победит; **he's leaving for ~** он навернякá уезжáет; **he has a ~ aim/hand** он цéлит навернякá, у негó твёрдая рукá; **you can be ~ of a good meal at her house** мóжешь быть увéрен, у неё хорошó поéшь/покóрмят; **I shouldn't be too ~ of that** я бы не слишком на это надéялся; **I think I locked the car, but I better make ~** по-мóему, я зáпер машину, но на всякий слýчай проверю; **I'm not ~ why he left** мне неясно, почемý он уéхал; **you should book in advance to make ~ of seats** чтóбы навернякá получить мéсто (*sing*), нýжно бронировать егó зарáнее; **I've made ~ of having enough food** я позабóтился зарáнее, чтóбы имéть достáточный запáс еды; **to be ~, he's not very intelligent** он, конéчно, не óчень умён.

sure *adv* (*US*) *CQ*: **he ~ is stupid/wealthy** ну и глуп/богáт же он!; **as ~ as eggs is eggs/fate he'll arrive on time** это уж тóчно, он придёт вóвремя; **he promised to write, and ~ enough, here's his letter** он говорил, что он напишет, и вот вам—от негó письмó; **~ enough, I forgot my money** ну конéчно же, я забыла взять дéньги.

surely *adv* **1** (*certainly*): **slowly but ~** мéдленно, но вéрно

2 (*expressing strong belief*): **we've ~ met somewhere** я увéрен, что мы гдé-то встречáлись; **~ there's some mistake** тут несомнéнно какáя-то ошибка; **~ he has come** (*hasn't he?*) конéчно же он пришёл

3 (*used negatively expressing incredulity*): **~ he didn't say such a thing!** он не мог такóго сказáть!; **he's over 70.—S. not!** емý за сéмьдесят.—Не мóжет быть!; **~ he hasn't come** (*has he?*) неужéли он пришёл?

surety *n* поручительство, порýка; **to stand ~ for smb** поручиться за когó-л.

surf *n* прибóй.

surface *n* повéрхность; **the road ~ is slippery** повéрхность дорóги скóльзкая; *fig*: **on the ~ she seems nice** на пéрвый взгляд онá кáжется óчень приятной; **under the ~ she is a sadist** по натýре онá прóсто садистка; *attr*: **~ noise** (*on record*) повéрхностный шум; *Phys* **~ tension** повéрхностное натяжéние; **~ work** (*of miners*) рабóта на повéрхности; (*on parcels, etc.*) **~ mail** простóй пóчтой.

surface *vti vt*: **to ~ a road with tarmac** покры|вáть дорóгу гудрóном (-ть)

vi всплы|вáть (-ть); **the diver/submarine ~d** водолáз всплыл, подлóдка всплылá; *fig*: **he suddenly ~d after 6 months away** он внезáпно появился пóсле шестимéсячного отсýтствия; **I'm just beginning to ~ after a month's slog** я тóлько начинáю приходить в себя пóсле мéсяца тяжёлой рабóты.

surface-to-air *adj*: **~ weapons** орýжие клáсса «земля—вóздух».

surfboard *n* доскá для сéрфинга.

surfeit *n*: **a ~ of food and drink** излишек еды и питья; *fig* **I've had a ~ of concerts lately** с меня довóльно концéртов.

surfing *n* сéрфинг.

surge *vi fig*: **the crowd ~d round the car/out of the cinema** люди толпились вокрýг машины, толпá хлынула из кинотеáтра.

surgeon *n* хирýрг.

surgery *n* хирургия; (*consulting room*) приёмная (врачá); **open chest ~** оперáция со вскрытием груднóй клéтки; (*act of consulting*) **when is his** (*the doctor's*) **~?** когдá у негó приём?; *attr*: **~ hours** приёмные часы.

surgical *adj* хирургический.

surly *adj* угрюмый.

surmise *n* предположéние.

surmount *vt* **1**: **a dome ~ed by a cross** кýпол с крестóм наверхý

2 (*overcome*): **to ~ difficulties** преодоле|вáть трýдности (-ть).

surmountable *adj fig* преодолимый.

surname *n* фамилия.

surpass *vt*: **to ~ smb in smth** пре|восходить когó-л в чём-л (-взойти); **he ~ed himself** он превзошёл самогó себя.

surplus *n* излишек, избыток.

surplus *adj* излишний, избыточный; лишний; **~ grain/copies** излишки зернá, лишние экземпля́ры; **this is ~ to our needs** э́то превыша́ет на́ши потре́бности.

surprise *n* (*of emotion*) удивле́ние; (*of a present, etc.*) сюрпри́з; (*of an event*) неожи́данность; **to my ~** к моему́ удивле́нию; **in ~** с удивле́нием; **to give smb a ~** сде́лать кому́-л сюрпри́з; **it came as a complete ~ to me** э́то бы́ло для меня́ по́лной неожи́данностью; **they took us by ~** они́ заста́ли нас врасплóх; *attr*: **a ~ attack** внеза́пная ата́ка; **a ~ gift** сюрпри́з; **a ~ visit** неожи́данный визи́т.

surprise *vt* **1** (*astonish*) удив|ля́ть (-и́ть); **I am ~d at you!** ты меня́ удивля́ешь!; **he was ~d at/by my reaction** он удиви́лся мое́й реа́кции (*D*), моя́ реа́кция удиви́ла его́; **he was ~d to hear/find that...** он удиви́лся, услы́шав, что..., он с удивле́нием узна́л, что...; **I shouldn't be ~d if...** меня́ бы не удиви́ло, е́сли бы...; **don't be ~d if...** не удивля́йтесь, е́сли...; **it is nothing to be ~d at** тут не́чему удивля́ться

2 (*catch unawares*): **we ~d the enemy/an intruder** мы захвати́ли врага́ врасплóх, мы спугну́ли во́ра; **we ~d them at breakfast** мы заста́ли их за за́втраком; **let's call in and ~ them** дава́й нагря́нем (*CQ*) к ним (*pf*).

surprising *adj* (*amazing*) удиви́тельный; (*unexpected*) неожи́данный.

surprisingly *adv* удиви́тельно; **he looked ~ happy for one who...** он вы́глядел на удивле́ние весёлым для челове́ка, кото́рый...; **I invited him but not ~ he refused** я пригласи́л его́, но он отказа́лся, что не о́чень-то меня́ удиви́ло; **~ enough I saw him only yesterday** удиви́тельно, но я его́ ви́дел то́лько вчера́.

surrender *n Mil* сда́ча, капитуля́ция; **unconditional ~** безоговоро́чная капитуля́ция; **they demanded the ~ of all firearms** они́ тре́бовали сда́чи всего́ ору́жия (*collect*).

surrender *vti vt Mil* сда|ва́ть (-ть); **they ~ed the town to the enemy/the documents** они́ сда́ли го́род проти́внику, они́ сда́ли *or* отда́ли докуме́нты; **they ~ed their rights** они́ отказа́лись от свои́х прав

vi Mil сдава́ться, капитули́ровать (*impf and pf*).

surreptitious *adj* та́йный.

surreptitiously *adv* укра́дкой, тайко́м.

surround *vt* окруж|а́ть (-и́ть), *also Mil and fig*; **the journalists ~ed him** журнали́сты окружи́ли/обступи́ли его́; **~ed by journalists** в окруже́нии журнали́стов; **the garden is ~ed by a moat/by poplars** сад окружён рвом/обса́жен тополя́ми; **the affair is ~ed in mystery** э́то де́ло окружено́ та́йной.

surroundings *npl*: **the ~ of London** окре́стности Ло́ндона; **when I am in strange ~** когда́ я в незнако́мой среде́/обстано́вке (*sings*); **animals in their natural ~** живо́тные в есте́ственной среде́.

surtax *n* доба́вочный подохо́дный нало́г.

surveillance *n* (*of suspect, patient*) наблюде́ние; **to keep smb under ~** держа́ть кого́-л под наблюде́нием.

survey *n* (*study*) обзо́р; *Geog* съёмка; (*of property*) обсле́дование, инспе́кция; **a general ~ of the situation** о́бщий обзо́р положе́ния/собы́тий (*pl*); **they are carrying out a ~ of public opinion/prices** они́ прово́дят опро́с обще́ственного мне́ния, они́ изуча́ют це́ны; **an aerial ~** аэрофотосъёмка; **they are doing a ~ of the east coast** они́ произво́дят съёмку восто́чного бе́рега; **the ~ showed several defects** инспе́кция обнару́жила не́сколько дефе́ктов; *attr*: **a ~ ship** гидрографи́ческое су́дно.

survey *vt* (*look at/on at*) осм|а́тривать (-отре́ть), обозре|ва́ть (-́ть); *Geog* произ|води́ть съёмку (-вести́); (*property*) обсле́довать (*impf and pf*); **he ~ed the landscape** он осмотре́л ме́стность; **they are ~ing the island** они́ произво́дят топографи́ческую съёмку о́строва; **the land is being ~ed with a view to building on it** уча́сток обсле́дуют с це́лью его́ застро́йки; **when the house was ~ed dry rot was discovered** при обсле́довании до́ма обнару́жили, что он поражён сухо́й гни́лью.

surveying *n* съёмочные рабо́ты (*pl*), съёмка.

surveyor *n Geog* топо́граф, геодези́ст; (*of property*) инспе́ктор зда́ний.

survival *n* выжива́ние; (*relic*) пережи́ток; **this custom is a ~ of the past** э́тот обы́чай—пережи́ток про́шлого.

survive *vti vt* пережи́ть (*usu pf*); **he ~d all his contemporaries/the illness** он пережи́л всех свои́х рове́сников, он вы́здоровел; **he is ~d by two children** он оста́вил двои́х дете́й; **only six people ~d the crash** то́лько шесть челове́к оста́лись в живы́х по́сле э́той ава́рии

vi вы|жива́ть (-́жить); **he alone ~d** то́лько он оди́н вы́жил; **this custom still ~s** э́тот обы́чай ещё существу́ет/соблюда́ется; **only a fraction of Latin literature ~s** до нас дошла́ [**NB** *tense*] лишь/то́лько небольша́я часть древнери́мской литерату́ры; *iron* **don't worry, he'll ~** не волну́йся, он суме́ет вы́карабкаться.

survivor *n*: **there were no ~s** никто́ не оста́лся в живы́х/уцеле́л.

susceptible *adj* (*to illness*) восприи́мчивый; (*to offence*) оби́дчивый; (*to women*) влю́бчивый; **he is ~ to colds/flattery/the influence of others** он скло́нен *or* восприи́мчив к просту́де (*sing*), он па́док на лесть, он поддаётся чужо́му влия́нию.

suspect *n* подозрева́емый.

suspect *adj* подозри́тельный; **his evidence is ~** его́ показа́ния (*pl*) подозри́тельны.

suspect *vt* **1** подозрева́ть (*impf*); (*doubt*) сомнева́ться в + *P* (*impf*); **he was ~ed of murder** его́ подозрева́ли в уби́йстве; **I ~ the truth of that statement** я сомнева́юсь в пра́вильности э́того утвержде́ния

2 (*think*): **I ~ (that) she knows more than she says** я подозрева́ю, что она́ зна́ет бо́льше, чем говори́т; **they are engaged?—I ~ed as much** они́ реши́ли пожени́ться?—Я так и ду́мал.

suspend *vt* **1** (*hang*) подве́|шивать (-сить); **the lamp was ~ed from the ceiling** ла́мпа была́ подве́шена под потолко́м

2 (*stop, defer*) приостан|áвливать (-ови́ть), прекра|щáть (-ти́ть); (*defer*) отмен|я́ть (-и́ть); **payment has been ~ed** платежи́ приостанóвлены; **publication has been ~ed** издáние приостанóвлено/прекращенó; **the weekly meetings have been ~ed** еженедéльные собрáния врéменно прекрати́лись; **this rule has been ~ed** э́то прáвило врéменно отмененó; **he will have his** (*driving*) **licence ~ed** егó врéменно лишáт води́тельских прав; *Law* **he received a ~ed sentence** емý вы́несли услóвный приговóр

3 (*from job, etc.*): **he has been ~ed from his job/from college** егó врéменно отстрани́ли от рабóты/не допускáют до заня́тий.

suspenders *npl* (*for stockings*) подвя́зки; (*US: braces*) подтя́жки; *attr*: **~ belt** пóяс.

suspense *n* (*uncertainty*): **in ~** в мучи́тельной неизвéстности; *CQ* **the ~ is killing me!** э́та неопределённость убивáет меня́.

suspension *n Aut, Tech* подвéс.

suspension bridge *n* вися́чий мост.

suspicion *n* **1** подозрéние; **he is under/above ~** он под подозрéнием, он вне подозрéний (*pl*); **~ fell on him** на негó пáло подозрéние; **I was right in my ~ that...** я был прав, подозревáя, что...; **I have my ~s about that/about his honesty** у меня́ есть подозрéния на э́тот счёт, я сомневáюсь в егó чéстности

2 *fig uses*: **with the faintest ~ of a smile** с едвá замéтной улы́бкой; **a ~ of aniseed** при́вкус/зáпах ани́са; **add just a ~ of cinnamon** добáвьте чýточку кори́цы.

suspicious *adj* (*feeling or causing suspicion*) подозри́тельный; **a ~ nature** подозри́тельная натýра; **I became ~ at once** у меня́ срáзу возни́кло подозрéние; **I am ~ of him** я егó подозревáю; **he looks ~** он вы́глядит подозри́тельно; **if you notice any ~ packages** éсли замéтите каки́е-нибудь подозри́тельные свёртки.

sustain *vt* **1** (*support*) поддéрж|ивать (-áть), *also fig*; *fig* подтвер|ждáть (-ди́ть); **these conditions cannot ~ life** э́ти услóвия непригóдны для жи́зни; *fig*: **he couldn't ~ the pretence** он не мог дóлго притворя́ться; *Law* **the court ~ed his claim** суд подтверди́л егó претéнзию; *Mus* **to ~ a note** тянýть нóту

2 (*suffer*): **they ~ed terrible injuries/severe losses** они́ бы́ли стрáшно изувéчены, они́ понесли́ тяжёлые потéри.

sustaining *adj* (*of food*) питáтельный, калори́йный.

sustenance *n*: **there is not much ~ in soft fruit** я́годы малокалори́йны; **he had no means of ~** у негó нé было никаки́х средств к существовáнию.

swab *n* (*mop*) швáбра; *Med* тампóн; **to take a ~** брать мазóк.

swab *vt*: **to ~ (down) a floor** мыть пол швáброй (по-); *Naut* **to ~ the decks** дрáить пáлубы (*impf*).

swaddle *vt* (*baby*) пеленáть (за-); закýт|ывать в одея́ло (-ать).

swag *n CQ* добы́ча.

swagger *vi*: (*walk*) **he ~ed round the room** он расхáживал по кóмнате с вáжным ви́дом; (*boast*) **to ~ about smth** хвáстаться/бахвáлиться чем-л (*impfs*).

swallow[1] *n Orn* лáсточка; *attr*: **~ dive** прыжóк лáсточкой.

swallow[2] *n*: **at a ~** одни́м глоткóм.

swallow[2] *vti vt* глотáть (*impf*), прогл|áтывать (-оти́ть), *also fig*; **he ~ed his beer in one gulp** он вы́пил пи́во зáлпом; **the fish/*fig* she ~ed the bait** ры́ба/онá попáлась на ýдочку; *fig*: **he ~s his words** он проглáтывает словá; **he ~ed the insult/his pride** он проглоти́л оскорблéние, он подави́л своё самолю́бие; **he was ~ed up in the crowd** он раствори́лся в толпé; *CQ* **I find that a bit hard to ~** мне трýдно э́то перевари́ть

vi: **he ~ed hard** он с трудóм сглотнýл.

swamp *n* болóто, топь.

swamp *vt* затоп|ля́ть (-и́ть); **the meadows were completely ~ed** лугá совершéнно затопи́ло (*impers*); **a huge wave ~ed the boat** огрóмная волнá окати́ла лóдку; *fig*: **the town is ~ed by tourists** гóрод наводнён тури́стами; **they were ~ed with requests** их завали́ли/засы́пали вопрóсами; **I am ~ed with work** я завáлен рабóтой.

swampy *adj* болóтистый, тóпкий.

swan *n* лéбедь (*m*); *attr fig*: **~ song** лебеди́ная пéсня.

swan *vi CQ*: **he is ~ning around in Italy somewhere** он разгýливает гдé-то по Итáлии.

swank *n CQ* чвáнство, бахвáльство; (*person*) хвастýн, бахвáл.

swank *vi CQ*: **to ~ about smth** хвáстаться/бахвáлиться чем-л (*usu impfs*).

swanky *adj CQ* (*of clothes, etc.*) шикáрный; **he wears ~ clothes** он шикáрно одевáется; (*boastful*) **he's very ~** он большóй хвастýн.

swap *n and vti see* **swop.**

swarm *n* (*of bees, insects*) рой; *fig* **tourists descended in ~s** тури́сты налетéли толпóй (*sing*).

swarm *vi* **1** (*of bees, insects*) рои́ться (*impf*); *fig*: **tourists were ~ing all over the place** вездé/всю́ду бы́ли тóлпы тури́стов; **the crowd ~ed round his car/through the gates** лю́ди толпи́лись вокрýг егó маши́ны, толпá хлы́нула в ворóта

2: to ~ with кишéть + *I* (*impf*); **the house is ~ing with cockroaches/*fig* children** дом киши́т таракáнами, в дóме полнó детéй

swarm up *vt* карáбкаться по + *D* (вс-).

swarthy *adj* смýглый.

swat *vt*: **to ~ flies** бить мух (*only in impf*).

swathed *ppp*: **~ in blankets/bandages/furs** закýтанный в одея́ла, обмóтанный бинтáми, одéтый в мехá *or* в мехáх.

sway *vti vt* **1** (*rock*) качáть (*impf*), (*violently*) раскáчивать (*usu impf*)

2 (*influence*): **the orator ~ed the crowd** орáтор склони́л толпý на свою́ стóрону; **he was ~ed by my argument** мои́ аргумéнты (*pl*) повлия́ли на егó решéние; **he is too easily ~ed by**

his colleagues он сли́шком поддаётся влия́нию свои́х колле́г

vi кача́ться, раска́чиваться.

swear *vti vt* кля́сться (по-); присяг|а́ть (-ну́ть); **to ~ allegiance to smb** покля́сться/присягну́ть в ве́рности кому́-л; **he swore vengeance/not to do it again** он покля́лся отомсти́ть/бо́льше э́того не де́лать; **to ~ an oath** прин|има́ть прися́гу (-я́ть), присяга́ть; **I could have sworn (that) he was there** я гото́в покля́сться, что он там был; **if he does it again I ~ I'll kill him** е́сли он ещё э́то сде́лает, кляну́сь/ей-бо́гу, я его́ про́сто убью́; **she swore me to secrecy** она́ заста́вила меня́ покля́сться, что я сохраню́ та́йну

vi **1** (*take oath*) кля́сться; **I'm sure I wrote to her but I couldn't ~ to it** я уве́рен, что я ей писа́л, но то́чно сказа́ть не могу́; **he swore to the truth of his statement** он кля́лся, что его́ заявле́ние соотве́тствует и́стине; *Law* **to ~ in a witness** приводи́ть свиде́теля к прися́ге; *fig* **he ~s by those pills** он о́чень ве́рит в э́ти табле́тки

2 (*curse*) руга́ться (вы́-); **don't ~ at me** не руга́й (ты) меня́.

swearword *n* руга́тельство.

sweat *n* пот; **he is dripping with ~** он облива́ется по́том, он весь в поту́; **by the ~ of his brow** в по́те лица́; *fig CQ*: **just thinking about it brings me out in a ~** от одно́й мы́сли об э́том меня́ прошиба́ет пот; **it was an awful ~** над э́тим пришло́сь попоте́ть; *attr*: **~ shirt** спорти́вный сви́тер.

sweat *vti vt*: **to ~ out a cold/fever** как сле́дует пропоте́ть; *CQ* **I ~ed my guts out (over that)** я труди́лся (над э́тим) до седьмо́го по́та

vi поте́ть (вс-, *fig pf* по-); **he ~s a lot** он си́льно поте́ет; **the cheese is ~ing** сыр со слезо́й; **he was ~ing over his homework** он поте́л над дома́шним зада́нием.

sweater *n* сви́тер.

sweat-stained *adj* пропоте́вший.

Swede *n* швед, шве́дка.

swede *n Bot* брю́ква.

Swedish *n* шве́дский язы́к.

Swedish *adj* шве́дский.

sweep *n* (*movement*) взмах; (*of lighthouse, beam*) диапазо́н, охва́т; (*curve*) изги́б; **with a ~ of his arm** взма́хом руки́; **the beam has a ~ of 180°** диапазо́н охва́та луча́ — 180 гра́дусов; **within the ~ of the searchlight** в преде́лах охва́та луча́ проже́ктора; **the ~ of the coastline** берегово́й изги́б.

sweep *vti vt* **1** (*with brush*) мести́ (*impf*) *and compounds*; (*with hands*) сма́х|ивать (-ну́ть); **to ~ the floor** мести́/под|мета́ть пол (-мести́); **to ~ out a room/a barn** подмета́ть ко́мнату/в сара́е; **to ~ a chimney** чи́стить трубу́ (по-); **to ~ up leaves/rubbish into a pile** сгре|ба́ть ли́стья/му́сор в ку́чу (-сти́); **he swept the path clear of snow** он расчи́стил доро́жку от сне́га; **he swept the crumbs off the table** он смёл/смахну́л кро́шки со стола́; *Naut* **to ~ a channel of mines** очи́стить кана́л от мин

2 (*carry away*): **a wave swept him overboard** его́ смы́ло (*impers*) волно́й за́ борт; **the boat was swept out to sea** ло́дку унесло́ (*impers*) в мо́ре; **he was swept off his feet by the wind** ве́тер сбил/сшиб его́ с ног

3 *fig uses*: **searchlights swept the sky** лучи́ проже́кторов мета́лись по не́бу; **the village was swept away by an avalanche** дере́вню снесло́ (*impers*) сне́жной лави́ной; **he swept aside all my objections** он отмёл все мои́ возраже́ния; **I was swept off my feet by his performance** я был в соверше́нном восто́рге от его́ выступле́ния; **he swept her off her feet** он ей совсе́м вскружи́л го́лову; **they swept the board in the elections** они́ одержа́ли убеди́тельную побе́ду на вы́борах; **they swept the district for the runaway** они́ прочеса́ли весь райо́н в по́исках беглеца́; **to ~ smth under the carpet** пря́тать концы́ в во́ду

vi: **to ~ up after the children** подмести́ пол по́сле дете́й; *fig*: **rain clouds swept across the sky** ту́чи несли́сь по не́бу; **the epidemic swept through the country** волна́ эпиде́мии прокати́лась по стране́; **she swept out of the room** она́ вели́чественно вы́плыла из ко́мнаты.

sweeper *n*: **road ~** (*person*) подмета́льщик у́лиц, (*machine*) подмета́льная маши́на.

sweeping *adj*: **a ~ gesture** широ́кий жест; *fig*: **~ generalizations/reforms** широ́кие обобще́ния, радика́льные рефо́рмы; **~ accusations** огу́льные обвине́ния.

sweepstake *n approx* тотализа́тор.

sweet *n* (*dessert*) сла́дкое; (*bonbon*) конфе́та; *fig* **my ~** моя́ ра́дость, мой дорого́й.

sweet *adj* **1** сла́дкий; **he likes ~ things** он лю́бит сла́дкое/сла́дости/сла́сти; **it isn't ~ enough for me** мне на́до посла́ще; *fig* **he/she has a ~ tooth** он/она́ сладкое́жка *or* сластёна *or* лю́бит сла́дкое

2 (*of air, milk*) све́жий; (*of water*) пре́сный; *CQ* (*nice*) ми́лый; **~ dreams** сла́дкие грёзы/мечты́; **the air is ~ with the scent of roses** во́здух напоён арома́том роз; **flattery is ~ to his ear** лесть ласка́ет его́ слух; **what a ~ child!** како́й преле́стный ребёнок!; **she is a ~ person** она́ о́чень ми́лый челове́к; **that's ~ of you** о́чень ми́ло с ва́шей стороны́; *CQ* **he'll come in his own ~ time** он придёт, когда́ ему́ заблагорассу́дится.

sweet corn *n* сла́дкая кукуру́за.

sweeten *vt* подсла́|щивать (-сти́ть); (*of room, air*) освеж|а́ть (-и́ть); *fig* **that will ~ the pill** э́то подсласти́т пилю́лю.

sweetheart *n* возлю́бленн|ый, -ая.

sweetie *n CQ* (*bonbon*) конфе́тка; *fig* **she's a ~** она́ ми́лочка.

sweetpea *n Bot* души́стый горо́шек.

sweet william *n Bot* туре́цкая гвозди́ка.

swell *n* (*of sound*) нараста́ющий звук; *CQ* (*person*) франт, щёголь (*m*); *Naut* **there's a big ~ today** сего́дня си́льно кача́ет.

swell *adj CQ* (*stylish*) шика́рный; (*US*) *CQ*: **he's a ~ guy** он па́рень что на́до; **that's ~!** сла́вно!

swell *vti vt*: **the rains have swollen the river** река́ взду́лась от дожде́й; **this should ~ our membership** э́то привлечёт но́вых чле́нов; **they came along to help ~ the numbers** они́ пришли́, что́бы попо́лнить на́ши ряды́/(*if of audience*) что́бы запо́лнить зал; **her eyes were swollen with crying** у неё глаза́ опу́хли от слёз

vi (*of sails, etc.*) на|дува́ться, (*of river*) вз|дува́ться (*pfs* -ду́ться); *Med* распух|а́ть (-нуть); **wood ~s in water** де́рево набуха́ет в воде́; **her leg ~ed (up)** у неё нога́ распу́хла; **the sound ~ed** звук/шум нараста́л.

swelling *n Med* о́пухоль, (*slight*) припу́хлость.

swelter *vi*: **I am ~ing** я изнемога́ю/умира́ю от жары́.

sweltering *adj* (*of weather, day, room, etc.*) ду́шный, о́чень жа́ркий.

swerve *vi* свора́чивать в сто́рону (сверну́ть): **she/the car ~d to avoid the child** она́/маши́на ре́зко сверну́ла, что́бы не сбить ребёнка; **the ball ~d** мяч отклони́лся; **the boxer ~d to avoid the blow** боксёр уклони́лся от уда́ра.

swift *n Orn* стриж.

swift *adj* бы́стрый; **he was ~ to react** он бы́стро/неме́дленно реаги́ровал; **he is ~ to anger/to take offence** он вспы́льчив/оби́дчив.

swig *n CQ*: **he took a ~ of whisky/at the bottle** он глотну́л ви́ски/из буты́лки.

swill *n* (*for pigs*) по́йло; (*slops*) помо́и (*pl*).

swill *vt, also* **to ~ out** опол|а́скивать (-осну́ть).

swim *n*: **let's go for a ~** пойдём купа́ться; **it is a long ~ to the far side** на ту сто́рону далеко́ плыть; *fig* **to be in the ~** быть в це́нтре собы́тий/в ку́рсе де́ла.

swim *vti vt*: **she swam three miles/the Channel** она́ проплыла́ три ми́ли, она́ переплыла́ Ла-Ма́нш; **he can ~ a few strokes/ten lengths** он мо́жет проплы́ть ме́тра два, не бо́льше/переплы́ть бассе́йн де́сять раз; **he can't ~ a stroke** он совсе́м не уме́ет пла́вать

vi пла́вать (*indet impf*), плыть (*det impf*) *and compounds*; **can you ~ under water?** ты уме́ешь пла́вать под водо́й?; **we swam round the island** мы спла́вали вокру́г о́строва; **she/the fish swam away** она́/ры́ба уплыла́; **he swam across the river** он переплы́л ре́ку; **he swam far out to sea** он заплы́л далеко́ в мо́ре; **we swam as far as the big rock** мы доплы́ли до большо́й скалы́; **he swam up to me** он подплы́л ко мне; *fig* **everything swam before his eyes** всё поплы́ло у него́ пе́ред глаза́ми.

swimmer *n* плов|е́ц, *f* -чи́ха.

swimming *n* пла́вание; *attr*: **~ baths/pool** бассе́йн; **~ costume/trunks** купа́льный костю́м, пла́вки.

swindle *n* надува́тельство, жу́льничество.

swindle *vt*: **to ~ smb** наду|ва́ть/обжу́ли|вать кого́-л (-́ть/-ть).

swindler *n* моше́нник, жу́лик.

swine *n fig CQ* свинья́.

swing *n* **1** (*movement, e.g. of pendulum*) кача́ние, колеба́ние; (*stroke*) разма́х, взмах, зама́х; (*in boxing*) свинг; **the needle gave a ~ to the right** стре́лка качну́лась впра́во; **with a full ~ of the racket** широ́ким взма́хом раке́тки; *fig*: **a ~ in public opinion** (ре́зкое) измене́ние обще́ственного мне́ния; (*in an election*) **a ~ to the right** укло́н впра́во; *attr*: **~ bridge/crane** разводно́й мост, поворо́тный кран; **~ door** дверь на пружи́не, открыва́ющаяся в любу́ю сто́рону

2 (*children's*) каче́ли (*pl*)

3 (*rhythm*) ритм; (*jazz music*) суи́нг; *fig*: **I'm just getting into the ~ of the work** я то́лько вхожу́ в ритм рабо́ты; **the party is going with a ~/is in full ~** весе́лье в по́лном разга́ре.

swing *vti vt* кача́ть *and compounds*; **to ~ a hammock** кача́ть/раска́ч|ивать гама́к (-а́ть); **to ~ one's arms/hips/legs** разма́хивать рука́ми, пока́чивать бёдрами, болта́ть нога́ми (*impfs*); **he swung the starting handle** он поверну́л ру́чку; **he swung the car round** он разверну́л маши́ну; **he swung his rucksack on to his shoulders** он заки́нул рюкза́к за пле́чи; *fig*: **that speech swung the elections** э́та речь реши́ла исхо́д вы́боров; *CQ* **he managed to ~ the deal** ему́ удало́сь обстря́пать э́то де́льце

vi **1** (*oscillate: of pendulum, etc.*) кача́ться (*impf*); (*of hammock, swing or of person on them*) кача́ться, раска́чиваться; **the lamp was ~ing in the wind** фона́рь кача́лся/(*violently*) раска́чивался на ветру́; **monkeys were ~ing from the branches** обезья́ны раска́чивались на ве́тках; **the needle swung sharply to the left** стре́лка ре́зко качну́лась вле́во; **a lamp was ~ing from the ceiling** ла́мпа свиса́ла с потолка́; **the door swung open/shut** дверь распахну́лась/захло́пнулась; *fig CQ* **he'll ~ for that** ему́ за э́то здо́рово влети́т

2 (*change direction*) по|вора́чивать (-верну́ть); **he swung round sharply** он ре́зко поверну́лся; **the car swung round the corner/swung round** маши́на сверну́ла за́ угол/разверну́лась; **the road ~s south at this point** тут доро́га повора́чивает на юг

3: he swung at the ball with his racket он уда́рил раке́ткой по мячу́.

swinging *adj*: **~ music** ритми́чная му́зыка; **a ~ rhythm** живо́й ритм.

swipe *vt* **1: he ~d the ball over the net** он вы́бил мяч за се́тку

2 *CQ, often joc* (*steal, take*) стяну́ть, стащи́ть (*pfs*).

swirl *vi* (*of dancers*) кружи́ться (*impf*); (*of water*) бурли́ть (*impf*); **in the ~ing snow** в сне́жных ви́хрях; **~ing skirts** развева́ющиеся ю́бки.

swish *n* (*of whip, cane*) свист; (*of skirts, etc.*) ше́лест, шурша́ние.

swish *adj CQ* шика́рный.

Swiss *n* швейца́рец, швейца́рка.

Swiss *adj* швейца́рский; *Cook* **~ roll** руле́т с варе́ньем.

switch *n* **1** *Elec* (*on/off switch*) выключа́тель (*m*); *Radio* (*to change wave band, etc.*) переключа́тель (*m*); **mains ~** гла́вный выключа́тель, руби́льник; **the light ~ is on/off** свет включён/вы́ключен

2 (*change*) измене́ние, перехо́д; **a ~ of opinion/plans** переме́на мне́ния, измене́ние пла́нов; **the ~ to the metric system** перехо́д на метри́ческую систе́му

3 (*of hair*) накла́дка; фальши́вая коса́

4 (*stick, etc.*) прут, хлыст.

switch *vti vt* **1** (*of controls*): **he ~ed the plane to the automatic pilot** он включи́л автопило́т; *Rail* **to ~ the points** пере|води́ть стре́лку (*sing*) (-вести́)

2 (*change*) меня́ть (*impf*) *and compounds*; переключа́ть, переводи́ть; **I ~ed my room/plan** я смени́л ко́мнату, я измени́л свой план; **he ~ed his allegiance to the other party** он перешёл в друго́й ла́герь; **to ~ the conversation to another topic** перевести́ разгово́р на другу́ю те́му; **we had to ~ taxis halfway** нам пришло́сь пересе́сть в друго́е такси́; **they ~ed the lecture to five o'clock** они́ перенесли́ ле́кцию на пять часо́в; **production has been ~ed to a new model** произво́дство перешло́ на но́вую моде́ль

vi пере|ходи́ть (-йти́); переключа́ться; **we've ~ed (over) to gas heating** мы перешли́ на га́зовое отопле́ние

switch off *vti Elec, etc.* вы|ключа́ть(ся) (-´ключить(ся)); **the oven ~es off automatically** духо́вка автомати́чески выключа́ется; *fig CQ* **when he's bored, he ~es off** когда́ ему́ ску́чно, он соверше́нно отключа́ется

switch on *vti Elec, etc.* включ|а́ть(ся) (-и́ть (-ся)); **is the radio ~ed on?** радиоприёмник включён (в сеть)?; **I left the radio ~ed on** я не вы́ключил/забы́л вы́ключить радиоприёмник

switch over *vti*: **he ~ed (the radio) over to medium wave** он переключи́л радиоприёмник на сре́дние во́лны (*pl*).

switchback *n* (*at fair*) америка́нские го́рки (*pl*).

switchboard *n Elec, Tel* коммута́тор; **to operate the ~** рабо́тать на коммута́торе; *attr*: **~ operator** телефони́стка.

swivel chair *n* враща́ющийся стул.

swizz *n CQ* обма́н, надува́тельство.

swollen *adj* опу́хший, распу́хший; взду́тый; **a ~ ankle/face/stomach** распу́хшая лоды́жка, опу́хшее лицо́, взду́тый живо́т; **~ eyelids** припу́хшие ве́ки; **her eyes were ~ with crying** у неё глаза́ опу́хли от слёз; **he has ~ glands** у него́ распу́хли гла́нды.

swoon *vi* па́дать в о́бморок (упа́сть); *fig CQ* **he ~s if he even sees her** он теря́ет го́лову при одно́м её ви́де.

swoop *vi*: **the hawk ~ed (down) on the mouse** я́стреб ри́нулся вниз и схвати́л мышь; **the planes ~ed low over the village** самолёты лете́ли ни́зко/шли на бре́ющем полёте над дере́вней.

swop *n CQ* обме́н; сде́лка; **that is a fair ~** э́то че́стный обме́н; **these stamps are ~s** э́ти ма́рки на обме́н; **we did a ~** мы обменя́лись.

swop *vti vt CQ* обме́н|ивать (-я́ть); **I ~ped my watch for a tennis racket** я обменя́л/сменя́л часы́ на те́ннисную раке́тку; **we ~ped places/stamps** мы поменя́лись места́ми, мы обменя́лись ма́рками

vi: **let's ~!** дава́й меня́ться!

sword *n* меч, шпа́га; **cavalry ~** са́бля, ша́шка; *attr*: **~ dance** та́нец с са́блями.

swordfish *n* меч-ры́ба.

sworn *adj*: **a ~ witness/statement** свиде́тель, приведённый к прися́ге, заявле́ние под прися́гой; **my ~ enemy** мой закля́тый враг.

swot *n CQ* зубри́ла (*m and f*).

swot *vti CQ* зубри́ть (вы́-, за-); **he's ~ting up his maths/for an exam** он зубри́т матема́тику/пе́ред экза́меном.

sycamore *n* я́вор.

sycophantic *adj* льсти́вый.

syllable *n* слог.

syllabus *n* учёбная програ́мма; **the exam ~** програ́мма экза́мена.

symbolic *adj* символи́ческий.

symmetrical *adj* симметри́чный.

sympathetic *adj* **1** (*pleasant*): **they're thoroughly ~ people** они́ о́чень располага́ют к себе́; **I find him/his philosophy ~** я чу́вствую к нему́ расположе́ние, мне близка́ его́ филосо́фия

2 (*showing pity, etc.*) сочу́вствующий; **he was ~, but he couldn't do anything** он сочу́вствовал мне, но ничего́ сде́лать не смог; **she gave me a ~ smile** она́ мне сочу́вственно улыбну́лась; **I am ~ to your point of view** я понима́ю ва́шу то́чку зре́ния.

sympathetically *adv*: **she listened ~** она́ слу́шала с уча́стием.

sympathize *vi* (*with people*) сочу́вствовать + *D* (по-); (*with grief, attitudes*) разделя́ть (*usu impf*); **I ~ with her** я сочу́вствую ей; **I ~ with you in your grief/your attitude** я разделя́ю ва́ше го́ре/ва́шу пози́цию; **I ~ with what you were saying** я понима́ю тебя́.

sympathizer *n*: **the liberals and their ~s** либера́лы и сочу́вствующие им.

sympathy *n*: **accept my deepest sympathy** приме́те мои́ глубо́кие соболе́знования (*pl*); **you have my ~** я вам сочу́вствую; **I have no ~ for him, he's just an idler** у меня́ нет к нему́ жа́лости — он про́сто безде́льник; **my sympathies are with the strikers** мои́ симпа́тии на стороне́ забасто́вщиков; **to strike in ~ with** бастова́ть в знак солида́рности с + *I*; **I'm in ~ with your proposals** я подде́рживаю/я за ва́ши предложе́ния.

symphony *n* симфо́ния.

symptom *n* симпто́м; **to show ~s of smth** обнару́живать симпто́мы чего́-л.

symptomatic *adj attr* симптомати́ческий; *predic*: **that was ~ of his nervous state** э́то бы́ло симптомати́чно для его́ не́рвного состоя́ния.

synagogue *n* синаго́га.

synchromesh *adj Aut*: ~ **gears** синхронизи́рующие переда́чи.

synchronize *vt Tech* синхронизи́ровать (*impf and pf*); (*of action*) координи́ровать (с-); ~ **your watches** све́рьте ва́ши часы́.

syncopation *n* синко́па.

syndicate *n* синдика́т, объедине́ние.

syndrome *n Med* синдро́м.

synonym *n* сино́ним.

synonymous *adj*: ~ **with** синоними́чный + *D*.

synopsis *n* сино́псис, кра́ткий обзо́р; (*of opera, film*) кра́ткое содержа́ние.

synoptic *adj* синопти́ческий, сво́дный, обзо́рный.

syntax *n* си́нтаксис.

synthesis *n* си́нтез.

synthesize *vt* синтези́ровать (*impf and pf*).

synthetic *adj* синтети́ческий.

syphilis *n* си́филис.

syphon *n* сифо́н.

Syrian *n* сири́ец, сири́йка.

Syrian *adj* сири́йский.

syringe *n* шприц.

syrup *n* сиро́п.

system *n* систе́ма; *Med* (**the** ~) органи́зм; **the solar/nervous** ~ со́лнечная/не́рвная систе́ма; **circulatory** ~ систе́ма кровообраще́ния; **railway** ~ железнодоро́жная сеть; **political** ~ госуда́рственный/полити́ческий строй; **his work lacks** ~ в его́ рабо́те нет систе́мы; *fig* **I need to get it out of my** ~ мне на́до от э́того отде́латься.

systematic *adj* системати́ческий; (*usu of people*) системати́чный; **he's a** ~ **worker** он системати́чен в рабо́те.

systematize *vt* систематизи́ровать (*impf and pf*); при|води́ть в систе́му (-вести́).

T

T: *CQ* **that suit fits you to a T** э́тот костю́м сиди́т на тебе́ как влито́й; **it suits me to a T** э́то меня́ вполне́ устра́ивает.

tab *n* (*on coat*) ве́шалка; *Mil* наши́вка, (*on collar*) петли́ца; (*US*) *CQ* (*café check*) счёт; *fig CQ* **to keep** ~**s on smb/on expenses** следи́ть за кем-л/за расхо́дами.

tabby *n*, *also* ~ **cat** полоса́тая ко́шка.

table *n* **1** (*furniture*) стол, *dim* сто́лик; **dining room/operating/folding/expanding** ~ обе́денный / операцио́нный / складно́й / раздвижно́й стол; **at** ~ за столо́м; **to sit down to** ~ сесть за стол; **to rise**/(*of children*) **get down from the** ~ встать/вы́йти из-за стола́; *fig*: **to drink smb under the** ~ спои́ть кого́-л; **now the** ~**s are turned** тепе́рь ситуа́ция ре́зко измени́лась; *attr*: ~ **lamp** насто́льная ла́мпа; ~ **tennis** насто́льный те́ннис; ~ **mat** подста́вка для таре́лок

2 (*of statistics, etc.*) табли́ца, *also Math*; **multiplication** ~**s** табли́ца (*sing*) умноже́ния; **log** ~**s** табли́цы логари́фмов; ~ **of contents** оглавле́ние.

table *vt*: **to** ~ **a motion** вы|двига́ть предложе́ние (´-двинуть).

tableau *n Theat* жива́я карти́на.

tablecloth *n* ска́терть.

table d'hôte *n attr*: **a** ~ **lunch** *approx* ко́мплексный обе́д.

tableland *n* плоского́рье.

tablespoonful *n*: **2** ~**s of flour** две столо́вые ло́жки муки́.

tablet *n* (*pill*) табле́тка; (*of stone*) плита́; (*of slate, wax, also of chocolate*) пли́тка; **a** ~ **of soap** кусо́к мы́ла.

taboo *n and predic adj* табу́ (*indecl*).

tabulate *vt* своди́ть в табли́цу (свести́).

tacit *adj* молчали́вый; ~ **consent, a** ~ **understanding** молчали́вое согла́сие.

taciturn *adj* неразгово́рчивый, молчали́вый.

tack *n* **1** (*nail*) гвоздь; (*US*) **thumb** ~ кно́пка

2 *Naut* галс; **on the port/starboard** ~ ле́вым/пра́вым га́лсом; *fig*: **to try another** ~ попро́бовать друго́й спо́соб; **to be on the right** ~ быть на пра́вильном пути́.

tack *vti vt* **1** (*nail*): **to** ~ **down a carpet** прибі|ва́ть ковёр (´-ть); **to** ~ **a notice to a board** при|ка́лывать объявле́ние к доске́ (-коло́ть)

2 *Sew* (*two things together*) смётывать (смета́ть), (*one thing to another*) при|мётывать к + *D* (-мета́ть)

vi Naut лави́ровать (*impf*).

tackle *n* **1** (*gear*) снасть (*collect*); *Naut* сна́сти (*pl*); **fishing** ~ рыболо́вная снасть; **shaving** ~ бри́твенный прибо́р

2 *Sport* блокиро́вка.

tackle *vt*: **I** ~**d the thief but he got away** я бро́сился на во́ра, но он убежа́л; **I will** ~ **him/that problem after lunch** я займу́сь им/э́той пробле́мой по́сле обе́да; **I don't know how to** ~ **the problem** я не зна́ю, как подойти́ к э́той пробле́ме; *Sport* блоки́ровать (*impf and pf*).

tacky *adj* ли́пкий, кле́йкий.

tact *n* такт, такти́чность.

tactful *adj* такти́чный.

tactical *adj* такти́ческий.

tactics *npl* та́ктика (*sing*).

tactless *adj* беста́ктный.

Tadjik *n* таджи́к, таджи́чка.

Tadjik *adj* таджи́кский.

tadpole *n* голова́стик.

tag *n* **1** (*label*) би́рка, этике́тка; (*on end of shoelace*) наконе́чник шнурка́; **name** ~ (*on clothes*) имення́я ме́тка; **price** ~ це́нник

2 (*quotation*) цита́та.

tail *n* (*of animal, aircraft, hair, comet, kite, procession, etc.*) хвост, *dim* хво́стик; (*of jacket*) фа́лда; *CQ* (~**s**) фрак: *CQ* (*detective*) сы́щик, «хвост»; **heads or** ~**s?** орёл и́ли ре́шка?; *fig* **they turned** ~ **and fled** они́ пусти́лись/бро́сились наутёк; *attr*: ~ **coat** фрак.

tail *vti vt* сле́довать за + *I* (по-); **they are** ~**ing us** за на́ми «хвост» *vi*: **to ~ away/off** (*of interest*, *attendance*, *etc*.) спа|да́ть (-сть); **he ~ed along after us/behind** он плёлся за на́ми/в хвосте́.

tail end *n* (*of conversation*, *of meat*, *roll of cloth*) коне́ц; (*of procession*) коне́ц, хвост.

tailgate *n Aut* за́дняя две́рца.

taillight *n Aut* за́дний свет.

tailor *n* портно́й.

tailored *adj*: **his suit is well ~** у него́ костю́м отли́чного покро́я; *fig* **the kitchen is ~ to her needs** в ку́хне вся ме́бель сде́лана по её зака́зу.

tainted *adj*: **the meat is ~** э́то мя́со не све́жее/с душко́м; **~ air/water** загрязнённый во́здух, загрязнённая вода́; *fig* **a ~ reputation** подмо́ченная репута́ция.

take *vti vt* **1** (*general*) брать (взять); **he took a pear/her by the hand** он взял гру́шу/её за́ руку; **he took the wheel** он сел за руль; **do you want to ~ the wheel?** хо́чешь сесть за ру́ль?; **he took the quotation from Chekhov** он взял цита́ту из Че́хова; **he took my father as his model** он брал приме́р с моего́ отца́; **which journals do you ~?** на каки́е журна́лы ты подпи́сываешься?

2 (*borrow or steal*) брать; **someboby has ~n my bicycle** кто́-то взял мой велосипе́д

3 (*capture*, *win*, *gain*) брать; **to ~ prisoners/a town/***Cards* **a trick/***Chess* **smb's queen** взять пле́нных/го́род/взя́тку/чьего́-л ферзя́; **he took all the prizes** он забра́л все призы́; **the shop ~s about 1,000 roubles a day** дневна́я вы́ручка магази́на о́коло ты́сячи рубле́й; **he ~s home £200 a month** он прино́сит домо́й две́сти фу́нтов в ме́сяц; *fig* **he was very ~n with her/the idea** она́/э́та иде́я ему́ о́чень понра́вилась

4 (*receive*, *accept*, *tolerate*) брать; при|нима́ть (-ня́ть); **he won't ~ less than £100 for the painting** он возьмёт не ме́ньше ста фу́нтов за карти́ну; **to ~ smth seriously/as a joke** приня́ть что-л всерьёз/в шу́тку; **she ~s (in) lodgers** она́ де́ржит жильцо́в; **to ~ an order for smth** приня́ть зака́з на что-л; **he took the news well/badly** он сто́йко/пло́хо перенёс э́то изве́стие; **he took it the wrong way and was offended** он не так э́то по́нял и оби́делся; **to ~ smth into consideration** взять/приня́ть что-л в расчёт; **he won't ~ no for an answer** для него́ «нет» не существу́ет; **he took the hint** он по́нял намёк; **you'll have to ~ us as we are/as you find us** принима́йте нас таки́ми, каки́е мы есть; **I took him at his word** я пойма́л его́ на сло́ве; **~ it from me** пове́рьте мне; **~ that!** (*hitting smb*) во́т тебе́!; **he couldn't ~ the strain** он не вы́держал тако́го напряже́ния; **he had to ~ a lot of teasing** ему́ пришло́сь вы́терпеть сто́лько насме́шек; **the lorry ~s weights up to 3 tons** грузови́к берёт груз до трёх тонн

5 *in combination with nouns* брать, принима́ть; *see also under particular nouns*: **to ~ a bath** приня́ть ва́нну; **to ~ British citizenship/part in smth/precautions/smb's side** приня́ть брита́нское по́дданство/уча́стие в чём-л/ме́ры предосторо́жности/чью-л сто́рону; **to ~ notes/(a note of) smb's address** де́лать за́писи, записа́ть чей-л а́дрес; **to ~ an opportunity** воспо́льзоваться слу́чаем

6 (*be in charge of*) вести́ (*det impf*); занима́ться (*usu impf*); **he ~s the older children for physics** он ведёт фи́зику в ста́рших кла́ссах; **he ~s the class three times a week** он занима́ется с кла́ссом три ра́за в неде́лю; **a young priest took the service** служи́л молодо́й свяще́нник

7 (*conduct*, *carry*) брать; (*on foot*) води́ть, (*in car*) вози́ть, (*carry*) носи́ть *and compounds*; **~ me with you** возьми́ меня́ с собо́й; **he took her to the doctor/theatre** он повёл её к врачу́, он пошёл с ней в теа́тр; **he ~s her to school every day** он отво́дит/он во́зит её в шко́лу ка́ждый день; **he was ~n to hospital by ambulance** ско́рая по́мощь увезла́ его́ в больни́цу; **he took the dog for a walk/the old woman across the road** он вы́вел соба́ку погуля́ть, он перевёл стару́шку че́рез доро́гу; **he/the tram will ~ you to the station** он/трамва́й довезёт тебя́ до вокза́ла; **she took us round the town/exhibition** она́ повози́ла нас по го́роду, она́ поводи́ла нас по вы́ставке; **it took us out of our way** мы из-за э́того сде́лали крюк; **his job ~s him abroad a lot** он по рабо́те ча́сто е́здит в загрaни́чные командиро́вки; **what took you there?** как ты там оказа́лся?; **I'll ~ the letter to the post/your case upstairs** я отнесу́ письмо́ на по́чту/твой чемода́н наве́рх; **he took her some flowers** он принёс ей цветы́

8 (*go by*): **let's ~ a taxi/the bus/the train** дава́й возьмём такси́, дава́й пое́дем авто́бусом/по́ездом; **~ the/a No 5 bus** сади́тесь на пя́тый авто́бус; **we took the wrong road/a short cut** мы пошли́ не по той доро́ге/напрями́к (*adv*)

9 (*negotiate*): **to ~ a fence** взять препя́тствие; **he took the bend too fast** он сли́шком ре́зко поверну́л

10 (*assume*): **I ~ it you have permission** у вас, разуме́ется, есть разреше́ние; **I took it you weren't coming** я по́нял так,/я реши́л, что вы не придёте; **I ~ her to be about 30** я ду́маю, ей лет три́дцать; **I took him for your brother** я при́нял его́ за твоего́ бра́та; **what do you ~ me for?** за кого́ ты меня́ принима́ешь?

11 (*consider*): **~ me, for example** возьми́ меня́, наприме́р; **he took Ireland as an illustration** он привёл в ка́честве приме́ра Ирла́ндию; **all things ~n together, the conference was a great success** в о́бщем и це́лом конфере́нция име́ла большо́й успе́х

12 (*ingest*) принима́ть; **to ~ medicine** приня́ть лека́рство; **"Not to be ~n internally"** «То́лько для нару́жного употребле́ния»; **he took neither food nor drink for three days** у него́ три дня ма́ковой роси́нки во рту́ не́ было; **I could ~ a little tea** хорошо́ бы чайку́ попи́ть; **how much alcohol has he ~n?** ско́лько он вы́пил?; **how much sugar do you ~?** ско́лько вам са́хару?; **do you ~ milk?** вам с молоко́м?

13 (*require*): **this recipe ~s six eggs** для приготовле́ния э́того блю́да ну́жно шесть яи́ц; **these windows ~ 10 m of curtaining** на занаве́ски для э́тих о́кон пойдёт де́сять ме́тров тка́ни; **it ~s courage to admit you are wrong** нужна́ сме́лость, что́бы призна́ть свою́ непра́воту́; **it doesn't ~ much to make her cry** чуть что—и она́ уже́ пла́чет; **it took two men to lift the trunk** пона́добилось дво́е (мужчи́н), что́бы подня́ть сунду́к; **it ~s two hours to get there** е́хать туда́ два часа́; **it took them an hour to find him** им потре́бовался час, что́бы найти́ его́; **I didn't ~ long to realize that...** я ско́ро по́нял, что...; **this verb ~s the dative** э́тот глаго́л тре́бует существи́тельного в да́тельном падеже́; **he ~s a bit of getting to know** его́ не сра́зу раску́сишь

14 (*accomodate*) брать; (*of hall, etc.*) вме|ща́ть (-сти́ть); **can you ~ two more?** (*in car, bus, etc.*) мо́жете взять ещё двои́х?; **the bus couldn't ~ any more passengers** в авто́бусе бо́льше не́ было свобо́дных мест; **the hall ~s 2,000 people** зал вмеща́ет две ты́сячи челове́к

15 (*occupy, engage*) за|нима́ть (-ня́ть); **is this seat ~n?** э́то ме́сто за́нято?; **all our rooms are ~n** у нас все ко́мнаты за́няты; **the sofa ~s (up) a lot of room** тахта́ занима́ет мно́го ме́ста; **~ a seat over there** ся́дьте там; **I have ~n a house for the summer/a room in the hotel** я снял да́чу на ле́то/но́мер в гости́нице

vi (*of vaccination, a plant*) принима́ться

take aboard *vt*: **the cargo has been ~n aboard** груз при́нят на́ борт; **only hand luggage may be ~n aboard the aircraft** на борт самолёта разреша́ется брать то́лько ручно́й бага́ж

take after *vt*: **he ~s after you in that respect** в э́том он пошёл в тебя́/весь в тебя́

take against *vt*: **he took against me at first sight** он меня́ сра́зу невзлюби́л

take apart *vt* (*to bits*) раз|бира́ть (-обра́ть)

take away *vti vt* (*clear away*) у|бира́ть, (*remove*) за|бира́ть (*pfs* -бра́ть); (*carry*) уноси́ть; (*on foot*) уводи́ть; (*by car*) увози́ть; (*deprive*) лиш|а́ть + *G* (-и́ть); **I took the dirty plates away** я убра́л/унёс гря́зные таре́лки; **they took her away from school** они́ забра́ли её из шко́лы; **they took him away** его́ увели́/увезли́; **"Not to be ~n away"** (*of library books*) «Не выноси́ть из за́ла»; **does this restaurant sell food to ~ away?** в э́том рестора́не даю́т обе́ды на́ дом?; **to ~ away smb's pension** лиши́ть кого́-л пе́нсии; **they have ~n away my pass** они́ отобра́ли у меня́ про́пуск; **it took away all my pleasure** э́то испо́ртило мне всё удово́льствие; **the tablets took away the pain** табле́тки сня́ли боль; **it took my breath away** от э́того у меня́ дух захвати́ло (*impers*); *Math* **~ away 3 from 5** от пяти́ отня́ть три, из пяти́ вы́честь три

vi: **that doesn't ~ away from his merit** э́то не умаля́ет его́ досто́инств (*pl*)

take back *vt* **1** (*return*) возвраща́ть (верну́ть), относи́ть/отводи́ть/отвози́ть обра́тно; **to ~ back books to the library** верну́ть/отнести́ кни́ги в библиоте́ку; **~ the tray back to the kitchen** отнеси́ подно́с (обра́тно) в ку́хню; **he was ~n back to his cell/home in a taxi** его́ увели́ (наза́д) в ка́меру, его́ отвезли́ домо́й в такси́; *fig* **it ~s me back to my childhood** э́то мне напомина́ет де́тство

2 (*receive*) брать обра́тно (взять); **the salesman took back the faulty goods** продаве́ц взял обра́тно брако́ванный това́р (*collect*); *fig* **I ~ back what I said** беру́ свои́ слова́ наза́д

take down *vt* снима́ть (снять); **to ~ down Xmas decorations** снять рожде́ственские украше́ния; **to ~ a book down from a shelf** взять кни́гу с по́лки; **to ~ down a building** сноси́ть зда́ние (снести́); **to ~ down (in writing)** запи́с|ывать (-а́ть)

take in *vt* **1** брать; **she ~s in washing/sewing** она́ берёт на́ дом сти́рку/шитьё; **I took in the washing when the rain began** я сняла́ бельё, когда́ пошёл дождь; *Sew*: **to ~ in a dress** уши|ва́ть пла́тье (-́ть); **to ~ smth in at the seams** убра́ть/забра́ть что-л в швах

2 (*include*): **our trip took in all the monasteries** мы осмотре́ли все монастыри́ во вре́мя экску́рсии; **will we have time to ~ in the zoo as well?** мы успе́ем посмотре́ть ещё и зоопа́рк?

3 (*comprehend*): **he took it all in at a glance** он с одного́ взгля́да всё по́нял; **at first I didn't ~ in his question** до меня́ не сра́зу дошёл смысл его́ вопро́са

4 (*in passive*: *be deceived*): **she was completely ~n in by his charm** её обману́ло его́ прия́тное обхожде́ние; **he was again ~n in by the same trick** он сно́ва попа́лся на ту́ же у́дочку

take off *vti vt* **1** (*remove*) снима́ть с + *G* (снять); **to ~ off one's hat/shoes/clothes** снять шля́пу/боти́нки, разде|ва́ться (-́ться); (*to guest on arrival*) **won't you ~ off your coat/things?** раздева́йтесь, пожа́луйста; **the builders/the wind took the roof off** строи́тели сня́ли кры́шу, ве́тром снесло́ (*impers*) кры́шу; **pheasant has been ~n off the menu** фаза́на вы́черкнули из меню́; **he's been ~n off the list** его́ вы́черкнули из спи́ска; **the play/that train has been ~n off** э́ту пье́су сня́ли с репертуа́ра, э́тот по́езд снят с расписа́ния; **I took a few days off** я не́сколько дней не выходи́л на рабо́ту; **he has to ~ off 10 kilos** ему́ на́до сбро́сить де́сять килогра́ммов; **he couldn't ~ his eyes off her** он не мог отвести́ от неё глаз

2 (*lead away*) забира́ть, отводи́ть, уводи́ть, отвози́ть, увози́ть; **he has ~n the children off to the zoo** он повёл (*on foot*)/повёз *or* отвёз (*by car*) дете́й в зоопа́рк; **they took him off to prison** его́ забра́ли в тюрьму́; **he took**

himself off in a huff он в негодова́нии удали́лся

3 (*imitate*): **he ~s off his professor to perfection** он так похо́же изобража́ет профе́ссора

vi Aer (*from a place*) вы|лета́ть (-лететь); (*from ground*) взлет|а́ть (-е́ть), отрыва́ться от земли́ (оторва́ться); (*of people*) **I grabbed my case and took off for the airport** я схвати́л чемода́н и помча́лся в аэропо́рт

take on *vti vt* **1** брать; **to ~ on extra work/an extra secretary** взять дополни́тельную рабо́ту/ещё одного́ секретаря́; **we've ~n him on for three months trial** мы взя́ли/при́няли его́ на трёхме́сячный испыта́тельный срок; **he ~s on too much** он сли́шком мно́го берёт на себя́; **his words took on a new meaning** его́ слова́ приобрели́ но́вый смысл

2 (*an opponent*): **to ~ smb on at chess/draughts** срази́ться с кем-л в ша́хматы/в ша́шки; **the government should be wary of taking on the unions** прави́тельство должно́ остерега́ться столкнове́ния с профсою́зами; **he could ~ on the lot of them single-handed** он оди́н мог бы спра́виться с ни́ми со все́ми

vi: **don't ~ on so!** не волну́йся!

take out *vt* **1** (*lead out, etc.*) вы|води́ть (-вести); (*remove*) брать, вы|нима́ть (-нуть); **she took him out of the room/for a walk** она́ вы́вела его́ из ко́мнаты/гуля́ть; **~ that dog out at once** сейча́с же вы́веди (*outside house*)/уведи́ (*remove*) э́ту соба́ку; **my husband never ~s me out** мой муж никуда́ со мной не хо́дит; **to ~ money out of the bank/a book out of the library/a quotation out of the Bible** взять де́ньги в ба́нке/кни́гу в библиоте́ке/цита́ту из би́блии; **~ your hands out of your pockets** вынь ру́ки из карма́нов; **the cost of the repair was ~n out of his wage** сто́имость ремо́нта вы́чли из его́ зарпла́ты; **he needs something to ~ him out of himself** его́ ну́жно че́м-то отвле́чь от его́ мы́слей

2 *Med*: **to ~ out smb's teeth/appendix** удал|я́ть кому́-л зу́бы/аппе́ндикс (-и́ть)

3 (*patent, etc.*): **to ~ out a patent/a gun licence/an insurance policy** взять пате́нт, получи́ть разреше́ние на ноше́ние ору́жия/страхово́й по́лис; **I've ~n out a subscription to Punch** я подписа́лся на «Панч», я выпи́сываю «Панч»

4 *CQ*: **the heat/journey took it out of me** меня́ изму́чила жара́/доро́га; **I know you are angry, but don't ~ it out on me** я зна́ю, ты не в ду́хе, но не срыва́й раздраже́ние на мне

take over *vti vt*: **he took over the firm from his father** он возгла́вил фи́рму вме́сто отца́; **the firm has been ~n over by an international company** фи́рма влила́сь в междунаро́дную компа́нию; **she took over the chairmanship after his resignation** она́ ста́ла председа́телем по́сле его́ ухо́да

vi: **I took over from him last month** (*permanently*) я занима́л его́ до́лжность/(*for a period*) я замеща́л его́ в про́шлом ме́сяце; (*on shift*) **I ~ over from him at 6 o'clock** я сменя́ю его́ в шесть часо́в

take to *vi*: **they took to the hills** они́ ушли́ в го́ры; **he has ~n to his bed with flu/to drink** он слёг с гри́ппом, он стал пить; **I didn't ~ to her** она́ мне не понра́вилась

take up *vti vt* **1** (*conduct, lift*) под|нима́ть (-ня́ть); **he/the lift took us up to the top floor** он повёл/лифт по́днял нас на ве́рхний эта́ж; **he took us up in his aeroplane for a spin** мы полете́ли на его́ самолёте; **to ~ up the floorboards/a carpet** подня́ть до́ски по́ла, снять (с по́ла) ковёр; **to ~ up a dress/hem** подши|ва́ть пла́тье/подо́л (-ть)

2 (*occupy*) за|нима́ть (-ня́ть); **it ~s up too much space/time** э́то занима́ет сли́шком мно́го ме́ста/вре́мени; **I won't ~ up any more of your time** я бо́льше не ста́ну отнима́ть у вас вре́мя

3 (*start, etc.*): **he has ~n up photography** он заня́лся́ фотогра́фией; **he left to ~ up a better job** он перешёл на лу́чшую рабо́ту; **to ~ up residence at** посели́ться в + *A*; **they took up my idea eagerly** они́ охо́тно подхвати́ли мою́ иде́ю; **I'll ~ up the matter with the director** я пойду́ с э́тим вопро́сом к дире́ктору; **I'll ~ you up on your offer** я воспо́льзуюсь ва́шим предложе́нием; **he took up the story at the point where...** он продолжа́л расска́з с того́ ме́ста, где...

vi: **he has ~n up with an undesirable crowd** он связа́лся с плохо́й компа́нией

take upon *vt*: **he took it upon himself to speak for us all** он стал почему́-то говори́ть за всех нас.

talc, talcum powder *ns* тальк.

tale *n* (*account*) расска́з; (*as title*) по́весть, сказа́ние; *CQ* **old wive's ~s** ба́бушкины ска́зки.

talent *n* тала́нт (*also of person*), тала́нтливость; **he is looking for new ~** он и́щет но́вые тала́нты (*pl*).

talented *adj* тала́нтливый.

talk *n* (*conversation*) разгово́р, бесе́да; **it's just ~** э́то всё одни́ разгово́ры (*pl*); **there is ~ of his going to America** говоря́т, что он пое́дет в Аме́рику; **to have a ~ with smb** поговори́ть с кем-л; (*lecture*) **he gave a ~ on his trip to Africa** он сде́лал сообще́ние о свое́й пое́здке в А́фрику; (*negotiations*) **to have ~s with smb** вести́ перегово́ры с кем-л.

talk *vti vt* говори́ть (*only in impf*); **to ~ sense/German/nonsense** говори́ть де́ло/по-неме́цки, нести́ чушь; **to ~ business** говори́ть о де́ле; **to ~ smb into/out of doing smth** уговори́ть кого́-л сде́лать что-л, отговори́ть кого́-л от чего́-л (*only in pfs*); **to ~ smth over** переговори́ть о чём-л (*only in pf*); **to ~ smb round** уговори́ть кого́-л; **he tried to ~ his way out of it** он всё опра́вдывался; **to ~ oneself hoarse** договори́ться до хрипоты́

vi говори́ть; (*converse*) разгова́ривать (*usu impf*); **to ~ on the subject of smth/to the point** говори́ть на каку́ю-л те́му/по существу́; **to ~ to smb about smth** говори́ть/разгова́ривать с кем-л о чём-л; **I'm not ~ing to him**

any more я с ним бóльше не разговáриваю; **he ~s down to his students** он разговáривает со студéнтами свысокá; **to get ~ing to smb** разговори́ться с кем-л (*pf*); **he's very interesting if you can get him ~ing** он óчень интерéсный собесéдник, éсли с ним разговори́ться; **the neighbours are beginning to ~** сосéди ужé нáчали [**NB** *tense*] поговáривать; **someone must have ~ed** должнó быть, ктó-то проговори́лся; *fig*: **you can't ~** не тебé бы говори́ть; **now you're ~ing!** тепéрь ты дéло говори́шь!; **~ of the devil!** лёгок на поми́не!; **~ing of him, did you know that..?** раз уж мы заговори́ли о нём, тебé извéстно, что..?

talkative *adj pejor* разговóрчивый, говорли́вый, болтли́вый.

talker *n* (*chatterer*) болтýн; **he's a good ~** он умéет говори́ть.

talking *n*: **he did all the ~** он оди́н говори́л; **no ~ in the library** в библиотéке не разговáривать; **all ~ ceased when he entered** когдá он вошёл, все разговóры прекрати́лись; **he tired me out with his ~** он заговори́л меня́.

talking-to *n CQ*: **he gave her a good ~** он её хорошéнько отчитáл.

tall *n* высóкий; **how ~ is he?/the mast?** у негó какóй рост?, какóй высоты́ мáчта?; **he is 2 m ~** он два мéтра рóстом; **how ~ you are!** какóй ты высóкий!; **he is ~er than I** он вы́ше меня́/, чем я; *fig*: **a ~ story** небыли́цы, вы́думки (*pls*); **a ~ order** трýдная задáча.

tally *vi*: **to ~ with** соотвéтствовать + *D* (*impf*).

talon *n* кóготь (*m*).

tambourine *n* бýбен, тамбури́н.

tame *adj* (*of birds, small creatures*) ручнóй, *also joc of people*; (*of animals, e.g. deer, bear*) прирýчённый; (*of fierce animals, e.g. lion*) укрощённый; *fig* (*boring*) скýчный.

tame *vt* (*of birds, animals*) прируч|áть (-и́ть); (*of fierce animals, fig of people*) укро|щáть (-ти́ть).

tamer *n* укроти́тель (*m*), дрессирóвщик.

tamper *vi*: **to ~ with** (*documents, accounts*) поддéл|ывать (-ать); **this lock has been ~ed with** ктó-то трóгал э́тот замóк.

tan *n* (*suntan*) загáр; **he has a marvellous ~** он так хорошó загорéл.

tan *adj* свéтло-кори́чневый.

tan *vti vt* (*of leather*) дуби́ть (вы́-); **his face was ~ned by the sun** егó лицó загорéло (на сóлнце)

vi (*with sun*) загор|áть (-éть).

tangent *n* (*in geometry*) касáтельная; (*in trigonometry*) тáнгенс; *fig* **he went off at a ~** он перескочи́л на другýю тéму.

tangerine *n* мандари́н.

tangible *adj* осязáемый, ощути́мый; *fig* **~ proof** реáльное доказáтельство.

tangle *vt* пýтать (с-, пере-), *usu pass*; **the threads are ~d** ни́тки спýтались; **~d hair** спýтанные вóлосы (*pl*); *fig*: **don't get ~d (up) in this affair** не впýтывайся ты в э́то дéло; **he got ~d up with the police**/*pejor* **with a gang of smugglers** у негó бы́ли неприя́тности с поли́цией, он спýтался с шáйкой контрабанди́стов.

tango *n* тáнго (*indecl*).

tank *n* **1** бак, (*larger*) цистéрна; **petrol ~** бензобáк

2 *Mil* танк.

tankard *n* пивнáя крýжка.

tanker *n Aut* автоцистéрна; *Naut* тáнкер.

tanned *adj* (*of leather; also fig: weather-beaten*) дублёный; (*by sun*) загорéлый.

tannic acid *n* дуби́льная кислотá.

tantalize *vt* терзáть (*impf*).

tantalizing *adj*: **a ~ smell from the kitchen** дразня́щий/соблазни́тельный зáпах из кýхни; **we had a ~ two days waiting for results** мы два дня мéста себé не находи́ли в ожидáнии результáтов.

tantamount *adj*: **~ to** равноси́льный + *D*; **that is ~ to murder/to killing her** э́то равноси́льно уби́йству, э́то всё равнó что уби́ть её.

tantrum *n*: **he's in one of his ~s** с ним опя́ть истéрика; **to throw a ~** закати́ть истéрику.

tap[1] *n* (*for water, gas, on barrel, etc.*) кран; **to leave the ~ running** остáвить кран откры́тым; **beer on ~** бóчковое пи́во; *fig* **he always has plenty of helpers on ~** у негó всегдá мнóго помóщников под рукóй.

tap[1] *vt* (*a tree for resin, etc.*) надрез|áть (-́ать); **to ~ new resources** разрабáтывать нóвые месторождéния (*usu impf*); **my phone is being ~ped** мой телефóнные разговóры подслýшиваются; *CQ* **to ~ smb for information/money** пытáться вы́удить у когó-л нýжную информáцию/дéньги (*pf*).

tap[2] *vti vt* стучáть (по-); **he ~ped his forehead/me on the shoulder** он постучáл себя́ пó лбу, он похлóпал меня́ по плечý; **he kept ~ping his foot on the floor** он тихóнько притóпывал ногóй (*impf*); **to ~ in a nail** вкол|áчивать гвоздь (-оти́ть); **to ~ out a message** (*in Morse*) выстýкивать сообщéние (*usu impf*)

vi: **to ~ on the door** (ти́хо) постучáть в дверь; **the blind man walked ~ping with his stick** слепóй шёл, постýкивая пáлкой.

tape *n* тесьмá; лéнта (*also for film or for recording*); *Med* плáстырь (*m*); *Sport* фи́нишная лéнточка; **sticky ~** ли́пкая лéнта, скотч; **to play back a ~** прослýшать магнитофóнную зáпись.

tape *vt* **1**: **to ~ up a parcel** заклé|ивать посы́лку скóтчем (-ить); *fig CQ* **I see you've got him/it all ~d** я ви́жу, ты егó раскуси́л/, ты всё устрóил как нáдо

2 (*record*) запи́с|ывать на магнитофóнную лéнту (-áть).

tape measure *n* (*of cloth*) сантимéтр; (*metal coil*) рулéтка.

taper *n* (*for lighting*) вощёный фити́ль (*m*); (*candle*) тóнкая воскова́я свечá.

taper *vti* (*of a cone*) заостр|я́ть(ся) (-и́ть(ся)); (*of a flat board, etc.*) су́живать(ся) (су́зить(ся)).

tape recorder *n* магнитофо́н.

tapering *adj* заострённый; су́женный.

tapestry *n* (*wall-hanging*) гобеле́н; *attr*: ~ **work** вы́шивка кре́стиком.

tar *n* дёготь (*m*); (*for road*) гудро́н; (*for boats*) смола́; *attr*: **a ~ barrel** бо́чка с дёгтем/со смоло́й.

tar *vt* (*a road*) покры|ва́ть гудро́ном (-́ть); (*a boat*) смоли́ть (о-, про-).

tardy *adj* (*slow*) ме́дленный; (*belated*) запозда́лый.

target *n* (*objective*) цель, *also fig*; (*for practice*) мише́нь, *also fig pejor*; **to hit/miss the ~** (не) попа́сть в цель/в мише́нь; **the rocket is (right) on ~ for Mars** ракéта нацéлена на Марс/идёт то́чно по за́данному ку́рсу к Ма́рсу; *fig*: **he is a ~ for ridicule/criticism** он мише́нь для насме́шек/для кри́тики; **we reached our ~ of £1,000** мы собра́ли, как и намерева́лись, ты́сячу фу́нтов; **production ~s for next year** произво́дственные зада́чи на сле́дующий год; **our export ~s** на́ши пла́ны по э́кспорту.

target practice *n* стрельба́ по мише́ням, учéбная стрельба́.

tariff *n Econ* тари́ф; *Comm* (*price list*) расце́нка, прейскура́нт.

tarmac *n* гудро́н; *attr*: **a ~ road** гудрони́рованное шоссе́.

tarnish *vti vt*: **the damp has ~ed the silver** серебро́ потускне́ло от сы́рости; *fig* **a ~ed reputation** запя́тнанная репута́ция

vi тускне́ть (по-).

tarpaulin *n* брезе́нт.

tarry *adj* смоли́стый; просмолённый; покры́тый дёгтем/(*on roads*) гудро́ном.

tart[1] *n* **1** (*large*) пиро́г; (*small*) пирожо́к; **apple ~** я́блочный пиро́г

2 *CQ* легкомы́сленная деви́ца.

tart[2] *adj* (*sour*) ки́слый; *fig* (*of remark, etc.*) ко́лкий, ре́зкий.

tartan *n* шотла́ндка, клéтчатая ткань.

Tartar *n* тата́рин, тата́рка, *pl* тата́ры; *fig CQ* **she is a regular ~** она́ про́сто мегéра.

tartar *n Chem* ви́нный ка́мень (*m*).

task *n* (*work set*) зада́ние; (*problem*) зада́ча, де́ло; **they gave me the ~ of persuading him** они́ да́ли мне зада́ние уговори́ть его́; **it's a hard ~** э́то тру́дное де́ло; *fig* **he took me to ~ for overspending** он руга́л меня́ за то, что я тра́чу мно́го де́нег.

taskmaster *n*: **he's a hard ~** он стро́гий нача́льник.

tassel *n* ки́сточка.

taste *n* **1** вкус, (*aftertaste*) при́вкус; **sense of ~** вкус; **sweet to the ~** сла́дкий на вкус; **this medicine has a strange ~/leaves a bad ~** у э́того лека́рства стра́нный вкус, от э́того лека́рства неприя́тный при́вкус во рту́; *fig*: **she has good ~** у неё хоро́ший вкус; **she dresses in good/bad ~** она́ одева́ется со вку́сом/безвку́сно; **the remark is in poor ~** э́то беста́ктное замеча́ние; **it is not to my ~** э́то мне не по вку́су; **what are your ~s in music?** кака́я му́зыка вам нра́вится?; **I am developing a ~ for prawns** я начина́ю понима́ть толк в креве́тках; **there is no accounting for ~** о вку́сах не спо́рят

2 (*sample*): **may I have a ~?** мо́жно мне попро́бовать?; *fig* **we had a ~ of his temper** мы узна́ли тепе́рь его́ нрав; **now he's had a ~ of freedom** тепе́рь он почу́вствовал свобо́ду

3 (*small amount*): **add a ~ of salt/brandy** доба́вьте чу́точку со́ли/коньяка́.

taste *vti vt* **1**: **I can ~ cinnamon in this pie** я чу́вствую за́пах кори́цы в пироге́; **I can't ~ anything when I have a cold** когда́ у меня́ на́сморк, я совсе́м не чу́вствую вку́са пи́щи

2 (*sample*) про́бовать (по-); **I haven't ~d salmon for years** я давно́ не про́бовал сёмги; **to ~ wines** дегусти́ровать ви́на (*impf and pf*); *fig* **to ~ power** почу́вствовать вкус вла́сти (*only in pf*)

vi: **it ~s good** э́то о́чень вку́сно; **the apples ~ sour** я́блоки ки́слые на вкус; **it ~s all right to me** мне ка́жется, э́то вку́сно; **the pie ~s of garlic** в пироге́ чу́вствуется чесно́чный при́вкус; **it doesn't ~ of anything** э́то совсе́м не вку́сно.

tasteless *adj* безвку́сный, *also fig*.

tasting *n*: **a wine ~** дегуста́ция вин.

tasty *adj* вку́сный.

tattered *adj* изо́рванный, истрёпанный, в лохмо́тьях.

tatty *adj CQ* потрёпанный.

taunt *n* зла́я насме́шка; *CQ* издёвка.

taunt *vt* дразни́ть (*impf*); (*scoff at*) издева́ться над + *I* (*impf*); **they ~ed him with cowardice/being a coward** его́ дразни́ли тру́сом, они́ издева́лись над ним за его́ тру́сость.

taut *adj* туго́й; натя́нутый, *also fig*; *fig* **~ nerves** взви́нченные не́рвы.

tavern *n* таве́рна.

tawdry *adj* (*of dress, jewelry*) безвку́сный, крича́щий.

tax *n* нало́г; **income ~** подохо́дный нало́г; **to levy a ~ on smth** обложи́ть что-л нало́гом; **to collect ~es** взима́ть нало́ги; **the ~ has been taken off tea** с ча́я нало́г сня́ли, чай сейча́с не облага́ется нало́гом; *attr*: **~ evasion** уклоне́ние от упла́ты нало́гов.

tax *vt* **1**: **to ~ whisky** об|лага́ть ви́ски нало́гом (-ложи́ть); *fig* **to ~ smb's patience/strength** испы́тывать чьё-л терпе́ние (*usu impf*), под|та́чивать чьи-л си́лы (-точи́ть)

2 (*accuse*): **he ~ed me with having broken my word** он обвини́л меня́ в том, что я нару́шил сло́во.

taxable *adj* облага́емый нало́гом, подлежа́щий обложе́нию нало́гом.

taxation *n*: **system of ~** нало́говая систе́ма, систе́ма обложе́ния нало́гом; **what is the rate of ~?** како́в разме́р налогообложе́ния?; **to grumble at high/heavy ~** жа́ловаться на высо́кие нало́ги.

tax collector *n* сбо́рщик нало́гов.

tax-free *adj* необлага́емый нало́гом.

taxi *n* такси́ (*indecl*); **to take a ~** взять такси́.

taxi *vi*: *Aer* **to ~ out** вы|ру́ливать (-́рулить); **to ~ up to** подру́л|ивать к + *D* (-и́ть); *CQ* **we taxied to the theatre** мы пое́хали в теа́тр на такси́.

taxi driver *n* води́тель (*m*) такси́, *CQ* такси́ст.

taxi rank *n* стоя́нка такси́.

taxpayer *n* налогоплате́льщик.

tea *n* чай; **strong/weak ~** кре́пкий/сла́бый чай; **a cup of ~** ча́шка ча́я/ча́ю.

tea bag *n* паке́тик с зава́ркой ча́я.

tea break *n approx* небольшо́й переры́в (в рабо́те).

tea caddy *n* коро́бочка для ча́я.

teach *vti vt* **1** (*a person smth*) учи́ть (вы́-, на-, об-), (*esp. of skills*) обуч|а́ть (-и́ть) (*both verbs take A of person and D or inf of subject*); **I taught him physics/to drive** я учи́л его́ фи́зике, я научи́л/обучи́л его́ води́ть маши́ну

2 (*a subject*) преподава́ть + *A* (*of subject*) (*impf*); **he ~s history** он преподаёт исто́рию; **the Greeks taught that...** гре́ки учи́ли, что...; *fig*: **I'll ~ him a lesson!** я проучу́ его́!; **he taught me a thing or two** он меня́ ко́е-чему́ научи́л

vi преподава́ть (*impf*).

teacher *n* учи́тель (*m*), *f* -ница, преподава́тель (*m*), *f* -ница; педаго́г; **a history ~** учи́тель исто́рии.

teacher(s') training college *n* педагоги́ческий институ́т.

teaching *n* **1** *usu pl*: **the ~s of Kant** уче́ние (*sing*) Ка́нта

2 (*profession*) преподава́ние; *attr*: **~ hospital** больни́ца с медици́нским учи́лищем; **the ~ profession** профе́ссия педаго́га, *as collect* преподава́тели (*pl*); **the ~ staff** преподава́тельский соста́в; **~ load** преподава́тельская нагру́зка.

teacloth *n* ча́йное полоте́нце.

teacup *n* ча́йная ча́шка; *fig* **a storm in a ~** бу́ря в стака́не воды́.

teak *n* (*tree*) тик, (*wood*) ти́ковое де́рево.

tea leaf *n* ча́йный лист.

team *n* **1** *Sport* кома́нда; **football/home/away ~** футбо́льная кома́нда, хозя́ева по́ля, кома́нда госте́й; *attr*: **~ events** кома́ндные соревнова́ния; **~ spirit** *approx* сы́гранность

2 (*of workers*) брига́да; (*group*) гру́ппа; **a ~ of inspectors, a research ~** инспекцио́нная/иссле́довательская гру́ппа

3 (*of sledge dogs, horses*) упря́жка.

team *vi*: **to ~ up** (*in work*) сотру́дничать, (*of colours*) гармони́ровать (*impf*); **I ~ed up with them on the excursion** на экску́рсии я присоедини́лся к ним; **this jacket ~s (up) with this skirt** жаке́т подхо́дит к э́той ю́бке.

team-mate *n* това́рищ по кома́нде.

teamwork *n* (*collaboration*) сотру́дничество; (*mutual aid*) взаимопо́мощь; *Sport* сы́гранность.

teapot *n* ча́йник для зава́рки [**NB** ча́йник *also* = *kettle*].

tear[1] *vti vt* (*rip*) рвать (по-́) *and compounds*; **to ~ one's shirt/a muscle** порва́ть руба́шку/мы́шцу; **he tore the paper into pieces** он порва́л/разорва́л бума́гу на кусо́чки; **the page is slightly torn** страни́ца немно́го надо́рвана; **to ~ one's hand on a nail** разодра́ть себе́ ру́ку о гвоздь (*only in pf*); **she tore herself from his arms** она́ вы́рвалась из его́ объя́тий; *fig*: **to ~ one's hair** рвать на себе́ во́лосы; **he was torn by conflicting emotions** его́ раздира́ли противоречи́вые чу́вства; **he was torn between them** он разрыва́лся ме́жду ни́ми; **to ~ smb's argument/work to pieces** разби́ть чей-л аргуме́нт, раскритикова́ть чью-л рабо́ту; *CQ*: **he tore a strip off me** он дал мне нагоня́й; **that's torn it!** тепе́рь всему́ коне́ц!

vi рва́ться *and compounds*; **this paper ~s easily** э́та бума́га легко́ рвётся; *fig* **he tore into the room/along the road** он ворва́лся в ко́мнату, он помча́лся по доро́ге

tear away *vt*: **I can't ~ myself away from this book** я не могу́ оторва́ться от э́той кни́ги

tear down *vt*: **to ~ down posters** срыва́ть плака́ты (сорва́ть); **to ~ down a building** снос́ить зда́ние (снести́)

tear off *vti* срыва́ть(ся); **he tore off the label/bandage** он сорва́л накле́йку/бинт; **he tore off** он сорва́лся с ме́ста

tear out *vt*: **to ~ a page out of a book** вы́рвать страни́цу из кни́ги

tear up *vt*: **to ~ up a letter** порва́ть письмо́; **to ~ plants up by the roots** вырыва́ть расте́ния с ко́рнем (*sing*).

tear[2] *n* слеза́; **in ~s** в слеза́х; **to burst into ~s** распла́каться; **to move/reduce smb to ~s** растро́гать/довести́ кого́-л до слёз.

tearful *adj* слезли́вый.

tearfully *adv* сквозь слёзы; (*whining*) плакси́во.

teargas *n* слезоточи́вый газ.

tear-off *adj*: **a ~ calendar** отрывно́й календа́рь (*m*).

tease *n* зади́ра (*m and f*).

tease *vti* дразни́ть (*impf*); **don't ~ the cat/your sister** не дразни́ ко́шку/сестру́; **they ~d him about his baldness** они́ подшу́чивали над его́ лы́синой; **I was only teasing** я про́сто пошути́л.

teaser *n CQ* (*puzzle*) головоло́мка.

tea set *n* ча́йный серви́з.

teasing *n* (*taunts*) насме́шки (*pl*); (*jokes*) шу́тки (*pl*); **he loves ~** он лю́бит иногда́ подшути́ть.

tea strainer *n* ча́йное си́течко.

teat *n* сосо́к.

tea towel *n* ча́йное полоте́нце.

tea urn *n* бак, тита́н.

technical *adj* техни́ческий; **~ college** техни́ческий институ́т; **due to a ~ hitch/fault** по техни́ческим причи́нам, из-за техни́ческих не-поля́док (*pls*); **a ~ difficulty** техни́ческая тру́дность.

technicality *n*: **a ~** техни́ческая дета́ль.

technician *n* те́хник.

Technicolor *n*: **a film in ~** цветно́й фильм.

technique *n* те́хника.

technological *adj* технологи́ческий.

teddy (bear) *n* плю́шевый ми́шка (*m*).

tedious *adj* ску́чный.

tee-hee *interj* хи-хи́!

teem *vi* кише́ть + *I*, изоби́ловать + *I* (*impfs*); **the streets were ~ing with people** на у́лицах бы́ло полно́ наро́ду; **the river was ~ing with fish** река́ изоби́ловала ры́бой; **the town was ~ing with life** в го́роде кипе́ла жизнь; **it is ~ing with rain** льёт как из ведра́.

teenage *adj*: **she has two ~ daughters** у неё дво́е де́вочек-подро́стков.

teenager *n* подро́сток.

teens *npl*: **he is in his ~** он ещё подро́сток.

teeny *adj CQ* малю́сенький, кро́шечный.

teethe *vi*: **baby is teething** у ребёнка прореза́ются/ре́жутся зу́бы.

teetotaller *n* тре́звенник, непьющий.

telecommunication(s) *n* телекоммуника́ции.

telegram *n* телегра́мма.

telegraph *n* телегра́ф; *attr*: **~ pole** телегра́фный столб.

telegraph *vti* телеграфи́ровать (про-).

telepathy *n* телепа́тия.

telephone *n* телефо́н; **by ~** по телефо́ну; **he is on the ~** (*subscribes*) у него́ есть телефо́н, (*is speaking*) он разгова́ривает по телефо́ну.

telephone *vti* звони́ть + *D* (по телефо́ну) (по-); **to ~ news to smb** сообщ|а́ть кому́-л но́вости (*pl*) по телефо́ну (-и́ть); **I'll ~ in the morning** я позвоню́ у́тром; *attr*: **~ directory** телефо́нный спра́вочник; **~ exchange** телефо́нная ста́нция; **~ number** но́мер телефо́на; **~ booth/box** телефо́н-автома́т *or* телефо́нная бу́дка; **I had a ~ call from him** он мне звони́л.

telephonist *n* телефони́ст(ка).

teleprinter *n* телета́йп.

teletype *n* (*US*) телета́йп.

televise *vt*: **the match was ~d** матч передава́лся по телеви́дению/*CQ* по телеви́зору.

television *n* телеви́дение; (*set*) телеви́зор; **colour ~** цветно́й телеви́зор; **to watch ~** смотре́ть телеви́зор; **he was/I saw him on ~** он выступа́л/я ви́дел его́ по телеви́зору; *attr* телевизио́нный.

tell *vti vt* **1** говори́ть (сказа́ть); (*relate*) расска́з|ывать (-а́ть); (*inform*) сообщ|а́ть (-и́ть); (*convey*) переда|ва́ть (-́ть); **has he told you of his decision?** он тебе́ сказа́л/сообщи́л о своём реше́нии?; **he told me a story/how it happened** он мне рассказа́л исто́рию/, как э́то случи́лось; [**NB** *in following examples note carefully constructions in indirect speech*]: **~ him (that) I'm not coming/how it's done/how to do it/how pleased I am** *or* **was/where to find me/where you left the money/why I can't come/why I didn't answer/when you are leaving** скажи́ *or* переда́й ему́, что я не приду́/, как э́то де́лается/, как э́то (с)де́лать/, как я дово́лен/, где меня́ найти́/, где ты оста́вил де́ньги/, почему́ я не могу́ прийти́/, почему́ я не отве́тил/, когда́ ты отправля́ешься; **I am told that...** мне сказа́ли/говоря́т, что...; **to ~ smb a lie** солга́ть кому́-л; **I'll ~ you all about it tomorrow** за́втра я вам всё об э́том расскажу́; **that ~s us a lot** э́то говори́т нам о мно́гом

2 *CQ uses*: **I told you so!** я же вам говори́л!; **~ me another!** что ты ещё ска́жешь?; **he won't come, I ~ you** говорю́ вам/пове́рьте мне, он не придёт; **you're ~ing me!** ты мне э́то говори́шь! (мне *emphasized*); **don't ~ me he's late again!** и не говори́ мне, что он опя́ть опозда́л; **I could ~ you a thing or two about him** я ко́е-что́ про него́ зна́ю; **I ~ you what!** ну зна́ешь (ли)!

3 (*order*) говори́ть, веле́ть (*impfs*); **do as you're told** де́лай, как тебе́ говоря́т/веля́т; **how many times have I told you not to interrupt?** ско́лько раз я проси́л тебя́ не перебива́ть!

4 (*know*) знать (*impf*); (*recognize*) узна|ва́ть (-́ть); (*distinguish*) отлич|а́ть, различ|а́ть (*pfs* -и́ть); **there's no ~ing what he'll do next** кто зна́ет, что он ещё вы́кинет; **I can ~ him by his height** я его́ узна́ю по ро́сту; **I can't ~ them apart/margarine from butter** я их не различа́ю, я не отлича́ю маргари́н от ма́сла; **it's hard to ~ what he thinks** тру́дно сказа́ть, что он ду́мает; **you can ~ at once he's a teacher** сра́зу ви́дно, что он учи́тель

5 *various*: **to ~ one's beads** перебира́ть чётки (*only in impf*); *CQ*: **he told me off for being late** он отруга́л меня́ за опозда́ние; **there were 20 of them all told** их всего́ бы́ло два́дцать челове́к

vi **1** говори́ть; *CQ* (*of children*: *sneak*) я́бедничать на + *A*; **you promised you wouldn't ~ on me** ты обеща́л не я́бедничать на меня́; **I never heard ~ of it** я никогда́ не слыха́л об э́том; **time will ~** вре́мя пока́жет

2 (*know*): **how can I ~?** отку́да мне знать?; **you can ~ from his face he's intelligent** по лицу́ ви́дно, что он у́мный челове́к; **we couldn't ~ from your letter when you'd be arriving** из твоего́ письма́ бы́ло не я́сно, когда́ ты приезжа́ешь/прие́дешь

3 (*have an effect on*) ска́з|ываться на + *P* (-а́ться); **his age is beginning to ~** (его́) во́зраст начина́ет ска́зываться/брать своё; **the strain told on him** напряже́ние сказа́лось на нём; **his lack of experience told against him** ему́ меша́л недоста́ток о́пыта.

teller *n* (*in bank*) касси́р; (*of votes*) подсчи́тывающий голоса́.

telling *n*: **the story did not lose in the ~** исто́рия ничего́ не теря́ла в переска́зе.

telling *adj*: **a ~ argument** си́льный аргуме́нт; **a ~ blow** эффе́ктный уда́р; **these are ~ figures** э́ти ци́фры говоря́т о мно́гом.

telling-off *n CQ*: **he gave me a ~** я получи́л от него́ нагоня́й/взбу́чку.
telltale *n* я́беда (*m and f*).
telltale *adj*: **a ~ blush** преда́тельский румя́нец; **the ~ ash** улича́ющий пе́пел.
telly *n CQ* телеви́зор.
temper *n* нрав, хара́ктер; **a sweet/an ill ~** мя́гкий/дурно́й нрав; **he has a quick ~** он о́чень вспы́льчив, у него́ горя́чий нрав, он челове́к горя́чий; **he lost his ~ with me** он рассерди́лся на меня́; **to keep one's ~** владе́ть собо́й; **in a good/bad ~** в хоро́шем/плохо́м настрое́нии.
temperament *n* хара́ктер; (*temperamental nature*) темпера́мент; **she has an artistic/a nervous ~** у неё артисти́ческий темпера́мент, она́ о́чень не́рвная.
temperamental *adj* темпера́ментный.
temperate *adj* уме́ренный; **a ~ climate** уме́ренный кли́мат; **he is ~ in his drinking** он не о́чень мно́го пьёт.
temperature *n* температу́ра; **I took his ~** я изме́рил ему́ температу́ру, я поста́вил ему́ гра́дусник; **he is running a ~** у него́ температу́ра; **the ~ is minus 5 today** сего́дня ми́нус пять (гра́дусов); *attr*: **~ chart** температу́рный листо́к.
tempest *n* бу́ря.
tempestuous *adj* бу́рный, *also fig*.
temple[1] *n Anat* висо́к.
temple[2] *n Rel* храм.
tempo *n Mus* темп, *also fig*.
temporarily *adv* вре́менно, на вре́мя.
temporary *adj* вре́менный.
temporize *vi* тяну́ть вре́мя (*impf*); **to ~ over answering** тяну́ть с отве́том.
tempt *vt* соблазн|я́ть (-и́ть), прель|ща́ть (-сти́ть), искуша́ть (*usu impf*); **to ~ smb to do smth** соблазни́ть кого́-л сде́лать что-л; **I was ~ed by/to accept his offer** его́ предложе́ние соблазни́ло/прельсти́ло меня́; **to ~ fate** искуша́ть судьбу́; **there were moments when he was ~ed to leave** бы́ли мину́ты, когда́ его́ так и подмыва́ло (*impers*) уйти́.
temptation *n* собла́зн, искуше́ние; **to lead smb into ~** вводи́ть кого́-л в собла́зн.
tempter *n* соблазни́тель (*m*), искуси́тель (*m*).
tempting *adj* соблазни́тельный, зама́нчивый.
ten *num* де́сять (*G, D, P* десяти́, *I* десятью́) [*see grammatical note under* **five**]; *collect* деся́ток (*not of people*); **10 black cats** де́сять чёрных ко́шек; **there were 10 of us** нас бы́ло де́сять челове́к; **a "10"** (*the number, also in cards, etc.*) деся́тка; **10 times 10** де́сятью де́сять [**NB** *stress*]; **~s of thousands** деся́тки ты́сяч; **chapter ~** деся́тая глава́; **in room 10** в ко́мнате (но́мер) де́сять; **10-year-olds** десятиле́тние; **he is 10** ему́ де́сять лет; **at 10 they are too young to understand it** в де́сять лет они́ ещё не понима́ют э́того—сли́шком малы́; **10 to 1 you'll lose** де́сять про́тив одного́, ты проигра́ешь.
tenable *adj*: **his theory is not ~** его́ тео́рия не выде́рживает кри́тики; **the post is ~ for 3 years** э́тот пост предлага́ется на три го́да.
tenacious *adj* це́пкий; **to be ~ of life/of one's rights** це́пко держа́ться за жизнь/за свои́ права́.
tenacity *n* це́пкость.
tenancy *n* аре́нда; **during my ~ of the farm** когда́ я арендова́л э́ту фе́рму; **he has a life ~ of the property** у него́ пожи́зненное пра́во аре́нды э́того владе́ния.
tenant *n* (*in house or room*) жиле́ц; (*of land, property*) аренда́тор, съёмщик; *attr*: **~ farmer** фе́рмер-аренда́тор.
tend[1] *vt* (*invalid, machine, sheep, etc.*) уха́живать за + *I* (*impf*).
tend[2] *vi* (*incline*) быть скло́нным к + *D or* + *inf*; **I ~ to agree with you/to be lazy** я скло́нен согласи́ться с ва́ми/к ле́ни; **he ~s towards radicalism in his thinking** по скла́ду мы́слей он скоре́е радика́л; **she ~s to agree with everything he says** она́ обы́чно соглаша́ется со всем, что он ска́жет; **this cloth ~s to shrink when washed** э́тот материа́л обы́чно сади́тся при сти́рке.
tendency *n*: **he has a ~ to** у него́ скло́нность/тенде́нция к + *D or* + *inf*.
tender[1] *n Comm* (*offer*) предложе́ние; **~s are invited for building the new theatre** тре́буется организа́ция-подря́дчик для строи́тельства но́вого теа́тра; *Fin* **this coin is not legal ~** э́та моне́та изъя́та из обраще́ния.
tender[1] *vti vt*: **to ~ one's resignation** пода|ва́ть в отста́вку (-́ть)
vi Comm: **our firm has ~ed for building the new bridge** на́ша фи́рма подала́ зая́вку на строи́тельство но́вого моста́.
tender[2] *adj* не́жный; **~ meat** не́жное мя́со; **a ~ age** не́жный во́зраст; **that's a ~ spot** э́то сла́бое ме́сто, *also fig*.
tender-hearted *adj* мягкосерде́чный.
tendon *n Anat* сухожи́лие.
tendril *n Bot* у́сик.
tenet *n* до́гмат; при́нцип.
tennis *n* те́ннис; *attr*: **~ court/player** те́ннисный корт, теннис́ист.
tenor *n Mus* те́нор (*of singer, voice, part*).
tense[1] *n Gram* вре́мя.
tense[2] *adj* напряжённый; **~ muscles/faces** напряжённые му́скулы/ли́ца; **he's always very ~** он всегда́ де́ржится о́чень напряжённо.
tense[2] *vti* напря|га́ть(ся) (-́чь(ся)).
tension *n* напряже́ние, *also Elec, Phys*; *fig* напряжённость; **to reduce the ~** снять/осла́бить напряже́ние; **the ~s of modern life** напряжённость (*sing*) совреме́нного ри́тма жи́зни; **~s in the family** нелады́ (*no sing*) в семье́; **racial ~s** ра́совые противоре́чия.
tent *n* пала́тка, (*very large*) шатёр; **oxygen ~** кислоро́дная пала́тка; *attr*: **~ peg/pole** ко́лышек/сто́йка для пала́тки.
tentacle *n Zool* щу́пальце.
tentative *adj* (*as trial*) про́бный; (*preliminary*) предвари́тельный; **to make a ~ suggestion** вы́двинуть предвари́тельное предложе́ние,

пусти́ть про́бный шар; (*hesitant*) **a ~ smile** ро́бкая улы́бка.

tenterhooks *npl*: **to be on ~** сиде́ть как на иго́лках; **to keep smb on ~** держа́ть кого́-л в мучи́тельной неизве́стности (*sing*).

tenth *adj* деся́тый; *as n* деся́тая (часть), одна́ деся́тая.

tenuous *adj* сла́бый.

tenure *n*: **farmers want security of ~** фе́рмеры тре́буют гаранти́рованного пра́ва на аре́нду; **the president's ~ of office is four years** срок полномо́чий президе́нта — четы́ре го́да.

tepid *adj* теплова́тый, *also fig*.

tercentenary *n* трёхсотле́тие.

term *n* **1** (*period*) срок; **~ of office/lease** срок пребыва́ния в до́лжности, срок аре́нды; **it will pay off in the long ~, but in the short ~...** в бу́дущем э́то принесёт по́льзу, но в настоя́щий моме́нт...

2 *Univ* семе́стр; *Law* се́ссия; *School*: **a 3-/6-months ~** че́тверть, полуго́дие; **during/in ~** во вре́мя уче́бного семе́стра; **out of ~** на кани́кулах

3 (*word*) те́рмин; **a technical ~** техни́ческий те́рмин; **a contradiction in ~s** противоре́чие в терминоло́гии; **in general/simple/philosophical ~s** в о́бщих черта́х, просты́ми слова́ми, на языке́ филосо́фии; **in ~s of production** в произво́дственном выраже́нии; **he spoke of you in very flattering ~s** он говори́л о вас в о́чень ле́стных выраже́ниях; **he sees everything in ~s of money** он на всё смо́трит с комме́рческой то́чки зре́ния; *Math* **A expressed in ~s of B** A, вы́раженное как фу́нкция B

4 *pl* (**~s**) (*conditions, prices*) усло́вия; **~s of surrender/payment** усло́вия капитуля́ции/опла́ты; **on one's own ~s** на свои́х усло́виях; **what are your ~s?** (*e. g. for lessons, rooms*) каковы́ ва́ши усло́вия?; **to come to ~s with smb/with one's position** прийти́ к соглаше́нию с кем-л, примири́ться со свои́м положе́нием

5 *pl* (**~s**) (*relations*) отноше́ния; **we are on familiar/easy ~s with them** мы с ни́ми в дру́жеских отноше́ниях; **we are not on speaking ~s** мы друг с дру́гом не разгова́риваем.

term *vt* на|зыва́ть (-зва́ть); **he ~s himself a doctor** он называ́ет себя́ врачо́м; **I ~ it a disgrace** я бы назва́л э́то безобра́зием.

terminal *n Rail* вокза́л; *Elec* кле́мма, зажи́м; **bus/air ~** автовокза́л, аэровокза́л.

terminal *adj* коне́чный; *Med* **he is a ~ case** он смерте́льно бо́лен.

terminate *vti vt* прекра|ща́ть (-ти́ть); **to ~ investigations/a contract/a marriage** прекраща́ть рассле́дования, расторг|а́ть контра́кт/брак (-нуть); **to ~ a pregnancy** пре|рыва́ть бере́менность (-рва́ть)

vi: *off* **the meeting will ~ at 6 o'clock** собра́ние зако́нчится в шесть часо́в; **words that ~ in a vowel** слова́, ока́нчивающиеся на гла́сную.

termination *n* прекраще́ние; оконча́ние; (*of pregnancy*) прерыва́ние бере́менности; (*of marriage*) расторже́ние бра́ка.

terminology *n* терминоло́гия.

terminus *n* (*of bus, tram*) коне́чная остано́вка, (*of train*) коне́чная ста́нция.

terrace *n* (*outside a dwelling, unroofed*) терра́са, *also Agric*; *Sport* (**the ~s**) трибу́ны стадио́на.

terrain *n* ме́стность.

terrestrial *adj* земно́й.

terrible *adj* ужа́сный, стра́шный, *also CQ*.

terrier *n* терье́р.

terrific *adj CQ* потряса́ющий, колосса́льный.

terrify *vt* ужас|а́ть (-ну́ть).

territory *n* террито́рия.

terror *n* (*fear*) у́жас; (*violence*) терро́р; **to strike ~ into smb** вселя́ть у́жас в кого́-л; *CQ* **that child's a holy ~** э́тот ребёнок про́сто наказа́ние.

terrorize *vt* терроризи́ровать (*impf and pf*).

terror-stricken *adj* объя́тый у́жасом.

terse *adj* сжа́тый, кра́ткий; *pejor* ре́зкий.

test *n* испыта́ние, *also fig*; (*check*) прове́рка; (*sample, audition*) про́ба; *Med* ана́лиз; *School* контро́льная рабо́та; **nuclear ~s** я́дерные испыта́ния; **a ~ of character** испыта́ние хара́ктера; **to put smth to the ~** подве́ргнуть что-л испыта́нию; **his theory has stood the ~ of time** его́ тео́рия вы́держала испыта́ние вре́менем; **to conduct ~s for radioactivity** проверя́ть на радиоакти́вность; **a voice ~, a ~ of strength** про́ба го́лоса/сил (*pl*); **an eye/intelligence ~** прове́рка зре́ния, прове́рка у́мственных спосо́бностей; **a driving ~** экза́мен по вожде́нию/на права́; **a Latin ~** контро́льная рабо́та по лати́ни; *attr*: **~ flight** испыта́тельный полёт; **~ case** показа́тельный слу́чай, *Law* показа́тельное де́ло.

test *vt* испы́т|ывать (-а́ть); (*try out*) опро́бовать (*pf*); (*check*) провер|я́ть (-́ить); **to ~ a new drug** проверя́ть но́вое лека́рство; **to ~ the microphones** опро́бовать микрофо́ны; **to ~ smth for radioactivity** проверя́ть что-л на радиоакти́вность; **to ~ smb's knowledge/eyesight** проверя́ть чьи-л зна́ния/чьё-л зре́ние.

testament *n Law* завеща́ние; *Rel* **New/Old T.** Но́вый/Ве́тхий заве́т.

testicle *n Anat* яи́чко.

testify *vti*: **to ~ that/to smth** свиде́тельствовать, что.../о чём-л (*only in impf*); **I ~/these facts ~ to his honesty** я руча́юсь за его́ поря́дочность, э́ти фа́кты — свиде́тельство его́ че́стности; *Law* **to ~ against/on behalf of smb** да|ва́ть показа́ния про́тив/в по́льзу кого́-л (-ть).

testimonial *n* о́тзыв, рекоменда́ция.

testimony *n Law* показа́ния (*pl*) свиде́теля; *fig* при́знак, свиде́тельство.

test match *n* междунаро́дный матч по кри́кету.

test pilot *n* лётчик-испыта́тель (*m*).

test tube *n* проби́рка.

test-tube baby *n* «проби́рочный» ребёнок.

testy *adj* раздражи́тельный, запа́льчивый.

tetanus *n Med* столбня́к.

tête-à-tête *n*: **we had a ~** у нас был разгово́р с глázу на глáз.

tether *n*: *fig CQ* **I'm at the end of my ~** я дошёл до то́чки.

text *n* текст; (*subject*) тéма.

textbook *n* учéбник.

textile *n* ткань; *pl* (**~s**) тексти́ль (*m, collect*); *attr*: **a ~ worker** тексти́льщик, ткач.

textual *adj* текстово́й; **a ~ error** текстовáя оши́бка; **~ criticism** текстолóгия.

texture *n* (*of cloth*) тексту́ра; (*of mineral, etc.*) структу́ра.

than *conj* **1** чем (*it may also be translated by G case, when things compared are in nom, but not after compound comparatives*); **I am taller ~ you** я вы́ше тебя́/, чем ты; **my car goes faster ~ yours** моя́ маши́на идёт быстрée твоéй/, чем твоя́; **he is more educated ~ his wife** он бóлее образóван, чем егó женá; **it is easier for me ~ for you** мне э́то лéгче, чем тебé; **that is easier said ~ done** э́то лéгче сказáть, чем сдéлать; **it is less ~ I expected** э́то мéньше, чем я ожидáл; **I would call it blue rather ~ green** я бы э́тот цвет назвáл скорée голубы́м, чем зелёным; **I'll do anything rather ~ give in** я сдéлаю всё, но не уступлю́; **he knows better ~ to deceive me** он не так глуп, чтóбы обмáнывать меня́; **you should know better ~ to say that** тебé слéдовало бы понимáть, что э́того говори́ть не нáдо

2 (*with numerals*) *usu G case*: **more ~ four** бóльше четырёх; **less ~ half** мéньше полови́ны; **I've seen her more ~ once** я не раз ви́дел её

3 other than: I couldn't do other ~ agree мне ничегó не оставáлось, как согласи́ться; **he turned out to be none other ~ my brother** он оказáлся не кем ины́м, как мои́м брáтом

4 no sooner... than: no sooner had I gone outside ~ it started to rain не успéл я вы́йти на у́лицу, как начался́ дождь; *CQ* **no sooner said ~ done!** скáзано—сдéлано!

thank *vt* благодари́ть (по-); **~ you (for your help)** спаси́бо (вам)/(*more formal*) благодарю́ вас (за пóмощь); **~ you very much** большóе (вам) спаси́бо, *iron* благодарю́ покóрно!; **I can't ~ you enough** я не могу́ вам вы́разить мою́ благодáрность; **he should ~ his lucky stars that...** он дóлжен благодари́ть судьбу́ за то, что...; *fig*: **you have him to ~ for the mess** благодари́те егó за всю э́ту пу́таницу; **he only has himself to ~ for it** он сам во всём виновáт.

thankful *adj* благодáрный; **let's be ~ it was no worse** бу́дем и за э́то благодáрны, ведь моглó быть ху́же; **I was ~ that you came/to rest after the journey** я был рад, что ты пришёл/отдохну́ть с дорóги; *CQ* **we must be ~ for small mercies** спаси́бо и на том!

thankfully *adv* благодáрно, с благодáрностью; (*with relief*) с облегчéнием.

thankless *adj* неблагодáрный.

thanks *npl* **1** благодáрность (*sing*); **to express one's ~ for smth** вы́разить благодáрность за что-л; **many ~!** большóе спаси́бо!; **that's all the ~ I get!** вот и вся благодáрность!

2 thanks to: ~ to you/your help благодаря́ вам/вáшей пóмощи; (*in neg sense*) **no ~ to you** вас нé за что благодари́ть; **~ to you/your inefficiency** из-за вас/вáшей нерастorо́пности.

thanksgiving *n* благодарéние; (*US*) **T. Day** день благодарéния.

that *dem adj* (*pl* **those**) тот, та, то, *pl* те; э́тот, э́та, э́то, *pl* э́ти; **not this book but ~ one** не э́та кни́га, а та; **I like ~ book better** мне бóльше нрáвится та (другáя) кни́га; **do you see ~ tower?** ты ви́дишь ту/э́ту бáшню?; **since ~ day** с тогó/э́того дня; **who is ~ man?** кто э́тот человéк?; **whose hat is ~?** чья э́то шля́па?; **in ~ case** в э́том/такóм слу́чае; **~ sort of book** кни́ги такóго рóда; *CQ*: **what about ~ money you owe me?** как насчёт тех дéнег, что ты мне дóлжен?; **how is ~ leg of yours?** как там вáша ногá?; **~ son of yours is a clever lad** а твой сын—у́мный пáрень.

that *dem pron* (*pl* **those**) тот, *etc.*; э́тот, *etc.* [**NB** э́тот, *esp. in form* э́то, *is used much more widely than* тот]; **this car is old but ~ is new** э́та маши́на стáрая, а та—нóвая; **after ~** пóсле тогó/э́того; **those are my children** э́то мои́ дéти; **we talked about this and ~** мы говори́ли о том, о сём; **I looked this way and ~** кудá тóлько я не смотрéл; **~'s true** э́то вéрно; **~'s right!** прáвильно!; **I didn't mean ~** я не то хотéл сказáть; **who/what is ~?** кто/что э́то?; **~ is...** то есть...; **all ~** всё э́то; **and all ~** и всё такóе; **as many as ~** стóлько; **~ I don't know** э́того я не знáю; **and ~ is ~!** вот и всё!; **~ is the train coming now** э́то подхóдит пóезд; **~ is how I met her** вот как я с ней познакóмился; **~ is what they all say** вот что все говоря́т; **~ is what I think** (*in agreement*) и я так ду́маю, (*after giving opinion*) вот что я ду́маю; **if it comes to ~ I shall resign** éсли дойдёт до э́того, я подáм заявлéние; **if it comes to ~ where were you yesterday?** éсли уж на то пошлó, где ты был вчерá?; **we left it at ~** на э́том мы останови́лись; **it's only a copy, and a poor one at ~** э́то тóлько кóпия, да к тому́ же плохáя; **will he come?—T. he will!** он придёт?—Непремéнно!; **did you see him?—T. I did!** ты ви́дел егó?—Ну конéчно!; **~'s just it** в тóм-то и дéло; **~ will do!** довóльно!, хвáтит!; **~'s a good boy!** вот молодéц!; **eat your porridge, ~'s a good boy** ешь кáшу, будь хорóшим мáльчиком.

that *rel pron* котóрый; **this is the man (~) I saw** вот человéк, котóрого я ви́дел; **where is the book (~) I was reading?** где кни́га, котóрую я читáл?; **it's the sort of film (~) I can't bear** э́то фильм из тех, котóрые я терпéть не могу́; **it was at the time (~) war broke out** э́то бы́ло, когдá начала́сь войнá; **not ~ I know of** наскóлько я знáю, нет.

that *adv*: **I have done ~ much** вот ско́лько я сде́лал; **he is only ~ high** он то́лько вот тако́го ро́ста; **I can't do ~ much** я не могу́ сде́лать сто́лько; **I didn't know he was ~ rich** я и не знал, что он так бога́т; **the hall doesn't hold ~ many people** зал вмеща́ет не так уж мно́го люде́й; **I have ~ much work to do** (*and then I'm ready*) мне вот э́то на́до сде́лать.

that *conj* **1** что [**NB** что *may very occasionally be omitted, e. g. after* ка́жется, несомне́нно *and after verbs* бою́сь, наде́юсь]; **I believe (~) you are right** я ве́рю, что ты прав; **~ he made a mistake is now clear** что он оши́бся, э́то тепе́рь я́сно; **it seems (~) he is lying** похо́же, что он лжёт, ка́жется, он солга́л; **supposing (~) he comes** предполо́жим, (что) он придёт; **I will come on condition ~...** я приду́ при том усло́вии, что...; **she was so weak (~) she fainted** она́ была́ так слаба́, что упа́ла в о́бморок; **who is he ~ everyone is afraid of him?** кто он тако́й, что его́ все боя́тся?; **if I seem indifferent it is merely ~ I have a lot on my mind** е́сли я кажу́сь равноду́шным, то э́то про́сто потому́, что у меня́ мно́го други́х забо́т; **it's not ~ I'm bored, but...** мне не то что́бы ску́чно, но...

2 (*indicating purpose*) что́бы; **I came early so (~) we could talk/I could find a place to park** я пришёл пора́ньше, что́бы мы смогли́ поговори́ть/, что́бы найти́ ме́сто для стоя́нки

3 (*in exclamations*): **~ he should treat me so!** что́бы он так посме́л обраща́ться со мной!; **would ~ he were here now!** е́сли бы он был сейча́с здесь!

4 in that: he is right in ~ nothing has been signed, but... он прав, ничего́ ещё не подпи́сано, но...

thatched *adj*: **a ~ roof** соло́менная кры́ша.

thaw *n* о́ттепель, *also fig*.

thaw, *also* **~ out** *vti vt* отта́|ивать (-ять) *vi* (*of snow, ice*) та́ять (рас-); (*of food, etc.*) отта́|ивать (-ять); **it is ~ing** сейча́с та́ет/о́ттепель; *fig*: **I sat by the fire to ~ out** я сел у ками́на, что́бы согре́ться; **after a bottle of wine he ~ed out** по́сле буты́лки вина́ он оживи́лся.

the *def article* **1 the + *noun***: *Russian has no def article, so "the" is often not translated; however for emphasis, and to avoid ambiguity, it is sometimes translated by the dem adjs* э́тот *or* тот; **~ sun is shining** со́лнце сия́ет; **where shall I put ~ table?** где мне поста́вить стол?; **~ owl hunts by night** сова́ охо́тится но́чью; **do you like ~ cake?** вам нра́вится э́тот торт?; **something of ~ kind** что́-то в э́том ро́де; **I was in Rome at ~ time** в то вре́мя я был в Ри́ме; **do you remember ~ time when...** вы по́мните, когда́... (*of an incident*)/то вре́мя, когда́... (*of a period*)

2 the + *adj*: **Catherine ~ Great** Екатери́на Вели́кая; (*forming noun*) **~ young** молодёжь; **within ~ bounds of ~ possible** в преде́лах возмо́жного

3 the + *adv*: **~ sooner ~ better** чем скоре́е, тем лу́чше; (*in reply*) **so much ~ better** тем лу́чше; **now it will be all ~ easier to deceive him** тепе́рь бу́дет ещё ле́гче обману́ть его́

4 *emphatic*: **you don't mean ~ Hemingway?** неуже́ли сам Хемингуэ́й?; **green was ~ colour last year** в про́шлом году́ мо́дным был зелёный цвет; **he's ~ man for ~ job** он са́мый подходя́щий челове́к для э́той рабо́ты

5 *special uses*: **oh ~ pain!** ой, (как) бо́льно!; **~ relief!** како́е облегче́ние!; **~ cheek of it!** на́глость кака́я!; **~ Smiths were here** Сми́ты бы́ли здесь; **he hasn't ~ sense to understand** у него́ не хвата́ет ума́ поня́ть; **how many apples are there to ~ kilo?** ско́лько я́блок в килогра́мме?

theatre, (*US*) **theater** *n* (*place or drama*) теа́тр; **lecture ~** аудито́рия; **operating ~** операцио́нная; *fig* **a ~ of war** теа́тр вое́нных де́йствий.

theatregoer, (*US*) **theatergoer** *n* театра́л.

theatrical *adj* театра́льный, *also fig*.

theft *n* кра́жа; (*abstract*) воровство́.

their *poss adj* **1** их; **~ house** их дом

2 *when the possessor is the subject of the sentence use reflex adj* свой *or omit if ownership obvious*: **they invited all ~ friends** они́ пригласи́ли всех свои́х друзе́й; **they sold ~ house** они́ про́дали дом

3 *referring to parts of body use* себе́ (*dative*), *reflex verb, or omit*: **they both broke ~ legs** они́ о́ба слома́ли себе́ но́ги; **they banged ~ heads on a beam** они́ сту́кнулись голово́й о ба́лку

4 *translated by pers pron + prep*: **I never went to ~ flat** я никогда́ не ходи́л к ним на кварти́ру; **they are still in ~ room** они́ всё ещё у себя́ в ко́мнате; **tears were rolling down ~ cheeks** слёзы кати́лись у них по щека́м.

theirs *poss pron* их; *if referring to the subject of the sentence or clause* свой; **is that record yours or ~ ?** э́то их пласти́нка и́ли ва́ша?; **it is no concern of ~** э́то не их де́ло; **I sold my paintings, but did they sell ~ ?** я про́дал свои́ карти́ны, а они́ свои́ про́дали?; *CQ* **that dog of ~ !** уж э́та их соба́ка!

them *pers pron* **1** (*oblique case of* **they**) *G, A* их, *D* им, *I* и́ми; *after preps* них, *etc.*; **I saw ~** я их ви́дел; **a message from ~** запи́ска от них

2 *when "them" refers to the subject of the sentence use reflex pron* себя́; **they took her with ~** они́ взя́ли её с собо́й

3 *translated by nominative* они́; **that's ~ !** вот они́!; **it wasn't ~** э́то бы́ли не они́; **let ~ come** пусть они́ приду́т.

theme *n* те́ма, *also Mus*; **variations on a ~** вариа́ции на те́му.

themselves 1 *pron of emphasis* са́ми; **they want to see for ~** они́ са́ми хотя́т уви́деть; (*alone*)

they were standing in a corner all by ~ они́ стоя́ли одни́ в углу́

2 *reflex pron* себя́, *etc. or use reflex verb*; **they bought ~ a new car** они́ купи́ли себе́ но́вую маши́ну; **they talked among ~** они говори́ли ме́жду собо́й; **they couldn't justify ~** они́ не могли́ оправда́ть себя́/оправда́ться; **they washed ~ hastily** они́ на́спех умы́лись

3 *phrases*: **they are not ~ today** сего́дня они́ са́ми не свои́; **they keep to ~** они́ де́ржатся за́мкнуто.

then *adj*: **the ~ President** тогда́шний президе́нт; **the ~ ruling party** пра́вившая в то вре́мя па́ртия.

then *adv* **1** (*at that time*) тогда́; в то вре́мя; **he was ~ a waiter** он тогда́/в то вре́мя рабо́тал официа́нтом; **I didn't notice him ~** я тогда́ не заме́тил его́; **from ~ on, since ~** с тех пор, с той поры́, с того́ вре́мени; **until ~** до тех по́р, до того́ вре́мени; **we shall have left by ~** к тому́ вре́мени мы уе́дем; **now and ~** вре́мя от вре́мени; **there and ~** тут же, сра́зу

2 (*next*) пото́м, *less often* зате́м; **and what ~?** а что пото́м?, а да́льше что?; **what did you do ~?** что ты де́лал пото́м?; **~ I went home** пото́м я пошёл домо́й; **he drank his milk and ~ went to bed** он вы́пил молока́ и зате́м лёг спать

3 (*concessive*): **they only gave us a plate of stew and (even) ~ it was cold** они́ по́дали нам то́лько таре́лку рагу́, да и то холо́дного; **it is too expensive, and ~ again I don't have time** э́то сли́шком до́рого, и кро́ме того́/, (да) и к тому́ же у меня́ нет вре́мени; **but ~ I'm not an expert** (да) я к тому́ же и не специали́ст

4 (*in that case*): **if not now ~ later** е́сли не тепе́рь, то попо́зже; **~ why did you come?** тогда́ заче́м ты пришёл?; **you're not coming ~?** зна́чит, ты не придёшь?; **my main idea, ~, is this** моя́ гла́вная мысль, ста́ло быть, такова́; **now ~, what are you doing?** ну́-ка, что ты там де́лаешь?; **well ~, are we all agreed?** ну так что, все согла́сны?; **all right ~, as you like** ну что ж, тогда́ как хоти́те.

thence *adv* (*from there*) отту́да; (*therefore*): **it follows, ~, that...** отсю́да сле́дует, что...

theological *adj* теологи́ческий, богосло́вский.

theorem *n* теоре́ма.

theoretic(al) *adj* теорети́ческий.

theory *n* тео́рия; **in ~** в тео́рии, теорети́чески; **my ~ is that...** по мое́й тео́рии...

therapeutic(al) *adj* терапевти́ческий.

therapy *n* терапи́я.

there *adv* **1** (*of place*) там; (*motion towards*) туда́; **I saw her over ~** я её ви́дел вон там; **put the box ~** поста́вь я́щик там/туда́; **~ and back** туда́ и обра́тно; **we left ~ yesterday** мы уе́хали отту́да вчера́; **so ~ you are!** вот вы где!; **here, ~ and everywhere** и там и сям, везде́, повсю́ду

2 (*indicating*) вот; **those men ~** вот э́ти мужчи́ны; **~ he is** вот он; **~ is the bus** вот и авто́бус, авто́бус идёт; **~ goes the bus—we'll have to wait** авто́бус ушёл—придётся подожда́ть; **~ we were, miles from anywhere, when the engine failed** и вот там, вдали́ от вся́кого жилья́, у нас загло́х мото́р

3 *various*: **you ~!** эй, вы там!; **move along ~!** проходи́те!; **~ you are wrong** тут/здесь вы непра́вы; **I'm always ~ if you need me** я всегда́ здесь, е́сли пона́доблюсь; **~'s gratitude for you!** вот тебе́ и благода́рность!; *CQ* **he is/isn't all ~** у него́ есть голова́ на плеча́х, у него́ не все до́ма

4 there is, there are *see* **be.**

there *interj*: **~, ~, don't cry** ну, ну, не плачь; **~, drink this** вот,/на, вы́пей э́то; **~ you are—I told you not to trust him** ви́дишь, говори́л тебе́—не верь ему́.

thereabouts *adv*: **in Oxford or ~** в О́ксфорде и́ли где́-то вблизи́ него́; **40 guests came or ~** пришло́ со́рок госте́й и́ли о́коло того́.

thereafter *adv* с того́ вре́мени, по́сле э́того.

thereby *adv* таки́м о́бразом; **~ hangs a tale** об э́том есть что порассказа́ть.

therefore *adv* поэ́тому, сле́довательно.

thereon, thereupon *adv* на э́том.

thermal *adj* теплово́й; **~ capacity** теплоёмкость; **~ springs** горя́чие/терма́льные исто́чники.

thermometer *n* термо́метр, гра́дусник.

thermonuclear *adj* термоя́дерный.

thermos *n* те́рмос.

thermostatically *adv*: **~ controlled** с термостати́ческим управле́нием.

thesis *n* (*dissertation*) диссерта́ция; (*proposition*) те́зис.

they *pers pron* (*see also* **them**) они́.

thick *adj* **1** (*of shape*) то́лстый; **a ~ slice** то́лстый ломо́ть; **a ~ book/neck** то́лстая кни́га/ше́я; **the ice is 5 cm ~** лёд толщино́й в пять сантиме́тров; **~ with dust** покры́тый то́лстым сло́ем пы́ли

2 (*of consistency*) густо́й; **~ soup/smoke, a ~ forest** густо́й суп/дым/лес; **the air was ~ with smoke/insults** бы́ло о́чень ды́мно, оскорбле́ния сы́пались со всех сторо́н; **in a ~ voice** хри́плым го́лосом; **a ~ German accent** си́льный неме́цкий акце́нт; **my head feels a bit ~** у меня́ голова́ поба́ливает

3 *CQ uses*: **he's pretty ~** он тупова́т; **they are very ~** они́ закады́чные друзья́; **that's a bit ~** э́то уж сли́шком/чересчу́р.

thick *adv* то́лсто; гу́сто; **he cut the bread ~** он наре́зал хлеб то́лстыми ломтя́ми; **don't put the paint on too ~** не клади́ кра́ску сли́шком гу́сто; **events followed ~ and fast** собы́тия развива́лись стреми́тельно; *fig CQ* **to lay it on ~** сгуща́ть кра́ски.

thicken *vti vt* (*soup, etc.*) де́лать гу́ще (с-), сгу|ща́ть (-сти́ть)

vi: **the fog is ~ing** тума́н сгуща́ется; **whip the cream until it ~s** взбе́йте сли́вки до густоты́; *fig* **the plot ~s** сюже́т усложня́ется.

thicket *n* ча́ща.

thickhead *n* тупи́ца (*m and f*).

thickly *adv*: ~ **cut** то́лсто наре́занный; ~ **spread with butter** гу́сто нама́занный ма́слом; ~ **populated** густонаселённый.

thickness *n* (*breadth*) толщина́; (*density*) густота́; (*layer*) слой; **one metre in** ~ толщино́й в оди́н метр; **three** ~**es of material** три сло́я мате́рии.

thickset *adj* кря́жистый, пло́тный.

thickskinned *adj fig* толстоко́жий.

thief *n* вор; **stop** ~! держи́те во́ра!

thieve *vti* вор*о*ва́ть (с-).

thieving *n* воровство́.

thigh *n* бедро́.

thimble *n* напёрсток.

thin *adj* **1** (*of people*) худо́й, худоща́вый; (*in breadth, etc.*) то́нкий; **a** ~ **face** худо́е лицо́; ~ **paper/wire** то́нкая бума́га/про́волока; **to grow** ~ худе́ть

2 (*in density: sparse*) ре́дкий, (*esp. of liquids*) жи́дкий; ~ **soup** жи́дкий суп; ~ **hair** жи́дкие/ре́дкие во́лосы; **he's getting** ~ **on top** у него́ во́лосы реде́ют; **the audience is a bit** ~ пу́блики малова́то; **doctors are** ~ **on the ground here** здесь ма́ло враче́й; **a** ~ **plot** бе́дный сюже́т.

thin *adv see* **thinly.**

thin *vti vt* (*paint, soup*) разбав|ля́ть (-́ить); *Agric* проре́|живать (-ди́ть); **to** ~ **smb's hair** вы|стрига́ть кому́-л во́лосы (-́стричь)

vi, also **to** ~ **out** (*of hair, crowds, population*) реде́ть (по-); рассе́иваться (*only in impf*).

thine *poss pron see* **yours.**

thing *n* **1** (*object*) вещь; **what's that** ~ **on the shelf?** что э́то (за предме́т) на по́лке?; **I like sweet** ~**s** я люблю́ сла́дкое/сла́дости; **a** ~ **of beauty** предме́т красоты́; **his best** ~**s have been translated into many languages** его́ лу́чшие ве́щи бы́ли переведены́ на мно́гие языки́; **you are seeing** ~**s** тебе́ помере́щилось [**NB** *tense*] (*impers*); *CQ*: **I haven't a** ~ **to wear** мне соверше́нно не́чего наде́ть; **I haven't eaten a** ~ **all day** я це́лый день ничего́ не ел; **I've got the tea** ~**s** я накры́л к ча́ю

2 *pl* (*belongings*) ве́щи; принадле́жности; **where are my** ~**s?** где мои́ ве́щи?; **my painting/shaving/swimming** ~**s** мои́ рисова́льные/бри́твенные/купа́льные принадле́жности

3 *expressions*: **it's a strange** ~ э́то стра́нно; **how are** ~**s?** как дела́?; **as** ~**s stand** при настоя́щем положе́нии дел; **that's how** ~**s are** вот как обстоя́т дела́; **the** ~ **is...** де́ло в том, что...; **that's just the** ~—**he won't listen** в то́м-то и де́ло, что он не жела́ет слу́шать; **one** ~ **led to another** одно́ тяну́ло за собо́й друго́е; **I don't like that sort of** ~ мне подо́бные ве́щи (*pl*) не нра́вятся; **all** ~**s considered, it's better to wait** всё обду́мав, пожа́луй лу́чше подожда́ть; **I have some** ~**s to attend to** мне на́до ко́е-что́ сде́лать, у меня́ есть ко́е-каки́е дела́; **to worry about every little** ~ беспоко́иться из-за ка́ждого пустяка́; **other** ~**s being equal** при про́чих ра́вных усло́виях; **among other** ~**s I don't like him because...** поми́мо всего́ про́чего, мне он не нра́вится, потому́ что...; **(I did) no such** ~! (я не де́лал) ничего́ подо́бного!; **it's a good** ~ **that...** хорошо́, что...; **the best/main** ~ **is to tell him** са́мое лу́чшее/гла́вное—сказа́ть ему́; **the first/next** ~ **he did was to undress** снача́ла/зате́м он разде́лся; **next** ~ **he knew...** он не успе́л опо́мниться, как...; **that's the last** ~ **we want** э́того нам хоте́лось бы ме́ньше всего́; **do it first** ~ **(in the morning)** сде́лай э́то у́тром, как вста́нешь; **the only** ~ **now is to wait** остаётся то́лько ждать; **he always says the wrong** ~ /**the first** ~ **that comes into his head** он всегда́ говори́т не то, что ну́жно/пе́рвое, что взбредёт в го́лову *or* на ум; **to do the right** ~ **by smb** хорошо́ обойти́сь с кем-л; **not a** ~ **escaped him** ничто́ не ускользну́ло от его́ внима́ния; **what a** ~ **to do!** ра́зве так де́лают?; **for one** ~**... and for another** (~)**...** во-пе́рвых..., во-вторы́х...; **he knows a** ~ **or two about cars** он разбира́ется в маши́нах; **that's just the** ~ **(we need)** э́то как раз/и́менно то, что ну́жно; **one can have too much of a good** ~ хоро́шенького понемно́жку; **it's not the done** ~ так не де́лают; **it's the** ~ **to do** так при́нято; *CQ* **he's got a** ~ **about planes** (*likes or hates*) самолёты—его́ пу́нктик

4 (*person*): **poor** ~! бедня́жка! (*m and f*).

think *vti vt* **1** ду́мать (по-); **he didn't** ~ **she had heard him** (*was unsure*) он не ду́мал, что она́ слы́шала его́, (*was unaware*) он ду́мал, что она́ не слы́шала его́; **is he still alive?**—**I** ~ **so** он ещё жив?—(Я) ду́маю, что да; **I thought as much** я так и ду́мал; **what do you** ~ **I should do?** как ты ду́маешь, что мне тепе́рь де́лать?; **so you** ~ **it can't be done** зна́чит, вы ду́маете,/счита́ете, что э́то невозмо́жно; **he** ~**s himself very clever** он счита́ет себя́ о́чень у́мным; **I thought her charming** я находи́л её очарова́тельной; **of course I didn't say anything.**—**I should** ~ **not!** коне́чно, я ничего́ не сказа́л.—Ну ещё бы!

2 (*imagine*): **I would never have thought it of him** я бы в жи́зни тако́е о нём не поду́мал; **to** ~ **that I didn't notice him!** поду́мать то́лько, я не заме́тил его́!; **I can't** ~ **where he might be** (я) не представля́ю себе́, где он мо́жет быть; **I can't** ~ **where I left the bike** не припо́мню/не по́мню, где я мог оста́вить велосипе́д; **who do you** ~ **you are to talk to me like that?** кто ты тако́й, что́бы так со мной говори́ть?

vi **1** (*abstractly*) мы́слить (*impf*); (*general*) ду́мать (по-); **I can't** ~ **clearly** я сейча́с не могу́ мы́слить я́сно; **to** ~ **aloud** размышля́ть/ду́мать вслух; **I accepted without** ~**ing** я согласи́лся, не ду́мая; ~ **twice before replying** поду́май два́жды, пре́жде чем отве́тить; **surely he can** ~ **for himself** разуме́ется, он в состоя́нии сам всё реши́ть; **don't tell him, let him**

~ **for himself** не говори́ ему́, пусть сам доду́мается

2 (*devote thought to*): **he ~s only about himself** он ду́мает то́лько о себе́; **give me time to ~ about it** да́йте мне вре́мя поду́мать над э́тим; **you have given me a lot to ~ about** ты меня́ заста́вил заду́маться о мно́гом; **what were you ~ing about/of to let her out alone?** о чём ты ду́мал, отпуска́я её одну́?; **it's time I was ~ing of leaving** пора́ мне поду́мать об ухо́де; **one has to ~ of the expense** ну́жно ду́мать о расхо́дах

3 (*imagine*): **just ~!, ~ of it!** поду́май!, поду́мать то́лько!; **I would never ~ of asking him** я бы и не поду́мал спроси́ть его́; **he never ~s to help/of helping** он и не поду́мает помо́чь; **you won't tell him?—I wouldn't ~ of it** ты не ска́жешь ему́?—И в мы́слях тако́го нет

4 (*devise*): **don't worry, we'll ~ of something** не беспоко́йся, мы что́-нибудь приду́маем; **what will he ~ of next?** что он ещё приду́мает/вы́думает?

5 (*remember*): **I can't ~ of her name** не могу́ припо́мнить её и́мя; **I'll ~ of it in a minute** сейча́с вспо́мню; **one can't ~ of everything** невозмо́жно всё упо́мнить; **I can't ~ of the right word** ника́к подходя́щее сло́во не прихо́дит на ум, не могу́ подобра́ть ну́жное сло́во

6 (*consider*): **I didn't ~ much of the play** пье́са мне не о́чень понра́вилась; **he ~s well/highly of her** он о ней хоро́шего/высо́кого мне́ния; **have you ever thought of marrying?** а ты не поду́мывал жени́ться?; **we thought better of it** мы переду́мали/разду́мали; **he ~s nothing of working till midnight** рабо́тать до полу́ночи для него́ в поря́дке веще́й

think out *vt* проду́м|ывать, обду́м|ывать (*pfs* -ать); **he likes to ~ things out for himself** он лю́бит сам всё проду́мать/обду́мать; **this problem needs ~ing out** над э́той пробле́мой на́до поду́мать

think over *vt* обду́мывать; **~ it over** обду́май всё хороше́нько

think up *vt*: **to ~ up an excuse** приду́м|ывать/вы́ду́мывать отгово́рку (-ать/вы́думать); **I'll ~ up something** я что́-нибудь приду́маю/*CQ* сообра́жу́.

thinking *n*: **to my way of ~...** на мой взгляд...; **I brought him round to my way of ~** я склони́л его́ к мое́й то́чке зре́ния; **that's wishful ~** э́то зна́чит принима́ть жела́емое за действи́тельное.

thinly *adv* то́нко; (*sparsely*) ре́дко; **~ spread** то́нко нама́занный; **sow the seeds ~** высева́йте/се́йте семена́ ре́дко; **~ populated** малонаселённый; **with ~ disguised contempt** с пло́хо скрыва́емым презре́нием.

third *n* треть; *Mus* те́рция.

third *adj* тре́тий; **the ~ largest** тре́тий по величине́; **~ party** тре́тья сторона́; *Gram* **the ~ person** тре́тье лицо́.

third *adv*: **he came ~** он пришёл тре́тьим, он за́нял тре́тье ме́сто.

thirdly *adv* в-тре́тьих.

third-rate *adj* третьесо́ртный, третьестепе́нный.

thirst *n* жа́жда, *also fig*; **a ~ for knowledge** жа́жда зна́ний (*pl*).

thirsty *adj*: **I am ~** мне хо́чется/я хочу́ пить; **this is ~ work** от э́того хо́чется пить.

thirteen *num* трина́дцать [*see* **eleven**].

thirteenth *adj* трина́дцатый.

thirtieth *adj* тридца́тый.

thirty *num* три́дцать (*G, D, P* тридцати́, *I* тридцатью́).

this *dem adj* (*pl* **these**) э́тот, э́та, э́то, *pl* э́ти; **~ new watch of mine** э́ти мои́ но́вые часы́ (*no sing*); **~ Tuesday I am busy** в э́тот вто́рник я за́нят; **~ time last year** в э́то вре́мя в про́шлом году́; **~ morning/afternoon/evening** сего́дня у́тром/по́сле обе́да/ве́чером; **he turned the handle ~ way and that** он верте́л ру́чку туда́ и сюда́; **he was watching her these ten minutes** он наблюда́л за ней э́ти де́сять мину́т; **everyone is so busy these days** тепе́рь все о́чень за́няты; **one of these days I will look him up** я ка́к-нибудь к нему́ загляну́.

this *dem pron* (*pl* **these**) э́тот, э́та, э́то, *pl* э́ти [**NB this is/these are** *often translated by* э́то]; **what is ~?** что э́то?; **these are my children** э́то мои́ де́ти; **~ is Nina speaking** э́то Ни́на говори́т; **there is my umbrella, but whose is ~?** вот мой зо́нтик, а э́то чей?; **what's all ~?** что э́то тако́е?; **what is all ~ I hear about your leaving?** что э́то я слы́шал—вы уезжа́ете?; **we talked of ~ and that** мы говори́ли о том, о сём; **~ is what I said** вот что я сказа́л; **~ is how I fell** вот как я упа́л; **do it like ~** де́лайте э́то (вот) так; **it was like ~** де́ло бы́ло так.

this *adv*: **I didn't know it was ~ far/as far as ~** я не знал, что так далеко́ идти́; **I can't do/I did ~ much** я не могу́ сто́лько сде́лать, вот ско́лько я сде́лал; **I have read ~ much** я вот доку́да дочита́л; **~ much is certain...** одно́ я́сно...

thistle *n* чертополо́х.

thither *adv mainly arch* туда́; **hither and ~** туда́ и сюда́.

thorn *n* шип, колю́чка; *attr*: **a ~ hedge** колю́чая и́згородь.

thorny *adj* колю́чий; *fig* **a ~ problem** сло́жная пробле́ма.

thorough *adj* (*careful*) тща́тельный; (*detailed*) подро́бный; **a ~ investigation/knowledge of a subject** тща́тельное рассле́дование, основа́тельное зна́ние како́го-л предме́та; **a ~ analysis** подро́бный/всесторо́нний ана́лиз; *CQ* **he's a ~ villain/gentleman** он зако́нченный негодя́й, он настоя́щий дже́нтльмен.

thoroughfare *n* у́лица, магистра́ль; **"No ~"** «Прохо́да/(*for cars*) Прое́зда нет».

thou *pers pron arch* ты, *see* **you.**

though *adv*: **it's not easy ~** э́то, одна́ко, нелегко́; **he's a good worker ~** и всё же/тем не ме́нее он хоро́ший рабо́тник.

though *conj* **1** (*although*) хотя́ и; **I agreed, ~ reluctantly** я согласи́лся, хотя́ и неохо́тно; **~ he is small, he is very strong** хотя́ он и невысо́к ро́стом, но о́чень силён; **strange ~ it may seem** как ни стра́нно

2 (*if*): **I'll do it (even) ~ it kills me** я э́то сде́лаю, хотя́ бы да́же цено́й жи́зни

3: as though как бу́дто; **he is hesitating, as ~ he were afraid** он колеблется, как бу́дто бои́тся чего́-то.

thought *n* **1** мысль; мышле́ние; (*contemplation*) размышле́ние; (*thoughtful mood*) разду́мье; **scientific ~** нау́чная мысль; **train of ~** ход мы́слей (*pl*); **abstract ~** абстра́ктное мышле́ние; **he was deep in ~** он был погружён в размышле́ния (*pl*)/в глубо́ком разду́мье; **after much ~** хороше́нько/серьёзно всё обду́мав...; **I have given it a great deal of ~** я мно́го ду́мал над э́тим; **he takes no ~ for the future** он не ду́мает о бу́дущем

2 (*idea, etc.*) мысль; **that's a ~** э́то мысль; **to collect one's ~s** собра́ться с мы́слями; **at the very ~ of it** при одно́й мы́сли об э́том; **he keeps his ~s to himself** он не де́лится свои́ми мы́слями; **the ~ never occurred to me that...** у меня́ и в мы́слях не́ было, что...; **you must give up all ~ of marrying her** ты и не ду́май жени́ться на ней; **my ~s were elsewhere** мои́ мы́сли вита́ли где́-то; **I didn't give it a second/another ~** я и ду́мать не стал об э́том; **on second ~s** раски́нув умо́м, по зре́лом размышле́нии; **I'm having second ~s about accepting the part** сомнева́юсь, сто́ит ли мне брать э́ту роль; **I was going to dismiss him but then I had second ~s** я уже́ реши́л бы́ло уво́лить его́, но пото́м переду́мал; **perish the ~!** бо́же упаси́!

thoughtful *adj* (*pensive*) заду́мчивый; (*serious*) вду́мчивый; (*considerate*) внима́тельный; **a ~ look** заду́мчивый взгляд; **a ~ student/piece of work** серьёзная/вду́мчивая студе́нтка, серьёзная рабо́та; **he is very ~ towards others** он о́чень внима́телен к други́м; **to become ~** заду́маться.

thoughtless *adj* невнима́тельный; (*careless*) беспе́чный; **it was ~ of you not to thank him** ты забы́л поблагодари́ть его́—как э́то некраси́во.

thousand *num and n* ты́сяча [**NB** *I sing num* ты́сячью, *n* ты́сячей; *for constructions see the following examples*]; **i)** *when used as a numeral*: **2,000/5,000 books** две ты́сячи/пять ты́сяч книг; **3,001/3,005 books** три ты́сячи одна́ кни́га/пять книг; **with two ~/several ~s of roubles** с двумя́/с не́сколькими ты́сячами рубле́й; **in the year 2000/1923** в двухты́сячном году́, в ты́сяча девятьсо́т два́дцать тре́тьем году́; **ii)** *when used fig*: **(with) a ~ apologies** ты́сяча извине́ний!; **a ~ thanks** ты́сяча благода́рностей; **they are produced by the ~** они́ произво́дятся ты́сячами; **I have a ~ and one things to do** мне ну́жно сде́лать ты́сячу дел; **she's one in a ~** така́я же́нщина—одна́ на ты́сячу.

thousandth *adj* ты́сячный; *as n* (**a ~**) одна́ ты́сячная (часть).

thrash *vti vt* изби|ва́ть (́-ть); *Sport* поби́ть (*usu pf*); *fig* **we must ~ out this problem** на́до подро́бно рассмотре́ть э́тот вопро́с

vi: **to ~ about** (*sleeplessly*) мета́ться (*impf*).

thread *n* ни́тка; нить, *also fig*; (*on screw*) резьба́; *fig*: **to lose the ~ of the conversation** потеря́ть нить разгово́ра; **he picked up the ~s of his story** он возобнови́л свой расска́з; **to hang by a ~** висе́ть на волоске́.

thread *vti*: **to ~ a needle** проде|ва́ть ни́тку в иго́лку (́-ть); **to ~ beads** нани́з|ывать бу́сы (-а́ть); **the motorbike ~ed its way through the traffic** мотоци́кл лави́ровал в сплошно́м пото́ке маши́н.

threadbare *adj* (*of clothes only*) изно́шенный, поно́шенный; **a ~ carpet** вы́тертый ковёр.

threat *n* угро́за; **a ~ of war/to civilization** угро́за войны́/цивилиза́ции; **under ~ of** под угро́зой + *G*.

threaten *vti vt* грози́ть (при-), угрожа́ть (*impf*); **he ~ed her with a knife/to leave her** он угрожа́л ей ножо́м, он грози́лся уйти́ от неё; **it is ~ing to rain** похо́же, что бу́дет дождь; **the roof is ~ing to cave in** кры́ша грози́т провали́ться; **pandas are ~ed with extinction** па́ндам грози́т/угрожа́ет вымира́ние

vi: **danger ~ed** нави́сла опа́сность; **a storm is ~ing** надвига́ется бу́ря.

threatening *adj*: **a ~ gesture/letter** угрожа́ющий жест, гро́зное письмо́.

three *num* три (*G*, *P* трёх, *D* трём, *I* тремя́); *collect* тро́е (*G*, *A*, *P* трои́х, *D* трои́м, *I* трои́ми) [*see grammatical notes under* **four**]; (*a 3 in cards, as school mark*) тро́йка; **the best 3 paintings** три лу́чшие/лу́чших карти́ны; **after 3 happy years** по́сле трёх счастли́вых лет; **I have 3 children** у меня́ тро́е дете́й; **with 3 friends** с тремя́ друзья́ми; **there were 3 of us** нас бы́ло тро́е; **a number 3 bus** тре́тий авто́бус; **3 times 3** три́жды три; **it's after 3** уже́ четвёртый час; **300** три́ста (*G* трёхсо́т, *D* трёмста́м, *I* тремяста́ми, *P* о трёхста́х); **3,000** три ты́сячи.

three-cornered *adj* треуго́льный; **a ~ hat** треуго́лка.

three-day *adj* трёхдне́вный.

three-dimensional *adj* трёхме́рный.

threefold *adj* тройно́й.

threefold *adv* втро́е, втройне́.

three-legged *adj* трено́гий.

three-sided *adj* трёхсторо́нний.

three-year *adj* трёхгоди́чный, трёхле́тний; **~ olds** трёхле́тние де́ти.

thresh *vt Agric* молоти́ть (с-).

threshing *n* молотьба́; *attr*: **~ machine** молоти́лка.

threshold *n* поро́г, *also fig*; **to cross the ~** переступи́ть поро́г.

thrift, thriftiness *n* бережли́вость, эконо́мность.

thrifty *adj* бережли́вый, эконо́мный.

thrill *n*: **with a ~ of expectation** в тре́петном ожида́нии; **to feel a ~ of pride** затрепета́ть от го́рдости.

thrill *vt*: **I was ~ed to get your letter** я был стра́шно рад твоему́ письму́.

thriller *n* приключе́нческий *or* детекти́вный рома́н/фильм.

thrilling *adj*: **a ~ film** захва́тывающий фильм; *CQ* **what ~ news!** потряса́ющая но́вость!

thrive *vi* процвета́ть (*impf*); преуспева́ть (*usu impf*); **the business/he is thriving** предприя́тие процвета́ет, он преуспева́ет; **he ~s on hard work** тяжёлая рабо́та ему́ по нра́ву.

throat *n* го́рло; **a lump in the ~** комо́к в го́рле; **to clear one's ~** прочища́ть го́рло, отка́шливаться; *fig*: **the words stuck in my ~** слова́ застря́ли у меня́ в го́рле; **he jumps down my ~ for the least little thing** он гото́в уби́ть меня́ из-за ка́ждого пустяка́.

throb *n* (*of engine*) бие́ние, пульса́ция; (*of music*) вибра́ция.

throb *vi*: **my head/arm/heart is ~bing** у меня́ стучи́т в голове́/рука́ но́ет/се́рдце бьётся; **a ~bing pain** пульси́рующая боль.

throes *npl CQ*: **I'm in the ~ of exams/of packing** я лихора́дочно гото́влюсь к экза́менам/упако́вываю ве́щи.

thrombosis *n Med* тромбо́з; **a coronary ~** инфа́ркт.

throne *n* трон, престо́л; **to come to the ~** вступи́ть на престо́л.

throng *vti vt* заполн|я́ть (-́ить); **the crowd ~ed the foyer/the market place** толпа́ запо́лнила фойе́, на ры́нке толкло́сь мно́жество наро́ду

vi: **people ~ed to see him** посмотре́ть на него́ лю́ди вали́ли то́лпами.

throttle *n Aut*, *Tech* дро́ссель (*m*); *CQ*: **give her a bit more ~** приба́вь газ; **at full ~** на по́лном газу́.

through *adj*: **a ~ train/ticket** прямо́й по́езд/биле́т; **no ~ road** нет (сквозно́го) прое́зда; **~ traffic** сквозно́е движе́ние; **a ~ draught** сквозня́к.

through *adv* **1** насквозь; (*to the end*) до конца́; *or conveyed by prefix* про-; **we got wet ~** мы промо́кли насквозь; **the wood rotted ~** де́рево прогни́ло насквозь; **he is evil ~ and ~** он олицетворе́ние зла; **I read the play (right) ~** я прочёл пье́су (до конца́); **I will see the project ~** я доведу́ э́тот прое́кт до конца́; **they wouldn't let us ~** они́ нас не пропусти́ли; **he got ~ to the second round** он прошёл на второ́й тур; **this jumper is ~ at the elbows** э́тот дже́мпер протёрся на локтя́х; **he heard my speech ~** он прослу́шал мою́ речь; **I'm staying ~ till Tuesday** я пробу́ду до вто́рника

2 *Tel*: **I'll put you ~ to him** я соединя́ю вас с ним; **I couldn't get ~ to him** я не мог до него́ дозвони́ться; **you're ~** говори́те

3 *CQ* (*finished*): **aren't you ~ yet?** ты ещё не ко́нчил?; **don't go, I'm not ~ with you yet** не уходи́те, я с ва́ми ещё не зако́нчил; **I am ~ with her** я порва́л с ней.

through *prep* **1** (*of place*: *through an obstruction*) сквозь + *A*; (*across*) че́рез + *A*, в + *A*; (*over area of*) по + *D*; **~ the smoke/noise of the crowd** сквозь дым/шум толпы́; **we pushed ~ the crowd** мы проти́снулись сквозь толпу́; **~ the keyhole** сквозь/че́рез замо́чную сква́жину; **to look ~ a window/~ a telescope** смотре́ть в окно́/в телеско́п; **he came in ~ the kitchen** он вошёл че́рез ку́хню; **a path ~ the forest** тропи́нка че́рез лес; **to wander ~ the streets** броди́ть по у́лицам; **I saw ~ him/his trick** я ви́дел его́ насквозь, я разгада́л его́ трюк

2 *conveyed by prefix* про-: **to look ~ the accounts** просмотре́ть счета́; **he drove ~ the lights at red** он прое́хал на кра́сный свет

3 (*of time*): **right ~ the night/his life** всю ночь, всю его́ жизнь; **we were half-way ~ supper when...** мы уже́ почти́ поу́жинали, когда́...; (*US*) **from Monday ~ Friday** с понеде́льника по пя́тницу

4 (*of means*) че́рез + *A*; по + *D*; **~ an interpreter** че́рез перево́дчика; **he found the flat ~ friends** он нашёл кварти́ру че́рез друзе́й; **~ ignorance** по неве́дению; **~ no fault of yours** не по твое́й вине́; **it was ~ you that we were late** мы опозда́ли из-за вас.

throughout *adv* (*of place*): **the house is furnished ~/needs painting ~** дом по́лностью обста́влен, дом нужда́ется в покра́ске; (*of time*): **the weather was good ~** всё вре́мя стоя́ла хоро́шая пого́да.

throughout *prep* (*of place*): **~ the world** по всему́ ми́ру; (*of time*): **~ the year** весь год, в тече́ние всего́ го́да.

throw *n* (*of dice*, *javelin*, *in wrestling*) бросо́к; *fig* **it is within a stone's ~ of here** э́то отсю́да руко́й пода́ть.

throw *vt* **1** брос|а́ть (-́ить), кида́ть (ки́нуть) *and compounds*; **the horse threw her** ло́шадь сбро́сила её; **he threw the ball into the air/his things into a case** он (под)бро́сил мяч вверх, он побросал свои́ ве́щи в чемода́н; **he threw open the door/window/the lid of the box** он распахну́л дверь/окно́, он отки́нул кры́шку сундука́; **she threw her arms round his neck** она́ бро́силась ему́ на ше́ю; **they were ~ing a ball about/to each other** они́ перебра́сывались мячо́м; **he threw the ball through the window** он забро́сил мяч в окно́; **he threw a plate at her** он бро́сил в неё таре́лкой; **he threw himself on to his knees** он бро́сился на коле́ни; (*with dice*) **he threw two sixes** он вы́бросил две шестёрки; *Sport*: **he threw his opponent** он бро́сил проти́вника на ковёр; **to ~ the discus/javelin** мет|áть диск/копьё (-нýть)

2 *fig uses*: **to ~ smb into jail** брóсить когó-л в тюрьмý; **to ~ a glance at** брóсить/кúнуть взгляд на + *A*; **to ~ a shadow** бросáть/отбрáсывать тень; **to ~ the blame on smb** валúть винý на когó-л (с-); **to ~ light on smth** проли|вáть свет на что-л (-́ть); **to ~ doubt(s)/suspicion on smth** стáвить что-л под сомнéние (*sing*) (по-), навле|кáть подозрéние на что-л (-́чь); **he threw himself wholeheartedly into the work** он с головóй ушёл в рабóту; *CQ*: **to ~ a party** устрóить вéчер; **I nearly threw a fit when I heard** я чуть в óбморок не упáл, когдá об э́том услы́шал

throw about *vt* (*toys, clothes, etc.*) разбр|áсывать (-осáть), раскúд|ывать (-áть); **to ~ one's money about** сорúть/швыря́ть деньгáми (*only in impfs*); **to ~ one's weight about** задавáться (*impf*)

throw away *vt* вы|брáсывать (-́бросить), *also fig*; **you are ~ing yourself away if you marry him** ты загýбишь свою́ жизнь, éсли вы́йдешь за негó (зáмуж); **to ~ away an opportunity** упус|кáть возмóжность (-тúть)

throw in *vt*: **with the spare wheel ~n in** с запасны́м колесóм в придáчу; *Cards* **to ~ in one's hand** брóсить кáрты (на стол), *fig* спасовáть (*pf*); **he threw in his lot with us** он связáл свою́ судьбý с нáми

throw off *vt* сбрáсывать (сбрóсить); **to ~ off one's clothes/the blanket** сбрóсить *or* скúнуть с себя́ одéжду/одея́ло; **to ~ dogs off the scent** сбить собáк со слéда; **to ~ off smb's influence/an illness** избáвиться от чьегó-л влия́ния/от болéзни (*usu pf*)

throw on *vt*: **to ~ on some clothes** набрóсить на себя́ одéжду; **~ some more wood on the stove** подбрóсь дров в пéчку

throw out *vt* **1** (*discard*) вы|брáсывать (-́бросить), вы|кúдывать (-́кинуть); **to ~ out rubbish** вы́бросить мýсор; **he was ~n out on to the street** егó вы́кинули на ýлицу; **to ~ out a suggestion** отверг|áть предложéние (-́нуть)

2 (*put forward*): **to ~ out a hint about smth** намек|áть на что-л (-нýть); **to ~ out ideas/suggestions** вы|двигáть идéи/предложéния (-́двинуть); *Bot* **to ~ out shoots** выбрáсывать побéги

3 (*upset*): **this threw out our calculations** э́то опрокúнуло нáши расчёты

throw over *vt*: **he has ~n her over for someone else** он брóсил её рáди другóй

throw together *vt*: **he threw his things together** он нáскоро собрáл свои́ пожúтки; **they were ~n together by circumstances** их свелú обстоя́тельства

throw up *vti vt*: **he threw the ball up** он подбрóсил мяч; **he threw up his hands in astonishment** он всплеснýл рукáми в изумлéнии; *fig* **to ~ up one's job** брóсить свою́ рабóту

vi: **he threw up** егó вы́рвало (*impers*).

thrush *n* дрозд.

thrust *vt* **1** (*insert*) совáть (сýнуть), за|сóвывать (-сýнуть); (*pierce*) втыкáть (воткнýть); (*push aside*) от|тáлкивать (-толкнýть); **he ~ a coin into my hand** он сýнул мне в рýку монéту; **he ~ his head out of the window** он вы́сунул гóлову в окнó; **to ~ a stick into the ground/a dagger into smb's back** втыкáть пáлку в зéмлю, втыкáть/вонзáть комý-л кинжáл в спúну; **I ~ him aside** я егó оттолкнýл

2 *fig* (*impose*) навя́з|ывать (-áть); **to ~ advice/responsibility on smb** навя́зываться *or* лезть к комý-л с совéтами (*only in impfs*), навязáть комý-л отвéтственность; **to ~ oneself on smb** навя́зываться комý-л; **he ~ aside all objections** он отбрóсил все возражéния.

thrusting *adj* (*of person*) напóристый.

thud *n* (глухóй) стук; **the ~ of hooves** стук копы́т; **to fall with a ~** упáсть с (глухúм) стýком; **the book dropped to the floor with a ~** книга грóхнулась нá пол.

thug *n* головорéз.

thumb *n* большóй пáлец (рукú); *fig*: **he's under her ~** он у неё под башмакóм; **my fingers are all ~s today** сегóдня у меня́ рýки как крю́ки.

thumb *vt*: **to ~ through a book** перелúст|ывать кнúгу (-áть); **he was trying to ~ a lift** он голосовáл на дорóге; **he ~ed a lift to London** он доéхал до Лóндона на попýтной машúне.

thumbnail *n* нóготь (*m*) большóго пáльца рукú; *fig* **a ~ sketch** крáткое описáние.

thump *n* (*blow*) удáр, тумáк; (*sound*) глухóй стук; **he gave me a ~ on the back** он дал мне тумакá, (*if in greeting, or to stop choking*) он хлóпнул меня́ по спинé.

thump *vti vt* сту|чáть (-́кнуть); **to ~ the table** стучáть по столý (по-); **to ~ out a rhythm** высту́кивать ритм (*impf*)

vi: **his heart/head was ~ing** у негó сéрдце колотúлось/в головé стучáло (*impers*); **he ~ed on the door** он колотúл в дверь.

thunder *n* гром; (*of traffic, guns, hooves*) грóхот.

thunder *vi* гремéть (*impf*); **it was ~ing** гремéл гром; **his voice ~ed in my ears** егó гóлос гудéл у меня́ в ушáх; **lorries ~ed past** грузовикú громыхáли мúмо.

thunderclap *n* удáр/раскáт грóма.

thundercloud *n* тýча.

thunderstorm *n* грозá.

thunderstruck *adj*: **~ by the news** ошеломлённый э́той нóвостью.

thundery *adj* (*of weather*) грозовóй.

Thursday *n* четвéрг.

thus *adv* так, такúм óбразом; (*resuming narrative*) итáк, такúм óбразом; **he sat ~** он сел вот так; **he began ~** он нáчал так/слéдующим óбразом; **~ I was unable to attend** стáло быть, я не мог там присýтствовать; **~ far everything is all right** покá всё нормáльно.

thwart *vt*: **to ~ smb's plans** меша́ть чьим-л пла́нам (по-); **I was ~ed at every turn** я встреча́л препя́тствия на ка́ждом шагу́.

thyroid *adj Anat*: **~ gland** щитови́дная железа́.

tic *n Med* тик.

tick[1] *n Zool* клещ.

tick[2] *n* **1** (*of clock*) ти́канье; **~-tock** тик-та́к

2 *CQ* (*moment*) мину́точка; **just a ~!** мину́точку!; **I'll be with you in a ~** я сейча́с приду́; **he'll do it in two ~s** он э́то сде́лает в два счёта.

tick[2] *vi* ти́кать (*impf*); *fig*: **the hours ~ed slowly away** вре́мя тяну́лось ме́дленно; **let the engine ~ over to warm it up** оста́вь мото́р на холосто́м ходу́, что́бы он прогре́лся.

tick[3] *n* (*mark*) га́лочка.

tick[3] *vt*: **to ~ the correct answer/items off a list** отме|ча́ть пра́вильные отве́ты/пу́нкты в спи́ске (-́тить); *CQ* **to ~ smb off** отруга́ть кого́-л (*pf*).

tick[4] *n CQ* креди́т; **to buy smth on ~** купи́ть что-л в креди́т.

ticket *n* биле́т; (*coupon*) тало́н; **bus/theatre/concert ~** авто́бусный биле́т, биле́т в теа́тр/на конце́рт; **complimentary ~** контрама́рка; **meal ~** тало́н на пита́ние; **cloakroom ~** номеро́к; **price ~** це́нник; *attr*: **~ collector** *or* **inspector/office** контролёр, биле́тная ка́сса.

ticking *n* (*of clock*) ти́канье.

tickle *n* щекота́ние; **I've a ~ in my throat** у меня́ в го́рле перши́т (*impers*).

tickle *vti vt* щекота́ть (по-), *also fig*; *fig* **it ~d his vanity** э́то щекота́ло его́ самолю́бие; **his story ~d us** (*CQ* **pink**) его́ расска́з нас о́чень позаба́вил

vi щекота́ть (*impers*); **my nose ~s** у меня́ щеко́чет в носу́; **it ~s!** щеко́тно!; **this wool ~s** э́та шерсть ко́лется.

ticklish *adj*: *fig* **a ~ problem** щекотли́вый вопро́с.

tidal *adj*: **~ wave** прили́вная волна́; **~ basin** прили́вный бассе́йн; **~ river** прили́во-отли́вная река́.

tiddler *n CQ* (*fish*) рыбёшка.

tiddly *adj* (*tiny*) кро́шечный; *CQ* (*drunk*) под му́хой, навеселе́ (*adv*).

tide *n*: **high ~** прили́в; **low ~** отли́в; **the ~ is coming in/going out** сейча́с прили́в/отли́в; **what time is high/low ~?** когда́ сего́дня по́лная/ма́лая вода́?

tide *vt CQ*: **this money will ~ me over till I get paid** на э́ти де́ньги я перебью́сь до зарпла́ты.

tidy *adj* (*of person*) опря́тный; (*of rooms, etc.*) при́бранный; **is your room ~?** у тебя́ в ко́мнате при́брано?; **a ~ desk/handwriting** аккура́тно при́бранный стол, чёткий по́черк; *CQ* **a ~ sum** изря́дная/прили́чная су́мма де́нег.

tidy *vt*, *also* **to ~ up** у|бира́ть, (*quickly*) при|бира́ть (*pfs* -бра́ть), при|води́ть в поря́док (-вести́); **to ~ a room** убра́ть/прибра́ть ко́мнату *or* в ко́мнате, привести́ ко́мнату в поря́док; **to ~ one's books away** убра́ть свои́ кни́ги; **to ~ oneself** привести́ себя́ в поря́док; **to ~ out a drawer** навести́ поря́док/прибра́ться в я́щике.

tie *n* (*necktie*) га́лстук; (*cord*) шнур; (*twine*) бечёвка; (*US*: *Rail*) шпа́ла; *fig* **~s of friendship, family ~s** дру́жеские/семе́йные у́зы.

tie *vti vt* **1** свя́з|ывать (-а́ть) *and other compounds*; **to ~ smb to a tree** привя́зывать кого́-л к де́реву; **to ~ smb's hands/smb hand and foot** связа́ть кому́-л ру́ки/кого́-л по рука́м и нога́м, *both also fig*; **to ~ a knot/bow in smth** завяза́ть что-л узло́м/ба́нтом; **to ~ a tie** завяза́ть/повяза́ть га́лстук; **to ~ one's shoelaces** завяза́ть шнурки́; **he ~d his things into a bundle** он связа́л/увяза́л свои́ ве́щи в у́зел

2 *fig uses*: **we are ~d by the rules/because of the children** мы свя́заны пра́вилами/детьми́; **I am ~d to these dates/to the house all day** в э́ти дни я за́нят, и ничего́ измени́ть нельзя́, я бу́ду за́нят(а́) хозя́йством це́лый день

vi Sport: **we ~d with them 3—all** мы сыгра́ли вничью́, 3:3; **I ~d with him for second place** мы с ним подели́ли второ́е ме́сто; *Polit* **the two candidates ~d** о́ба кандида́та получи́ли ра́вное число́ голосо́в

tie down *vt* свя́зывать; *fig*: **he won't be ~d down** он не жела́ет себя́ свя́зывать; **I am ~d down for several months** я бу́ду за́нят не́сколько ме́сяцев; **I am trying to ~ him down to next Tuesday** я постара́юсь заполучи́ть его́ к сле́дующему вто́рнику

tie in *vi fig*: **that doesn't ~ in with your theory** э́то не вя́жется с твое́й тео́рией; **can you ~ this in with your trip to London?** ты мо́жешь приуро́чить э́то к свое́й пое́здке в Ло́ндон?

tie on *vt*: **to ~ a label on (smth)** привяза́ть би́рку (к чему́-л)

tie up *vt*: **to ~ up a dog/prisoner** привяза́ть соба́ку, связа́ть плéнного; **to ~ up a dinghy/a parcel** привяза́ть ло́дку, перевяза́ть посы́лку; *fig*: **everything is ~d up now** тепе́рь всё решено́; **his money is all ~d up in property** все его́ де́ньги вло́жены в со́бственность; **he's ~d up with the director just now** он сейча́с у дире́ктора.

tie-on *adj*: **a ~ label** привязна́я би́рка, привязно́й ярлы́к.

tiepin *n* була́вка для га́лстука.

tier *n* я́рус.

tiff *n CQ* размо́лвка.

tight *adj* туго́й; (*stretched tight*) натя́нутый; (*cramped*) те́сный; **a ~ cork** туга́я про́бка; **a ~ knot** ту́го затя́нутый у́зел; **this jacket is ~ across the shoulders** э́тот пиджа́к те́сен в плеча́х; **these shoes are ~** э́ти ту́фли жмут; **is the screw/rope ~?** винт ту́го зави́нчен?, кана́т ту́го натя́нут?; **is the dinghy ~?** (*watertight*) ло́дка не течёт?; **a ~ hug** кре́пкое объя́тие; **to keep a ~ hold on smb** кре́пко держа́ть кого́-л; **it was a ~ squeeze to fit everyone into the car** пришло́сь потесни́ться, что́бы все помести́лись в маши́не; *fig*: **I have a ~ schedule** у меня́ напряжённый режи́м рабо́ты; **to keep a ~ rein on expenditure** стро́го контроли́ровать расхо́ды; **we're in a ~ spot** нам сейча́с ту́го прихо́дится; **money is ~ these days** с деньга́ми сейча́с тугова́то; **he is ~** (*with his money*/ *CQ drunk*) он прижи́мист, он си́льно навеселе́ (*adv*).

tight *adv*, *also* **tightly: to tie/draw smth ~** ту́го завяза́ть/затяну́ть что-л; **screw the cap on ~** ту́го завинти́ кры́шку; **to squeeze smb's hand ~** кре́пко жать чью-л ру́ку; **the door was ~ shut** дверь была́ пло́тно закры́та; *CQ*: **hold tight, we're off!** держи́тесь, мы пое́хали!; **just sit tight and see what happens** сиди́те и жди́те, как разверну́тся собы́тия.

tighten *vti vt*, *also* **~ up: to ~ a rope/ one's belt/a screw** натя́|гивать кана́т, затя́|гивать по́яс (*pfs* -ну́ть), зави́н|чивать винт (-ти́ть); **to ~ one's grip on smth** ещё кре́пче сжима́ть что-л (сжать); **to ~ restrictions** на|лага́ть бо́лее стро́гие ограниче́ния (-ложи́ть)

vi: **ropes ~ when wet** мо́крые кана́ты натя́гиваются; **to ~ up on discipline** стро́же соблюда́ть дисципли́ну (*impf*).

tight-fitting *adj* (*of lid*, *etc*.) туго́й, пло́тный; (*of clothes*) в обтя́жку.

tightly *adv see* **tight** *adv*.

tights *npl* колго́тки; *Theat*, *Sport* трико́ (*indecl*).

tile *n* (*for roof*) черепи́ца; (*for wall*, *stove*, *floor*) ка́фель (*m*), (*decorative*) изразе́ц.

tile *vt*: **to ~ a roof/wall** покры|ва́ть кры́шу черепи́цей/сте́ну ка́фелем (-ть).

tiled *adj* (*of roof*) черепи́чный; (*of wall*, *stove*, *floor*) ка́фельный, (*if with decorative tiles*) изразцо́вый.

till[1] *vt Agric* возде́л|ывать (-ать), обраб|а́тывать (-о́тать).

till[2] *n* ка́сса.

till[3] *prep and conj see* **until**.

tiller *n Naut* ру́мпель (*m*).

tilt *n*: **he ran full ~ into a wall** он на по́лном ходу́ вре́зался в сте́ну.

tilt *vti* (*of table*, *jug*, *chair*, *etc*.) наклон|я́ть(ся) (-и́ться).

timber *n* (*material*) лесоматериа́л, древеси́на; **standing ~** лес на корню́; **~s** (*beams*) брёвна (*pl*); *attr*: **~ merchant** лесопромы́шленник.

timbre *n Mus* тембр.

time *n* **1** (*general*) вре́мя; **as ~ goes on** с тече́нием вре́мени; **you will understand in ~** ты поймёшь со вре́менем; **since ~ immemorial** с незапа́мятных времён, испоко́н веко́в; **as old as ~** ста́рый как мир; **~ was when...** бы́ло вре́мя, когда́...; **he is playing for ~** он тя́нет вре́мя

2 (*free time*, *leisure*): **my ~ is my own** я хозя́ин своего́ вре́мени; **in my spare** *or* **free ~** в свобо́дное вре́мя, на досу́ге; **there's plenty of ~** вре́мени мно́го; **I've ~ on my hands** у меня́ есть вре́мя; **that doesn't leave much ~ for shopping** у нас остаётся ма́ло вре́мени на поку́пки; **I've no ~ to be bored**/*fig* **for him** у меня́ нет вре́мени скуча́ть, я не жела́ю его́ ви́деть; **there's no ~ to lose** нельзя́ теря́ть вре́мя; **he lost no ~ replying** он не заме́длил с отве́том; **you're wasting my ~** я тра́чу на тебя́ вре́мя впусту́ю (*adv*); **take your ~** не торопи́сь!; **it takes ~ to get to know him** ну́жно вре́мя, что́бы узна́ть его́ полу́чше; **they always take their ~ over meals** они́ всегда́ до́лго едя́т/ сидя́т за столо́м; **did you have a good ~ at the Smiths?** вы хорошо́ провели́ вре́мя у Сми́тов?; **we had the ~ of our lives** мы весели́лись как никогда́ в жи́зни

3 (*epoch*, *period*): **he was a famous singer in his ~** он был изве́стным певцо́м в своё вре́мя; **in former ~s** в пре́жние времена́; **at my ~ of life** в моём во́зрасте, в мои́ го́ды; **in ~s past/to come** в про́шлом *or* в старину́, в бу́дущем (*sings*); **in the ~ of Elizabeth I** при Елизаве́те I; **he's ahead of his ~** он опереди́л свою́ эпо́ху/свой век; **to keep up with the ~s** идти́ в но́гу со вре́менем (*sing*); **these are hard ~s** сейча́с наступи́ли тяжёлые времена́

4 (*period*, *interval*) вре́мя: **half the ~ he wasn't even listening** бо́льшую часть вре́мени он про́сто не слу́шал; **he knew all the ~** он всё вре́мя э́то знал; **I did it in half the ~** я э́то сде́лал в два ра́за быстре́е; **after a ~** че́рез не́которое вре́мя, спустя́ вре́мя; **we waited for a long/a short/some ~** мы жда́ли до́лго/недо́лго/не́которое вре́мя; **he's gone away for a ~/a long ~/some ~** он уе́хал на вре́мя/надо́лго/на не́которое вре́мя; **you were a long ~ making coffee** ты до́лго гото́вил ко́фе; **my spectacles were there all the ~** я иска́л очки́, а они́ всё вре́мя лежа́ли на ви́дном ме́сте; **we've been waiting a long ~** мы давно́ жда́ли; **for hours at a ~** часа́ми (подря́д); **for some ~ now** уже́ давно́; **a short ~ ago** неда́вно; **I'll stay here for the ~ being** я пока́/*CQ* пока́ что оста́нусь здесь; **in a short ~** ско́ро, в ско́ром вре́мени; **in two days' ~** че́рез два дня; **come/let me know in good ~** приходи́ пора́ньше, дай мне знать зара́нее; **we set off in good ~** мы отпра́вились зара́нее/заблаговре́менно; *CQ* **in no ~ at all** в два счёта

5 (*season*) вре́мя; **September is the ~ for plums/ to be in Scotland** сентя́брь—вре́мя созрева́ния слив/—са́мое вре́мя побыва́ть в Шотла́ндии; **it's a lovely ~ of year** э́то чуде́сное вре́мя го́да; **there's a ~ and place for everything** всему́ своё вре́мя и ме́сто

6 (*term*) срок; **when the ~ is up** по истече́нии сро́ка; **within the ~ agreed** к устано́вленному сро́ку; **he has done his ~ in the army** он отслужи́л свой срок в а́рмии; **to do ~** (*in prison*) отбыва́ть срок

7 (*point in time*) вре́мя; **the ~ has come to tell you** пришло́ вре́мя сказа́ть тебе́; **when the**

~ came, he was indifferent а когда́ подошло́ вре́мя, ему́ ста́ло безразли́чно; **a ~ came when...** наступи́ло вре́мя, когда́...; **at the present ~** в да́нное/в настоя́щее вре́мя; **at the/that ~** в то вре́мя, в ту по́ру, тогда́; **at one ~** одно́ вре́мя, когда́-то; **we've met him at various ~s** мы встреча́лись с ним в ра́зное вре́мя (*sing*); **at (certain) ~s** иногда́, времена́ми, по времена́м; **at all ~s** всегда́; **at the same ~** одновре́ме́нно, в то же вре́мя, *also fig*; **you came just at the right ~** ты пришёл как раз во́время; **by the ~ we got there/by that ~ he had left** когда́ мы прие́хали, его́ уже́ не́ было, к тому́ вре́мени он уже́ уе́хал; **by this ~ he should be there** к э́тому вре́мени он уже́ бу́дет там; **from that ~ on** с того́ вре́мени, с тех пор; **from ~ to ~** вре́мя от вре́мени; **until such ~ as he agrees** пока́ он не согласи́тся

8 (*appropriate time*) пора́; **it's high ~ you got up** тебе́ давно́ пора́ встава́ть; **he's had his hair cut, and about ~ too** он подстри́гся— давно́ пора́

9 (*occasion*) раз; **this/last/next ~** (на) э́тот/(в) про́шлый/(в) сле́дующий раз; **for the first/last ~** в пе́рвый/в после́дний раз; **the first ~ (that) I did it** пе́рвый раз, когда́ я э́то сде́лал; **I've been here several ~s** я не раз/я не́сколько раз быва́л здесь; **~ after ~, ~ and again** сно́ва и сно́ва; **many's the ~ I watched her** мно́го раз я наблюда́л за ней; **third ~ lucky** на/в тре́тий раз повезёт; **do you remember that ~ when...** ты по́мнишь, когда́ в тот раз...; **nine ~s out of ten he lost** в девяти́ слу́чаях из десяти́ он проигра́л; **one at a ~** по одному́; **don't try to do two things at a ~** не бери́сь за два де́ла сра́зу; **he took three oranges at a ~** он взял сра́зу три апельси́на; **he ran up the stairs two at a ~** он взбежа́л по ле́стнице, пры́гая че́рез ступе́ньку

10 (*on clock*): **to tell the ~** сказа́ть, ско́лько вре́мени; **what's the ~?** ско́лько (сейча́с) вре́мени?, кото́рый час?; **what ~ do you make it?** ско́лько (вре́мени) на ва́ших часа́х?; **he looked at the ~** он посмотре́л на часы́; **the ~ is 5.30** сейча́с полови́на шесто́го/*CQ* полшесто́го; **the time was 5.45** бы́ло без че́тверти шесть; **at this ~ of night** в э́тот час но́чи; **at any ~ of the day or night** в любо́е вре́мя дня и но́чи; **what ~ does the train leave?** когда́ отправле́ние по́езда?; **did you find out the ~s of the trains?** ты узна́л расписа́ние поездо́в?; **the train arrived on ~/five minutes ahead of/behind ~** по́езд при́был во́время/на пять мину́т ра́ньше, по́езд опозда́л на пять мину́т; **we were only just in ~ for the concert** мы е́ле-е́ле успе́ли на конце́рт; **were you in ~?** вы успе́ли?; **this watch keeps good ~** э́ти часы́ (*no sing*) хорошо́ иду́т; *fig* **to pass the ~ of day with smb** поздоро́ваться с кем-л

11 *Math*: **3 ~s 3 is 9** три́жды три—де́вять; **6 ~s 5 are 30** шесть на пять/ше́стью пять—три́дцать; **5 ~s faster/as big** в пять раз быстре́е/бо́льше

12 *Mus*: **to beat ~** отбива́ть такт; **in 3/4 ~** в те́мпе три четвёртых; **in ~ with the music** в такт му́зыке.

time *vt*: **he ~d his entrance well** он хорошо́ вы́брал моме́нт для своего́ появле́ния; **that remark was well ~d** э́то замеча́ние бы́ло своевре́менным/о́чень кста́ти (*adv*); **he ~d his journey so as to arrive before dark** он рассчита́л вре́мя на доро́гу так,/он подгада́л так, что́бы прие́хать до темноты́; **that was well ~d—we're just ready to eat** ты как раз во́время—мы собира́емся обе́дать; **the book was ~d to coincide with the release of the film** опубликова́ние кни́ги бы́ло приуро́чено к вы́ходу фи́льма на экра́н; *Sport* **to ~ smb/a race** засе|ка́ть чьё-л вре́мя/вре́мя го́нок (*pl*) (-'чь).

time bomb *n* бо́мба с часовы́м механи́змом.

time-lag *n* отстава́ние; заде́ржка.

timeless *adj* бесконе́чный, ве́чный.

time limit *n* преде́льный срок.

timely *adj* своевре́менный.

time-saving *adj*: **a ~ device** приспособле́ние, эконо́мящее вре́мя.

time sheet *n* та́бель (*m*) (учёта).

timetable *n* расписа́ние.

timework *n* почасова́я рабо́та.

timid *adj* ро́бкий, боязли́вый.

timing *n* (*Sport*, *in industry*) хронометри́рование, хронометра́ж; **the ~ of the elections is important** о́чень ва́жно назна́чить вы́боры в ну́жный моме́нт; **a good sense of ~** уме́ние вы́брать ну́жное вре́мя.

tin *n* **1** (*metal*) о́лово; *attr*: **~ soldier** оловя́нный солда́тик

2 (*container*) консе́рвная ба́нка, жестя́нка; **a sardine ~** жестя́нка из-под сарди́н; **a baking ~** про́тивень.

tin *vt* консерви́ровать (*impf and pf*).

tinfoil *n* фо́льга.

ting-a-ling *interj* динь-ди́нь.

tinge *n* окра́ска; *fig* тень, отте́нок.

tinged *adj*: **the sky was ~ with red** не́бо име́ло краснова́тый отте́нок; **his voice was ~ with envy** в его́ то́не звуча́ли/слы́шались зави́стливые но́тки.

tinker *vi CQ* вози́ться (по-), копа́ться (по-); **he's ~ing with the car/the radio** он во́зится с маши́ной, он копа́ется в приёмнике.

tinkle *n* звя́канье, звон; *CQ* **I'll give you a ~ tomorrow** я вам за́втра звя́кну.

tinkle *vti* звя́к|ать + *I* (-нуть); **he ~d the bell** он позвони́л/звя́кнул колоко́льчиком; **the door bell ~d** звя́кнул дверно́й звоно́к.

tinned *adj* консерви́рованный.

tin opener *n* консе́рвный нож.

tinplate *n* бе́лая жесть; полу́да; *attr* жестяно́й, лужёный.

tinsel *n* мишура́.

tint *n* (*dye*) кра́ска.

tint *vt*: **she ~s her hair red** она́ подкра́шивает во́лосы хной.

tintack *n* коро́ткий гвоздь (*m*).

tiny *adj* кро́шечный, малю́сенький.

tip[1] *n* (*of cigar, finger, etc.*) ко́нчик; (*if added—e. g. of walking stick*) наконе́чник; (*of mountain*) верши́на; *fig*: **from ~ to toe** с головы́ до ног; **I had it on the ~ of my tongue** э́то у меня́ верте́лось на ко́нчике языка́; **this is just the ~ of the iceberg** э́то то́лько нача́ло.

tip[2] *n* (*for rubbish*) сва́лка.

tip[2] *vt*: **he ~ped the contents of the drawer on to the table** он вы́валил содержи́мое (*sing*) я́щика на стол; **the lorry ~ped the rubbish on the dump** самосва́л вы́грузил му́сор на сва́лку; (*of liquids*) **to ~ water from a barrel into a jug** нали|ва́ть во́ду из бо́чки в кувши́н (-́ть); **he ~s the scales at 70 kg** он ве́сит се́мьдесят килогра́ммов

tip back *vt*: **he ~ped his chair back** он раска́чивался на сту́ле

tip out *vt* выва́ливать; **they ~ped out the rubbish** они́ вы́валили му́сор

tip over/up *vti* (*accidentally or on purpose*) опроки́|дывать(ся) (-нуть(ся)); **to ~ up the barrel to empty it** опроки́нуть бо́чку, что́бы вы́лить содержи́мое.

tip[3] *n* **1** (*gratuity*) чаевы́е (*pl*); **I gave him a ~** я дал ему́ на чай

2 (*hint*) намёк, (*advice*) сове́т; **I'll give you a ~** я вам дам ма́ленький сове́т.

tip[3] *vti vt* **1**: **he ~ped him a dollar** он дал ему́ до́ллар на чай

2 (*in racing, etc.*): **this horse is ~ped to win** э́та ло́шадь счита́ется фавори́том; *fig*: **Tom is ~ped for the job** говоря́т, что э́ту до́лжность полу́чит Том; **the police had been ~ped off about the robbery** поли́цию предупреди́ли о гото́вящемся грабеже́

vi: **he ~s generously** он ще́дро даёт на чай.

tipple *vi CQ* пить, выпива́ть (*only in impf*).

tippler *n CQ* пья́ница, выпиво́ха (*m and f*).

tipsy *adj CQ* подвы́пивший, под му́хой, навеселе́ (*adv*).

tiptoe *n*: **he stood/came in on ~** он стоя́л/вошёл на цы́почках.

tiptop *adj CQ* превосхо́дный, первокла́ссный.

tip-up *adj*: **a ~ lorry** самосва́л; **~ seats** откидны́е сиде́нья.

tire *vti vt* утом|ля́ть (-и́ть); **travelling ~s me** путеше́ствия (*pl*) утомля́ют меня́, я устаю́ от доро́ги

vi уста|ва́ть (-́ть), утомля́ться; **he ~s easily** он бы́стро устаёт/утомля́ется; **he never ~s of reminding me that...** он никогда́ не устаёт напомина́ть мне, что...; **I never ~ of the theatre** теа́тр мне никогда́ не надоеда́ет.

tired *adj* уста́лый; **I'm ~** я уста́л; **I'm ~ of him/of waiting** я от него́ уста́л *or* он мне надое́л [**NB** *past tense*], я уста́л *or* мне надое́ло ждать.

tireless *adj* неутоми́мый.

tiresome *adj* надое́дливый; **how ~!** кака́я доса́да!; **he can be very ~ at times** он иногда́ быва́ет надое́длив.

tiring *adj* утоми́тельный.

tissue *n* (*Anat, cloth*) ткань; (*paper*) то́нкая обёрточная бума́га; (*handkerchief*) бума́жная салфе́тка; *fig* **a ~ of lies** паути́на лжи (*sing*).

tit[1] *n* (*tomtit*) сини́ца; (*bluetit*) лазо́ревка.

tit[2] *n*: **~ for tat** зу́б за́ зуб.

titbit, (*US*) **tidbit** *n* (*of food*) ла́комый кусо́чек; (*of gossip*) пика́нтная но́вость.

title *n* (*of book, film*) загла́вие, назва́ние; (*of aristocracy, book*) ти́тул; *attr*: **~ page/role** загла́вный *or* ти́тульный лист, загла́вная роль.

title holder *n Sport* чемпио́н.

titter *vi* хихи́к|ать (-нуть).

tittle-tattle *n* спле́тни (*pl*).

titular *adj* номина́льный.

tizzy *n CQ*: **to be/get in a ~** всполоши́ться.

to *adv*: **~ and fro** взад и вперёд; **close/near ~** ря́дом; **to come ~** прийти́ в себя́, очну́ться; **push the door ~** прикро́й дверь.

to *prep* **1** *introducing indirect object: dative case, or various preps*: **to give/explain smth ~ smb** дать/объясни́ть кому́-л что-л; **to apologize ~ smb** извини́ться перед кем-л; **to confess ~ smth** призна́ться в чём-л; **to speak ~ smb** говори́ть с кем-л; **to agree ~ smth** согласи́ться на что-л; **susceptible ~ flattery** па́дкий на лесть; **what's that ~ me?** мне-то что до э́того?; **it's quite a mystery ~ me** для меня́ э́то зага́дка

2 *of direction*: (*with places*) в + *A or* на + *A*, (*with events*) на + *A*; (*with people*) к + *D*; (*as far as*) до + *G*; **to go ~ Italy/Moscow** е́хать в Ита́лию/в Москву́; [**NB** *with islands, or points of compass* на + *A*]: **to go ~ Cyprus/the south/the Moon** е́хать на Кипр/на юг, лете́ть на Луну́; **to go ~ school/the theatre** идти́ в шко́лу/в теа́тр; **to go ~ a concert/a play/the races/work** идти́ на конце́рт/на спекта́кль/на ска́чки/на рабо́ту; **to return ~ one's country/one's parents** верну́ться на ро́дину/к роди́телям; **to go ~ the doctor('s)** идти́ к врачу́; **have you been ~ London?** вы бы́ли в Ло́ндоне?; **to fall ~ the ground** упа́сть на зе́млю; **to point ~ smth** указа́ть на что-л; **the road ~ Kiev** доро́га на Ки́ев; **is this the road ~ the station?** э́та доро́га на ста́нцию?; **~ the north of Leeds** к се́веру от Ли́дса; **perpendicular ~/at right angles ~ the wall** перпендикуля́рно/под прямы́м угло́м к стене́; **~ the left/right** нале́во, напра́во (*advs*); **it's 100 km ~ Riga** до Ри́ги сто киломе́тров

3 (*up to, as far as*) до + *G*; **he saw her ~ the bus/the door** он проводи́л её до авто́буса/до две́ри; **~ the end of May/of one's life** до конца́ ма́я/свое́й жи́зни; **the tradition is carried on ~ this day** э́та тради́ция продолжа́ется и до сего́дняшнего дня/и по сей день; **they perished ~ a man** они́ поги́бли все до одного́; **~ some degree** до не́которой сте́пени; **moved ~ tears** тро́нутый до слёз; **to**

count ~ 20 считать до двадцати; **prizes ~ the value of 100 roubles** призы ценностью в сто рублей; **accurate ~ a millimetre** с точностью до миллиметра; **everyone was there down ~ the very youngest/up ~ the general himself** там были все, даже самые младшие/, даже сам генерал

4 (*of time*): **10 (minutes) ~ 5** без десяти (минут) пять; **a quarter ~ 3** без четверти три; **3 years ago ~ the day** три года назад в этот самый день; **it's only a week ~ the holidays** осталась только неделя до каникул [**NB** *tense*]

5 from... to: i) (*of place*) **from house ~ house** от дома к дому; **from east ~ west** с востока на запад; **ii)** (*of time*) **from morning ~ night** с утра до вечера; **from Monday ~ Friday** с понедельника по пятницу включительно (*including Friday*)/до пятницы (*not including Friday*)

6 (*in comparisons*): **a car inferior ~ mine** машина хуже качеством, чем моя; **I prefer beef ~ lamb** я предпочитаю говядину баранине; **that's nothing ~ what we'll see next** это пустяки/ничто по сравнению с тем, что мы сейчас увидим

7 (*of proportion*): **by a majority of 40 ~ 30** большинством в сорок против тридцати; **we won by 3 ~ 1** мы выиграли 3 : 1; **the odds are 5 ~ 1** шансы—пять к одному; **the ratio of students ~ teachers is 10 ~ 1** отношение числа студентов к числу преподавателей—десять к одному; **there are 100 kopecks ~ the rouble** в рубле сто копеек; **we got one rouble ~ the dollar** мы получили рубль за доллар; **100 people ~ the square mile** сто человек на одну квадратную милю

8 (*against*) к + *D*; **shoulder ~ shoulder** плечом к плечу; **to turn a mirror ~ the wall** повернуть зеркало к стене; **he put his ear ~ the keyhole** он приложил ухо к замочной скважине; *fig* **to talk man ~ man** говорить как мужчина с мужчиной

9 (*of dedications, etc.*): **a monument ~ smb** памятник кому-л; **to drink ~ smb's success** пить за чей-л успех

10 (*concerning*): **what would you say ~ a trip to Greece?** а что бы ты сказал о поездке в Грецию?; **that's all there is ~ it** вот и всё; *Comm* (*on bill*) **~ 3 tons of coal** за три тонны угля

11 (*according to*) по + *D*; **~ all appearances** по всей видимости; **it's not ~ my taste** это мне не по вкусу; **to work ~ a schedule** работать по расписанию; **~ my way of thinking** на мой взгляд; **it is sung ~ the tune of...** это поётся на мотив + *G*

12 (*to the accompaniment of*) под + *A*; **to dance ~ a band/records** танцевать под оркестр/под радиолу

13 (*introducing a complement*): **wife/secretary ~ the President** жена/секретарь президента; **he was a good friend ~ us** он был нам хорошим другом; **there's no end ~ it** этому нет конца; **the key ~ the door** ключ от двери; **ambassador ~ France** посол во Франции; **I want a room ~ myself** я хочу иметь отдельную комнату

14 *forming adverbial phrases*: **~ my surprise/shame** к моему удивлению/стыду; **~ this end** с этой целью.

to *particle with inf* **1** *with simple infinitive*: **~ run away is cowardly** убегать—трусливо; **it is impossible ~ forget it** невозможно это забыть; **everyone has ~ sign** все должны подписаться; **I want ~ tell him/you ~ tell him** я хочу сказать ему/, чтобы ты сказал ему [**NB** чтобы + *past tense is used with verbs of wishing, where subject of subordinate clause is different from subject of main clause*]

2 *expressing purpose* чтобы + *inf*; **I did it ~ help you** я это сделал, чтобы помочь тебе

3 *expressing result or outcome*: **he did nothing ~ deserve it** он ничего не сделал, чтобы заслужить это; **he didn't expect ~ see her/her ~ come** он не ожидал увидеть её/, что она придёт; **they parted never ~ meet again** они расстались, чтобы никогда больше не встретиться; **I returned ~ find everyone in bed** когда я вернулся, все спали; **if I live ~ see it** если я до этого доживу

4 *with ellipsis of verb*: **I don't want ~** я не хочу; **I should love ~** я бы очень хотел; **I meant to invite him but I forgot ~** я думал пригласить его, но забыл; **we didn't want ~ leave, but we had ~** нам не хотелось уходить, но мы должны были уйти

5 *after adjectives*: **he was the first ~ do it/~ arrive** он первый это сделал, он пришёл первым; **he was quick ~ agree** он быстро согласился; **the book is easy ~ understand** эта книга написана понятным языком; **he's too young ~ smoke** он слишком мал, чтобы курить; **the plates are too hot ~ hold** тарелки слишком горячие—не удержишь; **the box is too heavy ~ lift** ящик слишком тяжёлый—не поднимешь

6 *various*: **he was seen ~ enter the hotel** видели, как он вошёл в гостиницу; **he was often heard ~ say that...** часто слышали, как он говорил, что...; **he is believed ~ be in London** думают, что он в Лондоне; **~ look at him, one would think that...** посмотришь на него, так можно подумать, что...; **he's not ~ be trusted** ему нельзя доверять; **he's not the sort ~ lie** он не такой человек, чтобы лгать; **who is he ~ object?** кто он такой, чтобы возражать?; **what am I ~ do?** что мне делать?; **where's he ~ go?** куда ему идти?; **there was nobody ~ ask** некого было спросить.

toad *n* жаба.

toadstool *n* поганка.

toady *n CQ* подхалим.

toast *n* **1** *Cook* гренок

2 (*drink*) тост; **to propose a ~ to smb** провозгласить тост за кого-л; **here's a ~ to our guests!** выпьем за наших гостей!

toast *vt* **1** *Cook* поджа́ри|вать (-ть) **2** (*drink*) пить за + *A* (вы́-).

tobacco *n* таба́к; *attr*: ~ **pouch** кисе́т.

tobacconist *n*: (*shop*) **the** ~**('s)** таба́чная ла́вка.

toboggan *n* са́ни (*pl*); (*for children*) са́нки (*pl*).

toboggan *vi* ката́ться на саня́х/на са́нках (по-).

today *n* сего́дня (*adv*), сего́дняшний день; **what day is it** ~**?** како́й (у нас) сего́дня день?; **from** ~ с сего́дняшнего дня; ~**'s newspaper** сего́дняшняя газе́та; **a week** ~ че́рез неде́лю; **a year ago** ~ ро́вно год наза́д; **composers of** ~ совреме́нные компози́торы.

toddle *vi* ковыля́ть (про-); *CQ joc* **we must** ~ нам пора́ идти́.

toddy *n* пунш.

to-do *n CQ* (*commotion*) сумато́ха; (*row*) сканда́л; **he made a great** ~ **about...** он устро́ил сканда́л/он по́днял шум по по́воду + *G*.

toe *n Anat* па́лец (ноги́); (*of shoe, sock*) носо́к; **from top to** ~ с головы́ до ног; *fig*: **to tread on smb's** ~**s** наступи́ть кому́-л на люби́мую мозо́ль; **he keeps us all on our** ~**s** у него́ все по стру́нке хо́дят; **you have to keep on your** ~**s in this job** на э́той рабо́те на́до быть о́чень внима́тельным/(*if dangerous*) начеку́ (*adv*).

toecap *n* носо́к (о́буви).

toenail *n* но́готь (*m*) (на па́льце ноги́).

toffee *n* (**a** ~) (*hard*) ири́ска, (*soft*) тяну́чка; **to buy some** ~ (*collect*)/~**s** купи́ть ири́сок.

together *adv* вме́сте; ~ **with** вме́сте с + *I*; **to sit** ~ сиде́ть вме́сте; **I couldn't get seats for us** ~ я не мог доста́ть нам места́ ря́дом; **to tie smb's hands** ~ связа́ть кому́-л ру́ки.

toil *n* (тяжёлый) труд.

toil *vi*: **to** ~ **(at/over)** труди́ться (над + *I*) (по-); **we** ~ **ed up the hill** мы с трудо́м взобра́лись на холм.

toilet *n* (*dressing*) одева́ние, туале́т; (*W. C.*) туале́т, убо́рная; *attr*: ~ **paper/soap** туале́тная бума́га, туале́тное мы́ло.

token *n* (*symbol*) знак; (*disc*) жето́н; (*coupon*) тало́н; **as a/in** ~ **of** в знак + *G*; *fig* **by the same** ~ кста́ти (*adv*); *attr*: **a** ~ **payment** символи́ческая пла́та; **they put up a** ~ **resistance** они́ со́здали ви́димость сопротивле́ния.

tolerable *adj* (*bearable*) терпи́мый; (*quite decent*) прили́чный; **the food here is quite** ~ здесь непло́хо/прили́чно ко́рмят.

tolerably *adv*: **it's** ~ **certain that...** почти́ вероя́тно, что...

tolerant *adj* терпи́мый.

tolerate *vt* (*bear*) терпе́ть (по-, вы́-); (*support*) вы|де́рживать (-держать), *also Tech*; **I won't** ~ **your impudence/your leaving the room in such a mess** я не потерплю́ твоего́ ха́мства/тако́го беспоря́дка в твое́й ко́мнате; **I can't** ~ **him/heat** я его́ не выношу́, я не выношу́ жары́; **he can't** ~ **fat** ему́ вре́дно есть жи́рное.

toll[1] *n* (*road tax*) по́шлина, сбор; *fig* **the death** ~ **on our roads is heavy** у нас мно́го несча́стных слу́чаев на доро́гах.

toll[2] *vti* звони́ть (по-); **to** ~ **a bell** звони́ть в ко́локол; **the bell** ~**ed** ко́локол (за)звони́л.

tollbridge *n* мост, где взима́ется (доро́жный) сбор.

toll call *n* (*US*) = **trunk call.**

Tom *n*: **every** ~**, Dick and Harry** ка́ждый встре́чный (и) попере́чный.

tomato *n* помидо́р; *attr*: ~ **juice/sauce** тома́тный сок/со́ус.

tomb *n* моги́ла.

tomboy *n*: **she's a** ~ она́ сорване́ц.

tombstone *n* надгро́бный ка́мень (*upright*), надгро́бная плита́ (*flat*).

tomcat *n* кот.

tomfoolery *n* дура́чество.

tomorrow *n* за́втра (*adv*), за́втрашний день; **the day after** ~ послеза́втра (*adv*); ~ **morning** за́втра у́тром; **a week** ~ че́рез во́семь дней; **see you** ~ до за́втра.

ton *n* то́нна; *CQ* **we've** ~**s of time** у нас ма́сса вре́мени.

tone *n* тон (*pl* -ы *Mus*; *pl* -а́ *of colours and fig*); **his** ~ **was serious** он говори́л серьёзным то́ном; ~**s of green** зелёные тона́; **to set the** ~ задава́ть тон; *Mus*: **a** ~ **higher** то́ном вы́ше; (*of quality*) **the violin has a beautiful** ~ у э́той скри́пки краси́вый тембр; *attr Radio*: ~ **control** регуля́тор те́мбра.

tone *vti vt*: **to** ~ **down** смягч|а́ть (-и́ть); **exercises** ~ **up the muscles** физи́ческие упражне́ния укрепля́ют мы́шцы

vi: **to** ~ **down** смягча́ться; **to** ~ **in with** гармони́ровать с + *I* (*impf and pf*).

tone-deaf *adj*: **he is** ~ у него́ нет слу́ха.

tone poem *n Mus* симфони́ческая поэ́ма.

tongs *npl* щипцы́ (*no sing*).

tongue *n* (*Anat, Cook, Ling, of bell, shoe and fig*) язы́к; **mother** ~ родно́й язы́к; *fig*: ~**s of flame** языки́ пла́мени; **to hold one's** ~ придержа́ть язы́к, держа́ть язы́к за зуба́ми; *attr*: **that word is a real** ~ **twister** э́то сло́во — язы́к слома́ешь.

tongue-tied *adj*: **he was** ~ он как язы́к проглоти́л.

tonic *n Mus* то́ника; *Med* тонизи́рующее сре́дство, то́ник; *fig* **I find him a real** ~ он на меня́ де́йствует ободря́юще.

tonight *adv* сего́дня ве́чером.

tonnage *n* тонна́ж.

tonsil *n Anat* минда́лина; **I had my** ~**s out** мне удали́ли минда́лины.

tonsil(l)itis *n* тонзилли́т, анги́на.

too *adv* **1** (*excessively*) сли́шком; (*with size of clothes often not translated*); ~ **fast** сли́шком бы́стро; **the box is** ~ **heavy for me to carry** я́щик сли́шком тяжёл для меня́; **you are** ~ **kind** вы сли́шком добры́; **that was none** ~ **pleasant** э́то бы́ло не сли́шком прия́тно; **the holidays were over all** ~ **soon** кани́кулы сли́шком бы́стро ко́нчились; **this coat is** ~ **big for me** э́то пальто́ мне великó; **he gave me two roubles ~ much** он дал мне на два рубля́ бóльше; **that's ~ bad** дéло плóхо; **it was ~ bad of him not to tell me** плóхо то, что он не сказáл мне

2 (*also*) тáкже, тóже; и; **I lived in France and in Italy ~** я жил во Фрáнции, а тáкже в Итáлии; **tell your husband ~** мýжу тóже скажи́, скажи́ и мýжу

3 (*moreover*): **our products are just as good and cheaper ~** у нас товáры таки́е же хорóшие и к томý же дешéвле; **it snowed today, and in May ~!** сегóдня шёл снег, э́то в мáе-то!

tool *n* инструмéнт; *fig* орýдие; **machine ~** станóк; *fig* **he is just their ~** он прóсто орýдие в их рукáх.

toolbox *n* я́щик для инструмéнтов.

toolkit *n* набóр инструмéнтов.

toot *vti*: **he ~ed (his horn)** он дал гудóк, он погудéл, он посигнáлил.

tooth *n Anat* зуб; (*of saw, cog*) зубéц; **milk/false/wisdom teeth** молóчные/вставны́е зýбы, зýбы мýдрости; **to grit/clench one's teeth** скрежетáть зубáми, сти́снуть зýбы; **his teeth are chattering from the cold** у негó зýбы стучáт/зуб нá зуб не попадáет от хóлода; **I had a ~ out** мне удали́ли/у меня́ вы́рвали зуб; *fig*: **armed to the teeth** вооружённый до зубóв; **in the teeth of the wind/opposition** пря́мо прóтив вéтра, наперекóр сопротивлéнию.

toothache *n* зубнáя боль; **he has ~** у негó боля́т зýбы.

toothbrush *n* зубнáя щётка; *attr fig*: **a ~ moustache** усы́ (*pl*) щёточкой.

toothless *adj* беззýбый.

toothpaste *n* зубнáя пáста.

toothpick *n* зубочи́стка.

top[1] *n* **1** верх, вéрхняя часть; (*of mountain*) верши́на; (*of tree*) верши́на, верхýшка, макýшка; (*green tops of root vegetables*) ботвá (*collect*); *fig* верши́на; (*on bus*) **let's go on ~** пойдём навéрх (*adv*); **the fifth line from the ~** пя́тая строкá свéрху (*adv*); **he searched the house from ~ to bottom** он обыскáл дом свéрху дóнизу (*advs*); **on ~ of the cupboard** на шкафý, (*if inside*) на вéрхней пóлке шкáфа; **it's at the ~/near the ~ of the pile** э́то (лежи́т) на верхý стóпки, э́то в вéрхней чáсти стóпки; **at the ~ of the page** в начáле страни́цы; **at the ~ of the list/table** в начáле спи́ска, во главé столá; **at the ~ of the garden/street** в концé сáда/ýлицы; *School* **he's at the ~ of his form** он пéрвый учени́к в клáссе; **at the ~ of his voice** во весь гóлос; **he looked over the ~ of his spectacles** он взглянýл повéрх очкóв; **fat floats to the ~ of the soup** жир плáвает на повéрхности сýпа

2 (*lid, cap*) кры́шка; (*of pen*) колпачóк; (*of car*) верх; **table ~** кры́шка столá; **pyjama ~** пижáмная кýртка; **a skirt with matching ~** ю́бка с подóбранной к ней блýзкой

3 *fig uses*: **he has reached the ~ of his profession** он дости́г вéрхних ступéней (*pl*)/ верши́ны профессионáльного мастерствá; **on ~ of all that** в довершéние всегó; **I'm talking off the ~ of my head as I haven't the papers here** я говорю́ э́то на пáмять — у меня́ нет под рукóй докумéнтов; *CQ*: **I feel on ~ of the world** я чýвствую себя́ на верхý блажéнства/на седьмóм нéбе; **the work is getting on ~ of me** э́та рабóта дéйствует мне на нéрвы; **it's just one thing on ~ of another** всё однó за други́м.

top[1] *adj* вéрхний; *fig* вы́сший; (*best*) (наи-) лýчший; **~ storey** вéрхний этáж; **in the ~ left-hand corner** в вéрхнем лéвом углý; *fig*: **~ grade** вы́сший сорт; **the ~ men**/*CQ* **~ brass** верхи́, *CQ* верхýшка; **our ~ footballers** нáши лýчшие футболи́сты; **he got ~ marks in physics** он получи́л вы́сший балл по фи́зике.

top[1] *vt* **1** (*cut off*): **to ~ turnips** отрез|áть ботвý у рéпы (*collect*) (-́ать); **to ~ and tail gooseberries** чи́стить/общи́пывать крыжóвник (*collect*)

2 (*be top of*): **our team ~ped the league** нáша комáнда возглавля́ла турни́рную таблицу; *Theat CQ* **he ~s the bill** он гвоздь прогрáммы

top up *vti vt* подли|вáть (-́ть); **let me ~ up your glass**/*CQ* **~ you up** давáй я тебé подолью́

vi: **we ~ped up with petrol** мы дополнá заправились бензи́ном.

top[2] *n* (*toy*) волчóк.

top boots *npl* высóкие сапоги́.

top hat *n* цили́ндр.

top-heavy *adj*: **that pile of books is ~ — it will fall** э́та стóпка книг неустóйчива — сейчáс рýхнет.

topic *n* тéма.

topical *adj*: **a ~ question** актуáльный вопрóс.

top-level *adj*: **~ negotiations** переговóры на вы́сшем ýровне.

topple *vti, also* **~ over** опроки́|дывать(ся) (-нуть(ся)).

top-ranking *adj*: **a ~ officer** офицéр вы́сшего рáнга.

top-secret *adj*: **~ papers** совершéнно секрéтные докумéнты.

topsy-turvy *adv* ши́ворот-навы́ворот.

torch *n* (*electric*) кармáнный фонáрь (*m*), фонáрик; (*flaming*) фáкел.

torment *n* мýка, мучéние, *also fig*; **to be in ~** мýчиться.

torment *vt* мýчить (за-, из-), *also fig*; **to ~ smb with questions** замýчить когó-л вопрóсами; **to be ~ed by doubts/toothache** мýчиться сомнéниями/зубнóй бóлью.

tormenting *adj* мучи́тельный.

torpedo *n* торпéда; *attr*: **~ boat** торпéдный кáтер.

torrent *n* потóк, *also fig*; **the rain came down in ~s** дождь лил как из ведрá; **a ~ of abuse** потóк ругáтельств (*pl*).

torrential *adj*: **~ rain** проливнóй дождь.

torrid *adj* знóйный.

torso *n* торс.

tortoise *n* черепа́ха; *attr* черепа́ховый.

tortuous *adj* (*of path, etc.*) изви́листый; (*of argument, etc.*) запу́танный.

torture *n* пы́тка, *also fig*; *fig CQ* **it was ~!** э́то была́ про́сто пы́тка!

torture *vt* пыта́ть (*impf*), *also fig*; *fig* му́чить (за-, из-), терза́ть (ис-); **to be ~d by doubts** му́читься/терза́ться сомне́ниями.

Tory *n* (*UK*) *Polit* консерва́тор, то́ри (*indecl*); *attr* консервати́вный.

toss *n*: **he took a ~** (*from horse*) его́ сбро́сила ло́шадь; **he called heads and won the ~** он сказа́л «орёл» и вы́играл.

toss *vti vt* брос|а́ть (́-ить) *and compounds*; **to ~ a coin** подбр|а́сывать моне́ту (-о́сить); **the horse ~ed its mane** ло́шадь встряхну́ла гри́вой; **she ~ed her hair back** она́ отки́нула наза́д во́лосы; *CQ* **he ~ed off a whisky** он опроки́нул стака́нчик ви́ски

vi: **the boat was ~ing on the waves** кора́бль броса́ло (*impers*) на волна́х; **to ~ in one's sleep** воро́чаться/(*wildly*) мета́ться во сне (*impfs*); **to ~ and turn** воро́чаться с бо́ку на́ бок; **we ~ed up for who was to begin** мы бро́сили моне́ту, кому́ начина́ть.

tot[1] *n* (*child*) малы́ш; (*of drink*) глото́к, глото́чек.

tot[2] *vti CQ vt*: **to ~ up the bill/one's expenses** состав|ля́ть счёт/подсчи́т|ывать свои́ расхо́ды (́-ить/-а́ть); **I'll ~ it up** я подведу́ ито́г

vi: **it ~s up to 20 roubles** э́то составля́ет два́дцать рубле́й.

total *n* ито́г; **grand ~** о́бщий ито́г; **in ~** в ито́ге; **to work out the ~** подвести́ ито́г; **we spent a ~ of £100** мы потра́тили в це́лом сто фу́нтов; **the sum ~ of profits is over a million** при́были в совоку́пности превыша́ют миллио́н.

total *adj* о́бщий, по́лный; **the ~ number of participants** о́бщее число́ уча́стников; **the ~ population** о́бщая чи́сленность населе́ния; **in ~ agreement/ignorance** в по́лном согла́сии/неве́дении; **~ war** тота́льная война́; *Astron* **a ~ eclipse** по́лное затме́ние.

total *vi*: **our expenses ~ £1,000** на́ши расхо́ды в це́лом составля́ют ты́сячу фу́нтов; **the delegates ~led 100** делега́тов бы́ло сто челове́к.

totally *adv* вполне́, соверше́нно, по́лностью; **~ destroyed** по́лностью разру́шенный; **~ blind/helpless** соверше́нно слепо́й/беспо́мощный.

totter *vi* (*of child*) ковыля́ть (про-); (*of drunk, wounded, etc.*) шата́ться (*usu impf*); **he ~ed unsteadily upstairs** он, шата́ясь, пошёл наве́рх; **he ~ed towards us** он, шата́ясь, дви́нулся к нам; **the chimney ~ed and fell** труба́ пошатну́лась и упа́ла.

tottering, tottery *adj*: **~ steps** неуве́ренные шаги́; **~ gait** нетвёрдая похо́дка.

touch *n* **1** (*sense*) осяза́ние; **sense of ~** чу́вство осяза́ния; **smooth to the ~** гла́дкий на о́щупь; **to recognize smth by ~** узна́ть что-л на о́щупь

2 (*act*) прикоснове́ние; **at his/the slightest ~** при его́/мале́йшем прикоснове́нии; **it works at the ~ of a button** э́то приво́дится в де́йствие нажа́тием кно́пки; (*of typist, musician*): **she has a heavy ~** у неё тяжёлая рука́; **he has a light ~** (*of musician*) он мя́гко ста́вит ру́ку, *fig* у него́ лёгкая рука́

3 (*contact*) связь, конта́кт; **to keep in/lose ~ with smb** подде́рживать/потеря́ть связь *or* конта́кт с кем-л; **to be in ~ with smb** быть в конта́кте с кем-л; **I am out of ~ with her/events** я потеря́л [**NB** *tense*] её из виду, я не в ку́рсе собы́тий; **I will put you in ~ with my doctor** я предста́влю тебя́ моему́ врачу́; **I'll get in ~ with you soon** я ско́ро уви́жусь/свяжу́сь с тобо́й

4 (*of brush stroke*) штрих, мазо́к; *fig*: **to put the finishing ~es to smth** нанос́ить после́дние штрихи́; (*of writer*) **he has a bold ~** у него́ сме́лая мане́ра письма́; **here we can see the ~ of a great master** здесь видна́ рука́ большо́го ма́стера

5 (*small quantity*): **a ~ of irony** отте́нок иро́нии; **add a ~ of salt** доба́вьте чу́точку со́ли; **there is a ~ of frost in the air** в во́здухе чу́вствуется моро́зец; **I have a ~ of flu/of the sun** у меня́ лёгкий грипп, я немно́го перегре́лся.

touch *vti vt* **1** тро́|гать (-нуть); при|каса́ться (-косну́ться); дотр|а́гиваться до + *G*, притр|а́гиваться к + *D* (*pfs* -о́нуться); (*be contiguous with*) сопри|каса́ться с + *I* (-косну́ться); **don't ~ me/my papers** не тро́гай меня́/мои́ бума́ги, (*stronger*) не прикаса́йся ко мне/к мои́м бума́гам; **someone ~ed me on the arm** кто́-то тро́нул меня́ за́ руку; **his hand ~ed mine** его́ рука́ прикосну́лась к мое́й; **he ~ed my hand** он дотро́нулся до мое́й руки́; **the fire didn't ~ the pictures** ого́нь не тро́нул карти́н; **he hasn't ~ed his lunch** он не притро́нулся к обе́ду; *fig* **he hasn't ~ed his homework yet** он ещё не притро́нулся к дома́шним зада́ниям

2 (*reach*) доста|ва́ть до + *G* (́-ть); **can you ~ your toes?** ты мо́жешь доста́ть до свои́х носко́в?; **my feet are ~ing the bottom** я достаю́ (нога́ми) до дна; **the police can't ~ him now** тепе́рь поли́ции до него́ не добра́ться

3 *fig uses*: **nobody can ~ him as a violinist** как скрипачу́ ему́ нет ра́вных; (*concern*) **it ~es your interests closely** э́то каса́ется тебя́ непосре́дственно; (*move*) **I am ~ed by your concern** я тро́нут твое́й забо́той; *CQ*: **to ~ smb for a fiver** вы|пра́шивать у кого́-л пять фу́нтов (́-просить); **he is ~ed** (*mad*) он чо́кнутый, у него́ не все до́ма; **I wouldn't ~ it with a barge pole** я бы за э́то ни за что не взя́лся

vi тро́гать; **"Please do not ~"** «рука́ми не тро́гать»

touch at *vi Naut* за|ходи́ть в + *A* (-йти́)

touch down *vi Aer* приземл|я́ться (-и́ться)

touch off *vt*: **to ~ off an explosion**/*fig* **a crisis** вы|зыва́ть взрыв/кри́зис (-́звать)

touch on *vi*: **to ~ on a question** затр|а́гивать вопро́с (-о́нуть)

touch up *vt Photo, etc.* ретуши́ровать (от-); **to ~ up one's make-up** подкра́ситься (*usu pf*).

touch-and-go *n*: **it was ~ with the sick man** больно́й был на волосо́к от сме́рти; **it was ~, but I finally persuaded him** я до после́днего моме́нта не́ был уве́рен, уговори́л я его́ и́ли нет

touching *adj* тро́гательный.

touch-typist *n* машини́стка, печа́тающая по слепо́му ме́тоду.

touchy *adj* оби́дчивый; **he's ~ about his weight** он о́чень обижа́ется, когда́ шу́тят над его́ ве́сом.

tough *n CQ* хулига́н.

tough *adj* жёсткий, про́чный; (*hardy*) сто́йкий; *fig* тру́дный, тяжёлый; **~ meat/material** жёсткое мя́со, про́чный материа́л; **he's ~** (*physically*) он о́чень выно́слив, *fig* (*in his dealings*) он не идёт на усту́пки; *fig*: **a ~ problem** тру́дная пробле́ма; **~ conditions** тяжёлые усло́вия; **~ competition** жесто́кая конкуре́нция; **a ~ policy** жёсткая поли́тика; **~ measures** жёсткие ме́ры; *CQ*: **it was ~ on her** ей тяжело́ пришло́сь; **~ luck!** проклятое невезе́ние!; **he's a ~ guy** у него́ жёсткий хара́ктер.

tour *n* (*trip*) пое́здка, экску́рсия; *Sport* турне́ (*indecl*); *Theat* гастро́ли (*pl*); **a coach ~ of Scotland** авто́бусная экску́рсия по Шотла́ндии; **a walking ~** похо́д; **a sightseeing ~ of the town** осмо́тр го́рода; **a ~ of inspection** инспекцио́нный объе́зд; **the team enjoyed their ~ abroad** кома́нда была́ дово́льна свои́м загра́ничным турне́; **the ballet is on ~ in America** бале́т сейча́с на гастро́лях в Аме́рике.

tour *vti vt*: **to ~ France** путеше́ствовать по Фра́нции, *Theat* гастроли́ровать во Фра́нции (*impfs*)

vi: **the play is ~ing in the provinces** тру́ппа с э́той пье́сой уе́хала [**NB** *tense*] на гастро́ли в прови́нцию (*sing*).

tourist *n* тури́ст; *attr* туристи́ческий.

tournament *n* турни́р; **chess ~** ша́хматный турни́р.

tourniquet *n Med* жгут.

tousled *adj* взъеро́шенный.

tow *n* (*act*) буксиро́вка; **to have/take a car on ~** взять маши́ну на букси́р, тяну́ть маши́ну на букси́ре; *fig CQ* **he arrived with two pretty girls in ~** он пришёл с двумя́ красо́тками.

tow *vt* букси́ровать (*impf*) (*also of barge, caravan*); **they ~ed us away/off to the filling station** они́ на букси́ре довезли́ нас до бензоколо́нки.

toward(s) *prep* к + *D* i) (*of direction*) **they were driving ~ town** они́ е́хали к го́роду; **with one's back ~ the window** спино́й к окну́; ii) (*of time*) **he came ~ evening** он прие́хал к ве́черу/под ве́чер; **~ the end of the month** к концу́ ме́сяца; **~ two o'clock** к двум часа́м; iii) (*of attitude, purpose*) **they are hostile ~ us** они́ вражде́бно к нам отно́сятся; **his feelings ~ them** его́ чу́вства к ним; **we are saving ~ a new house** мы ко́пим на но́вый дом.

towel *n* полоте́нце; *attr*: **~ rail** ве́шалка для полоте́нца.

towel *vt* вы|тира́ть полоте́нцем (-́тереть); **to ~ oneself** вы́тереться полоте́нцем.

tower *n Archit* ба́шня; **watch/control ~** сторожева́я/диспе́тчерская ба́шня; *fig* **he was a ~ of strength to me** он был мне ве́рной опо́рой.

tower *vi, also* **~ up** возвыша́ться (*impf*), *also fig*; вы́ситься (*impf*); **the skyscrapers ~ above the city** небоскрёбы вы́сятся над го́родом; **he ~s above her** он намно́го вы́ше неё; *fig* **he ~s above them in intellect** он гора́здо вы́ше их по уму́/интеллектуа́льно.

towering *adj* высящийся; *fig* **in a ~ rage** в ди́кой я́рости.

town *n* го́род, *dim* городо́к; **they live out of ~** они́ живу́т за́ городом; **he is out of ~ just now** он сейча́с в отъе́зде, его́ сейча́с нет в го́роде; *fig*: **he really went to ~ on preparations for the party** он вовсю́ разошёлся с подгото́вкой к ве́черу; **to go out on the ~** кути́ть; *attr* городско́й; **~ council** городско́й/муниципа́льный сове́т; **~ centre** центр го́рода.

town-dweller *n* горожа́н|ин, *f* -ка.

town hall *n* (*not SU*) ра́туша, мэ́рия.

towrope *n* букси́р, кана́т.

toxic *adj* токси́ческий.

toy *n* игру́шка; *attr*: **a ~ soldier** игру́шечный солда́тик.

toy *vi*: **I'm ~ing with the idea of going to Finland** я поду́мываю, а не пое́хать ли мне в Финля́ндию.

toyshop *n* магази́н игру́шек.

trace *n* след, *also fig*; **her face showed ~s of tears** на её лице́ бы́ли следы́ слёз; **we've lost ~ of him** мы потеря́ли его́ и́з виду; **there is no ~ of her** её и след просты́л; **he vanished without ~** он исче́з бессле́дно; **so far there is no ~ of survivors** пока́ нет све́дений (*pl*), что кто́-либо оста́лся в живы́х; **without a ~ of malice** без те́ни зло́сти.

trace *vt* **1** (*with tracing paper*) калькирова́ть (с-); (*draw*: *of line, diagram, etc.*) черти́ть (на-); **he ~d the route on the map** он обозна́чил маршру́т на ка́рте

2 (*locate*): **the thief has been ~d by the police** (*and caught*) поли́ция вы́следила во́ра; **they ~d him to a small village** они́ разыска́ли его́ (*and found him*)/обнару́жили следы́ его́ пребыва́ния (*if he is no longer there*) в како́й-то дереву́шке; **the drugs were ~d back to their house** бы́ло устано́влено, что нарко́тики привезли́ в их дом; **to ~ the development of smth** просле́|живать разви́тие чего́-л (-ди́ть); **he came here to ~ his ancestors/sister** он прие́хал сюда́, что́бы установи́ть свою́ родосло́вную/, чтóбы разыскáть своЮ сестрý; **I cannot ~ any letter from him** я не могý найтú ни одногó письмá от негó; **to ~ back the source of a rumour** обнарýжить истóчник слýхов (*pl*); **this custom can be ~d back to Roman times** э́тот обы́чай восхóдит к эпóхе Дрéвнего Рúма.

tracing *n* (*copy*) (**a ~**) кáлька, калькúрованный чертёж; *attr*: **~ paper** кáлька.

track *n* **1** (*of animal, person*) след; (*of vehicle, etc.*) курс; (*on radar, screen, etc.*) траектóрия полёта; **they got/this put them on to his ~** онú напáли/э́то навелó их на егó след; **to throw smb off the ~** сбить когó-л со слéда; **to follow in smb's ~s** идтú по чьим-л следáм, *also fig*; **to cover one's ~s** заметáть следы́, *also fig*; **to keep ~ of smth** следúть за чем-л, *also fig*; **he had the police on his ~** за ним следúла/егó преслéдовала полúция; *fig*: **I have lost ~ of a lot of my books** я не знáю, кудá дéлись мнóгие моú кнúги; **I lost ~ of what he was saying/of events** я потеря́л нить егó мы́сли, я перестáл следúть за собы́тиями; **he lost all ~ of time** он (совсéм) потеря́л счёт врéмени; **I lost ~ of him during the war** я потеря́л с ним связь во врéмя войны́; *CQ*: **I must make ~s** мне порá идтú; **he was making ~s for the beach** он шёл в стóрону пля́жа

2 (*path*) тропúнка, тропá; **sheep ~** овéчья тропá; **the house is off the beaten ~** дом нахóдится в сторонé от дорóг; *fig* **to be on the right/wrong ~** быть на прáвильном/лóжном путú

3 *Sport* (*for running*) беговáя дорóжка, (*for cycle and motor racing*) трек

4 *Rail* колея́, рéльсовый путь; **double/single ~** двухколéйный/одноколéйный путь; **the train left the ~s** пóезд сошёл с рéльсов

5 (*on a record*) дорóжка

6 (*on tank*): **caterpillar ~** гýсеница.

track *vt* (*a person*) следúть за + *I*; (*a hunted animal or person*) вы|слéживать [**NB** *pf* ´-следить = *to track and find*]; **to ~ a satellite/an airplane/a missile** определ|я́ть орбúту спýтника/путь самолёта/траектóрию снаря́да (-úть)

tract[1] *n* **1: a ~ of land** (*strip*) полосá/(*stretch*) прострáнство землú; **huge uninhabited ~s** огрóмные ненаселённые прострáнства

2 *Anat*: **digestive/respiratory ~** желýдочно-кишéчный тракт, дыхáтельные путú (*pl*).

tract[2] *n* (*pamphlet*) трактáт.

traction *n* тя́га.

traction engine *n* трáктор-тягáч.

tractor *n* трáктор; **drawn by a ~** на трáкторной тя́ге; *attr*: **~ driver** тракторúст.

trade *n* **1** (*commerce*) торгóвля; **the furniture/building ~** торгóвля мéбелью, строúтельная промы́шленность; **the Board of T.** министéрство торгóвли; **balance of ~** торгóвый балáнс; **they did a brisk/*CQ* roaring ~ in umbrellas** у них шла бóйкая торгóвля зóнтиками

2 (*profession*) ремеслó, профéссия; **to learn a ~** учúться ремеслý; **a carpenter by ~** плóтник по профéссии.

trade *vti vt*: **to ~ a watch for a bicycle** обмéн|ивать часы́ на велосипéд (-я́ть); **I am buying a new car and trading in my old one** я покупáю нóвую машúну и отдаю стáрую в счёт частúчной оплáты

vi торговáть (*impf*); **to ~ with smb/in cotton** торговáть с кем-л/хлóпком; *fig* **to ~ on smb's credulity** злоупотреб|ля́ть чьей-л довéрчивостью (-úть).

trademark *n* фабрúчная мáрка.

trade mission *n* торгóвое представúтельство, *abbr* торгпрéдство.

trader *n* торгóвец.

tradesman *n* (*shopkeeper*) лáвочник.

trade union *n* профсою́з.

trade wind *n* пассáт.

trading *n* торгóвля.

tradition *n* традúция; **by ~** по традúции.

traditional *adj* традициóнный.

traffic *n* **1** движéние; трáнспорт; **road/one-way/air ~** ýличное/одностор́óннее движéние, движéние самолётов; **the town centre is closed to ~** центр гóрода закры́т для (движéния) трáнспорта; **~ coming in to London...** машúны, въезжáющие в Лóндон...; **a line of ~** верени́ца машúн; **be careful of the ~!** берегúсь автомобúля!; *attr*: **~ problems** проблéмы ýличного движéния

2 (*trade*): **the drug ~** торгóвля наркóтиками.

traffic circle *n* (*US*) *see* **roundabout.**

traffic island *n* островóк безопáсности.

traffic lights *npl* светофóр (*sing*).

traffic police *n* автоинспéкция; (*SU*) ГАИ (*abbr for* Госудáрственная автомобúльная инспéкция).

traffic sign *n* дорóжный знак.

tragedian *n* (*actor*) трáгик, трагúческий актёр; (*writer*) áвтор трагéдий.

tragedy *n* трагéдия, *also fig*; трагúчность; **the ~ is that...** трагéдия в том, что...; **the ~ of the situation** трагúчность ситуáции.

tragic *adj* трагúческий.

trail *n* **1** (*of animal, comet, rocket*) след; **vapour ~** след реактúвного самолёта; **he left a ~ of mud on the carpet** он остáвил гря́зные следы́ (*pl*) на коврé; **the hurricane left a ~ of destruction** ураѓан остáвил следы́ (*pl*) разрушéния на своём путú; **to be on/follow the ~ of smth** идтú по слéду чегó-л, выслéживать что-л; **to pick up/lose the ~** напáсть на/потеря́ть след

2 (*path*) тропúнка, тропá.

trail *vti vt* **1** (*track*) идтú по слéду (*impf*), вы|слéживать [**NB** *pf* ´-следить = *to trail and find*]

2 (*drag*) тащúть, волочúть (*impfs*); **the car was ~ing a caravan** машúна тащúла за собóй вагóнчик; **the tractor was ~ing a bulldozer** трáктор волочúл за собóй бульдóзер *vi* тащи́ться, волочи́ться; (*of plants*: *climbing*) ви́ться, (*on ground*) стла́ться (*impfs*); **her scarf ~ed in the mud** её шарф волочи́лся по грязи́; **he ~ed behind them** он тащи́лся за ни́ми; **ivy ~ed along the ground/over the walls** плющ стели́лся по земле́/обвива́л сте́ны.

trailer *n Aut* прице́п, тре́йлер; *Cine* рекла́ма фи́льма, ано́нс.

train[1] *n* **1** *Rail* по́езд; **freight/goods ~** това́рный соста́в; **a suburban ~** при́городный по́езд, электри́чка; **a through ~** по́езд прямо́го сообще́ния; **to go by ~** е́хать на по́езде/по́ездом

2: the king's ~ сви́та короля́; **baggage ~** (*carts or animals*) обо́з; **a ~ of camels** карава́н верблю́дов; *fig*: **the floods brought famine in their ~** наводне́ние (*sing*) вы́звало го́лод; **~ of thought/events** ход мы́слей/собы́тий; **~ of ideas** верени́ца мы́слей

3 (*of robe*) шлейф.

train[2] *vti vt* **1** (*to do smth*) обуч|а́ть (-и́ть); (*in smth*) учи́ть (на-, вы́-); (*prepare*) гото́вить (под-); (*coach*) тренирова́ть (на-); (*accustom*) приуч|а́ть (-и́ть); **to ~ smb to drive a tractor** обуча́ть кого́-л води́ть тра́ктор; **to ~ smb for the Navy/a new job** гото́вить кого́-л для слу́жбы во *or* на фло́те/для но́вой рабо́ты; **where were you ~ed?** где ты обуча́лся/учи́лся/прошёл подгото́вку?; **to ~ horses/footballers/one's memory** тренирова́ть лошаде́й/футболи́стов/па́мять; **to ~ lions** дрессирова́ть львов (*impf*); **he ~ed the dog to beg** он научи́л соба́ку служи́ть; **I ~ed myself not to think about it** я приучи́л себя́ не ду́мать об э́том

2 (*direct*): **to ~ a camera/gun on smth** на|води́ть ка́меру на что-л (-вести́), прице́ли|ваться во что-л из ружья́ (-ться); **to ~ a rose along a fence** сади́ть ро́зы вдоль забо́ра

vi обуча́ться, учи́ться, гото́виться, *Sport* тренирова́ться; **he is ~ing in accountancy/as a teacher** он у́чится на счетово́да, он гото́вится стать педаго́гом.

trained *adj* (*of teacher, nurse, etc.*) подгото́вленный; (*of circus animal*) дрессиро́ванный; **we need a ~ person** нам ну́жен подгото́вленный/квалифици́рованный специали́ст.

trainer *n Sport* тре́нер; (*in circus*) дрессиро́вщик.

training *n* (*of manual workers in practical skills*) обуче́ние; (*of teachers, engineers, etc.*) подгото́вка; (*of circus animals*) дрессиро́вка; (*upbringing*) воспита́ние; *Sport* трениро́вка; **to be in ~** тренирова́ться; **I'm in good ~ just now** я сейча́с в (хоро́шей) фо́рме; *attr*: **a ~ college** (*for teachers*)/**ship** педагоги́ческий институ́т, уче́бное су́дно.

traipse *vi CQ* тащи́ться (*impf*); **I had to ~ up to the top floor** мне пришло́сь тащи́ться на ве́рхний эта́ж.

trait *n* характе́рная черта́.

traitor *n* изме́нник, преда́тель (*m*); **a ~ to one's country** изме́нник ро́дины.

tram(car) *n* трамва́й, трамва́йный ваго́н.

tramp *n* **1** (*person*) бродя́га (*m*)

2 (*sound of feet*) то́пот

3 (*hike*): **to go for a ~ in the hills** идти́ в похо́д в го́ры; **after a ~ of many miles** по́сле до́лгого перехо́да.

tramp *vti vt*: **I ~ed the streets all day looking for a flat** я це́лый день мота́лся по го́роду в по́исках кварти́ры

vi: **we ~ed up and down the platform** мы ходи́ли взад и вперёд по платфо́рме; *CQ* **we ~ed six miles to the camp** мы протопа́ли шесть миль до ла́геря.

trample *vti vt* топта́ть (*impf*) *and compounds*; **to ~ smth into the mud** втопта́ть/затопта́ть что-л в грязь; **they ~d (down) the crops** они́ вы́топтали все посе́вы

vi: **to ~ about** топта́ться; **to ~ on a flower/on smb's toes** растопта́ть цвето́к, наступи́ть кому́-л на́ ногу; *fig* **to ~ on smb's feelings** заде|ва́ть чьи-л чу́вства (-́ть).

trampoline *n* трампли́н.

trance *n* транс; **to fall into a ~** впасть в транс.

tranquil *adj* споко́йный.

tranquillizer, (*US*) **tranquilizer** *n Med* успока́ивающее сре́дство, транквилиза́тор.

transact *vt*: **to ~ business with smb** вести́ де́ло с кем-л.

transaction *n* **1** (*deal*) сде́лка; **cash/shady ~s** сде́лки за нали́чный расчёт, сомни́тельные сде́лки

2 *pl*: **the ~s of a society** труды́/протоко́лы нау́чного о́бщества.

transcend *vt*: **it ~ed all my hopes** э́то превзошло́ все мои́ ожида́ния.

transcribe *vt*: **to ~ smth from shorthand notes** расшифро́|вывать стеногра́мму (-ва́ть).

transcript *n* (*of broadcast*) за́пись; (*of shorthand*) расшифро́вка.

transfer *n* (*act*) перемеще́ние; перенесе́ние, перено́с; перево́д; перехо́д; *see under verb*; (*of ownership, rights, etc.*) переда́ча; (*of money*) перево́д; (*to new premises*) перехо́д, перее́зд.

transfer *vti vt* пере|носи́ть (-нести́); пере|води́ть (-вести́); переме|ща́ть (-сти́ть); переда|ва́ть (-́ть); **he ~red his attention to other matters/the class to Tuesday** он заня́лся други́ми дела́ми, он перенёс уро́к на вто́рник; **he ~red his books to the other shelves** он перенёс/переста́вил свои́ кни́ги на други́е по́лки; **he is being ~red to another section** его́ перево́дят в друго́й отде́л; **he ~red money to his wife's account/the property to his brother** он перевёл де́ньги на счёт жены́, он переда́л иму́щество бра́ту; **the office is soon being ~red to another building** конто́ру ско́ро переведу́т в но́вое зда́ние

vi пере|ходи́ть (-йти́), переме|ща́ться (-сти́ться); (*of passengers*) пере|са́живаться (-се́сть); **he is ~ring to another team** он перехо́дит в другу́ю кома́нду; **the faculty is ~ring to a new site** факульте́т перево́дят в но́вое зда́ние; **can I ~ to another flight?** не могу́ ли я поменя́ть рейс?

transferable *adj*: **not** ~ без права передачи; **is this ticket** ~**?** можно передавать этот билет другому лицу?

transform *vt* преобразов|ывать (-ать), *also Phys*; **you'd never recognize their flat—it's quite** ~**ed!** их квартиры не узнать—там всё переделано.

transformation *n* преобразование; **he's shaved off his beard—what a** ~**!** он сбрил бороду—его просто не узнать!

transformer *n Tech* (*of frequency*) преобразователь (*m*); *Elec* трансформатор.

transfusion *n*: **a blood** ~ переливание крови.

transient *adj* преходящий, мимолётный.

transistor *n Radio* транзистор.

transit *n* (*of people*) проезд; (*of goods*) перевозка, транзит; **I was there in** ~ я был там проездом; **goods damaged in** ~ товары, испорченные при перевозке; *attr* транзитный; ~ **passengers/goods** транзитные пассажиры/товары; ~ **visa** транзитная виза.

transition *n* переход; **a period of** ~ переходный период.

transitional *adj* переходный.

transitive *adj Gram* переходный.

translate *vti vt* пере|водить (-вести); **how did you/do you** ~ **this word?** как ты перевёл/как переводится это слово?; *fig*: **to** ~ **ideas into actions** претвор|ять идеи в жизнь (-ить); **if you** ~ **our profits into figures...** если выразить наши прибыли в цифрах...

vi: **he** ~**s from English into Russian** он переводит с английского на русский; **this** ~**s easily** это легко переводится.

translation *n* перевод; **in** ~ в переводе.

translator *n* переводчик.

transmission *n* передача, *also Radio, TV*; *Radio, TV* трансляция; *Tech* передача, трансмиссия.

transmit *vt* переда|вать (-ть), *also Radio, TV*; *Radio, TV* транслировать (*impf and pf*); *Tech* **to** ~ **heat** проводить тепло (*only in impf*).

transmitter *n Radio, TV* передатчик; (*station*) передающая радиостанция, трансляционная станция.

transparency *n* прозрачность; *photo* диапозитив.

transparent *adj* прозрачный, *also fig*; *fig*: **a** ~ **hint/lie** прозрачный намёк, явная ложь; **a man of** ~ **honesty** человек кристальной честности.

transpire *vi*: **it** ~**d that...** (*turned out*) оказалось, что..., (*became known*) выяснилось, что...

transplant *n Hort, Med* пересадка; **he was given a kidney** ~ ему сделали пересадку почки.

transplant *vt Hort, Med* переса|живать (-дить).

transport *n* (*vehicles*) транспорт; (*action*) перевозка, транспортировка; **rail** ~ железнодорожные перевозки (*pl*); **I am without** ~ **today** я сегодня без машины; *fig* **in a** ~ **of delight/rage** в восторге, в гневе; *attr*: **a** ~ **café** дорожное кафе.

transport *vt* транспортировать (*impf and pf*); пере|возить (-везти); (*of convicts*) ссылать (сослать).

transpose *vt Mus* транспонировать (*impf and pf*).

transverse *adj* поперечный; **a** ~ **section** поперечное сечение.

transversely *adv* поперёк.

trap *n* **1** (*general*) ловушка, *also fig*; (*a spring trap for larger wild animals*) капкан, *also fig*; **to set a** ~ **for mice/***fig* **for smb** ставить мышеловку, приготовить для кого-л западню; **to fall into a** ~ попасть в ловушку/в капкан, *also fig*; **to catch a rabbit in a** ~ поймать кролика в капкан; *fig* **we were caught like rats in a** ~ мы попались как мыши в мышеловку

2 (*also* ~ **door**) люк.

trap *vt* **1** (*of animals*): **to** ~ **a wolf** (*set traps*) ставить капкан на волка (по-), (*catch*) поймать волка в капкан

2 (*cut off*): **they were** ~**ped for 3 hours underground** их завалило (*impers*), и они пробыли под землёй три часа; **they were** ~**ped in the lift/in the burning building/under the car** они застряли в лифте, они не могли выбраться из горящего дома/из машины; **it's a dead end—we're** ~**ped** это тупик—мы в ловушке.

trapeze *n* трапеция; *attr*: ~ **artist** акробат на трапеции.

trash *n* (*in dustbin*) мусор; (*rags, bones, etc.*) хлам; (*food refuse*) отбросы (*pl*); *fig CQ* чушь, дрянь; **that film is** ~ это дрянной фильм; **he talks a lot of** ~ он несёт/порет такую чушь; **that magazine is just** ~ этот журнал—дешёвое чтиво; *attr*: (*US*) ~ **can** мусорный ящик.

trashy *adj CQ* дрянной.

trauma *n Med, Psych* травма.

travel *n* путешествие; поездки (*pl*); **I find** ~ **tiring** я устаю от поездок (*pl*)/от дороги; **he has returned from his** ~**s** он вернулся из поездки (*sing*).

travel *vti* vt: **he** ~**led the country from top to bottom** он объездил всю страну вдоль и поперёк; **we have** ~**led thousands of miles/500 km today** мы проехали тысячи миль, сегодня мы наездили пятьсот километров (*usu pfs*)

vi **1** (*journey*) путешествовать (*impf*); ездить (*indet impf*), ехать (*det impf*); **we** ~**led round Europe** мы путешествовали/много ездили по Европе; **he** ~**s into London to work** он ездит на работу в Лондон; **we** ~**led by car/train/sea/air** мы ехали на машине/поездом, мы плыли морем, мы летели самолётом; **wine doesn't** ~ **well** вино портится при перевозке

2 (*move*) двигаться (*usu impf*); **light** ~**s faster than sound** свет движется быстрее звука; **the goods** ~ **along the conveyor** товары движутся по конвейеру; **the car was** ~**ling**

slowly towards us / at 100 m. p. h. машина медленно подъезжала к нам / шла со скоростью сто миль в час; **we were ~ling / he ~s too fast** мы ехали / он ездит слишком быстро; **gas ~s along this tube** газ проходит по этой трубе; **news ~s fast** новости (*pl*) быстро распространяются.

travel agency *n* туристическое бюро (*indecl*), бюро путешествий.

traveller, (*US*) **traveler** *n* путешественник; *Comm* коммивояжёр; **~'s cheque** туристский чек.

travelling, (*US*) **traveling** *n*: **he does a lot of ~ in his job** по работе ему приходится много ездить; *attr*: **~ expenses** дорожные расходы; **~ salesman** коммивояжёр; **~ exhibition** передвижная выставка; **~ rug** плед; *Theat* **~ company** гастролирующая труппа.

travel sickness *n*: **she suffers from ~** её тошнит в машине / в самолёте / на корабле.

traverse *vt* пересе|кать (-чь).

travesty *n* пародия; **a ~ of** пародия на + *A*.

trawl *vti* тралить (*impf*).

trawler *n* траулер.

tray *n* поднос; **a ~ of drinks** поднос с напитками.

treacherous *adj* предательский, *also fig*; *fig*: **~ weather** обманчивая / предательская погода; **the pavements are ~ after the snow** тротуары очень скользкие после снегопада.

treacle *n* патока.

tread *n* (*of feet*) поступь; (*of stair*) ступень; (*of shoe*) подошва; (*of tyre*) протектор; **a measured ~** мерная поступь; **I heard the heavy ~ of his feet** я услышал его тяжёлую поступь / его тяжёлые шаги.

tread *vti vt* топтать (*impf*) *and compounds*; **sheep have trodden a path across the field** овцы протоптали тропу через поле; **don't ~ ash into the carpet** не втаптывайте пепел в ковёр; **to ~ grapes** давить виноград (*impf*); **to ~ water** плыть стоя

vi ступ|ать (-ить); **to ~ softly / heavily** ступать мягко / тяжело; **don't ~ on the flowers / on my toe!** не наступи на цветы! / мне на ногу!; **he trod on the cockroach** (*to kill it*) он раздавил таракана; *fig*: **I was ~ing on air** я ног под собой не чуял; **we must ~ warily in this matter** мы должны быть осторожны в этом вопросе.

treason *n* измена; **high ~** государственная измена.

treasure *n* сокровище; **(buried) ~** клад, *both also fig of person*.

treasure *vt*: **she ~s the ring / their friendship** она дорожит этим кольцом / их дружбой (*impf*); **I shall always ~ the memory of today** я навсегда сохраню в памяти этот день.

treasurer *n* казначей.

treasury *n* *Fin* (*money, etc.*) казна; (*UK*) **the T.** государственное казначейство *or* министерство финансов; (*US*) **Department of the T.** министерство финансов.

treat *n* (*pleasure*) удовольствие; **it is a ~ to listen to him / to see you looking so well** слушать его — одно удовольствие, сегодня ты хорошо выглядишь — приятно посмотреть; **I want to give them a ~** я хочу доставить им удовольствие; *CQ*: **the roses are looking a ~** эти розы просто восхитительны; **it's my ~ today** сегодня я угощаю.

treat *vti vt* **1** (*behave towards*) обращаться с + *I* (*only in impf*), от|носиться к + *D* (-нестись), обходиться с + *I* (обойтись); **they ~ her like a child** они обращаются с ней как с ребёнком, они относятся к ней как к ребёнку; **they ~ed him badly** они плохо с ним обращались / обошлись; **he ~ed it as a joke** он принял это за шутку; **~ this as confidential** пусть это останется между нами; **the book ~s the problem of...** в книге рассматривается проблема + *G*

2 *Med*: **to ~ smb for cancer / smb's leg** лечить кого-л от рака / чью-л ногу (*impf*); **to ~ smb / smth with penicillin** лечить кого-л / что-л пенициллином; *Tech* **to ~ smth with chemicals** обраб|атывать что-л химикатами (-отать)

3 (*pay for, etc.*): **to ~ smb to an ice cream** уго|щать кого-л мороженым (-стить); **I ~ed myself to a new dress** я купила себе новое платье

vi: **the article ~s of...** в этой статье рассматривается...; **to ~ for peace with the enemy** вести переговоры о мире с противником.

treatise *n* трактат.

treatment *n* **1** обращение с + *I*, отношение к + *D*; обхождение с + *I*; **I received preferential ~** я был принят как почётный гость; **objective ~ of the subject** объективный подход к теме

2 *Med* лечение; **a new ~ for rheumatism** новый метод лечения ревматизма; **to undergo ~ for asthma** лечиться от астмы; **he received medical ~** ему оказали медицинскую помощь (*short term*), он прошёл курс лечения (*long term*); *Tech* **a method of ~ with acid** способ обработки кислотой.

treaty *n* договор.

treble[1] *n* *Mus* дискант (*of voice and singer*).

treble[2] *adj and vti see* **triple.**

treble[2] *adv* втрое больше.

tree *n* дерево; (*for shoe*) колодка; *fig* **family ~** родословное дерево, родословная.

tree-lined *adj*: **a ~ avenue / road** аллея, / дорога, обсаженная деревьями.

trefoil *n* трилистник.

trek *n* поход; *CQ* **it's a long ~ to the village** до деревни идти далеко.

trek *vi*: **we went pony ~king in Andorra** мы путешествовали на пони по Андорре; **we ~ked through the hills for days** мы долго бродили по горам.

tremble *vi* дрожать (*impf*); **to ~ with anger / fear / cold** дрожать от гнева / страха / холода; **she ~d for his safety / at the very thought of it** она за него боялась, она трепетала при одной мысли об этом; **I ~ to think what he might have done** меня бросает (*impers*) в дрожь при мысли о том, что он мог бы сделать.

trembling *n* дрожь; *fig* трепет; **in fear and ~** трепеща от страха.

tremendous *adj* огромный; *CQ* потрясающий.

tremendously *adv CQ* страшно, неимоверно, ужасно; **he is ~ strong/proud of his son** он неимоверно силён, он страшно гордится своим сыном.

tremor *n* дрожь; (*quaver*) трепет; **earth ~s** подземные толчки; **there was a ~ of excitement in his voice** его голос дрожал от возбуждения.

trench *n* ров; (*for drainage*) канава; *Mil* окоп, траншея; *attr*: **~ warfare** окопная война.

trenchant *adj*: **a ~ wit** острый ум; **a ~ style** резкий стиль; **~ comments** колкости.

trend *n* направление; тенденция; **new ~s in scientific thought** новые направления научной мысли; **the latest ~s in popular music** новейшие направления в популярной музыке.

trespass *vi*: **you are ~ing** *approx* здесь проход запрещён; *fig*: **to ~ on smb's time/hospitality** посяг|ать на чьё-л время (-нуть), злоупотреб|лять чьим-л гостеприимством (-ить).

trespasser *n*: **"Trespassers will be prosecuted"** «Проход запрещён — нарушение преследуется законом».

trestle *n* козлы (*no sing*); *attr*: **a ~ table** стол на козлах.

trial *n* **1** *Law* процесс; суд; **during his ~** во время процесса над ним; **his ~ has been postponed** суд над ним был отложен; **he is on ~** он (находится) под следствием; **he is on ~ for murder** его судят за убийство; **to bring smb to ~** привлечь кого-л к суду; **he will get a fair ~** его будут судить по закону; **~ by jury** слушание дела в суде присяжных

2 (*test*) испытание, проба; **a ~ of strength** испытание/проба сил; **to take smth/smb on ~** взять что-л на пробу/кого-л на испытательный срок; **he is on ~** он проходит испытательный срок; **to learn by ~ and error** учиться на своих ошибках (*pl*); *Sport* **sheep dog ~s** соревнования овчарок; *attr*: **~ period** (*for person*) испытательный срок; **they took the car for a ~ run** они взяли машину для пробного пробега

3 (*hardship*) испытание; **the ~s of old age** старческие немощи и огорчения; **he is a ~ to his mother** *CQ* матери с ним наказание.

triangle *n* треугольник.

tribal *adj* племенной, родовой.

tribe *n* племя, род; *CQ pejor* компания, шатия; **a ~ of Red Indians** племя индейцев; **a whole ~ of his relatives came** его родственники пришли скопом.

tribulation *n*: **trials and ~s** испытания и беды.

tribunal *n* трибунал.

tribune *n* (*stand*) трибуна; (*person*) трибун.

tributary *n* (*river*) приток.

tribute *n* дань, *also fig*; *fig*: **he paid ~ to the soldiers' bravery** он отдал должное мужеству солдат; **as a ~ to her loyalty** в награду за её верность.

trice *n*: **in a ~** мгновенно, *CQ* в два счёта.

trick *n* **1** (*practical joke*) шутка; (*prank*) шалость; (*ruse*) приём, проделка; уловка, хитрость; *pejor* трюк, выходка; **to play a ~ on smb** сыграть с кем-л шутку; **his memory played a ~ on him** его подвела память; **childish ~s** детские шалости; **a clever ~** ловкий приём; **a sly/dirty ~** хитрый/мошеннический трюк; **to play a dirty ~ on smb** сделать подлость/напакостить кому-л, *CQ* подложить кому-л свинью; **the children are up to their ~s again** опять дети шалят; **he is up to his old ~s again** опять он за свои фокусы; **he knows all the ~s (of the trade)** он знает все приёмы и уловки

2 (*entertainment*) фокус, трюк; **a conjuring ~** фокус; **a card ~** карточный фокус; **an acrobatic ~** акробатический трюк; **to do ~s** показывать фокусы; **to teach a dog to do ~s** дрессировать собаку; *fig* **this medicine should do the ~** это лекарство должно подействовать

3 (*peculiarity*): **certain ~s of style** некоторые особенности стиля; **he has a ~ of repeating himself** у него привычка повторяться; **a ~ of light** световой эффект

4 *Cards* взятка; **to take a ~** брать взятку.

trick *vt* (*deceive*) обман|ывать (-уть); *CQ* (*swindle*) наду|вать (-ть), провести (*only in pf*); **we were ~ed** нас обманули/надули/провели, *low CQ* нас взяли на пушку; **he ~ed her into signing the contract** он обманом заставил её подписать контракт; **he ~ed her out of the money** он выманил у неё эти деньги.

trickery *n* надувательство, обман.

trickle *n*: **a ~ of blood/water** струйка крови/воды; **the stream dried to a ~** поток высох до тоненького ручейка.

trickle *vi* (*ooze*) сочиться; (*drop*) капать; (*run away/down*) течь (*impf*) *and compounds*; *fig* про|сачиваться (-сочиться); **blood ~d from the wound** кровь сочилась из раны; **water is trickling** (*leaking*)/**only ~d from the tap** у нас кран течёт, вода едва капала из крана; **rain ~d down the back of his neck** капли дождя струйками стекали у него по спине; **tears ~d down her cheeks** слёзы текли у неё по щекам; **a stream ~d between the rocks** ручей струился меж камней; **the audience ~d into the hall** публика просочилась в зал; *fig* **news/donations ~d in slowly** сведения (*pl*)/пожертвования поступали медленно.

tricky *adj* хитрый; (*complicated*) сложный, мудрёный; **a ~ lock/politician** замок с секретом *or* мудрёный замок, хитрый политик; **a ~ problem/situation** запутанная проблема, сло́жная ситуа́ция; *CQ* **he's a ~ customer** он ско́льзкий тип.

tricolo(u)r *n* трёхцве́тный флаг.

tricycle *n* трёхколёсный велосипе́д.

trifle *n* **1** пустя́к, ме́лочь, *CQ* безде́лица; **he is upset by every ~** он расстра́ивается по вся́кому пустяку́; **£100 is a mere ~ for him** для него́ сто фу́нтов—су́щий пустя́к/су́щая безде́лица

2 *as adv CQ* немно́жко; **it's a ~ difficult** э́то трудновáто/немно́жко тру́дно; **could I have a ~ less?** мо́жно мне чу́точку поме́ньше?

trifle *vi*: **to ~ with one's food** ковыря́ться в еде́ (*impf*); **to ~ with smb's affections** игра́ть чьи́ми-л чу́вствами (*impf*); **he is not a man to be ~d with** с ним шу́тки пло́хи.

trifling *n* пустяко́вый, пустя́чный.

trigger *n* спусково́й крючо́к, куро́к; **to pull the ~** спусти́ть куро́к.

trigger *vt*: **it ~ed off a storm of protest/a whole series of events** э́то вы́звало бу́рю проте́стов, э́то повлекло́ за собо́й це́лую цепь собы́тий.

trigonometry *n* тригономе́трия.

trill *n* трель.

trim *n*: **her hair needs a ~** ей ну́жно подровня́ть во́лосы; **in (good) ~** (*of house, garden, etc.*) в поря́дке, (*of person*) в фо́рме.

trim *adj* аккура́тный, опря́тный; (*of figure*) аккура́тный, ла́дный.

trim *vt* **1** (*of hair, beard, nails, wick, etc.*) подрез|а́ть (-́ать); (*of beard, hedge, etc.*) под|ра́внивать (-ровня́ть); **to ~ dead branches off a tree** обрез|а́ть сухи́е ве́тки с де́рева (-́ать)

2 *Sew*: **to ~ a coat with fur** отде́л|ывать пальто́ ме́хом (-ать).

trimming *n* (*ribbon, etc.*) тесьма́; отде́лка; (*for dishes*) гарни́р; **with lace ~** с кружевно́й тесьмо́й, отде́ланный кру́жевом.

Trinity *n Rel* тро́ица.

trinket *n* безделу́шка.

trio *n* (*of people*) тро́йка; *Mus* три́о (*indecl*).

trip *n* пое́здка; (*tour, in car or on foot*) экску́рсия; **a business ~** делова́я пое́здка, командиро́вка; **a day ~** одноднéвная пое́здка; **a coach ~ to the seaside** авто́бусная экску́рсия к мо́рю; **we went on a boat ~ round the island** мы прокати́лись на ка́тере вокру́г о́строва; **the tour included a ~ to the theatre** в пое́здку входи́ло посеще́ние теа́тра; **we made a ~ to Stratford/to town** мы съе́здили в Стра́тфорд/в го́род; **he makes two ~s a year to Iceland** он два ра́за в год е́здит в Исла́ндию; **it cost £100 for the round ~** *approx* вся (туристская) путёвка сто́ила сто фу́нтов.

trip *vi* (*stumble*) спот|ыка́ться (-кну́ться); **he ~ped on/over a stone** он споткну́лся о ка́мень; *fig* **he ~ped up in his evidence/calculations** он сби́лся в свои́х показа́ниях (*pl*)/в (свои́х) расчётах.

tripartite *adj* трёхсторо́нний.

triple *adj* тройно́й, (*of political agreements*) тро́йственный; *Mus* **~ time** трёхдо́льный разме́р.

triple *vti* утр|а́ивать(ся) (-о́ить(ся)).

triplet *n Poet* трипле́т; *Mus* трио́ль; (*people*) (**~s**) тро́йня (*collect*).

triplicate *n*: **in ~** в трёх экземпля́рах.

tripod *n* трено́га, трено́жник.

tripper *n* экскурса́нт.

trite *adj* бана́льный, изби́тый.

triumph *n* торжество́; триу́мф; **a shout of ~** торжеству́ющий крик; **~ of justice/of man over nature** торжество́ справедли́вости/челове́ка над приро́дой.

triumph *vi*: **to ~ (over)** торжествова́ть (над + *I*) (вос-).

triumphant *adj*: **the ~ army** а́рмия-победи́тельница; **he was ~ at his success** он ликова́л, пра́зднуя свой успе́х.

trivia *npl* пустяки́, ме́лочи.

trivial *adj* (*trifling*) ме́лкий, пустяко́вый; (*insignificant*) незначи́тельный; **a ~ offence/scratch/injury** ме́лкое наруше́ние, пустяко́вая цара́пина, незначи́тельное поврежде́ние; **a ~ sum** ме́лкая/незначи́тельная су́мма; **~ matters** ме́лочи.

trolley *n* теле́жка; (*US*) трамва́й.

trolley bus *n* тролле́йбус.

trombone *n* тромбо́н.

troop *n* (*group*) гру́ппа; (*of scouts*) отря́д; (*US: of cavalry*) эскадро́н; *pl Mil* солда́ты, войска́.

troop *vi*: **hundreds of children ~ed past** со́тни дете́й проходи́ли ми́мо; **they all ~ed home** все разошли́сь по дома́м.

trooper *n*: (*US*) **state ~** резерви́ст; *CQ* **to swear like a ~** руга́ться как изво́зчик.

troopship *n* тра́нспорт (для перево́зки войск).

troop train *n* во́инский соста́в.

trophy *n* (*prize, booty*) трофе́й.

tropic *n* тро́пик; **in the ~s** в тро́пиках; **T. of Cancer/Capricorn** тро́пик Ра́ка/Козеро́га.

tropical *adj* тропи́ческий.

trot *n*: **at a ~** ры́сью; **the horse broke into a ~** ло́шадь пошла́ ры́сью; *fig CQ*: **he is always on the ~** его́ ве́чно где́-то но́сит (*impers*); **he keeps us on the ~** он не даёт нам поко́я/передышки.

trot *vi* (*of horse*) идти́ ры́сью; *CQ* **the dog/child ~ted along behind her** соба́ка бежа́ла/ребёнок едва́ поспева́л за ней.

trouble *n* **1** (*misfortune, difficulty*) беда́; непри́ятности (*usu pl*); **he told me all his ~s** он рассказа́л мне о всех свои́х бе́дах/непри́ятностях; **to be in ~** быть в беде́; **to get into ~** попа́сть в беду́; **the ~ is that...** беда́/де́ло в том, что...; **what a ~ you are!** беда́ мне с тобо́й!; **their son is a great ~ to them** сын о́чень их огорча́ет; **he has family/money ~s** у него́ до́ма нелады́, у него́ пло́хо с деньга́ми; **there's ~ enough without you** и без тебя́ забо́т хвата́ет (*impers*); *euph* **to get a girl into ~** соблазни́ть де́вушку

2 (*bother*) забо́та, беспоко́йство; **I am putting you to a lot of ~** я вам доставля́ю сто́лько забо́т/беспоко́йства; **it will save you the ~ of coming again** э́то изба́вит тебя́ от необходи-мости приходи́ть сно́ва; **it is no ~** меня́ нисколько не затрудни́т [**NB** *tense*]; **it is not worth the ~** не сто́ит труда́; **to take the ~ to** взять на себя́/дать себе́ труд + *inf*; **he took a lot of ~ over the posters** он мно́го труди́лся над э́тими плака́тами; **thank you for the ~ you took over my son** спаси́бо за ва́ши забо́ты о моём сы́не; **I hope my son wasn't too much ~ for you** наде́юсь, мой сын не доста́вил вам мно́го хлопо́т; **don't go to a lot of ~ for us** не беспоко́йтесь из-за нас; **he went to a lot of ~ over the preparations/to see that we were comfortable** он ума́ялся (*CQ*) с приготовле́ниями, он так хлопота́л, что́бы нам бы́ло удо́бно

3 (*upset*: *between people*): **there is always ~ between them** ве́чно они́ ссо́рятся; **there's ~ brewing!** быть беде́!; *Med* **he has heart/chest ~** у него́ боле́знь се́рдца *or* больно́е се́рдце, у него́ что-то нела́дно с лёгкими; *Tech*, *Aut*: **he has got engine ~** у него́ барахли́т мото́р; **the mechanic soon put the ~ right** меха́ник бы́стро устрани́л непола́дку

4 *pl Polit* волне́ния, беспоря́дки; **labour ~s** волне́ния среди́ рабо́чих; **after yesterday's ~s** по́сле вчера́шних беспоря́дков.

trouble *vti vt* **1** (*worry*) беспоко́ить (о-), трево́жить (вс-); **he was deeply ~d by what he heard** он был о́чень обеспоко́ен/встрево́жен тем, что услы́шал; **his leg is troubling him** его́ беспоко́ит нога́; **you look ~d** у тебя́ озабо́ченный вид; **his conscience ~d him** его́ му́чила со́весть

2 (*bother*) беспоко́ить (по-); **I won't ~ you if you're busy/with the details** не бу́ду вас беспоко́ить, е́сли вы за́няты, не бу́ду затрудня́ть вас подро́бностями; **don't ~ yourself** не затрудня́йте себя́; **may I ~ you for a light?** разреши́те прикури́ть?

vi беспоко́иться (*usu impf*); **don't ~ to write** не труди́тесь писа́ть; **he didn't ~ to explain/to take his boots off** он не потруди́лся объясни́ть/снять боти́нки.

troubled *adj*: **a ~ face** встрево́женное/озабо́ченное лицо́; **in these ~ times** в те беспоко́йные времена́; *fig* **to fish in ~ waters** лови́ть ры́бу в му́тной воде́.

troublemaker *n* (*causing unpleasantness*) наруши́тель (*m*) споко́йствия/поря́дка; (*of children*) забия́ка, зади́ра (*m and f*).

troublesome *adj* тру́дный; **a ~ child** тру́дный/беспоко́йный ребёнок; **a ~ affair** хлопотли́вое/*CQ* хло́потное де́ло; **a ~ problem** сло́жная пробле́ма; **he has a ~ cough** его́ беспоко́ит ка́шель; **the wasps are ~ this summer** о́сы досажда́ют нам э́тим ле́том.

trough *n* **1** (*for animals' food*) корму́шка, (*for food or water*) коры́то

2 *Meteorol*: **a ~ of low pressure** центр о́бласти ни́зкого давле́ния.

trouser leg *n* штани́на.

trousers *npl* брю́ки, штаны́; **a new pair/two pairs of ~** но́вые брю́ки, две па́ры брюк; *fig* **she wears the ~ in that house** в э́том до́ме она́ глава́ семьи́.

trousseau *n* прида́ное.

trout *n* форе́ль (*sing and collect*).

trowel *n* (*gardener's*) (садо́вый) сово́к; (*builder's*) лопа́тка; мастеро́к.

truancy *n* прогу́л.

truant *n* прогу́льщик; **to play ~** прогу́ливать.

truce *n* переми́рие; **to call a ~** объяви́ть переми́рие.

truck[1] *n* (*lorry*) грузови́к; (*barrow*) теле́жка; *Rail* **goods ~** откры́тая платфо́рма.

truck[2] *n*: **I want no ~ with him** я не хочу́ име́ть с ним ничего́ о́бщего.

truckdriver *n* (*US*) води́тель (*m*) грузовика́.

truck farm, truck garden *ns* (*US*) овощево́дческое хозя́йство.

truculent *adj* (*of person, behaviour*) агресси́вный, гру́бый; (*of manner, remark*) ре́зкий, гру́бый.

trudge *vti* таска́ться (*indet impf*), тащи́ться (*det impf*); **he ~d the streets all day** он таска́лся по у́лицам це́лый день; **he ~d wearily up the hill** он уста́ло тащи́лся в го́ру.

true *n*: **the wheel/door is out of ~** колесо́ пло́хо при́гнано, дверь перекоси́лась.

true *adj* **1** (*veracious*) правди́вый; (*correct*) ве́рный, пра́вильный; (*genuine*) и́стинный; **a ~ account** правди́вый расска́з; **~!** пра́вда!, ве́рно!; **it is ~ that...** э́то пра́вда,/э́то ве́рно, что...; **what is the ~ state of affairs?** каково́ и́стинное положе́ние веще́й?; **like a ~ scholar/Englishman** как и́стинный учёный/англича́нин; **~ value** и́стинная це́нность; **a ~ likeness** по́лное схо́дство; **this holds ~ for most cases** э́то справедли́во для большинства́ слу́чаев; **it's not ~ to life** э́то жи́зненно недостове́рный о́браз; **her dreams came ~** её мечты́ сбыли́сь

2 (*faithful*) ве́рный; **a ~ friend** ве́рный/пре́данный/и́стинный друг; **~ to one's word/ideals** ве́рный своему́ сло́ву/свои́м идеа́лам

3 (*used concessively*): **~, he is rarely here** пра́вда, он ре́дко быва́ет здесь; **he is not an expert, it is ~, but...** он вообще́-то не специали́ст, но...

4 (*accurate, accurately fitted*): **this wall/window frame is not ~** стена́ поста́влена ко́со, ра́ма кося́я; **his aim was ~** он то́чно прице́лился; *Mus* **the note is ~** э́та но́та взята́ ве́рно/чи́сто.

true *adv* правди́во; **his story rings ~** его́ расска́з звучи́т правди́во/правдоподо́бно; **his words ring ~** его́ слова́ звуча́т правди́во/и́скренне; (*accurately*) **to aim ~** це́литься то́чно.

truffle *n* трю́фель (*m*).

truism *n* трюи́зм, бана́льность, изби́тая и́стина.

truly *adv*: **~ good/grateful** по-настоя́щему до́брый, и́скренне благода́рный; **I am ~ happy for you** я действи́тельно рад за тебя́; **~ it was difficult** э́то бы́ло действи́тельно тру́дно; **tell me ~** скажи́ мне че́стно/по пра́вде; ~ **I tried to ring you** че́стное сло́во, я пыта́лся дозвони́ться до тебя́; **really and ~?** в са́мом де́ле?, пра́вда?; **do you ~ believe that?** ты и в са́мом де́ле ве́ришь э́тому?; (*in letters*) **yours ~** и́скренне Ваш, с уваже́нием.

trump *n* ко́зырь (*m*); **hearts are ~s** че́рвы— ко́зыри; **ace of ~s** козырно́й туз; **to lead ~s** ходи́ть с ко́зыря (*sing*).

trump *vt* крыть/бить ко́зырем (*pfs* по́-); *fig* **to ~ up charges against smb** фабрикова́ть обвине́ния про́тив кого́-л (с-).

trumpet *n Mus* труба́; **to sound the ~** труби́ть; **ear ~** слухова́я тру́бка; *fig* **to blow one's own ~** хвали́ться, бахва́литься.

trumpeter *n* труба́ч.

truncate *vt* усе|ка́ть (-́чь); (*of article, speech, etc.*) сокра|ща́ть (-ти́ть).

truncheon *n* дуби́нка.

trunk *n* (*of tree*) ствол; *Anat* ту́ловище; (*of elephant*) хо́бот; (*for travel*) кофр; (*US*) *Aut* бага́жник.

trunk call *n* междугоро́дный телефо́нный вы́зов.

trunk road *n* магистра́ль(ная доро́га).

trunks *npl* трусы́; **swimming ~s** пла́вки.

truss *n* (*bundle*) свя́зка; (*of hay*) пук; *Med* грыжево́й банда́ж.

trust *n* **1** (*faith*): **~ in smth** дове́рие к чему́-л, ве́ра во что-л; **to put one's ~ in smb/smth** доверя́ться кому́-л/чему́-л; **to take smb/smth on ~** ве́рить кому́-л на́ слово, принима́ть что-л на ве́ру

2 (*charge*): **to commit smth to smb's ~** дове́рить что-л кому́-л

3 *Law*: **the property is held in ~** иму́щество управля́ется по дове́ренности; **he is holding the money in ~ for his nephew** он распоряжа́ется деньга́ми племя́нника как опеку́н; **he left money in a ~ for his children's education** он оста́вил де́ньги на образова́ние дете́й опекуна́м

4 *Comm* (*organization*) трест, конце́рн.

trust *vti vt* довер|я́ть + *D* (-́ить); **he is not to be ~ed** ему́ нельзя́ доверя́ть; **I wouldn't ~ him with my car** я бы не дове́рил ему́ свою́ маши́ну; **you can't ~ a word he says** нельзя́ ве́рить ни одному́ его́ сло́ву; **you can ~ him to do the job properly** ему́ мо́жно дове́рить э́ту рабо́ту; *CQ*: **~ him to spoil things!** мо́жешь быть уве́ренным, он всё испо́ртит; **I seem to have lost the key.—T. you!** ка́жется, я потеря́л ключ.—Э́то на тебя́ похо́же!; **I ~ all was well** наде́юсь, всё обошло́сь хорошо́

vi: **to ~ in smb** доверя́ться/ве́рить кому́-л; **don't ~ to chance/luck** не наде́йся на счастли́вый слу́чай.

trusted *adj* надёжный.

trustee *n* (*of child*) опеку́н; (*of property, organization*) попечи́тель (*m*).

trustful, trusting *adj* дове́рчивый.

trustworthy *adj* надёжный, заслу́живающий дове́рия.

trusty *adj* ве́рный, пре́данный.

truth *n* пра́вда; правди́вость; *Philos* и́стина; **to speak/tell the ~** говори́ть пра́вду; **~ to tell** *or* **to tell the ~ ...** по пра́вде говоря́..., сказа́ть по пра́вде...; **in ~ I hardly know him** вообще́-то я его́ почти́ не зна́ю; **~ will out** пра́вды не скро́ешь; **there is not a word of ~ in it** в э́том нет и до́ли пра́вды; **it is the plain/honest ~** э́то су́щая/и́стинная пра́вда; **I told him a few home ~s** я вы́сказал ему́ пра́вду в глаза́; **people don't like home ~s** пра́вда глаза́ ко́лет.

truthful *adj* (*of people, statement, etc.*) правди́вый; **are you being quite ~?** ты пра́вду говори́шь?

try *n* попы́тка; **he had two tries** он сде́лал две попы́тки; **let me have a ~** дава́й я попро́бую/попыта́юсь; **it's worth a ~** сто́ит попро́бовать.

try *vti vt* **1** (*attempt*) про́бовать (по-); пыта́ться (по-); (*make effort*) стара́ться (по-); **I'll ~ to mend it** я попро́бую э́то почини́ть; **~ to understand** попыта́йтесь/постара́йтесь поня́ть; **he only tried two questions** он попро́бовал отве́тить то́лько на два вопро́са; **to ~ one's hand at smth** попро́бовать свои́ си́лы в чём-л; **he tried everything** он испро́бовал (*pf*) всё/все сре́дства; **he tried his best** он стара́лся изо всех сил; **it is ~ing to rain** собира́ется пойти́ дождь

2 (*test*) испы́т|ывать (-а́ть); провер|я́ть (-́ить); **to ~ one's strength/luck** испыта́ть *or* прове́рить свои́ си́лы, попыта́ть сча́стья (*G*) (*pf*); **all the goods have been tried and tested** все това́ры прошли́ контро́ль/прове́рку; **my patience was sorely tried by them** они́ испы́тывали моё терпе́ние

3 (*sample*) про́бовать (по-); **~ knocking** попро́буй постучи́; **do ~ my cake** попро́буй/отве́дай моего́ пирога́

4 *Law* суди́ть (*impf*); **he is being tried for murder** его́ су́дят за уби́йство

vi про́бовать; пыта́ться; стара́ться; **he is ~ing for a job in their firm** он пыта́ется получи́ть рабо́ту в их фи́рме; **~ as he would...** как бы он ни пыта́лся/стара́лся...; **he tried very hard** он о́чень стара́лся

try on *vt* (*of clothes, shoes*) пример|я́ть (-́ить); *fig*: **he's just ~ing it on** он про́сто притворя́ется; **you can't ~ that on with me** меня́ не проведёшь.

trying *adj* тру́дный, тяжёлый; **a ~ time/journey** тру́дное *or* тяжёлое вре́мя/путеше́ствие; **he can be very ~** с ним иногда́ о́чень тру́дно; **you are being very ~ today** ты сего́дня невыноси́м.

tsar *n* царь (*m*).

tsarevitch *n* царе́вич.

T-shirt *n* ма́йка (с коро́ткими рукава́ми).

T-square *n* уго́льник, рейши́на.

tub *n* (*large basin*) таз; (*bigger, for washing*) поха́нь, бадья́; (*vat, cask, also for plants*) ка́дка; (*bath*) ва́нна.

tubby *adj*: **a ~ little man/woman** коро́тышка.

tube *n* (*pipe*) трубка; *Anat* труба; (*of paint, toothpaste, etc.*) тюбик; *CQ* (*UK*) (**the ~**) метро (*indecl*); *Aut* **inner ~** камера, (*of bicycle*) велокамера; **I'm going by ~** я поеду на метро; *attr*: **~ station** станция метро.

tubeless *adj*: **a ~ tyre** безкамерная шина.

tuber *n* клубень (*m*).

tuberculosis *n* туберкулёз.

tubular *adj* трубчатый.

tuck *n* *Sew* складка; **to make a ~ in** сделать складку на + *P*.

tuck *vt* за|совывать (-сунуть); (*hide*) прятать (с-); **she ~ed the note into her bag** она засунула/спрятала записку в сумочку; **he ~ed his legs under him** он поджал под себя ноги

tuck away *vt* **1**: **to ~ smth away at the back of a drawer** засунуть что-л поглубже в ящик; **the key is ~ed away in my pocket** ключ спрятан у меня в кармане; **the house is ~ed away behind trees** домик прячется за деревьями

2 (*of food*) *CQ*: **he ~ed away two helpings** он уплёл две порции; **he can certainly ~ it away** ну и горазд же он поесть; **I can't think where he ~s it away** и куда только у него всё это помещается!

tuck in *vti vt*: **to ~ the sheets in** заправить простыни; **~ your shirt in** заправь рубашку

vi (*of food*) *CQ*: **~ in!** давайте-ка ешьте!; **they ~ed in hungrily** они уписывали за обе щёки

tuck up *vt*: **to ~ one's skirt up** под|бирать подол (-обрать); **to ~ one's sleeves up** засучи|вать рукава (-ть); **he is warmly ~ed up in bed** он лежит, хорошо укутанный одеялом.

Tuesday *n* вторник.

tuft *n* (*of feathers on bird, fig of hair on top of head*) хохол, хохолок; (*of hay, of hair sticking out*) клок, пучок; **a ~ of grass** кочка.

tug *n* **1** (*pull*) рывок

2 (*also* **~boat**) буксир.

tug *vti vt* (*pull*) дёр|гать (-нуть); **he ~ed the rope/her arm** он дёрнул (за) верёвку/её за руку

vi: **to ~ at/on smth** дёргать (за) что-л.

tug-of-war *n* перетягивание каната.

tuition *n* обучение; **he is having private ~ in maths** он берёт частные уроки по математике (*sing*); *attr*: **~ fees** плата за обучение.

tulip *n* тюльпан.

tulle *n* тюль (*m*).

tumble *vi* валиться (по-, с-) *and compounds*; (*overturn*) опроки|дываться (-нуться); (*of acrobats*) кувыркаться (*only in impf*); **he ~d off his horse/into the river** он свалился с лошади/в реку; **he ~d into/out of bed** он повалился на кровать, он упал с кровати; **the books ~d to the floor/out of the cupboard** книги свалились на пол/вывалились из шкафа; **the house is tumbling down** дом постепенно разваливается; **the children were tumbling about on the floor** дети катались по полу; **he ~d over the chair** он споткнулся (*stumbled*) о стул; **the pile of books/the lamp ~d down** *or* **over** стопка книг упала, лампа опрокинулась; *CQ*: **he has ~d to our plan** он разгадал наш план; **he hasn't ~d to it yet** до него это ещё не дошло.

tumbledown *adj* развалившийся.

tumbler *n* (*glass*) стакан.

tummy *n* *CQ* живот, животик.

tumour *n* опухоль.

tumult *n* суматоха.

tumultuous *adj* бурный; **a ~ meeting** бурное собрание; **~ applause** бурные аплодисменты (*pl*); **a ~ crowd** шумная/взволнованная толпа.

tundra *n* тундра.

tune *n* мелодия; мотив; **to sing in/out of ~** петь в лад, фальшивить; **the piano is in/out of ~** фортепьяно настроено/расстроено; *fig*: **to change one's ~** запеть на другой лад; **compensation to the ~ of £1,000** компенсация в размере тысячи фунтов; **they bought books to the ~ of £100** они купили книг на сумму сто фунтов.

tune *vti vt* *Mus* настр|аивать (-оить) (*also Radio, TV* **to ~ in**); *Aut* нала|живать (-дить); *Radio* **you are not ~d in properly** ты не настроил как следует

vi: *Radio* **to ~ in** настраиваться; **to ~ in to a station/to medium wave** настроиться на станцию/на среднюю волну; *Mus* **the orchestra is tuning up** оркестр настраивается.

tuneful *adj* мелодичный.

tuner *n* *Radio* механизм настройки; **piano ~** настройщик роялей.

tungsten *n* вольфрам.

tunic *n* (*blouse*) блуза; (*UK, US*) **a soldier's ~** куртка.

tuning *n* *Mus, Radio* настройка; *Aut* наладка; *attr*: **~ fork** камертон.

tunnel *n* тоннель (*m*), туннель (*m*); подземный ход; **to make a ~** проложить тоннель.

tunnel *vti vt*: **a mound ~led by rabbit burrows** холм, изрытый кроличьими норками; **shelters ~led into the hillside** убежища, вырытые в горе

vi: **to ~ into a hillside/under a wall/one's way out of prison** рыть тоннель в горе/лаз под стеной/подземный ход для побега из тюрьмы (*impf*); **to ~ down into the earth** зары|ваться в землю (-ться).

tunny fish *n* тунец.

turban *n* тюрбан; (*of Moslems*) чалма.

turbid *adj* мутный.

turbine *n* турбина.

turbojet *adj* турбореактивный.

turboprop *adj* турбовинтовой.

turbot *n* (белокорый) палтус.

turbulence *n* *Meteorol, Aer, of sea, etc.* турбулентность.

turbulent *adj* бурный, *also fig*; *fig* буйный.

turf *n* дёрн; (*peat*) торф; *Sport* (**the ~**) (*horse-racing circles*) скаковой спорт и люди, связанные с ним; (*races*) скачки (*pl*), бега (*pl*).

Turk *n* турок, турчанка.

turkey *n* индюк, *f* индейка.

Turkish *adj* туре́цкий; **a ~ bath** туре́цкая ба́ня; **~ delight** раха́т-луку́м.

Turkman *n* туркме́н.

Turkmenian *adj* туркме́нский; **a ~ woman** туркме́нка.

turmoil *n* смяте́ние; сумато́ха; **everything is in a ~** здесь по́лная неразбери́ха; **his thoughts were in a ~** его́ мы́сли смеша́лись.

turn *n* **1** (*turning movement*) поворо́т, *Tech* (*revolution*) оборо́т; **give the handle three ~s** сде́лай три поворо́та ру́чкой; **with a ~ of the key/hand** поворо́том ключа́/руки́; **give the screw another ~** ещё покрути́ винт; *fig*: **he never does a hand's ~** он и па́льцем не пошевельнёт; **the meat is done to a ~** мя́со поджа́рено как раз в ме́ру; **to do smb a good/bad ~** оказа́ть кому́-л до́брую/плоху́ю *or* медве́жью (*well-meant, but bad in result*) услу́гу

2 (*change of direction, bend*) поворо́т; **a ~ to the left** поворо́т нале́во (*adv*); **"No left ~"** «Ле́вый поворо́т запрещён»; **a sharp/sudden ~ in the road** круто́й поворо́т доро́ги; **a road full of twists and ~s** о́чень изви́листая доро́га; **to take a ~ in the garden** прогуля́ться/пройти́сь по са́ду; *Aer* **to make a ~** сде́лать разворо́т; *fig*: **a ~ of speech** оборо́т (ре́чи); **events have taken a dangerous ~** собы́тия при́няли опа́сный оборо́т; **a ~ for the better** переме́на к лу́чшему; **the patient/things took a ~ for the worse** больно́му ста́ло ху́же, положе́ние уху́дшилось; **at every ~** на ка́ждом шагу́; **at the ~ of the century** в нача́ле *or* в конце́ ве́ка

3 (*in queue, game, etc.*) о́чередь; **it's my ~** тепе́рь моя́ о́чередь; **to miss one's ~** пропусти́ть свою́ о́чередь; **out of ~** вне/без о́череди; **to speak out of ~** взять сло́во вне о́череди; **in ~, ~ and ~ about, by ~s** по о́череди (*sing*); **to take ~s at doing smth** де́лать что-л по о́череди (*sing*); **it's your ~ next** ва́ша о́чередь, вы сле́дующие; *fig*: **your ~ will come** придёт и твой черёд; **they were laughing and crying by ~s** они́ то смея́лись, то пла́кали; **let me take a ~ at the wheel** дава́й тепе́рь я поведу́ маши́ну

4 *Med* (*attack*) при́ступ, припа́док; *fig* **you gave me quite a ~** ну ты меня́ и напуга́л

5 *Theat* но́мер; **he is the star ~** его́ но́мер—гвоздь програ́ммы; **he did a comic ~** он испо́лнил коми́ческий но́мер.

turn *vti vt* **1** (*a tap, handle, key, etc.*) по|вора́чивать (-верну́ть); **~ the knob to "low"/to 300°** поверни́те ру́чку на «ни́зко»/на три́ста гра́дусов; **the belt ~s the wheel** реме́нь враща́ет колесо́ (*impf*)

2 (*in various directions, etc.*) повора́чивать *and compounds*; **to ~ a patient** перевора́чивать больно́го; **to ~ smth inside out** вы́вернуть что-л наизна́нку; **to ~ one's ankle** подверну́ть лоды́жку; **to ~ one's back on smb** от|вора́чиваться от кого́-л (-верну́ться), *also fig*; **as soon as my back was ~ed** как то́лько я отверну́лся; **to ~ one's/*fig* smb's head** поверну́ть го́лову, вскружи́ть кому́-л го́лову; *fig*: **it ~s my stomach (over)** меня́ от э́того тошни́т (*impers*); **he didn't ~ a hair** он и гла́зом не моргну́л

3 (*direct*) поверну́ть, направ|ля́ть (-ить), обра|ща́ть (-ти́ть); **he ~ed his face/the mirror to the wall** он поверну́лся лицо́м к стене́ [NB *reflexive*], он поверну́л зе́ркало к стене́; **he ~ed his steps homewards** он напра́вил свои́ стопы́ к до́му; **to ~ one's attention to smth** напра́вить своё внима́ние на что-л; *fig*: **to ~ smth to one's advantage** обрати́ть что-л себе́ на по́льзу; **he ~ed the conversation** он перевёл разгово́р на другу́ю те́му; **he ~ed them against us** он восстанови́л их про́тив нас; **he ~ed a deaf ear to my warnings/appeals** он пропусти́л моё предупрежде́ние (*sing*) ми́мо уше́й, он был глух к мои́м мольба́м

4 (*pass*) *CQ*: **he has/is ~ed 50** ему́ перева́лило (*impers*) за пятьдеся́т; **it has just/is ~ed 4 o'clock** то́лько что про́било (*impers*) четы́ре, уже́ пя́тый час

5 (*change*) превра|ща́ть (-ти́ть); **it ~ed him into an old man** э́то преврати́ло его́ в старика́; **to ~ a play into a film** экранизи́ровать пье́су (*impf and pf*); **the heat ~ed the walls black/the milk** сте́ны от жа́ра почерне́ли, от жары́ молоко́ ски́сло

6 (*on a lathe*): **to ~ wood** об|та́чивать де́рево (-точи́ть)

vi **1** повора́чиваться; (*revolve*) враща́ться (*impf*); **the tap/handle won't ~** кран/ру́чка не повора́чивается; **the Earth ~s on its axis** Земля́ враща́ется вокру́г свое́й оси́; **the wheels are ~ing** колёса враща́ются; *fig* **it will make him ~ in his grave** он от э́того в гробу́ перевернётся

2 (*change direction*) поверну́ть; (*turn round on the spot*) поверну́ться; **he/the bus ~ed right** он/авто́бус поверну́л напра́во; **he ~ed on his heel** он поверну́лся на каблука́х (*pl*); **the plane ~ed towards the sea** самолёт поверну́л к мо́рю; **we ~ed for home** мы поверну́ли к до́му; **left ~!** нале́во!; **about ~!** круго́м!; *fig*: **he didn't know which way to ~** он не знал, куда́ поверну́ться; **he ~ed to me for help** он обрати́лся ко мне за по́мощью; **her thoughts ~ed to...** её мы́сли обрати́лись к + *D*; **he ~ed to politics late in life** он стал занима́ться поли́тикой на скло́не лет; **the weather has ~ed** пого́да измени́лась; **our luck has ~ed** (*for better*) нам улыбну́лось сча́стье, (*for worse*) сча́стье измени́ло нам

3 (*become*): **to ~ blue/red/pale** сине́ть, красне́ть, бледне́ть (*pfs* по-); **he ~ed informer** он стал доно́счиком; **it's ~ing cold** стано́вится холодне́е; **the water has ~ed to ice** вода́ преврати́лась в лёд; **my admiration soon ~ed to scorn** моё восхище́ние ско́ро смени́лось презре́нием; **it ~ed into a joke** э́то обрати́ли в шу́тку

turn away *vti vt*: **they were ~ed away from the restaurant** их не пусти́ли в рестора́н; **he went to her for help but she ~ed him away**

он обрати́лся к ней за по́мощью, но она́ отказа́ла ему́

vi от|вора́чиваться (-верну́ться)

turn back *vti vt*: **he was ~ed back at the frontier** его́ не пусти́ли че́рез грани́цу; **today we ~ the clocks back an hour** сего́дня мы перево́дим часы́ на час наза́д

vi поверну́ть наза́д (*also fig*)/обра́тно

turn down *vt*: **to ~ down the corner of a page** за|гиба́ть страни́цу (-гну́ть); **to ~ down the coverlet** отогну́ть/отверну́ть покрыва́ло; **~ down the gas/radio/TV** уба́вь газ, сде́лай ра́дио/телеви́зор поти́ше; **to ~ down an offer/a suitor/smb's request** отказа́ться от предложе́ния, отказа́ть покло́ннику/кому́-л в про́сьбе; **he has already ~ed down three candidates** он уже́ отве́рг трёх кандида́тов

turn in *vti vt*: **to ~ in one's key/a piece of work** сда|ва́ть ключ/рабо́ту (-ть)

vi CQ ложи́ться спать (лечь)

turn inside out *vt*: **to ~ a coat inside out** вывора́чивать пальто́ наизна́нку; **he ~ed his pockets/drawers inside out** он вы́вернул карма́ны, он вы́тряхнул всё из я́щиков

turn off *vti vt* (*lights*, *gas*, *cooker*, *Radio*, *engine*) вы|ключа́ть (-´ключить); (*lights*) гаси́ть (по-); (*tap*) закры|ва́ть (-´ть)

vi: **we ~ed off the path** мы сверну́ли с тропи́нки; **where do we ~ off for Bristol?** где нам сверну́ть, что́бы дое́хать до Бристо́ля?

turn on *vti vt* (*lights*, *gas*, *cooker*, *Radio*, *engine*) включ|а́ть (-и́ть); (*tap*) откры|ва́ть (-´ть); **he left the tap ~ed on** он оста́вил кран откры́тым

vi: **to ~ on smb** набр|а́сываться на кого́-л (-о́ситься); *fig*: **the conversation ~ed on dogs** разгово́р (за)шёл о соба́ках; **everything ~s on his decision** всё зави́сит от его́ реше́ния

turn out *vti vt* (*drive out*) вы|гоня́ть (-´гнать); (*lights*) гаси́ть, выключа́ть; (*pocket*, *etc.*) вы|вора́чивать (-´вернуть); (*produce*) вы|пуска́ть (-´пустить); **to ~ cattle out to grass** выгоня́ть скот на па́стбище; **he was ~ed out of the bar** его́ вы́гнали из ба́ра; **the college ~s out good teachers** э́тот институ́т выпуска́ет хоро́ших педаго́гов; **the factory ~s out poor goods** э́та фа́брика выпуска́ет плохи́е това́ры

vi: **not many ~ed out for the meeting** на собра́ние пришло́ ма́ло люде́й; **people won't ~ out if it rains** е́сли бу́дет плоха́я пого́да, лю́ди не приду́т; **doctors don't like ~ing out at night** врачи́ не лю́бят ночны́е вы́зовы; **her dress did not ~ out well** её пла́тье не получи́лось; **it all ~ed out well** всё обошло́сь благополу́чно; **it ~ed out that he arrived first** оказа́лось,/так получи́лось, что он пришёл пе́рвым; **he ~ed out to be a doctor** он оказа́лся врачо́м; **as it ~ed out he already knew her** как оказа́лось,/вы́яснилось, он уже́ был с ней знако́м

turn over *vti vt*: **to ~ a page/patient over** перевора́чивать страни́цу/больно́го; **to ~ smb/smth over to the police** переда́ть кого́-л/что-л в поли́цию; **he ~ed the firm over to his son** он пе́реда́л дела́ фи́рмы сы́ну; **they ~ over a million a year** оборо́т у них миллио́н фу́нтов в год; **to ~ over smth in one's mind** обду́м|ывать что-л (-ать)

vi пере|вора́чиваться (-верну́ться)

turn round *vti vt*: **we ~ed the car round** мы разверну́лись; **~ your chairs round** поверни́те сту́лья

vi (*of person*) обора́чиваться (оберну́ться); (*revolve*) враща́ться (*only in impf*)

turn up *vti vt*: **to be ~ed up** (*of toes, corner of page or carpet*) за|гиба́ться (-гну́ться); **to ~ up one's collar/the hem of a dress** подня́ть воротни́к, подши́ть подо́л пла́тья; **~ up the gas** приба́вь газ/ого́нь; **~ up the volume** сде́лай (по)гро́мче; *fig* **she ~ed up her nose at the suggestion** она́ пренебрежи́тельно отнесла́сь к э́тому предложе́нию

vi (*appear*) появ|ля́ться (-и́ться); (*be found*) на|ходи́ться (-йти́сь); **he ~ed up two hours later** он появи́лся на два часа́ по́зже; **nobody ~ed up for the lecture** никто́ не пришёл на ле́кцию; **the pen ~ed up under the rug** ру́чка нашла́сь под ко́вриком; **something will ~ up** что́-нибудь да подвернётся.

turndown *adj*: **a ~ collar** отложно́й воротни́к.

turned-up *adj*: **a ~ nose** вздёрнутый нос; **with a ~ collar** с по́днятым воротнико́м.

turning *n* поворо́т; **the first ~ after the traffic lights** пе́рвый поворо́т по́сле светофо́ра; **a ~ off Gorky Street** переу́лок, иду́щий от у́лицы Го́рького; **we took the wrong ~** мы не там поверну́ли; *attr fig*: **~ point** перело́м.

turnip *n* ре́па, *also collect*.

turnout *n*: **there was a poor/good ~ at the match** на матч пришло́ ма́ло/мно́го наро́ду.

turnover *n Comm* оборо́т; (*of staff*) теку́честь; **our annual ~ is a million roubles** у нас годово́й бюдже́т в миллио́н рубле́й; **a quick ~ of goods/staff** бы́стрый товарооборо́т, больша́я теку́честь ка́дров.

turnstile *n* турнике́т.

turn-up *n* (*on trousers*) отворо́т.

turpentine, *CQ* **turps** *n* скипида́р, терпенти́н.

turquoise *n Min* бирюза́; (*colour*) бирюзо́вый цвет.

turtle *n* морска́я черепа́ха; *fig* (*of a ship*) **to turn ~** переверну́ться вверх дном, опроки́нуться.

turtledove *n* го́рлинка, го́рлица.

tusk *n* би́вень (*m*).

tussle *n* потасо́вка, сва́лка; (*verbal*) пере́бранка.

tussock *n* (*in marsh*) ко́чка.

tutor *n* (*coach*) репети́тор; *Univ* нау́чный руководи́тель (*m*).

tutor *vt*: **to ~ smb in Latin** учи́ть кого́-л лати́нскому языку́ (*usu impf*).

tutorial *n Univ* консульта́ция; **a physics ~** консульта́ция по фи́зике.

tuxedo *n* (*US*) смо́кинг.

twaddle *n CQ* чушь.

twang *n*: **he has a nasal ~** он гнуса́вит; **the ~ of a guitar** звон гита́ры.

tweak *vt*: **to ~ smb's ear** щипáть когó-л зá ухо (ущипнýть); **he ~ed the cloth off the table** он сдёрнул скáтерть со столá.

tweed *n* твид (*no pl*); **he is wearing ~s** он в тви́довом костю́ме (*sing*).

tweezers *npl* пинцéт (*sing*).

twelfth *adj* двенáдцатый.

twelve *num* двенáдцать [*see* **eleven**].

twenty *num* двáдцать (*G*, *D*, *P* двадцати́, *I* двадцатью́) [**NB** *in nom and A noun and adj are in G pl*; *in oblique cases nouns and adjs are plural*, *agreeing in case with numeral*]; **20 large houses** двáдцать больши́х домóв; **with 23 blue lorries** с двадцатью́ тремя́ си́ними грузовикáми; **there were 26 of them** их бы́ло двáдцать шесть; **a (number) 20/25 bus** двадцáтый/двáдцать пя́тый автóбус; **26/21 sheep were lost** пропáло двáдцать шесть овéц, потеря́лась двáдцать однá овцá; *as n*: **in the twenties** в двадцáтые гóды; **he is in his (early)/(late) twenties** емý чуть бóльше двадцати́, емý под три́дцать.

twice *adv*: **I told her ~** я говори́л ей двáжды/два рáза; **I have been there once or ~** я рáза два был там [**NB** *inversion of words to convey* "*once or twice*"]; **he doesn't have to be asked ~** егó не нýжно два рáза проси́ть; **she is ~ his age** онá вдвóе/в два рáза стáрше егó; **~ as much/long** вдвóе бóльше/длиннée; **think ~ before agreeing** подýмай хорошéнько, прéжде чем соглашáться.

twiddle *vti*: **to ~ (with) the knobs** вози́ться с кнóпками (*usu impf*); **to ~ with one's moustache/one's tie** крути́ть ус(ы́), тереби́ть гáлстук (*usu impfs*).

twig[1] *n* вéточка; (*without leaves*) прут.

twig[2] *vti CQ*: **I ~ged what they were up to** я разгадáл их намéрения; **did you ~ (what he meant)?** ты усёк?

twilight *n* сýмерки (*no sing*); **at ~** в сýмерках; *attr* сýмеречный.

twin *n* близнéц; **an identical ~** двойня́шка (*m and f*); **Siamese ~s** сиáмские близнецы́.

twin *adj*: **my ~ sister** моя́ сестрá-близнéц; **~ towns** городá-побрати́мы; **~ beds** две односпáльные кровáти.

twine *n* бечёвка.

twine *vti vt* (*weave*) вить (с-); (*encircle*) обви|вáть (-́ть); **to ~ flowers into a garland** плести́ венóк из цветóв (с-); **he ~d the string round his finger** он накрути́л бечёвку на пáлец

vi (*of plants*) ви́ться (*impf*).

twin-engined *adj* двухмотóрный.

twinge *n*: **I feel an occasional ~ (of pain) in my tooth** у меня́ иногдá возникáет (óстрая) боль в зýбе; **a ~ of conscience/regret** угрызéние сóвести, тень сожалéния.

twinkle *n* мерцáние, мигáние; *fig* **there was a ~ in his eye** у негó в глазáх мелькнýла и́скорка.

twinkle *vi* мерцáть (*impf*), мигáть (*only in impf*); *fig* **her eyes ~d mischievously** её глазá озорнó поблёскивали.

twinkling *n*: **in the ~ of an eye** в мгновéние óка.

twirl *vti vt* вертéть + *A or* + *I* (по-); **he ~ed his cane** он вертéл трость/трóстью; **to ~ one's moustache** крути́ть ус(ы́) (*usu impf*)

vi: **they ~ed around in the waltz** они́ кружи́лись в вáльсе.

twist *n* (*in road*, *river*) изги́б; **he gave the rope/his knee a ~** он скрути́л верёвку, он вы́вихнул колéно; **a ~ of paper** (*as bag*) кулёк; *fig* **the story has an unexpected ~** в э́том расскáзе есть неожи́данный поворóт.

twist *vti vt* **1** (*turn*) по|ворáчивать (-вернýть); (*turn to open*) крути́ть (с-), от|ворáчивать (-вернýть); (*in play or nervousness*) вертéть + *A or* + *I* (по-); **he ~ed his head to have a look** он повернýл гóлову, чтóбы посмотрéть; **to ~ the lid off a jar** отвернýть кры́шку бáнки; **~ the cap clockwise** поверни́ кры́шку вправо; **she was nervously ~ing her ring** онá, нéрвничая, вертéла кольцó на пáльце

2 (*make twisted*) крути́ть (с-); (*plait*) плести́ (с-) *and compounds*; **I've ~ed the thread/rope** я скрути́л ни́тку/верёвку; **to ~ straw into a rope** вить из солóмы верёвку (с-); **your belt is ~ed** у тебя́ ремéнь перекрути́лся; **she ~ed a scarf round her neck** онá намотáла на шéю шарф; **she ~ed her hair into a plait** онá заплелá вóлосы в кóсу; *fig* **she can ~ him round her little finger** онá вéртит/крýтит им как хóчет, онá из негó верёвки вьёт

3 (*wrench*) вы|ворáчивать (-́вернуть); (*bend*) из|гибáть (-огнýть); (*distort*) криви́ть (с-); искa|жáть (-зи́ть), *also fig*; **to ~ one's ankle/knee/smb's arm** вы́вихнуть лоды́жку/колéно, вы́вернуть комý-л рýку; **the key is ~ed** ключ изóгнут; **his face was ~ed with pain** егó лицó искази́лось от бóли; *fig* **to ~ the sense/the facts/smb's words** искажáть смысл/фáкты/чьи-л словá

vi (*of rope*) крути́ться; (*of road, river, snake*) ви́ться, извивáться (*usu impfs*); **the snake ~ed through the grass** змея́, извивáясь, ползлá в травé; **smoke was ~ing upwards** дым ви́лся над кры́шей; **the metal ~ed with the heat** метáлл корóбился от высóкой температýры.

twister *n CQ* мошéнник, обмáнщик.

twit *n CQ* дурáк, идиóт.

twitch *n*: **a nervous ~** нéрвное подёргивание; **with a ~ of his eyebrows** вздёрнув брóви; **he gave the reins a ~** он дёрнул вóжжи.

twitch *vi* подёргиваться; **his body/he was ~ing all over** он весь дёргался, егó всегó подёргивало (*impers*); **his eyebrows ~ed** он подёргивал бровя́ми; **the curtains ~ed at the window opposite** в окнé напрóтив шевельнýлись занавéски.

twitter *n* (*of birds*) щéбет, щебетáние.

twitter *vi* щебетáть (*impf*) (*also fig of little girls*).

two *num m and neut* два, *f* две (*G*, *P* двух, *D* двум, *I* двумя́); *collect* двóе (*G*, *A*, *P* двои́х, *D* двои́м, *I* двои́ми) [*see gram-*

matical notes under **four**]; **2 red apples** два кра́сных я́блока; **my 2 younger brothers** два мои́х мла́дших бра́та; **2 tabby cats** две полоса́тые ко́шки; **2 wide rivers** две широ́кие ре-ки́; **2 big bathrooms** две больши́е ва́нные; **after 2 long hours** по́сле двух до́лгих часо́в; **with 2 new friends** с двумя́ но́выми друзья́ми; **2 pairs of scissors** две па́ры но́жниц, дво́е но́жниц; **we have 2 sledges** у нас дво́е сане́й; **with 2 sledges** с двумя́ саня́ми; **a "2"** (*the number* 2, *a* 2 *in cards, school mark, also of a number* 2 *bus*) дво́йка; **the 2 of hearts** дво́йка черве́й; **he got a 2 in physics** он получи́л дво́йку по фи́зике; **chapter 2** втора́я глава́; **in room (number) 2** в ко́мнате (но́мер) два; **he is 2** ему́ два го́да; **2 times 2** два́жды два; **it is after 2** уже́ тре́тий час; **2-year-olds** двухле́тние де́ти; **200** две́сти (*G* двухсо́т, *D* двумста́м, *I* двумяста́ми, *P* о двухста́х); **2,000** две ты́сячи; **after ~ or three days** по́сле двух-трёх дней; **they arrived in ~s** они́ приходи́ли по́ двое; **they are ~ of a kind** они́ одного́ по́ля я́годы; *fig* **putting ~ and ~ together** сопоста́вив всё, поразмы́слив хороше́нько.

two-dimensional *adj* двухме́рный.

two-door *adj*: **a ~ car** маши́на с двумя́ дверя́ми.

two-edged *adj*: *fig* **a ~ compliment** двусмы́сленный комплиме́нт.

two-faced *adj fig* двули́чный.

twofold *adj and adv* двойно́й; вдво́е; вдвойне́.

two-seater *adj* двухме́стный.

two-storey *adj* двухэта́жный.

two-way *adj* двусторо́нний.

tycoon *n* магна́т.

type *n* тип; *Typ* шрифт; **a good champagne ~ of wine** хоро́шее вино́ ти́па шампа́нского; **he is an odd/not my ~** он стра́нный тип, он не в моём вку́се; **I don't like his ~** я не люблю́ таки́х люде́й; **what ~ of car does she have?** кака́я у неё маши́на?/ма́рка маши́ны?; **in bold/heavy ~** кру́пным *or* жи́рным шри́фтом.

type *vti* печа́тать на маши́нке (на-); **to ~ a letter** печа́тать письмо́ (на маши́нке).

typescript *n* машинопи́сный текст.

typesetter *n* (*person*) набо́рщик; (*machine*) набо́рная маши́на.

typesetting *n* (типогра́фский) набо́р.

typewriter *n* (пи́шущая) маши́нка.

typewritten *adj attr* машинопи́сный; *predic* напеча́танный на маши́нке.

typhoid *n* (брюшно́й) тиф.

typhoon *n* тайфу́н.

typhus *n* (сыпно́й) тиф.

typical *adj* типи́чный; **a ~ Frenchman** типи́чный францу́з; **it is ~ of him** э́то для него́ типи́чно; *CQ* **the train is late again—isn't that just ~?** по́езд опя́ть опа́здывает—э́то уже́ ста́ло но́рмой.

typify *vt*: **he/such behaviour typifies the youth of today** он типи́чный представи́тель совреме́нной молодёжи, тако́е поведе́ние характе́рно/типи́чно для совреме́нной молодёжи.

typing *n* печа́тание на маши́нке; (*in advertisement*) «перепи́ска на маши́нке»; **his ~ is awful** он ужа́сно печа́тает; *attr*: **~ classes** ку́рсы машинопи́си.

typist *n* машини́стка (*f*).

tyrannical *adj* тирани́ческий.

tyrant *n* тира́н.

tyre *n* ши́на; **a flat/burst ~** спу́щенная/ло́пнувшая ши́на.

U

U-bend *n Tech* двойно́й изги́б.

ubiquitous *adj* вездесу́щий, *often iron.*

ugh *interj* (*in disgust*) фу!

ugliness *n* уро́дливость.

ugly *adj* **1** некраси́вый, (*stronger*) уро́дливый; **poor soul, she's an ~ girl** бедня́жка, она́ така́я некраси́вая/дурну́шка; **she has grown old and ~** она́ постаре́ла и подурне́ла; **the new theatre is very ~** но́вое зда́ние теа́тра—верх уро́дства

2 *fig* безобра́зный, ме́рзкий, га́дкий; **an ~ scene** безобра́зная сце́на; **he's an ~ customer** он ме́рзкий/га́дкий тип; **his dismissal was an ~ business** его́ увольне́ние вы́глядело о́чень некраси́во; **the situation looks ~** положе́ние стано́вится серьёзным; **an ~ wound** опа́сная ра́на; **he is in an ~ mood** он в плохо́м/в дурно́м настрое́нии.

Ukrainian *n* украи́нец, украи́нка; (*language*) украи́нский язы́к.

Ukrainian *adj* украи́нский.

ulcer *n* я́зва; **stomach ~** я́зва желу́дка; **mouth ~s** лихора́дка/просту́да (*sings*) на губа́х.

ulterior *adj*: **he had an ~ motive in doing that** он поступи́л так не без за́дней мы́сли.

ultimate *adj* коне́чный; оконча́тельный; **his ~ destination is Rome** коне́чная цель его́ путеше́ствия—Рим; **my ~ aim** моя́ коне́чная цель; **the ~ decision depends on him** оконча́тельное реше́ние зави́сит от него́; **he bears the ~ responsibility** гла́вная отве́тственность лежи́т на нём.

ultimately *adv* в коне́чном счёте/ито́ге.

ultimatum *n* ультима́тум; **to deliver an ~** предъяви́ть ультима́тум.

ultimo, *abbr* **ult** *adv*: **your letter of the 5th ult** ва́ше письмо́ от пя́того числа́ истёкшего ме́сяца.

ultramodern *adj* ультрасовреме́нный, *CQ* супермоде́рн (*indecl*).

ultrasonic *adj* ультразвуково́й, сверхзвуково́й.

ultraviolet *adj* ультрафиоле́товый.

umbilical cord *n Anat* пупови́на.

umbrage *n*: **to take ~ at** обижа́ться на + *A*.

umbrella *n* зонт, *dim* зо́нтик; **to put up/take down an ~** раскры́ть/закры́ть зонт; *attr*: **~ stand** подста́вка для зонто́в.

umpire *n* (*in debate*) арби́тр; (*in football*) судья́ (на по́ле); (*in tennis*) судья́ на вы́шке.
umpire *vti*: **to ~ (a match)** суди́ть (матч) (*impf*).
umpteen *adj CQ*: **I've told you ~ times** я говори́л тебе́ сто раз; **I haven't seen him for ~ years** я сто лет его́ не ви́дел.
umpteenth *adj CQ*: **for the ~ time** в со́тый раз.
unabashed *adj*: **he continued, quite ~** он продолжа́л, нима́ло не смуща́ясь.
unabated *adj*: **with ~ enthusiasm** с неосла́бным энтузиа́змом; **the storm continued ~** бу́ря всё не утиха́ла/не ослабева́ла.
unable *adj*: **he is ~ to come** он не мо́жет прийти́; **he is still ~ to read** он ещё не уме́ет чита́ть; **I am ~ to advise you** я не в состоя́нии дать тебе́ сове́т.
unabridged *adj* несокращённый.
unaccented *adj* безуда́рный, неуда́рный.
unacceptable *adj* неприе́млемый; **these terms are ~ to me** э́ти усло́вия неприе́млемы для меня́.
unaccomodating *adj* неусту́пчивый.
unaccompanied *adj* (*alone*): **you shouldn't go out ~** тебе́ не сле́дует ходи́ть одному́/без провожа́того; **~ luggage** бага́ж, по́сланный вперёд; *Mus* без аккомпанеме́нта; **a piece for ~ violin** со́ло для скри́пки.
unaccountable *adj* необъясни́мый, непостижи́мый.
unaccountably *adv* по непоня́тной причи́не.
unaccounted for *adj*: **6 were reported dead and 3 ~** бы́ло сообщено́, что шесть челове́к поги́бло, а три пропа́ло бе́з вести; **£1,000 is ~ in the balance sheet** ты́сяча фу́нтов не пока́зана в бала́нсе.
unaccustomed *adj* необы́чный; *if predic use* не привы́к к + *D or* + *inf or* + что́бы; **I am ~ to being spoken to like that** я не привы́к, что́бы со мной так разгова́ривали.
unacknowledged *adj* (*of facts, people, etc.*) непри́знанный; **this letter is still ~** на э́то письмо́ так и не́ было отве́та.
unacquainted *adj predic*: **~ with** незнако́м с + *I*.
unadulterated *adj* (*of liquids*) неразба́вленный.
unaffected *adj attr* просто́й; (*genuine*) и́скренний; **with ~ pleasure** с и́скренним удово́льствием; *predic*: **he/his style is so ~** он/его́ стиль так прост и есте́ствен.
unafraid *adj*: **he is quite ~** он совсе́м не бои́тся, он ничего́ не бои́тся.
unaided *adj* без посторо́нней по́мощи; **it's his own ~ work** э́то его́ самостоя́тельная рабо́та.
unaltered *adj*: **this clause must stand/stands ~** э́тот пункт не подлежи́т измене́нию/не измени́лся.
unambiguous *adj* недвусмы́сленный.
unambitious *adj* (*of a person*) лишённый честолю́бия; **an ~ project** просто́й прое́кт.
unanimity *n* единоду́шие; (*in voting*) единогла́сие.
unanimous *adj* единоду́шный; (*in voting*) единогла́сный; **by a ~ vote** единогла́сно.
unanswerable *adj*: **an ~ argument** неопровержи́мый до́вод.
unanswered *adj*: **my letter is still ~** на моё письмо́ до сих по́р нет отве́та; **oh dear, these letters are still ~** бо́же мой, я забы́л отве́тить на э́ти пи́сьма.
unappetizing *adj* неаппети́тный, *also fig*.
unappreciated *adj*: **my efforts are not ~ by her** нельзя́ сказа́ть, что она́ не це́нит мои́х уси́лий; **his talent remained ~** его́ тала́нт не получи́л призна́ния.
unappreciative *adj attr* равноду́шный, холо́дный; *predic*: **he is not ~ of all you do for him** нельзя́ сказа́ть, что он не це́нит того́, что вы для него́ де́лаете.
unapproachable *adj* (*of people*) недосту́пный.
unarmed *adj* безору́жный.
unashamed *adj*: **he was quite ~** ему́ совсе́м не́ было сты́дно.
unasked *adj*: **they came ~** они́ пришли́ без приглаше́ния; **he did it ~** он э́то сде́лал доброво́льно/по со́бственной инициати́ве.
unassuming *adj* скро́мный, непритяза́тельный.
unattached *adj* (*of parts, etc.*) неприкреплённый; *fig* **he is ~ just now** у него́ сейча́с нет де́вушки.
unattainable *adj* недостижи́мый; **an ~ peak** непристу́пная верши́на.
unattended *adj*: **to leave a patient/one's children/luggage ~** оста́вить больно́го/дете́й/бага́ж без присмо́тра.
unattractive *adj* непривлека́тельный.
unauthorized *adj*: **an ~ version** неофициа́льная ве́рсия; **"~ persons not admitted"** «посторо́нним вход воспрещён».
unavailable *adj*: **he is ~ at the moment** его́ сейча́с нет (на ме́сте) (*not in*), он сейча́с за́нят (*busy*).
unavailing *adj* напра́сный, тще́тный.
unavoidable *adj* неизбе́жный.
unaware *adj*: **he was ~ of the danger** он не сознава́л опа́сности.
unawares *adv*: **to catch smb ~** заста́ть кого́-л врасплох.
unbalanced *adj* (*physically*) неусто́йчивый; (*mentally*) неуравнове́шенный.
unbandage *vt* разбинто́в|ывать (-а́ть).
unbaptized *adj* некрещёный.
unbearable *adj* невыноси́мый, нестерпи́мый.
unbeatable *adj*: **an ~ team** непобеди́мая кома́нда; *CQ* **this car is ~ value** за таки́е де́ньги лу́чше маши́ны не ку́пишь/не найдёшь.
unbeaten *adj Mil* непобеждённый; *Sport* **an ~ record** реко́рд, кото́рый до сих пор не поби́т.
unbeknown *adv*: **~ to me** без моего́ ве́дома.
unbelievable *adj* невероя́тный; **it is ~ that...** про́сто невероя́тно/пря́мо не ве́рится, что...
unbeliever *n* неве́рующий.

unbend *vi fig* (*of people*): **he can ~ among his friends** в кругу́ свои́х друзе́й он стано́вится про́ще.

unbias(s)ed *adj* (*impartial*) беспристра́стный; (*unprejudiced*) непредубеждённый.

unbleached *adj*: **~ linen** небелёное/суро́вое полотно́.

unblock *vt*: **to ~ a pipe/a sink** прочи|ща́ть тру́бку/ра́ковину (-́стить).

unblushing *adj*: **he tells the most ~ lies** он бессты́дно лжёт, он бессо́вестно/на́гло врёт.

unbolt *vt* от|пира́ть (-пере́ть).

unbreakable *adj* небью́щийся.

unbroken *adj*: **only one cup remained ~** то́лько одна́ ча́шка уцеле́ла; **the seal was ~** печа́ть не была́ сло́мана; **an ~ record** (*of service*) непреры́вный стаж, *Sport* реко́рд, кото́рый ещё не поби́т; **his spirit is ~** его́ дух не сло́млен; **the patient has had five hours of ~ sleep** больно́й спал пять часо́в не просыпа́ясь; **an ~ horse** необъе́зженная ло́шадь.

unbuckle *vt* рас|стёгивать (-стегну́ть).

unburden *vt fig*: **to ~ oneself to smb** изли|ва́ть ду́шу кому́-л (-́ть).

unbusinesslike *adj* неделово́й.

unbutton *vt* рас|стёгивать (-стегну́ть); **he ~ed his coat** он расстегну́л пальто́, он расстегну́лся; **his shirt was ~ed** руба́шка у него́ была́ расстёгнута.

uncalled-for *adj*: **that remark was quite ~** так не на́до говори́ть; **an ~ piece of rudeness** ниче́м не вы́званная гру́бость.

uncanny *adj* пуга́ющий, жу́ткий; **an ~ resemblance/feeling** пуга́ющее схо́дство, жуткова́тое ощуще́ние; **it is ~ how I always run into him** э́то о́чень стра́нно — мы с ним всё вре́мя встреча́емся.

unceasing *adj* беспреста́нный, беспреры́вный.

uncensored *adj*: **an ~ record of the meeting** неотредакти́рованный протоко́л собра́ния.

unceremonious *adj* бесцеремо́нный.

uncertain *adj* неопределённый, нея́сный; **it is ~ whether he will come** неизве́стно, придёт ли он; **I am ~ what to do** я не зна́ю, что де́лать; **I am ~ whether he is right** я не уве́рен, прав ли он; **he is ~ of himself** он не уве́рен в себе́; **~ weather** переме́нчивая/неусто́йчивая пого́да.

uncertainty *n* неопределённость, нея́сность; **in view of the ~ of the situation** ввиду́ неопределённости ситуа́ции; **there is some ~ about the date of...** пока́ нея́сно, когда́...; **to remove any ~** что́бы устрани́ть вся́кие сомне́ния (*pl*).

unchallenged *adj*: **I can't let that remark go ~** я не могу́ оста́вить без отве́та э́то замеча́ние.

unchanged *adj*: **the patient's condition is ~** состоя́ние больно́го не измени́лось.

unchanging *adj* неизме́нный.

uncharacteristic *adj*: **it is ~ of her not to leave any address** уе́хать, не оста́вив а́дреса — э́то на неё не похо́же.

uncharitable *adj* немилосе́рдный; **how ~ of you to say that!** как жесто́ко с твое́й стороны́ говори́ть так!

unchecked *adj* (*unverified*): **~ facts** непрове́ренные фа́кты.

uncivil *adj* неве́жливый.

uncivilized *adj*: **~ tribes** ди́кие племена́; **he is very ~** он о́чень груб/невоспи́тан.

unclaimed *adj*: **an ~ umbrella** невостре́бованный зо́нтик.

unclassified *adj* неклассифици́рованный; (*not secret*) несекре́тный.

uncle *n* дя́дя (*m*).

unclean *adj* нечи́стый, *also fig*.

unclouded *adj* безо́блачный.

uncoil *vti* (*rope, etc.*) раз|ма́тывать(ся) (-мота́ть(ся)); **the snake ~ed** змея́ разверну́лась.

uncoloured *adj fig*: **an ~ account of events** неприкра́шенное описа́ние собы́тий.

uncombed *adj* непричёсанный.

uncomfortable *adj* неудо́бный, *also fig*; **an ~ bed** неудо́бная крова́ть; **the water shortage is making life ~ for everybody** недоста́ток воды́ — большо́е неудо́бство для кого́ уго́дно; *fig*: **he felt ~ in her presence** он чу́вствовал себя́ нело́вко в её прису́тствии; **I had an ~ interview with the director** у меня́ был неприя́тный разгово́р с дире́ктором.

uncommon *adj* необы́чный; (*exceptional*) необыча́йный.

uncommunicative *adj attr* необщи́тельный; *predic*: **he was very ~ about what had happened** он ничего́ не говори́л о том, что случи́лось.

uncompleted *adj* незавершённый, незако́нченный.

uncomplimentary *adj* неле́стный; **an ~ remark** неле́стное замеча́ние; **he was very ~ about her playing** он весьма́ неле́стно отозва́лся о её игре́.

uncompromising *adj attr* бескомпроми́ссный; *predic*: **he is/was ~** он не идёт на компроми́ссы, он был непрекло́нен.

unconcerned *adj*: **he is ~ about the future** его́ не волну́ет бу́дущее; **everyone was panicking but he seemed quite ~** все до́ смерти перепуга́лись, а ему́ хоть бы что́.

unconditional *adj* безогово́рочный, безусло́вный.

unconnected *adj*: **he talks in ~ sentences** он говори́т несвя́зными фра́зами; **the two events are quite ~** э́ти два собы́тия ника́к не свя́заны ме́жду собо́й.

unconscionable *adj*: **you've been an ~ time dressing** го́споди, сто́лько вре́мени одева́ться!

unconscious *n Psych* (**the ~**) подсозна́ние.

unconscious *adj* бессозна́тельный, *also Med*; **he was ~ for three days** он три дня был без созна́ния; **~ tactlessness** нево́льная беста́ктность; **he was quite ~ of having offended her** он и не подозрева́л, что оби́дел её.

unconsidered *adj* необду́манный.

uncontrollable *adj* необу́зданный; бесконтро́льный; **~ sobbing** безу́держные рыда́ния (*pl*).

unconventional *adj*: **an ~ outlook** необы́чный взгляд на ве́щи; **he is very ~** он чужд усло́вностей; **it is ~ to go to an official function in jeans** неприли́чно идти́ на официа́льный приём в джи́нсах; *Mil* **~ weapons** осо́бые ви́ды вооруже́ния.

unconvinced *adj*: **I remain ~ by your arguments** твои́ до́воды не убеди́ли меня́; **he remained ~** его́ так и не убеди́ли, он так и оста́лся при своём мне́нии.

unconvincing *adj* неубеди́тельный.

uncoordinated *adj* несогласо́ванный, некоордини́рованный.

uncork *vt* отку́пори|вать, раску́пори|вать (*pfs* -ть).

uncorrected *adj* неиспра́вленный.

uncorroborated *adj* неподтверждённый.

uncouth *adj* гру́бый.

uncritical *adj* некрити́ческий.

uncrossed *adj Fin*: **an ~ cheque** некросси́рованный чек.

uncultivated *adj* (*of land*) необрабо́танный, невозде́ланный; (*of plants*) ди́кий, некультиви́рованный.

uncultured *adj* с ни́зкой культу́рой.

uncut *adj* (*of pages of a book*) неразре́занный; (*not abridged*) несокращённый; **an ~ diamond** нешлифо́ванный алма́з.

undamaged *adj* неповреждённый.

undated *adj* недати́рованный.

undaunted *adj*: **he was ~ by the sight of his opponent** его́ не смути́л/не устраши́л вид сопе́рника; **he carried on quite ~** он продолжа́л, ничу́ть не смуща́ясь/как ни в чём не быва́ло.

undecided *adj* нерешённый, неопределённый; **I'm ~ whether to go or not** я не реши́л, пойти́ и́ли нет.

undefeated *adj*: **our team is ~ this season** у на́шей кома́нды в э́том сезо́не ни одного́ пораже́ния.

undefended *adj* незащищённый; *Law* **the case is ~** у обвиня́емого нет защи́тника.

undefined *adj* неопределённый.

undemanding *adj* нетре́бовательный, непритяза́тельный.

undemonstrative *adj* сде́ржанный.

undeniable *adj* бесспо́рный.

undependable *adj* ненадёжный.

under *adv* внизу́, ни́же; **see ~ for details** подро́бности смотри́ ни́же; **children of 10 and ~** де́ти до десяти́ лет; **goods at £5 or ~** това́ры сто́имостью до пяти́ фу́нтов; **he went ~ and we feared he was drowned** он исче́з под водо́й, и мы испуга́лись, что он утону́л.

under *prep* **1** (*of place*) под + *I*, (*with motion*) под + *A*; **~ the window/the tree/one's arm** под окно́м/де́ревом, под мы́шкой (*adv*); **put the box ~ the bed** поста́вь я́щик под крова́ть; **we drove ~ the bridge** (*and through*) мы прое́хали под мосто́м, (*and stayed under*) мы въе́хали под мост; **from ~ the sofa** из-под дива́на; *fig*: **~ his very nose** у него́ под но́сом; **~ lock and key** под замко́м; **to sell ~ the counter** торгова́ть из-под полы́/прила́вка

2 (*of time*): **~ the Romans** во времена́ ри́мского госпо́дства, при ри́млянах

3 (*according to*) по + *D*, согла́сно + *D*; **~ the new rules** по/согла́сно но́вым пра́вилам; **~ the terms of the contract** по усло́виям контра́кта; **he was acting ~ orders** он де́йствовал по/согла́сно прика́зу

4 (*less than*): **children ~ 5** де́ти до пяти́ лет; **he is just ~ 40** ему́ под со́рок/о́коло сорока́; **he is ~ age** он несовершенноле́тний; **they did it in ~ an hour** они́ э́то сде́лали ме́ньше чем за час; **it costs ~£5** э́то сто́ит ме́ньше пяти́ фу́нтов

5 (*indicating various conditions*) под + *I*; **~ Roman rule** под вла́стью Ри́ма; **~ the command/chairmanship of** под кома́ндованием/председа́тельством + *G*; **I am working ~ Professor X** я рабо́таю у профе́ссора N/под руково́дством профе́ссора N; **he has 40 men ~ him** у него́ в подчине́нии со́рок челове́к; **~ the threat/influence/pretext of** под угро́зой/влия́нием/предло́гом + *G*; **~ pressure/suspicion/arrest** под давле́нием/подозре́нием/аре́стом; **~ the impression that...** предполага́я, что...; **the question is ~ discussion** вопро́с обсужда́ется; **the car/the theatre/the road is ~ repair** маши́на в ремо́нте, теа́тр закры́т на ремо́нт, иду́т доро́жные рабо́ты; **the house is still ~ construction** дом ещё стро́ится; **you are ~ no obligation to buy it** вы не обя́заны э́то покупа́ть; **~ an assumed name/a pseudonym** под вы́мышленным и́менем/псевдони́мом; **see ~ "Whales"** смотри́ в разде́ле «Киты́»; **~ article 42** в соотве́тствии со статьёй со́рок второ́й.

underarm *adv Sport*: **to serve ~** подава́ть сни́зу.

undercarriage *n Aer* шасси́ (*indecl*).

undercharge *vt*: **he ~d me by 5 roubles** он взял с меня́ на пять рубле́й ме́ньше, чем на́до.

underclothes *npl* ни́жнее бельё (*collect*).

undercoat *n* (*of paint*) грунто́вка; **to put on an ~** грунтова́ть.

undercurrent *n* подво́дное тече́ние; *fig* **I sensed an ~ of hostility** я чу́вствовал скры́тую вражде́бность.

undercut[1] *n* (*of meat*) вы́резка.

undercut[2] *vt*: **they are ~ting us** они́ сбива́ют нам це́ну; **the shops try to ~ each other** магази́ны стара́ются сбить друг дру́гу це́ны.

underdeveloped *adj* недора́звитый; *Econ* развива́ющийся.

underdog *n* горемы́ка, *CQ* бедола́га (*both m and f*).

underdone *adj* (*of meat*) недожа́ренный; (*of cakes*) непропечённый.

underemployed *adj*: **he is ~** у него́ сейча́с ма́ло рабо́ты; **the machines are ~** станки́ рабо́тают не на по́лную мо́щность.

underestimate *vt* недооце́ни|вать (-́ть).

underexposed *adj*: **the photo is ~** фо́то не додержа́ли.

underfed *adj*: **these children are ~** э́ти де́ти недоеда́ют.

underfoot *adv* под нога́ми.

undergo *vt* подверг|а́ться + *D* (-́нуться); **to ~ an operation/criticism/treatment for alcoholism** подверга́ться опера́ции/кри́тике/лече́нию от алкоголи́зма; **the area has ~ne a great change** э́тот райо́н си́льно измени́лся; **the house is ~ing major repairs** в до́ме идёт капита́льный ремо́нт.

undergraduate *n* студе́нт, *f* -ка; *attr* студе́нческий.

underground *n* метро́ (*indecl*); **I'm going by ~** я пое́ду на метро́; *Polit* **a member of the ~** член подпо́льной организа́ции.

underground *adj* подзе́мный; *Polit* подпо́льный, нелега́льный.

underground *adv* под землёй.

undergrowth *n* (*in forest*) подле́сок, мелколе́сье; (*in garden or forest*) куста́рник.

underhand *adj*: **~ methods/dealings** закули́сные ме́тоды, махина́ции; **an ~ trick** махина́ция.

underline *vt* подчёрк|ивать (-ну́ть), *also fig.*

underlying *n* основно́й; **the ~ cause** основна́я причи́на.

undermanned *adj*: **the factory is ~** на фа́брике не хвата́ет рабо́чей си́лы.

undermentioned *adj* нижеупомя́нутый.

undermine *vt*: **the sea is undermining the cliffs** мо́ре подмыва́ет ска́лы; *fig* **to ~ smb's authority/health** под|рыва́ть чей-л авторите́т/чьё-л здоро́вье (-орва́ть).

underneath *adj* ни́жний.

underneath *adv* внизу́, (*of motion*) вниз; **from ~** сни́зу.

underneath *prep* под + *I*, (*with motion*) под + *A*; **from ~** из-под + *G*.

underpaid *adj* (*of person or job*) низкоопла́чиваемый.

underpants *npl CQ* мужски́е трусы́ (*no sing*).

underpass *n* (*for cars*) тонне́ль (*m*); (*for pedestrians*) подзе́мный перехо́д.

underpay *vt* плати́ть ма́ло (*usu impf*).

underpopulated *adj* малонаселённый.

underpriced *adj*: **at £20 this picture is ~** два́дцать фу́нтов за э́ту карти́ну—э́то сли́шком дёшево.

underprivileged *adj* неиму́щий; *as n* **the ~** неиму́щие (кла́ссы).

underproduction *n Econ* недопроизво́дство.

underrate *vt* недооце́ни|вать (-́ть).

undersecretary *n* замести́тель (*m*)/помо́щник мини́стра.

underside *n* ни́жняя сторона́.

undersigned *adj*: **we, the ~...** мы, нижеподписа́вшиеся...

undersized *adj* (*of person*) низкоро́слый; (*of things*) ма́ленький.

understaffed *adj*: **the hospital/office is ~** в больни́це не хвата́ет медперсона́ла, отде́л не укомплекто́ван.

understand *vti* пон|има́ть (-я́ть); **to ~ smb/smth** понима́ть кого́-л/что-л; **do you ~?** понима́ешь?, (тебе́) поня́тно?; **to make oneself understood** объясн|я́ться (-и́ться); **I understood you to say that...** как я понима́ю, вы сказа́ли, что...; **he gave me to ~ that...** он дал мне поня́ть, что...; **he is understood to have refused/to be abroad at present** полага́ют, что он отказа́лся, говоря́т, что он сейча́с за грани́цей.

understandable *adj* поня́тный.

understanding *n* **1** понима́ние; **to achieve ~ between two countries** дости́чь взаимопонима́ния ме́жду двумя́ стра́нами

2 (*agreement*) договорённость; **I came to an ~ with her** мы с ней договори́лись; **on the ~ that...** при усло́вии,/на том усло́вии, что...

understanding *adj* понима́ющий; **an ~ father/look** понима́ющий оте́ц/взгляд; **he was very ~ when I told him about it** он прояви́л понима́ние, когда́ я сказа́л ему́ об э́том.

understate *vt* преуменьш|а́ть (-́ить).

understatement *n* преуменьше́ние; *iron* **he sometimes is not truthful.—Sometimes? That's the ~ of the year!** он иногда́ привира́ет.—Иногда́? Э́то мя́гко ска́зано!

understudy *n* дублёр.

understudy *vt* дубли́ровать (*impf*).

undertake *vt*: **he has ~n a new line of research** он на́чал но́вое иссле́дование/но́вую те́му; **to ~ responsibility for smth** брать на себя́ отве́тственность за что-л (взять); **he has ~n to proofread** он взял на себя́ чте́ние корректу́ры; **he undertook not to do it again** он обеща́л э́того бо́льше не де́лать; **I've mended your watch but I can't ~ that it will work** я почини́л ва́ши часы́, но не гаранти́рую, что они́ бу́дут хорошо́ ходи́ть.

undertaker *n* владе́лец похоро́нного бюро́.

undertaking *n* де́ло; *Comm, etc.* предприя́тие; **that's quite an ~** э́то це́лое предприя́тие; **a written ~** подпи́ска (о чём-л); **he gave an ~ not to see her again/to repay everything** он дал сло́во бо́льше не ви́деться с ней, он обяза́лся всё вы́платить.

undertone *n*: **to talk in ~s** говори́ть вполго́лоса (*adv*); **there was an ~ of hostility in all he said** в его́ слова́х сквози́ла недоброжела́тельность.

undervalue *vt* недооце́ни|вать (-́ть).

underwater *adj* подво́дный.

underwater *adv* под водо́й.

underwear *n collect* ни́жнее бельё.

underweight *adj*: **he is ~** он ве́сит ни́же но́рмы.

underworld *n* (*hell*) ад, преиспо́дняя; (*criminal*) престу́пный мир.

underwrite *vt* страхова́ть (за-).

undeserved *adj* незаслу́женный.

undesirable *adj* нежела́тельный.

undetected *adj* нераскры́тый.

undeterred *adj*: **he was ~ by the threats** его́ не останови́ли угро́зы.

undeveloped *adj* (*of buds, etc.*) нера́звитый; (*of land—not built on*) незастро́енный; *Agric* необрабо́танный; **this area is rich in minerals but so far ~** э́тот райо́н бога́т поле́зными ископа́емыми, но он ещё ма́ло осво́ен.

undies *npl CQ* ни́жнее бельё (*collect*).

undignified *adj* недосто́йный; **his behaviour was ~** он вёл себя́ недосто́йно.

undiluted *adj* неразба́вленный, неразведённый.

undiminished *adj* неуме́ньшённый.

undiplomatic *adj*: **it is ~ to...** недипломати́чно + *inf*.

undisciplined *adj* недисциплини́рованный.

undisclosed *adj*: **an ~ source** нена́званный исто́чник.

undiscovered *adj* (*of island, planet, etc.*) ещё не откры́тый; (*of crime*) нераскры́тый.

undiscriminating *adj* неразбо́рчивый.

undisguised *adj* нескрыва́емый.

undisputed *adj*: **the claim went ~** прете́нзия не была́ оспо́рена; **he was their ~ leader** он был их при́знанным вожако́м.

undistinguished *adj fig*: **he was an ~ headmaster** как дире́ктор шко́лы он про́сто посре́дственность.

undisturbed *adj*: **his papers were ~** его́ бума́ги бы́ли нетро́нуты; **he likes to be left ~** он не лю́бит, когда́ ему́ меша́ют; **he remained ~ by all the fuss** его́ весь э́тот шум не тро́гал; **the doctor hasn't had one ~ night this week** на э́той неде́ле у врача́ ни одна́ ночь не обошла́сь без вы́зова.

undivided *adj* неразделённый; **I want your ~ attention** я тре́бую от вас по́лного внима́ния.

undo *vt* (*of buttons, buckles, zips*) рас|стёгивать (-стегну́ть); (*of string, laces*) развя́з|ывать (-а́ть); **to come undone** расстегну́ться, развяза́ться; *fig*: **in one week he has undone everything we achieved in a year** за одну́ неде́лю он разру́шил всё, чего́ мы дости́гли за год; **what is done cannot be undone** сде́ланного не воро́тишь.

undoing *n*: **that was his ~** э́то погуби́ло его́.

undomesticated *adj*: **she/he is quite ~** она́ плоха́я хозя́йка, он ничего́ не уме́ет де́лать по до́му.

undoubted *adj* несомне́нный, бесспо́рный.

undreamt-of *adj*: **TV was ~ 200 years ago** две́сти лет наза́д о телеви́дении никто́ не мог и мечта́ть.

undress *vti* разде|ва́ться (-́ться).

undrinkable *adj* неприго́дный для питья́.

undue *adj* (*excessive*) чрезме́рный; **don't pay ~ attention to his criticism** не сли́шком обраща́й(те) внима́ние на его́ замеча́ния (*pl*).

unduly *adv* чрезме́рно, чересчу́р; **~ grateful/pessimistic** чрезме́рно благода́рный, чересчу́р пессимисти́ческий; **we were not ~ worried by what he said** нас не сли́шком обеспоко́ило то, что он сказа́л.

undying *adj fig*: **he's earned my ~ gratitude/hatred** я бу́ду до конца́ дней мои́х ему́ благода́рен, я всю жизнь бу́ду его́ ненави́деть.

unearned *adj*: **~ income** нетрудово́й дохо́д; **~ praise** незаслу́женная похвала́.

unearth *vt* обнару́жи|вать (-ть); **to ~ some interesting facts** обнару́жить/*CQ* раскопа́ть интере́сные фа́кты; *CQ joc* **where did you ~ that old suit?** где э́то ты откопа́л/вы́искал тако́е старьё?

unearthly *adj*: **a strange, ~ noise** стра́нный, ни на что не похо́жий звук; *CQ* **we had to get up at an ~ hour** нам пришло́сь встать ни свет ни заря́.

uneasy *adj*: **he had an ~ feeling that...** у него́ бы́ло трево́жное чу́вство, что...; **his conscience was ~** со́весть му́чила его́; **he passed an ~ night** он провёл беспоко́йную ночь; **he grew ~ when she hadn't returned by midnight** в по́лночь её всё ещё не́ было до́ма, и он на́чал беспоко́иться; **he gave an ~ laugh** он смущённо улыбну́лся; **he felt ~/~ about leaving her alone** он чу́вствовал себя́ нело́вко, ему́ бы́ло ка́к-то нело́вко оста́вить её одну́.

uneatable *adj* несъедо́бный.

uneconomic(al) *adj* (*of plans, etc.*) неэкономи́чный; (*of person*) небережли́вый, неэконо́мный.

uneducated *adj* необразо́ванный.

unemployable *adj* неработоспосо́бный.

unemployed *adj* безрабо́тный; *as n* **(the ~)** безрабо́тные (*pl*).

unemployment *n* безрабо́тица; **~ has risen/fallen this month** в э́том ме́сяце число́ безрабо́тных возросло́/сни́зилось.

unending *adj* бесконе́чный.

unenterprising *adj* непредприи́мчивый.

unenviable *adj* незави́дный.

unequal *adj* нера́вный; **of ~ length/weight** ра́зной длины́, ра́зного ве́са; **he was ~ to the job** э́та рабо́та была́ ему́ не под си́лу; **he felt ~ to telling her** он был не в си́лах сказа́ть ей об э́том; **~ marriage** нера́вный брак.

unequivocal *adj* недвусмы́сленный, я́сный.

unerring *adj* безоши́бочный.

uneven *adj* неро́вный.

uneventful *adj*: **we've had an ~ trip/week** на́ша пое́здка/э́та неде́ля прошла́ без вся́ких происше́ствий; **he leads an ~ life** он ведёт разме́ренную/споко́йную жизнь.

unexpected *adj* неожи́данный; **an ~ stroke of luck** неожи́данная уда́ча; **an ~ visitor** негда́нный гость.

unexpired *adj*: **the ~ period of a lease** оста́ток аре́ндного сро́ка.

unexplained *adj* необъяснённый.

unexploded *adj* невзорва́вшийся.

unexposed *adj Photo* неэкспони́рованный.

unexpurgated *adj*: **an ~ edition** по́лное изда́ние.

unfailing *adj*: **his ~ patience** его́ неистощи́мое терпе́ние; **his patience is ~** его́ терпе́ние безграни́чно; **an ~ supply of water** бесперебо́йное снабже́ние водо́й.

unfair *adj* несправедли́вый; **~ comment** несправедли́вое замеча́ние; **I won but I had an ~ advantage over him** я вы́играл, пра́вда, у меня́ бы́ло пе́ред ним преиму́щество; **by ~ means** нече́стными ме́тодами/сре́дствами.

unfaithful *adj* неве́рный; **he's been ~ to her** он ей измени́л.

unfamiliar *adj* незнако́мый; **I am ~ with their methods** я незнако́м с их ме́тодами.

unfashionable *adj* немо́дный.

unfasten *vt* (*of buttons, belts, zips, etc.*) рас|стёгивать, (*of clasps*) от|стёгивать (*pfs* -стегну́ть); **to ~ a bolt** отодви|га́ть задви́жку (-́нуть); **to ~ a knot** развя́з|ывать у́зел (-а́ть).

unfavourable, (*US*) **unfavorable** *adj* (*of weather, conditions, omens*) неблагоприя́тный; (*of reception, criticism*) неблагоскло́нный; **his reply was ~** он отве́тил отка́зом.

unfeeling *adj* (*insensitive*) нечувстви́тельный, (*hard-hearted*) бесчу́вственный.

unfeigned *adj* неподде́льный, непритво́рный.

unfeminine *adj* неже́нственный.

unfinished *adj* незако́нченный, незавершённый.

unfit *adj*: **the road is ~ for heavy traffic** доро́га неприго́дна для большо́го автомоби́льного движе́ния; **he is ~ to drive** по состоя́нию здоро́вья он не мо́жет води́ть маши́ну (*medically*), он не в состоя́нии вести́ маши́ну (*if drunk*); **he was declared medically ~ for service** он был при́знан не го́дным к вое́нной слу́жбе по состоя́нию здоро́вья.

unfitted *adj*: **he is ~ for this post** он не годи́тся/не подхо́дит для э́той до́лжности.

unflagging *adj* неослабева́ющий, неуста́нный.

unflattering *adj* нелéстный; **jeans are ~ to her figure** джи́нсы не иду́т ей/для неё неподходя́щий наря́д.

unfold *vti vt* раз|вёртывать (-верну́ть); **to ~ a map** разверну́ть ка́рту; *fig* **he ~ed his plans to me** он подели́лся со мной свои́ми пла́нами

vi (*of plants*) распус|ка́ться (-ти́ться).

unforeseen *adj* непредви́денный.

unforgettable *adj* незабыва́емый.

unforgivable *adj* непрости́тельный.

unforgiving *adj* непроща́ющий.

unforgotten *adj* незабы́тый.

unfortunate *adj* несча́стный, несчастли́вый; неуда́чный; **an ~ coincidence** неуда́чное совпаде́ние; **he made an ~ marriage** их [**NB** *pronoun*] брак был неуда́чным; **he was just ~** ему́ про́сто не везло́; **it is ~ that he saw you** пло́хо, что он тебя́ ви́дел; **how ~!** кака́я жа́лость!; **that was an ~ topic to raise** не сто́ило поднима́ть э́тот больно́й вопро́с.

unfortunately *adv* к несча́стью, к сожале́нию.

unfounded *adj* необосно́ванный.

unfrequented *adj*: **an ~ beach** пусты́нный пляж.

unfriendly *adj* недружелю́бный.

unfruitful *adj fig* бесплóдный.

unfulfilled *adj* (*of tasks, promises, etc.*) невы́полненный; (*of hopes, etc.*) неосуществлённый.

unfurnished *adj* без мéбели.

ungainly *adj* неуклю́жий.

ungodly *adj CQ*: **he got us up at an ~ hour** он разбуди́л нас в таку́ю рань.

ungrammatical *adj* граммати́чески непра́вильный.

ungrateful *adj* неблагода́рный.

unguarded *adj* незащищённый; *fig* неосторо́жный; **in an ~ moment he let out the secret** на каку́ю-то секу́нду он забы́л об осторо́жности и проговори́лся.

unhampered *adj*: **I like to travel ~ by heavy luggage** я люблю́ путеше́ствовать налегке́ (*adv*)/без большо́го багажа́; *fig* **the children are away so I can work ~** де́ти ушли́, так что я могу́ рабо́тать споко́йно.

unhappily *adv* (*miserably*) несчастли́во; (*unfortunately*) к несча́стью.

unhappiness *n* несча́стье.

unhappy *adj* несчастли́вый, несча́стный; неуда́чный; (*sad*) гру́стный, печа́льный; **an ~ translation** неуда́чный перево́д; **you look so ~** у тебя́ тако́й гру́стный/печа́льный/(*stronger*) несча́стный вид; **he is ~ in his marriage** у него́ не сложи́лась семе́йная жизнь; **I am ~ about present developments** меня́ огорча́ет сложи́вшаяся ситуа́ция (*sing*).

unharmed *adj* (*of things*) неповреждённый; (*of person*) невреди́мый.

unharness *vt* распря|га́ть (-́чь).

unhealthy *adj* нездоро́вый.

unheard-of *adj* неслы́ханный; **but that's ~!** э́то неслы́ханно!

unheeded *adj*: **my advice went ~** к моему́ сове́ту не прислу́шались.

unhelpful *adj*: **the shop assistant was most ~** продаве́ц был кра́йне невнима́телен; **her advice was not ~** её сове́т пригоди́лся.

unhesitating *adj*: **his reply was an ~ no** он не коле́блясь сказа́л нет.

unholy *adj CQ*: **an ~ row** жу́ткий сканда́л.

unhook *vt* отцеп|ля́ть (-и́ть); (*of a dress*) рас|стёгивать (-стегну́ть); **to come ~ed** отцепи́ться, расстегну́ться.

unhoped-for *adj* неожи́данный.

unhurried *adj* неторопли́вый, неспе́шный.

unhurt *adj* невреди́мый.

unhygienic *adj* негигиени́чный.

uniform *n* фо́рменная оде́жда, фо́рма; **nurses' ~** фо́рма медсестёр; *Mil*: **in full ~** в по́лной фо́рме; **in dress ~** в пара́дной фо́рме, в пара́дном мунди́ре; **he's (not) in ~** он в фо́рме, он в шта́тском.

uniform *adj* одина́ковый; **boxes of ~ size** я́щики одина́кового разме́ра; **to be kept at a ~ temperature** храни́ть при постоя́нной температу́ре.

unify *vt* объедин|я́ть (-и́ть).

unilateral *adj* односторо́нний.

unimaginable *adj* невообрази́мый.

unimaginative *adj* (*of people*) лишённый воображе́ния; **he is too ~ to understand it** ему́ не хвата́ет воображе́ния, что́бы поня́ть э́то; **an ~ colour scheme** ску́чная расцве́тка.

unimpaired *adj*: **his hearing is/his mental powers are ~** у него́ всё ещё отли́чный слух/я́сный ум (*sing*).

unimportant *adj* нева́жный; (*insignificant*) незначи́тельный.

uninformed *adj*: **there's too much ~ criticism these days** ста́ло мо́дным суди́ть о предме́те, то́лком его́ не зна́я; **he is ~ about current affairs** он не в ку́рсе после́дних собы́тий.

uninhabitable *adj* неприго́дный для жилья́.

uninhabited *adj* необита́емый.

uninhibited *adj* раско́ванный; **he is ~ in his conversation** он говори́т обо всём не стесня́ясь, он несде́ржан в разгово́ре.

uninjured *adj*: **he escaped from the crash ~** он не пострада́л в автомоби́льной катастро́фе.

uninspired *adj* невдохновлённый; **his writing is ~** он пи́шет без вдохнове́ния.

uninsured *adj* незастрахо́ванный.

unintelligent *adj* неу́мный.

unintelligible *adj* непоня́тный; (*of handwriting*) неразбо́рчивый.

unintended, unintentional *adj* ненаме́ренный, неумы́шленный.

uninterrupted *adj* непреры́вный.

uninvited *adj* неприглашённый; **an ~ guest** неприглашённый/*more pejor* незва́ный гость; **he came ~** он пришёл без приглаше́ния.

uninviting *adj* непривлека́тельный; (*of food*) неаппети́тный.

union *n* сою́з.

union card *n* профсою́зный биле́т.

unique *adj* уника́льный; **a ~ specimen** уника́льный образе́ц/экземпля́р; **he's ~ among writers** среди́ писа́телей он еди́нственный в своём ро́де.

unison *n*: **to sing in ~** петь в унисо́н; **they answered "No" in ~** «Нет»,— отве́тили они́ в оди́н го́лос.

unit *n* **1** едини́ца, *also Math*; *Mil* часть, подразделе́ние; **a ~ of heat/currency** теплова́я/де́нежная едини́ца

2 (*section, part*): **the research ~** иссле́довательский отде́л; **assembly ~** сбо́рочный цех; (*of furniture*): **a kitchen ~** ку́хонная се́кция; **a sink ~** мо́йка; *attr*: **~ furniture** секцио́нная ме́бель.

unite *vti* объедин|я́ть(ся) (-и́ть(ся)); **common interests ~ our (two) countries** на́ши стра́ны объединя́ет о́бщность интере́сов; **to ~ forces** объедини́ть си́лы; **to ~ against smb** объединя́ться про́тив кого́-л.

united *adj* объединённый; **the U. States (of America)** (*abbr* **US** *or* **USA**) Соединённые Шта́ты (Аме́рики) (*abbr* США); **the U. Nations Organization** (*abbr* **UN** *or* **UNO**) Организа́ция Объединённых На́ций (*abbr* ООН); **to present a ~ front** выступа́ть еди́ным/сплочённым фро́нтом; **~ action** совме́стные де́йствия (*pl*); **they are a ~ family** у них дру́жная семья́.

unity *n* еди́нство; **to live in ~** жить в дру́жбе.

universal *adj* всео́бщий; **~ approval** всео́бщее одобре́ние; **fridges have been in ~ use for some time** холоди́льники уже́ давно́ вошли́ в быт; *Tech* **~ joint** универса́льный шарни́р, карда́н.

universally *adv*: **this principle is ~ applicable** э́то универса́льный при́нцип; **it is ~ accepted that...** при́нято счита́ть, что...; **he is ~ popular** его́ все лю́бят.

universe *n* вселе́нная.

university *n* университе́т; **he is at/went to ~** он у́чится/учи́лся в университе́те; **to enter the ~** поступи́ть в университе́т; *attr*: **a ~ education/student** университе́тское образова́ние, студе́нт университе́та.

unjust *adj* несправедли́вый.

unjustifiable *adj*: **such behaviour is quite ~** тако́му поведе́нию нет никако́го оправда́ния.

unkempt *adj*: **with ~ hair** с растрёпанными волоса́ми; **he looks ~** у него́ неопря́тный/неря́шливый вид.

unkind *adj* недо́брый, недоброжела́тельный; **life has been ~ to him** судьба́ была́ к нему́ суро́ва/с ним нела́скова.

unkindly *adv*: **don't take it ~ if I say that...** не обижа́йся, е́сли я скажу́, что...

unknown *adj* неизве́стный; **the ~ soldier** неизве́стный солда́т; **an ~ disease** неизве́стная боле́знь; **~ to me** без моего́ ве́дома; *Math* **an ~ quantity** неизве́стное, неизве́стная величина́.

unlace *vt* расшнуро́в|ывать (-а́ть); **to come ~d** расшнуро́вываться.

unlawful *adj* незако́нный.

unleash *vt*: **to ~ a dog** спус|ка́ть соба́ку с поводка́ (-ти́ть); *fig* **the article ~ed a storm of protest** статья́ вы́звала бу́рю проте́ста.

unless *conj* е́сли не; **I'll expect you on Tuesday ~ I hear to the contrary** я бу́ду ждать вас во вто́рник, е́сли у вас ничего́ не изме́нится; **~ I am mistaken** е́сли я не ошиба́юсь; **I wouldn't have gone ~ it had been necessary** я бы не пошёл, е́сли бы не́ было необходи́мости.

unlike *adj and prep*: **he is quite ~ his sister** он совсе́м не похо́ж на сестру́; **it is ~ him not to phone** стра́нно, что он не позвони́л— э́то на него́ не похо́же; **~ his friends, he...** в отли́чие от свои́х друзе́й он...; **their flat is not ~ ours** их кварти́ра ма́ло чем отлича́ется от на́шей.

unlikely *adj* невероя́тный, неправдоподо́бный; маловероя́тный; **a most ~ story** соверше́нно невероя́тная исто́рия; **he is ~ to come** маловероя́тно, что/вряд ли он придёт; **the letter turned up in the most ~ place** письмо́ нашло́сь в са́мом неподходя́щем ме́сте; **it is not ~ that...** не исключено́, что...

unlimited *adj* неограни́ченный.

unlined *adj*: **~ paper** нелино́ванная бума́га; **her face is quite ~** у неё совсе́м нет морщи́н на лице́; **an ~ jacket** ку́ртка без подкла́дки.

unlit *adj* неосвещённый.

unload *vti vt*: **to ~ a lorry/a ship** разгру|жа́ть грузови́к/су́дно (-зи́ть)

vi выгружа́ться; разгружа́ться; (*of tip-up lorry*) свали|вать груз (-́ть).

unlock *vt* от|пира́ть (-пере́ть).

unlooked-for *adj* неожи́данный, непредви́денный.

unluckily *adv* к несча́стью.

unlucky *adj* **1** *attr* несчастли́вый; неуда́чный; **it has been an ~ year for her** э́тот год был для неё неуда́чным

2 *predic*: **you were ~** тебе́ не повезло́; **he is ~ in love** ему́ не везёт в любви́; **how ~!** како́е несча́стье!; **superstitious people consider black cats are ~** суеве́рные лю́ди счита́ют, что чёрные ко́шки прино́сят несча́стье.

unmade *adj*: **the beds are ~** посте́ли не застелены.

unmanageable *adj*: **these boxes/her children are ~** э́ти я́щики с ме́ста не сдви́нешь, её де́ти никого́ не слу́шают.

unmanly *adj* (*cowardly*) нему́жественный; (*effeminate*) **it's ~ to weep** мужчи́ны не пла́чут.

unmanned *adj*: **an ~ spaceship** автомати́чески управля́емый косми́ческий кора́бль.

unmannerly *adj* невоспи́танный, невежливый, гру́бый.

unmarried *adj* (*of man*) нежена́тый; (*of woman*) незаму́жняя.

unmask *vt fig*: **to ~ a traitor/a plot** разоблач|а́ть преда́теля (-и́ть), раскры|ва́ть за́говор (-́ть).

unmentionable *adj*: **such subjects are ~ in polite society** о таки́х веща́х не упомина́ют в прили́чном о́бществе.

unmerciful *adj* безжа́лостный.

unmerited *adj* незаслу́женный.

unmistakable *adj* безоши́бочный; **an ~ sign of rain** ве́рная приме́та бли́зкого дождя́; **he has very red hair—he's quite ~** у него́ я́рко-ры́жие во́лосы—его́ невозмо́жно не узна́ть.

unmistakably *adv* без сомне́ния, я́вно; **this handwriting is ~ his** э́тот по́черк я́вно его́.

unmitigated *adj*: **an ~ scoundrel** отъя́вленный негодя́й.

unmounted *adj*: **an ~ gem** ка́мень без опра́вы; **an ~ photo** ненакле́енное фо́то.

unmoved *adj*: **he was ~ by her pleading/tears** его́ не тро́нули её мольбы́/слёзы.

unnamed *adj*: **£100 was given by an ~ donor** сто фу́нтов бы́ли даны́ челове́ком, не назва́вшим себя́.

unnatural *adj* неесте́ственный; **it's ~ for a mother not to love her children** в ма́тери любо́вь к свои́м де́тям зало́жена само́й приро́дой; **an ~ crime** чудо́вищное преступле́ние.

unnaturally *adv*: **not ~** не без основа́ния.

unnavigable *adj* несудохо́дный.

unnecessarily *adv*: **they came ~ early** они́ пришли́ сли́шком ра́но; **the ring was ~ expensive** кольцо́ бы́ло сли́шком дорого́е.

unnecessary *adj* нену́жный, изли́шний; **an ~ expense/luxury** нену́жные расхо́ды (*pl*), изли́шняя ро́скошь; **it is ~ to add that...** не ну́жно/изли́шне добавля́ть, что...; **fur coats are ~ here** у нас здесь нет необходи́мости носи́ть зимо́й шу́бу (*sing*).

unnerving *adj*: **I found the interview ~** э́та бесе́да встрево́жила меня́.

unnumbered *adj*: **~ pages** ненумеро́ванные страни́цы; **~ generations** бесчи́сленные/мно́гие поколе́ния.

unobservant *adj* ненаблюда́тельный.

unobserved *adj* незаме́ченный; **he slipped away ~** он ушёл незаме́ченным.

unobtainable *adj*: **these goods are ~** э́ти това́ры невозмо́жно доста́ть.

unobtrusive *adj* (*of person, help, etc.*) ненавя́зчивый.

unobtrusively *adv*: **he ~ slipped a note into her hand** он незаме́тно вложи́л запи́ску ей в ру́ку; **I was trying to clear the table ~** я стара́лась убра́ть посу́ду со стола́, никому́ не меша́я.

unoccupied *adj* неза́нятый; *Mil* неоккупи́рованный; **an ~ seat** свобо́дное/неза́нятое ме́сто; **the house is ~/was ~ at the time of the burglary** в э́том до́ме никто́ не живёт, в до́ме никого́ не́ было, когда́ туда́ забра́лись во́ры.

unofficial *adj* неофициа́льный.

unopened *adj* неоткры́тый; **an ~ letter** неоткры́тое/нераспеча́танное письмо́; **the letter is ~** письмо́ не распеча́тано.

unopposed *adj*: **he was returned ~** он был и́збран как еди́нственный кандида́т.

unpack *vti* распако́в|ывать(ся) (-а́ть(ся)); **I'll ~** я распаку́ю свои́ ве́щи; **I'll ~ my dresses** я доста́ну/вы́ну пла́тья (из чемода́на).

unpaid *adj*: **an ~ debt** неупла́ченный долг; **~ work** неопла́чиваемая рабо́та; *joc* **I'm just an ~ servant in this house** я в э́том до́ме на положе́нии беспла́тной прислу́ги.

unpalatable *adj* невку́сный; *fig* неприя́тный.

unparalleled *adj*: **~ kindness** необыкнове́нная доброта́; **an ~ disaster** ни с чем не сравни́мое бе́дствие.

unpardonable *adj* непрости́тельный.

unpaved *adj* немощёный.

unperturbed *adj* невозмути́мый; **he carried on ~** он невозмути́мо продолжа́л.

unpick *vt Sew* рас|па́рывать (-поро́ть).

unpin *vt*: **to ~ a brooch** отцеп|ля́ть/от|ка́лывать бро́шку (-и́ть/-коло́ть); **to ~ one's hair** вы|нима́ть шпи́льки из воло́с (-́нуть).

unpleasant *adj* неприя́тный.

unplug *vt*: **to ~ the television** отключ|а́ть телеви́зор (от се́ти) (-и́ть).

unpolished *adj*: **an ~ stone** неотшлифо́ванный ка́мень; **~ shoes** нена́чищенные боти́нки; **~ oak** неполиро́ванный дуб; *fig* **an ~ style** неотто́ченный стиль.

unpolluted *adj* незагрязнённый.

unpopular *adj attr* непопуля́рный; *predic*: **he made himself ~ among his colleagues** он испо́ртил отноше́ния с колле́гами; **the decision is ~ with the students** э́то реше́ние не нашло́ благоприя́тного о́тклика у студе́нтов.

unpractical *adj* (*of person*) непракти́чный; (*of plan*) нереа́льный.

unprecedented *adj* беспрецеде́нтный.

unpredictable *adj*: **the results of the election are ~** результа́ты вы́боров тру́дно предсказа́ть; **she/the weather in England is ~** не зна́ешь, чего́ от неё и ждать, пого́ду в А́нглии тру́дно прогнози́ровать.

unprejudiced *adj* (*without prejudices*) непредубеждённый; (*impartial*) беспристра́стный.

unpremeditated *adj Law* непредумы́шленный.

unprepared *adj* (*of work, etc.*) неподгото́вленный; **the country was ~ for war** страна́ была́ не гото́ва к войне́; **I was ~ for rain/to find her so young** я не ду́мал, что бу́дет дождь/, что она́ так молода́.

unprepossessing *adj* нерасполага́ющий.

unpresentable *adj usu joc* непрезента́бельный.

unpretentious *adj* без осо́бых прете́нзий, просто́й.

unprincipled *adj* беспринци́пный.

unprintable *adj* нецензу́рный, непеча́тный.

unproductive *adj* непродукти́вный.

unprofitable *adj* невы́годный; **an ~ enterprise** невы́годное/нерента́бельное предприя́тие; *fig* **our discussions were ~** на́ши диску́ссии ни к чему́ не привели́.

unpromising *adj*: **the weather looks ~** хоро́шей пого́ды не ожида́ется; **after an ~ start** по́сле малообеща́ющего нача́ла.

unpronounceable *adj* непроизноси́мый.

unproved *adj* недока́занный; **your theory is ~** ва́ша тео́рия ещё не дока́зана.

unprovided for *adj*: **the widow was left ~** вдова́ оста́лась без средств; **such a case is ~ in the contract** э́тот слу́чай не предусмо́трен в контра́кте.

unprovoked *adj* ниче́м не вы́званный.

unpublished *adj* неопублико́ванный, неи́зданный.

unpunctual *adj* (*of person*) непунктуа́льный, нето́чный, неаккура́тный; **the trains are ~** поезда́ иду́т не по расписа́нию.

unpunished *adj*: **the thieves went ~** во́ры оста́лись ненака́занными.

unqualified *adj*: **he is an ~ teacher** он преподава́тель без дипло́ма; **he is ~** у него́ нет квалифика́ции; **~ praise** о́чень высо́кая похвала́; **the play was an ~ success** пье́са име́ла огро́мный/я́вный успе́х.

unquestionable *adj* несомне́нный, бесспо́рный; **~ authority/talent** бесспо́рный авторите́т, несомне́нный тала́нт.

unquestioned *adj* неоспори́мый; **his authority is/goes ~** его́ авторите́т неоспори́м; **I can't let that statement pass ~** я не могу́ приня́ть э́то утвержде́ние на ве́ру.

unquestioning *adj*: **~ obedience** беспрекосло́вное повинове́ние.

unravel *vti* (*of wool*) распу́т|ывать(ся) (-ать (-ся)); *fig* **to ~ a mystery** разга́д|ывать та́йну (-а́ть).

unreadable *adj* (*illegible*) неразбо́рчивый; *fig* **this book is quite ~** *CQ* э́та кни́га нечита́бельна.

unrealistic *adj* нереа́льный; **he's asking for an ~ price** он запра́шивает нереа́льную це́ну.

unrealized *adj*: **our hopes/plans are still ~** на́ши наде́жды не оправда́лись, на́ши пла́ны ещё не осуществи́лись.

unreasonable *adj* неразу́мный; безрассу́дный; **he is quite ~ about the amount he expects us to do** с его́ стороны́ про́сто неразу́мно ожида́ть, что мы смо́жем сде́лать/*CQ* провернуть таку́ю го́ру рабо́ты; **it's not ~ to expect him to pay half** вполне́ разу́мно ожида́ть, что он запла́тит полови́ну; **he is an ~ man to deal with** с ним тру́дно име́ть де́ло; **prices here are quite ~** *CQ* здесь сумасше́дшие це́ны.

unreceptive *adj*: **~ to** невосприи́мчивый к + *D*

unrecognizable *adj* неузнава́емый.

unrecognized *adj*: **his talent went ~ for a long time** его́ тала́нт до́лго остава́лся непри́знанным.

unrefined *adj*: **~ oil** неочи́щенная нефть, нефть-сыре́ц; **~ sugar** нерафини́рованный са́хар.

unrehearsed *adj Theat, Mus* неотрепети́рованный.

unrelated *adj*: **they are ~** они́ не ро́дственники; **the two matters are ~** э́ти два вопро́са не свя́заны (ме́жду собо́й); **his theory is quite ~ to Darwin's theory** его́ тео́рия не име́ет никако́го отноше́ния к тео́рии Да́рвина.

unrelenting *adj* неумоли́мый.

unreliable *adj* ненадёжный; **she/the car is quite ~** она́ ненадёжный челове́к, маши́на ненадёжна; **I heard it from an ~ source** я слы́шал э́то из ненадёжных/недостове́рных исто́чников (*pl*).

unrelieved *adj*: **three hours of ~ boredom** три часа́ невыноси́мой ску́ки; **heat ~ by even a breath of wind** нестерпи́мый зной без мале́йшего дунове́ния ветерка́; **~ misery** безысхо́дное го́ре.

unremitting *adj*: **~ efforts** неосла́бные уси́лия.

unremunerative *adj*: **the work is interesting but ~** рабо́та интере́сная, но не вы́годная.

unrepeatable *adj* неповтори́мый; **his stories are ~ in polite society** его́ анекдо́ты нельзя́ расска́зывать в прили́чном о́бществе.

unrepentant *adj*: **he is quite ~** он ни в чём не раска́ивается.

unrequited *adj*: **~ love** безотве́тная любо́вь.

unreserved *adj*: **~ seats** незаброни́рованные места́.

unresolved *adj* нерешённый.

unrest *n* волне́ния, беспоря́дки (*pls*).

unrestrained *adj* (*of language, behaviour*) несде́ржанный; ~ **tears** неудержи́мые слёзы.

unrestricted *adj* неограни́ченный.

unrewarding *adj* неблагода́рный; **the work is** ~ это неблагода́рная рабо́та.

unripe *adj* неспе́лый, незре́лый, недозре́лый.

unroll *vti* раз|вёртывать(ся) (-верну́ть(ся)).

unruly *adj*: ~ **children/hair** непослу́шные де́ти/во́лосы; **an** ~ **mob** беспоря́дочная толпа́.

unsaddle *vt* рас|сёдлывать (-седла́ть).

unsafe *adj* опа́сный; (*undependable*) ненадёжный; **the water here is** ~ **to drink** здесь вода́ непригo̸дна для питья́; **it is** ~ **to go out alone at night** но́чью небезопа́сно ходи́ть одному́; **the brakes are** ~ э́ти тормоза́ ненадёжны; **it's** ~ **to rely on taxis in the rush hours** нельзя́ рассчи́тывать на такси́ в часы́ пик; **he is an** ~ **driver** он неосторо́жно во́дит маши́ну.

unsaid *adj*: **that would have been better left** ~ бы́ло бы лу́чше э́то не говори́ть.

unsalaried *adj*: **he is an** ~ **worker, he gets paid by the hour** он не на твёрдом окла́де, а на почасово́й опла́те.

unsaleable *adj*: ~ **goods** неходово́й това́р (*collect*); **the house is in such bad repair, it's** ~ дом в тако́м плохо́м состоя́нии—его́ невозмо́жно прода́ть.

unsalted *adj* несолёный.

unsatisfactory *adj*: **this is** ~ **work** э́та рабо́та сде́лана пло́хо; **his work is** ~ его́ рабо́та весьма́ неудовлетвори́тельна; **we'll have to sack him—he's** ~ нам придётся его́ уво́лить—он нас не устра́ивает.

unsatisfied *adj* неудовлетворённый; **my appetite is still** ~ я ещё хочу́ есть.

unsatisfying *adj* неудовлетворя́ющий; **an** ~ **job/meal** рабо́та, не даю́щая удовлетворе́ния, несы́тный обе́д.

unsavoury, (*US*) **unsavory** *adj* (*of food*) невку́сный; *fig* **an** ~ **reputation** сомни́тельная репута́ция.

unscathed *adj* невреди́мый.

unscholarly, unscientific *adjs* нена́учный.

unscrew *vt* отви́н|чивать (-ти́ть); **to come** ~**ed** отвинти́ться.

unscrupulous *adj* беспринци́пный, неразбо́рчивый в сре́дствах.

unseal *vt* распеча́т|ывать (-́ать).

unseasoned *adj*: ~ **food** неприпра́вленная еда́; ~ **wood** невы́сушенное/невы́держанное де́рево.

unseaworthy *adj* неморехо́дный.

unseen *adj* неви́димый; **a plant hitherto** ~ расте́ние, неви́данное до сих по́р; **an** ~ **(translation)** перево́д с листа́ без подгото́вки.

unselfish *adj* бескоры́стный; **he is the most** ~ **person I know** бескоры́стнее челове́ка не найдёшь.

unsettle *vt* (*a person*) беспоко́ить (о-).

unsettled *adj*: **the weather is** ~ пого́да неусто́йчивая/изме́нчивая/капри́зная; **my plans are still** ~ мои́ пла́ны ещё нея́сны́; **the matter remains** ~ вопро́с остаётся откры́тым/нерешённым; **her account is still** ~ её счёт ещё не опла́чен; **her debts are still** ~ её долги́ ещё не упла́чены; **my stomach is** ~ у меня́ расстро́йство желу́дка; **I still feel** ~ **in my new job** я ещё не привы́к к но́вой рабо́те; **I have begun to feel** ~ **here—it's time I left** я начина́ю ощуща́ть беспоко́йство—зна́чит, пора́ в путь.

unsettling *adj*: ~ **news** трево́жная но́вость/весть; **she has an** ~ **influence on the others** *CQ* она́ всех баламу́тит.

unshakeable *adj* непоколеби́мый.

unshaken *adj*: **he was** ~ **by their threats** его́ не испуга́ли их угро́зы; **he was** ~ **by the accident** он перенёс ава́рию с невозмути́мым споко́йствием.

unshaven *adj* небри́тый.

unshrinkable *adj* безуса́дочный.

unsightly *adj* неприглядный.

unsigned *adj* неподпи́санный.

unsinkable *adj*: **rubber dinghies are virtually** ~ надувны́е ло́дки практи́чески непотопля́емы.

unskilful *adj* неуме́лый.

unskilled *adj* неквалифици́рованный; ~ **work** неквалифици́рованная/чёрная рабо́та.

unsociable *adj* (*of people*) необщи́тельный; **they lead a very** ~ **life** они́ веду́т за́мкнутый о́браз жи́зни.

unsold *adj* непро́данный.

unsolicited *adj*: **he gave me an** ~ **testimonial** он дал мне рекоменда́цию, хотя́ я и не проси́л об э́том; ~ **advice** непро́шеный сове́т.

unsolved *adj* нерешённый.

unsophisticated *adj*: **an** ~ **person** простоду́шный челове́к; **an** ~ **hair style** проста́я приче́ска.

unsound *adj*: **the theory is** ~ **in several respects** тео́рия не выде́рживает кри́тики по не́скольким пу́нктам; **this building is structurally** ~ у э́того зда́ния ненадёжная констру́кция; **his judgment is** ~ его́ сужде́ния (*pl*) ча́сто оши́бочны; *Law* **he is of** ~ **mind** он психи́чески бо́лен.

unsparing *adj*: **thanks to his** ~ **efforts** благодаря́ его́ неуста́нным уси́лиям; **he was** ~ **in his praise/efforts** он не скупи́лся на похвалы́, он не щади́л сил.

unspeakable *adj usu pejor*: **to my** ~ **horror/joy** к моему́ вели́кому у́жасу, к мое́й вели́кой ра́дости; **he is an** ~ **bore** он стра́шный зану́да; **his manners are** ~ его́ мане́ры неопису́емы.

unspecified *adj* неопределённый; **an** ~ **amount** неопределённое коли́чество; **at an** ~ **time** в неустано́вленное вре́мя.

unspoiled, unspoilt *adj* (*of people*) неизбало́ванный; **he is** ~ **by his success** он не избало́ван успе́хом; (*of scenery*): **the island is** ~ **by tourism** на о́строве почти́ не быва́ет тури́стов; **the countryside there is quite** ~ приро́да там почти́ в нетро́нутом ви́де.

unspoken *adj*: **an** ~ **agreement/reproach** молчали́вый угово́р/упрёк.

unsporting *adj* неспорти́вный; **he's very ~** в нём нет спорти́вного ду́ха; **that was very ~ of him** он себя́ вёл (в э́той исто́рии) не по-ры́царски.

unstable *adj* неусто́йчивый, *also Psych*; *Chem* нестóйкий.

unstamped *adj* (*of letter*) без ма́рки; (*of documents*) без печа́ти, без шта́мпа.

unsteadily *adv*: **he walked ~ towards the door** он, шата́ясь, пошёл к две́ри.

unsteady *adj*: **the chair is ~** э́тот стул шата́ется; **my legs feel ~** меня́ уже́ но́ги не де́ржат; **her hands are ~** у неё ру́ки трясу́тся; **he is ~ on his feet** он нетвёрдо де́ржится на нога́х, он е́ле на нога́х де́ржится.

unstick *vt* откле́и|вать (-ть); **to come unstuck** откле́иваться; *fig* **her plans have come unstuck** её пла́ны расстро́ились.

unstitch *vt* рас|па́рывать (-поро́ть); **to come ~ed** распоро́ться.

unstop *vt* **1** *see* **unblock**

2 (*a bottle*) отку́пори|вать (-ть).

unstressed *adj* (*of syllable*) безуда́рный.

unsubstantiated *adj* неподтверждённый.

unsuccessful *adj* неуда́чный, безуспе́шный; **an ~ business/attempt** неуда́чная сде́лка/попы́тка; **an ~ actor** актёр-неуда́чник; **an ~ novel** сла́бый/неуда́чный рома́н; **he was ~ in the audition/election** прослу́шивание прошло́ для него́ неуда́чно, он потерпе́л пораже́ние на вы́борах; **~ negotiations/efforts** безуспе́шные перегово́ры/попы́тки; **he was ~ in persuading her** он безуспе́шно пыта́лся/ему́ не удало́сь её уговори́ть; **the play was ~** пье́са не име́ла успе́ха.

unsuitable *adj* неподходя́щий; **a most ~ moment** са́мый неподходя́щий моме́нт; **that dress is quite ~ for the occasion** э́то пла́тье совсе́м не подхо́дит для э́того слу́чая.

unsuited *adj*: **they are ~ to each other** они́ не подхо́дят друг дру́гу; **he is ~ to teaching** он не мо́жет быть преподава́телем.

unsupported *adj* (*of structure*) без опо́ры; **an ~ statement** заявле́ние, не подтверждённое фа́ктами.

unsure *adj*: **she is ~ of herself** она́ не уве́рена в себе́; **I am ~ of the location of their house** я то́чно не зна́ю, где их дом.

unsurpassed *adj* непревзойдённый, превосхо́дный.

unsuspected *adj*: **he proved to have an ~ talent for acting** в нём неожи́данно откры́лся актёрский тала́нт; **he went ~ for a long time** до́лгое вре́мя он остава́лся вне подозре́ния.

unsuspecting *adj*: **his ~ partner** его́ ничего́ не подозрева́ющий партнёр; **the ~ girl believed every word** де́вушка простоду́шно ве́рила ка́ждому сло́ву.

unsweetened *adj* неподслащённый; **~ tea** несла́дкий чай.

unswerving *adj*: **~ loyalty** непоколеби́мая ве́рность.

unsympathetic *adj*: **I find him ~** он мне несимпати́чен; **I am not ~, but...** я всё понима́ю, но...; **he was ~ to our cause** он не сочу́вствовал на́шему де́лу; **he was ~ towards her/to her problems** он не прояви́л к ней до́лжного сочу́вствия, её пробле́мы не вы́звали в нём сочу́вствия.

unsystematic *adj* несистемати́чный.

untalented *adj* неталáнтливый, безда́рный.

untangle *vt* распу́т|ывать (-ать).

untapped *adj*: **~ resources** неиспо́льзованные приро́дные ресу́рсы.

untarnished *adj*: **an ~ reputation** незапя́тнанная репута́ция.

untaxed *adj* (*exempt from tax*) освобождённый от нало́гов; (*not liable to tax*) не облага́емый нало́гом.

unteachable *adj*: **these children are quite ~** э́тих дете́й ничему́ невозмо́жно учи́ть.

untenable *adj*: **that theory is ~** э́та тео́рия несостоя́тельна.

untested *adj* (*of new products, etc.*) неиспы́танный, неопро́бованный.

unthinkable *adj* немы́слимый; **it would be ~ not to invite him** немы́слимо не пригласи́ть его́.

unthinking *adj*: **in an ~ moment I blurted it out** в како́й-то моме́нт, позабы́вшись, я проболта́лся.

untidy *adj* неопря́тный, неаккура́тный; **he's very ~** он о́чень неопря́тен/неаккура́тен; **the room/your hair is ~** в ко́мнате беспоря́док, у тебя́ во́лосы растрепа́лись; **his work is quite good but very ~** он де́лает свою́ рабо́ту непло́хо, то́лько о́чень небре́жно.

untie *vt* развя́з|ывать (-а́ть); **to ~ smth from smth** отвя́з|ывать что-л от чего́-л (-а́ть); **to come ~d** развяза́ться, отвяза́ться.

until *prep* до + *G*; **~ now/then** до сих/тех по́р; **wait ~ tomorrow** подожди́ до за́втра; **I can't come ~ Saturday** я не могу́ прие́хать ра́ньше суббо́ты.

until *conj* пока́ (не); **wait ~ I call you** жди, пока́ я (не) позову́ тебя́; **I stayed in ~ he phoned** я остава́лся до́ма, пока́ он не позвони́л; **they didn't start playing ~ she came** они́ не начина́ли игры́, пока́ она́ не пришла́; **it was not ~ I saw her myself that I realized how ill she was** то́лько когда́ я сам её уви́дел, я по́нял, как серьёзно она́ больна́; **I didn't find her ring ~ after she had gone** я нашёл её кольцо́ уже́ по́сле её ухо́да; **she screamed ~ she was hoarse** она́ крича́ла до хрипоты́.

untimely *adj*: **he met an ~ death** он безвре́менно сконча́лся; **her ~ arrival** её несвоевре́менный прихо́д/прие́зд; **an ~ remark** неуме́стное замеча́ние; **he chose an ~ moment to...** он вы́брал неуда́чный/неподходя́щий моме́нт, что́бы + *inf*.

untiring *adj* (*of people*) неутоми́мый; **~ energy** неутоми́мая эне́ргия; **thanks to his ~ efforts** благодаря́ его́ неуста́нным уси́лиям.

untold *adj*: **the story will remain ~** расска́з так и оста́нется нерасска́занным; *fig*: **~**

wealth несме́тные бога́тства (*pl*); ~ **suffering** невырази́мое страда́ние.

untouched *adj* нетро́нутый; **he left his supper** ~ его́ у́жин оста́лся нетро́нутым, он не притро́нулся к у́жину.

untoward *adj*: **I hope nothing** ~ **has happened** наде́юсь, ничего́ плохо́го не случи́лось.

untrained *adj* (*of people*) нео́пытный; **an** ~ **nurse** нео́пытная медсестра́; **their dog is** ~ соба́ка у них не обу́чена; **an** ~ **eye cannot tell the difference between them** ненамётанный глаз ра́зницы ме́жду ни́ми не заме́тит.

untried *adj* неиспы́танный; *Law* **his case is still** ~ его́ де́ло ещё не слу́шалось.

untroubled *adj*: **he is** ~ **by worries about the future** его́ не трево́жат забо́ты о бу́дущем.

untrue *adj* неве́рный; **that is quite** ~ э́то неве́рно, э́то совсе́м не так, э́то непра́вда.

untruthful *adj*: **an** ~ **statement** ло́жное заявле́ние; **he is an** ~ **boy** э́тот ма́льчик ча́сто говори́т непра́вду.

untruthfully *adv*: **I answered** ~ **that I liked his performance** я покриви́л душо́й и сказа́л, что мне понра́вилась его́ игра́.

unusable *adj*: **this tablecloth is** ~ э́та ска́терть уже́ никуда́ не годи́тся.

unused *adj* **1** (*new*) неиспо́льзованный

2 (*unaccustomed*): **he is** ~ **to working/to the work** он не привы́к труди́ться, он новичо́к в рабо́те.

unusual *adj* необы́чный; необыкнове́нный; ~ **behaviour** необы́чное поведе́ние; **he is an** ~ **person** он челове́к необыкнове́нный; **it is** ~ **for him to be late** обы́чно он не опа́здывает, стра́нно, что он опа́здывает.

unusually *adv* необы́чно; необыкнове́нно; **he is** ~ **talented** он необыкнове́нно тала́нтлив; **he dresses rather** ~ он дово́льно стра́нно одева́ется.

unvaried *adj*: **an** ~ **diet** однообра́зная пи́ща/дие́та.

unventilated *adj*: **an** ~ **room** непрове́тренная ко́мната.

unverified *adj* непрове́ренный.

unvoiced *adj Ling* глухо́й.

unwanted *adj*: **I felt** ~ **there** я там чу́вствовал себя́ ли́шним; **the child was** ~ они́ не хоте́ли э́того ребёнка; ~ **advice** непро́шеный сове́т.

unwarranted *adj*: **his dismissal was quite** ~ его́ уво́лили несправедли́во; **such severe measures are** ~ таки́е стро́гие ме́ры не опра́вданы; **that criticism is** ~ э́то незаслу́женная кри́тика.

unwashed *adj* (*of fruit, etc.*) немы́тый; (*of person*) неумы́тый; (*of clothes*) нести́ранный.

unwavering *adj* непоколеби́мый; **under her** ~ **gaze** под её при́стальным взгля́дом.

unwelcome *adj*: **they were made to feel** ~ им да́ли поня́ть, что их прису́тствие нежела́тельно; **that is** ~ **news** э́то плоха́я но́вость; **an** ~ **guest** нежела́тельный гость; **a holiday would be not** ~ отдохну́ть бы не помеша́ло.

unwell *adj only predic*: **she is** ~ ей нездоро́вится; **I feel** ~ я пло́хо/нева́жно себя́ чу́вствую; **I felt** ~ **on the voyage** я пло́хо перенёс морско́е путеше́ствие.

unwholesome *adj*: ~ **food** нездоро́вая пи́ща; **an** ~ **influence** вре́дное влия́ние.

unwieldy *adj* (*of furniture, etc.*) громо́здкий.

unwilling *adj* неохо́тный; **an** ~ **helper** помо́щник понево́ле (*adv*); **he was** ~ **to help me/for me to come** он не хоте́л мне помо́чь/, что́бы я пришёл.

unwind *vti* (*of wool, twine*) раз|ма́тывать(ся) (-мота́ть(ся)); *fig only vi* расслаб|ля́ться (-иться).

unwise *adj* неблагоразу́мный, неразу́мный.

unwittingly *adv* (*unknowing*) не сознава́я; (*unintentionally*) нево́льно, ненаме́ренно.

unwonted *adj* необы́чный.

unworldly *adj*: **he's so** ~ *CQ* он пря́мо не от ми́ра сего́, он как с луны́ свали́лся.

unworn *adj* нено́шеный.

unworthy *adj* недосто́йный; **these remarks are** ~ **of you** вам не приста́ло так говори́ть.

unwrap *vt* раз|вора́чивать, раз|вёртывать (*pf for both* -верну́ть); **to come** ~**ped** разверну́ться.

unwritten *adj* (*of letter, etc.*) ненапи́санный: **an** ~ **law** непи́саный зако́н.

unzip *vt* рас|стёгивать (-стегну́ть); **to come** ~**ped** расстегну́ться.

up *n*: **we have our** ~**s and downs but generally we get on well** быва́ет ху́же, быва́ет лу́чше, но в о́бщем мы ла́дим; **he has had a lot of** ~**s and downs in his career** в его́ карье́ре бы́ли взлёты и паде́ния.

up *adv* (*for use with verbs see under verb entries*) **1** (*physically*) наверху́, (*if motion is implied*) наве́рх, вверх; **take your case** ~ отнеси́ свой чемода́н наве́рх; **"this side** ~**"** «верх»; **what are you doing** ~ **there?** что ты де́лаешь там наверху́?; **the mountain is very high—we had to rest half-way** ~**/we didn't go all the way** ~ гора́ о́чень высо́кая—нам пришло́сь отдыха́ть на полпути́/мы не дошли́ до верши́ны; **there's a good view from** ~ **there/here** отту́да/отсю́да све́рху хоро́ший вид; **my office is five floors** ~ моя́ конто́ра на шесто́м этаже́; **he lives two floors** ~ **from me** он живёт на два этажа́ вы́ше меня́; **"road** ~**"** «иду́т доро́жные рабо́ты»; **he walked** ~ **and down** он ходи́л взад и вперёд; **the ball bobbed** ~ **and down in the water** мяч пры́гал по воде́

2 (*out of bed*): **aren't you** ~ **yet?** ты ещё не встал?; **we were** ~ **by 7** к семи́ часа́м мы уже́ бы́ли на нога́х; **he was** ~**/stayed** ~ **all night** он всю ночь не ложи́лся; **he is** ~ **and about now** (*after illness*) он тепе́рь уже́ на нога́х

3 (*to a place of importance, universities, etc.*): **to go** ~ **to London** пое́хать в Ло́ндон; **when I was** ~ **at Cambridge** когда́ я учи́лся в Ке́мбридже; **he's staying** ~ **for the vacation** он оста́нется в университе́те на кани́кулы;

we're just ~ for the day мы здесь то́лько на́ день

4 (*of price*, *quantity*, *temperature*): **eggs are ~ this week** я́йца подорожа́ли на э́той неде́ле; **his temperature is ~** у него́ подняла́сь температу́ра; **pensions are ~ (by) 10%** пе́нсии увели́чили на де́сять проце́нтов; **our turnover is ~ £100,000 on last year** наш оборо́т на сто ты́сяч фу́нтов бо́льше, чем в про́шлом году́; **they've put the rent ~ to/by £20** квартпла́та возросла́ до двадцати́/на два́дцать фу́нтов; *Sport* **Liverpool are 3 goals ~** кома́нда Ливерпу́ля на три го́ла впереди́

5 (*of time*): **time is ~** вре́мя истекло́: **our lease is ~ in May** срок на́шей аре́нды истека́ет в ма́е; **our holiday is ~** наш о́тпуск ко́нчился

6 (*in court*): **he was ~ before the magistrate for dangerous driving** его́ вы́звали в суд за наруше́ние пра́вил доро́жного движе́ния; **he's ~ for trial** он ско́ро предста́нет пе́ред судо́м; **his case comes ~ on Tuesday** его́ де́ло бу́дет слу́шаться во вто́рник

7 *fig and CQ uses*: **he's high ~ in the army** он занима́ет высо́кий пост в а́рмии; **this is a step ~ for him** э́то для него́ шаг вперёд; **he's going ~ in the world** он преуспева́ет в жи́зни; **he sits with his feet ~ while she does the work** она́ всё по до́му де́лает, а он сиди́т сложа́ ру́ки; **he likes to be ~ and doing** он не мо́жет сиде́ть без де́ла; **he's gone ~ in my estimation** он вы́рос в мои́х глаза́х; **I'm sure there's something ~** я уве́рен, что что́-то здесь происхо́дит; **what's ~?** в чём де́ло?; **what's ~ with Jim?/with the car?** что с Джи́мом?/с маши́ной?

8 *in combinations with other advs and preps*: **we'll be ~ against him/a lot of difficulties/opposition** мы столкнёмся с ним/со мно́гими тру́дностями/со мно́жеством возраже́ний (*pl*); **now we're really ~ against it** тепе́рь нам действи́тельно тру́дно; **he's ~ for re-election** он опя́ть баллоти́руется; **the house is ~ for sale** дом продаётся; **he's well ~ in modern poetry** он хорошо́ зна́ет совреме́нную поэ́зию; **the water is ~ to our knees** вода́ нам по коле́но/до коле́н; **they advanced ~ to the frontier** они́ продви́нулись до грани́цы/к грани́це; **we read ~ to chapter 5** мы дочита́ли до пя́той главы́; **~ to a point** до не́которой/до изве́стной сте́пени; **cars cost ~ to £5,000** маши́ны сто́ят до пяти́ ты́сяч фу́нтов; **~ to now/that time** до сих/тех по́р; **~ to today the weather's been foul** до сего́дняшнего дня пого́да была́ ужа́сная; **~ to what age?** до како́го во́зраста?; **I can't get ~ to that note** я не могу́ взять э́ту но́ту; **the film isn't ~ to much** э́тот фильм не о́чень интере́сен; **this work is not ~ to her usual standard** э́та рабо́та не на её обы́чном у́ровне; **is he ~ to the job?** он годи́тся для э́той рабо́ты?; **I don't feel ~ to doing the washing today/to that sort of responsibility** я не в си́лах *or* не в состоя́нии стира́ть сего́дня/приня́ть таку́ю отве́тственность; **it's ~ to you to decide** тебе́ реша́ть; **it's ~ to you whether to tell her or not** э́то твоё де́ло—сказа́ть ей и́ли нет; **if it was ~ to me, I'd sack him** е́сли бы от меня́ зави́село, я бы его́ уво́лил; **what have you been ~ to all day?** чем ты весь день занима́лся?; **what are they ~ to?** что они́ затева́ют?; **what are you ~ to with that knife?** что ты собира́ешься де́лать э́тим ножо́м?; **you never know what that child will get ~ to next** никогда́ не зна́ешь, како́й но́мер э́тот ребёнок вы́кинет; **what do you think he is ~ to?** как по-тво́ему, что у него́ на уме́?; **I'm sure they are ~ to no good** я уве́рен, они́ затева́ют что́-то недо́брое.

up *prep* на + *A* (*of motion*), + *P* (*of position*); по + *D*; **the cat climbed ~/is ~ the tree** ко́шка взобрала́сь на де́рево/сиди́т на де́реве; **he went ~ the stairs** он подня́лся по ле́стнице; **he ran off ~ the street** он побежа́л по у́лице; **we sailed ~ the river** мы плы́ли вверх по реке́; **he stuffed his handkerchief ~ his sleeve** он су́нул плато́к себе́ в рука́в.

up *vti CQ*: **to ~ the price of smth** повы|ша́ть це́ну на что-л (-́сить); **he ~ped and ran** он вскочи́л и убежа́л.

up-and-coming *adj*: **he's an ~ young actor** он подаю́щий наде́жды молодо́й актёр.

upbringing *n* воспита́ние.

update *vt*: **the telephone directory is being ~d** в телефо́нную кни́гу вно́сятся измене́ния и дополне́ния.

upgrade *vt*: **to ~ the librarian/the librarian's job** повы́сить библиоте́карю зарпла́ту (*usu pf*).

upheaval *n*: **social/political ~s** социа́льные/полити́ческие сдви́ги; **I don't want to move again—it's such an ~** я не хочу́ бо́льше переезжа́ть—э́то о́чень тяжело́.

uphill *adj fig*: **it was an ~ task** э́то было тру́дное де́ло.

uphill *adv*: **to go ~** поднима́ться в го́ру; **it's ~ all the way** доро́га всё вре́мя идёт в го́ру.

uphold *vt* подде́рж|ивать (-а́ть); **the headmaster upheld the teacher's decision** дире́ктор поддержа́л реше́ние учи́теля; **the court of appeal upheld the verdict** апелляцио́нный суд подтверди́л пригово́р.

upholster *vt*: **to ~ a sofa in velvet** оби|ва́ть дива́н ба́рхатом (-́ть).

upholstery *n* оби́вка.

upkeep *n*: **the ~ of a house** содержа́ние до́ма; **the ~ of a garden/car** ухо́д за са́дом/за маши́ной.

uplift *vt*: **I felt ~ed after the concert** я испы́тывал подъём по́сле конце́рта.

upon *prep see* **on; once ~ a time there lived a king** (давны́м-давно́) жил-бы́л коро́ль.

upper *n* (*of shoe*) передо́к, верх.

upper *adj* ве́рхний; (*of class*, *rank*) вы́сший; **the ~ classes** вы́сшее о́бщество (*sing*); *fig* **to get the ~ hand of** взять/одержа́ть верх над + *I*.

uppermost *adj* са́мый ве́рхний; *fig* **these thoughts are ~ in his mind** э́то бо́льше всего́ занима́ет его́ мы́сли.

uppish, uppity *adjs CQ* надме́нный, спеси́вый.

upright *n* сто́йка, (*of goal posts*) бокова́я шта́нга.

upright *adj* прямо́й, *also fig*; **two ~ poles** два вертика́льных столба́; **an ~ piano** пиани́но; **an ~ man** прямо́й/че́стный челове́к.

uprising *n* восста́ние.

uproar *n* шум, гам; **the boys were creating an ~** ма́льчики по́дняли шум/гам; **his speech caused an ~** его́ речь вы́звала шум в за́ле; **the meeting ended in ~** заседа́ние ко́нчилось сканда́лом.

uproot *vt* вы|рыва́ть с ко́рнем (-рвать); *fig* **I don't want to ~ myself again** я не хочу́ бо́льше меня́ть ме́сто.

upset *n* расстро́йство, *also Med*; (*row*) сканда́л.

upset *adj* расстро́енный; **he was terribly ~ by the news** его́ ужа́сно расстро́ила э́та но́вость; **he has an ~ stomach** у него́ расстро́йство желу́дка.

upset *vt* (*overturn*) опроки́|дывать (-нуть); *fig*: **to ~ smb/smb's plans** расстр|а́ивать кого́-л/чьи-л пла́ны (-о́ить); **don't ~ yourself** не расстра́ивайся.

upsetting *adj*: **~ news** огорчи́тельная но́вость; **it was very ~ for us** нас э́то о́чень расстро́ило.

upshot *n*: **the ~ of it was that...** ко́нчилось тем, что...

upside down *adv* вверх дном, *also fig*; **the box is ~** я́щик стои́т вверх дном; **the chair is ~** стул стои́т вверх нога́ми; *fig CQ*: **the room is ~** в ко́мнате всё вверх дном; **he turned the room ~ looking for his keys** он всю ко́мнату переверну́л (вверх дном) в по́исках ключе́й; **because of him all our plans are ~** из-за него́ все на́ши пла́ны ру́хнули.

upstage *adj CQ* высокоме́рный.

upstage *adv*: **he was standing ~** он стоя́л в глубине́ сце́ны.

upstairs *adj*: **an ~ window** ве́рхнее окно́.

upstairs *adv* на ве́рхнем этаже́, наверху́; (*of motion*) наве́рх; **she lives ~** она́ живёт наверху́/на ве́рхнем этаже́; **to go ~** подня́ться наве́рх.

upstanding *adj* че́стный, прямо́й.

upstart *n* вы́скочка (*m and f*).

upstream *adv* вверх по тече́нию/по реке́; **we rowed ~** мы гребли́ вверх по тече́нию.

uptake *n CQ*: **he is quick/slow in the ~** он бы́стро схва́тывает, он ме́дленно сообража́ет.

up-to-date *adj* [**NB** *predicatively hyphens omitted*] совреме́нный; **~ furniture** совреме́нная ме́бель; **is this information ~?** э́то после́дние да́нные (*pl*)?; **an ~ car** автомоби́ль нове́йшей ма́рки; **I'm not ~ on the latest happenings** я не в ку́рсе после́дних собы́тий; **I must get ~ with my work before I go on holiday** мне ну́жно подогна́ть рабо́ту, что́бы уйти́ в о́тпуск.

upturned *adj*: **an ~ boat** перевёрнутая ло́дка; **an ~ nose** вздёрнутый нос.

upward *adj*: **an ~ glance** взгляд вверх; (*in a graph*) **an ~ curve** крива́я, иду́щая вверх; **prices are showing an ~ trend** намеча́ется повыше́ние цен.

upwards *adv* вверх; **to look ~** смотре́ть вверх; (*of material*) **facing ~** лицево́й стороно́й вверх; **children of three and ~** де́ти от трёх лет и ста́рше; **from childhood ~** с де́тства; **they cost from £20 ~** они́ сто́ят от двадцати́ фу́нтов и доро́же; **they found ~ of 500 ancient coins** они́ нашли́ свы́ше пятисо́т стари́нных моне́т; **~ of 1,000 people came** пришло́ бо́льше ты́сячи челове́к.

uranium *n* ура́н; *attr* ура́новый.

urban *adj* городско́й.

urbane *adj* учти́вый.

urchin *n* мальчи́шка (*m*), сорване́ц.

Urdu *n* (язы́к) урду́ (*indecl*).

urge *n* побужде́ние; жела́ние; **I felt the ~ to write** я испы́тывал пря́мо-таки потре́бность писа́ть; **I can work all night when I have/get the ~** когда́ есть вдохнове́ние, я могу́ прорабо́тать всю ночь.

urge *vt* подгоня́ть (*usu impf*); **to ~ on a horse/a team** подгоня́ть/понука́ть (*impf*) ло́шадь, под|ба́дривать кома́нду (-бодри́ть); *fig*: **I ~d her not to give in** я убежда́л её не сдава́ться; **he ~d patience** он сове́товал потерпе́ть; **he ~d this policy on the government** он настоя́тельно сове́товал прави́тельству проводи́ть и́менно таку́ю поли́тику.

urgency *n*: **a matter of great ~** сро́чное/неотло́жное де́ло; **do you understand the ~ of the situation?** ты понима́ешь всю остроту́ и сло́жность ситуа́ции?

urgent *adj* сро́чный, неотло́жный, безотлага́тельный; **that matter is ~** э́то сро́чное/неотло́жное *or* безотлага́тельное де́ло; **an ~ letter/message** сро́чное письмо́/сообще́ние; **it is ~ that I talk to you** мне необходи́мо сро́чно поговори́ть с ва́ми; **an ~ request** насто́йчивое тре́бование; **in an ~ tone** насто́йчивым то́ном; **that matter requires your ~ attention** де́ло настоя́тельно тре́бует ва́шего при́стального внима́ния.

urgently *adv* сро́чно; **they are ~ in need of supplies** им сро́чно необходи́мо продово́льствие (*collect*); **look into the matter ~** сро́чно рассмотри́те э́то де́ло.

urinal *n* писсуа́р.

urinary *adj Med*: **~ infection** инфе́кция мочевы́х путе́й.

urinate *vi* мочи́ться (по-).

urine *n* моча́.

urn *n* у́рна; (*for tea, etc.*) (электри́ческий) самова́р.

urogenital *adj* мочеполово́й.

us *pers pron* **1** (*oblique case of* **we**) *G, A* нас, *D* нам, *I* на́ми, *P* о нас; **don't forget ~** не забыва́йте (о) нас; **he advised ~** он сове́товал нам; **he came with ~** он пришёл с на́ми; **it's ~!** э́то мы!

2 (*imperative*): **let ~/let's go to the cinema** дава́й *or* дава́йте пойдём в кино́; **let's go** пойдём *or* пошли́, (*by car, etc.*) пое́хали

3 *where "us" refers to the subject of the sentence or clause it is translated by reflex pron* себя́; **we took him with ~** мы взя́ли его́ с собо́й.

use *n* **1** употребле́ние; по́льзование + *I*; (*application*) примене́ние; **it's for general ~** э́то для о́бщего по́льзования; **to come into/go out of ~** войти́ в употребле́ние/в обихо́д, вы́йти из употребле́ния/из обихо́да; **articles of household ~** предме́ты дома́шнего обихо́да; **for ~ in case of fire** применя́ть в слу́чае пожа́ра; **this tool has several ~s** э́тот инструме́нт применя́ется для разли́чных це́лей; **she doesn't care for him, she is just making ~ of him** она́ его́ не лю́бит, про́сто испо́льзует в свои́х це́лях; **this dictionary is in constant ~** э́тим словарём постоя́нно/ча́сто по́льзуются; **I made good ~ of my bicycle in Cambridge** в Ке́мбридже мне мно́го пришло́сь е́здить на велосипе́де; **is the telephone in ~ just now?** телефо́н за́нят?; **is this fishing rod fit for ~?** э́той у́дочкой мо́жно лови́ть ры́бу?

2 (*ability, right to use*): **he has lost the ~ of his right arm** у него́ отняла́сь пра́вая рука́; **he offered us the ~ of his library** он предложи́л нам по́льзоваться свое́й библиоте́кой, он предоста́вил свою́ библиоте́ку в на́ше распоряже́ние; **I have the ~ of the car when I want it** я могу́ по́льзоваться маши́ной, когда́ захочу́

3 (*usefulness*) по́льза; (*sense*) толк; **what's the ~ of talking about it?** что то́лку/како́й толк говори́ть об э́том?; **he/this is of no ~ to us** от него́/от э́того нам никако́й по́льзы; **there is little ~ in staying here** ма́ло то́лку/по́льзы остава́ться здесь; **there's no ~ asking him** бесполе́зно спра́шивать его́; **can I be of any ~?** могу́ ли я быть че́м-нибудь поле́зен?; **it's no ~ your objecting** ты зря возража́ешь; **they are of no further ~** они́ мне бо́льше не нужны́; **they are of no ~ to anyone/for anything** от них никому́ никако́й по́льзы, они́ никуда́ не годя́тся

4 (*habit*) привы́чка, обыкнове́ние; (*custom*) обы́чай.

use *vt* **1** употреб|ля́ть (-и́ть); испо́льзовать (*impf and pf*); по́льзоваться + *I* (вос-); **this word is no longer ~d** э́то сло́во бо́льше не употребля́ется; **which books did you ~?** каки́ми кни́гами вы по́льзовались?, каки́е кни́ги вы испо́льзовали?; **what sort of wood did you ~ for the house/for this table?** како́е де́рево вы испо́льзовали для постро́йки до́ма?, из како́го де́рева э́тот стол?; **the money is ~d to help the starving** э́ти де́ньги иду́т в фонд по́мощи голода́ющим; **I ~d six eggs in the pudding** я взяла́ шесть яи́ц для пу́динга; **may I ~ your phone?** мо́жно ли мне позвони́ть по ва́шему телефо́ну?; **have you ~d a rifle before?** ты когда́-нибудь стреля́л из винто́вки?; **I ~d a knife to open the tin** я откры́л ба́нку ножо́м; **may I ~ your name as a reference?** мо́жно мне сосла́ться на вас?; **be careful how you ~ that razor** будь осторо́жнее с э́той бри́твой; **we ~ a ton of coal a month** мы сжига́ем то́нну у́гля в ме́сяц; *CQ* **I could ~ a drink!** не меша́ло бы сейча́с вы́пить!

2 (*with abstract object*): **to ~ force** испо́льзовать си́лу; **~ your influence to get him to change his mind** повлия́й на него́—пусть он изме́нит своё реше́ние; **he ~d all possible means to attain his ends** он пошёл на всё, что́бы доби́ться своего́; **~ your discretion** поступа́йте по своему́ усмотре́нию; **~ your common sense!** поду́май/поразмы́сли хороше́нько!

3 (*treat*): **to ~ smb cruelly** жесто́ко обраща́ться/об|ходи́ться с кем-л (*only in impf*/-ойти́сь)

4 *as aux verb in past tense* **used to** + *inf, translated by impf aspect*: **I ~d to see him often** я ча́сто с ним ви́делся; **I ~d not to like him** ра́ньше он мне не нра́вился; **things aren't what they ~d to be** тепе́рь всё не так, как бы́ло ра́ньше

use up *vt*: **we have ~d up all our supplies/money** мы израсхо́довали все свои́ запа́сы/де́ньги; **it's time we ~d up this ham** пора́ бы уже́ съесть э́ту ветчину́.

used *adj* **1** *attr*: **a ~ car** поде́ржанный автомоби́ль; **a ~ stamp** гашёная ма́рка; **a ~ match** обгоре́лая спи́чка

2 *predic* (*accustomed*): **you will soon get ~ to it** вы ско́ро к э́тому привы́кнете; **I got/am ~ to the dark/to getting up early** я привы́к к темноте́/ра́но встава́ть; **we are not ~ to being treated like that** мы не привы́кли, что́бы с на́ми так обраща́лись.

useful *adj* поле́зный; **~ information** поле́зная информа́ция; **he has been very ~ to us** он был нам о́чень поле́зен; **make yourself ~ and get the tea** не сиди́ сложа́ ру́ки, принеси́-ка нам ча́ю; **I had a ~ visit to Bonn** моя́ командиро́вка в Бонн прошла́ успе́шно; **this string might come in ~** э́та бечёвка мо́жет пригоди́ться; **he is a ~ player** он результати́вный игро́к; **he is ~ with a gun** он уме́ет обраща́ться с ружьём.

usefulness *n*: **I question his ~ as a member of the committee** сомнева́юсь, бу́дет ли по́льза от его́ рабо́ты в комите́те; **these regulations have outlived their ~** э́тими пра́вилами уже́ не по́льзуются.

useless *adj* бесполе́зный; **a ~ attempt** бесполе́зная попы́тка; **it is ~ to shout** бесполе́зно крича́ть; **I feel ~ here** я здесь чу́вствую себя́ не у дел; *CQ* **he is ~ as a producer** никако́й он не режиссёр, како́й из него́ режиссёр!

user *n* (*consumer*) потреби́тель (*m*); **library ~s** чита́тели.

U-shaped *adj* U-обра́зный.

usher *vt*: **I was ~ed into the study** меня́ провели́ в кабине́т.

usherette *n Theat* билетёрша.

usual *adj* обы́чный; **he was sitting in his ~ place** он сиде́л на своём обы́чном ме́сте; **earlier than ~** ра́ньше, чем обы́чно; **more than ~** бо́льше, чем обы́чно; **he's late as ~** он, как обы́чно, опозда́л [**NB** *tense*]; **it is not ~ for people to leave so soon** обы́чно так ра́но не ухо́дят; **he said all the ~ things** он сказа́л всё, что в таки́х слу́чаях при́нято говори́ть.

usury *n* ростовщи́чество.

utensil *n*: **kitchen ~s** ку́хонные принадле́жности.

uterus *n Anat* ма́тка.

utility *n* **1** (*usefulness*) поле́зность

2 *pl* (*services*): **public utilities** коммуна́льные услу́ги; *attr*: **~ clothing** практи́чная оде́жда; **a ~ room** *approx* подсо́бное помеще́ние (в до́ме).

utilize *vt* испо́льзовать (*impf and pf*).

utmost *n*: **he did/tried his ~** он сде́лал всё, что мог, он стара́лся изо все́х сил.

utmost *adj* велича́йший; **a matter of the ~ importance** де́ло велича́йшей ва́жности; **with the ~ reluctance** с больши́м нежела́нием.

utter[1] *adj*: **~ rubbish** чисте́йший вздор, сплошна́я чушь/чепуха́; **it was ~ folly** э́то бы́ло чисте́йшее безу́мие; **he's an ~fool** он по́лный идио́т; **~ ruin** по́лное разоре́ние; **in ~ darkness** в полне́йшей темноте́.

utter[2] *vt* изда|ва́ть (-́ть), произ|носи́ть (-нести́); **to ~ a cry/groan** кри́кнуть, изда́ть стон; **he never ~ed a word** он сло́ва не произнёс/промо́лвил/пророни́л.

utterly *adv* соверше́нно; **he was ~ depressed** он был соверше́нно пода́влен; **I felt ~ lost there** я чу́вствовал себя́ там соверше́нно поте́рянным; **how ~ stupid!** кака́я ужа́сная глу́пость!

U-turn *n Aut* разворо́т; **"No ~s"** «Нет разворо́та».

Uzbek *n* узбе́к, узбе́чка.

Uzbek *adj* узбе́кский.

V

vacancy *n* **1** (*emptiness*) пустота́; **to stare into ~** уста́виться в пустоту́

2 (*for office job*) вака́нсия, ме́сто; **there is a ~/a ~ has come up for a typist in the department** в отде́ле есть/освободи́лось ме́сто машини́стки; **there's no ~ in this department** в э́том отде́ле нет вака́нтных мест (*pl*); **the ~ has been filled** (они́) нашли́ челове́ка на э́то ме́сто; (*of rooms in hotels*) **the hotel has no vacancies** в гости́нице нет свобо́дных мест/номеро́в.

vacant *adj* **1** (*empty*) пусто́й, *also fig*; **a ~ look** пусто́й/отсу́тствующий взгляд; **she sat there looking ~** она́ сиде́ла, уста́вившись в пустоту́

2 (*of post*) вака́нтный; (*of post, seat, room, etc.*) свобо́дный; **the post has become ~** э́та до́лжность вака́нтная; **have you any ~ rooms?** у вас есть свобо́дные номера́? **is this seat ~?** э́то ме́сто свобо́дно?; **the flat has been ~ for a month** э́та кварти́ра пусту́ет уже́ ме́сяц.

vacate *vt*: **to ~ a seat/the premises** освобо|жда́ть ме́сто/помеще́ние (*sing*) (-ди́ть).

vacation *n* (*Univ abbr* **vac.**) кани́кулы (*pl*); (*US*: *annual holiday*) о́тпуск; **the summer** *or* **the long vac.** ле́тние кани́кулы; (*US*) **he's going on ~** он ухо́дит в о́тпуск; **he's on ~** он в о́тпуске; *attr*: **vacation course** ле́тние ку́рсы (*pl*) обуче́ния.

vaccinate *vt* де́лать приви́вку (с-); **I was ~d against smallpox** мне сде́лали приви́вку от о́спы.

vaccination *n* приви́вка; **~ against cholera/smallpox** приви́вка про́тив холе́ры/от о́спы.

vaccine *n* вакци́на.

vacillate *vi* колеба́ться (*impf*); **he's still vacillating** (*about what to do*) он ещё не реши́л, что де́лать, он ещё коле́блется.

vacuous *adj*: **a ~ look** пусто́й взгляд.

vacuum *n* ва́куум; **in a ~** в ва́кууме, *also fig*; *attr* ва́куумный.

vacuum cleaner *n* пылесо́с.

vacuum flask *n* те́рмос.

vagary *n* причу́да, капри́з; **the vagaries of fashion/fortune** причу́ды мо́ды, превра́тности судьбы́.

vagina *n Anat* влага́лище.

vagrant *n* бродя́га (*m*).

vagrant *adj*: **~ musicians** бродя́чие музыка́нты.

vague *adj* нея́сный; неопределённый, сму́тный; **~ shapes of buildings** нея́сные очерта́ния зда́ний; **my future is still ~** моё бу́дущее ещё нея́сно; **~ rumours/promises** неопределённые слу́хи/обеща́ния; **he was ~ about the date of the meeting** он ничего́ определённого не сказа́л о да́те собра́ния; **I've a ~ idea I've seen him somewhere** я сму́тно припомина́ю, что ви́дел его́ где́-то; **I haven't the ~st idea of what physics is about/of what you mean** я не име́ю ни мале́йшего представле́ния о фи́зике/, о чём ты говори́шь; **she's terribly ~** она́ о́чень рассе́янна.

vaguely *adv* неопределённо; сму́тно; **he talked ~ about becoming an actor** он ка́к-то неопределённо говори́л о том, что собира́ется стать актёром; **I ~ remember him** я его́ сму́тно по́мню; **they are ~ alike in looks** вне́шне они́ че́м-то похо́жи друг на дру́га.

vain *adj* **1** (*useless*) напра́сный; **~ hopes** напра́сные/тще́тные наде́жды; **in ~** напра́сно (*adv*); **all our work was in ~** вся на́ша рабо́та пошла́ насма́рку (*adv*); **I tried to convince him but in ~** я напра́сно/впусту́ю стара́лся убеди́ть его́; **it is ~ to protest** возража́ть бесполе́зно; **all my efforts were in ~** я зря стара́лся

2 (*conceited*) тщесла́вный; **she's very ~** она́ о́чень тщесла́вна; **he's ~ about his successes with the fair sex** он лю́бит похва́статься своим успехом у прекрасного пола; **as ~ as a peacock** надутый как индюк.

vainglorious *adj* кичливый, хвастливый.

valedictory *adj*: **~ address/speech** прощальная речь.

valet *n approx* камердинер.

valetudinarian *n* мнительный человек, ипохондрик.

valiant *adj* доблестный; *CQ* **I made a ~ effort to arrive on time** я делал героические усилия (*pl*), чтобы поспеть вовремя/не опоздать.

valid *adj* действительный; **a ~ passport** действительный паспорт; **this ticket is ~ for one month** этот билет действителен на один месяц; **he made many ~ points** он привёл много убедительных доводов; **the objection was ~** возражение было обоснованным/правильным.

validate *vt*: **it will need a lot of evidence to ~ your claim** нелегко будет обосновать ваши претензии/доказать вашу правоту.

validity *n*: **this argument/document has no ~ at all** этот аргумент совсем необоснован, этот документ недействителен.

valise *n* плоский чемоданчик.

valley *n* долина.

valour, (*US*) valor *n* доблесть.

valuable *adj* ценный.

valuables *n* ценности, ценные вещи.

valuation *n* оценка; **the surveyor made a ~ of the property** инспектор произвёл оценку имущества; *fig* **don't take him at his own ~** не очень-то верь тому, что он говорит о себе—он себя явно переоценивает.

value *n* **1** ценность; *Econ, Comm* стоимость; *Math* значение; **it is a painting of great/no ~** это очень ценная картина, эта картина никакой ценности не представляет; **the ~ of discipline/of this discovery** важность дисциплины, ценность этого открытия; **his advice was of great ~ to us** он дал нам неоценимый совет; **it's of sentimental ~ only** это дорого для меня лишь как память; *Comm*: **the insurance paid us the full ~ of the car** страховое общество выплатило нам полную стоимость машины: **the market/face ~ of the goods** рыночная/номинальная стоимость товаров; **goods to the ~ of £5** товары стоимостью в пять фунтов; **my house is rising/going down in ~ all the time** стоимость моего дома всё время повышается/понижается; **I put its ~ at £100** я оцениваю это в сто фунтов; **this suit is good ~ for money** этот костюм—выгодная покупка; **he sets too high a ~ on his services** он слишком много хочет за свои услуги; *Mus* **give the note its full ~** играй полную длительность этой ноты; *fig* **to take smth at face ~** принимать что-л за чистую монету

2: spiritual/moral ~s духовные/моральные ценности; **he has a good sense of ~s** он знает, что в жизни действительно важно; **his scale of ~s** его шкала ценностей.

value *vt* оцен|ивать (-ить); *fig* ценить (*impf*); **he ~d the painting at £1,000** он оценил картину в тысячу фунтов; **he had the painting ~d by an expert** он отдал картину эксперту для оценки; *fig* **I ~ your opinion** я ценю ваше мнение.

valueless *adj*: **the brooch is ~** эта брошь ничего не стоит, это дешёвая брошь.

valuer *n* оценщик.

valve *n Tech* (*on water systems*) вентиль (*m*); (*pneumatic*) ниппель (*m*); (*hinged*) клапан, *also Anat, Mus*; *Radio* электронная лампа.

vampire *n* вампир; *fig* вампир, кровопийца.

van[1] *n Aut* автофургон; **furniture ~** мебельный фургон; *Rail* **goods ~** товарный вагон.

van[2] *n Mil* авангард, *also fig*; **in the ~** в авангарде.

vandal *n*: **young ~s** хулиганы.

vandalism *n* вандализм.

vandalize *vt*: **to ~ public property** варварски относиться к общественному имуществу (*impf*); **the telephone-booth has been ~d** телефон-автомат был поломан хулиганами.

vane *n* (*weather cock*) флюгер; (*of propeller*) лопасть.

vanguard *n Mil* авангард, *also fig*.

vanilla *n* ваниль; *attr* ванильный.

vanish *vi* исчез|ать (ʹнуть); **he ~ed from sight/into thin air** он исчез из виду, он как в воду канул.

vanity *n* тщеславие; **he did it out of ~** он сделал это из тщеславия; **her compliments tickled his ~** её комплименты тешили его самолюбие/льстили его самолюбию; **all is ~** всё суета сует.

vanity bag, vanity case *n* (сумочка-)косметичка.

vanquish *vt* побе|ждать (-дить).

vantage, *abbr* **van** *n* (*in tennis*): **~ in/~ out** больше/меньше (у подающего).

vantage point *n*: **from this ~ we can see the whole of Moscow** отсюда открывается вид на всю Москву; *Mil* **to gain a ~** захватить командную позицию.

vapid *adj* (*of style*) пресный; (*of remark, conversation*) пустой.

vaporize *vti* испар|ять(ся) (-ить(ся)).

vaporizer *n Tech* испаритель (*m*); (*for perfumes, etc.*) пульверизатор.

vapour *n* пар, испарения (*pl*).

variable *n Math* переменная (величина); *fig* **there are too many ~s to take any decision now** трудно сейчас принять решение, потому что много неясного.

variable *adj* переменчивый; **~ weather** переменчивая/неустойчивая погода; **they forecast ~ winds** согласно прогнозу ветер переменный; **his moods are very ~** у него семь пятниц на неделе.

variance *n*: **what you are saying now is at ~ with what you said yesterday** вчера ты говорил однó, сегóдня—совсéм другóе; **we are at ~ over this** мы расхóдимся в э́том вопрóсе/по э́тому вопрóсу.

variant *n* вариáнт.

variant *adj*: **a ~ spelling/reading** орфографи́ческий вариáнт, вариáнт тéкста.

variation *n* изменéние; *Mus* вариáция; **~s in temperature/in price** изменéние (*sing*) температу́ры/в цéнах (*pl*); **one finds great ~s in the prices of food in different parts of London** в рáзных райóнах Лóндона большáя рáзница в цéнах на продýкты; **~s on a theme by Haydn** вариáции на тéму Гáйдна; *fig* **that's another ~ on the same theme** ещё однá вариáция на тý же тéму.

varicose *adj Med* варикóзный.

varied *adj* разнообрáзный; **~ scenery** разнообрáзный ландшáфт; **the play had very ~ reviews** на э́ту пьéсу бы́ли сáмые разнообрáзные рецéнзии; **he's had a ~ career** кем он тóлько нé был (*had many jobs*), он ви́дел вся́кое на своём векý (*has seen much*).

variegated *adj* разноцвéтный, пёстрый.

variety *n* **1** (*diversity*) разнообрáзие; **~ in one's diet** разнообрáзие в пи́ще; **for the sake of ~** рáди разнообрáзия; **I've heard a very wide ~ of opinions on that** я слы́шал сáмые рáзные мнéния об э́том; **for a ~ of reasons** по рáзным причи́нам; **this can be done in a ~ of ways** э́то мóжно сдéлать по-рáзному; **they have a wide ~ of goods** у них большóй ассортимéнт товáров

2 (*sort*) сорт, разнови́дность, *also Bot*; **a new ~ of apple** нóвый сорт я́блок (*pl*)

3 *Theat* варьетé (*indecl*), эстрáда; *attr*: **~ artist/show** эстрáдный арти́ст/концéрт.

variety theatre *n* теáтр эстрáды.

various *adj* рáзный, различ́ный; **~ forms of transport** рáзные/различ́ные ви́ды трáнспорта; **eggs can be cooked in ~ ways** я́йца мóжно готóвить по-рáзному; **life is easier in ~ ways** жизнь стáла во мнóгом лéгче; **we saw her on ~ occasions** мы с ней не раз встречáлись.

variously *adv* по-рáзному; **this statement was understood ~** э́то заявлéние бы́ло воспри́нято по-рáзному.

varnish *n* лак; **nail ~** лак для ногтéй; **marine ~** лак для нарýжного покры́тия.

varnish *vt* покры|вáть лáком (-́ть); **to ~ a painting/a yacht/one's nails** покрывáть карти́ну/я́хту/нóгти лáком.

varsity *n CQ* (*UK*) университéт.

vary *vti vt* (*change*) измен|я́ть (-и́ть); (*diversify*) разнообрáзить (*impf*); **to ~ one's methods/diet** изменя́ть *or* разнообрáзить мéтоды, разнообрáзить диéту

vi: **the price varies with the season** ценá меня́ется в зави́симости от сезóна; **the price of coffee varies from £2 to £3 per kilo** кóфе стóит от двух до трёх фýнтов за килогрáмм; **opinions ~ on this point** мнéния по э́тому вопрóсу расхóдятся; **historians ~ in their opinions** истóрики расхóдятся во мнéниях; **how does their system ~ from ours?** чем отличáется их систéма от нáшей?; **to ~ from the norm** отклоня́ться от нóрмы.

varying *adj* рáзный, различ́ный; **with ~ results** с рáзными/различ́ными результáтами; **with ~ (degrees of) success** с перемéнным успéхом.

vase *n* вáза.

vaseline *n* вазели́н.

vast *adj* огрóмный; **a ~ area/undertaking** огрóмное прострáнство/предприя́тие; **on a ~ scale** в огрóмном масштáбе.

vastly *adv*: **the two things are ~ different** мéжду э́тими двумя́ вещáми огрóмная рáзница; **conditions have ~ improved** услóвия значи́тельно/намнóго улýчшились.

vat *n* чан, кáдка.

vault[1] *n Archit* свод; (*cellar*) пóгреб; **burial ~** склеп; **family ~** родовóй склеп; **the ~s of a bank** храни́лище (*sing*) цéнностей в бáнке.

vault[2] *vt*: **to ~ (over) a wall** пере|скáкивать чéрез забóр (-скочи́ть); **he ~ed into the saddle** он вскочи́л в седлó.

vaulted *adj Archit* свóдчатый.

vaulting horse *n* гимнасти́ческий конь (*m*).

vaulting pole *n Sport* шест.

veal *n* теля́тина; *attr*: **~ cutlets** теля́чьи отбивны́е.

veer *vi*: **the wind has ~ed (to the) north** вéтер задýл с сéвера; *fig* **he is ~ing round to my way of thinking** он постепéнно склоня́ется к моéй тóчке зрéния.

vegetable *n* óвощ (*usu pl*); **fresh ~s** свéжие óвощи.

vegetable *adj* расти́тельный; **~ soup/salad** овощнóй суп, салáт из овощéй; *fig* **she leads a ~ existence** онá ведёт расти́тельное существовáние.

vegetable garden *n* огорóд.

vegetable-growing *n* овощевóдство.

vegetable marrow *n* кабачóк.

vegetarian *n* вегетариáнец; *attr* вегетариáнский.

vegetate *vi* прозябáть (*impf*); **he just ~s in the country** он прóсто прозябáет в дерéвне.

vegetation *n* расти́тельность.

vehemence *n* горя́чность, стрáстность; **to speak with ~** говори́ть горячó/стрáстно.

vehement *adj*: **~ passions/protests** си́льные стрáсти, бýрные протéсты; **there was ~ opposition to his plan** егó план был встрéчен в штыки́.

vehicle *n*: **the road is closed to ~s** дорóга закры́та для трáнспорта; **motor ~s** автомоби́ли; *fig* **art may be used as a ~ for propaganda** искýсство мóжно испóльзовать как срéдство пропагáнды.

veil *n* вуáль; **bridal ~** свáдебная фатá; *fig*: **a ~ of mist** пеленá тумáна; **we'll draw a ~ over what happened** забýдем всю э́ту истóрию, бóльше не бýдем к э́тому возвращáться.

veil *vt*: **her face was ~ed** её лицó бы́ло спря́тано под вуáлью; (*of Moslem women*) to ~ oneself прятать лицо под чадрой; *fig* **the mountains are ~ed in clouds** горы окутаны облаками.

veiled *adj fig* скрытый, завуалированный; **~ hints/threats** скрытые *or* завуалированные намёки/угрозы; **~ irony** скрытая ирония; **with ~ hostility** с затаённой враждебностью.

vein *n Anat* вена; *Geol* пласт, жила; **a ~ of coal/ore** угольный пласт, рудная жила; **~s in a leaf/in marble** прожилки листа/в мраморе; *fig*: **there's a ~ of cruelty in his character** у него есть что-то жестокое в характере; **it's written in humorous ~** это написано с юмором; **when he's in the ~** когда у него есть настроение; **other comments in similar ~** другие замечания в том же духе.

vellum *n* пергамент.

velocity *n* скорость.

velour *n* велюр.

velvet *n* бархат; *attr* бархатный.

venal *adj* продажный.

vendor *n*: **street ~** уличный торговец; **news ~** продавец газет.

veneer *n* фанеровка; облицовка; *fig*: **his politeness is just a ~** его вежливость—чисто внешняя; **he's an uneducated man though he has a ~ of culture** он человек малообразованный, но не без налёта культуры.

veneered *adj*: **a ~ table** фанерованный стол.

venerable *adj* почтенный.

venerate *vt* почитать, чтить (*impfs*): **I ~ his memory** я чту его память.

veneration *n* почтение; **I hold my professor in ~** я отношусь к моему учителю [**NB** *Russian noun*] с большим уважением.

venereal *adj* венерический; **~ diseases** (*abbr* **VD**) венерические болезни; **a VD clinic** венерологический диспансер.

Venetian blinds *n pl* подъёмные жалюзи (*indecl*).

vengeance *n* месть, мщение; **to take ~ on smb for smth** мстить кому-л за что-л; *CQ*: **he paid me back with a ~** он отплатил мне с лихвой; **the rain came down with a ~** дождь полил вовсю/как из ведра.

vengeful *adj* мстительный.

venial *adj* простительный.

venison *n* оленина.

venom *n* яд; *fig* злоба; **he spoke about it with real ~** он говорил об этом, исходя злобой.

venomous *adj* ядовитый, *also fig*.

vent *n* (*opening*) отверстие; *Sew* (*in jacket, etc.*) разрез; *Tech* **air ~** отдушина; *fig* **to give ~ to one's feelings/one's anger** давать волю чувствам, излить свой гнев.

vent *vt*: **he ~ed his fury on his wife** он сорвал злобу на жене.

ventilate *vt* вентилировать (про-); *fig*: **to ~ a question** обсу|ждать вопрос (-дить); **they ~d their grievances** они высказали свои обиды.

ventilation *n* вентиляция.

ventilator *n* вентилятор.

ventriloquist *n* чревовещатель (*m*).

venture *n*: **a business ~** коммерческое предприятие; **he's been successful in all his ~s** ему сопутствовал успех во всех его начинаниях; **a very dubious ~** весьма сомнительная затея; **I would say at a ~ that ...** я бы рискнул сказать, что ...

venture *vti vt* риск|овать (-нуть); **I ~d the remarks that ....** я рискнул заметить, что ...; **if I may ~ an opinion** если позволите, я выскажу своё мнение

vi: **she did not ~ out of doors/further than the gate** она не рискнула высунуть нос/выйти за ворота; **don't ~ too near the edge of the cliff** не подходите слишком близко к краю скалы.

venturesome *adj*: **he's a ~ boy** он смелый парень; **a ~ journey/undertaking** рискованное путешествие/предприятие.

venue *n* место встречи.

veracious *adj* правдивый.

veranda(h) *n* веранда.

verb *n Gram* глагол.

verbal *adj*: **a ~ agreement** устное соглашение; **a good ~ memory** хорошая память на слова; **that's a common ~ error** это обычная ошибка в употреблении слова; *Gram* **~ adjective** отглагольное прилагательное.

verbatim *adv*: **I quote him ~** привожу его слова дословно, *CQ* я повторю то, что он сказал, слово в слово.

verbiage *n* многословие; **their assurances are so much ~** их заверения—одни слова.

verbose *adj* многословный.

verdict *n Law* приговор; **the jury brought in/returned a ~ of guilty** (*SU*) суд признал/(*UK, etc.*) присяжные признали подсудимого виновным; *fig*: **what's the doctor's ~?** что сказал врач?; **what's your ~ on the book?** что вы скажете об этой книге?

verdure *n* зелень.

verge *n* **1** край; **by the ~ of the road/the forest** на краю дороги, на опушке леса; **a grass ~** травяной бордюр

2 *fig uses*: **on the ~ of ruin** на краю гибели; **on the ~ of war/of a nervous breakdown** на грани войны/нервного расстройства; **we are on the ~ of a great discovery/of bankruptcy** мы на пороге великого открытия/на грани банкротства; **she was on the ~ of tears** она чуть не расплакалась; **it brought her to the ~ of insanity** она чуть с ума не сошла из-за этого.

verge *vi* граничить с + *I* (*impf*); **such views ~ on fanaticism** такие взгляды граничат с фанатизмом.

verifiable *adj*: **this statement is not ~** это утверждение не проверишь.

verify *vt* провер|ять (-ить); **we must ~ these figures/this quotation** нужно проверить эти цифры/эту цитату.

verisimilitude *n* правдоподобие.

veritable *adj*: **he's a ~ genius** он просто гений.

vermicelli *n* вермишéль.
vermilion *adj* ярко-крáсный, áлый.
vermin *n Agric* (*rats, etc.*) вреди́тели (*pl*); (*lice, etc.*) парази́ты (*pl*); **he was covered with ~** *CQ* он завши́вел.
verminous *adj* (*of prisoners, children*) вши́вый, завши́вевший; (*of animals*) **that cat/dog is ~** у э́той кóшки/собáки полнó блох.
vermouth *n* вéрмут.
vernacular *n* диалéкт; **he speaks in the ~** он говори́т на мéстном диалéкте.
versatile *adj* разносторóнний; **a ~ man/mind** разносторóнний человéк/ум; **~ a gadget** универсáльный прибóр.
verse *n* **1** (*poetry*) стихи́ (*pl*); **blank ~** бéлый стих; **a drama in ~** дрáма в стихáх.
2 (*stanza*) строфá; (*in Bible*) стих; **to quote smth chapter and ~** давáть тóчные ссы́лки/истóчники.
versed *adj*: **he is well ~ in Russian literature** он хорошó знáет рýсскую литератýру.
version *n*: **in the French ~ of the novel** во францýзском перевóде ромáна; **in his/according to his ~** соглáсно егó вéрсии; **a new ~ of the Bible** нóвый перевóд би́блии; **the film ~ of the play** экранизáция пьéсы.
versus, *abbr* **v** *prep Law* прóтив + *G*; *Sport* **France v Holland** матч Фрáнция—Голлáндия.
vertebra *n* позвонóк.
vertebrate *n* позвонóчное (живóтное).
vertex *n* верши́на, *also Math*.
vertical *n* вертикáль.
vertical *adj* вертикáльный.
vertigo *n* головокружéние.
verve *n* энтузиáзм; **she accepted it with ~** онá охóтно с э́тим согласи́лась; **he acted with ~** он игрáл с больши́м подъёмом.
very *adj* сáмый; **at that ~ moment** в тот сáмый момéнт; **the ~ man I was speaking of** тот сáмый человéк, о котóром я говори́л; **from the ~ beginning** с сáмого начáла; **on the ~ top** на сáмой верши́не; **her ~ manner was strange** самá её манéра былá стрáнной; **the ~ thought of it appalled me** однá мысль об э́том ужасáла меня́; **that's the ~ thing I meant** я и́менно э́то и имéл в видý/и хотéл сказáть; **that's the ~ thing** (*that's needed*) э́то и́менно то, что нýжно; **the ~ idea!** как ты мóжешь такóе говори́ть!, ну чтó ты говори́шь!
very *adv* **1** óчень; **~ good** óчень хорошó; **it wasn't ~ pleasant** э́то бы́ло не óчень прия́тно; **I ~ much like Proust** я óчень люблю́ Прýста; **are you hungry?—Yes, ~** ты гóлоден?—Да, óчень; **oh, ~ well** ну,/а, лáдно; **it's not so ~ surprising** э́то не так уж уди-ви́тельно
2 (*in emphasis*): **he is ~ much better** емý намнóго/горáздо лýчше; **his ~ first question** сáмый пéрвый егó вопрóс; **do your ~ best** сдéлай всё, что смóжешь; **£40 at the ~ most** сáмое бóльшее—сóрок фýнтов; **on the ~ next day** на слéдующий же день; **it's great to have a house of our ~ own** как хорошó имéть свой сóбственный дом; **he ~ nearly died** он чуть не ýмер.
vessel *n* **1** сосýд, *also Anat*; **drinking ~** сосýд для питья́
2 *Naut* сýдно.
vest *n* (*singlet*) мáйка; (*US*) жилéт.
vested *adj*: **he has a ~ interest in the deal/the outcome of this case** он ли́чно заинтересóван в э́той сдéлке/в исхóде э́того дéла.
vestibule *n* (*in hotel, etc.*) вестибю́ль (*m*).
vestige *n* след, остáток; **not a ~ of the old city remains** от стáрого гóрода не остáлось и следá; **there is not a ~ of truth in it** в э́том нет и дóли прáвды; **if there's any ~ of doubt** éсли есть хоть малéйшее сомнéние.
vet *n* (*CQ abbr of* **veterinary surgeon**) ветеринáр.
vet *vt CQ* про|веря́ть (-вéрить); **to ~ smb's work** проверя́ть чью-л рабóту; **he has been ~ted** (*by Security*) егó проверя́ли на благонадёжность.
veteran *n* ветерáн.
veterinary *adj* ветеринáрный; **~ medicine** ветеринáрия; **~ surgeon** ветеринáр.
veto *n* вéто (*indecl*); **right of ~** прáво вéто.
veto *vt*: **to ~ smth** на|лагáть вéто на что-л (-ложи́ть).
vex *vt* досáдовать (*impf*); **she was ~ed that I didn't help her/at her own stupidity** ей бы́ло досáдно, что я ей не помóг, онá досáдовала на себя́ за свою́ глýпость; **I was ~ed at not being able to come** я óчень досáдовал, что не смог прийти́; **I'm very ~ed that he repeated it to her** мне óчень неприя́тно, что он э́то ей передáл; **it's enough to ~ a saint** тут и у святóго лóпнет терпéние.
vexation *n*: **the petty ~s of life** мéлкие жи́зненные неприя́тности; **yet another ~** ещё однó досáдное обстоя́тельство.
vexatious *adj* досáдный.
vexed *adj* (*of people*) раздосáдованный; **a ~ question** спóрный вопрóс.
vexing *adj* досáдный; **how ~!** какáя досáда!; **it's most ~, we can't come** так досáдно, что мы не смóжем прийти́.
via *prep* чéрез + *A*; **we came ~ Berlin** мы éхали чéрез Берли́н.
viable *adj Biol and fig* жизнеспосóбный.
viaduct *n* виадýк, путепровóд.
vibrant *adj*: **the ~ notes of the cello** вибри́рующие звýки виолончéли; **his voice was ~ with emotion** егó гóлос дрожáл от волнéния.
vibrate *vi* вибри́ровать (*impf*).
vibration *n* вибрáция, колебáние.
vicarious *adj*: **I get a ~ delight from the children's enjoyment** рáдость детéй доставля́ет и мне рáдость.
vice[1] *n* порóк.
vice[2] *n Tech* тиски́ (*pl*); **to clamp smth in a ~** зажимáть что-л в тиски́.
vice-admiral *n* вице-адмирáл.
vice-chairman *n* заместитель председáтеля.
vice-chancellor *n Univ approx* рéктор.
vice-consul *n* вице-кóнсул.

vice-president *n* вице-президе́нт.

vice versa *adv* наоборо́т; **we can go first to the laundry and then to the market or ~** мы мо́жем пойти́ снача́ла в пра́чечную, а пото́м на ры́нок, и́ли наоборо́т.

vicinity *n*: **in the ~ of the station** побли́зости от/вблизи́ (*advs*) вокза́ла; **somewhere in the ~ of Moscow** где́-то под Москво́й.

vicious *adj* (*evil*) злой, зло́бный; (*depraved*) поро́чный, развра́тный; **a ~ dog** зла́я соба́ка; **a ~ remark/attack on** зло́бное замеча́ние/зло́бные напа́дки (*pl*) на + *A*; **he dealt her a ~ blow in the face** он в стра́шной зло́бе уда́рил её по лицу́; **a ~ life** поро́чная жизнь; *fig* **a ~ circle** поро́чный круг.

viciousness *n* зло́бность.

vicissitudes *npl*: **the ~ of life** превра́тности судьбы́.

victim *n* же́ртва; **the ~s of the crash/earthquake** же́ртвы ава́рии/землетрясе́ния; **a ~ of a hoax** же́ртва обма́на; **he fell a ~ to cholera/to her charms** он заболе́л холе́рой, он не устоя́л пе́ред её ча́рами.

victimization *n* пресле́дования, репре́ссии (*pls*).

victimize *vt* пресле́довать (*impf*).

victor *n* победи́тель (*m*).

Victorian *adj* викториа́нский.

victorious *adj* победи́вший; **the ~ team** победи́вшая кома́нда, кома́нда-победи́тельница.

victory *n* побе́да; **to win a ~ over smb** победи́ть/одоле́ть кого́-л, одержа́ть побе́ду над кем-л.

victuals *npl* продово́льствие, прови́зия (*sings*).

video(tape) *n* (*also* **~ recording**) видеоплёнка, видеоза́пись.

vie *vi*: **they are vying with each other for the first prize** они́ оспа́ривают пе́рвую пре́мию; **they ~d with each other to win her favour** они́ наперебо́й (*adv*) стара́лись доби́ться её расположе́ния.

Vietnamese *n* вьетна́мец, вьетна́мка.

Vietnamese *adj* вьетна́мский.

view *n* **1** (*sight*, *look*) вид; **in full ~ of everyone** у всех на виду́/на глаза́х; **he disappeared from ~** он скры́лся и́з виду; **we kept him in ~** мы не теря́ли его́ и́з виду; **we are in ~ of the sentry** часово́й мо́жет нас заме́тить; **the castle was now in ~/came into ~** показа́лся за́мок; **I'd like a closer ~** мне хоте́лось бы рассмотре́ть полу́чше; (*of exhibits*) **all our goods are on ~** здесь всё, что у нас есть; **the house is on ~ to the public** уса́дьба откры́та для широ́кой пу́блики; **a private ~** закры́тый просмо́тр

2 (*of scenery*, *photos*) вид; **a ~ of the hills** вид на го́ры; **you get a good ~ from here** отсю́да открыва́ется краси́вый вид; **an aerial ~ of the house** вид до́ма с самолёта

3 (*opinion*) взгляд, мне́ние; **in my ~** на мой взгляд, по-мо́ему; **he's a man of strong political ~s** у него́ твёрдые полити́ческие взгля́ды; **to state one's ~s** излага́ть свои́ взгля́ды; **point of ~** то́чка зре́ния; **to fall in with smb's ~s** соглаша́ться с чьим-л мне́нием (*sing*); **he takes the ~ that ...** он приде́рживается того́ мне́ния, что...; **I take a different ~** я смотрю́ на э́то ина́че; **I take a dim/poor ~ of his behaviour** мне не нра́вится его́ поведе́ние

4 (*consideration*): **in ~ of these circumstances** ввиду́ э́тих обстоя́тельств; **an overall ~ of the problem** всесторо́ннее рассмотре́ние пробле́мы; **at first ~** на пе́рвый взгляд

5 (*intention*) цель; **with this in ~** с э́той це́лью; **with a ~ to helping them** с це́лью/что́бы помо́чь им; **what had you in ~ when you said that?** что вы име́ли в виду́, говоря́ э́то?

view *vt* (*examine*) осма́тривать (осмотре́ть); (*consider*) смотре́ть (*only in impf*); **to ~ a house** осма́тривать дом; **how does he ~ the situation?** как он смо́трит на созда́вшееся положе́ние?; **I ~ the possible consequences with alarm** я с трево́гой смотрю́ на возмо́жные после́дствия; **~ed from the sea the island looks deserted** с мо́ря о́стров ка́жется необита́емым.

viewer *n* зри́тель (*m*); *TV* телезри́тель (*m*).

viewfinder *n Photo* видоиска́тель (*m*).

viewpoint *n* то́чка обзо́ра; *fig* то́чка зре́ния.

vigil *n Rel* все́нощная; *fig* **to keep ~ by a sick man's bedside** бо́дрствовать/проводи́ть ночь у посте́ли больно́го.

vigilance *n* бди́тельность.

vigilant *adj* бди́тельный.

vigorous *adj* энерги́чный; **a ~ man/protest/growth** энерги́чный челове́к/проте́ст, бы́стрый рост.

vigour, (*US*) **vigor** *n* эне́ргия.

vile *adj* гну́сный, ме́рзкий; **what a ~ thing to do!** кака́я гну́сность!/ме́рзость!; **~ weather** омерзи́тельная пого́да; **he's in a ~ mood** он в гнусне́йшем настрое́нии.

vilify *vt* поноси́ть, черни́ть (*impfs*).

village *n* дере́вня, (*rather larger*) село́; *attr* дереве́нский, се́льский.

villager *n* дереве́нский/се́льский жи́тель (*m*).

villain *n* негодя́й, злоде́й, *also Theat*; (*to child*) **you little ~** ах ты, разбо́йник!

villainy *n* злоде́йство.

vim *n CQ*: **put some ~ into it** поэнерги́чней!, поживе́й!

vinaigrette *n* сала́тный со́ус.

vindicate *vt* (*prove*) дока́з|ывать (-а́ть); (*justify*) опра́вд|ывать (-а́ть).

vindication *n*: **in ~ of one's actions** в оправда́ние свои́х посту́пков; **in ~ of his right** что́бы доказа́ть своё пра́во.

vindictive *adj* мсти́тельный.

vine *n* виногра́дная лоза́.

vinegar *n* у́ксус.

vinegary *adj* у́ксусный; **a ~ taste** у́ксусный при́вкус; **the wine's gone ~** вино́ прокис́ло.

vine grower *n* виногра́дарь (*m*).

vine-leaf *n* виногра́дный лист.

vineyard *n* виногра́дник.

vinous *adj* ви́нный.

vintage *n* сбор виногра́да; *attr*: ~ **wine** ма́рочное вино́; **1970 was a good ~ year** ви́на ты́сяча девятьсо́т семидеся́того го́да бы́ли превосхо́дны; *fig CQ* ~ **cars** маши́ны о́чень ста́рых ма́рок.

vinyl *n* вини́л; *attr* вини́ловый.

viola *n Mus* альт.

violate *vt* наруш|а́ть (-́ить); **to ~ a law/smb's privacy** наруша́ть зако́н/чьё-л уедине́ние.

violation *n* наруше́ние; ~ **of rights/an agreement** наруше́ние прав/догово́ра.

violence *n* наси́лие; **there has been an outbreak of ~** начали́сь беспоря́дки (*pl*); **to use/resort to ~** применя́ть наси́лие, прибега́ть к наси́лию; **robbery with ~** грабёж с примене́нием си́лы.

violent *adj* си́льный; неи́стовый; я́ростный (*usu of emotions*); ~ **emotions** си́льные чу́вства; **a ~ attack of fever/blow/explosion** си́льный при́ступ лихора́дки/уда́р, мо́щный взрыв; **a ~ storm** неи́стовая бу́ря; **a ~ quarrel** я́ростный спор; **in a ~ temper** в я́рости; ~ **colours** бу́йство кра́сок; **she took a ~ dislike to him** она́ его́ си́льно невзлюби́ла; **the drunken man got ~** пья́ный стал бу́йствовать; **he died a ~ death** он у́мер наси́льственной сме́ртью.

violently *adv* си́льно; **the boat rocked ~** ло́дку си́льно кача́ло (*impers*); **he was coughing ~** он си́льно ка́шлял; **he objected ~** он ре́зко возража́л; **they fell ~ in love** они́ стра́стно полюби́ли друг дру́га.

violet *n Bot* фиа́лка; (*colour*) фиоле́товый цвет.

violin *n* скри́пка; **to play the ~** игра́ть на скри́пке; **he plays first ~** он игра́ет пе́рвую скри́пку; *attr*: **a ~ case** футля́р для скри́пки.

violinist *n* скрипа́ч.

violoncellist *n* виолончели́ст.

violoncello *n* виолонче́ль.

viper *n* гадю́ка, *also fig*.

virago *n* мегéра.

virgin *n* де́вственница; *Rel* **the V. Mary** де́ва Мари́я, богоро́дица.

virgin *adj*: ~ **forest** де́вственный лес; ~ **land/lands** целина́, цели́нные зе́мли; ~ **snow** нетро́нутый снег.

virginity *n* де́вственность.

virile *adj* му́жественный.

virility *n* (*manliness*) му́жественность; (*potency*) мужска́я си́ла.

virtual *adj* факти́ческий; **the ~ ruler of the country** факти́ческий прави́тель страны́.

virtually *adv* факти́чески; **it's ~ impossible** э́то факти́чески/практи́чески невозмо́жно; **I'm ~ certain** я почти́ уве́рен.

virtue *n* **1** доброде́тель, досто́инство; **the path of ~** стезя́ доброде́тели; **tact is her chief ~** гла́вное её досто́инство—такт; **the great ~ of diesel ...** большо́е досто́инство ди́зеля в том, что...; **a woman of easy ~** же́нщина лёгкого поведе́ния

2 by/in virtue of: he won by ~ of his own efforts он победи́л благодаря́ свои́м со́бственным уси́лиям; **in ~ of what has just been said** в си́лу всего́ ска́занного.

virtuosity *n* виртуо́зность.

virtuoso *n* виртуо́з; *attr* виртуо́зный.

virtuous *adj* доброде́тельный; (*chaste*) целому́дренный.

virulent *adj* (*of poison*) смерте́льный; *Med* вируле́нтный; (*of hatred, abuse, etc.*) зло́бный, я́ростный; **a ~ green** ядови́то-зелёный цвет.

virus *n* ви́рус; *attr* ви́русный.

visa *n* ви́за; **entry/exit ~** въездна́я/выездна́я ви́за.

vis-à-vis *adv and prep* напро́тив + *G*; **they sat ~** они́ сиде́ли напро́тив друг дру́га.

viscera *npl* вну́тренности.

viscid, viscous *adj* вя́зкий.

vise *n* (*US*) *see* **vice**[2].

visibility *n* ви́димость; ~ **was down to 500 metres** ви́димость была́ то́лько пятьсо́т ме́тров.

visible *adj* ви́димый; **an island was ~ in the distance** вдали́ видне́лся о́стров; **the ship was no longer ~** корабля́ уже́ не́ было ви́дно; **with ~ embarrassment** с ви́димым смуще́нием.

visibly *adv* заме́тно, (*slightly stronger*) я́вно; **he was ~ moved** он был заме́тно/я́вно растро́ган; **she has aged ~** она́ заме́тно постаре́ла.

vision *n* **1** (*sight*) зре́ние; **his ~ is good** у него́ хоро́шее зре́ние; **field of ~** по́ле зре́ния; *fig*: **he is a man of ~** у него́ широ́кий кругозо́р; **he had the ~ to foresee the outcome** у него́ хвати́ло воображе́ния предви́деть после́дствия (*pl*)

2 (*dream*) грёза; **she had a ~ of the future/that ...** ей пригре́зилось бу́дущее, ей почу́дилось, что ...; *fig* **I had ~s of having to wait there all night** я предста́вил себе́, что придётся прожда́ть там всю ночь.

visionary *n* мечта́тель (*m*).

visit *n* посеще́ние, (*formal, official*) визи́т; (*excursion*) пое́здка; **our programme includes a ~ to the museum** в на́шу програ́мму вхо́дит посеще́ние музе́я; **the President has arrived in London on a (return) ~** президе́нт при́был в Ло́ндон с (отве́тным) визи́том; **the ambassador paid a ~ to the Minister** посо́л нанёс визи́т мини́стру; **a ~ to Paris** пое́здка в Пари́ж; **this is my first ~ to Greece** я пе́рвый раз в Гре́ции; **the doctor still has to make three ~s** у до́ктора ещё три вы́зова; **to pay a ~ to a friend in hospital** навеща́ть дру́га в больни́це; **she is on a ~ to her aunt** она́ гости́т у тётки; **we had a ~ from Nina** Ни́на была́ у нас в гостя́х; **we've had a ~ from the police** к нам приходи́ла поли́ция.

visit *vti vt* наве|ща́ть (-сти́ть), (*more off*) посе|ща́ть (-ти́ть); **the doctor ~s his patients every day** врач навеща́ет больны́х ка́ждый день; **the delegation is going to ~ Oxford** делега́ция посети́т О́ксфорд; **last year we ~ed the Soviet Union** в про́шлом году́ мы побыва́ли в Сове́тском Сою́зе; **I'm going to ~ friends** я собира́юсь навести́ть друзе́й (*length of visit unspecified*); **I'm going to ~ my sister** я собира́юсь (*to drop in*) зайти́ к сестре́/(*to stay*) навести́ть сестру́ *or* погости́ть у сестры́; **I'm going to ~ her in hospital** я иду́ к ней в больни́цу, я собира́юсь прове́дать её в больни́це; **do you know who ~ed us yesterday?** зна́ешь, кто вчера́ был у нас (в гостя́х)?; **when did you last ~ the dentist?/Paris?** когда́ вы в после́дний раз бы́ли у зубно́го врача́?/в Пари́же?

vi: **to go ~ing** ходи́ть в го́сти; **I'm just ~ing here** (*staying*) я здесь прое́здом, (*in answer to question on street*) я прие́зжий; (*US*) **to ~ with smb** навеща́ть кого́-л.

visitation *n joc*: **we've just had a ~ from our relatives** к нам понае́хали/к нам нагря́нули ро́дственники.

visiting *adj*: **~ hours** приёмные часы́; **a ~ lecturer** приглашённый ле́ктор; **~ card** визи́тная ка́рточка.

visitor *n* (*guest*) гость (*m*); (*to museum, etc.*) посети́тель (*m*); **we have a ~ from the US this evening** у нас сего́дня гость из Аме́рики; **I had lots of ~s in hospital** меня́ в больни́це навеща́ло мно́го наро́ду; **Cambridge is overrun with ~s in summer** ле́том в Ке́мбридже полно́ тури́стов.

vista *n* перспекти́ва, *also fig*.

visual *adj*: **~ images** зри́тельные о́бразы; **~ aids** нагля́дные посо́бия.

visualize *vt* представ|ля́ть себе́ (-́ить); **I can't ~ her doing that** я не могу́ себе́ предста́вить, что́бы она́ так поступи́ла.

vital *adj* **1** (*relating to life*) жи́зненный; **the ~ force** жи́зненная си́ла; **~ statistics** стати́стика продолжи́тельности жи́зни, *CQ* (*of woman's measurements for clothes*) разме́ры; *fig*: **a question of ~ importance** жи́зненно ва́жный вопро́с; **it is ~ to act at once** на́до де́йствовать незамедли́тельно

2 (*of person*) живо́й.

vitality *n* жи́зненная си́ла; **the children are full of/lack ~** де́ти полны́ жи́зни/вя́лые; **his style has great/lacks ~** у него́ живо́й/вя́лый стиль.

vitalize *vt* ожив|ля́ть (-и́ть).

vitally *adv*: **this is ~ important** э́то жи́зненно ва́жно.

vitamin *n* витами́н; *attr*: **~ pills** витами́нные табле́тки; **she suffers from a ~ deficiency** у неё авитамино́з.

vitiate *vt*: **this admission ~s your whole argument** э́то замеча́ние сво́дит на нет всю твою́ аргумента́цию.

vitreous *adj* (*of glass*) стекля́нный; (*glass-like*) стеклови́дный.

vitriol *n* купоро́с.

vitriolic *adj fig* ядови́тый, е́дкий.

vituperate *vt* брани́ть, поноси́ть (*impfs*).

vituperative *adj* бра́нный, руга́тельный.

vivacious *adj* живо́й, оживлённый.

viva voce, *abbr* **viva** *n* у́стный экза́мен.

viva voce *adv* у́стно.

vivid *adj* я́ркий; **~ colours** я́ркие цвета́; **a ~ description/imagination** я́ркое описа́ние, пы́лкое воображе́ние.

vividly *adv* я́рко, жи́во; **he described the scene ~** он я́рко описа́л э́ту сце́ну; **I remember it ~** я я́сно/жи́во по́мню э́то.

vixen *n* лиса́, лиси́ца.

V-neck *n* вы́рез мы́сиком.

vocabulary *n* (*at back of textbook*) слова́рь (*m*); (*of a dictionary*) сло́вник; (*of an individual*) слова́рный запа́с, запа́с слов; **he has a limited ~** у него́ ограни́ченный запа́с слов.

vocal *adj*: **the ~ chords** голосовы́е свя́зки; **there was some ~ opposition** бы́ли вы́сказаны возраже́ния (*pl*); *CQ* **he's pretty ~ after a drink or two** сто́ит ему́ вы́пить, как у него́ развя́зывается язы́к; *Mus* вока́льный.

vocalist *n* вокали́ст.

vocally *adv* (*orally*) у́стно; (*aloud*) вслух.

vocation *n* призва́ние; **she has a ~ for nursing** она́ медсестра́ по призва́нию; **to have a sense of ~** чу́вствовать своё призва́ние; **he missed his ~, he should have been a doctor** он занима́ется не свои́м де́лом, по призва́нию он врач.

vocational *adj*: **~ training** профессиона́льное обуче́ние.

vocative *n Gram*: **the ~ (case)** зва́тельный паде́ж.

vociferous *adj* шу́мный; гро́мкий; **a ~ crowd** шу́мная толпа́; **~ complaints** гро́мкие жа́лобы.

vodka *n* во́дка.

vogue *n* мо́да; **the ~ for miniskirts** мо́да на ми́ни-ю́бки; **to be in/come into ~** быть в мо́де, входи́ть в мо́ду; **the theory had a great ~ in the thirties** э́та тео́рия име́ла мно́го сторо́нников/хожде́ние в тридца́тые го́ды.

voice *n* го́лос; *Gram* зало́г; **in a low ~** ти́хим го́лосом; **with one ~** в оди́н го́лос; **to shout at the top of one's ~** крича́ть как оглаше́нный; **to raise/lose one's ~** повыша́ть/теря́ть го́лос; **I have no ~ in the affair** у меня́ в э́том де́ле нет пра́ва го́лоса; **he was in fine ~** он хорошо́ пел; *Gram* **the active/passive ~** действи́тельный/страда́тельный зало́г; *fig* **the ~ of reason** го́лос ра́зума.

voice *vt*: **to ~ a hope/feeling** вы|ража́ть наде́жду/чу́вства (*pl*) (-́разить).

voiced *adj Ling*: **~ consonants** зво́нкие согла́сные.

voiceless *adj*: **a ~ minority** беспра́вное меньшинство́; *Ling* **~ consonants** глухи́е согла́сные.

void *n* пустота́; (*gap*) пробе́л; **her death left a ~ in his life** её смерть образова́ла пустоту́ в его́ жи́зни.

void *adj* пусто́й; **an article ~ of interest** бессодержа́тельная/пуста́я статья́; *Law* **the agreement was declared (null and) ~** догово́р был объя́влен недействи́тельным.

voile *n* вуа́ль.

volatile *adj*: **he's ~** у него́ изме́нчивый/непостоя́нный хара́ктер; *Chem* лету́чий.

volcanic *adj* вулкани́ческий; **a ~ eruption** изверже́ние вулка́на.

volcano *n* вулка́н.

vole *n* мышь-полёвка.

volition *n* во́ля; **of his own ~** по свое́й во́ле.

volley *n*: **a ~ of fire/shots** залп; **to fire a ~** дать залп; **a ~ of stones/*fig* questions** град камне́й/вопро́сов; *fig* **he let fly a ~ of abuse** он разрази́лся бра́нью.

volley *vi Sport* (*in tennis*) бить с лёта (*impf, semel* уда́рить).

volleyball *n* волейбо́л.

volt *n Elec* вольт.

voltage *n Elec* вольта́ж, напряже́ние.

volte-face *n*: **he made a complete ~** он по́лностью перемени́л свою́ пози́цию.

voluble *adj* (*of person*) говорли́вый, разгово́рчивый.

volubly *adv* многосло́вно.

volume *n* **1** (*book*) том; **in three ~s** в трёх тома́х; **in V. III** в тре́тьем то́ме; **a dictionary in two ~s** двухто́мный слова́рь

2 (*liquid capacity*) ёмкость; **the ~ of a tank** ёмкость ба́ка; **~ in litres** литра́ж

3 (*quantity*) объём; **I'm appalled at the ~ of work in front of us** меня́ приво́дит в у́жас объём предстоя́щей рабо́ты; **~s of smoke** клубы́ ды́ма; *fig CQ* **it speaks ~s for her self-control** э́то говори́т о её большо́м самооблада́нии

4 *Radio* гро́мкость; **turn up the ~** сде́лай погро́мче; *attr*: **~ control** регуля́тор гро́мкости.

voluminous *adj*: **he's engaged on a ~ work** э́той его́ рабо́те конца́ не ви́дно; **he carried on a ~ correspondence with me** он вёл со мной большу́ю перепи́ску; **a ~ skirt** широ́кая ю́бка.

voluntary *n Mus* со́ло на орга́не.

voluntary *adj* доброво́льный.

volunteer *n* доброво́лец, *also Mil*; *attr*: **a ~ army** доброво́льческая а́рмия.

volunteer *vti vt*: **to ~ one's services** пред|лага́ть свои́ услу́ги (-ложи́ть); **he ~ed the remark that ...** он заме́тил, что ...

vi: **he ~ed** (*for the army*) он пошёл доброво́льцем (в а́рмию); **he ~ed for a mission/to wash the floor** он вы́звался вы́полнить зада́ние/помы́ть пол.

voluptuous *adj* сладостра́стный.

vomit *n* рво́та.

vomit *vti* рвать (вы́-); **he ~ed blood** его́ рвало́ (*impers*) кро́вью; **he/she ~ed** его́/её вы́рвало (*impers*).

voracious *adj*: **a ~ appetite** во́лчий аппети́т; *fig* **a ~ reader** ненасы́тный чита́тель.

voraciously *adv* жа́дно, с жа́дностью; **he ate ~** он ел с жа́дностью.

vortex *n* (*of wind*) вихрь (*m*); (*of water*) водоворо́т; *fig* **the ~ of politics** водоворо́т полити́ческой жи́зни.

vote *n* **1** (*franchise, right to vote*) избира́тельное пра́во; **women now have the ~** тепе́рь же́нщины по́льзуются избира́тельным пра́вом/име́ют пра́во го́лоса

2 (*ballot, process of voting*) голосова́ние; **a secret/free ~** та́йное/свобо́дное голосова́ние; **to decide by ~** реша́ть голосова́нием; **to take a ~ on a motion, to put a motion to the ~** ста́вить предложе́ние на голосова́ние; **the meeting proceeded to a ~** собра́ние приступи́ло к голосова́нию; **the ~ went against him** голосова́ли про́тив него́; **a ~ of no confidence** во́тум недове́рия; **to pass a ~ of censure on smb** принима́ть предложе́ние о вынесе́нии порица́ния кому́-л; **he proposed a ~ of thanks to the speaker** он предложи́л вы́разить докла́дчику благода́рность

3 (*vote cast*) го́лос; **to cast one's ~** подава́ть свой го́лос; **to cast one's ~ for smb/smth** голосова́ть за кого́-л/за что-л; **the casting/deciding ~** реша́ющий го́лос; **the total number of ~s cast** число́ по́данных голосо́в; **he got the most ~s** он получи́л большинство́ голосо́в; **he won by three ~s** он получи́л переве́с в три го́лоса; **an increase in the Labour ~** рост числа́ голосу́ющих за лейбори́стов; **the floating ~** голоса́ колеблю́щихся избира́телей

4 (*allocation in budget*) ассигнова́ния (*pl*); **the defence ~** ассигнова́ния на оборо́ну.

vote *vti vt*: **the meeting ~d that ...** собра́ние реши́ло, что ...; *Econ* **to ~ money for smth** ассигнова́ть де́ньги на что-л (*impf and pf*); *fig*: **the film was ~d a great success** по о́бщему призна́нию фильм действи́тельно уда́лся; **he was ~d to be a nice chap** его́ счита́ли хоро́шим па́рнем; *CQ* **I ~ (that) we go to the cinema** я за то, что́бы пойти́ в кино́

vi голосова́ть (про-); **the right to ~** избира́тельное пра́во; **which way did you ~?** за кого́ ты голосова́л?; **they ~d to impose the tax** они́ голосова́ли за введе́ние нало́га

vote against *vi*: **I ~d against the motion** я голосова́л про́тив э́того предложе́ния

vote down *vt*: **the proposal was ~d down** предложе́ние не прошло́

vote for *vi*: **I ~d for the motion** я голосова́л за э́то предложе́ние.

vote in/into/on to *vt*: **to ~ in a government** избира́ть прави́тельство; **to ~ smb into an office/on to a committee** избира́ть кого́-л на пост/в комите́т

vote on *vi*: **they ~d on the resolution** они́ поста́вили резолю́цию на голосова́ние

vote out of *vt*: **to ~ a party out of power** провали́ть пра́вящую па́ртию на вы́борах (*usu pf*)

vote through *vt*: **the bill was ~d through** законопрое́кт был при́нят.

voter *n* избира́тель (*m*).

voting *n* голосова́ние; уча́стие в вы́борах.

voting paper, voting slip *ns* избира́тельный бюллете́нь (*m*).

vouch *vi* руча́ться (поручи́ться); **to ~ for smb/smth** руча́ться за кого́-л/за что-л; **I can't ~ for the truth of what he says** я не могу́ поручи́ться, что он говори́т пра́вду.

voucher *n* (*receipt*) квита́нция, распи́ска; **a luncheon ~** тало́н на обе́д.

vow *n* обе́т, кля́тва; **marriage/monastic ~s** бра́чные/мона́шеские обе́ты; **to make a ~** дава́ть обе́т/кля́тву; **he's under a ~ of chastity** он дал обе́т безбра́чия; **she kept her ~** она́ не нару́шила кля́твы.

vow *vt* кля́сться (по-), да|ва́ть кля́тву (-ть); **to ~ vengeance on smb** дать кля́тву отомсти́ть кому́-л; **I ~ that...** кляну́сь/даю́ кля́тву, что...; **she ~ed she would never leave him** она́ покляла́сь, что никогда́ его́ не поки́нет; **to ~ to do smth** покля́сться сде́лать что-л.

vowel *n Ling* гла́сная; *attr* гла́сный.

voyage *n* (морско́е) путеше́ствие, пла́вание; (*of ship only*) рейс; **to go on a ~** отправля́ться в путеше́ствие; **a round-the-world ~** кругосве́тное путеше́ствие; **maiden ~** пе́рвое пла́вание корабля́; **on the homeward ~** в обра́тном ре́йсе.

voyage *vi* путеше́ствовать по мо́рю, пла́вать (*impfs*).

voyager *n* (морско́й) путеше́ственник.

vulcanize *vt* вулканизи́ровать (*impf and pf*).

vulgar *adj* вульга́рный; **a ~ expression** вульга́рное выраже́ние; **a ~ person** пошля́к.

vulgarism *n* вульгари́зм.

vulgarity *n* вульга́рность.

vulnerable *adj* уязви́мый; **a position ~ to attack** уязви́мая пози́ция; **he's ~ to criticism** он чувстви́телен к кри́тике; **she is so young and ~** она́ така́я молода́я и беззащи́тная.

vulture *n Orn* гриф.

W

wad *n* (*of wool, paper*) комо́к; **a ~ of (bank)notes** па́чка де́нег.

wadded *adj*: **a ~ jacket/quilt** подби́тая поролóном ку́ртка, ва́тное одея́ло.

wadding *n* (*in jacket, etc.*) подби́вка; (*for packing*) ва́та, *also Med*; **to pack smth in/with ~** переложи́ть что-л ва́той.

waddle *vi* идти́ вразва́лку (*adv*)/перева́ливаясь (*usu impf*).

wade *vi*: **to ~ across a stream** пере|ходи́ть ре́чку вброд (-йти́); **I ~d ashore** я добра́лся до бе́рега вброд; **to ~ through snow/mud** идти́ с трудо́м по сне́гу/по гря́зи; *fig CQ* **the book is so boring, I could hardly ~ through it** э́то така́я ску́чная кни́га, я с трудо́м её одоле́л.

wader *n Orn* (*in marshes*) боло́тная/(*coastal*) берегова́я пти́ца; *pl* (**~s**) (*boots*) боло́тные сапоги́.

wafer *n* то́нкая ва́фля (для моро́женого).

waffle *n Cook* (*US*) ва́фля; *fig CQ* **that article is just so much ~** э́та статья́—одна́ вода́.

wag[1] *vti vt* (*wave*) мах|а́ть + *I* (-ну́ть); (*of dog only*) ви|ля́ть + *I* (-льну́ть); **the dog was ~ging its tail** соба́ка виля́ла/маха́ла хвосто́м; **he ~ged his finger at me** он погрози́л мне па́льцем

vi: *fig* **be careful or tongues will ~** будь осторо́жнее, а то пойду́т слу́хи.

wag[2] *n* остря́к.

wage[1] *n* за́работная пла́та, *abbr* зарпла́та; **we get our ~s on Fridays** у нас зарпла́та по пя́тницам; **a living ~** прожи́точный ми́нимум; *attr*: **~ freeze** замора́живание за́работной пла́ты.

wage[2] *vt*: **to ~ war/a campaign against smb** вести́ войну́/кампа́нию про́тив кого́-л (*only in impf*).

wage-earner *n*: **she's the ~ of the family** она́ корми́лец в семье́.

waggish *adj* шутли́вый.

waggon, (*US*) **wagon** *n* пово́зка, фурго́н; **covered ~** кры́тая пово́зка; *Rail* **goods ~** това́рный ваго́н.

wagtail *n* трясогу́зка.

waif *n* беспризо́рник.

wail *n* (*of animal, wind*) вой; (*of person*) плач.

wail *vi* выть (за-).

waist *n* та́лия; **to let out a skirt at the ~** вы́пустить ю́бку в та́лии; **I put my arm round her ~** я о́бнял её за та́лию; **stripped to the ~** го́лый по по́яс.

waistband *n* по́яс, (*of skirt*) корса́ж ю́бки.

waistcoat *n* жиле́т.

waist-deep, waist-high *adj* по по́яс.

waistline *n* та́лия, ли́ния та́лии.

wait *n*: **we had a long ~ for our bus** мы о́чень до́лго жда́ли авто́буса; **the tiger lay in ~ for its prey** тигр подстерега́л добы́чу; **to lie in ~ for smb** подкарау́ливать кого́-л, (*of police, Mil*) устра́ивать заса́ду на кого́-л.

wait *vti vt*: **to ~ one's chance** вы|жида́ть удо́бного слу́чая (-ждать)

vi **1** ждать (*impf*) *and compounds*; **have you been ~ing long?** вы давно́ ждёте? [**NB** *tense*]; **sorry to keep you ~ing** извини́те, что заста́вил вас ждать; **this business can ~** э́то де́ло мо́жет подожда́ть; **~ a minute** подожди́/погоди́ мину́тку; **~ until you're sent for** жди́те, пока́ вас не вы́зовут; **we'll ~ until she leaves** мы подождём, пока́ она́ не уйдёт; **she ~ed behind after the others had gone** все ушли́, а она́ оста́лась ждать; **they fix watches while you ~** там/у них чи́нят часы́ в прису́тствии зака́зчика; **just you ~** ну, погоди́; **we'll have to ~ and see** поживём—уви́дим

2: **to ~ for smb/smth** ждать кого́-л/что-л *or* чего́-л (*usu impf*); **I'm ~ing for the/a train** я жду по́езд(а); **we're ~ing for you/for a letter** мы вас ждём, мы ждём письмо́ *or* письма́; **we'll not ~ for you for dinner** мы не бу́дем ждать тебя́ к обе́ду; **she ~ed up for them** она́ не ложи́лась, дожида́ясь их; **we didn't ~ (on) for the end of the film** мы не досиде́ли до конца́ сеа́нса; **to ~ for an opportunity** выжида́ть слу́чай/слу́чая

3 (*serve*): **to ~ at table/on smb** прислу́живать за столо́м (*impf*), обслу́жи|вать кого́-л (-́ть); *CQ* **she ~s on him hand and foot** она́ исполня́ет все его́ при́хоти.

waiter *n* официа́нт.

waiting *n* ожида́ние; *Aut* **"No W."** «Здесь нельзя́ остана́вливаться»; **I am tired of all this ~/of ~ for him** мне надое́ло э́то ожида́ние/его́ ждать.

waiting list *n* (*for house, hospital, etc.*): **he is first on the ~** он пе́рвый в спи́ске очередни́ков; **they put him on the ~** его́ поста́вили на о́чередь.

waiting room *n Rail, etc.* зал ожида́ния; (*doctor's, etc.*) приёмная.

waitress *n* официа́нтка.

waive *vt*: **to ~ a claim** отка́з|ываться от прете́нзии/от тре́бования (-а́ться); **he ~d the rule in my favour** он поступи́лся э́тим пра́вилом ра́ди меня́.

wake[1] *vti vt, also* **~ up** буди́ть (раз-), *also fig*; *fig* пробу|жда́ть (-ди́ть); **~ me at 7** разбуди́ меня́ в семь (часо́в); *fig*: **this woke unpleasant memories for him** э́то пробуди́ло в нём неприя́тные воспоминания; *CQ* **it's enough noise to ~ the dead** шум тако́й, что мёртвый проснётся

vi, also **~ up** про|сыпа́ться (-сну́ться); **~ up** просни́сь; **I woke (up) to find myself back in the ward** я очну́лся в пала́те; *fig*: **it's time for you to ~ up to reality** пора́ тебе́ спусти́ться на зе́млю; **he still hasn't woken up to the danger** он ещё не осозна́л опа́сности.

wake[2] *n Naut* кильва́тер; *fig* **war brought famine in its ~** война́ повлекла́ за собо́й го́лод.

wakeful *adj* (*sleepless*) бессо́нный; (*vigilant*) бди́тельный.

waken *vti see* **wake**[1].

waking *adj*: **during his ~ hours he suffers a lot of pain** когда́ он бо́дрствует, у него́ си́льные бо́ли.

walk *n* **1** (*walking*) ходьба́; (*stroll*) прогу́лка; **the shops are 10 minutes' ~ away** магази́ны в десяти́ мину́тах ходьбы́ отсю́да; **that's my favourite ~** я люблю́ там гуля́ть; **it's a lovely ~ to the woods** отсю́да до ле́са прия́тно прогуля́ться; **I'm going for a ~** пойду́ погуля́ю/пройду́сь; **she's taken the children/the dog for a ~** она́ вы́шла с детьми́/вы́вела соба́ку на прогу́лку; **it's just a short ~ from here** э́то в не́скольких шага́х отсю́да; *fig* **people from all ~s of life** лю́ди ра́зных профе́ссий

2 (*gait*) похо́дка; **I knew him by his ~** я узна́л его́ по похо́дке; **at a quick ~** бы́стрым ша́гом; **the horse dropped into a ~** ло́шадь перешла́ на шаг.

walk *vi* ходи́ть (*indet impf, pf* по-), идти́ (*det impf, pf* пойти́) [**NB** походи́ть *and* пойти́ *are not true pfs*; походи́ть = *to walk around for a while*, пойти́ = *to begin to walk*; *completed action of* идти́ *is expressed by pfs of compounds of* ходи́ть *with appropriate prefixes*]; **my son can't ~ yet** мой сын ещё не хо́дит; **I always ~ to work** я всегда́ хожу́ на рабо́ту пешко́м; **let's ~ round the shops a bit** дава́й похо́дим/пройдёмся по магази́нам; **we ~ed there and took the bus back** туда́ мы шли пешко́м, а обра́тно верну́лись на авто́бусе; **let's start ~ing, the car can catch us up** пошли́, маши́на нас дого́нит; **it's not far to ~** э́то пешко́м недалеко́; **we ~ed 5 miles** мы прошли́ пять миль; (*stroll*) **he's ~ing in the garden** он прогу́ливается по са́ду

walk about/around *vi*: **he was ~ing about the room** он ходи́л по ко́мнате; **let's ~ about till they come** дава́й погуля́ем, пока́ они́ не приду́т

walk away *vi*: **he ~ed away from the window** он отошёл от окна́; *fig* **our team ~ed away with the game** на́ша кома́нда о́чень легко́ одержа́ла побе́ду

walk in/into *vi* входи́ть в + *A* (войти́); *fig* **he ~ed into the trap** он попа́лся в лову́шку

walk off *vti vt*: **she ~ed me off my feet** она́ меня́ загоня́ла; **I want to ~ off my lunch/a few pounds** по́сле тако́го сы́тного обе́да мне на́до прогуля́ться, мне на́до мно́го ходи́ть, что́бы сбро́сить вес; **she soon ~ed off her headache** от ходьбы́ её головна́я боль ско́ро прошла́

vi: **he ~ed off in a huff** он расстро́ился и ушёл; **somebody ~ed off with my briefcase** кто́-то взял мой портфе́ль и унёс

walk out *vi*: **he ~ed out of the room/the meeting** он вы́шел из ко́мнаты, он ушёл с собра́ния; **the mechanics have ~ed out** меха́ники прекрати́ли рабо́ту; **his wife ~ed out on him** от него́ ушла́ жена́; **she's ~ing out with him** она́ встреча́ется с ним (*only in impf*)

walk over *vi*: **to ~ over a street/bridge** пере|ходи́ть у́лицу/(че́рез) мост (-йти́); **I ~ed all over the town** я обошёл весь го́род; **she ~ed over to the window** она́ подошла́ к окну́

walk up *vi*: **to ~ up to smb/smth** подходи́ть к кому́-л/к чему́-л; **he was ~ing up and down the corridor** он ходи́л (взад и вперёд)/он проха́живался по коридо́ру.

walker *n* ходо́к, *also Sport*.

walking *n* ходьба́; *Sport* спорти́вная ходьба́.

walking *adj*: **it's within ~ distance** туда́ мо́жно дойти́ пешко́м; **I'm going for a ~ holiday/tour** я ухожу́ в похо́д.

walking stick *n* трость, па́лка.

walk-on *adj*: **a ~ part** нема́я роль.

walkover *n*: *CQ* **the match was a ~ for us** мы их разби́ли на́голову (*adv*).

wall *n* (*high*: *of a house, etc.*) стена́, *dim* сте́нка; (*low outside wall*) (ка́менный) забо́р, (ка́менная) огра́да; **blank ~** глуха́я стена́; *fig*: **talking to him is like beating your head against a brick ~** говори́ть с ним—всё равно́, что би́ться голово́й о сте́нку; **with one's back to the ~** припёртый к стене́; **it's enough to drive you up the ~** от э́того на сте́нку поле́зешь; *attr*: **a ~ clock** стенны́е часы́ (*no sing*); **a ~ map** насте́нная ка́рта;

(*SU*) **a ~ newspaper** стенна́я газе́та, *abbr* стенгазе́та.

walled *adj*: **a ~ town** укреплённый го́род; **a ~ garden** сад, обнесённый стено́й *or* забо́ром.

wallet *n* бума́жник.

wall-eyed *adj* с бельмо́м на глазу́.

wallflower *n* желтофио́ль.

wallow *vi* валя́ться (*impf*); **to ~ in mud** валя́ться в грязи́; *fig*: **to ~ in a hot bath** полежа́ть в горя́чей ва́нне; *CQ* **she ~s in self-pity** она́ лю́бит себя́ пожале́ть.

wall painting *n* (*genre*) насте́нная жи́вопись; (*mural*) стенна́я ро́спись.

wallpaper *n* обо́и (*pl*).

wall socket *n Elec* (ште́псельная) розе́тка.

walnut *n* (*tree or nut*) гре́цкий оре́х.

walrus *n* морж.

waltz *n* вальс.

waltz *vi* танцева́ть вальс.

wan *adj*: **a ~ sky** бле́дное/ту́склое не́бо; **with a ~ smile** с ту́склой улы́бкой.

wander *vi* броди́ть (*indet impf*, *pf* по-); брести́ (*det impf*, *pf* по-); **he ~s round the park every day** он ка́ждый день бро́дит по па́рку; **he ~ed in the woods for a while** он поброди́л по ле́су; **he ~ed towards the sea** он брёл к мо́рю; **he ~ed off towards the village** он побрёл к дере́вне; **I ~ed into a bookshop** я загляну́л в кни́жный магази́н; **where have the children ~ed off to?** куда́ де́ти забрели́?; *fig*: **his thoughts began to ~** у него́ мы́сли на́чали разбреда́ться; **you're ~ing from the point** вы отклоня́етесь от те́мы; (*in fever*) **he is ~ing** он бре́дит.

wanderings *npl* (*travels*) стра́нствия; (*delirium*) бред (*sing*).

wane *n*: **the moon is on the ~** луна́ на ущёрбе/убыва́ет; *fig* **his influence is on the ~** его́ влия́ние ослабева́ет.

wangle *n CQ* блат; **he got the job by a ~** он получи́л э́ту рабо́ту по знако́мству/по бла́ту.

wangle *vt CQ*: (*get by influence*) **he ~d some tickets for them** он доста́л им биле́ты по бла́ту; (*fix*) **if I can ~ an extra week's holiday** е́сли я ухитрю́сь/изловчу́сь устро́ить себе́ ли́шнюю неде́лю о́тпуска.

want *n* **1** (*lack*) недоста́ток; нехва́тка; **people are dying for ~ of food** лю́ди умира́ют от недоеда́ния/(*stronger*) от го́лода; **he died for ~ of care** он у́мер из-за отсу́тствия ухо́да; **for ~ of something to do** от не́чего де́лать; **he lost, but not for ~ of trying** он проигра́л, но не потому́, что не прилага́л уси́лий

2 (*poverty*) нужда́; (*need*) потре́бность; **they live in ~** они́ живу́т в нужде́; **his ~s are few** его́ потре́бности невелики́.

want *vti vt* **1** (*need*) нужда́ться (*impf*); *usu translated by* ну́жно + *inf*; **what you ~ is a good wash/haircut** тебе́ ну́жно хорошо́ помы́ться/подстри́чься; **you ~ to turn left at the crossroads** на перекрёстке вам ну́жно поверну́ть нале́во; **the flat ~s repairing** кварти́ру на́до ремонти́ровать, кварти́ра нужда́ется в ремо́нте; **I'm in the kitchen if I'm ~ed** е́сли я пона́доблюсь, я бу́ду на ку́хне; **he is ~ed by the police** его́ разы́скивает поли́ция; **"Typist ~ed"** «тре́буется машини́стка»; **you're ~ed on the phone** тебя́ к телефо́ну

2 (*wish*) хоте́ть (за-), жела́ть (по-); **I ~ to talk to you** я хочу́ поговори́ть с тобо́й; **I ~ you to talk to her** я хочу́, что́бы ты поговори́л с ней; **the dog ~s out** соба́ка хо́чет погуля́ть; **your mother ~s you** ма́ма зовёт тебя́; **I ~ some carrots please** мне морко́ви, пожа́луйста; **he ~s £10 for it** он хо́чет за э́то де́сять фу́нтов

vi (*lack*): **he is ~ing in common sense** ему́ не хвата́ет здра́вого смы́сла; **she ~s for nothing** она́ ни в чём не нужда́ется (*impf*); **he does not ~ for helpers** он не нужда́ется в помо́щниках.

wanton *adj*: **~ destruction** бессмы́сленное разруше́ние; **a ~ woman** распу́тница, же́нщина лёгкого поведе́ния.

war *n* война́; **the First World W.** пе́рвая мирова́я война́; **before the ~** до войны́; **he was killed in the ~/in the civil ~** он поги́б на войне́/в гражда́нскую войну́; **he came back from the ~** он верну́лся с войны́; **he's gone to the ~** он ушёл на войну́; **to be at ~ with** воева́ть с + *I*; **to go to ~ with smb** начина́ть войну́ с кем-л; *fig CQ* **I see you've been in the ~s** ну, тебе́ и доста́лось; *attr* вое́нный; **~ correspondent** вое́нный корреспонде́нт; **~ memorial** па́мятник поги́бшим на войне́.

warble *vi* (*of birds, or person*) петь (*impf*).

ward *n* **1** *Law*: **the child was made a ~ of court** ребёнок был взят под опе́ку суда́; **she is his ~** он её опеку́н

2 (*UK*: *administrative area*) (городско́й) избира́тельный о́круг

3 (*in hospital*) пала́та; **maternity ~** роди́льная пала́та.

ward *vt*: **to ~ off a blow** защи|ща́ться от уда́ра (-ти́ться).

warden *n* (*of hostel*) коменда́нт; (*US*: *of prison*) нача́льник тюрьмы́; (*of game reserve, castle*) смотри́тель (*m*).

warder *n* (тюре́мный) надзира́тель (*m*).

wardrobe *n* (*cupboard*) платяно́й шкаф; гардеро́б; *CQ* (*of clothes*) **she has a large/magnificent ~** у неё большо́й гардеро́б/потряса́ющие туале́ты (*pl*).

warehouse *n* склад.

wares *npl* това́ры.

warfare *n*: **germ/nuclear ~** бактериологи́ческая/я́дерная война́.

warm *adj* **1** тёплый, *also fig*; **it's ~ here** здесь тепло́; **I'm ~** мне тепло́; **it's getting ~er** стано́вится тепле́е; **I put on a sweater to keep myself ~** что́бы не мёрзнуть, я наде́л сви́тер; **put the pie in the oven to keep ~** поста́вь пиро́г в духо́вку, что́бы не осты́л; *as n CQ*: **come and sit in the ~** иди́ посиди́ в тепле́

2 *fig uses*: **a ~ welcome/colour/person** тёплый приём/цвет, сердéчный человéк; **you're getting ~** (*in games*) горячée.

warm *vti vt* греть (*impf*) *and compounds*; **to ~ one's hands/oneself at the fire** греть рýки над огнём, грéться у огня́; **to ~ a house/a room** натопи́ть дом/кóмнату (*usu pf*); **to ~ up some milk** подогрéть/согрéть молокó; *fig* **it ~s the heart** э́то согревáет дýшу

vi грéться *and compounds*; **the air/the soup is ~ing up** вóздух нагревáется, суп подогревáется *or* разогревáется; **the athletes are ~ing up** спортсмéны дéлают размíнку/размина́ются; *fig*: **his heart/he ~ed to her** он почýвствовал к ней нéжность; **he is ~ing to his work** он вошёл [**NB** *tense*] во вкус, и тепéрь рабóта емý нрáвится.

warmed-up *adj* подогрéтый.

warm-hearted *adj* сердéчный.

warmth *n* теплó; теплотá; **the ~ of the air** теплотá вóздуха; **I was enjoying the ~ of the sun** я наслаждáлся сóлнечным теплóм; *fig*: **he spoke of her with ~** он теплó говори́л о ней; **he answered with some ~** он отвéтил с горя́чностью.

warn *vt* предупре|ждáть (-ди́ть); **I ~ed you not to go there/that...** я предупреждáл тебя́ не ходи́ть тудá/, что...; **I've been ~ed about him** меня́ предупреди́ли о нём; **she ~ed me off that subject** онá проси́ла меня́ не говори́ть об э́том; **he ~ed me against pickpockets at the station** он предупреди́л меня́, что на вокзáле нáдо остерегáться кармáнников.

warning *n* предупреждéние, предостережéние; **without ~** без предупреждéния; **he gave them ~ that...** он предупреди́л/предостерёг их, что...; **let that be a ~ to you** пусть э́то послýжит вам предостережéнием.

warped *adj*: **the door is ~ by the damp** дверь покоси́лась от сы́рости; **that record is ~** э́та пласти́нка погнýлась; *fig* **his mind is ~** у негó извращённый ум.

warrant *n* **1: there's no ~ for such behaviour** такóму поведéнию нет никакóго оправдáния

2 *Law* óрдер (на + *A*); **there's a ~ out for his arrest** полýчен óрдер на егó арéст; **search ~** óрдер на óбыск.

warrant *vt*: **the facts do not ~ such a conclusion** фáкты не даю́т никаки́х оснoвáний для такóго вы́вода; **he'll come back I ~ you** он вернётся, ручáюсь.

warranty *n* гарáнтия.

wart *n* бородáвка.

wartime *adj*: **his ~ experiences** óпыт (*sing*) егó воéнной жи́зни; **~ hardships** лишéния воéнного врéмени.

wary *adj* осторóжный, осмотри́тельный; **keep a ~ eye on him** погля́дывай за ним; **be ~ of strangers** остерегáйся незнакóмцев; **be ~ of speaking too plainly** смотри́, сли́шком не откровéнничай.

wash *n* **1** (*act*): **I must give the floor/my jersey a ~** (мне) нáдо помы́ть пол/постирáть сви́тер; **to have a ~** умывáться (*of face and hands*), помы́ться (*all over*)

2 (*clothes, etc.*) бельё; (*laundry*) сти́рка; **my undies are in the ~** моё бельё в сти́рке; **the ~ is back from the laundry** мы получи́ли бельё из сти́рки; **I sent my shirt to the ~** я óтдал мою́ рубáшку в сти́рку

3 (*from ship*) вóлны от пароxóда

4: mouth ~ полоскáние для рта; **eye ~** примóчка для глаз.

wash *vti vt* **1** (*clean*) мыть (по-, вы́-) *and compounds*; **to ~ the floor/dishes** помы́ть *or* вы́мыть пол/посýду (*collect*); **to ~ oneself** помы́ться; **to ~ one's face** умы́ть лицó; **to ~ one's face and hands** умы|вáться (-ться); **to ~ clothes** стирáть бельё (вы́-); *fig* **don't ~ your dirty linen in public** не выноси́ сор из избы́

2 (*of sea*): **the wreckage was ~ed ashore** облóмки корабля́ вы́несло (*impers*) на бéрег; **he/the mast was ~ed overboard** егó/мáчту смы́ло (*impers*) зá борт; **the raft was ~ed out to sea** плот унеслó (*impers*) течéнием в мóре; **the waves were ~ing the deck** вóлны заливáли пáлубу; **the west coast is ~ed by the Atlantic** зáпадное побережье омывáется Атланти́ческим океáном

vi (*have a wash*) мы́ться, умывáться; (*do the washing*) стирáть; **this material ~es well** э́та ткань хорошó стирáется; *CQ* **that excuse won't ~** э́то не оправдáние

wash away *vti* (*of stains, etc.*) смы|вáть (-ть); **the road has been ~ed away** дорóгу размы́ло (*impers*); **the rain ~ed the snow away** весь снег пóсле дождя́ сошёл

wash down *vt* (*of walls, paint-work, deck, etc.*) мыть, смывáть; **he ~ed the pills down with a glass of water** он запи́л таблéтки стакáном воды́; **he ~ed his lunch down with a glass of wine** он вы́пил за обéдом стакáн винá

wash off *vti* смывáть(ся)

wash out *vti vt* (*of stain, etc.*) отмы|вáть (-ть); **I ~ed out my tights/the bottles** я постирáла колгóтки, я вы́мыл буты́лки; **rain ~ed out play** из-за дождя́ игрá былá приостанóвлена; *fig* **she looks ~ed out** у неё утомлённый/измождённый вид

vi (*of stain*) отмывáться, отсти́р|ываться (-áться); (*of colours*) размы|вáться (-ться)

wash through *vt*: **I'll just ~ through the socks** я сейчáс вы́стираю носки́

wash up *vti vt*: **the barrels were ~ed up on the beach** бóчки вы́несло (*impers*) на бéрег

vi мыть пóсуду (по-).

washable *adj*: **is this ~?** э́то хорошó стирáется?

washbasin *n* умывáльник.

washer *n Tech* проклáдка.

washing *n* (*action*) сти́рка; (*things to be washed*) бельё; **I'm doing the ~ today** сегóдня у меня́ сти́рка; **she takes in ~** онá берёт бельё в сти́рку; **dirty ~** гря́зное бельё; **hard water is not nice for ~** в жёсткой водé плóхо стирáть; *attr*: **~ machine/soda/powder** стира́льная маши́на/со́да, стира́льный порошо́к.

washing-up *n* мытьё посу́ды; **to do the ~** помы́ть посу́ду; *attr*: **~ liquid** жи́дкость для мытья́ посу́ды.

wash-out *n CQ*: **the concert was a ~** конце́рт прошёл неуда́чно; **he's a ~** он пусто́е ме́сто.

washroom *n* (*US*) убо́рная.

washtub *n* таз.

wasp *n* оса́.

waste *n* **1: it's a ~ of time/money/energy** э́то напра́сная/пуста́я тра́та вре́мени/де́нег/сил (*pl*); **I don't like ~** я не люблю́ ничего́ выбра́сывать; **pick yourself some lettuces — they are just going to ~** нарви́ себе́ сала́та (*collect*), ина́че он про́сто пропадёт; **his talent is going to ~** он растра́чивает свой тала́нт по́пусту (*adv*)

2 (*waste products*: *domestic*, *Agric*) отбро́сы (*pl*); (*industrial*) отхо́ды (*pl*)

3: the frozen ~s of the Antarctic ледяны́е поля́/простра́нства Анта́рктики.

waste *adj*: **~ products** (*industrial*) отхо́ды; **the ~ land near the station** пусты́рь у ста́нции; **to lay ~** опустоша́ть.

waste *vti vt* тра́тить зря/впусту́ю (по-, рас-); **to ~ one's money/efforts** зря тра́тить де́ньги/уси́лия (по-); **you're wasting your time** вы тра́тите вре́мя впусту́ю; **don't ~ water** зря не трать во́ду; **we can't afford to ~ a minute** нельзя́ теря́ть ни мину́ты; *fig*: **the joke/caviare was ~d on him** он не по́нял шу́тки, он не оцени́л зерни́стой икры́; **don't ~ this opportunity** не упуска́й э́ту возмо́жность

vi: **one can see him wasting away** он ча́хнет на на́ших глаза́х; **our resources are wasting away** на́ши ресу́рсы истоща́ются.

wasteful *adj* неэконо́мный, расточи́тельный; **she's a good cook but very ~** она́ хорошо́ гото́вит, но о́чень не эконо́мна [**NB** не *separates from adj when predic*]/расточи́тельна.

waste paper *n* нену́жная бума́га; (*rubbish*) бума́жный/(*in office*) канцеля́рский му́сор; (*for pulping*) макулату́ра.

waste-paper basket *n* корзи́на для бума́жного му́сора.

waste pipe *n* сливна́я труба́.

wastrel *n* никчёмный челове́к.

watch[1] *n* **1: they kept a close ~ on him** за ним установи́ли постоя́нное наблюде́ние; **she keeps ~ over the patient day and night** она́ сиди́т с больны́м день и ночь; **to be on the ~ against smb/smth** остерега́ться кого́-л/чего́-л

2: to be on ~ *Naut* нести́ ва́хту, *Mil* стоя́ть в карау́ле; **officers of the ~** *Naut* ва́хтенные/*Mil* дежу́рные офице́ры; **our unit is going on ~** на́ше отделе́ние заступа́ет на дежу́рство.

watch[1] *vti vt* **1** смотре́ть; (*observe*) наблюда́ть, (*follow*, *shadow*) следи́ть (*impfs*); **I ~ed the match/him acting/how it was done** я смотре́л матч/, как он игра́ет/, как э́то де́лали; **~ me doing it** смотри́/понаблюда́й, как я э́то де́лаю; **to ~ smb's movements** следи́ть за чьи́ми-л передвиже́ниями; **I'm being ~ed** за мной наблюда́ют/следя́т; **to ~ developments** следи́ть/наблюда́ть за разви́тием собы́тий; **~ the milk** следи́ за молоко́м; **~ my case while I make a phone call** присмотри́те за мои́м чемода́ном, пока́ я позвоню́; **to ~ birds** наблюда́ть птиц

2 (*be careful of*): **~ him** с ним будь поосторо́жнее; **~ your language** поосторо́жнее в выраже́ниях; **~ your head** осторо́жно, не ушиби́ го́лову; **~ you don't scald yourself** осторо́жно,/смотри́, не обожги́сь; **one has to ~ one's step** на́до ду́мать, когда́ говори́шь; **~ that sharp knife** осторо́жно/поосторо́жнее с э́тим о́стрым ножо́м; **we must ~ the time** мы должны́ следи́ть за вре́менем; **we'll have to ~ the money carefully** на́до следи́ть за расхо́дами

vi: **~ out for that hole** осторо́жно,/смотри́, я́ма; **I ~ed by his bedside** я не отходи́л от его́ посте́ли; **we're ~ing (out) for our chance/for a signal** мы выжида́ем *or* ждём удо́бного слу́чая, мы ждём сигна́ла; **if you don't ~ out you'll find he has cheated you** с ним на́до гляде́ть в о́ба, а то ока́жетесь в дурака́х.

watch[2] *n* часы́ (*no sing*); **pocket/wrist ~** карма́нные/нару́чные часы́; **by my ~ it's 3 o'clock** по мои́м часа́м сейча́с три часа́.

watchdog *n* сторожева́я соба́ка, сторожево́й пёс.

watchful *adj* внима́тельный; **keep a ~ eye on him** внима́тельно следи́ за ним.

watchmaker *n* часовщи́к.

watchman *n* сто́рож.

watch strap *n* (*leather*) ремешо́к/(*metal*) брасле́т для часо́в.

water *n* вода́; **salt/fresh/boiling ~** солёная/пре́сная вода́, кипято́к; **tap/boiled ~** сыра́я/кипячёная вода́; **the street is under ~** у́лица зато́плена водо́й; **to turn on the ~** откры́ть кран, (*at the mains*) пуска́ть во́ду; *Naut* **high/low ~** прили́в, отли́в; *fig*: **she spends money like ~** она́ сори́т деньга́ми; **his explanation just doesn't hold ~** его́ объясне́ние кра́йне неубеди́тельно; *CQ*: **I got into hot ~ over that** ну и в передря́гу я попа́л из-за э́того; **an idiot of the first ~** по́лный/кру́глый идио́т; *attr*: **~ plants/birds** водяны́е расте́ния/пти́цы; **~ sports** во́дный спорт (*sing*); *Med* **~ on the brain/the knee** головна́я водя́нка, вода́ в коле́не; **to pass ~** мочи́ться.

water *vti vt*: **to ~ the garden/roses** поли|ва́ть сад/ро́зы (-́ть); **to ~ horses** пои́ть лошаде́й (на-); **to ~ down wine**/*fig* **one's remarks** разбав|ля́ть вино́ (-́ить), смягч|а́ть свои́ замеча́ния (-и́ть)

vi: **her eyes ~ed** у неё слези́лись глаза́; *fig* **it makes one's mouth ~** от э́того слю́нки теку́т.

water bottle *n* (*flask*) фля́жка; (*carafe*) графи́н.

water butt *n* ка́дка.

water closet, *abbr* **W.C.** *n* убо́рная, туале́т, ва́тер-клозе́т.

watercolour, (*US*) **watercolor** *n* акварéль; **to paint in ~s** писáть акварéлью (*collect*).
water-cooled *adj* с водяны́м охлаждéнием.
watercourse *n* рýсло.
waterfall *n* водопáд.
water heater *n* водонагревáтель (*m*); (*for cup, etc.*) кипяти́льник.
watering can *n* лéйка.
watering place *n* вóдный курóрт.
water lily *n* водянáя ли́лия, кувши́нка.
waterline *n* ватерли́ния.
waterlogged *adj*: **a ~ field** затóпленное водóй пóле; **the field is ~** луг заболóчен.
water main *n* водопровóдная магистрáль.
watermark *n* отмéтка ýровня воды́; (*on paper*) водянóй знак.
watermelon *n* арбýз.
water pipe *n* водопровóдная трубá.
waterproof *n* дождеви́к, плащ.
waterproof *adj* (*of material*) водонепроницáемый; (*of articles*) непромокáемый.
water rat *n* водянáя кры́са.
water rates *npl* плáта за вóду (*sing*).
watershed *n Geog* водораздéл, *also fig*.
water-skiing *n*: **to go ~** катáться на вóдных лы́жах (*pl*).
water supply *n* водоснабжéние.
water tank *n* цистéрна.
watertight *adj* водонепроницáемый; *fig* **a ~ argument** неопровержи́мый дóвод.
waterway *n* вóдный путь.
waterworks *n* водоочисти́тельная стáнция.
watery *adj* водяни́стый.
watt *n* ватт; *attr*: **a 20-~ bulb** двадцативáттная лáмпочка.
wave *n* **1** волнá, *also Phys, Radio, fig*; **sound ~s** звуковы́е вóлны; *Radio* **a programme on long ~** передáча на дли́нных волнáх
2 (*in hair*) зави́вка; **a permanent ~** перманéнт
3 (*action*) взмах; **she gave me a ~** онá махнýла мне.
wave *vti vt* **1** махáть (по-, *semel* махнýть) *and compounds*; **to ~ one's hand/handkerchief to smb** махáть комý-л рукóй/платкóм; **to ~ goodbye to smb** махáть комý-л на прощáние; **to ~ a flag/one's arms about** размáхивать флáгом/рукáми; **we ~d a car down** мы помахáли рукóй, и маши́на останови́лась; **the policeman ~d us on** полицéйский махнýл рукóй, и мы поéхали дáльше
2: she's had her hair ~d онá завилáсь, онá сдéлала зави́вку
vi: **she ~d from the window** онá помахáла рукóй из окнá; **I ~d back to her** я помахáл ей в отвéт; **the flags ~d in the wind** флáги развевáлись на ветрý.
wavelength *n Radio* длинá волны́; *fig CQ* **they are not on the same ~** они́ не нашли́ óбщего языкá.
waver *vi*: **his voice ~ed** егó гóлос дрóгнул; *fig*: **he's ~ing between going or staying** он колéблется—уйти́ и́ли остáться; **his courage began to ~** мýжество стáло покидáть егó.
wavy *adj* волни́стый; **~ hair/lines** волни́стые вóлосы/ли́нии.
wax[1] *n* воск; (*in ear*) сéра; *attr* восковóй.
wax[1] *vt*: **to ~ the floor** на|тирáть пол вóском (-терéть); **to ~ thread** вощи́ть ни́тку (на-).
wax[2] *vi* (*of moon*) прибывáть (*only in impf*); *fig* **to ~ enthusiastic/eloquent about smth** восторгáться чем-л (*impf*).
waxed *adj*: **~ floors** натёртые полы́; **~ paper** вощёная бумáга; **~ string** навощённая бечёвка.
waxwork *n* восковáя фигýра.
way *n* **1** (*road, route, etc.*) дорóга; путь (*m*), *also fig*; **we live just across the ~** мы живём чéрез дорóгу; **a covered ~** (*e.g. between two buildings*) кры́тый перехóд; (*road signs*) **"No Through W."** «Прохóда/(*for cars*) Проéзда нет»; **"W. Up"** «Навéрх»; **"W. Down"** «Вниз»; **we couldn't find the ~ out** мы не могли́ найти́ вы́ход; **on his ~ out he told me...** выходя́, он сказáл мне...; **pay on the ~ in** плати́те у вхóда/при вхóде; **I'll ask the ~** я спрошý дорóгу; **what is the quickest ~ to the market?** как пройти́ бли́же всегó к ры́нку?; **they went that ~** они́ пошли́ в ту стóрону/по э́той дорóге; **they went the wrong ~** они́ пошли́ не по той дорóге/не в ту стóрону; **they went the other ~** они́ пошли́ по другóй дорóге (*by a different route*)/в другýю стóрону (*in a different direction*); **I lost my ~** я сби́лся с дорóги/с пути́, *also fig*; **it rained the whole ~** всю дорóгу шёл дождь; **are you going our ~?** нам по пути́?; **they are already on their ~** они́ ужé в пути́; **I'll lead the ~** я пойдý впереди́; **I know my ~ about Moscow** я хорошó знáю Москвý; **I'll make my own ~ to the theatre** я сам доберýсь до теáтра; **we came by ~ of Minsk** мы éхали чéрез Минск; **the ship got under ~** корáбль отплы́л
2 *fig uses* (*in the sense of road, route*) путь; **they went their separate ~s** они́ пошли́ рáзными путя́ми; **he goes his own ~** он идёт свои́м путём; **he's on the ~ to success** он на пути́ к успéху; **this clears the ~ for negotiations** э́то расчищáет путь для переговóров; **this leaves the ~ open for further discussion** э́то открывáет путь для дальнéйшего обсуждéния; **we're at the parting of the ~s** мы (стои́м) на распýтье; **to choose the middle ~** вы́брать середи́ну; **it's the only ~ out** э́то еди́нственный вы́ход; **to make ~ for younger men** уступáть дорóгу молодёжи; **changes are on the ~** бли́зятся перемéны; **I kept well out of his ~** я держáлся от негó подáльше, я избегáл егó; **medicines should be kept out of the ~ of children** нáдо прятать лекáрства подáльше от детéй; **they wanted him out of the ~** они́ хотéли от негó отдéлаться; **I must get the ironing out of the ~ first** сначáла я должнá раздéлаться с глáжкой; **he went out of his ~ to help me/to be rude to me** он óчень старáлся помóчь мне, он был нарочи́то груб со мной; **her playing is nothing out**

of the ~ в её игре́ нет ничего́ осо́бенного/из ря́да вон выходя́щего; **am I in the** ~**?** я вам меша́ю?; **that child is in the** ~ **here** э́тот ребёнок ве́ртится здесь у всех под нога́ми; **to put difficulties in smb's** ~ чини́ть препя́тствия кому́-л; **I don't see my** ~ **to doing that** я не ви́жу возмо́жности сде́лать э́то; **she knows her** ~ **about** она́ зна́ет все ходы́ и вы́ходы; **she always pays her own** ~ она́ всегда́ пла́тит сама́ за себя́; **the factory isn't paying its** ~ э́та фа́брика не даёт при́были; **but that is by the** ~ но э́то так, к сло́ву; **by the** ~**, did you know..?** а кста́ти,/а ме́жду про́чим, знал ли ты..?

3 (*distance*): **it's a long** ~ **to London** до Ло́ндона далеко́; **we've still a long** ~ **to go** нам ещё далеко́ идти́/*fig* до конца́; *fig*: **he'll go a long** ~ он далеко́ пойдёт; **this is preferable by a long** ~ э́то гора́здо предпочти́тельнее; **not by a long** ~**!** отню́дь нет!

4 (*direction*): **look this/the other** ~ посмотри́ сюда́/в другу́ю сто́рону; **he lives out our** ~ он живёт где́-то в на́ших края́х; *fig*: **I didn't know which** ~ **to look** я не знал куда́ дева́ться; **if the opportunity comes your** ~ е́сли (вам) предста́вится возмо́жность

5 (*of position*): **your hat is on the wrong** ~ **round** ты наде́л шля́пу за́дом наперёд; **the box is the wrong** ~ **up** э́тот я́щик стои́т вверх дном; **he turned the table the right** ~ **up** он поста́вил стол на но́жки

6 (*custom*) обы́чай; **the** ~**s of the Romans** обы́чаи дре́вних ри́млян

7 (*manner*): **in a new/the usual** ~ по-но́вому, как обы́чно; **in the same** ~ таки́м же о́бразом; **it doesn't matter to me one** ~ **or the other** так и́ли э́так—мне всё равно́; **he's happy enough in his own** ~ он по-сво́ему счастли́в; **that's just his** ~**/his** ~ **of talking** про́сто у него́ така́я мане́ра/така́я мане́ра разгова́ривать; **to my** ~ **of thinking** на мой взгляд, по-мо́ему; **that's always the** ~ **with him** он всегда́ тако́й; **I like the** ~ **she said that** мне нра́вится, как она́ э́то сказа́ла; **it's not my** ~ **to bear a grudge** не в моём хара́ктере таи́ть оби́ду; **he has a** ~ **with people** он уме́ет располага́ть к себе́ люде́й; **to mend one's** ~**s** исправля́ться; **he's in business in a small** ~ у него́ есть небольшо́е де́ло; **he said it by** ~ **of an apology/an introduction** он сказа́л э́то как извине́ние/в ка́честве вступле́ния; **he brought me this by** ~ **of thanking me** он принёс мне э́то, жела́я меня́ отблагодари́ть; *CQ* **he fell for her in a big** ~ он по́ уши влюби́лся в неё

8 (*method*): **this is the** ~ **to do it** вот как на́до э́то де́лать; **the best** ~ **to do it** лу́чший спо́соб сде́лать э́то; **do it your own** ~ сде́лай э́то по-сво́ему; **to get one's** ~ доби́ться своего́; **he wants his own** ~ **in everything** он лю́бит, что́бы всё бы́ло, как ему́ хо́чется; **all right, have it your own** ~ хорошо́, пусть бу́дет по-тво́ему; **to get into/out of the** ~ **of doing smth** привыка́ть/отвыка́ть де́лать что-л; **the question of** ~**s and means** вопро́с путе́й и средств достиже́ния; **there are no two** ~**s about it** об э́том и спо́ру нет; **you can't have it both** ~**s!** за двумя́ за́йцами пого́нишься—ни одного́ не пойма́ешь!; (*encouragingly*) **that's the** ~**!** пра́вильно!

9 (*respect*): **in many** ~**s, in every** ~ во мно́гих/во всех отноше́ниях; **in a** ~ **I agree** в изве́стном/в како́м-то смы́сле я согла́сен; **in what** ~ **do they differ?** в чём (заключа́ется) ра́зница/кака́я ра́зница ме́жду ни́ми?; **she is in no** ~ **to blame** на ней нет никако́й вины́; **without in any** ~ **wishing to criticize him** нико́им о́бразом не жела́я критикова́ть его́; **what have we in the** ~ **of drink?** что у нас есть вы́пить?; **no** ~ (*as neg*) нико́им о́бразом

10 (*state*): **he is/things are in a bad** ~ с ним де́ло пло́хо, дела́ обстоя́т пло́хо; **the** ~ **things are now** при тепе́решнем положе́нии дел; **this is the** ~ **it was** э́то бы́ло так; **leave things the** ~ **they are** оста́вь всё как есть

11 give way *see* **give.**

way *adv CQ*: ~ **back in May** ещё в ма́е; **that was** ~ **back** э́то бы́ло давно́; ~ **down South** далеко́ на ю́ге; **they're** ~ **ahead of us** они́ намно́го опереди́ли нас.

wayfarer *n* пу́тник.

waylay *vt*: **he waylaid me on my way home** он подкарау́лил меня́, когда́ я шёл домо́й.

wayside *n* обо́чина; **by the** ~ у обо́чины; *attr*: ~ **flowers** придоро́жные цветы́.

wayward *adj* своенра́вный.

we *pers pron* мы; ~ **both know that...** мы о́ба зна́ем, что...; ~ **authors are often accused of that** нас, а́второв, ча́сто обвиня́ют в э́том.

weak *adj* сла́бый; **to grow** ~ слабе́ть; **I'm** ~ **in maths** я слаб в матема́тике; **he's** ~ **in the head** он слабоу́мный; **that's his** ~ **spot** э́то его́ сла́бое ме́сто.

weaken *vti vt* ослаб|ля́ть (-́ить); **the illness** ~**ed him** боле́знь осла́била его́; **his departure** ~**ed the team** его́ ухо́д осла́бил кома́нду

vi (*grow weak*) слабе́ть, ослабева́ть (*pf for both* ослабе́ть); *fig* **we must not** ~ **at this point** мы не должны́ здесь проявля́ть сла́бость.

weak-kneed *adj fig* трусли́вый, малоду́шный.

weakly *adj* хи́лый, боле́зненный.

weak-minded *adj* слабово́льный.

weakness *n* сла́бость; **in a moment of** ~ в мину́ту сла́бости; ~ **of will/of character** слабово́лие, слабохара́ктерность; **to have a** ~ **for smth** пита́ть сла́бость к чему́-л.

wealth *n* бога́тство; (*riches*) бога́тства (*pl*); *fig* **with a** ~ **of detail** со мно́жеством подро́бностей (*pl*).

wealthy *adj* бога́тый; *as n*: **the** ~ богачи́.

wean *vt*: **to** ~ **a baby** от|нима́ть ребёнка от груди́ (-ня́ть).

weapon *n* ору́жие, *also collect.*

wear *n* **1** (*clothes*) оде́жда; **men's/everyday** ~ мужска́я/повседне́вная оде́жда; **evening** ~ вече́рний туале́т

2 (*use*): **there's still a lot of ~ in the jacket** э́тот пиджа́к ещё до́лго мо́жно носи́ть; **this fabric stands up to hard ~** э́та ткань не зна́ет изно́са, э́той тка́ни изно́су нет; **the carpet is showing signs of ~** ковёр места́ми изно́сился/вы́терся; *Comm* **fair ~ and tear** проце́нт изно́шенности в преде́лах но́рмы; *fig CQ* **she's looking the worse for ~** у неё измождённый вид.

wear *vti vt* (*habitually*) носи́ть (*impf*); (*put on*) наде|ва́ть (-ть); **I never ~ a tie** я (никогда́) не ношу́ га́лстук; **I haven't worn that hat for ages** я давно́ не надева́л э́ту шля́пу; **she ~s glasses/her hair long** она́ но́сит очки́, у неё дли́нные во́лосы; **he was ~ing new spectacles** у него́ бы́ли но́вые очки́; **she always ~s black** она́ всегда́ но́сит чёрное/хо́дит в чёрном; **she was ~ing a black dress** она́ была́ в чёрном пла́тье, на ней бы́ло чёрное пла́тье; **I've nothing to ~** мне не́чего наде́ть; **he's worn his jersey into holes/those trousers threadbare** он износи́л сви́тер до дыр, э́ти брю́ки у него́ все обтрепа́лись; **the tyres are worn smooth** ши́ны совсе́м стёрлись/сноси́лись; *fig*: **he is worn to a shadow** он преврати́лся в тень; *CQ* **he won't ~ that** э́тот но́мер с ним не пройдёт

vi (*last*) носи́ться (*impf*); **this coat will ~ for years** э́то пальто́ бу́дет до́лго носи́ться; *fig*: **he's worn well** он хорошо́ сохрани́лся; **my patience is ~ing thin** моё терпе́ние конча́ется/ло́пается

wear down *vt*: **the heels/tyres are worn down** каблуки́ сноси́лись, ши́ны стёрлись

wear off *vi*: **the gilt has worn off** позоло́та стёрлась; *fig* **the novelty/pain will soon ~ off** пре́лесть новизны́ ско́ро пройдёт *or* исче́знет, боль ско́ро ути́хнет

wear on *vi*: **as time/the day wore on** с тече́нием вре́мени, к концу́ дня

wear out *vti vt*: **to ~ out clothes/shoes** из|на́шивать оде́жду/боти́нки (-носи́ть); *fig*: **I'm worn out with worry** я изму́чен забо́тами (*pl*); **I'm quite worn out** я соверше́нно измо́тан

vi: **his shoes ~ out quickly** у него́ бы́стро изна́шиваются боти́нки, *CQ* о́бувь гори́т на нём.

wearable *adj*: **this skirt is still ~** э́ту ю́бку ещё мо́жно поноси́ть.

weariness *n* уста́лость, утомле́ние.

wearing *adj* утоми́тельный.

wearisome *adj* (*boring*) ску́чный, надое́дливый; (*tiring*) утоми́тельный.

weary *adj* (*of people*) уста́лый, утомлённый; **I spent 3 ~ hours waiting at the station** я провёл на ста́нции три томи́тельных часа́ в ожида́нии; **he was ~ after his journey** он уста́л с доро́ги, доро́га его́ утоми́ла; **he is ~ of life** он уста́л от жи́зни.

weary *vti vt* утом|ля́ть (-и́ть)

vi: **he soon wearied of living alone** ему́ ско́ро наску́чило жить одному́.

weasel *n Zool* ла́ска.

weather *n* пого́да; **bad ~** плоха́я пого́да, непого́да; **foul ~** нена́стье; **in wet ~, in all ~s** в сыру́ю/в любу́ю пого́ду; **~ permitting** е́сли позво́лит пого́да; *fig*: **he's making heavy ~ of that job** он сам себе́ осложня́ет де́ло; **I'm a bit under the ~ today** мне сего́дня что́-то не по себе́.

weather *vti vt* (*of wood*) вы|де́рживать (-держать); **to ~ a storm/*fig* crisis** вы́держать шторм/кри́зис

vi (*of rocks, etc.*) вы|ве́триваться (-ветриться).

weather-beaten *adj* обве́тренный.

weather chart *n* синопти́ческая/метеорологи́ческая ка́рта.

weather cock *n* флю́гер.

weather forecast *n* прогно́з пого́ды.

weather station *n* метеорологи́ческая ста́нция.

weave *vti vt*: **to ~ cloth** ткать сукно́ (*usu impf*); **to ~ a basket** плести́ корзи́ну (с-); **to ~ flowers into a wreath** впле|та́ть цветы в вено́к (-сти́); *fig*: **he wove a story around the incident** э́тот слу́чай лёг в осно́ву его́ расска́за; **he was weaving his way through the crowd** он пробира́лся в толпе́

vi ткать; *fig*: **the road ~s through the valley** доро́га вьётся по доли́не; **the cyclists wove in and out of the traffic** велосипеди́сты лави́ровали ме́жду маши́нами; *CQ*: **get weaving!** поживе́е!; **it's time you got weaving on your homework** (тебе́) пора́ сади́ться за уро́ки.

web *n* (*of spider*) паути́на, *also fig*; **a ~ of intrigue** паути́на интри́г (*pl*).

webbed *adj*: **~ feet** перепо́нчатые ла́пы.

webbing *n* (*for upholstering*) брезе́нтовые ремни́ (для мя́гкой ме́бели).

web-footed *adj*: **~ birds** перепончатоно́гие пти́цы.

wed *vt*, *rarely vi* **1** (*take in marriage*) (*of woman*) вы|ходи́ть за́муж (за + *A*) (-йти), (*of man*) жени́ться (на + *P*) (*impf and pf*); (*of couple*) жени́ться (по-), *Rel* венча́ться (об-, по-)

2 (*join in marriage*): **they were ~ded** *or* **they ~ded in church/at a registry office/(*SU*) in the palace of weddings** они́ венча́лись в це́ркви, они́ зарегистри́ровали брак в мэ́рии, они́ расписа́лись во дворце́ бракосочета́ний; *fig* **he is ~ded to his pipe/his opinions** он неразлу́чен со свое́й тру́бкой, он твёрдо де́ржится своего́ мне́ния (*sing*).

wedding *n* сва́дьба; **a church ~** венча́ние; **silver/golden ~** сере́бряная/золота́я сва́дьба; **they were at our ~** они́ бы́ли на на́шей сва́дьбе; *attr* сва́дебный; **~ cake/present** сва́дебный пиро́г/пода́рок; **~ ceremony/night** бра́чная церемо́ния/ночь; **~ day** день сва́дьбы; **~ dress** сва́дебное пла́тье; **~ reception** сва́дьба; **~ ring** обруча́льное кольцо́.

wedge *n* клин; **to drive a ~ into smth** вбива́ть клин во что-л; *fig* **that's just the thin end of the ~** ему́/им то́лько па́лец дай.

wedge *vt*: **the book was ~d between the cupboard and the wall** книга застряла между шкафом и стеной; **he ~d the door open** он вставил клин под дверь, чтобы она не закрывалась; **I was ~d between two stout gentlemen** меня втиснули между двумя толстяками.

wedge-heeled shoes *npl* туфли на танкетке.

Wednesday *n* среда; **on ~** в среду; **on ~s** по средам.

wee *adj CQ* маленький, малюсенький; **I'm a ~ bit tired** я немного устал; **a ~ drop of water** глоток воды; **the ~ ones** малютки, крошки.

weed *n* сорняк, сорная трава.

weed *vt*: **to ~ the garden** полоть в огороде (вы-, про-); *fig* **we must ~ out the weakest candidates** надо исключить из списка слабейших кандидатов.

weeding *n* прополка.

weed-killer *n* гербицид.

weedy *adj*: **a ~ garden** сад, заросший сорняками; *fig* **a ~ youth** худосочный юноша.

week *n* неделя; **this/next ~** на этой/на будущей неделе; **for a ~** на неделю; **~ after ~, ~ in, ~ out** неделя за неделей; **for ~s on end** целыми неделями; **today ~** ровно через неделю; **on Tuesday ~** через две недели во вторник.

weekday *n* будний день; **on ~s** в будние дни; *attr*: **~ bus services** рейсы автобусов по будним дням.

weekend *n* уикенд; *approx* суббота и воскресенье; **at the ~** в субботу и воскресенье; **we spent a long ~ there** мы пробыли там с пятницы до понедельника; *attr*: **a ~ cottage** *approx* дача; **we have a lot of ~ visitors here** *approx* на выходные к нам сюда приезжает много народу.

weekly *adj*: **a ~ newspaper** еженедельная газета; **~ wage** недельный заработок.

weep *vti vt*: **to ~ bitter tears** проливать горькие слёзы (*usu impf*); **she wept herself to sleep** она заснула в слезах

vi плакать (*impf*) *and compounds*; **to ~ for joy** плакать от радости; **she wept over her broken vase/for her son** она плакала над разбитой вазой/по сыну.

weeping *n* плач; **I heard the sound of ~** я услышал плач.

weeping *adj*: **~ children** плачущие дети; **~ willow** плакучая ива.

weepy *adj* плаксивый.

wee-wee *n CQ*: **do you want to do ~?** хочешь на горшок?

weigh *vti vt* взве|шивать (-сить); **she ~ed the flour/herself** она взвесила муку, она взвесилась; *fig* **he ~ed his words** он взвешивал каждое слово (*sing*)

vi весить (*impf*); **this box ~s 10 kg** этот ящик весит десять килограммов; **what do you ~?** сколько ты весишь?; *fig*: **it is ~ing on my conscience** это лежит камнем на моей совести; **this evidence will ~ against you** эти показания (*pl*) будут не в твою пользу; **that argument doesn't ~ with me** для меня это не довод

weigh down *vt*: **the branches were ~ed down with snow** ветки гнулись под тяжестью снега; **he was ~ed down with suitcases** он еле волочил чемоданы; **the car was ~ed down with luggage** машина немного осела под тяжестью багажа; *fig* **he is ~ed down with cares** он обременён заботами

weigh in *vi Sport* про|ходить взвешивание (-йти)

weigh out *vt* отве|шивать (-сить)

weigh up *vt fig*: **to ~ up the pros and cons** взвесить все за и против; **to ~ smb up** состав|лять мнение о ком-л (-ить).

weighing machine *n* автоматические весы (*pl*).

weight *n* **1** вес; (*heaviness*) тяжесть; **table of ~s and measures** таблица мер и весов; **what's your ~?** какой у вас вес?; **will the platform take the ~ of the piano?** выдержит ли эта сцена рояль?; **a sack, 10 kg in ~** мешок весом десять килограммов; **to sell smth by ~** продавать что-л на вес; **he is over/under ~** он весит больше/меньше нормы; **to put on/lose ~** прибавлять/терять в весе, поправляться/худеть; **he reeled under the ~ of the box** он пошатнулся под тяжестью ящика

2 (*on scales, clock*) гиря; (*fishing, Naut*) **a lead ~** грузило; *Sport* **to put/lift the ~** толкать ядро, поднимать штангу

3 *fig uses*: **he/his opinion carries a lot of ~** с его мнением считаются; **that's a ~ off my mind** у меня словно камень с души свалился; **a good typist is worth her ~ in gold** хорошая машинистка—на вес золота; **he's feeling the ~ of his years** годы дают себя знать; **to give due ~ to smth** осознавать важность чего-л; *CQ* **to throw one's ~ about** важничать, задаваться.

weight *vt*: **he ~ed down the papers with an ashtray** он прижал бумаги пепельницей; **everything is ~ed in their favour** всё складывалось для них благоприятно.

weightless *adj* невесомый.

weight lifter *n* штангист.

weighty *adj* увесистый; *fig* веский; **~ considerations** веские соображения.

weir *n* плотина, запруда.

weird *adj* жуткий; *CQ* странный.

welcome *n*: **to bid smb ~** приветствовать кого-л; **they gave the team a rousing ~** команду восторженно приветствовали; **we were given a warm ~** нас тепло приняли; **to overstay one's ~** злоупотреблять чьим-л гостеприимством.

welcome *adj* **1**: **~ news** радостная/приятная новость; **that interruption was very ~** этот перерыв был очень кстати; **you're always ~/a ~ guest here** вам всегда здесь рады; **they didn't make us feel very ~** они нам не о́чень обра́довались; **a glass of beer would be very ~** кру́жка пи́ва сейча́с не помеша́ет; *as interj*: **~ (to Moscow)!** добро́ пожа́ловать (в Москву́)!; **~ back!/home!** с прие́здом!, с возвраще́нием!

2: you're ~ (*reply to thanks*) не́ за что; **you're ~ to borrow my bike** бери́ мой велосипе́д, когда́ захо́чешь; **you're ~ to try** мо́жешь попро́бовать; **if that's what you want, you're ~ (to it)** е́сли ты э́то хо́чешь—пожа́луйста.

welcome *vt* приве́тствовать (*only in impf*); **he ~d us warmly** он тепло́ нас приве́тствовал/при́нял; **he ~d the suggestion** он приве́тствовал э́то предложе́ние; **I'd ~ the opportunity to...** я был бы рад возмо́жности + *inf*.

welcoming *adj* приве́тливый.

weld *vti Tech* прива́ри|вать(ся), сва́ри|вать (-ся) (*pfs* -ть(ся)).

welder *n* сва́рщик.

welfare *n* (*of individual*) благополу́чие; (*the nation's*) благосостоя́ние; **to be concerned about smb's ~** забо́титься о чьём-л благополу́чии; **public ~** социа́льное обеспе́чение; (*US*) **to live on ~** жить на (госуда́рственное) посо́бие.

well[1] *n* коло́дец; **oil ~** нефтяна́я сква́жина; **to sink a ~** копа́ть (*dig*) коло́дец, бури́ть (*drill*) сква́жину.

well[2] *n*: **to wish smb ~** жела́ть кому́-л добра́; **why can't you leave ~ alone?** от добра́ добра́ не и́щут.

well[2] *adj* **1** (*healthy*) здоро́вый; **are you ~?** вы здоро́вы?; **she's not ~ today** ей сего́дня нездоро́вится; **you're looking ~ today** ты сего́дня хорошо́ вы́глядишь; **I'm feeling ~** я хорошо́ себя́ чу́вствую; **she'll soon get ~** она́ ско́ро попра́вится

2 (*satisfactory*): **all's ~ that ends ~** всё хорошо́, что хорошо́ конча́ется; **it would be (as) ~ to ask his advice** хорошо́ бы спроси́ть у него́ сове́та; **it was ~ for you that no one saw you** хорошо́, что вас никто́ не ви́дел; **it's all very ~ for him to say that** ему́ хорошо́ (э́то) говори́ть; **that's all very ~, but...** э́то всё хорошо́, но...

well[2] *adv* **1** хорошо́; **these colours go ~ together** э́ти цвета́ хорошо́ сочета́ются; **~ done!** хорошо́!, молоде́ц!; **oh, very ~** ну ла́дно; **he spoke ~ of your work** он хорошо́ отозва́лся о твое́й рабо́те; **they live very ~** они́ о́чень хорошо́ живу́т; **he's done very ~ for himself/out of the deal** он весьма́ преуспе́л, он хорошо́ зарабо́тал на э́том де́ле; **they did very ~ by him/him ~** они́ к нему́ о́чень хорошо́ отнесли́сь; **it all turned out ~** всё обошло́сь хорошо́/благополу́чно; **you would do ~ to listen to him** ты хорошо́ сде́лаешь, е́сли послу́шаешь его́; **you're ~ out of that** хорошо́, что ты с э́тим не име́ешь де́ла/, что ты вы́путался из э́того; **you know that perfectly ~** ты прекра́сно э́то зна́ешь; **our team was ~ and truly beaten** на́шу кома́нду разгроми́ли в пух и прах; **it's just as ~ he agreed** хорошо́, что он согласи́лся; **maybe it's just as ~** мо́жет быть, э́то и к лу́чшему

2 (*with good, equal reason*): **you may ~ say so** ещё бы; **it may ~ be so** вполне́ возмо́жно; **she told him off, as ~ she might** она́ отчита́ла его́, и подело́м; **he could ~ change his mind** вполне́ возмо́жно, что он переду́мает; **we might just as ~ have stayed at home** мы могли́ бы с таки́м же успе́хом оста́ться до́ма

3 (*intensive*): **~ over 1,000 people** бо́льше ты́сячи челове́к; **he's ~ over 50** ему́ далеко́ за пятьдеся́т; **~ into the night** далеко́ за́ полночь; **it was ~ worth the effort** ра́ди э́того сто́ило постара́ться; *sl* **he was ~ away** он был си́льно навеселе́ (*adv*)

4 (*in addition*) **as well (as): teachers as ~ as pupils want this** и учителя́, и ученики́ хотя́т э́того; **he gave me a book and a painting as ~** он подари́л мне кни́гу и ещё карти́ну вприда́чу; **he's a gossip and a liar as ~** он спле́тничает и к тому́ же ча́сто врёт; **she plays as ~ as sings** она́ поёт и к тому́ же игра́ет на роя́ле; **she plays the piano as ~ as she plays the violin** она́ одина́ково хорошо́ игра́ет и на роя́ле и на скри́пке.

well[2] *interj*: **~, look who it is!** бо́же мой, кого́ мы ви́дим!; **~ I never!** ну и ну́!; **~ here we are at last** ну вот, наконе́ц-то мы и прие́хали; **~, there's nothing we can do** что ж, ничего́ не поде́лаешь; **~ then, that's settled** ла́дно, договори́лись; **~, maybe you're right** ну что́ же, мо́жет, ты и прав; **~ then, let's get on with it** (ну) ла́дно, дава́й начнём.

well-behaved *adj*: **a ~ child** воспи́танный ребёнок; **he was ~** он хорошо́ себя́ вёл.

well-being *n* (*personal*) благополу́чие; (*public*) благосостоя́ние.

well-bred *adj* (хорошо́) воспи́танный.

well-built *adj* хорошо́ сложённый, ста́тный.

well-defined *adj*: **a ~ outline** чёткий/отчётливый ко́нтур.

well-fed *adj* (*of people*) упи́танный; (*of animals*) отко́рмленный.

well-founded *adj*: **~ suspicions** обосно́ванные подозре́ния.

well-groomed *adj* (*of horse or person*) ухо́женный.

well-heeled *adj CQ*: **he's ~** он состоя́тельный челове́к.

wellington boots, wellingtons *n* рези́новые сапоги́.

well-judged *adj*: **a ~ answer** проду́манный отве́т.

well-kept *adj*: **a ~ garden** ухо́женный сад; **a ~ secret** тща́тельно храни́мый секре́т.

well-known *adj* (хорошо́) изве́стный.

well-meaning *adj*: **at least he's ~** по кра́йней ме́ре, он никому́ не жела́ет зла.

well-off *adj*: **they're ~** они́ обеспе́ченные лю́ди; *CQ*: **we're quite ~ for vegetables/for shops here** у нас хорошо́ с овоща́ми, у нас здесь мно́го магази́нов; **he doesn't know when he's ~** он своего́ сча́стья не зна́ет.

well-proportioned *adj*: **a ~ room/woman** кóмната хорóших пропóрций, стрóйная жéнщина.

well-read *adj*: **he's ~ in Russian history** он хорошó знáет рýсскую истóрию.

well-spent *adj*: **it was time ~** врéмя бы́ло недáром потрáчено.

well-timed *adj* своеврéменный.

well-turned *adj*: **a ~ phrase/sentence/compliment** оттóченная фрáза, хорошó пострóенное предложéние, удáчный комплимéнт.

well-wisher *n* доброжелáтель (*m*).

well-worn *adj*: **~ clothes/shoes** понóшенная одéжда, стóптанные ботúнки; *fig* **~ phrases** избúтые фрáзы.

Welsh *n* (*language*) валлúйский/уэ́льский язы́к; **the ~** валлúйцы, уэ́льсцы.

Welsh *adj* валлúйский, уэ́льский.

Welshman *n* валлúец, уэ́льсец.

Welshwoman *n* валлúйка.

welt *n* (*of shoe*) рант; (*weal*) рубéц.

welterweight *n* (*boxer*) боксёр вторóго полусрéднего вéса.

west *n* зáпад; *Naut* вест; **in/from the ~** на зáпаде, с зáпада; **to the ~ of** к зáпаду от + *G*.

west *adj* зáпадный.

west *adv* на зáпад; **to sail ~** плыть на зáпад; **the house looks ~** дом выхóдит фасáдом на зáпад; **a village 20 km ~ of Prague** дерéвня в двадцатú киломéтрах к зáпаду от Прáги; *fig CQ* **all our plans went ~** все нáши плáны рýхнули.

westerly *adj* зáпадный.

western *n* (*of film*) вéстерн, ковбóйский фильм.

western *adj* зáпадный.

westward(s) *adv* на зáпад.

wet *n*: **don't stand out there in the ~** не стой под дождём.

wet *adj* мóкрый; **~ clothes/ground/weather** мóкрая одéжда/землякя, сырáя погóда; **we got ~ through/~ to the skin** мы насквóзь промóкли, мы вы́мокли до нúтки; **your coat is soaking/wringing ~** твоё пальтó мóкрое, хоть выжимáй; **he got his feet ~** он промочúл нóги; **it's too ~ to go out** идёт дождь—не до прогýлок; **"~ paint"** «осторóжно, окрáшено»; **the ink is still ~** чернúла (*pl*) ещё не вы́сохли; *fig CQ* **he's so ~** он занýда.

wet *vt*: **be careful, don't ~ the leaves** поливáй осторóжно, не облéй лúстья; **the child has ~ his trousers/his bed** ребёнок намочúл в штаны́/в постéль.

wet nurse *n* кормúлица.

wetting *n*: **we got a good ~** мы сúльно/насквóзь промóкли.

whacked *adj fig CQ*: **I'm ~** я вы́дохся.

whale *n* кит; **sperm ~** кашалóт; *CQ* **we had a ~ of a time** мы колоссáльно провелú врéмя; *attr*: **~ oil** китóвый жир.

whalebone *n* китóвый ус.

whaler *n* (*man*) китобóй; (*ship*) китобóйное сýдно.

wharf *n* причáл, прúстань.

what *pron* **1** *interrog* что?; **~ has happened?** что случúлось?; **~ did he say?** что он сказáл?; **then just ~ did he say?** тогдá что же он сказáл?; **~'s wrong with you?** что с тобóй?; **~'s that to you?** тебé-то что (за дéло)?; **is he joking or ~?** он что—шýтит?; **~'s his job?** кем он рабóтает?; **~'s the German for that?** как э́то по-немéцки?; **~ did you pay for it?** скóлько ты за э́то заплатúл?; **~ are your plans?** а какúе у тебя́ плáны?; **~ about a trip to the zoo?** как насчёт поéздки в зоопáрк?; **~'s this tool for?** для чегó э́тот инструмéнт?; **~'s this knife doing here?** зачéм здесь лежúт э́тот нож?; **~ did you do that for?** зачéм ты э́то сдéлал?; **~'s the weather like today?** какáя сегóдня погóда?; **~ more do you want?** что ещё тебé нýжно?; **and ~ of your brother?** а как ваш брат?; **well, ~ of it?/so ~?** ну и что?; **he knows ~'s ~** он знáет что к чемý; **they sell books, magazines and ~ not/and ~ have you** онú продаю́т кнúги и журнáлы и всё такóе/и что хотúте

2 *relative* что; то, что; **~ he said surprised me** то, что он сказáл, удивúло меня́; **that's ~ I was afraid of** вот чегó я боя́лся; **~ surprises me is that...** сáмое удивúтельное—то, что...; **~ I like is a good book** что я люблю́—так э́то хорóшую кнúгу; **I'm sorry about ~ happened** я сожалéю о том, что случúлось; **and ~ is more...** и бóлее тогó...; **~ with the rain and my cold I decided not to go** из-за дождя́ и нáсморка я решúл не идтú тудá; **say ~ you will, I'll never believe it** чтó бы ты ни говорúл, я всё равнó э́тому не повéрю.

what *adj* **1** *interrog* какóй?; **~ books do you want?** какúе кнúги вам нужны́?; **~ date is it?** какóе сегóдня числó?; **~ time is it?** котóрый час?, скóлько врéмени?; **~ time are you coming?** во скóлько вы придёте?; **~ sort of an excuse is that!** что э́то за объяснéние!

2 *relative* какóй; **I gave her ~ money/~ little money I had** я дал ей все дéньги, какúе бы́ли у меня́, я дал ей те грошú, котóрые у меня́ бы́ли; **I took ~ books I could find** я взял те кнúги, какúе нашёл

3 *exclamatory*: **~ a pity!** какáя жáлость!; **~ a pity he can't come** как жаль, что он не мóжет прийтú; **~ nonsense!** какáя чушь!; **~ a fool I am!** какóй же я дурáк!; **~ an actress!** какáя актрúса!

what-d'ye-call (her/him/it) *pron CQ*: **there's old ~ him** вот он, как бишь егó; **bring me the ~ it** принесú мне—я забы́л, как э́то называ́ется.

whatever *pron* **1** (*no matter what*) что бы ни; **~ happens, don't worry** что бы ни случúлось, не беспокóйся; **~ people say, I think he's right** что бы ни говорúли, по-мóему, он прав

2 (*anything*): **do/take ~ you like** дéлай как хóчешь, берú всё, что хóчешь; **~ I have is yours** всё, что у меня́ есть—твоё

3 *interrog*: **~ do you want that for?** зачéм тебé э́то?; **~ did you do that for?** зачéм/

почему́ ты э́то сде́лал?; ~ **can she/he/they mean?** что бы э́то могло́ зна́чить?

4: give me that drill, or ~ it's called дай мне э́ту дрель, и́ли как она́ там называ́ется; **everyone had a hammer, saw or ~** у ка́ждого был молото́к, пила́ и́ли что́-нибудь в э́том ро́де.

whatever *adj* **1** како́й бы ни; ~ **the reasons are/were** каки́е бы ни́ были причи́ны; **play ~ records you like** ставь каки́е хо́чешь пласти́нки; **he's lost ~ money he had** он потеря́л все де́ньги, каки́е у него́ бы́ли; **everyone of ~ age** лю́ди всех во́зрастов; **take ~ measures you think best** прими́те ме́ры, кото́рые сочтёте ну́жными

2: is there any hope ~? есть хоть кака́я-нибудь наде́жда?; **there is no doubt ~** нет ни мале́йшего сомне́ния.

whatsoever *pron and adj see* **whatever.**

wheat *n* пшени́ца; *attr* пшени́чный.

wheedle *vt*: **she ~d him into buying the car** она́ улома́ла его́ купи́ть маши́ну.

wheel *n* колесо́; **steering ~** рулево́е колесо́, руль; **potter's ~** гонча́рный круг; **a car passed with a woman at the ~** прое́хала маши́на с же́нщиной за рулём; *fig*: **to put one's shoulder to the ~** взя́ться за де́ло; **to put a spoke in smb's ~** сова́ть/вставля́ть кому́-л па́лки в колёса.

wheel *vti vt* вози́ть (*impf*) *and compounds*; ката́ть (по-); **she ~ed the baby/the patient around the park** она́ вози́ла/ката́ла ребёнка в коля́ске по па́рку, она́ ката́ла больно́го по па́рку; **the next patient was ~ed in** ввезли́ сле́дующего больно́го; **he ~ed his bike into the shed** он вкати́л велосипе́д в сара́й

vi: **the birds ~ed above him** пти́цы кружи́ли(сь) над ним; **he ~ed round** он кру́то поверну́лся.

wheelbarrow *n* та́чка.

wheelchair *n* инвали́дное кре́сло, кре́сло-ка́талка.

wheeze *vi* хрипе́ть (*usu impf*).

wheezy *adj* хри́плый.

when *adv* **1** *interrog* когда́?; ~ **is the train due?** когда́ прибыва́ет/прихо́дит по́езд?; **since ~ has he been director here?** когда́ его́ назна́чили дире́ктором?

2 *relative*: **Monday is ~ I do the washing** у меня́ сти́рка по понеде́льникам.

when *conj* когда́; **he always makes notes ~ reading** когда́ он чита́ет, он всегда́ де́лает вы́писки; ~ **he saw her, he got up** уви́дев её, он встал; **why invite him ~ you know he won't come?** заче́м приглаша́ть, когда́ ты зна́ешь, что он всё равно́ не придёт?; **I'll do it ~ I've had lunch/~ she's phoned** я сде́лаю э́то по́сле обе́да/по́сле её звонка́; **I read a lot ~ I was a child** в де́тстве я мно́го чита́л.

whence *adv mainly arch* отку́да.

whenever *adv* **1** *interrog* когда́ же?; ~ **can he have told her?** когда́ же он мог ей э́то сказа́ть?; ~ **will we have time to do that?** когда́ же мы успе́ем э́то сде́лать?

2 *relative* (*any time*): **I will meet her ~ she likes** я встре́чусь с ней, когда́ ей уго́дно; (*every time*): ~ **I see him, he's wearing that hat** когда́ бы я его́ ни уви́дел, он всегда́ в э́той шля́пе; **I go to the theatre ~ I can** я не упуска́ю слу́чая пойти́ в теа́тр, е́сли есть возмо́жность.

where *adv* **1** *interrog* где?; ~ **from?** отку́да?; ~ **are you?/are you going?/are you from?** где вы?, куда́ вы идёте?, отку́да вы ро́дом?; *fig* ~ **would I be if they hadn't helped me?** что бы со мной бы́ло, е́сли бы они́ мне не помогли́?

2 *relative* (*with antecedent*): **the town ~ we live** го́род, где мы живём; **the hotel ~ we stayed** гости́ница, в кото́рой/, где мы останови́лись; *CQ* **the resort ~ we're going (to)** куро́рт, куда́ мы е́дем; (*without antecedent*): **this is ~ we get off** нам здесь выходи́ть; **that is ~ you're mistaken** тут ты ошиба́ешься; **go ~ you like** иди́, куда́ хо́чешь; **you can see it from ~ I'm sitting** с моего́ ме́ста э́то хорошо́ ви́дно; ~ **I come from, people are very friendly** в мои́х родны́х места́х лю́ди о́чень приве́тливы.

whereabouts *adv* где?, куда́?; ~ **is this lake?** где э́то о́зеро?; ~ **do you think you put the scissors?** куда́ ты мог положи́ть но́жницы?

whereas *adv* а; *Law* (*since*) ввиду́ того́, что; **in France they drink coffee, ~ in England it's always tea** францу́зы лю́бят ко́фе, а англича́не—чай.

whereby *adv*: **an agreement ~...** догово́р, по кото́рому...; **a plan ~...** план, с по́мощью кото́рого...

whereupon *adv* (*as a result of which*) всле́дствие чего́; (*after which*) по́сле чего́.

wherever *adv* **1** *interrog* где же?; ~ **can my glasses be?** куда́ запропасти́лись мои́ очки́?; ~ **is he going?** куда́ э́то он идёт?

2 *relative* где бы ни; куда́ бы ни; ~ **he is, they'll find him** где бы он ни был, они́ его́ найду́т; ~ **he goes...** куда́ бы он ни пошёл...; ~ **he comes from...** отку́да бы он ни был ро́дом...; **go ~ you like** иди́те, куда́ хоти́те.

wherewithal *n*: **they haven't the ~ to buy it** им не́ на что э́то купи́ть.

whet *vt* точи́ть (на-); *fig*: **to ~ smb's appetite** возбу|жда́ть чей-л аппети́т (-ди́ть); **this only ~ted his curiosity** э́то то́лько возбуди́ло его́ любопы́тство.

whether *conj* ли; **ask him ~ he knows about it** спроси́ его́, зна́ет ли он об э́том; **I don't know ~ they'll come/agree to it or not** я не зна́ю, приду́т ли они́/, соглася́тся ли они́ на э́то; **the question is ~ he can be believed** вопро́с в том, мо́жно ли ему́ ве́рить; ~ **you like it or not, we must be there** хо́чешь ты и́ли нет, мы должны́ там быть.

whew *interj* (*in relief, exhaustion*) уф!; (*in surprise*) фью!

which *pron* **1** *interrog* что?, кото́рый?; како́й?; **~ do you want, a book or a magazine?** что ты хо́чешь взять — кни́гу и́ли журна́л?; **~ of the books do you need?** кака́я из э́тих книг вам нужна́?; **I can't tell ~ of the players is ~** я не могу́ разобра́ть, кто из э́тих игроко́в кто; **~ is cleverer, the boy or the girl?** кто из них умне́е — ма́льчик и́ли де́вочка?

2 *relative* (*with noun antecedent*) кото́рый; **the book ~ was lying on the shelf** кни́га, лежа́вшая/, кото́рая лежа́ла на по́лке; **the book ~ he was reading** кни́га, кото́рую он чита́л; **a poem ~ he had written as a boy** стихотворе́ние, напи́санное им/, кото́рое он написа́л в де́тстве; **the hotel at ~ we stayed** гости́ница, в кото́рой мы останови́лись

3 *relative* (*with clause antecedent*) что; **the train was late ~ annoyed everyone** по́езд опа́здывал, что раздража́ло всех; **from ~ we may conclude that...** из чего́ мо́жно заключи́ть, что...; **if it happens, ~ God forbid...** е́сли э́то случи́тся, что не дай бог...

which *adj* **1** *interrog* како́й?, кото́рый?; **~ way did she go?** в каку́ю сто́рону она́ пошла́?; **~ town is he from?** из како́го он го́рода?; **~ picture do you prefer?** кака́я из э́тих карти́н вам бо́льше нра́вится?

2 *relative*: **she got here at 3, by ~ time I had returned** она́ пришла́ в три, а к тому́ вре́мени я уже́ верну́лся; **she was here for an hour, during ~ time she talked non-stop** она́ пробыла́ здесь час, и всё э́то вре́мя не закрыва́ла рта.

whichever *pron*: **~ of you finds it will get a reward** кто из вас э́то найдёт, полу́чит награ́ду; **take ~ of the records you like** бери́ любы́е пласти́нки; **they are both good carpets — ~ you buy, you won't lose** о́ба ковра́ хоро́шие — како́й бы ты ни купи́л, в накла́де не оста́нешься.

whichever *adj* любо́й, како́й бы то ни́ было; **~ alternative you choose** како́й бы вариа́нт вы ни вы́брали; **I want to speak with ~ doctor is on duty** я хочу́ поговори́ть с дежу́рным врачо́м; **~ way you look at it, he's been lucky** как там ни говори́, а ему́ повезло́.

whiff *n*: **there was a ~ of garlic/tobacco about him** от него́ па́хло (*impers*) чесноко́м/табако́м; **I caught a ~ of gas** я улови́л за́пах га́за; **let me have a ~ of that scent** дай мне поню́хать э́ти духи́; **he took a few ~s** он сде́лал не́сколько затя́жек.

while *n*: **for a ~** на вре́мя; **after a ~** че́рез/спустя́ не́которое вре́мя; **in a little ~** ско́ро; **a little/long ~ ago** неда́вно, давно́; **it will take quite a ~** э́то займёт дово́льно мно́го вре́мени; **it's been a ~ since we saw him** мы его́ уже́ давно́ не ви́дели; **it will be a good ~ before he's better** он ещё не ско́ро попра́вится; **once in a ~ I do take a nip** иногда́ я вы́пью рю́мочку-другу́ю; **it's not worth your ~ asking him** не сто́ит да́же и спра́шивать его́; **I'll make it worth your ~ to do it** сде́лай э́то, не пожале́ешь.

while (*US sometimes* **whilst**) *conj* **1** (*of time*) пока́, в то вре́мя как; **~ all this was going on** пока́/в то вре́мя как всё э́то происходи́ло; **~ (he was) at university, he lived in a hostel** когда́/пока́ он учи́лся в университе́те, он жил в общежи́тии; **let's go ~ it's still day-light** пойдём, пока́ светло́; **~ you're away I'll stay with my mother** пока́ тебя́ не бу́дет, я поживу́ у ма́мы; **~ coming here** по доро́ге сюда́

2 (*concessive*) хотя́; **~ I admit that is so, I still think he's wrong** хотя́ я и признаю́, что э́то так, я всё же счита́ю, что он непра́в

3 (*implying contrast*) а; **he likes opera, ~ I like ballet** он лю́бит о́перу, а я (люблю́) бале́т.

while *vt*: **to ~ away the time** корота́ть вре́мя (с-).

whim *n* при́хоть, прихоу́да, каприз; **it's just a passing ~** э́то про́сто мимолётная при́хоть; **he satisfies her every ~** он исполня́ет все её при́хоти (*pl*).

whimper *vi* хны́кать, ныть, (*of dog*) скули́ть (*impfs*).

whimsical *adj* (*of story, idea, etc.*) причу́дливый; (*of look, smile*) зага́дочный.

whine *n* нытьё, (*of dog*) скулёж; **the ~ of bullets** свист пуль.

whine *vi* ныть, (*of dog*) скули́ть (*impfs*), *both also fig*; **he's always whining about something** он ве́чно на что́-нибудь жа́луется; **the dog was whining to be let in** соба́ка скули́ла под две́рью.

whip *n* (*riding crop*) плеть, плётка; (*long, for coach horses*) кнут; *attr fig*: **he's got the ~ hand over them** они́ у него́ в рука́х.

whip *vti vt* **1** хлест|а́ть (плётью) (-ну́ть); стег|а́ть (кнуто́м) (-ну́ть); (*punish*) поро́ть (вы́-); **to ~ cream** взби|ва́ть сли́вки (´-ть)

2 *with advs, preps*: **I ~ped the razor away from the baby** я вы́хватил бри́тву у ребёнка из рук; **he ~ped his jacket off** он сорва́л (с себя́) ку́ртку; **he was ~ped off to hospital** его́ сро́чно увезли́ в больни́цу; **he ~ped a gun out of his pocket** он вы́хватил револьве́р из карма́на; **the orator ~ped the crowd up to a frenzy** ора́тор довёл толпу́ до исступле́ния

vi fig CQ: **I'll just ~ round to the shop/upstairs** я то́лько сбе́гаю в магази́н/наве́рх.

whippet *n* го́нчая.

whipping *n* по́рка; **he got a ~ from his father** оте́ц за́дал ему́ по́рку.

whipping top *n* волчо́к, юла́.

whip-round *n CQ*: **his mates had a ~ for him** его́ това́рищи собра́ли для него́ де́ньги.

whirl *n*: **a ~ of dust** вихрь пы́ли; *fig*: **her life is a ~ of parties** она́ кру́жится в ви́хре све́тских развлече́ний; **my thoughts are in a ~** у меня́ все мы́сли перепу́тались в голове́.

whirl *vi* кружи́ться; **the dancers ~ed round the room** па́ры кружи́лись в та́нце; **towns and villages ~ed past the window** за окно́м пронос́ились дере́вни и города́.

whirlpool *n* водоворо́т.

whirlwind *n* вихрь (*m*).

whirr *vi* (*of propellers, insects*) жужжа́ть, (*click*) стрекота́ть (*usu impfs*); **the cameras began to ~** застрекота́ли кинока́меры.

whisk *n* (*small brush*) ве́ничек, мете́лочка; *Cook* (*also* **egg ~**) сбива́лка, муто́вка; **with a ~ of its tail** взма́хом хвоста́.

whisk *vt*: **the horse ~ed its tail** ло́шадь махну́ла хвосто́м; **the horse was ~ing away flies with its tail** ло́шадь отгоня́ла мух хвосто́м; **to ~ (up) egg whites** взби|ва́ть белки́ (-́ть); **she ~ed my plate away** она́ вы́хватила у меня́ таре́лку; *CQ* **they ~ed me off to the theatre** они́ затащи́ли меня́ в теа́тр.

whisker *n* ус; **~s** (*moustache*) усы́; **side ~s** бакенба́рды.

whisky, (*US*) **whiskey** *n* ви́ски (*indecl*).

whisper *n* шёпот; **in a ~, in ~s** шёпотом (*always sing*).

whisper *vti vt* шепта́ть (про-, шепну́ть)

vi шепта́ться; **they sat ~ing to each other** они́ сиде́ли и шепта́лись.

whispering *n* шёпот.

whist *n Cards* вист.

whistle *n* (*sound*) свист; (*instrument*) свисто́к; *fig CQ* **to wet one's ~** промочи́ть го́рло.

whistle *vti vt* свист|е́ть (-́нуть); (*tunefully*) насви́стывать (*impf*); **he ~d his dog/a tune** он сви́стнул соба́ку, он насви́стывал мело́дию

vi свисте́ть; **I ~d to him** я сви́стнул ему́; **the train/the referee ~d** по́езд/судья́ дал свисто́к; **the wind ~d in the chimney** ве́тер завыва́л в трубе́; **the bullets ~d over his head** пу́ли свисте́ли у него́ над голово́й.

white *n*: **she was dressed in ~** она́ была́ во всём бе́лом; **~ of an egg/of the eye** яи́чный бело́к, бело́к глаза́.

white *adj* бе́лый; (*of hair*) седо́й; **she was as ~ as a sheet** она́ была́ бе́лая/бле́дная как полотно́; **the walls are painted ~/gleamed ~ in the sun** сте́ны вы́крашены в бе́лый цвет/беле́ли на со́лнце; **her hair is beginning to go ~** у неё начина́ют седе́ть во́лосы, она́ начина́ет седе́ть; **we had a ~ Christmas** у нас на рождество́ вы́пал снег; **to turn ~ with anger/fear** побледне́ть от гне́ва/от стра́ха.

white-collar *adj*: **~ workers** слу́жащие.

white-haired *adj* седо́й.

white horses *npl* (*on sea*) бара́шки.

white-hot *adj* раскалённый добела́ (*adv*).

whitewash *n* побе́лка.

whitewash *vt* бели́ть (по-); *fig* **to ~ smb/smth** обел|я́ть кого́-л/что-л (-и́ть).

whither *adv mostly arch* куда́.

whiting *n* (*fish*) мерла́нг.

whitish *adj* белова́тый, белёсый.

whittle *vt*: **to ~ down a piece of wood** строга́ть (*impf*)/струга́ть кусо́к де́рева ножо́м (об-); *fig*: **our savings are being ~d away** на́ши сбереже́ния та́ют; **we have ~d down the number of candidates to 5** мы уме́ньшили коли́чество кандида́тов до пяти́.

whizz *vi*: **the bullets ~ed past** вокру́г свисте́ли пу́ли; **she ~ed past us in a car** она́ промча́лась ми́мо нас в маши́не; **the skiers ~ed down the slope** лы́жники несли́сь по скло́ну.

whizz kid *n sl* вундерки́нд.

who *pron* (*A* **whom,** *but CQ* **who,** *though not immediately following a prep*) **1** *interrog* кто? (*A/G* кого́?, *D* кому́?, *I* кем?, *P* о ком?); **~ is there?** кто там?; **~'s that speaking?** кто (э́то) говори́т?; **~ did you say was coming?** кто, ты сказа́л, придёт?; **~ is he anyway?, ~ does he think he is?** да кто он тако́й?; **I don't know ~'s ~ around here** я не зна́ю, кто здесь кто; **who(m) did you see?** кого́ ты ви́дел?; **who(m) were you speaking to?, to whom were you speaking?** с кем ты говори́л?; **~ should it be but Tom** э́то был не кто ино́й, как Том

2 *relative* кото́рый; **those ~** те, кото́рые *or* те, кто (*usu with sing verb*); **we saw her friend, ~ works in a shop** мы ви́дели её подру́гу, кото́рая рабо́тает в магази́не; **the man who(m) we met yesterday** челове́к, кото́рого мы встре́тили вчера́; **three women, none of whom I knew** три же́нщины, из кото́рых я не знал ни одно́й; **the man ~ was playing the piano** челове́к, кото́рый игра́л на роя́ле/, игра́вший на роя́ле; **those ~ have tickets** те, у кого́ есть биле́ты.

whoa *interj* тпру!

whoever *pron* **1** *interrog* кто?; **~ said that?** кто э́то сказа́л?; **~ would believe it?** кто э́тому пове́рит?; **~ do you mean?** кого́ ты име́ешь в виду́?

2 *relative*: **~ thinks that is mistaken** тот, кто так ду́мает, ошиба́ется; **~ comes will be welcome** кто придёт—бу́дет жела́нным го́стем; **I think you're right, ~ may criticize you** пусть тебя́ бу́дут критикова́ть, но, по-мо́ему, ты прав; **invite ~ you like** пригласи́ кого́ хо́чешь.

whole *n* це́лое; **these parts make up a ~** э́ти ча́сти составля́ют (одно́) це́лое; **if we take the novel as a ~** е́сли взять рома́н в це́лом; **society as a ~** о́бщество в це́лом; **as a ~, on the ~** в це́лом; **they sold the ~ of the estate** они́ про́дали всё име́ние; **this concerns the ~ of society** э́то каса́ется всего́ о́бщества.

whole *adj* **1** (*undamaged*) це́лый; **not a glass was left ~** не оста́лось ни одного́ це́лого стака́на

2 (*entire*) це́лый; весь; **the ~ world** весь мир, це́лый свет; **a ~ week** це́лую неде́лю; **a ~ series of mistakes** це́лый ряд оши́бок; **I want to know the ~ truth** я хочу́ знать всю пра́вду; **that's the ~ idea** в э́том весь смысл; **~ milk** це́льное молоко́; **they roasted a piglet ~** они́ зажа́рили поросёнка целико́м (*adv*); **to swallow smth ~** проглоти́ть что-л целико́м;

Math **a ~ number** це́лое число́; *CQ* **a ~ lot of money** це́лая ку́ча де́нег.

wholehearted *adj*: **you have my ~ support** я вас по́лностью (*adv*) подде́рживаю; **they were ~ in their approval of his idea** они́ по́лностью одо́брили его́ иде́ю.

wholemeal *n*, *also* **~ flour** мука́ из це́льного зерна́/гру́бого помо́ла.

wholesale *adj* опто́вый; *fig* огу́льный; **the ~ trade** опто́вая торго́вля; **at ~ prices** по опто́вым це́нам; **~ dealers** оптовики́; *fig* **~ criticism** огу́льная кри́тика.

wholesale *adv* о́птом; **to buy/sell smth ~** покупа́ть/продава́ть что-л о́птом; *fig* **he accused everyone ~** он обвини́л всех огу́лом (*adv*).

wholesaler *n* опто́вый торго́вец, оптови́к.

wholesome *adj* здоро́вый, поле́зный; (*of character*) положи́тельный; **~ food** здоро́вая пи́ща; **~ advice** поле́зный/здра́вый сове́т.

wholly *adv*: **I ~ agree** я по́лностью/вполне́ согла́сен; **that is ~ out of the question** об э́том не мо́жет быть и ре́чи; **to devote oneself ~ to smth** всеце́ло/целико́м посвяти́ть себя́ чему́-л; **he is not ~ without conscience** он ещё не совсе́м потеря́л со́весть.

whoop *n*: **a ~ of joy** ра́достный во́зглас.

whoop *vi* вскри́к|ивать (-нуть); **the children ~ed for joy** де́ти ра́достно закрича́ли.

whooping cough *n* коклю́ш.

whopper *n CQ*: **the fish was a ~** э́то была́ грома́дная ры́ба; (*lie*): **he tells some ~s** он врёт; **that's a ~!** како́е враньё!

whopping *adj CQ*: **a ~ great tree trunk** грома́дный ствол.

whore *n* проститу́тка.

whose *pron* **1** *interrog* чей?, чья?, чьё?, чьи?; **~ is this cup?** чья э́то ча́шка? [**NB** э́то]; **~ car did you come in?** на чьей маши́не ты прие́хал?

2 *relative* чей, кото́рый; **the lady ~ house we bought** та же́нщина, чей дом мы купи́ли; **the man ~ wife we helped** челове́к, чьей жене́ мы помогли́; **his son, for ~ sake he did it** сын, ра́ди кото́рого он э́то сде́лал; **the man in ~ pocket they found my wallet** челове́к, у кото́рого в карма́не нашли́ мой бума́жник.

why *n*: **never mind the ~s and wherefores** не спра́шивай, заче́м и почему́.

why *adv* **1** *interrog* (*for what reason*) почему́?; отчего́?; (*for what purpose*) заче́м?; **~ did you do that?** почему́/заче́м ты э́то сде́лал?; **~ did you come?** заче́м ты пришёл?; **~ didn't you come?** почему́ ты не пришёл?; **~ not?** почему́ (бы) нет?; **~ worry about that?** что об э́том беспоко́иться?

2 *relative* почему́; **I know ~ it happened** я зна́ю, почему́ э́то произошло́; **that's ~** вот почему́; **the reasons ~ he refused are obscure** причи́ны, по кото́рым он отказа́лся, неясны́.

why *interj* (*in surprise*): **~, there he is** а вот и он; (*in agreement*): **~ certainly** ну коне́чно же; (*in protest*): **~ what's wrong in that?** ну что́ же в э́том плохо́го?

wick *n* фити́ль (*m*).

wicked *adj* **1** (*evil*) плохо́й, дурно́й; (*immoral*) безнра́вственный; (*spiteful*) злой; **~ people** плохи́е/дурны́е/злы́е лю́ди; **what a ~ thing to do** как э́то жесто́ко (*cruel*)/бессо́вестно (*unscrupulous*); **he has a ~ temper** у него́ дурно́й нрав/скве́рный хара́ктер; *fig* **what a ~ waste to throw away good food** выбра́сывать еду́—грех

2 (*mischievous*): **he has a ~ sense of humour** он зло шу́тит; **you ~ child!** ах ты, него́дник/озорни́к э́такий!

wicker *adj*: **a ~ basket/chair** плетёная корзи́на, плетёный стул; **a ~ fence** плетéнь (*m*).

wide *adj* широ́кий, *also fig*: **a ~ river/path** широ́кая река́/тропи́нка; **how ~ is this road?** како́й ширины́ э́та доро́га?; **the lake is 2 km ~** о́зеро два киломе́тра шириной/в ширину́; *fig*: **a ~ choice** широ́кий вы́бор; **~ interests** широ́кие интере́сы; **a ~ knowledge of history** обши́рные позна́ния (*pl*) в исто́рии.

wide *adv* широко́; **he opened the gate ~** он широко́ распахну́л воро́та; **the door was ~ open** дверь была́ распа́хнута на́стежь; **with ~ open mouths** с рази́нутыми рта́ми; **the columns are set ~ apart** коло́нны стоя́т далеко́ друг от дру́га; **I looked far and ~** я везде́/повсю́ду иска́л.

wide-awake *adj*: **he was ~ within seconds** у него́ сон в оди́н миг как руко́й сня́ло; *fig* **you've got to be ~ when dealing with him** с ним на́до быть начеку́ (*adv*).

wide-eyed *adj* с широко́ раскры́тыми глаза́ми.

widely *adv* широко́; **the opinion is ~ held that...** широко́ распространено́/быту́ет мне́ние, что...; **he's ~ read** он весьма́ начи́тан (*of reader*), он изве́стный писа́тель (*of author*); **their opinions differ ~** их мне́ния ре́зко расхо́дятся; **it is ~ believed that...** мно́гие счита́ют, что...; **he has travelled ~** он мно́го е́здил по све́ту; **~ scattered farms** разбро́санные там и сям фе́рмы.

widen *vti* расшир|я́ть(ся) (-и́ть(ся)).

wide-screen *adj*: **a ~ film** широкоэкра́нный фильм.

widespread *adj*: **this opinion is becoming increasingly ~** э́то мне́ние завоёвывает всё бо́льше сторо́нников.

widow *n* вдова́; **she was left a ~** она́ оста́лась вдово́й.

widow *vt*: **to be ~ed** овдове́ть (*pf*).

widower *n* вдове́ц.

width *n* ширина́; *fig* широта́; **a plank 20 centimetres in ~** доска́ два́дцать сантиме́тров ширино́й; **a ~ of cloth** отре́з сукна́; *fig* **the ~ of his interests** широта́ его́ интере́сов.

wife *n* жена́, *off* супру́га; **the President and his ~** президе́нт с супру́гой.

wig *n* пари́к.

wiggly *adj* изви́листый; **a ~ line/road** изви́листая ли́ния/доро́га.

wild *n*: **animals living in the ~** живо́тные, живу́щие на во́ле; **he enjoys living in the ~** он лю́бит жить в глуши́; **the call of the**

~ зов пре́дков/приро́ды; **somewhere in the ~s of Australia** где́-то в са́мых ди́ких/глухи́х места́х Австра́лии.

wild *adj* **1** ди́кий; ~ **animals/tribes** ди́кие зве́ри/племена́; ~ **flowers** полевы́е цветы́; **a ~ apple tree/leek, ~ honey** я́блоня-дичо́к, ди́кий лук/мёд; **tulips grow ~ in Greece** в Гре́ции тюльпа́н—дикорасту́щее расте́ние; *fig*: **he was a ~ lad in his youth** в ю́ности он вёл разгу́льный о́браз жи́зни; **as children, we ran ~** в де́тстве мы росли́ на приво́лье

2 (*of weather, etc.*): ~ **weather** штормова́я пого́да; ~ **sea/coastline, a ~ country** бу́рное мо́ре, непристу́пный бе́рег, пусты́нное ме́сто; **it was a ~ night** но́чью была́ бу́ря

3 (*unrestrained, reckless*): ~ **enthusiasm/applause** горя́чий энтузиа́зм, бу́рные аплодисме́нты (*pl*); ~ **schemes/rumours** безу́мные пла́ны, невероя́тные слу́хи; **it was a ~ guess** э́то была́ дога́дка наобу́м (*adv*)

4 (*roused to anger or enthusiasm*) *CQ*: **she was ~ with me** она́ си́льно разозли́лась на меня́; **that made him ~** э́то разозли́ло его́ не на шу́тку; **everyone is ~ about the play** все без ума́/в восто́рге от э́той пье́сы; **he's ~ about her/opera** он без ума́ от неё, он поме́шан на о́пере.

wildcat *adj*: **a ~ strike** забасто́вка без разреше́ния профсою́за.

wilderness *n* ди́кая ме́стность, глушь; *fig* пусты́ня.

wildfire *n*: **the rumours spread like ~** слу́хи распространи́лись с быстрото́й мо́лнии.

wildfowl *n collect* дичь.

wild goose chase *n*: **it turned out to be a ~** э́то оказа́лось пусто́й зате́ей.

wiles *npl* хи́трости, ухищре́ния.

wilful *adj* (*capricious*) своенра́вный, своево́льный; (*deliberate*) умы́шленный, *also Law*.

will[1] *v modal aux* (*see also* **would**) (*in 1st person affirm, and in 1st and 2nd persons interrog used CQ for* **shall**; **NB won't** *CQ* = **will not; I'll, she'll, he'll, you'll, they'll** *CQ* = **I will,** *etc.*) **1** (*forming future tense*): **I'll do it/be staying with them** я э́то сде́лаю, я остановлю́сь у них; **who'll tell her?—I ~** кто ска́жет ей?—Я; **he ~ help us, won't he?—No, he won't** он ведь нам помо́жет, пра́вда?—Нет, не помо́жет

2 (*in requests, commands*): **won't you come in/sit down?** не хоти́те ли войти́?/сесть?; **~/won't you have some tea?** не хоти́те ли ча́ю?; ~ **you sit still!** сиди́ сми́рно!; ~ **you close the window, please** закро́йте, пожа́луйста, окно́

3 (*expressing willingness*): **come when you ~** приходи́, когда́ захо́чешь; **do as you ~** де́лайте, как хоти́те; **say what you ~, at least he's honest** что бы ты ни говори́л, а всё же он челове́к поря́дочный; **try as you ~ you won't open it** как бы ты ни стара́лся, тебе́ э́то не откры́ть; **he won't sing for us** он не хо́чет петь для нас

4 (*expressing conjecture*): **that ~ be the doctor now** э́то, должно́ быть, врач; **he ~ be about fifty** ему́, должно́ быть, лет пятьдеся́т; **he ~ have left by now** он, должно́ быть, уже́ ушёл

5 (*expressing habit, potentiality*) [**NB** *Russian often uses present tense*]: **he'll sit in front of the TV for hours on end** он часа́ми проси́живает у телеви́зора; **accidents ~ happen** быва́ют и несча́стные слу́чаи; **boys ~ be boys** мальчи́шки есть мальчи́шки; **the door won't shut** дверь не закрыва́ется; **on cold mornings the car won't start** в холо́дное у́тро маши́на ника́к не заво́дится; **the plane ~ seat 500** в э́том самолёте поме́стятся пятьсо́т челове́к; **his car ~ do 100 m.p.h.** его́ маши́на де́лает сто миль в час

6 (*in emphasis*): **I said I'd come and I ~** я сказа́л, приду́—зна́чит, приду́; **he ~ stay up late, so of course he's tired** коне́чно же, он уста́л—сиди́т ка́ждый ве́чер допоздна́; **he ~ have his little joke** он не упу́стит слу́чая пошути́ть; **I ~ be obeyed** меня́ бу́дут слу́шаться; **I won't have it** я э́того не допущу́/не позво́лю; **if you ~ listen to rumours...** е́сли ве́рить всем слу́хам...

will[2] *n* **1** во́ля; **free ~** свобо́да во́ли; **he did it of his own free ~/against his ~** он сде́лал э́то по до́брой во́ле/не по свое́й во́ле; **they can go out at ~** они́ мо́гут идти́ гуля́ть, когда́ хотя́т; **he has a ~ of his own** он своенра́вный челове́к; **has he no ~ of his own?** что, у него́ свое́й во́ли нет?; **they set to work with a ~** они́ с большо́й охо́той взяли́сь за рабо́ту; **with the best ~ in the world we can't be there for supper** как бы мы ни хоте́ли, мы туда́ к у́жину не попадём

2 *Law* завеща́ние; **in his ~** в своём завеща́нии; **to make one's ~** составля́ть завеща́ние.

will[2] *vti*: **I ~ed myself to keep awake** уси́лием во́ли я заста́вил себя́ не спать; **he ~ed her to keep silent** он о́чень не хоте́л, что́бы она́ говори́ла об э́том; *Law* **he ~ed his collection to the nation** он завеща́л свою́ колле́кцию госуда́рству (*pf*).

willing *adj* **1** (*helpful*) стара́тельный, усе́рдный; **he's a ~ worker** он хоро́ший/стара́тельный рабо́тник; **there are plenty of ~ hands** охо́тников хоть отбавля́й

2: **are you ~?** вы согла́сны?; **they are ~ for us to use the hall** они́ согла́сны предоста́вить нам зал; **he is ~/not very ~ to help** он гото́в помо́чь, он не рвётся помога́ть; **God ~** дай бог.

willingly *adv* охо́тно.

willow *n* и́ва.

willy-nilly *adv* во́лей-нево́лей, хо́чешь не хо́чешь.

wilt *vi* (*of flowers*) вя́нуть (за-, у-); *fig* **I ~ in the heat** я раски́с от жары́.

wily *adj* хи́трый.

win *n* (*victory*) побе́да; (*in gambling, lottery, etc.*) вы́игрыш.

win *vti vt* **1** побе|ждáть (-дить), вы|игрывать (-играть); **they won the war** они победили; **to ~ a victory/the day** одерж|ивать победу (-áть); **to ~ a battle/game** выигрывать сражение/игру; **to ~ a race/contest** выигрывать забег/соревнования (*pl*), побеждáть в забеге/в соревнованиях; **to ~ a prize/an award** получ|áть приз/премию (-ить); **they won the election** они одержáли победу/победили на выборах; **to ~ money at cards/in a lottery** выигрывать деньги в карты/в лотерее; **he won back the money** он отыгрáл деньги

2 (*gain, persuade*): **to ~ smb's confidence/respect** за|воёвывать чьё-л доверие/уважение (-воевáть); **this won him her gratitude** этим он заслужил её благодáрность; **he won her consent** он добился её соглáсия; **to ~ friends** располагáть к себе людей

vi побеждáть; выигрывать; **to ~ at cards** выигрывать в карты; **he won hands down** он легко одержáл победу; **he won on points** он победил по очкáм; **you'll ~ through in the end** ты в конце концов своего добьёшься.

wince *vi* (*for slight pain*) морщиться (по-); (*for severe pain*) содрог|áться (-нуться); **he ~d at what she said** он поморщился от её слов.

winch *vt*: **to ~ smth up** под|нимáть что-л лебёдкой (-нять).

wind[1] *n* **1** ветер; **a north/head/high ~** северный/встречный/сильный ветер; **a gust of ~** порыв ветра; **with the ~, with a following ~** с попутным ветром; **down ~** по ветру; **against the ~, up ~** против ветра; **the ~'s getting up** поднимáется ветер; **which way is the ~ blowing?** откуда ветер дует?, *also fig*; **we had a following ~/the ~ in our face** ветер дул нам в спину/в лицо; *fig*: **there's something in the ~** что-то назревáет/готовится; **he got ~ of their plan** он пронюхал об их плáне; **he's got the ~ up** он перепугáлся, *CQ* он сдрейфил; **it's an ill ~ that blows nobody any good** нет худа без добрá; **to throw caution to the ~s** отбрáсывать осторожность

2 (*breath*) дыхáние, дух; **I got my ~ back** я отдышáлся; **he was out of ~** он запыхáлся; *Sport* **he's got his second ~** к нему пришло второе дыхáние

3 *Med*: **the baby's got ~** у ребёнка гáзы; **to break ~** (*belch*) рыгáть, (*fart*) *euph* портить воздух

4 *Mus attr*: **~ instruments** духовые инструменты.

wind[1] *vt*: **the blow ~ed me** от удáра у меня перехвáтило дыхáние (*pf*).

wind[2] *vti vt* **1: the river ~s its way to the sea** рекá извилистым путём несёт свои воды к морю

2 (*wrap*) мотáть, смáтывать (*pf for both* смотáть) *and other compounds*; **to ~ wool** (*into a ball*) мотáть/смáтывать шерсть в клубок; **to ~ film on to a reel** на|мáтывать плёнку на кассету/на бобину (-мотáть); **the rope had wound itself round the axle** канáт намотáлся на ось; **the snake/ivy had wound itself round the branch** змея обвилáсь вокруг ветки, плющ обвил ветку; *fig* **she ~s him round her little finger** онá из него верёвки вьёт

3 (*turn*): **to ~ a handle** крутить ручку (*usu impf*); **to ~ up a clock/a toy** за|водить часы/игрушку (-вести)

4 *other uses with preps*: **to ~ back/on a tape** пере|мáтывать плёнку назáд/вперёд (-мотáть); **he wound down the car window** он спустил окно в машине; **to ~ in a (fishing) line** смáтывать удочку

5 *fig uses*: **to ~ up a meeting** закры|вáть собрáние (-ть); **to ~ up a story/a speech** за|кáнчивать рассказ/речь (-кончить); *Comm* **the company was wound up** компáния былá ликвидирована; *CQ* **she gets very wound up** онá такáя возбудимая

vi виться, извивáться (*impf*); **the road ~s along a valley** дорога вьётся по долине; **the procession wound round the town** процессия тянулась по улицам города; *CQ*: **we wound up in Aberdeen** мы закончили путешествие в Абердине; **he'll ~ up in gaol** он кончит тюрьмой.

windbag *n fig CQ* болтун, пустомеля.

windbreak *n* щит от ветра.

windcheater, (*US*) **windbreaker** *n* штормовка.

windfall *n* (*of fruit*) пáданец; *fig* **I've had a ~** мне эти деньги как с неба свалились.

wind gauge *n* анемометр.

winding *adj* извилистый.

windmill *n* ветрянáя мельница, ветряк.

window *n* окно; (*small, of cash desk, etc.*) окошко; **shop ~** витрина; **French ~** стеклянная дверь (, ведущая в сад или на верáнду); **to stand at the ~** стоять у окнá; **to look out of the ~** смотреть в окно/из окнá, (*out of open window*) выглядывать из окнá; **to throw smth out of the ~** выбрáсывать что-л за окно (*viewed from inside*)/из окнá (*viewed from street*).

window box *n* ящик для цветов на подоконнике.

window cleaner *n* мойщик окон.

window dressing *n* оформление витрин; *fig pejor* **it's all ~** это всё напокáз/*CQ* показуха.

window ledge, windowsill *ns* подоконник.

windpipe *n Anat* дыхáтельное горло.

windproof *adj* ветронепроницáемый.

windscreen, (*US*) **windshield** *n Aut* ветровое стекло.

windscreen wiper *n* стеклоочиститель (*m*), *CQ* «дворник».

windward *n*: **to ~** в наветренную сторону.

windy *adj* ветреный; **it's ~ today** сегодня ветрено; *fig CQ* **to be/get ~** перетрусить, сдрейфить.

wine *n* (*from grapes*) вино; (*from berries*) наливка.

wine *vt*: **to ~ and dine smb** кормить и поить кого-л (*pfs* на-).

wine cellar *n* ви́нный по́греб.
wineglass *n* рю́мка; (*large*) бока́л.
wine grower *n* виногра́дарь (*m*), виноде́л.
wine list *n*: **can I see the ~?** како́е у вас есть вино́?, что у вас есть из вин?
wine merchant *n* виноторго́вец.
wine taster *n* дегуста́тор вин.
wing *n* крыло́, *also Aer*, *Aut*, *Archit*; **birds on the ~** пти́цы в полёте; *Theat* **in the ~s** за кули́сами; *Sport* **he plays right ~** он пра́вый кра́йний; *fig*: **he's on the right ~ of the party** он принадлежи́т к пра́вому крылу́ па́ртии; **to take smb under one's ~** взять кого́-л под своё кры́лышко; **to clip smb's ~s** подреза́ть кому́-л кры́лья.
winged *adj* крыла́тый.
wing nut *n Tech* кры́льчатая га́йка, га́йка-бара́шек.
wingspan, wingspread *n* разма́х крыла́, *also Aer*.
wink *n*: **he gave me a ~** он подмигну́л мне; **he said with a ~** сказа́л он и подмигну́л; *fig*: **I'll tip you the ~ when he enters** я дам (тебе́) знак, когда́ он войдёт; **I didn't sleep a ~** я глаз не сомкну́л; **for him a ~ is as good as a nod** ему́ доста́точно намёка; *CQ* **he had forty ~s** он сосну́л/вздремну́л часо́к.
wink *vi* морга́ть, мига́ть ((под)моргну́ть, (под)мигну́ть); *fig* **to ~ at smth** закры|ва́ть глаза́ на что-л (-́ть), смотре́ть сквозь па́льцы на что-л (*usu impf*).
winner *n* победи́тель (*m*); пе́рвый призёр (*of all competitions except the following*); (*of Mus*, *Nobel Prize*, *Lenin Prize*, *etc.*) лауреа́т.
winning *adj*: **the ~ entrant** победи́тель; **the ~ team/horse** кома́нда-/ло́шадь-победи́тельница; **the ~ ticket** счастли́вый биле́т; **I drew the ~ ticket** я вы́играл в лотере́е; **a ~ smile** обая́тельная улы́бка.
winning post *n* фи́ниш, фи́нишный столб.
winnings *npl* вы́игрыш (*sing*), вы́игранные де́ньги.
winter *n* зима́; **in ~** зимо́й; *attr* зи́мний; **~ sports** зи́мние ви́ды спо́рта.
winter *vi* (*of birds*, *Arctic expedition*) зимова́ть (пере-); **they usually ~ in Nice** они́ обы́чно прово́дят зи́му в Ни́цце.
wintry *adj* зи́мний.
wipe *n*: **give the table/your mouth a ~** вы́три стол/рот.
wipe *vt* вы|тира́ть (-́тереть) *and other compounds*; **to ~ the dishes** вытира́ть посу́ду (*collect*); **to ~ one's brow/eyes/nose** вытира́ть лоб/глаза́/нос; **to ~ the floor** вы́мыть/протере́ть пол; **she ~d her hands on a towel** она́ вы́терла ру́ки полоте́нцем; **to ~ one's glasses/the windscreen** протира́ть очки́/ветрово́е стекло́; *fig*: **we'll ~ the slate clean** дава́й забу́дем про́шлое; **we ~d the floor with them** мы их про́сто стёрли в порошо́к
wipe away *vt*: **to ~ away tears/sweat** вытира́ть слёзы/пот
wipe off *vt*: **to ~ smth off a blackboard/the table** стира́ть что-л с доски́/со стола́ (стере́ть)
wipe out *vt*: **the earthquake ~d out whole villages** землетрясе́ние разру́шило це́лые дере́вни; **the epidemic ~d out half the population** в эпиде́мию поги́бла почти́ полови́на жи́телей; **our debt has been ~d out** наш долг нам прости́ли
wipe up *vt*: **she ~d up the spilt coffee** она́ вы́терла/подтёрла про́литый ко́фе.
wiper *n* (*cloth*) тря́пка; *Aut* «дво́рник».
wire *n* про́волока; (*usu insulated*) про́вод; *CQ* (*telegram*) телегра́мма; **telegraph/telephone ~s** телегра́фные/телефо́нные провода́; *Elec* **a live ~** про́вод под напряже́нием; *fig* **he's a live ~** он пря́мо жи́вчик, он тако́й живо́й; *attr* про́волочный.
wire *vt*: **to ~ a house** (*for electricity*) про|води́ть прово́дку в до́ме (-вести́); *CQ* **we ~d him to come** мы телеграфи́ровали, что́бы он прие́хал, мы вы́звали его́ телегра́ммой.
wire cutters *npl* куса́чки.
wireless *n* ра́дио (*indecl*); **on/over the ~** по ра́дио.
wireless operator *n* ради́ст, *f* -ка.
wire netting *n* про́волочная се́тка.
wire-tapping *n* подслу́шивание телефо́нных разгово́ров.
wiring *n* (электро)прово́дка.
wiry *adj*: **~ hair** жёсткие во́лосы; **a ~ person** жи́листый челове́к.
wisdom *n* му́дрость; **words of ~** му́дрые слова́; **I doubt the ~ of confiding in him** я сомнева́юсь, разу́мно ли бу́дет дове́риться ему́; *attr*: **~ tooth** зуб му́дрости.
wise[1] *adj* **1** му́дрый; у́мный; (*sensible*) разу́мный; **a ~ man/move** му́дрый/у́мный челове́к, разу́мный шаг; **it would be ~ to agree** разу́мнее бы́ло бы согласи́ться; **to grow ~r** поумне́ть; **nobody will be any the ~r** никто́ ничего́ не узна́ет; **he was ~ enough to...** (ему́) хвати́ло (*impers*) ума́ + *inf*
2 *CQ*: **he's a ~ guy** он у́мник; **I got ~/I put him ~ to their schemes** я раскры́л их махина́ции, я откры́л ему́ глаза́ на их проде́лки.
wise[2] *n*: **(in) no ~** нико́им о́бразом.
wisecrack *n* остро́та; **he's always making ~s** он ве́чно остри́т, ве́чно он со свои́ми шу́точками.
wish *n* **1** (*desire*) жела́ние; **in accordance with his ~es** по его́ жела́нию (*sing*); **they married against her father's ~** они́ пожени́лись про́тив во́ли её отца́; **he expressed the ~ that...** он вы́разил жела́ние, что́бы...; **it had long been her ~ to travel** она́ давно́ мечта́ла пое́хать куда́-нибудь
2: **to make a ~** загада́ть жела́ние
3 (*greetings*) пожела́ние; **give her my best/good ~es** переда́й ей мои́ наилу́чшие пожела́ния; **with best ~es for the New Year** (поздравля́ю) с Но́вым го́дом!

wish *vti vt* **1** *with inf* (*formal or emphatic*) желáть (по-); *more CQ* хотéть (за-); **the president ~es to see you** президéнт желáет вас ви́деть; **do you ~ the ambassador/her to be here?** вы желáете, чтóбы посóл присýтствовал?, ты хóчешь, чтóбы онá пришлá?

2 *with clause*: **(how) I ~ I could help you** éсли бы тóлько я мог вам помóчь; **I ~ I'd known about it** жаль, что я не знал об э́том; **I ~ to goodness that music would stop** гóсподи, хоть бы э́та мýзыка смóлкла!

3 *with noun*: **to ~ smb well/ill** желáть комý-л добрá/злá; **I ~ed him all the best/a good trip** я пожелáл емý всегó сáмого лýчшего/дóброго пути́; **to ~ smb a happy birthday** поздрав|ля́ть когó-л с днём рождéния (-́ить); **if he really ~es it** éсли он действи́тельно э́того хóчет; **he ~ed the job on me** он навязáл мне э́ту рабóту; **I wouldn't ~ my relatives on anyone** никомý не пожелáю таки́х рóдственников

vi желáть; **what more could one ~ for** чегó ещё мóжно желáть; **the weather was everything we could ~ for** погóда былá как на закáз.

wishful *adj*: **that's just ~ thinking on his part** он принимáет желáемое за действи́тельное.

wisp *n*: **a ~ of smoke/straw/hair** стрýйка ды́ма, пучóк солóмы, клок волóс.

wistful *adj* грýстный, задýмчивый.

wit[1] *n* **1** *often pl* (*intelligence*) ум (*sing*); **a battle of ~s** поеди́нок умóв; **he hadn't ~ enough/the ~ to realize this** у негó не хвати́ло (*impers*) умá поня́ть э́то; **he's out of his ~s** он с умá (*sing*) сошёл, *CQ* он спя́тил; **are you out of your ~s?** ты в своём умé?; **he has all his ~s about him** у негó есть головá на плечáх; **use your ~s** сам подýмай, подýмай-ка хорошéнько; **keep your ~s about you** не теря́й головы́, не теря́йся; **she was scared out of her ~s** онá испугáлась не на шýтку; **I'm at my ~s' end** я в пóлном недоумéнии

2 (*wittiness*) остроýмие; **he has a delightful ~** он так ми́ло остри́т; **he has a ready ~** он за слóвом в кармáн не полéзет.

wit[2] *vi*: **to ~** тó есть; а и́менно.

witch *n* вéдьма.

with *prep* **1** (*having*) с + *I*; **the man ~ a suitcase** мужчи́на с чемодáном; **a woman ~ grey hair** жéнщина с седы́ми волосáми; **a bottle ~ milk in it** буты́лка с молокóм; **a room ~ a bathroom** кóмната с вáнной; **a house ~ no garden** дом без сáда; **those ~ tickets** те, у когó есть билéты

2 (*together with*) с + *I*, у + *G*; **he was ~ me** он был со мнóй; **he took the book ~ him** он взял кни́гу с собóй; **he's ~ the headmaster** он у дирéктора (*in his room*); **we left the children ~ Mother** мы остáвили детéй с мáмой (*at our house*)/у мáмы (*at her house*); **leave the key ~ the porter** остáвь ключ у вахтёра; **I've no money ~ me** у меня́ нет с собóй дéнег; **he's been ~ the firm a long time** он давнó рабóтает в э́той фи́рме; **he was up ~ the sun** он встал на зарé; *CQ*: **I'm not ~ you** я тебя́ не пóнял; **I'm ~ you all the way** я во всём с вáми соглáсен; **I'm not ~ it today** я сегóдня не в фóрме; **I'll be right ~ you** я ми́гом/сейчáс

3 (*of instrument*) *I case*: **to write ~ a pencil** писáть карандашóм; **to cut ~ a knife** рéзать ножóм; **I saw it ~ my own eyes** я ви́дел э́то свои́ми сóбственными глазáми

4 (*of manner*): **~ difficulty/a smile** с трудóм, с улы́бкой; **~ all my heart** от всегó сéрдца, всем сéрдцем; **he stood ~ his head bowed** он стоя́л, опусти́в гóлову

5 (*with verbs*; *see also under verb entries*): **to fill ~ water** напóлнить водóй; **to speak ~ an American accent** говори́ть с американским акцéнтом; **he's in bed ~ flu** он лежи́т с гри́ппом; **to shiver ~ fear/cold** дрожáть от стрáха/от хóлода; **the decision rests ~ you** решéние за вáми

6 (*of condition*): **~ your permission** с вáшего разрешéния; **~ certain exceptions** с/за нéкоторыми исключéниями; **~ a good teacher that wouldn't happen** у хорóшего учи́теля такóго не случи́тся

7 *various*: **I came ~ the object of persuading you** я пришёл с однóй цéлью — уговори́ть вас; **~ these words he left the room** с э́тими словáми он вы́шел из кóмнаты; **as usual ~ them they were late** как обы́чно, они́ опоздáли; **it's a habit ~ me** у меня́ такáя привы́чка; **what do you want ~ him?** что ты от негó хóчешь?; **the trouble ~ him is you can't rely on him** бедá в том, что на негó нельзя́ положи́ться; **I can't do anything ~ him** я ничегó не могý с ним подéлать; **it's summer ~ us here** у нас здесь лéто.

withdraw *vti vt* убирáть (убрáть), снимáть (снять); **he withdrew his hand** он убрáл/óтнял рýку; **to ~ an application** снимáть свою́ кандидатýру; **to ~ money from the bank** брать дéньги из бáнка (взять); **to ~ smth from circulation/sale** изымáть что-л из обращéния (изъя́ть), снимáть что-л с продáжи; **to ~ an objection/one's support** снимáть возражéние, перестáть окáзывать поддéржку; **I ~ that remark** я берý свои́ словá (*pl*) обрáтно; *Mil* **to ~ troops from a country** вы|води́ть войскá из страны́ (-вести)

vi удал|я́ться (-и́ться); **after supper the ladies usually ~** пóсле ýжина дáмы обы́чно удаля́ются; **to ~ from society** удали́ться от óбщества; **to ~ from a competition** вы́быть из соревновáния (*usu pf*).

withdrawn *adj* (*of person*) зáмкнутый.

wither *vti vt*: **the drought has ~ed the crops** зáсуха погуби́ла урожáй; *fig* **he ~ed me with a glance** он посмотрéл на меня́ испепеля́ющим взгля́дом *vi* вя́нуть (*impf*), завя́ть, увя́ть (*pfs*); *fig* **the old traditions are ~ing away** ста́рые тради́ции исчеза́ют.

withered *adj*: **~ flowers** увя́дшие цветы́; **a ~ complexion** морщи́нистое лицо́; **a ~ arm** высохшая рука́.

withhold *vt*: **they withheld the information** они́ скры́ли э́ти све́дения (*pl*)/э́ту информа́цию; **he withheld his consent** он не дал согла́сия; **he is ~ing my pay/10% from my pay** он заде́рживает вы́плату мое́й зарпла́ты, он уде́рживает из мое́й зарпла́ты де́сять проце́нтов.

within *adv* внутри́; **from ~** изнутри́.

within *prep* **1** (*inside*) в + *P*; **~ the family circle** в семе́йном кругу́; **I'm fed up living ~ these four walls** мне надое́ло сиде́ть в четырёх стена́х; **~ the USSR** на террито́рии СССР

2 (*of distance, time*): **~ 20 km of the capital/the time allowed** в преде́лах двадцати́ киломе́тров от столи́цы/дозво́ленного вре́мени; **~ earshot/reach** в преде́лах слы́шимости/досяга́емости; **she'll be here ~ an hour** она́ бу́дет здесь че́рез час; **punctually to ~ a second** с то́чностью до секу́нды; **~ a year of their marriage he died** ме́ньше чем че́рез год по́сле их сва́дьбы он у́мер; **to live ~ one's income** жить по сре́дствам, по одёжке протя́гивать но́жки; **to keep ~ the law** не выходи́ть за ра́мки зако́на.

without *prep* **1** без + *G*; **~ money/a hat/doubt** без де́нег, без шля́пы, без сомне́ния; **to do ~ food** обходи́ться без пи́щи; **he's gone for three days ~ food** он три дня ничего́ не ел; **~ delay/fail** неме́дленно, непреме́нно

2 + *gerund* не; **he walked past ~ seeing me** он прошёл ми́мо, не ви́дя/, не заме́тив меня́; **he left ~ having seen her/~ saying a word** он ушёл, не повида́в её/, не сказа́в ни сло́ва; **never a minute passes ~ my thinking of you** и мину́ты не прохо́дит, что́бы я о тебе́ не ду́мал; **she couldn't have gone out ~ my noticing** она́ не смогла́ бы вы́йти незаме́ченной; **it goes ~ saying that...** само́ собо́й разуме́ется...

withstand *vt* вы|де́рживать (-держать), устоя́ть (*pf*).

witness *n* **1** (*person*) очеви́дец, свиде́тель (*m*), *also Law*; **there were no ~es to the accident** не́ было свиде́телей/очеви́дцев ава́рии; **~ for the prosecution** свиде́тель обвине́ния; **to call a ~/smb as a ~** вызыва́ть свиде́теля/кого́-л в ка́честве свиде́теля; **as God is my ~** ви́дит бог

2 (*testimony*) свиде́тельство; **to bear ~ to smth** свиде́тельствовать о чём-л; **these figures bear ~ to our achievements** э́ти ци́фры — свиде́тельство на́ших достиже́ний; *Law* **in ~ of which/whereof** в удостовере́ние чего́.

witness *vt* **1: the crash was ~ed by four people** четы́ре челове́ка бы́ли свиде́телями/очеви́дцами ава́рии

2 *Law*: **to ~ a document/signature** удостовер|я́ть докуме́нт/по́дпись (-ить)

3: ~ what happened last week возьми́те к приме́ру то, что случи́лось на про́шлой неде́ле.

witticism *n* остро́та.

wittingly *adv* созна́тельно.

witty *adj* остроу́мный.

wizened *adj*: **a ~ face** морщи́нистое лицо́; **a ~ apple/old man** смо́рщенное я́блоко, иссо́хший стари́к.

wobble *vi*: **this stool/the wheel ~s** э́та табуре́тка шата́ется, колесо́ вихля́ет (*usu impfs*); **her cheeks ~** у неё щёки трясу́тся.

wobbly *adj* ша́ткий; **~ furniture** ша́ткая ме́бель; **this chair has ~ legs** э́тот стул шата́ется; **I'm still a bit ~ after my illness** меня́ всё ещё пока́чивает по́сле боле́зни.

woe *n now usu only CQ*: **he told us all his ~s** он пове́дал нам о всех свои́х го́рестях; **~ betide anyone who believes her** го́ре тому́, кто пове́рит ей; **a tale of ~** печа́льная исто́рия.

woebegone *adj*: **the little girl looked so ~** у де́вочки был тако́й удручённый вид.

woefully *adv*: **he is ~ ignorant** он удруча́юще неве́жествен.

wolf *n* волк; **he's a lone ~** он одино́кий волк; **you've cried ~ too often** ты сли́шком ча́сто поднима́л ло́жную трево́гу.

wolf *vt CQ*: **he ~ed his supper and dashed off to the cinema** он на́спех проглоти́л у́жин и убежа́л в кино́.

woman *n* же́нщина, *pejor or low CQ* ба́ба; **a young/an old ~** молода́я же́нщина, стару́ха; **a ~'s magazine** журна́л для же́нщин; **women's liberation/*CQ* lib** фемини́стское движе́ние за освобожде́ние же́нщин; *fig* **he's an old ~** он как ста́рая ба́ба; *attr*: **a ~ doctor** же́нщина-врач; **her women friends** её подру́ги.

womanizer *n CQ* ба́бник.

womanly *adj* же́нский; (*feminine*) же́нственный.

womb *n Anat* ма́тка.

womenfolk *n collect*: **our ~** на́ши же́нщины.

wonder *n* **1** (*feeling*): **we were filled with ~ as we watched the sunset** красота́ зака́та изуми́ла нас

2 (*miracle*) чу́до; **the ~s of modern science** чудеса́ совреме́нной нау́ки; **the new drug works ~s** э́то но́вое лека́рство твори́т чудеса́; **he agreed, for a ~** каки́м-то чу́дом он согласи́лся; **~s never cease!** чудеса́м нет конца́!; **it was a nine-days' ~** э́то была́ кратковре́менная сенса́ция; **she was furious, and no ~** она́ пришла́ в я́рость, и не удиви́тельно; **the ~ of it is she understood him** что удиви́тельно — она́ поняла́ его́; **it's a ~ to me why she helps him** меня́ удивля́ет, почему́ она́ помога́ет ему́.

wonder *vti*: **I ~ who she is** интере́сно, кто она́; **that made me ~** э́то заста́вило меня́ призаду́маться; **sometimes I ~ where he gets all the money from** иногда́ я ду́маю, откуда у него такие деньги; **I ~ whether you can help me** не можете ли вы мне помочь?; **I don't ~ that she was angry** я не удивляюсь, что она рассердилась; **I shouldn't ~ if they got divorced** меня не удивит, если они разведутся.

wonderful *adj* чудесный, удивительный.

wont *n*: **as was his ~** по своему обыкновению; **he got up later than was his ~** он встал позже обычного.

wonted *adj*: **he rose at his ~ hour** он встал как обычно.

woo *vt* ухаживать за + *I* (*impf*).

wood *n* **1** (*material*) дерево; (*timber or material*) древесина; (*firewood*) дрова (*pl*); **a box made of ~** ящик из дерева; **there's plenty of ~ in the timberyard** на складе много леса/лесоматериала; **dead ~** сухостой; **to chop ~** колоть дрова; *fig CQ*: **he's ~ from the neck up** он дуб; **touch ~, (*US*) knock on ~** подержись за дерево, постучи по дереву, *equiv* плюнь через левое плечо; *attr*: **~ alcohol** древесный спирт

2 (*forest*) лес; **in the ~(s)** в лесу; *fig*: **we're not out of the ~ yet** нас ещё ожидают трудности; **he can't see the ~ for the trees** он за деревьями леса не видит.

woodcock *n* лесной кулик, вальдшнеп.

woodcut *n* гравюра на дереве.

woodcutter *n* лесоруб.

wooded *adj*: **a ~ area/park** лесистая местность, лесопарк.

wooden *adj* деревянный, *also fig*.

woodpecker *n* дятел.

woodpigeon *n* лесной голубь.

woodpile *n* (*in timberyard*) штабель (*m*) дров; (*beside house*) поленница; *fig* **he's the nigger in the ~** от него все напасти.

wood shavings *npl* стружка (*collect*), стружки.

woodshed *n* дровяной сарай.

woodwind *n Mus collect* (**the ~**) деревянные духовые инструменты (*pl*).

woodwork *n* (*carpentry*) столярная работа; **the ~ in our house all needs replacing** в нашем доме все деревянные части нуждаются в замене; **there's some beautiful ~ in the ballroom** в бальном зале красивые резные (деревянные) панели.

woodworm *n Zool* личинка древоточца; *CQ* **this table has ~** этот стол изъеден жуком(-древоточцем).

wool *n* шерсть; **a ball of ~** клубок шерсти; *attr* шерстяной; **the ~ trade** торговля шерстью.

wool-gathering *n and adj*: **he is ~ as usual** он, как всегда, витает в облаках.

woollen, (*US*) woolen *adj* шерстяной.

woolly, (*US*) wooly *adj* шерстяной; **~ jumpers/undergarments** (*CQ* **wool(l)ies**) шерстяные джемперы, шерстяное бельё; **a ~ poodle** пушистый пудель; *fig* **there's a lot of ~ thinking in his thesis** в его диссертации многое не продумано.

word *n* **1** слово; **in a ~** одним словом; **in other ~s** дру[illegible]ми словами; **to translate/repeat ~ for ~** переводить дословно (*adv*), повторять слово в слово *or* слово за словом; **he never said a ~ all evening** он за весь вечер ни слова не сказал; **not a ~ to anyone** никому ни слова; **by ~ of mouth** устно; **can I have a ~ with you?** можно вас на одну минуточку?; **~s fail me** у меня не хватает слов; **I won't hear a ~ against him** я не хочу слышать о нём ничего дурного; **a play on ~s** игра слов; **a man of few ~s** немногословный человек; **he hasn't a good ~ to say for her** он о ней слова доброго не скажет; **to eat one's ~s** взять свои слова обратно; **I didn't say so in so many ~s** я этого так прямо не сказал; **you took the ~s out of my mouth** вы перехватили мою мысль; **it's the last ~ in technology** это последнее слово техники

2 (*news, message*): **what ~ of his sister?** есть/какие новости о его сестре?; **we've had no ~ from her for ages** от неё давно нет никакой весточки; **~ came that he had arrived** нам сообщили о его приезде; **he left ~ that I was to phone him** он попросил передать, чтобы я позвонил ему

3 (*promise, etc.*) слово, обещание; **he's a man of his ~** он человек слова; **he was as good as his ~** он сдержал слово; **I give you my ~ (of honour) that...** даю вам слово, что...; **it's the truth, ~ of honour** это правда, честное слово; **to break one's ~** нарушать слово; **take my ~ for it** поверьте моему слову; **she took him at his ~** она поверила ему на слово; **it's my ~ against his** это он так говорит; *CQ* **my ~!** ну и ну!

4 (*command*) команда, приказание; **you only have to give the ~** вы только отдайте приказание.

word *vt* формулировать (с-); **a carefully ~ed answer** тщательно составленный ответ.

word-perfect *adj*: **all the actors were ~** все актёры знали текст своих ролей назубок (*adv*).

wordy *adj* многословный.

work *n* **1** работа; дело; (*labour*) труд; **he was sitting at his ~** он сидел за работой; **he is at ~ on his second novel** он работает над своим вторым романом; **we've done a good day's ~** мы неплохо поработали сегодня; **he set us to ~ (peeling potatoes) immediately** он тотчас (же) засадил нас за работу/чистить картошку (*collect*); **let's set/get to ~** давайте возьмёмся за дело; **it was the ~ of a minute to open the window** открыть окно было минутным делом; **it's all in the day's ~** дело обычное/привычное; **it will need a lot of ~ to repair that** отремонтировать это—нелёгкое дело; **I must do some ~ in the garden** мне надо кое-что сделать в саду; **manual ~** ручной труд; **this machine does the ~ of ten men** эта машина заменяет десятерых; **~ has begun on the new building** началось строительство нового здания; **you'll have your ~ cut out convincing him of that** вам придётся попотеть, чтобы убедить его в этом; *fig*:

I know whose ~ this is я зна́ю, чьих э́то рук де́ло; **there's been some dirty ~ here** тут что́-то нечи́сто

2 (*as employment*) рабо́та; **place of ~** ме́сто рабо́ты; **he is at ~** он на рабо́те; **he's off ~ today** он сего́дня не вы́шел на рабо́ту, его́ сего́дня нет на рабо́те; **he is out of ~** он безрабо́тный; **this has put a lot of people out of ~** из-за э́того мно́гие лиши́лись рабо́ты

3 (*product*) произведе́ние; **a ~ of art** произведе́ние иску́сства; **the complete ~s of Gogol** по́лное собра́ние сочине́ний Го́голя; **in Gogol's ~(s)** в тво́рчестве/в произведе́ниях Го́голя; **published** (*academic*) **~s** печа́тные труды́; **that painting is a ~ of genius** э́та карти́на отме́чена печа́тью ге́ния; **good ~s** благотвори́тельность (*sing*).

work *vti vt* **1: he ~s his staff too hard** он заставля́ет свои́х слу́жащих сли́шком мно́го рабо́тать; **she is ~ing herself to death** она́ вконе́ц изма́тывается на рабо́те; **he ~ed his passage to Australia** он отрабо́тал матро́сом свой прое́зд в Австра́лию; **he ~ed his way through University** он получи́л университе́тское образова́ние на де́ньги, кото́рые зараба́тывал сам; **he has ~ed his way up** он сам всего́ доби́лся в жи́зни; **the machines are ~ed by electricity** э́ти маши́ны приво́дятся в де́йствие электри́чеством; **can you ~ this gadget?** ты уме́ешь обраща́ться с э́тим прибо́ром?; **to ~ the soil** обраб|а́тывать зе́млю (-о́тать); **to ~ a mine/quarry** разраба́тывать рудни́к/карье́р

2 (*effect*): **to ~ miracles/wonders** твори́ть чудеса́ (со-); **I'll ~ it so that I get Friday off** я устро́ю так, что в пя́тницу у меня́ бу́дет отгу́л

3 (*manoeuvre*): **to ~ a boulder into a new position** перета́|скивать валу́н (-щи́ть); **he ~ed his hands free** он вы́свободил ру́ки; **he ~ed his way up the cliff** он взобра́лся на скалу́

4 (*shape, etc.*): **to ~ clay/dough** меси́ть гли́ну/те́сто (*impf*); *Sew* **she ~ed her initials in red** она́ вы́шила свои́ инициа́лы кра́сными ни́тками

vi **1** рабо́тать (*impf*); **he's not ~ing just now** он сейча́с не рабо́тает (*at the moment or is unemployed*); **she ~s part-time** она́ рабо́тает непо́лный рабо́чий день; **he ~s as a teacher/for a firm/in a factory** он рабо́тает учи́телем/в фи́рме/на заво́де; **he's ~ing under professor X** он рабо́тает под руково́дством профе́ссора N; **to ~ with one's hands** занима́ться физи́ческой рабо́той

2 (*of machines, etc.*) рабо́тать; **the lift isn't ~ing** лифт не рабо́тает; **the radio ~s off batteries** радиоприёмник рабо́тает на батаре́йках

3 (*have effect*): **the plan won't ~** э́тот план не годи́тся; **the medicine ~ed quickly** лека́рство бы́стро поде́йствовало; **that could ~ both ways** э́то мо́жет помо́чь, а мо́жет и навреди́ть

4 (*move*): **the wheel/his tie had ~ed loose** колесо́ отвали́лось, у него́ развяза́лся га́лстук

work off *vt*: **to ~ off a debt** отраб|а́тывать долг (-о́тать); **I'm trying to ~ off some fat** я пыта́юсь согна́ть вес; **I went for a walk to ~ off steam** я вы́шел погуля́ть, что́бы немно́го успоко́иться

work on *vi*: **to ~ on a thesis** рабо́тать над диссерта́цией; **they're still ~ing on the phone** (*repairing it*) они́ всё ещё чи́нят телефо́н; **I ~ on the principle that...** я рабо́таю по при́нципу, (что)...

work out *vti vt* **1: to ~ out a theory** разраб|а́тывать тео́рию (-о́тать); **to ~ out an agreement/plan** состав|ля́ть догово́р (-́ить), вы|раба́тывать план (-́работать); **we must ~ out what we want to say** нам на́до обду́мать, что нам сказа́ть; **to ~ out a problem** реша́ть пробле́му; **to ~ out the cost of smth/the position of a ship** вы|числя́ть сто́имость чего́-л/местонахожде́ние корабля́ (-́числить): **let her ~ things out for herself** пусть сама́ во всём разберётся; **I tried to ~ out what she meant** я пыта́лся поня́ть, что она́ име́ла в виду́

2: the mine has been ~ed out э́тот рудни́к истощён

vi: **the cost of a new door will ~ out at £100** но́вая дверь обойдётся в сто фу́нтов; **your share ~s out at £5** с тебя́ пять фу́нтов; **I don't know how it/their marriage will ~ out** не зна́ю, что из э́того полу́чится/, как сло́жится их семе́йная жизнь

work round *vti vt*: **to ~ the conversation round to...** под|води́ть разгово́р к + *D* (-вести́)

vi: **the wind has ~ed round to the east** ве́тер перемени́лся и стал дуть с восто́ка; **I was ~ing round to asking him about it** я всё собира́лся спроси́ть его́ об э́том

work up *vti vt*: **he ~ed up the material into an article** он обрабо́тал э́тот материа́л и на осно́ве э́того написа́л статью́; **he has ~ed the business up from nothing** он на́чал своё де́ло на пусто́м ме́сте; **I couldn't ~ up any enthusiasm for it** э́то не вы́звало у меня́ никако́го энтузиа́зма; **don't get so ~ed up** *CQ* не лезь в буты́лку

vi: **he ~ed up to the climax of his speech** он постепе́нно подходи́л к кульминацио́нному пу́нкту ре́чи.

workable *adj*: **a ~ scheme** осуществи́мый/реа́льный прое́кт *or* план.

work basket *n* корзи́нка для рукоде́лия.

work bench *n* верста́к.

workday *n* рабо́чий день; *attr*: **my ~ clothes** моя́ повседне́вная оде́жда.

worker *n* рабо́тник; (*manual*) рабо́чий; **a research ~** нау́чный рабо́тник; **he's a hard ~** он работя́га; **he's a fast ~** он вре́мени да́ром не теря́ет.

working *adj* рабо́чий; **a ~ day** рабо́чий день; **in ~ hours** в рабо́чее вре́мя; **a ~ drawing** рабо́чий чертёж; **in (good) ~ order**

в рабо́чем состоя́нии; **a ~ hypothesis** рабо́чая гипо́теза; **~ mothers** рабо́тающие ма́тери; **good ~ conditions** хоро́шие усло́вия труда́; (*in Parliament*) **a ~ majority** доста́точное большинство́ мест в парла́менте; *Econ*: **~ capital** оборо́тный капита́л; **~ costs** эксплуатацио́нные расхо́ды.

working class *n* (**the ~**) рабо́чий класс; *attr*: **~ families** се́мьи рабо́чих.

workmanlike *adj*: **that's a ~ job** э́то мастерски́ сде́ланная рабо́та.

workmanship *n*: **fine ~** то́нкая рабо́та.

works *npl* **1**: **the ~ of a watch** механи́зм (*sing*) часо́в

2 (*factory*) заво́д, (*usu in light industry*) фа́брика (*sings*).

workshop *n* (*in factory*: *shop floor*) цех; (*for repairing*, *tools*, *etc.*) мастерска́я, *also Art*.

world *n* **1** (**the ~**) мир, свет; **a map of the ~** ка́рта ми́ра; **from all parts of the ~** со всего́ све́та; **all over the ~** по всему́ ми́ру/све́ту; **since the ~ began** с сотворе́ния ми́ра; **to go round the ~** объе́хать весь свет; **he's seen the ~** он повида́л свет; **in this and in the next ~** на э́том и на том све́те; **he's not long for this ~** он не жиле́ц на э́том све́те

2 (*realm*) мир; **the ~ of art/music** мир иску́сства/му́зыки; **the scientific/literary ~** нау́чный мир, литерату́рные круги́ (*pl*); **in the animal ~** в ми́ре живо́тных

3 (*society*): **all the ~ (and his wife) knows that...** всем и ка́ждому изве́стно, что...; **he's a man of the ~** он зна́ет свет; **he's come down/up in the ~** он опусти́лся, он преуспе́л в жи́зни; **I don't belong to her ~** я не принадлежу́ к её кру́гу

4 *phrases*: **it's a small ~** мир те́сен; **you've got to take the ~ as you find it** такова́ жизнь; **that's the way of the ~** так уж повело́сь на све́те; **he lives in a ~ of his own** он живёт в своём ми́ре; **nothing in the ~ could make me do that** я э́того не сде́лал бы ни за что на све́те; **she is all the ~ to him** она́ для него́—всё; **I think the ~ of her** я о́чень высо́кого мне́ния о ней; **who in the ~ is he?** кто бы э́то мог быть?; **she walked past him for all the ~ as if she hadn't noticed him** она́ прошла́ ми́мо, как бу́дто его́ не замеча́я; **it did him a ~ of good** э́то принесло́ ему́ огро́мную по́льзу; *CQ*: **I'm the ~'s worst cook** нет на све́те ху́дшего по́вара, чем я; **I felt on top of the ~** я был на верху́ блаже́нства; **how's the ~ with you?** как ва́ши дела́?; **their flat is out of this ~** у них кварти́ра—не́что бесподо́бное

5 *attr*: **a ~ champion** чемпио́н ми́ра; **~ history** всеми́рная исто́рия; **the First W. War** пе́рвая мирова́я война́; **the W. Bank** Междунаро́дный банк реконстру́кции и разви́тия; **a ~ power** мирова́я держа́ва.

worldly *adj* мирско́й, земно́й; (*of the fashionable world*) све́тский; **~ pleasures** мирски́е/земны́е ра́дости; **all my ~ goods/possessions** всё моё иму́щество; **~ wisdom** жите́йская му́дрость; **he's very ~** он све́тский челове́к.

world-wide *adj* всеми́рный.

worm *n* червь (*m*), червя́к; **earth ~** земляно́й червь; **my dog has ~s** у моей соба́ки глисты́; *fig*: **he's a ~** он тако́е ничто́жество; **the ~ will turn** вся́кому терпе́нию есть преде́л.

worm *vt*: **he ~ed his way through the undergrowth** он пропо́лз сквозь за́росли; *fig*: **to ~ one's way into smb's confidence** вкра́сться к кому́-л в дове́рие (*usu pf*); **she ~ed the secret out of him** она́ вы́ведала у него́ та́йну.

worm-eaten *adj* изъе́денный/исто́ченный червя́ми.

worn, *also* **worn-out** *adj*: **a ~ coat** поно́шенное пальто́; *fig* **she looked ~** у неё был изможденный вид.

worried *adj* трево́жный, беспоко́йный; **you look ~** у вас встрево́женный вид; **to be ~ about smth** беспоко́иться о чём-л.

worrier *n*: **he's a terrible ~** он тако́й беспоко́йный.

worry *n* (*care*) забо́та; **financial/family worries** де́нежные/семе́йные забо́ты; **her son is a great ~ to her** сын доставля́ет ей большо́е беспоко́йство; **that's the least of my worries** об э́том я ме́ньше всего́ беспоко́юсь.

worry *vti vt* **1** беспоко́ить, волнова́ть (*only in impfs*); **to be worried about** беспоко́иться/волнова́ться о + *P*; **what is ~ing you?** что вас беспоко́ит?; **I am worried about his health** я беспоко́юсь о его́ здоро́вье; **I am worried about him—he hasn't done enough work for his exam/he should have been home two hours ago** я беспоко́юсь, что он пло́хо подгото́вился к экза́мену, я о́чень беспоко́юсь/волну́юсь—он до́лжен был быть до́ма два часа́ тому́ наза́д; **I'm worried about money/his future** меня́ беспоко́ят на́ши де́нежные дела́, меня́ беспоко́ит/забо́тит его́ бу́дущее; **to ~ smb with requests** беспоко́ить кого́-л про́сьбами; **he'll ~ himself to death** забо́ты (*pl*) сведу́т его́ в моги́лу

2: **the dog was ~ing a bone/a sheep** соба́ка гры́зла кость/покусала овцу́

vi: **I ~ about him** я беспоко́юсь о нём.

worrying *adj* беспоко́йный, трево́жный; **the ~ thing is...** что меня́ беспоко́ит,/трево́жит, так э́то...

worse *n* ху́дшее; **a change for the ~** переме́на к ху́дшему; **there's ~ to come** э́то ещё не са́мое ху́дшее; **things have gone from bad to ~** дела́ пошли́ ещё ху́же.

worse *adj* **1** *attr* ху́дший; **the ~ book of the two** ху́дшая из э́тих двух книг; **I must leave, ~ luck** о́чень жаль, но я до́лжен идти́; **we couldn't have had ~ weather** пого́да была́—ху́же не приду́маешь/ху́же не́куда

2 *predic* ху́же; **the patient is ~ today** больно́му сего́дня ху́же; **the situation is getting ~** положе́ние ухудша́ется; **and what's ~** и что ху́же; **it might have been ~** могло́ (бы) быть и ху́же; **so much the ~ (for you)** тем ху́же (для тебя́); **and to make matters ~** и в довершéние всех бед, и что сáмое ху́дшее; **he was the ~ for drink** он был я́вно пьян; **his suit was very much the ~ for wear** егó костю́м поизноси́лся; **he was none the ~ for these experiences** э́ти переживáния никáк не отрази́лись на нём.

worse *adv* хуже; **he's behaving even ~ than usual** он ведёт себя́ ху́же, чем обы́чно; **that may be, but I don't think any the ~ of him for that** пусть так, но я не ду́маю о нём ху́же из-за э́того; **it's raining ~ than ever** дождь льёт всё сильнée; **he could do ~ than marry her** жени́ться на ней — ещё не сáмое ху́дшее; **we're ~ off than we were** мы стáли (по)беднée.

worsen *vti* ухудш|áть(ся) (-ить(ся)).

worship *n Rel* богослужéние; **place of ~** храм, цéрковь; **forms of ~** религио́зные обря́ды.

worship *vt* поклоня́ться; **to ~ God/gods** моли́ться бо́гу, поклоня́ться богáм; *fig* **he ~s his father/the ground she walks on** он боготвори́т отцá/зéмлю, по котóрой онá хóдит.

worst *n* сáмое ху́дшее/плохóе; **if the ~ comes to the ~** в сáмом ху́дшем слу́чае; **we're past the ~** сáмое ху́дшее ужé позади́; **the ~ of it is that...** что ху́же всегó..., сáмое ху́дшее — то, что...; **at (the) ~** на худóй конéц; **when the storm was at its ~** в сáмый разгáр бу́ри; *Sport*, *Mil* **we got the ~ of it** мы потерпéли поражéние.

worst *adj* сáмый ху́дший, наиху́дший; **in the ~ possible conditions** в наиху́дших услóвиях; **his ~ fault** егó сáмый ху́дший недостáток; **it's the ~ book I've ever read** ху́дшей кни́ги я не читáл; **he came at the ~ possible time** он пришёл в сáмое неподходя́щее врéмя; **the ~ possible choice** сáмый неудáчный вы́бор; **his ~ enemy couldn't say he's not honest** егó злéйший враг не скáжет, что он непоря́дочный человéк.

worth *n*: **I bought £50's ~ of books** я купи́л книг на пятьдеся́т фу́нтов; **to know smb's true ~** знать кому́-л и́стинную цéну

worth *adj*: **the house is ~ about £10,000** дом стóит óколо десяти́ ты́сяч фу́нтов; **that table is not ~ much** за э́тот стол мáло даду́т; **your fur coat is well ~ the money** твоя́ шу́ба стóит э́тих дéнег; **it's a film ~ seeing** э́тот фильм стóит посмотрéть; **it's not ~ thinking about** не стóит об э́том ду́мать; **he must be ~ a lot of money** он, должнó быть, óчень богáт; **I'll make it ~ your while** вы не пожалéете; **I ran for all I was ~** я бежáл изо всех си́л; **that's my opinion, for what it's ~** э́то моё ли́чное мнéние, нрáвится онó вам и́ли нет; **it's more than my life's ~ to tell you** мне ху́до придётся, éсли я вам э́то скажу́; **he's ~ his weight in gold** емý цены́ нет.

worthless *adj*: **this painting is ~** э́та карти́на ничегó не стóит/не имéет никакóй цéнности; **a ~ book** пустáя кни́га.

worthwhile *adj*: **a ~ film/person** интерéсный фильм, достóйный человéк; **a ~ cause** стóящее дéло.

worthy *adj* достóйный; **a ~ opponent** достóйный проти́вник; **a husband ~ of her** муж, достóйный её; **that sort of behaviour is not ~ of you** такóе поведéние недостóйно вас; **any artist ~ of the name** кáждый настоя́щий худóжник.

would *v modal aux* (*see* **will**[1]) [**NB** *CQ* "*I'd, you'd, he'd,*" *etc. for* "*I/you/he etc. would*"] **1** (*conditional*): **if he knew, he ~ be glad** éсли бы он знал, он был бы рад; **if you had helped her, she ~ have done it** éсли бы ты помóг ей, онá бы э́то сдéлала; **if he were here he ~ tell you himself** éсли бы он был здесь, он бы сам тебé э́то сказáл; **if you were to leave tomorrow, you'd get there by Tuesday** éсли бы ты уезжáл зáвтра, ты был бы там ко втóрнику

2 (*in indirect speech*): **he said he ~ leave** он сказáл, что уйдёт; **she told me she'd be there** онá мне сказáла, что бу́дет там; **I thought they'd like it** я ду́мал, э́то им понрáвится; **I wonder whether he ~ object** интерéсно, стáнет ли он возражáть

3 (*in requests*): **~ you come in please?** входи́те, пожáлуйста; **~ you close the door?** закрóйте, пожáлуйста, дверь

4 (*expressing willingness*): **I ~ rather not meet her** мне бы не хотéлось с ней встречáться; **I asked him to play but he ~n't** я проси́л егó сыгрáть на пиани́но, но он не захотéл игрáть; **~ you like me to introduce you to him?** хоти́те, я вас емý представлю?; **~ you like a cup of coffee?** не хоти́те ли чáшку кóфе?; **~ you believe it, he was crying** вы не повéрите, но он плáкал; **try as she ~** как бы онá ни старáлась; **what ~ you have me do?** что, по-вáшему, я дóлжен дéлать?

5 (*expressing conjecture*): **she ~ be about forty** ей должнó быть лет сóрок; **it ~ be about six when she got here** онá пришлá, должнó быть, часóв óколо шести́; **you ~n't know her** вряд ли вы знáете её

6 (*expressing habit*): **he ~ visit her every Sunday** он, бывáло, заходи́л к ней кáждое воскресéнье

7 (*when emphasized*): **I told you you shouldn't, but you ~ do it** я говори́л тебé, что не нáдо э́то дéлать, а ты не послу́шал; **it ~ have to rain today of all days** нáдо же и́менно сегóдня быть дождю́; **she ~ be the one to answer the phone** и́менно ей нáдо бы́ло снять тру́бку; **that's just what he ~ say** э́то-то он и дóлжен был сказáть; **the window ~ not open** окнó никáк не открывáлось

8 (*in exclamations*): **~ that it were not so!** éсли бы э́то бы́ло не так!; **(I) ~ to God I'd been there!** éсли бы я тóлько там был!

would-be *adj*: **he's a ~ actor** он хо́чет стать актёром.

wound *n* ра́на; **a bullet/an open ~** пулева́я/откры́тая ра́на.

wound *vt* ра́нить (*impf and pf*); **to ~ smb in the arm with a knife** ра́нить кого́-л ножо́м в ру́ку; **he was ~ed in the war** он был ра́нен/его́ ра́нило (*impers*) на войне́; *fig* **his words ~ed her/her feelings** его́ слова́ бо́льно ра́нили её/её чу́вства.

wounded *adj* ра́неный; *as n* (**the ~**) ра́неные; *fig* **~ feelings** оскорблённые чу́вства.

wounding *adj fig* оби́дный, (*stronger*) оскорби́тельный.

wrangle *n* (*argument*) спор; **they're involved in a legal ~** у них тя́жба.

wrangle *vi*: **they're wrangling over who's to have the children** они́ спо́рят, у кого́ оста́нутся/, с кем бу́дут жить де́ти.

wrap *n* (*shawl or rug*) наки́дка; (*US*: *coat*) пальто́ (*indecl*).

wrap *vti vt* **1** завёртывать, завора́чивать (*pf for both* заверну́ть); уку́т|ывать (-ать); **she ~ped herself in the rug** она́ уку́талась в плед; **she ~ped the child in a blanket/the shawl round her shoulders** она́ заверну́ла *or* уку́тала ребёнка в одея́ло, она́ наки́нула на пле́чи шаль; **I ~ped the vase in cotton wool** я оберну́л ва́зу ва́той; (*in shop*) **do you want it ~ped?** вам заверну́ть?; **I ~ped a handkerchief round my finger** я об|мота́л па́лец носовы́м платко́м (*impf* -ма́тывать); **to ~ a scarf round one's neck** обмота́ть ше́ю ша́рфом; **the vine had ~ped itself round the post** лоза́ обвила́сь вокру́г столба́

2 *fig uses*: **an affair ~ped in mystery** де́ло, оку́танное та́йной; **hills ~ped in mist** го́ры, оку́танные тума́ном; **he's ~ped up in his work** он поглощён рабо́той; **he's ~ped up in himself/in his thoughts** он погружён в себя́/в свои́ мы́сли; **they're ~ped up in each other** они́ по́ уши влюблены́ друг в дру́га

vi: **~ up well when you go out** оде́нься потепле́е, когда́ пойдёшь на у́лицу.

wrapper *n* (*of book*) бума́га, в кото́рую обёрнута кни́га; **postal ~** бандеро́ль.

wrapping paper *n* обёрточная бума́га.

wreak *vt*: **to ~ revenge on smb** мстить кому́-л (ото́-); **the hurricane ~ed destruction** урага́н нанёс большо́й ущёрб; **the hail ~ed havoc with the harvest** гра́дом уничто́жило (*impers*) весь урожа́й.

wreath *n* вено́к (*also of funeral wreath*).

wreathe *vt*: **ivy had ~d itself round the tree trunk** плющ обви́лся вокру́г ствола́ де́рева; **a summit ~d in mist** верши́на горы́ оку́тана тума́ном; **faces ~d in smiles** ли́ца, расплы́вшиеся в улы́бке (*sing*).

wreck *n* **1** (*event*) *Naut* (кораблe)круше́ние; *fig* **the ~ of one's hopes** круше́ние наде́жд

2 (*remains*) обло́мки (*pl*); **the ~ of a ship/plane/car** обло́мки корабля́/самолёта/маши́ны; **his car was a ~ after the accident** его́ маши́на была́ вся искорёжена по́сле ава́рии; *fig*: **after the party his room was a ~** по́сле госте́й в его́ ко́мнате был по́лный разгро́м; **he's a nervous ~** у него́ не́рвы совсе́м сда́ли.

wreck *vt*: **the train/ship was ~ed** по́езд/кора́бль потерпе́л круше́ние; **I've ~ed my car** моя́ маши́на разби́лась; **the hooligans ~ed the telephone kiosk** хулига́ны разлома́ли телефо́нную бу́дку; **the bomb ~ed the building** взры́вом бо́мбы разру́шило (*impers*) зда́ние; *fig* **this ~ed my plans/my chances** э́то разру́шило мои́ пла́ны, э́то свело́ мои́ ша́нсы к нулю́.

wreckage *n* обло́мки (*pl*) круше́ния.

wren *n Orn* крапи́вник.

wrench *n* **1** (*act*): **he gave the handle a ~** он дёрнул за ру́чку; *fig* **leaving her was a ~** бы́ло о́чень тяжело́ с ней расстава́ться

2 (*tool*) га́ечный ключ.

wrench *vt*: **he ~ed the door off its hinges** он сорва́л дверь с пе́тель; **he ~ed the steering wheel round** он рывко́м поверну́л руль; **he ~ed the key out of my hands** он вы́рвал у меня́ из рук ключ; **to ~ one's ankle** вы́вихнуть себе́ лоды́жку.

wrestle *vi* боро́ться (*usu impf*); **to ~ with smb**/*fig* **one's conscience/a problem** боро́ться с кем-л, стара́ться заглуши́ть го́лос со́вести, би́ться над пробле́мой.

wrestler *n* боре́ц.

wrestling *n* (спорти́вная) борьба́.

wretch *n*: **poor ~** бедня́га; **you little ~** ах ты, несча́стный.

wretched *adj* жа́лкий; *CQ* ужа́сный; **a ~ hovel** жа́лкая/убо́гая лачу́га; **she looked ~** у неё был жа́лкий вид; **I feel ~** я ужа́сно себя́ чу́вствую (*either sick or unhappy*); **where's that ~ pen?** куда́ э́та злосча́стная ру́чка запропасти́лась?

wriggle *vti vt*: **to ~ one's toes** шевели́ть па́льцами ног (по-)

vi извива́ться (*only in impf*); **the snake ~d across the grass** змея́ извива́лась по траве́; **the worm ~d on the hook** червя́к извива́лся на крючке́; **sit still, don't ~!** сиди́ споко́йно, не ёрзай!; *fig*: **to ~ out of an invitation** увí|ливать от приглаше́ния (-льну́ть); **he knows how to ~ out of things** он уме́ет вы́крутиться.

wring *vt*: **to ~ (out) clothes** вы|жима́ть бельё (́-жать); **to ~ a hen's neck** сверну́ть ку́рице ше́ю (*usu pf*); **to ~ one's hands** зала́мывать ру́ки (*only in impf*); **he wrung my hand warmly** он тепло́ пожа́л мне ру́ку; *fig*: **the thought of it wrung her heart** мысль об э́том терза́ла (ей) ду́шу; **they wrung a promise out of him** они́ вы́рвали у него́ обеща́ние; *CQ* **I'll ~ his neck** я ему́ ше́ю сверну́.

wringing *adj*: **she/her blouse was ~ wet** она́/её блу́зка была́ мо́края, хоть выжима́й.

wrinkle[1] *n* (*on face, dress*) морщи́н(к)а.

wrinkle[1] *vti vt*: **to ~ one's brow** мо́рщить лоб (на-); **your tights/stockings are ~d** у тебя́ колго́тки/чулки́ пло́хо натя́нуты *vi* мо́рщиться (с-); **my dress has ~d under the arms** у меня́ пла́тье морщи́т под мы́шками.

wrinkle[2] *n CQ* (*hint*) намёк.

wrinkled *adj* (*of fruit, face*) смо́рщенный; (*of face*) морщи́нистый.

wrist *n* запя́стье; *attr*: **~ watch** нару́чные часы́.

wristband *n* (*on shirt*) манже́та.

wristlet *n* брасле́т.

writ *n Law* (*for arrest, etc.*) о́рдер; (*summons*) пове́стка (в суд); **to issue a ~ against smb** вы́дать кому́-л пове́стку в суд.

write *vti vt* писа́ть (на-); **to ~ a novel** писа́ть рома́н; **this word is written with a hyphen** э́то сло́во пи́шется че́рез дефи́с; **to ~ (out) a cheque** вы|пи́сывать чек (-писать); *fig* **guilt was written all over his face** у него́ бы́ло винова́тое выраже́ние лица́

vi писа́ть; **to ~ to smb about smth** писа́ть кому́-л о чём-л; **to ~ in ink/on paper** писа́ть черни́лами (*pl*)/на бума́ге; **this pen doesn't ~** э́та ру́чка не пи́шет; **we ~ to each other** мы перепи́сываемся; **she wrote (to) me to come** она́ написа́ла мне, что́бы я прие́хал; **he ~s for a living** он зараба́тывает на жизнь литерату́рным трудо́м; **he ~s for a newspaper/the cinema** он пи́шет *or* сотру́дничает в газе́те, он пи́шет сцена́рии для фи́льмов

write away *vi*: **to ~ away for goods** зака́з|ывать това́р по по́чте (-а́ть); **to ~ away for information** по|сыла́ть запро́с (-сла́ть)

write down *vt*: **to ~ down smb's address** запи́с|ывать чей-л а́дрес (-а́ть); **he wrote down a few notes** он сде́лал не́сколько заме́ток; **I wrote him down as a fool** я счёл его́ дурако́м

write into *vt*: **to ~ a name into a list** вноси́ть и́мя в спи́сок (внести́); **to ~ a new paragraph into a document** встав|ля́ть но́вый пара́граф в докуме́нт (-ить)

write off *vti vt*: **to ~ off a debt** спи́сывать долг; **to ~ off £500** списа́ть пятьсо́т фу́нтов; **to ~ the experiment off as failure** счита́ть экспериме́нт неуда́вшимся; **they wrote him off as stupid** они́ сочли́ его́ по́лным дурако́м; **I've written it off as a dead loss** я счёл э́то пусто́й зате́ей

vi see **write away**

write out *vt*: **to ~ out a poem from a book** перепи́сывать/выпи́сывать стихотворе́ние из кни́ги; **to ~ out a cheque/bill** выпи́сывать чек/счёт; **he has written himself out** он исписа́лся

write up *vt*: **to ~ up a report/an experiment** писа́ть докла́д, опи́сывать ход экспериме́нта; **I'm writing up my notes of the lecture** я подправля́ю свой конспе́кт ле́кции; **he wrote the film up for the paper** он написа́л для газе́ты реце́нзию на э́тот фильм.

write-off *n Comm* спи́санный това́р; *CQ* **his car was a complete ~ after the accident** по́сле ава́рии его́ маши́на годи́лась то́лько на слом.

writer *n* писа́тель (*m*), *f* -ница.

write-up *n*: **she got a ~ in the paper** о ней писа́ли в газе́те; **the play got a good ~** на э́ту пье́су бы́ли хоро́шие реце́нзии.

writhe *vi*: **to ~ in agony/with pain/***CQ* **with embarrassment** ко́рчиться в му́ках/от бо́ли/от стыда́.

writing *n* **1** (*handwriting*) по́черк; **his ~ is illegible** у него́ о́чень неразбо́рчивый по́черк; **it is in his own ~** э́то напи́сано его́ со́бственной руко́й; **there was some ~ on the paper** на бума́ге бы́ло что́-то напи́сано

2: **he earns a bit by ~** он подраба́тывает литерату́рным трудо́м; **in Marx's ~s** в труда́х Ма́ркса; **submit your proposals in ~** изложи́те свои́ предложе́ния в пи́сьменной фо́рме; **at the time of ~** в то вре́мя, когда́ пи́шутся/писа́лись э́ти стро́ки

3 (*as school subject*) чистописа́ние; **they do reading and ~** они́ у́чатся чита́ть и писа́ть.

writing desk *n* пи́сьменный стол.

writing pad *n* блокно́т.

writing paper *n* пи́счая бума́га.

written *adj*: **a ~ statement** пи́сьменное заявле́ние; **a ~ constitution** пи́саная конститу́ция.

wrong *n* зло; **to know right from ~** отлича́ть добро́ от зла; **to do smb a ~** де́лать кому́-л зло; **to right a ~** испра́вить зло; **I admit I was in the ~** призна́ю, я был непра́в/винова́т; **two ~s don't make a right** зло не попра́вить злом; **he can do no ~ in her eyes** в её представле́нии он всегда́ прав; **don't put yourself in the ~** не де́лайте э́того—бу́дете за э́то отвеча́ть.

wrong *adj* **1** (*morally*): **it is ~ to tell lies** лгать нехорошо́; **you were ~ to deceive her** нехорошо́ с твое́й стороны́ обма́нывать её; **what's ~ in the occasional drink?** *joc* что плохо́го, е́сли челове́к пропу́стит иногда́ рю́мку-другу́ю?

2 (*incorrect*) непра́вильный; оши́бочный; не тот; *predic* не пра́в; **a ~ answer** непра́вильный/неве́рный отве́т; **this statement is ~** э́то заявле́ние неве́рно; **you were ~ (in your calculations)** вы оши́блись (в вычисле́ниях); **that's just where you are ~** как раз здесь вы и ошиба́етесь; **we've come the ~ way** мы пошли́ не по той доро́ге; **I proved him ~** я доказа́л, что он не пра́в; **my watch is ~** у меня́ нето́чные часы́; **a ~ note** фальши́вая/не та но́та, *also fig*; **that's the ~ word** э́то не то сло́во; **I took the ~ suitcase by mistake** по оши́бке я взял не тот чемода́н; **we got off at the ~ stop** мы вы́шли не на той остано́вке; **to drive on the ~ side of the road** е́хать не по той стороне́ доро́ги; **you've done it the ~ way** вы сде́лали э́то непра́вильно; **he took what I said the ~ way** он не так меня́ по́нял; **it went down the ~ way** (*of food*) не в то го́рло попа́ло; **they came on the ~ day** они́ перепу́тали день; *Tel* **I got a ~ number** я не туда́ попа́л

3 (*unsuitable*): **you came at the ~ time** вы пришли́ не во́время/некста́ти; **to laugh in the ~ place** смея́ться невпопа́д; **it was the ~ thing to say** э́то бы́ло ска́зано не к ме́сту; **she was dressed in the ~ clothes for the occasion** она́ была́ оде́та не так, как на́до

4 (*amiss*): **is something ~?** что́-нибудь не так?; **what's ~ with you?** что с тобо́й?; **what's ~?** что случи́лось?; **I hope nothing's ~ at home?** наде́юсь, до́ма всё в поря́дке?; **there's something ~ with the engine** в мото́ре кака́я-то непола́дка; **there's nothing physically ~ with him** физи́чески он здоро́в.

wrong *adv*: **you did ~ to lie to me** ты пло́хо сде́лал, что солга́л мне; **did I do it ~?** я э́то сде́лал не так?; **I spelt this word ~** я непра́вильно написа́л э́то сло́во; **you've got it all ~** ты всё непра́вильно/преврáтно по́нял; **don't get me ~** пойми́те меня́ пра́вильно, не пойми́те меня́ превра́тно; **everything has gone ~ (for them)** всё (у них) пошло́ не так; **the plan went ~** план не уда́лся; **we went ~ in our calculations** мы оши́блись в расчётах; **something has gone ~/went ~ with the fridge** с холоди́льником что́-то случи́лось; **carry straight on, you can't go ~** иди́те пря́мо, не ошибётесь; **you can't go ~ with him** с ним не пропадёшь.

wrong *vt*: **she feels she has been ~ed** она́ чу́вствует себя́ оби́женной/, что с ней несправедли́во поступи́ли; **you ~ me in saying that** ты ко мне несправедли́в, говоря́ так.

wrongful *adj Law*: **~ dismissal** незако́нное увольне́ние.

wrongly *adv*: **he translated it ~** он непра́вильно э́то перевёл; **he understood it ~** он не так/непра́вильно э́то по́нял; **he maintains, ~ I think, that...** он утвержда́ет—на мой взгляд оши́бочно—что...; **he was ~ accused of the murder** его́ обвини́ли в уби́йстве соверше́нно несправедли́во.

wrought *adj*: **a ~ silver tray** серебряный подно́с с чека́нкой.

wrought-iron *adj*: **~ gates** ко́ваные чугу́нные воро́та.

wrought-up *adj*: **she was very ~** она́ была́ о́чень взволно́вана/возбуждена́; **don't get so ~** не волну́йся, не не́рвничай.

wry *adj*: **a ~ smile** крива́я улы́бка; **she made a ~ face** лицо́ её скриви́лось в грима́се; **he has a ~ sense of humour** у него́ стра́нный ю́мор; **a ~ comment** ирони́ческое замеча́ние.

X

x *n* **1** *Math* икс; **he earns x dollars a month** он зараба́тывает сто́лько-то до́лларов в ме́сяц; **Professor X** профе́ссор N

2 (*cross*) крест(ик); **the house is marked with an x on the map** дом отме́чен на ка́рте кре́стиком.

Xmas *n abbr see* **Christmas.**

X-ray *n pl* (**~s**) рентге́новы лучи́, рентге́н (*collect*); **an ~** (*photograph*) рентгеногра́мма, рентге́новский сни́мок; *attr*: **~ treatment/therapy** рентгенотерапи́я; **~ examination/room** рентгенологи́ческое иссле́дование, рентге́новский кабине́т.

X-ray *vt*: **they ~ed my hip** мне сде́лали рентге́новский сни́мок бедра́.

xylophone *n* ксилофо́н.

Y

yacht *n* я́хта; *attr*: **~ club** яхт-клу́б.

yachting *n*: **I love ~** я люблю́ пла́вать на я́хте; *attr*: **in ~ circles** среди́ яхтсме́нов.

yachtsman *n* яхтсме́н.

yale lock *n* автомати́ческий/«англи́йский» замо́к.

Yank *n CQ see* **Yankee.**

yank *vt*: *CQ* **I managed to ~ open the warped door** дверь закли́нило (*impers*), но мне удало́сь си́льным рывко́м откры́ть её; **to ~ out a nail** вы|дёргивать гвоздь (-дернуть); **he ~ed the handle off the door** он сорва́л ру́чку с две́ри.

Yankee *n CQ* я́нки (*m*, *indecl*).

yap *vi* (*of dog*) тя́вк|ать (*semel* -нуть).

yard[1] *n* (*measure*) ярд (= 0.914 *metres*); **a ~ away from the tree** в я́рде от де́рева; **to sell cloth by the ~** продава́ть ткань на я́рды (*pl*); *CQ* **with a face a ~ long** с вы́тянувшимся лицо́м.

yard[2] *n* (*courtyard*) двор.

yardstick *n fig* мери́ло; **money is not the ~ of success** де́ньги—не мери́ло успе́ха.

yashmak *n* чадра́, паранджа́.

yawn *n* зево́к.

yawn *vti* **1** зев|а́ть (*semel* -ну́ть); *CQ* **I was ~ing my head off the whole evening** я зева́л весь ве́чер; **just to look at her makes me ~** оди́н её вид нагоня́ет на меня́ зево́ту

2 (*gape open*) зия́ть (*impf*).

yawning *n* зево́та; **I had a fit of ~** на меня́ напа́ла зево́та.

yawning *adj*: **a ~ chasm** зия́ющая бе́здна.

yeah *particle* (*US*) да.

year *n* **1** (*calendar year*) год (*nominative pl* го́ды *and* года́, *G pl* лет); **4/5 ~s** четы́ре го́да, пять лет; **many ~s passed** прошло́ мно́го лет; **5 ~s later** пять лет спустя́; **in 2 ~s time** че́рез два го́да; **3 times a ~** три ра́за в год; **this/last/next ~** в э́том/в про́шлом/в бу́дущем году́; **the next ~** на сле́дующий год; **all the ~ round** кру́глый год; **£1,000 a ~** ты́сяча фу́нтов в год; **he comes here every ~** он приезжа́ет сюда́ ка́ждый год; **every ~ things get dearer** с ка́ждым го́дом всё дорожа́ет; **~ in, ~ out** из го́да в год; **in the ~ 1977** в ты́сяча девятьсо́т се́мьдесят седьмо́м году́; **he is 10 ~s old/about 10 ~s old** ему́ де́сять лет, ему́ лет де́сять; **he's getting on in ~s** он уже́ в года́х; **he looks young for his ~s** он мо́лодо вы́глядит для свои́х лет; **he's active for his ~s** он де́ятелен не по года́м

2 *School, Univ, etc.* год (*G pl* годо́в); **the school/financial ~** уче́бный/фина́нсовый год; *Univ* **he's in his first ~/in my ~** он на пе́рвом ку́рсе, он мой одноку́рсник; **he's doing fourth ~ French** он изуча́ет францу́зский язы́к четвёртый год

3 (*a period, an age*): **I don't see her for ~s at a time** я её не ви́жу года́ми; **we haven't met for ~s** мы давно́ не ви́делись; **that will take ~s** на э́то уйду́т го́ды.

yearbook *n* ежего́дник.

yearling *adj*: **a ~ colt** годова́лый жеребёнок.

yearlong *adj* годово́й.

yearly *adj* (*annual*) ежего́дный; (*for one year*) годово́й; **a ~ event/meeting** ежего́дное собы́тие/собра́ние; **~ income** годово́й дохо́д.

yearly *adv* ежего́дно; **thrice ~** три ра́за в год.

yearn *vi* тоскова́ть по + *D*, скуча́ть по + *D* (*impfs*); **I ~ for my children** я тоску́ю/скуча́ю по де́тям.

yearning *n* тоска́ по + *D*; **I have a ~ for home/to see Rome** я скуча́ю по до́му, я мечта́ю уви́деть Рим.

yeast *n* дро́жжи (*pl*); **brewer's ~** пивны́е дро́жжи.

yell *n* (*shout*) крик, вскрик; (*howl*) вопль (*m*).

yell *vti vt*: **to ~ instructions** выкри́кивать кома́нды; **I ~ed myself hoarse** я крича́л до хрипоты́ (*pf*)

vi (*shout*) кри|ча́ть (*semel* ́-кнуть), вскри́к|ивать (*semel* -нуть), вы|кри́кивать (́-крикнуть); (*howl*) вопи́ть (*impf*); **to ~ for help/at smb** крича́ть о по́мощи/на кого́-л; **the baby was ~ing** ребёнок гро́мко пла́кал.

yellow *adj* жёлтый; **rather ~** желтова́тый; *fig* **the ~ press** жёлтая пре́сса.

yellow *vi* желте́ть (по-).

yelp *vi* визжа́ть (*impf*), взви́згнуть (*semel pf*).

yelping *adj* визгли́вый.

yen *n CQ*: **I have a ~ to go swimming** мне страсть как хо́чется вы́купаться.

yep *particle CQ* (*esp. US*) да.

yes *n*: **I want a plain ~ or no** скажи́те пря́мо—да и́ли нет.

yes *particle* да; (*in contradiction*) нет; **do you love me?—Yes, I do** ты меня́ лю́бишь?—Да, люблю́; **you don't love me.—Yes, I do** ты меня́ не лю́бишь.—Нет, люблю́; **he says ~ to everything/to everyone** он со всем соглаша́ется, он всем подда́кивает.

yes man *n* подпева́ла (*m and f*).

yesterday *n* вчера́ (*adv*), вчера́шний день; **~ was Tuesday** вчера́ был вто́рник.

yesterday *adv* вчера́; **~ morning/afternoon/evening** вчера́ у́тром/днём/ве́чером; **the day before ~** позавчера́; **no later than ~** не да́лее чем вчера́.

yet *adv* **1** (*still*) ещё; (*already*) уже́; (*meantime*) пока́; **he hasn't come ~** он ещё не пришёл; **has he come ~?** он уже́ пришёл?; **it has ~ to be decided** э́то ещё предстои́т реши́ть; **he may surprise us all ~** он ещё всех нас удиви́т; **I'm not going as ~** я пока́ ещё не ухожу́; **need you go ~?** тебе́ уже́ пора́?

2 (*emphatic*): **he has failed his exam ~ again** он опя́ть провали́лся на экза́мене; **it rained ~ harder** дождь пошёл ещё сильне́е; **I don't care for him, nor ~ his brother** я не люблю́ ни его́, ни его́ бра́та.

yet *conj* но, одна́ко, всё же, всё-таки; **she may be stupid, ~ people like her** мо́жет, она́ не так умна́, одна́ко/но всё же её лю́бят; **he studied hard, ~ he failed** он мно́го занима́лся и всё-таки провали́лся; **it's strange, ~ true** как ни стра́нно, но э́то так.

yew, yew tree *ns* тис, ти́совое де́рево.

Yiddish *n* и́диш (*indecl*); **to speak ~** говори́ть на и́диш; *attr*: **a ~ newspaper** газе́та, выходя́щая на и́диш.

yield *n Econ* дохо́д; *Agric* (*harvest*) урожа́й; (*of milk*) надо́й, удо́й; **the ~ on his shares** дохо́д от его́ а́кций; **what is the ~ per hectare?** како́в урожа́й с гекта́ра?

yield *vti vt* **1** (*give*) при|носи́ть (-нести́), да|ва́ть (-ть); **how much fruit does the orchard ~?** како́й урожа́й фру́ктов прино́сит сад?; **the mine ~s 1,000 tons of coal per day** ша́хта даёт ты́сячу тонн у́гля в день; **the shares ~ 5% p.a.** а́кции прино́сят/даю́т пять проце́нтов в год

2 (*surrender*) сда|ва́ть (́-ть); уступ|а́ть (-и́ть); **to ~ a position/town to the enemy** сдать пози́цию/го́род проти́внику; (*in debate*) **I ~ that point to you** я уступа́ю вам в э́том вопро́се

vi сда|ва́ться, подда|ва́ться (*pfs* ́-ться); уступа́ть; **they will never ~** они́ ни за что́/никогда́ не усту́пят/не сдаду́тся; **to ~ to force/threats/temptation** поддава́ться си́ле/угро́зам/искуше́нию; **the door ~ed to a heavy push** от си́льного толчка́ дверь подала́сь; *iron* **I ~ to many in my admiration for him** я уж не в тако́м восто́рге от него́.

yoga *n* йо́га.

yog(h)ourt, yog(h)urt *n* йогу́рт, (*SU products very similar*: *thin*) кефи́р, (*thick*) простоква́ша.

yogi *n* йог.

yoke *n* (*on neck of oxen*) ярмо́, *also fig*; (*on shoulder for carrying buckets*) коромы́сло; **a ~ of oxen** (*pair*) па́ра воло́в; *Sew* **the ~ of a dress** коке́тка на пла́тье; *fig* **to throw off the ~** сбро́сить ярмо́; *Hist* **the Tartar ~** тата́рское и́го.

yokel *n* дереве́нщина (*m*).

yolk *n* желто́к.

you *pers pron* **1** *familiar sing* ты, *G* тебя́, *D* тебе́, *I* тобо́й, *P* о тебе́; *pl and polite sing* вы, *G* вас, *D* вам, *I* ва́ми, *P* о вас; **I saw ~** я ви́дел тебя́/вас; **what's wrong with ~?**

что с тобо́й/с ва́ми?; **they're talking about ~** они́ говоря́т о тебе́/о вас

2 *when it refers to the subject of the sentence "you" is translated by reflex pron* себя́, *etc.*; **close the door behind ~** закро́й(те) за собо́й дверь; **did you take my sister with ~?** вы взя́ли мою́ сестру́ с собо́й?

3 *in general, impersonal uses*: **~ can't smoke in the cinema** в кино́ нельзя́ кури́ть; **~ have to wind the toy up first** игру́шку снача́ла на́до завести́; **wherever ~ look, there are skyscrapers** куда́ (ты) ни посмо́тришь, везде́ небоскрёбы [**NB** *in impersonal uses always 2nd sing*]; **~'re only young once** молоды́м быва́ешь то́лько раз

4 *various*: **hey, ~ there!** эй, ты там!; **~ fool!** дура́к!; **poor ~!** бедня́жка! (*m and f*); **~ girls ought to be punctual** вы, де́вочки, не должны́ опа́здывать на рабо́ту; **so it was ~, was it?** так э́то был ты?; **between ~ and me** ме́жду на́ми (говоря́); **there's a real man for ~!** вот э́то настоя́щий мужчи́на!; **if I were ~, I'd choose the green tie** на твоём/ва́шем ме́сте я бы вы́брал зелёный га́лстук; **I'd like to invite ~ and your wife to dinner** я хочу́ пригласи́ть вас с жено́й к обе́ду.

young *n collect* (*people*): **the ~ of today** совреме́нная молодёжь (*collect*); *Zool* молодня́к (*collect*); (*sucklings*) детёныши (*pl*).

young *adj* молодо́й, ю́ный; **~ people** молодёжь (*collect*); **~ man!** молодо́й челове́к! (*in SU used also to older men to arrest attention*); **in my ~ days I...** в мо́лодости я...; **I'm not as ~ as I was** я уже́ не так мо́лод; **he's ~ at heart** он мо́лод душо́й; **16 is very ~ to get married** в шестна́дцать лет о́чень ра́но выходи́ть за́муж (*of a girl*)/вступа́ть в брак; **you look ~er** ты вы́глядишь помолоде́вшим; **that hat makes you look years ~er** э́та шля́па тебя́ о́чень молоди́т; **my ~(er) brother** мой мла́дший брат; **Ivan is the ~er of the two** Ива́н—мла́дший брат; *fig* **the night is still ~** ещё не так по́здно.

young-looking *adj* моложа́вый.

youngster *n* ма́льчик, мальчи́шка (*m*), де́вочка (*f*); **~s** ребя́та.

your *poss adj* **1** *familiar sing* твой, *pl and polite sing* ваш; **I admire ~ taste** я восхищён твои́м/ва́шим вку́сом

2 *in certain cases translated by oblique cases of pronouns* тебя́/вас, *etc., or, if referring to the subject of the sentence, by* себя́, *etc.*: **it's in ~ room** э́то у тебя́/у вас в ко́мнате; **are you going to stay in ~ room?** ты собира́ешься/вы собира́етесь оста́ться у себя́ в ко́мнате?

3 *if referring to the subject of clause, usu translated by* свой, *or, if sense is clear, omitted*; **you were with ~ sister** ты был с сестро́й; **you were telling me about ~ parrot** ты расска́зывал мне о своём попуга́е

4 *referring to parts of body, use* себя́, *or reflex verb, or omit*; **when you broke ~ leg** когда́ ты слома́л но́гу; **when you banged ~ head against the beam** когда́ ты сту́кнулся голово́й о ба́лку; **wash ~ hands!** вы́мой ру́ки!

5 *in generalizations use* свой *or omit*; **you should clean ~ teeth twice a day** зу́бы на́до чи́стить два ра́за в день; **it's hard to change ~/one's habits** тру́дно меня́ть свои́ привы́чки.

yours *poss pron*: *familiar sing* твой, *pl and polite sing* ваш; **is he a friend of ~?** он твой/ваш прия́тель?; **I've hung my coat next to ~** я пове́сил (моё) пальто́ ря́дом с твои́м/с ва́шим; (*in letters*) **Y. sincerely** и́скренне Ваш/Ва́ша.

yourself *pron of emphasis*: *familiar sing* сам(а́), *pl and polite sing* са́ми; **you told me so ~/yourselves** ты сам(а́)/вы са́ми мне э́то рассказа́л(а)/(-и).

yourself *reflex pron* **1** себя́, *etc., or use reflex verb*: **have you asked ~/yourselves why?** вы спроси́ли себя́ заче́м?; **you're too pleased with ~** ты сли́шком уж дово́лен собо́й; **you think only of ~/yourselves** ты ду́маешь/вы ду́маете то́лько о себе́; **help ~!/yourselves!** угоща́йся!, угоща́йтесь!

2 *phrases*: **you're not ~ today** ты сего́дня сам не свой; **make ~/yourselves at home!** бу́дь(те) как до́ма!; **I saw you standing by ~** я ви́дел, как ты стоя́л совсе́м оди́н.

youth *n* (*abstract*) мо́лодость, (*less commonly*) ю́ность; (*person*) ю́ноша (*m*); *collect* молодёжь; **in one's ~** в мо́лодости, в ю́ности; **he's past his first ~** он уже́ не так мо́лод; **a ~ of 25** ю́ноша/па́рень двадцати́ пяти́ лет; **modern ~** совреме́нная молодёжь; *attr* молодёжный; **~ hostel** *approx* молодёжная турба́за.

youthfulness *n* моложа́вость.

Yugoslav *n* югосла́в, югосла́вка.

Yugoslav *adj* югосла́вский.

Z

zeal *n* энтузиа́зм; рве́ние; **he shows great ~ for his work** он проявля́ет рве́ние в рабо́те.

zealous *adj* рья́ный, ре́вностный; **a ~ supporter** горя́чий сторо́нник, рья́ный защи́тник.

zebra *n* зе́бра; *attr*: **~ crossing** (пешехо́дный) перехо́д.

zenith *n* зени́т, *also fig*; *fig* **at the ~ of one's fame** в зени́те/в расцве́те сла́вы.

zero *n* нуль (*m*), ноль (*m*); **it's 5° below ~ today** сего́дня пять гра́дусов ни́же нуля́; **the temperature fell to ~** температу́ра упа́ла до нуля́; *attr* нулево́й; **~ visibility** нулева́я ви́димость; *Mil* **~ hour** час «Ч», вре́мя нача́ла наступле́ния/вы́садки деса́нта.

zigzag *n* зигза́г; *attr* зигзагообра́зный; **a ~ path/line** вью́щаяся тропи́нка, зигзагообра́зная ли́ния.

zigzag *vi*: **the drunkard ~ged along the street** пья́ный шёл по у́лице зигза́гами.

zinc *n* цинк; *attr* ци́нковый.

Zionism *n* сиони́зм.

zip *n* (*fastener*) (застёжка-)мо́лния; (*sound*) свист; *fig CQ* **put more ~ into it!** поэнерги́чней!, бо́льше жа́ру!

zip *vti vt*: **I ~ped up my dress/open my bag** я за|стегну́ла пла́тье, я рас|стегну́ла су́мку (*impfs* -стёгивать)

vi: **a bullet ~ped past my ear** пу́ля просвисте́ла у моего́ у́ха; *CQ* **my car may be old but it still ~s along** пусть моя́ маши́на и не но́вая, но бе́гает ещё будь здоро́в.

zip code *n* (*US*) почто́вый и́ндекс.

zip fastener, zipper *ns* (застёжка-)мо́лния.

zippy *adj CQ* бы́стрый, прово́рный; **look ~!** живе́е!

zodiac *n* зодиа́к.

zonal *adj* зона́льный.

zone *n Geog*, *Econ* зо́на, по́яс; (*strip*) полоса́; *Mil* **demilitarized/defence ~** демилитаризо́ванная зо́на, оборони́тельная полоса́.

zoo *n* зоопа́рк.

zoological *adj* зоологи́ческий; **~ gardens** зоологи́ческий сад, зоопа́рк (*sings*).

zoologist *n* зоо́лог.

zoom *n* гул, рёв; (*of insects*) жужжа́ние.

zoom *vi*: **the plane ~ed over our house** самолёт с рёвом пролете́л над на́шей кры́шей; **a bee ~ed past my ear** пчела́ прожужжа́ла у меня́ над у́хом.

NOTES

NOTES